The Handbook of Educational Theories

The Handbook of Educational Theories

Edited by

Beverly J. Irby
Sam Houston State University

Genevieve Brown
Sam Houston State University

Rafael Lara-Alecio
Texas A&M University

Shirley Jackson
Sam Houston State University

IAP

Information Age Publishing, Inc.
Charlotte, North Carolina • www.infoagepub.com

Library of Congress Cataloging-in-Publication Data

The handbook of educational theories / edited by Beverly J. Irby ... [et al.].
p. cm.
Includes bibliographical references.
ISBN 978-1-61735-865-4 (paperback)—ISBN 978-1-61735-866-1 (hardcover)—
ISBN 978-1-61735-867-8 (ebook) 1. Education—Philosophy. I. Irby, Beverly J.
LB14.7.H3636 2012
370.1—dc23

2012016438

Printed in the United States of America

The Handbook of Educational Theories

ALPHABETIZED CONTRIBUTORS LIST

Betty J. Alford, PhD, Professor and Chair, Department of Secondary Education and Educational Leadership, Stephen F. Austin State University, Nacogdoches, TX

Mary V. Alfred, PhD, Professor and Associate Dean, College of Education and Human Development, Texas A& M University, College Station, TX

Harlene Anderson, PhD, Consultant, Clinical Theorist and Author, Houston Galveston Institute (Houston, Texas), Taos Institute, and Access Success International

Barbara Applebaum, PhD, Associate Professor, School of Education, Syracuse University, Syracuse, NY

Juan Araujo, PhD, Assistant Professor, Bilingual and ESL Education, University of North Texas at Dallas, Dallas, TX

Colin Baker, PhD Professor and Pro Vice-Chancellor, Eifionydd, Normal Site and Main Arts School of Education, Bangor University, Wales, UK

Amy T. Banner, PhD, Codirector, Community Counseling Program, Assistant Professor NCC, Department of Counseling and Human Services University of Scranton, PA

JoAnn Danelo Barbour, PhD, Professor of Education Administration and Leadership, College of Professional Education, Texas Woman's University, Denton, TX

Richard Bates, PhD, Professor, School of Education, Deakin University, Melbourne, Australia

Gillian U. Bayne, PhD, Assistant Professor and Coordinator, Graduate Program in Science Education, Department of Middle and High School Teaching, Division of Education, Lehman College, City University of New York, New York, NY

Floyd D. Beachum, EdD, Bennett Professor of Urban School Leadership, Program Director Educational Leadership Program, Lehigh University, Bethlehem, PA

Doris Bergen, PhD, Professor, Department of Educational Psychology Miami University, Oxford, OH

Gert J. Biesta, PhD, Professor, School of Education, University of Stirling, Scotland, UK

Jill Blackmore, PhD, Director, Center for Research in Educational Futures and Innovation, School of Education, Deakin University, Melbourne, Australia

Cheryl L. Bolton, Senior Lecturer, Institute of Education Policy Review, Staffordshire University, Stoke-on-Trent, UK

Sandra Bosaki, PhD, Associate Professor, Brock University, St. Catherines, Ontario, Canada

Jacqueline Grennon Brooks, EdD, Professor, Science Education, Director, Institute for the Development of Education in the Advanced Sciences, School of Education, Health and Human Services, Hofstra University, Hempstead, NY

Jeffrey S. Brooks, PhD, Professor and PK-12 Educational Leadership Program Coordinator, Department of Educational Leadership and Policy Analysis, University of Missouri, Columbia, MO

Genevieve Brown, EdD, Dean College of Education, Sam Houston State University, Huntsville, TX

Kathleen M. Brown, EdD, Professor and Chair of Educational Leadership, University of North Carolina, Chapel Hill,

Chapel Hill, NC

Ric Brown, EdD, Adjunct Faculty, Northern Arizona University, Flagstaff, AZ

Rick Bruhn, PhD, Professor, Department of Educational Leadership and Counseling, Sam Houston State University, Huntsville, TX

Larry C. Bryant, PhD, Assistant Professor, Teacher Education/Special Education, University of North Texas at Dallas, Dallas, TX

John E. Burgette, PhD, Adjunct Graduate Faculty, Department of Counseling, Educational Psychology and Research, University of Memphis, Memphis, TN

Geoffrey Caine, LLM, Caine Learning Center, Idyllwild, CA

Renate N. Caine, PhD, Caine Learning Center, Idyllwild, CA

John A. Cassell, MLS, MA, Doctoral Candidate, University of the Pacific, Benerd School of Education, Stockton, CA

Thandeka K. Chapman, PhD, Associate Professor, Urban Education in the Department of Curriculum and Instruction, University of Wisconsin, Milwaukee, WI

Catherine A. Cherrstrom, MBA, MEd, Center for Teaching Excellence, Texas A&M University, College Station, TX

Paul Crawford, PhD Graduate Student, University of Victoria, Victoria, B.C., Canada

Emile Crevier-Quintin, Doctoral Program Student, Department of Psychology, University of Victoria, B.C., Canada

Gary M. Crow, PhD, Professor and Chair, Department of Educational Leadership and Policy Studies, Indiana University, Bloomington, IN

Autumn K. Cyprés, EdD, Professor and Director of The Center for Educational Leadership, University of Tennessee, Knoxville, TN

Darrel Davis, PhD, Assistant Professor, Department of Educational Psychology, Miami University, Oxford, OH

Kathryn A. Davis, PhD, Professor, Department of Second Language Studies, University of Hawaiì, Honolulu, HI

Kari Dehli, PhD, Professor, Department of Sociology and Equity Studies in Education, Ontario Institute for Studies in Education, University of Toronto, Canada

Adrienne Dixson, PhD, Associate Professor, Department of Educational Policy, Organization and Leadership, University of Illinois-Urbana Champaign, Champaign, IL

Ron Dumont, EdD, Professor and Director School of Psychology, Fairleigh Dickinson University Metropolitan Campus, Teaneck, NJ

Karen Dunlap, EdD, Assistant Professor, Curriculum and Instruction, Department of Teacher Education, Texas Woman's University, Denton, TX

Sarah Dykstra, MA, Doctoral Student University of British Columbia, Vancouver, B.C., Canada

Lily Dyson, PhD, Professor, Faculty of Education, Simon Fraser University, Burnaby, B.C., Canada

Patricia A. L. Ehrensal, EdD, Assistant Professor of Educational Administration, George Washington University, Alexandria, VA

Fenwick W. English, PhD, R. Wendell Eaves Senior Distinguished Professor of Education Leadership; Program Coordinator Department of Educational Leadership, University of North Carolina at Chapel Hill, Chapel Hill, NC

Rodney Evans, PhD, Independent Scholar, Seffner, FL

Vicky Farrow, PhD, Professor, Chair Department of Professional Pedagogy, Lamar University, Beaumont, TX

Patricia F. First, JD, EdD, Eugene T. Moore Distinguished Professor of Educational Leadership, Clemson University, Clemson, SC

Dawn P. Flanagan, PhD, Professor and School Psychology Program Director, Department of Psychology, St. John's University, Jamaica, NY

Pamela Fraser-Abder, PhD, Director Science Education, Department of Teaching and Learning, New York University, New York, NY

Rebecca Fredrickson, EdD, Assistant Professor, Curriculum and Instruction, Department of Teacher Education, Texas Woman's University, Denton, TX

Sonya Frey, BSc, Psychology, Research Assistant, University of Victoria, B.C. Canada

Alicia R. Friday, MEd, PhD Candidate, Texas A&M University, College Station, TX

Eugene E. Garcia, PhD, Professor and Vice President for Education Partnerships, Arizona State University, Phoenix, AZ

David Gillborn, PhD, Professor, Institute of Education, London, England, UK

Andrea M. Guillaume, PhD, Professor of Elementary and Bilingual Education, California State University, Fullerton, CA

James B. Hale, PhD, Associate Professor, Department of Psychology, University of Victoria, B.C., Canada

Susan Hansen, PhD, Associate Professor, National Louis University, Skokie, IL

Sandra Harris, PhD, Professor, Director Center for Doctoral Studies in Educational Leadership, Lamar University, Beaumont, TX

Carlene (Miki) Henderson, EdD, Assistant Professor, Language, Literacy and Special Populations, Sam Houston State University, Huntsville, TX

Richard C. Henriksen, Jr., PhD, Associate Professor, Department of Educational Leadership and Counseling, Sam Houston State University, Huntsville, TX

Hal Holloman, PhD, Associate Professor Department of Educational Leadership, East Carolina University, Greenville, NC

David L. Hough, PhD, Professor and Dean, College of Education, Missouri State University Springfield, MO

Kenneth R. Howe, PhD, Professor, School of Education, University of Colorado, Boulder, CO

Marcia B. Imbeau, PhD, Associate Professor, College of Education and Health Professions, University of Arkansas, Fayetteville, AR

Beverly J. Irby, EdD, Texas State University System Regents' Distinguished Professor and Associate Dean for Graduate Programs, College of Education, Sam Houston State University, Huntsville, TX

Shirley Jackson, EdD, Researcher, Center for Research and Doctoral Studies in Educational Leadership, Sam Houston State University, Huntsville, TX

Patrick M. Jenlink, EdD, Professor, Department of Secondary Education and Educational Leadership and Director, Educational Research Center, Stephen F. Austin State University, Nacogdoches, TX

Bryant Jensen, IES Postdoc Fellow, University of Oregon, Eugene, OR

Jennifer Job, Graduate Student, Research Assistant, University of North Carolina, Chapel Hill, NC

Timothy B. Jones, EdD, Associate Professor of Educational Law and Policy, Department of Educational Leadership and Counseling, Sam Houston State University, Huntsville, TX

Daniel L. Kain, PhD, Vice Provost, Academic Personnel, Northern Arizona University, Flagstaff, AZ

Alan S. Kaufman, PhD, Clinical Professor of Psychology, Yale University School of Medicine, Child Study Center, New Haven, CT

Lisa A. W. Kensler, EdD, Assistant Professor, College of Education, Auburn University, Auburn, AL

Janice Koch, PhD, Professor Emerita, Hofstra University, Hempstead, NY

William Allan Kritsonis, PhD, Professor, College of Education, Prairie View A&M University, Prairie View, TX

Hanna A. Kubas, BSc, Doctoral Program Student, Department of Psychology, University of Victoria, B.C., Canada

Amanda C. La Guardia, PhD, Assistant Professor, LPC-MHSP, NCC, Department of Educational Leadership and Counseling Sam Houston State University, Huntsville, TX

Susan Laird, PhD, Professor, Educational Studies, University of Oklahoma, Norman, OK

Gloria Ladson-Billings, PhD, Keller Family Chair in Urban Education, Department of Curriculum and Instruction, University of Wisconsin-Madison, Madison, WI

Lyse Langlois, PhD, Professor, Department of Industrial Relations, Laval University, Quebec City, Canada

Rafael Lara-Alecio, PhD, Professor and Director of Bilingual Programs, Department of Educational Psychology, College of Education and Human Development, Texas A&M University, College Station, TX

Cheu-jey Lee, PhD, Assistant Professor, School of Education Indiana University-Purdue University, Ft. Wayne, IN

Natasha Levinson, PhD, Associate Professor, Department of Foundations, Leadership, and Administration, College of Education, Health and Human Services, Kent State University, Kent, OH

Candise Y. Lin, BA, Doctoral Candidate, Department of Human Development and Quantitative Methodology, University of Maryland, College Park, MD

Fred C. Lunenburg, PhD, Merchant Professor of Education, College of Education, Sam Houston State University, Huntsville, TX

Susan Magun-Jackson, PhD, Associate Professor, Department of Counseling, Educational Psychology and Research, University of Memphis, Memphis, TN

Maria Lourdes Majdalani, ME, Lecturer, Majdalani Foundation, Center for Moral Development—Buenos Aires, Argentina

Catherine Marshall, PhD, Professor, Department of Educational Leadership, University of North Carolina-Chapel Hill, Chapel Hill, NC

Kevin S. McGrew, PhD, Director, The Institute for Applied Psychometrics, St. Joseph, MN

Martha McCarthy, PhD, President's Professor, Loyola Marymount University, Los Angeles, CA and Chancellor's Professor Emerita, Indiana University, Bloomington, IN

Sarah McMahan, PhD, Assistant Professor, Curriculum and Instruction, Department of Teacher Education, Texas Women's University, Denton, TX

Daniel C. Miller, PhD, Professor and Department Chair, Department of Psychology & Philosophy, Texas Woman's University, Denton, TX

Martin Mills, PhD, Professor, University of Queensland, Australia

Masahiko Minami, EdD, Professor, Foreign Languages and Literatures, College of Liberal & Creative Arts, San Francisco State University, San Francisco, CA/Visiting Professor, National Institute for Japanese Language and Linguistics, Tokyo, Japan

Jason R. Mixon, EdD, Director of the Online Doctoral Program in Educational Leadership, College of Education and Human Development, Lamar University, Beaumont, TX

Heather Mechler, PhD, Visiting Assistant Professor, Department of Education, Bucknell University, Lewisburg, PA

Glenda Moss, EdD, Chair, Department of Teacher Education & Administration, University of North Texas, Dallas, TX.

Carol A. Mullen, PhD, Professor and Chair, Department of Educational Leadership & Cultural Foundations, School of Education, University of North Carolina at Greensboro, Greensboro, NC

Ratna Narayan, PhD, Associate Professor, Science Education, Division of Education and Human Services, University of North Texas at Dallas, Dallas, TX

Thomas Nelson, PhD, Professor of Curriculum Studies and Teacher Education, University of the Pacific, Benerd School of Education, Stockton, CA

Thu Suong Thi Nguyen, PhD, Assistant Professor of Educational Leadership and Policy Studies, School of Education, Indiana University - Indiana, Indianapolis IN

Mary Nichter, PhD, Professor, Department of Educational Leadership and Counseling, Sam Houston State University, Huntsville, TX

Martina Nussbaumer, MA, Research Assistant, Department of Education, Paris Lodron; University of Salzburg, Salzburg, AUT

Samuel O. Ortiz, PhD, Professor, Department of Psychology, St. John's University, Jamaica, NY

Carlos J. Ovando, PhD, Professor, School of Transborder Studies, College of Liberal Arts and Sciences, Arizona State University, Tempe AZ

Karen D. Paciotti, EdD, Assistant Professor, Department of Teacher Education, College of Education, Texas A&M-Corpus Christi, Corpus Christi, TX

Rosemary Papa, EdD, Del and Jewell Lewis Endowed Chair, Learning Centered leadership, Northern Arizona University, Flagstaff, AZ

Daniel J. Parker, Undergraduate Honors Student—Psychology, Department of Psychology, University of Victoria, B.C., Canada

Jean-Luc Patry, PhD, Department of Education, Paris Lodron; University of Salzburg, Salzburg, AUT

Craig Peck, PhD, Assistant Professor, Department of Educational Leadership and Cultural Foundations, School of Education, University of North Carolina at Greensboro, Greensboro, NC

John E. Petrovic, PhD, Professor, Department of Educational Leadership, Policy, and Technology Studies, The University of Alabama, Tuscaloosa, AL

Steve Permuth, EdD, Professor, College of Education, University of South Florida, Tampa, FL

Joseph Renzulli, EdD, Director, The National Research Center on the Gifted and Talented, University of Connecticut, Storrs, CT

Kelly Rizzo, MEd, Brock University, St. Catherines, Ontario, Canada

Petra A. Robinson, PhD, Research Associate, Graduate School of Education, Department of Educational Psychology, Rutgers University, New Brunswick, NJ

Carol Robinson-Zañartu, PhD, Professor and Chair, Department of Counseling and School Psychology, College of Education, San Diego State University, San Diego, CA

Rebecca A. Robles-Piña, PhD, Professor, Educational Leadership and Counseling, Sam Houston State University, Huntsville, TX

Cynthia Rodriguez, PhD, Assistant Professor, Teacher Education and Reading Division of Education and Human Development, University of North Texas-Dallas, Dallas, TX

Linda Rodriguez, EdD, Area Superintendent Aldine ISD, Houston, TX, and Researcher, Center for Research and Doctoral Studies in Educational Leadership, Sam Houston State University, Huntsville, TX

Frances O'Connell Rust, EdD, Professor Emeritus, New York University; Visiting Professor, Interim Director of the Teacher Education Program, University of Pennsylvania Graduate School of Education, Philadelphia, PA

Eugenie Samier, PhD, Coordinator of EdD Program, British University in Dubai, United Arab Emirates

Kathryn Scantlebury, PhD, Professor and Secondary Science Education Coordinator, Department of Chemistry and Biochemistry, University of Delaware, Newark, DE

Andrea N. Schneider, BA, Doctoral Program Student, Department of Psychology, University of Victoria, B.C., Canada

W. Joel Schneider, PhD, Associate Professor, Psychology Department, Illinois State University, Normal, IL

Arthur Shapiro, PhD, Professor, College of Education, University of South Florida, Tampa, FL

Ali Shaqlaih, PhD, Assistant Professor, Math and Secondary Education, University of North Texas at Dallas, Dallas, TX

Carolyn M. Shields, PhD, Dean, College of Education, Wayne State University, Detroit, MI

Mark R. Shinn, PhD, Professor of School Psychology and Program Director, National-Louis University, Chicago, IL

Cecilia Silva, PhD, Professor, Bilingual/Multicultural Education, Texas Christian University, Fort Worth, TX

Eva E. A. Skoe, PhD, Professor, Department of Psychology, University of Oslo, Oslo, Norway

Stephen D. Sorden, EdD, Director of the Center for Teaching and Learning Excellence at Embry-Riddle Aeronautical University, Prescott, AZ

Pamela Spycher, PhD, Director, English Language and Literacy Acceleration (ELLA), WestEd, Sacramento, CA

Lynda Stone, PhD, Professor, Cultural Foundations, University of North Carolina, Chapel Hill, NC

Hayley Stulmaker, PhD student, Counselor Education and Supervision, University of North Texas, Denton, TX

Jeffrey M. Sullivan, PhD, Assistant Professor, Department of Educational Leadership and Counseling, Sam Houston State University, Huntsville, TX

Janet Tareilo, EdD, Associate Professor, Department of Secondary Education and Leadership, College of Education, Stephen F. Austin State University, Nacogdoches, TX

Janice L. Taylor, EdD, Executive Director, Human Resource Services, Klein Independent School District, Klein, TX, and Researcher, Center for Research and Doctoral Studies in Educational Leadership, Sam Houston State University, Huntsville, TX

Barbara J. Thayer-Bacon, PhD, Professor, Cultural Studies, University of Tennessee, Knoxville, TN

Stephen J. Thoma, PhD, Professor, Department of Educational Studies in Psychology, Research Methodology, and Counseling, The University of Alabama, Tuscaloosa, AL

Carol Ann Tomlinson, EdD, William Clay Parrish, Jr. Professor and Chair of Educational Leadership, Foundations, and Policy, Curry School of Education, University of Virginia, Charlottesville, VA

Fuhui Tong, PhD, Assistant Professor, Department of Educational Psychology, College of Education and Human Development, Texas A&M University, College Station, TX

Bruce Torff, EdD, Professor of Teaching, Learning and Literacy; Director, Doctoral Program in Learning and Teaching, School of Education, Health and Human Services, Hofstra University, Hempstead, NY

Rhonda Vincent, PhD, Lecturer and Director of Field Experiences, University of North Texas at Dallas, Dallas, TX

James A. Vornberg, PhD, Professor, College of Education and Human Services Texas A&M—Commerce, Commerce, TX

Min Wang, PhD, Associate Professor, Department of Human Development and Quantitative Methodology, University of Maryland, College Park, MD

Richard E. Watts, PhD, LPC-S University Distinguished Professor and Director Center for Research and Doctoral Studies in Counselor Education Sam Houston State University, Huntsville, TX

Alfred Weinberger, PhD, Private University College of Education of the Diocese of Linz, Austria

Molly Weinburgh, PhD, Professor and William L. and Betty F. Adams Chair of Education, Texas Christian University, Fort Worth, TX

Sieglinde Weyringer, PhD, University Assistant, Department of Education, Paris Lodron University of Salzburg, Salzburg, AUT

Patricia Williams, PhD, Professor (Retired), Department of Curriculum and Instruction, Sam Houston State University, Huntsville, TX

John O. Willis, EdD, Senior Lecturer in Assessment, Division of Education, Rivier University, Nashua, NH

Angie D. Wilson, Ph.D., Assistant Professor, Department of Psychology, Counseling, and Special Education, Texas A&M University – Commerce, Commerce, TX

Robert Wubbolding, EdD, Director, The Center for Reality Therapy in Cincinnati, OH; Senior Faculty for the William Glasser Institute in Los Angeles; Professor Emeritus, Xavier University, New Orleans, LA

Yael Wyner, PhD, Assistant Professor, Secondary, Middle School Science Program, City College of New York, NY

LingLing Yang, EdD, Director of the Language Lab, College of Humanities and Social Sciences, Sam Houston State University, Huntsville, TX

Peggy H. Yates, PhD, Assistant Professor, Elementary Education, East Carolina University, Greenville, NC

Michelle D. Young, PhD, Professor and Director of UCEA, Department of Leadership, Foundations, and Policy, University of Virginia, Charlottesville, VA

Anita Zijdemans-Boudreau, PhD, Assistant Professor and Flex Program Coordinator, School of Education, Pacific University, Portland, OR

CONTENTS

Preface xvii

SECTION 1: PHILOSOPHICAL EDUCATION—INTRODUCTION
Section Editor: Barbara J. Thayer-Bacon 1

1. On the Idea of Educational Theory
Gert J. J. Biesta 5

2. Epistemology and Education
Barbara J. Thayer-Bacon 17

3. Ethics and Moral Education
Lynda Stone and Jennifer Job 29

4. Aesthetics and Education
Susan Laird 43

5. Social Philosophy, Critical Whiteness Studies, and Education
Barbara Applebaum 57

6. Contemporary Political Theory and Education
Natasha Levinson 67

7. Philosophy of Social Science and Educational Research
Kenneth R. Howe 79

SECTION 2: LEARNING THEORY—INTRODUCTION
Section Editor: Patrick M. Jenlink 87

8. Behaviorism and Behavioral Learning Theory
Larry C. Bryant, Rhonda Vincent, Ali Shaqlaih, and Glenda Moss 91

9. Cognitivism: Ways of Knowing
Karen D. Paciotti 105

10. Experiential Learning Theory
Anita Zijdemans-Boudreau, Glenda Moss, and Cheu-jey G. Lee 115

11. Adult Learning Theory
Betty J. Alford 125

12. Transformative Learning Theory
Mary V. Alfred, Catherine A. Cherrstrom, Petra A. Robinson, and Alicia R. Friday 133

13. Stage Theory of Cognitive Development
Janet Tareilo 149

14. The Cognitive Theory of Multimedia Learning
Stephen D. Sorden 155

15. Constructivism—Constructivist Learning Theory
Ratna Narayan, Cynthia Rodriguez, Juan Araujo, Ali Shaqlaih, and Glenda Moss 169

16. Situated Cognition Theory
Patrick M. Jenlink 185

17. Cooperative Learning Theory
Rebecca Fredrickson, Karen Dunlap, and Sarah McMahan 199

18. Problem-Based Learning Theory
Rebecca Fredrickson, Sarah McMahan, and Karen Dunlap 211

19. Cultural-Historical Activity Theory
Patrick M. Jenlink 219

SECTION 3: INSTRUCTIONAL THEORY—INTRODUCTION
Section Editor: Janice Koch 237

20. Using Cogenerative Dialogues to Expand and Extend Students' Learning
Gillian U. Bayne and Kathryn Scantlebury 239

21. The Footsteps Project for Cultural Identity: An Instructional Theory for Teaching About Student Diversity in Public Schools
Pamela Fraser-Abder 251

22. Folk Belief Theory: Accounting for the Persistence of the Achievement Gap
Bruce Torff 259

23. Constructivism: Transforming Knowledge of How People Learn Into Meaningful Instruction
Jacqueline Grennon Brooks 271

24. Defining Teacher Action Research as an Instructional Theory in Teacher Education
Frances O'Connell Rust and Susan Hansen 277

25. Using Authentic Data to Teach Secondary Ecology: A Theory for Teaching the Nature of Science
Yael Wyner 283

26. An Instructional Theory for English Language Learners: The 5R Model for Enhancing Academic Language Development in Inquiry-Based Science
Molly H. Weinburgh and Cecilia Silva 293

SECTION 4: CURRICULUM THEORY—INTRODUCTION
Section Editor: Arthur Shapiro 305

27. A Theory and Practice of Curriculum
Arthur Shapiro 307

28. A Theory and Practice of Constructivist Curriculum
Arthur Shapiro 317

29. Does Practice Itself Know Nothing? Probing Teachers' Felt Experiences of Mandated Practice
Rodney Evans 329

30. School Board Control of the Curriculum: Democracy or Censorship?
Patricia F. First and Patricia A. L. Ehrensal 343

31. Maxwell's Demon: The Curriculum Structure as a Device to Generate Curriculum as a Routine and to Overcome the Evil Forces of Organizational Entropy
Arthur Shapiro 355

SECTION 5: LITERACY AND LANGUAGE ACQUISITION THEORY—INTRODUCTION
Section Editor: Fuhui Tong 367

32. Cross-Language Transfer in Bilingual and Biliteracy Development
Candise Y. Lin and Min Wang 369

33. The Development of Theories of Bilingualism and School Achievement
Colin Baker 385

34. Language and Literacy Acquisition Theories
Kathryn A. Davis, Carlos J. Ovando, and Masahiko Minami 395

35. (Post) Structural Analyses of Two Notions of Academic Language: Discourse, Dialect, and Deficit
J. E. Petrovic 419

36. Toward a Policy-Minded Sociocultural Theory of Student Literacy Learning
Bryant Jensen and Eugene Garcia 429

37. Meaning-Based Approaches to Literacy Education
Pamela Spycher 445

SECTION 6: COUNSELING THEORY—INTRODUCTION
Section Editors: Richard C. Henriksen Jr. and Mary Nichter 457

38. Adlerian Counseling
Richard E. Watts 459

39. Existential Counseling
Richard C. Henriksen, Jr. 473

40. Reality Therapy
Robert E. Wubbolding 481

41. Person-Centered Counseling
Jeffrey M. Sullivan and Hayley Stulmaker 491

42. Family Therapy
Mary Nichter and Rick Bruhn 503

43. Collaborative Learning Communities: A Postmodern Perspective on Teaching and Learning
Harlene Anderson 515

44. Feminist Counseling Theory
Amanda C. La Guardia and Amy T. Banner 529

45. Counseling From a Multiple Heritage Perspective: A Theoretical Framework
Richard C. Henriksen, Jr. 541

SECTION 7: MORAL DEVELOPMENT THEORY—INTRODUCTION
Section Editor: Rebecca A. Robles-Pinã 549

46. A Moral Conflict Development Theory Based on Child and Teacher Interactions: A Cross-Cultural Perspective
Maria Lourdes Majdalani and Rebecca A. Robles-Piña 553

47. Combining Values and Knowledge Education
Jean-Luc Patry, Alfred Weinberger, Sieglinde Weyringer, and Martina Nussbaumer 565

48. Moral Development
Susan Magun-Jackson and John E. Burgette 581

49. Social Cognitive Theory and Practice of Moral Development in Educational Settings
Kelly Rizzo and Sandra Bosacki 595

50. Moral Development and the Phenomenon of Absent Fathers
Angie D. Wilson and Richard C. Henriksen, Jr. 607

51. The Ethic of Care: Theory and Research
Eva E. A. Skoe 615

52. Making a Moral Decision: A Proposition for an Integrated Model of Cognition, Emotion, and Social Interaction
Lily Dyson, Paul Crawford, Sonya Frey, and Sarah Dykstra 629

53. Moral Development Theory: Neo-Kohlbergian Theory
Heather S. Mechler and Stephen J. Thoma 643

54. Playful Activity and Thought as the Medium for Moral Development: Implications for Moral Education
Doris Bergen and Darrel Davis 653

55. The Innocence of Experience Theory: Young Adolescent Encounters and Life-Long Moral Development
David L. Hough 667

SECTION 8: CLASSROOM MANAGEMENT THEORY—INTRODUCTION
Section Editors: Patricia Williams, Sandra Harris, and Vicky Farrow 679

56. Marzano's Evidence-Based Practices in Classroom Management: Four Management Factors for Moving Theory to Practice
Jason R. Mixon 681

57. Freedom Through Control: B. F. Skinner and Classroom Management Theory
Craig Peck 691

58. Control, Choice, and the Fulfillment of Fundamental Human Needs: William Glasser's Humanistic Vision of Individual, Classroom, and Schoolwide Positive Behavioral Support
John A. Cassell and Thomas Nelson 699

59. Beyond Compliance and Control: Creating Caring Classrooms—Alfie Kohn's Alternative to Discipline and Management
Andrea M. Guillaume 715

60. Haim Ginott-Congruent Communication
Peggy H. Yates and Hal Holloman 725

SECTION 9: ASSESSMENT THEORY—INTRODUCTION
Section Editors: Samuel O. Ortiz and Dawn P. Flanagan 735

61. Individual Norm-Referenced Standardized Assessment: Cognitive and Academic
John O. Willis, Ron Dumont, and Alan S. Kaufman 739

62. Luria and Learning: How Neuropsychological Theory Translates Into Educational Practice
Andrea N. Schneider, Daniel J. Parker, Emilie Crevier-Quintin, Hanna A. Kubas, and James B. Hale 751

63. School Neuropsychology Conceptual Model
Daniel C. Miller 761

64. Individual Differences in the Ability to Process Information
W. Joel Schneider and Kevin S. McGrew 767

65. Curriculum-Based Measurement
Mark R. Shinn 783

66. Dynamic Assessment: An Intervention-Based Approach
Carol Robinson-Zañartu 793

SECTION 10: ORGANIZATIONAL THEORY—INTRODUCTION
Section Editor: Fred C. Lunenburg 801

67. Systems Theory
James A. Vornberg 805

68. Complexity Theory
Timothy B. Jones 815

69. Ethical Sensitivity Unfolding in Educational Settings
Lyse Langlois 821

70. Legal Theory and Research
Martha McCarthy 829

71. Other Contemporary Organizational Theories
Fred C. Lunenburg 841

72. Organizational Theory in Light of Constructivist Thinking
Arthur Shapiro and Steve Permuth 855

73. Postmodernism—(The Antitheory)
Fenwick English 871

74. Ways of Knowing Through the Realms of Meaning: A Postmodernist Approach to Teaching Low-Income Students
William Allan Kritsonis 877

SECTION 11: LEADERSHIP AND MANAGEMENT THEORY—INTRODUCTION
Section Editor: Fenwick W. English 887

75. Classical Management Theory
Thu Suong Thi Nguyen and Gary M. Crow 891

76. Trait Theory
Kathleen M. Brown 897

77. Discourse Theories and School Leadership
Autumn K. Cyprés 903

78. Bureaucratic Theory : Myths, Theories, Models, Critiques
Eugenie A. Samier 909

79. Contingency Management and Situational Leadership Theories
JoAnn Danelo Barbour 917

80. Critical Race Theory and Educational Leadership
Floyd D. Beachum 923

81. Rational Choice Theories in Education Administration
Ric Brown and Rosemary Papa 929

82. Democratic Administration
Lisa A. W. Kensler and Jeffrey S. Brooks 935

83. The Aesthetics of Leadership and Administration
Eugenie A. Samier 945

84. Bourdieu's Theory of Misconnaissance or Misrecognition by Educational Leaders
Cheryl L. Bolton ... 953

85. Mentoring Theories for Educational Practitioners
Carol A. Mullen ... 959

86. Who Moved My Theory?: A Kitsch Exploration of Kitsch Leadership Texts
Rosemary Papa, Daniel L. Kain, and Ric Brown ... 969

87. Critical Feminist Theory
Michelle D. Young and Catherine Marshall ... 975

88. The Synergistic Leadership Theory: An Inclusive Theory in the Twenty-First Century
Beverly J. Irby, Genevieve Brown, and LingLing Yang ... 985

SECTION 12: SOCIAL JUSTICE THEORY—INTRODUCTION
Section Editor: Jill Blackmore ... 997

89. Social Justice in Education: A Theoretical Overview
Jill Blackmore ... 1001

90. Education and Social Justice: A Critical Social Theory Perspective
Richard Bates ... 1011

91. Critical Race Theory
Thandeka K. Chapman, Adrienne Dixson, David Gillborn, Gloria Ladson-Billings ... 1019

92. The Work of Nancy Fraser and a Socially Just Education System
Martin Mills ... 1027

93. Theorizing Democratic and Social Justice Education: Conundrum or Impossibility?
Carolyn M. Shields ... 1035

94. Michel Foucault: A Theorist of and for Social Justice in Education
Kari Dehli ... 1047

SECTION 13: TEACHING AND EDUCATION DELIVERY THEORY—INTRODUCTION
Section Editor: Shirley Jackson ... 1057

95. Teaching Through the Lens of Resilience Theory and Black Feminist Theory
Janice L. Taylor ... 1061

96. Teaching for How People Learn Naturally
Geoffrey Caine and Renate N. Caine ... 1071

97. The Reggio Emilia Approach to Early Childhood Education
C. Miki Henderson ... 1081

98. Montessori Philosophy, Education, and Bilingual Education
Linda Rodriguez, Beverly J. Irby, Rafael Lara-Alecio, and Genevieve Brown ... 1085

99. Differentiated Instruction: An Integration of Theory and Practice
Carol Ann Tomlinson and Marcia B. Imbeau ... 1097

100. What Makes Giftedness? A Four-Part Theory for the Development of Creative Productive Giftedness in Young People
Joseph S. Renzulli ... 1119

101. The Four-Dimensional Bilingual Pedagogical Theory
Rafael Lara-Alecio, Beverly J. Irby, and Fuhui Tong ... 1129

About the Editors and Section Editors ... 1139

Preface

Theory explains and predicts phenomena in a field, offers a guide for behavior, and provides structure to the knowledge base in the field. While numerous educational theories are presented in a variety of textbooks and in some discipline-specific handbooks and encyclopedias, no publications exist which offer a comprehensive, consolidated collection of some of the most influential and most frequently quoted and consulted educational theories. Some educational theories are casually addressed in encyclopedic volumes and texts related to content areas; however, such entries are lacking in detail and depth and often are authored by individuals not intimately related to the theories. As a result, many novice researchers, as well as experienced researchers, have a difficult time locating a single source that can aid them in the development of their line of inquiry. Thus, it was fitting that specific educational theories be compiled into a single, easily accessible volume.

Audience

As it is imperative that researchers base their research efforts on sound theory in order to move their investigations forward, most researchers seek appropriate theoretical frameworks to guide their work. The intent of the editors, section editors, and authors in this volume was to provide theories that can inform research perspectives. The primary audience for *The Handbook of Educational Theories* consists of researchers in the social sciences, particularly in education and counseling, including graduate students, university faculty, researchers at federal and state centers and agencies, and scholar-practitioners in school districts.

Scope

While it is virtually impossible to include every theory that might impact education in one volume, this handbook was designed to be as comprehensive in its coverage of educational theory as is possible. Although the scope is broad, some areas have more information than others. For example, more could be shared in terms of critical theory, feminist theory, theory related to minority students, curriculum theory, and higher education theory. Those are volumes to come. There is some overlap in the coverage of sections in this volume; however, this overlap is understandable and demonstrates the interrelatedness of educational theories.

A unique feature of the handbook is the way in which it conveys the theories, and it is initiated with the basis of philosophies which can also serve as the theoretical, conceptual, or philosophical frameworks for research. The organization of the chapters within each section makes the volume an easy-to-use and understandable reference tool as research and practitioners seek theories to guide their research and practice and as they develop theoretical frameworks. In addition to the traditional educational theories presented, the handbook includes theories for the twenty-first century as well as presents practical examples of the use of these theories in research from dissertations and published articles. Chapter authors were asked to describe (a) the specific theory with its goals, assumptions, and aspects particular to that theory; (b) the original development of and iterations of the theory; (c) generalizability of the theory across cultures, ethnicities, and genders; (d) the use and application of the theory; (e) critiques of the theory; (f) two to five particular studies exemplifying particular theories as individuals have used them in the theoretical framework of dissertations and/or published articles; and (g) any instruments associated with the theory.

Structure

Each section editor and author in this handbook took seriously the charge to produce the very best, first, and inclusive educational theory volume for their fellow researchers. Their willingness to respond positively to the invitation to participate by the individual section editors is commendable and noteworthy in light of these noted researchers' and editors' busy schedules. Their insights into their own theories or others' theories contribute to the quality and eminence of this handbook. In this volume, 101 theories are presented by 152 authors and 17 editors distributed among its 13 sections. These authors and editors represent 10 countries, including Argentina, Australia, Austria, Canada, Dubai (An Emirate of the United Arab Emirates), England, Norway, Scotland, the United States (28 states represented), and Wales. The first section, as indicated, is *Philosophical Education* (Section Editor, Dr. Barbara

The Handbook of Educational Theories, pp. xvii–xviii

Thayer-Bacon, University of Tennessee) and is composed of seven chapters; its focus is on what philosophers do and how their work contributes to educational theory. The next section is *Learning Theory* (Section Editor, Dr. Patrick Jenlink, Stephen F. Austin State University); its eight chapters consider the historical as well as contemporary origins of learning while challenging readers to rethink the acquisition of knowledge in contemporary society. Section Three, *Instructional Theory* (Section Editor, Dr. Janice Koch, Hofstra University) consists of seven chapters that represent a fusing of theories fundamental to teaching and learning with emerging instructional theories that rely on prior practices. Section Four, *Curriculum Theory* (Section Editor, Dr. Arthur Shapiro, University of South Florida) begins by acknowledging the difficulties surrounding the nature of theory and its relationship to practice when designing curriculum. Shapiro, in an effort to resolve these difficulties, expounds a social process theory of curriculum. This section's five chapters discuss not only a constructivist theory of curriculum design and delivery, but consider as well the outside influences that can influence curriculum decisions. The fifth section, *Literacy and Language Acquisition Theory* (Section Editor, Dr. Fuhui Tong, Texas A&M University), provides in its six chapters a comprehensive collection of the most consulted theories in language and literacy acquisition applied to meet the needs of linguistically and culturally diverse learners. Section 6, *Counseling Theory* (Section Editors, Drs. Richard Henriksen, Jr. and Mary Nichter, Sam Houston State University), includes eight chapters, divided among historical theories and family theories, as well as emanating theories that address counseling and psychotherapy constructs available to mental health clinicians. Section 7, *Moral Development Theory* (Section Editor, Dr. Rebecca A. Robles-Piña, Sam Houston State University) is comprised of 10 chapters which integrate established theories with the contemporary work of their authors to explain twenty-first century problems. Included with their integration of established theories and contemporary work are assessment instruments and techniques. Section 8, *Classroom Management Theory* (Section Editors: Drs. Patricia Williams, Sam Houston State University; Sandra Harris and Vicky Farrow, Lamar University) includes five chapters featuring the work of Marzano, Skinner, Glasser, Kohn, and Ginott. Believing classroom management is an essential component for effective teaching and learning, the authors in this section discuss the *why* behind the theories. Section 9, *Assessment Theory* (Section Editors: Drs. Dawn Flanagan and Samuel Ortiz, St. John's University) contains nine chapters whose authors discuss the relationship between evaluation and student success. With the current focus on standardized testing to measure student progress, an understanding of theoretical assessment models and their relevance in the education setting is essential to student improvement at every level. Section 10, *Organizational Theory* (Section Editor, Dr. Frederick C. Lunenburg, Sam Houston State University) is composed of eight chapters which set forth a variety of multidisciplinary approaches to organization analysis making fundamental assumptions about the nature and purposes of organizational theory. Section 11, *Leadership and Management Theory* (Section Editor: Dr. Fenwick W. English, University of North Carolina) contains 14 chapters with each one introducing a different study of leadership and management theory and blending science and art in an effort to advance educational administration and leadership. Section 12, *Social Justice Theory* (Section Editor, Dr. Jill Blackmore, Deakin University), includes six chapters to provide a range of epistemological and political perspectives on social justice in a time when educators are called upon to deliver greater equity to a society characterized by cultural diversity, mobility and fluidity. Section 13, *Teaching and Education Delivery Theory* (Section Editor, Dr. Shirley Jackson, Sam Houston State University) is the final section in the handbook. The focus of these seven chapters is to consider not just how individuals learn but how they learn best, addressing the concerns of educators as well as those of a variety of learners with identified special needs.

ACKNOWLEDGMENTS

Finalizing this handbook has taken longer than ever imagined. Despite unexpected pauses along the way created by, for example, personal and professional interruptions, job shifts, and section editor changes, the quality of the authors' and the section editors' work in this volume is unsurpassed.

We wish to thank George Johnson at Information Age Publishing for believing that this was a worthy endeavor for the field and for agreeing to publish such a large volume. We also want to thank each one of the section editors who volunteered their time to assist the authors in their sections and to write for the handbook as well. Their commitment and stature are extremely respected, and their time and expertise have been vital to the accomplishment of this important work. The depth of the authors' knowledge is impressive; their willingness to contribute to this volume in a way that can assist fellow researchers and students at the graduate and undergraduate levels who are interested in furthering research is commendable. This handbook stands as a unification of brilliance through the minds and words of stellar scholars represented herein.

Section 1: Philosophical Education

INTRODUCTION

SECTION EDITOR

Barbara J. Thayer-Bacon

University of Tennessee at Knoxville

When I was approached about the possibility of contributing to this project as the editor for a philosophical section for *The Handbook of Educational Theory,* I initially turned down the invitation due to the suggested categories. Unfortunately, philosophy has been taught to educators for more than half a century often by nonphilosophers who teach philosophy as *isms*, such as *idealism, realism, existentialism, pragmatism, postmodernism.* Students learn these basic categories for their course work, and then immediately forget them as soon as they leave the class. For those of us who have philosophy degrees, we have been scolded by our professors, please do not ever teach philosophy to educators that way! That approach is not a sign of good philosophical work. Presenting philosophy to educators as *isms* oversimplifies the complexity of philosophical positions and reduces the difficulty of the ideas and issues to overgeneralized categories that become meaningless. Philosophers do not usually fit into neat, simple schools of thought and are resistant to being described that way, and their work does not fit into basic categories easily. Or rather, their work can fit into multiple categories, not because the work is soft and mushy and ill defined, but rather because it is complex and crosses multiple boundaries. In fact, even the basic section divisions for this handbook are problematic for us as the work found in this section also could easily be placed in other sections, such as Ken Howe's essay fits nicely under the category of assessment theory, Barbara Applebaum's essay could easily be placed under the section for social justice theory, and Lynda Stone's essay fits well in the section for moral development theory.

When I turned down the invitation to edit this section and expressed my concerns, to my delight, the editors responded by asking me to suggest categories that were more appropriate for philosophers of educational theory. That was an invitation I could not resist. It is rare that philosophers of education have the chance to present ourselves the way we want to be presented, showing the world of education how philosophers do philosophy, rather than having a nonphilosopher describe our work to others. The categories I developed for this section are based on the traditional basic branches of philosophy and the key tools philosophers use to help them do their work. My original categories included: logic and critical thinking; epistemology and education; ethics and moral education; social and political philosophy; aesthetics and education; philosophy of social science and educational research; North American philosophy; and continental philosophy. I made a who's who list of the top philosophers of education currently contributing to these various categories, and explained in my invitation we were going to have a chance to do philosophy in these essays rather than just talk about the field in question. We were going to have the opportunity to show scholars and future scholars in education what philosophers of education do, and how our work is contributing to educational theory. Just as I could not resist such an invitation, neither could my colleagues, although, just like me, they made suggestions to continue to refine our basic subject categories for our section. Social and political philosophy became two separate categories as we decided that description was too broad, with Barbara Applebaum agreeing to write a social philosophical essay and Natasha Levinson agreeing to write a political philosophical essay. Gert Biesta asked if he could write an essay about educational theory itself, which also has turned out to be a good example of continental philosophy. I decided I should write the epistemology and education essay and that we did not need a logic and critical thinking category as well; my essay also represents an example of North American philosophy with

The Handbook of Educational Theories, pp. 1–3

its inclusion of key pragmatist philosophers. We all use logic and critical thinking to do our work, and many of us touch upon issues in regards to logic throughout our various essays. The reader will find in many of the essays the authors question within their separate essays even the basic branches of philosophy as they have been defined traditionally, including myself with epistemology.

I am so excited to introduce a stunning collection of essays written by some of the top scholars currently working in the philosophy of education, many who have been recent presidents of the Philosophy of Education Society, and many of whom are sure to be future presidents of Philosophy of Education Society. We are very grateful for the chance to do the work we love to do the way we think it should be done, and hope readers will agree, letting us shape the section the way we thought it should be was worth the risk our editors took.

Gert Biesta's essay on educational theory is the lead off essay, as he is questioning the basic way we think about educational theory in North America. Biesta is from The Netherlands, where he received his education, and he has taught in higher education in The Netherlands, England, and Scotland, as well as Sweden. He brings a strong continental perspective to our philosophical section and makes reference to numerous continental philosophers within his essay. Biesta claims that the academic study of *education* has developed quite differently in different geographical, national, linguistic, intellectual, and political contexts, and supports his claim by comparing two different constructions of the field of education. First we learn about the historical development of the academic study of education in the English-speaking world, especially the United Kingdom, and then we learn about the way in which the field has developed in the German-speaking context. By making these comparisons, Biesta shows us *that* the field of educational research can be constructed differently, as well as stimulates us to consider whether education can or should be a discipline in its own right or whether it is necessarily dependent upon input from elsewhere. His chapter sheds light on the very idea of educational theory and how we engage with theory in contemporary educational research. His recommendation is that if educational research wants to perform a critical role in relation to educational practice, it is important that it develops forms of theory that are properly *educational.*

My essay, "Epistemology and Education," follows Biesta's as it describes philosophy's basic branches of study as a way of positions *epistemology* within philosophy. I begin by explaining what epistemology is, as it has been defined historically by Euro-Western philosophers such as Plato and Aristotle, then I challenge this definition with the help of other present day philosophers. I am from the United States and my argument relies on North American philosophers predominantly, therefore it is able to serve as an example of current work by someone who is a feminist, pragmatist, and postmodernist in North America. I use the metaphor of casting a net in the ocean of experience, to help us understand the important role epistemology plays in educational research, as the warp of the net (the threads that run lengthwise), along with the weft (the threads that run across from side to side), our ontology, to form the net we use to develop theories about the experience (the fish) we catch up in our nets.

In Lynda Stone and Jennifer Job's essay, "Ethics and Moral Education," they seek to bring broad philosophical treatment of youth and adult ethics into contemporary educational relevance. The authors begin with the story of Phoebe Prince, a 15-year-old Irish immigrant high school student to the United States who committed suicide after several months of bullying triggered by dating and boyfriend issues. The powerful story reveals the students, teachers, and administrators of the school, as well as the parents, were well aware of the bullying Phoebe was experiencing and were unsuccessful at helping her stop the bullying, thus ending in tragedy. The three sections that follow focus on ethics, American moral education, and character education and school discipline. Stone and Job sketch a history of ethics that can be traced back to Plato and Aristotle, forward to more recent examples with Kant's categorical imperative and Mills' utilitarian ethics, before moving into a discussion of the history of moral education in America that leads to the current moral education model in America that is the character education movement. They then challenge major traditions of ethics and moral education with a presentation of Noddings's care theory. Phoebe's story is woven throughout the major theoretical sections and receives responses that attempt to connect ethics in society and especially the ethical lives of youth.

Susan Laird's essay, "Aesthetics and Education," begins by demonstrating the problem that a branch of philosophy known as aesthetics has with being conflated with the field of art and education, which is not merely or even primarily philosophical. Laird shows that the common category mistake of conflating aesthetics and art has more than logical or epistemological significance for educational studies today; it also has ethical and political consequences. Laird argues that aesthetics is often neglected, profoundly devalued, and underdeveloped as a field of philosophical inquiry, and that it merits a far more significant place than it enjoys currently in the scholarship and curriculum of philosophy of education. She describes some of the history of aesthetics as a major field within philosophy, and contrasts aesthetics to art. Some key historical philosophers of aesthetics theories are discussed (Dewey, Schiller,

Wollstonecraft) as well as current philosophers of education (Martin, Greene, Bogdan, Shusterman) who are contributing to a renovated role for aesthetics in educational thought, reminding educators that aesthetic experience is capable of functioning simultaneously as cultural asset and cultural liability.

In her essay "Social Philosophy, Critical Whiteness Studies, and Education," Barbara Applebaum demonstrates how social philosophy, a branch of philosophy that focuses on social issues, contributes to educational theory through the example of its contributions to an emerging field of research, Critical Whiteness Studies. Critical whiteness studies, that examine Whiteness and White privilege, has developed as a result of increased awareness that multicultural approaches to inequality that celebrate difference fail to give attention to the system that constitutes Whiteness as the hidden norm from which "difference" is determined. The starting point of critical Whiteness studies is the recognition that the normativity of Whiteness lies at the center of the problem of racism. Applebaum demonstrates how social philosophy and philosophy of education can contribute to our understanding of White privilege, White ignorance, and denials of complicity. Her focus is on pedagogy, as she shows how this work offers fruitful ways to reconsider how we teach about antiracism.

Natasha Levinson addresses the relationship between education and the state, in her essay titled "Contemporary Political Theory and Education." Political theory furnishes educational philosophers with a philosophical basis and a political framework for ascertaining the reach—and the limits—of the state's obligations for public education in liberal-pluralist democracies, for example. Levinson begins from a position that liberalism is now the predominant theoretical paradigm in the United States and United Kingdom and its influence is growing in Western European philosophical circles. She attributes this revival of liberal theory to the unexpected resurgence of religious fundamentalism in these countries as well as the realization that the values that shape liberal-pluralist democracies cannot be taken for granted. Her essay focuses on the idea of liberalism as a transformative project, what makes the liberal project educational as well as political. How liberals understand the tension between individual conceptions of the good and civic conceptions of the good is the main theme of her essay, as she considers the parameters of political liberalism (Rawls) and educational theorists' responses to Rawls (e.g., Macedo, Feinberg), and civic liberalism.

Ken Howe ends our collection of essays with "Philosophy of Social Science and Educational Research." Howe shows us that issues in the philosophy of social science have underlain disputes regarding the best understanding of and approach to educational research at least as far back as the debates between Dewey and Thorndike. His focus is on the more recent scene, in which the "paradigm wars" of the 1970s-1980s and the clamor for "scientifically-based" educational research that emerged in the past decade drew significant attention to several interlocking issues of concern to the philosophy of social science: about epistemology, appropriate research methods, conceptions of causation, the unity of science, and the place of values and politics in educational research. Howe sketches for us the paradigm wars, and what those debates entailed philosophically, and then moves to the current decade and the clamor for scientifically based educational research, to show us the current debate is the paradigm wars redux. He argues that just as we have seen a repeat of the paradigm wars at the level of philosophy of social science, we might very well see a repeat of parallel developments at the level of educational research practice. Howe predicts that the new methodology orthodox that attempts to regiment educational researchers in terms of a positivist-experimentalist framework will likely fail to produce results, and when this happens there will once again be impetus to rethink what constitutes *useful* educational research in much broader and more inclusive terms. He sees signs for this rethinking in the intensified efforts of mixed-methods within educational research.

I am already making copies of these essays and sharing them with my students and colleagues, to help them understand what philosophy in general and philosophers of education in particular have to contribute to education in general, and educational theory in particular. I predict others will want to do the same, and share these wonderful essays that are written in such as way that they will make sense to educational researchers from diverse fields of study.

Author Contact Information: Barbara J. Thayer-Bacon, PhD, University of Tennessee, 1126 Volunteer Blvd., 420 Claxton Bldg., Knoxville, Tennessee 37996-3456. Phone: 865-974-9505. Fax: 865-974-8301. E-mail: bthayer@utk.edu

CHAPTER 1

On the Idea of Educational Theory

Gert J. J. Biesta
University of Stirling—Scotland, UK

There can be no doubt that theory plays an important role in educational research and educational practice. But when we ask what kind of role theory plays or is supposed to play and also when we ask what kind of theory we actually need in the field of education, things become more complicated. One reason for this stems from the fact that the "field" of educational research is not one and the same across the world. The academic study of education has actually developed quite differently in different geographical, national, linguistic, intellectual and political contexts. In this chapter I compare two different "constructions" of the field: the way in which the study of education has been conceived in the English speaking world and the way in which the field has developed in the German speaking context. My reason for comparing these two "constructions" of the field is to show *that* the field of educational research can be constructed differently. The comparison also provides important insights into the question whether education can or should be a discipline in its own right or whether it necessarily is dependent upon input from elsewhere. Questions about the nature of distinctively educational forms of theory and theorizing play an important role in this discussion. My chapter is therefore also meant to shed light on the very idea of educational theory. While the discussion in this chapter may perhaps appeal most to those who are interested in the history of the field, I hope to be able to show that there are important lessons to be learned for how we engage with theory in contemporary educational research.

THE THEORY QUESTION IN EDUCATION AND THE EDUCATION QUESTION IN THEORY

Many would characterize educational research as the scientific study of educational processes and practices, both as they occur in designated institutions such as schools, colleges or universities, and as they happen in less formal settings such as the workplace or the community. Most of those working in the field of educational research would opt for a rather broad interpretation of what "scientific" stands for, thus encompassing a wide range of methods, methodologies and methodological or "paradigmatic" orientations (Biesta, 2010a). Theory plays an important role in this work and again many would highlight the large number of different theories and theoretical orientations that are being used in the conduct of educational research.

A common view in the English speaking world[1] is that the theoretical resources for educational research stem from a number of disciplines—most notably psychology, sociology, philosophy and history—thus giving rise to such subfields as the psychology, the sociology, the philosophy and the history of education (for a recent discussion see Lawn & Furlong 2009; for an earlier account see Tibble, 1966c). Although over the years other disciplines and approaches have joined the conversation—such as anthropology, economics, cultural studies and feminist theory—and although the relative influence of different disciplines on the study of education has fluctuated over time (McCulloch, 2002), the particular construction of the field of educational research as the inter- or multidisciplinary study of education has remained relatively constant. This has been supported by the social organization of the field, particularly through the existence of national and international societies and journals devoted to the contribution of particular disciplines to the study of education.

When we look at the role of theory in educational research from this angle it is not surprising to find a wide spectrum of theories with a wide range of different disciplinary *roots*. This makes any exploration of the

The Handbook of Educational Theories, pp. 5–15

role of theory in educational research exciting but also complex, as it has to navigate different and potentially conflicting disciplinary perspectives and agendas while at the same time having to keep an eye on how this theoretical multiplicity relates to and matters for education. Any attempt to explore the role of theory in educational research therefore not only needs to engage with the question how theories from a range of different disciplines pertain to the study of education—an angle to which we might refer as *the theory question in education*—but also needs to focus on what it means for particular theories to be used or applied within the context of educational research—an angle to which we might refer as *the education question in theory and theorizing*. One important aspect of the latter question is whether educational research *necessarily* has to rely on theoretical input from (other) disciplines or whether there are or ought to be distinctively *educational* forms of theory and theorizing. This, in turn, raises the question whether education can and should claim to be an academic discipline in its own right or whether it should be understood as an applied field of study, just like, for example business studies or sport studies.

While the idea of education as an academic discipline in its own right and with its own forms of theory and theorizing may be rather alien to the English speaking world, it is an important element of the way in which the academic study of education has developed in other settings, particularly under the influence of ideas and approaches developed in German speaking countries (Benner, 2005; Horn, 2003). The influence of this construction of the field has not only impacted on European countries such as Poland, Finland, or the Netherlands, but has also influenced developments in countries such as Japan, Korea and South Africa. To look at the role of theory in educational research through these different angles—that is, through the lens of two different constructions of the field—cannot only help to get a better sense of the different roles that theory can play, but also makes it possible to explore the case for distinctively *educational* forms of theorizing. In this chapter I wish to make a contribution to this.

The chapter is organized in the following way. I start with some brief observations about the idea of theory and discuss the different roles theory can play in research. I then focus on the question of the theoretical *resources* for educational research. I do this through a discussion of two different constructions of the field, one in which it is argued that the these resources necessarily have to come from (other) disciplines, and one in which the case is made that education is a discipline in its own right with its own forms of theory and theorizing. Based on this comparison I present, in the final step, a case for the idea of educational theory as a form of theory that is different from theories that have their origin in other disciplines.

THE ROLES AND FUNCTIONS OF THEORY

Although the word theory is easily used, it is actually quite difficult to identify what it refers to, not in the least because the meaning of the word has shifted significantly over time. If we go back to the Greek origins of the word—which, of course, always raises the further question where the Greeks got their words from—theory had to do with spectatorship: being a spectator of a performance or a festival, including religious festivals, being an official envoy to a festival, consulting an oracle, or making a journey in order to study something. Here the meaning of theory is firmly located within the domain of the empirical as it is about direct experience and witnessing. With Plato and Aristotle, however, theory became connected to the domain of the *non*empirical, that is, of Platonic forms and Aristotelian universals. Theory became knowledge of a permanent and unchangeable reality *behind* the empirical world of change, flux and appearances.

The distinction between empirical and theoretical knowledge gained further prominence with the raise of the worldview of modern science in which the main role of theory became that of the *explanation* of causal connections between empirical phenomena. The need for theory had to do with the insight that while correlations between phenomena can be perceived, underlying causal connections can not. Theory was therefore needed to account for or speculate about underlying processes and mechanisms. Here theory transformed into what Gaston Bachelard (1986, p. 38) has called "a science of the hidden." With the rise of hermeneutics and interpretivism in the late nineteenth century, theory also become a device for *understanding*, that is, for making intelligible *why* people say what they say and do what they do. The role of theory here is that of deepening and broadening everyday interpretations and experiences—something captured in Anthony Giddens's idea of double hermeneutics (Giddens, 1975). The primary interest of *critical* theory, developed by the philosophers of the Frankfurt School working in a tradition going back to Marx, lied in exposing how hidden power structures influence and distort such experiences and interpretations. The ambition here was that the exposure of the workings of power can contribute to *emancipation* (Biesta, 2010b; Carr & Kemmis, 1986).

Whereas from one angle there is a clear difference between the role of theory in research that aims at explanation, at understanding or at emancipation, what unites these approaches is that they all deploy theory in order to bring what is strange and not understood into the domain of understanding. This bigger gesture of making the strange familiar has been characterized as a typical modern conception of what research can and should achieve. Here research is depicted as a process that can help us to get better and deeper insights into the natural and social world. Research can, however, also operate in the opposite direction, that is with an ambition to make what is familiar strange. Such a more postmodern view has, for example, been espoused by Michel Foucault in his idea of *eventalization* (1991, p. 76). Foucault argues for an approach which aims at a "breach of self-evidence" by making visible "a singularity at places where there is a temptation to invoke a historical constant, an immediate anthropological trait, or an obviousness which imposes itself uniformly on all" (p. 76). Eventalization works "by constructing around the singular event … a polygon or rather a polyhedron of intelligibility, the number of whose faces is not given in advance and can never properly be taken as finite" (p. 77).

Eventalization thus requires that we complicate and pluralize our understanding of events, their elements, their relations and their domains of reference (Foucault, 1991). While eventalization does not generate the kind of insights that may lead to advice or guidelines for action, it is not without practical effect as it can bring about a situation in which people "'no longer know what they do,' so that the acts, gestures, discourses which up until then had seemed to go without saying become problematic" (p. 84). This is a situation in which people are spurred into thinking again about what they are doing and what they might do.

Such a practical effect can not only result from work that has its origin in empirical data, but can also stem from more autonomous forms of theorizing that aim at what, with Richard Rorty (1989), we might refer to as the *redescription* of educational processes and practices. Calling them redescriptions is to highlight the fact that educational processes and practices are always already described in some way by those involved in them. In this mode theoretical work can provide different and alternative descriptions of educational processes and practices. Theory can, for example, redescribe a classroom in terms of information processing, in terms of legitimate peripheral participation or in terms of the reproduction of class and gender inequalities. Theory can redescribe learning as a process of empowerment or a process of control. Theory can redescribe education as knowledge-transfer or as a concern for newness coming into the world. Although such redescriptions can function as hypotheses and therefore as starting points for empirical work, they do not necessarily or exclusively have to be understood as claims to truth. They can also be seen as possible interpretations of what might be the case—interpretations that can inform teachers' perceptions, judgments and actions by opening up possibilities for seeing things in new and different ways.[2]

With regard to the role of theory in empirical research there is a strong emphasis on the ways in which theory can be used for the analysis and interpretation of empirical data. Theory does indeed play a crucial role in making the shift from data to understanding (here used in the broad sense of the word). But this not only comes in after data have been collected, but also plays an important role in the initial phases of research. Two aspects are important here. First of all theory is indispensable for the *conceptualization of the phenomenon* one wishes to investigate. While a researcher may wish to study learning, it is only after one has engaged with the question how one wishes to conceptualize learning—for example, as information processing, as behavioral change, as acquisition, as participation, as social practice—that one can make decisions about *what* the phenomena are one should focus on and *how* one might go about in doing so (the question of design, methodology and methods). Some researchers, more often those working at the interpretative end of the spectrum, object to bringing in theory at the initial stages of research as they feel it would bias the research findings and would blind researchers from seeing potentially relevant aspects that fall outside of one's theoretical frame. While it is of course always important to be open in research, this particular objection fails to see that the world never appears unconceptualized, so that *not* to engage with conceptualization at all runs the risk of uncritically accepting existing definitions and conceptions of the object under investigation. Also, to conceptualize learning as, for example, participation in no way defines what one will find through empirical investigation, which means that theory's role in conceptualization never replaces empirical work.

The second way in which theory plays a role at the start rather than the end of research has to do with the *construction of the object* of research and the wider object of interest. As an educational researcher, one might say that the object of research and the wider object of interest is education—and this is probably the answer that most educational researchers would give if one were to ask them how to describe their work. But even if one were to agree that the object of research is to be found in schools—and many would question whether education can actually *only* be found in schools—there is still the difficult question what it actually is that happens within a building with the word "school" on it that would count as education. Is it about teachers talking? (And what would one already need to know when walking into the building to be able to identify some of the people there as teachers?) Or is it about teachers talking and students listening? Or is it about teachers talking, students listening and learning from such talk? Would punishment be part of education? And what about the hidden curriculum that, by definition, is not visible? Questions like these suggest that even the issue of what the object of investigation and interest of educational researchers and of education as an academic field or discipline is, requires further reflection in which theory also has a role to play (although, as I will argue below, it is not in all cases just a matter of theory).

These observations are in no way meant to serve as a history of theory (on the complexities of such a task see Hunter, 2005) or, even less, as an encompassing "theory of theory," but they can help to shed light on the different functions theory can perform in the conduct of empirical research. I now wish to focus more explicitly on the kind of theoretical resources that play a role in *educational* research. I will do this through a discussion of two different understandings or constructions of the field of educational research, one that has its roots in the English speaking world and one that has its roots in the German speaking world. This comparison not only helps us to get a sense of different views about the theoretical resources for educational research, but also provides insights in different views about what educational theory is or might be, and reveals different answers to the question of the object of educational research.

CONSTRUCTING THE FIELD (1): EDUCATIONAL STUDIES

As mentioned above, the idea that the study of education cannot proceed without contributions from a number of other disciplines has been a dominant idea in the way in which the academic study of education has developed in the English speaking world. In order to understand aspects of the history of this approach, some of the reasons given for it, and some of its social and sociological dimensions I will, in this section, focus on one particular articulation of this view which can be found in a book published in 1966 in Britain under the editorship of J.W. Tibble called *The Study of Education* (Tibble, 1966a). As McCulloch (2002, p. 106) has argued, this book is "probably the best known published work of the period to promote a disciplinary approach to educational studies." His reconstruction of the development of the field shows that the particular conception of educational studies presented in this book can be found in almost identical form in a number of key publications preceding and following the publication of Tibble's (1966a) book. Tibble's book is indeed a *paradigm case* of the construction of the field of educational studies as an interdisciplinary field based on theoretical input from four contributing disciplines: philosophy, history, psychology and sociology (Tibble, 1966b, p. vii) or fundamental (Hirst, 1966, p. 57). The book is also interesting because it provides an explicit rationale for this particular construction and for a particular notion of educational theory, arguing that the principles of educational theory "stand or fall entirely on the validity of the knowledge contributed by [the fundamental disciplines]" (Hirst, 1996, p. 50). This book is also interesting because it was intended as a deliberate intervention in the field of educational studies in the United Kingdom in order to give the field more structure and status (McCulloch, 2002).

The Development of the Study of Education

In Tibble's (1966c) own contribution to the book, a chapter called "The development of the study of education," Tibble locates the academic study of education firmly within the context of "the professional preparation of teachers" (p. 1). Although the connection with teacher education provides the study of education with an institutional context and a clear raison d'être, he emphasizes that because of the historically peripheral status of teacher education within the university—the main institutional setting for teacher education being nonuniversity colleges of education—the development of education "as a subject of study in its own right" has been limited (p. viii). This has not only impacted on the options for developing "close links between the study of education and the basic disciplines which contribute to it" (p. viii) but has also severely restricted the opportunities for doing higher degrees in education which, in turn, is a major cause of "a very serious shortage of adequately qualified lecturers in education" (p. 2). The weak identity and social structure of the field does not mean that education has not been studied at all, and the main part of Tibble's chapter is devoted to the development of the study of education in Britain "over the 120 years since the training of teachers was inaugurated in this country" (p. 3).

The picture that emerges from this is one where, until the first decades of the twentieth century, teacher education was mainly practice based—Tibble specifically mentions that so-called "pupil teacher system developed in Holland" (Tibble, 1966c, p. 3)—which some saw as a good thing and others not. While Andrew Bell early in the nineteenth century would argue that it is "by attending the school, seeing what is going on there, and taking a share in the office of tuition, that teachers are to be formed, and not by lectures and abstract instructions" (as cited in Tibble 1966c, p.4). C.H. Judd (1914) in his *The Training of Teachers in England, Scotland and Germany,* laments "the relative neglect of education theory" in teacher education, writing that "one is tempted to say that the teachers in English training colleges have not realized the possibility of dealing in a scientific way with the practical problems of school organization and the practical problems which come up in the conduct of recitations" (as cited in Tibble 1966c, p. 5). Tibble notes, however, that around the turn of the century some more theoretical strands were beginning to creep into "the embryonic study of education" (p. 6). These were the study of method, of the history of education and, increasingly, of educational psychology, a field which became more firmly established as a subject of study in the 1920s (p. 10), albeit that a first edition of the *Teacher's Handbook of Psychology* had already appeared in 1886 (p. 8).

The Herbartian theory of learning "with its 'scientific' prescription for the organization of the lesson" is listed as "a dominant influence" during this period (Tibble, 1966c, p. 9), also because of the influence of *The Herbartian Psychology Applied to Education*, published in 1897 by John Adams, first principal of the London Day Training College (Tibble, 1966c, p. 11). Another influential book was Percy Nunn's *Education, its Data and First Principles* (first published in 1920, with a second edition in 1930 and a third in 1945) which heavily relied on William McDougall's "hormic" psychology (Tibble, 1966c, pp. 11-12). There was also an emerging interest in child study, partly as a result of the rise of progressive education and further developed through the work of Jean Piaget, whose work became available in English translation in 1926. Psychology remained an important pillar of teacher education during this period (see Tibble, 1966c, pp. 12-19).

The second main strand Tibble identifies in the development of the study of education is that of the history of education, which includes comparative education and the study of great educators (Tibble, 1966c). Tibble documents a substantial amount of activity in this field from the late nineteenth century onwards, both in terms of book publications and with regard to the inclusion of history of education in the curriculum of teacher education programs. Nonetheless, "under the intense pressure of the 2-year course [for teacher education; GB], and with the main emphasis on educational psychology … historical studies were relatively meager" within the programs of teacher education colleges (p. 21).

From a more contemporary perspective it is also interesting to read Tibble's point that the sociology and philosophy of education "barely come within the scope of a historical survey" because their history is "too recent" (Tibble, 1966c, p. 21). This is not too suggest that no attention has been paid within teacher education curricula and programs to social and philosophical questions, but Tibble's reconstruction gives the impression that the development of sociology and philosophy of education as separate fields of study has only been of a recent date; a point confirmed by McCulloch (2002). Even so, Tibble does mention the presence of works by philosophers such as Dewey, Whitehead, Russell, Campagnac and Nunn on the booklists of department and college courses.

Three things stand out in Tibble's account. One is the fact that the context for the study of education is *teacher education*. This suggests that the field of education is mainly understood in terms of schooling and school education—which, as I will argue below, is significantly different from the location of the construction of the field in the German speaking world. Second, Tibble provides a number of reasons why the institutional reproduction of the study of education has been relatively weak, most notably the absence of education as an undergraduate subject in university programs. Third, Tibble's reconstruction is strongly framed in terms of four contributing disciplines. Of these, psychology seems to have had the strongest hold on the education of teachers, with history at a distance in second place. At the time of writing—the early 1960s—philosophy and sociology were only emerging as contributing disciplines for the study of education.

Educational Theory and the Disciplines

While Tibble provides a historical and, to a certain extent, sociological account of the development of the study of education, Paul Hirst (1966) takes a more systematic approach in that he aims to provide a rationale for a particular configuration of the study of education. Hirst does this under the heading of "educational theory" arguing that such questions as "What is educational theory, as a theoretical pursuit, trying to achieve? How does this theory relate to educational practice? What kind of theoretical structure has it got and how in fact do the various elements that are obviously a part of it fit in it?" have received "far too little sustained attention" (Hirst, 1966, p. 30). Hirst argues that, as a result, "educational studies have tended to become either a series of unrelated or even competing theoretical pursuits, or a confused discussion of educational problems where philosophical, psychological, sociological or historical and other issues jostle against one another, none being adequately dealt with" (p. 30), thus echoing Richard Peters' characterization of the field as an "undifferentiated mush" (Peters, 1963, p. 273). This is why Hirst aims to move toward "a more adequate framework within which research and teaching in this area can develop" (p. 30).

Hirst (1966) puts forward a very specific and very precise notion of educational theory. Starting from O'Connor's (1957) distinction between theory as "a set or system of rules or a collection of precepts which guide or control actions of various kinds" and theory as "a single hypothesis or a logically interconnected set of hypotheses that have been confirmed by observation" (Hirst, 1966, p. 38) he, unlike O'Connor, opts for the former rather than the latter as the most appropriate notion of theory for education. "Educational theory is in the first place to be understood as the essential background to rational educational practice not as a limited would-be scientific pursuit" (Hirst, 1966, p. 40). The reason for this has to do with his view about the function of theory in practical activities. Whereas "in the case of the empirical sciences, a theory is a body of statements that have been subjected to empirical tests and which express our understanding of certain aspects of the physical world," in the case of "a practical activity like education" theory "is not the end product of the pursuit, but rather it is constructed to determine and guide the activity" (p. 40). Hirst thus makes a distinction between educational theory in a narrow and a wider sense. The first concerns "the body of scientific knowledge on which rational educational judgments rest" while the second refers to "the whole enterprise of building a body of rational principles for educational practice" (p. 41).

Hirst (1966) is not arguing that one of these notions of theory is the correct one but that we neither should reduce educational theory to the former conception, nor that we should conflate the two types of theory. Hirst also believes that it is "on the development of the theory in its larger sense that educational practice depends, not simply on the development of scientific study" (p. 41). Educational theory in the wider sense is therefore "not concerned simply with producing explanations on the scientific model *but with forming rationally justified principles for what ought to be done in an area of practical activity* [emphasis added]" (p. 42). This is why the difference between scientific theory and educational theory is not a difference of degree or scale but expresses a *logical* difference between judgments about "what is the case" and "what ought to be the case" (p. 42)—or, to be more precise, about "what ought to be done in educational activities" (p. 53). This is why Hirst suggests that there is "a great deal to be said for characterizing these theories under moral knowledge" because he sees it as a fundamental task of theory to make "value judgments about what exactly is to be aimed at in education" (p. 52), not in a general sense but at a practical level and in *here-and-now* terms.

Hirst (1966) thus articulates a conception of educational theory as a form of practical theory the purpose of which is *not* the generation of scientific truth but the development of "rationally justified principles" for educational action. In this conception educational theory thus *mediates* between the contributions of "[philosophy], history, social theory, psychological theory and so on" (p. 33) and educational practice. This view has several important implications. One is that educational theory is not simply derivative of factual knowledge because factual knowledge in itself can never provide a sufficient justification for what ought to be done. In this sense the resources of educational theory are composite in that they consist of reasons for educational principles that are "of an empirical, philosophical, moral or other logical kind" (p. 51). This also means that educational theory is *not* "in the last analysis philosophical in character" (p. 30) because philosophy in itself cannot provide all that is needed to generate and justify principles for educational action. It can only provide one sort of reasons to inform such principles. The most important point for the discussion in this chapter, however, follows from Hirst's claim that the validity of the principles for educational action "turns on nothing 'educational' beyond these [reasons]" (p. 51). For Hirst the reasons that inform educational principles must be judged solely according to the standards of the particular disciplines from which they stem. "The psychological reasons must be shown to stand to the strict canons of that science. Equally the historical, philosophical or other truths that are appealed to must be judged according tot the criteria of the relevant discipline in each case" (p. 51). This lies at the very heart of Hirst's claim that educational theory is not and cannot be "an autonomous discipline" (p. 51) as it does not generate "some unique form of understanding about education" in addition to what is generated through the fundamental disciplines (p. 57). The principles of educational theory "stand or fall entirely on the validity of the knowledge contributed by ... [the fundamental disciplines]" (p. 50). Hirst summarizes his views by arguing, on the one hand, that educational theory "is not itself an autonomous form of knowledge or an autonomous discipline. It involves no conceptual structure unique in its logical features and no unique tests for validity," while on the other hand, educational principles "are justified entirely by direct appeal to knowledge from a variety of forms, scientific, philosophical, historical, etc. Beyond these forms of knowledge, it requires no theoretical synthesis" (p. 55).

Hirst's conception of educational theory thus provides a strong rationale for the construction of the field of educational studies prominent in the English speaking world, not only because he denies any autonomous disciplinary status to educational theory but also—and for this reason—because he locates all the "rigorous work" within the fundamental disciplines "according to their own critical canons" (Hirst, 1966, p. 55). He thus necessarily makes the study of education into the *interdisciplinary* study of the phenomenon of education to which educational theory itself has no cognitive contribution to make which, in turn, is the reason for it lacking a disciplinary status *among* other disciplines. Tibble (1971), in a book called *An Introduction to the Study of Education* summarizes this point of view in the following way.

> It is clear that "education" is a field subject, not a basic discipline; there is no distinctively "educational" way of thinking; in studying education one is using psychological or historical or sociological or philosophical ways of thinking to throw light on some problem in the field of human learning. (p. 16)

When from here we turn our attention to the development of the field in the German speaking world, a significantly different picture emerges.

CONSTRUCTING THE FIELD (2): PÄDAGOGIK

Whereas in the English language the word education suggests a certain conceptual unity, the German language has (at least) two different words—*Erziehung* and *Bildung*—and (at least) two different concepts to refer to the study of *Erziehung* and *Bildung*, namely *Pädagogik* and *Didaktik*. Although *Erziehung* and *Bildung* are not entirely separate concepts, they do represent different aspects of and approaches to educational processes and practices. As my aim in this chapter is to give a sense of different conceptions of educational theory in relation to different constructions of the field, I will focus, in what follows, only on the notions of *Erziehung* and *Pädagogik*.[3] For reasons that will become clear below, I have chosen not to translate these and other key terms.

The Idea of Erziehung

The concept of *Erziehung* became used as a noun in the German language from the Reformation onwards Oelkers (2001). With Luther, *Erziehung* came to refer to influences that in some way impact on the soul of the human being in order to bring about a virtuous personality, initially understood in terms of Christian virtues but later expanded so as to include secular virtues as well (p. 31). Although this is a central idea in the conceptual history of the notion of *Erziehung*, Oelkers emphasizes that the word *Erziehung* does not refer to one single reality. It can, for example, be used in relation to processes, institutions, situations or aims (p. 24), and can be characterized as dialogue or action, as communication, influence or development, as process or product, as restriction or expansion of possibilities, and so on (p. 33). What unites different usages of the word *Erziehung* is the idea that certain influences bring about certain effects—although there is a wide range of different views about the extent to which the effects that are supposed to be brought about by *Erziehung* can be contained and controlled. This is why Oelkers suggests that *Erziehung* always entails a certain hope or expectation about its efficacy, despite the fact that *Erziehung* often fails to achieve what it sets out to achieve (p. 32; Oelkers, 1993).

Within the plurality of views about the meaning, content and scope of *Erziehung*, Oelkers identifies three common characteristics of theories of Erziehung (Oelkers, 2001, p. 255). The first is that all theories of *Erziehung* focus on morality; the second is that they refer to interactions between human beings (*Personen erziehen andere Personen*—persons educate other persons); and the third is that *Erziehung* has to do with asymmetrical relationships, most notably between adults and children. In relation to this Oelkers argues that all theories of *Erziehung* therefore include the following three aspects: a definition of the *aims* of *Erziehung*, an account of the *process* of *Erziehung*, and a conception of the *object* of *Erziehung* (p. 263).

This brief account already reveals an important difference with the approach discussed above, in that here educational theorizing does not start from other disciplines and their perspective on education, but starts from a definition of what *Erziehung* is and is about, so that theoretical work needs to engage with the question of the object, the process and also the aims of *Erziehung*, thus combining descriptive and normative elements within educational theorizing.

Groothoff (1973) provides a similar definition of *Erziehung* as encompassing on the one hand any help toward the process of becoming a human being (*Menschwerdung*), and on the other hand any help toward becoming part of the life of society (p. 73). Whereas on this account *Erziehung* partly appears as a function of society, Groothoff emphasizes that in contemporary society *Erziehung* cannot be confined to an adaptation to the existing sociocultural order, but also needs to anticipate the independence of the thought and action of the ones being educated. It must include, in other words, an orientation toward maturity—or, with the much more specific German term which resonates with the English notion of autonomy, it must anticipate the *Mündigkeit* of the ones being educated.

Against this background—which Groothoff characterizes as a conception of *Erziehung* that has its roots in the Enlightenment (Biesta, 2006)—Groothoff argues that a theory of *Erziehung* needs to encompass the following elements: (1) a theory of becoming a human being; (2) a theory of interpersonal interaction; (3) a theory of emancipatory learning; (4) a theory of contemporary social life and its perspectives on the future; (5) a theory of the ends and means of education and their interrelationships; and (6) an account of the specific ends and means in the context of the different domains and institutions of *Erziehung* (Groothoff, 1973, p. 74). Groothoff argues that such a theory can be found in the work of Friedrich Schleiermacher and, to a lesser extent, that of Wilhelm Dilthey (p. 74). Groothoff, writing in 1973, no longer believes that such an encompassing theory of education is possible in our time, not only because the field of *Erziehung* has become much more complex, but also because society has lost its certainty about itself. Groothoff therefore presents the field of *Pädagogik* as a more fragmented field where individual theorists work on aspects of educational theorizing, rather than that they all engage with the development of an all-encompassing theory of *Erziehung*.

Padagogik as an Academic Discipline

An important question for the discussion in this chapter concerns the disciplinary status or identity of *Pädagogik*. What is important in this regard is that *Erziehung* is understood as a teleological process—a process with a particular *telos* or aim—and as a value-laden process—a process that is aimed at bringing about something that is considered to be desirable. Questions about the right way to educate, both in terms of the means and the ends of education, are therefore of central concern. In this reconstruction of the field König (1975) argues that questions about the right way to education, both in terms of the right ends and the right means, were not only the central concern for the practice of education but, at least up to the beginning of the twentieth century, were also the central questions for the scientific study of education, where *scientific* needs to be understood in the broad Continental sense of *Wissenschaft*, encompassing the sciences and the humanities. The theorists of *Erziehung* thus explicitly conceived of *Pädagogik* as a *normative* discipline as they saw it as their task to formulate aims for education and develop guidelines for educational practice (König, 1975, p. 34). In the initial stages of the development of the discipline, the ambition was to articulate ultimate educational aims that were considered to have universal validity. König's discussion of the different attempts to articulate such aims, for example, based on theological thinking such as Scheler's and Hartmann's philosophy of value, Herbart's moral conventions, or practical philosophy, all indicate that as a normative discipline *Pädagogik* was not confined to the simple formulation of educational aims but also engaged with its justification, and aimed to do so in a scientific manner.

This normative conception of *Pädagogik* is often seen as the first phase in the development of the discipline—and some would even characterize it as a prephase rather than as belonging to the establishment of the discipline itself. The idea that *Pädagogik* only came to maturity as a scientific discipline once it had overcome the traditional normative approach, was particularly promoted by a tradition which became known as *geisteswissenschaftliche Pädagogik* (sometimes translated as hermeneutic educational theory). The idea of *Pädagogik* as a *Geisteswissenschaft* (sometimes translated as human science or also moral science) was initiated by Wilhelm Dilthey, who argued that there was a fundamental distinction between the study of natural phenomena and the study of social and historical phenomena. While the world of natural phenomena is a world of cause and effect which for that reason is amenable to *explanation*, the sociohistorical world is a world in which human beings pursue aims and plan actions in order to achieve these aims. The main objective of the study of the sociohistorical world should therefore be to *clarify* the aims people pursue. This is not a question of explanation but requires *understanding*. Moreover, such understanding cannot be generated through observation from the outside but rather needs interpretation and an insider perspective. As education is a sociohistorical phenomenon, *Pädagogik* thus had to be conceived as a *Geisteswissenschaft*, and the main task of such a *geisteswissenschaftliche Pädagogik* became that of the *interpretation* of educational practices and the clarification of the normative orientations within such practices.

Against this background it is not too difficult to understand that Dilthey's design for a *geisteswissenschaftliche Pädagogik* entailed a rejection of normative *Pädagogik*—or to be more precise: it entailed a rejection of the ambition of normative *Pädagogik* to articulate *universal* or *external* educational aims. For Dilthey the aims of education are always relative to and internal to particular sociohistorical configurations. This means, however, that for Dilthey *Pädagogik* remained a normative discipline, but one with a hermeneutical structure, aiming at the *clarification* of the aims and ends implicit in particular settings. Dilthey's ideas provided the main frame of reference for the development of *geisteswissenschaftliche Pädagogik* in Germany in the first decades of the twentieth century, which became the main paradigm for academic work in education. It maintained its central position well into the 1960s (Wulf, 1978, p. 15), and still plays a role today (Benner, 2005; Oelkers, 2001).

Although the theorists of *geisteswissenschaftliche Pädagogik* rejected the idea of universal educational aims, they did see *Pädagogik* as a normative discipline, one aimed at the development of ideas about *right* ways to act in particular educational settings and situations. The normativity of *geisteswissenschaftliche Pädagogik* was closely connected to something which is perhaps one of the most interesting aspects of *geisteswissenschaftliche Pädagogik*, which is the idea of the *autonomy*—or, as it was phrased by the theorists of *geisteswissenschaftliche Pädagogik*, the *relative* autonomy—of education and of *Pädagogik* as the science of and for education.

The idea of the relative autonomy of *Pädagogik* first of all had to do with the intention to liberate *Pädagogik* from its dependence on ethics and psychology so as to be able to establish *Pädagogik* as a scientific discipline in its own right (Wulf, 1978, p. 35). To do so, the theorists of *geisteswissenschaftliche Pädagogik* connected the relative autonomy of *Pädagogik* to the relative autonomy of educational practice. The key idea here was that *Pädagogik* had a role to play in protecting the domain of education—and through this the domain of childhood more generally—from external influences from societal powers such the church, the state or the economy (Wulf, 1978, pp. 17, 35). The autonomy of *Pädagogik* as an academic discipline was thus articulated in terms of a particular educational *interest* which the theorists of *geisteswissenschaftliche Pädagogik* understood as an interest in the right of the child to a certain degree of *self-determination* (Wulf, 1978, p. 36).

Objects, Interests and the Case for Educational Theory

The foregoing comparison reveals some interesting differences between the ways in which the field of education has developed in the English speaking and in the German speaking world. Whereas in the English speaking world educational studies is conceived as an interdisciplinary field that focuses on the study of education through the application of theoretical frameworks from a number of disciplines, the key ambition of those working in the German speaking context was to establish *Pädagogik* as a discipline in its own right. Whereas someone like Hirst explicitly denied that education can be an academic discipline—his main argument being that educational theory can not generate any unique understanding about education but relies entirely on the knowledge generated through the disciplines—the theorists of *geisteswissenschaftliche Pädagogik* made a strong case for the autonomy of their discipline. Interestingly enough they did not argue for the disciplinary autonomy of *Pädagogik* on the basis of a particular object of study but instead they did so in terms of a particular *interest*, namely an interest in the right of the child to self-determination or, with a set of broader concepts, an interest in autonomy and freedom. Whereas the identity of educational studies can therefore be characterized as *objective* in that it is based on a particular object of study, the identity of *Pädagogik* might best be characterized as normative or *interested*, in that it is based on a particular interest in education—and in the case of *geisteswissenschaftliche Pädagogik* this interest is articulated as an interest in emancipation and freedom.

It is important to note that the idea that the identity of a discipline is based on a normative interest rather than an object of investigation is not unique for *Pädagogik*. One could argue that the identity of a field like medicine is also based on a particular interest, in this case an interest in health. It is also important to note that both with regard to *Pädagogik* and with regard to medicine, the interest that constitutes the discipline allows for different interpretations—and that part of the theoretical work going on within such disciplines is precisely focused on questions about the interpretation of the central interest of the discipline. This is why questions about freedom and autonomy remain a central aspect of contemporary discussions in education.

The reason why this constitutes a case for the idea of educational theory as a form of theorizing that is different from and cannot be reduced to the theoretical resources from other disciplines has to do with the fact that other disciplines have their own objects and interests that do not necessarily or automatically coincide with interests that are educational. To put simply: whereas psychology ask psychological questions about education, and sociology asks sociological question, and while philosophy asks philosophical questions about education and history historical questions, we need the perspective from education—and thus forms of educational theory—in order to generate *educational* questions about education, that is questions that articulate an educational interest, that is an interest in what education is *for*. While sociology, psychology, history and philosophy may all have something to contribute to, for example, the study of autonomy, it is only once autonomy has been identified as an educational interest and concern that it becomes possible to ask what other disciplines may have to contribute to its understanding.

This means that one important function of educational theory lies in what I have referred to as the construction of the object of research and more generally the object of educational interest. It is, after all, only if one would argue that education should always have an orientation toward the autonomy of those being educated that it becomes possible to identify certain processes and practices occurring within schools as *educational* processes and practices and thus as processes and practices. It is only then that such processes can become an object of investigation for educational research. The contribution of educational theory does not stop with the identification of potential objects for investigation but also plays an important role in processes of *conceptualization*. Where one educational theory might, for example, understand autonomy as a cognitive phenomenon having to do with the ability to argue in a logical and critical manner, another educational theory might see autonomy as fundamentally ethical and having to do with relationships of care and responsibility. While, in terms of the vocabulary introduced in this chapter, educational theory therefore starts on the autonomous end of the spectrum of theory and theorizing, such forms of theory and theorizing clearly feed back into empirical research. This means that although questions of definition—the question as what education 'is' or, preferably, how we might understand and articulate the educational dimension of education—are an important part of educational theory and theorizing, they are not the only form of what distinctively educational forms of theory and theorizing look like.

Conclusion

Whereas other disciplines definitely have important things to offer to the study of education, the conclusion of this chapter must be that in themselves such disciplines are not able to generate *educational* perspectives, *educational* ways of seeing, *educational* concerns, and *educational* ways of questioning. For this, as I have tried to argue in this chapter, we need *educational* theory. When this is overlooked in the ways in which we engage with theory in educational research, there is a real danger that such research will simply accept existing ideas of what education is or should be and is unable to expose such ideas and investigate them in a critical manner. If educational research wants to perform a critical role in relation to educational practice it is, therefore, of the utmost importance that it develops forms of theory and theorizing that are properly *educational*. In this chapter I have tried to articulate what such forms of theory and theorizing might look like and why we need them.

NOTES

1. I use this phrase as a very rough indication of a particular geographical area and loose intellectual network.
2. For more on the interconnections between theory, knowledge, judgement, and action see Biesta and Burbules (2003) and Biesta (2007, 2009, 2010c).
3. The literature on *Bildung* is vast. For a comprehensive introduction I recommend Hopmann (2007).

REFERENCES

Adams, J. (1897). *The Herbartian psychology applied to education: Being a series of essays applying the psychology of Johann Friedrich Herbart.* Lexington, MA: D. C. Heath & Co.

Bachelard, G. (1986). *Le rationalisme appliqué* [Applied rationalism]. Paris, France: Presses Universitaires de France. (Original work published 1949)

Benner, D. (2005). *Allgemeine Pädagogik* [General theory of education] Weinheim, Germany: Juventa.

Biesta, G. J. J. (2007). Why 'what works' won't work. Evidence-based practice and the democratic deficit of educational research. *Educational Theory, 57*(1), 1-22.

Biesta, G. J. J. (2006). *Beyond learning: Democratic education for a human future.* Boulder, CO: Paradigm.

Biesta, G. J. J. (2009). Values and ideals in teachers' professional judgement. In S. Gewirtz, P. Mahony, I. Hextall, & A. Cribb (Eds.), *Changing teacher professionalism* (pp. 184-193). London, England: Routledge.

Biesta, G. J. J. (2010a). Pragmatism and the philosophical foundations of mixed methods research. In A. Tashakkori & C. Teddlie (Eds.), SAGE *handbook of mixed methods in social and behavioral research* (2nd ed., pp. 95-118). Thousand Oaks, CA: SAGE.

Biesta, G. J. J. (2010b). A new 'logic' of emancipation: The methodology of Jacques Rancière. *Educational Theory 60*(1), 39-59.

Biesta, G. J. J. (2010c). Why 'what works' still won't work. From evidence-based education to value-based education. *Studies in Philosophy and Education 29*(5), 491-503.

Biesta, G. J. J., & Burbules, N. (2003). *Pragmatism and educational research.* Lanham, MD: Rowman & Littlefield.

Carr, W., & Kemis, S. (1986). *Becoming critical.* London, England: Routledge.

Foucault. M. (1991). Questions of method. In G. Burchell, C. Gordon, & P. Miller (Eds.), *The Foucault effect: Studies in governmentality* (pp. 73-86). Chicago, IL: The University of Chicago Press.

Giddens, A. (1975). *New rules of sociological method.* London, England: Hutchinson.

Groothoff, H. -H. (1973). Theorie der Erziehung [Theory of education] In H. -H. Groothoff (Ed.), *Pädagogik (Fischer Lexikon)* [Education: Fischer Dictionary] (pp. 72-79). Frankfurt am Main, Germany: Fischer Taschenbuch Verlag.

Hirst, P. H. (1966). Educational theory. In J. W. Tibble (Ed.), *The study of education* (pp. 29-58). London, England: Routledge and Kegan Paul.

Hopmann, S. (2007). Restrained teaching: The common core of Didaktik. *European Educational Research Journal 6*(2), 109-124.

Horn, K.-P. (2003). *Erziehungswissenschaft in Deutschland im 20. Jahrhundert. Zur Entwicklung der sozialen und fachlichen Struktur der Disziplin von der Erstinstitutionalisierung bis zur Expansion* [The study of education in Germany in the 20th century. On the development of the social and academic structure of the discipline from its original inception until its expansion]. Bad Heilbrunn, Germany: Klinkhardt.

Hunter, I. (2005). The history of theory. *Critical Inquiry, 33*, 78-112.

König, E. (1975). *Theorie der Erziehungswissenschaft. Band 1.* [Theory of the science of education. Vol. 1.] München, Germany: Wilhelm Fink Verlag.

Lawn, M., & Furlong, J. (2009). The disciplines of education in the UK: Between the ghost and the shadow. *Oxford Review of Education, 35*(5), 541-552.

McCulloch, G. (2002). Disciplines contributing to education? Educational studies and the disciplines. *British Journal of Educational Studies, 50*(1), 100-110.

Nunn, P. (1920). *Education, its data and first principles.* London, England: E. Arnold.

O'Connor, D. J. (1957). *An introduction to the philosophy of education.* London, England: Routledge and Kegan Paul.

Oelkers, J. (1993). Intention and development: Two basic paradigms of education. *Studies in Philosophy and Education 13*(2), 91-109.

Oelkers, J. (2001). *Einführung in die Theorie der Erziehung* [Introduction into the theory of education]. Weinheim & Basel, Germany: Beltz.

Peters, R. S. (1963). Education as initiation. In P. Gordon (Ed.), *The study of education* (Vol. 1, pp. 273-299). London, England: Woburn.

Rorty, R. (1989). *Contingency, irony, and solidarity.* Cambridge, MA: Cambridge University Press.

Tibble, J. W. (Ed.). (1966a). *The study of education.* London, England: Routledge and Kegan Paul.

Tibble, J. W. (Ed.). (1966b), Introduction. In *The study of education* (pp. vii-x). London, England: Routledge and Kegan Paul.

Tibble, J. W. (Ed.). (1966c). The development of the study of education. In *The study of education* (pp. 1-28). London, England: Routledge and Kegan Paul.

Tibble, J. W. (Ed.). (1971). *An introduction to the study of education.* London, England: Routledge and Kegan Paul.

Wulf, C. (1978). *Theorien und Konzepte der Erziehungswissenschaft* [Theories and concepts of the science of education]. München, Germany: Juventa.

Author Contact Information: Gert J. J. Biesta, PhD, School of Education, University of Stirling, Stirling, FK9 4LA, Scotland, UK. Phone: 44-1786-466136. Fax: 44-1786-466131. E-mail: gert.biesta@stir.ac.uk. Website: www.gertbiesta.com

CHAPTER 2

Epistemology and Education

Barbara J. Thayer-Bacon
University of Tennessee at Knoxville

As a philosopher and former elementary teacher who teaches in a college of education and works mainly with teachers and future teachers, as well as future professors in education, I am always in the role of translator, trying to translate abstract philosophical language and ideas into terms that make sense to students who do not have a strong background in philosophy. I can count on my two hands the number of students I have had in the past 20 years who had degrees in philosophy. This does not mean my students are not philosophers, for I think they are, and I seek to help them see themselves as philosophers too. It just means they have not been formally trained in the field of study. I do not want my students to be intimidated by philosophy, at the same time, I do not want to oversimplify or gloss over complex philosophical concepts. *Epistemology* is one of those concepts that students think is too abstract. In fact, it is just a fancy term that means "theories about knowledge." All educators have to be concerned with knowledge, with questions such as: what counts as knowledge (how to judge truth from fiction), how to measure knowledge (how to determine if a student knows something), and what to teach—what to leave in and what to leave out (how to decide what the curriculum should be). All researchers have to be concerned with knowledge as well, with questions such as: what counts as evidence in research problems, what criteria should we use to judge the quality of someone's reported results, and how do we avoid harmful biases in our judgments? My favorite story I tell students to help ease their concerns and make the topic more approachable is about the time that I had a student who thought I was saying "episiotomy" when I said "epistemology." As the mother of four children, I think of that misunderstanding every time I use the word now!

I tell my students, philosophy is the place where you can envision *how things should be* in education; what is the *best* way to offer schooling to children, for example, without any concern for resources and other limitations that we normally face on a daily basis as teachers. Philosophy is the place where we can argue for what the ideal classroom size should be, or what is the best way to try to measure what students have learned if we are trying to be fair and just. Here is the place where one can dream and make the case for what should necessarily be so, in order to have a fair, just, beautiful, truthful, and good educational system. Philosophers are poets, prophets, and soothsayers (Dewey, 1960; Rorty, 1989). Philosophy offers us ideals to strive for in our daily classroom practice. It gives us a guide that will help us in our daily decision making. And, it offers us ways to be able to critique what exists in education. While scientists wrestle with trying to figure out how things are, based on empirical evidence, and religious leaders make religious arguments based on faith, philosophers make arguments based on the use of logical reasoning, or what we call today "critical thinking." Elsewhere I have argued that philosophers use more than just reason to help us make our arguments, that we use our intuition, emotions, and imagination as well as our reasoning to help us (Thayer-Bacon, 2000). Still, for our purposes here, I think this distinction between philosophy, religion, and science will help readers make sense of the branch in philosophy known as epistemology.

Philosophers have historically divided their field of study into various branches, based on the kinds of questions they ask. In general, philosophers have tried to make the case for what is true, good, just, and beautiful for all of us, across time and place. Philosophical questions about virtue and goodness are the focus in the branch of philosophy known as ethics. Questions about what is beautiful represent the branch of aesthetics. Questions about essential, basic categories that we use to make sense of our world are metaphysical (a

The Handbook of Educational Theories, pp. 17–27

synonymous term is ontology), and questions about truth and knowledge are epistemological concerns.

Epistemological theories are theories about how it is we know what we know. It is important to draw attention to the use of the term *"knowledge"* because philosophers do not mean that knowledge is the same thing as what we *learn* yet these two terms are often treated as if they were synonymous. In philosophy, knowledge has historically been defined as that which is absolutely True, whereas what we learn can turn out to be false. We can believe that something is true, and even have good reasons to believe that something is true, but only things that are in fact True (in an absolute sense) do we get to count as knowledge. If we are not sure that something is True, we call it a *belief* instead of *knowledge*. There are different categories of beliefs, which depend on how close the beliefs are to being declared Knowledge, which is *True belief. Mere beliefs*, or right opinions, are stated as "S believes that p," with "S" symbolizing the subject of the belief, and "p" signifying the object of the belief. *Rational beliefs* are beliefs that are supported by compelling reasons ("S has good reason to believe that p"). We only call "p" Knowledge if what S believes about p, and S has compelling reasons to believe about p, is really True ("S knows that p"). It is similar to how in science scientists develop hypotheses and test them out, and even arrive at solutions, but very few scientific results become scientific laws. Knowledge, as it has been historically defined in philosophy, is that which is True for all times. Epistemologists, in their efforts to determine what counts as knowledge, look at questions about the *justification* of people's beliefs and they concern themselves with the normative status of knowledge claims. They attempt to *verify* claims that are made, and to prove the *validity* of arguments. Epistemologists attempt to establish the criteria and standards necessary to prove validity and truth. Epistemologists are concerned with what *warrants* the knowledge claims we make, therefore they ask normative questions such as what counts as good evidence, not causal questions concerning how beliefs are developed.

Let me give some examples of famous epistemological theories that philosophers have developed over time (from Thayer-Bacon, 1998, Chapter 2). Plato and Aristotle (Cahn, 1970), Plato's student, offer us examples of two different theories of knowledge that have had a tremendous impact on Euro-Western philosophy. The roots of more recent continental *and* North American epistemological theories can be traced back to Plato and Aristotle. Plato's theory, as presented in the *Meno*, is that we know "that p" because our souls are immortal and therefore know all knowledge. Knowing is an act of remembering what our souls already know. For Plato, knowledge is an Ideal, beyond the grasp of the world we experience as reality. It does not matter that each of us experiences the world in a different way; because our immortal souls inhabit our mortal bodies, we forget what we already know and become blind to what is true. We cannot trust our senses and be sure we really know what it is we are experiencing. We must tune in to what our souls know, due to their immortality. Only by tuning in to the knowledge our soul already possesses can we hope to eventually realize the truth of what we experience. Others, such as teachers, may act like midwives and help guide the soul on its journey, but ultimately each soul must find the answers by itself. Finding the answers, realizing the Ideals, is to have knowledge of what is True, according to Plato.

Aristotle argues, in disagreement with his teacher, that it is not enough to recollect Truth, thus relying on thought as reality and the origin of knowledge. Aristotle suggests that we must test out our ideas with our experiences to be sure they are true, thus asserting that material things are the reality, and the origin of knowledge. If our ideas correspond to our experiences then we can conclude they are True. Aristotle's correspondence theory follows a path that leads us to present day science and the scientific method. Following a similar vein as Plato, Descartes argues that what we know is what is beyond doubt. By using Descartes' doubting method to dismiss everything we can doubt, until we come to what we take to be self-evident, we can find Truth. Peirce follows Aristotle's path into the future, arguing that we will not know Truth until the end of time. Truth is something that we are getting closer to as we continue to test out our ideas with our experiences, but none of us can be guaranteed of certain knowledge in our own lifetimes. Thus, we find today that while epistemologists still strive for clarity and coherence, most have rejected certainty as a condition of knowledge, following Peirce's lead.

Foundational epistemologists seek to establish that we can ultimately justify our claims by relying on "foundational" beliefs that are justified, but not in terms of other beliefs. Coherentists seek to establish that claims fit coherently into the existing body of knowledge. Some describe foundationalists as embracing a pyramid model, and coherentists as embracing a raft model. The pyramid model attempts to establish basic "foundational" beliefs (undisputed Truths) and builds upon these. The raft model allows that specific truths may change over time, as we change in our understanding, so that individual logs on the raft may need repair or replacement, yet the raft continues to hold us and support us down the river of Truth.

Now that I have explained what *epistemology* is, as it has been defined historically by philosophers, I must move to challenging this definition of epistemology, for current philosophers, myself included, are bringing serious criticisms to bear on epistemological theories of the past. When I use the term "epistemology" in its traditional sense, I will capitalize it (Epistemology) so as to emphasize it relies on an assumption of absolute Truth. When I use it in a pragmatist, feminist, and postmodernist sense with an assumption of pluralistic truths I will write it so: (e)pistemology.

Casting Our Nets Into the Ocean of Experience

In past efforts to explain and explore epistemological theories I have used different metaphors to help me. In *Philosophy Applied to Education* (Thayer-Bacon, 1998), I turned to a famous poem from grade school, "The Blind Men and the Elephant," and described us, knowers, as the blind men, and the elephant as the world we are trying to understand. In *Transforming Critical Thinking* (Thayer-Bacon, 2000), I used the metaphor of a quilting bee to describe us, knowers, as quilters, and the knowledge we construct as the quilts. In *Relational "(e)pistemologies"* (Thayer-Bacon, 2003), I used the concept, *relations*, and turned to examples of: personal, social, w/holistic, ecological, and scientific relations to help me re/describe *(e)pistemology*. In the earlier work (1998) as well as the later work (2003) a shared metaphor is referred to that I would like to develop further here to see if it helps our understanding (Bateson, 1972; James, 1909/1977). Imagine that the world we experience is like a giant, endless ocean. We create fishing nets to cast into this ocean and catch up out of it what we can then research, study, and try to understand. Our fishing nets are woven from our epistemological and ontological theories. They determine what we will catch up in our nets, then name, and assign meaning to. No matter what net we create for our use, there will always be more in the ocean of experience then we can possibly catch up, more then our language can describe. When we cast our nets water will spill through (as well as microbes, seaweed, shells, small fish, et cetera, depending on how tightly woven each net is) and fish will spill out over the top of our nets, and back into the water. Our theories can never catch up all that is in this vast ocean, and language, our concepts, can never name all that is in the limitless ocean of experience. Also, it is very important to notice that the theories of knowing (epistemology) and being (ontology) we develop to help us "capture" this oceanic world influence what we catch up in our nets.

As a naturalist, Gregory Bateson (1972) effectively described the problem this way:

> In the natural world of living human being, ontology and epistemology cannot be separated. [One's] (commonly unconscious) beliefs about what sort of world it is will determine how [one] sees it and acts with it, and [one's] way of perceiving and acting will determine [one's] beliefs about its nature. The living [human] is thus bound within a net of epistemological and ontological premises which—regardless of ultimate truth or falsity—become partially self-validating for [her or him]. (p. 314)

Notice that even in this quote I have had to change Bateson's language so that it is gender neutral, for when he wrote, it was common practice to use the term "man" as if it were a universal concept that represented all human beings. Since then, feminists have critiqued this practice and shown that the net of assumed universality used to catch up and describe all experience was actually catching up males' experiences of the world and representing them as everyone's experiences, instead of as just males'. After this problem was brought to our attention, what we were losing out of our nets, we have created new nets that catch up women's experiences and include them in descriptions of human experiences. We continue to refine our nets and create new ones that include race, class, and sexual orientation as well as other descriptors such as ethnicity, religious orientation, and able-bodiedness, for example.

There are some key metaphysical assumptions embedded in traditional philosophy's definition of Epistemology, no matter which particular theory one embraces, that present day philosophers are showing to be problematic and dangerous. These assumptions are based on several dualisms, which we have already come across in my above description in the Introduction. We found out already that philosophy distinguishes itself from science, for example, based on the separation of theory from practice, and universality from particularity. Remember, I said that philosophy tries to answer general questions that apply to all of us across time and place, and science tries to answer causal questions about what exists, in its particularity. Philosophy has to do with theory, science with practice. Philosophy has to do with the general; science has to do with the particular. We also found out that Epistemology defines itself by drawing a sharp distinction between relative (individual) belief and absolute (universal) Truth. Epistemology has to do with absolute, universal Truth, and science has to do with hypotheses that are always being further tested. Third, when I described epistemologists as talking about knowers and the known (subjects/objects, S and p), this definition assumes a separation between S and p, knowers and what is known. Philosophy cares about the known, Truth, and speaks very little about the knowers. Philosophy assumes knowers are autonomous individuals who seem to sprout out of the ground as mature adults, already able to think for themselves. It is very rare for philosophers to even discuss children. Philosophy has been willing to let psychology worry about knowers as subjects/objects of inquiry.

Epistemologists believed that they could find what is True for all times and all people. That belief has now been shown to be one with tremendous power that looks like it is a neutral, harmless assumption, but is not. It has the power to determine who is heard and who is not, who is considered knowledgeable and who is not, who gets published or hired and who does not, who is judged to be a good teacher and who is not. It has been shown that the criteria and standards we use to judge what is true are fallible, and subject to change. They are not neutral and objective, but are based on particular values and beliefs, and we need to be able to continually critique and readjust our criteria and standards as we become more aware of our biases. We have learned that we cannot separate people's influences from their work, the questions they ask, and the theories they develop. Whatever theory a philosopher offers has their fingerprints all over it. We have learned that philosophers cannot jump out of their skins and rid themselves of their own perspectives. They do not have what feminists refer to as "a God's eye view" of Truth (Haraway, 1988; Harding, 1993). Instead they are embedded within their own setting and time, they are contextual beings, and they have their own unique experiences of the world, due to their own embodiment. They experience the world through their own eyes, ears, mouth, and skin.

For example, Aristotle's arguments for how things should be depended on what he called "natural causes" and these "natural causes" were based on how things were in Ancient Greece at the time of his writings. Ancient Greece was an elitist, racist, and sexist society where only Greek citizens (property owning males) were allowed to be educated and live the contemplative life, while noncitizens (women and slaves) did the laundry, cooking, and cleaning for those men. While Aristotle took this life to be the norm on which to base his philosophy, today we can critique it as not being a just or good model of how society should be. Rousseau made his arguments for what is natural based on his disdain for French society at the time of his writings, and his desire to be independent of that corrupt society. However, his education for Emile to help him develop into a self-made man was also dependent on an education for Sophie to learn how to be a homemaker who would take care of Emile's every domestic need, so that he could be an independent, free man. Today we can easily see the contradiction such a philosophy assumes, an independence for man that is based on the complete dedicated assistance of another, his wife, but it was not that long ago that a feminist philosopher brought Rousseau's contradiction to our attention and recovered the work of previous feminist philosophers in the process (Martin, 1985).

Feminists

Feminists have successfully made the case for philosophy's androcentrism (male-centric point of view) as well as Epistemology's androcentrism (Belenky, Clinchy, Goldberger, & Tarule, 1986; de Beauvoir, 1952/1989; Gilligan, 1982; Martin, 1994; Ruddick, 1989). A significant example of androcentrism in philosophy is demonstrated by the association of philosophy with the mind, which is linked to males, in contrast to the body, which is connected to females. Although Descartes usually gets blamed for splitting the mind from the body in Euro-Western philosophy (Bordo, 1987; Rorty, 1979), I (Thayer-Bacon, 2000) argue that we can go back to ancient Greece and find many examples of Plato severing the mind from the body, and assigning the body to a lesser status. A most vivid example of Plato's separation and assigned value can be found in his theory of knowledge. As we have already discovered, Plato describes each of us as having an immortal soul that knows all, and we forget what we know when our soul inhabits our body at birth. Thus, our bodies cause us to forget all knowledge, and we are doomed to spending our lifetimes trying to remember what we already knew.

Once the body is split from the mind, and given a lesser status as that which serves as a barrier, deceives us, and lures us away from seeking Truth due to its earthly passions; then, it is an easy next step to associate women with the body. Simone de Beauvoir (1952/1989) carefully makes the argument that there are only two things that distinguish women from men when we look at cultures around the world and throughout time, and yet these two things have been used to assign women an inferior, Other, status in many cultures. Given the inferior status of the body, it is not surprising to find that these two things that distinguish women from men have to do with women's physical bodies, that they have weaker muscles and they menstruate. de Beauvoir points toward the future when technology will help women compensate for their weaker muscles, and birth control will bring their reproductive systems within their control. When that day comes, de Beauvoir predicted that women may finally be given an equal status. That day that de Beauvoir predicted is here for many women, still women have not yet reached an equal status. Neutralizing bodily differences is not enough to change women's status; the status of the body must be raised, and it must be reconnected to the mind. Feminists realize now that in order to help put an end to the androcentrism in philosophy, we must call into question the body/mind split, and make the case for a holistic *bodymind*. That argument comes from many diverse camps.

Another good place to look for androcentrism in Epistemology is with the "subject," "S" in "S knows that p" statements. The subject, the knower, and the epistemic agent, are all quite objective, neutral terms that could represent anyone, so it seems. In fact, not only is the knower represented with neutral terminology, the importance and weight of considering "S's" contribution to "that p" is minimalized, thus devaluing the importance of "S" even more. Historically, Epistemology has been based on an assumption that subjects (S) do not need to be taken into consideration in determining "that p." As Epistemology has historically developed, the subject, S, has been severed from "that p" and the attention of epistemologists has been focused on "that p," at the expense of "S." Euro-Western Philosophy concerns itself with the product of knowers' efforts. Knowers are separated from what is known, and devalued in importance.

Lorraine Code (1987) argues that not taking subjects into account leads us to the following traditional Epistemological conclusions:

> (1) that knowledge properly so-called is autonomous in that it is of no epistemological significance whose it is; (2) that knowledge acquisition may be of psychological interest, but it is irrelevant to an epistemologist's quest for criteria of justification, validity, and verification; and (3) that knowledge is objective in the sense that discussion of the character and epistemic circumstances of subjects has nothing to contribute to the proper epistemological task of assessing the product. (pp. 25-26)

If we can ignore knowers in our quest for knowledge, then we can ignore questions such as how do we come to be knowledgeable, and for what purpose is such knowledge? We can ignore questions that draw our attention to the context of knowing, show the connection of knowledge with values, and point to issues of power. We can ignore gender, class, ethnicity, and race as categories of concern, for example. If we diminish the importance of subjects, then we can pretend to offer a neutral, general theory of knowledge, when what we really offer is an androcentric Epistemology. The androcentrism is visible in the objectification and neutralization of the subject.

Lorraine Code's work has contributed to a feminist effort to bring the subject, "S," more directly into discussions of epistemology. In *Epistemic Responsibility* (1987) her focus is on making the case that there are moral implications to knowledge claims, and that we need to understand how directly connected morality is to epistemology. In "Taking Subjectivity into Account," Code (1993) again takes up the topic of looking at "S" of "S knows that p" statements. Here she makes the case these statements are representative of a "received" knowledge model that is very narrow and limited in scoop. By "received" knowledge, she means "conditions that hold for any knower, regardless of her or his identity, interests, and circumstances (i.e., her or his subjectivity)" (p. 15). This dominant Enlightenment Epistemological theory relies on Ideals of objectivity and value neutrality to argue that Reason allows "S" to transcend particularity and contingency. Thus "S" is supposed to represent anyone and everyone (no one in particular). Code wants to seriously entertain a model of "constructed" knowledge, that

> requires epistemologists to pay as much attention to the nature and situation—the location—of *S* as they commonly pay to the content of *p*; ... [she maintains] that a constructivist reorientation requires epistemologists to take subjective factors—factors that pertain to the circumstances of the subject, *S*—centrally into account in evaluative and justificatory procedures. (p. 20)

Thus, gender, race, class, ethnicity become recognized as primary analytic categories as we move to take subjectivity into account.

Code (1993) makes the case that subjectivity is always there, hidden, despite disclaimers, and that we can always find the context that is being suppressed. Subjectivity is found in the examples selected for discussion, and the experiences used to represent "human thought," for example. Code argues that "taking subjectivity into account does not *entail* abandoning objectivity" (p. 36). What it does is help us guard against reductivism and rigidity. It allows us to accommodate change, by letting knowledge claims be provisional and approximate. Code describes herself as a "mitigated relativist," who argues that epistemology has no ultimate foundation, "but neither does it float free, because it is grounded in experiences and practices, in the efficacy of dialogic negotiation and of action" (p. 39). This is similar to my (Thayer-Bacon, 2003) *qualified relativist* position (*Relational "(e)pistemologies,"* Chapter 2).

PRAGMATISTS

Along with Epistemology's embracing of an absolutism/relativism dualism that values transcendental Truth instead of contingent truths, a mind/body dualism that values the mind at the expense of the body, and a subject/object dualism that separates knowers from what is known and assigns higher value to the objects of knowledge, we also find that Epistemology has historically embraced a theory/practice dualism. Epistemologists are supposed to be concerned with the judging of reasons and reasons (theories, ideas) are usually described as being in contrast to experiences (practice). Thus we find some philosophers argue that we cannot trust our experiences and must tune into our ideas (like Plato, Idealists), while others describe our experiences as our source of knowledge (like Aristotle, Empiricists). Overall, ideas have held a higher status in the Euro-Western world, as being more abstract, objective, and general than experience, which is judged to be more immediate, subjective, and concrete. Both types of argument still embrace a theory/practice dualism, favoring one side or the other. When treated as separate, contrasting entities then philosophers can ignore their transactional qualities, and again attempt to avoid issues concerning context, values, and power.

The classical pragmatists Peirce, James, and Dewey, contributed significantly to the collapse of the theory/practice categorical bifurcation. A place to look for classical pragmatism's contribution is in the two key concepts of *fallibilism* and *experience*. These two concepts form the epistemological and metaphysical netting that catches up the classic pragmatists philosophical ideas. Here I want to focus on Dewey's contributions to the dispersion of the theory/practice dualism through his development of the concept *experience*, which was significantly influenced by James' (1890/1950, 1907/1975, 1912/1976) writings on "experience.' Even though Dewey did not focus his discussions on power issues, the way current feminists and postmodernists do, his discussion of *the* philosophical fallacy of neglecting context moved us to a better understanding of philosophy's own limitations due to its own embeddedness. His discussion on context is also a way into understanding his concept of "experience."

In "Context and Thought," Dewey (1960) looks at language to demonstrate how words and sentences are saturated with context. He shows how the meaning of words and sentences are dependent on "the contextual situation in which they appear and are used" (p. 90). Dewey defines *context* as including background (which is both temporal and spatial) and selective interest. Contextual background is what we take for granted, which is tacitly understood, as we draw our attention to that which we are immediately thinking of, through our selective interest. Contextual background is like our nets we use to cast into the ocean and the fish we catch in that net are what draws our immediate attention.

> Surrounding, bathing, saturating, the things of which we are explicitly aware is some inclusive situation which does not enter into the direct material of reflection. It does not come into question; it is taken for granted with respect to the particular question that is occupying the field of thinking. Since it does not come into question, it is stable, settled. (p. 99)

Of course, background context can come into question, in fact that is one of the main contributions philosophers can make, helping to disturb what we take to be given, and causing us to bring an aspect of our background context to our selective interest (to look at what is in our nets). "Philosophy is criticism; criticism of the influential beliefs that underlie culture" (Dewey, 1960, p. 107). Dewey argues that while we can learn to question our background context, we can never completely escape our background context, anymore than we can step outside of our own skins in order to see them from an outsider perspective. We can only get partial glimpses of what all is falling out of our net.

Selective interest is the bias or attitude that exists for each of us in every particular thought we have. This attitude is what determines the questions we choose to ask and the way we choose to go about answering our questions. This bias is what causes us to notice certain qualities and not others, and to attend to certain experiences and not others. Selective interest is what we have discussed above in the feminist paragraphs as the "subjective." Dewey (1960) explains how interest is equivalent to individuality or uniqueness, when framed in modest terms, and it is genius and originality when framed in magnified terms. "Selective interest is a unique manner of entering into interaction with other things. It is not a part or constituent of subject matter; but as a manner of action it selects subject matter and leaves a qualitative impress upon it" (p. 102). The opposite of subjective is not objective, but rather the merely repetitive.

Dewey (1960) points out several different fallacies "that tend to haunt philosophizing" (p. 96). These fallacies are examples of ways that philosophers commit the fallacy of ignoring context, what Dewey sometimes calls "apart thought." In philosophical analysis, philosophers commit the analytic fallacy when they ignore "the context in which and for the sake of which the analysis occurs" (p. 93). The fallacy of unlimited extension or universalization occurs when philosophers try to move beyond the limiting conditions that set up a contextual situation to a single and coherent whole. "All statements about the universe as a whole, reality as an unconditioned unity, involve the same fallacy" (p. 95). Dewey warns us: "There exists at any period a body of beliefs and of institutions and practices allied to them. In these beliefs there are implicit broad interpretations of life and the world. These interpretations have consequences, often profoundly important" (p. 106).

Dewey (1960) tells us the significant business of philosophy is the disclosure of the context of beliefs, and he names *experience* "the last inclusive context. ... The significance of "experience" for philosophic method is, after all, but the acknowledgment of the indispensability of context in thinking when that recognition is carried to its full term" (p. 108). Dewey revealed his pragmatic leanings, which he called instrumental leanings, with his concept of experience for Dewey's logic of experience is one that argues meaning is "primarily a property of behavior" (Dewey, 1925/1981a, p. 141). Dewey adopted from Peirce his notion of meaning, that our conceptions are analyzed in terms of the consequences of our action. According to Peirce (1958), we cannot separate our ideas from our experiences. "A belief is that upon which a man is prepared to act" ("The Fixation of Belief," p. 91). Peirce argues that we determine how clear our concepts are by running them through a functional test, grounding them to experience. Thus, meaning is defined in terms of its effects.

Dewey's understanding of philosophy's own limitations due to its own embeddedness caused him to recommend the need to turn away from Epistemology because of its assumption of absolutism and neglect of context. He recommended we turn toward a theory of inquiry, which is best presented in his book *Logic: The Theory of Inquiry* (1938/1955). In *Logic*, Dewey points out that logic, as a branch of philosophy, is embedded in a context of philosophical assumptions. He argues that logic is a naturalistic theory and a social discipline (biological and cultural influences), that logic is a progressive discipline that involves a circular process. It is inquiry into inquiry. He argues that "all logical forms (with their characteristic properties) arise within the operation of inquiry and are concerned with control of inquiry so that it may yield warranted assertions" (pp. 3-4). Inquiry is due to doubts—when doubts are removed, inquiry ends. For Dewey, knowledge is "that which satisfactorily terminates inquiry" (p. 8). He tells us that he has no problem with the term "knowledge" if we mean by knowledge, the end of inquiry. That is a tautology, a truism. But if we take knowledge to have a meaning of its own *apart from inquiry*, then inquiry becomes subordinated to this meaning. This renders logic "subservient to metaphysical and epistemological preconditions" (p. 8). Dewey rejected *a priori* principles for logic that determine the character of inquiry. The conditions for logic are to be determined in inquiry. In other words, Dewey presented a contextual theory of logic as inquiry. His *Logic* is an account of what takes place in inquiry; he says he was "undertaking an inquiry into the facts of inquiry" (Dewey, 1960, p. 135). Logic is the method of intelligent behavior.

For Dewey (1960), "the unsettled, indecisive character of the situation with which inquiry is compelled to deal affects all of the subject matters that enter into all inquiry" (p. 136). The subject matters of the problem and the solution are both in question "since both are equally implicated in doubt and inquiry" (p. 137). Dewey perceived this as his original contribution in his theory of inquiry, his bringing the *problem* into question and declaring the problem belongs "in the context of the conduct of inquiry and not in either the traditional ontological or the traditional epistemological context," (p. 138). Dewey described, late in his life, how he used an historical approach to help elucidate his original contribution. In other words, he tried to give a larger, historical context to the philosophical ideas he was trying to bring into question. By taking a larger view, he hoped to make what we take for granted seem strange, and questionable. He looked at problems "in the context of the use they perform and the service they render in the context of *inquiry*" (p. 138). He tried "to convert all the *ontological*, as prior to inquiry, into the *logical* as occupied wholly and solely with what takes place in the conduct of inquiry as an ever going concern" (p. 142).

Dewey (1960) dissolved the bifurcation between theory and practice by showing that the subject matter of theory (the abstract) grows out of and returns to the subject matter of everyday concrete experiences. He showed that a problem that appears to be unsolvable if its terms are placed in an ontological context collapses when treated in the context of inquiry. "When the issue pertaining to and derived from this contrast is placed and treated in the context of different types of *problems* demanding different methods of treatment and different types of subject matter, the problem involved assumes a very different shape from that which it has when it is taken to concern ontological 'reality'" (p. 146).

Dewey's theory of inquiry, which was written within the context of Darwin's evolutionary theory and was affected by that context, still holds, not because it points us to absolute Truths, but because it is useful and purposeful for answering our questions and solving our problems. It helps us question our specific interests as well as our background assumptions. It stands up to the test of time as a way of establishing knowing and meaning, for it starts with experience and it is never beyond questioning itself. It represents a form of naturalistic (e)pistemology for it still strives to yield warranted assertions that are not arbitrary, yet it does not rely on a priori principles to do so. Dewey's theory of inquiry eliminates the need for an absolutist Epistemology by assuming justification relies on social practices and human needs, and nothing more.

We begin to understand how Dewey's concept of experience in relation to knowing opened up a space for feminists to argue for the need to examine the contextual qualities hidden in absolutist Epistemological theory, from different standpoints of experience. Feminists' insistence on the inclusion of women's experiences, and even more specifically Black women's, or Latina women's, or lesbian women's experiences in philosophical discussions, is an effort to underscore the importance of context. Clearly, Dewey does not embrace a transcendental view of Epistemology. In fact, he is very critical of Epistemology due to its *a priori* principles and its metaphysical assumptions. But this does not mean that Dewey does not use (e)pistemology, for certainly he gives reasons to justify his arguments and evidence to warrant his claims. Dewey's theory of inquiry relies on a rehabilitated (e)pistemology.

POSTMODERNISTS

The American pragmatists, Dewey and James in particular, helped push philosophers to let go of transcendental, universal arguments. Richard Rorty, as a contemporary pragmatist and postmodernist, continued to push against universalizing tendencies. Continental philosophers such as Lyotard, Foucault, Derrida, and Deleuze, influenced by Nietzsche and Heidegger, have also contributed significantly to efforts to undermine philosophy's tendency to legitimate itself with reference to a metadiscourse. These people, who hold significantly different views, share in common their focus on critiquing transcendental philosophical assumptions, and so they are usually categorized together as "postmodernists" or "deconstructionists." It is not easy to even call these people philosophers because they have each in their own way severely criticized philosophy's claims to transcendence, as well as philosophers' assumptions that they can accurately describe the world through their God's eye view. They each have declared philosophy dead, with the use of different methodologies and with different targeted focuses. However, they all serve as philosophers in the Deweyian sense of cultural critics who help to disturb influential beliefs that we take to be given. They all help to draw our attention to the nets we are using to cast into the vast ocean of experience, and help us see the flaws in our nets that need mending.

It seems that Rorty (1989) follows Dewey's lead, and describes philosophers as prophets, poets, and soothsayers. Rorty, like Hegel and Dewey before him, uses historical analysis to draw our attention to previous background assumptions, in an effort to contextualize philosophy. Foucault also uses historical analysis to do archeological digs on key social concepts, such as discipline and punishment, sexuality, and insanity, in order to demonstrate how these concepts become institutionalized and powerfully impact particular peoples' lives. Derrida turns to language, and Deleuze to literary analysis, to explore *différance* and the lack of any master word, any ultimate foundation of meaning. Each of these philosophers work to point out how our world is shifting, unstable and uncertain, lacking a center or a circumference. They break down the solid Metaphysical Categories and Epistemological Truths philosophers have worked so hard to build, creating ruptures, deconstructing and problematizing fixities, in an effort to affirm openness toward the other. We have already met the Other in the feminist discussion, she is the excluded, the marginalized, the one objectified and distanced from Us. Postmodernists share in common with feminists a desire to acknowledge what is different, to recognize what is left out, and to respect what is queer.

In *Philosophy and the Mirror of Nature* (Rorty, 1979), Rorty turns his focus specifically on the history of the development of Epistemology, in an effort to draw us to the conclusion that we no longer need Epistemology for we can access reality directly. Rorty dismantles the idea of the mind as a great mirror. In agreement with Wittgenstein, Heidegger, and Dewey, he recommends we abandon "the notion of knowledge as accurate representation, made possible by special mental processes and intelligible through a general theory of representation" (p. 6). Rorty places particular emphasis on the development of the concept of "mind" and the idea of a mental domain. As a pragmatist, Rorty looks at the functions that the different stages and developments of Epistemology have fulfilled. For example, he argues that Descartes's idea of a mental domain served the purpose of getting science out from under religion. Descartes sought certainty (that which he could not doubt), and he invented the mind/mental to give us a solid foundation (correspondence theory of truth). However, the concern for foundational knowledge is a holdover from Cartesian doubt, which has outlived its usefulness. Rorty proposes that philosophy's role now is not foundational, rather one of edifying discourse.

Rorty (1979) does not deny there is justification for knowledge, but he works to soften the distinction between justified belief and knowledge. Rorty argues that true is corrigible and fallible. Rorty does not even deny incorrigible knowledge (not open to doubt), for example the report that I am in pain, or that this paper is white. His point is just that these claims do not require us to have mental entities/minds. Rorty looks to sociology and history for justification and criteria for knowledge. Epistemology becomes descriptive science, not transcendental norms. He looks for causal links, not eminent norms. Rorty recommends we should continue to improve our criteria. This is because our only criteria are socially acceptable rules. Justification is in social practice, which is corrigible, self-correcting. Rorty wants us to have conversations with each other rather than confrontations. He describes philosophy's task as one of building bridges between disciplines, and opening communication.

Rorty's (1979) position is that language is contingent (therefore, there are no universal claims), and self is contingent (therefore there is no human nature, and other postmodernists add, the self is multiple and fractious). Truth is not *out there* or *in here* but *what is better for us to believe* (James's words, 1909/1977). True or right or just is whatever the outcome of undistorted communication happens to be. It is whatever view wins in a free and open encounter, not the accurate representation of reality. Rorty doubts the distinction between morality and prudence. These positions commit him to a lot of apparent paradoxes, and make him suspected of relativism, irrationalism, and immorality. But Rorty says these disadvantages of his position are outweighed by the advantages of being free of dogmatic universal claims of unchanging essences, of a historical natural kind with permanent sets of intrinsic features. Rorty emphasizes differences, over sameness, and accommodation over synthesis. Rorty describes the philosopher's role as one of telling new stories, using new metaphors, not relying on argumentation. Like Dewey, he recommends that we keep philosophy connected to culture and we learn to live with plurality.

Rorty (1977, 1979) has many good things to say about Dewey as a critic of philosophical tradition, and it is clear that Dewey and James have inspired Rorty, a self-described pragmatist. Yet Rorty is also critical of Dewey, and where he is particularly critical is in regards to Dewey's concept of *experience*. Rorty supports Dewey's strong renouncement of transcendental Metaphysics, but he thinks Dewey makes a mistake when he tries to rehabilitate metaphysics into an empirical metaphysics with the help of his concept of experience. Rorty recommends that Dewey should not have tried to offer a reform, a new program. Rorty accuses Dewey of becoming transcendental in his philosophy with his metaphysical discussion of experience in *Experience and Nature* (Dewey, 1925/1981).

Dewey avoided metaphysics as a topic for over 20 years. However, while at Teachers College, he came to realize his logic had ontological implications. But Rorty misunderstands Dewey when he accuses Dewey of becoming transcendental in *Experience and Nature* (1925/1981), similarly to the misunderstanding Dewey experienced about his *Logic: Theory of Inquiry*, due to his use of the term *Logic*. Dewey's metaphysics insists on the relativity of ontological commitments. Dewey attempts to establish a metaphysics of existence. He is a naturalist, not a super naturalist. He argues for a conception of nature as changing through the interaction of existences (Sleeper, 1986). Dewey's metaphysics is not transcendental, but he later realized that he should have never used the terms metaphysics, or experience, due to the confusion the words caused because philosophers attached traditional meanings to the two common terms, instead of being careful to use the terms as Dewey redefined them. This is a difficulty I may run into as well, if readers do not carefully read my explanation of the use of the term (e)pistemology, and instead make the false assumption that I mean the word in its traditional transcendental way. Dewey suggested later he should have used the word culture instead of experience to help avoid misunderstandings that he later had to clear up and defend his theory against.

Rorty thinks he can avoid ontology just as he tries to avoid epistemology, but he cannot. What he can do is avoid transcendental Metaphysics and Epistemology. However, I do not think philosophers can avoid ontology anymore than they can avoid epistemology, for the two together form the netting that we use to catch our ideas for our theories. They form our background context that we use to help us selectively attend to problems. Language becomes Rorty's ontological category, instead of experience. Relations is my ontological category. I think Dewey was on the right track with his efforts to rehabilitate metaphysics in *Experience and Nature* (1925/1981) and his efforts to rehabilitate epistemology in *Logic* (1938/1955). Dewey shows us how these concepts can retain their pragmatic uses while at the same time being held accountable for their potential misuses. This is exactly what I am trying to do with (e)pistemology.

The (e)pistemological theory I offer is steeped in a feminist and postmodern understanding of the need to address power and its effects on theories of knowledge. It is also steeped in the classic pragmatist focus on addressing context (background and selected interest). Like my pragmatic, feminist, and postmodern colleagues, I am working to dissolve dualisms traditional Philosophy and Epistemology embrace, such as theory/practice, subject/object, mind/body, and relative/absolute. I describe knowers as fallible human beings who are connected to knowledge, in a knowing relation. I question that a general account of knowledge, based on *a priori* standards for justification, is possible.

What I present is not a Transcendental Epistemology, for I do not have any Truth to offer. I do not have the Right Answer. I offer truths, that are assertions warranted by as much evidence as I can muster, with the understanding that our criteria and standards are socially constructed and therefore fallible, and corrigible. It is the need to warrant our assertions and justify our claims that causes me to continue to use the term epistemology in its altered form, (e)pistemology. I do not deny the need to justify claims, I just deny that any justification I can offer has transcendental force. (E)pistemology's legitimacy lies in the natural world, which is a contingent, ever-changing world in which we are active participants. It is important to address questions about what counts as good evidence, and criteria used to help us make decisions and solve our problems. As we continue to strive for solutions, to inquire, problem solve, and constructively think, (e)pistemological questions will continue to arise. Can we avoid these? I think not. I am not letting go of (e)pistemological concerns, just the concept of Epistemology that assumes absolutism, even in its nonvulgar form (Siegel, 1987). I present knowing as a relational process between the knower and the known, steeped in strong contextuality.

CONCLUSION

The controversial assumptions about epistemology that current philosophers are criticizing and bringing into question have triggered heated debates. For example: If we let go of the assumption of absolute Truth, the basis for how Philosophy and Epistemology originally were defined, what do we have? The death of Philosophy, as postmodernists such as Lyotard (1984) and Rorty (1979) argue? The end of Epistemology and a reign of terror in which anything goes for there will be no way to argue for what is right/wrong, good/bad, just/unjust? (Siegel, 1987). I do not think it is as bad as all that. In fact, I think the future looks bright for philosophy and epistemology, once we let go of an assumption of absolute Truth. After all, it is just an assumption, and it has not been able to stand up to the test of time and the critique of further philosophical arguments. This means we have already functioned for a long time without Truth, we just kept hoping and believing we had it to guide us. What we are left with to help us make decisions and solve problems is a naturalized theory of knowing that I call a relational (e)pistemology. I put brackets around the "e" to underscore that this theory is based on qualified truths, not absolute Truth. What we have is each other. We can argue and debate and defend what we think are the best descriptions of reality and truth until we settle on one we can live with. However, that one we settle on is not a description we can be sure is Right or True. Indeed, there are a variety of descriptions we could settle on as Right or True, depending on what lens we choose to use and which focus we want to emphasize. We can never settle comfortably on a description for long. We must continually re-search our findings. We will never find Certainty. But this does not mean we cannot make decisions and act. Whether we like it or not we must act. Even to decide not to decide is still a decision, and the decision to not act is still an action. What is important with a relational (e)pistemology is that we seek to act in ways that are as informed as we are able, realizing we can never get rid of ourselves, and that we are always implicated in our research findings. Knowing is not objective, neutral, certain, it is in a state of flux. What I point to here is a more humble theory of knowing that can never claim absolute knowledge. It is a theory of knowing that focuses on the process, not just the product, and recognizes that knowers and the known are directly connected. It is a pluralistic, inclusive theory that insists we must include others in our inquiring process, for we can never find the answer to our problems on our own. Others contribute to our thinking right from the start, and they help to enlarge our views beyond our own limitations.

We still need philosophers, as fallible social critics, for philosophers help us redescribe what has already been described, and they help us recreate and envision anew. With philosophy we learn how we can reform education, but we also learn that we need each other to help us in this process. Not one of us, alone, knows the Answers. I invite your contributions to the conversation, for as Dewey points out, inquiry only ends when we have solved all of our problems, and answered all of our questions, and we are a long way from there. Not only do I think we will never get to that point, I doubt it is even a desirable point in which to get. Disharmony, discontent, and diversity help us continue to grow and further our knowing.

References

Aristotle. (1970). Nichomachaen ethics. In S. Cahn (Ed.), *The philosophic foundations of education* (pp. 107-120). New York, NY: Harper & Row.

Bateson, G. (1972). *Steps to an ecology of mind*. New York, NY: Ballantine.

Belenky, M., Clinchy, B., Goldberger, N., & Tarule, J. (1986). *Women's ways of knowing*. New York, NY: Basic Books.

Bordo, S. (1987). *The flight to objectivity: Essays on Cartesianism and culture.* Albany, NY: State University of New York Press.

Cahn, S. (Ed.). (1997). *Classic and contemporary readings in the philosophy of education.* New York, NY: The McGraw-Hill.

Code, L. (1987). *Epistemic responsibility.* Hanover, NH: University Press of New England, for Brown University Press.

Code, L. (1993). Taking subjectivity into account. In L. Alcoff and E. Potter (Eds.). *Feminist Epistemologies* (pp. 15-48). New York, NY: Routledge.

de Beauvoir, S. (1989). *The second sex* (H. M. Parshley, Trans. and Ed.). New York, NY: Vintage Books Edition, Random House. (Original work published 1952)

Dewey, J. (1981). Experience and nature. In J. Boydston (Ed.). *John Dewey: The later works, 1925-1953, Vol. 1* (pp 1-326). Carbondale, IL: Southern Illinois University Press. (Original work published 1925)

Dewey, J. (1955). *Logic: The theory of inquiry.* New York, NY: Henry Holt and Company. (Original work published 1938)

Dewey, J. (1960). *On experience, nature, and freedom.* Indianapolis, IN: Bobbs-Merrill Co.

Gilligan, C. (1982). *In a different voice: Psychological theory and women's development.* Cambridge, MA: Harvard University Press.

Haraway, D. (1988). Situated knowledges: The science question in feminism and the privilege of partial perspective, *Feminist Studies, 14*(3), 575-599.

Harding, S. (1993). Rethinking standpoint epistemology: What is 'strong objectivity'? in L. Alcoff & E. Potter (Eds.), *Feminist epistemologies* (pp. 49-82). New York, NY: Routledge.

James, W. (1890, 1950). *The principles on psychology* (Vol. 1). New York, NY: Dover.

James, W. (1907, 1975). *Pragmatism.* Cambridge, MA: Harvard University Press. (Original work published 1907)

James, W. (1977). *A pluralistic universe.* Cambridge, MA: Harvard University Press. (Original work published 1909)

James, W. (1976). *Essays in radical empiricism.* Cambridge, MA: Harvard University Press. (Original work published 1912)

Lyotard, J. -F. (1984). *The postmodern condition: A report on knowledge.* Minneapolis, MN: University of Minnesota Press.

Martin, J. R. (1985). *Reclaiming the conversation: The ideal of the educated woman.* New Haven, CT: Yale University Press.

Martin, J. R. (1994). *Changing the educational landscape: Philosophy, women, and curriculum.* New York, NY: Routledge.

Peirce, C. S. (1958). *Values in an universe of chance: Selected writings of Charles Sanders Peirce (1839-1914)* (P. P. Wiener, Ed.). Garden City, NJ: Doubleday.

Plato. (1970). *Meno.* In S. Cahn (Ed.), *The philosophic foundations of education* (pp. 7-35). New York, NY: Harper & Row.

Rorty, R. (1977). Dewey's metaphysics. In S. Cahn (Ed.). *New studies in the philosophy of John Dewey* (pp. 45-74). Hanover, NH: University Press of New England, for University of Vermont.

Rorty, R. (1979). *Philosophy and the mirror of nature.* Princeton, NJ: Princeton University Press.

Rorty, R. (1989). *Contingency, irony, and solidarity.* Cambridge, England: Cambridge University Press.

Siegel, H. (1987). *Relativism refuted: A critique of contemporary epistemological relativism.* Dordrecht, The Netherlands: Reidel.

Sleeper, R. W. (1986). *The necessity of pragmatism: John Dewey's conception of philosophy.* New Haven, CT: Yale University Press.

Thayer-Bacon, B. (with Bacon, C.). (1998). *Philosophy applied to education: Nurturing a democratic community in the classroom.* Upper Saddle River, NJ: Prentice Hall.

Thayer-Bacon, B. (2000). *Transforming critical thinking: Thinking constructively.* New York, NY: Teachers College Press.

Thayer-Bacon, B. (2003). *Relational "(e)pistemologies."* New York, NY: Peter Lang. [Discussion of feminism, pragmatism, and postmodernism is from Chapter 1.]

Author Contact Information: **Barbara J. Thayer-Bacon**, PhD, University of Tennessee, 1126 Volunteer Blvd., 420 Claxton Bldg., Knoxville, Tennessee 37996-3456. Phone: 865-974-9505. Fax: 865-974-8301. E-mail: bthayer@utk.edu

CHAPTER 3

Ethics and Moral Education

Lynda Stone and Jennifer Job
University of North Carolina at Chapel Hill

In January 2010, Phoebe Prince, a 15-year-old immigrant high school student in the U.S. northeast, commits suicide after several months of bullying by both female and male schoolmates over dating and boyfriends. This event triggers a set of similar incidents across the nation but also makes international news. Youth bullying as well as suicide are not just American phenomena. In the year following, the event assumed a huge symbolic presence, principally of what is wrong with today's youth! In the chapter to follow, Phoebe's story is told as it relates to the issues surrounding ethics and moral education not only for youth but surely for adults as well.

In this handbook section on philosophical education, the purpose of the chapter is to introduce all too briefly the topics of ethics and moral education and their relationship to youth and schooling. Educators at all levels—and their students—should be concerned about the moral life of individuals and the societies in which they live. Even a globalized knowledge economy of international rankings, standardized test scores, information access, entrepreneurial opportunities and the like is not enough to establish and maintain a world that benefits all people. This understanding is especially important in the United States, a place privileged relative to great parts of the world, but in which the moral lives of many people appear adrift. For educators, one issue, and a premise for the chapter, concerns just how children and youth learn to be ethical and how this process prepares them for and carries into adulthood. Merely thinking of the many influences on morality is indicative of complexity: adult modeling, religious instruction, social networks, actions of peers, and the larger conditions of privilege and poverty, let alone the place of schooling in this process. Some youth do acquire what has been called a moral compass that guides their individual, and as conventionally recognized, good lives. However, all too often a public impression is that adolescents are a social and moral problem (Lesko, 2001). This belief seems more pronounced today than in ages past.

The chapter is organized as a set of sections, now outlined. The frame has already been introduced in the bullying and suicide of Phoebe Prince, of relationships among youth that have tragic consequences. A textual dialogue is set up as the chapter structure: First, Phoebe's story and an initial response, second, substantive sections on ethics, American moral education, character education and school discipline and its critique with a second response, and finally care theory and a third response and conclusion. In each response section, there is a return to Phoebe and the bullies as the unifying thread and focusing point of and for educational departure. It is hoped that the chapter is a contribution to philosophy of education and a useful teaching tool.

Given the severity of the Prince story, the stance of the chapter needs to be emphasized. This is not a diatribe against society or schools. This is not an account of blame that is all to easy to ascribe to youth, to particular groups in society, even to most adults who ought to be more engaged in a generalized ethical education. Because social and moral life today feels complicated, there are no easy answers or quick fixes. But, the answer is surely not to give up. Each and every family and community, each and every school, public and private, should be paying specific attention to ethics. As part of the chapter stance, moreover, underscored is the belief, with evidence such as widespread bullying, that the current character education movement seems to have had little positive effect (Stone, 2007). Unfortunately a history of past curricular efforts that include philosophical ideas offers scant guidance. The chapter does offer hope, however, in the introduction of care theory in a final substantive section. Surely if individuals and their society paid more attention to specific

The Handbook of Educational Theories, pp. 29–41

encounters and acts of caring, moral life in general would be better.

Before proceeding, a note on terminology and sources seems in order. Ethics as a domain is named as singular to allow for differentiation of plural formulations that are found across history. The term ethical education is used at times to encompass the various domains, influences on, and discourses of moral life, and as just indicated, of particular importance is the education of youth. Additionally, the phrase Phoebe and the bullies is employed with no intent to distance or objectify any young people. Lastly, to name the actions of the bullies and Phoebe's suicide a story is in no way to diminish seriousness. In addition to these conventions, specific philosophical terms are employed; readers are encouraged to read carefully for their meaning in the chapter context. Further, in several places classic texts are named for reader reference; these are not listed but are available everywhere. If books named are not familiar and have significant educational purpose, they are listed in the references.

PHOEBE'S STORY

When Phoebe Prince transferred to South Hadley High School in Massachusetts, in the fall of 2009, her aunt told the assistant principal that she had experienced bullying in her old school in Ireland and might need help adjusting to a new environment. At first, the fears seemed unfounded; the pretty girl was immediately popular among the other freshmen. She made friends and dated two high school seniors. Dating these boys, however, turned out to be her undoing as both had previous girlfriends. The girls were also older than Phoebe and were athletes and leaders.

When the girls learned that someone new was dating their boyfriends, they began to harass her. By December, the boys had broken off their relationships, returning to the girlfriends and joining in the bullying. Students later reported that the four students plus several others repeatedly accosted Phoebe at school, taunting and threatening harm. The girls posted menacing messages on her Facebook page and sent dozens of texts to her cell phone, warning that she was going to be hurt. They also called Phoebe names in the hallways, the cafeteria, and in classrooms, screaming, "Slut!" and posting notes about the "Irish whore" for others to see.

On January 14, 2010, Phoebe was walking home when one of the bullies drove by and threw a drink can at her head, shouting profanity and laughing; she was seen crying. Later that afternoon, her 12-year-old sister found her hanging by a scarf in the apartment stairwell. When students visited Phoebe's Facebook page in the days after her death, they saw that the bullies had posted a final message: "She deserved it" (Eckholm & Zezima, 2010).

The publicity surrounding Phoebe's death has shed light on how little the school had done to intervene in the situation. Reporters discovered that nearly the entire student body knew for months that she was being bullied. Also, it was common knowledge that the Mean Girls—as they were called in the press—were claiming responsibility for her death. Moreover, students asserted that Phoebe had tried to go to both teachers and administration for help; her mother also had contacted the principal. None of these efforts met with assistance.

In the months that followed, some in the community charged that the media's coverage of the bullying was hyperbolic. Several students said that there were conflicts, but that the girls did not gang up on Phoebe. School officials claimed that she had drawn unwanted attention by luring the boys away from their girlfriends. Also, they equivocated, Phoebe was known for being passive and not sticking up for herself. Moreover there is strong evidence that she was suffering from depression and had been describing such feelings to friends for months. She had been prescribed Seroquel, a medication for treating mood disorders. Reports also exist of Phoebe cutting herself and telling outlandish stories to teachers prior to the height of the bullying. The general implication is that it was difficult for teachers and other school personnel to know what to do.

Widespread observations of the case reveal rhetorical charges of ignorance, blame and irresponsibility. Targets for all three charges have encompassed to some degree the larger community but more directly the individuals involved, youth peers, school personnel, parents and relatives. The principal remedy has been legal: chief student participants have been charged and found guilty of crimes and a majority of American states now have antibullying laws. In a different vein, the Prince family also has started an educational foundation to combat bullying.

INITIAL RESPONSE

In this chapter, Phoebe's story is used to help explicate a current context of ethics for youth in American society, to determine significance of philosophical ethics, moral education, and contemporary character education as well as school discipline, and to offer concluding comments about the potential of care theory. The overall theme that connects youth to adults, to ethical education especially in school, is one of relevance.

At the outset, the introduction posited that the ethics of many youth and adults today seem adrift; drift also may characterize a current context and general societal condition. A widespread impression is that these times are ambiguous and uncertain, in which—at least nostalgically in memory—former anchors in social institutions and relationships no longer exist. In philosophical and educational terms, actual ethical practices that ought to originate in and benefit individuals as well as collectives, and especially the most vulnerable, which include youth, are missing. What is additionally missing is a common language for ethics that can build a unity in diversity that does describe present American society.

When a longer view is assumed, central to Phoebe's story is a relatively recent phenomenon of generational divide and emergence of a distinct youth culture, at least over the last 50 years. There are many explanations for change that differentiate traditional from late modern social life including new occupation, altered family structure, protracted adolescence, and a different significance of schooling. Youth culture today constitutes a lifestyle within which there is unity and diversity, unanimity and conflict. At the very least, adults often share a belief that kids are no longer just kids (as if they ever were).

The accused bullies have come to stand in for youth generally, at the least for good kids turned bad. They were athletes, leaders, and popular. All too easily, reflecting public confusion over youth, the immediate view was a puzzling negative: how could this have happened? In this first response to Phoebe, it surely must be repeated that many young people lead generally good lives. Suffice to say, a premise is that youth are neither born nor raised to harm others and/or themselves. Another basic idea is surely that societal conditions do contribute to lives of youth that entail benefit or harm. This chapter acknowledges but does not focus on these background beliefs and environments but instead embeds the tragedy within a theoretical context of specific ethics and moral education.

Of particular educational importance, Phoebe and the bullies demonstrate a set of issues facing today's youth. The first issue is identity. Youth and their world(s) revolve around matters that concern the relationship of the individual to the group even as they protest individuality—their personal identity, status, exercise of power along with a perception of invincible agency. Think here of the limiting lessons that adulthood brings! For many decades, one contributing factor has been an emphasis on consumption and the problems that its overimportance brings. What is significant too is that these matters also concern and characterize many adults. Besides consumption, a perception is that for an older generation an obsession exists with being young. Fewer and fewer mature persons, one might posit, grow old with grace.

Besides individual identity the other characteristic dimension is group membership. The primary ethical issue here concerns inclusion and exclusion. Scholars across disciplines have long described in and out as endemic to social order. Whether this is natural or not is beside the ethical point; the actual matter is benefit and harm. Those who are in surely benefit, especially around their security. At the least the group provides a kind of home, where one can be oneself within boundaries and with like persons. Of course this is complex as well. Moreover, sometimes, arguably often, belonging obligates positive commitment to one group at the cost of a negative response to those who do not belong. In Phoebe's story, clearly the bullies formed an in-group from which she was excluded. It does appear also that a result of bullying was an emergent isolation. There is no indication in case accounts that any peers at school came strongly to her defense.

In this first response, Phoebe's story emphasizes a society for both youth and adults in which identity and membership are crucial. The upshot all too often is that challenges and conflicts result in a mentality of us against them. The ethical education of youth includes early and persistent lessons of circling the wagons to protect what is mine and ours. The general theme of relevance figures prominently in subsequent responses; herein the relevant idea is that contemporary ethics must attend in positive and beneficial terms to both individual identity and group membership.

ETHICS

There is one other initial and troubling feature about Phoebe's story. This is that no where has ethics been connected to what happened. How the young treat each other, how adults react and, yes, enact a culture in which ill-treatment flourishes, have not been seen as salient. Before turning to a discussion of traditions in philosophical ethics, a good place to start is with common usage and commonsense. At the level of everyday life, the terms ethics and morality as well as moral philosophy are often synonymous. The basic conception concerns how individual persons live their lives and by extension their interactions with others. As Peter Singer (1994) puts it, "ethics is about how we ought to live. What makes an action the right, rather than the wrong, thing to do? What should our goals be?" (p. 3). Its form, he continues, is best understood as "ways of thinking" (p. 4), or according to Alasdair MacIntyre (1998/2002) is "encapsulated as changing moral concepts" (p. 2). Singer continues that ethics and morality are terms with roots in customs, ethos for the first and mores for the second. A connotative distinction, useful perhaps, is that ethics refers more so to individuals' lives per se and morality to their collectivity.

Across millennia, philosophers have been interested in ethics. The fathers of Western philosophy, Plato and Aristotle, wrote about ethics in the contexts of considering goodness and justice. In what philosophers name as the Classical era, the general idea was that man was to learn to be and practice being good as he contributed to a just society. Compared to modern specialists in distinct ethics traditions, their conceptions blurred ethics with metaphysics and epistemology, with asking great and universal questions such as about truth. Written near the end of his life that spans the fourth and third centuries B.C., Plato's *Republic* embedded ethics in a proposal for an ideal society, seeing individuals as naturally part of but differentiated in a state. Perhaps principled ethics began with him and especially his emphasis on rationality continues to this day. Writing a bit later, Aristotle focused more on individuals in the *Nichomachean Ethics* and started the centuries-long tradition in virtue ethics that has had a recent renaissance. He also began a tradition of considering ethics in particular cases. Two other historic periods with distinct ethics are the Scholastic and the Renaissance. In the first, ethics related to God's instruction and in the second ethics had a more down to earth emphasis.

More so than how ethics is defined, intuition, convention, and commonsense usage structure the reasons, the justifications, that persons offer for ethical attitudes, beliefs, and actions. This commonsense viewpoint arises out of Western history in sentiments for instance from culture, religion, and community. In modern ethics about which philosophers write, there are two prominent traditions, and of late, the virtues revival. The dominant two are based in principles, the first called deontological based in a rational law and the second called consequentialist based on a calculation of effects. The first is recognizable as a kind of golden rule and the second as a rational notion of individual relative to collective good. Because the two traditions seem familiar, a little philosophical unpacking helps raise issues of understanding and implementation that are taken up subsequently with regard to Phoebe and the bullies.

In a useful essay cited extensively in this chapter section, "Modern Moral Philosophy," J. B. Schneewind (2006) overviews modern, Western ethics. To begin, modernity is a long period stretching back to the late sixteenth century and reaching into the last third of the twentieth century. Schneewind asserts that there are three internal time and conceptual eras: the first two introduce and elaborate on the primary ethical viewpoint that "morality could be understood as human self-governance and autonomy," and the third moves "toward new issues concerning public morality" (p. 147). The first era is generally identified with Immanuel Kant (1724-1804) and the principal text, *Critique of Practical Reason,* from 1788. In understanding this view, it is important that even though Kant's terms may not be quite those of today, nonetheless, a general sense is possible. Here is Schneewind on Kant's German idealist position:

> He took the central point about morality to be that it imposes absolute duties on us, showing us what we have to do no matter what.... [The clue is freedom]. When we know we morally must do something, we know we can do it; and this can only be true if we are free. (p. 151)

Freedom, the capacity for reasoning, allows for recognition of duty. Here is the familiar aspect, in what Kant names as the categorical imperative. The principle is "to act in ways which we could rationally agree to have everyone act" (p. 151). Duty tells what is right and doing what is right is good. Doing one's duty, however, becomes problematic when it means acting in ways one does not prefer.

The second era of modern ethics sounds more group-oriented than the first but remains focused on an individualist ethic; it too is based in principle. Identified primarily with John Stuart Mill (1806-1873), its roots are in the economic theory of Jeremy Bentham and broader philosophical ideas of other British empiricists. Here the issues surround the consequences of action as they relate to pleasure, happiness, and goodness, and how to achieve the greatest amountS for the greatest number of persons. Taken from Mills's book, *Utilitarianism,* originally published in the mid-nineteenth century, Schneewind explains that this ethics arises thusly: "Commonsense morality ... which we all learn as children, represents the accumulated wisdom of mankind about the desirable and undesirable consequences of action" (p. 152). The philosophical problem for Mill is that commonsense may not easily offer conclusions. In response, he proposes an idea of inner motivation "as instrumental to our own happiness" (p. 152). Another related problem concerns what constitutes happiness. To address the latter, two lively essays are recommended. Bentham contributes a discussion first published in 1825 of the benefits of the game of push-pin relative to poetry and philosophy (Bentham, 1994). Mill poses differences in quality of higher and lower pleasures (Mill, 2004); his publication date is 1861. The latter's issue is whether happiness has universal features and/or particular ones relative to time and place.

The third era brings modern ethics into recent decades; exemplary here is the writings of the American philosopher, the late John Rawls (1921-2002). Beginning in *A Theory of Justice* from the early 1970s, he envisions morality for groups, for societies, as always political. This ethics works from individuals into their collective membership, and in a Kant-inspired view, unites the two principal modern traditions. Again, Schneewind offers interpretation:

> [The book] attempts to show how principles of right action, at least in the domain of justice, are justifiable independently of the amount of good that just action

> brings about.... [Further] no utilitarian account of justice can as adequately incorporate our strong commonsense convictions as can his Kantian view that the right is prior to the good. (p. 155)

Two central and philosophically unique principles from Rawls are the original position and the veil of ignorance. Applying reason once again, in a hypothetical experiment, individuals assume group interests in determining a just, stable society. In the process they do not know their own particulars or those of any other individual or group now or in the future. Thus they make ethical judgments out of shared interests because this is rational. A problem is whether interests are ever neutral—or indeed entirely rational.

American Moral Education

Ethical education of American youth has many sources and impacts. These do not generally include the reading of philosophy in school but there is a long-standing tradition of moral education. For purposes of this chapter, moral education is defined under the auspices of the school incorporating various interplays between curriculum and teaching. Beyond the scope of the chapter there remains a question of the value and effectiveness of moral education in schools. Given societal and moral complexity from the introduction, it may well be today that specific positive influence of the school is minimal at best.

In a U.S. context, moral education began with efforts at mass schooling in the early nineteenth century. Then as now, two emphases are present: one is individual development and the other is induction into an existing society. Three early, overt purposes focused on religion, literacy, and citizenship in which particular, curriculum was employed, most often delivered in direct instruction. In the first purpose, Protestant community values were taught such as hard work and thrift primarily in recitation from the Bible. In some communities direct attention to a connection between religion and schooling still exists; in others there appears more separation of church and state. Further, given a very diverse American society, whether the nation remains basically Protestant might be challenged.

In the second purpose, reading and writing were taught through such texts as *McGuffey's Readers* with general inculcation into Western culture a dominant theme. An example from Shakespeare's *Othello* concerns the value of keeping one's good name: "Good name ... in man or woman, dear my lord, is the immediate jewel of their souls" (McGuffey, 1879, p. 95, reformatted). At the least, secondary curriculum still includes an emphasis on Western civilization, often through Anglo-English texts.

Further, in the third purpose, students were taught to value a particular form of citizenship that is specifically democratic and American; it too largely had British origins. In the example to follow, one notes emphasis on rights but obedience sometimes as a dire price paid by immigrants. In a 1967 collection of historical sources and commentaries, *Turning Points in American Educational History,* David Tyack includes this illustration from a 1909 book on English for immigrants.

> Are you a citizen of the United States? The United States takes care of all its citizens and gives them many rights. A citizen has the right to life, liberty, and happiness. He has the right to buy and sell, to have a home, and to help in making the government under which he lives a good government.
>
> These rights are paid for by the men who enjoy them. A true citizen pays for his rights by obeying the laws, paying his taxes, and taking part in protecting the government of the United States. (Tyack, 1967, p. 242)

The three purposes evolved within specific pedagogical strategies; as indicated above, a universal strategy was direct, overt instruction of the curriculum. This was prevalent well into the twentieth century. In the last century also, a relatively recent purpose was introduced that focused on shaping youth values and actions. In another strategy, here moral education was program-based and existed alongside a hidden curriculum in schools. There are two important aspects of the hidden curriculum that continue to today: first, name a problem—create a curriculum program—and second, continue to teach traditional values embedded in more general school practices. From twentieth century mid-decades, the two best known programs were values clarification and cognitive moral development. In the first, Louis Rath, Merill Harmin, and Sidney Simon developed a program for teachers to "help people ... [especially youth] decrease value confusion and promote a consistent set of values through a valuing process" (Hersh, Miller, & Fielding, 1980, p. 75). Pedagogy included exercises of reasoned discussion and dialogue. While the origin of the first program was education practices, the second program was more theoretical, and from Lawrence Kohlberg (1981) had roots that included psychology and philosophy. Kohlberg's six stages (with changes and modifications) of moral development became the basis for curriculum projects. Pedagogy emphasized analysis of individual stages and presentation of moral dilemmas for reasoned discussion to promote stage change. Also, in this program a few experimental schools organized as communities of youth deliberation.

Thus far what can be named as two approaches to moral education have been set out, direct instruction in the general curriculum and student inquiry in special programs. A third approach also incorporated curriculum and arose from the efforts of philosophers of education. It targeted theorists, researchers, and teacher educators for application in schools. Two subtraditions operated, one focusing on educational concepts with an ethical connection and the other taking its lead from modern philosophical ethics. A principal source of the first subtradition was the writings of British analytical philosophers and philosophers of education, among them R. S. Peters and his influential book, *Ethics and Education* (1966). Concepts explored included equality, freedom, authority, and democracy. One notes for education the political orientation from this dominant philosophical tradition. The second subtradition was best exemplified in the text, *The Ethics of Teaching* (Strike & Soltis, 1985). Strike and Soltis's project was to teach principles from modern philosophy referring directly to Kant, Bentham and Mill. Through philosophical overviews, case studies, and a professional code of ethics, they hoped to infuse ethics especially into teacher preparation programs. Their cases concerned punishment, intellectual freedom, and the equality of student treatment. Today a strong cadre of philosophers of education continues to theorize ethics and moral education out of various philosophical traditions, analytic, pragmatist, and continental among them. Their efforts remain more focused on educating educators rather than students directly.

In summary, moral education for students in American schools has largely been an interplay of curriculum and teaching; the last approach has altered the basic model somewhat in a focus on educators. Specific moral purposes have been taught across the general curriculum, in particular programs, and in professional education. Teaching strategies have included direct instruction, and student/educator inquiry that incorporates discussion and decision training.

As introduced, American ethical education of youth takes place in many institutions and locales and indeed is always going on. One particular worry about moral education in schools today is that, for some segments of society, someone else's, different, values are being emphasized. For them, ethical education is best left to a private, familial, communal and often religious domain. Thus it is argued that morals are not the business of schools which have other responsibilities. Instead, they should focus on the acquisition of knowledge and the preparation of youths' economic and occupational lives. That there are ethical dimensions to current accountability, standardization and ubiquitous testing practices in schools seems not to enter consideration.

Character Education and School Discipline

The state of American moral education just presented is only part of the story, the largely historic account. What is extant today is a very widespread movement in character education again largely organized in specific curriculum and teaching programs. In a relatively recent study, *Moral Education in American Schools and the Shaping of Character from Colonial Times to the Present*, Edward McClellan (1999) identifies across several centuries the centrality of character. Indeed the two terms character and morality often have been used synonymously. Quoted frequently because of his public visibility, an early spokesperson for the present movement, former U.S. Secretary of Education, William Bennett (1992) places the need for moral education in response to social change beginning in the late sixties, to culture wars. He writes of serious conflicts that are ideological:

> The battle for culture refers to the struggle over the principles, sentiments, ideas, and political attitudes that define the permissible and impermissible … the preferred and the disdained in speech, expression, attitude, conduct and politics. (pp. 25, 27)

Given perceived societal excesses, especially of youth and their culture, in its day and since, Bennett's viewpoint has sharply divided Americans: many adults seem either to disapprove or to approve of youth and not surprisingly racial, class, gender, residence and other social factors figure in calculations. A concerted response across many positions has been encapsulated in the formation of the national Character Education Partnership. Composed of organizations and groups numbering in the hundreds, Character Education Partnership is "a nonpartisan national coalition dedicated to developing young people of good character who become responsible and caring citizens" (Berkowitz & Bier, 2005). Taken from the website, the coalition's vision relates that good character is based in "universal core ethical values" (Character Education Partnership, 2010), or virtues. The partnership has been particularly influential at the U.S. state level in promoting school programs. Their site in 2010 lists only five states and the District of Columbia without programs of some kind. It also lists numerous services. These include a set of organization publications; among them is a statement of eleven principles and their indicators. Other entries offer information about national prize winning and promising practices for districts and schools, on-site professional development, and an annual conference. What is important is that partnership members share common agreement on specific virtues and principles of enactment. At least in public documents there does not seem much room for disagreement within member organizations.

A bit more explication of the partnership's consensual model is in order to understand widespread, school-based popularity. In keeping with the present emphasis on accountability, character virtues are tied to academic achievement; individual students as well as schools are lauded for performance. Virtues, in effect, are to be performed and their practice leads to learning. Thomas Lickona, a central movement participant, describes key virtues in his book for a public audience, *How to Help Our Children Develop Good Judgment, Integrity, and Other Essential Values*:

> Two kinds of virtues are connected.... [We] need to be in control of ourselves in order to do right by others.... [Self-oriented] virtues ... [are] such as fortitude. self-control, humility, and putting forth our best effort rather than giving in to laziness.... [Other-oriented] virtues ... [are] such as fairness, honesty, gratitude, and love. (Lickona, 2004, pp. 12, 11)

Given rhetoric of character virtues to which any opposition seems immoral, supporters and critics do disagree over matters of movement conception and implementation; these are sometimes supported by philosophy or philosophically informed positions. An example of a movement supporter is Christina Hoff Sommers and of critics are Tainlong Yu and Deron Boyles. In her essay, "How Moral Education is Finding Its Way Back into America's Schools" (2002), Sommers turns to philosophy as she asserts that a major problem with modern child rearing and moral education is this:

> [Value-free] approaches to ethics have flourished at a time when many parents fail to give children basic guidance in right and wrong. The story of why so many children are being deprived of elementary moral training encompasses 3 or 4 decades of misguided reforms by educators, parents, judges.... Reduced to philosophical essentials, it is the story of the triumph of Jean-Jacques Rousseau over Aristotle. (p. 25)

Sommers's stance strongly favors directive moral education (2002, p. 34). She summarizes, "Children need standards, they need clear guidelines, they need adults in their lives who are understanding but firmly insistent on responsible behavior" (p. 35). In the essay she significantly contrasts the form of moral education of the Columbine killers with that of movement contributions. One elementary program cited by her is *Character Counts*, which asks schools to post core values on the walls of hallways and classrooms, and with an explicit agenda, to instruct for these values through student memorization and practice. Other components are daily recitation of the *Pledge of Allegiance* as well as a personal virtues pledge.

Two versions of critique, informed by ethics traditions in critical philosophy, focus on causes and elements of a hidden curriculum and on issues of pedagogy. First, in "Character Education for Adolescents: Pedagogy of Control," Yu (2010) begins with Bennett and his position supporters and makes the point that prevailing pedagogy is based in a fallacious rhetoric. He challenges a "seemingly logical rationale" (p. 413) about serious moral decline of America's youth. As he writes, "Morality does not develop in a vacuum.... The real causes may lie in the exploitation and oppression in ... [youth] lives and the resulting alienation from self and others" (p. 413). The conclusion of his argument is that children cannot be held responsible for societal moral deterioration. Second, Boyles's (2010) critique is exemplified in a state-funded program in Georgia in the essay, "Would You Like Values With That? Chick-fil-A and Character Education." The program, privately funded, is a curriculum package in which free food and other rewards are given out by teachers to students who are caught exhibiting specific monthly virtues. Elements of the hidden curriculum include fostering a specific capitalist and fundamentalist religious orientation through indoctrination and control. Boyles summaries,

> [A] nexus of Christianity and capitalism ... [as a] contrived optimism becomes an unquestioned foundation for docile, naïve workers. The nexus results in a kind of confused nationalist mythology that ... [lauds individualism] and pretenses of participating in a democracy. (p. 171)

This program is another example of employing core values when each school month emphasizes one of these: initiative, respect, uniqueness, peace, orderliness, kindness, courage, joy, and patience (p. 170). Boyles's point is that specific values underpin these virtues and are not acknowledged nor questioned; thus their enactment is often simplistic and even misleading.

Involved in the inculcation of youth morality, functioning alongside character education programs, is the pervasive presence of strict school discipline practices. An obvious irony exists overall: it is as if young people learning character cannot be trusted to exercise it. In a recent book, *Homeroom Security: School Discipline in an Age of Fear*, Aaron Kupchik (2010) provides this description: "Today's public schools are rife with strict rules and punishment, including zero tolerance policies, random searches by drug-sniffing dogs, high suspension rates, surveillance cameras, and the presence of police officers" (p. ix). Asserted as fair, schools employ systems that rhetorically are both positive and negative. But all, it is stressed, entail punitive practices.

A popular system is *School Wide Positive Behavior Supports*. The idea is to intervene in youth behavior before a student commits a wayward act (Osher, Bear, Sprague, & Doyle, 2010). School Wide Positive Behavior Supports is largely teacher-centered. It is based in a theory that if teachers provide positive modeling, teach actively, and reward what the school sees as good behavior, students are less likely to misbehave. Touted as responding to individual needs, but in strict application of the same standards, students who are not acting within school expectations are targeted for intensive intervention.

One previous generation of a schoolwide system was assertive discipline, again negative within a positive spin. Therein rules were pronounced for all to see—and sometimes students even had a hand in creating them! Infractions in classrooms led to a set of discipline steps. A student's name was put on a blackboard for a first one; checks were added with subsequent misbehaviors and each mark had a consequence. Among them were parent notification, in and out of school suspension, then expulsion. Boards in classrooms in which the system was not working were filled to the brim with names and checks, thus constituting a joke. In-school suspension, by the way, has always seemed the most illogical practice: students are kept out of classrooms they are supposed to be in to spend the same time sitting alone or with other offenders usually doing nothing and often ironically in the school library.

By far the most prevalent school discipline practice in recent years has been zero tolerance (Casella, 2003). The term describes any school policy that imposes the same severe consequences for a specific infraction regardless of circumstances. The widespread use of these policies originated prior to September 11 but has been intensified since. In order to combat youth and especially gang-related violent crime as well as school shootings, the legal initiation of zero tolerance was the *U.S. Gun-Free School Zones Act of 1990* (PL 101-647), which not only banned firearms from within 1,000 feet of school property but also mandated expulsion for anyone who brought a gun to school. In subsequent years, the word firearms was replaced with weapons, allowing schools to greatly expand the scope of zero tolerance policies. Over the past 15 years or so, weapons have been anything from brass knuckles to camping utensils to hair combs. Most schools have also enacted the same policies for drugs and alcohol infractions, and drug paraphernalia.

Significantly, zero tolerance has been applied to other kinds of rules such as tardiness. A case from a few years ago involved suspension from a high school football team of the entire first string because the youth were late suiting up for practice. They had been giving blood in a school-sponsored drive and required a short rest period. Once the story made the news, the coach had to suspend the policy and provide means for players to regain their team status. To a national audience, the specific policy appeared absurd and the conduct of the youth hardly serious. As Kupchik from above concludes, "Zero tolerance policies have repeatedly been shown to fail at their primary missions of reducing school misbehavior and increasing consistency in school discipline" (Kupchik, 2010, p. 199). At the time of this writing, there are a few, beginning indications that some political and educational minds may be seeking modification of zero tolerance policies.

Second Response

In addition to individual identity and group membership, the relevance of ethics for youth assumes two other categorical forms: their own experience and academic discourse and content. These two are seldom connected, let alone integrated. Moreover it seems clear in a present generational divide that there is no simple fitting of youth and their culture(s) to adults and theirs. Before turning to academic issues, a couple more experiential lessons beyond the initial response are relevant and instructive. A first takes up the importance of adult models and a related second concerns what youth see in adult moral conduct.

A central base in ethical education of the young is that adults—hopefully parents and community members—make positive moral decisions that are acted on before their eyes. Returning to the philosopher Singer, adults demonstrate right and wrong as well as what everyday customs and mores best benefit individuals and groups (Singer, 1994). Two general ideas follow: for a child, doing wrong feels bad intuitively; however, by the time children become adolescents, they begin to experience moral complexities. In effect, they come to recognize when it is all right to tell a little lie. For ethical adults, complications are expected and worked through, for instance, when it makes sense to circumvent a principle, to understand that fairness does not always mean sameness. Unfortunately, too many adults do not explain their actions and tell the young to do one thing while they do another.

What youth see in adult ethics is persons getting away relatively often with unethical behavior. The rich hire attorneys who obtain preferential legal treatment for offenders; parents cheat on their taxes and are proud of transgressions. The idea is to beat the system and best the other guy. A society in which competition above all matters surely contributes to what occurs. In schools, competition for grades or getting into a good college plays out this value. Thus youth experience unfairness and inequity, and in their broad ethical education, they come cynically to believe that this is the way things are. Long gone, albeit all too simply, is that a child's definitive moral lesson meant having to return a stolen candy bar to the corner grocery store. Daily, commonsense ethics are seen at best as naïve.

Getting away with unethical behavior means not getting caught and therefore escaping punishment. A larger societal belief is that punishment and its fear is supposed to deter crime or misbehavior, but it seems to do neither. The disciplinary trio is responsibility, consequence, and punishment—not fulfilling the first leads to the second and eventuates in the third. One wonders at the soundness of such a society when punishment, especially seen as unfair, never makes anyone feel good. Here experiential relevance, the lesson that youth do understand, takes a negative form.

The second category, academic relevance, is supposed to be positive and also is supposed to connect to youth lives and experiences. Disconnect is typical and for several problematic reasons. One problem concerns the formal content of philosophical ethics. For youth the language may well be confusing. Doing one's duty is often onerous, not something to be sought nor even appreciated. Consequences, as described above, are a far cry from utilitarian pleasures. Another problem concerns the training of rationality, what primarily is to guide adult ethics. This is certainly much easier said than done. Developing reason probably takes maturity as well as lots of practice. Then enter emotions, a third problem. Youth recognize that emotions are central to the daily practice of ethics but how to deal with them is often difficult; anger, resentment and the like are difficult for many adults as well.

In terms of moral education from above, it is important to note that experiences with values clarification and moral decision making both were school successes, the first because of the direct attention to youth issues and value orientations and the second probably because of the dilemma games. The most famous of these was the lifeboat situation when students had to argue for abandoning some persons in order to save others. Is this competition at its worst?

More specific to school practices today, academic relevance concerns the effectiveness of character education. It is difficult to imagine connections for the young of any time in memorizing virtue definitions; stories from literature or other times probably seem silly to them, but prizes do offer attraction. Unfortunately such prizes, remnants of behavior modification and its superficiality, have virtually nothing to do with the substance of ethics.

Another element of academic relevance concerns the standard curriculum and ethical issues inherent in it. A first question arises over whether it is moral to limit curricular offerings only to those students with specific aptitudes in college-oriented subjects—surely the dominant emphasis. A second question is whether a large number of school dropouts is itself not a matter of societal morality. Still another element that connects to the school's academic mission is the contemporary climate of discipline discussed above. The point here is that discipline at most levels of schooling is problematic at best. This has to do with who youth are: while learning to be both autonomous and live with others, often their existences entail various degrees of excess, evasion, and escape. To try to deal with today's youth, school and classroom discipline has become so strict, so invasive, and so based in fear, threat and punishment. The discourse of discipline then masks these aspects in the name of security. The result, often and interestingly, is youth learning to play the game of school often with passivity (but what thoughts abound?). A final question returns to lack of experiential relevance just described, of negative adult models, of unfair application of rules, of pervasive competition. It is not a great stretch to pose at least three effects: lack of trust, fractured community, and ineffective, appropriate authority and guidance.

A return to Phoebe and the bullies is again in order. From the introduction, a prior point: It accomplishes little to assign blame—the parents, the school, the community, the society, even in a direct sense the bullies—for the tragic events. The important issue is how all of this might never have happened and how elements of school life—including the interconnection of experiential and academic relevance—could have been turned from a very negative present to a very positive one for everyone. At South Hadley High, or any school, the three elements of trust, community, and guidance interrelate and certainly are relevant to the lives of youth. In the case of Phoebe and the bullies they appeared to be missing.

One factor that influenced events is Phoebe's family. Her mother did contact the school; her aunt's subsequent media appearances indicate that she was knowledgeable and involved. However, it does seem that school adults largely were clueless about what to do. This lack of school-based guidance had to contribute to Phoebe's general psychological condition. Typically when a school lets its students down, they turn inward and often to inappropriate actions toward each other. The other victims in this tragedy surely include the bullies. In many schools, beginning in early grades, students do form cliques that stand off against each other. By the way, once this does occur in a school, a grade level, or a classroom, it is very difficult to combat—and strict discipline is surely not the answer. One wonders, thus, what moral education including character education, can do. Unfortunately, the answer is often more strict discipline.

Care Theory

As previously illustrated, responses critical to character education, almost exclusively from the academic community, have largely focused on educational matters. One different stance to critique comes in a view recognizing educational problems but embedding them in an ethics philosophy. The approach is care theory developed by Nel Noddings in which a new philosophical language is created that is expressed here. Understanding of it requires some suspension of conventional ethics discourse—since this ultimately is what she questions. While she does raise issues of teaching and curriculum, her own philosophical position begins in agreement on the general intentions of the character education movement, although she would disagree with conservative, alarmist views of the culture wars and their supposed negative impact on youth. Her philosophical position begins in distinctions over traditional emphases on the acquisition of and types of virtues. Significantly societal values need to be added to those primarily for individuals. She also attends to specifics of context and condition rather than abstract universals, and along with these elements, the need for dealing with the ambiguities of ethical life.

Contextualizing for a moment, care theory is most often credited to two scholars, Noddings and Carol Gilligan. Working separately but simultaneously, Gilligan's book, *In A Different Voice: Psychological Theory and Women's Development* (1982), appeared 2 years before Noddings's *Caring: A Feminine Introduction to Ethics and Moral Education* (1984). With its roots in psychology, Gilligan's response to Kohlberg's cognitive moral development theory indeed changed the way women are perceived today as ethical decision makers. Differing from Noddings, Gilligan's morality is primarily embedded in cognition and in knowledge and is then posited in ways of knowing. This is important to keep in mind.

Noddings's care theory is initiated with persons born into an ethical life. In philosophical terms, relation is ontologically basic, a paired unit of persons named as one-caring and the cared-for. The model ideally is in the caring of the primary unit of mother and child. This means that persons, qua persons, begin their lives in connection with others and moreover that caring is first learned through being cared for. As one grows, life and encounters in what Noddings terms natural caring continue, and as well, ethical caring develops. The difference is that the first arises out of direct, often intimate, relations while the second occurs in more distanced, actual or potential relations, linked or not in society. In her writing, the caring relation is theoretically sophisticated in which openness, attentiveness, and affect operate for each self in the relational pair. What are named engrossment and motivational displacement from the one caring receives response as a form of reciprocity from the cared for. In summary, Noddings writes,

> We need … be reminded of our fundamental relatedness, of our dependence upon each other. We are both free—that which I do, *I* do—and bound—I might be far better if you reach out to help me and far, far worse if you abuse, taunt, or ignore me. (Noddings, 1984, p. 49, emphasis in original)

Moreover, as relation, caring is best understood as something different from conventional feelings either of empathy or sympathy; the latter are insufficient for the affect and action that a caring relation entails.

Two further ideas are important for educators to understand. One is that relations with students are asymmetrical and can be short term or of longer duration. Moreover while over time the cared for should respond to the one caring, the relation need not be responded to immediately. In schools, relation, perhaps difficult to maintain at times, is not primarily about the teacher. The important point of the teacher-student relation is to further what Noddings terms the projects of the student, the cared for, both educationally and ethically. In projects, one's educational interests and choices as well as responsibilities matter as does the facilitation of a developing ethical self. Note for emphasis: a project is anything of significance to the cared-for, even if it proves to be unreachable or even unimportant. Focusing on the cared-for's projects means that emphasis on, feelings of, and personal endeavors of the one-caring are not immediately primary. The one-caring puts her own interests in second place. However, an additional aspect is that because two ethical selves are involved, relations over time can become burdens. If so, with ethical diminishment and healthy guilt that are part of an ethical self, relations can be or must be terminated. This is not an ethic of self-sacrifice.

One additional element concerns Noddings's view of the relationship of a philosophical caring ethics and a psychological one. For her, when people meet, in encounters that are problematic sometimes, the pair moves in and out of affective and cognitive emphasis and discussion in order to foster a project. In a larger sense, too, epistemological aims such as gathering information to know about others are embedded in ethical concerns for the actual relations and realities of people. Whenever possible, ethics is highly personal or at least must be enacted as if so.

Developed by Noddings in more recent years, the form of ethical, singular paired relation extends into a societal model. Herein caring for becomes a focused caring about. Her premise is that a home rather than a state (as from Plato) might well provide the social starting point for ethical life. One dimension is that needs of individuals—that are not basically rights but can become so—are met; again the conventional language is purposefully altered. As her book, *Starting at Home: Caring and Social Policy* (2002b) describes, "beneath … [rights talk are] wants, desires, interests, and needs … [of individuals that give rise to rights of groups]" (pp. 54-55). Overall, all persons should have biological and social needs met, the latter that include growth and acceptability, as well as some nonbasic wants, that is, important personal things that individuals desire (p. 66). This opens possibility of life beyond mean subsistence.

With a history now of over 25 years, care theory has engendered a significant following within philosophy that includes valuable debate. Three issues within modern ethics concern the relationships of care theory: to virtue ethics implicated in critique of character education, to moral political theory based on principled justice, and back to the major ethics traditions. Again in her usual stance toward differences of opinion, Noddings recognizes the value of traditional and modern ethics. First, caring and virtue seem related as involving attributions and actions of persons. However, the possession of virtuousness and clearly the impositional teaching of character virtues miss the relational point of caring and become what might be termed selfish ends in themselves (Noddings, 2002a, p. 3). Second, distributive justice out of a conception of societal fairness also has a place, especially in social policy. But, a tradition of retributive justice, of desert and punishment, is seriously flawed (Noddings, 1999, pp. 8-9). What are commonly recognized as the problems of criminal justice systems are evident to all thoughtful persons. Third, modern ethics based on principles and procedures are problematic in their implementation; today they virtually invite noncompliance in finding ways to circumvent the system for individual or group advantage.

Given pedagogical criticisms of character education, a significant topic in care theory concerns suggestions for teaching and curriculum. Fostering both paired relations and broader extensions, strategies include teacher modeling, and open discussion and dialogue between teachers, students, and peers—as well as others related to schools and communities. One curriculum focus for frequent consideration is taking up issues central to student lives. These are matters that are often taboo in schools; controversial examples are sexuality and war. Another focus conceptualized by Noddings, in an early book primarily for teachers, is to divide by half the school curriculum into its traditional liberal model paired with integrated domains or centers of caring. She poses six illustrative centers of curriculum that range from caring for self to caring for ideas (Noddings, 1992).

Final Response and Conclusion

Noddings's care theory begins with the natural relations of being cared for. It is hoped that Phoebe and the bullies have shared this early experience as it presupposes the capacity to care. Caring then does grow in encounters with others in the world that include those not in natural relations, nonintimate others and strangers. In addition to engaging in caring relations with youth, one thing seems certain. Adults also ought to guide the young in their relations with others. All these endeavors of caring ethical education occur through modeling, discussion and other intimate pedagogies: guidance can come from many quarters, but if it is lacking, then developing caring individuals becomes more difficult. Significantly, for Noddings, there should always be the possibility for caring to begin and grow.

In the case of teacher and student, it is important to understand that relation is not equal and that focus of the caring pair is on the project of the student, the cared for. Often the most evident project is academic, for example in passing math class. The point is that the teacher steps into the perspective of the student and acknowledges that she might not like math, even as they together figure out what the student must do. As sensitive as is an academic project, one specifically moral is even more so. It is also important to understand that for Noddings relation is not relationship, which seems institutional and often superficial.

Additionally in furthering a substantive or enduring project, knowledge is often involved but is not the primary element. Establishing and maintaining ethical relations and projects is based primarily in affect, not in intellect and cognition. Further, with reference to the psychological formulation of care theory from Gilligan and others, in an experiential way, Noddings describes the process as moving in and out of subjective and objective discourse and thus on feeling and thinking where appropriate for furtherance.

In the case of Phoebe and the bullies, the ethical actions and lives of all the youth and indeed the adults who were involved—are projects to be facilitated through caring pairs. But bullying also affects larger social institutions, the school, the community, the society. First a general comment: Although people have always harmed others, bullying unfortunately has become an all-too-common occurrence both in school and out. Moreover it has taken on new more severe aspects in times of social media, and technological, communication and transportation advances. In cyberbullying it is now indirect and masked. The intensification of bullying into its present forms means that previous ways youth solved problems, such as putting on the boxing gloves in gym class, are gone.

Also gone—or never allowed to develop in contemporary social institutions that include many schools—are caring relations, sound friendships, between youth. So much of current conditions of schooling described in this chapter mitigate against caring. Even clique formation is not caring in Noddings's sense because these group relationships do not benefit the ethical growth of all involved. Caring might have altered the tragic events of Phoebe and the bullies; it appears that many involved adults and adolescents knew of the bullying problem but did nothing to stop it. Significantly, although family members tried to help, no teacher talked to the bullies about feelings and actions, and no administrator took a stand. Indeed, and this seems so significant, the event has not been considered a matter of ethics but only of law. To turn this to the courts lets all persons and other institutions, especially schools, off the hook.

The case of Phoebe and the bullies allows for an existential, largely concrete assessment of the potential of care theory. Important, further, are issues involving the relationship of care theory to standard ethics and moral education. A first is that traditionally caring is not part of philosophical, conventional ethics. It does not put principle or rationality first as do both classical and modern ethics. One cannot turn to rule when the ethical situation is difficult. Care theory is also different from the virtues tradition as it is not a matter of the possession of individual character attitudes, dispositions, and traits. Noddings asserts that both of these philosophically-based traditions have value but are not sufficient to get at the heart of caring for particular persons and projects. A second issue is that care theory is not part of conventional school discipline, itself largely rule-bound. In the chapter, current practices were described; especially significant is a system based on consequential punishment. Still another issue involves implementing caring by educators. In this latter regard, beginning teachers have been heard to say that they do not have time for this touchy-feely approach to classroom management. Noddings does not mean ethics to be discipline or management; relations should make the two easier in classrooms but the intent of student control, order and the like is not inherent in caring. Finally, in the greater social order today those who typically engage in caring relations or who promote a caring culture are sometimes seen as naïve, or worse foolish, unable to exercise their own sovereign power as individuals over others.

One other issue of care theory is that its language is seen as technical and not part of moral commonsense. A first matter here is that Noddings does offer a new philosophy but significantly it is out of a natural world, the world of individuals' intimacy. Caring is central to common life and therefore ultimately commonsensical. A central point about language is that to engage in caring relations does not entail memorizing a new discourse, but to change specific encounters and experiences. A second matter raised at the outset of the chapter concerns the need today for a shared language of ethics. Two past problems throw light on this issue. Previous attempts at one discourse such as from religion have proved ineffective and impossible, and at least in part because some persons spoke for some others without their participation or actual consent. Perhaps search for a language is not really the primary focus in a diverse contemporary world if shared caring relations and actions are undertaken. In this view ethics is analogous to a shared politics.

The closing matter is relevance, the thematic of responses throughout the chapter. To summarize, the principal purpose has been to bring broad philosophical treatment of youth and adult ethics into contemporary educational relevance. The actual story of Phoebe and the bullies has served as the principal and recurring vehicle and has been intended to make a philosophical exploration concrete. Youth and adults alike must see the seriousness today of bullying and other similar events of moral harm. Relevance is a general category by which to consider potential effects of any ethics especially for youth. In the chapter, the first form of relevance was individual identity and group membership. In a slightly different language from the response, security, inclusion, and acceptance of difference all are needed as part and parcel of current social life, again especially for youth. The second form of relevance was youth experience and academic context, discourse and content. One central element concerned the lack of their integration, in fact often their detrimental relationship. The important point was the negative modeling of ethics in adult lives, getting away with it, not getting caught, besting the other guy. The values and actions of adults carry over for youth into their own worlds but especially at school. A climate of strict discipline, of unequal treatment typically privileging some and not others, and as well, an often irrelevant curriculum coupled with ubiquitous standardization and accountability testing, surely do not make school positively relevant. In the third response, care theory has been posed as an alternative to traditional philosophical ethics, and to historical and current approaches to moral education, including character education and school discipline practices. As Noddings might put this, what could be more relevant to the everyday and always lives of youth and adults than to have persons who care for them and for whom they care. Actually living these relations is surely a sound basis for an ethical society.

REFERENCES

Bennett, W. J. (1992). *The de-valuing of America: The fight for our culture and our children*. New York, NY: Touchstone.

Bentham, J. (1994). Push-pin and poetry. In P. Singer (Ed.), *Ethics* (pp. 199-200). Oxford, England: Oxford University Press. (Original work published 1825)

Berkowitz, M. W., & Bier, M. C. (2005). *What works in character education: A research-driven guide for educators*. Washington, DC: Character Education Partnership.

Boyles, D. (2010). Would you like values with that? Chick-fil-A and character education. In J. L. DeVitis & L. Irwin-DeVitis (Eds.), *Adolescent education: A reader* (pp. 167-180). New York, NY: Peter Lang.

Casella, R. (2003). Zero tolerance policy in schools: Rationale, consequences, and alternatives. *Teachers College Record, 105*(5), 872-892.

Character Education Partnership. (2010). Retrieved from www.character.org.

Eckholm, E., & Zezima, K. (2010, April 8). Documents detail a girl's final days of bullying. *The New York Times*. Retrieved from www.nytimes.com/2010/04/09/us09bully.html?src=mv

Gilligan, C. (1982). *In a different voice: Psychological theory and women's development*. Cambridge, MA: Harvard University Press.

Hersh, R. H., Miller, J. P., and Fielding, G. D. (1980). *Models of moral education: An appraisal*. New York, NY: Longman.

Kohlberg, L. (1981). *Essays in moral development: The philosophy of moral development* (Vol. 1). Cambridge, MA: Harper & Row.

Kupchik, A. (2010). *Homeroom security: School discipline in an age of fear*. New York, NY: New York University Press.

Lesko, N. (2001). *Act your age! A cultural construction of adolescence*. New York, NY: Routledge Falmer.

Lickona, T. (2004). *Character matters: How to help our children develop good judgment, integrity, and other essential virtues*. New York, NY: Touchstone.

MacIntyre, A. (1998, 2002). Introduction. In S. M. Cahn & P. Markie (Eds.), *Ethics: History, theory, and contemporary issues* (2nd ed., pp. 1-3). New York, NY: Oxford University Press.

McClellan, B. E. (1999). *Moral education in America: Schools and the shaping of character from colonial times to the present*. New York, NY: Teachers College Press.

McGuffey, W. H. (1879). *McGuffey's sixth eclectic reader*. Cincinnati, OH: Van Antwerp, Bragg.

Mill, J. S. (2004). Higher and lower pleasures. In P. Singer (Ed.), *Ethics* (pp. 201-205). Oxford, England: Oxford University Press. (Original work published 1861)

Noddings, N. (1984). *Caring: A feminine approach to ethics & moral education*. Berkeley, CA: University of California Press.

Noddings, N. (1992). *The challenge to care in schools: An alternative approach to education*. New York, NY: Teachers College Press.

Noddings, N. (1999). Care, justice, and equity. In M. Katz, N. Noddings, & K. Strike (Eds.), *Justice and equity: The Search for common ground in education* (pp. 7-20). New York, NY: Teachers College Press.

Noddings, N. (2002a). *Educating moral people: A caring alternative to character education*. New York, NY: Teachers College Press.

Noddings, N. (2002b). *Starting at home: Caring and social policy*. Berkeley, CA: University of California Press.

Osher, D., Bear, G., Sprague, J., & Doyle, W. (2010). How can we improve school discipline? *Educational Researcher, 39*(1), 48-58.

Peters, R. S. (1967). *Ethics and education*. Oakland, NJ: Scott, Foresman.

Schneewind, J. B. (2006). Modern moral philosophy. In P. Singer (Ed.), *A companion to ethics* (pp. 147-157). Malden, MA: Blackwell.

Singer, P. (Ed.). (1994). Introduction. In *Ethics* (pp. 3-13). Oxford, England : Oxford University Press.

Sommers, C. H. (2002). How moral education is finding its way back into America's schools. In W. Damon (Ed.), *Bringing in a new era in character education* (pp. 23-41). Stanford, CA: Hoover Institution.

Stone, L. (2007). Should blame be part of the education of character? *Philosophy of Education*, 323-331.

Strike, K. A., & Soltis, J. F. (1985). *The ethics of teaching*. New York, NY: Teachers College Press.

Tyack, D. (1967). *Turning points in American educational history*. Waltham, MA: Blaisdell.

Yu, T. (2010). Character education for adolescents: Pedagogy of control. In J. L. DeVitis & L. Irwin-DeVitis (Eds.), *Adolescent education: A reader* (pp. 407-419). New York, NY: Peter Lang.

Author Contact Information: **Lynda Stone**, Professor, Philosophy of Education, University of North Carolina at Chapel Hill, CB#3500, Peabody Hall, Chapel Hill, NC 27599-3500. Phone: 919-962-1395. E-mail: lstone@email.unc.edu; **Jennifer Job**, Graduate Student, University of North Carolina at Chapel Hill, CB#3500, Peabody Hall, Chapel Hill NC 27599-3500. Phone: 919-962-1395. E-mail: jgjob@email.unc.edu

CHAPTER 4

Aesthetics and Education

Susan Laird
University of Oklahoma

Aesthetics and education is not in itself a theory, but a field of theoretical study within philosophy of education, variably pursued and disciplined, with practical value for educators across a broad range of roles, fields, and settings.

Most obviously, of course, arts educators are apt to regard *aesthetics* as the branch of philosophy whose subject matter is art, and therefore as important subject matter for students of the arts, so that they may learn to question how they and diverse others think about the arts they are studying. Their educational motivation for "doing aesthetics" derives typically from questions and problems that arise in their practical interactions with works of art, in their efforts to make, interpret, classify, evaluate, teach or learn about them (Parsons & Blocker, 1993). Largely because aesthetic ideas have so often been formulated thus, through experiences with works of art, or about appreciation, criticisms, and histories of artworks, the aesthetics and education field is often conflated with the field of *arts and education*, which has been acknowledged academically since the early twentieth century as one of the interdisciplinary "foundations of education" with especially strong ties also to the practical field typically called "curriculum and instruction." Indeed, aesthetics and education is so intimately related to arts and education that these two fields often do overlap and become indistinguishable from each other in practice. However, it can be a category mistake to draw a one-to-one correspondence between the aesthetics and education specialty within philosophy of education and the arts and education specialty within educational studies.

Arts and education is not merely or even primarily philosophical: for its thought and scholarship may become not only interdisciplinary, but sometimes primarily practical and actually artistic too. It may also be explicitly historical, sociological, anthropological, or psychological, or it may reflect rigorous interaction between two or more of these several foundational humanities and socioscience disciplines that take the arts as their topic, including philosophy. Concerned with theorizing educational questions, problems, values, and concepts related both to arts production and to arts reception, arts and education informs, and is informed by, philosophical inquiry in aesthetics and education. Although aesthetics and education does concern itself often with the multi-, inter-, and intradisciplinary subject matter of arts and education, especially with arguments theorizing arts' general educational value for learners, the subject matter of its philosophical inquiry is restricted neither to arts in education nor to education in and about arts (Higgins, 2010). Aesthetics and education poses philosophical questions that may concern moral educators, political educators, health and physical educators, religious and spiritual educators, environmental educators, even educational administrators, educational technologists, and educational psychologists, indeed many sorts of educators besides arts educators.

The common category mistake that conflates these two fields has more than merely logical and epistemological significance for educational studies in postmodernity, an era challenged by myriad technological and commercial developments of both aesthetic and educational consequence. Ethical and political concerns have become aestheticized in everyday life, almost everywhere, most often through mass media (Benjamin, 1955/1968; Berger, 1990; Bordo, 2004; Woolf, 1938). Pervasive contemporary aesthetic preoccupations with self-indulgence and keeping up appearances, entertainment and marketing, glamour and gore, comfort and luxury, apocalypse and terror, as well as with cultural and sexual politics, can give philosophical inquiry in this often neglected, profoundly devalued and underdeveloped field, aesthetics and education, some practical-ethical urgency and sociocultural complexity

The Handbook of Educational Theories, pp. 43–56

for twenty-first century educators outside the arts no less than for educators in arts (Abbs, 1994). This field merits a far more significant place than it enjoys typically now in the scholarship and in the curriculum of philosophy of education (Bogdan, 2010).

THE FIELD OF AESTHETICS AND EDUCATION

Along with logic, metaphysics, epistemology, and ethics, aesthetics is generally acknowledged as a major field within philosophy: as a branch of value theory that includes philosophy of art as well as philosophical inquiry concerning aesthetic experience of objects and phenomena not commonly recognized as art—for example, such as those encountered in nature or sport. First philosophically used by an eighteenth century German philosopher, Alexander Gottlieb Baumgarten, and subsequently cited by Kant (Kant, Walker, & Meredith, 2007), the term "aesthetics" derives from the Greek *aisthesis,* meaning sensory perception. Although some aestheticians have taken up educationally provocative philosophical questions about "taste" in its literal, sensory/perceptual sense related to food and drink (Korsmeyer, 2002, 2004; Laird, 2008a), aestheticians have theorized about matters of taste far more often in its metaphorical, critical sense, applied to objects or events seen, heard, experienced through multiple senses, or read—that is, about values that can and should ground sensory/perceptual judgments and about the conceptual meanings of terms invoked when discussing art or aesthetic experiences (Bourdieu & Nice, 1984; Korsmeyer, 1998; Tillman & Cahn, 1969).

Like philosophers of arts (Langer, 1977; McFee, 1992; Nussbaum, 1990; Scruton, 1979; Small, 1998), many theorists of aesthetics and education do take up philosophical questions concerning education in, about, and by specific and various fine arts—either taken collectively as a broad category or singly as a particular art form, or in particular combinations—such as literature, music, architecture, theater, dance, drawing, painting, sculpture, photography, and film. However, the meanings of *aesthetic* and of *art*—along with their epistemological status, their logical relationships to each other, and their contradistinction as well as their relationship to ethics, not to mention their political significance—are themselves topics of complex and intense philosophical analysis and debate (Korsmeyer, 1998, 2004)

Most obviously the term *art* is ambiguous insofar as it can refer broadly to any special skill whatsoever, such as cooking a meal, flying an airplane, raising a puppy, or arguing a point, no less than to the "high" and "fine" arts that have become proper curricular subject matter, often elite and aimed more at professionalizing and glamorizing artistry than at proliferating it. This ambiguity lends some credibility to arguments that art's conceptual meaning should be understood broadly, even if not so broadly as to include any skillful endeavor (Tillman & Cahn, 1969). Indeed one artistic preoccupation has often been to push the boundaries of art's philosophical definition, insofar as art is often understood definitively to require innovation or originality. Aestheticians have analyzed other various notions of art also, by which to test and theorize diverse understandings of it: for example, skillful making, creation of beautiful objects, significantly emotional or imaginative expression or communication (Parsons & Blocker, 1993). Through such analyses, theorists of aesthetics, arts, and education can consider questions about whether and why the term "art" should (not) extend to objects and phenomena such as top-40 hits and soap operas, teen fashions and hairdos, dolls and toys, trains and bicycles, parades and carnivals, slam-dancing and break-dancing, beat-boxing and crooning, blues and bluegrass, rap and rock, pottery-making and basket-making, tailoring and upholstering, quilting and lace-making. Aestheticians who embrace arts' democratic purposes and educational value have argued strongly for including many popular, folk, domestic, and commercial arts no less than fine arts within their definition of art (Beyer, 2008; Scruton, 1979; Sherman, 1984; Small & Walser, 1996). Indeed, contemporary aestheticians have generally discredited earlier distinctions between arts and crafts as no longer useful or defensible, although languages of "craft" have proven an especially useful topic for analytic philosophical inquiry concerning arts education (Howard, 1982).

The term *aesthetic,* both a noun and an adjective, is similarly ambiguous and dynamic in meaning. "An" aesthetic may refer to a distinctive taste, atmosphere, or style. An object, phenomenon, quality, criterion, attitude, point of view, experience, or wholly direct perceptual quality, unmediated by thinking, as in a color or as in an elicited pleasure or disgust, may be "aesthetic"; or the term may signify a quality that demands both perceptual and mindful attentiveness to meaning, or interpretation. Also, obviously, an object or phenomenon may be aesthetic in both senses simultaneously. In philosophical analysis, works of art are often considered paradigm (or intuitively clear) cases of aesthetic objects, but just as art's definition has broadened, so too a modern preoccupation with formulating the distinctiveness of aesthetic experience has given way to formulating more complex philosophical understanding of aesthetic experience in pragmatic relation to other values and concerns that may also be ethical, political, social, or otherwise practical (Bourdieu & Nice, 1984; Korsmeyer, 1998; Murdoch & Conradi, 1997; Parsons & Blocker, 1993).

These broadened understandings of art and aesthetic suggest far more educational consequence than the earlier, purer senses of these concepts. Given the vast historical significance of John Dewey's (1934) philosophical contributions to modern educational thought, as well as the conceptual centrality of *experience* within his democratic theory of education, his explicit aim in *Art As Experience* of "recovering the continuity" of aesthetic experience with "normal processes of living" has some pragmatic relevance for philosophical studies of learning, curriculum, and teaching in this media-saturated, appearance-obsessed postmodern era (Alexander, 1987; Garrison, 1997; Granger, 2006a, 2006b; Jackson, 1998). Indeed some theorists of aesthetics and education inspired by him have inquired whether we should think of teaching itself as an art that involves aesthetic practices and aims even when the curricular subject matter is not that of a fine art (Simpson, Jackson, & Aycock, 2005).

Philosophers of aesthetics and education not only analyze and define concepts that are useful to understand the practice of aesthetic education and various sorts of judgment that enter into it. They also pose and study questions concerning what should be taught, toward what ends, to and by whom, when and for how long, as well as questions about whether the purpose of aesthetic education should be the development of learners' knowledge, appreciation, imagination, or creativity, or perhaps some combination of these, whether aesthetic education should be considered general or specialized education or perhaps both. Educational aestheticians working in arts and education may pose and study particular questions concerning the educational justification for a particular art or for arts generally, concerning curricular censorship and selection of artworks as well as critical values and skills and pedagogical practices of particular arts, or concerning arts' educative integration with one another or into curricula in other subjects.

Aesthetics and education has particular epistemological significance for philosophy of education by, about, and for those social groups underrepresented by and within the field's scholarship (Green, 1997, 2002), who have suffered systematic miseducation and symbolic violence (Laird, 1989, 1999, 2002), whose embodied learning experiences have escaped philosophical notice (Bogdan, 1992; Greene, 1978; Laird, 2009; Martin, 2006), and whose own thought has been denied proper acknowledgment and full development within academic philosophy (Martin, 1985). Many of these underrepresented have composed their educational thought artistically, in diverse genres other than the philosophical treatise (Duran, 2007). Works of art by, about, and for such social groups—as well as their embodied experiences whose educational significance philosophers have neglected or otherwise devalued—may serve philosophers of education as primary sources and provocations for conceptual interpretation, critical evaluation, and original formulation to correct such gaps especially consequential for both philosophy and education (Laird, 1991, 1994, 1995, 1998, 2003; Milligan, 1998; Worley, 1999).

With such aims, modern analytic philosophers of education have tended to interpret works of literature mimetically, often as mere quasi-empirical cultural data, as cases for conceptual and logical analysis, without attention either to their formal or expressive artistry or to their pragmatics of reader response, even where such neglected aesthetic complexities may pose epistemological, ethical, logical, or political problems for their educational thought. However, theorists of aesthetics and education have explained and constructed aesthetic concepts, techniques, and practices for interpretation and evaluation of artworks and other significant sensory experiences, sensitive to such complexities, to inform processes of thinking philosophically about educational questions (Bogdan, 1992). In this way philosophical specialists in aesthetics and education have contributed significant resources vital to the new scholarship in cultural studies and in women's and gender studies.

No Philosophical History of Aesthetics and Education

A philosophical history of the aesthetics and education field has not yet been written—a project well worth undertaking. This section cannot offer a comprehensive gloss on any grand narrative, then, but will suggest some significant historical markers, sources, and gaps from which this field's future philosophical historians might begin tracing their own outlines of this project's possible shape with various present educational purposes in mind. These suggestions are necessarily limited and partial, however, and in this postmillennial age of globalization merit extensive amendment with comparative philosophical-historical studies of aesthetics and education from the continents of Asia, Latin America, and Africa as well. In Europe as well as postcolonial North America and Australia, academic consensus has it that aesthetic-educational inquiry's philosophical history begins with Plato (Plato, Cooper, & Hutchinson, 1997) and Aristotle (Aristotle, Roberts, & Bywater, 1984), as educational inquiry's philosophical history generally does, and owes much of its later modern development, as already noted, to Dewey (1934).

Those ancient Greek philosophers regarded music as an educational basic, for development of children's spirits as well as for development of philosophical minds, although in *Republic,* Plato (Plato, Cooper, &

Hutchinson, 1997) censored poetry for children and banished it completely from adult experience, whereas in *Poetics,* Aristotle (Aristotle, Roberts, & Bywater, 1984) theorized theatrical (also poetic) drama's power to evoke and educate difficult emotions with moral profundity. These ancient arguments may help to explain why philosophy of music education (with its own specialized journal, *Philosophy of Music Education Review*) is a more robust international academic field today than philosophy of education in other arts (Elliott, 1995; Jorgensen, 2002, 2008; Reimer, 2002; Woodford, 2004), with the possible exception of literature, whose value has enjoyed strong philosophical advocacy also (Bogdan, 1992; Frye, 1964; Nussbaum, 1990), often Aristotelian, against Plato's antiliterary arguments throughout modernity. Insofar as aesthetics and education claims its grounding exclusively in those ancient disputes about the meaning and value of music, poetry, and drama, disputes of undeniable curricular importance even today, the field is structured to neglect the most obvious primary sources of general aesthetic education: those spaces and places where learners learn and teachers teach (Gaines, 1991; Gomez, 2005). Such spaces and places are taken-for-granted metaphoric stage sets for the everyday dramas of educating and miseducating, environments that transmit cultural values by engendering countless meaningful unexamined sensory experiences of social consequence.

Such spaces and places do merit study by philosophical historians of aesthetics and education. Perhaps most famously, Thomas Jefferson's (Wilson, 2009) campus design for the University of Virginia represents an acknowledged major architectural concept of higher education for White republican statesmen. But also in *Alma Mater* historian Helen Lefkowitz Horowitz (1993) has analyzed another major architectural concept of higher education evident in U.S. college campuses designed explicitly for modern women. Both concepts have influenced U.S. campus design broadly. Also, rural one-room school-houses—representing an acknowledged major past architectural concept of public coeducation for children—have undergone historic preservation in many rural U.S. communities; the Blackwell History of Education Museum exhibits an actual rebuilt one-room school on the University of Northern Illinois campus along with design relics (furniture, implements, etc.) from the material culture of such one-room schools.[1] Yet today many of the newest high schools are—in stark contrast to those earlier well-known architectural icons of education—imposing, forbidding, massive, windowless, high-fenced, prisonlike structures without landscaping, organized for surveillance and security rather than for shared learning experiences of inspiration or curiosity. Meanwhile, many older schools still in use (as Jonathan Kozol has noted in his numerous popular books about urban education, most recently *The Shame of the Nation,* 2005) may have been elegantly designed, but are today dilapidated structures with live wires hanging from ceilings, many windows broken, painted over, filthy panes glued in with bubble gum, admitting little or no light (literally and metaphorically) to the learners within them (Worley, 1999).

Although building and furniture construction and architecture are typically arts curricula restricted to vocational and professional education programs (as if Home Depot lacked nationwide popularity), such taken-for-granted primary sources of general aesthetic education become hidden curricula for *all* learners when educators neglect them. Despite ubiquitous high school marching bands, school plays, required courses in English studies, and an admirable network of A+ Schools in North Carolina and Oklahoma that integrate arts across their academic and athletic curricula, could the philosophical history of aesthetics and education be constructed credibly as a narrative of such hidden curricula's consequential, but unnecessary neglect? Correcting that philosophical-historical neglect would entail learning to read such typical contemporary school buildings and their environing landscapes as material signs of educational thought's general ignorance of and indifference toward both arts and aesthetic experiences that, for worse as well as for better, shape and give meaning to learners' and educators' everyday lives.[2]

Although architecture clearly fits the several definitions of art surveyed above (Scruton, 1979), it has occasioned little philosophical scholarship in either aesthetics and education or arts and education that might address that corrective challenge. Yet the ancient Roman Vitruvius (Vitruvius Pollio & Granger, 1931, 1934; Vitruvius Pollio, Rowland, & Howe, 2001) theorized architecture as the art from which all other arts were developed, speculating its origins in organic human relations with the natural world. Indeed, experiencing architecture (Gauldie, 1968; Rasmussen, 1964; Scruton, 1979) is intensely aesthetic insofar as it involves engagement of *all* human senses, with the possible exception of taste (except in its metaphoric sense invoked by aestheticians): sight, hearing, touch, and smell, as well as other more complex sensory capacities such as kinaesthesia (proprioception, sensing position and movement of body) and synaesthesia (awakening one sense through another). Also, as an art that orders human-world relations at once conceptually and aesthetically, it may integrate examples or aspects of other arts and crafts into its own design work: drawing, photography, painting, sculpture, textiles, ceramics, furniture, and by suggestion or enclosure, if not by staging or other representation, even theater, music, dance, story, and film. Moreover, what other art form has a more ubiquitous and public-instructive, yet intimate and taken-for-granted, complex aesthetic presence in everyday life throughout the human lifespan?

Vitruvius's (Vitruvius Pollio & Granger, 1931, 1934; Vitruvius Pollio et al., 2001) *De Architectura,* a Latin treatise that teaches imperial Augustan-Roman architectural principles, practices, and aims—such as firmness (*firmitas*), commodity (*utilitas*), and delight (*venustas*)—has enjoyed significant historical influence in the theoretical curriculum for architects since its fifteenth century recovery. This earliest known text on architecture opens by theorizing architects' education as a multidisciplinary effort that involves both manual practice of craftsmanship of various sorts and theoretical studies—including philosophy, music, mathematics, astronomy, medicine, and law—for it theorizes architecture as a material expression of complex relationship between "man" [*sic*] and his environment. Its mathematical description of the human physique's perfect proportions—specifically those of a sculptural representation of emperor Augustus (McEwen, 2002)—informing the design of buildings' proportions inspired Leonardo da Vinci's famous drawing of the "Vitruvian man" (da Vinci, O'Malley, Saunders, and Saunders, 2003). That classic artistic image of the idealized adult male human outline with arms and legs apart, configured simultaneously within a perfect circle and a perfect square, entitled the *Canon of Proportions,* provided the visual-theoretical foundation from whose critical reexamination architectural proportion and scale have been redefined and reconfigured, reconstructed, taught, and learned, even in late modernity.

But perhaps even more importantly, Leonardo's Vitruvian image's maleness, adultness, static formality, and measured geometric perfection embody a vivid metaphor for still-commonplace modern metric conceptions of educational evaluation against ideal standards, which dominate much educational policy today. Yet the architectural notion critically derived from Vitruvius, of constructing an embodied reciprocal relationship between humans and their environments, through *multiple* senses and arts, suggests another conception of educational value—as rigorously aesthetic—with possible implications at the same time for environmental education as yet scarcely recognized by philosophers of aesthetic education.

Critical of classical philosophical preoccupations with static ideal forms, so vividly evident in Leonardo's image of Vitruvian man, Dewey (1934) puts a new democratic philosophical spin centuries later on the imperialistic Vitruvian architectural conception of aesthetic relationship. Although he (1934) never cites the

Note: Leonardo da Vinci [Public domain], via Wikimedia Commons: http://commons.wikimedia.org/wiki/File:Da_Vinci_Vitruve_Luc_Viatour.jpg. This widely reproduced and circulated image of Leonardo's "Vitruvian man," a drawing sometimes called the *Canon of Proportions,* is at the Gallerie dell'Academia in Venice, Italy, where it is only occasionally on exhibit, and appears on the cover of *Leonardo da Vinci on the Human Body: The Anatomical, Physiological, and Embryological Drawings of Leonardo da Vinci,* translated by O'Malley, Saunders, and Saunders (2003); it is also readily accessible via Google for viewing at many online sites, including "Vitruvian Man" on Facebook.

Figure 4.1. Leonardo da Vinci's "Vitruvian man" (ca. 1487).

Vitruvian man or *De Architectura*, he does cite works of architecture (e.g., the Parthenon), reflect upon architecture and space, and frame his thought in architectural and spatial metaphors in *Art as Experience.* There he premises his theory of aesthetic experience, significant also for his (1936) later theory of educational experience in *Experience and Education*, upon his conception of "the live creature," whose "life goes on in an environment; not merely *in* it, but because of it, through interaction with it" and whose "career and destiny ... are bound up with its interchanges with its environment, not externally but in the most intimate way" (Dewey, 1934, p. 13). This modern philosophical figure of the live creature is a sort of degendered Vitruvian man, not necessarily adult, not even necessarily human, removed from that perfect stasis, and not represented mathematically as a generic or imperial ideal. In contrast to Vitruvian man, the Deweyan live creature has needs and is responsive, active, and dynamic, with a history evolving as a consequence of that basic, constitutive, reciprocal, embodied, and at least potentially intelligent and emotive relationship to environment. Especially when perceived as a post-Darwinian philosophical figure revising radically the Vitruvian man, this Deweyan live creature signifies a paradigm shift of potentially vast significance for aesthetics and education, by calling attention to aesthetic experience not only in critical relation to high fine arts (including architecture as the matrix of all arts), but also with particular constructive and philosophical regard to any human-world relations at once embodied and mindful in ordinary everyday lives.

Throughout modernity, aesthetic education has focused mostly on the teaching and learning of specific arts, often in relation to liberal education or occasionally in relation to athletics, while only scarcely focusing on the educative construction of aesthetic human-environmental relations as suggested by the Vitruvian-Deweyan thinking glossed here. Indeed, since early modernity, aesthetic learning has occurred at the curricular margins of liberal education, as professionalized subject matter for elites' learning, as opportunity for display and publicity, and as mere "frill" entertainment, diversion, and decoration for ordinary learners. Leaving socially irresponsible aesthetic neglect of educational environments generally unchallenged, this curricular marginalization has diminished philosophical interest in aesthetic education even as it has imposed a burden of justification on the field.

Ironically, in early modernity, scarcely schooled, Mary Wollstonecraft (Laird, 2008b; Wollstonecraft, 1989) got much if not most of her own unusual self-education through aesthetic encounters with the nonhuman natural world and with arts of various media—literature, painting, theater, music, architecture—that were then flourishing with immense revolutionary significance. But in *A Vindication of the Rights of Woman* she (Wollstonecraft, 1989) theorized coeducation as a revolutionary alternative to the monarchist miseducation she had witnessed in Georgian England without questioning John Locke's (Locke, Grant, & Tarcov, 1996) placement of arts education at the curricular margins (Laird, 2008b). His (Locke, Grant, & Tarcov, 1996) seventeenth century educational thought had inspired Wollstonecraft and her eighteenth century revolutionary contemporaries with its acknowledgment of epistemological value in the human body's sense experiences and its theorizing that a learned disposition to sustain health was basic to the human mind's more highly valued intellectual (liberal) learning (Laird, 2008b). But Locke could scarcely have dreamed of the culturally transformative artistic developments and aesthetic experiences that would educate Wollstonecraft and her radically liberal cohort in the next century, so he located fine arts at the curricular margins—as subject matter merely for learning worthwhile leisure pursuits. (To his credit, he valued leisure pursuits as worthy of some philosophical and educational attention they are scarcely accorded today.)

Wollstonecraft's (Laird, 2008b; Wollstonecraft, 1989) experimental concept of coeducation did critique implicitly and constructively Locke's (Locke, Grant, & Tarcov, 1996) notion that cultivation of personal beauty was the one purpose that should distinguish girls' education from that of boys (Laird, 2008b). Highly critical of excessive educational emphasis on girls' concern with their own beautiful appearance and on fine arts as "accomplishments" that daughters of educated men were expected to learn for the everyday-life entertainments and comforts of their family, friends, and suitors, she was suspicious of education that fostered young women's sentimental sensibility and distanced young women from opportunities to develop their rational powers through the study of science. Those "female accomplishments" included arts such as music, drawing, poetry, story, dance, and theater as well as various forms of textile, ceramic, and culinary crafts and artistry within the domestic context. Apparently thinking only of those accomplishments associated with the construction of domesticated and weak femininity, Wollstonecraft neglected to consider other arts that women were generally denied opportunities to learn, such as architecture, for which mathematical and scientific studies were even then necessary (also evident in *De Architectura*), arts that contributed substantially to modern development of cultural imagination transformative for human-world relations of particular concern to her.

Sadly Wollstonecraft did not live to read and engage critically, in her own published writings, Friedrich Schiller's (1795/1994/2004) romantic argument in *On the Aesthetic Education of Man*. He theorized that art might have revolutionary cultural and educative power to free learners' senses and intellects from excesses and constraints of both pure rational mind and pure nature. Though Schiller was roughly Wollstonecraft's contemporary, aesthetic education became a major gap in her theory of coeducation (Laird, 2008b). It remains a major gap in American practices of coeducation in schools, colleges, and universities, where too often aesthetic education becomes primarily preprofessional, recreational, or privileged, and often gender specific, if not altogether absent. Because of such systematic devaluation, aesthetic education's justification has become perhaps the primary challenge for philosophical scholars in aesthetics and education throughout modernity.

In the early twentieth century, however, 3 decades before Dewey (1934) wrote *Art As Experience,* U.S. theorists in the material-feminist and home economics movements, which included Charlotte Perkins Gilman and some innovative teachers at the Laboratory School under Dewey's philosophical leadership at the University of Chicago, would take up practical questions that Wollstonecraft had neglected to theorize about aesthetic education in relation to scientific and liberal learning and gender—especially with regard to design education, to arts and education for everyday life, and to such aesthetic education's possible cultural consequences for social equality and well-being (Brown, 1985; Hayden, 1982). Concurrently with those women's movements, just as in *Up From Slavery* Booker T. Washington (1901) had theorized arts of building design and construction along with other practical arts and humanities as subject matter for African Americans' general education for survival and cultural development, W.E.B. DuBois (1903) was theorizing in *The Souls of Black Folk* that "story and song" and "spirit" were among African Americans' most significant "gifts" to U.S. culture, along with toil and brawn. At the same time, the Chicago Laboratory School (Mayhew & Edwards, 1936) was featuring an experimental coeducational curricular core of which both Vitruvius and Wollstonecraft might have approved: scientific and historical studies of human-world-making relations through a playful pedagogy of imaginary cultural formation that consisted in children's reasoning reenactment of design deliberations and constructions to meet live creatures' most basic needs in geographically diverse locales—needs such as food, clothing, and shelter that were profoundly aesthetic, often also artful. Such historical developments in educational thought and practice merit philosophical formulation and critique for aesthetics and education responsive to primary sources of aesthetic learning in taken-for-granted learning environments.

Over a half century later, in 1966, however, the inaugural issue of the *Journal of Aesthetic Education* highlighted the field's elitism as one of its constitutive problems requiring serious scholarly scrutiny. Since then, the *Journal of Aesthetic Education* has published studies of multicultural aesthetic education, of architecture in higher education, and of aesthetic education and gender, amid various special issues devoted to aesthetic education in one specific art or another (music, theater, etc.) and to questions about integrating arts and aesthetic education into curricula across the disciplines. For theorists of aesthetics and education, as for theorists in any valued field of study, understanding its structure of knowledge and its philosophical history is not a luxury. But such understanding awaits future construction, perhaps from resources such as those glossed here, especially the *Journal of Aesthetic Education.*

Cultural and Practical Studies in Aesthetics and Education

Postmillennial philosophers of education frame much, perhaps even most, of their inquiry across a wide range of specialties with a common critical concern that they name and formulate variously, which Jane Roland Martin (2002) has named "cultural miseducation," whose most obvious evidence is hatred, violence, and amoral indifference of various sorts that perpetuate suffering and social injustice. Racism, sexism, heterosexism, bigotry, terrorism, elitism, and abuse of children, elders, animals, and the environment are all familiar examples of cultural miseducation, although this short list does not begin to exhaust all possible forms that cultural miseducation may take. Only rarely, however, do philosophers of education engage aesthetic-educational inquiry in their own diversely conceived inquiries with regard to cultural miseducation (variously named and conceived) and its possible remedies.

For example, although Martin is a practicing and performing virtuosic amateur classical pianist herself, whose strong philosophical critiques aimed at education's radical redefinition value the arts emphatically, she is not an aesthetician and has not yet engaged the aesthetics and education field's thought in constructing her own, either. Her (2002) conceptual analysis of cultural miseducation and her proposed remedy for it merits reading specifically in the critical light of inquiry by some recent major philosophers of aesthetics and education that she has not yet engaged. Perhaps such reading may construct a helpful framework for explaining how this "aesthetics and education gap" (henceforth AEG) in philosophy of education generally, exemplified not only in Martin's own oeuvre but also in most others' as well, could render many of the field's critiques of cultural miseducation pragmatically naïve, insensitive to live creatures, despite abundant laudable moral intentions, even despite frequent reasonable turns toward the arts with educative intent. Such a reading may help explain how this AEG renders philosophers of education too often ignorant of subtle but vastly consequential practical problems that they will need to study if we are to understand live creatures' most ethically sensitive educational challenges of recognizing, preventing, diagnosing, mitigating, correcting, responding to, surviving, and recovering from cultural miseducation.

Martin (2002) theorizes that cultural miseducation begins with "a problem of generations" that results in one generation's transmitting its "cultural liabilities" to the next generation, or in one generation's failure to transmit its "cultural assets" to the next. The AEG signifies that twenty-first century philosophers of education and other professional educators confront such a problem of generations, whether most are aware of it yet or not. Within Martin's analytic frame, the (largely unacknowledged, as yet unformulated) philosophical history of aesthetics and education and recent contributions to that field constitute "cultural stock" that will either be preserved and transmitted as a "living legacy" of "cultural wealth" in the twenty-first century to correct AEG, or neglected, dismissed, and otherwise devalued as a chaotic heap of "dead relics," mere traces of AEG.

Also Martin (2002) theorizes that cultural miseducation occurs not only through schooling, whose reductive and essentialist equation with education remains a taken-for-granted commonplace in colleges of education, but also through a much broader "multiple educational agency" that may indeed constitute more powerful sources of learning than schooling itself. This latter notion is clearly not news to philosophers of arts, aesthetics, and education, inasmuch as they have long acknowledged that arts education and aesthetic education may occur within family and religious life, through gatherings of friends, at camps and nursing homes, at fairs and festivals, in community recreational groups and centers, at museums and libraries and concert halls, through a wide range of mass media, in parks or on streets, or in specialized studios and shops, not to mention private freelance instructors and organized master classes. Wherever public schools have cut their arts budgets, those who want aesthetic and artistic education for their children must depend privately often upon its multiple educational agency at large, which can be prohibitively costly, thereby rendering such education "elitist" regardless of its content, methods, or aims to the contrary. Schools' curricular devaluation of arts and aesthetics, implicitly endorsed by philosophy of education's AEG, may be characterized as cultural miseducation because it does foster such elitism. Yet few think of those many other agents of aesthetic education typically as agents of cultural miseducation, and rarely do evaluators of education assess aesthetic education by surveying the consequences of its multiple educational agency's configuration within a community. With respect to education generally, of course, the arts are themselves integral participants in multiple educational agency too. The AEG in philosophy of education denies reflection to such phenomena.

Against cultural miseducation, Martin (2002) recommends strategically thoughtful attention to multiple educational agency, evaluative studies that she has named "cultural book-keeping." She does not theorize this critical process's technical particulars, specifying only its general aim to ascertain what "cultural wealth" merits preservation and transmission to the next generation by examining all relevant "cultural stock" in order to classify each piece of it as either "cultural asset" or "cultural liability." When Locke (Locke et al., 1996) and Wollstonecraft (1989) consigned aesthetic education to the curricular margins of liberal education, they were practicing cultural book-keeping that became complicit in constructing AEG. When contemporary philosophers of education neglect to question that early modern philosophical move, and when philosophers of aesthetics and education neglect aesthetic experiences of spaces and places where teachers teach and learners learn, they are neglecting some of their field's most potentially consequential cultural book-keeping tasks and sustaining AEG. Martin's (2002) theoretical argument for the necessity of cultural book-keeping represents a general summons to philosophers of education to undertake thoroughgoing cultural studies as educational criticism. The practical value of such criticism's neglected technical particulars will depend upon extensive critical engagement of rigorous sorts that philosophers of aesthetics and education have begun to theorize with subtlety.

Many diverse and significant philosophical contributors to *Journal of Aesthetic Education* and *Philosophy of Music Education Review*, as well as *Philosophy of Education* proceedings and yearbooks, deserve recognition from philosophers of education and other educators for such efforts impossible to detail here. Maxine Greene (1973, 1978, 1995), Deanne Bogdan (1992, 2010), and Richard Shusterman (2000, 2008) stand out, however, among the most significant recent philosophical contributors to the aesthetics and education field in this regard. Although both Greene (1995) and Bogdan (1992, 2010) have acknowledged intellectual debts to Martin's gender critique of philosophy of education, and although Shusterman (2008) has engaged questions akin to hers, particularly in his study of Simone de Beauvoir's thought, none of these educational aestheticians has yet engaged her (2002) *Cultural Miseducation* directly. Yet their educational thinking could be cited as exemplifying distinctively aesthetic practices of cultural book-keeping. At the same time, their work demonstrates substantial further theoretical development of that process concept, pragmatically significant for post-millennial philosophy of education.

Neither Greene nor Bogdan has posed or engaged aesthetic questions about cultural book-keeping with regard to educational architecture or architectural education. But both Greene (1978) and Martin (1994) have called metaphoric attention to "landscapes" of learning and education as sites of necessary change, and both Greene (1995) and Bogdan (1992) have conceived philosophical texts themselves as material landscapes within which events occur. These two latter theorists may be nearly unique insofar as they call attention implicitly to the Vitruvian artistry evident in most modern philosophical prose, even in aesthetics and education, which constructs thoughts as perfectly composed logical structures for the anaesthetized ease of an idealized general reader, often presumed White and male. By contrast, the rational forms of Greene's and Bogdan's phenomenological prose are artfully textured to teach readers alertness to the aesthetic vitality of reasoning itself as a challenging self-educative art, by making their texts into pedagogical environments, where the written page becomes an eventful space for pursuit of that art's challenges. Their philosophical prose invites diverse readers as Deweyan live creatures, with their own needs and histories, into the complicated living stream of cultural book-keeping's eventful challenges and thinking processes, to be experienced through direct aesthetic engagement with the particular multiple educational agency that they cite as having prompted their own thinking. For both these phenomenological theorists of aesthetics and education, then, cultural book-keeping becomes an open-ended process that requires living readers' aesthetic engagement with the events of thinking, with the artfully signifying forms no less than with the signified logical content of their thought. They teach their readers that even philosophical thinking is not purely a mental, conceptual affair—but also an aesthetic one.

Over the past half century, Greene's (1973, 1978, 1995) prolific and monumental oeuvre as an existentialist phenomenologist in aesthetics and education has registered an influential philosophical alert to educators: to value both the arts and aesthetic experience as cultural wealth consequential for the education of Deweyan live creatures. Green (1978, 1995) has argued that the arts and aesthetic experience can arouse a moral "wide-awakeness" to "predicaments of women" and to many other cultural liabilities encountered in "the lived world," inspire questioning about their mystification within "landscapes of learning," and release learners' imaginations to resist and transform them in public spaces. In direct response to Greene's philosophical alert, Landon E. Beyer's (2000) recent curriculum theorizing about teacher education and schooling in *The Arts, Popular Culture, and Social Change* has applied her valuation of aesthetic experience as cultural wealth specifically to the curricular inclusion of popular arts as cultural assets useful for teaching diverse subjects with critical intent. Martin (1994) has premised her own half-century project of "changing the educational landscape" upon a tacit curricular valuation of the arts as cultural wealth without attempting to duplicate or revise Greene's defense of it. In *The Schoolhome*, for example, she (1992) argues for a "gender-sensitive" school curriculum rich in culturally and racially diverse world arts, which aims not just for children's "spectatorship," but also for their "learning to live" both at home and in the world. That thought experiment removes theater (together with newspaper) from the school's curricular margins to the schoolhome's curricular core, commends schoolchildren's joyful singing, and examines thought-provoking scenes of classroom cultural conflict that arise in forthright interpretive discussions of literature representing students' own most challenging lived realities such as racism, child abuse, sexism, violence, and poverty.

Critically examining her own pedagogical practices and experiences from a premise akin to Greene's, that literature has educational value as cultural wealth, Bogdan (1992) has made such classroom cultural conflict, along with literary theorist Northrop Frye's (1964) *The Educated Imagination,* the analytic focus of her earliest philosophical inquiry in aesthetics and education. Revisiting Plato's (Plato et al., 1997) theorizing in the *Republic* that poetry may function not as a cultural asset worthy of transmission to the next generation, but actually often as a cultural liability, a source of cultural miseducation, Bogdan (1992) has studied contemporary practices of cultural book-keeping as curricular censorship in *Re-Educating the Imagination.* Space does not permit comprehensive attention here to her microtheorizing of "the censorship problem," but most significantly it has included her aesthetic-educational conception of a "poetics of refusal" premised upon "the logical priority of direct response." She has derived those formulations from her phenomenological reflection upon women graduate students' refusal to read and discuss, even for philosophical purposes of studying feminist criticism of masculinist poetics, John Updike's (2003) story, "A & P," which narrates a coming-of-age male supermarket cashier's sexual-aesthetic response to a bikini-clad girl-customer's body. One student, Judy, responded directly to this seldom-questioned staple of the high-school literature curriculum, and her women classmates concurred: "I am not a censor, but burn the damned thing!" Bogdan (1992) analyzes the aesthetic logic in these intellectually sophisticated learners' "censorship as agnosis," from a pragmatic, gender-sensitive educational premise: that student readers cannot be approached ethically as generalized ideal readers (literary versions of Vitruvian man, merely studying literature in the abstract), but should be recognized as "real readers reading" (literary versions of Deweyan live creatures, coming to literature with their own needs). Inescapably, these real readers' experiencing bodies are as ethically and aesthetically relevant as their analytical minds to their reading responses and critical engagement as literary learners, Bogdan argues. Framing their aesthetic response as a problem of feeling, power, and location that demonstrates literary language's real-world consequences, she argues that literature education must be ethically accountable to such consequences, evident also in prominent censorship disputes about the teaching of Mark Twain's (1884) *The Adventures of Huckleberry Finn.*

Arguments justifying its curricular inclusion in school curricula on abstract grounds, such as its canonical status, its possible antiracist use, or even the value of its empathetic portrait of an abused, orphaned, runaway child, without regard to actually present African American students' feeling, power, and location problems as real readers reading this American classic's depictions of racism and White supremacist violence, become highly questionable from the perspective of Bogdan's (1992) theoretical argument for the logical priority of direct response. Thus Bogdan makes clear that an aesthetic experience may function as a cultural liability for one student or group of students even as it seems to function as a cultural asset for others. In response to this cultural book-keeping problem, she theorizes practices of "embodied" reading, criticism, and pedagogy that acknowledge its difficulties. Bogdan elaborates her aesthetic-educational theory of direct response's logical priority with even finer conceptual subtlety later, through her phenomenological studies of wordless musical experience in various practical contexts of multiple educational agency (e.g., classrooms, mass media, concert halls, church, home). Her (2002, 2010, 2011) latest thought in this vein enters the body most prominently by formulating a distinction between direct and critical responses to conceive aesthetic response as "shiver" or "shimmer." As unreflective aesthetic pleasure, shiver becomes a necessary condition of the more intricately reflective yet somatic, shimmer, which grounds aesthetic experience as spiritual, thus dissolving the Platonic body/spirit false dichotomy, and as having real-world consequences for learners as listeners embodied and embedded within contexts of cultural miseducation such as terrorism, bigotry, racism, professionalism, elitism, and commercial commodification.

Greene and Bogdan have situated their cultural book-keeping contributions to aesthetics and education primarily within arts and education, and some of Richard Shusterman's (1996, 2000) important cultural book-keeping contributions to aesthetics and education also fall within arts and education as he theorizes philosophical and educational value, for example, in the work of popular young rap artists. In the preface to his (2008) latest book *Body Consciousness,* moreover, he explains his confrontation with his publisher's choice of Ingres's (1806) painting *Baigneuse de Valpincon,* depicting a nude woman bather, for his book's cover. His exposition reflects substantial affinity with Bogdan's students' confrontation with her curricular choice of "A & P." Since Cambridge University Press's marketing department refused to heed his complaints about *Baigneuse,* he has argued that, in effect, this cover image is cultural miseducation, at odds with his book's educative purposes. Thus, implicitly Shusterman underscores Bogdan's critical insight that even a "great" work of art, presumed to be a cultural asset—like Updike's story or Ingres's nude—may foster aesthetic experience that makes it pragmatically a cultural liability.

That exposition exemplifies one branch of a new aesthetic-educational discipline Shusterman (2000) has formulated and proposed, which may concern fine arts as noted, but is more centrally concerned with the art of living well. He has named this new discipline "somaesthetics." Those philosophers of education who take seriously Martin's (1992) argument in *The Schoolhome* that "learning to live" should become a central curricular concern for educators of children will find in Shusterman's theory of somaesthetics many new cultural book-keeping questions to consider, particularly with regard to education for physical and spiritual health that philosophers of education have considered rarely if at all. Contemporary "problems of attention, overstimulation, and stress," along with "deceptive body images" (akin to those critiqued by Wollstonecraft) make this proposal pragmatically urgent for philosophers of education to engage. Shusterman has defined somaesthetics as "the critical, meliorative study of the experience and use of one's body as a locus of sensory-aesthetic appreciation (*aesthesis*) and creative self-fashioning" (Shusterman, 2000, 2008, p. 19). This discipline is complex in its conception, insofar as it may be practical, analytic, or pragmatic, in which case it may be experiential, representational, or performative.

For example, "practical somaesthetics" may include actual practices such as T'ai Chi Ch'uan, hatha yoga, Pilates, the Alexander Technique (which Dewey practiced and recommended), or the Feldenkrais Method (in which Shusterman is himself a licensed practicing instructor), as well as various martial arts, aerobics, calisthenics, athletics, dietetic regimens, clothing fashions, cosmetic techniques, and other body-decorative strategies and fads such as jewelry, tattoos, and so forth (Shusterman, 2000, 2008). Shusterman (2008) does not study Wollstonecraft's (1989) thought, but her discourse on the essentialist assumptions that weakness is feminine and strength is masculine presents an early clear case of "analytic somaesthetics," whose definitive purpose is descriptive and theoretical study of bodily perceptions and practices, including their epistemological consequences and politics. By contrast, "pragmatic somaesthetics" is theory and criticism focused on normative and prescriptive claims about specific practices like those enumerated above. Wollstonecraft's critique of early modern fashions that prevented girls' and women's freedom of movement and focused their minds on trivial rather than meaningful learning, exemplifies pragmatic somaesthetics which may include representational (externally focused), experiential (internally focused), and performative emphases. Critical concerns like those of Bogdan's students, or like his own about his book's cover, fall into his category of "representational somaesthetics."

Space limitations forbid full exposition of somaesthetics here, but even this brief conceptual summary could suggest many new cultural book-keeping questions concerning aesthetics and education in relation to a far broader range of consequential life-practices than those customarily classified as "arts"—including commonplace school and university practices that philosophers of education have scarcely considered worthy of examination heretofore: cheerleading, cafeteria meals, dress codes and uniforms, and sports. Philosophers of education who value "learning to live" may pursue somaesthetic inquiry to examine such taken-for-granted practices' and experiences' consequences for cultural miseducation (Laird, 2008a). Philosophers of education have neglected such topics, preferring a narrower focus on intellectualistic learning, probably because, as Shusterman (2008) has argued at length, the western philosophical tradition has devalued the body and bodily experience. He demonstrates how even many of those philosophers best-known for their thought about the body and bodily experience have in subtle ways devalued them. Shusterman has challenged that bias with sensitivity to the pervasively aesthetic character of postmodern life. By thus enlarging the range of philosophical study concerning cultural miseducation, his somaesthetics presents a significant agenda for aesthetics and education in the twenty-first century.

Both Bogdan's logical priority of direct response and Shusterman's somaesthetics show how aesthetic education can counter cultural miseducation. They show, too, where an accounting metaphor for cultural evaluation, even in curriculum, must inevitably break down in any empathetic concern for the vitality of Deweyan live creatures, or fail at its purpose by framing their aesthetically responsive lives in the calculating and generalizing terms of ideal Vitruvian standards aimed at their containment. At the heart of both Bogdan's and Shusterman's aesthetic-educational projects lies their differently formulated but similarly motivated sense that, in a world overwrought by cultural miseducation, which too often demands violence to self no less than to others, live creatures might learn through aesthetic engagements of/with their bodyminds or bodysouls to experience depth, luminosity, pleasure, health, meaning beyond words and calculations, which might enhance their conscientious resistance against cultural miseducation wherever they encounter or witness it.

Martin's (2002) other remedy for cultural miseducation (besides cultural book-keeping) is her proposed pedagogy of "circulating the gifts," a notion she derives from Lewis Hyde's (1999) cultural anthropology of arts. Although the thought of Greene, Bogdan, and Shusterman is far too complex, subtle, and prolific to summarize adequately here, their thought does suggest implicitly the postmodern necessity of circulating the gifts of aesthetics and education among philosophers and educators who aim to respond ethically to cultural miseducation. Philosophers of aesthetics and education can infer from Martin's theory of cultural miseducation a radically enlarged and more obviously significant role for their field in educational thought more generally than they have enjoyed recently, a role that requires broader and stronger attention to AEG. Greene, Bogdan, and Shusterman have laid vital philosophical groundwork for this renovated role, variously reminding educators that learners are live creatures to whom idealized and metric conceptions of educational value can do violence, that the arts merit recognition as cultural wealth for both philosophy and education, and that aesthetic experience is at once politically and pedagogically consequential, capable of functioning simultaneously as cultural asset and cultural liability. The field awaits further development by future philosophers of education, to correct AEG and to acknowledge finally that not just arts and body disciplines, but also taken-for-granted learning environments themselves, may educate learners' and educators' imaginations or function as cultural miseducation.

Notes

1. The College of Education at the University of Northern Illinois features a one-room schoolhouse exhibit, under the curatorship of Lucy F. Townsend, at the Blackwell Museum, the headquarters of the Country School Association of America. See http://www.cedu.niu.edu/blackwell/one-room/index.shtml.

2. L'Ecole des Beaux Arts in pre- and postrevolutionary Paris and the Bauhaus in high-modern Weimar Germany represent major schools with coherent theories of design education influential in the United States that merit critical study by scholars in aesthetics and education. In the late twentieth century architectural treatise *Learning from Las Vegas,* Robert Venturi, Stephen Izenour, and Denise Scott Brown (1977) theorize the curriculum implicit in the corporate, commercial

built landscape of the postmodern United States. The aesthetic practices of reading built structures and landscapes that aesthetic and educational theorists such as these teach could be generative for postmillennial scholars who aim to understand aesthetic hidden curricula in educational architecture and campus planning.

ACKNOWLEDGMENT

Special thanks to Sharon Peelor for her bibliographic assistance and also to Catherine Kinyon, Deanne Bogdan, Jim Garrison, Johnnie-Margaret McConnell, Joseph Bogdan, Julie Davis, and Thomas Cline for their helpful suggestions and for their critical readings and discussions of early drafts of this chapter. They have made it better, although its remaining gaps and other flaws are my fault alone.

REFERENCES

Abbs, P. (1994). *The educational imperative: A defense of Socratic and aesthetic learning.* London, England: Routledge.

Alexander, T. (1987). *John Dewey's theory of art, experience, and nature.* Albany, NY: State University of New York Press.

Aristotle, Roberts, R., & Bywater, I., (1984). *The rhetoric and the poetics of Aristotle* (I. Bywater, Trans.). New York, NY: McGraw-Hill, Modern Library.

Bailin, S. (1994). *Achieving extraordinary ends: An essay on creativity.* Norwood, NJ: Ablex.

Benjamin, W. (1968). *Illuminations* (H. Arendt, Ed.; H. Zohn, Trans.). New York, NY: Schocken Books. (Original work published 1955)

Berger, J. (1990). *Ways of seeing.* London, England: Penguin.

Beyer, L. E. (2000). *The arts, popular culture, and social change.* New York, NY: Peter Lang.

Bogdan, D. (1992). *Re-educating the imagination: Toward a poetics, politics, and pedagogy of literary engagement.* Portsmouth, NH: Boynton/Cook, Heinemann.

Bogdan, D. (2010). Betwixt and between: Working through the aesthetic in philosophy of education. *Educational Studies, 46*(3), 291-316.

Bogdan, D. (2011). The shiver-shimmer factor: Musical spirituality, emotion, and education. *Philosophy of Music Education Review, 18*(2): 111-129

Bordo, S. (2004). *Unbearable weight: Feminism, Western culture, and the body.* Berkeley, CA: University of California Press.

Brown, M. M. (1985). *Philosophical studies of home economics in the United States: Our practical intellectual heritage.* Lansing, MI: Michigan State University, College of Human Ecology.

Bourdieu, P., & Nice, R. (1984). *Distinction: A social critique of the judgement of taste.* Cambridge, MA: Harvard University Press.

da Vinci, L., O'Malley, C.D., Saunders, J. B., & Saunders, C. M. (2003). *Leonardo da Vinci on the human body: The anatomical, physiological, and embryological drawings of Leonardo da Vinci.* New York, NY: Gramercy.

Dewey, J. (1934). *Art as experience.* New York, NY: Continuum.

Dewey, J. (1936). *Experience and education.* New York, NY: Free Press.

DuBois, W. E. B. (1902). *The souls of Black folk.* New York, NY: Penguin classics.

Duran, J. (2007). *Women, philosophy, and literature.* Surrey, England: Ashgate.

Elliott, D. J. (1995). *Music matters: A new philosophy of music education.* New York, NY: Oxford University Press.

Frye, N. (1964). *The educated imagination.* Bloomington, IN: Indiana University Press.

Gaines, T. A. (1991). *The campus as a work of art.* Westport, CT: Praeger.

Garrison, J. (1997). *Dewey and Eros: Wisdom and desire in the art of teaching.* New York, NY: Teachers College Press.

Gauldie, S. (1969). *Architecture.* Oxford, England: Oxford University Press.

Gomez, D. S. (2005). *The space for good teaching* (Unpublished EdD dissertation). Teachers College, Columbia University.

Granger, D. A. (2006a). *John Dewey, Robert Pirsig, and the art of living: Revisioning aesthetic education.* Basingstoke, England: Palgrave Macmillan.

Granger, D.A. (2006b). Teaching Aesthetics and Aesthetic Teaching. *Journal of Aesthetic Education, 4*(2), 45-66.

Green, L. (1997). *Music, gender, and education.* Cambridge, England: Cambridge University Press.

Green, L. (2002). *How popular musicians learn: A way ahead for music education.* Surrey, England: Ashgate.

Greene, M. (1973). *Teacher as stranger: Educational philosophy for the modern age.* Los Angeles, CA: Wadsworth.

Greene, M. (1978). *Landscapes of learning.* New York, NY: Teachers College Press.

Greene, M. (1995). *Releasing the imagination: Essays on education, the arts, and social l change.* San Francisco, CA: Jossey-Bass.

Hayden, D. (1982). *The grand domestic revolution: A history of feminist designs for American homes, neighborhoods and cities.* Cambridge, MA: MIT Press.

Higgins, C. (2010). Educational aesthetics. In S. Tozer, B. P. Gallegos, A. Henry, & M. Bushnell Greiner (Eds.), *Handbook of research in the social foundations of education* (pp. 131-152). New York, NY: Routledge.

Horowitz, H. L. (1993). *Alma mater: Design and experience in the women's colleges from their nineteenth-century beginnings to the 1930s.* Amherst, MA: University of Massachusetts Press.

Howard, V. A. (1982). *Artistry: The work of artists.* Indianapolis, IN: Hackett.

Hyde, L. (1999). *The gift: Imagination and the erotic life of property.* New York, NY: Vintage.

Jackson, P. W. (1998). *John Dewey and the lessons of art.* New Haven, CT: Yale University Press.

Jorgensen, E. R. (2008). *The art of teaching music.* Bloomington, IN: Indiana University Press.

Jorgensen, E. R. (2002). *Transforming music education.* Bloomington, IN: Indiana University Press.

Kant, I. (2007). *Critique of judgment* (N. Walker., Ed.; J. C. Meredith, Trans.). Oxford, England: Oxford University Press.

Korsmeyer, C. (Ed.). (1998). *Aesthetics: The big questions.* Malden, MA: Wiley-Blackwell.

Korsmeyer, C. (2002). *Making sense of taste: food and philosophy.* Ithaca, NY: Cornell University Press.

Korsmeyer, C. (2004). *Gender and aesthetics: An introduction.* London, England: Routledge.

Kozol, J. (2005). *The shame of the nation: The restoration of apartheid schooling in America.* New York, NY: Crown.

Laird, S. (1989). The concept of teaching: Betsey Brown v. philosophy of education? In J. M. Giarelli (Ed.), *Philosophy of education 1988* (pp. 32-45). Normal, IL: Philosophy of Education Society.

Laird, S. (1991). The ideal of the educated teacher: Reclaiming a conversation with Louisa May Alcott. *Curriculum Inquiry, 21*(3), 271-297.

Laird, S. (1994). Teaching in a different sense: Alcott's Marmee. In A. Thompson (Ed.), *Philosophy of education 1993* (pp. 164-172). Urbana, IL: Philosophy of Education Society.

Laird, S. (1995). Who cares about girls? Rethinking the meaning of teaching. *Peabody Journal of Education: "Teacher Effectiveness," 70*(2), 82-103.

Laird, S. (1998). Learning from Marmee's teaching: Alcott's response to girls' miseducation. In J. Alberghene & B. L. Clark (Ed.), *'Little women' and the feminist imagination* (pp. 285-321). New York, NY: Garland.

Laird, S. (1999). Recapitulating. In S. Tozer (Ed.), *Philosophy of education 1998* (pp. 62-67). Urbana, IL: Philosophy of Education Society.

Laird, S. (2002). "The Meaning of Life as an Ultimate Justification for Education," in *Philosophy of Education 2001*, ed. S. Rice. Urbana, IL: Philosophy of Education Society, pp. 320-323.

Laird, S. (2003). "Befriending girls as an educational life-practice." In E. S. Fletcher (Ed.), *Philosophy of education 2002* (pp. 73-81). Urbana, IL: Philosophy of Education Society.

Laird, S. (2008a). Food for coeducational thought. In B. Stengel (Ed.), *Philosophy of education 2007* (pp. 1-13). Urbana, IL: Philosophy of Education Society.

Laird, S. (2008b). *Mary Wollstonecraft: Philosophical mother of coeducation.* London, England: Continuum.

Laird, S. (2009). Musical hunger: A philosophical testimonial of miseducation. *Philosophy of Music Education Review, 17*(1), 4-21.

Langer, S. K. (1977). *Feeling and form.* New York, NY: Prentice-Hall.

Locke, J., Grant, R. W., & Tarcov, N. (Eds.). (1996). *Some thoughts concerning education and of the conduct of the understanding.* Indianapolis, IN: Hackett.

Martin, J. R. (1985). *Reclaiming a conversation: The ideal of the educated woman.* New Haven, CT: Yale University Press.

Martin, J. R. (1992). *The schoolhome: Rethinking schools for changing families.* Cambridge, MA: Harvard University Press.

Martin, J. R. (1994). *Changing the educational landscape: Philosophy, women, and curriculum.* New York, NY: Routledge.

Martin, J. R. (2002). *Cultural miseducation: In search of a democratic solution.* New York, NY: Teachers College Press.

Martin, J. R. (2006). *Educational metamorphoses: Philosophical reflections on identity and culture.* Lanham, MD: Rowman & Littlefield.

Mayhew, K. C., & Edwards, A. C. (1936). *The Dewey school: The laboratory school of the University of Chicago, 1896-1903.* New York, NY: D. Appleton-Century.

McEwen, I. K. (2002). *Vitruvius: Writing the body of architecture.* Cambridge, MA: MIT Press.

McFee, G. (1992). *Understanding dance.* New York, NY: Routledge.

Milligan, J. A. (1998). *Negotiating the relationship between religion and public education: Conceptualizing a prophetic pragmatic teacher from Toni Morrison's Beloved* (Unpublished doctoral dissertation). University of Oklahoma.

Murdoch, I. (Ed.), & Conradi, P. (1997). *Existentialists and mystics: Writings on philosophy and literature.* New York, NY: Penguin.

Nussbaum, M. (1990). *Love's knowledge: Essays on philosophy and literature.* New York, NY: Oxford University Press.

Parsons, M. J., & Blocker, H. G. (1993). *Aesthetics and education.* Urbana, IL: University of Illinois Press.

Plato, Cooper, J. M., & Hutchinson, D. S. (1997). *Plato: Complete works.* Indianapolis, IN: Hackett.

Rasmussen, S. E. (1964). *Experiencing architecture.* Cambridge, MA: MIT Press.

Reimer, B. (2002). *A philosophy of music education: Advancing the vision.* New York, NY: Prentice-Hall.

Schiller, F. (2004). *On the aesthetic education of man* (R. Snell, Trans.). Mineola, NY: Dover Publications. (Original work published 1795; first translation 1994)

Scruton, R. (1979). *The aesthetics of architecture.* Princeton, NJ: Princeton University Press.

Sherman, A. (1984). Genderism and the reconstitution of philosophy of education. *Educational Theory, 34*(4), 321-325.

Shusterman, R. (1996). *Practicing philosophy: Pragmatism and the philosophical life.* New York, NY: Routledge.

Shusterman, R. (2000). *Pragmatist aesthetics: Living beauty, rethinking art.* Lanham, MD: Rowman & Littlefield.

Shusterman, R. (2008). *Body consciousness: A philosophy of mindfulness and somaesthetics* Cambridge, MA: Cambridge University Press.

Simpson, D., Jackson, M. J. B., & Aycock, J. C. (2005). *John Dewey and the art of teaching: Toward reflective and imaginative practice.* Thousand Oaks, CA: SAGE.

Small, C. (1998). *Musicking: The meanings of performing and listening.* Hanover, NH: Wesleyan University Press.

Small, C., & Walser, R. (1996). *Music, society, education.* Hanover, NH: Wesleyan.

University Press. (2007). *Tanglewood II declaration.* Retrieved from http://www.bu.edu/tanglewoodtwo/declaration /declaration.html

Tillman, F. A., & Cahn, S. M. (Eds.). (1969). *Philosophy of art and aesthetics: From Plato to Wittgenstein.* New York, NY: Harper and Row.

Twain, M. (1884). *Adventures of Huckleberry Finn* (1st ed.). Seattle, WA: First Edition Media.

Updike, J. (2003). A & P. In *The Early Stories: 1953-1975* (pp. 596-601). New York, NY: Ballantine.

Venturi, R., Izenour, S., & Brown, D. S. (1977). *Learning from Las Vegas—Revised edition: The forgotten symbolism of architectural form.* Cambridge, MA: MIT Press.

Venturi, R., Scully, V., & Drexler, A. (2002). *Complexity and contradiction in architecture.* New York, NY: Museum of Modern Art.

Vitruvius Pollio, M. (1931). *Vitruvius: On architecture* (Vol. 1, Books 1-5; F. Granger, Trans.). Cambridge, MA: Harvard College, Loeb Classical Library.

Vitruvius Pollio, M., & Granger, F. (Trans.). (1934). *Vitruvius: On architecture* (Vol. 2, Books 6-10; F. Granger, Trans.). Cambridge, MA: Harvard College, Loeb Classical Library.

Vitruvius Pollio, M. (2001). *Vitruvius: Ten books on architecture* (I. D. Rowland & T. N. Howe, Eds.). Cambridge, MA: Cambridge University Press.

Washington, B. T. (1901). *Up from slavery: An autobiography.* New York, NY: Elibron Classics.

Wilson, R. G. (2009). *Thomas Jefferson's academical village: The creation of an architectural masterpiece.* Charlottesville, VA: University of Virginia Press.

Wollstonecraft, M. (1989). *The works of Mary Wollstonecraft* (Vols. 1-7; J. M. Todd & M. Butler, Eds.). Washington Square, NY: New York University Press.

Woodford, P. (2004). *Democracy and music education.* Bloomington, IN: Indiana University Press.

Woolf, V. (1938). *Three guineas.* San Francisco, CA: Harper, Brace, Jovanovich.

Worley, V. A. (1999). *The educational place of "Metissage" in Colette's La Maison de Claudine: A two-fold pedagogy of place itself and of the place-teaching partnership* (Unpublished doctoral dissertation). University of Oklahoma.

Author Contact Information: Susan Laird, PhD, Educational Leadership and Policy Studies, University of Oklahoma, Jeannine Rainbolt College of Education, Room 117 SC Building #4, 555 East Constitution St., Norman, OK 73019.

CHAPTER 5

Social Philosophy, Critical Whiteness Studies, and Education

Barbara Applebaum
Syracuse University

Often graduate students in education ask me how philosophy, which is so theory based, can be of value to them. In this essay, I want to answer that question by demonstrating how social philosophy, a field of philosophy that focuses on social issues, contributes to an emerging field of research, *Critical Whiteness Studies*, as it relates to education.

Critical Whiteness Studies, a relatively new research area that examines Whiteness and White privilege, has developed as a result of the increased awareness that multicultural approaches to inequality that celebrate difference fail to give attention to the system that constitutes Whiteness as the hidden norm from which "difference" is determined (Ladson-Billings, 1996; Mills, 2007a). Scholars marginalized by race, who understand that the dynamics of racism cannot be fully comprehended by focusing solely on the victims of racism, are the precursors to this research area. Critical Whiteness Studies shifts the attention from an exclusive focus on "the racial object to the racial subject; from the described and imagined to the describers and imaginers; from the serving to the served" (Morrison 1992, p. 90). The starting point of Critical Whiteness Studies, thus, is the recognition that the normativity of Whiteness lies at the center of the problem of racism.

The call in teacher education programs to critically educate about Whiteness follows from the fact that the majority of teachers and preservice teachers are White (Zumwalt & Craig, 2005). Since most Whites have never had to consider their racial positioning because dominance operates by making Whiteness the normalized category that is taken for granted, Whiteness must be made visible to them. In order to ensure that all students have an opportunity to flourish, White teachers need to understand that even well-intended White people can reproduce racism and that they have a responsibility to acknowledge how racism is embedded in their own behavior. White teachers need to learn how race infuses their experiences so that they can recognize how Whiteness permeates their pedagogical practice and communication with students, families and communities. Teaching about Whiteness involves studying how the norm of Whiteness is constructed, naming Whiteness as the experience of privilege, and, how Whiteness can be unintentionally reproduced.

While the definition of Whiteness is difficult to pin down, there is widespread agreement that Whiteness is a socially constructed category that is normalized within a system of privilege that is taken for granted by those who benefit from it. Whiteness here is understood as a historically and socially produced construct—a construct that is the effect of systems of privilege and material advantage, not just a matter of physical markers such as skin color. Moreover, Whiteness is the hidden normative framework that mediates meaning. Toni Morrison (1992) uses the metaphor of a fishbowl containing fish and water to elucidate the invisibility of Whiteness as the condition from which meaning is made. If we focus on the water and the fish, we do not have to see how the fishbowl itself frames where and what happens within it. Charles Mills (1999), whose research in philosophy of race has been influential across many disciplines, highlights the systemic aspect of Whiteness when he advocates for the use of the term "White supremacy." While the term White supremacy has originally been used to refer to blatant racial prejudice, hatred and discrimination as exemplified in Jim Crow laws and slavery, Mills uses the term to refer to the political, economic and cultural *system* that is designed to privilege White people and

The Handbook of Educational Theories, pp. 57–65

that has not diminished even as racism has morphed from de jure to de facto forms (Mills, 1999, p. 14). Mills contends that understanding racism as *only* about prejudice obscures the true nature of racism and how it functions to protect White privilege.

In what follows, I will demonstrate how social philosophy and philosophy of education can contribute to our understanding of White privilege, White ignorance and denials of complicity. Although I maintain that philosophical analysis can enrich any investigation into the deep and enduring ways that White norms and White privilege have been taken for granted in curriculum policy and educational research, my focus will be directed at pedagogy. The recent philosophical work on Whiteness provides concrete illustrations of how theory can open up new possibilities for understanding the complexity of Whiteness and the way Whiteness functions to sustain systemic racism. Thus, this work offers fruitful ways to reconsider how we teach about antiracism.

White Privilege and White Being

In her analysis of the concept of oppression, Marilyn Frye (1983) offers a useful metaphor—the birdcage—that draws attention to the pattern of conditions and barriers that perpetuate systemic injustice. The experience of oppressed people, Frye maintains, "is that the living of one's life is confined and shaped by forces and barriers which are not accidental or occasional and hence avoidable, but are systematically related to each other in such a way as to catch one between and among them and restrict or penalize motion in any direction" (Frye, 1983, p. 4). Privilege, according to Alison Bailey (1998), is the flipside of oppression and is what systemically keeps the birdcage in place. Oppression and privilege are not only systemic but also relational; one does not exist without the other. This is what Peggy McIntosh (1997), in her oft-cited essay, means when she writes that privilege "confers dominance." The notion of privilege as conferring dominance is introduced by McIntosh when she explains how while some privileges should be extended to all (such as the privilege to walk around freely in stores), some privileges are entitlements that no one should have. As an illustration of the latter type of privileges, she points to the privilege "to be ignorant, oblivious, arrogant, and destructive" (McIntosh, 1997, p. 295).

One of the most significant features of privilege is that those who experience privilege take it for granted. This invisibility has consequences among which are not having to realize the pervasiveness of racism, becoming angry and defensive at being confronted by the fact that what one believes to be the product of merit is the consequence of privilege and the ability to unjustly universalize privileged experience to all. Philosophers have directed attention to additional ways that White privilege confers dominance.

That White people are not being followed around in stores is not *only* about the ability to walk through a store freely but also about *a presumed moral standing*. The presumption of White moral integrity is a privilege that is contingent upon the coconstruction of Black as morally suspect. As Cynthia Kaufman (2002) explains,

> The image of the Black thief helps stabilize the image of the average good citizen (who of course is coded as White). When I walk into a store and the clerks look at me with respect and assume that I am not going to steal anything, the trust that I receive is at least partially built upon the foundation of my distance from the image of the savage. When an African American walks into the store that unconscious material comes into play in the opposite way. (p. 32)

White privilege, therefore, protects and supports White moral standing and this protective shield depends on there being an "abject other" that constitutes White as "good." Whites benefit from White privilege in a very deep way. This point is intimated when Zeus Leonardo (2004) contends that all Whites are responsible for White dominance since their "very being depends on it" (p. 144).

George Yancy (2008) employs philosophical analysis to elucidate how the meaning of the White body is constituted on the back of the Black body in the quotidian, everyday level of social transactions—like being in an elevator. Yancy enters the elevator well-dressed and without any threatening action on his part. Yet the White woman who "sees" his Black body reacts with apprehension and brings her purse closer to her body. The White woman "sees" Yancy as a criminal and, as he explains, despite what he thinks of himself "her perspective, her third-person account, seeps into my consciousness" (p. 5).

While the White woman thinks that her "seeing" is an unmediated act of "knowing" who he is and what he will do, Yancy insists that such "seeing" is really "a form of reading" (2008, p. 22) that is "actually a cultural achievement, a racist sociohistorical schematization, indeed, an act of epistemic violence" (p. 17). This reading of his body is not her personal reading but the product of centuries of White hegemony that have structured and shaped the reading of Black bodies. Yancy describes this reading as one that "ruminates over my dark flesh and vomits me out in a form not in accordance with how I see myself" (p. 2). The White woman in the elevator, thus, "Blackens" Yancy's body because she "sees" his Black body through a framework of historically structured forms of "knowledge" (that is really a lack of knowledge, as will be subsequently explained).

In this example, it is not enough to focus on the White woman's beliefs for it is more that she constitutes the Black body by her practices than any specific conscious belief. Practices of Whiteliness, as Marilyn Frye (1992) highlights, is an orientation that manifests "a deeply ingrained way of being in the world" (p. 151). Whiteliness involves the ways in which Whiteness is performatively enacted. Similarly, Shannon Sullivan (2006) addresses White ways of being when she explains White privilege as unconscious habits that function invisibly in the way that Whites do things and what they say "without thinking" (p. 4). As an illustration of such habits of White privilege, Sullivan points to what she refers to as "White ontological expansiveness" or the tendency for White people "to act and think as if all spaces—whether geographical, psychical, linguistic, economic, spiritual, bodily, or otherwise—are or should be available for them to move in and out of as they wish" (Sullivan, 2006, p. 10).

In drawing attention away from White beliefs and attitudes and toward White practices, these philosophers are able to unfold how Whites enact their privilege even when they are well-intentioned. As an illustration of "White ontological expansiveness" Sullivan discusses the antiracist White person who makes a choice not to live in an all-White neighborhood. Sullivan explains that "the sheer fact that she is able to make a choice about which neighborhood in which she lives, is … an effect of the privilege she has because of her race and economic class" (Sullivan, 2006, p. 10). White ontological expansiveness involves, among other things, an unconscious arrogance in which White people presume they would be welcomed in all spaces. Even antiracist White action, Sullivan demonstrates, can reinforce the very White privilege that the White antiracist is trying to disrupt.

Building on the work of Judith Butler, John Warren (2003) appends Frye's concept of Whiteliness when he argues that *we become White through White practices*. According to Butler, the subject is discursively constituted through power—that is, we become subjects through the process of subjection or what Foucault (1977) referred to as *assujettissment*, the paradoxical process of becoming a subject through subjection. What is meant by this is that the subject is an effect of power. It is not that one is an individual and then power comes along and shapes the individual in particular ways. Rather, bodies are *discursively* constituted—subjects become intelligible as subjects through norms or discursive regimes.

Butler draws to our attention how the linguistic act of naming, for instance, is a process of subject formation that interpolates (calls into being) the subject through socially sanctioned forms of address that "put us in our place even as they make us feel at home" (Butler, 1997, p. 1). The subject is compelled to repeat norms because gender, the case that Butler focuses on, is not achieved in one isolate moment of interpellation (the doctor's announcement at birth, "it is a girl") but rather is achieved in a performance of gender norms that the subject continually repeats. Performativity, therefore, implicates the subject in its own constitution. Warren applies the concept of performativity to Whiteness and claims that White subjects are constituted by the repetition of White norms in daily practice. Such discursive practices have a historicity that produce and reproduce the White body. It is through gestures, movements and other kinds of discursive communications that raced bodies come to exist. As Warren highlights,

> Butler wants to argue that my White subjectivity is not something 'I' underwent, but rather, by undergoing the process of White subjectivity my 'I' was formed—an 'I' that is, in and of itself, a product of the social, political, and cultural possibilities generated through history. People constitute their racial subjectivity through the maintenance and regulation of racial norms. (Warren, 2003, p. 33)

Race as constituting difference is not *in* the body but is produced *through* the body. What Warren and Butler emphasize is the notion that raced bodies are *effects* of power. Warren underscores how as White, "I am part of a social system that continually, through both strategic means and mundane enactments, reiterates my Whiteness" (Warren, 2003, p. 32).

Back to the White woman in the elevator with Yancy—how is her privilege manifest? As Yancy accentuates, not only does the White women "ontologically freeze" his Black body but she also

> becomes ontologically frozen in her own embodied (White) identity.... She "sees," but does not necessarily reflect upon, herself as normative, innocent, pure. Her performances reiterate the myth of the proverbial White victim at the hands of the Black predator. (Yancy, 2008, p. 19)

As such, her White innocence is procured on the back of Black criminality, whether she intends this or not. *Her White body* is constituted as "nonthreatening" even when it becomes threatening to Yancy as a Black man. Yancy notes how his movements become constrained as he fights the label her White practices force upon him. She displays a nervous smile, perhaps, as Yancy surmises, to draw a flicker of humanity from her darkened traveler. Yancy, though, does not return the smile lest it be interpreted as a sexual advance. Becoming super conscious of his movements, he does not want to play into her fears. "Within this space," Yancy realizes, "she 'controls' the 'truth' of my intentions" (Yancy, 2008, p. 13).

"Bullshit!" a White student cries in response to Yancy's telling of this story during a presentation about racism that he was invited to give. Yancy acknowledges the interesectionality of race and gender in this story and possible counter readings. Nevertheless, according to Yancy, the White student positions himself as the "discerner of bullshit, and so as the one who ought to be believed" (Yancy, 2008, p. 228). The White student's "Bullshit!" not only erases Yancy's credibility but also erases all other Black men who have had similar experiences in elevators. Yancy's interpretation of what is happening to him in the elevator is grounded in a pattern of such experiences and in the role that Black criminality has played in the history of Whiteness. Even if the White woman's intention was otherwise, and even is she is unaware of the consequence of her behavior, such White practices can have negative implications for non Whites (Yancy, 2008, p. 24).

What Yancy and other philosophers contribute to our understanding of how to teach about systemic White privilege to White students is the insight that racism must be challenged not only at the level of beliefs but also at the level of unconscious practices. Educators must help White students examine the ways in which they perform their Whiteness and how White being is deeply engrained in habituated somatic practices. Moreover, White students must be encouraged to consider how their unconscious White practices are complicit in sustaining White supremacy.

The Privilege of Ignorance

Cris Mayo (2005) intimates that White ignorance is a type of privilege that protects White innocence when she writes, "Privilege ... gives Whites a way to not know that does not even fully recognize the extent to which they do not know that race matters or that their agency is closely connected with their status" (p. 309). Charles Mills' (2007b) discussion of the *epistemology* of ignorance helps to expand this point. In his early work, *The Racial Contract,* Mills (1999) argues that a racial contract underwrites the modern social contract. According to Mills, the racial contract is a *covert* agreement or set of meta-agreements between White people to create and maintain a subperson class of non-Whites. The purpose of the racial contract is to "secur(e) the privileges and advantages of the full White citizens and maint(ain) the subordination of nonWhites" (Mills, 1999, p. 14). To achieve this purpose, there is a need to perpetuate ignorance and to misinterpret the world as it really is.

The racial contract, thus, is an agreement to not know and *an assurance that this will count as a true version of reality* by those who benefit from the account. Mills refers to such lack of knowledge as an "inverted epistemology" and contends it is an *officially sanctioned* reality (that) is divergent from actual reality.... one has an agreement to *mis*interpret the world. One has to learn to see the world wrongly, but with the assurance that this set of mistaken perceptions will be validated by White epistemic authority, whether religious or secular" (Mills, 1999, p. 18, emphasis added). White ignorance, thus, will *feel* like knowledge to those who benefit from the system because it is supported by the social system *as knowledge.*

Mills (2007b) distinguishes White ignorance from individual and personal ignorance in people who happen to be White. Moreover, he emphasizes that White ignorance is not exclusively about overtly White racists that some may claim are just not educated. According to Mills, White ignorance involves the type of *not knowing* existing in even those who are well-intended and "educated" which "after the transition from de jure to de facto White supremacy, it is precisely this kind of White ignorance that is most important" (Mills, 2007b, p. 21).

White ignorance has a number of characteristic features that can enhance our understanding of the intractable White resistance to learning about Whiteness that educational researchers have documented. First, White ignorance involves a "not knowing" that is *intimately* connected to racial positionality. As such, White ignorance is part of an epistemology of ignorance, "a particular pattern of localized and global cognitive dysfunctions (which are psychologically and socially functional), producing the ironic outcome that Whites will in general be unable to understand the world they themselves have made" (Mills, 1999, p. 18). A good illustration of such White ignorance can be found in Yancy's (2004) description of a White philosopher whom he deeply respected and who, out of seemingly deep concern, cautioned him not to get pegged as someone who pursues issues in African American philosophy. Yancy finds himself instantaneously reflecting,

> "Pegged! I'm doing philosophy!" It immediately occurred to me that the introductory course in philosophy that I had taken with him some years back did not include a single person of color. Yet, *he did not see* his own philosophical performances—engagements with European and Anglo-American philosophy as "pegged"; he simply taught philosophy qua philosophy. Such a philosophy only masquerades as universal. (Yancy, 2004, p. 1, emphasis added)

In this illustration, race is a fundamental factor in the type of ignorance exhibited by the White philosopher.

Mills further explains how White ignorance is connected to the White conceptual framework that White people have at their disposal. What the White philosopher "sees" (or, in this case, does not "see") is mediated. Such ignorance is made possible because the conceptual framework from which one interprets one's social world "will not be neutral but oriented toward a certain understanding" (Mills, 2007b, p. 24). Whatever one perceives, it is the "concept (that) is driving the perception" (Mills, 2007b, p. 27).

A second feature of White ignorance is that it is not passive. Systemic ignorance is not a passive lacking as the term "ignorance" might lead one to suppose but rather, as Eve Sedgwick (1980) contends, an activity. Building upon Sedgwick's insights, Cris Mayo (2002) argues that such ignorance does not equate with "lack of knowledge" but is "a particular kind of knowledge" (p. 85) that does things and, more specifically, protects racial injustice from challenge. Which leads to a third feature of White ignorance—its benefit to White people.

Mills argues that it is White group interest that is a "central causal factor in generating and sustaining White ignorance" (Mills, 2007b, p. 34). Such ignorance functions to mystify the consequences of such unjust systems so that those who benefit from the system do not have to consider their complicity in perpetuating it. There are benefits for the dominant social group of such ignorance. Members of the dominant group, for instance, have *a vested interest* in not knowing. Linda Alcoff (2007) emphasizes that White people not only have less interest in understanding their complicity in social injustice than those who are victimized by such systems but also that White people have a *positive interest* in remaining ignorant.

To summarize, White ignorance involves not just "not knowing" but also "not knowing what one does not know and *believing that one knows.*" White ignorance is a form of White knowledge. It is a type of ignorance that arrogantly parades as knowledge. Rather than an absence of knowledge, White ignorance is a particular way of everyday knowing or thinking that one knows how the social world works that is intimately related to what it means to be White (Leonardo, 2008). Moreover, such "ignorance as knowledge" is socially sanctioned. Thus White people tend not to hesitate to dismiss and rebuff the knowledge of those who have been victims of systemic racial injustice rather than engaging with them, inquiring for more information and having the humility to acknowledge what they do not know.

White knowledge of the social world that is really White ignorance fuels a refusal to consider that one might be morally complicit and further promotes a resistance to knowing. White people have a positive interest in remaining ignorant because such ignorance serves to sustain White moral innocence while at the same time protects systems of privilege and oppression from being interrogated. Mills cautions that it is crucial that White people take these "recognition problems" (1999, p. 150) seriously since, "it becomes easier to do the right thing if one knows the wrong things that, to one's group, will typically *seem* like the right thing" (1999, p. 149). It is not easy to get White people to consider their complicity, however, when denials of complicity masquerade as White "common sense."

Discourse and Denials of Complicity

Sandra Bartky (2002) delineates a typology of denial of complicity in which she includes the culpably ignorant or those who fail to know what they ought to know because such knowledge would morally implicate them. The ideologies of color ignorance and meritocracy are examples of discourses of denials that help Whites dismiss the prevalence of racism and, consequently, relieve them from having to consider their complicity. Color ignorance is a widespread position of moral belief but is also a strategy of denial (Bonilla-Silva, 2003). A refusal on the part of White students to "see" color may seem to White students as common moral sense; yet, it actually functions as a way in which to establish their moral, nonracist credentials. Often what appears to be White resistance to educators is read by White students as just expressing their moral belief. Thus, to consider any challenge to their belief would impute their moral status.

Peg O'Connor (2002) offers an instance of such a refusal to consider race when she describes the response of some of her White students when she asks them to consider statistics that show that people of color are refused mortgages to a significant degree more than White people. She notes how some of her White students

> may seek out and then parade a variety of explanations for the refusal—the person may have bad credit history, the refusal does not have anything to do with the race of the person, but only with that person's financial history. Or the refusal may have nothing to do with the person but rather with the neighborhood. The neighborhood is the problem, not race. It just wouldn't make good business sense to give homeowners' loans for houses in certain neighborhoods. Banks have obligations to their customers. (pp. 123-124)

The point is not to reject the possibility that in isolated cases one of these explanations might be relevant but instead to focus on how such discursive practices are connected to not only colorblind ideology but also a belief in the myth of meritocracy. No matter what one produces to try to engage this student with the possibility that financial history and race are systemically related, the student continues to refuse to even consider that race might be a factor. The student may even come back with the allegation that Black people are always "playing the race card."

According to Tim Wise (2006), "playing the race card" is so often a play of the White denial card. Even if some people do play the "race card," Wise compellingly contends that White people play the White denial card even more frequently. White people have always doubted people of color when they claim that racism exists. In fact, this is why playing the race card is usually futile. White people, Wise notes, often continue to deny the racial aspects of incidents even when they are compelled to recognize the strong evidence that is produced before them. Wise concludes that whatever the benefits of "playing the race card" may be for people of color, "playing the White denial card" will usually be the trump and Whites play it far more regularly.

Educational researchers, especially researchers who study how White students engage in social justice education, have given serious attention to such denials. Kim Case and Annette Hemmings (2005) refer to "distancing strategies" to describe how White women preservice teachers avoid being positioned as racist or implicated in systemic oppression. Kathy Hytten and John Warren's (2003) outstanding ethnography of the rhetorical moves their White students performed in courses that attempt to teach about systemic oppression and privilege offers many examples of such tactics. Among the types of discursive strategies that Hytten and Warren discuss are: remaining silent, evading questions, resorting to the rhetoric of ignoring color, focusing on progress, victim blaming and focusing on culture rather than race. Hytten and Warren emphasize that these discursive moves are culturally sanctioned discourses of evasion that "were not original—that is, they are already available, already common forms of asserting dominance" (p. 66). These rhetorical strategies work to obstruct engagement so that deliberations about one's complicity in systemic oppression can be avoided. Along similar lines, Alice McIntyre (1997) coined the phrase "White talk" to name discourse that functions to "insulate White people from examining their/our individual and collective role(s) in the perpetuation of racism" (p. 45).

What becomes apparent throughout this scholarship is that White ignorance is not only sustained by denials of complicity but White ignorance also authorizes such denials. In effect, "resisters" believe they are just disagreeing with the material. Consequently, their disagreement also functions as a "justified" reason to dismiss and to refuse to engage with what is not compatible with their beliefs. One can disagree and remain engaged in the material, for example, by asking questions and searching for clarification and understanding. Denials, however, function as a way to distance oneself from the material and to dismiss *without engagement*. Hytten and Warren explain that such strategic denials are not only already available in the sense that they are socially authorized but also that they serve to protect the center, the location of privilege. Such discursive strategies of denial are an "implicit way of resisting critical engagements with Whiteness" (Hytten & Warren, 2003, p. 65).

All these studies depend on an understanding of White denials as performative that philosophical scholarship can help us to comprehend. In order to appreciate what White denials of complicity do, one has to make a shift from understanding language as representational to language as discourse. Traditional accounts of the self, inherited from the Enlightenment, conceive persons as beings with an essential core whose authentic qualities can be found underneath a contingent surface. Such an account presumes that if you dig deeply enough into this subjectivity and peel away its contingent aspects, for instance, if you ignore their race, gender, sexuality, you will find who that person *really* "is." Autonomy based on rationality is the hallmark of such a notion of personhood. When the person is a rational agent, the person is the author or originator of the meaning of subjective experience and, as free, uses language to represent one's internal world to others. Under this traditional account, the subject first exists in the world and then uses language as a tool to communicate one's inner world to other beings.

Language as representation assumes that language is a *passive representation* of some reality external to it. I point to a cup on the table and say, "This is a cup." According to the representational approach of language, the statement "This is a cup" functions as a picture of reality that can be studied for the truth or accuracy of its portrayal of a mind-independent reality. Language, in other words, is a tool that *mirrors* reality and when people use this tool they are not themselves affected by it. Language as representation also presumes that the world, language and persons are distinct entities, with language mediating between the world and people. As passive, language not only has no affect on the person using language but also adds *nothing* to the world.

Finally, because language is assumed to be an unmediated tool, people *use* language to communicate what the speaker *intends* to communicate. "Language," as representational, "is the neutral servant of the people" (Wetherell, 2001, p. 15). Language as representation presumes that words are transparent instruments by which people transmit the ideas that they *want* to communicate to others (Bingham, 2002, p. 354). And it is assumed that we always understand ourselves because we are the source of meaning of our own speech (Hall, 2001, p. 79).

In contrast to accounts of language as representation and notions of autonomous, rational selves, some philosophers have been concerned with exposing how language or utterances are related to larger social patterns of power and the ways in which language may do things *through us* without our knowledge or consent. In this scholarship, attention is drawn to the linguistic space within which statements are uttered in order to uncover what our utterances do. What exactly does language do?

First, language constructs and constrains meaning. Language does things in the sense that it is the framework from which our conceptions of reality are constructed. Ferdinand de Saussure (1974) maintains that words are signs in a system that structures the possible ways in which we understand ourselves, others and the world around us. Challenging the representational account of language, Saussure argued that signs only have meaning in relationship to other signs whose entire system is part of a particular worldview. Paying attention to the relationship between signs in a system highlights how language systems organize and give meaning to our experiences. The concepts that are available to us (or not available to us) provide the horizons that give meaning to our interpretation of our experiences.

Second, language is also performative. In his celebrated work, *How To Do Things With Words,* J. L. Austin (1962) discerns a type of speech act that does not merely describe but that actually does something. The minister's recitation, "I now pronounce you man and wife," in a marriage ceremony, does not merely describe the world but actually does something at the time of its utterance. While Austin recognized that conditions must be met in order for the speech act to be successful, he insisted that when those conditions are met, it is the intention of the minister that makes the performative utterance successful.

Jacques Derrida (1988), however, challenges Austin exactly on this point insisting that the force of performative utterances and what makes them successful is not derived from the speaker's intentions but rather from the citationality of conventions that preexist the speaker who utters them. Derrida has long maintained that all language depends on the repetition of linguistic signs and conventions and that "there is nothing outside of the text" (Derrida, 1976, p. 158). This is not to imply that Derrida denies the existence of a nondiscursive reality but instead emphasizes that our engagement with the world is contingent on the meanings that discourse make possible. For Derrida, discourse is not a founding act by an originating subject but a derivative citation. This is not a rejection of intentions but instead a rejections of intentions as the foundational force of utterances. Judith Butler (2008) concurs when she emphasizes that even as one uses discourse to affect certain intentional ends, one is also used by the history of that discourse. Discourse always constrains the field of what can and cannot be intended or said. Thus, discourse may have effects that are not consonant with our intentions because discourse may do things *through us* without our knowledge or consent.

Derrida's insight parallels Michel Foucault's contention that power works through discourse that constitutes the subject. Discourse, as Foucault puts it, involves "practices that systematically form the objects of which they speak" (Foucault, 1969/1972, p. 49). Discourse actively functions to construct and maintain particular versions of social reality and also constitutes who we can understand ourselves to be. One way to highlight this is to note that there are many ways to describe things and events and one description often competes with a variety of alternatives. Those who reject language as representation are interested in interrogating why one version can be uttered but another is unthinkable. Why this version or this utterance? What does it do? What does it accomplish and in whose interests? Does it constitute subjects in a particular way and how?

Why is this so important for social justice pedagogy? In order for White students to understand how their utterances can be distancing strategies they must not be "stuck on the cup."[1] White students must be encouraged to make a shift from understanding language as *only* about representation and to recognize that discourse "does" things above and beyond their intentions. Acknowledging how discourse exceeds intention can lead to a heightened vigilance and reflection for White students. Charles Bingham demonstrates such vigilance about his own speech.

> While I, as a White man, ask simple questions while listening to, and trying to understand, an African American student's point of view, the *effect* of my questioning and listening may be on another plane altogether than representation. It is very possible that the social act of dialogue is itself a stage for racist hierarchies to be played out, for example. If the *effect* of speech is oppression, then a genealogical skepticism toward dialogue causes me to wonder if representation really took place at all. Let us say that my questioning and listening enacted racist codes that I do not condone, but that were in the air nonetheless.... At such a point, it is not so useful to make up a convoluted description of the limits of representational dialogue. It is more useful to follow Foucault's linguistic pragmatism and admit that what just happened was a discursive act. And that act was oppressive. (Bingham, 2002, p. 363)

It is important to expose students to the problem of language as representation and to have them engage with the idea that discourse is a site of power. Only then can will it make any sense that "distancing strategies" are not merely individual opinions but part of a pattern of beliefs and practices that benefit certain groups of people and are socially sanctioned.

CONCLUSION

Social philosophy can offer much to enrich educators' understanding of how to teach about Whiteness to White students but that is beyond the scope of this essay. Social philosophy can also help us to appreciate the deep ways that White norms are embedded in school policy, curriculum and in educational research. I hope in this essay to have provided some compelling illustrations of the usefulness of social philosophical thought for educators.

NOTE

1. I thank Dan Cutler for articulating this point in this way.

REFERENCES

Alcoff, L. (2007). Epistemologies of ignorance: Three types. In S. Sullivan & N. Tuana (Eds.), *Race and epistemologies of ignorance* (pp. 39-58). Albany, NY: State University of New York Press.

Austin, J. L. (1962). *How to do things with words* (2nd ed.). Oxford, England: Oxford University Press.

Bailey, A. (1998). Privilege: Expanding on Marilyn Frye's 'Oppression.' *Journal of Social Philosophy, 29*(3), 104-119.

Bartky, S. (2002). *"Sympathy and solidarity": And other essays.* Lanham, MD: Rowman & Littlefield.

Bingham, C. W. (2002). A dangerous benefit: Dialogue, discourse, and Michel Foucault's critique of representation. *Interchange, 33*(4), 351-369.

Bonilla-Silva, E. (2003). *Racism without racist: Color-blind racism and the persistence of racial inequality in the United States.* New York, NY: Rowman & Littlefield.

Butler, J. (1997). *Excitable speech: A politics of the performative.* New York, NY: Routledge.

Butler, J. (2008). Conversation with Judith Butler IV. In B. Davies (Ed.), *Judith Butler in conversation: Analyzing the texts and talk of everyday life* (pp. 187-216). New York, NY: Routledge.

Case, K., & Hemmings, A. (2005). Distancing strategies: white women preservice teachers and antiracist curriculum. *Urban Education, 40*(6), 606-626.

Derrida, J. (1976). *On grammatology.* Baltimore, MD: John Hopkins University Press.

Derrida, J. (1988). Signature event context. In G. Graff (Ed.), *Limited, Inc.* (pp. 1-24). Evanston, IL: Northwestern University Press.

Foucault, M. (1972). *The archaeology of knowledge* (S. Smith, Trans.). London, England: Travistock. (Original work published 1969)

Foucault, M. (1977). *Discipline and punish: The birth of the prison* (A. Sheridan, Trans.) London, England: Penguin.

Foucault, M. (1980). Truth and power. In C. Gordon (Ed.), *Power/knowledge: Selected interviews and other writings 1972-1977* (pp. 109-133). New York, NY: Pantheon.

Frye, M. (1983). *The politics of reality: Essays in feminist theory.* Trumansburg, NY: The Crossing Press.

Frye, M. (1992). *Willful virgin: Essays in feminism 1976-1992.* Freedom, CA: Crossing Press.

Hall, S. (2001). Foucault: Power, knowledge and discourse. In M. Wetherell, S. Taylor, & S. Yates (Eds.), *Discourse theory and practice: A reader* (pp. 72-18). London, England: SAGE,

Hytten, K., & Warren, J. T. (2003). Engaging Whiteness: How racial power gets reified in education. *Qualitative Studies in Education, 16*(1), 65-89.

Kaufman, C. (2002). A user's guide to White privilege. *Radical Philosophy Review, 4*(1-2), 30-38.

Ladson-Billings, G. (1996). 'Your blues ain't like mine': Keeping issues of race and racism on the multicultural agenda. *Theory into Practice, 35*(4), 248-255.

Leonardo, Z. (2004). The color of supremacy: Beyond the discourse of 'White privilege.' *Educational Philosophy and Theory, 36*(2), 137-152.

Leonardo, Z. (2008). Reading whiteness: Antiracist pedagogy against White racial knowledge. In W. C. Ayers, T. Quinn & D. Stovall (Eds.), *Handbook of social justice in education* (pp. 231-248). New York, NY: Routledge.

Mayo, C. (2002). Civility and its discontents: Sexuality, race, and the lure of beautiful manners. In S. Rice (Ed.), *Philosophy of education 2001* (pp. 78-87). Urbana, IL: Philosophy of Education Society.

Mayo, C. (2005). Certain privilege: Rethinking White agency. In C. Higgins (Ed.), *Philosophy of education 2004* (pp. 308-316). Urbana, IL: Philosophy of Education Society.

McIntosh, P. (1997). White privilege and male privilege: A personal account of coming to see correspondences through work in women's studies. In R. Delgado & J. Stefancic (Eds.), *Critical White studies: Looking behind the mirror* (pp. 291-299). Philadelphia, PA: Temple University Press.

McIntyre, A. (1997). *Making meaning of Whiteness: Exploring racial identity with White teachers.* Albany, NY: State University of New York Press.

Mills, C. W. (1999). *The racial contract.* Ithaca, NY: Cornell University Press.

Mills, C. W. (2007a). Multiculturalism as/and/or anti-racism? In A. S. Laden & D. Own (Eds.), *Multiculturalism and political theory* (pp. 89-114). Cambridge, England: Cambridge University Press.

Mills, C. W. (2007b). White ignorance. In S. Sullivan & N. Tuana (Eds.), *Race and epistemologies of ignorance* (pp. 13-38). Albany, NY: State University of New York Press.

Morrison, T. (1992). *Playing in the dark: Whiteness and the literary imagination.* New York, NY: Vintage Books.

O'Connor, P. (2002) *Oppression and responsibility: A Wittgensteinian approach to social practices and moral theory.* University Park, PA: Pennsylvania State University Press.

Saussure, F. d. (1974). *Course in general linguistics.* London, England: Fountana.

Sedgwick, E. K. (1980). *Epistemology of the closet.* New York, NY: Oxford University Press.

Sullivan, S. (2006). *Revealing Whiteness: The unconscious habits of racial privilege.* Bloomington, IN: Indiana University Press.

Warren, J. T. (2003). *Performing purity: Whiteness, pedagogy, and the reconstitution of power.* New York, NY: Peter Lang.

Wetherell, M. (2001). Themes in discourse research: The case of Diana. In M. Wetherell, S. Taylor, & S. Yates (Eds.) *Dis-*

course theory and practice: A reader (pp. 14-29). London, England: SAGE.

Wise, T. (2006). *What kind of card is race? The absurdity (and consistency) of White denial.* Retrieved from http://www.lipmagazine.org/~timwise/whatcard.html

Yancy, G. (2004). Fragments of a social ontology of Whiteness. In *What White looks like: African-American philosophers on the Whiteness question* (pp. 1-24). New York, NY: Routledge.

Yancy, G. (2008). *Black bodies, White gazes: The continuing significance of race.* Lanham, MD: Rowman & Littlefield.

Zumwalt, K., & Craig, E. (2005). Teachers' characteristics: Research on the demographic profile. In M. Cocchran-Smith & K. M. Zeichner (Eds.), *Studying teacher education: The report of the AERA Panel on Research and Teacher Education* (pp. 111-156). Mahwah, NJ: Erlbaum.

Author Contact Information: Barbara Applebaum, PhD, Syracuse University, 350 Huntington Hall, Syracuse, New York 13244. Phone: 315-449-1514. E-mail: bappleba@syr.edu

CHAPTER 6

Contemporary Political Theory and Education

Natasha Levinson
Kent State University

When philosophers of education think about matters having to do with the relationship between education and the state, they engage with the field of political theory. Political theory furnishes educational philosophers with a philosophical basis and a political framework for ascertaining the reach—and the limits—of the state's educational obligations in liberal-pluralist democracies. In the field of philosophy of education, as in the field of political theory, liberalism is now the predominant theoretical paradigm in the United States and the United Kingdom, and its influence is growing in Western European philosophical circles as well. This revival of liberal theory can be attributed to the unexpected resurgence of religious fundamentalism in these countries, and the concomitant realization that the values that shape liberal-pluralist democracies cannot be taken for granted. These values were hard won, but because they took shape over a long period of time, they seem to have always been part of our political framework. Educational theorists are increasingly concerned to articulate more clearly the virtues of liberalism in relation to the fact of cultural and religious plurality. These theorists rightly take education to be central to the shift from the condition of plurality "as such," that is the mere fact of difference, to a recognition of pluralism as a political and educational value that requires careful and considered cultivation (Feinberg, 2006). Contemporary liberal theorists make the case that pluralism is not antithetical to liberalism; the two values go hand in hand. Nonetheless, as I will show, there is quite a bit of debate about how to conceive of the relationship between the two. What are the parameters of the liberal project? What does liberalism demand of cultural and religious groups whose values are at odds with the liberal project? And what concessions are liberal theorists willing to make to these groups, with what consequences, and for whom? This chapter will focus on an aspect of contemporary liberal theory that is of particular interest to philosophers of education, and indeed, that philosophers of education have done much to foreground; the idea of liberalism as a transformative project. While the parameters of liberalism's transformative ambitions are hotly disputed within liberal theory, there is general agreement that liberalism "will not leave everything as it is" (Callan, 1997, p. 13). This is what makes the liberal project an educational endeavor as well as a political one (Blacker, 2007).

There are two reasons for focusing our attention on the liberal tradition. First, there is the degree to which liberalism as a political theory has struggled over the centuries, in various ways, and with varying degrees of success, to accommodate value pluralism. Liberal political theories emerged in response to the hard won recognition that there are multiple conceptions of the good, and that the role of the state is to ensure that citizens can pursue their vision of the good with a minimum of interference. But liberalism is not simply a negative political project that leaves individuals and communities entirely to their own devices. Precisely because people have different conceptions of the good, citizens need to learn to live together. The idea that liberalism is a positive political project that has an interest in the formation of particular kinds of citizens is the second and more important reason for attending to liberal theories of education. It is increasingly clear (Callan, 1997; Macedo, 2000) that liberalism is not simply a matter of "statecraft," but also of "soulcraft." This is no doubt what makes it a controversial undertaking, and it is why the liberal state has to proceed with care in mat-

The Handbook of Educational Theories, pp. 67–78

ters of educational policy. Nonetheless, as educational theorists are starting to point out (Feinberg, 2006; Nussbaum, 2010), the political project of liberal-pluralism cannot be taken for granted. As Feinberg (2006) explains, we cannot "assume that the attitudes, skills and dispositions required to produce liberal, democratic society can be placed on automatic and grow themselves…. The skills required for liberal democracy is multifaceted, the dispositions deep, and the attitudes complex" (p. xiv). The success of a liberal democracy "depends on a general citizenry who is committed to advancing its principles as robustly as any one citizen is to advancing any one particular set of beliefs and commitments" (Feinberg, 2006, p. xiv).

The idea of liberalism as a positive political project makes it clear that we are not talking here about the laissez-faire approach to the public good—and indeed, to public goods in general—advocated by neoliberals. Far from being a hands-off endeavor, contemporary liberal political theorists are unabashed in enjoining the state to efforts to see to it that education serves individuals well without sacrificing a view of the common good. How liberals understand this tension between individual conceptions of the good and civic conceptions of the good is the main theme of this paper. I should make clear at the outset that liberal political theorizing today falls under the umbrella of normative political theory. The theorists I write about below are talking about how the state *ought* to conceive of its role in education and how it *ought* to justify its involvement in educational considerations. This normative view is quite often at odds with the way the state works "on the ground," so to speak. But this is precisely why normative theorizing matters. If we have a sense of how education ought to be and why it ought to be this way, we have a lens through which to critique actually existing practices. While normative perspectives are guided by ideals, they are not idealistic in the sense of being unrealizable or unfeasible. Indeed, part of the appeal of liberal political theorizing is its recognition that this approach is antiutopian. Liberal theorizing that is true to the spirit of liberalism's history recognizes that is an approach to political life that is cognizant of its limitations: not everyone will buy into the liberal educational project as I describe it in what follows to the same degree or for the same reasons. These theories are perhaps best understood as the most likely to succeed under the conditions of plurality. Normative political theorizing then does not claim to solve the difficult problems of humans living together. It can, at best, help us to come to grips with the difficulties in order to better navigate them.

The debate over the parameters of liberalism's educational project hinges on questions of authority, legitimacy and justification, on the one hand, and respect for individual liberty and "value pluralism" on the other. As we will see, the nature of the debate changes quite a bit when children are added to the equation. As beings in formation, children's life possibilities are circumscribed by the moral commitments, interests and investments of their parents. The state has to balance the interests of parents with the interests of children, and this is no easy task. The state also has to determine how far its interest in questions of the good life may legitimately go. On one view of the state's positive educational project, the state is expected to maximize the liberties of individuals, which means that it has to restrict its involvement in the education of children to the *civic* dimensions of education. But on another view, this emphasis on the civic puts some children at a disadvantage because it essentially allows their life possibilities to be subsumed by the interests of their parents. From this perspective, the issue is not simply a matter of civic stability, but a more fundamental matter of *fairness*: appeasing various faith communities should not trump the state's obligation to see to it that every child has the opportunity to develop the capacity to shape their own conception of the good. On this view, the state has an obligation to promote the development of autonomy in citizens, even though the state must temper its interest in autonomy promotion with the recognition that an autonomous life is one possible conception of the good life. In other words, it is quite possible that citizens will decide that a heteronomous life is better for them, and this has to be recognized as an acceptable life choice of citizens in a liberal state.

Indeed, liberal political theorists are increasingly conceding that a heteronomous life (i.e., a life in service of God, or in an institutional framework that requires a certain amount of unquestioned obedience to authority) is perfectly compatible with the liberal project as long as such a life is freely chosen (i.e., not coerced), and as long as the right to exit this life is protected by the state. Liberal theorists have tempered the liberal ideal of the self-directed citizen considerably in response to the pluralist challenge. They now talk about the liberal state as *weakly perfectionist* (Levinson, 1999), a phrase that acknowledges that not everyone wants to live in accordance with the liberal philosophical ideal of autonomy. Some people are more fulfilled living in traditionalist cultural communities, or in orthodox or similarly restrictive faith communities. Other theorists (Brighouse, 2000) describe education as facilitating the development of autonomy rather than promoting autonomy. This distinction protects the rights of citizens to opt for seemingly illiberal ways of life. Others ratchet down the concept of autonomy in various other ways. Reich (2002), for example talks about *minimalist autonomy* rather than strong autonomy. Whereas strong autonomy suggests that people ought to be self-governing, minimalist autonomy proposes instead that people should be able to choose the kind of life they want to live. On this view, liberalism is not opposed to restrictive cultural contexts, as long as the conditions that make such a life freely chosen are met. This softening of the liberal project is deeply attentive to the paradoxical position in which some parents are placed, but it is equally concerned that the alternative fails to protect the (future) liberties of children and violates the liberal principle of equality in the process. This chapter will explore each of these approaches to the liberal project in turn.

Repositioning Liberal Political Theory

Before I situate the debate between civic liberalism and autonomy-facilitating liberalism in its contemporary theoretical context, I should explain first why liberal political philosophies of education are the focus of this paper. Within the field of political theory, there is wide agreement that "liberalism has become the dominant position" (Dryzek, Honig, & Phillips, 2006, p. 17). This is not to say that there aren't alternatives to this position, or that liberal political philosophy is immune from philosophical scrutiny, but liberalism has shown itself to be remarkably resilient. It has also shown itself to be surprisingly responsive to the various critiques it has weathered over the years, from communitarians, multiculturalists, feminists and democratic theorists in academic circles, and in response to the claims of cultural and religious minority groups "on the ground." The editors of the *Oxford Handbook of Political Theory* (Dryzek et al., 2006) explore some of these "concessions" in their introductory essay, noting three important shifts in liberal conceptions of the person in relation to the state:

1. Equality is now regarded not simply as a formal right but as a substantive right. This is why liberal political theorists attend increasingly to questions of access to resources and the fair distribution of basic goods. The handbook editors are not altogether satisfied with the trajectory of this new emphasis, because theorists tend to deal mainly with differences between individuals (talents, interests, "aspiration and effort") and not with the more pressing questions about structural inequality and political oppression (race, gender, class and caste) (Dryzek et al., 2006, p. 18). Nonetheless, they concede that liberals are now writing about inequality, and the fact that equality is now given equal footing with liberty "can be read as a radicalization of liberal theory" (p. 18).

2. Liberals still place ethical primacy on the individual, but individuals are now understood as situated beings rather than as abstracted ones. People become who they are in relation to a social context; they are formed in relationship with others, and these formative experiences condition our life chances and choices in ways that we do not always comprehend. Liberals are also increasingly attentive to the claims of culture (Benhabib, 2002), although they do not concede everything to culture. The individual is still ethically primary. Nonetheless, liberalism has made important adjustments in response to the feminist and communitarian critique of liberal conceptions of the self in relation to others (Dryzek et al., 2006).

3. Finally, the conception of the citizen has changed as liberalism has shifted from an emphasis on the "negative liberties" (freedom from the state) to a new emphasis on citizens as participants in the political process. The nature of this participation has changed too, with the older notion of politics as the pursuit of self-interest giving way to a more public minded, deliberative conception of politics. The new conception of citizenship goes beyond the more traditional understanding of a citizen as one who obeys the law and fulfills their civic duty by voting, usually based on their own interests and values. The new civic ideal is that of the reasonable citizen who understands that part of the "burden" of citizenship is to recognize that political decisions cannot simply be based on self-interest. A political decision has to seek to be broadly representative, which means that the perspectives of others have to be taken into account and factored in to the decision-making process. This is a thicker conception of citizenship than the traditional one, and it explains why contemporary liberal political theorists focus more concertedly on education than they did before.

The Parameters of Political Liberalism

Each of these shifts is in some way indebted to the groundbreaking work of John Rawls (1971/1999), whose first major work, *A Theory of Justice,* is credited with having revived the egalitarian tradition within liberal political philosophy. Rawls was interested in moving beyond the *negative* liberties traditionally associated with liberalism, to a more *public minded* framework through which citizens could reach agreement about the fair distribution of primary goods in a liberal society. *A Theory of Justice* put forward a framework for thinking about justice that Rawls thought most people would be able to endorse, no matter what their particular interests and circumstances. The conception of justice hinges on two *devices* that require individuals to abstract themselves from their actual circumstances (thereby assuming the original position) and proceed as though they have no specific knowledge of their circumstances or social position in the new, more fair system they are asked to imagine (this is the famous *veil of ignorance*).

Rawls' (1971/1999) book received a great deal of attention, much of it critical. Communitarian and feminist critics were bothered by the assumption that individuals can abstract themselves from the values that are typically brought to bear on decisions of such a magnitude. The gist of their criticism is that people are not as rational as Rawls thinks; we are constrained by our circumstances and bound by our beliefs. While liberal individualists might regard this embeddedness as a limitation, communitarian and feminist critics regard it as a source of fulfillment and meaning. These kinds of complexities are reflective of value pluralism, and they help us understand why it is so hard to create the conditions for a fair distribution of primary goods. Rawls recognized that a more nuanced framework for solving difficult social problems would be required; one that could take into account the extent to which people come at important political considerations from within their particular comprehensive world-views. He was also at pains to underscore the limited reach of the political realm. For liberals, the political is not the whole of life; politics is essential for social cohesion and cooperation, but it is not coextensive with all of life. This means that there is much that lies beyond the reach of the political as Rawls understands it. I will say more about this shortly because this is a difficulty for thinking about the relationship between education and political theory. Education is not as easily *bounded* as Rawls seems to think it is. The "line" between educating for citizenship and educating for personhood is far from clear.

Twenty-two years after *Theory,* Rawls (1993) published *Political Liberalism,* which offers a new framework for thinking about the ways in which people can establish *fair terms of cooperation* in the midst of differing and even conflicting comprehensive beliefs. Shortly after he died, *Justice as Fairness: A Restatement,* was published (Rawls, 2001). This text (Rawls, 2001) sought to bring the original ideas of *Theory* in line with the new conception of political decision making of *Political Liberalism. A Restatement* begins with a reflection on the *four roles of political philosophy.* This section is worth exploring in some detail because it gives us insight into the predicament that gives rise to political liberalism. Rawls (2001, p. 3) explains that political philosophy *orients* us to the kind of society in which we find ourselves. It reminds us of the particular history of the society in question—in the case of liberal societies, this history would address the religious conflicts out of which these societies generally emerged. The other orienting feature of political philosophy is that it foregrounds the basic aims and purposes of the society as a society (as opposed to a community or an aggregate of individuals). In this sense, political philosophy helps to situate us, but it also *enlarges* us by drawing our attention to the many others with whom we need to learn to live.

Political philosophy also has an *existential* dimension, although Rawls does not name it as such. Rawls (2001) refers to this function of political philosophy as *reconciliation.* Reconciliation is required because few of us have chosen to be in the place where we find ourselves, and we do not choose who else is there with us. They too are simply *there.* This is the given from which Rawls's approach to the political begins, and this is the phenomenon to which political philosophy must reconcile us. When political institutions are understood in their historical context and in relation to present social conflicts, we are less likely to "rage against our society" and are more likely to understand and "affirm" these institutions (p. 3). This quirky formulation of the problem, rooted in Rawls's (2001) reading of Hegel's *Philosophy of Right* (p. 3), alerts us to the most important feature of political liberalism, which is that not everyone is going to buy into it wholeheartedly. Reconciliation is the best we can expect in these instances. It becomes clear that political liberalism is not a utopian philosophy. It does not claim to make everyone happy. The most that can be said for it is that it is a philosophy that we can all live with because it is the best we can do under the circumstances of moral and philosophical plurality.

Political philosophy also plays an important *practical* role in relation to political conflicts. It can guide us through "deeply disputed" territory with a view to either finding "some underlying basis" for agreement or narrowing the disagreement in such a way that "mutual respect among citizens" can be preserved (Rawls, 2001, p. 2). This process is not easy. It is sustained by the final role of political philosophy—the normative dimension—which encourages us to "[probe] the limits of practicable political possibility." It is important to remember here that political liberalism does not aim at political perfection. What is wanted instead is the less lofty pursuit of "a decent political order," one that most of us could live with, in part because we are all simply "here" and have to learn to live together.

The premise of *Political Liberalism* (Rawls, 1993) is that precisely because we live in a society that is populated by people who have religious and philosophical differences (some of which are more profoundly divergent than others), there is a need to construct a way of thinking about politics that is cognizant of these differences at the same time as it is careful to create a basis for political cooperation. In the absence of such a space, society collapses into an array of relatively insular cultural communities. Rather than asking citizens to set aside their comprehensive beliefs, which is what Rawls (2001) came to realize that he was in effect asking in *A Theory of Justice,* political liberalism instead suggests that most people will be able to sign on to the project of political liberalism from within their comprehensive beliefs. The Amish, for example, have a circumscribed view of the state that allows them to sign on conditionally to political liberalism even though they reject the basic tenets of liberalism as a philosophical system. While they are weary of those aspects of state coercion that overstep their understanding of what they themselves are required to do to provide for the material and spiritual well being of their own community (Yoder, 1993), the Amish acknowledge that their community is one of many. This makes the state a necessary source of order and stability in the broader society, a view that the Amish endorse from within the tenets of their faith (Joireman, 2009; Yoder, 1993). Others might find the philosophical and theological resources to sign on less conditionally to political liberalism from within their particular comprehensive view of life. Christians of many denominations might, for example, agree to "render unto Ceasar the things that are Ceasar's, and unto God the things that are God's" (Mathew 22:21). Other people, religious and nonreligious, have a stronger overlap, either because their comprehensive beliefs are *weaker* (i.e., less comprehensive) than others, or because their comprehensive beliefs are more complex, in which case, they will overlap at multiple points with the political sphere. The important thing about this view is that it recognizes that people engage in politics for a variety of reasons, and they do so in a variety of ways. Some people will have more minimal engagements than others. Political liberalism seeks to accommodate both those who regard the political sphere as a necessary evil, and those who regard the political sphere as a source of value in and of itself. This is because it has a delimited conception of politics. Political liberals (and liberals more generally) do not think that the political sphere is the whole of life, although it is not inconsequential either. A healthy political sphere is essential for the stability, coherence and continuity of a liberal-pluralist society.

What distinguishes political liberalism from stronger versions of liberalism is that it is, in Rawls's (1993) pithy formulation, "political, not metaphysical" (pp. 97-98). This distinction is subtle and not without difficulties. Rawls is trying to find a way, within the broad parameters of liberal political philosophy, to be more accommodating of people who do not endorse liberalism as a moral philosophy. The basic idea is that one does not have to be philosophically liberal in order to sign on to the project of political liberalism; one can endorse the basic structure of political liberalism from within one's comprehensive world view. But one does have to accept that our society allows for a range of ways of conceiving of the good life, and one has to be willing to support the construction of a conception of political life that strives to be fair to all. Political liberalism does thus require that one be a kind of liberal, albeit in only one sphere of life. Citizens can be as closed to alternative possibilities as they like in other aspects of their lives, but political life requires a willingness to develop and exercise a different set of virtues. In short, for political liberalism to work, citizens have to learn to be liberal in political life. Thus conceived, political liberalism is educative, although Rawls does not make this point explicitly.

Actually, Rawls says very little about education, which is strange given the distance between the idea of plurality as such—for example, the mere fact of value diversity—and the notion of reasonable pluralism. Reasonable pluralism is an altogether different notion because it is not a given. It has to be cultivated. It requires a degree of exposure to other points of view, an ability to imagine what absent others might think of a particular proposal, and an ability to weigh potentially conflicting claims before coming to a decision that counts as reasonable. In short, reasonable pluralism is a *political* and an *educational* achievement.

When Rawls (1993) does briefly address education, he is careful to stipulate that it take place entirely within "the political conception" (p. 200). In other words, an education for political liberalism must not set out to make children philosophically liberal: it need not aim to foster their autonomy (following the liberalism of Kant) nor cultivate their individuality (following the liberalism of John Stuart Mill). Political liberalism, Rawls (1993) writes, "has a different aim and requires far less" (p. 199). Under the parameters of political liberalism, children must learn about the rights they have as individuals under the Constitution of the United States; they must learn enough to be self-supporting should the need arise; and they must also learn the political virtues that will enable them to be "fully cooperating members of society" (p. 199). These are the virtues of "civility and tolerance, of reasonableness and the sense of fairness" (p. 194). Again, Rawls insists that these political virtues are stand alone virtues that can be restricted to the political sphere. He stipulates that these political virtues cannot be imposed on various associational ideas, nor should they filter into familial relationships. Rawls could be right here: many people belong to selective associations, and we are able to square this phenomenon with an understanding that political engagements require a greater degree of openness to diversity. But it is not easy to cordon off the values of one sphere from those of another. This suggests a paradox: the strength of political liberalism lies in its recognition of its own boundedness. But at the same time, the virtues of political liberalism are likely to spill over into other spheres of life—the very ones that Rawls appears to want to protect.

Rawls (1993, p. 199) recognizes this to some degree when he acknowledges that civic education could lead to a loosening of ties with one's constitutive community. Knowing one's constitutional rights gives members of closed communities the confidence to follow their conscience and the security of knowing that they have certain legal rights that trump the claims of their religious community. Even the basic and seemingly benign stipulation that all children are educated well enough to become self-supporting will mean that a closed community has less of a hold on a child who may be nervous about their prospects for survival should they leave the community. The primacy placed on the rights we bear as individuals makes political liberalism liberal as well as pluralist, and Rawls grants that an education that tries to take place solely within the political conception may lead some children down the road of comprehensive liberalism. But he makes it clear that this is not something that liberals should advocate or celebrate: "the unavoidable consequences of reasonable requirements for children's education may have to be accepted, often with regret" (p. 200).

EDUCATIONAL THEORISTS RESPOND TO RAWLS: FROM POLITICAL LIBERALISM TO CIVIC LIBERALISM

In educational theory, the debate over Rawls's work hinges on the question of how liberal citizens have to be for the project of political liberalism to work. Some theorists (Blacker, 2007; Macedo, 2000) argue that Rawls should be more forthcoming about the degree to which political liberalism is a "transformative enterprise" (Macedo, 2000, p. 10), although they agree with Rawls that the scope of this transformation is more or less restricted to the political sphere. Others (Callan, 1997; Levinson, 1999; Reich, 2002) argue that political liberalism is simply a closeted comprehensive liberalism, and that political liberals should come clean about this. I will explore this debate in the remainder of this paper. This debate is not simply theoretical; it has serious implications for educational policy. We will see that both sides are essentially making an argument for expanded state involvement in education, although they offer different rationales for increased state regulation of schooling, whether public or private (Brighouse, 2005; Feinberg, 2006), including homeschools (Kunzman, 2009; Reich, 2002, 2008).

In *Diversity and Distrust: Civic Education in a Multicultural Democracy,* Stephen Macedo (2000) argues that Rawls has not attended sufficiently to the educational project that is essential to the success of political liberalism. Macedo's work shows how central education is to the success of the overall project of political liberalism and is thus a good example of the seriousness with which liberal political philosophers are now attending to questions of the state's role in the formation of citizens. Macedo agrees that liberals have tended to treat citizens as though we are born rather than made. Libertarians who argue against public schools mistakenly assume "that liberal citizens—self-restrained, moderate and reasonable—spring full blown from the soil of private freedom" (p. 21). Similarly, citizens capable of living in the predicament of plurality that Rawls takes to be the starting point of political liberalism "are not simply born that way, they must be educated by schools and a variety of other social and political institutions" (p. 16). Much has to be accomplished on the road from pluralism *as such* to "reasonable pluralism." Macedo mounts a case for an approach to education that is more forthcoming about the extent to which political liberalism is a "transformative enterprise" (p. 10). Political liberalism cannot be understood to be a matter of statecraft alone; soulcraft of a certain sort is required (p. 34). This is the task of *civic liberalism.* Civic liberalism is not simply an extension of the project of political liberalism into the educational sphere; it also alerts us to a problem with Rawls's attempt to cordon off the political sphere from the moral sphere, i.e. the sphere of comprehensive belief. The idea of a civic liberalism is thus an important corrective to the idea that political liberalism extends only to the domain of the political sphere and does not deliberately intrude into the rest of life.

An example will help explain how the parameters of political liberalism change when one starts to understand it as a civic project. Macedo (2000) returns to a pivotal moment in the history of liberalism: John Locke's *Letter Concerning Toleration.* This letter, which laid the groundwork for thinking about the separation of church and state, takes us back to a period in which the tensions of religious diversity were far more serious than they are today (a testament in itself to the success of the liberal project). Macedo's reading of the letter shows that Locke was susceptible to a similar misconception about the extent to which it is possible to cordon off the work of the church from the business of the state. Locke argues that the church should limit its concerns to the souls of parishioners, while the state should devote itself solely to securing the stability of the commonwealth. However, in the course of his letter, it becomes evident the soul is not only the proviso of the church. The state too has a vested interest in a "certain ordering of the soul," although it has to make sure that its intervention is motivated by public rather than particularist reasons, and it has to apply equally to everyone. At the same time, the church is not left completely to its own devices. Locke urges religious leaders to take it upon themselves to foster the kinds of Christian virtues that will lend themselves to religious coexistence. He urges church leaders to remind their flock of the "duties of peace, and good-will toward all men; … the erroneous [and] the orthodox" (p. 33). Macedo's larger point (p. 34) is that a certain convergence of values is essential for the long term survival of the liberal state. Political liberalism does not take a hands-off approach to the various faith communities that have to figure out how to live in the condition of plurality; it expects that these communities will take it upon themselves to bring the flock "in line" with the liberal-pluralist project.

Of course, the thin moral values promoted by Locke have since been supplanted by a thicker set of values. While it is true that many schools are still most comfortable promoting the relatively thin political virtues of civility and tolerance advocated by Locke, some schools seek to promote mutual respect and reciprocity. It's important not to underestimate the value of *thin* political virtues, although it is true that they do not require much engagement with specific differences of beliefs and values; the general understanding that some people are different is all that is necessary. Mutual respect and reciprocity, however, require a deeper understanding of these differences so that matters of public concern can be discussed in terms that others can understand. Mutual respect and reciprocity are thus more deeply educative. We learn about other ways of understanding the world, and we take this learning *on board* in order to generate a public language that is broadly acceptable. But this taking on board has a delimited rationale. Members of specific faith/cultural communities are not being asked to subject their beliefs to critical scrutiny, but simply to recognize how their views might differ from those of others, and to grant that any public policies that emerge from these deliberations will have to take these differences into account. The trouble is that this seemingly small conceptual shift from the "one true belief" to the possibility that there might be another way of understanding the world is not as straightforward as one might think. For true believers, such a move is laden with religious anxieties because this kind of attention to alternative beliefs might sow the seeds for a reevaluation of one's own beliefs. Nonetheless, Macedo (2000) is careful to stipulate that this is not the purpose of public reasonableness. The aim is not to change the religious beliefs of individuals but simply to cultivate their capacity for civic mindedness.

This is not to say that there won't be spill over from the public/political domain to the private/religious domain. It is quite possible—and Macedo (2000) thinks it is actually desirable—that citizens will reevaluate aspects of their beliefs that are in some way at odds with the civic project. Walter Feinberg (2006) observes this process at work in a Catholic school he visited while researching the civic dimensions of religious schooling. He found that while the church is quite categorical in its opposition to homosexuality, divorce and birth control, the teachers he encountered approached these issues with a surprising amount of discretion and sympathy for students who did not adhere to church doctrine on these issues. Although he acknowledges the creativity of teachers in light of the difficulties their actions pose to the Catholic identity of these schools (p. 118), Feinberg is ultimately not happy with the degree of subterfuge in which they had to engage. While Feinberg regards this as a shortcoming of the school, Macedo might see it as a sign of the liberal settlement in progress. One by one, teachers are recognizing the difficulties their students face as they navigate the school as children of divorced parents, as gay students, or as sexually active adolescents, and the teachers are finding ways to accommodate their emotional needs in the school within ideological constraints. Whether this will affect church doctrine is another question entirely, one that must be left to the church to decide. But from Macedo's transformative perspective, it is interesting that the strategies Feinberg observes are taking place voluntarily in a Catholic school. It shows the extent to which the transformative liberal project is a two way street. Public policies have to be formulated in ways that allow religious schools to set their own policies in relation to sexuality education, but the schools in turn find that they are not able to draw the boundaries of acceptable practice as tightly as Church doctrine expects. Importantly, the schools accommodate students not because the state stipulates that they have to, but because they themselves see a need to respond to the conflicting societal pressures on their students.

Civic liberalism is clear about its transformative aims in a way that political liberalism is not. But like political liberalism, it is reluctant to press these aims too far. The political domain is still understood to be a bounded sphere. It is not, "the whole of the human good" (Macedo, 2000, p. 138). It does not require that citizens subject their deepest beliefs to scrutiny, only that they work toward enough of an understanding of other beliefs to be able to offer reasons for their points of view on civic matters that are in keeping with the political ideal of reciprocity. This idea that there are moral limits to politics is one of the attractions of political liberalism. It is not a totalizing view of politics; it does not take politics to be "the entire realm of moral value" (Macedo, 2000, p. 219). This would seem to be what makes political liberalism the most fair minded and inclusive approach to the political realm. But Macedo goes on to explain that this is actually not the case. Political liberalism operates with a particular conception of the self in view—a divided self that is able to move with relative ease between the potentially different moral demands of the private sphere (generally, the sphere of one's deepest moral commitments), and the demands of the public sphere. Participation in the public sphere requires one to essentially let go of the idea that the values one holds dear *ought* to have the same hold on others. This is not to say that people attracted to political liberalism will be starkly divided selves who are willing to cordon off their strongest beliefs for the sake of a civic compromise. If anything, writes Macedo (2000), political liberalism takes advantage of a certain "loosejointedness" in matters of belief (p. 215). Many of us do not have particularly coherent moral beliefs. Our moral values are more likely to be an amalgamation of disparate philosophical and/or religious perspectives, not all of which are altogether compatible. Political liberalism capitalizes on this moral fragmentation precisely because the goal isn't consistency of belief but rather a willingness to forge common ground with others who are similarly "at ease" in the condition of value pluralism.

Political liberalism is not then perfectly neutral, and nor does it claim to be (Rawls, 1993, p. 191). It is biased toward a particular kind of self—one who is "prepared to live with a certain fragmentation of authority and purpose" (Macedo, 2000, p. 144), and/or one who is comfortable with "complexity" (Blacker, 2007, p. 193). It is biased against those who are unable to set aside the "totality of their beliefs" for the sake of the civic project. Macedo is more forthright than Rawls here about the limits of liberalism's ability to accommodate all points of view. Religious fundamentalists like Vicki Frost, who was one of the families in the *Mozert* case, is the focal point of this discussion (Macedo, 2000). The *Mozert* plaintiffs objected to a particular set of readers because the content of the series conflicted with their fundamentalist Christian beliefs. They asked that their children be exempt from having to read these books on these grounds. It is significant that they were not demanding that the books be removed from the school, simply that the children be exempted from exposure to the books because they were thought to contain ideas that contradicted their faith. The decision found against the plaintiffs on the grounds that "mere exposure" does not constitute a burden to their beliefs. The court pointed out that the plaintiff's children were not forced to agree with what they were reading. As the court saw it, the school was acting within its bounds because it did seek to change the ideas of children. Macedo finds this somewhat disingenuous, and argues that the court should have been more forthright about the civic responsibilities of schools and more careful to explain the distinction between the parameters of civic life and the sphere of private religious belief.

To illustrate this point, Macedo (2000) refers to the poem about the six blind men and the elephant, one of many readings that the plaintiffs found objectionable. In the poem, each man has access to one part of the elephant and concludes from this the kind of animal it is. The poem concludes with a section entitled "Moral" which goes like this (p. 177):

> So oft in theologic wars
> The disputants, I ween
> Rail on in utter ignorance
> Of what each other mean,
> And prate about an Elephant
> Not one of them has seen!

Macedo sees how the Mozert families concluded that the poem is making an argument about religious truth (or the lack thereof), but he nonetheless asserts that the poem is better understood to be making a civic point about the futility of engaging in theological disputes in the public realm. He grants that this distinction between the demands of the civic sphere and the demands of the religious sphere probably wouldn't have persuaded the Mozert families to abandon their claim, but it would have articulated more clearly the civic values at stake. More specifically, it would have made clear that the civic realm requires the development of distinctive skills and attributes, and it would have reinforced the idea that the schools have a role to play in their cultivation.

In contrast with political liberalism, civic liberalism is much more forthright about liberalism's transformative inclinations: in order to move from the condition of "pluralism as such" to the thicker notion of "reasonable pluralism," the state, through its educational institutions, must be willing to engage in soul craft. In other words, civic liberalism does not leave citizens unchanged. But civic liberals temper their transformative impulses by restricting their reach to the admittedly porous boundary of the civic realm. This has led some educational theorists (e.g. Callan, 1997) to wonder whether civic liberals aren't perhaps failing to "'fess up" to the full significance of the transformative project. Others worry that civic liberals are insufficiently attentive to the circumstances of children in closed, or "totalizing" communities. Either way, civic liberals are criticized for not being liberal enough. I turn to these arguments now.

Comprehensive Liberalism: From Shaping the Civic to Shaping Selves

Civic liberalism is primarily concerned about pluralism as a political project that aims to shape civic life by cultivating particular kinds of citizens. While "selves" are bound to change in the process, civic liberalism does not set its sights on the formation of selves, but on the formation of citizens. The understanding here is that citizenship is part of personhood, but it is not the whole of it, and it is not even the most important part of life—although neither is it the least important. The state, working through its educational institutions, is understood to have a legitimate interest in the formation of citizens. This interest is not restricted to public schooling but extends to religious schools also (Feinberg, 2006). While civic liberals seek to cordon off the moral commitments of citizens from the broader and perhaps deeper moral commitments of persons, others in the liberal tradition take a more extensive view of the state's interest in education. On their view, the liberal state must see to it that each individual is capable of a degree of self-formation that might otherwise be unavailable to young people, especially children living in relatively closed cultural or religious communities. Because they regard liberalism as a comprehensive moral philosophy, they are called *comprehensive liberals*.

Interestingly, comprehensive liberals do not regard the liberal project to be at odds with pluralism, because liberalism recognizes a range of conceptions of "the good." The good in question could be the good of modern liberal individualism, or it could be a more communal, or even traditional conception of the good. As long as individuals are able to determine "the good" for themselves, i.e. autonomously, they can be said to be living within the purview of comprehensive liberalism. The emphasis on autonomy distinguishes comprehensive liberalism from civic liberalism. Civic liberalism recognizes that some communities adhere to ways of life that do not prize autonomy. As long as these communities are willing to recognize that there are other ways of life, they can be said to be in accordance with the project of political liberalism. For comprehensive liberals, "mere recognition" of a range of conceptions of the good in political life is not sufficient. Comprehensive liberals have a more stringent demand that these conceptions of the good be made available to *all* children. While most children might, in the end, decide to endorse the way of life mapped out for them by their parents or faith community, they ought, at the very least, to be given an education that would enable them to "try on" other possibilities. Under the stipulations of comprehensive liberalism, educational institutions have a deeper reach than the view of schools put forward by civic liberalism. They are not simply concerned with the formation of liberal citizens but with the formation of liberal selves, which is to say, selves that are capable of determining for themselves a view of "the good." For comprehensive liberals, it is a matter of justice to say that the state needs to ensure that each child has this opportunity. Justice is construed here as giving each child in a liberal society their due.

Autonomy-Facilitating Liberalism: Questions of Fairness and Liberty

To autonomy-facilitating liberals, the problem with political liberalism is not just that it does not recognize its transformative inclinations but that it does not take them far enough. They contend that in its bid to attend to the diversity of the public sphere, civic liberalism is insufficiently attentive to the interests of children (Reich, 2009), especially those who are growing up in the context of relatively closed communities. The tradeoff (Brighouse, 2009) is two fold. First, the (future) liberty of children is traded off with the rights of their parents to exercise their religious freedom. Second, they worry that the emphasis on liberty—in this case, the liberty of parents to shape the direction of their children's education—takes precedence over the liberal commitment to equality, understood here to mean that each person should have an opportunity to decide for themselves the kind of life they wish to lead. As autonomy-facilitating liberals see it, political liberalism should not worry about being "too liberal"; it should worry about being insufficiently liberal.

Autonomy-promoting liberals recognize a paradox at the heart of liberalism. The attraction of liberalism is that it makes room for a range of conceptions of the good, including the desire to live a "heteronomous" life. It also promises not to intrude into the private sphere. To insist that children receive an education in autonomy would seem to counter the very basis of liberalism's appeal, violating pluralism and "[infringing] the public/private divide by interfering with the family" (Levinson, 1999, p. 41). This seeming paradox hinges in part on a misunderstanding of the liberty proviso, but it also reflects a deeper failure to recognize the distinctive position of children in a liberal society. The misunderstanding of the liberty proviso can be cleared up with a reminder that liberty does not attach to "spheres" but to persons (Brighouse, 2005, p. 11). It is one thing to say, as liberalism does, that adults have the right to live a life that accords with their vision of the good, but granting adults this right should not foreclose the interests of children in exercising the same right at some future point. If liberty rights are applied to spheres, the risk is that children will not be afforded the opportunity to develop the capacities needed to ascertain their own view of the good life.

Because children are dependent beings, autonomy-facilitating liberals are attentive to the particularities of the parent-child relationship. At the same time, they want to make sure that the life the child is living is the right life for them, which is to say, a life they can identify with (Brighouse, 2005, p. 16) and live "from the inside" (Brighouse, 2000, p. 70). While many parents similarly hope that their children will be in a position to live authentically, this is not always a priority. Some parents put primacy on cultural continuity, or on a vision of what God wants for their children. From the perspective of autonomy-facilitating liberals, this puts some children at a serious disadvantage. The life mapped out for them may or may not be the life that is best for them, but they will not have the opportunity to think about it deeply; nor will they know that there are other ways of life that might be good for them given the type of person that they are or hope to become. Autonomy-facilitating liberals (Brighouse, 2000; Reich, 2009) are thus attuned to the possibility that the interests of particular children may be at odds with the interests of their parents. At the same time, they acknowledge that taking away a parent's right to share their religious values with their children, or to pass along a traditional way of life would overstep the bounds of the liberal state. Autonomy-facilitating liberals navigate this with care, although they concede that the primacy they place on the rights of children to ascertain for themselves what matters most will not satisfy critics who do not share this ethical commitment.

First, they address the question of how to divide the authority over children's education carefully. Rather than simply talking about parents' rights versus state's rights over children, they parse the two responsibilities. Normatively speaking, parents are in the best position to raise their children, while the neutral liberal state is in the best position to determine the broad content of education. On this view (Brighouse, 2009; Reich, 2009), parents are understood to have extensive interests in the upbringing of their children, and this obviously extends to their right to pass along their cultural traditions or religious commitments to their children. But this does not preclude the state from seeing to it that their children will be exposed to other valuable ways of life. This takes us to the second consideration with which autonomy-facilitating liberals grapple: what counts as a valuable way of life? Because liberals are sometimes perceived to have antipathy toward religion, autonomy-facilitating liberals make clear their rejection of the view that religion has no place in public schooling. Brighouse (2005), for example, proposes that religious people from a variety of faiths be invited into the classroom to put forward the best arguments for their particular worldviews. Similarly, de Ruyter and Merry (2009) make a case for the inclusion of religious ideals in the curriculum, arguing that religious ideal give students a better sense of why religion matters to people than does the study of religious doctrines and practices. Religious ways of life are thus not beyond the purview of an autonomy-facilitating education. The key is that such a way of life be chosen knowingly, which is to say, based on a careful appraisal of the value of the worldview in question, and on an equally considered appraisal of other valuable ways of life. Needless to say, this new openness to religion on the part of liberal educational theorists will not necessarily endear them to religious communities. Critics include both those who prefer that religious remain a private familial concern beyond the purview of the school (or the state) and those who would like to see their own religious beliefs manifest in the public realm without having to contend with the risks of exposing their children to potentially conflicting beliefs.

Third, I mentioned earlier that autonomy-facilitating liberals have ratcheted down an earlier insistence on the liberal ideal of autonomy as a way of life. Autonomy-promotion has ceded to a more nuanced emphasis on autonomy-facilitation, the idea being that not everyone will be happy living a life that is completely self-determined. Some people are more fulfilled and find more meaning leading heteronomous lives, be this a life lived in deference to God's will, or in accordance with cultural or institutional strictures that limit autonomy in some way. Autonomy-facilitation does not reject the value of these ways of life, but it seeks to ensure that such life choices are considered and not coerced. Exposure to other life possibilities is one way to address the criterion of noncoercion, although from the perspective of heteronomous ways of life, this criterion is a bit of a challenge, to say the least. Religious people often speak of having been called to the faith, and while of course, they often say that they chose to answer the call (i.e. they could have refused; they have free will), to true believers, there is also a sense in which they could not resist the call. Autonomy-facilitating liberals do not engage this question at this level, although I suspect that the coercion they are most concerned about is decidedly *earthly*—it is not the power of God that is at issue, but the power of parents to constrain the education of their children in ways that might work against the child's interest in developing the capacity for autonomy.

Whereas civic liberalism stipulates that the state's interest in education must remain entirely within the civic realm, autonomy-facilitating liberals think that this view stops short of taking children seriously as individuals in their own right. The overriding criterion for autonomy-facilitating liberals is an understanding of educational justice that is premised on a notion of "ethical individualism" (Brighouse, 2000, p. 6). In a liberal state, justice is not accorded to adults alone; it must extend to children. Each child, as a distinct being, has an interest in an autonomy-facilitating education, and the state is obligated to ensure that each child has access to such an education. This argument is both pragmatic and principled. On the principled side, it is a matter of justice in the sense of seeing to it that each child has an opportunity to choose a way of life that makes sense to them. This argument, at present, proceeds somewhat pragmatically on economic grounds that the state as we know it can comprehend: the state has an interest in seeing to it that students who exit "closed" faith communities have the wherewithal to support themselves once they leave. If the education provided by their community of origin does not enable them to do this, the state can legitimately insist that the community improve its educational provision in light of costs that accrue to the state when young people exercise their right of exit. At present the debate hinges on the cost of vocational training for adolescents and emerging adults, but those who make these arguments are motivated by the principle that the state owes equal educational provision to each child as an individual in their own right. For autonomy-facilitating liberals, the focal point is the individual rather than the group. The group is valuable to the extent that it contributes to the flourishing of individuals.

Robert Kunzman's (2009) recent ethnographic exploration of homeschooling suggests that many, and perhaps even most, religiously based homeschoolers do this very well, but not all do. In these instances, the state must be willing to protect those who are vulnerable, even though this will be seen as overstepping the boundaries of both parent's rights and traditional conceptions of religious liberty. Tightening regulations on educational provision is one form that this protection takes, although there is some question over the reach of these regulations. Kunzman, for example, concludes that "a liberal democratic society needs to tread lightly when it comes to defining the boundaries of possible good lives, and even in specifying the virtues of good citizenship" (p. 220). He favors persuasion over compulsion, adding that the challenge is to find a way to "foster an identification and commitment to a broader public that connects all of us while also recognizing that it is our narrower communities and private identities that sustain us in ways at least as powerful and important" (p. 220).

Tensions in the Liberal-Pluralist Project

Liberal-pluralist societies are characterized by a certain amount of tension *at the hyphen*. The liberal side of the equation prioritizes the individual, while the pluralist side gives credence to the value of the cultural group/religious community. Tensions emerge when concerns about cultural identity/continuity take precedence over the individual's right to shape their own identity and vice versa. An added source of tension has to do with the transformation from plurality *as such* to pluralism, wherein groups can no longer expect to be left entirely to their own devices. They are expected to cultivate the dispositions and skills that will enable them to move beyond a *modus vivendi* by engaging with one another on a range of matters of shared public concern. How are these skills to be conceptualized and how are they best cultivated? Space limitations permit only the briefest consideration of these questions.

The value of civic liberalism lies in its attempt to maximize space for diverse communities to live in accordance with their view of the good while insisting that the communities in question work toward the cultivation of civic values as a "second-order" set of commitments (Feinberg, 2006, p. 44). These second-order commitments are quite demanding, but they stop short of requiring *true believers* to subject their views to critical scrutiny. Instead, what is required is a willingness to acknowledge that others have different beliefs, even though, from the perspective of the *True faith* in question, these beliefs might be considered to be wrong or misguided. Civic liberals like Feinberg (2006) make it clear that they are not asking that the capital T "Truth" of the other faith(s) be accepted, but rather that the significance of that faith for the faithful be acknowledged. This is a crucial distinction, and a very helpful one. It is not that one is expected to loosen one's own beliefs, but rather that one is expected to recognize that others take their own beliefs equally seriously (p. 163). Thus, the respect in question is for other people, and not so much for the faith in question (although one might, through serious engagement with it, develop such respect over time). This requires a willingness to distance oneself from one's own commitments just enough to recognize that others might have different moral commitments that are equally important to them (p. 42), but not so much that one is forced to engage with the substance of these ideas.

This disengagement/distantiation worries comprehensive liberals, who are in many ways arguing for a more robust political culture. Brighouse (2000), for example, wants students to not only be exposed to a range of religious, nonreligious and antireligious ethical systems but he also wants to encourage students to engage seriously with the best arguments for these worldviews. As de Ruyter and Merry (2008) note, this emphasis on exposure to a range of religious ideals is important for the project of reasonable pluralism; it is an essential first step in the movement from mere plurality to reasonable pluralism, i.e. the ability to take into account other conceptions of the good with a view to formulating public policies that are more representative and thus, more just. This sort of exposure is important for the liberal project also. Engagement with these ideals also presents individual students with an opportunity to formulate their own conception of the good, one that accords with their sense of what would make for a flourishing life (Brighouse, 2005, de Ruyter & Merry, 2008).

Civic liberals stop short of this aim. Although they grant that this sort of openness to ideas may well lead to a deeper transformation at the level of the *self*, they argue that the state has to exercise restraint here. It can insist only on the sorts of transformations necessary to protect the political realm. This puts them in some tension with the liberal side of the hyphen. Again, it is not that civic liberals are more pluralist than liberal. I hope that by now it is clear that the two conceptions are connected: pluralism requires a certain liberal sensibility, and liberalism wouldn't be necessary if societies were homogenous and without the sorts of moral conflicts that follow from value diversity. But the civic liberal project does stop short of advocating that the purpose of education in a diverse society is to shape the whole self. Civic liberals concede that education has a partial role to play in this project, but they argue that it is best that the state maintain a certain distance in questions of the ultimate good for individuals and limit its interest in education to the challenges of creating a viable conception of common good.

My bias toward civic liberalism is probably clear, but I must end by addressing a legitimate concern that children who live in communities that liberals take to be *closed* will be disadvantaged by this more minimal state involvement in education. My response to this very real worry is a pragmatic one. It's important to bear in mind that the fall out from the Mozert case was that many of the children left the public school system as a result of the district's unwillingness to accommodate the families' request for an exemption to the reading series (Macedo, 2000). Some went to Christian schools while others were homeschooled. Even though autonomy-facilitating liberals would not object to the demand that their religious ideals be included in the curriculum, religious fundamentalists are likely to reject the idea that their view is somehow being regarded as equivalent to other religious ways of life, let alone nonreligious ones. And they would certainly reject the state's rationale for this exposure, i.e. that their children have the right to determine for themselves their view of the good life. Putting the state in opposition to the parents in this way would likely do their children a grave disservice, especially if it propels them more deeply into a faith community that is already uncomfortable with pluralism. This doesn't mean that these families would sign on wholeheartedly to the civic project either. But of the two options—civic versus comprehensive liberalism—the civic project is more likely to be regarded as the legitimate purview of schooling. At least, the general public is likely to regard it as such, even though a few religious communities may not. At this point, liberals have to say simply that this is the best that can be hoped for. The liberal-pluralist project will not win everybody over. Neither will it leave everything as it is (Callan, 1997, p. 13). Herein lies its educational significance and political potential, although it also explains why it is that even in its thinner, civic dimensions, liberal-pluralism is not an easy undertaking.

REFERENCES

Benhabib, S. (2002). *The claims of culture: Equality and diversity in the global era.* Princeton, NJ: Princeton University Press.

Blacker, D. J. (2007). *Democratic education stretched thin: How complexity challenges a liberal ideal.* Albany, NY: State University of New York Press.

Brighouse, H. (2000). *School choice and social justice.* Oxford, England: Oxford University Press.

Brighouse, H. (2005). *On education.* London, England: Routledge.

Brighouse, H. (2009). Moral and political aims of education. In H. Siegel (Ed.), *The Oxford handbook of philosophy of education* (pp. 35-52). Oxford, England: Oxford University Press.

Callan, E. (1997). *Creating citizens.* Oxford, England: Clarendon Press.

de Ruyter, D. J., & Merry, M. S. (2009). Why education in public schools should include religious ideals. *Studies in Philosophy of Education, 28*, 295-311.

Dryzek, J. S., Honig, B., & Phillips, A. (2006). Introduction. In *The Oxford handbook of political theory* (pp. 3-35). Oxford, England: Oxford University Press.

Feinberg, W. (2006). *For goodness sake: Religious schools and education for a democratic citizenry.* New York, NY: Routledge.

Joireman, S. F. (1993). Anabaptists and the state: An uneasy coexistence. In S. F. Joireman (Ed.), *Church, state, and citizen* (pp. 73-91). Oxford, England: Oxford University Press.

Kunzman, R. (2009). *Write these laws on your children: Inside the world of conservative Christian homeschooling.* Boston, MA: Beacon Press.

Levinson, M. (1999). *The demands of liberal education.* Oxford, England: Oxford University Press.

Macedo, S. (2000). *Diversity and distrust: Civic education in a multicultural democracy.* Cambridge, MA: Harvard University Press.

Nussbaum, M. (2010). *Not for profit: Why democracy needs the humanities.* Princeton, NJ: Princeton University Press.

Rawls, J. (1999). *A theory of justice* (Rev. ed.). Cambridge, MA: The Belknap Press of Harvard University Press. (Original work published 1971)

Rawls, J. (1993). *Political liberalism.* New York, NY: Columbia University Press.

Rawls, J. (2001). *Justice as fairness: A restatement* (E. Kelly, Ed.). Cambridge, MA: The Belknap Press of Harvard University Press.

Reich, R. (2002). *Bridging liberalism and multiculturalism in American education.* Chicago, IL: The University of Chicago Press.

Reich, R. (2008). On regulating homeschooling: A reply to Glanzer. *Educational Theory, 58*(1), 17-24.

Reich, R. (2009). Educational authority and the interests of children. In H. Siegel (Ed.), *The Oxford handbook of philosophy of education* (pp. 469-488). Oxford, England: Oxford University Press.

Yoder, P. (1993). The Amish view of the state. In D. B. Kraybill (Ed.), *The Amish and the state* (pp. 23-40). Baltimore, MD: Johns Hopkins University Press.

Author Content Information: Natasha Levinson, PhD, School of Foundations, Leadership and Administration, College of Education, Health and Human Services, Kent State University, Kentm, OH. Telephone: 1-330-672-0592. E-mail: nlevinso@kent.edu

CHAPTER 7

Philosophy of Social Science and Educational Research

Kenneth R. Howe
University of Colorado

Issues in the philosophy of social science have underlain disputes regarding the best understanding of and approach to educational research at least since the Thorndike-Dewey divide in the early twentieth century (Condliffe-Lageman, 2000). Arguably, offshoots of the very same fault lines that existed then continue to divide the educational research community to this day. But the focus of this chapter will be the more recent scene, in which two events—the *paradigm wars* (Gage, 1989) that emerged in the late 1970s to early 1980s and the clamor for *scientifically based* educational research that emerged at the turn of the twenty-first century—drew significant attention to several interlocking issues within the purview of the philosophy of social science: about epistemology, appropriate research methods, conceptions of causation, the unity of science, and the place of values and politics in educational research.

THE PARADIGM WARS

In his classic *The Structure of Scientific Revolutions*, historian-cum-philosopher of science Thomas Kuhn (1962) contends that the breakdown of a scientific paradigm and subsequent "revolution" is propelled by an increasing stock of problems (anomalies) that eventually leads to questioning and abandoning core premises, including epistemological premises. Although educational research has never truly exemplified scientific paradigms or revolutions in the senses described by Kuhn, his framework can nonetheless be fruitfully applied to characterize the so-called paradigm wars in educational research.

CLASSICAL EXPERIMENTALISM

Bearing in mind that I am taking some liberties with Kuhn's framework, the dominant paradigm in educational research in the 1970s was *classical experimentalism* (Howe, 2004). It is exemplified well by Donald Campbell and Julian Stanley (1963), in which they declare in their seminal monograph *Experimental and Quasi-Experimental Designs for Research* (1963) that the experiment is "the *only* means for settling disputes regarding educational practice, as the *only* way of verifying educational improvements, and as the *only* way of establishing a cumulative tradition" (p. 2, italics added).

Campbell and Stanley (1963) advocated implementing this general experimentalist stance using quantitative data and statistics. They dismissed the kind of close-up engagement with research participants associated with so-called qualitative methods (common in cultural anthropology, for example) as committing the "fallacy of misplaced precision" and dismissed the associated focus on a single context, the "one-shot case study," as "well nigh unethical" to use (p. 7).

Although often identified with *positivist* philosophy of social science by the broader educational research community, the task of explicating the tenets of positivism, the ways and extent to which it was exemplified by classical experimentalism and how it might be criticized fell primarily to philosophers (e.g., Garrison, 1986; Howe, 1985, 1988; Phillips, 1983). Among the central tenets of positivism brought under scrutiny were *verificationism*, the fact/value dichotomy, the regularity conception of causation, and the unity of science.

Verificationism is an empiricist epistemological principle whose function is to demarcate scientific statements from other kinds of statements, particularly metaphysical ones. Verificationism stipulates that for a

The Handbook of Educational Theories, pp. 79–86

statement to be genuinely scientific, it must be possible to determine whether it is true or false or to specify how this determination could be made. There are only two kinds of statements that satisfy this requirement: (1) *synthetic* statements, in which it is possible to specify what observations would render a statement true or false, at least *in principle*; and (2) *analytic* statements, in which it is possible to determine whether a statement is true or false by appeal to (a) logic or (b) synonymy. An example of a synthetic statement is "There are craters on the dark side of the moon." Uttered before the dark side of the moon could be observed by satellites and moon walkers, this claim was synthetic by virtue of the *in principle* qualification, and its actual truth or falsity was unknown. In general, yet to be tested scientific statements have this status. An example of the a-type analytic statement is "All moon walkers are moon walkers;" an example of the b-type is "All bachelor moon walkers are unmarried." Analytic statements seem uninformative or *empty*, which is accounted for by the fact they are without observational (empirical) content. But long lines of logical inference and complex relationships among concepts are not obvious in the way the straightforward moon walker examples are. The function of analytics statements in science is to organize its observational content and sanction logical inferences from and to observational content, as in scientific explanations and scientific predictions, respectively.

Verificationism is most clearly exemplified in behaviorist social science, which, when ascendant, was also prevalent in educational research. In its purest form, behaviorism jettisons any theoretical or metaphysical terms that cannot be directly tied to observable human behavior. Thus, to be part of legitimate science, minds, thoughts, intentions, and other mental concepts must be recast in terms of observable behavior (movements) in order for claims involving them to be verifiable/falsifiable. This effectively requires eliminating them as distinct descriptive and explanatory elements of observable human behavior. In this vein, Sigmund Freud's psychoanalytic theory, which posits an unobservable unconscious mind underlying observed behavior, was criticized for failing to be verifiable or falsifiable and, thus, contrary to Freud's aspirations, for being unscientific (Thornton, 2005).

The principle of the *unity of science* adds to verificationism the idea that all areas of scientific investigation have the same structure. Physics, which provides explanations and predictions in terms of identified laws of nature, was taken to be the paragon. Thus, other candidates deserving of the designation *science*, including the social sciences, were required to model themselves on physics.

The *fact/value dichotomy* is a corollary of verificationism. Value statements, often characterized by words such as *good, ought*, and *right*, are not capable of meeting the requirements of verificationism. Consider "All Americans ought to be provided with an education that enables them to flourish, regardless of race, gender, special needs, or ability to pay." This statement is not true (or false) in virtue of logic or the meanings of the words that make it up. But neither is it synthetic, for we cannot specify the observations that would render it true or false. Thus, according to positivist epistemology, value statements lack "cognitive significance." Being incapable of verification or falsification, they occupy a different (or non) epistemic realm. As Donald Campbell (1982) put it in the context of social and educational research: "The tools of descriptive science and formal logic can help us implement values which we already accept or have chosen, but they are not constitutive of those values. Ultimate values are accepted but not justified" (p. 123).

The *regularity conception of causation*, often associated with the eighteenth century Scottish philosopher David Hume, identifies causal relationships with a *constant conjunction* in which the cause is temporally prior to the effect (Morris, 2009). Put most simply, "A causes B," means that whenever A is observed, the observation of B will follow. For example, "Increasing heat causes gas to expand." Of course, causal relationships are typically much more complicated than this. In the above example, for instance, there are assumptions that there is no concomitant increase in pressure that would prevent expansion, that the gas container is not rigid, and so on. A central feature of the regularity conception that is particularly relevant to social science is that it requires causes and effects to be related only contingently, and not conceptually. This rules out intentional causation. For example, "Jane intends to buy a book" (I) cannot be the cause of "Jane buys a book" (B) because I is not contingently related to B. Rather, I is *contained in* the description provided by B: as a conceptual matter, Jane can't satisfy the description "buys a book" without intending to buy a book. This is different from the relationship that exists between increasing heat and the expansion of gas, which is contingent and had to be discovered empirically.

Classical Experimentalism Criticized

Although positivism does not entail the adoption of classical experimentalism and the elevation of quantification, strictly speaking, it is certainly very congenial to them. In education, *quantitative methods* and the *quantitative paradigm* often served as umbrella terms for the more general positivist stance of classical experimentalism. Over time the dominant quantitative paradigm fell under increasing criticism for failing to adequately illuminate educational practice and to provide findings that could drive its improvement, helping to ignite the *paradigm wars* (Gage, 1989). Eventually, a state of détente was reached (Smith & Heshusius, 1986) in which qualitative methods and the qualitative paradigm won general acceptance, either as standing on their own or as a necessary adjunct to quantitative methods. Among those who came to embrace a role for qualitative methods were several very prominent and influential thinkers of the classical experimentalist paradigm, for instance, Phillip Jackson (1968), Lee J. Cronbach (Cronbach et al., 1980), and Donald Campbell (1974) himself.

In addition to on-the-ground criticisms concerning the fruits (the lack thereof) of classical experimentalism, more general developments in the philosophy of social science challenged the fundamental principles of positivist social science in which classical experimentalism was rooted. Numerous modifications of the principle of verificationism failed to remedy problems that emerged in specifying its requirements. As Denis Phillips (1983) put it, verificationism "became a contorted monstrosity" that "choked under its own weight" (p. 7). At a more fundamental level, pragmatist philosophers such as W.V.O. Quine (1951) and Hilary Putnam (1962) advanced decisive criticisms of the synthetic-analytic distinction that underpinned verificationism. The general and far-reaching result was the undermining of the empirical/conceptual bifurcation that the synthetic-analytic distinction was supposed to capture. It was displaced by the view that the observational content of science is inextricably entangled with its conceptual content such that scientific observations are unavoidably *theory-laden* in a *web of belief* (Quine & Ullian, 1978). Beliefs become progressively less subject to direct empirical testing and revision as the center of the web is approached. Near the center is where so-called analytic truths are found. But these truths are less subject to revision because of their interconnectedness with other beliefs throughout the web and the associated ripple effects of altering them, not because they are true *come what may*.

The abandonment of verificationism helped spur the abandonment of the idea of social scientific language of behavior stripped of all reference to (unobservable) mental events. Such a language proved inadequate for social and educational research (MacKenzie, 1977; Scriven, 1969; Strike, 1974; Taylor, 1964). There emerged a growing recognition among philosophers that *intentionalist* explanations were required, suitable for describing and explaining the norm-regulated behavior in which human beings, unlike the particles in motion of physics, engage (Dennett, 1989; Searle, 1984, 1995). For example, a marriage cannot be described solely in terms of the movements and noises emitted by the participants because the intentional states of those involved—the contents of their minds—are required to distinguish, say, a real marriage from a marriage acted out in a play.

Embracing this picture means rejecting the regularity conception of causation in social scientific investigation, as least as the primary or only kind. John Searle (1984), for example, who embraces intentionalist causation, claims that contrary to the positivist view sketched earlier, regularities do not provide explanations. Rather, they require them. For example, the mere observed regularity that automobiles stop when traffic lights are red, by itself, tells us very little about what is going on. It is not like the regularities associated with billiard balls. We need some kind of conception of people observing or obeying traffic laws and the reasons they might have for doing (avoiding bodily harm, property damage, fines, etc.) to grasp what is going on. Billiard balls *obey* laws only in a metaphorical sense.

Searle (1984) brushes off the idea that cause and effect cannot be conceptually linked. In general, causation involves the idea that "something makes something else happen" (p. 65). Intentionalist causation is typically much more illuminating and complex than vacuous examples such as "Jane bought a book because she intended to buy a book." Consider "Jane bought a book because she wanted to keep her mind sharp." In philosophical work the idea of "intentionality" includes intentions to act but also encompasses a much broader domain of mental concepts that have the characteristic of *aboutness*. Springs of behavior such as beliefs, doubts, and knowledge, are always about something; fears and worries usually are. Intentional concepts are of particular interest because that they go into descriptions of the *actions* people perform, as distinct from the mere *movements* of physical bodies, where intentionality has no place. So, Jane had the belief that reading a book would keep her mind sharp, which caused her to form the intention to buy a book, which ultimately resulted in her buying a book.

This remains an exceedingly simplistic example, and things become quite complicated when we move toward a comprehensive framework of causal explanation in the social sciences. Searle's (1995) framework incorporates a complex array of concepts, but three are of particular importance: *collective intentionality, social facts*, and the *background*.

When humans cooperate in the pursuit of goals, they exhibit collective intentionality. And via collective intentionality humans construct a special class of social facts that, unlike the *brute facts* of the physical world, would not exist without the activities of human beings. Searle's favored illustration is money. Its value and function have nothing to do with the brute fact physical form it takes, but is to be found in our collective acceptance of, and behavior in accord with, the rules of exchange.

The idea of collective intentionality does not require that agents always or even usually consciously follow rules. The idea of consciously following rules applies to learning certain activities, such as balancing a bicycle or reading, but only to the early stages of learning such that once a certain level of skill is reached, after which following rules is no longer necessary and can actually become an impediment to performance. In other cases, such as speaking grammatically, agents often just *catch on* to the rules without at any point consciously appealing to them, using criteria such as what sounds right. In each of these cases, we might say that rather than *following* the rules (consciously or unconsciously), agents are *tracking* them.

Searle (1995) introduces the background to help account for the phenomenon that just described as *tracking* the rules. He describes the background as "the set of nonintentional or preintentional capacities that enable intentional states to function" (p. 129). These capacities include abilities, dispositions, and know-hows, and among the things they do is to enable linguistic and perceptual interpretation, structure motivation, and dispose persons to certain kinds of behavior.

> One develops skills and abilities that are, so to speak, functionally equivalent to the system of rules, without actually containing any representations or internalizations of those rules....
>
> There is a parallelism between the functional structure of the Background and the intentional structure of the social phenomena to which the background capacities relate. That strict parallelism gives the illusion that the person who is able to deal with money, cope with society, and speak a language must be [consciously or] unconsciously following rules. (Searle, 1995, p. 142)

In many situations, Searle (1995) says, we just know what to do, and it's an unwarranted stretch to say we are following rules, either consciously or unconsciously. Of course, we do follow rules in many situations—the civil law, institutional by-laws, and so forth—but the applicable rules are never self-interpreting and are never exhaustive. So even in cases of consciously following rules we have to exercise the kind of interpretive and creative capacities associated with the Background.

Under Searle's (1995) account, humans typically have little or no say in what the social facts and rules are. Rather, through accident of birth they find themselves enmeshed in social life circumscribed by facts and rules that they (often unreflectively) accept in learning to how to act and shape their identities. This may make it appear that humans are shaped by external forces and not by their own intentions, and are thus products of causes beyond their control. In the end, are they then not like physical entities being pushed to and fro by external causes?

There are two responses to this challenge. First, humans do sometimes play an active, intentional role in shaping the course of their existence in a way that physical entities clearly do not. Second, the *social shaping* of individuals from outside forces is not a species of the *mechanical shaping* that characterizes how the wind, rain and snow shape a mountainside. Mechanical accounts of how nature shapes things are nonnormative and must be revised if their predictions are not born out. For example, a mountainside does not violate a norm and thus behave *wrongly* if it does not erode as predicted. And the geologic formulae, measurements, and so on, that led to the inaccurate prediction of how much erosion would occur would have to be revised. By contrast, social shaping is normative and its rules do not have to be revised when violated. A student who plagiarizes a paper, for example, behaves *wrongly*, but the occurrence of such an event does not invalidate the rule that plagiarism is forbidden. The rule remains in place, subject to *enforcement* by moral criticism, punishment, and the like.

The intentionalist framework is wholly consistent with, in many ways equivalent to, the more far-reaching *interpretive turn* that occurred in philosophy of social science in the mid to late twentieth century away from positivism. In his seminal *Interpretation and the Sciences of Man,* Charles Taylor (1987) pointedly criticized the view that there can be any scientifically neutral, impersonal language (à la positivism's verificationism) with which to describe and interpret human activities. Rather, he says, "we have to think of man [*sic*] as a *self-interpreting* animal ... there is no such thing as the structure of meanings for him independently of his interpretation of them" (p. 46, emphasis added).

As part of this general upheaval in the philosophy of social science, it had become increasingly recognized that exclusive reliance on the formalized, quantitative inference associated with classical experimentalism was inadequate for social research, which, combined with the central role assigned to intentionality-interpretation in understanding human behavior, fundamentally challenged the principle of the unity of science. From the perspective of the interpretive turn, the idea that the social sciences should closely emulate the natural sciences had run its course. As Anthony Giddens (1976) declared, "those who are still waiting for a Newton of social science aren't only waiting for a train that won't come in, they're waiting in the wrong station altogether" (p. 13). The related idea of demarcating science from other forms of inquiry on the basis of its purported grounding in theory-free observation, uncontaminated by prior conceptual-theoretical presuppositions also fell by the wayside. Finally, the fact/value bifurcation, which lay at the bottom of the idea of science as *objective* in the sense of being *value-free,* was opened to serious challenge.

As a consequence of the undermining of empirical/conceptual bifurcation, "*the whole argument for the classical fact/value dichotomy was in ruins*" (Putnam, 2002, p.

30, emphasis in original). Just as social and educational research is theory laden, it is also value laden—in at least three ways. First, many concepts in social and educational research have both descriptive and evaluative dimensions, for instance, achievement, oppression, motivation, defiance, and an indefinite number of others. Such terms are "two-edged" (Howe, 1985) in that they simultaneously describe and evaluate. Thus, when someone offers the description "GLBT youth are oppressed in schools," they do not have to add the value claim "and that's a bad thing." Likewise, if someone offers the description "Achievement is on the rise across all groups," they do not have to add the value claim "and that's a good thing." Without having to decide on the merits of claims such as these, it is apparent that value commitments about what is worth aiming for and investigating are built into them as well as the vocabulary of social and educational research generally.

Second, in the design and conduct of their research, social and educational researchers unavoidably "fix" certain elements of the background (Root, 1993). Educational researchers, for example, often fix income levels in investigating achievement as opposed to actually manipulating income levels or suggesting they should be manipulated. Though income levels are often correlated with achievement, the idea of making recommendations based on their research findings that large income gaps ought to be remedied in order to remedy large achievement gaps is often (though by no means always) taken to be beyond the purview of educational researchers. Thus, income level is treated differently from variables such as teacher professional development, the length of the school day, pedagogical methods, and so forth, where educational researchers do see it to be within their purview to make recommendations based on their research. The point here is not to suggest that educational researchers should be more (or less) activist, more (or less) progressive, and so on, but only that some stance toward the social, economic, and political status quo is unavoidable in the conduct of educational research.

In a related vein, third, some commitment to the political function of educational research is also unavoidable. Two alternatives are the technocratic and deliberative-democratic conceptions (House & Howe, 1999). The technocratic approach holds that educational researchers should remain politically neutral; they should investigate *means and their effects* but remain silent regarding *ends*. On this view ends are *external* to educational research (Howe, 2009). For example, whether to value parental choice of schools as an end over school desegregation as an end, is a matter to be addressed by political process. The purview of the educational researchers is limited in this example to investigating the effects of parental choice on desegregation. The deliberative democratic approach (House & Howe, 1999), by contrast, holds that educational researchers have an obligation to remain consistent with and promote democratic principles in the conduct of their research. This requires designing research so as to provide a background characterized by defensible political principles, such as the principle of including the perspectives of various groups in research on an equal footing—including and especially the marginalized and disenfranchised. Parental choice policy, for example, would be investigate both as a means and an end (House & Howe, 1999) with the input and due consideration of the views of all relevant stakeholders. The point here is not to suggest what conception of the political function of educational research is best, but only that *some* conception is unavoidable. In this vein, an advocate of neutrality is just that: she cannot be neutral toward neutrality.

One can only speculate about what influence the appropriation of developments in the philosophy of social science had on the larger educational research community. For example, despite growing acceptance of the idea of theory ladeness and other postpositivist principles, the idea of value-free (or at least "value-neutral") social and educational research seems to have remained resilient. It can be stated with some confidence, however, that the paradigm wars had subsided by the late 1980s. As indicated previously, the qualitative-interpretative paradigm gained considerable prominence and security vis-a-vis the quantitative-experimentalist paradigm, both as a legitimate alternative and when combined with quantitative-experimental methods to form a mixed-methods approach.

The Clamor for Scientifically Based Educational Research (The Paradigm Wars Redux)

The peace was short lived. By the turn of the twenty-first century there was a clamor for scientifically based educational research. The emergent conception championed by various influential social and educational researchers in and out of the Federal Government (e.g., Boruch, 2002; Coalition for Evidence-Based Policy, 2002; Cook, 2002; Whitehurst, 2003) differed little from classical experimentalism. Partly in an effort to advance a moderate approach more congenial to interpretive-qualitative methods, the National Research Council (NRC) assembled a committee charged with providing a detailed articulation of *scientific research in education*. It published a report by that name in 2002, which gained widespread attention and influence and provided the impetus for NRC's subsequent implementation document (2004), as well as the American Educational Research Association's *Standards for Reporting on Empiri-*

cal Research (2006). Arguably, this combination of documents was exemplary of a new methodological orthodoxy in educational research (Howe, 2009).

Scientific research in education (SRE) also prompted much discussion in education journals, both pro and con. The influence this had on the actual conduct of educational research is a question to which there is probably no clear answer. From the perspective of the philosophy of social science, however, whatever the extent of SRE's influence, its direction was retrograde. For SRE is a positivist throwback. It incorporates versions, albeit tacitly, of each of the tenets of positivism examined in the previous section—verificationism, the fact/value dichotomy, the regularity conception of causation, and the unity of science.

At the outset SRE adopts a version of the principle of the unity of science as follows: "at its core, scientific research is the same in all fields" (NRC, 2002, p. 2). It subsequently fleshes out this principle in terms of the "epistemological or fundamental principles that guide the scientific enterprise" (pp. 51-52), which it distills into six (p. 52):

1. pose significant questions that can be investigated empirically;
2. link research to relevant theory;
3. use methods that permit direct investigation of the question;
4. provide a coherent and explicit chain of reasoning;
5. replicate and generalize across studies; and
6. disclose research to encourage professional scrutiny and critique.

Principles 1 and 3 are particularly germane to the issue of verificationism and the demarcation of science from other intellectual pursuits. Little direct guidance is provided by SRE on how to determine whether the two principles are satisfied. SRE makes no mention of the synthetic-analytic distinction that underpins the empirical/conceptual distinction, for example. But there are good reasons to attribute tacit versions on these distinctions based on what SRE does say.

Philosophy, for instance, is explicitly excluded by SRE from the domain of scientific educational research (NRC, 2002, p. 131, note). But because it fits SRE's general characterization of scientific research as "a continuous process of rigorous reasoning supported by a dynamic interplay among methods, theories, and findings" (NRC, 2002, p. 2), empirical testability, principle 1, is the additional requirement that philosophy apparently lacks. But philosophy can lack empirical testability only if some bright line can be drawn between the empirical and the conceptual, with philosophy falling on the conceptual side. Drawing such a line is exactly what the critique of verificationism undermined. True, philosophy is a highly conceptual discipline, but that is a matter of degree. In terms of the web of belief described earlier, the questions philosophy asks tend to be more at the center than the periphery web, which does not mean that they are nonempirical. For example, no political theory with a fantastical view of human psychology could pass philosophical muster.

History is another discipline explicitly excluded from the domain of science by SRE. History (historiography) clearly makes empirical claims. Is SRE's reasoning that Principle 1 is not satisfied because historiography's claims aren't testable; that Principle 5 is not satisfied because historiography's claims are not replicable and generalizable (which they surely are not)? This is not made clear. Perhaps history and philosophy shouldn't be conceived as science. But if so, more is required to make this case than (positivist) intuitions, which, it seems, are all SRE has as a justification.

SRE's Principle 3 also emphasizes the value of employing a variety of methods, properly tailoring them to individual research questions. This is a recurrent theme in SRE that some of its advocates point to as evidence that SRE explicates a moderate position in comparison with more extreme experimentalist views (Phillips, 2006).

According to SRE, programs of education research proceed cumulatively—from describing and conjecturing, to establishing causal relationships, to understanding the mechanisms underlying such relationships. Although qualitative methods are embraced throughout, they are assigned a subsidiary epistemological and methodological role. Qualitative methods are employed in the initial describing and conjecturing phase of scientific research, and can also "illuminate important nuances, identify potential counterhypotheses, and provide additional sources of evidence for supporting causal claims in complex educational settings" (NRC, 2002, pp. 125-126). But "if research is to be used to answer the question about 'what works' ... it must advance to other levels of research" (p. 108). The other levels are experimental, the ideal of which is "randomized trials ... for establishing whether one or more factors caused change in an outcome" (p. 110). As in classical experimentalism, quantitative–experimental methods do the real work of science: the testing of hypothesis. Though SRE is more congenial to qualitative-interpretive methods than classical experimentalism, it nonetheless relegates them to the subsidiary role of exploration and conjecture.

The high epistemic status that SRE affords experimental methods is rooted in its adoption of the regularity conception of causation. SRE is pretty much silent on the concept of intentionalist causation. It mentions the *volitional* features of human behavior but construes this as a problem for experimental research design: "Education is centrally concerned with people: learners, teachers, parents, citizens and policy makers. The volition, or will, of these individuals decreases the level of control that researchers can have over the process" (NRC, 2002, p. 86). SRE reduces the difference between causal inference in physics and human behavior to the precision with which regularities can be determined. Because people behave more erratically than protons do, education research has to cope with more sources of "noise" and larger "error limits" than physics (NRC, 2002, p. 83).

For SRE, the sine qua non of scientific educational research is establishing causal relationships (regularities) associated with what works. Largely glossed over in SRE is that the question "What works?" is elliptical for "What works to produce valued education outcomes?" And the valued outcomes of interest are picked out by means of the kind of two-edged concepts described previously, such as literacy, achievement, motivation, citizenship, cooperativeness, and the like. As indicated before, by employing such concepts, education researchers unavoidably introduce their values of education and those of policy makers, curriculum designers, and so on, into the descriptive vocabulary of education research. Value commitments are uniformly woven into the fabric of educational research into *what works*, however infrequently they may be appreciated and acknowledged.

In general, SRE has little to say about values and the issue of value-ladeness. It mildly protests the ways that education research is often buffeted by changes in political winds and recommends that it be better shielded. The third of its "design principles for fostering science in federal education research agencies" reads "Insulate the agency from inappropriate political interference" (NRC, 2002, p. 127). Types of inappropriate political interference include "micromanagement of decision making, the distortion of the research agenda to be solely short-run, and the use of the agency as a tool to promote a particular policy or position" (pp. 139-140). SRE's relative silence on values, combined with its generally positivist tenor, suggests that SRE adopts the technocratic conception briefly described earlier. At the heart of this conception is the idea that education science and democratic politics (moral-political values in general) occupy separate epistemic domains, consistent with the positivist fact/value bifurcation. Investigating questions such as whether, to what extent, and at what monetary cost a given educational intervention works to produce a given outcome is in the domain of education science; deciding what outcomes ought to be investigated and pursued in light of the information provided by education researchers is in the domain of values.

Conclusion

Just as we have seen a repeat of the paradigm wars at the level of the philosophy of social science, we might very well see a repeat of parallel developments at level of educational research practice. The new methodological orthodoxy (Howe, 2009) that attempts to regiment educational researchers in terms of a positivist-experimentalist framework could—and very likely will—fail, even in terms of its own limited way of focusing on what works.

There exists an ongoing mutual adjustment between methodology and practically applied research methods, between *reconstructed logic* (e.g., the new orthodoxy) and *logic-in-use* (randomized field trials; Kaplan, 1964). Both must be adjusted when research programs fail to produce useful results, typically beginning with logic-in-use. The forerunner of the new orthodoxy failed in the 1970s and 1980s, giving rise to the first paradigm war and the eventual acceptance of qualitative research, in particular, and much broader interpretivist logic, in general. If and when the logic-in-use of the new orthodoxy fails to produce results, there will once again be impetus to rethink what constitutes *useful* educational research in much broader and more inclusive terms.

Some signs of this are evident in the intensified efforts in the arena of mixed-methods research, accompanied by the appearance of several new journals and a number of new books. Whether it is fruitful to create a new "mixed-methods paradigm" alongside quantitative and qualitative paradigms, as some have suggested (Johnson & Onwuegbuzie, 2004), is debatable. And so is the question of whether, in general, it is fruitful to think of paradigms in terms of methods—quantitative, qualitative, and mixed— in isolation from larger epistemological and political frameworks. In any case, things seem to be moving in a positive direction, away from the narrow constraints imposed by the new orthodoxy. And there are many issues here about which the philosophy of social science will have (and had has) much to contribute.

References

American Educational Research Association. (2006). *Standards for reporting on empirical social science research in AERA publications.* Retrieved from http://www.aera.net/publications/Default.aspx?menu_id=32&id=1850

Boruch, R. (2002). The virtues of randomness. *Education Next*, 2(3), 36-42.

Campbell, D. (1974, September). *Qualitative knowing in action research.* Kurt Lewin Award Address, Society for the Psychological Study of Social Issues, presented at the meeting of the American Psychological Association, New Orleans, LA.

Campbell, D. (1982). Experiments as arguments. In E. R. House, S. Mathison, J. A. Pearsol, & H. Preskill (Eds.), *Evaluation studies review annual* (Vol. 7, pp. 117–128). Beverly Hills, CA: SAGE.

Coalition for Evidence-Based Policy. (2002). *Bringing evidence-driven progress to education: A recommended strategy for the U.S. Department of Education*. Retrieved from http://www.excelgov.org/displayContent.asp?NewsItemID=4541 &Keyword =prppcEvidence

Condliffe-Lageman, E. (2000). *An elusive science: The troubling history of education research*. Chicago, IL: University of Chicago Press.

Cook, T. (2002). Randomized experiments in educational policy research: A critical examination of the reasons the educational evaluation community has offered for not doing them. *Education Evaluation and Policy Analysis, 24*(3), 175-199.

Cronbach, L., Ambron, S., Dornbusch, S., Hess, R., Hornik, R., Phillips, D.C., … Weiner, S. (1980). *Toward reform of program evaluation*. San Francisco, CA: SAGE.

Dennett, D. (1989). True believers. In *The intentional stance* (pp. 13-35). Cambridge, MA: The MIT Press.

Gage, N. (1989). The paradigm wars and their aftermath: A historical sketch of research on teaching since 1989. *Educational Researcher, 18*, 4-10.

Garrison, J. (1986). Some principles of postpositivistic philosophy of science. *Educational Researcher, 15*(9), 12-18.

Giddens, A. (1976). *New rules of sociological method*. New York, NY: Basic Books.

House, E., & Howe, K. (1999). *Values in evaluation and social research*. Thousand Oaks, CA: SAGE.

Howe, K. (1985). Two dogmas of educational research. *Educational Researcher, 14*(8), 10-18.

Howe, K. (1988). Against the quantitative-qualitative incompatibility thesis (or dogmas die hard). *Educational Researcher, 17*(8), 10-16.

Howe, K. (2004). A critique of experimentalism. *Qualitative Inquiry, 10*(4), 42-61.

Howe, K. (2009). Positivist dogmas, rhetoric, and the education science question. *Educational Researcher, 38*, 428-440.

Jackson, P. (1968). *Life in classrooms*. New York, NY: Holt, Rinehart, & Winston.

Johnson, R., & Onwuegbuzie, A. (2004). Mixed methods research: A research paradigm whose time has come. *Educational Researcher, 33*(7), 14-26.

Kaplan, A. (1964). *The conduct of inquiry*. San Francisco, CA: Chandler.

Kuhn, T. (1962). *The structure of scientific revolutions*. Chicago, IL: University of Chicago Press.

MacKenzie, B. (1977). *Behaviorism and the limits of scientific method*. Atlantic Highlands, NJ: Humanities Press.

Morris, W. (2009). David Hume. Retrieved from http://plato.stanford.edu/entries/hume/#CauIndInfNegPha

National Research Council. (2002). *Scientific research in education*. Washington, DC: National Academy Press.

National Research Council. (2004). *Advancing scientific research in education*. Washington, DC: National Academy Press.

Phillips, D. C. (1983). After the wake: Post-positivistic educational thought. *Educational Researcher 12*(5), 4-12.

Phillips, D. C. (2006). A guide for the perplexed: Scientific educational research, methodolatry, and the gold versus platinum standards. *Educational Research Review, 1*, 15-26.

Putnam, H. (2002). *The collapse of the fact/value distinction and other essays*. Cambridge, MA: Harvard University Press.

Quine, W. V. O. (1951). Two dogmas of empiricism. *The Philosophical Review, 60*, 20-43.

Quine, W. V. O., & Ullian, J. (1978). *The web of belief* (2nd ed.). New York, NY: Random House.

Root, M. (1993). *Philosophy of social science: The methods, ideals and politics of social inquiry*. Oxford, England: Blackwell.

Scriven, M. (1969). Logical positivism and the behavior sciences. In P. Achenstein & S. Barker (Eds.), *The legacy of logical positivism* (pp. 195-210). Baltimore, MD: John Hopkins Press.

Searle, J. (1984). *Minds, brains and science*. Cambridge, MA: Harvard University Press.

Searle, J. (1995). *The construction of social reality*. New York, NY: The Free Press.

Smith, J. K., & Heshusius, L. (1986). Closing down the conversation: The end of the quantitative-qualitative debate among educational researchers. *Educational Researcher, 15*(1), 4-12.

Strike, K. (1974). On the expressive potential of behaviorist language. *American Educational Research Journal, 11*(2), 103-120.

Taylor, C. (1964). *The explanation of behavior*. New York, NY: Humanities Press.

Taylor, C. (1987). Interpretation and the sciences of man. In P. Rabinow & W. Sullivan (Eds.), *Interpretive social science: A second look* (pp. 33-81). Los Angeles, CA: University of California Press.

Thornton, S. (2005). Retrieved from http://www.iep.utm.edu/freud/august 23 2010)

Whitehurst, G. (2003, April). *The Institute of Education Sciences: New wine and new bottles*. Presentation at the annual meeting of the American Educational Research Association, Chicago, IL.

Author Contact Information: Kenneth R. Howe, PhD, School of Education, Room 245, University of Colorado at Boulder, 249 UCB, Boulder, CO 80309-0249. Phone: 303-492-7229. E-mail: ken.howe@colorado.edu

Section 2: Learning Theory

INTRODUCTION

SECTION EDITOR
Patrick M. Jenlink
Stephen F. Austin State University

> I believe that all education proceeds by the participation of the individual in the social consciousness of the race.... I believe that this educational process has two sides—one psychological and one sociological—and that neither can be subordinated to the other, or neglected. (Dewey, 1897, p. 77)

> It is impossible to understand the subtler and more planful learning of cultural men without clear ideas of the forces which make learning possible in the first form of directly connecting some gross bodily response with a situation immediately present to the sense. (Thorndike, 1913, Vol. II, p. 16)

> For meaningful learning to occur in a multimedia environment, the learner must engage in five cognitive processes (1) selecting relevant words for processing in verbal working memory, (2) selecting relevant images for processing in visual working memory, (3) organizing selected words into a verbal mental model, (4) organizing selected images into a visual mental model, and (5) integrating verbal and visual representations as well as prior knowledge. (Mayer, 2001, p. 54)

What is learning theory? How do the behavioral theorists view learning? The cognitivists? The constructivists? The humanists? Each school of thought on learning theory views learning very differently. Setting out to edit a section on learning theories prompts one to consider the context within which an examination of learning theories is situated, in this case that context is educational theories. And, editing a section on learning theories draws into specific relief the need to consider the historical as well as contemporary origins of different theories of learning in educational settings. As well, it requires a consideration of new, emerging theories that are redefining our thinking about learning and at the same time challenging us to rethink education in contemporary society.

Reflecting on the tasks and responsibilities of serving as a section editor, I was initially drawn to John Dewey and his numerous contributions to educational philosophy. In revisiting Dewey's many and varied works, I settled on his work titled, "My Pedagogic Creed," originally published in 1897. In that work, Dewey laid out five articles of faith that gave form and meaning to his understanding of education. The first epigraph opening this introduction is taken from Article I of "My Pedagogic Creed" to frame a deeper meaning of "What Education Is." It is worth noting that in addition to the social and psychological dimensions of education, Dewey also discussed what might be framed as the existential dimensions of education, the idea that education and life are inseparable: that schools should not be insular training grounds or ivory towers, but rather parts of an organic playing field of life. He saw education not so much as preparation for life but as life itself. In that sense, education, and therein how we define learning as a theory and a social practice, determines, in part, the nature of educational experiences for the learner.

The second epigraph opening this introduction is from Edward L. Thorndike's (1913) *The Psychology of Learning* (Vol. 2). Thorndike believed that research on learning should begin at the most elemental level and build up. As a researcher and theorists, Thorndike was the first person to codify the concepts related to reinforcement-based influences on behavior, naming this theory "instrumental conditioning," with its main tenet being the "law of effect." For Thorndike, language and other aspects of social behavior were constructed from—and understandable as—primitive associations of stimuli and responses, that is habits instinctive and acquired. I chose the first two epigraphs, each focusing on theorists that were contemporaries of each other at the turn of the twentieth century. It was Dewey who

The Handbook of Educational Theories, pp. 87–90

envisioned a special connection between learning theory and educational practice, whereas it was Thorndike who investigated principles of learning that could be directly applied to the teaching process (i.e., the law of effect and the law of exercise).

The third epigraph opening this introduction is drawn from Richard Mayer's (2001) book, *Multimedia Learning*. In surveying the evolution of learning theories from the early part of the twentieth century and into the first decade of the twenty-first century, Mayer's thoughts were selected to present a contrast to Dewey and Thorndike, focusing on the world of multimedia and the need for advances in how we think about learning theory. The complexity of cognition and the implications of living in a technology enriched world presents particularly aggressive challenges for individuals designing learning environments, not only in P-20 educational settings but in all settings of human learning. As technology becomes increasingly ubiquitous in daily life, the integration of text, visual imagery, graphic representation, and auditory stimulus challenges the theoretical principles of learning set forth in the twentieth century.

The three framing epigraphs each contribute to an understanding of the variant relationship between education as a social institution in society and learning as a process that is enacted within that institution. The three theorists, respectively, have introduced important philosophical and theoretical principles and understandings of learning, spanning historical and contemporary theories of learning. It is important to take note of as well as understand how learning theories have contributed to shaping the practices within the different levels—P-20 educational settings—of the institution of education. In particular, embracing the early history of learning theory along its evolutionary path forward from behaviorism to cognitivism, and onward to constructivism and beyond. The technological advances that are redefining society and its social institutions and practices in today's contemporary society have had no less of an impact on education than on other aspects of society, and certainly on the nature of learning theory with the advances of theoretical fields like multimedia learning theory.

It is important to acknowledge that the scope of education as an institution in the twenty-first century has become so expansive it can overwhelm one's understanding of education's role, and equally important overwhelm one's understanding how learning theory relates to the changing landscape of education. And the pace of change is only accelerating as society moves outward on the edge of technological innovation. One need only look at the impact of social networking to understand that the demands on education are exponentially compounded by technology's influence and innovation, and simultaneously the needs of learners are compounding exponentially in a rapidly changing society.

Retrospectively, it is against a backdrop of a changing society that the foundation of learning theory, as it applies to education, can be traced to early work on the part of educational psychologists to develop connections between psychology, as a science, and the application of learning theory in educational settings. Dewey, Thorndike, and Mayer symbolize, in part, an evolution path in learning theory. That evolutionary path, over the last century, can be divided into two essential parent movements, behaviorism and cognitivism. Over the course of decades, these two movements gave way to a continuum of specific learning theories that continue to evolve and extend into the twenty-first century.

Four broad schools of thought, evolving from the two parent movements in learning theory, include behaviorism, cognitivism, constructivism, and humanism. Within each school of thought there have been, and continue to be, evolutionary offshoots of the parent theories within the four schools (i.e., stage theory of cognitive development and cognitive theory of multimedia learning each evolved, respectively, from cognitivism; social learning theory evolved from behaviorism; situated learning theory evolved from constructivism; experiential learning theory evolved from humanism). As well, descriptive and meta theories of learning have emerged on the theoretical landscape, including cultural historical activity theory and distributed cognition. Along the way, cooperative learning and problem-based learning evolved within educational settings, contributing to perspectives of learning as forms of social or situational theories.

Making sense of the many theories of learning is not easy, nor should it be. Answering the question: What is learning? is no less easy. Simply stated, drawing from Ormrod (1999) in her text *Human Learning*, "learning is a means through which we acquire not only skills and knowledge but values, attitudes, and emotional reactions" (p. 3). Ormrod is instructive in her work, in consideration of the how theories of learning have evolved within education. She notes that educational psychologists have defined the concept of learning in two different ways. First, learning is a relatively permanent change in behavior due to experience and, second, learning is a relatively permanent change in mental associations due to experience. The difference between the two is what changes when learning occurs. One supports a change in behavior (behaviorism) and the other supports a change in thought processes (cognition). That said, "both the behaviorist and the cognitivists perspectives have something important to say about human learning and … both provide useful suggestions for helping people learn more effectively" (Ormrod, 1999, p. 4). That said, the different learning theorists across the four schools of thought will continue to argue along differing lines of reasoning what kinds of experiences cause what kinds of changes. Such argument is necessary to the evolution of learning theory, questioning and examining existing theoretical perspectives as well as advancing new perspectives.

Reflecting on the evolution of learning theories from the early part of the twentieth century to current decade of the twenty-first century, it is important to accentuate the interconnected nature of learning theories within and across schools of thought. Where one might easily look to behaviorism and cognitivism as the parent movements in learning theory, in turn it is important to understand the evolutionary connection between the two. Along that path it was the social learning theory of Bandura (1969, 1986) that symbolizes a transition theory connecting the two parent movements. Social learning theory provided the theoretical bridge between the behaviorists, which eschewed mental events, and the cognitivists, which embraced mental events. Social learning theory provides a perspective on learning that includes the individual, cognitive influences, and the environmental, social influences. Suffice to say, as the evolutionary path of learning theory has continued over time and through much research, the four schools of thought emerged and within and across those schools of thought new theoretical perspectives have presented variant responses to the question: What is learning?

The chapters in this section contribute to an understanding of learning theories and the respective theorists that given voice to theorizing about human learning. As well, the authors of the chapters situate the reader within the four schools of thought on learning theory and the evolutionary path that learning theory has taken within and across the varied education settings of society.

The section begins with the two schools of thought, behaviorism and cognitivism, reflecting the two parent movements in learning theory. Larry Bryant and his coauthors Rhonda Vincent, Ali Shaqlaih, and Glenda Moss examine the theoretical roots of behaviorism in their chapter *Behaviorism and Behavioral Learning Theory*. Karen D. Paciotti examines the theoretical roots of cognitivism in her chapter *Cognitivism: Ways of Knowing*.

Drawing on the metaphor of evolutionary path of learning theory, the section is organized by schools of thought. It is important to note for the reader that the contributions to the section are representative of the four schools of thought but do not present an exhaustive survey of each school or the myriad theories within. Anita Zijdemans-Boudreau, Glenda Moss, and Chey-jey Lee examine the evolution of *Experiential Learning Theory* as an offshoot from the humanist school of thought. Betty J. Alford, in her chapter *Adult Learning Theory*, examines the nature of andragogy and adult learning. Mary V. Alfred, Catherine A. Cherrstrom, Petra A. Robinson, and Alicia R. Friday, in their chapter *Transformative Learning Theory*, introduce a rich discussion of an adult education based theory that suggests ways in which adults make meaning of their lives. It looks at "deep learning," not just content or process learning, and examines what it takes for adults to move from a limited knowledge of knowing what they know without questioning (usually from their cultures, families, organizations and society).

Janet Tareilo gives thoughtful attention to a discussion of cognitivism's evolution in her chapter *Stage Theory of Cognitive Development*. Stephen D. Sorden follows with his chapter on The *Cognitive Theory of Multimedia Learning* as an evolution of the cognitivist school of thought. One might consider Tareilo's chapter as representative of an earlier evolutionary branch of cognitivism whereas Sorden's chapter is representative of how cognitivism is evolving as technological innovation has influenced society and its educational institution.

Ratna Narayan, Cynthia Rodriguez, Juan Araujo, Ali Shaqlaih, and Glenda Moss examine constructivism in their chapter *Constructivism—Constructivist Learning Theory*, illuminating the theoretical underpinnings of the constructivist school of thought. Next, in *Situated Cognition Theory*, I delve into the emergence of situated cognition as an evolutionary offshoot of cognitivism and a form of situational theory. Rebecca Fredrickson, Karen Dunlap, and Sarah McMahan examine a theory learning evolving from the constructivist school of thought in their chapter *Cooperative Learning Theory*. Continuing along the evolutionary path of constructivist theories, Rebecca Fredrickson, Sarah McMahan and Karen Dunlap examine problem-based approaches to learning in their chapter *Problem-Based Learning Theory*.

The final chapter in the section is titled *Cultural Historical Activity Theory (CHAT)*, authored by myself, and offers an examination of activity theoretical perspectives within a framework of what is often termed meta theory. This theoretical perspective has historical origins in the early movements of learning theory. Many of the theoretical principles align with the constructivist school of thought.

As one reads the chapters prepared by the contributing authors, it might be helpful to center on the opening question for this introduction: What is learning theory? As editor, reading and rereading the chapters, one major challenge is in evidence. Within the schools of thought on learning theory and across the many theoretical perspectives of learning, the challenge for theories of learning is to understand how particular kinds of learning experiences develop adaptive expertise. There is something most profound in Dewey's words when he stated the "educational process has two sides—one psychological and one sociological—and that neither can be subordinated to the other, or neglected" (1897, p. 77).

REFERENCES

Bandura, A. (1969). *Principles of behavior modification*. New York, NY: Holt, Rinehart, & Winston.

Bandura, A. (1986). *Social foundations of thought and action: A social cognitive theory.* Englewood Cliff, NJ: Prentice-Hall.

Dewey, J. (1897). My pedagogic creed. *School Journal, 54*, 77-80.

Mayer, R. E. (2001). *Multimedia learning*. Cambridge, England: Cambridge University Press.

Ormrod, J. E. (1999). *Human learning* (3rd ed.). Upper Saddle River, NJ: Merrill Prentice-Hall.

Thorndike, J. E. (1913). *The psychology of learning: Educational psychology* (Vol. II). New York, NY: Teachers College Press.

Author Contact Information: Patrick M. Jenlink, Department of Secondary Education, and Educational Leadership, Stephen F. Austin State University, PO Box 13018-SFA Station, Nacogdoches, TX 75962-3018. Phone: (936) 468-1756. E-mail: pjenlink@sfasu.edu

CHAPTER 8

Behaviorism and Behavioral Learning Theory

Larry C. Bryant, Rhonda Vincent, Ali Shaqlaih, and Glenda Moss
University of North Texas at Dallas

The age of educator accountability has powered standardized testing and student achievement to the forethought of educational discourse. During this era, many theories have evolved around educational best practices; one such theory is behaviorism. While very few other theories have responded to the urgency of proficient educational outcomes, behaviorism has enjoyed an illustrious relationship with education; in many instances it has extended and expanded to address the unique needs of the educational institution. The purpose of this section is to explore goals, assumptions and aspects of behaviorism.

The primary goal of behaviorism is to promote the scientific study of human behavior (Mills, 1998). Iversen (1992) asserts that secondary goals include designing reliable methods and valid parameters so the discipline is based on scientific reasoning with human learning as a major influence on development and behavior (Rilling, 2000). In fulfilling its goals, it was imperative that the field advance its theory, methodology, and practice. In doing so, the field (especially as it relates to education) has borne witness to two significant changes so as to reengage its connection with education. Table 8.1 outlines the development of behaviorism in education.

It is widely accepted that Behaviorism began with Ivan Pavlov and the Associationism period, which established classical conditioning. Mills (1998) describes classical conditioning as involving the pairing of a neutral stimulus before a naturally occurring reflex. For example, a school bell softly chimes, the teacher prompts the class to stand for the Pledge of Allegiance; over time the class begins to stand whenever they hear the chimes. The bell softly chiming is the neutral stimulus, the students standing without prompting is the naturally occurring reflex. While most of this early work was conducted with animal subjects, human trials eventually occurred.

When associationism failed to fully explain the maintenance of human behavior, neobehaviorism presented the field with operational models that analyzed motivation of behavior. These models would later form the basis of operant conditioning. Although operant conditioning was able to define stimulus/response

Table 8.1. History of Behaviorism and its Evolutionary Path as a Theory of Learning From 1897 to Present

1897-1930	1930-1960	1960-Present
Associationism	Neobehaviorism	Sociobehaviorism
Connectionism	Operationalism	Social cognitive theory
Classical Conditioning	Operant conditioning	Functional behavioral analysis
	Applied behavior analysis	Positive behavioral supports

Note: Schools of thought aligned with behaviorism theory are denoted by three time periods that demarcate the origin of behaviorism (beginning with associationism) to current theoretical thought of behavioral learning theory.

The Handbook of Educational Theories, pp. 91–103

correlations with respect to human behavior, it was limited in addressing the ecology of the individual. Where operant conditioning failed to distinguish the individual in isolation of behavior, sociobehaviorism addressed this paradigm by way of explaining the structures and dynamics of the individual's environment and the intricate connections between it and the individual's life changes, which is defined by and through social cognitive theories. As a point of reference, all the periods are invaluable to the growth of behaviorism; one may not have been as successful as the other without the work that preceded it. With that said, current behaviorism in education continues to utilize many aspects developed during the transitional periods to aid in the science of learning.

Aspects and Assumptions of Behaviorism

As associationism gave way to neobehaviorism and later sociobehaviorism, overall behaviorism assumptions remained constant. Behaviorism assumes that behaviors must be (a) both observable and measurable, (b) can be predicted and controlled, and (c) individuals respond to and operate with their environment to produce desired behaviors (Cooper, Heron, & Heward, 2007). Many contemporary behaviorism assumptions applied in education are derivatives of fundamental operant conditioning principles. Domjan (2003) explained that operant conditioning is based on the modification of voluntary behavior and the maintenance of that behavior by virtue of its consequence; whereas, behaviors that are conditioned using methods from the Associationism period, (i.e., classical conditioning) are more likely not to be maintained by consequences. However, for the purpose of education, it is expected that behaviors (whether academic of social) be maintained versus being shaped.

Baum (2003) asserts that contemporary behaviorism grew out of B. F. Skinner's (1938) work on experimental analysis of behavior. In this work, Skinner sought to explore behaviorism utilizing scientific methods. Furthermore, he wanted to establish constructs that identified external and internal observable behavioral patterns, which included thinking, and feeling (noting that they were behaviors as well). Although Skinner receives much of the credit for how behaviorism is conceptualized in the field of education, a number of researchers (e.g., John B. Watson, Ivan Pavlov, Edward Lee Thorndike, Ole Ivar Lovass, and Albert Bandura) made significant contributions to the overall understanding and application of behaviorism. Most notable, classical conditioning researcher John B. Watson, who in 1925 concluded that behavior are the function of learned responses and reflexes (O'Donnell, 1986). More importantly, Watson paved the way for the evolution of behaviorism through the introduction of two influential theories: (a) all behavior is observable and can be correlated with other observable behavior and (b) all behavior precedes as well as follows an event (Watson, 1925). As Watson (1913) set the foundation for behaviorism, Skinner (1938) led the neobehaviorism period, which was the dominant behavioral discourse between the years 1930 and 1960 (Hergenhahn, 2005). During this period, Skinner introduced the concept of operationalism, which eventually gave birth to operant conditioning.

In accordance with behaviorism philosophy, operant conditioning assumes behavior that is followed by a reinforcer strengthens the probability of that behavior reoccurring (Cooper et al., 2007). Additionally, operant conditioning employs the model of positive and negative reinforcement and punishment and extinction. Table 8.2 outlines the four dimensions of operant conditioning.

Here, the expressions positive and negative are not used in their traditional definitions; instead they are used to explain the scientific thought of adding or subtracting a pleasant or unpleasant stimulus in effort to affect directional change of a behavior. For instance, if an educator wanted to increase a student's on task behavior they may select a positive reinforcement to increase the student's on task behavior (i.e., adding a pleasant stimulus, such as giving candy for completing independent seatwork); and if the educator wanted to decrease a student's off task behavior, they could use a positive punishment (i.e., adding an unpleasant stimu-

Table 8.2. Four Dimensions of Operant Conditioning Premised on the Model of Positive and Negative Reinforcement, Punishment, and Extinction

	Directional Change of Behavior	
	Increase Behavior	Decrease Behavior
Pleasant Stimulus (Appetitive)	Positive Reinforcement (Add appetitive)	Positive Punishment (Add aversive)
Unpleasant Stimulus (Aversive)	Negative Reinforcement (Remove aversive)	Negative Punishment (Remove appetitive)

lus, such scorning a student for not completing seatwork). Likewise, if an educator wanted to increase a student's on task behavior, they may select to use negative reinforcement to address the student's on task behavior (i.e., subtracting an unpleasant stimulus, such as quieting down the class during independent seatwork); or an educator could employ a negative punishment to decrease a student's excessive off task behavior (i.e., subtracting a pleasant stimulus, such as taking away free time). Although Azrin and Holz (1966) argued that there would be ongoing debate surrounding the usage of the expressions (e.g., positive and negative reinforcement and positive and negative punishment), Baum (2005) viewed this innovation of terminology as critical to the field, as it advanced behaviorism language, thus allowed for behaviorism to be recognized as more scientific than not.

BEHAVIORAL LEARNING THEORY OPERATIONALIZED IN EDUCATION

Behavioralism has an enormous responsibility in the field of education. Thus it is defensible to tease out the most consumed verse of the theory—operant conditioning. An original development, operant conditioning introduced the concept of reinforcer to affect behavior change (Montana & Charnov, 2008). The concept describes the effects that control the frequency of a behavior (Azrin & Holz, 1966). Blackman (1974) argues that a reinforcer is the stimulus, event, or situation that is presented when the response behavior is performed and that serves to strengthen the behavior (i.e., make it more likely to reoccur or to reoccur more frequently). In addition to the reinforcer "test," Michael (2005) argues there are three conditions of a reinforcer; (1) must follow the response; (2) must be immediate; and (3) must be paired with the response.

For example, a second grader (in art class) makes a piece of art for his homeroom teacher. He asks, "Can I give this to my homeroom teacher?"

The art teacher responds, "Yes."

The second grader leaves the class and proceeds to take the art to his homeroom teacher. Upon his return, his art teacher, who was very angry he had left, meets him at the door yelling, "Where have you been?"

The youngster begins to sob and physically shrink inward due to the public humiliation. The art teacher's responds, "I didn't mean for you to take the art at that moment."

Examining this dialogue through the lens of operant conditioning, yelling is the reinforcer (a negative stimulus to decrease behavior). It occurred when the child returned to the class as soon as he entered the doorway, and it was paired with him leaving without clear permission. This is an example of an incident rather than a repetitive behavior that requires scheduled reinforcements over time to change a behavior.

Reinforcement schedules are primarily designed to control and alter problematic behavior (Flora, 2004). According to Ferster and Skinner (1957), a reinforcement schedule is a deliberate program that establishes when and how often a reinforcer will be administered upon the occurrence of appropriate behavior. For the purposes of education, simple reinforcement schedules have remained prominent. The two major forms of schedules are continuous and intermittent schedules (Zirpoli & Melloy, 1993).

CONTINUOUS REINFORCEMENT SCHEDULE

A continuous reinforcement schedule is enacted when an educator wants to reinforce the behavior each and every time that behavior occurs. For example, each and every time (continuous reinforcement schedule) a young child spells/writes their name correctly (behavior), the educator gives the young child verbal praise (reinforcer). Kerr and Nelson (1989) contends that continuous reinforcement schedules are best utilized when introducing a new behavior. Although, continuous reinforcement schedules are known to create an association between the behavior and the reinforcement, they are limited in producing long-term changes in behavior (Kerr & Nelson, 1989). Thus, educators may consider pairing this schedule with another type of reinforcement schedule.

INTERMITTENT REINFORCEMENT SCHEDULES (INTERVALS AND RATIO)

Intermittent reinforcement schedules are administered in intervals or ratios and are used when it is necessary to measure (in terms of duration) behavior. Intermittent interval schedules are based on the elapse of time. Skinner (1974) argues that there are two types of interval reinforcements. The first is fixed interval schedule, which assigns a specific interval of fixed time that a behavior must be observed prior to it be reinforced (i.e., verbally praising students after every 5 minutes of quietly working on worksheets). The second is variable interval schedule, which varies the amount of time (shorter or longer) within the interval of time; however, the time will equal a predetermined specific number (i.e., verbally praising students after 4 minutes for quietly working on a worksheet, then again after 6 minutes of working on the same worksheet). Intermittent ratio schedule relies on the number of times the behavior occurs. As with interval schedules, ratio schedules also employ fixed and variable component. A fixed ratio schedule is used when a behavior has to occur a set amount of times before it can be reinforced (i.e., a student has to complete three worksheets before they can have free time). A variable ratio schedule changes the number of times the before has to occur after the initial reinforcement has been administered (i.e., a student completed three worksheets, they were reinforced, the next reinforcer will occur once the student has complete four additional worksheets). In addition to reinforcer schedules, educators can elicit the behavior strength and assess it through measuring its count, frequency, duration, latency, accuracy, and intensity: (a) count, the number of times the behavior occurs; (b) frequency, how often the behavior occurs over a unit of time; (c) duration, how long the behavior episode last; (d) latency, the amount of time between the stimulus and the response; (e) accuracy, how the rate changes over time; and (f) intensity, the measure of the strength of the behavior (Flora, 2004).

Although the era of accountability appears to remain the focal point of current educational discourse, educators can rely on the core principles of behaviorism to assist in achieving proficient outcomes. Synthesizing the components of behaviorism marks for high reliability of predicting and controlling for behavior (Cooper et. al., 2007); thus the educational institution will continue to embrace key aspects of behaviorism. However, it will be incumbent upon educators to create innovative ways of implementing behaviorism throughout the academic and social curriculums. Moreover, it is the educator who has to employ the skill set to determine which dimension of operant conditioning and reinforcement schedule will provide for optimal behavior modification.

VALIDATION OF THE THEORY

As a philosophy, behaviorism is very simple. It embodies the notion that behavior can be explained as a reaction to environmental rewards or punishments. All learning, according to behaviorist theories, is a result of the connection between the behavior and an environmental response. Because behaviorism focuses only on observable events, it posits a direct connection between those events and subsequent environmental changes. Validating such a straightforward theory is not so easy.

RADICAL BEHAVIORISM VERSUS SOCIAL BEHAVIORISM

There are several problems associated with validation of behaviorism. In outlining these issues, it is important to understand that there are different forms of behaviorism. Radical behaviorism, associated with B. F. Skinner, contends that internal states, such as thinking or feeling, are impossible to observe, and therefore irrelevant to the study of behavior. In fact, in order to qualify as a scientific theory, radical behaviorism requires "repeatable, verifiable, observable events that everyone [can] agree had taken place" (Svinicki, 1999, p. 5). A contrasting view is held by social behaviorists who accept the premise that such internal states are involved in the stimulus-response connection, therefore influencing behavior. Social behaviorists believe that in "the study of man it is not necessary to denude [him] of his dynamism, his creativity, his self-determination and freedom, his values, attitudes, feelings and cognitions, and other aspects of his personality" (Staats, 1976, p. 59). Social behaviorists argue that human behavior is influenced by complex gestures, such as language, which require the influence of hidden mental states (Chomsky, 1959; Mead, 1934).

The clash between behaviorist viewpoints complicates an otherwise straightforward approach to validation. Radical behaviorists argue that the observable outcomes of Skinnerian experiments validate the theory. Skinner's work featured a variety of animal experiments including rats that learned to successfully navigate mazes and pigeons that learned to peck at particular lights on a pegboard. While social behaviorists do not deny the validity of the theory in these instances, they argue that such validity applies mostly to animals that learn in artificially controlled environments (Francis, 1975). While falling short of complete dismissal of the theory, some experts assert that radical behaviorism and the tenets of conditioning are too limited to provide adequate explanations for human behavior (Greenwood, 1999). This position addresses the philosophy undergirding behavioral theories like operant and classical condition. For example, in arguing that the theory does not adequately account for complex human behavior Hunter and Benson (1997) assert that "behaviorism is a misapplication of positivistic philosophy" (p. 87).

CHALLENGES TO VALIDATION: HUMAN DEVELOPMENT

In order to understand the criticism of radical behaviorism, it is important to identify the elements of human complexity that interfere with a direct connection between behavior and the environment. One element is human development. Cognitive scientists contend that learning is achieved when an individual is exposed to an appropriate environment and has acquired the developmental maturation required to interact meaningfully within that environment (Greenwood, 1999). Such development includes both physical and cognitive maturation. Radical behaviorists, however, contend that because humans are born with the ability to interpret and react to their environments, there essentially "is no development, only learning" (Strauss, 1993, p. 193). Such a position rests on the classical laws of learning developed in the early 1900s by

Edward L. Thorndike. Two of Thorndike's laws, the law of frequency and the law of contiguity, emphasize the importance of the environment on strengthening the stimulus-response association, resulting in subsequent learning. A second challenge to the validity of the theory as it relates to development is that radical behaviorism does not account for the "biological limits on conditioning" (Breland & Breland, 1961; Garcia & Koelling, 1966, as cited in Greenwood, 1999, p. 2). For example, the theory does not address the universal nature of language development, in relation to age. If chronological age does not influence facility with language, then infants could learn to speak if environmental reinforcement was sufficiently powerful. It is evident that some areas of development like language acquisition cannot be explained by the influence of conditioning alone. Human development, which proceeds in a predictable sequence, is also characterized by a wide range of variance between individuals. According to the principles of radical behaviorism, "different individuals would exhibit the same behaviors if … given the same stimuli and reinforcements" (Romberg, 2010, p. 61). However, some individuals learn faster and retain more than their counterparts, even if they are similar in respect to age, gender, or ethnicity. Such variance in individual behavior is not explained by this theory which hinders validation.

Disposition

Another element of human complexity that is at odds with theory validation is personal disposition. Villegas (2007) defined disposition as "tendencies for individuals to act in a particular manner under particular circumstances, based on their beliefs" (p. 373). Other factors of disposition include "values, commitments, and professional ethics" (National Council for Accreditation of Colleges of Teacher Education, 2002). Dispositions are generally measured by observation of behaviors, which fits nicely into the positivist tradition embraced by behaviorists. At issue again is making a direct connection between behavior and the environment. As stated previously, radical behaviorism denies the existence of internal states. Exclusion of internal influences makes it difficult to explain individual behavior in similar situations. For example, consider the behavior of two children attending the same birthday party at which a clown is performing. Upon seeing the clown, one child bursts into tears while another dances in delight. It is difficult to explain such disparate behaviors without considering differences unrelated to the environment. The social behaviorist has a completely different perspective. According to this view, it is impossible to explain why an individual's behavior varies in different situations without attention to his disposition. Because disposition includes values, moral behavior becomes an observable event applicable to tests of validation. Like disposition, though, the genesis of moral behavior is found in internal processes. Because moral behavior is an outcome of moral decisions, such behavior must be considered in light of "the observable behavior and the psychological process that give rise to it" (Walker, 2002, p. 354).

Motivation

A construct closely related to disposition is motivation and this presents another challenge to validating radical behaviorism. As Svinicki (1999) explains,

> Because behaviorists originally believed that behavior was caused solely by past contingencies, motivation, which implied a looking ahead or anticipation of future consequences, couldn't really exist. A learner engaged in a behavior not in anticipation of being reinforced when he finished but rather because that behavior had been reinforced in the past. (p. 19)

The obvious flaw in validation rests in explaining novel behavior. Logically, every behavior is novel when it is first performed. Radical behaviorism cannot explain the existence of any behavior, exhibited for the first time, because it necessarily lacks any type of past reinforcement. It becomes equally problematic for radical behaviorists to explain task perseverance irrespective of punishment. A good example of this phenomenon is the athlete who endures strenuous training despite fatigue and physical pain. Indeed, there is evidence that intrinsic reward (motivation) is more powerful than the extrinsic rewards described by radical behaviorists. Strickler (2006) contends that extrinsic rewards in the workplace actually decrease creativity, innovation, and productivity. She notes that employers who rely on behaviorist tactics establish a culture in which workers are willing to do only what is rewarded, demanding ever greater rewards as time passes. In another study, nursing students who expressed intrinsic motivation for taking a course outperformed their extrinsically motivated classmates (Simons, Dewitte, & Lens, 2004). The author of this study describes the extrinsically rewarded students as "less interested in the course, less motivated … [who] use more surface level strategies and receive lower exam results" (p. 356).

Social and Cultural Interaction

A final obstacle to validation of this theory is that radical behaviorism ignores the influence of social interaction and culture in the learning process. As Corsaro and Eder (1990) explain, behaviorism places "emphasis on simplistic processes (imitation and reinforcement) to explain complex phenomenon" (p. 198). Such a stance minimizes the intangible, but powerful influence wielded by groups that the individual values. Behaviorists do recognize the importance of modeling and reinforcement of imitating modeled behavior. However, this limits the learner to a passive role in the learning process. This is especially the case in the behaviorists' perspective regarding children because the adult model is thought to have the greatest level of influence on the child (Corsaro & Eder, 1999). The adult-child relationship provides a simple framework for observing empirical evidence of learning. More complex relationships, like the individual's interaction with social, peer, or cultural groups are more complicated to study. This is because interaction in these groups consists of active engagement on the part of the learner who functions as both a model and a receiver of modeled behavior, a reinforcer and a recipient of reinforcement, an imitator and an instigator of behavior. When roles are interchangeable and conflated, validation becomes more difficult.

Validation

While obstacles to validation exist, it is important to note that behaviorism has been validated, though such validation is limited in context and scope. The tenets of behaviorism, specifically articulated in classical and operant conditioning, have been successfully applied to the study of animal behavior. As noted previously, the experiments conducted by behaviorists like B. F. Skinner were very successful in using manipulated environments (punishment and reward) to affect animal behavior. Success, though not at the same level, can be found in the use of operant conditioning in humans. Traditional approaches to classroom management have successfully employed systems of reward and punishment characteristic of operant conditioning. The same approaches have been validated in teaching young children simple tasks and routines. Faulkner (2002) describes how nurses, perhaps unconsciously, employ punishment and reward to encourage dependent behaviors in their elderly patients. Little success, however, has been achieved in shaping more complex behaviors such as use of language or other symbolic gestures via conditioning (Hunter & Benson, 1997). Finally, gender may contribute to susceptibility to behaviorist approaches. In a study of pedagogical approaches in university classes, "males were more oriented to extrinsic goals and less oriented to intrinsic goals that are females" (Roeser, Midgely, & Urdan 1996 as cited in Edens, 2007, p. 172). As these examples demonstrate, it can be argued that validation of behaviorism is limited in context.

Romberg (2010) notes how traditional mathematics instruction is based on "drill-and-practice routines" (p. 61). Using such methods for low-level mathematics skills, like memorization of multiplication tables, is successful, but it is less so when applied to more complex mathematic operations involving problem-solving and critical reasoning. As McKeachie (1974) explains, "the classical laws of learning so laboriously developed over the years have generally failed in their application to human learning of any but the most structured and relatively low-level kind" (p. 8). For this reason, the validation of the theory is limited in scope. Such limited validity may warrant a tentative approach to radical behaviorism as expressed in Graubard's (1968) warning, "treatment, research, and educational reforms which fail to take the system into account are liable to do more damage than good" (p. 388).

Instruments Associated With Behaviorism

Behavioral assessments are meant to measure "differences in the rates or other dimensions of behavior across different contexts and settings and as a function of different response contingencies" (Helby & Haynes, 2003, p. 11). While such purposes are closely aligned to the positivist tradition to which behaviorists adhere, behavioral assessments are widely used across disciplines and theoretical paradigms. Although such measurements are used broadly and in different fields, all behavioral assessment instruments share a core of common characteristics. In the opening section of this chapter, we discussed the role that reinforcement plays in the use of behaviorism, but how are behavioristic practices assessed?

Instruments associated with behaviorism generally employ four basic formats: (1) direct observation, (2) self-report, (3) interviews, and (4) questionnaires. Direct observation of behavior can be recorded in myriad forms, including anecdotal notes, behavior checklists, task analysis, and time-sampling. Direct observation can yield a great deal of data, but is frequently time consuming, labor intensive, and subjective. Self-report allows the individual under study to contribute to data collection. Because behavioral instruments emphasize observable behaviors, self-reports feature low-inference items such as frequency counts of objective actions (McConnell & Bowers, 1979). Interviews allow the assessor to gather abundant data that is contextualized in time and setting. However, like direct observation, interviews are time consuming and are often characterized by inference and unnecessary explanatory mechanisms (Helby & Haynes, 2003). In addition, data collected via interview is susceptible to the subjectivity of the interviewer during the process of data coding. Questionnaires are constructed to elicit information related only to the behavior under study and offer a relatively quick and easy way to gather data. In addition, questionnaires are easily structured so that the data is aligned with specific constructs associated with the behavior.

Functional Behavioral Assessment

Functional behavioral assessments (FBA) are most commonly used in educational settings, particularly with exceptional children. The assessment is based on the premise that behavior is a function of environmental conditions. Functional behavioral assessment begins with a description of behavior that is problematic and, thus, targeted for change or elimination. The next steps of functional behavioral assessments involve multiple observations during which the clinician describes the setting in which the behavior occurs. Observation also includes notation of antecedent and subsequent events in relation to the target behavior. A variety of tools are available to document observation. These include the Functional Assessment Checklist for Teachers and Staff (March, 2000, as cited in Carter & Horner, 2007) and the Functional Assessment Observer Form (O'Neill, 1997, as cited in Carter & Horner, 2007). When analysis is complete an intervention plan is drafted to replace maladaptive behaviors with those deemed appropriate for the child and setting.

Motivated Strategies for Learning Questionnaire

This assessment, developed by Pintrich, Smith, Garcia, and McKeachie (1991, as cited in Edens, 2008), is also used in educational settings. The assessment is designed to "measure prior knowledge of course content and to obtain information on students' self-regulatory skills and motivational goal" (Edens, 2008, p. 167). The Motivated Strategies for Learning Questionnaire has two broad sections: (1) motivation, and (2) learning strategies. Each has several subscales which can be used individually or collectively. In addition, there is a multiple choice section that measures prior knowledge. This measurement has been used in a variety of educational settings and is designed to support students' learning by making the instructor aware of possible areas of deficiency.

The Rokeach Value Scale

This instrument has been used in a variety of settings to determine how one's values relate to his attitudes and behaviors (Rokeach, 1973, 1974, as cited in Welch, Pitts, Tenini, Kuenlen, & Wood, 2010). The scale consists of 18 terminal and 18 instrumental values. The participant is instructed to rank the listed values in order of importance. This assessment has allowed researchers to study the connection between consumerism, personal habits, and the use of leisure time (Welch et al., 2010).

Defining Issues Test (DIT)

The DIT was developed in 1974 as a response to Lawrence Kohlberg's Moral Judgment Interview (MJI). The DIT is a multiple-choice test designed to determine the development of four components of morality: (1) moral sensitivity, (2) moral judgment, (3) moral motivation, and (4) moral character. The DIT instructs participants to respond to five moral dilemmas by answering multiple-choice questions. It also requires participants to rate and rank moral stage-typed items. Wide use of this instrument has confirmed its construct and discriminant validity (Walker, 2002). Limitations to the assessment, however, include an inability to assess moral development in children due to the advanced reading level of the dilemmas. In addition, the test does not measure Stage I development, which would be developmentally consistent with most young children.

Generalizability of Behaviorism Across Cultures, Ethnicities, and Genders

"Give us a dozen healthy infants, well-formed, and my own specified world to bring them up in and I'll guarantee to take any one at random and train him to become any type of specialist I might select—doctor, lawyer, artist, merchant-chief and, yes, even beggarman and thief, regardless of his talents, penchants, tendencies, abilities, vocations, and race of his ancestors" (Watson, 1930, p. 104). Then the question is how do we see brothers grown in the same family, same environment, have different desires, abilities and different reactions to same matter? Research on acculturation and ethnic-minority health indicates that acculturation has opposite effects on the same behavior among different ethnic groups; opposite effects on the same health behavior for the women vs. the men of most ethnic groups (Landrine & Klonoff, 2004). This means that people from different cultures and different ethnicities might react differently under the same circumstances, reinforcement or punishment. The focus of behavioral learning theory traditionally has been behavior at the individual-level. In recent years however, the theory has been used at the population-level to explain the similarity of the behavior of members of a Population (Landrine & Klonoff, 2004). Then the natural questions becomes is the behavioral learning theory generalizable across cultures, ethnicities, and genders?

Skinner (1969) proposed that "a culture is the contingencies of social reinforcement which generate and maintain its members' behaviors" (p. 13). According to the theory of planned behavior, an individual's behavior is largely dependent on his or her intention to perform that behavior (Ajzen, 1991). According to behaviorism, behavior can be studied in a systematic and observable manner with no consideration of internal mental states. One of the assumptions of many behaviorists is that the behavior is determined by a combination of forces (Merriam & Caffarella, 1999). It assumes that change in behavior is due to external forces and totally neglects the internal thought process. Since the goal, under the behavioral theory, is to transform the learner's behavior to a desired behavior, it does not give weights to differences in gender, cultures and ethnicities. Given the fact that different people with different background react differently, behavioral theory fails to find reasonable explanations for all these differences.

From an educational perspective, according to the behavioral theory, the teachers are the center of learning. Educators look at many of the current teaching approaches and see most of them stress an active learning style in which the student plays the major rule in the learning process. Educators also see that behaviorism does not account for other types of learning, especially learning that occurs without the use of reinforcement and punishment. There are many examples in which students learn by themselves without looking for rewards or fairing from punishments. How can educators explain the successful results in the classrooms when instructors use discovery learning in teaching science and mathematics?

In discovery learning, students learn by themselves under the supervision of their instructor. Of course the instructor gives guidance and suggestions; but for most, learning is taking place without reinforcement and punishment. From an educational perspective, behaviorism supports the "direct" teaching model in which the teacher plays the major role in the classroom, "teacher-centered" instruction. This means that the teacher should direct the learning process and hence the students will not be given the chance to face the challenges and improve their thinking. Even though direct instruction is highly used in many classrooms, there are many other modern approaches in teaching including discovery learning, inquiry based learning that give better results.

According to behaviorism, knowing is giving the correct response when exposed to a particular stimulus. Therefore behaviorists are not concerned with how the knowledge is obtained, but rather if the correct response is given. If educators look at the learning process from the behavioral point of view, they see that the learning process tends to be passive. The learner uses low level processing skills to understand material and the material is often isolated from real-world contexts or situations. Little responsibility is placed on the learner concerning education and previous knowledge or experience. It is assumed that students have learned the concepts only if they learn the correct response, which reduces all the learning processes to remembering information and memorizing rather than logical and critical thinking. Many educators do not want the learning process to be seen as pattern and imitation of the instructor.

Criticism of Behaviorism and Behavioral Learning Theory

Not only progressive teachers have criticized behavioral learning theory for its constraints on learning. Researchers have criticized the foundational research base in animal experimentation, which ignores the critical thinking capacity of human beings. Therefore, one of the weaknesses of the behavioral theory is that much of its experimentation is done on animals and then generalized to humans; however, humans are different from animals in their interior thinking. Pazimino (1988) criticized behaviorist research, pointing out that "persons are more than well-conditioned animals" and "freedom and dignity have a place" (p. 108). In fact this is why behavioral theory is good to be applied in skills training but not in the learning process that require interior thought processes. Although behavioral theory adequately explains skills training, it does not have a reasonable explanation to many of the critical thinking processes. It does not explain why people act in a certain ways and why people act differently even if they have the same experiences. For example, it doesn't explain why criminals commit crimes and why children tend to be quite while others voice their opinions.

One if the implication of behaviorism is that learning is evidenced by a behavior change but that is not always the case. For example, a student in elementary school might understand the concept of addition but at the same time does not reflect on his behavior in answering a related problem in the test because of test anxiety. To understand learning processes from behaviorism perspective, instructors need to focus on stimulus and responses which deviates them from teaching the concepts to looking for ways of rewards or punishments. Behaviorism heavily stresses reward and punishment and that may make the student lose the interest in the subject and will only be concern about getting the reward or avoiding the punishments. Furthermore given more reward to some students and not others may affect the feelings of the other students in the classroom that might be not able to get the desired solution. Alfie Kohn (1993) has criticized behaviorism in classrooms, pointing out that children are not animals to be confined to boxes.

With all that has been said above, it does not mean behavioral theory is not used and not applicable. In fact, it has some strength that make many people believe in it. For example, since behaviorism is based upon observable behaviors, it is easier to quantify and hence to conduct research. In conclusion, there is no learning theory that can explain all the learning process or can be applicable in all situations. To be realistic, we should accept all the strength of any theory and try to apply it where it is applicable and avoid the weaknesses of the theory. This will take us to a strong combination of learning theories that will enable us to improve our educational system.

USE AND APPLICATION OF BEHAVIORAL LEARNING THEORY

Teachers have traditionally translated behaviorism into classroom practice in the form drill, lecture, memorization, and reproduction of information. Freire (1970) labeled this the banking system of education. Engelmann (1980) referred to such teaching as direct instruction. With the onset of standards and accountability testing, teachers have been encouraged to adopt Madeline Hunter's (1976) lesson cycle with a focus on mastery learning. Many teacher preparation programs still require the use of Hunter's lesson plan template. In more recent years, behaviorism is seen in direct instruction. Magliaro, Lockee, and Burton (2005) recently took a look at direct instruction, defined as "teacher-directed actions in a classroom (p. 43) and technology based instruction. They presented the following components as key to effectiveness:

1. Materials and curriculum are broken down into small steps and arrayed in what is assumed to be the prerequisite order.
2. Objectives must be stated clearly and in terms of learner outcomes or performance.
3. Learners are provided with opportunities to connect their new knowledge with what they already know.
4. Learners are given practice with each step or combination of steps.
5. Learners experience additional opportunities to practice that promote increasing responsibility and independence (guided and/or independent; in groups and/or alone).
6. Feedback is provided after each practice opportunity or set of practice opportunities (p. 44).

For beginning teachers, the lesson cycle provides an outline to ensure that curriculum, instructional strategies, and assessment are addressed; and direct instruction is the best practice in some contexts.

Behavioral learning theory has been applied to the field of special education in the form of behavior modification. For teachers who are reading this, we would caution you to not immediately think in terms of classroom management issues and discipline. In a case study (Blairs, Slater, & Hare, 2007) of a 31-year-old man "whose ASD was not recognized until he was 29," "deep touch pressure," defined by the use of "bedclothes tucked in tight around him" (p. 216) when the clinical patient showed signs of anxiety or being upset. In the context of treating the subject "with moderate learning disabilities" in a clinical setting, behavioral learning theory was applied as a stimulus-response model. The use of deep touch produced by tucking sheets around the man while he lay in a bed resulted in relaxation in the man. We could not help but notice the pattern that developed as the man's episodes of anxiety and state of being upset resulted in some staff tucking the man in bed. Who was doing the learning here? Did the man actually learn to control his anxiety, or did the clinical staff learn to respond to the man's discomfort with an action that comforted the man?

Behavioral theories have informed classroom management and continue to be prevalent in many schools. Hardin (2008) presents a range of approaches to classroom management, beginning with behavioral approaches and ending with judicious discipline. She divides her text into three major divisions: (1) classroom management as discipline, (2) classroom management as a system, and (3) classroom management as instruction. The first section, classroom management as discipline, is strongly framed by behavioral learning theory. Hardin discusses behavior modification, assertive discipline, positive classroom discipline, and logical consequences, all strategies that draw on positive and negative reinforcement.

Behavioral theories have been applied with students do not complete homework because of reading and writing difficulties (Margolis & McCabe). The use of extrinsic rewards to reinforce students doing homework, which they find hard, is one place to begin.

Preservice teachers are asked to document their knowledge, skills, and dispositions in teaching portfolios (Interstate New Teacher Assessment and Support Consortium, 1992; National Council for Accreditation of Colleges of Teacher Education, 2002; Moss, 2003). Although National Council for Accreditation of Colleges of Teacher Education did not explicitly prescribe that teacher education programs adopt a portfolio assessment system for teacher certification, many interpreted the call for performance-based assessment as a call for portfolios. The portfolio assessment process provided the context for teacher educators to adopt behavioral practices by designing portfolio systems with rubrics that result in preservice teachers writing three-part portfolio reflections to describe their artifact, tell what they learned, and make connections to the Interstate New Teacher Assessment and Support Consortium standards (Moss, 2003). The same system provided a context for critical pedagogy within a social reconstructivist framework (Moss, 2010). Teachers and teacher educators work within an era of standardization that resembles a framework of behaviorism. The way one works within the system determines if behaviorism is sustained or critiqued through other learning theories.

As teacher educators engaged in the process of documenting teachers' knowledge, skills, and dispositions, attention grew in the area of dispositions. The body of literature concerning the definition of, development of, and assessment of dispositions continues to grow (Dotger, 2010; Duplass & Cruz, 2010; Jung & Rhodes, 2008; Stooksberry, Schussler, & Bercaw, 2009). Each study cites the National Council for Accreditation of Colleges of Teacher Education (2002) standards as a mandate for accreditation. This begs the question, is standardization framed by behavioral learning theory? Does this set teacher educator programs up for taking a behavioral approach?

Dispositions can be documented by lesson plans and modifications for students. Dispositions are also assessed by preservice teachers and their teacher educators (Coughlin, Moss, Zijdemana-Boudreau, Matschiner, & Bailey, 2011). In the effort to advance teacher education toward a rigorous profession that prepares intelligent, culturally competent, and caring teachers, are we trying to influence behaviors? Although few would disagree with the goal of shifting preservice teachers' racist dispositions toward humane and democratic dispositions, when preparation programs present desired dispositions and ask students to complete self-assessment surveys and goals for changed behaviors, are we using behavioral learning theory? Where is the division between behaviorism and constructivism? Is constructivism sometimes implemented in behavioristic ways? Thus is the complexity of education and use of various learning theories.

EXAMPLE STUDIES

- Mitchell, W. S., & Stoffelmayr, B. E. (1973). Application of the Premack principle to the behavioral control of extremely inactive schizophrenics. *Journal of Applied Behavior Analysis, 3*, 419-423.

In the article "Application of the Premack principle to the behavior control of extremely inactive schizophrenics" by William Mitchell and Bertram Stoffelmayr, we find the introduction of reinforcements to be pivotal in the modification of behavior. The article chronicles the behavior of participants on a hospital unit designated for individuals with severe schizophrenia. The unit housed 42 long-stay patients, however, of the 42 patients, 9 patients where identified as being extremely inactive (i.e., where not employed on or off the unit). Of the nine inactive patients, four were concluded as extremely inactive and unmotivated and thus selected for the experiment. Although the unit staff attempted many reinforcements, none proved successful. The four participants were introduced to a reinforcement sampling consisting of candies, cigarettes, biscuits, and fruit. Two of the four participants repeatedly accepted cigarettes and fruit; one occasionally accepted candy and the other refused to accept any form of reinforcement. The two participants who accepted the tangible reinforcers formed the control group, while the other two participants formed the experimental group. Principles of the Premack response-reinforcement were utilized with the experimental group. Premack principle (a product of operant conditioning) suggests that behaviors that are more pleasant to an individual can control for behaviors that are less pleasant to that individual. Using this notion, observers determined the target behavior for the experimental group was to perform the coil-stripping job, while the response-reinforcement was sitting while working versus standing. During the experiment the observers measured the experimental group's performance using an intermittent fixed interval reinforcement schedule (i.e., 30 seconds intervals per 30 minute session). In addition, to assure reliability of their findings, the observers employed interrater reliability checks. As a result, they concluded their observations generated high reliability.

Concluding the experiment, the observers found when using the reinforcer, participants were more inclined to perform work at a high frequency. Thus, patients with severe schizophrenia who previously refused any tangible reinforcements were found to have their behaviors influenced by the reinforcer. During the baseline period and instruction-only phases, work frequency was not observed. However, in the shaping phase where instruction was paired with reinforcement, the participants exhibited substantial growth in the frequency of work. Next, during the reversal-conditioning phase, observers determined the desired behavior decreased to baseline levels. However, in the reinstatement phase, the observers noted an increase in the work frequency. As a result, this study illustrated that aspect (i.e., Premack principle) of operant conditioning reinforcement schedule has the capacity to shape, control for, and maintain targeted behaviors.

- McAllister, L. W., Stachowiak, J. G., Baer, D. M., & Conderman, L. (1969). The application of operant conditioning techniques in a secondary school classroom. *Journal of Applied Behavioral Analysis, 4*, 277-285.

In the McAllister article, we find the application of operant conditioning in a seconding English classroom. A unique characteristic of this article is the use of operant conditioning as the framework of a dissertation. The article features the outcomes of an experiment, which sought to modify the behavior of high school students in an English class. The teacher, who was a second year teacher, observed behavioral trends that were inappropriate, thus elicited the support of an intervention. An experiment was conducted in effort to control for the inappropriate behavior and outcomes were successful.

McAllister et al. (1969) investigated the usage of contingent social teacher reinforcer on selected targeted behaviors. To set up the experiment, the participants were one second-year secondary English teacher and two classes with a minimum of 26 students per class. The classes were considered "low track" classes, which enrolled juniors and seniors. The teacher held a bachelor's degree but felt she did not have adequate classroom behavior management skills. She believed she had established rapport with some students, and she believed this rapport assisted in their academic instruction. In addition, she believed if she attempted to discipline students she might inadvertently compromise her rapport with the particular students.

Both classes (which were under roll of the teacher participant) were observed for 2 weeks to gain baseline data. Outcomes of the observations noted several inappropriate incidences, however inappropriate talking and turning around were the selected targeted behaviors. After the targeted behaviors were identified, they were next defined. Additionally, classes were randomly selected into experimental and control groups. Each class was observed and initiated under the same conditions and interrated reliability checks were conducted with multiple observers in order to gain trustworthiness. The teacher was trained to offer positive praise or disapproval for the occurrences of targeted behavior. The outcomes of the study found the control group's targeted behavior of inappropriate talking decreased substantially from baseline levels. The teacher contingent reinforcer was successful in reducing and controlling for the behavior. In addition, the second targeted behavior of turning around was also decreased in the control group. However, given both targeted behaviors, it cannot be determined if the intervention was solely controlling for the behavior as the study did not include a reversal-conditioning phase. Thus it is not absolutely clear if the praise/disapproval stimulus prompted the behavior change. Regardless, during the experiment, the teacher participant gained valuable insight in regards to classroom management. The teacher's behavior was also measured and the data notes an increase in overall positive management of student's inappropriate targeted behaviors.

REFERENCES

Ajzen, I. (1991). The theory of planned behavior. *Organizational Behavior and Human Decision Processes, 50*, 179-211.

Azrin, N. H., & Holz, W. C. (1966). Punishment. In W. K. Honig (Ed.), *Operant behavior: Areas of research and application* (pp. 380-447). New York, NY: Appleton-Century-Crofts.

Baum, W. M. (2003). The molar view of behavior and its usefulness in behavior analysis. *Behavior Analyst Today, 4*, 78–81.

Baum, W. M. (2005). *Understanding behaviorism: Behavior, culture and evolution.* Malden, MA: Blackwell.

Blairs, S., Slater, S., & Hare, J. (2007). The clinical application of deep tough pressure with a man with autism presenting with severe anxiety and challenging behaviour. *British Journal of Learning Disabilities, 35*, 214-220.

Blackman, D. (1974). *Operant conditioning: An experimental analysis of behaviour.* London, England: Methuen.

Breland, K., & Breland, M. (1961). The misbehavior of organisms. *American Psychologist, 16*, 681-684.

Carter, D. R., & Horner, R. H. (2007). Adding functional behavioral assessment to first step to success: A case study. *Journal of Positive Behavior Interventions, 9*, 229-238.

Chomsky, N. (1959). A review of B. F. Skinner's verbal behavior. *Language, 35*(1), 26-58.

Cooper, J. O., Heron, T. E., & Heward, W. L. (2007). *Applied behavior analysis.* Upper Saddle River, NJ: Merrill.

Corsaro, W. A., & Elder, D. (1990). Children's peer cultures. *Annual Review of Sociology, 16*, 197-220.

Coughlin, E., Moss, G., Zijdemana-Boudreau, A., Matschiner, A., & Bailey, M. (2011). *Developing dispositions among pre-service teachers.* Poster session at the fourteenth annual conference of Oregon Association of Teacher Educators, Kennedy School, Portland, OR.

Domjan, M. (2003). *The principles of learning and behavior* (5th ed.). Belmont, CA: Thomson/Wadsworth.

Dotger, B. H. (2010). "I had no idea": Developing dispositional awareness and sensitivity through a cross-professional pedagogy. *Teaching and Teacher Education, 26*, 805-812.

Duplass, J. A., & Cruz, B. C. (2010). Professional dispositions: What's a social studies professor to do? *The Social Studies, 101*, 140-151.

Edens, K. M. (2008). The interaction of pedagogical approach, gender, self-regulation, and goal orientation using student response system technology. *Journal of Research on Technology in Education, 41*(2), 161-177.

Faulkner, M. (2002). Instrumental passivity: A behavioural theory of dependence. *Nursing Older People, 14*(2), 20-21.

Ferster, C. B., & Skinner, B. F. (1957). *Schedules of reinforcement.* New York, NY: Appleton-Century Crofts.

Flora, S. R. (2004). *The power of reinforcement.* Albany, NY: State University of New Your Press.

Francis, J. B. (1975). Theory vs. practice in high-level learning: A response to behaviorism. *Journal of Individual Psychology, 31*(1), 3-12

Freire, P. (1970). *Pedagogy of the oppressed.* New York, NY: Seabury.

Garcia, J., & Koelling, R. A. (1966). Relation of cue to consequence in avoidance learning. *Psychometric Science, 4*, 123-124.

Graubard, P. S. (1968). Training, research, and systems change. *Exceptional Children, 34*(6), 388-389.

Greenwood, J. D. (1999). Understanding the "cognitive revolution" in psychology. *Journal of the History of the Behavioral Sciences, 35*(1), 1-22.

Hardin, C. J. (2004). *Effective classroom management models and strategies for today's classrooms.* New York, NY: Pearson/Merrill/Prentice Hall.

Helby, E. M., & Haynes, S. N. (2003). Introduction to behavioral assessment. In S. N. Haynes & E. M. Helby (Eds.), *Comprehensive handbook of psychological assessment: Behavioral assessment* (pp. 3-18). Hoboken, NJ: Wiley.

Hergenhahn, B. R. (2005). *An introduction to the history of psychology* (5th ed.). Belmont, CA: Wadsworth.

Hunter, W. J., & Benson, G. D. (1997). Arrows of time: The misapplication of chaos theory in education. *Journal of Curriculum Studies, 29*(1), 87-100.

Interstate New Teacher Assessment and Support Consortium. (1992). *Model standards for beginning teacher licensing and development: A resource for state dialogue.* Washington, DC: Council of Chief State School Officers.

Iverson, I. H. (1992). Skinner's early research: From reflexology to operant conditioning. *American Psychologist, 47*(11), 1318-1328.

Jung, E., & Rhodes, D. M. (2008). Revisiting disposition assessment in teacher education: Broadening the focus. *Assessment & Evaluation in Higher Education, 33*(6), 647-660.

Kerr, M. M., & Nelson, C. M. (1989). *Strategies for managing behavior problems in the classroom* (2nd ed.). New York, NY: Macmillan.

Kohn, A. (1993). *Punishment by rewards: The trouble with gold stars, incentive plans, A's, praise, and other bribes.* Boston, MA: Houghton Mifflin.

Landrine, H., & Klonoff, E (2004). Culture change and ethnic-minority health behavior: An operant theory of acculturation. *Journal of Behavioral Medicine, 27*(6), 737-745.

Magliaro, S. G., Lockee, B. B., & Burton, J. K. (2005). Direct instruction revisited: A key model for instructional technology. *Educational Technology Research & Development, 53*(4), 41-55.

Margolis, H., & McCabe, P. P. (1997). Homework challenges for students with reading and writing problems: Suggestions for effective practice. *Journal of Educational and Psychological Consultation, 8*(1), 41-74.

McAllister, L. W., Stachowiak, J. G., Baer, D. M., & Conderman, L. (1969). The application of operant conditioning techniques in a secondary school classroom. *Journal of Applied Behavioral Analysis, 4*, 277-285.

McConnell, J. W., & Bowers, N. D. (1979, April). *A comparison of high-inference and low-inference measures of teachers behaviors as predictors of pupil attitudes and achievements.* Paper presented at the annual meeting of the American Educational Research Association, San Francisco, CA.

McKeachie, W. M. (1974). The decline and fall of the laws of learn. *Educational Researcher, 3*(3), 7-11.

Mead, G. H. (1934). *Mind, self, and society.* .Chicago, IL: University of Chicago Press.

Merriam, S. B., & Cafferella, R. S. (1999). *Learning in adulthood,* (2nd ed.). San Francisco, CA: Jossey-Bass.

Michael, J. (2005). Positive and negative reinforcement, a distinction that is no longer necessary; or a better way to talk about bad things. *Journal of Organizational Behavior Management, 24*, 207-222.

Mills, J. A. (1998). *Control: A history of behavioral psychology.* New York, NY: New York University Press.

Mitchell, W. S., & Stoffelmayr, B. E. (1973). Application of the Premack principle to the behavioral control of extremely inactive schizophrenics. *Journal of applied behavior analysis, 3*, 419-423.

Montana, P. J., & Charnov, B. H. (2008). *Management* (4th ed.). Hauppauge, NY: Barron's Educational Series.

Moss, G. (2003). Critical self-reflective narrative of portfolio assessment in teacher preparation. *Scholar-Practitioner Quarterly, 2*(1), 45-60.

Moss, G. (2010). Working within accountability models—With vision! Vision of standardization and vision of critical pedagogy. In T. Swim, J. Nichols, K. Murphey, G. Moss, A. Merz, D. Lindquist, B. Kanpol (Eds.), *Teacher national accreditation as community dialogue: Transformative reflections* (pp. 101-126). Cresskill, NJ: Hampton Press.

National Council for Accreditation of Colleges of Teacher Education. (2002). *Professional standards for the accreditation of schools, colleges, and departments of education.* Washington, DC: Author.

O'Donnell, J. (1986). *Origins of behaviorism. American Psychology, 1870–1920.* New York, NY: New York University Press.

Pazmino, R. W. (1988). *Foundational issues in Christian education.* Grand Rapids, MI: Baker Book House.

Rilling, M. (2000). John Watson's paradoxical struggle to explain Freud. *The American Psychologist, 55*(3), 301-312.

Romberg, T. A. (2010). Wittrock's influence on mathematics education: Some personal comments. *Educational Psychologist, 45*(1), 61-63.

Roeser, R. W., Midgely, C., & Urdan, T. C. (1996). Perceptions of the school psychological environment and early adolescents' psychological and behavioral functioning in school: The mediating role of goals and belonging. *Journal of Educational Psychology, 88*, 408-422.

Simons, J., Dewitte, S., & Lens, W. (2004). The role of different types of instrumentality in motivation, study strategies, and performance: Know why you learn, so you'll know what you learn! *British Journal of Educational Psychology, 74*, 343-360.

Skinner, B. F. (1938). *The behavior of organisms: An experimental analysis.* New York, NY: Appleton-Century.

Skinner, B. F. (1969). *Contingencies of reinforcement.* Englewood Cliffs, NJ: Prentice-Hall.

Skinner, B. F. (1974). *About behaviorism.* New York, NY: Knopf.

Staats, A. W. (1976). Skinnerian behaviorism: Social behaviorism or radical behaviorism? *The American Sociologist, 11*(1), 59-60.

Stooksberry, L. M., Schussler, D., & Bercaw, L. A. (2009). Conceptualizing dispositions: Intellectual, cultural, and moral domains of teaching. *Teachers and Teaching: Theory and Practice, 15*(6), 719-736.

Strauss, S. (1993). *Theories of learning an d development for academics and educators, 28*(3), 191-203.

Strickler, J. (2006). What really motivates people? *The Journal for Quality & Participation,* 29(1), 26-28.

Svinicki, M. D. (1999). New directions in learning and motivation. *New Directions for Teaching and Learning, 80*, 5-27.

Villegas, A. M. (2007). Dispositions in teacher education: A look at social justice. *Journal of Teacher Education, 58*(5), 370-380.

Walker, L. (2002). The model and the measure an appraisal of the Minnesota approach to moral development. *Journal of Moral Education, 31*(3), 353-367.

Watson, J. B. (1913). Psychology as the behaviorist views it. *Psychological Review, 20*, 158-177.

Watson, J. B. (1925). *Behaviorism*. New York, NY: People's Institute.

Watson, J. B. (1930). *Behaviorism* (Rev. ed.). Chicago, IL: University of Chicago Press.

Welch, F. C., Pitts, R. E., Tenini, K. J., Kuenlen, M. G., & Wood, S. G. (2010). Significant issues in defining and assessing teacher dispositions. *The Teacher Educator, 45*(3), 179-201.

Zirpoli, T. J., & Melloy, K. J. (1993). *Behavior management: Applications for teachers and parents.* New York, NY: Macmillan.

Author Contact Information: Glenda Moss, University of North Texas, Department of Teacher Education & Administration, 7300 University Hills Blvd., Dallas, TX 75241-4600. Phone: 972-338-1373. E-mail: glenda. moss@unt.edu

CHAPTER 9

Cognitivism

Ways of Knowing

Karen D. Paciotti
Texas A&M University

Cognitive science, as defined by Gardner (1985), is "a contemporary, empirically based effort to answer long-standing epistemological questions—particularly those concerned with ... efforts to explain human knowledge" (p. 6). Cognitivism differs from behaviorism, which was prevalent in the first half of the twentieth century, and which held that learning occurs when there is an observable behavioral change as a reaction to environmental stimuli. Cognitivists maintain that learning takes place through unobservable mental actions within the mind/brain, that are influenced by the learner's own thoughts and experiences (Martinez, 2010).

Considered in the 1950s and 1960s to be a "cognitive revolution" (Overskeid, 2008, p. 131) against behaviorism, Neisser (1967) notes that cognitivism considers learning to be "all processes by which the sensory input is transformed, reduced, elaborated, stored, recovered, and used" (p. 4) by the mind/brain. Brunig, Schraw, and Norby (2011) add that later cognitivism holds that humans are active processors of information, based on "human perception, thought, and memory" (p. 1). In other words, unlike a computer, which was at one time the main metaphor for cognitive learning theorists, humans not only mentally construct their own learning and build new schemata, or structures that organize comprehension, as they experience new information and process the stimuli that are received by the brain, but they use prior knowledge, social/cultural experiences, and emotions as they subconsciously select which sensory information to accept or adapt, and which to ignore. To cognitivists, learning is not merely a matter of an external reaction to stimuli, but also consists of planning within the mind/brain if, when, and how to react to stimuli; placing information into memory; mentally acting on it, and then retrieving well-learned knowledge back to working memory to construct new schemata or expand old schemata to solve problems (Brunig et al., 2011).

Original Development of and Interactions of the Cognitivist Theory

According to Woolfolk (1998), the mid-twentieth century ascendance of the cognitive perspective, which acknowledges that humans do not merely react to the environment, but actively plan responses to changes in their environment, problem solve, use systems for memory, and uniquely organize learning into structures that make sense to the individual, was due to three major events: (a) the knowledge gained from high-level research during World War II that focused on complex human skill development, (b) the modern advances of the computer age, and (c) the development of new language acquisition theories. The cognitive revolution signaled the waning of the mechanistic era and turned the balance toward the humanistic era, as it transformed educators' previous reliance on the behaviorist belief that learning exists as a change in observable behavior through the processes of stimulus, response, and reinforcement and posited the idea that learning happens during unobservable mental phenomena that occur as humans solve inconguencies (Martinez, 2010; Overskeid, 2008).

Furthermore, the advent of Chomsky's (1959) internalist theory of generative grammar occurred with the

The Handbook of Educational Theories, pp. 105–113

context of the cognitive revolution and increasingly weakened behaviorists' views that language was acquired primarily through behaviorism's mechanistic "imitation, shaping, and reinforcement" (Brunig et al., 2011, p. 4) and suggested that language is innately human within the mind/brain. Chomsky (1959) claims that the human brain is biologically structured, or prewired, for language. In fact, Chomsky (2000) argues that, "The faculty of language can reasonably be regarded as a 'language organ' in the sense in which scientists speak of the visual system, or immune system, or circulatory system, as organs of the body" (p. 4). Chomsky (1965) writes:

> language acquisition is based on the child's discovery of what from a formal point of view is a deep and abstract theory—a generative grammar of his language—many of the concepts and principles of which are only remotely related to experience by long and intricate chains of unconscious quasi-inferential steps. (p. 58)

According to Chomsky (1965), this concept of generative grammar consists of mental processes "that are far beyond the level of actual or even potential consciousness" (p. 8). In addition, furthering the views of cognitivism that biological factors affect the unobservable mental actions that take place upon experiences, Chomsky (2000) writes that the "language organ is an expression of the genes [and] each language is the result of the interplay of two factors: the initial state and the course of experience" (p. 4). In fact, in congruence with information processing theory, discussed later in this chapter, Chomsky (2000) writes of that initial state as "a 'language acquisition device' that takes experience as 'input' and gives the language as an 'output'—an 'output' that is internally represented in the mind/brain" (p. 4).

Chomsky's theory (1959) gave credence to nativism, which posits that the human brain possesses innate knowledge of language, and that, as children mature, they internalize rules of grammar, enabling the production of infinite sentences. They begin to create new rules for language and continue to develop ever-increasing complexity of language patterns (Morrow, 2012).

In contrast to behaviorism, cognitive learning theory seeks to understand the complexity of human learning processes (Brunig et al., 2011) as they occur in the mind/brain within the entire scope of the human context (Overskeid, 2008). As Woolfolk (1998) explains, "The cognitive approach suggests that one of the most important elements in the learning process is what the individual brings to the learning situation" (p. 247). Furthermore, cognitive learning theory suggests that learning does not need to be externally observable, but occurs internally, as changes take place in mental processes that operate as the mind tries to make sense of the world (Eggen & Kauchak, 2004; Nath & Cmajdalka, 2011). In addition, newer cognitivist approaches stress the mind/brain's construction of knowledge over the acquisition of knowledge (Woolfolk, 1998). Cognitivists now theorize that mental operations lead to constructing models of thinking, or schemata, in integration with the influences of environmental and biological contexts that include individual and cultural affective nuances such as "beliefs, expectations, and feelings" (Woolfolk, 1998, p. 282), social factors (Vygotsky, 1978), motivation, agency, and self-efficacy (Bandura, 1989) and neurological processes (Brunig et al., 2011) that influence how humans think and learn.

The major developments of cognitivism that have impacted the field of education are discussed in this chapter, such as Piaget's cognitive developmental model (1964/1997), Vygotsky's sociocultural model, Bandura's (1989) social cognitive theory, the information processing model, and the metacognitive model.

Piaget's Developmental Stage Cognitive Model

Jean Piaget's (1964/1997) stage theory of cognitive development explained his view that learning occurs from internal biological forces of the developing child (Martinez, 2010) within the interaction of "maturation, social experiences, ... activity, and the process of equilibration" (Rackley & Knight, 2011, p. 8). Through various life experiences, a child builds increasing knowledge that is adapted to prior experiences through accommodation or assimilation (Woolfolk, 1998), thus arranging and rearranging thoughts and experiences into schemata, or mental structures, that enable humans to make sense of their world (Rackley & Knight, 2011). Assimilation occurs when current experiences match or make sense with prior knowledge, and a child uses existing schemata to integrate new experience into prior knowledge (Rackley & Knight, 2011), even though, as Woolfolk (1998) writes, "We may have to distort the new information to make it fit" (Woolfolk, 1998, p. 29). Woolfolk (1998) illustrates assimilation through the following example, "The first time many children see a skunk, they call it a 'kitty.' They try to match the new experience with an existing scheme for identifying animals" (p. 29). Accommodation occurs when new situations or experiences do not match a person's schema and the schema is adjusted to fit the new data. Woolfolk (1998) illustrates accommodation with the example of the skunk, "Children demonstrate accommodation when they add the scheme for recognizing skunks to their other systems for identifying animals" (p. 29). However, when a "mismatch" (Martinez, 2010, p. 198) between prior knowledge and current experience occurs, and neither assimilation nor accommodation is enough for a child to adapt prior knowledge to current experiences, disequilibrium occurs. According to Gibbs (2006), disequilibrium is the motivating force of learning, because, as Martinez (2010) explains,

> The mind's tendency is toward equilibration, toward regaining the mental balance or homeostasis that will result in a harmonious relationship between our knowledge and the world as we experience it. (p. 198)

Equilibration is the Piagetian term for the active process of self-regulation (Piaget, 1964/1997) in which equilibrium is restored as the mind continually seeks to make sense of the new experience through accommodation, assimilation, and adaptation (Gibbs, 2006; Piaget, 1964/1997). Through these recursive cognitive processes, a child actively strives to incorporate prior knowledge and current experience into new schemata (Martinez, 2010).

Piaget (1964/1997) identified four developmental stages through which humans progress as they assimilate, accommodate, and actively construct new schemata: (a) the sensorimotor stage (0-2 years); (b) the preoperational stage (2-7 years); (c) the concrete operational stage (7-11 stage); and (c) the formal operational stage (11 years-adult). During the sensorimotor stage, a child primarily constructs knowledge in the present, through senses, manipulation of objects, and movement. At this stage a child lacks the understanding of object permanence. If an object is hidden from view, he or she does not realize that it still exists. As he or she progresses to the preoperational stage, the child understands the concept of object permanence. The child starts to internalize symbolic function, using language to name things, and to make requests. Furthermore, egocentrism is a prominent characteristic of this stage; the child sees the world only from his or her own point of view. In addition, the child is not able to complete or reverse an operation, which Piaget (1964/1997) identifies as "the essence of knowledge ... an interiorized action which modifies the object of knowledge" (p. 20), and thus does not understand the conservation of quantity. In the concrete operational stage, a child can perform operations on objects, such as classifying, ordering, and counting, but it is not until the fourth stage, formal operational, that Piaget (1964/1997) writes that the child can "reason on hypotheses, and not only on objects [but] constructs new operations ... operations of propositional logic" (p. 21).

Challenges to Piaget

Some of Piaget's generalizations from the developmental stage model have been challenged, particularly his beliefs that children at the same developmental level perform consistently across developmental tasks. According to Martinez (2010), the phenomenon of *decalage*, which occurs when children sometimes reason in more adult ways on some tasks, but in more childlike ways on other tasks, has been an important criticism. In addition, critics have noted that Piaget's theories have not accounted enough for the different effects that external factors, such as specialized content knowledge and extra instruction could have on performance, regardless of age and developmental stage (Woolfolk, 1998). Furthermore, critics have written that Piaget's theory has not considered sufficiently the influences of cultural and social groups on levels of thinking. For example, basic concrete operational tasks in Western cultures, such as classification, may not be viewed in the same light in other cultures (Woolfolk, 1998). Maynard (2008) writes that although Piaget's theory "accommodates aspects of cultural variation in cognitive development ... his methods ... did not" (p. 63).

Recent Research on Piaget's Theory

Nevertheless, as methodologies have improved for studying the development model, the congruence of Piaget's theories have become more apparent with more recent thinking (Maynard, 2008). Recently, more stringent studies in cognitive developmental neuroscience have found that cultural environment affects brain development (Fox, 2006), and that experiences affect timing of brain development (Hammock & Levitt, 2006; Nelson, Moulson, & Richmond, 2006).

Maynard (2008) concludes that Piaget's theories are congruent with "cultural variation in cognitive development" (p. 63), that cross-cultural research has been significantly influenced by Jean Piaget, and that new researchers must "reveal the pathways of development that exist in and across cultures and to use data to strengthen the theoretical and methodological foundations of our field" (p. 63). Therefore, as researchers continue to study human learning, Piaget's theories have provided valuable insights on the ways that humans build cognitive knowledge through actively constructing knowledge and building schemata (Martinez, 2010).

Vygotskyan Sociocultural Cognitive Model

Similarly to Piaget, Vygotsky (1978) proposed that children learn as they actively build new schemata, or mental structures that organize information. However, Vygotsky (1978), as a social constructivist, theorized that social relationships and cultural factors influence when and how new schemata are built rather than ascribing to Piaget's view of a developmental progression through internal biological stages. According to Woolfolk (1998), Vygotsky (1978) thought that language was the critical symbolic system for supporting learning (Woolfolk, 1998). Through verbal self-talk, children interact verbally with themselves to guide their thinking, and as they mature, they internalize self-talk, rather than speak the words aloud. The progression from audible speech cues to inner speech cues within the mind/brain is a basic process of Vygotsky's (1978) theory of cognitive development (Woolfolk, 1998).

In addition, Vygotsky's (1978) theory of socially mediated learning emphasizes the importance of verbal feedback and modeling from more knowledgeable people, or *experts*, to assist students, or *novices*, to complete tasks they could not complete alone. This assistance is called scaffolding, and it is central to Vygotsky's (1978) theory of socially mediated learning and his concept of the zone of proximal development (ZPD). This theory holds that the optimal range for cognitive change lies just beyond the level of difficulty in which the child can perform independently, but below the level of difficulty in which it is impossible for the child to succeed independently. Rather, the zone of proximal development lies within the level of difficulty of problem solving that the novice can accomplish with the aid of other, more knowledgeable experts (Brunig et al., 2011; Morrow, 2012). These experts, either adults or peers, mediate the construction of knowledge through the use of scaffolding, using both modeling of the task and social interaction to help learners perform new tasks. Then, as the novices start to increasingly internalize, practice, and become adept at the new skill, the experts gradually decrease scaffolding. As novices learn and internalize more information through the social interaction of scaffolding, they develop increasingly complex schemata and become experts (Morrow, 2012). Then, additional scaffolding is provided to assist the novice in advancing to new and more complex understandings, then gradually withdrawn as the novice becomes more expert, and the process continues, expanding knowledge during each reiteration (Woolfolk, 1998).

Bandura's Social Cognitive Theory

Illustrating the additive nature of cognitivist research, Bandura's (2006) research is in congruence with aspects of Vygotsky's sociocultural theory. Bandura (2006) writes, "Most human functioning is socially situated" (p. 165). Social cognitive theory holds that the human mind/brain is not viewed as merely reactive to outside and internal factors, but it is considered to be generative and interactive; people make choices that generate their environments. Then they interact with their environments, whether they were constructed through their own agency, or whether through fortuitive events that might interact with each other to change life courses, as in chaos theory (Bandura, 1999). However, Bandura (2006) also states, "To be an agent, is to influence intentionally one's functioning and life circumstances" (p. 164).

Social cognitive theory is built on a model of "emergent interactive agency" (Bandura, 1989, p. 1175) in which humans are agents who make "causal contribution to their own motivation and action within a system of triadic reciprocal causation" (Bandura, 1989, p. 1175), which represents human functioning as a "product of a reciprocal interplay of intrapersonal, behavioral, and environmental determinants" (Bandura, 2006, p. 165) which include the actions and self-reflection of the human agent (Bandura, 1989, p. 1175). Bandura (2006) explains further:

> In this model of reciprocal causality, internal personal factors in the form of cognitive affective and biological events; behavioral patterns, and environments events all operate as interacting determinants that influence one another bidirectionally. (p. 23)

Bandura (1993) identifies self-efficacy as "people's beliefs about their capabilities to exercise control over their own level of functioning and over events affect their lives" (p. 118), and as "the foundation of human agency" (Bandura, 1999, p. 28), it is critical to the level of human functioning that can be achieved. Illustrating this, he writes

> Unless people believe that they can produce desired effects by their actions they have little incentive to act or persevere in the face of difficulties. Whatever other factors serve as motivators, they are rooted in the core belief that one has the power to produce changes by one's actions. (p. 28)

According to Bandura (2006), self-efficacy is important to social cognitive theory because not only does it affect action directly, but it affects goal setting. Bandura (2006) notes that people choose "which challenges to undertake, how much effort to invest in the pursuits and how long to persevere in the face of difficulties" (p. 28) based on their efficacy beliefs. These choices have ripple effects, as self-efficacy beliefs affect choices people make whether or not to engage in challenging tasks and problem solving, which can have negative or positive effects on the individual's self-efficacy beliefs, which interact continually with the affective beliefs and choices of others, and can lead to gains or losses in performance, which lead to positive or negative changes in the intrapersonal, interpersonal, and behavioral aspects of both people and the environment (Bandura, 2006).

Bandura (1993, 1999, 2006) continues to contribute to the additive research of the cognitive model through his social cognitive theory, in which there occurs an increasingly complex interaction among internal and external factors that lead to learning. Bandura (2006) describes the interactions of environment, biology, cognition, personal agency, motivation, self-efficacy and other affective behaviors and beliefs as they can affect human functioning. In addition, Schauffele and Baptiste (2000) posit that a person's spiritual dimension should be included within Bandura's (1989, 2006) concept of triadic reciprocality, which explains human functioning as "a product of a reciprocal interplay of intrapersonal, behavior, and environmental determinants" (Bandura, 2006).

The Internet and other advances in social and global communication have advanced social cognitive theory by extending the impact of triadic reciprocality, allowing people to instantaneously use personal and collective agency to influence human functioning across a global scale, crossing cultures, genders and connecting disciplines in ways that were not envisioned before (Bandura, 2006).

Information Processing Cognitive Model

Information processing models of cognition are based upon the metaphor of the computer. Woolfolk (1998) writes,

> The human mind takes in information, performs operations on it to change its form and content, stores the information, retrieves it when needed, and generates responses to it. Thus, processing involves gathering and representing information, or *encoding*; holding information, or *storage*; and getting at the information when needed, or *retrieval*. The whole system is guided by control processes that determine how and when information will flow through the system. (p. 250)

One component of the information processing cognitive model is memory (Brunig et al., 2011; Martinez, 2010; Nath & Cmajdalka, 2011). Countless stimuli enter the mind through the senses and are held in the sensory memory, also called the sensory register, which is the first memory structure that "perceives, recognizes, and assigns meaning to incoming stimuli" (Brunig et al., 2011, p. 13). Once held in the sensory memory, either the stimuli are given attention by the brain and transferred to the short-term memory, now called working memory (Baddeley, 1986; Martinez, 2010), or they are ignored. If ignored, the information remains in the sensory memory for only a second or two, and then it is lost. (Nath & Cmajdalka, 2011; Woolfolk, 1998). Once attended to and stored in the working memory, the brain actively processes and stores the information (Baddeley, 1986; Brunig et al., 2011). However, the information must keep receiving attention through repetition or rehearsal, or it will be lost within a short duration of 20-30 seconds. That is one reason educators must be sure to gain students' attention before instruction and keep students engaged throughout instruction. Once attention is lost, the information will be lost from working memory (Nath & Cmajdalka, 2011). Miller (1956) posited that the storage capacity of working memory is limited to seven items, plus or minus two of new information; trying to store more new information results in overload and the information is lost (Woolfolk, 1998). One way to store more information in working memory is through chunking, or grouping small bits of information into chunks. One such example is the arrangement of phone numbers and social security numbers. Each long number is chunked into groups of three or four, thus allowing more items to be stored in working memory (Nath & Cmajdalka, 2011).Working memory is often called the workbench, where the brain not only stores information, but actively works with it. It is here that mental work is conducted (Baddeley, 1986) by holding new information, using it, such as in mathematical computations, and making connections with knowledge from long-term memory (Martinez, 2010). However, the duration of storage is only about 5 to 20 seconds (Woolfolk, 1998). Mental rehearsal is one way of keeping information activated so that it can be retained long enough to be transferred to long-term memory, the brain's permanent storage system. This process is called encoding (Nath & Cmajdalka, 2011). Two types of rehearsal are maintenance rehearsal, the repetition of the information in the mind, and elaborative rehearsal, the connection of new information with old information from long-term memory. According to Woolfolk (1998), maintenance rehearsal is useful for retaining information that is useful for only a short time, and then forgotten, like a telephone number. However, elaborative rehearsal is connection-making. It not only helps retain information in working memory but helps the transfer to long-term memory, which holds well-learned information that may be retrieved indefinitely, depending upon representation and organization of the information (Woolfolk, 1998). Therefore teachers must ensure that students transfer, or encode, information from working memory into long-term memory, which is permanent memory storage (Nath & Cmajdalka, 2011).

Long-term memory differs from working memory in several ways. Although information enters working memory very quickly, it is transferred to long-term memory relatively slowly. While the capacity of working memory to hold new information is limited, the capacity of long-term memory is unlimited. Also, while the retrieval of information from working memory is immediate, access to information in long-term memory requires more time and effort (Woolfolk, 1998).

Criticisms of Information Processing Theory

Although the computer is useful to use as a metaphor for the human mind because they both store memory, they are both durable and temporary, they both transform or act upon information, and they are both open systems that can receive input and transform it as output, it is not an exact comparison, because there are differences that must be considered (Martinez, 2010). First, computers do not have the humanistic qualities of personality, purpose, beliefs, and affect. Next, computers do not possess the consciousness of self-awareness that humans have. Although these differences do not preclude the usage of the computer as the model for information processing (Martinez, 2010), the additive nature of cognitive research necessitates that the computer model be integrated with the developmental, self-regulatory, social, cultural, and self-efficacy components of Piaget, Vygotsky, and Bandura's theories. The metacognitive model, as described in the next section, provides an avenue to incorporate all of these concepts.

Metacognition Cognitive Model

Metacognition adds a humanistic emphasis to the concepts from information processing theory and has been described as "cognition about cognition" (Woolfolk, 2010, p. 267). Morrow (2012) writes, "*Metacognition* is one's own awareness of how his or her learning is taking place" (p. 207). Nath and Cmajdalka (2011) define metacognition as "a complex cognitive process that requires knowledge of and control over one's own mental processes" (p. 151) to enable students to problem solve by learning and selecting strategies that enable them to gain knowledge. Metacognition stresses the importance of the explicit teaching of learning strategies. Students must be taught different types of thinking strategies, and then be taught how to recognize and choose which ones to use, depending upon their needs and the content of the information to be learned (Gaskins & Pressley, 2010).

Metacognitive strategies include *metamemory* (Martinez, 2010). According to Martinez (2010), students with good metamemory have an accurate appraisal of what they do and do not know. Research shows that superior metamemory is correlated to superior achievement (Tobias & Everson, 1996). Self-regulation is important in comprehension of new learning because students who are metacognitively aware continually ask themselves whether or not they understand what they are reading. This self-regulation monitors comprehension, and, based on their awareness of their understanding, students can choose various metacognitive strategies, such as pausing, rereading, discussing content with peers, attending tutoring session, or seeking clarification from teachers. However, students who have a lack of self-regulation, may continue to read text without realizing that they are not comprehending text. These students do not register their lack of comprehension, so they continue their ineffective reading, assuming that this lack of comprehension is their normal state. Teachers must explicitly teach metacognitive skills so that their use becomes ingrained within students' arsenals of learning strategies (Martinez, 2010).

Recent Research on Metacognition

Piaget's (1964/1997) concept of self-regulation is important to metacognitive theory. McMillan (2010) incorporates the lens of self-regulation theory in qualitative research on how effective students learn. McMillan (2010) recognizes that self-regulation theory within metacognition "synthesizes cognitive, motivational, affective and social-contextual factors in the construction of explanations of learning" (p. 1), an important component of metacognition. McMillan (2010) writes, "Metacognition strategies, such as planning, monitoring, and self-regulating cognition, manifest as information-seeking, time management, and critical thinking" (p. 1). Other metacognitive and self-regulative strategies used by students in this research include (a) rehearsal, (b) highlighting main ideas, (c) repetition, (d) summarizing, and (e) paraphrasing (McMillan, 2010).

Validation of Cognitivism

Cognitive science is a rapidly developing field that is constantly being affected by advances in methodology, neuroscience, and other areas (Woolfolk, 1998). Rather than refuting the various aspects of cognitivism, newer research seems to add to the constantly growing base of evidence that humans have the innate faculty to construct knowledge through building and adjusting schemata as they continue to interact with their environment.

Bandura's (1989) research enhances the understanding of cognitive science with his addition of social cognitive theory, in which human agency is increasingly important to the mental processing of information, and is integrated with environmental contexts through "the model of reciprocal causation [through which] people partly determine the nature of their environment and are influenced by it" (p. 1182). Scribner (1985) adds to the validity of this theory with her work on situated learning, writing that the active learning process is "a synthesis of mental and behavioral processes" (p. 452), calling attention to "the apparent reciprocity of influence between the subject and the environment" (Schauffele & Baptistse (2000, p. 452).

Mestre, Thaden-Koch, Dufresne, and Gerace (2004) revealed another aspect of cognition that continues to add to the knowledge of cognitivism: the theory that misconceptions often occur throughout domains, and that educators must consider how to address these misconceptions through questioning and reteaching (Martinez, 2010). In addition, Howard Gardner's (1985) research on multiple intelligences has changed the way that people view intelligence. Rather than reliance on earlier beliefs that intelligence is fixed at birth, Gardner (1985) shows that intelligence can be enhanced, and he emphasizes that a person's strengths in one or more of nine different intelligences can be enhanced through experience and the use of instructional strategies to enable humans to use several pathways to learning. In addition, neuroscience has influenced cognitivism additively by further delineating the differences between the brain and the mind. According to Martinez (2010), the field of mind/brain connection has now assigned

> importance both to the abstraction of the mind and to the biological substrate of the mind—the human brain. The mind depends on the brain ... [and] the development of the brain also depends on the mind and its activity. (p. 233)

From an integrative, holistic point of view, the metacognitive model is a useful structure in which to integrate the previous theories. This model is in congruence with Bandura's (1989) statement on the importance of self-efficacy beliefs, "Among the mechanisms of personal agency, none is more central or pervasive than people's beliefs about their capabilities to exercise control over events that affect their lives" (p. 1175). The use of metacognitive strategies that allow students to learn how to learn boost their self-perceptions of self-efficacy, which leads to higher achievement (Martinez, 2010). In addition, the metacognition model includes the explicit modeling and scaffolding techniques integral to Vygotsky's (1978) theory of socially mediated learning for higher cognition. Furthermore, the scaffolded teaching that occurs within Vygotsky's (1978) zone of proximal development is congruent with what later cognitive researchers have added to Piaget's biological stage development theory, that although learning tasks are dependent upon a child's developmental level, completion of higher-level tasks can be affected by outside environmental influences, such as high exposure to content and extra instruction, which in turn is in congruence with the knowledge and use of metacognitive strategies from the metacognitive model, as well as the importance of the performance of mental action upon stimuli from information processing theory to encode and transfer information from working memory to long-term memory (Nath & Cmajdalka, 2011), as well as the scaffolding and guided practice that is important to Vygotsky's theory, and the self-efficacy of Bandura's theory.

Generalizability Across Cultures, Ethnicities, and Genders

The majority of cognitive research is additive, rather than subtractive. For example, although some researchers have found that certain cognitive abilities may become apparent earlier than Piaget's developmental stages indicate (Cohen & Cashon, 2006), and that Piaget's stages are not only biological, and developmentally dependent, but they are more dependent upon cultural influences than Piaget originally conceived (Maynard, 2008), and cognition can be heavily influenced by environmental factors such as precocious, extremely high content knowledge, diverse personal experiences and cultural influences, and additional instruction (Rackley & Knight, 2011).

Bandura (1989) adds to this additive perspective of cognitivism through his research on social cognitive theory, which stresses the importance of self-efficacy beliefs of the individual in the learning process. According to Bandura (1989)

> Persons are neither autonomous agents nor simply mechanical conveyers or animating environmental influences. Rather they make causal contribution to their own motivation and action within a system of triadic reciprocal causation. In this model of reciprocal causation, action, cognitive, affective, and other personal factors, and environmental events all operate as interacting determinants. (p. 1175)

Additive Nature of Cognitivism

From an integrative, holistic point of view, current applications of the cognitive model are useful structures in which to integrate previous theories. Cognitivism, especially as viewed through the lens of metacognitive theory, is in congruence with Bandura's (1989) statement on the importance of self-efficacy beliefs that, "among the mechanisms of personal agency, none is more central or pervasive than people's beliefs about their capabilities to exercise control over events that affect their lives" (p. 1175). The use of metacognitive strategies that allow students to learn how to learn boosts their self-perceptions of self-efficacy, which leads to higher achievement (Martinez, 2010). In addition, the metacognition model includes Piaget's concept (1967/1997) self- regulation, and the explicit modeling and scaffolding techniques integral to Vygotsky's (1978) theory of socially mediated learning for higher cognition. Furthermore, the scaffolded teaching that occurs within Vygotsky's (1978) zone of proximal development is congruent with what later cognitive researchers have added to Piaget's biological stage development theory, that although learning tasks are dependent upon a child's developmental level, completion of higher-level tasks can be affected by outside environmental influences, such as high exposure to content and extra instruction, which in turn is in congruence with the knowledge and use of metacognitive strategies from the metacognitive model, as well as the importance of the performance of mental action upon stimuli from information processing theory to encode and transfer information from working memory to long-term memory (Nath & Cmajdalka, 2011), as well as the scaffolding and guided practice that is important to Vygotsky's theory, and the self-efficacy of Bandura's theory.

Relatedly, neuroscience and neural imagery have begun to open new research areas in the area of cognitive neuroscience as new technologies continue to enable scientists to locate specific areas of the brain that affect short-term and working memory, mathematical activity, and language, allowing cognitive scientists to "map cognitive functioning to specific brain anatomy" (Martinez, 2010). These advances have led to the generalizability of cognitivism across cultures, ethnicities, and genders (Bandera, 2002; Martinez, 2010; Maynard, 2008).

Critiques of Cognitivism

As stated earlier in this chapter, the majority of research is additive, rather than subtractive. Gibbs (2006) writes that cognitivism has neglected to consider *embodiment*, which he defines, as "understanding the role of an agent's own body in its everyday, situated cognition" (p. 1). Some researchers have shown that the ability to transform mental images is linked to motor processes, and specifically concerning Piaget's (1964/1997) developmental stages, they have found that concepts may occur from bodily actions, as well as felt experiences (Stenlund, 1997). Others have posited that although cognitivism has failed to provide a detailed account of the mental activities it purports to study (Erneling, 1997) rather than focusing on the early cognitive focus of the "model inner structural aspects of the mind" (p. 381) that additive work should augment cognitivism, with the addition of ecological work, such as "studies of discourse, actions and interpersonal networks, [and] historical developments" (Erneling, 1997). As mentioned earlier in the chapter, the critiques have been additive in nature, leading to an integration of mind, brain, thought, body, and action within the framework of mental processes, illustrating Mandler's (2008) agreement with Hegel that there is a "spiral of thought, with topics recurring repeatedly in the history of a discipline, often at a more sophisticated or developed level" (p. 351).

Instruments Associated With Cognitivism

Cognitive assessments may include IQ tests, achievement tests, and learning styles tests. However, one instrument used to measure cognition is the Cognitive Assessment Interview, which is a 10-item, interview based instrument that measures cognitive functioning (Ventura et al., (2010). Another instrument used in a study of self-efficacy of Hispanic college students, the 20-item, College Self-Efficacy Instrument, was found to have internal consistency and convergent and discriminant validity (Solberg, O'Brian, Villarreal, Kennel, & Davis, 1993).

References

Baddeley, A. (1986). *Working memory.* Oxford, England: Clarendon.

Bandura, A. (1989). Human agency in social cognitive theory. *American Psychologist, 44*(9), 1175-1184.

Bandura, A. (1993). Perceived self-efficacy in cognitive development and functioning. *Educational Psychologist, 28*(2), 117-148.

Bandura, A. (1999). Social cognitive theory: An agentic perspective. *Asian Journal of Social Psychology, 2*, 21-41.

Bandura, A. (2002). Social cognitive theory in cultural context. *Applied Psychology: An International Review, 51*(2), 269-290.

Bandura, A. (2006). Toward a psychology of human agency. *Perspectives on Psychological Science,* 1(2), 164-180. doi10.1111/j.1745-6916.2006.00011.x

Brunig, R. H., Schraw, G. J., & Norby, M. M. (2011). *Cognitive psychology and instruction* (5th ed.). Boston, MA: Allyn & Bacon.

Chomsky, N. (1959). A review of B. F. Skinner's "Verbal behavior." *Language, 35*(1), 26-58.

Chomsky, N. (1965). *Aspects of theory of syntax.* Cambridge, MA: The M.I.T. Press.

Chomsky, N. (2000). *New horizons in the study of language and mind.* New York, NY: Cambridge Press.

Cohen, L. B., & Cashon, C. H. (2006). Infant cognition. In W. Damon & R. M. Lerner (Series Eds.) & D. Kun & R. S. Siegler (Vol. Eds.), *Handbook of child psychology: Vol. 2. Cognition, perception, and language* (6th ed., pp. 214-251). New York, NY: Wiley.

Eggan, P., & Kauchak, D. (2004). *Educational psychology: Windows on classrooms* (6th ed.). Upper Saddle River, NY: Merrill Prentice Hall.

Erneling, C. (1997). Cognitive science and the future of psychology. In D. M. Johnson & C. E. Erneling (Eds.), *The future of the cognitive revolution* (pp. 376-382). New York, NY: Oxford University Press.

Fox, N. A. (2006). How can research on the brain inform and expand our thinking about human development? *Human Development*, 49, 257-259.

Gardner, H. (1985). *The mind's new science.* New York, NY: Basic Books.

Gaskins, I. W., & Pressley, M. (2007). Teaching metacognitive strategies that address executive function processes within a schoolwide curriculum. In L. Meltzer (Ed.), *Executive function in education: From theory to practice* (pp. 261-286). New York, NY: Guilford Press.

Gibbs, R. W., Jr. (2006). *Embodiment and cognitive science*. Cambridge, England: Cambridge University Press.

Hammock, E. A. D., & Levitt, P. (2006). The discipline of neurobehavioral development: The emerging interface of processes that build circuits and skills. *Human Development, 49,* 294-309.

Martinez, M. E. (2010). *Learning and cognition: The design of the mind*. Upper Saddle River, NJ: Pearson Education.

Maynard, A. E. (2008). What we thought we knew and how we came to know it: Four decades of cross-cultural research from a Piagetian point of view. *Human Development, 51,* 56-65.

Mestre, J., Thaden-Koch, T., Dufresne, R., & Gerace, W. (2004). The dependence of knowledge deployment on context among physics novices. In E. Redish & M. Vicentini (Eds.), *Proceedings of the International School of Physics "Enrico Fermi," Course CLVI, research on physics education* (pp. 367-408). Amsterdam, The Netherlands: IOS Press.

McMillan, W. J. (2010). "Your thrust is to understand": How academically successful students learn. *Teaching in Higher Education, 15*(1), 1-3.

Miller, G. A. (1956). The magical number seven, plus or minus two: Some limits on our capacity for processing information. *Psychological Review, 63,* 81-97.

Morrow, L. M. (2012). *Literacy development in the early years: Helping children read and write*. Upper Saddle River, NJ: Pearson Education.

Nath, J. L., & Cmajdalka, S. (2011). Understanding learning theory and other factors that impact learning. In J. L. Nath & M. D. Cohen (Eds.), *Becoming an EC-6 teacher in Texas* (pp. 140-184). Belmont, CA: Cengage Learning.

Nelson, C. A., Moulson, M. C., & Richmond, J. (2006). How does neuroscience inform the study of cognitive development? *Human Development, 49,* 260-272.

Overskeid, G. (2008). They should have thought about the consequences: The crisis of cognitivism and a second chance for behavior analysis. *The Psychological Record, 58,* 131-151.

Piaget, J. (1997). Development and learning. In M. Gauvain & M. Cole (Eds.), *Readings on the development of children* (pp. 19-28). New York, NY: W. H. Freeman. (Reprinted from *Piaget rediscovered: A report of the Conference on Cognitive Studies and Curriculum Development* (pp. 7-20), by R. E. Ripple & V. N. Rockcastle, Eds., 1964, Ithaca, NY: Cornell University Press).

Rackley, R. A., & Knight, S. L. (2011). Understanding development in children in grades EC through 6. In J. L. Nath & M. D. Cohen (Eds.), *Becoming an EC-6 teacher in Texas* (pp. 4-42). Belmont: CA: Cengage Learning.

Schaufelle, S., & Baptiste, I. (2000). Appealing to the soul: Towards a Judeo-Christian theory of learning. *International Journal of Lifelong Education, 12*(3), 448-458.

Scribner, S. (1985). Knowledge at work. *Anthropology & Education Quarterly, 16,* 199-206.

Solberg, V. S., O'Brien, K., Villarreal, P., Kennel, R., & Davis, B. (1993). Self-efficacy and Hispanic college students: Validation of the College Self-Efficacy Instrument. *Hispanic Journal of Behavioral Sciences, 15*(1), 80-95. doi:10.1177/07399863930151004

Stenlund, S. (1997). Language, action, and mind. In D. M. Johnson & C. E. Enerling (Eds.), *The future of the cognitive revolution* (pp. 302 -316). New York, NY: Oxford University Press.

Tobias, S., & Everson, H. T. (1996). *Assessing metacognitive knowledge monitoring* (College Board Report No. 996-1). New York, NY: College Board.

Ventura, J., Reise, S. P., Keefe, R. S. E., Baade, L. E., Gold, J. M., Green, M. F., ... Bilder, R. M. (2010). The Cognitive Assessment Interview (CAI): Development and validation of an empirically derived, brief interview-based measure of cognition. *Schizophrenia Research, 121,* 24-31. Retrieved from www.elsevier.com/locate/schres

Vygotsky, L. S. (1978). *Mind in society: The development of psychological processes*. Cambridge, MA: Harvard University Press.

Woolfolk, A. E. (1998). *Educational psychology* (7th ed.). Needham Heights, MD: Allyn & Bacon.

Author Contact Information: Karen D. Paciotti, EdD, Assistant Professor, Department of Teacher Education, College of Education, Texas A&M University-Corpus Christi, Faculty Center 220, 6300 Ocean Drive, Corpus Christi, TX 78412-5818. E-mail: Karen.paciotti@tamucc.edu

CHAPTER 10

Experiential Learning Theory

Anita Zijdemans-Boudreau
Pacific University

Glenda Moss
University of North Texas at Dallas

Cheu-jey G. Lee
Indiana University-Purdue University Fort Wayne, Indiana

Learning has been a major area of research attention for decades. Researchers have become interested in understanding the process of learning and its implications for pedagogical approaches. According to Bergsteiner, Avery, and Neumann (2010), Coffield, Moseley, Hall, and Ecclestone (2004) did a comprehensive review of the experiential learning field and identified 71 learning styles models, 13 of which were regarded as major contributions. Among them is the highly influential model developed by David Kolb (1984). In formulating his model of experiential learning, Kolb primarily built on the work of Dewey (1938), who stressed the importance of experience in the process of learning; Lewin (1951), who underlined active participatory learning; and Piaget (1970), who conceived of intelligence as largely a result of the interaction of the individual with the environment. Kolb defines learning in his experiential learning theory as "the process whereby knowledge is created through the transformation of experience" (cited in Lee, McCullouch, & Chang, 2008, p. 158). Knowledge results from the combination of obtaining and transforming experience. Specifically, Kolb (1984) posits that learning is a process involving constant adaptation to, and engagement with, one's environment. Individuals create knowledge from experience rather than just from received instruction. Conflicts, disagreements, and differences are inevitable in the learning process.

Kolb (1976, 1984) refers to learning as four modes: concrete experience (CE), reflective observation (RO), abstract conceptualization (AC), and active experimentation (AE), based on the bipolar dimensions of cognitive growth and learning, which can be represented by the concrete-abstract continuum and the reflective-active continuum. The concrete-abstract continuum corresponds to how individuals obtain information from their environment based on their preference for involvement with particular and concrete events in CE as opposed to conceptual analysis or logical thinking and evaluation based on basic theories in AC. The reflective-active continuum, which represents how individuals process the information they obtain, ranges from learners who take a more observational role in learning as in RO to those who prefer active participation in AE. Immediate or concrete experiences are the basis for observations and reflections. These reflections are assimilated and distilled into abstract concepts, from which new implications for action can be drawn. These implications can be actively tested and serve as guides in creating new experiences.

Kolb suggests that as a result of repeated person-environment interactions in particular types of learning environments, individuals develop preferred ways of processing information from the world, that is, characteristic learning styles. Kolb (1999a, 1999b) created the Learning Style Inventory (LSI) to assess individual learning styles. Whereas individuals tested on the LSI show many different patterns of scores, research on the instrument has identified four prevalent learning

The Handbook of Educational Theories, pp. 115–123

styles: divergers, assimilators, convergers, and accommodators.

Divergers

Divergers have strong CE and RO skills and prefer concrete people-oriented learning experiences. They tend to be imaginative and emotional, have broad cultural interests, and tend to specialize in the arts. In formal learning situations, people with the diverging style prefer to work in groups, listening with an open mind, and receiving personalized feedback. This learning style is characteristic of counselors, personal managers, and others with humanities and liberal-arts backgrounds.

Assimilators

Assimilators have highly developed RO and AC competencies. They are best at understanding a wide range of information and putting it into concise, logical form. Assimilators are less focused on people and more interested in ideas and abstract concepts. This learning style is characteristic of persons in the basic sciences and mathematics.

Convergers

Convergers have strong AC and AE learning skills and are good at testing out theories or ideas in practical situations. They prefer to deal with technical tasks and problems rather than with social and interpersonal issues. These learning skills are important for effectiveness in specialist and technology careers.

Accommodators

Accommodators have highly developed AE and CE learning competencies and excel at carrying out plans and seeking out new experiences. They learn primarily from "hands-on" experience. They tend to act on "gut" feelings rather than on logical analysis. In solving problems, accommodators rely on people for information more than on their own technical analysis. Accommodators are prone to be more of risk takers than persons in other learning style categories. They tend to solve problem in a trial-and-error manner. This learning style is important for effectiveness in action-oriented careers such as marketing or sales.

Validation of the Theory

The literature provides a number of opportunities for validating experiential learning theory. Kolb and Kolb's (2009) bibliography of research on ELT includes 1,004 studies that were conducted across multiple fields, many of them providing "empirical support for the constructs of ELT using the Learning Styles Inventory, and more recently, the Learning Skills Profile and Adaptive Styles Inventory. About 55% of this research has appeared in refereed journal articles, 20% in doctoral dissertations, and 10% in books and book chapters" (Mainemelis, Boyatzis, & Kolb, 2002, p. 12). The Kolb's experiential learning theory (KELT) literature further shows that a vast proportion exists on the contribution of ELT, a large amount relates to reliability and validity studies of the LSI and its revisions, and finally a smaller percentage provides analyses of the theory itself (Bergsteiner et al., 2010). Here, validation of KELT is discussed in relation to its contribution to the learning theory discourse, key strengths, and psychometric features.

Kolb's comprehensive three-part experiential learning theory—the experiential learning theory (ELT); a learning cycle model; and the Learning Styles Inventory (LSI)—has stimulated considerable engagement in learning theory discourse. Laschinger (1990), for instance, endorses ELT have having potential for guiding "whole brain education" or a holistic view of learning that emphasizes the affective as well as cognitive aspects of learning. With respect to action learning, Kolb's learning cycle model is described as significant in that it "provides a step by step sequence which ought to be followed if the full potential for learning is to be created from the action learning process" (Mumford, 2006, p. 72).

Dyke (2009) posits that ELT should emphasize the role of reflection and learning with others to "encourage people to critically engage with other forms of expertise, reflect upon the received wisdom of others, test it in practice and be open to the creation of knowledge that works in a given time and place, without compromising the lives and futures of others" (p. 295). Finally, Quay (2003) advises moving beyond the practical focus by establishing conceptual structures to formalize and validate experiential education theory. As context plays an intricate role in learning, consideration of the situated nature of learning will shift the focus from the individual learner to learning as participation in the social world. He proposes a more holistic philosophical approach that contemplates learning through experience at the levels of the individual [constructivism], the small group [social constructionism], and culture [cultural discourse] will support a deeper analysis of experiential education within learning discourses.

Because ELT presents a wide-ranging theory of learning style differences, its implementation spans across multiple disciplines seeking to understand the dynamics of learning, education, and the workplace. Of the 1,004 studies noted in the bibliography of research on ELT, 207 were conducted in the field of management, 430 in education, 104 in computer studies, 101 in psychology, 72 in medicine, as well as others in nursing, accounting, and law (Mainemelis et al., 2002). The use and application of theory are described in detail elsewhere; however, in relation to the issue of validation ELT can be summarized as having the following key strengths:

First, it provides insights into students' learning style preferences that can help instructors to better match their teaching methods to the strengths of their students (Baker, Simon, & Bazeli, 2001), as well as determine appropriate curriculum planning, implementation, and evaluation strategies (Sugarman, 1985). Second, by enabling individuals to understand their own preferences, ELT can help empower them to become more self-directed in setting skills development goals for learning or work (Kluge, 2007) or, provide a means for evaluating career choices that might best fit with their styles (Atkinson & Murrell, 1988; Baker et al., 2001). Last, programs and organizations can use KELT to promote higher learner engagement through the development of simulation-based learning environments that allow individuals to learn by doing (Kluge, 2007, Laschinger, 1990), and—in the case of Kolb Team Learning Experience—learn how to work more effectively in teams (Kayes, Kayes, & Kolb, 2005).

Bergsteiner et al. (2010) note that a large amount of ELT literature relates to reliability and validity studies of the LSI and its revisions. In the Mainemelis et al. (2002) review of Hickox's qualitative analyses of 81 studies, results indicated "overall 61.7% of the studies supported ELT, 16.1% showed mixed support, and 22.2% did not support the theory [and] a meta-analysis of 101 quantitative studies of ELT and LSI ... found that 49 studies showed strong support for the LSI, 40 showed mixed support and 12 studies showed no support" (p. 12).

Although a number of studies criticize KELT (see section on critiques of the theory), many examples can be found validating Kolb's work whether it be his cycle of learning (Sugarman, 1985), his technical manual replete with split-half and test-retest reliability measures (Baker et al., 2001), support for the model's orthogonal factors (Sadler-Smith, 2001), or statistical interpretations showing that "ipsative procedure are not always inferior to normative procedures" (Brew, 2002, p. 375).

Overall, it is not uncommon to find studies in education and health professions expressing findings similar to the following by Laschinger (1990), "In this review, the results of studies in a variety of nursing samples have provided encouraging support for the validity of experiential learning theory in nursing education settings" (p. 992). Also worth noting are some newer explorations such as Brew's (2002) evidence suggesting that "interpretation of the LSI is sensitive to gender and that the construct validity of the instrument's scores varies for females and males in this sample" (p. 386).

Use and Application of Experiential Learning Theory

Sugarman (1985) perceived that Kolb's experiential learning theory would be useful for trainers, students, counselors, and clients. Accounting for differing learning styles could inform the kinds of learning activities to engage trainers and students, and counselors and clients in effective learning relationships. During the past three decades, experiential learning theory has been used to actively engage learners in the process of identifying their learning styles, understanding discipline concepts, and constructing meaningful connection to practice as professional development and/or to effect change in communities. This bridge between classroom learning for living in society and learning through community experiences appears in the form of teamwork (Kayes et al., 2005), Socratic seminars and process drama (Baer & Glasgow, 2010), simulations (Kluge, 2007; Xu & Yang, 2010), clinical practice, field trips (Rone, 2008), ee-learning (Donovan, 2008) and service-learning (Permaul, 2009; Levesque-Bristol, Knapp, & Fisher, 2010). It has been applied to learning in a number of fields, including business education (Nees, Willey, & Masfield, 2010; Xu & Yang, 2010), construction engineering education (Lee et al., 2008), chemistry education (Pedrosa de Jesus, Almeida, Teixeira-Dias, & Watts, 2000), music education (Schmidt, 2010), nursing education (Laschinger, 1990), career counseling (Atkinson & Murrell, 1988; Turesky & Mundhenk, 2008), communication skill development (Stokes-Eley, 2007), and enterprise education (Dorasamy, 2009). In a study of undergraduate medical students, experiential learning was found to be the dominant learning process (Niemantsverdriet, van der Vleuten, Majoor & Scherpbier, 2005).

Although Kolb (1984) came to the conclusion that all learning is experiential, educators have found value in examining the learning process through the framework of ELT to create learning activities that provide students with concrete experiences, giving them a basis for deeper reflection and construction of knowledge. It is in the creation of learning experiences that educators ask questions concerning the generalizability of experiential learning theory across cultures, ethnicities, and genders. Anderson (1988) and Boud and Walker (1993) critiqued experiential learning theory for a lack of attention to cultural and gender specific learning preferences. Kolb and Kolb (2005) found that age, gender, level of education and area of expertise were significant influences on learning styles. Kluge (2007) found that positive learning outcomes resulting form experiential learning methods is connected to the participating learners. Experiential learning theory, then, is generalizable across cultures, ethnicities, and gender if the target population's values and goals are closely considered when designing learning experiences.

Learning styles inventories that have resulted from Kolb's (1985, 1985) experiential learning theory may assist instructors and facilitators in constructing meaningful activities. Knowing that Kolb's LSI is sensitive to gender (Brew, 2008; Knight, Elfenbein, & Messina, 1995), attention can be given to the differences in the way that males and females interpret the LSI items. Joy and Kolb (2009) used experiential learning theory to assess differences in how individuals learn across cultures in comparison by gender, age, level of education and educational specialization. Culture plays an important role in learning styles.

Critiques of the Theory

Although experiential learning theory is widely endorsed, mixed support and nonsupport as cited by Mainemelis et al. (2010) and others suggest that a lively debate exists in the literature. This section considers criticisms of ELT more generally then focuses on Kolb's theory, cyclical model, and LSI instrument.

- At a broader level, there is some skepticism regarding the validity of learning preference styles research and its contribution to the discourse.
- Theories of learning in experiential education lack an "embeddedness" in the world creating a gulf between learning *theory* and experiential learning as *practice*. Understanding of learning in experiential education needs to be advanced in order to encompass a practice of experiential education, which is based very firmly in the social and cultural world. (Quay, 2003, p. 111)
- Illeris (2007) also notes that in coming to the conclusion that all learning is experiential learning, Kolb himself has made "this reference rather meaningless or empty" (p. 84).

With respect to KELT, the approach has been criticized for simplifying the complexities of the learning process and presenting an eclectic theoretical model that inadequately represents its Lewinian and Deweyan foundations (Dyke, 2006, 2009). Miettinen (2000) elaborates, "It appears to me that the concept of experiential learning, in the form used by Kolb and the adult education tradition, represents the kind of psychological reductionism that Dewey considered a misinterpretation of his antidualist conception of experience" (p. 70).

The validity of Kolb's cyclical model of the learning process is well accepted with some advocating its abstract feature as being a strength as it allows for more flexible applications (Sugarman, 1985; Baker et al., 2001). Others, however, judge the model as flawed, presenting an inflexible structure, and failing to meet the test of graphic sufficiency and simplification (Bergsteiner et al., 2010).

Similarly, while many applaud LSI's success in demonstrating differences in an individual's preferred learning style, others list a host of weaknesses related to its: forced-choice ranking and scoring method; use of an ipsative scaling; questionable classifications of some items; test-retest reliability; volatility of individual scores; lack of relational consistency and correlation; and sequential framework (Baker et al., 2001; Bergsteiner et al., 2010; Sadler-Smith, 2001; Brew, 2002; Mumford, 2006).

In response to these criticisms, Kolb and colleagues quote authors who have effectively addressed problems associated with the free-choice method, ipsative scaling, and the like. In addition, they have conducted their own research which has subsequently led to the release of newer LSI versions that they argue are more psychometrically sound (Brew, 2002; Kolb & Kolb, 2005). In his defense, Kolb further states that the LSI was developed as a starting point for gaining insights into an individual's approach to learning, and was not intended for use without support by other learning theory research.

In summary, as the mixed response to ELT is notable in the literature it too warrants some mention. Mumford (2006), for example, faults the model for creating too rigid a formulation of individual differences, and yet suggests that Kolb's work presents a means of understanding and acting upon the consequences of those individual differences within action learning programs. Additionally, Baker et al. (2001) provide a review of several studies that speak to the strengths and weaknesses of ELT. They refer to a Wunderlich and Gjerde follow-up study that critiques the LSI or learning style approach, but only to the extent to which an individual's learning style preferences may be associated with specific career choices. Two additional studies endorse the validity of ELT at the group level, nevertheless, question the application of the instrument on an individual-by-individual basis due to variance in an individual's learning process.

Instruments Associated With the Theory

Though the notion of individual differences is often linked to Binet's first intelligence tests in the early 1900s, the concept of learning style preferences is commonly associated with Kolb, Dunn, Honey and Mumford, and others. A number of instruments have been developed to measure learning styles, many of them adaptations of Kolb's model for different contexts. This section provides a brief overview of a sampling of instruments most commonly associated with ELT, with a view to assisting the reader in understanding some of their general similarities and differences.

Learning Styles Inventory

Of the three components that comprise Kolb's experiential learning theory (KELT)—the experiential learning theory (ELT); a learning cycle model; and the Learning Styles Inventory (LSI)—the LSI instrument was developed as a construct validation of the ELT and self-assessment to test the theory (Bergsteiner et al., 2010; Mainemelis et al., 2002). The LSI was first implemented in 1969 for a MIT curriculum development project as "an experiential educational exercise designed to help learners understand the process of experiential learning and their unique individual style of learning from experience" (Kolb & Kolb, 2005, p. 8). It has evolved over several versions since the 1980s, largely in response to critiques about its psychometric soundness in areas such as construct validity and reliability (Brew, 2002).

The LSI is a 9- to 12-item, self-ranking questionnaire that uses a forced-choice method structure. Six variables are assessed, the individual preferences among the four abstract, concrete, active and reflective orientations, as well as two combination scores that measure preference for abstractness over concreteness (AC-CE), and action over reflection (AE-RO) (Baker et al., 2001; Kolb & Kolb, 2005). To that end, the instrument tests the theoretical assumption that "the more balanced a person is in their dialectic preference, the more they will experience a creative tension or attraction to both poles opening a wider space for flexible adaptation and development of learning skill" (Mainemelis, Boyatzis & Kolb, 2002, p. 8).

Learning Styles Questionnaire

Honey and Mumford developed the Learning Styles Questionnaire as an alternative to Kolb's LSI that would be more relevant to industry and management, though it has since also been applied to education. They propose that their version of the learning cycle can be applied to all kinds of learning, not just the hands-on experiences generally associated with ELT (Mumford, 2006). The instrument is an 80-item self-report inventory that measures an individual's tendency or preferred learning style as indicated by their ratings of behavioral and preference orientations. The four learning styles measured by the learning styles questionnaire are: (a) activist (Kolb's active experimentation); (b) reflector (Kolb's reflective observation); (c) theorist (Kolb's abstract conceptualization); and (d) Pragmatist (Kolb's concrete experience) (Cassidy, 2004, p. 432).

Grasha-Riechmann Student Learning Style Scales

Grasha defines learning style as "a child's preferences in thinking and interaction with other children in different classroom environments and experiences" (Baykul et al., 2010, p. 177). The Grasha-Riechmann Student Learning Style scales was created to determine college students' styles of classroom participation focusing on their attitudes toward learning, classroom activities, teachers, and peers. The original scale had three learning styles, but in 1976 was extended to include six styles each of which is composed of 10 items. Students are separated into six groups: (a) independent; (b) dependent; (c) collaborative; (d) competitive; (e) contributive or participative; and (f) avoidant (Baker et al., 2001; Baykul et al., 2010).

Dunn Learning Styles Inventory

Dunn and Dunn define learning style as the way in which each learner begins to concentrate, process and retain new and difficult information. The original 1978 Dunn and Dunn 228-item Learning Style Questionnaire was created for school aged students in grades 3 through 12. In 1989, it was redesigned as the Dunn Learning Styles Inventory to identify an individual's strengths and preferences via an assessment of 22 factors representing five categories that determine how we learn: (a) environmental; (b) emotional; (c) sociological; (d) physical; and (e) psychological or processing. An adult version of the Dunn Learning Styles Inventory, called the Productivity Environmental Preference Survey, was also developed. It consists of 100 items measuring 20 factors (Baker et al., 2001).

Johnson Decision Making Inventory

The Decision Making Inventory provides a measure of typologies regarding decision making based on five characteristics: (a) goal orientation; (b) selecting among alternatives; (c) thinking patterns; (d) Speed of commitment to new ideas; and (e) reaction to events. These are used to differentiate between spontaneous and systematic dimensions of gathering information. The premise of the theory is that individuals can adapt behaviors associated with another style. As such, this approach has been used in helping people make use of their preferred styles in decision making and to understand individual differences (Baker et al., 2001; Coscarelli, 1983). The inventory has undergone 12 revisions since

1978 and in its current version consists of 36 questions (Vaught, 2007).

Adaptive Styles Inventory

The Adaptive Styles Inventory is an adaptation of Kolb's ELT designed to help employees or students understand their preferred learning styles, and improve or become more flexible in their approach to learning and problem solving situations. The instrument uses a 48-item, paired comparison method to rank learning preferences for four learning modes: (a) acting situations; (b) valuing situations; (c) thinking situations; and (d) deciding situations—in eight personalized learning contexts. It is particularly effective for newly created teams where members are just learning to work together, or with individuals who are new to a position or an organization. The goal is to help them assess their relative use of the learning styles, and how they apply and adapt each style to different situations (Mainemelis et al., 2002).

Learning Skills Profile

The Learning Skills Profile, another adaptation of ELT, is designed to help individuals identify areas of strength and weakness so that they can compare skill level with job demands and set goals for learning skills development. It has been used most commonly in learning needs assessment and program evaluation. The self-scoring inventory is a 72-item, modified Q-sort method for assessing levels of skill development in four skills areas that are related to four learning modes: (a) interpersonal skills (CE); (b) informational skills (RO); (c) analytical skills (AC); and (d) behavioral skills (AE) (Mainemelis et al., 2002).

The Kolb Team Learning Experience

The Kolb Team Learning Experience is an integrative, holistic approach to team learning based on ELT and Mill's (1967) developmental stages. The Kolb Team Learning Experience provides a structured step-by-step simulation where members of new or ongoing teams learn to manage the six aspects of team functioning: (a) shared purpose; (b) roles; (c) context; (d) process; (e) composition or membership; and e) actions. This approach "helps teams realize the importance and potential of team learning without falling prey to the problems that often plague teams during the learning process" (Kayes et al., 2005, p. 352).

Adaptive Competence Profile (ACP)

Developed by Kolb and Wolfe (1981, cited in Laschinger, 1990), the ACP has been used in the fields of engineering, social work and nursing to measure learning style and environmental press in order to determine a person's fit with the environment. The ACP requires learners to rate their level of skill on learning competences associated with each learning style. Ratings on these competencies are then applied to calculate a characteristic profile (Laschinger, 1990).

Environmental Press Questionnaire

Closely associated to the ACP is the Environmental Press Questionnaire, which determines learners' ratings of the importance of each learning competency for success in a specific learning environment. The instrument is scored in the same manner as the ACP in that scores assigned to each competency are then mapped to generate a visual representation of style and environmental press. Kolb used this instrument to "investigate differential contributions of different types of learning environments in the development of adaptive learning competences and to compare the effects of educational programmes and work environments on the development of these competences in engineers and social workers" (Laschinger, 1990, p. 987).

The instruments described here—a number of them theoretically similar but methodologically different from the LSI (Mainemelis et al., 2002)—have been applied both in numerous studies with a variety of populations such as medicine, dentistry, occupations, therapy, education, business administration, and the nursing professions (Laschinger, 1990), as well as at the individual, group or team, and organizational level. Many of the models use a bipolar continuum, whilst a smaller number are grounded in decades of history and research. Fewer yet are based on limited research, the quality of which is widely debated in the literature. Dunn (1990) further points out that many learning styles models are relatively new and cannot be observed in a variety of geographically, socioeconomically, and ethnically different schools or districts; whereas others are well established and can be observed in diverse programs.

Common to these approaches, nonetheless, is the acknowledgement that diversity exists amongst individuals and that consideration of individual differences across varied sectors and circumstances can yield multiple benefits making it a worthwhile endeavour. New directions in learning style preferences research, such as Brew's (2002) application of the LSI to gender studies, further suggest that exploration in heretofore unchartered territory is likely to continue into the future. In the final section, we provide example studies using experiential learning theory.

Example Studies Using Experiential Learning Theory

Experiential and Electronic Learning in a Graduate Education Course

Donovan (2008) taught a graduate level education course that utilized ee-learning (the combination of experiential and electronic learning) to break down barriers between theory and practice, and knowledge and experience. Donovan wanted to measure the effectiveness of an electronic class format combined with experiential learning, in terms of meeting course goals and student satisfaction with the class. The research questions were: "Was the ee-learning class successful?" and "If so, what ee-learning factors contributed to the successful outcomes of the course?"

A major assignment in the course was for students to donate a minimum of ten hours at a P-12 school site as different from their work site as possible, in terms of race, class, gender, and standardized state test scores. Students teaching at a suburban school with middle class white students could volunteer to work at a lower income urban or rural school with a predominantly minority student body. Conversely, students teaching in a mostly minority urban school needed to find a suburban or rural placement.

The electronic components of the course allowed students to record and share experiences, thoughts, and reactions in journals and discussions, view videos and explore web sites to learn about inequities in schools and society, and complete interactive web exercises designed to help users recognize their biases and misconceptions. The experiential learning component brought students into schools and community centers to observe and confront inequities first hand. These two pedagogies worked together to provide students with the knowledge and opportunity to move from passive observers to active proponents for educational equity. Students shared and reflected on experiences at volunteer sites, their personal lives, their individual school settings, and coursework, to create a powerful, integrated learning experience.

Results show that ee-learning can be an effective pedagogy for classes consisting of controversial, personal, and sensitive subject areas such as the exploration and discussion of beliefs concerning race, class, and gender. Donovan (2008) questioned if the results are generalizable to "other populations" and "other subject areas" (p. 76). She was not questioning the generalizability of ee-learning, but specifically engaging "students to explore issues of race, class and gender" (p. 76).

Field Trip Experience

In this study, Rone (2008) used the field trip in her course Language and Culture as a teaching pedagogy that draws on experiential learning. Rone aimed to demonstrate how a field trip to Sea Islands, South Carolina, presented an opportunity for undergraduate anthropology students to experience a learning continuum from course readings and films to a firsthand experience. The primary aim of the course was to introduce undergraduates to the core concepts and methods in linguistic anthropology. Secondary aims included (1) increasing student knowledge about the Gullah region, its people, and their culture; (2) challenging students to think critically about the tensions between representations of preserving culture and preserving culture; and (3) increasing student understanding of the linkages between the social sciences and policy.

Data were drawn from participant observations supplemented by field notes, photography, student discussion, and assignments and reflective essays completed by students enrolled in the course. Findings indicated that the field trip enriched students' learning experiences with practical, experiential learning that connected classroom experiences with firsthand experiences outside the classroom. Intellectually, these experiences contributed directly to how students (1) increased their knowledge and developed an appreciation for a cultural region, group, way or life, and Creole language, with which most knew little about before enrolling in the course; (2) concretized abstract core concepts in cultural and linguistic anthropology; (3) developed their skills in reflective observation and ability to substantiate general claims with specific evidence and examples; and (4) reached a better understanding through firsthand knowledge of the interface of theory, practice, and policy.

References

Anderson, J. A. (1988). Cognitive styles and multicultural populations. *Journal of Teacher Education, 39*(1), 2-9.

Atkinson, G., Jr., & Murrell, P. (1988). Kolb's experiential learning theory: A meta-model for career exploration. *Journal of Counseling and Development, 66*, 374-377.

Baer, A. L., & Glasgow, J. N. (2010). Negotiating understanding through the young adult literature of Muslim cultures. *Journal of Adolescent & Adult Literature, 54*(1), 23-32.

Baker, R. E., Simon, J. R., & Bazeli, F. P. (1986). An assessment of the learning style preferences of accounting majors. *Issues in Accounting Education, 4*, 1-11.

Baykul, Y., Gürsel, M., Sulak, H., Ertekin, E., Yazici, E. Dülger, O., … Büyükkarci, K. (2010). A validity and reliability study of Grasha-Riechmann Student Learning Style Scale (GRSLSS). *International Journal of Human and Social Science, 5*(5), 3-26. Retrieved from www.waset.org/journals/ijhss/v5/v5-3-26

Bergsteiner, H., Avery, G. C., & Neumann, R. (2010). Kolb's experiential learning model: Critique from a modeling perspective. *Studies in Continuing Education, 32*(1), 29-46.

Boud, D., & Walker, D. (1993). *Using experience for learning.* Buckingham, England: Open University Press.

Brew, C. R. (2002). Kolb's learning style instrument: Sensitive to gender. *Educational and Psychological Measurement, 62*(2), 373-390.

Cassidy, S. (2004). Learning styles: An overview of theories, models, and measures. *Educational Psychology, 24*(4), 419-444.

Coffield, F., Moseley, D., Hall, E., & Ecclestone, K. (2004). *Learning styles and pedagogy in post-16 learning: A systematic and critical review.* London, England: Learning and Skills Research Center.

Coscarelli, W. C. (1983). Development of a decision-making inventory to Assess Johnson's Decision-Making Styles. *Journal of Measurement and Evaluation, 16*(3) 149-60.

Dewey, J. (1938). *Experience and education.* New York, NY: Macmillan.

Donovan, J. (2008). Effective use of ee-learning in a graduate education course. *Journal of the Scholarship of Teaching and Learning, 8*(3), 61-78.

Dorasamy, N. (2009). Diverse enterprising needs and outcomes: a case for experiential learning. *Industry & Higher Education, 23*(5), 405-412.

Dunn, R. (1990). Rita Dunn answers questions on learning styles. *Educational Leadership, 48*(2), 15-19. Retrieved FROM www.ascd.org/ASCD/pdf/journals/ed_lead/el_199010_dunn

Dyke, M. (2006). The role of the 'other' in reflection, knowledge formation and action in a late modernity. *International Journal of Lifelong Education, 25*(2), 105-123.

Dyke, M. (2009). An enabling framework for reflexive learning: Experiential learning and reflexivity in contemporary modernity. *International Journal of Lifelong Education, 28*(3), 289-310.

Illeris, K. (2007). What do we actually mean by experiential learning? *Human Resources Development Review, 6*(1), 84-95.

Joy, S., & Kolb, D. (2009). Are there cultural differences in learning style? *International Journal of Intercultural Relations, 33*, 69-85.

Kayes, A. B., Kayes, D. C., & Kolb, D. A. (2005). Experiential learning in teams. *Simulation & Gaming, 36*(3), 330-354.

Kluge, A. (2007). Experiential learning methods, simulation complexity and their effects on different target groups. *Journal of Educational Computing Research, 36*(3), 323-349.

Knight, K. H., Elfenbein, M. H., & Messina, J. A. (1995). A preliminary scale to measure connected and separate knowing: The Knowing Style Inventory. *Sex Roles, 33*, 499-513.

Kolb, D. (1976). *Learning style inventory: Technical manual.* Boston, MA: McBer & Company.

Kolb, D. (1984). *Experiential learning: Experience as the source of learning and development.* Englewood Cliffs, NJ: Prentice-Hall.

Kolb, D. A. (1999a). *Learning style inventory, version 3.* Boston, MA: TRG Hay/McBer Training Resources Group.

Kolb, D. A. (1999b). *Learning style inventory, version 3: Technical specifications.* Boston, MA: TRG Hay/McBer Training Resources Group.

Kolb, A. Y., & Kolb, D.A. (2005). The Kolbe Learning Style Inventory–Version 3.1 2005 Technical Specifications. Retrieved from http://www.whitewaterrescue.com/support/pagepics/lsitechmanual.pdf

Kolb, A., & Kolb, D. A. (2009). *Experiential learning theory bibliography* (Vol. 2, 2006–2011). Retrieved from EBLS Web site: http://learningfromexperience.com/research-library/experiential-learning-theory-bibliography-volume-2/

Laschinger, H. (1990). Review of experiential learning theory research in the nursing profession. *Journal of Advanced Nursing, 15*, 985-993.

Lee, J. H., McCullouch, B. G., & Chang, L. M. (2008). Macrolevel and microlevel frameworks of experiential learning theory in construction engineering education. *Journal of Professional Issues in Engineering Education and Practice, 134*(2), 158-164.

Levesque-Bristol, C., Knapp, T. D., & Fisher, B. J. (2010). The effectiveness of service-learning: It's not always what you think. *Journal of Experiential Education, 33*(3), 208-224.

Lewin, K. (1951). *Field theory in social science.* New York, NY: Harper & Row.

Mainemelis, C., Boyatzis, R., & Kolb, D. (2002). Adaptive flexibility: Testing experiential learning theory of development. *Management Learning, 33*(1), 5-33.

Miettinen, R. (2000). The concept of experiential learning and John Dewey's theory of reflective thought and action. *International Journal of Lifelong Education, 19*(1), 54-72.

Mumford, A. (2006). Action Learning: nothing so practical as a good theory. *Action Learning: Research and Practice* 3(1), 69-75.

Nees, A. T., Willey, S., & Mansfield, N. R. (2010). Enhancing the educational value of experiential learning: The Business Court Project. *Journal of Legal Studies Education, 27*(2), 171-208.

Niemantsverdriet, S., van der Vleuten, C. P. M., Majoor, G. D., & Scherpbier, A. J. J. A. (2005). An explorative study into learning on international traineeships: Experiential learning processes dominate. *Medical Education, 39*, 1236-1242.

Pedrosa de Jesus, H. T., Almeida, P. A., Teixeira-Dias, J. J., & Watts, M. (2000). Students' questions: Building a bridge between Kolb's learning styles and approaches to learning. *Education and Training, 48*(2/3), 97-111.

Permaul, J. S. (2009). Theoretical bases for service-learning: implications for programs design and effectiveness. *New Horizons in Education, 57*(3), 1-7.

Piaget, J. (1970). *Genetic epistemology.* New York, NY: Columbia University Press.

Quay, J. (2003). Experience and participation: Relating theories of learning. *The Journal of Experiential Learning, 26*(2), 105-116.

Rone, T. R. (2008). Culture from the outside in and the inside out: Experiential education and the continuum of theory, practice, and policy. *College Teaching, 56*(4), 237-245.

Sadler-Smith, E. (2001). Does the learning styles questionnaire measure style or process? A reply to Swailes and Senior (1999). *International Journal of Selection and Assessment, 9*(3), 207-214.

Schmidt, M. (2010). Learning from teaching experience: Dewey's theory and preservice teachers' learning. *Journal of Research in Music Education, 58*(2), 131-146.

Stokes-Eley, S. (2007). Using Kolb's experiential learning cycle in chapter presentations. *Communication Teacher, 21*(1), 26-29.

Sugarman, L. (1985). Kolb's model of experiential learning: Touchstone for trainers, students, counselors, and clients. *Journal of Counseling and Development, 64*, 264-268.

Turesky, E. F., & Mundhenk, L. G. (2008). Going beyond traditional career development theories: Individualizing counseling using cognitive stage and experiential learning theories. *Canadian Journal of Career Development, 7*(2), 3-7.

Vaught, D. R. (2007) *Classroom seating: Applying Johnson's decision making inventory* (Unpublished doctoral dissertation). University of Missouri-Columbia.

Xu, Y., & Yang, Y. (2010). Student learning in business simulation: An empirical investigation. *Journal of Education for Business, 85*, 223-228.

Author Contact Information: **Glenda Moss**, University of North Texas at Dallas, Department of Teacher Education & Administration, 7300 University Hills Drive, Dallas, Texas 75241-4600. Phone: 972-338-1373. E-mail: Glenda.Moss@unt.edu

CHAPTER 11

Adult Learning Theory

Betty J. Alford
Stephen F. Austin State University

In current educational leadership preparation program recommendations (Young, 2011) as in professional development recommendations for educators (Loughridge & Tarantino, 2005), adult learning theory is often referred to as if it was a single, consistent body of knowledge that serves as a foundation of recommended tenets to serve as guidelines for effective practices of working with adults. For example, Young (2011), the University Council of Educational Administration's executive director stated, "[University Council of Educational Administration] stresses the use of adult learning theory in instructional approaches" (p. 8). She further pointed out that the standards for effective school leadership preparation would include "use of adult learning theory and active learning strategies" (p. 8). However, adult learning theory is not a singularly agreed upon theory, universal in application and timespan (Brookfield, 1986; Jarvis, 1992; Merriam, 2001; Merriam & Cafferella, 1991). In 1986, Brookfield argued, "It is evident, then, that the last 20 years have witnessed a mounting challenge to our stereotypical views of the nature and extent of adult learning and the appropriate roles for professional educators" (p. 66). Jarvis (1992) further explained, "Educators of children are beginning to recognize that there is not a large divide between the education of children and adults" (p. 55). He further shared, that all educators could gain more in sharing knowledge rather than to "seek to draw laborious and even false distinctions between andragogy and pedagogy" (p. 55). As Merriam (2001) stressed:

> The central question of how adults learn has occupied the attention of scholars and practitioners since the founding of adult education as a professional field of practice in the 1920s. Some 80 years later, we have no single answer, no one theory or model of adult learning that explains all that we know about adult learning, the various contexts where learning takes place and the process of learning itself. What we do have is a mosaic of theories, models and explanations that, combined, compose the knowledge base of adult learning. (p. 3)

The historical adult learning theoretical framework consists of varying assumptions and guidelines that have been criticized widely in the last 2 decades (Merriam, 2001; Merriam & Cafferella, 1991). However, when adult learning theory is offered as the explanation of the theoretical framework guiding instruction to adults, the theories being proposed are often the ones that were publicized most widely by Malcolm Knowles from the 1950s to mid-1980s emphasizing informal learning, andragogy, differences in instruction due to adults' developmental stages versus children's developmental stages, and roles for adult educators as facilitators of learning. Transformational learning (Mezirow, 1991, 2000) and self-directed learning (Brookfield, 1986) also are part of the framework of adult learning tenets that are often proposed. This chapter will discuss the historical underpinnings of adult learning theories and the key authors who advanced these theories, the aspects most frequently emphasized by key theorists in the field, current criticisms of adult learning theory and current research.

Historical Underpinnings of Adult Learning Theory

Adult learning theories are relatively recent in the history of American education (Merriam, 2001). An early emphasis of the 1920s was the question whether adults could learn followed by behavioral and psychological perspectives focusing on how and when adults could learn (Merriam, 2001). In citing the history of adult learning theory, Merriam (2001) stated, "Until the mid-twentieth century, adult educators relied on research in

The Handbook of Educational Theories, pp. 125–131

psychology and educational psychology for an understanding of adult learning" (p. 4). Drawing on the 1830s European concept of andragogy which identified the way adults learn as distinctively different from the way children learn, Lindeman (1926) is credited as articulating the theory of adult learning to a wider audience in the United States through his book, the *Meaning of Adult Education.* In the book, Lindeman (1926) described the process of adult learning as a liberating experience of personal growth. Malcolm Knowles (1989), an influential theorist in the field of adult education and former executive director of the Adult Education Association of the United States, recounted in his autobiography that he had attended Harvard on a scholarship and upon graduation had taken a job with the National Youth Administration in Massachusetts where after 3 months on the job, he met Lindeman. Knowles (1989) described Lindeman as his "first real mentor" (p. 8). Having read Lindeman's *Meaning of Adult Education*, Knowles (1989) commented, "I was so excited in reading it that I couldn't put it down. It became my chief source of inspiration and ideas for a quarter of a century" (p. 8).

Other theorists who influenced Knowles included his advisor at the University of Chicago where he had completed his master's degree and PhD, Cyril O. Houle, a leading educator of this time period who emphasized the value of scholarship, as well as Carl Rogers, whose associate, Authur Shedlin, taught a course that Knowles completed (Knowles, 1989). Knowles commented about this class that when he finished the first class session, he

> ran to the library and checked out all the books and periodicals I could find by or about Carl Rogers. I never read so many books and worked so hard in any course I had ever been in.… It was exhilarating. I began to think about what it means to become a facilitator of learning rather than a teacher. (p. 13)

Knowles (1989) explained that the three things that he valued most from Rogers' theories were his "unqualified positive regard for the helpee, a deep ability to empathize, and absolute authenticity" (p. 32).

Knowles (1989) also acknowledged the importance of John Dewey's work by stating, "Perhaps the most impactful system of ideas about effective teaching was propounded by John Dewey during the first half of the century" (p. 87). Although Knowles (1989) emphasized the value of Dewey's discussions of the importance of experience, democracy, continuity, and interaction to learning, from the 1960s through the 1980s, Knowles (1984) continued to posit that education for children largely did not reflect Dewey's ideals and differed from the conditions for learning needed by adult learners. These conditions included:

- The learners feel a need to learn.
- The learning environment is characterized by physical comfort, mutual trust and respect, mutual helpfulness, freedom of expression, and acceptance of differences.
- The learners perceive the goals of a learner's experience as their goals.
- The learners accept a share of the responsibility for planning and operationalizing a learning experience and therefore have a feeling of commitment toward it.
- The learners participate actively in the learning process.
- The learning process is relevant to and makes use of the experiences of the learner.
- The learners have a sense of progress toward their goals (pp. 85-87).

Knowles (1989) acknowledged, "John Dewey's *Experience and Education* gave me a theoretical justification for emphasizing the role of learners' experiences in learning" (p. 75). Knowles (1989) also explained that Freire's (1970) *Pedagogy of the Oppressed* "made me aware of the importance of 'consciousness raising' as a part of the learning process" (p. 81) and described Freire as "a highly innovative, socially concerned, activist adult educator. I have gained a good deal of inspiration and many methodological suggestions from his writings" (p. 85). Knowles (1989) also added that Freire is for "changing the existing system. And I am too" (p. 96).

Other theorists who influenced Knowles were Kolb who emphasized learning styles; Kenneth Benne, Leland Bradford, and Ronald Lippett, who founded the National Training Laboratories and emphasized group facilitation and social action; and Kurt Lewin, a leading theorist on change (Smith, 2002). Knowles (1950) stated, "Every adult group, of whatever nature, must become a laboratory of democracy, a place where people may have the experience of learning to live cooperatively" (p. 9). Knowles (1989) was influenced by his experiences in attending the National Training Laboratory in 1952 and 1954. In addition, Knowles (1989) credited Maslow's (1970) book titled *Motivation and Personality* as providing him "the framework of the hierarchy of student needs, a deeper understanding of the meaning of readiness to learn as well as the concept of the self-actualized person" (p. 81). Knowles modeled life-long learning, and as he (1989) stated, "This, then, is where my thinking about adult learning stands at this time" (p. 85). He (1989) acknowledged his certainty "that if this book is revised in 10 years, it will report substantial changes in my thinking" (p. 85).

Just as theorists influenced other theorists in the development of adult learning theories, Jesson and Newman (2004) pointed out that the "field of adult education is continuously shaped by the broader political and economic environment" (p. 252). Race relations and social action issues also influenced the understandings that were developed concerning adult learning (Jesson & Newman, 2004). For example, the Highlander Folk School in the Appalachian Mountains of Tennessee offered workshops for community activists while citizenship schools in the South were designed to assist people in learning to read in order to vote (Jesson & Newman, 2004). Environmental issues, contextual issues, and political issues continue to influence our understanding of adult learning and historically impacted the field of adult education (Jesson & Newman, 2004).

KEY THEORISTS IN THE FIELD AND ASPECTS MOST FREQUENTLY EMPHASIZED BY THEM

Three key theorists whose work has been instrumental in shaping theories of adult learning are Malcolm Knowles, Stephen Brookfield, and Jack Mezirow. Although many other theorists have influenced and continue to influence the field of adult learning, this chapter will focus on a discussion of Malcolm Knowles's life and aspects most frequently discussed by him. This discussion will be provided followed by sharing ways that Brookfield and Mezirow further clarified important tenets of adult learning theories.

MALCOLM KNOWLES

Knowles's educational and professional career extended from Harvard as an undergraduate to his master's degree at the University of Chicago and his thesis in which he described informal learning as a key attribute of adult learning (later the basis of his first book in 1950 titled *Informal Adult Education*) to a PhD at the University of Chicago in 1960 at the age of 47. Knowles completed his master's degree in 1949 and in 1951, became executive director of the Adult Education Association of the United States. Following his 9 years as director of the Adult Education Association, he taught at Boston University beginning in 1949 for 14 years followed by a faculty appointment at North Carolina State University in 1974 until he retired in 1979. Key texts by Knowles included *The Modern Practice of Adult Education* (1970) and *The Adult Learner: A Neglected Species* (1973) in which he continued to write about the concept of andragogy. Convinced that there were key differences between learning by adults versus learning by children, he is credited as "first to chart the rise of the adult education movement in the United States, first to develop a statement of informal adult education practice, and first to develop a comprehensive theory of adult education (via the notion of andragogy)" (Smith, 2002, p. 11). Although Knowles retired from university teaching at the age of 65 as required by the university, until shortly before his death in 1997, Knowles continued to serve as a consultant for adult education emphasizing important concepts of adult learning theories.

In his work with adults after World War I, Knowles noted that the didactic methods that he associated with the art and science of education of children (pedagogy) were not effective with adults. However, he noted that many adults were being taught as dependent, submissive children with the teacher as the sole authority for instruction. Knowles commented that the Greek word *paid* meaning children was part of the origin of the word pedagogy and explained that pedagogy was based on beliefs and assumptions about teaching and learning that derived from the education of boys in cathedrals in the seventh and twelfth centuries (Knowles, 1990). Knowles (1990) attributed a Yugoslavian adult educator who was attending a summer institute at Boston University as providing his primary introduction to andragogy. Using the concept of andragogy as an organizing term, Knowles postulated that andragogy, the art and science of working with adults, was the opposite of pedagogy. With andragogy, Knowles (1990) argued, "Adults need to know why they need to learn something before undertaking to learn it" (p. 57). He (1990) further stated, "Their self-concept is that they are responsible for their decisions, their lives. They have both a greater role of experience and different qualities.... The richest resources for learning reside in the adult learners themselves" (p. 59). Five assumptions about the characteristics of adult learners as different from children were in "self-concept, experience, readiness to learn, the orientation of learner, and in the motivation to learn" (Knowles, 1984, p. 12). In fact one of Knowles's books included the subtitle *Pegagogy Versus Andragogy*. Later, as Knowles recognized that andragogy could include principles of pedagogy such as when teaching a physics lesson, he changed the book's subtitle to *From Pedagogy to Andragogy* eliminating the dichotomy between the two terms. Knowles's (1989) two cardinal principles of adult learning were; "(1) You always start with learners where they are starting from in terms of their interests, problems and concerns, and (2) You engage the learners in a process of active inquiry with you" (p. 41). The foundation stones of modern adult learning theory as proposed by Knowles (1990) included, "(1) Adults are motivated to learn as they experience needs and interests that learning will satisfy, (2) Adults' orientation to learning is life-centered, (3) Experience is the richest resource of adult learning, (4) Adults have a deep need to be self-directed, and (5) Individual differences among individuals increase with age" (p. 31).

Stephen Brookfield and Jack Mezirow

Two other theorists who were very influential in the field of adult learning were Stephen Brookfield and Jack Mezirow, contemporaries who published separatively as well as collaboratively. Brookfield is known best for his work with self-directed learning while Mezirow is known best for his work in explaining transformational learning theory. Stephen Brookfield (1988) emphasized the varied contexts for adult learning but stressed that a common element is that the individuals are all adults, they often are engaged in purposeful learning, learning often occurs in group settings, and adults bring a diverse set of knowledge, skills, and experiences. Brookfield (1986) acknowledged the voluntary nature of adult learning as compared to compulsory attendance laws for children to attend school. His principles of effective practice included:

> (1) Participation is voluntary, (2) Effective practice is characterized by respect among participants for each other's self-worth, (3) The facilitation is collaborative, (4) Praxis is placed at the heart of effective facilitation. Learning and facilitation is a continual process of action, reflection, action, reflection. (5) The facilitator aims to foster in adults a spirit of critical reflection. (6) The aim of facilitation is nurturing self-directed empowered adults. (p. 100)

The influence of Dewey and Freire is evident in Brookfield's work. He (1988) proposed that a goal is to develop self-directed learners. As Brookfield (1986) stated, "In an effective teaching-learning transaction all participants learn, no one member is regarded as having a monopoly on insight, and dissension and criticism are regarded as inevitable and desirable elements of the process" (p. 105).

In 1991, Jack Mezirow developed the theory of transformational learning. He postulated that he did not seek to "interpret systematically what Habermas or any other single theorist has to say about adult learning" (p. xiv). Further, Mezirow (1991) stated that he

> adopted some of Habermas's ideas such as his distinction between instrumental and communicative learning and his description of the ideal conditions for rational discourse, but I have freely changed others; for example, I have extended the process of emancipatory learning to include the instrumental domain. (p. xv)

Mezirow (1991) was also influenced by Freire's "calls for social transformation" (p. 137) and by a sabbatical with psychiatrist Roger Gould who proposed adult stages of development whereas "Piaget had cited emergence into adolescence as the final developmental stage" (p. 73). Other theorists who contributed to Mezirow's (1991) theories included Donald Schon's recognition of the power of metaphors to learning, John Dewey's emphasis on experiential learning, reflection, and critical inquiry, Kolb's (1984) experiential learning theory in his design of transformational learning with its emphasis on the "personal meanings that we attribute to our experiences" (p. xiv), and Maxine Greene's (1978) description of "meaningful learning as involving a process of disclosure, reconstruction, and generative" (p. 197). Mezirow (1991) posited, "Learning is a dialectical process" (p. 11), and stated, "All reflection involves a critique" (p. 15). Mezirow (1991) emphasized, "Any major challenge to an established perspective can result in a transformation" (p. 168). Mezirow (1991) further described the role of the adult learner as to "help learners to look critically at their beliefs and behaviors, not only as these appear at the moment but in the context of their history (purpose) and consequences in the learner's life" (pp. 197-198) with the goal of "critical discourse and reflective action" (p. 199). Critical reflection is a key component of transformational learning and "freedom, democracy, equity, justice are necessary conditions for optimal participation in critical discourse" (p. 226). The facilitator of adult learning is encouraged to foster the critical reflection through respectful dialogue that will, in turn, lead to new action.

Criticisms of Adult Learning Theory

Much of Knowles's work has been criticized as largely descriptive, linear-based, and technical in addition to not recognizing the importance of consideration of context to any theory (Brookfield, 1993). Brookfield further argued that conditions that impact self-directed learning are political as much as pedagogical. In short, context matters in learning. Merriam and Cafferella (1991) argued against the linear process for learning that Knowles advocated recognizing that "adults don't follow a defined set of steps" (p. 46). Chance and circumstance also influence learning (Merriam & Cafferalla, 1991). Incidental learning, informal learning, formal education, transformative learning, and self-directed learning are all concepts that serve to reinforce that there cannot be a single theory of adult learning.

The emphasis on experience as a tenet for adult learning (Knowles, 1990; Lindeman, 1926) has also been criticized with arguments that many children also have rich experiences to draw upon while not all adults have rich experiences to use as a foundation for learning (Merriam, 2001). As many of the research studies of the mid-twentieth century, most of Knowles' research studies were conducted with middle class White participants rather than reflecting the diversity of race, gender, or socioeconomic group (Brookfield, 1993). The theories of learning have grown "more sophisticated and international with growing recognition of the central role of learning in our lives" (Brookfield, 1995, p. 252). Knowles's views on informal learning have also been criticized (Merriam, 2001). Moreover, as constructivist learning theories have been more widely advocated for school-age students as well as for adults, the distinctions from pedagogy and andragogy have diminished. Constructivist teaching is advocated for children as well as for adults. Freire (1970) argued against the banking model of education in which deposits in learning were made. Instead, the learner is to be an active participant in the learning process with dialogue characterizing the primary mode of instruction. Although Freire primarily worked with adults, his theories have been advocated in K-12 settings. P-16 teachers are recommended to serve as facilitators of learning as Knowles and Freire had advocated for roles in fostering adult learning. In short, the distinctions between adult learning theories and learning theories have diminished.

Current Research

Current researchers in the field of adult learning have not engaged in an attempt to create one unifying theory for adult learning. Instead, current researchers have focused on particular dimensions of adult learning including incidental learning, transformative learning and informal learning. Greater awareness of the importance of the context wherein learning is studied is evident with current research conducted with a more diverse range of participants. Recent research on adult learning has also moved from a positivist approach with an attempt to provide explicit steps for the learning process to consideration of the interwoven, dialectical process of learning. New forms of technology in adult learning have also triggered additional research questions concerning how adults learn best online.

Cranton (1994) pointed out that the last decade has seen radical changes in adult education, and "Perspectives on adult learning have changed dramatically over the decades" (p. 3). Rather than considering adult education and adult learning as one large field, the field is subdivided such as human resource development or vocational education. There is also growing recognition in research studies that learning can occur in many settings both formal and informal, and each setting may have different characteristics. In addition, current research has moved away from issues of pedagogy versus andragogy. Instead, constructivist learning is accepted as appropriate for both adults and children.

Discussion

Called into question is whether adult learning theory in the twenty-first century still has merit as a singularly advanced set of assumptions. If we are to use adult learning theory and active learning theory as the *standards for effective school leaders* recommended by stressing the "use of adult learning theory in instructional approaches" (p. 8), what does this really mean?

To consider adult learning theory as a nonchanging set of assumptions to guide best practice in the instruction of adults reminds me of the difficulty in departing from Maslow's hierarchy of needs as the basis of motivation. In introductory education and educational psychology courses, young educators learn the stages of Maslow's hierarchy of needs and often accept them unquestioningly because on some basic level, they make sense. For example, if a child is very hungry, he or she probably will be thinking more about acquiring some food than seeking self-actualization. If an adult is being pushed out of an airplane, within that moment, he or she is probably thinking more about basic survival than which college he or she may attend next. However, many adults can remember being in graduate school without extra income when they were seeking goals of self-actualization even though financial resources were scarce. The stages of Maslow's hierarchy were first proposed as very linear just as Knowles's stages in adult learning. Maslow later admitted that the stages may overlap just as Knowles later admitted that the steps of adult learning theory may not be linearly based.

In the twenty-first century, criticisms of both of these theories have continued; yet, the theories remain widely acknowledged. Criticisms include recognition of the importance of context to learning and the interrelatedness of many factors influencing a person's motivation and informing a person's learning. When adult learning theory is stressed in professional development for educators, these concepts may be recommended to promote the opposite of the instructional practice of lecture-oriented professional development largely practiced in the 1970s. Professional development was criticized as a passive event that was irrelevant to specific needs, the antithesis of tenets of adult learning theories as discussed in this chapter. In the last 3 decades, tremendous advances in professional development have occurred influenced widely by the National Staff Development Standards and a body of literature criticizing the traditional, lecture-dominated mode of instruction for adults.

These changing practices reflect tenets of traditional adult learning theories of Knowles, Brookfield, and Mezirow emphasizing the role of the facilitator as promoting individual's personal growth in knowledge and skills and resulting in a change in actions. New forms of delivery for professional development experiences have occurred that emphasize adult students' involvement in learning through dialogue, experiential activities, and action research. Adult learning theories as guides for actions provide an argument for the change in delivery and interaction from the lecture-dominated mode of delivery that characterized professional development that was offered in the 1970s. While there are criticisms of the tenets of adult learning theory as being equally true for children, adult learning theories do continue to offer insights that are useful for adult educators. As educators, it is important to recognize that adult learning theory is not a single theory or a linear process. There are multiple theories with overlap into areas that characterize all successful learning experiences. However, some truths prevail. For the most part, children do face compulsory attendance laws if they drop out of schools while adults do not. Children may not have experienced the range of experiences of adults. Adults do have multiple responsibilities that children who are preadolescent often do not. There are always exceptions, such as children who care for other children and assume adult responsibilities at an early age. However, positive relationships and relevance are vitally important for both.

The true test of the usefulness of educational theories is whether the theories serve to guide practice in a productive way. While not a linear process to follow in fostering learning, collectively encouraging reciprocal learning, transformational learning, reflective learning, constructive leadership, self-directed learning, and incidental learning are worthy goals. It is important to consider that adults learn what they need to know, that they have multiple responsibilities and priorities, that they often bring a depth of experience to the learning experience, that reflective and reflexive practice can enhance learning, and that active engagement enhances learning. For some children, particularly early adolescents, most of the adult learning concepts are equally true as those who have criticized the theories proposed.

Self-directed learning should be encouraged as well as incidental learning. In short, human growth in knowledge, skills, and dispositions is important as a life-time quest. Learning contributes to the richness of life and can be fostered by conditions that optimize it. Adult learning theories describe learning characteristics and illuminate ways that conditions to foster learning can be nurtured. For this reason, the usefulness of considering the theories endures not as an exact science or a linear process, but as guiding principles for action. Knowles, in 1990, stated, "For more than 4 decades I have been trying to formulate a theory of adult learning that takes into account what we know from experience and research about the unique characteristics of adult learners" (p. 54).

While formulating one theory of adult learning was not achieved by Knowles, those who desire to serve as facilitators of adult learning can draw both inspiration and ideas from considering tenets of adult learning including those proposed by Lindeman, Knowles, Brookfield, and Mezirow. As Jarvis (1992) postulated, "Perspectives on adult learning have changed dramatically over the decades.... The phenomenon of adult learning is complex and difficult to capture in any one definition" (p. 3). We are still in the process of understanding the art and science of promoting learning, but the timeless wisdom of adult learning theories can serve not as absolutes but as guides for practice. As learning is a voluntary process and not guaranteed, considering the importance of establishing a learning environment wherein mutual respect is realized, meaning is evoked, purposeful actions result, and individuals' lives are transformed, merits our strong consideration. As Knowles (1990) proposed, "Learning is fundamental to our own humanity, whatever our age—it is central to life itself—and only by facilitating others learning can we enrich their lives and demonstrate that we really care for them as persons" (p. 147).

Exhilarating, invigorating, and transformational are all words used by theorists to describe what adult learning can be. Whether these goals are achieved can be influenced by the facilitator of adult learners who, in turn, can experience the same concepts through the reciprocal process of learning that can result when dialogue occurs in a context of mutual respect characterized by critical inquiry and reflective processes. Therein lies the heart of adult learning theories and the challenge of education for all learners, regardless of age.

REFERENCES

Brookfield, S. D. (1986). *Understanding and facilitating adult learning*. San Francisco, CA: Jossey-Bass.

Brookfield, S. D. (1993). Self-directed learning, political clarity, and the critical practice of adult education. *Adult Education Quarterly, 43*(4), 227-242.

Brookfield, S. D. (1995). *Becoming a critically reflective teacher.* San Francisco, CA: Jossey-Bass.

Cranton, P. (1994). *Understanding and promoting transformative learning*. San Francisco, CA: Jossey-Bass.

Freire, P. (1970). *Pedagogy of the oppressed.* New York, NY: Continuum.

Greene, M. (1978). *Landscapes of learning*. New York, NY: Teacher's College Press.

Jarvis, P. (1992). Leaders of adult and continuing education should come from outside the field. In M. W. Galbraith & B. R. Sisco (Eds.), *Confronting controversies in challenging times: A call for action* (pp. 53-58). San Francisco, CA: Jossey-Bass.

Jesson, J., & Newman, M. (2004). Radical adult education learning. In G. Foley (Ed.), *Dimensions of adult learning:*

Adult education and training in a global era (pp. 251-264). Berkshire, England: Open University Press.

Knowles, M. S. (1950). *Informal adult education*. New York, NY; Association Press.

Knowles, (1970). *The modern practice of adult education: Andragogy versus pedagogy*. New York, NY: Association Press.

Knowles, M. S. (1973). *The adult learner: A neglected species*. Houston, TX: Gulf.

Knowles, M. S. (1984). *The adult learner: A neglected species* (3rd ed.). Houston, TX: Gulf.

Knowles, M. S. (1989). *The making of an adult educator: An autobiographical journey*. San Francisco, CA: Jossey-Bass.

Knowles, M. S. (1990). *The adult learner: A neglected species* (4th ed.). Houston, TX: Gulf.

Kolb, D. A. (1984). *Experiential learning: Experience as the source of learning and development*. Englewood Cliffs, NJ: Prentice-Hall.

Loughridge, M., & Tarantino, L. R. (2005). *Leading effective secondary school reform: Your guide to strategies that work*. Thousand Oaks, CA: Corwin Press.

Lindeman, E. (1926). *The meaning of adult education*. New York, NY: New Republic.

Maslow, A. H. (1970). *Motivation and personality*. New York, NY: Harper & Row.

Merriam, S. B. (2001). Andragogy and self-directed learning: Pillars of adult learning theory. *New Directions for Adult and Continuing Education*, 89, 3-13.

Merriam, S. B., & Cafferalla, R. S. (1991). *Learning in adulthood: A comprehensive guide*. San Francisco, CA: Jossey-Bass.

Mezirow, J. (1991). *Transformative dimensions of adult learning*. San Francisco, CA: Jossey-Bass.

Mezirow, J. (2000). *Learning transformation: Critical perspectives on a theory in progress*. San Francisco, CA: Jossey-Bass.

Smith, M. K. (2002). Malcolm Knowles, informal adult education, self-direction and andragogy. *The Encyclopedia of Informal Education*. Retrieved from http://www.infed.org/thinkers/et-kknowl.htm

Young, M. (2011). From the director: Quality assurance in educational leadership preparation. *UCEA REVIEW: University Council for Educational Administration, 5*(2), 6-9.

Author Contact Information: Betty J. Alford, Department of Secondary Education and Educational Leadership, Stephen F. Austin State University, P.O. Box 13018-SFA, Nacogdoches, TX 75962. Phone: 936-468-1865. E-mail: balford@sfasu.edu

CHAPTER 12

Transformative Learning Theory

Mary V. Alfred and Catherine A. Cherrstrom
Texas A&M University

Petra A. Robinson
Rutgers University

Alicia R. Friday
Texas A&M University

Transformative learning theory is an adult education theory about how adults make meaning in their lives. As a theory, transformative learning continues to be discussed, experienced, and applied after 3 decades of formation, development, and evolution. Taylor (2007) contends transformative learning theory is the most researched and discussed theory in adult education. A review of scholarly books, journal articles, research studies, dissertations, and conferences confirms transformative learning is a frequent and popular subject.

This chapter's purpose is to describe transformative learning theory, including constructs, development, evolution, critiques, application, and use as theoretical framework in research. The chapter begins with an overview of transformative learning theory as conceptualized by Mezirow, including his 10-phased transformative learning process. It continues with a review of the theory's main constructs, including meaning making, frames of reference, habits of mind, points of view, domains of learning, critical reflection, and disorienting dilemmas. After an overview of the theory's 3 decades of development and evolution, critiques of transformative learning theory are identified and discussed using research from the literature. Finally, the chapter explores recent dissertations to highlight how transformative learning theory is being used as a research framework.

Transformative Learning Theory's Development and Evolution

Transformative learning theory first emerged in the 1970s with Mezirow's work about how adults make sense of their life experience. Mezirow (2000) defined transformative learning as "the process by which we transform our taken-for-granted frames of reference (meaning schemes, habits of mind, mindsets) to make them more inclusive, discriminating, open, emotionally capable of change, and reflective so that they may generate beliefs and opinions that will prove more true or justified to guide action" (p. 8). Frames of reference define our world and include the assumptions and expectations we use to filter and understand our experiences (Mezirow, 1997). Transformative learning is manifested in the constructivist orientation to learning, in which meaning is made through learning, reflection, and dialogue (Merriam, Caffarella, & Baumgartner, 2007). While all learning may not be transformative, all learning has the opportunity to be transforming.

Mezirow's Transformative Learning Process

Transformative learning is a process. When new learning and experiences contradict prior learning and experiences, the result may be a disorienting dilemma. As adults deal with disorienting dilemmas, they gather new information and experiences, reflect, dialogue, wrestle with meaning, and work to integrate the new

The Handbook of Educational Theories, pp. 133–147

learning into their changing perspectives. Mezirow (1975) concluded 10 possible phases of transformation based on his qualitative research of women's experiences returning to college after an extended period of time:

- a disorienting dilemma;
- self-examination with feelings of fear, anger, guilt, or shame;
- a critical assessment of assumptions;
- recognition that one's discontent and the process of transformation are shared;
- exploration of options for new roles, relationships, and actions;
- planning a course of action;
- acquiring knowledge and skills for implementing one's plans;
- provisional trying of new roles;
- building competence and self-confidence in new roles and relationships; and
- a reintegration into one's life on the basis of conditions dictated by one's new perspective.

The 10-phased transformative learning process encompasses four main components: experience, critical reflection, reflective discourse, and action (Merriam et al., 2007). Triggered by experience resulting in a disorienting dilemma, the process continues with critical reflection, defined by Brookfield (2004) as a reflective process which includes identifying and challenging assumptions and imagining alternatives. Critical reflection includes understanding power and its impacts and questioning hegemonic assumptions and practices. Next, adults share their discontent and explore new roles, relationships, and actions through critical discourse. Critical discourse, like critical reflection, involves assessment of assumptions and can lead to clearer understanding by using collective experience to form a best judgment (Mezirow, 2000). Finally, the process may lead to action, such as acquiring new knowledge and skills, trying on new roles, building competence and confidence, and ultimately a reintegration into life based on a new perspective's conditions.

Transformative Learning Theory's Constructs

Transformative learning theory emphasizes meaning making, or how adults make sense of their experiences and make meaning. Mezirow (2000) defined learning as a process in which we use prior experiences and interpretations to form new or revised interpretations to make meaning and guide future action. He describes three types of meaning structures, a *frame of reference* (or meaning perspective), which is comprised of *habits of mind* and *points of view* (Mezirow, 1997).

A *frame of reference* is a meaning perspective, consisting of assumptions and expectations, through which we view and filter the world and our experiences. A meaning perspective is "the structure of assumptions within which one's past experience assimilates and transforms new experience" (Mezirow, 1991, p. 42). Meaning perspectives are shaped, limited, and distorted by a variety of epistemic, sociolinguistic, and psychological factors and are often acquired uncritically, from childhood, through socialization and acculturation (Mezirow, 1991, 2000). Examples of epistemic factors include developmental stage perspectives, cognitive/learning/intelligence styles, sensory learning preferences, and reflectivity; sociolinguistic factors include social norms/roles, cultural/language codes, and ethnocentrism; and psychological factors include self-concept, locus of control, and tolerance of ambiguity (Mezirow, 1991). "One's frame of reference may include intentionally or incidentally learned philosophical, economic, sociological, and psychological orientations or theories as well" (Mezirow, 2000, p. 17).

Frames of reference, or meaning perspective, include habits of mind and points of view. A *habit of mind* is a broad, generalized set of assumptions used to filter and interpret our experiences and meaning making (Mezirow, 1997). Habits of mind include moral, ethical, philosophical, psychological, and generalized predispositions (Merriam et al., 2007). A *point of view* is comprised of meaning schemes, or sets of knowledge, beliefs, values, and feelings (Merriam et al., 2007). Mezirow's (2000) transformative learning is described as transformations in our habits of mind or points of view:

> Through transformative learning we are freed from uncritical acceptance of others' purposes, values, and beliefs. Transformation in our habits of mind may be sudden and dramatic (epochal) or they may be slower, incremental changes in our points of view (meaning schemes), which eventually lead to a change in our habits of mind (meaning perspective). (Merriam et al., 2007, p. 133)

Transformative learning fits within the larger framework of Habermas's domains of knowledge, or three kinds of knowledge (see Table 12.1): technical or instrumental, practical or communicative, and emancipatory (Cranton, 1994, 2002; Habermas, 1971). Mezirow (1990) contended critical reflection triggers learning and distinguishes between Habermas's domains of learning in terms of reflection's role. In instrumental learning, reflection looks back on content and procedural assumptions to reassess the effectiveness of implemented strategies and methods, including relevance, accuracy, consequences, and consistency with values;

Table 12.1. Domains of Knowledge

Domain	Description	Goal of Learning in Study of
Technical or instrumental	• Cause and effect • Objective • Derived from scientific methodologies	• Trades • Technologies • Science
Practical or communicative	• Understanding of ourselves, others, and the social norms of our community or society • Derived through language • Validated through by consensus	• Human relations • Political and social systems • Education
Emancipatory	• Self-awareness that frees us from constraints • Product of critical reflection, including self-reflection • Transformative	• All areas of adult education, including o Life skills learning o Literacy programs o Self-help groups o Women's studies o Community action groups

Source: Compiled from Cranton (1994, 2002) and Habermas (1971).

while in communicative learning, reflection is an assessment of the problem solving process (Mezirow, 1990). Reflection is critical to transformative learning and may occur within the instrumental or communicative learning domains (Mezirow, 1990):

> Transformative learning involves a particular function of reflection: reassessing the presuppositions on which our beliefs are based and acting on insights derived from the transformed meaning perspective that results from such reassessments.... It may involve correcting distorted assumptions—epistemic, sociocultural, or psychic—from prior learning. (p. 18)

In emancipatory learning, reflection impels us to identify and challenge distorted meaning perspectives. Emancipatory knowledge is gained through critical self-reflection, distinct from technical interest in the objective world and practical interest in social relationships.

Transformative learning occurs by elaborating existing frames of reference, learning new frames of reference, transforming points of view, or transforming habits of mind (Mezirow, 2000). Critical reflection is essential to the transformative learning process and Mezirow identifies three kinds of reflection (Cranton, 1996):

- Content reflection: thinking about the problem's content or description;
- Process reflection: thinking about problem-solving strategies; and
- Premise reflection: questioning the problem's relevance.

Premise reflection or questioning the problem's relevance, including the underlying assumptions, believes, and values, can lead to transformative learning (Cranton, 1996).

Frames of reference, or meaning perspective, act as filters, helping us organize new experiences and meaning making. Some new experiences reinforce or complement our past experiences and resulting frame of reference. However, other experiences may conflict with our prior experiences and frame of references, resulting in a disorienting dilemma, causing us to reject the new experience or transform our frame of reference. Mezirow's (1991) 10-phased transformative learning process begins with a disorienting dilemma. Disorienting dilemmas may be epochal or incremental events, but often result from a major life transition or crisis—loss of a loved one or job, marriage, divorce, illness, going back to school, changing jobs, moving, experiencing new cultures, war, et cetera. When a current experience does not match our prior experiences and assumptions, we experience a disorienting dilemma, causing us to question and possibly shift our assumptions and expectations, changing our frame of reference and meaning perspective.

Three Decades of Development and Evolution

The transformative learning theory is not static, but has developed and evolved for 3 decades. "The theory continues to evolve through the inclusion of new perspectives on adult learning and development" (Cranton, 2002, p. 65). Mezirow first introduced transformative learning theory in 1978, heavily influenced by Kuhn's paradigms, Freire's conscientization, and Habermas's domains of knowledge (Kitchenham, 2008). In the 1980s, Mezirow adapted Habermas's domains of knowledge—technical, practical, and emancipatory—to domains of learning—instrumental, communicative, and emancipatory; expanded the theory to include instrumental, dialogic, and self-reflective learning; defined meaning scheme and meaning perspective; then used the terms in three new learning processes—learning within meaning schemes, learning new meaning schemes, and learning through meaning transformation (Kitchenham, 2008). In the 1990s, Mezirow stressed the importance of altering existing and forging new relationships; expanded the idea of distorted meaning perspectives; argued three types of meaning perspectives—epistemic, sociolinguistic, and psychological; presented three types of reflection—content, process, and premise; stressed the role of critical reflection in perspective transformation; and stressed the importance of critical reflection of assumptions (Kitchenham, 2008). In this century, Mezirow continued to revise and elaborate, including acknowledging the affective, emotional, and social aspects of transformative learning theory; introducing habits of mind and points of view; and expanding in relation to constructivist theory, psychic distortion, schema therapy, and individuation (Kitchenham, 2008).

Transformative learning theory focuses on "how we learn to negotiate and act on our own purposes, values, feelings, and meanings rather than those we have uncritically assimilated from others—to gain greater control over our lives as socially responsible, clear-thinking decision makers" (Mezirow, 2000, p. 8). Transformative learning "*transforms problematic frames of reference to make them more inclusive, discriminating, reflective, open and emotionally able to change*" (Mezirow, 2009, p. 22, emphasis in original). Over the years, transformative learning theory, as first conceptualized my Mezirow, has been met with various critiques as scholars use the theory to frame their research, thus expanding its utility as a theoretical framework.

Critiques of Transformative Learning Theory

In a 2007 review of scholarly literature about transformative learning theory, Taylor concluded recent research predominantly appears in settings of higher education and situations in which adult learning is already a desired outcome. This finding is important for understanding how Mezirow's transformative learning theory has shaped the body of research regarding adult learning, as well as understanding what gaps exist in the literature. According to Taylor (2007), the literature on transformative learning has taken on several new trends in the areas of methods, views about reflection, transformative relationships, epistemological change, and cultivating transformative learning in practice.

While the literature on transformative learning offers greater insight into how the theory has been used to understand adult learning experiences, gaps exist. Based on Taylor's (2007) critique of the current literature, four questions emerge related to transformative learning theory and the need for additional research:

- How does transformative learning take place in *contexts* outside of formal education?
- What are the roles of *emotion and relationships* in creating a transformative learning experience?
- How do we know *critical reflection* has taken place?
- How do *learners* play a part in rendering their own transformative learning?

Transformative learning appears as a consistent theoretical and conceptual framework in many studies and we present specific examples of research that address these critiques.

Context and Transformative Learning

One critique launched against transformative learning theory is that the theory as conceptualized by Mezirow negates the role of context beyond formal education. Taylor (2007) argues recent scholarly research on transformative learning lacks an in-depth investigation into a variety of contexts beyond formal educational settings. In 1991, Clark utilized a qualitative phenomenological approach to study the impact of context on transformative learning and the restructuring of meaning. Phenomenological research identifies the essence of human experiences, based on the descriptions of a small number of study participants collected over time (Creswell, 2003). Clark explored how the participants' sociocultural context affected their transformative learning experiences. The participants came from a variety of backgrounds and learning experiences, such as "recovery from alcoholism; religious conversion; becoming a parent; marrying later in life; and adjusting to physical disability" (Clark, 1991, p. 60). By interviewing participants with a mixture of transformative learning experiences, Clark was able to consider the specific context of the individual's learning experience.

One of Clark's (1991) main findings is context's important role in shaping each participant's transformative learning experience. Context is critical to understanding how participants make meaning from learning experiences because it informs their epistemological perspective, or the way they interpret their world. In addition, Clark identifies two dimensions of context, "the more distant or background context, consisting primarily of personal and familial history; and the more immediate context surrounding the learning event, particularly the personal and professional situation of the individual at that time" (Clark, 1991, p. 126). These two dimensions of context affect a participant's transformative learning experience, providing insight into how a participant interprets learning and ultimately assign meaning to the experience. Additionally, the participants' transformative learning experiences were all outside of formal education and training settings, offering a contrast to the preponderance of the research focused on formal educational environments (Taylor, 2007).

Clark's (1991) findings illuminate how participants made meaning from learning experiences and illustrate context does not operate discretely, but instead directly informs how learning is interpreted. The participants called upon their previous experiences, such as how they grew up and where they lived, and their current settings. Context's important role in the participants' transformative learning process aligns with Mezirow's (1996) original thought that learning takes place through using existing learning to inform, interpret, and reorganize present learning. The context individuals pull from to make sense of learning inevitably informs the transformative learning experience.

Another study uses transformative learning theory to explore meaning making within the context of living with chronic illness. Courtenay, Merriam, and Reeves (1998) studied 18 people living with HIV/AIDS. The participants' meaning making process included an initial reaction to the diagnosis, or disorienting dilemma, followed by a "catalytic" event, often involving others, propelling them away from the initial reaction to a period of exploration and experimentation (Baumgartner, 2011). In the first phase, participants "had a perspective transformation and realized that people, not things, were important. Participants wanted to make a meaningful contribution, had a continued sensitivity to life, and had a continued need to be of service to others" (Baumgartner, 2011, p. 10). In the second phase, they consolidated new meaning.

Follow-up studies offer additional insights into transformative learning theory and people living with chronic illness. Two years after the original study, Courtenay, Merriam, Reeves, and Baumgartner (2000) interviewed 14 of the original 18 people living with HIV/AIDS. The study confirmed the irreversibility of the original perspective transformation and continued meaning scheme changes including having a sense of the future, greater care for the self, and an increased integration of HIV/AIDS into one's self. Two years later, Baumgartner (2002) interviewed 11 of the original 18 participants and the perspective transformation still held. Participants expressed greater appreciation of the human condition, less judgment of self and others, and expanded views of intimacy (Baumgartner, 2002, 2011). "Social interaction, namely through support groups, was integral to the transformative learning process" (Baumgartner, 2011, p. 10).

Courtenay et al.'s studies contribute to the transformative learning theory literature by providing a longitudinal examination of transformative learning in a nonacademic environment. The diagnosis of a chronic is a disorienting dilemma, potentially triggering the transformative learning process. Meaning making and perspective transformation were confirmed and, very importantly, confirmed over time.

Culture and Transformative Learning

Continuing the discussion of context, transformative learning theory has also been critiqued for its lack of attention to culture as a factor in the learning process. Merriam and Ntseane (2008) conducted a study in Botswana, Africa, where they interviewed 12 adult participants about transformational learning experiences. The study highlights the Afrocentric paradigm, questioning African identity from an African perspective (Merriam & Ntseane, 2008, p. 186). Using the lens of African context, the researchers were able to understand the participants' learning experiences from a culturally relevant viewpoint.

The 12 study participants, eight women and four men, ranged in age from 25 to 60 years, with educational levels from seventh grade to master's degree. Their disorienting dilemmas encompassed a variety of life events, including husband's death, orphaned, lover married to another, death of a child, witnessed death in a car accident, marital abuse, HIV/AIDS patient, husband committed suicide, abused by father, called to be a Sangoma (spiritual leader), and mother's illness and death (Merriam & Ntseane, 2008). Similar to Clark's research focused primarily on the importance of context, Merriam and Ntseane's research provides insights into the formation of transformative learning through the intersection of different contexts and a person's cultural lens.

Merriam and Ntseane's (2008) main findings include how spirituality, community responsibilities, relationships, and gender affect the transformative learning experience. From a spiritual perspective, the participants interpreted their learning experiences based on what originally prompted the event to take place. For example, one participant who witnessed his daughter's death explains how a disagreement caused his brother to seek revenge "by having a traditional doctor use his powers to 'silence' [him]" (Merriam & Ntseane, 2008, p. 189). He describes how the spiritual nature of his daughter's death ultimately brought peace to his family through reconciliation with his brother. Merriam and Ntseane (2008) also discuss how several participants in the study viewed their learning experiences with direct consideration of spirituality: "In the African context, for perspective transformation to occur, a connection is made to the myths, stories, and proverbs that bind people together. From here, new myths, stories, and proverbs may emerge, offering an opportunity to create new interpretations" (p. 190). The interconnectedness of spirituality and the transformative learning process was critical to understanding the experience. Ultimately, the learning was not fully accepted until a connection was made back to "God" and the metaphysical world (Merriam & Ntseane, 2008).

Another study relates to culture and the significance of community responsibilities, relationships, and gender roles (Merriam & Ntseane, 2008). Participants often cited their consideration of learning with regard to family and community responsibilities, such as caring for a dying parent and educating the community about HIV/AIDS. In both examples, participants felt they could explain their learning as a part of cultural responsibility and ultimately translate the learning into an integrated part of their daily lives. Similarly, gender roles affected how participants framed transformative learning experiences, such as the cultural view of women. Two participants in abusive marriages explained an abused woman is expected to remain in the relationship and is often blamed for causing the abuse. The cultural norms associated with their learning were called upon as they questioned the relevance to their personal experience (Merriam & Ntseane, 2008).

These findings offer an important update to transformative learning theory because learning can be more deeply understood through the lens of culture. The role culture plays in our view of transformative learning may influence parts of Mezirow's 10-phase process, such as how an individual questions cultural norms related to learning experiences and generates a new framework (Merriam & Ntseane, 2008). Consideration of culture in the transformational learning process showed less orientation toward a rational processing of transformative learning experiences in favor of a more private and internal development of learning (Merriam & Ntseane, 2008). The distinction between Mezirow's rational and predominantly Western interpretation of a learning event, and Merriam and Ntseane's findings from an Afro-centrism perspective, highlight how culture can influence the mental frameworks we use to inform our learning.

EMOTIONS AND RELATIONSHIPS IN TRANSFORMATIVE LEARNING

The research on transformative learning theory has also made strides to understand how emotion can affect the learning process. Taylor's (2007) critique of the transformative learning literature emphasizes the need to seek further analysis about the impact of emotion. While Mezirow (2000) notes emotion could affect transformative learning, the original theory did not expand on the management and development of emotion during a transformative learning experience. Recent research, however, attempts to address the function of emotion as an integral part of transformative learning (Roberts, 2009; Stevens, Gerber, & Hendra, 2010). Emotion is defined as the feelings simultaneously associated with cognitive processes, physical reactions, and a variety of performances that can be behavioral in nature (Goleman, 1997).

In Roberts' (2009) study of spirituality's role in transformative learning, emotions appeared at various times throughout the process and played an important role in transformative learning experiences. The translation of emotion occurred when participants described moving through Mezirow's ten phases of transformative learning. All but one participant experienced more than one emotion during the process. At various points in time, the participants felt negative or positive emotions, or both: frustration, depression, excitement, amazement, fear, inadequacy, happiness, gratitude, disappointment, anger, loneliness, apathy, grief, pain, regret, sadness, jealousy, guilt, devastation, acrimony, confusion, shock, and resentment (Roberts, 2009). They did not experience shame and experienced more emotions than anger, fear, and guilt, contrasting with Mezirow's original findings. The finding that individuals who have experienced transformative learning describe more emotions than Mezirow originally identified offers an expansion to transformative learning theory.

Scoffham and Barnes (2009) also found emotion is an important component of transformative and deep learning, as experienced by U.K. students participating in an intercultural study visit to India. The qualitative study included eleven participants, ten female and one male, who were all racially White and from middle- to upper-class socioeconomic backgrounds (Scoffham & Barnes, 2009). The researchers describe students' expressed deep emotions in response to the transformative learning that took place as a result of the visit:

> Some students expressed their anger and irritation at the demands being placed upon them. One felt "frustrated" when her roommate woke her up by sleep-talking, another found herself "irritated" when the rest of the group made simplistic judgments, a third, more self-critically, noted that she was "shocked and disappointed" by her own response to a difficult situation. (Scoffham & Barnes, 2009, p. 264)

Similar to Roberts (2009) findings, the students describe a variety of emotions influenced their learning, such as shock. Both studies note the role of emotions appears to influence the transformation as participants called upon their old and new frameworks to make sense of their learning.

While emotions have been shown to affect individuals in a variety of ways in a transformative learning event, a gap remains in understanding how different emotions might appear at different phases of the transformative learning process. For example, individuals might be more likely to experience positive or negative emotions as a result of fitting a new worldview into their life during the theory's action phase. In a study of daughters learning to care for elderly parents, Owens (2004) pointed out the emotional process of caring for a parent needs to be considered. The women in the study were actively engaged in the new role of caregiver, rather than being the person cared for, which could provide a multifaceted understanding about the emotions associated with learning process.

Implications for further research about how emotions affect the transformative learning process exist as possible ways to further develop the theory. As Taylor (2007) points out, cultivating an emotional response to help facilitate a transformative learning experience continues to be an important area; little is known about engaging emotion in practice and the relationship to critical reflection. The findings from Roberts (2009) and Scoffham and Barnes (2009) underscore how emotions can be explained by a preexisting frame, such as spirituality, or influenced by a new experience, such as visiting another country.

Critical Reflection in Transformative Learning

Critical reflection is central to the transformative learning process, to identify why, how, and to what extent a transformative learning experience has taken place. The literature about transformative learning often notes reflection took place for participants, but does not describe how they understood the reflection to be critical as opposed to a surface-level reflection (Taylor, 2007). This view of reflection stems from the issue that categorizing, or measuring reflection, can be deeply subjective in nature. Because individuals are often asked to describe their transformative learning, they must call upon their personal understanding of the experience and definition of what it means to be reflective. Kreber (2004) and Liimatainen, Poskiparta, Karhila, and Sjogren (2001) discuss the need to identify consistent ways to determine whether individuals have reached the level of critical reflection. While the attempt to measure the concept of reflection airs toward a Western perspective for positivist practices, the literature reveals reflection is considered as an area for further study.

Merriam (2004) posited research methods to capture critical reflection will likely be criticized for validity and reliability, because the measures are often subjective in nature. Additionally, she calls for an expansion to Mezirow's theory "to include more 'connected,' affective, and intuitive dimensions on an equal footing with cognitive and rational components" (Merriam, 2004, p. 67), which may come in the form of qualitative research. Stevens et al. (2010) offer an answer to Merriam's call for qualitative approaches to assess critical reflection in the form of an approach to *prior learning assessment* and student development of a *prior learning portfolio*. The study involved an in-depth review of student-submitted PLPs, used to determine if college credit should be earned for a prior learning experience. The 45 study participants ranged in age from 26 to 61 years and were predominantly female (91%) and racially White (71%) (Stevens et al., 2010).

According to Stevens et al. (2010), the portfolios were reviewed for critical reflection on the learning experience, using a process resembling triangulation in qualitative research through reviewing data from multiple angles. The researchers describe the evaluation process of students' transformative learning:

> We then independently and carefully reviewed each transcript and decided if the respondent described her or his [prior learning portfolio] experience in ways that fit within the framework of our definition [of Mezirow's transformative learning].... They (selected reviewers) were then asked to code the transcripts by denoting which phase, if any, was reflected in the transcript content and whether the content indicated no change; a change in degree, affirmation, or validation; or a dramatic change in how the respondent saw himself or herself alone or in relation to others or the world (Stevens et al., 2010, p. 386).

The description of the researchers' process to determine if transformative learning had taken place depended upon the students' written reflections about their learning. By using a method often utilized in qualitative research, they were able to compare their interpretations about the depth of the students' reflections.

While the research findings indicate certain levels of written reflection could be evaluated through a qualitative approach, the process did not ensure the absence of critical reflection if the participant failed to meet the written requirements (Stevens et al., 2010). One of the limitations was a student may not have fully responded to the open-ended question in a manner matching the established criteria for transformative learning. As Merriam (2004) cautions, the ability to find quantitative notions of validity and reliability from the reflective data may not provide an accurate measure of the construct.

Learners' Role in Transformative Learning

Taylor (2007) argued the transformative learning literature has not successfully provided an in-depth consideration about how students impact their own process of transformative learning. Much research is geared toward how to foster transformative learning, but the process can be helped or hindered by the students themselves (Young, Mountford, & Skrla, 2006). Specifically important to understanding the role of students in their own transformative learning is the ability for students to select the learning they choose to pursue.

Young et al. (2006) conducted a qualitative study of 27 students using open-ended questioning methods to study reflections about their introduction to feminist literature in educational leadership. The researchers sought to understand how students were transformed by reading and learning about feminist literature and whether or not they ultimately acted on the learning: "Most students believed that their beliefs had changed to some degree as a result of exposure to feminist literature, though fewer appeared to have changed their behaviors. Results also demonstrated the existence of student resistance to transforming beliefs and behaviors about gender issues" (Young et al., 2006, p. 270). The study's findings suggest students often put up roadblocks to full transformative learning by choosing not to act on their new learning; resistance to transformative learning played a part in this study's results (Young et al., 2004).

Young et al. (2004) found distancing, opposition, and intense emotions reoccurred as themes in student responses to learning about diversity and gender issues. Distancing behaviors included instances when male students expressed a clear understanding of gender privilege, but would not express they themselves were recipients of such privileges (Young et al., 2004). The use of opposition as a resistance behavior was evident when students attempted to undermine new learning about gender issues in order to keep the status quo in place (Young et al., 2004). The researchers also found students used intense emotions as a barrier to transformative learning and chose to stop their own progress when the emotional burden became uncomfortable (Young et al., 2004). This study's findings suggest transformative learning experiences are directly tied to the individual's desire, or developmental capacity, to undergo a transformative learning experience, aligning with previous recommendations to research this cognitive process (Merriam et al., 2007; Taylor, 2007).

Summary

The literature on transformative learning has captured the attention of a variety of scholars, especially in formal educational settings (Taylor, 2007). The use of Mezirow's transformative learning theory has been successful in providing insight into how people make meaning of their learning experiences, but research in particular areas remains limited (Taylor, 2007). Four areas of limited research on transformative learning include transformative learning in different contexts, the role and impact of emotion and relationships in the transformative learning process, how critical reflection is identified, and the learner's role in a transformative learning experience (Merriam, 2004; Taylor, 2007).

The context of a transformative learning experience was found to impact individuals' meaning making frameworks because they often pulled information from past familial experiences and current experiences in their personal and professional worlds (Clark, 1991). Context was also examined in a series of studies of people living with chronic illness. The diagnosis of HIV/AIDS was a disorienting dilemma, triggering the transformative learning process, leading to sustained meaning making (Courtenay et al., 1998; Courtenay, Merriam, Reeves, & Baumgartner, 2000; Baumgartner, 2002, 2011). Culture was studied as one element of context that can impact the transformative learning process because individuals use culturally relevant frameworks and assumptions to guide their thinking (Merriam & Ntseane, 2008). The role of emotions was found to impact transformative learning as participants gained a deeper understanding about the happenings in another country (Scoffham & Barnes, 2009). Emotions were relevant to transformative learning that took place in the context of spirituality and participants expressed many more emotions than originally noted by Mezirow (Roberts, 2009). Finally, the power of individuals to foster or resist a transformative learning experience was addressed through a study of students who were introduced to feminist perspectives in the educational administration literature (Young et al., 2006). Students could often express they had learned something transformative, but rarely acted on the new knowledge by employing a variety of resistance techniques.

While the research on transformative learning theory has begun to address some gaps proposed by scholars, there is a need for more research in the aforementioned areas. Much research continues to be situated in formal educational settings, although some studies have broadened into community settings in the Western and international contexts. The intersection of context, emotion, resistance, and reflection offers an in-depth look at the various ways transformative learning takes place because learning often takes place across the contexts.

Transformative Learning Theory as Research Framework

Over the years, scholars have explored transformative learning theory through a variety of theoretical and practical perspectives (Dirkx, 1998). This speaks to the theory's generalizability across cultures, ethnicities, genders, and disciplines. Transformative learning theory remains applicable and relevant across disciplines in studies using varied methodological approaches. While most studies utilize a qualitative methodology, the research methods have evolved into more creative applications, including "longitudinal designs, action research, scales, surveys, content analysis of various documentation (e.g., e-mails, journals, portfolios) and the use of stimulated recall via video recordings and photo-elicitation interviews" (Taylor, 2007, p. 176). Transformative learning theory continues to be popular as evidenced by the large number of peer-reviewed journal publications and a dedicated international conference, namely, *Transformative Learning Conference.*

A literature search conducted on the ProQuest Dissertations and Theses database indicated a multitude of studies using transformative learning theory as the primary theoretical framework or related theory conceptions. These studies were generated by scholars from all over the world and range from topics of leadership and church spiritual maturity, to healthcare education and even quantum mechanics.

In this section, we highlight how transformative learning theory is used in five recent dissertation studies (see Appendix). The studies exemplify the theory's generalizability across disciplines using varied research methods. For each study, we describe the overall purpose and methodology, summarize the findings, discuss how the study contributes to the literature on transformative learning theory, and, where applicable, highlight recommendations for further research.

- ***Examining Teacher Beliefs About Diverse Students Through Transformative Learning: The Common Beliefs Survey and the Disorienting Dilemma* (Grand, 2011)**

In this study, Grand (2011) examined teachers' beliefs about their students who are ethnically, racially, and/or socioeconomically different from themselves. The study uses the transformative learning framework to explore the phenomenon of the disorienting dilemma, by studying the education students' experiences using the Common Beliefs Survey (CBS). As part of a Teaching Diverse Students Initiative (TDSi), the CBS is a tool theoretically aligned with Mezirow's (1991) concept of the disorienting dilemma as the "kick off" to the transformation process (Grand, 2011). The survey was designed, in part, to create a response much like a disorienting dilemma, in order to move teachers into the process similar to perspective transformation for teaching diverse students.

The research was conducted among three cohorts of education students enrolled at different postsecondary institutions. Two of the cohorts were comprised of graduate students and the third cohort of undergraduate students. The study also involved two teacher educators connected to the two graduate student cohorts. Both teacher educators were registered users on the Teaching Diverse Students Initiative website and had incorporated the CBS into their courses.

The study used a combination of survey, interview, and case study methods to collect, analyze, and report the data from the three respondent types: teacher educators, graduate students who experienced the CBS in a facilitated environment, and undergraduate students who experienced the CBS in an unfacilitated environment. The study also explored variables that may contribute to CBS users' disorienting dilemmas, specifically CBS content, course facilitation, and user attributes. Several surveys were created to capture different slices of data, in order to understand the disorienting dilemmas and the variables contributing to them. After completing the surveys, all participants were interviewed using a semistructured interview format. The teacher educator data provided context for the two graduate cohorts and information about the type and quality of CBS-imbedded course facilitation. The student data was used to validate reported disorienting dilemmas. Processes for analyzing and categorizing the data were created, and the reported disorienting dilemmas and a case study format were used to report the findings.

Grand (2011) concurred with Taylor's (2000, 2007) critiques of transformative learning and suggestions for further research about theoretical comparisons, in-depth component analysis, strategies for fostering transformative learning, and the use of alternative methodological designs. However, Grand (2011) posits the current study makes a contribution toward filling in at least one research gap in the form of in-depth component analysis related to disorienting dilemmas by suggesting "this study's descriptions of participant's disorienting dilemmas provided confirmation to the assertions that disorienting dilemmas can be related to an epochal event, the accretion of experiences and knowledge or anywhere in between" (p. 205). Based on the study's findings, transformative learning can be used as a framework to examine teachers' beliefs about race, ethnicity, and socioeconomic status, and the changes in meaning perspective over time. Overall, the theory's applicability speaks to how it can be used as a framework to explore strategies and methods to improve teacher preparation and professional development about teaching diverse students.

- ***Developing Executives Through the Exploration of Personal Histories: A Phenomenological Study of Transformative Learning in the Executive Development Process* (Hamilton, 2011)**

This study's focus is the executive development process within a corporate environment context. Hamilton

(2011) used a phenomenological approach to examine how developing executives experienced an intense psychologist-led executive-feedback session and the impact on them as leaders. The study examined the participants' developing self-awareness, to enhance deeper understanding of themselves as individuals and the source of their patterns of behavior and motivations. Essentially, Hamilton (2011) used transformative learning theory as the framework to guide the study, focusing on the executives' development experiences and the process by which their learning may be characterized as transformative. To better understand the developing executives' mental models and how these models influence their daily behaviors and beliefs, Hamilton (2011) used Mezirow's (1981, 1991) transformative learning theory, specifically perspective transformation, as the framework to examine the executive development process.

Using the phenomenological approach supported the study's purpose of understanding the developing executives' learning experiences, especially from an intense feedback session. The session was designed to connect significant childhood experiences and various psychological assessment results to present-day leadership behaviors. Three main questions guided the study:

- What is the lived experience of developing executives who progress through a feedback session designed to connect early-childhood and young-adult experiences, beliefs, and marker events to present-day leadership behaviors?
- In what ways do these developing executives experience this process as transformative?
- What has been the impact of this executive-feedback experience on them as leaders?

In the study, 11 developing executives were interviewed and, using a phenomenological approach, extensive coding and clustering were completed for interpretation, followed by a thematic analysis to address the study's inquiry area. The study's findings suggest a deep internal struggle existed within each developing executive. The transformative learning theory was useful in highlighting the ways in which the executives developed their intrapersonal skills. In addition, the study contributes to the literature by providing an avenue for an organization to address the deep development process involved in executive development, particularly as it relates to self-learning and the development process.

- ***A Grounded Theory of Behavior Transformation Among Filipino Christian Women (Snider, 2011)***

This study's purpose was to discover and understand the process by which Filipino women, who each self-identify as born-again Christians, changed their behavior to align with what they perceived as acceptable biblical behavior, sometimes in ways they recognized as counter-cultural. One main research question guided the study: How does behavior transformation occur in born-again urban Filipino Christian women coming from a Roman Catholic tradition?

This grounded theory study sought to understand and describe the process by which self-identified born-again Filipino women change their behavior after conversion. Grounded theory uses multiple data collections and the refinement and interrelationships of information categories "to derive a general, abstract theory of a process, action, or interaction grounded in the views" of study participants (Creswell, 2003, p. 14). The study proposed a substantive theory about the transformation process and was grounded in data from 24 semistructured interviews with Filipinas, ranging in age from 22 to 62 years, who became born-again as adults. The interviews were done in the context of the role of women as the "heart of the Filipino family." Snider (2011) also utilized participant-observation methods and open-ended interviews to capture the meanings ascribed to the participants' experiences within their entire context.

Participants were selected through grounded theory sampling to ensure they could build informative interpretation toward the construction of a theory of explanation. As such, the women were required to be over the age of 21 years, self-identified as first generation Christians, and endorsed by a pastor or credible Christian lay-leaser, in addition to having lived most of their lives in the Philippines and able to speak English. Snider (2011) emphasized Mezirow's work and the intersection of the participants' behavioral changes in relation to transformative learning theory.

Using an inductive strategy, data analysis in this study involved reflection, axial coding, comparative analysis, and theory formulation. The participants explained their transformational journey was personal and far reaching, extending to impact the larger sociocultural context. As such, Snider (2011) shows the intersection of Freire's (1997) sociocultural transformation theory and how Filipinos transform their individual behavior. In addition, although Snider reports minor discrepancies between Mezirow's ideas and the study, the theory is workable, practically and theoretically as the study's framework.

The findings suggest context and culture affected transformation in the Philippine framework and the participants agree with Mezirow that a rational analytical process does not depend on cultural mores. As such, they reported the process as being a holistic one, involving cognition and emotion. Overall, transformative learning theory is highlighted in this study as a means of understanding the change process and, therefore, compatible in many ways with the behavior change process after conversion in Filipino women.

In terms of contribution to the literature on transformative learning theory, this study, and the substantive theory generated from it, conforms to transformative learning precepts. It confirms the tenets are applicable in contexts outside of the traditional educational ones into those embracing religion or spirituality.

- ***Transformational Learning Experiences Among Latina who Have Attained Tenure Status (Salazar, 2011)***

Using transformative learning theory as a mechanism to explore how Latinas operate within academia, Salazar (2011) designed a qualitative study to understand their transformational learning experiences and impact on academic experience and teaching styles. Four research questions guided the data collection and analysis:

- How do Latinas that reach a tenure status interpret their journey and experiences within academia?
- How do they describe their working and teaching organizational culture?
- What types of leadership skills do they possess?
- How do they describe their experiences in relation to their larger community?

To address the research questions, the methodological approach was based on a qualitative interpretive design. This design held the focus on the women's narratives of their experiences in a multicultural learning organization. Participants were selected based on their affiliation with diversity programs and committees on campus. The recruitment strategy's main criteria for participants included Latina scholars, U.S. citizens, and attended U.S. colleges and universities.

Using a phenomenological research design with purposive and criterion-based sampling, the participants had an opportunity to challenge their mental states and explore convictions through a series of semi-structured one-on-one interviews, 1-month personal reflections (captured via digital recorders), focus group interviews, class observations, and document analysis of curriculum vitas and published works. Using narrative and performance analysis, Salazar (2011) used a grounded theory approach to identify themes, code the interview data, and perform a content analysis.

In studying the participants' life stories, the tenured-Latinas' transformational experiences were examined to explore how those experiences affected leadership and teaching styles. The findings suggest each Latina professor had transformational learning experiences, some of which were negative and challenging. According to Salazar (2011), the negative and challenging experiences may not lie in tandem with Goleman's (1997) critical components of transformational learning: trustworthiness, emotional intelligence, honesty, and integrity. Given the experiences and context of discrimination against the participants within academia, the Latina professors were skeptical of White people. The findings suggest transformational learning can occur without Goleman's critical components. This study contributes to the transformative learning literature with implications for resilience theory.

Overall, the study finds the Latina women showed great resiliency and commitment to diversity and promoting social change. Despite the challenging experiences on the journey to achieve tenure, these experiences were described as part of a transformation process, speaking directly to transformative learning theory's applicability to the study.

- ***A Phenomenological Study: Educational Experiences of International Doctoral Students of Education at a Midwestern University (Unyapho, 2011)***

In this phenomenological study, Unyapho (2011) used transformative learning theory as a complementary theory to examine the educational experiences of six international doctoral students of education at a Midwestern university. Interested in understanding international doctoral education students as learners and how they narrate their educational experiences, he examined their experiences in American academic culture, paying attention to how they negotiated identities, engaged in critical reflection, and made meaning (Unyapho, 2011).

One main research question guided the study, followed by two subquestions:

- How do international doctoral students in the field of education in a U.S. university critically reflect on their experiences as learners?
- How do international doctoral students describe their academic experience during their doctoral studies at a college of education?
- How do international doctoral students in a college of education negotiate their identities as learners in a U.S.-dominant academic culture?

To address these research questions, critical theory was used to explore issues related to knowledge, power, and human agency from the participants' perspectives, especially as they developed critical consciousness. Cocultural theory was used to explore how the international students participating in the study negotiated their learner identities in their classes and, for some, as teaching assistants. The concept of cultural scripts was another theoretical concept used to drive the study, by guiding the discussion and interpretation of the reported educational experiences. These theories were used in conjunction with transformative learning theory.

Data collection included a series of three in-depth, semistructured interviews with each participant and two focus group interviews. The data were coded, looking for three central topics of self-reflection, transformative experiences, and meaning making.

The study's findings revealed much of the transformation and meaning making related to the students' instrumental learning. As a result, a major implication from this study is the need for learning facilitators to encourage students to expand their frames of reference, by encouraging meaningful discussion beyond instrumental learning, resulting in critical thinking, accountability, and development of critical consciousness. In addition to contributing to the literature on international students studying in the United States, particularly related to their identity negotiation as learners in an American context, this study contributes to the literature on transformative learning theory regarding how participation in the research process can trigger a perspective transformation.

Conclusion

In this chapter, we provided an overview of transformative learning theory as conceptualized by Mezirow, including his 10-phased transformative learning process. We reviewed the theory's main constructs, including meaning making, frames of reference, habits of mind, points of view, domains of learning, critical reflection, and disorienting dilemmas. After summarizing the theory's development and evolution, critiques of transformative learning theory were identified and discussed using research from the literature. Finally, we explored recent dissertations used highlight transformative learning theory as a research framework. For more than 3 decades, transformative learning theory has been discussed, experienced, applied, formed, developed, expanded, and evolved. We look forward to continued scholarly discussion about transformative learning theory as a viable framework for understanding how adults learn and develop from the disorienting dilemmas that confront them as they live their personal and professional lives.

References

Allen, G. (2008). Practicing teachers and web 2.0 technologies: Possibilities for transformative learning (Doctoral dissertation). , Teachers College, Columbia, University, New York, NY. Available from ProQuest Dissertations and Theses database. (UMI No. 3327101)

Baumgartner, L. M. (2002). Living and learning with HIV/AIDS: Transformational tales continued. *Adult Education Quarterly, 53*(1), 44-59.

Baumgartner, L. M. (2011). The role of adult learning in coping with chronic illness [Part of a special issue: Adult education for health and wellness]. *New Directions for Adult and Continuing Education, 130*, 7-16.

Brookfield, S. D. (2004). Critical thinking techniques. In M. G. Galbraith (Ed.), *Adult learning methods: A guide for effective instruction* (3rd ed., pp. 341-360). Malabar, FL: Krieger.

Clark, M. C. (1991). *The restructuring of meaning: An analysis of the impact of context on transformational learning* (Unpublished doctoral dissertation). University of Georgia, Athens.

Courtenay, B. C., Merriam, S. B., & Reeves, P. M. (1998). The centrality of meaning-making in transformational learning: Flow HIV-positive adults make sense of their lives. *Adult Education Quarterly, 48*(2), 65-84.

Courtenay, B. C., Merriam, S. B., Reeves, P. M., & Baumgartner, L. M. (2000). Perspective transformation over time: A 2-year follow-up study of HIV-positive adults. *Adult Education Quarterly, 50*(2), 102-119.

Cranton, P. (1994). *Understanding and Promoting Transformative Learning*. San Francisco, CA: Jossey-Bass.

Cranton, P. (1996). *Professional development as transformative learning*. San Francisco, CA: Jossey-Bass.

Cranton, P. (2002). Teaching for transformation. *New Directions for Adult & Continuing Education*, 93, 63-71. Retrieved from http://web.ebscohost.com/ehost/pdfviewer/pdfviewer?sid=cdaf67ee-cf10-452c-8999-d48a28036509%40sessionmgr4&vid=2&hid=13

Creswell, J. W. (2003). *Research design* (2nd ed.). Thousand Oaks, CA: SAGE.

Cuddapah, J. (2005). *Exploring first-year teacher learning through the lens of Mezirow's transformative learning theory* (Doctoral dissertation). Columbia University Teachers College, New York, NY. Available from ProQuest Dissertations and Theses database. (UMI No. 3175680)

Dirkx, J. (1998). Transformative learning theory in the practice of adult education: An overview. *PACE Journal of Lifelong Learning*, 7, 1-14.

Freire. P. (1997). *Pedagogy of the oppressed*. New York, NY: The Continuum.

Goleman, D. (1997). *Emotional intelligence: Why it can matter more than IQ*. New York, NY: Bantam Books.

Grand, D. (2011). *Examining teacher beliefs about diverse students through transformative learning: The common beliefs survey and the disorienting dilemma* (Doctoral dissertation). University of Maryland, College Park, MD. Available from ProQuest Dissertations and Theses database. (UMI No. 3461621)

Habermas, J. (1971). *Knowledge and human interests*. Boston, MA: Beacon Press.

Hamilton, R. (2011). *Developing executives through the exploration of personal histories: A phenomenological study of transformative learning in the executive development process* (Doctoral dissertation). George Washington University, Washington, DC. Available from ProQuest Dissertations and Theses database. (UMI No. 3426448)

Kitchenham, A. (2008). The evolution of John Mezirow's transformative learning theory. *Journal of Transformative*

Education, 6, 104-123. Retrieved from http://jtd.sagepub.com/content/6/2/104.full.pdf+html

Kreber, C. (2004). An analysis of two models of reflection and their implications for educational development. *International Journal for Academic Development, 9*, 29-49.

Liimatainen, L., Poskiparta, M., Karhila, P., & Sjogren, A. (2001). The development of reflective learning in the context of health counseling and health promotion during nurse education. *Journal of Advanced Nursing, 34*, 648-658.

Merriam, S. B. (2004). The role of cognitive development in Mezirow's transformational learning theory. *Adult Education Quarterly, 55*(1), 60-68.

Merriam, S. B., Caffarella, R. S., & Baumgartner, L. M. (2007). *Learning in adulthood: A comprehensive guide.* San Francisco, CA: Jossey-Bass.

Merriam, S. B., & Ntseane, G. (2008). Transformational learning in Botswana: How culture shapes the process. *Adult Education Quarterly, 58*(3), 183-197.

Mezirow, J. (1975). *Education for perspective transformation: Women's reentry programs in community colleges.* New York, NY: Center for Adult Education, Teachers College, Columbia University.

Mezirow, J. (1981). A critical theory of adult learning and education. *Adult Education, 32*(1), 3-24.

Mezirow, J. (1990). *Fostering critical reflection in adulthood: A guide to transformative and emancipatory learning.* San Francisco, CA: Jossey-Bass.

Mezirow, J. (1991). *Transformative dimensions of adult learning.* San Francisco, CA: Jossey Bass.

Mezirow, J. (1996). Contemporary paradigms of learning. *Adult Education Quarterly, 46*, 158-172.

Mezirow, J. (1997). Transformative learning: Theory to practice. *New Directions for Adult and Continuing Education, 74*, 5-12.

Mezirow, J. (2000). Learning to think like an adult. In J. Mezirow and associates (Eds.) *Learning as transformation* (pp. 3-33). San Francisco, CA: Jossey-Bass.

Mezirow, J. (2009). Transformative learning theory. In J. Mezirow & E. W. Taylor (Ed.), *Transformative learning in practice* . San Francisco, CA: Wiley.

Owens, M. N. (2004). *The lived experience of daughters who care for frail, elderly parents in the parents' home* (Doctoral dissertation). Available from ProQuest Dissertations and Theses database. (UMI No. 3146516)

Roberts, N. A. (2009). *The role of spirituality in transformative learning* (Doctoral dissertation). Florida International University, Miami, FL. Available from ProQuest Dissertations and Theses database. (UMI No. 3377924)

Salazar, A. (2011). *Transformational learning experiences among Latinas who have attained tenure status in* academia (Doctoral dissertation). University of New Mexico, Albuquerque, NM. Available from ProQuest Dissertations and Theses database. (UMI No. 3460999)

Scoffham, S., & Barnes, J. (2009). Transformational experiences and deep learning: The impact of an intercultural study visit to India on UK initial teacher education students. *Journal of Education for Teaching, 35*(3), 257-270.

Snider, K. (2011). *A grounded theory of behavior transformation among Filipino Christian women* (Doctoral dissertation). Available from ProQuest Dissertations and Theses database. (UMI No. 3462038)

Stevens, K., Gerber, D., & Hendra, R. (2010). Transformational learning through prior learning assessment. *Adult Education Quarterly, 60*(4), 377-404.

Taylor, E. (2000). Analyszing research on transformative learning theory. In J. Mezirow & Associates (Eds.) *Learning as transformation: Critical perspectives on a theory in progress* (pp. 285-328). San Francisco, CA: Jossey Bass.

Taylor, E. (2007). An update of transformative learning theory: A critical review of the empirical research (1999-2005). *International Journal of Lifelong Education, 26*(2), 173-191.

Unyapho, P. (2011). *A phenomenological study: Educational experiences of international doctoral students of education at a midwestern* university (Doctoral dissertation). Available from ProQuest Dissertations and Theses database. (UMI No. 3460462)

Whitney, A. (2006). *The transformative power of writing: Teachers writing in a national writing project summer institute* (Doctoral dissertation). University of California, Santa Barbara. Available from ProQuest Dissertations and Theses database. (UMI No. 305348096

Young, M., Mountford, M., & Skrla, L. (2006). Infusing gender and diversity issues into educational leadership programs: Transformational learning and resistance. *Journal of Educational Administration, 44*(3), 264-277.

Author Contact Information: Mary V. Alfred, PhD, Texas A&M University, College Station, TX, 804 Harrington Tower, 4222 TAMU, College Station, TX 77843-4222. Telephone: 979-845-2718. E-mail: malfred@tamu.edu

(Appendix appears on next page)

Appendix: Transformative Learning Theory as Theoretical Framework for Research

Author (Year) Themes	Dissertation	Research Study	Findings	Implications
Grand (2011) • Diversity • Teacher professional development	Examining teacher beliefs about diverse students through transformative learning: The common beliefs survey and the disorienting dilemma	Qualitative study of three student cohorts at different institutions, using surveys, interviews, and case studies to examine beliefs about diverse students and disorienting dilemmas	• Disorienting dilemmas can be related to an epochal event, the accretion of experiences and knowledge, or anywhere in between.	• Transformative learning theory can be used as a framework to deal with teacher beliefs about race, ethnicity, and socioeconomic status. • Expanded use of the theory as a framework can include improving teacher preparation and professional development around teaching diverse students.
Hamilton (2011) • Executive/leadership development • Corporate context	Developing executives through the exploration of personal histories: A phenomenological study of transformative learning the executive development process	Qualitative phenomenological study to examine how 11 developing executives experience an intense executive-feedback session, led by a psychologist, and the impact of this session on them as leaders	• Developing executives experienced a deep internal struggle. • Transformative learning theory highlighted the ways in which the executives developed their intrapersonal skills.	• Provides an avenue for an organization to address the deep development process involved in executive development, particularly as it relates to self-learning and the related development process.
Snider (2011) • Cultural context • Religion/spirituality	A grounded theory of behavior transformation among Filipino christian women	Qualitative study of 24 Filipinas to discover and understand the process by which the women, who each self-identify as born-again Christians, change their behavior to align with what they perceive as acceptable biblical behavior, sometimes in ways they recognize as counter-cultural	• Context and culture affected transformation in the Philippine framework • Participants agree with Mezirow that a rational analytical process does not depend on cultural mores. • As such, participants reported the process as being a holistic one, involving cognition and emotion.	• Transformative learning theory tenets are applicable beyond the traditional educational context to contexts embracing religion or spirituality.
Salazar (2011) • Diversity • Emotions	Transformational learning experiences among Latina who have attained tenure status	Qualitative phenomenological study of U.S. Latina scholars to understand their transformational learning experiences and how they affect academic experience and teaching styles	• Each Latina professor had transformational learning experiences, some of which were negative and challenging. • Negative and challenging experiences may not lie in tandem with Goleman's (1998) critical components of transformational learning: trustworthiness, emotional intelligence, honesty, and integrity.	Transformational learning can occur without Goleman's critical components of trustworthiness, emotional intelligence, honesty, and integrity. Contributes to transformative learning literature with implications for resilience theory.
Unyapho (2011) • Diversity • Research as transformation trigger	A phenomenological study: Educational experiences of international doctoral students of education at a midwestern university	Qualitative phenomenological study of six international doctoral students of education at a Midwestern University to examine how they make meaning of their educational experiences	• Much of the transformation and meaning making related to the students' instrumental learning. • Participation in the research process triggered a perspective transformation.	• Frames of reference may be expanded by encouraging meaningful discussion beyond instrumental learning, resulting in critical thinking, accountability, and development of critical consciousness. • Transformative learning can be triggered by the research process.

(Appendix continues on next page)

Appendix (Continued)

Author (Year) Themes	Dissertation	Research Study	Findings	Implications
Additional Dissertations Not Discussed in the Text				
Allen (2008) • Technology • Teacher professional development	Practicing teachers and Web 2.0 technologies: Possibilities for transformative learning	Qualitative case study of five K-12 public school teachers to determine if Web 2.0 technology tools prompted significant changes in role perception in and out of the classroom	• Four participants experienced transformative learning in the classroom • Three participants experience transformative learning out of the classroom • Two participants were in emerging states of transformative learning out of the classroom	• Researchers can benefit from using transformative learning theory as a framework for changes in teacher practice.
Cuddapah (2005) • New teacher development	Exploring first year teacher learning through the Lens of Mezirow's transformative learning theory	Qualitative study of 10 teachers using a variety of methods to explore the extent to which first-year teaching experiences were connected to transformative learning theory	• Eight of the 10 teachers experienced transformative learning with different alignments to the multi-phased transformative learning process • Participants experiences unique triggering events • Timing of disorienting dilemmas varied	• In order to support new teacher development it is important to keep in mind learning occurs in context, in community, and through teaching experiences. • Providing support to new teachers can be enhanced by recognizing learning is triggered at different times, in different ways.
Whitney (2006) • Writing • Teacher professional development	The transformative power of writing: Teachers writing in a national writing project summer institute	Qualitative study of seven K-12 teachers using interviews, observation, and writing analysis to examine the relationship between teachers' writing experiences and transformative professional development	• Writing played a critical role in several phases: • Self-examination • Trying new roles • Building confidence and competence • Self-monitoring was increased through the writing group and contributed to transformative learning	• Researchers can benefit from using transformative learning theory as a framework for professional development • Writing may play a critical role in supporting and contributing to transformative learning.

CHAPTER 13

Stage Theory of Cognitive Development

Janet Tareilo
Stephen F. Austin State University

Children develop their concept of the world around them based on their own understandings, their age, and their ability to process incoming information. Knowledge and learning result from this interchange. Each level of understanding then results in a continued complexity of thought (Brooks & Brooks, 2001). Slavin (2000) contends that "development refers to how people grow, adapt, and change through physical, personality, socioemotional, cognitive, and language development" (p. 28) and that by understanding that this occurs in and through various stages helps to define how learning takes place. The person who understood this phenomenon the most was Jean Piaget (1896-1980) who became a leading voice in the area of cognitive development of children by using skills of observation, having simple conversations, and listening attentively to children's responses (Atherton, 2011). Biehler (1978) suggests that Piaget "exerted more influence on theoretical discussions of development and on educational practices than any other [living] psychologist" (p. 150).

Though not an educator at heart, Piaget's work with Alfred Binet, who was studying the commonality of children's responses on a testing instrument, led him to question not only how the children responded but how they derived at their answers (Sadker & Sadker, 2005). His observations began by watching his own children grow and learn and broadened into an epistemological stance of understanding the acquisition of knowledge. His exploration into discovering the concept of cognitive development occurred because he proposed as a child aged, there were four distinct stages that allowed a child to receive new information and then process that information into learning (Slavin, 2000). Piaget's theory of cognitive development actually presented learning in such a way that parents and educators could understand a child's readiness to learn new skills as well as the type of experiences that would impact learning at each of the four stages (Seifert, 2011).

While learning is the result of an individual child's interactions with his world and certain stimuli, Piaget believed that development and learning were dissimilar in fact due to the creation of distinct structures that enabled a child to process specific information (Siegler, 2005). Siegler (2005) further asserts that developmental sequences occur that enable a child to accept or adapt to new learning. The idea that the process of learning could be different but the path taken to learn was the same supported Piaget's conceptualization of cognitive development.

Stages of Cognitive Development

Piaget's four stages of cognitive development stood as collective reflections of his observations of what children had the capacity to learn and when certain skills and knowledge could be learned. He perceived that the stages never changed and every child passed through these stages in a sequential order. At each stage, children demonstrated new intellectual abilities and these abilities increased their levels of understanding (Wood, Smith, & Grossniklaus, 2001). The stages of cognitive development included (1) sensorimotor, (2) preoperational, (3) concrete operational, and (4) formal operational and stipulated that at each stage a child required specific experiences to ensure learning (Wood, et al., 2001). The progressive nature of each stage examined how age and cognitive abilities influenced learning and the acquisition of skills (see Table 13.1).

The Handbook of Educational Theories, pp. 149–153

Table 13.1. Piaget's Stages of Cognitive Development

Sensorimotor	Preoperational	Concrete Operational	Formal Operational
Birth–2 years of age	2–7 years of age	7–11 years of age	Adolescence to adulthood

Every stage involves a child's encounter with stimuli, his or her ability to process information, and then a follow through with the organization of those thoughts to understand the world (Biehler, 1978). Brooks and Brooks (2001) view Piaget's stages as different places of thought processes that every child passes through according to the experiences provided at that particular time of growth as well as the actions taken by the child.

Sensorimotor Stage

During the first identified stage of cognitive development (birth to 2), a child primarily deals with his or her world through the use of their senses. Children experience trial and error thinking that leads to problem solving abilities appropriate for their age. Included in this stage is the concept of object permanence that allows a child to understand that an object, though out of sight, still exists. This ability leads a child to his or her learning of symbolic representation (Slavin, 2000).

Preoperational Stage

At approximately 2 years of age and until the age of 7, a child uses their concepts of symbols to make sense of objects. During this phase of development, the child acquires a great deal of language which in turn helps to stimulate his cognitive development. A major concept at this time is the principle of conservation that signifies an object stays the same regardless of other variables associated with the object. This stage also entails egocentric thinking in that everyone in the child's world thinks the way he or she does (Slavin, 2000).

Concrete Operational Stage

Many children enter school during this stage of cognitive development. This stage occurs between the ages of 7 and 11 and provides the child with experiences that develop his sense of reversibility and problem solving. Children during this stage are able to think logically but not abstractly. The child moves away from the importance of self (decentering) to being in the development of an imagination. Because of the age of the child, his world revolves around school, social interaction, and forming individual patters of thinking (Slavin, 2000).

Formal Operational Stage

The cognitive development at this stage includes a child's ability to move beyond the need for concrete objects to have an understanding of the world around them. Abstract and symbolic thinking are constantly in use as problem-solving and decision-making skills increase. This learning time brings children acceptances of things around them that help make acquire, process, and master new knowledge (Slavin, 2000).

Awareness of these stages of development provides a picture into the cognitive abilities of a child. Piaget realized there was a clear distinction in the differences that existed between the stages when objects were introduced, actions were required, and the thought process moved from a concrete to an abstract frame (Gardner, 1980). Seagal and Horne (1997) relate that recognition and understanding differences in the way children learn and acquire knowledge allow parents and educators to examine life and school experiences as well as instructional practices at the appropriate time when a child can accept what he or she is expected to learn.

Additional Piagetian Concepts Related to Cognitive Development

Cognitive development, as explained by Jean Piaget's four stages, includes additional concepts of learning that Piaget found equally important: (a) schemata; (b) assimilation; (c) accommodation; and (d) equilibration. These principles are ingrained into the learning experience based on Piaget's interest in biology and epistemology (Biehler, 1978).

Schema

In regards to Piagetian theory as defined by Wadsworth (2004), schemata are "the cognitive mental structures by which individuals intellectually adapt to and organize the environment" (p. 14). It is through the development of these schemes that children organize and process cognitive structures that determines their behaviors (Slavin, 2000). As a child moves through the cognitive stages of development, schema mature and change to allow children to develop necessary concepts related to their age and experiences. These changes occur through the ability a child has to assimilate and accommodate information.

Assimilation

Because each stage involves experiences that are varied and understood differently, a child must find a way to process incoming information. Assimilation allows children to comprehend the experiences by using existing schemata (Slavin, 2000).

Accommodation

When a child does not have a schema to make sense of the incoming information, he must modify or adjust an existing schema. This process is referred to as accommodation. By using this skill, children are able to understand new experiences (Slavin, 2000).

Equilibration

A key point in the discussion of developmental stages concerns the fact that children are constantly trying to remain balanced in their thinking and understanding. With equilibration, a child possesses the ability to remain in a state of stability and coherence to comprehend any inconsistency that arises in their experiences (Biehler, 1978).

Validation of the Theory Through an Educational Lens

Key to Piaget's foundation of cognitive development was the fact that the acquisition of knowledge was more important than being able to define knowledge (Campbell, 2006) and understanding this point was an essential element in the planning and implementation of instruction. Learning was a process that developed on a continuum with children taking an active role in the acquisition of skills and abilities because of a delineated readiness based on their ages (Duffy, 1996).

The goal of education then was not to consider results-based outcomes but to incorporate this belief with a child's eagerness to learn (Duffy, 1996). By addressing learning in developmental terms, Piaget contended that teaching and instructional strategies need to be addresses in relation to the child's level of cognitive ability (Wood et al., 2001). The concept of developmental and appropriate education could directly influence a teacher's use of resources, instructional materials, and the learning atmosphere (Slavin, 2000).

Seagal and Horne (1997) support these views when they discuss the importance of recognizing that learning does indeed occur in stages and children would acquire lasting knowledge by incorporating this thinking. Sadker and Sadker (2005) contend that using Piaget's theories could provide teachers with in depth ways to analyze a child's abilities and limitations to accept information based on their experiences.

Using Piagetian thinking, teachers should provide opportunities for the child to take an active role in their learning by presenting a variety of experiences, using open-ended questioning techniques, and individualizing instruction as much as possible (Biehler, 1978). The curriculum and materials used during the learning process would also be reflective of a child's abilities to absorb incoming information. Instruction and content should reflect a child's developmental level if mastery of subject matter and the acquisition of basic skills is expected (Wood et al., 2001). As a child progresses through school, Piaget's stages of cognitive development bring awareness to the most beneficial time to teach certain concepts, when to introduce abstract thinking, and give a child's ability to assess and process new information. With this in mind, a child will be given several opportunities to "discover and transform" knowledge on their own and by doing that a child discovers meaning, experiences a continual revision of existing knowledge, and plays as an active participant in their own learning (Slavin, 2000, p. 256).

The realization of this translates into specific practices for teachers (Berk, 1997):

1. provide appropriate learning opportunities;
2. ask students to explain their reasoning techniques;
3. provide discovery learning opportunities such as centers;
4. teach for mastery learning according to the specific stage of development; and
5. be prepared to accept children's individual differences.

Wood et al. (2001), using Piaget's stage theory advocate further suggestions for instruction:

1. use of hands-on learning;
2. provide learning situations that require a child to explore and experiment to develop new knowledge;
3. introduce complex terms at the appropriate time; and
4. encourage students to work together in problem-solving exercises.

In addition, Duffy (1996) recommends that teachers accept a Piaget frame of thinking by:

1. allowing students to discover answers on their own;
2. create learning situations that prompt the exploration of new concepts;
3. consider the individual intellectual abilities of each child; and
4. use teaching strategies that are appropriate and meaningful.

These beliefs about how children learn were instrumental in influencing the idea of constructivist learning (Brooks & Brooks, 2001) and led many to place the child at the center of cognition regardless of a prescribed curriculum or a predetermined grade level.

Constructivist thinking borrowed from the works of Piaget his idea that cognitive change occurs through a process and that process is determined by a child's age and his or her ability to use existing information to think in a more complex way (Slavin, 2000). Simply put, a child will learn what they need to know through self-discovery and student-centered instruction. A teacher acts as a facilitator during this process. Piaget's influence continues to be reflected in the use of Howard Gardner's Seven Intelligences and Marie Montessori's Method of Discovery Learning (Duffy, 1996). Munari (1994) suggests that Piaget's experimental data serves as a building block for Gardner, Montessori, and others who insisted a relationship existed between learning, knowledge, and readiness.

CRITICISMS OF PIAGET AND HIS STAGE DEVELOPMENT THEORY

The works of Jean Piaget regarding the stages of cognitive development created as many questions as it did inquiry into how children learned and formulated understanding about themselves and their world. Because of his background in biology, he viewed the process of cognitive development as a systemic reaction to receiving and translating incoming stimuli. However, not all of his contemporaries agreed with his methods or his findings.

As a researcher, Piaget's methods of collecting data came under much scrutiny. He lacked a control group, his sample size was small, and his disregard for statistical analysis of his findings led to the belief that his research was limited and created additional concerns about the generality of his findings (*Criticisms of Piaget's Theories*, n.d.). By using different groups of children for different studies, Piaget failed to consider a child's individual differences such as gender, socioeconomic status, or family patterns. Continued criticism arose because it appeared that there was far too much theorizing about the stages and not enough evidence to support the theories as well as the concern that Piaget excluded any alternative explanations for his findings (*Criticisms of Piaget's Theories*, n.d.). The merging of his findings from various studies also led to many questions about the reliability and validity of those studies.

The idea that children could not acquire advanced skills because they had not reached a certain stage of cognitive development falls as one of Piaget's shortcomings. Critics argue that the tasks children were asked to complete were too difficult, it was inconceivable to accept that thinking would be the same through each of the stages regardless of the task, and trying to teach advanced thought processes to children early would prove unsuccessful (Wood et al., 2002). Wood et al. (2002) maintain that continued research in this area has produced a deeper understanding of children's abilities to accept and process advanced skills when the instructional level is appropriate, the learner is considered as an individual, and a wide scope of learning opportunities are provided.

Additional controversy developed over Piaget's beliefs that the stages of development were fixed and that development actually preceded learning (Slavin, 2000). In contrast to Piagetian theory, Slavin (2000) cited several studies that addressed these concerns:

1. Some of the skills presented by Piaget that developed at certain stages could be introduced at an earlier time (Black, 1991; Donaldson, 1978; & Kusaka, 1989).
2. If similar language was used in addressing certain skills, children could perform those skills at earlier stages (Gelman, 1979).
3. Cognitive abilities of children develop differently based on the task at hand and a child's previous experiences (Byrnes, 1988; Gelman & Baillargeon, 1983; & Overton, 1984).

If anything, Piaget caused fellow researchers to question the factors that influenced the way children learned and how that learning took place.

Probably Piaget's greatest criticism came from Jerome Bruner. Instead of four succinct stages in cognitive development, Bruner suggested that there were actually only three systems of representation and that language played a key role in the development of thought (Biehler, 1978). Bruner believed that Piaget's thoughts centered on maturation while his theories of cognitive development concentrated on the concept of internalization (Biehler, 1978). In terms of readiness, Bruner and Piaget also differed. Bruner did not agree that children should learn through their own experiences; instead, he thought that a child's experiences should be specific in their design to allow for later learning (1978).

Regardless of the criticisms placed on Piaget and his stages, he is still regarded as a scientist and psychologist whose innate interests regarding cognition opened doors of exploration and discovery on how children learn and acquire knowledge.

PIAGET'S INFLUENCE

The Russian psychologist, Lev Vygotsky (1896-1934), adopted several of Piaget's concepts regarding the process of learning. While Piaget and Vygostsky were interested in intellectual development, Vygotsky was concerned with how social and cultural factors influenced the cognitive development of children (Wadsworth, 2004). Piaget saw learning as a result in the development of a child's abilities while Vygotsky purported that learning was the driving force for cognitive development (Wadsworth, 2004). He did veer from some aspects of Piaget's thoughts regarding cognition because he maintained that "cognitive processes [were] determined by the subject's interactions with his/her social environment rather than emanating from his/her internal functioning" (Santiago-Delefosse & Delefosse, 2002, p. 728).

As children grown and begin to make sense of their world and their surroundings, explanation about their patterns of thought became essential. Piaget introduced a sense of reasoning as to what the child was experiencing. Gardner (1980) contends that Piaget's observations regarding children remains "without peer" (para. 5). Gardner (1980) continues with his praise for Piaget's efforts by crediting him with "more thought about what he had to say about cognition than what Skinner posited on overt behaviors or Freud's focus on motivation, personality, or the unconscious" (para. 4).

When faced with trying to explain certain phenomenon, scientists utilize various methods of inquiry and research techniques. The research process allows individuals to question, seek out additional information, and formulate new thinking from an original idea or hypothesis. From Piaget's simple observation of his children at play, he set in motion years of study and research that influenced how parents interacted with their children and even the educational system.

Through approximately 13 years of formal education, a child experiences a variety of teaching styles, a multitude of social interactions, and an assortment of learning opportunities. These occur in different settings with many variables that also influence how a child learns. Piaget's research recognized the importance of each stage of development and made a lasting impression on the area of early childhood education as well as influences a child needed during formative years (Sadker & Sadker, 2005).

Piaget looked at cognitive development as a result of the formation of knowledge that was a result of certain stages and times that a child experienced (Valsiner, 2005). The belief that the child was an active participant in his or her learning and that a child does possess cognitive abilities still remain valuable Piaget contributions to understanding how a child acquires lasting knowledge (Gardner, 1980). Piaget said (as cited in Feldman, 2008), "the only knowledge that is truly worthwhile is knowledge that each of us creates for our own purposes, that helps achieve goals that are important to us, that seeks answers to verify important questions, and that ultimately enriches the collective experiences of humankind" (p. 200).

REFERENCES

Atherton, J. S. (2011, February). *Learning and teaching: Piaget's developmental theory.* Retrieved from http://www.learningandteaching.info/learning/piaget.htm

Berk, L. E. (1997). *Child development* (4th ed.). Boston, MA: Allyn & Bacon.

Biehler, R. F. (1978). *Psychology applied to teaching* (3rd ed.). Boston, MA: Houghton Mifflin.

Brooks, J. G., & Brooks, M. G. (2001). *In search of understanding: A case for constructivist classrooms.* Upper Saddle, NJ: Prentice-Hall.

Campbell, R. L. (2006). *Jean Piaget's genetic epistemology: Appreciation and critique.* Retrieved from http://hubcap.clemson.edu/~campber/piaget.html

Criticisms of Piaget's theory. (n.d.). Retrieved from http://ehlt.flinders.edu.au/education/DLit/2000/Piaget/critics.htm

Duffy, K. (1996). *Jean Piaget: The man behind the lab coat.* Retrieved from http://www.users.muohio.edu/shermalw/honors_2001_Fall/honors_papers_2000/duffy.html

Feldman, D. H. (2008). Darwin? Lamarck? Piaget? All of the above. *Human Development, 51*, 196-201.

Gardner, H. (1980, September 21). Jean Piaget: The psychologist as renaissance man. *The New York Times*, p. E20.

Munari, A. (1994). Jean Piaget. *International Bureau of Education, 24*(1/2), 311–327.

Sadker, M. P., & Sadker, D. M. (2005). *Teachers, schools, and society* (7th ed.). New York, NY: McGraw Hill.

Santiago-Delefosse, M. J., & Delefosse, J. M. O. (2002). *Spielrein, Piaget and Vygotsky: Three positions on child thought and language.* Retrieved from http:tap.sagepub.com/content/12/6/723

Seagal, S., & Horne, D. (1997). *Human dynamics: A new framework for understanding people and realizing the potential in our organizations.* Waltham, MA: Pegasus Communications.

Seifert, K. (2011). *The learning process: Major theories and models of learning.* Retrieved from http://cnx.org/content/m38002/1.2

Siegler, R. S. (2005, November). Children learning. *American Psychologist, 60*(8), 769-778.

Slavin, R. E. (2000). *Educational psychology: Theory and practice.* Needham Heights, MA: Allyn & Bacon.

Valsiner, J. (2005, January/February). Participating in Piaget. *Society, 42*(2), 57-61.

Wadsworth, B. J. (2004). *Piaget's theory of cognitive and affective development* (5th ed.). New York, NY: Pearson Education.

Wood, K. C., Smith, H., & Grossniklaus, D. (2001). Piaget's stages of cognitive development. In M. Orey (Ed.), *Emerging perspectives on learning, teaching, and technology.* Retrieved from http://projects.coe.uga.edu/epltt/index/php?title=Piaget%27s_Stages

Author Contact Information: Janet Tareilo, EdD, Stephen F. Austin State University, Nacogdoches, TX 75962. Phone: 936-468-1592. E-mail: tareiloj@sfasu.edu

CHAPTER 14

The Cognitive Theory of Multimedia Learning

Stephen D. Sorden
Embry-Riddle Aeronautical University

The cognitive theory of multimedia learning was popularized by the work of Richard E. Mayer and other cognitive researchers who argue that multimedia supports the way that the human brain learns. They assert that people learn more deeply from words and pictures than from words alone, which is referred to as the multimedia principle (Mayer, 2005a). Multimedia researchers generally define multimedia as the combination of text and pictures; and suggest that multimedia learning occurs when we build mental representations from these words and pictures (Mayer, 2005b). The words can be spoken or written, and the pictures can be any form of graphical imagery including illustrations, photos, animation, or video. Multimedia instructional design attempts to use cognitive research to combine words and pictures in ways that maximize learning effectiveness.

The theoretical foundation for the cognitive theory of multimedia learning (CTML) draws from several cognitive theories including Baddeley's model of working memory, Paivio's dual coding theory, and Sweller's theory of cognitive load. As a cognitive theory of learning, it falls under the larger framework of cognitive science and the information-processing model of cognition. The information processing model suggests several information stores (memory) that are governed by processes that convert stimuli to information (Moore, Burton & Myers, 2004). Cognitive science studies the nature of the brain and how it learns by drawing from research in a number of areas including psychology, neuroscience, artificial intelligence, computer science, linguistics, philosophy, and biology. The term *cognitive* refers to perceiving and knowing. Cognitive scientists seek to understand mental processes such as perceiving, thinking, remembering, understanding language, and learning (Stillings, Weisler, Chase, Feinstein, Garfield, & Rissland, 1995). As such, cognitive science can provide powerful insight into human nature, and, more importantly, the potential of humans to develop more efficient methods using instructional technology (Sorden, 2005).

Key Elements of the Theory

The cognitive theory of multimedia learning centers on the idea that learners attempt to build meaningful connections between words and pictures and that they learn more deeply than they could have with words or pictures alone (Mayer, 2009). According to CTML, one of the principle aims of multimedia instruction is to encourage the learner to build a coherent mental representation from the presented material. The learner's job is to make sense of the presented material as an active participant, ultimately constructing new knowledge.

According to Mayer and Moreno (1998) and Mayer (2003), CTML is based on three assumptions: *the dual-channel assumption*, the *limited capacity assumption*, and the active processing assumption. The dual-channel assumption is that working memory has auditory and visual channels based on Baddeley's (1986) theory of working memory and Paivio's (1986; Clark & Paivio, 1991) dual coding theory. Second, the limited capacity assumption is based on cognitive load theory (Sweller, 1988, 1994) and states that each subsystem of working memory has a limited capacity. The third assumption is the active processing assumption which suggests that people construct knowledge in meaningful ways when they pay attention to the relevant material, organize it

The Handbook of Educational Theories, pp. 155–167

into a coherent mental structure, and integrate it with their prior knowledge (Mayer, 1996, 1999).

The Three Store Structure of Memory in CTML

CTML accepts a model that includes three memory stores known as sensory memory, working memory, and long-term memory. Sweller (2005) defines sensory memory as the cognitive structure that permits us to perceive new information, working memory as the cognitive structure in which we consciously process information, and long-term memory as the cognitive structure that stores our knowledge base. We are only conscious of information in long-term memory when it has been transferred to working memory. Mayer (2005a) states that sensory memory has a visual sensory memory that briefly holds pictures and printed text as visual images; and auditory memory that briefly holds spoken words and sounds as auditory images. Schnotz (2005) refers to sensory memory as sensory registers or sensory channels and points out that though we tend to view the dual channel sensors as eye-to-visual working memory and ear-to-auditory working memory, that it is possible for other sensory channels to introduce information to working memory such as "reading" with the fingers through Braille or a deaf person being able to "hear" by reading lips.

Working memory attends to, or selects information from sensory memory for processing and integration. Sensory memory holds an exact sensory copy of what was presented for less than .25 of a second, while working memory holds a processed version of what was presented for generally less than 30 seconds and can process only a few pieces of material at any one time (Mayer 2010a). Long-term memory holds the entire store of a person's knowledge for an indefinite amount of time. Figure 14.1 is a representation of how memory works according to Mayer's cognitive theory of multimedia learning.

Mayer (2005a) states that there are also five forms of representation of words and pictures that occur as information is processed by memory. Each form represents a particular stage of processing in the three memory stores model of multimedia learning. The first form of representation is the words and pictures in the multimedia presentation itself. The second form is the acoustic representation (sounds) and iconic representation (images) in sensory memory. The third form is the sounds and images in working memory. The fourth form of representation is the verbal and pictorial models which are also found in working memory. The fifth form is prior knowledge, or *schemas*, which are stored in long-term memory.

According to CTML, content knowledge is contained in schemas which are cognitive constructs that organize information for storage in long term memory. Schemas organize simpler elements that can then act as elements in higher order schemas. As learning occurs, increasingly sophisticated schemas are developed and learned procedures are transferred from controlled to automatic processing. Automation frees capacity in working memory for other functions. This process of developing increasingly complicated schemas that build on each other is also similar to the explanation given by Chi, Glaser, and Rees (1982) for the transition from novice to expert in a domain.

The Development of the Theory of Working Memory

The current conception of working memory in CTML grew out of Atkinson and Shiffrin's (1968) model of short term memory. The Atkinson and Shiffrin model was viewed primarily as a structure for temporarily storing information before it passed to long-term memory. Eventually, researchers began to question some of the assumptions of short-term memory and a few started to look for better explanations. Baddeley and Hitch (1974) subsequently proposed a more

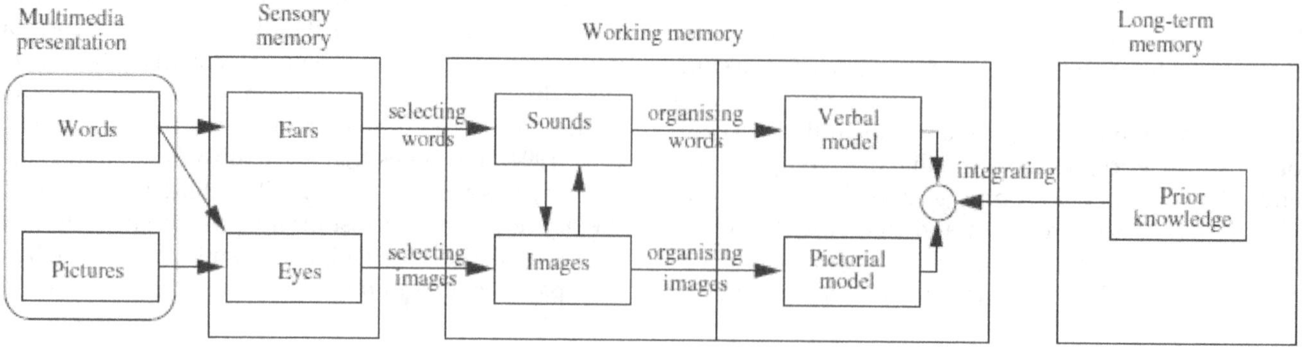

Source: Mayer (2010a).

Figure 14.1. Mayer's cognitive theory of multimedia learning.

complex model of short-term memory which they called working memory. Their model for working memory was a system with subcomponents that not only held temporary information, but processed it so that several pieces of verbal or visual information could be stored and integrated.

Baddeley (1986, 1999) later proposed that there was an additional component in working memory called the central executive. According to the theory, the central executive controlled the two subcomponents of working memory, known as the *visuo-spatial sketch pad* and the *phonological loop*. The *central executive* also was responsible for controlling the overall system and engaging in problem solving tasks and focusing attention. Baddeley theorized that the central executive could transfer storage tasks to the two subcomponent systems in working memory, so that the central executive would continue to have capacity for performing more demanding selection and information processing tasks.

The visuo-spatial sketch pad is assumed to maintain and manipulate visual images. The phonological loop stores and rehearses verbal information. It has also been suggested that the phonological loop has an important function of facilitating the acquisition of language by maintaining a new word in working memory until it can be learned (Baddeley, Gathercole, & Papagno, 1998). Baddeley (2002) eventually proposed the addition of a third subsystem known as the *episodic buffer*, which has acquired some of the tasks that were originally attributed to the central executive (now seen as a purely attentional system). The episodic buffer functions as a storage structure which acts as a limited capacity interface to integrate multiple sources of information from other slave systems.

Sweller (2005) and Yuan, Steedle, Shavelson, Alonzo, and Oppezo (2006) suggest that while there is strong evidence for the two main subcomponents in working memory, that there is less evidence for a central executive that consciously attends to information in sensory memory. Rather, Sweller suggests that schemas which exist in long-term memory serve as the executive function, ultimately directing working memory to attend to information that fits preexisting schemas. Schemas determine which information enters working memory because we tend to pay attention to information that fits the knowledge that we already have. This would support the idea that our paradigms cause us to focus on information that fits our existing beliefs, while ignoring information that does not fit neatly into our understanding of the world.

Meaningful Learning

Mayer (2010a) argues that meaningful learning from words and pictures happens when the learner engages in five cognitive processes:

1. selecting relevant words for processing in verbal working memory;
2. selecting relevant images for processing in visual working memory;
3. organizing selected words into a verbal model;
4. organizing selected images into a pictorial model; and
5. integrating the verbal and pictorial representations with each other and with prior knowledge.

These cognitive processes in working memory determine which information is attended to or selected, which knowledge is retrieved from long-term memory and integrated with new the information to construct new knowledge, and ultimately, which bits of new knowledge are transferred to long-term memory. Knowledge that is constructed in working memory is transferred to long-term memory through the process of *encoding* (Mayer, 2008). However, Dwyer and Dwyer (2006) caution that proper encoding requires rehearsal and since rehearsal takes time, the multimedia lesson must allow an adequate period for incubation or it can be ineffective. Hasler, Kersten, and Sweller (2007) add that this is why learner control is important when using animation in multimedia learning.

Mayer (2009) distinguishes meaningful learning from "no learning" and "rote learning" and describes it as active learning where the learner constructs knowledge. Meaningful learning is demonstrated when the learner can apply what is presented in new situations, and students perform better on problem-solving transfer tests when they learn with words and pictures. Mayer (2008) also identifies two types of transfer: *transfer of learning* and *problem-solving transfer*. Transfer of learning occurs when previous learning affects new learning. Problem solving transfer occurs when previous learning affects the ability to solve new problems. Mayer defines learning as a "change in knowledge attributable to experience" (2009, p. 59). Learning is personal and cannot be directly observed because it happens with the learner's cognitive system. It must be inferred through a change in behavior such as performance on a task or test.

Cognitive Load

The limited capacity assumption states that there is a limit to the amount of information that can be processed at one time by working memory. In other words, learning is hindered when cognitive overload occurs and working memory capacity is exceeded (De Jong, 2010). DeLeeuw and Mayer (2008) theorize that there are three types of cognitive processing (essential, extraneous, and generative) and place them in the *triarchic model of cognitive load*. Mayer (2009) made this model the organizing framework for the cognitive theory of multimedia learning and stated that a major goal of multimedia learning and instruction is to "manage essential processing, reduce extraneous processing and foster generative processing" (p. 57). The model is heavily based on Sweller's cognitive load theory (Chandler & Sweller, 1991; Sweller, 1988, 1994).

According to Sweller, Van Merrienboer, and Paas (1998), there are three types of cognitive load: intrinsic, extraneous, and germane. Intrinsic cognitive load occurs during the interaction between the nature of the material being learned and the expertise of the learner. The second type, extraneous cognitive load, is caused by factors that aren't central to the material to be learned, such as presentation methods or activities that split attention between multiple sources of information, and these should be minimized as much as possible. The third type of cognitive load, germane cognitive load, enhances learning and results in task resources being devoted to schema acquisition and automation. Intrinsic cognitive load cannot be manipulated, but extraneous and germane cognitive load can.

In the triarchic model of cognitive load, essential processing (intrinsic load) relates to the essential material or information to be learned. Extraneous processing (extrinsic load) does not serve the instructional goal or purpose and reduces the chances that transfer of learning will occur. Generative processing (germane cognitive load) is aimed at making sense of the presented material. It is the activity of organizing and integrating information in working memory.

De Jong (2010) has called into question whether there is truly a distinction between intrinsic (essential) and germane (generative) cognitive load, writing that if "intrinsic load and germane load are defined in terms of relatively similar learning processes, the difference between the two seems to be very much a matter of degree, and possibly nonexistent" (p. 111). Deleeuw and Mayer (2008), however, did report finding that extraneous, essential, and generative processing appear to be able to be measured by different assessment instruments, suggesting that they are three distinct constructs.

The Science of Instruction

The previous sections describe what Mayer (2009) calls the *science of learning*, while this section explains what Mayer calls the *science of instruction* and defines as the "creation of evidence-based principles for helping people learn" (2009, pp. 29), or more simply as the "scientific study of how to help people learn" (Mayer, 2010a, p. 543). Mayer insists that research on multimedia instruction must be *theory-grounded* and *evidence-based*. Theory-grounded means that each principle, method and concept is derived from a theory of multimedia learning. Evidence-based means that each principle, method and concept is supported by an empirical base of replicated findings from rigorous and appropriate research studies, which yields testable predictions. Mayer (2011a) subsequently adds the *science of assessment* to the sciences of learning and instruction to form what he calls the "big three" (p. 2).

As part of his evidence-seeking efforts for the science of instruction, Mayer (2009) identifies the following 12 multimedia instructional principles which were developed from nearly 100 studies over the past 2 decades:

- Coherence principle: People learn better when extraneous material is excluded rather than included.
- Signaling principle: People learn better when cues that highlight the organization of the essential material are added.
- Redundancy principle: People learn better from graphics and narration than from graphics, narration, and printed text.
- Spatial contiguity principle: People learn better when corresponding words and pictures are placed near each other rather than far from each other on the page or screen.
- Temporal contiguity principle: People learn better when corresponding words and pictures are presented at the same time rather than in succession.
- Segmenting principal: People learn better when a multimedia lesson is presented in user-paced segments rather than as a continuous unit.
- Pretraining principle: People learn more deeply from a multimedia message when they receive pretraining in the names and characteristics of key components.
- Modality principle: People learn better from graphics and narration than from graphics and printed text.
- Multimedia principle: People learn better from words and pictures than from words alone.
- Personalization principle: People learn better from a multimedia presentation when the words are in conversational style rather than in formal style.
- Voice principle: People learn better when the words in a multimedia message are spoken by a friendly human voice rather than a machine voice.
- Image principle: People do not necessarily learn more deeply from a multimedia presentation when the speaker's image is on the screen rather than not on the screen.

As mentioned earlier, these 12 principles are grouped in a framework based on the three types of cognitive load (Mayer, 2009):

- reducing extraneous processing: coherence, signaling, redundancy, spatial contiguity, temporal contiguity;

- managing essential processing: segmenting, pre-training, modality; and
- fostering generative processing: multimedia, personalization, voice, image.

In addition to these instructional principles, Mayer (2009) includes boundary conditions that can determine the effectiveness of some of the principles. These boundary conditions are a recent addition to the theory, and they suggest that the instructional principles in CTML are not universal, absolute rules. Some have criticized the existence of boundary conditions in CTML as an indicator that the theory has inconsistencies (De Jong, 2010), but Mayer (2010b) views boundary conditions as a healthy evolution in CTML that allows the theory to continue to develop and be implemented realistically, rather than as a set of immutable rules that have to be followed in all situations.

One example of a boundary condition is that of *individual-differences*, which states that some instructional methods or principles may be more effective for low-knowledge learners than for high-knowledge learners (Mayer, 2009; Schnotz & Bannert, 2003). Kalyuga, Ayres, Chandler, and Sweller (2003) have called this the *expertise-reversal effect*. Paas, Renkl, and Sweller (2004, pp. 2-3) similarly stated this from a CLT point of view when they wrote: "A cognitive load that is germane for a novice may be extraneous for an expert. In other words, information that is relevant to the process of schema construction for a beginning learner may hinder this process for a more advanced learner." Another example of a boundary condition is the *complexity and pacing condition*, which suggests that some of these methods may be more effective when the material of the lesson is complex or the pace of the presentation is fast. Each principle in CTML is subject to boundary conditions as illustrated by Mayer (2009).

Although they have not appeared in recent CTML literature, Mayer suggests several "advanced" principles for multimedia learning in his 2005 book, *The Cambridge Handbook of Multimedia Learning*, which are listed as chapters by various authors. These should be considered as possible areas for future CTML research and not necessarily evidence-based principles.

- Animation and interactivity principles: People do not necessarily learn better from animation than from static diagrams.
- Cognitive aging principle: Instructional design principles that effectively expand the capacity of working memory are particularly helpful for older learners.
- Collaboration principle: People learn better when involved in collaborative online learning activities.
- Guided-discovery principle: People learn better when guidance is incorporated into discovery-based multimedia environments.
- Navigation principles: People learn better in environments where appropriate navigational aids are provided.
- Prior knowledge principle: Instructional principles that are effective in increasing multimedia learning for novices may have the opposite effect on more expert learners.
- Self-explanation principle: People learn better when they are encouraged to generate self-explanations during learning.
- Site map principle: People learn better in an online environment when presented with a map showing where they are in a lesson.
- Worked-out example principle: People learn better when worked-out examples are given in initial skill learning.

In addition to the 12 principles and the advanced principles listed in this chapter, Mayer (2011a) discusses several more principles that have appeared in CTML literature over the years. This demonstrates once again that the cognitive theory of multimedia learning is dynamic. Therefore, the 12 principles should not be taken as a rigid canon, but rather a starting point for discussion. Mayer (2011b), for example, only lists ten principles just 2 years after he published the 12 principles, having dropped the multimedia and image principles. In fact, this number seems to vary from publication to publication, so the focus should be on understanding what the latest research suggests about the effectiveness of the various instructional methods, rather than memorizing a codified set of 12, or any other number of principles.

Development of the Theory

The evolution of CTML literature and research is evident in the body of work published by Mayer and his colleagues over the past 20 years (Mayer, 2005a). Mayer reminds us that even though the name has changed over the years, the underlying elements of the theory have not changed. In fact, the theory appears to have matured as it enters its third decade of active research and is finally reaching a consistently recognizable state.

See Moore et al. (2004) for an excellent overall accounting of the theoretical and research foundations of multimedia learning and Yuan et al. (2006) for the extensive history of working memory. The actual cognitive theory of multimedia learning first begins to emerge as a distinct theory at the end of the 1980s when Mayer (1989) introduced the theory as the "model of meaningful learning" and then shortly thereafter as the "cognitive conditions for effective illustrations" (Mayer & Gallini, 1990). It has also been called the "dual-coding model" (Mayer & Anderson, 1991, 1992), "generative theory" (Mayer, Steinhoff, Bower, & Mars, 1995), the "generative theory of multimedia learning" (Mayer, 1997; Plass, Chun, Mayer, & Leutner, 1998), and the "dual-processing model of multimedia learning" (Mayer & Moreno, 1998).

The name "cognitive theory of multimedia learning" was first used in Mayer, Bove, Bryman, Mars, and Tapangco (1996), but did not become the standard name for Mayer's theory until the year 2000 and beyond. The various models over the years focused on different aspects of the current model, but the underlying assumptions remained unchanged. Elements such as cognitive processes and mental representations were slowly added and refined until we have the model currently described by Mayer (2009).

It is important to note that before her death, Roxana Moreno, a former student of Mayer's, had begun to develop a *cognitive-affective theory of learning with media* (Moreno, 2005, 2006b, 2007). Moreno (2005) includes factors of self-regulation and motivation in this theory and explained that this new model extends the cognitive theory of multimedia learning by "integrating assumptions regarding the relationship between cognition, metacognition and motivation and affect" (2007, p. 767). Moreno and Mayer (2007) assert that the cognitive-affective theory of learning with media "expands the cognitive theory of multimedia learning to media such as virtual reality, agent-based, and case-based learning environments" (p. 313).

Moreno's model integrates three assumptions. The first assumption is that humans have a limited working memory capacity (Baddeley, 1992). The second assumption is that long-term memory consists of past experiences and general domain knowledge, which is similar to Tulving's (1977) distinction between episodic and semantic memory systems. The third assumption is that motivational factors affect learning by increasing or decreasing cognitive engagement (Pintrich, 2003). Paas (1992) discussed a similar distinction between mental load and mental effort from a CLT perspective nearly 2 decades ago.

Measurement and Instruments

There is no one single measurement instrument that is associated with CTML research. Mayer (2009) states that since the goal is to make a causal claim about instructional effectiveness, one of the most useful approaches in CTML research is quantitative experimental comparisons, with random assignment and experimental control being two important features. The main question in this type of research is whether a particular instructional method is effective. CTML researchers generally try to identify instructional methods that cause large effect sizes of .8 or greater across many different experimental comparisons. Learning is generally measured through tests of retention and transfer, and much of the recent research has focused on the instructional methods discussed earlier in this chapter.

Because of its central role in CTML research, cognitive load theory research is also of interest. De Jong (2010) provides a lengthy criticism of the instruments and tests of measurement in cognitive load theory. He points out that one of the most frequently used methods for measuring CLT is self-reporting in a one-item questionnaire where learners indicate their perceived amount of mental effort. De Jong asserts that this approach often leads to inconsistency in the outcomes of studies that use this type of questionnaire. Another way that cognitive load has been measured is physiologically using indicators such as heart rate, blood pressure, and pupillary reactions. A third way of measuring cognitive load has been through the dual-task or secondary-task approach which indicates increased consumption of cognitive resources in the primary task when slower or inaccurate performance on the on the secondary task occurs (Brünken, Plass, & Leutner, 2003). De Jong criticizes the measurement of cognitive load as a single construct, as most of these approaches tend to do. He calls for the development of better instruments and multidimensional scales that can reliably measure intrinsic, extraneous, and germane load separately.

Applying the Cognitive Theory of Multimedia Instruction

Once we understand the science of learning and the science of instruction, the next question becomes how to apply the principles in order to foster meaningful learning. See Mayer's (2011a) *Applying the Science of Learning* for a good overview of what to consider when applying the methods described in this chapter, as well as others,

This section looks at what to keep in mind as the instructional methods in CTLM are implemented. In addition to applying the 12 principles and the advanced principles presented in this chapter and in Mayer (2005a, 2009, 2011b), the instructional designer should be aware of the information presented in this section when creating multimedia instruction. These theories come from the cognitive theory of multimedia learning, cognitive load theory, and cognitive science in general. It should be remembered that they are theories, and as such should be applied with caution, but all of them have research and a theoretical background that make them worth considering as guidelines for creating better instruction.

The principles of multimedia learning should be viewed as instructional methods whose primary goal is to foster meaningful learning. An instructional method is a way of presenting a lesson; it does not change the content of the lesson—the covered content is the same. As discussed previously, the principles should not be viewed as absolute rules that have to be applied equally in every situation. They are guidelines that should be adjusted depending on the intended audience, the goals of the instruction, and boundary conditions such as the expertise level of the learner. Most important, the theory is a learner-centered learning theory (Mayer, 2009).

Learner-Centered Focus

A critical perspective to maintain while designing multimedia lessons according to CTML is that the multimedia instructional methods are learner-centered—they are not technology-centered approaches. Mayer (2009) reminds us that multimedia can be as simple as a still image with words and that it is the instructional method, not the technology that matters. Multimedia instructional designers often fall victim to letting the technology drive the instructional design, rather than looking at the design from the perspective, and limitations, of the learner.

Moreno (2006a) expressed this idea when she distinguished between a *method-affects-learning* hypothesis versus a *media-affects-learning* hypothesis. A media-affects-learning approach could best be described as what occurred in the twentieth century when state-of-the-art technologies such as radio, television, computers, and the Internet were introduced into education with the assumption that they would improve education simply because they were better tools than had previously been available.

Managing Cognitive Load

Because the principles of CTML are organized around the three types of cognitive load, designing instruction according to cognitive load theory (CLT) research findings is important if you are designing according to CTML. Mayer, Fennell, Farmer, and Campbell (2004) cite evidence that two important ways to promote meaningful learning are to design activities that reduce cognitive load, which frees working memory capacity for deep cognitive processing during learning, and to increase the learner's interest, which encourages the learner to use this freed capacity for deep processing during learning. CLT suggests that for instruction to be effective, care must be taken to design instruction in a way as to not overload the brain's capacity for processing information.

CLT suggests that instructional techniques that require students to engage in activities that aren't directed at schema acquisition and automation can quickly exceed the limited capacity of working memory and hinder learning objectives. In simple terms, this means that you shouldn't create unnecessary activities in connection with a lesson that require excessive attention or concentration that may overload working memory and prevent one from acquiring the essential information that is to be learned. This is an important guideline in any form of instruction, but it is an essential rule in multimedia instruction because of the ease with which distractions can be incorporated. Instructional designers should not fill this limited capacity with unnecessary, flashy bells and whistles (Sorden, 2005).

An example of what this means for multimedia instructional design is that the layout should be visually appealing and intuitive, but that the activities should remain focused on the concepts to be learned, rather than trying too much to entertain. This is especially true if the entertainment is time consuming to construct and complicated for the learner to master. Working memory can be overloaded by the entertainment or activity before the learner ever gets to the concept or skill to be learned. Mayer (2009) states that effective "instructional design depends on techniques for reducing extraneous processing, managing essential processing, and fostering generative processing" (p. 57).

Schnotz and Kürschner (2007) echo this idea by stating that techniques to simply reduce cognitive load can be counterproductive. They argue that learning tasks should be adapted to the learner's zone of proximal development which in turn depends on the learner's level of expertise, and that intrinsic and germane cognitive load should be promoted while extraneous cognitive load is reduced. De Jong (2010) states that the three main recommendations that cognitive load theory has contributed to the field of instructional design are: "present material that aligns with the prior knowledge of the learner (intrinsic load), avoid non-essential and confusing information (extraneous load), and stimulate processes that lead to conceptually rich and deep knowledge (germane load)" (p. 111). These cognitive load processes occur simultaneously in working memory, are limited in capacity, and can only occur at the expense of the other two. If true, this creates important considerations for multimedia learning.

Task Analysis

Task analysis is tied to the concepts of schemas and levels of expertise. The multimedia lesson should try to ensure that the learner has sufficiently automated key core knowledge or tasks. The learner should do this before trying to tackle an overall task that may be beyond the learner's current ability range, which could cause unnecessary frustration and possibly even cause the learner to drop out of the activity. The theories of Vygotsky's zone of proximal development and Piaget's concept of scaffolding can be applied here. This suggests that a task analysis should be done during the instructional design of a multimedia lesson in order to breakdown the skills and information that are needed to learn or perform the educational objective.

Guided Instruction

According to CTML, guided instruction and worked examples are preferable to discovery learning, even though other learning theories often support discovery learning as a useful component of multimedia instruction. Mayer (2004, 2011a) and Kirschner, Sweller, and Clark (2006) caution against using discovery learning and argue that guided instruction is much more effective. Mayer (2011a) presents four principles for "studying by practicing" that support this idea. The four principles supporting guided instruction are spacing, feedback, worked example, and guided discovery.

Interactivity

While the principle of interactivity still requires more research, much of the literature suggests that infusing interactivity such as learner control, feedback, and guidance into a multimedia lesson will increase the affective conditions that will improve learning transfer and performance (Mayer, 2009; Piaget, 1969; Renkl & Atkinson, 2007; Wittrock, 1990). Domagk, Schwartz, and Plass (2010) define interactivity as "reciprocal activity between a learner and a multimedia learning system, in which the [re]action of the learner is dependent up the [re]-action of the system and vice versa" (p. 1025). They propose a model of interactivity called the Integrated Model of Multimedia Interactivity which consists of six principal components of an integrated learning system: the learning environment, behavioral activities, cognitive and metacognitive activities, motivation and emotion, learner variables, and the learner's mental model (learning outcomes). Moreno and Mayer (2007) also describe an interactive multimodal environment that is based on the cognitive affective theory of learning with media and include five design principles of guided activity, reflection, feedback, pacing, and pretraining.

Animation and Screencasts

Hasler, Kersten, and Sweller (2007) suggest that animation can be more effective when learners are allowed to stop and start the animation instead of having it just play through in one pass, however this still leaves the question of whether still images are ultimately just as affective and much easier and cheaper to produce.

Regarding the use of animation to improve student achievement, Dwyer and Dwyer (2006) suggest that animation is not a viable instructional tool for improving achievement when the content to be learned is hierarchically structured. They go on to state that previous research does indicate that animation can be effectively used to teach both factual and conceptual types of information, but that this content can be taught equally well at less cost with other instructional strategies. Schnotz (2008) raises similar questions. This does not necessarily discount CTML studies, as CTML researchers have argued that simple graphical images can be highly effective when combined with words, and have already called into question whether animation is superior to still images in the "advanced" principles of animation and interactivity (Betrancourt, 2005).

Evaluation of the Theory

Validation

Theories are meant to be advanced upon and ultimately cast aside as new information is integrated and new understanding is developed. Moreno (2006a), for example, writes that "we should concede as cognitive scientists, that valid criticisms can be raised against any existing theory of cognition and that such criticism is essential to progress. Theories and constructs are useful only as long as they evolve in their heuristic, explanatory, and predictive functions" (p. 179). While the cognitive theory of multimedia learning has generally met with acceptance, there remains questions by various learning and education theorists in certain quarters about its validity, as well as the validity of other cognitive theories upon which it is based. Mayer and his colleagues, however, counter that there is an extensive body of research that does validate this theory.

In recent years there have been several prominent researchers who have continued to develop the cognitive theories of multimedia learning and cognitive load. Among these are Richard E. Mayer, Roxana Moreno, John Sweller, Jan Plass, and Wolfgang Schnotz. Significant studies have included Mayer and Anderson (1991); Moreno and Mayer (2000); Schnotz and Bannert (2003); Pass et al. (2004); and Plass et al. (2004). Gall (2004) points out that much of Mayer's research has been published in top peer-reviewed journals such as the *Journal of Educational Psychology* and is available for deeper study and critique. Dacosta (2008) provides a detailed table of almost 70 published studies by CTML researchers on instructional principles, along with the number of experiments and the particular principle each study measured. For a substantial listing of dozens of CTML studies that support each of the 12 multimedia instructional principles presented in this chapter, see Mayer (2009). Finally, Yuan et al. (2006) also cite a series of studies that suggest that working memory performance correlates with cognitive abilities and academic achievement.

Mayer (2009) states that his research goal is to contribute to the cognitive theory of multimedia learning, and ultimately to practical applied instructional practice. While criticizing the technology-centered use of multimedia for instruction and the misapplication of cognitive load theory, Mayer (2005b), Ballantyne (2008), and Schnotz (2008) have all stated that it is the instructional method that is important, not the technology, no matter how sophisticated. Ultimately, the validation of the theory lies in the fact that it has a large body of studies and literature to support it, that it has exhibited "staying power" and that it continues to demand attention and exert influence in the fields of education and training. The power of the theory lies in its dynamic structure, in which it is expected and even driven to constantly change and morph as new information is discovered and tested in the field of cognitive science.

CRITIQUE

There are critics of the theory, however, and the use of multimedia for instruction has been challenged (Clark & Feldon, 2005; Tufte, 2003). Ballantyne (2008) has criticized the narrowness of some of the CTML studies and whether the principles derived from CTML research can be applied in broader, more realistic settings. Additionally, striking at the very heart of the cognitive theory of multimedia learning, Rasch and Schnotz (2009) were not able to show that students actually learned better from text and pictures than from text alone, calling the multimedia principle itself into question. They also could not show that students learned better from interactive pictures than from noninteractive ones.

Gall (2004) points out that Mayer's research has tended to focus mainly on the understanding of physical and mechanical systems, and thus raises the question of how applicable his results are to nondidactic, immersive learning environments. This criticism of whether results obtained in controlled experimental situations can be applied to dynamic classrooms and learning environments is an old complaint that has been leveled at psychology since psychologists first began studying and trying to measure learning. Often, these charges of nonrelevance to real-life learning and instruction have been justified. But Mayer is careful not to claim that his research should be seen as the final word on instruction in the situations he is trying to measure. Rather, it is obvious in the evolution of the cognitive theory of multimedia learning that they are only trying to determine what appears to make a difference in learning situations, hypothesize about it, and then continue to look for better explanations and hypotheses. The theory is dynamic and the expectation that it will continue to grow, adapt, and change appears frequently in the literature.

There has also been general criticism of information-processing theory and cognitive science on which CTML is based, and there have also been some negative critiques of certain aspects of cognitive load theory. Gerjets, Scheiter, and Cierniak (2008) for example, state that according to the traditional critical rationalism of Popper, CLT cannot be considered a scientific theory because some of its fundamental assumptions cannot be tested empirically. However, Gerjets et al. go on to suggest that in spite of this limitation, CLT can still be viewed as a scientific theory under Sneed's structuralist view of theories. De Jong (2010) asserts that many studies supporting CLT make speculative interpretations of what happened, but that only when a suitable measure of cognitive load is developed can these interpretations be considered valid. Several cognitive and CTML researchers have also challenged CLT as they attempt to evolve the theory and address perceived shortcomings (Moreno, 2006b; Gerjets et al., 2009; Schnotz & Kürschner, 2007). De Jong (2010) provides an excellent critical analysis of cognitive load theory which discusses many problematic areas that currently exist in the existing body of research and literature.

De Jong (2010) points out that cognitive load theory is used to suggest guidelines for instructional design, which assumes that CLT research results are applicable to real-life situations, which de Jong questions. For example, de Jong cites several recent studies that could not find support for the modality principal when learner control is increased. In response to de Jong's article, Mayer (2010b) responds that criticism such as de Jong's is welcome and can only strengthen the cognitive theory of multimedia learning as weaknesses are exposed and researched in ways that contribute to the ongoing evolution of the theory.

CURRENT TRENDS AND FUTURE DIRECTIONS

As has already been pointed out, the field of research for the cognitive theory of multimedia learning is very active; new studies and literature are being added every year. While Richard Mayer, Jan Plass, John Sweller, and the late Roxanna Moreno continued to publish research and books in support of their theories, many others have also contributed to the growing and maturing field. Dissertations, for example, are a way to gauge general trends and the overall vitality of the field.

As a quick search in the ProQuest database will attest, there are dozens of dissertations that have been added in the last 5 years which have studied some aspect of Mayer's cognitive theory of multimedia learning. The following are just a few examples of recent dissertations and their findings. Lu (2008) found that animated instructions with narration lead to better performance on retention tests, possibly due to less cognitive load on the learner. Lu also found that levels of learner control may not benefit learners when learners do not have enough prior experience. Dong (2007) found that when positive emotions are elicited through an aesthetically pleasing interface design, it can result in deeper learning, at least for low prior knowledge learners. Dacosta (2008) tentatively reported that his study was not able to reproduce the modality effect reported by Mayer and Moreno (Mayer, 1998, Experiments 1 and 2; Moreno & Mayer, 1999a, Experiments 1 and 2; 2002a, Experiments 1 and 2; Moreno et al., 2001, Experiments 4a and 4b and 5a and 5b), stating that it did not appear that middle-aged learners attained a higher degree of meaningful learning from animation with concurrent narration than animation with concurrent printed text. Um (2008) reported that positive emotions induced before learning begins, facilitate cognitive processes and other affective experiences in a multimedia-based learning environment and that the positive mood state continued until the end of the learning and made significant effects on learning performance, cognitive load, motivation, satisfaction and perception of the learning. Finally, Musallam (2010) found that students who received pretraining through a screencast prior to instruction reported a statistically significant decrease in perceived mental effort, as well as an increase in performance when compared to students who did not receive pretraining.

Major trends at the moment appear to be continued research on the various CTML principles as well as identifying possible new ones. The focus on the affective domain in multimedia learning also seems to be strengthening as noted in the recent dissertations by students of CTML researcher Jan Plass (Dong, 2007; Um, 2008) and recent research by Moreno and Mayer (2007) on interactivity and the cognitive-affective theory of learning with media; and McLaren, DeLeeuw, and Mayer (2011) on whether learning is enhanced when web-based intelligent tutors use polite language instead of direct language in instruction. Another promising area for future research is that of interactivity, especially as intelligent tutoring system technology continues to improve (Domagk et al., 2010; McLaren et al., 2011; Moreno & Mayer, 2007).

Possibly a holy grail for CTML and CTL researchers in the near future will be the quest to find evidence of three separate cognitive load processes (essential, extraneous, generative) and how to measure them reliably (Brünken et al., 2003; Antonenko, Paas, Grabner, and Van Gog, 2010). A recent study by Antonenko and Niederhauser (2010) found that measuring overall cognitive load with self-reports may not be adequate. Instead, they suggest that cognitive load should be viewed as a dynamic process and assessed with electroencephalogram-based measures to provide a more complete picture for explaining the causes and effects of cognitive load.

While not directly focusing on the cognitive theory of multimedia instruction, the use of electroencephalography, or brain waves, to measure increased cognitive load as learners engage in tasks provides an interesting new development in CTML and CLT theory. The use of electroencephalography has been around for many years (Gerlic & Jausovec, 1999; Klimesch, 1999), but it is only recently that the technology has advanced to the point of possibly being able to non-obtrusively and reliably measure what appears to be cognitive load while learners engage in normal learning activities. Jaeggi et al. (2007), for example, observed specific patterns of brain activity when cognitive load was thought to be high. This neuroscientific approach may also eventually be able to help with distinguishing between intrinsic, extraneous, and germane cognitive load, which has not been possible up to this point. Since CLT is a central concept of CTML, a breakthrough in CLT measurement technology as this study suggests could be very significant for the future of CTML research.

Mayer (2011b), states that more research is needed including "(a) the continued discovery of evidence-based principles for multimedia design particularly in authentic learning situations; and (b) research that pinpoints the boundary conditions of multimedia design principles" (p. 441). Mayer notes that new multimedia technology is emerging faster than the science of instruction is developing, and that more research in these new areas is needed, especially as textbooks migrate to computer-based media, instructional multimedia games and simulations become more prevalent, and mobile learning on hand-held devices becomes common. He reiterates that it is the instructional method that matters, not the sophistications of the technology and believes that we do not need more comparison research between technologies or unscientific studies on the development of new multimedia technologies for instruction.

As de Jong (2010) and Mayer (2010b) point out, there are many, many unresolved issues in CLT and CTML research, which means that the field continues to be wide open and should provide a challenging and stimulating area of research for many years to come. De Jong suggests that research in CLT should now turn to finding load-reducing approaches for intensive knowledge-producing strategies such as learning from multiple representations, self-explanations, inquiry learning, or game-based learning which all stimulate germane (generative) processes. While speaking to cognitive load theory, de Jong's recommendation for future research can be applied as easily to the cognitive theory of multimedia learning in determining:

> (1) which instructional treatments lead to which cognitive processes (and how), (2) what the corresponding effects are on memory workload and potential overload, (3) what characteristics of the learning material and the student mediate these effects and (4) how best to measure effects on working memory load in a theory-related manner. (p. 127)

CONCLUSION

The cognitive theory of multimedia learning has progressed over the past 2 decades and is poised to become a mature, robust theory as it enters its third decade. Fortunately, the theoretical cognitive foundations upon which the theory is based go much further back and have contributed heavily to its framework of the "big three" sciences, as well as the structure given to its principles by the triarchic theory of cognitive load. Together, these two areas of study form what we generally understand today to be the cognitive theory of multimedia learning.

The theory is expanding into exciting new areas that will allow it to continue to evolve. Its learner-centered and cognitive-constructivist orientation makes it very relevant in current educational applications. The fact that it focuses on finding effective instructional methods rather than a specific technology makes it a dynamic theory that will allow it to expand well beyond the life cycle of any particular technology.

While the theory continues to have problematic and unanswered areas, the researchers acknowledge this and expect that the theory will continue to develop and change as new and better research techniques are developed for the study of how we learn and how the human brain works. It is an exciting field that is developing very quickly due to advances in technology and neuroscience, and there is a great need for new researchers to contribute new scientific studies to the development of the theory, the principles, the boundary conditions, and finally, the "big three" sciences of learning, instruction, and assessment themselves.

REFERENCES

Antonenko, P., & Niederhauser, D. (2010). The effects of leads on cognitive load and learning in a hypertext environment. *Computers in Human Behavior, 26,* 140-150.

Antonenko, P. D., Paas, F., Grabner, R., & Van Gog, T. (2010). Using electroencephalography to measure of cognitive load. *Educational Psychology Review, 22,* 425-438.

Atkinson, R. C., & Shiffrin, R. M. (1968). Human memory: A proposed system and its control processes. In K.W. Spence (Ed.), *The psychology of learning and motivation: Advances in research and theory* (pp. 89-195). New York, NY: Academic Press.

Baddeley, A. D. (1986). *Working memory.* Oxford, England: Oxford University Press.

Baddeley, A. D. (1992). Working memory. *Science, 255,* 556-559.

Baddeley, A. D. (1999). *Human memory.* Boston, MA: Allyn & Bacon.

Baddeley, A. D. (2002). Is working memory still working? *European Psychologist,* 7(2), 85-97.

Baddeley, A. D., Gathercole, S. E., & Papagno, C. (1998). The phonological loop as a language learning device. *Psychological Review,* 105, 158-173.

Baddeley, A. D., & Hitch, G. J. (1974). Working memory. In G. A. Bower (Ed.), *Recent advances in learning and motivation* (Vol. 8, pp. 47-90). New York, NY: Academic Press.

Ballantyne, N. (2008). Multimedia learning and social work education. *Social Work Education,* 27(6), 613-622.

Betrancourt, M. (2005). The animation and interactivity principles in multimedia learning. In R. E. Mayer (Ed.), *The Cambridge handbook of multimedia learning.* New York, NY: Cambridge University Press.

Brünken, R., Plass, J. L., & Leutner, D. (2003). Direct measurement of cognitive load in multimedia learning. *Educational Psychologist, 38*(1), 53-61.

Chandler, P., & Sweller, J. (1991). Cognitive load theory and the format of instruction. *Cognition and Instruction, 8*(4), 293-332.

Chi, M. T. H., Glaser, R., & Rees, E. (1982). Expertise in problem solving. In R. Sternberg (Ed.), *Advances in the psychology of human intelligence* (pp. 7-75). Hillsdale, NJ: Erlbaum.

Clark, J. M., & Paivio, A. (1991). Dual coding theory and education. *Educational Psychology Review, 3,* 149-210.

Clark R. E., & Feldon, D. F. (2005). Five common but questionable principles of multimedia learning. In R. E. Mayer (Ed.), *The Cambridge handbook of multimedia learning.* New York, NY: Cambridge University Press.

Dacosta, B. (2008). *The effect of cognitive aging on multimedia learning* (Doctoral dissertation). Retrieved from Dissertations & Theses Database.

DeLeeuw, K. E., & Mayer, R. E. (2008). A comparison of three measures of cognitive load: Evidence for separable measures of intrinsic, extraneous, and germane load. *Journal of Educational Psychology, 100,* 223-234.

De Jong, T. (2010). Cognitive load theory, educational research, and instructional design: Some food for thought. *Instructional Science, 38,* 105-134.

Domagk, S., Schwartz, R. N., & Plass, J. L. (2010). Interactivity in multimedia learning: An integrated model. *Computers in Human Behavior, 26,* 1024-1033.

Dong, C. (2007). *Positive emotions and learning: What makes a difference in multimedia design* (Doctoral dissertation). Retrieved from Dissertations & Theses Database.

Dwyer, F., & Dwyer, C. (2006). Effect of cognitive load and animation on student achievement. *International Journal of Instructional Media, 33*(4).

Gall, J. E. (2004). Reviewed work(s): Multimedia learning by Richard E. Mayer and The cognitive style of PowerPoint by Edward R. Tufte. *Educational Technology Research and Development, 52*(3), 87-90.

Gerjets, P., Scheiter, K., & Cierniak, G. (2009). The scientific value of cognitive load theory: A research agenda based on the structuralist view of theories. *Educational Psychology Review*, 21, 43-54.

Gerlic, I., & Jausovec, N. (1999). Multimedia: Differences in cognitive processes observed with EEG. *Educational Technology Research and Development*, 47(3), 5-14.

Hasler, B. S., Kersten, B., & Sweller, J. (2007). Learner control, cognitive load and instructional animation. *Applied Cognitive Psychology, 21*, 713-729.

Jaeggi, S. M., Buschkuehl, M., Etienne, A., Ozdoba, C., Perrig, W. J., & Nirkko, A. C. (2007). On how high performers keep cool brains in situations of cognitive overload. *Cognitive Affective & Behavioral Neuroscience*, 7, 75-89.

Kalyuga, S., Ayres, P., Chandler, P., & Sweller, J. (2003). The expertise reversal effect. *Educational Psychologist, 38*, 23-32.

Klimesch, W. (1999). EEG alpha and theta oscillations reflect cognitive and memory performance: A review and analysis. *Brain Research Reviews, 29*, 169-195.

Kirschner, P. A., Sweller, J., & Clark, R. E. (2006). Why minimal guidance during instruction does not work: An analysis of the failure of constructivist, discovery, problem-based, experiential, and inquiry-based teaching. *Educational Psychologist, 41*(2), 75-86.

Lu, T. (2008). *Effects of multimedia on motivation, learning and performance: The role of prior knowledge and task constraints* (Doctoral dissertation). Retrieved from Dissertations & Theses Database.

Mayer, R. E. (1996). Learning strategies for making sense out of expository text: The SOI model for guiding three cognitive processes in knowledge construction. *Educational Psychology Review, 8*, 357-71.

Mayer, R. E. (1997). Multimedia learning: Are we asking the right questions? *Educational Psychologist, 32*, 1-19.

Mayer, R. E. (1989). Systematic thinking fostered by illustrations in scientific text. *Journal of Educational Psychology, 81*, 240-246.

Mayer, R. E. (1998). *The promise of educational psychology: Learning in the content areas* (Vol. 1). Upper Saddle River, NJ: Prentice Hall.

Mayer, R. E. (1999). Research-based principles for the design of instructional messages: The case of multimedia explanations. *Document Design, 1*, 7-20.

Mayer, R. E. (2003). Elements of a science of e-learning. *Journal of Educational Computing Research, 29*(3), 297-313.

Mayer, R. E. (2004). Should there be a three-strikes rule against pure discovery learning? The case for guided methods of instruction. *American Psychologist, 59*, 14-19.

Mayer, R. E. (Ed.). (2005a). Cognitive theory of multimedia learning. In *The Cambridge handbook of multimedia learning*. New York, NY: Cambridge University Press.

Mayer, R. E. (Ed.). (2005b). Introduction to multimedia learning. In *The Cambridge handbook of multimedia learning*. New York, NY: Cambridge University Press.

Mayer, R. E. (2005c). Principles for managing essential processing in multimedia learning: Segmenting, pretraining, and modality principles. In *The Cambridge handbook of multimedia learning*. New York, NY: Cambridge University Press.

Mayer, R. E. (2008a). Applying the science of learning: Evidence-based principles for the design of multimedia instruction. *American Psychologist, 63*(8), 760-769.

Mayer, R. E. (2008b). *Learning and instruction* (2nd ed.). Upper Saddle River, NJ: Pearson Merrill Prentice Hall.

Mayer, R. E. (2009). *Multimedia learning* (2nd ed). New York, NY: Cambridge University Press.

Mayer, R. E. (2010a). Applying the science of learning to medical education. *Medical Education, 44*, 543-549.

Mayer, R. E. (2010b). Seeking a science of instruction. *Instructional Science, 38*, 143-145.

Mayer, R. E. (2011a). *Applying the science of learning*. Boston, MA: Pearson.

Mayer, R. E. (2011b). Instruction based on visualizations. In R. E. Mayer & P. A. Alexander (Eds.), *Handbook of research on learning and instruction*. New York, NY: Routledge.

Mayer, R. E., Fennell, S., Farmer, L., & Campbell, J. (2004). A personalization effect in multimedia learning: Students learn better when words are in conversational style rather than formal style. *Journal of Educational Psychology, 96*(2), 389-395.

Mayer, R. E., & Anderson, R. B. (1991). Animations need narrations: An experimental test of the dual-coding hypothesis. *Journal of Educational Psychology, 83*, 484-490.

Mayer, R. E., & Anderson, R. B. (1992). The instructive animation: Helping students build connections between words and pictures in multimedia learning. *Journal of Educational Psychology, 84*, 444-452.

Mayer, R. E., Bove, W., Bryman, A., Mars, R., & Tapangco, L. (1996). When less is more: Meaningful learning from visual and verbal summaries of science textbook lessons. *Journal of Educational Psychology, 88*, 64-73.

Mayer, R. E., & Gallini, J. K. (1990). When is an illustration worth ten thousand words? *Journal of Educational Psychology, 82*, 715-726.

Mayer, R. E., & Moreno, R. (1998). A split-attention effect in multimedia learning: Evidence for dual processing systems in working memory. *Journal of Educational Psychology, 90*, 312-320.

Mayer, R. E., Steinhoff, K., Bower, G., & Mars, R. (1995). A generative theory of textbook design: Using annotated illustrations to foster meaningful learning of science text. *Educational Technology Research & Development, 43*, 31-43.

McLaren, B. M., DeLeeuw, K. E., & Mayer, R. E. (2011). Polite web-based intelligent tutors: Can they improve learning in classrooms? *Computers & Education, 56*, 574-584.

Moore, D. M, Burton, J. K., & Myers, R. J. (2004). Multiple-channel Communication: The theoretical and research foundations of multimedia. In D. H. Jonassen (Ed.), *Handbook of research on educational communications and technology* (2nd ed., pp. 981-1005). Mahwah, NJ: Erlbaum.

Moreno, R. (2005). Instructional technology: Promise and pitfalls. In L. Pytlik Zillig, M. Bodvarsson, & R. Bruning (Eds.), *Technology-based education: Bringing researchers and practitioners together* (pp. 1-19). Greenwich, CT: Information Age.

Moreno, R. (2006a). Learning with high tech and multimedia environments. *Current Directions in Psychological Science, 15*, 63-67.

Moreno, R. (2006b). When worked examples don't work: Is cognitive load theory at an impasse? *Learning and Instruction, 16*, 170-181.

Moreno, R. (2007). Optimizing learning from animations by minimizing cognitive load: Cognitive and affective consequences of signaling and segmentation methods. *Applied Cognitive Psychology, 21*, 765-781.

Moreno, R., & Mayer, R. E. (1999). Cognitive principles of multimedia learning: The role of modality and contiguity. *Journal of Educational Psychology, 91*(2), 358-368.

Moreno, R., & Mayer, R. E. (2000). A learner-centered approach to multimedia explanations: Deriving instructional design principles from cognitive theory. *Interactive Multimedia Electronic Journal of Computer Enhanced Learning*

Moreno, R., & Mayer, R. E. (2002). Learning science in virtual reality multimedia environments: Role of methods and media. *Journal of Educational Psychology, 94*(3), 598-610.

Moreno, R., & Mayer, R. E. (2007). Interactive multimodal learning environments. *Educational Psychology Review, 19*, 309-326.

Moreno, R., Mayer, R. E., Spires, H. A., & Lester, J. C. (2001). The case for social agency in computer-based teaching: Do students learn more deeply when they interact with animated pedagogical agents? *Cognition and Instruction, 19*(2), 177-213.

Musallam, R. (2010). *The effects of using screencasting as a multimedia pre-training tool to manage the intrinsic cognitive load of chemical equilibrium instruction for advanced high school chemistry students* (Doctoral dissertation). Retrieved from Dissertations & Theses Database.

Paas, F. (1992). Training strategies for attaining transfer of problem-solving skill in statistics: A cognitive load approach. *Journal of Educational Psychology, 84*, 429-434.

Paas, F., Renkl, A., & Sweller, J. (2004). Cognitive load theory: Instructional implications of the interaction between information structures and cognitive architecture. *Instructional Science, 32*, 1-8.

Paivio, A. (1986). *Mental representations: A dual coding approach.* Oxford, England: Oxford University Press.

Piaget, J. (1969). *Mechanisms of perception*. New York, NY: Basic Books.

Pintrich, P. R. (2003). Motivation and classroom learning. In W. M. Reynolds & G. E. Miller (Eds.), *Handbook of psychology: educational psychology* (pp. 103-122). New York, NY: Wiley.

Plass, J. L., Chun, D. M., Mayer, R. E., & Leutner, D. (1998). Supporting visual and verbal learning preferences in a second-language multimedia learning environment. *Journal of Educational Psychology, 90*, 25-36.

Rasch, T., & Schnotz, W. (2009). Interactive and non-interactive pictures in multimedia learning environments: Effects on learning outcomes and learning efficiency. *Learning and Instruction, 19*, 411-422.

Renkl, A., & Atkinson, R. K. (2007). Interactive learning environments: Contemporary issues and trends. An introduction to the special issue. *Educational Psychology Review, 19*, 235-238.

Schnotz, W. (2005). An integrated model of text and picture comprehension. In R. E. Mayer (Ed.), *The Cambridge handbook of multimedia learning.* New York, NY: Cambridge University Press.

Schnotz, W. (2008). Why multimedia learning is not always helpful. In J. F. Rouet, R. Lowe, & W. Schnotz (Eds.), *Understanding multimedia documents* (pp. 17-41). New York, NY: Springer.

Schnotz, W., & Bannert, M. (2003). Construction and interference in learning from multiple representation. *Learning and Instruction, 13*, 141-156.

Schnotz, W., & Kürschner, C. (2007). A reconsideration of cognitive load theory. *Educational Psychology Review, 19*, 469-508.

Sorden, S. D. (2005). A cognitive approach to instructional design for multimedia learning. *Information Science Journal, 8*, 263-279.

Stillings, N. A., Weisler, S. E., Chase, C. H., Feinstein, M. H., Garfield, J. L., & Rissland, E. L. (1995). *Cognitive science: An introduction* (2nd ed.). Cambridge, MA: MIT Press.

Sweller, J. (1988). Cognitive load during problem solving: Effects on learning. *Cognitive Science, 12*, 257-285.

Sweller, J. (1994). Cognitive load theory, learning difficulty, and instructional design. *Learning and Instruction, 4*, 295-312.

Sweller, J. (2005). Implications of cognitive load theory for multimedia learning. In R. E. Mayer (Ed.), *The Cambridge handbook of multimedia learning.* New York, NY: Cambridge University Press.

Sweller, J., Van Merrienboer, J. J. G., & Paas, F. G. W. C. (1998). Cognitive architecture and instructional design. *Educational Psychology Review, 10*(3), 251-29.

Tufte, E. R. (2003). *The cognitive style of PowerPoint.* Cheshire, CT: Graphics Press.

Tulving, E. (1977). Episodic and semantic memory. In E. Tulving & W. Donaldson (Eds.), *Organization of memory* (pp. 381-403). New York, NY: Academic Press.

Um, E. (2008). *The effect of positive emotions on cognitive processes in multimedia-based learning* (Doctoral dissertation). Retrieved from Dissertations & Theses Database.

Wittrock, M. C. (1990). Generative processes of comprehension. *Educational Psychologist*, 24(4), 345-376.

Yuan, K., Steedle, J., Shavelson, R., Alonzo, A., & Oppezo, M. (2006). Working memory, fluid intelligence, and science learning. *Educational Research Review, 1*, 83-98.

Author Contact Information: Stephen D. Sorden, EdD, Mohave Community College, Lake Havasu City, AZ. Phone: 928-527-2718. E-mail: steve@sorden.com

CHAPTER 15

Constructivism—Constructivist Learning Theory

Ratna Narayan, Cynthia Rodriguez, Juan Araujo, Ali Shaqlaih, and Glenda Moss
University of North Texas at Dallas

Constructivism is a learning theory that posits that learners actively construct knowledge and make meaning, based on their experiences, individually or socially. Confrey (1990, p. 108) describes constructivism as a belief that all knowledge is necessarily a product of our own cognitive acts. The active role the learner takes in constructivist learning sharply contrasts with one in which learning is the passive transmission of information from one individual to another (Brooks & Brooks, 1993, Duffy & Cunningham, 1996). Constructivism is a theory that posits knowledge must be constructed by a person, not just transmitted to the person. Two simple but important ideas highlight the notion of constructed knowledge: (a) prior knowledge always influences the formation of new knowledge and (b) learning is an active process (Hoover, 1996). Learners are not blank slates, they bring prior cultural knowledge and/or experiences to learning situations that impact the new knowledge they will construct or modify (Merriam & Caffarella, 1999). If the new knowledge emerging is not in agreement with their current schema, the learner can evaluate both and modify their knowledge and schema. Hence meaning making is interpretive and dependent on the learner's experiences and understanding (Jonassen, 1992). People construct knowledge by taking new information and integrating it with their own preexisting knowledge (Cooper, 2007; Woolfolk, 2007).

OBJECTIVISM AND CONSTRUCTIVISM: OPPOSING PARADIGMS

Constructivism arose as a response to objectivism as a contrasting philosophical paradigm, and researchers express varying opinions as to their relationship. Although Marra and Jonassen (1993) describe them as mutually exclusive, Cole (1992) places them on opposite ends of the epistemological continuum. Cronje (2006) describes a more integrative approach where the two opposing theories are placed at right angles to each other enriching the learning experience without diminishing either. According to Lakoff (1987), objectivism "is one version of basic realism" (p. 158) that holds reality exists independent of humans. The real world is completely and correctly structured in terms of its entities, properties and relationships (Vrasidas, 2000). Hence the meaning of the world exists objectively and is external to the knower (Jonassen, 1992), and structure can be modeled for the learner. Constructivists hold opposing views positing there is no ultimate shared reality, it is independent of human thought and is determined by the interpretation of the learner (Crotty, 1998).

Objectivists believe objects have intrinsic meaning (Jonassen, 1991) determined by the structure of the world and is independent of the understanding of the learner. The mind is the processor of abstract symbols. For a constructivist, meaning is indexed by experience (Brown, Collins, & Duguid, 1989), imposed on the world and dependent on the understanding and experiences the learner is able to construct meaning from. Objectivists adopt a behaviorist role in education. According to Jonassen (1991, p. 28),

> Learning therefore consists of assimilating that objective reality. The role of education is to help students learn about the real world. The goal of designers or teachers is to interpret events for them. Learners are

The Handbook of Educational Theories, pp. 169–183

told about the world and are expected to replicate its content and structure in their thinking.

Constructivists on the other hand assert that knowledge resides in individuals and cannot be transferred intact from the head of a teacher to the heads of students (Lorsbach & Tobin, 1997). According to Gergen (1995) teachers in a constructivist learning experience take on the roles of coordinators, facilitators, resource advisors, tutors or coaches. Constructivists foster authentic learning via contextual learning methods such as inquiry and experiential learning, role playing and case studies.

Assumptions of Constructivism

According to Guba and Lincoln (1989), constructivism is based on three fundamental assumptions that are ontological, epistemological and methodical. The basic ontological assumption of constructivism is relativism, a philosophical theory that postulates there is no absolute truth, only truth construed relative to the individual, or to a particular time or culture, or both. The epistemological assumption of constructivism is transactional subjectivism where the "investigator and the object under investigation are assumed to be linked so the "findings" are literally created as the investigation proceeds (Guba & Lincoln, 1994, p. 111).

Collay and Gagnon (2004) delineate epistemological assumptions upon which constructivist learning is centered: (a) knowledge is physically constructed by learners who are involved in active learning, (b) knowledge is symbolically constructed by learners who are making their own meaning to others, and (c) knowledge is theoretically constructed by learners who try to explain things they do not completely understand. The basic methodological assumption of constructivism is hermeneutic-dialecticism, suggesting varying individual constructions are interpreted using conventional hermeneutic techniques and then compared and contrasted by dialectical techniques (Guba & Lincoln, 1994, p. 111)

Bruner (1966) describes three key principles of constructivism. The first principle "readiness" relates to the instruction that makes a learner willing and able to learn by providing appropriate experiences and contexts. The principle of "spiral organization" suggests that not only must the content be structured so that it can be grasped by the learner; it must also be sequenced effectively. The principle of "generation" pertains to instruction "going beyond the information given" (p. 225) ether to further extrapolate or fill in the gaps.

Constructivist Conditions for Learning

Driscoll (2000) summarizes Umberto Eco's "rhizome" metaphor: "The rhizome models the unlimited potential for knowledge construction, because it has no fixed points and no particular organization. Eco also spoke of a jar full of marbles, which, when shaken, will produce a new configuration and a new set of connections among marbles" (p. 378). Cunningham (1992) stated that "the rhizome concept alerts us to the constructed nature of our environmental understanding and the possibilities of different meaning, different truths, and different worlds" (p. 171).

Building on the basic assumptions of constructivism, Driscoll (1994, pp. 382-833) generated five conditions for constructivist learning. These include the following: (a) providing complex learning environments that incorporate authentic activity. Reiser and Dempsey (2007) stress instruction must engage students in authentic activities that will prepare them in solving complex real life problems; (b) providing for social negotiation as an integral part of learning. Bruner (1986) believes learning is a cultural exchange between members of a group. Social negotiation allows for the variance between members of a group to be tested against each other (Hay & Barab, 2001) as new knowledge is being constructed; (c) supporting multiple perspectives and use multiple modes of representation. Constructivists believe examining material through multiple perspectives and multiple modes of representation will enhance the understanding of the learner. According to Spiro et al. (1991), to "revisit the same material, at different times, in rearranged contexts, for different purposes, and from different conceptual perspectives is essential for attaining the goals for advanced knowledge acquisition" (p. 28); (d) nurturing reflexivity. Reflexivity is an important tenet of constructivism and is explained as the process by which a learner develops an awareness how their own thought processes work. Driscoll (1994) believes that reflexivity and critical thinking will assist learners in comprehending how they arrive at conclusions and help developing new schema; (e) emphasizing student-centered learning, also termed as "discovery learning" by Bruner (1966). A method of inquiry-based instruction, discovery learning believes it is best for learners to discover facts and relationships for themselves which they are more likely to remember in contrast to transmissionist models (Bruner, 1967). According to Hannafin (1992), the learner is "the principal arbiter in making judgments as to what, when, and how learning will occur" (p. 51). The idea of student ownership of the learning process arises from this idea.

> Honebein (1996) delineates seven goals for the design of constructivist learning environments: (1) provide experience with the knowledge construction process; (2) provide experience in and appreciation for multiple perspectives; (3) embed learning in realistic and relevant contexts; (4) encourage ownership and voice in the learning process; (5) embed learning in social experience; (6) encourage the use of multiple modes of representation; (7) Encourage self-awareness in the knowledge construction process. (p. 11)

DEVELOPMENT OF CONSTRUCTIVIST LEARNING THEORY

As a theory of learning, constructivism can be traced to the eighteenth century work of the philosopher Giambattista Vico, who postulated humans can understand only what they have themselves constructed. Jean Piaget, John Dewey and Jerome Bruner were among the founding thinkers of constructivist theory. Piaget's (1896-1980) constructivism was based on the psychological stages of development of children; the basis of learning was discovery. He believed intellectual growth involved three processes, assimilation, accommodation and equilibration. Assimilation occurs when a learners' new experience aligns with and is incorporated into a preexisting cognitive structure. Accommodation occurs when existing structures are modified to accommodate new information (Block, 1982).

> No behavior, even if it is new to the individual, constitutes an absolute beginning. It is always grafted onto previous schemes and therefore amounts to assimilating new elements to already constructed structures. (Piaget, 1970, p. 707)

When a child experiences a new event, disequilibrium sets in until the child is able to assimilate and accommodate the material into his schema, hence attaining equilibrium. Achieving the equilibrium necessitates self-regulating activities by the subject to respond correctly to the external intrusion (Piaget, 1972). Hence each learner over the course of his or her development constructs knowledge and reality through assimilation and accommodation. Piaget's constructivist theory is also called cognitive constructivism.

John Dewey (1859-1952) was a constructivist theorist who believed education depended on action and emphasized the place of experience in education. According to Dewey, meaning construction was mental, and children needed to be provided activities that engaged their hands and minds. He termed this reflective activity (1916/1966), a central tenet of the constructivist theory.

> Processes of instruction are unified in the degree in which they center in the production of good habits of thinking. While we may speak, without error, of the method of thought, the important thing is that thinking is the method of an educative experience. The essentials of method are therefore identical with the essentials of reflection. They are first that the pupil have a genuine situation of experience – that there be a continuous activity in which he is interested for its own sake; secondly, that a genuine problem develop within this situation as a stimulus to thought; third, that he possess the information and make the observations needed to deal with it; fourth, that suggested solutions occur to him which he shall be responsible for developing in an orderly way; fifth, that he have opportunity and occasion to test his ideas by application, to make their meaning clear and to discover for himself their validity. (Dewey, 1916/1966, p. 192)

Dewey believed that students must be provided opportunities to think and articulate their thoughts. He was against rote memorization and suggested students engaged in real-world practical workshops through which they could collaboratively and creatively demonstrate their knowledge.

Vygotsky's (1896-1934) theories stressed the fundamental role of social interaction in the development of cognition (Vygotsky, 1978) and unlike Piaget who stressed that children's development must precede learning, Vygotsky believed that social learning preceded development. Vygotsky's constructivist theory is better known as social constructivism because he emphasized the critical importance of culture and the importance of the social context for cognitive development. Culture provides the child cognitive tools needed for development such as language, cultural history and social context. Vygotsky was best known for his "zone of proximal development." He observed when children were working on a task alone, they seldom did better than when they were working in collaboration with an adult. This did not imply that the adult was doing the task for them or teaching them how to do the task. The processes of engaging with the adult allowed the child to refine his thinking to make his performance more effective. Four principles related to teaching and learning immediately become evident: (1) learning and development is a social, cognitive activity, (2) the zone of proximal development can serve as a guide to curricular development, (3) learning extends beyond the school to home and other environments, and (4) classroom activities should always be related to real life.

George Kelly's (1905-1967) theory of personal constructs was based on a single metaphor "Man is a scientist" (Kelly, 1955/1991). Key features of this theory were that the individual creates his own way of seeing and interpreting the world that he lives in by building constructs. Kelly defined constructs as

> patterns which are tentatively tried on for size. They are ways of construing the world. They are what enables man ... to chart a course of behavior, explicitly formulated or implicitly acted out, verbally expressed or utterly inarticulate, consistent with other courses of behavior or inconsistent with them, intellectually reasoned or vegetatively sensed. (Kelly, 1963, p. 33)

Kelly emphasized that the individual perceived the world by whatever meaning they applied to it and that the individual had the freedom to choose an alternate meaning if they preferred. This implied the individual was capable of applying alternate constructions or meanings to events in the past, present or future reinterpreting and redefining them. Kelly suggested the personal construction theory was based on the philosophy of constructive alternativism. While some personal construct theorists have suggested Kelly's personal construct psychology to be a form of constructivism (Niemeyer; 1993), it is widely accepted nowadays that constructivism has subsumed Kelly's theory (Botella, 1995).

Jerome Bruner's (1915-) theoretical framework for constructivism was based on the notion that learning is an active process and learners construct new concepts based on existing knowledge. His views were similar to that of Piaget though he placed more emphasis on the social influences impacting development. Bruner's theory (1966) includes four primary features: predisposition, structure of knowledge, sequencing, consequences: (a) predisposition toward learning refers to experiences which direct the learner toward learning in general or learning something specific. Bruner believed these experiences were impacted by social factors as well as parental and teacher influence, especially during the early years; (b) structure of knowledge relates to the different ways in which a body of knowledge can be structured so it can be most readily grasped by the learner. This can be connected to ideas of learning styles theory; (c) effective sequencing of the material to be learned refers to the scaffolding process in which knowledge and skills build from one to another; (d) the nature and pacing of rewards and punishment was also a consideration, bridging behaviorism and constructivism. Bruner gave much attention to categorization of information in the construction of internal cognitive maps. He believed that perception, conceptualization, learning, decision making, and making inferences all involved categorization.

> The concept of prime numbers appears to be more readily grasped when the child, through construction, discovers that certain handfuls of beans cannot be laid out in completed rows and columns. Such quantities have either to be laid out in a single file or in an incomplete row-column design in which there is always one extra or one too few to fill the pattern. These patterns, the child learns, happen to be called prime. It is easy for the child to go from this step to the recognition that a multiple table, so called, is a record sheet of quantities in completed multiple rows and columns. Here is factoring, multiplication and primes in a construction that can be visualized. (Bruner, 1973, p. 428)

Ernst von Glaserfeld (1917-2010) was a proponent of radical constructivism whose central tenet is that knowledge is a self-organized cognitive process of the human mind. Von Glaserfeld was influenced by Piaget's child development and cognition and Cybernetics, the study of self-contained systems. In contrast to social constructivism, knowledge is actively constructed by the mind of the individual. Von Glaserfeld (1995) believed that as knowledge was subjectively constructed it could not be passively received and hence cannot be transferred from one person to the other. Thus knowledge has to be constructed by the individual who interprets and constructs a reality based on his experiences and interactions with his environment. This has important implications for classroom practice. Von Glaserfeld defines radical constructivism as

> an unconventional approach to the problems of knowledge and knowing. It starts from the assumption that knowledge, no matter how it is defined, is in the heads of persons, and that the thinking subject has no alternative but to construct what he or she knows on the basis of his or her own experience. What we can make of experience constitutes the only world we consciously live in ... all kinds of experience are essentially subjective, and though I may find reasons to believe that my experiences may not be unlike yours, I have no way of knowing that it is the same.... Taken seriously, this is a profoundly shocking view. (Von Glasersfeld, 1995, p. 1)

Von Glasersfeld focused on individual self-regulation and the building of conceptual structures through reflection and abstraction (von Glasersfeld, 1996).

TYPES OF CONSTRUCTIVISM

Various types of constructivism have emerged. Ernest (1995) points out that "there are as many varieties of constructivism as there are researchers" (p. 459). Dougimas (1998) delineated seven "faces" of constructivism on the basis of "points of view perspectives" defined by the individual's writings.

- Trivial or cognitive constructivism is the root of all other shades of constructivism credited to Piaget where knowledge is actively constructed by the learner not passively received from the environment.

- Radical constructivism, here the focus is still on the individual learner as the constructor. However, the learner's constructions do not necessarily reflect knowledge of a real world. Knowledge does not represent or correspond to external reality, but it is viable (von Glaserfeld, 1996).
- Social constructivism emphasizes the social nature of an individual's learning. The theory can be traced back to Piaget and Vygotsky who focused on the role society plays on an individual's development. An important concept for social constructivists is that of scaffolding which is a process of guiding the learner from what is presently known to what is to be known.
- Cultural constructivism encompasses the wider context of cultural influences beyond the immediate social environment of the learning situation. Cobern (1993) describes the internal mental world of the student as competing conceptual "ecologies," an image which invokes pictures of competing constructs, adaptation and survival-of-the-fittest. Dougimas (1998) considers this more complex than radical constructivism as it highlights the need to consider both the student as well as the knowledge to be learned.
- Critical constructivism examines constructivism within a social and cultural environment but with an added dimension of reforming these environments to improve the success of constructivism applied as a referent. This has broader implications for education, and Taylor (1996) suggests that teachers need to work collegially toward reconstructing the education culture together rather than heroically on their own.
- Constructionism, a theory developed by Seymour Papert asserts that learning is effective when it is a reconstruction rather a transmission of knowledge and when the learner is constructing a meaningful product.

Other types of constructivism such as physical, evolutionary, postmodern constructivism, social constructionism, information-processing constructivism and cybernetic systems have been identified (Heylighen, 1993; Prawat, 1996; Steffe & Gale, 1995). According to Tobin and Tippins (1993), constructivism is a way of thinking about knowing, a referent for building models of teaching, learning and curriculum. It thus functions as a philosophy of learning as well as a philosophy of teaching.

Validation of Constructivist Learning Theory

In recent years, constructivism has received attention in educational settings as well as with regards to policy formation (MacKinnon & Scarff-Seatter, 1997; Richardson, 1997; Teets & Starnes, 1996). Proponents call it a "more natural, relevant, productive, and empowering framework" for instructing both PreK-12 students and higher education students (Cannella & Reiff, 1994). Constructivist approaches are considered critical to producing deeper understanding and internalizing material.

The notion of active learning (Tudor, 1996) is a key facet in this learning theory. The teacher's role shifts from being the "keeper of the knowledge" that he/she transmits into students to being a facilitator of the activities and classroom discussions. The constructivist teacher coaches, mediates, prompts, and helps students develop and assess their understanding and learning. Students who use simplified versions of the tools and methods of professionals in the subject area to actively construct their own knowledge have superior generalization skills and transfer of learning to novel contexts (Cobb, 1999). Furthermore, students who cooperate in small groups develop superior critical thinking skills and have longer retention of learning than those working alone (Johnson & Johnson, 1986). Involving students and requiring their participation has shown positive results in diverse learners. English language learners and students with learning differences are able to perform at a higher level when given support by peers and actively engaging in the activity (Gibbons, 2003). The connection to real life makes the content areas more accessible to girls, peoples of color, and the economically disadvantages, and is an important step toward demystification (Gibbons, 2003).

Critiques on Constructivism

Reviewing the relevant literature yields several overarching critiques on constructivism. The most prevalent concern seems to be the "fragmented and incoherent character of the literature on constructivism" (Davis & Sumara, 2002, p. 410) and this lack of clarity has contributed to a misunderstanding of the major tenets of the theory. A primary misconception is the fact that it is a theory of learning, not a theory of teaching (Wolfe & McMullen, 1996), and translating theory to practice is both difficult and imprecise (MacKinnon & Scarf-Seatter, 1997). Teachers are challenged to balance the objective specific curriculum with the more open-ended constructivist methods valued in teacher preparation programs. Furthermore, there is a common misunderstanding that constructivism does not have a wide body of knowledge associated with it and therefore, teachers have an "anything goes" attitude toward learning (Gordon 2009). Baines and Stanley (2000) believe "with constructivism, the teacher is supposed to set up the learning environment, know student preferences, guide student investigations, and then get out of the way" (p. 753).

Richardson (1997) discussed the dangers of accepting students' carrying understandings perspectives at the expense of "right" answers. There is a concern that constructivism is encouraging diversity of thought where conformity is required and that overuse of this method may lead to the "abandonment" style of teaching (MacNinnon & Scarff-Seatter, 1997). As discussed later in the chapter, it is recommended that some classroom assessments be formative in nature in order to inform classroom instruction. Teachers must have knowledge in developing assessments, so that they may be considered valid and reliable data for the students. As Zane (1999) points out, "the constructivist's world is complex, multifaceted, ill-structured, and contextually based" (p. 84). This makes it difficult and time consuming for teachers to produce performance assessments that adhere to the rigorous expectations for learning placed on students in today's classrooms.

Martin (1994) and Vadeboncoeur (1997) explored the need to "deconstruct and scrutinize cultural assumptions that underlie various interpretations of constructivism to expose how social beliefs have influenced the development of theory and practices" (p. 47). Without this examination, inequalities and other forms of oppression may inadvertently perpetuate itself into a constructive classroom where the exact opposite goal was trying to be achieved.

Fox (2001) observed that in its emphasis on learners' active participation, it is often seen that constructivism "too easily dismisses the roles of passive perception, memorization, and all the mechanical learning methods in traditional didactic lecturing" (p. 29). Biggs (1998) and Jin and Cortazzi (1998) noted that while constructivist teaching approaches, including one-to-one or small group classroom interaction, do not always guarantee teaching effectiveness, traditional didactic lecturing in large classes of 50 to 70 students in China has not always meant the "doom" of teaching efforts.

Instruments Associated With Constructivism

As discussed throughout this chapter, the constructivist theory promotes learning contexts in which students play an active role in learning. Roles of the teacher and student are therefore shifted, as a teacher should collaborate with his or her students in order to help facilitate meaning construction. Learning is a reciprocal experience for the students and teacher. With this concept underpinning teaching and learning, it inherently impacts assessment as well. Instruments used in constructivist settings do provide critical quantitative data on student progress, however, perhaps a more valuable resource of these instruments are the specific qualitative information regarding shifts in individual learning. Constructivist educators believe that assessments should measure what teachers teach and what students learn. Traditional assessments rely on student's ability to recall learned items. Wiggins (1990) contends that valid inferences about a students' performance cannot be made based on their ability to recall or "plug in" items. He identifies the following positive attributes of authentic assessment:

- requires students to be effective performers with acquired knowledge,
- presents the student with a full array of tasks that align with the priorities and challenges found in the best instructional activities,
- attend to whether the student can craft polished, thorough and justifiable answers, performances, or products,
- achieves validity and reliability by emphasizing and standardizing the appropriate criteria for scoring such varied products,
- "test validity" depends in part on whether the test simulates real-world "tests" of ability, and,
- involve "ill-structured" challenges and roles that help students rehearse for the complex ambiguities of the "game" of adult and professional life (Wiggins, 1990).

Such authentic assessments help teachers to discover what is working and what is needed in the teaching-learning interactions (Farr, 1992). Because authentic assessment is based on students' actual experiences and interactions throughout each content area, it makes sense that the instruments are often teacher created and maintained. Using constructivist theory as a basis for assessment design places a greater emphasis on cognitive processing (versus content topics or visible behaviors) as assessments are designed. This greater emphasis on cognitive processing could then lead to the specification of more robust performance measures that focus more on enduring traits than on content knowledge (Zane, 2009). There are three critical factors to consider in development of performance assessments (Zane, 2009). First, learning and assessment should be based on the complex and integrated nature of the real world. Second, boundaries of the real world should be reduced to a manageable size. Finally, domains should utilize appropriate theoretical foundations to help define cognitive processing and enduring characteristics of examinees.

Although the requirement to translate assessments into grades continues to be an issue for many teachers, the following assessment instruments provide constructivist teachers with an alternative to more standardized grading systems provided within behaviorist models.

Running Records

Running records (Clay, 2006) are a method of assessing reading in primary grades that can be done quickly and frequently. It is an individually conducted formative assessment that is ongoing and curriculum based. Through a running record, a teacher can learn about a student's strengths and weaknesses in their use of reading strategies. An accuracy rate and a self-correction ratio can also be obtained. A running record provides a detailed representation of a student's oral reading and a teacher's analysis of the record informs subsequent reading instruction. Running records will also provide data for the teacher, child, and their parents that clearly shows progress over time.

Miscue Analysis

Miscue analysis (Goodman, 1973) is similar to the running records described above. Miscue analysis is a more effective way of monitoring intermediate grade students' progress in reading. Although it is less detailed in its recording method, a teacher is still able to learn about students' reading behaviors and to monitor the development across time.

Anecdotal records

Anecdotal records are used for recording significant incidents or specific, observable behaviors (Heibert, Valencia, & Afflerbach, 1994; Wiggins, 1993, 1998). They provide cumulative information about students' development across learning objectives in all curriculum areas as well as their physical and social growth and development. By systematically collecting and analyzing anecdotal comments, teachers can evaluate students' progress and abilities to use language and then plan appropriate instruction.

Rubrics

Rubrics are used to measure various aspects of students' work (Heibert et al., 1994, 1998; Wiggins, 1993, 1998). Rubrics are scoring guides that assess student performance based on a range of criteria, rather than one numerical score. A rubric serves as a guide for students and teachers, often distributed prior to the assignment so that students understand the grading criteria. Rubrics can be used in any content area. The rubric is also a formative type of assessment because it utilized as part of the whole teaching and learning process. As students become more familiar with rubrics, they can become more involved with their construction and also in self and peer evaluating (Alesandrini & Larson, 2002). Critical to using rubrics constructively is to include students in the construction of the rubrics or insuring the rubrics are a guide and not a summative high-stakes evaluation.

Gibbons Evaluation Instrument for Elementary Science Teachers

The Gibbons Evaluation Instrument for Elementary Science Teachers (Gibbons, 2003) can be used by school administrators to facilitate constructivist teaching of elementary science through effective supervised instruction. This model involves three components: preobservation conference, observation, and postobservation conference. Again, the complexity of creating a professional learning process within mandated evaluation processes is ongoing.

Recursive Inquiry Cycle

The recursive inquiry cycle (Short & Harste, 1996) includes exploring (reading, prewriting, discussing, etc.), focusing (framing issues and questions, etc.) searching (gathering information from many sources), synthesizing and evaluating (putting the information together, making sense of it all), creating, publishing, and presenting (composing a message, drafting, revising, editing, publishing/presenting to authentic audiences), reflecting, assessing, and moving forward (evaluating the product and the process of the inquiry; looking for new questions). Taking an inquiry stance provides students and their teachers a tool to answer their particular questions about the topic at hand in an authentic way.

Generalizability of Constructivist Learning Theory

Constructivist learning theory has made significant contributions to the way educators see the learner, the teacher, and the use of their resources as they construct meaning. Today, it is widely believed that learning is a subjective, active and constructive process (Vygotsky, 1978) by involved learners (Kucer, 2005). That is to say, we construct knowledge and make our individual unique realities through activity (Wells & Chang-Wells, 1992), previous experiences (Moll, Amanti, Neff, & Gonzalez, 1992) and reflection with the world around us. Recently, studies have focused on students from culturally and linguistically diverse populations. The purpose of this section of the chapter is to provide a discussion about how the constructivism learning theory applies to culture, ethnicity, gender, and socioeconomic status.

The learner's background and culture is essential to the constructivism learning theory because of its importance on how it shapes the learner's local and global views of themselves and the world. Culture is a process (Spindler, 1997) that is frequently informed by our experiences; while we may find a strategy or activity that is engaging for one set of learners, it does not necessarily mean that it will engage all learners, including those who may have the same background. It is a combination of symbolic, linguistic and meaningful aspects of human collectivities (Kroeber & Kluckhohn, 1954). It is embedded in every second of our lives. Our family, friends, community, and television update our cultural view of how we see the world around us. We are in a constant process of cultural renewal. Constructivist learning theory suggests, therefore, that each learner is unique with their individual strengths and needs.

Constructivism Across Cultures

The constructivism theory is applicable across cultures. Recently, studies relating to the constructivism perspective have been conducted in Australia (Golding, 2011), Ireland (Girvan & Savage, 2009), and United Arab Emirates (Blaik-Hourini, 2011) just to name a few. Golding (2011) studied the difference between teacher directed and unstructured discussions. From his findings he suggested that a community of inquiry was a suitable middle ground between student and teacher directed discussions. From a constructivism perspective, a community of inquiry provides the learner the flexibility to explore topics of their personal interests and simultaneously have support as needed from other members of the group.

Girvan and Savage (2009) studied constructivism as it pertains to learning in virtual worlds. They found that communal constructivism is a possible answer to enhance learning. The participants in this study provided some evidence through semistructured interviews that they did take advantage of the virtual resources at their disposal and made them affordances during the construction of their knowledge. The authors of this chapter exemplify the diversity of cultures and genders and the many applications the constructivism learning theory invites.

Constructivism Across Communities and Gender

Cippolleta (2011) studied the self-construction and interpersonal distances of youth living in residential communities in Sicily, Italy. Using a repertoire grid (Fransella, Bell, & Bannister, 2003; Kelly, 1963) with 59 participants she studied their self-constructions. From the grids three distinct profiles emerged. The first group considered themselves "far" from the group. This self-characterization created an environment of low self-esteem and low self-fulfillment. The author suggested that this group would find it difficult to adjust their construction of their identities since they were expected to adopt the norms of their communities. The second group considered themselves "close" to the group. They findings suggested that they had the possibility to adopt alternative constructions of themselves. This group found it difficult to differentiate among each other and had difficulty seeing self-change.

The third group was similar to the "close" group but was able to better tell apart individuals and were also able to see change in themselves (p. 136). Cippolleta (2011) commented on the prevalence of females within the third profile and their low identification with their mothers. She suggested that this "could imply a difficulty in construing a gender image" (p. 136).

Overall, the author writes that constructing identity should be considered "situated" (Zimmerman, 1998) and, therefore, should be preserved and necessary as youth construct meaning. In other words, the learner's self-perception and gender possess a role in the way they construct knowledge.

Use and Application of Constructivism as a Learning Theory

Dewey's perspective, best known for the experiential and reflective components, influenced what is best known in the field of education as the Progressive Movement. Some call him the father of the Progressivism, which is seen as the antecedent to constructivism. Constructivism has been used and applied in the field of teacher education and educational leadership. As we have pointed out, one of the key components of constructivism is learning through reflection. For Dewey, reflection had not occurred unless the learner had used thinking to make a change that could be seen in action (Rodgers, 2002). Based on this theory, the learner theorizes based on current experience, imagines another course of action, and takes action. Without the follow-up action, reflection has not occurred. This is one of the key lessons that teacher educators try to engage preservice teachers to entertain as they consider the complexity of context with accountability testing, multiple languages spoken, differing life styles (based on race, culture, gender, and social class) diverse learning styles, and diverse needs of students (including learning disabilities, talents, gifts, interests, and values). Critical reflection and participatory dialogue with learners is essential to classroom learning.

Using authentic assessments, such as portfolios, have been used in teacher preparation programs, counseling programs, and doctoral programs (Stephen F. Austin State University, n.d.). Stephen F. Austin State University posts the following statement concerning the use of portfolio assessment: "through their own portfolio assessment experience, learn to assess for purposes of promoting growth instead of for the purposes of ranking and sorting."

Some require professional presentations while others use electronic systems such as Taskstream and TK20. Electronic systems use scoring rubrics, which may be antithetical to the constructivist perspective. In considering the application of constructivist principles, educators must pay attention to whether the instruments foster constructivist practices or reduce them to behaviorism in practice.

The use of rubrics in education can be controversial in terms of moving from behaviorist practices to constructivist practices. Although some view rubrics as a bridge to constructivism, when applied through a behaviorist perspective, they can also have a minimizing affect, resulting in students not thinking beyond the criteria. If the criteria include a template, like using a behaviorist lesson plan template, the product is not authentic in the full sense of the meaning and does not bridge to a constructivist stance. Without students having input into the construction of an authentic product and assessment rubrics, they are often seen as a traditional grading measure. This has seen in the scoring of portfolios for teacher certification, where some students viewed it as a narrow assessment system (Moss, 2003). One student in Moss's study commented,

> Honestly, I feel as if I'm taking a standardized test. There's one way to put together your portfolio, and those that are assessing them are grading the portfolios with a number system. So, I ask myself the question, how can I get more points, currency, for my portfolio? (p. 57)

The key is to create instruments, such as portfolios, to provide students with space to authentically make visible their insights and creative endeavors without using a scoring system that defeats the constructivist process. When a scoring system is required, the key is to engage the students to focus on critical self-reflection rather than the rubric (Moss, 2010).

Constructivist has also been used in the peer-coaching model for professional development. Using narrative methods and action research, Moss, Sloan, and Sander (2009) worked with classroom teachers to implement writer's workshop in an elementary school. The peer-coaching model created space for professional conversations, inquiry, reflection, and transformation of teaching writing.

Constructivism frames the project approach in Reggio Emilia early childhood and elementary classrooms (Forman, 2005). The children design their projects and the teacher supports them. Similarly, project-based instruction in a middle school setting engages students in rich conversations as they negotiate and codesign (DePew, Moss, & Swim, 2009).

Finally, constructivism has been used in educational leadership. Walker (2005) constructivist leadership "as a reciprocal process" through which the school members identify goals "based upon values, beliefs, and individual and shared experiences" (p. 14). Constructivist leaders engage members in active participation and expressing values and beliefs. Inquiry is an important tool in maintaining an organization based on constructivism. Lambert (1998) developed a process for school leaders to use in this process of developing constructivist learning communities.

During the last 40 years education researchers have tried to study the effectiveness of utilizing a constructivism learning perspective. Below are a few recent research studies that focus on the enactment of the constructivism perspective in literacy, social studies, science, and higher education. These examples show that it behooves teachers to allow students to coconstruct knowledge. In this perspective, teachers become mediators instead of deliverers of information. This learning stance allows students to create their own connections and truths about what they are learning.

Example Studies Exemplifying Constructivism

In Literacy Education

One of the most recognizable versions of constructivism is the sociocultural perspective formulated by Vygotsky (1978) in the 1930s and reintroduced in the United States in the 1970s. In this perspective, learning is shaped not only by the learner's prior learning experiences, but also by tapping into the learner's social capital (e.g., Bourdieu, 1972; Dewey 1899; Moll et al., 1992), linguistic knowledge and culture, educational experiences, motivation, and individual learning patterns (Gardner, 1987). In this perspective, each learner is distinctive from one another and therefore, brings with them their own strengths, background knowledge and needs (Moll et al., 1992). Unlike the behaviorist perspective (Skinner, 1952) constructivism believes that each learner is an active participant in the learning process.

A recent research initiative funded by the National Writing Project (2007-2013) provides a good example of how culturally mediated writing instruction (Wickstrom, Araujo, & Patterson, 2011, p. 145) was achieved by teachers who took a sociocultural stance and embraced the following practices. The teachers provided students the opportunity to create empathetic, caring and responsive relationships with other students and the teacher (e.g., Freire, 1978; Noddings 2005). The teachers encouraged meaningful connections between, and among ideas, text, and previous experiences (Moll et al., 1992). Throughout the tasks the students were expected to take an inquiry stance about their learning (Wilhelm, 2007). Once the project was complete, the teachers provided students audiences that the students perceived as authentic like principals, parents and other students (e.g., Atwell, 1998; Jago, 2008; Romano, 1987). The teacher meanwhile provided students appropriate support and mediation to help them become proficient (e.g., Ball, 2006; Freeman & Freeman, 2008; Fu, 2009).

These culturally mediated writing instruction practices were enacted from an inquiry stance and were organized as a recursive set of inquiry cycles (Short, Harste, 1996). The overlapping phases or components of this recursive cycle allowed students the ability to take advantage of their background knowledge to inquire about specific academic knowledge they were interested in exploring. From a constructivist learning theory perspective, the inquiry cycle took advantage of the students' ability to gather information about their specific topic, organize the information in a way that made sense to them, and then provide the learners the opportunity to present their findings to others in an authentic way.

For example, in one of the classrooms the freshman and sophomore students inquired, "What do I need to do to be the person I want to be in 15 years?" At first, they searched and wrote about possible careers, housing, family, cars, and luxuries (e.g., phones, suits, swimming pools, etc.). From this information they created a monthly budget that included all their needs and wants. Next, they focused and wrote about one career (i.e., video game designer, police officer, nurse). They searched online for the educational requirements, potential salary, job opportunities and potential for advancement. Then, they analyzed where they stood academically, and planned what they needed to do in high school during the next 2 to 3 years to be ready for college, career and life. At the end of the unit, they found that they needed to compromise between their needs, their careers, and where they presently stood academically.

As these students coconstructed knowledge about their career and life interests they were immersed in reading, writing, and mathematic activities. This authentic exercise allowed the teacher to informally assess the students' literacy skills through observations, questions, and conferencing and simultaneously allowed students to construct knowledge with regard to their present and future interests.

In Social Studies Education

Social studies education teachers often use the constructivist learning theory to allow students learn about, study, and analyze historical events through role play, debates, and multigenre projects. Rather than simply ask students to provide facts and dates related to events, these engaging activities provide students a way to make meaning of the content and then make direct connections to today's events.

As noted earlier, other parts of the world outside of the United States are finding it beneficial to implement a constructivism learning stance. Blaik-Hourini (2011), a practicum supervisor in the United Arab Emirates, suggests that the constructivism learning theory needs implementation to improve the social studies curriculum and pedagogy.

Through naturalistic, qualitative case studies he found that, indeed, 18 of the 21 study participants' satisfactory understood constructivism, and 17 of 21 were familiar with its learning strategies. However, only two of the participants integrated the constructivism learning theory into their daily activities. The participants spoke of the difficulties of implementation. The topics ranged from readiness of school facilities, and willingness of administrators and students.

Blaik-Hourini (2011) suggests that more training is needed about constructivism uses and application in real classrooms environments. The author also suggests that the education council develop a curriculum that invites constructivism perspectives instead of rote memorization exercises.

In Science Education

Science education teachers use constructivist learning theory when they allow students to conduct hands-on observations, experimentation, and reporting of findings. Rather than simply write a hypothesis about what would happen, these activities allow students to make active meaning and make connections to what they are reading in their textbooks. One recent science education action research study (Oliver, 2011) examined the ways students explored the topic of evolution using a qualitative, naturalistic methodology over a period of 4 weeks. The researcher wondered if "problems generating cognitive conflict can be used to challenge students' prior conceptions" and whether, "taking part in construction of knowledge with the teacher and others students can aid in creating conceptual change" (p. 14). Oliver (2011) found that "the group work in class activities provided students the opportunity for individuals to verbalize and justify their own ideas" and that in using the students' prior conceptions about evolution teachers provided a space where "students can clarify their understanding." Importantly, Oliver commented about the unevenness of the learning process, at times the learners reverted back to their misconceptions. Oliver found that learning is indeed a complex undertaking that "takes time" (p. 18).

IN MATHEMATICS EDUCATION

Constructivists argue that mathematics is a human intervention with a long history. Culturally embedded schools of thought compete, fashion change, and accept some questions may be irresolvable (Fosnot, 2005, p. 85). A more recent view of doing mathematics is to conjecture, to invent and extend ideas, to test and revise ideas. Currently, most modern approaches look at the mathematics classroom as a community of inquiry and problem solving. Creating teaching practice guided by constructivist principles requires a qualitative transformation of every aspect of mathematics teaching (Fosnot, 2005, p. 90). There is no doubt that the constructivist approach is applied in mathematics teaching. We present here two examples in which constructivism are essential in understanding the process of teaching some mathematical concepts.

The first example is Anne Hendry in her approach of teaching measurement to a first grade class (Fosnot, 2005). She wondered how she could start teaching the measurement concepts and what children know about measurements. Do students have any previous experience that could be related to the measurements? She thought there must be something that the students know that has something to do with measurements. Then she decided to connect it to their upcoming holiday. Hendry's lesson approach was based on constructivism in that she began with the concept that students learn through social interaction. Hendry did not follow traditional teaching. In fact she gave the students the chance to discuss and try different answers; she listened to all their suggestions and tried to avoid answering the problem but rather followed their questions with questions. This approach made the students more attached to the problem and, therefore, more involved in the discussion (Hendry, 1996). The inquiry and the logical thinking were more important goals in the classroom than getting right answers.

The second example is Carol Mosesson teaching fractions to fourth grade. Traditionally most teachers will teach fractions as shaded parts of a whole (Fosnot, 2005). In the traditional approach it is assumed that the teacher is source of knowledge and mathematics is thought of as algorithms and formulas. In Carol's class, students share knowledge and information to create a context in which the students can generate mathematical ideas related to fractions. Students in Carol's class constructed meaning, found relations and explored concepts. Carol's classroom displayed evidence of many views of mathematics. One is surely constructing meaning in which children notice relations and put explanations and conjectures (Fosnot & Dolk, 2005, p. 181).

This view was put forth by Hans Freudenthal when he argued that mathematics was a human activity (Fosnot & Dolk, 2005, p. 182). The question is what does it mean to understand a concept in mathematics such as fractions? Carol made the students get involved in discussion about many views for fractions and had them response to some questions. She pushed the students toward comparing fractions and realizing for example that one fourth is more than one fifth. She pushed toward critical thinking that goes beyond just answers. She continues to encourage development and she created what is so called math congress in which all students gather, present and discuss their strategies/solutions with one another (Fosnot & Dolk, 2005, p. 184). We can look at the math congress idea as a form of cooperative learning and hence it is important to realize the importance of exchanging ideas between students. Carl has successfully used the math congress to support students' growth (Fosnot & Dolk, 2005, p. 186). In math congress, when the students construct their own strategy and then present and defend their ideas, all the students can see all the ideas and hence improve their ways of thinking of the problem and then possibly build a new strategy for future problems.

There are many students who solve mathematical problems without understanding the concepts. For example, a student might be able to find the derivative of a given function but without understanding that the derivative is a form of rate of change of the function. In that case the student is just imitating the instructor and applying the formulas. This is not the mathematics that we want our students to learn. That is why making the student to construct their own strategies is important. As Reuben Hersh stated, "It's the questions that drive mathematics. Solving problems and making up new ones is the essence of mathematical life. If mathematics is conceived apart from mathematical life, of course it seems dead (Hersh, 1997, p. 18). The connection between what students know and are learning is essential in constructivist approach.

For example, a student will learn that the equation $x + 6 = 2$ does not have a solution in the set of natural numbers, but it does have one in the set of integers. From this understanding the instructor can take the student to the equation like $2x + 5 = 7$ that does not have a solution in the set of integers but does have a solution in the set of rational numbers. Then extend to an equation like $x2 - 2 = 0$, which does not have a solution in the set of rational numbers but does have a solution in the set of real numbers. Then an equation like $x2 + 2 = 0$ which doesn't have a real solution but has a complex one. In this setting we introduced a constructivist approach in which the students construct on their knowledge of not able to solve the equation in a certain set to solving the same equation in different settings.

Teachers need to make mathematics meaningful students by connecting it to their world. Encourage communication between the teacher and the students and also between the students is essential in any constructivist approach. When mathematics becomes meaningful to students, they will value it, like it and enjoy doing it. This will take us to the most important goal of teaching mathematics to our children, which is improving their thinking and become more creative in their lives.

In Higher Education

The constructivism learning theory applies to undergraduate and graduate education. In an action research project (Patterson, Baldwin, Araujo, Shearer, & Stewart, 2010) one author used a constructivism learning stance to improve the students' knowledge base relating to bilingual and English as a second language education. Araujo (2011) used a reflective journaling technique to allow students to actively coconstruct with themselves and with other students and the teacher. Araujo asked "What can I change in my practice so that I create a culture that elicits content ownership and that rewards meaningful sustained learning?" (p. 152).

The findings of this action research project suggested that allowing students to take an inquiry, coconstructive stance allowed students to question what they were reading and to validate what they were learning. "This stance afforded us (teacher and students) the opportunity to move our conversations to a global and critical perspective" (Patterson et. al, 2010, p. 154).

In sum, the constructivism learning theory provides learners the opportunity to take advantage of the many resources (i.e., culture, ethnicity, gender, and language proficiency) at their disposal as they coconstruct knowledge.

References

Alesandrini, K., & Larson, L. (2002). Teachers bridge to constructivism. *The Clearing House, 75*(3), 118-122.

Araujo, J. J. (2011). *Teacher decision making: Cultural mediation in two high school English language arts classrooms* (Unpublished doctoral dissertation). University of North Texas, Denton, TX.

Atwell, N. (1998). *In the middle: New understandings about writing, reading, learning* (2nd ed.). Portsmouth, NH: Boynton/Cook.

Ball, A. R. (2006). Teaching writing in culturally diverse classrooms. In C. A. MacArthur, S. Graham, S., & J. Fitzgerald (Eds.), *Handbook of writing research* (pp. 293-310). New York, NY: The Guilford.

Baines, L. A., & Stanley, G. (2000). 'We want to see the teacher': Constructivism and the rage against expertise. *Phi Delta Kappan, 82*(4),327–330.

Biggs, J. (1998). Learning from the Confucian heritage: So size doesn't matter? *International Journal of Educational Research, 29*, 723-738.

Blaik-Hourani, R. (2011). Constructivism and revitalizing social studies. *The History Teacher, 44*(2), 227-249.

Block, J. (1982). Assimilation, accommodation, and the dynamics of personality development. *Child Development, 53*, 281-295

Botella, L. (1995). Personal construct psychology, constructivism and postmodern thought. In R. A. Neimeyer & G. J. Neimeyer (Eds.), *Advances in personal construct psychology* (Vol. 3, pp. 3-35). Greenwich, CT: JAI Press.

Bourdieu, P. (1972). *Outline of a theory of practice.* Cambridge, England: Cambridge University Press.

Brooks, J. G., & Brooks, B. G. (1993). *The case for constructivist classrooms.* Alexandria, VI: Association for Supervision and Curriculum Development.

Brown, J. S., Collins, A., & Duguid, P. (1989). Situated cognition and the culture of learning. *Educational Researcher, 18*(1), 32-41.

Bruner, J. S. (1966) *Toward a theory of instruction.* Cambridge, MA: Harvard University Press.

Bruner, J. S. (1967). *On knowing: Essays for the left hand.* Cambridge, MA: Harvard University Press.

Bruner, J. S. (1973). *Going beyond the information given.* New York, NY: Norton.

Bruner, J. S. (1986). *Actual minds, possible worlds.* Cambridge, MA: Harvard University Press.

Cannella, G. S., & Reiff, J. C. (1994). Individual constructivist teacher education: Teachers as empowered learners. *Teacher Education Quarterly, 21*(3), 27-38.

Cippolleta, S. (2011). Self-construction and interpersonal distances of juveniles living in residential communities. *Journal of constructivist psychology, 24*(2), 122-143.

Clay, M. M. (2006). *Observation survey of early literacy achievement.* Portsmouth, NH. Heinemann.

Cobb, P. (1999). Where is the mind? In P. Murphy (Ed.), *Learners, learning and assessment* (pp. 135-150). London, England: Open University Press.

Cobern, W. (1993) Contextual constructivism: The impact of culture on the learning and teaching of science. In K. Tobin (Ed.), *The practice of constructivism in science education* (pp. 51-69). Hillsdale, NJ: Erlbaum.

Cole, P. (1992). Constructivism revisited: A search for common ground. *Educational Technology, 33*(2), 27-34.

Collay, M., & Gagnon, G. (2004). Constructivist learning design. Retrieved from http://www.prainbow.com/cld/cldp.html

Confrey, J. (1990). What constructivism implies for teaching. *Journal for Research in Mathematics Education Monographs, 4*, 107-122

Cooper, R. (2007). *Those who can, teach* (11th ed.). New York, NY: Houghton Mifflin.

Cronjé, J. (2006). Paradigms regained: Toward integrating objectivism and constructivism in instructional design and the learning sciences. *Association for Educational Communications and Technology, 54*(4), 387-416.

Crotty, M. (1998). *The foundations of social research: Meaning and perspective in the research process.* London, England: SAGE.

Cunningham, D. J. (1992). Beyond educational psychology: Steps toward an educational semiotic. *Educational Psychology Review, 4,* 165-194.

Davis, B., & Sumara, D. (2002). Constructivist discourses and the field of education: Problems and possibilities. *Educational Theory, 52,* 409-428.

DePew, J., Moss, G., & Swim, T. (2009). Engaging rural-urban students in creative writing. *scholarlypartnershipsedu, 4*(2), 52-67.

Dewey, J. (1899). *School and society.* Chicago, IL: University of Chicago Press.

Dewey, J. (1966). *Democracy and education: An introduction to the philosophy in education.* New York, NY: McMillan. (Original work published 1916)

Dougiamas, M. (1998). *A journey into constructivism.* Retrieved from http://dougimas.com/writing/constructivism.html

Driscoll, M. P. (1994). *Psychology of learning for instruction.* Boston, MA: Allyn & Bacon.

Driscoll, M. P. (2000). *Psychology of learning for instruction* (2nd ed.). Needham Heights, MA: Allyn & Bacon.

Duffy, T. M., & Cunningham, D. J. (1996). Constructivism: Implications for the design and delivery of instruction. In D. H. Jonassen (Ed.), *Educational communications and technology* (pp. 170-199). New York, NY: Simon & Schuster Macmillan.

Ernest, P. (1995). The one and the many. In L. Steffe & J. Gale (Eds.), *Constructivism in education* (pp. 459-486). Hillsdale, NJ: Erlbaum.

Farr, R. (1992). Putting it all together: Solving the reading assessment puzzle. *Reading Teacher, 46*(1), 26-37.

Forman, G. (2005). The project approach in Reggio Emilia. In C. T. Fosnot, (Ed.). *Constructivism: Theory, perspectives, and practice* (pp. 212-221). New York, NY: Teachers College Press.

Fosnot, C. T. (Ed.). *Constructivism: Theory, perspectives and practice* (2nd ed.). New York, NY: Teachers' College Press.

Fosnot, C. T., & Dolk, M. (2005). "Mathematics" or "mathematizing"? In C. T. Fosnot (Ed.), *Constructivism: Theory, perspectives, and practice* (pp. 175-192). New York, NY: Teachers College Press.

Fox, R. (2001). Constructivism examined. *Oxford Review of Education, 27*(1), 23-35.

Fransella, F., Bell, R., & Bannister, D. (2003). *A manual for repertoire grid techniques.* West Sussex, England: Wiley.

Freeman, Y., & Freeman, D. E. (2008). *Academic language for English language learners and struggling readers: How to help students succeed across content areas.* Portsmouth, NH: Heinemann.

Freire, P. (1978). *Pedagogy of the oppressed.* New York, NY: Seabury.

Fu, D. (2009). *Writing between languages: How English language learners make the transition to fluency, Grades 4-12.* Portsmouth, NH: Heinemann.

Gardner, H. (1987). The theory of multiple intelligences. *Annals of Dyslexia, 37,* 19-35.

Gergen, K. (1995). Social construction and the education process. In L. D. Steffe & J. Gale (Eds.), *Constructivism in education* (pp. 17-40). Hillsdale, NJ: Erlbaum.

Gibbons, B. A. (2003). Supporting elementary science education for English learners: A constructivist evaluation instrument. *Journal of Educational Research, 96*(6), 371-380.

Girvan, C., & Savage, T. (2010). Identifying an appropriate pedagogy for virtual worlds: A communal constructivism case study. *Computers and Education, 55,* 342-349.

Golding, C. (2011). The many faces of constructivist discussion. *Education Philosophy and Teaching, 43*(5), 467-483.

Goodman, K. (1973). Miscues: "Windows on the reading process." In F. Gollasch (Ed.). *Language and literacy: The selected writings of Kenneth Goodman* (Vol. 1, pp. 93-102). Boston, MA: Routledge & Kegan Paul.

Gordon, M. (2009). The misuses and effective uses of constructivist teaching. *Teachers and Teaching: Theory and Practice, 15*(6), 737-746.

Gordon, M. (2009). Toward a pragmatic discourse of constructivism: Reflections on Lessons from Practice. *Educational Studies, 45,* 39-58.

Guba, E. G., & Lincoln, Y. S. (1989). *Fourth generation evaluation.* Newbury Park, CA: SAGE.

Guba, E. G., & Lincoln, Y. S. (1994). Competing paradigms in qualitative research. In N. K. Denzin & Y. S. Lincoln (Eds.), *Handbook of qualitative research* (pp. 105-117). London, England: SAGE.

Hannafin, M. J. (1992). Emerging technologies, ISD, and learning environments: Critical perspectives. *Educational Technology Research and Development, 40,* 49-64.

Hay, K. E., & Barab, S. A. (2001). Constructivism in practice: A comparison and contrast of apprenticeship and constructionist learning environments. *The Journal of the Learning Sciences, 10*(3), 281-322

Heibert, E. H., Valencia, S. W., & Afflerbach, P. P. (Eds). (1994). Understanding authentic reading assessment. Definitions and perspectives. In *Authentic reading assessment: Practices and possibilities* (pp. 6-21). Newark, DE: International Reading Association.

Hendry, A. (1996). Math in the social studies curriculum. In D. Schifter (Ed.), *What's happening in the math class? Vol 1. Envisioning new practices through teacher narratives* (pp. 9-13). New York, NY: Teachers College press.

Hersh, R. (1997). *What is mathematics, really?* London, England: Oxford University Press.

Heylighen, F. (1993). Epistemology, introduction. Retrieved from http://pespmc1.vub.ac.be/EPISTEMI.html

Honebein, P. (1996). *Seven goals for the design of constructivist learning environments.* In B. Wilson (Ed.), *Constructivist learning environments* (pp. 17-24). Englewood Cliffs, NJ: Educational Technology Publications.

Hoover, W. A. (1996, August). The practice implications of constructivism. *SEDL Letter, 9*(3). Retrieved from http://www.sedl.org/pubs/sedletter/v09n03/practice.html

Jago, C. (2008). *Come to class: Lessons for high school writers.* Portsmouth, NH: Heinemann.

Jin, L. X., & Cortazzi, M. (1998). Dimensions of dialogue: large classes in China. *International Journal of Educational Research, 29,* 739-761.

Johnson, R. T., & Johnson, D. W. (1986). Action research: Cooperative learning in the science classroom. *Science and Children, 24*, 31-32.

Jonassen, D. H. (1991). Evaluating constructivist learning. *Educational Technology, 36*(9), 28-33.

Jonassen, D. H. (1992). Objectivism versus constructivism: Do we need a new philosophical paradigm? *Educational Technology Research and Development, 39*(3), 5-14.

Kelly. G. (1963). *A theory of personality: The psychology of personal constructs*. New York, NY: Norton

Kelly, G. A. (1991). *The psychology of personal constructs* (Vols. 1 & 2). London, England: Routledge. (Original work published 1955)

Kroeber, A., & Kluckhohn, C. (1954). *Culture: A critical review of concepts and definitions*. New York, NY: Random House.

Kucer, S. B. (2005). *The dimensions of literacy: A conceptual base for teaching reading and writing in schools*. Mahwah, NJ: Erlbaum.

Lakoff, G. (1987). *Women, fire, and dangerous things: What categories reveal about the mind*. Chicago, IL: University of Chicago Press.

Lambert, L. (2003). *Building leadership capacity*. New York, NY: McGraw-Hill International.

Lorsbach, A., & Tobin, K. (1997). Constructivism as a referent for science teaching. Retrieved from http://www.exploratorium.edu/ifi/resources/research/contsructivism.html

MacKinnon, A., & Scarff-Seatter, C. (1997). Constructivism: Contradictions and confusion in teacher education. In V. Richardson (Ed.), *Constructivist teacher education: Building new understandings* (pp. 38-55). Washington, DC: Falmer Press.

Marra, R., & Jonassen, D. (1993). Whither constructivism. In D. Ely & B. Minor (Eds), *Educational media and technology yearbook* (pp. 56-77). Englewood, CO: Libraries Unlimited.

Martin, R. J. (1994). Multicultural social reconstructionist education: Design for diversity in teacher education. *Teacher Education Quarterly, 21*(3), 77-89.

Merriam, S. B., & Caffarella, R. S. (1999). *Learning in adulthood: A comprehensive guide* (2nd ed.). San Francisco, CA: Jossey-Bass.

Moll, L. C., Amanti, C., Neff, D., & Gonzalez, N. (1992). Funds of knowledge for teaching: Using a qualitative approach to connect homes and classrooms. *Theory into Practice, 31*(2), 132-141.

Moss, G. (2003). Critical self-reflective narrative of portfolio assessment in teacher preparation. *Scholar-Practitioner Quarterly, 2*(1), 45-60.

Moss, G. (2010). Working within accountability models-With vision! Vision of standardization and vision of critical pedagogy. In T. Swim, J. Nichols, K. Murphey, G. Moss, A. Merz, D. Lindquist, & B. Kanpol (Eds.), *Teacher national accreditation as community dialogue: Transformative reflections* (pp. 101-126). Cresskill, NJ: Hampton Press.

Moss, G., Sloan, L., & Sandor, J. (2009). Peer coaching and action research as professional development. *scholarlypartnershipsedu, 4*(2), 68-81.

Neimeyer, R. A. (1993). Constructivism and the problem of psychotherapy integration. *Journal of Psychotherapy Integration, 3*(2), 133-157.

Noddings, N. (1992). *The challenge to care in schools: An alternative approach to education*. New York, NY: Teachers College Press.

Oliver, M. (2011). Teaching and learning evolution: Testing the principals of a constructivism approach through action research. *Teaching Science, 57*(1), 13-18.

Patterson, L., Baldwin, S., Araujo, J., Shearer, R., & Stewart, A. (2010). Look, think, act: Using critical action research to sustain reform in complex teaching ecologies. *Journal of Inquiry and action in education, 3*(3), 139-157.

Piaget, J. (1970). Piaget's theory. In P. H. Mussen (Ed.), *Carmichael's manual of child psychology* (Vol. 1, 3rd ed., pp. 703-732). New York, NY: Wiley.

Piaget, J. (1972). *To understand is to invent*. New York, NY: The Viking Press.

Prawat, R. (1996). Constructivisms, modern and postmodern. *Educational Psychology, 31*(3/4), 215-225.

Reiser, R. A. & Dempsey, J. V. (2007). *Trends and issues in instructional design* (2nd ed.). Upper Saddle River, NJ: Pearson Education.

Richardson, V. (1997). Constructivist teaching and teacher education: Theory and practice. In V. Richardson (Ed.), *Constructivist teacher education: Building new understandings* (pp. 3-14). Washington, DC: Falmer Press.

Rodgers, C. (2002). Defining reflection: Another look at John Dewey and reflective thinking. *Teachers College Record, 104*(4), 842-866.

Romano, T. (1987). *Clearing the way: Working with teenage writers*. Portsmouth, NH: Heinemann.

Short, K., & Harste, J. (with Burke, C.). (1996). *Creating classrooms for authors and inquirers* (2nd ed.). Portsmouth, NH: Heinemann.

Skinner, B. F. (1952). *Verbal behavior*. Acton, MA: Copley.

Spindler, G. (1997). *Education and the cultural process*. Prospect Heights, IL: Waveland Press

Sprio, R. J., Feltovich, P. J., Jacobson, M. J., & Coulson, R. L. (1991). Cognitive flexibility, constructivism, and hypertext: Random access instruction for advanced knowledge acquisition in ill-structured domains. *Educational Technology, 31*, 24-33.

Stears, M. (2009). How social and critical constructivism can inform science curriculum design: A study from South Africa. *Educational Research, 51*(4), 397-410.

Steffe, L., & Gale, J. (Eds.) (1995). *Constructivism in education*. Hillsdale, NJ: Erlbaum.

Stephen F. Austin State University. (n.d.). Retrieved from http://www.sfasu.edu/education/departments/secondaryeducation/doctoral/corevalues.asp

Taylor, P. (1996) Mythmaking and mythbreaking in the mathematics classroom. *Educational Studies in Mathematics, 31*, 151-173

Teets, S. T., & Starnes, B. A. (1996). Foxfire: Constructivism for teachers and learners. *Action in teacher education, 18*(2), 31-39.

Tobin, K., & Tippins, D (1993). Constructivism as a referent for teaching and learning. In K. Tobin (Ed.), *The practice of constructivism in science education* (pp. 3-21). Hillsdale, NJ: Erlbaum.

Tudor, I. (1996). *Learner-centeredness as language education*. Cambridge, MA: Cambridge University Press.

Vadeboncoeur, J. (1997). Child development and the purpose of education: A historical context for constructivism in teacher education. In V. Richardson (Ed.), *Constructivist teacher education: Building new understandings* (pp. 15-37). Washington, DC: Falmer Press.

von Glasersfeld, E. (1995). *Radical constructivism: A way of knowing and learning*. London, England: Falmer Press.

von Glasersfeld, E. (1996). Introduction: Aspects of constructivism. In C. Fosnot (Ed.), *Constructivism: Theory, perspectives, and practice* (pp. 3-7). New York, NY: Teachers College Press.

Vrasidas, C. (2000). Constructivism versus objectivism: Implications for interaction, course design, and evaluation in distance education. *International Journal of Educational Telecommunications, 6*(4), 339-362.

Vygotsky, L. S. (1978). *Mind in society: Development of higher psychological processes* [M. Cole, V. John-Steiner, S. Scribner, E. Souberman (Eds.). Cambridge, MA: Harvard University Press.

Walker, D. (2005). Constructivist leadership: Standards, equity, and learning—Weaving whole cloth from multiple strands. In L. Lambert, D. Walker, D. P. Zimmerman, J. E. Cooper, M. D. Lambert, & M. Szabo (Ed.), *The constructivist leader* (2nd ed., pp. 1-33). New York, NY: Teachers College Press.

Wells, G., & Chang-Wells, G. L. (1992). *Constructing knowledge together: Classrooms as centers of inquiry and literacy.* Portsmouth, NH: Heinemann.

Wickstrom, C., Araujo, J., Patterson, L. (with Hoki, C., & Roberts, J.). (2011). I can see you, therefore I can teach. In P. Dunston, K. H. Gambrell, P. Stecker, S. Fullerton, V. Gillis, & C. C. Bates (Eds.), *60th Literacy Research Association yearbook* (pp. 144-157). Oak Creek, WI: Literacy Research Association.

Wiggins, G. (1990). The case for authentic assessment. *Practical Assessment, Research & Evaluation,* 2(2). Retrieved from http://PAREonline.net/getvn.asp?v=2&n=2

Wiggins, G. (1993). Assessment: Authenticity, context, and validity. *Phi Delta Kappan, 75*(3), 200-214.

Wiggins, G. (1998). *Educative assessment: Designing assessments to inform and improve student performance.* San Francisco, CA: Jossey Bass

Wilhelm, J. D. (2007). *Engaging readers and writers with inquiry: Promoting deep understandings in language arts and the content areas with guiding questions.* New York, NY: Scholastic.

Wolffe, R. J., & McMullen, D. W. (1996). The constructivist connection: Linking theory, best practice, and technology. *Journal of Computing in Teacher Education, 12*(2), 25-28.

Woolfolk, A. (2007). *Educational psychology* (10th ed.). Boston, MA: Pearson Education.

Zane, T. W. (2009). Performance assessment design principles gleaned from constructivist learning theory (part 1). *TechTrends, 53*(1), 81-88.

Zimmerman, D. H. (1998). Identity, context and interaction. In C. Anataki & S. Widdicombe (Eds.), *Identities in talk* (pp. 87-106). London, England: SAGE.

Author Contact Information: Glenda Moss, University of North Texas, Department of Teacher Education & Administration, 7300 University Hills Blvd., Dallas, TX 75241-4600. Phone: 972-338-1373. E-mail: glenda.moss@unt.edu

CHAPTER 16

Situated Cognition Theory

Patrick M. Jenlink
Stephen F. Austin State University

Learning as cognitive only was the dominant approach to the study of learning throughout much of the twentieth century, that is, as a cognitive process within the mind of the individual learner, decontextualized from the lived-in world. However, in the latter part of the twentieth century there was, and continues to be, a growing interest in the study of cognition and learning as "situated" in a specific time, place, and social activity —as "situated cognition and learning"—and to view the locus of learning not as in the brain of the single individual learner but as situated in a sociocultural context or activity, wherein cognitive processes and learning are distributed among person, language, artifact, activity, and environment (Brown, Collins, & Duguid, 1989; Lave & Wenger, 1999; Salomon, 1993).

The concept of situated cognition and its implications for learning were explicitly set forth, in the context of contemporary research, in a 1989 article by Brown, Collins, and Duguid. After observing that the prevailing approach to knowledge acquisition in schools concerns activity and context as "pedagogically useful" but "fundamentally distinct and even neutral with respect to what is learned" (p. 32), the authors stated their basic thesis as follows:

> The activity in which knowledge is developed and deployed ... is not separable from or ancillary to learning and cognition. Nor is it neutral. Rather it is an integral part of what is learned. Situations might be said to co-produce knowledge through activity. Learning and cognition, it is now possible to argue, are fundamentally situated. (p. 32)

Learning then, from this perspective, is a process of "enculturation" wherein the opportunity to observe and to practice *in situ* allows the development of contextualized competencies incorporating the tools and forms of social interaction that are valued in a given cultural community.

SITUATED COGNITION THEORY—GOALS, ASSUMPTIONS, AND ASPECTS

Situated cognition theory, varied in its forms and names (i.e., cognitive apprenticeship, situated learning, legitimate peripheral participation, etc.) share a common idea that cognition is situated, and that learning is inseparable from doing *in situ*; that cognition and learning are processes of enculturation. Historically, situated cognition draws upon the work of Dewey (1938), Vygotsky (1978, 1926/1997), Leont'ev (1978, 1981), and Luria (1976, 1979) in the area of early theory and research on cognition and learning, as well as the work of Lave (1988, 1993), Lave and Wenger (1991), and Reynolds, Sinatra, and Jetton (1996) in the area of anthropological studies.

What is meant by "situation" as it relates to situated cognition is relatively unclear. However, in *Experience and Education*, Dewey (1938) suggested the following: Any normal experience is an interplay of these two sets of conditions (objective and internal). Taken together, or in their interaction, they form what we call a situation" (p. 42). Learning within the situation, then, became a point divergence from more traditional educational psychology perspectives. It was during the latter part of the twentieth century that situated cognition gained recognition in the field of educational psychology (Brown, Collins, & Duguid, 1989), sharing many principles with older fields such as critical theory, (Frankfurt School [see Wiggershaus, 1986]; Freire, 1970) anthropology (Lave & Wenger, 1991), philosophy (Heidegger, 1968), critical discourse analysis (Fairclough, 1989), and sociolinguistics theories (Bakhtin, 1981) that

The Handbook of Educational Theories, pp. 185–198

rejected the notion of truly objective knowledge and Kantian empiricism principles.

Situated cognition draws on a variety of perspectives, from an anthropological study of human behavior within communities of practice (Lave & Wenger, 1991) to the ecological psychology of the perception-action cycle (Gibson, 1979) and intentional dynamic (Shaw, Kadar, Sim, & Reppenger, 1992), and even research on robotics with work on autonomous agents at NASA and elsewhere (e.g., work by Clancey, 1993). Early attempts to define situated cognition focused on contrasting the emerging theory with information processing theories dominant in cognitive psychology (Bredo, 1994a).

In concert with the evolution of situated cognition theories, in the latter part of the twentieth century Greeno (1997) introduced the term "situativity" to describe cognition and learning that is situated. This designation was fostered to include situated cognition that is both human and nonhuman in nature (i.e., cognition as related to computer and artificial intelligence). In general, situated cognition and situativity theorists explain cognition in terms of the relations among learners and the properties of specific environments (Bredo, 1994c; Clancey, 1993; Greeno, 1997; Lave, 1997; Young, Barab, & Garret, 2000). From a situated cognition or situativity perspective, learning as a process, through knowing about, is described as a dynamic process distributed across the knower, that which is known, the environment in which knowing occurs, and the activity through which the learner is participating when learning or knowing occurs (Barab & Plucker, 2002). In this way, situativity theory allows for "unification of the world, the individual, and the relations among these reciprocal components" (Barab et al., 1999, p. 360).

Choi and Hannafin (1995) explained that in situated cognition, learning cannot be separated from the context in which it occurs, and emphasize the importance of learning in real-life contexts, whereby knowledge is acquired by embedding the subject matter in the experiences of the learner and by creating the opportunity for the learner to interact in the context of real life situations. Transfer of learning then occurs when the natural learning environment that is created engages the learner in solving authentic, complex, nonroutine problems, which they would likely encounter in a professional or work-life situation.

Brown, Collins, and Duguid (1989) contended that learning involves more than acquiring a set of self-contained entities. It actually involved building a contextualized appreciation of these entities as tools, as well as for the situations through which these tools have value (Barab & Plucker, 2002).

Goals of Situated Cognition

In situated cognition, the primary goal of cognitive activity is to guide the learner to think like a professional (or more experienced other) who would solve a problem within a given context (Brown et al., 1989). Simply stated, the goal is have the learner become part of a community of learners and members of a "culture of learning" (p. 39). Interpreting the goal further, the focus is on assisting the learner to move from novice to more capable and independent expert, a person who learns to use their expertise, intuition, and deep understanding to solves problems of their choosing. This requires authentic experiences with opportunities to examine ideas, develop underlying concepts, and engage in activities to successfully complete a learning experience.

Given the nature of this goal, the learner, in attempting to become more like an experienced professional (or expert), would establish his or her own goals within specific learning contexts and in relation to other learners and/or more experienced others. Thus, cognition, as it is understood from a situativity theoretical perspective, is a process distributed among individuals within a social-cultural context. Learning is foundationally connected with and reflexively constitutive of the cultural and context through which learning occurs (Barab & Kirshner, 2001; Cobb & Yackel, 1996).

Premised on learner set goals, the "learner's ultimate understanding of any object, issue, concept, process, or practice," in relation to the cognitive goals set for specific activities related to learning,

> as well as his or her ability to act competently with respect to using these, can be attributed to ... the physical, temporal, and spatial occurrences through which his or her competencies have emerged. It is in this sense that cognition is embodied, situated. (Barab & Plucker, 2002, p. 170)

The intellectual goal of situated cognition is acquiring cognitive skills and strategies; this occurs through sustained participation and engagement within a community of practice (Brown et al., 1989; Collins, Brown, & Newman, 1989; Lave, 1988, 1990; Lave & Wenger, 1991; Prawat & Floden, 1994). Within situated contexts of cognitive activity, learners are able to observe and experience how experts or more experienced others examine and undertake daily problems, and they learn to define and solve problems in similar ways by "learning-through-guided-experience (Brown et al., 1989, p. 457). Simply stated, the focus, for the learner, is on attaining problem-solving strategies or ways of analyzing and acting in relation to a problem; learning through authentic activities, situated in sociocultural contexts, which can be used to solve problems encountered in everyday situations. Through the lens of situated cognition or situativity theories, the problem represents an authentic situation that allows 'real world' problem solving to be experienced.

In examining the goal(s) of situated cognition, it is important to note that, with respect to cognition as situated in nature, although the cognitive development of the individual is emphasized, a primary emphasis is placed on the theoretical underpinnings of context, rather than the individual or a group. The context may be any form of a sociocultural or organizational environment and does not necessarily have to be in relation to another person. However, it is also important to note that, although situated cognition does not place emphasis on the individual or the group, it does not reject them. One could argue that the environment or the context will be highly influenced by the individuals or the group that it is made up of, and therefore knowledge is situated within environment influenced by individuals or groups.

There is a related note concerning the goal of situated cognition, set forth by the Cognition and Technology Group at Vanderbilt (1990) in their work with anchored instruction. With regard to everyday cognition, apprenticeships, and authentic tasks, there is a need for, over time,

> the establishment of semantically rich, shared environments that allow students and teachers to find and understand the kinds of problems that various concepts, principles, and theories were designed to solve, and that allow them to experience the effects that new knowledge has on their perception and understanding of these environments. (p. 9)

Situated cognition lends to the experience of growing from the novice learners who have "rudimentary knowledge to relatively sophisticated experts who have explored an environment from multiple points of view" (p. 11).

Basic Assumptions

Drawing from the work of situated cognition researchers and theorists (Bredo, 1994a, 1994b; Brown et al., 1989; Clancey, 1993, 1995, 1997; Dewey, 1938; Greeno, 1998; Hall, 1996; Lave, 1988, 1991, 1997; Lave & Wenger, 1991; Lemke, 1997; McLellan, 1995; Resnick, Levine, & Teasley, 1991; Rogoff, 1990; Roth, 2001; Salomon & Perkins, 1998; The Cognition and Technology Group at Vanderbilt, 1990; Wenger, 2003; Wertsch, 1985, 1991, 1998), the following set of assumptions represent contemporary thought:

- The ultimate goal of learning is to produce meaning —an ability to experience the world in a way that makes sense.
- Human thought is situated, adapted to the environment—what people perceive, how they conceive of their experience in activity, and what they physically do all develop together.
- Human learning is fundamentally influenced by the fact that human beings are social and negotiate meanings with one another.
- The actions of individuals and the context in which they operate are inseparable—there is a dialectical ontology.
- Knowledge means competence with respect to valued enterprises and accrues through lived practices and active engagement within a community.
- Learning means increasing participation and competency in the interactions that are valued by the community.
- Reasoning is observable in the form of socially structured and embodied activity.

Aspects of Situated Cognition

Drawing again from the work of situated cognition researchers and theorists a set of principles can be identified that build upon the basic assumptions previously outlined (Bredo, 1994a, 1994b; Brown et al., 1989; Clancey, 1993, 1995, 1997; Dewey, 1938; Greeno, 1998; Hall, 1996; Lave, 1988, 1991, 1997; Lave & Wenger, 1991; Lemke, 1997; McLellan, 1995; Resnick, Levine, & Teasley, 1991; Rogoff, 1990; Roth, 2001; Salomon & Perkins, 1998; The Cognition and Technology Group at Vanderbilt, 1990; Wenger, 2003; Wertsch, 1985, 1991, 1998). A set of eleven principles further explaining situated cognition as it relates to learning (see Table 16.1) builds on the work of Wilson and Madsen Myers (2000). The principles illuminate key insights from situated cognition in considerations for the design of authentic, situated learning experiences. Building on the basic assumptions of situated cognition, the principles further delineate and explain the substantive aspects of situated cognition.

Original Development and Major Contributors to the Theory

The original development of situated cognition theory is typically associated with three primary contributors, Jean Lave and Etienne Wenger who worked both independently and collaboratively, and three researchers who worked closely together, John Seely Brown, Allan Collins, and Paul Duguid. Certainly there are others that have made significant contributions, such as Eric Bredo, William J. Clancey, James G. Greeno, and Wolf-Michael Roth to mention a few. For purposes of this section, the original three primary contributors will be the focus.

Table 16.1. Principles of Situated Cognition Relating to Learning Environments

Learning in context: Thinking and learning make sense only within particular situations. All thinking, learning, and cognition are situated within particular contexts; there is no such thing as nonsituated learning.
Communities of practice: People act and construct meaning within communities of practice. These communities are powerful repositories and conveyors of meaning and serve to legitimate action. Communities construct and define appropriate discourse practices.
Learning as active participation: Learning is seen in terms of belonging and participating in communities of practice. Learning is seen as a dialectical process of interaction with other people, tools, and the physical world. Cognition is tied to action—either direct physical action or deliberate reflection and internal action. To understand what is learned is to see how it is learned within the activity context.
Knowledge in action: Knowledge is located in the actions of persons and groups. Knowledge evolves as we participate in and negotiate our way through new situations. The development of knowledge and competence, like the development of language, involves continued knowledge-using activity in authentic situations.
Mediation of artifacts: Cognition depends on the use of a variety of artifacts and tools, chiefly language and culture. These tools and constructed environments constitute the mediums, forms, or worlds through which cognition takes place. Problem solving involves reasoning about purposes in relationship to the resources and tools, which a situation affords.
Tools and artifacts as cultural repositories: Tools embody the history of a culture. They enable thought and intellectual processes and constrain or limit that thought. They also provide powerful means of transmitting culture.
Rules, norms, and beliefs: Cognitive tools include forms of reasoning and argumentation that are accepted as normative in society. Using a tool in a certain manner implies adoption of a cultural belief system about how the tool is to be used.
History: Situations make sense within an historical context, including the past experiences and interactions of participants, as well as anticipated needs and events. Cultures, through tools, artifacts, and discourse practices, embody the accumulated meanings of the past.
Levels of scale: Cognition can best be understood as a dynamic interplay between individual and social levels. Focus on one level, while assuming constancy or predictability at the other, is bound to at least partly misinterpret the situation.
Interactionism: Just as situations shape individual cognition, individual thinking and action shape the situation. This reciprocal influence constitutes an alternative conception of systemic causality to the more commonly assumed linear object causality.
Identities and constructions of self: People's notion of self—of continuing identity, separate from others yet belonging to various groups—is a constructed artifact with many uses. People have multiple identities, which can serve as tools for thinking and acting.

Source: Adapted from Wilson and Madsen Myers (2000).

JEAN LAVE

In contemporary theory and research, Jean Lave is often recognized as the originator of situated cognition theory. In *Cognition in Practice*, Lave (1988) discussed the transfer problem in school learning, and argued that learning in natural setting, contrast with most of classroom learning, occurs is a function of the activity, context and culture in which it is situated. Lave studied cognition in everyday situations and gave descriptions of the following findings:

- Cognition is socially defined, interpreted, and supported.
- Social context constrain and aid cognition—examining cognition in everyday situates is important to determining the generality of cognitive skills and articulating the role of culture in the development of these skills.
- People devise satisfactory opportunistic solutions—people do not employ formal approaches to solving problems in everyday thinking.
- Participation in interaction results in adaptivity of successful reasoning and learning.

Instead of seeing individuals in containers, Lave (1988) argued that learning contexts are socially dynamic and dialectically performed: "social practices are produced and reproduced in activity in the world, dialectally, rather then exclusively within or between persons" (p. 193).

Lave (1988) presented a theory of cognition as a socially situated process whereby practice is "distributed—stretched over, not divided among—the mind, body, activity and culturally organized settings (which includes other actors)" (p. 1). Lave's analysis of arithmetic as cognitive practice in schools and "everyday contexts," such as grocery stores, suggests that the appropriate unit of analysis necessary to understand the highly relational phenomenon of people learning in the social world is the "whole person in action, acting with the settings of that activity" (p. 8).

Breaking away from functionalist views of cognition, this framework clearly characterizes the dialectical nature of individuals learning within and from a socially ordered world, thus emphasizing the ways in which human activity is dynamically linked to social and political structures or institutions (Kirshner & Whitson, 1998). At the heart of the analysis, Lave argues for a broadening view of learning in "context" to better theorize this new unit of analysis (e.g., characterizing "arenas" and "settings"). To do so, Lave draws upon theories of social action and cultural reproduction to explain how, albeit with different theoretical claims, the sociocultural order as one element of the dialectical relation, works to constitute human agency, as the other term of the relation, as well as the reverse. Such a view makes it difficult, according to Lave (1988), to "argue for the separation of cognition and the social world, form and content, persons acting and the settings of their activity, or structure and action" (p. 16).

John Seely Brown, Allan Collins, and Paul Duguid

John Seely Brown, Allan Collins, and Paul Duguid (1989) are recognized for their major contribution to clearly articulating and delineating the salient aspects of situated cognition. The authors capture the thesis of situated cognition by the "folk categories of 'know what' and 'know how'" (p. 32). Knowing what describes factual recall, conceptual relationships, and even theories of practice, but it does not make anything happen. Conversely, knowing how is the demonstration of knowledge. Demonstration is the production of something useful to people. Brown et al. further articulated the foundation upon which situated cognition and learning, as a theory, is based:

> A theory of situated cognition suggests that activity and perception are importantly and epistemologically prior—at a nonconceptual level—to conceptualization and that it is on them that more attention needs to be focused. An epistemology that begins with activity and perception, which are first and foremost embedded in the world, may simply bypass the classical problem of reference—of mediating conceptual representations. (p. 35)

The epistemology underlying situated cognition is that learning entails the process of doing. Simply stated, individuals do not first learn all of the steps to a complex social task before undertaking the task. Rather, individuals start with the artifacts and tools in hand and then proceed to learn to use them. Whether it is a task such as riding a bicycle or learning to use a computer, the individual engages in "knowing how" as situated in a particular place, time, and activity.

According to Brown, Collins and Duguid (1989), the different instructional goals of *knowing what* and *knowing how* result in different structures and practices of the education system. The authors criticized the decontextualized learning resulted from separation between learning and doing. They suggested that "activity and situations are integral to cognition and learning" and that cognitive apprenticeship can provide "the authentic practice through activity and social interaction in a way similar to that evident—and evidently successful—in craft apprenticeship" (p. 37). Brown et al. argued the importance of authentic learning; authentic experiences and activities within real-world contexts. Key points expounded upon by Brown et al. focused on situated cognition and cognitive apprenticeship and include:

Situated cognition

- Knowledge, as a product of a meaning-making process, cannot be separated from the context of its use.
- Learning is a continuous, lifelong process from acting in situations.
- Tools and their use reflect the particular accumulated insights of communities.
- Learning is an enculturation process—it is through observation and practice *in situ,* as members of a culture, that people acquire language, imitate behavior, and gradually start to act in accordance with the cultural or community norms.

Cognitive apprenticeship

- By beginning with a task embedded in a familiar activity it shows the students the legitimacy of their implicit knowledge and its availability as scaffolding in apparently unfamiliar tasks.
- By pointing to different decompositions it stresses that heuristics are not absolute but assessed with respect to a particular task—and that even algorithms can he assessed in this way.
- By allowing students to generate their own solution paths, it helps make them conscious creative members of the culture of problem-solving mathematicians.
- Also, it helps students, in enculturating through this activity, acquire some of the culture's tools—a shared vocabulary and the means to discuss, reflect

upon, evaluate and validate community procedures in a collaborative process.

Etienne Wenger

Etienne Wenger (1998) first worked with Jean Lave in her earlier studies of situated learning. Together, they conceptualized the idea of "situated learning" and advanced the notion of "legitimate peripheral participation" (Lave & Wenger, 1991) as foundational to situated cognition and learning. Etienne Wenger initially posed the term "community of practice" while studying with Jean Lave. He furthered developed the concept in his book, *Communities of Practice: Learning, Meaning and Identity*, and also introduced the importance of apprenticeship (which emerged in his earlier work with Lave) as a more complex set of social relationships through which learning is situated and takes place.

Wenger's work revealed two important implications for learning theory. The first is that learning can take place among people who are closer to being peers than master and apprentice (i.e., teacher and student). This is in contrast to the traditional model where knowledge moves only in one direction, which directly relates to the second implication. The second is that the relationships are more complex than that of a traditional learning setting, where each learner (student) has a hierarchical relationship with the master or more experienced other (teacher), but not with each other. In Lave and Wenger's (1991) research, they revealed a web of relationships between apprentices and more experienced others, drawing into specific relief the earlier work of Vygotsky (1978) and the conception of his zone of proximal development. Wenger's (1998) work with communities of practice illuminates how direct instruction as seen in the classroom can be effectively supplanted by teams of workers of varying skill, i.e. apprentice and more experienced other. As they work alongside one another in a community of practice, learning takes place as work is done and products are produced. In this way, refinements of practice can take place over weeks and years and generations, refinements of use and practice of technique and tool passed on from user to user.

In his research, Wenger (1998) identified five learning trajectories for individuals' participation, over time, in communities of practice (CoP) (see Table 16.2). The trajectories reflect the nature of variation in the level of participation in the activities of the community.

Generalizability of the Theory

As Clancey (1997) notes, situated cognition spans many disciplines, which relates social, behavioral/psychological, and neural perspectives of knowledge and action (p. 343). Concerning generalizability, Lave (1991) clarifies:

> "Situated" ... does not imply that something is concrete and particular, or that it is not generalizable, or not imaginary. It implies that a given social practice is multiply interconnected with other aspects of ongoing social processes in activity systems at many levels of particularity and generality. (p. 84)

Therefore, situated cognition should not be characterized as only allowing for tangible learning in localized situations. Rather, situated cognition emphasizes the complex, dynamic web of social and activity systems within which authentic practice takes shape.

Lave and Wenger (1991) state that, "learning is an integral part of generative social practice in the lived-in world" (p. 35). In their writing they describe the concept of legitimate peripheral participation as a "descriptor of engagement in social practice that entails learning as an integral constituent" (p. 35). Further explained: "Participation in social contexts becomes a way of engaging the learner that involves both absorbing and being absorbed in—the culture of practice" (p. 95). Viewed from a sociologic view of community, each learner within a group or community negotiates his or her own role that is played out in the learning community.

A major issue related to situated cognition is the construct of learning transfer. Generalizability of acquired information to other situations, from a sociological view, is relatively rare and unpredictable (Detterman, 1993; Greeno, 1997; Lave & Wenger, 1991). The authors are not arguing that transfer does not exist. In fact, they have adopted the perspective of Sternberg and Frensch (1994) that teaching should promote learning in a context that is as close as possible to the one where the acquired information will be applied so that there is a better chance of it being activated when needed.

Critiques of the Theory

Several researchers have challenged the theoretical assumptions or underpinnings of situated cognition. Boaler (1993) disagreed with Lave's (1988) assumptions, first arguing against her point that school learning is bound to the context in which it occurs. Second, Boaler argued against Lave's contention that transfer cannot be improved through any factors in the learning environment. Renkl, Mandl, and Gruber (1996) criticized the difficulty in studying situated cognition as lacking the characteristics of a clearly articulated and empirically testable theory. Anderson, Reder, and Simon (1996), in addressing ethnographic studies of learning within context stated that: "Even if those claims are valid and transferable beyond these specific cases, they

Table 16.2. Learning Trajectories

Peripheral	Inbound	Insider	Boundary	Outbound
Learner never engages in full participation— may choose not to seek full participation, or is excluded from full participation.	Learner as newcomer has invested in the CoP—headed toward full membership	Learner's practices are continually evolving within a CoP—fully participates and seeks new ways of defining new practices.	Learner maintains full membership in multiple CoPs— promotes interaction between them.	Learner is in the process of leaving a CoP—develops new relationships and looks for other CoPs.

These trajectories further delineate the relationship between novice and more experienced other as learners in the community of practice.

demonstrate at most that particular skills practiced in real-life situations do not generalized to school situations. They assuredly do not demonstrate the converse" (p. 6).

Bereiter (1997) notes that the main weakness of situated cognition is related to "problems of transfer"; the problem lies with the limitations of situatedness of cognition. What an individual learns in one situation her/she often fails to apply in another. Simply stated, the progress of situated learning consists of increasingly fine attunement to the constraints and affordances of the particular situation (physical, temporal, tool, etc.). Thus, as learning progresses it tends to become less and less generalizable to other situations. Bereiter goes on to note that in advanced stages of situated learning, the learner may in fact begin to experience a negative transfer yield, particularly as habits are acquired that will need to be overcome in a new situation.

Salomon and Perkins (1998) note concern for situated approaches, in particular drawing attention to how interactions between individual and collective learning can go bad:

> What is learned by an individual may upset or even subvert rather than abet collective ends, as with the student taking advantage of his or her team members' work or the corporate climber being more interested in personal advancement than in the overall success of the organization. In such cases, the collective has "learned," but what it has learned happens to be profoundly limiting both for itself and for the participating individuals. (p. 21)

Learning within sociocultural contexts, like communities of practice or school classrooms, may foster and convey wrong values, or individual learners may not fit the culture or may be naïve to messages within the context that work against academic learning goals.

Kirshner and Whitson (1998) take the position that most approaches to situated cognition and learning are limited by their tendency to treat "situation" as an entity located in time and space; what is needed, they believe, are "ways to theorize about cognition and community that transcend such physiotemporal domination" (p. 25). They advocate a "reconceptualization" of situated cognition theory based on a broader range of supporting disciplines, a reconceptualization that "probes the physiological, psychoanalytical and semiotic constitution of persons" (p. 9).

FLAWED CLAIMS

Anderson et al. (1996) identified what they believe are the four central claims of a situated learning perspective, arguing each is flawed. These claims and respective arguments are situated in an educational setting.

- Action is grounded in the concrete situation in which it occurs. Objection: It is true that Brazilian street sellers, who correctly calculate the cost of items, which they sell in the streets, are unable to answer similar questions at school. However, this is a demonstration that skills practiced outside of schools do not generalize to schools, not that arithmetic procedures taught in the classroom cannot be used by shopkeepers. Indeed, skills like reading clearly transfer from one context to another.
- Knowledge does not transfer between tasks. Objection: The psychological literature contains both success and failures to achieve transfer. Transfer between tasks depends on the amount of practice in the initial domain and the degree of shared cognitive elements. For example, subjects who learned one text editor learned subsequent editors more rapidly, with the number of procedural elements shared by two text editors predicting the amount of transfer.
- Training in abstraction is of little use. Objection: This, Anderson et al. (1989) argue, has been extended into an advocacy for apprenticeship training by those taking a situated perspective. In contrast, Anderson, et al, advocate a combination of

abstract instruction and concrete examples. When they introduced real-world-like problems to situate high school algebra, they felt much class time was wasted on such clerical tasks as tabling and graphing, while relatively little time was spent relating algebraic expressions to the real-world situations.

- Instruction must be done in complex, social environments. Objection: Research in psychology shows training is often more effective when nearly independent parts are practiced first, before combining them. In team sports and orchestras, more time is spent on individual practice than group practice, although both are necessary. (Shouldn't the kind of knowledge, whether procedural or conceptual, matter? Learning how to factor and understanding the nature and uses of functions seem quite different.) Anderson, et al, also question the efficacy of cooperative learning when applied without requisite structuring or scripting.

Interestingly, Greeno (1997), in responding to the claims and arguments set forth by Anderson et al. (1996) for what is flawed in situated cognition and learning approaches, noted that the purported claims are *not* those of situated cognition. Also Greeno notes that the critique by Anderson et al. seems to have missed the point about what adherents of situated cognition are actually studying and claiming—Anderson et al. present a straw man, or caricature, which they knock down.

The counter argument Greeno (1997) makes is worth exploring in more detail. Whereas the cognitive perspective attempts to explain processes and structures at the level of individuals, the situated perspective focuses on interactive systems and the resulting "trajectories" of individual participation. Knowledge is not just "in the head," as Greeno explains, rather knowledge consists in the ways a person interacts with other people and situations. The situated perspective does not say that group learning will always be productive, regardless of how it is organized, or that individual practice cannot contribute to a person's becoming a more successful participant in social practices. It does call for more varied learning situations. For mathematics, this means more than collective watching and listening, doing exercises individually, and displaying individual knowledge on tests. Students need opportunities to participate actively by formulating and evaluating problems, questions, conjectures, conclusions, arguments, and examples. Greeno argues that situated experiences of learning, within practical, authentic cognitive activities, offer the learner real-world examples with more experienced others, demonstrating that reasoning is adaptive in ways that are not well explained by more traditional views of cognitive theory.

Learning in authentic settings, as viewed through the situativity perspective, as Greeno (1997) explains, suggests that successful transfer means improved participation. Whether transfer occurs depends on how the situation is transformed. Whether it is difficult or easy for the learner depends on how the learner is 'attuned' to the constraints and affordances in the initial learning activity. For example, when students are given instruction about refraction prior to shooting targets under water, they are more likely to become attuned to the apparent angular disparity of a projectile's trajectory before and after entering the water, and hence, perform better. Greeno also distinguishes between abstraction and generality using an example from mathematics. If students learn correct rules for manipulating symbols without learning that mathematical expressions represent concepts and relationships, what they learn may be abstract, but it is not general (i.e., cannot be widely used).

UNRESOLVED ISSUES

Following specific critiques of situated cognition and learning theory, there are, according to Allal (2001, pp. 46-471), three unresolved issues that require attention in the scope designing instruction sensitive to situated cognition and learning.

Issue 1

It is a postulate of the situated perspective that all human cognition and learning are embedded in situations that permeate psychological processes. As Greeno et al. (1998) state, the issue is not "whether learning is situated or not, but how it is situated" (p. 14). Bereiter (1987), in a critical discussion of this perspective, raises a different question: "Are there aspects of situated cognition and learning that, however much a part of human culture, need to be overcome?" He suggests that the specificity of schooling, as a community of practice, is that the work to be accomplished is "work with knowledge" (p. 298), moreover, the primary characteristic of school work with knowledge is that it needs to go "beyond what the situation calls for" (p. 288). Bereiter also points to the role of individual intentionality in determining how, in a same learning situation, constraints and affordances may differ from one learner to another. We can restate this concern as follows: The notion of agency has yet to find a clearly defined place in theories of situated cognition and learning.

Issue 2

At a conceptual level, the notion of learning as participation offers a promising, new way of looking at instructional processes. It needs to be recognized, however, that the implications of this notion have not yet been thoroughly explored in classroom-based research. Several questions under investigation in an ongoing study by Mottier Lopez (2001) include the following preoccupations: Is participation in the classroom microculture sufficient for appropriation of social practices and for progression of conceptual understanding? Do all students participate in the coconstitution of classroom culture? By participating do students learn to participate? More generally speaking, it is difficult to study the activity of participation without looking for individual cognitive and/or social competencies produced through this activity. Participation is a particularly slippery notion when confronted with social demands for accountability in teaching. Is it sufficient, for example, for a teacher to tell parents that a student has participated consistently in classroom activities without any further statement about competence manifested with respect to the objects of knowledge dealt with in the activities?

Issue 3

In Schoenfeld's 1999 presidential address to the American Educational Research Association, he stated that one of the challenges for the twenty-first century is the creation of a unified theory of cognitive and social processes that explains thinking, acting and being. Although many would agree that learning implies a "reciprocal spiraling relationship" between these processes (Salomon & Perkins, 1998), the mechanisms of the spiral have yet to be adequately uncovered. The situated perspective offers some fruitful starting points for this endeavor. We also think it allows, as described elsewhere (Allal, 2001), a renewal of the concept of a spiral curriculum (Bruner, 1960) in which complex, authentic learning activities are articulated with more specific skill-oriented tasks in instructional sequences that help learners move into new realms of practice and understanding.

Instruments and Measurements Associated with Situated Cognition

With respect to measurement of situated cognition, such as job knowledge, tacit knowledge, or knowledge structure in organizations, there are two important issues for consideration. First, measurement of situated cognition accompanies situational characteristics in addition to cognition. Second, since situated cognition is accrued when a person participates in the surrounding situations/environment in an active manner, environment is not discernible from cognitive process.

In more traditional learning settings, measuring cognition and learning typically follow cognitive style inventories, learning inventories, and basic forms of written and performance-based assessment. The most familiar form of assessment or measurement is most often designed by teachers in classrooms in the form of pen and paper or computer-based assessment (i.e., discipline-specific items in multiple formats that attempt to measure knowledge). As well, performance assessment based on assessor observation of performance of skills in specific problem-related contexts is a more traditional form of measuring skill and knowledge.

Situated cognition models or approaches to learning present interesting challenges to the dynamics of both the learning experience and the requisite forms of measuring learner cognition and/or learning. Given the various assumptions and principles of situated cognition and learning, instruments for measurement of situated cognition appear to be based in specific disciplines or related to specific research interests guiding field studies. What is of particular interest in measurement and assessment of social cognition is the recognition that knowledge is not objective or independent of the knower. Also of interest is the realization that performance is situated; the situation, activity, or task requires the ability to elicit elaborated performance that can be observed. Simply stated, there are many implications of situated cognition and learning for assessment. Examples of instruments are offered for consideration in the remaining paragraphs of this section.

Student Evaluation of Clinical Education Environments (SECEE) Inventory

Sand-Jecklin (1998), in her dissertation research, refined and tested the Student Evaluation of Clinical Education Environment (SECEE) inventory, an instrument designed to measure nursing students' clinical experience. The inventory contains 29 forced-choice items divided among four scales: communication and feedback, learning opportunities, learning support, and department atmosphere. The SECEE inventory appears to be a reasonably valid and reliable instrument for measuring clinical experience of nursing students.

Situational Judgement Test

Recent developments of situational judgment tests (SJTs) as low-fidelity simulations (e.g., Motowidlo, Dunnette, & Carter, 1990; Pulakos, Schmitt, & Chan, 1996) have contributed to such instruments' popularity in industrial and organizational settings as tools for measuring situated cognition such as judgment competencies encountered with problem situations. A situational judgment test is comprised of situational scenarios and a number of response alternatives or multiple-choice questions following them. Situational judgement tests have several advantages including (a) high face validity (Motowidlo et al., 1990) due to the items reflecting practical situations and behaviors, and (b) good criterion validity ($p = .34$ in McDaniel Morgeson, Finnegan, & Campion, 2001) for the relatively low expense of development and the convenience of management (Motowidlo et al., 1990; Motowidlo & Tippins, 1993).

Situational judgment tests have a long history of being used for measuring situated cognition; they have been used forward from the 1920s (McDaniel et al., 2001). Although the situational judgment test has been originated from the conception of measuring dimensions, it has been viewed as a measurement method (e.g., McDaniel et al., 2001; Weekly & Jones, 1999) rather than a specific instrument, largely because it is difficult to delineate the dimensions and situations. The situations represented by scenarios in SJTs, while reflecting practical situations and behaviors are viewed as method in nature from a psychometric sense, meaning that situation effect, scenario effect, or method effect are each interchangeable, respectively.

Sense of Classroom Community Index (SCCI)

The Sense of Classroom Community Index (SCCI) has been developed by Alfred Rovai (2002) to explore the development of learning communities in both traditional and online environments. Rovai identified four essential elements in such communities—spirit (the recognition of community membership), trust, interaction, and learning. The SCCI measures students' sense of each of these elements, such that comparisons between learning communities can be made both in terms of overall sense of community and/or on each of the subscales. Using the SCCI, Rovai compared classroom communities among adult learners enrolled in a mix of fourteen traditional and asynchronous online undergraduate and graduate courses at two urban universities. While Rovai found no differences in overall sense of community between the two media formats, he found greater variability in overall SCCI scores among the online courses. Indeed, the five (of seven) online courses with the highest SCCI scores had significantly higher sense of community ratings than did the seven traditional courses. Similar dropping of low scoring traditional classes did not result in significant differences between these and the entire group of online classes. Rovai suggests that this indicates that the development of community in online courses is more sensitive to course design and pedagogical factors than its development is in traditional environments.

Research Studies Exemplifying Situated Cognition and Learning

Within the social sciences, the past decade is hallmarked by an increase in educational research focusing on situated cognition and learning, and applications of the theoretical assumptions and principles within and across a number of disciplines. Interestingly, there is a particular increase in applications in the field of technology and computer and artificial intelligence. Concerning educational research studies, within this section a set of five studies are examined that range from 1985 to 2008, denoting paths of evolution in application of situated cognition theory within disciplines including mathematics, science, and web-based design of learning communities.

- **Carraher, T. N., Carraher, D. W., & Schliemann, A. D. (1985). Mathematics in the streets and in schools.** ***British Journal of Developmental Psychology, 3,*** **21-29.**

Carraher, Carraher, and Schliemann (1985) incorporated a situated cognition approach in their study, observing Brazilian children solving simple mathematical problems as they sold produce on the street. The situated learning experience within authentic contexts revealed that the same children failed to solve the same problems when they were presented out of context in conventional mathematical form. One 9-year-old child answered a customer's question regarding the price of three coconuts by counting aloud, 40, 80, 120. Yet, this same child arrived at a result of 70 when confronted with 3×40 on a formal test. The situated or authentic nature of context and cultural artifacts seemed to support the child's ability to work through the same problem more effectively, again speaking to the situated nature of human knowledge and learning.

- **Roth, W-M., & Roychoudhury, A. (1993). The development of science process skills in authentic contexts.** ***Journal of Research in Science Teaching, 30,*** **127-152.**

Roth and Roychoudhury (1993) conducted a study focused on science process skills, following an iterative process of situated cognition learning theory. The situated cognition model enabled the authors to generate findings to show student growth, within authentic contexts of experience, in science knowledge, skills, and dispositions via extended inquiry. Their qualitative data indicated that student interpretation of results evolved from simplistic formulations to being able to identify complex relationships using multiple representations and analyses of experimental data. Following their own interests was motivating, and students were able to generate new ideas from previous results. Perhaps one of the most significant results Roth and Roychoudhury's study produced was that students were able to define concepts, events, and actions to design their own experiments and communicate the results.

- **Park, S. (1999). A study of situated cognition and transfer in mathematics learning. *Journal of the Korea Society of Mathematical Education Series D: Research in Mathematics Education*, *3*(1), 57-68.**

Sungsun Park (1999) investigated the comparative effectiveness of two kinds of instructional methods in transfer of mathematics learning: one based on the situated cognition, i.e. situated learning (SL) and the other based on traditional learning (TL). Five research questions were developed to investigate the issues related to situated cognition: (1) Is there any significant difference between SL group and traditional learning (TL) group in the computational test? (2) Is there any significant difference between SL group and TL group in the problem-solving test? (3) Is there any significant difference between SL group and TL group in the real situation test? (4) Is there any difference between SL group and TL group in the method of computation and problem solving? and (5) Is there any difference between SL group and TL group in the recognition of context resources given in the story problems?

A nonequivalent control group design was used in the study. The two classes of second grade students (the class assigned to SL group and the class assigned to TL group) studied addition and subtraction of 3-digit numbers. After studying, the two groups completed two written tests (Written Test 1 included computation problems, Written Test 2 included computation problems and story problems) and a real situation test. Three types of instruments were used: a questionnaire, pretest and posttest, and interview.

As a result, no significant differences were found between the two groups' performance on computation skill in Written Tests 1 and 2. But the SL group performed significantly better on the performance of story problem and real situation test than TL group. This result indicated that the SL made improvement in transfer of mathematics learning.

The study supports the argument that cognition is situated in the context and knowledge is developed in the interaction between individual and situation; cognition is not separated from the situation. Consequently, the children as situated learner (SL group) were able to connect the knowledge acquired in shopping situation to school-based problems. This suggests that the ability of using context resources in one situation be transferred to that in another situation.

- **Hung, D. W. L., & Chen, D. (2001). Situated cognition, Vygotskian thought and learning from the communities of practice perspective: implications for the design of web-based e-learning. *Educational Media International*, *38*, 3-12.**

Hung and Chen (2001) examined the development of online learning communities, which they noted can be related to situated cognition and Vygotskian thought, including the idea that "even when mental functioning is carried out by an individual in isolation, it is inherently social, or sociocultural, in that it incorporates socially evolved and socially organized tools" (p. 5). One of the benefits of learning in context is that the individual can pick up situated meanings tacitly. Hung and Chen argue that communities of practice bring back "this emphasis on embedded learning in the workplace, of which, we argue that e-learning on the web may be a possible platform for situated or contextual learning" (p. 5) because it is not constrained by physical location.

The authors outline four factors that contribute to a successful online community of practice: "*situatedness, commonality, interdependency,* and *infrastructure*" (Hung & Chen, 2001, p. 7, emphasis in original). Situatedness means that the learning takes place in rich, social situations, where the learner can develop both explicit and implicit knowledge; commonality involves the participants working together toward a real-world common goal; interdependency means that the community exploits the differing expertise and needs of its members, with the result that the community can achieve more than any individual member would alone; infrastructure involves having a structure to the way that the community functions, whereby participants understand the processes and rules, and mechanisms and accountability facilitate the process.

Hung and Chen (2001) argue that "chatrooms and discussion forums are too primitive to manage complexity" (p. 10), that is, complex interactions between members of a community. This is particularly relevant when both the information flow and participants' involvement are dynamic. Hung and Chen go on to note that "unless these online communities are structured appropriately with the four factors, we would just end up with empty communities" (p. 11). What becomes apparent from a Vygotskian perspective, is that "infrastructure considerations are the social cultural dimensions of cognition" (p. 11).

- **LaBanca, F. (2008). Impact of problem findings on the quality of authentic open inquiry science research projects. (Unpublished doctoral dissertation, Western Connecticut State University, Danbury, CT, 2008). *Dissertation Abstracts International, 71*(06), UMI No. 577640566).**

LaBanca (2008), in his dissertation study, examined problem finding as a creative process whereby individuals develop original ideas for study. Specifically, LaBanca examined problem finding strategies employed by students who successfully completed and presented the results of their open inquiry research at the 2007 Connecticut Science Fair and the 2007 International Science and Engineering Fair. The thesis of the study was that secondary science students who successfully participate in authentic, novel, open inquiry studies must engage in problem finding to determine viable and suitable topics.

A multicase qualitative study was framed through the lenses of creativity, inquiry strategies, and situated cognition learning theory. LaBanca triangulated data by methods (interviews, document analysis, surveys) and sources (students, teachers, mentors, fair directors, documents). The data demonstrated that the quality of student projects was directly impacted by the quality of their problem finding. Effective problem finding was a result of students using resources from previous, specialized experiences. They had a positive self-concept and a temperament for both the creative and logical perspectives of science research. Successful problem finding was derived from an idiosyncratic, nonlinear, and flexible use and understanding of inquiry. Finally, problem finding was influenced and assisted by the community of practicing scientists, with whom the students had an exceptional ability to communicate effectively.

LaBanca (2008) concluded that, as a result of engaging in open inquiry within communities of practice, there appears to be a juxtaposition of creative and logical/analytical thought, by learners, for open inquiry that may not be present in other forms of inquiry. Instructional strategies are suggested for teachers of science research students to improve the quality of problem finding for their students and their subsequent research projects. LaBanca also concluded that considering the instructional implications, and therefore applications, a situated cognition model parallels well with an inquiry approach. Furthermore, students, it was argued, should engage in cognitive apprenticeships; apprenticeship methods that attempt to enculturate students into authentic practices through activity and social interaction such as the open inquiry experiences of the students in the LaBanca study.

CONCLUSION

While the research to date has demonstrated that a situated approach to cognition is of import as a theoretical perspective of learning, much research remains to be done. However, it is important to note that prevailing assumptions about learning, in particular those that underlie the design of learning experiences and environments are now being reconsidered in light of the theoretical arguments set forth in situated cognition. The notion of communities of practice, cognitive apprenticeship, and legitimate peripheral participation present salient theoretic perspectives that advance both the meaning of learning as well as its complexities, adding a new level of thoughtful pursuit to the question What is learning?

REFERENCES

Allal, L. (2001). Situated cognition and learning: From conceptual frameworks to classroom investigations. *Revue Suisse des Scienecs de L'éducation*, *23*(3), 407-422.

Anderson, J. R., Reder, L. A., & Simon, H. A. (1996). Situated learning and education. *Educational Researcher, 25*(4), 5-11.

Bakhtin, M. M. (1981). *The dialogic imagination: Four essays*. (M. Holquist, Ed.; C. Emerson & M. Holquist, Trans.). Austin, TX: University of Texas Press.

Barab, S. A., & Kirshner, D. (2001). Guest editors' introduction: Rethinking methodology in the learning sciences. *The Journal of the Learning Sciences*, *19*(1&2), 5-15.

Barab, S. A., & Plucker, J. A. (2002). Smart people or smart contexts? Cognition, ability, and talent development in an age of situated approaches to knowing and learning. *Educational Psychologist*, *37*(3), 165-182.

Barab, S. A., Cherkes-Julkowski, M., Swenson, R., Garret, S., Shaw, R. E., & Young, M. (1999). Principles of self-organization: Ecologizing the learner-facilitator system. *The Journal of the Learning Sciences*, *8*(3&4), 349-390.

Bereiter, C. (1987). Situated cognition and how to overcome it. In D. Kirshner & J. A. Whitson (Eds.), *Situated cognition: Social, semiotic and psychological perspectives* (pp. 281-300). Mahwah, NJ: Erlbaum.

Boaler, J. (1993). The role of contexts in the mathematics classroom: Do they make mathematics more "real?" *For the Learning of Mathematics*, *13*, 12-17.

Bredo, E. (1994a). Reconstructing educational psychology: Situated cognition and Deweyian pragmatism. *Educational Psychologist*, *29*(1), 23-35.

Bredo, E. (1994b). Cognitivism, situated cognition, and Deweyian pragmatism. *Philosophy of Education Yearbook 1994*. Retrieved from http://www.ed.uiuc.edu/EPS/PES-Yearbook/94-docs/BREDO.THM

Bredo, E. (1994c). Reconstructing educational psychology: Situated cognition and Deweyian pragmatism. *Educational Psychologist*, 29(1), 23-35.

Brown, J. S., Collins, A., & Duguid, P. (1989). Situated cognition and the culture of learning. *Educational Researcher, 18*(1), 32-42.

Bruner, J. S. (1960). *The process of education*. New York, NY: Vintage.

Carraher, T. N., Carraher, D. W., & Schliemann, A. D. (1985). Mathematics in the streets and in schools. *British Journal of Developmental Psychology, 3*, 21-29.

Choi, J., & Hannafin, M. (1995). Situated cognition and learning environments: Roles, structures, and implications for design. *Educational Technology Research and Development*, *43*(2), 53-69.

Clancey, W. J. (1993). Situated action: a neuropsychological interpretation. Response to Vera and Simon. *Cognitive Science*, *17*, 87-116.

Clancey, W. J. (1995). Practice cannot be reduced to theory: Knowledge, representations, and change in the workplace. In S. Bagnara, C. Zuccermaglio, & S. Stuckey (Eds.),

Organizational learning and technological change (pp. 16-46). Berlin, Germany: Springer-Verlag.

Clancey, W. J. (1997). *Situated cognition: On human knowledge and computer representations.* Cambridge, MA: Cambridge University Press.

Cobb, P., & Yackel, E. (1996). Constructivist, emergent, and sociocultural perspectives in the context of developmental research. *Educational Psychologist, 31*, 175, 190.

Collins, A., Brown, J. S., & Newman, S. (1989). Cognitive apprenticeship: Teaching students the craft of reading, writing, and mathematics. In L. Resnick (Ed.), *Knowing, learning, and instruction: Essays in honor of Robert Glaser* (pp. 453-493). Hillsdale, NJ: Erlbaum.

Cook, S., & Brown, J. S. (1999). Bridging epistemologies: The generative dance between organizational knowledge and organizational knowing. *Organization Science, 10*(4), 381-400.

Detterman, D. K. (1993). The case for the prosecution: Transfer as an epiphenomenon. In D. K. Detterman and R. J. Sternberg (Eds.), *Transfer on trial: Intelligence, cognition and instruction* (pp. 25-38). Norwood, NJ: Ablex.

Dewey, J. (1938). *Experience and education* (Kappa Delta Pi Lecture Series). New York, NY: Collier Books.

Fairclough, N. (1989). *Language and power.* London: Longman.

Freire, P. (1970). *Pedagogy of the oppressed.* New York, NY: Herder and Herder.

Gibson, J. J. (1979). *The ecological approach to visual perception.* Boston, MA: Houghton Mifflin.

Gibson, J. J. (1986). *The ecological approach to visual perception.* Boston, MA: Houghton Mifflin.

Greeno, J. G. (1997). Response: On claims that answer the wrong questions. *Educational Researcher, 26*(1), 5-17.

Greeno, J. G. (1998). The situativity of knowing, learning, and research. *American Psychologist, 53*, 5-26.

Greeno J. G., Smith, D. R., & Moore, J. L. (1993). Transfer of situated learning. In D. K. Detterman & R. J. Sternberg (Ed.), *Transfer on trial: Intelligence, cognition, and instruction* (pp. 99-167). Norwood, NJ: Ablex.

Hall, R. (1996). Representation as shared activity: Situated cognition and Dewey's cartography of experience. *The Journal of the Learning Sciences, 5*, 209-238.

Heidegger, M. (1968). *What is called thinking*? New York, NY: Harper & Row.

Hung, D. W. L., & Chen, D. (2001). Situated cognition, Vygotskian thought and learning from the communities of practice perspective: implications for the design of web-based e-learning. *Educational Media International, 38*, 3-12.

Kirshner, D., & Whitson, J. A. (1997). Editors' introduction to situated cognition: Social, semiotic, and psychological perspectives. In D. Kirshner & J. A. Whitson (Eds.), *Situated cognition: Social, semiotic, and psychological perspectives* (pp. 1-16). Mahwah, NJ: Lawrence Erlbaum Associates.

Kirshner, D., & Whitson, J. A. (1998). Obstacles to understanding cognition as situated. *Educational Researcher, 27*(8), 22-28.

LaBanca, F. (2008). *Impact of problem findings on the quality of authentic open inquiry science research projects* (Unpublished doctoral dissertation, Western Connecticut State University). *Dissertation Abstracts International, 71*(06). (UMI No. 577640566)

Lave, J. (1988). *Cognition in practice. Mind, mathematics and culture in everyday life.*

Lave, J. (1990). The culture of acquisition and the practice of understanding. In J. W. Stigler, R. A. Shweder, & G. Herdt (Eds.), *Cultural psychology: Essays in the comparative human development* (pp. 309-327). Cambridge, MA: Cambridge University Press.

Lave, J. (1991). Situated learning in communities of practice. In L. B. Resnick, J. M. Levine, & S. D. Teasley (Eds.), *Perspectives on socially shared cognition* (pp. 63-82). Washington, DC: American Psychological Association.

Lave, J. (1993). The practice of learning. In S. Chaiklin & J. Lave (Eds.), *Understanding practice: Perspectives on activity and context* (pp. 3-32). New York, NY: University of Cambridge Press.

Lave, J. (1997). The culture of acquisition and the practice of understanding. In D. Kirshner & J. A. Whitson (Eds.), *Situated cognition: Social, semiotic, and psychological perspectives* (pp. 17-36). Mahwah, NJ: Lawrence Earlbaum Associates.

Lave, J., & Wenger, E. (1991). *Situated learning: Legitimate peripheral participation.* Cambridge, MA: Cambridge University Press.

Lemke, J. L. (1997). Cognition, context, and learning: A social semiotic perspective. In D. Kirshner & J. A. Whitson (Eds.), *Situated cognition: Social, semiotic and psychological perspectives* (pp. 37-55). Mahwah NJ: Erlbaum.

Leont'ev, A. (1978). *Activity, consciousness, and personality.* Englewood Cliffs, NY: Prentice-Hall.

Leont'ev, A. (1981). The problem of activity in psychology. In J. Wertsch (Ed.), *The concept of activity in Soviet psychology* (pp. 37-71). Armonk, NY: M. E. Sharpe.

Lopez, M. L. (2001, September). L'interaction collective dans la classe de mathématiques: Observation de la participation aux pratiques sociales de la communauté classe en 3ème année primaire. Canevas de thèse en sciences de l'éducation, Université de Genève [The collective interaction in the mathematics classroom: Observation of participation in social practices of the community in the 3rd year primary class. Canvas thesis presented to the College of Doctors of Sciences Section of Education, Canvas thesis presented to the College of Doctors of Sciences Section of Education, University of Geneva].

Luria, A. R. (1976). Cognitive development: Its cultural and social foundations (M. Lopez-Morillas & L. Soltaroff, Trans.). Cambridge, MA: Harvard University Press.

Luria, A. (1979). *The making of mind: A personal account of Soviet psychology.* Cambridge, MA: Harvard University Press.

McDaniel, M. A., Morgeson, F. P., Finnegan, E. B., & Campion, M. A. (2001). Use of situational judgment tests to predict job performance: A clarification of the literature. *Journal of Applied Psychology, 86*, 730-740.

McLellan, H. (1995). *Situated learning perspectives.* Englewood Cliffs, NJ: Educational Technology Publications.

Motowidlo, S. J., Dunnette, M. D., & Carter, G. W. (1990). An alternative selection procedure: The low-fidelity simulation. *Journal of Applied Psychology, 75*, 640-647.

Motowidlo, S. J., & Tippins, N. (1993). Further studies of the low-fidelity simulation in the form of a situational inventory. *Journal of Occupational or Organizational Psychology, 66*, 337-344.

Park, S. (1999). A study of situated cognition and transfer in mathematics learning. *Journal of the Korea Society of Mathematical Education Series D: Research in Mathematics Education, 3*(1), 57-68.

Prawat, R. S., & Floden, R. E. (1994). Philosophical perspectives on constructivist views of learning. *Educational Psychology, 29*, 37-48.

Pulakos, E. D., Schmitt, N., & Chan, D. (1996). Models of job performance ratings: An examination of ratee race, ratee gender, and rater level effects. *Human Performance, 9*, 103-119.

Renkl, A., Mandl., H., & Gruber, H. (1996). Inert knowledge: Analyses and remedies. *Educational Psychology, 31*, 115-121.

Resnick, L., Levine, J., & Teasley, S. D. (Eds.). (1991). *Perspectives on socially shared cognition.* Washington, DC: American Psychological Association.

Reynolds, R. E., Sinatra, G. M., & Jetton, T. L. (1996). Views of knowledge acquisition and representation: A continuum from experience centered to mind centered. *Educational Psychologist, 31*(2), 93-94.

Rogoff, B. (1990). *Apprenticeship in thinking: Cognitive development in social context.* New York, NY: Oxford University Press.

Roth, W. -M. (2001). Situating cognition. *The Journal of the Learning Sciences, 10*(1 & 2), 27-61.

Roth, W. -M., & Roychoudhury, A. (1993). The development of science process skills in authentic contexts. *Journal of Research in Science Teaching, 30*, 127-152.

Rovai, A. P. (2002). A preliminary look at the structural differences of higher education classroom communities in traditional an ALN courses. *Journal of Asynchronous Learning Networks, 6*(1), 41-56.

Salomon, G. (1993). *Distributed cognitions: Psychological and educational considerations.* New York, NY: Cambridge University Press.

Salomon, G., & Perkins, D. N. (1998). Individual and social aspects of learning. In P. D. Pearson & A. Iran-Nejad (Eds.), *Review of research in education* (Vol. 23, pp. 1-25). Washington, DC: American Educational Research Association.

Sand-Jecklin, K. (1998). Student evaluation of clinical education environment (SECEE): Instrument development and validation (Unpublished doctoral dissertation, West Virginia University). *Dissertation Abstracts International, 60*(6). (UMI No. 304464573).

Schoenfeld, A. H. (1999). Looking toward the 21st century: Challenges of educational theory and practice. *Educational Researcher, 28*(7), 4-14.

Shaw, R. E., Kadar, E., Sim, M., & Repperger, D. W. (1992). The intentional spring: A strategy for modeling systems that learn to perform intentional acts. *Journal of Motor Behavior, 24*(1), 3-28.

Sternberg, R., & Frensch, P. A. (1993). Mechanisms of transfer. In D. K. Detterman and R. J. Sternberg (Eds.), *Transfer on trial: Intelligence, cognition and instruction* (pp. 25-38). Norwood, NJ: Ablex.

The Cognition and Technology Group at Vanderbilt. (1990). Anchored instruction and its relationship to situated cognition. *Educational Researcher, 19*(6), 2-10.

Vygotsky, L. S. (1978). *Mind in society: The development of higher psychological processes.* Cambridge, MA: Harvard University Press.

Vygotsky, L. S. (1997). *Educational psychology.* St. Lucia Press, Florida. (Original work published 1926)

Weekly, J. A., & Jones, C. (1999). Further studies of situational tests. *Personnel Psychology, 52*, 679-700.

Wenger, E. (1998). *Communities of practice: Learning, meaning and identity.* Cambridge, MA: Cambridge University Press.

Wenger, E. (2003). *Communities of practice: Learning, meaning, and identity.* Cambridge, England: Cambridge University Press.

Wertsch, J. V. (1985). *Vygotsky and the social formation of mind.* Cambridge, MA: Harvard University Press.

Wertsch, J. V. (1991). *Voices of the mind: A sociocultural approach to mediated action.* Cambridge, MA: Harvard University Press.

Wertsch, J. V. (1998). *Mind as action.* New York, NY: Oxford University Press.

Wiggershaus, R. (1986). *Die Frankfurter Schule.* Munich, Germany: Care Hanser Verlag.

Wilson, B., & Madsen Myers, K. (2000). Situated cognition in theoretical and practical contexts. In D. H. Jonassen & S. M. Land (Eds.), *Theoretical foundations of learning environments* (pp. 57-88). Mahwah, NJ: Lawrence Erlbaum Associates.

Young, M. F., Barab, S. A., & Garret, S. (2000). Agent as detector: An ecological psychology perspective on learning by perceiving-acting systems. In D. Jonassen & S. M. Land (Eds.), *Theoretical foundations of learning environments* (pp. 147-173). Mahwah, NJ: Earlbaum.

Author Contact Information: Patrick M. Jenlink, EdD, Station Stephen F. Austin State University Nacogdoches, Texas 75962-3018. Phone: 936-468-2908. E-mail: pjenlink@sfasu.edu

CHAPTER 17

Cooperative Learning Theory

Rebecca Fredrickson, Karen Dunlap, and Sarah McMahan
Texas Woman's University

Constructivist theory focuses on the idea that students gain understanding and value through their relationships, interactions, and encounters with others. Cohen (1994) defines cooperative learning as "students working together in a group small enough that everyone can participate on a collective task that has been clearly defined, and without direct and immediate supervision of the teacher" (p. 3). Cooperative learning builds upon the concepts in constructivism in that it focuses on meaningful collaborative interactions between students where students are actively engaged in learning though working with their peers seeking a common goal. This gives students the opportunity to build their own knowledge as they simultaneously engage in making meaning through shared dialogue with their peers.

Initially, teaching by having students working with one another in cooperative groupings was not something that was heavily researched or taught as an instructional methodology to preservice teachers. As a matter of teacher training, most of the preservice teacher instruction dealt with teachers having meaningful interactions with their materials (curriculum, textbooks, etc.) and their students (Johnson & Johnson, 2009b). The idea that students would work cooperatively was counter to what was the current philosophy of the time, individual achievement. Based upon the aspects of Darwin's "survival of the fittest," the students were expected to compete with one another for academic enhancement and achievement. The concept behind this idea that society would become a stronger and better society and would lead to "continued improvement" (Hofstadter, 1992, p. 6).

Through the years, educational practices have changed and the concepts of competition have evolved to the concepts favoring cooperation (Detusch, 1949). Although individual and competitive structures still appear in schools, cooperative learning has become a preferred instructional methodology that has been proven to enhance student learning both academically and socially (Johnson & Johnson, 2009a). Cooperative learning theory is grounded in the concept that active learning happens through academic and social grouping encounters. When students are given the appropriate supports and structures, students are able to master shared objectives and goals thus creating an atmosphere for effective cooperative learning (Johnson & Johnson, 2009b).

VALIDATING COOPERATIVE LEARNING

Since the 1970s research has increased dramatically that examines the effects of cooperative learning as well as its effectiveness compared to that of independent or competitive learning (Esmonde, 2009; Sharan, 1980; Slavin, 1980, 1995). As the research as increased, so has the validity of cooperative learning as an effective teaching tool, "from being discounted and ignored, cooperative learning has steadily progressed to being one of the dominant instructional practices throughout the world" (Johnson & Johnson, 2009b, p. 365). Slavin (2011) addressed the idea that there have literally been hundreds of studies validating the use of cooperative learning as a successful educational methodology. Over half of the studies that have examined the effectiveness of cooperative learning have demonstrated that it is a successful teaching methodology:

> approximately 65% of the research that has been conducted on cooperative learning represents field studies demonstrating its effectiveness in a wide range of classes, subject areas, grade levels, and students. The use of cooperative learning procedures in so many different subject areas and setting, in preschool through adult education, with so many varies tasks and stu-

The Handbook of Educational Theories, pp. 199–210

dents, and in so many different countries and cultures validates the theory. (Johnson & Johnson, 2009b, p. 374)

There have been many articles and studies citing information about the positive impacts of cooperative learning. Most of the literature cites the research completed by Johnson and Johnson (1994). In a meta-analysis of cooperative learning methods by Johnson, Johnson, and Stanne (2000), there was a significant positive student impact through the use of cooperative grouping in classrooms.

The positive aspects of cooperative learning have been addressed by Slavin (1980, 1995, 2011). Slavin cited that group goals and individual accountability are vital aspects in cooperative grouping. Self-esteem and self-efficacy of students, especially students with special needs, has been shown to rise through the use of cooperative learning. Students who have struggled in school academically also showed signs of being more socially and academically successful after working in cooperative groupings.

IMPLEMENTING SUCCESSFUL GROUPINGS

It must be realized, however, that cooperative learning is more than just group work. The idea of moving desks into groups is just not enough. To be effective, cooperative learning groups must be constructed in a purposeful and deliberate manner (Johnson & Johnson, 2009b). Effective cooperative learning groups have students that are "placed in groups that are mixed in performance level, gender, and ethnicity. The percentage of high, middle, and low learners in each group should represent the appropriate population of each group in the whole class" (Moore, 2009, p. 203). When created appropriately, group dynamic benefits for student participants include: cohesive feelings as a result of group interdependence, enhanced senses of student self-efficacy, enriched multicultural interactions, and improved student academic achievement.

GROUPINGS

The impetus of collaborative groups originates in the actual group composition. Teachers should strive to create groups reflective of the classroom membership. Purposely placing a finite number of differing ability leveled students together in a group setting creates potential for meaningful dialogue and interaction among all members. To achieve that goal, all group members must have a job to do for which they are held personally accountable. Jobs are typically set at the discretion of the teacher, depending upon the requirements of the collaborative endeavor (Johnson & Johnson, 2009a). It is common for groups to function utilizing positions such as leader, recorder, checker, presenter, materials manager, et cetera. For example, the recorder might be the person responsible for any written portion of the required project; while the checker ensures all members not only have a voice, but that all voices are heard as the each participant completes his/her part of the project. Every job, therefore, insures each participant is a contributing group member with an integral role to play in the successful completion of the collaborative endeavor (Moore, 2009).

One of the positive individual gains resulting from an effective cooperative learning experience is the resulting group interdependence. By holding the entire group accountable for each member's learning, the group, as a unit, works together to achieve the project's goal(s) that have been set ahead of time (Nam, 2011). Because each group member holds a unique and contributory function or job, all group members are necessary if the project's ultimate goal is to be successfully reached. Thus, in cooperative learning, the group, as an entity, will "sink or swim" together.

ENHANCED SELF-EFFICACY

How a student perceives his/her ability to successfully complete a given project can translate into how he/she acts, feels, thinks, and/or behaves in situations both inside and outside the classroom. In cooperative groups, students have opportunities to interact with different people depending on group composition and membership. By creating heterogeneous groups (with respect to ability grouping, gender, and ethnicity), ideas from a variety of perspectives may be discussed through a variety of perspectives as each student negotiates his/her own meaning. This gives each member of the group an equal opportunity for success. A student's self-esteem and self-efficacy have been shown to have a strong effect on their academic achievement. Students who work in cooperative groupings often demonstrate a stronger sense of self-efficacy.

ENRICHED MULTICULTURAL INTERACTIONS

Today's classrooms may truly be described as a cultural "melting pots." As global boundaries blur, American classrooms must also adjust to the variety of cultures represented within their walls. Cooperative learning offers a process by which multicultural knowledge may be shared and acceptance nurtured. As students from varying backgrounds work together in their groupings, they are able to bring many different ideas and thoughts can be investigated and discussed through a myriad of perspectives as together as they learn (Hall, Cabrera, & Milem, 2011). By making sure that the cooperative groups are multiculturally diverse, teachers open lines of communication for students of differing cultures. Cooperative learning provides a vehicle for students who are not English proficient to have meaningful interaction with their English speaking peers. This can only help strengthen their grasp and delivery of English.

With the current emphasis on inclusion in the classroom, cooperative learning is a powerful tool that teachers can employ to help students of all ability levels, gain knowledge and information. Additionally, the groupings should include both male and female students and students of different ethnicities as well as differing social classes. Group interdependence is created due to the entire group working to the same goal. With this in mind, cooperative learning serves as a way for teachers to incorporate inclusion in the classroom both academically and multiculturally.

English language learners also benefit greatly from cooperative learning. It has been shown to help students improve their ability to speak and use English. Cooperative learning also allows for students to develop their language proficiency. Calderon, Slavin, and Sanchez (2011) site that students who are not fluent in English often are afraid to ask or answer questions in class. By working in cooperative groups all students have the ability to discuss the lesson with their peers in a less threatening manner without fear of ridicule.

Improved Academic Achievement

Cooperative learning takes the knowledge of one student and transmits that knowledge to the group. In this way, group participants are able to not only enhance their own knowledge and academic achievement; but also increase their problem-solving and decision-making skills. Cognitive growth occurs because students model the information for one another thus creating a more advanced way of thinking.

Types of Cooperative Learning Groups

There are a variety of cooperative grouping strategies that teachers can employ to help their students work effectively in cooperative learning. Johnson, Johnson, and Holubec (1998) describe three distinct types of cooperative learning groups: formal, informal and base groups. Each of these groupings offers the teacher an instructional model that they may use to enhance the cooperative learning activity within their classroom.

Formal Grouping

In a formal cooperative learning group setting, student groupings and learning activities are more highly structured and designed for group members to meet as a unit over a period of time ranging from a single class period to a series of weeks or months. Every member of the group comes to know their specific roles and responsibilities and attempts to fulfill them as they work over a designated time period to complete requirements for a specific assignment or task. During formal cooperative learning, the teacher has several roles:

1. Planning: the teacher must make decisions in the planning phase before implementing formal cooperative learning activities. These decisions include developing the objectives, planning the groupings in the class including the size of the groups, student members of each group, the roles of each student and how students will be selected for each group. They will also need to have planned the arrangement of the room and how or where the materials are stored or to be located by the students.
2. Communication: the teacher needs to be able to effectively communicate the plans for the lesson. This includes explaining the assignment itself, criteria for mastery, their individual and group goals to be attained, the roles for each student. They also need to make sure that each student understands not only their role but the roles of the rest of the group thus increasing accountability.
3. Monitoring: the teacher needs to be monitoring the students and intervene only if it is necessary. Necessary reasons would include to help the group stay on task, help the group improve meeting instructional objectives, and to help with teamwork. By monitoring the students, the teacher helps to foster an air of individual accountability. Teachers may also use this monitoring to collect data to help them with their assessment.
4. Assessment: the teacher will help the students provide their own assessment as well as offer group and/or individual assessment for work completed. By doing this the teacher is able to complete the closure part of the lesson, allow the students to assess not only their own growth but that of the group and that of the group process. The students will also need to create a plan to improve the group process.
5. Celebration: the teacher and the students should reflect upon the growth and achievement of the groups and their accomplishments. This also allows for the development of the social aspects of the group process. The group celebration may also be considered a reward to celebrate the interdependence gained from the process (Johnson & Johnson, 2009b).

The teacher carefully monitors each group throughout the project's progression; from initiation through completion of the work. This type of grouping is especially useful for skill development in areas such as group decision making, group problem solving, or peer review (Johnson et al., 1998).

Informal Grouping

In contrast to formal cooperative learning, informal cooperative grouping is more loosely structured. Often these ad hoc groupings are temporary and created quickly. For example, a teacher may ask students to group by proximity (turn to the person next to you) in an effort to give students the opportunity to explore briefly the topic under discussion by sharing responses with one another. In this manner, students are able to draw from their own thoughts as well as those of their peers. Such groups may last only for a few moments, or for the entire class period. Informal groupings often happen during the direct instruction phase of the lesson being taught. Baloche (1998) suggests that it may resemble this format:

1. The teacher provides the focus or the anticipatory set for the lesson. This may take the form of a question or a statement. The students have a few minutes within their groups to discuss possible thoughts or answers.
2. The teacher begins the direct instruction part of the lesson. This may be done through several mediums (text, story, video, lecture, etc.). The teacher will stop approximately every 10 minutes and ask students previously prepared questions and allow the students time to discuss this in their groups.
3. The teacher allows the students to then synthesize the information that was taught by asking questions and guiding them though the closure part of the lesson.

Regardless, the teacher monitors each grouping throughout the process. Informal grouping is especially useful for focusing student attention on the material covered during direct teaching, lectures, or demonstrations.

Base Groups

Base groups are long term heterogeneous collaborative groupings (Johnson et al., 1998). Membership in base groups is stable; allowing for the development of committed relationships. Base group participants learn to support, aid, encourage, and assist one another as they academically progress through the school year. The group members have the responsibility to:

1. Help assess that each member is continuing to grow academically and hold one another accountable for this continued growth.
2. Be a constant encourager and supporter for the other group members.
3. Assist the group when needed.

Base groups will usually meet on a regular basis and the groupings last usually for the entire class (year[s] or semester). Base group construction usually occurs after the instructor has an opportunity to know his/her students to insure social supportive pairings exist within each group (Johnson & Johnson, 2009a).

THE JOHNSON AND JOHNSON MODEL

From data collected from research focusing on their cooperative learning work, Johnson and Johnson (1994) developed five criteria indicative of properly functioning cooperative groups. Appropriately named the Johnson and Johnson model (1999), the five elements include: positive interdependence, individual accountability, face-to-face interaction, social skills, and group processing. The following discussion examines each of Johnson and Johnson's essential group characteristics.

POSITIVE INTERDEPENDENCE

Positive interdependence is the belief by each group participant that there is value in working with other members and that both individual learning and task outcomes will be better as a result of collaboration (Gillies & Boyle, 2009). Stated simply, the first component of effective group interaction, positive interdependence, means group members need each other to succeed. In order for a high degree of positive interdependence to occur, all group members must participate in face to face interactions and be accountable for their portion of the overall task.

INDIVIDUAL AND GROUP ACCOUNTABILITY

In effective cooperative learning groupings, each member is held accountable at both the group and individual level. While individual and group accountability's primary focus is the group as a whole, each member within the group is held accountable for the successful completion of his/her specific task. In this way, information sharing contributes to learning. Thus, no one person is allowed to "freeload "off the work of others; rather each member must master his/her assigned material for the achievement of the group's goal. Each individual performance is also assessed and the results given back to the group. This enables both teacher and group members to offer additional support/encouragement to individuals when necessary.

Participation in cooperative learning groups which function effectively contributes to students becoming stronger individuals. Johnson et al. (1999) maintain that when students learn together they actually perform better individually. Examples of activities which mesh individual and group accountability include asking individual students to summarize ideas discussed in the group setting and randomly calling on individual group members to speak for the team in a given situation. The instructor may also use peer evaluations to determine progress made within the group. Such opportunities help students stay engaged in the learning.

Face-to-Face Interaction

Face-to-face interactions promote active rather than passive learning. Through this process, group members in a smaller setting are given opportunities to overcome feelings of shyness and improve self-confidence. Relationships developed among team members foster feelings of respect and caring which in turn feed the group's motivation to finish the task at hand. Group members encourage each other by promoting team success (Johnson & Johnson, 2009).

Teams encourage discussion of ideas. Face-to-face peer assistance aids concept clarification for both the student inquiring and the student answering the inquiry. Feedback between members allows each individual to test ideas as they build knowledge and create relevant meaning. Cooperative learning teams help students learn to value individual differences as they participate in critical discussions (Slavin, 1995). Instructors encourage face-to-face conversation by placing groups at round tables so each member is clearly visible to the rest of the team or designating specific areas on the floor (with sufficient space between) for team meetings.

Social Skills

For cooperative groups to work together successfully, prerequisite social skills should be intentionally taught. Some teachers encounter failure when implementing cooperative learning strategies because students have not been trained in social skills that promote cooperative learning, such as giving and receiving feedback, listening, sharing, trusting, decision making, and conflict resolution (Goodwin, 1999; Owens, 1986).

From the onset, students should be made aware of the need for particular social skills. Classroom rules can be positively written and framed as social skills. Social skills can also be integrated into academic lessons. Students might role play what good "listening" is and what it is not or how they felt when someone ignored them or their response. Cooperative group functionality will benefit from regular student participation in activities where they learn, practice, and are assessed on their mastery of prescribed group social skills.

Group Processing

Johnson and Johnson (2009b) state that groups need an intentionally structured time span that is set aside for reflective purposes such as reviewing data, progress monitoring, and maintenance of team member relationships. Through group processing, students reflect upon the degree to which they were successful in working together, completing the assigned task, and using social skills.

It is also beneficial for group members to debrief at the end of the project to assess the effectiveness of group dynamics set goals for future endeavors. Student assessment may be informal such as indicating a "thumbs up" or "thumbs down" response, an observer may simply discuss or give feedback to the group. More direct assessments may involve asking group members for specific information such as *Name three things your group did well* or *Write a sentence explaining what someone in your group did that let you know they were listening to you*. This helps students become reflective regarding both group process and project outcome.

Cooperative Learning: From Then Until Now

With its roots deeply embedded within constructivist theory, cooperative learning certainly considers itself a student centered instructional model. The idea of students working collaboratively with one another on projects is not a novel concept. Social theorists and philosophers such as John Dewey, Morton Deutsh, and Kurt Lewin have long purported the advantages of group think over independent isolation. Dewey (Niell, 2005) believed students should be actively engaged in dialogue with one another as they developed social skills needed for proper participation within a democratic society. Through this type of dialogue, students were seen as active participants in their own learning; gaining information through collaborative engagement in the learning process. Deutsh (Johnson & Johnson, 2009b) explored the idea of social interdependence among group members. Social interdependence examines the relationship existing between project goal structure, student interaction patterns and project outcome Lewin's (Smith, 2001) investigated two ideas critical to successful group dynamics: interdependence of fate and task independence. Interdependence of fate is similar to the "one for all and all for one" adage of yesteryear; the group works more cohesively when each member realizes his/her fate is dependent upon group action. Task interdependence also speaks to this concept. If the task is constructed so that its successful resolution is dependent upon the success of each individual member, a powerful group dynamic emerges. Shared responsibility becomes the foundation upon which group achievement rests.

In recent years, additional authors and theorists have provided updated material pertaining to cooperative learning classroom practices. Most notably is the work of Slavin (1995) and Johnson and Johnson (2009b). Slavin built upon the older idea of task interdependence by espousing the value of creating tasks in which the group's success was dependent upon the individual learning expertise of each group member. It was Slavin's belief that students are more motivated to help each other learn when they perceive they have a valued stake in each other's success. Johnson and Johnson (1999b) suggest students must be instructed in the functionality of roles within collaborative projects for optimum achievement to occur and therefore placed a greater emphasis on teaching students how to work together collaboratively.

Why Use Cooperative Learning

There have been many articles and studies citing information about the positive impacts of cooperative learning. Most of the literature cites the research completed by Johnson and Johnson (1994). In a meta analysis of cooperative learning methods by Johnson et al. (2000), significant positive student impact was seen through the use of cooperative grouping in classrooms.

Many positive aspects of cooperative learning have been addressed by Slavin (1980, 1995). Slavin cited that group goals and individual accountability are vital aspects in cooperative grouping. Self-esteem and self-efficacy of students, especially students with special needs, has been shown to rise through the use of cooperative learning. Students who have struggled in school academically also showed signs of being more socially and academically successful after working in cooperative groupings.

Benefits of Cooperative Learning

Cooperative learning is a powerful approach to learning that teachers can employ to help students of all ability levels gain knowledge. Recent literature targeting cooperative learning includes studies which support the use and describe the benefits of the strategy in today's diverse classroom climates. In a study by Slavin (1995), students who were taught through cooperative learning pedagogy were more willing to listen to classmates' perspectives than those of their counterparts taught in noncooperative groupings. Marzano, Pickering, and Pollock (2001) reported significant increases in learning occurred when students of both genders had opportunities to work in heterogeneous cooperative groups at least once a week.

Furthermore, in an age of increased accountability and high stakes testing demands, Tsay and Brady (2010) examined the relationship between students working in collaborative groups and the potential impact that arrangement had on their academic achievement. The study's result showed students who worked in collaborative teams had greater probabilities of receiving high test scores.

Cooperative learning has been shown to benefit special populations of students as well. Slavin (1995) suggested self-esteem and self-efficacy of students, especially students with special needs, has been shown to rise through the use of cooperative learning. Students who have struggled in school academically also showed signs of being more socially and academically successful after working in cooperative groupings. Zhang (2010) addressed the positive impact responsible teaming had on the language proficiency development of English language learners. Hart (2009) praised cooperative learning's utilization of a participatory approach, high levels of engagement and variety of routes by which content may be accessed among students with disabilities.

Cooperative Learning Challenges

A word of caution is needed here, however. It should be noted that, as with all instructional approaches, one size does not fit all. Cooperative learning does have its critics. Sharan (2010) acknowledged that while responsibly executed cooperative learning groups improved both student achievement and social skills; the process did not always live up to its promise of skill translation from the theoretical to actual practice outside the classroom. In Sharan's view, a disconnect exists between cooperative learning's theory and its practice. Educators are not stereotypically trained in cooperative learning methodologies; therefore, confusion surrounding effective strategies and methods exists.

The hallmark of cooperative learning, heterogeneous grouping, has also met with some resistance. Students who are functioning higher academically may be resistant to working with their colleagues who may struggle with the material. While attitudes of gifted and talented students *improved slightly* in classrooms where cooperative learning was used on a limited basis; when this approach was used more consistently, one study highlighting gifted students' academic achievement in mathematics and another underscoring students with special needs' social skill acquisition showed *no difference in skill attainment* from that of peers taught in a traditional manner (Hecox, 2010; Pratner, 1998; Ramsey & Richards, 1997).

Other studies have also noted that students who actively participate in cooperative groupings achieve higher academically. Cooperative grouping has been shown to yield positive results for all students. In a study by Long and Bai (2011), they addressed the impact of cooperative grouping on English language learners as well.

There have also been studies that demonstrated the limitations of cooperative learning. In 2010, Sharan discussed the problem of the constant evolving of cooperative learning. As previously stated, there are many different ideas and theories addressing cooperative learning. Because of this, there is a concern that teachers may become confused. Additionally, some students who are slower at grasping the material may feel neglected or demeaned by the rest of their group. When seeking the validity of cooperative learning, concurred with the following statement:

> There may be no other instructional strategy that simultaneously achieves such diverse outcomes as cooperative grouping. The amount, generalizability, breadth, and applicability of the research on cooperative, competitive, and individualistic efforts provides considerable validation of the use of cooperative learning to achieve diverse outcomes, including achievement, time on task, motivation, transfer of learning, and other benefits. (p. 1)

The grouping itself is of importance as well. It was also demonstrated that heterogeneous grouping is far superior to homogeneous grouping for lower performing students.

One of the reasons cited by teachers for not using cooperative learning is because of assessment. Teachers often do not know how to appropriately assess students who have been in cooperative groupings (Gillies & Boyle, 2009). Most often, teachers assume that each student participated equally within the group and they assign a group grade for each student within that group. By using this method, it is hard to assess how hard each student worked or participated within the group. Another strategy used is to have the students complete a rubric assessing the contributions of the other group members. Using this method has its difficulties as well because of the perceived "fairness" issues raised by not only the students but by parents and administration as well. Other teachers use a self-assessment method for evaluation where each student will self-evaluate their performance in the group. Where this may cause some deep self-reflection, this may also be based on each student's self-confidence level or level of self-perception. Another method includes a combination of group performance and individual performance. The students will be assigned a group grade but they will also do a follow-up activity to determine their individual understanding. By using this method it, "blends both participation and contribution with subject matter learning in a way that helps the teacher know what each pupil has learned" (Airasian, 2005, p. 301).

How to Use Cooperative Learning

Often teachers are reluctant to begin using cooperative groups in their classrooms because they are unsure how to begin the process. From Northwest Educational Technology Consortium's website, *Focus on Effectiveness* (2005) the seven strategies listed are intended to assist teachers in the facilitation of responsible cooperative learning groups:

1. Make sure the group type meets the lesson's need or objective. The teacher needs to already know what the expected outcome of the lesson should be so that they know how best to create or develop the groupings. Based upon the expected student outcome, the teacher may create informal, formal or base collaborative teams Johnson et al. (1998).
2. The size of the group needs to be a key consideration. It is best to keep the cooperative groups to a small size (Gillies & Boyle, 2009). For informal groupings try to maintain a membership of four. At times, formal and base groups may require up to six members. Cooperative groups should ideally have between 4-6 members (Cohen, 1994; Johnson et al., 1994).
3. Create heterogeneous rather than ability groups if at all possible. Groups should include students from different ethnicities, genders, abilities, and languages. All students benefit from working with students of different ability levels. Keep ability grouping to a minimum (Marzano et al., 2001).
4. Do not just use cooperative learning in all instances. While cooperative learning is a powerful instructional approach, students need time to work independently and competitively as well (Johnson & Johnson, 2009a). This way the students have the time to work and develop by themselves to achieve a goal that is independent of the other students, they have the ability to compete for enjoyment, and they are able to grow and learn with others through cooperation. Where all opportunities should be employed, the students should spend the majority of their time cooperatively.
5. Randomly select students for groupings when having informal groups. Use a variety of options in the membership selection process (shirt color, birthday, letters in name, poker chip color, etc.). By making different types of groups, the students never feel that they are being singled out. This strategy works at all grade levels but is especially important in the middle school levels where the students are chal-

lenged at new social, academic, and biological degrees (Johnson, Johnson, & Roseth, 2010).

6. Develop a structure for success for all groups. Make sure that students have access to all necessary forms and organizational tools that they need. Borich (2011) cited that there are many roles that students may take in the cooperative groupings that assist in making each group successful. By assigning these roles to students, the students know what they are supposed to do and are able to participate fully in the group experience. The student may be responsible for more than one role during each session depending on the roles that are required for each activity and the number of people in the group. The student roles may include a student to: (a) summarize the material that the group is to present, (b) check the material for accuracy, (c) research the material that is to be studied and provide additional information as necessary, (d) gather the materials that are needed including equipment, reference materials, et cetera, (e) be a writer for the group when writing up major findings, and (f) keep the group on track and encourage all members to actively participate in the process. At times, many of the members will act as the group "leader" however, it is not always necessary to state that as a role to be filled.
7. Continually create new teams. Monitoring and adjustment will be required as successful facilitation of cooperative learning is an acquired skill. The students need to be taught how to work cooperatively. The students also need to learn how to fill each role (as listed above). By changing the groupings and the roles the students represent, they are all able to learn to work in a cooperative environment. Students will need specific instruction in how to work cooperatively. This may include learning how to listen to their fellow group members, discuss the findings and make a consensus, encouraging each other, seek information from all stakeholders within the group, not to criticize others for offering an incorrect answer, and to encourage the group to look in different places to seek their answers or solve their goals (Borich, 2011). Take time to meet with groups and provide guidance as needed.

As previously discussed, many positive attributes are attributed to the use of cooperative learning in the classroom. Teachers occasionally struggle, however, finding collaborative activities that effectively blend social and academic skills in a manner which successfully accomplishes project objectives. The following discussion describes cooperative activities developed initially by Kagan (2001) and used/adapted by others for classroom use.

Partner Working

Kagan (2001) established the idea of *partner working* as a cooperative learning activity. Partner working is a fast and simple way for teachers to begin engaging their class in the cooperative grouping process. Initially students are divided into groups of four. Each foursome is further divided into partners of two. At this point,-each set of partners moves to opposite sides of the room where a task is assigned. All students on the same side of the room address the same question or assignment and have the ability to work together. At the task's conclusion, each pair must rejoin their original partners in their original group and teach the concept/information discussed. Each set of partners has the ability to quiz and question other group members making sure everyone understands the material. This activity allows students to be both the learner (by exploring the same topic with another group of students) and the expert (by presenting material learned to other members of the group).

Think–Pair–Share

Think–Pair–Share consists of three cooperative steps. Initially, students are asked by the instructor to think individually about a question or questions. Second, students pair up with a partner and share their thoughts and ideas with one another. Finally, the pair exchanges their thoughts and responses with another pair or the entire class. By using this method, students are given the opportunity to work with the material both independently and with a partner in a low stress, low risk environment. Thus, for the student, this activity has only minimal risk of embarrassment or failure. This has been shown to be helpful for students who are English language learners as it gives them the opportunity to communicate in an environment with less risk or stress (De Jong & Estrada, 2011).

Jigsaw

In a jigsaw, the students work together to investigate a shared issue. The class members are divided into original (or base) groups consisting of five to six students with each group member possessing a unique number from one to five (1-5/6 depending upon the number of students per group). Class members then form subsequent groupings in which all 1s come together, the 2s come together, etc. in order to explore a specific and distinct idea or topic. Subgroups are expected to learn the material; in short they are expected to become the expert on their particular topic. Once subgroups have had a sufficient amount of time to interact with the information and feel they understand it well enough to instruct others, members return to their original or base groups and one at a time present their unique information to their peers. Every member of the group is expected to know all of the information about the issue by the end of the jigsaw activity. Once the jigsaw is completed, it is important to assess the students' knowledge of task objectives (Moore, 2009).

Team–Pair–Solo

Team–Pair–Solo is an activity in which students first work with their group members to solve a given problem or task. Next, teams break into pairs and work on the same or similar type of problem. Finally, students work independently on either the same or related task (Kagan, 2001). By using this method, students may develop self confidence levels which allow them to attempt problems which initially may be viewed as beyond their abilities. Team–Pair–Solo is based on the idea of mediated learning. Through the use of the group, students are able to progress to a point that they may not have been able to independently. This method is extremely useful for students who struggle academically or do not have the self-confidence to be an academic risk-taker. It may also be helpful for students who are struggling learning new concepts, special needs learners, or English language learners as it helps to build the student's academic knowledge as well as their self-confidence (Hall et al., 2011).

Round-Robin Brainstorming

In a round-robin brainstorming activity, the class works within their cooperative groups of four to six members. One of the group members is selected to act as the recorder. The teacher, either orally on paper, then poses a divergent question, one with many possible answers. After the students have had time to think about the question asked, group members exchange their answers with each other in a "round-robin" style where from one member to the next each, in turn, shares his/her information or ideas. The group member sitting next to the designated recorder initiates the round robin session as the recorder writes down all ideas as they are stated. This process continues multiple times around the group until time is up or until everyone is out of ideas. By using a round-robin style, every person has an equal voice within the group with no one person dominating the conversation (Putman & Paulus, 2009).

Student Teams Achievement Division

Student Teams Achievement Division is a frequently used cooperative learning activity because it may readily be used in so many different grade levels and subject areas. Combining cooperative learning with a competitive quality, Student Teams Achievement Division is the idea of teams of 4-5 students competing with other teams in the class (Moore, 2009). However, the teams are not necessarily competing for an end product but based on individual improvement in skill test scores. Slavin (1995) created the steps involved in the implementation of Student Teams Achievement Division include:

1. The student's initial knowledge must be measured either by a pretest or from previous work.
2. The students must then be ranked by score from top to bottom.
3. Each team must be divided equally based on the score, ethnicity, and gender.
4. The lesson is taught by the teacher.
5. The students are then allowed to work in their groups building upon the material that was taught through text, worksheets, handouts, etc.
6. The teacher should continue to monitor the groups helping guide the students if necessary.
7. Each student is then assessed on an individual basis (quiz, test, etc.)
8. The groups are then each given a score based upon the growth of each member from step one to step seven.

Circle the Sage

Circle the sage is a collaborative strategy which allows students to play the role of the expert. Initially, with the class grouped in original or base groups, the teacher asks who has a special skill or possesses special knowledge about a particular topic (Kagan, 2001). For example, the teacher may ask who in the class has visited Europe, who can successfully complete a complex math problem, or who has read a certain book. Those students are then designated as sages and asked to take positions in various places around the room. Next, students are asked to form groups around the sage who has pertinent information for them. Teachers need to monitor student selection of topic and sage to make sure each sage has approximately the same number of students listening to him/her and that no base group has two students circling a particular sage. Sages then present what they know about their topic as students ask questions, take notes, and gather information about the subject from their sage. Finally, students return to their base groups and gathered from their sage. Circle the sage highlights class members as resident experts and gives group members opportunities to instruct their peers.-This may also be a helpful activity for students who are English language learners or special needs students as it enhances and reinforces the knowledge that they already have acquired. Additionally, it gives them the opportunity to be the teacher and the leader within their classroom setting (Hall et al., 2011).

Three-Step Interview

The three-step interview helps students personalize their learning by critically listening to others. For this collaborative strategy, the students work in pairs with one student acting as the interviewer, the other as the interviewee. The interviewer asks the questions and then actively listens and paraphrases the responses. In the second step of this activity, partners reverse roles and repeat the process. The final phase has each pair joining another pair to create a group of four. Students then share what their partner had to share with the rest of their group or class (Kagan, 2001).

Numbered Heads Together

Numbered heads together is a group investigation technique that places students in groups of four with each student possessing a unique number (1-4). The teacher poses a question and the group *puts its collective head together* to research and determine the answer. Once a sufficient amount of time has passed, the teacher calls out a number and the member with that number becomes the group's spokesperson and answers the question. Since all students in the group have discussed the topic, theoretically it should not matter which student the teacher calls on to answer; all should be prepared. With this cooperative learning strategy, higher level learning is promoted. Moore (2009) identifies six steps that have been recognized that promote and foster this:

1. topic identification and understanding;
2. cooperative planning time within the group;
3. implementation of the research;
4. analysis and synthesis of the research;
5. the selected student's presentation of the material; and
6. group evaluation.

Numbered heads together is a powerful tool as all students in a group are held accountable for all information learned.

Three-Minute Review

Three-minute review is a simple technique that teachers can use to clarify information and help students assess their knowledge of the material under discussion. To utilize this technique, teachers are encouraged to stop at various points during a discussion or lecture and give student groups three minutes to discuss among themselves certain ideas, review presented concepts, or ask questions about the topic (Moore, 2009). The Three Minute Review gives teachers an opportunity to quickly reinforce salient points for students.

The Role of the Teacher

Teachers are often resistant to using cooperative learning because of the unanswered questions that surround it. What is the role of the teacher in cooperative learning? If the students are working together in groups, what is the teacher supposed to be doing? How are teachers supposed to monitor and assess cooperative groups? In 2009, Johnson and Johnson (2009b) addressed these questions in reference to working in formal cooperative group settings:

1. Teachers are responsible for making all of the decisions before instruction begins. Teachers make the determination of academic and social objectives to be taught. Teachers establish the method used for group assignments, determine the number of students needed per group, and decide which roles students will portray. Teachers are responsible for arrangement of the room and materials. It is important to make sure the room arrangement is conducive to group work.
2. Teachers need to explain to students both the-cooperative roles and structure of the cooperative learning process. Students need to clearly understand the assigned task and the manner by which they will be assessed. The teacher also needs to make sure that roles are assigned for interdependence and accountability. Teachers also need to stress the interdependence required so that group members understand that they are a part of team and they succeed as a team. The behaviors and expectations for each member also need to be addressed. The social skills and interactions that are expected in the assignment should also be addressed with the students.
3. Teachers must closely and actively monitor students to ensure the task is successfully completed and both academic and social skills are addressed. Often active teacher oversight encourages student engagement and increases accountability.
4. Teachers need to carve time after the cooperative task is complete to debrief student groups and guide them in learning to reflect on their behavior both academically and socially. By reflecting upon the group process, students learn to recognize their successes and understand areas needed for future growth
5. The teacher's role does not change substantially from the traditional one when working with informal groups of students as this type of group func-

tions in a more temporary capacity. Instructions and expectations of the task must be clearly understood by the students. Informal groups may be teacher initiated or teacher directed during instruction involving film, lecture, or demonstration, for example to help students focus on the more salient instructional points. Or, perhaps informal groupings may be used during the closure of a lesson to garner student understanding. Regardless of when it is used, successful informal cooperative teams have members who are actively engaged and focused on the topic or lesson.

Although no method of instruction is full proof, cooperative learning has been shown to improve student retention, promote social skills, assist in the inclusive process, help students academically, and increase learning in students. Cooperative learning is a tool that can be used with students of all ages and across all subject areas. Cooperative learning can be a powerful instrument for teachers to employ to improve student learning in their classroom.

REFERENCES

Airasian, P. W. (2005). *Classroom assessment: Concepts and applications* (5th ed). New York, NY: McGraw Hill.

Baloche, L. (1998). *The cooperative classroom: Empowering learning*. Upper Saddle River, NJ: Prentice Hall.

Borich, G. D. (2011). *Effective teaching methods: Research-based practice* (2nd ed). Boston, MA: Pearson Education.

Calderon, M., Slavin, R., & Sanchez, M. (2011). Effective instruction for English learners. *Immigrant Children, 21*(1), 103-127.

Cohen, E. G. (1994). Restructuring the classroom: Conditions for productive small groups. *Review of Educational Research, 64*(1), 1-35.

De Jong, E. J., & Estrada, P. L. (2011). The role of a teachers in promoting language use through Think–Pair–Share interactions. *Sunshine State TESOL Journal, 10*(1), 8-14.

Deutsch, M. (1949). A theory of cooperation and competition. *Human Relations, 2*, 129-152,

Esmonde, I. (2009). Ideas and identities: Supporting equity in cooperative learning mathematics learning. *Review of Educational Research, 79*(2), 1008-1043.

Gillies, R. M., & Boyle, M. (2009). Teachers' reflections on cooperative learning: Issues of implementation. *Teaching and Teacher Education, 26*(4), 933-940.

Goodwin, M. (1999). Cooperative learning and social skills: What skills to teach and how to teach them. *Intervention in School and Clinic, 35*(1), p. 29-33.

Hall, W. D., Cabrera, A. F., & Milem, J. F. (2011). A tale of two groups: Differences between minority students and non-minority students in their predispositions to and engagement with diverse peers at a predominately White institution. *Research in Higher Education, 52*(4), 420-439.

Hart, J. (2009). Strategies for culturally and linguistically diverse students with special needs. *Preventing School Failure, 53*(3), 197-206.

Hecox, C. C. (2010). Cooperative learning and the gifted student in elementary mathematics (Doctoral dissertation). Retrieved from http://digitalcommons.liberty.edu/doctoral/365/

Hofstadter, R. (1992). *Social Darwinism in American thought*. Boston, MA: Beacon Press.

Johnson, D., & Johnson, R. (1994). *Learning together and alone, cooperative, competitive, and individualistic learning*. Needham Height, MA: Prentice-Hall.

Johnson, D., Johnson, R. & Holubec, E. (1998). *Cooperation in the classroom*. Boston, MA: Allyn & Bacon.

Johnson, D. W., & Johnson, F. (2009). *Joining together: Group theory and group skills* (10th ed.). Boston, MA: Allyn & Bacon.

Johnson, D. W., Johnson, R. T., & Roseth, C. (2010). Cooperative learning in middle schools: Interrelationship of relationships and achievement. *Middle Grades Research Journal, 5*(1), 1-18.

Johnson, D. W., Johnson, R. T., & Stanne, M. B. (2000). *Cooperative learning methods: A meta-analysis*. University of Minnesota.

Johnson, D. W., & Johnson, R. T. (2009a). Energizing learning: The instructional power of conflict. *Educational Researcher, 38*(1), 37-51.

Johnson, D. W., & Johnson, R. T. (2009b). An educational psychology success story: Social interdependence and cooperative learning. *Educational Researcher, 38*(5), 365-379.

Kagan, S. (2001). Kagan structures for emotional intelligence. *Kagan Online Magazine, 4*(4).

Long, Y., & Bai, X. (2011). The validation of cooperative learning based on ICARE strategy training. *Contemporary Foreign Languages, 361*(10), 32-38.

Marzano, R. J., Pickering, D. J., & Pollock, J. E. (2001). *Classroom instruction that works: Research-based strategies for increasing student achievement*. Alexandria, VA: Association for Supervision and Curriculum Development.

Moore, K. D. (2009). *Effective instructional strategies: From theory to practice* (2nd ed). Los Angeles, CA: SAGE.

Nam, C. W. (2011). The relative effects of positive interdependence and group processing on student achievement and attitude in online cooperative learning. *Computers and Education, 56*(3), 680-688.

Niell, J. (2005). John Dewey: Philosophy of education. Retrieved from http://wilderdom.com/experiential/JohnDeweyPhilosophyEducation.html

Northwest Regional Educational Laboratory. (2005). Focus on effectiveness. Retrieved from http://www.netc.org/focus/strategies/coop.php

Owens, L. (1986). Cooperation. In M. J. Duncan (Ed.). *The international encyclopedia of teaching and teacher education*. (345-349). New York, NY: Pergamon.

Pratner, M. J. (1998). Acquiring social skills through cooperative learning and teacher directed instruction. *Remedial and Special Education, 19*(3), 160-172.

Putman, V. L., & Paulus, P. B. (2009). Brainstorming, brainstorming rules and decision making. *The Journal of Creative Behavior, 43*(1), 23-39.

Ramsay, S. G., & Richards, H. C. (1997). Cooperative learning environments: Effects of academic attitudes of gifted students. *Gifted Child Quarterly, 41*(4), 160-168.

Sharan, S. (1980). Cooperative learning in small groups: Recent methods and effects on achievement, attitudes, and ethnic relations. *Educational Research, 50*(2), 241-271.

Sharan, S. (2010). Cooperative learning for academic and social gains: Valued pedagogy, problematic practice. *European Journal of Education, 45*(2), 300-313.

Slavin, R. E. (1980). Cooperative learning. *Review of Educational Research, 50*(2), 315-342.

Slavin, R. E. (1995). *Cooperative learning: Theory, research, and practice* (2nd ed.) Englewood Cliffs, NJ: Prentice-Hall.

Slavin, R. E. (2011). Instruction based on cooperative learning. In R. E. Mayer & P. A. Alexander (Eds.), *Handbook of research on learning and instruction* (pp. 344-360). New York, NY: Routledge.

Smith, M. K. (2001). Kurt Lewin: Groups, experiential learning and action research. Retrieved from The Encyclopedia of Informal Education website: http://www.infed.org/thinkers/et-lewin.htm

Tsay, M., & Brady, M. (2010). A case study of cooperative learning and communication pedagogy: Does working in teams make a difference? *Journal of the Scholarship of Teaching and Learning, 10*(2), 78-89.

Yael, S. (2010). Cooperative learning for academic and social gains: Valued pedagogy, problematic practice. *European Journal of Education, 45*(2), 300-313.

Zhang, Y. (2010). Cooperative language learning and foreign language learning and teaching. *Journal of Language Teaching and Research, 1*(1), 81-83.

Author Contact Information: Rebecca Fredrickson, EdD, Assistant Professor, Curriculum and Instruction, Texas Woman's University. Telephone: 940-898-2238. E-mail: RFredrickson@mail.twu.edu

CHAPTER 18

Problem-Based Learning Theory

Rebecca Fredrickson, Sarah McMahan, and Karen Dunlap
Texas Woman's University

Aspects of Problem-Based Learning

The term problem-based learning (PBL) encompasses different meanings depending on the paradigm. Within the educational paradigm, the meaning of the word depends upon the objective of the lesson, the lesson design, the age and ability of the students and the skills of the teacher. PBL consists of student-centeredness, teachers acting as facilitators, small group learning, and beginning with problems that are ill structured and authentic (Barrows, 1986, 1992, 1996).This method is focused on the student learner. The student centered methodology is multifaceted and uses complex problems to find various solutions. This simultaneous format allows for students to develop a content knowledge foundation while using academic skills and problem-solving strategies to work through the problems seeking a solution.

Since PBL is a student-centered pedagogy, it is considered a fundamental shift in philosophy of teaching. The focus from the teacher moves from that of a disseminator of knowledge to that of a facilitator of knowledge (Merrill, 2007). The paradigm shift moves from teaching (responsibility of the teacher) to that of student learning.

Recent research (Jonassen, 2000; Spector, 2004) have probed into the aspects of student centered research and most notably, problem-based learning. The PBL structures can vary widely and the amount of support provided for the students within their study is just as broad. There are the two extremes of students being given little to no guidance, little support, and a minute amount of information that is needed to complete the assignment. With this small amount of guidance, the PBL format is often ineffective (Mayer, 2004). Contrasting this extreme would be a support system that is provided for students as they seek to find a solution to the problem they are presented. For students who have experience with PBL, often little supervision or guidance is necessary however, when students are first entering a PBL situation, a great deal of scaffolding and guidance is necessary.

The History of Problem-Based Learning

There are multiple theories regarding the initial development of PBL. Some scholars have put the dates back in the early 1950s with the research done by the medical faculty at Case Western Reserve University and others have stated that PBL initially was started in the late 1950s at McMaster University as a practice in their medical school (Savery & Duffy, 1996). Other medical schools have since adopted this teaching philosophy for their programs (Barrows, 1986, 1992). Medical school professors used PBL as an instructional technique in the beginning stages of a medical education, generally the first 2 years, as a replacement for the teacher-driven option of lecture only. Through the years, PBL has been used in many other areas of instruction at the collegiate level as well as moving across the curriculum through the K-12 levels (Savery & Duffy, 1996).

Within the medical environment, PBL encompasses groups of students identifying and working on a problem collaboratively. While discussing the problem, it is each student's goal to come up with a rationale, discuss key elements, and critically exam all the components related to the problem. Additionally, each student them is instructed to research and find out different information related to the problem individually (self-directed learning). Once each student has had an opportunity to study the problem individually, the group reconnects to discuss the problem systematically and use everyone's information to work through the problem.

The Handbook of Educational Theories, pp. 211–217

Often this is repeated to flush out non relevant information to the problem. This continued search through data may continue on several times before a solution to the problem is reached (Savery & Duffy, 1996).

Initially the validation of PBL resided in medical schools with medical students and practicing doctors who studied medicine utilizing the methodology of PBL. Multiple studies demonstrate the effectiveness of PBL within the medical environment (Albanese & Mitchell, 1993; Barrows, 2002; Vernon & Blake, 1993). Other theorists have validated the use of PBL in the classroom through the lens of a constructivist perspective. A study by Hmelo-Silver and Barrows (2006) demonstrated that PBL within the constructivist learning method to be a very successful methodology. A later study (Walker & Leary, 2009), a meta-analysis, examining the use of PBL outside of the medical field, demonstrated that the students who used a PBL method "did as well or better than their lecture-based counterparts" (p. 24).

Similar to the medical environment design, the constructivist-learning by-product of PBL focuses on student centered learning pedagogy that allows the student to be an active participant in the learning process. Within PBL, students are actively engaged in constructing new knowledge instead of using the direct lecture from the teacher to gain new knowledge. PBL allows for creativity and abstract thinking regarding a problem. Often time, PBL engages students to think "outside of the box" (Barrows, 2006).

Student engagement with PBL, includes students usually working in groups to discuss the problem to determine the knowledge they already have, and then process of discovering what knowledge they might need, and then divide up individually to seek the knowledge. Once the knowledge is obtained, the students rejoin the group and together to present knowledge and draw conclusions and solutions to the original problem presented. Gregory and Chapman (2007) developed the KND model as a way for teachers to begin using PBL within their classrooms. Within the KND model the students define what they already (K) know, then they look at what they (N) need, and finally, what will they need to (D) do to get the information. Although this is a very simplified version of a PBL, it also offers a starting point for both students and teachers as they enter into the PBL classroom (Freiberg & Driscoll, 2004). A more advanced model for using PBL states that the steps to follow include:

1. Identify, clarify, and describe the problem with everyone involved in the PBL.
2. Identify what is already known about the problem. This can be through previous experiences, personal knowledge, or through various resources.
3. Identify what is unknown at this point in the process. Begin by addressing these questions and finding the resources to do this.
4. Identify possible solutions with the information that has been generated thus far. Examine these solutions to determine if the answers seem correct.
5. Identify the solution that is the best answer for the problem presented. If there is not one, continue to search and develop possible solutions.
6. Identify the solution to be presented and assess this solution.

Although both models vary from one another, the basic steps of the PBL may be found in both of these.

Like the various models for implementation of a PBL, the attributes of a PBL learning community can vary slightly as well. Barrows (1992, 2006) states that the attributes of a PBL learning community should be a place where:

- Students accept responsibility for their own learning. In a PBL environment, the students seek and gather their own information in seeking a solution to their problem. The students are also responsible for evaluating the outcomes they establish (Borich, 2011).
- Student learning within the PBL is an authentic experience. Students spend time working on real life problems and tasks. The information that they seek provides relevance only when analyzed and applied in an authentic environment (Stepien, Senn, & Stepien, 2008).
- Students master many social skills as well as finding the academic answers they are seeking. Students learn to work within a collaborative process by sharing their own thoughts while respecting the thoughts of their peers (Gallow, 2001). The socialization process in PBL allows students to learn valuable problem-solving skills as they work through the process with their group (Barrows, 1986).
- The roles of the teacher and the student take on many similarities in a PBL environment. The students and teachers both become critical thinkers, planners, evaluators, and instructors as they work their way through the problems (Freiberg & Driscoll, 2004).
- Student learning in PBL is driven by problems that lack structure and definition (Stepien, Senn, & Stepien, 2008). Until the students begin collectively working on the problem, the structure of the learning environment is vague at best. The students work together to facilitate an organization and structure to the teaching and learning process.

Why Use Problem Based Learning

Although the medical environment is far different from a traditional educational environment, it still utilizes the same approach. In the late 80s and early 90s, scholars in education begin to see the paradigm shift to that of student learning experience, where the teacher became the facilitator and students discovered their own learning. Within the discipline of education, PBL was developed because traditional, teacher-centered teaching practices produced students who were often disillusioned and disappointed with their education. A great deal of the instruction came in the format of the "sage on the stage" where teachers disseminated information to students and students were expected to be empty vessels waiting to be filled. Students were not retaining the information they were taught. All of the instruction was done in a competitive format where students were rewarded based on their individual contributions and performances.

There have been many articles and studies citing information about the positive impacts of problem based learning. In 1993, Albanese and Mitchell completed a comprehensive literature review of the outcomes and implications of PBL. The results of the review demonstrated that most students who used PBL scored higher on their standardized exams and faculty evaluations. Additionally, students found PBL courses to be more enjoyable and nurturing then traditionally taught classes. The faculty who taught the PBL courses also tended to enjoy teaching using this methodology (Albanese & Mitchell, 1993).

In another study, Vernon and Blake (1993) conducted a meta-analysis to determine if problem based learning is a superior teaching methodology to that of a traditional classroom. This study consisted of five different meta-analyses conducted on 35 independent studies. Overall, the results for the study demonstrated that PBL is a superior approach to teaching then that of traditional teacher centered pedagogy. Based on student evaluations, there was a significant difference between PBL courses and traditionally taught classes. Students believed that PBL courses were superior to traditionally taught classes. In unstandardized measures such as faculty attitude, student attendance, and student feelings, the PBL courses were also seen more favorably than that of their traditional counterparts. However, there was no difference demonstrated between PBL and traditional classroom methods on students' demonstration of on faculty testing of factual knowledge. Traditional methodology however did show a more favorable response then PBL when it came to standardized testing (Vernon & Blake, 1993).

Vygotsky (1978) states that learning is a social process between student and the teacher. Research has shown that students learn and retain more information when they work in collaborative groupings. Johnson and Johnson (1994) demonstrated that student learning is more effective in collaborative groups. In a later study by Johnson, Johnson, and Stanne (2000), the authors were able to demonstrate that student learning was dramatically increased through the use of cooperative grouping in classrooms.

Other positive aspects of collaborative working include enhanced self-efficacy and self-esteem of students. Students who are special needs see a great deal of growth when working in a cooperative grouping. They have shown to have improved social skills when working with their peers as well as improved academic skills. Additionally, personal accountability increases when students work collaboratively with one another (Slavin, 1995, 2011).

There are three major complaints that employers have about students entering the workforce: they do not know how to write, problem solve, or work collaboratively with other professionals (Gallow, 2001). In the technology rich twenty-first century, students need to be able to work collaboratively (Boss & Krauss, 2007). By working with others during their formal schooling years, students are prepared to work collaboratively in the workforce. By solving problems through the PBL framework, using the technology in a meaningful way, students are exposed to real world problem-solving strategies to help make them workforce ready upon graduation (Keller, 2007)

Student Diversity

With the recent trend toward inclusion, problem based learning is a natural alternative for teachers to embrace. Since the majority of the time spent in PBL is within collaboration, students are supported by their peers throughout the process (Freiberg & Driscoll, 2004). This support, as well as the small group process, allows for all students to actively participate in the learning activity which may be more difficult independently for students with special needs or students who are English language learners.

Students With Special Needs

Problem-based learning is deemed a helpful teaching tool to use with special needs students. It is important that when teachers are establishing the PBL groupings, students of all ability levels are represented and learning from each other. Differing perspectives may be presented as all students need to have the ability to present their perspectives on the information. Additionally, since PBL groups are working collaboratively with one another, special needs students continue to receive instruction as they work within their groups. Through PBL, students are working in a community with one another where they take on the responsibility and ownership of their own learning. Through this process, students gain more than just academic knowledge, they also make social gains as they interact with their peers and self-esteem gains as they take responsibility for their own learning (Keller, 2007).

Students Who Are English Language Learners

Research suggests that working in collaborative group environments allows English language learners positive learning experiences (Calderon, Slavin, & Sanchez, 2011). By working with a PBL model, students are not only interacting with their peers academically but also socially. Within these groupings, students are free to address their concerns or have questions answered in a less stressful environment compared to having the entire class watching students speak in front of the class. Through the PBL process, students begin to take ownership of their own learning as they have to first determine their personal knowledge, and then determine what knowledge is still needed to begin seeking possible solutions to the problem presented (Freiberg & Driscoll, 2004). Since students work to construct their own learning, they are bringing in differing perspectives to the group from their previous learning or experience. This time spent searching for knowledge already known by the group allows for all students within the group to contribute to the group's knowledge base. As the students share the information that they already have and the information that they have sought out through the PBL process, they are having to create a continuous dialogue with the members of the group. This sharing process allows students without a firm grasp on the English language to take a part in the dialogue with their peers thus helping their language acquisition—both understanding and speaking (Calderon, Slavin, and Sanchez, 2011).

Students of Differing Cultures

Today's classrooms truly reflect the diversity of the society. As the global community becomes more reflected in the diversity of society, the classroom must adjust to the diversity of cultures represented within their walls (Price & Nelson, 2011). Because students are working collectively and bringing their unique perspective to the group, they may begin to dialogue with their peers about the cultural aspects of the lesson. As questions in PBL are authentic, there are often aspects of culture and community that may be derived and discussed through the PBL process. Students then have the ability to gather data and bring own knowledge to the group for discussion, thus fostering aspects of multicultural diversity within the classroom (Hall, Cabrera, & Milem, 2011).

Using PBL in the Classroom

Many teachers resist using PBL in their classroom simply because they do not know how to use it or fear letting the students have to much control in the classroom. Teachers must be effectively trained on how to implement PBL in the classroom in order for it to be a successful learning experience (Park & Ertmer, 2008).

Teachers must be taught the essential elements of PBL including group management techniques, how to communicate clear and concise directions and giving each group a problem that requires critical thinking for all group members (Freiberg & Driscoll, 2004). With the PBL model, the students are not given a predetermined outline or objective to be met. Instead, as the students discuss the problem and theorize possible solutions, they generate the objective of the problem based on their own analyses.

Implementing PBL in the Classroom

There are several guidelines that teachers can share with students so that PBL will be an effective learning experience for all students. Teachers are encouraged to:

1. Students must comprehend and understand the problem. Students have been given a problem that lacks structure and definition. Students need to discuss the problem with their groups and list the significant parts.
2. Each group needs to make a list of the knowledge that your group has about the subject (Amador, Miles, & Peters, 2007). Discuss with each other what you know about the problem as well as how to begin finding solutions. Make sure that all members have an equal opportunity to share information.
3. Within their assigned group, the leader of the group must a statement of the problem. Take the time to actually write out the group's assessment of the problem. Initially students may want to seek teacher input about the perceived problem by the group. The problem statement may be revised and revisited as new information is gathered and more knowledge is gained.
4. Assignments need to be made for gathering information. This can be done independently or as partners. After the assignments are given, the students need to go and seek the information they are looking for (Amador, Miles, & Peters, 2007).
5. After all of the individuals (or partners) have assembled their information, all of the information needs to be brought to the group for general discussion and evaluation. It is important that everyone's research be given careful consideration and thought (Freiberg & Driscoll, 2004).
6. As a group, make a listing of all of the possible solutions. Make sure that everyone in the group con-

tributes a possible solution. Once a list has been compiled, as a group, rank the solutions in order from strongest to weakest (Amador, Miles, & Peters, 2007).

7. Each group must choose the best solution or the one that is the most likely to be successful.
8. Once a solution has been established, begin compiling a list of what actions need to occur to meet with success. Begin gathering more information and making assignments with deadlines for completion.
9. After your group has completed the work, write up your solution and provide all supporting documents and data.
10. Begin presenting the material in the way established by your teacher. This could take the form of making a class presentation, presenting to the teacher, or simply making a formal presentation that is submitted to the teacher (Berk, 2010). It is not enough to simply present the conclusions, the foundation and supporting evidence must be presented as well. Make sure that all members of the group understand the process and solution so that if challenged, all members of the group are able to address any concerns.
11. After the presentation, assess the group. Assess not only the solution but also the process. Look at the behaviors that were beneficial to the process and those that were not (Amador, Miles, & Peters, 2007).
12. Celebrate! After completing a PBL, take some time to celebrate the accomplishments of the group, the interactions that occurred, and the knowledge that was gained (Freiberg & Driscoll, 2004). It is important to take the time to recognize the completion of a project like this!

The Role of the Teacher

In a PBL classroom, the roles of the teacher and student vary from those within a traditional classroom. Students are largely responsible for their learning in a PBL classroom where the role of the teacher in PBL is that of a facilitator. The teacher makes sure that they are available for consultation during the class meeting times and helps to guide the students when necessary. This role is often challenging for teachers as they have been taught to be disseminators of knowledge rather than facilitators of knowledge acquisition (Rhem, 1998). However, Gallow (2001) states that the teacher is active throughout the lesson. The three main activities for the teacher in the PBL process include planning the instruction, implementing the PBL, and finally, assessing student achievement.

Planning

As with all good instruction, the teacher must first establish the goal or objective that they are trying to help the students master (Kauchak & Eggen, 2011). The teacher provides the problem for the students as well as the underlying supports for the group to find the answers to their problems. When developing the problem for the groups, it is important to make sure that the solution method is not too clear. When this happens, the students loose the problem-solving opportunity (Bransford, Brown, & Cocking, 2000). The students need to have a well-defined problem to address in order for the PBL to be of value to the student. Kauchak and Eggen (2012) define a well-defined problem having "only one correct solution and a prescribed method for finding it exists, whereas an ill-defined problem has more than one solution and no generally agreed-upon strategy for reaching it" (p. 349). Another activity for the teacher is the development of the PBL groups. Although it may be preferable for the students to place themselves into their groups, often this creates homogenous groupings. Groups should include students from all ability levels, socioeconomic backgrounds, ethnicities, and genders (Marzano, Pickering, and Pollock, 2001). The final act in planning is making sure that there are resources and materials available for the students to access. The teacher may provide organizers for the groups to use as well as have resources available for the groups to seek their solutions. Additionally, the teacher may also serve as a resource for the students as they are gathering their information to take back to their group.

Implementation

The teacher must first familiarize the students with the problem they will be finding a solution for. The students need to understand how this problem is meaningful for them. Students also need to understand method they will to present their solutions (research paper, exhibit, oral report, etc.). The teacher may also guide students in making their solutions accessible to others as a means for developing perspective and the life-skill of presenting solutions to problems (Berk, 2010).

The teacher also provides support throughout the process as the students work within their problem to find the solution. The teacher may ask guiding questions to help the students if they are struggling or veering off of the path (Amador, Miles, & Peters, 2007). The teacher also may also choose to help the students as they work to assess their progress. Often the students are initially leery of assessing their own progress and solution. The teacher provides guidelines for the students as they begin learning how to self-assess and reflect upon their work as a group as well as independently (Kauchak & Eggen, 2012).

Assessment

Teachers often express concern over how to assess problem-based learning since the students perform a self-assessment and a group processing assessment (Gillies & Boyle, 2009). In PBL, assessment is not separate from the learning. Assessment is an integral part of the learning process (Amador, Miles, & Peters, 2007). Normative comparisons have no place in PBL. Assessment is an unbroken process that guides instruction.

In the traditional, teacher-centered instruction, the assessment is the culminating activity or experience of teaching. It is a marking of the ending of instruction. Instead of providing a test or an exam for the students to demonstrate knowledge, the students are a part of a continuous assessment that constantly examines the learning processes and aspects of their understanding (Rhem, 1998).

Students are expected to be active participants in not just their learning but also in the evaluative process. The teachers may perform informal evaluations along the way but, the formal assessment that is a part of PBL resides with the student. Students work to evaluate not only their own contributions to the knowledge base but also that of their peers. Students should assist in setting the accomplishments and goals to be determined at each stage of PBL thus making assessment a multidimensional process.

LIMITATIONS OF PBL

Some scholars suggest a limitation of PBL is that teachers may not know how to create real-life problems or assess students work within a PBL framework (Amador, Miles, & Peters, 2007; Keller, 2007; Park & Ertmer, 2008). Additionally, most teachers are not trained in how to teach students to work cooperatively (Sharan, 2010). It is imperative that teachers who implement PBL have an understanding of their student's current knowledge and ability levels so that when the teachers are establishing their groups, they make sure that they are representative of their classroom. Also, teachers need to be cognizant of their student's levels so that they keep the problem within reach of the student's academic levels (Marzano, Pickering, & Pollock, 2001). If the teacher does not have this understanding, the learning may become an activity of frustration or of little to know importance to the students.

Many educators are afraid of using PBL strategies in the classroom. Often these teachers are not trained in how to initiate PBL activities in the classroom as well as terrified of giving students too much control of their own learning (Rhem, 1998). With PBL, students must already come armed with foundational knowledge of the problem statement. In fact, students must have background fact and comprehension of aspects that involve the problem. PBL is hard to instigate in the classroom if the teacher has not taught foundational issues regarding the problem. PBL requires that learners are self-motivated and willing to take ownership of their learning. If students have not been taught how to participate in democratic problem solving then commitment to learning will not be achieved. Teachers must be willing to train students to socially interact and learn together in a democratic environment. In addition, many teachers have to model the style they want students to emulate in their groups (Gallow, 2001).

Teachers are notorious for ownership of the learning environment. It is often difficult for teachers to let students have too much control of their learning. In order to establish a PBL learning community, teachers much entrust their students in the learning process. Teachers need a solid management plan in order for PBL to be successful. Teachers must now when to release the reins when opportunities arise for teaching and learning (Rhem, 1998).

With PBL, students must take responsibility for their own problem. With this ownership, there is no a guarantee that all learning objectives will be covered in a given problem (Fenwick & Parsons, 1997). PBL requires students to have the cognition and emotional maturity to focus on the learning the content and the learning how to critically reflect on the problem (Amador, Miles, & Peters, 2007). Another limitation with PBL is that often times the content is learned by a few group members, but often not everyone critically examines the issue.

CONCLUSIONS

The role of teacher is very important for the success of PBL and as pointed out by Gordon, Rogers, and Comfort (2001) that the role of the teacher as facilitator is very important to success of PBL. Teacher whom take on the role of facilitator instead of direct control allow for flexibility in planning, implementing and assessing learning. It is imperative that preservice be trained in PBL as a way of teaching in the classroom.

PBL is an effective way of having students critically examine problems. PBL focuses on individuals own knowledge construction as well as applying knowledge to solve a problem. PBL allows students to transfer knowledge into problems while critically examining all pieces of the puzzle. PBL allows for students to actively engage in meaningful learning experiences by problem solving as a team effort.

REFERENCES

Albanese, M. A., & Mitchell, S. (1993). Problem-based learning: A review of literature on its outcomes and implementation issues. *Academic Medicine*, 68(1), 52-81.

Amador, J. A., Miles, L., & Peters, C. B. (2007). *The practice of problem-based learning: A guide to implementing PBL in the college classroom*. Boston, MA: Anker.

Barrows, H. S. (1986). A taxonomy of problem-based learning methods. *Medical Education, 20*, 481-486.

Barrows, H. S. (1992). *The tutorial process.* Springfield, IL: Southern Illinois School of Medicine.

Barrow, H. S. (1996). Problem-based learning in medicine and beyond: A brief overview. In L. Wilkerson & W. H. Gijselaers (Eds.), *New directions for teaching and learning* (Vol. 68, pp. 3-12). San Francisco, CA: Jossey-Bass.

Barrows, H. S. (2002). Is it truly possible to have such a thing as dPBL? *Distance Education, 23*(1), 119-122.

Barrows, H. S. (2006). Problem-based learning in medicine and beyond: A brief overview. *New Directions for Teaching and Learning, 1996*(68), 3-12.

Berk, L. (2010). *Development through the lifespan* (5th ed.). Boston, MA: Allyn & Bacon.

Borich, G. D. (2011). *Effective teaching methods: Research-based practice* (2nd ed.). Boston, MA: Pearson Education.

Boss, S., & Krauss, J. (2007). *Reinventing project-based learning: Your field guide to real-work projects in the digital age.* OR: International Society for Technology in Education.

Bransford, J. D., Brown, A. L., & Cocking, R. R. (Eds.). (2000). *How people learn: Brain, mind, experience, and school.* Washington DC: National Academy Press.

Calderon, M., Slavin, R., & Sanchez, M. (2011). Effective instruction for English learners. *Immigrant Children, 21*(1), 103-127.

Fenwick, T., & Parsons, J. (1997). *A critical investigation of the problems with problem-based learning.* ERIC Document: ED 409272.

Freiberg, H. J., & Driscoll, A. (2004). *Universal Teaching Strategies* (4th ed). Boston, MA: Pearson Education.

Gallow, D. (2001). What is problem-based learning? A faculty guide. Retrieved from http://www.pbl.uci.edu/whatispbl.html

Gillies, R. M., & Boyle, M. (2009). Teachers' reflections on cooperative learning: Issues of implementation. *Teaching and Teacher Education, 26*(4), 933-940.

Gordon, P., Rogers, A., & Comfort, M. (2001). A taste of problem-based learning increases achievement of urban minority middle-school students. *Educational Horizons,* 79(4), 171-175.

Gregory, G., & Chapman, C. (2007). *Differentiated Instructional Strategies: One Sized Doesn't Fit All.* Thousand Oaks, CA: Corwin Press.

Hall, W. D., Cabrera, A. F., & Milem, J. F. (2011). A tale of two groups: Differences between minority students and non-minority students in their predispositions to and engagement with diverse peers at a predominately white institution. *Research in Higher Education, 52*(4), 420-439.

Hmelo-Silver, C. E., & Burrows, H. S. (2006). Goals and strategies of a problem-based learning facilitator. *The Interdisciplinary Journal of Problem-Based Learning, 1*(1), 21-39.

Johnson, D., & Johnson, R. (1994). *Learning together and alone, cooperative, competitive, and individualistic learning.* Needham Height, MA: Prentice-Hall.

Johnson, D. W., Johnson, R. T., & Stanne, M. B. (2000). *Cooperative learning methods: A meta-analysis.* Minneapolis, MN: University of Minnesota.

Jonassen, D. H. (2000). Toward a design theory of problem solving. *Educational Technology Design and Development, 48*(4), 63-85.

Kauchak, D., & Eggen, P. (2011). *Introduction to teaching: Becoming a professional* (4th ed.). Upper Saddle River, NJ: Pearson.

Keller, B. (2007). No easy project. *Education Week, 27*(4), 21-23.

Marzano, R. J., Pickering, D. J., & Pollock, J. E. (2001). *Classroom instruction that works: Research-based strategies for increasing student achievement.* Alexandria, VA: Association for Supervision and Curriculum Development.

Mayer, R. E. (2004). Should there be a three-strikes rule against pure discovery learning? *American Psychologist, 59*(1), 14-19.

Merrill, M. D. (2007). A task-centered instructional strategy. *Journal of Research on Technology in Education, 40*(1), 33-50.

Park, S. H., & Ertmer, P. A. (2008). Examining barriers in technology-enhances problem-based learning: Using a performance support systems approach. *British Journal of Educational Technology, 39*(4), 631-643.

Price, K. M., & Nelson, K. L., (2011). *Planning effective instruction: Diversity response methods and management* (4th ed.). CA: Wadsworth, Cengage Learning.

Rhem, J. (1998). Problem–based learning: An introduction. *National Teacher and Learning Forum, 8*(1). Retrieved from http://www.ntlf.com/html/pi/9812/pbl_1.htm

Sharan, S. (2010). Cooperative learning for academic and social gains: Valued pedagogy, problematic practice. *European Journal of Education, 45*(2), 300-313.

Slavin, R. E. (1995). *Cooperative learning: Theory, research, and practice* (2nd ed.) Englewood Cliffs, NJ: Prentice-Hall.

Slavin, R. E. (2011). Instruction based on cooperative learning. In R. E. Mayer & P. A. Alexander (Eds.), *Handbook of research on learning and instruction* (pp. 344-360). New York, NY: Routledge.

Savery, J., & Duffy, T. (1996). Problem Based Learning: An instructional model and its constructivist framework. *In Constructivist learning environments: Case studies in instructional design* (pp. 135-149). Engelwood, NJ: Educational Technology Publications.

Spector, J. M. (2004). Problems with problem-based learning: Comments on model-centered learning and instruction in SEEL (2003). *Technology, Instruction, Cognition and Learning, 1*(4), 35-374.

Stepien, W. J., Senn, P., & Stepien, W. C. (2008). *The internet and problem-based learning: Developing solutions through the web.* Waco, TX: Prufrock Press.

Vernon, D. T., & Blake, R. L. (1993) Does problem-based learning work? A meta-analysis of evaluative research. *Academic Medicine, 68*(7), 550-563.

Vygotsky, L. S. (1978). *Mind in society: The development of higher psychological processes.* Cambridge, MA: Harvard University Press.

Walker, A., & Leary, H. (2009). A problem based learning meta analysis: Differences across problem types, implementation types, disciplines, and assessment levels. *Interdisciplinary Journal of Problem-Based Learning, 3*(1), 6-28.

Author Contact Information: Rebecca Fredrickson, EdD, Texas Woman's University. Phone: 940-898-2238. E-mail: RFredrickson@mail.twu.edu

CHAPTER 19

Cultural-Historical Activity Theory

Patrick M. Jenlink
Stephen F. Austin State University

Cultural-historical psychology, as a theory of psychology, was founded by L. S. Vygotsky at the end of the 1920s and developed by his students and followers in Eastern Europe and worldwide. Cultural psychology, an interdisciplinary field, emerged at the interface of anthropology, psychology, and linguistics. Its aim, in part, has been that of examining ethnic and cultural sources of psychological diversity in relation to emotional functioning, moral reasoning, social cognition and human development (Holland & Cole, 1995). A central thesis of cultural psychology, originating in the Russian cultural-historical school of thought (Valisner, 1988) is "that structure and development of human psychological processes emerge through culturally mediated, historically developing, practical activity" (Cole, 1996, p. 108). In his conceptualizing a second cultural psychology, Cole elected to bring cultural artifacts, both ideal and material, to the foreground of understanding learning. In this perspective, artifacts are viewed as products of human history, situated socially and culturally: culture is moved to the center in relation to artifact-mediated action within human activity systems. Explicating his theoretical perspective of cultural psychology, Cole was concerned with a conception of culture adequate to the theories and practices related to an artifact mediated perspective of learning as activity, adopting an activity theory framework to further elaborate his cultural-historical notion of learning.

A retrospective examination of the intellectual roots of cultural-historical psychology extend back to eighteenth and nineteenth century German philosophy (particularly Kant to Hegel), the sociological and economic writings of Marx and Engels (specifically *Theses on Feuerbach* and *The German Ideology*) (Tolman, 2001) and most directly to the research of Lev Semyonovich Vygotsky and his colleagues Alexander Romanovich Luria and Alexei Nikolaevich Leont'ev (Chaiklin, 2001). Marx (1945) framed the principle that praxis, everyday activity, produces and transforms the material and social world. Marx also put forward the claim that the interaction between human beings and the material world is dynamic, cumulative, and transformative (Volosinov, 1973). Cultural-historical psychology seeks relational, historical, and nondualist ways of reconceptualizing "learning" and "behavior" as "development" and "practice." Within education broadly, cultural-historical psychology has stimulated a shift from a focus on brain-local cognitive function to an appreciation of human developmental processes as interrelated with and contingent upon historical, cultural, institutional, and discursive contexts.

In the field of cultural psychology, cultural-historical activity theory (CHAT) is associated with the writings of the Russian "troika," Lev Semyonovich Vygotsky (Reiber, 1997; Reiber & Carton, 1987, 1993; Reiber & Wollack, 1997; Vygotsky, 1934/1962, 1978), Alexei Nikolaevich Leont'ev (1978, 1981a, 1981b, 1982) and Alexander Romanovich Luria (1932, 1961, 1966, 1976, 1979a, 1979b; Luria & Tsvetkova, 1990). Western interest in CHAT began with the English translations of Vygotsky's works, *Thought and Language* (1934/1962), *The Psychology of Art* (1971), and *Mind in Society* (1978). *The Concept of Activity in Soviet Psychology* (Wertsch, 1981) introduced many western scholars to seminal concepts.

A distinctive notion of CHAT is that learning is mediated within/by culture and its products/artifacts. Learning is also understood as being historical and having social origins. Suggested as a main discipline to the cultural-historical psychology approach is human activity that is constructive. As summarized by Davydov (1995), "the genuine, deep determinants of human activity, consciousness and personality lie in the historically developing culture, embodied in various sign and symbol systems" (p. 15). Cultural-historical theory, then, suggests that individuals engage in goal-directed activities within cultural contexts while relying on "oth-

The Handbook of Educational Theories, pp. 219–236

ers" who are more experienced, and using artifacts to mediate learning.

CHAT has experienced three generational shifts in its theoretical foundation. In its origin, CHAT was conceived of as a concrete psychology immersed in everyday praxis (Vygotsky, 1989). It was over seven decades ago that Vygotsky (1934/1962) posited that psychology was in a state of crisis because of the "atomistic and functional modes of analysis ... [that] treated psychic processes in isolation" (p. 1). Specifically, he pointed out that the separation of intellect and affect

> as subjects of study [was] a major weakness of traditional psychology, since it [made] the thought process appear as an autonomous flow of "thoughts thinking themselves," segregated from the fullness of life, from the personal need and interests, the inclinations and impulses of the thinker. (p. 10)

These analytic challenges remained unresolved for years, leading Vygotsky's student Leont'ev (1978) to continue expressing dissatisfaction over the eclectic state of psychology.

Vygotsky developed what is referred to as first-generation activity theory. It was further developed, substantially by two of his students, Luria and Leont'ev, to incorporate societal, cultural, and historical dimensions into an explication of human mental functioning (Eilam, 2003; Stetsenko, 2003), leading to what constituted the second-generation activity theory. Whereas Vygotsky formulated practical human labor activity as a general explanatory category of psychology, he did not fully clarify the nature of this category. It was left to Leont'ev to make historically evolving object-practical activity the fundamental unit of analysis and the explanatory principle that determines the genesis, structure, and contents of the human mind. By taking the practical labor activity as coextensive with cognition, it is the work of the latter that is recognized as the cornerstone for present forms of activity theory, together with its broader application to classroom learning, linguistics, and speech act theory (Langner, 1984). Engeström (1996a, 1996b, 2001) describes a third-generation activity theory that is concerned with applications of activity systems in developmental research, wherein activity systems is introduced with minimally two interacting activity systems included. The third-generation model of activity theory places emphasis on multiple perspectives distributed across networks of intersecting activity systems.

CHAT—Goals, Assumptions, and Aspects

CHAT is a psychological metatheory or theoretical framework, with its philosophical and theoretical roots in the early work of Vygotsky's cultural-historical psychology. Building on the tradition of Vygotsky, Leont'ev and Luria evolved much of the foundation for the current generation of CHAT. Contemporary theorists and researchers propose that activity is the appropriate unit of analysis for observing and explaining learning and development. Activity is defined by the cultural-historical interpretations of roles, goals, tools, and other means of participating in institutional contexts (Wertsch, 1985a, 1985b). Among the different units of analysis that have been presented are mediated action (Wertsch, 1991, 1994), activity or event (Rogoff, 1990, 1994), activity system, (Cole & Engeström, 1993), and activity setting (Tharp & Gallimore, 1988). Although these researchers define units differently, there is commonality in their use of the term *activity*, which they agree is the point for inquiry and simultaneously the basic context in which learning and development occur.

Goal of CHAT

CHAT examines human behavior and consciousness in terms of activity systems, which represent goal-directed, historically-situated, cooperative human interactions. The goal of activity theory may be concisely stated as understanding the mental capabilities of a single individual. However, activity theory rejects the isolated individual as an insufficient unit of analysis, rather it analyzes the cultural and technical aspects of human actions (Bertelsen & Bødker, 2002). Expanding on the nature of understanding mental capabilities, activity theory serves as a theoretical/analytical framework to describe actions in a sociotechnical system through six related elements (Engeström, 1987) of a conceptual system (see Figure 19.2 that follows later for a graphic representation of the six elements):

- ***Object-orientedness***. The object (objective or goal or common task) of the activity system refers not only to persons or objects in a passive state (what is acted upon) but also to the goal of an intentional activity. Object refers to the objectivness of the reality; items are considered objective according to natural sciences but also have social and cultural properties.
- ***Subject or internalization***. Individuals engaged in the activities; the traditional notion of mental processes. Internalization, change in human behavior and consciousness, individual or collective, is mediated by other human beings through the use of tools. Internalization of external experiences is derived from social interactions that are mediated through use of tools and artifacts, and, as such, internalization is simultaneously an individual and social process.

- *Community or externalization.* Externalization is an individual and social process through which the application of schemas and cognitive processes work to create/transform existing semiotic, ideal/conceptual, and material artifacts, and animate learning. Within the cultural-historical context of community, individuals as actors/members of a community engage in activities that are part of large human activity systems.
- *Tool or artifact mediation.* The artifacts (tools, semiotic systems, or concepts) used by individuals in the system mediate social interaction and learning. Mediational tools/artifacts influence human-structure interactions, changing with accumulating experience. In addition to physical and social change, knowledge also evolves. Tools are influenced by culture, and their use is a way for the accumulation and transmission of social knowledge. Tools influence both the agents and the structure. Mediational means (tools) may consist not only of tools in the usual sense (hammers, computers) but also semiotic tools: speaking and writing, as well as gestures, music, architecture, physical position, naturally occurring objects, and so on (Engeström, 1990; Smagorinsky & Coppock, 1994).
- *Division of labor.* Within the external, community of practice, there is a social strata, or hierarchical structure of activity that reflects a division of labor within and across activities according to the individuals in the activity system. Community members divide work related tasks, differentiating tasks often based on skill and proficiency with respect to tools and mediational artifacts.
- *Rules.* Sociocultural conventions, guidelines and rules regulating activities in the system reflect cultural norms. Rules shape the interactions of subject and tools with the object (objective or goal) within the activity system. It is important to note that rules are forms of cultural artifacts that change as the human activity system changes and evolves according to the needs with the community of practice.

Activity theory helps explain how social artifacts and social organization mediate social action, and therein the demonstration of mental capacities of individuals.

Basic Assumptions of CHAT

Activity theory is a philosophical framework and descriptive tool focusing on understanding human activity and work practices. Premised, in part, on the anthropological and psychological theory of Leont'ev (1978) and Vygotsky (1978), CHAT acknowledges the sociocultural origin and nature of human subjectivity (i.e., broadly conceived human psychological processes that include cognition, self-regulation, emotion and self). Emerging from a rich, extensive body of theoretical work a number of assumptions have been identified that help to understand CHAT (Brown & Cole, 2002; Cole, 1988, 1995a, 1995b, 1996, 1998; Cole & Engeström, 1993; Cole & Scribner, 1981; Davydov, 1975a, 1975b, 1995; Davydov & Markova, 1983; Engeström, 1987, 1990, 1991a, 1991b, 1996a, 1996b, 1996c, 2001; Engeström & Miettinen, 1999; Engeström, Engeström, & Suntio, 2002; Engeström, Miettinen, & Punamäki, 1999; Griffin & Cole, 1984; Kuutti, 1996; Lave, 1988; Lave & Wenger, 1991; Leont'ev, 1975, 1978, 1981a, 1981b; Luria, 1932, 1961, 1966, 1976, 1979a, 1979b; Nardi, 1996a, 1996b; Newman, Griffin, & Cole, 1984; Reiber, 1997; Reiber & Carton, 1987, 1993; Reiber & Wollack, 1997; Ratner, 2002, 2006; Smagorinsky & Coppock, 1994; Stetsenko & Arievitch, 2004; Vygotsky, 1934/1962, 1978, 1981, 1989; Vygotsky & Luria, 1993; Wertsch, 1985a, 1985b, 1991, 1994; Wenger, 1998; Wertsch & Bivens, 1992; Wertsch & Rupert, 1993). Following are eight of the core assumptions that inform our understanding of CHAT.

Human Activity Is Object-Oriented

Activity it is directed towards a physical or conceptual object, which is manipulated or transformed by the activity. It is the object of activity and not the goal that allows distinguishing different activities from one another.

Activities Are Mediated

Activities are always mediated by tools and signs, which are constitutive elements of the activity. From simple material instruments to more complex ones, such as human knowledge and technological know-how, tools reflect ways of mastering specific classes of tasks experienced in collaborative or community-based practices. Tools and signs are mediators, which range from material tools over less tangible artifacts like plans and spreadsheets to scientific theories and languages. Tools capture and preserve the socially shared knowledge developed in a given community and mediate the subjects' relation with the object of the activity as well as with other human beings (Leont'ev, 1978; Stahl, 2003).

Activities Are Shaped by Context

Activities are shaped by contextual conditions and circumstances. The subject has to continuously adapt its actions and operations to external events and circumstances. As a consequence human activity is guided but not predefined and determined by the plans of those engaged in the activity (Bardram, 1997). The variability of contextual conditions and circumstances inevitably results in a variation of the way the activity is carried out and can result in the evolution of the activity system if improper variations are selected and proper variations stabilized (Scheunpflug, 2001).

Relationships Are Reciprocal

The relationship between subjects, objects, and tools is reciprocal. These elements are mutually interdependent, which means that a change in one of them will inevitably alter the other ones. In this sense the constituents of an activity form a system where each component is defined in relation to the other components.

Activities Are Hierarchically Structured

According to (Leont'ev, 1978) three levels of activities can be distinguished, namely collective activities which are carried out on a communal level often involving multiple actors, actions that are performed by a single subject to achieve a certain goal relevant to the collective activity, and operations in the form of fine grained automated routines. But even though activities are structured hierarchically the relation between operations and actions as well as actions and activities is not an additive one (Leont'ev, 1978). Therefore it is not possible to simply decompose an activity into a set of actions.

Activities Evolve

Activities are never static but evolve when contradictions or tensions emerge between the elements in an activity system. Human activity whether carried out by an individual or collectively cannot be detached from its social context as its meaning is bound to its interpretation within a collective.

Historical Origins of Self

The historical origins of self and social interactions are situated in collective or communal practices of material or artifact production. The primacy of material production interprets as the richness and agency of human subjectivity need to keep in sight their ultimate origination from and embededness in material processes of human practice (Leont'ev, 1978; Stetsenko & Arievitch, 2004, p. 483).

Nonreductionist Ontology

CHAT is nonreductionist in nature, that is, CHAT understands human nature and development as rooted in material social practices. These practices are viewed as both producing and engendering social interactions and human subjectivity and simultaneously are themselves reciprocally produced by these interactions and subjectivity (Stetsenko & Arievitch, 2004, p. 476).

Aspects (Principles) of CHAT

Drawing again from the work of cultural-historical activity researchers and theorists a set of principles can be identified that build upon the basic assumptions previously outlined

(Brown & Cole, 2002; Cole, 1988, 1995a, 1995b, 1996, 1998; Cole & Engeström, 1993; Cole & Scribner, 1981; Davydov, 1975a, 1975b, 1995; Davydov & Markova, 1983; Engeström, 1987, 1990, 1991a, 1991b, 1996a, 1996b, 1996c, 2001; Engeström & Miettinen, 1999a, 1999b; Engeström, Engeström, & Suntio, 2002; Engeström, Miettinen, & Punamäki, 1999; Griffin & Cole, 1984; Kuutti, 1996; Lave, 1988; Lave & Wenger, 1991; Nardi, 1996a, 1996b; Newman et al., 1984; Reiber, 1997; Reiber & Carton, 1987, 1993; Reiber & Wollack, 1997; Leont'ev, 1975, 1978, 1981a, 1981b; Luria, 1932, 1961, 1966, 1976, 1979; Ratner, 2002, 2006; Smagorinsky & Coppock, 1994; Stetsenko & Arievitch, 2004; Vygotsky, 1934/1962, 1978, 1981, 1989; Vygotsky & Luria, 1993; Wertsch, 1985a, 1985b, 1991, 1994; Wertsch & Bivens, 1992; Wertsch & Rupert, 1993).

The principles of CHAT can be divided into two subsets, one that reflects the earlier work of cultural psychologists and theorists forward up to what is considered to be second-generation CHAT, and one that reflects third generation CHAT principles. In each subset, the principles illuminate key insights from cultural-historical activity theorists. It is noted that the first subset of principles (first-second generation CHAT) do not exclude the second subset of principles (third generation CHAT), rather the second subset build upon the first.

First Generation Principles

The first generation activity theorists laid the foundation for what was to evolve as CHAT under the guidance of Leont'ev and Luria. The principles aligned with first generation reflect the early work of Vygotsky (1978) and Leont'ev (1978).

- Consciousness emerges out of socially organized practical activity (labor), the intentional goal-directed activity of humans who possess the ability to reflect on their progress toward the attainment of their goals. Engaging in the labor of practical activity, human beings use instrumental and psychological tools to transform material objects, such as lumber and stone, and ideal objects, such as plans, into socially valued outcomes. In doing so, they transform their own physical characteristics and thinking processes.

- Social processes give rise to individual processes. Rather than emerging from within the individual, cognitive activity has a cultural and social origin. In the beginning stages of development, the purposeful acts of the individual are accomplished through the joint activity of the learner and another person performing together as a working social system (Luria, 1932). Vygotsky's (1978) general law of cultural development poses that higher order thinking processes appear on two planes, first between people on the interpsychological plane, then within the individual on the intrapsychological plane.
- The zone of proximal development (ZPD) accounts for movement between the interpsychological and intrapsychological planes. This is the distance between learning and development as a result of independent problem solving and potential learning and development as a result of problem solving under adult or more capable peer guidance (Vygotsky, 1978). The processual mechanism for activity in the ZPD is internalization/externalization (Leont'ev, 1987; Vygotsky, 1978; Wertsch & Stone, 1985): For individuals and groups, moments of external activity transform internal cognitive processes and knowledge structures and moments of internal activity organize and regulate external social processes. Given these ideas, a central issue for teacher preparation is how computers and telecommunications can be used to co-construct individual and group ZPDs and mediate internalization/externalization processes.
- Consciousness evolves through tool-mediated activity that unites the mind with the real world of objects and events (Cole, 1995a, 1995b, 1996; Ilyenkov, 1977a, 1977b, 1982). Vygotsky (1978) appropriated Marx's idea of material tools, adding a psychological tool. Material tools or instruments are directed outward and bring about external effects on material objects. Psychological tools, such as language, number systems, plans, and concepts, on the other hand, are aimed inward and outward, producing internal effects on both individuals and social groups. For individuals, the effects are self-regulation and the regulation of others, for social groups shared thinking, negotiated meaning and practices. Cole (1996) adds that tools carry the reified social practices, cognitive activities, and codes for how they were used by their creators, mediating a connection between the user and the culture of prior generations. From the perspective of teacher preparation, a vital question is how do computers and telecommunications mediate learning activity and affect thinking processes of individuals and social processes of groups.
- There is a distinction between scientific and spontaneous concepts (Vygotsky, 1978). Each kind of concept has different origins and courses of acquisition. Scientific concepts, such as the scientific knowledge on teaching, are systemically organized bodies of knowledge, are flexible and can be generalized to contexts other than the one in which they are acquired. Concepts of this kind are embedded in cultural systems and transmitted through formal schooling. We are consciously aware of the scientific concepts we possess; we think with and apply them intentionally. Because scientific concepts are linguistic entities, they are acquired through verbal explanation, and become contextualized as they move "downward" and are applied to spontaneous objects and events. Spontaneous concepts are acquired in the course of participation in the activities in which they are typically used. Spontaneous concepts are less flexible and are limited in their application to the situated context in which they are acquired. Spontaneous concepts begin with a grasp of concrete events and phenomena and develop as they move upward and are integrated into formal knowledge systems.

Second-Generation Principles

The second-generation of activity reflects the evolution forward as CHAT emerged more in its contemporary theoretical aspects. As an evolving theory, there are several basic principles shared by its proponents. The principles are transitional, moving forward form first-generation activity theory. It is important to note that the second-generation principles do not replace first-generation principles; rather they clarify and advance understanding of cultural-historical psychology and therein CHAT.

- Human behavior is social in origin, and human activity is collective. Human-computer interactions are also social in origin.
- Human consciousness—"mind"—grows out of people's joint activity with shared tools. Individual minds are in a sense coconstructed and distributed among others. One's thoughts, words, and actions are always potentially engaged with the thoughts, words, and actions of others. Through involvement in collective activity, however widely distributed, learners are always in contact with the history, values, and social relations of a community—or among communities—as embedded in the shared cultural tools used by that community(ies).
- Activity theory emphasizes tool-mediated action in context. Human beings not only act on their environment with tools, they also think and learn with tools. At a primary level these tools are material, "external"—hammers, books, clothing, computers, social networks (advancing the concept of external-

ization). But as humans we also fashion and use tools at a secondary or "internal" level—language, concepts, scripts, schemas (advancing the concept of internalization). Both kinds of tools are used to act on the environment collectively (Wartofsky 1979). This suggests that distributed learning must take into account *all* the tools members of a community use, as well as the relations among tools—both "external" and "internal"—of variant kinds as they mediate collective activity.

- Activity theory is interested in development and change, which it understands broadly to include historical change, individual development, and moment-to-moment change.
- Activity theory grounds analysis in everyday life events, the ways people interact with each other using tools over time.
- Activity theory assumes that individuals, within a community, are agential or active agents in their own self-development, acting in variant experiential settings not always of their own choosing. Individual learners learn, of course, but they do so in environments that involve others, environments of people-with-tools that both afford and constrain their actions.
- Activity theory, as Cole (1996) states, "rejects cause and effect, stimulus response, explanatory science in favor of a science that emphasizes the emergent nature of mind in activity and that acknowledges a central role for interpretation in its explanatory framework" (p. 104).

THIRD GENERATION PRINCIPLES

Engeström (1993, 1995, 1999a, 1996b, 2000, 2001) has set forth five principles that build upon the earlier principles (first and second generation) and define, in large part, third-generation CHAT. It is instructive to quote extensively from Engeström (2001, pp. 136-137) in stating these principles.

- *First principle.* A collective, artifact-mediated and object-oriented activity system, seen in its network relations to other activity systems, is taken as the prime unit of analysis. Goal-directed individual and group actions, as well as automatic operations, are relatively independent but subordinate units of analysis, eventually understandable only when interpreted against the background of entire activity systems. Activity systems realize and reproduce themselves by generating actions and operations (Engeström, 2001, p. 136).
- *Second principle.* Activity systems are multivoiced. An activity system is always a community of multiple points of view, traditions and interests. The division of labor in an activity creates different positions for the participants, the participants carry their own diverse histories, and the activity system itself carries multiple layers and strands of history engraved in its artifacts, rules and conventions. The multivoicedness is multiplied in networks of interacting activity systems. It is a source of trouble and a source of innovation, demanding actions of translation and negotiation (Engeström, 2001, p. 136).
- *Third principle.* Activity systems are subject to historicity. Activity systems take shape and get transformed over lengthy periods of time. Their problems and potentials can only be understood against their own history. History itself needs to be studied as local history of the activity and its objects, and as history of the theoretical ideas and tools that have shaped the activity. Thus, medical work needs to be analyzed against the history of its local organization and against the more global history of the medical concepts, procedures and tools employed and accumulated in the local activity (Engeström, 2001, pp. 136-137).
- *Fourth principle.* Contradictions have a central role as sources of change and development. Contradictions are not the same as problems or conflicts. Contradictions are historically accumulating structural tensions within and between activity systems. The primary contradiction of activities in capitalism is that between the use value and exchange value of commodities. This primary contradiction pervades all elements of our activity systems. Activities are open systems. When an activity system adopts a new element from the outside (for example, a new technology or a new object), it often leads to an aggravated secondary contradiction where some old element (for example, the rules or the division of labor) collides with the new one. Such contradictions generate disturbances and conflicts, but also innovative attempts to change the activity (Engeström, 2001, p. 137).
- *Fifth principle.* There is a possibility of expansive transformations in activity systems. Activity systems move through relatively long cycles of qualitative transformations. As the contradictions of an activity system are aggravated, some individual participants begin to question and deviate from its established norms. In some cases, this escalates into collaborative envisioning and a deliberate collective change effort. An expansive transformation is accomplished when the object and motive of the activity are reconceptualized to embrace a radically wider horizon of possibilities than in the previous mode of the activity (Engeström, 2001, p. 137).

Original Development and Major Contributors to the Theory

CHAT (first termed activity theory AT) evolved from the work of Alexei Nikolaevich Leont'ev, at Moscow State Lomonosov University during the 1960s, based largely on Lev Semyonovich Vygotsky's particular theories of cognition and learning. In more recent years the implications of activity theory in organizational development have been promoted through the work of Yrjö Engeström's team at the Centre for Activity Theory and Developmental Work Research at the University of Helsinki, and Mike Cole at the Laboratory of Comparative Human Cognition at the University of California San Diego campus. The developmental focus is on how individuals develop understandings of the real world, draw meanings from that understanding, create learnings from those meanings and are motivated to respond to those learnings. These cognitive "mental models" correspond to how individuals think about the real world and engage with it, not necessarily how the world actually works in a physical or biological sense.

Activity theory and its development, while originating within the cultural-historical tradition of Soviet psychology, is credited largely to Leont'ev (1979, 1981a, 1981b). Leont'ev evolved Vygotsky's formulation of mediation: how practical activity shapes and is shaped by cognitive functioning. A growing international community has developed around this theory and excellent analyses of its intellectual origins are available in the work of several scholarly domains, including education (Engeström & Miettinen, 1999a, 1999b), cultural psychology (Ratner, 2006), human-computer interaction (Kaptelinin & Nardi, 2006; Kuutti, 1996) and information science (Wilson, 2006).

CHAT, as it has evolved as a third-generation activity theory, is grounded in the work of Yrjö Engeström and his Developmental Work Research program at the University of Helsinki. Engström and his colleagues drew on the mediational theories of Leont'ev (1978) and Vygotsky (1978). In its evolution, CHAT reflects a theoretical position of the socially distributed activity system as the fundamental unit of analysis. Activity becomes the least meaningful context for understanding individual actions, but at a higher level it can be used to describe and evaluate systemic interactions and relationships. In this approach, the activity system is composed of "the individual practitioner, the colleagues and coworkers of the workplace community, the conceptual and practical tools and the shared objects as a unified dynamic whole" (Engeström, 1991a, p. 267). The systemic view of activity posits that each element is related to all other elements dialectically; that is, they are distinct yet interdependent (Ratner 2002, 2006).

Important contributors to CHAT include Karl Marx, Lev Semyonovich Vygotsky, Alexei Nikolaevich Leont'ev, Alexander Romanovich Luria, Michael Cole, and Yrjö Engeström. Each theorists will be discussed in the remaining paragraphs to this section.

Karl Marx

Activity theory is philosophically rooted in Karl Marx's (1945) concept of reality as "sensuous human activity, practice," explicated in his *Theses on Feuerbach* (pp. 659-660). Engeström and Miettinen (1999a) argued that in the first and third theses, Marx showed that "the concept of activity opens up a new way to understand change.... The key is 'revolutionary practice,' which is not to be understood in narrowly political terms but as joint 'practical-critical' activity" (p. 3). Marx also pointed out that activity is always riddled with internal contradictions, which are the driving force of history; in capitalism, the contradiction between the use value and exchange value pervades all activities.

Lev Semyonovich Vygotsky

Vygotsky is credited with creating the foundation of cultural-historical psychology, based on the concept of mediation. Human action is not a direct response to the environment—it is mediated by culturally meaningful tools and signs which make the human being able to control him- or herself from the outside. Collaboration with other humans creates zones of proximal development for individuals, enabling them to go beyond their current capacity by grasping and constructing new mediating tools and signs. According to Vygotsky, to uncover human potential, we must first conduct formative experiments, which induce zones of proximal development. Vygotsky, argued: "The social dimension of consciousness is primary in time and in fact. The individual dimension of consciousness is derivative and secondary" (Vygotsky, 1979, p. 30, cited in Wertsch & Bivens, 1992). From this perspective, mental functioning of the individual is not simply derived from social interaction; rather, the specific structures and processes revealed by individuals can be traced to their interactions with others. Vygotsky distinguished between two lines of development—the natural line of development and the cultural line of development. Vygotsky initially advanced a model that included a subject and his or her object of activity. The subject cannot act directly on the object but rather employs tool mediation to carry out cognitive functions. The diagram often used to illustrate this relationship is the basic triangle. In Vygotsky's work, tool mediation, located at the vertex of the triangle, affords and constrains cognition. The common reformulation of Vygotsky's model of mediated action is depicted in Figure 19.1 (see also Engeström, 1999). The

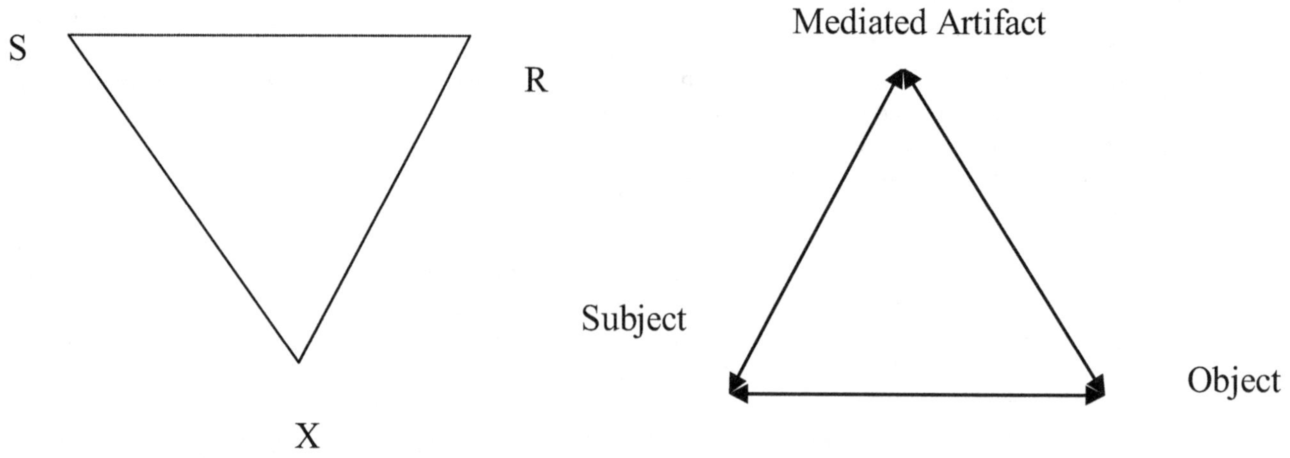

Figure 19.1. (A) Vygotsky's model of mediated act and (B) its common reformulation.

first generation of activity theory was centered on Vygotsky's idea of mediation. Figure 19.1A represents mediation, in which the conditioned direct connection between stimulus (S) and response (R) was transcended by "a complex mediated act." Vygotsky's idea of cultural mediation of action is more commonly expressed in contemporary work as the triad of subject, object, and mediating artifact (Figure 19.1B).

Vygotsky formulated "the genetic law of cultural development" according to which the child's cultural development appears twice or on two planes (Vygotsky, 1981, p. 163). First it appears interpsychologically, in interaction between people, and secondly within the child as an intrapsychological achievement. For Vygotsky, "Social relations or relations of people genetically underlie all higher functions and their relations" (p. 163).

Vygotsky (1978) used the concept of internalization to explain how individuals processed what they learned through mediated action to develop individual consciousness through social interactions. In his explanation of internalization, he stated: "Every function in a child's cultural development appears twice: first, on the social level, and later, on the individual level: first *between* people (*interpsychological*), and then *inside* the child (*intrapsychological*)" (p. 57). Following Vygotsky's foundational work, the cultural-historical theoretical approach has been very much a discourse of vertical development toward "higher psychological functions."

Alexei Nikolaevich Leont'ev

Leont'ev developed Vygotsky's notions of mediated social processes into what is known as activity theory. He formulated the concept of activity as a systemic formation and unit of analysis for human sciences. His work helped to formulate the elements of a second generation of activity theoretical development. Leont'ev distinguished between actions, operations, and activity. Actions, he proposed, are conscious, tool-mediated, and goal-oriented, whereas operations are routinized and therefore unconscious components of actions subject to concrete conditions. Operations are "the methods for accomplishing actions" (Leont'ev, 1978, p. 65). An activity is a molar unit that manifests itself in actions. While operations and actions are discussed as the constituent characteristics of an activity, Leont'ev maintained that they must not be conceptualized as special "units" that are included in the structure of the activity, because "human activity does not exist except in the form of action or a chain of actions.... If the actions that constitute activity are mentally subtracted from it, then absolutely nothing will be left of activity" (Leont'ev, 1978, p. 64). He believed that to understand and facilitate development, it was necessary to study and change entire collective activity systems, their objects and motives, not just isolated actions and skills.

Alexander Romanovich Luria

Luria was interested in Utopian socialism and, particularly, the problem of change: What was the source of ideas about society? How can one use such ideas to bring about social change? His social thinking was, from the beginning, focused on the individual. How can the individual be linked to larger social units? Luria demonstrated that individuals' ways of thinking and reasoning are indeed culturally mediated and change when ways of life undergo historical transformations. He also showed that our brain is a flexible organ, which, working together with cultural tools and signs, enables us to remediate our activities even when we are seriously impaired by injury.

In the early 1930s Luria undertook a pioneering study in Soviet Central Asia to grasp the historical transformation of human psychological functions under the influence of changing psychological tools. Luria (1976) showed that implementation of written language and logico-mathematical operations, typically connected to formal schooling, had significant influence on how people categorized objects of the environment.

Luria made advances in many areas, including cognitive psychology, the processes of learning and forgetting, and mental retardation. One of Luria's most important studies charted the way in which damage to specific areas of the brain affect behavior. Today, Luria is honored as the father of neuropsychology.

Michael Cole

Cole demonstrated that in activity theory there is a need to understand the simultaneous coexistence and interaction of various different cultures and activities—not just the historical evolution of a single culture. Michael Cole (1988; see also Griffin & Cole, 1984) was one of the first to clearly point out the deep-seated insensitivity of the second-generation activity theory toward cultural diversity. Cole is recognized for his theoretical work in cultural psychology, advancing Vygotsky's earlier work with respect to cultural psychology.

Central to Cole's elaboration of cultural psychology is the notion of artifacts and the mediation of human behavior. Advancing on the Russian cultural-historical conception of tool-mediated action (Leont'ev, 1978; Vygotsky, 1978), Cole situated tool-use within a larger conception of artifact-based mediation. Much like Dewey, Cole defines an artifact as a cultural object that is modified over the course of human history for the purposes of goal-directed behavior. For Cole (1996), artifacts are simultaneously ideal (i.e., conceptual) and material: Artifacts "are ideal in that their material form has been shaped by their participation in the interactions of which they were previously a part and which they mediate the present" (p. 117). As Cole explains, all artifacts embody a cultural purpose- an ideal form- that is made concrete in their particular design and application. Whether we consider physical artifacts such as tables or abstract artifacts such as language, it is the purpose-driven manufacture of these artifacts that gives them significance.

Yrjö Engeström

Engeström (1987, 1990) built upon Vygotsky and Leont'ev's work, and other theorists, in developing the concept of activity as a unit of analysis. Based on Vygotsky's requirements, Engeström elucidated a definition of activity as a unit of analysis that fulfills the following demands: it is representative of the complexity of the whole, it is analyzable in its contextuality, it is specific to human beings by being culturally mediated, and it is dynamic rather than static. Engeström critiqued Leont'ev on the basis that the instrumental and communicative aspects of activity were not brought into a unified complex model; that is, Leont'ev did not extend Vygotsky's basic triangular model (subject-object-mediator) to account for social relations. Engeström expanded the unit of activity to include three additional components that explicate the social structure of activity: (a) rules that regulate the subject's actions toward an object, and relations with other participants in the activity; (b) the community of people who share a interest in and involvement with the same object; and (c) the division of labor – what is being done by whom toward the object, including both the relatively horizontal division of tasks and the vertical division of power, positions, access to resources, and rewards. this expanded unit is referred to as an activity system by Engeström and his colleagues (see Figure 19.2.) The top triangle presents Vygotsky's original mediated action. In articulating an activity system, Engeström demonstrates in the lower right and left triangles, respectively, the interactions within the system. The limitation of the first generation of activity, as Engeström (2001) notes, was the unit of analysis remained individually focused. With the expansion of Vygotsky's mediation idea, Leont'ev envision the difference between individual and collective activity. Engeström's model in Figure 19.2 demonstrates how mediated activity is expansive into the community, and in relation to the differentiation of labor.

Engeström's model of CHAT as a third generation of theory, makes possible the analysis of a multitude of relations within the triangular structure of activity. In activity theory terms, one or more members of a group engaged in collective activity at any given moment may be viewed as a subject engaging the object of the activity through a particular action.

Critiques of the Theory

Ratner (1997) notes that while activity theorists know that activity has particular social characteristics, they often fail to analyze the manner in which the latter comprise psychological characteristics. Instead, activity theorists commonly treat activity as having intrinsic general characteristics. Reading, writing, attending school, and communicating are portrayed as activities that have an intrinsic, general character apart from particular social systems. The manner in which tools mediate psychological processes is also described quite generally. Tools are said to foster planning, deliberation, and self-control because one uses an instrument to accomplish a goal instead of achieving it directly. Such

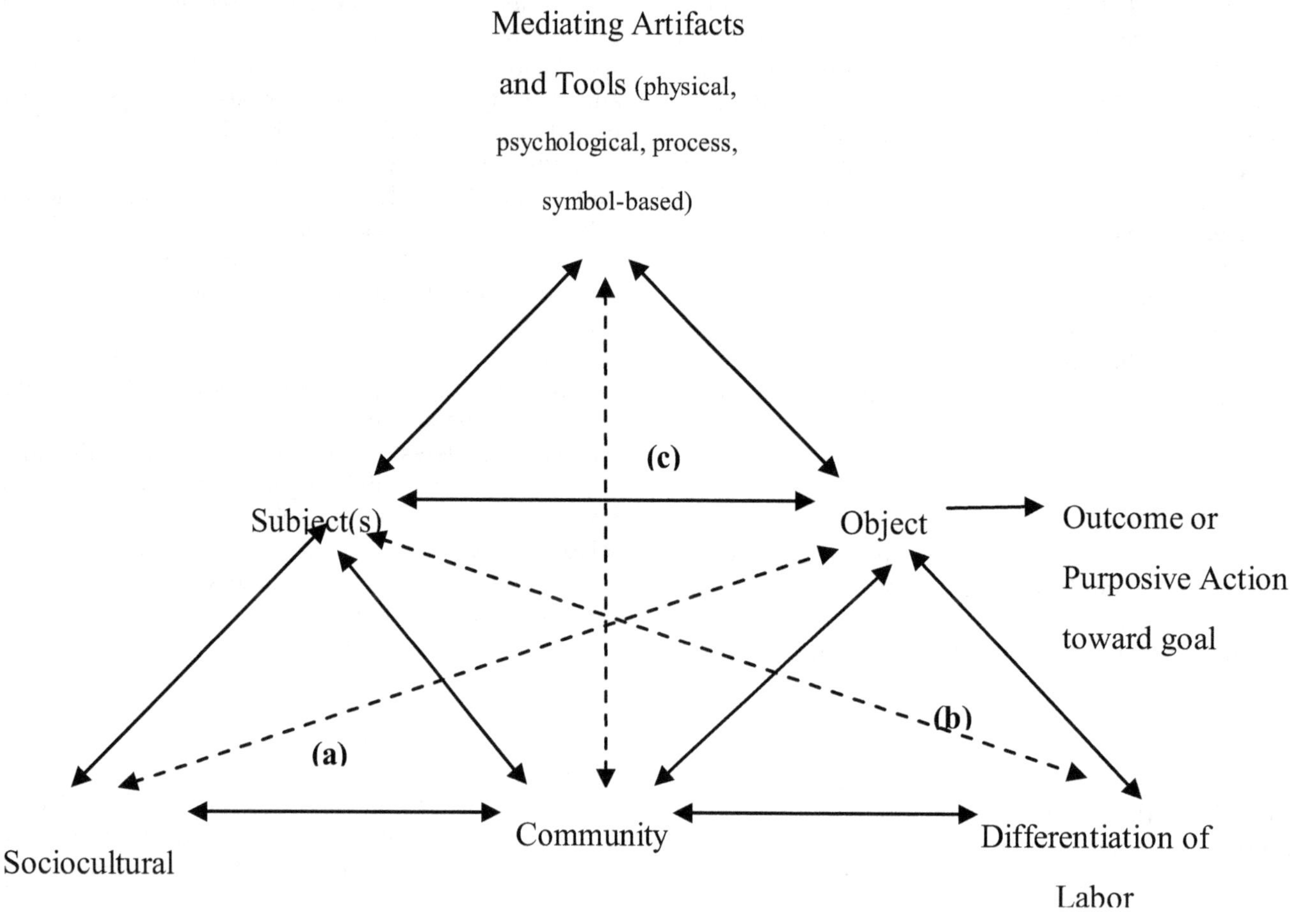

Source: Adapted from Engeström (1987) and Cole and Engeström (1993).

Figure 19.2. The structure of a human activity system.

a general description overlooks the particular features and functions of instruments, which reflect the needs of particular social activities.

Aaro Toomela (2000, 2008) has offered two works, which critically assess the contents and potential of activity theory. According to Toomela, there are five fatal faults in activity theory:

1. It relies on unidirectional instead of a dialectical view of culture-individual relationships.
2. It focuses on analyses of activities without taking into account the individual involved in the activity at the same time.
3. It underestimates the role of signs and the importance of focusing on sign meaning.
4. It approaches mind fragmentally, without understanding the holistic nature of mind.
5. It is fundamentally a developmental and therefore not appropriate for understanding emerging phenomena, including mind.

Countering the arguments set forth by Toomela (2000, 2008) is the increasing number of theorists advancing activity theory and in particular CHAT (Cole & Engeström, 1993; Cole & Scribner, 1981; Engeström, 1987, 1990, 1991a, 1991b, 2001; Engeström & Miettinen, 1999; Engeström, Engeström, & Suntio, 2002; Engeström, Miettinen, & Punamäki, 1999; Kuutti, 1996).

Perhaps more telling is a positive critique offered by Nissen (2008) in an article wherein the author examines CHAT in consideration of contemporary critical psychology. Nissen notes that adding to a psychology and ideology critique the positive dimension of "foundational" theory is important. Contemporary critical psychology shares the same problem with the German-Scandinavian theorists that have contributed to the origin of CHAT, where, as Nissen explains, "where quite sketchy general notions of the 'societal formation' of 'bourgeois society' were sometimes considered sufficient to historicize psychological analysis" (p. 11). CHAT attempts to resolve this problematic.

Instruments and Measurements Associated with Situated Cognition

CHAT, as it has evolved as a third-generation activity theory, presents a framework for analysis. That said, it is in the application of CHAT as an analytic framework that researchers and theorists are able further understand the nature of human activity; activity that is characteristic of human activity a first-generation, second-generation, and third-generation sociocultural interactions. The unit analysis in activity systems analysis is the object-centered activity itself (see Figure 19.2) (Engeström, 1987, 2001; Rogoff, 1994; Rogoff, Radziszewska, & Masiello, 1995; Wertsch, 1991; Wertsch, del Rio, & Alvarez, 1995). The instrument of analysis is the CHAT framework, with the framework guiding assessment of each respective element of activity system, and affording an analytic frame for understanding the relationship of the six interacting elements.

Amaro-Jimenez (2008) provides a working model for the use of CHAT as a macroanalytic framework. In her study of Latino students and English as a second language, she used the macrotheoretical framework to examine subject-matter appropriation through technology-mediated activities. Other researchers (Fernandez, 2010; Forbes, 2009; Seaman, 2006) have also used CHAT to guide analysis within activity systems, each adapting the macrotheoretical framework within their respective studies.

Betts (2006), in her research, provides an example of instrumentation with the Perceived Self-Efficacy And Attitude Questionnaire (PSE&A). The PSE&A questionnaire was created to measure perceived self-efficacy, frequency and types of arts experiences, and attitudes towards the arts and related activities were included. There were also literacy skills items to determine student's language abilities.

Code (2010), in her research on agency for learning, developed the Agency for Learning Questionnaire (AFLQ) using item response theory (IRT) to assess agency within the context of student's self-regulation, motivation, and self-efficacy in learning environments. She conducted a study of agency for learning (AFL) with 850 second-year undergraduate chemistry students. Results from the study indicate that agency mediates the effect of various affective-volitional, environmental-social, and cognitive-behavioral processes on academic achievement.

Research Studies Exemplifying CHAT

Within the social sciences, the past decade is hallmarked by an increase in educational research focusing on CHAT, and applications of the theoretical assumptions and principles within and across a number of disciplines. Interestingly, there is a particular increase in applications in the field of technology and education. Concerning educational research studies, within this section a set of five studies are examined that range from 2001 to 2010, denoting paths of evolution in application of CHAT within disciplines including teacher education, arts and multimedia learning, adventure education, English as a Second Language, role negotiation of front-line supervisors in a union setting, and Latino/a parent and family outreach.

- **Blanton, W. E., Simmons, E., & Warner, M. (2001). The fifth dimension: Application of cultural-historical activity theory, inquiry-based learning, computers, and telecommunications to change prospective teachers' preconceptions. *J. Educational Computing Research*, *24*(4), 435-463.**

Blanton, Simmons, and Warner (2001) examine the application of CHAT in understanding the learning of prospective teachers (PSTs). The authors noted that individuals often enter teacher preparation with flawed preconceptions of teaching, learning, and pupils. The specific focus the research study related to a programmatic effort to change PSTs preconceptions by participation in a learning system designed to promote learning interactions mediated through computer technology and telecommunications.

Blanton et al. (2001) predicted that CHAT might prove to be a robust tool for designing technology based learning systems for the preparation of teachers. As well, the authors noted to that teacher preparation occurs within two communities of practice, a college of education and the public schools. In their preliminary research and review of related literature, the authors derived a set of guiding principles used to redesign an introduction to teaching course (CI 2800). Participants for this study were 37 undergraduate PSTs enrolled in two sections of the CI 2800 course. The core activities of CI 2800 were: (a) participating in class devoted to lecture, reading discussion, student presentations; (b) participating in the Fifth Dimension after-school program two times per week; (c) writing detailed field-notes on experiences and observations in the Fifth Dimension; (d) interacting with undergraduates at other campuses about the Fifth Dimension through e-mail and distance learning; and (e) participating in a web-based learning system. A ten-item test was designed to determine attitudes and beliefs toward teaching, learning, and pupils. Data analysis was a comparison of responses on the pretest and posttest and triangulated with articulation from field-notes and notes.

Blanton et al. (2001) note that existing research suggesting that teacher education candidates' preconceptions are impervious to change was challenged by their research. In particular, results of the study suggest that teacher education students who participated in the learning system began to take steps to transform their beliefs about education. This transformation was a movement away from a view of learning as a linear process toward a view of learning as a social process involving the active participation of children.

- **Betts, J. D. (2006). Multimedia arts learning in an activity system: New literacies for at-risk children.** ***International Journal of Education & The Arts*, 7(7).** **Retrieved September 15, 2011, from http://ijea.asu.edu/v7n7/.**

Betts (2006), studied a multi-year after school arts technology program, the Multimedia Arts Education Program (MAEP) for low-income youth sponsored by The Tucson Pima Arts Council (TPAC). This program was designed to meet three objectives: job skills, art technology skills, and multimedia literacy. Initial funding for pilot programs came through the federal Job Partnership Training Act that supported school-to-work training. A five-semester curriculum was developed to introduce multimedia literacies in the electronic arts workplace and provide tools for students to become creators as well as consumers of new literacies. Through the duration of the 6-year study, formative data on an early cohort of participants was collected from students and their parents or guardians. A pre- and posttest questionnaire measured changes in perceived self-efficacy and attitudes about art, technology and learning. This study also looked at long-term effects of participation in MAEP. Program graduates were contacted 4 years later and asked about their high school success (defined as graduation) and career directions. The study findings were reviewed and analyzed using CHAT as a framework for retrospective analysis.

According to Betts (2006), CHAT is a useful framework for analyzing a complex human endeavor in the arts. Activity theory takes human activity as the basic unit of analysis. It focuses on the subject, an individual or group, with an objective, and the mediating tools they use. An activity system exists in the context of a community or culture with a division of labor and rules. Through the artist's efforts the objective is transformed into an outcome. The system moves through time and each change in one aspect is reflected in all the others.

As Betts (2006) notes, MAEP was a learning activity that evolved over time, adjusting to meet the changing needs and abilities of each cohort of students and each new technological affordance that became available. This dynamic aspect of the program lent itself to analysis through CHAT, based on the understanding that human interactions change and evolve over time as conditions in the activity setting are changed.

The study examined students' success in high school, the impact of the program on extended families, and the impact of the program on students' college and/or career goals. An anticipated outcome of MAEP was to encourage new, multimodal, literacies to middle school students. The program was successful for many of the participants, certainly it was for those who completed the five semesters and received a computer along with skills to use it.

- **Seaman, J. (2006). Adventure education as cultural-historical activity theory: A study of experience, learning and social processes in project adventure workshops. (Published doctoral dissertation, Durham, NH, University of New Hampshire, 2006).** ***Dissertation Abstracts International*, 67(05), UMI No. 305279676.**

Seaman (2006), in his dissertation study, examined the way participant learning in adventure experiences intersects with broader social, cultural and institutional contexts. The study was guided by the following questions: How is participant experience constructed in a facilitated, small group adventure setting? How is the construction of the adventure experience related to the intentions and orchestrations of the trainer? How is the construction of the adventure experience related to the institutional and social context in which it occurs? The study used grounded theory methodology (Strauss & Corbin, 1998) and CHAT (Engeström, 1987; Leont'ev, 1978; Vygotsky, 1978).

Activity as an analytic device facilitates the mapping of historical, social and cultural influences on local action, while grounded theory helps maintain close attention to local phenomena. Seaman developed several major concepts. First, he identified the object of adventure education as the morally improved and socially interdependent subject. It is this object that defines and establishes the conditions toward which the activity is oriented and must be understood. Second, he determined that participation frameworks position the subjects as interested actors who negotiate and align with one another through the course of different exercises. As an analytic device, participation frameworks help identify the way subjects expect the workshop to conform with their goals, and act on the basis of their expectations. Third, Seaman established that collaborative ideation is the process through which the object of adventure education is realized. There are two subparts to collaborative ideation: vertically mediated action, or the ways participants' encounters with speech, kinesthetic poses, and physical instruments are orchestrated by the trainer for particular effect; and horizontally mediated action, or the ways participants' become resources for each other's learning. According to Seaman (2006) these factors reflect a complex process of interaction in which participants experience contradictions between the actions required for involvement in the adventure, and the social expectations they have for situations.

- **Amaro-Jimenez, C. (2008). Latino children's English as a Second Language and subject-matter appropriation through technology-mediated activities: A cultural historical activity theory perspective. (Unpublished doctoral dissertation, Cincinnati, OH: University of Cincinnati, 2008).** ***Dissertation Abstracts International, 69*****(08). UMI No. 304666719.**

Amaro-Jimenez (2008), in her dissertation research, focused on Latino children appropriation of English as a Second Language through technology-mediated activities. Specifically, she focused on the implementation of technology-mediated activities (TMA) and what TMA provides third grade language minority children, in general, and Latino children, in particular, with respect to opportunities to appropriate the second language (L2) skills and subject-matter knowledge that they need before the fourth grade slump. The purpose of the study was to investigate how and why the implementation of TMA in public schools provided third grade Latino children with opportunities to appropriate the L2 skills and subject-matter knowledge that they so much need to achieve academic success in public schools in the U.S. Amaro-Jimenez documented the ways in which the TMA implemented provided affordances and constraints to not only the Latino children but to their English as a Second Language (ESL) and content area teachers as well. Furthermore, she investigated the impact that the implementation of such TMA had on the Latino children's academic achievement. The participants in the study were 21 third grade Latino children and six teachers (four content area teachers and two ESL teachers) from three public schools (two urban schools and one suburban school) in the Midwest United States. To achieve the research purpose, Amaro-Jimenez used CHAT as a macrotheoretical framework, supplemented with a concurrent triangulation mixed-method design for data collection and analyses. Data collection techniques included interviews with students and teachers, observations in ESL and content area classrooms, documents and artifacts, think-aloud protocols performed by the children participants in the study, and formative and summative evaluation data.

Findings indicate that the utilization of various kinds of TMA provided the Latino children with opportunities to appropriate both L2 and subject-matter skills and knowledge when these were enacted in and out of their classrooms. To appropriate such skills and knowledge, the third grade Latino children attempted to connect the new knowledge they were learning in the classroom with a vast array of prior and present experiences.

Findings revealed that the affordances and constraints experienced from enacting TMA were dependent on the kind of instructional approach that was used to meet the needs of these Latino learners, on who the agent was, and on where the agent was positioned in the larger context. The impact that enacting the TMA had on the Latino children participants included coconstructing knowledge with more and less knowledgeable others, using their L2 as a semiotic tool to explain their thinking, and activating the children's zone of proximal development, among others.

Furthermore, findings revealed that the Latino children who were mainstreamed and had access to various kinds of TMA in school outperformed those who were pulled out of the regular classroom to receive English language learning instruction and remediation services. Moreover, findings suggest that certain kinds of TMA could be used for "forecasting" the Latino children's performance on achievement tests.

- **Lord, R. J. (2009). Managing contradictions from the middle: A cultural historical activity theory investigation of front-line supervisors' learning lives. (Unpublished doctoral dissertation, University Park, PA, The Pennsylvania State University, 2009).** ***Dissertation Abstract International, 70*****(11), UMI No. 304985385.**

Lord (2009), in this dissertation study, examined front-line supervisors in a union shop, steel-production plant and how they learn to successfully negotiate their role with in the corporation's division of labor. Negotiating their role means continued practice in how issues of standpoint, agency, power, oppression, habits, knowledge, related business concerns, mediating instruments integrity, etc, intersect in ways that shape, inform, and guide how one engages, conducts, discusses, confers, consults, bargains, agrees, and settles the various issues bounded within the workplace environment. Six front-line supervisors were interviewed and observed in their work-environment over a four-month period. CHAT was used as the analytical framework that informed data analysis.

The following research questions guided the study: (a) What shapes and informs front-line supervisors learning? (b) What do front-line supervisors draw upon to develop and use supervisory skill? (c) How can informal instances of learning be empirically described in light of the full, complex range of artifacts, interactions, and shop-floor situations?

CHAT provided the comprehensive and exhaustive framework allowing for analyzing both the manifest and latent shop-floor processes. In particular, Lord (2009) focused on analyzing how front-line supervisors addressed and resolved role negotiation, empirically describing how the front-line supervisors experienced learning. The use of CHAT permitted investigating the hidden world of front-line supervisors learning lives in respect to their accessing and grasping the latent aspects related to the division of labor, the unspoken rules, and the development and use of mediating instruments.

Lord (2009) notes in his findings and discussion that front-line supervisors drew upon their ability to convert primary contradictions into peripheral ones and for generating mediating instruments for future use through addressing the present contradictions. They also drew upon their ability to use the artifacts in the three way of mediation. They were using an artifact as designed, using an artifact through appropriation of an existing one, and by creating new mediating artifacts. The specific mediation employed rises from their access to and grasp of the underlying conditions as well as the latent shop-floor aspects.

- **Forbes, C. T. (2009). Preservice elementary teachers' development of pedagogical design capacity for inquiry---An activity-theoretical perspective. (Published doctoral dissertation, Ann Arbor, MI, 2009). *Dissertation Abstracts International, 70*(10). UMI No. 304937963.**

Forbes (2009) examines preservice elementary teachers need to begin developing their pedagogical design capacities for inquiry by learning how to translate their conceptions of inquiry into classroom practice through the adaptation and enactment of curriculum materials. Using both qualitative and quantitative research methods, Forbes draws upon CHAT to investigate preservice elementary teachers' curriculum design and development of pedagogical design capacity for inquiry during the final year of their teacher education program. The study concerned analysis of curricular artifacts and survey data from 46 prospective elementary teachers in two sections of an undergraduate elementary science teaching methods course, as well as interviews, observational fieldnotes, reflective journals, and other artifacts from four preservice teachers from this larger group studied during the methods and student teaching semesters.

Results show that preservice teachers were able to translate their espoused inquiry frameworks into planned and enacted science lessons. This involved adapting existing curriculum materials to better promote specific inquiry practices, but also to fundamentally shift the nature of classroom science. The preservice teachers' curriculum design efforts were constrained, however, by features of their institutional contexts and subject to emergent tensions. Forbes (2009) notes that in attempting to resolve these tensions through curriculum design for inquiry, the preservice teachers ultimately articulated a fundamental contradiction between two distinct and competing visions for classroom inquiry: traditional classroom science, which promotes students' reproduction of scientific explanations by objectifying students, and a novel form of classroom inquiry that repositions students as contributing community members involved in the coconstruction of knowledge through lesson-specific shared problem-spaces. For each of the preservice teachers, this contradiction had important implications for the design of science learning environments and remained unresolved at the end of the study.

Forbes (2009) argues that the findings have implications for practice and theory. While they illustrate the important role both formal teacher education and science curriculum materials play in supporting teachers to engage in inquiry-oriented science teaching, they also highlight the need for schools to foster inquiry practices in the classroom. Findings also provide novel insights into the teacher-curriculum relationship, teacher learning, the nature and goals of inquiry-oriented science teaching and learning, and CHAT-based research on teachers.

- **Fernandez, G. (2010). Abriendo Caminos para la Educacion: A Case Study of a Parent Outreach Initiative Building on the Knowledge, Skills, and Resources of the Latina/o Community. (Published doctoral dissertation, Santa Barbara, CA, 2010). *Dissertation Abstracts International, 72*(01). UMI No. 815732436.**

Fernandez (2010) examined the Latina/o Family, School and Community Avanzando Project, which supported the development of parent and family outreach initiatives to strengthen the Latina/o pathways to college. This case study focused on Abriendo Caminos para la Educación, a program that was supported by the Avanzando Project to promote parent engagement in the Central Coast of California. The program was based on the Parent School Partnership curriculum, which was designed to introduce parents to the U.S. educational system and promote their leadership development to advocate for their children's educational attainment.

Fernandez used an embedded case study research design and employed ethnographic research methods as a participant observer (program coordinator and graduate student researcher). She investigated the 3-year (2005-2008) implementation of the program at a dual language immersion elementary charter school. Fernandez made ethnographic observations, wrote fieldnotes, video recorded the meetings, and collected artifacts. In the analysis of the qualitative research data, she drew from cultural historical activity theory

(Engeström, 1987; Engeström, 2001; Vygotsky, 1978; Wertsch, 1985a, 1985b) and critical pedagogy (Freire, 1970; Wink, 2000) to examine how the parent participants used their community cultural wealth (Yosso, 2005) as mediational tools to name, reflect, and act upon their goals and objectives.

Fernandez (2010) found that parents drew from their aspirational capital (Yosso, 2005) as the primary source of motivation to participate in the program and increase their involvement in the education and schooling of their children. In addition, they shared and developed social and navigational capital (Yosso, 2005) to explore their role in the education and schooling of their children and to address some of the challenges and barriers to Latina/o college access. Through their participation in the program, parents developed a greater sense of place in the U.S. educational system and the responsibility to develop into a parent-led organization and continue supporting their children and other parents in the school and the community.

CONCLUSION

The evolution of first-generation activity to third-generation CHAT has transformed Vygotsky's early work of cultural mediation into a macroframework for analysis of complex human activity systems. There is, embedded within CHAT shared assumptions and principles that reflect a rich activity-theoretic approach to examining human learning. CHAT presents a theoretic approach to understanding the situated nature of learning as transformative, reflexively shaping and being shaped by the learner's cognitive and cultural processes and practices; presenting a theoretic -view of reality as the learners participate within and across communities of diversity and difference.

REFERENCES

Amaro-Jimenez, C. (2008). Latino children's English as a Second Language and subject-matter appropriation through technology-mediated activities: A cultural historical activity theory perspective. (Unpublished doctoral dissertation, Cincinnati, OH: University of Cincinnati, 2008). *Dissertation Abstracts International, 69*(8). UMI No. 304666719.

Bardram, J. E. (1997). Plans as situated action: An activity theory approach to workflow systems. *Proceedings of the 5th European Conference on Computer Supported Cooperative Work* (ECSCW'97) (pp. 1732-1740). Lancaster, England: Kluwer Academic Publishers.

Bertelsen, O., & Bødker, S. (2002). Activity theory. In H. Carroll (Ed.), *HCI Models, theories and frameworks* (pp. 291-324). Waltham, MA: Morgan Kaufmann

Betts, J. D. (2006). Multimedia arts learning in an activity system: New Literacies for at-risk children. *International Journal of Education & The Arts, 7*(7). Retrieved September 15, 2011, from http://ijea.asu.edu/v7n7/.

Blanton, W. E., Simmons, E., & Warner, M. (2001). The fifth dimension: Application of cultural-historical activity theory, inquiry-based learning, computers, and telecommunications to change prospective teachers' preconceptions. *J. Educational Computing Research, 24*(4), 435-463.

Brown, K., & Cole, M. (2002). Cultural historical activity theory and the expansion of opportunities for learning after school. In G. Wells & G. Claxton, (Eds.), *Learning for life in the 21st Century*, (pp. 225-238). Malden, MA: Blackwell.

Chaiklin, S. (2001). The institutionalization of cultural-historical psychology as a multinational practice. In S. Chaiklin (Ed.), *The theory and practice of cultural-historical psychology* (pp. 15-34). Aarhus, Denmark: Aarhus University Press.

Code, J. (2010). *Agency for learning*. Burnaby, British Columbia: Simon Fraser University.

Cole, M. (1988). Cross-cultural research in the socio-historical tradition. *Human Development, 31*, 147-157.

Cole, M. (1995a). The supra-individual envelope of development: Activity and practice, situation and context. *New Directions for Child Development, 67*, 105-118.

Cole, M. (1995b). Socio-cultural-historical psychology: Some general remarks and a proposal for a new kind of cultural-genetic methodology. In J. V. Wertsch, P. Del Rio, & A. Alvarez (Eds.), *Sociocultural studies of mind* (pp. 187-214). Cambridge, MA: Harvard University Press.

Cole, M. (1996). *Cultural psychology: A once and future discipline*. Cambridge, MA: Harvard University Press.

Cole, M. (1998). Can cultural psychology help us think about diversity? *Mind, Culture, and Activity, 5*(4), 291-304.

Cole, M., & Engeström, Y. (1993). A cultural-historical approach to distributed cognition. In G. Salomon (Ed.), *Distributed cognition: Psychological and educational considerations* (pp. 1-46). Cambridge, England: Cambridge University Press.

Cole, M., & Engeström, Y. (1993). A cultural-historical approach to distributed cognition. In G. Salomon (Ed.), *Distributed cognition: Psychological and educational considerations*. Cambridge, England: Cambridge University Press, 1-46.

Cole, M., & Scribner, S. (1981). *The psychology of literacy*. Cambridge, MA: Harvard University Press.

Davydov, V. V. (1975a) Logical and psychological problems of elementary mathematics as an academic subject. *Soviet Studies in the Psychology of Learning and Teaching Mathematics, 7*, 55-108.

Davydov, V. V. (1975b) The psychological characteristics of the prenumerical period of mathematics instruction. *Soviet Studies in the Psychology of Learning and Teaching Mathematics, 7*, 109-206.

Davydov, V. V., & Markova, A. A. (1983) A concept of educational activity for school children. *Soviet Psychology*, 2(2), 50-76.

Davydov, V. (1995). The influence of L. S. Vygotsky on education theory, research, and practice (S. Kerr, trans.). *Educational Researcher, 24*(1), 12-21.

Eilam, G. (2003). The philosophical foundations of Alexksandr R. Luria's neuropsychology. *Science in Context, 16*, 551-577.

Engström, R. (1995). Voice as communicative action. *Mind, Culture, and Activity*, 2(3), 192-215.

Engeström, Y. (1987). *Learning by expanding: An activity-theoretical approach to development research.* Helsinki, Finland: Orienta-Konsultit.

Engeström, Y. (1990). *Learning, working and imagining: Twelve studies in activity theory.* Helsinki, Finland: Orienta-Konsultit Oy.

Engström, Y. (1991a). Non scolae sed vitae discimus: Toward overcoming the encapsulation of school learning. *Learning and Instruction, 1*(3), 243-259.

Engeström, Y. (1991b). Developmental work research: reconstructing expertise through expansive learning. In M. Nurminen & G. Weir (Eds.), *Human jobs and computer interfaces* (pp. 265-290). New York, NY: North-Holland.

Engeström, Y. (1996a). Developmental work research as educational research: Looking ten years back and into the zone of proximal development. *Nordisk Pedagogik/Journal of Nordic Educational Research, 16*, 131-143.

Engeström, Y. (1996b). Development as breaking away and opening up: A challenge to Vygotsky and Piaget. *Swiss Journal of Psychology, 55*, 126-132.

Engeström, Y. (1996c). Interobjectivity, ideality, and dialectics. *Mind, Culture and Activity, 3*, 259-265.

Engeström, Y. (1999a). Activity theory and individual and social transformation. In Y. Engeström, R. Miettinen, & R-L. Punamäki (Eds.), *Perspectives on activity theory* (pp. 19-38). Cambridge, MA: Cambridge University Press).

Engeström, Y. (1999b) Innovative learning in work teams: Analyzing cycles of knowledge creation in practice. In Y. Engeström, R. Miettinen, & R. -L. Punamäki (Eds.), *Perspectives on activity theory* (pp.). Cambridge, MA: Cambridge University Press.

Engeström, Y. (2000). Activity theory as a framework for analyzing and redesigning work. *Egronomics, 43*(7), 960-974.

Engeström, Y. (2001). Expansive learning at work: Toward an activity theoretical reconceptualization. *Journal of Education and Work, 14*(1), 133-156.

Engeström, Y., & Miettinen, R., (1999). Introduction. In Y. Engeström, R. Miettinen, & R. Punamäki (Eds.), *Perspectives on activity theory* (pp. 1-16). New York, NY: Cambridge University Press.

Engeström, Y., Miettinen, R., & Punamäki, R. (1999). *Perspectives on activity theory.* New York, NY: Cambridge University Press.

Engeström, Y., Engeström, R., & Suntio, A. (2002). Can a school community learn to master its own future? An activity-theoretical study of expansive learning among middle school teachers. In G. Wells & G. Claxton (Eds.), *Learning for life in the 21st Century* (pp. 211-224). Malden, MA: Blackwell.

Fernandez, G. (2010). Abriendo caminos para la educacion: A case study of a parent outreach initiative building on the knowledge, skills, and resources of the Latina/o community. (Published doctoral dissertation, Santa Barbara, CA, 2010). *Dissertation Abstracts International, 72*(01). UMI No. 815732436.

Forbes, C. T. (2009). Preservice elementary teachers' development of pedagogical design capacity for inquiry—An activity-theoretical perspective (Published doctoral dissertation, Ann Arbor, MI, 2009). *Dissertation Abstracts International, 70*(10). UMI No. 304937963.

Freire, P. (1970). *Pedagogy of the oppressed.* New York, NY: Herder and Herder.

Griffin, P., & Cole, M. (1984). Current activity for the future: The zo-ped. In B. Rogoff & J. V. Wertsch (Eds.), *Children's learning in the zone of proximal development: New Directions for child development* (No. 23). San Francisco, CA: Jossey-Bass.

Holland, D., & Cole, M. (1995). Between discourse and schema: Reformulating a cultural–historical approach to culture and mind. *Anthropology & Education Quarterly, 26*, 475-490.

Ilyenkov, E. V. (1977a). The concept of the ideal. In *Philosophy in the USSR: Problems of dialectical materialism* (pp. 71-99) (R. Daglish Trans.). Moscow, Russia: Progress.

Ilyenkov, E. V. (1977b). *Dialectic logic: Essays on its history and theory.* Moscow, Russia: Progress.

Il'enkov, E. V. (1982). *The dialectics of the abstract and the concrete in Marx's "Capital".* Moscow, Russia: Progress.

Kaptelinin, V., & Nardi, B. (2006). *Acting with technology: Activity theory and interaction design.* Cambridge, MA: MIT Press.

Kuutti, K. (1996). Activity theory as a potential framework for human-computer interaction research. In B. A. Nardi (Ed.), *Context and consciousness* (pp. 17-44). Cambridge, MA: MIT Press.

Langner, (1984). Tätigkeitstheory—Sprechtätigkietstheorie [Activity theory—Speech act theory]. *Deutsche Sprache, 2*, 110-140.

Lave, J. (1988). *Cognition in practice.* New York, NY: Cambridge University Press.

Lave, J., & Wenger, E. (1991). *Situated learning: Legitimate peripheral participation.* Cambridge, MA: Cambridge University Press.

Leont'ev, A. N. (1978). *Activity, consciousness, and personality.* Englewood Cliffs, NJ: Prentice-Hall.

Leont'ev, A. N. (1975). *Activity, consciousness and personality* (M. J. Hall, Trans.). Englewood Cliffs, NJ: Prentice-Hall.

Leont'ev, A. N. (1982). *Problems of the development of mind.* Moscow: Progress Publishers.

Leont'ev, A. M. (1981a). The problem of activity in psychology. In J. Wertsch, (Trans. and Ed.), *The concept of activity in Soviet psychology* (pp. 37-70). Armonk, NY: M.E. Sharpe.

Leont'ev, A. N. (1981b). *Problems of the development of the mind.* Moscow: Progress.

Lord, R. J. (2009). Managing contradictions from the middle: A cultural historical activity theory investigation of front-line supervisors' learning lives. (Unpublished doctoral dissertation, University Park, PA, The Pennsylvania State University, 2009). *Dissertation Abstract International, 70*(11), UMI No. 304985385.

Luria, A. R. (1932). *The nature of human conflicts.* New York, NY: Liveright.

Luria, A. R. (1961). *The role of speech in the regulation of normal and abnormal behavior.* New York, NY: Liveright.

Luria, A.R. (1966). *Human brain and psychological processes.* New York, NY: Harper and Row.

Luria, A. R. (1976). *Cognitive development: Its cultural and social foundations.* Cambridge, MA: Harvard University Press.

Luria, A. R. (1979a). *The making of mind: A personal account of Soviet psychology.* Cambridge, MA: Harvard University Press.

Luria, A. R. (1979b). *Higher cortical functions in man*. New York, NY: Basic Books.

Luria, A. R., & Tsvetkova, L . S. (1990). *The neuropsychological analysis of problem solving*. Orlando, FL: Paul M. Deutsch Press.

Marx, K. (1945). Theses on Feuerbach. In R. Tucker (Ed.), *The Marx and Engels reader* (pp. 143-145). New York, NY: W. W. Norton.

Nardi, B. (Ed.). (1996a). *Context and consciousness: Activity theory and human-computer interaction*. Cambridge, MA: MIT Press.

Nardi, B. A. (1996b). Studying context: A comparison of activity theory, situated action models, and distributed cognition. In B. A. Nardi (Ed.), *Context and consciousness: Activity theory and human-computer interaction* (pp. 69-101). Cambridge, MA: MIT Press.

Newman, D., Griffin, P., & Cole, M. (1984). *The construction zone: Working for cognitive change in school*. New York, NY: Cambridge University Press.

Nissen, M. (2008). The place of a positive critique in contemporary critical psychology. *Critical Social Studies, 10*(1), 49-66.

Ratner, C. (1997). *Cultural psychology and qualitative methodology: Theoretical and empirical considerations*. New York, NY: Plenum.

Ratner, K. (2002). *Cultural psychology: theory and method*. New York, NY: Kluwer Academic.

Ratner, K. (2006). *Cultural psychology: a perspective on psychological functioning and social reform*. Mahwah, NJ: Lawrence Erlbaum Associates.

Rieber, R. W. (1997). *The collected works of L. S. Vygotsky: Vol. 4. The history of the development of higher mental functions: Cognition and language*. New York, NY: Plenum.

Rieber, R. W. & Carton, A. S. (1987). *The collected works of L. S. Vygotsky. Volume I: Problems of general psychology*. New York, NY: Plenum Press.

Rieber, R. W., & Carton, A. S. (1993). *The collected works of L. S. Vygotsky. Volume II: The fundamentals of defectology*. New York, NY: Plenum Press.

Reiber, R. W., & Wollack, J. (Ed.). (1997). *The collected works of L. S. Vygotsky: Vol. 3. Problems of theory and history of psychology* (pp. 345-369). New York, NY: Plenum.

Rogoff, B. (1990). *Apprenticeship in thinking: Cognitive development in social context*. New York, NY: Oxford University Press.

Rogoff, B. (1994). Developing understanding in the idea of communities of learners. *Mind, Culture, and Activity, 1*, 209-229.

Rogoff, B., Radziszewska, B., &Masiello, T. (1995). Analysis of developmental processes in sociocultural activity. In L. M. W. Martin, K. Nelson, & E. Tobach (Eds.), *Sociocultural psychology: Theory and practice of doing and* knowing (pp. 125-149). New York, NY: Cambridge University Press.

Scheunpflug, A. (2001). *Evolutionäre Didaktik: Unterricht aus system- und evolutionstheoretischer perspektive*. Weinheim, Germany: Beltz Verlag.

Seaman, J. (2006). Adventure education as cultural-historical activity theory: A study of experience, learning and social processes in project adventure workshops. (Published doctoral dissertation, Durham, NH, University of New Hampshire, 2006). *Dissertation Abstracts International*, 67(05), UMI No. 305279676.

Smagorinsky, P., & Coppock, J. (1994). Cultural tools and the classroom context: An exploration of an alternative response to literature. *Written Communication, 11*, 283-310.

Stetsenko, A. (2003). Alexander Luria and the cultural-historical activity theory: Pieces for the history of an outstanding collaborative project in psychology. *Mind, Culture, and Activity, 10*, 93-97.

Stetsenko, A., & Arievitch, I. M. (2004). The self in cultural-historical activity theory: Reclaiming the unity of social and individual dimensions of human development. *Theory & Psychology, 14*(4), 475-503.

Stahl, G. (2003). Meaning and interpretation in collaboration. In B. Wasson, S. Ludvigsen, & U. Hoppe (Eds.), Designing for change in networked environments (pp. 523-532). Dordrecht, The Netherlands: Kluwer.

Tharp, R. G., & Gallimore, R. (1988). *Rousing minds to life: Teaching, learning, and schooling in social context*. New York, NY: Cambridge University Press.

Tolman, C. W. (2001). The origins of activity as a category in the philosophies of Kant, Fichte, Hegel, and Marx. In S. Chaiklin (Ed.), *The theory and practice of cultural-historical psychology* (vol. 22, pp. 84-92). Aarhus, Denmark: Aarhus University Press.

Toomela, A. (2000). Activity theory is a dead end for cultural psychology. *Culture and Psychology, 6*, 353-364.

Toomela, A. (2008). Activity theory is a dead end for methodological thinking in cultural psychology. *Culture and Psychology, 14*, 289-303.

Valisner, J. (1988). *Developmental psychology in the Soviet Union*. Bloomington, IN: Indiana University Press

Volosinov, V. N. (1973). *Marxism and the philosophy of language*. Cambridge, MA: Harvard University Press

Vygotsky, L. S. (1962). *Thought and Language* (Eds. & Trans., E. Hanfmann & G. Vakar). Cambridge, MA: MIT Press. (Original work published 1934).

Vygotsky, L. S. (1971). *The psychology of art*. Cambridge, MA: MIT Press.

Vygotsky, L. S. (1978). *Mind in society: The development of higher psychological processes*. Cambridge, MA: Harvard University Press.

Vygotsky, L. S. (1981). The instrumental method in psychology. In J. V. Wertsch (Ed.), *The concept of activity in Soviet psychology* (pp. 124-144). Armonk, NY: Sharpe.

Vygotsky, L. S. (1989). Concrete human psychology. *Soviet Psychology, 27*(2), 53-77.

Vygotsky, L. S. & Luria, A. R. (1993). *Studies in the history of human behavior: Ape, primitive, and child*. Hillsdale, NJ: Erlbaum.

Wartofsky, M. (1979). *Models: Representation and the scientific understanding*. Dordrecht, Holland: Reidel.

Wenger, E. (1998). *Communities of practice: Learning, meaning, and identity*. Cambridge, MA: Cambridge University Press.

Wertsch, J. V. (Ed.) (1981). *The concept of activity in Soviet psychology*. Armonk, NY: Sharpe.

Wertsch, J. V. (1985a). *Vygotsky and the social formation of mind*. Cambridge, MA: Harvard University Press.

Wertsch, J. V. (1985b). *Culture, communication and cognition: Vygotskian perspectives*. Cambridge, MA: Cambridge University Press.

Wertsch, J. V. (1991). *Voices of the mind: a sociocultural approach to mediated action.* Cambridge, England: Harvard University Pres.

Wertsch, J. (1994). The primacy of mediated action in sociocultural studies. *Mind, Culture, and Activity, 1*(4), 202-208.

Wertsch, J. V., & Bivens, J. A. (1992). The social origins of individual mental functioning: Alternatives and perspectives. *Quarterly Newsletter of the Laboratory of Comparative Human Cognition, 14*(2), 35–44.

Wertsch, J. V., & Rupert, L. J. (1993). The authority of cultural tools in a sociocultural approach to mediated agency. *Cognition and Instruction, 11*(3 & 4), 227-239.

Wertsch, J. V., Stone, C. A. (1985). The concept of internalization in Vygotsky's account of the genesis of higher mental functions. In J. V. Wertsch (Ed.), *Culture, communication, and cognition: Vygotskian perspectives* (pp. 162-179). New York, NY: Cambridge Press.

Wertsch, J. V. (1991). *Voices of the mind: A sociocultural approach to mediated action.* Cambridge, MA: Harvard University Press.

Wertsch, J. V., del Rio, P., & Alvarez, A. (Eds.). (1995). *Sociocultural studies of mind.* New York, NY: Cambridge University Press.

Wilson, T. D. (2006). A re-examination of information seeking behaviour in the context of activity theory. *Information Research, 11*(4), paper 260. Retrieved from http://InformationR.net/ir/11-4/paper260.html

---

Author Contact Information: Patrick M. Jenlink, Stephen F. Austin State University Nacogdoches, Texas 75962-3018. Phone: 936-468-2908. E-mail: pjenlink@sfasu.edu

Section 3: Instructional Theory

INTRODUCTION

SECTION EDITOR
Janice Koch
Hofstra University

The instructional theories presented in this section of the *Handbook of Educational Theories* represent a significant blend between theories that are considered fundamental to teaching and learning, such as constructivism and multistage models for science instruction, with important emerging instructional theories that rely on prior practices, such as teacher action research and the understanding of the nature of science. Common to these chapters are the ways in which these theories are informed by and inform practice, in precollege and postsecondary education.

An instructional theory can provide direction in helping people to learn, understand and/or apply a predetermined set of principles, concepts and/or procedures. Bayne and Scantlebury help us to understand how to engage students in meaningful educational experiences that are situated in the specific contexts of the learners' economic, cultural, ethnic and social status. They examine *cogens*, an abbreviation for cogenerative dialogues, an instructional process that acknowledges the ways in which the students' lives are brought to bear upon classroom discourse. As Bayne and Scantlebury illustrate, cogens offer us insight into conditions that may improve teaching and learning. They help us to allocate individual and collective responsibility for learning, and establish a research agenda based upon local knowledge and experiences. Although used extensively in science education, they most certainly apply to instruction in any content area. Research on cogens reveals their importance in under-served communities where students' social capital is often different from that which is traditionally recognized and valued. In addition to Bayne and Scantlebury's work on cogens, Fraser-Abder explores an instructional theory that enables teachers to examine their own tacitly held beliefs about students who they often see as *other.* Torff examines how these same tacitly held beliefs influence pedagogical strategies by persisting in offering disadvantaged students fewer opportunities for critical thinking. His research examines the instructional practices that will help teachers to confront these beliefs and create opportunities for all students to experience higher order thinking activities.

What these studies share is the convergence of theory and practice and the mutuality of their existence. Brooks examines the significance of constructivist learning theory in the form of its influence on instruction while Rust and Hansen examine teacher action research as its own instructional theory, rendering a separation between theory and practice artificial. Embedded in this section is the importance of fusing theory and practice; in some ways they are indistinguishable and conversely, their separation is artificial and inauthentic. For example, Wyner illustrates that what seems natural to practicing scientists, that evidence based on data should inform our conclusions about nature, has become an instructional theory and practice as she demonstrates the impact of using authentic scientific studies to teach secondary science.

The authors in this section reflect upon theory while making the case for practices based on the theories. This is exemplified by Weinburgh and Silva's emergent theory making the ground breaking instructional 5R theory a model for science instruction for English language learners. It is in this emergent theory that we see how instruction may unfold when language is emphasized within an inquiry-based science lesson. As with all the theories in this section, this new, emergent theory provides an instructional framework, a set of general propositions used to help explain a class of phenomena.

The Handbook of Educational Theories, pp. 237–238

It is a privilege and a profound learning experience to be the midwife to these exemplary studies as they provide new lenses for instruction.

Author Contact Information: Janice Koch, PhD, Professor Emeritus, School of Education, Health and Human Services Hofstra University. Phone: 301-617-4399 E-mail: Janice.koch@hoftsra.edu

CHAPTER 20

Using Cogenerative Dialogues to Expand and Extend Students' Learning

Gillian U. Bayne
Lehman College, City University of New York

Kathryn Scantlebury
University of Delaware

Over the past decade, instructors at all levels have used *cogenerative dialogues* (*cogens*) to research issues impacting the teaching and learning of science through the generation of local knowledge. Cogens' pedagogy|research dialectic provides a structure for teachers and students to identify conditions that may improve teaching and learning, to allocate individual and collective responsibility for learning, to generate optimal learning conditions and to establish a research agenda based upon local knowledge and experiences. Cogens can provide empowerment to disenfranchised students and teachers. This chapter will discuss the theoretical basis for cogens, provide details on their use in different learning environments and document how using cogens' pedagogy|research dialectic can improve science learning and teaching.

THEORY DESCRIPTION

Cogenerative dialogues (cogens) have developed into a powerful tool for teachers and students at all education levels. Cogens allow for participants to examine the local context for improving teaching and learning through a dialectic structure of pedagogy research. The success of cogens in improving students' learning is due to the emphasis and importance placed upon participants' shared responsibility to prioritize the classroom conditions that promote learning, and to generate agreed upon successful outcomes. The relationship between pedagogy and research within cogens is dialectical, where each constituent informs the other, without having to presuppose the other. This pedagogy|research[1] relationship provides cogens the structural resources to generate local knowledge about teaching and learning in science. In this chapter we will examine the theoretical underpinnings of cogens, discuss and critically assess their advancement and the generalizability of their applications, and describe three studies that detail differing contexts while employing aligned methodologies.

THEORY DEVELOPMENT

COGENS: AN APPLICATION OF SOCIOCULTURAL THEORY IN EDUCATION SETTINGS

In cogenerative dialogues (cogens), the dynamic interactions of cultural, social and symbolic capital are concurrently examined through sociocultural theoretical lenses (Bourdieu, 1986; Roth, Tobin, & Zimmermann, 2002). A sociocultural framework addresses the salient features of social life. It also addresses how those features mediate in-depth understandings about what unfolds in the cogens participants' lives and/or participants who benefit directly or indirectly from

The Handbook of Educational Theories, pp. 239–249

cogens. Social life, as experienced in cogens, classrooms, laboratory settings and the like, are explored through the dialectical relationship of agency and structure (Sewell, 1992). This recursive relationship, agency|structure, implies that there is a back and forth nature whereby the pair, "mutually presuppose or constitute one another ... although they are radically different entities" (Roth, 2005 p. xxi). We view agency as the power to act by accessing and appropriating resources in order to meet varying individual and collective motives and goals; structure is comprised of scheme and resources that can be human and/or material. Schema and resources are those commodities that aid in meeting an individual's motives and goals.

Cogens as Social Fields

Cogens are social fields within which new culture is produced. Within cogens, participants engage in critical reflection by making meaning of shared experiences through polysemic and polyphonic opportunities, by generating agreed upon measures to address concerns through a developed sense of solidarity, and by catalyzing change at the individual and collective levels. The production of new culture warrants further examination, and it is in this context that cogens are tools for pedagogy|research. For when cogen participants discuss the unconscious practices and underlying structures that are restricting the teaching and learning of science, they are reflecting on their practices, the structures that may be impeding their learning and/or teaching and their agency in changing those structures. As structures are situated historically and socially, a discussion of where they have come from and how they are sustained through cultural practices is a form of research. When cogen participants generate strategies and implement practices to improve the teaching and learning experiences, an example of the pedagogy|research dialectic emerges. There are examples when cogen participants have moved from examining how local structures (that is at the meso level) influence the teaching and learning of science to macro (federal/state/district mandated testing, assessments, curriculum schedules).

Fields are sites for cultural production and enactment that have resources (i.e., material, human and temporal) that promote structure. Cogens, like science classrooms, are dynamic fields and exist without boundaries. That is, culture that is enacted in one field can also be enacted in others; culture is fluid. Social life within a field (i.e., teaching and learning in an urban science classroom) is mediated by both agency and structure.

Defining Culture

Culture is regarded as that which is *done* by participants, and exists as an agency|structure relationship (Sewell, 1999). Culture influences action by shaping a collection of symbols, stories, rituals and worldviews. When enacted, culture is said to be *once occurrent*. As such, any act of reproduction of culture simultaneously is an act of transformation. Thus, teaching and learning science are forms of culture. The utilization of cogens to address the shaping and creation of new culture can lead to successful interactions across sociocultural boundaries (Tobin, Elmesky, & Seiler, 2005). The production of new culture to promote success is fundamental to the pedagogy|research relationship and is a key consideration in striving towards the alignment of schema and practices in science teaching and learning. In addition to addressing successful interactions, cogens afford the examination of contradictions in participants' actions, including those displayed through body language and speech. The flow of talk in science education fields commonly becomes an important feature of cogenerative dialogue research (Tobin, Elmesky, & Seiler, 2005). When flow of talk is optimal in a cogen, others in the dialogue commonly anticipate an individual's actions. These actions can become resources in expanding others' opportunities to act. Such activity is said to be fluent—a successful result of fluent flow of talk. Fluency encompasses actions that are anticipated, appropriate, and timely. The occurrence of widespread fluency and the unfolding of structural resources are indicative of entrainment, which is characterized by the presence of resonant conditions that support success, fluency and participation (Tobin & Roth, 2006). Synchrony, an indication of the potential for the development of solidarity, is evidenced through a variety of indicators. Evidence may include the appropriation of another's practices in verbal and/or physical encounters such as facial expressions, head nods, body sways, etc. Successful encounters give rise to positive emotional energy that, as Collins (2004) describes, can generate and sustain feelings of solidarity. This notion is extremely important when we consider the connection that exists between learning and emotions. Flow of talk, fluent actions, evidence of entrainment, the development of solidarity and agency are all examined in cogen pedagogy|research. When considered at the individual and collective levels, these indicators may point to areas in need of support or improvement, or serve as indicators of where improvements have already been addressed. Our view of social life respects a variety of perspectives. In increasingly diverse teaching and learning environments, a sociocultural framework allows educators, students and researchers to become aware of, and become more responsive to, the needs of students that often go unaddressed. For example, in a ninth grade urban science class, where issues involving race, ethnicity, socioeconomic status, learning styles and language differences are not explicitly dealt with in a mutually agreeable manner by the participants involved in the class, the success of teaching and learning the content could be jeopardized. A heuristic generated early on in setting up cogens, and adhered to by participants, provides for optimal opportunities to assure participants that their voices will be heard and that a communal effort will be made to change the field appropriately (see Figure 20.1).

Enacting Culture: Cogens as Conversation

Cogens unfold as conversations between participants within the enactment of culture in a particular field. The cogen field can be envisioned as an 'in-between space' or *third space,* (Bhabha, 1994) because it affords the production of and the enactment of a newly transformed, hybridized culture—one that acknowledges the value of difference and the acceptance of insurgent personalities and dispositions. Consequently, cogens encourage successful interactions across sociocultural differences, including those related to race, ethnicity, class, language and learning differences, gender and age. Cogens also encourage mutual understandings through discourse. That discourse can occur between participants in a graduate science education classroom, where a discussion around the relevance of including the historical foundations of a scientific discovery in a high school science classroom is being contested, or in one where participants are discussing the possibilities of creating innovative techniques for an upcoming science activity. Such examples of opportunities for interactions are resources for helping science educators, students and other stakeholders, to develop better understandings of the complexities of science education and the dynamic nature of the formation, reformation and transformation of culture and identity. Of significance is that the new culture produced during cogens can and does become integrated into participants' *habitus* (Bourdieu, 1986), mediating an individual's *core self,*

1. **Respect and rapport**
2. **Inclusion of stakeholders**
3. **Ways to participate**
    1. Listening attentively
    2. Initiating dialogue/ideas around critical questions/concerns
    3. Staying on topic
    4. Utilizing free writes as a springboard to meaningful conversation
    5. Providing evidence
        a. Expressing an opinion
        b. Speaking freely; not privileging any voice or hurting others' feelings
        c. Clarifying and elaborating on ideas
        d. Suggesting alternatives for actions
        e. Evaluating ideas and practices
4. **Opportunities to participate**
    1. Contributing to an equitable playing field
    2. Listening attentively
    3. Making space to participate
    4. Showing willingness to participate
    5. Making invitations to participate
    6. Refusing all forms of oppression
5. **Discussion topics**
    1. Learning to teach
    2. Teaching and learning
    3. Curriculum
    4. Equitable and ethical teaching opportunities
    5. Coteaching
    6. Transformative potential of individuals and activities/curriculum

Source: Adapted from Roth, Tobin, and Zimmermann (2002, p. 10).

Figure 20.1. Sample heuristic for the establishment and unfolding of cogenerative dialogues.

sub and *role* identities (Turner, 2002). More specifically, the self (identities) has three distinct levels. The first level is the *core self* and encompasses trans-situational cognitions and feelings about who a person is. The second level, referred to as the *subidentity* level, deals with cognitions and feelings about self in classes of situations generally associated with institutional domains (for example, family, work, citizenship, legion, education, and so on). The third level is one that involves *role identities* or cognitions and feelings about the self in particular roles (p. 101).

Identities are coproduced with the interaction of others, while being involved with differing forms of work and in a variety of fields within which social life gets enacted. An important component of cogen work, within the pedagogy|research relationship, deals with identity formation and the development of science teachers, students and researchers. Deep understandings into how identities and personal histories shape experiences and dispositions toward science emerge, and inform how teaching and learning can occur. Identity is not something that is fixed or stable but rather, is constantly being formed and reformed. It is recognized as being socially constituted, both at an individual and collective level (Roth & Tobin, 2005). We view identity as consisting of interrelated ways by which an individual is viewed as s/he participates in social communities and, is formed as a life is lived in a particular *lifeworld*. While social class, gender and ethnicity play roles in identity, they do not determine identity. By utilizing a sociocultural framework we understand identity issues as they present themselves within varied contexts, such as the classroom, cogens, and laboratory. Cogens provide participants the opportunities to construct identities as learners within multiple fields. By building solidarity through experiencing positive emotional energy and mutual understanding around shared experiences in a variety of fields—whether that field is a high school science laboratory, a university classroom, an informal lunchtime cogen or by being involved as a participant in the research itself—opportunities arise through cogens for participants to reflect upon and come to learn about the intricacies inherent to teaching and learning science, as well as identity formation, reformation and transformation.

Cogens and Freirean Culture Circles

A critical liberatory education enables students and teachers to confront, "the contradiction in which banking education seeks to maintain them, and then engage themselves in the struggle for their liberation" (Freire, 1972, p. 56). Cogens reinforce this emancipatory notion because a key assertion for their use is that there is a need for dialogue between students, teachers and other stakeholders to enable the implementation of positive changes in the teaching and learning process. Cogens are reminiscent of Freire's *culture circles*, which were used as a liberatory means to transcend illiteracy. Groups of poor illiterate adults in Brazil (and elsewhere) have become empowered through engaging in equitable dialogic exchanges, grounded in practices of mutual respect, with teachers and each other. The culture circle, a field constructed outside of the traditional classroom, encouraged the sharing of experiences and the understanding of individual and collective ways of being through dialogue versus monologic practices (p. 124). The result of these discussions led to a collective charge to improve the participants' oppressive living situations. Of note is the remarkable impact that the circles had on improving literacy rates during a very short period of time. Freire's contributions to the education and liberation of those who are, and have been oppressed, continue to reverberate within the many domains of science education. When we envision the urban high school, for example (whether low performing, high performing, charter or magnet type), the notion that students are becoming empowered to know, understand and confront ineffective power structures, helps to set the stage for transformation. Freire's emphasis on dialogue founded upon respect, involving people working with each other, instead of one person *acting on another* is a theme that runs throughout cogen pedagogy|research.

By being engaged in dialogue that critically examines the unfolding of social life in the science learning environment, opportunities for reflecting upon and transforming culture emerge. Cogens provide the context within which connections of the lived experience to sociocultural theory are made. Diagram 1 identifies some salient issues discussed in cogens that urban high school students found to mediate their science learning (Bayne, in press). Issues related to, and involving both students and teachers in reflecting upon curricular content, its delivery, and how teaching and learning are enacted, synergistically afford the integration of critical science pedagogy and cogens (see Figure 20.2).

Critical Science Pedagogy and the Bricolage

The diverse complexities of science classrooms have required stakeholders to question, reflect upon, and take action toward understanding and improving issues involving difference and power dynamics between participants. Critical pedagogies suggest that changes to contemporary science classes must involve educators taking an active role in creating critical consciousness and utilizing critical science pedagogy, in order to effectuate meaningful outcomes (Kincheloe,

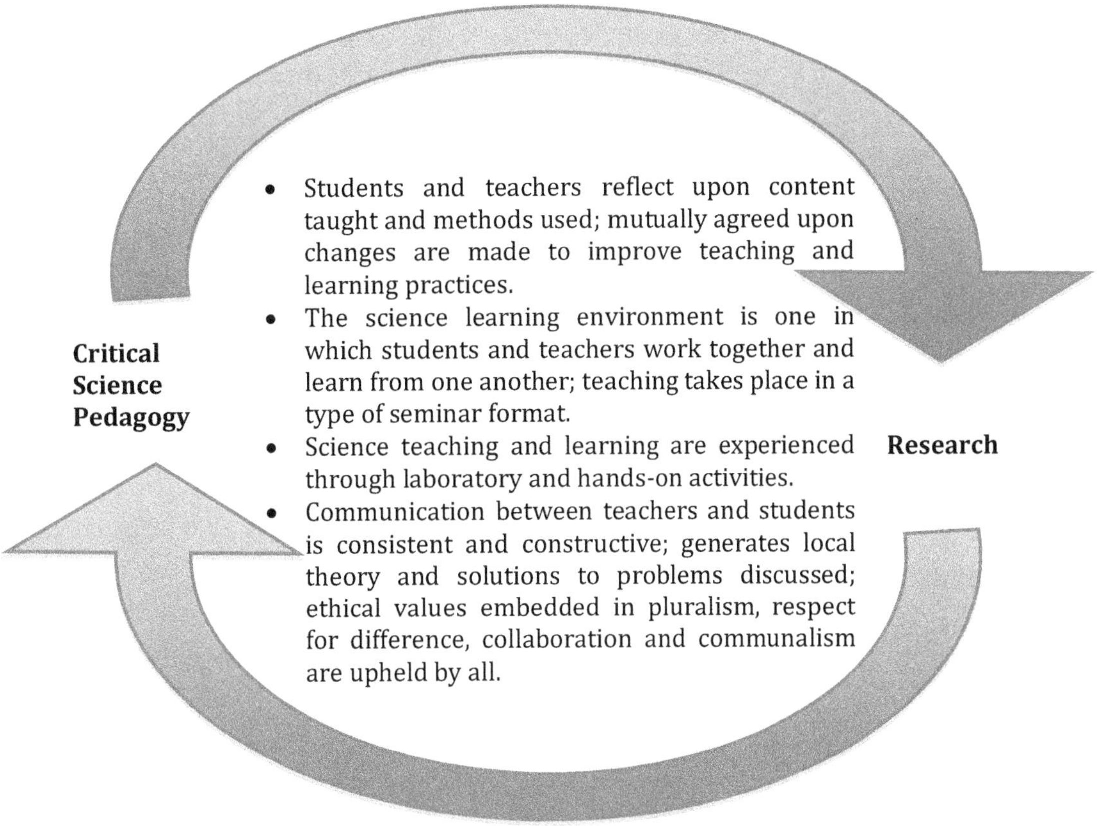

Figure 20.2. Salience of issues raised in cogens and their relationship to the recursive nature of critical science pedagogy | research.

1998). Such an examination incorporates a multimethodological, multitheoretical, and multidisciplinary informed lens that incorporates social, cultural, political, economic, and cognitive dynamics—known as a *bricolage* (Kincheloe, 2004). Cogen research | pedagogy has provided a compelling understanding of, and insights into, the intricate forces that shape teaching and learning science and science education. It does so by insisting that science educators endeavor to understand the conditions and effects of scientific knowledge production while at the same time being a part of the knowledge production. Critical science pedagogy has implications in improving science education policies, in developing actions that challenge and in cultivating the intellect, while operating in a manner that is understanding of difference and is socially just.

Kincheloe (2005) posits that through becoming critically conscious we are encouraged to seek value in contradictions and in the nontraditional, so long as that which is different is not harmful to the welfare and/or interests of others. He additionally emphasizes the need to expose unexamined power relations that shape cognitive theory and educational psychology in an effort to encourage autonomy and an expansion of human agency. When researchers, teachers and other stakeholders recognize the necessity to discern the unique ways that historical and social context make for special circumstances—whether they involve, for example, the academic development of high school students, the personal histories of developing science teachers, or the desire to have control over boisterous, defiant students in a large urban science inclusion class —guarding against a reductionist form of knowledge that impoverishes understanding of everything connected to the circumstance is of significant importance.

Validation of the Theory

For over three decades, researchers have used Likert scales surveys to examine and quantify the classroom environment. Students respond to statements about their perceptions of the actual classroom environment and their preferred classroom environment (Fraser, 1998). When those two environments are closely aligned, students' attitudes and achievement increases. A majority of the studies on cogens are qualitative, and a few, utilizing quantitative data to support, or validate the assumption that providing students power and voice with regard to the learning environment, improve student affective and achievement outcomes. The strength of cogens is their development and implementation at a local level. The participants articulate their classroom perceptions and their preferred environment through reflective discussions rather than responding to written items on previously developed scales. Many classroom environment scales are usually developed by researchers and not by teachers and/or students. Cogens encourage multiple voices and perspectives producing a bricolage of understanding of the classroom environment. Cogen participants have generated multiple outcomes and solutions to improve the teaching and learning in science classes. Tobin and Llena's (2010) work point to students' science achievement on standardized exams increases when they have participated in cogens.

Generalizability of the Theory Across Culture, Ethnicity, and Gender

The use of cogens began in urban schools as a structure for teachers, who were often culturally and ethnically *other* from their students, to learn about their students' learning needs and preferences. However, cogens also afforded teachers the opportunity to learn about their students' lifeworlds and how those worlds impact students' learning. For example, the boy who explained that the evenings he spent at his father's home he had no space to complete homework. Girls labeled as tardy by school officials had *other-mothering* responsibilities that included escorting children to school and the elementary school began at a later time than the high school (Scantlebury, 2005).

Cogens as pedagogy|research can reflect a critical science pedagogy, and with particular characteristics they can be considered a feminist pedagogy|research (Scantlebury & LaVan, 2006). Those structures include a focus on the macro-, meso- and micro-sociocultural issues impacting girls and women, and/or having a female only cogen to enhance the opportunity and possibility of participants developing their female voice and focusing the discussions on issues that impact females' science learning. Other researchers noted the high dropout and truancy rates for African American male students in urban schools and have utilized cogens as a way for teachers to connect with their students across racial, cultural and age boundaries (Seiler, 2001). Through cogens, teachers and students discussed which science concepts would interest the boys and developed a curriculum that engaged the students. Cogens provide the opportunity to dismantle power hierarchies between teachers and students, and can also identify and generate strategies for teachers and students to deal with different learning needs.

Critiques of the Theory

Cogens endeavor to restructure power relations with education settings. However, without active monitoring and reflection from participants cogens can also reproduce power dynamics and stereotypes within the field. For example, target students within a class setting can also transfer these practices to the cogen. And although cogens are a shared responsibility, teachers may need to *step up* and remind students to listen to each other and share the space. Cogens rely upon individuals assuming responsibility for enacting the knowledge generated through the shared discourse. Also, there is a collective responsibility for cogen participants. One difficulty is when students', empowered through the use of cogens in science, enact their agency and look to improve their learning and teaching in other content areas where teachers may not agree with the redistribution of power among the class participants. Students in these circumstances have had to learn how to *code switch*; that is, practices that are acceptable and encouraged through cogens may not transfer into another field. Also, in most education settings an instructor/teacher cannot fully divest her/himself of the individual responsibilities that are bestowed upon by institutional structures.

Applications of the Theory

The sites for cogen research have included a variety of settings—in urban middle and high school science and mathematics classes, university science and science education classrooms, math adult education learning environments and elementary classrooms. The findings from each site inform and direct the research in other cogen settings. Cogens are routinely introduced at the onset of a new academic calendar, the beginning of a student teaching internship, or at the start of a new teaching cycle, unit, strand or module. Their use and analysis, and the work that results occur in an emergent fashion. Many cogen sessions actively engage participants in making meaning of shared experiences and providing opportunities for engaging in discussions around the application of theory to understand the unfolding of social life in a variety of related settings (e.g., classroom, school, playground, home, and neighborhood). They also are sites where new theoretical insights and their application occur. Many educators have established cogen participation as a normal pedagogical practice. Students, parents or guardians, teachers, university researchers and school administrators routinely discuss the goals of cogens generally and, once there is agreement to participate, sign approved informed consent and institutional review board (IRB) forms. Usually cogens occur once a week (or as needed) on a day that is mutually convenient to the participants. Commonly, the unfolding of a science class, science education class or elementary school science lesson, is documented using videotape and audiotape and is followed by a discussion in the cogen field about the occurrences that unfolded. Cogens are often organized outside of the structured class time—at lunch, during a free period, before or after class/school.

Researchers and their students/student researchers are represented in cogens hermeneutically. That is, they differ greatly in many regards so as to ensure a variety of perspectives and a balance for gender and ethnic backgrounds. Successful interactions of different participants result in the production of hybrid or interstitial forms of culture. Difference may be represented through the participation of a special education student, a physically challenged student, a student who is a high achiever in science, a recent immigrant with little proficiency in the English language, a popular football player, and a student who has an average academic history in all classes. On average, the number of cogen participants is between four and six. Historically, however, there have been circumstances where only one student and his/her teacher participated in the cogen or others that involved half a class, approximately 16 students. Planned versus impromptu cogens differ according to the dynamic structures of the research field, the methodology employed, and the research foci. Researchers videotape and audiotape lessons, including laboratory activities and, presentations during the week, while capturing salient aspects of social life, as well as the cogens. Researchers collaborate with teachers and students to select specific vignettes for whole class and small group discussions—at the meso-, micro- and macrolevel, and for reminding participants about agreed upon individual and collective responsibilities to enact cogen outcomes. Computer software, such as, iMovie HD and the professional version of QuickTime Player (Macintosh OS X) allow cogen participants to modify the recording speeds, thus providing the possibility to interpret images by each frame. Researchers are able to capture phenomena at the microlevel—something that is difficult to observe as the normal rate by which social life unfolds. It is through careful observation at the micro level that we become conscious of patterned actions in real time. Transcription of vignettes using conventions identified by Roth (2005), and prosody analysis using PRAAT conventions are employed as well. Researchers[2] traditionally hold discussions around specifically selected vignettes/episodes. Both video and audiotapes produce a record that detail understandings of specific occurrences, and identify, articulate and clarify problems.

Within the cogen field, options that promote the creation of new and/or increased choices for enacting teaching and learning afford stakeholders opportunities to participate in discussions involving almost any issue related to teaching and learning. These discussions can impact a learner's identity. Science teachers and students may have an open discussion, for example, about a problem in an elementary school science activity, following a laboratory protocol, or how to structure university exams to help students more clearly demonstrate their knowledge around a biochemical pathway. Following the heuristic generated by stakeholders, teachers and students, within the context of a cogen, might agree upon new ways to cocreate ways to allocate time towards engaging in inquiry (Siry & Lang, 2010), organize how labs are executed in a more student-friendly manner (Bayne, 2007), or provide good exam response samples that detail acceptable ways to describe *de novo* synthesis of purines (Gilmer & Cirillo, 2007)—essentially collectively creating new classroom/laboratory/examination cultures.

During cogen research, multiple data sources are collected and analyzed. Participants are usually interviewed at varying times. Video data are collected regularly within research fields—during classroom lectures, laboratory assignments and group activities. Weekly lesson plans, journal entries, teacher and student made artifacts and field notes serve as additional data resources. Interviews are commonly transcribed and video reviewed, generating short clips, vignettes or episodes. Teacher and student researchers participate in data analysis that provides an *emic* or insider's perspective on the data constructions and interpretations.

The benefits of cogens for participants are evaluated using four authenticity criteria: ontological, educative, catalytic and tactical authenticity (Guba & Lincoln, 1989). These criteria are adhered to largely due to the standpoint of not privileging theoretical knowledge and to learn from local knowledge. Ontological authenticity encompasses the extent to which an individual's constructions are improved upon, have matured and expanded, and elaborated upon as a result of research participation. The extent to which individual participants' understandings of and appreciation for the constructions of others are enhanced are evaluated through the educative authenticity criterion. Evidence of catalytic authenticity is judged by the extent to which action has been stimulated and facilitated due to the research. The standard by which tactical authenticity is measured involves assessing the degree to which those who are not directly involved in and/or those who participate marginally in the research reap rewards from it. This may present itself in ways by which those who cannot access the necessary resources to act on their own behalf, are helped because of the research rewards.

Using Cogens With Undergraduate Biochemistry Students: The Case of a Seasoned Biochemist

Cogens assume that leveling of power dynamics in learning environments poses questions around the popularly held notion that teachers should have *control over* their students. Such notions of *control over* students —whether they be elementary school children learning how to become socialized in the classroom and on the playground, competitive premedical students who need to do well an advanced biochemistry class in order to master questions on entry exams and much of the first year curriculum in medical school, or urban middle and high school students who are often viewed through deficit lenses—run counter to the tenets of cogens, where collaboration with students is fundamental to the work and affords successful participation in science.

Penny Gilmer, a professor of chemistry and biochemistry at Florida State University, has documented her cogen research that focused on improving the learning environment (Gilmer, 2010). This cogen research is important because the focus at the university level, and specifically in the science disciplines, has significant potential in fostering students' interest to pursue, and become involved professionally in science, technology, engineering and mathematics fields. Penny, her students, cogen participants, and a student researcher, Jennifer (who videotaped and audio-taped each session and transcribed salient episodes) examined the patterns of coherence within the culture of the class and cogen fields, as well as the contradictions experienced. Penny used formative feedback from, and with, her students to implement and test ideas for improvement of the class, and to help guide the development of individual and collective strategies of action during the class.

Penny became involved in this research when she *tag-team* taught two intensive biochemistry course sections with another colleague, Thomas. Tag-team teaching involved the co-planning of a course, and an equitable division of labor to present materials to the students—Penny in the early part of the course, Thomas the later part of the course. The course, which included pre-medical students, and emphasized such topics as biosynthesis, biodegradation, and regulation of advanced metabolism, met three times per week and had between 70-90 students enrolled in it. The research focused on whether tag-team teaching the course would reduce the faculty's time commitment, thereby affording faculty more time for research. Penny introduced cogens to both sections and invited students to participate in a weekly cogen group at lunchtime. About half of the students indicated an interest in participating. After the first quiz and second week of class, Penny and Jennifer selected two students from each of the biochemistry course sections to participate in cogens. The students were selected hermeneutically to produce a balanced group that included students with high and low quiz scores, as well as one that had a good representation of gender and ethnic diversity. The four students participated in the cogen throughout the semester (Gilmer & Cirillo, 2007).

Results garnered from Penny's 2007 study informed subsequent studies (Gilmer, Al-humiari, & Bratton 2008). In her 2007 study, Penny discussed the dynamics, challenges, rewards and constraints of tag-teaching an upper level biochemistry course at a major American university (while working with another colleague) and implementing cogens. From her research, Penny's findings noted that (a) she needed to generate focal points for the lectures when she used PowerPoint to help students understand the content and prepare for exams, (b) student agency helped in the implementation of technical modifications related to Penny's lecturing styles, and the need to accommodate the large class size so that students could benefit from the visual representation of biochemical pathways; this was also important when considering the physical limitations of the classroom, (c) students liked having opportunities to demonstrate their understandings on quizzes in between those times when exams were given; students requested study guides, (d) through feedback from Blackboard and cogen discussions, agreements were made to create and incorporate alternative assessment strategies, (e) conflicts between Penny and her biochemistry tag-team colleague, Thomas, were related largely to the extent to which material was expected to be learned by students. Differing views and values systems held by Penny and Thomas resulted in differing ways of addressing conflicts related to the lectures, assignments and exams.

During the course of this study, Penny saw herself as a professor who, while understanding and valuing the Cartesian methods traditionally employed by those in the scientific field, viewed herself as a rational, postmodern biochemist. It was noted that Thomas, on the other hand, was aligned to a more authoritarian value system. These differing of views by the professors attributed to contradictions in the biochemistry course that led students to *play* off of the two faculty members in vying for higher grades on quizzes and tests. Valuable lessons were learned throughout the course of this semester-long research project, greatly influencing the growth of Penny, a seasoned faculty member. As such, "faculty members can learn to address these issues by utilizing theoretical perspectives that fit the situation, thereby improving students' learning and interest in science" (Gilmer & Cirillo, 2007, p. 8.).

Cogenerating Pedagogy|Research for Improved Teaching and Learning in Second Grade Science

In an effort to include children's voices and perspectives in the teaching and learning of elementary science classrooms, Christina Siry, preservice teachers and elementary school children incorporated cogens as a regular part of their classroom practice. During a 10-week science field-based methods course in a second grade urban elementary school in the metropolitan New York area, the use of cogens revealed to teacher participants (preservice teachers, classroom teachers, and professors) that structures could, "create or hinder opportunities for [young] children to gain agency, and, in turn, consider how their agency ... impact[ed] the structures of the classroom" (Siry & Lang, 2010, p. 150). As such, the field based methods course provided opportunities for sharing experiences of children's growing understandings about learning science, and created a space for them to voice their frustrations with classroom practices, and offering suggestions for change. Findings revealed that by having critical conversations with young children, their agency was supported in the classroom, and their detailed desires and needs were made known, including having more time to be involved in science inquiry. The value of and the need for children to have opportunities to demonstrate, "their ways of knowing and developing interpretations of the practice of science," and "address the way that science is taught in their classroom" were evidenced (p. 154), affording opportunities for changes to be made accordingly.

Three vignettes were highlighted within this research study. The first details children's desires to be more physically involved in science activities versus hearing and/or talking about science. The second grade children shared specific examples of how teachers could come to know when it was time to go to the tables after being spoken to on the rug; all indicators pointed to physical demonstrations by children of their readiness to do so. One student, Marcos, succinctly spoke for the collective by saying, "we want more time at the tables with the science and less time at the rug listening about the science" (p. 156). Cogens created opportunities for children to speak about how to improve the classroom climate to enhance their learning and afforded students access to appropriate the necessary structures to enact their agency. The second vignette is an example of how students can come to know and to interpret science on a personal level—important components needed to foster curiosity about science, while affording the support of deeper understandings around canonical terms and concepts inherent to conventional science. This vignette gives us insights into how teachers can learn to embrace students' understandings of science, and expand upon them. The third vignette provides another illustration of connecting science experiences (around the topic of decomposition) in the second grade classroom to students' personal knowledge and experiences. The value of seizing opportunities to address children's' understandings of the content and then subsequently strengthening these understandings through cogens participation is underscored in this research example.

Using Cogenerative Dialogue and Coteaching in Middle School Science

While much work on cogens has taken place within the context of urban secondary public schools (Bayne, 2009; Tobin, Elmesky, & Seiler, 2005), Nicole Grimes, a teacher researcher in a coeducational private college preparatory school located in New York City, was involved in a year-long research project that involved tenth grade students as coteachers working with her, in her sixth grade class (Grimes, 2010). Nicole and three of her 10th-grade students were in a special position to use cogens in ways that generated affordances into understanding many of the complexities of students' lifeworlds that manifested in the science classroom, affecting the teaching and learning. Nicole's principal asked her how to accommodate three tenth grade students (girls from varied ethnic and socioeconomic backgrounds), who recently transferred into the school, and had completed 10th grade science. Nicole and the girls decided to develop a course that would involve both science education and Nicole's sixth-grade classes. One of Nicole's sixth grade classes (she taught two) consisted of six girls and four boys. Nine of the students had individualized education plans (IEPs[3]). It was for this class and within the cogens, that Nicole and the student researchers designed curricula, created authentic coteaching plans, and discussed the best teaching practices that met students' needs. In this research, Nicole documented the reflective practices she generated with each researcher, including ontological shifts, the transformations that took place in both the sixth-grade students and her coteachers, and the changes in other social fields. A culminating event of the classroom research occurred in a professional forum, where the student researchers and Nicole gave an oral presentation, which documented the coteachers' progress, both individually and collectively, while working with the sixth grade students.

CONCLUSION

Cogens are a pedagogy|research tool that educators can use to generate deep understandings about the local context for teaching and learning. Although initially developed by researchers in urban settings as an approach for teachers to connect with students who were culturally different and diverse from themselves, researchers and educators have utilized cogens in a wide range of education settings with a variety of goals and purposes—from elementary children to science undergraduates. When framed as an example of critical science pedagogy, cogens can facilitate the dismantling of power hierarchies, provide students the opportunity to develop a voice regarding their science education, and have stakeholders examine the sociocultural structures that impact students' and teachers' agency and identities.

Research has shown the importance of attaining solidarity between learners and instructors. Cogens can play a key role in establishing solidarity among participants by providing successful, positive interchanges and learning experiences in science. These circumstances can produce fluency of language and action that indicate solidarity among cogen participants with a resultant identity for students that includes "science learner."

Cogens focus on the production of local knowledge to understand the sociocultural issues that impact science teaching and learning. As the K-12 student population becomes increasingly diverse, while the teaching population does not keep pace and is often predominantly White and female, educators need various strategies to connect with their students, understand learning needs and devise successful pedagogical strategies. Students are often culturally different from their teachers, and each other. Cogens provide a mechanism where students can examine the culture that impacts their, and their peers', learning; assume individual and collective responsibility for their learning and the classroom environment to promote that learning; as well as, develop an understanding of the meso- and macro-structures that impact their lives, within the cultural fields of the science classroom, the school, and their neighborhoods and communities. This instructional theory increases the possibilities for authentic student learning in a context of trust and mutual respect.

NOTES

1. Roth (2005) indicates a dialectical relationship by the using of the Sheffer stroke.
2. Researchers includes students, teachers and/or university based science educators
3. An IEP is a legal document that is developed for every student who has been determined to meet federal and state requirements for special education. Services are provided as needed, goals are set and assessments are made at specific times during the school year.

REFERENCES

Bayne, G. (in press). Capturing essential understandings of the urban science learningenvironment. *Learning Environments Research.*

Bayne, G. (2009). Cogenerative dialogues: The creation of interstitial culture in the New York metropolis. In W. -M. Roth & K. Tobin (Eds.), *World of science education: North America* (pp. 513–528). The Netherlands: Sense.

Bayne, G. (2007). *Identity, culture and shared experiences: The power of cogenerative dialogues in urban science education.* Doctoral dissertation, The Graduate School and University Center, City University of New York, New York.

Bhabha, H. (1994). *The location of culture.* New York, NY: Routledge.

Bourdieu, P. (1986). The forms of capital. In J. G. Richardson (Ed.), *Handbook of theory and research for the sociology of education* (pp. 241-258). New York, NY: Greenwood Press.

Collins, R. (2004). *Interaction ritual chains.* Princeton, NJ: Princeton University Press.

Fraser, B. (1998). Science learning environments: Assessment, effects and determinants. In B. J. Fraser & K. Tobin (Eds.), *International handbook of science education* (pp. 527–564). Dordrecht, The Netherlands: Kluwer.

Freire, P. (1972). *Pedagogy of the oppressed.* New York, NY: Herder and Herder.

Gilmer, P. (2010). *Transforming university biochemistry teaching using collaborative learning and technology: Ready, set, action research.* New York. NY: Springer.

Gilmer, P., & Cirillo, J. (2007). *Using cogenerative dialogue with undergraduate biochemistry students to improve the learning environment,* Paper presented at the National Association of Research in Science Teaching Annual Meeting, New Orleans, LA.

Gilmer, P., Al-humiari, M., & Bratton, D. (2008, April). *Cogenerative dialogue: Improving undergraduate biochemistry teaching and learning,* Paper presented at the National Association of Research in Science Teaching Annual Meeting, Baltimore, MD.

Grimes, N. (2010). Exploring multiple outcomes: Using cogenerative dialogues and coteaching in a middle school science classroom. In C. Murphy & K. Scantlebury (Eds.), *Coteaching in international contexts: Research and practice.* (pp. 303-326). New York, NY: Springer.

Guba, E., & Lincoln, Y. S. (1989). *Fourth generation evaluation.* Beverly Hills, CA: SAGE.

Kincheloe, J. L. (1998). Critical research in science education. In B. J. Fraser & K. Tobin (Eds.), *International handbook of science education* (pp. 1191–1205). Dordrecht, The Netherlands: Kluwer.

Kincheloe, J. L. (2004). *Critical pedagogy primer.* New York, NY: Peter Lang.

Kincheloe, J. L. (2005). Auto/biography and critical ontology: Being a teacher, developing a reflective teacher persona. In W. -M. Roth (Ed.), *Auto/biography and auto/ethnography: praxis of research method* (pp. 155-174). Rotterdam, The Netherlands: Sense.

Roth, W. -M. (2005). *Doing qualitative research: Praxis of method.* Rotterdam, The Netherlands: Sense.

Roth, W. -M., Tobin, K., & Zimmermann, A. (2002). Coteaching/cogenerative dialoging: Learning environments research as classroom praxis. *Learning Environments Research, 5,* 1-28.

Scantlebury, K. (2005). Meeting the needs and adapting to the capital of a Queen Mother and an Ol' Head: Gender equity in urban high school science. In K. Tobin, R.

Elmesky, & G. Seiler, (Eds.), *Improving urban science education: new roles for teachers, students, and researchers* (pp. 201-212). New York, NY: Rowman & Littlefield.

Scantlebury, K. & LaVan, S. -K. (2006). Re-visioning cogenerative dialogues as feminist research|pedagogy [32 paragraphs]. Forum Qualitative Sozialforschung/Forum: Qualitative Social Research [On-line Journal], 7(2). Retrieved from http://www.qualitative-research.net/fqs-texte/2-06/06-2-41-e.htm

Seiler, G. (2001), Reversing the "standard" direction: Science emerging from the lives of African American students. *Journal of Research in Science Teaching, 38*, 1000–1014.

Sewell, W. H. (1992). A theory of structure: Duality, agency and transformation. *American Journal of Sociology, 98*, 1-29.

Sewell, W. H. (1999). The concept(s) of culture. In V. E. Bonnell & L. Hunt (Eds.), *Beyond the cultural turn: New directions in the study of society and culture* (pp. 35-61). Berkeley, CA: University of California Press.

Siry, C., & Lang, D. (2010). Creating participatory discourse for teaching and research in early childhood science. *Journal of Science Teacher Education, 21*, 149-160.

Tobin, K., & Llena, R. (2010). Producing and maintaining culturally adaptive teaching and learning of science in urban schools. In C. Murphy & K. Scantlebury (Eds.), *Coteaching in international contexts: Research and practice* (pp. 79-99). New York, NY: Springer.

Tobin, K., & Roth, W. M. (2006). *Teaching to learn: A view from the field*. Rotterdam, The Netherlands: Sense.

Tobin, K., Elmesky, R., & Seiler, G. (Eds.). (2005). *Improving urban science education: New roles for professors, students and researchers*. New York, NY: Rowman and Littlefield.

Turner, J. (2002). *Face to face: Toward a sociological theory of interpersonal behavior.* Stanford, CA: Stanford University Press.

Author Contact Information: **Gillian U. Bayne**, PhD, assistant professor and coordinator, Graduate Program in Science Education in Science Education Department of Middle and High School Teaching, Division of Education Lehman College, City University of New York, 250 Bedford Park Boulevard West, Carman Hall 232, Bronx, New York 10468-1589. Phone: 718-960-2486. E-mail: gillian.bayne@lehman.cuny.edu. **Kate Scantlebury**, PhD, Professor &Secondary Science Education Coordinator Department of Chemistry & Biochemistry, University of Delaware, Newark, DE, 19716. Phone: 302-831-4546. E-mail: kscantle @udel.edu

CHAPTER 21

The Footsteps Project for Cultural Identity

An Instructional Theory for Teaching About Student Diversity in Public Schools

Pamela Fraser-Abder
New York University

This instructional theory is a tool for teacher educators to develop strategies for enabling teachers to better understand the lives of their students. These teachers will use this cultural understanding to inform their pedagogy in order to foster increased student interest, participation and achievement. Teachers come from cultures that are often different from those of their students, and need to develop an understanding of their students' cultures' in order to develop more appropriate pedagogical instruction.

BACKGROUND

The academic achievement of minority students continues to be a topic of immense interest in the research, policy and education communities. A consistent finding seems to be that European American and Asian Pacific students continue to perform at higher levels on mathematics, science and reading standardized tests compared with African American and Hispanic students (Perie, Grigg, & Dion, 2005). Historically, poor and minority students have experienced a significantly lower rate of academic achievement than their White middle-class peers (Gordon, 2006; Ratts, DeKrufy, & Chen-Hayes, 2007). This low achievement creates a cycle of failure for these students. When students fail in school, it is not because of their inabilities to learn, but because of failure of the school to provide the expertise to foster academic success (Hanley & Noblit, 2009; Ladson-Billings, 1994). Additionally poor students and those from culturally diverse backgrounds tend to encounter cultural discontinuity at school on a daily basis (Gay, 2000; Ladson-Billings, 1994). The disconnection between children's home, street and school environment and the school can have a deleterious effect on their dispositions, behaviors, attitudes, achievement and participation in school (Boykin, 2001; Fraser-Abder, 2001, Jenks, Lee, & Kanpol, 2001). Banks and Banks (2007) argue that successful programs respond to the cultural and language experiences of poor and minority students and such programs create learning environments in which students and teachers interact with each other and that in such environments, student academic interest and achievement escalate.

The teacher is considered to be the most important variable in the child's learning environment because the teacher's attitudes and beliefs have a profound impact on a student's perceptions, academic ability, self-concepts, and attitude toward learning (Banks, 2006; Shade, Kelly, & Oberg, 1997;). Teachers also set the learning climate by their verbal and non-verbal messages, personal relationships with their students and respect for students' cultural differences and cultural styles.

Culturally based differences in communication styles and language patterns between culturally diverse minority students and their teachers can often result in misinterpretations of students' intelligence

The Handbook of Educational Theories, pp. 251–258

and academic ability (Coleman, 2000; Delpit, 2004; Lovelace & Wheeler, 2006). While numerous teachers recognize cultural differences and use the persistent life situations of their students to connect students' home lives and experiences to school, far too many teachers' own dispositions toward cultural diversity often prevent them from incorporating student's funds of knowledge into the teaching and learning experience (Gay, 2000; Jenks et al., 2001; King, 2004; Ladson-Billings, 1994). By acknowledging the legitimacy of the cultural heritage of different ethnic groups both as legacies that affect students' dispositions, attitudes, and approaches to learning and as worthy content to be taught in the formal curriculum, students perceive the learning as having meaning in their lives (Gay, 2000). Successful schools for minority students are schools in which teachers integrate aspects of their students' culture, history and experiences into their programs (Banks, 2004; Shade et al. 1997).

Academic achievement has consistently been linked with culturally responsive teachers (Irvine & Armento, 2001; Pasch, Sparks-Langer, Gardner, Starko, & Moody, 1991). Culturally responsive teachers recognize that those students who do not feel valued in school settings are likely to have lower self-esteem, thereby further alienating them from school learning (Phuntsog, 1999). These teachers use the students' cultural experiences to affirm their identity, foster their interest in learning and to develop meaningful pedagogy. Varying instructional pedagogy to meet students' needs and changing classroom interactions to build strong teacher-student-peer relationships can improve students' academic success (McKinley, 2003; Sleeter, 2001; Villegas & Lucas, 2002). Villegas and Lucas further claim that teachers who hold a culturally responsive view of learning might be expected to use a culturally sensitive pedagogy which involves them being socioculturally conscious, having an affirming view of students from diverse backgrounds, seeing themselves as responsible and capable of making schools more equitable, understanding how diverse students learn, being capable of promoting knowledge construction, being involved in their students' lives, and designing instruction that builds on what students already know to expose them to the unknown.

Ladson-Billings' (1994) conception of cultural responsiveness suggests that schools are better for minority students if they provide opportunities for educational self-determination, honor and respect for students' home culture, foster opportunities for students to try to make the world a better place to live and to see themselves to be an important part of that world. Cultural responsiveness is embodied in critical consciousness, a type of learning that helps students develop awareness about the world in which they live (Banks & Banks, 2007; Gay, 2000; Ladson-Billings, 1995). Rebell (2007), Villegas and Lucas (2002) and Walsh (2005), suggest that when poor and minority students are perceived as capable of learning like their White peers, they are just as likely to achieve success. Studies on home culture, street culture and school-classroom culture (Banks, 2006; Banks & Banks, 2007; Fraser-Abder, 2001; Gay, 2002; Shade et al., 1997), culturally responsive teaching (Foster, 1992; Irvine, 1991, Ladson-Billings, 1994), culturally responsive pedagogy (Ladson-Billings, 1995; Phuntsog, 2001), cultural awareness (Gay, 2002; Grant & Secada, 1990; Ladson-Billings, 1994), and teachers' expectations (Irvine, 1991; Rosenthal & Jacobson, 1968) suggest that these elements are critical in the development of a culturally responsive and effective learning environment.

Development and Iteration of the Theory

As I reflect on the past decades I have come to understand that the theory evolved slowly within the context of developing culturally responsive science teachers. I did not begin with a plan to develop a theory of pedagogical instruction. Intuitively I worked towards such a goal utilizing strategies which I had read about or discussed with fellow science educators. The evolution was not based on an initial literature review or the development of a research based plan. To a large extent it evolved as I responded to the experienced and observed tensions around intercultural communications and understandings in my graduate program. This led me to develop a philosophy of teaching which revolved around sensitization to issues of diversity. As I used this philosophy in my teaching, students began to communicate about their own culture and to develop some cultural understanding of other cultures represented in the classroom. As I worked towards the development and implementation of this teaching theory I used my past personal experience, my knowledge and global experience in science teacher professional development, my intuition of what would work as we attempted to teach science in large multi-cultural urban settings and the then slowly evolving theoretical literature on cultural border crossings, professional development in a community of practice, dynamic transformations and identity transformation and reflection.

Cultural Border Crossings

The decision to migrate from one's country of birth brings with it many unforeseeable emotions and border crossings. Border crossings refer to both the political border crossings and also the cultural border crossings explained by Costa (1995), Aikenhead and Jegede (1999) and Giroux (1992). Most of the students in the urban schools bring the effects of first or second generation cultural border crossings into their classroom.

To travel between worlds is to cross cultural borders (Aikenhead & Jegede, 1999). Traveling between worlds forces one to shift from being one person in one context to being another person in a different context, while maintaining self-identity from the most familiar world. Students experience varying degrees of success in moving between the culture of their home and the culture of the school-classroom (Fraser-Abder, 2001). According to Costa (1995), these transitions are smooth when the home culture and school culture are congruent. Transitions are manageable when the cultures are somewhat different. Transitions are hazardous when the two cultures are diverse, and they are virtually impossible when the cultures are very different. Success in school depends on (a) the degree of cultural differences that students perceive between their life-world and their classroom, (b) how effectively students move between their life-world culture and the culture of the school/classroom, and (c) the assistance students receive in making those transitions easier (Aikenhead & Jegede, 1999). In addition to directly experiencing border crossings, I have used this knowledge base to inform my theory for developing cultural understanding.

Professional Development in a Community of Practice

Models of professional development of teachers in the United States have focused primarily on content acquisition and more recently on pedagogical knowledge. According to Howe and Stubbs (2003), a broader view of professional development has only been adopted by a small number of educators who have incorporated a sociocultural or social constructivist perspective with attention to social and personal development as well as the more traditional area of content and pedagogy. In the professional development for teachers in this program social development occurred as preservice and in-service teachers interacted with each other while jointly developing a better understanding of what is involved in teaching and learning in the urban context. Their personal development evolved as they constructed meaning out of their interactions with each other and the urban students in their respective classrooms. Their professional development revolved around the change in their teaching practice as they reflected on the following questions: *Who am I? Who are my students?* and subsequently they slowly revised their initial teaching philosophy.

Communities of Practice (CoP) as described by Lave and Wenger (1991) involve learning brought about by a shared practice, social, and collaborative interaction binding members together, around an area of knowledge or activity. I used the following shared practice and social and collaborative interactions, which according to Lave and Wenger, are essential to an effective CoP to inform my theory for developing cultural understanding. All participants in the program were involved in a common course in which they were required to:

- Learn as much about and become sensitive to and as aware as they can be of racial, ethnic, cultural and gender groups other than their own.
- Avoid stereotyping: Never make assumptions about an individual based on their perceptions of that individual's race, ethnicity, culture or gender.
- Get to know each student as an individual.

Participants were encouraged to:

- Begin to assess their own conscious and subconscious biases about people who are different from themselves in race, ethnicity, culture, gender or socioeconomic status.
- Plan their curriculum within a multicultural framework while making their classroom a safe and secure haven for all students.
- Infuse multicultural instructional materials and strategies in their teaching.
- Foster collaboration and cooperation among students, parents, teachers and administrators.

Students were engaged in group work, classroom observations, self and group reflection and action research. The preservice teachers who were all white were now in groups with the minority in-service teachers. They were meeting outside of class to complete class projects; they were going to ethnic restaurants; they were attending church together. They had started cross cultural sharing. This sharing was not limited to black and white integration. In one group, for example, a Dominican Republic teacher was sharing with a teacher from Puerto Rico and one from Belize. We were building interethnic communities within our classroom comprised of White preservice teachers and in-service teachers from minority groups. The in-service teachers were guiding and slowly directing the preservice White teachers on their paths to cultural awareness, sensitization and understanding. This shared practice fostered increased awareness and sensitization to cultural diversity and the challenges of border crossing.

Dynamic Transformations and Identity Transformation

Transformations are dynamic processes that occur through social practice when participants carry out an authentic activity or a meaningful life project (Stetsenko & Arievitch, 2004). Social practice leads to transformations, and transformations lead to the creation of new social practices. This can occur when an activity is meaningful, authentic, and dynamic and involves participants in collaboratively constructing their world through the use of cultural tools with the goal of augmenting social practices. Through this process identity is fostered (Stetsenko, 2010). Identity is transformed through learning and understanding. According to Lave and Wagner (1991) learning and a sense of identity are inseparable. Learning occurs between individuals through activity while using artifacts and tools within a community of practice. Stetsenko theorizes that education is not about acquiring knowledge for the sake of knowing, but an active process of creating one's identity.

Identity is fluid, being continuously produced and reproduced within a community of practice; it shapes and is shaped by activity. Teacher candidates enter with an identity which continuously develops and transforms based on their experiences and interactions with instructors, peers and their prospective students. They never come away from an activity with identical meaning however they share the process of engagement and development of their perceptions as they uniquely contribute to the collective within the activity (Engeström, 2009). Self-perception and the perceptions of others shape their engagement during the reflections. The activity engaged in was dynamic, shaped and reshaped by the enacted identities. Participation in this activity allowed teacher candidates to gain knowledge and experience about cultural diversity and to shape their teaching philosophy.

Reflection

Teaching and learning are activities that are mediated by cultural tools, and can lead to collective and individual transformations (Stetsenko, 2010). The process of reflection manifests itself as a cultural tool. Reflection is a form of mediation that contributes to the development of new beliefs and practices through the use of evidence to inform the new beliefs. Reflective thought consists of active, persistent, and careful consideration of any belief or perception in the light of evidence that support or does not support it, and the further conclusions to which it leads reflective thought targets beliefs when individuals combine new information, based on evidence, with their current beliefs or perceptions, as they refine their way of thinking and acting (Dewey, 1910/1997). The collective reflection meditated through the in class discussions in the activity ultimately lead to changes in cultural understanding. The unique design of the activity attempted to facilitate learning through collective reflection on a common experience within a community of practice. An integral part of the aim of the activity was to overcome negative perceptions about other cultures, develop sensitization to issues of diversity in the school/classroom and enable participating teachers to use this new understanding to enhance their cultural knowledge about their students.

In the activity, participants were learning and knowing in relation to understanding the home and street culture of their students. Through this social process, participants produced, reproduced, and developed their knowledge and understanding of teaching to diverse students. The process of prospective teachers *walking in the footsteps of their students*, and then reflecting on the experience with their colleagues encouraged legitimate peripheral participation in a community of practice. Situated learning occurred as members of a class engaged in the activity and as they used shared tools (reflection) to reach a common goal of sensitization to issues of diversity. The activity is designed to promote interaction and engagement between peers because of the belief that mastery of teaching and learning is fostered by social interactions in the community (Lave & Wegner, 1991), and not by the professor lecturing about content in the classroom. This moves the focus from the teaching and onto the structure of the learning resources within a community of practice (Lave & Wenger, 1991). Within this framework participants can share their unique understanding of teaching and learning and how that impacts their identity and their profession (Lave & Wenger, 1991).

Walking in the Footsteps of Culturally Diverse Strangers Leads to a Theory of Pedagogical Instruction

Before teachers can assist students in making the transition between the home culture and the school science culture (a form of border crossing), they need to become familiar with the students' home cultures. The activity that led to the Footsteps Project began in a course for teacher candidates that directly explored the role of race, ethnicity, and culture in science education. Described below, *Walking in the Footsteps of Strangers* was designed to sensitize participants to the home cultures of urban students, and engage them in reflective journaling and group discussion to come to terms with tensions about cultures and to develop new understandings (Fraser-Abder, 2001, 2002, 2009). The activity represents an example of situated learning (Lave & Wenger, 1991) where the focus is on knowledge creation through participation in meaningful activities. The goal is to help participants develop a better understanding of students, students' lives and home environment, and the cultural contextual framework that each student brings to the classroom.

Walking in the Footsteps of Strangers: Science Teacher Barrier Crossing Activity

When you walk in the footsteps of a stranger, you learn things you never knew you did not know. The following instructions allow you to walk in the footsteps of a stranger.

- Spend one hour interviewing a struggling student. Your interview should gather information on:
  - Student's future plans,
  - Life situation,
  - The influence of friends and significant others on their learning,
  - Attitude and achievement in science
  - Family perceived views on education, science, future careers, jobs.

- Travel to the home area of the student paying close attention to:
  - Street environment,
  - Interaction with peers, people on the street,
  - Safety.

- Talk to parents at a school meeting or by telephone about:
  - Expectations for students,
  - Education,
  - Discipline,
  - Homework rules.

- Pay special attention to TV viewing time, study area, cultural norms, gender roles and expectations.
- What can you do? Use your journal to reflect on what you have learned about this student and develop a plan for integrating what you have discovered into developing teaching and learning strategies for that student. Remember you cannot wear their skin, because at this point in their lives it is their time to wear that skin and to deal with the pressures involved in so doing, but you can walk in their steps and begin to understand what they experience as they wear that skin.
- Prepare a 5-10 minute presentation in which you will share your reflection on what you learned about this student. DO NOT include student's name in presentation.
- After all participants have shared their reflection the class will engage in collective reflection on what they have learned as a result of this activity.

Many culturally diverse, urban students often find themselves misplaced in our school system as they try to navigate cultural border crossings between home life and school environments. They struggle to survive in their new environment while dealing with the realities of their own life situations. It is within this context that the private reflections of teachers and students are shared. Although life circumstances are often hidden, they have a profound impact on the teaching and learning of science. This activity (Fraser-Abder, 2001, 2002, 2009) focuses on the powerful cultural forces both within and outside the classroom which shape the work of teachers and reflect the tensions between their two worlds. The school often provides the forum for conflict between the teacher and student. Often teachers are unaware of the problems faced by their culturally diverse students and also do not have teaching models for providing the required support.

This activity also provides teachers with a model for understanding cultural differences which helps them to create classroom organization and management from the inside out, instead of responding only to students' external behaviors and guessing what might be going on inside their minds and hearts (Rothstein-Fisch & Trumbull, 2008). According to Cabello and Burstein (1995) and Delgado-Gaitan (1996), teachers who are knowledgeable about the culture of school and the cultures of students' homes can serve as cultural brokers helping their students to negotiate a new cultural school environment thus becoming biculturally proficient. These teachers can also share their cultural knowledge about the home culture of their students with other school personnel and help to develop school policies that are more culturally congruent for their students. These teachers are also better prepared to use this acquired information to inform their curriculum development using strategies that are specifically geared to their culturally diverse student body.

Uses and Applications of the Theory

Reorganizing One's Thinking

The journaling, reflection and group presentation strategies found in the *Walking in the Footsteps of Strangers* activity enable participants to be involved in what Palus and Drath (1995) described as the reorganization of an individual's thinking. These pedagogical strategies provide opportunities to experience five interwoven processes: experience and disequilibrium, equilibrium and construction, and potentiation.

- *Experience and Disequilibrium*. Individuals engage in meaning making, stretching the capacity to accept and assimilate the experience within their existing framework of reality. They experience confusion, initial lack of acceptance, or surprise at seeing their world in a new light. They are exposed to the realities of the persistent life situations of the urban child. This experience initially causes disequilibrium, and individuals can feel threatened and anxious as they resist accepting the experience as meaningful. They may not believe that this is the life experience of their footstep student. The feeling of losing one's balance is part of the Palus and Drath (1995) process. For example, one female preservice teacher's reflective daily journaling revealed her struggles with believing that students could come to school without food and that they sometimes had to work to support their family. She came from a wealthy family, had attended a top rate private school, and had never experienced poverty. She was only convinced that it existed after observing her footstep student and talking to the grandmother of the student who was on welfare and supported ten grand-children, whose parents had died of HIV/AIDS.
- *Equilibrium and Construction*. Each individual experienced this activity and the disequilibrium differently. Individuals living in the community are at a different stage of disequilibrium than those who come from homogenous white communities. Within the supportive environment of a CoP it is possible for each individual to rethink past assumptions, frame and reframe, vision and revision new possibilities, both personally and for the community of learners. Through this process, new meaning structures are built; ideas or events that did not previously make sense are now accepted. An effective program must provide an environment in which individuals are supported as they explore new avenues of understanding and eventually reestablish equilibrium. The preservice teachers often used the in-service teachers as their support system and reality check when they encountered issues which they thought were unreal.
- *Potentiation*. This term refers to the potential for future growth and development in the individual. Developmental change is never a straightforward progression through stages but involves back-and-forth movement between the old and the new until a fresh perspective is attained. Individuals who undergo the process of disequilibrium followed by the attainment of a new equilibrium become sensitized to the possibility that new perspectives and new ways of knowing can be found. They thus develop the potential for continuing development. At the end of this activity one preservice teacher commented, "I now want to follow in the footsteps of all my students." This statement reflects the feelings of numerous participants over the 20 years in which I have engaged students in this activity.

CONCLUSION

Both in-service and preservice teachers were surprised by how much better they understood their footstep student on completion of the activity. Not only did they gain a more personal relationship with that student, but they were also able to relate to the student, understand the student's persistent life situation, and adapt lessons in order to help the student succeed. All of our students have a story to tell. By listening to these stories, teachers can better understand and support their students. Like Hodson (1992), I believe that the task of teaching is to help all students acquire knowledge, interest, skills, attitudes and ways of thinking without ignoring their particular cultural beliefs and experiences. Sensitizing teachers to the border crossings their students may be navigating is essential to developing effective pedagogical instruction.

This instructional theory has been employed with over 1500 participants over a period of 20 years. It has been presented and written about in multiple venues for teachers and teacher educators and at least ten doctoral students have used aspects of this theory with similar results. In a recent presentation at a national conference I had in the audience a middle school teacher who ten years ago had heard me talk about this activity and was so excited about its potential that she returned to her school district and successfully implemented it. Since I was in her state, she brought some of her students who had taken part in the activity. They all acknowledged the positive difference it had made in their lives. The disequilibrium experienced by participants requires a resetting and reorientation of prior beliefs and practices. This instructional theory provides a critical tool as teachers prepare for the journey in shifting the paradigm from thinking of those who are different as "other" or "lesser."

REFERENCES

Aikenhead, G. S., & Jegede, O. J. (1999). Cross-cultural science education: A cognitive explanation of a cultural phenomenon. *Journal of Research in Science Teaching, 36*(3), 269-287.

Banks, J. A. (2004). Multicultural education: Historical development, dimensions, and practice. In J. A. Banks & C. A. M. Banks (Eds.), *Handbook of research on multicultural education* (2nd ed., pp. 3-29). San Francisco, CA: Josey-Bass.

Banks, J. A. (2006). *Cultural diversity and education: Foundations, curriculum, and teaching* (5th ed.). Boston, MA: Allyn & Bacon.

Banks, J. A., & Banks, C.A.M. (2007). *Multicultural education: Issues and perspectives* (6th ed.). Hoboken, NJ: Wiley/Josey-Bass.

Boykin, A. W. (2001). The challenges of cultural socialization in the schooling of African American elementary school children: Exposing the hidden curriculum. In W. H. Watkins, J. H. Lewis, & V. Chou (Eds.), *Race and education: The roles of history and society in educating African American students* (pp. 190-199). Needham Heights, MA: Allyn & Bacon.

Cabello, B., & Burstein, N. (1995). Examining teachers beliefs about teaching in culturally diverse classrooms. *Journal of Teacher Education, 46*(4), 285-294.

Coleman, T. J. (2000). *Clinical management of communication disorders in culturally diverse children.* Boston, MA: Allyn & Bacon.

Costa, V.B. (1995). When science is "another world": Relationships between worlds of family, friends, school and science. *Science Education, 79*, 313-333.

Delgado-Gaitan, C. (1996). *Protean literacy: Extending the discourse on empowerment.* Washington, DC: Falmer Press.

Delpit, L. (2004). The silenced dialogue: Power and pedagogy in educating other people's children. In G. Ladson-Billings & D. Gillbom (Eds.), *The RoutledgeFalmer reader in multicultural education* (pp. 225-242). New York, NY: Routledge-Falmer.

Dewey, J. (1997). *How we think.* Mineola, NY: Dover. (Original work published 1910)

Engeström, Y. (2009). The future of activity theory. In A. Sannino, H. Daniels, & K. D. Gutierrez (Eds.), *Learning and expanding with activity theory* (pp. 303-328). New York, NY: Cambridge University Press.

Foster, M. (1992). Sociolinguistics and the African American community: Implications for literacy. *Theory into Practice, 31*, 303-311.

Fraser-Abder, P. (2001). Preparing science teachers for culturally diverse classrooms. *Journal of Science Teacher Education, 12*(3), 287-313.

Fraser-Abder, P. (2002). *Professional development of science teachers: Local Insights with lessons for the global community.* New York, NY: RutledgeFalmer.

Fraser-Abder, P. (2009). Developing intercultural communication and understanding through a community of practice. In M. Weinburgh & K. Weiseman (Eds.), *Becoming and being: Women's experiences in leadership in K-16 science education communities* (pp. 95-109). New York, NY: Springer.

Gay, G. (2000). *Culturally responsive teaching: Theory, research, & practice.* New York, NY: Teacher's College Press.

Gay, G. (2002). Preparing for culturally responsive teaching. *Journal of Teacher Education, 53*(2), 106-116.

Giroux, H. A. (1992). *Border crossings: Cultural workers and the politics of education.* Minneapolis, MN: University of Minnesota Press.

Gordon, E. W. (2006). Establishing a system of public education in which all children achieve at high levels and reach their full potential. In T. Smiley (Ed.), *The covenent with Black America* (p. 23). Chicago, IL: Third World Press.

Grant, C. A., & Secada, W. G. (1990). Preparing teachers for diversity. In J. Sikula (Ed.), *Handbook for research on teacher education* (pp. 403-422). New York, NY: McMillan.

Hanley, M. S., & Noblit, G.W. (June 2009). *Cultural responsiveness, racial identity and academic success: A review of literature.* Pittsburgh, PA: Heinz Endowments.

Hodson, D. (1992). Towards a framework for multicultural education. *Curriculum, 13*, 15-18.

Howe, A. C., & Stubbs. H. S. (2003). From science teacher to teacher leader: Leadership development as meaning making in a community of practice. *Science Education, 87*, 281-297.

Irvine, J. J. (1991). *Black students and school failure: Policies, practices, and rescriptions.* New York, NY: Praeger.

Irvine, J. J., & Armento, B. J. (2001). *Culturally responsive teaching. Lesson planning for elementary and middle grades.* New York, NY: McGraw-Hill.

Jenks, C., Lee, J. 0., & Kanpol, B. (2001). Approaches to multicultural education in pre-service teacher education: Philosophical frameworks and models for teaching. *The Urban Review, 33*, 87-105.

King, J. (2004). Culture-centered knowledge: Black studies, curriculum transformation, and social action. In J. A. Banks & C. A. Banks (Eds.), *Handbook of research: Multicultural education* (2nd ed., pp. 628-634). San Francisco, CA: Josey-Bass.

Ladson-Billings, G. (1994). *The dreamkeeper: Successful teachers of African American children.* San Francisco, CA: Josey-Bass.

Lave, J., & Wenger, E. (1991). *Situated learning: Legitimate peripheral participation.* New York, NY: Cambridge University Press.

Lovelace, S., & Wheeler, T. (2006). Cultural discontinuity between home and school language socialization patterns: Implications for teachers. *Education, 127*, 303-309.

McKinley, J. H. (2003). Leveling the playing field and raising African American student achievement in twenty-nine urban classrooms. *New Horizons for Learning.* Retrieved from http://education.jhu.edu/newhorizons/strategies/topics/Differentiated%20Instruction/playing-field/index.html

Palus, C., & Drath, W. (1995). *Evolving leaders: A model for promoting leadership development in programs.* Greensboro, NC: Center for Creative Leadership.

Pasch, M., Sparks-Langer, G., Gardner, T. G., Starko A. J., & Moody, C. D. (1991). *Teaching as decision making: instructional practices for the successful teacher.* White Plains, NY: Longman.

Perie, M., Grigg, N. S., & Dion, G. S. (2005). *The nation's report card: Mathematics 20005* (NCES-2006-453). Washington, DC: US Department of Education, Institute of Education Sciences, National Center for Education Statistics.

Phuntsog, N. (1999, Summer). The magic of culturally responsive pedagogy: In search of the Genie lamp in multicultural education. *Teacher Education Quarterly*, 97-111.

Phuntsog, N. (2001). Culturally responsive teaching: What do selected United States elementary school teachers think? *Intercultural Education, 12*(1), 51-64.

Ratts, M. J., DeKrufy, L., & Chen-Hayes, S. F. (2007).vThe ACA advocacy competencies: A social justice advocacy framework for professional school counselors. *Professional School Counseling, 11*, 90-97.

Rebell, M. A. (2007). From adequacy to comprehensive educational equity: Toward a realistic agenda for equity and excellence. *Annenberg Institute for School Reform*, 3-5.

Rosenthal, R., & Jacobson, L. (1968). *Pygmalion in the classroom. Teacher expectation and pupils' intellectual development.* New York, NY: Holt, Rhinehart, & Winston.

Rothstein-Fisch, C., & Trumbull, E. (2008). *Managing Diverse Classrooms: How to build on students' cultural strengths.* Alexandria, VA: Association for Supervision and Curriculum Developments.

Shade, B. J., Kelly, C., & Oberg, M. (1997). *Creating culturally responsive classrooms.* Washington, DC: American Psychological Association.

Sleeter, C. (2001). Preparing teachers for culturally diverse schools: Research and the overwhelming presence of whiteness. *Journal of Education, 52*(2), 94-106.

Stetsenko, A. (2010). Teaching-learning and development as activist projects of historical Becoming: Expanding Vygotsky's approach to pedagogy. *Pedagogies: An International Journal, 5*(1), 6-16.

Stetsenko, A., & Arievitch, I. (2004). The self in cultural historical activity theory: Reclaiming the unity of social and individual dimensions of human development. *Theory Psychology, 14*(4), 475-503.

Villegas, A. M., & Lucas, T., (2002). *Educating culturally responsive teachers: A coherent approach.* Albany, NY: State University of New York Press.

Walsh, K. (2005). Educational equity in Marin. Marin County Fund. *Springboard to School.* Retrieved from http://www.marineducationfund.org/downloads/EECP_TL.pdf

---

Author Contact Information: Pamela Fraser-Abder, PhD, Director of Science Education Department of Teaching and Learning, New York University, 239 Greene Street, 637 East Building, New York, NY 10003. Phone: 212-998-5208 E-mail: Pamela.Fraser-Abder@nyu.edu, pa1@nyu.edu

CHAPTER 22

Folk Belief Theory

Accounting for the Persistence of the Achievement Gap

Bruce Torff
Hofstra University

"Folk belief theory" describes how socially-shared beliefs about learning and teaching, part of the "folk psychology" of our culture (Bruner, 1990), contribute to teachers' instructional strategies. These commonly held, default beliefs hold that learning is a hierarchical process, such that higher-order cognitive processes (e.g., critical thinking) are understood to grow out of lower-order ones (e.g., retrieval from a knowledge base). Low-advantage learners are thought to lack the lower-order fundamentals, and are thus unable to handle higher-order challenges, so they ought to receive a curriculum that goes back to basics. Because of these beliefs, teachers support a curriculum that emphasizes higher-order skills more for high-advantage learners than low-advantage ones, introducing a systematic, seemingly unconscious, bias into the nation's schools. This bias results in impoverished pedagogy for low-advantage learners, limiting their academic growth. But beliefs are resistant to change, as with other kinds of socially-shared "folk" beliefs, even in the face of considerable efforts to counter them. Hence the achievement gap persists despite overwhelming efforts to overcome it, in part because teachers believe in pedagogy that provides low-advantage learners inequitable access to rigorous curriculum and instruction. Evidence collected in a series of survey-research projects lends support to folk belief theory. This chapter describes the research and the development of this theory.

BACKGROUND

Even in the divisive world of educational policy and practice, there is widespread agreement that the most troublesome problem in our nation's schools remains the achievement gap between disadvantaged learners and their more affluent peers. The achievement gap has persisted despite the well-intentioned efforts of tens of thousands of educators, sweeping educational reform initiatives such as No Child Left Behind, a cornucopia of state and local programs, the grant-making priorities of the federal government and a plethora of foundations interested in educational improvement, and a blizzard of educational theory, research, and discussion.

A variety of possible causes for the achievement gap have been discussed in the educational literature. For example, Barton (2004) identified 14 factors linked to the achievement gap, including in-school factors such as teacher experience and out-of-school factors such as birth weight. Heading this list was *rigor of curriculum*: the practice of giving disadvantaged learners less rigorous curriculum and instruction compared to more privileged learners. This "rigor gap" is widely thought to curtail disadvantaged learners' achievement levels by providing them with too few opportunities to face academic challenges and rise to the occasion.

This reasoning is in keeping with the zeitgeist on the national scene in education, emphasizing "raising the bar" as a primary objective for educational reform. The zeitgeist finds its roots in the widely heralded "Pygmalion" effect, which holds that people tend to rise to the

The Handbook of Educational Theories, pp. 259–270

level of expectations set out for them by teachers, supervisors, or other authority figures (Rosenthal & Jacobsen, 1992). Belief in the Pygmalion effect lies at the core of the signature educational reform initiative of our time, No Child Left Behind, which endeavors to raise the bar with standards, tests, and accountability.

The clear implication here is that the bar needs to be raised because educators ostensibly support rigorous curriculum and instruction more for high-advantage learners than low-advantage ones suppressing educational outcomes in low-advantage schools. Do educators actually hold such beliefs? Is it certain that such beliefs are problematic? What obstacles stand in the way of belief change, if needed, and what might be done to promote this change? Answers to these questions are presented in this chapter, in the form of an instructional theory with accompanying evidence and discussion.

History and Development of Folk Belief Theory: Cultural Psychology

A more detailed treatment of folk belief theory begins with the general theoretical perspective of cultural psychology, or cultural-historical psychology (Bruner, 1990; Cole, 1996; Daniels, Cole, & Wertsch, 2007; Shore, 1996; Shweder, 1991; Triandis, 1989; Vygotsky, 1978). "Cultural psychology is the study of the way cultural traditions and social practices regulate, express, and transform the human psyche, resulting less in psychic unity for humankind than in ethnic divergences in mind, self, and emotion" (Shweder, 1991, p. 72). In this view, human cognition results less from endogenously-regulated, genetically-specified structures and functions, and results more from exogenously-regulated, culturally-specified structures and functions. Cultures provide cognitive "tools" through which individuals make sense of the world and organize their behavior (Kozulin, 1998).

An example will illustrate this point. To conceptualize distances in most cases, people in the United States employ a culturally provided unit of distance, the mile, which acts as a useful cognitive tool. "Thinking in miles" allows people to understand that Los Angeles is quite far from New York City (when driving, and especially when walking!). However, if people are deprived of the culturally provided unit of distance and asked to use a different one (e.g., during the abortive attempt to instill the metric system in the 1970s), figuring out how far away things are becomes nearly impossible. Most Americans can think in miles, but not in kilometers, so hearing that Paducah, Kentucky is 1531 kilometers from New York City does not immediately bring to mind just how far Paducah is. For cultural psychologists, three terms, often seen as separate—learning, socialization, and enculturation—actually connote the same thing: the process through which individuals appropriate the cognitive tools of their culture and use these to accomplish tasks in the world they live in. Cognitive tools are typically implicitly held (with little conscious awareness) and seldom reflected upon; as the saying goes, the fish will be the last to discover water. Patterns of cognitive tool use tend to be robust and resistant to change, even when an individual attempts to do so (hence the difficulties switching to the metric system).

The term "folk psychology" has been used to describe the canon of culturally provided cognitive tools through which people make sense of learning, teaching, thinking, and related matters in psychology and education (Bruner, 1990). People conceptualize what learning is, and therefore, how teaching should proceed, with the help of cognitive tools that describe how the human mind works and consequently, how best to teach. All educational interventions are predicated on one or another conceptualization of the mind, so the tenets of a culture's folk psychology go a long way to explain the culture's classroom practices.

Evidence for Folk Belief Theory

Our culture's folk psychology helps to explain the rigor gap, and with it the persistence of the achievement gap. In particular, folk belief theory sets out three claims with supporting evidence, presented below. The survey instrument that was used to provide the evidence is referred to as the critical thinking belief appraisal (CTBA).

The Critical Thinking Belief Appraisal

Much of the research reported in this chapter employed the survey instrument, the CTBA (Torff & Warburton, 2005). Based on a four-factor model, the CTBA was designed to assess teachers' beliefs concerning the effectiveness of (a) high-CT activities for high-advantage learners (high-CT/high-advantage), (b) high-CT activities for low-advantage learners (high-CT/low-advantage), (c) low-CT activities for high-advantage learners (low-CT/high-advantage), and (d) low-CT activities for low-advantage learners (low-CT/low-advantage). The scale is comprised of a series of 12 prompts—vignettes describing classroom activities in English, mathematics, science, social studies, and languages other than English. The prompts are divided equally between high-CT and low-CT activities. Below are examples of each.

> High-CT: A social-studies class is studying the Treaty of Versailles signed at the end of World War I. The teacher assigns learners to write "letters from the future" to

President Wilson arguing why the United States should or should not support the treaty.

Low-CT: A social-studies class is studying the industrial revolution. The teacher provides learners with a list of inventions, explains the impact of these inventions during this period, and describes how they continue to influence the modern world.

The CTBA was designed to allow teachers' beliefs to be assessed separately for high-advantage and low-advantage learners. To avoid response bias caused by leading questions, a contextualized assessment scheme was designed drawing on the characteristics that teachers have been shown to take into consideration as they judge learners' SES advantages. Three such "advantage characteristics" were used: (a) *ability* (learners' capacity for academic achievement when dealing with the specific topic to which a given prompt refers); (b) *prior knowledge* (the extent of learners' knowledge about the specific topic to which a given prompt refers before learners participate in additional activities); and (c) *motivation* (how much interest and attention learners demonstrate when dealing with the specific topic to which a given prompt refers) (Archer & McCarthy, 1988; Dweck, 1986; Edwards, 1999; Givvin, Stipek, Salmon, & MacGyvers, 2001; Nolen & Nichols, 1994; Madon, Jussim, Keiper, Eccles, Smith, & Paolumbo 1998; Moje & Wade, 1997; Pintrich & Schunk, 1996; Tollefson, 2000).

Using 6-point Likert-type scales, each of the instrument's 12 prompts is followed by either a high-advantage item or a low-advantage one for each advantage characteristic—for example, prompt #1 is followed by a low-ability item, a low prior-knowledge item, and a high-motivation item. The 36-item instrument is balanced as follows: it has a total of 12 prompts, 6 high-CT and 6 low-CT; it presents 18 items for high-advantage learners and 18 for low-advantage ones; and it includes 12 of each of the 3 advantage characteristics, 6 for high-advantage learners and 6 for low-advantage ones.

Results of a sequence of five validation studies support the theoretical and practical utility of the construct and measure of teachers' beliefs about classroom use of high-CT and low-CT activities for high- and low-advantage learner populations (Torff & Warburton, 2005). The scale produced scores with high internal-consistency reliability, with an overall alpha level of .89. The CTBA was found to have a stable factor structure comprised of four factors that collectively accounted for 62% of the within-group variance and individually yielded alpha levels of .88, .76, .90, and .88. A replication study produced similar internal-consistency reliability and factor-analytic results. The scale's scores demonstrated satisfactory discriminant validity, producing low correlations (ranging from .02 to .28, $p < .05$) between each of the four factors and measures of CT ability (the California Critical Thinking Skills Test; Facione, Facione, & Giancarlo, 2000), CT disposition (the Need for Cognition scale; Cacioppo & Petty, 1982; Cacioppo, Petty, Feinstein, & Jarvis, 1996), and social desirability (The Marlowe-Crowne Social Desirability scale; Crowne & Marlowe, 1964). Finally, the scale yielded scores with acceptable predictive validity, with an overall correlation of .72 ($p < .05$) between ratings of observed classroom use of CT activities and the subset of CTBA items that matched the learner characteristics of the classroom observed (as judged by the teacher). Validation research also supported the use of the three advantage characteristics: factor-analytic results and internal-consistency correlations (ranging from .74 to .96, $p < .05$) indicated that ability, prior knowledge, and motivation collectively were reliable indicators of teachers' perception of learner advantages but had little effect as independent factors. Taken together, the results of the five validation studies support the theoretical utility of the CTBA for assessing teachers' beliefs about critical thinking.

Use and Application of the Theory

Claim #1: Critical Thinking Activities are More for High- than Low-Advantage Learners

With validity and reliability of the scores produced by the CTBA satisfactorily established, the instrument was used to put folk belief theory to the test. The initial claim of this theory is that our folk psychology's beliefs about cognition and learning are largely hierarchical, such that higher-order cognitive processes (i.e., critical thinking in all its forms, such as problem solving and decision making) are thought to grow out of lower-order ones (i.e., a knowledge base and basic cognitive/learning skills). On this view, learners must develop a base of prior knowledge, accompanied by some basic learning skills, before they can successfully engage in more rigorous tasks (that is, ones requiring higher-order thinking). Beliefs as such result in curriculum based on a progression from lower-order to higher-order; when learners lack the fundamentals, these must be remediated before complex critical-thinking activities are attempted.

These beliefs make learners' level of socioeconomic advantages an important factor in educational decision-making. Low-advantage learners are often judged to lack the needed fundamental knowledge and skills to complete high-order thinking tasks, and are thus deemed to require a remedial regimen of lower-order ones to catch up. A self-fulfilling prophecy may result; high-advantage learners receive a rich, rigorous curriculum, which enhances their academic performance, which leads to more rigorous curriculum in subsequent lessons; but low-advantage learners receive watered-down curriculum, which restricts their academic growth, leading to still more impoverished curriculum down the road (Zohar, Degani, & Vaakin, 2001). Accordingly, folk belief theory predicts that educators support use of rigorous curriculum and instruction, featuring such challenges as critical-thinking activities, more for high-advantage learners than low-advantage ones, introducing a systematic bias into educational practice.

Teachers really do believe in a hierarchical structure of human cognition and learning according to research using both interviews and survey methods. Research in this area began with the work of Raudenbush and colleagues, who asked 303 teachers of four secondary subjects (English, math, science, and social studies) in 16 schools in California and Michigan to identify instructional objectives for upper- and lower-track classes and complete specially designed scales that assessed teachers' emphasis on high-CT activities in these classes (Raudenbush, Rowan, & Cheong, 1993). Instructional objectives and emphasis on high-CT activities differed significantly across academic tracks, such that teachers were more likely to focus on high-CT activities in upper-track classes. Attempts to analyze teachers' beliefs about low-CT activities were unsuccessful because of low reliabilities produced by the researchers' low-CT scales, precluding analyses comparing beliefs about high-CT and low-CT activities. Based on the data for high-CT activities, however, the researchers concluded that teachers favored differentiation of high-CT instruction based on academic track (i.e., a "tracking effect").

Obtaining similar results, Zohar and colleagues conducted semistructured interviews in which 40 Israeli secondary teachers discussed their instructional goals for high- and low-achieving learners (Zohar et al., 2001). The researchers divided these goals into three categories, two corresponding to low-CT activities ("knowledge" and "comprehension") and one corresponding to high-CT activities ("higher-order thinking"), although no attempt was made to compare beliefs in these categories. Participants' levels of educational attainment and teaching experience were reported but not entered into analyses of instructional goals. Results indicated that 19 of 40 teachers (47.5%) judged high-CT activities to be inappropriate for low-achieving learners. The researchers interpreted this finding as evidence of an "achievement effect" comparable to the tracking effect reported by Raudenbush et al. (1993). However, with 21 of 40 teachers (52.5%) judging high-CT activities to be appropriate for low-achieving learners, it appears that considerable variability obtains in teachers' beliefs about use of high-CT activities in the classroom.

Results reported by Raudenbush et al. (1993) and Zohar et al. (2001) indicate that at least some teachers judged high-CT activities to be more appropriate for high-advantage learners than low-advantage ones. Based on these data, the researchers have suggested that teachers prefer low-CT activities to high-CT ones when teaching low-advantage learners. But the researchers did not assess beliefs about low-CT activities (or compare low-CT and high-CT ones), and thus their results do not speak to the extent to which the reported tracking effect and achievement effect are unique to high-CT activities or obtain with low-CT activities as well. This seems a crucial issue to investigate, because it concerns the extent to which teachers hold beliefs consistent with differentiation of instruction across advantage levels in ways that result in less rigorous curriculum and instruction for low-advantage learners.

Designed to move into the gap, the CTBA was used in three studies investigating in-service teachers' beliefs about high-CT and low-CT activities for different learner populations (Torff, 2005, 2006; Warburton & Torff, 2005). In the three studies, a total of 350 in-service secondary teachers in over 100 schools in New York State and South Carolina completed the CTBA (N = 145, 103, and 102, respectively). (See Table 22.1.)

Within-participants MANCOVA procedures (see Table 22.2) indicated that in-service teachers rated high-CT activities as significantly more effective for high- than low-advantage learners, with large effect sizes (eta-squared statistics) of .63, .58, and .67 in the three studies. (Effect sizes less than .20 have been categorized as "small," between .20 and .40 as "moderate," and above .40 as "large;" Cohen, 1988). This robust "advantage effect" is similar to the tracking effect (Raudenbush et al., 1993) and achievement effect (Zohar et al., 2001) found previously. However, in results not shown in prior research, teachers also rated low-CT activities as considerably more effective for high-advantage learners than low-advantage ones (also with large effect sizes of .53, .52, and .48). Low-CT activities as well as high-CT ones were associated with strong advantage effects.

In other findings, not revealed in prior research, teachers produced "pedagogical-preference effects" in which high-CT activities were rated as significantly more effective than low-CT ones for both learner populations. For high-advantage learners, the effects were moderate to weak, with effect sizes of .24, .20, and .08 in the three studies. For low-advantage learners, the effect was weaker and less consistent: in the initial study, the effect size was a small .09 (Warburton & Torff, 2005); a subsequent study produced an effect size of .05 (Torff, 2005); and a third study found no statistically significant effect (Torff, 2006).

These findings call into question an earlier claim that teachers judge low-CT activities to be preferable to high-CT ones for low-advantage learners (Raudenbush et al., 1993; Zohar et al., 2001). But neither do the results

Table 22.1. Means and Standard Deviations in CTBA Responses, by Group

	Variable							
	HH		*HL*		*LH*		*LL*	
Group	*Mean*	*SD*	*Mean*	*SD*	*Mean*	*SD*	*Mean*	*SD*
Expert***	4.59	.45	4.20	.76	2.84	1.08	2.49	.76
In-service***	4.44	.60	3.06	.59	4.19	.92	3.05	.79
In-service**	4.59	.86	3.28	.77	4.11	.93	2.91	.67
In-service*	4.62	.94	3.15	.78	4.10	.93	2.89	.79
Preservice*	4.60	.71	3.34	.71	3.99	.98	3.07	.67
Prospective*	4.89	.59	3.33	.66	4.46	.76	3.41	.73

Note: CTBA = Critical Thinking Belief Appraisal; HH = high-CT activities for high-advantage learners; HL = high-CT activities for low-advantage learners; LH = low-CT activities for high-advantage learners; LL = low-CT activities for low-advantage learners.
* Results reported in Torff (2005).
** Results reported in Warburton & Torff (2005).
*** Results reported in Torff (2006).

Table 22.2. Within-Group Differences: Probability Values and Effect Sizes, by Group

	Effect			
	Advantage Effect		*Pedagogical-Preference Effect*	
Group	*High-CT*	*Low-CT*	*High-Adv.*	*Low-Adv.*
Expert	$p < .0001$	$p < .01$	$p < .0001$	$p < .0001$
Teachers***	*eta* = .28	*eta* = .09	*eta* = .65	*eta* =. 69
In-service	$p < .0001$	$p < .0001$	$p < .01$	n.s
Teachers***	*eta* = .68	*eta* = .52	*eta* = .08	
In-service**	$p < .0001$	$p < .0001$	$p < .0001$	$p < .01$
Teachers	*eta* = .63	*eta* = .53	*eta* = .24	*eta* = .09
In-service	$p < .0001$	$p < .0001$	$p < .0001$	$p < .01$
Teachers*	*eta* =. 58	*eta* = .48	*eta* = .20	*eta* = .05
Preservice	$p < .0001$	$p < .0001$	$p < .0001$	$p < .01$
Teachers*	*eta* = .67	*eta* = .38	*eta* = .22	*eta* =.07
Prospective	$p < .0001$	$p < .0001$	$p < .0001$	n.s.
Teachers*	*eta* = .78	*eta* = .51	*eta* = .30	

Notes: CT = critical thinking; Adv. = advantage; n.s. = not significant; Advantage effect = comparison of high-advantage learners versus low-advantage learners for either high-CT or low-CT activities; pedagogical preference effect = comparison of high-CT activities versus low-CT activities for either high-advantage learners or low-advantage learners. All advantage effects indicate advantage of high-advantage learners over low-advantage learners.
All advantage effects indicate advantage of high-advantage learners over low-advantage learners.
^ Preference for low-CT activities over high-CT activities; other pedagogical-reference effects indicate preference for high-CT activities over low-CT activities.
* Results reported in Torff (2005).
** Results reported in Warburton and Torff (2005).
*** Results reported in Torff (2006).

suggest that teachers believe that high- and low-advantage learners should receive equal access to high-CT activities. The advantage effect was stronger for high-CT activities than low-CT ones, and the pedagogical preference effect was considerably stronger and more consistent for high-advantage learners than low-advantage ones. Teachers preferred high-CT activities to low-CT ones for all learners, but apparently still judged it appropriate that low-advantage learners receive fewer high-CT activities than high-advantage learners. Results as such are consistent with folk belief theory, which predicts that teachers support a rigorous curriculum more for high- than low-advantage learners, because the higher-order skills are thought to depend on a basis of lower-order skills that low-advantage learners are believed to lack.

Claim #2: Impoverished Curriculum for Low-Advantage Learners

The results summarized above show that teachers favored differentiated use of high-CT activities according to learners' academic track, achievement level, and/or SES advantages. But these studies do not demonstrate that teachers' beliefs are in any way problematic. It is possible that instructional practices are optimized when high-CT activities are directed more often to high-advantage learners than low-advantage ones, because low-advantage learners need remedial work. If so, expert teachers – individuals unlikely to hold beliefs that aggravate educational problems such as the rigor gap—would produce similar CTBA responses to the ones produced by the randomly selected in-service teachers in the studies summarized above. But if in-service teachers' beliefs are impoverished (as folk belief theory predicts), their responses can be expected to differ from those of expert teachers.

To investigate these possibilities, the CTBA was administered to 110 randomly selected in-service teachers and 92 expert teachers in New York State (Torff, 2006). Teachers in the expert group (from 27 different schools) were nominated by supervisors in the role of principal or assistant principal. Teachers in the in-service group were picked at random from 30 schools similar in socioeconomic status (SES) to the schools at which the expert teachers were employed, with data on housing costs used for SES matching. In this study, *experts* were the group of teachers with the highest level of teaching skill (even though they worked as in-service teachers) and *in-service teachers* were the group representing the full range of levels of teaching skill (even though some teachers classifiable as experts were likely also included in such a group).

Table 22.1 presents means and standard deviations for the two groups. In between-participants MANCOVA procedures (see Table 22.3), the groups did not differ in ratings of high-CT activities for high-advantage learners, indicating that experts and in-service teachers were similarly supportive of high-CT instruction for high-advantage learners. However, experts exceeded in-service teachers in ratings of high-CT activities for low-advantage learners (with a large effect size of .48)—experts were considerably more likely to ask low-advantage learners to think critically in the classroom. In addi-

Table 22.3. Between-Group Differences: Probability Values and Effect Sizes

	Variable			
Group	*HH*	*HL*	*LH*	*LL*
Pros-Pres*	Pros > Pres $p < .05$ *eta* = .05	n.s.	Pros > Pres $p < .01$ *eta* =. 06	Pros > Pres. $p < .05$ *eta* = .06
Pres-Ins*	n.s.	Pres > Ins $p < .05$ *eta* = .02	n.s.	n.s.
Ins-Exp**	n.s.	Ins < Exp $p < .0001$ *eta* = .48	Ins > Exp $p < .0001$ *eta* = .36	Ins > Exp $p < .0001$ *eta* = .15

Notes: n.s. = not significant; eta = eta-squared statistic; Pros = prospective teacher group; Pres = preservice teacher group; Ins = in-service teacher group; Exp = expert teacher group; CT = critical thinking; HH = high-CT activities for high-advantage learners; HL = high-CT activities for low-advantage learners; LH = low-CT activities for high-advantage learners; LL = low-CT activities for low-advantage learners.
* Results reported in Torff (2005).
** Results reported in Torff (2006).

tion, in-service teachers evinced support for didactic instruction not shared by experts, producing higher ratings for low-CT activities for both learner populations (with effect sizes of .36 for high-advantage learners and .15 for low-advantage learners).

Within-participants MANCOVA procedures (Table 22.2) showed that each group rated both high-CT and low-CT activities as more effective with high-advantage learners than low-advantage ones, indicating that experts as well as in-service teachers demonstrated the advantage effects obtained in prior research (Raudenbush et al, 1993; Warburton & Torff, 2005; Zohar et al., 2001). However, the effect sizes produced by in-service teachers (.68 and .52 for high-CT and low-CT activities, respectively) were considerably larger than those yielded by expert teachers (.28 and .09), indicating that in-service teachers expressed much stronger advantage effects relative to expert teachers. Both experts and in-service teachers produced a pedagogical-preference effect favoring high-CT activities over low-CT ones for high-advantage learners. This effect was far stronger for experts (effect size of .65) than for in-service teachers (.08). For low-advantage learners, experts (but not in-service teachers) demonstrated a pedagogical-preference effect (with a large effect size of .69).

These results indicate that experts were generally more supportive of high-CT activities and less supportive of low-CT ones, relative to randomly selected in-service teachers. Experts were also less inclined to differentiate use of high-CT and low-CT activities based on learner advantages, suggesting that experts are less likely to contribute to the rigor gap. These discrepancies between expert and in-service teachers indicate that the less rigorous pedagogy supported by in-service teachers for low-advantage learners does not constitute appropriate curriculum and instruction matched to learners in need of remedial studies. Rather, the discrepancies point to impoverished teaching for low-advantage learners, who should be challenged to the same extent as high-advantage learners. Teacher-education initiatives are needed to promote belief change concerning high-CT and low-CT instruction for different learner populations, with emphasis on high-CT activities for low-advantage learners (strategies for so doing are discussed below). The results also lend support to folk belief theory, which holds that culturally-provided folk beliefs about the human mind prompt teachers to support educational practices that provide impoverished curriculum and instruction for low-advantage learners, fomenting a rigor gap that contributes to the achievement gap.

Claim #3: Teachers' Beliefs Are Resistant to Change

To what extent do teachers' beliefs change as they participate in preservice teacher education? And how do they change afterward, as teachers gain in-service education and teaching experience? To answer these questions, research on the development of teachers' beliefs was conducted (Torff, 2005). Folk belief theory predicts that observed changes over time will be small, if any, since socially-shared beliefs tend to be stable and resistant to change.

In this study, the CTBA was administered in New York State to several groups including (a) *in-service teachers*—practitioners with a minimum of five years of teaching experience; (b) *preservice teachers*—undergraduates who had completed preservice teacher education but had yet to begin teaching; and (c) *prospective teachers*—undergraduates who had indicated an intention to enter the teaching profession but had yet to begin pre-service teacher education (N = 408). The research was designed to explore differences associated with pre-service education and the combination of teaching experience and in-service education. (See Table 22.3 for a summary of results.)

Effects of preservice education. Between-participants analyses showed that preservice and prospective teachers did not differ in ratings for high-CT activities for low-advantage learners. However, the groups did differ slightly in support for high-CT activities for high-advantage learners and low-CT activities for both student populations—and in all three cases pre-service teachers produced lower ratings than did prospective teachers. Preservice teachers were somewhat lower than prospective ones in ratings for high-CT activities for high-advantage learners (with a very small effect size of .05), indicating a modest loss of support for use of high-CT activities with high-advantage learners. Preservice teachers were also marginally lower than prospective ones in ratings for low-CT activities for both high- and low-advantage learners (each with an effect size of .06). Preservice education evidently had the effect of encouraging learners to rethink their support for low-CT instruction for all learners, although the effects were weak.

This pattern may be linked to learners' experiences in preservice teacher-education programs. These programs vary in philosophy and methods, but typically support student-centered, constructivist teaching emphasizing such methods as hands-on activities and student inquiry (e.g., Lambert & McCombs, 1998). Curriculum-centered pedagogy (e.g., lecture, note copying) is often derided as less effective in promoting learners' learning and well-being in school. Given this widely held view among teacher-educators, it is not surprising that pre-service teachers in this study tended to devalue low-CT activities after they have been enrolled in a teacher-education program for an extended period.

Within-participants analyses showed that preservice education was associated with reductions in advantage-effect sizes. Preservice teachers produced weaker advantage effects (.67 for high-CT activities and .38 for low-CT ones) relative to prospective teachers (.78 and .51). The groups also differed in pedagogical-preference effect sizes. For high-advantage learners, preservice teachers produced a pedagogical-preference effect size of .22, relative to .30 for prospective teachers. For low-advantage learners, preservice teachers yielded a pedagogical-preference effect size of .07, while prospective teachers produced no significant effect. With the declining advantage effect for high-CT activities combined with the emerging pedagogical preference effect favoring high-CT activities for low-advantage learners, the conclusion may be drawn that preservice education reduced teachers' inclination to differentiate the level of CT in instruction according to learners' SES advantages—but not by much.

Effects of Teaching Experience and In-Service Education

Teachers often say that classroom experience is the single most powerful influence on their work, much more so than preservice education. But this judgment is inconsistent with the findings of this study, which revealed the combination of teaching experience and in-service education to be associated with virtually no change in teachers' beliefs. One extremely small change was obtained: in between-participants analyses, in-service teachers were marginally lower than preservice ones in ratings for high-CT activities for low-advantage learners, with a negligible effect size of .02. Support for high-CT activities for low-advantage learners diminished following pre-service education—but with an effect size this small, it can hardly be seen as a meaningful shift. The groups did not differ in ratings for high-CT activities for high-advantage learners. Neither were differences obtained for low-CT activities for either student population. These results suggest that teachers' beliefs about CT in the classroom are largely stable of during the in-service years.

All groups in this study produced CTBA responses consistent with a rigor gap between high- and low-advantage learners. Moreover, the minute changes in beliefs during preservice education, and the absence of change afterward, indicate considerable stability in teachers' beliefs. These beliefs changed very little over time, despite circumstances that might be expected to induce substantial belief change (such as classroom experience). Results as such are consistent with folk belief theory, which suggests that beliefs about learning and teaching, as with other kinds of beliefs, tend to be robust and resistant to change (Bruner, 1990; Cole, 1996). Such a situation stacks the deck against the kinds of belief change teacher educators might wish to encourage, but it does render this change impossible. In the following section strategies for fostering belief change are considered.

Fostering Belief Change

A large body of literature is focused on strategies for facilitating change in teachers' beliefs (e.g., Blumenfeld Krajcik, Marx, & Soloway, 1994; Calderhead, 1996; Feinman-Nemser, McDiarmid, Melnick, & Parker, 1989; Hollingsworth, 1989; Holt-Reynolds, 2000; Morine Dershimer, 1993; Nespor, 1987; Patrick & Pintrich, 2001; Putman & Borko, 2000; Richardson, 1990, 1994; Richardson & Placier, 2002). This literature does not include discussions specifically about beliefs related to higher-order thinking, but many of the strategies described therein have potential for initiating change in these beliefs.

Professionals involved in facilitating belief change do not espouse telling people what they ought to believe. There is considerable evidence that people tend to tell teachers or researchers what they want to hear—and later revert to what they previously believed (e.g., Carey, 1985; Gardner, 1989; Gardner, Torff, & Hatch, 1996/2006). Hence, it is preferable to induce belief change by employing techniques that encourage people to question their existing beliefs and consider alternatives. These techniques typically involve *reflective thinking*, which can be defined as the act of careful consideration of previous conceptions, decisions, or actions—especially one's own (Conway, 2001; Iran-Nejed & Gregg, 2001; King & Kitchener, 1994; Richardson, 1996; Roskos, Vukelich, & Risko, 2001; Westbury, Hopmann, & Riquarts, 2000). Beliefs about CT, as with beliefs on other topics, are seldom carefully reasoned entities for which teachers have detailed rationales or even much conscious awareness; more often, beliefs are tacitly and uncritically held and involve unexamined assumptions (Sternberg et al., 2000; Torff & Sternberg, 2001; Wagner & Sternberg, 1986). Consequently, initiatives to promote reflection shed light on what teachers believe but have not actively contemplated.

Issues on which to focus teacher reflection. The design of these reflection activities can be informed by research on the specific issues that teachers take into account in deciding what kind of teaching to support for low-advantage students. A study was conducted combining qualitative and quantitative methods (Torff & Sessions, 2006). Initially, interviews were conducted with secondary social-studies teachers (N = 20), who were asked to review and comment on high-CT and low-CT activities included in the CTBA, particularly with respect to how effective these activities would be for teaching low-advantage students. A set of 11 issues were mentioned as important to classroom decision-making, including *students' level of prior knowledge, time constraints, influence of parents, influence of colleagues, students' level of motivation, students' level of ability, high-stakes tests, influence of administrators, nature of the subject* (social studies), *classroom management,* and *ease of assessment.*

These 11 issues were further examined using a survey instrument that included two prompts from the original CTBA (presented above). Each prompt was followed by 11 items—6-point Likert-type scales asking respondents to rate their level of agreement with a statement describing one of the eleven issues. For example, the issue *students' level of prior knowledge* is described in the statement, "Low-advantage students have sufficient prior knowledge to participate successfully in the activity." To make their ratings, respondents used the following scale: 1= *strongly agree*; 2 = *agree*; 3 = *agree more than disagree*; 4 = *disagree more than agree*; 5 = *disagree*; and 6 = *strongly disagree*. The instrument was administered to 120 secondary social-studies teachers in New York State. To determine the extent to which each issue was associated with a statistically significant pedagogical-preference effect (i.e., a difference between the high-CT prompt and the low-CT one for a given issue), within-subjects MANCOVA procedures were performed on the dependent variables.

The variables *classroom management* and *ease of assessment* yielded no statistically significant pedagogical preference effects. Three variables were associated with significant preferences for high-CT activities over low-CT ones when teaching low-advantage students. These include *influence of high-stakes tests* (partial eta-squared effect size of .12), *influence of administrators* (.09), and *the nature of the subject* (social studies) (.05).

Statistically significant preferences for low-CT activities over high-CT ones (for low-advantage students) were obtained with respect to six variables. These include, in order of effect size: *students' level of prior knowledge* (effect size of .15); *time constraints* (.13); *influence of parents* (.08); influence of colleagues (.08); *students' level of motivation* (.07); and *students' level of academic ability* (.04). Teachers were least supportive of high-CT activities when they perceive students to lack prior knowledge of the topic being taught. Such a result is consistent with the claim that teachers see a knowledge base as a necessary precondition for successful participation in high-CT activities, not something that can be gained through these activities. It is difficult to argue with the claim that high-CT activities are more time-consuming that low-CT ones, so it is no surprise that the variable *instructional time* was associated with diminished support for using high-CT activities with low-advantage students. Also associated with reduced use of high-CT for low-advantage students were two variables involving teachers' social environment, *influence of parents* and *influence of colleagues*; and two variables involving students' characteristics, *motivation* and *academic ability.*

For advocates of equitable access to high-CT activities in schools, these six issues provide topics of relevance for preservice and in-service teacher education. There are at least four strategies for inducing teachers to engage in reflection about these issues, with the goal of encouraging them to reconsider their beliefs about high-CT activities.

Reflection on existing beliefs. First, teachers can be encouraged to reflect on their existing beliefs about high-CT activities or personal histories regarding these activities (as learners and teachers) by responding, either verbally or in writing, to specially crafted questions. Some teacher educators advocate use of interview processes and/or class discussions to induce reflection (e.g., Hollingsworth, 1989; Holt-Reynolds, 1992; Manouchehri, 2002; Moyer & Milewicz, 2002; Peressini & Knuth, 1998). Other teacher educators ask their charges to write journal entries or response papers (sometimes requiring responses to specific questions and sometimes in an unrestricted format), or compile a portfolio (Bain, Mills, Ballantyne, & Packer, 2002; Hoover, 1994; Loughran & Corrigan, 1995; Spalding & Wilson, 2002). Questions growing out of the six issues described above (issues associated with differentiation of use of high-CT activities according to learner advantages) have potential to encourage teachers to reflect on the rationale for such differentiation. For example, should learners with a low level of academic ability be made to engage in debate (a high-CT activity)? Why or why not? What is likely to happen should these learners be engaged in such an activity? What could these learners gain from the activity, if anything? Questions as such ask teachers to ponder what they believe, develop a rationale for their beliefs, and possibly consider how their beliefs might be reexamined.

Reflection on case studies. Second, teachers can be asked to reflect on cases—the analysis of which prompts beliefs to be pressed into action (Cochran-Smith & Lytle, 2001; Trundle, Atwood, & Christopher, 2002). A teacher educator may provide scenarios of classroom situations and ask teachers to comment. Preservice teachers may be asked to consider issues growing out of the field observations that many teacher education programs require prior to student teaching. Similarly, practicing teachers may be asked to discuss situations from their classrooms. In each of these instances, the six issues found to be associated with differentiation of CT activities by learner advantages can be brought into play. Questions that may arise include: Why did learners in the low-track class fail to solve the biology problem correctly? Can learners short on motivation be expected to succeed in such tasks? Why? How to teach this content? As with interviews and journals, case-based questions require teachers to reflect on their beliefs and determine if changes to these beliefs are warranted.

Reflection on models of best practice. The third technique is actually a variation of the second. Teachers can be asked to analyze and evaluate models of the sorts of classroom activities that the teacher educator advocates (i.e., "best practices") (Basile, Olson, & Nathenson-Mejia, 2003; Jones & Vesilund, 1996; Sykes & Bird, 1992). For example, it is common to hear pre-service teachers say that it is impossible to use high-CT activities with learners who have little prior knowledge—for example, "the learners are in first-year Spanish; they don't know any Spanish yet—you just have to show them the conjugation rules and make them practice." As a response, the teacher educator might say: "Put a fully conjugated regular verb on the board and a non-conjugated one next to it, and start asking questions. If this is the *yo* form here, what's the *yo* form over there?" After the learners respond correctly, ask, "How did you come up with that?" After the learners state the conjugation rule, you can restate it with accuracy and clarity, and move on. Now learners are in the driver's seat, not the back seat.

Once teachers are exposed to this model, they can be asked to reflect on it in relation to the six issues described above. Can learners with little prior knowledge be made to think for themselves? What happens if you try? What can you hope to gain from such an attempt? What do you conclude about the role of learners' prior knowledge in use of high-CT and low-CT activities? Providing a model of the kind of activities precluded by teachers' existing beliefs may encourage a change in these beliefs. Videos of expert teachers may be helpful in this regard, as might field placements (prior to student teaching) in which carefully selected expert teachers demonstrate successful lessons using high-CT activities with low-advantage populations.

Curriculum design. Fourth, once teachers have been exposed to (and reflected upon) such models, they can be asked to create their own classroom activities along these lines. Instructional planning has been explored as a way to teach concepts in teacher education (Baylor, 2002; Blumenfeld, Hicks, & Krajcik, 1996). In this instance, teachers may be asked to develop an instructional unit for a disadvantaged class, with the goal of using high-CT activities appropriately. Once these activities are designed, and perhaps also implemented in actual K-12 classrooms (likely during student teaching), a laudable goal is to engage in reflective practice—systematic inquiry into one's own teaching and learning experiences with the goal of improving teaching practice (e.g., Artzt, 1999; Dunn & Shriner, 1999; Osterman & Kottkamp, 2005; Reiman, 1999; Westbury, Hopmann, & Riquarts, 2000). Reflective practice focused on the six issues associated with differentiation of high-CT activities by learner advantages may increase the likelihood that future instructional planning and lesson implementation will not exclude low-advantage learners from participating in high-CT activities.

These four vehicles for reflection can be useful ways to induce belief change when implemented generally, but they become more effective when based on the six issues known to be associated with differentiation of high-CT activities according to learner advantages (Torff & Sessions, 2006). Belief-change interventions that have been targeted in this way have potential to help teacher educators influence the instructional practice of future teachers and work for solutions to the rigor gap.

CONCLUSION

The achievement gap likely has many causes. But the evidence supporting folk belief theory makes the case that socially shared beliefs about learning and teaching in our culture go a long way to explain the rigor gap, which is widely seen as a primary cause of the achievement gap. Growing out of our culture's folk psychology, these beliefs prompt teachers to support a pedagogy in which classroom activities rich in higher-order thinking challenges are more often directed to high-advantage learners than lower-order ones. The research also supports the claim that the less rigorous pedagogy afforded low-advantage learners is not a pedagogically appropriate leveling of curriculum and instruction for learners in need of remedial work, but instead constitutes a regimen of impoverished teaching for learners who deserve to be challenged as much as their more affluent peers. The theory and accompanying research account for the persistence of the achievement gap, by showing how little teachers' beliefs change as they participate in pre-service and in-service education and as they accrue teaching experience. Difficult as fostering belief change may be, strategies for so doing have been suggested, including various forms of reflective thinking, analysis of models, and use of curriculum-development activities. Taking aim at the beliefs underlying the rigor and related instruction gap, addresses the root causes of the problem. The instructional strategies described in this chapter have the promise to ameliorate the achievement gap, the most vexing problem in our nation's schools.

REFERENCES

Archer, J. & McCarthy, B. (1988). Personal biases in student assessment. *Educational Research, 30,* 142-145.

Artzt, A. (1999). A structure to enable preservice teachers of mathematics to reflect on their teaching. *Journal of Mathematics Teacher Education, 2,* 143-166.

Barton, P. (2004). Why does the gap persist? *Educational Leadership, 62,* 8-13.

Bain, J., Mills, C., Ballantyne, R., & Packer, J. (2002). Developing reflection on practice through journal writing: Impacts of variations in the focus and level of feedback. *Teachers & Teaching: Theory & Practice, 8,* 171-196.

Basile, C., Olson, F., & Nathenson-Mejia, S. (2003). Problem-based learning: Reflective coaching for teacher educators. *Reflective Practice, 4*, 291-302.

Baylor, A. (2002). Expanding preservice teachers' metacognitive awareness of instructional planning through pedagogical agents. *Educational Technology Research & Development, 50*, 5-22.

Blumenfeld, P., Hicks, L., & Krajcik, J.S. (1996). Teaching educational psychology through instructional planning. *Educational Psychologist, 31*, 51-62.

Blumenfeld, P. C., Krajcik, J.S., Marx, R.W., & Soloway, E. (1994). Lessons learned: How collaboration helped middle-school science teachers learn project-based instruction. *Elementary School Journal, 94*, 539-551.

Bruner, J. (1990). *Acts of meaning*. Cambridge, MA: Harvard University Press.

Caccioppo, J., & Petty, R. (1982). The need for cognition. *Journal of Personality and Social Psychology, 42*, 116-131.

Cacioppo, J. T., Petty, R. E., Feinstein, J. A., & Jarvis, W. B. (1996). Dispositional differences in cognitive motivation: The life and times of individuals varying in need for cognition. *Psychological Bulletin, 119*, 197-253.

Calderhead, J. (1996). Teachers: Beliefs and knowledge. In D. Berliner & R. Calfee (Eds.), *Handbook of educational psychology* (pp. 709-725). New York, NY: Macmillan.

Carey, S. (1985). *Conceptual change in childhood.* Cambridge, MA: MIT Press.

Cochran-Smith, M., & Lytle, S. L. (2001). Beyond certainty: Taking an inquiry stance on practiced A. Lieberman & L. Miller (Eds.), *Teachers caught in the action: Professional development that matters* (pp. 45-58). New York, NY: Teachers College Press.

Cole, M. (1996). *Cultural psychology: A once and future discipline.* Cambridge, MA: Harvard University Press.

Conway, P. (2001). Anticipatory reflection while learning to teach: From a temporally truncated to temporally distributed model of reflection in teacher. *Teaching & Teacher Education, 17*, 89-106.

Crowne, D. & Marlow, D. (1964). *The approval motive.* New York, NY: Wiley.

Daniels, H., Cole, M., & Wertsch, L. (Eds.). (2007). *Cambridge companion to Vygotsky.* Cambridge, MA: Cambridge University Press.

Dunn. T., & Shriner, C. (1999). Deliberate practice in teaching: What teachers do for self improvement. *Teaching & Teacher Education, 15*, 631-651.

Dweck, C. (1986). Motivational processes affecting learning. *American Psychologist, 41*, 1040-1048.

Edwards, D. C. (1999). *Motivation and emotion.* Thousand Oaks, CA: SAGE.

Facione, P., Facione, N., & Giancarlo, C. (2000). *The California critical thinking skills test.* Millbrae, CA: California Academic Press

Feinman-Nemser, S., McDiarmid, G. W., Melnick, S. L., & Parker, M. (1989). *Changing beginning teachers' conceptions: A description of an introductory teacher education course* (Research Report 89-1). East Lansing, MI: National Center for Research on Teacher Education, College of Education, Michigan State University.

Gardner, H (1989). *The unschooled mind.* New York, NY: Basic Books.

Gardner, H., Torff, B., & Hatch, T. (1996). The age of innocence reconsidered: Preserving the best of the progressive traditions in psychology and education. In D. R. Olson & N. Torrance (Eds.), *The handbook of education and human development: New models of learning, teaching and schooling* (pp. 28-55). Cambridge, MA: Blackwell. Translated into French, Reprinted: *Revue Francaise de Pedagogie, 111*(95), 35-56.

Gardner, H., Torff, B., & Hatch, T. (2006). The age of innocence reconsidered: Preserving the best of the progressive tradition in psychology and education. In D. Olson & N. Torrance (Eds.), *Handbook of psychology in education: New models of learning, thinking, and teaching* (pp. 28-55). Cambridge, MA: Basil Blackwell. (Original work published 1996)

Givvin, K. B., Stipek, D. J., Salmon, J. M., & MacGyvers, V. L. (2001). In the eyes of the beholder: Students' and teachers' judgments of students' motivation. *Teaching and Teacher Education, 17*, 321-331.

Hollingsworth, S. (1989). Prior beliefs and cognitive change in learning to teach. *American Educational Research Journal, 26*, 160-189.

Holt-Reynolds, D. (2000). What does the teacher do? Constructivist pedagogies and prospective teachers' beliefs about the role of a teacher. *Teaching & Teacher Education, 16*, 21-32.

Holt-Reynolds, D. (1992). Personal history-based beliefs as relevant prior knowledge in coursework. *American Educational Research Journal, 29*, 325-349.

Hoover, L. (1994). Reflective writing as a window on preservice teachers' thought processes. *Teaching & Teacher Education, 10*, 83-93.

Iran-Nejad, A., & Gregg, M. (2001). The brain-mind cycle of reflection. *Teachers College Record, 103*, 868-895.

Jones, M. G., & Vesilind, E. (1996). Putting practice into theory: Changes in the organization of preservice teachers' pedagogical knowledge. *American Educational Research Journal, 33*, 91-117.

King, P. M., & Kitchener, K. S. (1994). *Developing reflective judgment: Understanding and promoting intellectual growth and critical thinking in adolescents and adults.* San Francisco, CA: Jossey-Bass.

Kozulin, A. (1998). *Psychological tools.* Cambridge, MA: Harvard University Press.

Lambert, N., & McCombs. B. (Eds.) (1998). *How learners learn: reforming schools through learner-centered instruction.* Washington DC: American Psychological Association.

Loughran, J. & Corrigan D. (1995). Teaching portfolios: A strategy for developing and teaching in preservice education. *Teaching & Teacher Education, 11*, 565-577.

Madon, S., Jussim, L., Keiper, S. Eccles, J., Smith, A., & Paolumbo, P. (1998). The accuracy and power of sex, social class, and ethnic stereotypes: A naturalistic study in person perception. *Personality and Social Psychology Bulletin, 24*, 1304-1318.

Manouchehri, A. (2002). Developing teaching knowledge through peer discourse. *Teaching &Teacher Education, 18*, 715-737.

Moje, E. B., & Wade, S. E. (1997). What case discussions reveal about teacher thinking. *Teaching and Teacher Education, 13*, 691-712

Morine Dershimer, G. (1993). Tracing conceptual change in preservice teachers. *Teaching and Teacher Education, 9*, 15-26.

Moyer, P., & Milewicz, E. (2002). Learning to question: Categories of questioning used by preservice teachers during diagnostic mathematics interviews. *Journal of Mathematics Teacher Education, 5,* 293-315.

Nespor, J. (1987). The role of beliefs in the practice of teaching. *Journal of Curriculum Studies, 19,* 317-28.

Nolen, S. B., & Nicholls, J. G. (1994). A place to begin (again) in research on student motivation: Teachers' beliefs. *Teaching and Teacher Education, 10,* 57-69.

Osterman, K., & Kottkamp, R. (2005). *Reflective practice for educators: Professional development to improving student learning* (2nd ed.). Thousand Oaks, CA: Corwin Press.

Patrick, H., & Pintrich, P. (2001). Conceptual change in teachers' intuitive conceptions of learning, motivation, and instruction: The role of motivational and epistemological beliefs. In B. Torff & R. Sternberg (Eds.), *Understanding and teaching the intuitive mind: Student and teacher learning* (pp. 117-144). Mahwah, NJ: Erlbaum Associates.

Pintrich, P., & Schunk, D. (1996). *Motivation in education.* Upper Saddle River, NJ: Prentice Hall.

Peressini, D., & Knuth, E. (1998). Why are you talking when you could be listening? The role of discourse and reflection in the professional development of a secondary mathematics teacher. *Teaching & Teacher Education, 14,* 107-125.

Putman, R., & Borko, H. (2000). What do new views of knowledge and thinking have to say about research on teacher learning? *Educational Researcher, 29,* 4-15.

Raudenbush, S. W., Rowan, B., & Cheong, Y. F. (1993). Higher order instructional goals in secondary schools: Class, teacher, and school influences. *American Educational Research Journal, 30,* 523-553.

Reiman, A. (1999). The evolution of the social roletaking and guided reflection framework in teacher education: Recent theory and quantitative synthesis of research. *Teaching & Teacher Education, 15,* 597-612.

Richardson, V. (1990). Significant and worthwhile change in teaching practice. *Educational Researcher, 19,* 10-18.

Richardson, V. (1994). The consideration of beliefs in staff development. In V. Richardson (Ed.), *Teacher change and the staff development process: A case of reading instruction* (pp. 90-108). New York, NY: Teachers College Press.

Richardson, V. (1996). The role of attitudes and beliefs in learning to teach. In J. Sikula (Ed.), *Handbook of research in teacher education* (2nd ed., pp. 102-119). New York, NY: Macmillian.

Richardson, V., & Placier, P. (2002). Teacher change. In V. Richardson (Ed.), *Handbook of research on teaching* (4rd ed., pp. 905-947). Washington, DC: American Educational Research Association.

Rosenthal, R., & Jacobson, L., (1992). *Pygmalion in the classroom: Expanded edition.* New York, NY: Irvington.

Roskos, K., Vukelich, C., & Risko, V. (2001). Reflection and learning to teach reading: A critical review of literacy and general teacher education studies. *Journal of Literacy Research, 33,* 595-635.

Shore, B. (1996). *Culture in mind: Cognition, culture and the problem of meaning.* New York. NY: Oxford University Press.

Shweder, Richard (1991). *Thinking Through Cultures.* Cambridge, MA: Harvard University Press.

Sykes, G., & Bird, T. (1992). Teacher education and the case idea. In G. Grant (Ed.), *Review of research in education* (Vol. 18, pp. 457-521). Washington, DC: American Educational Research Association.

Spalding, E., & Wilson, A. (2002). Demystifying reflection: A study of pedagogical strategies that encourage reflective journal writing. *Teachers College Record, 104,* 1393-1421.

Sternberg, R. J., Forsythe, G. B., Hedlund, J., Horvath, J. A., Wagner, R. K., Williams, W. M., et al. (2000). *Practical intelligence in everyday life.* New York, NY: Cambridge University Press.

Tollefson, N. (2000). Classroom applications of cognitive theories of motivation. *Educational Psychology Review, 12,* 63-83.

Torff, B. (2005). Developmental changes in teachers' beliefs about critical-thinking activities. *Journal of Educational Psychology, 97,* 13-22.

Torff, B. (2006). Expert teachers' beliefs about critical-thinking activities. *Teacher Education Quarterly, 33,* 37-52.

Torff, B., & Sessions, D. (2006). Issues influencing teachers' beliefs about use of critical-thinking activities with low-advantage learners. *Teacher Education Quarterly, 33,* 77-92.

Torff, B., & Sternberg, R. (2001). Intuitive conceptions among learners and teachers. In B. Torff & R. Sternberg (Eds.), *Understanding and teaching the intuitive mind: Student and teacher learning* (pp. 3-26). Mahwah, NJ: Erlbaum Associates.

Torff, B., & Warburton, E. (2005). Assessment of teachers' beliefs about classroom use of critical-thinking activities. *Educational and Psychological Measurement, 65,* 155-179.

Triandis, H. C. (1989). The self and social behavior in differing cultural contexts. *Psychological Review, 96,* 506–520.

Trundle, K., Atwood, R., & Christopher, J. (2002). Preservice teachers' conceptions of moon phases before and after instruction. *Journal of Research in Science Teaching, 39,* 633-658.

Vygotsky, L. (1978). *Mind in society.* Cambridge, MA: Harvard University Press.

Wagner, R. K., & Sternberg, R. J. (1986). Tacit knowledge and intelligence in the everyday world. In R. J. Sternberg & R. K. Wagner (Eds.), *Practical intelligence: Nature and origins of competence in the everyday world* (pp. 51-83). New York, NY: Cambridge University Press.

Warburton, E., & Torff, B. (2005). The effect of perceived learner advantages on teachers' beliefs about critical-thinking activities. *Journal of Teacher Education, 56,* 24-33.

Westbury, I., Hopmann, S., & Riquarts, K. (Eds.) (2000). *Teaching as a reflective practice: The German didaktik tradition.* Mahwah, NJ: Lawrence Erlbaum Associates.

Zohar, A., Degani, A., & Vaakin, E. (2001). Teachers' beliefs about low-achieving students and higher-order thinking. *Teaching and Teacher Education, 17,* 469-485.

Author Contact Information: **Bruce Torff**, PhD, professor of curriculum and teaching, director, Doctoral Program in Learning and Teaching, Department of Teaching, Literacy and Leadership School of Education, Health and Human Services Hofstra University Hempstead, NY 11549. Phone: 516-463-5803. E-mail: Bruce.A.Torff@hofstra.edu

CHAPTER 23

Constructivism

Transforming Knowledge of How People Learn Into Meaningful Instruction

Jacqueline Grennon Brooks
Hofstra University

This chapter presents *constructivism* as a powerful instructional theory, one that requires rich understanding of the theory, deep content knowledge, and creative capacities to transform learning theory and content knowledge into problem based instructional sequences. The discussions in this chapter intersect with theories of literacy and language acquisition, classroom management, and assessment, all of which are discussed in other sections of this volume. In this chapter, we focus on constructivism as an instructional theory emerging from what we know about how people learn.

While teachers can offer constructivist-based instruction within many modalities and structures, there are certain classroom practices consistent with constructivist pedagogy and others that are not. Generally speaking, teachers cannot fully and authentically offer constructivist instruction within classroom management systems based on token economies, language acquisition programs based on solely rote repetition, and assessment processes ruled by fill-in-the-blank sheets and grading designed to generate a bell curve. This chapter describes the teaching practices that effectively offer students opportunities to think, build conceptual knowledge and develop academic and social skills.

THE THEORY'S GOALS AND ASSUMPTIONS

Constructivism is a learning theory that includes discussions of deep issues within the human search for understanding. Constructivism asks the psychological question: How does the mind work? It poses the epistemological query: What is knowledge? And it enters the controversial philosophical debate: What is real? Embedded within these discussions are the theory's instructional goals and assumptions.

Constructivism assumes that learners generate meaning though mental activity that satisfies a search for understanding. The theory is often associated with the work of the twentieth century psychologist Jean Piaget. However, historians typically credit the eighteenth century philosopher, Giambattista Vico, with the first use of constructivism as a word to describe the notion that people can know only what their cognitive structures allow them to know (Lo, 1996).

The goal of education rooted in constructivist learning theory is to offer students opportunities to construct understandings at the leading edge of their current functioning. These opportunities are designed, offered and managed by a teacher with understandings of how people forge new concepts, including both the individual and collaborative nature of concept formation. An assumption of this theory is that there are common teaching practices that are observable across contexts and developmental levels. What are those practices? The rest of the chapter discusses the foundational research from which these practices emerge, and then describes the practices.

FOUNDATIONAL RESEARCH

Constructivist learning theory is described by countless behavioral studies of children's thinking. Today,

The Handbook of Educational Theories, pp. 271–275

there exists an ever increasing production of neuroscientific studies documenting how the human brain is always changing in relationship to experience. These studies tie the learning experiences described by constructivist theory with brain growth and development. We know much more today than we did years ago about the brain as an organ of the body and the mind as an ongoing process of awareness (Pinker, 1999, 2007).

Neuroplasticity refers to the process by which experiences last as anatomical and physiological changes to the physical brain (Tortora & Grabowski, 1996). Our interaction with the environment shapes our brain structure by strengthening some of our neuronal connections and pruning others. Anatomical changes in the brain have dramatic effects because they influence future learning (Gopnic, Meltzoff, & Kuhl, 1999). "The mind uses the brain to create itself" (Siegel, 2010, p. 261).

Although researchers are cautious to equate any specific form of specific learning environment with any specific type of physical brain development, the past decade has witnessed the rise of educational programs based on inferences from research and marketed as brain-based (Krakovsky, 2005). Even under the umbrella of caution, there are reasonable approaches to programs aligned with both neuroscientific research and behavioral development research. Emerging data suggest a link between brain development and the type of education within constructivist classrooms (Michaels, Shouse, & Schweingruber, 2007).

Engaging children in meaningful educational activities provides a viable foundation for physical brain development, the capacity for mindful reason, and positive emotions toward learning. The National Scientific Council on the Developing Child (2007) reinforces the importance of the learning experiences associated with constructivist theory. They acknowledge that novel learning experiences actually stimulate the growth of new neurons (Siegel, 2010). Thus, the definition of what constitutes brain-based education is increasingly pointing to the provision of a constructivist learning environment.

Validation of the Theory

There exist literature and existing frameworks aimed at measuring the essential practices of high quality teaching and learning. MacGregor (2007) identifies the underlying assumptions of the major frameworks, many of which are observation instruments that include student work and structured interviews, and generates a list of essential observable practices that can be systematically measured and fostered. Shulman (2004) points out that observation protocols can be limited. He uses the example of photographing a great work of art with an instant camera or recording a fine opera with an office dictation machine. Much of the artistry is lost in capturing the moment with a blunt instrument. Yet, over time and across race, ethnicity, and socioeconomics, patterns of instructional success in high performing schools emerge.

While improved student learning depends on and is associated with a range of school characteristics (Goldstein & Noguera, 2006), this chapter focuses on the instructional components of those characteristics, those aligned with constructivist instructional theory. Two examples are the Teaching Attributes Observation Protocol (Abbott & Fouts, 2003) that looks at how teachers engage students in building knowledge through reflection and applying knowledge in real word problems, among many other activities, and the STAR Protocol (Baker, Olzendam, Gratama, & Arington, 2005) that looks at how teachers guide students in building conceptual knowledge and engaging in substantive communication, including as well, other activities. Both of these protocols and others like them, all of which are associated with improved student learning, share a common focus: deep alignment of the content, context, and cognitive demands of curriculum, instruction, and assessment (Shannon & Byisma, 2007).

Instruction based on understandings of the cognitive demands of the curriculum and the leading edge cognitive functioning of the learner is the iconic description of constructivist instructional theory. The protocols reviewed here, and the others like them, serve as a mechanism to link instruction to learning. The learning measured in these studies was largely based on scores on standardized tests. Thus, these protocols substantiate constructivism as a mechanism to improve student test scores, as well as generate other learning as evidenced by classroom discourse and student generated artifacts.

Critiques of the Theory

For many, constructivism is viewed as an inclusive instructional theory, informing practices that offer equitable learning opportunities across diverse populations (Atwater, 1996; Cobern, 1996). Yet, there also exist critiques of constructivism on many levels, some of which serve the important function of pressing the study of constructivism forward and others of which are based on misinterpretations and do not further discussion.

In some studies, constructivism is viewed as a theory of instruction that asks teachers to allow learners free reign to explore topics with minimal teacher input (Kirschner, Sweller, & Clark, 2006). This is a misinterpretation of the carefully orchestrated teaching activity in which competent constructivist teachers engage. In other critiques, comparisons of teaching models find constructivist teaching as falling behind not only direct instruction schools, but behind schools categorized as the comparison no-treatment control group (W. J. Matthews, 2003). Matthews reports on a highly funded large scale study, but without measures of fidelity of practice to the tenets of categorized models and with no description of the activities in which the *no-treatment* children engaged; therefore, he fails to critique constructivism on a basis from which we can learn how to better offer instruction.

Contrary to the nature of the above critiques, there are reasoned critiques of constructivist instructional theory that center on its relativist principles, which lead to discussions of larger issues. Some critiques of constructivist theory question the definition of *truth*. In these critiques, constructivism is characterized as acknowledging the notion that culture influences perceptions, and thus influences what is construed as true or accurate, and this notion of relativistic truth is not valued (M. R. Matthews, 1998).

Richardson (2003) offers the perspective that today's descriptions of constructivist pedagogy are too narrow and calls for an instructional theory of constructivism that reaches beyond what we presently see. She contends that there currently exist only meager descriptions of teaching practices consistent with constructivist learning theory and advocates for more empirical research linking student learning and cultural responsiveness.

The next section of this chapter looks at an instructional sequence as a teacher analyzes a student's meaning making process and transforms her analysis into meaningful instruction.

Application of the Theory

Third grader, Imani, had an idea during a science lesson. She wanted to put water in a Ziploc bag to tape to the window to see what would happen. Her teacher, Ms. Rivera, asked Imani and her partner to put the same amount of water in each of their bags, so it would be *fair.* Knowing that there were only 100 milliliter graduated cylinders available, Ms. Rivera purposely suggested that they use 200 milliliters of water, in order to prompt the necessity for the children to engage in a sequential task with some type of record keeping required.

After much contemplation while looking at all the supplies, Imani asked Ms. Rivera whether or not she could pour water twice from the 100 milliliter cylinder. Ms. Rivera told her that it sounded reasonable, encouraged her to go ahead with her plan, and asked her to let her know how it turned out.

When Imani poured the second 100 ml into the zippered bag, she was disappointed that it did not work. The teacher asked her why she thought it did not work. Imani pointed and said that there was less water in the bag. The teacher asked her how much water she thought was in the bag, and, to the teacher's surprise, she replied, "About 25." Together, Ms. Rivera and Imani poured the water back and forth a couple of times, but each time Imani viewed the 200 ml of water in the bag, Imani claimed the water was now "About 25."

Understanding the Confusion

Initially, Imani had the idea that she might be able to apply what she knew about adding two numbers to real life water in a cylinder. But, her mathematical idea proved, in her eyes, to be wrong. Even though she, on her own initiation, correctly reasoned that 100 ml of water added to 100 ml of water would generate 200 ml, her perception of the amount of water took over her reasoning, and led her to conclude that her very correct idea was not correct.

When a child reasons that a given volume of water remains the same when poured, without any spilling, into another container, we call this reasoning a process of conserving continuous quantity. In this case, the continuous quantity is water. When a child can pour a volume of water from a narrow container into a wide container, or in this case a plastic zippered bag, and allows her *reasoning* that there is the same amount of water to take over her *perception* that the amount of water *looks* less, we call this reasoning a process of conserving volume. Imani was not conserving volume. To her, the 200 mls of water in the zippered bag *looked* less, and although she had just poured the water herself from one container to the zippered bag, she concluded that it *was* less.

Addressing the Confusion

Ms. Rivera was quite surprised by Imani's response and had to think on her feet about how to proceed. Many thoughts raced through her mind:

- If I had not drawn Imani's attention to the question of whether the bag really contained 200 mls of water, would she have gone on with her experiment, thinking her 100 + 100 = 200 idea was a good one?
- Did my question inadvertently plant seeds of misconceptions?
- Would it be a good idea now to invite Imani to pour her 100 ml samples into equal cups, and provide her the opportunity to potentially confirm her reasoning that 100 + 100 = 200?
- Would it be a good idea to ask Imani to develop a way to use the cups in her experiment instead of the problematic zippered bag?

Ms. Rivera decided that Imani was on the verge of changing her thinking, given Imani's reasoning before she looked at the outcome of her pouring. Ms. Rivera brought out various containers with volume markings, and presented some problems to Imani. Ms. Rivera made a contextual decision that this instruction may result in more meaningful learning than proceeding with the intended direction of the lesson.

In her school, the administration and state tests force a good deal of drill and practice of arithmetic problems, with 100 + 100 being one of the simple ones. Conservation of volume is a benchmark cognitive conquest in later childhood, about 11-14 years of age, but the beginnings of conserving principles usually begin at about age 7.

A visitor to Ms. Rivera's room may see Imani engaged in what looks like Kindergarten water play. Perhaps it is. Perhaps Imani did not have the kindergarten water play experiences that often afford young children a background for the type of thinking to come. But, perhaps it is not kindergarten water play. Perhaps Imani is engaging in experiences that are timely and well suited for her current, eight-year-old water conservation or water non-conservation.

Transitioning From Confusion

In Ms. Rivera's case, she listened to Imani's questions *and* answers, and realized that Imani's currently *missing* cognitive scheme may interfere with her success in much of the math curriculum to follow. Ms. Rivera made the professional decision that, due to her inference that Imani was in a transitional time in her thinking with regard to quantity and amount, offering Imani multiple experiences to measure and pour may be fruitful in bridging the transition to conserving volume.

Ms. Rivera knew that cognitive schemes cannot be directly taught. But, she could provide the types of experiences out of which Imani's brain and mind could construct the cognitive scheme.

CONCLUSION

How people learn is an ongoing study as education, philosophy, epistemology and neuroscience converge in studies that spill from one discipline to the next. Using what we know about how people learn to design instruction defines the leading edge of good education. Sadly, today's educational world is focused on test preparation, not learning through meaning making. But, happily, today's research is opening up a new lens with which to refocus education on meaning making.

Constructivism is a learning theory based on the premise that learners generate meaning triggered by interactions with the world around them. Through mental formulation and reformulation of theories that satisfy the search for understanding, learners grow and develop. Alliances between researchers conducting cognitive science investigations on how people learn and researchers conducting brain-mapping studies of brain cell communication are setting the stage for a new era in learning about learning (Tokuhama-Espinosa, 2010). Early advances in the field offer neurological evidence of the power of constructivist pedagogical approaches.

Making sense of the world and choosing correct answers on standardized tests do not exist at cross purposes. While this article posits that meaning making is more important, it also recognizes that choosing the correct answers on exams is a form of meaning making. Thus, teaching with constructivist approaches is consistent with the outcome of fostering students' success on standard measures of academic performance. And, lastly, neuroscience is supporting the educational argument that the building of conceptual knowledge and the development of academic and social skills necessitates instruction rich in problem-solving opportunities.

REFERENCES

Abbott, M. L., & Fouts, J. T. (2003) *Constructivist teaching and student achievement: The results of a school level classroom observation study in Washington.* Seattle, WA: Washington Research Center, Seattle Pacific University.

Atwater. M. M. (1996). Social constructivism: Infusion into the multicultural science education research agenda. *Journal of Research in Science Teaching, 33*(8), 821-837.

Baker, D. B., Olzendam, A. M., Gratama, M. S., & Arington, S. R. (2005). *The STAR classroom protocol: a measure of powerful teaching and learning in Washington State.* Bothell, WA: The BERC Group.

Cobern, W. W. (1996). Constructivism and non-Western science education research. *International Journal of Science Education, 4*(3), 287-302.

Goldstein, J., & Noguera, P. A. (2006). A thoughtful approach to teacher evaluation. *Educational Leadership, 63*(6), 31-37

Gopnic, A., Meltzoff, A., & Kuhl, P. (1999). The scientist in the crib: What early learning tells us about the mind. New York, NY: HarperCollins.

Kirschner, P. A., Sweller, J., & Clark, R. E. (2006). Why minimal guidance during instruction does Not work: An analysis of the failure of constructivist, discovery, problem-based, experiential, and inquiry-based teaching. *Educational Psychologist, 41*(2), 75-86. Retrieved from http://www.cogtech.usc.edu/publications/kirschner_Sweller_Clark.pdf

Krakovsky, M. (2005, February 2). Dubious 'Mozart Effect' remains music to many Americans' ears. Stanford Report. Retrieved from http://news-service.stanford.edu/news/2005/february2/mozart-020205.html

Lo, H. N. (1996). *Giambattista Vico.* Georgia Institute of Technology.

MacGregor, R. R. (2007, February). *The essential practices of high quality teaching and learning.* Bellevue, WA: The Center for Educational Effectiveness. Retrieved from http://www.effectiveness.org/files/EssentialPracticesofHighQualityTeaching%20and%20Learning.pdf

Matthews, M. R. (1998). *Constructivism in science education: A philosophical examination.* Norwell, MA: Kluwer.

Matthews, W. R. (2003, Summer). Constructivism in the classroom: Epistemology, history, and empirical evidence. *Teacher Education Quarterly*, 51-64. Retrieved from http://www.teqjournal.org/backvols/2003/30_3/matthews.pdf

Michaels, S., Shouse A. W., & Schweingruber H. A. (2007). *Ready, set, science!: Putting research to work in K-8 science classrooms.* Washington, DC: National Academies Press.

National Scientific Council on the Developing Child. (2007). *The science of early childhood development.* Retrieved from http://www.developingchild.net

Pinker, S. (1999). *How the mind works.* New York, NY: W. W. Norton.

Pinker, S. (2007). *The stuff of thought: Language as a window into human nature.* New York, NY: Viking; London: Penguin.

Richardson, V. (December 2003). Constructivist pedagogy. *Teachers College Record, 105*(9), 1623-1640.

Shannon, G. S., & Bylsma, P. (2007). *The nine characteristics of high-performing schools: A research-based resource for schools and districts to assist with improving student learning* (2nd ed.). Olympia, WA: OSPI.

Shulman, L. S. (2004). *The wisdom of practice: Essays on teaching, learning, and learning to teach.* San Francisco, CA: Jossey-Bass.

Siegel, D. J. (2010). *Mindsight: The new science of personal transformation.* New York, NY: Bantam.

Tokuhama-Espinosa, T. (2010). *Mind, brain, and education science: A comprehensive guide to the new brain-based teaching.* New York, NY: W. W. Norton.

Tortora, G., & Grabowski, S. (1996). *Principles of anatomy and physiology* (8th ed.), New York, NY: HarperCollins College.

Author Contact Information: Jacqueline Grennon Brooks, EdD, Department of Teaching, Literacy and Leadership, School of Education, Health and Human Services, Hofstra University, 105 Hagedorn Hall, Hempstead, NY 11549 Phone: 516-463-5777 E-mail: Jacqueline.grennon.brooks@hofstra.edu

CHAPTER 24

Defining Teacher Action Research as an Instructional Theory in Teacher Education

Frances O'Connell Rust
University of Pennsylvania

Susan Hansen
National Louis University, Chicago, Illinois

Teacher research, action research, practitioner inquiry—each of these describes a type of qualitative research that draws on the rich traditions of qualitative research in anthropology, education, and social work (Eisner & Peshkin, 1990; Ely, Anzul, Freidman, Garner, & Steinmetz, 1991; Erickson, 1986; Lewin, 1948; Miles & Huberman, 1984; Spindler, 1982; Spradley, 1979; Wolcott, 1973). Cochran-Smith and Lytle (1999) define *teacher research*

> in the broadest possible sense to encompass all forms of practitioner inquiry that involve systematic, intentional, and self-critical inquiry about one's work in K-12, higher education, or continuing education classrooms, schools, programs, and other formal educational settings. (p. 22)

The data collection tools used in this work are already part of the instructional tool kit of many practitioners: observation protocols, interviews, anecdotal records, work samples, test scores, video- and audiorecordings, photographs, journals, and other similar hands-on techniques. Hence, while not a new form of research, its increased use in teacher education (Cochran-Smith & Lytle, 1999; Korthagen, Loughran, & Russell, 2006; Lampert & Ball, 1999), teacher professional development (Little, 2007; Putnam & Borko, 2000), as an integral aspect of lesson study (Hiebert, Gallimore, & Stigler, 2002), and in assessing the impact of education policy (Erickson & Christman, 1996; Zeichner, 1993) has given it increasing visibility as a powerful form of inquiry for teachers examining the effectiveness of various interventions, for researchers trying to discern the impact of research on practice, and for education policy-makers curious about the ways in which policy is understood and enacted.

Theory Description

Our experience as teacher educators has led us to situate action research as a core instructional process in our teacher education programs and to move beyond Cochran-Smith and Lytle's (1999) definition toward a framing of action research as an instructional theory that has the potential to put teachers directly in touch with data that informs thoughtful teaching. In taking this stance, we draw not only on the traditions of qualitative research described above but also on theories about reflection in action (Dewey, 1904, 1929, 1933/1998; Schön, 1983; Lyons, 2010; Van Veen & Van de Ven, 2008; Zeichner & Tabachnick, 1991), recent research on how the brain works and its implications for both teaching and learning (Bransford, Brown, & Cocking, 1999; Rogoff & Lave, 1999; Vygotsky, 1968, 1978), and on theoretical frames about the ways in which teacher education is or could be structured as professional development (Dewey, 1904; Hawkins, 1973; Hiebert, Morris, Berk, &

The Handbook of Educational Theories, pp. 277–281

Jansen, 2007; Feiman-Nemser, 1983). In earlier work (Rust, 2009), we have positioned teacher action research as a bridge between theory/research and practice—the place where practitioners can see their initiatives and interactions with learners in the context of the prior research on the topic of interest, while at the same time taking a clear-sighted look at the success or not of what they are doing in their classrooms. We described action research as the means through which teacher educators could engage prospective teachers in shaping inquiry around their efforts to implement in their student teaching experiences the research and theory that were introduced in their methods courses. We also suggested that action research could serve as an important frame for teacher professional development (Rust, 2009; Rust & Meyers, 2006), and, following Berk and Hiebert (2009) and Rust (2009), for the professional development of teacher educators themselves. Teacher research, as we conceive of it and as we teach it, is informed by the broad field of educational research that includes psychology, sociology, and literacy, mathematics, science, social studies, arts education and, also by data drawn from the day-to-day interactions that influence teachers' decision making.

Development and Iteration of Action Research as an Instructional Theory

Reflection

Dewey (1933/1998) describes two aims for teacher education:

> Two controlling purposes may be entertained so different from each other as radically to alter the amount, conditions, and method of practice work. On one hand, we may carry on the practical work with the object of giving teachers in training working command of the necessary tools of their profession; control of the technique of class instruction and management; skill and proficiency in the work of teaching. With this aim in view, practice work is, as far as it goes, of the nature of apprenticeship. On the other hand, we may propose to use practice work as an instrument in making real and vital theoretical instruction; the knowledge of subject matter and of principles of education. (p. 2)

The move toward the second aim is informed by the development in the teacher of the capacity for reflective inquiry that Dewey (1933/1998) claims to be essential to education which he describes as "the formation of wide-awake, careful, thorough habits of thinking" (p. 78). Dewey identifies five qualities of reflective thought:

> In between, as states of thinking, are (1) suggestions, in which the mind leaps forward to a possible solution; (2) an intellectualization of the difficulty or perplexity that has been felt (directly experienced) into a problem to be solved, a question for which the answer must be sought; (3) the use of one suggestion after another as a leading idea, or hypothesis, to initiate and guide observation and other operations in the collection of factual material; (4) the mental elaboration of the idea or supposition (reasoning, in the sense in which reasoning is a part, not the whole inference); and (5) testing the hypothesis by overt or imaginative action. (p. 107)

Building on Dewey's work, Schön (1983) focused on how professionals know through practice and describes this as *knowing in action*:

> ordinary people and professional practitioners often think about what they are doing, sometimes while they are doing it. Stimulated by surprise, they turn back on action and on knowing, which is implicit in action. They may ask, "What features do I notice when I recognize this thing? What are the criteria by which I make this judgment? How am I framing the problem?" As (the practitioner) tries to make sense, he also reflects on the understandings which have been implicit in his (prior) understandings. (p. 52)

Often, suggests Lyons (2010) in describing Schön's work, "the task for the professional (is) to know how to frame the problem, not even to solve it but to frame it so it could be solved" (p. 15). Zeichner and Tabachnich (1991) describe identify three types of reflection:

- *Instrumental reflection*, which refers to the organization of the lesson, the effective application of methods, skills, and technical knowledge, the interaction, etc. In general, it refers to acting in the classroom.
- *Academic reflection*, which refers to the use of subject pedagogical and educational theories to understand the content, the underlying principles and mechanisms of teaching and learning, and the implications of certain teaching strategies and curricula. In general, it refers to the use of theory in the reflection process.
- *Critical reflection*, which refers to moral, ethical, and esthetical reflections and other normative criteria to think about such aspects as the social function of education and the consequences of one's teaching for the well-being of others.

Reflection has become an essential underpinning of most teacher education programs. In some programs that we will describe later, the press toward reflective practice has moved the program toward the adoption of teacher research as a core pedagogy that enables both prospective and experienced teachers to engage more fully in inquiry around their instructional interactions with students and so to use inquiry as a type of formative assessment that guides and enhances instruction.

How Adults Learn and Implications for Learning and Instruction

Thanks to Vygotsky (1968, 1978), we now know that much of our understanding of self, of one another, of the world is shaped in culture and community. *Everyday cognition* is the way that Rogoff and Lave (1999) describe the development of knowing, and we are learning that the *funds of knowledge* (Moll, 1992) that individuals develop are quite complex and idiosyncratic even as children and certainly by the time that they enter adulthood. Bransford, Brown, and Cocking (1999) show that adults, as much as children, are constructors of knowledge. They draw on what they already know to make sense of new material. They need to be scaffolded (supported) as they learn; they need to be able to engage in trial and error; they need to be able to practice new skills and receive feedback from respected others; and they need to have models of practice.

In teaching as in other fields, we now understand that ways of knowing are informed by one's own lived experience as well as by interaction with others who are trying similar things and confronting similar issues. However, what happens all too often in preservice teacher education is a disconnect of prospective teachers from their own experience as students as well as an isolation of the individual as a student and then as a student teacher. For in-service teachers, opportunities for collaborative inquiry are often similarly constrained.

Rust (2009) suggests teacher research done in a *community of practice* (Wenger, 1998) can be a powerful form of professional development for it is in such settings that pre-service and experienced teachers can share ideas, experiment with practice, and receive appropriate and meaningful commentary regarding their findings. It is in such settings that teachers can begin to surmount the barrier of privatism that Lortie (1975) found to be so constricting of teacher professional development. As Rust writes,

> When teachers work together as colleagues (Wenger, 1998) in focused, collaborative inquiry (Hiebert, Gallimore, & Stigler, 2002; Lewis & Tsuchida, 1998; Stigler & Hiebert, 1999), they are likely to be successful at substantively changing their practice—the ultimate goal of most educational innovation and professional development. (p. 1889)

For teacher education, the implications seem obvious. First, it is essential to develop programs in ways that enable new and experienced teachers to draw on their own lived experience as students, what Lortie (1975) describes as the *apprenticeship of observation*. They should be able to reflect on that experience consciously weighing and analyzing it relative to the research and theory with which they are coming in contact as well as with their classroom practice. As Van Veen and Van Der Ven (2008) write:

> Practice needs theory, as theory needs practice. Reflection needs theory because it raises questions, undermines long-held beliefs, introduces ambiguities, reveals complexities, and sets new tasks. Theory assists the process of analyzing and understanding practice and opens new possibilities. At the same time, practice also contributes to theory because it can function as a laboratory where theory is tested, refined, adapted and criticized. (p. 47)

Second, both preservice and experienced teachers should have the opportunity to work collaboratively with one another. Such collaboration should be focused around inquiry, for example, the careful study of children's work that Carini (1971, 1972, 1975, 1979, 1984) and her colleagues have modeled or the action research studies that Rust (2007) and Hansen and her colleagues (Beane, 2005; Muldowney, 2010) help their students to shape. And, teacher research itself should be informed by relevant research and theory. Inquiry that exists in its own little bubble changes nothing; inquiry that is informed by reference to research, that is seen as part of a larger inquiry can both raise the level of individual practice (Rust & Meyers, 2006) and contribute to the larger conversation about teaching and learning (Hiebert, Gallimore, & Stigler, 2002).

Bringing Theory and Practice Together in Learning to Teach and Refining Teaching Practice: Application of Teacher Research as an Instructional Theory

"Teachers are always asking questions about their work" (Meyers & Rust, 2003, p. 1). The process of teacher research begins from this natural teacher activity, when the teacher intentionally chooses one of these classroom-based questions for further study. Using the question as a guide, the teacher collects classroom data that will contribute to exploring the question. The data is then carefully and thoughtfully examined. That is one cycle of teacher research, and the second begins when the findings from the first cycle are implemented, and further data is collected and examined. The resulting reflection on practice has the capability of being instrumental (improving teaching practices and student learning), academic (referencing and adding to the work of experts in the field) and critical (as teachers examine their values, frames of reference and their concerns for their students) (Zeichner & Tabachnich, 1991).

Further, teacher research placed at the core of teacher education has the potential to support self-initiated professional development that enables professional autonomy. Hawkins (1973) suggests that such a placement could result in what Hiebert, Morris, Berk, and Jansen (2007) describe as "a long term learning process" (p. 48). "It may be possible," writes Hawkins, "to learn in two or three years the kind of practice which then leads to another 20 years of learning" (p. 7). Hiebert et al. (2007)

> believe that the core of teaching—interacting with students about the content—is not learned well through automatizing routines or even through acquiring expert strategies during a teacher preparation program. Rather, it is learned through continual and systematic analysis of teaching. (p. 49)

There are an increasing number of teacher education programs that have brought together the frame of teacher research and the concept of communities of practice. Korthagen (2001) and his colleagues have shaped what they describe as realistic teacher education around a model of reflective practice that relates preservice students' prior experience with the competencies required in their field and enables them to study and inquire around the meeting of the two in the field of practice. Similarly, and drawing on Zeichner and Tabachnick's (1991) concept of critical reflection, Van Veen and Van der Ven (2008) developed a theoretical framework for a teacher education program that is used by their student teachers to understand and examine their teaching. This approach is demonstrated in a final task completed by their student teachers: an analysis of their own teaching, using key incident analysis. McVarish and Rust (2006) describe an integrated curriculum for elementary teachers that used inquiry in the form of increasingly sophisticated case studies done by each student teacher over the course of the two-year program. Hansen and her colleagues (Beane, 2005; Muldowney, 2010) have shaped a master's level teacher education program for experienced teachers that has inquiry at its core and, as its final project, the development of a teacher research project by each teacher. While each of these programs is unique, all draw their strength from their combined emphasis on critical reflection (as defined by Zeichner & Tabachnick, 1991) and inquiry around practice that is situated within a community of practice.

CONCLUSION

While teacher research/action research is not a new form of research, its use in teacher education has the potential to radically shift instructional practice in schools as well as in teacher education programs. We have found that teacher research that is situated at the nexus of research and practice and developed in community enables a *mindfulness* (Langer, 1979) that pushes our prospective teachers beyond the rote implementation of practice to careful examination of their students' individual needs as well as comprehensive instructional goals. At the same time, those who embrace teacher research seem to situate themselves as inquirers in a community of learners who seek greater understanding of how to teach so that children will learn, and how to practice in ways that acknowledge the very specific, contextual nature of learning and, therefore, of teaching. Their practice, then, embodies action research as an instructional theory. As well, those for whom teacher research is a core value also find that the flexibility and insight gained through their ongoing inquiry leads them toward becoming activists in shaping and reshaping education. With this work of inquiry, teacher research becomes the bridge between research/theory and practice.

REFERENCES

Beane, J.A. (2005). *A reason to teach: Creating classrooms of dignity and hope.* Portsmouth, NH. Heinemann.

Berk, D., & Hiebert, J. (2009). Improving the mathematics preparation of elementary teachers, one lesson at a time. *Teachers and Teaching: Theory and Practice, 15*(3), 337-356.

Bransford, J. D., Brown, A. L., & Cocking, R. R. (1999). *How people learn: Brain, mind, experience, and school.* Washington, DC: National Academy Press.

Carini, P. (1971). *Recordkeeping.* North Bennington, VT: The Prospect Center.

Carini, P. (1972). *Documentation: An alternative approach to program accountability.* Bennington, VT: The Prospect Center.

Carini, P. (1975). *Observation and description: An alternative method for the investigation of human phenomena.* Grand Forks, ND: North Dakota Study Group on Evaluation.

Carini, P. (1979). *The art of seeing and the visibility of person.* Grand Forks, ND: North Dakota Study Group on Evaluation.

Carini, P. (1984). *The lives of seven children.* Grand Forks, ND: North Dakota Study Group on Evaluation.

Cochran-Smith, M. (2002). Learning and unlearning: The education of teacher educators. *Teachers and Teacher Education, 19*(1), 5-28.

Cochran-Smith, M., & Lytle, S. (1999). The teacher research movement: A decade later. *Educational Researcher, 28*(7), 15-25.

Dewey, J. (1904). Part I—The relation of theory to practice in the education of teachers. *The Third Yearbook For The Scientific Study Of Education.* Chicago, IL: University of Chicago.

Dewey, J. (1929). *The sources of a science of education.* New York, NY: Horace Liveright.

Dewey, J. (1998). *How we think: A restatement of the relation of reflective thinking to the educative process.* Boston, MA: Houghton-Mifflin. (Original work published 1933)

Eisner, E. W., & Peshkin, A. (Eds.). (1990). *Qualitative inquiry in education: The continuing debate.* New York: Teachers College Press

Ely, M., Anzul, M., Freidman, T., Garner, D., & Steinmetz, A. M. (1991). *Doing qualitative research. Circles within circles.* New York, NY: Falmer.

Erickson, F. (1986). Qualitative methods on research on teaching. In M. Wittrock (Ed.), *Handbook of research on teaching* (3rd ed., pp. 119-161). New York, NY: Macmillan.

Erickson, F., & Christman, J. B. (1996). Taking stock/making change: Stories of collaboration in local school reform. *Theory into Practice, 35*(3), 149-157.

Feiman-Nemser, S. (1983). Learning to teach. ERIC Education Index: ED234043.

Hawkins, D. (1973). What it means to teach. *Teachers College Record, 75*(1), 7-16.

Hiebert, J., Gallimore, R., & Stigler, J. W. (2002). A knowledge base for the teaching profession: What would it look like and how can we get one? *Educational Researcher, 31*(5), 3-15.

Hiebert, J., Morris, A. K., Berk, D., & Jansen, A. (2007). Preparing teachers to learn from teaching. *Journal of Teacher Education, 58*(1), 47-61.

Korthagen, F. (2001). *Linking practice and theory. The pedagogy of realistic teacher education.* New York, NY: Routledge.

Korthagen, F. A., Loughran, J., & Russell, T. (2006). Developing fundamental principles for teacher education programs and practices. *Teaching and Teacher Education, 22*(8), 1020-1041.

Lampert, M., & Ball, D. (1999). Aligning teacher education with contemporary K-12 reform visions. In L. Darling-Hammond & G. Sykes (Eds.), *Teaching as the learning profession: Handbook of policy and practice* (pp. 33-53). San Francisco, CA: Jossey-Bass.

Langer, S. K. (1979). *Philosophy in a new key: A study in the symbolism of reason, rite, and art.* Cambridge, MA: Harvard University Press.

Lewin, K. (1948). *Resolving social conflicts.* New York, NY: Harper and Row.

Lewis, C., & Tsuchida, I. (1998). A lesson is like a swiftly flowing river: How research lessons improve Japanese education. *American Educator, 22*(4), 12-17, 50-52.

Little, J. W. (2007). Teachers' accounts of classroom experience as a resource for professional learning and instructional decision making. In P. A. Moss (Ed.), *Evidence and decision making. The 106th Yearbook of the National Society for the Study of Education* (Part I, pp. 217-241). Malden, MA: Blackwell.

Lortie, D. C. (1975). *Schoolteacher: A sociological study.* Chicago, IL: University of Chicago Press.

Lyons, N. (Ed.). (2010). *Handbook of reflection and reflective inquiry.* New York, NY: Springer.

McVarish, J., & Rust, F. O'C. (2006). Un-squaring teacher education: Reshaping teacher education in the context of the Research I university. In C. Kosnik, C. Beck, A. R. Freese, & A. P. Samaras (Eds.), *Making a difference in teacher education through self-study: Personal, professional, and program renewal* (pp. 185-201). Dordrecht, The Netherlands: Springer.

Meyers, E., & Rust, F. (Eds.). (2003). *Taking action through teacher research.* Portsmouth, NH: Heinemann.

Miles, M., & Huberman, A. M. (1984). *Qualitative data analysis: an expanded sourcebook.* Thousand Oaks, CA: SAGE.

Moll, L. (1992). Bilingual classroom studies and community analysis: Some recent trends. *Educational Researcher, 21*(2), 20-24.

Muldowney, K. P. (2010). *Teaching from the heart: The Interdisciplinary Studies Program of National-Louis University as a Vehicle for Professional Development of Teachers* (Unpublished dissertation). National-Louis University, Chicago, IL.

Putnam, R. T., & Borko, H. (2000). What do new views of knowledge and thinking have to say about research on teacher learning? *Educational Researcher, 29*(1), 4-15.

Rogoff, B., & Lave, J. (1999). *Everyday cognition: Development in social context.* Cambridge, MA: Harvard University Press.

Rust, F. O'C. (2009). Teacher research and the problem of practice. *Teachers College Record, 111*(8), 882-1893. Retrieved from http://www.tcrecord.org ID Number: 15506

Rust, F. O'C. (2007). Action research in early childhood contexts. In A. Hatch (Ed.), *Qualitative Research in Early Childhood Education* (pp. 95-108). New York, NY: Routledge.

Rust, F. O'C., & Meyers, E. (2006). The bright side: Teacher research in the context of educational reform and policy-making. *Teachers and Teaching: theory and practice, 12*(1), 69-86.

Schön, D. (1983). *The reflective practitioner: How professionals think in action.* New York, NY: Basic Books

Spindler, G. (Ed.). (1982). *Doing the ethnography of schooling: Educational anthropology in action.* New York, NY: Holt, Rhinehart, & Winston.

Spradley, J. (1979). *The ethnographic interview.* New York, NY: Holt, Rhinehart, and Winston.

Stigler, J. W., & Hiebert, J. (1999). *The teaching gap.* New York, NY: Free Press.

Van Veen, K., & Van de Ven, P. H. (2008). Integrating theory and practice. Learning to teach L1 language and literature. *L1-Educational Studies in Language and Literature, 8*(4), 39-60.

Vygotsky, L. (1968). *Thought and language.* Cambridge, MA: MIT Press.

Vygotsky, L. (1978). *Mind in society: The development of higher psychological processes.* Cambridge, MA: Harvard University Press.

Wenger, E. (1998). *Communities of practice.* New York, NY: Cambridge University Press.

Wolcott, H. F. (1973). *The man in the principal's office: An ethnography.* New York, NY: Holt, Rhinehart, & Winston.

Zeichner, K. (1993). Action research: personal renewal and social reconstruction. *Educational Action Research, 1*(2), 199-219.

Zeichner, K., & Tabachnick, B. R. (1991). Individual, institutional and cultural influences on the development of a teacher's craft knowledge. In J. Calderhead (Ed.), *Exploring teachers' thinking* (pp. 21-59). London, England: Cassell.

Author Contact Information: Frances O'Connell Rust, EdD, Visiting Professor and Interim Director of Teacher Education, University of Pennsylvania Graduate School of Education, Professor Emeritus, New York University Steinhardt School of Education, 96 Round Hill Drive Briarcliff Manor, NY 10510. Phone: 914-414-8171. E-mail: francesrust49@gmail.com. Susan Hansen, PhD, Associate Professor, National Louis University, North Shore Campus at Skokie, 5202 Old Orchard Road, Skokie, IL 60077. Phone: 224-233-2467. E-mail: SHansen@nl.edu

CHAPTER 25

Using Authentic Data to Teach Secondary Ecology

A Theory for Teaching the Nature of Science

Yael Wyner
City College of New York

This instructional theory posits that using authentic scientific studies and their relevant data to teach science in the secondary classroom increases student understanding of the nature of science, including the ways scientists collect and analyze data and draw conclusions based on those data.

The Importance of Bringing Authentic Science Practice to Classrooms

In today' s knowledge driven world, where access to information is no longer a barrier, but where the ability to scrutinize and filter is paramount, students need to learn how to evaluate data (Leu, Kinzer, Coiro, & Cammack, 2004). Yet, Americans are falling behind in science (National Academy of Science [NAS], 2006). Fewer American students are choosing to pursue careers in the sciences than have done so in the past (NAS, 2006). At the same time, many Americans fail to use evidence when making conclusions about complex problems. In fact, a large percentage of even the college-educated do not differentiate between scientific and nonscientific explanations of natural events like evolution (Alberts, 2009). Furthermore, even as our perception of science and scientific practice remains mired in misunderstanding, the growing impact of human activity on the Earth increases the necessity of scientific thinking skills amongst the general public (Pfirman & AC-ERE, 2003; NSF Advisory Committee for Environmental Research and Education, 2005).

Science educators and more recently cognitive scientists have been seeking to address this crisis in science thinking for decades. Since the 1960s, educators have emphasized the importance of bringing authentic scientific process and practice to the classroom (Duschl, Schweingruber, & Shouse, 2007). In 2007, building on the call for authentic science and recognizing the newfound importance of student prior knowledge, the National Academy of Sciences issued a framework that identifies four important strands of student science proficiency. Accordingly, all students should:

1. know, use, and interpret scientific explanations of the natural world;
2. generate and evaluate scientific evidence and explanations;
3. understand the nature and development of scientific knowledge; and
4. participate productively in scientific practices and discourse (Duschl et al., 2007).

Students should gain proficiency in these four strands by doing activities and participating in lessons that intertwine them. In the same way that these strands are interconnected in science practice, they are also linked for student learning. Student learning of both scientific knowledge and process will be inhibited if the strands are artificially separated from one another (Duschl et al., 2007; Lehrer & Schauble, 2006).

The Handbook of Educational Theories, pp. 283–291

USING PUBLISHED DATA TO BRING AUTHENTIC SCIENCE PRACTICE TO THE CLASSROOM

Bringing published data to the classroom can achieve the goals of student science proficiency advocated by the recent National Academy of Sciences' report (Duschl et al., 2007). In a proper framework, analysis of authentic published data can help students develop proficiency in the National Academy's four strands of science practice by helping student learning of science content, the value of empirical evidence, the nature of scientific knowledge, and how to actively participate in scientific discussion.

The use of published research for learning science is already an essential tool for teaching graduate science and medical students how to "think" scientifically (Cave & Clandinin, 2007; Iyengar et al., 2008; Kohlwes et al., 2006). This tool is so useful that a number of scientists and educators have developed courses for undergraduates that rely on in-depth analysis of journal articles. The courses that use this approach have been shown to humanize scientists and lead to positive impacts on student learning of scientific inquiry skills and the scientific concepts studied in the journal articles (Hoskins, 2008; Hoskins, Stevens, & Nehm, 2007).

In a twist on the journal club approach, researchers have also offered "seminar deconstruction" courses for first and second year undergraduates. Students in these courses spent the semester deconstructing two 1-hour full-scale research seminars by invited faculty speakers. Researchers found that students who participated in these courses showed major gains in the depth of their understanding and in the growth of their critical thinking skills (Clark et. al, 2009).

The effectiveness of using published research at the college and graduate level has inspired researchers and educators to bring scientific data sets to secondary school classrooms (Cary Institute, 2010; Cook, Swan, & Vahey, 2008; Griffis Thadani & Wise, 2008; Hammerman, 2008; Urban Advantage, 2010) including researchers at Oregon Health and Science University who incorporated analysis of journal articles into a multi-faceted class that they created for Portland high school students. They found that 73% of class graduates were planning careers in health and science and that they were seven times more likely to rank this class as influencing their career or life choices than other more traditional science classes like chemistry and biology (Rosenbaum, Martin, Farris, Rosenbaum, & Neuwelt 2007).

DEVELOPMENT OF THE THEORY

Science educators since the 1960s have recognized the need for bringing authentic scientific practice into the science classroom. Originally, this recognition took the form of new curriculum written to influence the type of instruction. The goal of the new curricula was to bring science practice to schools by designing materials that asked students to develop science process skills like making observations and hypotheses, designing experiments, and collecting data. The thrust of the reform was very teacher centered. Improve the curriculum and the students will learn (Duschl et al., 2007). In the past 15 years there has been a growing recognition of the importance of student prior knowledge and experience for influencing science learning. Therefore, today's recommended instructional practices seek to build on student's prior knowledge and conceptual understanding (Bransford, Brown, & Cocking, 2000). Teachers need to actively engage students in the process of science and guide students to reflect and discuss their explanations.

The two themes of authentic practice and the importance of student prior knowledge inform best practices for science education today. Emphasis on inquiry seeks to engage students in the authentic activities of scientists by asking students to investigate research questions by developing hypotheses, designing experiments to test their hypotheses, and collecting and analyzing data (Chinn & Malhotra, 2002; Roth & Roychoudhury, 1993; Singer, Marx, & Krajcik, 2000). Students are asked to use their prior knowledge to inform their discussions about their proposals and findings (Bransford et al., 2000). These combined tactics have been shown to successfully counteract some of didactic practices common in poor urban areas (Thadani, Cook, Griffis, Wise, & Blakey, 2010).

Growing out of this impulse to utilize student prior knowledge has been a movement to use inquiry in real world contexts (Bransford et al., 2000; Lee & Songer, 2003; Singer et al., 2000) Real life contexts in which students are familiar will better engage and connect them with scientific practice. For example, Lee and Songer (2003) show that an activity that requires students to use pressure and front data to forecast local weather patterns in real time is successful for promoting student learning of disadvantaged urban sixth graders. Singer et al. (2000), describe the importance of using topics that are of interest to middle school students like, "What is the water quality in my river?" and "Can my friend make me sick?," for successful learning of science practice and content skills in long-term student centered inquiry projects. The NSF funded, Science Education for Public Understanding Program (SEPUP, http://sepuplhs.org/) curricular resources developed by the Lawrence Hall of Science, includes modules that ask students to investigate familiar everyday items like food safety and household chemicals. Also, GLOBE, a worldwide science education program has been engaging students in authentic scientific practice in students' local environment since its inception in 1992 (Means, 1998; http://www.globe.gov/).

Closely connected to the use of real world contexts for inquiry learning is the relatively recent exploration of using social dilemmas linked to science and technology, socioscientific issues, to develop student critical reasoning skills; particularly in how students evaluate evidence, conceive of the relationship between the nature of science and society, and how students structure their arguments, all learning goals that overlap with the student proficiencies outlined by the National Academy of Sciences (Duschl et al., 2007; Sadler, 2004). The emphasis on society engages students in science within a context, society, with which they have prior knowledge (Sadler, 2004). Although surprisingly, researchers have found that students seem to have difficulty integrating the scientific knowledge they learn through their exploration of socioscientific issues with the personal knowledge that they bring to the issue (Sadler, Chambers, & Zeidler, 2004; Zeidler, Walker, Ackett, & Simmons, 2002). Nevertheless, researchers still view engagement in these issues as critical for developing the necessary scientific thinking skills for tackling the world's complex problems (Driver, Newton, & Osborne, 2000; Kolstø, 2001; Zeidler, Sadler, Simmons, & Howes, 2005), a crucial issue identified by the National Academy and others (Alberts, 2009; NAS, 2006; Pfirman & AC-ERE, 2003).

Studies of student learning of socioscientific issues elucidate some of the difficulties that students have when approaching scientific evidence. A number of studies show that even though students recognize the importance of scientific evidence or data, they still show difficulty evaluating and relying on the evidence for making decisions (Sadler, Chambers, & Zeidler, 2004; Tytler, 2001). Furthermore, in a study focused on global warming, many high school students were unsure of what type of information to identify as data (Sadler, Chambers, & Zeidler, 2004).

Using Published Data About Environmental Issues for Learning the Nature of Science

The difficulties in identifying and evaluating published scientific data that students show while exploring socioscientific issues point to the importance of activities that more thoroughly delve into the data behind real world issues. These activities place students in the context of authentic science, as published data by their very nature are part of the community of scientific exploration. This chapter will describe two modules that use media and authentic published data to link ecological processes and environmental issues to daily life. The modules, constructed to follow the four-strand framework put forth by the National Academy (Duschl, et al., 2007), work to help student learning of science content, the value of empirical evidence, the nature of scientific knowledge, and how to actively participate in scientific discussions. To achieve the goals of science learning summarized by the National Academy, these modules build upon years of research and findings on science learning by using real world issues that engage student prior knowledge and by immersing students in the authentic practice of science through the analysis published research.

Use of the Theory: The Ecology Disrupted Framework

While connecting students to the nature of science, these curriculum modules, titled *Ecology Disrupted*, are designed to help students learn the importance and complexity of normal *ecological* processes, by studying the environmental issues that result when people *disrupt* them. As such, media and published scientific data are used to connect a focused environmental issue to daily life and ecology.

The goal of implementing these curriculum modules is to enhance student learning of the nature of science, particularly the role of evidence in making scientific conclusions and the work of science as a human endeavor. Further, students will gain understanding and appreciation of the connection between daily life, environmental issues, and ecological processes.

Testing the Theory

The curriculum modules were pilot-tested in northeastern urban communities three times over the course of the 2007-2010 school years and redesigned after each implementation. Teacher training, prior to teacher implementation, emphasized the goals of enhancing student understanding of the nature of science and the connections between daily life activities and environmental impact. In total, 30 teachers implemented the modules in the middle and high school classrooms of a large urban public school system. Pre/post testing in the classrooms of 60 control/experimental teachers is ongoing and will be completed in a year. The different rounds of pilot-testing were designed to improve the use of the modules, test pre/post assessment items for the controlled testing, and to elicit teacher feedback on the effectiveness of the units at achieving the two learning goals described above, enhancing student understanding of the nature of science and the connections between daily life activities and environmental impact.

MODULE ORGANIZATION

Each module is a case study based upon data from published ecology research (Epps et al., 2005; Kaushal, et al., 2005). Each case study is constructed around a question that asks students to use data and prior knowledge to link everyday human actions to an environmental issue. One case study asks students, "How might snowy and icy roads be connected to Baltimore area's water supply?" and the other asks, "How might being able to drive from Los Angeles and Las Vegas in just four hours put the bighorn sheep at risk?"

Students are introduced to each topic from the perspective of the scientist who conducted the research. In the case of the first example, students are asked to use their prior knowledge with snow and ice to consider why the scientist, Dr. Sujay Kaushal, might wonder if snowy and icy roads affected the water supply. After students describe their own experience slipping on ice and walking through salt crystals, students watch a short digital slideshow, *Winter Roads Make Salty Streams*, produced by the American Museum of Natural History (*Biobulletins Snapshots*; http://www.amnh.org/sciencebulletins/biobulletin/index.html) that describes Dr. Kaushal's research that shows that freshwater supplies are getting saltier due to salting of roads in winter. The students now know the conclusions of the research, but they have not examined the data. Before they do so, they watch a video profile of the scientist showing his research site and explaining his motivation and personal connection to the research. During the next two lessons, students explore water and salt, necessary topics for understanding the implications of the data. Then during the following three lessons, they explore and make meaning from the published data. Finally, in the last lesson, students use case study specific data to learn how salting roads for safe travel disrupts the ecological processes of water runoff and abiotic factors. They consider solutions like using alternative solvents to melt snow and ice and they apply the same methodology to other environmental issues that are caused by different human actions that disrupt the same ecological processes.

The bighorn sheep example follows the same format as the winter roads example. Students are asked to consider why the scientist, Dr. Clinton Epps, might wonder if the ability to travel by car between Los Angeles and Las Vegas in just four hours might impact the bighorn sheep. Since, students have little experience with bighorn sheep or wide open spaces, students immediately watch a short digital slideshow, *Highways Block Bighorn Sheep*, produced by the American Museum of Natural History (*Biobulletins Snapshots*; http://www.amnh.org/sciencebulletins/biobulletin/index.html) that describes Dr. Epps' research that shows that highways, built to make travel easier, block the movement of sheep between mountaintops, thereby leading to inbreeding. Students then discuss their own experience with their neighborhood boundaries to learn how roads, highways, train tracks, and parks can also act as barriers to people. In this module too, student watch a video profile of the scientist showing the research site, the sheep, and explaining his motivation and personal connection to the research. During the next two lessons students explore genetic analysis and inbreeding, necessary topics for understanding the implications of the data. Then during the following three lessons, they explore and make meaning from the published data. Finally, in the last lesson, students use case study specific data to learn how building highways for easy travel disrupts the ecological processes of populations and habitat. They consider solutions like building raised highways to allow movement of the sheep, and they apply the same methodology to other environmental issues that are caused by different human actions that disrupt the same ecological processes.

LEARNING THE NATURE OF SCIENCE

SCIENCE AS HUMAN ENDEAVOR

Students often have difficulty thinking of science as an activity undertaken by people (Bell, Blair, Crawford, & Lederman, 2003). These modules work to incorporate the scientist into the scientific process. Through video and verbal and written questions students view the research from the perspective of the scientist who conducted the research. Students explore why the scientist chose to study the topic and any personal connections the scientist may have with the work. Also, students act like scientists, throughout the process of investigating and analyzing the data. This behavior in the context of the video of the scientist who conducted the research serves to personalize the scientific experience to the student.

THE EVIDENCE-BASED NATURE OF SCIENCE

One of the most important elements of science for students to understand is that all scientific conclusions are based upon evidence. The ability to analyze evidence and to use evidence to make and defend conclusions is central to the practice of science. It is also increasing in importance in today's knowledge driven world, where the impact of people on the complex ecology of our world is ever growing (Leu et. al, 2004; Pfirman & AC-ERE, 2003). Evidence and data analysis are at the heart of these activities. The students experience through multiple steps in their analysis of the data. First, before students view the published data, they need to understand the type of data that would be useful for making the conclusions described in the digital slide show. Second, the students need to represent their data in a format that will allow easy analysis. Third, students use the data to make and support their conclusions. Fourth, students watch media on other scientific research about environmental issues and pull out the type of evidence needed to support the research claims described by the media.

Analyzing the Data: Determining How to Investigate, Representing the Data, and Making Meaning From Data

In the Winter Roads example, after students watch the digital slideshow and the video profile of the scientist, Dr. Kaushal, who studied Baltimore area streams, the students determine the type of data that need to be collected in order to make the claim that road salt is entering into Baltimore's water. Through scaffolded questioning, students determine that they must compare seasonal and annual data from sites with few roads to sites with many roads. They also decide that graphs would be the best way to represent the data for comparison. Students graph the data and then discuss their graphs. Multiple teachers described the "aha" moment when students looked at the data and saw significantly higher levels of salt in urban versus forested areas.

As in the Winter Roads example, the Bighorn Sheep example asks students to determine the type of data that need to be collected to show that highways block sheep from different mountaintops from mating. In this case, the data in their original form, genetic distance data, are very difficult to interpret. However, when applied to a map with mountaintop populations, they are much easier to understand. In this example, students determine that if highways are blocking inbreeding, then geographically close sheep populations that are separated from one another by a highway will show less sign of breeding, that is, share less genes, than sheep that are further away and have no highway separating them. Using maps that show the range of the mountaintop sheep populations, students measure geographic distance with rulers and overlay the genetic breeding data onto maps. They then use the data to support their claims about the affect of highways on bighorn sheep.

For both modules, after students analyze and use data to support scientific claims, students apply what they have learned to media about other environmental issues. They use a graphic organizer to analyze the environmental issues that they watch and deconstruct them into the elements of daily life that contribute to the environmental issue, how the associated ecological principle is disrupted, the solutions to the environmental issues, and the evidence on which the conclusions of the research are based. This activity is an important application of scientific thinking to videos of popular science research studies. Assertions do not have meaning without data. Yet often conclusions are put forth without the supporting data. In this experience, students must point out the evidence that give the conclusions meaning.

Testing the Theory: Student Testing

During pilot-testing in the classrooms of six teachers in the winter of 2010, students, most of whom qualified for free or reduced lunch, completed pre/post assessments before and after they used the *Ecology Disrupted* units. The goal of the student testing was to develop validated and reliable tests for the controlled testing that is now ongoing. However, analysis of the pre/post assessment data shows preliminary evidence for the effectiveness of the modules for student learning of the nature of science and how daily life impacts basic ecological processes.

Pre-/Postassessment Design and Grading

In total, teachers submitted graded multiple-choice assessments from 214 students. Constructed response items were scored as yes/no. Two graders scored the same two classes of constructed response items to calibrate acceptable answers. Since interrater reliability was calculated to be very high, 90%, only one person graded each constructed response item for the rest of the exams.

Prior to pilot testing, 20 New York City public school teachers of biology evaluated 56 multiple choice items and four multipart constructed response items using a 4-point Likert scale for validity at assessing content knowledge: (a) that is important in the teaching of biology, (b) that is included in New York State standards for biology, (c) that might be included (or in the past has been included) on the state biology exam in these content areas—how humans disrupt ecological processes, how daily life contributes to human impact, and how science is used to learn about the natural world. Results from this analysis helped narrow the items selected for use in pilot-testing. In total, four multiple-choice items and four multipart (36 components) constructed response items were selected for use in the pre/post tests. Of the 34, multiple-choice items, 12 were designed to measure understanding of the nature of science. The other items were designed to measure understanding of ecological principles in the context of human impact and the relationship between daily life and human impact. The four constructed response items consisted of 50 multiple parts designed to measure understanding of ecological principles in the context of human impact, the relationship between daily life and human impact, and the nature of science. However, due to the structure of the questions, only four out of those 50 parts were designed specifically to test the nature of science.

FINDINGS

Results from the pre/post tests indicate that these modules are effective for increasing student learning of ecological principles in the context of human impact, human impact in the context of daily life, and of the nature of science. *T* tests showed that students made significant gains ($p < 0.05$) in all content areas in both the multiple choice and constructed response items, except for the nature of science constructed response items. However, this is probably due to the few constructed response items ($N = 4$) included that were designed to measure the nature of science and the exam fatigue reported by many of the teachers that drastically reduced the sample size by disproportionately impacting the completion of the constructed response section at the end of the test.

A Closer Look at a Sample of the Nature Of Science Test Items

The 12 multiple choice items, built to measure understanding of the nature of science, emphasized many different elements of the process of science including the role of evidence in making scientific conclusions and scientific process skills like reading data tables, graphing, and making measurements. All four constructed response items about the nature of science, measured student learning of how scientists use evidence to make conclusions. Figure 25.1 includes a sample of three multiple choice and one constructed response item. Students showed gains in all items (multiple choice 1 = 33.8%, 2 = 16.7%, 3 = 14.9%, and 131.2% for the constructed response item.)

Testing the Theory: Teacher Feedback

In each iteration of pilot-testing, the testing teachers were asked to list the parts of the units that worked and the parts of the units that did not work. Time and again teachers stated that working with the data was the most rewarding aspect of the units. It was the most consistent feedback that we received regarding the units. Below are some comments from teachers:

- "I like how it [a module] uses real world data.... Keep it up."
- "The part that worked best for the students is making connections to real life data. They were able to experience what scientist had to go through by working in groups, finding a hypothesis, evaluating results to come up with a conclusion for their group. This activity also allowed my students to review their graphing skills and make numbers become significant in proving their hypothesis."
- "Students really responded to working with the data sets such as creating graphs with the Winter Roads unit and plotting the lines and roads on the maps for the Bighorn sheep unit."
- "Actually, I have enjoyed teaching this material to my students. Their graphing accomplishments were absolutely magnificent. Many of the graphs, which contrasted and compared Baltimore's forested, suburban and urban areas were done by hand and with colors. At least two of my students utilized technology in order to generate bar graphs for each studied area."
- "What worked for winter roads:
  – Getting the students involved by having them talk about their own experiences with ice during the winter.
  – Looking at the data and having students graph it. There were a lot of "lights" that went on when they saw the urban data graphed next to the suburban and forested data."
- "These units are amazing! They contain a ton of information and your goal for these units can be any number of things-human impact, how scientists conduct work, the scientific method, factors that affect the ecosystem."

CONCLUSION

The two *Ecology Disrupted* case studies are just two examples of using published research to help student learning of the nature of science. The first round a pre/post student assessment data and the positive feedback from teachers is the first indication that this approach is useful for enhancing student learning of the nature of science. Further, controlled pre/post testing on student learning is ongoing. These case studies show how published research about real world issues can engage students' prior knowledge, immerse students in the authentic practice of science, and significantly increase student learning of the nature of science.

ACKNOWLEDGMENTS

I thank S. Gano, J. Koch, R. DeSalle, J. Becker, B. Torff, A. Bickerstaff, M. Chin, S. Bothra, and R. Thorne for their contributions in developing and testing the *Ecology Disrupted* curriculum. I also thank the many teachers who tested and used this curriculum in their classroom. This work was supported by the National Science Foundation (grant #s 733269, 0918629). Any views expressed in this manuscript are those of the author and not of the National Science Foundation.

1. The analysis of data gathered during a particular experiment is necessary in order to
   a. Formulate a hypothesis for the experiment
   b. Develop a research plan for the experiment
   c. Design a control group for the experiment
   d. Draw a valid conclusion for the experiment
2. Graphs of the data from laboratory investigations are used to
   a. Observe patterns in the data
   b. Prevent errors in measuring data
   c. Make the observed data more accurate
   d. Change the experimental hypothesis
3. Which statement most accurately describes scientific inquiry?
   a. It ignores information from other areas of study.
   b. It does not allow scientists to judge the reliability of their sources
   c. It does not involve ethical decisions based on research findings
   d. It may lead to explanations that combine data with what people already know

Constructed Response Item:

In a small town upstate that supplies food to New York City, people are falling sick with stomach illnesses and ear infections. Scientists tested Lake Ruby Reservoir, which is the water supply in the area. Testing of the deep and cold water, which is home to animals like fish and insects, identified the cause of the illnesses. Nitrogen-rich animal waste that farmers had spread onto their food crops as fertilizer got into the drinking water.

There are three farms (A, B, and C) that are on three different rivers that feed into the town's reservoir, Lake Ruby. What data would support the claim that farm A and not farm B or C is responsible for the animal waste in the reservoir?

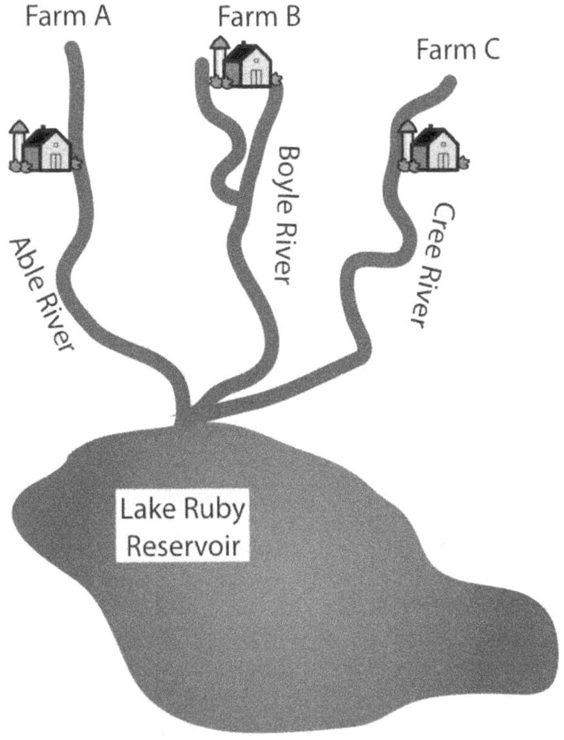

Figure 25.1. A sample of three multiple choice and one constructed response item.

REFERENCES

Alberts, B. (2009). Redefining science education. *Science, 323*, 427.

Bell, R. L., Blair, L., Crawford, B., & Lederman, N. G. (2003). Just do it? Impact of a science apprenticeship program on students' understanding of the nature of science and scientific inquiry. *Journal of Research in Science Teaching, 40*(5), 487-509.

Bransford, J. D., Brown, A. L., & Cocking, R. R. (Eds.). (2000). *How people learn: Brain, mind, experience, and school.* National Washington, DC: Academy Press.

Cary Institute of Ecosystem Studies. (2010). *The changing Hudson project.* Retrieved from http://www.ecostudies.org/chp.html

Cave, M. T., & Clandinin, D. J. (2007). Revisiting the journal club. *Medical Teacher, 29*, 365-370

Chinn, C. A., & Malhotra, B. A. (2002). Epistemologically authentic inquiry in schools: At heoretical framework for evaluating inquiry tasks. *Science Education, 86*, 175-218.

Clark, I. E., Romero-Calderón, R., Olson, J. M., Jaworski, L., Lopatto, D., & Banerjee, U. (2009). Deconstructing scientific research: A practical and scalable pedagogical tool to provide evidence-based science instruction. *PLoS Biology,* 7(12), e1000264.

Cook, D. Swan, K., & Vahey, P. (2008) Thinking with data: A cross-disciplinary approach. NSF Program DR-K12 Grant # 0628122. Retrieved from http://www.nsf.gov/awardsearch/showAward.do?AwardNumber=0628122

Driver, R., Newton, P., & Osborne, J. (2000). Establishing the norms of scientific argumentation in classrooms. *Science Education, 84*, 287–312.

Duschl, R. A., Schweingruber, H. A., & Shouse, A. W. (2007). *Taking science to school: Learning and teaching science in grades K-8.* Washington, DC: National Academies Press.

Epps, C. W., Palsbøll, P. J., Wehausen, J. D, Roderick, G. K., Ramey, R. R., & McCullough, D. R. (2005). Highways block gene flow and cause a rapid decline in genetic diversity of desert bighorn sheep. *Ecology Letters, 8*, 1029-1038.

Griffis, K., Thadani, V., & Wise, J. (2008). Making authentic data accessible: The sensing the environment inquiry module. *Journal of Biological Education*, 42, 119-122.

Hammerman, J. K. L. (2008). *Educating about Statistical Issues in Large Scientific Data Sets NSF Program DR-K12 Grant # 0822178.* Retrieved http://www.nsf.gov/awardsearch/showAward.do?AwardNumber=0822178

Hoskins, S. G. (2008). Using a paradigm shift to teach neurobiology and the nature of science—A C.R.E.A.T.E.-based approach. *The Journal of Undergraduate Neuroscience Education,* 6(2), A40-A52.

Hoskins, S., Stevens, L., & Nehm, R. (2007). Selective use of primary literature transforms the classroom into a virtual laboratory. *Genetics, 176*, 1381-1389.

Iyengar, R., Diverse-Pierluissi, M. A., Jenkins, S. A., Chan, A. M., Devi, L. A., Sobie, E. A., Ting, A. T., & Weinstein, D. C. (2008). Inquiry learning: Integrating content detail and critical reasoning by peer review. *Science, 319*(5867), 1189-1190.

Kaushal, S., Groffman, P. M., Likens, G. E., Belt, K. T., Stack, W. P., Kelly, V. R., Band, L. E., & Fisher, G. T. (2005). Increased salinization of fresh water in the northeastern United States. *Proceedings of the National Academy of Sciences, 102*(38), 13517-13520.

Kohlwes, R. J., Shunk, R. L., Avins, A., Garber, J., Bent, S., & Shlipak, M. G. (2006). The PRIME curriculum: Clinical research training during residency. *Journal of General Internal Medicine, 21*(5), 506-509.

Kolstø, S. D. (2001). Scientific literacy for citizenship: Tools for dealing with the science dimension of controversial socioscientific issues. *Science Education, 85*, 291-310.

Lee, H. S., & Songer, N. B. (2003). Making authentic science accessible to students. *International Journal of Science Education, 25*(8), 923-948.

Lehrer, R., & Schauble, L. (2006). Scientific thinking and science literacy. In W. Damon, R. Lerner, K.A. Renninger, & I. E. Sigel (Eds.), *Handbook of child psychology, 6th ed.* (Vol. 4). Hoboken, NJ: Wiley.

Leu, D. J., Kinzer, C. K., Coiro, J. L., & Cammack, D. W. (2004). Toward a theory of new literacies emerging from the internet and other information and communication technologies In R. B. Ruddell & N. J. Unrau (Eds.), *Theoretical models and processes of reading* (pp. 1570-1613). Newark, DE: International Reading Association.

Means, B. (1998). Melding authentic science, technology, and inquiry-based teaching: Experiences of the GLOBE program. *Journal of Science Education and Technology, 7*, 97-105.

National Academy of Science, National Academy of Engineering, Institute of Medicine, Committee on Prospering in the Global Economy of the 21st Century: An Agenda for American Science and Technology. (2006). *Rising above the gathering storm: Energizing and employing America for a brighter economic future.* Washington DC: National Academy Press.

NSF Advisory Committee for Environmental Research and Education (2005). Complex Environmental Systems: Pathways to the Future. Retrieved from http://www.nsf.gov/geo/ere/ereweb/acere_synthesis_rpt.cfm

Pfirman, S. & the AC-ERE (2003). *Complex environmental systems: Synthesis for earth, life, and society in the 21st century, A report summarizing a 10-year outlook in environmental research and education for the National Science Foundation.* Retrieved from http://www.nsf.gov/geo/ere/ereweb/acere_synthesis_rpt.cfm

Rosenbaum, J. T., Martin, T. M., Farris, K. H., Rosenbaum, R. B., & Neuwelt, E. A. (2007). Can medical schools teach high school students to be scientists? *The FASEB Journal, 21*(9), 1954-1957.

Roth, W. M., & Roychoudhury, A. (1993).The development of science process skills in authentic contexts. *Journal of Research in Science Teaching, 30*, 127-152.

Sadler, T. D. (2004). Informal reasoning regarding socioscientific issues: A critical review of research. *Journal of Research in Science Teaching, 41*, 513-536.

Sadler, T. D., Chambers, F. W., & Zeidler, D. L. (2004b). Student conceptualisations of the nature of science in response to a socioscientific issue. *International Journal of Science Education, 26*, 387-409.

Singer, J., Marx, R. W., & Krajcik, J. (2000). Constructing extended inquiry projects: Curriculum materials for science education reform. *Educational Psychologist, 35*, 165-178.

Thadani, V., Cook, M. S., Griffis, K., Wise, J., & Blakey, A. (2010). The possibilities and limitations of curriculum-based science inquiry interventions for challenging the "pedagogy of poverty." *Equity for Excellence in Education, 43,* 21-37.

Tytler, R. (2001). Dimensions of evidence, the public understanding of science and science education. *International Journal of Science Education, 23,* 815-832.

Urban Advantage. (2010). *Urban Advantage Middle School Science Initiative.* Retrieved from http://www.urbanadvantagenyc.org/home.aspx

Zeidler, D. L., Walker, K. A., Ackett, W. A., & Simmons, M. L. (2002). Tangled up in views: Beliefs in the nature of science and responses to socioscientific dilemmas. *Science Education,* 86, 343-367.

Zeidler, D. L., Sadler, T. D., Simmons, M. L., & Howes, E. V. (2005). Beyond STS: A research-Based framework for socioscientific issues education. *Science Education, 89,* 357–377.

Author Contact Information: Yael Wyner, PhD, assistant professor, secondary education, City College of New York, 160 Convent Avenue, New York, NY 10031. Telephone: 212-650-5869. E-mail: ywyner@ccny.cuny.edu

CHAPTER 26

An Instructional Theory for English Language Learners

The 5R Model for Enhancing Academic Language Development in Inquiry-Based Science

Molly H. Weinburgh and Cecilia Silva
Texas Christian University

The 5R instructional model discussed in this chapter is in its infancy and is a significant emerging framework (Silva, Weinburgh, Smith, Malloy, & Marshall, 2012; Weinburgh & Silva, 2011) that integrates sheltered instruction language strategies into inquiry-based science lessons. As with any theory, it is a coherent set of general propositions used to help explain a class of phenomena. In this case the set is the acquisition of academic language and scientific concept development, especially for students for whom the language of instruction is not the home language. As a conceptual model, the 5Rs provides an image for teachers of how instruction may unfold when language is emphasized within an inquiry-based science lesson.

In the United States, a common goal of all educational programs is to ensure that English language learners (ELLs) attain English language proficiency and achieve academically. The 5R Instructional Model sets forth five features found embedded within a unit of study which, joined with other strategies, help build academic language and scientific discourse (Gee, 2004) while developing science concepts and habits of mind. The emergence of a new model which expands and unites two current models is predictable "because the construction of curricula proceeds in a world where changing social, cultural, and political conditions continually alter the surroundings and the goals schools and their students" (Bruner, 1977, p. 8).

The 5R instructional model for academic language acquisition for ELLs emerged from the perceived conflict between the widely implemented Sheltered Instruction Observation Protocol (SIOP) (Echevarría, Vogt, & Short, 2008; Short, Vogt, & Echevarría, 2011) and inquiry-based science (Bybee, 1997, 2000; Schwab, 1958, 1960, 1966). Settlage, Madsen, and Rustad (2005) found teachers struggling with the "misalignment between the thirty-item SIOP checklist" (p. 51) and inquiry-based science instruction. They suggested that "a fresh conceptualization of the interface between inquiry-based science teaching and sheltered instruction seems necessary" (p. 39). The 5R instructional model provides such an interface.

The chapter begins with assumptions about learning which serve as the foundation for the 5R instructional model. This is followed by the history of research in inquiry-based science and language acquisition instruction and the need for a new model. Next we discuss the development of the model and finally we provide is a detailed description of the model.

THEORY BACKGROUND AND DEVELOPMENT

The 5R instructional model is grounded in sociocultural constructivist learning theory and based on the belief that (a) social connections and cultural practice

The Handbook of Educational Theories, pp. 293–303

mediate cognition and (b) language, literacy, and discourse are simultaneously tools and products of cognitive, social, and cultural practice (Weinburgh & Silva, 2011).

Sociocultural constructivist learning theory brings together features of leaning suggested by genetic (developmental) epistemology (Piaget, 1929, 1972) and social learning theory (Bruner, 1977, 1990; Vygotsky, 1968, 1978). Piaget suggested a theory about how various factors, including maturation, interaction with objects, people, language and culture, and internal regulators, produce cognitive growth. He saw learning as an internal process of construction and subordinated to development. He saw experience as indispensable in order for learning to occur but not guaranteeing it. In his theory, assimilation and accommodation account for the construction of new knowledge.

Vygotsky put forward the idea that human mental abilities develop through interactions with the world. Learning is deemed as a process of negotiating meaning using culturally based signs, symbols, and tools. Vygotsky posited that one of the most important cultural tools is language. In examining how people learn, he suggested that there is a *zone* between the cognitive tasks that are at the upper limits of the learner's abilities to accomplish alone and the cognitive tasks that are at the limits of the learner's abilities to accomplish with help. Within this zone, learners actively negotiate meaning with the help of more knowledgeable others. The socialization between adults and children helps scaffold or support the children toward problem solving. What is most important for teaching basic concepts is that the child be helped to pass progressively from concrete thinking to the utilization of more conceptually adequate modes of thought. Language is a tool for thinking and for expressing thought. Therefore, what a student is able to conceptualize is intrinsically coupled to the types of language capital available to articulate that understanding.

Others see cognition as distributed or *stretched over* (Lave, 1988) the learner, the group and various artifacts such as symbolic tools. Discourse communities provide cognitive tools that learners appropriate as their own as they construct meaning from experience. Sociocultural constructivist learning theory combines these theories by stressing the individual construction of knowledge through social and cultural negotiation and validation (O'Loughlin, 1992). "Learning is always about learning a 'language' and real learning. Learning that leads to understanding and the ability to apply one's knowledge is always 'situated understanding'" (Gee, 2010, p. 1). When learners develop situated understanding of words or concepts, they go beyond verbal or dictionary-like definitions and are able to associate these words or concepts to specific images, actions, feelings, values and dialogues. Situated meanings are associated with different contexts or situations (Gee, 2002).

While children develop their primary discourse within the communities in which they are socialized, as they enter school they acquire new styles of language as well as new ways of acting, feeling and thinking. To succeed in school, ELLs must acquire the language of the academic disciplines they encounter in this new setting. When discussing academic language, classroom teachers—particularly in the upper grades—are quick to identify vocabulary as a key component of an academic discipline. Academic vocabulary—the lexical component of academic language—though critical, is only one of the complex features involved in academic language. Over the past two decades researchers have developed a better understanding of the complex nature of academic English.

When ELLs develop academic English proficiency, they gain control of the linguistic systems of academic language as well as develop the social competence necessary to appropriately use these systems within academic contexts (Bailey & Butler, 2003; Freeman & Freeman, 2009; Kucer, 2005; Scarcella, 2003; Schleppegrell, 2004). The development of competence using the linguistic dimension requires the language user's understanding of how the various systems of language interact in order to produce meaning: pragmatics (functions and uses of academic language), text types (text genres and structures), semantics (roles and meanings of words within a sentence), syntax (arrangement of words in a sentence), morphological (forms and meaning of words), orthographic (spelling conventions), phonological (sounds, patterns, stress, and intonation), and graphophonic (relation between letters and sounds).

In a science class, for example, ELLs must be able to appropriately use oral language to participate in discussions regarding science investigations or present investigation findings to peers in their class. To make a point, students in this context might need to develop expressions to make inferences ("I predict …") or negotiate consensus ("I agree with …"). In terms of written language, academic science texts typically require that readers and writers engage in expository text. Expository texts present factual information and generalizations and often include compare/contrast, cause/effect or problem/solution structures. Such text structures generally require that ELLs utilize *signal words* to indicate conceptual relations among the idea presented in the text. Compare/contrast text structures might employ signal words less familiar to children such as *however, on the other hand,* and *although.* Furthermore, academic texts are often written from a third person perspective and make use of nominalizations—where verbs and adjectives are used as nouns (e.g., the process of moving earth materials becomes *erosion*).

Science Education

During the early part of the 1900s, Dewey (1902, 1910, 1938) argued that education and learning are social and interactive processes. He further argued that students thrive when they are allowed to experience and interact with phenomenon, and that all students should have the opportunity to become involved in their own learning. He "noted that developing thinking and reasoning, formulating habits of mind, learning science subjects, and understanding the process of science were the objectives of teaching science through inquiry" (Demir & Abell, 2010, p. 717). This idea of hands-on, experiential science was expanded during the 1950 and 1960s by Schwab (1958, 1960, 1966) who advocated that science should not be taught as revealing stable truths about nature but should be taught as a process of inquiry. Schwab thought that early laboratory experiences were essential if students were to learn to ask questions, collect evidence and devise explanations.

During the late 1980s, the science community continued to work toward curriculum that was more inquiry-based. In an attempt to help teachers, the Biological Science Curriculum Study (BSCS) program, supported by the National Science Foundation, produced materials which introduced teachers to inquiry-based instruction using the 5E model (Bybee, 1997). The 5E model for science instruction has its origins in learning theory research and is a direct descendent of the learning cycle used with the Science Curriculum Improvement Study (Atkin & Karplus, 1962). This model begins with *engaging* students in the learning task. Successful engagement "results in students being puzzled by, and actively motivated in, the learning activity" (Bybee, 1997, p. 177). This is followed by a period of *exploration* in which the students develop first-hand experience and collect data. This phase is often accomplished in small groups with students talking, listening, and writing about their experience. The experience and data are expanded during the *explain* period as the teacher helps students draw conclusions and develop canonical knowledge of the topic. Large group discussions often characterize this phase. The students then deepen their new understanding (*elaborate*) and finish by *evaluating* their work or having the teacher assess them.

Inquiry has continued as a major theme in science education reform research. Pedagogically, inquiry-based teaching is often distinguished from more traditional expository, chalk-and-talk, transmission methods by its active and constructivist nature. In its core, inquiry-based teaching engages students in ways of satisfying curiosities. The *National Science Education Standards* (National Research Council, 1996) outline five essential features of inquiry for teachers to use as a framework when developing lessons. These features include learning to ask scientific questions, gathering evidence to use in answering the questions, formulating explanations using the evidence, evaluating alternative conclusions and communicating findings. Because the purpose of inquiry is to channel students toward the construction of their own knowledge, the process moves back and forth depending on whether the teacher or student is most responsible for each of the five essential features. Inquiry is not the linear process often learned as the *scientific method* (Weinburgh, 2007, 2008; Windschitl, 2004) by students in science classrooms but a reiterative, active process.

Language Education

The research distinguishing conversational and academic language has had much impact in the development of instructional models to support ELLs. Cummins (1981, 1996) put forward the distinction between basic interpersonal communication skills (BICS) and cognitive academic language proficiency (CALP). The BICS/CALP distinction served to explain why children who were proficient in conversational language—BICS—were not able to perform on school tasks that required the use of academic language—CALPS. Based on this distinction, Cummins also provided a framework to support teachers in helping students cope with the linguistic and cognitive demands involved in developing academic proficiency (see Figure 26.1). The horizontal line relates to the range of contextual support available to ELLs to express or receive meaning. The vertical line relates to the cognitive demands that the information places on ELLs and is dependent on the language user's experience.

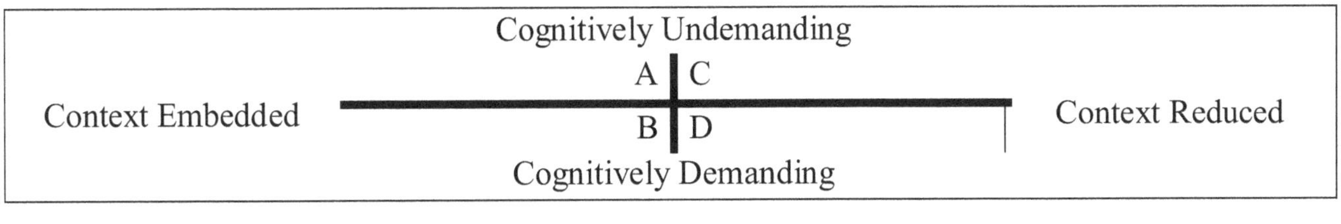

Source: Adapted from Cummins (1981, p. 12).

Figure 26.1. Cummins' contextual support and degree of cognitive involvement in communicative activities.

Conversational language develops quickly because this type of communication is supported with interpersonal and context cues and is cognitively undemanding (Quadrant A). In Quadrant A, for example, an ELL might rely on the teacher's gestures and an object within the physical setting—a book—to understand a relatively undemanding command: *Open your book.* Quadrant D, on the other hand, solely relies on linguistic cues to accomplish a cognitively demanding task. An ELL, for example, might be asked to read a science text or listen to a lecture on *mitosis*. In this case the student has to rely on the written or oral language to understand a topic that is cognitively demanding. Though the progression of academic tasks naturally flows from Quadrant A to Quadrant D, teachers should target Quadrant B for teaching. In this quadrant, ELLs are cognitively challenged while provided with the contextual support needed to cope with the challenge. The contextual scaffolding that teachers provide for ELLS supports the development of the situated meaning found through inquiry science.

Cummins' work on BICS and CALP laid the foundation for the development of sheltered instruction (SI), an approach that emerged in the late 1980s to make academic instruction in English understandable to LEP [limited English proficient] students (Freeman & Freeman, 1988). SI is also known under the name of Specially Designed Academic Instruction in English (SDAIE). However, most teachers recognize SI as the trademarked protocol of SIOP. Commonly associated with SI are the uses of a variety of strategies that serve to magnify meaning and support academic language acquisition within the content classroom: extra linguistic cues (e.g., use of manipulatives, visuals, props, body language), linguistic modifications (e.g., enunciation, repetition, pauses), content and language objectives, hands-on experiential learning activities, cooperative learning, thematic curriculum, explicit teaching of literacy and learning strategies (Díaz-Rico & Weed, 2010; Freeman & Freeman, 1988; Hansen-Thomas, 2008; Herrera & Murry, 2005). The SIOP was developed in the early 1990s to train classroom teachers in using SI (Echevarría, Vogt, & Short, 2008). Grounding the model is its theoretical underpinning "that language acquisition is enhanced through meaningful use and interaction" (p. 16).

CRITIQUES

The overlap between SIOP and inquiry-based science is perceived as a positive step in making high quality science instruction accessible to ELLs (Fathman & Crowther, 2006; Pray & Monhardt, 2009; Settlage et al., 2005; Short, Vogt, & Echevarría, 2011). However, differences in each model's theoretical stance—linguistic vs. inquiry—raise questions as to their compatibility in terms of implementation. The pedagogical lens through which the lesson is approached in the SIOP emphasizes linguistic features, therefore, entering the lesson from a language and texts stance (Lemke, 2004). In contrast, inquiry-based instruction proponents approach a lesson by asking students to develop understanding through the manipulation of phenomena; thus entering the lesson through an inquiry stance (Lemke, 2004). Of particular interest to this discussion is the point at which students are to be introduced to new vocabulary within the lesson. Anne, one of the participants in Settlage et al.'s (2005) research, struggled with whether to present new vocabulary at the beginning of the lesson—as emphasized in SIOP—or after the students had participated in the hands-on science experience component of the lesson—as advocated within an inquiry approach:

> This inclination to begin with definitions and follow this with experiences to contextualize the knowledge is in direct conflict with inductive instruction. The inductive, inquiry-based approach she had successfully employed reserved the formal vocabulary instruction until after the students had participated in a hands-on activity. (p. 52)

In their discussion, Settlage et al. recognize that the conflict they identified could be attributed to their misinterpreting of what the SIOP authors intended. The SIOP training materials, Settlage at al. note, give high ratings to teaching practices where vocabulary is explicitly taught at the beginning of the lesson.

In a response to the concerns raised by Settlage et al. (2005), Echevarría (2005), one of the developers of the SIOP, clarifies that the SIOP "allows for variation in classroom implementation—including inductive learning—while at the same time providing teachers with specific lesson features that, when implemented consistently and to a high degree, lead to improved academic outcomes for English language learners" (p. 60). Explicitly addressing the presentation of vocabulary, she further states: "We advocate specific vocabulary instruction, and it can come where it makes the most sense" (p. 61). Echevarría then makes a case for the apparent lock-step procedures of the SIOP lessons by arguing that such procedures would be of benefit to less experienced teachers. She states, "More experienced teachers know where in the lesson to teach the terms but novice teachers may benefit from structuring lessons in a particular way, especially since many teachers of ELLs are new to the profession, particularly in urban schools." (p. 61)

Developing the Instructional Theory

Here we present the 5R instructional model for enhancing academic language development in inquiry-based science. Many science teachers are aware that "science inquiry, as a central tenet of science, and the learning of science need to address the importance of language" (Hand, 2008, p. 3). As experienced teachers, and teacher educators, we recognize the benefits of overlapping SI and inquiry science and aspire to support novice as well as experienced teachers in considering multiple ways of scaffolding academic language within an inquiry lesson to create the situated meanings that Gee (2002) discusses.

Critical to our model is the assumption that inquiry-based instruction provides ELLs a shared experience for thinking, talking, listening, reading and writing. We view the exploration phase of inquiry-based science as important because the exploratory language that emerges at this phase contributes to vocabulary and content learning (Staples & Helselden, 2002). In the exploration phase of inquiry we begin by drawing on what students bring to the classroom: "Instead of regarding student backgrounds as a challenge to overcome, teachers use children's 'funds of knowledge' as a resource to ground and extend science instruction, thereby reducing the discontinuities between school science and everyday life" (Settlage et at, 2005, p. 46).

As researchers and classroom practitioners, we too have wrestled with the point at which to embed language instruction within an inquiry lesson. As teacher educators we want to support novice teachers entering the field in developing the attitudes, beliefs and pedagogical tools they will need to provide ELLs with opportunities to acquire language while achieving academically. The 5R instructional model blends SI and Inquiry-based science in a way that brings language needs to consciousness.

The model, emerging as an instructional theory, is grounded in studies investigating the acquisition of academic language and inquiry-based science begun in 2006. More than 268 hours (17,040 minutes) of science and mathematics instruction emphasizing academic language acquisition were video- and audiotaped. Instruction occurred in 7 classrooms over 4 years with 9-11 year old ELLs. These students had lived in the United States for no more than 2 years. As we examined the video and audio looking for evidence of student change, the features of the 5R model became evident.

The 5R model was developed within the framework of culturally relevant instruction for helping ELLs as they try to acquire academic language in science as well as learning to conduct investigations in inquiry-based classrooms. Since 2007, the model has been used with children from a variety of countries. In addition, more than 21 languages have been represented as the children's first language. Equal numbers of males and females have been instructed using the model and both seem to respond well to it.

The 5R instructional model has also been used with ELLs during mathematics instruction. The same emphasis on reloading language and of repositioning language into the discourse of mathematics appears to be equally effective as was seen in science. All indications are that the 5R instructional model is equitable, working well with a variety of ethnic backgrounds, cultural and linguistic differences and genders.

The research on this model is only 3 years old and has not yet been validated. The focus is on a way to help teachers become conscious of the features that together can help integrate science and language instruction at multiple points during the lesson. More research is needed to show the strength of the model in other disciplines.

The 5R Model

The 5R instructional model is nonlinear; consisting of a set of five features that can be use throughout a unit of study to facilitate the incorporation of scientific language within science content instruction (see Figure 26.2). The 5R Instructional Model provides a perspective on how and when academic language should be introduced into inquiry science (Silva et al., in press; Weinburgh, 2009; Weinburgh, Silva, Oliver, & Wielard, 2009).

Through the inquiry-based science lesson, new language emerges as students discuss the concept being studied. The teacher introduces and interjects new vocabulary either by *replacing* or *revealing*. After introducing the new vocabulary, he/she emphasizes the words by *repeating* them throughout the lesson. In addition, discourse typically found in science, is modeled through *repositioning* student talk into a more complex sentence structure. Though these four Rs appear to surface spontaneously, in reality, they emerge because the teacher artfully planned how to weave them into a lesson. *Reloading* (the 5th R of the model) is a purposeful act that occurs after the initial language introduction, usually as the opening activity of a subsequent lesson.

Although the 5R instructional model does not occur in a hierarchical-ordered manner, it does require the teacher to think about the content objectives in science and language prior to the lesson. The simplistic title/name given to each area of language/concept development is attractive to teachers because it appears doable in a regular classroom. However, each R has a research base as well as a teacher's craft knowledge base that makes it complex. Some features are at the word level and some are at the sentence/text level. All the features

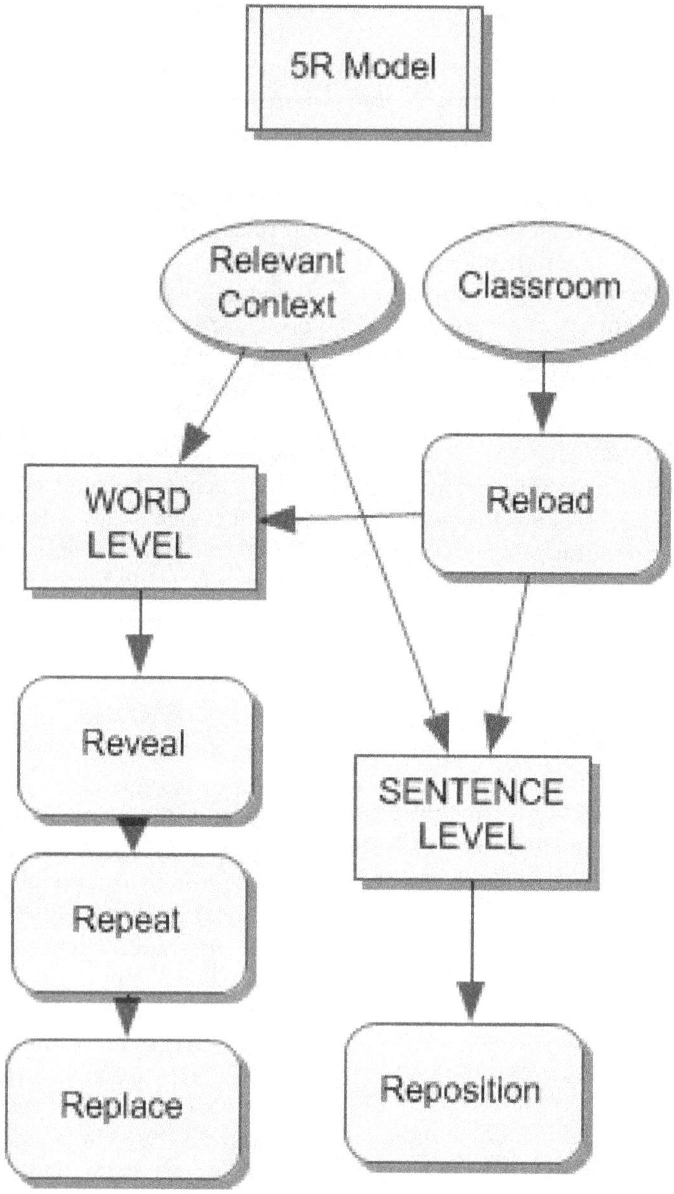

Figure 26.2. 5R model.

can be oral or written. The over-riding concept of the 5R Instructional Model is that language should emerge in context from the experiences that children have, build on language they already know, and push them to use new academic language.

Replace

The strategy of *replacing* is used while the children talk and write about their experience using their social language. The teacher scaffolds the development of language, helping the student move from common to academic language (Buchanan & Helman, 1997; Watts-Taffe & Truscott, 2000), by substituting an academic word for the common word. *Replace* is usually a one-to-one correspondence and is always at the word level. This strategy can be used with oral or written language. Once a common word is *replaced*, the students are reminded to use the academic word when talking or writing. An example from a conversation would be the *replacement* of "line" and "ditch" with "gully" during an erosion lesson using a stream table model.

T: What did you see happening when you poured the water?
S1: The sand moved.
T: What do you see that lets you know sand has moved?
S1: The line.

S2: A ditch.

T: When sand moves and leaves a line or ditch, we call the line a *gully.* You see the gully.

The teacher can use *replacing* when helping a student with writing about an experience. An example from a student journal is seen in Figure 26.3. In this example the student rereads her work and edited it by *replacing* "goggles" for "glasses."

Reveal

In science, understanding word meaning often demands grasping a concept. "Words like *density* or *compression* are not simply a matter of translation from another language (low literacy students often do not have these words in their first language in any case)" (Miller, 2009, p. 575). When there is no corresponding common language, the teachers must use the strategy of *revealing* the new language. Backward planning allows the teacher to identify potential concepts and language that must become a part of the students' language in order to fully participate in meaning making. Commonly, the name of a piece of equipment or object must be *revealed* to the students. If this unveiling of the words occurs within the context of the lesson, rather than as an aside, the student is more likely to remember them. Like *replace,* this strategy can be oral or written and is at the word level. An example of *reveal* is providing the name of a structure such as *petiole* during a plant lesson or *Golgi apparatus* during a cellular structure lesson and the name of equipment such as the *triple beam balance* or *distillation tube.*

T: I am going to show you pictures, and I want you to tell what the picture is showing. [shows first picture]

S: hair

T: [shows second picture]

S: nails

T: [shows third picture]

S: oil gland

T: The body system that includes these structures as well as dermis and epidermis cells is called the integumentary system. We will explore how important the integumentary system is to our survival.

Revealing may occur in writing as seen in this students' journal on plant growth (see Figure 26.4). The student has drawn a picture without knowing the technical word. The teacher uses the margin of the journal to *reveal* its name. In this case, the student did not know that science used specific words for orientation—lateral view and bird's eye view.

The strategy of *repeating* new and important words is not a new concept in the literacy research. It is a strategy many teachers know but may not use to its full advantage. Beginning language learners rely heavily on the cognitive strategy of *repetition* while intermediate and advanced level student rely less heavily but continue to use *repeat* (Chamot & Kupper, 1989). "Say-

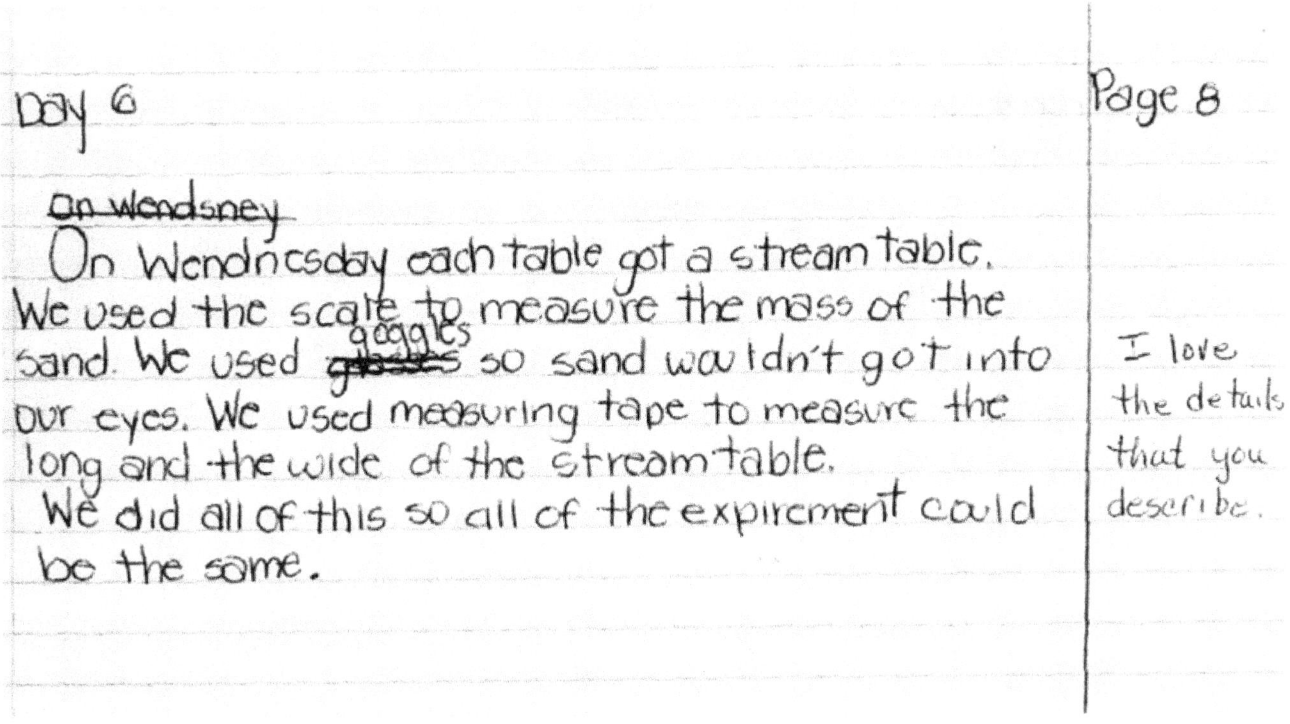

Figure 26.3. Replace.

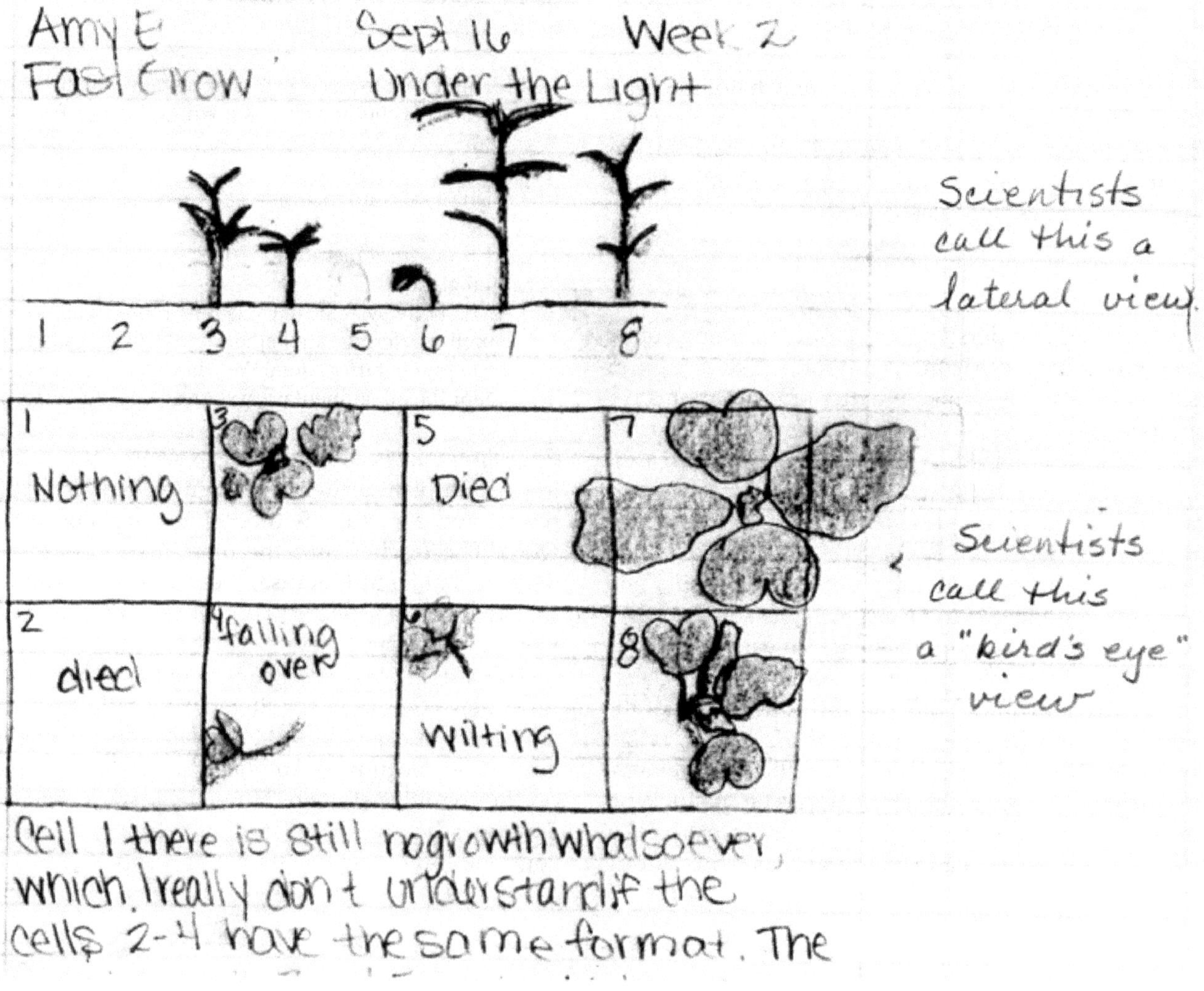

Figure 26.4. Reveal.

ing the same thing more than once gives a child more than one opportunity to catch on to what is being said" (Tabors, 2008, p. 92). The teacher may emphasize the word as he/she says it as a way to draw attention to it. *Repeat* is demonstrated in the following conversation with fourth grade ELL students who were studying erosion.

T: I want us to think about what we know about *models*. Earlier, we were talking about the 3-D *models* you made with clay. Let's look at the *model* that one group made. I can tell where you were on the campus from looking at the *model*. What is this a *model* of?

S: The creek.

T: Yes it is. Scientists also make another kind of *model*. They make a *model* to see if they can answer their question. We will make a *model* using the stream table to help answer our question about what effect the rain will have on the sandy hill.

Reposition

"A guiding principle of science education is that engaging in the canonical discourse—meaning language, genre, textual forms, and the use of symbolic conventions—of a discipline is critical for science learning" (Grimberg & Hand, 2009, p. 504). Talking science is not as easy as just using the correct words. In order to *talk science* a student must hear others talk science (Lemke, 1990). Apprenticeship into the complex vocabulary and syntax of science is accomplished as students hear a teacher talk science and try to mimic the talk. Because the meaning of words in scientific discourse often differs from the common use, some researchers argue for the explicit attention to language use and practice (Dawes, 2004; Fang, 2006). The strategy of *repositioning* is a way for the teacher to help "make the patterns of scientific discourse more explicit (Miller, 2009, p. 575).

This strategy requires the teacher to rephrase student utterances to be structured as scientific discourse and to use scientific discourse (talk science) in conversations with students. Repositioning is important because subject specific discourse is needed to develop the students' abilities to think and reason scientifically and mathematically (Buchanan & Helman, 1997; Dong, 2002; Fang, 2006). Gibbons (2009) points out that "language is heard and used in a real context" (p. 39) and teachers can give students opportunities where "ideas are reworded and revised, key words and phrases are repeated, problems are restated, and meanings are refined" (p. 39). Repositioning can occur at the oral or written language and is always at the sentence/text level. This conversation is helping sixth grade students as they discuss *mitosis*.

T: Look on page 40. What is happening in picture 3 and picture 4?
S1: A cell is dividing.
S2: The things are in a line. And then they move. Some go one way and some go another.
T: Can you give me a name for the 'they'?
S: Chromosomes?
T: Yes, chromosomes. In cell division, chromosomes aligned at the equator, separate and move to the poles.

Written repositioning occurs when a student uses the notes written during a laboratory experience and converts them to a formal lab report.

RELOAD

The model stresses the *reloading* rather than front-loading (Echevarría, Vogt, & Short, 2008) of words and sentence structure. When a sociocultural frame is applied to science language, individuals' thinking and social negotiation of meaning are critical for students to fully grasp language. The strategy of *reloading* language encourages both personal and social negotiation as students interact with words that have previously emerged within a rich context. The reloading occurs as the teacher or students pronounce words, give definitions, use them in a sentence, and connect them to other words. The reloading of the vocabulary can help develop word consciousness, the interest in and awareness of words (Graves & Watts-Taffee, 2002), by giving students a time to *play* (Blachowicz & Fisher, 2004) with words and sentence construction. Interesting features of the word may be introduced such as homophone or cognate or *funny* pronunciation. Students may work alone or in groups to complete tasks that require the use of words that were used in prior lessons.

CONCLUSION

The 5R instructional model can help practitioners looking for theories to guide practice. This model links the research in language education and the research in science education to help teachers as they strive to make high quality science instruction accessible to English Language Learners. The teacher uses the five components—replace, repeat, reveal, reposition, reload—to strengthen the link between language acquisition and science inquiry. Replacing, revealing, and repeating support the development of new vocabulary. More complex science discourse is encouraged through the use of repositioning and reloading. The model provides a framework for teachers as they plan for the purposeful teaching of language at various points throughout an inquiry science lesson. This inclusion is nonlinear and may occur in multiple ways.

REFERENCES

Atkin, J. M., & Karplus, R. (1962). Discovery or invention. *The Science Teacher, 29*(2), 121-143.

Bailey, A. L., & Butler, F. A. (2003). An *evidentiary framework for operationalizing academic language for broad application* to *K-12 education: A design document* (CSE Report 61). Los Angeles, CA: University of California, Los Angeles, Center for the Study of Evaluation, National Center for Research on Evaluation, Standards, and Student Testing, Graduate School of Education & Information Studies. Retrieved from http://www.cse.ucla.edu/products/rsearch.asp

Blachowicz, C. L. Z., & Fisher, P. (2004). Keep the "Fun" in fundamental: Encouraging word awareness and incidental word learning in the classroom through word play. In J. F. Baumann & E. J. Kame'enui (Eds.), *Vocabulary instruction: Research to practice* (pp. 210-238). New York, NY: Guilford Press.

Bruner, J. (1977). *The process of education.* Cambridge, MA: Harvard University Press.

Bruner, J.S. (1990). *Acts of meaning.* Cambridge, MA: Harvard University Press.

Buchanan, K., & Helman, M. (1997). *Reforming mathematics instruction for ESL literacy students.* Digest. Retrieved from http://www.cal.org/resources/digest/digest_pdfs/buchan01.pdf

Bybee, R. (1997). *Achieving scientific literacy: From purposes to practices.* Portsmouth, NH: Heinemann.

Bybee, R. (2000). Teaching science as inquiry. In J. Minstrell & E. H. van Zee (Eds.), *Inquiring into inquiry learning and teaching in science* (pp. 20-46). New York, NY: American Association for the Advancement of Science.

Chamot, A. U., & Kupper, L. (1989). Learning strategies in foreign language instruction. *Foreign Language Annals, 22*(1), 13-22.

Cummins, J. (1981). The role of primary language development in promoting educational success for language minority students. In California State Department of Education (Ed.), *Schooling and language minority students: A theoretical framework* (pp. 3-50). Los Angeles, CA: Evaluation,

Dissemination and Assessment Center, California State University, Los Angeles.

Cummins, J. (1996). *Negotiating identities: Education for empowerment in a diverse society* (1st ed.). Ontario, CA: California Association for Bilingual Education.

Dawes, L. (2004). Talk and learning in classroom science. *International Journal of Science Education, 26*(6), 677-695.

Díaz-Rico, L. T., & Weed, K. Z. (2010). *The crosscultural language, and academic development handbook* (4th ed.). Boston: MA: Allyn & Bacon.

Demir, A. & Abell, S. K. (2010). Views of inquiry: Mismatches between views of science education faculty and students of an alternative certification program. *Journal of Research in Science Teaching, 47*(6), 716-741.

Dewey, J. (1902). *The child and the curriculum.* Chicago, IL: University of Chicago.

Dewey, J. (1910). *How we think.* Mineola, NY: Dover.

Dewey, J. (1938). *Experience and education.* New York, NY: Macmillan.

Dong, Y. R. (2002). Integrating language and content: How three biology teachers work with non-English speaking students. *International Journal of Bilingual Education and Bilingualism, 5*(1), 40-57.

Echevarría, J. (2005). Using SIOP in science: Response to Settlage, Madsen, and Rustad. *Issues in Teacher Education, 14*(1), 59-62.

Echevarría, J., Vogt, M., & Short, D. (2008). *Making content comprehensible for English learners. The SIOP Model.* Boston, MA: Pearson.

Fang, Z. (2006). The language demands of science reading in middle school. *International Journal of Science Education, 28*(5), 491-520.

Fathman, A. K., & Crowther, D. T. (2006). Teaching English through science and science through English. In A. K. Fathman, & D. T. Crowther (Eds.), *Science for English Language Learners: K-12 Classroom Strategies* (pp. 3-21). Arlington, VA: National Science Teachers Association Press.

Freeman, D., & Freeman, Y. S. (1988). Sheltered English instruction. ERIC Identifier: ED301070. *ERIC Digest*, Washington DC: ERIC Clearinghouse on Languages and Linguistics. Retrieved from http://www.ericdigests.org/pre-9210/english.htm

Freeman, Y. S., & Freeman, D. E. (2009). *Academic language for English language learners and struggling readers.* Portsmouth, NH: Heinemann.

Gee, J. P. (2002). Literacies, identities , and discourses. In M. J. Schleppegrell & M. Cecilia Colombi (Eds.), *Developing advanced literacy in first and second languages* (pp. 159-175). Mahwah, NJ: Lawrence Erlbaum Associates.

Gee, J. P. (2004). Language in the science classroom: Academic social languages as the heart of school-based literacy. In. E. W. Saul (Ed.), *Crossing Borders in Literacy and Science Instruction* (pp. 13-32). Arlington, VA: NSTA Press.

Gee, J. P. (2010). Science, literacy, and video games. In A. J. Rodrigues (ed.), *Science education a pathway to teaching language literacy,* p 1-22. Rotterdam: Sense.

Gibbons, P. (2009). *English learners, academic literacy, and thinking: Learning in the challenge zone.* Portsmouth, NH: Heinemann.

Graves, M. F., & Watts-Taffee, S. (2002). The place of word consciousness in a research-based vocabulary program. In A. Farstrup & S. J. Samuels (Eds.), *What research has to say about reading instruction* (3rd ed., pp. 140-165). Newark, DE: International Reading Association.

Grimberg, R. I., & Hand, B. (2009). Cognitive pathways: analysis of students' written texts. *International Journal of Science Education, 31*(4), 503-522.

Hand, B. M. (2008). Introducing the science writing heuristic approach. In B. M. Hand (Ed.), *Science inquiry, argument and language* (pp. 1-12). Rotterdam: Sense.

Hansen-Thomas, H. (2008, Summer). Sheltered instruction: Best practices for Ells in the mainstream. *Kappa Delta Pi Record*, 165-169.

Herrera, S. G., & Murry, K. G. (2005). *Mastering ESL and bilingual methods.* Boston, MA: Pearson.

Kucer, S. B. (2005). *Dimensions of literacy: A conceptual base for teaching reading and writing in school settings* (2nd ed.) Mahwah, NJ: Lawrence Erlbaum Associates.

Lave, J. (1988).*Cognition in practice: Mind, mathematics and culture in everyday life.* Cambridge, MA: Cambridge University Press.

Lemke, J. L. (1990). *Talking science.* New York, NY: Ablex.

Lemke, J. L. (2004). The literacies of science. In. E. W. Saul (Ed.). *Crossing borders in literacy and science instruction.* Arlington, VA: NSTA Press.

Miller, J. (2009). Teaching refugee learners with interrupted education in science: Vocabulary, literacy and pedagogy. International *Journal of Science Education, 31*(4), 571-592.

National Research Council. (1996). *National Science Education Standards.* Washington, DC: National Academy Press.

O'Loughlin, M. (1992). Rethinking science education: Beyond Piagetian constructivism toward a sociocultural model of teaching and learning. *Journal of Research in Science Teaching, 28*(8), 791-820.

Pray, L., & Monhardt, R. (2009). Sheltered instruction techniques for ELLs. *Science and Children, 46*(7), 34-38.

Piaget, J. (1926). *The language and thought of the child.* New York, NY: Harcourt.

Piaget, J. (1972). *Psychology and epistemology.* New York, NY: Viking.

Scarcella, R. (2003). *Academic English: A conceptual framework* (Technical Report 2003-1). Irvine, CA: The University of California Linguistic Minority Institute.

Schleppegrell, M. J. (2004). *The language of schooling: A functional linguistic perspective.* Mahwah, NJ: Lawrence Erlbaum Associates.

Schwab, J. J. (1958). The teaching of science as inquiry. *Bulletin of the Atomic Scientists. 14,* 374-379.

Schwab, J. J. (1960). Enquiry, the science teacher, and the educator. *The Science Teacher,* 6-11.

Schwab, J.J. (1966). *The teaching of science.* Cambridge, MA: Harvard University Press.

Settlage, J., Madsen, A. & Rustad, K. (2005). Inquiry science, sheltered instruction, and English language learners: conflicting pedagogies in highly diverse classrooms. *Issues in Teacher Education, 14*(1), 39-57.

Short, D.J., Vogt, M., & Echevarría, J. (2011). The SIOP model for teaching science to English learners. Boston, MA: Pearson.

Silva, C., Weinburgh, M. H., Smith, K., Malloy, R., & Marshall, J. (2012). Toward integration: A model of science and literacy. *Childhood Education, 88*(2), 91-95.

Staples, R., & Heselden, R. (2002). Science teaching and literacy, Part 3: Speaking and listening, spelling and vocabulary. *School Science Review, 84*(306), 83-95.

Tabors, P. O. (2008). *One child, two languages* (2nd ed.). Baltimore, MD: Paul H. Brooks.

Vygotsky, L. S. (1968). *Thought and language*. Cambridge, MA: MIT Press.

Vygotsky, L. S. (1978). *The mind in society*. Cambridge MA: Harvard University Press.

Watts-Taffe, S., & Truscott, D. M. (2000). Using what we know about language and literacy development for ESL student in the mainstream classroom. *Language Arts, 77*(3), 258-265.

Weinburgh. M. H. (2007). Challenging elementary preservice teachers' beliefs about scientific methodology. In D. F. Berlin & A. L. White (Eds.), *Global issues, Challenges, and opportunities to advance science and mathematics education* (pp. 181-188). Columbus, OH: International Consortium for Research in Science and Mathematics Education.

Weinburgh, M. H. (2008). How middle childhood in-service teacher view the scientific method. *California Journal of Science Education, 9(1)*, 87-102.

Weinburgh, M. H. (2009, October). *Reloading Science academic Language for ELL Students*. Paper presented at the annual meeting of School Science and Mathematics Association, Reno, NA.

Weinburgh, M. H., & Silva, C. (2011). Integrating language and science: The 5Rs for English language learners. In D. F. Berlin & A. L. White (Eds.), *Science and mathematics: International innovations, research, and practices* (pp. 19-32). Columbus, OH: International Consortium for Research in Science and Mathematics Education.

Weinburgh, M. H., Silva, C., Oliver, T., & Wielard, V. (2009, April). *Reloading and repositioning science language for ELL students: A new look at sheltered instruction*. Paper presented at the annual meeting of the National Association for Research in Science Teaching, Orange Grove, CA.

Windschitl, M. (2004). Fold theories of "inquiry": How preservice teachers reproduce the discourse and practices of a theoretical scientific method. *Journal of Research in Science Teaching. 1*(5),481-512.

Author Contact Information: **Molly Weinburgh**, PhD, professor and William L. & Betty F. Adams Chair of Education, Andrews Institute of Mathematics and Science Education, director, College of Education, Texas Christian University, Fort Worth, TX 76129. Phone: 817-257-6115. E-mail: m.weinburgh@tcu.edu. **Cecilia Silva**, PhD, professor, Texas Christian University, TCU Box 297900, Fort Worth, TX 76129. Phone: 817-257-6769. E-mail: c.silva@tcu.edu

Section 4: Curriculum Theory

INTRODUCTION

Section Editor
Arthur Shapiro
University of South Florida

To use an anthropomorphic metaphor, as Josesph Schwab (1983) criticized the field of curriculum for its inverterate reliance on theory, yet the field of curriculum has been strangely resistant to the development of theory). Fortunately, however, the small team of Arthur Shapiro, William F. Benjamin, and John J. Hunt undertook such a quest, which resulted in a book titled *Curriculum and Schooling, A Practitioner's Guide* (1995), in which a social process theory of curriculum emerged.

The first chapter in this section by Shapiro summarizes and analyzes the theory, and explores its use. The chapter then deals with the nature and properties of theory. For example, for a theory to be a theory, it must be descriptive of the phenomena with which it seeks to deal, it must be analytic, and, it must be predictive. In any work dealing with theory, it must contain a great deal of material directly pertaining to the nature of theory, such as its necessity to be comprehensive, objective, to differ from models and taxonomies, its relationship to practice and to so-called "reality" et cetera.

This theory in Chapter 31 consists of four phases, which the authors labeled PINC, with which any enterprise attempting to develop a curriculum must contend. They are: sensing an issue and developing a *Plan*; generating *Interactions* among parties; entering into a process of *Negotiating*, and perceiving *Consequences*, or outcomes. Thus, the acronym, PINC. The practitioner now has a tool by which he or she can predict which phases will emerge and thus, to utilize in developing any curriculum.

The following quotation keyed Arthur Shapiro's decision to develop a constructivist theory of curriculum:

> The overwhelming consensus as the twentieth century closed has been that knowledge is constructed. (Phillips, 2000, p. viii)

Taking a cue from philosopher Phillips, the second chapter in this section, "A Theory and Practice of Constructivist Curriculum," represents an attempt to construct a constructivist theory of curriculum. First, we delve into the development of constructivist thinking (amazingly, started by French renaissance genius Bishop Nicole D'Oresme in 1377!) and next dealing with the two major forms of constructivist theory and practice, psychological and social constructivism, each of which has generated moderate and radical schools of thought. The approach taken is that curriculum development comprises a social process in which curriculum is generated and developed. As such, it is highly individualized tending to be based first, as Tyler insisted, on the needs and interests of students, second on those of society, and last on the insights of subject matter specialists. This contrasts with present attempts to develop common core standards for an entire nation and with ever more strict testing to ensure accountability, thus increasingly nationalizing curriculum and basing it on the recommendations of subject matter specialists.

Rodney Evans' chapter, "Does Practice Itself Know Nothing? Probing Teachers' Felt Experiences of Mandated Practice," follows, fitting neatly into the previous chapter's focus on constructivist approach to curriculum design and delivery. He severely criticizes the present trend toward developing mandated and prepackaged curriculum and equally mandated high stakes testing which divests teachers of their ownership of and ability to shape curriculum to the needs and interests of their students. This consists of a takeover the entire fabric of teaching of unprecedented

The Handbook of Educational Theories, pp. 305–306

proportions. The purpose is to ensure top-down accountability, being foisted on teachers nationwide. Evans' approach combines philology with philosophical hermeneutics and is influenced by the work of the twentieth century German philosopher Hans-Gorge Gadamer. His interpretive analysis is based on in-depth interviews and focus group sessions with teachers.

The following chapter, "School Board Control of Curriculum: Democracy or Censorship," by Patricia F. First (who is also an attorney) and Patricia A. L. Ehrensal, points to another layer of the complexity of the American educational system by dealing with the power of school boards over curriculum via discussion of court cases where this power has been questioned. In this chapter, the place of the local school board and its powers and responsibilities within the governance system of the United States is discussed; therefore, concepts of power, democracy, the role of the state, academic freedom, the expertise of educators in making curricular decisions, the prerogatives of the state to determine curriculum, and the role of censorship are involved in this discussion. The authors explore the existence and power of local school boards as part of what Galbraith in 1996 termed "the good society," a society with a humane agenda with excellence in public education as a vehicle of opportunity for all. The belief in openness and expansiveness rests upon the "marketplace of ideas," a phrase used in *Keyishian v. Board of Regents* in 1967 as a rationale for freedom of expression and academic freedom. The belief is that the truth or the best policy arises from the open expression of various and competing ideas in the classroom as in public life. In the decades since this case, the courts have supported a wide-ranging and robust exchange of ideas at all levels of the educational system, considering such freedom for students and faculty a special concern of the First Amendment of the U.S. Constitution. In U.S. elementary and secondary schools, it is the local school board that bears the responsibility for protecting this freedom.

The next chapter, "Maxwell's Demon: The Curriculum Structure as a Device to Generate Curriculum as a Routine and to Overcome the Evil Forces of Organizational Entropy," by Arthur Shapiro is an antidote to the inevitable decline of our educational organizations into an unproductive phase in their careers. This is based upon the tripartite theory of organizational change and succession (1969), which predicts that all organizations careen through three phases in their careers. From a long period of organizational senescence, whoever has the power recruits a charismatic leader who breaks the school or system or department out of its slumber and generates an organization that bustles with ideas, energy, vigor. As this phase, person-orientation, wanes, the organization then recruits a planner to carry out the ideas of the former leader, which results in plan-orientation. However, as this phase slowly fades in energy and ideas, the organization often just sits complacently, not doing very much at all, labeled position-orientation. Shapiro then points to a structure he and Superintendent Ronald Simcox developed to finesse this proclivity for schools and systems to become moribund. The organization is designed to stabilize a school system or school in the planning phase of its career. Maxwell's Demon is based on nineteenth century prominent physicist, James Clark Maxwell, who proposed a clever approach to beat the second law of thermodynamics to stop physical systems from running downhill. The curriculum structure was designed to do precisely that and succeeded. The chapter discusses several structures and processes needed to pull it off.

REFERENCES

Galbraith, J. K. (1996). *The good society: The humane agenda.* Boston, MA: Houghton Mifflin.

Keyshain v. Board of Regents. 385 U.S. 589 (1967).

Phillips, D. C. (Ed.). (2000). *Constructivisim in education: Opinions and second opinions on controversial issues. Ninety-ninth Yearbook of the National Society for the Study of Education, Part I.* Chicago, IL: University of Chicago Press.

Schwab, J. J. (1983). The practical 4: Something for curriculum professors to do. *Curriculum Inquiry, 13*(3), 239-265.

Shapiro, A., Benjamin, W. F., & Hunt, J. J. (1995). *Curriculum and schooling: A practioner's guide.* Palm Springs, CA: ETC.

Author Contact Information: Arthur Shapiro, PhD, College of Education, University of South Florida, Tampa, FL 33620. Preferred mailing address: 1301 Trimaran Place, Trinity, FL 34655. Phone: 727-807-7599. E-mail: ashapiro@tampabay.rr.com

CHAPTER 27

A Theory and Practice of Curriculum

Arthur Shapiro
University of South Florida

The days of a teacher getting a curriculum and putting her independent spin on it—those days are over.
—Reading supervisor, large school system (2009)

It is because modern education is so seldom inspired by a great hope that it so seldom achieves a great result.
—Bertrand Russell, *Why Men Fight*

The accountability movement sweeping over American public education to reform it, as mandated by the Federal No Child Left Behind Act and various implementing knockoff state tests, has morphed into a testing mania (Bracey, 2005). Principals are being threatened with loss of income and dismissal if their kids do not show improvement in passing test standards being raised yearly and also to meet the complex Annual Yearly Progress formulas mandated by the act. So are teachers. Whole schools have been closed and new faculties and administrators have been assigned to improve them based on a single test. Indeed, Florida has developed a system to hammer its schools by developing four categories indicating that they had better improve—or else. Grades of A through F are being awarded to schools based on that single test, with the public and the school personnel *actually believing* that the letter grade is a valid indicator of the quality of the school.

This is in complete contrast with the Scandinavian and other European nations who are moving in another direction. Oldroyd (2003) pointed to two major trends internationally. The first he terms "educational leadership for results," that is, "new public management," being followed by the United States and the United Kingdom in their accountability focus. The second direction he calls "educational leadership for learning," or "progressive humanistic leadership." This second direction is being pursued by Scandinavian and other European countries, with excellent results educationally, which we in the United States are steadfastly and resolutely, even stubbornly ignoring.

Because Grades 3 and 4 in the United States are those in which the tests start, many teachers have opted out of those grades because they do not want to face the pressures any more, leading to new teachers filling the positions. Being ignored in this movement is the enormous role poverty and parenting play in school achievement (Berliner, 2006). Thus, testing has become not only a frenzy, but also has become a driving force (when people's livelihoods are threatened over their kids' scores on a single test).

We need another driving force to assist in reforming our schools, not coercion through threats of tests, but the entire raison d'etre, a central purpose for administration, supervision, and teaching—quality curriculum and quality instruction. A central purpose of leadership is quality instruction—to generate high quality teaching. Obviously, then, a central purpose of schooling is to develop and deliver first rate curriculum, which, with quality teaching and administration, should result in effective learning.

Education, however, has long lacked a theory of curriculum to guide its efforts. As early as 1976, Zais pointed to the lack of a theory of curriculum to guide teaching and learning. Since we have not had such a base, we could not develop the quality we need and want to improve and to reform education. This paper presents such a theory.

The Handbook of Educational Theories, pp. 307–316

Why a Theory of Curriculum? Why Is it Necessary?

Most Americans think theory is worse than useless. I am told even by graduate classes, "Do not give us theory. We want ideas and processes which are useful." So, I promise faithfully not to confuse folks with theory. We make certain agreements in running the class, such as "Everything said in here stays in here" (the Las Vegas norm), so that people feel safe. When the students walk in, we start setting up the class to work in groups, which helps to meet their social needs. Then we agree that we will not criticize people's ideas negatively, but will consider them as interesting contributions to class thinking, which helps to meet their esteem needs. Rosalind Driver (1973) in her seminal research on how students thought, discovered that their thinking was well grounded in what she realized were *"coherent frameworks of ideas."* She realized that the students' thinking were based on those ideas, were legitimate, and certainly not mistakes.

Pretty soon, some smart alec will say, "Isn't that based on Maslow?" Of course, I ask why s/he is coming up with that conclusion. The student indicates that safety is Maslow's (1952) second step, working in groups meets social needs, his third step, and no destructive criticism is his fourth step, esteem. To which I firmly assert that we will absolutely not utilize any theory any more, that this was merely an accident, for which I apologize and indicate that I was quite unaware of that. Of course, some of the sharp people become suspicious, and begin to watch for other theories coming into play. We make agreements publicly, that we'll read all assignments (which will be reasonable). After a while, someone asserts that that is based on Lewin (of course, I give them Lewin's [1952] seminal study regarding social change to read at the opportune time).

Why a Theory? It Guides our Behavior.

Because theory guides our behavior, it guides our actions. As the above example shows, it certainly guides my running my classes. As an example, it absolutely guides our behavior when we feel sick, or when someone in our family becomes sick. We head off to a physician, and if we actually are sick, then we know an antibiotic is heading our way because most of us in the West subscribe to the germ theory of disease. This is how important theory is in our daily lives. Can you imagine any parent not taking a sick child to an medical doctor for help? We would immediately be suspicious of child abuse.

Before the germ theory guided our behavior, what did we do to deal with illness and disease: bled people to reduce their fever (thereby killing George Washington); tried to eliminate evil spirits; used superstition, such as night air causes illness (the reason why beds were so high); used magic potions, incantations, and charms? And note that theory involves an "if-then" statement. If we decentralize our school into small learning communities, then we expect to reduce social distance, the achievement gap and school dropouts (Shapiro, 2009). How is that as guide to a leader's behavior? Theory as a guide to develop curriculum points up the possibility of looking for structure, or for such processes as decision making, or for different models of curriculum, or for other phenomena that may be useful.

Theory as a Guide to Collecting Facts

This is a no-brainer. If we conclude that our child is sick, we look for a flushed face, we feel the forehead, we even use a thermometer. We are collecting data, facts. If we find temperature, and it is high enough, we either call the doctor's office for medication, or call and ask if we should head over to the office. We are collecting facts. So, theory is not only inordinately useful, but it also is critical in determining our behavior. If we want to reduce the achievement gap, what studies do we want to find that substantiates such a result (Bickel & Howley, 2002)? If we want to reduce dropping out, it seems a good idea to look for research regarding that phenomenon. (Actually, all we have to do is to look for literature on decentralizing schools [Pittman & Haughwout, 1987].)

As for a definition of fact, several appear to be useful: "a piece of information about circumstances that exist or events that have occurred;" "an event known to have happened or something known to have existed" (wordnetweb Princeton edu/peri/webwn). Johnson's (1958) approach adds precision to our recognizing a fact when we stumble across one. He notes four properties relating to any fact:

1. it is necessarily incomplete;
2. it changes;
3. it is a personal affair since it depends upon one's perception; and
4. its usefulness depends upon the degree to which others agree with one concerning it.

Summing up, a fact can be defined as an event or a happening that two or more competent observers can agree upon. Consequently, facts tend to be tentative and subjective, depending upon human observation, as anyone who reads two descriptions of an accident can conclude.

So, let's digress for a moment in the pursuit of the value of theory (even in education), and ask what makes a theory a theory.

What Makes a Theory a Theory: First, a Definition, Then, Its Three Key Characteristics

Hoy and Miskel (2008) cited Kerlinger (1986) in defining theory as "a set of interrelated concepts, assumptions, and generalizations that systematically describes and explains regularities in educational organizations" (p. 3). Griffiths' (1959) approach is more general in that he noted that his definition of theory is based on Feigl (1951),

> A theory is essentially a set of assumptions from which a set of empirical laws (or principles) may be derived. A theory cannot be proved by direct experiment.... The Copernical Theory of the Solar System was accepted some 150 years before there was direct evidence of its truth. (p. 28)

Griffiths is stating that a theory can only substantiated, but cannot be proved.

For an idea or a generalization to be a theory it has to have the following three characteristics:

1. descriptive;
2. analytic; and
3. predictive.

Descriptive

Using the germ theory of disease, we have a slam dunk. The germ theory describes a whole slew of diseases, including measles, tuberculosis, whooping cough, et cetera. Using this as a takeoff for our proposed theory of curriculum, it should be broad enough to describe its structure, and/or its process, and/or the large number of existing curricula, or models, or other properties. We will have a section on comprehensiveness in due course.

Analytic

It is not enough merely to describe some symptoms. We must be able to analyze them and be able to make a generalization. "Your child has strep throat. So, here is a prescription for an antibiotic." And, we rush off to the pharmacy. Not only is theory a guide to action, but it also is a guide to our doctor analyzing the data. Similarly, our theory of curriculum must enable us to analyze the data. Does the curriculum meet student needs and interests if it only uses worksheets all day long, with kids supposedly working alone (but actually copying from each other)? Probably not. (That actually is a major curriculum used in some private schools.) What different results seem to be generated by different curriculum models?

Predictive

This is the kicker—and the key to differentiating curriculum from a model or a taxonomy. We use a theory to predict. We predict that if we do not get our child some help in the form of antibiotics, he or she may get sicker; it may even turn into pneumonia, which is really dangerous, so we act. We predict really bad consequences if we do not act. We are predicting that we must destroy the germs in order to terminate the disease. And, a whole host of antibiotics have been developed to do that. We also have learned that theory tells us that we must take all of the prescribed dosage, or we may develop an immunity to that antibiotic, not a healthy choice.

As cited by Lunenburg and Ornstein (2008), Van Dalen (1979) notes that this is a major function of theory. Therefore, we might ask, what about a theory of curriculum? For any proposed theory of curriculum to be predictive, it must be able to predict structural aspects in developing the curriculum such as stages that curriculum development undergoes, and/or process elements such as involvement strategies, if the focus is on implementation. We will revisit this later.

How Do Models and Taxonomies Differ From Theories?

Zais (1976, pp. 91-93) defines models as,

> miniature representations that summarize data and/or phenomena and thus act as an aid to comprehension. In other words, "models in science act like metaphors in language: they enlighten us by suggesting arguments by analogy from known resemblances to resemblances so far unnoticed." (O'Connor, 1957, p. 90)

Although numerous authors have developed typologies of models, Zais' analysis of four kinds of models seems to be useful for our purposes:

1. a physical or working model, often three-dimensional, to show how something works;
2. a conceptual or verbal model such as the industrial model of schooling;
3. a mathematical model, such as in chemistry and physics (Ohm's Law [amperes = volts/ohms]) which describes the relationships of three constructs in electricity; and
4. a graphic representation, such as maps, grammatical diagrams of sentences, and other graphs which describe the components of the objects, and which explain the relationships among its parts.

Models tend to be descriptive, and can be explanatory or analytical. Taxonomies are classification devices since they point to relationships, which can be analyzed. An example consists of the periodic table of elements. Another is Bloom's (1956) Taxonomy. However, neither the model nor the taxonomy can be predictive, nor can they produce principles.

Further Uses of Theory

Comprehensiveness

Any decent theory covers a lot of phenomena. For example, the germ theory covers a whole host of diseases, not just one or two. What good would a germ theory prove if it only covered one illness? We could not develop medications which deal with other germs. In research on small schools, we deal with dropping out, student and faculty norms of behavior, graduation rates, scheduling models, and many other phenomena. Therefore, we would expect any theory of curriculum to deal with a wide range of curriculum issues, and/or processes (such as steps in curriculum development), and/or structures—and/or models.

Objectivity

Generally, scientists want their results to be objective, so that using the same methodology will produce the same results. And for a big chunk of time, that was the prevailing wisdom among scientists. Then, along came Thomas Kuhn (1962) who pointed out that science experiences a revolution sporadically, which he called a paradigm shift. Think Einstein and relativity, think Newtonian physics and then quantum mechanics. In education, we have not had a theory of curriculum, perhaps until now.

Casti (1989) picks up the first point made above, "what is taken to be true at any moment is more a matter of social convention in the scientific community than it is a product of logical methods and procedures." Scientists generally tend to conform to general beliefs, concepts, constructs, and, certainly, the paradigms in vogue in their disciplines. Mavericks who deviate are generally not appreciated (somewhat of an understatement) by those in the mainstream of thought, until that mainstream may change. Thus, objectivity appears to be somewhat of an illusion, since scientific fields will change over the long run since the core of scientific inquiry will make new discoveries, which changes the field.

A Guide to New Knowledge

Science has enormous value in guiding us to new knowledge. The germ theory points us to look for germs as the cause of a disease. The theory of tectonic plates leads us to look for them as a cause for earthquakes, rather than the gods being jealous of human tranquility and shaking us up in a fit of jealous rage. Weick's notion that some organizations are loosely coupled points us in the direction of inquiring how schools are organized, and to inquire into the "tightness" of their organization. Similarly, if a theory regarding curriculum decision making is our focus, we can look for or develop potential structures to generate curriculum, or we can seek out processes that have potential to generate curriculum. Or, we can look for stages in the process of curriculum development, or we can search for barriers and supports in the processes of developing different curriculum models. Note that developing a theory gives us a jumping off platform, or a fulcrum to guide us in our thinking and subsequent action.

Classifying Phenomena

As noted by Lunenburg and Ornstein (2008), Van Dalen (1979) mentions as one of the functions of theories (in addition to those cited above) that they classify phenomena. He mentions the study by Halpin and Crofts (1963) of organizational climate in which they classify six organizational climates from eight dimensions. Benne and Sheats (1948) classified a number of constructive and not-so-constructive role functions in organizations that are extremely useful in working with groups. What could a theory of curriculum provide us in terms of classifying various models of curriculum?

Formulating Constructs

Another Van Dalen perception consists of the idea that theory can lead to generating constructs to describe, to analyze and to predict individual, group and organizational behavior. He mentions Lewin's force-field analysis as a theoretical construct, which can be inordinately useful in changing people's behavior in an organization. For curriculum, we can take constructivist philosophy, theory and practice and try to develop a theory and practice of constructivist curriculum. (See Chapter 28 for such a theory.)

Revealing Needed Research

Another of Van Dalen's perceptions is that since theories are predictive, they can predict areas that need further research, which seems quite plausible. For example, of late, a "small schools movement" has developed. What kind of personality styles seem to fit better into running a small unit? Can we use the Gregorc Personality Style Delineator (1982) to help us research this interesting question? What different personalities using Gregoric's model seem to prosper and which have trouble with different curriculum models?

Is Theory Practical?

If so, we need some illustrations. Going to our old reliable germ theory of disease, we have been developing medications, these days, antibiotics, whose sole mission in life is to kill and maim specific germs. In medicine, researchers found that using Boyle's Law to predict that when gasses expand, they will be cooled. The field of cryotherapy resulted, using frozen nitrogen to treat skin diseases, such as warts. In administration, Griffiths (1959) established a theory that administration itself is decision making, which leads us to explore the process of decision making in organizations.

Taking a cue from Griffiths' theory, we can begin to ask some key questions. Who should be involved in decision making? What does involvement mean to the people involved? Does such a process generate a degree of buy-in to decisions? Do we want buy-in? Should we study the process of decision making? Perhaps, we should defer that a bit later when we attempt to delineate a theory of curriculum, which, if Griffiths is correct, could be a process of decision making. This will be discussed later.

In discussing the relationship of theory to practice, (as noted in the second section of this chapter), Americans think not only that the two are separate, but the twain can never meet. We face difficulty in trying to show that the two are practically one. Let us turn to Dewey for his insights, which, to the average American, will prove shocking. In *Experience and Education* (1938), he wrote about "a theory and practice of education which proceeds." A bit further down the page, he states, "any theory and set of practices is dogmatic which is not based upon critical examination of its own underlying principle" (p. 8). Clearly, Dewey is deliberately using the singular here, and obviously perceives theory and practice as one, as unified, as one and the same.

Parton (2000), a professor of social work, argue that "to explore the nature of the discipline of social work … that perhaps its central and unique characteristic is the way theory and practice are closely interrelated" Coladarci and Getzels (1955) note in their paper on the relationship of theory to practice that "theory is a guide to practice" (p. 7). Hoy and Miskel (2008) noted the relationship of theory to practice "in at least three ways. First, theory forms a frame of reference to the practitioner. Second, the process of theorizing provides a general mode of analysis of practical events. And third, theory guides decision making" (p. 7). Apparently, a number of scholars perceive the close if not unitary relationship of theory and practice. So does the author of this paper. If this holds water, then a theory of curriculum will prove inordinately in our practice of designing and implementing curriculum models.

The Relationship of Theory to "Reality": A Good Fit? Or Not?

Can Theory Map Reality?

Since different philosophies treat so-called reality differently, this is a question long entertained in human thinking. For education, the models, theories, constructs attempt to describe and analyze reality, but, as Mintzberg (1989) noted, the words we use to try to get a handle on reality are just that, not reality itself. Mintzberg felt that the organizations we are trying to describe and to analyze are more complex than any of our representations. As Hoy and Miskel (2008) noted, "Our choice is not usually between reality and theory, but rather between alternative theories" (p. 4). If we look at the above thinking about describing and defining a fact, we immediately see how personal and possibly idiosyncratic it is, that it is difficult to achieve a solid degree of objectivity.

Thus, "reality, however, is not in our heads; we learn what it is the course of coping and responding, acting and adjusting, and testing and refining our theories" (Hoy, 1996, p. 368; Selznick, 1982). Some literature has suggested that theory can map reality. But, since our personalities and our culture influences one's maps, it is clear that our maps are both personally and culturally impacted. Conant (1952), a respected scientist and resident of Harvard, noted

> Scientific theory should not be regarded as an objective map that describes and explains reality, but rather, as a "policy—an economical and fruitful guide to action by scientific investigators." (p. 97)

Percy Bridgeman (1952), another highly respected physicist, treats this relationship in the following manner:

> Scientific, empirical-rational methods had shown that scientific theory was not, as had been thought, a value-free, objective description of reality, but a construct invented to advance human endeavors. (p. 97)

> Theory regarded as a map, as mentioned earlier, purports to tell us what the world is really like. It implies *discovered* knowledge, which literally represents an uncovering of the nature of reality. By contrast, modern scientific theory—that is, theory regarded as a policy for action—claims only to tell us what the best *representations* of the work in terms of present experience. Knowledge from this point of view is regarded as *constructed*, that is, fabricated on the basis of human experience for particular ends-in-view … theory may vary accordingly as purposes for which it is constructed may vary.
>
> As we noted in a previous paragraph, all of the evidence available seems to indicate that the revolution in

> modern physics has rendered the "map" concept of scientific theory both an illusion and a presumption. Scientific theory not only *does not* describe the nature of reality, but it *cannot*. The reason, some physicists contend, is that theory is a product of human thought processes, and modern physics suggests that human thought processes may not correspond sufficiently to the structure of nature to permit us to think about it at all. (pp. 86-87).

VALIDITY AND RELIABILITY

The above discussion should give us pause regarding the difficulty of obtaining validity, inasmuch as cultural perceptions may affect the process. Nonetheless, scientists try to seek validity. It consists of evidence that gives us some confidence that what we think we are measuring we are measuring. Reliability consists of an estimation that the measurements or results obtained will be achieved again if we use the same procedures. One of my favorite examples is that if we measure an object with a rubber band which stretches out of shape after we measure it and does not return to its original shape, and we use the rubber band to measure the same object again, the second results will not be too reliable.

Validity and reliability are a major basis for scientific knowledge. Without it, we have literature, not science. Without both, we cannot point to the certainty of the knowledge, the findings we have developed. It may be interesting, but it is not science.

A SUMMARY OF THINKING ABOUT THEORY—SO FAR

In this chapter, we pointed out the huge change the accountability movement is imposing on American schools in comparison with the Scandinavian and several European systems which focus on leadership for learning, instead. We indicated that we need another driving force, a theory of curriculum, inasmuch as a key focus of education is the development of quality curriculum to drive instruction. However, we noted that education has lacked a theory of curriculum to be that force. Consequently, we focused on the nature of and function of theory which both guides behavior and acts as a guide to new knowledge. We indicated that it is a guide to collecting facts, not the reverse. We took a look at what makes a theory a theory and pointed to three major properties: It describes, analyzes and predicts, differentiating it from models and taxonomies.

We then noted some additional functions of theory: (a) It is comprehensive in that it describes a wide range of phenomena; (b) it is objective; (c) it can classify phenomena; (d) it can formulate constructs; and (e) it can point to the need for additional research. We next considered the generalization that theory is extremely practical because it guides us in our trying to solve problems. Next, we looked at the relationship of theory to reality and found serious limitations, indicating that theory has considerable difficulty mapping so-called reality. We note that theory is a construct created by human beings based on their experiences, and influenced by their culture, their beliefs, their paradigms, their personalities, among other factors. We then took a brief glance at the necessity of validity and reliability in developing scientific thinking and in evaluating research.

CONSEQUENCES OF A LACK OF THEORY IN ANY FIELD, INCLUDING CURRICULUM

Just looking at the literature in curriculum reveals the consequences of the lack of a theoretical base. For example, a common terminology and common definitions still defy the field, leading to considerable confusion. Since the terminology has not been established, its definitions not set, how can practitioners communicate clearly? Benjamin Lee Whorf (1947, 1956), a revolutionary linguist, pointed out that even with standard terminology and meaning, communication is often difficult. He notes that communication is difficult even among people from the same socioeconomic classes and profession. Lacking a common theoretical base, as is true in the field of curriculum, exacerbates the difficulty in communicating.

While we do have Tyler's (1950) rationale and Bloom's (1956) taxonomy, neither is a curriculum theory to guide our practice, so we are at sea in the field. Fortunately, a theory has been developed, a process theory.

PINC, A SOCIAL PROCESS THEORY OF CURRICULUM

Theories come in many shapes and guises. Some focus on structure, some on relationships, others on processes that seem to take place in a field, others on models. This theory of curriculum is a decision-making theory, a theory of process, actually, a theory of *social* processes. Incidentally, after it is delineated, we will follow up with its use in organizational decision making.

"STEP 1: SENSING AN ISSUE, CONCERN, PROBLEM, NEED, OR SITUATION—AND, DEVELOPING A *PLAN*" (SHAPIRO, BENJAMIN, & HUNT, 1995, P. 38)

The process of dealing with an issue resulting in decision making starts with one or more people, usually in the organization, sensing or perceiving that something is not quite right, or sensing a discontinuity, or a concern, or an issue, or a problem. One or more people begin to recognize this. It is a situation in which people feel a sense of unrest, of feeling that something may not be right (Blumer, 1946). People feel that their program needs improving. Generally, this leads to someone proposing a course of action to do something about it, that is, a *plan*, which may be very loosely or very precisely conceived. Of course, people can also decide it is not worth dealing with, or it is too explosive to face, so they may do nothing. If a plan gets started, it can take almost any form, a vague intention to do something, or at the other end of the continuum, a more concrete model.

"Step 2: Generating *Interactions* Among People Involved" (Shapiro, Benjamin, & Hunt, 1996, p. 38)

If the people in the organization, in this case, a school, are not involved, the plan is essentially imposed. A colleague, very close to a president of a small and prestigious university, described the president as dumbfounded when he decided to reorganize "his" (he thought) organization, did it over a weekend, and discovered that his reorganization was not followed. He asked, "Can't I reorganize my own university?" It was clear that people had no idea what to do, so they merely continued their own routines. If we do not generate interactions, we ultimately do not get involvement, or understanding or buy-in, which, generally is the death knell of even very good ideas.

In terms of something as complex as curriculum, it makes sense to involve people to obtain their take, their perceptions, their ideas, their input. So, obviously, we are talking about the second step in developing curriculum as getting faculty (including aides, etc.), supervisors, administrators, hopefully, students and community involved to work on these intended outcomes. Therefore, we begin to generate a series of *interactions* among the various reference groups and individuals involved in developing, and, hopefully, implementing any curriculum or program of instruction.

Note that we are proposing a theory and practice of curriculum that is a social enterprise. In actuality, we also are presenting a theory of organizational decision making *as a social enterprise*, but that will be discussed (albeit briefly) after the process theory has been delineated.

This process is really usually quite informal, with interactions beginning as people begin communicating their unrest, or their feelings, or their perceptions, and begin thinking about ways to deal with the situation or condition, or issue. If the focus is on curriculum, people begin to think about what to do, such as studying their students' needs, or processes to involve different stakeholders in developing a unit, or a lesson plan, or an entire program. Since this theory describes a series of processes, these processes are not linear necessarily, but people can go back and forth. Of course, such 'slight' issues, often hidden to the outside, as power, influence, various social system's takes and perceptions on how this might affect them begin to emerge. That is, people's and various social systems' perceptions and concerns begin to be raised.

This leads to the next step:

"Step 3: The Process of *Negotiating*" (Shapiro, Benjamin, & Hunt, 1996, p. 39)

As concerns, issues, purposes (often hidden), viewpoints, interests emerge, so do various individual's and social systems' perceptions of institutional concerns and limitations. As interactions continue, as ideas emerge, people begin to negotiate about a variety of concerns, and potential lines of action may begin to surface. If the teachers are fortunate enough to become involved, their voice may be heard. Various social systems' voices may become heard in the potential din of interactions—or, if not heard early enough, may not make it to the table.

Power issues begin to be played out if and when people begin to realize that something may actually happen, that there may be serious *outcomes or Consequences* (Step 4), that something may become of the process. For example, I was working with an elementary school in which the administration had bought into the idea of decentralizing into small learning communities with teams as the basis of the reorganization. Most of the key people had stayed away in droves, perceiving it as another empty effort which would not be pulled off, so they were quite unwilling to spend any time on it.

The folks in the task force were actually quite serious and accepted a change strategy that I developed at that meeting (Shapiro, 2003, 2008, 2009), which I called *"the analysis of dynamics of change."* After the task force also had bought into the idea of really forming small teams and decentralizing into small learning communities, when I arrived quite early at the school for the next meeting to schmooze with key reference persons, the other key social systems people who hadn't bothered to show up previously, were waiting somewhat anxiously and asked to talk for a few minutes before the meeting. I kind of figured out their agenda and was really very interested in what they were up to. They apologized for not coming to the earlier meetings, indicated that previously they had a goodly number of initiatives at which nothing of substance had happened, and they thought that this was another fruitless enterprise. So, when the people at the previous meeting reported on the success of the planning, which was followed up by minutes which the task force sent out immediately after the meeting, they realized that this was a serious change, indeed, and that it was going to be carried out. They requested us to revisit our efforts at the last meeting, only this time with their involvement, and, I gathered, their support.

The point is that at this point some people begin to realize that the decisions being made may have serious consequences for them. It may serve as a motivation to participate rather seriously. In terms of curriculum, the focus of this paper, this leads to the fourth step.

"Step #4: Consequences, Outcomes" (p. 40)

The fourth step in the process consists of the *consequences or outcomes*, which are the consequences of the negotiations. However, obviously, this does not end with one and all euphorically basking in the results. Hard work, then, is necessarily to build the curriculum. Usually, my model involves having small work parties build the curriculum in the summer.

To summarize, four steps in the process are proposed

1. sensing a problem, issue, concern, need, or situation and developing a *Plan;*
2. generating *Interactions;*
3. *Negotiating* by various players, social systems; and
4. resulting *Consequences*, outcomes.

Hence the acronym, PINC.

This Process of Decision Making in Curriculum—Not Fixed, but an Ongoing Cycle

Even when a curriculum has been developed, people and social systems change the negotiated consequences and outcomes. For example, readings may change. So may audiovisuals and/or examples on the internet. State mandates may change, regulations may be added or dropped, or reinterpreted—or, ignored. This process of change simply continues, since things never seem to become fully fixed. Many people seem to tinker and to adjust their programs to improve them.

Obviously, this process theory is not one with clear cut, fixed stages. It is a *social process theory* which focuses on the patterns of interactions involved in the very complex and lengthy process of initiating, developing and implementing curriculum. It constitutes *a social enterprise* in nature.

Interestingly, Whitehead (1946) explored a construct regarding the phases of teaching a unit or a lesson plan:

- romance;
- precision; and
- generalization.

For Whitehead, one phase may dominate in the lesson or unit, but more may be present at any time. In developing clear information about data, the teacher may still want the kids to be able to develop generalizations as they go along. Obviously, this social process theory tries to grasp the processes people and social systems use in developing curriculum. From the standpoint of this theory, curriculum may be conceived as the process of negotiating agreements individuals and social systems make in organizations as they interact and develop agreements about what is to be learned and how it is to be delivered. In short, *it is a process theory of curriculum as a social enterprise.*

The Big Picture: A Theory of Organizational Decision Making

Looking at the big picture provides a larger scale conception of the theory—as a theory of organizations, or, more precisely, as a theory of organizational decision making. We have focused in this case on its application as a theory of curriculum decision making. By expanding its purview, we have moved it to a wider level of application than that of curriculum decision making. It may be useful in examining the processes people and social systems undertake to make decisions in the organization itself. That is, it may be used to understand, to describe and to predict the processes people in and outside the organization or organizations make as they sense issues and problems, begin to interact, and then negotiate to develop lines of actions to deal with these issues, concerns and problems.

An example may be illuminative. A school district may begin to sense that it needs to come to grips with a national trend to increase accountability and the fact that most (but not all) of its schools are not meeting the Annual Yearly Progress mandated by the No Child Left Behind Act. Should it insist that all schools focus on readying for the state No Child Left Behind Act test, or should it follow the models being used by the schools who are actually achieving Annual Yearly Progress criteria? Perhaps some of them may be following the Scandinavian model of 'Educational Leadership for Learning' following the Scandinavian model, as is true of an elementary school in Orange County, Florida, described by Isaacson (2004), and later Brown (2006). Obviously, they are sensing a major problem. They must begin to interact about this with key social systems and stakeholders. As they consider options, these systems begin to negotiate, which eventually lead to consequences or outcomes.

SUMMARY

This chapter introduced its subject by noting that two large international trends are transforming and driving education: one is the accountability movement, that is, "new public management," or "leadership for results," being pursued by the United States and the United Kingdom leading to our accountability mania, and the other is "progressive leadership," or "leadership for learning" by the Scandinavian and some European nations. We then noted that curriculum reform and development has been and can be used as a driving force to improve education, but that we have no theory of curriculum to assist us in this process. We indicated, as is true of any field, illustrated by the field of medicine, that theory is necessary for it to prosper, and that the process of curriculum development could be vastly improved with a theory of curriculum to guide us in our travails in this rather complex process. We then noted several advantages of having a theory, that it guides and shapes our behavior, that it is a guide to collecting facts, and we even defined what a fact might look like if we could find one.

We then digressed to define theory and noted its three characteristics as descriptive, analytic and predictive, which distinguish theory from models and taxonomies, with both lacking a predictive capacity. Theory, we then noted, is comprehensive, objective and functions as a guide to new knowledge. We discovered that theory and practice are practically one and the same in contrast to the American predilection of separating the two (while actually enjoying the fruit of the close relationship by using theory in everyday life, such as using the germ theory of disease daily, etc.).

We then investigated the relationship of theory to so-called "reality" and discovered that we have a difficult, really, an impossible time trying to map reality. We discussed trying to make sure that our theories and data were both valid and reliable, and summarized our thinking about theory to that point. We noted the problems in any field that lacked theory to guide it, and launched into the theory of curriculum, noting that it is a social process theory, we labeled PINC. We also considered it a process theory of curriculum *as a social enterprise*.

We then described each phase, "P" for sensing concerns and issues, and then developing a plan to take some sort of action. This is followed by people and social systems interacting (the "I") to tease out issues and concerns and potential solutions or lines of action. This is followed by negotiations (the "N") in PINC to come up with action to deal with the concerns, which culminates in the fourth step consequences (the "C") or outcomes. We then indicated that was not fixed so much as an ongoing process. Last, we noted that the theory is in reality a process theory of organizational decision making as a social enterprise, ending with an illustration of a school system deciding to try to meet the testing demanded by the No Child Left Behind Act either by focusing on practicing for the test, or by following the Scandinavian model of continuing to focus on learning.

Acknowledgment: This chapter is modified from an original chapter titled, "A Theory and Practice of Curriculum," and was published in *Curriculum and Schooling: A Practitioner's Guide* by Shapiro, Benjamin, and Hunt, assisted by Sue Shapiro (1995).

REFERENCES

Berliner, D. (2006, February). *Fixing school isn't everything.* Washington, DC: NEA Today.

Benne, K. D., & Sheats, P. (1948). Functional roles of group members. *Journal of Social Issues 4*, 242-247.

Bickel, R., & Howley, C. B. (2002, March). The influence of scale. *American School Board Journal, 189*(3), 28-30.

Bloom, B. (Ed.). (1956). *Handbook of educational objectives: The classification of educational goals: Handbook I. Cognitive domain.* New York, NY: David McKay.

Blumer, H. (1946). Part four: Collective behavior. In A. M. Lee, (Ed.), *Principles of sociology* (pp. 167-222). New York, NY: Barnes & Noble.

Bracey, G. W. (2005, Oct.). The 15th Bracey report on the condition of public education. *Phi Delta Kappan, 87*(2), 138-153.

Bridgeman, P. W. (1952). Philosophical implications of physics. *American Academy of Arts and Sciences Bulletin*, 86-87.

Brown, J. C. (2006). A case study of a school implementing a constructivist philosophy (Unpublished doctoral dissertation). University of South Florida.

Casti, J. L. (1989). *Paradigms lost: Images of man in the mirror of science.* New York, NY: William Morrow.

Coladarci, A. P., & Getzels, J. W. (1955). The nature of the theory-practice relationship. In A. P. Coladarci & J. W. Getzels (Ed.), *The use of theory in educational administration* (pp. 49-54). Stanford, CA: Stanford University Press.

Conant, J. B. (1952). *Modern science and modern man.* New York, NY: Columbia University Press.

Dewey, J. (1938). *Experience and education.* New York, NY: Macmillan.

Driver, R. (1973). The representation of conceptual frameworks in young adolescent science students (Unpublished doctoral disseration). University of South Florida.

Feigl, H, (1951). Principles and problems of theory construction in psychology. In W. Dennis, R. Leeper, H. F. Harlow, J. J. Gibson, D. Krech, D. M. Krioch, … H. Feigl (Eds.), *Current trends in psychological theory* (pp. 179-208). Pittsburgh, PA: University of Pittsburgh Press.

Gregorc, A. (1982). *Gregorc Personality Styles Indicator.* Columbia, CT: Gregorc Associates.

Griffiths, D. E. (1959). *Administrative theory.* Englewood Cliffs, NJ: Prentice-Hall.

Hoy, W. K. (1996). Science and theory in the practice of educational administration: A pragmatic perspective. *Educational Administration Quarterly, 32*, 366-378.

Hoy, W. K., & Miskel, C. G. (2008). *Educational administration: Theory, research, and practice* (8th ed.). Boston, MA: McGraw-Hill.

Isaacson, L. L. (2004). Teacher perceptions of constructivism as an organizational change model: A case study. *Dissertation Abstracts International.*

Johnson, J. D. (1958). Modern approaches to theory in administration. In A. Halpin (Ed.). *Administrative theory in education.* Chicago, IL: Midwest Administration Center.

Kerlinger, F. N. (1986). *Foundations of behavioral research* (3rd ed.). New York, NY: Holt, Rinehart & Winston.

Kuhn T. (1970). *The structure of scientific revolution* (2nd ed.). Chicago, IL: University of Chicago Press.

Lewin, K. (1952). Group decision and social change. In T. M. Newcomb & E. L. Hartley (Eds.). *Readings in social psychology* (Rev. ed.) New York, NY: Holt.

Lunenburg, F. C., & Ornstein, A. C. (2008). *Educational administration: Concepts and practices.* (5th ed.). Belmont, CA: Thomson/Wadsworth.

Maslow, A. H. (1954). *Motivation and personality.* New York, NY: Harper & Row.

Mintzberg, H. (1989). *Mintzberg on management.* New York, NY: Free Press.

O'Connor, D. J. (1957). *An introduction to the philosophy of education.* New York, NY: Philosophical Library.

Oldroyd, D. (2003). Educational leadership for results or for learning? Contrasting directions in times of transition. *International Research Journal: Managing Global Transitions, 1*(1), 40-67.

Parton, N. (2000). Some thoughts on the relationship between theory and practice in and for social work. *British Journal of Social Work, 30*(4), 449-463.

Pittman, R., & Haughwout, P. (1987). Influence of high school size on dropout rate. *Educational Evaluation and Policy Analysis, 9*, 337-343.

Selznick, P. (1992). *The moral commonwealth.* Berkeley, CA: University of California Press.

Shapiro, A. (2003). *Case studies in constructivist leadership and teaching.* Lanham, MD: Scarecrow.

Shapiro, A. (2008). *The constructivist leader: A guide to the successful approaches.* Lanham, MD: Rowman & Littlefield.

Shapiro, A. (2009). *Making large schools work: The advantages of small schools.* Lanham, MD: Rowman & Littlefield.

Shapiro, A. S., Benjamin, W. F., & Hunt, J. J., assisted by Shapiro, S. (1995). *Curriculum and schooling: A practitioner's guide.* Palm Springs, CA: ETC.

Tyler, R. (1950). *Basic principles of curriculum and instruction.* Chicago, IL: University of Chicago Press.

Van Dalen, D. B. (1979). *Understanding educational research* (4th ed.). New York, NY: McGraw-Hill.

Whitehead, L. A. N. (1946). *The aims of education: And other essays.* London, England: Williams & Northgate.

Whorf, B. L. (1947). Science and linguistics. In T. M. Newcomb & E. L. Hartley (Eds.). *Readings in social psychology.* New York, NY: Holt.

Whorf, B. L. (1956). Language, thought, and reality. In J. B. Carroll (Ed.), *Selected writings of Benjamin Lee Whorf.* Cambridge, MA: Technology Press.

Zais, R. S. (1976). *Curriculum: Principles and foundations.* New York, NY: Crowell.

Author Contact Information: Arthur Shapiro, PhD, College of Education University of South Florida Tampa, FL. 33620. Preferred mailing address: 1301 Trimaran Place, Trinity, FL 34655. Phone 727-807-7599. Fax: 813-905-9980. E-mail: ashapiro2@tampabay.rr.com

CHAPTER 28

A Theory and Practice of Constructivist Curriculum

Arthur Shapiro
University of South Florida

The overwhelming consensus as the twentieth century closed has been that knowledge is constructed.
—D. C. Phillips, *Constructivism in Education*

Constructivism has become the reigning paradigm in teacher education in America today.
—S. Hausfather, *Educational Horizons*

Constructivism and constructivist thinking have exploded onto our educational stage with a suddenness and strength that was hardly imaginable a decade or so ago, (but not yet clearly understood widely). This chapter will get at that, hopefully, in a down-to-earth way.

In order to achieve the goal of developing an understandable theory and practice (what good is theory without practice?) of constructivist curriculum, we will look at what makes a theory a theory, even looking at the possibility that theory can map "reality" (which gives us a strong thrust into the underlying basis for constructivist thinking). The next logical step we face is to uncover constructivist thinking by peering into its philosophic roots (where we will be utterly amazed at how very long ago the first instance of solid constructivist thinking appeared), and then its two major schools of thought, psychological and social constructivism, which again provide clues as to how we actually learn. Each school of thought is divided into moderate and radical subdivisions (of course).

Two brief examples will illustrate the differences between a constructivist classroom and a traditional teacher-centered classroom, which emphasizes the considerable distance constructivist practices have moved from traditional models. The entire constructivist approach is based on understanding not only how children learn, but also on how everyone learns, which is the fundamental basis that led to the development of constructivist thinking and its considerable impact on approaches to teaching. A social process theory and practice of curriculum next will be explored for its insights into a constructivist theory of curriculum, with an acronym, PINC.

Then, we examine the sources of constructivist curriculum, using Tyler as a point of reference with its critical implications for No Child Left Behind (NCLB), followed by Maslow's contribution to our thinking with his Hierarchy of Needs. As we will see, this impacts our thinking regarding systems of delivering curriculum, which will be followed by illustrations of interest-based curriculum. Lewin's contribution to effective decision-making is the next topic, followed by Thelen's insights into the limits of size of groups in terms of their effectiveness and the distribution of roles in groups. The just concluded Menard study pushes those insights further and points to the use of a technological model of laptop computers for each student and teacher in an experimental program which led to major role changes among teachers and students. In the study, normal teacher-student roles became blurred, with students becoming partners with teachers, students even tutoring teachers, and actually taking charge of their learning.

Calvin Taylor's model of human talents is next addressed, further adding to understanding of constructivist curriculum, as is Shapiro's take on creating effective cultures supporting constructivist curriculum and classroom practices. Bloom's taxonomy is just mentioned, as is Gregorc's Personality Style Delineator's insights into the thrust of this chapter. The next topic is the seminal study on trust by Bryk and Schneider and

The Handbook of Educational Theories, pp. 317–328

its impact on constructivist curriculum and classroom achievement, which is followed by several illustrations of empirically-based constructivist curriculum models. Last, are a summary, conclusions, and implications.

THEORY, AND (BY IMPLICATION) PRACTICE, AND THE RELATIONSHIP OF THEORY TO "REALITY"

Although a thorough definition of theory and its relationship to practice is provided in another chapter, "A Theory and Practice of Curriculum Development," in this section on curriculum, we will provide a brief foray into establishing the nature of theory. Griffiths (1959) uses Feigl (1951, p. 182) for his take on theory by stating:

> A theory is essentially a set of assumptions from which a set of empirical laws (or principles) may be derived.... A theory cannot be proved by direct experiment.... (An) illustration of this from the history of science demonstrate(s) this point. The Copernican Theory of the Solar System was accepted 150 years before there was direct evidence of its truth. (p. 28)

And, since the above-mentioned chapter also provides a more fulsome analysis of the succeeding three characteristics of theory analyzed below, we will deal with them in a fairly brief manner. What are the key properties, components of any theory? And how can we tell if something is a theory or a model? For a theory to be a theory it has to be:

- descriptive
- analytic
- predictive

An example? In medicine, the germ theory permits us to predict that if certain germs infect us (say, cold germs), we probably will start sneezing and infecting those friends and family who, unfortunately, have been too close to us. Very predictive. It should be somewhat obvious that we consider theory to be quite practicable, since if we become infected (using the germ theory of disease), we usually think it is a good idea to take some steps to kill off the germs—for many diseases with an antibiotic.

A model, although exceedingly useful, only is descriptive and analytic. An example? Bloom's taxonomy. Very useful, very helpful, in that it describes objectives, and then helps us analyze on what level the objective is. But, is it predictive? Obviously, not. A theory is. Hopefully, we will be able to tease out some elements of a theory of curriculum that is constructivist in nature and has properties that are predictive. As for theory mapping "reality," we can turn to a highly regarded scientist, James Conant (1952), who pointed out:

> Scientific theory should not be regarded as an objective map that describes and explains reality, but rather, as "a policy—and economical and fruitful guide to action by scientific investigators." (p. 97)

Since we are heading into dealing with constructivism as a way of looking at the world, noted physicist Percy Bridgman's take on the issue of theory being able to map reality is a segue into the theory and philosophy. Bridgman (1952) took apart the notion that with scientific method we can acquire a one-for-one or exact knowledge of "reality."

> Scientific, empirical-rational methods had shown that scientific theory was not, as had been thought, a value-free, objective description of reality, but a *construct* [added emphasis] invented to advance human endeavors.
>
> Theory regarded as a map, as mentioned earlier, purports to tell us what the world is really like. It implies *discovered* knowledge, which literally represents an uncovering of the nature of reality. By contrast, modern scientific theory—that is, theory regarded as a policy for action—claims only to tell us what are the best *representations* of the work in terms of present experience. Knowledge from this point of view is regarded as *constructed*, that is, fabricated on the basis of human experience for particular ends-in-view ... theory may vary accordingly as purposes for which it is constructed may vary. As we noted in a previous paragraph, all of the evidence available seems to indicate that the revolution in modern physics has rendered the "map" concept of scientific theory both an illusion and a presumption. Scientific theory not only *does not* describe the nature of reality, but it *cannot*. The reason, some physicists contend, is that theory is a product of human thought processes, and modern physics suggests that human thought processes may not correspond sufficiently to the structure of nature to permit us to think about it at all. (pp. 86-87)

Now that our two noted scientists have laid the groundwork for thinking about constructivist thought, we can proceed.

THE CONSTRUCTIVIST LANDSCAPE

THE PHILOSOPHERS

The Introduction in the opening of this chapter made a somewhat rash promise that we would be amazed at finding how long ago the first source for legitimate constructivist thinking occurred, although the actual use of the word itself is quite recent. Heretofore, most people peering back into the first stirrings of constructivist thought had seized on Immanuel Kant (1734-1804), an eighteenth century philosopher, as the originator, but I discovered an earlier source. Fully four centuries earlier, renaissance genius Bishop Nicole D'Oresme in *1377* articulated constructivist thinking, as Taschow (2003) noted:

> In his classical aesthetics, (D')Oresme formulated a modern subjective "theory of perception," which was not the perception of objective beauty of God's creation, but the constructive process of perception, which causes the perception of beauty or ugliness in the senses. Therefore, we can see that every individual perceives another "world." (p. 3)

Astoundingly, D'Oresme preceded Immanuel Kant, the first philosopher, by four hundred years. Philosopher D. C. Phillips (2000, p. 8) noted that Kant:

> argued that certain aspects of our knowledge of the physical universe (time and space, for example) were the products of our own cognitive apparatus—thus, we 'construct' the universe to have certain properties, or, rather, our facility of understanding imposes those temporal and spatial properties on our experience.

Descarte, Rousseau, and Pestalozzi all contributed to the development of constructivist thought with Descarte famously noting that he cast away all of his beliefs to the foundational thought, "I think, therefore, I am." So, he attempts to begin thinking and developing knowledge from his perceptions of unquestioning thought. Rousseau believed that students learn through their senses, as well as from their experience and their activity (a forerunner of constructivist instruction). Marlowe and Page (1998) stated,

> Pestalozzi ... believed that the student's mind receives impressions through observations and experience and that these impressions produce ideas and an organized mental structure that the student uses to compare, examine, separate, and conclude. (p. 17)

The Scientists

We have to wait a couple of centuries, namely, the twentieth, for the next major contributor, Jean Piaget, who founded the field of empirical development psychology. The title of his epic work, *The Construction of Reality in the Child* (1954), asserts that the child is in charge of constructing his/her own reality, although Piaget did not use the term constructivist as we use it today. Obviously, Piaget is a constructivist. Bruner (1962), who followed closely , thought that discovery is at the core of people's thinking. Marlowe and Page (1998) indicate that Bruner noted, "Whatever a person discovers himself is what he truly knows. From discovery ... comes increased intellectual ability, including the ability to solve problems" (p. 18).

Although none of the contributors to constructivist thinking and philosophy used the term constructivist, Dewey, George Herbert Mead (Dewey's colleague at the University of Chicago) who founded the field of symbolic interactionism, and also contemporary social psychology, Lev Vygotsky and Howard Gardner, among others are key contributors to the field. Sociologists Peter Berger and Thomas Luckman in 1966 published a book titled *The Social Construction of Reality*, although not really using the word constructivism. Yet the key thinking is clear and present—we construct our social reality.

A key and early contributor to constructivist thought, and one of the earliest employers of the word, constructivist, was Rosalind Driver, an English researcher in science education. Driver was interested in "the development of approaches to work with teachers to consider research findings and their applications for science classrooms and curricula ... (later) she expanded her work to consider ... students' perceptions of science and the impact of these on their learning" (Gumstone, 2000, as cited in Phillips, 2000, p. 261). Students' perceptions she considered as *coherent frameworks of ideas*, and as a consequence she *did not* perceive them as mistakes. They were simply what they brought to the table, not errors. This viewpoint is crucial to developing an effective classroom in which students' viewpoints are respected.

Brooks and Brooks (1993) were early pioneers in education arguing for using constructivist practices in the classroom, and Linda Lambert et al. (1995) were the earliest to focus on constructivist leadership.

Major Forms of Constructivism

The major forms of constructivism exert not only *fundamental* implications, but also applications for a theory of curriculum and for education in general. Philosopher D. C Phillips was commissioned by the National Society for the Study of Education (NSSE) to produce a book titled *Constructivism in Education: Opinions and Second Opinions on Controversial Issues* (2000). In it he points to two differing constructivist approaches, psychological and social constructivism.

Psychological Constructivism

Psychological constructivism, Phillips notes

> refers to a set of views about how individuals learn (and about how those who help them learn ought to teach). Roughly, this ... type of constructivist view is that learners actively construct their own ("internal," as some would say) sets of meanings or understandings;

> knowledge is *not* [emphasis added] a mere *copy* of the external world, nor is knowledge acquired by passive absorption or by simple transference from one person (a teacher) to another (a learner or knower). In sum, knowledge is *made*, not *acquired* (p. 7).

Phillips then indicates why he perceives this approach to be psychological constructivism:

> Some constructivists of this broad type go on to stress that we cannot be certain any two individuals will construct the same understandings; even if they use the same linguistic formulations to express what they have learned, their deep understandings might be quite different.... I n previous papers I have used the expression *psychological constructivism*, because the center of interest is the psychological understandings of individual learners. (p. 7)

We now are into the heart of constructivist thinking, in that each of us sees the world surrounding us differently depending on our differing experiences, personalities, cultures and subcultures in which we live and in which we are raised. We develop different life experiences, different opportunities, some of which we construct, which lead to different expectations, different perceptions of the world—from even our siblings. Some of us might believe that twins develop the same personalities, perceptions and world view because their experiences are roughly the same. But, are they? My wife, an older twin, is acutely aware of subtle differences in twins' behavior so that she can recognize nine out of ten times which twin is the older. Her younger twin is absolutely unaware of these phenomena. And, I, with no twin experience, hardly recognize twins even when I supposedly see them. They are not significant symbols to me. Therefore, by this example, it should be clear that many individual twins do not perceive the world similarly to their twin siblings. In part, this occurs because family expectations often differ for the older and younger twin. And expectations help in driving behavior. Thus, we begin to realize that each of us constructs his/her own world differently, often quite differently.

As is true with every academic discipline, different schools of thought emerge—in this case, a more moderate psychological constructivism, generally described above—and a more radical version. The guru of this latter form is Ernst von Glasersfeld (1995), who explained radical psychological constructivism as follows:

> Radical constructivism ... starts from the assumption that knowledge, no matter how it is defined, is in the heads of persons, and that the thinking subject has no alternative but to construct what he or she knows on the basis of his or her own experience. What we can make of experience constitutes the only world we consciously live in.... All kinds of experience are essentially subjective, and although I may find reasons to believe that my experience may not be unlike yours, I have no way of knowing that it is the same.... Taken seriously, this is a profoundly shocking view. (p. 1)

Von Glasersfeld hit the constructivist perception of how we know in the heart, dead center. We really do not know what the other person's knowledge is until s/he communicates with us, and even then, meaning is sometimes uncertain. Another perception by von Glasersfeld was that I cannot be sure that his concept of the color blue and mine are the same, struck home to me. When my very color-conscious wife unthinkingly sent me out to get a can of primary blue paint to paint a piece of sculpture, I was in somewhat of a panic, so I called her from a Sherman Williams and said that there were a lot of different shades of blue, and that I was out of my league. To which she responded, "Just get a can of primary blue." I did receive an apology when I returned because she had realized that my sense of color was leagues away from hers, and I needed help in figuring out primary blue (and red, and yellow, as well).

So, von Glasersfeld *is* right in asserting that because we never share the same experiences, we can never perceive the same phenomena similarly. However, he misses the key processes that any society and culture generate—its language. Culture and its underpinning vehicle, language, exert enormous impact on every single person in any and every society. For example, we speak the same language—obviously, no accident. We share many of the same customs, such as Thanksgiving feasts and, driving on the right side of the road. Thus, not only are we socially formed, but as George Herbert Mead (1934) wrote, the mind, the self, and society are socially formed.

Social Constructivism

As with psychological constructivism, social constructivism also has developed into two fields, moderate and radical social constructivism (although other category systems have been developed, such as by Matthews [2000]). Phillips (2000) captured the essence of this school of thought:

> "Constructivism" embodies a thesis about the disciplines or bodies of knowledge that have been built up during the course of human history. I have described this thesis as, roughly, that these disciplines (or public bodies of knowledge) are human constructs, and that the form that knowledge has taken in these fields has been determined by such things as politics, ideologies, values, the exertion of power and the preservation of status, religious beliefs, and economic self-interest. This thesis denies that the disciplines are the objective reflections of an "external world." (p. 6)

This statement, if taken seriously, has enormous implications for the fields of science, some of which we tend to treat as sacrosanct. It is noteworthy that Phillips indicates that these sciences consist of *constructed fields of knowledge*. Therefore, it is important to examine this area rather carefully. Thus, we will deal first with the more moderate form of social constructivism.

Moderate Social Constructivism, Relatively Briefly

A more moderate form of social constructivism holds that the sciences dealing with the *social world* are socially constructed. This is fairly evident. For example, in one of earliest books using the word constructivism, as noted earlier, sociologists Berger and Luckman (1966) titled their book, *The Social Construction of Reality*. Thus, the authors are contending that we construct our social worlds, that they are *not* ready-made by nature to be put on like a t-shirt or a pair of jeans. That this is self-evident is obvious, in that many of our rituals have been developed quite recently. For example, homecoming in high schools developed after World War II. Some or many people text while they drive (probably not a particularly good idea), but this has only developed in this first decade in the new millennium. Use of e-mail has exploded in the last 15 years or so.

Thus, the social world, manifestly, is socially constructed. These and virtually all customs only have come into existence relatively recently. Even long time customs (Thanksgiving dinner, celebration of Christmas) have developed at some time in the past (probably not originating in the time of the Big Bang).

Radical Social Constructivism—A Serious Threat to The Assumed Objectivity of Science

While moderate social constructivism is moderate, the more radical social constructivists really push the envelope quite a bit further to the consternation of those in the so-called "hard sciences." These sociologists, who are in the Strong Program in the sociology of knowledge, state:

> that the form that knowledge takes in a discipline can be *fully explained* or *entirely accounted for*, in sociological terms. That is, ... what is taken to be knowledge in any field has been determined by sociological forces including the influence of ideologies, religion, human interests, group dynamics, and so forth ... this group of thinkers wishes to deny that so-called knowledge is in any sense a reflection or copy of that "external reality" that the community in question is investigating. (Phillips, 2000, pp. 8-9)

To sum up, what the radical social constructivists are asserting is that even the hard sciences are socially constructed, and, as a result, cannot claim to be objective. They are claiming that the structure and knowledge of the sciences and mathematics are determined by social forces, and that, as a consequence, the objectivity our culture ascribes to the sciences and mathematics is a delusion. That this has serious implications is an understatement, since if we take this viewpoint, how can you tell science from utter nonsense? This viewpoint is asserting that science has no validity or objectivity. If so, what does this do to the foundation of our cultural understandings?

Consequently, natural scientists and mathematicians have not applauded this viewpoint. But, if one sits back and takes a long view, it is clear that the major concepts of science have not always been with us. They were, and they still are, in process of being developed, as Phillips (2000) notes:

> The concepts we use in everyday life or in the scholarly disciplines, did not descend—fully formed—out of the blue. There was a time when the concepts of "energy" or "mass" or "molecule" or "psychosis" or "working class" did not exist; and the halting and interactive process can be traced whereby these concepts and the very things or categories themselves were developed. (p. 88)

A Classical Versus a Constructivist Teaching Approach

The approach taken by classical teachers was described by Claudia Geocaris (1996-97), who taught ninth grade biology. Note *who made every single* decision (all italics of the word, *I*, are mine):

> In the past years *I* took a traditional approach with a complex but vitally important scientific concept: What is DNA and how does it contribute to genetics and the diversity of life? *I* usually presented material to students through lectures and labs. *I* explained key scientific discoveries and told students about the theories that resulted from the research. After presenting the material, *I* expected the students to understand the relationship among DNA, RNA, proteins, and genetics. Although many students did, other did not; moreover, my students did not exhibit high levels of student engagement. (p. 72)

To give Ms. Geocaris credit, she abandoned this model afterward. Note who is making all decisions. This presents Ms. Geocaris with the illusion that she is in control, but is she? Some kids are jumping to her tune, but lots aren't, and she was so frustrated that she changed her model. The second case study is constructivist (obviously).

Sue Shore left her teammates at the end of their middle school meeting, and steamed into the room. She typed into the computer, which then appeared on the screen on the wall the following:

Today's goals:

Schedule for:

- The Celts
- The Horsemen
- The Vikings
- The Armorers
- The Magicians

Review today's objectives:

- Work
- Dates of presentations

Wrap-up, evaluation of day's activities on the Group Planning (Postmeeting Reaction Form)

Development of objectives, resources, and time needed for tomorrow.

Sue asked the first members of each group entering the room if they wanted to change any of their plans for today from those handed in yesterday. Four of five groups stuck with their plans, with the Celts modifying their plan with an additional objective: Marissa wanted to focus on home-building techniques. Sue asked if the rest of the group was ok with that, and they were. As students entered, they immediately joined their group and worked intensely. Sue sat with each group as they worked on their project of early village life in Britain. Sue was impressed with the energy, thought, the range of materials and studies the kids had collected, their focus and creativity. She thought that the laptops were inordinately useful in exploring and locating materials and information.

"A Constructivist View of Learning" ala Driver's Research

Although Driver and Bell (1986) focused on learning science, their conclusions appear to be generalizable:

1. Learning outcomes depend not only on the learning environment, but also on the knowledge of the learner.
2. Learning involves the construction of meanings. Meaning constructed by students from what they see or hear may or may not be those intended. Construction of a meaning is influenced to a large extent by our existing knowledge.
3. The construction of meaning is a continuous and active process.
4. Meanings, once constructed are evaluated and can be accepted or rejected.
5. Learners have the final responsibility for their learning.
6. There are patterns in the types of meanings students construct due to shared experiences with the physical world and through natural language. (pp. 453-454)

Clearly, Driver is arguing that learning consists of the social construction of knowledge, and that we form connections among new concepts, ideas, processes with our previous understandings. Various activities can be suggested to promote learning. Active learning is obvious; however, it is the *meaning* we make of it that matters. Such activities include students writing a play or skit, writing a poem or short story, conducting an experiment, planning and carrying out an activity to accomplish a goal, students planning the goal itself, developing a report, and/or designing and building a model, all comprise active learning. Driver does distinguish between discovery learning and constructivist learning, in that she discovered that students often need concepts or processes to be suggested that they might not conjure up in their own efforts.

Impact on Curriculum, or, a Constructivist Theory of Curriculum: Theoretical Elements

A Social Process Theory Of Curriculum Decision Making

Shapiro, Benjamin, and Hunt (1995) may have developed the first theory of curriculum cited in the chapter titled "A Theory and Practice of Curriculum," essentially a process theory of curriculum decision-making, which was expanded into a theory of organizational decision making. The theory envisions four steps in the process:

- "Step One: Sensing an Issue, Concern, Problem, Need, or Situation—and Developing a *Plan*" (p. 38). In this step, someone or a group sense some sort of need and develop some sort of intention or plan to start to cope with it. Recognizing an issue begins the process. This leads to the second step,
- "Generating *Interactions* among People to be Involved." To get anywhere, people have to become involved, which, in turn, generates interactions among people. If people become serious, they have to figure out which key reference groups have to become involved, or any initiative will go down in flames. The interactions have to consist of people thinking and communicating about their purposes and goals.
- "The Process of *Negotiating*," the third step, commences as people become more serious and they

define their expectations, purposes, viewpoints, interests. As they interact, people begin to negotiate, and all sorts of issues and concerns begin to emerge among participants. Power issues and social systems with more or less power and authority begin to emerge and become factors. When players begin to realize that Outcomes or Consequences may emerge, people may tend to become much more serious.

- "Outcomes, *Consequences*," the fourth step, begin to emerge, with the negotiations ending with some consequences. Thus, the authors called this process: PINC. Obviously, this cycle can start all over as consequences emerge that may or may not be intended, leading the authors to conclude that the process of curriculum development comprises an ongoing process.

This theory of curriculum decision making is a social process theory, and, therefore, quite constructivist in nature.

Tyler's Three Sources and How They Fit Into Constructivist Curriculum

Tyler (1950) suggested three sources for developing curriculum: The needs and interests of learners, the needs and concerns of society, and the contribution of subject matter specialists to the general education of the learners. Interestingly, the Greeks, in discussing curriculum, referred to subjects, such as mathematics and poetry, the impact of which is felt to today. Laymen (including so-called expert panels supposed to reform schools) and educators almost invariably talk of subjects. The Committee of Ten in 1893 focused on subjects as its take on secondary education, for example, laying out the science sequence of subjects, and not on their contribution to the general education of adolescents. Incidentally, since they had no frame of reference to decide in what grade each science should be taught, they settled on ordering them alphabetically: biology, chemistry, and physics, pointing up the necessity of a research-based rationale to guide our thinking, or another rationale insidiously appears.

The recommendations of the National Education Association (NEA) in 1917 also focused on subjects, although their recommendation of Civics in ninth grade was to instill some civic knowledge so people would vote and be good citizens, inasmuch as huge numbers of kids stopped going to school during that grade. Still the focus was on subjects: civics, history (American and European) and government. Today's reform movements, such as NCLB and developing a national set of standards, also focus on subjects, although citing national needs to reform education as the rationale. Both sit on opposite ends of the continuum from the focus of constructivism.

Constructivism, clearly, puts its money on the first source of curriculum, the needs and interests of learners. In the example of Sue Shore's constructivist classroom above, while the students were working on an early British settlement, student interests were driving the curriculum. All one has to do is to look at the topics (the Celts, Horsemen, Viking, Armorers, Magicians) to see that it is the interests of the students that led to these choices. I suspect this is the reason that Driver (1981) placed the structure of the learner's thinking over that of the discipline in her thinking about "implications for classroom practice" (the first two of which state):

1. In organizing learning experiences science curriculum development needs to consider the structure of the child's thinking as much as considering the structure of the discipline. The specific content is significant rather than Piagetian operations.
2. The logical order of a topic derived from views of the structure of the discipline may not correspond to appropriate psychological order of learning (pp. 93-101).

In a couple of systems in which I worked, we exploded the high school curriculum into an interest-based approach, providing 80 plus courses in both the social studies and in the English/language arts, numbers of them interdisciplinary in nature, depending upon the interests and expertise of faculty. First, faculty were asked for their interests, hobbies, and then students were consulted. Students responded by wanting to teach a course they called "Black Humor" (which was accommodated by having a teacher supervise it), and peoples' interests were plumbed for their input, leading to quarter courses (9 weeks in length) called The Old West, The Civil War and others with an interdisciplinary focus by having English offerings provided (such readings as *Andersonville, The Red Badge of Courage*).

Thus, a huge variety of courses were provided, fitting into constructivist theory and practice by providing options galore for student and faculty interests. About 22 courses in history were offered in a high school of 1200, as much or more than in a small college. This model stimulated the creative juices of the faculty, which responded by developing simulations, one of which was called Stones and Bones, an archaeological dig (proudly asserted by the developer as the very best in the country). The school early on adopted the Ropes course, and other simulations. Adolescent Love was a course cooked up by a shrewd Language Arts teacher, which featured Hamlet as one play. And, Criminology, as well as Adolescent Psychology, were other courses. In the practical arts department of Industrial Processes, one of the faculty developed a simulation similar to the Junior Achievement model, in that the students decided on planning and manufacturing a product, and then organized to produce it. In the process, they visited industrial plants to compare and to improve their organizational structure and processes to manufacture the product (vice president for manufacture, for safety, for marketing, etc.). A local paper called these "Zingy Courses", so the adult education program asked why the adult education program couldn't follow suit and not be so stodgy.

Years later, my wife and I met a couple of students from that high school at a cocktail party, whereupon I asked them separately what they learned in that high school. The young woman, Pam, now about 26, thoughtfully responded that she learned to manage her time and to make better decisions (students had to pick among the huge number of courses, obviously). The young man indicated that he had learned to take responsibility. I asked them if it carried over into college, and they both noted that since kids had to take responsibility for their time (we had no study halls), graduates told them they had a much easier time buckling down to work in college, since the high school was essentially a college. Because the courses were so rich, the dropout rate declined, and disciplinary problems were fairly well reduced since kids were not forced for a year into a course with a teacher with whom they had problems. We also structured a lot of labs into settings where kids could sign in during their "free" time, which proved highly attractive. Interestingly, a department which decided not to expand its offerings (huffily indicating that they would not play "fun and games") did not fare too well in this relative free-for-all (although each department could and did establish a structure, obviously, as graduation requirements had to be met). When the student selections were made, such a department lost a lot of its enrollment, and one foreign language group tried to maintain that a foreign language with 60 students in 3 years of courses was the ideal size.

Maslow and Curriculum

Maslow's (1954) Hierarchy of Needs can prove beneficial in thinking about curriculum. Since at least half or more of Americans tend to be Abstract Random (Gregorc, 1982), that is, they are audio learners, want to work with others and learn best that way. They do not think sequentially, but rather are people-people first, so that organizing the classroom into groups makes a great deal of sense (Maslow's third level: Social Needs). Maslow's second level, Safety, is essential to develop a productive class, since people have to trust the instructor and each other, otherwise interaction is shut down. Trust will be discussed later.

Esteem is Maslow's (1954) fourth level, which is easily achieved by remembering Driver's astute perception that each student approaches a course with a series of concepts, understandings, ideas, and so on, that are their "coherent frameworks of ideas," not mistakes, and are, therefore, to be respected (Phillips, 2000, p. 261). Once students pick up this attitude on the part of teachers, life becomes a lot easier. People quickly pick up if they are respected or not. Maslow's fifth level, Self-Actualization, as he notes, is difficult to define and to reach, but, perhaps, might be a goal for a constructivist class.

Lewin and Thelen

Lewin's (1952) seminal experiments in decision-making inform us to this day about classroom practice and organizational functioning. He discovered that when *individuals* indicated they would change behavior, they usually did not carry through. However, when they committed publicly *in a group* to make a change in behavior, such as feeding their newborns orange juice or milk, even if completely isolated from each other after a meeting, they would follow through and do what they had committed. Thus, working groups (also supported by Gregorc's studies), are a major tool in working with people, not only in classes, but also in most organizations. People who agree to do something publicly will do so.

Thelen (1949) gives us insight into the optimal size of those work groups: Never fewer than four, or creativity will suffer, and never more than seven, because that is the largest number of roles that can be developed in a small work group. If the number of people exceeds seven, people will start to compete for roles, and the less aggressive will be shoved out and will participate less fully, if at all. This work stands as the rationale for size of work groups, teaching teams, et cetera.

The Menard Study

The Menard (2010) study is a research project that focused on determining whether a technology model of having each student and each teacher in 33 classes in 12 elementary schools having a laptop 24/7 stimulated teachers to move into developing both constructivist practices and curriculum. The more experienced teachers (with technology) did so more rapidly than the novice teachers who had 0 to 2 years experience.

What was so interesting, however, was that the traditional roles of student and teacher became blurred, with elementary students helping teachers with technological and instructional problems and techniques. In the process of development of constructivist practices, many students began to take charge of their own learning, a major finding, and a considerable stimulation of the value of constructivist approaches. Students became partners with teachers, even became tutors, which most faculty appreciated. Motivation was extremely high with kids and teachers working at projects for hours and hours. Teachers reported that when the laptops were opened in the classrooms, other faculty came out of their rooms on hearing the screams of excitement from the students. Kids worked with kids in other classrooms, in other schools, in other cities, and even in other countries. This research provided an example of self-regulated learning.

Menard (2010) recommended that in-service and mini-courses in constructivist theory and practices would have been quite helpful in teachers' development, could have avoided floundering and overcoming obstacles to effective functioning.

Calvin Taylor and Human Talents

Taylor (1968) rejected the notion that we humans are unidimensional, as most high schools treat their students. By the time kids get into high school, we narrow the curriculum into mostly academic areas. Taylor argued that humans display an array of talents, including academic (to be sure), artistic (such as musical, painting, acting), physical (including dance), planning, communicating, decision making, human relations talents, and others. He then noted that we may be above average in one talent, but if we take into account six of these talents and others, virtually 95% of people are above average. All one has to do is see what talents people have, and we are virtually always working with people who are above average in at least one or more talents. This is a profound approach to working with people—and, certainly fits into the constructivist paradigm.

Creating Culture for a Constructivist Classroom and Team, and an Emergent Curriculum

Shapiro (2000) delineated the major dimensions of developing a constructivist classroom and team. Obviously, establishing a culture by creating norms is something every teacher develops in his/her classroom, as does every group, every organization, and every family, although we may be unaware that we do so. Creating constructive norms, such as respecting everyone and every viewpoint (Driver's "coherent frameworks of ideas") probably works to everyone's advantage (Phillips, 2000, p. 261). Such a norm also follows Maslow's (1954) Hierarchy. Indeed, following Maslow was a centerpiece of the article, which includes making sure that everyone feels safe ("what's said in here stays in here"), working in groups to satisfy social needs (both Maslow and Gregorc), and respecting all contributions follows Maslow's Esteem Needs level. In actuality, once the students realize that they have a role in creating the norms and the culture, an empowerment process is created that can energize students and instructors.

The article also points out that establishing the norms, and, thus, the culture, as described above can be treated as establishing a *social compact*, to which everyone can agree. Once this step is taken, a class can move on, since the instructor and students can refer to the social compact in dealing with classroom issues. I have found the social compact to be an invaluable tool in developing consensus and dealing with potential disruption and outlier behaviors. Since everyone agreed, which includes such matters as reading reasonable assignments, this makes running such an operation much easier. Additionally, as groups develop, a process of bonding begins to develop, a considerable asset in creating a constructivist classroom.

Active learning is a must in a constructivist classroom and to implement a constructivist curriculum, which is why previous discussion focused on simulations. Role play, sociodrama are other active learning models are utilized. An *emergent curriculum* is probably at the heart of a constructivist curriculum development process. In my classes, this is facilitated by asking students what they want to learn. Interestingly, in the numerous years I've used this (and as numbers of people who have utilized this constructivist approach found), students invariably do want to learn what the general focus of the class aims at, but their recommendations also are invariably more creative than mine.

Bloom's Taxonomy

It is extremely useful to use Bloom (1956)—and, constructivist, as well. His six levels of cognitive thinking provide a schemata for helping us become more aware of the levels we use in our teaching practice. And, it provides an antidote to the urge to "drill and kill" in order to increase scores for state level NCLB-driven tests. Working at the higher levels pushes us toward reflection, much needed in our haste to increase scores. Reflection, obviously is constructivist since it asks learners to make meaning from class discussions and proceedings.

The Uses of Gregorc's Personality Style Delineator

Gregorc (1982) contributed greatly to a constructivist curriculum and classroom, since his four major personality styles generate preferred learning styles, which means that we have to satisfy all learning styles and needs.

The four styles, briefly, consist of:

- Concrete sequential, who want structure, and tend to be black and white in outlook, tend to be loners, are very time-focused and well-organized
- Abstract random, who are people persons, who want to be liked, learn best in groups
- Abstract sequential—the intellectuals, "big picture" people, who can learn in any mode, want to work alone
- Concrete random, who tend to be problem solvers, highly creative, need autonomy, respond to challenge, innovators

Stanton Leggett (Personal communication, May, 1977) once noted that the small group is the vehicle to pull that off, since in the group, people can take different roles and satisfy their learning proclivities (shades of Thelen's findings).

Trust

A seminal ten year study of social trust by Bryk and Schneider (2002) studying effective and ineffective elementary schools in Chicago focused on the impact of relational trust on student achievement. Relational trust is based on social respect and interpersonal regard for others, as well as on perceptions of competence and integrity. When high levels of relational trust are present, according to the authors, schools have a one in two chance of improving academic achievement in mathematics and reading. When relational trust is low, schools have a one in seven chance of in improving such scores. The authors note, "virtually no chance of showing improvement in either math or reading" (Gewertz, 2002). In addition, small school size was found crucial in that building trusting relationships is much easier in small schools (Shapiro, 2009).

Examples of Constructivist Curriculum Models

Isaacson (2004) moved her large elementary school into a decentralized team-based constructivist model, in which all teachers supported and utilized constructivist teaching practices. As these practices worked, the school moved toward developing a constructivist curriculum while meeting the state of Florida's Sunshine State Standards. Teachers developed units with much student input of various artifacts which were placed into large plastic containers, which included all materials, books, photographs, videos, DVDs necessary to develop the unit. The containers were stored in the school's curriculum storeroom, so that people could access them at will and as necessary. The constructivist practices and curriculum were supported by the small learning communities (SLCs) the school developed and its supporting professional learning communities (PLCs), which met regularly and in which all new teachers were involved on a biweekly basis.

Brown (2006) did a follow-up study, which indicated that teachers, indeed, were teaching using constructivist practices, but needed in-service work to make sure that they understood the theoretical basis for their practices. He also found teachers were using the curriculum model and working to improve it. Menard also indicated that most teachers had moved into developing constructivist curriculum approaches. Other illustrations of constructivist curriculum are provided by Summerhill (Neill, 1977) and the Sudbury Valley School (Greenberg, 1995), in which students constructed their own curriculum.

Shapiro's (2000) curriculum is based on student needs and interests, and has been referred to previously. Using this model, students facilitate creating the culture of the class, as well as developing the goals and objectives, and bringing in resources for the class. This is also evident in the Menard study.

Summary, Conclusions, and Implications

This chapter dealt with a number of topics starting with defining and describing the three properties of theory, while the relationship of theory to practice was dealt with in a previous chapter, "A Theory and Practice of Curriculum." Some effort was spent in exploring the validity of theory being able to map "reality," with the conclusion that it could not be done because the inherent nature of human thought is not able to pull this off. We next peered into the philosophical and scientific roots of constructivist thinking, finding that a medieval bishop, Bishop Nicole D'Oresme, actually started constructivist thinking in 1377, 400 years before Kant formulated such thinking.

The chapter then described and analyzed the two schools of thought, psychological and social constructivism, characterizing the field, each with two subschools of thought, moderate and radical constructivist thinking. Two brief examples of classroom models were presented, the first of a traditional classroom and the second of a constructivist classroom. This segued into a section analyzing research, started by Rosalind Driver, on how people learn science, the fundamental basis of constructivism. Next, the first theory of curriculum was presented, a social process theory of curriculum development, also a theory of organizational decision-making, with four steps in the process: sensing and planning, interacting, negotiating, and consequences or outcomes. The authors called this PINC after the four stages.

We next examined sources of constructivist curriculum, starting with Tyler's three sources, and concluded that the major source for building curriculum constructivistically is to consider the needs and interests of learners first, then needs and interests of society, and last, the contributions of subjects to the general education of the learner. We also concluded that No Child Left Behind and the drive to develop national standards focus on subjects (and not on their contribution to the general education of children), and on society's needs. Since needs of learners are quite diverse, this appears to be moving in the wrong direction.

We next analyzed Maslow's (1954), contributions to constructivist curriculum development and to effective constructivist classroom practice. Without meeting Maslow's Hierarchy of Needs, teachers have difficulty first, making the class safe, and then meeting the social and esteem needs of students (including their own). This means that teachers have to establish groups as an organizing vehicle, as is indicated by Gregorc's findings, and be concerned for supporting everyone emotionally, so that their needs are met.

Lewin (1952) was cited as supporting the use of groups to develop buy-in and as a vehicle for effective decision making. Thelen was cited for his insights into the size ranges needed for effective groups, and the Menard study was discussed for its technology model which facilitated both developing constructivist teaching practices and curriculum. Its revelations regarding the blurring of formerly distinct teacher/student roles, with students taking charge of their learning and becoming partners and tutors to and with faculty, are major findings. Calvin Taylor's model of human talents was delineated for its importance in valuing human beings' numerous talents, with the upshot being that virtually everyone is above average in talents.

Bryk and Schneider's (2002) seminal study on the importance of trust in student achievement is profound in its implication that without trust, it is almost impossible to increase student achievement as measured by tests (which appears to be a present American cultural proclivity, and, obviously, the present National reform paradigm). Last, we cited two illustrations of constructivist curriculum.

Several conclusions are worthwhile mentioning. A constructivist curriculum is practicable, as is evident from the Isaacson/Brown study, the Menard study and the Shapiro model. Obviously, others exist in the field. A constructivist approach tends to develop high motivational levels, as the Isaacson and Menard studies reveal (as do others in the literature), and supports developing constructivist curriculum models. This type of approach also stimulates high levels of creativity. The Menard study points to the development of teacher/student partnerships, of blurring traditional student/teacher roles into much more productive models, even to the point of students tutoring teachers.

A major implication is the United States' increasing emphasis on accountability through ever more rigorous testing and increasing the test bar for higher standards appears to be diametrically opposite to meeting students' and teachers' needs. The same can be said for the recent stress on developing national standards for most academic fields. It is contrary to meeting student needs as well as local community needs. Driver's finding that students are not making mistakes in articulating their scientific knowledge, but merely expressing their "coherent frameworks of ideas" has great implication for listening to students' ideas in all fields as a prelude to facilitating their grasping more realistic concepts and theories in terms of the academic fields' present understandings. As Gregorc's work substantiates, listening, accepting, and respecting are not only necessary, but also the underpinning to working effectively with people (which obviously includes students).

A constructivist curriculum clearly appears to be considerably more rewarding, motivating, and eliciting more creativity for students, teachers and administrators. Learning to teach takes time, and so does learning to use constructivist teaching practices and developing constructivist curriculum approaches and models. But, it certainly is worthwhile, according to those who have moved into these approaches.

REFERENCES

Berger, P., & Luckman, T. (1966). *The social construction of reality.* Garden City, NY: Doubleday.

Bloom, B. S. (Ed.). (1956). *Handbook of educational objectives: The classification of educational goals: Handbook I: Cognitive domain.* New York, NY: David McKay.

Bridgman, P. W. (1952, February). Philosophical implications of physics. *American Academy of Arts and Sciences Bulletin,* 86-87.

Brooks, M. G., & Brooks, J. G. (1993). *In search of understanding: The case for constructivist classrooms.* Alexandria, VA: Association for Supervision and Curriculum Development.

Brown, J. C. (2006). *A case study of a school implementing a constructivist philosophy* (Unpublished doctoral dissertation). University of South Florida.

Bruner, J. S. (1962). *On knowing: Essays for the left hand.* Cambridge, MA: Harvard University Press.

Bryk, A. S., & Schneider, B. (2002). *Trust in schools: A core resource for improvement.* New York, NY: Russell SAGE.

Commission on the Reorganization of Secondary Education. (1918). *Cardinal Principles of Secondary Education* (Bulletin 35). Washington, DC: U.S. Office of Secondary Education.

Conant, J. B. (1952). *Modern science and modern man.* New York, NY: Columbia University Press.

Driver, R., & Bell, B. (1986). Students' thinking and the learning of science: A constructivist view. *School Science Review, 679*(240), 453-454.

Driver, R. (1981) Pupil's alternative frameworks in science. *European Journal of Science Education, 3*, 93-101.

Feigl, H. (1951). Principles and problems of theory construction in psychology. In *Current trends of psychological theory* (pp. 179-208). Pittsburgh, PA: University of Pittsburgh Press.

Geocaris, C. (1996-97). Increasing student engagement: A mystery solved. *Educational Leadership, 54*(4), 72-75.

Gewertz, C. (2002, October). Trusting school community linked to student gains. Bethesda, MD: Education Week on the Web. Retrieved from http://www.edweek.com/ew/ewstory.cfm?slug=07trust.h22

Greenberg, D. (1995). *Free at last: The Sudbury Valley School.* Norfolk County, MA: The Sudbury School Press.

Gregorc, A. F. (1982). *An adult guide to style.* Columbia, CT: Gregorc Associates.

Griffiths, D. E. (1959). *Administrative theory.* New York, NY: Appleton-Crofts.

Gumstone, R. F. (2000). Constructivism and learning research in science education. In D. C. Phillips (Ed.), *Constructivism in education: Opinions and second opinions on controversial issues. Ninety-ninth Yearbook of the National Society for the Study of Education. Part I.* Chicago, IL: University of Chicago Press.

Isaacson, L. S. (2004). *Teachers' perceptions of constructivism as an organizational change model: A case study* (Unpublished doctoral dissertation). University of South Florida.

Lambert, L., Walker, D., Zimmerman, D. P., Cooper, J. E., Lambert, M. D., Gardner, M. E., & Ford Slack, P. J. (1995). *The constructivist leader.* New York, NY: Teachers College Press, Columbia University.

Lewin, K. (1952). Group decision and social change. In S. E. Swandon, T. M. Newcomb, & E. L. Hartley (Eds.), *Readings in social psychology* (Rev., pp. 459-473). New York, NY: Holt.

Marlowe, B. A., & Page, M. L. (1998). *Creating and sustaining the constructivist classroom.* Thousand Oaks, CA: Corwin.

Maslow, A. H.(1954). *Motivation and personality.* New York, NY: Harper & Row.

Matthews, M. R. (2000). Appraising constructivism in science and mathematics education. In D. C. Phillips (Ed.), *Constructivism in education: Opinions and second opinions on controversial issues.* Ninety-ninth Yearbook of the National Society for the Study of Education. Part I. Chicago, IL: University of Chicago Press.

Mead, G. H. (1934). *Mind, self, and society.* Chicago, IL: University of Chicago Press.

Menard, L. B. (2010). *Elementary teachers' perceptions of technology as a catalyst for constructivist practices in the classroom: A case study* (Unpublished doctoral dissertation). University of South Florida.

Neill, A. S. (1977). *Summerhill: A radical approach to child rearing.* NY: Pocket Books.

Phillips, D. C. (Ed.). (2000). *Constructivism in education: Opinions and second opinions on controversial issues. Ninety-ninth Yearbook of the National Society for the Study of Education. Part I.* Chicago, IL: University of Chicago Press.

Piaget, J. (1954). *The construction of reality in the child.* New York, NY: Basic Books.

Shapiro, A. (2000, May). Creating culture for a constructivist classroom and team. *Wingspan 13*(1), 5-7.

Shapiro, A. (2009). *Making large schools work: The advantages of small school.* Lanham, MD: Rowman & Littlefield.

Shapiro, A. S., Benjamin, W. F., & Hunt, J. J. (1995). *Curriculum and schooling: A practitioner's guide.* Palm Springs, CA: ETC.

Taschow, U. (2003). *Nicole Oresme und der fruhling modern* [Nicole Oresme and the birth of modernism]. Retrieved from http://www.nicole-oresme.com/seiten/oresme-biography.html.

Taylor, C. W. (1968, February). Nearly all students are talented —Let's teach them! *Utah Parent Teacher*, 9-10.

Thelen, H. A. (1949, March). Group dynamics in instruction: The principle of least group size. *School Review*, 139-48.

Tyler, R. (1950). *Basic principles of curriculum and instruction.* Chicago, IL: University of Chicago Press.

Von Glasersfeld, E. (1995). *Radical constructivism: A way of knowing and learning.* London, England: Falmer.

Author Contact Information: Arthur Shapiro BA, MA, PhD, College of Education, University of South Florida Tampa, FL. 33620. Preferred mailing address: 1301 Trimaran Pl., Trinity, FL 34655. Phone: 727-80-7599. E-mail: ashapiro2@tampabay.rr.com. Fax: 813-905-9980

CHAPTER 29

Does Practice Itself Know Nothing?

Probing Teachers' Felt Experiences of Mandated Practice

Rodney Evans
Independent Scholar

> Reading has not had a [mandated] curriculum for years and years—when I first started teaching, and that's why I liked teaching reading, because I didn't have to follow a curriculum. (Alexis, reading coach)
>
> But if they gave me [name of program] and said, "This is how you're going to teach this topic" I would come unglued. (Janice, social studies teacher)
>
> I'm pretty smart and I'm pretty capable and I have a lot of energy ... and I work just as hard as anybody. But I can't do it! I can't do it and I'm frustrated! I want to be the best teacher but I feel like a crappy one! (Jackie, science teacher)
>
> But teaching [name of program]—we were told we had to be positive about it—if we didn't teach it as given, we could be fired for insubordination ... I have a bachelor's degree and a master's degree in secondary English education and I received a teacher-proof curriculum! (Jayne, language arts teacher)

Across North America, the shift in the locus of control of teaching—from out of the hands of teachers and into the hands of an administrative and research policy-making elite—is well advanced and constitutes a de facto *takeover* of teaching that is without precedent in modern times. The mechanisms behind this *takeover* are subtle, and designed to appeal to the professional identity and scientific predispositions of the well trained, data-proficient, modern teacher. Although these mechanisms take various forms, they all begin by assuming that teaching is made more efficacious when it is treated as an applied scientific activity, and that theory developed outside or beyond the classroom is better positioned to govern classroom practices than knowledge arising from within. Whether the mechanisms underlying this *takeover* are enacted through the growing use of prepackaged curriculum programs, the expanded application of a regime of *high-stakes* testing, or the ongoing surveillance of teachers via intensified regimes of curriculum inspection, the result is the same—the space available for teachers and for teaching has narrowed to the vanishing point. When these curricular "innovations" are then combined with externally developed learning standards—which is to say *both* content *and* student performance standards—little is left for teachers other than to implement the externally designed curriculum as dutifully as possible. The question to be asked is: Can teaching as we know it, that is a teaching that is genuinely and substantively educative, survive the onslaught of an enforced process of curricular control and predetermination? Or in more personal terms: Can teachers thrive in a climate of enforced (mandatory) practice?

In what follows I wish to examine these questions, not admittedly with any pretense of neutrality (one can hardly be neutral in the face of what is happening to teaching these days), but with the intention of bringing to light important aspects of the task of teaching that

The Handbook of Educational Theories, pp. 329–341

are being dismissed in the project to bring teaching to heel, to turn the complex and difficult task that is teaching into a wholly preplanned and predeterminable process. Along the way I shall present the voice of Jackie, a midcareer, Florida middle-school science teacher with whom I had the opportunity to converse on the topic of mandated practice; but first a little more detail on what is meant and what is included in the phrase *mandated practice.*

TOWARD A DEFINITION OF MANDATED PRACTICE

In employing the phrase mandated practice I am referring to the changes taking place in the way teaching is thought about and practiced—with specific reference to the manner in which local, state and federal policies are altering the classroom practices of qualified, competent, experienced teachers. In this regard, I use the phrase to refer to the growing use of curriculum packages in the form of externally prescribed, often prescripted programs, which teachers are mandated to use across an increasingly broad range of subject matter content. The tightly sequenced and highly specified content of these curriculum programs has been designed or aligned to fit as seamlessly as possible with externally derived curriculum standards. The practical professional problem for teachers is that they are occupationally bound to implement the prescribed content with minimal deviation from the predetermined sequencing and/or pacing of such content. Aptly known as *teacher proofing*, this curriculum practice is based on the assumption that a linear relationship exists between strict adherence to the curriculum makers' preestablished instructional design on the one hand, and increased student performance on the other. In many jurisdictions such teacher proofing practices are monitored and enforced via the use of curriculum audits or classroom walk-throughs carried out to monitor and ensure fidelity to the preestablished program. Such totalizing practices are more and more promoted by curriculum designers and for-profit curriculum makers aided by state and federal policymakers and by school and district level administrators. Thus, as I use the term, the phrase mandated practice refers to any effort on the part of the administrative apparatus of schools to reshape the classroom conduct and pedagogic practices of teachers via externally enforced means—including the use of externally developed a priori learning standards, benchmarking, externalized high-stakes testing—to drive classroom instruction. The authoritative standard behind the enforced implementation of the paradigm of mandated practice is that it be *research based* in its desire to lay claim to the mantra of research and aura of science. Today, the term research based has become a powerful slogan by means of which far-reaching changes in teaching practices are justified and enforced. I will argue that this has been at the cost of distancing/dispossessing teachers and placing them in an oddly removed and *alien* situation vis-à-vis their own practice. In many parts of North America teachers are more and more expected to implement prepackaged curriculum programs with which they feel little connection and little ownership. At this point we should ask: Has a point been reached where teaching no longer belongs to teachers? In the transcribed sections that follow, Florida middle school science teacher, Jackie, describes her experience with the mandated program of science in her district.

> I teach science and every year it has gotten a little more scripted and then a little more and a little more.... You used to be able to grow plants where you could actually grow a garden and you had the whole growing season and now you have to do [indoor] plants like there's only two weeks left of school.... You can't plant anything now because you need time for things to grow.
>
> In science we have a county made exam every 9 weeks—I'm giving the one for the past 9 weeks that ends this Friday—it's all on scantrons and we have a new computer program in the district and the scores go downtown to the science department, and she [school superintendent] gets everybody's scores to look at. At this point nothing is done with them but I imagine in the future that will change.
>
> So I can either do that [i.e. give students a meaningful hands-on learning experience] and have lower 9-week test scores because I didn't get to Chapter 7, Section 3! I do that because I know ... its part of my responsibility to the student. That's a great opportunity for them and that's something they'll remember and have a felt experience about forever. So in the big picture that's what I would like—that they will like science and become good stewards of the environment.

Such statements, interesting and revealing though they may be, are clearly at odds with today's climate of opinion as it relates to the work of teachers. In Jackie's account, the modern accountability movement collides with a very different way of thinking (about) and practicing the craft of teaching; her remarks regarding the pervasive use of scantrons stand in marked contrast to her own understanding of the importance of the task before her. Of course, as a purely statistical matter her comments are easy to dismiss—the voice of a single teacher having difficulty reconciling her 20 plus years of teaching experience with the newly imposed demands for more technical and standardized teaching. And yet despite arguments in favor of mandatory practice, Jackie seems to have caught something necessary and important to teaching. This necessary and important thing seems to lie less in the mechanics of her teaching than in the particular aims and intentions she brings to her work as her students' science teacher, namely that her pupils will like science and become good stewards of the environment. With these basic but nevertheless important aims, it seems as if Jackie has found something worthy of her efforts as a science teacher insofar as these aims connect her work with something she deems socially valuable and meaningful and which provide her with an aim or purpose that is outside or above her teaching and to which her teaching aims to be responsive. In an age which glamorizes the trivial and exalts the inconsequential and where all things are, so to speak, downgraded and graded from below as Heidegger (1968) put it, getting middle school students to like science and become good stewards of the planet is no small matter with no small long term consequences—as we are all now very much aware. These are desirable, meaningful, humanly necessary ends—ends which make teaching an activity worthy of our best efforts and concerted abilities.

It is not farfetched to say that what Jackie's teaching strives to make contact with, that is what her teaching aims to be responsive to, is beyond the reach of tests and measurement devices of whatsoever kind. In her unrehearsed and spontaneous remarks, the lowly scantron acquires semiotic significance and serves as a potent emblem of a way of life very much at odds with Jackie's deeper sense of the task she is there to perform as her middle school students' science teacher.

In What Sense Can Teaching Be Called a Task?

It is, admittedly, somewhat strange today to speak of teaching as a *task*. As moderns, we are much more likely to speak of teaching as a *process*, and by use of this term intend, in a general way, to allude to the internal ordering and sequencing of the various acts (parts) that constitute the act of teaching. To speak of a teaching *task* is different. One is *given* a task, and whatever the nature of the task at hand it has to be accomplished, it has to be fulfilled. So to speak of teaching as a *task* is to recognize that something outside the activity itself needs to be achieved, needs to be fulfilled—and that this *something* resides beyond the nature of the actual teaching task itself. Today the notion that teaching, in the sense of educating, is in the service of something outside itself meets with outright resistance when all things are measured with respect to their functional utility. And yet this hostility to the transcendent aims that education seeks to serve does not deny the existence of such aims—for Jackie such aims/intentions clearly do exist and constitute for her (but not just for her) the full measure of the meaning and significance of her work with her pupils.

> I don't care at this stage in the game if my [test] scores are lower than someone else's.... This [science curriculum] is so crammed full that we are almost prohibited from doing these extra things like the Tampa Bay Grasses program that I do—we had a pond where we grew salt marsh grass and harvested it and when they reclaim an area around Tampa Bay we get to go out and plant it. So we're out there monitoring the marsh pond which is making a difference.... The students are learning about PH because they're checking it all of the time—it's not the same as in the textbook.... So they might not recognize the question on the exam on PH but sometime later it'll make sense to them.

But, something else is noticed, seldom discussed in the mainstream research literature, about Jackie's intentions for her teaching and that is the utter impossibility of ever being in a sufficiently commanding position to ensure the full realization of these aims—either in whole or in part. Clearly, whether students will like science, or whether they will become good stewards of the environment, is not within the purview of the teacher no matter how technically adept or dedicated to her craft she may be. This is part of the unwritten law of teaching—that the strongest and most motivating hopes we harbor for our teaching rest on nothing more substantial than that—that in the end they are merely hopes and rather flimsy ones at that. Does this mean that their flimsiness (i.e., their unenforceability) outlaws them as legitimate aims or purposes for our teaching and that as experienced professionals we should accede to the popular wisdom that insists that our aims be delimited and delimitable, made more concrete, more measurable, more achievable? Still more we can ask, are measurable "results" the only thing that count in education? The curious thing about teaching—but perhaps curious only in terms of its complete neglect—is that what *moves* teachers in a fundamental sense (over and above various motivational devices, e.g., teacher of the month, car parking privileges, merit pay schemes, etc.), is the deep desire to contribute to socially ameliorative ends for the society they serve and to personally ameliorative ends for the pupils they teach; only this motive is powerful enough to move teachers to the heights of which they are fully capable. This means that the actual *de facto* accomplishment of such ends, if not insignificant, is much less significant than the desire (wish) to work on behalf of their *possible* accomplishment. It is the existence of this desire (i.e., its actuality, its facticity) to work towards, on behalf of, the *possible* realization of such ends that inspires true teachers, and if the *actual* accomplishment lies just slightly over the horizon this has no bearing on the motivating force of the desire itself. As a genuine and committed teacher, all of this Jackie realizes in a personal and deeply intuitive way.

At the same time it is important to realize how far such nontechnical aims fall outside the cognitive ambitions and technocratic framework of modern educational theory as educational theorists such as Dylan Wiliam (2008) recently have pointed out. Wiliam draws upon Aristotle's distinction between production and action to argue that technical knowledge alone is unable to *move* teachers and other education workers to engage in work of a genuinely educational nature because it lacks a focus on action (rather than production). This insight might help to explain the odd spectacle of an increasing number of school jurisdictions hiring motivational speakers at the start of each new school year to fire-up teachers, especially new teachers, for the work that lies ahead. Such a practice makes sense only in a professional and academic milieu where the idealism and sense of communal service that supports and sustains teaching at its theoretical core has been eroded or downgraded or, in Jackie's version, scantronized. In Jackie's defense of her teaching (and we should ask why such a defense is needed) we see an *upgrading* in the form of authentic, life-world intentions for her pupils that the dismal practice of bubbling-in scantron sheets can never hope to replicate.

Jackie's Dilemma is Not of Her Own Making

It is important to note that the importance Jackie ascribes to her work as her students' science teacher is not at the expense of any type of theoretical or methodological sophistication regarding her teaching style or methodology. Jackie is anything but a *backwards* teacher. Although she does not speak the overburdened language of strategies or techniques, she nevertheless seems to understand (as many teachers do not) that the realization of her long term goals requires students to actually *experience* the curriculum, that is to *undergo* a type of lived or felt experience if the acquired understanding is to be more than skin deep, i.e. if the learning is to acquire genuine educational significance. She also seems to have an intuitive feel for the way in which in all truly educational endeavor the effects are seldom if ever immediate but reveal themselves (or not) over a much longer time horizon. The patience of a lifetime may not be too long to wait.

> So we're out there monitoring the marsh pond which is making a difference.... The students are learning about PH because they're checking it all of the time—it's not the same as in the textbook ... so they might not recognize the question on the exam on PH but sometime later it'll make sense to them.

Yet in recognizing the importance of Jackie's intentions for her teaching we ought not assume that as a bona fide science teacher she is in any way dismissive of the historical accumulation of facts, scientific knowledge, scientific theories and so forth that comprise the subject matter and enterprise of science she is honor bound to teach, only that these facts and accumulated scientific knowledge are not ends in and of themselves, they are not the main reason she is there as her pupils' science teacher and ultimately as their educator. Jackie's teaching reaches for something higher, for something qualitatively different, and while any number of quasi-psychological theories of learning might be brought forward in an attempt to account for her *hands-on* teaching style, they would be wholly unable to account for the obvious tension that underlies her words as a teacher. The tension Jackie is experiencing is hardly the result of a collision between one type of teaching style or learning theory as against another, rather it is the more fundamental conflict between her own self-understanding of her role and purpose as a teacher and the type of teacher she is confronted with being/becoming. This is Jackie's dilemma as a teacher but not just as a teacher.

> There was a point several years ago when they [county officials] said that sixth grade science was simply "exposure" and that all we were doing was just showing them all of the different areas of science. You learned a little stuff and that was fine ... now we're giving them 9-week tests that are conceptually pretty tough. I spent a couple of years complaining and asking, "Do you want me to just expose the students to information—or am I supposed to teach it so they can take the test?" So we go to the department meeting and compare notes—everyone has to be at the same place ... so it's like: "Are you in Chapter 6?"
>
> We went to a meeting the other day and I left in tears. The next day we had a department meeting and I refused to go ... I boycotted a meeting which is not like me at all!
>
> I get frustrated because I can't do it all, and I might feel guilty because I like to be good at what I'm doing and I know I can be good ... I am enthusiastic about what I'm doing ... I'm here because I like to be here ... I'm creative and if you let me alone I can think of a way to get Johnny to do this whether he's inclined or not ... so I'm frustrated because I could teach them.

As a specialized craft, teaching is a highly individualized and personal endeavor. It is this way because of the endlessly varied and variable nature of the "raw material" on which the teacher plies her craft. Not only are no two students the same, but more apropos to the work of teachers, the same student can be utterly different on different days and even at different points on the same day with the same teacher. Nor does the teacher inhabit the same dispositional space day in and day out or even from one moment to the next; teachers not only have moods they *are* their moods and so find themselves in constantly changing "felt-space" as their work unfolds, a change precipitated in large part by the twists and turns, false starts, new beginnings and so forth that are the natural accompaniment of teaching. So it is difference rather than sameness that characterizes the work of teachers and makes the work of teaching far more art (craft) than science.

But the demoralizing and destructive reality is that Jackie is being pulled in two very different directions in her role as science teacher and this is why it is correct to designate her situation as a *predicament*. Should she abandon the knowing resident in her practical experience, her 20 plus years of on-the-job training, the knowledge sutured into her flesh as the teacher she *is*, someone who knows her subject, her students, her milieu—knowledge that taken collectively constitutes her ability and capability as a teacher. What happens when such knowing is denied? What happens to identity and the sense of oneself as a teacher? The knowing that makes Jackie the teacher she *is*, is no externalized store-bought knowledge, this is no *standing reserve* ready to be *on call* whenever the occasion requires. There is no false dualism here, only the recognition that it is *her* knowing that makes Jackie the confident self-assured teacher she is, and that she *is* the knowing—or as Aoki (1992/2005, p. 197) once unforgettably remarked, "[s]he *is* the teaching." This is predominantly a form of craft knowledge—knowledge acquired through patient doing, laborious practice, each year starting over, trying something different, holding fast to what works, discarding what does not, getting a feel for the subtle rhythms of teaching, for her subject, for how it can be made teachable, for the pulse of the (age) group with whom she needs to connect and for whom she serves as their teacher. And slowly, painfully, by fits and starts building up a repertoire of teachable lessons and associated knowledge and skills that can be drawn upon at appropriate times throughout the school year. It is this intensely personal knowledge that gives the teacher who has acquired it an unmistakable air of confidence in the classroom and in her work with students—such a teacher is truly *at home* in her knowledge, in her classroom, and in her work as a teacher. It would not be too far fetched to say that this confidence and the self-assured manner it enables is what allows the teacher to be (or become) a genuine and truly effective teacher. All this Jackie seems to understand albeit in a dialectical or roundabout way.

> I'm hugely frustrated and I try not to think about it.... If I start talking about it I get angry, I get frustrated because I *am* a good teacher and after 20+ years of practice I should be *very* good. I should be able to walk into my room and be so comfortable that I don't have to spend all of this time preparing. I should know what I'm doing.... I have a lot of things that have worked in the past in here. I've gone to training and gotten a lot of things, and I'm pretty creative. And even if they show me some training that seems irrelevant ... I can still twist it and use it and get it to work. And yet every morning I walk into the room I'm so stressed! And the poor kids ... they come into the room and ask me for a pencil and I'm practically screaming at them ... I'm thinking, "Good God what's wrong with me?" So I'm hugely frustrated with being unable to do everything I'm mandated to do.

These are again interesting and revealing lines in which Jackie's felt experience of her teaching predicament comes bubbling to the surface. There is nothing abstract about the felt and very real dilemma in which she finds herself (German, *sich befinden*) and which constitutes for Jackie what Heidegger refers to as her *befindlichkeit* (Heidegger, 1968, cited in Gendlin, 1978/79), by which he avers to the fact that beneath or below the threshold of her cognitive awareness of her current predicament (brought vividly to speech in the transcribed text before us), there lingers a vast and complex tapestry of sensed and originally unsymbolized felt-feelings that give rise to the text before us. Heidegger and later Gendlin establish the philosophical primacy of such "unsymbolized felt-feelings" in the formation of "concepts" and in the development of cognitive schemas of various kinds. However, the horns of Jackie's dilemma, her *befindlichkeit*, are clear enough. On the one hand her practical wisdom born of her years of thoughtful, on-the-job experience confidently informs her teaching practice, which if it does not rise to the level of providing her with detailed specifications, a blueprint if you will, of what to say or do and when, it nevertheless provides her with a general outline and sense of direction for her teaching, informing her in a nonspecific way of what needs to be done, and where, as a teacher, she needs to go next and why. This is the personally and locally and intuitively developed knowledge that is indispensable to her as a teacher. Yet on the other hand there is the insistent and, for Jackie at least, intrusive voice of state and local mandates prescribing for her in precise and highly specific detail the exact nature of the work to be done. For Jackie (but not just for Jackie) these are contradictory forces. Yet what is also undeniable is that in Jackie the collision of these forces is causing profound ambivalence and doubt—indeed a demoralizing form of self-doubting—regarding her abilities as a teacher and her fitness for teaching. The irony of this situation should not be missed, as despite her intense discomfort her words reveal affection for her students and a genuine enthusiasm for the work of (science) teaching without which nothing of long-term consequence can be achieved. Again we can ask, is this just Jackie or are there deeper structural issues involved? It is also worth noting as a point of pedagogic practice that the end result of her work as science teacher is nothing scientific—it is not so much that her students will become miniscientists or that they will begin to think in the way scientists think—rather it is the more personalistic goal that students will like science and become good stewards of the environment. These are normative life-world aims that have nothing to do with the production of scientific consciousness and everything to do with the production of a form of ethical consciousness and the fostering of broadly spiritual qualities. For Jackie, the curriculum and its contents are not the *be-all and end-all* of her teaching, or in Husserlian terms, the curriculum itself is not the thing. Jackie seems to understand her task as science teacher more broadly and for her the formal curriculum becomes a means, or a way—a *via*—by which more transcendent ends can be striven for. This does not diminish the importance of curricular content, quite the contrary—only now such content is placed in the service of larger, more overarching goals. This brings Jackie's teaching in line with the broader educational purpose of schools, especially middle schools, in promoting life-affirming goals that serve the *sunum bonum* of individual and collective life, indeed of all life forms. It need hardly be said that this is a far cry from the obsessive use of scantrons and with what, with only slight exaggeration, we might describe as the scantronization of teaching. When we read in news reports that in the South Pacific there is an area of floating plastic debris roughly the size of Texas, Jackie's goals for her teaching assume major significance.

Does Practice Itself Know Nothing?

Increasingly today research-based knowledge presents itself as superior (i.e., more efficacious) to non research-based knowledge and as the only knowledge capable of producing the *effects* demanded by policymakers and educational bureaucrats. In this model, Jackie's steadily accumulating stock of practical knowledge/wisdom derived from her engagement with her students and her subject matter in the context of middle school life, is downgraded, and in some cases dismissed outright, in favor of strategic (evidence-based) knowledge imported from beyond the horizon of her experience—knowledge from foreign parts. In answer to the question raised by the philosopher, H-G. Gadamer, and incorporated into the title of this article, "does practice itself know nothing?" (Gadamer 1998, p.24), the answer would appear to be "Yes!"

For many in the educational hierarchy, the choice *for* mandated practice is increasingly viewed as a choice between research-based knowledge or the alternative which is coming to be seen as an *anything goes* approach to practice, a pedagogic wild, wild West as Levine (2005) would have it, with every teacher teaching in his or her own way according to his or her own lights—as if the alternative to a research-based practice of teaching was a teaching practice unregulated by—and ungrounded in—anything other than the teacher's own personal preferences and predilections. In short an ungoverned and ungovernable practice. But this is hardly the reality of teaching. The alternative to a research-based practice of teaching is hardly anything goes, teachers have their reasons for doing as they do—for doing *this* rather than *that*, for going *here* rather than *there*—they have their practical knowledge/wisdom built up over years, their sense of what can/cannot work in present circumstances. This noncodified and ultimately noncodifiable knowledge is neither a lesser, nor a weaker, nor a less trustworthy form of knowledge for all its private, nonobjective character. The idea that practice (i.e., teaching practice) must be predicated on a solid foundation of codified and publicly available research-based knowledge misunderstands something vital (about teaching) that belongs to teaching at its existential core, namely the highly personalistic and idiosyncratic nature of all good teaching. Teaching is this way—not because I might *like* it to be this way or because I *want* or for some reason might *prefer* it to be this way, but because it *is* this way. Those who know teaching from the inside, who know its nature by living its nature, know that it cannot be reduced to rules, external prescriptions, official mandates and so forth, without jeopardizing the crucial balance between intellect and instinct on which all good practice relies. This realization will come as good news to teachers but perhaps not-so-good-news to educational researchers, policymakers, administrators and others who yearn for a complete makeover of teaching into a practice that is a more stable, predictable and controllable practice of teaching. Speaking in the context of the inexorable erosion of freedom that is the inescapable accompaniment of the ever-increasing specialization of the modern world, Gadamer (1998) wrote: "Instead of having the kind of control over things allowed by abilities, which leaves space for the creative play of self-expression, a new kind of slavery has come over mankind.... With this development, all our human capabilities lose their equilibrium, as does the balance that seems so natural between instinct and intellect" (Gadamer 1998, p. 117). I will argue that it is precisely this loss of *balance* between instinct and intellect that is so much a part of Jackie's predicament.

Between What We Make and What We Do Not Make: Deciding For a Practice

It is a tough sell today to argue that something *belongs to* a practice and that as self-conscious agents we are somehow not in charge of, nor ultimately determinative of the basic features of the practice in its essential outlines, contours et cetera. This seems to be more an admission of weakness than a robust assertion of our unlimited ability to mold/manage things in *our* image of how we feel they should be. Yet Jackie's clear and compelling description of her predicament (her *befindlichkeit*) seems to point to just this problem, namely of *there-being* something outside *our* ability to decide, *our* ability to make, to something that belongs or exists intrinsically and is *native* to the practice itself. As a seasoned science teacher we can see from Jackie's transcripts that mandates notwithstanding, she has established a clear and coherent sense of her pedagogic role and task as her students' science teacher, and although we cannot be definitive it seems unlikely that her teaching sensibilities are derived from textbook accounts of teaching, lofty mission statements, pious ethical codes and so forth, all of which attempt to define for her where she must go, what she must do, and how she must conduct herself with her students. Jackie's intuitive *teacherly* sense does not seem to be derived from higher authorities at all (for instance, her discourse is refreshingly free of contemporary education jargon); rather her practical intuitiveness (we might call it her teacherly instinct) appears to have evolved from her own personal praxis, from within her own praxis-based understanding of what it means to be a middle school science teacher in the living context in which she finds herself—an understanding in which felt-feelings play an unacknowledged but highly formative role. And yet in the face of official mandates and massive curricular intrusion, Jackie experiences professional and personal dislocation, suffers an erosion of confidence, loss of personal efficacy and becomes predictably less surefooted in her ways as a teacher. I will let Jackie describe her teaching predicament in her own words:

> I just thought of a quote: "Teaching is not just a vocation, it's an avocation." You walk into this profession with this "felt sense" ... that you love the kids and learning and you want the kids to succeed. You sit there with those little faces looking at you and you feel the importance or the gravity of what you're supposed to do. You understand that all the way to your core or else you should be in the business world! And there are moments when you look at your kids and your feet are hooked to the floor because you realize all those little platitudes, "I touch the future, I teach" and they are all right there! It's true! And you turn around and you pick up the book and it's about isotopes! These are 12-year-old boys and they are enthralled with animals.... These kids just came in, and there's a slug on the sidewalk and they're like: "Oh, wow, could we go places now!" But, "Oh, no! We have to teach isotopes because the county test is next week!" And you feel all of this gravity and importance and you have to chuck it out the window because they sit down and take out their paper and do isotopes which does not have much to do with anything! It certainly doesn't have anything to do with them because conceptually they cannot get there no matter how hard you pull them. And so there's that sense of banging your head against the wall all the time!

Again, it would be easy to dismiss Jackie's words as the exaggerated rhetoric of a late-career teacher giving vent to little more than her *feelings* over the rapid pace of change in an occupation and teaching environment to which she has been long acclimatized. Change never comes easily and, as we are constantly reminded, there is a price to be paid for progress. But even if this were the case only the most obtuse could miss the sincerity of her sentiments or the depth and the density of the disillusion she is feeling. For better or worse these *are* her feelings and constitute the facts-on-the-ground so to speak—facts with which current reforms including and especially mandated practice must in the end contend.

> I get so conflicted because I'm here because I believe that I can handle this all-important job ... I have the insanity it takes ... I have the sense of humor it takes ... I have the creativity it takes ... I have it all ... and I have an education that cost me a fortune and nobody will let me use it! They gave me this book [*Jackie taps on the cover of the science text book in front of her*] that anybody off the street could come in my room, open the book, and say, "Read about isotopes, Johnnie." I have this conflict all the time about what I *should* be doing and what I *am* doing, and I'm sick to my stomach ... well, not literally sick to my stomach! I just want to teach! I just want to do my job!

Jackie's account of her teaching predicament raises many issues but especially it raises the question of the status of feelings or of teachers' felt experience in the stampede for reform and, far more broadly, it raises the question of the status of "feelings" in the age of science itself. What can be attributed to such feelings, anything or nothing? Although current research orthodoxy attempts to limit knowledge to that which can be proven, to that for which there is clear and compelling objective evidence, we would still want to ask about the *evidence of feeling*—after all feelings are real, they exist, they are neither imaginary nor especially mysterious; indeed so much are they a part of the fabric of ordinary existence that we are fully entitled to speak of the facticity of feeling. For Jackie, the question to be asked is whether it is the expressed (symbolized) content or contents of her feeling (feeling frustrated about *this*, disappointed about *that*) that is decisive in terms of her understanding—or whether it is the entire, vast, complex, presymbolic interweaving of felt-feeling arising out of her encounter with the world's facticity, that is, Jackie's *befindlichkeit* understanding of how things stand teachingwise for her—that is the decisive factor. And instead of saying that Jackie *has* these feelings—as if her feelings are merely *in* Jackie, that is, as if Jackie and her feelings are two separated things—it would be more accurate to say that Jackie *is* her feelings. A whole different way of relating to the world and of thinking and acting arise in consequence.

The point I am making is that felt feeling—not to be conflated with sheer emotionality—is not just the affective residue left over from perceptual awareness and its resultant cognitions. The *conceptual* distinction often made between the so-called cognitive and affective aspects of experience is simply that—a conceptual distinction ungrounded in experiential reality. This is one of the reasons why Gendlin (1978/79) spoke of the *implicit wisdom* to be found in feelings. This brings us back to Jackie's descriptive account of her felt experience of her teaching predicament and to the implicit wisdom lodged therein. In short, can there be knowledge in feeling?

Teachers' Practical Wisdom Contains Ethical and Aesthetic Content

It seems important to state that what we call teachers' practical knowledge or practical wisdom is practical in more than a technically practical sense—good teachers are about more than simply what works in a merely technical sense of production (seeking to produce only predetermined outcomes). All truly educational outcomes are not so much *produced* as *educed*—they are not the outcome of a form of making which makes the work of teaching vastly different from economic-productive activities which are essentially processes of making, producing, manufacturing, and so forth. To the extent that teachers have ethical ideals in mind as ends or aims of their teaching (for instance that students will become *good* stewards of the environment), their teaching cannot rest on purely logical arguments but must in the end make an *appeal* to something (in the student) that is and remains beyond logic—call it the growing child's sense of right/wrong, his emerging sense of goodness/badness, his growth in empathy, sympathy, compassion et cetera, generally what we imply by the nurturing of conscience. But the making of an *appeal* presupposes a particular kind of relationship in which the teacher is an admired figure, able to exercise influence, trusted as someone who would not lead astray. Such qualities have nothing whatever to do with technical prowess *per se*, rather they are *virtues*, features of the person himself/herself, less issues of personality than of the character of the teacher. And as virtues they do not operate mechanically as in the manner of cause and effect. This is a big issue for mandated practice with its focus on the *made* or *produced* or *doing* aspect of education—it cannot deal with the ethical dimension of teaching, that is with its educing (appeal-making) character.

Although she does not say as much in words it seems that Jackie has an intuitive feel for the ethical aspects of her work with her sixth- and seventh-grade pupils; she desires more than a mere "instructional" relation with them as their (science) teacher and educator. Yet these deep-seated teacherly instincts collide head-on with the requirements of an accountability-driven, research-based practice of teaching, a practice which views teaching largely as a production function in which teachers are held responsible for the production of prespecified outcomes but little else. Thus to raise the question of *mandated* practice is to see more and more clearly the manipulated character of efforts aimed at (re)forming and (re)shaping practice. [Note: *to mandate*, has etymological affinities with other modern English words, such as manual, manufacture, manipulate—all of which contain the Latin root word, *manus* or hand, and have the sense of something made, notably handmade or man-made]. But an important question for teachers and for those who conduct (re)search to support the work of teachers is: Can a human practice be constructed (made) from nothing, from ground zero so to speak? This is the fundamental assumption on which mandated practice stands, that is, that nothing exists, and that the world is indeed without form and void and absent of *meaning* other than those meanings *we* so graciously choose to bestow upon an otherwise empty landscape (in our time, evidence-based research attempts to do this *bestowing*). But science—in the form of evidence-based research—is entirely unable to generate or regenerate meanings other than those fabricated meanings on which it relies and methodologically depends; in this sense science is non-generative, literally ungenerous. Science may be able (or close to being able) to (re)generate limbs, organs, tissue et cetera, but it cannot generate *meaning* and it is upon teachers' ability to grasp and interpret meaning that all good teaching practice ultimately depends.

The flipside to a teaching (practice) based on experimentally manipulated sensory evidence is first and foremost a responsive and responsible practice of teaching; it is a practice that does not begin with the assumption that its practitioners know nothing and from there goes about attempting to fill the void with its well-laundered, sanitized, scientized knowledge; it is a practice that recognizes that evidence takes many forms and that there is no higher form of evidence than self-evidence whereby the inner truthfulness of a thing manifests itself *in-itself* and needs no external confirmation of its truthfulness. The Greeks knew this as *ekphanestaton* which Gadamer (1998, p. xii) defined as "the most radiant, most manifest … [i]t needs no validation other than itself, no signs that could err or lie, because it offers itself in evidence of its own truth." The alternative to a made or mandated practice (of teaching) is a practice that grasps the distinction between "what we make and what we do not make," and that the deepest impulses of our teaching—amongst which one could cite the normatively driven pedagogic impulse which animates the work of many teachers—respond to what we *do not make*, to what is already given, coincident as it were, with the nature of the practice itself. It seems almost (but not quite) superfluous to add that there is nothing mystical nor especially clairvoyant about such practices and that in demarcating the grounds of a self-evident practice of teaching we do not enter a realm of mere metaphysical speculation; the move away from an evidence-based practice or theory of teaching hardly points in the direction of a practice shrouded in mystery. So we should clarify: The grounds for what is self-evident in the practice of teaching are empirically available—albeit in a more original sense of empirical ("empirical" derived from the Greek, *empeiria*, literally, *en- peira*, in trial).

The point I am making is that as a seasoned teacher, Jackie's carefully honed pedagogic instincts are a better guide to her practice than the prescriptive mandates she is obliged to follow. The implementation of administratively sanctioned teaching practices means that teachers' work is less and less their own, their words (and increasingly their purposes) are scripted for them—they are being *ventriloquated*—mouthing words that are not their own, engaging in practices over which they have less and less control. Such practices are obstacles to growth, denying teachers the possibility of acquiring the insight that comes from engaging with practice in their own way and on their own terms. Of course, none of this denies the importance of engaging with theory—which Gadamer defined as the taking of a certain distance from oneself—or with colleagues or other education professionals in the pursuit of greater and greater understanding of the nature of one's practice. The complexities of teaching are such that no single individual, left to his or her own devices, can approach mastery much less achieve it. But it is to say that each individual teacher must have the freedom to teach in a manner that seems right to her and towards ends she finds pedagogically fulfilling. This implies what is generally thought of as judgment. Yet it is the teacher's power of judgment (*erfahrung*) that is not only neglected, but as Jackie's comments show, actively compromised when teaching is made subservient to externally imposed rules per mandated practice. So we can ask: Where in the paradigm of mandated practice is there space for the free exercise of teacher judgment and the creative play of self-expression that is so essential to inspired and inspiring teaching?

Moving Beyond a Concern for "What Works" in Teaching

Today, a major thrust of much university based research is aimed at uncovering *what works* in the concrete practice of teaching. As a popular if somewhat utopian research paradigm, it is an approach which once more cashes out in the development of "rules" as a way to further rationalize teaching, and by extension, the work of teachers. By virtue of this paradigm teachers become rule-followers, and in an entirely parallel manner it is becoming more and more common for university-based preparation programs to deliberately foster the cultivation of a narrowly defined scientific mindset in pre- and in-service teachers. This is justified as part of the training needed to produce graduate-level "scientific" research; less transparently, such training is *de rigueur* because it inclines teachers and future educational leaders to become more receptive to rule-governed forms of educational practice. But teachers have to discover what works for themselves; they have to discover the *how* and the *why* beneath the what—otherwise the practice is hollow, lacking substance and meaning; this discovery cannot be done for them; it must be the product of one's own experimenting and reflective engagement with practice. Thus the attempt to develop practice-dependent rules for teachers means that the capacity for the exercise of teacher judgment is thereby downgraded and with it the last vestige of claims to genuine professional status, for what is genuine professional status if not the ability and opportunity to exercise personal pedagogical judgment? The problem with rules is not only that there could never be enough of them, but that an approach that begins by assuming the rule-governed nature of teaching neglects and omits the development of the *personhood* of the teacher—and it is the cultivation of the personhood of the teacher (a type of *bildung*) that is the prerequisite for the exercise of sound pedagogical judgment. The utopian desire for what works and the attempt to extrapolate what works into a generalized program (rules-for-teaching) is, ironically, a repudiation of education and its deep and lasting value, and the triumph of a mechanistic training approach to teaching. In short, the rules-based approach—including all so-called *problem-finding* and *problem-solving* approaches to research and practice—means that teachers are being trained but not educated. This is neither a small nor an insignificant distinction and much hangs on the difference that is at stake here. For the teacher who is ready and prepared to exercise his or her pedagogic judgment, the encounter with mandated practice in the form of programmatic rules must be experienced as a type of mental and spiritual imprisonment as the verbatim comments from teachers included at the outset of this paper tend to suggest. The origin of modern English *program* is from the Greek, *prographein* (*pro-* before and *graphein* to write) and contains at its semantic core a sense of the preplanned and preplannable nature of the work to be done. Again we can ask: Where is the space for the free exercise of teacher judgment and the creative play of self-expression that is so essential to inspired and inspiring practice?

How Does Educational Leadership Contribute to Jackie's Predicament?

In the last decade or so, educational leadership has come under fire from numerous quarters as lacking the wherewithal to move education into the twenty-first century. This reference to the twenty-first century—now almost a constant refrain in teacher in-service and preservice sessions—is intended to designate the hyperrationalized, ultraspecialized and historically unprecedented new world order or global village for which the phrase world-wide-web is apt. In Western democracies at least, educational systems are generally viewed as functional components of such systems and judged according to their capacity to prepare young people to enter the market-driven, technocapitalist productive system or ownership-society. Sitting astride what could be regarded as a natural, even inevitable gulf, between schools and the economic order of society—today's educational leadership interprets its task as ensuring that schools and their instructional production function align with the goals and economic aspirations of the parent polity. Whereas in the past this alignment has been quite loose, with schools much less enamored of the economic consequences of their educative mission, today that situation has changed. With the threatened loss of economic dominance, American education has fallen back on its ideologically charged, imperialist impulses whereby the school and the curriculum are used—less for the cultivation of humane and ecologically sustainable educational goals and a generalized concern for the *commons* (having students monitor and *care* about the growth or destruction of salt marsh grass for example), than for reasserting the dominance of neoliberal, consumerist and market-based values. In this context, today's obsessive preoccupation with student *achievement*—as opposed, let us say, to a broader concern for student *accomplishment*—should be seen as a thinly disguised surrogate for education for economic competitiveness. Given this reality it should not be so surprising that conflicting viewpoints characterize the relation between teachers and their in-school supervisors.

> My frustration and my anger—my two words—comes in when I ask myself "Why isn't there somebody above me here that when that mandate comes down or the county says do this ... that whoever is supposed to be watching my back above me (because I'm on the front lines) turns around and says "No, that's ridiculous!" Nobody does say that ... and I'm angry that people don't protect my little sanctum of learning ... and then I get frustrated that I cannot comply with all of the stuff that's on my plate. I'm pretty smart and I'm pretty capable and I have a lot of energy ... and I work just as hard as anybody! But I can't do it! I can't do it and I'm frustrated! I want to be the best teacher but I feel like a crappy one!

Today, the notion of educational leadership is undergoing major redefinition at the hand of the newly formed alliance between mainstream educational research and the policymaking elite. Previously, the label *educational leadership* was understood as a shorthand way of designating someone with extensive practical in-school experience, an understanding and empathy for boys and girls at so-and-so stage of development, above average teaching skills, organizational know-how, and a feel for the importance of education in its educing, conscience-forming sense. In short, educational leadership is/was a largely *un*specialized endeavor, not without certain skills of course, but primarily an activity requiring an abundance of common sense, good judgment and a related set of nonspecialized pedagogic virtues—of which Bollnow (1979) provides just three examples, namely, love of educating, patience and trust. Today these time worn virtues seem strangely out of place in today's overspecialized, acronym-driven version of teaching or leading in which only the technically minded are encouraged to apply.

Jackie's honest admission of her dilemma brings to the surface a veritable universe of problems regarding the prescriptive, top-down approach to teaching (and learning) that are concealed in a contemporary discourse that focuses exclusively on measurable outcomes to the detriment of any other type of outcome. Part of the problem inherent in the paradigm of mandatory practice lies in the attempt to make schools and classrooms fully transparent places, nothing hidden, nothing concealed, everything out in the open, every moment of adult-child interaction to be accounted for and justified according to externally fabricated criteria of excellence. In this modality very little of the teacher-student relation can be spontaneous, very little can be allowed to arise spontaneously from the ground on which both student and teacher stand—but this means that if nothing can arise spontaneously nothing can be authentic, for authenticity requires the ability to be spontaneous, to be fully present to the other. In a sense, something must be between the teacher and her students, something must serve to distinguish the relationship, mark it off as somehow different from other relationships, some part of the relation must remain hidden, out-of-sight, so that full transparency—even if it were possible—would negate the meaning of relationship. As Hannah Arendt (1968) long ago pointed out, nothing can survive the full glare of constant exposure and this is as true of teaching as anything else. So Jackie is right in thinking that some part of who we are and what we are about as teachers must remain sacrosanct, out of the glare of constant scrutiny. So her notion of the classroom as a sanctum of learning needing the protection of, and increasingly *from,* those above her, contains more intuitive wisdom than first meets the eye (so to speak).

Today the notion of something needing to remain hidden, a private realm concealed from general view meets with resistance from all sides. The new accountability movement seems especially hostile to the idea that some part of the teacher's work should remain inscrutable and hidden, and modern psychology itself seems determined to lift anything and everything out from hiddenness into the bright light of day. It is not hard to see how accountability and transparency go hand in hand, and how many contemporary administrative practices (e.g., classroom walk-throughs, curriculum audits, the demand that teachers post lesson objectives or learning standards at the beginning of every lesson) are all practices designed to make teaching a more transparent, see-through process on the assumption that transparency is *ipso facto* a good thing and that greater transparency equals greater controllability, equals greater accountability, equals greater teaching effectiveness. But as Jackie's description of her predicament makes clear, this is not how teachers experience such things.

Teachers' Felt-Experience Grounds Our Knowledge of Teaching

How teachers experience such things is far from irrelevant to the debate about teaching. Here again language is important. It is not so much the sheer *having* of experience that is the decisive factor, such as having an experience of this, having an experience of that, as if the mere *having* of experience can vouchsafe for anything beyond the experience itself; rather it is the *mode* or *manner* of experiencing that allows us insight into the thing experienced and provides grounds for grasping its inner falsity or truthfulness. There is a frisson of affect, of something sensed or felt that is the inevitable accompaniment of experience such that we are fully entitled to speak of felt-experience as something eminently real and no mere epiphenomenon. Borrowing from the lingo of contemporary educational research, we could perhaps speak of the evidence of felt-experience and posit such evidence over against the more hard-core evidence of positivistic science. The point I am making is that when there is no echo of familiarity in the felt-experience of knowledgeable practitioners, when such (mandatory) reforms find no resonance in the living understanding of teachers, when teachers say, in effect, "This is not how I experience this or that particular aspect of teaching," then we have grounds to question and indeed to doubt the efficacy of such proposals. University of Chicago philosopher and psychologist, Eugene Gendlin, puts it this way:

> If we speak of *Befindlichkeit* not merely as something about humans, but as basic to the way humans are open to anything, much more than psychology is affected. A basic method results, in which inquiry articulates what is first only sensed, found implicitly. One must not forget that, as if to begin with sharp conceptions. The beginning is always how we sense ourselves, find ourselves already with ... whatever we study, in an implicitly "understood" way, in our living. *Whatever conceptions are developed, in any science, they need to be related back to the implicit lived understanding we already have of the topic, and need to be viewed as articulations of that.* Much changes if one employs such a method. (Gendlin, 1978/79, p. 48, emphasis added)

These are important comments that point away from (teaching) policy based on political or economic desiderata, towards policy initiatives grounded in the lived experience of capable, caring, knowledgeable professionals. To do otherwise is to run the risk of alienating teachers from the transcendent purpose(s) of their craft and of substituting a fabricated mission unrelated to the deeply felt and intuited reasons for their work. In *Praise of Theory,* philosopher Hans-Georg Gadamer addresses these questions and provides a compelling analysis of the current world situation and what he calls the "dominant superstition" of our time, namely "the unwarranted belief that the life-world can and should be rationalized, that is, reordered according to a technological model of applied knowledge." In the teaching field of education such "reordering" is well underway. Under an administratively dominated program of research-based practice, teaching is rapidly devolving into a technical, low-level, applied scientific activity as teachers' *in situ* praxis-based knowledge is relegated to inferior status and is replaced by anonymous (research-based) knowledge. Under this regime (of mandated practice) teachers become little more than curricular factotums implementing the curricular dictates of others. But more than a loss of prestige is involved; it is a fundamental transformation of teaching practice such that teachers' work is not their own. Again, we are entitled to ask: Are teachers becoming distanced, that is, alienated from their own practice?

Listening to the voices of teachers is one way to gain insight into this question.

> **RESEARCHER:** How does someone who feels this tension—and we all do—between what you want to do and what you're being made/expected to do? How is that experienced? How do you experience that tension?
>
> **JACKIE:** I carry a flask and I smoke a lot—I'm just kidding! I feel so bad that I feel that way. I'm here because I like this job. I know I'm going to be stuck in a room with 24 kids ... I volunteered for this! And when everything makes me so frustrated, that's when I have a problem! I'm frustrated because I'm not allowed to do it [i.e. teach my way]. Sometimes it's a feeling of panic but you can't let it out ... if you walk in here and you're panicked, you don't get anything done that day ... so I think like everything else you compensate for those feelings, you shove them in a corner or in a box and I run up and talk to my buddy on campus who feels the same way I do.
>
> I do a lot of closing the door and do what you want. And at the next staff meeting you don't say anything ... you just nod your head and keep your mouth shut ... which makes me feel bad or guilty because I was brought up not to lie ... that's a bad thing!

Despite Jackie's ego-defending attempts at humor, a strain of self-suppressive anxiety runs through her words and it is entirely reasonable to suppose that the self-doubting and discomforture hearable in her response—and experienced by Jackie as a panicked narrowing of the (otherwise endless) possibilities for her teaching—stems from a felt sense of impotence, that is, from a personally felt sense of powerlessness to control the inner and outer circumstances of her teaching life. In the face of an ever-increasing flood of administratively sanctioned curriculum mandates, Jackie nods her head and keeps her mouth shut. Such acts of self-abnegation are matters of concern; they are symptomatic of a repressive world of teaching in which the teacher feels less and less secure, less and less at home.

FINAL THOUGHTS AND CONCLUSIONS

The remaking and reordering of teaching as a preeminently rule-bound and rule-governed enterprise is well advanced and in this sense the mandated practice movement dovetails with the scientific and technological ethos of the modern era. As older teachers move on we can expect their place to be taken by more pliable, data-trained, and data-driven teachers for whom the idea of mandated practice will provoke no resistance and no alarm. In some quarters this will be hailed as a sign of progress, of teaching moving into the more controlled and controlling twenty-first century. But for those with *memoria* it is not just nostalgia that obliges them to recollect more powerful and more authentic modes of teaching. Unless memory is given voice it too remains mute and impotent.

The question, "[d]oes practice itself know nothing?" thus encapsulates the crux of the problem we are facing, namely the denial of teachers' practical wisdom at the hand of various "research-based" practices and policies now being enforced upon teachers. This is Gadamer's question (taken from *Praise of Theory*) a collection of essays and speeches in which Gadamer's central purpose is to free theory from its postenlightenment habitat—that is, as the systematic and controlled application of scientific knowledge to the so-called problems of practice. In this deeply thoughtful text, Gadamer seeks to reinstate philosophical and historical knowledge as *theory*, i.e. as guides to action, and to restore the integrity of practice from out of the shadow of technical rationality by reasserting the primacy of practical wisdom and practical decision making and its basis in practical reason(ing). The historical basis for Gadamer's question, "does practice itself know nothing?" is the entirety of modern enlightenment thought, which as Gadamer points out "ushered in a new sense of the world that also changed the ideal of the theoretical life: knowledge became research."

> By subscribing to the logic of research and so presenting itself as self-certifying, the interest in theoretical knowledge understands itself as extending humankind's power by way of knowledge. It is a matter of course that precisely in the age of science the tension intensifies between abstract and universal theory ... and established practices that have become firmly rooted through long habituation. It becomes the struggle of tomorrow's science against yesterday's science, which is supported by the practice of administration. *Does practice itself know nothing?* (Gadamer, 1998, pp. 23-24, emphasis added)

Despite its rhetorical quality the question points rather clearly in the direction of its own answer, and in this respect Gadamer's work in philosophical hermeneutics seems indispensable in the context of today's landscape of education. In the foreword to *Praise of Theory,* Joel Weinsheimer quoted a hitherto unpublished statement by Gadamer in which Gadamer sums up the chief significance of his life-long philosophical endeavor. It is a summation that reveals the relevance of Gadamer's philosophical thinking for the modern condition of education:

> To put it the way Jaspers did, we wanted to grasp in what way reason was incarnate in existence itself. And it is that search which has determined my entire philosophical work. Right to my very last years that impulse has held through.... We were in search of a way to think in which we could see the truth of things, to discover the truth that was there in each thing before us in

the world. *And that meant we were utterly distanced from … efforts to control things, to make things, to manage things.* (Gadamer, 1998, p. vii, emphasis added).

The distancing that Gadamer spoke of is nowhere in sight (in education) and everywhere the contrary circumstance prevails. In its deep desire to control things, make things, manage things, mandated practice shows itself as it is in-itself; there is no sense that there *can be* something outside the things of our own making; it denies and makes vastly more difficult educators' efforts to be responsive in their teaching; it has no sense of ontology. More practically and pragmatically it constrains teachers and stymies them from employing the full range of their creative powers.

Jackie's teaching—and the practical wisdom on which it relies—deserves a better fate than to be tossed aside at the hand of what is widely assumed to be a superior knowledge form. Older and more durable conceptions of competence are at stake. The conception of evidence that now prevails—as something entirely dependent on processes of external verification and confirmation—needs rethinking, and the importance of rediscovering forms of *self-evident understanding* is quite urgent. Along the way we will need to learn, or relearn, once again to trust in ourselves. As Gadamer (1998, p. viii) said, "A new Enlightenment is needed … to overcome the old Enlightenment superstition that we can make our world anything we would have it."

REFERENCES

Aoki, T. (2005). Layered voices of teaching: The uncannily correct and elusively true. In W. F. Pinar & R. L. Irwin (Eds.), *Curriculum in a new key: The collected works of Ted T. Aoki* (pp. 187-197). Mahwah, NJ: Erlbaum. (Original work published 1992)

Arendt, H. (1983). *Between past and future.* New York, NY: Penguin Books.

Bollnow, O. F. (1979a). On the virtues of the educator. *Education, 20,* 69-79.

Gadamer, H. -G. (1998). *Praise of theory.* New Haven, CT: Yale University Press.

Gendlin, E. T. (1978/79). Befindlichkeit: Heidegger and the philosophy of psychology. *Review of Existential Psychology and Psychiatry, 16*(1-3), 43-71.

Heidegger, M. (1968). *What is called thinking?* New York, NY: Harper Colophon.

Levine, A. (2005). *Educating school leaders.* New York, NY: Education Schools Project.

Wiliam, D. (2008). What should education research do, and how should it do it? *Educational Researcher, 37(7), 432-438.*

Author Contact Information: Rodney Evans, PhD, Independent Scholar, 308 Cactus Road, Seffner, FL 33584. Telephone: 813-689-3594. E-mail: rod.evans@verizon.net

CHAPTER 30

School Board Control of the Curriculum

Democracy or Censorship?

Patricia F. First
Clemson University

Patricia A. L. Ehrensal
George Washington University

Local school boards are said by some researchers, and are seen by some members of the public, as the last level of governance practicing the democratic ideal, while others see school boards as outdated and as comprising an unnecessary level of government. And some see school boards in the worst possible light as inhibitors in the march of educational rights for all children (Ehrensal & First, 2008). But whatever view one holds of local school boards, the power of these boards over the curriculum remains undisputed. Though guided and sometimes mandated by state and federal statutes, our local school boards do control our children's freedom to access the "marketplace of ideas" (*Keyishian v. Board of Regents,* 1967). The role of local school boards and the relationship of the school board to the curriculum is explored in this chapter.

THE COURTS, SCHOOL BOARDS, AND THE CURRICULUM

For decades courts have addresses specific questions about the power of school boards over the curriculum. In general the courts will not intervene in school matters unless there is shown to be a "flagrant abuse of discretion" on the part of school officials. In *Zykan v. Warsaw* (1980) the court said, "Nothing in the Constitution permits the courts to interfere with local discretion until local authorities begin to substitute rigid and exclusive indoctrination for the right to make pedagogic choices regarding matters of legitimate dispute." In living up to this standard the courts often support the discretion of the school district in curricular matters.

In 2008 in *Parker v. Hurley,* the First Circuit ruled that instructional materials that seek to reduce sexual orientation prejudices do not deny either religious freedom or the due process rights of students and parents. The parents who brought this suit objected to two books used in kindergarten and first grade which included same gender couples and gay marriages in units concerning diverse families. The parents' religious beliefs were offended by gay marriage and homosexuality, but the Court dismissed their complaint for failure to state a federal constitutional claim upon which relief could be granted. The Court used the Massachusetts statewide curricular standards for context around the school board's decisions and state statutes specifying responsibility for book selection and curricular decisions. The school board's decisions about this curriculum rested upon firm ground.

As long ago as 1886 in *State ex rel. Andrews v. Webber* (1886) a court ruled that a school board has the power to enforce reasonable rules prescribing specific curriculum. A hundred years later the Fourth Circuit Appeals

The Handbook of Educational Theories, pp. 343–353

Court in *Sandlin v. Johnson* (1981) ruled that once having prescribed the curriculum, the school board has the power to deny promotion for failure to complete requisite reading levels. In the intervening years and up to the present time the courts have sought to strike a balance between not interfering in conflicts that arise in the daily operation of the schools that do not involve constitutional protections, but at the same time not tolerating laws which cast "the pall of orthodoxy" over education as described in *Keyishian*. The courts look to support the school boards but as Justice Jackson observed in his dissent in *McCollum v. Board of Education* (1948), "If we are to eliminate everything that is objectionable to any of these warring sects or inconsistent with any of their doctrines, we will leave public education in shreds." At the time over 250 separate religious groups were listed in the United States. There are many more today. State statutes regarding the curriculum have also been addressed by the courts. In *Meyer v. Nebraska* (1923) the Supreme Court of the United States struck down a Nebraska statute restricting the teaching of languages other than English. In the incident at hand, the issue of the language was German. In the opinion of the Court, "No emergency has arisen which renders knowledge by a child of some language other than English so clearly harmful as to justify its inhibition with the consequent infringement of rights long freely enjoyed." The court went on to say that the statute was arbitrary and unrelated to legitimate state purposes.

Parents of course do have rights regarding the education of their children and the curriculum to which they are exposed. They may choose private schooling, religious schooling, home schooling, and various other manifestations and combinations of these options. The courts recognize the primacy of the parents in the custody, care, and nurture of their own children (*Pierce v. The Society of Sisters*, 1925; *Meyer v. Nebraska*, 1923) but this right does not give parents the power to control or limit what is offered in the public school curriculum to all children.

> If all parents had a fundamental constitutional right to dictate individually what the schools teach their children, the schools would be forced to cater a curriculum for each student whose parents had genuine moral disagreements with the school's choice of subject matter. We cannot see that the Constitution imposes such a burden on state educational systems, and accordingly find that the rights of parents as described by *Meyer* and *Pierce* do not encompass a broad-based right to restrict the flow of information in the public schools. (*Brown v. Hot, Sexy, and Safer Productions, Inc.*, 68 F. 3d 525, 533 (1st Cir. 1995))

The curricular power of the school board includes choice of activities as well as the information flow. For example the Second Circuit in 1996 ruled that mandatory community service as a graduation requirement does not violate students' Constitutional rights. Parents had argued, among other things, that because the mandatory community service program required students to serve others in order to graduate from high school the program was a form of slavery.

In addition to complaints about textbooks, books available in the school library are often the subject complaints to the school board and subsequently the subject of court cases. In 1982 the Supreme Court ruled that a local school board may not remove books from school libraries simply because it dislikes the ideas contained in the books (*Board of Education, Island Trees Union Free School District N. 26 v. Pico)*. But the book banning battles continue. In 2003 a U.S. District Court needed to decide that a school board restriction of access to *Harry Potter* violated the Constitution (*Counts v. Cedarville*). And the battles still continue. In the four years between 2006 and 2010 The National Coalition Against Censorship (2001) reported that school districts attempted to ban books over 250 times in 31 states.

Whether these attempts by school boards to ban books are examples of democracy in action or blatant censorship of divergent ideas is what the courts are called upon to decide. The various federal appeals court circuits are appealed to about a variety of school board curricular decisions. For example, the Ninth Circuit has supported a school board against complaints that discussing witchcraft and sorcerers violated the constitutional prohibition against establishing religion (*Brown v. Woodland*, 1994). The 11th Circuit supported a school board's removal of Aristophanes and Chaucer from the curriculum because the removal was found to be "reasonably related to legitimate pedagogical concerns," a key criterion for school boards in defending their actions (*Virgil v. School Board of Columbia County, Florida*, 1989). And the Sixth Circuit supported a school district's requirement that students study the basic reader series chosen by the school for its curriculum (*Mozert v. Hawkins County Board of Education*, 1987).

Regarding issues of health, sexuality, and obscenity, arguments about the school board's right to choose curriculum can get very heated. In supporting a school board on a matter of attendance in a health education class the Second Circuit opined, as have circuits around the country, that a parent does not have a fundamental right to mandate school curriculum (*Leebaert v. Harrington*, 2003). In the selection and production of a play the Fourth Circuit supported the school board, again emphasizing that the school board has legitimate pedagogical interest in curriculum (*Boring v. Buncombe County Board of Education*, 1998).

Perhaps the curricular issue most known to the public at large is the debate over evolution versus creationism. As early as 1968 the Supreme Court of the United

States struck down as unconstitutional an Arkansas statute forbidding the teaching of evolution (*Epperson v. State of Arkansas*, 1968). The Court referred to the words in *Keyishian* (1967) that

> The First Amendment "does not tolerate laws that cast a pall of orthodoxy over the classroom." There is and can be no doubt that the First Amendment does not permit the State to require that teaching and learning must be tailored to the principles or prohibitions of any religious sect or dogma.

In 1987 the Supreme Court ruled that a Louisiana statute requiring balanced treatment of creation science and evolution science violates the First Amendment (*Edwards v. Aguillard*, 1987). But the aggressive efforts of some parents to insert religion into the public school curriculum continue.

The curriculum for children whose primary language is other than English is also loudly contested. But the law is clear that a school's curriculum must provide special instructional services for limited-English-proficiency students. In *Lau v. Nichols* (1974) the Supreme Court found that the San Francisco school systems failure to provide English language instruction to Chinese speaking children violated the Civil Rights Act of 1964. "There is no equality of treatment merely by providing students the same facilities, textbooks, teachers and curriculum; for students who do not understand English are effectively foreclosed from any meaningful education" (*Lau*, 1974). The details of curricular implementation of *Lau* are heavily litigated to the present day.

As a general rule the courts have upheld openness and the expansiveness of knowledge, while at the same time being supportive of the expertise of educators in making curricular decisions and recognizing the prerogative of the state to determine the school curriculum (Alexander & Alexander, 2011.) The belief in openness and expansiveness rests upon the "marketplace of ideas," a phrase used in *Keyishian* in 1967 as a rationale for freedom of expression and academic freedom in higher education. This belief is that the truth or the best policy arises from the open expression of various and competing ideas in the classroom as in public life. In the decades since this case the courts have supported a wide ranging and robust exchange of ideas at all levels of the educational system, considering such freedom for students and faculty a special concern of the First Amendment of the U.S. Constitution. In our elementary and secondary schools it is the local school board that bears the responsibility for protecting this freedom.

THE PLACE OF THE SCHOOL BOARD IN K-12 EDUCATION

The role of the school board in the governance of education both regarding curriculum and in other aspects of board responsibility is both contested and misunderstood. From a legal perspective, school boards are created by the state for the sole purpose of administering a public school district, and thus have only that authority vested by state legislatures (Alexander & Alexander, 2011; Briffault, 2005). Ryan (2004) emphasizes, that local school boards have "little to no constitutional authority or responsibility over education" (p. 43). Given this legal construction, the role of the school board is only to ensure that state policies are carried out at the local level. However, from an organizational perspective boards are one level in multiple levels of school governance. What happens in schools can be traced for causation and implementation across and up and down the levels. Additionally, most school boards are locally elected bodies, which complicates their role. Local citizens often depend upon the boards to carry out local wishes and in conceptualizing the school board as a democratic ideal believe the boards have this power, a difficult image to maintain (First, 2001). "School boards are, and are seen by many citizens, as symbols of our democratic processes and as providers of future opportunity and access to the good life for the community's children" (First, 1992a, p. 209).

Local boards have real powers, such as hiring and firing and our concern in this chapter, approving curriculum, even though they must operate within state and federal directives. It is a huge responsibility and the requirements to stand for election are minimal. It is perhaps a myth that once elected board members learn what they need to know to do the job well. Sarason (1995) writes that in his experience he has "never known a board member, however bright, motivated and well-intentioned, who sought actively, truly to acquire knowledge about the substance of the important educational issues" (p. 10).

People have various motives for standing in a school board election or when seeking a slot on an appointed board. Often these motives are tied to a negative view of some part of the district's curriculum. Sex education and evolution are frequent examples. These motives influence their behavior when they are elected or appointed to these bodies (Mountford & Brunner, 2001). When they are members of locally elected political bodies, school board members are logically viewed as accountable to their local constituencies and thus a direct example of democracy in action. After all, elected board members can be, and often are, replaced in the next election. Even the appointed members are seen as responsible to their communities or section of the city. However, it is well documented that better schools are controlled by upper middle and upper class parents. Consequently, few school boards resist their demands, given the threat that such parents will remove their children to private schools (Kohn, 2006). Yet the belief persists, perhaps now only as a myth, that the existence of local school boards is part of what Galbraith (1996) terms "the good society." The "good society" is one with a humane agenda, with public education as a vehicle of opportunity for all. Education is necessary to ensure a knowledgeable electorate and a knowledgeable electorate is necessary for the preservation of the "good society." Control of public school boards by the upper classes may be changing. There are ways for school board membership to respond to changing school district demographics and changing community wishes (Hochschild, 2005). Non-White and underrepresented ethnic groups can increase their representation on the school board through elections from single member voting districts rather than at-large elections (Marschall, 2005, Meier & Juenke, 2005). In our increasingly diverse society the importance the diverse membership on the school boards cannot be overemphasized.

It is a growing problem for school boards that the usefulness of these bodies has been called into question, and recently in urban districts such as New York City, mayors have disbanded school boards and replaced them with parent councils. Other cities that have experienced mayoral takeover of the school district include Boston, Chicago, Philadelphia, Cleveland, Baltimore and Washington DC (Wong & Shen, 2005). Such changes further complicate both the lay role in educational governance and research about school governing boards. There have also been calls, some strident, some reasoned, for the total elimination of school boards from the educational governance system (Finn, 1992; National Center on Education & the Economy [NCEE], 2007). But there continue to be defenders of local school board governance of education (Glover, 2004; Shannon, 1992).

The traditional literature on school boards fall into two major categories: the board's relationship with the superintendent (see, for e.g., Alsbury, 2003; Cox & Malone, 2003; Glass, 2002), and how superintendents view and manage the board (see, e.g., Dawson & Quinn, 2001; Glass, 2001; McAdams, 2003; Smoley, 1999). There is also a small body of literature in impact study methodology on school board implementation of federal and state statutes (see, e.g., Bingenheimer-Rendahl, 2006; Nowakowski & First, 1989). Additionally, there is literature on how school boards do and should manage community relationships (Glass, 2000). Many of these works are targeted to helping the school districts enact a particular policy, such as a curricular change. Others document successes and failures in policy development, much of it in the area of curriculum.

What is lacking in the traditional literature is an understanding of the political characteristic of school boards (First, 1992b). But challenges to the curriculum and/or proposals that some may see as censorship are intertwined with the political life of the nation, state, and local community.

The belief underlying the exploration of school board politics in these pages is that public education is a public good necessary to ensure the continuation of a democratic society, not a product for private consumption subject to the caprice of the market place. Consequently, educating citizens is a public undertaking, which must be subject to public scrutiny and financed with public dollars. The education of citizens is vital for the future of democracy. Researchers have questioned whether local school boards are essential for this educational process. Local school boards act as an arm of the state legislature and also as the representatives of the local community to ensure that these local publics have a voice in the education process of its citizens. In this representative role, school boards can contribute to the concept of "active liberty," (Breyer, 2005) for when a school board makes a decision, it is "possible to trace without much difficulty a line of authority for the making of governmental decisions back to the people themselves" (p. 15). Nowhere is this more evident than in the realm of curricular decisions.

A Confused Role for a Misunderstood Layer of Government

"A school board is a legislative body of laypeople elected locally by their fellow citizen who serve as agents of the state legislature" (Pennsylvania School Board Association, 1979, p. 7). This is a rather simple definition for what is a complex and often misunderstood body. Within the school district organization, school boards have several roles (valid, invalid, and often conflicting), and relationships (cooperative and adversarial). The statutes of some states are specific and prescriptive regarding what a school board may and/or must do. In Arizona, for example, the school district governing boards respond to no less than 37 detailed statutory mandates from prescribing curricula and criteria for promotion and graduation, through establishing a bank account, to employing a real estate attorney or broker. The range of specificity in the statutes directed at school boards varies across the states. Somewhere in the lists control over the curriculum usually appears as just one of the many tasks.

Clearly, there is a difference between what is statutorily required of school boards and what activities they can and do perform. McAdams (2006) addresses what urban school boards can do regarding educational reform. Hayes (2001) writes of what board members do and how they can be both effective and ethical while doing it. Hochschild (2005) culls from the literature a variety of things school boards do such as hiring and firing the superintendent, overseeing budgets, negotiating with teachers, and many others. She asks, "Is the accomplishment of those tasks sufficiently important to justify maintaining boards even though they do poorly at promoting democracy and equality?" (p. 333). But these do not represent the heart of the educational process and they are far from what most people think school boards do, that is, decide what shall be taught to the children of the community. Hochschild suggests that even within the present organization of school districts, boards can do better in the distribution of resources toward equality of educational opportunity for all children and in promoting genuine deliberation among all the district's residents.

Given their assumed "lay" status in a professional organization, plus the confusion over volunteerism in their own and the public's minds, compounded by having to represent both the state legislature and the local community that elected them, it is easy to understand why there are confusion and misunderstandings on the part of board members, the community and even teachers and administrators. School board members are usually thought of by their fellow citizens as lay leaders of a professional organization, that is, a school district. However, when they are elected officials they are "lay" in the same sense as state legislators and members of Congress, though with power and influence limited to their local district. But legally they are not volunteers. Yet "volunteer" status of school board members is an issue and in the eye of the public differs from their more formalized elected or appointed role in states like Arizona and Pennsylvania to the small town atmospheres of rural New England and the less populous western part of the United States. Their status may be akin to a view analogous to that expressed by Rabbi Harold S. Kushner (2006) about synagogue leadership: "they are volunteers, men and women who have limited time and limited insight; they are not villains but people simply trying to do the best they can for their community, even though they will often be misguided in their efforts" (p. 41). This softer view might be more practical and leading to more cooperation and understanding from a community struggling with curricular concerns. Though not strictly a legal interpretation, it could be considered more legally realistic.

Community members do think it is important that we have local school boards even though the same people confess to not knowing very much about what school boards really do (Institute for Educational Leadership, 1986). These confusions and misunderstanding of the board's role are due, and contribute to, misinterpretation of the role of the superintendent and her/his relationship to and with the board. In the literature on school boards this role confusion and misunderstanding clusters around the issues of representation, policymaking, and management (of the school district and the board). These confusions and misunderstandings also contribute to curriculum controversy over the authority of the school board in these matters.

School Board as Representative, Policymaker, and Micromanager

Board members can be seen acting in three politically charged roles: representative, policymaker and manager, or as many characterize the management of school boards, micromanager.

Whose representative? School boards are "creatures of the legislature" which handle "the administrative functions necessary to properly implement legislation" (Alexander & Alexander, 2011, p. 104). Statutes dictate the operation of school districts in either expressed or implied language. Thus, according to these legal definitions, local school boards are representatives of the state, and school board members are state, not local officials (*Board of Education of Louisville v. Society of Alumni*, 1951). They possess only that power bestowed by the state to ensure that state laws and policies are carried out in the local district (Alexander & Alexander, 2011; Briffault, 2005). In expressing that delegated power school boards have attributes of all three branches of government, executive, quasi-judicial and regulatory or quasi-legislative. In pausing to consider whose representative school board members are the critical legal fact is that school boards are state bodies. The school board member, as a public officer, is in "a position to which a portion of the sovereignty of the state attaches for the time being, and which is exercised for the benefit of the public" (*Shelmadine v. City of Elkhart*, 1921).

Most school board members are elected by the local community (those who live within the boundaries of the school district). They campaign on local issues (Bolman, Deal, & Rallis, 1995). "In many respects, local school boards are one of the last bastions of meaningful local government" (Danzberger & Usdan, 1992, p. 92). It is of little wonder then, that many members of the local community view school board members as their representatives in the public schools. But power in educational governance is increasingly centralized at state and national levels. Given this centralization, Epstein (2004) contends that local school boards are increasingly "implementing other people's goals and priorities" (p. 3). And Kirst (2004) declares, "it appears likely that traditional local governance structures will be overwhelmed by the trend toward increased nonlocal power over schools" (p. 15).

As part of its community relations role, the school board acts as an advocate of the public schools (Mathews, 2006; Smoley, 1999). Thus, in a sense, the school board represents the public school organization to the community. They do so by structuring community input, explaining actions, and facilitating information flow to the community (Smoley, 1999). In the ideal operation of a school board, regardless of an individual member's view, after taking a decision the board presents a unified front to the public (Bolman, Deal, & Rallis, 1995; Smoley, 1999). This is especially difficult after a board has publicly debated a contentious curricular issue. The reality is often different in politically divided and conflicted communities. School boards have the complex task of representing several, and potentially conflicting, interest groups. Again, in the ideal the best interest of the children comes first and they are to negotiate this terrain in harmony, i.e. without squabbling or bickering (McAdams, 2006). The best interest of all the children ought to come first. Thus, school board members must undertake the balancing of all interest groups and their statutory responsibilities in a way which will best serve the needs of all the children attending the public schools of their district.

Policymaker. One of the primary roles of the school board is to enact policies for the school district including curricular policy (Bolman, Deal, & Rallis, 1995; Conley, 2003; First, 1992a, 1992b; Mathews, 2006; McAdams, 2006), but research tells us "that boards spend less than one-tenth of their time developing and overseeing policy" (Hochschild, 2005, p. 325) and only a small percentage of the one-tenth of their time spent on policy is available for attention to curriculum. Chait and Taylor (1989) saw boards as unavailable for policy and strategy, their time "frittered away on operations" (p. 45). However, a school board's policy making ability is constrained by policy discourses imposed upon it from outside the school district (Ehrensal, 1999), that is, the state and national levels. Local policy decisions are also constrained by Federal laws such as the No Child Left Behind Act (NCLB) (2002) and The Individuals With Disabilities Education Improvement Act (IDEIA) (2004). These policy and legislation discourses include the influence of many interests groups. Thus, local school district policy is shaped by interests groups external to, and unaware of the norms, values, beliefs and needs of the local community and these groups are usually interested in more comprehensive issues of curriculum.

In the recent history of the United State, however, the values of some local districts clashed (and still clash) with national policy choices of great magnitude such as school desegregation. Hochschild (2005) writes that "local district governance in the American public school system sustains racial, ethnic, and class hierarchies in the society as a whole" (p. 328). Further, in its capacity as representative of the state legislature, school boards pass policies to ensure that state legislation and policies are implemented. Whether they do so in the totality and spirit of the statutes is questionable (Nowakowski & First, 1989). Also the influence of the superintendent of schools must be factored into considerations of school board policy making (First, 2001). Through supplying the materials (research, district data, etc.) needed (Smoley, 1999) and setting the agenda (Petersen & Williams, 2005), the superintendent has a great deal of influence in shaping policy decisions.

Micromanaging. Much has been written concerning boards' penchant for micromanaging schools (Conley, 2003; Mathews, 2006; McAdams, 2006; Mountford & Brunner, 2001; Smoley, 1999). Much of this literature is a critique of such behavior including, serving self-interest of individual board members (Mountford & Bruner, 2001), narrow interests of a particular constituency (McAdams, 2006) or a particular board member (Carver, 1990) and the practice being generally injurious to board-superintendent relationships (Conley, 2003; Smoley, 1999). Such views and behaviors are also detrimental to reasoned consideration of curricular policy. Mathews (2006) however, offers insight into the reasons for micromanagement on the part of school boards.

People run for school boards because they want to make a contribution to the schools and the community. They run because of incidents involving their own children or children of their neighbors. They run because they care about what is taught to their children and the children of the community. As a school board member they are told that their chief duty is policy making, however they quickly realize that their ability to make policy is constrained by many factors, including the superintendent's role of policy advisor. Board members then come to believe that they cannot contribute (or contribute very little) in the policy arena and consequently look for a way to play a role. Micromanaging then, becomes that contributing role, instead of leadership on issues such as curriculum, which are of importance to the community as a whole.

Stakeholder Theory

Stakeholder theory (Freeman & Reed, 1983; Phillips, Freeman, & Wicks, 2003) is useful in understanding the complex roles and relationships of school boards. Stakeholders are "those groups who have a stake in the actions of the [school organization]," as well as "those groups without whose support the organization would cease to exist" (Freeman & Reed, 1983, p. 89). Stakeholder theory, then "maintains that the objectives of the [school organization] should be derived by balancing the conflicting claims of the various 'stakeholders' of the [organization]" (Ansoff, 1990, p. 89).

"Stakeholder theory is a theory of organizational management and ethics" (Phillips, Freeman & Wick, 2003, p. 480), that is the subject matters of the theory are inherently moral topics.

> Stakeholder theory is distinct [from other managerial theories] because it addresses morals and values explicitly as a central feature of managing organizations. The ends of a cooperative activity and the means of achieving these ends are critically examined in stakeholder theory in a way that they are not in many theories of strategic management. Stakeholder theory is conceived in terms that are "explicitly and unabashedly moral." This is evidenced in the branch of stakeholder theory literature examining the moral foundations of the theory. (p. 481)

Consequently, in managing for stakeholders, "Attention to the interests and well-being of those who cans assist or hinder the achievement of the organization's objectives is the central admonition of the theory" (p. 481).

Stakeholders

Freeman and Reed (1983) define two broad categories of stakeholders. The "wide sense of stakeholder" is "any identifiable group or individual who can affect the achievement of an organization's objectives or who is affected by the achievement of an organization's objectives" (p. 91). In the school organization these would include government agencies, public interest groups (including adversary groups), unions, local community, employees, parents and pupils. The narrow sense of stakeholder is "any identifiable group or individual on which the organization is dependent for its continued survival" (p. 91). This group includes governmental agencies (the state department of education) employees, parents, pupils, and local tax payers.

Stakeholder analysis is an important strategy in terms of governance. "It implies looking at public policy questions in stakeholder terms and trying to understand how the relationships between an organization and its stakeholders would change given the implementation of certain policies" (Freeman & Reed, 1983, p. 93). A two-dimensional grid map is offered by Freeman and Reed as an analytic tool for assessing stakeholders.

"The first dimension is one of 'interest' or 'stake' and ranges from an equity interest to an economic interest or marketplace state to an interest or stake as a 'kibitzer' or influencer" (Freeman & Reed, 1983, p. 93). In terms of school district organizations, employees and vendors certainly have an economic interest, and homeowners and realtors have a market interest. *Kibitzers* are those who are politically motivated but at a distance, such as the chamber of commerce and homeschooler's associations. Influencers include parents, PTAs, band and athletic booster clubs, employee's unions, and local tax payer groups.

"The second dimension of a stakeholder is its power" which includes economic power "the ability to influence due to marketplace decisions" and, political power which is "the ability to influence due to the use of the political process" (Freeman & Reed, 1983, p. 93). An example of marketplace power would be the publishing of districts' standardized test results (league tables) in newspapers and homebuyers basing decisions to (not) purchase in a district based on its standing. Political power is particularly salient to local school boards. Alsbury's (2003) work on dissatisfaction theory demonstrates how local communities use the voting booth to demand change in school district organizations. Often it is dissatisfaction with the curriculum that feels these demands of change.

School Boards and Balancing Stakeholder Demands

"The board must decide not only whether management is managing the affairs of the [school district organization], but indeed, what are to count as the affairs of the [organization]" (Freeman & Reed, 1983, p. 96). In a public school organization, boards cannot make this determination either in isolation or with the sole consultation of the professional administrators. "It is important for the sake of ethics, psychological well-being, and organizational success that stakeholders be accorded some say in determining … how [the organizational] outputs are created" (Phillips, Freeman, & Wick, 2003, p. 490). Stakeholder analysis promotes and understanding of the school organization's stakeholders, as well as acknowledging the importance of including their participation in the policy decision-making process (Freeman & Reed, 1983). Minimally, "this implies that [school boards] must be aware of the impact of their decisions on key stakeholder groups" (Freeman & Reed, 1983, p. 96).

This is not to say that all stakeholders are to be treated equally. Rather, it is the task of the school board to balance the interests of the various stakeholders (Phillips, Freeman, & Wick, 2003). One means of doing this is to determine whether a stakeholder is normative or derivative (Phillips, Freeman & Wick, 2003). "Normative stakeholders are those to whom the organization has a direct moral obligation to attend to their well-being" (p. 489). In a public school organization, children are the primary normative stakeholders. It is their present and future well-being for which the school organization has a moral obligation. Employees, too fall in this category. "Alternatively, derivative stakeholders are those groups or individuals who can either harm or benefit the organization, but to whom the organization has no direct moral obligation as a stakeholder" (p. 489). The local press would be an example of a derivative stakeholder in a school district.

In balancing the interests of the various stakeholders under this rubric, boards need to negotiate the multiple ethical paradigms justice, caring, and critique (Shapiro & Stefkovich, 2005), as well as the norms, values and beliefs of the community to which the children belong. In such cases, the board would be well to adopt the "ethic of the profession," "to serve the 'best interests of the student'" (Shapiro & Stefkovich, 2005, p. 25). In doing so, however the board would need to be mindful of how it constructs students, as well as not imposing its interests on the children (Ehrensal, 2002).

BALANCING PUBLIC VOICE AND PROFESSIONAL POWER

Stakeholder theory, then, repositions the school board in the school district organization. As the board is the entity charged with balancing various stakeholder interests, board roles and relationship would need to alter. Board members could no longer be the conduit of state policy and legislation. This huge shift confronts established law in every state. Operating within stakeholder theory, policies would have to be considered in light of the needs of the various stakeholders. Thus, board members would need to take more active roles in state level politics. Working through regional school board committees and state school board associations, board members can actively represent the local stakeholders, ensuring that state level politicians and department of education professionals understand the local context.

Board members would also need to be more approachable by community members, both at board meetings and at various community functions (e.g., fraternal organizations, social clubs, fairs, and yes even the aisle in the supermarket). Good (2003) writes,

> It is an unofficial but important part of my responsibilities as a school board member to listen to the concerns of parents about their children's teachers. Their stories, when they stop me in the supermarket parking lot or at the soccer field, are alarming. (p. 74)

While legally, no one member can speak or act unilaterally on behalf of the board, individual board members can be open to listening to stakeholders concerns and bring these back to the board. This openness and accessibility is vital for building trust so that the public reengages with the public schools. If the public understands that they have a voice in public schools—even if they do not have children attending those schools—they will be more inclined to vote in school board elections, attend meetings and support the schools politically and financially (Mathews, 2006). Additionally, charged with balancing the interests of stakeholders in policy decision making, the board would need to adopt strategies of analysis, such as dividing stakeholders into normative and derivative stakeholders. Consequently, single issue campaigns would become a less effective strategy in school board elections. And hopefully, boards could attend more thoroughly to comprehensive curriculum issues for the good of all the children in their care.

Repositioning the school board in the school district organization also means altering its relationship with the superintendent. Under stakeholder theory, employees of the school organization, including the professional staff (teachers and administrators) are another set of stakeholders whose interests "must be viewed in terms of the entire grid of stakeholders" (Freeman & Reed, 1983, p. 96). This is not to say that the superintendent's power would diminish, indeed that position would remain quite powerful. Rather, the superintendent could no longer regard the board as an entity to be managed. In a district operating under the tenets of stakeholder theory it would not be the task of the superintendent to manage the board meeting agenda or construct the reality on which the board will base its policy decisions. Kowalski (2001) sees the superintendent's role becoming broader as political and social conditions will eventually lead to the transformation of school boards into local educational policy boards. In the ideal the superintendent would be freed to operate as the guardian of justice and care for all students (First, 2001) and as the leader for the public good as discussed in Gardner (1990).

However, superintendents need to understand the limits of their professional perspective. The duty of the board to balance their power with local voices if social justice and democratic ideals are to be fostered in the school organization (First, 2001). That is, the superintendent, and indeed board members, need to practice an "ethic of community" (Furman, 2003).

> In its simplest terms, an ethic of community means that [school board members] administrators, teachers, school staffs, students parents, and other community members interested in schools *commit to the process of community*; in other words, they feel that they are *morally responsible to engage in communal processes* as they pursue the moral purpose of schooling and address the ongoing challenges of daily life and work in schools. (p. 4)

This process of community can only be done through an open political process, where the interests of the various stakeholders are acknowledged and weighed. Indeed, if a superintendent aspires to be a democratic and ethical educational leader (s)he would embrace the process that stakeholder theory offers.

Will There Still Be School Boards Tomorrow?

As we have indicated in this chapter, the role and indeed nature of school boards are points of contention. However, in an era of ever increasing centralization of control of public education, one could easily ask: "What difference does it make?" "Are school boards relevant or even needed?" Indeed, reports such as *Tough Choices or Tough Times* (NCEE, 2007) call for the abolishment of local school boards and the centralizing of school policy and funding at the state level.

However, there is another point to consider. While there has been a trend for increased centralized control of school policy and curriculum, the funding schemes for schools have remained the same. That is, the larger part of school funds are raised at the local level based on local property taxes. If local governance is removed, communities will not have a body to take their concerns and grievances. Exclusion of these community voices will lead to a sense of disenfranchisement and possibly resulting in taxpayer revolt movements, especially in those communities where few households have children enrolled in the public schools and/or where school budgets are subject to referendum votes.

Finally, there are pedagogical consequences to be considered if local school boards are disbanded. We have maintained here that the most important mission of public education is to prepare citizens for their roles in a democratic society. Further, as children learn as much by example as by exposition, citizens need to consider what lessons would be taught by the abolishment of local school boards. What would children learn about the democratic process if the public is allowed little voice in something as basic as the education of its citizens? What lessons would be taught about the relationship between citizens and their government if this important governmental function is given over to unelected education professionals? Finally, would we be actually telling children about the importance of education if it becomes just one of many issues vying for attention and resources at the state level?

Local school boards then, are important and complex governmental bodies. Rather, for those who aspire to be democratic and ethical educational leaders, school boards are the bodies that keep them honest by challenging their assumptions and constructs, as well as preserving these leaders' grounding in the communities that they serve. While local school boards have a long standing tradition in the educational system, the debate on whether or not these bodies continue to serve a useful purpose is yet to be resolved. The useful purpose could be the preservation of "the marketplace of ideas" (*Keyishian*, 1967).

> It could be preserving the freedom of literature. Freedom of literature is the lifeblood of a democratic state. Exposing the nation's children to different and sometimes uncomfortable viewpoints is what stimulates them towards success. It encourages critical thinking instead of blind obedience. Without it society would be in a far worse place. (Brenyo, 2011, p. 549)

The public still sees local school boards as a piece of the "good society" (Galbraith, 1996).

> Any useful identification of the good society must therefore take into consideration the institutional structure and the human characteristics that are fixed, immutable. They make the difference between the utopian and the achievable, between the agreeably irrelevant and the ultimately possible. (p. 3)

If local school boards do disappear there will need to be created some system, mechanism or institutional structure open to all stakeholders, including the general public, to voice their concerns and ideals. Only then will reform of the educational governance system be achievable and ultimately possible. Only then will good curriculum decisions be made. As for now the debate can continue as to whether the local school board is the guardian of a democracy or the imposer of censorship.

References

Alexander, K., & Alexander, M. D. (2011). *American public school law (*8th ed.). Belmont, CA: Thomson West.

Alsbury, T. L. (2003). Superintendent and school board member turnover: Political versus apolitical turnover as critical variable in the application of disaffection theory. *Education Administration Quarterly, 39*(5), 667-698.

Ansoff, H. I. (1990). *Implanting strategic management*. Boston, MA: Longman.

Beingenheimer-Rendahl, F. (2006). *The impact of NCLB on staff development reform in small rural school districts in Arizona* (EdD Dissertation). University of Arizona.

Board of Education of Louisville v. Society of Alumni of Louisville Male High School, 239 S.W. 2d. 931 (Ky. 1951).

Board of Education, Island Trees Union Free School District No. 26 v. Pico, 457 U.S. 853, 102 S.Ct. 2799, 73 L.Ed.2d 435 (1982).

Bolman, L. G., Deal, T. E., & Rallis, S. F. (1995). *Becoming a school board member.* Thousand Oaks, CA: Corwin Press.

Boring v. Buncombe Board of Education, 136 F.3d 364, 368 (4th Cir. 1998).

Brenyo, M. (2011). Censored: Book banning in the US education system. *Journal of Law and Education, 40*(3), 541-549.

Breyer, S. (2005). *Active liberty: Interpreting our democratic constitution.* New York, NY: Knopf.

Briffault, R. (2005). The local school district in American law. in W. G. Howell (Ed.), *Besieged: School boards and the future of education politics* (pp. 24-55). Washington, DC: Brookings Institution Press.

Brown v. Hot Sexy and Safer Productions, Inc. 68 F. 3d 525, 533 (1st Cir. 1995).

Brown v. Woodland Joint Unified School District, 27 F.3d 1373 (9th Cir. 1994).

Carver, J. (1990). *Boards that make a difference.* San Francisco, CA: Jossey-Bass.

Chait, R. P., & Taylor, B. E. (1989). Chartering the territory of non-profit boards. *Harvard Business Review, 89,* 44-54.

Conley, D. T. (2003). *Who governs our schools: Change roles and responsibilities.* New York, NY: Teachers College Press.

Counts v. Cedarville School District, 295 F.Supp.2d 996 (W.D. Ark. 2003).

Cox, E. P., & Malone, B. (2003). New superintendents' perception of their jobs: Is the honeymoon over? *ERS Spectrum. 21*(1) 8-11.

Danzberger, J. P., & Usdan, M. D. (1992). Strengthening a grass roots American institution: The school board. In P. F. First & H. J. Walberg (Eds.), *School boards: Changing local control* (pp. 91-124). Berkeley, CA: McCutchan.

Dawson L. J., & Quinn, R. (2001). Moving boards out of operations, into results. *The School Administrator, 58*(3), 54.

Edwards v. Aguillard, 482 U.S. 578 (1987).

Ehrensal, P. A. L. (1999, July). *Calling the shots: How elite discourses constrain local strategic actors.* Paper presented at the Critical Management Studies Conference, Manchester, England.

Ehrensal, P. A. L. (2002, October) *Are we doing what is best for the children? Towards a radical ethical critique. Profiling New Scholarship Keynote Address.* Paper presented at the 7th annual Values and Leadership Conference, OISE/UT Centre for the Study of Values and Leadership, Toronto, Canada.

Ehrensal, P., & First, P. (2008).Understanding school board politics: Balancing public voice and professional power. In B. Cooper, J. Cibulka, & L. Fusarelli (Eds.), *Understanding the politics of K-12: A Handbook of theory & practice applications & reform.* Mahwah, NJ: Lawrence Erlbaum Associates.

Epperson v. Arkansas, 393 U.S. 97 (1968).

Epstein, N. (2004). *Who's in charge here? The tangled web of school governance and policy.* Denver CO: Education Commission of the States.

Finn, C. E. (1992). Reinventing local control. In P. F. First & H. J. Walberg (Eds.), *School boards: Changing local control* (pp. 21-25). Berkeley, CA: McCutchan.

First, P. F. (1992a). *Educational policy for school administrators.* Boston, MA: Allyn & Bacon.

First, P. F. (1992b). Evaluating school boards: Looking through the next-generation lenses, in P. F. First & H. J. Walberg (Eds.), *School boards: Changing local control* (pp. 177-195). Berkeley, CA: McCutchan.

First, P. F. (2001). The new superintendent as guardian of justice and care. In C. C. Brunner and L. G. Bjork (Eds.), *The new superintendency* (pp. 249-266). London: Elsevier.

Freeman, R. E., & Reed, D. L. (1983). Stockholders and stakeholders: A new perspective on corporate governance. *California management review, 25*(3), 88-106.

Furman, G. C. (2003). Moral leadership and the ethic of community. *Values and Ethic in Educational Administration, 2*(1), 1-8.

Galbraith, J. K. (1996). *The good society: The humane agenda.* Boston, MA: Houghton Mifflin.

Gardner, J. W. (1990). *On leadership.* Boston, MA: The Free Press.

Glass, T. E. (2000). The politics of school board evaluation. *The School Community Journal, 10(2),* 83-98.

Glass, T. E. (2001). *Superintendent leaders look at the superintendency, school boards and reform. ECS Issue Paper.* Denver, CO: Education Commission of the States.

Glass, T. E. (2002). *School boards presidents and their view of the superintendency. ECS Issue Paper.* Denver, CO: Education Commission of the States.

Glover, S. (2004). School boards as leaders of reform. *Education Next, 4(3),* 11-13.

Good, H. (2003). *Educated guess: A school board member reflects.* Lanham, MD: Scarecrow Press.

Hayes, W. (2001). *So you want to be a school board member.* Lanham, MD: Scarecrow Press.

Hochschild, J. L. (2005). What school boards can and cannot (or will not) accomplish. In W. G. Howell (Ed.), *Besieged: School boards and the future of education politics* (pp. 324-338). Washington, DC: Brookings Institution.

Institute for Educational Leadership. (1986). *School boards: Strengthening grass roots leadership.* Washington DC: Author.

Individuals with Disabilities Education Improvement Act of 2004 (Pub. L. 108-446, Dec. 3, 2004, 118 Stat. 2647).

Keyishian v. Board of Regents, 385 U.S. 589 (1967).

Kirst, M. (2004). Turning points: A history of American school governance. In N. Epstein (Ed.), *Who's in charge here? The tangled web of school governance and politics* (pp. 14-41). Denver, CO: Education Commission of the States.

Kohn, A. (2006). *Beyond discipline: From compliance to community.* Alexandria, VA: Association for Supervision & Curriculum Development.

Kowalski, T. J. (2001). The future of local school governance: Implications for board members and superintendents. In C. C. Brunner & L.G. Bjork (Eds.), *The new superintendency.* (pp. 183-201). London, England: Elsevier.

Kushner, H. S. (2006). *Overcoming life's disappointments.* New York, NY: Knopf.

Lau v. Nichols, 414 U.S. 563 (1974).

Leebaert v. Harrington, 332 F.3d 134, 142 (2d Cir. 2003).

McAdams, D. R. (2003). Training your board to lead. *School Administrator, 60*(10), 7.

McAdams, D. R. (2006). *What school boards can do: Reform governance for urban schools.* New York, NY: Teachers College Press.

McCollum v. Board of Education, 333 U.S. 203, 68 S.Ct. 461 (1948).

Marschall, M. J. (2005). Minority incorporation and local school boards. In W. G. Howell (Ed.), *Besieged: School boards and the future of education politics* (pp. 173-198). Washington, DC: Brookings Institution.

Mathews, D. (2006). *Reclaiming public education by reclaiming our democracy.* Dayton, OH: Kettering Foundation Press.

Meier, K. J., & Juenke, E. G. (2005). Electoral structure and the quality of representation on school boards. In W. G. Howell (Ed.), *Besieged: School boards and the future of education politics* (pp. 199-227). Washington, DC: Brookings Institution.

Meyer v. Nebraska, 262 U.S. 390 (1923).

Mountford, M., & Brunner, C. C. (2001). Motivations for school board membership: Implications for decision making. In C. C. Brunner & L. G. Bjork (Eds.), *The new superintendency* (pp. 135-152). London: Elsevier.

Mozert v. Hawkins County Board of Education, 827 F.2d 1058 (1987).

National Center on Education and the Economy. (2007). *Tough choices or tough times: The report of the new commission on the skills of the American workforce.* San Francisco, CA: Wiley

National Coalition Against Censorship, The Kids' Right to Read Project (2011). Retrieved from http://www.abffe.com/KR2R.pdf

No Child Left Behind Act of 2001 (NCLB) (Pub. L. 107-110, Jan. 8, 2002, 115 Stat. 1425).

Nowakowski, J., & First, P. F. (1989). A study of school board minutes: Records of reform. *Educational Evaluation & Policy Analyses, 11(4),* 389-404.

Parker v. Hurley, 474 F. Supp. 2d 261 (D. Mass. 2008).

Pennsylvania School Board Association. (1979). Public guide to Pennsylvania School Boards. In *Mastering the basics of effective school board service* (pp. 7-10) New Cumberland, PA: Pennsylvania School Boards Association.

Petersen, G. J., & Williams, B. M. (2005). The board president and superintendent: An examination of influence through the eyes of the decision makers. In G. J. Petersen & L. D. Fusarelli (Eds.), *The politics of leadership: Superintendents and school boards in changing times* (pp. 23-50). Greenwich, CT: Information Age Publishing.

Phillips, R., Freeman, R. E., & Wicks, A. C. (2003). What stakeholder theory is not. *Business ethics quarterly, 13*(4) 479-502.

Pierce v. Society of Sisters, 268 U.S. 510 (1925).

Ryan, J. E. (2004). The Tenth Amendment & other paper tigers: The legal boundaries of education governance. In N. Epstein (Ed.), *Who's in charge here? The tangled web of school governance and policy* (pp. 42-74). Denver, CO: Education Commission of the States.

Sandlin v. Johnson, 643 F. 2d 1027, Court of Appeals, 4th Circuit (1981).

Sarason, S. B. (1995). *Parental involvement and the political principle: Why the existing governance structure of schools should be abolished.* San Francisco, CA: Jossey-Bass.

Shelmadine v. City of Elkhart, 75 Ind. App. 493, 129 N.E. 878 (1921).

Shannon, T. (1992). Local control and "organizacrats." In P. F. First & H. J. Walberg. In *School boards: Changing local control.* (pp. 27-33). Berkeley, CA: McCutchan.

Shapiro, J. P., & Stefkovich, J. A. (2005). *Ethical leadership and decision making in education: Applying theoretical perspective to complex dilemmas* (2nd ed.). Mahwah, NJ: Lawrence Erlbaum Associates.

Smoley, E. R., Jr. (1999). *Effective school boards: Strategies for improving board performance.* San Francisco, CA: Jossey-Bass.

State. ex. rel. Andrews. v. Webber. Supreme Court of Indiana, 108 Ind. 31, 8 N.E. 708(1886).

Taylor, S., Rizvi, F., Lingard, B., & Henry, M. (1997). *Educational policy and the politics of change.* New York, NY: Routledge.

Virgil v. School Board of Columbia County, 862 F.2d 1517 (11th Cir. 1989).

Wong, K. K., & Shen, F. X. (2005). When mayors lead urban schools: Assessing the effects of takeover. In W. G. Howell (Ed.), *Besieged: School boards and the future of education politics* (pp. 81-101). Washington, DC: Brookings Institution.

Zykan v. Warsaw Community School Corp., 631 F.2d 1300, 1306 (7th Cir. 1980).

Author Contact Information: Patricia F. First, JD, EdD, Eugene T. Moore Distinguished Professor of Educational Leadership Eugene T. Moore School of Education, Clemson University 404G Tillman Hall Clemson, SC 29634. Phone: 864-656-032. E-mail: pfrist@clemson.edu

CHAPTER 31

Maxwell's Demon

The Curriculum Structure as a Device to Generate Curriculum as a Routine and to Overcome the Evil Forces of Organizational Entropy

Arthur Shapiro
University of South Florida

At some time in the life cycle of virtually every organization, its ability to succeed in spite of itself runs out.
—Brien's First Law, *Murphy's Law*

If you have knowledge, let others light their candles at it.
—Margaret Fuller

Every physical system in the universe (your car, your clocks, the solar system itself) falls prey to entropy, that is, slowly runs downhill, loses its energy, eventually stops functioning. Shockingly, so do all organizations. The pages of history are littered with the rusting hulks of organizations long past their productive lives. They begin with energy, pizzazz, slowly change, and in the long run, slow down, decay, go to pot. Evidence? General Motors, Chrysler, Ford, big city school systems, Lehman Brothers Bank bankruptcy.

As a matter of fact, organizations (which, of course, include school systems and individual schools) generate a career of three phases, and almost inevitably careen uncontrollably through these phases: The first is person-orientation led by a charismatic leader, next is plan-orientation led by a planner, and last is position-orientation led by a bureaucrat. The first two are productive. The last is a kind of senescence, where the school or district slowly loses its energy, purpose, just exists—and runs downhill. Can anything be done to counteract this disastrous scenario?

This chapter lays out a theoretically-based curriculum structure designed to stabilize a school district or school in the planning phase in its career in order to prevent the forces of organizational entropy from emasculating it, as is virtually inevitable—unless.... The models presented provide a structure and processes to *generate curriculum as a routine* to maintain the district or school in the planning phase. All have worked.

In order to do that, this article first delineates an empirically-based theory, the tri-partite theory of organizational change and succession (Shapiro, 2009; Shapiro, Benjamin, & Hunt, 1995; Wilson, Byar, Shapiro, & Schell, 1969) that predicts the virtually inevitable three phases that all organizations careen through uncontrollably in their careers, usually without us realizing it. The first two phases are productive, but the last, position-orientation, is essentially a wasteland. The theory points to this inevitable cycle of organizational entropy in which organizations lose their effectiveness in a relatively short time—unless—a solution can be found to stabilize the organization in one of its two productive phases. We briefly note that entropy in the physical world relates to the second law of thermodynamics, that entropy inexorably increases over time, so that all physical systems (from your auto, to your plumbing, to your clock battery) all run downhill, all run out of energy. Prominent nineteenth century physicist James

The Handbook of Educational Theories, pp. 355–365

Clark Maxwell came up with a droll solution to beat the Second Law, a nano-demon—thus, called "Maxwell's Demon." His solution, however, relies upon an individual, but since we deal with organizations, we search instead for an actual structure or structures and processes focusing on how schools can break this virtually inevitable outcome of organizational decay and dysfunction.

The article proposes tested solutions for schools to construct an internal organization, a mechanism, an organizational Maxwell's Demon, by which it can continue in a productive phase of its career—the planning phase. These mechanisms comprise planning structures and/or a development laboratory by which the school or school system can continue to remain viable and highly productive, since *they make change routine*, as has occurred in several districts in which the author and others worked as administrators, rather than succumb to the forces of entropy.

The five models are carefully delineated and include recommended structures and operating procedures for practitioners' use. These include a centralized, district-wide model, the DeKalb, IL model. Model 2 is a decentralized, building-based model established in the Hinsdale, IL school system. The third model was used in a New York district, Long Beach, where high levels of distrust existed and involved faculty, paraprofessionals, students, and community. The fourth model was an adaptation of these structures into a long range planning structure. The last model is a curriculum development laboratory developed in the Newport-Mesa district in California.

A summary, conclusions and implications conclude the paper, pointing out that with these models, *change can be made routine*, that these are devices to defeat the forces of organizational entropy and maintain the organization in the productive planning phase of its career.

THE THEORY—AND ITS USES

The tri-partite theory of organizational change and succession, which predicts that all organizations virtually inevitably careen through three successive phases or cycles, comprises essentially a theory of organizational entropy. Entropy in the physical universe states that every physical system runs down, runs out, from plumbing to brakes to the solar system itself.

Similarly, organizations run out of steam as they cycle through three phases in their careers: person, plan, and position. Briefly, an organization that has once been dynamic has fallen on sad times, resting on its laurels, drifting, being reactive, unproductive (like our once proud auto companies). The top levels of administration recognize that it is in trouble and cast around for a forceful, dynamic executive to resuscitate their failing enterprise. They locate a charismatic leader, one who is dynamic, who can develop programs, ideas, which can stir the imaginations of the folks in the organization, one who generates excitement. Programs begin to develop, people get involved, ideas get communicated, lots of initiatives start to develop, the place becomes forward-looking. The charismatic leader develops loyalty as people buy into his/her plans and ideas, the rationale for calling this phase of the organization's career, person-oriented, due to their attitudes of loyalty toward the leader. Examples? Moses, Christ, Bill Clinton, Barack Obama, Sara Palin, Franklyn Delano Roosevelt, John Dewey, Ted Sizer, Churchill, Generals David Petraeus and Robert E. Lee, Martin Luther King, Lee Iacocca. Unfortunately, this phase usually is relatively short-lived, with the charismatic either being shot out of the saddle, or leaving for another organization or district wanting to experience the excitement and accomplishment which the leader has generated. Thus, because people feel left in the lurch, they seize on the latter ideas on which they and the charismatic leader have been working and look to someone who can implement these plans and ideas—in short, a planner.

Plans come in all sorts of sizes and shapes. In education, examples are middle schools, small learning communities (SLCs), professional learning communities (PLCs), No Child Left Behind, state testing models, state standards, reading programs, national standards, charter schools, vouchers, and so on. In the process of carrying them out, people become loyal to the plan, sometimes passionately so. Since planners usually are nowhere as charismatic as their predecessors, loyalty becomes attached to the ideas; therefore, this phase is called Plan-Orientation. Fortunately, this phase lasts longer than Person-Orientation. Examples of planners? Lyndon Johnson, Generals Omar Bradley and Douglas MacArthur, Bill Gates, John Dewey, Albert Shanker of the American Federation of Teachers.

However, plans can also experience the same fate as charismatic leadership, unless people can develop a planning process or structure that can assist it to remain in this stage to resist the forces of entropy. This is precisely the intention of this article, namely, to present several planning structures and a development laboratory that have stabilized the schools or systems in a planning phase for quite some time. These structures can prevent the plan from dying out as new people enter the organization who are not too familiar with the plan, or who have different ideas. Indeed, plans often unravel as administrators develop procedures to implement the plan, such as specific role descriptions to guide new arrivals (which, in many cases, limit what people do), and bit-by-bit incremental procedures to accomplish the plan. In this process, red tape, rules and regulations increase and, typically, after three years or so, people talk about the "Good Old Days" as new folks enter and do not understand fully, nor share the goals the old-timers have adopted and slowly drift from the purpose.

Eventually, the planner leaves, often frustrated by the red tape the organization has developed to achieve the plan, which often increasingly blocks attainment of the plan. He or she is replaced by someone who is more interested in stabilizing the organization, in short, a bureaucrat who increasingly relies on red tape, regulations and rules to control people. The organization becomes backward-looking with loyalty to the person or the plan changing to loyalty to the position, thus, position-orientation. ("Well, our principal doesn't inspire loyalty, but we think the position is important"). Examples of bureaucrats? Gerald Ford, George H. W. Bush, the presidents of General Motors watching their market share dwindle from over 50% of the U.S. market to under 20%. The organization is headed at best by tinkerers, who resist change, and are usually interested in increasing their power and control—and importance.

However, once in a blue moon, an organization is able to locate a *synergist*, a relatively rare person who is both a planner *and* a charismatic leader. Synergists are able to break an organization out of its doldrums formerly led by a position-oriented leader. Examples include some of the people mentioned earlier. They include Presidents Obama and Clinton, Generals Robert E. Lee and Petraeus, Mahatma Ghandi, Lee Iacocca, John Dewey, Martin Luther King. Since synergists are rare, a planner and a charismatic who are mature and secure may be able to team together to generate this rare combination of talents, avoiding the jealousy that a less popular planner may experience as the charismatic generates more popularity and attention. Figure 31.1 illustrates the tri-partite theory.

How Maxwell's Demon Overcame Physical Entropy

To review, in the physical world, Newton's second law of thermodynamics states that an object will change velocity if it is pushed or pulled. The problem with the physical world (and with the organizational world, as well) is that all the systems eventually run down. Allison (1971), in his introduction to J. A. Morton's *Organizing for Innovation* delineated Morton's use of Maxwell's whimsical solution to break the Second Law. He notes,

> the clock on your mantle, the brakes on your car, the entire car itself, our entire solar system, for all these things, the Second Law holds. Some day ... they are going to run down...
>
> A century ago ... Maxwell proposed a way to beat the Second Law. Maxwell did it with a demon. Imagine, he said, an intelligent creature small enough to see molecules, a sort of tiny demon. And imagine the demon as the custodian of a gate between two tanks of gas at equal temperature and pressure. By opening and closing the gate at just the right time, the demon allows the swifter molecules to pass in one direction, and slower molecules to pass in the other. And the available energy —the difference in temperature between one tank and other—increases! That Demon has busted the Second Law!
>
> Jack Morton suggests that the effective manager can operate as a sort of Maxwell Demon himself, encouraging the "hot" creative ideas, and discouraging the "cold" ones. He can defeat the Second Law insofar as a human system is concerned. More to the point, the Demon Manager can improve the odds that the adaptive responses of his system will enhance its growth and its chance for survival. (pp. vi-vii)

Voila! He has broken the Second Law.

While a variety of approaches to this interesting problem can be developed in the organizational world of the school, most of which heavily involve teachers and administrators, here and there a single administrator can perform the Maxwell's Demon function. In this personalized and authoritarian approach, a single administrator slowly cycles in new ideas, tests them, and expels what does not work. Superintendent J. Lloyd Michaels of the Evanston Township High School District (Illinois) operated in this manner. He would bring in programs and ideas, some competing with those in place, and would implement them, such as a combined social studies-English program. While neither of the departments was particularly enthusiastic about the interdisciplinary program, the competing program stimulated both, with all three surviving and prospering.

The Curriculum Structure as a Synergistic Plan—A Maxwell's Demon

Allison (1971), in his introduction to Morton's book noted, "Morton's innovation process is nothing but a means by which strong people with a variety of talents can work together toward a common objective—in his case, toward enhancing communication" (p. ix). Allison seems to be referring to a synergy in which human talents are combined for a purpose. This is precisely what is being advocated here, but with a significant difference. Individuals trying to introduce change into almost any organization, almost any system, need to develop internal structures within the organization to stimulate and to monitor the processes, or they often will suffer the slings and arrows hurled their way by their colleagues, who often become jealous of their

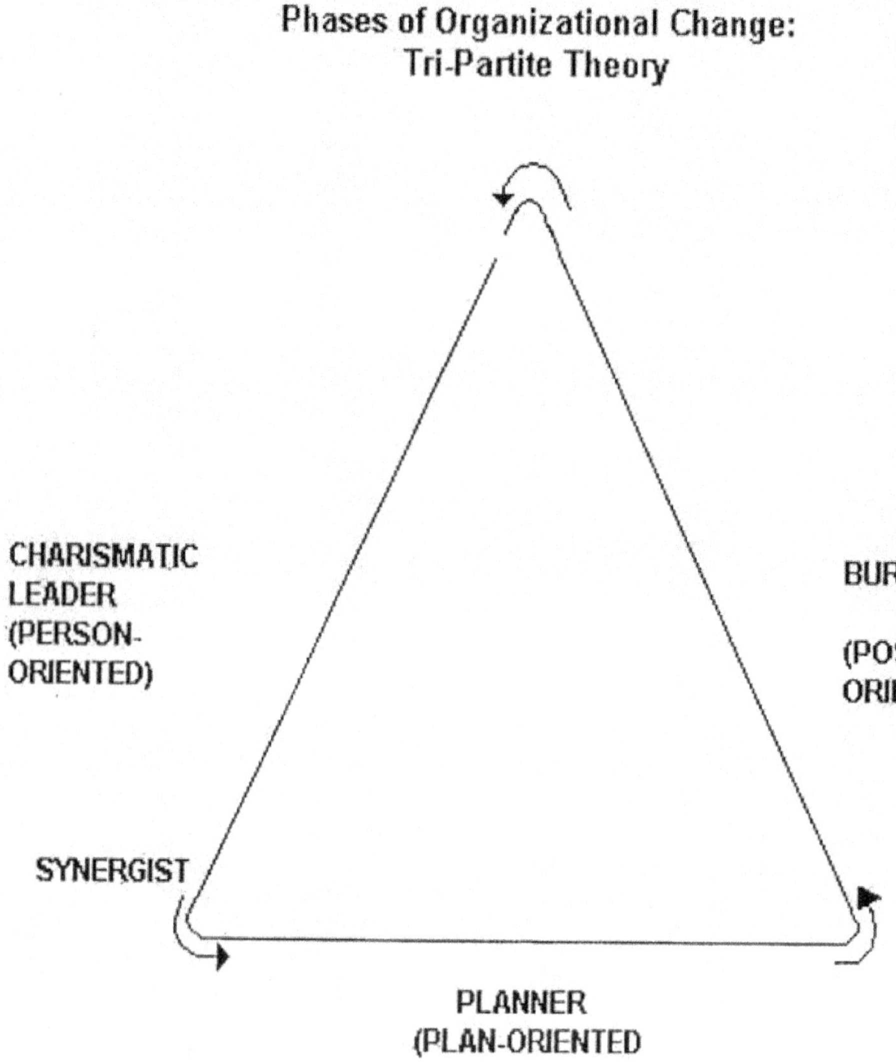

Figure 31.1. The tri-partite theory.

prominence. Working alone without a structure and process increases the difficulty considerably and the change usually disappears once the individual leaves. A curriculum structure which is developed to generate and to monitor change continually enhances the chances for success considerably.

The author worked in two systems in two states utilizing several such structures to stabilize them into the planning phase (as described by the tri-partite theory). The purpose of these structures was essentially *to introduce change as a routine* into the schools with heavy staff involvement. Indeed, in one community, students, aides, noncertified staff and community participated.

A curriculum structure properly operated functions as a vehicle to:

1. Establish a channel for developing and implementing programs
2. State that organizational approval and sanction at the highest levels that program change is legitimate in the eyes of the organization
3. Collect the adventurous, the interested, the motivated, the dissatisfied to work within the legitimate channels of the organization constructively on change
4. Funnel ideas to improve programs to top levels of administration
5. Remove normal blocking forces against changes, such as:

   a. Principals who do not wish changes

b. Coordinators who do not support changes
c. Department chairs who want to maintain the *status quo*
d. Eliminating the norm of making changes through personal influence ("whom you know")

6. Eliminate normal excuses, such as

a. "They'll never let us"
b. State curriculum requirements block changes

7. Support those who have ideas
8. Promote staff professionalism
9. Generate a motivational system that is *intrinsic* and is at Maslow's (1954) and Herzberg's (1966) higher levels—self-esteem and self-actualization
10. Establish a system that recognizes and rewards ability, initiative, creativity and interest in designing and developing programs. In short, it establishes a new reward and recognition system for people for professional competence in designing and developing curriculum and program

11. Establish a structure and a variety of new norms in the organizational and even community culture relating to professionalism and productivity related to constructive change considered as normal and expected of competent people

The trick, of course, is to design a curriculum producing system that works—and then support it vigorously at top levels. The first system follows.

Model 1—The DeKalb Model: A Centralized District Curriculum Generating Structure

A curriculum generating structure can involve large numbers of teachers, administrators, and, if desired, aides, students and parents. Figure 31.2 presents a centralized, system-wide model. (Appropriate adjustments could be made in large systems using clusters of feeder schools or a subdistrict if it is the right size.) The structure works as follows: If a person or group has an idea, the Assistant Superintendent for Instruction forms a work group, if needed, to formulate a proposal with appropriate elements and format. The format includes a:

- rationale
- budget
- summer curriculum writing organization with a timetable
- in-service provisions for teachers and administrators
- methods of evaluation and dissemination

The proposal is first considered by an area committee (humanities, special areas, math-science, and applied arts in this model). After rigorous examination, if approved, it is sent to the curriculum steering committee's (see Figure 31.2) chairperson who distributes it to committee members at least two weeks ahead of the monthly meeting. There, proponents present the proposal and respond to questions.

If the proposal is recommended for adoption to the Assistant Superintendent, it is placed in the file for a spring meeting where proposals are rated 1 (high), 2, or 3 (low) for implementation. It is wise to schedule this prioritizing meeting early enough, usually in April, for faculty and administration to plan budgeting and summer curriculum workshop commitments. Where budgetary requirements exceed capacity, proposals may be phased in over two or three years. A K-8 reading program might be implemented in K-2 the first year, 3-5 the next, and 6-8 the third year.

In Figure 31.2, the curriculum steering committee structure is first laid out, followed by the four (4) Area committees consisting of humanities, special areas, math-science and applied arts. Work groups are formed by the assistant superintendent to support people with proposal ideas.

The job of the assistant superintendent for instruction is to develop and to implement (not block) first rate programs. If s/he blocks, the entire structure will slowly disintegrate as quality people will refuse to serve. Commitment of top administration is imperative. The author used the above structure in two states with a good deal of success. Interestingly, considerable prestige accrued by being asked to serve or by being elected to these groups. The principals were selected by the assistant superintendent and superintendent with the advice of the principals.

Committee members who were unable to evaluate proposals perceptively clearly became an embarrassment, and were not selected again. Professional recognition also occurred when a person or a group was able to get a proposal approved (minutes of the curriculum steering committee went to the board of education, all schools, the classroom teachers' association board, building representatives), and then wrote the curriculum during the summer. These proposals were publicized in both the school newsletter and community papers. Consequently, many of the most talented and committed people in the organization were attracted to the point that several passed up coaching assignments to work on their proposals.

The curriculum, once written, was implemented first by in-service workshops for inclusion into the regular program. The person who suggested and honchoed the idea usually chaired the process. If possi-

A Centralized District Curriculum Structure

Curriculum Steering Committee

(5) 2 representatives appointed by Classroom Teachers' Association (CTA) President and 3 teachers to be selected at large (1 elementary, 1 middle school, 1 high school) by Ass't Supt. for instruction, one Principal & CTA President

(4) Chairman of Area Committees (all teachers)

(3) Principals

(1) Director of Research

(1) Assistant Superintendent for Instruction

(1) Assistant Superintendent for Students

(1) Superintendent (Ex-Official)

Humanities	Special Areas	Math-Science	Applied Arts

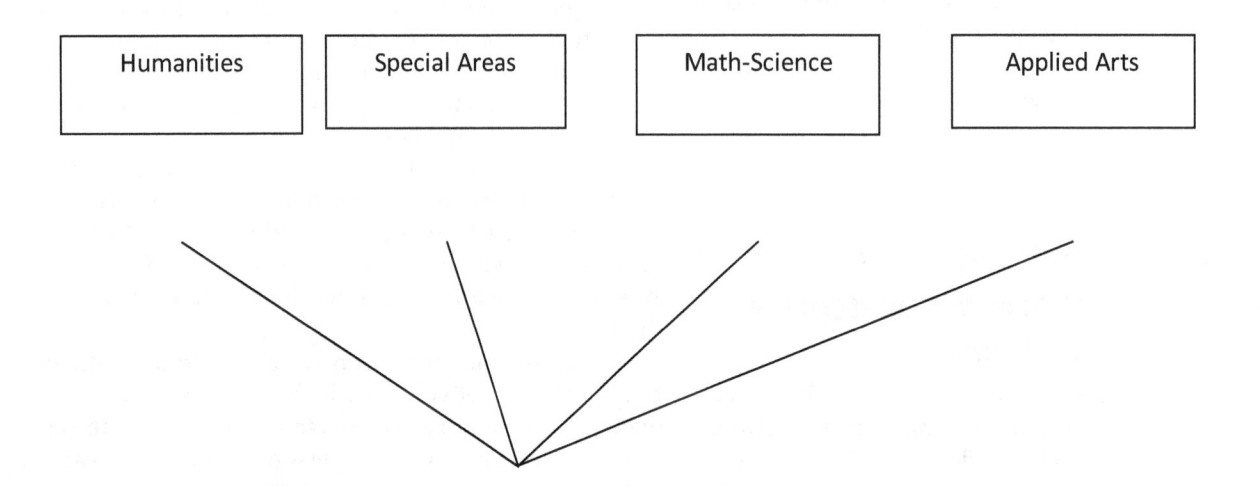

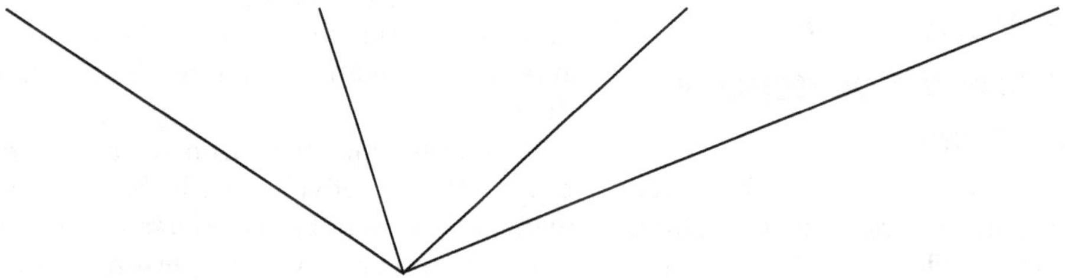

Each Area Committee is composed of:

(9) Teachers—(3 from each of : elementary, middle and high school), and

(1) Principal and (1) Assistant Supt. for Instruction

Work Groups ⟶ ⟵ Assistant Superintendent ⟶ ⟵ Work Groups

Figure 31.2. Centralized district curriculum structure.

ble, this individual could attend a workshop for the program run by a national or regional group. In addition, summer curriculum workshop writing was paid, but the workday ran no more than four hours (we took that from Earnest Hemingway, who wrote that he could write no more than four hours daily). Interestingly, neighboring school systems began to request consultation and workshops from people who developed proposals. In several instances, teachers were offered administrative positions in those districts. High levels of competency were an avenue for ascent within the school district also. On which of Maslow's (1954) levels did these focus? Social needs, esteem, obviously, and, hopefully, self-actualization. The process through its design (producing a great deal of intense committee and subcommittee work) met staff social needs. Those involved received a great deal of recognition and esteem not only within the schools, but also from the board of education, the faculty, the classroom teachers' association, the larger community. People felt trusted as professionals. Those who were self-starters, who developed quality programs, or who were creative could utilize the process. The individual or group who developed a proposal had major impact for years. About 20 major proposals a year were implemented, some over several years. People were self-selected, so the process was perceived as fair. Job performance and rewards were closely linked, and rewards were highly valued (Rand, 1977). Indeed, the value of rewards appreciated, opening career doors.

To add to the effectiveness of the process, the author found two other supporting practices invaluable. The first is a "Hot Idea" fund, a small amount of venture capital in the account of the assistant superintendent for instruction to support people with interesting ideas who need help with modest expenses (visiting an outstanding program, buying modest resource materials). Another interesting notion is the "pilot" idea. A program might be tried out for a short time—never for more than a year—as a pilot. After that time, to be continued, it would have to go through the process described above.

Model 2—A Decentralized, Building-Based Curriculum Structure

A decentralized building-based model is portrayed in Figure 31.3. Committees are organized by building but the process is the same. This model was developed by Dr. Ronald Simcox, Superintendent of Hinsdale Elementary School District, Hinsdale, IL, who also was involved in developing Model 1, with similar results.

Model 3

A third model is possible. In areas of high distrust, a committee might be composed of eight staff, eight community members, and eight or nine students (see Figure 31.4). Situations will arise which will require the coordination of both committees. In such cases, a subcommittee (consisting of representation from both committees) would be drawn together. The potential benefits of such a structure are manifold. This plan provides for awakening and utilizing available resources which have heretofore not been utilized. Obviously, the involvement is considerable—both from within and from without—the schools. Opportunity is structured for interaction and exchange of ideas, followed by systematic study and evaluation. *No idea or innovation will be permitted to be killed or censored before it has a chance to be born.* Manifestly, this process was established to avoid the heavy politicizing which characterized the district in previous years.

Model 4—The Long-Range Planning Structure as a Synergistic Plan

Model 1, the centralized curriculum generating structure used in DeKalb, IL, Model 2, the decentralized, building-based approach used in Hinsdale, IL, and Model 3, which was used in Long Beach, NY, may be used for general planning and implementing purposes such as long-range planning structures and processes. Often called strategic planning approaches or school improvement plans, their mission can be expanded beyond that of the area of curriculum to focus on one area or even the entire school or district. In short, the long range planning structure can be considered as a synergistic structure—a sort of Maxwell's Demon.

Model 5—The Development Laboratory

The development laboratory operates within a school district to assist staff in developing and implementing curriculum. The development laboratory's personnel consist of an instructional system analyst and clerical staff whose functions are to provide technical planning and development assistance for "problem identification, planning and (development of solutions)" (Newcomer & Schuck, 1967). Superintendent Newcomer and Schuck note that personnel spend their time on four major functions:

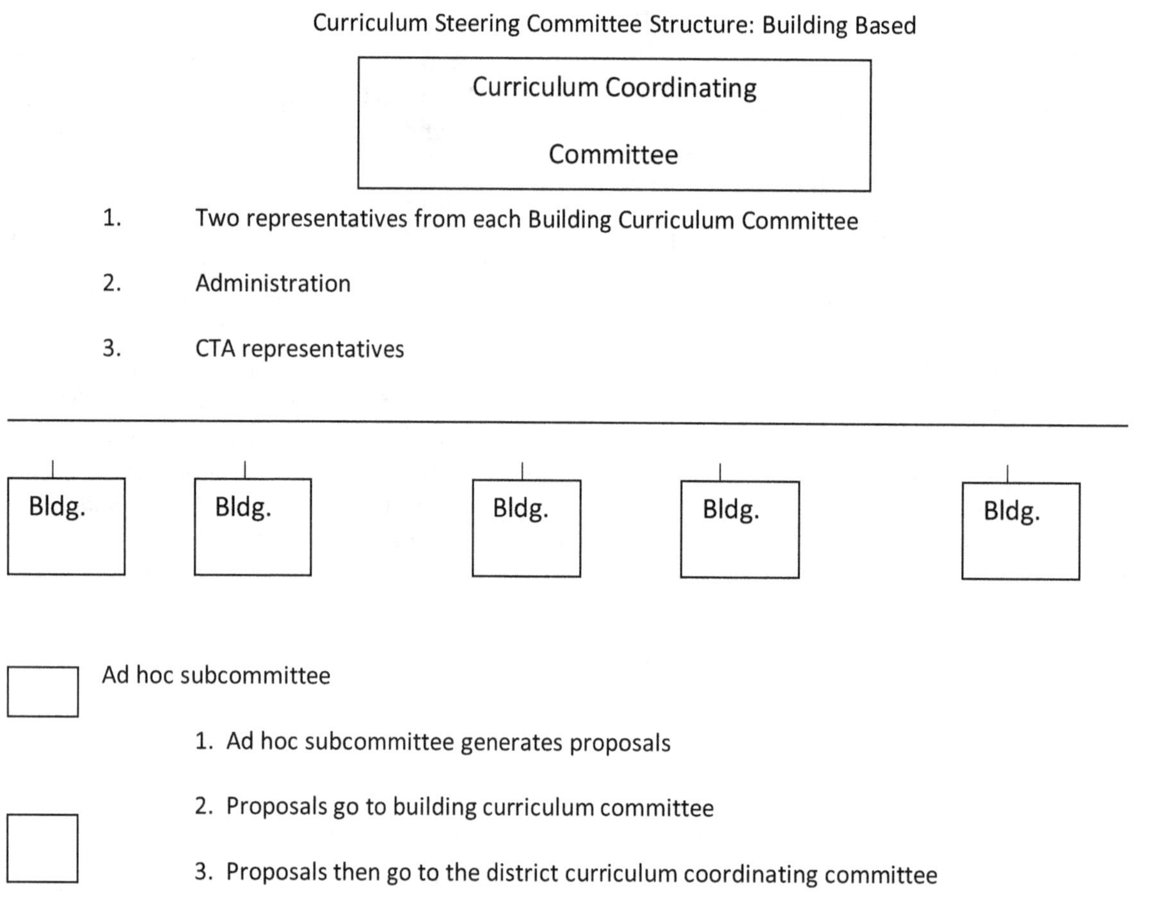

The District Curriculum Coordinating Committee

2 representatives from each building curriculum committee

2 administration

classroom teachers association representatives

Bldg A   Bldg B   Bldg C   Bldg D   Bldg E

The process:

1. An ad hoc subcommittee generates proposals
2. Proposals go to building curriculum committee
3. Proposals then go to the district coordinating committee following the process in the first model, the DeKalb model

Figure 31.3. Model 2: A decentralized building-based model.

Elementary	Secondary
Membership:	Membership:
5 teachers, 1 from each school	5 teachers
4 students, 2 senior high, 2 middle school	4 students, 2 senior high, 2 middle school
1 administrator	1 administrator
1 coordinator/supervisor	1 coordinator/supervisor
1 student services	1 student services

Figure 31.4. Model 3: The Long Beach Public Schools, Long Beach, NY model.

1. Anyone introduces an idea to the elementary or secondary committee, whichever is applicable
2. A *ad hoc* work group (including the originator) is formed by the committee to study the suggestion and develop a proposal
3. The proposal is submitted to the curriculum committee for further study, evaluation, recommendation, and priority rating to the central committee
4. Central administration delivers a final decision after considering the proposal, evaluation, and recommendation
5. When the verdict is "GO" and the idea is ready for implementation, appropriate administrators and faculty become involved

Figure 31.5. How an idea moves through this structure.

1. "maintaining the *status quo* of instructional programs that are desirable and accomplish what is required;
2. sensing (gaining) information to be used for evaluation and ultimate decision making concerning

   a. Programs and operations that are required;
   b. Areas where there are no current programs and operations;
   c. Developing solution(s) (and) plans to solve problems in areas where requirements are not being met, and
   d. Evaluating and revising plans to fit program and operations requirements ascertained during the sensing stage."

Noting that 99% of staff *cannot* perform all four functions, that staff "supermen" are very rare (as are synergists), this model specializes by utilizing those staff who are competent in program design and evaluation within the system and calling on additional outside expertise when necessary. Hence, "the plan to combine these resources is called the development laboratory." The system analyst functions as a planner and developer who can work with people who have a good idea. Budget and space are provided to preclude financial restraints from blocking ideas. This model was established in the Newport-Mesa Unified School District, Newport-Mesa, CA. As with the DeKalb, Hinsdale, and Long Beach curriculum structures, this meets Rand's (1977), Maslow's (1954) and Herzberg's (1966) criteria.

SUMMARY, CONCLUSIONS, AND IMPLICATIONS

The purpose of this chapter was to present solutions to the devastating and virtually inevitable onset of entropy that destroys the viability and vitality of all organizations in a surprisingly short time. First, we discussed the tri-partite theory of organizational change and succession which points to these inevitable three phases in their careers that all organizations tend to careen through uncontrollably. we cited first the person-oriented phase with its charismatic leader, and provided examples. We noted that the next phase was that of plan-orientation in which a plan is developed to implement some of the plans of the departed charismatic leader, with a planner in the leadership role. Examples also were cited. This is followed by the organization slowly losing its viability and essentially becoming backward-looking, essentially position-oriented, led by a bureaucrat, and remaining unproductively senescent for long periods of time. Unfortunate examples were mentioned. We then cited the possibility of the organization finding a synergist, a rare combination of both a charismatic and a planner both to lead and to plan, with notable representatives noted.

We then pointed out that entropy is an equal disaster to effectiveness and viability in the physical universe, in that all physical systems inevitably decay, run out of energy. We noted that nineteenth century physicist James Clark Maxwell created a whimsical approach to break Newton's second law by having a nano-demon open and close a gate between two tanks of gas so that he allows the hot gas molecules to pass through into one tank and the cold molecules into the other tank. Maxwell's Demon, then, is able to break the second law of thermodynamics.

We then proposed using an organizational Maxwell Demon to counter the virtually inevitable decay that organizations suffer by stabilizing it in the tri-partite theory's second phase—planning. We proposed establishing a curriculum structure as a Maxwell's Demon to stabilize the school or district and delineated three such structures, plus a take-off of a long range planning structure as the fourth suggestion, and a development laboratory as a fifth structure.

Well thought out curriculum-producing processes and structures and/or a development laboratory can produce highly effective programs and a quality system *if* strongly supported by the top of the organization attitudinally and with staff and resources. Through it, *change can be made routine*, instead of exceptional. The structure can function as a synergy by harnessing the organization, its resources, and its staffs', students', and community's resources into a productive combination. It creates a professional process to introduce expectations into the organization's culture that curriculum change, professionally produced, is not only supported, but is also one of the highest priorities of the district. Such an expectation and a structure can result in producing professional and personal satisfaction simultaneously. Commitment and loyalty to the process can generate not only high degrees of productivity, but also high levels of personal and professional satisfaction leading to high commitment and motivation. The structures establish new reward systems relatively free of influence and capable of being professionally productive. For example, for Maslow, these would be on social esteem and self-actualization levels.

The basis of program development rests on the quality of people chosen and trust that the process is legitimate and strongly supported by top echelons. Otherwise, people will go through the motions, little will happen, and eventually, they will opt out. Several fundamental questions remain: How long can an organization be stabilized in the planning phase? If not stabilized, it will careen out of control and endure position-orientation for much of its career. The author obviously believes that we should and can take action to bring our organizations under our control and not be enslaved by a nonproductive, bureaucratic dominating system. Last, do these structures operate as a buffer between faculty and administrators, permitting both parties to utilize a vehicle to improve their capabilities to cooperate, to function, and to communicate more effectively?

While other approaches (such as personal charisma) have been employed to take control and bring productivity into our organizations, making them viable for short periods, the author found that a curriculum structure uses such a structure and process rather than the more evanescent personal power and influence to accomplish those ends to harness people's creativity and to generate professionally and personally rewarding experiences and processes. Such a structure and process provide opportunity for organizations to stimulate creativity and satisfaction while simultaneously improving their programs, and to foster keeping organizations in their productive planning phases.

REFERENCES

Allison, D. (1971). *Introduction* In J. A. Morton (Ed.), *Organizing for innovation.* New York, NY: McGraw-Hill.

Herzberg, F. (1966). *Work and the nature of man.* New York, NY: World.

Maslow, A. H. (1954). *Motivation and personality.* New York, NY: Harper & Row.

Morton, J. A. (1971). *Organizing for innovation.* New York, NY: McGraw-Hill.

Newcomer, L. B., & Schuck, L. E. (1967). *Development laboratory—A staff utilization plan to make better use of existing resources.* Newport-Mesa, CA: Newport-Mesa Unified District.

Rand, T. (1977, Sept.). Diagnosing the valued reward orientations of employees. *Personnel Journal,* 451-54, 464.

Shapiro, A. (2009). *Making large schools work.* Lanham, MD: Rowman & Littlefield.

Shapiro, A. S., Benjamin, W. F., & Hunt, J. J. (1995). *Curriculum and schooling: A practitioner's guide.* Palm Springs, CA: ETC.

Wilson, L. C., Byar, T. M., Shapiro, A. S., & Schell, S. H. (1969). *Sociology of supervision.* Boston, MA. Allyn & Bacon.

Author Contact Information: Arthur Shapiro, PhD, College of Education University of South Florida Tampa, FL. 33620. Preferred mailing address: 1301 Trimaran Place, Trinity, FL 34655. Phone 727-807-7599. Fax: 813-905-9980. E-mail: ashapiro2@tampabay.rr.com

Section 5: Literacy and Language Acquisition Theory

INTRODUCTION

SECTION EDITOR
Fuhui Tong
Texas A&M University

This section, as the title suggests, covers a comprehensive, consolidated collection of the most influential and most frequently quoted and consulted theories in language and literacy acquisition. It aims to provide an easy-to-use and understandable reference tool as researchers and practitioners seek theories to guide their research and practice, and as they develop theoretical frameworks. A brief introduction of this section follows.

Chen and Wang, in Chapter 32 on cross language transfer in bilingual/biliteracy development, review the competing theories upon which the definition of transfer is drawn, including Cummins' Developmental Interdependence Hypothesis, which predicts that transfer occurs when a learner reaches a certain level of L1 competence; and the contrastive analysis hypothesis, which argues that transfer occurs when there are structural similarities or differences between L1 and L2. The authors then provide empirical evidence of cross language transfer in phonology, morphology, and orthography. In conclusion the chapter recognizes the limitations of the theories and research in the literature and discusses the implication of cross language transfer in bilingual education.

In Chapter 33, Baker conducts a comprehensive review of theories that guide, as well as are refined by, researches in bilingualism and bilingual children's school achievement. He attempts to address two overlapping language issues: (a) do children with two languages have disadvantages or advantages in thinking and in school achievement due to their bilingualism? and (b), why do some bilingual children fail in school, for example when they move from a home language that is different from the school? The theories covered in this chapter follow a progressive order including common underlying proficiency; threshold theory; the developmental interdependence hypothesis; basic interpersonal communication skills (BICS)/ cognitive and academic language proficiency (CALP), and the refinement of BICS/CALP theory, from a simplistic and minimalistic sense to a more advanced and multidimensional representation that encapsulates research findings.

Davis, Ovando, and Minami (Chapter 34) explore the development of theoretical paradigm for understanding language and literacy acquisition from three eras namely, modernity (when language learning was viewed as stimulus-response connection or innate abilities), modernism (when sociocognitive theory prevailed, suggesting that language structures emerge as a result of social interaction), and postmodernism (when theorization shifted to the investigation of multimodality in terms of linguistic and cultural diversity). The last section of this chapter grounds language and literacy theories within the sociopolitical contexts in which educational policies and practices are formed.

Chapter 35 presents an original view of *academic language* as socially constructed by particular users in particular times and contexts. Petrovic starts his argument by first highlighting the reductive consequences of Cummins' work and further extended this discourse from non-English languages to varieties of English language, more specifically, Ebonics. He situates his discussion within the Foucauldian and Saussurean framework. The chapter concludes with recommendations for further development of a theory that can account for both the poststructural and structural aspects of language.

Drawing from recent research in cognition and literacy learning, Jensen and Garcia in Chapter 35 argue for a more robust, policy-oriented, and pragmatic sociocultural theory to accommodate the educational needs of an increasing number of linguistically and culturally diverse students. Advocating for a convergence of

The Handbook of Educational Theories, pp. 367–368

anthropological and psychological approaches in student literacy learning for educational policymakers and practitioners, Jensen and Garcia offer examples of literacy learning on such convergence based on three strands of research in human cognition: implicit learning, designs for formal learning, and informal learning.

With the same focus of literacy research, Spycher in Chapter 36 discusses meaning-based approaches to literacy education that derive from the sociolinguistic theory of systemic functional linguistics, also referred to as functional grammar or functional linguistics, which suggests that language can be deconstructed and constructed at word, sentence (or clause), and text levels. In meaning-based approaches, teachers can demonstrate to their students how to analyze linguistically challenging texts for better comprehension and independent writing. Case studies are introduced exemplifying how systemic functional linguistics theory has been applied to meaning-based models in a variety of public school settings in United States, Australia, and the United Kingdom.

Author Contact Information: Fuhui Tong, PhD, Assistant Professor, Department of Educational Psychology, College of Education and Human Development, Texas A&M University, 1071 Harrington Tower, College Station, TX 77843-4225. Phone: 979-845-7979. E-mail: fuhuitong@tamu.edu

CHAPTER 32

Cross-Language Transfer in Bilingual and Biliteracy Development

Candise Y. Lin and Min Wang
University of Maryland

It is estimated that 60 to 75% of the world's population speak two or more languages. In other words, there are more bilingual or multilingual individuals than monolinguals in the world (Tucker, 2003). In addition, the numbers of children who are being educated via a second language (L2) are much more than those who are educated exclusively via the first language (L1). As a result of this bilingualism approach to education, many children throughout the world are learning to speak and read in two different languages simultaneously. Therefore, it is important to identify and examine the factors that may influence bilingual and biliteracy development. Learning to read in two languages is fundamentally different from learning to read in exclusively one language because learners may bring their existing linguistic knowledge in their L1 to the process of learning to read in their L2 (Koda, 2008). In addition, knowledge acquired through learning to read in the L2 may also facilitate literacy development in the L1. The transfer of knowledge from one language to the other during the learning process is called cross-language transfer. The current chapter will examine the theories of cross-language transfer in biliteracy development. Furthermore, whether cross-language transfer occurs and what is being transferred are determined by many linguistic factors such as proficiency in L1 and L2, print input and exposure in L2, typological similarities and differences between the two languages, and metalinguistic awareness of the learner. The current chapter will focus on the transfer of awareness in three major constituent processes in learning to read: phonology, morphology, and orthography .

The chapter opens with the definition of the term *transfer* and discussion of the competing theories. Then empirical evidence of cross-language transfer in phonology, morphology, and orthography is presented and examined in terms of support or invalidation of the theories. The instruments used in the empirical studies to assess each constituent process are analyzed. Finally, the chapter recognizes the limitations of the theories and research in the literature and discusses the implication of cross-language transfer in bilingual education.

Definitions and Theories of Cross-Language Transfer

Definitions of Transfer

Despite the large amount of research conducted on the topic of cross-language transfer, there is still no consensus among researchers for a definition of transfer. Overall, there are two camps of views on how to define transfer. In one camp, researchers viewed transfer as a reliance on L1 knowledge when L2 is not sufficiently developed (Gass & Selinker, 1983; Krashen, 1983). In addition, transfer is influenced by the structural similarities and differences between L1 and L2 (Oldin, 1989). There are three assumptions underlying these views (Koda, 2007, 2008). First, linguistic knowledge is transferred as a set of rules. Second, learners fall back on L1 knowledge because of the lack of understanding of L2 rules. Third, transfer ceases to occur when learner acquires high proficiency in L2 because reliance on L1

The Handbook of Educational Theories, pp. 369–383

rules is no longer necessary. Essentially, transfer is narrowly defined as a set of rules governed by language typology in which structural similarity may entail positive transfer while difference may result in negative transfer. In addition, transfer only occurs in the direction from L1 to L2 and it stops as soon as the learner develops a sufficient understanding of the rules in L2.

In contrast, the second camp endorsed a broader definition of transfer and considered transfer as a continuously evolving process. Researchers in this camp defined transfer as the ability to use prior learning experience as a source of knowledge and skills when learning to speak and read in a new language (Genesee, Geva, Dressler, & Kamil, 2006; Riches & Genesee, 2006). An important distinction between this perspective and the previous viewpoint is that transfer does not cease to occur at any point of L2 development. Instead, transfer is a dynamic process that matures as the knowledge and skills for language learning accumulate and become more refined. Thus, transfer is no longer constrained by typological differences. Learners can take advantage of the general learning mechanisms they acquired from one language and apply to literacy acquisition in the other language.

THEORIES OF TRANSFER

In addition to the controversy surrounding the definitions of transfer, there are also a number of competing theories relevant to the concept of cross-language transfer. One of these theories is the competition model which is based on the views of functionalism and connectionism (Bates & MacWhinney, 1989, MacWhinney, 1987). The functionalists view language as a set of mappings between forms and functions (Bates & MacWhinney, 1981; MacWhinney, 1987). For example, in the word *cats*, its phonological form (e.g., /kæt/) and syntactic form (e.g., the plural suffix *-s*) serves the communicative function of expressing the meaning of more than one domesticated feline. On the other hand, the Connectionists view the language learning mechanisms as a network of interconnected units (Rumelhart & McClelland, 1986). The units have activation level and transmit signals to one another through the weighted connections. Learning takes place when the weight of the connections and the activation threshold are adjusted. Strengthened connections and lower activation level would result in more efficient and less error-prone output.

Built upon the premises of functionalism and connectionism, the competition model postulates language learning as internalizing the connections between forms and functions (MacWhinney, 1992; MacWhinney & Bates, 1989). In language production, forms compete to express the speakers' underlying intentions or meanings; in comprehension, functions compete to be interpreted by the reader based on the surface forms (MacWhinney, 2005), hence the name, the Competition Model. For example, the association of *cat* and /kæt/ involves the connection between one unit to another. The connection becomes stronger over repeated practice and a speaker intended to express the concept *cat* would always produce its phonological form /kæt/. In terms of cross-language transfer, the Competition Model assumes that all language processing takes place in a common, interactive networks of cognitive structures and predicts that all aspects of L1 that can possibly be transferred to L2 will transfer (MacWhinney, 1997, 2005). In other words, all the internalized form-function mappings from L1, whether they facilitate or interfere with L2 learning, will be massively transferred to L2. For example, at the beginning of L2 acquisition, learners tend to transfer L1 articulatory patterns to L2 (Flege & Davidian, 1984). Despite the benefits of being able to communicate in L2, learners will have long-term difficulties in correcting pronunciation errors. On the other hand, massive transfer will also result in facilitation in L2 learning when the conceptual and linguistic worlds of the two languages are similar (MacWhinney, 2005). For example, in both English and Spanish, the word *tomato* refers to the same meaning, a red and round vegetable. Thus, for a native-English speaker learning Spanish as a L2, lexical transfer will occur smoothly without producing errors.

However, transfer will not occur if mapping skills in L1 have not been well-established. In fact, one of the factors that determine the occurrence of transfer is L1 proficiency. According to Cummins' (1979) developmental interdependence hypothesis, the level of L2 competence which a bilingual child attains is partially a function of the level of competence the child has developed in L1. In other words, transfer may not occur if the child has not reached a certain level of L1 proficiency when mapping skills have been internalized and automaticized (Koda, 2007). Previous research has shown that transfer of phonemic awareness (e.g., the ability to recognize and manipulate the smallest unit of sounds) did not occur in children with below-average L1 skills (Atwill, Blanchard, Gorin, & Burstein, 2007). Thus, the existing theories in the literature (e.g., the competition model and the interdependence hypothesis) appear to suggest that during L1 learning, a bilingual child internalizes the mapping between forms and functions; when the mapping skills becomes automatic and L1 competence has been reached, the child will be able to transfer these skills to L2 learning. Reading entails mapping graphic symbols onto the speech sounds they represent (Perfetti, 2003) and interpreting the meanings of words. Therefore, the mapping skills of grapheme to phoneme and morpheme are critical for literacy development in every language. The connectionist theory predicts that the transfer of phonological, morphological, and orthographic awareness, which are linguistic knowledge acquired through prior L1 literacy experience, will transfer to the L2 reading acquisition process. Many studies have observed effects of cross-language transfer in phonology, morphology, and orthography in children learning to read two typologically distant languages (e.g., Chinese and English: Cheung, Chan, & Chong, 2007; Wang, Yang, & Cheng, 2009; Korean and English: Kim, 2009) and in children learning to read two typologically similar languages (e.g., Spanish and English: Lindsey, Manis, & Bailey, 2003; Ramirez, Chen, Geva, & Kiefer, 2010; Sun-Alperin & Wang, 2010; see Durgunoglu, 2000; Durgunoglu & Oney, 2000, for reviews).

In addition to the empirical evidence for the theory of mapping skills transfer, there are also research findings supporting the transfer theory based on language typology (e.g., Wade-Woolley & Geva, 2000; Wang & Geva, 2003; Wang, Yang, et al., 2009). The contrastive analysis hypothesis (Lado, 1964) involves identifying the structural similarities and differences between the learners' L1 and L2. This theory predicts that, when learners encounter structures in the L2 that differ from or are unfamiliar to them in the L1, interference will occur and learners will make errors in the L2 (Genesee et al., 2006). On the other hand, transfer from the L1 can facilitate literacy development in the L2 when the two languages share similar features such as phonological forms or cognate vocabulary. Facilitation resulting from typological similarity is referred to as positive transfer while interference due to typological difference is called negative transfer (Gass & Selinker, 1983). For example, Wang, Yang, et al. (2009) have found positive transfer of onset awareness in Chinese-English bilingual children's literacy development. Onset awareness in Chinese contributes to English word reading because onset is a shared phonological unit in both languages. Similarly, negative transfer occurs in English-Hebrew bilingual children's discrimination of phonemic contrasts /s/ and /ts/. Children made more errors when /ts/ occurred in the syllable onset position because /ts/ is an illegal candidate for English onsets but it is legal in Hebrew onsets. The empirical evidence supported the contrastive analysis hypothesis by demonstrating that whether facilitation or interference occurs in cross-language transfer is determined by the structural similarity or difference between L1 and L2.

To recapitulate, the developmental interdependence hypothesis together with the functionalist and connectionist theories, and the competition model (hereby refer to as the interdependence hypothesis) predicts that transfer occurs when mapping skills becomes automatic and a certain level of L1 competence has been reached. What is being transferred are the linguistic knowledge and learning abilities acquired through prior literacy experiences. In contrast, the contrastive analysis hypothesis predicts that transfer occurs when there are structural similarities or differences between L1 and L2. What transferred are the specific phonological units, morphological forms, spelling patterns, cognate vocabulary, and grammatical structures. In the following sections, empirical evidence supporting or invalidating both theories will be examined.

Phonological Transfer

Phonological awareness is defined as the ability to perceive and manipulate the sound units in spoken language (Goswami & Bryant, 1990). Previous research has shown that phonological awareness is an important predictor of literacy development in bilingual children learning to read various combinations of L1-L2 (e.g., Chinese-English: Wang, Yang, et al. 2009; Korean-English: Cho & McBride-Chang, 2005; Spanish-English: Manis, Lindsey, & Bailey, 2004; Turkish-Dutch: Verhoeven, 1994; Oriya-English: Mishra & Stainthorp, 2007). The emergence of phonological awareness follows a continuum in which sensitivity to large phonological units develops first, following by smaller phonological units (Ziegler & Goswami, 2005). According to the linguistic structure hypothesis, (e.g., Bruck, Treiman, & Caravolas, 1995; Treiman, 1995; Treiman, Mullennix, Bijeljac-Babic, & Richmond-Welty, 1995), the syllable is the largest phonological unit and at the highest of the hierarchical structure. At the intermediate level is the onset and rime while at the bottom is phoneme, which is the smallest unit of sound. In biliteracy development, effects of cross-language transfer can be observed at each of these levels of phonological units if the units are shared across L1 and L2.

Transfer of Syllable Awareness

Transfer of syllable awareness has been identified in Chinese-English biliteracy development (Chow, McBride-Chang, & Burgess, 2005; McBride-Chang et al., 2008). In a longitudinal study (McBride-Chang et al., 2008), native Cantonese-speaking children who are learning to read in English were tested twice within 1 year. Analyses showed that Chinese syllable awareness assessed at Time 1 uniquely predicted English word reading after controlling for age, oral vocabulary, nonverbal IQ, short term memory, and Chinese character recognition at Time 1. The positive transfer of syllable awareness from Chinese L1 to English L2 supports the contrastive analysis hypothesis. Chinese has a morphosyllabic orthography in which each character maps onto a morpheme, which is also a syllable. In other words, Chinese represents sounds at the largest phonological unit. On the other hand, English follows the alphabetic principal in which each grapheme maps onto a phoneme. However, since the grapheme-phoneme correspondence is inconsistent in English in which one grapheme can be pronounced in different ways (e.g., "a" in "apple," "woman," "ladle," and "father") or vice versa, children may need to rely on larger phonological units such as rime and syllable in the early stages of reading acquisition (Ziegler & Goswami, 2005). The bilingual children in McBride-Chang and colleague's (2008) were 4.5 years of age at the time of testing. The transfer of syllable awareness observed in these beginning readers demonstrated that syllable awareness is important for early literacy development and the syllable is a shared phonological unit between Chinese L1 and English L2.

However, Cho and McBride-Chang (2005) did not find transfer effects at the syllable level in Korean-English bilingual children. Using a similar longitudinal design, the researchers administered measurements of syllable, onset, and phonemic awareness and word reading in both Korean and English to their 8-year-old participants twice within 1 year. After controlling for age, short term memory, oral vocabulary, and Korean reading at Time, the strongest predictor for Korean reading at Time 2 is syllable awareness whereas the strongest predictor for English reading at Time 2 is phonemic awareness. In other words, there was no cross-language transfer of syllable awareness. These results were inconsistent with McBride-Chang et al. (2008). The writing system of Korean, Hangul, is alphabetic in which each grapheme maps onto a phoneme. However, graphemes are organized into a square block to form a syllable. Like Chinese, each syllable represents both a phonological unit and a morpheme. Due to this unique characteristic of the Hangul, the Korean writing system is considered an alphasylalbary. Therefore, the syllable should be shared phonological unit between L1 Korean and L2 English. However, the absence of syllable transfer may be explained by the age of the Korean children. The Chinese children in McBride-Chang et al. (2008) were 4.5-year-old beginning readers whereas the 8-year-old Korean children in Cho and McBride-Chang (2005) had been receiving literacy instruction for a longer time. The older children may have developed phonemic awareness as a result of being taught how to read and write in English, thus, they no longer need to rely on the larger phonological unit. The results from these two studies implied that similarities in phonological representations may encourage positive transfer whereas the lack of such similarity results in absence of cross-language interaction.

Transfer of Onset and Rime Awareness

Following syllable awareness, onset and rime awareness are at the intermediate level of the hierarchical structure (Treiman, 1995). In Chinese-English biliteracy acquisition, transfer has been observed for both onset (Wang, Yang, et al., 2009) and rime awareness (Gottardo, Siegel, Yan, & Wade-Woolley, 2001). Wang, Yang, et al. (2009) assessed onset awareness using an oddity task in which children were presented with three syllables and they had to determine which one syllable begins with a different onset than the other two. The researchers found that Chinese onset awareness accounted a significant amount of unique variance in both English real word and pseudoword reading after controlling for age, oral vocabulary, phonological and morphological awareness in English. Since onset is a shared phonological unit between Chinese English, these results supported the contrastive analysis hypothesis. However, the researchers (Wang, Yang, et al., 2009) did not find a significant correlation between Chinese rime awareness and English reading measures. This is probably due to the simplicity of the Chinese syllable structure. With only two ending consonants "n" and "ng." most Chinese syllables are opened syllables. Therefore, onset is a more prominent phonological unit than rime, which is consists of the vowel and the final consonant. On the other hand, English allows a large number of consonant and consonant clusters at the syllable-final position. Due to the inconsistent grapheme-phoneme correspondence in English orthography, the use of small-unit reading strategy is not as efficient as a larger unit strategy because the correspondence is more consistent at the rime level (Treiman et al., 1995). For example, the vowel "a" is usually pronounced as /æ/ when followed by the final consonant "t" as in "cat," "pat," and "mat." Therefore, rime is a prominent phonological unit in English but not in Chinese, explaining the absence of rime awareness transfer in Wang, Yang, et al. (2009).

However, Gottardo et al. (2001) have found that rime awareness in Chinese L1, using a similar oddity task, was a significant predictor for English real word and pseudoword reading after controlling for English phonemic awareness. The researchers reasoned that what was being transferred was an underlying process that is not specific to the bilingual children's L1 phonology but that is related to the children's ability to reflect on all levels of phonological information regardless of structural differences. This argument of transfer of general linguistic knowledge rather than rules governing specific structures resonated with the interdependence hypothesis. Since Gottardo et al. (2001) did not assess onset awareness in their study, it is difficult to compare the results from this study to that from Wang, Yang, et al. (2009). If a measurement of onset awareness is included, it is possible that onset awareness may emerge as a stronger predictor of English reading than rime awareness in support of the contrastive analysis hypothesis.

Transfer of Phonemic Awareness

In the previous sections of syllable and onset-rime awareness, only studies examining transfer between an alphabetic (e.g., English) and a nonalphabetic writing system were discussed because Chinese and Korean uses larger unit of phonological representation. Therefore, transfer of phonemic awareness may only be observed between two alphabetic languages such as Spanish and English (e.g., Sun-Alperin & Wang, 2010), Turkish and Dutch (e.g., Verhoeven, 1994), or French and English (e.g., Comeau, Grandmaison, & Lacroix, 1999) et cetera. Compared to the English orthography, the Spanish orthography is highly consistent. There is almost a one-to-one grapheme-phoneme correspondence as the 29 graphemes in Spanish map onto approximately 25 phonemes (Fashola, Drum, Mayer, & Kang, 1996). Therefore, children can reliably use the small-unit decoding strategy to read Spanish. However, since both English and Spanish use the alphabetic writing system, phoneme is the unit of phonological representation in both languages. The contrastive analysis hypothesis would predict transfer of phonemic awareness in Spanish-English biliteracy acquisition. Indeed, a bidirectional transfer effect was observed in Sun-Alperin & Wang (2010). Phonemic awareness was measured by phoneme deletion in which children were asked to remove a sound from a word and pronounce the new word (e.g., say "mab" without "b"). Analyses showed that Spanish phonemic awareness accounted for unique variance in both English real word and pseudo-word reading after taken into consideration age, oral vocabulary, English phonemic awareness, and English orthographic awareness. Similarly, English phonemic awareness is a significant predictor of Spanish reading after controlling for the Spanish measures. These results supported and extended the contrastive analysis hypothesis by showing that cross-language transfer can occur from L1 to L2 as well as from L2 to L1.

In contrast to the positive transfer of phonemic awareness found in Spanish-English bilingual children (Sun-Alperin & Wang, 2010), Wade-Woolley and Geva (2000) reported negative transfer in English-Hebrew bilingual children with Hebrew as their L2. In the phoneme identification task, children listed to Hebrew pseudo-words and were asked to select the item they had just heard from a printed array of three choices, comprising the target, the phonological distracter and a visual distracter. Each pseudo-word contained one phoneme of the minimal pair /ts/ and /s/. For each item (e.g., /lartsad/), the phonological distracter contained the competing member of the minimal pair in the same location (e.g., /larsad/) while the visual distracter contained a visually similar grapheme in the same location. Both phonemes /s/ and /ts/ appear in English rimes (e.g., *house*, *cats*), but only /s/ is a legal candidate for English onsets. However, there is no such positional constraint in Hebrew. Results of Hebrew L2 phoneme identification task showed that English-Hebrew bilingual children made more errors when /s/ appeared in the onset position while they found it easier when both /ts/ and /s/ occurred in the rime position. There results supported the contrastive analysis hypothesis because positive transfer occurred when the phonotactic constraints are similar in both L1 and L2 and negative transfer occurred when the constraints are different.

Transfer of Phonological Awareness

Previous research focusing on the awareness of specific phonological units such as syllable, onset-rime, and phoneme have shown that cross-language transfer occurs when L1 and L2 share the same units of phonological representations and these results supported the contrastive analysis hypothesis. On the other hand, studies that have examined phonological awareness as a distinct set of skills have provided evidence for the interdependence hypothesis. A consistent result reported in these studies was that L1 phonological awareness is a unique predictor of L2 reading and transfer occurs between two alphabetic writing systems (Spanish-English: Durgunoglu, Nagy, & Hancin-Bhatt, 1993; French-English: Comeau et al., 1999), between an alphabetic system and an alphasyllabary (Korean-English: Kim, 2009; Wang, Park, & Lee, 2006), as well as between an alphabetic and a logographic writing systems (Chinese-English: Tong & McBride-Chang, 2010)

Unlike previous studies in which L2 was a language spoken by the majority of the population in the country (e.g., Durgunoglu et al., 1993; Lindsey et al., 2003; Wang, Park, et al. 2006; Wang, Ko, et al., 2009; Wang, Yang, et al., 2009), Saiegh-Haddad and Geva's (2008) study examined cross-language transfer in a group of native-English speaking children attending an English-Arabic bilingual school in Canada where L2 is the minority language. The bilingual children had relatively little exposure to Arabic outside of school and parents all reported to speak English at home. Phonological awareness was measured by an elision test which required children to delete phonological units of varying size (e.g., consonant vowel consonant, syllables, consonant clusters, and phonemes) embedded in monosyllabic, disyllabic, and trisyllabic words. Despite limited exposure, phonological awareness in English was a significant predictor for Arabic real word and pseudo-word reading and phonological awareness in Arabic was also a significant predictor for English reading. These results suggested that children can transfer the skills of identifying and manipulating phonological units at varying sizes from L1 to L2 as well as from L2 to L1. These findings also supported the interdependence hypothesis because children transferred their phonological sensitivity acquired through literacy experience with English to assist in their literacy acquisition in Arabic. Since interdependence hypothesis viewed transfer as a dynamic process, as children's proficiency in Arabic develops, the higher level of L2 competence may enable the transfer of phonological skills back to L1.

Instruments of Phonological Awareness

The measurements of phonological awareness vary by size of the phonological units. For example, researchers have used the deletion task to assess syllable awareness (Cho & McBride-Chang, 2005; McBride-Chang et al., 2008). In the syllable deletion task, children were asked to delete a syllable from words or short phrases. An example of this task is saying the phrase *one flower vase* without saying *flower* (i.e., *one vase*). To measure onset-rime awareness, researchers have often used the oddity task (Gottardo et al., 2001; Wang, Yang, et al., 2009). Typically, children were presented with three syllables, and they had to select one syllable that did not share the same onset or the same rime with the other two. For example, in the set *bag, top,* and *boy, top* is the correct answer in an onset oddity task. To assess phonemic awareness, both phoneme deletion (Sun-Alperin & Wang, 2010) and phoneme discrimination (Verhoeven, 1994) have been used. In phoneme deletion, children were asked to delete a sound from a word and pronounce the new word (e.g., say *stop* without /t/ and the correct answer is *sop*). The phoneme discrimination task required children to distinguish between minimal pairs of words that differ in only one phoneme. Children would make same-different judgments to spoken word pairs such as *bag-tag* or *sheep-ship*.

Most of the instruments described previously were designed and developed by the researchers. However, researchers have also used standardized instruments to assess phonological awareness. For example, Saiegh-Haddad and Geva (2008) used the Auditory Analysis Test which was an elision test that required children to delete phonological units of varying sizes. Similarly, Kim (2009) used the blending, matching, and segmenting subtests of the Comprehensive Test of Phonological Processing to measure phonological awareness. In the blending task, children were asked to combine sounds together to make a new word (e.g., /s/, /i/, and /t/ make *sit*). In the matching task, children were presented with a target syllable and two candidates and they had to select one candidate that shared the same sound as the target (e.g., /hat/: /cat/ vs. /dad/). In the segmenting task, children were required to spell out the sounds in a word (e.g., *man:* /m/, /æ/, and /n/). Regardless of the instruments used, previous research has consistently observed cross-language transfer of phonological awareness between typologically distant or typologically similar languages in biliteracy development.

One limitation of the instruments is the lack of consistency in task format. For example, the oddity task is a perception task in which children were presented with three spoken syllables and asked to pick, rather than produce, the correct answer. In contrast, other tasks such as phoneme deletion and segmentation are production tasks in which children were required to say aloud the correct answer. Perception tasks tend to be easier than production tasks because in the former children only need to recognize the correct answer among the choices provided whereas in the latter children must generate the answer based on their knowledge. This difference in task difficulty between perception and production tasks may reduce comparability of the results across studies. One possible solution to this problem is to use an instrument of phonological awareness that involve both perception and production components. For example, administering both the phoneme deletion and phoneme discrimination tasks would overcome this limitation.

Morphological Transfer

Morphological awareness is defined as an individual's awareness of the morphemic structures of words and the ability to reflect on and manipulate those structures (Carlisle, 1995). A morpheme is the smallest unit in a language that can be associated with semantic and syntactic functions. Words can be divided into monomorphemic words (e.g., *berry*) and multimorphemic words (morphologically complex words) (e.g., *berries* and *blueberry*). Morphemes can be divided into free morphemes that can stand alone (e.g., *happy* in *happiness*) and bound morphemes that cannot stand alone (e.g., *-ing* in *eating*). There are three types of morphologically complex words. Derivational words are formed by adding a bound morpheme to a free morpheme to change the meaning of the free morpheme without reference to the specific grammatical role a word might play in a sentence (e.g., the noun *nation* becomes an adjective *national* by adding a suffix –al whereas the adjective *happy* remains an adjective *unhappy* after adding a prefix –un). Inflectional words are formed by adding a bound morpheme to a free morpheme to express the grammatical role of the word in a sentence (e.g., add the suffix *–s* to pluralize the noun *dog* or add the suffix *–ed* to change the tense of the verb *study*). Compound words are formed by combining two free morphemes (e.g., *bedroom* or *housekeeping*). Cross-language transfer of awareness to each morphological structure will be examined in the following sections.

Transfer of Awareness to Derivational Morphology

Cross-language transfer of awareness to derivational morphology has been observed between bilingual readers of two alphabetic systems (Spanish-English: Ramirez et al., 2010) and between an alphabetic system and an alphasyllabary (English-Hebrew: Saiegh-Haddad & Geva, 2008; Korean-English: Wang, Ko, & Choi, 2009). Wang, Ko, et al. (2009) examined transfer of derivational awareness in Korean-English biliteracy development. Similar to English, Korean derivational morphology is very productive. For example, the suffix 넓 (*wide*) can be added to an adjective or a verb to form a noun (e.g., 넓이 *width*). Similarly, in English the suffix –er is added to a verb to form a noun that denotes the agent performing the action (e.g., *teacher* is a person who teaches) and the suffix –ness is added to an adjective to form a noun (e.g., *happy – happiness*). The contrastive analysis hypothesis would predict cross-language transfer as a result of his typological similarity. Indeed, Wang, Ko, et al. (2009) found that awareness to Korean derivational morphology accounts for unique variance in English word reading after controlling for age, English oral vocabulary, English phonological and morphological awareness and Korean phonological awareness.

On the other hand, Wang, Cheng, and Chen (2006) did not find transfer of derivational awareness in Chinese-English bilingual children. The researchers reasoned that transfer is less likely to occur because derivation morphology is not a common word formation strategy in Chinese. For example, the fixed suffix –*er* signifies the agent for an action in English. However, a fixed suffix that denotes the agent performing an action is absent in Chinese; the noun for the verb 写作 (write) is 作家 (writer) and the noun for the verb 射击 (shoot) is 射手 (shooter). Their results concurrently supported the contrastive analysis hypothesis in which structural similarity resulted in positive transfer of derivational awareness in Korean-English biliteracy development whereas transfer did not occur due to the absence of shared derivational structures between Chinese and English.

Transfer of Awareness to Inflectional Morphology

Transfer of inflectional awareness has not been studied extensively in the literature; only one study of biliteracy development has included measurements of inflectional morphology. This is probably because, in English, inflectional morphemes are limited in number but high in frequency. In addition, inflectional morphology carries relatively transparent phonological changes (e.g., *eye-eyes*) whereas derivational morphology involves more complicated phonological changes (e.g., *nation-national*) (Kuo & Anderson, 2006). Therefore, inflectional morphology is less challenging for school-age children compared to derivational morphology. Children's ease with acquiring inflectional morphology may result in less individual variation in inflectional awareness, thus attracting less attention from researchers.

Deacon, Wade-Woolley, and Kirby (2007) examined transfer of inflectional awareness in a group of native-English speaking children enrolled in a French immersion program by using a 3-year longitudinal design. The researchers manipulated past and present tense of verbs to assess children's sensitivity to inflectional morphology. Children were presented with a pair of example sentences that reflected a tense change, such as "Chris bought a car" and "Chris buys a car" and they were asked to make the same kind change to another sentence, such as "Chris ate the noodles." Results showed that inflectional awareness in English measured in Grade 1 predicted French reading in Grades 1-3 after verbal and nonverbal IQ, phonological awareness and French inflectional awareness had been controlled. French inflectional awareness in Grade 1 also made unique contribution to English reading in Grades 2 and 3. These results can be explained by the typological similarity in tense marking between English and French. In English, past tense was indicated by adding the auxiliary *–ed* to a verb (e.g., the past tense of *look* is *looked*). Similarly, past tense modification in French involves adding two fixed auxiliaries, word initial *a* and word-final é as in *a* étudié (studied). Although these results are consistent with the contrastive analysis hypothesis, the fact that French inflectional awareness in Grade 1 did not predict English reading measured in any grades also provided evidence for the interdependence hypothesis. In order for transfer to occur, bilingual children must achieve a certain level of competence in L1. Although French was the participants' L2, transfer to English L1 occurred when their proficiency in French grew as they reached Grade 2.

Transfer of Awareness to Compound Morphology

Transfer of compound awareness has been consistently found in Chinese-English biliteracy development (Wang, Cheng, et al. 2006; Wang, Yang, 2009; Zhang et al., 2010). Unlike derivational morphology, Chinese is similar to English in terms of compound morphology. In both languages, compound is formed by combining two free morphemes (e.g., snow 雪 + ball 球 = snowball 雪球). Both Chinese and English allow a variety of lexical categories such as nouns, verbs, and adjectives to appear in compounds (Zhou & Marslen-Wilson, 2000). Here are examples for noun-noun compounds in English *wristwatch* and in Chinese

手表, and examples for adjective-noun compounds in English *blueprint* and in Chinese 蓝图. This typological similarity would result in transfer of compound awareness, according to the contrastive analysis hypothesis. The measurement for compound awareness in Wang, Cheng, et al. (2006) involved asking children to choose the better compound candidate to answer a given riddle. An example item is, "What is a better name for the flower that grows in a tree: a *tree flower* or a *flower tree*?" The researchers found that English compound morphology predicted unique variance in Chinese reading comprehension after controlling for age, vocabulary knowledge, and English phonemic awareness. However, the correlation between Chinese compound morphology and English compound morphology was not significant. In other words, English compound awareness did not contribute to learning to read in Chinese via transfer of awareness to similar compound structures, invalidating the contrastive analysis hypothesis. Wang, Cheng, et al. (2006) proposed that what transferred was a general form of metalinguistic awareness to morphemic structures. This explanation is in line with the interdependence hypothesis. The absence of transfer from the L1-L2 direction also supported this hypothesis. Although the bilingual children in this study learned Chinese as their L1, their language of dominance was in fact English. Their competence in L1 Chinese has not reached a certain level that enables transfer.

In contrast to results reported by Wang, Cheng, et al. (2006), Zhang and colleagues (2010) actually found transfer of compound awareness in Chinese-English bilingual children. In the training study conducted by Zhang et al. (2010), Chinese children learning English as a L2 were randomly assigned to the experimental group or the control group. The experimental group received a 45 minutes intervention on Chinese or English compound morphology, aiming to improve children's sensitivity to compound structure such as noun+noun, verb+noun, and noun+verb (e.g., *baseball, playground, role play,* respectively). The word structure analogy task was administered to both groups of children before and after the intervention. Children were presented with a pseudo-compound target followed by three choices. Their task was to circle the choice that was most similar to the target word (e.g., *handcar*: *handout*, *handbook*, and *handover*). Results showed that evidence of compound transfer in which the Chinese intervention group performed significantly better in the English analogy task than the control groups and the English intervention group performed better in the Chinese analogy task than the control group. In other words, children's knowledge about compound structure acquired through training in one language facilitated the development of compound awareness in another language. These results supported both the interdependence hypothesis and the contrastive analysis hypothesis because the general awareness toward compound structure acquired through L1 linguistic experience was transferred and the similarity of compound structures between Chinese and English resulted in the positive transfer.

INSTRUMENTS OF MORPHOLOGICAL AWARENESS

Many different instruments have been used to measure awareness to derivational morphology. For example, Wang et al. (Wang, Cheng, et al., 2006; Wang, Ko, et al., 2009) and Ramirez et al. (2010) used a sentence completion task in which children were asked to fill in the sentence "my uncle is a ____" based on a clue word such as *farmer*. On the other hand, Saiegh-Haddad and Geva (2008) used two tasks to assess awareness to derivational structures. In the morphological relatedness task, children were presented with pairs of words and asked to determine whether the pairs were morphologically related, such as *speak-speaker* or *but-butter* (e.g., phonologically related foils). In the morphological decomposition task, both derived words and foil words were presented to children and their task was to decide whether the word could be broken down into smaller units. On the other hand, Wang et al. (Wang, Cheng, et al., 2006; Wang, Yang, et al., 2009) used the compound structure task to measure compound awareness. Children's task was to choose the better two-morpheme compound as an answer to a riddle (e.g., which is a better name for a tree that grows flower: A tree flower? Or a flower tree?). The word structure analogy task was employed by Zhang and colleagues (2010) to assess compound awareness. Children were given a target compound and three candidate compounds and they had to select one that matches the structure of the target.

To assess awareness to inflectional morphology, Deacon et al. (2007) manipulated the tense of verbs in the sentence context. Children were presented with pairs of sentences such as "Amy tries to study" and "Amy tried to study" and they were asked to modify the verb in the same way in a new sentence "Amy listens to music." One limitation of this inflectional morphology task is that it only tested children's awareness to verb tenses. There are many other types of inflectional suffixes in English including third person singular present tense (e.g., *-s* in *looks*), plurals, (e.g., *-s* in *books*), comparative (e.g., *-er* in *stronger*), and superlative (e.g., *-est* in *strongest*). In other words, the task used by Deacon et al. (2007) was not a comprehensive assessment of inflectional awareness and children's performance on the task does not reflect their full knowledge on inflectional morphology. For future studies, measurements of inflectional awareness should include items from each type of inflectional suffix.

Orthographic Transfer

Orthographic awareness is defined as children's understanding of the conventions used in the writing system of their language (Trieman & Cassar, 1997). Writing systems can be classified into three types: alphabetic, syllabic, and logographic (Gelb, 1952). In an alphabetic system, each graphic symbol represents a phoneme while in the syllabary, each grapheme maps onto a syllable. In the logographic system, each character represents the meaning and sound of an entire morpheme. Script is defined as the graphic symbols of a writing system while orthography is the language-specific details in which graphic symbols are placed in word formation. For example, although both English and Russian use the alphabetic systems, the former employs the Roman script while the latter uses the Cyrillic. In addition, both English and Spanish are alphabetic and use the roman script. However, according to the Orthographic Depth Hypothesis, the Spanish orthography is more transparent in which the grapheme-phoneme correspondence is relatively consistent whereas English has a deep orthography in which one grapheme corresponds to multiple sounds and one phoneme can be written in many different ways (Katz & Frost, 1992). Therefore, Spanish is typologically closer to English than Russian while Chinese (e.g., a logographic writing system) is more distant to English than Russian.

Transfer between alphabetic writing systems

Researchers have examined orthographic transfer between two typologically similar alphabetic writing systems (e.g., Spanish and English: Sun-Alperin & Wang, 2008, 2010) and between two typologically distant alphabetic writing systems (e.g., English and Hebrew: Wade-Woolley & Geva, 2000). In Sun-Alperin and Wang's (2010) study, orthographic awareness in both Spanish and English was assessed by a homophone choice task. Children were presented with a pair of words, one real word and one pseudohomophone word (e.g., *brain* and *brane*) and children determined which word was spelled correctly. Results showed that orthographic awareness in Spanish contributed to English real and pseudoword reading after controlling for age, oral vocabulary, English and Spanish phonological awareness and English orthographic awareness. The researchers attributed the cross-language transfer to the similarity between the two orthographies. Both Spanish and English follow the alphabetic principal and use the Roman script with a linear writing system. Several of the shared graphemes in both languages map onto the same phonemes, such as /s/ in *sit* and *seis* ("six" in Spanish) or /m/ in *man* and *mano* ("hand" in Spanish). These results were consistent with the contrastive analysis hypothesis which predicts that typologically similar structure results in positive transfer in Spanish-English bilingual reading development.

Despite this positive transfer in reading, Sun-Alperin-Wang (2008) observed negative transfer in Spanish-English bilingual children's spelling. English real word and pseudoword spelling tests were administered to Spanish immigrant children learning English as a L2 and monolingual English children. Only spelling errors of vowel sounds were coded because spelling English vowels is especially difficult. In English, each vowel phoneme can be spelled in multiple different ways (e.g., consider the vowel /i/ in *seed, meat, believe, ceiling,* and *impede*). However, in Spanish the vowel /i/ can only be spelled as "i." Due to this difference in the consistency of phoneme-grapheme correspondence, the contrastive analysis hypothesis would predict interference in bilingual children's spelling development. Indeed, results showed that the Spanish-speaking children made significantly more spelling errors that conform to the Spanish orthography than their English-speaking counterparts. For example, bilingual children spelled *meat* as *mit*, which is an incorrect in English but phonologically legitimate in Spanish.

Transfer Between Alphabetic and Syllabic Writing Systems

Orthographic transfer between an alphabetic system and a syllabary has not been studied extensively in the literature. To the best of the current authors' knowledge, Wang, Park, and Lee's (2006) study of Korean-English bilingual children was the only published study on this topic. The nature of the Korean writing system, Hangul, is alphabetic in which each grapheme maps onto a phoneme. However, the composition of letters is shaped into a square like syllable block. Each syllable block is separated by a clear boundary (e.g., 한국어). Thus, an accurate name for Hangul is alphasyllabary. Compared to Spanish, Korean is typologically more distant from English. Orthographic awareness was measured by the orthographic choice task which assessed children's sensitivity to the legality of vowel and consonant positions in Korean. Hangul is a nonlinear orthographic system. A horizontal vowel is always placed under the initial consonant (e.g., in 오) while a vertical vowel is always placed to the immediate right of the initial consonant (e.g., in 어). Since English uses a linear writing system and the Roman alphabets, there is little similarity between the English orthography and Korean Hangul. Therefore, the contrastive analysis hypothesis would predict no orthographic transfer. Indeed, Wang, Park, et al. (2006b) found that only English orthographic awareness was a significant predictor of English real word and pseudo-word reading after controlling for age, nonverbal IQ, and English phonological awareness. Korean orthographic awareness did not account for any additional unique variance. These results supported the contrastive analysis hypothesis. In addition, the interdependence hypothesis was invalidated because orthographic knowledge acquired through prior L1 literacy experience did not facilitate L2 reading development despite the fact that the bilingual children had decent competence in Korean.

Transfer Between Alphabetic and Logographic Writing Systems

Similar to the study with Korean-English bilingual children, researchers have also reported no effect of orthographic transfer in Chinese-English biliteracy development (Gottardo et al., 2001; Wang, Perfetti, & Liu, 2005; Wang, Ko, et al., 2009). Gottardo and colleagues (2001) used the orthographic legality task to assess orthographic awareness. Children were presented with pairs of pseudo-words and they had to determine which one of the two looked more like a real word. An example pair is *filv* and *filk* and the correct answer is *filk* because it had some orthographic neighbors (e.g., *milk*). The researchers found that orthographic awareness in Chinese did not significantly associate with English reading. Similarly, Wang et al. (2005; Wang, Perfetti, et al., 2009) reported that Chinese orthographic awareness did not contribute to real word and pseudo-word reading in English. Conversely, English orthographic awareness also did not predict Chinese character reading. These results all supported the contrastive analysis hypothesis which predicts that no transfer would occur due to typological differences between alphabetic and logographic writing systems.

However, Cheung et al. (2007) have found positive transfer of orthographic knowledge in reading by Chinese-English bilingual children. The researchers manipulated the three structural regularity underlying Chinese orthography to assess children's orthographic awareness. Over 90% of Chinese characters are compound characters (Li, 1993) and the majority of which follow the left-right or top-bottom composition rule. Compound characters consist of two or more radicals, which are meaningful components of characters. Radicals that provide clues to the character's pronunciation are called phonetic radicals while radicals that give clues to the meaning of the character are known as semantic radicals. In left-right structured compound characters, the semantic and phonetic radicals are placed on the left and right position, respectively. For example, the character 清 /qing/1 "clear" is composed of a semantic radical, 氵, which is not a character by itself and unpronounceable but denotes the meaning of "something related to water," and a phonetic radical 青 /qing/1 "green." In top-bottom structured compound characters, the semantic and phonetic radicals are placed on the top and bottom positions, respectively. Most of Chinese compound words are modifier compounds in which the second character provides broad categorical information about the word while the first character offers specific information for narrowing down the interpretation of the first. For example, 飞机 "airplane" is a machine (机) that flies (飞). In the novel object labeling task, children were presented with a picture of a novel object followed by four written nonwords, each containing two noncharacters. Children were asked to choose the nonword that was most likely to be the name of the object and read out loud the word they chose. Children's selection of the correct nonword reflected their ortho-semantic knowledge because they took advantage of the characteristics of the modifier compounds and the semantic radicals in compound characters to answer the question. On the other hand, children's ortho-phonological knowledge was indicated by their pronunciation of the phonetic radicals in each noncharacter.

Analyses showed that ortho-phonological knowledge was a significant predictor of English reading after controlling for age, nonverbal IQ, and short term memory (Cheng et al., 2007). Chinese ortho-phonological knowledge also accounted for unique variance in English reading comprehension. The absence of cross-language transfer for ortho-semantic knowledge in fact was consistent with the contrastive analysis hypothesis because there is no exact equivalent of semantic radicals in English. Therefore, the rules that some components in a character or word represent semantic cues do not get transferred to English. However, the transfer of ortho-phonological knowledge supported the interdependence hypothesis. Children who were good at using phonetic cues to derive character pronunciation may apply part of their ortho-phonological knowledge to read English words. Since grapheme-phoneme correspondence occurs at different levels in Chinese and English (e.g., syllable versus phonemes), what transferred was a script-independent skill of finding cues in the orthography to derive pronunciations.

Instruments of Orthographic Awareness

While Cheung et al. (2007) reported transfer of ortho-phonological knowledge, Gottardo et al. (2001) and Wang et al. (2005; Wang, Perfetti, et al., 2009) did not find any evidence of cross-language transfer in Chinese-English biliteracy development. One possible explanation is the difference in the instruments used to measure orthographic awareness. Both Wang et al. (2005; Wang, Perfetti, et al., 2009) and Gottardo et al. (2001) used the orthographic legality task in which children are presented with pairs of noncharacter in which one of them contained a component radical in an illegal position or an illegal radial in a legal position. Children had to choose which one of the two noncharacters looked more like a real word. This task did not assess children's ortho-phonological knowledge because they were not asked to pronounce the noncharacters. Therefore, they did not need to look for pronunciation cues in the phonetic radicals. However, Cheung and colleagues' (2007) novel object labeling task requires children to read out lout the nonwords, encouraging children to use to their ortho-phonological knowledge. Therefore, it is possible that researchers who used the orthographic legality task did not find transfer because ortho-phonological knowledge was not measured.

Researchers have also used the homophone choice task to assess orthographic awareness (Sun-Alperin & Wang, 2010). In this task, children were presented with pair of words in which one was a real word and the other was a pseudohomophone (e.g., *brain* and *brane*). Children were to point out the word that was spelled correctly. Real word and pseudoword spelling was another instrument of orthographic knowledge (Sun-Alperin & Wang, 2010; Wang & Geva, 2003). Children were asked to spell words in their L2 and errors were examined in terms of transfer of spelling convention or phonotactic constraints from L1. For example, Spanish-speaking children spelled *mit* for the English target *meat* and *mit* is a phonological legitimate spelling in Spanish. Cantonese children also made more mistakes spelling the word *teeth* because the phoneme /?/ is absent in Chinese phonology.

One limitation of the object labeling task used by Cheung et al. (2007) is that, in addition to orthographic awareness, it also measured children's phonological and semantic knowledge. In order to correctly label a novel object, children must know the meaning and pronunciation of the radicals. Therefore, children's performance on the task may reflect their metalinguistic awareness to orthography, phonology, and semantics. In contrast, an advantage of the orthographic choice task employed by Wang et al. (2005; Wang, Perfetti, et al., 2009) is that it only measured children's sensitivity to the legality of various orthographic patterns. In other words, no phonological or semantic knowledge is needed to complete the task. Children's performance on the task truly represents their orthographic awareness that is not confounded with their awareness to other constituent processes in learning to read. In addition, results obtained from the orthographic choice task is more generalizable because the task has been used with many different scripts, including alphabetic (e.g., English: Gottardo et al., 2001), alphasyllabary (e.g., Korean: Wang, Ko, et al., 2009), and logographic scripts (e.g., Chinese: Wang et al., 2005; Wang, Perfetti, et al., 2009). Therefore, researchers may consider using the orthographic choice task to assess orthographic transfer in biliteracy development.

Limitations and Future Direction

Limitations of the Theories

Overall, the literature reviewed above supported both the interdependence hypothesis and the contrastive analysis hypothesis in biliteracy development. Previous studies have consistently shown that while structural similarities facilitate positive transfer and typological differences results in interference, general metaglinguistic awareness also gets transferred as a result of prior literacy experience. Despite these findings, there are a number of limitations associated with both hypotheses.

First, neither the interdependence hypothesis nor the contrastive analysis hypothesis accounts for transfer from L2 to L1. Researchers have observed transfer from L2 to L1 when children's L2 competence has reached a certain level (Saiegh-Haddad & Geva, 2008; Sun-Alperin & Wang, 2010). For bilingual children whose L1 literacy skills are still developing, knowledge of the specific structures that are similar in both L1 and L2 as well as metaglinstuic awareness acquired through literacy experience in L2 are both facilitative resources for L1 reading development. Therefore, both cross-language transfer hypotheses must take into account the bidirectional transfer frequently observed in bilingual children.

The second limitation is that both hypotheses do not make predictions regarding how transfer changes as children's literacy skills develop in both L1 and L2. One group of researchers defined transfer as the reliance on L1 knowledge and transfer ceases to occur when L2 proficiency has been achieved because reliance on L1 knowledge is no longer necessary (Koda, 2007, 2008). On the other hand, the definition of transfer put forth by Riches and Genesee (2006) assumes that transfer is a dynamic process that does not stop at a certain point but rather continues to evolve as children acquire new skills and abilities through literacy experiences. However, neither the Independence Hypothesis nor the contrastive analysis hypothesis predicts that transfer ends at a certain point or evolves continuously. However, previous research showing transfer from the L2-L1 direction (e.g., Saiegh-Haddad & Geva, 2008; Sun-Alperin & Wang, 2010; Zhang et al., 2010) appears to suggest transfer does not cease to occur despite achievement of L2 competence. In other words, transfer is a continuously evolving process that is influenced by the literacy skills and proficiencies acquired in both languages.

Limitations of the Research

One methodological limitation of the research in the cross-language transfer literature is the lack of experimental design and training studies. Most of the studies in the literature employed a cross-sectional (e.g., Wang, Cheng, et al., 2006; Wang, Park, et al., 2006; Wang, Ko, et al., 2009; Wang, Yang, et al., 2009) or longitudinal design (Comeau et al, 1995; Cho & McBride-Chang, 2005; Deacon et al., 2007; McBride-Chang et al., 2008). One disadvantage of cross-sectional design is cohort effect. In addition, both cross-sectional and longitudinal designs do not allow researchers to draw conclusion about causal relationships. In other words, it is impossible to conclude that structural similarities between L1 and L2 cause cross language transfer or positive transfer causes L2 reading development. Only a few studies in the literature have employed an experimental design (e.g., Cisero et al., 1995; Friesen, 2007; Jared & Kroll, 2001; Wang, Koda, & Perfetti, 2003). To the best of the current authors' knowledge, only one training study has been conducted on the topic of cross-language transfer (e.g., Zhang et al., 2010). The researchers administered a 45-minute session on Chinese compound structures and found that children in the experimental group outperformed their peers in the control group in measures of both Chinese and English compound structure. Since the only difference between the control and the experimental group is that the latter have received the intervention, the researchers can safely conclude that the knowledge of Chinese (L1) compound structure acquired during the training session cause the transfer of this knowledge to English (L2). In light of the advantage of being able to claim causal relationships, researchers should consider conducting more training studies like Zhang et al. (2010) to examine the transfer of specific linguistic structures as well as general metalingusitic awareness.

Another limitation in the transfer literature, specifically concerning transfer of phonological awareness, is that the topic of suprasegmental awareness has received relatively little attention. A segment is defined as any discrete unit that can be identified in the stream of speech sounds such as consonants and vowels. Suprasegmentals, such as stress and tone, are speech features that accompany consonants and vowels and are not limited to single sounds but often extend over syllables, words or phrases (Crystal, 2003). Previous studies involving Chinese-English biliteracy development have shown that children's awareness to Chinese tone predict their English reading (Wang et al., 2005; Wang, Perfetti, et al., 2009). There are four tones in standard Mandarin Chinese. The first tone is called the high-level tone and labeled as 1 and the second tone, 2, is called the high-rising tone. The third tone, 3, is the falling-rising, and the fourth tone, 4, is the high-falling. Tone s attached to the vowel and an alternation in the tone of a syllable results in the change in its meaning. For example, the syllable /ma/ can have four possible meanings when a different tone is attached to it: /ma/1 妈 "mother," /ma/2 麻 "hemp," /ma/3 马 "horse," /ma/4 骂 "scold." Wang, Yang, et al. (2009) used an oddity task to measure Chinese-English bilingual children's tone sensitivity. Children were presented with three syllables and asked to choose one that has a different tone from the other two (e.g., /hua/1, /hua/2, and /hua/1). Results showed that children's Chinese tone sensitivity contributed unique variance to English reading after controlling for age, oral vocabulary, English phonological, morphological, and orthographic awareness.

The researchers proposed the "prosodic transfer" hypothesis to explain this result. Both Chinese tone and English stress are prosodic features and previous research has found that stress plays an important role in reading development for monolingual English-speaking children (Goodman, Libenson, & Wade-Woolley, 2010; Holliman, Wood, & Sheehy, 2008, 2010; see Wood, Wade-Woolley, & Holliman, 2009 for a review). Therefore, it is possible that awareness to Chinese tone transfer to the sensitivity to English stress which in turn facilitates reading development in English. Similarly, research with monolingual Spanish-speaking children has shown that stress is an important predictor of reading development (Gutierrez-Palma & Palma-Reyes, 2007; Gutierrez-Palma, Raya-Garcia, & Palma-Reyes, 2009). Since stress is both English and Spanish is lexical (e.g., minimal pairs of words that differ in stress alone such as REcord and reCORD[1]), this structural similarity may result in transfer of stress sensitivity in Spanish-English biliteacry development. However, Gutierrez-Palma and colleagues (Gutierrez-Palma et al., 2009; Gutierrez-Palma & Palma-Reyes, 2007) only studied monolingual Spanish children. Thus, future research should closely examine the transfer of prosodic sensitivity, between Spanish and English as well as other L1-L2 combinations, by administering measures that target suprasegmental awareness in both L1 and L2.

Educational Implications

Although more carefully controlled experimental studies and training studies is needed to confirm the causal relationship between cross-language transfer and biliteracy development, the current research appears to suggest that positive transfer does have an facilitative effect on reading development. Therefore, it is important for educators to keep up-to-dated with the most current research in the cross-language transfer literature. Second language teachers should familiarize themselves with the linguistic characteristics of their students' L1. Teachers should take advantage of the structural similarities between the students' two languages and encourage the students to utilize their knowledge of the L1 to the L2 learning process. On the other hand, teachers should prevent students from transferring their L1 knowledge by teaching them new strategies to approach the typologically different linguistic structures. Furthermore, bilingual educators may want to delay introduction of a second language until children reach a certain level of proficiency in their L1 because children with a lower level of L1 competence may not benefit from cross-language transfer.

Since approximately 60 to 75% of the people in the world speak two or more languages, biliteracy development is a topic that impacts about two thirds of the world's population. Cross-language transfer, as one of the important factors that influence biliteracy acquisition, warrants more research in the future. Particularly, empirical studies using both correlational and experimental designs needs to be conducted to examine how different L1-L2 combinations interact. Better understanding of how transfer works and what is being transferred will benefit both biliteracy learners and educators.

NOTE

1. Capitalized letters indicate stress location.

REFERENCES

Atwill, K., Blanchard, J., Gorin, J. A., & Burstein, K. (2007). Receptive vocabulary and cross-language transfer of phonemic awareness in kindergarten children. *Journal of Educational Research, 100*, 336-345.

Bates, E., & MacWhinney, B. (1981). Second language acquisition from a functionalist perspective: Pragmatic, semantic and perceptual strategies. In H. Winitz (Ed.), *Annals of the New York Academy of Sciences conference on native and foreign language acquisition* (pp. 190-214). New York, NY: New York Academy of Sciences.

Bates, E., & MacWhinney, B. (1989). Functionalism and the competition model. In B. MacWhinney & E. Bates (Eds.), *The crosslinguistic study of sentence processing* (pp. 3-73). New York, NY: Cambridge University Press.

Bruck, M., Treiman, R., & Caravolas, M. (1995). The syllable's role in the processing of spoken English: Evidence from a nonword comparison task. *Journal of Experimental Psychology: Human Perception & Performance, 21*, 469-479.

Carlisle, J. (1995). Morphological awareness and early reading achievement. In L. B. Feldman (Ed.), *Morphological aspects of language processing* (pp. 189–209). Hillsdale, NJ: Erlbaum.

Cheung, H., Chan, M., & Chong, K. (2007). Use of orthographic knowledge in reading by Chinese-English biscriptal children. *Language Learning, 57*, 469-505.

Cho, J. -R., & McBride-Chang, C. (2005). Levels of phonological awareness in Korean and English: A 1-year longitudinal study. *Journal of Educational Psychology, 97*, 564-471.

Chow, B. W. -Y., McBride-Chang, C., & Burgess, S. (2005). Phonological processing skills and early reading abilities in Hong Kong Chinese kindergarteners learning to read English as a second language. *Journal of Educational Psychology, 97*, 81-87.

Comeau, L., Cormier, P., Grandmaison, E., & Lacroix, (1999). A longitudinal study of phonological processing skills in children learning to read in a second language. *Journal Educational Psychology, 91*, 29-43.

Crystal, D. (2003). *A dictionary of linguistics and phonetics* (5th ed.). Malden, MA: Blackwell.

Cummins, J. (1979). Linguistic interdependence and the educational development of bilingual children. *Review of Educational Research, 49*, 222-251.

Deacon, S. H., Wade-Woolley, L., & Kirby, J. (2007). Crossover: The role of morphological awareness in French immersion children's reading. *Developmental Psychology, 43*, 732-746.

Durgunoglu, A. Y. (2002). Cross-linguistic transfer in literacy development and implications for language learners. *Annals of Dyslexia, 52*, 189-204.

Durgunoglu, A. Y., Nagy, W. E., & Hancin-Bhatt, B. J. (1993). Cross-language transfer of phonological awareness. *Journal of Educational Psychology, 85*, 453-465.

Durgunoglu, A. Y., & Oney, B. (2000, April). *Literacy development in two languages: Cognitive and sociocultural dimensions of cross-language transfer.* Paper presented to A Research Symposium on High Standards in Reading for Students from Diverse Language Groups: Research, Practice & Policy, Department of Education, Office of Bilingual Education and Minority Language Affairs, Washington, DC.

Fashola, O. S., Drum, P. A., Mayer, R. E., & Kang, S. (1996). A cognitive theory of orthographic transitioning: Predictable errors in how Spanish-speaking children spell English words. *American Educational Research Journal, 33*, 825–843.

Flege, J., & Davidian, R. (1984). Transfer and developmental processes in adult foreign language speech production. *Applied Psycholinguistics, 5*, 323-347.

Gass, S., & Selinker, L. (1983). *Language transfer in language learning.* Rowley, MA: Newbury House.

Gelb, I. J. (1952). *A study of writing.* Chicago, IL: University of Chicago Press.

Genesee, F., Geva, E., Dressler, C., & Kamil, M. L. (2006). Synthesis: Cross-linguistic relationships. In D. August, T. Shanahan, & L. Shanahan (Eds.) *Developing literacy in second-language learners: Report of the national literacy panel on language-minority children and youth* (pp. 153-174). Mahwah, NJ: Erlbaum.

Goodman, I., Libenson, A., & Wade-Woolley L. (2010). Sensitivity to linguistics stress, phonological awareness and early reading ability in preschoolers. *Journal of Research in Reading, 33*, 113-127.

Goswami, U., & Bryant, P. (1990). *Phonological skills and learning to read.* New York, NY: Psychology Press.

Gottardo, A., Siegel, L. S., Yan, B., & Wade-Woolley, L. (2001). Factors related to English reading performance in children with Chinese as first language: More evidence of cross-language transfer of phonological processing. *Journal of Educational Psychology, 93*, 530-542.

Gutierrez-Palma, N., & Palma-Reyes, A. (2007). Stress sensitivity and reading performance in Spanish: A study with children. *Journal of Research in Reading, 30*, 157-168.

Gutierrez-Palma, N., Raya-Garcia, M., & Palma-Reyes, A. (2009). Detecting stress patterns is related to children's performance on reading tasks. *Applied Psycholinguistics, 30*, 1-21.

Holliman, A. J., Wood, C., & Sheehy, K. (2008). Sensitivity to speech rhythm explains individual differences in reading ability independently of phonological awareness. *British Journal of Developmental Psychology, 26*, 357-367.

Holliman, A. J., Wood, C., & Sheehy, K. (2010). The contribution of sensitivity to speech rhythm and non-speech rhythm to early reading development. *Educational Psychology, 30*, 247-267.

Katz, L., & Frost, R. (1992). The reading process is different for different orthographies: The orthographic depth hypothesis. In R. Frost & L. Katz (Eds.), *Orthography, phonology, morphology and meaning* (pp. 67–84). Amsterdam, The Netherlands: Elsevier Science.

Kim. Y. -S., (2009). Crosslinguistic influence on phonological awareness for Korean-English bilingual children. *Reading and Writing, 22*, 843-861.

Koda, K. (2007). Reading and language learning: Crosslinguistic constraints on second language reading development. *Language Learning, 57*, 1-44.

Koda, K. (2008). Impacts of prior literacy experience on second-language leaning to read. In K. Koda & A. M. Zehler (Eds.), *Learning to read across-languages: cross-linguistic relationships in first- and second-language literacy development* (pp. 68-96). New York, NY: Routledge.

Krashen, S. (1983). Newmark's "ignorance hypothesis" and current second language acquisition theory. In S. Gass & L. Selinker (Eds.), *Language transfer in language learning*. Rowley, MA: Newbury House.

Kuo, L. J., & Anderson, R. C. (2006). Morphological awareness and learning to read: A cross-language. perspective. *Educational Psychologist, 41*(3), 161–180.

Lado, R. (1964). *Language teaching*. New York, NY: McGraw-Hill.

Li, D. (1993). *A study of Chinese characters*. Beijing, China: Peking University Press.

Lindsey, K. A., Manis, F. R., & Bailey, C. E. (2003). Prediction of first-grade reading in Spanish-speaking English-language learners. *Journal of Educational Psychology, 95*, 482-494.

MacWhinney, B. (1987). Applying the competition model to bilingualism. *Applied Psycholinguistics, 8*, 315-327.

MacWhinney, B. (1992). Competition and transfer in second language learning. In R. Harris (Ed.), *Cognitive processing in bilinguals* (pp. 371-390). Amsterdam, The Netherlands: Elsevier.

MacWhinney, B. (1997). Second language acquisition and the competition model. In A. M. B. de Groot & J. F. Kroll (Eds.), *Tutorials in bilingualism: Psycholinguistic perspective* (pp. 113-143). Mahwah, NJ: Erlbaum.

MacWhinney, B. (2005). A unified model of language acquisition. In J. F. Kroll & A. M. B. de Groot (Eds.), *Handbook of bilingualism: Psycholinguistic approaches* (pp. 49-67). New York, NY: Oxford University Press.

MacWhinney, B., & Bates, E. (Eds.). (1989). *The crosslinguistic study of sentence processing*. New York, NY: Cambridge University Press.

Manis, F. R., Lindsey, K. A., & Bailey, C. E. (2004). Development of reading in Grades K-2 in Spanish-speaking English-language learners. *Learning Disabilities Research & Practice, 19*, 214-224.

McBride-Chang, C., Tong, X., Shu, H., Wong, A. M. -Y., Leung, K. -W., & Tardif, T. (2008). Syllable, phoneme, and tone: Psycholinguistic units in early Chinese and English word recognition. *Scientific Studies of Reading, 12*, 171-194.

Mishra, R., & Stainthorp, R. (2007). The relationship between phonological awareness and word reading accuracy in Oriya and English: A study of Oriya-speaking fifth-graders. *Journal of Research in Reading, 30*, 23-37.

Oldin, T. (1989). *Language transfer*. New York, NY: Cambridge University Press.

Perfetti, C. A. (2003). The universal grammar of reading. *Scientific Studies of Reading, 7*, 3-24.

Ramirez, G., Chen, X., Geva, E., & Kiefer, H. (2010). Morphological awareness in Spanish-speaking English language learners : Within and cross-language effects on word learning. *Reading and Writing, 23*, 337-358.

Riches, C., & Genesee, F. (2006). Cross-language and cross-modal influences. In F. Genesee, K. Lindholm-Leary, W. Saunders, & D. Christian (Eds.), *Educating English language learners: A synthesis of research evidence*. New York, NY: Cambridge University Press.

Rumelhart, D. E., & McClelland, J. L. (Eds.). (1986). On learning the past tense of English verbs. In *Parallel distributed processing: Explorations in the microstructure of cognition: Vol. 2. Psychological and biological models* (pp. 216-271). Cambridge, MA: MIT Press.

Saiegh-Haddad, E., & Geva, E. (2008). Morphological awareness, phonological awareness, and reading in English-Arabic bilingual children. *Reading and Writing, 21*, 481-504.

Sun-Alperin, M. K., & Wang, M. (2008). Spanish-speaking children's spelling errors with English vowel sounds that are represented by different graphemes in English and Spanish words. *Contemporary Educational Psychology, 33*, 932-948.

Sun-Alperin, M. K., & Wang, M. (2010). Cross-language transfer of phonological and orthographic processing skills from Spanish L1 to English L2. *Reading and Writing, 24*, 591-614.

Tong, X., & McBride-Chang, C., (2010). Chinese-English biscriptal reading: Cognitive component skills across orthographies. *Reading and Writing, 23*, 293-310.

Treiman, R. (1995). Errors in short-term memory for speech: A developmental study. *Journal of Experimental Psychology: Learning, Memory, and Cognition, 21*, 1197-1208.

Treiman, R., & Cassar, M. (1997). Spelling acquisition in English. In C. A. Perfetti, L. Rieben, & M. Fayol (Eds.), *Learning to spell: Research, theory, and practices across languages* (pp. 61-80). Hillsdale, NJ: Erlbaum.

Treiman, R., Mullennix, J., Bijeljac-Babic, R., & Richmond-Welty, E. D. (1995). The special role of rimes in the description, use, and acquisition of English orthography. *Journal of Experimental psychology: General, 124*, 107-136.

Tucker, G. R. (2003). A global perspective on bilingualism and bilingual education. In C. B. Paulson & G. R. Tucker (Eds.) *Sociolinguistics: The essential readings* (pp. 464-471). Malden, MA: Blackwell.

Verhoeven, L. (1994). Transfer in bilingual development: The linguistic interdependency hypothesis revisited. *Language Learning, 44*, 381–415.

Wade-Woolley, L., & Geva, E. (2000). Processing noval phonemic contrasts in the acquisition of L2 word reading. *Scientific Studies of Reading, 4*, 295-311.

Wang, M., & Geva, E. (2003). Spelling performance of Chinese children using English as a second language: Lexical and visual-orthographic processes. *Applied Psycholinguistics, 24,* 1-25.

Wang, M., Cheng, C., & Chen, S. -W. (2006). Contribution of morphological awareness to Chinese-English biliteracy acquisition. *Journal of Educational Psychology, 98,* 542-553.

Wang, M., Ko, I. Y., & Choi, J. (2009). The importance of morphological awareness in Korean-English biliteracy acquisition. *Contemporary Educational Psychology, 34,* 132-142.

Wang, M., Park, Y. J., & Lee, K. R. (2006). Korean-English biliteracy acquisition: Cross-language phonological and orthographic transfer. *Journal of Educational Psychology, 98,* 148-158.

Wang, M., Perfetti, C. A., & Liu, Y. (2005). Chinese-English biliteracy acquisition: Cross-language and writing system transfer. *Cognition, 97,* 67-88.

Wang, M., Yang, C., & Cheng, C. (2009). The contribution of phonology, orthography, and morphology in Chinese-English biliteracy acquisition. *Applied Psycholinguistics, 30,* 291-314.

Wood, C., Wade-Woolley, L., & Holliman, A.J. (2009). Phonological awareness: Beyond phonemes. In C. Wood & V. Connelly (Eds.), *Contemporary perspectives on reading and spelling* (pp. 7-23). London, England: Routledge.

Zhang, J., Anderson, R. C., Li, H., Dong, Q., Wu, X., & Zhang, Y. (2010). Cross-language transfer of insight into the structure of compound words. *Reading and Writing, 23,* 311-336.

Zhou, X., & Marslen-Wilson, W. (2000). Lexical representation of compound words: Cross-linguistics evidence. *Psychologia, 43,* 47-66.

Ziegler, J. C., & Goswami, U. (2005). Reading acquisition, developmental dyslexia, and skilled reading across languages: A psycholinguistic grain size theory. *Psychological Bulletin, 131,* 3-29.

Author Contact Information: Candise Y. Lin, BA, 3304 Benjamin Building, Department of Human Development, University of Maryland, College Park, MD 20742. Phone: 626-222-6685. E-mail: candisec@umd.edu

CHAPTER 33

The Development of Theories of Bilingualism and School Achievement

Colin Baker
Bangor University

There are two predominant and intriguing language issues that relate to bilinguals in school. First, do children with two languages have disadvantages or advantages in thinking and in school achievement due to their bilingualism? Second, why do some bilingual children fail in school, for example when they move from a home language that is different from the school's (e.g. Spanish to English in the United States)?

The answers were historically discouraging. From the 1920s to the 1950s, the belief was that bilingual children suffered mental deficits from this bilingualism. This was particularly supported by research using IQ tests where bilinguals from *manual* social classes performed lower than English monolingual speakers from the more middle classes (Baker, 2011). Recent research has shown the opposite: bilinguals competent in two languages outperform monolinguals on various dimensions of cognition (Bialystok, 2001) and in their curriculum achievement (Lindholm-Leary, 2001).

Research from many different countries, different age groups, varying ability levels, socioeconomic classes and immigrant and heritage language speakers became voluminous from the early 1960s onwards, and allowed theories to develop and be refined. The progress of such theories that relate bilingualism to cognition and school achievement will be outlined in this chapter. This outline commences with the development from *naïve* theories that are still publicly and politically popular, and then moves to theories that encapsulate research and variations in research findings.

THE BALANCE THEORY OF BILINGUALISM

Early twentieth century research found bilinguals to be inferior to monolinguals on IQ and school attainment. This was commonly explained by a naïve theory of bilingualism that sees the two languages as a balance—as one rises the other falls. A second language increases at cost to the first language. An alternative naïve analogy is of two language balloons inside the head. The monolingual has one well-filled balloon: the bilingual has two less filled or half filled balloons in the same space. As the second language balloon increases in size (e.g., English), the first language balloon (e.g., Spanish) decreases proportionately, leading to a less well-functioning cognitive system and no transfer between the two balloons.

The balance and balloon theories of bilingualism and thinking/school achievement were subsumed into the separate underlying proficiency model of bilingualism. This theory of bilingualism is that the first and second languages operate separately in the brain. Recent research on cognition and the brain shows this notion to be false (Bialystok, 2001). Even when only one language is being spoken, the other remains activated and not dormant (Kroll & De Groot, 1997). When children develop into relatively balanced bilinguals, there tend to be cognitive advantages rather than disadvantages (Cummins, 2009). Also certain types of bilingual education (e.g., Early Total Immersion and Heritage Language bilingual education) appear to result in attainment advantages over monolingual education (Baker, 2011).

The Handbook of Educational Theories, pp. 385–394

The assumption of the separate underlying proficiency theory of bilingualism is that the first and second languages are activated separately in cognitive functioning. To the contrary: transfer readily occurs, as a simple example will illustrate. When a lesson is in Spanish, it does not just feed a Spanish part of the brain. Rather concepts learnt through one language transfer into use by the other language. Teaching a child about evolution in one language does not mean that it has to be retaught in a second language. The idea learnt through one language is then available in the other language to the extent that this other language is sufficiently developed to express that concept. Such an easy transfer of ideas, understandings and knowledge across languages is called common underlying proficiency (Cummins, 1981a).

In contrast to the separate underlying proficiency theory, and to better encapsulate early research, Cummins (1981a) defined the common underlying proficiency model of bilingualism. This is pictorially explained in the form of two icebergs, separate above the surface but joined underneath into one entity. For example, two languages are typically separate and distinct in speaking, but both languages operate through the same underlying cognitive processing. For education, this has implications for additive bilingual classroom approaches rather than subtractive monolingual approaches (e.g., for immigrants). That is, using two languages for learning seems viable as opposed to monolingual education for all.

The common underlying proficiency theory of bilingualism has five implications:

1. Irrespective of the language in which a person is operating, the thoughts that accompany talking, reading, writing and listening come from the same integrated source and process of thinking.
2. Children have the cognitive capacity to store and function in two or more languages.
3. Concepts, understandings and knowledge may be developed through two languages and not just one. School achievement can prosper through monolingual learning or equally successfully through two well-developed languages.
4. If children are expected to learn through an insufficiently developed second language, they may fail to understand and progress.
5. If education is monolingual through a weaker language, or bilingual, the language(s) need to be sufficiently advanced (e.g., in vocabulary, syntax) for the child to be able to understand the increasingly complex nature of classroom learning, otherwise academic performance may be negatively affected.

Is the common underlying proficiency theory tenable? Later in this chapter, it will be shown that it is too simplistic and minimalistic, and more advanced and multidimensional theories are presented. Also, the Sapir-Whorf hypothesis (e.g., that different languages contain different views of the world) challenges the idea that bilinguals have one integrated source of thought (Pavlenko, 2005). Each particular language may influence both the content and process of thinking. Thus varied languages can influence thought differently through their concepts, understandings and inner meanings. The common underlying proficiency theory of bilingualism therefore has been refined, extended, and replaced, as this section will show. The first refinement has been termed the Thresholds Theory, and has been influential and impactive on the international education of bilinguals (e.g., Canada, Basque Country in Spain, and Wales in the United Kingdom).

The Thresholds Theory

The term *bilinguals* encompasses a considerable range of language competences. At one end of the spectrum there are children who are very competent in two (or more) languages and function with ease in both languages, including in the classroom. At the other end of the spectrum there are children who have just started to learn a second language. In between, there are numerous variations. There is also more than one language dimension, with children varying across understanding, speaking, reading and writing. One particular variation is children who are immigrants and may be fluent in a home language but find it difficult (for whatever reason) to work in a different mainstream school language (e.g., English in the United States and United Kingdom). The common underlying proficiency theory cannot account for these variations and dimensions. A step forward came with the thresholds theory.

Many research studies have suggested that the further the child moves toward balanced bilingualism, the greater the likelihood of cognitive advantages (Bialystok, 2001; Clarkson, 1992; Cummins, 2000b; Dawe, 1983). However, the term *balanced bilingualism* is more idealistic than real, as few bilinguals are equally balanced in their two languages. Nevertheless, the term has been found to be valuable when, for example, it refers to children whose two languages are both sufficiently well developed to cope in the classroom in either or both languages. A considerable volume of research suggests such children have distinct cognitive and school achievement advantages (Baker, 2011).

Thus the questions have become: (a) Under what conditions does bilingualism have positive, neutral and negative effects on cognition and school achievement? (b) How far does someone have to travel up the metaphorical two language ladders to obtain cognitive and achievement advantages from bilingualism? (c) What degree of competence in one or both languages is required to avoid potential negative outcomes, perform similarly to monolinguals, and obtain the positive advantages of bilingualism? Long-standing and research-supported answers have been given in the thresholds theory.

The thresholds theory was devised by Cummins (1976) and Toukomaa and Skutnabb-Kangas (1977). They suggested the idea of two thresholds as the best explanation of the research findings on cognition and bilingualism. This idea is that each threshold is a level of language competence that has important implications for a bilingual child. The first threshold is a level which a child must attain to avoid the negative consequences of bilingualism. The second threshold is a level which enables a child to experience the potential advantages of bilingualism. This theory therefore provides a basis for determining which children will be likely to obtain cognitive benefits, and which children may suffer cognitive disadvantages, from their bilingualism.

The thresholds theory can be pictured as a house with three floors. Two language ladders are placed up the sides of the house, indicating that a bilingual child will usually be moving upward and not stationary on a floor. But those children whose current competence in both their languages is insufficiently developed, especially by comparison with their age group, will be stuck on the ground floor of the house. A low level of competence in both languages may have negative or detrimental cognitive consequences. A child who cannot cope in the classroom in either language is likely to fall behind with their educational development. Those children with age-appropriate competence in one of their languages but not in both may reside at the middle level, the second floor of the house. At this level, a partly-bilingual child is unlikely to have any significant positive or negative cognitive differences from a monolingual child. Those children who are close to being *balanced* bilinguals, that is, those who have age-appropriate competence in two or more languages, reside at the top of the house, the third floor. At this level, for example, children can cope with curriculum material in either of their languages. Children with age-appropriate ability in both their languages may therefore have cognitive advantages over their monolingual peers.

The thresholds theory is supported by research from, for example, Bialystok (1988), Clarkson and Galbraith (1992), Clarkson (1992), Dawe (1983) and Cummins (2000b). Dawe examined bilingual Panjabi, Mirpuri and Jamaican children aged 11 to 13 on tests of deductive mathematical reasoning, and found evidence for both the lower and the higher threshold. Deductive reasoning skills in mathematics increased in proportion to competency in two languages, while limited competence in both languages appeared to equate to negative cognitive outcomes.

The thresholds theory helps to explain one of the issues raised at the beginning of this chapter—why do minority language children taught through a second language (e.g., immigrants in the United States) sometimes fail to achieve adequate competency in their second language (e.g., English) and thus gain little benefit from mainstream education where only English is used in the classroom? Their lack of proficiency in English makes it difficult to cope with the curriculum. That is why dual education programs, whereby children are taught in their more developed home language as well as in another language (e.g., English), can achieve better results than mainstream or transitional bilingual education.

The thresholds theory does however present one particular problem. How precisely can one define the level and nature of language proficiency a child must obtain in order, first to avoid the negative effects of bilingualism, and second, to obtain its positive advantages? At what language *height* do the ceilings of the house become floors? What language skills does a bilingual child need to develop, and to what degree, before they can climb to a higher floor? Indeed, it may be counterproductive to construct artificial "critical stages" or levels, because in practice transition between levels tends to be gradual and smooth. The following section will expand on this point.

The Developmental Interdependence Hypothesis

The thresholds theory is relatively rudimentary. Consequently, more elucidatory theories developed. One advancement of the Thresholds Theory has considered the relationship between the two languages of a bilingual by outlining the language developmental interdependence hypothesis (Cummins (1978, 2000a, 2000b).

According to this hypothesis, a child's competence in a second language depends in part on the level of competence they have already reached in their first language. Huguet, Vila, and Llurda (2000) found that this developmental interdependence hypothesis was borne out by research on the language competence of Spanish/Catalan speakers of varying degrees of balance. For example, those 12-year-old students who were more proficient in Catalan were also more proficient in Spanish, and vice versa. Similarly, research on 952 Miami, Florida, students in dual language and English immersion schools found that this hypothesis helped to explain their achievements in reading and writing (see Oller & Eilers, 2002). For example, "children did not tend to excel in one language at the expense of the other" (Cobo-Lewis, Eilers, Pearson, & Umbel, 2002, p. 120) and there was evidence that skills and concepts were transferred from one language to another. Proctor (2003) analyzed Spanish/English 4th grade data from Boston, Chicago and El Paso to show that students with well-developed Spanish and English vocabularies performed better than their less balanced bilingual counterparts (i.e., those whose Spanish or English was their dominant language) in English reading achievement. These findings appear to apply equally in situations where trilingual students are involved (Cenoz, 2003; Errasti, 2003).

The possession of simple communication skills, such as holding a straightforward conversation with a shopkeeper, does not necessarily mean that a child's language proficiency is sufficient to deal with the cognitive and academic demands of the classroom. The language used when playing with a ball in the school playground is very different from the complexities of mathematics terminology.

The BICS and CALP Theory

A distinction has been drawn between 'surface fluency' and the more evolved language skills required to benefit from the education process (Cummins, 1984). Cummins (1979) found that children could acquire everyday conversational skills in 2 years, whereas it could take them 5 to 7 or even more years to develop the more complex language abilities needed to cope with the curriculum. In California, Hakuta et al. (2000) found that it takes 3 to 5 years to develop oral proficiency in English, as against 4 to 7 years to develop proficiency in academic English. This resulted in criticism of English mainstream schooling for immigrants in the United States, where children are expected to acquire English almost immediately and learn curriculum content solely through English.

The distinction between (a) the language used for basic everyday conversation *in the street and shop* and (b) the more complex and abstract language of the classroom led to a distinction: BICS and CALP (Cummins, 1984, 2008). It became a distinction that became famous and fought over, influential among teachers yet a battleground among scholars. This remarkable theory, that has been persuasively dominant yet publically disputed, will now be considered.

Cummins (1984, 2008) expressed a language distinction in terms of basic interpersonal communicative skills (BICS) and cognitive/academic language proficiency (CALP). BICS is said to occur when there are contextual supports and props for language delivery. Face-to-face *context embedded* situations provide, for example, nonverbal support to secure understanding. Actions with eyes and hands, instant feedback, cues and clues support verbal language.

CALP, on the other hand, relates to context reduced academic situations. Where higher order thinking skills (e.g., analysis, synthesis, evaluation, hypothesizing, inferring, generalizing, predicting, and classifying) are required in the curriculum, language is *disembedded* from a meaningful, supportive context. Where language is *disembedded,* the situation is often referred to as *context reduced.* CALP is specific to the context of schooling.

One illustration of the difference is to compare playground with classroom language. The language of the playground and street is face-to-face, with plenty of physical and visual supports to language, many gestures and other forms of body language. The purpose is often to engage in friendly, playful, and social activities. In contrast, classroom language is often more abstract, using a curriculum language to help learning in mathematics, technology, science, humanities and the arts.

The BICS/CALP distinction has been influential and valuable for policy, provision and practice, not only in terms of instruction but also in assessment. Teachers, possibly more than academics, have found the distinction illuminating and informative, allowing more sensitivity to the kind and amount of language support many children need. Also, for teachers, it has led to an awareness of the dangers of high-stakes testing of bilingual children, for example in the United States.

Critiques of the BICS/CALP Theory

The BICS/CALP distinction has received criticism (MacSwan & Rolstad, 2003; Wiley, 1996, 2005, with a response by Cummins, 2008).

First, the distinction between BICS and CALP has intuitive appeal and does appear to fit the case of children who are seemingly fluent in their second language, yet cannot cope in the curriculum in that language. However, it only paints a two-stage idea. A large number of dimensions of language competences exist. Children and adults may move forward on language dimensions in terms of sliding scales rather than in big jumps. A bilingual's language competences are evolving, dynamic, interacting and intricate. They are not simple dichotomies, easily compartmentalized and static.

Second, Martin-Jones and Romaine (1986) suggested that the distinction does not exactly indicate how the two ideas may be precisely defined and accurately tested. Thus the distinction becomes difficult to operationalize in research. Third, terms such as BICS and CALP can become overcompartmentalized, simplified and misused. Such terms may be used to label and stereotype students, especially if BICS is seen as inferior to CALP (Wiley, 1996, 2005).

Fourth, CALP may relate to an ability to perform well on school tests (test-wisdom). This relates to specific, traditional, school-based literacy practices. Such practices favor the middle-class groups that control institutions. Such tests favor *standard* academic language with a bias against speakers of dialects, Creoles and non-standard language (e.g., Black English). MacSwan and Rolstad (2003) argue that the theory gives special status to educated, middle class language styles and hence belittles working class oral language styles. This could relate to a deficit view of language that stigmatizes nonacademic language. This was certainly not Cummins' intention (Baker & Hornberger, 2001) and given that this theory has persuaded many educators not to mainstream prematurely English language learners especially in the United States, the theory has not had this effect.

The distinction between BICS and CALP helps explain the relative failure within the educational system of many minority language children. For example, in the United States, various programs aim to give language minority students sufficient English language skills to enable them to converse with peers and teachers and to operate in the curriculum. The transfer occurs because children appear to have sufficient language competence (BICS) to cope in mainstream education. Cummins' (1984) distinction between BICS and CALP explains why such children tend to fail when mainstreamed. Their cognitive academic language proficiency is not developed enough to cope with the demands of the curriculum. What Cummins regards as essential in the bilingual education of children is that a child's language-cognitive abilities need to be sufficiently well developed to cope with the curriculum processes of the classroom. This underlying ability could be developed in the first or the second language, but also in both languages simultaneously.

Refinements to the BICS/CALP Theory

The BICS/CALP theory became refined by being two dimensional (Cummins, 1981b, 1983, 1984). This extension is represented in Figure 33.1.

Both dimensions are about communicative proficiency. The first dimension refers to the amount of contextual support available to a student. Context embedded communication exists when there is a good degree of support, particularly using body language. For example, people give and receive plenty of clues and cues to help the content of the message to be understood by pointing to objects, using the eyes, head nods, hand gestures and intonation. It is not infrequent to see two young children of different languages playing together without difficulty. In context reduced communication, by contrast, there may be very few nonverbal cues to the meaning that is being transmitted. The words of the sentence are almost the sole means of conveying the meaning. Context reduced communication often occurs in the classroom where the meaning is restricted to words, with a subtlety and precision of meanings in the vocabulary of the teacher or the book.

The second dimension is the level of cognitive demands required in communication. Cognitively demanding communication often occurs in a classroom where much information at a demanding level must be processed quickly. Cognitively undemanding communication occurs where a person's language skills are sufficient to enable easy communication. An example might be holding a conversation in the street, shop, or stadium, where the information to be processed is relatively simple and straightforward.

Surface fluency or basic interpersonal communication skills will fit into the first quadrant (see diagram above). That is, BICS (basic interpersonal communication skills) is context embedded, cognitively undemanding use of a language. Language that is cognitively and academically more advanced (CALP) fits into the fourth quadrant (context reduced and cognitively demanding). Cummins' (1981b) theory suggests that second language competency in the first quadrant (surface fluency) develops relatively independently of surface fluency in the *first* language. By contrast, context reduced, cognitively demanding communication develops interdependently and can be promoted by either language or by both languages in an interactive way. Thus, the theory suggests that bilingual education will be successful when children have sufficient first or second language proficiency to work in the context reduced, cognitively demanding situation of the classroom.

In Cummins' (1981b, 2000b) view it often takes 1 or more years for a child to acquire context embedded second language fluency, but 5 to 7 years or more to acquire context reduced fluency. This is illustrated in Figure 33.2.

Research by Hakuta and D'Andrea (1992) with Mexican Americans found that English proficiency reaches asymptotic performance after about 8 years. This agrees quite well with Cummins' (1984) estimate, based on a heterogeneous L1 population in Canada (p. 96), of 5 to 7 years required for attainment of the full range of second language acquisition. Shohamy (1999) found that immigrant students in Israel need 7 to 9 years to catch up with native speakers in Hebrew literacy. It must be remembered that native speakers are

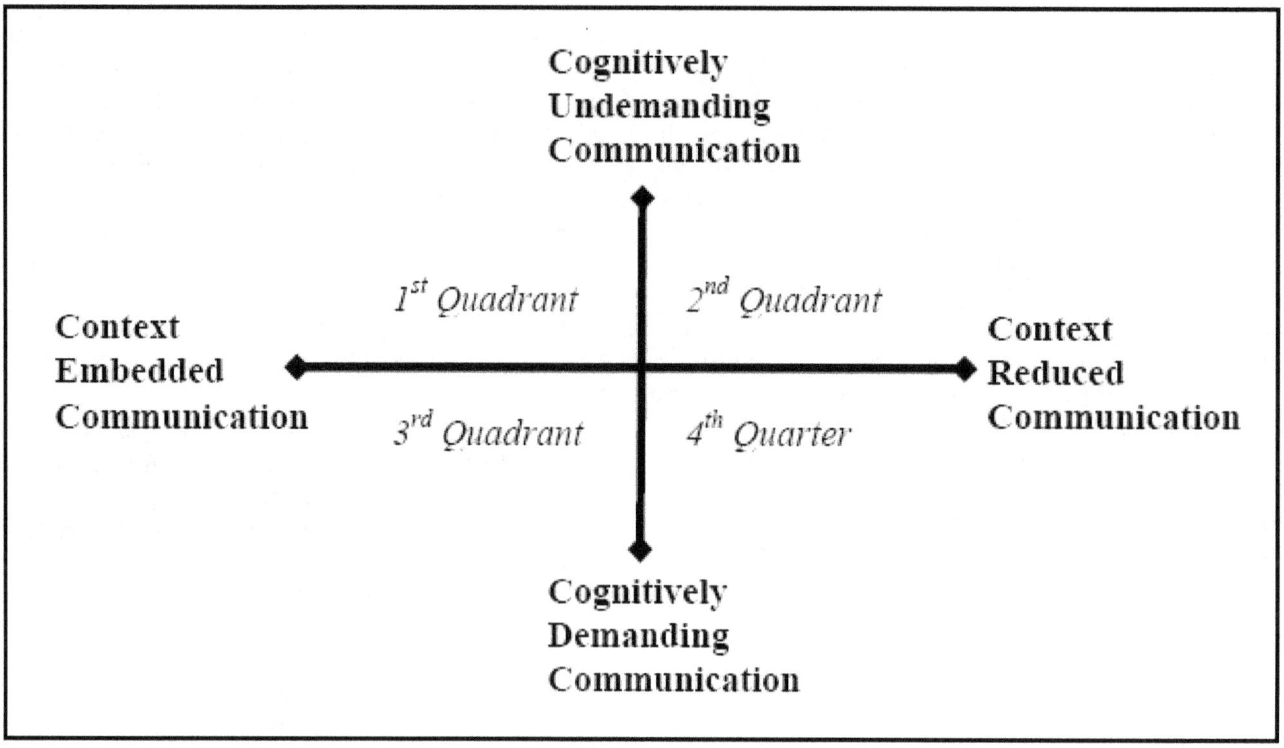

Figure 33.1. Contexts and cognitive demands in communication.

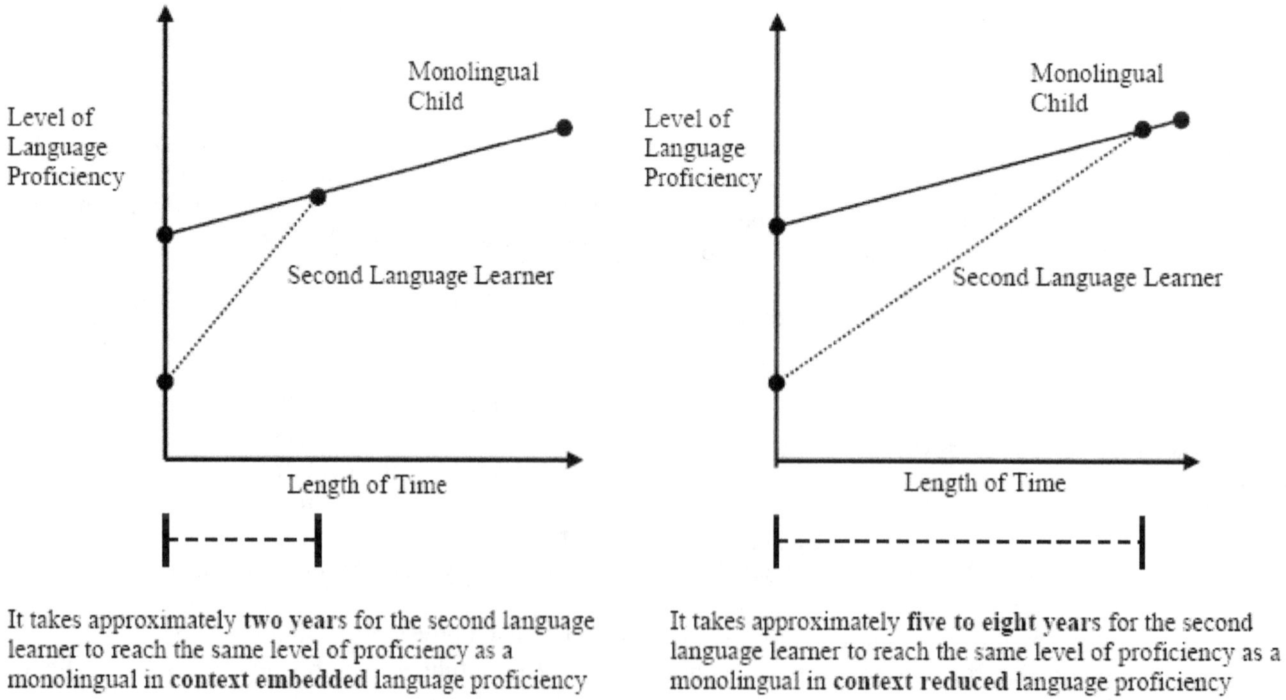

Figure 33.2. Level of language proficiency across time.

not standing still in their language development. The immigrants are therefore chasing a moving target.

Spada and Lightbown (2002) found that Inuit students in northern Québec fail when they experience a sudden transition from their home language (used in Kindergarten to Grade 2) to education almost solely in French or English. This results in many students working in classrooms where the cognitively demanding language is beyond their grasp. The problems are particularly serious at high school level because of its needs for more abstract academic language. The lack of age-appropriate competence in the French language is identified as the principal cause of academic failure.

This two-dimensional (four quadrant) model helps to explain a number of research findings. First, in the United States, language minority children are sometimes reclassified from LEP (limited English proficiency) or EL (English learners) to FEP (fluent English proficient) as soon as they are deemed to have sufficient conversational ability in English (Linquanti, 2001). Subsequently, these children often achieve poorly. The two-dimensional theory explains this poor performance by attributing it to their lack of facility in *curriculum* or *grade level* English (or their home language), resulting in an inability to operate in a more cognitively and academically demanding environment.

Second, immersion students in Canada tend to lag behind their monolingual peers for a short period, but they usually catch up with them once they have attained the necessary degree of proficiency in their second language. Third, Heritage Language education in the United States, Canada and parts of Europe allow minority language children to use their minority language for much or most of their elementary schooling. These experiments demonstrate that such children do not suffer delays in school achievement or in majority language proficiency. Instead, they develop the ability to achieve success in the cognitively demanding and context reduced classroom environment through the medium of their minority language (Baker, 2011). This ability then *transfers* to the majority language when that language is sufficiently well developed. Cummins (1984) observed that transfer is much more likely to occur from minority to majority language because of the greater exposure to literacy in the majority language and the strong social pressure to learn it.

Application and Relevance of the Theory

The importance of Jim Cummins' (1984, 2008, 2009) ideas is that they relate directly to "creating instructional and learning environments that maximize the language and literacy development of socially marginalized students" (Cummins, 2008, p. 81). A student's reservoir of knowledge, understanding and experience is a crucial starting point for the teacher and can provide a meaningful context on which the teacher can build. A teacher who dramatizes a story by adding gestures, pictures, facial expressions and other acting skills can make it much more context embedded. It is cognitively less demanding for a student to talk about something familiar than to discuss culturally or academically unfamiliar. Therefore any curriculum task presented to the student needs to be considered against the following criteria: (a) the cognitive demands inherent in the task (as found by an individual child); the "entry skills" that a task necessitates; (b) What form of presentation will be meaningful to the child; use of visual aids, demonstration, modeling, computers, oral and written instructions; amount of teacher assistance ("scaffolding"); (c) The child's language proficiencies; (d) The child's previous cultural and educational experience and knowledge, individual learning style and learning strategies; expectations and attitudes, confidence and initiative; the child's familiarity with the type of task. These are illustrated in Figure 33.3.

Critiques of Theories of Bilingual Students and Their Curriculum Achievement

There have been criticisms of the development of theories outlined in this chapter regarding the relationship between language and school achievement (Edelsky, 1991; Edelsky et al., 1983; Frederickson & Cline, 1990, 2002; MacSwan & Rolstad, 2003; Martin-Jones & Romaine, 1986; Rivera, 1984; Robson, 1995; Wiley, 1996). Cummins (2000a, 2000b, 2008) provides his perspective on these criticisms. The critique can be summarized as follows:

1. Cummins' (1981b) initial theory may have reduced and fragmented certain ingredients in a bilingual's cognitive or classroom experience. Many factors other than those presented in this theory influence the attainment of bilingualism and the relationship between bilingual education and school achievement. The theory took little account of socioeconomic or sociocultural differences. Bilingualism and bilingual education do need to give due weight to other variables, including cultural, social, political, community, teacher expectations and home factors. Every one of these variables helps to explain bilingualism as an individual and societal phenomenon. Cummins (1986, 2000b, 2008) has subsequently addressed these issues in further studies.

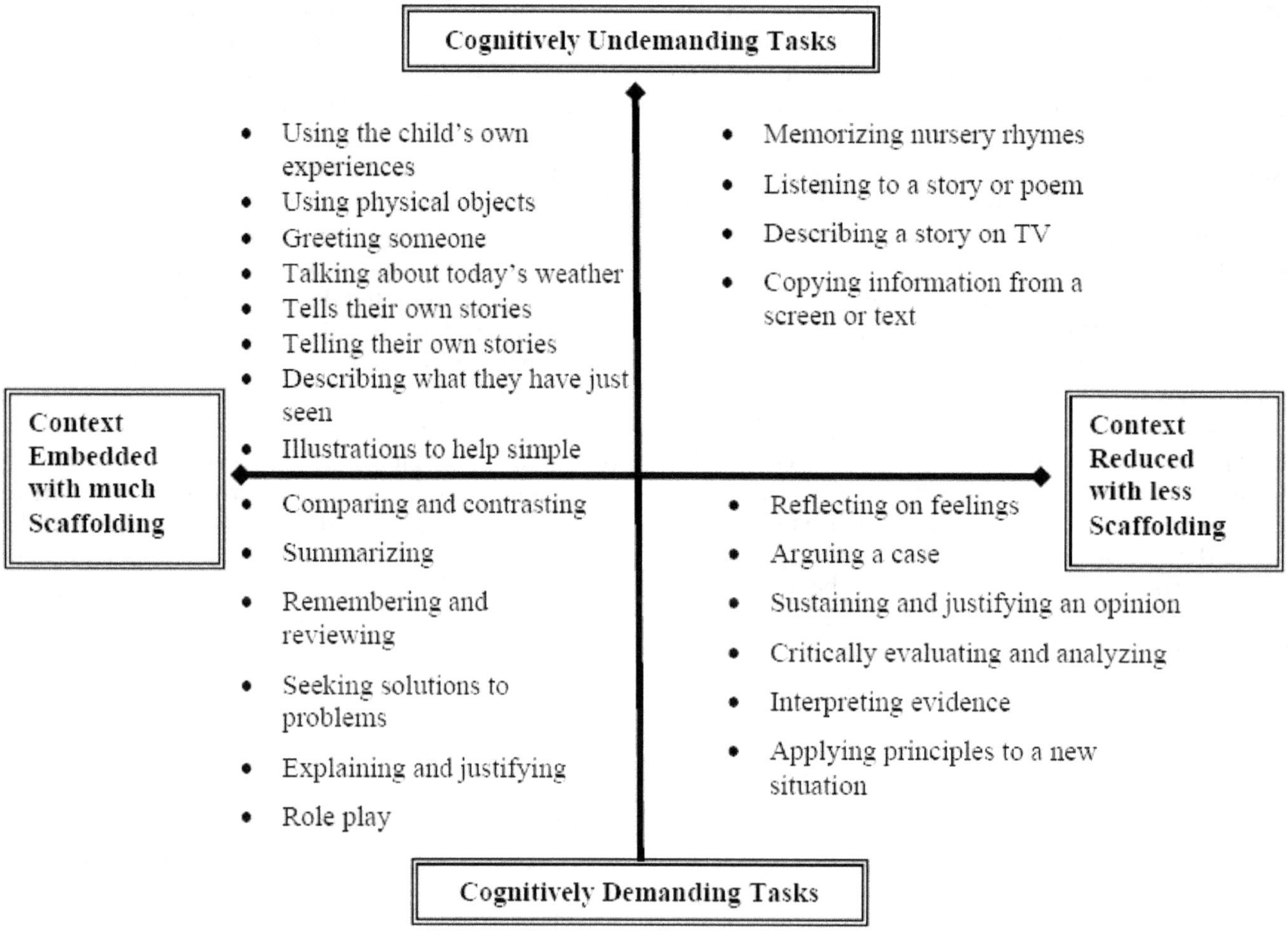

Figure 33.3. Contexts and cognitive demands of activities.

2. Cummins (1981b) tended to center on dominant, middle-class indices of achievement when setting the criteria for educational success. Thus, he placed importance on language skills, literacy and formal educational achievement. He did not initially consider alternative outcomes of schooling such as self-esteem, social and emotional development, divergent and creative thinking, long-term attitude to learning, employment or moral development.
3. The two dimensions are not necessarily distinct from each other, and may not best be represented by two axes 90 degrees apart. When applying Cummins' two dimensions to curriculum tasks, Frederickson and Cline (1990) found it "difficult to disentangle the 'cognitive' from the 'contextual.' In some cases, movement along the contextual dimensions has actually been represented on the model as a diagonal shift [on the diagram from top left to bottom right], as it was found in practice that making tasks or instructions more context embedded also made them somewhat less cognitively demanding. Similarly, changes in cognitive demand may result in tasks actually being presented with greater context embeddedness" (p. 26)
4. The distinction between de-contextualized and contextualized communication may be too simplistic, since all communication appears in some kind of context. For example, teachers' use of the language in mathematics is classroom-based within a mathematics lesson.

CONCLUSION

The chapter began by indicating that there are two overlapping language issues that relate to bilinguals in the classroom: first, do children with two languages have disadvantages or advantages in thinking and in school achievement due to their bilingualism? Second, why do some bilingual children fail in school, for example when they move from a home language that is different from the school (e.g., Spanish to English in the United States)?

The answers given in this chapter derive from the development of a simple theory about common underlying proficiency in a person's two languages. For educationalists, that served as a simple statement that bilingualism can be beneficial as both languages feed a central think tank. The later development of the developmental interdependence hypothesis refined such cognitive integration.

The extension of that early theory was the thresholds theory. This has provided teachers with a simple guide. A language used in the classroom must be well developed to enable learning to occur; when two languages can be used, there are likely to be benefits and achievement advantages. The basics of the theory are now widely supported by research, reason and experience.

The imagination of teachers has been most fired by the notion of BICS and CALP. It is possibly the most influential theory as the distinction is neat, and the terms have become part of the language of bilingual education. Its explanatory power for the failure of some children (e.g., immigrants) in classrooms secured its place among educational theories. Bilingual children who fail often do so because their school language is not nearly so developed as their home language, and is not at the level to cope with the increasingly complex language of the classroom.

The simplicity of the BICS/CALP distinction was soon critiqued by scholars. It led to the refinement by creating dimensions of (a) context reduced and context embedded communication and (b) cognitively demanding and cognitively undemanding communication. This, in turn, gave teachers of bilingual children an organizing tool for curriculum activity, especially with those who are emerging bilinguals (Garcia, 2009).

That has been the ultimate value of these theories. They are about empowering bilingual children. They relate to a dismantling of prejudices about the supposed cognitive deficits of bilingualism. Instead, these theories have been influential in a new vision about bilingual children. The effect has been to seek empowerment of emerging bilinguals. This is about developing the cognitive and curriculum potential of those children fortunate enough to share the potential advantages of bilingualism: communication, cultural, cognitive, curriculum, character, and cash.

REFERENCES

Baker, C. (2011). *Foundations of bilingual education and bilingualism*. Bristol, England: Multilingual Matters.

Baker, C., & Hornberger, N. H. (2001). Jim Cummins: A biographical introduction. In C. Baker & N. H. Hornberger (Eds.), *Introductory reader to the writings of Jim Cummins* (pp. 1-15). Clevedon, England: Multilingual Matters.

Bialystok, E. (1988). Levels of bilingualism and levels of linguistic awareness. *Developmental Psychology, 24*(4), 560-567.

Bialystok, E. (2001). *Bilingualism in development: Language, literacy and cognition*. Cambridge, England: Cambridge University Press.

Cenoz, J. (2003). The additive effect of bilingualism on third language acquisition: A review. *International Journal of Bilingualism, 7*(1), 71-87.

Clarkson, P. C. (1992). Language and mathematics: A comparison of bilingual and monolingual students of mathematics. *Educational Studies in Mathematics, 23,* 417-429.

Clarkson, P. C., & Galbraith, P. (1992). Bilingualism and mathematics learning: Another perspective. *Journal for Research in Mathematics Education, 23*(1), 34-44.

Cobo-Lewis, A. B., Eilers, R. E., Pearson, B. Z., & Umbel, V. C. (2002). Interdependence of Spanish and English knowledge in language and literacy among bilingual children. In D. K. Oller & R. E. Eilers (Eds.), *Language and literacy in bilingual children* (pp. 118-134). Clevedon, England: Multilingual Matters.

Cummins, J. (1976). The influence of bilingualism on cognitive growth: A synthesis of research findings and explanatory hypotheses. *Working Papers on Bilingualism, 9,* 1-43.

Cummins, J. (1978). Metalinguistic development of children in bilingual education programs: Data from Irish and Canadian Ukrainian–English programs. In M. Paradis (Ed.), *Aspects of bilingualism* (pp. 127-138). Columbia, NY: Hornbeam Press.

Cummins, J. (1979). Cognitive/academic language proficiency, linguistic interdependence, the optimum age question. *Working Papers on Bilingualism,* 19, 121-129.

Cummins, J. (1981a). *Bilingualism and minority language children.* Ontario, Canada: Ontario Institute for Studies in Education.

Cummins, J. (1981b). The role of primary language development in promoting educational success for language minority students. In California State Department of Education (Ed.), *Schooling and language minority students. A theoretical framework* (pp. 3-49). Los Angeles, CA: California State Department of Education.

Cummins, J. (1983). Language proficiency, biliteracy and French immersion. *Canadian Journal of Education, 8*(2), 117-138.

Cummins, J. (1984). *Bilingualism and special education: Issues in assessment and pedagogy.* Clevedon, England: Multilingual Matters.

Cummins, J. (2000a). *Language, power and pedagogy: Bilingual children in the crossfire.* Clevedon, England: Multilingual Matters.

Cummins, J. (2000b). Putting language proficiency in its place: Responding to critiques of the conversational/academic language distinction. In J. Cenoz & U. Jessner (Eds.), *English in Europe: The acquisition of a third language* (pp. 54-83). Clevedon, England: Multilingual Matters.

Cummins, J. (2008). BICS and CALP: Empirical and theoretical status of the distinction. In B. Street & N. H. Hornberger (Eds.), *Encyclopedia of Language and Education, 2nd Edition, Volume 2: Literacy* (pp. 71-83). New York, NY: Springer.

Cummins, J. (2009). Fundamental Psychological and Sociological Principles Underlying Educational Success for Linguistic Minority Students. In A. K. Mohanty, M. Panda, R. Phillipson & T. Skutnabb-Kangas (Eds.), *Multilingual educa-*

tion for social justice: Globalising the local (pp. 21-35). New Delhi, India: Orient BlackSwan.

Dawe L.C. (1983). Bilingualism and mathematical reasoning in English as a second language. *Educational Studies in Mathematics, 14*(1), 325-353.

Edelsky, C. (1991). *With literacy and justice for all: Rethinking the social in language and education*. London: Falmer.

Edelsky, C., Hudelson, S., Flores, B., Barkin, F., Altwerger, B., & Jilbert, K. (1983). Semilingualism and language deficit. *Applied Linguistics, 4*(1), 1-22.

Errasti, M. P. (2003). Acquiring writing skills in a third language: The positive effects of bilingualism. *International Journal of Bilingualism,* 7(1), 27-42.

Frederickson, N., & Cline, T. (1990). *Curriculum Related Assessment with Bilingual Children.* London: University College London.

Frederickson, N., & Cline, T. (2002). *Special Educational Needs, Inclusion and Diversity: a Textbook.* Buckingham, England: Open University Press.

Garcia, O. (2009). *Bilingual education in the 21st century: A global perspective*. Oxford, England: Blackwell.

Hakuta, K., & D'Andrea, D. (1992). Some properties of bilingual maintenance and loss in Mexican background high-school students. *Applied Linguistics, 13*(1), 72-99.

Huguet, A., Vila, I., & Llurda, E. (2000). Minority language education in unbalanced bilingual situations: a case for the linguistic interdependence hypothesis. *Journal of Psycholinguistic Research,* 29(3), 313-333.

Kroll, J. F., & De Groot, A. M. (1997). Lexical and conceptual memory in the bilingual: Mapping form to meaning in two languages. In A. M. De Groot & J. F. Kroll (Eds.), *Tutorials in bilingualism: Psycholinguistic perspectives* (pp. 169-200). Mahwah, NJ: Erlbaum.

Lindholm-Leary, K. J. (2001). *Dual language education.* Clevedon, England: Multilingual Matters.

Linquanti, R. (2001). *The redesignation dilemma: Challenges and choices in fostering meaningful accountability for English learners.* Santa Barbara, CA: Linguistic Minority Research Institute, University of California.

MacSwan, J., & Rolstad, K. (2003). Linguistic diversity, schooling and social class: Rethinking our conception of language proficiency in language minority education. In C. B. Paulston & G. R. Tucker (Eds.), *Sociolinguistics: The essential readings* (pp. 329-340). Oxford, England: Blackwell.

Martin-Jones, M., & Romaine, S. (1986). Semilingualism: A half baked theory of communicative competence. *Applied Linguistics,* 7(1), 26-38.

Oller, D. K., & Eilers, R. E. (Eds.). (2002). *Language and literacy in bilingual children.* Clevedon, England: Multilingual Matters.

Pavlenko, A. (2005). Bilingualism and thought. In J. Kroll & A. De Groot (Eds.), *Handbook of bilingualism: Psycholinguistic approaches* (pp. 433-453). Oxford, England: Oxford University Press.

Proctor, P. (2003, April). *Degree of bilingualism and English reading achievement.* Paper presented at the Fourth Symposium on Bilingualism, Arizona State University.

Rivera, C. (Ed.). (1984). *Language proficiency and academic achievement.* Clevedon, England: Multilingual Matters.

Robson, A. (1995). The assessment of bilingual children. In M. K. Verma, K. P. Corrigan, & S. Firth (Eds.), *Working with bilingual children* (pp. 28-47). Clevedon, England: Multilingual Matters.

Shohamy, E. G. (1999, August). *Unity and diversity in language policy.* Paper presented at the AILA Conference, Tokyo.

Spada, N., & Lightbown, P. M. (2002). L1 and L2 in the education of Inuit children in northern Quebec: Abilities and perceptions. *Language and Education, 16*(3), 212-240.

Toukomaa, P., & Skutnabb-Kangas, T. (1977). *The intensive teaching of the mother tongue to migrant children at pre-school age* (Research Report No. 26). Department of Sociology and Social Psychology, University of Tampere.

Wiley, T. G. (1996). *Literacy and language diversity in the United States.* McHenry, IL: Center for Applied Linguistics and Delts Systems.

Wiley, T. G. (2005). *Literacy and language diversity in the United States* (2nd ed.). McHenry, IL: Center for Applied Linguistics and Delts Systems.

Author Contact Information: **Colin Baker**, PhD, professor and pro vice chancellor, Bangor University, Wales, United Kingdom. Phone: +44 (0) 1248 351151. E-mail: c.r.baker@bangor.ac.uk

CHAPTER 34

Language and Literacy Acquisition Theories

Kathryn A. Davis
University of Hawaiì

Carlos J. Ovando
Arizona State University

Masahiko Minami
San Francisco State University/National Institute for Japanese Language and Linguistics

> I come back to theory and politics, the politics of theory. Not theory as the will to truth, but theory as a set of contested, localized, conjunctural knowledges, which have to be debated in a dialogical way. But also as a practice which always thinks about its intervention in a world in which it would make some difference, in which it would have some effect. (Hall, 1992, p. 286)

Theories concerning the acquisition and meanings of language and literacy have proliferated in Western scholarship since the early twentieth century. While varying theories and associated research methodologies are historically situated in and influenced by major philosophical eras, scholars have engaged in debate over the efficacy of particular perspectives that cross time and thought. This chapter explores the development of language and literacy theories arising from modernity, modernism, and postmodernism as these have impacted past and present educational policies and teaching practices. Thus, we take up Hall's call for fostering dialogic debate while recognizing theory as "a practice which always thinks about its intervention in a world in which it would make some difference." In acknowledging contested contributions that span theoretical and research epistemologies, this chapter also explores the politics of theory in terms of the learning and social equity outcomes of practices arising from particular theoretical stances.[1]

Modernity and the Rise of Scientific Rationality

Although modernity and modernism are often linked, Grbich (2004) describes key distinctions between these two philosophical eras. Modernity emerged during the period in eighteenth century European history known as the Enlightenment. This era of scientific knowledge based in logic was intended to displace the perceived predominance of ignorance and superstition. Modernity philosophical thought and social transitions that spanned the Enlightenment and industrialization promoted narratives of progress gained through scientific measurement, technological processes, and rationalism (Grbich, 2004). Specialist disciplines with defined boundaries were established and defended while scientific principles such as causality, logical determinism, and analytical analysis came to define empirical research. These philosophical and institutional premises subsequently formed the basis for positivist and postpositivist research, which is concerned with internal and external validity, grounded in logical-deductive theory, and represented through scientific reports

The Handbook of Educational Theories, pp. 395–418

(Denzin & Lincoln, 2005). Although subsequent positivistic theoretical and methodological approaches have not strictly adhered to modernity tenets, this philosophical era greatly influenced language learning research and theories.

During the first half of the twentieth century, the field of behaviorism in Western societies and especially the United States took a positivist view of social psychology that involved scientific study of complex forms of mental activity (Watson, 1913, 1924, 1928). Behaviorists, also known as learning theorists or environmentalists, viewed the environment as molding the child. In suggesting language as a representative case of learning theory, the behaviorist B. F. Skinner (1957) argued that language development is largely determined by establishing connections between stimuli and verbal responses. While the behaviorist approach claimed that the learning principle of reinforcement plays a central role in the process of language acquisition, Noam Chomsky (1959) argued that because the linguistic environment cannot account for the structures that appear in children's language, aspects of language rules and structure must be innate. N. Chomsky (1959) specifically criticized Skinner's behaviorist claim that language learning is based on experience. Instead, N. Chomsky (1965) held that because patterns of language development are similar across different languages and cultures, the environment plays a relatively minor role in language maturation. He emphasized that humans have a biological endowment, which he called a *language acquisition device,* which contains innate abilities concerning grammar in general and syntax in particular. In other words, the language acquisition device contains fundamental knowledge about the basic nature and structure of human language, which N. Chomsky identified as universal grammar. Although grammatical rules of sentence structure are limited, when triggered by input, this internalized system of rules can generate an infinite number of grammatical sentences. In this way, the language acquisition device enables normally developing children in any culture to learn language and use it fluently. Believing in a self-charged "bioprogram" whereby language acquisition is autonomous, N. Chomsky (1985) hypothesized that in the language acquisition process, children move from an initial learning state to language facility, as though by flipping a series of switches. This parameter setting is considered to occur at a very early age through prosodic cues; that is, infants find important clues to the basic configuration of their language in the prosodic characteristics of the speech they hear (Mazuka, 1998; J. L. Morgan & Demuth, 1996).

For nearly 5 decades, the linguistic revolution originated by N. Chomsky exerted an influence on child language studies, particularly research into children's acquisition of syntax (e.g., Slobin, 1985; Wanner & Gleitman, 1982). Drawing on modernist assumptions, Brown and Bellugi (1964) stressed the rule-governed nature of language acquisition as opposed to behaviorist theory, which holds that children's speech is not rule-governed but is shaped by external contingencies and reinforced by caretakers' approval. While acknowledging the significant influence of environmental or parental interactions (e.g., mothers modify their speech to their children by simplifying, repeating, and paraphrasing), Brown and Bellugi emphasized that the process of language acquisition could not be explained by the behaviorist stimulus-response-reinforcement system alone. Rather they believed that the child's ability to engage in inductive processing would aid language acquisition. These researchers paid particular attention to inductive processes that characterize the child's acquisition of syntactic structures. In analyzing toddlers' language acquisition, Brown and Bellugi concluded that mother-child interaction, which is a cycle of imitations, reductions, and expansions, would help the child's inductive processing of the latent structure and rules of the target language. Likewise, Carol Chomsky (1969, 1972) examined elementary school children's language development and found a relationship to literacy activities such as reading. With a particular emphasis on the innate mechanism for language learning, she suggested that this natural process of children's language development would continue actively into their elementary school years. According to C. Chomsky, the degree of sophistication in language acquisition is reflected in the ability to understand grammatically complex sentences, such as "John told Bill to leave" versus "John promised Bill to leave." Furthermore, according to a number of theorists (e.g., Nelson, 1981), despite diverse individual differences particularly in terms of the rate of development, all children construct implicit grammatical rules and pass through a developmental sequence of linguistic stages.

While first language (L1) acquisition research theories were developing during the modernist era, parallel theories/hypotheses in the field of second language (L2) acquisition began to emerge. Up until the late 1960s, the behaviorist conception of language acquisition prevailed (e.g., Fries, 1945/1972; Lado, 1957). While Fries's and Lado's contrastive analysis hypothesis incorporated behaviorist views, they argued that L1 and L2 acquisition differ because L2 learners use the structure of the L1 in learning an L2. Thus, according to the contrastive analysis hypothesis, L2 errors originate from differences between the learner's L1 and the target language. However, on conceptual grounds, Corder (1967, 1971) and Selinker (1972) claimed that, like children learning their L1, learners of a second language could be characterized as proceeding through a series of intermediate grammars. On empirical grounds,

Dulay and Burt (1974) proposed the notion of *L2 creative construction*, a subconscious process that, rather than relying on L1 rules, resembles the L1 acquisition process itself. That is, L2 learners gradually organize the language they hear, and understand and generate sentences according to the rules they hypothesize. Following Brown's (1973) L1 study, which reported remarkable similarity among his three subject children in the order in which fourteen functor morphemes (e.g., present progressive *–ing*, plural *–s*) were acquired, Dulay and Burt conducted a series of L2 studies to examine the question of whether developmental sequences, regardless of the L1 or the L2, could be identified in terms of a common/invariant sequence of acquisition for functor morphemes in English. Dulay and Burt attributed the observed discrepancy between L1 and L2 acquisition to the different cognitive abilities of children at different stages of their development. Likewise, these researchers concluded that the observed similarity among L2 learners from different L1 backgrounds (Chinese, Spanish) provided a strong indication that universal cognitive mechanisms (the L2 system rather than the child's L1) would serve as the basis for the child's organization of the target English language.

Given the focus on modernist and positivist forms of research, scholars began to propose alternative paradigms for understanding language acquisition to address concerns that the environmental influence on language development not be overlooked. For example, the emergentist approach (MacWhinney, 1999) claimed that although an innate, domain-specific mechanism might allow for the initial emergence of language, domain-general cognitive mechanisms, such as working memory, statistical learning, and pressures on memory organization and retrieval, contribute to evolving language acquisition. More specifically, in the emergentist framework, domain-general cognitive mechanisms utilize environmental stimuli to realize complex and elegant structures of language. Thus, the emergentist view suggests the surfacing of a constructivist perspective in emphasizing the interaction between the organism and the environment; i.e., children gradually learn through interacting with environmental factors such as parents' speech patterns. Snow and Ferguson (1977) further suggested that parents play a far more important role in their children's language acquisition than simply modeling the language and providing input for language acquisition device.

While early linguists were influenced by modernist scientific rationality that guided theories of innate language acquisition abilities (N. Chomsky) and positivist first and second language acquisition research that was predominantly conducted in Western English-dominant situations, researchers became increasingly aware of the roles that social context plays in language development.[2] Subsequent overlapping modernist and postmodernist philosophies have further promoted social constructivist, context-embedded, and diversity theories of language/literacy development and use.

Language and Literacy in the Modernist Era

Movement from a positivist and postpositivist ontology of realism toward social constructivism reflected the modernist philosophical view that reality is multiple and locally constructed through social practices. The following account first describes the emerging intersection of language, environment, and mind in sociocognitive approaches to language development. This section then focuses on first and second language and literacy acquisition research and theories that arose through the philosophical influences of modernism, leading into the postmodernist era.

In contrast to behavioristic or linguistic approaches, Piaget (1926/1959) was among the first to argue that the complex structures of language seem neither innate nor learned. Rather, Piaget's interactive approach suggests that language structures emerge as a result of continuing interaction between the child's current level of cognitive functioning and his or her linguistic as well as nonlinguistic environment. The relationship between cognitive and linguistic development is reflected in Piaget's earliest stage of sensorimotor intelligence (from birth to approximately 2 years of age). For example, the most important achievement of the sensorimotor stage is the acquisition of object permanency, which is closely related to the emergence of language. Early in the sensorimotor stage, Piaget suggested that children appear to assume that objects no longer exist when they cannot be seen. That is, children at this stage understand the world only through direct sensation (i.e., sensory) and the activities they perform upon it (i.e., motor). Piaget proposed that once an object is outside a child's immediate perceptual environment, it ceases to exist, and thus no labels (or names) are necessary to refer to such objects. During the second year of life, however, Piaget stated that children gradually acquire the concept of object permanence. As a consequence, objects need labels/names so that children can refer to those objects apart from their own perception of them. Thus, children progress through cognitive stages that correspond to language development.

Vygotsky (1978) was instrumental in furthering sociocognitive theory through viewing language as a socioculturally mediated product. Vygotsky (1962) argued that language is at first only a tool for social interaction, but that the role of language changes over the course of development from a social tool to a private tool as the child internalizes linguistic forms. More generally, Vygotsky (1978) hypothesized that children learn from other people, and particularly that children's problem-solving skills, which include language, first develop through social interactions with more capable members of society—adults and peers—that become internalized after long practice. Specifically, Vygotsky interpreted the acquisition of children's cognitive skills in terms of the "zone of proximal development." For Vygotsky, the zone of proximal development is determined by the relationship between the following two types of children's problem-solving behaviors: (a) the behaviors children exhibit when they solve a problem by interacting with adults who can provide them with some guidance, such as structuring the problem, solving part of the problem, or providing suggestions—i.e., interpsychological behavior corresponding to the potential level of development; and (b) the behaviors children exhibit when they can solve the problem by themselves—that is, intrapsychological behavior in accordance with the actual level of development. As the child matures, the relationship between interpsychological and intrapsychological behaviors changes for a given task, so that children gradually come to solve on their own problems that previously they could solve only partially, or not at all, except through interpersonal supportive interactions provided by adults.

Vygotsky's zone of proximal development is principally a construct that helps explain how interaction contributes to children's development. Through the process of social interaction, adults provide children with the tools to establish complex series of actions in problem-solving situations. The zone of proximal development holds that because the process of social interaction occurs before children have the mental capacity to take appropriate actions to solve the problem on their own, adults need to regulate children's actions. Through the process of interaction, these regulatory behaviors exhibited by adults gradually become part of the children's own behavior. The relationship between cognitive development and social interaction, particularly early social interactions between children and more mature members of society, can be summarized by Vygotsky's claim that all higher mental functions appear twice in development: first as social or interpsychological functions during interactions with other social agents, and only later through the internalization of social-interactive processes as individualized or intrapsychological functions.

While sociocognitive theories of language evolved, anthropological and sociological researchers were also exploring diverse language, social, and cultural behavior. Sociologist Erving Goffman suggested a modernist perspective as early as 1956 in holding that individuals actively construct their social identities rather than passively perform particular cultural prescriptions for social behavior. Goffman argued for studying how individuals construct identities and mutually negotiate meaning in face-to-face interaction. Based on Goffman's work, Sacks, Schegloff, and Jefferson (1974) and Sinclair, McHardy, and Coultard (1975) studied the organization of turn-taking in conversation and classroom discourse, respectively. Anthropologist Dell Hymes (1974) directly opposed purely cognitive language theories and decontextualized communicative studies in proposing the ethnography of communication approach to language research. This approach argues that speech acts and other communicative events cannot be fully understood without attending to culture and context. In challenging de Saussure and N. Chomsky in their dichotomous definitions of *competence* and *performance*, Hymes (1974) introduced the concept of *communicative competence*, the ability not only to apply the grammatical rules of a language in order to construct a grammatically correct sentence, but also to know when, where, and with whom to use these correct sentences in a given sociocultural situation. Gumperz (1981) further clarified the definition of *communicative competence* as "the knowledge of linguistic and related communicative conventions that speakers must have to initiate and sustain conventional involvement" (p. 325). Thus, whereas N. Chomsky focused on the universal nature of language acquisition, interactional sociolinguists Hymes and Gumperz contended that language is largely shaped by culture-specific experiences and beliefs, and emphasized characteristic features of the outcome of language acquisition in specific sociocultural contexts.

Gumperz (1982) further bridged the study of interaction and culture through his "crosstalk" research, which explored how taken-for-granted social norms affect negotiation of meaning in intercultural encounters. Theories of "contextualization cues" emerging from this research played a significant role in the development of interactional sociolingustics, a combined sociology and linguistics approach to examining discourse strategies across cultural, ethnic, racial, and gender backgrounds. Both interactional sociolingustics and ethnography of communication influenced the emergence of studies and theories concerning cross-cultural communication in everyday life and classrooms. Most notably, Cazden, John, and Hymes's (1972) landmark publication *Functions of Language in the Classroom* initiated a theoretical shift in explanations for school failure. For example, Philips's work on the Warm Springs Indian Reservation revealed differences in participation structure between community and classroom interactive norms that led to student-teacher miscommunication (Philips, 1972, 1983). Gumperz and Hernandez-Chavez (1972) also contributed a study of Spanish-English code-switching among Chicanos/Chicanas and in which they argued for teacher understanding of social meanings of cultural identities and values conveyed through the use of multiple linguistic codes. And the British sociologist Basil Bernstein's research on language use and development resulted in theories of restricted (working-class) and elaborated (middle-class) language codes as these relate to school performance (e.g., 1973). More specifically, Bernstein posited that whereas British middle-class speakers do not assume prior or shared understanding or knowledge in interaction, working-class speakers tend to presuppose shared knowledge that is connotatively referenced in interaction. Although critics (e.g., de Castell & Walker, 1991) held that this sociolinguistic perspective suggested linguistic deficiency among restricted code speakers, Bernstein argued that his research emphasized ways in which working-class students are disadvantaged by school expectations for an elaborated code. Bernstein saw his work as contributing to a theory of sociolinguistic and sociocultural difference (as opposed to genetic or sociocultural deficit) as an explanation for school failure.

While modernist philosophy undergirded early constructivist oral language acquisition and cross-cultural communication theories, literacy acquisition was also undergoing similar philosophical, methodological, and theoretical transformations.[3] Since the early twentieth century, language researchers had engaged in theorizing the cognitive effects of literacy. The "great literacy-orality theoretical divide" arose from modernity-era (post-Fordian) theorists who held that higher and more complex mental functions such as logical and analytical thinking resulted from the invention of writing systems and subsequent text production (Goody & Watt, 1963). Bruner (1966) further asserted that writing promotes cognitive development. Since, in his view, oral language relies on context for communication, written language requires that meaning be clear and independent of immediate reference. Olson (1977) specifically linked literacy-related logical operations to Piaget's final stage of formal operational thought and further contends that literacy and education drive cognitive growth. In contrast to development theory, Scribner and Cole (1981) utilized a functional approach in proposing that literacy skills promoted by schooling are not necessarily applied in social contexts unrelated to school practices. They further explored the possible consequences of literacy apart from schooling. They conducted a longitudinal study among the Vai people of Liberia, who were unschooled but literate in a syllabic writing system they had invented and used for nearly 200 years. Rather than starting from a developmental premise, these researchers engaged in situated theory-building by conducting observations of how literacy was actually socially organized and used by the Vai. Scribner and Cole's (1978) research generally suggests a theory of literacy as practice, whereas engagement in particular functions has interrelated cognitive and social outcomes: "Carrying out critical analyses of text, for example, might promote certain analytic operations with language, whereas rote learning from the same text, or reading it for some other purposes, is not likely to do so" (Scribner & Cole, 1978, p. 244). They conclude that "the effects of literacy, and perhaps schooling as well, are restricted—perhaps to the practice actually engaged in or generalized only to closely related practices" (1978, p. 243). These researchers also theorize that neither literacy nor schooling is a requisite for or necessarily results in abstract thinking, as was suggested by the developmental theorists.

Anthropological work that further challenged the literacy theories advanced by scholars such as Goody and Watt (1963) included the work of Ruth Finnegan, who wrote a series of articles culminating in her volume *Literacy and Orality* (1988). Through drawing on her ethnographic fieldwork, Finnegan illustrated how the Limba of Sierra Leone had a heightened awareness of language use through proximity with speakers of mutually unintelligible languages. Their elaborated philosophy of language and understanding of the nature and uses of language discredited claims by Olson, Goody and Watt, and others that nonliterates were incapable of abstract thought. Finnegan (1988) further challenged the notion of literature as solely written text in portraying Limba storytelling and poetry as oral performance that comprises a legacy of Limba literature. Finnegan's work additionally goes beyond a functional approach in indirectly suggesting that metalinguistic and metacognitive awareness can arise from situated practices, such as multilingualism, that create the conditions for philosophical and creative expression.

During the 1980s, an increasing number of anthropological studies explored the social meaning of literacy.[4] Most notable among these was Heath's study of three communities in the U.S. southeast. This 10-year-long study drew on the inquiry theories and methods of Hymes (1974) and other modernist sociolinguists and ethnographers to examine "the actual forms and functions of oral and literate traditions and coexisting relationships between spoken and written language" (Heath, 1983, p. 93). Through this comparative study of White and African American working-class neighborhoods and White and African American middle-class townspeople, Heath not only went beyond the orality-literacy divide to understand the intersecting roles of both, but also explored the meaning of situated patterns of language and literacy practices for school achievement. For example, Heath addressed mainstream teachers' assessment that African American working-class students could not respond appropriately to the "simplest questions or instructions," resulting in diagnoses of these children as "nonverbal" and "a bit slow." In documenting adult-child interaction routines across communities, Heath illustrated how working-class children's language socialization differed greatly from mainstream teachers' expectations regarding the initiation-response-evaluation pattern of questioning generally found in classrooms (Cazden, 1988; Mehan, 1979). Essentially, Heath asserted that the acquisition of communicative competence occurring through immersion in social practices, including those associated with oral interaction and literacy, results in advantaging or disadvantaging children in school depending on the degree of similarity between home and classroom expectations for social behavior. Although Heath established that interactional routines and social expectations surrounding literacy in middle-class homes paralleled those in school, she also found that children from the African American working-class community mastered environmental forms of print (e.g., names of cereal, meanings of railroad names) without being taught. For these children, comprehension became the context rather than the outcome of learning to read (Heath, 1986).

Collins and Blot (2003) summarize Heath's ethnographic work (1982, 1983) as demonstrating that "the complex mix of oral and literate means of communication in the communities undermines any claim to a set of universal uses and functions of literacy" (p. 44). More specifically, they state:

> What we learn from Heath's work is that there is no universality to literacy; there are many illiteracies. To describe only one set of uses and functions (those associated with school or essayist literacy) is to miss the myriad other uses and functions found among the literacies of communities throughout the world. This is no mere academic issue. An acceptance of Olson-like essayist literacy as normative condemns those whose ways of making meaning and of taking meaning from text vary from the norm to a perpetual struggle to legitimate their own practices. (p. 44)

This struggle to legitimate multiple language and literacy practices as realized in schools serving socially, linguistically, and/or culturally diverse student populations has been documented by a number of educational researchers and theorists. Scholars (e.g., Cummins, 1979; Nieto, 1992; Ovando, Combs, & Collier, 2006; Zentella, 1997) have long argued for bilingual education programs that support immigrant students' multiple sociointeractional, literacy, and cultural resources while they acquire the second/dominant language of the school.

At the same time that ethnographic studies of language/literacy socialization/use and the coconstruction of meaning were contributing to language education theory-building, first language acquisition psycholinguistic case studies (e.g., Brown, 1973) and N. Chomsky's (1975) cognitive-based language acquisition theories had led to the development of the field of second language acquisition. While contributing to an understanding of the cognitive nature of language development, the field has resisted inclusion of social context in learning theories (Block, 2003; Firth & Wagner, 1997). Firth and Wagner suggested that, since the 1960s, tension has existed between "on the one hand, acknowledgement of the social, contextual dimensions of language, language acquisition and learning, and on the other, the centrality of the individual's language cognition and mental process" (p. 288). These authors concluded that while language is a cognitive function, it is also "fundamentally a social phenomenon, acquired and used interactively, in a variety of contexts for myriad practical purposes" (p. 296). Watson-Gegeo (2004) further advanced the social-anthropological position by stating that "cognition originates in social interaction and is shaped by cultural and sociopolitical processes: These processes are central rather than incidental to cognitive development" (p. 331). While there was general movement toward the theoretical centrality of language and literacy as social practice, scholars were also increasingly challenging researchers to include analyses of sociopolitical processes embedded in situated practices and impacted by policies. For example, although acknowledging sociolinguists and ethnographers for their contributions to complexity theories of language and literacy acquisition, researchers such as Heath were criticized (e.g., Collins & Blot, 2003; de Castell & Walker, 1991) for not attending to power relations. In *Ways with Words*, Heath (1983) included descriptions of how teachers involved in her study integrated emerging theories of situated language and literacy use into their pedagogical practices to mitigate inequitable schooling. However, she concludes with the revelation that some of the theoretical insights and curricula illustrated in the book were dismantled through federal and state educational policies that effectively removed institutional spaces for school reform.

A notable exception to the lack of attention to sociopolitical issues during late modernism was the "pedagogy of the oppressed" theories and practices of Paulo Frère. As a result of postindustrial economic shifts, large portions of populations had been identified as illiterate and thus as poorly equipped to meet newly created labor demands. Adult literacy campaigns subsequently emerged, and schools were charged with providing all students with a "functional" level of reading and writing ability. In response to literacy campaigns in Brazil and Peru, Freire (1982) developed a critical approach to literacy learning that involved "reading the word and reading the world." Freire's "pedagogy of the oppressed" model went beyond decoding and encoding by engaging groups in a cyclical process of reflection and action regarding the social equity issues that impacted their lives.

In sum, fundamental to the modernist and evolving postmodern eras of social constructivism is the view that languages and literacies are social practices (Barton, Hamilton, & Ivanič, 2000; Cope & Kalantzis, 2000; Gee, 1996; Lankshear & Knobel, 2003; Street, 2003, 2005). While second language acquisition arising from the cognitivist theories of Chomsky sought ever-increasing refinement of acquisition theories based on positivist and postpositivist research, sociolinguists and linguistic anthropologists held that cognition resides in sociocultural interaction and sociopolitical processes. In addition, although psychology skills-based approaches to teaching reading and writing continued throughout this era, the social practice theories that dominated education theory at this time argued that, rather than a set of static, decontextualized, and discrete skills, literacy is always instantiated, dynamic, situated, and multifaceted through local practices that are "embedded in socially constructed epistemological principles" (Street, 2003, p. 1).

In many ways, the language and literacy theories that arose during modernism reflect Bakhtin's notion of dialogism (Bakhtin, 1981) as articulated by Kristeva (1980). Kristeva coined the term *intertextuality* to describe the idea that "any text is constructed as a mosaic of quotations; any text is the absorption and transformation of another" (1980, p. 66). In other words, various linkages exist between texts or between different discourse events. While modernist philosophy of the twentieth century involved increasing refinement of social constructivist theories, they also melded into and foreshadowed postmodern philosophical and theoretical thought. Early studies of relationships between abstract thought and literacy intersected with the emerging social practices theories of Goffman, Gumperz, Geertz, and Hymes, which in turn impacted educational research and theory-building. The research of scholars such as Cazden, Heath, and Philips moved theories concerning differential student performance from genetic and cultural deficit to home/school difference explanations for school failure. Activists and theorists Freire (1982) and Boal (1979) directly addressed sociopolitical structures of social inequity surrounding literacy and discourse through the pedagogy and theatre of the oppressed, respectively. Yet, rather than a historical progression, philosophical and theoretical intertextuality supports the ongoing crossover of epistemological, ontological, methodological, and sociopolitical thought and action. Scribner and Cole's theories of interrelated cognitive and social outcomes of literacy functions along with Finnegan's theories of metalinguistic and metacognitive awareness arising from situated practices are reflected in postmodern language and literacy theories. These social practice theories proved to hold significant implications for late twentieth and early twenty-first century politically and economically motivated educational policies that imposed psychological skill-based language and literacy models.

Language and Literacy in the Postmodern Era

Grbich (2004) defines postmodernism as "the identifiable ideological position that developed from modernism, including further development of the ideas, stylistic communications and the perceptions and beliefs, which began to dominate this era" (p. 17). Postmodern researchers have sought new models of truth, method, and (multimodal) representation while increasingly engaging in reflexivity and calling into question static social constructions such as gender, class, race, and borders (disciplinary, cultural, and geographic). A number of scholars publishing during late modernism and early postmodernism formulated theories that were to have a significant impact on language and literacy perspectives associated with schooling.

Bourdieu (1991) describes three primary concepts illustrative of the mutually reinforcing and regulatory social relationships that characterize the human social environment. *Fields* are semiautonomous, structured social spaces characterized by discourse and social activity. Schools are just one of many intersecting and/or competing social spaces that an individual may encounter (Carrington & Luke, 1997). *Habitus* involves the notion that through socialization, one develops particular class, culture-based, and engendered ways of seeing, being, occupying space, and participating in history. The various language and literacy practices of individuals and groups are articulations of the linguistic habitus. *Capital,* defined by Bourdieu as the cultural, economic, social, and linguistic indexes of relative social power, is such only if it is authoritatively recognized in a particular social field. Since middleclass mainstream habitus is commonly embedded in educational practices, familiarity with these ways of knowing and being commonly holds capital in school settings (Delpit, 2006; Heath, 1983). Gee (1996) also explored the distribution of social power and hierarchical social structures through his theory of Discourse. In contrast to "discourse" with a lowercase *d* that simply stands for language in use, Gee defines Discourse with an uppercase *D* as ways of "thinking, feeling, believing, valuing, and acting that can be used to identify oneself as a member of a socially meaningful group" (p. 131). Gee holds that Discourses are "always and everywhere ideological" and further argues that power accrues to dominant Discourses (p. 132), such as those found in schools as well as the governing bodies who set educational policies. Carrington and Luke (1997) suggest that how and whether cultural capital can make a difference for individuals or groups is contingent on a number of factors, including whether or not there is "institutional recognition of the value of the student's various capitals *qua* symbolic capital" (p. 106). Lankshear and McLaren (1993) further argue that theorization of literacy (and language) socialization in terms of its potential consequences for the individual and her/his community depends on its connections to the operation of both local and systemic power relationships.

Theorization of language and literacy during the postmodern era "signal multiple communication channels, hybrid text forms, new social relations, and the increasing salience of linguistic and cultural diversity" (Hull & Schultz, 2002, p. 26). This social practice approach, known as new literacy studies, explores how literacies are multiple, ideological, and both locally and globally situated (Street, 2003, 2004). More specifically, new literacy studies scholars are investigating associated theories of multimodality (Hull & Nelson, 2005; Stein, 2004) and hybridity (Anzaldúa, 1987; Arteaga, 1994; Bhabha, 1994). Hull and Nelson (2005) define multimodality in view of recent technological trends. They suggest that

> It is possible now to easily integrate words with images, sound, music, and movement to create digital artifacts that do not necessarily privilege linguistic forms ... but rather that draw on a variety of modalities—speech, writing, image, gesture, and sound—to create different forms of meaning. (2005, pp. 224-225)

Kress (2003) also indicates the need for investigating multimodality across cultures, ages, and modes of representation. Stein (2004, p. 95) describes local forms of multimodality in South Africa, including the visual, the gestural, and the performative, as deeply embedded in ways of being in and viewing the world. Directly connected to multimodality is the concept of hybridity or complex identity formation as reflected in what Anzaldúa (1987) refers to as living a mosaic of multiple languages and cultures—always in a state of transition, ambivalence, and conflict, and yet also a potentially rich and enriching resource.

In sum, the philosophical and theoretical intertextuality of thought and action across modernism and postmodernism described here provides a view toward educational practices that are responsive to current and future needs of students. Yet, shifting sociopolitical ideologies regarding diverse populations in the United States have fostered debate (Wiley & Wright, 2004) over what constitutes effective language and literacy education. The final section of this chapter is intended to ground language and literacy theories within the sociopolitical contexts in which educational policies and practices are formed. This discussion offers a decidedly pluralistic position that arises from our reading of the theoretical literature and our own sociopolitical stances.

Grounding Modernism and Postmodernism

Central to grounding modern and postmodern language and literacy theories in schooling practices is the need to explore assimilation and pluralism as underlying ideologies that drive language policies, curriculum planning, and pedagogical approaches. Yet, as postmodern philosophy suggests, binary positions fail to capture the complex meanings of these and related ideologies. The multifaceted and interrelated nature of the assimilation versus pluralism debate in the United States is highlighted by the legislative ideologies and minority schooling that dominated schooling in the mid- to late twentieth century. The landmark 1974 Supreme Court *Lau* decision held that a "sink or swim" instructional approach to the education of children who arrive in school with little or no English-speaking ability is a violation of their civil rights (Title VI of the Civil Rights Act of 1964). In the *Martin Luther King Junior Elementary School Children et al. v. Ann Arbor School District* ruling (73 F.Supp. 1371, E.D. Mich. 1979), this principle of equal educational opportunity was extended to children who speak a minority dialect of English. In both cases, the courts assumed the need for an equitable means for students to transition from their home language into standard English. The sociolinguist William Labov, who testified in the Ann Arbor case, proposed the principle of linguistic autonomy, which holds that "Linguists support the use of a standard dialect (or language) in so far as it is an instrument of wider communication for the general population, but oppose its use as a barrier to social mobility" (Labov, 1982). At this historical moment, an assimilationist perspective tempered by recognition of language and literacy acquisition theories and the moral obligation to provide equal opportunity rights provided the means for more equitable education.

While U.S. court decisions opened the way for schools to acknowledge the language and literacy needs of minority students, extensive research by scholars such as Cummins (1979), Thomas and Collier (1997), Ovando et al. (2006; Ovando & Combs, 2012), and many others concerned with the bilingual educational needs of second language speakers of English subsequently contributed to the growth of bilingual education programs in school districts serving immigrant students across the United States and elsewhere. Linguists such as Rickford (1998) and Baugh (2008) further supported the development of instructional programs that address the needs of bidialectal students.

These bilingual/bidialectal programs increasingly moved toward a pluralistic model of education that recognized the cognitive, social, and educational benefits of bilingualism and pluralism. Ruiz (1984) summarized the ideological debate concerning assimilation and pluralism by suggesting that language-in-education policies in the United States and globally tend to reflect a language as problem, language as right, or language as resource ideology. Although U.S. educators have drawn on civil rights legislation to argue for bilingual education, these court decisions are essentially based on a language as problem ideology. Bilingual schooling activists (Fishman, 2006; Nieto, 1992; Ovando et al., 2006) subsequently argued for a language as right position and increasingly suggested multiple ways in which language and social diversity are resources.

Based on right and resource ideologies, scholars (e.g., Nieto, 1992; Ovando et al., 2006; Ovando & Combs, 2012) have drawn on a range of language and literacy theories from the modernist and postmodernist philosophical eras in informing bilingual and multicultural programs. As teachers faced the challenges of teaching two or more languages and dialects for social interactional and academic purposes in classrooms, educational researchers began to explore the range of language and literacy theories that could inform first and second language/dialect development in situated educational settings. In the following discussion of grounding theories in practice, rather than make explicit links to specific theories, the range of perspectives described earlier are assumed in the complex integration of cognitive, social, and cultural empirical findings and ideological positions on language and literacy learning.

Theory-Based Language and Literacy Education[5]

Designing quality programs for language-minority students can profit from examining effective teaching and learning classroom climates for students in general, taking into account ongoing school reform movements. In summarizing and endorsing the case for constructivist classrooms in the reform efforts of the 1990s, Fosnot (1993) suggested that:

> Constructivism is not a theory about teaching. It's a theory about knowledge and learning. Drawing on a synthesis of current work in cognitive psychology, philosophy and anthropology, the theory defines knowledge as temporary, developmental, socially and culturally mediated, and thus, nonobjective. Learning from this perspective is understood as a self-regulated process of resolving inner cognitive conflicts that often become apparent through concrete experience, collaborative discourse, and reflection. (p. vii)

Fosnot identifies five key principles of such constructive psychology: (a) posing problems of emerging relevance to learners; (b) structuring learning around "big ideas" or primary concepts; (c) seeking and valuing students' points of view; (d) adapting curriculum to address students' suppositions; and (e) assessing student learning in the context of teaching (Fosnot, 1993, pp. vii-viii). While these principles provide an important reminder of certain basic pedagogical practices that may have validity for all students, regardless of language background, a variety of language issues in classroom instruction are unique to addressing the needs of language-minority students.

Constructivist approaches to the education of languages and language varieties other than Standard English pose particular pedagogical questions. For example, should speakers of language varieties, such as Black English, Appalachian English, and Hawai'i Creole English, be trained to be bidialectal, that is, to be able to switch from their home variety of English to standard English according to the situation? Some educators interpret bidialectalism as a waste of educational effort, suggesting that students need to discard their home language and replace it with Standard English, preferably by the time they leave kindergarten. Yet most linguists remind us that suppressing such dialects is confusing and detrimental to the academic and social well-being of students. As evidenced by the repeated attempts over the last 50 years to eradicate nonstandard varieties of English from the schools, such efforts have been negatively correlated with achievement gains among language-minority students (Ovando & Collier, 1998). The use of nonstandard English itself cannot be singled out as the cause of school failure. Instead, among the sources of poor academic performance are the school's reaction and approach to nonstandard English. A more positive pedagogical position, states Torrey (1983), is one that:

> affirms the importance of home dialect and its appropriate use within the community in which it is spoken while at the same time students are taught the standard variety. Affirming home language means that students may produce utterances in the classroom in native dialect without being told that they are wrong or that what they say is vulgar or bad. Instead, the teacher analyzes with the students the differences between their dialect and the standard variety; grammatical patterns, pronunciation, vocabulary items, varying social contexts, and so on. (p. 627)

Siegel (1999) further describes some of the educational inequities and obstacles faced by speakers of creoles, which he notes are often mislabeled "nonstandard" or minority dialects. He also outlines proposals for dealing with these problems and describes initiatives that have already taken place, such as developing resources for teachers, running public awareness campaigns, and using the students' home varieties in the classroom (also see Davis, 2009; Davis, Cho, Ishida, Soria, & Bazzi, 2005).

In addition to addressing the needs of speakers of languages, dialects, and creoles, a variety of instructional approaches have been developed to meet the unique needs of speakers of languages other than English. Current curricular approaches to English language learning support the idea that creating bridges between the world of the language-minority student and the world of the school will produce positive cognitive, linguistic, and cultural outcomes. In 1980, for example, the California Office of Bilingual Education launched a case studies project, based on leading theories of cognitive development, second language acquisition, and cross-cultural communication. The resulting integrated curriculum, incorporating home language instruction, communication-based sheltered English, and mainstream English, has subsequently produced excellent results in reading, language arts, and mathematics for language-minority students. Five principles serve as the pedagogical platform for the case studies project:

> (1) Language development in the home language as well as in English has positive effects on academic achievement; (2) Language proficiency includes proficiency in academic tasks as well as in basic conversation; (3) English Language Learners should be able to perform a certain type of academic task in [their] home language before being expected to perform the task in English; (4) Acquisition of English language skills must be provided in contexts in which the student understands what is being said; (5) The social status implicitly ascribed to students and their languages affects student performance. Therefore, majority and minority students should be in classes together in which cooperative learning strategies are used. English speakers should be provided with opportunities to learn the minority languages, and teachers and administrators should model using the minority languages for some noninstructional as well as instructional purposes. (Crawford, 1999, p. 161)

A two-way bilingual program is specifically designed to give both languages equal status. The English-speaking children learn the minority language at the same time that the language-minority students are learning English. Collier (1995) found the following five elements to be important for effective two-way bilingual instruction. Implicit in this approach are attention to sociocultural issues and inclusion of community involvement to ensure a successful bilingual program.

> (1) Integrated schooling, with English speakers and language minority students learning academically through each other's languages; (2) perceptions among staff, students, and parents that it is a "gifted and talented" program, leading to high expectations for student performance; (3) equal status of the two languages achieved, to a large extent, creating self-confidence among language minority students; (4) healthy parent involvement among both language minority and language majority parents, for closer home-school cooperation; and (5) continuous support for staff development, emphasizing whole language approaches, natural language acquisition through all content areas, cooperative learning, interactive and discovery learning, and cognitive complexity for all proficiency levels. (pp. 15-16)

Bilingual programs by definition include an English as a second language (ESL) component, since a main goal is to develop the language-minority student's proficiency in English. Many communities, however, do not or are unable to provide bilingual instruction for all language-minority students. This occurs for a variety of reasons, including such factors as politics, the availability of bilingual teachers, and demographics. In such situations, English language learners are provided with ESL instruction alone, without any significant instruction in their home language. Among the skills important to ESL teachers are (a) a sound knowledge of theory and methods of language acquisition; (b) an understanding of the relationships among culture and language, identity, and adjustment to the new school environment; and (c) the ability to design instruction in such a way that students are helped to become as proficient as possible in content areas such as math, science, and social studies at the same time that they are learning English.

Regarding knowledge of language acquisition, the ESL teacher strives to enable the English language learner to develop phonology, morphology, syntax, and vocabulary primarily through real communicative activities rather than through such approaches as lecture and drills (Heath, 1986). Crawford (1987) describes such language-rich instruction as follows:

> (1) Content is based on the students' communicative needs; (2) instruction makes extensive use of contextual clues; (3) the teacher uses only English, but modifies speech to students' level and confirms student comprehension; (4) students are permitted to respond in their native language when necessary; (5) the focus is on language function or content, rather than grammatical form; (6) grammatical accuracy is promoted, not by correcting errors overtly, but by providing more comprehensible instruction; and (7) students are encouraged to respond spontaneously and creatively. (p. 43)

With respect to cultural knowledge, studies (e.g., Ovando et al., 2006) show that effective ESL teachers do not necessarily have to speak the first languages of their students, but they do need to have as broad an understanding as possible of the history, folklore, traditions, values, attitudes, and current sociocultural situation of the cultural groups with which they work. This knowledge gives the teacher a better understanding of the behavior of ESL students as they adjust to school not as blank slates, but rather as unique individuals with rich linguistic, social, and cultural backgrounds.

The role of ESL teachers in enabling English language learners to develop cognitive-academic language proficiency is also a primary need. Two such curricular and instructional approaches are communication-based sheltered English classes and the cognitive academic language learning approach (CALLA). Sheltered English is an immersion type of methodology that "shelters" English language learners from "input beyond their comprehension, first in subjects that are less language-intensive, such as mathematics, and later in those that are more so, such as social studies" (Crawford, 1987, p. 43). In sheltered English classes, teachers, who may be familiar with the students' first language and cultures, adjust subject matter content and methodology for students who represent a variety of linguistic backgrounds and who are at about the same level of competence in the target language (Richard-Amato, 1998). As reflected in the case studies design, sheltered English classes require that

> teachers change their speech register by slowing down; limiting their vocabulary and sentence length; repeating, emphasizing, and explaining key concepts, and using examples, props, visual clues, and body language to convey and reinforce meaning carried by the language of instruction. (Crawford, 1999)

Like sheltered English, CALLA is a content-based ESL instructional model originally developed by Chamot and O'Malley (1986) in response to the lack of academic success of English language learners. The model supports the notion that by adding academic content to the ESL curriculum and following a specific set of instructional strategies, English language learners can be prepared for grade-level content classrooms (Chamot & O'Malley, 1994). Buttressed by cognitive theory, research, and ongoing classroom use, CALLA is aimed at English language learners who are at the advanced beginning and intermediate levels of English language proficiency. As developed by Chamot and O'Malley (1994), CALLA is compatible with such instructional approaches as language across the curriculum, language experience, whole language, process writing, cooperative learning, and cognitive instruction.

Reflecting the bilingual and ESL principles discussed throughout this section, the California Commission on Teacher Credentialing (1993) has adopted a design for the preparation of teachers who serve English language learners. The design includes two credential variations—a cross-cultural, language, and academic development emphasis for nonbilingual contexts, and a bilingual cross-cultural, language, and academic development emphasis for bilingual contexts. The cross-cultural, language, and academic development/bilingual cross-cultural, language, and academic development credentials include the following six domains of knowledge and skills in which teachers must show competence: (1) language structure and first and second language development; (2) methodology of bilingual, English-language development and content instruction; (3) culture and cultural diversity; (4) methodology for primary language instruction; (5) the culture of emphasis; and (6) the language of emphasis. (Culture and language of emphasis refer to the particular group with whom the teacher is preparing to work, such as Vietnamese, Korean, or Chinese.)

Two common threads run through this entire section on how to address the language needs of speakers of nonstandard varieties of English and second language learners within bilingual education, ESL programs, or mainstream classrooms. First, the languages that children bring to the classroom must be respected and used as a valuable cognitive tool and as a bridge to the development of the language skills that will enable them to succeed academically. Second, all language-minority students need opportunities to develop the complex language skills they will use in literacy-related school activities and throughout their lives as lifelong learners and thinking, active citizens. In other words, it is not enough for students to be able to converse with their peers on the playground or in the halls, or to be able to recite a few rules about standard English. They need to be able to use the context-reduced language associated with extracting meaning from the printed word, for synthesizing and evaluating materials, and for writing. The importance of the development of such high-level skills is illustrated in Collier's (1987) research on non-English-speaking students who entered school in the United States at seventh grade and who were not provided with native-language content instruction. Even though they may have had a solid academic background in their home language, in the U.S. school system they tended to fall behind in standardized test norms, except in mathematics, by the time they reached the eleventh grade. Collier (1987) points out that:

> as they master enough BICS and develop a wide enough range of vocabulary in English to move into deeper development of CALP in second language, they have in the meantime lost 2-3 years of CALP development at their age-grade level. This puts them significantly behind in mastery of the complex material required for high school students. (p. 12)

An important general principle to keep in mind when working with language-minority students—either English-speaking or non-English-speaking—is that their cognitive development must be launched from within the existing sociolinguistic context (Ovando et al., 2006). A number of scholars have suggested that there is no such thing as an exportable model that works everywhere without adaptation. For example, Heath (1986) points out that while language arts curricula are based on an assumption of a path of language development that is the same for all children, regardless of their ethnic origin, the research that establishes such lines of development is based predominantly on middle-class English-speaking families. Only in the last 3 decades have ethnographers working in language-minority communities begun to identify culturally different patterns of language socialization experienced by children. One implication of this variation in language development is that the academic success of language-minority students may hinge to some degree on how these children are able to manipulate language in a variety of contexts and for different purposes, rather than on the specific language they use.

Thus, in addition to phonology, morphology, syntax, and vocabulary, culturally influenced domains such as body language, degrees of formality, genres, and styles of speaking and listening must also be considered in curriculum design. Related to these domains is the need to explore genres. Regarding the specific linguistic elements that are essential for academic success in school regardless of language background, Heath (1986) argued for inclusion of genre, which she defines as the

> kind of organizing unit into which smaller units of language, such as conversations, sentences, lists, or directives may fit. Each cultural group has fundamental genres that occur in recurrent situations; and each genre is patterned as a whole that listeners can anticipate by the prosody of opening formulae what is coming—a joke, a story, or a recounting of shared experiences. Moreover, each sociocultural group recognizes and uses only a few of the total range of genres that humans are capable of producing. (pp. 168-170)

Heath (1986) argues that in order to function well in formal U.S. school settings, students must be able to use a variety of genres typical of U.S. pedagogy, such as label quests, meaning quests, recounts, accounts, event casts, and stories. She indicates that such genres exist in mainstream U.S. school-based activities in a predictable and consistent manner, but that genres may or may not be consistently present in the same way in the language-minority child's home context. Heath suggests that it is the school's responsibility to help students acquire these genres by working closely with the ethnolinguistic community. She recommends that teachers work in a creative partnership with ethnolinguistic communities in a sustained and creative effort to expose students to school-based genres while capitalizing on available community genres.

In addition to the genres identified by Heath, a number of scholars have expanded the notion of genre analysis in efforts to help students develop metalinguistic awareness of complex uses of oral and written texts for multiple purposes. For example, Davis et al. (2005) draws on McComiskey's (2000) framework for student-centered analyses of textual, discursive, and rhetorical aspects of home/school multilingual/bidialectal oral and written texts. Thus, genres are expanded to include a vast array of situated oral, literacy, and multimodal ways of meaning-making across diverse local, global, and educational environments. Gebhard, Willet, Caicedo, and Piedra (2011) have alternatively directly addressed recent structuralist pedagogical demands (standardized curriculum, texts, and tests) in U.S. schools by utilizing Holliday's systemic functional linguistic analysis of genre. This approach to student analysis of the structure of school-oriented genres allows for the systematic approaches to assessment demanded by recent shifts in U.S. education. In the following section, we describe the impact of language-in-education policy changes since the late twentieth century on the education of both minority and mainstream public school students.

Diversity and Standards in the Age of Accountability[6]

Decontextualized approaches to schooling and an attack on bilingual education began in the late 1990s. Despite growing evidence that schooling in immigrants' native languages and English was the most effective form of education for second language learners (e.g., Thomas & Collier, 1997), Ronald Unz, a software entrepreneur, funded and led a crusade to end bilingual education. Unz legislative initiatives, prohibiting classes taught in languages other than English and replacing them with 1 year of ESL classes, were passed in California in 1998, Arizona in 2000, and Massachusetts in 2002. A more comprehensive measure affecting immigrants and other minorities is the federal No Child Left Behind Act (NCLB), which was signed into law in 2002. The stated purpose of NCLB legislation is "to ensure that all children have a fair, equal, and significant opportunity to attain a high-quality education and reach, at a minimum, proficiency on challenging state academic achievement standards and state academic assessments" (NCLB, 2002). Yet, contrary to this proposed intent, NCLB has come under extreme criticism by educators across the United States, especially in relation to emerging consequences for marginalized students (e.g., Cochran-Smith, 2005; Crawford, 2004; Evans & Hornberger, 2005; Lather, 2004; Meier & Wood, 2004; Moore, 2006; Wiley & Wright, 2004; Wright, 2005).

Most of the criticism of NCLB lies with Title I and Title III accountability provisions and sanctions components of the bill. As a member of the National Research Council's Committee on Teacher Education, Cochran-Smith (2002) suggests that the act virtually mandates assessment instruments "using experimental or quasi-experimental designs ... with a preference for random-assignment experiments" (p. 188) that disadvantage minority students. Lather (2004) further argues that the "disciplining and normalizing effort to standardize educational research in the name of quality and effectiveness" (p. 26) shows, as Hall (1996) notes, an "aggressive resistance to difference (and) an assault, direct and indirect, on multiculturalism" (p. 468). A study from the Harvard Civil Rights Project (Orfield, Losen, Wald, & Swanson, 2004) supports these observations in reporting recent nationwide student outcome data that indicate a "national crisis" in graduation rates of minority students, even in those states with the worst overall records of student graduation.

Not only do recent draconian initiatives put a negative spin on biculturalism, bilingualism, and biliteracy in U.S. society, they also denigrate the positive value that first language instruction can have on the academic achievement for language-minority students. In addition, both NCLB and antibilingual education measures reject the accumulated knowledge base generated for the past 25 years by linguists, cognitive psychologists, and bilingual educators that supports the idea that quality-controlled bilingual programs do yield positive outcomes (Crawford, 2000; Ovando & Collier, 1998; Ovando & Pérez, 2000). Yet, given the challenges of these recent policies, educators have found the spaces to draw on modern and postmodern theories in developing and implementing diverse and equitable school practices.

A Postmodern Case Study of Diversity Education

Comprehensive use of postmodern theories during NCLB reform is illustrated through the studies of heritage and academic languages and literacies (SHALL) school program, described by Davis et al. (2005). Over the course of 3 years, teachers at a high school in Hawai'i created a "third space" (Bhaba, 1994) in which Filipino and Samoan students who were fluent speakers of Hawaii Creole English and had varying degrees of Ilokano, Samoan, and English proficiency could explore social, cultural, linguistic, and ideological discourses in heritage and academic English courses. The tools teachers utilized in providing space for student reflection involved students as critical researchers approaches, which included critical ethnography (Davis, 2009; Davis et al., 2005); Duncan-Andrade, 2004; Ginwright, Cammarota, & Noguera, 2005; Ginwright, Noguera, & Cammarota, 2006; Mahiri, 2004; Morrell, 2004), critical language awareness, and critical discourse analysis (Cope & Kalantzis, 1993; Fairclough, 1989, 1992, 1995; Janks, 1993; Luke, 1996; Pennycook, 2001; Wallace, 1992). By emphasizing and legitimizing the knowledge that exists in local discourse communities, research projects encouraged students to view home knowledge as a resource for their academic learning.

More specifically, the SHALL high school program is designed to meet the needs of Filipino and Samoan students at Farrington High School by drawing on recent cross-disciplinary theoretical and ideological developments intended to redress inequitable schooling for linguistic minorities. First, teachers acknowledge heritage language and cultural resources through language courses in Ilokano for Filipinos and Samoan for Samoans. These courses are designed to allow student exploration of multiple language and cultural identities while promoting linguistic proficiency. Second, academic English courses are offered to Filipino, Samoan, and Hawaiian students that are designed to help them develop an improved understanding of the social and educational expectations of teachers within classrooms and across disciplines. Third, in both the heritage and English language courses, students are provided with "third spaces" in which to negotiate or resist the hidden meanings of dominant discursive practices and knowledge frameworks. The strategies teachers use to accomplish goals are based on a number of theoretical considerations. Recent literature on the identity of the learner (Canagarajah, 1993; Norton, 1997; Norton & Toohey, 2002) views contexts and identities as multiple and varied (Bourdieu, 1991; Gee, 1996; Wenger, 1998). Such contexts extend beyond narrowly defined language and literacy skills to include the socially constructed values, understandings, and behaviors associated with language use. Wenger refers to these contexts as "communities of practice," which he defines as

> A historical and social context that gives structure and meaning to what we do ... it includes the language, tools, documents, images, symbols, well-defined roles, specified criteria, codified procedures ... that various practices make explicit for a variety of purposes. But it also includes all the implicit relations, tacit conventions, subtle cues, untold rules of thumb, recognizable intuitions ... and shared world views. (1998, p. 47)

In SHALL courses at Farrington High School, teachers begin with student experiences of communities of practice within their own neighborhoods. However, within local communities, students commonly navigate multiple and complex identities. The Kalihi neighborhood where they live consists of strong Filipino and Samoan communities. A constant influx of relatives from the home countries provides a continuum of cross-generational linguistic abilities and cultural practices. In addition, interaction among numerous ethnic cultural communities (e.g., Hawaiian, Japanese, Chinese, Pacific Islanders, Portuguese, Southeast Asians, Americans) has resulted in a unifying local language (Hawaiì Creole English) and culture (local). U.S. mainstream English is considered the language of schooling.

The SHALL program utilized a student as ethnographer approach in examining multiple layers of both cultural and linguistic practices. At the intercultural level, students explore what "family" or "community" means within their cultural milieu in terms of how these meanings are lived in the routine practices of everyday life and how these relate to their peer group and school communities of practice. Students then engage in a critical examination of their own identity formation through exploring who they are and how others within and outside their communities view their emerging multiple identities. For example, there may be tension between the families' attempts to maintain traditional Samoan cultural practices and students' need to "fit in" by adopting local culture and Hawai`i Creole English (known as Pidgin in the Islands). This exploration not only aids students in considering a possible hybrid cultural and language identity, but it can also contribute to parents' and teachers' valuing of students' ability to draw on a repertoire of cultural and linguistic knowledge for appropriate language use in particular interactional situations. Through community explorations, students begin to develop metalinguistic and metacognitive awareness of how language is structured and used, which they then can transfer to understanding school communities of practice.

Many of the students in the program also had not been provided with an understanding of "how to do school" in the United States. Students utilize the metacognitive awareness developed through community explorations of language use to gain explicit knowledge of how school tasks are performed. To enhance academic metacognitive abilities, teachers draw from the work of Bourdieu (1991), Gee (1996), Wenger (1998), and Wertsch (1991) on a process approach to teaching and learning. Churchill (2003) describes a process approach as follows:

> The negotiation between context and learner is first and foremost a process of apprenticeship. This process is largely determined by the accessibility afforded to the newcomer by the context, field, or community of practice. Thus, rather than passively awaiting the incorporation of the newcomer, the community of practice strongly suggests "trajectories of participation, and exclusion.... Negotiation along the trajectory, or from one proposed trajectory to another more desirable course of involvement, is by definition a process.... The process-oriented approach focuses on strategies, learning processes, study skills and other mechanisms that enhance learners' ability to teach themselves outside of the context of the classroom. (pp. 13, 9).

The curricular purpose of SHALL is to apprentice students to the discourses of schooling by providing "trajectories of participation." While acknowledging students' rich repertoires of cultural and linguistic abilities, teachers provide the infrastructure for linguistic and ethnographic analyses of expectations for school practices. Teachers bring into play McComiskey's (2000) suggestion that successful language and literacy learning involves focusing on three interrelated levels of analysis: textual, rhetorical, and discursive. At the textual level, the focus is on appropriate grammar and structural usage. At the rhetorical level, genres of use are examined in terms of particular purposes, audiences, and situations. At the discursive level, learners investigate and critically reflect on their learning processes. Students utilize student as ethnographer strategies for observing classroom interaction and collecting classroom documents to determine both oral and literacy expectations in school communities of practice. Through careful analyses of reading material and writing assignments at the textual and rhetorical levels, students begin to "notice," and thus have the capacity to reproduce, teacher expectations for classroom behavior and written work. Yet this curriculum rejects a purely "apprenticeship to" or "socialization into" the school community of practice. Rather, a central component of the school program is a critical discursive analysis of texts and practices to provide students with a voice in their own schooling.

Norton (2000), drawing from the theoretical work of Bourdieu (1977), suggests that communicative competence should include the power to "impose reception." As illustrated by previous research on schooling in Hawaiì (Kadooka, 2001; Talmy, 2001), many immigrant and otherwise marginalized students have been treated in dehumanizing ways, considered illegitimate members of the community, and subjected to a kind of censorship that excludes them from the right to have a voice in school and other communities. But similarly to what McKay and Wong (2000) found in their study of Chinese adolescent immigrants, these students commonly resist positioning, and employ counterdiscourses. Churchill (2003) theorizes that this process of resistance suggests "the need for learners to find a means of negotiating firmly with the communities in which they find themselves" (p. 18). One way in which we engage in discursive practices is to teach students how to "talk back" to the text. Students are encouraged to draw from their own experiences in responding to written texts, and thus learn to cross-reference their own experiences and theories with so-called "experts," and use these sources to develop cohesive academic critiques of the texts they encounter.

Integrated throughout the curriculum are assessment procedures that reflect the SHALL project process and discursive orientations. Through developing individual electronic portfolios of their work, students learn sophisticated technological applications such as PowerPoint and iMovie; reflect on their own literacy progress; and engage in critical analyses of school and society. Oral heritage language assessment focuses on examination of communicative language ability in a variety of contexts at different times and includes appreciation for a wide range of abilities not usually recognized in language tests, such as skill in code-switching in the heritage language, Hawai'i Creole English, and standard English; interactional competence with friends and family; and self-assessment of language abilities. The purposes of these procedures are to provide students with tools to assess their own learning while contributing information to teachers on how to improve the curriculum so as to meet students' self-identified goals.

In sum, the theoretical perspectives described above represent a critical participatory approach to education. Current practices serving low-income and/or linguistic-minority students tend to include low expectations for academic success and school work representing low cognitive demands that fail to challenge students or allow them to acquire higher-order thinking skills. Rather than hold low expectations and employ rote memorization practices commonly found in low-income schools (Moll, Amanti, Neff, & Gonzalez, 1992), these researchers assume high levels of student achievement and provide for use of higher order cognitive skills through project-centered work. The community and school research projects allow students to develop a flexible strategy repertoire that enables them to plan, monitor, and evaluate their own learning. Students further conducted ethnographic investigations of their school discourses and ultimately made connections between home and school communities. Critical language awareness and critical discourse analysis approaches were also used to highlight the notion that text can be deconstructed and, through this process, unmask text laden with values associated with power while providing what Cope and Kalantzis (1993) consider an explicit pedagogy for inclusion and access.[7]

While bilingual/multilingual education provides the optimal conditions for immigrant students in the United States to succeed in school, postmodern theories can provide "spaces" for bilingualism, multiculturalism, and other forms of diversity. These theories can also offer students the opportunity to engage with critical analyses of marginalization and agency as well as gain expertise in academic English to further political, individual, and collective goals. In addition to the positive effects realized by linguistic minorities, all students can benefit from the approaches described here through becoming researchers of the multiple linguistic, literacy, social, and multimodal discourses they encounter and/or need for full participation in twenty-first century social and economic endeavors. Given the need to address current and future educational needs in situated and global ways, the pedagogical approaches presented in this section reflect the power of cognitive, social, cultural, and political theories that cross the modernist and postmodernist eras.

CONCLUSIONS

We end where we began, with Hall's (1992) vision of theory that is not the *truth,* but rather "a set of contested, localized, conjunctural knowledges" (p. 286). This reflects the notion of intertextuality (Kristeva, 1980) as the ongoing crossover of epistemological, ontological, methodological, and sociopolitical thought and action that resound throughout this chapter. As previously described, cognitivists and sociocognitivists, including N. Chomsky, second language acquisition researchers, and Vygotsky, have had an enduring impact on language learning endeavors. The paradigm shift by scholars such as Cazden, Heath, and Phillips has greatly contributed to the education of social, economic, linguistic, and cultural minorities in the United States and elsewhere. The focus on power relations in education now promoted by postmodernists built on the theories and activism of Freire (1982), who is considered by many to be the first and foremost scholar to directly address sociopolitical structures of social inequity surrounding literacy and socioeconomic conditions. Drawing from burgeoning research and theories concerning bilingualism (Hakuta, 1986) and the positive effects of bilingual schooling (Cummins, 1979; Minami, 2011; Thomas & Collier, 1997), scholars (e.g., Ovando et al., 2006; Ovando & Combs, 2012) incorporated ongoing theoretical findings into teacher education practices. Postmodern educational researchers subsequently contributed to changing notions of diversity by calling into question static social constructions of gender, class, race, and borders (disciplinary, cultural, geographic, and political) as these interrelate with pedagogical practices. In addition, Scribner and Cole's early theories of interrelated cognitive and social outcomes of literacy functions along with Finnegan's theories of metalinguistic and metacognitive awareness arising from situated practices suggest important implications for current politically and economically motivated educational policies that impose psychological skills-based language and literacy models. While standardized curriculum and assessment suggest restricted cognitive and social outcomes, diversity theories hold promise for effective twenty-first century schooling practices in the United States and globally.

With a recent shift in global geopolitics (i.e., economic and technological globalization), cultural and linguistic diversity has become a central and critical issue in schooling for all students around the world. According to the New London Group (2000),

> Local diversity and global connectedness mean not only that there can be no standard; they also mean that the most important skill students need to learn is to negotiate regional, ethnic, and/or class-based dialects; variations in register that occur according to social context; hybrid cross-cultural discourses; the code switching often to be found within a text among different languages, dialects, or register; different visual and iconic meanings; and variations in the gestural relationships among people, language, and material objects. (p. 14)

The New London Group and others (Cope & Kalantzis, 1993) have further argued that cultural and linguistic diversity can operate as a classroom resource in profound ways. Reminiscent of Finnegan's (1988) work with the Limba, which suggested that metalinguistic and metacognitive awareness can arise from multilingualism, the New London Group (2000) assert that "When learners juxtapose different language, discourses, styles, and approaches, they gain substantively in metacognitive and metalinguistic abilities and in their ability to reflect critically on complex systems and their interactions" (p. 15). Cope and Kalantzis (1993) further argue for a replacement of the monocultural, nationalistic sense of "civic" toward a notion of civic pluralism. Civic pluralism implies a space in which differences are negotiated in ways that complement each other and provide the opportunity for all to expand their cultural and linguistic repertoires so that they can access a broader range of cultural and institutional resources. Critical researchers and theorists (e.g., Benesch, 2001; Canagarajah, 2004; Morgan & Ramanathan, 2005) further suggest syllabus design that encourages students' critical negotiation of identities and validates their experiences and forms of resistance to systemic discrimination.

Finally, this chapter first and foremost considers theories "as a practice which always thinks about its intervention in a world in which it would make some difference, in which it would have some effect" (Hall, 1992, p. 286). We consequently sought to portray a mosaic of theories that always and everywhere are embedded in situated practices and social, political, and educational ideologies (Pennycook, 2010). Ongoing refinement of the meanings of language as practice through philosophical and research explorations of linguistic and literacies flows (Pennycook, 2010) promise to inform diversity toward schooling practices that are profoundly knowing, humanizing, and equitable.

Recommended Reading Sources

- Banks, J. A., & Banks, C. A. M. (Eds.). (2004). *Handbook of research on multicultural education* (2nd ed.). San Francisco, CA: Jossey-Bass.

> The second edition of this volume describes and analyzes changes such as increased immigration to the United States and new developments in theory and research related to race, culture, ethnicity, and language. It addresses new issues such as findings on the increase in the number of interracial children and the characteristics of children of immigrant families. The educational implications of new research trends are also discussed. (From the inside front cover of the book)

- Bourne, J., & Reid, E. (Eds.). (2003). *World yearbook of education 2003: Language education.* London, England: Kogan Page.

> The issues raised by the role of language in education are some of the most important and contentious faced by education systems across the globe. Language is embedded in the concepts of nationhood and identity, and is therefore directly linked to the very social and political fabric of a country. In a climate of increasing globalization, development and mobility of populations, nations around the world are concerned with the tension between cultivating a sense of cultural and linguistic cohesion and making use of the linguistic diversity that exists in every country and region. This book examines the implications and impacts, the dilemmas and potential for language education in relation to education systems and wider society. (From the back cover of the book)

- Canagarajah, A. S. (1999). *Resisting linguistic imperialism in English teaching.* Oxford, England: Oxford University Press.

> Canagarajah juxtaposes *reproduction theories* against *resistance theories* in exploring agency in English language teaching. He describes educational reproduction as somewhat deterministic in explaining school failure as socialization into behavior that ultimately serves dominant groups. In contrast, Canagarajah states that *resistance theories* suggest how students either refuse to collude in their own oppression by resisting authority or are provided with the opportunity to gain agency, engage in critical thinking, and initiate change. The book focuses on the politics and pedagogy of achieving agency through appropriating dominant discourses.

- Crawford, J., & Krashen, S. (2007). *English learners in American classrooms: 101 questions & 101 answers*. New York, NY: Scholastic.

  This small book provides a concise but comprehensive introduction that serves as a state-of-the art guide to the field, written to focus sharply on the major issues facing English language learners and the educators who work to help them. The book includes 11 sections: Students, Programs, Research, Heritage Languages, Criticisms of bilingual Education, Public Opinion, Legal Requirements, Assessment and Accountability, Politics of Language, History, and Language Policy.

- Davis, K. (Ed.). (2011). *Critical qualitative research in second language studies: Agency and advocacy*. In T. Osborn (Series Ed.), Contemporary research in education series. Greenwich, CT: Information Age.

  This volume begins by locating critical inquiry within the epistemological and methodological history of second language study. Subsequent chapters portray researcher-participant exploration of identity and agency while challenging inequitable policies and practices. Research on internationalization, Englishization, and/or transborder migration addresses language policies and knowledge production at universities in Hong Kong, Standard English and Singlish controversies in Singapore, media portrayals of the English as an Official Language movement in South Korea, transnational advocacy in Japan, and Nicaraguan/Costa Rican south-to-south migration. Transnational locations of identity and agency are foregrounded in narrative descriptions of Korean heritage language learners, a discursive journey from East Timor to Hawaiʻi, and a reclaimed life history by a Chinese peasant woman. Labor union and GLBT legal work illustrate discourses that can hinder or facilitate agency and change. Hawaiian educators advocate for indigenous self-determination through revealing the political and social meanings of research. California educators describe struggles on the front lines of resistance to policies and practices harmful to marginalized children. A Participatory Action Research (PAR) project portrays how Latina youth in the United States "resist wounding inscriptions" of the intersecting emotional and physical violence of homes, communities, and antiimmigrant policies and attitudes. Promoting agency through drawing on diversity resources is modeled in a bilingual undergraduate PAR project. The volume as a whole provides a model for critical research that explores the multifaceted and evolving nature of language identities while placing those traditionally known as participants at the center of agency and advocacy.

- Freire, P. (2007). *Pedagogy of the oppressed*. New York, NY: Continuum.

  Freire criticizes what he terms the *banking* concept of education, which views teaching as depositing facts into the empty vessels of students' minds. His theories of an alternative teacher-student interactive approach to learning form the basis of critical pedagogy. He describes how critical pedagogy promotes teacher engagement of students in active reflection on the social contexts in which their experiences of oppression and privilege take place. Freire theorizes that achieving consciousness (*conscientization*) concerning power relations allow students to engage in "praxis" or a cycle of theorizing, application, evaluation, reflection, and theory. He concludes that at the collective level, the product of praxis is social transformation.

- Grbich, C. (2004). *New approaches in social research*. Thousand Oaks, CA: SAGE.

  Grbich provides an overview of the movement of social science research and theory from modernism to postmodern philosophical perspectives. She explains that while modernism holds that truth and knowledge are rational, universal, objective, and unified, postmodernism considers knowing as multifaceted, locally situated, and time and context bound. Grbich indicates that poststructuralism specifically refutes the notion that language can be understood in structuralist terms as a network of systematically linked propositions and coherent and organized ideas. Instead, she provides explanations of Foucauldian philosophy that warn against assuming structure, coherence, intention, and systematicity. She further discusses postmodern opposition to modernist assumptions of political neutrality that argue for the examination of power relations. Grbich reviews how postmodern research approaches such as critical discourse analysis and critical narrative studies are used to explore power relations from ever-evolving, changing, locally and politically situated perspectives.

- Harste, J. C., Short, K. G., & Burke, C. (Eds.). (1988). *Creating classrooms for authors: The reading-writing connection*. Portsmouth, NH: Heinemann.

  In an attempt to develop a practical theory of literacy instruction, Jerry Harste and his colleagues Kathy Short and Carolyn Burke began working with teachers in first- through sixth-grade classrooms. Their aim was to create the best literacy-learning environment possible given what is currently known about how young children learn to read and write. *Creating Classrooms for Authors: The Reading-Writing Connection* is a result of that involvement. Written in response to teachers' requests for a practical reference or guide to organizing process-centered classrooms, this volume presents a curricular frame around which teachers can plan classroom activities that help students understand what reading and writing have to do with reasoning and learning. Through this curriculum, students come to see reading and writing as composing, composing as learning, and learning as a form of authorship. Here, readers will find Harste, Short, and Burke at their practical best: sharing their lesson ideas and demonstrating how teachers might set up a process-centered reading and writing classroom. (From the back cover of the book) Though not directed specifically at English language learners, this book is a gold mine of creative and innovative curricular strategies that can be modified for second language literacy acquisition contexts.

- Hinkel, E. (Ed.). (2005). *Handbook of research in second language teaching and learning*. Mahwah, NJ: Erlbaum.

Intended for researchers, practitioners, graduate students and faculty in teacher education and applied linguistic programs … and other professionals in the field of second language teaching and learning, this volume provides a broad-based, state-of-the-art overview of current knowledge and research into second language teaching and learning. The tome includes eight thematic sections: social contexts of second language learning; research methodologies in second language learning, acquisition, and teaching; contributions of applied linguistics to the teaching and learning of second language skills; second language processes and development; teaching methods and curricula; issues in second or foreign language testing and assessment; identity, culture, and critical pedagogy in second language teaching and learning; and important considerations in language planning and politics. (From the back of the book cover)

- hooks, b. (1994). *Teaching to transgress. Education as the practice of freedom*. London, England: Routledge.

bell hooks draws on Freire in arguing for progressive, holistic, and engaged pedagogy relevant to multicultural contexts. She argues that *engaged pedagogy* is more demanding than conventional critical or feminist pedagogy in that it emphasizes well-being (or agency). She specifically suggests "that teachers must be actively committed to a process of self-actualization that promotes their own well-being if they are to teach in a manner that empowers students." (hooks, 1994, p. 15)

- Minami, M. (2011). *Telling stories in two languages: Multiple approaches to understanding English-Japanese bilingual children's narratives*. Charlotte, NC: Information Age.

The topic of bilingualism has aroused considerable interest in research on language acquisition in recent decades. Researchers in various fields, such as developmental psychology and psycholinguistics, have investigated bilingual populations from different perspectives in order to understand better how bilingualism affects cognitive abilities like memory, perception, and metalinguistic awareness. *Telling Stories in Two Languages* contributes to the general upsurge in linguistically related studies of bilingual children. The book's particular and unique focus is narrative development in a bilingual and multicultural context. The book is particularly important in an increasingly pluralistic and multicultural United States, where there are large numbers of children from increasingly diverse cultural and linguistic backgrounds. Telling stories is important in the context of language and communication development because it is often by means of this activity that children develop the skill of presenting a series of events both in speech and writing. However, varying concepts of literacy exist in different societies, and literacy has different social and personal implications in different social and cultural contexts. In our schools, teachers are expected to teach what is relevant for students in the dominant cultural framework, but it would benefit those teachers greatly to have an understanding of important differences in, for example, narrative styles of different cultures. Bilingualism or even multilingualism is all around us. Even in the United States, where a single language is clearly predominant, there are hundreds of languages spoken. Speaking more than one language may not be typical, but is so common in modern times that it would be senseless to ignore its many implications. The study of narratives told by children in both English and Japanese that are presented in this book will provide an important point of reference for research aimed at teasing apart the relative contributions of linguistic abilities and cultural conceptions to bilingual children's narrative development. (From the back cover of the book)

- Minami, M., & Kennedy, B. P. (1991). Language issues in literacy and bilingual/multicultural education (Reprint Series No. 22). *Harvard Educational Review*.

This collection contains some of the most impactful articles on language acquisition, literacy, and bilingual and multicultural education that have appeared in the *Harvard Educational Review*. The volume is organized into three parts. Part I provides an overview of the classic theoretical approaches to literacy with particular attention to psycholinguistic studies. In addition, a theoretical discussion of second language acquisition is included. Part II considers literacy as a sociocultural product. More specifically, the articles in this section discuss issues related to literacy in different societies, such as the United States, Liberia, and Brazil. Part III further extends the issues discussed in Part II to bilingual and multicultural education settings within a culturally diverse society such as the United States. The book concludes with the section "Notes on Books," which contains brief reviews of recent books on language acquisition, literacy, and bilingual/multicultural education. (From Introduction by Masahiko Minami and Bruce Kennedy)

- Ortega, L. (2009). *Understanding second language acquisition*. London, England: HODDER Education.

  Understanding Second Language Acquisition (SLA) offers a wide-encompassing survey of this burgeoning field, its accumulated findings and proposed theories, its developed research paradigms, and its pending questions for the future. The book zooms in and out of universal, individual, and social forces, in each case evaluating the theories and research findings that have been generated across diverse naturalistic and formal contexts for second language acquisition. It assumes no background in SLA. (From the back cover of the book) [Note that the conceptual framework formulated in the book later evolved into Minami and Ovando's chapter in Banks and Banks (2004).]

- Ovando, C. J., & Combs, M. C. (2012). *Bilingual and ESL classrooms: Teaching in multicultural contexts* (5th ed.). Boston, MA: McGraw-Hill.

  Demographic predictions are that students with close connections to their bilingual/bicultural heritages (now labeled "language minority students" by the federal government) will be very large in number in the near future, becoming the majority in many states over the next 3 decades. The authors feel it is the responsibility of all educators, not just specialists, to prepare themselves to work with language minority students. This time-tested classic text (not an edited volume) integrates theory and practice and provides comprehensive coverage of bilingual and ESL issues. The text integrates the fields of ESL, bilingual, and multicultural education and provides rich examples of effective practices and their underlying research knowledge base and provides an extremely clear and balanced overview of research on teaching in multilingual and multicultural contexts. (From www.mhhe.com/ovando5e)

- Street, B. (Ed.). (2005). *Literacies across educational contexts*. Philadelphia, PA: Caslon.

  In the introduction to this edited volume, Street describes how, since the early 1990s, new literacy studies has greatly influenced first language reading/writing research and curriculum development. He explains the new literacy studies argument that everyday literacy practices vary in significant cultural and discursive ways across communities, contexts, and domains. In acknowledging educational practices as socially constructed, varying across time and space, and representing societal power relations, the authors of chapters in this volume explore first and second language rhetorical, discursive, and technological literacy abilities and transformations in and out of school.

- Valdés, G. (1996). *Con respeto: Bridging the distances between culturally diverse families and schools*. New York, NY: Teachers College Press.

  In this book Guadalupe Valdés presents a study of ten Mexican immigrant families, with a special focus on mothers, that describes how such families go about the business of surviving and learning to succeed in a new world. The author examines what appears to be a lack of interest in education by Mexican parents and shows, through extensive quotations and numerous anecdotes, that these families are both rich and strong in family values, and that they bring with them clear views of what constitutes success and failure. The book's conclusion questions the merit of typical family intervention programs designed to promote school success and suggests that these interventions—because they do not genuinely respect the values of diverse families—may have long-term negative consequences for children. (From the back cover of the book)

NOTES

1. Although framed within the modernist and postmodernist philosophical eras, this exploration of language and literacy acquisition theories assumes the ongoing crossover of epistemological and research methodology perspectives.

2. We have provided here only a sample of the extensive first and second language research that emerged during this era. For a detailed account of second language acquisition research, see Ortega (2009).

3. A major influence in the modernist era is the theories of anthropologist Clifford Geertz (1973, 1983), who called into question the nature of reality and the centrality of local studies. More specifically, he argued that all anthropological writings are interpretations of interpretations, and thus the observer has no special insight into reality. Geertz suggested that ethnographers explore local situations and acknowledge the interpretive nature of analyses and presentation of findings. He also argued that an interpretive approach implies the blurring of boundaries between the social sciences and humanities.

4. Szwed (1981) specifically called for research on "the roles these abilities [reading and writing] play in social life; the varieties of reading and writing available for choice; the contexts for their performance; and the manner in which they are interpreted and tested, not by experts, but by ordinary people in ordinary activities" (p. 14).

5. Parts of this section first appeared in a chapter titled "Language Diversity in Education" (pp. 268-291) written by Carlos J. Ovando for *Multicultural Education: Issues & Perspectives* (4th ed., 2001), edited by James A. Banks and Cherry A. McGee Banks, published by John Wiley and Sons. This material is used with permission from John Wiley and Sons.

6. Parts of this section are drawn from Davis (2009) and Davis et al. (2005).

7. Elective enrollment in the program grew from 30 students in the first year to 234 students by the third year of the project. Of these 234 students, 38% received "honors" for their academic work as compared to 11% of the general student population. Compared to the national public school average of high school graduation of just over 50% for marginalized student populations (Green, 2002), nearly 90% of our student participants graduated from high school and went on to community colleges or universities.

REFERENCES

Anzaldúa G. (1987). *Borderlands/La frontera: The new mestiza.* San Francisco, CA: Aunt Lute Books.

Arteaga, A. (1994). *An other tongue: Nation and ethnicity in the linguistic borderlands.* Durham, NC: Duke University Press.

Bakhtin, M. (1981). *The dialogic imagination: Four essays.* Austin, TX: University of Texas Press.

Barton, D., Hamilton, M., & Ivanič, R. (Eds.). (2000). *Situated literacies: Reading and writing in context.* London, England: Routledge.

Baugh, J. (2008). Valuing nonstandard English. In M. Pollock (Ed.), *Everyday antiracism* (pp. 102-106). New York, NY: The New Press.

Benesch, S. (2001). *Critical English for academic purposes: Theory, politics, and practice.* Mahwah, NJ: Erlbaum.

Bernstein, B. (1973). *Class, codes and control: Applied studies towards a sociology of language.* London, England: Routledge and Kegan Paul.

Bhabha, H. K. (1994). *The location of culture.* New York, NY: Routledge.

Block, D. (2003). *The social turn in second language acquisition.* Washington, DC: Georgetown University Press.

Boal, A. (1979). *Theatre of the oppressed.* London, England: Pluto Press.

Bourdieu, P. (1977). *Outline of a theory of practice.* New York, NY: Cambridge University Press.

Bourdieu, P. (1991). *Language and symbolic power.* Cambridge, MA: Harvard University Press.

Brown, R. (1973). *A first language: The early stages.* Cambridge, MA: Harvard University Press.

Brown, R., & Bellugi, U. (1964). Three processes in the child's acquisition of syntax. *Harvard Educational Review, 34*(2), 133-151.

Bruner, J. S. (1966). *Toward a theory of instruction.* Cambridge, MA: Belknap Press.

California Commission on Teacher Credentialing. (1993, May 19). *CLAD/BCLAD: California's new design for the preparation and credentialing of teachers of limited-English-proficient students.* Sacramento, CA: Author.

Canagarajah, A. S. (1993). Cultural ethnography of a Sri Lankan classroom: Ambiguities in student oppositions to reproduction through ESOL. *TESOL Quarterly, 27*(4), 601-626.

Canagarajah, A. S. (Ed.). (2004). *Reclaiming the local in language policy and practice.* Mahwah, NJ: Erlbaum.

Carrington, V., & Luke, A. (1997). Literacy and Bourdieu's sociological theory: A reframing. *Language and Education, 11*(2), 96-112.

Cazden, C. (1988). *Classroom discourse.* Cambridge, MA: Harvard University Press.

Cazden, C., John, V., & Hymes, D. (Eds.). (1972). *Functions of language in the classroom.* New York, NY: Teachers College.

Chamot, A. U., & O'Malley, J. M. (1986). A cognitive academic language learning approach: An ESL content-based curriculum. Washington, DC: National Clearinghouse for Bilingual Education.

Chamot, A. U., & O'Malley, J. M. (1994). *The CALLA handbook: Implementing the cognitive academic language approach.* Reading, MA: Addison-Wesley.

Chomsky, C. (1969). *The acquisition of syntax in children from 5 to 10.* Cambridge, MA: MIT Press.

Chomsky, C. (1972). Stages in language development and reading exposure. *Harvard Educational Review, 42*(1), 1-33.

Chomsky, N. (1959). A review of B. F. Skinner's *Verbal Behavior. Language, 35*(1), 26-58.

Chomsky, N. (1965). *Aspects of the theory of syntax.* Cambridge, MA: MIT Press.

Chomsky, N, (1975). *Reflections on language.* New York, NY: Random House.

Chomsky, N. (1985). *Knowledge of language: Its nature, origin, and use.* New York, NY: Praeger.

Churchill, E. (2003). *Construction of language learning opportunities for Japanese high school learners of English in a short term study abroad program* (Unpublished doctoral dissertation). Temple University, Philadelphia.

Cochran-Smith, M. (2002). What a difference a definition makes: Highly qualified teachers, scientific research, and teacher education. *Journal of Teacher Education, 53*(3), 187-189.

Cochran-Smith, M. (2005). No Child Left Behind: 3 years and counting. *Journal of Teacher Education, 56*(2), 99-103.

Collier, V. P. (1987, April). *Age and rate of acquisition of cognitive-academic second language proficiency.* Paper presented at the American Educational Research Association Meeting, Washington, DC.

Collier, V. P. (1995). Second language acquisition for school: Academic, cognitive, sociocultural, and linguistic processes. In J. E. Alatis, J. E. Alatis, C. A. Straehle, B. Gallenberger, & M. Ronkin (Eds.), *Georgetown University Round Table on Languages and Linguistics* 1995 (pp. 311-327). Washington, DC: Georgetown University Press.

Collins, J., & Blot, R. K. (Eds.). (2003). *Literacy and literacies: Texts, power, and identity.* Cambridge, England: Cambridge University Press.

Cope, B., & Kalantzis, M. (Eds.). (1993). *The powers of literacy: A genre approach to teaching writing.* Pittsburgh, PA: University of Pittsburgh Press.

Cope, B., & Kalantzis, M. (Eds.). (2000). *Multiliteracies: Literacy learning and the design of social futures.* New York, NY: Routledge.

Corder, S. P. (1967). The significance of learners' errors. *International Review of Applied Linguistics, 5,* 161-170.

Corder, S. P. (1971). Idiosyntactic dialects and error analysis. *International Review of Applied Linguistics, 9,* 147-160.

Crawford, J. (1987, April 1). Bilingual education: Language, learning, and politics (Special report). *Education Week*, p. 43.

Crawford, J. (1999). *Bilingual education: History, politics, theory, and practice* (4th ed.). Los Angeles, CA: Bilingual Education Services.

Crawford, J. (2000). Language politics in the United States: The paradox of bilingual education. In C. J. Ovando & P. McClaren (Eds.), *The politics of multiculturalism and bilingual education* (pp. 106-125). Boston, MA: McGraw-Hill.

Crawford, J. (2004, September). *No child left behind: Misguided approach to school accountability for English language learners.* Paper presented at forum sponsored by Center on Education Policy. Retrieved from http://users.rcn.com/crawj/langpol/Crawford_NCLB_Misguided_Approach_for_ELLs.pdf

Crawford, J., & Krashen, S. (2007). *English learners in American classrooms: 101 questions & 101 answers.* New York, NY: Scholastic.

Cummins, J. (1979). Linguistic interdependence and the educational development of bilingual children. *Review of Educational Research, 49,* 222-251.

Davis, K. (2009). Agentive youth research: Towards individual, collective, and policy transformations. In T. G. Wiley, J. S. Lee, & R. Rumberger (Eds.), *The education of language minority immigrants in the USA* (pp. 202-239). London, England: Multilingual Matters.

Davis, K. (Ed.) (2011). *Critical qualitative research in second language studies: Agency and advocacy.* Charlotte, NC: Information Age.

Davis, K. A., Cho, H., Ishida, M., Soria, J., & Bazzi, S. (2005). "It's our Kuleana": A critical participatory approach to language-minority education. In L. Pease-Alvarez & S. R. Schecter (Eds.), *Learning, teaching, and community: Contributions of situated and participatory approaches to educational innovation* (pp. 3-25). Mahwah, NJ: Erlbaum.

de Castell, S., & Walker, T. (1991). Identity, metamorphosis and ethnographic research: What kind of story is "Ways with Words"? *Anthropology and Education Quarterly, 22,* 3-20.

Delpit, L. D. (2006). *Other people's children: Cultural conflict in the classroom.* New York, NY: New Press.

Denzin, N. K., & Lincoln, Y. S. (Eds.). (2005). *The Sage handbook of qualitative research* (2nd ed.). Thousand Oaks, CA: Sage.

Dulay, H. C., & Burt, M. K. (1974). Natural sequences in child second language acquisition. *Language Learning, 24,* 37-53.

Duncan-Andrade, J. M. R. (2004). Your best friend or your worst enemy: Youth popular culture, pedagogy, and curriculum in urban classrooms. *The Review of Education, Pedagogy, and Cultural Studies, 26*(4), 313-337.

Evans, B., & Hornberger, N. H. (2005). No child left behind: Repealing and unpeeling federal language education policy in the United States. *Language Policy, 4,* 87-106.

Fairclough, N. (1989). *Language and power.* London, England: Longman.

Fairclough, N. (1992). *Discourse and social change.* Cambridge, England: Polity Press.

Fairclough, N. (1995). *Critical discourse analysis.* London, England: Longman.

Finnegan, R. (1988). *Literacy and orality.* New York, NY: Basil Blackwell.

Firth, A., & Wagner, J. (1997). On discourse, communication, and (some) fundamental concepts in SLA research. *The Modern Language Journal, 81*(3), 285-300.

Fishman, J. (2006). *Joshua A. Fishman's contributions to international sociolinguistics.* In O. Garcia, R. Peltz & H. Schiffman (Eds.), *Language loyalty, continuity and change: Joshua A. Fishman's contributions to international sociolinguistics* (pp. 126-176). Clevedon, England: Multilingual Matters.

Fosnot, C. T. (1993). Preface. In J. G. Brooks & M. G. Brooks (Eds.), *In search of understanding: The case for Constructivist classrooms* (pp. vii-viii). Alexandria, VA: ASCD.

Freire, P. (1982). *Pedagogy of the oppressed.* New York, NY: Continuum.

Fries, C. (1972). *Teaching and learning English as a foreign language.* Ann Arbor, MI: University of Michigan Press. (Original work published 1945)

Gándara, P., & Hopkins, M. (Eds.). (2010). *Forbidden language: English learners and restrictive language policies.* New York, NY: Teachers College Press.

Gebhard, M., Willet, J., Caicedo, J., & Piedra, A. (2011). Systemic functional linguistics: Teachers' professional development, and ELL's academic literacy practices. In T. Lucas (Ed.), *Teacher preparation for linguistically diverse classrooms* (pp. 91-110). New York, NY: Routledge.

Gee, J. P. (1996). *Social linguistics and literacies: Ideology in discourses.* Bristol, PA: Taylor & Francis.

Geertz, C. (1973). *The interpretation of cultures.* New York, NY: Basic Books.

Geertz, C. (1983). *Local knowledge: Further essays in interpretive anthropology.* New York, NY: Basic Books.

Ginwright, S., Cammarota, J., & Noguera, P. (2005). Youth, social justice, and communities: Toward a theory of urban youth policy. *Social Justice, 32*(3), 24-40.

Ginwright, S., Noguera, P., & Cammarota, J. (Eds.). (2006). *Beyond resistance! Youth activism and community change: New democratic possibilities for practice and policy for America's youth.* New York, NY: Taylor & Francis.

Goffman, I. (1956). *The presentation of self in everyday life.* New York, NY: Anchor Books.

Goody, J., & Watt, I. (1963). The consequences of literacy. *Comparative Studies in Society and History, 5*(3), 304-345.

Grbich, C. (2004). *New approaches in social research.* Thousand Oaks, CA: SAGE.

Green, J. P. (2002). *High school graduation rates in the United States.* Paper prepared for the Black Alliance of Education Options, The Manhattan Institute for Policy Research, New York, NY.

Gumperz, J. J. (1981). The linguistic bases of communicative competence. In D. Tannen (Ed.), *Analyzing discourse: Text and talk* (pp. 323-334). Washington, DC: Georgetown University Press.

Gumperz, J. J. (1982). *Discourse strategies.* Cambridge, MA: Cambridge University Press.

Gumperz, J., & Hernandez-Chavez, E. (1972). Bilingualism, bidialectualism and classroom interaction. In C. Cazden, V. John, & D. Hymes (Eds.), *The functions of language in the classroom* (pp. 84-108). New York, NY: Teachers College Press.

Hakuta, K. (1986). *Mirror of language: The debate on bilingualism.* New York, NY: Basic Books.

Hall, S. (1992). Cultural studies and its theoretical legacies. In L. Grossberg, C. Nelson, & P. Treichler (Eds.), *Cultural studies* (pp. 277-294). London, England: Routledge.

Hall, S. (1996). What is this "Black" in Black popular culture? In D. Morley & K. H. Chen (Eds.), *Stuart Hall: Critical dialogues in cultural studies* (pp. 465-476). London, England: Routledge Kegan Paul.

Heath, S. B. (1982). What no bedtime story means: Narrative skills at home and school. *Language in Society, 11*(1), 49-76.

Heath, S. B. (1983). *Ways with words: Language, life and work in communities and classrooms.* New York, NY: Cambridge University Press.

Heath, S. B. (1986). The functions and uses of literacy. In S. de Castell, A. Luke, & K. Egan (Eds.), *Literacy, society, and schooling* (pp. 209-229). New York, NY: Cambridge University Press.

hooks, b. (1994). *Teaching to transgress: Education as the practice of freedom.* New York, NY: Routledge.

Hull, G. A., & Nelson, M. E. (2005). Locating the semiotic power on multimodality. *Written Communication, 22*(2), 224-261.

Hull, G. A., & Schultz, K. (Eds.). (2002). *School's out: Bridging out-of-school literacies with classroom practice.* New York, NY: Teachers College Press.

Hymes, D. (1974). *Foundations in sociolinguistics: An ethnographic approach.* Philadelphia, PA: University of Pennsylvania Press.

Janks, H. (Ed.). (1993). *Critical language awareness.* Johannesburg, South Africa: Hodder and Stoughton and Wits University Press.

Kadooka, J. (2001). ESL: "A different kind of academics": An ethnographic study of a public high school ESLL program in Hawaii (Unpublished manuscript.) University of Hawaii at Manoa.

Kress, G. (2003). Multimodality. In B. Cope & M. Kalantzis (Eds.), *Multiliteracies: Literacy learning and the design of social futures* (pp. 182-202). New York, NY: Routledge.

Kristeva, J. (1980). *Desire in language: A semiotic approach to literature and art.* New York, NY: Columbia University Press.

Labov, W. (1982). Objectivity and commitment in linguistic science: The case of the Black English trial in Ann Arbor. *Language in Society, 11*(2), 165-201.

Lado, R. (1957). Linguistics across cultures. Ann Arbor, MI: University of Michigan Press.

Lankshear, C., & Knobel, M. (2003). *New literacies.* Buckingham, England: Open University Press.

Lankshear, C., & McLaren, P. (1993). *Critical literacy: Politics, praxis, and the postmodern.* Albany, NY: State University of New York Press.

Lather, P. (2004). This is your father's paradigm: Government intrusion and the case of qualitative research in education. *Qualitative Inquiry, 10*(1), 15-34.

Lau, et al. v. Nichols, et al. (Alan Nichols- President of the school board), No. 72-6520, Supreme Court of the United States, 414 U.S. 56 (1974).

Luke, A. (1996). Text and discourse in education: An introduction to critical discourse analysis. *Review of Research in Education, 21,* 3-48.

MacWhinney, B. (Ed.). (1999). The *emergence of language.* Mahwah, NJ: Erlbaum.

Mahiri, J. (Ed.). (2004). *What they don't learn in school: Literacy in the lives of urban youth.* New York, NY: Peter Lang.

Martin Luther King Junior Elementary School Children et al., v. Ann Arbor School District, 73 F.Supp. 1371 (E.D. Mich. 1979).

Mazuka, R. (1998). *The development of language processing strategies: A cross-linguistic study between Japanese and English.* Mahwah, NJ: Erlbaum.

McComiskey, B. (2000). *Teaching composition as a social process.* Logan, UT: Utah State University Press.

McKay, S. L., & Wong, S. C. (2000). *New immigrants in the United States: Readings for second language educators.* New York, NY: Cambridge University Press.

Mehan, H. (1979). *Learning lessons.* Cambridge, MA: Harvard University Press.

Meier, D., & Wood, G. (2004). *How the No Child Left Behind Act is damaging our children and our schools.* Boston, MA: Beacon Press.

Minami, M. (2011). *Telling stories in two languages: Multiple approaches to understanding English-Japanese bilingual children's narratives.* Charlotte, NC: Information Age.

Minami, M., & Ovando, C. J. (2004). Language issues in multicultural contexts. In J. A. Banks & C. A. M. Banks (Eds.), *Handbook of research on multicultural education* (2nd ed., pp. 567-588). San Francisco, CA: Jossey-Bass.

Moll, L. C., Amanti, C., Neff, D., & Gonzalez, N. (1992). Funds of knowledge for teaching: Using a qualitative approach to connect homes and classrooms. *Theory into Practice, 31*(2), 132-141.

Moore, H. A. (2006). Testing whiteness: No child or no school left behind? *Washington University Journal of Law and Policy, 18,* 173-202.

Morgan, B., & Ramanathan, V. (2005). Critical literacies and language education: Global and local perspectives. *Annual Review of Applied Linguistics, 25,* 151-169.

Morgan, J. L., & Demuth, K. (1996). *Signal to syntax: Bootstrapping from speech to grammar in early acquisition.* Mahwah, NJ: Erlbaum.

Morrell, E. (2004). *Linking literacy and popular culture: Finding connections for lifelong learning.* Norwood, MA: Christopher-Gordon.

Nelson, K. (1981). Individual differences in a language development: Implications for development and language. *Psychological Bulletin, 17,* 170-187.

New London Group. (2000). A pedagogy of multiliteracies: Designing social futures. In B. Cope & M. Kalantzis (Eds.), *Multiliteracies: Literacy learning and the design of social futures* (pp. 9-37). New York, NY: Routledge.

Nieto, S. (1992). We have stories to tell: A case study of Puerto Ricans in children's books. In V. Harris (Ed.), Teaching *multicultural literature in Grades K-8* (pp. 171-202). Norwood, MA: Christopher-Gordon.

No Child Left Behind (PL 107-110, 115 Stat.1425, 2002)

Norton, B. (1997). Language, identity, and the ownership of English. *TESOL Quarterly, 31,* 409-430.

Norton, B. (2000). *Identity and language learning: Gender, ethnicity and educational change.* Harlow, England: Longman/ Pearson Education.

Norton, B., & Toohey, K. (2002). Identity and language learning. In R. B. Kaplan (Ed.), *Oxford handbook of applied linguis-*

tics (pp. 115-123). Oxford, England: Oxford University Press.

Olson, D. (1977). From utterance to text: The bias of language in speech and writing. *Harvard Education Review, 47,* 257-281.

Orfield, G., Losen, D., Wald, J., & Swanson, C. B. (2004). *Losing our future: How minority youth are being left behind by the graduation rate crisis.* Cambridge, MA: Harvard University, The Civil Rights Project; contributors: Advocates for Children of New York, The Civil Society Institute.

Ortega, L. (2009). *Understanding second language acquisition.* London, England: Hodder Education.

Ovando, C. J. (2001). Language diversity and education. In J. A. Banks & C. A. M. Banks (Eds.), *Multicultural education: Issues and perspectives* (4th ed., pp. 268-291). New York, NY: John Wiley & Sons.

Ovando, C. J., & Collier, V. P. (1998). *Bilingual and ESL classrooms: Teaching in multicultural contexts* (2nd ed.). New York, NY: McGraw-Hill.

Ovando, C. J., & Pérez, R. (2000). The politics of bilingual immersion programs. In C. J. Ovando & P. McLaren (Eds.), *The politics of multiculturalism and bilingual education: Students and teachers caught in the cross fire* (pp. 148-165). Boston, MA: McGraw-Hill.

Ovando, C. J., & Combs, M. C. (2012*). Bilingual and ESL classrooms: Teaching in multicultural contexts* (5th ed.). Boston, MA: McGraw-Hill.

Ovando, C. J., Combs, M. C., & Collier, V P. (2006). *Bilingual and ESL classrooms: Teaching in multicultural contexts* (4th ed.). Boston, MA: McGraw-Hill.

Pennycook, A. (2001). *Critical applied linguistics: A critical introduction.* Mahwah, NJ: Erlbaum.

Pennycook, A. (2010). *Language as a local practice.* New York, NY: Routledge.

Philips, S. U. (1972). Participant structures and communicative competence: Warm Spring children in community and classroom. In C. Cazden, V. John, & D. Hymes (Eds.), Functions *of language in the classroom* (pp. 370-394). Prospect Heights, IL: Waveland Press.

Philips, S. (1983). *The invisible culture: Communication in classroom and community on the Warm Springs Indian Reservation.* New York, NY: Longman.

Piaget, J. (1952). *The origins of intelligence in children* (M. Cook, Trans.) New York, NY: International Universities Press. (Original work published 1936)

Piaget, J. (1959). *The language and thought of the child.* London, England: Routledge & Kegan Paul. (Original work published 1926)

Richard-Amato, P. A. (1998). *World views: Multicultural literature for critical writers, readers, and thinkers.* Belmont, CA: Wadsworth.

Rickford, J. (1998). The Ebonics controversy in my backyard: A sociolinguist's experiences and reflections. Retrieved from http://www.stanford.edu/~rickford/papers /EbonicsInMyBackyard.html

Ruiz, R. (1984). Orientations in language planning. *NABE Journal, 8*(2), 15-34.

Sacks, H., Schegloff, E. A., & Jefferson, G. (1974). A simplest systematics for the organization of turn-taking for conversation. *Language, 50,* 696-735.

Scribner, S., & Cole, M. (1978). Literacy without schooling: Testing for intellectual effect. *Harvard Educational Review, 48*(4), 448-461.

Scribner, S., & Cole, M. (1981). *The psychology of literacy.* Cambridge, MA: Harvard University Press.

Selinker, L. (1972). Interlanguage. *International Review of Applied Linguistics, 10,* 219-231.

Siegel, J. (1999). Creoles and minority dialects in education: An overview. *Journal of Multilingual and Multicultural Development, 20*(6), 508-531.

Sinclair, J. M., & Coulthard, M. R. (1975). *Towards an analysis of discourse: The English used by teachers and pupils.* London, England: Oxford University Press.

Skinner, B. F. (1957). *Verbal behavior.* Englewood Cliffs, NJ: Prentice-Hall.

Slobin, D. I. (Ed.). (1985). Introduction: Why study acquisition crosslinguistically. In *The crosslinguistic study of language acquisition: Vol. 1. The data* (pp. 3-24). Hillsdale, NJ: Erlbaum.

Snow, C. E., & Ferguson, C. (Eds.). (1977). *Talking to children: Language input and acquisition.* New York, NY: Cambridge University Press.

Stein, P. (2004). Representation, rights, and resources: Multimodal pedagogies in the language and literacy classroom. In B. Norton & K. Toohey (Eds.), Critical *pedagogies and language learning* (pp. 95-115). New York, NY: Cambridge University Press.

Street, B. (2003). What's "new" in new literacy studies? Critical approaches to literacy in theory and practice. *Current Issues in Comparative Education, 5*(2), 77-91.

Street, B. (2004). Futures of the ethnography of literacy? *Language and Education, 18*(4), 326-330.

Street, B. (Ed.). (2005). *Literacies across educational contexts: Mediating learning and teaching.* Philadelphia, CA: Caslon.

Szwed, J. F. (1981). The ethnography of literacy. In M. F. Whiteman (Ed.), *Writing: The nature, development, and teaching of written communication: Vol. 1. Variation in writing: Functional and linguistic-cultural differences* (pp. 13-23). Hillsdale, NJ: Erlbaum.

Talmy, S. (2001, December). *Historical and political contexts for educational transformation.* Paper presented at the American Anthropological Association Conference, Washington, DC.

Thomas, W. P., & Collier, V. P. (1997). *School effectiveness for language minority students.* Washington, DC: National Clearinghouse for Bilingual Education.

Torrey, J. W. (1983). Black children's knowledge of Standard English. *American Educational Research Journal, 20*(4), 627-643.

Vygotsky, L. S. (1962). *Thought and language.* Cambridge, MA: MIT Press.

Vygotsky, L. S. (1978). *Mind in society: The development of higher psychological processes.* Cambridge, MA: Harvard University Press.

Wallace, C. (1992). *Reading.* Oxford, England: Oxford University Press.

Wanner, E., & Gleitman, L. R. (Eds.). (1982). *Language acquisition: The state of the art.* New York, NY: Cambridge University Press.

Watson, J. B. (1913). Psychology as the behaviorist views it. *Psychological Review, 20,* 158-177.

Watson, J. B. (1924). *Behaviorism.* Chicago, IL: University of Chicago Press.

Watson, J. B. (1928). *Psychological care of infant and child.* New York, NY: Norton.

Watson-Gegeo, K. A. (2004). Mind, language, and epistemology: Toward a language Socialization paradigm for SLA. *Modern Language Journal, 88*(2), 331-350.

Wenger, E. (1998). *Communities of practice: Learning, meaning, and identity.* New York, NY: Cambridge University Press.

Wertsch, J. (1991). *Voices of the mind: A sociocultural approach to mediated action.* Cambridge, MA: Harvard University Press.

Wiley, T. G. (1996). Language planning and language policy. In S. McKay, & N. Hornberger (Eds.), *Sociolinguistics and language teaching* (pp. 103-147). Cambridge, England: Cambridge University Press.

Wiley, T. G., & Wright, W. E. (2004). Against the undertow: Language-minority education policy and politics in the "age of accountability." *Educational Policy, 18*(1), 142-168.

Wright, W. E. (2005). English language learners left behind in Arizona: The nullification of accommodations in the intersection of federal and state policies. *Bilingual Research Journal, 29*(1), 1-29.

Zentella, A. C. (1997). *Growing up bilingual: Puerto Rican children in New York.* New York, NY: Oxford University Press.

Author Contact Information: Kathryn Davis, PhD, Associate Professor, Department of Second Language Studies, University of Hawai'i, 1890 East-West Rd., Honolulu, HI 96822. Phone: 808-956-8610. E-mail: kathrynd@hawaii.edu

CHAPTER 35

(Post) Structural Analyses of Two Notions of Academic Language

Discourse, Dialect, and Deficit

J. E. Petrovic
The University of Alabama

In the literature and discussions about language diversity in K-12 education, references to something called "academic language"—purportedly the language that children need and use in schools, especially to complete academic tasks—are commonplace. In the field of bilingual education, the discourse of "academic language" owes probably most notably to the work of Jim Cummins. His theories of language proficiency have been highly influential (consider the regurgative review by Martinez, 2001; May, Hill, & Tiakiwai's, 2004, use of Cummins in their report to the New Zealand Ministry of Education) and strongly critiqued (see, e.g., Commins & Miramontes, 1989; Edelsky, 1983, 1996; MacSwan, 2000; Petrovic & Olmstead, 2001; Wiley, 1996). For both reasons, it cannot be denied that he has advanced the field in significant ways. As his work has become part of the common parlance among educators, it has indeed provided an important tool for teachers to make a case against the premature mainstreaming of English language learners (ELLs)—one of Cummins' stated purposes. Nevertheless, academics must recognize the simultaneity of productive and reductive consequences of our work. This, I would argue, Cummins has not done.

Academic discourses and their regulative ideal of rational inquiry are the product of ongoing social and historical processes. Further, within the broad category of "academic language" we find the discipline of linguistics, or the academic language for talking about language—academic language having itself become part of the taken for granted parlance of the field. Again, not only is the idea of linguistics a product of social and historical processes, but so is the object of its study. The result is that, by the time we travel far enough down the rabbit hole of academia to find ourselves perusing linguistics journals, the social construction of our analyses have been doubled and redoubled, to the point that any original practical intent for paying close attention to language has almost always receded from view.

This, of course, might be said of any academic discipline. However, I am concerned here to examine the implications of certain practices of linguistics scholarship for language education policy. This analysis will require looking at language through a poststructural lens employing Michel Foucault's notion of discourse. However, I also want to argue, somewhat ironically perhaps, that the application of a poststructural lens is required by and reveals the importance of structuralism, more specifically the linguistic structuralism of Ferdinand de Saussure. I apply these frameworks separately to the issues raised in this chapter: "decontextualized" language and "Ebonics," respectively. Both of these issues speak in different ways to the larger issue of "academic language," the construct that I seek most to problematize. It should be noted at the outset that academic language has actually been defined as decontextualized language in the literature. Not to put a fine point on it, there is no such thing as decontextualized language. The occlusion of this point by the received discourse reveals the need for the Foucauldian lens.

The Handbook of Educational Theories, pp. 419–428

In this chapter, I first discuss Cummins' work as discourse. I highlight its reductive consequences and broaden its implications beyond non-English speakers (the primary focus of Cummins' work) to speakers of language varieties, namely Ebonics.[1] In this move, I distinguish between two manifestations of academic language: academic language as defined by Cummins (decontextualized language) and academic language as a variety of language privileged in school (standard English as opposed to other varieties of English). I note, however, that the former is implicated in the construction of the latter. At first blush, this might strike as misplaced critique to Cummins and his followers. For the notion of academic language was meant to refer to the language proficiency[2] necessary for success in school. But this presumes that academic language simply *is*. My point, however, is that academic language is a signifier: a symbol that takes on meaning as part of a system of socially constructed conventions. Interestingly, in this case, the thing which academic language signifies is itself a social construction.

Thus, my overarching arguments are as follow: (1) the thing signified by academic language is a social construction (in both manifestations named above). It is neither natural nor universal, but socially constructed from a point of view, in particular contexts and times, by particular users. Since academic language or "appropriate" language varieties (in the case of Ebonics) are sociohistorical constructions, they are, therefore, contested; (2) the language of language, the signifiers that we draw on to talk about language, contributes to this process, despite its arbitrariness, constructing as superior and, therefore, privileging certain language varieties, forms, and repertoires.

Discourse

A brief definition of discourse is that it refers to "ways of constituting knowledge, together with the social practices, forms of subjectivity and power relations which inhere in such knowledges and relations between them" (Weedon, 1997, p. 105). Ultimately, discourse is a means of authority and social control, an institutionalized way of thinking. In setting the bounds of speech, discourse constructs "truth" and defines our reality in certain ways. Ways of thinking are always historical and contingent, that is, dependent upon discourse. As Foucault (2003) illustrates in his *Society Must Be Defended*, a discourse is not attached to any one subject; it is productive of that subject.

Discourse produces what Foucault calls regimes of truth which facilitate normalization. These regimes of truth come to be through social systems and are a source of power since they regulate the conceptual categories of what is, what matters, and what is true. Take, for example, neoliberalism, an ideology that permeates our language.[3] This permeation refers to the idea that the ideology tacks taken-for-granted meanings to the words and ideals we employ and naturalizes them. "Democracy" and "capitalism" or the "market order" become a matched set. Or, worse yet, they become synonyms. Not a poststructuralist in the same way as Foucault, Bourdieu (1998) is nonetheless elucidating here, arguing,

> This fatalistic doctrine [of neoliberalism] gives itself the air of a message of liberation, through a whole series of lexical tricks around the idea of freedom, liberation, deregulation, etc.—a whole series of euphemisms or ambiguous uses of words ... designed to present a restoration as a revolution, in a logic which is that of all conservative revolutions. (p. 50)

This thesis is similarly laid out, albeit more broadly, by Chet Bowers (1987) who argues that "the invisible hand of language appears to be at work in organizing the most basic conceptual coordinates used by nearly all liberal educational theorists" (pp. 5-6). On the one hand, "the power to establish the legitimacy of new names, explanations, and sources of authority involves a partial escape from the embeddedness of tradition" that liberalism requires (Bowers, 1987, p. 12). On the other hand, this "escape" simply becomes an instantiation of the larger political aspect of the cultural milieu, limited, in this case by the frame of liberalism. This frame is a unique epistemological code that not only shuts out other ways of thinking but also provides the illusion that we are thinking differently.

Similarly, the language of academic language organizes the conceptual coordinates of how other linguistic notions are constructed, "proficiency," e.g. (see footnote (2) or "decontextualized language" (to be discussed), further reinscribing itself yet more deeply into the discourse, becoming a taken-for-granted and, therefore, unquestioned construct. The process of this reinscription is explained by Foucault as the discursive construction of bodies of thought united by an object of study. Thus, the basic definition of discourse already provided, in order to be more accurate, must also state that

> Discourses are ways of referring to or constructing knowledge about a particular topic of practice: a cluster (or formation) of ideas, images and practices, which provide ways of talking about, forms of knowledge and conduct associated with a particular topic, social activity or institutional site in society. (Hall, 1997, p. 4)

To reiterate, scientific or professional discourses and their regulative ideal of rational inquiry are the product of ongoing social and historical processes. Even though Foucault did not address fields dealing with language such as, for the purposes of this chapter, linguistics or language policy, this same kind of analysis can certainly be applied to these fields. For, the signifier "academic language" is created, supported, and reinscribed by these disciplines. Therefore, the theoretical framework of "discourse" must also be applied to language. The coordinates already stated set into place a discourse, a regime of truth, that operates around and constructs "language" in ways that reinscribe status quo power relations vis-à-vis language forms and varieties.

Contextualizing the Decontextual

The notion of decontextualized language describes the idea that meaning is conveyed primarily by linguistic cues that are independent of the communicative context. Reading expository text without pictures would be an example of this. In the area of language minority education, this construct has arguably been most promoted by the continuum of basic interpersonal communicative skills (BICS) and cognitive academic language proficiency (CALP) introduced by Jim Cummins (1979, 1980).

Cummins (1980) uses BICS to refer to "cognitively undemanding manifestations of language proficiency in interpersonal situations" and CALP "to refer to the dimension of language proficiency that is related to literacy skills" (p. 28). Drawing on the image of an iceberg, Cummins explains that the former is represented by that portion of the iceberg visible above the water (pronunciation, grammar, and vocabulary). The latter is represented by that portion of the iceberg that is submerged: the level of proficiency required in the "manipulation of language in decontextualized academic situations" (p. 29). Cummins (2000) explains the original purpose of the constructs which was "to warn against premature exit of ELL students (in the United States) from bilingual to mainstream English-only programs on the basis of attainment of surface level fluency in English" (p. 58). Decontextualized or "academic language," characterized, according to Cummins (2000, pp. 35-36), by such things as "low frequency vocabulary," "complex grammatical structures" and greater knowledge of "language itself," takes longer to develop.

Later, Cummins (1981) elaborates the BICS/CALP distinction along intersecting continua of context-embedded/context-reduced and cognitively demanding/undemanding language. The former refers to "the range of contextual support available for expressing and receiving meaning"; whereas, the latter "is intended to address the developmental aspects of communicative competence in terms of the degree of active cognitive involvement in the task or activity" (pp. 11 and 12, respectively). This intersection creates four language quadrants: (a) Context-embedded and cognitively undemanding (e.g., a face-to-face conversation, following directions); (b) context-embedded and cognitively demanding (e.g., conducting science experiments, doing demonstrations); (c) context-reduced and cognitively undemanding (e.g., telephone conversation); and (d) context-reduced and cognitively demanding (e.g., standardized test, following a lecture).

As regards these two theorizations, it is important to point out that for Cummins, the quadrant model represents the evolution of his original BICS/CALP continuum, not its abandonment (Cummins, 2003). Thus, the coordinates of the discourse do not change. Context-reduced simply massages decontextualized which is still the definition of academic language. As such, these notions remain open to evolving critique. Specifically, the quadrant model—even though it has been argued to provide a practical tool to inform educational practice and policy (Cline & Fredrickson, 1996; Cummins, 2003)—becomes a nest of hidden assumptions about language, proficiency, school culture, and power similar to Cummins' original constructs of BICS and CALP, becoming an error of commission toward deficit model thinking.

This is so because of the neutrality implicit in the construct. Language, even the so-called decontextualized language of schools, is never neutral, culture free, or value free as if education were occurring through some purified medium. School language or academic language is a distinctly middle and upper middle class, mainly white, language variety. This is true from communicative styles to vocabulary.

In her classic work on communicative styles, Shirley Brice Heath (1983), for example, documents culturally embedded child-rearing practices wherein parents from middle and upper middle class homes stress what might be called decontextualized language under the quadrant model. For example, Heath found that middle class students have much more exposure to the kinds of questions teachers ask in school. In general, what such research reveals is a "transmission model of socialization" which reinscribes a particular knowledge form (academic language) as natural and neutral against other equally rich forms. As Heath (2000) reviews, research has shown,

> Textbooks and tests were for the most part structured around decontextualized discrete-point knowledge as the only type that can determine grade-level achievement. Getting at creative, independent thought that either went beyond expected answers or raised further questions had to be left largely to certain types of classroom activities and to the extra credit sections of textbooks. Sociolinguists showed that the usual text book question called for straightforward answers, drawing inappropriate responses from children whose early socialization and peer interactions had taught them to value heavy use of metaphor and sociodramatic bids that asked others to join in imaginative and hypothesized scenarios. The logic of these and other nonstan-

> dard ways of telling stories, arguing a claim, or illustrating generalizations did not fit the standard in classroom discussion or answers called for in many tests and general end of the chapter questions of textbooks. (p. 52)

Lisa Delpit (1988) similarly discusses the communicative styles of African American parents. Lexical items also often differ for historical and cultural reasons. For example, the historical development of the acceptability of "ain't" and "won't" is illustrative here. Neither makes much sense as a contraction. However, only the latter is considered to be acceptable and school-worthy. This is due to the use of that contraction by the upper classes. "Ain't," on the other hand, came to be used more frequently by lower classes.[4]

The signifier academic language (my use of the term from this point on should be considered to subsume both "decontextualized" and "context-reduced" language) is a product of social and historical processes and linguistic activity is a major part of this process. In other words, the language of language, the ways that we talk about language, construct as superior and, therefore, privilege certain language varieties and forms. The meanings of academic language or the meanings of "appropriate" language forms, as sociohistorical constructions, are naturally contested. Academic language is neither natural nor universal, but arrived at from a point of view, in particular contexts, by particular users. It has been called into being through the development of schools, an unnatural institution which is also a product of social and historical processes.

To the extent that the socially constructed nature of academic language is hidden in the supposed neutrality of the quadrant model, the model helps to reinscribe taken for granted norms of school language (re)inscribing a regime of truth. It also then reinscribes privilege to children who come to school with this repertoire[5] largely intact and deficit model thinking for other children who lack what school is supposed to provide them in the first place.

Lacking this specific repertoire, children, especially language minority children, are frequently identified as not being "fluent," sometimes even in their first language, a linguistic impossibility. On the adult level, this would be equivalent to saying that Ernest Hemingway was more fluent or proficient in English than, say, a high school drop out. Here Cummins (2000) makes an equally mistaken comparison between Toni Morrison and a 5 year old, claiming that "The argument that language development is largely complete by age five essentially claims that Nobel Literature laureate Toni Morrison has no more language proficiency than a five-year-old child" (Cummins, 2000, p. 108). The problem for Cummins here is that this statement is linguistically true (cf. Macswan, 2000).[6] As Petrovic and Olmstead (2001) argue,

> To the extent that this can be read as blaming the five year old for not having the literary repertoire that schooling has yet to give her, one could indeed interpret it as a deficit model. We could take Cummins' comparison a step further and compare a fifty-year-old monolingual Mexican peasant woman and Toni Morrison. Could we possibly claim that this peasant woman is not proficient in her language? And could we possibly make such a claim because she did not hold the same linguistic repertoire as Toni Morrison? To do so would be elitist at best. (p. 254)

Lachman Khubchandani (2003), although not in specific reference to Cummins, similarly argues:

> The literate world [here we could change literate to "educated," since this involves assimilation to a specific language form generally and not just the technology of reading and writing] seems to be circumscribed by the myth of treating language in everyday life as a "crystallized" entity characterized by a distinct "tradition" embodied in its literary heritage. This myth is shared by many "underdeveloped" speech communities in their drive for modernization ... by accepting language as a social artifact (as in a literary creation), instead of as an ongoing activity. This leads to crystallizing the preferred speech more or less arbitrarily, guided mainly by literary styles and pressures from the elite, and proclaiming the 'autonomy' of the variety (or varieties) in all domains of communication. (pp. 241-242)

To be fair, Cummins' point is not to arbitrarily crystallize a preferred speech but to argue that there is a certain level of proficiency required of language minority students in the second language to accomplish academic tasks. My point is that, as a social construction, academic language is not a level of proficiency and Cummins fails to contextualize it. Once it is contextualized, it becomes apparent that the lack of such academic language "proficiency" is not exclusive to language minority students, as noted earlier in my citation of Heath. And, it is here that Cummins helps reinscribe another problematic, socially constructed language category: dialect.

WHY CONSTRUCT LANGUAGES *AND* DIALECTS?

As a social construction, the lack of academic language cannot be the exclusive domain of language minority students; it must be the case that many native speakers of Xish enter classrooms with only BICS. So how do these students demonstrate CALP? Edelsky (1996) notes how the construct is problematically based on test results measuring atomized skills. In this critique, Edelsky reveals what Cummins means by "academic," a meaning that is a far cry from what Heath describes, but probably portrays accurately how schooling has been constructed. Furthermore, it seems to me that there is a slippage here from academic language as decontextualized school language to particular ways of expressing oneself that reveal or not a mastery of that narrow skill set. In other words, children are forced to express themselves in "school ways," ways that mirror assessment procedures derived from the construct of academic language. (These, of course, function in recursive legitimation.) I do not think it a stretch to argue that this process feeds into a reification of standard English as the dominant mode of academic expression. Of course, some children come to school already speaking dominant varieties of English. These varieties are often called "languages." Thus, the regime of truth around language which arbitrarily crystallizes a preferred speech is also expressed in naming "languages" and "dialects." Note that I am arguing neither that Cummins embraces a distinction between language and dialect nor that he seeks to devalue dialects. My argument is that his theoretical constructs inadvertently help to reinscribe such a distinction to the extent that Cummins' academic language does not exist in a vacuum but is descriptive or replicative of traditional schooling, its rules, goals, procedures, and accepted modes of expression. While I see them in recursive relation, I am, admittedly, shifting here from Cummins' notion of academic language to a different use of "academic language" as language, modes of expression, or *parole* that is deemed to be school-worthy. This notion of academic language is equally problematic and requires an analytic shift to which I turn subsequently.

The signifier "dialect" tends to refer to stigmatized varieties of a given "language" and inevitably fall into the nonacademic category and, thus, become non-school-worthy. However, as famed sociolinguist Joshua Fishman (1977) pointed out long ago, "basically, there is no way to distinguish between a dialect and a language on the basis of objective linguistic discriminada alone, whether phonological, lexical, or morphosyntactic. There is no linguistic tattle-tale gray that gives the dialect away" (p. 316). In other words, we cannot reach up into Plato's cabinet and pull out the form of "English."

Even though there is no real linguistic distinction, anyone on the street will tell you that there is. Furthermore, they will tell you that language but not dialect is school-worthy. A false belief in a pure English (or any other language) form is exactly what any distinction between language and dialect must be based on. The perpetuation of this false belief, this regime of truth, is a sociopolitical, not a linguistic, project. It is precisely for sociopolitical reasons that the discursive categories of "language" and "dialect" must exist. For without the regime of truth they create on what would linguistic power rest? Dominant groups would be forced to recognize the linguistic privilege gained by the subsequent "truths" that the language/dialect truth generates: a language is standard, and a dialect is "non," nonstandard, non-school-worthy, nonexistent except from the mouths of substandard people.

While this position is applicable across a number of linguistic boundaries, for example speakers of southern or Native American varieties of English, the debate is brought into its most stark relief around the issue of Ebonics. Reactions to the Ebonics debate stirred up by the resolution of the Oakland School Board to recognize Ebonics as a language in 1996 have demonstrated the colonial nature of this particular regime of truth. Recall the reactions of Jesse Jackson and Maya Angelou to the Resolution. Jackson opined, "you don't have to go to school to learn to talk garbage." Angelou was "incensed" by "the very idea that African-American language is a language separate and apart."[7] The paradox of Angelou's position is revealed in her poetry of the 1970s in which she employs many of the rules and structures of African American vernacular that linguists long ago identified as consistent, stable aspects of the language that John and Russell Rickford (2000) refer to as "Spoken Soul."[8] By the 1980s, these structures had all but disappeared from Angelou's poetry. To my mind, the reactions of Angelou and Jackson provide glaring examples of how the "disciplinary power" of discourse (Foucault, 1995) manifests. Through the discourse of language, they have come to "understand" that some language forms are superior, or right, or correct, or standard, as compared to other forms.

To this point I have focused on the repressive nature of power (as discourse) vis-à-vis language. Nevertheless, power is both repressive and productive simultaneously. This is especially true to the extent that we can view language as discourse. By this, I mean to say that language, as a medium of communication, shapes individual identity and thought as much as discourse generally and that shaping should be seen as a source of empowerment. Here we need to dig into Foucault's intellectual roots and reconsider the work of Ferdinand de Saussure.

Language as Discourse

Arguably, Foucault's project was to "Saussurize" social systems, that is, to treat entire systems of social meaning the way de Saussure treated language. Thus, my naming of "language as discourse" reflects the Foucauldian frame from which I began. However, much of this work had already been done in de Saussure's notion of *langue*. In his seminal *Course in General Linguistics*, de Saussure (2002) makes several key arguments. First, the distinction I began this chapter with between signifier and signified owes to de Saussure. Put simply, a signifier is the sequence of sounds used to refer to things or ideas and to communicate. The sequence of sounds that comprise the signifier is arbitrary. One might just as easily make the sound "nasha" to refer to a "chair." The things to which it refers is the signified. Signifiers and signifieds together form and make sense only as parts of the sign, the language. Second, he divides language into *la langue* and *parole*. Parole refers to actual utterances as external manifestations of language. But there are no meaningful utterances without *la langue*.

La langue refers to the semiotic system, the system of signs, developed within the social system. "[Language] is a system of signs in which the one essential is the union of sense [signifieds] and sound pattern [signifiers]" (de Saussure, 1986, p. 14). The importance of language as discourse is driven by the ideas that this union is developed within language communities, and communities differ in the ways that matrices of signifieds are constructed. For signifieds have meaning only by their relation to other signifieds.

Extending this, it must also be the case that, as signifieds differ, the ways that different peoples understand their worlds and linguistically organize these understandings differ. Take for example the different set of relations that lead to different understandings of "river" in French and English. The French words *rivière* and *fleuve*, which have different meanings in French, both translate simply to *river* in English. Thus, the distinction between *rivière* and *fleuve* (the latter flows into the sea but not the former) is lost in translation. Or, we might consider the extent to which the two ways of "knowing" in Spanish (*saber, conocer*) lead to very different psycho-social organizations of otherwise basic information. *Conocer* is a knowing that can never be "known" for it is situational and relational. It is the sense of being acquainted with something and depends on interactivity. *Saber*, however, is to know a fact. It claims a level of universal certainty and/or objectivity.[9] The two verbs here open a "bifurcated epistemological space," "epistemological spaces that are difficult to think about in English alone" (Padilla, 2004, pp. 4 and 3, respectively). More to de Saussure's point, we cannot tell the difference between *rivière* and fleuve and *saber* and *conocer* without referring to the other. They are locked in meaning-constructing relationships.

Another philosopher influenced by Saussure, John Dewey, extends this logic, drawing explicit links between language and culture. "Culture and all that culture involves, as distinguished from nature," he argued,

> is both a condition and a product of language. Since language is the only means of retaining and transmitting to subsequent generations acquired skills, acquired information and acquired habits, it is the latter. Since, however, meanings and the significance of events differ in different cultural groups, it is also the former. (Dewey, 1938, p. 56)

Being a product of language, the culture that remains once a group has experienced a shift from the historical language to another language is invariably different.

Joshua Fishman (1991) is worth citing at some length to illustrate this causal relationship between language shift and cultural shift. He claims that

> the traditionally associated language of any ethnocultural collectivity is associated with the total ethnocultural pattern of that collectivity at a particular time and place. Jews who have lost their familiarity with Hebrew have lived a different daily life-pattern (a different Jewishness) than have Jews who did not, regardless of whether both groups continued to call themselves Jews and to be so called by others. The discontinuance of Hebrew in daily life was often lamented by rabbis and other Jewish community leaders (rabbis are not merely religious spokesmen; they are often community leaders in all other respects as well), because this discontinuance was associated with other profound changes as well: with a greater incidence of leaving the historic homeland, with a greater incidence of non-observance of then-current traditions, with a greater incidence of intermarriage, with a greater incidence of new customs (not hallowed as were the original ones), with a greater incidence of mispronunciation of hallowed ritual texts —all in all, therefore, with a greater incidence of culture change. (p. 16)

In addition to the cultural change effected by language shift, we may also need to consider language shift involves tacit acceptance of the regimes of truth that membership in the new language community entails.

Understanding the issue of Ebonics (or any so-called dialect) from this Saussurean frame begs the question: Is the choice for Maya Angelou to accept language shift and become Clarence Thomas or reject it and become Snoop Dog? Or must she forever exist in a liminal space, being neither fully here nor there? The answer here is not as Faustian as it might seem, that is if Angelou accepts that a rap (typically nonstandard) is as culturally-laden, academically rich, and linguistically school-worthy as a Shakespearean soliloquy.[10] Otherwise, the language and, thus, the culture of the community is undermined. In the end, it is stable linguistic and cultural communities, not individuals, that speak different truth to power.

Speaking truth to power here should involve the possibility of changing what counts as academic language (in both senses discussed), how that has been constructed, and toward what ends. This requires critical or transformative pedagogy. Cummins (2000) embraces such pedagogy "to foster collaborative relations of power" (p. 246) in order to empower students and affirm their identities. As regards language in these collaborative relations, Cummins' position is, rightly, that variation in command of academic registers exists both within and between groups and that differences between groups are the result of coercive relations of power operating in both school and society. Yet, his own notion of academic language is left unchallenged. As such, his iteration of transformative pedagogy serves to maintain the linguistic status quo. His answer is for all students, regardless of language background, to accept and adopt academic language proficiency as it currently exists. As Petrovic and Olmstead (2001) argue, "'Cummins' pedagogy is transformative only in that it demands respect for other languages and language varieties for the overly utilitarian purpose of acquiring CALP" (p. 410), which, thusly, becomes a tool of prescriptivism.

CONCLUSION

In order to conceptualize the different aspects of analysis that need to be recognized here, let me summarize by drawing on an example provided by E. F. Schumacher (1977, p. 1):

> On a visit to Leningrad some years ago I consulted a map to find out where I was, but I could not make it out. From where I stood, I could see several enormous churches, yet there was not a trace of them on my map. When finally an interpreter came to help me, he said, "We don't show churches on our maps." Contradicting him, I pointed to one that was very clearly marked. "That is a museum," he said, "not what we call a living church. It is only living churches that we don't show."

To overlay this example on my discussion, consider that discourse generally speaking in the Foucauldian sense is this map. It in fact limits what we can see, and tells us what is real and shapes our understanding of the social context. The discursive field for the purpose of this chapter has been school.

The next aspect is the language used on the map. My argument has been that the medium of the discourse (i.e., the language in which the map is written) contributes to and is inseparable from the formation of discourse. I have referred to this as "language as discourse;" Foucault refers to it as the "enunciative field" (Foucault, 1972). It provides us the vocabulary (or not) to name what is real. The lexical item "Academic language," then, reinscribes school in particular ways.

Finally, the third aspect is the discourse of language. This refers to the discourse, the regime of truth, that socially constructs our ideas about language as a medium, as in the false distinction between language and dialect or between academic language and non-academic language or a description of school language as decontextualized (when it is, in fact, hypercontextualized, recognition of which is occluded in the recursive functioning of the first two aspects). To continue with the map example, this would involve discussions around which language form or variety the map should be written in. Ultimately, this is not a linguistic question, but a question of power and politics. It is suggested that schools be "written" in "academic language." However, once we admit that schools are discursive fields, we must also admit that the concept (the signified) to which the signifier "academic language" refers has no materiality, although it certainly has material consequences for certain groups of children.

To conclude, I summarize my argument in five recommendations that rehearse the critiques revealed in the discussions above.[11] From a poststructural perspective, we must, firstly, analyze schools as discursive fields. The "field" consists of the complex relationship among language, social institutions (in this case, school), subjectivity, and power. "Academic language" becomes a "disciplinary power" that creates, justifies, and continuously reinscribes linguistic privilege. This disciplinary power enforces narrow, prescriptivist notions of language and recreates schools in their own (traditional, elitist) image. The result is that privilege is simply a hidden part of the "natural" order of schools.

Second, we must recognize that what is presented as *neutral* academic language is just as culturally laden as other communication patterns. This is because schools are not natural. "School" is a social construction and, as such, it is a unique and often foreign discourse. This discourse has its own system of meaning into which students are more or less or not at all socialized. The meaning system of school has predetermined whose knowledge, ideas, experiences, and language(s) will be valued. A Foucauldian analysis reveals that the only reason to make distinctions between normal and abnormal or any other binaries—school language and home language or academic language and non-academic language—is to keep people in check, to regulate them so as not to upset the social order.

Third, while the quadrant model presents as universal a particular school language, we must recognize the heteroglossic nature of schools. Heteroglossia speaks to the multiplicity of languages, language forms, language varieties, language styles, etc. that exist within some apparently unified language. In his discussion of the novel, for example, Bakhtin (1981) argues,

> The novel can be defined as a diversity of social speech types (sometimes even diversity of languages) and a diversity of individual voices, artistically organized. The internal stratification of any single national language into social dialects, characteristic group behavior, professional jargons, generic languages, languages of generations and age groups, tendentious languages, languages of authorities, of various circles and of passing fashions, languages that serve the specific sociopo-

> litical purposes of the day, even of the hour (each day has its own slogan, its own vocabulary, its own emphases)—this internal stratification present in every language at any given moment of its historical existence is the indispensable prerequisite for the novel as genre. (pp. 262-263)

Here Bakhtin is not engaging in some simplified notion of "celebrating diversity" or the mere coexistence of languages. He is speaking to the tension within which they coexist and the resultant disruption of some stable language form, a disruption without which the genre dies. The question to consider is the extent to which the quadrant model privileges the language of authorities, languages that serve the specific sociopolitical purposes of the day, or languages that enforce disciplinary power.

Building on this notion of heteroglossia, we must, fourthly, recognize that as James Paul Gee (2003) argues,

> learning in school, from the primary grades on, is a matter not of learning "English" or "literacy" in general, but, rather, of learning specific social languages tied to specific communicative tasks and functions. In turn, these tasks and functions are tied to specific discourse communities, social practices, interests, norms, and values.

(e.g., those of certain branches of science or, in some cases, just "school science"). Here Gee is speaking to a different kind or perhaps different level of nondecontextualization. I have addressed mainly the fact that schools and their languages of operation are socially constructed and that, on that broad level, there can be no such thing as decontextualized language. Gee is arguing that "decontextualized language" is "a problem, not a solution" since in order for students to really get a handle on the repertoires of language used in schools they must be supercontextualized: within the specific discourse community of history, science, and so on.

On the one hand, I am suggesting that this is merely a problem of terminology. "Academic language" or "decontextualized language" and the way that they are defined is simply imprecise. Perhaps we might use "school repertoire(s)" instead or, as MacSwan and Rolstad (2003), "second language instructional competence" (although this is directed toward English language learners and, therefore, would also be imprecise for speakers of varieties of English). On the other hand, it is imperative to recognize the importance of this imprecision. The importance of the need to contextualize the quadrant model as attempted above is seen in the materialist dimension, in the material consequences, of "academic language" as discursive practice. Language creates meaning around itself, privileging certain forms or varieties both universally and context specifically (e.g., in schools). "Academic language" becomes a discourse of deficit since it has already been socially constructed through uneven power relations, reflecting, therefore, the language of the dominant group.

Finally, given that language creates meaning around itself, privileging certain forms or varieties both universally and context specifically, teachers must be made aware of the beliefs and practices that exacerbate privilege and reify dominant language forms as natural and neutral. They must understand the processes by which bilingualism or bidialecticalism becomes an operation of language forms as discursive practice, becoming signifier and signified. The use of nonstandard language varieties or of "foreign" languages can signify resistance to school authority. It is a signifier of racial or ethnic or cultural difference. Even though their use is an inherent form of subversion, this use can also reinscribe difference, the normalcy and necessity of privileged "proficiencies." To avoid this, teachers must be taught how to exploit strategically the inherent heteroglossic contexts of schools and classrooms, challenging received notions of academic language.

Now the questions are: what does an education that empowers students to exist in and navigate liminal spaces look like? How do we ensure that the primary medium of their education (standard English) does not become an overwhelming form of authority? What I have argued is that the medium of discourse (discourse in the Foucauldian sense) is itself discourse (in the de Saussurean sense) and further development of a theory that can account for both the poststructural and structural aspects of language is required to address these questions.

For poststructuralism reveals the power relations and processes behind how and why language is policed in schools. For its part, structuralism, on the one hand, helps to reveal further the political (and nonlinguistic) nature of this policing given the arbitrary nature and constant flux of all language (from a synchronic analysis). On the other hand, structuralism also reveals the material consequences of linguistic privilege and oppression since, from a diachronic analysis, systems of signs, whether referring to different languages or to varieties of a given language, are indeed different in linguistically and culturally interesting and important ways. In short, notions of decontextualized language and academic language become errors of commission toward deficit model thinking, revealed through a poststructural analysis, with important curricular and pedagogical implications (to the extent that one believes curriculum and pedagogy must be both culturally sensitive and critical), revealed through a structural analysis

NOTES

1. My argument is applicable to any language variety. I use Ebonics merely as a case in point given its wide notoriety in the U.S. context.

2. Note that Cummins' imprecise use of the term "proficiency" is also a point of critique. Specifically, he has been taken to task to the extent that his distinctions confuse language proficiency with the ability to engage in academic tasks, literacy activities, for example (see, e.g., MacSwan, 2000; Petrovic & Olmstead, 2001).

3. I do not mean to suggest here that Foucault, himself, was providing a theory of ideology. His project was, in fact, to theorize against the notion that power operates through ideology in the Marxist sense. Nevertheless, the effects of discourse and ideology can be quite similar.

4. While it is certainly documented in a number of places, my awareness of this example owes to Macswan and Rolstad (2003).

5. I deliberately employ "repertoire" here as a substitute for academic language proficiency to avoid the mistake of confusing "academic language" as being a component or measure of proficiency.

6. Macswan convincingly argues that Cummins' views on "proficiency" represent a reintroduction of the widely discredited theory of semilingualism.

7. Both quotes owe to "'Black English' Proposal Draws Fire." Retrieved from www.cnn.com/us/9612/22/black.english/

8. Compare, for example, Angelou's (1994) "The Pusher" and "Little Girl Speakings."

9. Similar distinctions exist in other languages as well (e.g., *connaître* and *savoir* in French and *kennev* and *wissen* in German).

10. Of course, not every song will be "academically rich." However, for critical pedagogues, many of the songs by rap artists are offering stirring commentaries of political resistance. The primary point here, excluding debates about the age-appropriateness of some of the more "colorful" language, is that the vernacular structures employed by these artists are legitimate both linguistically and culturally and, therefore, school-worthy.

11. These recommendations owe to Petrovic (2006).

REFERENCES

Angelou, M. (1994). *The complete collected poems of Maya Angelou.* New York, NY: Random House.

Bakhtin, M. M. (1981). *The dialogic imagination.* Austin, TX: University of Texas Press.

Bowers, C. A. (1987). *Elements of a post-liberal theory of education.* New York, NY: Teachers College Press.

Bourdieu, P. (1998). *Acts of resistance: Against the tyranny of the market.* New York, NY: The New Press.

Cline, T., & Frederickson, N. (Eds.). (1996). *Curriculum related assessment, Cummins and bilingual children.* Clevedon, England: Multilingual Matters.

Commins, N., & Miramontes, O. (1989). Perceived and actual linguistic competence: A descriptive study of four low-achieving Hispanic bilingual students. *American Educational Research Journal, 26*(4), 443-472.

Cummins, J. (1979) Cognitive/academic language proficiency, linguistic interdependence, the optimum age question and some other matters. *Working papers on bilingualism,* No. 19, 121-129.

Cummins, J. (1980). The entry and exit fallacy in bilingual education. *NABE Journal, 4*(3), 25-59.

Cummins, J. (1981) The role of primary language development in promoting educational success for language minority students. In California State Department of Education (Ed.), *Schooling and language minority students: A theoretical framework* (pp. 3-49). Los Angeles, CA: Evaluation, Dissemination and Assessment Center, California State University.

Cummins, J. (2000). *Language, power, and pedagogy.* Lianbadarn Rd Aberystwyh, England: Cambrian Printers.

Cummins, J. (2003). *Putting language proficiency in its place: Responding to critiques of the conversational/academic language distinction.* Retrieved January 4, 2011, from http://www.iteachilearn.com/cummins/converacademlangdisti.html

Delpit, L. (1988). The silenced dialogue: power and pedagogy in educating other people's children. *Harvard Educational Review, 58,* 280-298.

de Saussure, F. (1986). *Course in general linguistics.* Chicago, IL: Open Court.

Dewey, J. (1938). *Logic: The theory of inquiry.* New York, NY: Henry Holt.

Edelsky, C. (1983). A critical look at several versions of a popular theory: Plus ca change, plus c'est la meme chose. In H. Trueba & B. Blair (Eds.), *Advances in second language literacy* (pp. 31-69). San Diego, CA: Center for Ethnographic Research, San Diego State University.

Edelsky, C. (1996). *With literacy and justice for all: Rethinking the social in language and education.* Bristol, PA: Taylor & Francis.

Fishman, J. (1977). "Standard" versus "Dialect" in bilingual education: An old problem in a new context. *The Modern Language Journal, 61*(7), 315-325.

Fishman, J. (1991). *Reversing language shift.* Clevedon, England: Multilingual Matters.

Foucault, M. (1972). *The archeology of knowledge & the discourse on language* (A. M. Sheridan Smith, Trans.). New York, NY: Pantheon Books.

Foucault, M. (1995). *Discipline and punish: The birth of the prison.* New York, NY: Vintage Books.

Foucault, M. (2003). *Society must be defended.* New York, NY: Picador.

Gee, J. P. (2003, April). *Decontextualized language: A problem, not a solution.* Paper presented at the 4th International Symposium on Bilingual Education, Tempe, Arizona State University.

Heath, S. B. (1983). *Ways with words: Language, life, and work in communities and classrooms.* Cambridge, England: Cambridge University Press.

Heath, S. B. (2000). Linguistics in the study of language in education. *Harvard educational review, 70*(1), 49-59.

Hall, S. (Ed.). (1997). *Representation: Cultural representations and signifying practices.* London: SAGE.

Khubchandani, L. (2003). Defining mother tongue education in plurilingual contexts. *Language Policy, 2*(3), 239-254.

MacSwan, J. (2000). The threshold hypothesis, semilingualism, and other contributions to a deficit view of linguistic minorities. *Hispanic Journal of Behavioral Sciences, 22*(1), 3-45.

MacSwan, J., & Rolstad, K. (2003). Linguistic diversity, schooling, and social class: Rethinking our conception of language proficiency in language minority education. In C. B. Paulston & R. Tucker (Eds.), *Sociolinguistics: The essential readings* (pp. 329-340). Oxford, England: Blackwell.

Martinez, G. (2001). [Review of Language, power, and pedagogy: Bilingual children in the crossfire]. Linguist list, 12.489. Retrieved from http://www.linguistlist.org/issues/12/12-489.html#1.

May, S., Hill, R., & Tiakiwai, S. (2004). *Bilingual/immersion education: Indicators of good practice*. Wellington, New Zealand: Ministry of Education.

Padilla, R. V. (2004, February). *Epistemology, knowledge production, and social change.* Paper presented at the conference Abriendo Brecha/Opening a Path: A Workshop & Conference on Activist Scholarship in the Humanities and Social Sciences, Austin, TX.

Petrovic, J. E. (2006, April). *Contextualizing "decontextualized language": Poststructural cautions to Cummins' quadrant model.* Paper presented at the American Educational Research Association, San Francisco, CA.

Petrovic, J. E., & Olmstead, S. (2001). [Essay Review of Language, power, and pedagogy: Bilingual children in the cross fire]. *Bilingual research journal, 25*(3), 405-412.

Rickford, J. R., & Rickford, R. J. (2000). *Spoken soul: The story of black English*. New York, NY: Wiley.

Schumacher, E. F. (1977). *A guide for the perplexed.* New York, NY: Harper & Row.

Weedon, (1997). *Feminist practice and poststructuralist theory* (2nd ed.). Malden, MA: Blackwell.

Wiley, T. (1996). *Literacy and language diversity in the United States.* Washington, DC: Center for Applied Linguistics.

Author Contact Information: John E. Petrovic, PhD, Professor, Department of Educational Leadership, Policy, and Technology Studies, The University of Alabama, 323C Graves Hall, Tuscaloosa, Alabama 35487. Phone: 205-348-0465. E-mail: petrovic@bamaed.ua.edu

CHAPTER 36

Toward a Policy-Minded Sociocultural Theory of Student Literacy Learning

Bryant Jensen
University of Oregon

Eugene Garcia
Arizona State University

Although classroom management issues are still moderately important to new teachers, they are no longer the dominant concern.... New concerns focus on dealing with the increasing diversity of students' instructional needs. New teachers express the clear need for insight and practical strategies to successfully address the diverse learning needs of their students. Not surprisingly, they also want more information about how to best communicate with the parents of their students. Parents often come from cultures that differ from that of the teacher, and teachers often need to interact with parents who speak languages other than English.

—Good and Brophy (2008)

There is, at present, no agreed-upon way to deal with the difficulties that arise from the interaction of presumably universal school content and manifestly variable socio-cultural values.

—Cole (2005)

The evolution of qualitative methods in the study of language in education will surely be more influenced by cognitive psychology than has been the case in the past three decades. Such a link will insist on more attention to learning over time and contexts and less to classifying what happens in highly specific classrooms.... Necessary to this evolution ... is the substantial recognition that methods of research cannot sit totally in the service of advocacy of particular ideologies, teaching methods, approaches o assessment, or evaluation of school reform efforts.

—Heath (2000)

Schooling has had multiple purposes in our nation's history, some intended and others not. From a policy perspective, however, the clear purpose of schooling is preparing citizens for the modern economy. The challenge, from a policy perspective, is to know exactly what civil society and the economy of the twenty-first century, will demand of its citizens and workers to know and do. This can be difficult to ascertain when the technologies that drive economic advancement change so rapidly, as is currently the case. Rapid change leads to new demands on workers, on companies, and on schools. How can we train today for the jobs and communities of tomorrow? Indeed, the top 10 in-demand jobs projected for 2010 did not exist in 2004 (Gunderson, Jones, & Scanland, 2004). And what about the compatibility between the knowledge and skills demanded by changing economies, on the one hand, and the competences demanded by civil society, on the other?

While addressing these larger questions is outside the scope of this chapter, they serve as an important backdrop to our discussion. There are actually some things we do know about schooling to prepare tomorrow's citizens and workers. This knowledge leads us to compelling questions whose answers remain unknown, yet incredibly timely. We know that today's children and youth will be expected to access, produce, manipulate, and organize greater quantities of written

The Handbook of Educational Theories, pp. 429–444

information in increasingly diverse forms—more than in any previous generation (Wagner, 2008). We also know that reading, writing, and math performance of U.S. students are insufficient—increasingly lagging those of other industrialized nations (Darling-Hammond, 2010). We know that the fastest growing segment of the U.S. population—low-income and racial/ethnic minority students—perform substantially lower on standardized tests than middle-class, White, and Asian students whose scores are consistent with industrialized norms. And we know that culturally and linguistically diverse students bring a wealth of knowledge and abilities that fall under the radar of teachers, school administrators, and policymakers.

What we are less sure of is how policy should address the sociocultural dimension of the literacy dilemma for low-income minority students. Policy suggestions have been made that orient around the family, school, and students, each to quite different degrees. Some suggest a complete overhaul of the curriculum to reflect the cultural values and beliefs of students and their families. Others suggest intensive language instruction in the classroom to catch students to speed. Very little discussion, however, comprehensively addresses literacy learning at home and in the classroom. We have plenty of "high-minded" theory to account for complex processes in student literacy learning, but little of it is leads to the sort of research accessible by education policymakers.

Indeed, in 2006 the National Literacy Panel published a synthesis of research on literacy development for second language learners (August & Shanahan, 2006). Three chapters and an entire section of the book were devoted to "sociocultural contexts and literacy development." While a rich body of descriptive (and to a much lesser degree experimental and quasi-experimental) work was categorized and interpreted for common trends that might lead to policy recommendations, very few final conclusions were rendered because of methodological incoherence between studies (Goldenberg, Rueda, & August, 2006). We argue that addressing this incoherence requires a more policy-minded sociocultural theory of literacy learning.

To date most sociocultural theory has been "high-minded" rather than policy-minded. This is not meant as a criticism. Indeed rich intellectualism in many cases must precede meaningful pragmatism. Yet given the pragmatic nature of policy, in conjunction with the demographic imperative in U.S. schools (Garcia, Jensen, & Scribner, 2009), we argue that a more robust, comprehensive, and pragmatic sociocultural theory is needed. It does not mean dismissing complexity, but it does mean using multiple tools to ascertain the most important social and cultural processes to student literacy learning.

Any sociocultural theory must consider learning across contexts, including activity setting in schools and homes. To frame our discussion, we draw heavily from the burgeoning science of learning (Meltzoff, Kuhl, Movellan, & Sejnowski, 2009), which increasingly is finding forms of merging historically discrepant and isolated perspectives on how humans learn. It includes neurological, anthropological, psychological, and educational perspectives. An emergent "synergy" (Bransford et al., 2006) between these perspectives, we contend, is a valuable way of framing a policy-minded sociocultural approach to student literacy learning. While yet incomplete, we hope the theory we sketch will make a contribution toward a more robust and consequential approach.

Problems With Theories of Student Literacy Learning

Ways in which social and cultural processes are associated with aspects of human learning have been addressed primarily by anthropologists for several decades. Due to the research methods that tend to be employed, most of the information we have, however, is descriptive. We know, for example, that parenting practices, particularly with young children, can differ quite extensively across cultural communities, with a variety of combinations between what researchers call warmth and control (Chao, 1994). Parents also induce different amounts of responsibility at different ages (Rogoff, Sellers, Pirrotta, Fox, & White, 1975), and expect children to participate in cultural activities (e.g., sibling caregiving, food preparation, free play) in different ways and at different ages (Rogoff, Mistry, Göncü, & Mosier, 1993). These expectations are central to the types of skills (e.g., letter naming, word recognition, addition, subtraction, listening, cooperating, observing, imitating) developed in cultural communities, and in understanding how literacy learning develops across groups of children and youth.

A variety of studies have converged on the finding that cultural practices are associated with different reading and writing outcomes of U.S. students (Risley & Hart, 2006; Snow, Griffin, & Burns, 2005). The reasons for these outcomes, however, are less known and highly contested. Some researchers and practitioners in education point to inferior classroom practices that favor children from highly schooled families (Gonzalez, Moll, & Amanti, 2005; Gutierrez & Rogoff, 2003), while others attribute differences largely to inadequate home practices (Risley & Hart, 2006; Snow, Barnes, Chandler, Goodman, & Hemphill, 1991), or even biological differences in cognition among groups of students (Herrnstein & Murray, 1994). While we reject outright the notion that differences in literacy learning are attributed to group differences in students' genetic makeup, engaging the debate between the other two positions—historically anthropological versus psychological studies of literacy learning—can be much more slippery. Ultimately the contestation is difficult because these two camps—attributing student literacy gaps to schools (anthropological) versus homes (psychological)—tend embrace different definitions of student literacy learning, making interdisciplinary dialogue quite challenging. Psychologists tend to see literacy learning simply as the incremental and universal acquisition of reading and writing skills. Students first learn letter names and sounds, followed by the blending of sounds, word recognition, word knowledge, reading fluency, and then comprehension. Anthropologists, on the other hand, accentuate the "situatedness" of literacy (Heath, 1983; Street, 1993). They describe in great detail the person-to-person interactions in cultural activities that incorporate words and letters through text and oral dialogue. The activity setting itself becomes an important unit of analysis, as are the identity, agency, and power of individuals involved (Lewis, Enciso, & Moje, 2009).

So, on the one hand we might say that psychologists accentuate the *form* of literacy learning, while the anthropological perspective spotlights its *functions*. A question we raise in this chapter is whether one aspect of student literacy learning should take precedence over the other. Our position is that it should not. We contend that there is much yet untapped richness in describing functions while at the same time inferentially unpacking skill development across cultural communities. As we discuss in this chapter, this underexplored middle ground better lends itself to educational policymaking, and it requires deeper combinations of qualitative and quantitative research methods—the cyclical process of deduction *and* induction.

We recognize that at present ours is a minority stance, as heated debates between literacy camps and research disciplines continue. If the issue was merely academic or scholarly, perhaps challenging the literacy dichotomy would not be as compelling or timely. But the issue is not simply intellectual. As discussed in other chapters in this *Handbook*, the demographic landscape of students in U.S. schools is rapidly changing to include more children and youth from language and cultural minority groups (Garcia, Jensen, & Scribner, 2009). It is estimated that by 2030 more than half of all Pk-12 students in U.S. schools will be from a racial/ethnic minority group, including Hispanics, Blacks, Asians, and Native American students. Moreover, due in part to burgeoning immigration figures and birth rates among lower socioeconomic groups, increasing numbers of students (absolute and proportional numbers) come from families with limited experiences in formal schooling (Bradley & Corwyn, 2002). And national data show that literacy gaps between classes and racial/ethnic groups decrease only very slowly from year to year—hardly quick enough to prepare U.S. adolescents for the modern information economy (Carnegie Council on Advancing Adolescent Literacy, 2010).

Given this scenario, should we not be sophisticated enough to attend to the forms *and* functions of student literacy learning vis-à-vis education policy? By pitting function against form in essence we are saying that walking to the grocery store (a cultural activity) is more important than taking steps (a developmental skill), or vice versa. In this example we could agree that the dichotomy is absurd, especially when so many thousands of students in U.S. schools are sedentary, so to speak. Indeed, U.S. students should not have to choose between skill development and finding value, relevance, and meaning in literacy activities at school. They should be able to do both, and ultimately the success of one is contingent on the other. Indeed, a theoretical convergence between the forms and functions of reading and writing in everyday life should more nuanced, better account for its actual nature, and address policy more directly.

Even a standard (or psychological, if you will) model of reading performance brings to bear concepts and considerations from cultural studies of literacy. Figure 36.1, for example, includes specific skills considered by psychologists to be central to the development of measured reading performance. How well a child reads depends on the acquisition of skills (or aptitudes), and their subsequent execution. This includes the umbrella skills of phonemic awareness and oral language, yet it also includes the prior knowledge (or experiences) of students, as well as noncognitive attributes such as emotional regulation, motivation, interest, sustained attention, and so on (Morrow, Rueda, & Lapp, 2009). How can we understand these latter aptitudes without considering the cultural contexts in which they necessarily develop? What is it we should know about out-of-school learning opportunities in order to inform and enhance cultural ways of literacy learning in classrooms? To draw on the terminology of the "New Literacy Studies" (Lewis, Enciso, & Moje, 2009; Street, 2005), how can cultural identities of children and youth be understood by classroom teachers so as to leverage student agency and enhance writing and reading through meaningful activities?

To date there is no underlying, unitary, policy-oriented theory to explain how cultural and social variables are associated with the literacy learning trajectories of students in primary and secondary education. To be fair, this is partly because said processes are inherently complex, and the theoretical and methodological work required to simply describe practices in situ can be very labor intensive. But we argue that it

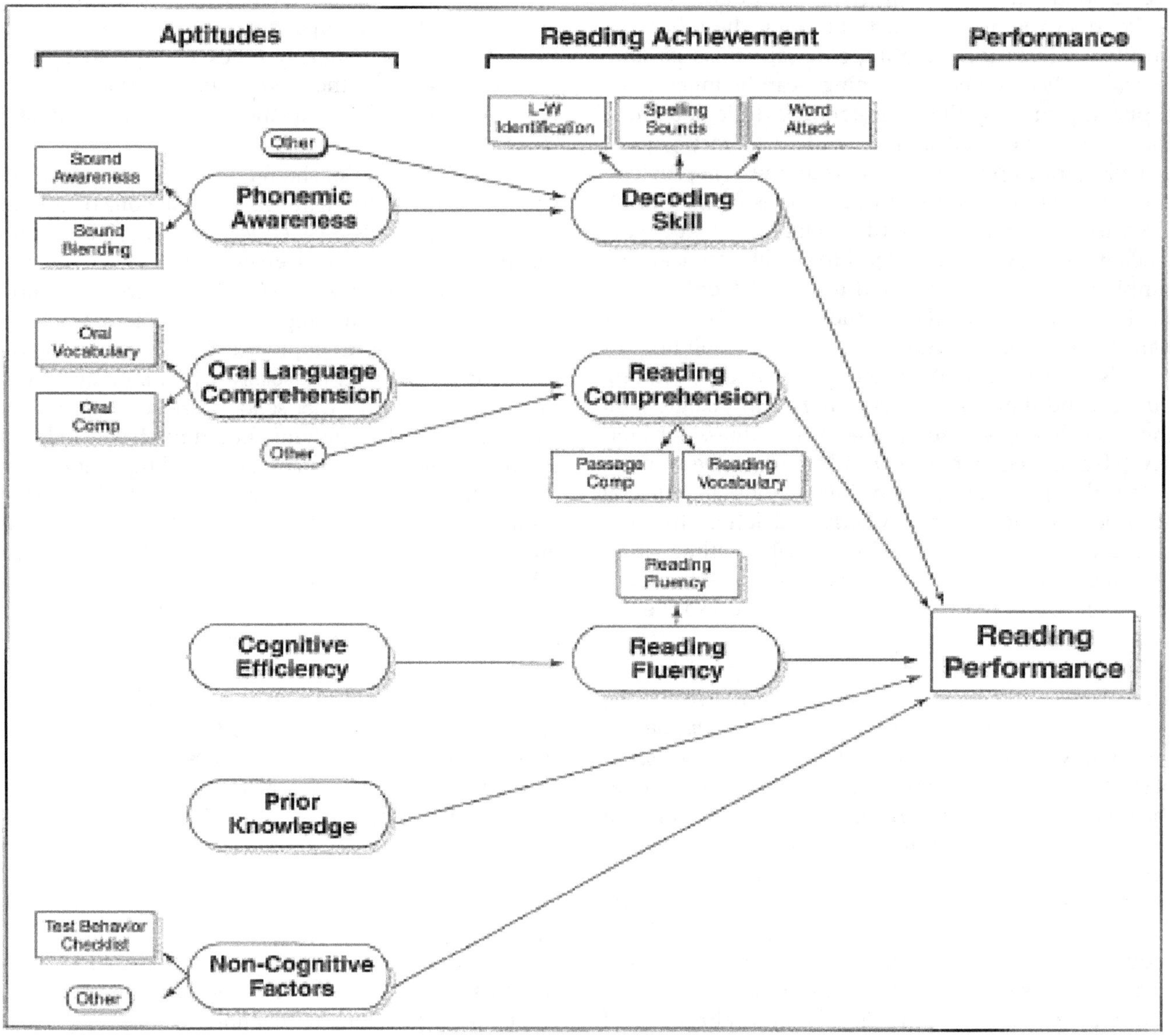

Figure 36.1. Standard model of reading performance.

is also because the work of literacy researchers tends to be narrow, focusing on *either* its forms (or skills) in formal learning environments, *or* (though less frequently) its functions (specifically the learning dynamics in out-of-school settings).

Just as science education researchers are drawing on concepts and principles from the new "science of learning" (Bransford et al., 2006) to understand how schools can be more responsive to student learning of science concepts in informal settings like museums, after-school programs, media enterprises, aquariums, zoos, state parks, and botanical gardens (Bell, Lewenstein, Shouse, & Feder, 2009), we submit that similar efforts are needed in the study of student literacy learning.

To this end, our chapter draws from recent research in cognition and literacy learning, from multiple perspectives, to argue for a more policy-oriented theory of sociocultural literacy. We make the argument that theorists and researchers in education should be more mindful of our audience, which includes those who devise laws, policies, and procedures for students, families, teachers and administrators. Unfortunately education policymakers, to date, have found little utility in the New Literacy Studies, not because concepts addressed are not compelling or considered important, but because the studies simply describe phenomena. They do not (tend to) produce inferential information applicable to students beyond the sample studied. And current policy-minded theories underemphasize (or simply do not address) the social and cultural aspects of literacy learning (e.g., Gersten et al., 2007), to the detriment of low-income and minority students—the most under-served in schools and classrooms. These social processes include the discourse patterns (Moje, Collazo, Carrillo, & Marx, 2001), observation demands (Paradise & Rogoff, 2009), cooperation opportunities (Leseman & de Jong, 1998), listening demands (Beals, DeTemple, & Dickinson, 1994), autonomous involvement (Hamre & Pianta, 2001), and requirements for empathy (Eisenberg & Mussen, 1989) and other social competences (Fuller & Garcia-Coll, 2010) across settings. Cultural processes include symbolic (i.e., ideas, beliefs, values) and behavioral (i.e., rituals, practices) knowledge across communities (Shonkoff & Phillips, 2000), as well as fluid changes in these forms of knowledge due to economic (e.g., maternal employment) and societal (e.g., nonparental care) changes.

We must confess that there are considerable conceptual and methodological challenges to convergence between anthropological and psychological approaches in student literacy learning. While we do not pretend to provide all the answers (or questions for that matter) to this awesome dilemma, we provide some suggestions that move us toward a more policy-minded sociocultural theory of student literacy learning. Namely, we suggest that researchers should make greater efforts to (a) understand literacy activities of students outside of school, (b) highlight what and how teachers should learn about out-of-school literacy activities, (c) underscore what and how parents should learn about literacy activities in classrooms and schools, (d) and incorporate a creative blend of research methods to provide descriptive and inferential information. From this concerted research effort, teachers and administrators should know (a) how literacy takes shape for children and youth across settings outside of school, (b) what activities in classroom can build on students' out-of-school literacy, and (c) how to learn from and incorporate parental involvement in literacy learning.

Given these assertions, we contend that objectivity in sociocultural research in student literacy learning is not only possible (Snow, 2006), it is also necessary to providing more useful insights for policymakers, administrators, and teachers to meet the educational needs of a growing body of students from culturally and linguistically minority backgrounds. This is not the same as saying we should search out ways by which all children across all cultural communities acquire literacy in the same, linear fashion. It does mean, however, that we seek to uncover means through which all parents and teachers can discover particular paths of success for their teachers and students, respectively.

In the following sections we base a discussion of student literacy research on the work of Bransford and colleagues (2006), who call for greater convergence (or "synergy") in the study of human learning, across social science disciplines. It has been debated by anthropologists in the education (e.g., Bartlett, 2007) that the impoverished psychological approaches to literacy learning derive narrowly from research in cognition. This argument, however, fails to address recent efforts by researchers and scholars from several disciplinary backgrounds to merge conceptual and methodology approaches in the science of learning (Banks et al., 2007a; Meltzoff et al., 2009). These studies, all under the expanding umbrella of cognitive research, seek to understand particular aspects of learning (i.e., skills, understanding, interactions, settings, timescales), and Bransford et al. (2006) suggest categorizing and synthesizing them as a way of creating more useful theories of how, when, where, and why people learn. They argue that we should be able to find "synergy" between the three major strands of research in human cognition: (a) implicit learning, (b) designs for formal learning, and (c) informal learning. Following a discussion of each of these bodies of research, and how they relate to studies and theories of literacy learning, we provide examples of literacy learning on the cutting edge of convergence. We envision an education policy environment in which mixed method research in student literacy is more widely financed and referenced, and offer some suggestions in doing so.

Implicit Learning

The first strand of research Bransford and colleagues consider in cognitive study is what we learn effortlessly, or implicitly, often without conscious recollection. Our differentiation and understanding of many visual patterns (DeSchepper & Treisman, 1996), for example, is implicit, as are many of our motor responses (Nissen & Bullemer, 1987). Other research refers to this sort of understanding as "tacit knowledge". That is, we know, but we do not necessarily know we know. We demonstrate we know by doing, which is an important point from a sociocultural standpoint, which argues that mind cannot be separated from activity (Bruner, 1996; Cole, Engestrom, & Vasquez, 1997). Matthew might not be able to verbally explicate how to dribble a basketball through the swiping hands of defenders, but he can demonstrate this sort of competence by actually doing it (Nasir, Rosebery, Warren, & Lee, 2006). Much of our learning, therefore—not only recreational but academic as well—can be very difficult to assess or understand without providing meaningful opportunities for demonstration. The extent to which the apparently ubiquitous human capacity to implicitly know and do are nurtured or innate, or both, is not as compelling for applied researchers (e.g., education researchers) as are their implications for ongoing learning—student literacy in our case.

While applications to school settings remain limited (Bruer, 1997, 1999), much brain research in human learning would fall also into this "implicit learning" category (Bransford et al., 2006). This field of behavioral neuroscience grew tremendously in the 1990s with new neuroimaging technologies and is currently providing important insights regarding these biological mechanisms for *how* and *why* we learn, not only *when* (Bransford, Brown, & Cocking, 2000). It has been established that neurological changes (e.g., synaptic, cellular) clearly precede behavioral changes, and that behaviors that appear similar across persons can have quite different neural networks associated with these behaviors (Tremblay, Kraus, & McGee, 1998). That is, the same behaviors can have a variety of neurological causes and consequences between persons. Singing The Beatles tune *Let It Be*, for example, might trigger a very different array of synaptic networks between cortical regions in the brain across a group of 12-year old children, depending on their varied experiences with singing in general, and with this tune, more specifically.

So what does the study of implicit learning (and behavioral neuroscience) have to do with sociocultural theory and/or student literacy? First, it is important to note that the transmission of many of the social and cultural processes related to learning have powerful neurological bases. For example, neuroscientists have recently identified "mirror neurons" to account for ways we learn simply through observing other people, like a parent, sibling, or a friend (Meltzoff & Decety, 2003). This includes learning how to participate in a cultural activity like dish washing, car repair, or basket weaving (Paradise & Rogoff, 2009)—activities which include limited explicit instruction through elaborate verbalization. Cultural psychologists have been interested in forms of participation in activities associated with the cognitive development of children, but have not considered, per se, how such might have neurological underpinnings. Understanding the biological basis for learning through observation could extend the audience and evidence for the argument of observation as a social and cognitive skill. Furthermore, it could lead to the design and development of classroom activities that improve learning opportunities and academic performance of children whose parents have limited formal schooling, families in which learning from "observing and pitching in" is the dominant form (Paradise & Rogoff, 2009).

Second, many of the underlying skills central to reading and writing development—even those less understood to date—are learned implicitly. Stanislas Dahaene (2009) and others have shown how young learners commit neural networks to reflect their natural language environments. This includes early phonemic learning, which are the building blocks not only to speaking words and sentences, but also learning to connecting symbols (i.e., letters, and groups of letters) with sounds (Kuhl, 2004). With such wide discrepancies in the quality and quantity of verbalization (through social conversation) suspected in homes of young children across socioeconomic groups (e.g., Hart & Risley, 1999), finding ways to delve into the early social environments of young children should continue to be a major policy consideration (Neuman & Celano, 2006).

And third, the developmental proficiency of reading and writing needs to be understood in the contexts in which they develop. Emergent research in implicit learning supports the long-standing assertion by cultural psychologists that pervasive problems emerge when we try to separate *what* is learned from *where*, *how*, and *with whom* it is learned (Scribner & Cole, 1973). The constraints *and* affordances of literacy learning environments for diverse students need to be better understood, not only in terms of the cognitive skills in literacy learning, but also those social (Fuller & Garcia-Coll, 2010; Morrow, Rueda, & Lapp, 2009). This includes having a better grasp of the daily routines of students in and out of school, and their varied activities (e.g., school recess, playing video games, homework, watching TV, cooking meals, football practice, visiting relatives, Sunday school, etc.; Weisner, 2002).

DESIGNS FOR FORMAL LEARNING

Most of the learning research in cognitive science falls into the category of "formal learning"—learning in formal settings like classrooms—which probably contributes to stereotypes among some anthropologists that cognitive scientists ignore cultural ways of knowing in out-of-school settings. Indeed, several research journals are devoted singly to how children and youth acquire academic content in formal academic settings. Certainly much has been studied and written about the instructional features in classrooms that are associated with the acquisition of literacy skills among diverse learners (e.g., cooperative learning [Slavin, Hurley, & Chamberlain, 2003]). But these studies have tended to speak very little to how, precisely, classroom teachers can leverage different social and cultural forms of learning availed to students outside of school. Moreover, classroom "strategies", to date, have not demonstrated a capacity to markedly decrease the historic and pervasive gap in reading and writing performance between student groups by race, ethnicity, language background, and class (Ladson-Billings, 2006; Lee, 2007; Miller, 1995).

Important classroom strategies that have emerged from this work include regular screening and progress monitoring, intensive small-group interventions, structured academic conversations with students, explicit literacy instruction across content areas, regular scaffolding for reading and writing tasks, peer-assisted learning, and explicit teaching of academic vocabulary (Carnegie Council on Advancing Adolescent Literacy,

2010; Gersten et al., 2007; Shanahan & Beck, 2006). While promising, these strategies routinely fail to address the notion that literacy learning often occurs during all waking hours for children and youth, not only in formal settings (which only accounts for about a fifth of a student's daily waking time). We might say, therefore, that students whose learning environments outside of school more closely reflect the social and cultural norms of classrooms (e.g., use of external rewards to motivate, quality of collaboration between children and adults, division of responsibility; Rogoff et al., 2007) are inordinately advantaged over those students for whom learning opportunities outside of school are very different, thus perpetuating the aforementioned achievement gaps (Schauble, Banks, Coates, Martin, & Sterling 2007a). Out-of-school learning can often be powerfully associated with school learning (including literacy; Lee, 2007), but these associations are inadequately understood by researchers (namely through the inclusion of inferential data), and tend to be overlooked by teachers, school administrators, and policymakers (Schauble et al., 1996). We cannot help but think that an advancement of research designs and studies that address school and nonschool learning in tandem, specifically around literacy development, would provide useful insights for practitioners as well as more responsible policymaking.

This sort of bridge building will continue to battle with age-old questions in education research. What should students know and be able to do? What configuration of attitudes, skills, and knowledge structures support education goals? What forms of assessment can be used to identify "success?" What do we know about the processes involved in helping students to meet learning goals? And how can learning objectives (or standards) be aligned across schools, districts, and states (Bransford et al., 2006)? But studies of formal learning environments point to less-traditional questions as well—questions that address learning in nonschool environments, which are equally important to enhancing engagement and learning in classrooms. These questions are based heavily on the notion that meaningful instruction should not be a one-size-fits-all proposition. A central, burgeoning principle in classroom learning on which these questions are based is that instruction should be "student-centered" (Wertsch, 1991). This means gauging not only what students know and/or do not know, but *how* they know what they do and *why*. For example, it might not be as important to assess whether Juan knows the dictionary definition of the word "transmit", but to understand *why* he decided to associate the word with car engines in his short essay. His understanding of car "transmissions" could lead to an array of relevant classroom activities that unveil his "prior knowledge" (Schwartz & Bransford, 1998) of gas-powered motors, their parts, and functions. Such an effort could have a consequential impact on Juan's literacy development, in addition to his cognitive, emotional, *and* behavioral engagement in the classroom (Fredricks, Blumenfeld, & Paris, 2004).

The idea that all classroom learners begin with preconceptions in order to develop understanding (Bereiter & Scardemalia, 1993) means that regular efforts should be made by teachers to construct school content (including literacy learning) immediately applicable to the lives and current understanding of individual students. Correcting misconceptions, therefore, should not simply be about providing students with correct answers, but making student thinking more explicit, to draw out the *reasons* for their misunderstanding which may help teachers learn more about other forms of student understanding (Smith, diSessa, & Roschelle, 1993). Moreover, understanding the reasons for misconceptions rather than simply correcting them is more likely to lead to the *transfer* of understanding across environments (Bransford & Schwartz, 1999)—or generalization—which is arguably the goal of schooling. Transfer is about moving knowledge and skills from training to action, from declarative to procedural understanding, and back again. Transfer, therefore, constitutes learning, and cannot be indifferent to what happens in the day-to-day activities of students (Detterman & Sternberg, 1993). Letter, word, sentence, and text learning in schools and classrooms should be deeply mindful of ways in which the individual student participates in literacy outside of the classroom to promote this sort of transfer.

An approach based on individual differences of student understanding and transfer requires a high degree of flexibility on the part of the teacher. The sort of flexibility in classrooms, that regularly assesses, deconstructs, and builds on the understandings of individual students, however, is not the norm. Schwartz, Bransford, and Sears (2005) argue that this is the case because teachers are largely encouraged to be "routine experts" in their classrooms, rather than "adaptive experts." Teachers considered routine experts are primarily concerned with efficiency. Minutes are counted, standards addressed, and teachers are to control the rhythm of the classroom (Brophy & Good, 1986; Emmer & Stough, 2001). Adaptive expert teachers, on the other hand, respond to two dimensions of teaching expertise: innovation *and* efficiency. Adaptive expert teachers regularly struggle to balance the administrative demands while finding ways to engage the understandings of individual learners. At times this may mean being less "efficient" than their colleagues, or even getting frustrated in trying to attend to differences in student understanding while failing to address the classroom standards and schools procedures. Yet this tension between efficiency and innovation, Schwartz and colleagues argue, is more conducive to student learning over the long term. Teachers who work in the "optimal corridor" between innovation and efficiency are more likely to nurture engaged thinkers who find rich connections between home and school learning activities.

The extent research literature on formal learning environments does not currently provide a clear path to adaptive expertise in teaching, nor does it communicate its impacts on student literacy learning for diverse learners. This body of work, nonetheless, is exciting and promising given the increasing importance being placed on "learner-centered" teaching (Darling-Hammond & Bransford, 2007) and literacy learning across academic subjects (Carnegie Council on Advancing Adolescent Literacy, 2010; Graham & Perin, 2007). One thing is certain: adaptive expertise entails a degree of discomfort as it requires teachers to "restructur[e] core ideas, beliefs, and competencies" (Bransford et al., 2006, p. 223). Such restructuring is certainly pivotal for teachers working with students whose parents have little or limited formal schooling experiences, where values, practices, and forms of competence often vary a great deal from those of school staff (Banks et al, 2007b). It may require some inefficiency of teachers in the short run, but can increase important flexibility in the classroom and student academic outcomes over the long term (Gopnik & Meltzoff, 1997).

Rather than distract from tried and tested classroom strategies shown to be associated with literacy gains for diverse students, future studies of classroom learning should build on them to explore, develop, and test classroom approaches that are more responsive to cognitive notions of transfer, prior knowledge, and metacognition (Bransford, Brown, & Cocking, 2000; Bransford & Donovan, 2005). This will mean incrementally designing classrooms in which student perspectives are highly regarded (Hamre & Pianta, 2005), and it will involve a better understanding of developmental processes at the personal, interpersonal, and institutional planes (Rogoff, 1995).

So while "culturally responsive pedagogies" (Au, 2005; Garcia, 2005; Gay, 2000; Ladson-Billings, 1995) in their current forms provide useful notions to guide teacher thinking around student learning differences in the classroom, inferential data regarding how, and the extent to which, the application of these concepts actually lead to specific academic gains (forms of literacy, for example) for students are limited (Goldenberg, Rueda, & August, 2006). Lee (2007), for example, describes how she found ways of drawing on her students' social and linguistic competencies inherent in African American Vernacular English (AAVE) to address literature and literacy learning in the classroom. She provides a rich account of how cultural understandings from her students' everyday experience can be thoughtfully integrated into the curricular and instructional life of the classroom. She demonstrates how cultural word referents can be incorporated into the classroom, and how this sort of activity led to an increased sense of belonging, ownership, and confidence in school work among her students. This is consistent with the work of Noddings (2005) on caring, and speaks to the importance of teacher flexibility and relationship building with students and their cultural histories. It also speaks to the powerful role of students' "identities" in the classroom—that literacy learning in the classroom has meaning for them beyond school walls (Gee, 2001).

Moreover, culturally responsive pedagogies call for teachers to have deeper understandings of second language development (for English learners; Garcia, 2005), cultural histories (Roth & Lee, 2007), interpersonal interactions (Au & Mason, 1981; Tharp, 1982), and the values, beliefs (Delgado-Gaitan & Trueba, 1991) and cultural practices (Gutierrez & Rogoff, 2003; Hull & Shultz, 2001) availed to students outside of school. The theoretical notions linking student culture to literacy learning indeed are numerous, yet they are also diffuse (Warikoo & Carter, 2009) and have not led to research findings on classroom designs accessible to policymakers. This is because sociocultural studies in student literacy are largely descriptive (e.g., Jimenez, 1997; Kenner, 1999; Moje et al., 2004), while policymakers continue to require inferential (and experimental) information to inform policy and practice (Slavin, 2002). Of course it can difficult—conceptually and instrumentally—to quantify cultural elements of (literacy) learning (Rogoff & Angelillo, 2002), but we argue that by mixing research methods and building on frameworks that link school and nonschool learning environments (Hull & Shultz, 2001), a more robust body of research and classroom strategies can be provided policymaker, teachers and students alike to markedly improve teaching and learning of literacy.

We should note that some inferential research on sociocultural interventions in the classroom has been done. In a well-known study, Au and Mason (1981), for example, studied adult-child interactions for native Hawaiian children in and outside of classrooms. They found that when the sort of spontaneity in participation—including self-selected and overlapping speech—characteristic in students' homes was promoted in the classroom, students were more engaged in reading instruction. Additional analysis (Tharp, 1982) found that students participating in this programmatic "intervention", called the Kamehameha Early Education Project (KEEP), performed significantly better on tests reading achievement than their nonparticipating peers. The research design employed, however, could not ascertain the extent to which the instructional accommodation of children's native interactions actually contributed to the gains in reading performance. But the hypothesis was quite plausible, and the work of Au and colleagues is a wonderful example of the sort of mixed-method research needed to understand how sociocultural processes can be understood and applied to formal learning environments as a way to bridge home and school literacy learning.

More robust sociocultural research of the kind we advocate should also embrace a comprehensive approach to classroom quality. Obviously because this chapter centers on literacy learning, many of the classroom strategies discussed orient around the academic instructional supports rendered by teachers. They include the quality, frequency, and timing of questions teachers pose to students, as well as ways by which teachers model language learning and provide opportunities for academic conversation with their students (Walqui & van Lier, 2010). But there are other important aspects of classroom quality associated with literacy learning, over and above the richness of instruction (Pianta & Hamre, 2009). They include the extent to which teachers communicate social and emotional support to students through praise, proximity, flexibility, sensitivity, and a high regard for student opinion and perspective (Greenberg, Weissberg, & O'Brien, 2003; Hamre & Pianta, 2005; Raver, 2004; Roeser, Eccles, & Sameroff, 2000). A comprehensive approach to classroom quality should also take into account the extent to which teachers provide clear expectations, routines, redirection, and efficient use of time (Emmer & Stough, 2001). Pianta and Hamre (2009) maintain that these three broad aspects of classroom quality—what they refer to as instructional support, emotional support, and classroom organization—should be represented in more classroom research designs, using standardized instruments.

INFORMAL LEARNING

Informal learning can simply be understood as learning that takes place outside of formal settings. We should make clear that designed and formal settings are not necessarily synonymous, nor are their respective opposites. Indeed, some informal learning environments—such as museums, zoos, and after-school clubs—are designed for specific types of learning (Bell, Lewenstein, Shouse, & Feder, 2009; Bransford et al., 2006), while others—such as playgrounds, peer play, and other family activities (referred to as emergent settings)—are not. Designed environments have an agenda, so to speak, while emergent settings do not, even though learning opportunities in these settings can be the most meaningful. Indeed, around four-fifths of a child's waking time is spent in nonschool pursuits. Thus, understanding the forms and functions of learning outside of the classroom becomes paramount, particularly for teachers who are expected to build on their students' prior knowledge.

Given its importance it is surprising how understudied informal learning actually is (Bransford et al., 2006). Not only do we lack data, but we lack comprehensive frameworks to understand how literacy learning, for example, takes shape outside of school. With its origins in Margaret Mead's (1928, 1930) early twentieth century studies of childrearing and adolescent development in South Pacific (McDermott, 2001), the study of informal learning grew most notably in the 1970s when a greater emphasis was being placed on learning ecologies. This included the work of Howard Becker, Jerome Bruner, Sylvia Scribner, Michael Cole, and Urie Brofenbrenner. Based on the work of Lev Vygotstky, 1970s scholars of informal learning were largely interested in comparative cognition—how cultural groups differed in their performance on specific cognitive tasks (e.g., categorization, memory) associated with their daily routines (e.g., Scribner & Cole, 1973). And in the 1980s, scholars became increasingly interested in how cognition actually developed in daily activities through differing forms of socialization and participation of children (e.g., Rogoff, 1991; Rogoff & Lave, 1984).

Currently, work in informal learning is expanding rapidly, as scholars and policymakers are finding applications to contemporary economic and workforce needs. For example, a recent report by the National Academy of Sciences (Bell, Lewenstein, Shouse, & Feder, 2009) positions informal learning as a very promising field for science education. The gist is that U.S. students need to be better prepared for an increasingly sophisticated technological society by leveraging the quality of science learning outside of the classroom. Authors of the report challenge classroom activities to better reflect science learning outside of school, as a way of producing greater student interest in and understandings of concepts in biology, chemistry, physics, earth science, computer science, and so on. Their push is to design more meaningful and engaging science learning in informal settings, and to partner with communities, schools, and teachers in doing so.

How would similar research and development efforts in literacy education enhance the general quality and meaningfulness of literacy learning for minority and low-income students across the country? Of course, the question is not simply a matter of institutional will. Unlike science education, there is less of a groundbreaking movement in literacy education to understand and leverage informal learning to improve policy and practice, than exists in science education. Though we hope this will change, the groundswell needed will depend on our ability to articulate an approachable framework of social and cultural processes associated with student abilities to read and write. Certainly we must draw on the frameworks availed in the sociocultural studies of learning to do so, but we must also find ways of making clearer and more robust applications to classroom settings, as discussed earlier.

So what contributions can be gleaned from an informal learning perspective to furnish such a groundswell? First, it must be clear that real learning happens outside of the classroom, even when its goals and means differ substantially from those of formal schooling. The work of Barbara Rogoff (2003) makes this clear. She demonstrates how learning in indigenous Central American villages takes place as apprenticeships between children and adults. Children learn how to weave at an early age through close observation and guided participation (Paradise & Rogoff, 2009). In these settings, there is a clear collaboration between child and adult, unlike the hierarchal structure common in U.S. classrooms. Children take their own initiative, rather than being given explicit directives, and communication between the adult and child is mostly through joint action, rather than verbal instruction and Socratic questioning. Rewards for the activity are inherent to the completion of the task in traditional Mayan communities, rather than through praise or an external reward. Listening, observing, and participation are critical competencies in and of themselves, but also to the acquisition of valuable cognitive abilities.

Second, studies in informal learning provide important, fine-grained tools for analysis. These include activity types, forms of participation, and types of interactions. Activities are found in the daily routines of children and youth (Weisner, 2002). Simply, what do students tend to do with their time outside of school—where do they spend it, and in what endeavors (e.g., playing video games, homework, watching TV, cooking meals, football practice, visiting relatives, Sunday school, babysitting)? What is the purpose of these activities, and what values and goals do they communicate? What resources are needed to make them happen, and what scripts define appropriate engagement in the activities? This leads us to questions of how children and youth are expected and socialized to participate in activities. To what extent are they expected to take initiative, listen, observe, speak, or inquire? Indeed, some research has demonstrated quite different expectations for participation between home and school settings. Philips (1983), for example, found that a wide variation between home and school participation structures and speech practices of Native American children. At home, the elders of the community expected more silence and keen listening of the children, while teachers at school expected more talking and self-initiated turn-taking. This difference led teachers to misinterpret the students' abilities.

And finally, it is important to understand what, in addition to mental processes, changes occur when/as children and youth from different cultural communities learn. Research has found that learning in some cultural communities is defined less by what is known (or declared) than changes in how children and youth identify themselves (Holland, Lachicotte, & Skinner, 1998; Lave & Wenger, 1991; Wenger, 1999). Other work finds that learning is primarily indicated by changes in the way children/youth participate in activities (Lave & Wenger, 1991; Paradise & Rogoff, 2009). For example, learning might be considered complete when a child takes immediate initiative to "pitch in" rather than taking more time to observe, and fumble without guidance (Paradise & Rogoff, 2009).

Certainly sociocultural literacy research has applied these concepts from studies of informal learning to understand how children and youth acquire and use reading and writing outside of school. It is a relatively extensive and quite diverse body of literature that considers ways in which discourse and interaction characteristics (e.g., Gregory, 1998), attitudes and beliefs at home (e.g., Volk & De Acosta, 2001), oral language and literacy experiences at home (e.g., Mulhern, 1997), and language status (e.g., Moll & Diaz, 1987), and other sociocultural characteristics (e.g., Blake, 2001; Jimenez & Gersten, 1999; Moll, Saez, & Dworin, 2001; Reyes & Azuara, 2008) shape engagement in and learning from literacy activities outside of school. The "new literacies" movement (Lewis, Encisco, & Moje, 2007; Street, 2005), moreover, has provided additional concepts by exploring the functions of literacy beyond written texts, to understand how the negotiation of identity (Bartlett, 2007; McCarthey & Moje, 2002), power (Lewis, 2001), and agency (Holland, Lachiotte, Skinner, & Cain, 1998) between students, adults, and practices develop alongside activities broadly applied to literacy learning.

All of this work provides useful concepts and frameworks for understanding the development of reading and writing uses and capabilities outside of school. It is difficult, however, to devise a synthesis or evaluation of the current literature in informal literacy learning in ways that inform policy and practice, for three broad reasons. First, there are limited applications to classroom practice. Policymakers are ultimately interested in institutional processes—what happens in the schools. This is what they can control through programs, policies, and other initiatives. If the study of informal learning somehow speaks to institutional domain, policymaker interest is much more likely. Within the context of studies of informal literacy learning, this means addressing classroom practice, or some program that falls in the purview of the school (e.g., afterschool learning; Schauble et al., 1996).

Second, even when some connections to classroom practice have been made in sociocultural studies of literacy learning (Heath, 1983, 2000; Pahl & Roswell, 2005), the work draws largely on ethnographic and case study methods, which makes inference difficult. Certainly descriptive aspects of sociocultural processes (through ethnography and other qualitative research tools) in literacy learning are pivotal (Gutierrez & Rogoff, 2003), simply because of their inherent complexity and deep associations with context. Yet we reject the notion that research should somehow choose between providing descriptive and inferential information (Fuller & Clarke, 1994). At the end of the day policymakers at the local, state, and federal levels ask about trends, means, and variation. We argue that we can provide this information about populations, while also honoring cultural complexity, ethnic difference, and the sort of nuance that matters to learning in and out of schools.

Finally, common frameworks for the forms and functions of reading and writing in and outside of school are needed. This means more interdisciplinary work and, again, the combination of research methods. It also means finding connections between concepts in psychological and anthropological studies of literacy. For example, there are certainly overlaps between what anthropologists call power (Fairclough, 1989) and what psychologists label autonomy (Pianta, 2006) in literacy learning. Researchers from diverse disciplines will have to work together on the same problems, and with the same goals, to build—or refine—broader conceptual understandings.

The good news is that sound parameters already exist. We can agree that sociocultural studies linking nonschool and school learning will require teachers to be learners. And much of what they learn will be unexpected. In many cases teacher learning will require shifts—or expansions—in their definitions of knowledge, competence, and ability (Gonzalez, Moll, & Amanti, 2005). We can also agree that the social capacities of students are not incidental to their interest and abilities to engage with texts and other forms of literacy. This means having a deeper understanding of the ways in which students cooperate, communicate, listen, observe, and empathize. Literacy learning also has an emotional face (Guthrie, Rueda, Gambrell, & Morrison, 2009; Pekrun, 1992, 2006), which is in need of further study. The social and emotional aspects of literacy learning need to be understood in terms of the daily practices by which they develop, which requires an understanding of language uses (Cazden, 1988).

Toward Convergence

There is wide agreement that the ways literacy learning tends to take shape in schools and classrooms for low-income minority students are inadequate, and that the persistent gap in reading and writing proficiency is highly problematic. A key contributor to the problem has been the failure to assert a framework by which researchers can study—and policymakers can respond to—important social and cultural processes in classrooms, homes, and other settings. Without such an assertion, it is difficult to develop a necessarily comprehensive understanding of student literacy required to provide needed recommendations to teachers, administrators, and policymakers working with/on behalf of diverse students. While we do not address all of the difficult answers (or questions) in this chapter, we hope to have paved a path toward convergence. Policy matters quite a bit to the literacy learning opportunities of low-income minority students (Garcia & Wiese, 2009), and should afford rather than constrain ongoing learning.

In this chapter we have drawn from the emergent "science of learning" (Meltzoff et al., 2009) to argue for a more policy-minded sociocultural theory of literacy learning, by establishing that:

- literacy learning is an inherently social (and emotional) process;
- teachers are necessarily social and cultural brokers, not only the bearers of information;
- social and cultural aspects of literacy learning are implicit, and have a neurological basis;
- literacy learning requires understanding the array of activities in which aspects of reading and writing are regularly practiced (in and outside of school);
- ways in which children and youth participate in day-to-day activities should inform literacy learning in the classroom;
- classroom quality should be understood in terms of the structural, affective, and instructional nature of learning opportunities;
- teacher and parent education is pivotal to understanding and bridging school-home divides in literacy learning opportunities; and
- teacher training may entail some discomfort and inefficiency in the short run, but can lead to increased student interest and performance in the long term.

A helpful way to think about the sociocultural processes in literacy learning is to consider the three levels, or planes, of human development (Rogoff, 1995): personal, interpersonal, and the community/institutional. Interpersonal processes are obviously nested within community/institutional processes, and personal within interpersonal. Institutional processes could consider what school-wide initiatives, for example, might lead to deeper parent-teacher collaborations to bridge forms of literacy learning between homes and classrooms. This may mean requiring home visits in which teachers are prompted in meaningful ways to learn what children actually do at home, how these activities relate to literacy learning, and ways in which the organization of classrooms can more thoughtfully reflect learning in the home.

Interpersonal processes, probably the most important plane, consider how children actually participate with others in home activities. How do they tend to interact with their family members, in comparison with teachers? Anthropology and cultural psychology have provided several useful concepts and research tools to understand these interactions. Indeed, because of this work, we are able to understand how roles, forms of communication, modes of learning, and structure in person-to-person interactions matter (Rogoff et al., 2007). In terms of literacy learning, however, we need to know which interpersonal aspects predict literacy learning, and the extent to which they are malleable (among teachers, students, and parents).

Finally, the personal means through which sociocultural processes are associated with literacy learning are less understood. Some work exists demonstrating ways by which social competencies like cooperation, helping, and sharing (Caprara, Barbaranelli, Pastorelli, Bandura, & Zimbardo, 2000; DiPerna, Volpe, & Elliott, 2001; Galindo & Fuller, 2010)—and emotions like enjoyment, relief, and boredom (Pekrun, 2006; Pekrun, Goetz, Titz, & Perry, 2002)—are associated with literacy learning, but it is not clear the extent to which these processes are mediated by the interpersonal (or cultural) processes cited above. We need to know the reasons, internal to the student, by which "culturally responsive pedagogy" (Gay, 2000), for example, makes a difference in literacy engagement and learning of individual students (Guthrie, Rueda, Gambrell, & Morrison, 2009; Zins, Weissberg, Wang, & Walberg, 2004).

The work of Goldenberg, Gallimore, and Reese (2005) is a wonderful example of the sort of sociocultural work needed to understand and improve policy and practice in literacy learning. Even though Goldenberg and colleagues do not incorporate classroom data in their work—or addresses processes at the personal level—they have managed over several years to combine qualitative with quantitative methods to understand, in an iterative way, how aspects of the home, community, and home-school connections shape literacy learning for urban Latino children. At the community level, for example, they have found that church attendance and parental familiarity with the university system, over and above socioeconomic differences, are positively correlated with literacy learning in the early grades. And at the interpersonal plane, they found in a longitudinal study that early literacy practices in Spanish correlated with seventh-grade reading performance in English.

We should make quite clear that we do not envision a grand consensus theory in sociocultural studies of literacy at the expense of the varied approaches now existent. Such is neither feasible nor desirable. We do, however, advocate for a convergence of historically isolated paradigms to provide an accessible framework for educational policymakers and practitioners. This will mean simplifying our vocabulary to work out a common language (the example of "power" in anthropological studies, and "autonomy" in psychology, was cited earlier). It will also mean combining research methods—providing descriptive and inferential information about institutional/community, interpersonal, and personal processes associated with student literacy learning. Granted, not all studies should implement the same designs. Some will be more exploratory, and others (quasi-) experimental. But all should be mindful of limitations inherent in design and method. This should lead us toward a stronger knowledge-base over the coming years, as well as a greater interest and commitment from foundations and federal grant programs to finance this sort of work.

REFERENCES

Au, K. (2005). *Multicultural issues and literacy achievement*. Mahwah, NJ: Lawrence Erlbaum Associates.

Au, K., & Mason, J. (1981). Social organization in learning to read: The balance of rights hypothesis. *Reading Research Quarterly, 17*, 115-152.

August, D., & Shanahan, T. (Eds.). (2006). *Developing literacy in second language learners: Report of the national literacy panel on language minority youth and children*. Mahwah, NJ: Lawrence Erlbaum Associates.

Banks, J., Au, K., Ball., A. E., Bell, P., Gordon, E. W., Gutierrez, K. D., ... Zhou, M. (2007a). *Learning in and out of diverse environments: Life-long, life-wide, life-deep*. Seattle, WA: Center for Multicultural Education, University of Washington.

Banks, J., Cochran-Smith, M., Moll, L., Richert, A., Zeichner, K., LePage, P., ... McDonald, M. (2007b). Teaching diverse learners. In L. Darling-Hammond & J. Bransford (Eds.), *Preparing teachers for a changing world: What teachers should learn and be able to do* (pp. 232-274). San Francisco, CA: Jossey-Bass.

Bartlett, L. (2007). To seem and to feel: Situated identities and literacy practices. *Teachers College Record, 109*(1), 51-69.

Beals, D. E., DeTemple, J. M., & Dickinson, D. K. (1994). Talking and listening that support early literacy development of children from low-income families. In D. K. Dickinson (Ed.), *Bridges to literacy: Children, families, and schools* (pp. 19-40). Cambridge, MA: Blackwell.

Bell, P., Lewenstein, B., Shouse, A. W., & Feder, M. A. (2009). *Learning science in informal environments*. Washington, DC: National Research Council.

Bereiter, C., & Scardamalia, M. (1993). *Surpassing ourselves: An inquiry into the nature and implications of expertise*. Chicago, IL: Open Court.

Blake, B. E. (2001). Fruit of the devil: Writing and English language learners. *Language Arts, 78*(5), 435-441.

Bradley, R. H., & Corwyn, R. F. (2002). Socioeconomic status and child development. *Annual Review of Psychology, 53*, 371-399.

Bransford, J. D. et al. (2006). Learning theories and education: Toward a decade of synergy. In P. Alexander & P. Winne (Eds.), *Handbook of Educational Psychology* (2nd Ed.). Mahwah, NJ: Erlbaum.

Bransford, J. D., Brown, A. L., & Cocking, R. R. (Eds.). (2000). *How people learn: Brain, mind, experience, and school.* Washington, DC: National Academies Press.

Bransford, J. D., & Donovan, M. (Eds.). (2005). *How students learn: History, mathematics, and science in the classroom.* Washington DC: The National Academies Press.

Bransford, J. D., & Schwartz, D. L. (1999). Rethinking transfer: A simple proposal with multiple implications. In A. Iran-Nejad & P. D. Pearson (Eds.), *Review of Research in Education* (pp. 61-101). Washington, DC: American Educational Research Association.

Bransford, J. D., Stevens, R., Schwartz, D., Meltzoff, A., Pea, R., Roschelle, J., … Sabelli, N. (2006). Learning theories and education: Toward a decade of synergy. In P. Alexander & P. Winne (Eds.), *Handbook of educational psychology* (2nd ed., pp. 207-244). Mahwah, NJ: Erlbaum.

Brophy, J., & Good, T. (1986). Teacher behavior and students achievement. In M. C. Wittrock (Ed.), *Handbook of research on teaching* (3rd ed.). New York, NY: Macmillan.

Bruer, J. (1997). Education and the brain: A bridge too far. *Educational Researcher, 26*(8), 4-16.

Bruer, J. (1999). In search of … brain-based education. *Phi Delta Kappan, 80*(9), 648-654.

Bruner, J. (1996). *The culture of education.* Cambridge, MA: Harvard University Press.

Caprara, G. V., Barbaranelli, C., Pastorelli, C., Bandura, A., & Zimbardo, P. (2000). Prosocial foundations of children's academic achievement. *Psychological Science, 11*(4), 302-306.

Carnegie Council on Advancing Adolescent Literacy. (2010). *Time to act: An agenda for advancing adolescent literacy for college and career success.* New York, NY: Carnegie Corporation of New York.

Cazden, C. B. (1988). *Classroom discourse: The language of teaching and learning.* Portsmouth, NH: Heinemann.

Cole, M. (2005). Cross-cultural and historical perspectives on the developmental consequences of education. *Human Development, 48,* 195-216.

Cole, M., & Engeström, Y., & Vasquez (Eds.). (1997). *Mind, culture, and activity: Seminal papers from the laboratory of comparative human cognition.* New York, NY: Cambridge University Press.

Chao, R. K. (1994). Beyond parental control and authoritarian parenting style: Understanding Chinese parenting through the cultural notion of training. *Child Development, 65*(4), 1111-1119.

Dahaene, S. (2009). *Reading in the brain: The science and evolution of a human invention.* New York, NY: Viking.

Darling-Hammond, L. (2010). *The flat world and education: How America's commitment to equity will determine our future.* New York, NY: Teachers College Press.

Darling-Hammond, L., & Bransford, J. (Eds.). (2007). *Preparing teachers for a changing world: What teachers should learn and be able to do.* Washington, DC: National Academy of Education.

DeSchepper, B., & Treisman, A. (1996). Visual memory for novel shapes: Implicit coding without attention. Journal of *Experimental Psychology: Learning, Memory, and Cognition, 22,* 27–47.

Delgado Gaitan, C., & H. Trueba. (1991). *Crossing cultural borders: Education for immigrant families in America.* London: Falmer.

Detterman, D. K., & Sternberg, R. J. (1993). *Transfer on trial: Intelligence, cognition and instruction.* Norwood, NJ: Ablex.

DiPerna, J. C., Volpe, R. J., & Elliott, S. N. (2001). A model of academic enablers and elementary reading/language arts achievement. *School Psychology Review, 31*(3), 298-312.

Eisenberg, N., & Mussen, P. H. (1989). *The roots of prosocial behavior in children.* New York, NY: Cambridge University Press.

Emmer, E. T., & Stough, L. (2001). Classroom management: A critical part of educational psychology, with implications for teacher education. *Educational Psychologist, 36*(2), 103-112.

Fairclough, N. (1989). *Language and power.* New York, NY: Pearson.

Fredricks, J. A., Blumenfeld, P. C., & Paris, A. H. (2004). Student engagement: Potential of the concept, state of the evidence. *Review of Educational Research, 74*(1), 59-109.

Fuller, B., & Clarke, P. (1994). Raising school effects while ignoring culture? Local conditions and the influence of classroom tools, rules, and pedagogy. *Review of Educational Research, 64*(1), 119-157.

Fuller, B., & Garcia-Coll, C. (2010). Learning from Latinos: Contexts, families, and child development in motion. *Developmental Psychology, 46*(3), 559-565.

Galindo, C., & Fuller, B. (2010). The social competence of Latino kindergartners and growth in mathematical understanding. *Developmental Psychology, 46*(3), 579-592.

Garcia, E. (2005). *Student cultural diversity: Understanding and meeting the challenge* (3rd ed.). Boston, MA: Houghton Mifflin.

Garcia, E., Jensen, B., & Scribner, K. (2009). The demographic imperative, *Educational Leadership, 66*(7), 8-13.

Garcia, E., & Wiese, A. (2009). Policy related issues to diversity and literacy: Implications for English learners. In L. M. Morrow, R. Rueda, & D. Lapp (Eds.), *Handbook of research on literacy and diversity.* New York, NY: The Guilford Press.

Gay, G. (2000). *Culturally responsive teaching: Theory, research, & practice.* New York, NY: Teachers College Press.

Gee, J. P. (2001). Language, class, and identity: Teenagers fashioning themselves through language. *Linguistics and Education, 12*(2), 175-194.

Gersten, R., Baker, S.K., Shanahan, T., Linan-Thompson, S., Collins, P., & Scarcella, R. (2007). *Effective Literacy and English Language Instruction for English Learners in the Elementary Grades: A Practice Guide* (NCEE 2007-4011). Washington, DC: National Center for Education Evaluation and Regional Assistance, Institute of Education Sciences, U.S. Department of Education. Retrieved from http://ies.ed.gov/ncee

Goldenberg, C., Gallimore, R., & August, D. (2006). Synthesis: Sociocultural contexts and literacy development. In D. August & T. Shanahan (Eds.), *Developing literacy in second* language learners: Report of the national literacy panel on language minority youth and *children.* Mahwah, NJ: Lawrence Erlbaum Associates.

Goldenberg, C., Gallimore, R., & Reese, L. (2005). Using mixed methods to explore Latino children's literacy development. In T. S. Weisner (Ed.), *Discovering successful pathways in children's development* (pp. 20-46). Chicago, IL: The University of Chicago Press.

Good, T. L., & Brophy, J. E. (2008). *Looking in classrooms* (10th ed.). Boston, MA: Allyn & Bacon.

Gopnik, A., & Meltzoff, A. N. (1997). *Words, thoughts, and theories.* Cambridge, MA: MIT Press.

Graham, S., & Perin, D. (2007). *Writing next: Effective strategies to improve writing of adolescents in middle and high schools.* New York, NY: Carnegie Corporation of New York.

Greenberg, M. T., Weissberg, R. P., & O'Brien, M. U. (2003). Enhancing school-based prevention and youth development through coordinated social, emotional, and academic learning. *American Psychologist, 58*(6-7), 466-474.

Gregory, E. (1998). Siblings as mediators of literacy in linguistic minority communities. *Language and Education, 12*(1), 33-54.

Gonzalez, N., Moll, L., & Amanti, C. (2005). *Funds of knowledge: Theorizing practices, households, communities, and classrooms.* Mahwah, NJ: Lawrence Erlbaum Associates.

Gunderson, S., Jones, R., & Scanland, K. (2004). *The jobs revolution: Changing how America works.* Austin, TX: Copywriters.

Guthrie, J. T., Rueda, R., Gambrell, L. B., & Morrison, D. A. (2009). Roles of engagement, valuing, and identification in reading development of students from diverse backgrounds. In L. M. Morrow, R. Rueda, & D. Lapp (Eds.), *Handbook of research on literacy and diversity* (pp. 195-215). New York, NY: The Guilford Press.

Gutierrez, K., & Rogoff, B. (2003). Cultural ways of learning: Individual traits and repertoires of practice. *Educational Researcher, 32*(5), 19-25.

Hart, B., & Risley, T. (1999). *The social world of children learning to talk.* Baltimore, MD: Paul H. Brookes.

Hammerness, K., Darling-Hammond, L., Bransford, J., Berliner, D., Cochran-Smith, M., McDonald, M., & Zeichner, K. (2005). How teachers learn and develop. In L. Darling-Hammond & J. Bransford (Eds.), *Preparing teachers for a changing world: What teachers should learn and be able to do* (pp. 358-389). San Francisco, CA: Jossey-Bass.

Hamre, B. K., & Pianta, R. C. (2001). Early teacher-child relationships and the trajectory of children's school outcomes through eighth grade. *Child Development, 72*(2), 625-638.

Hamre, B. K., & Pianta, R. C. (2005). Can instructional and emotional support in the first grade classroom make a difference for children at risk of school failure? *Child Development, 76*(5), 949-967.

Heath, S. B. (1983). *Ways with words: Language, life, and work in communities and classrooms.* New York, NY: Cambridge University Press.

Heath, S. B. (2000). Linguistics in the study of language in education. *Harvard Educational Review, 70*(1), 49-59.

Herrnstein, R. J., & Miller, C. (1994). *Bell Curve: Intelligence and class structure in American life.* New York, NY: Free Press Paperbacks.

Holland, D., Lachicotte, W., Skinner, D., & Cain, C. (1998). *Identity and agency in cultural worlds.* Cambridge, MA: Harvard University Press.

Hull, G., & Shultz, K. (2001). Literacy and learning out of school: A review of theory and research. *Review of Educational Research, 71*(4), 575-611.

Jimenez, R. T. (1997). The strategic reading abilities and potential of five low-literacy Latina/o readers in middle school. *Reading Research Quarterly, 32*(3), 224-243.

Jimenez, R. T., & Gersten, R. (1999). Lessons and dilemmas derived from the literacy instruction of two Latina/o teachers. *American Educational Research Journal, 36*(2), 265-301.

Kenner, C. (1999). Children's understandings of text in a multilingual nursery. *Language and Education, 13*(1), 1-16.

Kuhl, P. K. (2004). Early language acquisition: Cracking the speech code. *Nature Reviews Neuroscience, 5*, 831–843.

Ladson-Billings, G. (1995). Toward a theory of culturally relevant pedagogy. *American Journal of Educational Research, 32*(3), 465-491.

Ladson-Billings, G. (2006). From the achievement gap to the education debt: Understanding achievement in U.S. schools. *Educational Researcher, 35*(7), 3-12.

Lave, J., & Wenger, E. (1991). *Situated learning: Legitimate peripheral participation.* New York, NY: Cambridge University Press.

Lee, C. D. (2007). *Culture, literacy, and learning: Taking Bloom in the midst of the whirlwind.* New York, NY: Teachers College Press

Leseman, P. M., & de Jong, P. F. (1998). Home literacy: Opportunity, instruction, cooperation and socioemotional quality predicting early reading achievement. *Reading Research Quarterly, 33*(3), 294-318.

Lewis, C. (2001). *Literacy practices as social acts: Power, status, and cultural norms in the classroom.* Mahwah, NJ: Lawrence Erlbaum Associates.

Lewis, C., Enciso, P., & Moje, E. B. (Eds.). (2009). *Reframing sociocultural research on literacy: Identity, agency, and Power.* New York, NY: Routledge.

McCarthey, S., & Moje, E. B. (2002). Identity matters. *Reading Research Quarterly, 37*, 228-237.

McDermott, R. (2001). A century of Margaret Mead. *Teachers College Record, 103*(5), 843-867.

Mead, M. (1928). *Coming of age in Samoa.* New York, NY: Morrow.

Mead, M. (1930). *Growing up in New Guinea.* New York, NY: Morrow.

Meltzoff, A., et al. (2009) Foundations for a new science of learning. *Science, 325*, 284-288.

Meltzoff, A. N., & Decety, J. (2003). What imitation tells us about social cognition: A rapprochement between developmental psychology and cognitive neuroscience. *Philosophical Transactions of the Royal Society of London: Biological Sciences, 358*, 491–500.

Miller, L. S. (1995). *An American imperative: Accelerating minority educational advancement.* New Haven, CT: Yale University Press.

Moje, E. B., Ciechanowski, K. M., Kramer, K., Eliis, L., Carrillo, R., & Collazo, T. (2004). Working toward third space in content area literacy: An examination of everyday funds of knowledge and discourse, *Reading Research Quarterly, 39*(1), 38-70.

Moje, E. B., Collazo, T., Carrillo, R., & Marx, R. W. (2001). "Maestro, what is quality?": Language, literacy, and discourse in project-based science. *Journal of Research in Science Teaching, 38*, 469-496.

Moll, L., & Diaz, S. (1987). Change as the goal of educational research. *Anthropology and Education Quarterly, 18*(4), 300-311.

Moll, L., Saez, R., & Dworin, J. (2001). Exploring biliteracy: Two student case examples of writing as social practice. *Elementary School Journal, 101*(4), 435-449.

Morrow, L. M., Rueda, R., & Lapp, D. (Eds.). (2009). *Handbook of research on literacy and diversity*. New York, NY: The Guilford Press.

Mulhern, M. M. (1997). Doing his own thing: A Mexican-American kindergartner becomes literate at home and school. *Language Arts, 74*(6), 468-476.

Nasir, N. S., Rosebery, A. S., & Lee, C. D. (2006). Learning as a cultural process: Achieving equity through diversity. In K. Sawyer (Ed.), *Cambridge handbook of the learning sciences* (pp. 489-504). New York, NY: Cambridge University Press.

Neuman, S. B., & Celano, D. (2006). The knowledge gap: Implications of leveling the playing field for low-income and middle income children. *Reading Research Quarterly, 41*(2), 176-201.

Nissen, M. J., & Bullemer, P. T. (1987). Attentional requirements for learning: Evidence from performance measures. *Cognitive Psychology, 19*, 1-32.

Noddings, N. (2005). *The challenge to care in schools: An alternative approach to education* (2nd ed.). New York, NY: Teachers College Press.

Paradise, R., & Rogoff, B. (2009). Side by side: Learning by observing and pitching it. *Ethos, 37*(1), 102-138.

Pahl, K., & Roswell, J. (Eds.). (2005). *Travel notes from the new literacy studies in the classroom.* Clevedon, England: Multilingual Matters.

Pekrun, R. (1992). The impact of emotions on learning and achievement: Towards a theory of cognitive/motivational mediators. *Applied Psychology, 41*(4), 359-376.

Pekrun, R. (2006). The control-value theory of achievement emotions: Assumptions, corollaries, and implications for educational research and practice. *Educational Psychology Review, 18*(4), 315-341.

Pekrun, R., Goetz, T., Titz, W., & Perry, R. P. (2002). Academic emotions in students' self-regulated learning and achievement: Qualitative and quantitative research. *Educational Psychologist, 37*(2), 91-105.

Philips, S. (1983). *The invisible culture: Communication in classroom and community on the Warm Springs Indian Reservation*. Prospect Heights, IL: Waveland Press.

Pianta, R. C. (2006). Teacher-child relationships and early literacy. In D. Dickinson & S. Neuman (Eds.), *Handbook of early literacy research* (Vol. 2, pp. 149-162). New York, NY: The Guilford Press.

Pianta, R. C., & Hamre, B. K. (2009). Conceptualization, measurement, and improvement of classroom processes: Standardized observation can leverage capacity. *Educational Researcher, 38*(2), 109-119.

Raver, C. C. (2004). Placing emotional self-regulation in sociocultural and socioeconomic contexts. *Child Development, 75*(2), 346-353.

Reyes, I., & Azuara, P. (2008). Emergent biliteracy in young Mexican immigrant children. *Reading Research Quarterly, 43*(4), 374-398.

Risley, T. R., & Hart, B. (2006). Promoting early language development. In N. F. Watt et al. (Eds.), *The crisis in young mental health: Early intervention programs and policies*. Westport, CT: Praeger.

Roeser, R. W., Eccles, J. S., & Sameroff, A. J. (2000). School as a context of early adolescents' academic and social-emotional development: A summary of research findings. *Elementary School Journal, 100*(5), 443-471.

Rogoff, B. (1991). *Apprenticeship in thinking: Cognitive development in social context.* New York, NY: Oxford University Press.

Rogoff, B. (1995). Observing sociocultural activity on three planes: Participatory appropriation, guided participation, and apprenticeship. In J. V. Wertsch, P. del Rio, & A. Alvarez (Eds.), *Sociocultural studies of mind* (pp. 139-163). Cambridge, MA: Cambridge University Press.

Rogoff, B. (2003). *The cultural nature of human development.* New York, NY: Oxford University Press.

Rogoff, B., & Angelillo, C. (2002). Investigating the coordinated functioning of multifaceted cultural practices in human development. *Human Development, 45*, 211-225.

Rogoff, B., & Lave, J. (1984). *Everyday cognition: Development in social context.* Cambridge, MA: Harvard University Press.

Rogoff, B., Mistry, J., Göncü, A., & Mosier, C. (1993). Guided participation in cultural activity by toddlers and caregivers. *Monographs of the Society for Research in Child Development, 58*(8), 1-179.

Rogoff, B., Moore, L., Najafi, B., Dexter, A., Correa-Chavez, M., & Solis, J. (2007). Children's development of cultural repertoires through participation in everyday routines and practices. In J. Grusec & P. Hastings (Eds.), *Handbook of Socialization* (pp. 490-515). New York, NY: Guilford.

Rogoff, B., Sellers, M. J., Pirrotta, S., Fox, N., & White, S. H. (1975). Age of assignment of roles and responsibilities to children: A cross cultural survey. *Human Development, 18*(5), 353-369.

Roth, W. M., & Lee, Y. J. (2007). Vygotsky's neglected legacy: Cultural-historical activity theory. *Review of Educational Research, 77*(2), 186-232.

Schauble, L., Banks Beane, D., Coates, G. D., Martin, L. M., & Sterling, P. V. (1996). Outside the classroom walls: Learning in informal environments. In L. Schauble & R. Glaser (Eds.), *Innovations in learning: New environments for education* (pp. 5-24). Mahwah, NJ: Lawrence Erlbaum.

Schwartz, D. L., & Bransford, J. D. (1998). A time for telling. *Cognition & Instruction, 16*(4), 475–522.

Schwartz, D., Bransford, J., & Sears, D. (2005). Efficiency and innovation in transfer. To appear in J. Mestre (Ed.), *Transfer of learning: Research and perspectives* (pp. 1-51). Greenwich, CT: Information Age.

Scribner, S., & Cole, M. (1973). Cognitive consequences of formal and informal education. *Science, 182*(4112), 553-559.

Shanahan, T., & Beck, I. (2006). Effective literacy teaching for English language learners. In D. August & T. Shanahan (Eds.), *Developing literacy in second language learners: Report of the national literacy panel on language minority youth and children* (pp. 415-488). Mahwah, NJ: Lawrence Erlbaum Associates.

Shonkoff, J., & Phillips, D. (Eds.). (2000). *From neurons to neighborhoods: The science of early childhood development.* Washington, DC: National Academy Press.

Slavin, R. E. (2002). Evidence-based education policies: Transforming educational practice and research. *Educational Researcher, 31*(7), 15-21.

Slavin, R. E., Hurley, E. A., & Chamberlain, A. M. (2003). Cooperative learning and achievement: Theory and research. In W. M. Reynolds & G. E. Miller (Eds.), *Handbook of psychology: Educational psychology* (pp. 177-198). New York, NY: Wiley.

Smith, J. P., diSessa, A. A., & Roschelle, J. (1993). Misconceptions reconceived: A constructivist analysis of knowledge in transition. *The Journal of the Learning Sciences, 3*(2), 115–163.

Snow, C. E. (2006). Cross-cultural themes and future research directions. In D. August & T. Shanahan (Eds.), *Developing literacy in second language learners: Report of the national literacy panel on language minority youth and children* (pp. 631-651). Mahwah, NJ: Erlbaum.

Snow, C. E., Barnes, W. S., Chandler, J., Goodman, I. F., & Hemphill, L. (1991). *Unfulfilled expectations: Home and school influences on literacy.* Cambridge, MA: Harvard University Press.

Snow, C. E., Griffin, O., & Burns, M. S. (Eds.). (2005). *Knowledge to support the teaching of reading: Preparing teachers fir a changing world.* Washington, DC: The National Academy of Education.

Street, B. V. (Ed.). (1993). *Cross-cultural approaches to literacy.* New York, NY: Cambridge University Press.

Street, B. V. (Ed.) (2005). *Literacies across educational contexts: Mediating learning and teaching.* Philadelphia, PA: Caslon Publishing.

Tharp, R. G. (1982). The effective instruction of comprehension: Results and descriptions of the Kamehameha Early Education Program. *Reading Research Quarterly, 17,* 503-527.

Tremblay, K., Kraus, N., & McGee, T. (1998). The time course of auditory perceptual learning: neurophysiological changes during speech-sound training. *NeuroReport, 9,* 3557–3560.

Volk, D., & De Acosta, M. (2001). "Many differing ladders, many ways to climb…": Literacy events in the bilingual classroom, homes, and community of three Puerto Rican kindergartners. *Journal of Early Childhood Literacy, 1*(2), 193-224.

Wagner, T. (2008). *The global achievement gap.* New York, NY: Basic Books.

Warikoo, N., & Carter, P. (2009). Cultural explanations for racial and ethnic stratification in academic achievement: A call for a new and improves theory. *Review of Educational Research, 79*(1), 366-394.

Walqui, A., & van Lier, L. (2010). *Scaffolding the academic success of adolescent English language learners: A pedagogy of promise.* San Francisco, CA: WestEd.

Weisner, T. (2002). Ecocultural understanding of children's developmental pathways. *Human Development, 45,* 275-281.

Wenger, E. (1999) *Communities of practice: Learning, meaning and identity.* Cambridge, England: Cambridge University Press.

Wertsch, J. V. (1991). *Voices of the mind.* Cambridge, MA: Harvard University Press.

Zins, J. E., Weissberg, R. P., Wang, M. C., & Walberg, H. J. (2004). *Building academic success on social and emotional learning: What does the research say?* New York, NY: Teachers College Press.

Author Contact Information: **Bryant Jensen**, Bryant Jensen, PhD, IES Postdoc Fellow, University of Oregon, Riverfront Research Park, 1600 Millrace Drive, 5292 University of Oregon, Eugene, OR 97403-5292. Phone: -541-346-8057. E-mail: bjensen@uoregon.edu

CHAPTER 37

Meaning-Based Approaches to Literacy Education

Pamela Spycher
West Ed

This chapter focuses on meaning-based approaches to literacy education that derive from the sociolinguistic theory of language systemic functional linguistics (SFL), also referred to as functional grammar or functional linguistics. SFL was originally developed by Michael Halliday (1975, 1993) and has been elaborated over several decades by a growing number of scholars (including Christie & Derewianka, 2008; Coffin, 2006; Halliday & Matthiessen, 1994; Hammond & Gibbons, 2005; Hasan & Williams, 1996; Martin & Rose, 2005; and Schleppegrell, 2004) to form a robust theory of language and, in particular, language in education. In this chapter, the theory of SFL is explained, and the application of the theory to educational research is examined with a particular focus on four studies of meaning-based approaches to literacy in elementary, middle, and high school in South Africa, Australia, and the United States.

Educational scholars working from a functional linguistics perspective are interested in understanding the most effective ways for students to learn about language while they are also learning language and learning through language. Meaning-based approaches to literacy education are designed to support students to become more conscious of how language is used to construct meaning in different contexts by providing them with a wide range of linguistic resources, enabling them to make appropriate grammatical choices so that they can effectively comprehend and construct meaning in text. This is achieved not by simplifying the curriculum, as is often the approach with "underachieving" students, but rather, by using intellectually challenging content, making the features of academic text explicit, and providing time and opportunities for students to analyze and construct academic text and discuss how meaning is realized through language. From this perspective, "grammar is seen as a resource for making meaning ... as a network of interrelated meaningful choices" (Halliday & Matthiessen, 1994, p. 31).

Among the theoretical assumptions underlying meaning-based approaches to literacy education is that learning is essentially a social process and that teachers play a key role in socializing students into the language and knowledge valued in schooling. Learning is a collaborative activity in which the language interactions between teachers and students mediate cognitive and linguistic development. This perspective resonates with language socialization theories, which are often defined as "socialization through the use of language and socialization to use language" (Schieffelin & Ochs, 1986, p. 163) and highlight the central role that language and interaction play in education as the medium in which teaching and learning take place. Meaning-based approaches also draw from Vygotsky's (1978) notion of the "zone of proximal development," the ideal instructional place that exists between what the learner can do independently and that which is too difficult for the learner to do without strategic support, or scaffolding (Bruner, 1978; Cazden, 1983).[1]

Functional linguists note that in school settings, particularly for culturally and linguistically diverse students, scaffolding "does not just spontaneously occur" (Hammond, 2006, p. 271). In order for scaffolding to occur, teachers need "a clear understanding of the nature of the curriculum challenges faced by students ... to provide the context in which effective support becomes possible" (p. 271). This supportive context requires a sophisticated understanding of the particular ways that meaning is construed in different types of

The Handbook of Educational Theories, pp. 445–456

text (Schleppegrell, 2004) and the role that language itself plays in the learning process, as well as the delineated pedagogical moves within the zone of proximal development that are necessary for literacy learning to occur.

A related assumption is that there are conditions in traditional education that produce unequal outcomes. Multiple studies have shown how traditional schooling enhances the opportunities of some students while also disadvantaging others, particularly cultural and linguistic minorities and low-income students who may not be familiar with the type of language that is highly valued in school (Berenstein, 1971 & 1990; Hart & Risley, 1995; Heath, 1983; Michaels, 1986). This research has shown how parent-child interactions in middle-class families positions young children for success in school, and some research has even identified the specific language moves used in middle-class families that mirror the literacy practices privileged in schooling.[2] Hasan's (1989) research on mother-child interactions revealed that there is semantic variation in the way that mothers interact with their children and that the two main factors that account for this variation are the gender of the child and the social class of the family. Painter (1999) extended Hasan's work when she analyzed her son Stephen's language development over the course of 2.5 years, from age two to five, in order to document how language develops in a young middle-class child before school entry. By the time he was 5, Painter reports, Stephen "had been inducted into a meaning style with an orientation to five features:

1. learning from definitions,
2. attending to principles underlying categories,
3. specifying contextual information in language,
4. privileging textual (over perceptual) information and inferencing, and
5. construing information exchange as a means of learning" (p. 72).

In her description of Stephen's language development over time, Painter shows how family members prepare him, through common middle-class home interactions, for formal learning and educational knowledge.

In a study of language use by families from different social classes, Williams (1999) showed how, although both working-class and middle-class parents in the study read to their children in highly interactive ways to prepare them for schooling, the nuanced ways in which these two groups interacted through language around text favored middle-class families because those nuances, such as prompting for elaboration, were similar to school interactions around text. Williams suggests that, rather than attempting to get parents to master these nuances, which is akin to asking them to change entire ways of interacting with their children, a more effective approach is to educate teachers to recognize that the language used in homes is functional for that context but that expectations for language use in school are different and that not all children come to school prepared to meet those expectations. Meaning-based approaches to literacy education are designed to mediate differences in language use that students bring to school by showing teachers how to make the linguistic features of school language explicit to their students.

Description of the Theory

The foundations of meaning-based approaches to literacy education are found in SFL, which provides insights into how meaning is construed in language and how language is organized on multiple levels: at the text, sentence, clause, group/phrase, and word levels. Because the point of departure in SFL is meaning, the text level is "the fundamental unit of analysis" (Christie, 1999, p. 2). This is one of the ways in which SFL differs from traditional grammar, which tends to view the sentence as the central unit of analysis. Another difference between traditional notions of grammar and SFL is that grammar is seen not as a finite set of rules, but as an endless meaning-making resource. The "functional" in SFL denotes the ways that language functions to construe meaning. The theory illuminates how meaning and knowledge are realized through language, and it provides tools for interpreting and explaining language, as well as the nature of language development over time (Christie & Derewianka, 2008).

SFL emphasizes the interrelatedness between grammar, meaning, and social context, or what Halliday (1993) called a social semiotic. In this framework meaning and language are inextricably linked, and language, as a social semiotic, is functional for the social context in which it occurs. Context is viewed in two ways. First, the context of culture has to do with the genres, or social processes, for achieving specific purposes within a culture. Genres are socially recognized ways of using language that enable people to say things about the world, establish relationships, organize spoken and written text in certain ways, and accomplish things. Successful readers and writers are conscious of the expectations participants in social contexts (lawyers or chemists, for example) have for language use and also to have the linguistic resources available to them to meet those expectations.

The second aspect of context is context of situation, a term first used by the anthropologist Malinowski and then by the linguist Firth.[3] In specific situations within cultures, linguistic variables combine to form registers, the lexical and grammatical resources that constitute particular genres. Christie and Misson (1998) note that "just as a singer changes register from time to time, so too, metaphorically, a language user is said to change register depending upon the context" (p. 10). The linguistic resources we use and the language choices we unconsciously make when communicating vary depending upon the context in which we are communicating. For example, the language choices we make to discuss a work-related problem with an employer will be different from the choices we make when talking about a movie with a friend or telling a child to stop misbehaving. Similarly, chemists have a way of using language when they present a research paper in a peer-reviewed journal that differs from the language used by a fifth grade teacher who is describing a chemical reaction.

Halliday identified three variables in the contexts in which language is used—*field, tenor,* and *mode*—to explain how variation in register is responsive to context and how different linguistic choices realize different social contexts. The field dimension refers to what the text is about and the social activity in which people are involved, the tenor dimension involves the relationships between participants in the interaction, and the mode dimension refers to how language is used (written, oral, visual, etc.). The grammatical choices (ideational, interpersonal, and textual choices), or metafunctions,[4] that correspond with each of these register variables help writers/speakers to meet the expectations of particular genres. Ideational choices (in the field dimension) help present ideas about the world through the use of linguistic resources such as noun and verb phrases, technical vocabulary, etc. Interpersonal choices (in the tenor dimension) allow one to take a stance and establish relationships through linguistic resources such as various modal verbs ("could," "should," "would") or adverbs ("probably," "certainly") used for tempering statements or hedging. Textual choices (in the mode dimension) help to structure texts coherently through the use of linguistic resources such as conjunctions ("although," "however," "because"), clause combining, or rhetorical organization to create cohesion. In every clause, these ideational, interpersonal, and textual metafunctions work simultaneously to make meaning and realize context.

SFL provides additional metalanguage that enables both linguists and students as young as the elementary grades to analyze and talk about language in order to understand how it is constructed and achieves specific purposes. The term *participant* helps discourse analysts of all ages identify who is involved in a process (an *actor, agent,* or *receiver* of a process). The term *process* helps identify the types of events that occur or the relationships being established. *Processes* can be *action* or *doing* verbs (e.g., dissect, explode, shift), *thinking/feeling* verbs (e.g., detest, reflect, imagine), *saying* verbs (e.g., suggest, indicate, state), or *relating* verbs (e.g., is, have, include).[5] The term *circumstances* helps the discourse analyst talk about details presented in text that provide information about who, what, when, how, et cetera. These can be *circumstances of time* (e.g., recently, long ago, while), *circumstances of place* (e.g., in the center, elsewhere), and *circumstances of concession* (e.g., despite the fact that), to name a few. Additional metalinguistic terms allow students to discuss the nuances of language even further.

In a meaning-based approach, language can be deconstructed and constructed at multiple levels: at the text level, at the sentence level, at the clause level, at the group/phrase level (e.g., noun group), and at the word level. At the text level, whole text types/genres can be deconstructed to reveal how, for example, a narrative (e.g., retelling, story, biography, memoir) is constructed differently than a scientific explanation. A narrative, the purpose of which is to retell events or to create entertaining stories about people and experiences, is organized temporally by sequence of event. A predictable story structure is: orientation, complication, resolution with, of course, a sequence of events filling out the stages). In the orientation phase of a story, readers are oriented through information about the setting (where, when) and the characters (who). In the complication phase, a problem is introduced and set in motion. In the resolution phase, the problem is resolved, and sometimes there is a coda, or commentary on the events that have taken place.

In contrast, a scientific explanation is organized logically and is structured by first identifying the phenomenon of interest and then explaining it. Christie and Derewianka (2008) explain how the explanation phase varies depending on the type of explanation. For example, in a sequential explanation, the phenomena is explained by establishing the order in which things occur. In a causal explanation, the causes for the phenomenon are outlined, and the explanation explains how or why the phenomenon occurs. In a factorial explanation, the factors responsible for the phenomenon are explained. Making the organization and structure of different types of texts explicit, or transparent, can help students comprehend the texts better because they can anticipate what to look out for, and it can help them write similar texts because they know what to include.

At the sentence or clause level, text can be deconstructed to help students identify the meaningful constituents in sentences (including noun and verb groups, dependent clauses, etc.) and discuss how the sentences are organized, who is doing what in the sentences (participants) and how they are getting things done (processes), and how ideas are connected and how the text flows (e.g., text organization and cohesion). This can lead to discussions about how writers present their points of view by choosing how people are represented (e.g., as actors or receivers of actions in history texts), how patterns of language reoccur throughout particular types of text (e.g., the use of timeless verbs in science, as in "Bats *are* mammals"), and to pick out detailed information about events in a story (e.g., how, what, why, who, where) that may otherwise be difficult to disentangle from densely packed text. At the word level, students learn new meanings of words, begin to understand how whole concepts or processes can be condensed into one word (e.g., photosynthesis or democracy), and identify what a writer really thinks through her or his deliberate selection of verbs (e.g., "She claims that the research is valid" versus "She clearly demonstrates that the research is valid"). Understanding how writers take advantage of different language resources when constructing sentences and when linking sentences together to make whole texts provides scaffolding for students' construction of similar texts.

Research on academic written registers from a functional perspective has demonstrated how, as students move into the secondary grades, the language used in the texts they encounter becomes increasingly distanced from everyday language (Christie & Derewianka, 2008; Schleppegrell, 2004). As students move from stories and more personal genres, which are closer to everyday language, to analytical genres, which are more academic in nature, the texts they are asked to read and write become more densely packed and take on the features, including the vocabulary, grammar, and discourse structures that are functional for constructing meaning in the different disciplines. Christie and Derewianka's (2008) extensive research on student writing in three school subjects—English, history, and science—provides a rich explanation of the trajectory that students make as they move through schooling (from early primary through the end of secondary) and transition from everyday ways of expressing knowledge to more advanced ways that provide them with opportunities for full participation in literate contexts.

One linguistic resource students must learn to control as they advance into and through secondary schooling is grammatical metaphor, which Halliday and Matthiessen (1999) referred to as wording used to express ideas in unexpected or "incongruent" ways, typically through the use of nominalization (e.g., turning verbs into nouns, or processes into things). Halliday (1993) describes grammatical metaphor as follows: "The experience has been reconstrued, in metaphorical terms; but with the metaphor being in the grammar, instead of in the vocabulary like metaphor in its traditional sense" (p. 111). This linguistic resource enables writers to use abstraction to both densely pack ideas into clauses and link them logically to other clauses. Christie and Derewianka (2008) describe how students develop control over grammatical metaphor as they move up through the grades. In the first example presented here, a young adolescent boy (age 13/14) begins to make use of the resource in a history essay on ancient Rome. A congruent (or everyday language) version of the same idea is also presented.

Using grammatical metaphor

> "The Roman religion was a savage one **which arose from the warring tribes and the need for protection**" (p. 110).

A congruent (everyday language) version

> "The Roman religion was a savage one **which arose because the tribes were constantly fighting and people needed to be protected**" (p. 110).

The second example shows how an adolescent girl (age 15/16), writing a science report on Down syndrome, uses grammatical metaphor in a more sophisticated way:

Using grammatical metaphor

> "Its cause is directly related to a mutation or abnormality of chromosome 21" (p. 193).

A congruent (everyday language) version

> "Chromosome 21 mutates so that it becomes abnormal [clause of result] and (so that) this produces a person with Down Syndrome. [clause of result]" (p. 193).

In both of these instances, grammatical metaphor is used to condense a great deal of information in the sentence. Nominalization contributes to the lexical density (the number of lexical, or content, words per total number of words in an unembedded clause) of texts where grammatical metaphor occurs, which not only allows the writer to "pack in" more information but also to use the nouns as points of departure (e.g., its cause) and to evaluate abstractions as things. Understanding how to recognize grammatical metaphor and how to "unpack" lexically dense text can help students, particularly English learner (EL) students and students with low literacy, to comprehend difficult texts and utilize this linguistic resource in their own writing.

Meaning-Based Approaches in the Classroom

In the United States, Australia, and the United Kingdom, schools face a persistent challenge responding to the academic and linguistic needs of students who have achieved proficiency with conversational English but who lack the linguistic resources to successfully understand and produce academic text. Meaning-based approaches offer ways for teachers to make the linguistic features of academic text explicit to students and support them to develop their knowledge of the subject-specific language they need to fully participate in academic communities. Research on the implementation of meaning-based approaches in postsecondary settings (Burns & Knox, 2005; Rose, Rose, Farrington, & Page, 2007); middle and high school English (Christie, 2002; Culican, 2007), science (Halliday & Martin, 1993; Schleppegrell, 1998), history (Schleppegrell & de Oliveira, 2006; Veel & Coffin, 1996), and mathematics (Veel, 1999); and elementary grades language arts (Acevedo & Rose, 2007; Derewianka, 1990; Dufficy, 2004; Schleppegrell, 2010; Williams, 1999), social studies (Reppen, 1994), and science (Matthiessen, Slade, & Macken, 1992; Spycher, 2009) have shown how teachers can use meaning-based approaches to literacy education to analyze the texts they use for linguistic challenges, engage their students in conversations about the language to support comprehension, show their students how to analyze the language in the texts to better understand them, and provide scaffolding so that students can independently write in ways that meet the expectations of specific genres. The following four studies exemplify how SFL theory has been applied to meaning-based models in a variety of public school settings in three countries.

Reading to Learn in High School History

Reading to Learn (Martin & Rose, 2005; Rose, 2005, 2007) has been the subject of multiple, long-term action research projects in Australia at the elementary, secondary, and postsecondary levels. The model was developed as an alternative to traditional literacy intervention models that tend to do a poor job of scaffolding-up low literacy adolescents to the mainstream curriculum, primarily due to the low literacy rigor of the texts used in these programs:

> Often attributing literacy failure to individual deficit, many intervention programs, albeit well-intentioned, led to a differentiated curriculum which potentially compounds educational disadvantage and maintains stratified outcomes. (Rose & Acevedo, 2006, p. 35)

In addition to the low level texts used in some intervention programs, Martin and Rose found that in many classrooms, the typical type of pedagogical interaction, the initiation-response-feedback (IRF) process (Wells, 1999) was ineffective for certain students, particularly culturally and linguistically diverse students. In the IRF process, the teacher poses a query (usually unplanned) to the class (initiation). Often, at least one student in the class is able to provide enough information (response) so that the teacher can move to the next step of the lesson, and the teacher affirms the student's response (feedback) and moves on. The fact that one student manages to provide enough information for the teacher to move to the next phase of the lesson can lead the teacher to believe that most students are on board and that anyone who is not on board is a "slow" learner. In fact, many students may not have been on board in the first place either because they are unfamiliar with the expected styles of interaction, or they have been underprepared by previous lessons or previous years of schooling, or the query was vague (or all of the above). Alternatively, when teachers pose queries to students who are unprepared to infer what information the teacher is asking for and are therefore unable to provide the expected response, the teacher may infer that the student is in some way deficient. Either scenario can lead to an oversimplification of literacy tasks for some students, based on the perception that the students are low on the "ability" scale and must therefore need remediation. This, Martin and Rose argue, serves as a significant barrier to academic learning as students are prevented from participating in intellectually challenging coursework and from learning to use the increasingly abstract and specialized academic language of this coursework.

In contrast, in the Reading to Learn model, teachers carefully and deliberately prepare classroom interactions to scaffold students' use of the mainstream academic text in order to ensure that all students are successful with literacy tasks. The approach uses a six-stage curriculum cycle:

1. Preparing before reading: The teacher orients students to the topic as it unfolds in the text.
2. Detailed reading: The teacher guides students to analyze and understand each sentence in a short passage from the text.
3. Preparing before writing: The students plan together what they'll write, based on the modeling and discussion of the passage they analyzed in detailed reading.
4. Joint reconstruction/rewriting: The teacher guides the students to write a new text that uses the language patterns of the text read in the detailed reading.
5. Individual reconstruction/rewriting: Students practice writing a new text, based on the detailed reading and joint reconstruction texts.
6. Independent writing: Students practice writing their own texts, based on what was learned and practiced in the preceding steps.

In the model, the "scaffolding learning cycle" (elsewhere referred to as the "scaffolding interaction cycle") puts a spin on the IRF process by putting into practice Vygotsky's social model of learning and delineating the moves that are necessary within the zone of proximal development to push students up to increasingly more challenging literacy tasks. The cycle consists of three steps:

1. Prepare (the teacher orients the students to the general meaning of a sentence, paraphrases it, and provides prompts for the students to identify sentence wordings),

2. Identify (students identify the sentence wordings and the teacher affirms the response, the teacher guides the students to highlight specific wordings), and
3. Elaborate (the teacher leads the class in a discussion of language meanings, defining terms, explaining key ideas, and discussing ideas).

Martin and Rose (2005) provide an example of how a high school history teacher in the South African township of Sobantu[6] uses the scaffolding learning cycle during the detailed reading step in their model to provide students with access to the academic history textbook and support them to jointly reconstruct the text using detailed notes. The dense text students are reading in the excerpt is from the history textbook, *From Apartheid to Democracy: South Africa 1948-1994* (Nuttal et al., 1889, p. 117):

Prepare:	(position) Then it tells us that (commonsense meaning) South African politics blew up. Can you see the word that tells us South African politics blew up? (position) South African politics ...? (empty tonic)
Identify:	Erupted.
Affirm:	Erupted! Is he right? (students) Yes.—Can you see the word that says erupted? Let's do that one, erupted (repeating pronunciation).
Elaborate:	(unpack metaphor) The reason they use the word erupted is because that's what volcanoes do. Have you heard that before? (students) Yes.—A volcano erupts? (students) Yes.—So what were the townships like? They were like ...? (students) Volcanoes.— Exactly right, they were like a volcano, and there was all this pressure inside, waiting to blow up and erupt, with all this anger the people were feeling about the government's repression (Martin & Rose, 2005, pp. 12-13).

Here, the IRF process is transformed into a scaffolding interaction cycle and used strategically for the purpose of supporting understanding of the text and, ultimately, independent writing of similar texts. The teacher moves from familiar language to unfamiliar (academic) language, which is made transparent and explicit. Queries about the text are carefully planned to include discussion about the text (e.g., who, what, where questions), phases of the text are paraphrased using more everyday language, metaphors and dense language is unpacked, and connections are made to students' background knowledge about the content. Culican (2007), who implemented the reading to learn model in her research, shares the following sentence stems teachers can use in each phase of the cycle:

Prepare:	"The first/next part of the sentence tells us ..." (sentence preparation) "It starts by saying (position cue) that ..." (meaning cue)
Identify:	"Can you see the words that tell us ...?" "That's right" (affirm). "Let's highlight ..." (highlight)
Elaborate:	(discuss) "That means ..." "Why do you think ..." "Have you ever ...?" etc. (Cullican, 2007, p. 15).

Rose (2007) suggests that because the meaning-making resources in the language are made transparent to students, the academic text is demystified, and every student, no matter what their social class or cultural background, can access the text:

> There is no mystery, no quasi-religious realm of "higher order consciousness," "transformation," or "critical consciousness," no pious angst about valuing learners' voices; there are just meanings—useful, and so economically valuable meanings—that can be taught and learnt by anyone. (Rose, 2007, p. 14)

Culican (2006) reports on an independent evaluation of the reading to learn model used with indigenous children in Australia, which showed that in 1 year, the average improvement in reading and writing was 2.5 levels. In another study, literacy gains were double what were expected, and 20% of students made four times the expected literacy growth (McRae et al., 2000).

UNPACKING THE GRAMMAR OF HISTORY IN MIDDLE SCHOOL

In the United States, content-based instruction is an approach commonly used with English learner (EL) students to make content more accessible, typically through the use of graphic organizers, highlighting disciplinary vocabulary, and cooperative learning techniques. Schleppegrell, Achugar, and Oteiza (2004) describe a study conducted with secondary history teachers in California where functional grammar analysis was used to enhance content-based instruction for EL students at intermediate to advanced levels of English proficiency struggling with academic English.[7] The researchers sought to provide teachers with pedagogical tools, through a linguistic focus on the language in their grade-level textbooks, that would move beyond beginning English as a second language (ESL) methods in order to help students develop advanced literacy: "The alternative view presented here, based on a functional theory of language, sees how the linguistic features of disciplinary texts construe particular kinds of meanings. This makes a focus on language central to the teaching of disciplinary content" (p. 70).

Over the course of 3 years, Schleppegrell et al. (2004) worked with 79 middle and high school history teachers in California in a professional development project designed to give them tools to help their EL and low literacy-students gain greater access to the grade level history content while also improving their academic language skills. The first part of the project involved identifying the challenges students face when approaching the history textbook, such as the tendency for cause-effect relationships to be expressed through verbs such as "established" or "resulted in" rather than the everyday "because," as well as the limited elaboration provided in the textbook when new terms are introduced.

The researchers found that teachers in the project had few strategies for addressing these linguistic challenges in the classroom. Consequently, they designed a series of activities to raise teachers' awareness of how meaning is constructed in history textbooks and to give them pedagogical tools to help their students better understand the grade-level text. At the same time, the pedagogical tools were designed to enable students to develop a critical awareness of historical explanations while simultaneously improving their academic language skills.

Schleppegrell et al. (2004) highlight the case of a middle school history teacher with 29 students (4 were EL students, and many others were identified as low literacy students and language minority students with Spanish as the most prevalent language represented). One of the texts the teacher taught her students to analyze addressed the Missouri Compromise of 1820, which resulted in the admittance of the state of Missouri as a slave state. Functional language activities, designed to complement the instruction the teacher regularly implemented, focused on a variety of linguistic features used to construct the text and convey meaning. Analysis of the processes (verbs) found in the text (e.g., action, thinking/feeling, saying, relating) was designed to help students determine how the historian selected the events presented, provided background information, and commented on the events. Analysis of the connectors (e.g., verbs such as "result in" to establish causality or adverbs such as "meanwhile" to establish circumstances of time) used in the text was designed to help students understand how the text unfolded.

Participant analysis was designed to help students determine who the main actors, agents, and receivers in the text were and to identify points of view. For example, in the following excerpt, Schleppegrell et al. (2004) note that "slavery" and "African Americans" only appear as receivers, and not as agents, of the action:

Agent	Action	Receiver of the Action
Missouri settlers	had brought	enslaved African Americans
Missouri	applied to	Congress
Its constitution	allowed	slavery
Eleven states in the Union	permitted	slavery
Eleven (states)	did not (permit)	(slavery)

The admission of a new state would upset that balance (Schleppegrell et al., 2004, p. 79)

This type of discourse analysis, Schleppegrell et al. (2004) argue, can enable students to discuss possible reasons why the content has been conveyed through language in such a manner, opening a pathway for critical reading of text:

> Looking at the agents and the receivers of the actions, students identify the goings on in this passage, developing an understanding of what the nominalization balance stands for and what is in balance, as a way of understanding the basis of the Missouri Compromise. In addition, students are asked to reflect on who the agents are. As they see that African Americans and slavery are not presented as agents in this text, students recognize that the historians' language choices shape what we learn about history. (p. 80)

Teachers in the study were encouraged to maintain the content-based instruction strategies they regularly implemented, such as having students work in pairs or cooperative groups to complete activities, rather than working in isolation, so that they would be actively engaged in the learning. In this way, language analysis supplemented, rather than supplanted, what teachers were already doing in instruction. The researchers of this study suggest that in order to scaffold EL and low-literacy students' development of advanced English literacy, a stronger focus on language itself is required. In helping students see how language choices construe meaning in grade-level history texts, teachers can support reading comprehension and facilitate the choices that students make as they begin to appropriate the linguistic resources in their own writing. The instructional strategies in this study provide ways for teachers to talk with students about the abstract and specialized language of the history textbook, practices which have the potential to push students to advanced levels of academic English.

HIGH-CHALLENGE, HIGH-SUPPORT IN MIDDLE SCHOOL ENGLISH LITERATURE

Arguing for "high-challenge and high-support" approaches to literacy education for culturally and linguistically diverse students, Hammond (2006) reports on a study of an English literature unit on *Romeo and Juliet* in Australia. The study was part of a larger research project that investigated teachers' experiences with "quality teaching" initiatives in Sydney schools with significant numbers of ESL students and how the notion of "intellectual quality" plays out in these schools (Gibbons, 2006, 2008; Hammond, 2008; Hammond & Gibbons, 2005). The 8-week-long *Romeo and Juliet* unit took place in a public school for boys ages 12-13. The students in the study were classified as ESL students, most of whom had been in Australia for no more than 1-3 years, who were enrolled in mainstream classes. These "second phase" students were beyond the beginning stages of English and capable of performing academically, as evidenced by the competitive selection process to gain entry to the school. However, they were placed in "English focused class" because beginning of year assessments showed they needed extra support in academic English.

The teacher provided a variety of activities to build understanding of the Shakespeare play and of the language used in the text. Students viewed a film of the play, discussed the plot and details of specific scenes, participated in a range of drama activities (including rephrasing specific scenes of the play in their own words, thereby "playing with" content and language), analyzed rhetorical structures and patterns in the language, and constructed their own texts. The curriculum was not simplified or modified for the ESL students; rather, the students were "supported-up to enable their participation" (Hammond, 2006, p. 273).

In an effort to interweave curriculum content and deliberate academic language instruction, the teacher in the study implemented a "double-field" focus during lessons, shifting between the teaching of content and language and also showing their relationship within and between tasks. For example, in one lesson early on in the unit, the teacher began with a review of the genre of a news report, focusing on the genre's rhetorical structure and major language features (language focus). This was followed by a task where students identified topics for news reports based on a review of specific sequences of events in *Romeo and Juliet* (curriculum focus). Next, the teacher engaged the students in an analysis of a model news report, focusing on the metalanguage used in the analysis and the language choices made in the model (language focus). Finally, the teacher provided an opportunity for students to work in pairs or individually to brainstorm ideas for their own texts (curriculum focus).

Transcripts from lessons reveal that there was much class discussion *about* language during the *Romeo and Juliet* unit, and this talk ranged from discussions about genre and text structure to the characteristics of noun groups and their role in character description to the meaning of new vocabulary, punctuation, and spelling. The use of a metalanguage (nouns, vocabulary, alliteration, voice) to talk about language enabled students to analyze the language choices that Shakespeare made in writing the play, and it gave them a new way to think about their own language choices in the texts they wrote. In the following excerpt, the teacher guides the students to talk *about* language as the class discusses the significance of "voice" in their own rephrasing of a *Romeo and Juliet* scene:

Teacher: You need to develop a particular voice. Now we all know what voice means, don't we? When we say we have a voice for a character, it's not how they speak aloud. What do we mean by voice?

Student: Like personality.

Teacher: Their personality. Now how would their personality come through?

Student: What language, like how they think, like…

Teacher: How they think, so their actual choice of vocabulary, what might be the difference, perhaps, between Juliet's vocabulary and Tybalt's vocabulary?

Student: Juliet would be more formal than him.

Teacher: Maybe more formal, yes. Anything else?

Student: Tybalt would be, like, use a lot of slang and not…

Teacher: He could be using slang, he may not because he's a high status character. Remember, don't slide into the modern idea that once it's male, it's a man of action, they all have to be swear words. But we have his language within the play, which is, although it's formal, it's got a lot of very strong action type words. Yes?

Student: He uses more rough language, like he's not always, like his voice doesn't sound kind.

Teacher: He's not gentle so a lot of his language would be in commands. He could have threats, right? He could have promises of violence in it. What are some of the words that we can use that would make his language sound violent, there are a couple of things that we've talked about. One of the things that we used in the newspaper article would work here. What was one of the language devices we used in the headline?

Student: Alliteration.

Teacher: Alliteration. Now if we look at alliteration, we can use alliteration in Tybalt's speech but this time, if you wanted to do it to make it sound very harsh, you can use what we call onomatopoeia. Do you all know what that means?

Students: (general) Yes.

Teacher: Yeah? Sound echoing sense. So we've got a lot of plosive sounds like b, p, t, d, f. They're all harsh sounds. Right? You can use those sounds, look for words that begin with those sounds and have a lot of those sounds in them, and you'll find that a lot of the thing he said sound more harsh. Short vowels and more plosive consonants (pp. 278-279).

Again, the IRF process was reconstructed to provide strategic support to students to better understand the text—how particular wordings were deliberately used by Shakespeare to establish the voice of characters. This enabled students to move beyond "everyday" statements about the text (e.g., I liked it) to more academic stances using technical language. The metalanguage (voice, alliteration, onomatopoeia) supported students to discuss and evaluate the language Shakespeare used to convey particular meanings, which in turn gave them a linguistic awareness they would be able to draw upon when constructing their own texts. Hammond reports that the "English focused" literature class served to begin to socialize students into using the specialized language of English literature. Further, the outcome assessments administered at the end of the year indicated that ESL students who participated in the "English focused" literature class had performed better than many of their English proficient peers in the traditional English literature class.

Language Dissection in Elementary Grades Science

In the United States, De Oliveira, a linguist and university professor, and Dodds, an elementary school classroom teacher, collaborated on an action research project in which Dodds implemented an approach to help her EL students at the intermediate to advanced levels of language proficiency access science content and the language of science. De Oliveira and Dodds (2010) explain that teachers often implement "general" instructional strategies for teaching EL students (e.g., creating collaborative groups, using visuals, etc.), but that these general strategies, while helpful, have not provided enough specific support when students must understand their densely packed science textbooks. The "language dissection in science" approach was designed as a way for teachers to discuss scientific meanings within a text and help students analyze the science text so that students understand the content.

In the study, Dodds implemented five "language dissection in science" lessons in her fourth-grade general education classroom. The lessons were designed collaboratively by De Oliveira and Dodds by discussing the particular science texts that Dodds had found to be challenging for her EL students from previous classes and by identifying the particular linguistic demands in the science text that present challenges for EL students. For example, words that have specialized meanings in science but also everyday meanings that may be more familiar to EL students (e.g., stage) appear frequently in science texts, and this may confuse students if their attention is not drawn to these new meanings.

During the lessons, Dodds taught her students a metalanguage for talking about the language in the science textbook. For example, the students learned the terms "connector," "participant," "process," and "scientific description," and then, using a table with the metalinguistic terms as the column headers, deconstructed and analyzed the sentences in whole paragraphs from the text. A final column titled "questions to promote science discussion" enabled Dodds to pose strategic queries about the science content that students would be able to answer from their sentence deconstruction. This task enabled the students to see patterns in the way science knowledge is construed in language and also to gain greater access to the science concepts embedded in the language, thereby creating greater access to the science textbook.

De Oliveira and Dodds make several recommendations to teachers interested in using this meaning-based approach to content literacy instruction in their own classrooms. They suggest setting aside ample time to:

- consider the language challenges that EL students face when using the science textbook,
- identify how the textbook is organized and how the patterns of language can be revealed to students,
- determine the best methods to actively engage students so that they are interested in learning about both the language and the science content, and
- carefully decide how often to provide the activity and how much language dissection to include in each lesson (2010, p. 11).

With careful preparation, the authors suggest, rather than simplifying the language used in science, an amplification model (Walqui & Van Lier, 2010) can be adopted where EL students are supported to read the difficult language of science textbooks.

Discussion

Among the central themes of meaning-based approaches to literacy education is that students are simultaneously learning language, learning through language, and learning about language. Meaning-based approaches derived from SFL offer a metalanguage that teachers can use to talk about language with their students, which serves as an opening to conversations about how meaning is construed in language. The approach also recognizes that there are particular ways of using language and interacting in school that favor middle class students who have been socialized in these ways. Instead of positioning students in "ability levels," which is largely based on their language socialization prior to entering school, as well as throughout schooling, functional linguists place the responsibility of literacy success on the socialization that occurs within school. Texts can be analyzed and questioned in order to understand their underlying notions and how particular linguistic features come together to construct different genres and meanings. Academic text is demystified and made transparent, revealing the meaning-making resources that are available to anyone, as long as they know they are there. In this way, meaning-based approaches differ from traditional, or behaviorist, ideas of literacy development that place the responsibility of literacy failure on learner weaknesses and that present text as natural and uncontestable truth.

This does not mean that meaning-based approaches reject the teaching of phonics or decoding. On the contrary, teachers must attend to each stratum of language —discourse (text, phrase, message), lexicogrammar (clause, group, word), and phonology/graphology (word, syllable, onset/rhyme) in order to provide a comprehensive literacy education. Rose and Acevedo (2006) provide a critique of approaches that ignore the complexity inherent in learning to read and write:

> Phonics programs treat reading as primarily "decoding" letter patterns, and ignore the higher level complexity of real texts. Basal reading programs may focus on the level of words and phrases in sentences, but ignore higher levels of meaning. At the other extreme, whole language programs treat texts as lakes of meanings for readers to "immerse" in, and ignore the complexity of patterns at the levels of the text, the sentence and the word. So called critical literacy approaches focus on a few higher level meanings in texts, but ignore the complexity of patterns in which they are expressed. (pp. 41-42)

In response to ongoing debates about which method is best to teach literacy, Martin and Rose (2005) explain that "in Halliday's stratified model of language, this polarization dissolves into different perspectives on the same phenomenon.... The answer flowing from the systemic functional model is of course both" (p. 5). Learning to read and write is a complex process requiring multilayered instructional approaches. In a meaning-based model, students learn to identify the sounds that letters make and the spelling patterns of syllables. They also learn to recognize linguistic differences between conversational language and academic language and to use the specialized language in which discipline-specific forms of knowledge is embedded. With access to academic language and the tools to deconstruct it, students can develop an understanding that knowledge is "a social construction that is open to scrutiny, challenge, and change" (Hammond, 2006, p. 272). This takes the reader/writer out of a passive and compliant role and into an active and critical one, in which texts are seen as "discursive constructs rather than windows on reality" (Macken-Horarik, 1998, p. 75).

Ultimately, the goal of meaning-based approaches to literacy, whether explicitly stated or implied, is to alter unequal power relations between groups by making both teachers and students aware of privileged discourses and providing tangible ways to teach students the literacy processes necessary for full participation in these discourses. As Rose[8] has suggested,

> The goal of the pedagogy is overtly political: redistribution of the symbolic resources that are the basis of middle class occupations, to social groups that are currently excluded by middle class pedagogic practices. This is achieved by transmitting skills in reading the privileged discourses of schooling, grounded in the genre-based approach to language. However, the focus of change is equally on the consciousness of learners, as they become critically aware of written ways of meaning, and develop confidence through continual experience of success in recognizing and using them. (Rose, 2007, 15)

Meaning-based approaches to literacy education have the potential to provide teachers with tangible tools and practical pedagogy to demystify the academic language that students are expected to understand and produce on a daily basis in schools (Schleppegrell, 2004).

As this chapter is being prepared, school districts across the United States are determining how best to implement their state's version of the Common Core State Standards (National Governors Association Center & Council of Chief State School Officers, 2010), a set of rigorous national educational standards for English language arts and mathematics that most states have adopted. The common core state standards for English language arts and literacy in history/social science, science, and technical subjects set ambitious goals for the literacy knowledge and abilities that all students are expected to achieve by the end of high school. Ensuring that all students master the advanced levels of academic English literacy delineated in the new standards will require a significant shift in the way literacy is taught. It will also require a significant investment in teacher professional learning, one that extends beyond the typical staff development teachers are provided, namely, the "quick fix" 2-hour workshop. The promise of meaning-based approaches for advanced literacy education for culturally and linguistically diverse students and low literacy students has been established in multiple studies, including those described in this chapter. If the true goal of public education is to close opportunity and achievement gaps that persistently plague schools in the United States and elsewhere, looking to examples of the effectiveness of meaning-based approaches to literacy education may provide the guidance sorely needed for long-term solutions.[9]

NOTES

1. In addition, Hyland (2002) highlighted the similarities between two schools of genre theories—English for specific purposes and SFL. While English for specific purposes research has focused on postsecondary education and SFL has included K-12 education and research on parent-child interaction prior to school entry, both perspectives have emphasized the lexico-grammatical and rhetorical features of text and have proposed intervening in literacy development through a "transparent curriculum which makes the genres of power visible and attainable through explicit induction" (Hyland, 2002, p. 125).

2. SFL theory and research has been greatly influenced by the work of the sociological research in education of Basil Berenstein and his doctoral students, who sought to understand the relationship between social class and pedagogic

practice (Christie, 1999). In his work on pedagogic practice and discourse, Berenstein presented an analysis of how schools reproduce social-class advantages and disadvantages through the way certain kinds of knowledge is validated, transmitted, and evaluated through the "pedagogic device." Ironically, Berenstein's work has been characterized by some as a form of "cultural deficit" theory. However, closer examination of Berenstein's work reveals this claim to be a false one.

3. Halliday studied under Firth at the University of London and elaborated on the foundations established by Firth to develop SFL.

4. Functional linguists have suggested that the term "function" is limited in that it refers simply to the purpose or way of using language. Instead, the term "metafunction" was adopted to demonstrate how "the systemic analysis shows that functionality is intrinsic to language: that is to say, the entire architecture of language is arranged along functional lines" (Halliday & Matthiessen, 1994, p. 31).

5. There is some variation within SFL in how various areas of meaning are divided. For example, Halliday and Matthiessen (2004) discuss six process types, while others (e.g., Martin & Rose, 2003) use four.

6. Martin and Rose (2005) report that only about 2% of such students from black township schools matriculate into university.

7. A critique of content-based instruction is the focus on making content comprehensible for students at the expense of focusing on academic language itself.

8. For an elegant explanation on how meaning-based approaches synthesize multiple contrasting theories of literacy development, including progressive, behaviorist, social-psychological, and critical pedagogies, see Rose (2007).

9. In Australia, for example, SFL serves as the foundation theory for the national literacy curriculum.

REFERENCES

Acevedo, C. & Rose, D. (2007). Reading (and writing) to learn in the middle years of schooling. *Primary English Teaching Association, 157*, 1-8.

Bruner, J. (1978). The role of dialogue in language acquisition. In A. Sinclair, R., J. Jarvelle, & W. J. M. Levelt (Eds.), *The child's concept of language*. New York, NY: Springer-Verlag.

Burns, A., & Knox, J. (2005). Realisation(s): Systemic-functional linguistics and the language classroom. *Applied Linguistics and Language Teacher Education Educational Linguistics, 4*(4), 235-259.

Cazden, C. (1983). Adult assistance to language development: scaffolds, models and direct instruction. In R. P. Parker & F. A. Davies (Eds.), *Developing literacy*. Delaware: International Reading Association.

Christie, F. (1999). *Pedagogy and the shaping of consciousness: Linguistic and social processes*. New York, NY: Continuum.

Christie, F. (2002). The development of abstraction in adolescence in subject English. In M. C. Colombi & M. Schleppegrell (Eds.), *Advanced literacy in first and second languages* (pp. 45-66). Mahwah, NJ: Erlbaum.

Christie, F., & Derewianka, B. (2008). *School discourse: Learning to Write across the years of schooling*. London, England: Continuum.

Christie, F., & Misson, R. (1998). *Literacy and schooling*. London, England: Routledge.

Coffin, C. (2006). *Historical discourse*. London, England: Continuum.

Culican, S. J. (2006). *Learning to read, reading to learn: A middle years literacy intervention research project, final report 2003-4*. Melbourne, Australia: Catholic Education Office Melbourne.

Culican, S. J. (2007). Troubling teacher talk: The challenge of changing classroom discourse patterns. *The Australian Educational Researcher, 34*(2), 7-27.

de Oliveira, L. C., & Dodds, K. N. (2010). Beyond general strategies for English language learners: Language dissection in science. *The Electronic Journal of Literacy Through Science, 9*(1), 1-14.

Derewianka, B. (1990). *Exploring how texts work*. Rozelle, New South Wales, Australia: Primary English Teaching Association.

Dufficy, P. (2004). Predisposition to choose: The language of an information gap task in a multilingual primary classroom. *Language Teaching Research. 8*(3), 241-261.

Firth, J. R. (1957). *Papers in linguistics* 1934-1951. London, England: Oxford University Press.

Gibbons, P. (2006). *Bridging discourses in the ESL classroom: Students, teachers and researchers*. London, England: Continuum.

Gibbons, P. (2008). "It was taught good and I learned a lot": Intellectual practices and ESL learners in the middle years. *Australian Journal of Language and Literacy, 31*(2), 155-173.

Halliday, M. A. K. (1993). Toward a language-based theory of education. *Linguistics and Education 5*, 93-116.

Halliday, M. A. K., & Martin, J.R. (1993). *Writing science: Literacy and discursive power*. London, England: Falmer Press.

Halliday, M. A. K., & Matthiessen, C. M. I. M. (1994). *An introduction to functional grammar* (3rd ed.). London, England: Arnold.

Halliday, M. A. K., & Matthiessen, C. M. I. M. (1999). *Construing experience through meaning: A language-based approach to cognition*. London, England: Cassell.

Hart, B., & Risley, T. (1995). *Meaningful differences in the everyday experience of young American children*. Baltimore, MD: Brookes.

Hammond, J. (2006). High challenge, high support: Integrating language and content instruction for diverse learners in an English literature classroom. *Journal of English for Academic Purposes, 5*, 269-283.

Hammond, J. (2008). Intellectual challenge and ESL students: Implications of quality teaching initiatives. *Australian Journal of Language and Literacy, 31*(2), 128-154.

Hammond, J., & Gibbons, P. (2005). Putting scaffolding to work: The contribution of scaffolding in articulating ESL education. *Prospect Special Issue, 20*(1), 6-30.

Hasan, R. (1989). Semantic variation and sociolinguistics. *Australian Journal of Linguistics, 9*, 221-275.

Hasan, R., & Williams, G. (1996). *Literacy in society*. New York, NY: Longman.

Heath, S. B. (1983). *Ways with words: Language, life, and work in communities and classrooms.* New York, NY: Cambridge University Press.

Hyland, K. (2002). Genre: Language, context, and literacy. *Annual Review of Applied Linguistics, 22*, 113-135.

Macken-Horarik, M. (1998). Exploring the requirements of critical school literacy: A view from two classrooms. In F. Christie & R. Misson (Eds.), *Literacy and schooling* (pp. 74-103). London, England: Routledge.

Malinowski, B. (1923). The problem of meaning in primitive languages. In C. K. Ogden & I. A. Richards (Eds.), *The meaning of meaning: A study of influence of language upon thought and of the science of symbolism* (pp. 296-336) New York, NY: Harcourt, Brace and World.

Martin, J. R., & Rose, D. (2003). *Working with discourse: Meaning beyond the clause.* London, England: Continuum.

Martin, J. R., & Rose, D. (2005). Designing literacy pedagogy: Scaffolding asymmetries. In R. Hasan, C. M. I. M. Matthiessen, & J. Webster (Eds.), *Continuing discourse on language* (pp. 251-280). London, England: Equinox. .

Matthiessen, C., Slade, D., & Macken, M. (1992). Language in context: A new model for evaluating student writing. *Linguistics and Education, 4*, 173-193.

McRae, D., Ainsworth, G., Cumming, J., Hughes, P., Mackay, T., Price, K., ... Zbar, V. (2000). *What has worked, and will again: The IESIP strategic results projects.* Canberra, Australia: Australian Curriculum Studies Association.

Michaels, S. (1986). Narrative presentations: An oral preparation of literacy with first graders. In J. Cook-Gumperz (Ed.) *The social construction of literacy* (pp. 94-116). Cambridge, England: Cambridge University Press.

National Governors Association Center for Best Practices & Council of Chief State School Officers. (2010). *Common core state standards.* Washington DC: Author.

Nuttall T., Wright J., Hoffman J., Sishi N., & Khandlhela, S. (1998). *From Apartheid to democracy: South Africa 1948-1994.* Pietermaritzburg, South Africa: Shuter & Shooter.

Painter, C. (1999). Preparing for school: Developing a semantic style for educational knowledge. In F. Christie (Ed.), *Pedagogy and the shaping of consciousness: Linguistic and social processes* (pp. 66-87). London, England: Continuum.

Reppen, R. (1994). A genre-based approach to content writing instruction. *TESOL Journal, 4*(2), 32-35.

Rose, D. (2005). Democratising the classroom: A literacy pedagogy for the new generation. *Journal of Education, 37*, 132-167.

Rose, D. (2007). A reading based model of schooling. *Pesquisas em Discurso Pedagógico, 4*(1), 1-22.

Rose, D., & Acevedo, C. (2006). Closing the gap and accelerating learning in the Middle Years of Schooling. *Australian Journal of Language and Literacy, 14*(2), 32-45.

Rose, D., Rose, M., Farrington, S., & Page, S. (2007). Scaffolding academic literacy with indigenous health sciences students: An evaluative study. *Journal of English for Academic Purposes, 7*(3), 165-179.

Schieffelin, B. B., & Ochs, E. (1986). Language socialization. In B. Siegel (Ed.), *Annual Review of Anthropology* (pp. 163-191). Palo Alto, CA: Annual Reviews.

Schleppegrell, M. J. (1998). Grammar as resource: Writing a description. *Research in the Teaching of English, 32*(2), 182-211.

Schleppegrell, M. J. (2004). *The language of schooling: A functional linguistics perspective.* Mahwah, NJ: Erlbaum.

Schleppegrell, M. J. (2010). Functional grammar in the classroom. In M. Olofsson (Ed.), *Symposium 2009: Genrer och funktionellt språk i teori och praktik* (pp. 79-95). Stockholm, Sweden: Stockholms universitets förlag.

Schleppegrell, M. J., Achugar, M., & Oteíza, T. (2004). The grammar of history: Enhancing content-based instruction through a functional focus on language. *TESOL Quarterly, 38*(1), 67-93.

Schleppegrell, M. J., & de Oliveira, L. C. (2006). An integrated language and content approach for history teachers. *Journal of English for Academic Purposes, 5*, 254-268.

Spycher, P. (2009). Learning academic language through science in two linguistically diverse classrooms. *Elementary School Journal, 109*, 3.

Veel, R. (1999). Language, knowledge and authority in school mathematics. In F. Christie (Ed.), *Pedagogy and the shaping of consciousness: Linguistic and social processes.* London, England: Continuum.

Veel, R., & Coffin, C. (1996). Learning to think like an historian: The language of secondary school history. In R. Hasan & G. Williams (Eds.), *Literacy in society* (pp. 191-231). Harlow, Essex, England: Addison Wesley Longman.

Vygotsky, L. (1978). *Mind in society: The development of higher psychological processes.* Cambridge, England: Cambridge University Press.

Walquí, A., & Van Lier, L. (2010). *Scaffolding the academic success of adolescent English language learners: A pedagogy of promise.* San Francisco, CA: WestEd.

Wells, G. (1999). *Dialogic inquiry: Towards a sociocultural practice and theory of education.* New York, NY: Cambridge University Press.

Williams, G. (1999). The pedagogic device and the production of pedagogic discourse: A case example in early literacy education. In F. Christie (Ed.), *Pedagogy and the shaping of consciousness: Linguistic and social processes* (pp. 88-122). London, England: Continuum.

Author Contact Information: Pamela Spycher, PhD, Director, English Learners and the Language Arts, WestEd, 1107 9th St., 4th Floor, Sacramento, CA 95814-3607. Phone: 916-492-4026. E-mail: pspycher@wested.org

Section 6: Counseling Theory

INTRODUCTION

SECTION EDITORS

Richard C. Henriksen Jr. and Mary Nichter

Sam Houston State University

Over 60 years ago, Gestalt psychologist Kurt Lewin stated, "There is nothing so practical as a good theory." This statement offered by Dr. Lewin reflects a foundational assumption in the field of counseling and psychotherapy. Theory informs practice of counseling and psychotherapy and provides clinicians with a model or foundation from which to offer their professional services. In fact, theory is so important to the practice of mental health services that a course or courses in theory is often part of the core curriculum in counselor education programs. Further, according to the Council for Accreditation of Counseling and Related Educational Programs (CACREP) 2009 Standards, accredited counselor education programs are required to include learning experiences for students focusing on counseling theories and models.

In a review of textbooks, research articles, and other publications, we found claims that the number of counseling and psychotherapy theories available to mental health clinicians ranges from 130 to 450. However, we take the position that most of these theories have their roots in one or more of the more historical theories. Therefore, we have included in this section on counseling theories a review of *historical theories* including Adlerian, existential, cognitive-behavioral, and person-centered. Next, we present a chapter on *family theories* and then finally, move to more *contemporary theories* including collaborative language and feminist theories.

Historical counseling theories have provided counselors and other mental health professionals a foundation for conceptualizing the many challenges individuals, couples, and families face. There are many different theories and we present four key theories that serve as foundations for many other theories. The first theory presented by Dr. Richard E. Watts is Adlerian Theory. Alfred Adler developed the first holistic theory of personality, psychopathology, and psychotherapy that focused on the individual's development of optimal mental health. His theory was also connected to a humanistic philosophy of living and is viewed as foundational to the development of other humanistic theories. From an Adlerian perspective, a basic goal is to help clients increase their social interest through the use of encouragement resulting in optimal living. Dr. Watts provides an overview of the theory and addresses many of the key tenants of the theory. Dr. Richard C. Henriksen Jr. presents existential theory from a relationship perspective with an emphasis on authentic living. Rather than focusing on the inevitability of death and dying, this theory is presented from the perspective of a fear of authentic living that leaves the person without a life based on meaning and purpose. Dr. Henriksen presents key components of Existential Theory in a manner that is relevant to twenty-first century counselors. Dr. Robert Wubbolding describes cognitive-behavioral theory through his focus on reality therapy. On his website Dr. Wubbolding states,

Reality therapy is a practical method of helping people take better control of their lives. It assists people in identifying what they want and what they need and then in evaluating whether they can realistically attain what they want. It helps them examine their own behaviors and evaluate them with clear criteria.

In the chapter on reality therapy, Dr. Wubbolding provides a complete overview of the theory and a thorough description of the implementation of the WEDEP system.

The final theory presented in the historical section is person-centered theory by Jeffrey M. Sullivan and Haley Stulmaker. Often considered the foundation for all counseling theories, person-centered theory provides a focus on the counseling relationship and the counseling environment. Person-centered therapy,

The Handbook of Educational Theories, pp. 457–458

considered one of the founding theories in the humanistic school of psychotherapies, began with Carl Ransom Rogers and continues to have a major influence on counseling today. In this chapter, the basic tenants of person-centered theory are presented along with a discussion of its application to counseling process.

The second section provides a focus and emphasis on system theories. In the chapter on family therapy, Drs. Nichter and Bruhn present 12 prominent approaches developed and practiced within a family systems framework. Unlike individual therapy, the focus is on the entire family system rather than on one family member. Family therapies share an emphasis on process rather than content and believe the communication patterns within the family are at the root of most family dysfunction. From this perspective, the goal of therapy is to eliminate the problem by conceptualizing the family system as creating and maintaining the problem, thereby, placing responsibility for change on the entire unit.

The final section of theories focuses on contemporary theories of counseling and their application in a modern society. Dr. Harlene Anderson presents a chapter on collaborative learning communities. From this perspective, education and learning is viewed as a collaborative approach based on the assumptions of postmodern philosophy, which include social construction, narrative, and dialogue theories. She states that the purpose of collaborative learning is, "Creating the kinds of relationships and conversations that allow all participants to access their creativities and develop possibilities where none seemed to exist before." In this chapter, Dr. Anderson presents a description of collaborative learning communities, a discussion of the basic tenants of the theory, and a description of the collaborative learning training process.

Dr. Amanda C. Healey and Dr. Amy T. Banner provide a theoretical framework that is focused on Feminist Theory. These authors state that, "The feminist theoretical perspective emerged and continues to develop as an approach designed to address the societal and systemic inequity that exists as a result of culturally defined gender normative expectations." Through this chapter, the authors present the basic tenants of feminist theory using a multicultural lens and describe how feminist theory can be applied in diverse settings.

The final theory is presented by Dr. Richard C. Henriksen Jr. and focuses on the concept of multiple heritage identity. This theory is based on work that is focused on helping counselors understand the challenges of individuals with cultural identities that come from multiple heritages that include race, ethnicity, religion, language, national origin and other characteristics of one's identity. Through the presentation of the multiple heritage identity development model Revised, Dr. Henriksen provides counselors with an overview of the identity development process and a discussion of effective ways of helping clients.

Each of the theory authors have provided perspectives of counseling that even though they are from different perspectives provide positive and purposeful means for helping clients achieve their goals. Each theory is focused on helping and is presented with a positive view of human growth and potential. From the historical to the contemporary, there is a clear and distinct message, counselors care about people and want to help them reach their potentials and realize their dreams.

Author Contact Information: Richard C. Henriksen, Jr., PhD, LPC-S, ACS, NCC, associate professor of education, Sam Houston State University, College of Education, Department of Educational Leadership and Counseling, Box 2119, Huntsville, TX 77341-2119. Telephone: 936-294-1209. E-mail: rch008@shsu.edu

CHAPTER 38

Adlerian Counseling

Richard E. Watts
Sam Houston State University

Adlerian counseling views humans as holistic, creative, and responsible beings. Persons are not static but forward moving toward subjective, self-created goals within one's cognitive life-map known as the *lifestyle* or *style of life*. Feelings of inferiority, a common thread among all human beings, may lead to faulty convictions about oneself, others, and the world, which can result in self-defeating behaviors. In the Adlerian view, maladjusted persons are not sick but "discouraged." That is, they lack sufficient courage to face the tasks of life. The counselor's role is to encourage the person, to activate social interest, and to help the individual develop a socially useful style of living through relationship, investigation, and action methods. Adlerians are not interested in curing "sick" individuals, groups, or communities, but in reeducating individuals and in reshaping society so that all people can live together as equals (Carlson, Watts, & Maniacci, 2006; Mosak & Maniacci, 2011).

Individual Psychology, or Adlerian psychological theory, is often misunderstood as primarily focusing on individuals; however, Adler chose the name Individual Psychology (from the Latin, "individuum" meaning indivisible) for his theoretical approach because he disdained reductionism. He emphasized that persons cannot be properly understood as a collection of parts but rather should be viewed as a unified whole. An integration of cognitive, existential, psychodynamic, and systemic perspectives, Adlerian theory is a holistic, phenomenological, socially oriented, and teleological (goal-directed) approach to understanding and working with people. It emphasizes the proactive, form-giving and fictional nature of human cognition and its role in constructing the "realities" that persons know and to which they respond. Adlerian theory asserts that humans construct, manufacture, or *narratize* ways of viewing and experiencing the world and then takes these *fictions* for truth. It is an optimistic theory affirming that humans are not determined by heredity or environment. Rather, they are creative, proactive, meaning-making beings, having the ability to choose and to be responsible for their choices (Carlson et al., 2006; Watts & Eckstein, 2009).

Alfred Adler was born in 1870 in a suburb of Vienna. He attended public school in Vienna and then trained as a physician at the University of Vienna. Adler entered private practice as an ophthalmologist. A short time later he switched to general practice and then to neurology. In 1902, he was invited by Sigmund Freud to join the Vienna Psychoanalytic Society. Due to significant theoretical disagreement with Freud, Adler resigned from the Society in 1911. He spent the remainder of his life developing a personality theory and approach to counseling and psychotherapy so far ahead of his time that Albert Ellis (1970) declared, "Alfred Adler, more than even Freud, is probably the true father of modern psychotherapy" (p. 11). Ansbacher and Ansbacher (1979) noted that after Adler's death in 1937, his name vanished for quite some time, except among small groups of Adlerians. Adler's ideas, however, were not antiquated. In fact, many were simply ahead of their time and have subsequently reappeared in contemporary approaches to counseling and psychotherapy with different nomenclature and typically without reference to Adler (Watts & Critelli, 1997). Prochaska and Norcross (2010), echoing Ellenberger (1970), noted that many of "Adler's ideas have quietly permeated modern psychological thinking, often without notice. It would not be easy to find another author from which so much as been borrowed from all sides without acknowledgment than Alfred Adler" (p. 91). According to Corey (2005), Adler's most important contribution was his influence of other theoretical perspectives. Adler's influence has been acknowledged by—or his vision traced to—neo-Freudian approaches, existential therapy, person-centered therapy, cognitive-

The Handbook of Educational Theories, pp. 459–472

behavioral therapies, reality therapy, family systems approaches, and, more recently, constructivist and social constructionist (e.g., solution-focused and narrative) therapies (Carlson et al., 2006; Watts, 1999).

Philosophical Underpinnings of Adlerian Counseling

The epistemological roots of Adlerian theory are primarily found in the critical philosophy of Immanuel Kant and the "as if" philosophy of Hans Vaihinger. Both Kant and Vaihinger emphasized the proactive, form-giving, and fictional character of human knowledge and its role in constructing the "realities" we know and to which we respond. Adlerian theory asserts that humans construct, manufacture, or narratize ways of looking and experiencing the world and then takes these *fictions* for truth (Adler, 1956; Ellenberger, 1970; Watts, 2003b; Watts & Shulman, 2003).

Adler also acknowledged the influence of Karl Marx and Friedrich Nietzsche on his theory. From Marx and Nietzsche, Adler gleaned ideas such as the socially-embedded and fictional nature of human knowledge, the abilities and creativity of human beings, the necessity of egalitarian relationships and equal rights for all persons, and the socially useful and socially useless political and power issues involved in human relationships (Ansbacher, 1977; Ansbacher & Ansbacher, 1956, 1979; Ellenberger, 1970; Watts, 2003b; Watts & Shulman, 2003). Social constructionist therapies, via the writings of poststructural/postmodern theorists such as Derrida and Foucault, also have roots in the philosophies of Marx and Nietzsche. Consequently, many ideas Adler gleaned from Marx and Nietzsche are among the prevalent themes discussed in social constructionist therapies.

Adlerian Counseling: Personality Theory

Adlerian counseling theory affirms that humans are characterized by unity across the broad spectrum of personality—cognitions, affect, and behavior. *Style of life*, the Adlerian term for personality, is a cognitive blueprint or personal metanarrative containing the person's unique and individually created convictions, goals and personal beliefs for coping with the tasks and challenges of living. The style of life is uniquely created by each person, begins as a prototype in early childhood, and is progressively refined throughout life. Shulman (1973; Shulman & Mosak, 1988) described the functions of the style of life: It organizes and simplifies coping with the world by assigning rules and values; it selects, predicts, anticipates; its perceptions are guided by its own "private logic"; it selects what information it allows to enter, what it will attend to, what affects will be aroused and what its response will be. According to Shulman (1985), the style of life contains certain key elements. These include "a set of constructs about the self, the world, and the relationship between the two; a construct about what the relationship should be; an image of the ideal self; and a plan of action" (p. 246).

Human Agency

According to Adlerian theory, humans are proactive—versus reactive and representational—in regard to the development of the style of life. This idea is inherent in the Adlerian construct known as the *creative power of the self* or *the creative self*. In discussing the creative self, Adler (1913/1956) stated,

> Do not forget the most important fact that not heredity and not environment are determining factors. Both are giving only the frame and the influences which are answered by the individual in regard to his styled creative power (p. xxiv).... The individual is both the picture and the artist. He is the artist of his own personality. (p. 177)

Because of this creative power, people function like actors authoring their own scripts, directing their own actions, and constructing their own personalities within a socially-embedded context. Humans coconstruct the realities to which they respond. According to Carlson and Sperry (1998), the realization that individuals coconstruct the *reality* in which they live and are also able to "question, deconstruct, or reconstruct reality for themselves" is a fundamental tenet "not only of Adlerian psychotherapy but also of other constructivist psychotherapies" (p. 68).

Motivation

According to Adler (1913/1956), the central human directionality is toward competence or self-mastery, what Adler called *striving for perfection or superiority*. Adler's understanding of "striving" evolved over time and he used various words like completion, mastery, perfection, and superiority to describe how humans seek to move from "the present situation, as observed and interpreted, to a better one, one that was superior to the present status" (Manaster & Corsini, 1982, p. 41). Striving for perfection or superiority is the individual's creative and compensatory answer to the normal and universal feelings of insignificance and disempowerment, and the accompanying beliefs that one is less that what one should be (i.e., *feelings of inferiority*). Thus, striving for perfection or superiority is the natural human desire to move from a perceived negative position to a perceived positive one. This concept of striving or teleological/ teleonomical movement is seen in the writings of various personality theorists including Kurt Goldstein, Karen Horney, Carl Jung, Abraham Maslow, Otto Rank, Carl Rogers, and Robert White (Jorgensen & Nafstad, 2004; Manaster & Corsini, 1982). One can find similar ideas in various contemporary theoretical perspectives, including constructivist, evolutionary, and positive psychologies (Linley & Joseph, 2004; Mahoney, 2003; Rasmussen, 2010; Snyder, Lopez, & Pedrotti, 2011). For example, in discussing happiness and human potential, Ryan and Deci (2001) described optimal functioning and development as "the striving for perfection the represents the realization of one's true potential" (p. 144).

SOCIAL EMBEDDEDNESS

Adlerian psychology is a relational theory. It asserts that humans are socially-embedded and that knowledge is relationally distributed. Adler stressed that persons cannot be properly understood apart from their social context. Consequently, the Adlerian perspective on the tasks of life—love, society, work, self and spirituality—is a strongly relational one. These tasks of life address intimate love relationships, relationships with friends and fellow beings in society, our relationships at work, our relationship with self, and our relationship with God or the universe (Carlson et al., 2006; Watts, 2003a; Watts, Williamson, & Williamson, 2004).

Manaster and Corsini (1982) stated that human personality or *style of life* "evolves from a biological being in a social context creating a sense of self in the world in which he (or she) acts" (p. 77). This social context of the child includes both the cultural values of the child's culture of origin and his or her experiences within his or her *family constellation*, Adler's phrase for the operative influences of the family structure, values, and dynamics (Shulman, 1985). Thus, "the child sees the world in general as paralleling his (or her) home environment and eventually the wider world on the basis of his (or her) initial perceptions" (Manaster & Corsini, 1982, p. 91).

According to Mosak (1989), the cardinal tenet of Adlerian psychology is *gemeinschaftsgefuhl*. It is typically translated social interest or community feeling, and emphasizes the relational, social-contextual nature of the theory. According to Watts and Eckstein (2009), both community feeling *and* social interest are needed for a holistic understanding of *gemeinschaftsgefuhl*; that is, "community feeling" addresses the affective and motivational aspects and "social interest" the cognitive and behavioral ones. Thus, true community feeling (i.e., sense of belonging, empathy, caring, compassion, acceptance of others, etc.) results in social interest (i.e., thoughts and behaviors that contribute to the common good, the good of the whole at both micro- and macrosystemic levels); true social interest is motivated by community feeling. Interestingly, the development of Adler's community feeling/social interest appears to remarkably parallel the development of the attachment motive in attachment theory. Both are innate, both have to be developed in interaction with primary caregivers, and the degree to which both are present in an individual's life impacts the degree to which that person moves toward or against/away from fellow human beings (Peluso, White, & Kern, 2010; Watts, 2003b; Watts & Shulman, 2003).

> The tendency of human beings to form attachments (social feelings) was considered by Adler to be a fact of life. The striving of the human is always in some way connected with human bonding. Social interest is the expression of this tendency in a way that promotes human welfare. Some aspects of social interest are innate as in the infant's tendency to bond with its mother. However, social interest is a potential that must be developed through training in cooperation with productive endeavor. (Shulman, 1985, p. 248)

A significant difference between Adler and other personality theorists regarding the aforementioned "striving" is the role of community feeling/social interest. Adler emphasized that striving for perfection or superiority occurs in a relational context and this striving may occur in either a socially useful or a socially useless manner. How one strives, and the manifest behaviors, are predicated on one's community feeling/social interest. Thus, in Adler's (1933/1979) mature theoretical formulation, *striving for perfection* means that one is striving toward greater competence, both for oneself and the common good of humanity. This is a horizontal striving that is useful both for self and others, seeking to build both self- and other-esteem. *Striving for superiority* means to move in a self-centered manner, seeking to be superior over others. This is a vertical striving that primarily pursues personal gain without contribution to or consideration of others and the common good. The manner one chooses to strive constitutes the Adlerian criterion for mental health: healthy development follows the goal of community feeling and social interest; maladjustment is the consequence of pursuing narcissistic self-interest (Manaster & Corsini, 1982).

ADLERIAN COUNSELING: PRACTICE CONSIDERATIONS

MALADJUSTMENT

Adlerian counseling embraces a nonpathological perspective. Clients are not viewed as sick and in need of a cure. Rather clients are viewed as discouraged, as lacking the courage to engage in the tasks of living. As noted earlier, all persons struggle with feelings of inferiority—feelings of insignificance and disempowerment and the accompanying beliefs that one is less that what one should be. Thus, all persons are striving to move from a perceived *minus* position to a perceived *plus*. When persons creatively respond with courage and community feeling/social interest to the challenges of life and the concomitant feelings of inferiority, they are considered well-functioning. When they do not respond with courage, or if they respond without community feeling/social interest, they are discouraged and may develop what Adler called an *inferiority complex*. Persons with an inferiority complex are more concerned with how others perceive them than they are with finding solutions to problems. The *superiority complex* is a socially useless attempt to overcome an inferiority complex; it is a variation on a theme. Persons with an inferiority complex tend be passive and withdrawing. Persons compensating for inferiority feelings by the superiority complex tend to be arrogant and boastful. In both cases, the persons are discouraged but responding to overwhelming feelings of inferiority in different ways.

Adlerians affirm that early existential decisions about self and the world—decisions made within and in relation to the first sociological environment, the family—form the core convictions of a client's style of life, his or her "Story of My Life" (Adler, 1931/1992, pp. 70-71). Many of the early formed convictions may have been useful for a child to belong and survive in his or her early environment but later prove no longer useful for productive living.

The Adlerian position on maladjustment resonates with that described by narrative counselors Parry and Doan (1994):

> The experiences that bring individuals or families to therapy represent, in our view, a "wake up call"—a message that the stories that have formed them and shaped their emotional reactions have reached their limit. Although these stories made sense to children dependent upon adults, they are no longer adequate to help individuals handle present challenges effectively. It is now time for them to question the beliefs and assumptions that their stories have coded, in order to free themselves from the constraints upon capacities that maturity and responsibility have since made available to them. (p. 42)

Adlerians also agree with Littrell (1998), a solution-focused counselor, who stated that clients present for counseling because they are "demoralized" or "discouraged," not because they are sick and in need of a cure. Clients "lack hope.... One of our tasks as counselors is to assist in the process of restoring patterns of hope" (p. 63).

Whereas Adlerians view clients as discouraged rather than sick, they thus view client symptoms from a proactive rather than merely reactive perspective. According to Mosak and Maniacci (1999), symptoms are selected and chosen because they are perceived as facilitating movement toward a desired goal. In other words, symptoms are not merely reactions to situations, but rather attempted solutions.

Client Hesitancy to Change

Adlerian counseling espouses a "self-protective" view of client reluctance to change. According to Shulman (1985), the core convictions of a person's style of life are essentially unconscious and are less accessible and amenable to change. When these core style of life convictions are challenged (in life or in therapy), the client often responds by use of *compensation*. Adler used the word compensation as an umbrella to cover all the problem-solving devices the client uses to "safeguard" his or her self-esteem, reputation, and physical self. Adlerians view client reluctance to change in terms of the client *self-protecting* or *safeguarding* his or her sense of "self" (Mosak, 1989; Shulman, 1985).

In addition, Adlerian counseling views client reluctance to change in terms of goal misalignment. According to Dreikurs (1967),

> Therapeutic cooperation requires an alignment of goals.... What appears as "resistance" constitutes a discrepancy between the goals of the therapist and those of the [client]. In each case, the proper relationship has to be reestablished, differences solved, and agreement reached. (p. 7)

Thus, as Dreikurs noted, when there is disagreement between clients and counselors regarding the goals of counseling, clients will be reluctant to engage in the therapeutic process. It is the responsibility of counselors to ensure that they understand and are aligned with the goals of clients.

The Four Phases of Adlerian Counseling

Adlerian counseling typically proceeds in a series of logical phases. The four phases of Adlerian counseling include: relationship, analysis/assessment, insight/interpretation, and reorientation/reeducation.

Client-Counselor Relationship

Adlerian counseling is commonly viewed as consisting of four phases. The first and most important phase is entitled *relationship*. Counseling occurs in a relational context. The client-counselor relationship in Adlerian counseling is variously described as cooperative, collaborative, egalitarian, optimistic, and respectful. Success in the other phases of the Adlerian approach is predicated on the development and continuation of a strong counselor-client relationship based on the aforementioned characteristics (Watts & Pietrzak, 2000).

The client-counselor relationship in Adlerian counseling is an *encouragement-focused* one. Encouragement is often incorrectly described in secondary source textbooks as a "technique." Adlerians place strong emphasis on developing a respectful therapeutic relationship, they emphasize strengths and resources, and they are optimistic and future-oriented. These characteristics describe what Adlerians have historically called *encouragement*, or the therapeutic modeling of social interest (Watts, 1999, Watts & Pietrzak, 2000). Thus, for Adlerians, encouragement is not merely a technique; it is both an attitude and a way of being with clients. According to Watts and Pietrzak, Adler (1956) and subsequent Adlerians consider encouragement a crucial aspect of human growth and development. This is especially true in the field of counseling. Stressing the importance of encouragement in therapy, Adler stated: "Altogether, in every step of the treatment, we must not deviate from the path of encouragement" (p. 342). Dreikurs (1967) agreed: "What is most important in every treatment is encouragement" (p. 35). In addition, Dreikurs stated that therapeutic success was largely dependent upon "(the therapist's) ability to provide encouragement" and failure generally occurred "due to the inability of the therapist to encourage" (pp. 12-13).

> Encouragement focuses on helping counselees become aware of their worth. By encouraging them, you help your counselees recognize their own strengths and assets, so they become aware of the power they have to make decisions and choices.... Encouragement focuses on beliefs and self-perceptions. It searches intensely for assets and processes feedback so the client will become of aware of her (or his) strengths. In a mistake-centered culture like ours, this approach violates norms by ignoring deficits and stressing assets. The counselor is concerned with changing the client's negative self concept and anticipations. (Dinkmeyer, Dinkmeyer, & Sperry, 1987, p. 124)

As noted previously, clients present for counseling because they are discouraged and, consequently, lack the confidence and "courage" to successfully engage in the tasks or problems of living. The process of encouragement helps build hope and the expectancy of success in clients. In addition to developing and maintaining a cooperative, collaborative, egalitarian, optimistic, and respectful client-counselor relationship by active listening, empathic understanding, and communicating respect, Adlerians use encouragement throughout the counseling process to help clients create new patterns of behavior, develop more encouraging perceptions, and access resources and strengths. These skills of encouragement include, but are not limited to communicating confidence in clients' strengths, assets, and abilities, including identifying and drawing upon past successes; helping clients distinguish between what they do and who they are (deed vs. doer); assisting clients in generating perceptual alternatives for discouraging fictional beliefs; focusing on clients' efforts and progress; and communicating affirmation and appreciation to clients (Watts, Lewis, & Peluso, 2009; Watts & Pietrzak, 2000).

ASSESSMENT

Adlerians take a process view of individuals and, consequently, do not see assessment as an event that categorizes clients with static diagnostic labels. Assessment is ongoing, a continual process. Although they may or may not use many traditional assessment instruments and procedures, most Adlerians do some from of *style of life analysis* as a part of their assessment, either formally or informally. This assessment occurs in the second phase of Adlerian counseling—the analysis/assessment phase—and usually includes eliciting information about the client's childhood *family constellation* and asking the client for *early recollections*, a projective assessment whereby clients share memories of specific childhood events. According to Adlerian psychology, early memories are seen as invented, selected, and altered by the individual to reflect his or her current attitudes and perspectives (Watts & Eckstein, 2010).

There are several different ways for counselors to conduct a style of life analysis. Some conduct the interview in the first session, while others take 2-3 sessions to complete. Some interviewers utilize a standard format for the assessment, while others may collect the information more informally. However, Adlerian counselors typically include an interview that leads to a formulation or summary of the client's style of life (Watts et al., 2009). These interviews, based on clients' memories of their family-of-origin, have many common subject areas that are explored. Interviewers first ask about *siblings* and how similar or different clients were relative to their siblings. Next, clients are asked about the influence of their *parents*. This gives the counselor information about the client's perceived ordinal position (or psychological birth order), the family constellation (how each person related to other family members), and the family atmosphere (the overarching "mood" of the family). Next Adlerian counselors ask about the client's childhood *physical development*, *sexual development*, *social development*, and *school experience*. Counselors also ask about clients' local *community* and *socioeconomic* status to help determine their view of themselves and the family's position in the larger world (Watts et al., 2009).

The final phase of the interview is the collection of early childhood recollections. Each early recollection elicited by the counselor should be a single, specific incident preferably occurring before the age of 10. Early memories are not coincidences; they are often projections. In large measure, what we selectively attend to from the past is reflective of what we believe and how we behave in the present, and what we anticipate for the future. Clients may have difficulty accessing or sharing these beliefs when asked directly; however, by asking for early childhood memories, counselors are often able to bypass potential safe-guarding measures by clients. Interviewers collect anywhere from three to eight early memories (Watts et al., 2009).

Insight/Interpretation

Having gathered all the aforementioned data in the *analysis* phase of Adlerian counseling, the counselor has sufficient information to create tentative hypotheses about a client's style of life (i.e., patterns of behavior, way of viewing himself or herself, and his or her world, etc.). Next the counselor presents these hypotheses to the client (the *insight/interpretation* phase of the Adlerian counseling process). In this third phase, the Adlerian counselor helps the client gain self-understanding and insight by communicating *hypothesis interpretations* of basic themes that are self-defeating and impede client growth (*basic mistakes* or *misperceptions*). The purpose of using hypothesis interpretation is to convey to the client that more than one explanation for behavior exists, and that the counselor wants to check out his or own hunches to see if they are on the mark. The phrasing of hypothesis interpretation is important. For example, after reviewing the style of life assessment, a counselor may start the interpretation process with, "Could it be that …" or "Is it possible that …" Interpretations phrased in this way provide the client an opportunity to let the counselor know if he or she is on the right track. Observing an "ah-ha" moment in the client's expression (*recognition reflex*), or a quick glance of disapproval in response to the interpretation, would be enough for the counselor to continue or move in a different direction. Phrasing interpretations as hypotheses is also an effective way to diminish resistance in the counseling relationship. The message to the client is, "I have something to offer you, but I acknowledge that you are the expert on you. I am interested if this fits with you or not" (Carlson et al., 2006; Watts et al., 2009)

It is important at this juncture to clarify what Adlerians mean by insight and how the Adlerian notion of insight has been misunderstood and misrepresented. Insight, as understood by Adlerians, is more than mere intellectual assent to facts. Rather, it is "understanding translated into constructive change" (Mosak & Maniacci, 2011, p. 89). True insight results in useful changes in cognitions, affect, and behavior. Given that one of the phases of Adlerian counseling is entitled insight/interpretation, one might erroneously assume that Adlerian counseling asserts that *insight* always precedes any behavioral change. To the contrary, Adlerians assert that insight can be facilitated by encouraging clients to do something different. Adlerians often use action-oriented procedures common to the reorientation phase of Adlerian counseling (e.g., acting as if) in order to facilitate insight (Watts & Pietrzak, 2000; Watts, Peluso, & Lewis, 2006).

Reorientation

This last phase of Adlerian counseling is an action-oriented one in which clients are encouraged to *put feet to their insight*; that is, to make the constructive changes necessary to reach their desired goals. Clients particularly need encouragement in this phase of counseling because discouraged clients are often fearful of taking risks and making necessary changes. Clients must be encouraged and challenged to courageously engage the tasks of living and the relationships therein. This process of reorientation must, however, be done in a culturally sensitive manner; that is, it should be compatible with the client's context and culture. Adlerian counselors create and modify procedures and interventions so as to be culturally and personally attuned to their clients (Carlson & Englar-Carlson, 2008; Carlson et al., 2006).

Goal of Adlerian Counseling

The fundamental goal of Adlerian counseling is to help clients experience and assimilate new information that is discrepant with existing cognitive structures (style of life). Thus, clients have opportunity to create perceptual alternatives and modify or replace growth-inhibiting beliefs or personal narratives with ones that are growth-enhancing and thereby overcome overwhelming feelings of inferiority and discouragement. Adlerians seek to help clients develop the courage to engage in the tasks of living in useful and healthy ways. The ultimate goal for Adlerians is the development or expansion of clients' community feeling/social interest. Congruent with Adlerian personality theory, the goals of Adlerian counseling are relationally focused (Carlson et al., 2006; Watts & Eckstein, 2009).

Techniques

Adlerians are technical eclectics and *multimodal* in the sense that they use a variety of cognitive, behavioral, and experiential techniques for achieving the aforementioned goals of counseling. Adlerian counseling is immensely flexible and, consequently, Adlerians select techniques based on the unique needs and problems of each client or client system. That is not to say, however, that there are no techniques originally developed by Adlerians. Some have already been addressed in this chapter (encouragement, hypothesis interpretation, and style of life analysis and early recollections). The following are techniques original to Adlerian counseling commonly addressed in the Adlerian literature (Carlson et al., 2006; Mosak & Maniacci, 2011; Dinkmeyer & Sperry, 2000).

The Question

In using *The Question*, counselors ask a variation of the question, "How would your life be different if, all of a sudden, you didn't have this problem anymore?" There are variations for dramatic or explanatory purposes (i.e., "Suppose I gave you a pill…" "What if you had a magic wand…" "What if you woke up in the morning and no longer had this problem…," etc.). There are three possible responses to The Question. One type of response reflects a clearly psychogenic symptom, meaning that the cause and relief from the symptom are purely psychological in nature (i.e., malingering, avoiding responsibility, or trying to "save face"). The second type reflects a somatogenic symptom meaning that the cause and relief from the symptom are purely physical in nature (i.e., chronic pain, condition, or illness). The third type of response is a combination of the psychogenic and somatogenic responses. The Question forces clients to think in terms of a new reality where they are no longer burdened by their presenting problem. As a result, clients will either be unable to hide what their symptom is doing *for* them (i.e., the usefulness, or "purpose" of the behavior), or they will feel a sense of encouragement because they begin to understand that they have the resources and abilities to overcome the problem (Watts et al., 2009).

Acting As If and Reflecting As If

In the traditional approach to using the acting as if technique, counselors ask clients to begin acting as if they were already the person they would like to be; for example, a confident individual. Using this procedure, counselors ask clients to pretend and emphasize that they are only acting. The purpose of the procedure is to bypass potential resistance to change by neutralizing some of the perceived risk. The counselor suggests a limited task, such as acting as if one had the courage to speak up for oneself. The expectation is that the client will successfully complete the task. If the task is unsuccessful, then the counselor explores with the client what kept him or her from having a successful experience (Watts et al., 2009).

A more reflective approach to acting as if asks clients to take a "reflective" step back prior to stepping forward to act "as if." The *Reflecting As If* process encourages clients to reflect on how they would be different if they were acting "as if" they were the person they desire to be.

By using reflective questions, counselors can help clients construct perceptual alternatives and consider alternative behaviors prior to engaging in acting as if tasks (Watts et al., 2009).

Catching Oneself

This technique involves encouraging clients to catch themselves in the act of performing the presenting problem. Clients may initially catch themselves too late and fall into old patterns of behavior. However, with practice, clients can learn to anticipate situations, recognize when their thoughts and perceptions are becoming self-defeating, and take steps to modify their thinking and behavior. Catching oneself involves helping clients identify the signals or triggers associated with one's problematic behavior or emotions. When triggers are identified, clients can then make decisions that stop their symptoms from overwhelming them (Watts et al., 2009).

Pushbutton

This technique helps clients become aware of their role in maintaining, or even creating, their unpleasant feelings. The pushbutton technique has three phases. In phase one, clients are asked to close their eyes and recall a very pleasant memory, a time when they felt happy, loved, successful, and so on. Clients are to recreate the image in their minds in as specific detail as possible and strongly focus on the positive feelings generated by the pleasant memory. In phase two, clients are asked to close their eyes and recall a very unpleasant memory, a time when they felt sad, unloved, unsuccessful, and so on. As in phase one, clients are to recall the memory in all its clarity and, this time, strongly focus on the unpleasant feelings created by the memory. In phase three, clients are asked to retrieve another very pleasant memory, or return to the one used in phase one. Again, they are to recall the memory in specific detail and strongly focus on the positive feelings. After they have relived the pleasant memory and positive feelings, clients are instructed to open their eyes. They are then asked to share what they learned from the exercise. Clients usually make the connection between beliefs and feelings. If they fail to do so, counselors should help them understand that certain thoughts or images usually generate certain types of feelings. After making sure the connection is made, counselors then give clients two make-believe *pushbuttons* to take for a homework assignment. These pushbuttons control the images clients create. When they push the *negative pushbutton*, they create unpleasant images that negatively impact how they feel. When they push the *positive pushbutton*, they create pleasant images that positively affect how they feel. These pushbuttons affirm that feelings or behaviors are typically a choice. When they return for the next counseling session, the discussion with the counselor can focus on which button clients have been pushing, and the purpose of the choice (Mosak & Maniacci, 2011; Watts et al., 2009).

VALIDATION OF ADLERIAN COUNSELING

Watkins and Guarnaccia (1999) correctly noted that although there is a solid body of research literature supporting central constructs of Adlerian psychological theory, research studies on Adlerian psychotherapy are "few, far between, and hard to find" (p. 226). They suggested that Adlerian counseling research might benefit by the development of an Adlerian treatment manual that could be used in therapist training and as a guide to research. Watkins and Guarnaccia further stated, "Such manuals are not a panacea, and problems attendant to them must be borne in mind…. Yet they could be one viable means of allowing [Adlerians] to … research the Adlerian therapy process, its effects, its outcome" (p. 227). The above comments by Watkins and Guarnaccia regarding Adlerian research remain valid. There is a wealth of research supporting specific Adlerian theoretical constructs but very little research specifically on Adlerian counseling.

This not to say, however, that there is no research supporting Adlerian counseling. There is a wealth of current research that clearly, albeit indirectly, supports the process and practice of Adlerian therapy. For example, the results of the research described by Prochaska and Norcross (1994, 2003, 2010) are remarkably similar to the contemporary theory and practice of Adlerian counseling. For example, in their most recent study, Prochaska and Norcross (2010) asked a panel of 62 experts in the field to predict trends regarding the practice of counseling and psychotherapy for the near future. Prochaska and Norcross describe the results as follows:

> In terms of theoretical orientations, cognitive, cognitive-behavioral, multicultural, integrative, eclectic, and systems perspectives will thrive…. In terms of methods and modalities, the consensus is that psychotherapy will become more directive, psychoeducational, technological, problem-focused, and briefer in the next decade…. In terms of therapy formats, psychoeducational groups, couples therapy, and group therapy are seen as continuing their upward swing. The largest transformation is expected in the length of therapy. Short term is in, and long term is on its way out. (p. 519)

Anyone familiar with the Adlerian approach will see the remarkable similarity between Prochaska and Norcross's results and the contemporary practice of Adlerian counseling. Adlerian counseling is a psychoeducational, present/future-oriented, time-limited (or brief) and integrative and eclectic approach. Furthermore, the Adlerian model clearly integrates cognitive, systemic, and multicultural counseling perspectives, and solidly resonates with postmodern approaches (Carlson et al, 2006; Watts, 2000; Watts & Pietrzak, 2000). Thus, Prochaska and Norcross's results are consistent with and provide support for the fundamental tenets of Adlerian counseling.

Perhaps even more remarkable is the significant common ground between Adlerian therapy and the research addressing the transtheoretical *factors* commonly identified in the successful psychotherapy outcome literature (e.g., Duncan, Miller, Wampold, & Hubble, 2010; Hubble, Duncan, & Miller, 1999a; Norcross, 2002, Prochaska & Norcross, 2003; Wampold, 2001). Prochaska and Norcross (2003) stated,

> Despite theoretical differences, there is a central and recognizable core of psychotherapy … [that] distinguishes it from other activities … and glues together variations of psychotherapy. The core is composed of *common factors* or nonspecific variables common to all forms of psychotherapy and not specific to one. More often than not, these therapeutic commonalities are not specified by theories as being of central importance, but the research suggests exactly the opposite. (p. 6)

Adlerian counseling resonates enormously with the common factors of successful outcomes and these common factors are indeed specified by Adlerian therapy *as being of central importance*. Below is a brief description of the points of common ground between Adlerian counseling and the common factors of successful psychotherapy outcomes.

EXTRATHERAPEUTIC/CLIENT FACTORS

According to the research literature, client factors make the greatest impact on psychotherapy outcome. These factors consist of what clients bring to therapy and the influences and circumstances in clients' lives outside of it.

Adlerian therapy stresses the importance of attending to what clients bring to therapy; especially their strengths, assets, and resources. According to Adler (1913/1956), "The actual change in … the patient can only be his own doing" (p. 336). Consequently, therapists must believe that clients have the requisite capabilities to solve their problems (Mosak, 1979). Hubble, Duncan, and Miller expressed (1999c) it well:

> It is perhaps best summarized by Alfred Adler when he said he approached all clients, "fully convinced that no matter what I might be able to say ... the patient can learn nothing from me that he, as the sufferer, does not understand better" [Adler, 1913/1956, p. 336]. Approaching clients in this manner not only helps to combat discouragement and instill hope but, as Adler also noted, "make[s] it clear that the responsibility for ... cure is the patient's business" [Adler, 1913/1956, p. 336]. (p. 411)

Therapeutic Relationship Factors

Extratherapeutic/client factors have arguably had the most significant influence on the results of psychotherapy. It is clear, however, that therapeutic relationship factors play a crucial role in successful outcomes, perhaps as crucial as client factors (Duncan et al., 2010). Research indicates that positive outcomes in psychotherapy are clearly related to therapist relationship skills and are essential for building and maintaining a strong therapeutic alliance.

Of all the common factors, Adlerian counseling most strongly resonates with the emphasis on the therapeutic relationship. Adlerian counseling, a relational approach, consists of four phases. The first and most important phase, entitled "relationship," clearly focuses on establishing a strong client-therapist alliance. Furthermore, and consistent with the positive outcome research literature, Adlerians believe that therapeutic efficacy in other phases of Adlerian counseling is predicated upon the development and continuation of a meaningful therapeutic alliance (Carlson et al., 2006).

Placebo, Hope, and Expectancy

Asay and Lambert (1999) noted that clients come to therapy because they have lost hope; they are not only "demoralized about having problems" but also they "have lost hope about being able to solve them" (p. 44). They note that expectancy of success generated in therapy is powerful because it helps provide clients with hope that their problems can be solved.

Mosak and Maniacci (2011) described the Adlerian therapeutic process in terms of "faith, hope, and love" (p. 83). That is, expressing faith in the client, developing the client's faith in himself or herself, and both the client and therapist having faith the therapeutic process; engendering hope in clients who present with varying levels of hope of improvement; and love, in the broadest sense, in that the client experiences a relationship with a caring, empathic, nonjudgmental, genuine human being. Adlerian counseling therapy is an optimistic and encouragement-focused approach to helping people.

Model/Technique Factors

Prochaska and Norcross (2003) stated that there is a pervasive misconception suggesting that psychotherapists who align themselves with a specific theoretical orientation are dogmatic and antiquated and refuse to adapt their counseling practices to the needs and situation of the client. According to Hubble, Duncan, and Miller (1999c), affirming that common factors do account for the majority of change in psychotherapy does not mean that one must practice a "'model *less*' or technique*less*' therapy" (p. 408). Rather, they suggest that therapeutic models informed by the common factors attend to and implement what works to facilitate change. Furthermore, as Lambert and Barley (2001) suggested, improvement of psychotherapy may more readily occur when therapist increase their ability to relate to clients and tailor treatment to individual clients.

The Adlerian model of counseling clearly includes a rationale, offers an explanation for client's difficulties, and possesses strategies or procedures to prepare clients to take some action to help themselves. In agreement with Hubble, Duncan, and Miller (1999b), Adlerian therapists "expect their clients to do something different—to develop new understandings, feel different emotions, face fears, or alter old patterns of behavior" (p. 10). Furthermore, Adlerians are *technical eclectics* and *therapeutic chameleons*. Different clients may require different therapeutic relational emphases and different therapeutic metaphors. Adlerian counseling allows the therapist to tailor therapy to the client's unique needs and expectations, rather than forcing the client into one therapeutic or technical framework.

Finally, the validation of Adlerian counseling is supported by the large number of Adlerian concepts used by other counseling approaches (although typically not acknowledged), especially those with significantly more empirical support (e.g., cognitive-behavioral therapies). According to Corey (2009), a non-Adlerian author:

> It is difficult to overestimate the contributions of Adler to contemporary therapeutic practice. Many of his ideas were revolutionary and far ahead of his time. His influence went beyond counseling individuals, extending into the community mental health movement.... One of Adler's most important contributions is his influence on other therapy systems. Many of his basic ideas have found their way into other psychological schools, such as family systems approaches, Gestalt therapy, learning theory, reality therapy, rational emotive behavior therapy, cognitive therapy, person-centered therapy, existential therapy, and the postmodern approaches to therapy are based on a similar concept of the person as purposive, self-determining, and striving for growth. In many respects, Adler seems to have paved the way for current developments in both the cognitive and constructivist therapies.... A study of

> contemporary counseling theories reveals that many of Adler's notions have reappeared in these modern approaches with different nomenclature, and often with giving Adler the credit that is due him.... It is clear that there are significant linkages of Adlerian theory with most present-day theories. (p. 125)

Adlerian Counseling: Multicultural Considerations

The demographics of North America—especially in the United States—are changing rapidly. Thus, if any approach is to be considered a relevant psychotherapy for contemporary society, it must successfully address multicultural and social equality issues (Watts, 2000).

With the increasing emphasis on multiculturalism, many counselors have been drawn to postmodern approaches because of their focus on the social embeddedness of humans and, consequently, human knowledge. Adlerians and Adlerian theory addressed social equality issues and emphasized the social embeddedness of humans and human knowledge long before multiculturalism became a focal issue in the helping professions. Adler campaigned for the social equality of women, contributed much to the understanding of gender issues, spoke against the marginalization of minority groups, and specifically predicted the Black Power and Women's Liberation movements (Ansbacher & Ansbacher, 1978; Dreikurs, 1971; Hoffman, 1994; LaFountain & Mustaine, 1998; Mozdzierz, 1998; Watts, 2000). In addition, Adlerian theory played an influential positive role in the outcome of the historic *Brown v. Board of Education* decision of May 17, 1954:

> Kenneth B. Clark headed a team of social scientists who called on Adlerian theory to explain the need for equality in American society. Their argument against separate-but-equal schools swayed the highest court in its decision that ruled in favor of the plaintiffs. (LaFountain & Mustaine, 1998, p. 196)

Adlerian psychotherapy is clearly relevant for working with culturally diverse populations in contemporary society. According to Gerald Corey, the Adlerian approach is "certainly compatible with many of the macrostrategies for future delivery of service to culturally diverse populations" (as cited in Sweeney, 1998, pp. 33-34). Arciniega and Newlon (1999) noted that the characteristics and assumptions of Adlerian psychology are congruent with the cultural values of many minority racial and ethnic groups and affirm that the Adlerian therapeutic process is respectful of cultural diversity. Adlerian therapy goals are not aimed at deciding for clients what they should change about themselves.

> Rather, the practitioner works in collaboration with clients and their family networks. This theory offers a pragmatic approach that is flexible and uses a range of action-oriented techniques to explore personal problems within their sociocultural context. It has the flexibility to deal both with the individual and the family, making it appropriate for racial and ethnic groups. (p. 451)

The Adlerian psychology and psychotherapy literature addresses a wide range of multicultural issues including culture, ethnicity, gender, racism, sexual orientation, and social equality.

A rapidly growing dimension of multiculturalism includes attention to and appreciation of the role of religion or spirituality in the lives of clients. The field of counseling and psychotherapy has made a 180-degree turn, from a position of disdain and avoidance, to one appreciating the influence of spiritual issues on cognition, emotion, and, ultimately, behavior.

Historically, most systems of psychology have had either a neutral or negative position toward religion and spirituality. Adlerian therapy, however, has been quite open to addressing religious and spiritual issues. The topic is addressed somewhat regularly by authors in the *Journal of Individual Psychology* (e.g., Mansager, 2000).

According to Manaster and Corsini (1982), "the most common Adlerian position toward religion is positive, viewing God as the concept of perfection.... For Adler, religion was a manifestation of social interest" (p. 63). Mosak (1995) notes that "Adler's psychology has a religious tone. His placement of social interest at the pinnacle of his value theory is in the tradition of those religions that stress people's responsibility for each other" (p. 59). Mosak mentioned that when Adler introduced the concepts of *value* and *meaning* into psychology via his 1931 book *What Life Should Mean to You*, the concepts were unpopular at the time. The cardinal tenet of Adlerian theory is social interest, and Adler equated it with the mandate to "love one's neighbor as oneself" and the Golden Rule. Furthermore, Mosak identifies *spirituality* as one of the five major tasks of life:

> Although Adler alluded to the *spiritual*, he never specifically named it. But each of us must deal with the problems of defining the nature of the universe, the existence and nature of God, and how to relate to these concepts. (p. 54)

Applications

Adler addressed the application of Adlerian psychology via his writings, lectures, and demonstrations with an impressive array of problems and settings. He addressed counseling with at-risk children, especially those struggling with delinquency; woman's right and gender equality; adult education; teacher training; community mental health and the establishment of family counseling and child guidance clinics; experimental schools for public school students; and brief counseling and psychotherapy.

Because it is a strength-based, growth model, as opposed to a medical model, Adlerian counseling is widely applicable to many areas of people helping. Adlerians have developed useful models for teacher education and classroom management based on the principles delineated by Adler and his foremost student, Rudolf Dreikurs. There are many Adlerian-based child and family guidance clinics throughout the world and most of the leading parent education programs and literature are based on Adlerian principles (e.g., *Systematic Training for Effective Parenting, Active Parenting, Positive Discipline, Raising Kids Who Can,* etc.) and Adlerians have also developed couple-enrichment programs (e.g., Dinkmeyer & Carlson, 2003). In the family therapy literature, Adler is often mentioned as the first *systems-oriented* theory. In the 1920s, Dreikurs began using Adlerian principles in group therapy and Adlerian group therapy has remained an important counseling modality among Adlerians. Dreikurs was the first therapist to use group therapy in private practice.

Because Adler and his colleagues maintained 28 child guidance clinics in Vienna prior to World War II, and because of the success of Adlerian-oriented parent education materials, some may assume that Adlerian counseling is only useful for working with children. This would be an unfortunate assumption. Adlerian counseling is used in a wide variety of formats and with diverse client populations and problems. Adlerians practice with individuals, couples and families, in group counseling settings, and career/employment counseling settings, as well as others. The client problems addressed by Adlerian counselors and authors range from normal developmental struggles through the various conditions described listed in the *Diagnostic and Statistical Manual* published by the American Psychiatric Association (Mosak & Maniacci, 1999).

CRITIQUE OF ADLERIAN COUNSELING

Adler focused more on helping people by counseling practice and training others than on developing a formal and systematic theory. His writings, therefore, are sometimes difficult to read (especially those translated from German). Adler seldom wrote for professional audiences and many of his writings were notes transcribed from his lectures to lay audiences. This often gave the sense that his ideas were simplistic and unsystematic (Carlson et al., 2006; Mosak & Maniacci, 1999).

Regarding work with culturally diverse clients, there are several potential issues that Adlerian counselors may need to address. First, Adlerian counseling emphasizes choice and responsibility. Adlerian counselors must take into consideration the role and impact of oppression on client choice and oppression when working with clients from minority populations. Second, some culturally diverse clients may be uncomfortable with the personal and family questions Adlerians often ask in securing the personal and family information during the assessment phase of counseling. Adlerian counselors may need to gather the information more informally using a brief questionnaire and interview techniques to obtain information. Third, the Adlerian model is based on principles of democracy and egalitarianism. Clients from cultures that view counselors as experts, however, come to counseling with a strong desire for structure and direction; they want the counselor to advise them regarding decisions they must make. In sum, Adlerian counselors may need to adapt their style of counseling to be maximally effective with culturally diverse clients. As noted earlier, Adlerians tailor treatment to clients' needs and contexts, a particularly useful idea when working with culturally diverse clients (Carlson & Englar-Carlson, 2008).

Finally, as noted earlier, direct research supporting Adlerian counseling is limited. Although there is an exponentially growing body of research in support of Adlerian theoretical concepts, more research addressing the effectiveness of Adlerian counseling would be very useful. Given that Adlerians have historically preferred an idiographic or case study method, the recommendation by Edwards, Dattilio, and Bromley (2004)—that clinical practice and case-based research be included as a significant contributor to evidence-based practice—may be of particular interest to Adlerians. Similarly, the burgeoning qualitative research methodologies may also prove useful for studying Adlerian psychotherapy. Whatever methodologies chosen by researchers, Adlerian counseling will benefit from additional research.

RECENT STUDIES USING ADLERIAN THEORY

Watkins (1982, 1983, 1986, 1992, Watkins & Guarnaccia, 1999) provided excellent summaries of Adlerian research over the three decades immediately preceding the twenty-first century. In recent years, there has been exponential growth in the Adlerian research literature and discussion of this research is beyond the present scope; however, immediately below are brief descriptions of three recent studies investigating Adlerian theory and practice concepts.

Peluso, Stoltz, Belangee, Frey, and Peluso (2010) conducted a confirmatory factor analysis of the BASIS-A inventory. The purpose of the study was to test the five-factor model of the BASIS-A using confirmatory factor analysis. The study's sample included 917 participants from three southern and one northern university locations in the United States. According to Peluso et al., the BASIS-A asks respondents to report early childhood memories and classifies responses to style of life themes (belonging/social interest, going along, taking charge, wanting recognition, being cautions). The results support the existing five scale structure and the overall validity of the instrument. In addition, the authors reported high Cronbach's alpha coefficients (.81 – .88) supporting the consistency and reliability of the BASIS-A. The results support the validity of the Adlerian style of life construct and the BASIS-A as a valid and reliable measure of style of life.

According to McVittie and Best (2009), a large body of research indicates that an *authoritative parenting style* most positively affects adolescent development. McVittie and Best investigated whether Adlerian-based parent education influenced parental behavior in a more authoritative direction. Over 1,250 participants who participated in 110 Adlerian parenting classes in the United States and Canada completed a retrospective comparison method questionnaire developed for the study that assessed parents-guardians' perceptions of their behavior prior and subsequent to the 6-10 week Adlerian parent education course. Using repeated measures ANOVA and ANCOVA statistics, McVittie and Best found that the parent-guardians reported statistically significant changes in their parenting behavior indicative of movement toward a more authoritative parenting style. Specifically, the parent-guardians reported statistically significant changes in setting clear limits, increasing their sense of positive connection, and decreasing harshness in their interactions with their children. The greatest amount of change occurred with younger parents, women, persons with the lowest income, and parents-guardians with few children. The results support Adlerian parent education as an evidence-based approach for helping families.

Using the BASIS-A Inventory and selected items from the alcohol and other drug survey, Lewis and Watts (2004) examined the predictability of Adlerian lifestyle themes for college alcohol consumption. Two hundred and seventy-three undergraduates completed the instruments and the results of the multiple regression analysis indicated that "Adlerian lifestyle combinations accounted for more variance in alcohol related behaviors than other variables commonly found to be predictive of alcohol consumption (i.e., grade of first drinking experience, gender, fraternity/sorority membership, and religious participation)" (p. 245). Overall, according to Lewis and Watts, the combined Adlerian lifestyle themes "accounted for more variability in frequency of binge drinking and frequency of alcohol consumption than the additional variables" (p. 245).

CONCLUSION

Adlerian counseling theory is an integration of cognitive, psychodynamic, existential, and systems perspectives. H. L. Ansbacher, a noted Adlerian scholar, described Adlerian psychology as a:

> holistic, phenomenological, teleological, field-theoretical, and socially-oriented approach to psychology and related fields. This approach is based upon the assumption of the uniqueness, self consistency, activity, and creativity of the human individual (style of life); an open dynamic system of motivation (striving for a subjectively conceived goal of success); and an innate potentiality for social life (social interest). (Manaster & Corsini, 1982, p. 2)

The beauty of the Adlerian approach to counseling is its flexibility and applicability in a variety of settings. Adlerians can be both theoretically integrative, albeit consistent, and technically eclectic. Different clients may require different therapeutic metaphors. One client may prefer a narrative oriented approach, another a solution-focused orientation, and yet another a cognitive-behavioral or systemic one. Adlerian counseling allows the counselor to do whatever is in the best interest of his or her client, rather than forcing the client—and his or her unique situation—into one therapeutic framework (Carlson et al., 2006; Watts, 2000).

REFERENCES

Adler, A. (1956). *The individual psychology of Alfred Adler* (H. L. Ansbacher & R. R. Ansbacher, Eds.). New York, NY: Harper Torchbooks. (Original work published 1913)

Adler, A. (1979). *Superiority and social interest* (3rd ed.) (H. L. Ansbacher & R. R. Ansbacher, Eds.). New York, NY: Norton. (Original work published 1933)

Adler, A. (1992). *What life could mean to you* (C. Brett, Trans.). Oxford, England: Oneworld Publications. (Original work published 1931)

Ansbacher, H. L. (1977). Individual psychology. In R. J. Corsini (Ed.), *Current personality theories* (pp. 45-82). Itasca, IL: F.E. Peacock.

Ansbacher, H. L., & Ansbacher, R. (Eds.). (1978). *Cooperation between the sexes: Writings on women, love, and marriage.* New York, NY: Norton.

Ansbacher, H. L., & Ansbacher, R. R. (Eds.). (1979). *Superiority and social interest* (3rd ed). New York, NY: Norton.

Arciniega, G.M., & Newlon, B.J. (1999). Counseling and psychotherapy: Multicultural considerations. In D. Capuzzi & D.F. Gross (Eds.), *Counseling & psychotherapy: Theories and interventions* (2nd ed., pp. 435-458). Upper Saddle River, NJ: Merrill/Prentice-Hall.

Asay, T. P., & Lambert, M. J. (1999). The empirical case for the common factors in therapy: Quantitative findings. In M. A. Hubble, B. L. Duncan, & S. D. Miller (Eds.), *The heart & soul of change: What works in therapy* (pp. 33-55). Washington, DC: American Psychological Association.

Carlson, J., & Englar-Carlson, M. (2008). Adlerian therapy. In J. Frew & M Spiegler (Eds.), *Contemporary psychotherapies for a diverse world* (pp. 93-140). Boston, MA: Lahaska.

Carlson, J., & Sperry, L. (1998). Adlerian psychotherapy as a constructivist psychotherapy. In M. F. Hoyt (Ed.), *The handbook of constructive therapies: Innovative approaches from leading practitioners* (pp. 68-82). San Francisco, CA: Jossey-Bass.

Carlson, J., Watts, R. E., & Maniacci, M. (2006). *Adlerian therapy: Theory and practice.* Washington, DC: American Psychological Association.

Corey, G. (2005). *Theory and practice of counseling and psychotherapy* (7th ed.). Pacific Grove, CA: Brooks/Cole.

Corey, G. (2009). *Theory and practice of counseling and psychotherapy* (8th ed.). Pacific Grove, CA: Brooks/Cole.

Dinkmeyer, D., & Carlson, J. (2003) *Training in marriage enrichment (TIME).* Bowling Green, KY: CMTI Press.

Dinkmeyer, D. C., Dinkmeyer, D. C., Jr., & Sperry, L. (1987). *Adlerian counseling and psychotherapy* (2nd ed.). Columbus, OH: Merrill.

Dinkmeyer, D., Jr., & Sperry, L. (2000). *Counseling and psychotherapy: An integrated, Individual Psychology approach* (3rd ed.). Upper Saddle River, NJ: Merrill/Prentice Hall.

Dreikurs, R. (1967). *Psychodynamics, psychotherapy, and counseling.* Chicago, IL: Alfred Adler Institute of Chicago.

Dreikurs, R. (1971). *Social equality: The challenge of today.* Chicago, IL: Regnery.

Duncan, B. L., & Miller, S. D., Wampold, B. E., & Hubble, M. A. (Eds.). (2010). *The heart & soul of change: What works in therapy* (2nd ed.). Washington, DC: American Psychological Association.

Edwards, D. J., Dattilio, F. M., & Bromley, D. B. (2004). Evidence-based practice: The role of case-based research. *Professional Psychology: Research and Practice, 35,* 589-597.

Ellenberger, H. (1970). *The discovery of the unconscious: The history and evolution of dynamic psychiatry.* New York, NY: Basic Books.

Ellis, A. (1970). Humanism, values, rationality. *Journal of Individual Psychology, 26,* 11.

Hoffman, E. (1994). *The drive for self: Alfred Adler and the founding of individual psychology.* Reading, MA: Addison-Wesley.

Hubble, M. A., Duncan, B. L., & Miller, S. D. (Eds.). (1999a). *The heart and soul of change: What works in therapy.* Washington, DC: American Psychological Association.

Hubble, M. A., Duncan, B. L., & Miller, S. D. (1999b). Introduction. In *The heart & soul of change: What works in therapy* (pp. 1-19). Washington, DC: American Psychological Association.

Hubble, M. A., Duncan, B. L., & Miller, S. D. (1999c). Directing attention to what works. In *The heart & soul of change: What works in therapy* (pp. 407-447). Washington, DC: American Psychological Association.

Jorgensen, I. S., & Nafstad, H. E. (2004). Positive psychology: Historical, philosophical, and epistemological perspectives. In S. Joseph & P. A. Linley (Eds.), *Positive psychology in practice* (pp. 15-34). New York, NY: Wiley.

LaFountain, R. M., & Mustaine, B. L. (1998). Infusing Adlerian theory into an introductory marriage and family course. *The Family Journal, 6,* 189-199.

Lambert, M. J., & Barley, D. E. (2001). Research summary on the therapeutic relationship and psychotherapy outcome. *Psychotherapy: Theory, Research, Practice, Training, 38,* 357-361.

Littrell, J. M (1998). *Brief counseling in action.* New York, NY: Norton.

Lewis, T. F, & Watts, R. E. (2004). The predictability of Adlerian lifestyle themes compared to demographic variables associated with college student drinking. *Journal of Individual Psychology, 60,* 245-264.

Linley, P. A., & Joseph, S. (Eds.). (2004). *Positive psychology in practice.* New York, NY: Wiley.

Mahoney, M. J. (2003). *Constructive psychotherapy: A practical guide.* New York, NY: Guilford.

Manaster, G. J., & Corsini, R. J. (1982). *Individual psychology: Theory and practice.* Itasca, IL: Peacock.

Mansager, E. (2000). Holism, wellness, spirituality. *Journal of Individual Psychology, 56,* 237-242.

McVittie, J., & Best, A. M (2009). The impact of Adlerian-based parenting classes on self-reported parental behavior. *Journal of Individual Psychology, 65,* 264-285.

Mosak, H. H. (1979). Adlerian therapy. In R. J. Corsini (Ed.), *Current psychotherapies* (2nd ed., pp. 44-94). Itasca, IL: Peacock.

Mosak, H. H. (1989). Adlerian therapy. In R. J. Corsini & D. Wedding (Eds.), *Current psychotherapies* (4th ed., pp. 64-116). Itasca, IL: Peacock.

Mosak, H. H. (1995). Adlerian psychotherapy. In R. J. Corsini & D. Wedding (Eds.), *Current psychotherapies* (5th ed., pp. 51-94). Itasca, IL: Peacock.

Mosak, H. H., & Maniacci, M. (2011). Adlerian therapy. In R.J. Corsini & D. Wedding (Eds.), *Current psychotherapies* (9th ed., pp. 67-112). Belmont, CA: Brooks/Cole.

Mosak, H. H., & Maniacci, M. (1999). *A primer of Adlerian psychology: The analytic-behavioral-cognitive psychology of Alfred Adler.* Philadelphia, PA: Accelerated Development/Taylor and Francis.

Mozdzierz, G. J. (1998). Bridging intellectual and cultural gaps: The challenge and heritage of individual psychology. *Journal of Individual Psychology, 54,* 1-3.

Norcross, J. C. (Ed.) (2002). *Psychotherapy relationships that work: Therapist contributions and responsiveness to patients.* New York, NY: Oxford.

Parry, A., & Doan, R. E. (1994). *Story revisions: Narrative therapy in a postmodern world.* New York, NY: Guilford.

Peluso, P. R., Stoltz, K. J., Belangee, S., Frey, M. R., & Peluso, J. P. (2010). A confirmatory factor analysis of a measure of the Adlerian lifestyle, the BASIS-A Inventory. *Journal of Individual Psychology, 66,* 152-165.

Prochaska, J. O., & Norcross, J. C. (1994). *Systems of psychotherapy: A transtheoretical approach* (3rd ed.). Pacific Grove, CA: Brooks/Cole.

Prochaska, J. O., & Norcross, J. C. (2003). *Systems of psychotherapy: A transtheoretical approach* (5th ed.). Pacific Grove, CA: Brooks/Cole.

Prochaska, J. O., & Norcross, J. C. (2010). *Systems of psychotherapy: A transtheoretical analysis* (7th ed.). Belmont, CA: Brooks/Cole.

Rasmussen, P. R. (2010). *The quest to feel good.* New York, NY: Routledge/Taylor & Francis.

Ryan, R. M., & Deci, E. L. (2001). On happiness and human potentials: A review of research on hedonic and eudaimonic well-being. *Annual Review of Psychology, 52,* 141-166.

Shulman, B. H. (1973). *Contributions to Individual Psychology.* Chicago, IL: Alfred Adler Institute.

shulman, b. h. (1985). cognitive therapy and the individual psychology of Alfred Adler. In M. J. Mahoney & A. Freeman (Eds.), *Cognition and psychotherapy* (pp. 243-258). New York, NY: Plenum.

Shulman, B. H., & Mosak, H. H. (1988). *Manual for life style assessment.* Muncie, IN: Accelerated Development.

Snyder, C. R., Lopez, S. J., & Pedrotti, J. T. (2011). *Positive psychology: The scientific and practical explorations of human strengths* (2nd ed.). Los Angeles, CA: SAGE.

Sweeney, T. (1998). *Adlerian counseling and psychotherapy: A practitioner's approach* (4th ed.). New York, NY: Routledge.

Wampold, B. E. (2001). *The great psychotherapy debate: Models, methods, and findings.* Mahwah, NJ: Lawrence Erlbaum.

Watkins, C. E., Jr. (1982). A decade of research in support of Adlerian psychological theory. *Individual Psychology: Journal of Adlerian Theory, Research & Practice, 38,* 90-99.

Watkins, C. E., Jr. (1983). Some characteristics of research on Adlerian psychological theory, 1970-1981. *Individual Psychology: Journal of Adlerian Theory, Research & Practice, 39,* 99-110.

Watkins, C. E., Jr. (1986). A research bibliography on Adlerian psychological theory. *Individual Psychology: Journal of Adlerian Theory, Research & Practice, 42,* 123-132.

Watkins, C. E., Jr. (1992). Research activity with Adler's theory. *Individual Psychology: Journal of Adlerian Theory, Research & Practice, 48,* 107-108.

Watkins, C. E., Jr., & Guarnaccia, C. A. (1999). The scientific study of Adlerian theory. In R. E. Watts & J. Carlson (Eds.), *Interventions and strategies in counseling and psychotherapy* (pp. 207-230). Philadelphia, PA: Accelerated Development

Watts, R. E. (1999). The vision of Adler: An introduction. In R. E. Watts & J. Carlson (Eds.), *Interventions and strategies in counseling and psychotherapy* (pp. 1-13). Philadelphia, PA: Accelerated Development/Taylor & Francis.

Watts, R. E. (2000). Entering the new millennium: Is Individual Psychology still relevant? *Journal of Individual Psychology, 56,* 21-30.

Watts, R. E. (2003a). Adlerian therapy as a relational constructivist approach. *The Family Journal: Counseling and Therapy for Couples and Families, 11,* 139-147.

Watts, R. E. (Ed.). (2003b). *Adlerian, cognitive, and constructivist psychotherapies: An integrative dialogue.* New York, NY: Springer.

Watts, R. E., & Critelli, J. (1997). Roots of contemporary cognitive theories and the Individual Psychology of Alfred Adler: A review. *Journal of Cognitive Psychotherapy, 11,* 147-156.

Watts, R. E., & Eckstein, D. (2009). Individual Psychology. In American Counseling Association (Ed.), *The ACA encyclopedia of counseling* (pp. 281-283). Alexandria, VA: American Counseling Association.

Watts, R. E., Lewis, T. F., & Peluso, P. (2009). Individual Psychology counseling techniques. In American Counseling Association (Ed.), *The ACA encyclopedia of counseling* (pp. 283-285). Alexandria, VA: American Counseling Association.

Watts, R. E., & Pietrzak, D. (2000). Adlerian "encouragement" and the therapeutic process of solution-focused brief therapy. *Journal of Counseling and Development, 78,* 442-447.

Watts, R. E., & Shulman, B. H. (2003). Integrating Adlerian and constructive therapies: An Adlerian perspective. In R.E. Watts (Ed.), *Adlerian, cognitive, and constructivist psychotherapies: An integrative dialogue* (pp. 9-37). New York, NY: Springer.

Watts, R. E., Williamson, J., & Williamson, D. (2004). Adlerian psychology: A relational constructivist approach. *Adlerian Yearbook: 2004* (pp. 7-31). London, England: Adlerian Society (UK) and Institute for Individual Psychology.

Author Contact Information: Richard E. Watts, PhD, LPC-S University Distinguished Professor and Director Center for Research and Doctoral Studies in Counselor Education, Sam Houston State University, Huntsville, TX. Phone: 936-294-4658. E-mail: watts@shsu.edu

CHAPTER 39

Existential Counseling

Richard C. Henriksen, Jr.
Sam Houston State University

Existentialism dates back to the days and times when Socrates provided counseling to individuals seeking to learn the meaning of their own existence. As Längle (2005) stated, "existence means having a chance to change things for the better, to experience what is of value and to avoid or to eliminate what could be damaging or harmful" (p. 3). The roots of existential thought can also be found in the works of Martin Buber, Victor Frankl, Martin Heidegger, Søren Kierkegaard, Friedrich Nietzsche, Blaise Pascal, Jean-Paul Sartre, Clement Vontress, and Irvin Yalom. The frameworks established by each of those early and contemporary existential philosophers can be summed up in the words of Rollo May (1953) who stated," joy, rather than happiness, is the goal of life, for joy is the emotion which accompanies our fulfilling our natures as human beings. It is based on the experience of one's identity as a being of worth and dignity" (p. 67).

Existentialism is not a theory of personality like many other theories used in counseling, psychology, and the other social sciences. It is a philosophy that attempts to answer the basic questions of life and living, which include the nature of anxiety, despair, grief, loneliness, isolation, and social instability. Existentialism is a philosophy that is based on the "assumption that we are all free and therefore responsible for our choices and actions" (Corey, 2009, p. 132). Rather than focusing on death, existentialism focuses on living and the challenges all people face as they live inauthentic lives rather than lives focused on creativity and the love we all seek for self and others. By focusing on living, existential counselors seek to help individuals and those with whom they have relationships to focus on developing meaning and purpose for their lives out of the nothingness that life presents to each of us. The key idea is that the client's ability to take responsibility for his or her own actions and his or her own life rather than to place blame on various scapegoats is the essence of responsible living.

Heidegger (1962), considered one of the leaders of modern existential perspectives, believed that it is the way in which each individual lives that life has meaning and purpose. He noted that each person has the ability to live an inauthentic life or an authentic life. The person who lives an *inauthentic life* lives by allowing the external world to define him or her both as an individual and in relation to the world around him or her. In contrast, the individual who lives an *authentic life* takes personal responsibility for the creation of his or her life activities and the consequences of those activities and does this in spite of the anxiety provoking nature of being responsible. In the words of Bugental (1965), "a person is authentic in the degree to which his [or her] being in the world is in accord with the givenness of his [or her] own nature and of the world" (pp. 31-32). Heidegger (1962) also pointed out that the individual living an authentic life is able to see his or her uniqueness and strives to become what the individual desires. Yalom (1980) described this as being able to identify one's self-creation and ultimately be able to bring about personal changes in response to ones uniqueness and desire to self-create. The end result is that each person who lives an authentic life is seeking the answer to what it means to exist rather than living a life in fear of death, which is at the core of anxiety.

PHILOSOPHICAL UNDERPINNINGS OF EXISTENTIAL COUNSELING

Existentialism does not have a concrete definition because of its philosophical nature and because the contributions to existential perspectives come from a wide and diverse group of people from different academic and professional disciplines and who had differ-

The Handbook of Educational Theories, pp. 473–480

ent views on the meaning of life and to the question, What does it mean to exist? Some of the key individuals who have influenced existential thought include: Søren Kierkegaard (1813-1855), Friedrich Nietzsche (1844-1900), Edmund Husserl (1859-1938), Martin Heidegger (1889-1976), Jean-Paul Sartre (1905-1980), Martin Buber (1878-1965), Ludwig Binswanger (1881-1966), Paul Tillich (1886-1965), Clemmont Vontress (Born 1930), Viktor Frankl (1905-1997), Rollo May (1909-1994), and Irvin Yalom (born 1931). Their contributions have helped to move existentialism and existential counseling forward. Significant contributions were made by Søren Kierkegaard (1954), who believed that individuals could best be understood by their emotional expressions and that the expression of love for one's self was necessary for the individual to express love for others; Irvin Yalom (1980), who developed one of the first and most comprehensive psychotherapeutic approaches using existentialism; Clemmont Vontress (1979), who expanded the use of existentialism to multicultural contexts; and Viktor Frankl (1959), who viewed existentialism as a therapeutic means to help individuals find meaning in life even in the face of great trauma and tragedy.

One of the key philosophical components of existential counseling is the ability to describe the basic tenants of human existence. Binswanger (1991) used three German words to describe three basic aspects of being human. First, the *Umwelt*, or physical world, represents the individual's relationship to the environment from which life sustaining resources are obtained. May and Yalom (1995) described the *Umwelt* as the biological world or the world around us. It is the relationship we have with the world we occupy. The second aspect of the human condition is the *Mitwelt* or the social environment. Vontress (2008) described the *Mitwelt* as a way of being that "protects, nourishes, socializes, and contributes to the individual's psychological well-being" (p. 143). Additionally, May and Yalom (1995) defined the *Mitwelt* as the world in which we interact with other human beings. It is the relationships we have with other people. The third concept identified by Binswanger (1991) was the *Eigenwelt* or the world of the self or the individual. This world "consists of each person's private thoughts, experiences, and uniqueness' (Vontress, 2008, p. 143). It can also be described as the world in which each individual has a relationship with himself or herself. It is the world in which the individual "presupposes self-awareness and self-relatedness" (May & Yalom, 1995, p. 265).

Existential therapy is viewed as a holistic approach to helping that includes all aspects of the individual. However, Binswanger's (1991) typology of the human condition did not include the spiritual aspects of the person. In an effort to address this exclusion, Emily van Deurzen-Smith (1988) added the *Uberwelt* to Binswanger's typology. The *Uberwelt* identifies the transcendent or spiritual world of the individual. It is more than religion because it represents the individuals ideal world. The individual is able to organize the physical, social, and personal worlds into one ideal world that leads to an individual philosophy or definition of life. These four aspects of the human condition or better identified as relationships are at the core of the individuals ability to develop meaning and purpose in life. Without the four healthy relationships, individuals are likely to live life with despair, hopelessness, and anxiety.

THEORETICAL DESCRIPTION

ASSUMPTIONS

Existential counseling focuses on understanding the ultimate concerns of life and how they intersect with the concept of being. Rollo May (1983) described being as the person's "pattern of potentialities" (p. 17) meaning that to be is to work to achieve the potential that one has to live in a manner that allows for the achievement of goals and to maximize the potential to make meaning and purpose in the lived experience and then establish and move toward new goals that focus on overcoming the fears that interfere with the ability to maximize those potentialities for meaning creation. Yalom (1980) focused his attention to being on describing the fears that can interfere with meaning and purpose creation and achievement.

THE ULTIMATE CONCERNS

Yalom (1980) believed that there exists an "existential dynamic effect" (p. 8) that leads to internal conflicts that bring about anxiety and moves people away from the ability to live meaningful and purposeful lives. Längle (2005) described these internal conflicts as "four fundamental conditions for fulfilled existence" (p. 6). He described them as "the world in its factuality and potentiality; life with its network of relationships and its feelings; 'being oneself': existing as a unique, autonomous person; and the future which we shape = our development through our activities" (p. 6). Yalom (1980) pointed out that "existential psychotherapy is a dynamic approach to therapy which focuses on concerns that are rooted in the individual's existence" (p. 5). The intersections of the four ultimate concerns are at the core of each individual's existence and provide the foundation for descriptions of each individual's definition of life's meaning and purpose and are at the root of existential conflict (Yalom, 1980). In a similar thought, Frankl (1969) suggested that "there is no psychotherapy without a theory of man [people] and a philosophy of life underlying it" (p. 15). The basic philosophy of life leads each individual to his or her fears. Yalom (1980) described these fears as the four ultimate concerns of living: death, freedom, isolation, and meaninglessness.

Death is presented as the first concern because it is something that is inescapable and will be faced at some point by every person. Yalom (1980) described the anxiety related to death as a core existential conflict because of the "tension between the awareness of the inevitability of death and the wish to continue to be" (p. 8). The focus was not so much on not wanting to die but on wanting to continue to live in the face of death and dying. Yalom (1980) stated that "the fear of death plays a major role in our internal experience; it haunts as does nothing else; it rumbles continuously under the surface; it is a dark, unsettling presence at the rim of consciousness" (p. 27). May and Yalom (1995) pointed out that "a core inner conflict is between awareness of inevitable death and the simultaneous wish to continue to live" (p. 273). From a counseling perspective, the problem involves helping clients learn to live authentic lives in the face of impending death.

The second ultimate concern is existential *freedom*. From an existential perspective, freedom is the absence of external structure (Yalom, 1980). The focus is on recognizing that the world we enter at birth is not clearly structured and that the individual is responsible for giving life structure. Yalom (1980) described freedom as having the ability to author ones world, to create a design to the lived experience, and to have the ability to make choices and be held accountable for the choices made. Additionally, each of us is held responsible for the actions taken in response to the choices we make. This concept focuses on the belief that we are not grounded by structure but instead life is a void or an abyss without meaning and purpose and that as individuals we have the freedom to provide our lives with the structure that then grounds our existence (Yalom, 1080). May (1953) defined freedom as the "capacity to take a hand in his [our] own development. It is our capacity to mold ourselves" (p. 138). Freedom is a concept that is universal and available regardless of culture or gender because it allows each individual the opportunity to define for himself or herself how he or she will experience the unstructured nature of living. According to May and Yalom (1995), existential freedom encompasses the idea that:

> the human being doe not enter and ultimately exit from a structured universe with a coherent, grand design. Freedom refers to the fact that the human being is responsible for and the author of his or her own world, own life design, own choices, and actions. (p. 274)

While the concept of freedom in and of itself is not necessarily anxiety provoking, when looked at from the perspective of personal responsibility and the responsibility to being willing to act on one's choices (Yalom, 1980), we can see the anxiety provoking nature of freedom. It is the idea that each individual is responsible for the world he or she makes. For existential counselors, working to help clients to become willing to accept that change is natural and that it is the responsibility to act upon the choices he or she faces that will bring about a resolution of anxiety is at the core of the counseling process. Clients often experience high levels of anxiety when they work to pass onto others the responsibility of acting on their choices rather than acting upon them themselves.

Existential isolation is the third ultimate concern. People often feel isolated from themselves and from other people. As was pointed out earlier, each of us are engaged in four different relationships that move us toward the creation of meaning and purpose in our lives. Isolation then moves us away from our relationships and steers us toward aloneness. Yalom (1980) identified three types of isolation that are of existential concern: interpersonal, intrapersonal, and existential. Interpersonal isolation is often referred to as loneliness and is the experiences and isolation from other people. Cultural factors can affect interpersonal isolation due to how our relationships are affected by culture. Cultural influences include the use of technology for primary communication, religious affiliations, the decline in associations with extended family, the lack of stable neighborhoods, and the changing demographics of our society. Counselors are challenged to find new and innovative ways to encourage individuals to increase their social interactions as a means to reduce interpersonal isolation. Yalom (1980) described intrapersonal isolation as the partitioning of oneself resulting in the exclusion of different painful thoughts from consciousness. Finally, Yalom (1980) identified the third type of isolation as existential isolation. This type of isolation involves being an individual and being separated from the world. It is the idea that you can be in a crowded room socializing and integrating with others and still feel alone. This is one of the major challenges counselors face; helping clients feel a part of the greater community of people. However, existential isolation is based on the reality that, no matter how close each of us becomes to another, there remains a final, unbridgeable gap; each of us enters existence alone and must depart from it alone (May & Yalom, 1995). This is what makes this concern such a challenge.

The final ultimate concern is *meaninglessness*. Vontress (2008) stated that "feeling that one's life has meaning is basic to being human" (p. 158). If each of us must first deal with our impending death, existential freedom, and our isolation from ourselves and others, then we must ask the question, how do we get meaning in life? Where does meaning come from? How can we create meaning? These questions are at the core of the concern of meaninglessness. May and Yalom (1980) pointed that each of us are born into a world that lacks meaning and purpose and that "in an unpatterned world an individual is actually unsettled and searches for a pattern, an explanation, a meaning of existence" (p. 276). May and Yalom also pointed out that we need meaning in life because the values we hold as individuals come from life's meaning: "Values provide us with a blueprint for life conduct; values tell us not only *why* we live but *how* we live" (p. 276). They suggest that each individual experiences anxiety as she or he attempts to find meaning in a meaningless world. In the words of Frankl (1984),

> The meaning of life differs from man to man, from day to day and from hour to hour. What matters, therefore, is not the meaning of life in general but rather the specific meaning of a person's life at a given moment. (pp. 130-131)

The above descriptions of the four ultimate concerns can leave us with a sad and dark view of existence. We may see that life is hopeless and without merit. However, Längle (2005) gives us hope in his comparison of the ultimate concerns with the "fundamental conditions for fulfilled existence" (p. 6) and our fight for existence,

> Groundlessness implies the world with its supporting structures; death means having a life with growth and temporality; loneliness arises from the uniqueness of each person; and meaning relates to a contextual understanding of one's own existence and of one's activities which are directed towards a worthwhile future. (p. 6)

This view of existentialism and the ultimate dilemmas each individual faces places an optimistic perspective on living and existence. It is a hopeful perspective and implies that it is not death that creates anxiety it is living.

ANXIETY

Anxiety serves to "protect us from dangers that threaten ... our existence or values we identify with existence" (May, 1977, p. 363). Thus, anxiety is a normal reaction to the perceived dangers to our sense of being. It is our being confronted with nonbeing (May, 1977) and an intense feeling of apprehension and tension. May and Yalom (1995) described two types of anxiety: normal anxiety and neurotic anxiety.

Faced with the challenge of being or nonbeing the individual seeks ways to live authentically facing the daily issues of existence and anxiety. "Anxiety arises from our personal need to survive, to preserve our being, and to assert our being" (May & Yalom, 1995, p. 264). Through the day to day process of surviving we encounter normal anxiety and use our existing coping skills and neurotic anxiety where we lack coping skills.

Normal anxiety has three characteristics: (a) it is appropriate to the situation, (b) it does not lead to repressed thoughts, and (c) it can lead to the developing of coping skills (May & Yalom, 1995). The individual is able to face impending death without becoming paralyzed and is able to find the root causes of his or her anxiety and is able to find solutions to the dilemma. In contrast, neurotic anxiety can leave one paralyzed and without hope.

Neurotic anxiety, "is not appropriate to the situation, ... is repressed, ... and is destructive, not constructive" (May & Yalom, 1995, p. 264). Vontress (2008) suggested that neurotic or existential anxiety stems from the challenges of living in an unpredictable world that confronts us with the death, freedom, and choice. Corey (2009) pointed out that existential counselors see existential anxiety as outside of the consciousness of the individual. Through therapy, counselors are able to help clients gain insight into the causes of their existential anxiety so that they can identify the choices they have when facing that anxiety. The goal is not to rid oneself of all anxiety; rather, it is to learn how to cope with anxiety in the normal process of living.

THE EXISTENTIAL COUNSELING PROCESS

Existential counselors seek to help clients to identify their beliefs about life and living. They focus on the development of a relationship that can be viewed as collaborative and one in which both the client and counselor will be changed through the process of facing life (Corey, 2009). The focus is not on the past but instead on the present and how the client views himself or herself in present circumstances.

THE RELATIONSHIP

Vontress (2008) described several characteristics endemic to the counselor-client relationship: (a) two individuals striving to be authentic, (b) recognizes the responsibility each has to the other, (c) both share the same or similar Umwelt (environment) and Mitwelt (social environment or system), and (d) they both exert influence upon the other. "I-Thou reflects the spiritual nature of the existential counselor-client working relationship" (Vontress, 2008, p. 159). Through the relationship, "existential psychotherapy provides the forum for the challenge of encounter with self, other, and world: a broadening of possibilities over and above symptomatic cure" (Mendelowitz & Schneider, 2008, p. 310). According to Mendelowitz and Schneider (2008), the most important aspect of the existential approach to counseling is the relationship where the counselor serves as a guide. The relationship is the place where clients can experience caring and friendship and move toward meaning creation.

Goals

Bugental (1990) identified three primary goals for existential counseling: (a) to help clients see their inauthentic actions during the therapeutic process and how that my impact their sense of living in daily life, (b) to assist clients with the challenge of facing normal and neurotic anxiety, and (c) assisting clients with the ability to define themselves in relationship to themselves, others, and the world around them. According to Mendelowitz and Schneider (2008), another goal of existential counseling involves helping clients come to terms with the neurosis in their lives, to get stuck clients moving toward a healthier existence. They go on to note that "it can also lead to an awareness of one's own inner resources in coexisting with the world, with its tribulations and challenges" (p. 314). Corey (2009) pointed out that the primary goal of existential counseling is to help clients see that they have choices that they did not recognize prior to counseling.

Techniques

Existential counseling is a technique neutral process of helping. May (1964) suggested that placing too much emphasis on the use of techniques could lead counselors to miss the life story of the client. The emphasis in counseling is on gaining insight into the clients' world. "Existential psychotherapists prefer to be thought of as philosophical companions, not as people who repair psyches" (Vontress, 2008, p. 161). The view is that the client and counselor are on a journey together seeking to understand the world of the client.

Counseling Process

"What differentiates existential therapists from other therapists is their overarching philosophical attitude toward human existence. Their focus is on the Dasein, the human being and the environments that influence the personal journey" (Vontress, 2008, p. 162). Vontress pointed out that through the development of a therapeutic relationship, existential counselors work alongside clients to find solutions to the clients' problems, which are believed to be found within the client. The Socratic dialogue is used to help clients explore their inner world, without imposing "knowledge, advice, and direction" (Vontress, 2008, p. 161). May and Yalom (1995) noted that the process of counseling involves helping clients explore areas in which they avoid responsibility and helping the client to become aware of those instances. This new awareness allows the client to develop new ways of being personally responsible. Listening is a key to the process of counseling because it allows the counselor to gain clear insights into the clients' struggles (Mendelowitz & Schneider, 2008).

Like other counseling theories, existential counseling can be viewed as a process that often passes through different phases. It is important that we remember that because existentialism and existential counseling is philosophical based, a step wise way of processing client issues existentially is in most cases avoided. The focus should be on creating a relationship and then exploring the client's phenomenological world. However, to aid in the process of learning to become an existential counselor, Corey (2009) put forth a process of existential counseling. In the first phase, clients identify and clarify their basic assumptions of the world and their relationships. The focus is on discovering ones values, morals, beliefs, assumptions and all other aspects of the person that affect their perceptions of their world. There is an effort to help the client overcome the need to blame problems on external sources. The focus is on learning what role the client plays in the creation of the problems that result in inauthentic living. During the second or middle phase "clients are encouraged to more fully examine the source and authority of their present value system" (Corey, 2009, p. 151). Corey also pointed out that during this phase clients are able to gain new insights and begin the process of restructuring their lives including their values and attitudes. During the final phase, clients put into action the things they have learned about themselves. The focus shifts to helping clients apply what was learned in the counseling session to life outside counseling. Through this process, clients learn to create their own meaning and purpose to their life experiences.

Validation of the Theory Across Cultures, Ethnicities, and Genders

Because existential theory is multidisciplinary and there is no one comprehensive description of the philosophy that is largely accepted by the majority of existential therapists and counselors, it is difficult to identify research that directly validates the constructs of existential theory (Sousa, 2004). There are a wide variety of studies available that demonstrate the usefulness of the theory; however, "contemporary advocates of existential therapy draw on different aspects of Heidegger's work and in differing degrees" (Daitz, 2011, p. 140).

It is common to see existential theory described in most theory and abnormal psychology textbooks as a humanistic approach to counseling. Burston (2003) compared existentialism to humanism and identified several areas of convergence. First, suffering caused by the problems clients encounter present an opportunity to assist the client in a collaborative exploration leading to the elucidation and restoration of meaning that was lost in the process of coping with inauthentic living. Second, both existential therapy and humanistic therapy helps clients author and experience self-determination as they develop character and coping strategies for authentic living. Finally, both perspectives focus on the phenomenological world view of the client as being central to meaning and purpose making. The duality of these approaches points to their belief that each person is the author of his or her life and not predetermined.

Rather than studies designed to specifically validate the constructs of existential counseling and psychotherapy, studies have been conducted looking at the efficacy of using psychotherapy with different populations. Three examples of the application of existential psychotherapeutic principles are presented here. First, Suri (2010) applied the concepts of existential psychotherapy to working with the elderly and demonstrated the efficacy of exploring presence, spirituality, and meaning. Second, Taylor and Nanney (2011) applied the Hideggerian concepts of existentialism to multiracial individuals as means of gaining insight into the existential themes of being multiracial in a race conscious society. Finally, Crabtree (2009) used existentialism to gain existential insight to sexual identity particularly as it relates to gays and lesbians. These and other studies demonstrate the validity of using existential therapeutic approaches when working with a wide cross section of individuals.

MULTICULTURAL APPLICATION

Vontress (1979) described the need for a "philosophical orientation that enables counselors to transcend culture" (p. 117). He proposed that existentialism was a means by which counseling professionals could "discontinue their preoccupation with analyzing cultural differences and concentrate instead on the commonality of people" (p. 117). Vontress noted that by focusing on the clients Umwelt, Mitwelt, and Eigenwelt the concepts of race, ethnicity, and culture could be overcome and that counselors could become effective in cross-cultural therapy. Vontress (1985) also pointed out that existentialism takes a global view of human existence and "transcends cultural and national boundaries" (p. 207). Corey (2009) suggested that there are several strengths when using existential counseling in cross-cultural counseling. First, he noted that existential counseling allows counselors to examine social and cultural conditioning. Second, clients can explore their individual perspective of existential freedom and discover the internal limits that each client places on the freedom. From that point, client can be encouraged to identify choices and take responsibility for enacting choices that can lead to life with a greater sense of existential freedom. Finally, Corey pointed out that existential therapy is an international philosophy and is not bound by geographical definitions therefore allowing for its use with individuals from around the world.

EXISTENTIAL QUESTIONNAIRES

Research using instruments based on existential practices are limited and have not received widespread use. However, efforts to understand the existential qualities of life have been developed and are continuing to be developed. One of the first instruments developed to assess neurosis as defined by Viktor Frankl was the *Purpose in Life Test* (Crumbaugh & Maholick, 1996). Frankl (1969) believed that what led to anxiety and was the basis for individuals seeking counseling was the lack of having a clear purpose in life and living, which was manifested by boredom and the lack of meaning in personal existence. This early instrument had be used in subsequent research and has proved to be a helpful tool for counselors to use when helping clients who are exploring what life means and how they can find purpose in life.

The Existential Loneliness Questionnaire (Mayers, Khoo, & Svartberg, 2002), was developed to assess existential loneliness. The questionnaire consists of 22 items that are internally consistent and performed well in measuring the construct existential loneliness. Existential loneliness moves beyond the experience of not having someone to love and toward the idea that the lonely individual seeks to grasp meaning in the face of life's impermanence, the dread, despair, and anguish of human freedom, and the inevitability of death. lonely individual faces death not as the consequence of living but as the bane of lived experiences. Understanding the depth of loneliness experienced by the individual client can provide insight into the counseling needs of the client.

Existentialists often seek to understand how individuals are effected the many relationships they become involved in during the course of their lived experiences. One of the important relationships to existential is the marital dyad. Charny and Asineli (1996) developed the Existential/Dialectical Marital Questionnaire to assess marital functioning in the areas of family management, companionship, relationship and communication, attraction and sexuality, and parenting. They also used this instrument to assess five areas of the marital relationship: competence, commitment, respect, power, and closeness. By gaining insight into the way married couples experience the strengths and weaknesses as well as the contradictions and tensions experienced in all relationships, counselors are to gain increased insights into the experiences of the couple and are able to help the couple explore the nature of their relationship and the meaning and purpose of the relationship. Through this understanding the counselor and the couple can explore the nature of the relationship and work to overcome obstacles the couple may be facing.

USE AND APPLICATION OF THE THEORY

Existential therapy has been applied to counseling in a many different ways. Corey (2009) described the use of existential counseling in brief therapy. Corey stated that existential therapy could "focus clients on significant areas such as assuming personal responsibility, making a commitment to deciding and acting, and expanding their awareness of their current situation" (p. 153). Existential therapy can be used in a time limited fashion that encourages the client to be active in the therapy process (Strasser & Strasser, 1997). Langdridge (2006) expanded the work of Strasser and Strasser and applied the principles of existential therapy to solution focused therapy. Through the use of the solution focused approach, counselors are able to incorporate elements of the client's past, present, and future in a time limited manner and still retain the flavor of an existential approach.

Corey (2009) also posited that existential therapy can be effectively used in group counseling. According to van Deurzen (2002), existential group counseling could lead clients to (a) gaining the ability to become honest in their communications about themselves, (b) gain the ability to see their world in relation to themselves (Eigenwelt), others (Mitwelt), and the world around or environment (Umwelt), and (c) gaining greater insight into the creation of meaning and purpose to present and future living. Yalom (2005) put forth a comprehensive look at the use of existential therapy in his book *The Theory and Practice of Group Psychotherapy*. With this work, existential therapy has gained foothold in the counseling profession and has had a major influence on the development of group therapy. Yalom (2005) identified the therapeutic factors of group counseling and they have become the foundation for effective group practice and development.

CRITIQUES OF THE THEORY

Existentialists focus on meaning and purpose creation and understanding the phenomenological perspectives of their clients. Little attention is paid to the use of techniques because the counseling wants to stay in the moment with each client. Corey (2009) noted that a major limitation of existential therapy is its lack of a "systematic statement of the principles and practices of psychotherapy. Langdridge (2006) also pointed out that this is a limitation of the practice when trying to apply existential therapy to other therapeutic modalities. Because of the lack of a coherent description of existential therapy, it has been difficult for researchers to conduct research demonstrating the efficacy of the therapy (Corey, 2009). Mendelowitz and Schneider (2008) suggested that there are limits to the use of existential therapy because there are no clear answers to the ultimate concerns. The ultimate concerns can be faced but not conquered.

Vontress (2008) identified four limitations in the use of existential therapy. First, existentialism is often viewed as Eurocentric and lacking use in cross-cultural counseling. Second, existential concepts are often difficult to describe and viewed as complicated thus turning away many counselors whose clients could benefit from existential therapy. Third, Existentialists frown upon the use of techniques if they are viewed as overshadowing the client's story and problems. Finally, many counseling professionals view existential therapy as only beneficial to the well educated.

Finally, van Deurzen (2002) noted that the challenge with becoming an effective existential counselor lies in the process of becoming trained. Counselors need to be mature in their own development, have a wide variety of life experiences, and be willing to experience training over an extended period of time. Existential counselors need to be well read and find learning as the key to understanding the human condition.

CONCLUSION

Existential counseling focuses on the Dasein or the human being. It takes a holistic look based on relationships with self, others, the world around, and the spiritual. Through these relationships clients are able to gain insights into the fours ultimate concerns of life, death, freedom, isolation, and meaninglessness that bring about anxiety. Through the counselor-client relationship, clients are able to explore their inner lives and move toward a life that has greater meaning and purpose. In the words of Clemmont Vontress (2008), "when applied therapeutically, existentialism offers hope for the hopeless" (p. 145).

REFERENCES

Binswanger, L. (1991). Existential analysis and psychotherapy. In J. Ehrenwald (Ed.), *The history of psychotherapy* (pp. 374-379). Northvale, NJ: Aronson.

Bugental, J. F. (1965). *The search for authenticity: An existential-analytic approach to psychotherapy.* New York, NY: Holt, Rinehart and Winston.

Bugental, J. F. T. (1990). Existential-humanistic psychotherapy. In J. K. Zeig & W. M. Munion (Eds.), *What is psychotherapy?*

Contemporary perspectives (pp. 189-193). San Francisco, CA: Jossey-Bass.
Burston, D. (2004). Existentialism, humanism, and psychotherapy. *Existential Analysis, 14*, 309-319.
Charny, I. W., & Asineli, S. (1996). A validity study of existential/dialectical marital questionnaire [EDMQ]: A psychometric questionnaire for assessing marital interaction. *Contemporary Family Therapy, 18*, 41-59.
Corey, G. (2009). *Theory and practice of counseling and psychotherapy* (8th ed.). Belmont, CA: Thomson.
Crabtree, C. (2009). Rethinking sexual identity. *Existential Analysis, 20*, 248-261.
Crumbaugh, J. C., & Maholick, L. T. (1996). An experimental study in existentialism: The psychometric approach to Frankl's concept of noogenic neurosis. *Journal of Clinical Psychology, 20*, 200-207.
Daitz, L. (2011). Understanding, truth or resolve? Considering the 'aim' of existential psychotherapy and the approaches of van Deurzen and Spinelli. *Existential Analysis, 22*, 140-149.
Frankl, V. E. (1969). *The will to meaning: Foundations and applications of logotherapy.* New York, NY: Penguin Books.
Frankl, V. E. (1984). *Man's search for meaning.* Boston, MA; Washington Square Press.
Heidegger, M. (1962). *Being and time* (J. Macquarrie & E. Robinson, Trans.). New York, NY, Basic Books.
Kierkegaard, S. (1954). *Fear and trembling and the sickness unto death.* Garden City, NY: Doubleday.
Langdridge, D. (2006). Solution focused therapy: A way forward for brief existential therapy? *Existential Analysis, 17*, 359-370.
Längle, A. The search for meaning in life and the existential fundamental motivations. *Existential Analysis, 16*, 2-14.
May, R. (1953). *Man's search for himself.* New York, NY: Norton
May, R. (1964). Existential basis of psychotherapy. In M. Friedman (Ed.), *The worlds of existentialism: A critical reader* (pp. 440-462). Chicago, IL: University of Chicago Press.
May, R. (1977). *The meaning of anxiety* (Rev. Ed.). New York, NY: Norton.
May, R. (1983). *The discovery of being: Writings in existential psychology.* New York, NY: Norton.
May, R., & Yalom, I. (1995). Existential psychotherapy. In R. J. Corsisni & D. Wedding (Eds.), *Current psychotherapies* (5th ed., pp. 262-292). Itasca, IL: F.E. Peacock.
Mayers, A. M., Khoo, S. T., & Svartberg, M. (2002). The existential loneliness questionnaire: Background, development, and preliminary findings. *Journal of Clinical Psychology, 58*(9), 1183-1193.
Mendelowitz, E., & Schneider, K. (2008). Existential psychotherapy. In R. J. Corsini & D. Wedding (Eds.), *Current psychotherapies* (8th ed., pp. 295-327). Itasca, IL; F.E. Peacock.
Suri, R. (2010). Working with the elderly: An existential humanistic approach. *Journal of Humanistic Psychology, 50*, 175-186.
Sousa, D. (2004). A short note underlying reflection on psychotherapy research. *Existential Analysis, 15*, 194-202.
Strasser, F., & Strasser, A. (1997). *Existential time-limited therapy: The wheel of existence.* Chichester, West Sussex, England: Wiley.
Taylor, M. J., & Nanney, J. T. (2011). An existential gaze at multiracial self-concept: implications for psychotherapy. *Journal of Humanistic Psychology, 51*, 195-215.
van Deurzen, E. (2002). *Existential counseling and psychotherapy in practice* (2nd ed.). London, England: SAGE.
van Deurzen-Smith, E. (1988). *Existential counseling in practice.* Beverly Hills, CA: SAGE.
Vontress, C. E. (1979). Cross-cultural counseling: An existential approach. *Personnel and Guidance Journal, 58*, 117-122.
Vontress, C. E. (1985). Existentialism as a cross-cultural counseling modality. In P. Pederson (Ed.), *Handbook of cross-cultural counseling and therapy* (pp. 207-212). Westport, CT: Greenwood Press.
Vontress, C. E. (2008). Origins and evolution of existential therapy. In J. Frew & M. D. Spiegler (Eds.), *Contemporary psychotherapies for a diverse world* (pp. 141-176). Boston, MA: Lahaska Press.
Yalom, I. D. (1980). *Existential psychotherapy.* New York, NY: Basic Books.
Yalom, I. D. (2005). *The theory and practice of group psychotherapy* (5th ed.). New York, NY: Basic Books.

Author Contact Information: Richard C. Henriksen, Jr., PhD, LPC-S, ACS, NCC, Associate Professor of Education, Sam Houston State University, College of Education, Department of Educational Leadership and Counseling, Box 2119, Huntsville, TX 77341-2119. Telephone: 936-294-1209. E-mail: rch008@shswu.edu

CHAPTER 40

Reality Therapy

Robert E. Wubbolding
The Center for Reality Therapy

In many ways reality therapy and its underlying theory represent a revolution in educational thinking. While some of the principles are common to other theories reality therapy is at odds with the widespread popular notion that educators can control students' behavior by force. W. Glasser (1990) asserts that the use of coercion has created many educational problems such as the failure of students to derive maximum benefit from their education. On the other hand, he states, "The persuasive, lead management approach (reality therapy) is not known well enough" (p. 29). Implementing its principles means not merely using innovative ways to teach students and manage the educational enterprise. It includes a redefinition and re-evaluation of such concepts as human motivation, the role of choice and personal responsibility, how to deal with problem behaviors and abandoning punishment (except in obviously heinous cases). It also embraces the adoption of a delivery system for intervening and communicating with students and with all stake holders, as well as employing the same formulation for organizational development and for staff supervision. It even means infusing choice theory into an already glutted curriculum, teaching the same ideas and skills to parents, initiating and maintaining an ongoing training program for all staff. For this purpose, teaching materials are available for conducting brief lessons aimed at helping students satisfy their needs thereby enabling educators to utilize their classroom time more effectively (C. Glasser, 1996a, 1996b, 2008). And finally, a credibility enhancing component consists in an unflagging commitment to researching the effectiveness of this entire effort.

Choice Theory

Choice theory explains human motivation as a need system driving human behavior. All behavior is an attempt to satisfy five motivators or needs common to all human beings: survival or self-preservation, love and belonging, power or inner control, freedom or independence, and fun or enjoyment. These five motivators are universal, general and genetic (W. Glasser, 1998). All human beings regardless of race, ethnicity, age or other characteristics have a need to continue living, to connect with other people, to feel a sense of inner control or achievement, to be autonomous—at least to some degree, and to have fun. Schools provide an exemplary setting for developing a sense of belonging, gaining a sense of accomplishment or power, making choices and enjoying life.

According to choice theory the human mind operates similar to a thermostat. This mechanism controls its environment by maintaining the room temperature at a specific level. It sends a signal to its air conditioning or heating unit to generate "behaviors" designed to impact the world outside of itself. By analogy the thermostat is said to have a goal: to create a match between the desired temperature and the current room temperature. Similarly, when human needs are unmet the mind sends a signal to the behavioral system to make choices for the purpose of impacting the world, that is, molding the world so that the person sees the external world as congruent with his/her desires. These desires are specific wants related to each generic need.

Human needs are general or generic. They are not therefore specific as are wants. Wants are precise desires such as mental pictures of people, ideas, possessions and situations that satisfy the general universal needs. The collection of pictures is referred to as a "mental picture album" or "quality world" because its content consists only of need-satisfying and therefore quality images (W. Glasser, 1998, 2005).

Though it is impossible to prove, W. Glasser (2005) believes that the need system is genetic. And yet, whether the practitioner sees the needs as genetic or learned makes little difference in the implementation

The Handbook of Educational Theories, pp. 481–489

of the principles of reality therapy. For operational purposes the need system, as well as the quality world, are best seen as a series of motivators for human behavior.

The goal of the educator is to be part of the students' quality worlds. The delivery system of reality therapy assists teachers and administrators to be seen as helpful, as caring, as competent and as ethical. If the educator can establish and develop healthy relationships with students, they are more inclined to put into their quality worlds the content taught by the firm, fair and friendly (approachable) teacher. They are more likely to insert into their quality worlds ethical and altruistic behaviors if they see the adults modeling such behavior.

An interesting sidelight is that the control system can be fooled. If a match is held under the thermometer the thermostat will read an inaccurate message and will mistakenly adjust the room temperature. For instance, when students abuse drugs or alcohol they can have a superficial and temporary sense of wellbeing. They often make such conclusions as: they are well functioning individuals; everybody else has a problem and they are being unfairly harassed; their needs are satisfied effectively or would be satisfied if people would "leave us alone." The role of the educator using reality therapy is to help students see that lighting a match under the thermostat, that is, abusing substances, only fools their motivational and behavioral systems and results in greater pain.

ORIGIN

Though reality therapy is understood as based on choice theory, it has a separate origin. In the 1950s and 1960s, William Glasser worked in a mental hospital under the supervision of his professor G. L. Harrington. They both believed that patients should be held responsible for their behavior and need not be victimized by their debilitating conditions. Out of this experience Glasser formulated the original principles of reality therapy. He asserted that mental health is a consequence of effective need satisfaction (1960). In 1965 he published his more controversial book *Reality Therapy: A New Approach to Psychiatry* insisting that clients' outside environments such as parental influence or past personal history need not determine their current choices. He stated that the role of the helper is to assist people to see a range of options previously unimagined. As he lectured on reality therapy it became clear that the most receptive audiences were educators, counselors, social workers and psychologists. Because teachers readily saw the value in holding students responsible he was asked to train educators in the Los Angeles area schools. Based on this experience he published *Schools Without Failure* in 1968. Much later the organizational implications became clear (W. Glasser, 1990). Not only do teachers use reality therapy interventions in their classrooms, the entire philosophy of the efficacy of enhanced human relationships which is the result of the school wide use of reality therapy principles, creates a genuine learning community that is characterized by joy, self discipline and motivation to learn. The William Glasser Institute currently provides a training program for educators who wish to implement the principles of reality therapy. After the school has achieved a high level of quality they declare themselves a "Glasser Quality School." Only after reaching the following levels of quality do they qualify for this title (W. Glasser, 2008):

1. Relationships are based upon trust and respect, and all discipline problems, not incidents, have been eliminated.
2. Total learning competency is stressed and an evaluation that is below competence or what is now a "B" has been eliminated. All "schooling" as defined by Dr. William Glasser has been replaced by useful education.
3. All students do some quality work each year that is significantly beyond competence. All such work receives an A grade or higher, such as an A+.
4. Students and staff are taught to use choice theory in their lives and in their work in school. Parents are encouraged to participate in study groups to become familiar with the ideas of Dr. William Glasser.
5. Staff, students, parents and administrators view the school as a joyful place.

Throughout the quality journey students learn the art of self-evaluating their work, their behavior and their relationships. Wubbolding (2007) states, "They evaluate their own behavior and seek ways to improve it" (p. 255). He emphasizes that belonging has eliminated fears, threats and external control. "Human relationships continuously improve and lead management (reality therapy) has replaced boss management (coercion)" (p. 255).

Clearly the journey to quality is gradual and sometimes arduous. Nevertheless, relying on a deep commitment to the school as well as to choice theory and the practice of reality therapy provides a need satisfying experience for teachers. When they see students behaving more appropriately, making fewer harmful choices, improving grades and enhancing their interpersonal relationships with other students, staff and parents they lessen their own frustrations and see their own careers and parenting as more worth while.

The roots of choice theory lie in a cybernetic theory of brain functioning originally called control theory or control system theory (MacColl, 1946; Powers, 1973; Wiener, 1948, 1952). This theory postulates that the human mind attempts to maneuver the external world with behaviors that originate within the organism.

W. Glasser (1981, 1985, 1998) adapted the theory to therapy and education and changed the name of his version of it to *choice theory.* Wubbolding (2000) states,

> Because of the additions made by Dr. Glasser, he changed the name of the theory to choice theory in 1996 to fit its clinical and educational use and because of its emphasis on human choice. These changes are more than mere accessories or appendages. (p. 11)

Differences Between Choice Theory and Reality Therapy

Individuals learning reality therapy often ask for clarification regarding the differences between choice theory and reality therapy. The phrase reality therapy is often used to include both the delivery system—reality therapy as well as the underlying theory—choice theory. Nevertheless there are differences. Choice theory explains human behavior and describes its purpose: to satisfy quality world pictures or wants thereby fulfilling the needs for survival, belonging, power or inner control, freedom and fun. It furthermore includes the foundational principle that people choose most of their behaviors. Consequently, it answers questions that focus on why people do what they do, where behavior originates and the purpose of behavioral choices. More specifically, human beings choose behaviors especially actions to gain something from the world around them. This "something" is not merely an external reward. It is the internal satisfaction resulting from need fulfillment.

Recently, Wubbolding and Brickell (2005) have added another purpose for human behavior. They state that behavior is an attempt to communicate with the world around us. Our behavior sends a message or a signal to our surroundings. For instance, an angry, resistant and acting out adolescent attempts to communicate the message, "I want to be left alone to do as I please." The practical implication for the educator who seeks to communicate with the student is addressed by the skillful implementation of choice theory through the use of reality therapy. They add: "In fact, it might be said that our actions *are* a language, [that is], a means of communication and the primary vehicle for maintaining or destroying human relationships" (p. 19). In speaking of the language component of human actions W. Glasser & C. Glasser (1999) state, "Choice theory language helps us to work out problems with one another; external control language increases them" (p. viii).

In summary, choice theory explains why and how people generate behavior. Reality therapy is the "how to," the delivery system, the train or the vehicle that delivers the product. In schools it is more properly called lead management. Wubbolding and Brickell (2007) state

> It operationalizes, applies and conveys choice theory principles to clients, students, parents, educators, employees or any other consumer of services. Choice theory focuses on knowledge of how the mind works. Reality therapy focuses on skills for dealing with human minds, [that is], behaviors or choices generated by human beings. (p. 29)

Reality Therapy in Practice

The delivery system is divided into two major components: environment or atmosphere in a classroom or throughout the school and procedures or specific interventions used in a classroom or on an organizational basis. Linked together these components express reality therapy as a pedagogical tool and are called the "Cycle of Counseling, Coaching, Managing and Supervision" (see Figure 40.1) (Wubbolding, 2010).

Environment

Educators seeking to implement reality therapy, i.e., lead management, create a noncoercive, friendly but not permissive atmosphere in the classroom. This is accomplished by establishing clear rules or boundaries, consequences and by avoiding toxic behaviors. Teachers make every attempt to shun *a*rguing with students, *b*laming or *b*elittling, *c*riticizing, *demeaning,* colluding with *e*xcuses, instilling *f*ear, and *g*iving up either on the students or on the reality therapy/lead management system expressed as the Cycle of Counseling, Coaching, Managing and Supervision.

A popular but mistaken notion is that "caring" equates with permissiveness. As noted in Figure 40.1, creating the proper learning atmosphere (tonic behaviors) means setting boundaries (F) and utilizing consequences (K). All human behavior, that is, choices, has consequences, either positive or negative and sometimes neutral. In education, when students learn how to study effectively they generally have the favorable consequence of success. Failure to learn course material results in the negative consequence of failure or, in a Glasser Quality School, the requirement of repeating or redoing the assignment until at least some quality is achieved.

Students demonstrating a lack of discipline or respect for people around them are subject to consequences that are often undesired. Such consequences are usually spelled out early in the school year before crises or incidents arise. At the same time, the range of consequences for rule violations should be limited and can be determined in individual schools and classrooms. And yet it is not possible to identify specific con-

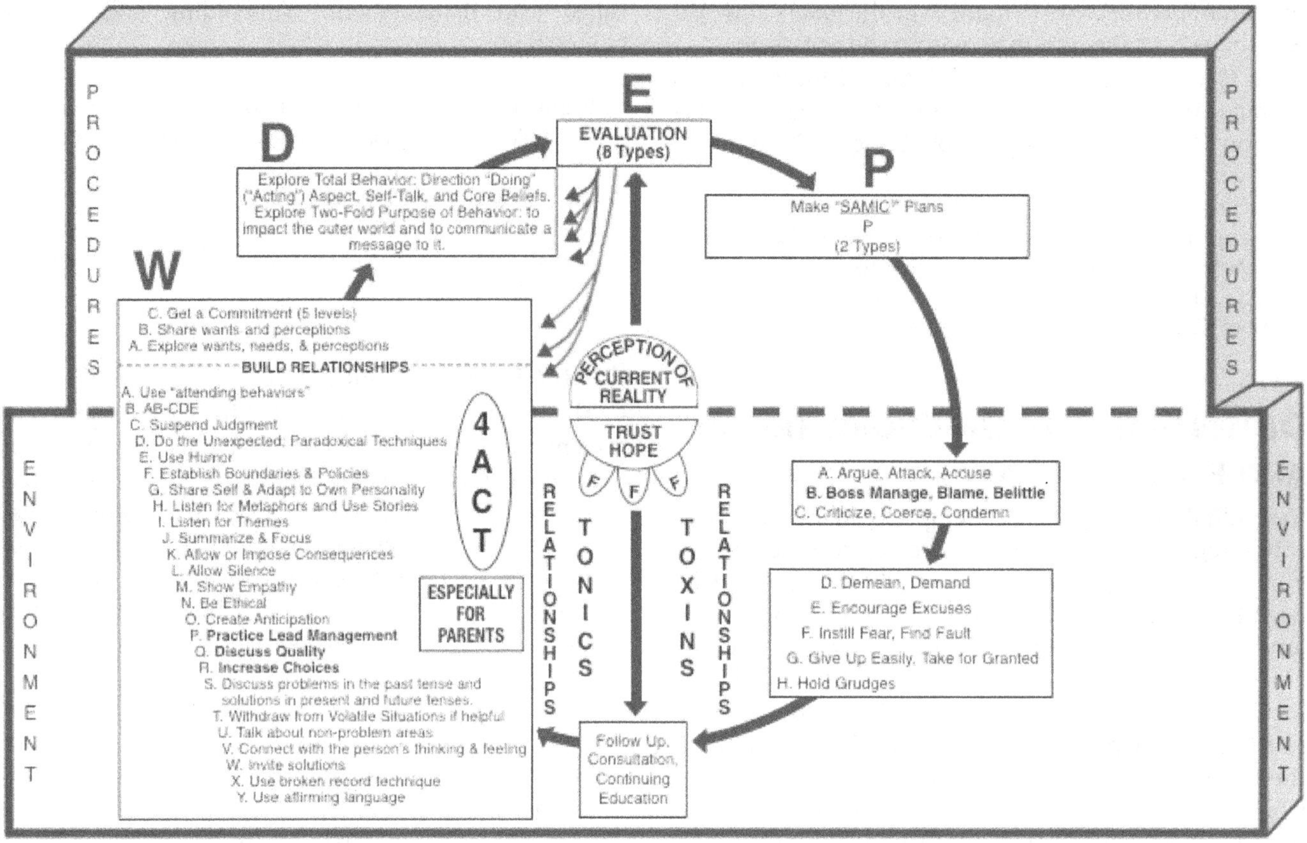

Source: Wubbolding (1986).

Figure 40.1. Cycle of counseling, coaching, managing and supervising (Figure continues on next page).

sequences for every ingenious rule violation that emerges from the creativity of students.

On the other hand, punishment is often vindictive, imposed with harsh words and often not promulgated to students in advance. Consequences for infractions are calmly administered with such statements as, "You chose to fight and now you will not be part of the group today." "You flunked the test and your grade is ...." The attitude of the adult is analogous of the basketball referee who calls the fifth foul on a player. Five fouls results in sitting on the bench for the remainder of the game. The fans might become punitive. The coach might be angry. But the referee is independent and neutral.

Consequences are connected to the infraction. On the other hand, corporal punishment is punitive because it is unconnected with a previous behavior. Disrespect shown to a teacher has little connection with the imposition of swats. Repairing the damage in the relationship is, in some way, consequential. In mending the connection between teacher and student the student learns how to communicate more effectively rather than learning that the person who is more powerful can use a bigger stick to get his/her way.

PROCEDURES

More characteristic of reality therapy are specific interventions grouped into four general categories summarized by the acronym WDEP with each letter representing a cluster of concepts and skills.

W represents exploring the quality worlds of students by helping them define what they want from school, from the classroom, from teachers and from various specific lessons. Most importantly, they learn to define what they want from themselves or how hard they are willing to work at achieving their goals. Wubbolding (2000, 2011a) listed five levels of commitment: (1) "I don't want to be here, leave me alone" (this represents no commitment). (2) "I'd like the outcome but not the effort." (3) "I'll try, I might." (4) "I will do my best." (5) "I will do whatever it takes." Also included in the *W* are questions and explorations about perceptions especially the perceived locus of control. Students in the classroom and staff in their own meetings distinguish between the controllable and the uncontrollable. From the point of view of reality therapy human beings have control *only* over their own behavior.

Learning that reality therapy is not an innovative way to control other people or to maneuver them into

SUMMARY DESCRIPTION OF THE "CYCLE OF COUNSELING, COACHING, MANAGING, AND SUPERVISING"

The Cycle is explained in detail in books by Robert E. Wubbolding:
Employee Motivation, 1996; *Reality Therapy for the 21st Century*, 2000
A Set of Directions for Putting and Keeping Yourself Together, 2001
Reality Therapy in APA's *Theories of Psychotherapy Series*, 2010

Introduction:

The Cycle consists of two general concepts: Environment conducive to change and Procedures more explicitly designed to facilitate change. This chart is intended to be a **brief** summary. The ideas are designed to be used with employees, students, clients as well as in other human relationships.

Relationship between Environment & Procedures:

1. As indicated in the chart, the Environment is the foundation upon which the effective use of Procedures is based.
2. Though it is **usually** necessary to establish a safe, friendly Environment before change can occur, the "Cycle" can be entered at any point. Thus, the use of the cycle does **not** occur in lock step fashion.
3. Building a relationship implies establishing and maintaining a professional relationship. Methods for accomplishing this comprise some efforts on the part of the helper that are Environmental and others that are Procedural.

ENVIRONMENT:

Relationship Tonics: a close relationship is built on TRUST and HOPE through friendliness, firmness and fairness.

A. Using Attending Behaviors: Eye contact, posture, effective listening skills.
B. AB = "Always **B**e . . ." **C**onsistent, **C**ourteous & **C**alm, **D**etermined that there is hope for improvement, **E**nthusiastic (Think Positively).
C. Suspend Judgment: View behaviors from a low level of perception, i.e., acceptance is crucial.
D. Do the Unexpected: Use paradoxical techniques as appropriate; Reframing and Prescribing.
E. Use Humor: Help them fulfill need for fun within reasonable boundaries.
F. Establish boundaries: the relationship is professional.

4 A C T
- Affirm feelings
- Accept
- Show affection
- Action consequences
- Conversation (WDEP)
- Time together

G. Share Self: Self-disclosure within limits is helpful; adapt to own personal style.
H. Listen for Metaphors: Use their figures of speech and provide other ones. Use stories.
I. Listen to Themes. Listen for behaviors that have helped, value judgements, etc.
J. Summarize & Focus: Tie together what they say and focus on them rather than on "Real World."
K. Allow or Impose Consequences: Within reason, they should be responsible for their own behavior.
L. Allow Silence: This allows them to think, as well as to take responsibility.
M. Show Empathy: Perceive as does the person being helped.
N. Be Ethical: Study Codes of Ethics and their applications, e.g., how to handle suicide threats or violent tendencies.
O. Create anticipation and communication hope. People should be taught that something good will happen if they are willing to work.
P. **Practice lead management, e.g., democracy in determining rules.**
Q. **Discuss quality.**
R. **Increases choices.**
S. Discuss problems in the past tense, solutions in present and future tenses.
T. Withdraw from volatile situations if helpful.
U. Talk about non-problem areas.
V. Connect with the person's thinking and feeling.
W. Invite solutions.
X. Use broken record technique.
Y. Use affirming language.

Relationship Toxins:

Argue, **Boss Manage,** or Blame, Criticize or Coerce, Demean, Encourage Excuses, Instill Fear, or Give up easily, Hold Grudges.

Rather, stress what they **can** control, accept them as they are, and keep the confidence that they can develop more effective behaviors. Also, continue to us "WDEP" system without giving up.

Follow Up, Consult, and Continue Education:

Determine a way for them to report back, talk to another professional person when necessary, and maintain ongoing program of professional growth.

PROCEDURES:

WDEP

Build Relationships:

A. Explore **W**ants, Needs & Perceptions: Discuss picture album or quality world, i.e., set goals, fulfilled & unfulfilled pictures, needs, viewpoints and "locus of control."
B. Share Wants & Perceptions: Tell what you want from them and how you view their situations, behaviors, wants, etc. This procedure is secondary to A above.
C. Get a Commitment: Help them solidify their desire to find more effective behaviors.

Explore Total Behavior:

Help them examine the **D**irection of their lives, as well as specifics of how they spend their time. Discuss core beliefs and ineffective & effective self talk. Explore two-fold purpose of behavior: to impact the outer world and to communicate a message to it.

Evaluation – The Cornerstone of Procedures.

Help them evaluate their behavioral direction, specific behaviors as well as wants, perceptions and commitments. Evaluate own behavior through follow-up, consultation and continued education.

Make **P**lans: Help them change direction of their lives.

Effective plans are **S**imple, **A**ttainable, **M**easurable, **I**mmediate, **C**onsistent, **C**ontrolled by the planner, and **C**ommitted to. The helper is **P**ersistent. Plans can be linear or paradoxical.

Note: The "Cycle" describes specific guidelines & skills. Effective implementation requires the artful integration of the guidelines & skills contained under Environment & Procedures in a spontaneous & natural manner geared to the personality of the helper. This requires training, practices & supervision. Also, the word "client" is used for anyone receiving help: student, employee, family member, etc.

For more information contact:

Robert E. Wubbolding, EdD, Director
Center for Reality Therapy
7672 Montgomery Road, #383
Cincinnati, Ohio 45236
(513) 561-1911 • FAX (513) 561-3568
E-mail: wubsrt@fuse.net • www.realitytherapywub.com

The Center for Reality Therapy provides counseling, consultation, training and supervision including applications to schools, agencies, hospitals, companies and other institutions. The Center is a provider for many organizations which award continuing education units.

Figure 40.1. (Continued.)

doing "the right thing" is the most difficult part of applying the WDEP system. However, it is a creative system for structuring relationships, creating a positive learning environment and thereby extending our hands to students, parents and other stakeholders. This effective extension facilitates more efficacious choices. In short, it is based on the ability of educators to regulate their own behavior.

D stands for direction and doing. Teachers help students focus on their own behaviors by asking them how they spend their time, what specifically happened when they faced a disagreeable situation such as a major or minor altercation. The school faculty discusses the overall direction of the school or their specific classrooms. Are they on a quality journey and how do they identify benchmarks along the way?

E represents self-*e*valuation, the cornerstone in the practice of reality therapy/lead management. Students and faculty examine whether their behavior is helping or hurting them, whether it is congruent with the goals of the classroom or the mission of the school. Students are asked to conduct a searching self-assessment of whether their actions are within the rules of the classroom or school. Subject to self-evaluation also is the realistic attainability of wants or goals. A student who communicates the message that "I want to be left alone" is asked to explore the realistic attainability of such a want.

Evaluating the quality of relationships constitutes the core of self-evaluation. This principle is based on the assumption that the success of most endeavors in education or in life is based on the quality of human relationships. Individuals succeed in families, business, athletics and in every aspect of life if they function as a team characterized by harmonious relationships. Developing and maintaining satisfying relationships is an ongoing effort. It is analogous to rowing a canoe upstream. It requires sustained effort and continuous monitoring. Students, staff and all who wish to implement the principles of reality therapy continually evaluate how they are interacting with others: peers, subordinates, supervisors and the public at large. This self-evaluation involves a major paradigm shift. For staff the focus moves from "How can I get them to do what I want them to do?" to "How can I improve my relationship with the students?" Student learning and better behavior become a by-product of satisfactory human relationships.

In summary, the effective use of reality therapy has as its cornerstone the use of self-evaluation. People do not change behavior until they decide that their current behaviors are unhelpful. Wubbolding (2009a) states,

> It is emphasized because many people do not conduct this searching inner evaluation. Have you ever misplaced your car keys? Did you ever look repeatedly in the same place, your pocket s, purse, between the seats in the car, etc., with the knowledge that the keys were not there? It seems clear that human beings sometimes generate behaviors which are not effective. (p. 20)

Consequently, both educator and student are well served by the ability and skill in self evaluating their choices, their wants and their perceptions.

P highlights the significance of effective planning. With the help of the teacher, students formulate SAMIC plans. The plan should be:

S = simple, uncomplicated;

A = attainable, realistically doable;

M = measurable, precise, answers the question "when will you do it?";

I = immediate, carried out as soon as possible; and

C = controlled by the planner, not dependent on the behavior or others.

The saying, "To fail to plan is to plan to fail" is integral to the WDEP system of reality therapy. The objective of the reality therapy process is the formulation and subsequent follow through of efficacious planning leading to the fulfillment of the goal: the satisfaction of wants and needs.

In summary, the reality therapy system provides interventions for classroom use, counseling, managing and all relationships connected to education (W. Glasser, 1990; Glasser & Wubbolding, 1997; Wubbolding, 2009b, 2011b). Its long-term application leads to a successful educational experience for students and staff, positive community living and enhanced mental health.

VALIDATION

A major criticism of choice theory and reality therapy occasionally presented, is that there has been a dearth of studies validating its use. For many years this criticism has been obsolete and even false. The effectiveness of reality therapy as a counseling system applied to severe mental health issues was shown from the very beginning of Glasser's work in a mental hospital. Along with his supervisor G. L. Harrington, Glasser applied the initial and seminal techniques of reality therapy to mental patients resulting in the release of large numbers of patients with very few relapsing (Glasser & Wubbolding, 1995). Greene and Uroff (1991) described the application of reality therapy to the Apollo Continuation School in California for at-risk secondary students. They reported that after several years student attendance improved 78%. Weekly drug use declined from 80% to 20% and the number of students on probation decreased from 30% to 5%.

In 1997 the first Glasser Quality School, Huntington Woods in Michigan, witnessed the mainstreaming of all but two students from special education and the near cessation of vandalism. According to Ludwig and Mentley (1997), students judged the quality of their own work and figured out ways to improve it within boundaries established by the teacher.

During the 1994-95 school year, Dr. Glasser worked with his wife Carleen in Schwab School, a public junior high inner city school in Ohio. By the end of summer school 147 out of 170 students who had failed regularly and were over age were promoted to high school. They also demonstrated a 20% increase in their math scores.

Hinton and Warnke (Personal communication, May 15, 2010) investigated the effect of choice theory and the WDEP system with high school freshman having approximately the same grade point average. They divided the class into three teams each with the same number of students. Among the results was a 69.5% reduction in office referrals for offenses in the choice theory/WDEP group. While the study is still in progress, results seem to indicate the positive influence of reality therapy on students.

Passaro, Moon, Wiest, and Wong (2004) studied the effect of reality therapy with emotionally disturbed students who also qualified as attention deficit hyperactive disorder and oppositional defiant disorder. The authors state,

> Results were measured in three domains: changes in daily behavioral ratings over the school year; changes in the numbers of out of school suspensions compared to the previous academic year; and changes in the amount of time students participated in general education courses, within the current school year. (p. 508)

Students' daily behavioral rating improved by an average of 42%. There was an increase in their overall participation in general education courses by over 62% and a 12% decrease in out of school suspensions. In summarizing the study Passaro (Personal communication, June 23, 2009) states, "Reality therapy is widely regarded by professionals working with oppositional and defiant youth as one of a few highly effective methodologies that can be successfully employed with this treatment resistant population."

Generalizability Across Cultures

Reality therapy has been taught on every continent except Antarctica. Indigenous instructors teach choice theory in Japan, Korea, Singapore, India, South Africa, Colombia, Kuwait, as well as throughout Europe and North America.

More specifically reality therapy has been extensively researched in Korea. Kim and Hwang (2006) state,

> Since 1986 reality therapy and choice theory have been introduced to the counseling and business fields in Korea followed with much research ... it is embraced by professionals, including counselors, educators, psychologists, psychiatrists, social workers and others, as well as parents. (p. 25)

Similarly, Jazimin Jusoh, Mahmud, and Mohd Ishak (2008) cite several research studies in the Malaysian language and state, "These works are testimony that reality therapy, when applied in suitable modules, can be beneficial for clients of various backgrounds" (p. 5).

Moreover, evidence of the universality of reality therapy and its relevance to many ethnic and cultural communities is the existence of 16 reality therapy institutes outside of the United States from Korea to South Africa to Bosnia-Herzegovina. Each year representatives from around the world attend the international conference of the William Glasser Institute and describe how they are adapting reality therapy to their respective cultures. Moreover, individual countries sponsor their own conferences (Wubbolding, 2005). Finally, the European Association for Reality Therapy sponsors the international conference every four years (Wubbolding, 2009c).

Critiques of the Theory

Even though reality therapy has been shown to apply cross culturally several authors find that it contains a short coming in that it does not fully take into consideration environmental forces faced by minorities. According to several authors, the emphasis on internal control, choices and the explicit rejection of a habitual victimhood world view presents a problem to people whose environment prevents them from getting what they want (Corey, 2009). Murdock (2004) states,

> Reality therapy does not seem to take these phenomena into account. Glasser would probably say that going along with the crowd is more a result of a failure to wake up and make choices than to any magical power of social forces. (p. 273)

Wubbolding (2011b) adds that because reality therapy contains an explicit delivery system (WDEP), adults might mistakenly believe that it is a step-by-step mechanical system designed for correcting other people's behavior by imposing their own values on them.

A final limitation consists in language used to convey concepts and methodology. Free of most technical language reality therapy seems simplistic to the casual observer. It describes human motivation as conscious and current. It speaks of needs and wants, choices and perceptions. It shuns discussion about the subconscious. Individuals practicing reality therapy in school settings believe that students are responsible for their behavior and cannot blame external forces such as early childhood, intrapsychic conflicts, environment or society in general. And yet, far from superficial, human options can be very complicated in that choice can be impacted but not removed by external influences as well as by internal influences such as emotions. Experience has shown that the effective implementation of the WDEP system requires study, practice, feedback and supervision, as well as the more personal qualities of empathy, compassion and understanding.

INSTRUMENTATION

Instruments unique to reality therapy that demonstrate both reliability and validity have been lacking. On the other hand, numerous teacher and counselor made instruments have been published such as "Pete's Pathogram" (Peterson & Truscott, 1988). This instrument along with Brickell's Choice Theory Needs Satisfaction Rating scale (2008) are self-reporting measures focusing on the strength of love and belonging, power, freedom, fun and survival. Clients or students rate the intensity of their inner need satisfaction. The need for belonging measures the self-perception of the degree of satisfaction of relationships ranging from intimacy through friendships and acquaintanceships. The self-perception of power focuses on feelings ranging from unworthiness to a high sense of inner control. The self-perception of freedom indicates a sense of being trapped versus unrestricted self-determination. Fun measures a perception ranging from boredom to activities that are absorbing and stimulating. And finally, the clients and students are asked to judge the satisfaction of their need for survival or whether their physiological needs are met to a lesser or greater degree.

SUMMARY

Reality therapy began in a mental hospital and a correctional institution in the 1950s and 1960s. Because of the success in these institutions, William Glasser, MD, the founder, then applied the ideas to education, management and supervision and family life. Originally formulated as eight steps and now described as the WDEP system, the principles of reality therapy are now based on a theory of brain functioning choice theory derived from the world of cybernetics. The William Glasser Institute sponsors a certification program providing a credential "Choice Theory/Reality Therapy Certified." Individuals seeking more training in this specialty can contact the following organizations:

The William Glasser Institute
22024 Lassen Street, Suite 118
Chatsworth CA 91311
USA
Tel: 1-800-899-0688
E-mail: wginst@wglasser.com
Website: www.wglasser.com

or

Center for Reality Therapy
7672 Montgomery Road #383
Cincinnati OH 45236
USA
Tel: 1-513-561-1911
E-Mail: wubsrt@fuse.net
Website: www.realitytherapywub.com

REFERENCES

Brickell, J. (2008). *Choice theory needs satisfaction rating scale.* Romsey, England: Centre for Reality Therapy.

Corey, G. (2009). *Theory and practice of counseling and psychotherapy.* Belmont, CA: Thomson Brooks/Cole.

Glasser, C. (1996a). *My quality world workbook.* Los Angeles, CA: William Glasser.

Glasser, C. (1996b). *The quality world activity set.* Los Angeles, CA: William Glasser.

Glasser, C. (2008). *Glasser class meeting kit.* Los Angeles, CA: William Glasser.

Glasser, W. (1960). *Mental health or mental illness.* New York, NY: HarperCollins.

Glasser, W. (1965) *Reality therapy.* New York, NY: HarperCollins.

Glasser, W. (1968). *Schools without failure.* New York, NY: Harper-Collins.

Glasser, W. (1981). *Stations of the mind.* New York, NY: HarperCollins.

Glasser, W. (1985). *Control theory.* New York, NY: HarperCollins.

Glasser, W. (1990). *The quality school.* New York, NY: HarperCollins.

Glasser, W. (1998) *Choice theory.* New York, NY: HarperCollins.

Glasser, W. (2005). *Defining mental health as a public health issue.* Chatsworth, CA: The William Glasser Institute.

Glasser, W. (2008). *Criteria for a quality school.* Retrieved from http://wglasser.com/index.php?option=com_content&task=view&id=15&Itemid=30

Glasser, W., & Glasser, C. (1999). *The language of choice theory.* New York, NY: HarperCollins.

Glasser, W., & Wubbolding, R. (1995). Reality therapy. In R. Corsini (Ed.), *Current psychotherapies* (pp. 293-321). Itasca, IL: Peacock.

Glasser, W., & Wubbolding R. (1997). Beyond blame: A lead management approach. *Reaching Today's Youth, 1*(4), 40-42.

Greene, B., & Uroff, S. (1991). Quality education and at risk students. *Journal of Reality Therapy, 10*(2), 3-11.

Jazimin Jusoh, A., Mahmud, Z., & Mohd Ishak, N. (2008). The patterns of reality therapy usage among Malaysian counselors. *International Journal of Reality Therapy, 28*(1), 5-14.

Kim, R. -I., & Hwang, M. (2006). A meta-analysis of reality therapy and choice theory group programs for self-esteem and locus of control in Korea. *International Journal of Choice Theory, 1*(1), 25-30.

Ludwig, S., & Mentley, K. (1997). *Quality is the key.* Wyoming, MI: KWM Educational Services.

MacColl, L. A. (1946). *Fundamental theory of servo-mechanism,* New York, NY: Van Nostrand.

Murdock, N. (2004). *Theories of counseling and psychotherapy: A case approach.* Upper Saddle River, NJ: Merrill/Prentice Hall.

Passaro, P., Moon, M., Wiest, D., & Wong, E. (2004). A model for school psychology practice: Addressing the needs of students with emotional and behavioral challenges through the use of an in-school support room and reality therapy. *Adolescence, 39*(155), 503-517.

Peterson, A. V., & Truscott, J. (1988). Pete's pathogram: Quantifying the genetic needs. *Journal of Reality Therapy, 8*(1), 22-32.

Powers, W. (1973). *Behavior: the control of perception.* New York, NY: Aldine.

Wiener, N. (1948). *Cybernetics.* New York, NY: John Wiley & Sons.

Wiener, N. (1952). *Nonlinear problems in random theory.* New York, NY: The Technology Press of MIT and John Wiley & Sons.

Wubbolding, R. (2000). *Reality therapy for the 21st century.* Philadelphia, PA: Brunner Routledge.

Wubbolding, R. (2005). *Cultural adaptations of reality therapy* (CD). Cincinnati, OH: Center for Reality Therapy.

Wubbolding, R. (2007). Glasser quality school. *Group Dynamics: Theory, Research, and Practice, 11*(4), 253-261.

Wubbolding, R. (2009a). *Reality therapy training.* Cincinnati, OH: Center for Reality Therapy.

Wubbolding, R. (2009b). Applying reality therapy approaches in schools. In R. Christner & R. Mennuti (Eds.), *School-based mental health* (pp. 225-250). New York, NY: Routledge.

Wubbolding, R. (2009c). 2029: Headline or footnote? Mainstream or backwater? Cutting edge or trailing edge? Included or excluded from the professional world? *International Journal of Reality Therapy, 29*(1), 26-29.

Wubbolding, R. E. (2010). *Reality therapy.* Washington, DC: American Psychological Association.

Wubbolding, R. (2011a). Reality therapy/choice theory. In D. Capuzzi & D. Gross (Eds.), *Counseling and psychotherapy* Alexandria, VA: American Counseling Association.

Wubbolding, R. (2011b). *Reality therapy: Theories of psychotherapy series.* Washington, DC: American Psychological Association.

Wubbolding R., & Brickell, J. (2005). Purpose of behavior: Language and levels of commitment. *International Journal of Reality Therapy, 25*(1), 39-41.

Wubbolding R. & Brickell, J. (2007). Frequently asked questions and brief answers: Part I, *International Journal of Reality Therapy, 27*(1), 29-30.

Author Contact Information: Robert E. Wubbolding, EdD, Senior Faculty for the William Glasser Institute in Los Angeles, professor emeritus, Xavier University, Director, The Center for Reality Therapy in Cincinnati, OH, 7672 Montgomery Road #383, Cincinnati, OH 45236. Phone: 513-561-1911.

CHAPTER 41

Person-Centered Counseling

Jeffrey M. Sullivan
Sam Houston State University

Hayley Stulmaker
University of North Texas

Carl Rogers developed person-centered counseling in the United States roughly between the years of 1940-1990 (Raskin, Rogers, & Witty, 2008). The dominant theories of psychotherapy of that time emphasized interpretation of the client by the therapist (i.e., psychoanalysis) or the molding of behavioral patterns (i.e., operant conditioning). In contrast, Rogers viewed directive and interpretive models of therapy as potentially disavowing the phenomenal and essentially human experience of the client (Rogers, 1968). Rogers deeply believed that only the client truly knows him or herself. Rogers' believed that all people are essentially trustworthy and good, and this positive view of human nature shaped the development of person-centered counseling tremendously.

Rogers maintained that allowing the client to lead in the counseling relationship frees the client to develop toward his or her full potential. According to Rogers, "Only in the individual can alternative courses of action be most deeply and consciously tested as to their enriching or destructive consequences" (Rogers, 1989, p. 266). Rogers emphasized the reflective process of the counselor to foster self-awareness and generate positive self-regard for the client. He based the role of the person-centered counselor upon the deep trust that all people to possess everything necessary within them to grow and develop. Rogers stressed, "that the client has the right to select his own life goals, even though these may be at variance with the goals that the counselor might choose for him" (Rogers, 1942, p. 86).

Rogers' belief in the fundamentally positive and forward moving direction of all humans places him among the leaders of the humanistic movement in counseling. Rogers developed person-centered therapy through three major phases. The first, *nondirective* phase focused largely on explaining how nondirective counselors differed from directive counselors. It was at this time that Rogers wrote of the directive counseling relationship, "An understated implication is that the counselor is superior to the client, since the latter is assumed to be incapable of assuming full responsibility for choosing his own goal" (Rogers, 1942, p. 86). Conversely, for Rogers, every individual has the right to be psychologically independent and the right to maintain that integrity. The 1951 publication of *Client Centered Therapy* marked the beginning of the second phase of Rogers' theory development. Rogers shifted his focus away from the counselor and to the client. During this period, Rogers began to emphasize the client role as "the responsible agent whose nature provided the rationale for the counselor's therapeutic conduct" (Fall, Holden, & Marquis, 2010). It was during this middle phase that Rogers developed a formalized theory of development and a structured therapeutic approach that emphasized the client's phenomenological experience as leading the counseling relationship. Rogers later expanded the basic therapeutic principles of client-centered counseling beyond the counseling relationship into all other areas of human relationship. This generalization of client-centered principles marked the third and final evolution of Roger's theory, *person-centered theory.*

PHILOSOPHICAL UNDERPINNINGS

Rogers (1957) maintained that he developed person-centered therapy largely through his own professional work with clients. His training as a therapist began in

The Handbook of Educational Theories, pp. 491–501

New York City where he enrolled in several psychology classes while attending the Union Theological Seminary. Rogers soon transferred to Teachers College at Columbia University to pursue further study in psychology where he was exposed to a "contradictory mixture of Freudian, scientific, and progressive educational thinking" (Rogers & Sanford, 1985, p. 1374; as cited in Raskin et al., 2008). This training included testing, measurement, diagnostic interviewing, and interpretative treatment (Raskin et al., 2008). After attending Teachers College, Rogers worked for 12 years at a psychoanalytically oriented child-guidance center in Rochester, New York as a practicing psychologist. This experience served as among the most powerful influences on Rogers in developing person-centered therapy. Rogers found that the training he had received was not effective in helping his clients. On his own, Rogers altered his approach and began listening and following the client's lead rather than assume a role as the expert, an approach he found more effective in helping his clients. This began a period for Rogers in which he began to explore and formalize the experiences and principles that would shape the development of person-centered counseling.

While Rogers cites his own experiences as contributing to the development of person-centered counseling, he does acknowledge the influence of Otto Rank (1884-1939) in shaping his view of the counseling relationship. Rogers' exposure to the views of Rank occurred while Rogers attended a 3-day seminar in Rochester. Rank articulated a belief in the creative power of each person, importance of self-acceptance, and focus of the client as being imperative to the therapeutic process. Rank shunned the notion that therapists impose a particular theory upon a client, suggesting that such practice will never address what is wrong with *this* client (Rychlak, 1981). Rank went on to say, "In each separate case it is necessary to create, as it were, a theory or technique made for the occasion without trying to carry over this individual solution to the next case" (Rank, 1968, p. 3; as cited in Rychlak, 1981, p. 575). For Rank, it is the uniqueness and spontaneity of the counseling relationship that helps the client rather than the theory espoused the counselor (Raskin et al., 2008). Rogers also developed a professional relationship with a Rankian trained social worker, Elizabeth Davis (Raskin et al, 2008). It was this relationship to which Rogers remarked, "I first got the notion of responding almost entirely to the feelings being expressed. What later came to be called reflection of feeling sprang from my contact with her" (Rogers & Haigh, 1983, p. 7; as cited in Raskin et al., 2008, p. 148).

In addition to the influence of Rank, Rogers' belief that all people possess a subjective, or phenomenological, experience is quite consistent with that of Edmund Husserl (1859-1938). Husserl, often called the father of phenomenology, wrote of the phenomenological experience that the only way for a science of psychology to understand anything is to see it from person's subjective view. According to Husserl, individuals cannot hope to find an independent reality that exists objectively. Objectivity is merely the agreement people reach through subjective experience. Similarly, For Rogers, a person cannot have an experience outside of their phenomenological reality. Moreover, because a person cannot have experience anything beyond his or her own phenomenological perception, Rogers also maintained that the phenomenological experience of another person could never be known fully. It could only be approximated. Therefore, each individual is the only one capable of truly understanding his or her own phenomenological experience.

Another important philosophical precursor to Rogers was Kurt Lewin (1890-1947), a gestalt theorist whose primary contribution was the development *field theory.* In field theory, Lewin described a *phenomenal field* that constructs a person's subjective reality. According to Lewin, people's focus constantly shifts between what he termed the *figure* and *ground.* The ground represents the full experience of a person in a given moment, while the figure represents the point of interest for the person within the ground. Imagine a colorful painting with swirling colors of blue, red, and gold. When focusing on the blue of the painting, the red and gold blend into the background and the blue stands apart. The blue represents the figure, the focus of the individual, while the red and gold represent the ground, the background that helps shape and define the blue on the painting. Shifting the figure from blue to will cause the blue and gold to blend into the background. Thus, the meaning of the colors of the painting changes depending upon the focus of the observer.

Lewin believed that people experience all things this same way—a subjectively determined point of interest, the figure, shapes perception of the whole experience, the ground. For Lewin, the figure's relationship to the ground changes according to the needs of the person. Consequently, human behavior is directed toward self-determined goals defined by the perceived relationship between the field and ground. People thus set their own expectations of what they consider success or failure depending upon the figure/ground relationship of their subjective experience. The relationship of figure and ground resonates throughout Rogers' presentation of person-centered theory and, as will be demonstrated, is central in defining Rogers' view of human development.

THEORETICAL DESCRIPTION

ASSUMPTIONS

The key assumption for Rogers in developing person-centered therapy is that all people possess intrinsic motivation to grow toward their full potential (Raskin et al., 2008). This belief stemmed from his view that within all of nature there is an innate tendency, which Rogers termed the *formative tendency* (Rogers, 1980), toward growth, development, and enhancement of the organism (a term used by Rogers to describe all living things). The formative tendency represents a creative force that motivates organisms to move beyond mere survival and toward greater complexity, harmony, and wholeness. Because people possess and experience this formative tendency, they also possess within them the necessary and sufficient resources needed to achieve healthy functioning and to become what Rogers termed a fully functioning person (Rogers, 1957b). Consequently, Rogers considered all humans to be at a fundamental level good, trustworthy, and forward moving in development.

EARLY DEVELOPMENT

Rogers believed that all people possess an *actualizing tendency* to grow, to heal, and to develop to one's full potential (Rogers, 1951, 1957b). For Rogers, the actualizing tendency is intrinsic and innate. It is not learned or developed. It manifests in the infant as particular needs, such as basic survival needs (i.e., sustenance, sleep), as well as needs for love, affection, aggression, and affiliation. Some needs of the actualizing tendency are innate and present at birth. However, people also possess an innate ability to develop additional needs through learned experience. The actualizing tendency motivates the infant to seek ways to meet these needs. The actualizing tendency also motivates the infant to seek order and consistency in the environment (Rogers, 1957b).

Rogers selected the term *tendency* carefully to indicate a general movement toward higher levels of development rather than a striving to meet particular developmental goals. The less forceful nature of the actualizing tendency means that people are more likely to stray from it. In fact, Rogers believed that all people deviate from their actualizing tendency at some point. However, Rogers stressed that the actualizing tendency is always present and accessible. The only way to destroy the actualizing tendency is to destroy the organism.

Rogers also believed that people possess an innate ability to accurately symbolize sensory phenomena in the environment and visceral experiences within the body. For the developing infant, the perception of experience interacts with the actualizing tendency to motivate the infant to meet particular needs generated by the actualizing tendency. For instance, an infant experiencing a growling stomach will accurately symbolize this sensation as hunger. Because of the actualizing tendency, the infant will experience hunger as a need that must be satisfied.

The infant's actualizing tendency interacts with the infant's direct experience through what Rogers termed the *organismic valuing process.* Through the organismic valuing process, the infant possesses the innate capacity to determine whether an object or experience in the environment satisfies, thwarts, or neither satisfies or thwarts the needs of the actualizing tendency. For the infant experiencing hunger, the organismic valuing process allows the infant to recognize which objects in the environment will satisfy hunger. Through the organismic valuing process, the infant may recognize that milk satisfies the hunger need, while chewing on the corner of a blanket or sucking a thumb fail to satisfy the need.

Based upon how the infant values experiences to meet particular needs, the infant will move toward experiences perceived as satisfying a need and move away from experiences perceived as thwarting the satisfaction of a need. According to Rogers, "behavior is the goal-directed attempt of the organism to satisfy the need experienced needs for actualization in the reality as perceived" (Rogers, 1959, p. 244). Staying with the example of the poor, hungry infant, because the infant values milk as satisfying the hunger need, the infant, when hungry, may cry, grab at a bottle, and suck on the bottle to satisfy that need. However, the hungry infant may kick and pull away from mom if the bottle is removed before the hunger need is met.

The *organismic valuing process* also endows the infant with an *internal locus of evaluation.* The needs of the infant at a given moment determine the value the infant ascribes to a particular object or experience. For example, an infant desiring affection may smile and laugh when her mother lovingly picks her up. However, the same infant, when exhausted after a long day of being picked up by adoring relatives, may cry loudly when picked up in the same loving manner by her mother. In this moment, the infant is tired and in need of rest. The need of the infant, either for affection or rest, determines how she evaluates the same loving behavior. Thus, the organismic valuing process is fluid rather than fixed. The infant is an active agent in determining the value of objects or experiences in the environment and constantly evaluating them regarding their value in meeting or thwarting the actualizing tendency.

Over time, as the infant experiences success or failure in meeting needs, the infant receives feedback regarding the best way to meet needs as they emerge. For instance, an infant may initially cry to meet the need for affection, but find that her parents mistake her crying as wanting food, which misses the need for affection. Conversely, the infant finds that smiling often results in her being picked up, meeting her need for affection. According to Rogers, the infant will cry less for affection when her parents are close and smile instead, as smiling meets the need of child for affection from her parents. Thus, the feedback received by the infant regarding the success of past behaviors to achieve a desired outcome will help the infant adjust future behaviors. This feedback leads to an increasing awareness on the part of the infant as to which behaviors best meet the needs of the actualizing tendency.

In summary, the infant's actualizing tendency interacts with the infant's perceived experience to identify needs necessary for growth and development. Through the organismic valuing process, the infant determines which objects or experiences in the environment are most conducive to meeting these needs. The infant then organizes behavior to move toward objects and experiences perceived as satisfying a need or move away from objects and experiences perceived as thwarting a need. Feedback received by the infant will help the infant organize behaviors that are more effective in meeting the needs of the self-actualizing tendency.

During this early period of development, Rogers postulated that the infant perceives experiences in the body and environment directly. There is no distinction between experience and self. The infant's perception of reality *is* reality, so that when the infant experiences hunger, the infant literally is hunger. However, Roger's theorized that as part of the actualizing tendency, the infant will move toward a differentiation between self and environment, leading to the emergence of the infant's *self-concept.*

The Emerging Self-Concept

Just as the infant is able to symbolize experiences, such as symbolizing hunger as a need for food, the infant comes to symbolize a portion of individual experience into an *awareness of feeling* or an *awareness of being* (Rogers, 1957b). According to Rogers this experience is recognized as an *awareness of self.* Through interactions with the environment, particularly an environment composed of significant others, the infant becomes his or her own perceptual object, which Rogers termed the infant's *self-concept.* The self-concept represents an important psychological distinction between self and other. Prior to developing a self-concept, the infant experienced needs directly with no awareness of being distinct from the perceived environment. With an emerging serf-concept, the infant now perceives the self as someone experiencing the need. The infant has a distinct psychological identity. She now perceives herself as someone *who* experiences, someone *who* behaves.

Early in the development of the self-concept, the infant's self-concept is *congruent* with the infant's experience. Who the infant imagines herself to be is accurately experienced in the environment. However, as the infant's self-concept emerges, so too does the infant's *need for positive regard.* Rogers does not specify whether the need for positive regard is innate or learned, but Rogers believed it to be a universal experience. Through the need for positive regard, the infant experiences a need to feel accepted and valued by significant others, particularly primary caregivers. The infant's need for positive regard is strong and remains a powerful motivator throughout the lifespan. In fact, Rogers believed it to be as powerful, if not more so, then the actualizing tendency.

Rogers believed that significant others provide experiences that feed the child's need for positive regard. The child tries to attain positive regard by relinquishing the internalized locus of evaluation and converting it to an external process, an *external locus of evaluation.* By externalizing the locus of evaluation, the child learns to distrust her own experience and avoids using it to guide behavior. Instead, the child uses the opinions of others as a guide, which pulls her away from her actualizing tendency and limits her personal development (Rogers, 1959, 1964).

In seeking positive regard, the child experiences interactions from primary caregivers that range from complete *unconditional positive regard* (complete empathic understanding and acceptance of the child) to *conditional positive regard* (empathy and acceptance of the infant only if the child meets certain conditions). It is unlikely that caregivers are able to provide either condition absolutely. Rather caregivers provide varying degrees of either level of empathy and acceptance.

When caregivers provide conditional positive regard, they also communicate *conditions of worth,* particular expectations that the infant must meet to receive acceptance and feel valued. The child internalizes conditions of worth as part of the self-concept and gradually comes to believe that they must behave, feel, and think in certain ways to experience acceptance. If these conditions are not consistent with the child's actualizing tendency, the child will experience *incongruence* between the self-concept of the domain of experience. Rogers labeled this process *self-regard.* However, the more the child experiences from caregivers high levels of acceptance and empathy that are in accord with the child's self-concept, then the child manifests *unconditional self-regard,* a sense of being worthwhile no matter what experience comes along.

Healthy Versus Unhealthy Functioning

For Rogers, healthy functioning occurs when the person experiences higher levels of congruence between the self-concept and actual experience. The use of the organismic valuing process is the healthiest way to function because people are operating from an internal locus of evaluation. People using the organismic valuing process tend toward higher levels of congruence because their actual feelings match their awareness of their feelings. They are not influenced by conditions of worth and are able to trust their experience and live in the moment. They live in accord with their actualizing tendency.

When experiencing healthy functioning, the person experiences a heightened sense of integration. The person's perceived self matches perceived experiences in the environment. The more similar the perceived self and perceived experience, the more congruent the people will be. In this state of congruence, people are able to continuously evaluate their experience to create unique and adaptive behavior for each situation (Rogers, 1959). They are open to new experiences, flexible, and non defensive. Rogers termed this state of congruence the *fully functioning person* (Rogers, 1961a).

Unhealthy functioning occurs when people lose sight of their innate positive direction for growth, their *actualizing tendency*. With unhealthy functioning, people operate primarily out of their need for positive regard, seeking experiences that satisfy their internalized conditions of worth. They discount their own beliefs and values to gain positive regard from others. When the conditions of worth are not consistent with the actualizing tendency, people experience *incongruence* between the self-concept and perceived experience. People may create rigid ideas or perceptions about themselves based primarily on other people's beliefs. As people seek to conform to the perceived expectations of others, they may feel lost and alienated from themselves.

When experiencing incongruence, people also develop an *external locus of evaluation* that often leads to maladaptive behavior. Rather than organizing behavior to satisfy the actualizing tendency, people organize behaviors to satisfy the conditions of worth they perceive from others. Because people are trying to fulfill others' perceived expectations, their behavior often results in unrecognized, unclaimed, and unexpressed feelings. In addition, when operating through conditions of worth, people develop fixed values that are rarely examined and typically reside beyond self-awareness. People begin to perceive themselves in a way that is incongruent to the actualizing tendency, which they experience as feelings of anxiety, depression, and psychological tension. For Rogers, the greater the incongruence between the self and perceived experience, the more disorganized the behavior that will emerge (Rogers, 1961a, 1961b, 1964).

To move from unhealthy functioning to healthy functioning, the client needs to experience an environment that is free of conditions of worth. When a person experiences unconditional acceptance and empathic understanding from another person, they become aware of the incongruence between self and experience, which leads to greater awareness the actualizing tendency. Because all people possess a tendency to move toward actualizing their full potential, the actualizing tendency is always accessible. When reconnected with the actualizing tendency, the person will naturally tend toward living in a way that is congruent with the actualizing tendency and experience higher levels of freedom, as well as diminished levels of anxiety and psychological tension.

THE PERSON-CENTERED COUNSELING PROCESS

Roger's believed the sole purpose of the counseling was to provide the conditions necessary for clients to understand their own experience, develop self-awareness, and recognize internalized barriers impeding the actualizing tendency. According to Rogers, all people have the innate ability to understand themselves, change their self-concept and attitudes, and produce self-directed behavior. When people experience higher levels of congruence, they move toward a more constructive and complete development to enhance not only themselves, but also other members of society (Kutash & Wolf, 1986; Rogers, 1957a). In person-centered therapy, the most significant facilitator of change and factor in developing congruence is the relationship between counselor and client.

Essentially, the goal of counseling is for the clients to become the person they truly are. Clients create their goals, which ultimately encompass an understanding of themselves. Clients discontinue operating out of conditions of worth and strive toward self-actualization. They develop a freedom to make decisions, leaving behind the desire to please others. In reaching congruence, clients are able to take responsibility for their lives and become more complex human beings who are open to new experiences. They begin to trust others and accept themselves more fully (Rogers, 1961a).

THE NECESSARY AND SUFFICIENT CONDITIONS

Rogers (1957c) believed that there are six conditions that must be present over a period of time to produce therapeutic change. For Rogers, "if these six conditions exist and continue over a period of time, this is sufficient" (Rogers, 1957c, p. 221). Thus, the six conditions identified by Rogers are necessary and sufficient for producing positive psychological change for the client. No other conditions are needed. Rogers identified the six conditions as the following:

1. Two persons are in psychological contact.
2. The first person, the client, is in a state in incongruence, being vulnerable or anxious.
3. The second person, the therapist, is congruent in the relationship.
4. The therapist is experiencing unconditional positive regard toward the client.
5. The therapist is experiencing an empathic understanding of the client's internal frame of reference.
6. The client perceives, at least to a minimal degree, the unconditional positive regard of the client and the empathic understanding of the client.

The first of these conditions means that a relationship must be formed. There needs to be an awareness of both the client and counselor being in psychological contact with each other in order for this condition to be met. The relationship is the basis for the remaining five conditions. According to Rogers, "(t)he first condition of therapeutic change is such a simple one that perhaps it should be labeled an assumption or a precondition in order to set it apart from those that follow. Without it, the remaining items would have no meaning, and that is the reason for including it" (Rogers, 1957c, p. 222). For Rogers, this first condition is the only condition that is dichotomous, meaning that it either exists or does not exist. The remaining conditions may exist to varying degrees in the counseling relationship.

The second condition is that the client in the relationship needs to experience some form of incongruence. When clients enter therapy, there needs to be some discrepancy between their experience and self-concept, which creates a sense of vulnerability and susceptibility to anxiety within the client. A person needs to be in a state of distress and aware of being in that state in order to be helped.

The third, fourth, and fifth conditions represent the attitudes of the counselor toward the client. With the third condition, Rogers believed that the therapist needs to be in a state of congruence and genuineness with the client. Counselors need to be aware of themselves in the present moment and not present a façade. Although counselors' feelings toward clients are not always positive, they should be aware of these feelings, using them to creating immediacy within the therapeutic relationship (Rogers, 1957c).

With the fourth condition, the counselor also needs to experience unconditional positive regard for the client. Having unconditional positive regard for clients gives them permission to own their feelings and experiences while still feeling accepted. Experiencing unconditional positive regard creates an open environment for the client to move toward positive self-regard, congruence, and an internal locus of control (Rogers, 1957c). The counselor should always strive to accept the client unconditionally, which includes accepting the client's feelings and motivations to behave in certain ways. However, the client's behavior does not have to be accepted unconditionally. Roger's believed strongly that a person was more than their behaviors such that one could have unconditional positive regard for the person and not be accepting of particular behavior.

The fifth condition is that counselors express empathy with clients' experience and successfully communicates this understanding to the client. Counselors need to sense clients' feelings as if they were their own without losing themselves in the clients' emotions. When therapists have true feelings of empathy toward clients, they are able to communicate their understanding to the clients and help them feel truly understood and accepted for who they are (Rogers, 1957c).

The final condition is that the client needs to perceive counselor's empathy and unconditional positive regard. If the client does not feel accepted or understood, then those two conditions have technically not been met. Therefore, it is not enough for the counselor to experience unconditional positive regard and acceptance of the client. The counselor must successfully communicate these conditions to the client and the client must perceive them from the counselor. If the client and counselor successfully meet these six conditions, then these conditions are necessary and sufficient to produce personality change (Rogers, 1957c).

Resistance can occur on behalf of the therapist and the client. The main source of resistance results from the therapist being unable to meet one of the six therapeutic conditions. If the therapist incorrectly reflects to the client, resistance is likely to occur. Another form of resistance occurs when clients are directed to a place where they are unprepared to be. Most resistance can be avoided by allowing clients to lead while constantly ensuring that the six conditions are present (Rogers, 1957c).

In person-centered therapy, it is the clients' responsibility to direct sessions where they need them to go. They need to trust the therapist and feel comfortable enough to express their feelings in the relationship. When the client experiences the therapist as a part of the relationship, through that rapport the client experiences higher levels of congruence and genuineness.

Clients are also responsible for increasing their self-concept, self-regard, and internal locus of control (Rogers, 1959). The primary role of the counselor is to create an environment that allows for a therapeutic relationship to form within the parameters of the six conditions. The counselor takes on a nondirective role and goes along with clients on their counseling journey toward change. Unconditional positive regard, congruence and genuineness, and empathy are the three attitudes the counselor must possess in therapy to make it successful (Rogers, 1957c).

A person-centered counselor does not require techniques or specific treatment for therapy to be successful. For Rogers, counselors should avoid techniques and focus instead on building relationships with clients to bring about change (Elliott & Freire, 2007; Rogers, 1957c). Through the use of the basic skills of therapy (reflecting content, reflecting feelings, minimal encouragers, clarification, and active listening, coupled with empathy, unconditional positive regard, and congruence), the client is free to move toward self-actualization and congruence. The relationship between the counselor and client is the most important healing modality. Using these skills and meeting the conditions necessary and sufficient for change and will allow for clients to meet their goals (Elliott & Freire, 2007; Rogers, 1957c).

Validation of Person-Centered Theory

Person-centered theory has been researched and thoroughly scrutinized throughout the more than 60 years of its existence. Before Rogers's death, he was the primary publisher and creator of person-centered theory. He discouraged the formation of organizations and institutes because of the importance of individuality of the therapist in the therapeutic relationship. Therefore, after his death other person-centered therapists began publishing and forming organizations, increasing the prevalence and research base of person-centered theory in a wide variety of journals and publications. Currently, more than 200 organizations and training centers have been developed specifically for the propagation of person-centered theory (Kirschenbaum & Jourdan, 2005).

Many research studies have been conducted to determine the efficacy of person-centered theory through examining the core conditions and their impact on therapeutic outcome (e.g., Bergin & Suinn, 1975; Mitchell, Bozarth, & Krauft, 1977; Parloff, Waskow, & Wolfe, 1978). Instead of describing each research study's findings, it may be more meaningful to discuss several meta-analyses researchers have conducted on person-centered theory and the core conditions. Truax and Mitchell (1971) examined 14 studies that examined at the core conditions as measured through instruments such as the *Relationship Inventory* (Barrett-Lennard, 1962). They found 66 statistically significant correlations between positive outcome in therapy and core conditions while only one statistically negative correlation was found.

Orlinsky and Howard (1986) reviewed factors in process-outcome studies, such as empathic resonance, mutual affirmation, therapist role-investment, and overall quality of the relationship as measured by client observation of the therapeutic relationship. They also examined therapist and outside observer measures. Positive outcomes were found when using client perspectives, affirming Rogers's view that clients need to perceive and experience the conditions from the therapist in order for change to occur.

Sexton and Whiston (1994) reviewed 12 studies with similar results in regard to empathy in the relationship and therapeutic outcome. Orlinsky, Grawe, and Parks (1994) confirmed Sexton and Wiston's (1994) outcomes after reviewing 10 additional studies. Additionally, Bohart, Elliott, Greenberg, and Watson (2002) included 47 studies in their meta-analysis on empathy and therapy success, and found a medium effect size, which they interpreted as a meaningful correlation between empathy and positive outcomes in therapy. Furthermore, Orlinsky, Grawe, and Parks (1994) reviewed 24 studies and confirmed the notion that therapists' affirmation of clients, including acceptance, warmth, and unconditional positive regard, is positively linked to successful therapeutic outcomes.

Lambert (1992) examined factors that contribute to the success of psychotherapy, regardless of theory. He concluded that approximately 45% of success of therapy can be attributed to psychotherapy itself, including the relationship and therapist's techniques. He attributed 15% of positive change to the client's expectations of therapy and 40% to other factors outside of the therapeutic relationship, such as client family support and extraneous events. Although not all of therapeutic success can be attributed to the therapeutic relationship and the conditions inherent in the relationship, the evidence is compelling toward the usefulness of these conditions, further enhanced by the prevalence of the use of the conditions by other theorists.

Recent developments in neuroscience help to further validate person-centered theory. Many of the concepts detailed by Rogers, such as self-concept, incongruence, empathy, and unconditional positive regard can be explained by brain functions. Implicit and explicit memory processes contribute to the development of self-concept and impact the way people code and symbolize their experiences. Incongruence occurs as a result of the inconsistency between implicit and explicit systems in coding and storing information from experiences (Lux, 2010).

Gallese, Fadiga, Fogassi, and Rizzolatti (1996) are credited for discovering mirror neurons, which enable empathy to occur. Mirror neurons are activated when people witness an action occurring and trigger a response within the people who are observing as if they experience it happening to them (Ferrari & Gallese, 2007; Hatfield, Rapson, & Le, 2009; Siegel, 2010). Watson (2007) explained that empathy is used in therapy to establish relationships through addressing clients' concerns, supporting clients in regulation of emotions through labeling and symbolizing, and facilitating a reshaping of clients' world views and inner frameworks. These uses describe the process of change through person-centered theory with the support of neuroscience. Further, oxytocin levels have been found to lower blood pressure and stress levels, and oxytocin can be released by social interactions marked by love, warmth, and empathy (Uvnas-Moberg, 2003). Genuineness occurs and breeds trust within the therapeutic relationship, allowing for social connection, and therefore, higher levels of oxytocin (Lux, 2010).

Generalizability Across Cultures, Ethnicities, and Genders

Inherent in person-centered theory is an acceptance of clients for who they are as people, regardless of culture, ethnicity, and gender. Person-centered therapy is focused around the relationship created between two people. All clients, regardless of diversity from counselors should be able to benefit from engaging in this relationship built on equality, acceptance, and unconditional positive regard. However, Proctor (2008) argues that multicultural, specifically gender, concerns need to be addressed when using person-centered theory. She states that gender dynamics should be considered when two people come into contact. Bringing in the knowledge of these differences and implications that can occur could help therapists build better relationships. Gillon (2008) asserts that masculine men tend to want a "quick fix" and are focused more on cognitive thought processes, which seemingly opposes the person-centered approach to counseling. He continues to stress that person-centered theory is based on thoughts, feelings, and behaviors and these three constructs are interwoven and interdependent. Similarly, it is important for therapists to be aware of their personal biases and their clients' biases that may impede the therapeutic alliance.

This concept can be applied to clients who experience cultures that are different from their counselors. Power differentials may affect the strength of the relationship, and the dynamics of the relationship may be discussed during the course of therapy. Counselors can best approach these issues by continuing to provide the core therapeutic conditions in an attempt to help clients feel accepted and understood regardless of differences (Cheung & Leung, 2008).

In collectivist cultures, such as in Japan, person-centered theory has struggled to break through. In Japan, person-centered therapy was presented as non-directive counseling to align more with the nature of Japanese culture. After client-centered therapy became a source of academic study, it became the more prominent term in Japan. Slowly, the theory has grown in popularity among people in Japan. However, the progress is slow based on the image of an individual approach based on the sole client (Shimizu, 2010). The prevalence of person-centered theory in collectivistic cultures speaks to the possibility of success with clients who may not value individualistic thinking, which tends to dominate person-centered theory.

Despite cultural and gender considerations, person-centered theory seems to be an effective and sensitive approach given the client-centered nature of the theory. Counselors using this theory need to be aware of the potential dynamics in the counseling process that may impede development of a strong therapeutic relationship. However, by remaining theoretically consistent, these differences may be handled in a way that promotes further therapeutic progress.

Use and Application

In addition to individual counseling, Rogers applied the principles of person-centered therapy to facilitate group counseling. Rogers spent considerable time working with clients in group settings, developing what he termed *encounter groups*. Of his views on group counseling, Rogers said, "I usually have no specific goal or direction for a particular group and sincerely want it to develop in its own direction" (Rogers, 1970, as cited in Kirschenbaum & Henderson, 1989, p. 340). When describing the group process, Rogers affirmed his trust in the group to move toward its full potential when he wrote, "The group will *move*—of this I am confident – but it would be presumptuous of me to think that I can or should *direct* that movement toward a *specific* goal" (p. 340). As with individual counseling, Rogers believed that group counseling required only the six conditions and that these conditions were necessary and sufficient for the group to move toward higher levels of growth and development.

Person-centered theory also has been adapted by Axline (1969) and Landreth (2002) for therapy with children though child-centered play therapy (CCPT). CCPT shares the philosophical foundation of person-centered theory that the client needs to experience congruence, genuineness, and unconditional positive regard from the counselor for therapeutic growth to occur. CCPT is based on the belief that children, when in a relationship with a warm, empathic, and accepting person, innately know what they need, possess within them the ability to grow, and intrinsically move toward the self-actualizing tendency. However, CCPT is developmentally suited for use with children based on the use of toys and play as children's most effective way of communicating. As with person-centered counseling, CCPT has been adapted for use with individual and group settings.

More recently, throughout the literature, person-centered theory seems to be paired with many other theories or techniques (Kim, 2010; Knight, 2007; Tursi & Cochran, 2006; van Blarikom, 2008). Bozarth (1998) argues for the use of techniques if they are developed from clients' points of view and are chosen by clients. Other theorists utilizing person-centered principles to justify their techniques seem to not believe fully in the construct that people will strive toward their actualizing tendency if the conditions are met. Most of these theorists appear to be utilizing the conditions as necessary but not sufficient components of successful therapy.

Critiques of Person-Centered Theory

As mentioned previously, person-centered counseling focuses extensively on the self, which may lack cultural sensitivity for individuals from collectivist cultures. According to Fall et al. (2010), the emphasis on the individual in person-centered counseling may render the approach incompatible with cultures that value a collectivist wisdom. In addition, Rogers stated that when the six conditions are present over a period of time, they are necessary and sufficient for therapeutic change. However, because the process of change is client led, the time frame is often unspecified. In addition, because the person-centered counselor resists determining specific goals for their client, the goals of counseling are often hard to define and evolve over time depending upon the needs of the client. In an era when the emphasis often is on time-limited interventions, the person-centered approach may be viewed as too open-ended to be viable in many settings.

Finally, theorists from other counseling perspectives tend to view the person-centered approach as limited (Fall et al., 2010). Research over the past 2 decades suggest the six conditions described by Rogers may be neither necessary nor sufficient for therapeutic change (Kirschenbaum, 2007). While Kirschenbaum agrees with this position, he also stated that the conditions "are helpful to extremely helpful with virtually all clients" (p. 592). In the past decade, however, the view that the six conditions comprising the therapeutic relationship was again endorsed by the findings of an American Psychological Association task force (Fall et al., 2010; Norcross, 2001). The difference between person-centered therapists and other practitioners from other theoretical perspectives is the view that the six conditions are necessary and sufficient for therapeutic change and positive outcome (Norcross, 2002).

Conclusion

Rogers developed person-centered counseling in the mid-to-late twentieth century. According to Rogers, all people have an inherent potential to move toward self-actualization because they are all inherently good natured, forward-moving, unique, and socialized creatures. People need to enter a safe relationship in order to move toward self-actualization. Humans have the ability to understand themselves, change their self-concept and attitudes, and produce self-directed behavior. Furthermore, when people are congruent, they are constantly moving toward a more constructive and complete development to enhance not only themselves, but also other members of society. This flow of behavioral development exists in every person and is a product of congruence (Kutash & Wolf, 1986; Rogers, 1957a). Person-centered counseling focuses on the relationship between the client and counselor as the necessary and sufficient component to help people realign with their inner wisdom and reconnect with their actualizing tendency. In the words of Rogers, "Yet the deeply exciting thing about human beings is that when the individual is inwardly free, he chooses as the good life this process of becoming" (Rogers, 1957b, p. 420).

References

Axline, V. (1969). *Play therapy.* Boston, MA: Houghton-Mifflin.

Barrett-Lennard, G. T. (1962). Dimensions of therapist response as causal factors in therapeutic change. *Psychological Monographs, 76*(43), 1-33.

Bergin, A. E., & Suinn, R. M. (1975). Individual psychotherapy and behavior therapy. In M. R. Rosenzweig & L. W. Porter (Eds.), *Annual review of psychology* (pp. 509-556). Palo Alto, CA: Annual Reviews.

Bohart, A. C., Elliott, R., Greenberg, L. S., & Watson, J. C. (2002). Empathy. In J. C. Norcross (Ed.), *Psychotherapy relationships that work: Therapist contributions and responsiveness to patients* (pp. 89-108). New York, NY: Oxford University Press.

Bozarth, J. D. (1998). *Person-centered therapy: A revolutionary paradigm.* Ross-on-Wye, United Kingdom: PCCS Books.

Cheung, M., & Leung, P. (Eds.). (2008). Client-centered theory. *Multicultural Practice & Evaluation: A Case Approach to Evidence Based Practice.* Denver, CO: Love.

Elliott, R., & Freire, E. (2007). Classical person-centered and experiential perspectives on Rogers (1957). *Psychotherapy: Theory, Research, Practice, Training, 44*(3), 285-288.

Fall, K. A., Holden, J. M, & Marquis, A. (2010). Person-centered counseling. *Theoretical models of counseling and psychotherapy* (2nd ed., pp. 169-200). New York, NY: Routledge.

Ferrari. P. F. & Gallese, V. (2007). Mirror neurons and intersubjectivity. In S. Braten (Ed.), *On being moved* (pp. 73-88). Amsterdam, The Netherlands: John Benjamins.

Gallese, V., Fadiga, L., Fogassi, L., & Rizzolatti, G. (1996). Action recognition in the premotor cortex. *Brian, 119,* 593-609.

Gillon, E. (2008). Men, masculinity, and person-centered therapy. *Person-Centered and Experiential Psychotherapies, 7*(2), 120-134.

Hatfield, E., Rapson, R. L., & Le, Y. L. (2009). Emotional contagion and empathy. In J. Decery & W. Ickes (Eds.), *The social neuroscience of empathy* (pp. 19-30). Cambridge, MA: MIT Press.

Kutash, I., & Wolf, A. (Eds.). (1986). *Psychotherapist's casebook.* San Francisco, CA: Jossey-Bass.

Kim, S. (2010). A story of a healing relationship: The person-centered approach in expressive arts therapy. *Journal of Creativity in Mental Health, 5,* 93-98.

Kirschenbaum, H., & Henderson, V. L. (1989). *The Carl Rogers reader.* New York, NY: Houghton Mifflin.

Kirschenbaum, H., & Jourdan, A. (2005). The current status of Carl Rogers and the person-centered approach. *Psychology: Theory, Research, Practice, Training, 42*(1), 37-51.

Kirschenbaum, H. (2007). *The life and works of Carl Rogers.* Ross-on-Wye, United Kingdom: PCCS Books.

Knight, T. A. (2007). Showing clients the doors: Active problem-solving in person-centered psychotherapy. *Journal of Psychotherapy Integration, 17*(1), 111-124.

Lambert, M. J. (1992). Psychotherapy outcome research: Implications for integrative and eclectic therapists. In J. C. Norcross & M. R. Goldfried (Eds.), *Handbook of psychotherapy integration* (pp. 94-129). New York, NY: Basic Books.

Landreth, G. L. (2002). *Play therapy the art of the relationship* (2nd ed.). New York, NY: Brunner-Routledge.

Lux, M. (2010). The magic of encounter: The person-centered approach and the neurosciences. *Person-Centered and Experiential Psychotherapies, 9*(4), 274-289.

Mitchell, K. M., Bozarth, J. D., & Krauft, C. C. (1977). A reappraisal of the therapeutic effectiveness of accurate empathy, nonpossessive warmth, and genuineness. In A. S. Gurman & A. M. Razin (Eds.), *Effective psychotherapy: A handbook of research* (pp. 482-502). New York, NY: Pergamon Press.

Norcross, J. C. (2001). Purposes, processes and products of the task force on empirically supported therapy relationships. *Psychotherapy, 39,* 345-356.

Norcross, J. C. (2002). *Psychotherapy relationships that work: Therapist contributions and responsiveness to patients.* New York, NY: Oxford University Press.

Orlinsky, D. E., Grawe, K., & Parks, B. K. (1994). Process and outcome in psychotherapy. In S. L. Garfield & A. E. Bergin (Eds.). *Handbook of psychotherapy and behavior change* (4th ed., pp. 270-376). New York, NY: Wiley.

Parloff, M. B., Waskow, I. E., & Wolfe, B. E. (1978). Research on therapist variables in relation to process and outcomes. In S. L. Garfield & A. E. Bergin (Eds.), *Handbook of psychotherapy and behavior change* (2nd ed., pp. 233-282). New York, NY: Wiley.

Proctor, G. (2008). Gender dynamics in person-centered therapy: Does gender matter? *Person-Centered and Experiential Psychotherapies, 7*(2), 82-94.

Raskin, N., Rogers, C., & Witty, M. C. (2008). Client-centered therapy. In R. J. Corsini & D. Wedding (Eds.), *Current psychotherapies* (8th ed., pp. 141-186). Belmont, CA: Thomson Brooks/Cole.

Rogers, C. R. (1942). *Counseling and psychotherapy.* Boston, MA: Houghton Mifflin.

Rogers, C. (1951). *Client-centered therapy: Its current practice, implications, and theory.* Boston, MA: Houghton Mifflin.

Rogers, C. R. (1957a). A note on the nature of man. *Journal of Counseling Psychology, 4*(3), 199-203.

Rogers, C. R. (1957b). A therapist's view of the good life: The fully functioning person. *The Humanist, 17,* 291-300.

Rogers, C. R. (1957c). The necessary and sufficient conditions of therapeutic personality change. *Journal of Consulting Psychology, 21*(2), 95-103.

Rogers, C. R. (1959). A theory of therapy, personality and interpersonal relationships as developed in the client-centered framework. In S. Koch (Ed.). *Psychology: A study of a science: Vol. 3. Formulations of the person and the social context* (pp. 184-256). New York, NY: McGraw-Hill.

Rogers, C. R. (1961a). *On becoming a person.* Boston, MA: Houghton Mifflin.

Rogers, C. R. (1961b). The loneliness of contemporary man as seen in the case of Ellen West. *Review of Existential Psychology and Psychiatry, 1*(2), 94-101.

Rogers, C. R. (1964). Toward a modern approach to values: The valuing process in the mature person. *Journal of Abnormal and Social Psychology 68*(2), 160-167.

Rogers, C. R. (1968). *Some thoughts regarding the current presuppositions of the behavioral sciences.* In W. Coulson. & C. R. Rogers (Eds.), *Man and the science of man.* (pp. 55-72). Columbus, OH: Charles E. Merrill.

Rogers, C. R. (1970). *Carl Rogers on encounter groups.* New York. NY: Harper and Row.

Rogers, C. R. (1980). *A way of being.* Boston, MA: Houghton Mifflin.

Rogers, C. R. (1989). The necessary and sufficient conditions of therapeutic personality change. *TACD Journal, 17*(1), 53-65.

Rychalk, J. F. (1981). *Introduction to personality and psychotherapy: A theory-construction approach.* Boston, MA: Houghton Mifflin.

Sexton, T. L., & Whiston, S. C. (1994). The status of the counseling relationship: An empirical review, theoretical implications, and research directions. *The Counseling Psychologist, 22*(1), 6-78.

Shimizu, M. (2010). The development of the person-centered approach in Japan. *Person-Centered and Experiential Psychotherapies, 9*(1), 14-24.

Siegel, D. J. (2010). *Mindsight: The new science of personal transformation.* New York, NY: Random House.

Truax, C. B., & Mitchell, K. M. (1971). Research on certain therapist interpersonal skills in relation to process and outcome. In A. E. Bergin & S. L. Garfield (Eds.), *Handbook of psychotherapy and behavior change* (pp. 299-344). New York, NY: Wiley.

Tursi, M. M, & Cochran, J. L. (2006). Cognitive-behavioral tasks accomplished in a person-centered relational framework. *Journal of Counseling and Development, 84,* 387-396.

Uvnas-Moberg, K. (2003). *The oxytocin factor: Trapping the hormones of calm, love, and healing.* Cambridge, MA: Da Capo Press.

van Blarikom, J. (2008). A person-centered approach to borderline personality disorder. *Person-Centered and Experiential Psychotherapies, 7*(1), 20-36.

Watson, J. C. (2007). Facilitating empathy. *European Psychotherapy, 7*, 61-76.

Author Contact Information: Jeffrey M. Sullivan, PhD, LPC, NCC, assistant professor of counselor education, Department of Educational Leadership and Counseling, Sam Houston State University, 1932 Bobby K Marks Dr, CEC 118, Huntsville, TX 77341. E-mail: jms107@shsu.edu

CHAPTER 42

Family Therapy

Mary Nichter and Rick Bruhn
Sam Houston State University

The systemic framework for family therapy has its roots in general systems theory; a theory introduced in 1945 by biologist, Ludwig von Bertalanffy (1968). According to Bertalanffy, general systems theory is a basic reorientation in scientific thinking challenging the application of principles of natural science models to all living systems. He explained that traditional closed system models based on classical science principles, such as reductionism and mechanism, are inapplicable to living systems. Bertalanffy postulated that living systems are open to and interact with other components and the environment, and he emphasized the nonlinearity of those interactions, described man as an active organism, and thereby challenged "the model of man as a robot" (p. 205) depending on a stimulus-response model to explain human behavior.

The systemic frame has been embraced by family therapists. Focusing on understanding relationships and interactions between family members rather than the individual's symptomatic behavior, family therapists "shift" their view of the source of the problem from the individual to the entire family unit. From a systemic perspective, families are conceptualized as an integrated system comprised of members whose interactions with one another influences the family experiences of all members. According to Goldenberg and Goldenberg (2008), a family therapist regards all behavior within the family as part of ongoing, interactional, recursive events with no obvious beginning or end; consequently, the notion of linear causation is not part of the family systems model.

Basic concepts of general systems theory contribute to an understanding of the family as a system and are common factors shared across most family therapy approaches:

1. Organization. A family is organized around the relationships between the members and the members interact with each other in a patterned or "predictable 'organized' fashion" (Goldenberg & Goldenberg, 2008, p. 79).
2. Wholeness. The family as a unit or whole is greater than the sum of its individual parts or members. With this in mind, in therapy even when working with an individual, the therapist does not consider the person in isolation (Becvar & Becvar, 2009) rather considers the interactions within the family and between family members as the focus in therapy.
3. Circular causality. Any change within one family member affects the system as a whole and, thereby, affects each individual member. This idea, referred to as circular causality describes the idea that events within a relationship context occur in a circular manner rather than a one-way, linear one (Watts, Nelson, Bruhn, & Nichter, 2011).
4. Morphogenesis. Morphogenesis is the system's ability to make adjustments, modifications, and adaptations to meet the changing needs of the family in response to internal and external demands. In all families there is an ongoing dynamic tension between trying to maintain stability even as things change (Goldenberg & Goldenberg, 2008).
5. Homeostasis. Family therapists define homeostasis as the development of recurring patterns of interaction in the attempt to maintain stability and resist change. When the balance of the system is disturbed, family members tend to return to a previous level of balance or homeostasis by using internal and ongoing interactional mechanisms that maintain a balance of relationships (Watzlawick, Weakland, & Fisch, 1974).
6. Subsystems. Families usually contain a number of coexisting subsystems that are assigned to carry out particular functions within the system (Minuchin & Fishman, 1981). These subsystems

The Handbook of Educational Theories, pp. 503–513

include the parental subsystem, sibling subsystem, and other subsystems that are made up of various family members such as, mother-child and father-son. Subsystems may be created by generation, interests, intellect, or function.

7. Feedback. Feedback is the process whereby information about past behaviors is entered back into the system in a circular manner (Becvar & Becvar, 2009). The feedback can be "positive" which leads to accommodating new information and changing one or more aspects of the family's system or it can be "negative" which leads to maintaining the status quo.
8. Rules. Family rules are rarely explicit but are well known to the family members and are shaped by family values. The rules within the family help stabilize the family to function as a unit and control or limit behaviors. According to Goldenberg and Goldenberg (2008), "rules are frequently carried over from previous generations and often have a powerful cultural component" (p. 81).

History of Family Therapy

As the social currents in Europe shifted in the late 1800s and early 1900s (Crankshaw, 1963), and political systems shifted in response to changes in both the industrial revolution and the increasing philosophical emphasis on the rights of individuals, classes, and nationalities, there was a corresponding shift toward looking at not only the internal experience of individuals, but the relationships between individuals and larger social groups (Adler, 1931; Freud, 1963, 1965; Ramsland, 1969). A strong voice emphasizing the importance of relationships and responsibility in social interactions was that of Alfred Adler (1938). Adler believed that individual's personalities were developed in the context of relationships, that children thrived when they felt successful, and that children become pervasively discouraged when they consistently experience failure. These fundamental beliefs were built upon by other psychologists, social workers, psychiatrists, and counselors, in Europe, America, and around the world, laying the foundation for the constructs and professional beliefs now known as family therapy.

Early History of Marriage Counseling and Family Therapy

Following Adler's footsteps, influential psychologists such as Harry Stack Sullivan and Kurt Lewin noted the importance of interpersonal relationships (Hall & Lindzey, 1957). In the 1930s and 40s marriage counselors, practitioners of Moreno's group psychodrama, and therapists delivering group therapy to traumatized veterans of World War II all broadened the understanding of interactions between individuals in various contexts (Broderick & Schrader, 1981; Goldenberg & Goldenberg, 2008). Numerous postwar researchers, often trained in psychoanalysis, observed the value of seeing parents together with children, and treating married couples conjointly, contravening the status quo of the day, which was to see only the individual, no matter what the presenting problem (Framo, 1996; Goldenberg & Goldenberg, 2008).

Panels at the American Orthopsychiatric Association and American Psychiatric Association conferences in 1957 were devoted to families, bringing together a number of researchers and psychiatrists interested in studying and treating more than one patient at a time (Guerin, 1971). Noted researchers such as Murray Bowen, Lyman Wynne, Theodore Lidz, Gregory Bateson, and Don Jackson looked at family influences on patients, communication patterns of disturbed families, and ways to treat families through bringing groups of families together and applying group therapy techniques (Goldenberg & Goldenberg, 2008). As further research on families was presented in the early 1960s and written for professional examination, an excitement for treating whole families grew. By the late 1960s and 70s, books and monographs were published by early writers in the family therapy field, and researchers translated the implications from early studies with families into pragmatic suggestions for therapeutic practice (Framo, 1996).

By the early 1970s, training programs devoted to marriage and family therapy were sprouting up in East Coast, Midwestern, and West Coast locales. Academic programs started to offer master's degrees with a marriage and family therapy focus. The American Association for Marriage Counselors and family therapists joined together to create the American Association for Marriage and Family Counselors (AAMFC). Another group, the American Family Therapy Association remained a separate and strong voice for family therapy practice. Upon discovering Ludwig von Bertalanfy's genetic research describing systemic interactions, the field embraced "systems" as a defining term, shifting terminology to emphasize practice as marriage and family systems therapy. By the mid-1970s strong and charismatic leaders such as Jay Haley, Virginia Satir, Salvador Minuchin, Murray Bowen, and others were writing books, presenting to conferences, producing video tapes of therapy sessions, and leading training programs in California, Philadelphia, and Washington D.C (Framo, 1996). As excitement grew and mental health practitioners identified with systemic marriage and family therapy, others flocked to workshops, training institutes, read books, or sought master's or doctoral level training in the field. By the late 1970s there was a rush to practice, with therapists excitedly trying new (and often poorly researched) ideas to their work with couples and families in therapy. By the early 1980s, family systems therapy was being practiced for practice's sake.

Marriage and Family Systems Therapy as a Stand-alone Profession

Realizing that marriage and family therapists could be subsumed under other practitioner identifications such as psychologist, social worker, psychiatrist, or counselor, and striving to establish the legitimacy of marriage and family therapy, the AAMFC changed its name to the American Association for Marriage and Family Therapy (AAMFT,) and continued to emphasize theoretical and practical applications of "systems" thinking, until approaches to family therapy became known as systemic, for example, Bowen Family Systems Therapy. As AAMFT strove to strengthen the legitimacy of marriage and family therapists (MFTs), the headquarters was moved to Washington DC and efforts to gain recognition coalesced around the notion that "systemic" therapists where a separate field of study. This was done by lobbying for inclusion of MFTs as mental health providers for the poor, the military, and veterans. At the same time, efforts were made to create an accrediting body, the Commission for Accreditation for Marriage and Family Therapy Education (COAMFTE), setting standards for master's, doctoral, and postdegree training programs, and ultimately winning recognition by the U.S. Department of Health, Education, and Welfare as the body to accredit training for a core mental health practice.

By the mid-1980s there was a growing concern by the leading minds of the field regarding the lack of research to support the legitimacy of family therapists' claims for effectiveness. Simultaneously feminist psychologists offered a sharp critique of male dominant views, occurring while the membership of AAMFT shifted from predominantly male to its eventual (and current) status as predominantly female. The field increased its focus on research on a range of issues related to couples and family therapy, including effectiveness of the approach (Goldenberg & Goldenberg, 2008). Today, a large number of doctoral programs, including those accredited by COAMFTE and the Commission on Accreditation for Counseling and Related Educational Programs, are generating research that not only supports the notion of systemic couple and family therapy as a stand alone field, but also connects the practice of couples and family therapy with other mental health practitioners and researchers.

Family Therapy Approaches

Several prominent approaches, developed and utilized by clinicians practicing within a family systems framework, are commonly acknowledged by the field. These include Adlerian, Bowen Family Systems, Structural, Strategic, Cognitive-Behavioral, Psychodynamic, Experiential, Emotionally-focused, Solution-focused, Narrative, Gottman, and Integrated.

Adlerian Family Therapy

Most family therapy approaches were developed in last half of the twentieth century. However, "the Adlerian approach pre-dates the formal development of marriage and family therapy (and in fact was a forerunner to the field)" (Sperry, Carlson, & Peluso, 2006, p. 172).

Overview of Goals, Assumptions, and Aspects of Alderian Therapy

The general goal of Adlerian family therapy is to encourage change in family members, as well as the family as a whole (Carlson, Watts, & Maniacci, 2005). Basic Adlerian goals are (a) to offer new understanding and awareness about family members' purposes, goals, and behavior; (b) to teach skills in communication, problem solving, and conflict resolution; (c) to improve social interest and cooperation; and (d) to encourage continued growth.

Consistent with the systemic perspective, Adlerian theory emphasizes the internal unity of all organisms and their unified functioning as integral parts of larger systems (Sherman & Dinkmeyer, 1987). Adlerian family therapists work from an interpersonal approach and focus on the family system to understand an individual's behavior. As LaFountain and Mustaine (1998) stated, "Adler emphasized the importance of examining individuals within their social context and regarded the family as the primary context" (p. 190). Another basic assumption in Adlerian family therapy is that family members often become stuck in repetitive, negative interactions based on mistaken goals that motivate all parties involved (Bitter, 2009).

Adlerian Family Therapy Approach

The Adlerian family therapist's work begins with a lifestyle assessment. Family lifestyle includes family atmosphere, family constellation, birth order, early memories, beliefs, values, goals, and ways family members attempt to reach their goals (Bitter, 2009; Sherman & Dinkmeyer, 1987). Therapists start with the tentative hypothesis that family interactions are influenced by the family lifestyle. Family members are helped to gain insight into their life style by asking questions in the form of "Could it be ... ?" or "I'm wondering if ... ?" (Dinkmeyer, Dinkmeyer, & Sperry, 1987).

Bowen Family Systems

Overview of Goals, Assumptions, and Aspects of Bowen Family Systems

The Bowen Family Systems (BFS) approach, developed by Murray Bowen in the 1950s is among the first, if not the first, systemically based approaches for working with families (Gladding, 2011). The core goal underlying BFS is to understand and address family-of-origin relationship problems that manifest in one's current family. Kerr and Bowen (1988) identified the reduction of anxiety and symptom relief, and an increase in each family member's level of differentiation of the self as the two specific goals for the practice of family systems theory.

Family systems theory conceptualizes the family as an emotional unit, a network of interlocking relationships, best understood when analyzed within a multigenerational framework (Bowen, 1985). Anxiety and emotional response patterns are transmitted from generation to generation until unresolved emotional attachments with family-of-origin members are confronted and resolved effectively. Dysfunction in the family results when members of the marital dyad have poor differentiation of self and respond to each other in an emotionally fused manner, meaning that high levels of anxiety lead to emotional reactions overcoming the capacity to respond to problems rationally.

Bowen Family Systems Approach

Early in therapy, BFS therapists address presenting issues and assess the transmission of anxiety and emotional patterns through the construction of a three generation genogram. A genogram is a graphic layout that provides a visual picture of a family tree (McGoldrick & Gerson, 1985). The genogram helps family members see patterns and relationships in a new light creating a more objective assessment of their families of origin. Other techniques of BFS include detriangulation, asking questions, defining the roles and relationships in the family, defusing emotions, avoiding blame, and coaching clients as they change their behavior in the family-of-origin.

Structural Family Therapy

Overview of Goals, Assumptions, and Aspects of Structural Family Therapy

Salvador Minuchin is most frequently credited for the development of structural family therapy, an active problem-solving therapeutic approach (Sperry, Carlson, & Peluso, 2006). The structural approach to family therapy originated in the early 1960s when Minuchin worked with delinquent boys and their families in New York and later was further developed by Minuchin and his colleagues at the Philadelphia Child Guidance Clinic (Bitter, 2009). The goal of structural family therapy is to establish an effective hierarchical structure within the family. Family members relate to each other according to certain structures, which form an "invisible set of functional demands that organizes the ways in which family members interact" (Minuchin, 1974, p. 51). Structural family therapists attempt to modify verbal and nonverbal interactional sequences by changing the rules (often unstated) that govern interactions. Doing this helps family members develop clearer boundaries. Consequently, symptoms are understood as resulting from dysfunctional family structures. Structural therapists assume that symptoms are not only indicative of dysfunctional family organization but may also serve important regulatory functions such as maintaining emotional contact among members, detouring conflict elsewhere in the family, or protecting members from the difficulties of structural transformation (Lopez, 1986).

Structural Family Therapy Approach

Structural family therapists are active and directive leaders, utilizing a range of techniques to facilitate change in family structures. According to Goldenberg and Goldenberg (2008),

> the major therapeutic thrust is to actively and directly challenge the family's patterns of interaction, forcing the members to look beyond the symptoms of the identified patient in order to view all of their behavior within the context of family structures. (p. 224)

To help the family accomplish this, the structural therapist joins the family and participates in a high degree of interaction (Aponte, 1992), wherein the therapist "uses himself to transform the system" (Minuchin & Fishman, 1981, p. 2). To this end, the therapist may utilize disequilibrium techniques to create change within the family system. "Some of them, like enactment and boundary making, are primarily employed in the creation of a different sequence of events, whereas others, like reframing, punctuation, and unbalancing, tend to foster a different perception of reality" (Colapinto, 2000, p. 154).

Strategic Family Therapy

Overview of Goals, Assumptions, and Aspects Of Strategic Family Therapy

Strategic family therapy is a "method-oriented" (Gladding, 2011, p. 220) approach focusing on behavioral change rather than on gaining insight and understanding of problems. Development of strategic family therapy was significantly influenced by Jay Haley (1973,

1976) who claimed that the approach has strong roots in the ideas and teachings of Milton Erickson, a psychiatrist specializing in the use of hypnosis in mental health treatment. Haley, like Erickson, believed in utilizing the resources of clients to solve their own problems.

Haley's contention that current interaction of the family rather than historical events or family of origin issues are the cause of a family's problems, distinguishes this approach from others that view an understanding of the past as a necessary prerequisite for changing current behavior. The goal of strategic therapy, therefore, is to resolve presenting problems by focusing on behavioral sequences and interactions (Bitter, 2009) and to determine the function the problem or symptom serves to maintain the family "system." According to Haley (1976), the problem is a metaphor for the real problem or issue the family is experiencing, and brings an ironic payoff to a family system that isn't ready for change. To this end, strategic therapists focus on creating interventions formed to shift the family organization or structure so that the symptom no longer serves its previous function for the family (Goldenberg & Goldenberg, 2008).

Strategic Family Therapy Approach

Interventions used by strategic therapists are change oriented and include reframing or therapist-ascribing meaning (Duncan & Solovey, 1989) in which problem behaviors are more positively interpreted, directives such as homework to encourage family members to behave differently outside the therapy room, and paradoxical tasks such as prescribing the symptom. Paradoxical interventions take several forms, such as reframing behaviors or patterns, or prescribing a family member or members to engage in the symptomatic behavior. These prescriptions may take the form of the injunction to "go slow" as it is too soon to change, or an ordeal, which the family member finds arduous and will oppose. Family members either rebel against the directive and give up the symptom or obey the request and continue in the symptom, "thus putting the maintenance of the symptom under his or her conscious, voluntary control" (Sperry, Carlson, & Peluso, 2006, p. 159). The strategic family therapists works as a consultant or expert and serves as an agent of change to help the family resolve the presenting problem (Corey, 2005).

Cognitive-Behavioral Family Therapy

Overview of Goals, Assumptions, and Aspects of Cognitive-Behavioral Family Therapy

Cognitive-behavioral family therapy (CBFT) takes its shape from traditional cognitive and behavioral therapies that emphasize the way cognitive components of beliefs, attitudes, and expectations influence behavior (Goldenberg & Goldenberg, 2008). CBFT emphasizes the exploration of cognitive components or schemas that, according to Dattilio (2005) are long held beliefs and attitudes about people, relationships, and events that shape thoughts, perceptions, and emotions within individuals and families. Long held beliefs may become spontaneous cognitions labeled as automatic thoughts (Dattilio, 2005) and may consequently, lead to behaviors without cognitive awareness or logical thought. According to Bitter (2009), "the overall goal of cognitive-behavioral family therapy is to address automatic thoughts, cognitive distortions, and schemas that lead to antagonistic interactions and to plan modifications of emotions and behaviors that will lead to more harmonious family lives" (p. 310). Maladaptive behaviors resulting from faulty schemas have been learned, and according to cognitive-behavioral therapist, can be unlearned (Dattilio, 2005, Goldenberg & Goldenberg, 2008).

Dattilio (2005) pointed out that behaviors of one member of the family affect the emotions, perceptions, and behaviors of the other family members. Consistent with family systems thinking, Dattilio (2001, 2005) described the family members as intertwined, creating something larger than themselves. Consequently, change in one family member results in change in other members.

Cognitive-Behavioral Family Therapy Approach

CBFT is a short-term, structured treatment approach focusing on here-and-now problems, rather attempting to uncover or reconstruct the past. A CBF therapist begins therapy with an assessment exploring the thinking processes of each family member in treatment and focuses on how these thoughts result in negative interactions within the family. The assumption is that once family members understand and improve their information processing and cognitions, positive changes in behavior and emotions will occur (Baucom & Epstein, 1990). The therapist will help family members accomplish this by using behavioral interventions and cognitive restructuring techniques such as reworking family schemas, communication training, problem-solving training, identifying automatic thoughts, and challenging and restructuring maladaptive schemas (Bitter, 2009; Dattilio, 2005; & Sperry, Carlson, & Peluso, 2006).

Psychodynamic Family Therapy

Overview of Goals, Assumptions, and Aspects of Psychodynamic Family Therapy

Nathan Ackerman, a psychoanalytically trained child psychiatrist, has been credited as the founder of psychodynamic family therapy, shifting from therapy with one patient at a time to treating an entire family, departing from the traditionally approach of Freudian analysts (Gladding, 2011). Through the integration of psychoanalytic theory and systems theory, Ackerman viewed the family as a system of interacting individual personalities each a subsystem of the system. Ackerman resolved problems in relationships in the clients' current family or in their lives through intrapsychic exploration and the resolution of unconscious object relationships internalized from early parent-child relationships. He assumed that these early influences affect and explain the nature of present interpersonal difficulties. Psychodynamic family therapists focus on helping clients deal with issues influenced by the dynamics experienced in the family of origin. Psychodynamic family therapy is most often described in the current literature as object relations couples therapy (Scharff & Scharff, 2008).

Psychodynamic Family Therapy Approach

The family therapist working from a psychodynamic approach modifies the traditional view of understanding symptoms as biologically driven, unconscious, intrapsychic conflict to include a consideration of context within which the symptoms occur (Goldenberg & Goldenberg, 2008). Therapists carefully set a psychodynamic frame for the therapy, assessing unconscious and early experiences of each family member, and utilizing intuition and a well tuned awareness of countertransference to understand how past experiences impact the present and current relationships with family members (Scharff & Scharff, 2008). To accomplish this, the therapist takes on the role of a catalyst and plays a wide range of roles—"from activator, challenger, and confronter to supporter, interpreter, and integrator" (Goldenberg & Goldenberg, 2009, p. 159).

Experiential Family Therapy

Overview of Goals, Assumptions, and Aspects of Experiential Family Therapy

Experiential family therapy includes the pragmatic and atheoretical approaches developed by Carl Whitaker and Virginia Satir, who emphasized the experiential nature of therapy and the significance of human interaction for the process of change and personal growth (Becvar & Becvar, 2009). Experiential family therapists rely on their abilities to be spontaneous, intuitive, and creative. This model embraces the notion that individuals in families are typically not aware of their emotions and, if aware, tend to suppress them creating emotional deadness and resulting in the expression of symptoms within one or more family members (Gladding, 2011). "The primary goal of experiential therapy is growth and creativity, rather than mere symptom reduction, because individual growth and creative freedom will reduce the need for the symptom" (Watts, Nelson, Bruhn, & Nichter, 2011, p. 351). Freedom to safely own and express emotions within the context of family provides a sense of belonging to an integrated whole and "it is through the sense of belonging to the whole that the freedom to individuate and separate from the family is derived" (Becvar & Becvar, 2009, p. 158).

Experiential Family Therapy Approach

Experiential family therapy frames therapeutic interventions in the here and now experiences and interactions of the family. This involves an exploration of family members' covert world beneath the surface words of thinking and reasoning (Whitaker & Keith, 1981) and surface level interactions (Satir, 1988). Experiential therapists develop a close personal relationship with all family members, join and separate from the family, and "tend to create family turmoil and then coach the members through the experience" (Bitter, 2009, p. 153). The primary technique utilized in experiential family therapy is the therapist's use of self. From Whitaker's view, this requires practitioners to be actively engaged with the family and go beyond the surface level of interactions by sharing his or her own impulses, fantasies, and symbolic meanings of what evolves between him or her and family members. From Satir's view, this involves touch, movement, family sculpting, modeling and teaching clear communication skills, and emphasizing the strengths and resources of not only individuals, but the entire family. For Whitaker's approach, therapeutic techniques include redefining symptoms as efforts for growth and change, modeling fantasy alternatives to real-life stress through role play, promoting family member's confrontation of their own emotions prior to examining behaviors, and using silence as an opportunity for therapists and family members to be introspective with freedom to think and feel (Bitter, 2009; Gladding, 2011; Goldenberg & Goldenberg, 2008).

Narrative Family Therapy

Overview of Goals, Assumptions, and Aspects of Narrative Family Therapy

Narrative family therapy, a language based approach developed by Michael White and David Epston, is informed by social constructionism and postmodern worldviews and is a relatively significant departure from traditional systems thinking (Walsh & Keenan, 1997). The narrative model of family therapy makes explicit the power of language, how language as stories can shape the "truth" as the family comes to understand it, and how lives and relationships are shaped by the stories developed to give meaning to family member's experiences (Rasheed, Rasheed, & Marley, 2011). Meanings assigned to the stories by families are strongly influenced by sociocultural practices, beliefs, and values. "Narrative therapy is one of the few psychotherapeutic theories that integrates societal and cultural issues into its core conceptualizations of how problems are formed and resolved" (Gehart, 2010, p. 420). Further, Gehart described problems from the narrative therapy view as generated in the failure of families to create experiences and life stories that follow the dominant-cultural narratives of how life should be lived in order to be happy and successful. Families often integrate the dominant-cultural narratives and act as if these are the only acceptable stories for their lives even when they are not useful to the family (Bitter, 2009). This results in oppressive narratives in which family stories are problem-saturated and deficit. From the narrative family therapy position, change occurs by challenging dominant-cultural narratives that do not reflect the life experiences, multiple realities, belief, and values of family members, leading to the expression of "subjugated knowledges [sic] that fit more closely with an individual's lived experience" (Gehart & Tuttle, 2003, p. 215).

Narrative Family Therapy Approach

Narrative family therapists approach their work with families from a non-expert stance and view themselves as collaborators, asking questions to facilitate the knowledge and experience carried in the stories of the families with whom they work (Walsh & Keenan, 1997). The goals of narrative therapists are to listen closely to the stories that support the problem, and collaborate with family members to coconstruct narratives that better fit individual family members and align with a family's goals and objectives (Miller & Forrest, 2009). Narrative therapists listen with a "deconstructing ear" (Walsh & Keenan, 1997, p. 332) and ask reflection-oriented questions tied to the process of deconstruction or reconstruction of family stories (Rasheed, Rasheed, & Marley, 2011). Deconstruction of oppressive narratives often begins with the therapist asking questions that help to separate the problem from the family and identify the influence of the problem in the family's lives. This type of questioning brings about a shift in language used by the therapist and begins to externalize the problem and deconstruct the original narrative in which family members have become problem saturated (Bitter, 2009). The therapist now questions the family about times the problem is not present and beings to engage in re-authoring conversations (Goldenberg & Goldenberg, 2008) leading to the discovery of unique outcomes. The family, collaborating with the therapist, is now positioned to coconstruct alternative stories that provide freedom from the problematic stories. Narrative family therapists encourage families to tell and retell the preferred stories, thickening them by going into greater and greater detail for the purpose of encouraging families to begin living the preferred rather than the problematic story.

Solution-Focused Family Therapy

Overview of Goals, Assumptions, and Aspects of Solution-focused Family Therapy

Steve de Shazer, Insoo Kim Berg, and others developed the solution-focused family therapy SFFT approach in the 1970s and 1980s (DeShazer et al., 1986). Due to it's adoption by insurance companies as a preferred treatment approach due to the focus on solutions rather than problems, SFFT became prominent in the field of family therapy. According to de Shazer, solution-focused therapy offers a paradigm shift from the traditional psychotherapy approaches with a focus on problems and client deficits to a focus on solutions and client strengths (Trepper, Dolan, McCollum, & Nelson, 2006). A major assumption underlying this approach is that individuals and families are the experts in their life situations and have the resources they need to find solutions to resolve their problems (Rasheed, Rasheed, & Marley, 2011). Specifically, central to the SFFT model is the notion that effective solutions are present but are often hidden to the families (Bitter, 2009). Trepper et al. stated, "de Shazer held an abiding belief in clients' abilities to know what is best for them and to effectively plan how to get there" (p. 134).

Solution-focused family therapy has roots in social constructionism and, similar to other models influenced by this philosophy, believe that problems are problems because they are described as problems (Bitter, 2009). Acknowledging the power of language is a foundational concept and frames the overall goal of the solution-focused model, helping families move from problem talk to solution talk (Rasheed, Rasheed, & Marley, 2011).

Solution-Focused Family Therapy Approach

Solution-focused brief therapy is a future-focused, goal-directed approach that utilizes questions designed to identify exceptions, solutions, and scales (Trepper et al., 2006). According to Walter and Peller (2000), these are questions of difference and encourage families to think of times when the problem did not exist. Remembering together times of difference restores hope in families and shifts them to sharing conversations of solutions with the family therapist. When families cannot recall exceptions to the problem, a solution-focused therapist may ask the miracle question (e.g., "If you woke up in the morning and the problem no longer existed, what would be different?") to create a hypothetical solution (Andrews & Clark, 1996).

The scaling question is another technique used by solution-focused family therapists and is aimed at helping families create a hypothetical solution. Scaling questions ask family members to quantify their own perceptions (Goldenberg & Goldenberg, 2009) and "imagine when their problem was at a low point—a 'one' and to think about what things might look like when they are at a 'ten' and the problem is no longer a problem" (Andrews & Clark, 1996, p. 245). Scaling questions invite dialogue between family members as to why each one assigned a specific number assessing the problem to be more or less problematic than other family members. This discussion can focus on strengths of the family and move members forward toward more solution talk (Rasheed, Rasheed, & Marley, 2011). Since SFFT focuses on resiliency, clients' own previous solutions, and exceptions to their own problems, this approach is seen as applicable to problems faced by clients across a range of cultures (Trepper et al., 2006).

Gottman Method Couple Therapy

Overview of Goals, Assumptions, and Aspects of Gottman Method Couple Therapy

John and Julie Gottman and others have developed an approach to treating couples that is strongly supported by research (Gottman & Gottman, 2008; Jencius & Duba, 2003). Through rigorous research, Gottman and his associates have studied elements of live couple's interactions as predictors of marital satisfaction. These researchers have demonstrated the capacity to analyze a couple's dialogue and behaviors and to then predict the likelihood a couple will divorce or stay together. Among the constructs and behavior patterns studied are conflict and capacity for conflict resolution, the ratio of positive exchanges between partners compared to negative exchanges and the impact on relationship satisfaction, the capacity to share goals and dreams, predictors of disaster in relationships, overall attitudes toward the relationship as well as fundamental beliefs about the partner's attitudes toward the relationship, techniques for decreasing physiological arousal at times of conflict, and statistical estimates of conflicts seen in couples which are not likely to be resolved (Gottman & Gottman, 2008).

Gottman Method Couple Therapy Approach

The techniques of the Gottman Method Couple Therapy (Gottman & Gottman, 2008) include a thorough assessment of problematic issues as well as couple strengths. They collect data through both individual and couple sessions. This includes the history of the relationship, the goals of the couple, and information about each of the partner's parent's relationship. Combining cognitive-behavioral strategies with techniques of emotionally focused therapy (Greenberg & Johnson, 1988), the Gottman method uses therapy to prepare couples for psycho-education about affect-regulation, conflict resolution, and shared beliefs and couple long-range goals.

Integrated Approaches to Family Therapy

Most experienced marriage and family therapists have studied and practiced several approaches to either couples therapy and/or family therapy. These therapists have come to know that certain MFT techniques are identified with specific approaches, and are the creations of specific, well known pioneer(s) of MFT. For example, sculpting families into *communication stances* is a technique identified with Virginia Satir. Using *counterparadox* or *prescribing rituals* is identified with the Milan Team (Tomm, 1984). Discussing the *four horseman of the apocalypse* is an activity associated with the Gottman approach. Coaching one member of a family to *go back to their family-of-origin* while acting in a different, prescribed, and consistent manner is associated with Bowen Family Systems.

All of these techniques work in some instances and not in others. Some are researched and others are the intuitive creations of the originators of the technique. It is useful to understand that experienced MFTs typically utilize a range of techniques, from a variety of approaches within their work with couples and families (Gurman, 2008) and sometimes use multiple techniques, identified with multiple approaches in one or more sessions with specific clients. Ultimately, experienced therapists know that one approach does NOT fit all, and they shift "approaches" in response to variations in presenting issues, the characteristics of the couples or families, or in response to agency requirements.

Furthermore, some therapists specialize in working with families, some with couples. The location of the practice, the populations served, and the billing practices all influence approaches are used with each client. For example, in agencies that serve low income families, the therapist may specialize in SFFT or cognitive-behavioral family therapy. On the other hand, in a private practice where most of the clients are upper middle-class couples, the therapist may use Gottman's (Gottman & Gottman, 2008) approach ("Building the Sound Marital House"), Bret Atkinson's (2005) pragmatic/experiential therapy for couples, or a variation of emotionally focused therapy (Johnson, 2008) as a primary approach. However, in a private practice where clients pay through insurance, the therapist may primarily use SFFT. If a knowledgeable MFT were to observe any of the sessions in the settings described above, he or she would likely see an experienced MFT using a range of techniques from disparate approaches.

CULTURAL SENSITIVITY IN FAMILY THERAPY

Rasheed, Rasheed, and Marley (2011) described the family identity as the unique definition a family holds of itself which may be strongly influenced by ethnic, racial, cultural, and subcultural values for some families. The family's identity includes themes and organizing narratives that provide the lens through which families view themselves within a broader social context. The family identity narrative for some ethnic minority families may include a theme of powerlessness based on experiences of discrimination and oppression that have robbed them of self-affirming powers that result in a state of vulnerability. According to Rasheed, Rasheed, and Marley,

> As ethnic minority families present themselves for family therapy, a culturally attuned therapist must have the clinical skills that allow the therapist to enter into the family's narrative world to uncover with the family the interplay of those ethnic themes and broader sociocultural metanarratives. (p. 85)

This charge to family therapists is echoed by the American Association for Marriage and Family Therapy (AAMFT, 2004) in the *Marriage and Family Therapy Core Competencies* in which core competencies for clinicians "encompass behaviors, skills, attitudes, and policies that promote awareness, acceptance, and respect for differences, enhance services that meet the needs of diverse populations, and promote resiliency and recovery" (p. 1). In addition, *AAMFT Code of Ethics* (AAMFT, 2001) Principle I, Responsibility to Clients, 1.1 states that marriage and family therapist are to provide services without discrimination on the basis of race, age, ethnicity, socioeconomic status, disability, gender, health status, religion, national origin, or sexual orientation.

To practice as a culturally sensitive and competent marriage and family therapist, a clinician must work with families in ways that promote understanding and respect, making therapy meaningful for all members of the family system. Therefore, therapists must be sensitive to how families give meaning to the presenting problem, relationships, and interactions within their cultural framework. To this end, therapists must be willing to learn from the family and if needed seek cultural consultation to establish a culturally sensitive therapeutic relationship and safeguard the welfare of the family.

ASSESSMENT IN FAMILY THERAPY

The use of assessments in family therapy is moderated by the therapist's theoretical approach, the context in which the therapist works, and the training the therapist received (Boughner, Hayes, Bubenzer, & West, 1994; Goldenberg & Goldenberg, 2008; Gurman, 2008; Lavee & Yitzhak, 2006). Formal and informal assessments are used at the therapist's discretion, and in most cases, therapists use informal assessment techniques to identify presenting issues, generate hypotheses and diagnoses, and track issues that need to be addressed in therapy with couples and families.

The typical family therapist conducts a brief intake assessment prior to seeing the couple of family. This takes the form of the clients filling out intake data forms collecting information such as problems to be addressed, history of prior treatment, medications, substance use, family members in prior treatment, and high stress events such as divorce or a death in the family. Therapists may also include a brief checklist where the client identifies thinking, feeling, and behavior patterns. The number of therapists using pencil and paper (or computer-based) assessments following intake procedures are in the minority. Instead, therapists tend to use assessment techniques that are related to their preferred approach to therapy. For example, Bowen Family Systems therapists are likely to use a genogram to track emotional functioning across several generations. Structural family therapists use family mapping followed by enactments to assess and treat dysfunctional family structures. Solution focused family therapists use scaling questions and crystal ball techniques to assess client strengths, willingness to work toward solutions, and to assess progress toward therapeutic goals. Intergenerational therapists will collect data on the family-of-origin to assess the influence of dynamics on current functioning. Strategic family therapists may assess each family member's position in the *family life cycle*.

Other therapists developed techniques that involved experiential involvement as a combined assessment and intervention. For example, Satir (1964) used the *Family Life Chronology*, a set of questions asked within early sessions of therapy, and family sculpting to assess and teach about communication in relationships. Peggy Papp (1972) also used techniques adapted from psychodrama to assess and treat simultaneously.

Behavioral and cognitive behavioral therapists are most likely to collect base line data on behaviors, and utilize tests to identify satisfaction, adjustment, violent behaviors, substance use, and rating scales to measure parenting skills and attitudes. There are a number of nonstandardized assessments which may be found in Corcoran and Fischer's (1987) *Measures for Clinical Practice*, or in Sherman and Fredman's (1986) *Handbook of Structured Techniques in Marriage and Family Therapy*.

REFERENCES

Adler, A. (1931). *What life should mean to you* (A. Porter, ed.) New York, NY. Blue Ribbon Books.

Adler, A. (1938). *Social interest: A challenge to mankind* (J. Linton, & R. Vaughan, trans.) London, England: Faber and Faber.

Andrews, J., & Clark, D. (1996). In the case of a depressed woman: Solution-focused or narrative therapy approaches? *The Family Journal: Counseling and Therapy for Couples and families 4*, 243-250.

Aponte, H. J. (1992). Training the person of the therapist in structural family therapy. *Journal of Marital and Family Therapy, 18*(3), 269-281.

American Association for Marriage and Family Therapy. (2001). *AAMFT code of ethics.* Alexandria, VA: AAMFT.

American Association for Marriage and Family Therapy. (2004). *Marriage and family therapy core competencies.* Alexandria, VA: AAMFT.

Atkinson, B. (2005). *Emotional intelligence in couples therapy: Advances in neurobiology and the science of intimate relationships.* New York, NY: W. W. Norton.

Baucom, D. H., & Epstein, N. (1990). *Cognitive-behavior marital therapy.* New York, NY: Brunner/Mazel.

Becvar, D., & Becvar, R. (2009). *Family therapy: A systemic integration* (7th ed.). Boston, MA: Allyn & Bacon.

Bertalanffy, V. L. (1968). *General systems theory: Foundation, development, applications.* New York, NY: Braziller.

Bitter, J.R. (2009). *Theory and practice of family therapy and counseling.* Belmont, CA: Brooks/Cole.

Boughner, S., Hayes, S., Bubenzer, D., & West, J. (1994). Use of standardized assessment instruments by marital and family therapists: A survey. *Journal of Marital and Family Therapy, 20*(1), 69-75.

Bowen, M. (1985). *Family therapy in clinical practice.* Northvale, NJ: Jason Aronson.

Broderick, C., & Schrader, S. (1981). The history of professional marriage and family therapy. In A. Gurman, & D. Kniskern (Eds.), *Handbook of family therapy* (pp. 5-35). New York, NY: Brunner/Mazel.

Carlson, J., Watts, R. E., & Maniacci, M. (2005) *Adlerian therapy theory and practice.* Washington, DC: Love.

Colapinto, J. (2000). Structural family therapy. In A. M. Horne (Ed.), *Family counseling and therapy* (3rd ed., pp. 140-169). Itasca, IL: F. E. Peacock.

Corcoran, K., & Fischer, J. (1987). *Measures for clinical practice.* New York, NY: Free Press.

Corey, G. (2005). *Theory and practice of counseling and psychotherapy.* Belmont, CA: Brooks/Cole–Thomson Learning.

Crankshaw, E. (1963). *The fall of the house of Habsburg.* New York, NY: Viking.

Dattilio, F. M. (2005). Restructuring family schemas: A cognitive-behavioral perspective. *Journal of Marital and Family Therapy, 31*(1), 15-30.

Dinkmeyer, D. C., Dinkmeyer, D. C., Jr., & Sperry, L. (1987). *Adlerian counseling and psychotherapy* (2nd ed.). Columbus, OH: Merrill.

Duncan, B. L., & Solovey, A. D. (1989). Strategic-brief therapy: an insight-oriented approach? *Journal of Marital and Family Therapy, 15*(1), 1-9.

Framo, J. (1996). A personal retrospective of the family therapy field. *Journal of Marital and Family Therapy, 22*, 289-316.

Freud, S. (1963). *A general introduction to psycho-analysis* (J. Riviere, Trans.). New York, NY: Liveright.

Freud, S. (1965). *New introductory lectures on psycho-analysis* (J. Strachey, Trans.). New York, NY: W. W. Norton.

de Shazer, S., Berg, I., Lipchik, E., Nunnally, E., Molnar, A., Gingerich, W., & Weiner-Davis, M. (1986). Brief therapy: Focused solution development. *Family Process, 25*, 207-222.

Gehart, D. (2010). *Mastering competencies in family therapy.* Belmont, CA: Brooks/Cole.

Gehart, D., & Tuttle, A. (2003). *Theory-based treatment planning for marriage and family therapists.* Pacific Grove, CA: Brooks/Cole.

Gladding, S. (2011). *Family therapy: History, theory, and practice* (5th ed.) Upper Saddle River, NJ: Pearson Education.

Goldenberg, H., & Goldenberg, I. (2008). *Family therapy: An overview* (7th ed.). Belmont, CA: ThomsonBrooks/Cole.

Gottman, J. M., & Gottman, J. S. (2008). Gottman method couple therapy. In A. Gurman (Ed.), *Clinical handbook of couple therapy* (4th ed., pp. 138-164). New York, NY: Guilford.

Greenberg, L., & Johnson, S. (1988). *Emotionally focused therapy for couples.* New York, NY: Guilford.

Gurman, A. (2008). A framework for the comparative study of couple therapy. In A. Gurman (Ed.), *Clinical handbook of couple therapy* (4th ed., pp. 1-26). New York, NY: Guilford.

Guerin, P. (1971). Family therapy: The first twenty-five years. In P. Guerin (Ed.), *Family therapy: Theory and practice* (pp. 2-22). New York, NY: Gardner Press.

Haley, J. (1973). *Uncommon therapy: The psychiatric techniques of Milton H. Erickson, M.D.* New York, NY: W.W. Norton.

Haley, J. (1976). *Problem-solving theory: New strategies for effective family therapy.* San Francisco, CA: Jossey-Bass.

Hall, C., & Lindzey, G. (1957). *Theories of personality.* New York, NY. Wiley.

Jencius, M., & Duba, J. (2003). The marriage of research and practice: An interview with John M. Gottman. *The Family Journal: Counseling and Therapy for Couples and Families, 11*(2), 216-223. doi:10.1177/1066480702250432

Johnson, S. (2008). Emotionally focused couple therapy. In A. Gurman (Ed.), *Clinical handbook of couple therapy* (4th ed., pp. 107-137). New York, NY: Guilford.

Kerr, M., & Bowen, M. (1988). *Family evaluation.* New York, NY: W. W. Norton.

LaFountain, R.M., & Mustaine, B.L. (1998). Infusing Adlerian theory into an introductory marriage and family course. *The Family Journal, 6*, 189-199.

Lavee, Y., & Yitzhak, A. (2006). Use of standardized assessment instruments in couple therapy: The role of attitudes and professional factors. *Journal of Marital and Family Therapy, 32*(2), 233-244.

Lopez, F. G. (1986). Family structure and depression: Implications for the counseling of depressed college students. *Journal of Counseling and Development. 64*, 508-511.

McGoldrick, M., & Gerson, R. (1985). *Genograms in family assessment.* New York, NY: W. W. Norton.

Miller C. P., & Forrest, A. W. (2009). Ethics of family narrative therapy. *The Family Journal: Counseling and Therapy for Couples and Families, 17*(2), 156-159.

Minuchin, S. (1974). *Families and family therapy.* Cambridge, MA: Harvard University Press.

Minuchin, S., & Fishman, C. H. (1981). *Family therapy techniques.* Cambridge, MA: Harvard University Press.

Papp, P. (1976). Family choreography. In P. Guerin (Ed.), *Family therapy* (pp. 465-479). New York, NY: Gardner Press.

Ramsland, K. (1989). *Engaging the immediate: Applying Kierrkegaard's theory of indirect communication to the practice of psychotherapy.* Toronto, Canada: Associated University Presses.

Rasheed, J. M., Rasheed, M. N., & Marley, J. A. (2011). Family therapy models and techniques. Los Angeles, CA: SAGE.

Satir, V. (1964). *Conjoint family therapy.* Palo Alto, CA: Science and Behavior Books.

Satir, V. (1988). *The new peoplemaking.* Mountain View, CA: Science and Behavior Books.

Scharff, J., & Scharff, D. (2008). Object relations couple therapy. In A. Gurman (Ed.), *Clinical handbook of couple therapy* (4th ed., pp. 167-195). New York, NY: Guilford.

Sherman, R., & Dinkmeyer, D. (1987). *Systems of family therapy: An Adlerian integration.* New York, NY: Brunner/Mazel.

Sherman, R., & Fredman, N. (1986). *Handbook of structured techniques in marriage and family therapy.* New York, NY: Bruner/Mazel.

Sperry, L., Carlson, J., & Peluso, P. (2006). *Couples therapy integrating theory and technique.* Denver, CO: Love.

Trepper, T. S., Dolan, Y., McCollum, E. E., & Nelson, T. (2006). Steve de Shazer and the future of solution-focused therapy. *Journal of Marital and Family Therapy, 32*(2), 133-139.

Tomm, K. (1984). One perspective on the Milan systemic approach: Part I. Overview of development, theory and practice. *Journal of Marital and Family Therapy, 10*(2), 113-125.

Walsh, W., & Keenan, R. (1997). Narrative family therapy. *The Family Journal: Counseling and Therapy for Couples and Families, 5*(4), 332-336.

Walter, J., & Peller, J. (1992). Becoming solution-focused in brief therapy. New York, NY: Brunner/Mazel.

Watts, R., Nelson, J., Bruhn, R., & Nichter, M. (2011). Couple and family counseling. In S. Nassar-McMillan & S. Niles (Eds.), *Developing your identity as a professional counselor: Standards, settings, and specialties* (pp. 336-362). Belmont, CA: Brooks/Cole Cengage.

Watzlawick, P., Weakland, J., & Fisch, R. (1974). *Change: Principles of problem formation and problem resolution.* New York, NY: W. W. Norton.

Whitaker, C., & Keith, D. (1981). Symbolic-experiential family therapy. In A. Gurman, & D. Kniskern (Eds.), Handbook of family therapy (pp. 187-225). New York, NY: Bruner/Mazel.

Author Contact Information: Mary Nichter, PhD, Sam Houston State University College of Education, Department of Educational Leadership and Counseling. Box 2119 Huntsville, TX 77341-2119. Telephone: 936-294-1209. E-mail: edu_msn@shsu.edu

CHAPTER 43

Collaborative Learning Communities

A Postmodern Perspective on Teaching and Learning

Harlene Anderson
Houston Galveston Institute

New landscapes require changing perspectives that in turn call for new practices. The new landscape of education—and collaborative teaching and learning discussed in this chapter—is our fast-changing world, characterized by social, cultural, political, and economic transformations including the influence of the internet and media on the decentralization and dissemination of information and knowledge. Our traditional perspectives on education and mainstream practices of producing knowledge, solving problems and creating change no longer meet the unavoidable contemporary complexities inherent in these changes and the challenges they present. People in every corner of the world demand the opportunity to have a voice in decisions that affect their lives: they want to participate, to contribute and to share ownership. Increasingly, they no longer want to be treated as numbers and categories that ignore their humanness and uniqueness. This can be said of educators and learners.

In addressing these changes educators are pressed to reassess our traditions and the language of our traditions—how we understand the world around us including our educational philosophies, our psychological theories, our students and our roles as educators. We are simultaneously pressed to continually consider what education demands to keep in sync with our fast changing world and create new perspectives that address these demands. In this chapter, I present and discuss my perspective of education and learning: a collaborative approach based in the assumptions of postmodern philosophy including social construction, narrative and dialogue theories. Postmodern assumptions provide an alternative language that in turn provides a particular orientation to educational practices: practices that are germane to students and in which students are actively and intimately engaged in their learning and have a voice in determining and evaluating the what and how of it. In earlier writings I refer to it as *collaborative learning* and *collaborative learning communities* (Anderson, 1998, 2000; Anderson & Swim, 1993, 1994). A story describing a collaborative learning community and collaborative learning—a course for psychotherapy supervisors—will illustrate the approach.

Collaborative learning entails a partnership in which the wisdom, knowledge and customs of the members of a local learning community, for example, education classrooms, business teams, faculty senates, neighborhood citizen associations and parenting groups are acknowledged, accessed and utilized. This requires creating an environment for transformative dialogue in which newness occurs. In turn, the environment requires particular educator values and attitudes: (a) the transformative nature of dialogue and collaboration; (b) trust and confidence in each member's expertise and judgment about, and what is critical to, their daily and future lives; (c) the knowledge and experiences that the students brings as equal to theirs, and (d)

The Handbook of Educational Theories, pp. 515–527

self-reflection and remaining open to their perspectives being examined and challenged. Foremost this requires that the one designated as "teacher" expresses these values and attitudes and invites others to consider them by living them.

Fertile Means to Creative Ends

Collaboration is the fertile means to creative ends. Collaborative partners in their dynamic exchanges generate knowledge and other newness far more creative and abundant and specific to the local context and needs than any member of the partnership could accomplish alone. The notion of collaborative learning is not new. Well documented in fields of art and science (John-Steiner, 2000), for more than 3 decades a growing body of literature suggests in one way or another the importance of collaboration in education, variously referred to as collaborative, collective, cooperative, action, peer, partner, group and team learning (Anderson, 1998, 2000; Anderson & Swim, 1993, 1994; Astin, 1985; Bonwell & Eison, 1991; Bosworth, 1994; Bruffee, 1993; Freire, 1970; Goodsell, Maher, Tinto, Smith, & MacGregor, 1992; Johnson, Johnson & Holubec, 1994; Mezirow, 2000; Peters & Armstrong, 1998; Slavin, 1990; Weiner, 1986).

Collaborative learning is a relational, collective and nonhierarchical approach to education in which each member of the learning community, including educator and student, contributes to the production of new learning and knowledge, its integration and application and shares responsibility in these. It is based on the supposition that knowledge is a communal construction, created in social exchange rather than instructive interaction. In other words, knowledge is a fluid construction rather than a static one than can be passed from one person to another. It is also based on the supposition that the collective learning experience is transformative: what is being learned changes (is altered, modified, extended) in the learning process; likewise, the learning or knowledge-making process itself is transformed in its making as are the persons involved in the learning. Transformative or transforming refers to the generative process in which people engage with each other and with themselves in the sharing and inquiring into their experiences and critically considering and reflecting on familiar and new reference frames and assumptions. Transformative learning is not informational learning in the manner that many of us are accustomed to. Instead, as Harvard University educator and psychologist Robert Kegan suggests, "genuinely transformational learning is always to some extent an epistemological change rather than merely a change in behavioral repertoire or an increase in the quantity or fund of knowledge" (2000, p. 48). Similar to Kegan's notion of epistemological change, educator Jack Mezirow (2000) suggests that it is a change in habits of mind that lead to a change of reference or perspective. We can conclude then that transformational learning has implications beyond the educational space, that it is an opportunity to think differently about ourselves and others and to live differently in our world.

As noted above, the concept and practice of collaborative learning is not new. What is often lacking is its presentation is a discussion of the theoretical or philosophical assumptions on which it is based. This chapter will present a collaborative learning approach based in postmodern philosophical assumptions. It will discuss these assumptions and their implications for collaborative learning and will describe the formation of a collaborative learning community to illustrate how the one designated as the teacher can be consistent with and perform this philosophy in their way of thinking and being.

The Influence of Postmodern Philosophy on the Development of the Collaborative Learning Approach

My interest in collaboration in education came through my years of focus on collaboration in my practices as a psychotherapist, consultant and trainer in various clinical, university and postgraduate training contexts (Anderson, 1998; Anderson & Gehart, 2007; Anderson & Goolishian, 1988). My philosophy of education is based in a body of assumptions that form a world view of understanding human beings as unique, active and engaged participants in the construction of knowledge that has local relevance and fluidity. I am strongly influenced by a set of abstract assumptions associated with postmodern philosophy which support the notion of collaboration in education. Maintaining congruence between my philosophy of psychotherapy and my philosophy of education and being able to perform consistently with these has been of primary importance to me. This requires being what learning systems theorist Donald Schön (1983) describes as a reflective practitioner. Schön refers to the practitioner's reflecting in action: reflecting, pausing and inquiring into to understand one's theoretical underpinnings and to describe one's practice as one does it. In doing so, theory and practice are reciprocally influenced as the practitioner makes new sense of these and thus the practitioner becomes more thoughtful and accountable regarding their work. Based on his research about how professionals learn, Schön suggests that incorporating reflective practice in education leads to learning that is more profound. To paraphrase Schön, self-discovered, self-appropriated learning or learning that belongs to the learner is the only learning that significantly influences behavior. I would add, the way that one lives in both one's professional and personal worlds.

Reexamining the Traditions of Knowledge

We are born and socialized in a world based on the classical world view of the autonomous, bounded and rational self: the individual who thinks and constructs knowledge. Knowledge in this view is an individual accomplishment; it can be transmitted from one person to another and from one generation of discourse to the next, and it can be verified through observation. In this classical world view, we inherit assumed and often obscured knowledge that is centralized, fixed, discoverable and rediscoverable, and we automatically carry out our professional and personal lives in the distant, dualistic, hierarchical relationships and static structures that can flow from this view. Furthermore, we are guided for the most part by theories (e.g., educational, psychological) that we have become heirs to; theories that often seductively lead us to understand human beings (e.g., students, clients) and their lives and behaviors as standardized categories, types and kinds (e.g., students as academic, vocational, motivated, unmotivated).

For more than 3 decades an increasing assembly of scholars and practitioners in the social and human sciences have contributed alternative perspectives to this classical view of knowledge and the autonomous knowledge constructing individual (Berger & Luckman, 1966; Gergen, 1999; Hacking, 1999; Sampson, 1993; Shotter, 1993). Writing under banners such as social construction, hermeneutic, dialogue, language and narrative theories, all are influenced and inspired to some extent by foregoing critical thinkers such as Mikhail Bakhtin (1981, 1984), Gregory Bateson (1972), Jacques Derrida (1978), Hans-George Gadamer (1975), Harold Garfinkel (1967), Jean-Francios Lyotard (1984), Merleau-Ponty (1992), Michael Foucault (1972), Ludwig Wittgenstein (1922/1961), and Lev Vygotsky (1934/1962, 1978). Some of these critical thinkers served as imaginary conversational partners for the assembly of scholars and practitioners, helping each to reflect, to see and to understand differently and thus to further develop their unique contributions that increasingly challenged mainstream psychology, education and related fields of study. You might say that these scholars and practitioners worked in collaboration with the written words of their predecessors, yielding irreverent contributions and creating a rhizome effect at the edge of a move from the classical worldview to a world view of understanding human systems (singular and plural) and their lives and behaviors, as unique, active, engaged participants in the construction of knowledge that has local relevance and fluidity (Anderson & Gehart, 2007).

Similar themes run through the works of these critical thoughts that collectively create the threads of what I suggest as a postmodern philosophy tapestry. Postmodern refers to a set of abstract assumptions, a collage of contemporary hermeneutics philosophy and social construction, narrative and dialogue theories that challenge and provide a contemporary alternative to our inherited and often taken-for-granted and invisible classical traditions of knowledge and language that were from a different age and for a different culture. The central challenge is to reexamine these traditions in which (a) knowledge is fundamental and definitive; (b) knowledge systems have a centralized top-down structure; (c) knowledge is the product of an individual mind; (d) knowledge is fixed, discoverable and re-discoverable; (e) language is descriptive and representational, and (f) meaning is stable.

Six Interconnected Guiding Assumptions: Threads of a Postmodern Tapestry

Meta-Narratives and Knowledge Are Not Fundamental and Definitive

We are born, live and educated within grand knowledge narratives and discourses and the traditions they have produced that we mostly accept without question. We unwittingly buy into and reproduce such institutionalized knowledge that can lead to forms of practice that risk being out of sync with our contemporary societies and possibly alien to them as well. Lyotard (1984) for instance called attention to the seductive nature of the grand narratives – established dominant discourses, universal truths and rules—as privileging, legitimizing and oppressing. Correspondingly, Foucault (1972) called attention to the not-so-visible and often fully invisible power discrepancies that inhabit our language, our words, our relationships and our societies. Words, for instance, he suggests, have hidden mechanisms of coercion and predefinition of relationships of power.

This does not suggest that we abandon our inherited knowledge or discourses (i.e., educational theories, a priori criteria), or that these can be discarded for that matter: any and all knowledge can be useful. Nor does it suggest that postmodernism is a meta-knowledge narrative: it is not. The invitation is simply to question, to be skeptical of and to critically analyze any discourse's claim to truth, including the postmodern discourse itself. In regards to education, "know" why a particular philosophy of education appeals, what does it permit or not permit.

The Generalization of Dominant Discourses, Meta-Narratives and Universal Truths Is Seductive and Risky

Inherent in Lyotard (1984 and Foucault's (1972) warnings about the potential seduction and oppression of grand narratives is a warning about the risks of deliberately and unintentionally assuming the validity of likeness among and across peoples, cultures, situations or problems. In other words, skepticism is suggested regarding the probability that dominant discourses, meta-narratives and universal truths can be generalized and applied across peoples, cultures, situations, or problems.

Thinking in terms of ahead-of-time knowledge (e.g., theoretical scripts, predetermined rules) can lead us to look for similarities and thus we may create categories, types and classes (e.g., people, problems, solutions) that may inhibit our ability to learn about the uniqueness and novelty of each person or group of people. Instead, the invitation is to learn about the distinctiveness of others and their lives directly from them and see the familiar or what we take for granted in an unfamiliar or fresh way. Thus we are challenged to relinquish the custom of viewing, wittingly or unwittingly, the people and the events of their lives encountered in our professional practices as familiar and instead to develop a habit of viewing them as exceptional. Familiarity tempts us to find what we think we know and assumingly fill in the gaps and then proceed based on these. This knowing can put us at risk of depersonalizing the student for instance and can prevent us from learning about each student's specialness, limiting our and their possibilities.

Knowledge and Language Are Interactive and Generative Social Processes

A common assumption of postmodernism is the centrality of knowledge and language (verbal and nonverbal) as contextualized social, cultural, historical and communal processes in which knowledge and language are relational and generative and therefore inherently transforming. That is, we participate in constructing the world we live in. Though this perspective is evident in the writings of critical thinkers such as those mentioned above, it is not as new a perspective as it may appear. As far back as the 1700s Italian philosopher Giambattista Vico denounced the Cartesian method that truth can be verified through observation. He alternatively suggested that the observer participates in the construction of what he observes, attributes their descriptions to it and wears multiple interpretive lenses regarding the same. More contemporarily, constructivists such as Heinz von Foerster (1982) called attention to the notion of observing systems claiming that believing is seeing. Maturana and Varela (1986) suggested that everything said is said by an observer to another observer.

Put differently, embedded as it is in culture, history and language, knowledge is a product of social discourse. The creation of knowledge (e.g., theories, ideas, truths, beliefs, realities or how tos) is an interactive interpretive process that occurs within the discourses of knowledge communities in which all parties contribute to its development, sustainability and transformation. Its creation is a dialogic activity in which there is not a dichotomy between "knower" and "not-knower." Knowledge is not the product of an individual or a collective mind; it is not fundamental or definitive, nor is it fixed or discovered. As Maturana and Varela (1986) suggested there is no such thing as instructive interaction in which preexisting knowledge (including meanings, understandings, etc.) can be taken from the head of one person (be it the voice of a teacher in person or the words of an author on the pages of a book) and placed into the head of another (e.g., a student in a classroom or a reader). Knowledge acquisition by one person is not and cannot be determined by another person; the teacher cannot determine what the student will learn. Knowledge creation is relational, and it is fluid and changeable in its making. Yet personalized: when we share our knowledge with one another, we cannot know what each person brings, we cannot predetermine how each will interact with the shared knowledge nor can we predict what each will create with it. The learning outcome will be something different than either started with, something more than either could have created alone, something socially constructed.

Language in its broadest sense is any means by which we try to communicate, articulate or express with ourselves and with others, verbally or otherwise. It is the medium through which we create knowledge, the tool that we use to construct the realities of our everyday lives. Language, like knowledge, is viewed as active and creative rather than as static and representational. Words, for instance, are not meaning mirrors; they gain meaning as we use them and in the way that we use them. This includes a number of things such as the context in which we use them, our purpose in using them and how we use them such as our tone, our glances and our gestures.

Language and words are relational. Bakhtin (1984) called attention to a new way of understanding language and words and their relationship. In his words, the use of language is "always individual and contextualized in nature." Although a word is an "Expression of some evaluative position of an individual person that person cannot determine how that word will affect another person, what it expresses for that person." Bakhtin suggested that "No utterance in general can be attributed to the speaker exclusively; it is the *product of the interaction of the interlocutors* and broadly speaking, the product of the whole complex *social situation* in which it has occurred" (p. 30). He further suggested that we do not own our words:

> The word in language is half someone else's. The word becomes "one's own" only when the speaker populates it with his own intention ... the word does not exist in a neutral and impersonal language ... but it exists in other people's mouths, in other people's contexts. (1984, pp. 293-294)

Bakhtin's perspective of knowledge and language as interactive social processes that are inherently transforming suggest that students are active agents in their own learning. And if this is so, it calls upon educators to create learning environments that help encourage and enhance this agency to its fullest.

Privilege Local Knowledge

Local knowledge—the wisdom, expertise, truths, values, customs, narratives, et cetera—that is created within a community of persons (e.g., family, classroom, board room, factory team) who have first-hand experience (e.g., unique meanings and understandings from personal experience) of themselves and their situation is important. Knowledge formulated within a community will be more relevant, pragmatic and sustainable for its members. Local knowledge, of course, always develops against the background of dominant discourses, meta-narratives and universal truths (as mentioned above) and is influenced by these conditions. This influence cannot be, nor is it suggested that it should be, avoided.

Knowledge and Language Are Inherently Transforming and Therefore Intrinsically Transforming

Transformation—whether in the form of a shift, modification, difference, movement, clarity, et cetera—is a natural consequence of the fluid and creative aspects of knowledge and language. Just as knowledge is produced in dialogue or conversation so is what is typically called change. Change is not a from-to phenomenon produced from the outside or occurring within a person; it is not an intervening-into process but an ongoing one within the dialogic space. When engaged in the use of language and in the creation of knowledge one is involved in a living dialogic activity (i.e., dialogue with oneself or another) and cannot remain unchanged. From this perspective, in education, both educator and learner are at risk for change.

Self Is a Relational Dialogical Concept

Central in the writings of the above is a challenge and alternative to the traditional notion of the self as a bounded or contained autonomous individual—the essential "me." The alternative proposed is that the person, the self, is a dialogic being who speaks, thinks and acts not as one voice but as the multiplicity of voices that inhabit the person. We, our self identities and those we attribute to others, are constructed in dialogue, in conversation. What a dialogic construction of self or human nature permits according to psychologist Sampson (2008) is not the essence of a person

> but rather will unfold an emerging, shifting and open horizon of human possibilities, which cannot be readily known in advance or outside the dialogue but emerges as a property of the ongoing dialogue itself. (p. 24)

Gergen (2009) who is at the forefront of this contemporary challenge to the traditional notion of the self suggests

> My attempt is to generate an account of human action that can replace the presumption of bounded selves with a vision of relationship. I do not mean relationships between otherwise separate selves, but rather, a process of coordination that precedes the very concept of the self ... that all intelligible action is born, sustained, and/or extinguished within the ongoing process of relationship. (p. 88)

In a similar view on learning, Vygotsky (1962) called attention to the linguistic, social and historical context of creative thinking and cognition and the interdependent nature of their processes as social and individual. He challenged established theories of learning and development, proposing such activities as social, dialectical processes occurring not within the minds of an individual nor transmitted from the teacher to the learner but within social relationships in which the learner plays an active role in the how and what of learning and in which the teacher is likewise a learner. Neither Gergen and nor others mentioned above (such as Bahktin, 1981, 1984; Hermans, 1992; Mead, 1934; Resnick, 1991; Sampson, 1993; Vygotsky, 1934/1962; Wittgenstein, 1922/1961) suggest that the traditional notion of self is false. Instead, the suggestion is that there is an alternative perspective or construction that is more useful, permitting more freedom and flexibility in our thinking and acting and thus our increased possibilities for our futures.

Implications for Pedagogy

How do the above philosophical assumptions and the challenges that flow from them contribute to a different way of thinking about our world and our construction of it and particularly the way we conceptualize and organize our pedagogic practices? Foremost, they inform a philosophical stance: *a way of being*. A way of being refers to a way of orienting with—how we approach—the people we meet in our educational practices and the doing of it. This includes a way of thinking with, being in relationship with, talking with, acting with and responding with. The important word here is *with*. *With* puts us and the other in a *shared engagement* in which the other becomes our *conversational partner* with whom we connect, collaborative and construct (Anderson, 1998). Education is one kind of conversational partnership endeavor.

Central to this philosophical stance is the notion of collaborative relationship and generative conversation that involve dynamic two-way exchanges, sharing, criss-crossing and weaving of ideas, thoughts, opinions and feelings through which newness emerges. St. George and Wulff (in press) at the University of Calgary suggested that collaborating entails

> a way of interacting with others such that everyone contributes in his/her preferred way(s) and a new understanding, idea, or process is developed that would be unlikely by any individual actor. This dialogue is *threaded*, meaning that comments/actions are connected to the other comments/actions. The beauty of collaborating is that there are no set roles; there is a flexibility and fluidity that allows for leading and following to be in motion. In collaborating all participants appreciate the variety of ideas and strive to be inclusive. (Personal communication, 2011).

For collaboration to occur there must be room for each person and their voice to be unconditionally present. What each contributes must be equally appreciated and valued. Having a full sense of being appreciated and valued leads to a sense of belonging (e.g., to the educational community). A sense of belonging to the community leads to a sense of participation which in turn leads to a sense of ownership thus a sense of shared responsibility. All combine to promote contribution to the product (learning) and its sustainability.

Dialogue or dialogic conversation refers to a dynamic form of talk in which participants engage with each other (out loud) and with themselves (silently)—in words or gestures—in a mutual or *shared inquiry*—jointly examining, questioning, wondering, reflecting and so forth about the issues at hand (e.g., a discourse, subject content, opinions). What is put forth in dialogue is interacted with and interpreted, entailing two-way exchanges and crisscrossing of ideas, thoughts, opinions and feelings. Participants are engaged in a shared inquiry in which they try to understand each other, try to learn the uniqueness of their language and their meanings whether expressed in words or without words. In other words, participants engaged in dialogue do not assume they know what the other intends; they do not try to fill in meaning gaps. Through these dialogic exchanges, through the shared inquiry, participants engage in a process of trying to understand each other, through which new meanings, viewpoints and perspectives (e.g., learning) are created.

In education, the goal of collaborative relationships and dialogic conversations is the generation of new learning—such as, new knowledge, expertise, skills—that has relevancy and usefulness beyond the classroom. The process of achieving this goal has several features. Foremost, the one designated as the teacher must trust the collaborative-dialogic process and must trust the students. They must act and talk consistent with the philosophy of collaborative learning. In other words, they must live it, being genuinely and naturally collaborative. This includes respecting, inviting and valuing each voice from the time educator and student first meet and through the duration of the learning program (e.g., course, workshop). This requires that the educator is flexible, responsive and creatively responds to what the occasion calls for at any moment. What begins to be created are relationships and learning that are different from the familiar hierarchical and dualistic teacher-student relationships and learning processes that students have come to know.

Student and teacher and student and student develop connections in which what is learned—for example, knowledge, expertise, and skills—is jointly selected and created in contrast to a so-called knower (e.g., a teacher) bestowing knowledge that is predetermined (e.g., by a teacher, learning institute or larger learning context) upon the one (e.g., student) who does not know.

The collaborative educator wants to create and facilitate learning relationships and processes where participants can identify, access, elaborate and produce their own unique competencies, cultivating seeds of newness in their personal and professional lives outside the learning context. They want to talk and act to invite and encourage participants to take responsibility for, and to be the architects of, their learning.

To illustrate some of the necessary features of collaborative learning and collaborative learning communities and how to create and sustain a collaborative learning community and collaborative learning, I will describe a course for supervisors and how I orient myself to the task and the participants to invite collaborating. I will make comments on how my actions and the structure of the course connect to the assumptions that I talked about earlier. The structure that I will describe serves as an example of a general template and is modified for each course, and as each course evolves, according to the participants and their responses. This is to say that although collaborative learning is often mistaken as unstructured learning, it is simply a particular kind of structure that shifts in response to the learners and the context.

Inviting, Facilitating and Sustaining Collaboration by Doing: A Course for Psychotherapy Supervisors

I conduct a course for psychotherapy supervisors that is required by state licensing boards and professional associations for a therapist, counselor or social worker to be credentialed as a supervisor. The institutional host is the Houston Galveston Institute, a nonprofit psychotherapy training and clinical center. As with any education event, the course takes place within a nest of stakeholders and their expectations. The course is designed to meet each stakeholder's content requirements. It is a 40-hour course comprised of a combination of opportunities and contexts for learning including in-class study, independent study assignments and online exchanges. Course participants meet for two, 2-day sessions scheduled 4 to 6 weeks apart; the out-of-class study assignments and online exchanges are accomplished between the two sessions. The combination of study structures provides multiple opportunities for generative learning.

In the in-class study, I provide brief didactic lectures that I weave throughout the various content topics, discussions and questions. I conduct demonstration supervision consultations with participants and with supervisor-supervisee duos who volunteer to come to the course as guests. During the consultations participants are assigned reflecting roles so that they are not merely observers (Andersen, 1995). Participants may also schedule to invite their supervisees to participate in a consultation session with them. Throughout all of the above, I provide ample time for participants to be involved in conversations with each other and with me. For example, I frequently have participants convene in small conversational clusters to inquire into our various topics, generated questions and assigned readings; they also participate in whole course membership discussions.

The out-of-class assignments include: (a) following each in-class session day participants submit, to me and to each other, a reflection on the day. They note their experience and what struck or surprised them. They also include new questions and topics of interest that they want to address as well as any other suggestions for the next meeting; (b) between the two, 2-day sessions they submit brief reflecting essays on selected required readings, and they write a philosophy of supervision essay; (c) also between the two sessions participants are required to observe two supervision sessions and submit a paper in which they reflect on the observations, compare and contrast the two experiences and note what they learned and if and how the experience has influenced their supervision philosophy or daily performance.

Heterogeneity in Learning Groups

Typically, homogeneity in the membership of the learning group, largely based on a developmental theory of learning, is valued over heterogeneity. In collaborative learning, diversity among participants provides a richness of perspectives and realities that enhance the quality and quantity of the learning that is produced. The supervision course might include experienced and rookie supervisors with degrees in different disciplines, who practice in various clinical settings and who come for distinct reasons. Often participants who have previously completed the course attend again because they value the learning and collegial experience. Each person brings a difference in terms of age/life stage, personal/professional experience, degree/discipline, learning style/agenda and theoretical and practice experience. These differences, I have found over time, help enhance the richness of the learning experience.

Getting Started

Meetings and Greetings

After registering for the course, participants receive a letter welcoming them to it along with copies of suggested precourse readings. On the first day, I greet and introduce myself to each person as they arrive and provide name tags and course folders. I offer them refreshments and ask them to begin to introduce themselves to each other while waiting for the full membership to arrive. I also try to help the participants begin to connect with each other based on what I may know about some of them before they arrive. The chairs are arranged in a circle though depending on the number of participants the seating might be configured otherwise (e.g., concentric circles, chevron). The important thing is that participants can see each other and are not seated in rows where they see only the backs of heads of the others and the face of the course leader in the front of the room. This arrangement is preferred for at least two reasons: (a) when people face each other the opportunity for conversation is enhanced, and (b) because I place myself in the circle as well, it is a less hierarchical arrangement.

Once all have arrived, I welcome the group and briefly introduce myself and say a few words about the Houston Galveston Institute and practicalities of the building. I then tell them that since we will be together for 4 days and that the format will be very interactive, I have found that it helps to take time for each person to introduce themselves. During the introductions I express my curiosity and interest in each person. I comment on or ask a question about something that each person has said.

Creating the Agenda

The course syllabus includes content topics required by the external credentialing institutions and topics I consider important. I want participants, however, to have a voice regarding the course content and the learning structure. After the group introductions, I introduce myself more fully, talking some about my professional history and me as a person. In other words, I think it is just as important to the development of a learning community—one that is more egalitarian and less hierarchical—for them to learn about me as it is for me to learn about them and them about each other.

I then briefly talk about my philosophy regarding the course and its organization. I tell them that I have a lot of experiences and biases about supervision to share with them but I do not assume that we are all here for the same reasons. I tell them that I need their help in selecting out what to emphasize. I ask them to think for a moment why they are in the course: What is their expectation of the course, of me? What would they like to leave with at the end of the fourth day? What are some of the most important things that you think it would be helpful for us to know about them and their everyday work? I then ask them to form small conversational clusters of three to five persons and to share their expectations and so forth. I only designate the number for each cluster, they are free to arrange themselves and to choose spaces available in or outside the building to meet. I trust that each cluster will find their unique way to organize themselves and respond to my request. I find that clusters might discuss all of the questions, address only one, or talk about something different. I do not expect certain kinds of answers or even answers: the questions serve as starters for conversations. I give each cluster a large tablet and markers to share what their conversation generated, a small pragmatic action that enhances engagement and conveys my serious interest in the task and their voices.

I walk around and visit each cluster though I do not participate in the conversations. I do this partly to signal my sincere interest and to have an indication of the content and tone of their talking. Some cluster quickly become energized and engaged with each other, others will have a slower start. What I consistently notice however is that all end up having lively and serious discussions as they learn more about each other and talk about their supervision interests. Collaborative learning has begun.

I reconvene the larger membership and each cluster shares the highlights—what they would like for us to know—of their conversations. I simply ask them to tell us; I do not designate how they should do so. Nor do I use the language of "reporting". First of all, trying to reiterate a conversation can lose the richness of it; second, I hope that the telling about the talk will be generative in itself; and third, I hope that they will experience that when one person tells about the talking how it is that person's interpretation. (This I connect later when I discuss the importance of keeping in mind that when a supervisee "reports" on a therapy session that they are giving their description, experience and interpretation of it.) As each cluster shares, I ask questions to make sure that I understand what they are telling us, what they want us to know about their talking. I then post the tablet sheets on the wall. Through this process, and at the beginning of each session meeting thereafter, participants similarly help create the course content and agenda for each day.

The Learning Continues

Following the agenda collecting on day one, I give an overview to postmodern philosophy and its implications for collaborative learning and supervision. During the presentation I keep their beginning agendas, interests and questions in mind and weave in responses to them as appropriate. After the introduction, I invite participants to form conversational clusters to discuss what I have talked about and to pose new questions that emerged from the overview or their discussion of it. We then reconvene in the large group for a general discussion.

Content is seldom entirely covered in a discrete time frame or as a discrete entity. Instead, various aspects of course content weave throughout each session in various ways. The content agenda (that proposed in the course syllabus now expanded with their added agenda items) is always so full that each session day participants have working lunches. As one participant put it, "Agenda building is a great tool … to state what is important, puzzling, exciting … so that everyone's needs are stated, even though there may be too many items to address!"

Relationships and Conversations Are Inseparable and Reciprocally Influence Each Other

We all know the importance of relationship building though we often short-cut it, failing to give it deserved attention. The way in which an educator greets and meets the learners is critical to setting the tone for a collaborative and dialogical process and to sustaining it.

Beginning to Create Relationships

The quality of the relationship begins before student and teacher meet. It is influenced by each party's preconceived ideas and expectations of the other. These are attributed reputations that might be influenced by personal experience, hearsay, or stereotypical categories and groups of people such as undergraduate psychology students, graduate philosophy students, math professors and so forth. From the collaborative perspective, educators want students to meet and experience them in the present moment. Though educators cannot unilaterally influence how students will experience and describe them, they can take care in what they do and say that will set the stage for collaborating.

To invite and maximize collaborative learning, I must maintain coherence with my philosophy in my acting and speaking. In other words, I must live it, being genuinely and naturally collaborative. This includes respecting, inviting and valuing each voice, being flexible and responsive and creatively doing what the occasion calls for on the spot. This includes trusting the other and our process and trusting the uncertainty that accompanies people walking along together determining the path and destination instead of one person determining it. I want to create and facilitate learning relationships and processes, in which participants can identify, access, elaborate and produce their own unique competencies, cultivating seeds of newness in what they learn and the translation of the newness to their professional and personal lives. I want to talk and act to invite and encourage participants to take responsibility for and to be the architects of their learning. I also want each participant to experience our task and relationship differently from the familiar hierarchical and dualistic teacher-student relationships and learning processes they may have experienced.

Hosts and Guests

In emphasizing the importance of relationship and its association with generative dialogue, I find it helpful to talk about hospitality. I use a host–guest metaphor: it is as if the teacher or supervisor is the host who meets and greets the student or client as a guest while simultaneously being their guest. I ask the participants to take a moment and think about how they like to be received as a guest. What does a host do that makes them feel welcomed or not, at ease or not, special or not and importantly, that they would be invited back. I ask them to describe the quality of the meeting and greeting, what was it like? Likewise, I ask them to think of a time that they had a guest in their home, office, et cetera that was the kind of guest who they would invite back. What were the qualities of the guest? These are not rhetorical questions. I do not expect particular answers. Rather, I want the participants to think about the *sense* of their experience in the relationship and conversation—what it communicated to them, how it invited them to feel welcomed, valued and so forth.

Once they have had an opportunity to think for a moment I ask each to put a few words or phrases about the qualities on a piece of paper. I then ask them to form conversational clusters and talk with each other (sometimes in clusters, sometimes in pairs) about some of their experiences and the qualities of preferred guests and hosts that they have identified. I organize the task with these three steps (thinking, writing, talking) with the following intents in mind. One, I want them to learn to slow down and take the time to be reflective. Two, I want them to experience the generative nature of putting silent thoughts into written and then spoken words. Three, I want them to experience the further generative nature of communicating one's thoughts with another and engaging in process of trying to learn and understand each other's meanings.

We reconvene and hear from each cluster. I make a list of the qualities they have identified, and while doing so I take the opportunity to discuss and relate their comments to the some of the material covered in my earlier introductory comments about postmodern philosophy and its application to supervision. As well, participants' talk always serves as an opportunity to revisit and expand on my previous didactic moments as well as introduce new material.

I conclude by highlighting that they have just created a vision of the kind of guest and host they want to be as a supervisor. I emphasize however the importance of keeping in mind that even though we may have shared visions and values, how we each perform those will be influenced by our individual unique "style," the person(s) we are supervising, the occasion and the context. Additionally, we must be able to spontaneously adapt to each new and continuing relationship and conversation and its circumstances. Each conversational partnership is distinctive; it forms and evolves, mutually and periodically readapting and redefining itself over time.

Authority and Power in the Relationship

Questions about authority and power never fail to arise when discussing collaborative learning. Does not the teacher have power over the students? Does not the teacher evaluate the student? My response is "yes" and "no" to such questions. Inequities are inherent in and supported by our societies and its institutions and unfortunately the traditions of these inequities are passed on from generation to generation. An educator—the role of a teacher or supervisor—is granted power and authority by the multiple cultural and organizational contexts in which they perform and the discourses they participate in. They are automatically placed in a hierarchical position. Each person however holds the personal freedom to choose how to exercise that power and authority. What I am most interested in is how I can position myself within these cultural and organizational contexts to best offer my knowledge in an environment in which the learner can summon his or her voice and be in charge of his or her own learning.

One of the discussion questions that participants in the supervision course always add to the agenda is how to go back to their everyday work settings and begin not only to supervise from a collaborative perspective but to position themselves and perform collaboratively with their colleagues in hierarchically arranged organizations. In conjunction with a brief didactic piece, I find it effective to use the participant's own material in such discussions. For example, I might ask a participant to briefly tell us about a recent or imagined experience related to this concerning question. Using their material makes the discussion more relevant and useful as they begin to engage in exploring putting what they are learning in the course into their everyday work.

Collaborative learning and participation in collaborative learning communities gives participants—*citizens*—the opportunity to have their taken-for-granted assumptions about education challenged. They experience the opportunity to think reflectively and critically, to be curious about others' assumptions, to have their assumptions examined by others and to share in the responsibility for learning. This in itself is empowering.

EVALUATION

Closely associated with the notion of power and authority is evaluation. In the supervision course, participants either complete or do not complete the course. They receive a certificate of completion if they have attended all of the sessions and submitted the documentation for the out-of-class assignments (reflections, essays, etc.). I do not judge the quality of their products. I find that they become their own evaluators. Because they share what they have produced with the other participants, I find that they compare their products with the others'. They comment on the new thoughts, perspectives and learning that emerge from these exchanges.

When I teach in a context where I must assign a grade, I make every effort to have a collaborative evaluation. For instance, if I am supervising a university therapy team, I must turn in an evaluation for each student and assign a grade. I create a forum of co/self-evaluation. I ask students to evaluate themselves and I evaluate them (using the university form in both instances). We then meet and compare and discuss our evaluations. I then complete the form a second time based on our discussion and mutual agreement regarding the rankings. In addition to this process I conduct a team evaluation. In a team meeting I have each member of the team evaluate themselves, noting areas in which they think they have development as a therapist and areas where they want to further develop. I also ask them to tell how the team members and I can help them achieve these learning goals. Once each member of the team has had a turn, I then ask the members to discuss how they think we are doing as a team, what has really helped their growth and development as a therapist, what they would like for us to do differently. Sometimes I ask the team to comment on each other, noting areas of growth and development that they have seen in each other. The students also evaluate me. I leave the room and they anonymously complete an evaluation form as I do as well. We then discuss what they want me to do more of, less of and in addition to. All of the above engage students in being reflective, assessing and responsible for their own learning as well as the teams.

RELATIONAL EXPERTISE

Being collaborative means that I too must be a learner; I must believe that I can learn as much as the participants. This does not mean that I discount my wealth of so-called knowledge nor do I think that I can leave it behind when I enter the classroom or web course. This does not mean that I ignore or do not use my knowledge whether in the form of ideas, opinions or experiences. The difference is the intention and manner with which I use it: my intent is to help the other person learn and to learn alongside them.

REFLECTING PROCESS

As mentioned above, an important part of learning and especially collaborative learning is the opportunity for reflecting—reflecting with oneself and others, putting silent thoughts into spoken or written words. This encourages learners to be active and purposeful in their learning and in determining its direction. My hope is that the reflecting experiences for instance of the supervision course will encourages reflection as part of everyday practice: reflecting with one's self, reflecting among supervisors and supervisees and among therapists and clients. The reflection process consistently builds in continuous self, other, course and teacher evaluation as well. Importantly, the reflecting processes help me continually learn the participants' changing needs and improve my teaching by adjusting my style and the course structure to best serve their individual and combined needs—to accommodate to what each group, occasion, circumstance and relationship calls for at any one time.

It is equally important for me to reflect as well. I offer my reflections at the end of a session and at the beginning of the next. I share my inner thoughts perhaps about what we have done together, about what struck me that day, what I now think I might have done differently. As well I periodically reflect during the session itself.

Learner's Feedback About Collaborative Learning

Participants overwhelmingly report in their reflections and end of course evaluations that though they feel they have learned more than they ever expected to learn, that the learning process is more important than the content. Participants consistently report amazement at the richness and meaningfulness of the process. They comment on how the communication of the conversations transpires, the emergence of new learning and the surprising changes in their thoughts and practices. They express gratefulness for the opportunity to be thoughtful active learners, although at first the experience is unfamiliar and challenging. They appreciate and develop the richness of possibilities as they move from a need for certainty and closure to a sense of comfortableness with uncertainty and the yet to come. In one participant's words, "it [collaborative learning experience] gave me a new sense of self-confidence." As another learner put it, "The atmosphere beckoned to me, 'Take a chance.' "

Participants report ways that the new learning is useful in their everyday work. They begin to appreciate what their supervisees bring to the table—listening and hearing their stories differently. As one participant said, "respect for the supervisor-supervisee relationship as well as for each of their positions—that no one position is of greater importance than another." Another one said she valued learning to talk about supervisees and clients with "critical thinking and compassion" rather than with a pejorative and judgmental attitude. Another describes a shift in her perspective of her therapy clients,

> I am constantly amazed at how my supervisees change, as they are willing to learn more about their client's lives, their struggles, their histories. Their negativity usually reduces in proportion to their openness. I amaze myself when I am willing to be more open-minded as well.

Another told of her supervisees' experience of collaboration,

> My supervisees have reported that my nonhierarchical and collaborative model of supervision is refreshing compared to previous supervision in which the supervisee feels intimidated and judged.

Also noteworthy is that participants express pride of ownership in the course and accountability for their learning. They also describe a new sense of responsibility to each other. That is, as one positions oneself differently with another—as I position myself differently with the learners—we boldly experience that no one holds sole responsibility. When responsibility is shared—as participants connect, collaborate and construct with each other—the learning relationship and process are more mutually gratifying and rewarding. These experiences with supervision as collaborative learning reported by supervision course participants and their supervisees are consistent with other accounts of supervision from a postmodern perspective (Caldwell, Becvar, Bertolino, & Diamond, 1997).

What seems to most surprise and delight them are the personal transformations they experience. They report thinking differently about themselves and experiencing and acting differently with family and friends. They report feeling more confident and competent in all aspects of their lives.

Conclusion

You can neither teach someone to be collaborative nor how to learn collaboratively. Educators can however create environments in which students learn to learn collaboratively. The essential relationships and conversational processes spontaneously emerge out of the experience itself, learning by doing rather than through be lecturing and so forth. Students move from a tradition of individualized competitive learning to a new experience of shared inquiry and construction. In so doing, students become more active agents in their learning, they enhance each other's learning and they share with each other the responsibility for their own and each other's learning. Students report satisfaction and amazement at not only what and how the learning has applicability in other areas of their lives. In other words, learning is a transforming experience from fertile means to creative ends.

References

Andersen, T. (1995). Reflecting processes, acts of informing and forming: You can borrow my eyes but you can't take them away from me. In S. Friedman (Ed.). *The reflecting team in action: Collaborative practice in family therapy* (pp. 11-37). New York, NY: Guilford.

Anderson, H. (1998). Collaborative learning communities. In S. McNamee & K. J. Gergen (Eds.). *Relational responsibility: Resources for sustainable dialogue* (pp. 65-70). Newbury Park, CA: Sage Publications.

Anderson, H. (2000, Fall). Supervision as a collaborative learning community. *American Association for Marriage and Family Therapy Supervision Bulletin*, 7-10.

Anderson, H. & Gehart, D. (2007). *Collaborative therapy: Relationships and conversations that make a difference.* New York, NY: Routledge.

Anderson, H., & Goolishian, H. (1988). Human systems as linguistic systems: Evolving ideas about the implication of theory and practice. *Family Process, 27*, 371-393.

Anderson, H., & Swim, S. (1993). Learning as collaborative conversation: Combining the student's and the teacher's expertise. *Human systems: The Journal of Systemic Consultation and Management, 4*,145-160.

Anderson, H., & Swim, S. (1994). Supervision as collaborative conversation: Combing the supervisor and the supervisee voices. *Journal of systemic Therapies, 14*(2), 1-13.

Astin, A. W. (1985). *Achieving educational excellence.* San Francisco, CA: Jossey-Bass.

Bakhtin, M. M. (1981). *The dialogic imagination: Four essays* (M. Holquist, Ed.; C. Emerson & M. Holquist, Trans.) Austin, TX: University of Texas Press.

Bakhtin, M. M. (1984). *Rabelais and his world* (H. Iswolsky, Trans.). Bloomington, IN: Indiana University Press.

Bateson, G. (1972). *Steps to an ecology of the mind.* New York, NY: Ballantine Books.

Berger, P. L., & Lukermann, T. (1966). *The social construction of reality: A Treatise in the sociology of knowledge.* Garden City, NY: Anchor Books.

Bonwell, C. C., & Eison, J. A. (1991). *Active learning: Creating excitement in the classroom* (ASHE-ERIC Higher Education Report 1). Washington, DC: The George Washington University, School of Education and Human Development.

Bosworth, K. (1994). Developing collaborative skills in college students. *New Directions for Teaching and Learning, 59*, 25-31.

Bruffee, K. (1993). *Higher education, interdependence and the authority of knowledge.* Baltimore, MD: The John Hopkins University Press.

Caldwell, K., Becvar, D. S., Bertolino, R., & Diamond, D. (1997) A postmodern analysis of a course on clinical supervision. *Contemporary Family Therapy, 19*, 269-287

Derrida, J. (1978). *Writing and difference.* (A. Bass, Trans.). Chicago, IL: University of Chicago Press.

Foucault, M. (1972). *The archeology of knowledge.* Sheridan, London: Tavistock.

Freire, P. (1970). *Pedagogy of the oppressed.* New York, NY: Herder and Herder.

Gadamer, H-G. (1975). *Truth and method* (G. Burden & J. Cumming, Trans.) New York, NY: Seabury Press.

Garfinkel, H. (1967), *Studies in Ethnomethodology.* Englewood Cliffs, NJ: Prentice-Hall.

Gergen, K. L. (1999). *An invitation to social construction.* Thousand Oaks, CA: SAGE.

Gergen, K. L. (2009). *An invitation to social construction* (2nd ed.) London, England: SAGE.

Goodsell, A., Maher, M., Tinto, V., Smith, B., & MacGregor, J. (1992). *Collaborative learning: A sourcebook for higher education.* University Park, PA: Pennsylvania State University.

Hacking, I. (1999). *The social construction of what?* Cambridge, MA: Harvard University Press.

Hermans, H. J. M. (1992). The limitations of logic in defining the self. *Theory and Psychology, 5*, 375-382.

John-Steiner, V. (2000). *Creative collaboration.* New York, NY: Oxford University Press.

Johnson, D. W., Johnson, R. T., & Holubec, E. J. (1994). *The nuts and bolts of collaborative learning.* Edina, MN: Interaction Book.

Keagan, R. (2000). What form transforms? A constructive-developmental perspective on transformational learning. In J. Mezirow (Ed.) *Learning as transformation: Critical perspectives of a theory-in-progress* (pp. 3-34). San Francisco, CA: Jossey-Bass.

Lyotard, J. -F. (1984). *The post-modern condition: A report on knowledge.* Minneapolis, MN: University of Minneapolis Press.

Maturana, H., & Varela, F. (1986). *The tree of knowledge.* New York, NY: Shambhala.

Mead, G. H. (1934). *Mind, self, and society* (C. W. Morris, Ed.). Chicago, IL: University of Chicago Press.

Merleau-Ponty, M. (1992). *Phenomenology of perception* (C. Smith, Trans.) London, England: Routledge.

Mezirow, J. (2000). *Learning as transformation.* San Francisco, CA: Jossey-Bass.

Peters, J., & Armstrong, J. (1998). Collaborative learning: People laboring together to construct knowledge. *New Directions for Adult and Continuing Education, 79*, 75-85.

Resnick, L. B. (1991). Shared cognition: Thinking as social practice. In L. B. Resnick, J. M. Levine, & S. D. Teasley (Eds), *Perspectives on socially shared cognition* (pp 1-20). Washington, DC: American Psychological Association.

Sampson, E. E. (1993). *Celebrating the other.* Boulder, CO: Westview Press.

Sampson, E. E. (2008). *Celebrating the other: A dialogic account of human nature.* Chagrin Falls, OH: The Taos Institute Publications.

Schön, D. (1983). *The reflective practitioner: How professionals think in action.* New York, NY: Basic Books.

Shotter, J. (1993). *Conversational realities: Constructing life through language.* London, England: KCC Foundation.

Slavin, R. E. (1990). *Cooperative learning: Theory, research and practice.* Needham Heights, MA: Allyn & Bacon.

Smith, B. L., & MacGregor, J. T. (1992). What is collaborative learning? In A. Goodsell, M. Mahe, & V. Tinto (Eds.), *Collaborative learning: A sourcebook for higher education* (pp. 10-30). University Park, PA: The National Center on Postsecondary Teaching, Learning and Assessment at Pennsylvania State University.

St. George, S. & Wulff, D. (in press). Frequently asked questions: What is collaboration? *International Journal of Collaborative Practices.*

von Foerster, H. (1982). *Observing systems.* Salinas, CA: Intersystems Publications.

Vygotsky, L. S. (1962). *Thought and language* (E. Hanfmann & G. Vakar, Trans.). Cambridge, MA: MIT Press. (Original work published in 1934)

Vygotsky, L. S. (1978). *Mind in society: The development of higher psychological processes.* Cambridge, MA: Harvard University Press.

Wiener, H. S. (1986). Collaborative learning in the classroom: A guide to evaluation. *College English, 48*, 52-61.

Wittgenstein, L. (1961). *Tractatus logico-philosophicus* (D. Pears & B. McGulness, Trans.). London, England: Routledge and Kegan Paul. (Original work published in 1922).

Author Contact Information: Harlene Anderson, PhD, Houston Galveston Institute, 3316 Mount Vernon St., Houston, TX 77006. Telephone: 713-522-7122. E-mail: harleneanderson@earthlink.net

CHAPTER 44

Feminist Counseling Theory

Amanda C. La Guardia
Sam Houston State University

Amy T. Banner
University of Scranton

The feminist theoretical perspective emerged and continues to develop as an approach designed to address the societal and systemic inequity that exists as a result of culturally defined gender normative expectations. Feminist theorists in counseling, higher education and other fields of study envision themselves as advocates for change and challengers of the status quo. Therefore, in practice, feminist theory is a way of highlighting societal injustice, gender inequity, and the needs of women and other marginalized populations. The three main tenets of feminist theory are (1) the personal is political; (2) empowering and valuing of the female voice; and (3) fostering egalitarian relationships. Within feminist counseling, there are several schools of thought ranging from radical feminist theory to liberal or cultural feminist perspectives. While all of the varying viewpoints within feminist theory differ slightly with regard to their practical focus, each situates itself around the three core values of empowerment, personal and societal intersection, and the privileging of marginalized experiences.

With regard to counseling and education, the main feminist frameworks professionals tend to identify with are radical, liberal and cultural and those will be reviewed here. Some others include the queer and lesbian feminist perspective, feminist women-of-color, and transnational feminists (Enns, 2004). As feminism has become aligned with postmodernist philosophical thinking (or vice versa as both movements have influenced one another) each of these frameworks will be presented with postmodernism as a foundational guide.

History and Development

Feminist theory, as it is understood and practiced today, includes constructs influenced by historical events that began with the women's suffrage movements occurring in several industrialized countries throughout the world between the late 1800s and the early twentieth century. As a social movement feminism is currently in a postmodernist phase. This period in the development of the theory has followed the three typically known "waves" of feminist philosophy, thought, and political action. The postmodernist perspective is also sometimes associated with third wave feminist thinking. While the first and second waves of the feminist movement focused on establishing equal rights, discrimination, and liberation the third wave served to develop feminist thinking within a variety of realms with a focus on cultural issues as a whole, rather than just attending to specific issues such as suffrage or pay disparities. Snyder (2008) defines the third wave movement as being centered on intersectional and personal versions of feminism, valuing action over theoretical justification, and emphasizing inclusivity of the possible dynamic perspectives present concerning issues of gender equity. The postmodernist perspective, as separate from the third wave definition, sets the stage for a global view on women's issues and is not solely situated within the historical context of the United States.

Goals and Assumptions

The tenets that make up feminist theory are generally regarded to fall within postmodernist philosophical

The Handbook of Educational Theories, pp. 529–540

thinking. Feminist teleology is centered in the diversity of women's experiences of oppression. This may come in the form of gender bias, but may also be experienced within the realm of other marginalized societal positions (i.e., ethnicity, SES [social economic status], sexual orientation). Congruent with the postmodernist teleological perspective, each individual creates her or his purpose, truth, or personal meaning as a result of the intersections of individual experience with dominant cultural expectations or messages. In essence, a collective reality exists as created through the dominant cultural messages each society or the world ethos perpetuates. Given this perspective, the individual experience of society through one's unique perspective is considered essential to understanding a person's life. Therefore, feminist theory is grounded in the idea of social constructivism or the belief that a person creates her or his own values and beliefs related to society, which is based on her or his interpretation of societal norms, messages, culture, and family atmosphere through her or his unique positioning within these realms. The overarching goal of feminist counseling or any application of feminist theory is to give voice to those who experience marginalization as a result of the dominant culture and to empower action towards affirming a self authorized perspective on life (Belenky, Clinchy, Goldberger, & Tarule, 1997; Brown, 1994).

Radical feminists tend to work from the perspective that in order for women to achieve equality in society, fundamental change must occur within our social and political constructs and that this change should be facilitated through the counseling or pedagogical relationship. Gender-role distinctions are seen to perpetuate inequality and patriarchy and are actively undermined, confronted, and discussed openly by feminist practitioners. Radical feminists believe that ending the oppression of women is cannot be easily addressed by achieving equality or gaining a "bigger piece of the pie" because the "pie" of society "itself is rotten" (as cited in Enns, 2004, p. 99). Clients and students are encouraged to question traditional and emerging gender-role distinctions and transgress societal boundaries associated with being male or female.

Liberal feminism began with the suffrage movement of the early twentieth century and continues today through feminist empiricism; a focus on change in societal policy through feminist empirical research. The liberal feminist perspective seeks to create equality for women by considering their unique life experiences on the macro level through the development of public policy and on the microlevel through counseling and within the classroom. One of the most notable liberal feminists is Betty Friedan who focused on the processes by which women internalize their own oppression. A person working from this particular feminist framework would likely focus on providing the support necessary for women to realize their own potential, abilities, and options so that they could create goals based on their unique strengths rather than the societal messages that may limit them.

Finally, cultural feminist and indeed feminists focusing on women-of-color and queer theory seek to value all aspects of women's lives, traditional and otherwise, while considering a context of intersectional oppression. Women are encouraged to discover their own truth based on their own values and experiences rather than adhering to the external *shoulds* or expectations created by others. A feminist acting from this perspective would focus on the complexity of individual experience and attempt to understand a person's unique social context prior to supporting students or clients in determining and achieving their goals (be them academic or otherwise). For example, bell hooks (1994) describes intersections of race and feminism in the feminist classroom through a report of a common student experience she encountered when teaching:

> Their [black students] relentless efforts to link all discussions of gender with race may be seen by white students as deflecting attention away from feminist concerns and thus contested. Suddenly, the feminist classroom is no longer a safe haven ... confronting one another across differences means that we must change ideas about how we learn; rather than fearing conflict we have to find ways to use it as a catalyst for new thinking, for growth. (p. 113)

This sentiment highlights the need for feminist instructors and practitioners to value the differing perspectives that each individual may bring to the content being discussed as each viewpoint comes from a unique and equally important positioning in society. Cultural feminism and indeed all feminist perspectives value the sharing of personal narratives or experiences in the process of knowing. In the classroom, these narratives would be linked with the subject being discussed and in a counseling session, the sharing of experiences would be used to build a relationship and help the client develop new perspectives when working toward her or his stated goals.

Application to Diverse Populations

The intersection of oppression, experience, and personalized perspective is a key to understanding individuals within a cultural and systemic context. Essentially, this means that a counselor or educator must focus on the way in which clients or students perceive their own cultural norms through the lens of their individually developed life experiences. In order to highlight how cultural intersectionality is important to diversity from a feminist perspective, the case of Jalbala will be evaluated from a global, gender specific, ethnic, spiritual and holistic framework. Jalbala, or Bala for short, is a 35 year-old Indian-American female who identifies as being a lesbian. She immigrated to the United States with her family when she was five and is estranged from her parents, although she is still close with her older brother and younger sister. She states that she was raised Buddhist, but has not practiced since her partner died three years ago. Bala has decided to return to school to finish her bachelor's degree at the urging of her siblings. Currently, she is struggling with her spirituality as well as her feelings of rejection from her culture due to her sexuality. In order to help highlight the feminist perspective on diversity, Bala's case will be used to exemplify certain aspects of the theory.

Because a primary goal of feminist counseling theory is liberation from oppression (Brown, 1994), the approach is appropriate for every person who has experienced oppression; thus, it is applicable across all genders, ethnicities, cultures, and abilities. In feminist counseling theory, the personal is political. In essence, this means that the personal pain of oppression cannot be separated from the specific cultural, social, and political environment in which each individual exists. Therefore, we are able to discuss the application of feminist counseling theory to the diverse social, cultural, and political realities related to the case of Bala for illustration of certain theoretical concepts.

Gender Issues

Women can certainly benefit from feminist counseling theory as it was originally developed to address women's needs related to sexism. Many dominant societies and cultures tend to devalue women and their experiences whereas feminist counselors view women and their experiences as important and central (Brown, 1994). Feminist counselors assume that all women have been negatively affected by patriarchy and that, as a group, women have been silenced and ignored to the point where many have forgotten the importance of their voice and how to listen to and trust their own wisdom (Belenky et al., 1997; Brown, 1994). In response to patriarchical oppression, feminist counselors encourage women to value their experiences, give voice to their perspectives, trust their own wisdom, and resist those who would repress these processes.

In therapy with Bala, a feminist counselor would begin by establishing an equal, respectful, and open relationship. The counselor would listen for and ask questions about the ways in which Bala has been negatively affected by patriarchy and sexism within her culture of origin and within the current culture and cultural subgroups to which she belongs. For example, the counselor may ask, "How have you been treated as less valuable because of your gender?" and "How have your experiences as a woman been ignored or painted as abnormal?" Using education, encouragement, and empowerment, the counselor would help Bala value and trust herself, her experiences, and her wisdom. The counselor could accomplish these goals by asking Bala about her unique experience, by encouraging Bala to listen to her own voice when seeking answers, and by sharing her perspectives during the counseling process. The counselor might use any number of techniques to enhance this work; the essence of feminist counseling is not the technique used but the way in which the counselor thinks about and approaches her or his work (Brown, 1994). Whereas Bala's experiences as a woman contribute to the likelihood of a good fit between her needs and the goals of feminist counseling theory, people of other genders are likely to benefit from the approach as well.

Men

Because of feminist counseling theory's origins and its primary focus on women's experiences, it may seem surprising to some that the theory can also be useful for men in counseling. Indeed, the question of whether men should be involved in feminist work has been and remains controversial (Good, Gilbert, & Scher, 1990; Holmgren & Hearn, 2009; Jardine & Smith, 1987). Nonetheless, feminist counseling theory posits that all human beings are influenced by patriarchy and sexism even those who benefit from patriarchal privilege (Brown, 1994). Men are held to a very narrow set of standards that require them to be individualistic, independent, separatist, stoic, strong, and powerful; these norms are limiting and destructive as they create boundaries for acceptable societal behavior (Keller, 1986). A feminist counselor might educate a male client about these processes and encourage him to become more aware of and to voice vulnerabilities, insecurities, fears, and longings for genuine connection that have been labeled not to be masculine by dominant social and cultural expectations (Good et al., 1990). In addition, a feminist counselor would discuss the male client's involvement in privilege and patriarchy and encourage him to make changes that would benefit him, finding ways to be active in society to perpetuate this change and encourage others. Unfortunately, due to expectations of strength and independence, men are less likely to seek counseling and are therefore less likely to benefit from this approach (Good et al., 1990; McCarthy & Holliday, 2004).

Transgendered Individuals

Although not always recognized as a distinct gender group, transgendered individuals do not fit within the traditional dichotomous social distinction of gender afforded by the labels *man* and *woman*. In broad terms, transgendered individuals experience a disconnect between their biological sex and their self-perceived gender (Wester, McDonough, White, Vogel, & Taylor, 2010). It is important to note that this basic description does not indicate the immense diversity among transgender individuals, nor the fact that these individuals are involved in an ongoing process to describe themselves (Carroll, Gilroy, & Ryan, 2002). Because of these two internal realities, it is imperative that counselors recognize the specificity of each transgender individual (Halberstam, 1998) and employ culturally appropriate counseling when working with this group (American Counseling Association [ACA], 2005). Feminist counselors are well-prepared to meet both of these requirements given their focus on the singularity of personal knowledge. Further, transgendered individuals face many challenges including sexism, homo-prejudice, abandonment and rejection by loved ones, dangers of violence associated with disclosure, and the need for social and political activism for themselves (Carroll et al., 2002). In addition, transgendered individuals often are viewed as traitors by those who share their biological sex and as unwelcome imposters by those who share their self-perceived gender (Halberstam, 1998).

Feminist counselors are well-prepared to encourage and empower these individuals as they struggle with oppression and the devaluing of their experience by dominant social, political, and cultural groups. More specifically, feminist counselors argue that reality (including gender) is constructed by individuals within a social context (Brown, 1994). This nonessentialist view provides the space that transgendered individuals need to explore their specific, constructed realities and to self-identify in a way that fits for them (Carroll et al., 2002). This constructivist approach of feminist counseling theory applies to clients interested in exploring their personal spirituality, as well.

Spirituality

In the past, spirituality was not a topic that was embraced or even tolerated by many feminists (Plaskow & Christ, 1989), counselors (Cashwell & Young, 2005), or feminist counselors (Funderbunk & Fukuyama, 2002). Unfortunately, patriarchal religion has been used to oppress, suppress, subordinate, separate, silence, devalue, and shame many women (Banner, 2009; Briggs & Banner, 2011; Flinders, 1998; Fukuyama, Siahpoush, & Sevig, 2005; Plaskow & Christ, 1989; Spretnak, 1982), causing emotional, psychological, and spiritual pain (Fukuyama et al., 2005; Briggs & Banner, in press). Because of this, feminists have worked to reform and transform patriarchal religion in such a way that welcomes, values, affirms, and heals women (Plaskow & Christ, 1989) and many women have set aside or modified traditional religion in order to seek a spiritual path that better meets their needs (Borysenko, 1999; Briggs & Banner, in press). Central to these processes has been a valuing of each woman's unique spiritual experience and recognition that there are common themes across women's spirituality (Banner, 2009; Briggs & Banner; Spretnak; Ruth, 1994). Further, there is the recognition that spirituality is innate and may be an important aspect of women's overall well-being and therefore useful to the work that counselors and clients do together (Briggs & Banner, in press).

Two of the themes of women's spirituality that may be the most pertinent and useful to Bala from a feminist counseling perspective are *immanent power* and *embodied divinity*. The view of power as immanent instead of external and hierarchical emphasizes the precedence of a woman's experience over external authority (Spretnak, 1982; Ruth, 1994). The view of divinity as embodied emphasizes the availability of the divine to all without rules or restrictions (Spretnak, 1982; Banner, 2009). When women believe that power and divinity dwell within themselves, they may be more likely to trust, value, respect, and appreciate their experiences, their strength, their bodies, and themselves (Christ, 1982; Spretnak, 1982; Ruth, 1994; Banner, 2009; Briggs & Banner, in press), all outcomes that are essential goals of feminist counseling (Brown, 1994). Thus, a feminist counselor might weave the themes of immanent power and embodied divinity into her work with Bala in order to address the pain that Bala feels related to her culture's rejection of her and her sexuality. Considering Bala's expressed struggle with spirituality and the fact that she has not practiced her religion for three years, a feminist counselor would encourage and empower Bala to construct her own spirituality based on her personal experiences and unique needs. One aspect of Bala's experience that is likely to be a factor in her preferred approach to spirituality is her race and ethnicity.

Race and Ethnicity

Early feminist theorists focused on gender as the most salient personal characteristic only to learn that whereas this may be true for some women, it is not true for all women (Brown, 1994). They were criticized for using "white-oriented models" (p. 59) that ignored the experiences of women of color and issues associated with racism (Combahee River Collective, 1977). Women of color, like Bala, are members of two oppressed groups, and thus have a unique standpoint not shared by all women (Combahee River Collective, 1977). Bala's standpoint is even more complex, however, in that Bala is not only a woman, not only a non-White woman, but also a non-white woman who originates from an ethnic group and nation outside of the United States. Thus, Bala has experienced oppression as a woman, as a woman of color, and as an immigrant from South-Asia (Patel, 2007). Further, Bala may have experienced a unique combination of racism and sexism often encountered by South-Asian-American women who are stereotyped and objectified as either asexual and unattractive or hypersexual and exotic (Patel, 2007).

Considering these factors, a feminist counselor may ask questions designed to help Bala explore her unique experience and internalization of racism and sexism such as, "What's been your experience of racism and sexism?" and "How have these experiences shaped your view of yourself?" Because stereotypes and objectification may have denied Bala the right to define herself, her counselor may ask questions that give Bala the opportunity to voice her own identity such as, "How do you describe yourself?" and "What do you value about yourself?" In addition, a feminist counselor may encourage Bala to identify a powerful South-Asian-American woman with whom she might relate such as Urvashi Vaid, a past leader of the National Gay and Lesbian Taskforce (Patel, 2007). Given the fact that Bala may never be fully accepted as "American" because she is not white or does not fit into dominant cultural norms and because she has been rejected by her culture of origin, such personal identification could be empowering and encouraging.

Sexual Orientation

Unfortunately, Bala's experience of rejection based on her sexuality is not uncommon. Lesbian, gay, bisexual, and questioning (LGBQ) individuals often are ostracized by their loved ones because of their sexuality. Feminist counseling theory asserts that heterosexuality is a dominant institution (Brown, 1994) that is presented as "normal" thereby rendering all other forms of sexuality deviant (Rich, 1980). In reality, the problem lies in the dominant social and cultural norms (Brown, 1994) and in the oftentimes severe penalties for not complying with heterosexuality (Rich, 1980). Sometimes, LGBQ individuals internalize this heterosexism and the expectations of women's gender role socialization resulting in emotional and psychological pain. Szymanski and Gupta (2009) examined the relationships among internalized racism, internalized heterosexism, self-esteem, and psychological distress among African American LGBQ individuals and reported that both internalized racism and heterosexism were significantly associated with lower self-esteem whereas internalized heterosexism was associated with increased psychological distress. As this study and the personal experience of non-White LGBQ individuals suggests, belonging to multiple marginalized groups exacerbates the negative results of oppression.

A feminist counselor working with Bala, therefore, would be interested in the affects of such oppression in her life. A counselor might ask Bala to voice the pain of rejection that she has experienced. As Bala may have been denied social support for the loss of her partner, her counselor may ask about injustices experienced by her and her partner when they were together and how that may influence her grieving process. Bala has many reasons to feel anger and may have experienced powerlessness, as well. To help Bala move towards a feeling of personal empowerment, her counselor might encourage Bala to explore her anger and, if appropriate, to use the energy associated with that anger to work for equal rights for LGBQ individuals, such as the right to adopt (Baumgardner & Richards, 2000).

Global Perspective

Globalization seems as though it is a macrocosm of a process that has been occurring throughout history. As our population grows, so does our concept of community and our willingness to live in a world of increasing complexity and ambiguity. This has been historically true in that 500 years ago, the idea of instantaneously being able to communicate with someone thousands of miles away seemed impossible and the influence of drastically different cultures was minimal. Now, the majority of children grow-up with the knowledge of the existence of societies very different than their own and possibilities for communication never conceived of in previous generations. This will influence their style of living, their values, and their beliefs related to their own competency in functioning within what is now perceived as insurmountable complexity. Bringing a gendered lens to this process allows for an awareness of diversity and a valuing of differing voices that will influence the future. If the complexity of cultural interactions and the intersections of self, gender, and society were a function of life that was realized and valued, then the process of globalization might be realized as a process that could create positive change.

The addition of a feminist framework can help to mediate the needs and goals of the individual with the changing complexities of the global society. By highlighting the processes that occur as a result of hierarchical views currently permeating globalization, a path towards an egalitarian framework can be found. In order to create awareness and bring a differing perspective, it is first important to allow the presence of women and other oppressed groups into the global arena. Women play an integral role in the development of societies as well as the maintenance of their functioning. This role is determined by the larger patriarchy and manifests itself in different forms depending on cultural and family values. However, when these roles are regarded as biologically created or not worthy of attention there are deleterious effects and change is hindered (Enloe, 1989). In order for the voice of women to be heard, it must first be found. Feminist methodological research from an ethnographic tradition or framework has been proposed by Harrison (2007) as a way to bring the experiences of women who are living with the repercussions of globalization to the forefront. This process can allow for a scientific presentation of women's experiences in a way that also emphasizes the value of the context related to the circumstances of women. Research into women's experiences of globalization can help to bring an awareness of the repercussions of global decision making to the table of the corporations and governments involved in perpetuating the current system.

The final step in creating a sense of personal importance for understanding the diversity of human experience involves this process of creating awareness. Through consciousness raising (Worell & Remer, 2005), the concerns related to feelings of incompetence associated with increased complexity can be outweighed by the need to enhance the wellbeing of the community. When a connection can be made between what happens to a woman in a sweat shop in India and the livelihood of a corporate executive's family, then real change can happen (Enloe, 1989). It is important for those in power to see how their decisions affect the lives of others, and how the consequences of others can come to affect them and the way of life that they value. The personal is political, and when that idea is realized and understood, the institutions that control commerce and political agenda can begin to value the diversity of the individual and how their actions affect that diversity. Further, gaining an awareness of the effects of globalization can assist counselors and educators in understanding the experiences of those with whom they work.

Intersectional View

As stated throughout the discussion of Bala above, lives are not shaped by gender alone (Brown, 1994; Kolmar & Bartkowski, 2005). Instead, gender, spirituality, race, ethnicity, culture, sexuality, and many other social constructs intersect to create a unique standpoint in each individual's life (Brown, 1994; Kolmar & Bartkowski, 2005). One person may experience oppression based upon any number of the aspects of her identity; therefore, there is no one "women's experience" (McCann & Kim, 2003). This leaves women like Bala with the task of identifying, naming, and making meaning of their multiple identities. Bala is a nonwhite, Indian-American, lesbian woman who is struggling with her spirituality but these labels only begin to describe her unique experiences. A counselor working with Bala might help her make meaning of each of these identities in such a way that allows Bala to name herself and to use her voice to reclaim the power that has been taken from her.

Application in Diverse Settings

There are several techniques associated with the use of feminist theory in counseling. Interventions include assertiveness training, power analysis, biblio-therapy, gender-role or socially embedded identity analysis, self disclosure, and women's consciousness raising or support groups. All interventions used are approached from an encouraging, affirming perspective with process-transparency and egalitarian communication driving the discussion between the counselor and client or educator and student.

Counseling and Mental Health

Counseling and mental health settings were not designed with the assumptions of feminist theory in mind and, often, do not operate in a way that is congruent with feminist goals (Brown, 1994). Nonetheless, feminist counselors are making change from within these systems in ways that affect client services. Some of these changes, and feminist approaches to working in counseling agencies in general, will be discussed in this section.

Informed Consent

Before the counseling process begins, counselors must seek client's informed consent (ACA, 2005). Feminist counselors assert that the common practice of informed consent does not provide enough information to allow clients to make fully informed and empowered decisions about the counseling process (Brown, 1994). In order for clients to fully understand what they can expect from counseling and how their lives may be affected, counselors must provide full descriptions of themselves as a profession, what approach will be used, and how using insurance to cover counseling may affect the client, to name a few. Related to informed consent is the feminist belief that counselors should share their personal values about issues discussed in counseling with their clients because clients have a right to know and because it is impossible for counselors to practice value-free counseling (Enns, 2004). In education, this consent process would be reflected in the development and communication of the course syllabus.

A Feminist Approach to Diagnosis and Conceptualization

Following informed consent, counselors in mental health agencies often begin the process of diagnosis immediately. The assumptions of "normalcy" and the "pathological nature of distress" that underlie traditional diagnosis conflict with the feminist assertion that personal problems are a product of oppression (Brown, 1994, p. 126). Further, diagnoses have the potential to harm clients in indirect and direct ways; for this reason, many feminist counselors have refused to participate in diagnosis or in discussions about the usefulness of diagnosis. Brown argues, however, that feminist counselors must work towards changing diagnosis by contributing a feminist approach that will serve as an alternative option.

A feminist approach to diagnosis is simply a way for the counselor and client to work together to name the client's distress, to begin to understand its origin, and to place it within the appropriate social and political context so that informed choices may be made about how to move towards healing (Brown, 1994; Enns, 1997). By taking part in naming her own distress, the client exercises her voice and takes back some of her power. By uncovering the external origins of her pain, the client begins to value her distress as resistance to or attempts to cope with oppression, and, thereby to begin to name and further utilize her strengths.

A Feminist Approach to Healing

After conceptualizing a client's distress, the counselor and client can begin to work together to reclaim the client's power and sense of personal value. In the beginning of the counseling process, this may mean that the counselor helps the client to honor the goals or purposes (e.g., safety, power) associated with the symptoms of distress by finding more empowered ways to meet these goals. Specifically, the counselor may encourage the client to develop new coping skills that fit her experience as an empowered person (Enns, 1997). A piece of this work may be to acknowledge that the client's specific and unique methods of resisting oppression which may have aided in her survival and are indications of her resiliency (Brown, 1994), thereby increasing the client's value of self (Enns, 1997). Feminist counselors often explore the specifics of clients' experiences as a way of helping the client to re-claim and re-write their own stories.

For example, if a client has experienced pain within her family of origin, a feminist counselor may avoid placing blame on the mother or central parental figure by highlighting the family's place within the larger social and political context and by conceptualizing the parent(s) as having internalized heterosexist beliefs (Brown, 1994). This may serve to help the client do the same and preserve the relationship with her mother, preventing patriarchy from severing this important women's relationship. Related to this modeling process, feminist counselors help clients break free from restrictive gender (and other) roles by educating them about gender inequality and by brainstorming ways to increase role flexibility (Enns, 1997). These are merely two examples of content that may be examined in feminist counseling. Regardless of the specifics of the content of feminist counseling, the process always serves to increase the personal power of the client and to decrease the power of patriarchy.

As the client's personal power is reclaimed and her consciousness is raised, she may feel compelled to become involved in efforts to produce social change (Brown, 1994). This type of activity further empowers the client while connecting her to other women who can relate to her unique personal experiences of oppression. Regardless of the specific activities undertaken, feminist counselors work to understand and affirm clients' experiences over their own expertise (Enns, 1997). Therefore, feminist counselors will encourage their clients' to share the work and the power of the counseling relationship, in an egalitarian partnership.

SCHOOL COUNSELING AND CLASSROOM GUIDANCE

Unfortunately, the oppression and inequality that exists within the dominant culture of society also exists within the school system (Hipilito-Delgato & Lee, 2007). Students, especially those of marginalized groups, experience oppression daily and throughout their educational experiences. Classism, sexism, racism, able-ism, and heterosexism operate to ensure unequal opportunities for learning, success, and growth; the result of these oppressive experiences may last a lifetime (Hipilito-Delgato & Lee, 2007).

For these reasons, Hipilito-Delgato and Lee (2007) call for feminist principles of social justice to be applied in schools by school counselors. They argue that by empowering individual students, they may liberate them from oppression and internalized oppression. This can be accomplished by using a strengths-based approach when working with students, by valuing students' perspectives and experiences, and by empowering students to make choices for themselves (Brown, 1994). School counselors can use their position to create consciousness-raising opportunities among students by including curricula that embraces non-Western perspectives, informs students of oppression, and places oppression within the current sociopolitical context. In addition, school counselors may develop consciousness-raising groups in which students can connect and share their life experiences with peers (Hipilito-Delgato

& Lee, 1997). Because students of oppressed groups are less likely to be exposed to empowered individuals from their own cultural group, school counselors may want to consider inviting empowered men and women from various backgrounds to speak at school events or to interact with students in the classroom. By taking steps to educate students about oppression and to empower them to resist, feminist school counselors can have a significant impact on our children and our society.

Higher Education

Institutions of higher education can continue the oppression that students experience during their K-12 education. Colleges and universities are typically patriarchal and thus structurally hierarchical; these institutions value certain types of knowledge and information over others, value certain types of contributions over others, and commonly approach learning from a mono-cultural perspective. Belenky et al. (1997) share the stories of women who felt belittled, discouraged, and disempowered by their experiences in higher education through their qualitative study women's development of personal knowledge. Specifically, these women reported that they were taught to mistrust their own senses and to be dependent upon external authority for knowledge. Although they recognized the need for some structure, they expressed that the effort to conform to rigid and specific requirements thwarted their ability to think for themselves, to prioritize, and to draw their own conclusions about the material covered; in essence, "the effort to be good had prevented the development of a more authentic voice" (p. 209).

In order for students (particularly women) to believe that they are capable of learning, they need to know that they are intelligent and that they already possess valuable knowledge that is uniquely their own. Once they accept this, they will be more willing to trust that they will be successful in their learning endeavors and will take more risks in their educational development (Belenky et al., 1997). Therefore, teachers must help students discover and express this knowledge and ability that they already possess. This can be accomplished when instructors allow students to witness the imperfect process of thinking and re-thinking lectures, papers, and ideas that often occurs in private prior to a fully conceived and perfectly delivered lecture (Belenky et al., 1997). When students see only the finished process of thought, they may not be able to believe that they are capable of such a product. If teacher and students talk through ideas together, in community students may begin to see that they can come to their own knowledge. This focus on community over hierarchy is essential to feminist teaching.

Leadership

Similar concepts are important to feminist leadership, as well, however, there is a marked dearth of literature and empirical research on the topic (Chin, 2004; Strachan, 1999). The available literature is consistent in its description of feminist leadership. One characteristic of feminist leadership is collaboration and consensus-building as a way to determine direction (Irby & Brown, 1995). Feminist leaders admit that this process can be more time-consuming than the dominant, hierarchical, independent method of decision making; however, they emphasize the value and strength of working collaboratively. This style of decision making is an example of the egalitarian nature of feminist leadership. It is important to note, however, that displaying merely a collaborative, egalitarian style of leadership does not make leadership feminist. In order for leadership to by truly feminist, it must aim to achieve feminist goals. For example, feminist leadership resists and challenge injustice, strives to change oppressive social and political policies, empower women to be feminist leaders, and promotes feminist policies such as those that increase gender equality within organizations (Chin, 2004; Strachan, 1999). In a word, feminist leadership can be described as empowerment; extending through the self to others and the greater community.

Research

Similar to the feminist leadership style, research from this perspective focuses on highlighting the voices of participants, valuing that voice, and empowering them to become involved in the process of discovery along-side the researcher. When considering the female voice in particular, this type of research is seen to be a next step in the process of allowing women to contribute uniquely to the body of knowledge available and to provide a forum that represents women's interests. Feminist methodologies are largely focused on qualitative research (ethnography, case studies, and action research) however this perspective can be applied to meta-analysis, experimental or survey research as well. The core of this philosophy is a process of affirming diversity which can take on many forms. With regard to statistical analysis, sometimes feminist researchers take the position that the results should not be viewed as "hard facts" and that nothing is truly generalizable. A quantitative feminist researcher will seek to highlight all facets of the populations involved in a study, be deliberate about seeking diversity, and frame their results within the population of respondents who contributed to the work rather than attempting to make broad societal statement about behavior. Feminists often make the critique that statistical methodologies can serve to feed into an oppressive dominant culture, and therefore tentative reporting is not only imperative to the recognition of constructed personal meaning but it is ethically appropriate within a diverse cultural context. According to Reinharz (1992) it is important to note that researchers may attempt to get close to the "natural setting" of their participants, but "social life cannot adequately be comprehended through the detached objectivity demanded by the experimental method" and rather should be "comprehended through the method of *verstehen*, or empathic understanding" (p.106).

CURRENT RESEARCH

Relatively few researchers have performed outcome studies related to feminist counseling and pedagogy. The available research focuses on the relationship between feminist counseling principles and various aspects of the mental health of women. One of the most influential studies related to women's experiences was conducted by Belenky et al. (1997), which revealed information about the development of knowledge as based on a qualitative study with 135 women from diverse backgrounds. This study derived five themes of development ranging from received knowing to self-authorized learning. These concepts now commonly associated with women's learning have influenced work with women, be it in counseling, the classroom, or student affairs. In focusing on research specific to counseling, three current research studies will be reviewed below.

LaFave, Desportes, and McBride (2009) performed both a quantitative and a qualitative study to assess the outcomes of a day treatment program for women with substance abuse problems that was based on the feminist counseling principles of empowerment, choice, and client/counselor collaboration. For the quantitative portion of the study, participants were 50 women who were either currently enrolled in or who had recently completed the day treatment program. Participants completed a survey prior to beginning the treatment program and again following completion of the program. The survey examined clients' perceptions of their life skills, finances, leisure, relationships, living arrangements, occupational/educational status, health, internal resources, and recovery. Results of paired t-tests indicated that following completion of the day treatment program, participants reported statistically significant improvements for all but one variable, occupational/educational status.

For the qualitative portion of the study, six participants completed a structured interview of open-ended questions about their experience in the program, their perceptions about the program's effectiveness, and what changes they would recommend be made to the program. Participants included women who had completed the program and were not reporting substance abuse problems, women who had returned to the program after having relapsed, and women who had left the program before its completion. Analysis of participants' responses revealed several feminist themes; participants reported that the treatment program helped them realize they had choices, feel empowered to make choices, learn to have healthier relationships, accept responsibility, express feelings, and value themselves. The results of both the quantitative and qualitative portions of this study suggest that a substance abuse program based on feminist principles has the potential to improve female clients' quality of life and to be effective for helping women struggling with substance abuse to heal.

Another study that examined the relationship between feminist principles and women's mental health was performed by Hurt et al. (2007). Although not based upon the outcomes of feminist counseling per se, Hurt et al. performed an internet survey to examine the relationship between feminist identity and factors of women's mental health. Participants were 282 women with an average age of 25. Participants completed a survey in which they were asked to respond "Yes" or "No" to the statement, "I consider myself to be a feminist" and to answer questions about their conformity to feminine norms, eating attitudes, body consciousness, self-esteem, and depression. Bivariate correlations indicated that those who self-identified as feminist were significantly less likely to place high importance on being in a romantic relationship than were those participants who self-identified as nonfeminist. They also were significantly less likely to report feeling shame and self-consciousness about their bodies than were those participants who self-identified as non-feminist. Further, results of structural equation modeling indicated that feminist identity indirectly and negatively predicted negative eating attitudes, depressive symptoms, and poor self-esteem. These results suggest that young women who identify as feminist are less likely to struggle with negative body-image and to base their self-worth upon their relationship status, and that feminist identity may play a role, albeit indirect, in decreasing the likelihood of depression and poor self-esteem.

Sinclair (2006) also addressed women's body-image in her study of 190 traditional aged female undergraduate students. Specifically, Sinclair asked participants to complete questionnaires about their experiences of gender-based objectification, their awareness and internalization of sociocultural attitudes toward appearance, and their own body self-consciousness. Results of multiple regression analyses indicated that awareness of sociocultural attitudes toward appearance predicted body shame, internalization of sociocultural attitudes toward appearance predicted body self-consciousness and body shame, and objectification experiences predicted body shame. These results highlight the significance of the damage done to young women by the dominant sociocultural expectations about female appearance and by the misogyny of objectification of women.

The research studies performed by Sinclair (2006) and Hurt et al. (2007) indicate that women continue to suffer the emotional and psychological effects of sexism, misogyny, and the oppressive norms of dominant society and culture. The research study performed by LaFave et al. (2009) demonstrates the potential for healing that can be accomplished when feminist principles are used in therapy with women. The dearth of research on the outcomes of feminist counseling indicates that more information is needed. Specifically, it has been established that women suffer from internalized oppression (Hurt et al., 2007; Sinclair, 2006) and that feminist counseling increases women's sense of their own empowerment (LaFave et al., 2009); what is needed, then, are both qualitative and quantitative analyses of a broad variety of women's experiences during and following feminist counseling.

Critiques

The feminist movement as whole has been criticized for a lack of inclusivity, and more recently, people who refer to themselves as postfeminists have been most vocal in the criticism; many times embracing and encouraging traditional roles and values for women. While some postfeminists state a belief that feminism no longer has any social justification as a movement, others attempt to use this term to highlight a repositioning of the movement to focus on the realities of women's marginalization (Wright, 2000). The call for a repositioning of the feminist movement may in part be due to the lack of a cohesive philosophical foundation, which has been noted as lacking with regard to feminist theory. As this perspective evolved from a social movement as a response to historical societal inequities that women faced, the philosophical underpinnings of this process were not fully developed and communicated until after action was taken. Recently, feminist theory has been firmly couched within the postmodernist and constructivist philosophies of counseling and teaching.

The critic that feminist theory lacks a philosophical framework directly relates to the belief that feminism is a movement rather than a theory of counseling or a teaching approach. Feminism, as framed within a political movement, is thought to be value-based and therefore it has been argued that because of this there is no place for the perspective within mental health and education. Feminist theorists certainly do not contend that their approach is not value-oriented, but rather argue that every counselor or educator functions from their own value system. Feminists take time to understand their own biases and determine how their beliefs may be beneficial or detrimental to their work. Awareness of one's personal values and beliefs is essential to the process of creating therapeutic transparency and using self disclosure to assist in helping a client or student in their own development. Self disclosure, as a technique, has also been critiqued as being unnecessary and possibly detrimental to work with clients and students. However, when implemented properly it is designed to build a trusting and egalitarian relationship focused on client and student personal growth and awareness.

With regard to feminist research, it has been said that the approach does not result in conclusive findings, especially quantitative studies, and is therefore lacking a solid contribution to the body of knowledge available. As the feminist perspective works to empower the voices of oppressed groups often this subversion against the dominant culture is viewed as lacking strength or creating an unnecessary sense of ambivalence. However, it can be argued that feminist methodology seeks to highlight the complexity that exists within our world by framing results within the postmodernist idea of individual truth rather than universal truth. This philosophy does not make results less valid, less rigorous, or reliable but simply takes into account the possibility that findings may not be true for everyone but are indeed true for some, and that truth should be equally valuable to policy decisions, future research, and considerations in counseling or education. Feminist theoretical approaches and interventions also lack outcome data to support its use in education and in counseling. This may be due to misunderstandings of feminist methodology just mentioned which could result in lower publication rates of this information in widely accessible and well-known professional journals. Also, as feminist theory in itself is meant to be subversive to dominant culture, its use is sometimes seen as divisive and it therefore not widely embraced. While feminist theorists, counselors, educators and researchers seek to empower those experiencing oppression, value social action to create equity, and seek to highlight cultural issues that may be harmful, it is important to note that such considerations occur within a collaborative, egalitarian, and encouraging atmosphere, not a divisive one.

References

American Counseling Association (2005). *ACA code of ethics*. Alexandria, VA: Author.

Banner, A. T. (2009). *The effects of spirituality on anxiety and depression among breast cancer patients: The moderating effects of alexithymia and mindfulness* (Doctoral dissertation). Retrieved from ProQuest. (3387583)

Baumgardner, J., & Richards, A. (2000). Third wave manifesta. In W. K. Kolmar & F. Bartkowski (Eds.), *Feminist theory: A reader* (2nd ed.). New York, NY: McGraw-Hill.

Belenky, M. F., Clinchy, B. M., Goldberger, N. R., & Tarule, J. M. (1997). *Women's ways of knowing: The development of self, voice, and mind* (10th anniversary ed.). New York, NY: BasicBooks.

Borysenko, J. (1999). *A woman's journey to God: Finding the feminine path.* New York, NY: Putnam.

Briggs, M. K., & Banner, A. T. (2011). Working with the divine feminine. In C. S. Cashwell & J. S. Young (Eds.), *Integrating spirituality and religion into counseling: A guide to competent practice* (2nd ed., pp. 261-278). Alexandria, VA: American Counseling Association.

Brown, L. S. (1994). *Subversive dialogues: Theory in feminist therapy.* New York, NY: Basic Books.

Carroll, L., Gilroy, P. J., & Ryan, J. (2002). Counseling transgendered, transsexual, and gender-variant clients. *Journal of Counseling and Development, 80,* 131-139.

Cashwell, C. S., & Young, J. S. (Eds.). (2005). Integrating spirituality and religion into counseling: An introduction. In *Integrating spirituality and religion into counseling* (pp. 1-9). Alexandria, VA: American Counseling Association.

Chin, J. L. (2004). 2003 Division 35 Presidential Address: Feminist leadership: Feminist visions and diverse voices. *Psychology of Women Quarterly, 28,* 1-8.

Christ, C. P. (1982). Why women need the goddess: phenomenological, psychological, and political reflections. In C. Spretnak (Ed.), *The politics of women's spirituality* (pp. 71-86). New York, NY: Anchor Books.

Combahee River Collective. (1977). A black feminist statement. In W. K. Kolmar & F. Bartkowski (Eds.), *Feminist theory: A reader* (3rd ed., pp. 254-259). New York, NY: McGraw-Hill.

Enloe, C. (1989). Gender makes the world go round. In *Bananas, beaches and bases* (pp. 1-18). Berkeley, CA: University of California Press.

Enns, C. Z. (2004). *Feminist theories and feminist psychotherapies : origins, themes, and diversity* (2nd ed.). New York, NY: Haworth Press.

Flinders, C. (1998). *At the root of this longing: Reconciling a spiritual hunger and a feminist thirst.* San Francisco, CA: HarperCollins.

Fukuyama, M. A., Siahpoush, F., & Sevig, T. D. (2005). Religion and spirituality in a cultural context. In C. S. Cashwell & J. S. Young (Eds.), *Integrating spirituality and religion into counseling* (pp. 123-142). Alexandria, VA: American Counseling Association.

Funderbunk, J. R., & Fukuyama, M. A. (2002). Feminism, multiculturalism, and spirituality. *Women and Therapy, 24*(3), 1 - 18.

Good, G. E., Gilbert, L. A., & Scher, M. (1990). Gender aware therapy: A synthesis of feminist therapy and knowledge about gender. *Journal of Counseling and Development, 68,* 376-380.

Halberstam, J. (1998). Transgender butch: Butch/FTM border wars and the masculine continuum from female manscculinity. In W. K. Kolmar & F. Bartkowski (Eds.), *Feminist theory: A reader* (3rd ed., pp. 502-507). New York, NY: McGraw-Hill.

Harrison, F. (2007). Feminist methodology as a tool for ethnographic inquiry on globalization. In N. Gunewardena & A. Kingsolver (Eds.), *The gender of globalization: Women navigating cultural and economic marginalities* (pp. 23-34). Sante Fe, NM: School for Advanced Research Press.

Hipilito-Delgato, C. P., & Lee, C. (2007). Empowerment theory for the professional school counselor: A manifesto for what really matters. *Professional School Counseling, 10*(4), 327-322.

Holmgren, L. E., & Hearn, J. (2009). Framing "men in feminism": Theoretical locations, local contexts and practical passings in men's gender-conscious positionings on gender equality and feminism. *Journal of Gender Studies, 18*(4), 403- 418.

hooks, b. (1994). *Teaching to transgress: Education as the practice of freedom.* New York, NY: Routledge.

Hurt, M. M., Nelson, J. A., Turner, D. L., Haines, M. E., Ramsey, L. R., Erchull, M. J., & Liss, M. (2007). Feminism: What is it good for? Feminine norms and objectification as the link between feminist identity and clinically relevant outcomes. *Sex Roles, 57,* 355-363.

Irby, B. J., & Brown, G. (1995, April). *Constructing a feminist-inclusive theory of leadership.* Paper presented at the annual meeting of the American Educational Research Association, San Francisco, CA. Retrieved from https://unx1.shsu.edu:9443/login?url=http://search.ebscohost.com/login.aspx?direct=true&db=eric&AN=ED384103&site=ehost-live&scope=site

Jardine, A., & Smith, P. (1987). *Men in feminism.* New York, NY: Routledge.

Keller, C. (1986). *From a broken web: Separation, sexism, and self.* Boston, MA: Beacon Press.

Kolmar, W. K., & Bartkowski, F. (2005). *Feminist theory: A reader* (2nd ed.). New York, N:Y: McGraw-Hill.

LaFave, L., Desportes, L., & McBride, C. (2009). Treatment outcomes and perceived benefits: A qualitative and quantitative assessment of a women's substance abuse treatment program. *Women and Therapy, 32(1),* 51-68.

McCann, C. R., & Kim, S. K. (2003). *Feminist theory reader: Local and global perspectives.* New York, NY: Routledge.

McCarthy, J., & Holliday, E. L. (2004). Gender role: An examination from a multicultural perspective. *Journal of Counseling and Development, 82*(1), 25-30.

Patel, N. R. (2007). The construction of South-Asian-American womanhood. *Women and Therapy, 30*(3), 51-61.

Plaskow, J., & Christ, C. P. (1989). *Weaving the visions: New patterns in feminist spirituality.* San Francisco, CA: HarperCollins.

Reinharz, S. (1992). *Feminist methods in social research.* Oxford, England: Oxford University Press.

Rich, A. (1980). Compulsory heterosexuality and lesbian existence. In W. K. Kolmar & F. Bartkowski (Eds.), *Feminist theory: A reader* (2nd ed.). New York, NY: McGraw-Hill.

Ruth, S. (1994) *Take back the light.* Lanham, MD: Rowman & Littlefield.

Sinclair, S. L. (2006). Object lessons: A theoretical and empirical study of objectified body consciousness in women. *Journal of Mental Health Counseling, 28(1),* 48-68.

Snyder, R. C. (2008). What is third-wave feminism? A new directions essay. *Signs: Journal of Women in Culture & Society, 34*(1), 175-196.

Spretnak, C. (1982). *The politics of women's spirituality.* New York, NY: Anchor Books.

Strachan, J. (1999). Feminist educational leadership: Locating the concepts in practice. *Gender and Education, 11*(3), 309-322.

Szymanski, D. M., & Gupta, A. (2009). Examining the relationship between multiple internalized oppressions and African American lesbian, gay, bisexual, and questioning persons' self-esteem and psychological distress. *Journal of Counseling Psychology, 56*(1), 110-118.

Wester, S. R., McDonough, T. A., White, M., Vogel, D. L., & Taylor, L. (2010). Using gender role conflict theory in counseling male-to-female transgender individuals. *Journal of Counseling and Development, 88,* 214 -219.

Worell, J., & Remer, P. (2003). *Feminist perspectives in therapy: Empowering diverse women* (2nd ed.). Hoboken, NJ: Wiley.

Wright, E. (2000). *Lacan and postfeminism (Postmodern encounters).* Duxford, Cambridge, England: Totem Books.

Author Contact Information: Amanda C. Healey, PhD, Department of Educational Leadership and Counseling, Sam Houston State University.

CHAPTER 45

Counseling From a Multiple Heritage Perspective

A Theoretical Framework

Richard C. Henriksen, Jr.
Sam Houston State University

The year 2000 brought with it many advances and a renewed hope for the future. With this new decade came the first time that those with multiracial and multiethnic backgrounds could identify the full range of their racial and ethnic backgrounds (Jones & Smith, 2001). It was in the U.S. Census that the multiple heritage population gained acceptance for the first time by a governmental institution. Over 6 million individuals identified the true range of their racial backgrounds (Jones & Smith, 2001).

The 2010 U.S. Census brought about a new change for the multiple heritage population. The U.S. Census Bureau added a new category "Some Other Race" (Humes, Jones, & Ramirez, 2011, p. 3). This new term is defined as including

> all other responses [on the census form] not included in the White, Black or African American, American Indian or Alaskan Native, Asian, and Native Hawaiian or Other Pacific Islander.... Respondents reporting entries such as multiracial, mixed, interracial, or Hispanic or Latino group (for example, Mexican, Puerto Rican, Cuban, or Spanish) in response to the race section are included in this category. (Humes et al., 2011, p. 3)

The creation of this new category is a departure from the 2000 census and a further recognition of this growing population. The change in the U.S. population is due in part to the growth in the some other race group. The two or more race group grew from 6,826,228 in 2000 to 9,009,073 (Humes et al, 2011). This is a growth rate of 32% and suggests that counselors need to be prepared to work with the members of this growing population and be able to meet their unique cultural needs. Focusing on only meeting the cultural needs of the dominant racial and ethnic groups has left this group to largely fend for themselves resulting in an exacerbation of their struggles (Henriksen & Paladino, 2009a). The challenges of constructing a comprehensive developmental theory that could help counselors and other helping professionals provide effective services to this population has been challenging and has undergone many changes over the decades (Rockquemore, Brunsma, & Delgado, 2009). This chapter focuses on an identity development theory that can help counselors who work with multiple heritage individuals and their families and couples and their families.

Philosophical Underpinnings of Multiple Heritage Theory Development

Studies focused on the identity development and other developmental processes among the multiple heritage population gained popularity in the 1990s. Prior to that time most studies were small and were focused on psychiatric populations (Henriksen & Paladino, 2009a). Jackson (2009) noted that early research was "often based on speculation and nonrepresentative case histories" (p. 310). The resulting models had little utility with a growing and changing population.

The Handbook of Educational Theories, pp. 541–548

The first and most widely used early look at multiple heritage development was from the work of Stonequist (1937) who focused on studying multiple heritage individuals with one Black and one White parent. This model was referred to as the *marginal man*. The underlying premise of this model of development was that multiple heritage individuals suffered from psychological issues because they could not identify with one racial/ethnic group and therefore were stuck on a fence never knowing which side they fit. This idea of psychological dissonance dominated the literature focused on the multiple heritage population until the 1990s when a more positive view came into prominence.

Following the work of Stonequist (1937), many models of racial/ethnic identity development were created focusing on the many diverse cultural groups. Cross (1971) developed the first and most widely used model of identity development from his research involving African Americans. This model was a stage model that focused on African Americans moving from shame to acceptance to pride. This model of nigrescence (the Negro-to-Black conversion experience) has five stages that have established the foundation for racial/ethnic identity development models: (a) preencounter, (b) encounter, (c) immersion-emersion, (d) internalization, and (e) internalization-commitment. The Cross model has gone through several revisions; however, the revision in 2001 was the first indication that at each stage of development African Americans experience "multiple identity clusters" (Worrell, Cross, & Vandiver, 2001, p. 201). This finding would also impact research focused in identity development models for multiple heritage individuals because of their experience with multiple identities throughout their lives. As a result of the work of Cross, other models of racial/ethnic identity development were created including the minority identity development model of Atkinson, Morten, and Sue (1979) and the White identity development model created by Helms (1995).

Jackson (2009) pointed out several philosophical issues that have historically provided a foundation for research focused on understanding the identity development process for multiple heritage individuals: (a) multiple heritage individuals were viewed as emotionally unstable because of the challenge of existing in multiple identities, (b) multiple heritage individuals faced adjustment problems due to not fitting into one racial/ethnic group, and (c) that multiple heritage individuals' identity development was influenced by their social relationships including family.

Multiracial Identity Development Models

In the 1990s, research involving the multiple heritage population began to take a different focus and became much more positive with an emphasis on understanding the process of identity development. In 1990, Poston conducted research that focused on multiracial individuals as a reaction to research that was focused on Black and minority identity development. He wanted a model that would reflect the experiences of biracial and multiracial individuals. Poston's *biracial identity development model* includes five stages: (a) personal identity, (b) choice of group categorization, (c) enmeshment/denial, (d) appreciation, and (e) integration. While this model moved beyond the earlier models to focus on the biracial and multiracial population, it did not uncover the idea that multiple heritage individuals could complete the identity development process with one of several different identities and could have different identities in different situations. Tizard and Phoenix (1995) conducted extensive research that led to realizing that multiple heritage individuals have a variety of racial and ethnic identities that are influenced by both their family and social environments. The outcome was an expansion of the model developed by Poston.

Maria P. P. Root (1990) also began to conduct research during this time period seeking to understand the identity issues associated with multiple heritage identity development. She found a similar process to that of Poston (1990) and also identified the influences found by Tizard and Phoenix (1995) but she added positive resolutions to the overall models. Root (1990) found that multiracial individuals could resolve the identity development process in one of four ways: (a) acceptance of the identity society assigns, (b) identification with both racial groups, (c) identification with a single racial group, and (d) identification as a new racial group. Root was able to account for the racism experienced by multiracial individuals in her model and was the first researcher to introduce the idea of identifying oneself as biracial or multiracial. Root (2001) revised her model to add two additional positive resolutions to the identity development process. These two additions resolutions are (a) identifying with a symbolic race or ethnicity, and (b) identifying with a particular racial or ethnic identification depending on circumstances present of the given situation. Root's work freed the multiple heritage population to become better able to identify healthy ways of living and the ability to decide how each person chooses to self-identify.

The research that has led to an expansion of racial/ethnic identity development models to the multiple heritage population continues to move toward understanding the overall developmental issues faced by multiple heritage individuals. Hall (2005) developed the identity across the lifespan: biracial model. This is both an ecological and human development model with a focus on understanding the multiple heritage individual in context. This model focuses on the notion that multiple heritage individuals actively experience the identity development process and that their experiences take place with the individual's social reality. Each of the models presented have provided foundational information that is included in the multiple heritage identity development model (Henriksen & Paladino, 2009a).

The Multiple Heritage Identity Development Model

Ongoing efforts to understand the multiple heritage identity development process focusses not only on the process but also focuses on ways of helping. Each of the theories we have discussed helps us to better understand this population and provides some insight into effective helping practices. The multiple heritage identity development model (MHID) (Henriksen & Paladino, 2009a) provides a framework for understanding the complexity of the identity development process and a means for identifying and developing ways to help multiple heritage individuals with the identity development process.

Henriksen (2000) developed the *Black/White biracial identity development model* as a way to begin the development of a model of multiple heritage identity development that could help the multiple heritage population with their identity issues by giving the participants in the study a voice. The model was based on extensive interviews with seven participants who told their stories of developing a racial/ethnic identity and the challenges they faced in the process. From the qualitative data collected and analyzed, a model of identity development was created. However, Henriksen found that this model has limited use if it was only based on individuals with one Black and one White parent. During the next 5 years, Henriksen and others used the model with other populations and in other research. The knowledge gained from the application of the model to a wider cross section of multiple heritage individuals demonstrated its utility with multiple heritage individuals with a wide range of backgrounds and with transracially adopted individuals (Henriksen & Paladino, 2009a). The continuation of this process during the past 5 years has led to the development of the revised MHID that is presented in this chapter (see Figure 45.1).

The MHID included six nonlinear periods that could be revisited by the individual dependent upon the individual's family and social experiences (Henriksen & Paladino, 2009a). The MHID revised includes the same six periods but one has been renamed. Several of the periods intersect with several additional identities that are part of the multiple heritage identity of the individual. The periods are not necessarily distinct and are not linear. The process does not necessarily have a specific beginning but the periods do provide a means to help the individual identify where the identity development process began. There is also no specific age at which an individual will begin the identity development process. This is important because each individual engages the identity development process differently. Experience has also indicated that the early periods (neutrality and acceptance) are only experienced; however, the remaining period can be revisited by the individual throughout his or her lifetime. The six periods of identity development are neutrality, acknowledgment, awareness, experimentation, transition, and recognition.

Neutrality, the first period of multiple heritage identity development, is defined as the period during which the individual is unaware of the concept of race or ethnicity (Henriksen, 2000; Henriksen & Paladino, 2009a). It is important to note that not all multiple heritage individuals experience this period in the same way. Some experience this period as the time when they are not aware of how one's race or ethnicity affects social interactions. For example, I once had a multiple heritage tell me about growing up in Germany and having a friend who was German and did not speak English (Henriksen, 2000). The two children did not realize they were different until their parents told them about their differences.

Acknowledgment (formally referred to as acceptance) is the second period of development period and occurs when a multiple heritage individual is able to acknowledge that he or she is different from other people but is not aware of why (Henriksen, 2000; Henriksen & Paladino, 2009a). This period was renamed because more and more clients described this period as a time of being able to acknowledge their existence as a racial being. It is during this time that the individual sees himself or herself as a racial being because family, friends, and other social acquaintances refer to the person in terms of racial names such as biracial and multiracial or negative names such as half-breed or mixed. This often occurs when the individual first enters school. The individual does not see this as a problem unless it is coupled with a negative interaction. Because the individual is now becoming aware of his or her identity as a racial being, the family takes on a greater role in the identity development of the individual and this may be a time when the family has its greatest influence. Many clients indicated that this period was the first time their families pointed out that they had two different racial identities and that they were identified with one. For many clients, this is the first time they remember being confused about their racial identity because they were different from their parents and their friends.

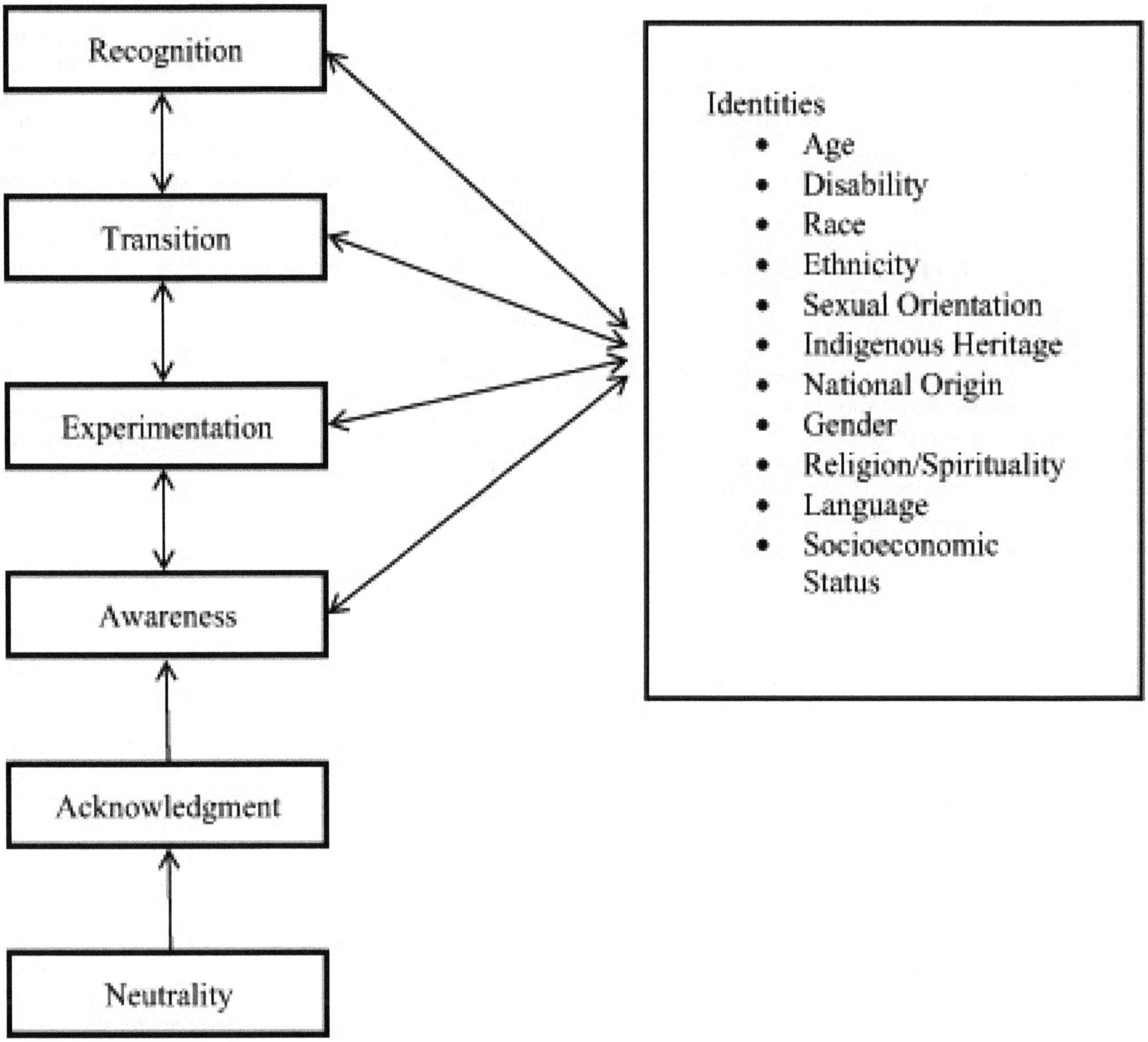

Figure 45.1. The multiple heritage identity development model revised.

Individuals who experience the first two periods of development tend to move from one to the other. That can occur at the same time or can happen over a period of time. However, some individuals may not experience these two periods at all. I once had a client who was adopted and always saw herself as Black. When she turned 18, she found out that she had a White mother and was biracial. She went directly into the third period of development awareness.

Awareness is the third period of development and occurs when a multiple heritage individual recognizes that he or she is racially different from others and begins to understand what that means (Henriksen, 2000; Henriksen & Paladino, 2009a). This period is often encountered through a negative interaction that often results in the person feeling alone and isolated because the person realizes that there is not a racial group that includes him or her. Many people have described experiencing both the acknowledgment and awareness phase at the same time. A client once told me that he never realized that he was different from other people racially until he was called a "wetback" who wanted to be White. He described going from not seeing himself as someone different than other people to becoming aware that not only was he different but that there was no one else like him except his brother. This period also ushers in the realization that each person has multiple identities and the individuals begin the process of incorporating those identities into his or her overall identity.

The fourth period of identity development is referred to as *experimentation* (Henriksen 2000; Henriksen & Paladino, 2009a) and is viewed by many multiple heritage individuals as the most challenging time of the identity development process. During this period, multiple heritage individuals are facing the challenge of finding out where they fit in society from a racial and or ethnic perspective. The multiple heritage individual tries on each racial identity trying to see if he or she fits into one of them. The pressure is on at this time to begin to find a racial and/or ethnic identity so that the person can more easily fit into society and develop a clear connection with other people. During this time the individual is much more aware that he or she has other identities and tries to find a way to fit into each of the different identities as well. These additional identities include: age, disability, race, ethnicity, sexual orientation, indigenous heritage, national origin, gender, religion/spirituality, language, and socioeconomic status. During this period, the multiple heritage individual asks, "How do I become the person I want to be when there are so many different parts of me?"

Following the experimentation period, the individual moves into the fifth period of identity development referred to as *transition* (Henriksen, 2000; Henriksen & Paladino, 2009a). This period of transition is the time when many multiple heritage individuals move toward self-recognition and the development of a way to identify themselves racially. It is a time of great turmoil because the individual has to make choices about his or her identity and the person realizes that he or she does belong to multiple groups. I recently worked with a couple that had a 27-year-old child who was moving toward his own racial identity. They asked, "How do we help him choose which racial identity to identify with when it is his life and not ours?" The struggle during the transition period is often a family struggle and one that was often not discussed prior to the couple having children. The challenge is to move toward the recognition of all parts of the individual's multiple heritage identity, which is made more challenging by the intersection with the additional identities of the person.

Recognition is the final period and the time during which the individual makes a decision about his or her identity and develops a way of sharing that identity with others (Henriksen, 2000; Henriksen & Paladino, 2009a; Root, 1990; Root, 2001). It is during this time that the individual is able to proclaim his or her identity with pride. Not only are individuals able to identify themselves racially or ethnically but they are also able to include other parts of their identities in their self-descriptions. As noted earlier, Root (1990, 2001) identified six ways that multiple heritage individuals could self-identify: (a) acceptance of the identity society assigns, (b) identification with both racial groups, (c) identification with a single racial group, (d) identification as a new racial group, (e) identifying with a symbolic race or ethnicity, and (f) identifying with a particular racial or ethnic identification depending on circumstances present of the given situation. Henriksen and Trusty (2004) pointed out that each of these ways of self-identifying are healthy when they include all aspects of the individual's identity.

The MHID revised model provides helping professionals with a starting place to gain insight into the identity development process each multiple heritage individual faces. From this beginning point, the helping professional can help clients identify where they are in the process and develop appropriate interventions that will help the individual move toward a resolution of the identity development process. It is important to remember that many multiple heritage individuals will recycle through many of the cycles multiple times throughout their lives.

THE COUNSELING PROCESS

Harris (2009) pointed out that because of the unique backgrounds of multiple heritage individuals; counselors need a thorough understanding of the multicultural counseling competencies (Sue, Arredondo, & McDavis, 1992) prior to beginning work with this population. This is especially important in the area of self-awareness. Counselors need to understand their own personal views of the multiple heritage population and how they intersect with the helping process. Paladino and Davis (2006) also pointed that when counseling multiple heritage students "it is important to note that some multiracial students' counseling issues are not related to their racial identity and they are not at a psychological disadvantage concerning their self-esteem" (p. 25). The process of counseling is therefore is the same as it would be with any other client. The major difference is that helping professionals need to have insight into the unique challenges faced by multiple heritage individuals.

THE RELATIONSHIP

Like other ways of helping, the relationship between client and counselor should be one of a collaborative nature where both the client and counselor share a relationship of mutual respect, congruence, and goal orientation. Multiple heritage clients need to feel safe and accepted with and by the counselor. Maxwell and Henriksen (2009) suggested that a key to developing a therapeutic relationship with a multiple heritage client is the inclusion of empathy and understanding. Clients who feel connected with their counselors are more likely to be open and to explore the true nature of the challenges they face. "A therapeutic intervention attempted without previously established rapport, empathy, and trust can be perceived as a covert endeavor" (Maxwell & Henriksen, 2009, p. 74) to manipulate the client.

Goals

Clients come to counseling for a wide range of reasons and when facing a wide range of challenges. Many times multiple heritage clients come to counseling for reasons other than identity development issues. When this is the case, the counselor and client would establish goals leading to the resolution of the issues being presented by the client. When the client presents an issue related to his or her identity development, the goal of counseling is to help the client resolve the identity development challenge and to establish a healthy identity.

Techniques

Several techniques have been identified as being effective when working with multiple heritage clients. First, Maxwell and Henriksen (2009) noted that the establishment of a working relationship with the client is imperative if a positive outcome from counseling is to be achieved. Kazdin (1994), for example, pointed out that the relationship was key to successful therapeutic interventions with adolescents. A second technique involves allowing the client to vent and explore his or feeling about being multiple heritage. For many multiple heritage clients, they report not ever having been able to just plain tell their stories. Allowing their stories to be told can lead to a healthy and healing cathartic release. Another technique is the my multiple heritage identity (Henriksen & Paladino, 2009b) activity. This activity helps clients explore all aspects of their multiple heritage identity by allowing them to draw a picture that reflects all aspects of their identity. Clients then process the picture and reflect up the unique nature of their identity. A final activity that can help children is bibliotherapy. In a study conducted by Henriksen, Irby, and Frels (2011), they found that there are many multiple heritage children's books available that can assist young children and their families with the identity exploration of the child. Bibliotherapy can also be used with transracially adopted children. There are even more resources available for this multiple heritage population.

Counseling Process

Smith (1991) proposed a four phase process of counseling when the focus is the racial/ethnic identity development of the client. It is important to note that this process is not linear and that work with the client can be conducted based on any one of the three phases. Phase 1 begins after the client has experienced an identity crisis. For example, a Puerto Rican and Chinese male client seeking a date with a female Korean friend has been rejected because he is not Korean. This event has upset the balance of the client's identity and propelled him into a search for his own identity. He now questions his group membership and wonders where he fits in. The search for an identity often includes experimentation that is like that experienced by individuals in the MHID revised model.

Phase 2 is centered on exploring the unhealthy attitude toward the ethnic group that is the focus of the conflict. In this case, the client would have become angry with Koreans and would be expressing a negative view of them. Even though both individuals share an Asian background, the differences are made the focus so that the client can minimize self-reflection. It is during Phase 3 that the client works to resolve the conflict in a manner similar to that found during the transition period of the MHID revised model. Smith (1991) pointed out that clients are unable to "continue indefinitely in a state of heightened tensions or heightened awareness" (p. 185).

During the final phase, Phase 4, the individual moves toward and often achieves recognition (Henriksen, 2000; Henriksen & Paladino, 2009a). Recognition is achieved when the client is able to describe his or her multiple heritage identity in a healthy manner as noted earlier in this chapter.

Use of the Theory With a Variety of Multiple Heritage Populations

The MHID model (Henriksen & Paladino, 2009a) has been used across the multiple heritage population. In the book, *Counseling Multiple Heritage Individuals, Couples, and Families* (Henriksen & Paladino, 2009a), the MHID model was applied to working with children, adolescents, college students, adults, families, and individuals with additional intersecting identities such as sexual orientation. Baden, Thomas, and Smith (2009) have also applied the MHID model to working with transracially adopted children. The model has proven to be useful in each of these instances and has provided helping professionals with a place to begin work with multiple heritage identity issues. The MHID model is not designed to provide all of the challenges faced by multiple heritage individuals, couples, and families but it does provide all involved to gain insight into the challenges they face.

Henriksen, Watts, and Bustamante (2007) used the MHID as the basis for developing the Multiple Heritage Couple Questionnaire. This questionnaire provides counselors with a tool to help couples explore their views of multiple heritage relationships and the impact that their beliefs have upon the couple and their families. As a tool, this questionnaire allows counselors to help clients explore their relationships in the manner that meets their specific needs.

Conclusion

Theories focused on the multiple heritage population continue to be developed and explored. Unfortunately, little research has been conducted with these theories so that they have a wider evidence base. This does not diminish the usefulness and utility of the theories. The MHID is the culmination of more than 15 years of research and practice. The model has evolved into its present articulation and continues to be revised. The usefulness of the model is found in its adaptability to the changing characteristics of the multiple heritage population. This growing population will continue to present challenges for counselors seeing to help them with identity development issues. The MHID revised model can provide the foundation for the work.

References

Atkinson, D., Morten, G., & Sue, D. W. (1979). *Counseling American minorities: A cross cultural perspective*. Dubuque, IA: Little, Brown, & Company.

Baden, A. L., Thomas, L. A., & Smith, C. (2009). Navigating heritage, culture, identity, and adoption: Counseling transracially adopted individuals and their family. In R. C. Henriksen, Jr., & D. A. Paladino (Eds.), *Counseling multiple heritage individuals, couples, and families* (pp. 125-144). Alexandria, VA: American Counseling Association.

Cross, W. E. (1971). The Negro-to-Black conversion experience. *Black World, 20*, 13-27.

Hall, R. E. (2005). Eurocentrism in social work education: From race to identity across the lifespan as biracial alternative. *Journal of Social Work, 5*, 101-114.

Harris, H. L. (2009). Counseling multiple heritage children. In R. C. Henriksen, Jr., & D. A. Paladino (Eds.), *Counseling multiple heritage individuals, couples, and families* (pp. 45-63). Alexandria, VA: American Counseling Association.

Helms, J. E. (1995). An update of Helm's White and people of color racial identity development models. In J. G. Ponterotto, J. M. Casas, L. A. Suzuki, & C. M. Alexander (Eds.), *Handbook of multicultural counseling* (pp. 181-198). Thousand Oaks, CA: SAGE.

Henriksen, R. C., Jr. (2000). Black/White biracial identity development: A grounded theory study. *Dissertation Abstracts International, 61*/07, 2605.

Henriksen, R. C., Jr., Irby, B., & Frels, R. (2011). A text analysis of multiple heritage young children's literature. *National Forum of Applied Educational Research Journal*, 24, 1-18.

Henriksen, R. C., Jr., & Paladino, D. A. (2009a). *Counseling multiple heritage individuals, couples, and families*. Alexandria, VA: American Counseling Association.

Henriksen, R. C., Jr., & Paladino, D. A. (2009b). My multiple heritage identity. In C. F. Salazar (Ed.), *Group work experts share their favorite multicultural activities: A guide to diversity-competent choosing, planning, conducting, and processing* (pp. 202-205). Alexandria, VA: Association for Specialists in Group Work.

Henriksen, R. C., Jr., & Trusty, J. (2004). Understanding and assisting Black/White biracial women in their identity development. *Women & Therapy: A Feminist Quarterly, 27*, 65-83.

Henriksen, R. C., Jr., Watts, R. E., & Bustamante, R. (2007). The multiple heritage couple questionnaire. *The Family Journal, 15*, 405-408.

Humes, K. R., Jones, N. A., & Ramirez, R. R. (2011). *Overview of race and Hispanic origin: 2010*. Retrieved from http://www.census.gov/prod/cen2010/briefs/c2010br-02.pdf

Jackson, K. F. (2009). Beyond race: Examining the facets of multiracial identity through a life-span developmental lens. *Journal of Ethnic & Cultural Diversity in Social Work, 18*, 309-326.

Jones, N. A., & Smith, A. S. (2001). *The two or more races population: 2000*. Washington, DC: U.S. Census Bureau.

Kazdin, A. E. (1994). Psychotherapy for children and adolescents. In A. E. Bergin & S. L. Garfiled (Eds.), *Handbook of psychotherapy and behavior change* (4th ed., pp. 543-594). New York, NY: Wiley.

Maxwell, M., & Heneriksen, R. C., Jr. (2009). Counseling multiple heritage adolescents. In R. C. Henriksen, Jr., & D. A. Paladino (Eds.), *Counseling multiple heritage individuals, couples, and families* (pp. 65-81). Alexandria, VA: American Counseling Association.

Paladino, D. A., & Davis, H., Jr. (2006). Counseling and outreach strategies for assisting multiracial college students. *Journal of College Student Psychotherapy, 20*(3), 19-31. doi:10.1300/J035v20n03_03

Poston, W. S. C. (1990). The biracial identity development model: a needed addition. *Journal of Counseling & Development, 69*, 152-155.

Rockquemore, K. A., Brunsma, D. L., & Delgado, D. J. (2009). Racing to theory or rethorizing race? Understanding the struggle to build a multiracial identity theory. *Journal of Social Issues, 65*, 13-34.

Root, M. P. P. (1990). Resolving other status: Identity development of biracial individuals. *Women & Therapy, 9*, 185-205.

Root, M. P. P. (2001). *Loves revolution: Interracial marriage*. Philadelphia, PA: Temple University Press.

Smith, E. J. (1991). Ethnic identity development: Toward the development of a theory with the context on minority/majority status. *Journal of Counseling and Development, 20*, 181-188.

Stonequist, E. V. (1937). *The marginal man: A study in personality and culture and conflict*. New York, NY: Russell & Douglas.

Sue, D. W., Arredondo, P., & McDavis, R. J. (1992). Multicultural competencies and standards: A call to the profession. *Journal of Multicultural Counseling and Development, 20*, 64-88.

Tizard, B., & Phoenix, A. (1995). The identity of mixed parentage adolescents. *Journal of Child Psychology & Psychiatry & Allied disciplines, 36*, 1399-1410.

Worrell, F. C., Cross, W. E., Jr., & Vandiver, B. (2001). Nigrescence theory: Current status and challenges for the future.

Journal of Multicultural Counseling & Development, 29, 201-213.

Author Contact Information: Richard C. Henriksen, Jr., PhD, LPC-S, ACS, NCC, associate professor of education, Sam Houston State University, College of Education, Department of Educational Leadership and Counseling, Box 2119, Huntsville, TX 77341-2119. Telephone: 936-294-1209. E-mail: rch008@shswu.edu

Section 7: Moral Development Theory

INTRODUCTION

SECTION EDITOR
Rebecca A. Robles-Pinã
Sam Houston State University

It is fitting that a section on moral development be included in a handbook covering educational theories as the work of many moral developmental theorists is the backbone on which education theory has been developed. Seminal works contributed by such authors such as Piaget, Kohlberg, and Vygotsky have filled entire pages of textbooks and handbooks. Rarely, however, have the works of these authors been used in a compendium of all educational theorists where established theories are integrated with contemporary work for the development of twenty-first century theories that can explain twenty-first century problems. This section on moral development proposes to fill in this gap by presenting a section on how its authors used traditional theories as a backdrop for proposing new theories that are based on their most recent empirical work. Further, this section includes discussions of instruments and techniques for the assessment of the proposed theories.

Ten chapters are included in this section and we are fortunate to have contributors that bring both U. S. and international perspectives. We expect that this section will be beneficial as a guide for using moral development perspectives to explain the empirical findings of educational research conducted by graduate students, researchers, and professors in the social sciences.

In the first chapter, titled "A Moral Conflict Development Theory Based on Child and Teacher Interactions: A Cross Cultural Perspective," Majdalani and Robles-Piña propose a new conflict moral development theory. The theory is based on Hoffman's work of the development of primary and secondary emotions, such as guilt and shame. Further, the new theory builds on the existing work which has primarily focused on child and parent interactions for the development of a new theory which explains child and teacher interactions. This work has several educational implications. For one, it can be used to assist teachers in interacting with students so that feelings of guilt, which have a reparative component, can be developed in students. Second, the instrument developed can be used by others who are interested in gathering data from students regarding moral conflict experienced in schools. Third, the authors explain moral development from an international context, since this work was conducted in Argentina.

In the second chapter, "Combining Vales and Knowledge Education, Patry," Weinberger, Weyringer, and Nussbaumer propose a theory that explains how students can learn values while receiving traditional instruction. The authors explain how they used existing constructivist theories to develop their own theory known as VaKE (values and knowledge education). Further, this theory provides an international perspective since it was developed in Austria. This chapter will be of special interest to educators who wish to develop moral education while also building knowledge in students. A step-by-step approach of implementing this program is provided by the authors. Assessment techniques used to teach VaKE, such as the lesson interruption method, WALK, and sociograms, are discussed. Additionally, several empirical studies are cited that were used in validating the theory using cross cultural populations, gender, and various age groups.

In the third chapter titled "Moral Development," Jackson and Burgette, provide a very comprehensive overview of Lawrence Kohlberg's moral development theory. Specifically, a very thorough historical perspective is provided and integrated with recent developments of contemporary neo-Kolbergian theories. Of special interest was the authors' discussion of Kohlberg's emphasis on Piaget's stages of cognitive development which lead to an inclusion of the social aspects of moral development. Educators interested in instruments that can be used for the collection of quantitative

The Handbook of Educational Theories, pp. 549–551

and qualitative data will find this chapter useful. Most notably, the following instruments were discussed as a means of gathering data on moral development: *Moral Judgment Interview, Defining Issues Test, Defining Issues Test (2),* and the *Moral Judgment Test.*

In the fourth chapter titled "Social Cognitive Theory and Practice of Moral Development in Educational Settings," Rizzo and Bosacki propose the use of social cognition theories, also known as domain theories, be integrated with existing moral development theories in moral development. Educators interested in a theory that questions whether children in earlier stages of development can make moral judgments, whether moral development in children consists of stages, and the role of social conventions and personal preferences will be interested in this chapter. The authors suggest that this theory is more in line with twenty-first century skills that includes emphasis on acquisition of knowledge and competencies such as an integration of moral judgments, social norms, and personal preferences. The authors provide extensive empirical evidence for how educators can apply this theory to classroom settings.

In the fifth chapter titled "Moral Development and the Phenomenon of Absent Fathers" Wilson and Henriksen propose the need for a moral development theory that is based on culturally and linguistically diverse populations. Specifically, their interest is in developing a moral development theory that explains the absent father phenomenon among African American fathers. The authors use existing theories of Piaget, Kohlberg, and Gilligan as a basis for their model, however, add that a lack of definitions and descriptions of morality and immorality have not been applied to cross-cultural populations. The authors critique existing theories and empirical work to highlight the need for a culturally based moral development theory. It was generalized that aspects of religion, spirituality, poverty, ethics, and trust all need to be included in a moral development model that explains why there are so many absent fathers in all cultures, but especially in African American populations. Noteworthy, was the lack of instruments for collecting data that have been normed on culturally diverse groups.

In the sixth chapter titled "The Ethic of Care: Theory and Research," Skoe develops her moral development of care by building on Gilligan's existing theory of moral orientations and positive contributions to care and justice. Various empirical studies are cited and mention is made of the lack of empirical evidence supporting Gilligan's claim that Kohlberg's theory was biased again women. Starting with her dissertation in Norway, Skoe presents ample empirical work supporting her thesis. Educators who are interested in the interaction between ethic of care and gender, culture, emotions, and contextual factors will be very well served in reading this chapter. The instrument, *Ethic of Care Interview,* was used for gathering the vast empirical data collected on the ethic of care.

In the seventh chapter titled "Making a Moral Decision: A Proposition for an Integrated Model of Cognition, Emotions, and Social Interaction," Dyson, Crawford, Frey, and Dykstra, propose that moral decision making is a *process* that includes a discussion of cognitions, emotions, and social interaction. Educators who are looking for explanations to their empirical findings that explain moral orientation via examining prosocial reasoning and empathy will be interested in reading this chapter. The authors have gone beyond examining work by Piaget and Kohlberg and examined Hoffman's work on development of empathy as having an impact on moral decision making and socialization practices as studied by Grusec and Bandura. The authors provide several empirical studies to validate their theory including studies on students with disabilities. Instruments introduced were *The Primary Student Survey of Handicapped Persons: An Index of Empathy for Children and Adolescents* which assesses empathy and the modified *Chedoke-McMaster Attitudes towards Children with Handicaps Scale* (CATCH). Finally, this work presents an international perspective as it was developed in Canada.

In the eighth chapter titled "Moral Development Theory: Neo-Kohlbergian Theory," Mechler and Thoma propose a neo-Kohlbergain theory to moral development that does not strictly adhere to one based on stages and that is more in line with with-in person variability. Further, this chapter is based on the development of schemas that move from simple to complex as well as the role of affect in moral functioning. Some of the measurements that are suggested for measuring the precepts outlined in neo-Kohlbergian theory are the *Defining Issues Test* and the *Defining Issues Test (2).* The validity of this theory has been based on some empirical research including moral judgment related to political choices.

In the ninth chapter titled "Playful Activity and Thought as the Medium for Moral Development: Implication for Moral Education," Bergen and Davis propose a theory of moral development based on play, specifically Paidia theory. This theory is based on the work of traditionalists such as Piaget, Erikson, and Vygotsky in addition to psychoanalytic theorists such as Sigmund Freud and Anna Freud. The theory seeks to integrate three major moral dimensions - moral emotion, moral behavior, and moral reasoning both in early and later years of life. New concepts such as culture and technology were considered in the development of the theory. Assessments discussed included observational methods, clinical experiments, interviews, and surveys.

In the tenth chapter titled "The Innocence of Experience Theory: Young Adolescent Encounters and Life-Long Moral Development," Hough proposes that early experiences have a very strong effect on adults' moral development in later life. The theory developed is based on the interactions between physical, psychosocial, emotional, and cognitive/intellectual domains used in Kohlberg's six stages; however, this particular theory does not measure moral development in stages, but as a continuum. Validity for the theory was developed by a couple of retroactive studies conducted on adults' perceptions of their adolescent experiences. Most of the adults indicated that experiences based on their adolescent experiences assisted them in forming how they view moral dilemmas in adulthood. Interviews were the basis of collecting data for this theory.

In conclusion, this chapter presents new theories and assessments from a variety of international perspectives while also honoring traditional moral developmental theorists.

Author Contact Information: Rebecca A. Robles-Piña, PhD, Sam Houston State University, Department of Educational Leadership & Counseling. P.O. Box 2119 Huntsville, Texas, 77341. Phone: 936-294-1118. E-mail: edu_rar@shsu.edu

CHAPTER 46

A Moral Conflict Development Theory Based on Child and Teacher Interactions

A Cross Cultural Perspective

Maria Lourdes Majdalani
Majdalani Foundation—Center for Moral Development

Rebecca A. Robles-Piña
Sam Houston State University

The purpose of this chapter is to explain the development of a moral conflict development theory that uses child/child and teacher/child interactions and that is based on a cross-cultural perspective. The goal of the moral conflict development theory is to make specific contributions to teachers' practice by: (a) providing a theoretical and practical framework concerning children's moral development based on the unfolding of certain moral emotions such as guilt and shame and (b) assisting teachers to become aware of the fact that they do make a difference in children's moral development that is dependent on how they intervene in moral mishaps and antisocial behavior that arise among children during school time.

The development of the moral conflict development theory can be traced back to the work of several developmental theorists. Initially, Hume (1888) first proposed the idea that emotions were of necessary importance in moral development and character building, placing sympathy and empathy at the center of his theory. Other researchers such as Hauser (2006), Le Doux (1999) and Frijda (1993) agreed that emotions should be given a special place when it comes to observing human behavior. Additionally, the moral conflict development theory builds on Hoffman's (2000) theory of induction concerning parents and the way in which they contribute to children's moral and emotional development and the internalization of moral rules. Building on Piaget's (1965) work about child development, this theory proposes that adults do shape the way in which children develop in the moral domain, especially in the way they shape certain moral emotions. The socialization process between child and parent is important because as Harter and Whitesell (1989) have proposed "the ability to experience these self-affects (emotions) is highly dependent upon one's socialization history" (p. 94).

Guilt and Shame—Parent/Child Interactions

Specifically, the moral conflict development theory is based on techniques that indicate that parents and teachers use certain socialization practices that contribute to the unfolding of guilt and shame, in children. Ferguson and Stegge (1995) pose that "since guilt and shame are self-evaluative emotions, socialization expe-

The Handbook of Educational Theories, pp. 553–564

riences provided by significant others should be primary contributors to the development of these emotions" (p. 182). Most of the research indicates that guilt is positively related to empathy and responsibility in the reparation of harm (Barrett, 1998, Eisenberg, 2000, Ferguson & Stegge, 1995; Frijda, 1993, Hoffman, 2000, Lewis, 2000; Tangney, Burgraff, & Wagner, 1995; Williams, 1998). Guilt can be defined as a "painful feeling of disesteem for oneself, usually accompanied by a sense of urgency, tension and regret that results from empathic feelings for someone in distress, combined with awareness of being the cause of that distress" (Hoffman, 2000, p. 114). Shame, on the other hand, is positively related to personal distress and fear of punishment, and sometimes to anger. It is a "highly negative and painful state that also results in the disruption of ongoing behavior, confusion in thought and inability to speak" (Lewis, 2000, p. 629). As opposed to guilt, shame does not lead to the reparation of the harm. We could assume, then, that if children learn to repair the harm they committed because they feel guilty and responsible for what they have done, they would be on a development track towards the internalization of moral rules.

Parents contribute with children's moral and emotional development by means of their parenting styles. There are several ways in which parents contribute to children's moral and emotional development. Fergusson and Stegge (1995) state four major ways: (a) direct parental modeling of affective styles; (b) parental feedback to the child in emotion-eliciting situations; (c) parental communication to the child about how the parent perceives the child; and (d) "parental attributional, emotional, and behavioral reactions to the child when the parent perceives that an *ideal* or *ought* has been violated" (p. 183). That is, whenever a child violates certain moral standards, parents will react in a way that in turn will elicit certain moral emotions.

When parents use inductive methods, they guide the child towards a deeper insight of the situation and of the consequences of his or her behavior and the result is that the child is prone to develop empathy and guilt. When parents assist their child on focusing on their actions and consequences, the child is more likely to develop empathy for the victim and more likely to repair the harm committed. In time, the child internalizes these transgression-reparation scripts and starts to process the information, eventually detaching the rule from the parent. The rule starts to prevail by itself and is related to others' suffering rather than to the disciplinary agent. This is what we call *moral internalization*. "Induction highlights both the victim's distress and the child's action that caused it and has been found to contribute to the development of guilt and moral internalization in children" (Hoffman, 2000, p. 10).

By contrast, when parents do not give any types of explanation and instead focus on the child's entire self and punish him or her, either by power assertion or love withdrawal, the child is more prone to develop shame. In research conducted by Ferguson and Stegge (1995), shame responses were predicted by the absence of induction—parents not responding at all to a moral mishap or engaging in love withdrawal, and power assertion. In general, Kochanska, Gross, Lin, & Nichols (2002) have found that children of mothers who used (or reported using) more power-assertive discipline showed less guilt, that is, less reparative social behavior.

Shame does not lead to the reparation of harm or to moral internalization. The experience of shame is more painful than that of guilt because the child does not see the possibility of repairing the harm committed. The child does not feel that a wrong was committed based on behavior, but that the whole self is regarded as bad or damaged. Consequently, the child cannot make the link between transgression, consequences regarding others and the moral rule, due to the overwhelming feelings of personal distress. In this state of behavior, the child is more likely to fear abandonment due to the experience of shame and feel sorry for himself or herself rather than focusing on the victim and the reparation of the harm.

GUILT AND SHAME—TEACHER/CHILD INTERACTIONS

The special aspect and contribution of our theory is that it concerns teachers because they are also very important in contributing to children's moral development. We are actually transferring to schools what we know happens at homes and given that the child spends a significant amount of time with adults who are not their parents (Ryan & Bohlin, 1999). We focus on the assumption that the way in which teachers intervene after a moral mishap or antisocial action involving children is related to children's experience of guilt and shame, two important secondary emotions which will eventually contribute to the child's moral development. In particular, the manner in which teachers judge either the child's conduct, by either focusing on emotions or on rules and how they provide or fail to provide positive feedback regarding reparation of harm, will ultimately shape the child's experience of guilt or of shame.

The moral conflict development theory is original in as much as it concerns teacher-child interaction while building on the established literature of both guilt and shame which has been researched by authors like Eisenberg (2000), Hoffman (2000) and Lewis (2000).

Assumptions

The research described above specifically addresses parent-child interactions; the paucity of research is related to teacher-child interactions at school. However, based on the research about parent-child interactions using shame and guilt as means of developing moral development, several assumptions can be made about teacher/child interactions and the effect on moral development. Some of the assumptions are: (a) teachers´ manner of judging the child's conduct is similar to that of parents, (b) teachers who reprimand children by judging the child's self rather than the behavior can elicit shame, (c) teachers who reprimand children by judging the child's behavior can elicit guilt feelings which are likely to lead to repairing harm, and (d) teachers, who are made aware of proper parenting styles, can make use of those during school hours.

Original Development and Interactions of Theory

The moral conflict development theory was based on the following research on emotions. Authors divide emotions into two large groups: primary and secondary. Primary emotions—joy, fear, anger, sadness, disgust, and surprise—appear throughout the first year of life and are so called primary because they need practically no cognitive support (Lewis, 2007). They are also accompanied by prototypic facial expressions, which make them easily recognizable (Ekman, 1999). Babies, for instance, can not only feel and express fear, which includes brows raising and widening and tensing of mouth as well as fixation on stimulus, but also recognize it in other people.

Secondary emotions such as pride, shame, guilt, embarrassment, empathy, or envy, appear later in life because they are somewhat more complex. They are also called *moral*, *self-conscious* or *social* emotions. There are several characteristics that researchers attribute to these emotions. Lewis (2000) sustains that the emergence of *self-conscious* emotions, as he calls them, is due to some cognitive processes that involve the notion of self. "It is the way we think or what we think about that becomes the elicitor of pride, shame, guilt or embarrassment" (p. 623).

Lewis (2000) points out three typical characteristics of self-conscious emotions. In the first place, these emotions appear together with the notion of self as independent from others. Between 15 and 24 months, when children recognize themselves as separate from their mother, they are already capable of feeling empathy, shame, or guilt. In the second place, Lewis adds that these emotions involve a set of standards, rules, and goals (SRGs). These are normative standards that are passed on to children via culture and that refer to the behavior that is acceptable within a social group. In most cultures, for instance, hitting others is considered an antisocial action that hurts others. Children, thus, are raised with the rule *We do not hit each other*, which they already understand by age two. These SRGs must be known and incorporated into the child's cognition (Lewis, 2007). In the third place, Lewis (2000) points out the evaluation of one's actions, thoughts and feelings vis-à-vis these SRGs. Evaluation has to be internal, as opposed to merely external, in order for the self-conscious emotion to arise. That is, the child has to evaluate if his or her behavior, compared with the standards or rules he or she was raised in, falls short of them or, on the contrary, that it coincides with them.

But how does a child evaluate his or her own behavior? Hoffman (2000) sustains that it is a matter of responsibility. Once a child empathizes with the victim, and by casual attribution knows he or she is to blame, then he or she will feel responsible for what has happened. Stipek (1995) proposes that before a child can evaluate his or her own behavior vis-à-vis some normative standards set beforehand, a socialization process has been necessary. This means, according to Stipek that caretakers are constant sources of information when children need to know what is acceptable and what is not acceptable in the social group to which he or she belongs.

Children constantly refer to the adult in order to know whether his or her behavior is in tune with the normative standards. With repeated feedback from the adult, in the form of approval or disapproval, praise, or punishment, the child will anticipate the adult's reaction and start to feel the emotion without needing the actual presence of the adult. In time, the child will internalize a pattern about what is socially and morally accepted in the culture he or she was raised in and will feel the emotion without the presence of an external audience. It is interesting to see that most authors agree with the idea that the presence of an audience is still necessary in the experience of secondary emotions. Only now the audience has been internalized, *Nobody sees me, but I see myself.*

Emergence of Moral Emotions in Development

What about the ages in which secondary emotions appear? Do all of these secondary emotions appear together developmentally speaking? Hoffman's (2000) theory is that the precursor of one of these secondary emotions—guilt—is another secondary emotion: empathy. Although it is true that empathy as a moral emotion may appear at around age two, there are features of this emotion that appear earlier. When a baby sees somebody else in distress, he or she experiences a similar distress by means of mimicry, conditioning or association. The baby is feeling empathy for the victim. This is supported by Frijda (1993) who, referring to empathy, asserts that distress may well be a necessary condition. In time, and together with the ability to differentiate the self from others—as becomes clear when children recognize themselves in the mirror—and casual attribution, the child will experience the awareness that he or she has caused the other's distress and will want to do something in order to repair the harm. In this way, Hoffman holds that for the child to feel guilt there must be a previous feeling of empathy towards the victim. Only if the child can feel empathy, will he or she be able to feel guilt and be able to repair the harm. Guilt, and not shame, is therefore related to empathy, and apparently follows it (Tangney, Suewig, & Mashek, 2007). Shame, on the other hand, may be negatively related to empathy and positively related to personal distress and aggressive antisocial behavior. Together, both empathy and guilt are predictors of responsibility and reparation of harm.

Authors like Barrett (1995) and Eisenberg (2000) have suggested that the precursors of secondary emotions are already observed around the second year of life. There is evidence that 2- and 3-year-olds have already formed an idea of right and wrong and respond to mishaps with prosocial behavior. Barrett (1998) observed 2-year-olds' reactions to an apparent mishap. The toddlers were left to play with the experimenter's rag doll, and the leg fell off. Some children, the "avoiders", showed shame, thus averting their gaze from the experimenter's and delaying their reporting on the mishap. Others, the "amenders," in contrast, showed guilt; they tried to repair the rag doll and told the experimenter what had happened right away. In coincidence with these results, parents of the guilt-prone children reported that, at home, these felt more guilt as compared to shame as well.

Also, parents have reported that guilt in their children increases from 14 to 24 months of age. "Thus, it appears that precursors or rudimentary forms of guilt are evident before age three and that guilt increases with age in the early years" (Eisenberg, 2000, p. 679). Barrett (1998) also sustains that these emotions appear with more frequency as the child grows. "Children become likely to experience most emotions in a wider array of contexts as they grow older" (p. 79).

Critics from the more cognitive approaches, like those of Harris (1989), Harter and Whitesell (1989), Thompson (1989) and Griffin (1995), suggest that only from 7/8 years of age do secondary emotions appear. Some of them have argued that what the child starts to experience are only precursors of pride, shame or guilt, and not yet the emotions in themselves. Authors like Frijda (1993) do not conceive of the feeling of an emotion without the "awareness of the event as appraised" (p. 358). This means that although emotions may be experienced without its thorough awareness, cognitive awareness induces a different emotional experience altogether. What these authors argue is that cognitive impairments make the experience of certain secondary emotions doubtful.

Harris (1989), however, does not deny the experience of secondary emotions but instead suggests that there is a natural delay between the experience of emotion and the thorough understanding of it by the child. In fact, Harris's interpretation indicates that although children are already capable of feeling pride, shame, or guilt, they do not fully understand their meaning until around age 7 or 8. To prove this, Harris and colleagues (1989) studied the answers of Dutch and English children ranging from 5 to 14 years of age to see whether they understood a set of 20 terms dealing with emotion. The children were presented with the emotion term and then asked to describe a situation that may have elicited that emotion. The study included both primary and secondary emotion terms. Five-year-olds correctly described situations that would elicit primary emotions such as joy, anger or sadness. But only from 7 years of age were children able to describe situations that elicited secondary emotions such as pride, shame, or guilt. Thus, Harris concluded that the understanding of complex emotions is positively correlated to age and that children under 7 are not yet capable of understanding them. Young children are inclined to mix up guilt with sadness and pride with happiness, thus providing situations that may elicit happiness for pride and situations that may elicit sadness for guilt.

Harter and Whitesell (1989) suggest that the experiencing of secondary emotions by the child depends on the existence of an audience. "The young child would require an actual audience that witnesses, and reacts to, behaviors that are shameful or, alternatively, worthy of pride" (p. 95). In order to feel pride, for instance, the child must be able to know he or she is seen by a parent who will be happy for the child's performance. In time, the child will internalize this audience, and will be able to experience these emotions without the actual presence of a parent.

Thompson's (1989) work explains emotional development in children with the use of the *attribution-emotion* model. The author argues that children begin by experiencing *outcome-dependent* emotions resulting from a primary appraisal. Later, as their cognitive skills become more elaborate, they experience *attribution-dependent* emotions resulting from a secondary appraisal. That is, younger children will begin by experiencing happiness, sadness, or frustration depending on fulfilling or not fulfilling a desire (outcome), regardless of what caused that outcome. Older children will also experience pride, guilt, surprise, or gratitude, depending on what caused a certain outcome. Attribution-dependent emotions are more complex because they are triggered not only by positive or negative outcomes—success or failure—but also by the causes of those outcomes. For example, when failure is due to lack of effort, the child may feel guilty. If, on the other hand, success is due to hard work, the child will experience pride. Causes can be divided into three dimensions: (a) internal or external locus; (b) stability, and (c) controllability. Stability may give rise to the experience of shame, as when the child feels that *I am always a bad person*. Controllability is very important for the experience of guilt because the child who feels in control will feel responsible for what he or she has done.

This cognitive approach proposes that secondary appraisals need the working memory capacity. In order for the child to simultaneously bear in mind both outcomes and the causes of those outcomes, the working memory capacity is needed. Along these lines, but somewhat different, Griffin (1995) suggests that the child needs the working memory capacity in order to represent two variables of social reality: evaluating success or failure vis-à-vis some moral standards and anticipating what an audience would say.

Berti, Garattoni, and Venturini (2000), on the other hand, suggest that researchers have been underestimating children's experience of secondary emotions. Contrary to Harris, who suggests that children are not ready to thoroughly understand secondary emotions until age 7 or 8, these authors suggest that 5- and 6-year-old children are ready. To prove their hypothesis, they carried on two studies in Italy that were not only limited to the children being presented with different emotion terms and then asked to say which situation may have provoked that emotion. Instead, they carefully interviewed children ranging from 5 to 10 years old to see whether they understood the differences between sadness, guilt and shame.

The first study dealt with sadness and guilt; the second with guilt and shame. The interviewer showed the children a picture of ET—the character of Spielberg's film—and invited them to pretend that they had to help ET understand what humans are like. Children were thus presented with situations in which ET met a boy or a girl who told him, to begin with, that he or she was feeling *sad*. The same was done with the other emotions. The children were then asked to provide, for each emotion, a definition, its antecedents, the thoughts characterizing the emotion, the action tendencies, the role of the audience and the emotion regulation. In the case of the comparison between sadness and guilt, the first study showed that 5-year-olds already differentiated between these two emotions. Although children could not give a clear definition of guilt—they did in the case of sadness—they were very good at describing, for both emotions, the antecedents, the thoughts, the action tendencies, the role of the audience and the emotion regulation. In the case of sadness, children described the aggression from peers and the scolding by adults as antecedents of the emotion; they described misdeeds and disobedience to adults as antecedents of guilt. The thoughts and action tendencies described by the children in the case of sadness were related to mourning, the will to do nothing, to take revenge or to do something nice; in the case of guilt, children described remorse, fear of punishment and the need to repair the harm committed. As regards the role of the audience, children associated the presence of parents with the reduction of sadness and with the increase of guilt. Finally, regarding emotion regulation, children proposed distraction in the case of sadness and reparation and apologizing in the case of guilt. The first study, thus, shows that even though 5-year-olds are still not good at defining, guilt, they understand all its components and clearly differentiate it from sadness.

In the second study, guilt and shame were compared with the same procedure, except for the question of the definition of these two emotions, which was eliminated. The answers given for guilt were very similar to the previous study. For shame, children related its antecedents to failure in performance—at school or at sports—to being refused or scolded and to embarrassing situations. As regards the thoughts associated with shame, children made reference to the need to be somewhere else, to feeling blocked or unable to think. When questioned about the action tendencies, most children denied that there was a way of coping with shame, and instead referred to the need to escape, hide, cry, withdraw, or seek comfort, answers that coincide with the regulation of the emotion. Regarding the role of the audience, children associated the presence of parents with the reduction of shame. The second study, thus, shows that children understand shame and clearly differentiate it from guilt. "At all ages, there was overall very little overlap between the answers about shame and guilt. An understanding of shame and the distinction between shame and guilt therefore appears to be already achieved at age five-six years" (Berti et al., 2000, p. 314). In sum, the literature regarding exactly when children are capable of expressing primary and secondary emotions is mixed. Thus, the need for a theory that serves to integrate the existing empirical work.

Shame and Guilt

Evaluation of personal behavior is crucial to the emergence of secondary emotions. But different ways of evaluating personal behavior may lead to different emotional experiences. Children and people in general may make specific or global attributions when evaluating their behavior. When the child evaluates success and focuses on the whole self, he or she will feel hubris; by contrast, if the child evaluating success focuses on a single action, he or she will feel pride. Likewise, when the child feels responsible for an action that goes against the SRGs and focuses on the whole self, then he or she will feel shame. "In shame, the focus of the negative evaluation is on the entire self ... the entire self is painfully scrutinized and found lacking" (Tangney et al., 1995, p. 344). If, by contrast, the child feeling responsible for a bad action, only focuses on that action, then he or she will feel guilt. "Guilt seems to result when one has some sense of a "should" or a "shouldn't" that was violated" (Barrett, 1998, p. 78). A typical shameful assertion would be *I am a bad person because I have done something wrong.* A typical guilty assertion would be *I have done something wrong and I need to repair it.* Niedenthal, Tangney, and Gavanski (1994) assert that shame is associated with the counterfactual thinking involving the desire to undo aspects of self; whereas guilt is associated with the counterfactual thinking involving the desire to undo aspects of behavior. The shameful person rarely does something to rectify the antisocial action he or she committed. By contrast, the guilty person usually tries to repair the harm or apologize.

It is interesting to see how the bodily postures of a child feeling shame as opposed to a child feeling guilt vary. Lewis (2000) describes shame as

> a highly negative and painful state that also results in the disruption of ongoing behavior, confusion in thought and an inability to speak. The physical action accompanying shame is a shrinking of the body, as though to disappear from the eye of the self or the other. (p. 629).

Barrett (1995) adds that the shameful person "avoids looking at others, hides the face, slumps the body, lowers the head and/or withdraws from contact with others" (p. 41). Along the same lines, Stipek (1995) describes shame as "characterized in the literature by blushing and universal facial expressions consisting of eyes lowered, lips rolled inward, mouth corners depressed, and lower lip tucked between the teeth" (p. 241). Guilt, on the other hand, makes the child look up and move as if trying to repair the harm. Once the reparation is done, guilt disappears.

For Barrett (1995) guilt and shame are *social emotions* because they involve somebody else, in this case, the socialization agent who eventually will become the internalized audience. Social emotions are endowed with significance by social communication, are connected with social interaction and are related to appraisals regarding self and others. Also, guilt and shame help in the development of the self by showing the child how he or she should behave and how he or she is seen by others. Tracy and Robins (2007) propose that the social status of these emotions influences the way in which the person represents him or herself vis-à-vis others.

The functionalist approach presented by Barrett (1998) describes that social emotions serve three functions: social communication, behavior regulation, and internal regulation. Tangney et al. (2007) suggests that social emotions function as emotional moral barometers "providing immediate and salient feedback on our social and moral acceptability" (p. 22). From this point of view, also supported by Frijda (1993), Baumeister, Stillwell, and Heatherton (1995) and Tracy and Robins (2007), guilt is helping the person protect relationships by communicating to the other that he or she did not wish to harm the other and that something is being done to correct the wrongdoing. This is why the guilty person will often want to explain what happened or apologize. The guilty child might refer to the adult as if seeking help. The function of shame, on the other hand, is to distance the self from the evaluation of others. Barrett proposes that frequent guilt experiences, in time, might empower the child to control antisocial behavior, and help him or her internalize moral standards by providing the knowledge of ways to repair the harm. The same does not apply to shame. Frequent shame experiences, in time, might tell the child he or she *is bad.*

The present study aims at observing adult-child interaction at schools to see whether it is possible to make a connection between what adults tell children and these children's emotional reactions, especially, those emotional reactions depicting the experience of shame and guilt.

VALIDATION OF THE MORAL CONFLICT DEVELOPMENT THEORY AND INSTRUMENT

The moral conflict development theory has been validated by the literature discussed above. What follows is a description of the validation of the theory based on the description of a program, an instrument, and some preliminary data.

There have been several phases to the development of the moral conflict development theory. In the first phase, The *Values Project,* a 10-year program was developed and implemented and the goal is to teach children moral values, such as responsibility, honesty, respect, and justice. The *Values Project* has been implemented in several provinces in Argentina. The didactic material includes a teacher training manual and activities for children aged 4-9. It became increasingly evident that the *Values Project* needed to be evaluated for its effectiveness in promoting the use of prosocial skills in children. In order to assess the effectiveness of the

Values Project, the *Moral Conflict Situation Questionnaire* [*MCSQ*] (Majdalani, 2010) was developed.

The purpose of the *MCSQ* is to rate: (a) children's behavior to a moral conflict, (b), teacher's interventions to the moral conflict in which a child is engaged, (c) and child's reaction to the intervention provided by the teacher. The *MCSQ* was originally developed in Spanish to collect data in Argentina and was later translated into English. The *MCSQ* assesses spontaneous moral conflicts among children as a way of making a diagnosis of what happens at schools while simultaneously observing the teacher/child reactions to the conflict. The dynamics observed between teacher and child to a child's moral conflict are deemed essential in the development of the moral conflict development theory.

Development of the MCSQ

Validity. The *MCSQ* was developed in several steps. In the first step certain procedures were followed to assure the instrument was valid. They were: (a) developing items for the *MCSQ* which were based on the moral development literature on shame and guilt, (b) subjecting items to two experts' advice, (c) conducting a pilot test, and (d) soliciting opinions from teachers about behaviors that assist in resolving conflict.

Evidence of validity was provided by several sources. For example, two experts on moral emotion theory were asked to assess the items developed to determine whether they reflected the literature on conflict resolution using shame and guilt responses in both teachers and children. After providing the experts with a complementary paper on the description of both shame and guilt, we asked them to select "S" for shame and "G" for guilt for each item on both teachers´ intervention and children's reactions. We also indicated to the experts that we wanted to use the information gathered for developing an instrument to determine teachers´ roles in resolving conflict in children and the development of shame and guilt. The experts agreed with the way in which we did this, but suggested making the instrument simpler in terms of the way in which we expressed both teachers´ interventions and children's reactions.

On the survey, we had 189 responses and wished to increase the numbers in order to provide more information for validating the Moral Conflict Development Theory. The results of the survey indicated that teachers felt that the most common antisocial behavior observed in children aged 4-9 is *aggression* (22.8%). Included in this behavior, other antisocial actions such as hitting, pushing, grabbing hair, and spitting were noted. The next most frequent behavior noted was *subduing* (13%), followed by *insulting* (10.2%) and *bothering* (8.8%). The least common behaviors were *lying* (2.3%), *stealing* (1.4%) and *threatening* (0.5%). Further, the results indicated that most conflicts (57.1%) take place among children. Additionally, the results of the survey indicated that conflicts between children and teachers (16.4%) were less than those both among children and between children and teachers (26.5%).

The pilot test was conducted to further improve the validity of the study and the following procedures were used. Monitors (persons who actually observed the moral conflicts and filled in the questionnaire) where asked to test the instrument, and provide suggestions. We previously gave monitors the complementary paper which described shame and guilt in detail. Monitors were especially asked to provide more detail on moral conflicts. This resulted in a list of 15 antisocial actions, partly provided by the monitors and partly provided by the literature. Also, monitors suggested adding whether the conflicts were among children or between children and teachers. Monitors finally suggested the possibility of qualitatively describing the moral conflicts and of writing any other child reactions different from those apparently belonging to guilt and shame. This pilot test (106 protocols) was conducted in 4 different cities (San Carlos de Bariloche, Malargüe, Ushuaia, and Río Grande) and described moral conflicts in groups at schools.

Reliability. In regards to reliability, the *MCSQ* is still in stages of development. At this point, the instrument is a rating scale, where observers indicate whether the behaviors are occurring or not at the time of the moral conflict. We are in the process of gathering inter-rater reliability. Future plan are to add a Likert-scale to the items to collect interval data that will permit analysis for determining a reliability coefficient, such as a Cronbach's alpha. Moreover, once our data collection improves and more data are collected, it is our plan to use factor analysis to determine the construct validity and factors specific to the *MCSQ*.

Description of the Instrument-MCSQ

There are six parts to the *MCSQ* (see Appendix). The first part requests demographic information such as school, course, and type of school. The second part requests qualitative information about the moral conflict situation observed. The third part requests information on whether the conflict was between child/child, child/teacher or both. The fourth part requests information on the action that generated the moral conflict in the child. The fifth part requests information on the teacher's intervention to the moral conflict. The sixth part requests information on the child's reaction to the teacher's intervention. The MCSQ was developed in Spanish and has recently been translated to English.

Items were developed to measure teachers' pedagogical style regarding moral conflict. Six items were developed to measure whether the teacher was operating from a shame style and 10 items were developed to measure whether the teacher was operating from a guilt style. Examples of an item measuring a teacher operating from a shame style is "You are a bad boy" or "Get out of the classroom" and an example of an item measuring a teacher operating from a guilt style is "What you said is not true". The former items lead to a child feeling shame, while the latter leads to a child feeling guilt and leading to reparation of harm.

Items were also developed to measure the type of interventions provided by teachers. For example the items "Look how sad Jamie is" and "What can we do to make Jamie feel better?" were included to determine if the teacher uses this type of statements to elicit empathy in the child. Use of this type of statements by teachers result in reparation of the harm committed and guides the child in apologizing. Information from our survey indicated that teachers who used interventions that elicited guilt in children were more likely to foster empathy and help children repair harm, give moral advice, lead moral reflection with groups of children, ask about moral intentions, and talk about emotions.

Finally, 23 items were developed to measure children's feelings of guilt and shame in reaction to a teacher's interventions. Examples of items that measured shame were "Looks down," "Face gets red," while some of the items that measured guilt were "Looks up," "Looks for teacher," and "Apologizes."

Generalizability of the Theory Across Cultures, Ethnicities, and Gender

The moral conflict development theory was developed in Argentina, a Spanish-speaking country. An instrument (*MCSQ*) was developed to gather data in order to validate the theory; it was developed originally in Spanish and has now been translated into English. Data have been gathered from children ages 4-9 in four cities Argentina in children. Thus, generalizability remains limited to demographic characteristics shared by this sample. It is our intention to continue to collect data in Argentina and extend the data gathering to other cities in Argentina and the United States. A next step would be to analyze the data by gender to investigate if there are gender differences.

Conclusion

The development of the moral conflict development theory was developed as a means of helping teachers interact in a more positive manner with the children they teach and to help them in developing prosocial behaviors such as honesty, respect, and responsibility. The literature on which this theory was developed came from studies that have investigated the development of primary and secondary emotions and whether young children who are four or five are capable of expressing emotions related to guilt and shame. It is important to study children's feelings of guilt and shame because they are the precursors to whether children will develop emotions such as guilt which leads to acts of repairing the harm they have committed. The literature indicates that parents are the first role models who help their children develop the feelings of guilt and shame by the way the interact with them. Statements that indicate to children that they are okay but that their behaviors are not are more likely to elicit feelings of guilt in children. Conversely, statements that indicate to children that they are not okay versus their behavior being the target of criticism are more likely to elicit feelings of shame which do not lead to feelings of empathy and behaviors such as apologizing to repair the harm committed.

The moral conflict development theory was developed based on the theories and assumptions discussed above. The purpose of this theory is to take this information and transfer it to how school teachers interact with children to develop their moral education and specifically feelings of guilt and shame. To this end, a 10-year *Values Project* was developed and evaluated to assess the degree to which children had learned prosocial behaviors. The *MCSQ* in Spanish was developed to assess the project in Argentina and has most recently been translated to English. Some preliminary data have been collected from four provinces in Argentina and the hopes are to continue collecting data to further validate the theory. Ultimately, the goal is that information from this theory will be used by school teachers to develop prosocial skills in children.

References

Barrett, K. (1995). A functionalist approach to shame and guilt. In J. Tangney & K. Fischer (Eds.), *Self-conscious emotions: The psychology of shame, guilt, embarrassment, and pride* (pp. 25-63). New York, NY: The Guilford Press.

Barrett, K. (1998). The origins of guilt in early childhood. In J. Bybee (Ed), *Guilt and children* (pp. 75-90). San Diego, CA: Academic.

Baumeister, R. F., Stillwell, A. M., & Heatherton, T. F. (1995). In J. Tangney & K. Fischer (Eds.), *Self-conscious emotions: The psychology of shame, guilt, embarrassment, and pride* (pp. 255-273). New York, NY: The Guilford Press.

Berti, A., Garattoni, C., & Venturini, B. (2000). The understanding of sadness, guilt, and shame in 5-, 7-, and 9-year-old children. *Genetic, Social and General Psychology Monographs, 126*, 293-318.

Eisenberg, N. (2000). Emotion, regulation and moral development. *Annual Reviews Psychology, 51*, 665-697.

APPENDIX: MORAL CONFLICT QUESTIONNAIRE

City:

Demographic data (teacher):

Seniority in teacher performance:

Seniority in current school:

Current course:

Number of children in current course:

Type of school:

- Public
- Secular
- Private
- Religious

Describe in detail the moral conflict situation observed:

Specify:

a. Subjects involved in the moral conflict situation described above:

Child/Children—Child/Children
Teacher/s—Child/Children

b. Action/s identified as generators of the moral conflict situation described above:

1.	The child speaks louder or makes annoying noises.
2.	The child insults or uses aggressive language.
3,	The child hits or pushes.
4.	The child pulls other's hair.
5.	The child takes out his/her tongue or spits.
6.	The child verbally quarrels (over something or about the rules of a game).
7.	The child bothers or provokes other with words or actions, trying to make him/her react.
8.	The child takes or ruins other's belongings or productions (copybooks, backpacks) or wishes to impose his/her will over others.
9.	The child is intentionally indifferent to other's asking for help or does not listen to other.
10.	The child criticizes or laughs at other because of physical or intellectual limitations, looks, actions, belongings or productions (drawing, grades). The child might disqualify other by giving him/her nick-names.

(Appendix continues on next page.)

APPENDIX: MORAL CONFLICT QUESTIONNAIRE CONTINUED

11.	The child puts other aside (says "You go", "You don't play with us", "You are nobody", "You are not my friend").
12.	The child makes gestures as if trying to hurt other, or says something like "I'm gonna kill you" or "I'm gonna hit you".
13.	The child says things which are not true, exaggerates, slanders, denies or unfairly accuses other.
14.	The child takes away other's belongings –stuff, money- in order to intentionally keep them with the other's consent.
15.	The child does not abide by a promise or a task and hams others.
c.	Teacher's intervention in the moral conflict situation described above:
1.	The teacher refers negatively to the child's person saying phrases such as "You are a liar" or "You are a bad boy/girl".
2.	The teacher reinforces a negative name previously given to the child saying phrases such as "You are always the same" or "What could we expect from you?"
3.	The teacher refers to a moral rule saying phrases such as "We do not hit each other", "We do not lie" or "We do not say bad words" without providing further explanation.
4.	The teacher leaves the child without the break, sends him/her to the corner or punishes him/her in an unrelated way to the conflict.
5.	The teacher expels the child out of the classroom.
6.	The teacher does not provide any suggestion to the child so that he/she can repair the harm committed.
7.	The teacher refers negatively to the child's conduct saying phrases such as "What you did was wrong" or "What you said is not true".
8.	The teacher refers to the moral damage –real or hypothetical- and to the emotions implied in the conflict saying phrases such as "Would you like XX done to you?", "Look how sad Jamie is" or "We should not hurt each other".
9.	The teacher helps the child repair the harm committed saying phrases such as "What can we do to make Jamie feel better?", "Ask Jamie to forgive you" or "Give back what you took away from him."
10.	The teacher explains the spirit of a moral rule saying phrases such as "We do not hit each other because we would hurt others and be disrespectful to them."
11.	The teacher tries to find out about the child's intentions saying phrases such as "Did you want to hurt him or was it unintended?"
12.	The teacher leads a moral reflection with the group of children about the moral conflict situation.
13.	The teacher talks about the emotions the children had.
14.	The teacher helps the children elaborate moral judgments posing questions such as "Why is it wrong to hit each other?"
15.	The teacher uses didactic material to work on the moral conflict situation (story, movie, game, role-playing).
16.	The teacher gives moral advice for future episodes (reinforces a moral rule by writing it on the blackboard)
d.	Child's reaction after teacher's intervention:
1.	The child lowers his/her head in order to avoid the teacher's or somebody else's sight.
2.	The child looks down or covers his/her eyes in order to avoid the teacher's or somebody else's sight.
3.	The child blushes.
4.	The child bends his/her back o shrinks his/her body.
5.	The child is unable to speak.

6.	The child stops doing what he/she was doing or freezes.
7.	The child gets away of the victim.
8.	The child lies in order to elude responsibility.
9.	The child looks up as if looking for a solution to the moral conflict situation.
10.	The child looks for the teacher as a reference to what he/she should do.
11.	The child is reflective and/or takes responsibility on what he/she has done.
12.	The child talks with the victim.
13.	The child shows empathy, sympathy, help or comfort towards the victim.
14.	The child gives back to the victim what he/she took away from him/her.
15.	The child spontaneously apologizes to the victim or because teacher says so.
16.	The child cries.
17.	The child says he/she did not do it on purpose.
18.	The child justifies his/her behavior.
19.	The child finds trouble apologizing.
20.	The child is indifferent to the teacher's intervention.
21.	The child seems surprised with the teacher's intervention.
22.	The child responds with a threat.
23.	The child increments his/her anger.

Ekman, P. (1999). Facial expressions. In T. Dalgleish & M. Power (Eds.), *Handbook of cognition and emotion* (pp. 301-320). New York, NY: Wiley.

Ferguson, T. J., & Stegge, H. (1995). Emotional states and traits in children: The case of guilt and shame. In J. Tangney and K. Fischer (Eds.), *Self-conscious emotions: The psychology of shame, guilt, embarrassment, and pride* (pp. 174-197). New York, NY: The Guilford Press.

Frijda, N. H. (1993). The place of appraisal in emotion. *Cognition and Emotion, 7* (3-4), 357-387.

Griffin, S. (1995). A cognitive-developmental analysis of pride, shame, and embarrassment in middle childhood. In J. Tangney & K. Fischer (Eds.), *Self-conscious emotions: The psychology of shame, guilt, embarrassment, and pride* (pp. 219-236). New York, NY: The Guilford Press.

Harris, P. L. (1989). *Children and emotion.* New York, NY: Blackwell.

Harter, S., & Whitesell, N. R. (1989). Developmental changes in children's understanding of simple, multiple, and blended emotions concepts. In C. Saarni & P. L. Harris (Eds.), *Children's understanding of emotions* (pp. 81-116). Cambridge, England: Cambridge University Press.

Hoffman, M. L. (2000). *Empathy and moral development*. Cambridge, MA: Cambridge University Press.

Hauser, M. D. (2006). *Moral minds.* New York, NY: HarperCollins.

Hume, D. (1888). *A treatise of human nature.* New York, NY: Oxford University Press.

Kochanska, G., Gross, J. N., Lin, M. -H, & Nichols, K. E. (2002). Guilt in young children: Development, determinants, and relations with a broader system of standards. *Child Development, 73,* 461-482.

LeDoux, J. (1996). *The emotional brain.* New York, NY: Simon & Schuster.

Le Doux, J. (1999). *El cerebro emocional.* Bs. As.: Planeta.

Lewis, M. (2000). Self-conscious emotions: Embarrassment, pride, shame and guilt. In M. Lewis & J. M. Haviland-Jones (Eds.), *Handbook of emotions* (2nd ed., pp .623-636). New York, NY: The Guilford Press.

Lewis, M. (2007). Self-conscious emotional development. In J. L. Tracy, R. W. Robins & J. P. Tangney (Eds.), *The self-conscious emotions* (pp. 134-149). New York, NY: Guilford Press.

Majdalani, L. (2010). *Moral Conflict Situation Questionnaire [MCSQ]*. Unpublished instrument.

Niedenthal, P. M., Tangney, J. P., & Gavanski, I. (1994). If only I weren't versus If only I hadn't: Distinguishing shame and guilt in counterfactual thinking. *Journal of Personality and Social Psychology, 67,* 585-595.

Piaget, J. (1965). *The moral judgment of the child.* New York, NY: The Free Press.

Ryan, K., & Bohlin, K. (1999). *Building character in schools.* San Francisco, CA: Jossey-Bass.

Stipek, D. (1995). The development of pride and shame in toddlers. In J. Tangney & K. Fischer (Eds.), *Self-conscious emotions: The psychology of shame, guilt, embarrassment, and pride* (pp. 237-252). New York, NY: The Guilford Press.

Tangney, J. P., Burgraff, S. A., & Wagner, P. E. (1995). Shame-proneness, guilt-proneness, and psychological symptoms. In J. Tangney and K. Fischer (Eds.), *Self-Conscious emotions: The psychology of shame, guilt, embarrassment, and pride* (pp. 237-252). New York, NY: The Guilford Press.

Tangney, J. P., Stuewig, J., & Mashek, D. J. (2007). What's moral about the self-conscious emotions? In J. L. Tracy, R. W. Robins, & J. P. Tangney (Eds.), *The self-conscious emotions* (pp. 21-37). New York, NY: Guilford Press.

Thompson, R. A. (1989). Causal attribution and children's emotional understanding. In C. Saarni & P. L. Harris (Eds), *Children's understanding of emotion* (pp. 117-150). Cambridge, England: Cambridge University Press.

Tracy, J. L. & Robins, R. W. (2007). The self in self-conscious emotions. In J. L. Tracy, R. W. Robins & J. P. Tangney (Eds.), *The self-conscious emotions* (pp. 3-20). New York, NY: Guilford Press.

Williams, C. (1998). Guilt in the classroom. In J. Bybee (Ed.), *Guilt and children* (pp. 233-243). San Diego, CA: Academic.

Author Contact Information: María Lourdes Majdalani, Majdalani Foundation—Center for Moral Development—Argentina. Phone: 5411-4771-3231. E-mail: educacion@fundacionmajdalani.org. **Rebecca A. Robles-Piña,** PhD, professor, Department of Educational Leadership & Counseling, Sam Houston State University, P. O. Box 2119, Huntsville, TX 77341. E-mail: edu_rar@ shsu.edu

CHAPTER 47

Combining Values and Knowledge Education

Jean-Luc Patry
University of Salzburg, Austria

Alfred Weinberger
Private University College of Education of the Diocese of Linz, Austria

Sieglinde Weyringer and Martina Nussbaumer
University of Salzburg, Austria

In school, content learning and values education are usually taught in separate lessons, if the latter is taught at all. Values and moral education in school have often been hampered by the teachers' lack of consensus on topics, goals and methods of value education and insufficient conceptualization and guidelines, the primacy of curricular subjects contrasted by low status of value education, the large amount of curricular subjects, pressure resulting from exams and grading, and several other reasons (Gruber, 2009). On the other hand, values and moral education are legally required from the teachers (although usually only to be seen in the prefaces of the curricula), and politicians, parents, et cetera, increasingly call for values and moral education in school to compensate for the deficits in the society.

The present chapter presents an approach that aims to overcome this problem and to carry out values and moral education without risking the problems mentioned above; in fact the research shows that knowledge education can even be increased by some of these approaches.

Description of the Theory With Goals, Assumptions, and Aspects Particular to the VaKE-Theory

V*a*KE (Values *and* Knowledge Education; Patry, Weyringer, & Weinberger, 2007) is a teaching method that integrates constructivist value education (e.g., Blatt & Kohlberg, 1975) and constructivist knowledge acquisition (e.g., Glasersfeld, 1995) (see Figure 47.1). This approach is based on problem solving using moral dilemma stories and the discussion of related issues as a challenge for the development of moral judgment and for self-organized knowledge acquisition (e.g., searching for information in the internet). The moral dilemma discussion fosters the development of moral judgment in the sense of Kohlberg (1984), and it triggers questions on the content level that the students want to get a response to (for details of this "mechanism," see p. 567 constructivist theories: disequilibrium). Evaluations have shown this approach to be quite effective.

An example of such a dilemma is the following story (Weinberger, 2006, p. 52, shortened):

> Mr. Bauer, an unemployed construction worker, cannot find work. His wife looks after the three children. The youngest, Peter, is 3 years old; he suffers from a life-threatening illness and needs expensive medicines. The allowance is barely sufficient to cover their basic needs, and if Mr. Bauer does not find work soon Peter's life is seriously threatened.
>
> The family learns that close to their place a nuclear plant is to be built. Construction would start within two months, and the company is looking for construction workers. However, before construction begins, the population is to be consulted about its opinion.
>
> What should the family do in this situation? Why?

The Handbook of Educational Theories, pp. 565–579

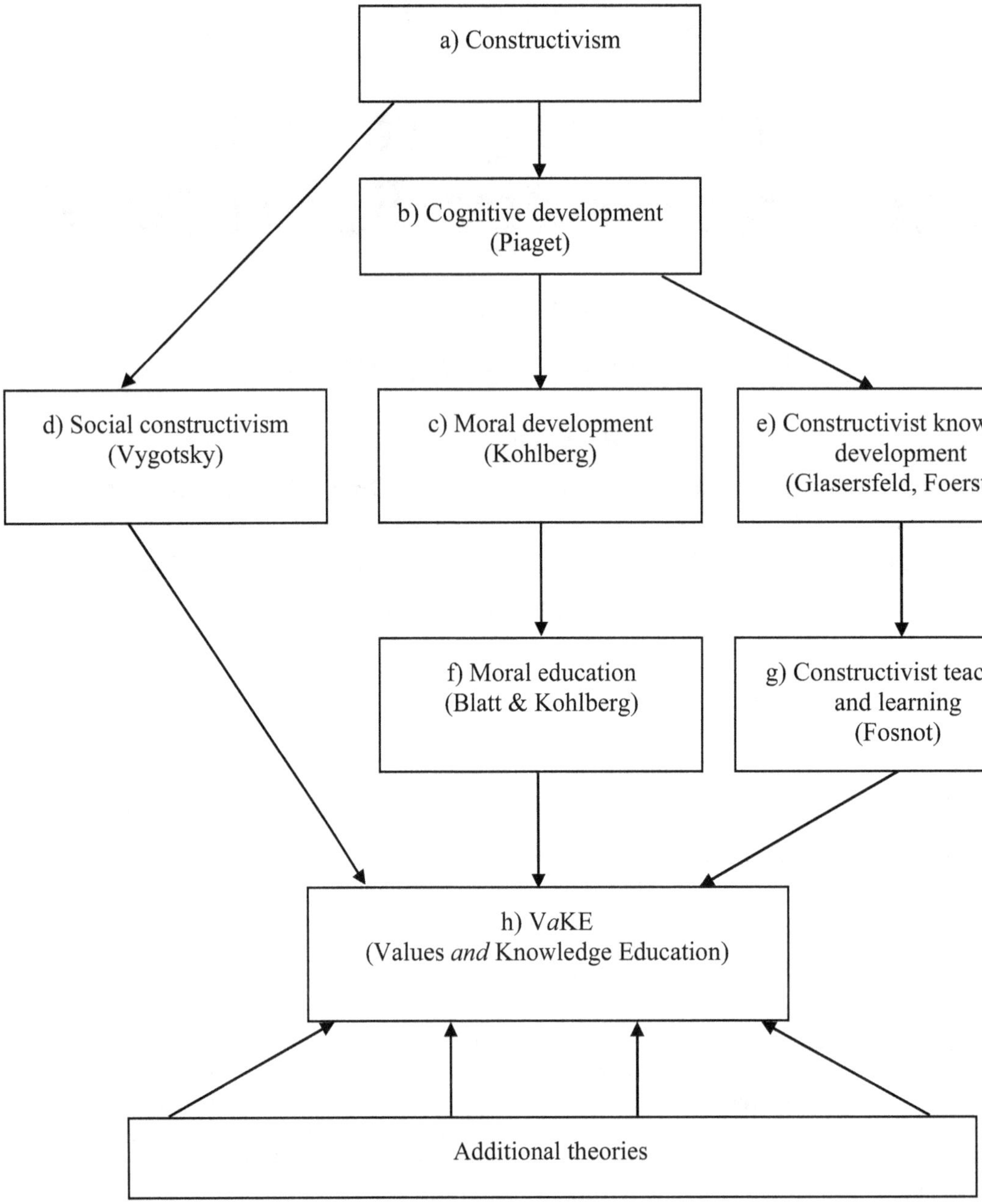

Figure 47.1. Background theories and their interaction for the development of VaKE.

The students, about 13 years old, start to discuss what the family should do but soon discover that they do not know enough about nuclear plants to be able to argue substantially. They spontaneously decide that they must search for the necessary information, and for this they use the internet or other appropriate information sources. In a second dilemma discussion they provide much more sophisticated arguments. After several periods of dilemma discussions and information gathering, the students are quite knowledgeable about nuclear plants and they have improved their argumentation skills; one can assume that their development of moral judgment has been fostered.

*Va*KE consists of at least 11 steps (plus a preparation and clarification step), as depicted in Table 47.1; to satisfy specific purposes (e.g., for research or to foster and encourage particular behavior such as reflection) additional steps can be included. Very briefly, the steps can be described as follows:

Preparation and Clarification: If it is the students' first experience with *Va*KE, they need to be prepared since most of them are not familiar with open teaching and

Table 47.1. Minimal Steps in a VaKE Process; Italics: Values Education; Underlined: Knowledge Acquisition

	Step	Action	
	Preparation and clarification	Students' understanding of values; abilities in the working techniques; rules of interaction	Class
1	*Introduce dilemma*	Understanding dilemma and values at stake	Class
2	*First decision*	Who is in favor, who against?	Group
3	*First arguments (dilemma discussion)*	Why are you in favor, why against? Do we agree with each other? (moral viability check)	Group
4	Exchange experience and missing information	Exchange of arguments; what more do I need to know to be able to argue further?	Class
5	Looking for evidence	Get the information, using any source available!	Group
6	Exchange information	Inform the other students about your constructions; is the information sufficient? (content related viability check)	Class
7	*Second arguments (dilemma discussion)*	Why are you in favor, why against? (moral viability check)	Group
8	*Synthesis of information*	Present your conclusions to the whole class (moral and content related viability check)	Class
9	*Repeat 4 through 8 if necessary*		Group/Class
10	*General synthesis*	Closing the sequence capitalizing on the whole process	Class
11	*Generalization*	Discussion about other but related issues	Group/Class

the freedom it provides. They must be informed about the principles of VaKE (including the 11 steps) and possibly learn to deal appropriately with each other, to argue and to focus on arguments, to search for information on the internet and elsewhere, et cetera.

1. *Introducing the dilemma:* The dilemma is presented in a form adequate for the target group, and the teacher ascertains that the students know what values are at stake.
2. *First decision:* The students have to communicate what they think the protagonist should do. This decision is taken with the students knowing very little and based on their common knowledge; it is the first opportunity to recognize that they should base their decisions more on facts.
3. *First arguments (dilemma discussion):* The students argue in favor and against the different solutions to the dilemma; this corresponds to the dilemma discussion in the Blatt and Kohlberg (1975) tradition.
4. *Exchange of experiences and missing information:* The groups' experiences concerning the results of the argumentation are exchanged, although the dilemma discussion may not be finished yet. More importantly, at this stage of learning, there is the exchange about what kind of knowledge is necessary to be able to discuss the dilemma more deeply. The students set their individual learning goals (e.g., dangers of a nuclear power plant, radioactivity).
5. *Looking for evidence:* The students organize themselves so as to obtain the necessary information and to exchange the evidence they have acquired, while the teacher is a manager and counselor of the whole endeavor; if clearly stated in this phase, the teacher can also serve as source of information and respond to the students' content questions—as an expert among others.
6. *Exchange of information:* After this phase of information acquisition, there is once again a phase of exchange of information in the whole class so that all students have the same level of knowledge.
7. *Second arguments (dilemma discussion):* With this new knowledge in mind, the students turn back to the dilemma discussion itself, as in Step 3.
8. *Synthesis of information:* There then follows a general discussion with the presentation of the results (current state of the negotiations). This can be done in anticipation of the task to be performed in Step 10.
9. *Repeat 4 through 8 if necessary:* If the knowledge base is not yet sufficient, the phases 4 through 8 are reviewed once again, with additional material and internet research and maybe with a new focus (e.g., to satisfy curricular needs); this can be done several times, depending on the time constraints of the course.
10. *General synthesis:* The final synthesis presents the *solved problem* or the current state of the solution (including, if appropriate, new problems) of the group. This can be done in didactically sophisticated ways such as through role plays, writing a newspaper, etc.

11. *Generalization:* The generalization consists of dealing with similar issues to broaden the perspective. Very often, this does not need to be conceived; rather the students do it spontaneously. Sometimes they decide to act in some way (e.g., writing letters to newspapers or politicians, collecting money for a certain cause, etc.).

It is characteristic for this approach are that the students often spontaneously decide what to do, and this is usually in agreement with the step sequence. The teacher's roles vary depending on the steps (Weyringer, Patry, & Weinberger, in press) and include organizing and initiating learning situations, managing learning situations, being an expert in certain phases, particularly when asked for by the students, and last but not least, the teacher may be a learner just like the students, since the students may know more about the subject matter after the course than the teacher had known before. In his or her role as participant, the teacher's argument has the same weight as the students': The teacher's argument will be accepted or declined based on its quality, not because of the person who introduced it. In not enforcing one's argument based on hierarchical grounds, but on discussion activities, the teacher is a role model.

Original Development of and Interactions of the Theory

In our research on *Va*KE, we have a series of specific meta-theoretical concepts. Furthermore, *Va*KE is based on constructivist theories following Piaget (e.g., 1985) and Kohlberg (e.g., 1984), but the approach also has close relationships with or capitalizes on other theories. *Va*KE is an element of the methodological pool of teaching; therefore all theories of learning and instruction as well as classroom management are involved and can be addressed using the *Va*KE theory. Some theories that go beyond traditional didactics will be addressed briefly, but it is not possible to do this for all theories that have been used, due to space restrictions.

Meta-Theoretical Concept

First, it is necessary to mention the meta-theoretical bases underlying both the theory and the research on *Va*KE. It is not possible here to give a full account of these bases; rather we want to present the main features.

Postpositivist Concept

A *postpositivist concept* is embraced (Phillips, 2000; Phillips & Burbules, 2000). In particular, the research follows the principle of what Dewey (1938) has called "warranted assertibility":

> When knowledge is taken as a general abstract term related to inquiry in the abstract, it means "warranted assertibility." The use of a term that designates a potentiality rather than an actuality involves recognition that all special conclusions of special inquiries are parts of an enterprise that is continually renewed, or is a going concern. (Dewey, 1938, p. 9)

A warranty, in this context, is a support of a statement or its credibility. Every statement that is claimed to be scientific, needs to be backed up in a reasoned way. The more arguments that are provided which are in favor of a statement and the more substantial they are, the more credible the statement is (see also Phillips & Burbules, 2000, p. 3).

Critical Multiplism

This provision is best done following the principles of critical multiplism (Cook, 1985; Patry, 1989; Shadish, Cook & Campbell, 2002). Hetherington (1997) distinguished two dimensions of research (Table 47.2): Thoughtless versus thoughtful research and single vs. multiple methods. Critical multiplism refers to thoughtful multiplism, which means systematic, rational multiplism, well aware of the problems and biases, and theory driven. The attempt is to compensate the biases which a given theory or method has or may have, by using a different theory or method that has different biases. This means the use of multiple theories, including presumably incompatible ones, (e.g.,

Table 47.2. Types of Research

	Thoughtless	Thoughtful
Single Method	Mindless Monism • Poor science • Rear-end validity	Rigid Monism • Newtonian Science • MAX-MIN-CON
Multiple Methods	Mindless Multiplism • Poor science • Anything goes	Critical Multiplism

Source: Hetherington (1997).

cognitive theories as well as ones with behaviorist backgrounds such as the social learning theories; see next section) and systemic instead of linear relationships.

Constructivist Theories

The *Va*KE approach is based on constructivism and in particular on Piaget (intelligence) and Kohlberg (moral) for its developmental concepts, on Vygotsky for its social interaction and zone of proximal development approach, on Glasersfeld and Fosnot (content) and on Blatt and Kohlberg (moral) for its educational concepts; Particularly, this theory combines the latter two (see Figure 47.1):

a. Constructivism means that the students construct their knowledge. In other words, they invent knowledge (Foerster, 1997), in contrast to a knowledge transmission concept where knowledge is more or less directly transferred from the teacher to the student.
b. According to Piaget (1985) this construction process follows the principles of assimilation if the proposed information fits well into the preexisting cognitive structure. Otherwise, that is, if this information does not prove to be viable but is still regarded as important, there is disequilibrium between the proposed content and the cognitive structure. In this case the person aims at reducing the disequilibrium by changing ("accommodating") the relevant cognitive structure.
c. Kohlberg (1984) has adapted these principles into moral judgments and their development. When confronted with a dilemma, the students argue in favor or against a certain option; however, it is possible that the problem cannot be solved to the individual's satisfaction (the argument is not viable) and disequilibrium in the individual's moral cognitive structure ensues. To accommodate this, the individual has to invent new argumentation principles which are more viable. Kohlberg (1971) has proposed a series of five or six stages of moral argumentation, which individuals successively reach.
d. Disequilibrium is very often provoked in social encounters, particularly through interactions with peers, and the creation of new concepts is accomplished as a common group endeavor. This corresponds to Vygotsky's (1978) social constructivism.
e. Glasersfeld (e.g., 1995) and other researchers have applied this principle to knowledge construction through disequilibrium and accommodation as a didactical tool, for instance in mathematics (e.g., Lampert, 1992) with students commonly inventing mathematical concepts.
f. Similarly, Blatt and Kohlberg (1975; see also Lind, 2003) have developed a dilemma discussion procedure that fosters the development of moral judgment.
g. Constructivist theory of learning have been developed and applied in many different teaching-learning settings; evidence exists regarding positive effects on knowledge acquisition (Fosnot, 1996).
h. *Va*KE combines the two procedures of moral education and knowledge acquisition and additionally integrates the education of social behavior.

These constructivist theories have been forming the base of the *Va*KE approach since the beginning of its conceptualization. Its implementation into school lessons, as well as into other educational programs and the evaluation of this practical experience have shown evidence of additional theories.

Additional Theories

These relevant theories can be classified as nonconstructivistic, and they focus not only on issues related to learning and teaching, but additionally on technological, cultural, psychological and developmental aspects. These issues are: learning in groups (e.g., Johnson & Johnson, 1991); critical thinking (e.g., Paul, 1993); individualized and web-based learning (e.g., Hron & Friedrich, 2003); the interaction between formal, nonformal and informal learning (e.g., Belle, 1982); subjective theories (e.g., Groeben, Wahl, Schlee, & Scheele, 1988); personal development and identity (e.g., Blasi & Glodis, 1995; Erikson, 1968; Gurucharri & Selman, 1982; Kegan, 1982; Redmore & Loevinger, 1979); discourse ethics (e.g., Habermas, 1990); culture (e.g., Parsons, 1970); wisdom (e.g., Sternberg, 2003). We have not yet finished investigating the relevance of each of the above theories for the *Va*KE approach; nevertheless results of several studies on other theories can already be presented. These studies are on care, on discursive learning and on problem solving.

Theory of Care

While Kohlberg's theory of the development of moral judgment is oriented on justice as guiding principle, Gilligan (1982) proposed that care might be another (in her view, particularly female) main criterion for morality. The focus, then, is not that all people have to be treated equally, but that each person deserves to be cared for in cases of need. We have responsibility for the well-being of those individuals of whom we are in charge of or are in contact with.

However, Lyons (1983) and Walker (1984), among many others, have shown that there is not a one to one relationship between moral perspective and gender. Furthermore, Döbert and Nunner-Winkler (1986) have also demonstrated that gender is less important than concern. If the individual feels emotionally concerned by the dilemma or by the fortune of the protagonist, it is more likely that he or she will tend to judge with a focus on care, whereas in case of emotional distance, a justice judgment will be more likely.

The findings above are consistent with our own research related to *Va*KE. For example, Patry and Schaber (2010) assessed whether participants felt concern with the protagonist of a given dilemma (an abortion dilemma) and whether they judged their argumentation being more focused on justice or on care. Care and justice judgments did not correlate. The subjects' gender played no role at all. Concernment had no or slightly negative correlations with justice ($.03 > r > -.31$) and high positive correlations with care ($.32 < r < .70$). This shows that in *Va*KE the participants use arguments of both types (justice and care) and that their priority depends on their level of concern.

It must be mentioned here, that the classical Kohlbergian dilemmas, like the famous Heinz dilemma, are constructed in such a way that concernment is avoided. It remains to be seen whether concernment has an impact on the interest and hence on the motivation to construct new knowledge. In our dilemma construction we have tended to personalize the situation as much as possible, with much semblance between the protagonist and the students, thus trying to increase concernment; it might well be that this is one of the key features for the success of knowledge construction which is part of the *Va*KE process.

The Theory of Discursive Learning

In *Va*KE, the aim of the argumentations is to find arguments in favor of or against one of the options of the dilemma's protagonist. The individual's learning process deepens with each additional argument whose viability is acknowledged. For this reason it seems to be appropriate to analyze the structure of such debates. Beyond content and moral judgment, most individuals also learn the use of argumentation and reasoning by arguing with other individuals. In both domains (moral and content) the acquired disposition depends not only on the person's individual ability to argue but also on that of the whole social group. Miller (2006) provides the framework for analyzing the structure of group argumentation in a *Va*KE process.

In Miller's terminology, an *argument* is a series of statements that relate to each other. Such an argument can be described with a structure tree (Miller, 2006, p. 15; see Figure 47.2 for an example) that describes the statements (P1 through P10) and the transitions from one statement to another (arrows). Some of these statements are accepted directly (P4, P5, P8, P9, and P10) while the other statements are deduced from these using temporary regulations and inference rules: P6 follows from P8 and P2 follows from P4, P5 and P6, et cetera. The last statement, (the conclusion, P1), is the answer to a question (or partial question). The *logic of an argument* refers to the principles used in the transitions from one statement to another.

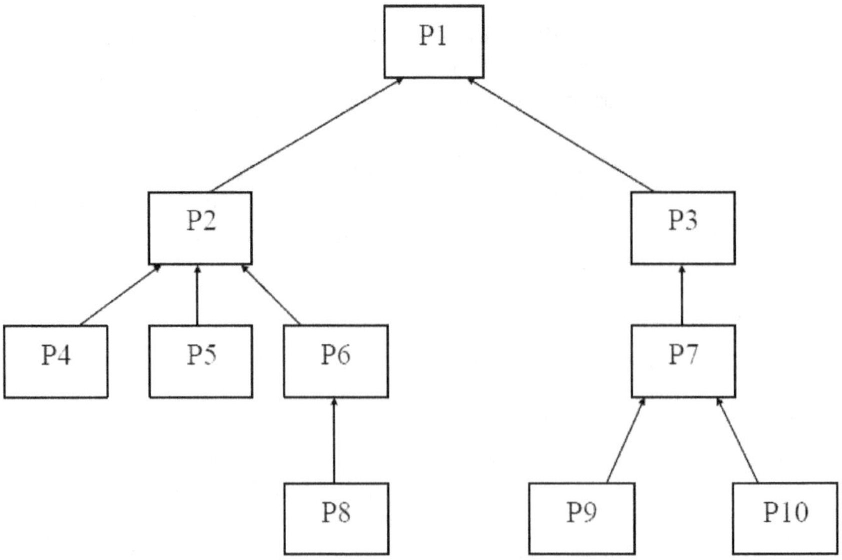

Note: Compare Miller (2006).

Figure 47.2. Example of a structure tree.

An *argumentation* consists of a sequence of statements produced by various individuals in a collective argument; the chronology of the statements is indicated by the following digits: P1 was the first statement, P2 the second, etc. Based on the statements and the relation expressed by the participant (e.g., P2 is used to support P1), it is possible to develop a collective argument to answer the question of the argumentation. According to Miller (2006) an argumentation is considered successful if the participants manage to elaborate a collective argument whose aim is the answer to a question (or partial question).

Miller's approach has been used successfully to describe *Va*KE argumentations (Kircher, 2008; Nussbaumer, 2007, 2009). To represent the discussion in a *Va*KE argumentation it is important to address both arguments in favor and against a certain decision. Therefore two structure tees; one with a positive conclusion P1 ("The protagonist should do X.") and one with a negative conclusion ("The protagonist should not do X.") are used.

The statements can also be classified; for instance, one can distinguish whether a statement belongs to the morality domain (normative statements) or to the subject matter domain (descriptive statements). Hence, structure trees can be a useful tool, for instance, to analyze whether the participants commit the naturalistic fallacy, i.e., whether the students agree that a normative statement follows from a descriptive one—it turned out that such a logic is rare but in a few cases is accepted (Nussbaumer, 2009; Patry, Weyringer & Weinberger, 2010b).

Theory of Problem Solving and Problem-Based learning

Essential characteristics of problem-based learning (e.g., Barrows & Tamblyn, 1980) are consistent with *Va*KE principles: Students must have the responsibility for their own learning. In *Va*KE, the teacher's primary responsibility is to create an appropriate learning atmosphere, e.g., preparing the problem, providing information resources (Weyringer et al., in press). The students are responsible for setting their learning goals, to select the resources for their information research and to check their learning achievement. The teacher prepares a content-related moral dilemma, facilitates the students' constructive work (e.g., by asking challenging questions), offers different sources of information, and gives the students the opportunity to check if their moral argument and their constructed knowledge are viable.

The problem situation (in *Va*KE: the dilemma) is illstructured. It stimulates the learner to generate multiple hypotheses about possible approaches and solutions. A typical content related moral dilemma is illstructured because the protagonist's options can be supported with several arguments and diverse facts from different fields which can support different moral arguments.

Learning in *Va*KE is *interdisciplinary* (Patry, Weinberger, & Weyringer, 2010a). During self-directed learning, students should integrate information from all the disciplines that are relevant in order to solve the problem. Usually content-related moral dilemmas are relevant to different school subjects. For example, the dilemma "Family Bauer's decision" has relevance to biology (e.g., diseases caused through radioactivity), physics (e.g., nuclear power plant, radioactivity), and geography (power generation in different countries).

Collaboration: The students work together helping each other to gain an understanding of what they are learning and its application to the problem. Student collaboration occurs during the group's dilemma discussion (Steps 3 and 7), the acquisition and processing of information (Step 5), and the presentation of the group's solution to the problem (Step 10).

Application of the acquired knowledge to the problem: The students apply their new knowledge by using it to support their moral argument in the dilemma discussion (step 8).

Closing analysis: The students reflect on what has been learned. This usually happens during Step 11 in *Va*KE, when the students discuss similar issues to broaden the perspective.

Self and peer assessment: The students learn to assess their individual learning process and that of their peers. In Step 6, for example, the students present and discuss their findings; they compare their acquired knowledge with each other and give accurate feedback to their colleagues.

Realistic problems: The problems must be as realistic as possible. The stories of *Va*KE-dilemmas often deal with current controversial issues (e.g., the building of a nuclear power plant close to the student's home).

Validation of the Theory

Many studies additional to those described above were performed to test the validity of the *Va*KE approach and its basic constructivist theories. Before addressing the results of these studies we need to describe the methods and the instruments used, some of which have been newly developed.

Methods and Instruments Used

For validation we used specific and newly developed assessment tools, as well as traditional instruments such as questionnaires etc.

The Lesson Interruption Method. To study the educational processes, we have used the lesson interruption method (Patry, 1997): The teacher interrupts the lesson at a predetermined moment (e.g., before a new step according to Table 47.1 has been started), and the students answer a short questionnaire, (typically we have used about 12 questions), about their observations during the last phase, (e.g., the last step). Those who are most concerned by the lesson—the students—report their observation of what, in their view, has actually been going on in the given situation, (the last step). Once the students are accustomed with this method, they will respond very quickly; the experience shows that this observation does not disturb the course of the lesson. The studies using this method (e.g., Patry, 1979, Patry & Schaber, 2010) have shown that the students answer quite homogenously (high interobserver agreement). Typically, the internal consistencies (Cronbach's α) are higher than .80, which is very high, compared to traditional assessments of social behavior with questionnaires; this is due to the fact that specific situations are being observed while normally in questionnaires the responders have to aggregate their experiences in many situations.

WALK. The *WALK* ("W" assessment of latent knowledge) is a summative assessment of knowledge based on a constructivist theoretical framework. It consists of several pictures dealing with the content of the *Va*KE lesson (Patry, 2001; Patry & Weinberger, 2004). "W" refers to the five "W" questions (who, what, where, when, why), that guide the students during the first WALK phase, where they write down as many key words as possible to each picture. In the second phase they frame the key words as questions and in the last phase they try to answer these questions. The achievement score is determined by the number of responses in each phase, after a content analysis based on a differentiated coding handbook. Experiences showed that the students can perform the WALK very well after they have become acquainted with the instrument. They do not show any test anxiety in contrast to traditional knowledge tests. Interrater-reliability proved to be very high (Cohen's Kappa = .936, $p < .01$) and internal consistency between the pictures was satisfactory (Cronbach's $\alpha > .70$, Patry, Zlöbl & Felber, 2009). Studies revealed high correlations ($r > .6$, $p < .01$) between the WALK and traditional tests examining applicable knowledge; this indicates high concurrent validity (Weinberger, 2010). The advantage of this kind of instrument is that it is open to the ideas and interests of the students and no questions or content are imparted by the teacher. Since in *Va*KE, the content to be constructed is not determined by the teacher in advance, he or she cannot anticipate what to ask in a knowledge test of the traditional questionnaire type. In the WALK, the students can respond on any knowledge level and be as specific as they can and want to be in the domain of their specialization. For instance after a *Va*KE unit on nuclear plants, the students may have concentrated on the consequences of radioactivity; the responses to pictures that refer to radioactivity will be much more detailed compared to students who have focused on other issues, such as the problem of nuclear waste, which is addressed in another picture.

Sociograms. In several studies we examined the classroom atmosphere using a sociometric questionnaire. This instrument provides information about the level of sympathy (positive social relationship) and antipathy (negative social relationship) among the students (cf. Coie, Dodge, & Coppotelli, 1982). Each student provides a sympathy/antipathy rating for each of his or her classmates accordingly. The retest reliabilities of the positive social relationship ranged from $r = .61$ to $r = .89$ and for the negative social relationship from $r = .64$ to $r = .98$ (Weinberger, 2006).

Crossover designs. Many studies with *Va*KE use a quasi-experimental crossover design (Campbell & Stanley, 1963). Two classes get both treatments (*Va*KE and traditional teaching) in sequence. Therefore each class serves as its own control group. In the first phase, class A is the experimental group and taught with *Va*KE while class B is the control group, which is taught traditionally. In the second phase class A is taught traditionally (control group) while class B serves as the experimental group. In both phases the content is different.

Knowledge. When schools consider implementation of a new method, the teachers' and parents' most important concern is that the students do not learn less curricular content than with the traditional method. The thinking is that moral judgment development should be secondary to knowledge construction. This is due to society's main focus on knowledge that has to be respected in implementation attempts. Therefore, we have put much effort into studying the students' knowledge construction. In general, we have found that in this regard, *Va*KE is even better than anticipated; among others, we have seen repeatedly again that after *Va*KE units, the students have more knowledge about the topic than the teacher had before the units (Patry & Weinberger, 2010).

The first studies were conducted in the regular classroom. The participants were mainly Secondary I, but also primary and Secondary II. *Va*KE was compared with traditional teaching and results indicated that the students constructed at least as much knowledge as the control groups (crossover design). For instance, Weinberger (Patry & Weinberger, 2004) studied *Va*KE for students, aged 13, compared with moderate constructivist teaching by the same teacher. The topics were nuclear power plants (the dilemma of the Bauer family presented in section 1), in Phase 1 and Jewish life and religion (hiding Anne Frank's family during World War II). The instruments were teacher-made tests with 30 items of different levels according to Bloom's taxonomy (Bloom, Englehart, Furst, Hill, & Krathwohl, 1956) used in the pre- and posttests and WALK (posttest only). The results of the teacher-made tests showed main effects for "time" and no interaction with teaching type. This means that the students acquired knowledge with both teaching methods, and they did not learn less with *Va*KE teaching than with normal teaching. The WALK results indicated that the students constructed more applicable knowledge with *Va*KE than with normal teaching, at least in some cases and in any case not less (Weinberger, 2006).

In the second study *Va*KE was used in a 3-day summer course for gifted students. In this extracurricular enrichment course Weinberger, Kriegseisen, Loch, and Wingelmüller (2005) used Büchner's drama "Woyzeck," the dilemma being whether Woyzeck should be pronounced guilty of murdering his girlfriend Marie. The *Va*KE process was analyzed in detail based on a content analysis of video recordings (230 minutes of discussion). The arguments were analyzed with respect to the depth of knowledge construction: superficial, reflected, and differentiating and reflective. It turned out that the longer the process lasted, the more the superficial arguments decreased and the reflected arguments increased. Furthermore, after the units the students knew much more about the content (e.g., the impact of a pea diet on mental health due to a lack of iodine) than the four workshop leaders would ever have imagined. Similar experiences—though not documented in detail—were made in many more studies in summer camps (yearly since 2004, see http://platon.echa-oesterreich.at/english/index.html). In self-reports the students agreed that they had acquired substantial knowledge (discussed in detail in Weyringer, 2008).

In a seminar at a children's university with a dilemma about recycling in opposition to friendship, Patry and Weyringer (2005) observed that the children (aged 9 and 10) participated in the discussion in a lively manner, and some of them had a pause of reflection before making their statements. It was obvious that the children had acquired new knowledge. Using methods of content analyses and comparing the numbers of arguments before and after the search, show that after the web-based research, most of them strengthened their position by using very specific information and details of facts they had found during their self-directed exploration of the problem and not by pointing out the value of friendship. After the course, some of them reported that they had realized that using facts in an argumentation can convince a friend, without harming the friendship.

Moral Judgment Competence. For the validation of *Va*KE we have concentrated not on moral judgment competence but on knowledge construction as discussed above; we have two reasons for this in addition to the lower practical importance mentioned there:

It has already been repeatedly shown, (with many replications), that dilemma discussions foster moral judgment development (Blatt & Kohlberg, 1975; Lind, 2003). These results can be generalized to *Va*KE discussions, since one of their core elements does not differ significantly from the dilemma discussions in the Kohlberg tradition.

The influence on moral development is not an instant effect; rather, it takes several months of repeated dilemma discussions until significant changes in moral stages can be seen. Furthermore, the instruments for measuring moral stages, particularly the moral judgment interviews, are very time consuming for the participants and we have preferred to invest the available time—which was very restricted—in more important studies, than to provide yet another replication of the studies mentioned above.

Generalizability of the Theory Across Cultures, Ethnicities, and Genders

Besides in Austria, the approach was used in several European countries (Spain, Norway and Germany), and its success was confirmed. Furthermore, it was used in international summer camps with students from different countries speaking different languages, and the impact of the native language was studied (Patry, Weyringer, & Weinberger, 2010c).

One study (Ali, 2006) was conducted outside of Europe, in Egypt. Ali found that both the teachers and the students had very little experience with open teaching such as *Va*KE. However, they soon adapted to the requirements and *Va*KE could be practiced successfully. It is then a question of preparation (see Table 47.1), the introduction and clarification of the method and the procedure; the students need to be prepared for *Va*KE. Finally, gender differences were studied with respect to the focus on justice and care, but no difference was found (Patry & Schaber, 2010). Hence we assume that there are no differences with regard to culture, ethnicity, and gender.

We have used *Va*KE in many age groups. There have been some attempts even to use *Va*KE in Kindergarten with adapted procedures (Hörtenhuber, 2008; Lebersorger & Linortner, 2008; Linortner, 2008). It turned out that the children understand the dilemma; the decision (Step 2; taking one's own stance) was difficult because the children are not used to deciding independently without the opinion of other people. The justification, however, was easier for them; they could articulate clearly the reasons for their decision. Searching for information and exchanging information were again difficult. Although the children were quite motivated, they did not really understand the meaning of these activities. Further activities (Steps 7 and beyond) could not be performed because the children could no longer concentrate; only the final product (Step 10, general synthesis), realized through a role-play, turned out to be quite practicable. Whether it achieved its goal could not be tested, however. It was recommended that the information should be provided through stories, which were read to the children, or through picture books or films. These procedures can still be described as constructivist, because from this material each child picks out what is important to him or her. However, further research is required at Kindergarten level.

From primary school onwards, *Va*KE can be used according to Table 47.1. The dilemmas must be adapted to the age group; for instance, for younger children, social relationships (friendship) can be a value to which they are very sensitive. If the dilemmas are personalized the children can deal with them very well and argue quite appropriately even if they are on Stage 2 of moral judgment, according to Kohlberg's theory. However, the more generalized statements, such as principles, were observed to be only made by children from the secondary level up. The search for information, on the other hand, was not a problem, although the primary school children sometimes had some difficulties to extract the information they needed from the available sources and in some cases they lacked the necessary computer skills. In general, though, the students were more skilled in handling the computers and the internet than the teachers; they were quite familiar with the search engine, although it was certainly pertinent to tell them that there are other search services apart from Google. It is appropriate thus, to provide the students with lists of available tools.

Use and Application of the Theory

As previously described, the theory has been implemented in schools, in teacher trainings, and in summer camps. Several adaptations of the concept have been performed and tested, and these developments are continuing.

Secondary School. Implementation of *Va*KE in a secondary school was adapted to fit the requirements of very heterogeneous achievement groups. In this case *Va*KE was used with additional viability checks (repeating Steps 5 and 6 several times), school implementation of a specific curriculum for the *Va*KE-classes with regular *Va*KE-projects, weekly dilemma discussions, and constructivist teaching in each subject.

University Colleges. Implementation of *Va*KE in university colleges for teacher training; *Va*KE-units are taught in particular lessons (e.g., didactics, moral education) or students can choose a whole course.

Teacher Training. At teacher training institutions all over Austria, already qualified teachers have the possibility to learn *Va*KE; usually courses last one day; teachers reflect on the theory after they themselves have participated in a *Va*KE-unit; in some institutions teachers get counseling during the implementation of *Va*KE in class.

Red Cross Youth. The Red Cross Youth offers material with dilemma stories promoting the core values of this organization including an algorithm how to work on the particular topic with *Va*KE (Weyringer, Patry, & Weinberger, 2005). Additionally, in a training program, teachers can learn the method.

Platon Youth Forum. Platon Youth Forum is an international summer camp for highly gifted adolescents (age 15 to 20 years) from all European countries. The intention is to nurture European citizenship by discussing current problems of the European Union from the perspective of different points of view. All courses and seminars use *Va*KE to realize this educational objective.

Critiques of the Theory

There are several sources for critique. We distinguish critiques with respect to the ethics of applying the theory, to the theoretical foundations and to the use and application of the theory.

Ethical Critics

Some critiques have mentioned that moral education is not viewed as one of the major goals of education. An anonymous reviewer mentioned, for instance, that in many countries the curricula are more narrowly constructed and focus on memorizations of decontextualized factual information. Our answers are as follows.

First, there is no doubt that in many curricula, the focus is on knowledge, mostly at a low level in Bloom's taxonomy. However, prefaces of national curricula explicitly address values as goals of education, for example, humanity, solidarity, tolerance, justice and respect for nature, which are named as main goals of school education in Austria (see Lehrpläne für die Schulen Österreichs, n.d.).

Teachers aim at both goals—the transmission of knowledge and the education of an ethical behavior in the way they interpret the given values in the curricula. Hence teachers report excessive demands on themselves in integrating values education into their regular teaching (Patry & Hofmann, 1998), because they do not know how to do it.

Second, even if moral education is deemed important by the curricula as well as by the teachers, we believe that moral education is justified because of additional reasons. Many of them are addressed in this volume and need not to be described here in detail. For the additional reasons a few indications might be useful. There is a broad agreement that humanity is threatened by many challenges like food availability (insufficient food supplies in some countries while there is food waste in other countries). Most of these challenges are moral in nature. In the case of food availability, for instance, the people in industrialized countries could improve the situation in the needy countries if they wanted to; the main arguments to do so, however, are ethical. This is an example for the desperate need for moral competence in our societies (see Patry et al., 2011). We think that it is the duty of schools to provide a moral education.

Third, it has been argued that it is up to the parents to provide moral education and schools and teachers must not take a stance in ethical issues. We definitely agree that moral education should be conducted by families; nevertheless schools cannot abstain from moral education because school matters are values laden, whether the teachers and other educators acknowledge it or not (Patry, 2002). It is much better that teachers are aware of this and include it in the education they practice, instead of presuming values to be unimportant, because in that case values enter school education through the backdoor. Another example is the hidden curriculum (Snyder, 1971), which necessarily is value laden. Again we prefer that the teachers address the respective issues instead of enforcing it without being aware of it.

Fourth, it has been argued that school must not interfere with parents' values systems (see Gruber, 2009). In the Kohlbergian tradition, one can answer that the focus is not on the values per se; instead it is on the people's arguments and their underlying structure. The interference, then, is with respect to the justification of values and not with respect to the values themselves. Our experience is that the children transport the values from discussions with their families and that this might have an impact on whether values should be the sole responsibility of the family. This indeed is interference. We think that this is justified; the impact is not on the values themselves but on the rationale behind them, and more rational arguments are seen as an improvement.

Theoretical Critics

The following critiques have been already addressed; in this section they will be summarized. It has been criticized that the integration of norms and facts is weak, if existing at all. It is important to recognize that there is no relationship between these two components per se. However, as expressed in the previous section, teachers cannot teach content without addressing values issues, whether implicitly or, preferably, explicitly. Hence, a relationship must be established in practice. This is done through argumentation, and it is the students who address these questions. However, the students are aware to some degree that the conclusions from facts to further goals and development can become problematic. The background of this problem is the question whether facts can develop the power to set norms for further development, and—if the answer is yes, to which extent? In our view it would be necessary to sensitize the students even more on this issue. Furthermore, since the dilemmas explicitly address contents that relate to the curriculum, the values of these contents and particularly their justification become a central focus of the argumentation.

In the same vein critics asked the question about the relationship between the focus on procedures (justification) in the values domain as opposed to the propositional knowledge that is constructed. In our view, both procedural as well as propositional issues are relevant in both domains. The propositional perspective in the values domain is present insofar as values, in order to be discussed, must be made explicit. For this, specific tools have been developed. One of them is the structure tree analysis after Miller (2006), others are Schulz von Thun's Values Square (Schulz von Thun, 1990) and the Potter Box (Potter, 1965) that make the values explicit. The procedural perspective in the knowledge domain is addressed through the knowledge construction procedure. The students learn how to gather information, and in particular, they become very critical toward the information that is offered, such as, on the internet because they become aware that the facts that are reported there may be contradictory. We assume, hence, that the students change from an objectivist position about science (knowledge is given and true and unchangeable)—if they defended this position at all—to a postmodern position (knowledge viability depends on the use one wants to make of it; science develops); this hypothesis has not yet been tested.

The approach has been criticized for not being new. This is certainly correct: *Va*KE is to be seen within a tradition, as described above, particularly in the one initiated by Kohlberg and followed up by Blatt and Kohlberg. Many studies have been conducted that deal with one or the other issues related with processes like those in *Va*KE. We certainly do not claim to have developed a wholly new concept; rather we hope that we have gone a small step further than previous approaches by implementing *Va*KE in schools and by addressing a series of other issues similar to the ones discussed in the section about interactions of the theory.

*Va*KE faces the same opposition as all constructivist theories do; we cannot address all issues that are relevant in this regard. Let us just take one of the most influential ones. For example, Kirschner, Sweller, and Clark (2006) argue that guided instruction is superior to unguided methods of instruction, for which constructivist teaching may be seen as a prototype. Weinberger (2006) has proposed the use of viability checks to control the lack of structure the students are faced with in *Va*KE. He could show that at least in some regards, less able students improve compared to only a few viability checks, while for the able students it does not make a difference (it is to be assumed that the students with high ability do viability checks whether suggested by the teacher or not). This hypothesis needs to be further investigated.

One critique has been that affect is not sufficiently taken into account. We argue here that concernment as addressed in the study by Patry and Schaber (2010) is closely related with affect. Frewein (2009) has shown that *Va*KE yields higher values in achieving the affective teaching goals according to Boekarts, Koenig, and Vedder (2006) such as pleasure in learning, avoiding stress, wellbeing, et cetera. But again, we agree that this issue requires further studies.

Overall we can say that several of the critiques are not valid from the onset, while for others we propose at least some hypotheses that can be tested, so the answer is still open.

From our point of view it must be underlined that even if *Va*KE is viable one cannot assume that the theory is correct. But from our point of view *Va*KE is primarily a practical concept that is based on scientific theories and is not a scientific theory for itself.

Further, the concept is too complex to be tested as a whole; rather it is necessary to test it element by element within a research program. This is what we aim to do.

Practical Critics

From the practical point of view *Va*KE has been criticized in several regards. Practitioners have criticized that *Va*KE is not a rule that can strictly be applied. In our view this is not a problem, but rather an asset of the method. However, the different steps (Table 47.1) clearly require different actions from the teacher; some are fairly clearly determined whereas others are quite open (Weyringer et al., in press), but in any case there is a lot of freedom. The freedom, however, is also given to the students, and it is up to the teacher to react to the situations created by the students. This requires flexibility. To be able to react appropriately, though, it is necessary that the teachers know not only the steps but are fully aware of the underlying theoretical rational. This means that the teacher keeps the responsibility for what is happening but has a strong framework in the background that helps him or her know how to intervene in a given situation.

This freedom and the uncertainties of what is going to happen in the course of *Va*KE units is in clear contrast to the teachers' roles in traditional teaching. The teachers may experience a loss of control, which is something many of them have difficulties in handling.

These two issues need to be addressed in teacher training. Therefore, we are in the process of developing a teacher training program. This is more necessary for experienced teachers because both approaches are new to them and it is quite likely that they will fall back into their earlier habits linked with traditional teaching.

When first confronted with *Va*KE, the students—who typically have mainly experienced direct teaching—do not really know what to do. But they soon become accustomed to the freedom that they are provided with and work with much enthusiasm. We have very rarely had the experience that students misused the freedom, and if so, there were clear reasons for that (particularly personal needs that override the motives to practice *Va*KE). It is suggested though, that students should be prepared for open teaching.

Teachers have claimed that although *Va*KE is interesting, it is difficult to fit it into the curriculum and it might be too time consuming. To this we can answer that (a) the curriculum often allows much more freedom than teachers tend to recognize, (b) the dilemmas can be adapted to the specific curricular needs and the teachers can regulate the direction of the debate through subtle (yet transparent!) indications, and (c) the time structure of *Va*KE can also be managed by the teacher—and often the students use their leisure time to continue the discussions.

Discussion

*Va*KE is an attempt to capitalize on scientific theories (Piaget, Kohlberg) for implementing a teaching approach that combines values education and content construction. This endeavor is justified by the need that we perceive that schools must not only address content issues but also moral education; this is required because humanity desperately needs more morality in decision making and actions because the lack of ethics in daily and professional life has led societies all over the world into huge difficulties. It is assumed that moral education in the tradition of Kohlberg will provide a small but maybe significant improvement in practiced ethics. But such an endeavor will only be successful if content learning is not jeopardized, since in our societies this kind of learning is seen as much more important than moral development. *Va*KE, we hope, can provide moral education without neglecting knowledge construction. Quite the opposite in fact: Learning of content is improved, and particularly the acquired knowledge is more sustainable in both senses of the term: It lasts longer, and it is more applicable but the application, we assume, is guided by responsibility—this is where the values domain connects with the content domain.

VaKE relates also with many other theories, some of which could be described here. We were surprised to see how these other theories can be integrated in the theoretic framework. It turned out then, that applying *VaKE* is not only beneficial with respect to morality and content knowledge but also in other fields like social competence and critical thinking, to mention only two of them.

Hence *VaKE* and the connecting theories has become an extremely complex framework. It is not possible to account for all its facets in the present paper. And there are still more issues that need to be addressed.

Further research is required in all these regards. However, in any case *VaKE* has been shown to be successful to achieve its two main aims, moral and content education. We do not claim, however, that *VaKE* should fully replace traditional teaching. Instead we suggest that *VaKE* would be an interesting supplement to traditional teaching, with a healthy mix of different approaches.

We also do not claim that *VaKE* is the only approach that fulfills the aims discussed above. There are certainly other possibilities, and maybe these are more successful. On the other hand we also do not claim that *VaKE* itself cannot be improved—here again, further research is necessary.

ACKNOWLEDGMENT

This chapter is financially supported by the FWF (Fonds zur Förderung der wissenschaftlichen Forschung, Austria).

REFERENCES

Ali, S. N. A. (2006). *The values and knowledge education (VaKE) approach and its impacts on teaching and moral judgment competences of pre-service primary school science teachers* (Unpublished doctoral dissertation). Gesellschafts- und Kulturwissenschaftliche Fakultät der Universität Salzburg, Austria.

Barrows, H. S., & Tamblyn, R. M. (1980). *Problem-based learning: An approach to medical education*. New York, NY: Springer.

Belle, T. J. (1982). Formal, non-formal and informal education: A holistic perspective on lifelong learning. *International review of education, 8,* 159-175.

Blasi, A. & Glodis, K. (1995). The development of identity. A critical analysis from the perspective of the self as subject. *Developmental Review, 15,* 404-433.

Blatt, M. & Kohlberg, L. (1975). The effects of classroom moral discussion upon children's moral judgement. *Journal of Moral Education, 4,* 129-162.

Bloom, B. S., Englehart, M. B., Furst, E. J., Hill, W. H. & Krathwohl, D. R. (1956). *Taxonomy of educational objectives. The classification of educational goals: Handbook I. Cognitive domain.* New York, NY: Longmans Green.

Boekarts, M., Koening, E., & Vedder, P. (2006). Goal-directed behavior and contextual factors in the classroom: An innovative approach to the study of multiple goals. *Educational Psychologist, 41,* 31-52.

Campbell, D. T., & Stanley, J. C. (1963). Experimental and quasi-experimental designs for research on teaching. In N. L. Gage (Ed.), *Handbook of research on teaching* (pp. 171-246). Chicago, IL: Rand McNally.

Coie, J. D., Dodge, K. A., & Coppotelli, H. (1982). Dimensions and types of social status: A cross-age perspective. *Developmental Psychology, 18,* 557-570.

Cook, T. D. (1985). Postpositivist critical multiplism. In R. L. Shortland & M. M. Mark (Eds.), *Social science and social policy* (pp. 458-499). Beverly Hills: CA: SAGE.

Dewey, J. (1938). *Logic: The theory of inquiry.* New York, NY: Holt, Rinehart & Winston.

Döbert, R., & Nunner-Winkler, G. (1986). Wertewandel und Moral. In H. Bertram (Ed.), *Gesellschaftlicher Zwang und moralische Autonomie* (pp. 289-321). Frankfurt am Main, Germany: Suhrkamp.

Erikson, E. H. (1968). *Identity, youth and crisis.* New York, NY: Norton.

Foerster, H. V. (1997). Entdecken oder Erfinden. Wie läßt sich das Verstehen verstehen? In C. Friedrich von Siemens Stiftung (Ed.), *Einführung in den Konstruktivismus, 3. Aufl* (pp. 41-88). München, Germany: Oldenbourg.

Fosnot, C. T. (Ed.) (1996). *Constructivism: Theory, perspectives, and practice.* New York, NY: Teachers College Press.

Frewein, K. (2009). *VaKE – Die Verbindung affektiver und kognitiver Lehrziele oder Kognitive Lehrziele müssen erfüllt werden – affektive auch* [VaKE—The alliance of affective and cognitive teaching goals, or cognitive goals must be achieved—Affective ones as well] (Unpublished master's thesis). Paris Lodron Universität Salzburg, Austria.

Gilligan, C. (1982). *In a different voice: Psychological theory and women's development.* Cambridge, MA: Harvard University Press.

Glasersfeld, E. V. (1995). *Radical constructivism. A way of knowing and learning.* London, England: The Falmer Press.

Groeben, N., Wahl, D., Schlee, J., & Scheele, B. (1988). *Das Forschungsprogramm Subjektive Theorien. Eine Einführung in die Psychologie des reflexiven Subjekts* [The research program subjective theories]. Tübingen, Germany: Francke.

Gruber, M. (2009). Barriers to value education in schools—What teachers think. *Newsletter from EARLI SIG 13 Moral and Democratic Education* [On-line serial], *5,* 26-30. Retrieved from http://www.earli.org/resources/sigs/Sig%2013/Newsletters%20SIG%2013/Newsletter_5_SIG13.pdf

Gurucharri, C., & Selman, R. L. (1982). The development of interpersonal understanding during childhood, preadolescence, and adolescence: A longitudinal follow-up study. *Child Development, 53,* 924-927.

Habermas, J. (1990). *Moral consciousness and communicative action.* Cambridge, MA: MIT Press.

Hetherington, J. (1997). Lecture 16: *Advanced research design.* Retrieved from http://mccoy.lib.siu.edu/projects/psyc/hetherington/lect16.ppt

Hörtenhuber, B. A. (2008). *VaKE im Kindergarten* [VaKE in the kindergarten] (Unpublished bachelor's thesis). Paris Lodron Universität Salzburg, Austria.

Hron, A., & Friedrich, H. F. (2003). A review of web-based collaborative learning: factors beyond technology. *Journal of Computer Assisted Learning, 19,* 70-79.

Johnson, D. W., & Johnson, R. T. (1991). *Cooperation in the Classroom.* Edina, MN: Interaction Book Company.

Kegan, R. (1982). *The evolving self: problem and process in human development.* Cambridge, MA: Harvard University Press.

Kircher, J. (2008). *Argumentationen im VaKE-Unterricht. Dargestellt mit der Argumentationsstruktur von Max Miller* [Argumentation in VaKE teaching: The structure of argumentation according Max Miller] (Unpublished bachelor's thesis). Paris Lodron Universität Salzburg, Austria.

Kirschner, P. A., Sweller, J., & Clark, R. E. (2006). Why minimal guidance during instruction does not work: an analysis of the failure of constructivist, discovery, problem-based, experiential, and inquiry-based teaching. *Educational Psychologist, 41,* 75-86.

Kohlberg, L, (1971). From 'is' to 'ought': How to commit the naturalistic fallacy and get away with it in the study of moral development. In T. Mischel (Ed.), *Cognitive development and epistemology* (pp. 151–284). New York, NY: Academic Press.

Kohlberg, L. (1984). *Essays on moral development: Vol. 2. The psychology of moral development.* San Francisco, CA: Harper & Row.

Lampert, M. (1992). Practices and problems in teaching authentic mathematics. In F. Oser, A. Dick, & J. -L. Patry (Eds.), *Effective and responsible teaching: The new synthesis* (pp. 295-314). San Francisco, CA: Jossey-Bass.

Lebersorger, K., & Linortner, L. (2008). *Vergleich der Konzentration bei Kleinkindern mittels LUM zwischen Regelunterricht und VaKE-Unterricht* [Comparing small children's concentration in regular and VaKE teaching using the Lesson Interruption Method] (Unpublished paper). Paris Lodron Universität, Salzburg, Austria.

Lehrpläne für die Schulen Österreichs [Curricula of the schools in Austria]. (n.d.). Retrieved from http://www.bmukk.gv.at/schulen/unterricht/lp/Volkschullehrplan3911.xml

Lind, G. (2003). *Moral ist lehrbar: Handbuch zur Theorie und Praxis moralischer und demokratischer Bildung* [Morality can be learned: Handbook of theory and practice of moral and democratic education]. München, Germany: Oldenbourg.

Linortner, L. (2008). *VaKE im Kindergarten* (Unpublished bachelor's thesis). Paris Lodron Universität Salzburg, Austria.

Lyons, N. (1983). Two perspectives on self, relationships, and morality. *Harvard Educational Review, 53,* 125-145.

Miller, M. (2006). *Dissens. Zur Theorie diskursiven und systemischen Lernens* [Dissent: About the theory of discursive and systematic learning]. Bielefeld, Germany: Transcript.

Nussbaumer, M. (2007). *Das Unterrichtskonzept VaKE in Verbindung mit der Argumentationsstruktur von Max Miller* [The teaching concept VaKE in connection with the argumentation structure of Max Miller] (Unpublished bachelor's thesis). Paris Lodron Universität Salzburg, Austria.

Nussbaumer, M. (2009). *"Argumentieren geht über studieren." Wie Schülerinnen und Schüler im didaktischen Konzept VaKE argumentieren* ["Argumentation instead of studies:" How students argue in the teaching method VaKE] (Unpublished master's thesis). Paris Lodron Universität Salzburg, Austria.

Parsons, T. (1970). *The social system.* London, England: Routledge & Kegan Paul.

Paul, R. (1993). *Critical thinking. What every person needs to survive in a rapidly changing world.* Santa Rosa, CA: Foundation for Critical Thinking.

Patry, J. -L. (1989). Evaluationsmethodologie zu Forschungszwecken - Ein Beispiel von "kritischem Multiplizismus" [Evaluation methodology for research goals—An example of critical multiplism]. *Unterrichtswissenschaft, 17,* 359-337.

Patry, J. -L. (1997). The lesson interruption method in assessing situation-specific behavior in classrooms. *Psychological Reports, 81,* 272-274.

Patry, J. -L. (2001). WALK: A summative assessment of constructivist teaching. *Salzburger Beiträge zur Erziehungswissenschaft, 5*(2), 49-63.

Patry, J. -L. (2002). Science is not values-free—Neither in research, nor in school. *Salzburger Beiträge zur Erziehungswissenschaft, 6*(1), 5-14.

Patry, J. -L. & Hofmann, F. B. (1998). Erziehungsziel Autonomie – Anspruch und Wirklichkeit [Educational goal autonomy – aspiration and reality]. *Psychologie in Erziehung und Unterricht, 45,* 53-66.

Patry, J. -L., Pnevmatikos, D., Tapola, A., Veugelers, W. M. M. H., Tirri, K., & Fritzén, L. (2011). *SIG 13 International Projects.* Paper presented at the 14th Biennial Conference EARLI 2011, Exeter, England.

Patry, J. -L., & Schaber, K. (2010). *Fürsorge versus Gerechtigkeit: Argumentieren Frauen anders als Männer? Eine Untersuchung zur Geschlechtsspezifität in moralischen Entscheidungssituationen* [Care versus justice: Are women's arguments different from men's? A study of sex specificity in moral decision situations]. Paper presented at "Moral und Beruf 2010" conference, Basel, Switzerland.

Patry, J. -L. & Weinberger, A. (2004). Kombination von konstruktivistischer Werterziehung und Wissenserwerb [Combination of constructivist values education and knowledge acquisition]. *Salzburger Beiträge zur Erziehungswissenschaft, 8*(2), 35-50.

Patry, J. -L., & Weinberger, A. (2010). Leistungsmessung im konstruktivistischen Unterricht: WALK [Achievement assessment in constructivist teaching: WALK]. In K. Zierer (Ed.), *Schulische Werteerziehung* (pp. 220-230). Hohengehren, German: Schneider.

Patry, J. -L. & Weyringer, S. (2005). Forschendes und konstruktivistisches Lernen [Inquiry and constructivist learning]. In Österreichisches Zentrum für Begabtenförderung und Begabungsforschung (Eds.), *Die Forscher/ innen von morgen. Bericht des 4. Internationalen Begabtenkongresses in Salzburg* (pp. 18-22). Innsbruck, Austria: StudienVerlag.

Patry, J. -L., Weyringer, S., & Weinberger, A. (2007). Combining values and knowledge education. In D. N. Aspin & J. D. Chapman (Eds.), *Values education and lifelong learning* (pp. 160-179). Dordrecht, The Netherlands: Springer.

Patry, J. -L., Weinberger, A., & Weyringer, S. (2010a). Fächerübergreifende Ansätze: Atmosphäre, Dilemma-Diskussionen, VaKE und Just Community [Interdisciplinary approaches: Atmosphere, dilemma discussions, VaKE, and just community]. In K. Zierer (Ed.), *Schulische Werteerziehung* (pp. 178-194). Hohengehren, Germany: Schneider.

Patry, J. -L., Weyringer, S., & Weinberger, A. (2010b). Kombination von Moral- und Werterziehung und Wissenserwerb mit *Va*KE – Wie argumentieren die Schülerinnen und Schüler? [Combining moral and values education and knowledge acquisition with *Va*KE—How do students argue?]. In B. Latzko & T. Malti (Eds.), *Moralische Entwicklung und Erziehung in Kindheit und Adoleszenz* (pp. 241-259). Göttingen, Germany: Hogrefe.

Patry, J. -L., Weyringer, S., & Weinberger, A. (2010c). Values and knowledge education (*Va*KE) in European summer camps for gifted students: Native versus non-native speakers. In C. Klaassen & N. Maslovaty (Eds.), *Moral courage and the normative professionalism of teachers: Moral development and citizenship education* (pp. 133-148). Rotterdam, The Netherlands: Sense.

Patry, J. -L., Zlöbl, S., & Felber, M. (2009). *Assessing students' knowledge about environmental issues on higher levels in Bloom's taxonomy: Validation of the Environment WALK Test (EWT)*. Paper presented at a round-table discussion at the EARLI Conference, Amsterdam.

Phillips, D. C. (2000). *The expanded social scientist's bestiary: A guide to fabled threats to, and defenses of, naturalistic social science*. Lanham, MD: Rowman & Littlefield.

Phillips, D. C., & Burbules, N. C. (2000). *Postpositivism and educational research*. New York, NY: Rowman & Littlefield.

Piaget, J. (1985). *The equilibration of cognitive structures*. Chicago, IL: University of Chicago Press.

Potter, R. B. (1965). *The structure of certain American Christian responses to the nuclear dilemma* (Unpublished doctoral dissertation). Harvard University. Cambridge, MA.

Redmore, C. D., & Loevinger, J. (1979). Ego development in adolescence: Longitudinal studies. *Journal of youth and adolescence, 8*, 1-20.

Schulz von Thun, F. (1990). *Miteinander reden. Stile, Werte und Persönlichkeitsentwicklung* (Bd. 2) [Speaking with each other: Stiles, values and personality development]. Hamburg, Germany: Reinbeck.

Shadish, W. R., Cook, T. D., & Campbell, D. T. (2002). *Experimental and quasi-experimental designs for generalized causal inference*. Boston, MA: Houghton Mifflin.

Snyder, B. R. (1971). *The hidden curriculum*. New York, NY: Alfred A. Knopf.

Sternberg, R. J. (Ed.). (2003). *Wisdom: Its nature, origins, and development* (2nd ed.). New York, NY: Cambridge University Press.

Vygotsky, L. S. (1978). *Mind in society: The development of higher psychological processes* (M. Cole, V. John-Steiner, S. Scribner, & E. Souberman, Eds.). Cambridge, MA: Harvard University Press.

Walker, L. J. (1984). Sex differences in the development of moral reasoning: A critical review. *Child Development, 55*, 677-691.

Weinberger, A. (2006). *Kombination von Werterziehung und Wissenserwerb. Evaluation des konstruktivistischen Unterrichtsmodells VaKE (Values and Knowledge Education) in der Sekundarstufe I* [Combination of values education and knowledge acquisition. Evaluation of the constructivist teaching model VaKE (Values *and* Knowledge Education on the secondary level I]. Hamburg, Germany: Kovac.

Weinberger, A. (2010). *Kritischer Multiplizismus: Der Viabilitätscheck im VaKE-Unterricht* [Critical multiplism: The viability check in *Va*KE teaching]. Paper presented at the 74th AEPF conference, Jena, Germany.

Weinberger A., Kriegseisen, G., Loch, A., & Wingelmüller, P. (2005). Das Unterrichtsmodell *Va*KE (Values *and* Knowledge Education) in der Hochbegabtenförderung: Der Prozess gegen Woyzek [The teaching model *Va*KE (Values and Knowledge Education) in the education of gifted students: The case of Woyzeck]. *Salzburger Beiträge zur Erziehungswissenschaft, 9*(1), 23-40.

Weyringer, S. (2008). *Die Anwendung von VaKE in internationalen Sommercamps für besonders begabte Jugendliche* [Applying *Va*KE in international summer camps for particularly gifted students] (Unpublished doctoral dissertation). Gesellschafts- und Kulturwissenschaftliche Fakultät der Universität Salzburg, Austria.

Weyringer, S., Patry, J. -L. & Weinberger, A. (2005). Das bessere Argument [The better argument]. *Arbeitsblätter. Magazin des Österreichischen Jugendrotkreuzes, 58*, 15-23.

Weyringer, S., Patry, J. -L., & Weinberger, A. (2012). Values and knowledge education. Experiences with teacher trainings. In D. Alt & R. Reingold (Eds.), *Changes in teachers' moral role. From passive observers to moral and democratic leaders* (pp. 165-179). Rotterdam, The Netherlands: Sense.

Author Contact Information: **Jean-Luc Patry**, University of Salzburg, Erzabt-Klotz-Strasse 1, 5020 Salzburg, Austria. Phone: +43 (0)662 8044 4225. E-mail: jean-luc.patry@sbg.ac.at

CHAPTER 48

Moral Development

Susan Magun-Jackson and John E. Burgette
University of Memphis, Tennessee

The focus of this chapter will be on moral development, and more specifically, Kohlberg's theory of moral development. Within higher education and especially psychology, moral development is highly researched and cited. While there are several moral development theories, it is fair to say that Lawrence Kohlberg's theory of moral development is the most dominant and most frequently cited and consolidated theory in this domain. In a half of a second, a Google search of moral development will produce 95,000,000 results. A majority of the results either directly explain or refer to Kohlberg's theory or refer to research related to moral development that cites his theory.

Starting with a brief biography of Lawrence Kohlberg and how his activities and experiences led to the development of his theory, the interactions with earlier cognitive theories and philosophers that influenced the development of his theory will also be considered. His theory will be described in terms of the hierarchical relationship of its three-level, six stage development with the assumptions of reasoning at each stage. In addition, major instruments that measure and support the theory will be described. These will include the development and advance of qualitative instruments as well as the growth of more quantitative measures, the validity of these instruments as well as their overall validity and the generalizability of these instruments to his theory.

The chapter will also provide an overview of the use and application of Kohlberg's theory, including a summary of studies that show the relationships between moral development theory and other domains. Several studies and dissertations that have used Kohlberg's theory and related measurements to further explore and apply its principles will also be presented. The final section of this chapter will consider the future directions, as well as other major theories that have emerged from Kohlberg's Framework including, but not limited to, neo-Kohlbergian studies.

THEORY DEVELOPMENT AND INTERACTIONS

KOHLBERG'S EARLY BACKGROUND

For 30 years of his life, Lawrence Kohlberg shaped the direction of American psychology in the field of morality, primarily in how individuals think and study this phenomenon. A year after his death, a special issue of *Counseling and Values* was published in which researchers and project directors in morality commented on Kohlberg's strong influence on their work and the direction they thought morality was heading. James Rest (1988), who had worked primarily in moral judgment assessment instruments and their interpretations, devoted an entire chapter on Kohlberg's legacy.

Lawrence Kohlberg, born in Bronxville, New York, in 1937, was the son of a wealthy businessman. Instead of following the life of a privileged person, he joined the Merchant Marines after high school and travelled the world. Later on, he signed up with a ship smuggling Jewish refugees, who had survived the Holocaust in Europe, into Palestine through the British blockade. It was at this time that he first encountered the struggle of how one could defend going against genuine authorities and the law. This struggle shows up in the research questions posed in his dilemmas about "Heinz and the Drug" and "The Escaped Prisoner" (Rest, 1988).

Kohlberg eventually attended the University of Chicago, where the heart of the curriculum was in the "Great Books," from which he became completely absorbed with Plato, Kant, Dewey, Mead, and others (Rest, 1988). He earned his PhD in psychology at the

The Handbook of Educational Theories, pp. 581–594

University of Chicago, and it was during this time that he became familiar with Jean Piaget's work, which was a scholarly approach where morality decisions were made based on the significance of the individual's reasoning (Kohlberg, 1958). In the middle 1950s, American psychologists were still debating about the psychological nature of cognition, and Piaget had not yet even been discovered. Psychological approaches to morality at that time were based on the influence of socialization. Kohlberg found that his own personal moral experiences resembled more of the Piagetian view. Consequently, his theory was strongly influenced by Piaget's cognitive development and moral development theories.

Piaget's Cognitive and Moral Development Theories

Piaget maintained that children develop more sophisticated schemas as they grow from infancy through adolescence. They actively move through four orderly stages of cognitive maturation: sensorimotor, preoperations, concrete operations, and formal Operations (Piaget & Inhelder, 1966/1969). The first stage, sensorimotor, takes place during the approximate ages from birth to 2 years where the infant/toddler thinks through actions. By the time the toddler advances from this stage, he has acquired object permanence which is the understanding that things exist even if they cannot be seen. The second stage, preoperations, takes place during the approximate ages of 2 to 6/7 years where the type of thinking is representational. It is during this stage that there is an increase in language development and the child is very egocentric in that he can only see things through his own perspective. Around the age of 6 or 7 the child enters the third stage, concrete operations, which lasts until the ages of 11 to 13. In this stage thinking is based strictly upon the organization of the physical surroundings. It is called concrete in that there is little or no abstract thinking. It is interesting to note, that many people never advance from concrete operations. The last stage, formal operations, is divided into two different substages. Early formal operations take place during adolescence where thinking is based upon possible organization of the physical surrounding. Here thinking is restricted to the individual's social life and generally the thinking is rather inconsistent. It is during this substage that individuals are again egocentric which has led to the term adolescent egocentrism whereby adolescents are totally concerned with themselves: how they look; how they think others are seeing them; and how they think they are immortal. Full formal operations, the second subheading takes place at the earliest at 11 to 13 years of age, if at all. As stated earlier, some individuals never advance from the concrete operations stage and, therefore, cannot think abstractly about the organization of the physical surroundings because in this substage the individual is capable of consistently applying hypothetical, deductive reasoning as well as thinking abstractly.

Piaget (1932) expanded his cognitive developmental approach to the social development of children. He was specifically concerned with how they begin to reason and make moral judgments, with moral judgments representing the child's understanding of what is right and wrong, fair or unfair. "It is the moral judgment that we propose to investigate not the moral behavior or sentiments" (p. vii). His clinical method for his research on children's social development included observations of children in groups and alone, children who were at play and with some structured activity. He developed stories where the child was asked to make a judgment as to the fairness or unfairness of an act. Piaget was not concerned with the specific judgment or decision of the child; he was more interested in the reasoning and rationale the child gave for the judgment.

Using this method, he developed his stage theory of moral development. It is important to note that he identified a premoral stage that lasts from birth to about the age of three. In this particular stage, children have no concept of morality because they basically do not understand the concept of rules. The first moral stage, the heteronomous stage, takes place between the approximate ages of 3 and 9. This stage roughly coincides with the sensorimotor and preoperational stages of his cognitive theory in that the child has no ability to carry out complex mental operations and has a poor understanding of other people's perceptions. In this stage, children understand the concept of rules, but these rules are seen as immutable and external. Rules are obeyed because they exist and because a rule tells an individual what he or she is not supposed to do. Children do not evaluate the intentions of the wrongdoer, but the consequences. In addition, this stage is governed by external controls, usually the parent.

The second moral stage, the autonomous stage, takes place from approximately age 10 and continues through life. In this stage, the child recognizes that rules can be changed based upon mutual consent (usually between the parent and child). External rules are not rigid as they develop their own internal morality. Intentions play a larger role in moral development as actions are evaluated in a more sophisticated manner. According to Piaget (1932), children at this stage also develop a firm concept that punishment specifically fits the crime. Because children are more able to carry out complex mental operations (concrete and perhaps abstract), this stage corresponds to Piaget's concrete and formal operations stages.

These two theories heavily influenced Kohlberg in his own research. He saw Piaget's work as a rational, individualistic side of moral development. Moreover, his own personal life and moral experiences were more in-line with the Piagetian view (Rest, 1988); like Piaget's two theories, Kohlberg's theory of moral development was a stage theory.

Stage Theory

According to Kohlberg (1968), the nature of Piaget's theory of development implies several strong properties. The first is that the stages form an invariant sequence, which means that the order does not change. An individual must progress through each stage in the order given; there is no skipping of a stage. The first stage is very simple and logical. Subsequent stages are more complex and abstract. Developmental progress is orderly even within stages with one type of operation, developing prior to another. Within Piaget's model, regression does not exist. For example, once an individual has the capability of abstract thinking, he or she always has that capability. The capability may not always be used, but it is not lost. This is why the stages are called "hard stages," because once achieved, that cognitive capability is not lost. On the other hand, "soft stages" are those stages that an individual could visit for a while and then move backward or forward.

The second property is that of universalization. Piaget and Kohlberg relate to how the human species has developed and evolved, and the same stages and the same invariant sequence among people around the world would be expected. The cultural differences that would be found on a world basis would affect how a researcher tested for a specific stage or sequence, but not the form of the thought or reasoning.

The third property is that progression through the stages is not based upon chronological age. Everybody must mature to a certain extent within each of the stages prior to the emergence of the next stage. This consists of a certain progression of logical operations, which when people begin a stage, they are quite new at the use of those logical operations. To apply the logical operations to a variety of tasks, the individual should be ready and practiced. Note that in the discussion of ages or ones given on the chart that the ages are not concrete; they are approximate ages.

The fourth property is that the stages are qualitatively different. Thinking at different stages is structured along qualitatively different connections. There is a genuine, inherent difference between the stages. For example, an individual in concrete operations cannot use abstract thinking as a way to solve a problem.

The fifth property is that stages are structured as wholes, which means that the stages are general patterns of thought that are consistently confirmed across many different kinds of issues. Kohlberg found that individuals score at their dominant stage across nine dilemmas about two thirds of the time (Colby, Kohlberg, Gibbs, Lieberman, Fischer, & Saltzstein, 1983).

The sixth property is that stages are hierarchically integrated, meaning that as one goes into higher stages, individuals do not lose whatever insights they had integrated at earlier stages. The earlier stages become integrated into the higher stages. Researchers have suggested that individuals in higher stages have some intuitive sense of greater competency at the higher stage (Rest, 1973; Rest, Turiel, & Kohlberg, 1969).

Kohlberg's Moral Development Theory

Kohlberg's dissertation methodology consisted of interviewing participants and asking and presenting them with some moral problems. The initial participants consisted of 72 middle and lower class boys aged 10, 13, and 16 (Kohlberg, 1958). Later he added males and females, younger children, adolescents, adults and delinquents in other parts of the United States, as well as other countries (Kohlberg, 1963, 1970). Like Piaget, he was not concerned with the selected answer, but in what individuals said in justifying their decisions. Also like Piaget, he noted people judged fairness by interpreting actions and drawing inferences, not just those given by the moral problems. He originally described six basic patterns in people's moral reasoning. He refined these patterns over the next 30 years while his procedures for scoring material became more complicated and explicit. Although he finished his dissertation in 1958 (Kohlberg, 1958), it took him 5 years to publish an article from it (Kohlberg, 1963).

He had a brief appointment at Yale before returning to teach at the University of Chicago (1962-1968), where he instituted the Child Psychology Training Program, which generated much interest in the growing field of developmental psychology. Kohlberg's main agenda in the 1960s was to expand upon the cognitive developmental position. Using his own morality research, he reinterpreted personality and social development according to a cognitive developmental view (Kohlberg, 1969). His contention that cognitive development was the key, not only to the psychology of morality, but also to early education, sex role identity, personality development, identification processes as well as all topics in social development, was not only an alternative to the behaviorist and psychoanalytical approaches popular at that time, but also the major contribution to American psychology's interest in Piaget, cognition, and social cognition.

While Kohlberg was strongly influenced by Piaget's theories, he was also struck by the limitations of Piaget's research in moral judgments. As noted, Piaget only studied children, and he used games and rules as the basis for his moral development theory. Kohlberg believed that adding dilemmas would aid in the clarification about different hypothetical moral situations. Children and others would be forced to choose between opposing issues, as the dilemmas would pose a conflict between two goods or two evils. The most famous of Kohlberg's dilemmas is the Heinz dilemma. This is the story of a man named Heinz whose wife is dying and he has to choose as to whether or not he should steal a drug that may save her life (Kohlberg, 1971a).

To further probe the child's rationale and thought process, Kohlberg (1971a) also added an extensive interview format. Through his research, Kohlberg incorporated Piaget's two stages of moral development and described more stages of moral thinking and judgment. In addition, he found that the stages of moral development are based upon one's cognitive capabilities. Thus, his stages of moral judgment and thinking are "grounded by" Piaget's extensive cognitive developmental research, as well as moral development theory.

In essence, Kohlberg (1971a) found that Piaget's stages of cognitive development are prerequisites to an individual's social role-taking capabilities. That is, individuals must have a certain level of perspective-taking ability before being able to understand the various social roles that are presented. This means that cognitive development lays the foundation for social role-taking and social cognition. In turn, social cognition becomes a prerequisite to moral understanding, thinking, and judgment. However, moral development in this context is not moral action. Individuals do not necessarily act in accord to the way that they think.

While cognitive development is necessary for moral development and action, it does not necessarily guarantee moral action. A person's stage of cognitive development is necessary to conceptualize and understand the reasoning in a specific stage of moral development, but it is not enough to assure that the individual is within that stage of moral reasoning. The person easily could be in a lower developmental stage of moral reasoning. On the other hand, individuals cannot be in a higher stage of moral development than what they can understand cognitively.

Furthermore, Kohlberg's (1971a) cognitive moral development theory was primarily justice-based, meaning that the highest level and stages are the highest measure of morality, based upon justice. The concept of justice is grounded in the principles of respect, equality, and autonomy of the dignity of all human beings as individuals (Self, Baldwin, & Wolinsky, 1992). Therefore, measuring moral development essentially assesses the individual's use of "justice" reasoning.

Kohlberg's theory maintains that individuals will develop through three levels of moral development, with two stages within each level (Kohlberg, 1984). These stages occur as a result of role-taking opportunities that give individuals the chance to consider other viewpoints and perspectives. As with the properties of stage theories, his stages are qualitatively different ways of thinking, are structured wholes (general patterns of thought), progress in an invariant sequence (no skipping of stages) and are cross-cultural universals (the same for all cultures) (Magun-Jackson, 2004). Like Piaget, Kohlberg's model starts with a stage 0 that represents the moral thought of an infant. Level I is called the preconventional level because the individuals' reasoning is according to their own needs and desires, which is a very selfish or egocentric perspective. The focus in Level I is totally on the self, with little to no thought of others. Stage 1, often referred to as the punishment and obedience orientation, corresponds to the cognitive prerequisite of the preoperational stage of reasoning. This stage is also similar to Piaget's heteronomous stage. Morally, the individual will do what is expected to avoid punishment. Individuals in this stage are egocentric and thus unable to see things from a different perspective. In regard to the Heinz dilemma, an individual in this stage would decide on stealing or not stealing the drug based upon whether or not they might be caught. Criminals and convicts are often stuck in this stage. Stage 2, the instrumental relativist orientation, corresponds to the cognitive prerequisite of the concrete operations stage of reasoning. Morally, the reasoning is still very self-oriented but has now progressed to individuals making deals or exchanges in order to maximize positive outcomes for themselves. If there is mutual agreement, rules can be changed. Often, trial and error is used to resolve conflicts. In regard to the Heinz dilemma, the individual might reason that Heinz should steal the drug so as not to lose his wife or not steal the drug so as not lose his own life for that of his wife. Many adult criminals and con-artists never get out of stage 2 reasoning even if they have developed full formal operations cognitively. It's their crimes and criminal activity that becomes quite sophisticated.

Level II is called the conventional level because individuals in this level reason from the perspective of the status quo. That is, the individual in this level reflects moral thinking generally found in one's society, family, and peers. No longer is the self the focus of the stage. The cognitive prerequisite for both stages in this level is early formal operations. Stage 3, the Interpersonal concordance orientation, is dominated with individuals concerned with living up to other's expectations. This stage is all about conforming with the group, whether friends or parents. Therefore, these individuals avoid conflicts; they want to be "good" for everyone. Regarding the Heinz dilemma, a person would respond as to "what would a good … (fill in the blank) do?" Stage 4, the law and order orientation, is dominated by rules, regulations, the way things have always been done, etc. This stage is about the maintenance of law and order. Everything is black or white; there is no grey. Regarding the Heinz dilemma, a person in this stage would make the decision based upon protecting the family structure or "what if everyone did it?"

Kohlberg (1984) added a "soft stage" to his model called Stage 4 1/2. It is between one level and the next level (Levels II and III). It is a transitional level in that one can stay in this stage the rest of his or her life, or move back to stage 4, or move up to stage 5. The individual in this stage does not yet have the full operations capability to move to Level III. This person is what one might call a "fence sitter," an individual who does not want to get involved. In this stage, individuals find everything relative, and therefore, feel that "who are they to make a decision?"

Level III is called the postconventional level because the individual in this level is concerned with, and can fully analyze and implement, abstract social issues and principles. This is the only level that has an age requirement, which is at least the late 20s. The cognitive prerequisite for both stages within this level is full formal operations because of the need to mentally manipulate abstract concepts. Both stages in this level are quite abstract and complex. Moral issues at this level have been completely internalized and are no longer based on others' standards. Stage 5, the social contract-legalistic orientation, is concerned about the greatest good for the greatest number of people. This stage is identified with values and principles that underscore basic rights and the democratic process. A good example of reasoning at this stage is the judicial system. In regard to the Heinz dilemma, an individual in this stage might use the law as the reasoning in that the law either does not protect the wife's life or the law needs to be respected. Stage 6, the universal ethical principles orientation, is based upon the ethical tenets of all the great religions regarding how to treat one another. Individuals in this stage are concerned with universal principles and the demands of individual conscience, which act as a personal guide and personal philosophical construct. Martin Luther King and his 1963 speech from the Birmingham Jail is a good example of this stage. In regard to the Heinz dilemma, an individual in this stage might reason about the sacredness of life. It is important to note that only 20-25% of the population ever reaches the last two stages (Ishida, 2006). This is understandable, considering that most adults never reach full formal operations of cognitive development and this is a prerequisite for both stages.

After Kohlberg's Dissertation

Kohlberg made daring inroads in philosophy and education. After his move to Harvard in 1968 as Full Professor, he developed the Center for Moral Development and Education. He advocated a form of moral education, which was not using indoctrination or values that could be used in any American public school. He also took the stance that psychologists should not be value relativists where all values are the same (Kohlberg, 1971b). He consequently angered the philosophical community by suggesting that philosophers should recognize the facts of moral development as relevant to their philosophical theories, and that for better conceptual decision-making, higher stages of moral development were needed and therefore higher stages of philosophy were more defensible (Rest, 1988).

Kohlberg's timing was in-tune with what was going on in America. The civil rights movement was growing, the Vietnam War protests were increasing, and the women's movement was gaining energy. Morality in America was an extremely important topic. Kohlberg's concentration on justice, on autonomous decision-making, and the defense of principled civil disobedience was most timely. It is no surprise that by the mid-1970s the cognitive development approach, as well as Kohlberg's theory of moral development, had generated tremendous interest. This, in turn, led to critics and others requesting more evidence and demonstrations of the theory. It took the Harvard group 10 years to successfully undertake a drastic revision of stage definitions and the scoring system, which also led to hundreds of studies that confirmed the usefulness of his methods and theory (Rest, 1988).

During this time, Kohlberg was also very involved in moral education. His first programs followed the hypothetical dilemmas to provide group discussions whereby participants were provided practice in moral problem solving, as well as feedback and new ideas from others. However, he was displeased with the discussions and that the programs did not reflect the moral environment of the institution. While in Israel in a kibbutz school with a strong sense of community, Kohlberg discovered the model that would become his vision of a "just community" approach to moral education, and which he implemented in several schools and prisons (Rest, 1988).

As he grew older, Kohlberg completed many writing projects on moral philosophy and moral psychology. He was highly recognized by international scholars, who regularly consulted with him about moral development programs and research in their own countries. However, Kohlberg's health was deteriorating due to a disease he contracted in 1973 during a trip to Central America. It caused him to always be dizzy, nauseated and tremendously lethargic. In addition, he suffered from pain, disability, and depression. And so, in 1987 at the age of 59, it is highly speculated that he committed suicide by drowning (Rest, 1988).

Although Kohlberg was gone, the use and application of his theory continued. Additional instruments were developed that measured and supported the theory. Assessment was a key to measure moral development and resulted in several instruments.

Measuring Moral Development

In order to research moral development—for example, to understand the differences between groups of people (e.g., age, gender, ethnicity, education) or the impact of educational interventions—it is necessary to have instruments that can be used to measure moral reasoning and levels of moral development. Moreover, these instruments need to be designed in such a way that they can be administered consistently, over time, and can be assured of being reliable and consistent in their interpretation. The following section considers three major instruments that have been developed for measuring moral development: the Moral Judgment Interview (Colby, Kohlberg, Gibbs, & Lieberman, 1983), the Defining Issues Test (Rest, 1990) and the Moral Judgment Test (Lind, 1998).

Moral Judgment Interview

Through the 1970s, Kohlberg worked to develop an instrument for effectively determining an individual's moral development, and by the early 1980s this work led to the Moral Judgment Interview (MJI), which used a method called Standard Issue Scoring (Colby, Kohlberg, Gibbs, Lieberman, Fischer, et al., 1983). According to Colby, Kohlberg, Gibbs, and Lieberman (1983), the MJI presents the subject with three moral dilemmas (e.g., Heinz and the drug), followed with nine to twelve standard questions, which are used to justify and clarify the subject's moral perspective toward two moral issues from the dilemma (e.g., save Heinz's wife or obey the law). From the subject's answers, the interviewer determines specific moral elements that basically represent a moral stage that supports the reasoning; the stage scores for each issue is then combined to build a moral maturity score for the interview (Colby, Kohlberg, Gibbs, & Lieberman, 1983). The MJI requires subjects to *produce* responses, either verbal or written, which are then interpreted by trained interviewers (Elm & Weber, 1994).

Colby, Kohlberg, Gibbs, and Lieberman (1983) report that construct validity was shown during longitudinal studies in that a primary aspect of the moral development theory was supported: individuals moving through the correct, invariant, sequences. In regard to the test-retest reliability of the MJI, in reviewing interviews scored by two raters, there was found to be a 70% to 80% agreement; analysis of inter-rater reliability yielded results that were very similar to the test-retest analysis (Colby Kohlberg, Gibbs, & Lieberman 1983). Colby, Kohlberg, Gibbs, and Lieberman also reported a Cronbach's Alpha in the low-to-mid .90s for the three interview forms. Although a reasonably reliable instrument, a major concern with any interview method is that it assumes that subjects can understand and explain their own reasoning (Rest, Narvaez, Bebeau, & Thoma, 1999). Although subjects might be able to *recognize* a high level of moral reasoning, it may be more difficult for them to *produce* the appropriate response at that same level. Rest et al. argue that this may be part of the reason that level III reasoning is rarely reported from interview data.

Defining Issues Test

According to Rest, Narvaez, Thoma, and Bebeau (1999), the Defining Issues Test (DIT) was first introduced in the 1970s as another way to understand moral reasoning. Although it is built from Kohlberg's framework, it is different than the MJI; while the MJI works toward having the subject *produce* a level of moral reasoning when presented with a dilemma, the DIT only asks the subject to *recognize* a level of moral reasoning (Elm & Weber, 1994; Rest, Thoma, & Edwards, 1997). Assuming that a person will rationalize moral dilemmas within the context of Kohlberg's three levels of moral reasoning, the DIT presents several statements, which represent different levels or stages, and the individual ranks these statements, based on how closely each one matches his or her moral viewpoint (Elm & Weber, 1994; Rest, Narvaez, Bebeau, et al., 1999). Examples of the six dilemmas of the DIT are: (a) a man contemplates stealing a drug to save his gravely ill wife (Heinz and the drug); (b) students contemplate taking over the administration building of a university because of an army ROTC program; (c) an old neighbor contemplates reporting an escaped convict to the police and have him sent back to prison (The Escaped Prisoner); (d) a doctor contemplates a patient's request for more morphine to end her life as she is dying of incurable cancer that is excruciatingly painful; (e) a mechanic must decide whether or not to hire a good mechanic of Chinese descent while knowing that many of his customers would take their business elsewhere; and (f) a principal contemplates stopping the production of a high school newspaper because in two editions students took a stand against some contemporary social issues (e.g., the Viet Nam War, boys wearing long hair) (DIT Manual, 1986/1990).

Rest, Thoma, and Edwards (1997) contend that the DIT exceeds other methods for measuring moral decision-making. Unlike instruments that may require extensive knowledge of a methodology (e.g., interviewing), the DIT requires little or no training and is fairly easy to administer (Elm & Weber, 1994). Along with the instrument, the following administration process is provided through the DIT Manual (Rest, 1990). The DIT can be administered through either a set of six or three questions, and each question represents a hypothetical moral dilemma. The subject is first asked to answer a "yes/no" question for the dilemma. The subject is then provided with a list of issues and statements, which may be related to the decision just selected for the dilemma, and ranks these in the order of importance for the selected decision. Finally, the subject ranks the four most important statements, those that most impacted the selected decision. A stage of moral development might be represented by each of the statements. However, there are some statements that are included purposely, are considered meaningless, and are not related to any stage of moral development. For any of the statements that are deemed meaningless, subjects are instructed to rank these very low. It is the four rankings from all the stories that are used to derive a *P score*, and this score provides a measurement for the subject's level of moral development. Stage five and six statements that were included in the final list are used to derive this score. The *P score* is reported as a percentage (0-95%), and it represents the percentage of the subject's reasoning that is at the post-conventional level. Also, preliminary analysis for both of the ranking lists is done specifically to verify both the validity and consistency of responses. Tests that have too many of the meaningless statements ranked high are considered invalid. Too many inconsistencies between final rankings and the individual statement rankings, or when too many individual statements are ranked the same, will also be considered invalid. At least under normal circumstances, subjects that intentionally try to imitate a morally, higher answer should not result in higher *P scores* (Rest, 1990).

According to Elm and Weber (1994), because the DIT has been used, internationally, in thousands of studies, many of which include tests for reliability and validity, the instrument is a good choice when construct validity is important. Rest, Narvaez, Bebeau, et al. (1999) report that consistent validity and reliability have been shown through hundreds of studies. Many studies have been conducted that consider moral developmental in the context of professions, higher education, types of institutions, and gender (Bebeau, 2002; King & Mayhew, 2002, 2004). Schlaefli, Rest, and Thoma (1985) reviewed 55 studies that used the DIT to analyze the impact of moral development from education interventions (with overall, modest effects), while Restm Narvaez, Thoma, and Bebeau (2000) report an assessment from over 50 studies that also showed moderate gains. Most studies have found age to have a positive relationship with moral development (King & Mayhew, 2002, 2004). According to Rest (1990), the DIT has been used in many studies that compare differences in age and education, and has shown statistically high criterion group validity in explaining DIT score variance (about 50%). In studies that used the DIT with a large number of samples, 30-50% of the variance in *P scores* could be explained by education (Rest et al., 2000). Studies have shown that the DIT has also been used to demonstrate longitudinal gains in stage progression for moral development (Rest, Thoma, & Edwards, 1997). One longitudinal study of college students showed effect sizes of 0.80 (Rest et al., 2000). Rest (1990) reports that measures of life experience correlates with the DIT, around 0.60 for young adults. Overall, the Cronbach's Alpha for the DIT has been reported to be in the high .70s or .80s, which is a sufficient level of consistency (Rest 1990; Rest et al., 2000; Rest, Thoma, & Edwards, 1997).

Although the DIT is a reliably consistent instrument, there are some considerations when using it. Although the administration of the DIT is relatively simple, if subjects do not complete the instrument correctly or do not understand the instructions, it can result in their score not being used in the analysis, which can be very problematic for studies that may already have a small sample (Elm & Weber, 1994). Also, the DIT is designed for subjects with a reading level of no less than 12 years; as such, it has not been used for studies that seek to understand preadolescent moral reasoning (Rest et al., 1999a). According to Rest (1990), the DIT should also have face validity in that it considers the subject's reasoning for addressing a moral dilemma. However, Elm and Weber (1994) caution that this type of validity might not be as high in some contexts: for example, none of the dilemmas occur in a business organization setting, therefore using the DIT for measuring the moral development of business people might not have as high a face validity as in other contexts (e.g., sociopolitical).

Defining Issues Test, Version 2 (DIT2). In the late 1990's, work began on a new version of the DIT, the DIT2. First, the number of dilemmas for the DIT2 is reduced from six to five, and the verbiage of the dilemmas is reworded (Rest, Narvaez, Thoma, & Bebeau, 1999). Although the overall structure of the DIT2 is very similar to the original DIT, in that subjects are presented with a dilemma and then asked to recognize and rank statements that best fit their moral perspective, the wording for the dilemmas having been updated from when the original DIT was first developed. For example, the five DIT2 dilemmas are: (a) a father of a starving family must decide whether or not to steal food from a rich man's warehouse in which food is being hoarded; (b) a newspaper reporter contemplates reporting a detrimental story about a political candidate; (c) a school board chair must decide whether or not to conduct a controversial and risky open meeting; (d) a doctor contemplates giving an overdose of a pain-killer to an anguished, but fragile, patient; and (e) college students protest against U.S.

foreign policy (Center for the Study of Ethical Development, 2004). In addition, the method and criteria for eliminating unreliable or meaningless statements has been updated to allow fewer participants to be excluded from the final analysis, and finally, the inclusion of a new index (*N2*) has been included in the final analysis (Rest, Narvaez, Thoma, et al., 1999).

Rest et al. (1997) argue that the need for a new index is based on the realization that individuals are not limited to just a single stage—that their moral reasoning may depend on many reasons—and that the *P score* from the DIT1 does not fully consider lower stage selections for the subject. As such, the *N2* is derived from two major factors: a value that is nearly the same as the original *P score*, as well as a new variable that is computed from the subject's rejection of stages two and three in their selections. Although the *P score* might still be best when only considering level III reasoning, the *N2* might provide a more comprehensive understanding of the individual's overall reasoning. In other words, the *N2* represents a more complete picture: not only of the individual's recognition of level III reasoning, but also for the rejection of lower stages of moral reasoning. In computing and comparing the *N2* with the *P score* from earlier studies, Rest et al. found the *N2* to be about the same as the *P score* in relationship to longitudinal trends and moral comprehension, but having a more positive relationship with educational interventions, as well as slightly higher internal reliability (Cronbach's Alpha): *P score* (higher .70s); *N2* (lower .80s).

In the first study of the DIT2, Rest, Narvaez, Thoma, et al. (1999) compared the new instrument with the DIT. Because this was the first study to use the DIT2, its validity could not be reported. However, comparisons of reliability were made. For the preliminary reliability of subject responses, the DIT2 retained more subjects (96%), than the DIT (77%). Cronbach's Alpha for the DIT was .76, while the DIT2 was .81. The correlation of the DIT's *P Score* with the DIT2's *N2* value was .71. Overall, the well-established DIT still compared reasonably well with the DIT2. Whether using the DIT or DIT2, Rest, Narvaez, Thoma, et al. recommend using the *N2* variable, however, unlike the hand-calculated *P score*, the *N2* is much more complicated and it is recommended that a computer be used to derive the value, as well as perform the new reliability checks (if using the DIT2).

Moral Judgment Test

Since 1976, the Moral Judgment Test (MJT) has been used to derive a *C-Index*, which is used to measure moral development (Lind, 1998). There are several factors that the DIT and MJT share in common in that, following the description of a dilemma, a group of subjects are asked to recognize and rank statements that can then be used to quantitatively measure their moral reasoning within the context of Kohlberg's stages; however, while the DIT can be used to measure moral preference, the *C-Index* represents moral consistency (Rest, Thoma, & Edwards, 1997). A study that compared the two instruments concluded that subjects who scored high on the DIT are focused on principles for their moral reasoning, while a high MJT score shows a consistent moral characteristic for those subjects; as such, which instrument to use depends on what the research is intended to address (Ishida, 2006).

Lind (1998) provides an overview of the MJT. Using two stories that each present a dilemma, the subject is asked to address statements that represent the different stages of moral development. Basically, there are six arguments that support a decision and six counter-arguments for the decision in which the subjects rank their agreement or disagree. The total of all twenty-four rankings can then be used to derive the *C-Index*, which is a percentage (1 to 100) of a person's variation in responses, in regard to concern for the morality of an argument. Although other indices can be used to understand the person's moral attitudes, a high score on the *C-Index* represents the consistency of moral reasoning or competencies, not an attitude.

Lind (2000) reports that, between 1976 and 2000, the MJT has been used in many studies (over 38,000); many in Europe, and several studies validated its use in different languages (e.g., Flemish, French, Hungarian, Italian, Portuguese, Spanish, and Turkish). He argues that, because of a thorough review of the research literature, including the MJI, the MJT is theoretically valid. In considering the empirical validity of the MJT, Lind (1998, 2000) argues that studies have shown that moral preferences are logically aligned with Kohlberg's stages, that the correlations between adjoining stages are higher than more distance stages, there is a logical correlation between moral attitudes and the *C-Index*, and there appears to be equivalency between the pro/counter-arguments for each moral dilemma. In measuring the validity of MJT translations, the *C-Index* was found to be correlated (over 0.4) with education (Lind, 1998).

The MJT should be easy to administer and score, and can be used for large samples of subjects for program evaluations (Lind, 1999). Rest, Thoma, and Edwards (1997) argue that the MJT does not have sufficient checks for testing unreliable data at the individual level. Because subjects might not correctly interpret dilemmas and arguments, Lind (2000) warns that the MJT should not be used for studying individual scores, but rather, groups of subjects.

With more assessment instruments available, more research on moral development has been conducted. Hundreds of articles have been produced. At the same time, some of the research raised concerns and issues regarding the theory, resulting in a variety of criticism.

CRITICISM OF THE THEORY

In spite of numerous research articles confirming Kohlberg's cognitive moral development theory, many researchers took issue that his theory is primarily justice-based. That is, justice is the highest principle of morality. Other principles (e.g., autonomy, equality, and respect for the dignity of all human beings as individuals) are centered in the principle of justice (Self et al., 1992). However, many disagreed with this concept.

Carol Gilligan (1982) was perhaps the most vocal researcher who argued that moral development is based on the commitment of care for others, not on justice. Gilligan had been a research assistant for Kohlberg and had worked with him on many studies. Because Kohlberg initially based his theory by primarily studying males, Gilligan maintained that his research was gender biased. Her research claims became very popular perhaps because of the timing of her research results, when women's studies were gaining strength in the research area. There are not many educational psychology or lifespan textbooks that do not include her claim when discussing moral development and Kohlberg's theory. Her assertion that there is a difference between males and females using Kohlberg's model because of the bias was unsubstantiated as hundreds of subsequent studies revealed that there were no significant differences between males and females on moral reasoning (Rest, 1994). Currently, most psychologists dispute Gilligan's empirical claim of gender bias in Kohlberg's theory. Many studies have found that both genders use care and justice dimensions in their moral reasoning. In addition, the results from four different studies suggest that females scored significantly higher than males in moral reasoning (see Latif & Berger, 1997; Self & Olivarez, 1993; Self, Safford, & Shelton, 1988; Self, Olivarez, & Baldwin, 1998). In addition, there have been serious criticisms of Gilligan's research methodology. Her greatest critic has been Christina Sommers (2001) who maintains that Gilligan failed to produce the data for her research and instead used anecdotal evidence that has been impossible to replicate.

Kohlberg also maintained that, as for all stage theories, his theory is the same in all cultures. Critics thought differently. While different cultures hold different belief systems, his stage theory is not about beliefs, it's about moral reasoning (Kohlberg & Gilligan, 1971). Moral reasoning is based upon the cognitive component, which matures regardless of cultural influences. Thus, according to Kohlberg, cognitive development is shaped by thought, not necessarily by culture. To examine this further, Kohlberg expanded his research to other countries (e.g., India, Kenya, Mexico, and Israel) where he and his researchers interviewed children and adults. These studies supported his stage theory order (Gibbs, Basinger, Grime, & Snarey, 2007). Yet, in the United States most individuals living in an urban environment reach stage 4, while in some underdeveloped countries where many people live primarily in small villages, attaining stage 4 is very infrequent and stage 5 is nonexistent (Gibbs et al., 2007). However, Cortese (1989) found no substantive ethnic or gender differences in 70 British, Mexican American, Black American, and White American men and women who were given Kohlberg's Moral Judgment Interview.

Another criticism of Kohlberg's theory has to do with the invariant sequencing (no skipping stages, no going backwards). Initially Kohlberg's research was based on cross-sectional studies where the data supported the stage sequencing. However, for those unfamiliar with different methods of research, cross-sectional studies are problematic in that generalizations about changes due to aging cannot be made. To determine evidence that changes occur due to aging (in this case going from one stage to the next), longitudinal studies should be conducted. Kohlberg conducted two longitudinal studies and found the results uncertain. This caused him to change his method of scoring. New longitudinal studies were conducted and the results were as expected insofar as invariant sequencing was concerned. However, the new scoring procedure indicated that very few individuals demonstrated stage 6 reasoning, and Kohlberg dropped stage 6 from his studies.

As discussed earlier, Kohlberg's theory of moral development is in the cognitive domain, which means that it addresses moral reasoning, not moral action or behavior. Kohlberg, like many researchers (Bandura, 2002; Bergman, 2002), wanted a relationship between the two. Thus far, such a connection is still uncertain, although several studies have suggested that moral reasoning may affect ethical behavior (Cummings, Dyas, Maddux, & Kochman 2001; Duckett & Ryden, 1994; Rest, 1986; Thoma, 1994). Meanwhile, there are many researchers still looking for the relationship. On the other hand, the theory has been applied to a variety of other domains.

APPLICATIONS OF THE THEORY

Despite the criticism of his theory, Kohlberg remains among the most influential of the cognitive developmental theorists (Pascarella & Terenzini, 2005). Hundreds of research articles have been published based upon his theory of moral development. Initially, the framework of these studies was in the cognitive development domain. This direction changed through time whereby researchers were interested in studying Kohlberg's theory in other areas and domains (e.g., education, business, psychology). Given the controversy and the length of time since the development of his theory, it might be assumed that interest in utilizing his theory would diminish. This is not the case.

In just the last few years, there have been multiple research studies employing Kohlberg's theory of moral development in an assortment of areas. These include, but are not limited to, the areas of higher education (Enright, Schaefer, Schafer, & Schaefer (2008); Mayhew & Engberg, 2010), education (Hooli & Shammari, 2009), faith development (Fowler, 1981), accounting (Frank, Ofobike, & Gradisher, 2010); Welton & Guffey, 2009), business (Coleman & Wilkins, 2009; Kracher & Marble; 2008; Lieber, 2008; O'Donohue & Nelson, 2009; Xu & Ziegenfuss, 2008), the environment (Karpiak & Baril, 2008), psychology (Crowson & DeBecker, 2008; Cushman & Young, 2009; Malti, Keller, Gummerum, & Buchmann, 2009; Maxwell, 2010;), and moral reasoning (Robinett, 2008).

In addition, there have been many dissertations that have utilized Kohlberg's theory. These dissertations also reflect the change in areas of study. For example, Beerman (2008) wrote her dissertation using moral development dilemmas to teach American history in postsecondary schools. Burgette's (2007) dissertation focused on determining whether there was a relationship between moral development and transformational leadership and found that there was none. Meanwhile, Heron's (2007) dissertation examined the moral development and ethical decision making of information technology (IT) professionals. He examined the factors of gender, age, career stages, education and ethics training on the moral development of IT professionals and found that none of the factors were predictors of the *P-scores* results or the level of moral development. However, he found a significant correlation between *P-scores* and age, career stage, highest education, and ethics training. Murrell's (2006) dissertation focused on examining moral development of medical students at various stages of their medical education. She found no significant differences between medical students in any of the separate graduating years, nor were there any differences based upon those who had participated in a different course of study that included more attention on ethics. In addition, she found no differences based on gender.

As seen, there have been many challenges to Kohlberg's theory including gender bias, the universality of the theory, the connection between moral judgment and action, to name a few. However, the academic conversation surrounding his theory has not harmed the reputation of Kohlberg's research, but instead has pointed to the need to refine and develop research in this domain. Consequently, his theory has had an impact on other moral theories.

IMPACT OF KOHLBERG'S THEORY AND BEYOND

NEO-KOLBERGIAN THEORIES

While there have been criticisms of Kohlberg's theory, as previously discussed, many researchers have used his theoretical framework as a foundation for their own research in the area of morality. This has created a shift in the definition of moral development from a strictly Kohlbergian cognitive development theory to that of neo-Kohlbergian theories of moral development. These theories emphasize cognition, personal construction, development and postconventional thinking. For the focus of this chapter, the main theorists to be discussed are Bandura (2002), Turiel (1983), and Rest (1979).

Albert Bandura, a Canadian psychologist, is best known for his research on social cognitive theory, an expansion of social learning theory. He suggests that, like social learning theory, moral development occurs as human beings observe each other in a social context. That is, individuals learn by watching other individuals and that the thinking process develops accordingly. He believes that learned behavior from one's environment influences development, as does the individual person's way of thinking (cognition) (Bandura, 2002). This phenomenon is classified as modeling, where individuals observe the behavior and imitate that behavior. Social cognitive theory, therefore, is based upon learning directly from the observation of models and around the process of knowledge acquisition (Bandura, 1988).

Bandura (1989) maintains that within the social cognitive theory there is greater insight into the complex concept of morality. Consequently, learning will most likely occur when there is a closer identification between the model and the observer especially if the observer has a high degree of self-efficacy. Self-efficacy is the beliefs that individuals have in their abilities, although one must note that these beliefs may not be realistic. Individuals with high self-efficacy feel a strong connection with the model (the imitated) and will more likely feel that they have the ability to achieve the imitated action. In terms of moral development, within the social cognitive domain, one's moral development is based upon the modeling of morality.

Early in Kohlberg's research there were anomalies in his theory (see previous subheading, Criticisms in the Theory). At that time, one of the members of Kohlberg's research team, Elliot Turiel (1983), disagreed that the changes to the stage descriptions were sufficient and developed a new theoretical base to understand moral development, which was called domain theory. According to domain theory, there is a distinction between a child's development of morality and social convention. The foundation of moral cognition is the consideration of the effects that actions have on the well-being of individuals. Consequently, morality is based upon the notions of fairness, harm, and welfare. On the other hand, there are social conventions that have no interpersonal consequences. That is, there are some conventions that are important only because it keeps the social group functioning efficiently. These concepts are structured by a child's understanding of social organization.

Another researcher in domain theory is Larry Nucci (2001). He has conducted much research with children and adolescents across cultures. He has found that for this group there is a set of common moral concerns for human welfare and fairness that differ from their concepts of the religious norms and conventions specific to their particular cultural and social settings. His research has formed the basis for programs in moral and character education that are now utilized in the construction of an alternative assessment of moral growth.

James Rest admired the work of Kohlberg (Rest, 1988; Rest, Thoma & Edwards, 1997) and used Kohlberg's theory to guide his research. As noted earlier, his research led to the development of the DIT. Ultimately, he broke from his mentor, engaging in his own research on morality (Rest, Narvaez, Thoma, et al., 1999). Rest (1986) proposed an initial question for analyzing an individual's moral development: When a person is behaving morally, what must we suppose has happened psychologically to produce that behavior?

By researching this question, Rest (1984) found that the answer could be explained in his *Four Component Model of Moral Development*, whereby a moral agent must perform four psychological processes. The first component is that the moral agent must be able to make some sort of interpretation of the particular situation in terms of what actions are possible, who (including oneself) would be affected by each course of action, and how the interested parties would regard such efforts on their welfare. For the second component, the moral agent also must be able to make a judgment about which course of action is morally right, thus labeling one possible line of action as to what a person ought to do in that situation. The third component requires that the moral agent must give priority to moral values above other personal values such that a decision is made to intend to do what is morally right. The fourth and final component is that the moral agent must have sufficient perseverance, ego strength, and implementation skills to be able to follow through on his/her intention to behave morally, to withstand fatigue and flagging will, and to overcome obstacles.

Typically, morality researchers are divided amongst moral thought, moral emotion, and moral behavior. Rest (1984) maintained that these dimensions interact with his four-component model. He also projected adequate functioning in the four components as necessary for moral behavior and that his four components were interactive, not linear.

Future Areas of Interest

Kohlberg is still a major influence in moral development in terms of the relationship between moral development and other research areas. For example one of the recent growing areas of research is in empathy. Hoffman (2010) has tied moral development and empathy research in terms of implications for justice and caring. Contrary to Piaget's and Kohlberg's moral development theories whereby babies and infants are considered premoral, Gopnik (2010) has conducted a considerable amount of research on pre-Kindergarten children and has found them to be empathic even at these early years.

Gibbs (2009) has continued research in moral development by utilizing Kohlberg's and Hoffman's works in a different perspective. He utilizes the new research in evolutionary biology, affectivity as well as motivation and empathy while at the same time looking at moral development from these different perspectives. And, as another example, the topic of education and moral development continues to be studied by Nucci and Turiel (2009) who are examining the challenges for effective moral education.

Summary

This chapter has emphasized the tremendous impact of Kohlberg's theory of moral development on psychology and education. It has included the development, application, and limitations of the theory as well as the development of major instruments that have validated and helped further the understanding of the theory. In addition, this chapter has highlighted studies as well as dissertations that have utilized the theory in a variety of domains while discussing other major theories that have emerged from Kohlberg's work.

References

Bandura, A. (1988). Organizational application of social cognitive theory. *Australian Journal of Management, 13(2)*, 275-302.

Bandura, A. (1989). Human agency in social cognitive theory. *American Psychologist, 44*, 1175-1184.

Bandura, A. (2002). Selective moral disengagement in the exercise of moral agency. *Journal of Moral Education, 31*(2), 101-119.

Bebeau, M. J. (2002). The defining issues test and the four component model: contributions to professional education. *Journal of Moral Education, 31*(3), 271-295.

Beerman, J. (2008). *The use of moral dilemmas derived from feature films to teach American history in secondary schools* (Doctoral dissertation). Retrieved from ProQuest Dissertations and Theses. (3329859).

Bergman, R. (2002). Why be moral? A conceptual model from developmental psychology, *Human Development, 45,* 104-124.

Burgette, J. E. (2007). *Transformational leadership and moral development: A study of college students as future leaders* (Doctoral dissertation). Retrieved from ProQuest Dissertations and Theses. (3293755).

Center for the Study of Ethical Development. (2004). DIT-2. Minneapolis: University of Minnesota. Retrieved from http://www.centerforthestudyofethicaldevelopment.net/DIT2.htm

Colby, A., Kohlberg, L., Gibbs, J., & Lieberman, M. (1983). A longitudinal study of moral judgment. *Monographs of the Society for Research in Child Development* (serial No. 200).

Colby, A., Kohlberg, L., Gibbs, J., Lieberman, M., Fischer, K., & Saltzstein, H. D. (1983). A longitudinal study of moral judgment. *Monographs of the Society for Research in Child Development, 48*(1/2), 1-124.

Coleman, R., & Wilkins, L. (2009). The moral development of public relations practitioners: A comparison with other professions and influences on higher quality ethical reasoning. *Journal of Public Relations Research, 21(3),* 318-340. doi:10.1080/10627260802520462

Cortese, A. J. (1989). The interpersonal approach to morality: A gender and cultural analysis. *Journal of Social Psychology, 129, 4,* 429-443.

Cummings, R., Dyas, L., Maddux, C., & Kochman, A. (2001). Principled moral reasoning and behavior of preservice teacher education students. *American Education Research Journal, 38* (1), 143-158.

Crowson, H. M. & DeBacker, T. K. (2008). Political identification and the defining issues test: Reevaluating an old hypothesis. *Journal of Social Psychology, 148,* 43-61.

Cushman, F. & Young, L. (2009). The psychology of dilemmas and the philosophy of morality. *Ethical Theory and Moral Practice, 12,* 9-24.

DIT Manual. (1990). Center for the Study of Ethical Development. University of Minnesota. (Original work published 1986)

Duckett, L. J., & Ryden, M. B. (1994). Education for ethical nursing practice. In J. Rest & D. Narvaez (Eds.), *Moral development in the professions: Psychology and applied ethics* (pp. 51-69). Hillsdale, NJ: Erlbaum.

Elm, D. R., & Weber, J. (1994). Measuring moral judgment: The moral judgment interview or the defining issues test? *Journal of Business Ethics, 13*(5), 341-355.

Enright, M. S., Schaefer, L. V., Schafer, P. S., & Schaefer, K. A. (2008). Building a just adolescent community. *Montessori Life, 20,* 37-42.

Frank, G., Ofobike, E., & Gradisher, S. (2010). Teaching business ethics: A quandary for accounting educators. *Journal of Education for Business, 85,* 132-138.

Fowler, J. W. (1981). *Stages of faith.* New York, NY: Harper and Row.

Gibbs, J. C. (2009) *Moral development and reality: Beyond the theories of Kohlberg and Hoffman, Second Edition.* New York, NY: Pearson.

Gibbs, J. C., Basinger, K. S., Grime, R. L., & Snarey, J. R. (2007). Moral judgment development across cultures: Revisiting Kohlberg's universality claims. *Developmental Review, 27,* 443-500.

Gilligan, C. (1982). *In a different voice.* Cambridge, MA: Harvard University Press.

Gopnik, A. (2010, Feb. 24). 'Empathic civilization': Amazing empathic babies. *Huffington Post.* Retrieved from http://www.huffingtonpost.com/alison-gopnik/empathic-civilization-ama_b_473961.html

Heron. W. T. (2007). *The examination of the moral development and ethical decision-making of information technology professionals* (Unpublished doctoral dissertation). Nova Southeastern University, Florida.

Hooli, A. A., & Shammari, Z. A. (2009). Teaching and learning moral values through kindergarten curriculum, *Education, 129,* 382-400.

Hoffman, M. L. (2010). *Empathy and moral development: Implications for caring and justice.* Cambridge, MA: Cambridge University Press.

Ishida, C. (2006). How do scores of DIT and MJT differ? A critical assessment of the use of alternative moral development scales in studies of business ethics. *Journal of Business Ethics, 67,* 63-74.

Karpiak, C., & Baril, G. (2008). Moral reasoning and concern for the environment. *Journal of Environmental Psychology, 28*(3), 203-208.

King, P. M., & Mayhew, M. J. (2002). Moral judgment development in higher education: Insights from the defining issues test. *Journal of Moral Education, 31(3),* 247-270.

King, P. M., & Mayhew, M. J. (2004). Theory and research on the development of moral reasoning among college students. In J. C. Smart (Ed.), *Higher education: Handbook of theory and research* (Vol. 19, pp. 375-440). The Netherlands: Kluwer.

Kohlberg, L. (1958). The development of modes of thinking and choice in the years 10 to 16 (Unpublished doctoral dissertation). University of Chicago, Chicago, IL.

Kohlberg, L. (1963). The development of children's orientation toward a moral order: I. Sequence in the development of moral thought. *Human Development, 6,* 11-33.

Kohlberg, L. (1968). Early education: A cognitive-developmental approach. *Child Development, 39,* 1013-1062.

Kohlberg, L. (1969). Stage and sequence: The cognitive-developmental approach to socialization. In D. A. Goslin (Ed.), *Handbook of socialization theory and research* (pp. 347-3480). Chicago, IL: Rand McNally.

Kohlberg, L. (1970). The child as a moral philosopher: *Readings in developmental psychology today.* Del Mar, CA: CRM Books.

Kohlberg, L. (1971a). Stages of moral development as a basis for moral education. In C. M. Beck, B. S. Crittenden, & E. V. Sullivan (Eds.), *Moral education: Interdisciplinary approaches* (pp. 23-92). Toronto, Canada: University of Toronto Press.

Kohlberg, L. (1971b). From is to ought: how to commit the naturalistic fallacy and get away with it in the study of moral development. In T. Mischel (Ed.), *Cognitive development and epistemology.* New York, NY: Academic Press.

Kohlberg, L. (1984). *Essays on moral development. Volume II. The psychology of moral development.* New York, NY: Harper & Row.

Kohlberg, L., & Gilligan, C. (1971). The adolescent as philosopher. *Daedalus, 100,* 1051-1086.

Kracher, B., & Marble, R. (2008). The significance of gender in predicting the cognitive moral development of business practitioners using the sociomoral reflection objective measure. *Journal of Business Ethics, 78,* 503-526. DOI:10.1007/s10551-007-9365-9

Latif, D. A., & Berger, B. A. (1997). Moral reasoning in pharmacy students and practitioners. *Journal of the Society of Administrative Pharmacy, 14,* 166-179.

Lieber, P. S. (2008). Moral development in public relations: Measuring duty to society in strategic communication. *Public Relations Review, 34,* 244-251.

Lind, G. (1999). *An introduction to the moral judgment test (MJT).* Konstanz, Germany: Psychology of Morality & Democracy and Education. Retrieved from http://www.uni-konstanz.de/FuF/SozWiss/fg-psy/ag-moral/pdf/Lind-1999_MJT-Introduction-E.pdf

Lind, G. (2000). *Review and appraisal of the moral judgment test (MJT).* Konstanz, Germany: Psychology of Morality & Democracy and Education. Retrieved from http://www.uni-konstanz.de/ag-moral/pdf/Lind-2000_MJT-Review-and-Appraisal.pdf

Magun-Jackson, S. (2004). A psychological model that integrates ethics in engineering education. *Science and Engineering Ethics, 10,* 219-224.

Malti, T., Keller, M., Gummerum, M., & Buchmann, M. (2009). Children's moral motivation, sympathy and prosocial behavior. *Child Development, 80,* 442-460.

Maxwell, B. (2010) Does ethical theory have a place in post-Kohlbergian moral psychology? *Educational Theory, 60,* 167-88.

Mayhew, M. J. & Engberg, M. E. (2010). Diversity and moral reasoning: How negative diverse peer interactions affect the development of moral reasoning in undergraduate students, *Journal of Higher Education, 81,* 459-488.

Murrell, V. (2005). *Moral judgment in medical students* (Doctoral dissertation). Retrieved from ProQuest Dissertations and Theses. (3199487).

Nucci, L. (1989). Challenging conventional wisdom about morality: The domain approach to Values education. In L. Nucci (Ed.), *Moral development and character education: A dialogue* (pp. 183-203). Berkley, CA: McCutchan.

Nucci, L. (2001). *Education in the moral domain.* Cambridge England: Cambridge University Press.

Nucci, L., & Turiel, E. (2009). Capturing the complexity of moral development and education. *Mind, Brain and Education, 3(3),* 151-159.

O'Donohue, W., & Nelson, L. (2009). The role of ethical values in expanded psychological contract. *Journal of Business Ethics, 90,* 251-263.

Pascarella, E. T., & Terenzini, P. T. (2005). *How college affects students: A third decade of research* (Vol. 2). San Franscisco, CA: Jossey-Bass.

Piaget, J. (1932). *The moral judgment of the child.* London, England: Routledge and Kegan Paul.

Piaget, J., & Inhelder, B. (1969). *The psychology of the child* (H. Weaver, Trans.) New York, NY: Basic Books. (Original work published 1966)

Rest, J. R. (1973). The hierarchical nature of moral judgment: The study of patterns of preference and comprehension of the moral judgment of others. *Journal of Personality, 41,* 86-109.

Rest, J. R. (1979). *Development in judging moral issues.* Minneapolis, MN: University of Minnesota Press.

Rest, J.R. (1984). The major components of morality. In W. M. Kurtines & J. L. Gewirts (Eds.), *Morality, moral behavior, and moral development.* New York, NY: Wiley.

Rest, J. R. (1986). *Moral development: Advances in research and theory.* New York, NY: Praeger.

Rest, J. R. (1988). The legacy of Lawrence Kohlberg. *Counseling and Values, 32,* 156-162.

Rest, J. R. (1990). *DIT manual: Manual for the defining issues test* (3rd ed.). Minneapolis, MN: University of Minnesota.

Rest, J. R. (1994). Background theory and research. In D. Narvaez & J. R. Rest (Eds.), *Moral development in the professions: Psychology and applied ethics.* Hillsdale, NJ: Erlbaum.

Rest, J. R., Narvaez, D., Bebeau, M. J., & Thoma, S. J. (1999). A neo-Kohlbergian approach: The DIT and schema theory. *Educational Psychology Review, 11(4),* 291-324.

Rest, J. R., Narvaez, D., Thoma, S. J., & Bebeau, M. J. (1999). DIT2: Devising and testing a revised instrument of moral judgment. *Journal of Educational Psychology, 91(4),* 644-659.

Rest, J. R., Narvaez, D., Thoma, S. J., & Bebeau, M. J. (2000). A neo-Kohlbergian approach to morality research. *Journal of Moral Education, 29*(4), 381-395.

Rest, J., Thoma, S., & Edwards, L. (1997). Designing and validating a measure of moral judgment: stage preference and stage consistency approaches. *Journal of Educational Psychology, 89*(1), 5-28.

Rest, J., Thoma, S. J., Narvaez, D., & Bebeau, M. J. (1997). Alchemy and beyond: Indexing the defining issues test. *Journal of Educational Psychology, 89(3),* 489-507.

Rest, J., Turiel, E., & Kohlberg, L. (1969). Relations between level of moral judgments and preference and comprehension of the moral judgment of others. *Journal of Personality, 37,* 225-252.

Robinett, T. L. (2008). A comparison of moral reasoning stages using a model of hierarchical complexity. *World Futures, 64,* 468-480.

Schlaefli, A., Rest, J. R., & Thoma, S. J. (1985). Does moral education improve moral judgment? a meta-analysis of intervention studies using the defining issues test. *Review of Educational Research, 55*(3), 319-352.

Self, D. J., & Olivarez, M. (1993). The influence of gender on conflicts of interest in the allocation of limited critical care resources: Justice versus care. *Journal of Critical Care, 8,* 64-74.

Self, D. J., Baldwin, D.C., Jr., & Wolinsky, F. D. (1992). Evaluation of teaching medical ethics by assessment of moral reasoning. *Medical Education, 26,* 178-184.

Self, D. J., Olivarez, M., & Baldwin, D. C. (1998). Clarifying the relationship of medical education and moral development. *Academic Medicine, 73,* 517-520.

Self, D. J., Safford, S. K., & Shelton, G. C. (1988). Comparison of the general moral reasoning of small animal veterinarians vs. large animal veterinarians. *Journal of Veterinary Medical Education, 19,* 1509-1512.

Sommers, C. H. (2001). *The war against boys: How misguided feminism is harming our young men.* New York, NY: Simon & Schuster.

Thoma, S. J. (1994). Moral judgments and moral action. In J. Rest & D. Narvaez (Eds.), *Moral development in the professions.* Hillsdale, NJ: Erlbaum .

Turiel, E. (1983). *The development of social knowledge: Morality and convention.* New York, NY: Cambridge University Press.

Welton, R., & Guffey, D. (2009). Transitory or persistent? The effects of classroom ethics interventions: A longitudinal study. *Accounting Education, 18*(3), 273-289. doi:10.1080/09639280802217990.

Xu, Y., & Ziegenfuss, D. E. (2008). Reward systems, moral reasoning, and internal auditors' reporting wrongdoing. *Journal of Business Psychology, 22,* 323-331. doi:10.1007/s10869-008-9072-2

Author Contact Information: Susan Magun-Jackson, Phd, Department of Counseling, Educational Psychology and Research, University of Memphis, Memphis, TN 38152. Phone: 901-678-4859.

CHAPTER 49

Social Cognitive Theory and Practice of Moral Development in Educational Settings

Kelly Rizzo and Sandra Bosacki
Brock University

The current landscape of developmental moral and social cognitive theory is complex and contradictory. Over the past 10 years, in particular, a disconnect between thought and action, the ability of young children to reason at a moral level, and the instability of stages has troubled moral development theories in general and structural cognitive theories specifically. The following chapter will outline these issues within the framework of a current developmental social cognitive theory, focusing on both theoretical and methodological issues. This chapter will provide an overview of the social cognitive theory known as domain theory, including the theory's development, its generalizability, characteristics which make it unique, and evidence to support it. The chapter will discuss the educational implications of a developmentally and culturally appropriate social cognitive and moral theory. Finally, this chapter will make recommendations for its application in practice within the context of character education delivered in school environments. Such applications will be discussed with an emphasis on the promotion of healthy adult-child and child-child relationships as a foundation for sociomoral learning at various stages of development.

Social cognitive theory known as domain theory began in an effort to address issues identified in the seminal work of Lawrence Kohlberg (Nucci & Turiel, 2009) including disconnect between thought and action (Colby & Damon, 1992) and the apparent ability of younger children to reason morally (Carpendale & Krebs, 1992). In contrast to structural cognitive stage theory that claims children develop in a unilateral direction, domain theory argues for the existence of three distinct domains: moral universal, social convention, and personal. Based on domain theory capacity in each of these three domains exist simultaneously. Children then do not reason at a level of social convention or rules and then mature to have that reasoning ability replaced with moral based thinking, as was claimed in the earlier work of Kohlberg (1968, 1973, 1981) and Piaget (1965).

The ability to coordinate and or subordinate domains may be related to the experiences and maturity of the child (Nucci, 2006; Lapsley, 2006; Turiel, 1983). Failure to act in ways consistent with moral reasoning may in fact be due to an inability to prioritize conflicting domains present in the situation rather than failure to have reached a postconventional level of reasoning (Nucci, 2006). For example, a child in junior elementary grades may determine that it is his prerogative who he befriends (a personal matter), and as such chooses to intentionally exclude a specific student from his social network physically and or virtually (i.e., with Internet or texting). To this end he tells others in that circle he does not think they should be friends with this individual (moral matter, causing harm to another) because he thinks the individual is not the right kind of person for their group. It is not, however,

The Handbook of Educational Theories, pp. 595–606

his intent to cause harm, but rather to exercise his personal preferences to choose with whom to be friends.

Based on domain theory, children are assumed to construct their morality, rather than acquire it; experiences of children are directly related to their abilities to coordinate and or subordinate simultaneously occurring domains (Nucci, 2008). Ideally, an individual learns to shift the weight given to each of the three domains to reflect the circumstances of the situation, including differences in cultural norms (Turiel, Hildebrandt, & Wainryb, 1991). Relationships between children and adults form the basis for this sociomoral learning and are therefore of great significance in furthering children's abilities to manage the complexities they experience.

Domain Theory

Theory Development and Description

Social domain theory began as a study into apparent directionality difficulties with Kohlberg's (1968, 1973) stage theory. Kohlberg discovered some older adolescents and young adults reverting back to earlier preconventional stages of reasoning which was cause for some concern to the validity of his research. There was concern as this progression in reverse is contradictory to principles of structural stage theory (Nucci, 2008) which claims that once established the stages are stable and do not allow for regression. In 1974, Turiel examined the reasoning exercised by these young adults and determined that interactions between social conventions (rules governing a group) and moral matters (concepts of fairness and human welfare), may account for the apparent regression found by Kohlberg (1968, 1973). Perhaps even more importantly, Turiel found that children, regardless of age, judged moral transgressions differently from social convention transgressions. Where social transgressions were judged based on the presence or absence of a rule to govern such behavior (i.e., forms of address, running in school halls), moral transgressions (i.e., hitting a peer without provocation), were judged on the impact these decisions had upon the welfare of others (Nucci, 2008). This discovery is a contradiction to both Piaget 's (1965) and Kohlberg's (1968, 1973, 1984) claims that young children were not capable of moral reasoning until more advanced levels of cognition were constructed.

Piaget (1965) argued that while children may start their sociomoral understanding as accepting the teachings (rules) of adults they also engage in relationships with others, specifically peers, and it is through a growing understanding of reciprocity facilitated by these relationships that children learn first hand about what is just, or fair. While they may appreciate that rules govern certain things (i.e., a game), it is through their experiences playing the game that they come to appreciate the idiosyncratic nature of play and the need to at times, be flexible, and cooperate to make the game fit the needs of the players. This flexibility is valued when choosing who will play the next time. In this way they develop cooperative spirits and their understanding of reciprocal relations separate from the rules imposed by authority figures (Lapsley, 2006). Relationships between peers and teachers can support student academic achievement (Crosnoe, Johnson, & Elder, 2004), their sense of belonging (Furrer, & Skinner, 2003), and improve peer relations (Hughes, Cavell, & Willson, 2001). It will also be argued here, that relationships are key to sociomoral development.

The third domain to be distinguished in social domain theory is that of personal preference and is known as the personal domain. According to Nucci (2008) this element is critical to the establishment of autonomy and individual identity, as well, it is necessary to maintain boundaries between self and others. Parents typically communicate items for personal choice with children from very young ages, i.e., "What would you like to wear today?" as a means for developing an early sense of autonomy and decision making ability. Parents will typically negotiate these types of items with children where such latitude is not usually exercised when the matter is a convention or moral issue (Nucci, 2008). This development of autonomy is of significance as a means for children to develop their sense of self and identity as separate from rules.

Lagatutta, Nucci, and Bosacki (2010) examined the perception of parental regulation of activities for children which were believed to be essential to their identity. This research found children as young as 4 years of age were able to distinguish between rules which govern moral and personal domains, and considered the relevance of the rule to the individual's identity when deciding whether the rule could or should be disobeyed. Within schools, this domain may present challenges where there is perceived overlap with social conventions. This is particularly applicable to periods of adolescence when students are required to follow a rule (social convention) which they see as infringing upon their personal freedoms or rules (i.e., a dress code), however, based on Lagattuta and colleagues' (2010) research, this thinking and its potential challenges cannot be discounted as a potential reality for children much younger as well.

Patterns of Development Within Domain Theory

Within each of the three domains there is development which follows a characteristic pattern. Changes to the moral domain are concerned with underlying conceptions of human welfare and principles of justice, or what is considered fair (Damon, 1977; Nucci & Turiel, 2009). Changes to the social convention realm are based on understanding of social systems and organization (Turiel, 1983) and with a greater sense of self identity for the personal domain (Nucci, 1996). With maturation and experience children learn to coordinate each of the elements in increasingly complex situations. In complex multi domain situations the child is required to subordinate or coordinate the domains (moral, social convention and personal). For example, is a child able to coordinate their own interests with those of another, when faced with an issue containing both moral principles of justice, and social convention? The coordination of these two domains proves a challenge for younger children who may not yet have the conceptual understanding that what is just or fair forms the basis for a reciprocal relationship (Nucci, 2008). Damon (1977) argues this challenge to coordination is particularly true when there are multiple people whose needs require consideration. This understanding of reciprocity is later replaced with a more advanced understanding of the principles of equity and equality (Damon, 1977) such that a child is able to reason that what is fair is not necessarily the same for everyone. An example of which could be an assessment situation in a classroom, where certain students, to be successful, require a modified or different form of assessment than is given to other students, or recognition that someone who is visually impaired is not subject to the same rules regarding bringing dogs into a supermarket.

Reasoning about human welfare presents the greatest challenges, particularly where harm may be indirect, as it proves to be highly multifarious following a more U shaped pattern than understanding of justice (what is considered fair). This pattern means that where an indirect form of harm is concerned for the younger child (i.e., age 7 or 8) and the older adolescent (i.e., age 16 or 17) the course of action is clear. In a situation where money has been dropped for example and the owner is unaware, such young people are clear in their reasoning about the need to return the money, where a 13-year-old is not as clear in his reasoning (Nucci, 2008). The exception to this based on Nucci and Turiel (2007) occurs when the individual who has unknowingly dropped the money is known to be handicapped in some way. In these instances all the participants were as likely to return the money.

Understanding of the role/purpose of conventions, relative to the functioning of an organization or group, form the basis for change in levels of social convention reasoning in children (Turiel, 1983). Advancement of social convention understandings can be identified at one of seven different levels (Turiel, 1983). For example, typically a 10-year- old will describe the reason for rules in school as necessary to maintain order and that those responsible for everyone's safety generally make up the rules to be followed (Nucci, 2008). This perspective shifts in adolescence to one of arbitrariness; a sense that rules are essentially representative of what persons in positions of authority, such as teachers or parents desire (Nucci, 2008). Finally the older adolescent and young adult transitions into a more global or holistic perspective recognizing that such conventions of practice are important to social system structure (Nucci, 2008).

According to Gershkoff and Thelen, (2004) such U shaped patterns as those identified in both the moral and social convention domains are typical of other developmental areas including language, cognition, and physical ability, and signify growing competence with more complex matters. Given the complexity of today's world, with growing access to technological advances which facilitate easy and often nearly instant communication around the world, the global interrelatedness of economies and the increasing multicultural nature of communities, it is imperative our youth be provided with opportunities within the context of their schooling to develop into sociomorally caring and competent responsible beings, able to think critically and respond effectively to the multifaceted issues they will encounter.

From the perspective of social cognitive domain theorists the understanding of moral development is not limited to moral reasoning alone (Turiel, 2008), but rather needs to incorporate simultaneous, not consecutive relation with social convention and personal preferences (Nucci, 2001). This approach also assists in the appreciation of the difficulties with the dilemmas used by Kohlberg (1981) and the apparent regression of adolescents to earlier stages of reasoning which troubled Kohlberg's structural stage theory of moral development. Adolescents in these studies appeared to regress to an earlier stage of reasoning (Nucci, 2008) as they were perhaps consolidating their ability to coordinate competing domains. The dilemmas used by Kohlberg were also structured so as to pit issues of justice or welfare against social standards. This finding, in conjunction with social domain theory has implications for pedagogical practices in general, and character education practices specifically. For example, where the distinction is made between social convention and morality in educator modeling of problem solving and expectations of students, understanding that situations may incorporate social convention and or moral principles among students may be reinforced.

According to Wainryb (2006), children are not passive recipients of their socialization but actively process and reflect upon their experiences to arrive at their understanding of what is the right course of action. Through guided practice with adults and peers, using these experiences, and school curriculum content as a basis, children come to know how to first distinguish matters of convention and personal preference from moral matters, and can then be guided as to how to prioritize their relative importance. Educators help to create the context for these experiences in the establishment of classroom and school culture which is determined in part by the nature of the relationships within.

THEORETICAL IMPLICATIONS

Thornberg (2010) supports the claim that children judge moral situations differently than matters of convention or personal preference, based on the impact of these choices on others. Thornberg extends this understanding with research exploring levels of distinction within matters of convention among school age children. Thornberg (2010) categorizes school rules into five different categories (relational rules, structuring rules, protecting rules, personal rules, and etiquette rules). In many instances, the five different categories of rules were found to overlap. For example, a rule about running in the halls or classroom may be viewed as both a structuring—maintaining order, as well as a protecting rule—preventing harm from falls or collisions with others. To correlate these rules with social domain theory, rules pertaining to relational matters align more with the moral domain, while structuring and etiquette rules would relate more closely to the social convention domain.

Thornberg's (2010) study suggests need for further refinement of the social convention domain. Findings indicate that children further differentiate the purpose of social convention type rules (i.e., to provide structure, or serve as etiquette expectation within the group) when judging the seriousness of violations to these rules. Since they reasoned that rules intended to provide structure, when broken, could disturb the learning of others, these transgressions were judged more harshly than those governing etiquette, which were viewed as more arbitrary (Thornberg, 2010). When it comes to matters pertaining to personal rules, children are generally less accepting of adult limits unless the behavior is something which could cause harm to themselves, in which case they see adult regulation as necessary (Smetana & Bitz, 1996). Recommendations from this research for educators may include a need to justify the need for a convention type rule to help children make sense of it, and to recognize that some rules may be seen as arbitrary because they do not affect anyone else directly (i.e., wearing a hat indoors). The extent to which children see that justification as trustworthy and reasonable will likely influence their level of compliance with established rules of convention. Such research serves to illustrate the complexity of the experiences of children and the level of reasoning present among children navigating their environment.

GENERALIZABILITY OF DOMAIN THEORY

Domain theory then, recognizes three realms within which the individual functions and develops: (a) moral universal, based on principles of justice, welfare and rights; (b) social convention, and (c) personal choice, although not all three may be developed or applied simultaneously. Social convention serves the purpose of coordinating interactions within a social system. They are established by, and embedded within the social system they serve. According to Nucci (1997) strong evidence supports the distinction made between matters of morality and those of convention. This distinction has been found to hold true outside North American countries in numerous studies (Turiel, 1998; Nucci, 2001) and regardless of religious affiliation (Nucci, 1985; Nucci & Turiel, 1993). For example, when children and adolescents of various faiths were questioned about the permissibility of a moral act such as stealing or unprovoked harm to another, over 80% maintained that even if there were no religious ruling (i.e., a rule about it in the holy book for the particular faith) on the act, it would still be wrong. This conclusion did not apply for social convention matters, such as working on the Sabbath or allowing priests to marry. With respect to social convention practices the majority of children and adolescents felt they would be acceptable if there were no rule in their faith to say otherwise. Based on domain theory framework, familiarity with the conventions of the society or the doctrine of a faith is not a precursor to morality. Rather, moral understanding coexists with understanding and application of social conventions.

Morality and social convention exist simultaneously within the individual, and outside the individual. That is, the individual is subject to and understands the social conventions of the society to which they belong, but also responds to these conventions on a personal or individual basis, some of which may incorporate or interfere with their sense of morality. In this way, an overlap of domains is established and potential conflict created. Whether an individual is able to reconcile any conflict between what is viewed as a personal preference, or a convention of society with their moral judgment of what is fair or just, helps to explain inconsistencies in actions (Nucci, 1997). Generally, situations where moral understanding and social convention overlap positively, at least within western society, are viewed as the mannerly or respectful course of action and are not usually controversial. Perhaps, it is not a coincidence then; that this is the aspect of development that many character education programs purport to serve.

Interpretation of a matter as belonging to the social convention or personal domains varies with maturational development. During early adolescence, as youth are expanding their decision making in what they consider personal matters (such as the right to wear whatever they want to school as a sign of individuality), marks a time for conventions, such as dress codes, to be challenged. By midadolescence youth are more apt to recognize convention as a necessary means for providing structure in social situations whether they are within the context of the school/classroom environment or greater society (Nucci, 2009). Moral reasoning follows a similar pattern of development based on principles of human welfare and justice. In early childhood, reasoning is based on concrete understandings of harm, for example, it is wrong to hit another because you would hurt them (Smetana, 1981). This reasoning later evolves to understandings of reciprocity and equality and finally, in later adolescence, to an ability to recognize ambiguity and complexity of moral circumstances (Nucci, 2009). Each of these patterns of development has implications for classroom/school practices as well as the nature of relations within that environment, and would suggest that singular approaches are not suitable. Possible approaches, based on this theoretical understanding and school environment experience as both teacher and administrator, will be explored in the following section.

Domain Theory in Practice

Youth around the world today are growing up in a unique time with respect to the level of technology and accessibility of information. Twenty-first century realities, or as they are popularly known—twenty-first century fluencies (see http://www.fluency21.com/fluencies.cfm) require both knowledge and competence, an ability to think critically in a multi media world, and thus call for different educational measures. Youth culture today differs from past in significant ways with respect to methods and speed of communication, access to vast amounts of information, levels of diversity in communities, and growing concern about the effective management of resources, to name just a few. Youth today, who have been raised with cellular telephones and social networks on the Internet expect near constant electronic communication with others based on their experiences growing up. Through technological advances they have been exposed to resources which allow access to more information than ever before in history. Local and global communities are growing in diversity and call for greater recognition and understanding of ethical issues including equity, fairness, compassion, and social justice for a peaceful coexistence. Economies around the world are closely linked and impacted by collapse, something which unarguably impacts human welfare, and appears through the media to have been brought on by excessive greed and immoral (or at the very least irresponsible) management of resources. What some might call moral decay, others recognize as a period of significant rapid change for which members of society may not be fully prepared or comfortable to embrace. Given these significant differences in the societal collective consciousness, there is perhaps greater need than ever before to promote sociomoral competence among today's youth. For this task schools are called upon to act. The educational measures called for apply not only to the content, or material covered in school curricula but also to the context, or the school culture that is developed and how that culture is maintained when transgressions occur.

Culture can been described as, "historical constructs created and sustained in the context of collaborations, disagreements, power clashes, and contested meanings among individuals," (Wainryb, 2006, p. 211) and is inclusive of a diverse, rather than homogeneous, harmonious group. Both anthropologists and developmental psychologists have argued that within a culture there is need of both autonomy and interdependence (Killen & Wainryb, 2000). Within the context of school, *culture* has been defined as, the underlying values and ideology (Anderson, 1982; Creemers & Reezigt, 1999) and *climate*, the practices and lived experiences of these values (Creemers & Reezigt). Levels of autonomy and interdependence in this sense are realized through the relationships between adults and children, and peer groups which form the core of a school culture. The social relationships that students engage in on a daily basis (including relationships with peers, teachers, administrators and parents) are vital to the process for character development (McClellan, 1999). Accordingly, classroom practices; classroom management strategies as well as instructional strategies and content, should serve to reinforce positive relationships while allowing for autonomous growth. The establishment of trust embodied in positive relationships is critical to developing positive, supportive and safe learning environments for all. Where school culture and climate are positive, members of the learning community should feel a sense of belonging and safety which in turn may reinforce commitment to that community and individual feelings of worth (Wu, Hughes, Kwok, 2010).

Educational Implications

Character education, an umbrella term to describe school based activities intended to develop character of youth, can vary greatly in terms of understanding of purpose and accomplishment (Berkowitz & Bier, 2004). Character, is the everyday language used to describe the moral worthiness of individuals and their actions.

That is, a person of "good" character is usually cognizant of the moral implications of their actions and chooses to act in accordance with what is moral (Nucci, 2001). Hunter (2000) defines character as the amalgamation of three properties: (a) *moral discipline*, which refers to an ability to inhibit and direct individual needs and wants within the greater moral order; (b) *moral attachment*, is the commitment one feels to a community including its moral principles and; (c) *moral autonomy*, which refers to ethical decision making of individuals. Character education, based on social cognitive domain theory incorporates not only the moral aspects (moral domain) of one's character, but also their inter- (social domain) and intra- (personal domain) personal development.

The approach taken in the construction and delivery of character education varies, and is linked directly to how morality is defined, and developed. Some traditional character education proponents (see Bennett 1996; 1998; Ryan, 1989 for examples) see morality as residing outside the individual, such that morality is viewed as the transmission or acquisition of the correct values gleaned from moral models of society (people in positions of authority including parents and teachers). Such a traditional approach requires teachers to maintain power in their relationships with students and to establish themselves as "experts" who teach the less educated in matters of curricula, rules of society and moral values. Such lessons tend to take the form of instruction on rules to be followed by the passive learner.

Social cognitive domain theory provides a framework for a more contemporary approach which is aligned with current constructivist educational pedagogical practices and recognizes the differences between matters of convention which *can* be learned through application and practice with rules, moral principles, which are not governed by rules, and personal preferences, which expand with maturation (Nucci, 2009). It is also more readily able to handle both diverse and complex circumstances and encourages a questioning of the status quo (Nucci, 2006) rather than a transmission of predetermined values or virtues. Recognition of these differences calls for different practices; practices which also need to differ based on the maturation of the students. In all applications the child is required to be an active participant in the construction of his knowledge, and not a passive receptor to be filled with the correct interpretations of his world. Such understandings, it will be argued here, are reinforced with dynamic relationships between and among peers and their teachers.

In classrooms where pedagogy is based on social cognitive domain theory, teachers also work to establish and maintain relationships with and between students. These relationships form the foundation for classroom culture to be established. This claim is based on the premise that through these interactions youth construct their understanding and skill in applying sociomoral decision making (Piaget, 1932/1965). It is also through continual and qualitatively different interactions with peers and adults that students develop their understanding of the differences between social, moral and personal domains (Horn, Daddis, & Killen, 2008) including recognition of the need for social conventions to help maintain order and positive learning environments for all and an appreciation for matters which are personal in nature. Skills in coordinating and or subordinating each of these domains in increasingly complex situations evolve with maturation and experience; experience which is influenced by the nature of classroom practices employed by the teacher to establish culture, maintain order, and deal with transgressions. As such, the practices of teachers of primary grade levels (Kindergarten to Grade 3) will differ somewhat from teachers of junior (Grades 4 to 6) and more so again from intermediate grade levels (Grades 7 to 9) as moral, social convention and personal domain situations occur, whether through curriculum content or as part of the lived experience in the classroom, and levels of student autonomy advance.

At the primary stage of development (approximately 4 to 9 years of age), from school entry to grade three, children tend to look to adults for guidance and reassurance of safety as they enter a new world, the classroom (Reavis, Keane, Calkins, 2010). The relationship that is formed between child and teacher is critical in establishing trust and a social emotional climate suited to early risk taking in learning and may have both immediate and longer term implications for the child's social adjustment (Reavis, Keane, Calkins, 2010). However, a relationship which reinforces that the adult (parent/teacher) has all the control and the child is powerless has been shown to impact the likelihood of peer victimization (Reavis, Keane, Calkins, 2010) and should be avoided. The strategies employed in the primary classroom to advance sociomoral reasoning, as well as deliver content material will tend to be very concrete, are taught directly to match developmental stages of its occupants, and should serve to reinforce positive peer and adult relations. Tyson (2000) found that positive and nurturing type relationships can encourage self regulatory skills in children. The level of autonomy at this stage, while still present, will be lower than at any other of the two general educational stages discussed here.

Even though children at the primary stage of development are not fully cognizant of the need for social convention to maintain order within the class/society, teachers can begin to instill this appreciation by involving children in the construction of routines and rules to govern the class (Watson, 2003). In this way, children begin to develop a sense of ownership and responsibility to the group. Based on the findings from Thornberg (2010), justifying the need for such rules so that children can make sense of them, may also assist in their development of understanding and levels of responsiveness. Children are learning early on, what is expected to belong to a group through their experiences in relationships involving individuals other than members of family. Teacher-student relations may be considered an extension of parent-child relations, in such dyads, the need for rules to govern social interactions may be somewhat limited. As children join larger groups (i.e., classrooms), their circle of peers is expanded and as such the need for social conventions to maintain order increase.

The need to identify rules which govern the operation of such groupings as social conventions, rather than moral imperatives to ensure domain concordant understanding is framed early on in children (Nucci & Weber, 1991) and has longer term implications. Nucci and Weber (1991) explored domain concordant instruction in the context of grade eight history and English classes. In this study students were assigned to one of three groups, the first studied all historical events as conventions, the second treated the facts as moral issues, and finally the third group matched discussion to the nature of the fact being discussed and they were taught how to integrate issues of morality with normative conventions. Findings indicated that instruction does impact student learning. Students who received instruction in only one of the domains developed skills only in that domain. Only students who received domain appropriate instruction were able to coordinate both domains when situations of domain mixing arose. Based on this finding, teachers must be able to identify (in lesson material as well as everyday situations) moral, social convention and personal choice examples and use developmentally appropriate methods of instruction for children to begin to recognize the differences between these domains, and most importantly develop their ability to reason for themselves.

Transgressions, or wrongdoings, involving social convention at the primary school age stage of development may result more out of a lack of understanding of the need for the rule than desire to challenge it. Such an example is when children are required to line up for school entry, and someone cuts into the front of the line. The teacher is often looked toward by the child to resolve the conflict for the child. The teacher is also required to maintain a safe learning environment. This is imperative to the child-adult relationship, an extension of the parent-child relationship, at this time which has a great emphasis on safety and nurturing. Children at this stage are developmentally equipped to view situations in terms of fairness and are in the early phases of being able to take the perspective of another (Piaget, 1932/1965). Teachers can assist with this development by modeling mediation, including the active listening necessary to hear the all viewpoints rather than simply providing a solution for the child. This practice can be approached a number of ways, including dramatic representations, such as role play, as well as through use of literature. According to Nucci (2009) the first step in this process is helping children identify the emotions and motivators of others, either with characters in stories or lived experiences, and to provide alternative viewpoints than the eye for an eye attitude typical at this stage. Such an alternate viewpoint should emphasize the importance of the relationship between individuals and not reinforce that it is through the application of power that one gets what one desires.

Children in the junior grades (Grades 4 to 6) continue to depend on their teacher to maintain a safe (learning) environment (free from physical, social and emotional harm), although what they expect from their teacher to accomplish this has evolved based on their sociomoral understanding, their growing level of autonomy, and their changing relationship with peers and adults. In junior classrooms children tend to recognize the need of conventions to maintain order. Teachers can empower students at this educational stage by engaging them in practices to determine the conventions necessary (i.e., again establishing rules in a classroom/school). By extension, monitoring their application among younger students, (i.e., peer mediators) may help to create a greater sense of ownership and belonging (Gregory & Chapman, 2007) as members of the group. Developmentally, children from grades four to six are more skilled in perspective taking (Piaget, 1932/1965; Flavell, Miller, & Miller, 2002), more autonomous, and socially engaged. Acceptance from others becomes pronounced, as children are further defining their sense of self, relative to others; asking themselves "Where do I fit in?" Children who are excluded from activities may be viewed as unskilled either in the activity or the social skills required (i.e., cooperation). Feeling as though they do not fit in or are not part of the group will have greater implications as the risk taking in learning more complex curriculum increases (Nucci, 2009). Teachers are relied upon to maintain a culture in the classroom where children feel safe to make mistakes, without being excluded from the group, and children are required to accept responsibility for their learning (Gregory & Chapman, 2007).

Through use of school curriculum and lived experiences of the classroom, teachers can again, reinforce perspective taking, advance understanding of justice as being what is fair (Nucci, 2009) and maintain a positive supportive culture in the classroom. According to McTighe (1990), teachers can ensure their classes have a welcoming culture by demonstrating in their actions, they accept diversity, originality and different perspectives and dealing with transgressions in conduct promptly. This will require teachers to be flexible in their instructional strategies, meeting the learner where they are, and differentiating practices for students to experience success. As well, providing opportunity where it is expected that students "try on" the perspective of others, connecting these perspectives to what they know, to further their understanding of what is fair and just are key to their learning. Practices including, small group instruction (or guided practice), student led conferences, and literature circles would all serve to reinforce the need for positive, supportive relationships with others, as each scenario requires a cooperative spirit, something which Narvarez (2006) argues is fundamental to advancing sociomoral development within the context of schools.

While the dependency on adults for basic necessities of life (Maslow, 1968) may be somewhat diminished at the junior school age, peer relations and sense of belonging become more pronounced (McLaughlin & Clarke, 2010) and as such peer judgment can influence positively or negatively, the reasoning of these students. Recent work by, Hanley and Abell (2002) has argued that more important than relationship utility (its usefulness in meeting one's needs) is the substance of the relationship. Further, that for true self-actualization, individuals must see their connection to their environment, and the impact of their choices on both it and those with whom they share it. A literature review of the impact of the school experience on mental health conducted by McLaughlin and Clarke (2010) revealed relationships as a significant factor in the mental health of children aged 10-13. Further, their investigation indicated that early adolescent youth in the United States, when compared to their same aged peers from other countries, have negative perceptions of their learning environment, stating there are higher levels of emotional and physical problems including having a peer culture which is largely unsupportive and mean spirited. Conversely, children who have a feeling of belonging or connectedness feel cared for and have a positive sense of well-being (Resnick et al., 1997). It is thus desirable to limit the impact of negative influences through a greater number of positive experiences and relationships, appreciating the reciprocal nature of these relations.

According to Nucci (1984) students use their knowledge of social, moral and personal domains to evaluate their classroom learning experiences. Students in fifth grade, for example, evaluate teacher effectiveness on their ability to consistently address transgressions in domain specific ways. Such that teachers who consistently address moral transgressions using principles of human welfare, justice and fairness and social convention transgressions with rules to govern operations, were viewed more knowledgeable and effective than teachers who did not respond in domain concordant ways (Nucci, 1984). It is reasonable to expect that where teachers use domain concordant classroom management strategies, students will be treated fairly helping to maintain and enhance a positive trusting relationship with the teachers and among peers who come to expect certain conduct from one another, while at the same time reinforcing these understandings in students. According to McLaughlin and Clarke (2010) caring, fairness, mutual respect, trust, having a voice (engaged in making meaningful decisions), and being positive are the valued characteristics in relationships, as children transition through early adolescence.

When children reach early adolescence, ages 13-15, they are among the intermediate grades of schooling. It is at intermediate grade levels (Grades 7-9) that children are consolidating their understanding of justice and expanding their abilities to manage complex situations taking into account the needs of others. This occurs in tandem with their developing sense of self and growing need of autonomy. It is possibly these aspects of development which provide the greatest challenge in managing overlap between personal and social convention domains. In intermediate years, children view conventions as more arbitrary and at times infringing upon their personal domains (for example, a dress code). As such transgressions at this stage of maturation are more reasonably thought to be challenges to the rules, something which could be interpreted by some as a lack of respect toward authority (Nucci, 2009). Involving students more at a school level of decision making, as members of committees, providing an avenue for student voices to be heard are advisable strategies to help reinforce the need for adherence to socially accepted (conventional) practices within the school culture, while at the same time, maintaining open lines of communication and greater insight into the attitudes of adolescents by their teachers. Such committees may have responsibilities for determining needs to maintain a safe and inviting school culture (i.e., a safe schools committee), or determining projects/special events for students to engage in (i.e., a student leadership committee).

During the period of adolescence both parents and peers are particularly important sociomoral influences (Dodge et al. 2006). Teachers spend, in some cases, more time with children on a day to day basis than parents. This adult-child relationship with adolescents; again, an extension of the parent-child relationship, is expected to continue to influence student understanding and application of sociomoral reasoning. For example, a study of adolescents' perceptions of parental response to antisocial actions indicated that where adolescents believed their parents would disapprove fewer antisocial acts were noted in the adolescents (Wyatt & Carlo, 2002). This is somewhat contradictory to earlier arguments which suggested that peers have increasing influence during this developmental period (Erikson, 1968; Steinberg & Monahan, 2007). Findings by Cook, Buehler and Henson (2009) suggest that both peers and parents were looked toward to deter negative or antisocial conduct. The implication being relationships between and among students and the teacher (as parent in absentia) in the intermediate classroom continue to be important and need to evolve with this developmental phase. Of paramount import to this developing relationship is ongoing, meaningful, open communication (Cook, Buehler, & Henson, 2009). Such open communication contributes to student understanding of the social function of these norms (Nucci & Weber, 1991), and may also serve to increase levels of motivation which have been found to suffer when adults maintain all the power in schools (Eccles, Wigfield, & Schiefele, 1998). Such levels of involvement can be increased further with support from school board or Ministry of Education initiatives such as the Ontario Ministry of Education Speak Up initiative, which invites children from Grades 7-12 to develop and implement initiatives to improve their school and environments beyond their ideas (Ontario Ministry of Education, 2010a). With the ever growing access to and ability to communicate information through technological advances, such positive relations, and opportunities to contribute meaningfully to decisions made in and outside of the school context would seem of great importance during this stage of development.

At the adolescent level (ages 13-15), application of moral judgment often expands beyond the immediacy of the school context and focuses on more global social justice. Issues of poverty, human dignity, economic collapse, ethical use of technology, and the environment for example are in the forefront of the minds of many who do not see the world as a just place. What will move adolescents to action however, is their sense of responsibility to others (Haynes, 2009), something which must have been nurtured through their various relationships with others (teachers, parents, and peers) up to the time of adolescence. It is perhaps during adolescence that children can be best engaged in meaningful action and, as such expand their knowledge and skills in the sociomoral domains (Moshman, 2009). Meaningful service learning type projects, such as sponsoring a family in need (from the immediate community or abroad), volunteering at a food drive depot, or helping to increase understanding of inequalities in access to education worldwide, are all examples of how adolescents can be engaged to practice applying principles of human welfare and justice within their immediate communities and well beyond.

Although this chapter focuses more on the relationships between and among peers and their teachers it is worth mentioning there has also been research to support the need for positive relations between teachers and parents. Weissbourd (2009) has argued that positive relations between teachers and parents are paramount to problem solving sociomoral challenges faced by children as a unified team; each learning from the other. Without positive relationships between adults and students, understanding of students, interests, skills, and sociomoral development will allude educators, making it more challenging for educators to partner with parents in developing the whole child. This is a topic worthy of further exploration but is beyond the scope of the current chapter.

Transgressions in student conduct, at any age, require domain concordant responses. Teachers distinguish responses to transgressions in behavior which cross moral boundaries differently than they do a transgression of a conventional nature. Children recognize moral transgressions; matters involving principles of justice, human welfare, and individual rights (Smetana, 2006) as qualitatively different from social conventions. Where social conventions refer to group functionality, they are best learned through transmission of rules, traditions and conventions applicable to the group (Nucci, 2001). For example, where a student has yelled out a response rather than raise their hand, the teacher might remind the student about the rule, and the need for the rule to maintain order in the classroom. However, if a student strikes another student without provocation the teacher would not refer to a rule, but rather the principle of human welfare, and the consequences to others, to address the issue with that student. Were educators to use moral principles to admonish transgressions which are social conventions it might be expected that students would always look for a rule, or someone in a position of authority, to govern their behavior rather than be able to critically evaluate and respond to novel and complex situations independently.

It is important to establish relationships between and among students and the teacher to create a positive and supportive culture where risk taking for learning is reinforced (it is safe to make a mistake) and understanding that what is fair is not necessarily the same for all. Within the context of schools in Ontario, Canada, where communities are highly diverse, ethnically and economically, this understanding is paramount to practices within schools. Students are met where they are, provided the support they require to meet with success with the established criteria through differentiation in program, and are assessed fairly (Ontario Ministry of Education, 2010b). The underlying premise to this pedagogical approach is that every child is valued, unique and must be given opportunity to be successful. The reality in the classroom is that children begin to understand that fair or just is not necessarily the same for everyone. This understanding is enhanced when individuals in the context of the classroom/school can trust one another, and come to care about one another as unique human beings. Where it is safe to make mistakes and choices are made which acknowledge the welfare of others, as well as the need of rules to maintain a safe and orderly environment. Democratic principles are applied consistently as both teacher and students work together to solve problems, students practice their decision making skills, and are encouraged to resolve conflicts that arise out of their interactions with peers using negotiation and principles of cooperation (Devries & Zan, 1994). To assist in development of reasoning skills necessary to manage more complex social and moral situations teachers use developmentally appropriate social experiences of children as a basis for discourse, as well as lived experiences of the class. This adult supervised exposure and practice provides valuable experience for students to develop critical thinking skills necessary to coordinate the domains. This is particularly important given that some peer interactions can influence negatively, including exclusion and bullying practices (Horn, Daddis, & Killen, 2008).

CONCLUSIONS

This chapter describes two main points pertaining to the application of social cognitive domain theory. The first suggests that there are distinct differences between matters of social convention, personal preferences and moral principles; the understanding of which advances with developmental maturity and experience and have implications for educational practice cross culturally. The second point suggests that relationships between and among peers and their teachers in these socioculturally diverse environments are paramount to advancing understanding and application of the personal, social convention and moral domains as well as maintaining good mental health. It is through the establishment and maintenance of a positive classroom/school culture that relationships flourish which facilitate exposure to meaningful contextualized experiences and practice applying principles of domain distinction and or coordination. Children must feel safe to risk being different, or even make mistakes if they wish to learn at any age. Respect for autonomy and interdependent relationships are keys to the establishment of a positive and supportive classroom/school culture. As children progress through developmental phases, their understanding of and agreement with established norms, particularly those which touch on personal freedoms, such as sexuality and friendships may become issues for conflict (Nucci, 2009) within the dynamic of the school environment. These should be viewed critically by educators to reflect the developmental stage of the child and to ensure responses to such challenges are domain and developmentally appropriate.

Children progress in their ability to subordinate and or coordinate matters of convention and morality with experience and opportunity to develop a sense of autonomy (Nucci, 2008). Social cognitive domain theory recognizes the need for sociomoral education to be contextualized and developmentally suited to the students. Central to this development are the relationships that form between children and adults. Educators at all levels of the educational and developmental continuum can model, and provide guided practice with these skills. Making use of school curriculum, such as literature study, history and science content, as well as lived experiences from the students, (i.e., an interpersonal conflict between students on the playground), for discussion of the social, moral and personal aspects of issues, drawing distinctions between elements which are moral, social convention and/or personal preferences, and dealing with transgressions in behavior with domain concordant responses are all advisable strategies for sociomoral development. Social cognitive domain theory mirrors the complexity of today's world and may serve as a flexible framework for educators to apply in the context of elementary and secondary schools to advance students' abilities to critically evaluate issues and develop their course of action in novel situations. As the name, social cognitive domain theory suggests, it is by its nature a social and cognitive process, at the foundation of which lies human relations.

REFERENCES

Anderson, C. (1982). The search for school climate. *Review of Educational Research, 52,* 368-420.

Bennett, W. (1996). *The book of virtues: A treasury of great moral stories.* New York, NY: Simon & Schuster.

Bennett, W. (1998). *The death of outrage: Bill Clinton and the assault on American ideals.* New York, NY: Simon & Schuster.

Berkowitz, M., & Bier, M., (2004, January). Research-based character education. *The Annals of the American Academy, AAPSS, 591,* 72-85.

Carpendale, J., & Krebs, D. (1992). Situational variation in moral judgment: In a stage or on a stage? *Journal of Youth and Adolescence, 21,* 203-224.

Colby, A., & Damon, W. (1992). *Some do care: Contemporary lives of moral commitment.* New York, NY: Free Press.

Cook, E., Buehler, C., & Henson, R. (2009). Parents and peers as social influences to deter antisocial behavior. *Journal of Youth and Adolescence 38,* 1240-1252.

Creemers, B., & Reezigt, G. (1999). The role of school and classroom climate in elementary school learning environments. In H. J. Freiberg (Ed.), *School climate: Measuring, improving, and sustaining learning environments* (pp. 30-47). Philadelphia, PA: Falmer Press.

Crosnoe, R., Johnson, M. K., & Elder, G. H. (2004). Intergenerational bonding in school: The behavioral and contextual correlates of student–teacher relationships. *Sociology of Education, 77,* 60-81.

Damon, W. (1977). *The social world of the child.* San Francisco, CA: Jossey-Bass.

DeVries, R., & Zan, B. (1994). *Moral classrooms, moral children: Creating a constructivist atmosphere for early education.* New York, NY: Teachers College Press.

Dodge, K., Malone, P., Lansford, J., Miller-Johnson, S., Pettit, G., & Bates, J. (2006). Toward a dynamic developmental model of the role of parents and peers in early onset substance use. In Clarke-Stewart & J. Dunn (Eds.), *Families count: Effects on child and adolescent development* (pp. 104-135). New York, NY: Cambridge University Press.

Eccles, J., Wigfield, A., & Schiefele, U. (1998). Motivation to succeed. In W. Damon (Series Ed.) & N. Eisenberg (Vol. Ed.), *Handbook of child psychology: Vol. 3. Social, emotional and personality development* (5th ed., pp. 1017-1095). New York, NY: Wiley.

Erikson, E. (1968). *Identity, youth, and crisis.* New York, NY: W.W. Norton.

Flavell, J., Miller, P., & Miller, S. (2002). *Cognitive development.* Norwood, NJ: Prentice Hall

Gershkoff, L., & Thelen, E. (2004). U-shaped changes in behavior: A dynamic systems perspective. *Journal of Cognition and Development, 5,* 11-36.

Hanley, S., & Abell, S. (2002). Maslow and relatedness: Creating an interpersonal model of self-actualization. *Journal of Humanistic Psychology, 42*(4), 37-58.

Haynes, C. (2009). Schools of conscience. *Educational Leadership, 66*(8), 6-13.

Horn, S. Daddis, C., & Killen, M. (2008). Relationships and social groups: Implications for moral education. In L. Nucci & D. Narvaez (Eds.), *Handbook of moral and character education* (pp. 267-287). New York, NY: Routledge.

Hughes, J. N., Cavell, T. A., & Willson, V. (2001). Further evidence for the developmental significance of teacher–student relationships: Peers' perceptions of support and conflict in teacher–student relationships. *Journal of School Psychology, 39,* 289-301.

Hunter, J. D. (2000). *The death of character: Moral education in an age without good or evil.* New York, NY: Basic Books.

Killen, M., & Wainryb, C. (2000). Independence and interdependence in diverse cultural contexts. In S. Harkness & C. Raeff (Eds.), *New directions for child development: Vol. 87. Individualism and collectivism as cultural contexts for development* (pp. 5-22). San Francisco, CA: Jossey-Bass.

Kohlberg, L. (1968). Stage and sequence: The cognitive developmental approach to socialization. In D. A. Goslin (Ed.), *Handbook of socialization theory and research* (pp. 347-480). Chicago, IL: Rand McNally.

Kohlberg, L. (1973). Continuities in childhood and adult moral development revisited. In P. B. Baltes & K. W. Schaie (Eds.), *Life-span developmental psychology: Personality and socialization* (pp. 180-204). New York, NY: Academic Press.

Kohlberg, L. (1981). *Essays on moral development: Vol. 1. The philosophy of moral development.* San Francisco, CA: Harper & Row.

Kohlberg, L. (1984). *Essays on moral development: Vol. 2. The psychology of moral development.* New York, NY: Harper & Row.

Lagattuta, K., Nucci, L., & Bosacki, S. (2010). Bridging theory of mind and the personal domain: Children's reasoning about resistance to parental control. *Child Development, 81*(2), 616-635.

Lapsley, D. (2006). Moral stage theory. In M. Killen & J. Smetana (Eds.), *Handbook of moral development* (pp. 37-66). Mahwah, NJ: Erlbaum.

Maslow, A. (1968). *Toward a psychology of being.* New York, NY: Van Nostrand Reinhold.

McClellan, B. E. (1999). *Moral education in America: Schools and the shaping of character from colonial times to the present.* New York, NY: Teachers College Press.

McLaughlin, C., & Clarke, B. (2010). Relational matters: A review of the impact of school experience on mental health in early adolescence. *Educational and Child Psychology, 27*(1), 91-103.

McTighe, J. (1990). *Better thinking and learning: Building effective teaching through educational research.* Retrieved from http://www.eric.ed.gov/PDFS/ED353561.pdf

Moshman, D. (2009). Identity, morality and adolescent development. *Human Development 52,* 287-290.

Narvaez, D. (2006). Integrative ethical education. In M. Killen & J. Smetana (Eds.), *Handbook of moral development* (pp. 703-732). Mahwah, NJ: Erlbaum.

Nucci, L. (1984). Evaluating teachers as social agents: Students' ratings of domain appropriate and domain-inappropriate teacher responses to transgressions. *American Educational Research Journal, 21,* 367-378.

Nucci, L. (1985). Children's conceptions of morality, societal convention, and religious prescription. In C. Harding (Ed.), *Moral dilemmas: Philosophical and psychological issues in the development of moral reasoning* (pp. 115-136). Hillsdale, NJ: Erlbaum.

Nucci, L. (1996). Morality and the personal sphere of actions. In E. Reed, E. Turiel, & T. Brown (Eds.), *Values and knowledge* (pp. 41-60). Hillsdale, NJ: Erlbaum.

Nucci, L. (1997). Moral development and character formation. In H. J. Walberg & G. D. Haertel (Eds.), *Psychology and educational practice* (pp. 127-157). Berkeley, CA: MacCarchan.

Nucci, L. (2001). *Education in the moral domain.* Cambridge, England: Cambridge University Press.

Nucci, L. (2006). Education for moral development. In M. Killen & J. Smetana (Eds.), *Handbook of moral development* (pp. 657-681). Mahwah, NJ: Erlbaum.

Nucci, L. (2008). Social cognitive domain theory and moral education. In L. Nucci & D. Narvaez (Eds.), *Handbook of Moral and Character Education* (pp. 291-309). New York, NY: Routledge.

Nucci, L. (2009). *Nice is not enough: Facilitating moral development.* Upper Saddle River, NJ: Pearson Education.

Nucci, L., & Turiel, E. (1993). God's word, religious rules, and their relation to Christian and Jewish children's concepts of morality. *Child Development, 64*(5), 1475-1491.

Nucci, L., & Turiel, E. (2009). Capturing the complexity of moral development and education. *Mind, Brain, and Education, 3*(3), 151-159.

Nucci, L., & Weber, E. (1991). Research on classroom applications of the domain approach to values education. In W. Kurtines & J. Gerwirtz (Eds.), *Handbook of moral behavior and development: Vol. 3. Applications* (pp. 251-266). Hillsdale, NJ: Erlbaum.

Ontario Ministry of Education. (2010a). Speak up campaign. Retrieved from http://www.edu.gov.on.ca/eng/students/speakup/index.html

Ontario Ministry of Education. (2010b). Growing success assessment, evaluation, and reporting in Ontario schools. Retrieved from http://www.edu.gov.on.ca

Piaget, J. (1965). *The moral judgment of the child* (M. Gabain, Trans.). New York, NY: The Free Press. (Original work published 1932)

Reavis, R., Keane, S., & Calkins, S. (2010). Trajectories of peer victimization: The role of multiple relationships. *Merrill-Palmer Quarterly, 56*(3), 303-332.

Resnick, M., Bearman, P., Blum, R., & Bauman, K. (1997). Protecting adolescents from harm. Findings from the National Longitudinal Study on Adolescent Health. *Journal of the American Medical Association, 278*, 823-832.

Ryan, K. (1989). In defense of character education. In L. Nucci (Ed.), *Moral development and character education: A dialogue* (pp. 3-17). Berkeley, CA: McCutchan.

Smetana, J. (1981). Preschool children's conceptions of moral and social rules. *Child Development, 52*(4), 1333-1336.

Smetana, J. (2006). Social cognitive domain theory: Consistencies and variations in children's moral and social judgments. In L. Nucci (Ed.), *Conflict contradiction and contrarian elements in moral development and education* (pp. 69-91). Mahwah, NJ: Erlbaum.

Smetana, J., & Bitz, B. (1996). Adolescents' conceptions of teachers' authority and their relations to rule violations in school. *Child Development*, 67, 1153-1172.

Steinberg, L., & Monahan, K. (2007). Age differences in resistance to peer influence. *Developmental Psychology, 43*, 1531-1543.

Thornberg, R. (2010). A study of children's conceptions of school rules by investigating their judgements of transgressions in the absence of rules. *Educational Psychology, 30*(5), 583-603.

Turiel, E. (1983). *The development of social knowledge: Morality and convention.* Cambridge, England: Cambridge University Press.

Turiel, E. (1998). The development of morality. In W. Damon (Series Ed.) & N. Eisenberg (Vol. Ed.), *Handbook of child psychology: Vol. 3. Social, emotional, and personality development* (5th ed., pp. 863-932). New York, NY: Wiley.

Turiel, E. (2008). The development of children's orientations toward moral, social, and personal orders: More than a sequence in development. *Human Development, 51*(1), 21-39.

Turiel, E., Hildebrandt, C., & Wainryb, C. (1991). Judging social issues: Difficulties, inconsistencies and consistencies. *Monographs for the Society for Research in Child Development, 56* (Serial No. 224).

Tyson, K. (2000). Using the teacher-student relationship to help children diagnosed as hyperactive: An application of intrapsychic humanism. *Child & Youth Care Forum, 29*, 265-289.

Wainryb, C. (2006). Moral development in culture: Diversity, tolerance and justice. In M. Killen & J. Smetana (Eds.), *Handbook of moral development* (pp. 211-240). Mahwah, NJ: Erlbaum.

Watson, M. (2003). *Learning to trust: Transforming difficult elementary classrooms through developmental discipline.* San Francisco, CA: Jossey-Bass.

Weissbourd, R. (2009). The schools we mean to be. *Educational Leadership, 66*(8), 27-31.

Wu, J., Hughes, J., & Kwok, O. -M. (2010). Teacher-student relationship quality type in elementary grades: Effects on trajectories for achievement and engagement. *Journal of School Psychology, 48*(5), 357-387.

Wyatt, J., & Carlo, G. (2002). What will my parents think? Relations among adolescents' expected parental reactions, prosocial moral reasoning, and prosocial and antisocial behaviors. *Journal of Adolescent Research, 17*, 646-666.

Author Contact Information: Kelly Rizzo, MEd, Brock University, St. Catherines, Ontario, Canada, 1 Short Street, Freelton, Ontario L0R1K0. Telephone: 905-628-1588. E-mail: Kelly.rizzo@hwdsb.on.ca

CHAPTER 50

Moral Development and the Phenomenon of Absent Fathers

Angie D. Wilson
Texas A&M University

Richard C. Henriksen, Jr.
Sam Houston University

Moral education and moral development are popular topics in the psychology and education fields today. There are several things that contribute to the state of our society such as, absent fathers, violent crime, teen pregnancy, substance abuse, and addiction to violent video games. These are not problems simply brought about by nature, but at some point each of the persons that participate in these types of activities justify or convince themselves that their behavior is acceptable. Today, our society has become accepting of situations that were not acceptable in earlier times. There appears to be a moral crisis in our nation, and moral education may help in reducing some of the aliments experienced in today's society. One area that has received attention because of the potential effects it can have on children's moral development is absent father homes.

The United States is the world's leader when it comes to fatherless homes (Horn & Sylvester, 2002), and absent fathers are one of the largest issues plaguing our society (Baskerville, 2004). Over the last four decades there has been a drastic increase in the number of children growing up in fatherless homes, and today approximately 25% of children are being reared in homes led primarily by mothers and grandmothers (Kissman, 2001; Snyder, McLaughlin, & Findeis, 2006). According to Kissman, 50% of divorced fathers fail to see their children and even fewer never married fathers see their children. DeBell (2008) noted 69% of Black students in kindergarten through 12th grades live in fatherless homes. The fatherhood crisis creates several issues for society as a whole including the moral development of children (Wallerstein & Lewis, 2008). The absence of fathers is a major factor in many issues such as crime and delinquency, premature sexuality, poor educational achievement, and poverty, which have negatively impacted society (Popenoe, 1996). Fatherless children have been linked to more violent crime, substance abuse, truancy, unwed pregnancies, and psychological disorders than children whose fathers are an active part of their life (Baskerville, 2004). The fatherhood crisis in America impacts the moral development of children in several aspects, and in this chapter the authors will explain the moral development theories, discuss the moral development theories in relationship to the fatherhood crisis in America, and explore the impact of absent fathers on the moral development of children.

MORAL DEVELOPMENT

Morality is the ability to follow rules and a system of rules that regulate the flow of communication and interaction on an interpersonal level (Biggs, 1976). Morality also encompasses morals, values, ethics, trust, and the rights of individuals, families, and society at large. The ability to do "the right thing," is often described as being moral. However, there is really no one true definition of morality. It is impossible to define morality and put it in a box. In order to truly understand morality, individuals must complete an introspective search of themselves, their ethics, and their

The Handbook of Educational Theories, pp. 607–614

values. According to Kohlberg (1964), we judge people as being "good" or "bad," and some people are not as good as others, and that being good or being evil is a part of who we are. Both Piaget and Kohlberg conducted research studies involving children with moral dilemmas, and one may wonder how the moral development and education of today's children has been impacted by the absence of fathers and the presence of a strong parental unit.

The moral development theories of Jean Piaget, Lawrence Kohlberg, and Carol Gilligan will be discussed in relationship with the moral and social dilemma of absent fathers in society. The overall goal of moral development theory is to explain how morality is observed and to understand the development of people's movement into different developmental stages. The question becomes can moral development and moral reasoning be improved? If moral development and moral education can be improved, the challenge is for researchers to find innovative ways to educate the children of today's society with hopes of providing a better future for the children of tomorrow.

Cognitive Aspects of Moral Development

The development of moral principles based also on cognitive development involves the development of the ability to philosophize about what is considered right and wrong in the abstract. For example, Krebs and Denton (2006) noted that "when people philosophize about morality, they reflect on hypothetical moral issues and attempt to explicate ideal moral principles" (p. 673). To understand the cognitive aspects of moral development, therefore, means that it is necessary to understand the overall cognitive development of the individual and how the individual moves from concrete thinking to abstract thinking. Carroll and Rest (1982) indicated that there are four steps regarding moral behavior. According to Carol and Rest, the first step to moral behavior is recognizing the dilemma and understanding the severity of the issue. Second, the individual makes a decision on what intervention should be made and what is considered appropriate or inappropriate. The third step includes determining a plan of action considering norms and values. Last, the individual implements the plan of action. The work of Carroll and Rest, Piaget, and Kohlberg are based on cognitive development and understanding moral situations and dilemmas from a cognitive perspective (Lefrancois, 1999).

Piaget's Two-Stage Approach

Jean Piaget is one of the first psychologists to work with moral development theories. Much of his work focused on the lives of children and his studies of children's interactions and play in order to learn about their beliefs. After years of research and experience with the moral development of children, Piaget concluded that schools should incorporate and emphasize tools that would assist children in being moral beings and being fair. He focused on how children developed moral thinking patterns and how they acted on those thoughts. Piaget's moral development theory is often explained from a cognitive perspective; however, moral development occurs at a slower pace than cognitive development (Biggs, 1976).

Piaget's moral development theory encompasses two stages, and his work was later expanded by Kohlberg. The two stages of Piaget's (1932) moral development theory are heteronomy and autonomy. He developed these two stages by exploring moral development with children by telling stories with a moral dilemma and asking for their opinions and judgment. For example, the young child hears the story that a boy broke 15 cups trying to help his mother in the kitchen, while another boy broke one cup trying to take a snack from the kitchen. The young children based their judgments on which child's behavior was worse based on the amount of damage created or the negative consequences of the behavior. A child that has moved into the second stage of autonomy would base his or her response on the intentions and meaning of the behavior being described in the story (Piaget, 1932).

According to Piaget (1932), children between the ages of 5 and 10 years old view the world and things that take place in it through a heteronymous lens of morality. The term heteronymous means directed by others, and in this case rules are told and given to the child by authority figures (parents, adults, and teachers) and the rules are seen as absolute. This would be consistent with the children at this age being concrete thinkers. The relationship between authority figures and children are viewed as authoritarian, and the children obey and follow rules based on the negative consequences that are associated with breaking rules.

The second stage of Piaget's (1932) moral development theory is autonomy. Toward the latter years of middle childhood (10 to 12 years old), children gain the ability to view situations from other people's perspectives. In the process of doing this, children are able to put themselves in someone else's shoes and morality begins to become more self-directed. Piaget referred to children becoming more autonomous and self directed as learning. Children in this stage still find the rules to be important, but their view of rules shifts from being absolute to negotiable. Children begin to make their decisions based on their overall view of the situation unlike children in the heteronomy stage who base their decisions on punishment or negative consequences. Piaget suggested that there is a shift from authoritarian to obedience oriented parenting (DeVries, 1997) that affects the moral development of the child; however, he did not take cultural differences into account in the development of his theory. Piaget made major contributions to moral development theory, and other theorists like Kohlberg and Gilligan have expanded his work.

Kohlberg's Theory of Moral Development

Lawrence Kohlberg is one of the major contributors to moral development theories, and some would argue that he stands at the forefront of moral development theories and research. He took an interest in Piaget's (1932) moral development theoretical model while completing graduate work at the University of Chicago. Kohlberg (1958) expanded Piaget's stages of moral development from two stages into three levels with two stages within each level in his doctoral dissertation. Kohlberg identified six stages of moral reasoning and grouped them into three major levels. He completed this task by asking children a series of questions and presenting situations and moral dilemmas to them. One of the famous examples of Kohlberg's (1969) scenarios was the case of Heinz:

> Heinz's wife was dying from a rare form of cancer, and a druggist from town recently discovered a cure for the rare form of cancer. The druggist could make the drug for about $200, but is charging ten times that amount for the actual drug. Heinz borrowed money from all of his friends and everyone he knew, but he was only able to collect $1000. Heinz asked the druggist to sell him the drug for a reduced rate or to allow him to pay half now and pay the other later. The Druggist refused. Heinz desperately broke into the drugstore and stole the drug needed to save his dying wife. Should Heinz have done that? Why? (p. 379)

Kohlberg's research was not based on the responses of yes or no, but he was more concerned with the explanation behind the children's responses. Based on the children's responses, Kohlberg developed six stages of moral development which are separated by three levels. The three levels of moral development are: (a) Level 1 (preconventional), (b) Level 2 (conventional), and (c) Level 3 (postconventional).

Level One: Preconventional Morality

The preconventional level, like the other levels of moral development, encompasses two stages: (a) *punishment and obedience orientation* and (b) *naïve instrumental hedonism*. At the preconventional level of moral development, children's responses to rules are based on labels of good and bad, right or wrong. For children in the preconventional level, good and bad are interpreted by the consequences of their behavior and are absolute. Kohlberg and Hersh (1977) developed descriptions of the two stages found at the preconventional level.

Stage 1: punishment and obedience orientation. Kohlberg's first stage of moral development is similar to Piaget's (1932) first stage. The child makes the assumption that authority figures are all knowing and that he or she must obey the orders of adults. The avoidance of negative consequences or punishment is the determining factor of "good" versus "bad" behavior. Children in this stage do not actually understand the underlying moral principles; they merely understand the consequences associated with behaviors. Referring back to the example with Heinz, a child in this stage may respond with "If he steals the drug he may go to jail." This response is associated with punishment, and there is no understanding of the principle. Stage one is called punishment and obedience because children are not speaking as members of society, and they see morality as something outside of themselves and enforced on them by authority figures (Kohlberg & Hersh, 1977).

Stage 2: instrumental relativist orientation. At this stage, children view right actions as actions that satisfy their individual needs. They act as individuals without paying attention to society, and they do not make a connection between values. Kohlberg (1963) stated that in this stage each person pursues his or her individual wants, and when asked about Heinz one boy responded that Heinz might steal the drug if he wanted his wife to live, but he may not steal the drug if he wanted to marry someone younger or better looking. This is an example of how a child makes decisions based on individual wants. Though children do have some sense of right and wrong at this stage, they continue to base moral decisions on the idea of fair exchange "If you scratch my back, I'll scratch yours."

Level Two: Conventional Morality

Conventional morality is typical of the period of adolescence into young adulthood and involves comparing one's view of morality to that of the larger society with its moral expectations. During this level of morality development, most children are approaching their teenage years and they believe that their values should be in line with their family, peers, and community (Kohlberg & Hersh, 1977). Immediate consequences or punishment do not play a role in their judgment of morality like children in the preconventional level. The two stages in this level are stage three, *good boy-nice girl* orientation and stage four, *law and order* orientation.

Stage 3: good boy-nice girl orientation. During this stage children are moving into their early teenage years and are beginning to think of themselves as a part of a community or larger system. They identify good behavior as behavior that helps others and behavior that receives approval from those that are important to them such as their parents, teachers, and peers (Kohlberg, 1963). During this stage of moral development, the behavioral intentions of others is identified for the first time, and teenagers in this phase may respond with a comment like "he means well" (Kohlberg & Hersh, 1977). During this stage, love, trust, empathy, and concern for others arises and the adolescent begins to equate good behaviors with these feelings. It is the druggist's fault, and he should not let someone die. Heinz loved his wife and wanted to save her and anyone would. The judge would look at the situation and see that the druggist is over charging, would be a typical response for someone in stage three (Kohlberg, 1963).

Stage 4: law and order orientation. During the process of developing a law and order orientation, adolescents become aware of the laws that govern society, and they become focused on obeying those laws and respecting the different levels of authority. Adolescents begin to look at society as a whole and conforming to the law becomes an important aspect of their moral decision making process. When asked about Heinz's situation, those in stage four made reference to Heinz's story and stated that they understood that his intentions were good, but stealing is wrong and could not be condoned (Kohlberg, 1963). It is important to note that individuals in stages one and four give similar responses to the Heinz dilemma. According to Kohlberg, it is important to understand the reasoning behind the answer given and to explore each person's reasoning. Those in stage four have a basic understanding of the laws of society; whereas, younger children are much more focused on individual punishment and how that affects them.

Level Three: Postconventional Morality

Kohlberg (1963) described postconventional morality as the principled level where individuals develop a clear vision of their separate identity for that of the greater society. Individuals realize that their view of moral behavior can take precedence over what society might expect of the individual. During this highest level of morality, morals and values become clearly defined. Individual rights, cultural norms, values, and laws are all taken into consideration when making decisions. The two stages of the postconventional level of morality are *social contract and individual rights* orientation and *universal ethical principle* orientation. Though these stages are a part of Kohlberg's model, he noted that it is rare for people to reach these two stages.

Stage 5: social contract and individual rights orientation. When someone enters this stage of moral development, he or she begins to look at individual rights and standards that are acceptable by society and those that may be in conflict with the individual's perceptions of morality. Individuals begin to think about society as a whole and examine the values they think society should uphold (Kohlberg, 1963). At stage five, people may ask themselves "What makes for a good society?," and they begin to make an individualized effort to think about what it means to live in a moral society. Individuals in this stage may respond to the Heinz dilemma by explaining that Heinz has a responsibility to save his wife's life and to value life over property (Kohlberg, 1963).

Stage 6: universal ethical principle orientation. This stage is often associated with martyrs such as Martin Luther King Jr., Gandhi, and Mother Theresa. Those in this stage attempt to define the principles to reach and maintain justice. There is some doubt that stage six should be included as a stage in the moral development process, and there has also been mention of a seventh stage regarding logic of contemplation and mystical logic but it is not recognized in the literature as being a stage of moral development (Colby & Kohlberg, 1984).

Like Piaget, Kohlberg was an influential theorist and researcher, but his research consisted of only White male children. The result is that moral development models have not clearly addressed issues of moral development based on race/ethnicity, culture, and gender. Carol Gilligan conducted moral development research with women, and adapted Kohlberg's stages of moral development to be applicable to women (Gilligan, 1982).

Gilligan's Theory of Gender and Moral Development

In response to Kohlberg's moral development theory that was based on research with White males, Gilligan (1982) conducted moral development research utilizing females in an attempt to capture their experiences. Gilligan (1982) described female morality in terms of selfishness and responsibility or the concept of caring; whereas, Kohlberg viewed male morality as justice oriented. Gilligan proposed that female morality encompasses more compassion and caring, and those women's concerns for society and humanity may be similar to those of males, but for different reasons. Gilligan proposed that men may move towards being moral beings because they are compelled to follow rules and principles; while women become more compassionate for society as a whole. However, the lack of focus on cultural issues that can have an effect on moral development has led to many questions about the applicability of the three moral development models.

Summary of Moral Development Models

The overall goal of moral development theory is to explain how morality is observed and to understand the development of people's movement into different developmental stages. According to Kohlberg (1964), we judge people as being "good" or "bad," and some people are not as good as others, and that being good or being evil is a part of who we are. Piaget's (1932) two stage approach encompasses the two stages of heteronomy and autonomy. The term heteronymous means directed by others, and in this case rules are told and given to the child by authority figures. Autonomy is described as children being able to put themselves in someone else's shoes and when morality begins to become more self-directed. Kohlberg expanded on Piaget's theory, and he developed his moral development theory. Kohlberg's (1958) moral development theory consisted of six stages divided into three levels: (a) preconventional, (b) conventional, and (c) postconventional. At the preconventional level of moral development, children's responses to rules are based on labels of good and bad, right or wrong. During conventional morality most children are entering their teenage years and their values are most likely aligned with those important to them (Kohlberg & Hersh, 1977). The two stages in this level are stage three, *good boy-nice girl* orientation and stage four, *law and order* orientation. The third stage of postconventional morality is when values and morals become clearly defined (Kohlberg, 1958). According to Kohlberg it is rare for people to reach this level. The two stages within postconventional morality are *social contract and individual rights* orientation and *universal ethical principle* orientation. Colby and Kohlberg (1984) stated that this stage is often associated with peacemakers and martyrs. As a way to include women's morality issues with moral development theories Carol Gilligan (1982) conducted moral development research utilizing females in an attempt to capture their experiences. Gilligan proposed that female morality encompasses more compassion and caring, and those women's concerns for society and humanity may be similar to those of males, but for different reasons. Gilligan proposed that women's moral development issues are geared toward compassion for society.

Culturally Based Moral Development: A Model

The current moral development models fail to address the characteristics involved with the moral development of individuals from different ethnic and cultural backgrounds. Because of the continued growth of the culturally diverse members of society, a moral development model that addresses cultural diversity is necessary and could be referred to as *culturally based moral development: a model*. This model would include characteristics from each of the previous models that are relevant to individuals from diverse cultural backgrounds. In Cohen's (2006) dissertation, she took several concepts from the Jewish religion and used them to adapt Piaget's and Kohlberg's models to this population. The result was a moral development model that could be applied to members of the Jewish faith. A culturally based moral development model could encompass a variety of issues including gender, ethnicity, sexual orientation, and religion. A grounded theory approach could be utilized to adapt Piaget's and Kohlberg's models, thus making their theories relevant to individuals from diverse cultural backgrounds. The model could also provide for individualism and flexibility in regards to sexual orientation and the individual rights of others. Researchers interested in adapting current models may find it rewarding to create scenarios to assess levels and stages of moral development. The use of the scenarios has been utilized by moral development theorists and is a valuable method of collecting data. Adapting scenarios to include culturally based dilemmas could help to provide empirically based research to fill this gap in the current literature.

Moral Development Theories and Diverse Populations

Understanding moral development is more complex than just looking at how Kohlberg, Piaget, and Gilligan described and examined the development of moral identities. There are several issues that affect moral development that are not addressed by the primary theories of moral identity development. Some of the issues addressed in the following sections include a short discussion of moral development and absent fathers, cultural issues and moral development, and critiques of the moral development models from a multicultural perspective. As noted by Gibbs, Basinger, Grime, and Snarey (2007), models of moral development are controversial and need further research to determine their utility with culturally diverse groups. There are several issues regarding moral development of children reared in absent father homes and cultural issues of moral development. The authors highlight important facts and identify key areas for future research of moral development and diverse populations in the following sections.

Absent Fathers and Moral Development of Children

The application of moral development theories to diverse populations is challenging because none of the theories available were developed based on the moral development of members of different ethnic groups or based on different family types. For example, there is the challenge of absent father homes and the moral development of their children. Early research on this topic (Santrock, 1975), proposed that "the age of onset of father absence has little or no impact on the moral development of pre-adolescent boys" (p. 757). However, Barclay (1980) pointed out that moral development in boys is positively fostered by the presence of the father especially as it relates to the model of masculine behavior and the development of masculine behavior. The results of these two early studies do not provide a clear picture of how moral development is affected by the presence of the father versus homes where the father is not present. Direct research involving single parent homes is scare as noted in this section and there is no research found that addresses the moral development of girls in absent father or single parent homes. Research that addresses issues of the moral development of both boys and girls in single parent families is necessary if we are to have a better understanding of the overall moral development of children.

Cultural Issues and Moral Development

Helping children with their moral development is made even more complex when children come from homes that are culturally diverse. DiMartino (1989) noted that when culture is added to the discussion of moral development the results are mixed. She found that to understand a child's moral development the child must be placed in a cultural context because there is an underlying sense of right and wrong established within differing cultural groups. In a study conducted by Chang (1996), she challenged Carol Gilligan's gender constructed adaptation of Kohlberg's moral development model by pointing out that the manner in which Chinese individuals make moral decisions is in large part based on power relations based on culture rather than gender. Nasir and Kirschner (2003) developed a 3-level framework to understand how culture influences moral decision making. The three levels include: (a) institutional context, (b) cultural practices, and (c) social interactions. The outcome of the implementation of this framework is the understanding that moral development moves from the local (moral development based on social interactions that include cultural practices of families) to the general (moral development is influenced by the greater society). Fu, Xu, Cameron, Heyman, and Lee (2007) also found that children's moral decision making is influenced by group versus individual values and local definitions of truth and deception. The complexity of culture and cultural differences provides challenges to understanding the moral development process for members of culturally diverse groups. This complexity of moral development understanding has led to many critiques of the moral development models.

Critiques of Moral Development Theory

Moral development models have historically been based on Caucasian males. The primary adaptation to these models has been the work of Carol Gilligan who adapted Kohlberg's moral development model to meet the needs of the moral development of women. However, there have been no adaptations of the models to meet the needs of members of diverse racial and ethnic groups. For example, a review of moral development literature did not lead to the identification of research that included studies involving Piaget and African Americans. Without any research available, the application of Piaget's moral development model to the African American population is challenging at best.

According to Rorty (2010), moral developmental theories serve two purposes. First, moral development models provide descriptions and explanations of what is defined as moral versus that which is defined as immoral. Second, moral development models are viewed as normative meaning that the available models "provide criteria for evaluating, and sometimes radically revising and correcting the practices with which it is initially presented" (p. 30). Moral development models are said to provide a critique of what constitutes moral and immoral behavior. However, Rorty also pointed out that there is no uniform or widely accepted, across cultures, definition of morality and immorality. Thus, without a commonly held description of both morality and immorality and the infusion of cultural definitions, the ability to apply moral development models cross-culturally is limited.

In a study conducted by Hart, Atkins, and Ford (1998), they found that socioeconomic status was a predictor of moral development and that because many who come from a lower socioeconomic level feel powerless, they are less likely to accept the moral imperatives from the greater more powerful parts of society and are more likely to have their own code of morality. Hart and Ford also pointed out that "disorganized families, poverty, an inability to sympathize with others, a lack of personal resiliency" (p. 517) and other factors influence the development of a moral identity and would not foster the development of moral reasoning as proposed by Kohlberg and Piaget. However, they point out those adolescents who come from poor neighborhoods can and do develop healthy moral identities when they believe that their actions are respected. It is through the interactions of positive social institutions such as church and community centers that adolescents from poor neighborhoods develop the skills necessary for the development of healthy moral identities. Moral development models have also been criticized because of the lack of attention to the moral development of women.

Gilligan's (1982) adaptation of Kohlberg's moral development model is based on feminist theory and the application of feminist theory. However, controversy has surrounded Gilligan's model of moral development for women because of the primary inclusion of feminist theory (Jorgensen, 2006; Peeples, 1991; Puka, 1991). The debate over how to describe moral development continues and there do not appear to be any clear cut answers.

Assessments

There is a lack of information and literature on current literature regarding moral development assessments and measurements. According to the *17th Mental Measurements Yearbook* (Buros Institute of Mental Measurements, 2007), Kohlberg's Moral Judgment Interview (MJI) and the Measurement of Moral Judgment (MMJ) are the only two assessment instruments that were identified that measure moral development. Kohlberg's moral judgment scale (MJS) helped launch researchers to create additional moral judgment instruments (Wilmoth & McFarland, 1977). The Sexual Moral Judgment Scale (SMJS) (Gilligan, Kohlberg, Lerner, & Belenky, 1971), objective form of Moral Judgment Scale (OMJS) (Maitland & Goldman, 1974), and the Defining Issues Test (DIT) (Rest, Cooper, Coder, Masanz, & Anderson, 1974) were developed from Kohlberg's MJS. Of these instruments, DIT is used today and has offered significant contributions to the field, unlike the MJI the DIT is a multiple choice questionnaire (Rest et al., 1974). The MJI must be administered and scored by a trained professional; it is comprised of six ethical moral dilemmas (Kohlberg, 1958). The ethical dilemma of Heinz was presented previously in this chapter, and is one of the dilemmas from the MJI. Though these assessments have been used as a means of measuring moral development and moral issues, a limitation is that they have not been used with culturally diverse groups and populations. Having assessments and tests that were not normed on the populations they are used for can be an issue for assessment and testing because the test may be invalid for the cultural groups if the assessments were not normed on that specific group or population.

Conclusion

Moral development is impacted by several aspects of life including peer associations, parents, teachers, and environmental circumstances. Our society continues to be more acceptable of circumstances and issues that were not acceptable years ago. The United States is the world leader regarding fatherless homes (Horn & Sylvester, 2002), and the absence of fathers is a major factor in many decisions that children and adolescents make (Popenoe, 1996). Morality encompasses morals, values, ethics, trust, and the rights of individuals, families, and society at large. The ability to do "the right thing," is often described as being moral.

The moral development theories of Jean Piaget, Lawrence Kohlberg, and Carol Gilligan were explored and cultural aspects of the theories were addressed in detail. Future areas of research include: addressing issues of the moral development of both boys and girls in single parent families, moral development theories being researched with culturally diverse populations, moral development and sexual orientation, the effects of religion and spirituality on moral development, and a greater depth of understanding regarding the moral development of women assist those in helping professions with understanding the moral development process of children reared in absent father homes, culturally diverse populations, and women.

References

Barclay, J. R. (1980). Values in adolescent males and father son relationships. *Personnel and Guidance Journal, 58*, 627-629.

Baskerville, S. (2004). Is there really a fatherhood crisis? *The Independent Review, 8*, 485-508.

Biggs, J. B. (1976). Schooling and moral development. In V. P. Varma & P. Williams (Eds.), *Piaget, psychology, and education* (pp. 155-177). Itasca, IL: Peacock.

Buros Institute of Mental Measurements (2007). *The 17th Mental Measurements yearbook.* Highland Park, NJ: Author.

Carroll, J. C., & Rest, J. R. (1982). Moral development. In B. B. Wolman, G. Stricker, S. J. Ellman, P. Keith-Spiegel, & D. S. Palermo (Eds.), *Handbook of developmental psychology* (pp. 434-450). Englewood Cliffs, NJ: Prentice-Hall.

Chang, K. A., (1996). Culture, power and the social construction of morality: Moral voices of Chinese students. *Journal of Moral Education, 25*, 141-157.

Cohen, D. M. (2006). *Children's views of basic concepts of morality* (Unpublished doctoral dissertation). Yeshiva University, New York.

Colby, A., & Kohlberg, L. (1984). Invariant sequence and internal consistency in moral judgment stages. In W. M. Kertines & J. L. Gewirtz (Eds.), *Morality, moral behavior, and moral development* (pp. 41-55). New York, NY: Wiley.

DeBell, M. (2008). Children living without their fathers: Population estimates and indicators of educational well-being. *Social Indicators Research, 87*(3), 427-443. doi: 10.1007?s11205-007-9149-8

DeVries, R. (1997). Piaget's social theory. *Educational Researcher, 26*, 4-18.

DiMartino, E. C. (1989). The growth of moral judgment in young children: The role of culture. *Education, 109*, 262-267.

Fu, G., Xu, F., Cameron, C. A., Heyman, G., & Lee, K. (2007). Cross-cultural differences in children's choices, categorizations, and evaluations of truths and lies. *Developmental Psychology, 43*, 278-293. doi: 10.1037/0012-1649.43.2.278

Gibbs, J. C., Basinger, K. S., Grime, R. L., & Snarey, J. R. (2007). Moral judgment development across cultures: Revisiting Kohlberg's universality claims. *Developmental Review, 27*, 443-500.

Gilligan, C. (1982). *In a different voice: Psychological theory and women's development.* Cambridge, MA: Harvard University Press.

Gilligan, C., Kohlberg, L., Learner, J., & Belenky, M. (1971). Moral reasoning about sexual dilemmas: The development of an interview and scoring system. In *Technical Report of the Commission on Obscenity and Pornography* (Vol. 1). Washington, DC: U.S. Government Printing Office.

Hart, D., Atkins, R., & Ford, D. (1998). Urban America as a context for the development or moral identity in adolescence. *Journal of Social Issues, 54*, 513-530.

Horn, W. F., & Sylvester, T. (2002). *Father facts* (4th ed.). Gaithersburg, MD: National Fatherhood Initiative.

Jorgensen, G. (2006). Kohlberg and Gilligan: Duet or duel? *Journal of Moral Education, 35*, 179-196. doi:10.1080/03057240600681710

Kissman, K. (2001). Interventions to strengthen noncustodial father involvement in the lives of their children. *Journal of Divorce & Remarriage, 35*, 135-148.

Kohlberg, L. (1958). *The development of modes of moral thinking and choice in the years ten to sixteen* (Unpublished doctoral dissertation). University of Chicago, Chicago, IL.

Kohlberg, L. (1963). Moral development and identification. In H. Stevenson (Ed.), *Child psychology: 72nd yearbook of National Society for the Study of Education* (pp. 277-332). Chicago, IL: Chicago University Press.

Kohlberg, L. (1964). Development of moral character and moral ideology. In M. L. Hoffman & L. W. Hoffman (Eds.), *Review of child development research* (Vol. 1). New York, NY: Russell Sage

Kohlberg, L. (1969). Stage and sequence. The cognitive developmental approach to socialization. In D. Gosslin (Ed.), *Handbook of socialization theory and research* (pp. 347-480). Chicago, IL: Rand McNally.

Kohlberg, L., & Hersh R. (1977). Moral development: A review of the theory. *Theory into Practice, 16*, 53-59.

Krebs, D. L., & Denton, K. (2006). Explanatory limitations of cognitive-developmental approaches to morality. *Psychological Review, 113*, 672-675.

Lefrancois, G. (1999). *The lifespan* (6th ed.). Belmont, CA: Wadsworth Publishing Company.

Maitland, K., & Goldman, L. (1974). Moral judgment as a function of peer group interaction. *Journal of Personality and Social Psychology, 30*, 699-704.

Nasir, N. S., & Kirshner, B. (2003). The cultural construction of moral and civic identities. *Applied Developmental Science, 47*(3), 138-147.

Piaget, J. (1932). *The moral judgment of the child.* New York, NY: Harcourt, Brace Jovanovich.

Peeples, S. E. (1991). Her terrain is outside his "domain." *Hypatia, 6*, 192-200.

Popenoe, D. (1996). *Life without fathers.* New York, NY: Kessler Book.

Puka, B. (1991). The science of caring. *Hypatia, 6*, 200-210.

Rest, J., Cooper, R., Coder, R., Masanz, J., & Anderson, D. (1974). Judging the important issues on moral dilemmas. *Developmental Psychology, 10*, 491-501.

Rorty, A. (2010). Questioning moral theories. *Philosophy, 85*, 29-46.

Santrock, J. W. (1975). Father absence, perceived maternal behavior, and moral development in boys. *Child Development, 46*, 753-757.

Snyder, A. R., McLaughlin, D. K., & Findeis, J. (2006). Household composition and poverty among female-headed households with children: Differences by race and residence. *Rural Sociology, 74*, 597-624.

Wallerstein, J. S., & Lewis, J. M. (2008). Divorced fathers and their adult offspring: Report from a twenty-five-year longitudinal study. *Family Law Quarterly, 42*, 695-711.

Wilmoth, G., & McFarland, S. (1977). A comparison of four measures of moral reasoning. *Journal of Personality Assessment, 41*, 396-401.

Author Contact Information: Angie D. Wilson, PhD, Department of Psychology, Counseling, and Special Education, Texas A&M University-Commerce, Box 3011, Commerce, Texas 75429-3011. Phone: 903-886-5510. E-mail: dr.angiewilson@gmail.com

CHAPTER 51

The Ethic of Care

Theory and Research

Eva E. A. Skoe
University of Oslo

In her famed book, *In a Different Voice*, Carol Gilligan (1982) connected the recurrent problems in interpreting women's development to the repeated omission of women from the critical theory-building studies of psychological research. She put forth a critique of Kohlberg, pointing out that in the research from which Kohlberg derived his theory on the development of justice-based moral thought, females simply were excluded. Consequently, Gilligan claimed, Kohlberg's model and measurement are insensitive to women's voice or views on moral issues, with the result that men typically score higher in their moral reasoning levels on Kohlberg's justice measure.

> Since moral judgments pertain to conflicts in the relation of self to others, a difference in the construction of that relationship would lead to a difference in conception of the moral domain.... If women's moral judgments reflect a different understanding of social relationships, then they may point to a line of social development whose presence in both sexes is currently obscured. (p. 201)

In this chapter, Gilligan's theory of two distinctive sex-related moral orientations, care and justice, is briefly expounded, followed by a review of the empirical evidence regarding her allegations and some critiques of her theorizing. In the final section, Skoe's *Ethic of Care Interview*, which assesses Gilligan's proposed developmental levels of care reasoning, and research findings with use of this instrument are presented.

Gilligan's Theory of Moral Orientation

On the basis of her own work with women, Gilligan proposed an alternate theory of moral development to Kohlberg's. In her view, there are two sex-related (but not sex-specific) moral orientations—justice and individual rights, which are more representative of men's moral judgment, and interpersonal responsibility and care for self and others, which are more representative of women's judgment. According to Gilligan and colleagues (Brown, Tappan, & Gilligan, 1995), the ethic of care develops from the person's early childhood experiences of attachment to others and reflects an ideal of love, connection and mutual responsiveness; the ethic of justice develops from the person's early experiences of inequality and reflects an ideal of fairness, equality, and reciprocity. Because children are born into a position of inequality and cannot survive without an attachment figure, all children are exposed to the conditions that form the basis of both moral orientations (Jaffee & Hyde, 2000). Traditionally, however, women are urged toward a morality of care and responsibility in relationships, whereas men are socialized toward a morality of rights, a concern for autonomy in judgment and action as well as for freedom and noninterference with the rights of individuals. Thus, moral conflicts typically are regarded as entailing issues of conflicting rights by men and conflicting responsibilities by women. These two patterns, of rights and justice versus responsibility and care as foci, are distinct approaches to moral reasoning, Gilligan (1982) argued, and maturity entails a greater understanding of both perspectives. Just as inequality adversely affects both parties in an unequal relationship, so too violence or harm is in the end destructive for everyone involved in interpersonal relations.

Many theorists (e.g., Chodorow, 1978; Gilligan, 1982, Josselson, 1987; Noddings, 1984) have argued that due to interactions between biologically-determined roles and cultural norms, women value the maintenance of relations with others more than do men. Social norms

The Handbook of Educational Theories, pp. 615–628

for men, in contrast, have defined their roles as securing provisions and protecting family members from outside dangers (Zahn-Waxler, Cole, & Barrett, 1991). In tracing the origins of the proposed two different moral points of view, Gilligan relies on Chodorow's (1978) neopsychoanalytical account of gender identity development with reference to early parent-child relationships. The differences that characterize feminine and masculine personality are attributed to the fact that women are the primary caretakers in most cultures. Being parented by a person of the same sex, girls identify with their mothers and stay longer in close physical proximity to them than do boys. In this way, creating and continuing close connection with others becomes more central to girls' gender identity and self-esteem; girls also emerge with a stronger basis for empathy due to more flexible self-other boundaries. Boys, on the other hand, focus more on the experience of inequality, and separation or independence becomes more salient for their identity and self-esteem.

Empirical Evidence Regarding Gilligan's Theory

There is little empirical evidence supporting Gilligan's claim that Kohlberg's moral reasoning measure is biased against women in terms of stage level. In his extensive meta-analyses Walker (e.g., 1984, 2006) observed that nonsignificant sex differences were reported in most studies (86%). In early adolescence, a small percentage of studies found a stage difference favoring girls. With adults, in the few studies where women scored lower than men, they also tended to have less formal education. In every case where researchers controlled for education and/or occupation, Walker (2006) stated, sex differences in justice reasoning disappeared; he therefore concluded that the overall review pattern is one of nonsignificant sex differences on Kohlberg's stage measure.

In contrast to the rather unequivocal findings for Kohlbergian stages of justice reasoning, research has provided some mixed support for Gilligan's claim of sex differences in *moral orientation* (preference for care or justice reasoning, regardless of stage or level). Unlike Kohlberg's moral stages, as noted by Jaffee and Hyde (2000), moral orientations do not represent cognitive structures that develop in a stage sequence. Instead, they represent distinctive frameworks that can be modified by experience and through which people perceive and resolve moral conflicts. Lyons (1983), a student of Gilligan, developed in her doctoral dissertation a coding scheme for analyzing moral considerations presented by participants when discussing moral conflicts in their own lives. Considerations (i.e., scorable thought units) were categorized as either response (care) or rights (justice). In her system, concern with maintaining or restoring relationships, and the promotion of the welfare of others or prevention of hurt, are defined as care-oriented, whereas concern with the maintenance of impartial rules, principles and standards, especially fairness and reciprocity, are defined as justice-oriented. In support of Gilligan's theory, Lyons observed that the majority of women (75%) used care considerations, whereas the majority of men (79%) used justice considerations. With more refined analyses, Gilligan and Attanucci (1988) found that most people used both care and justice perspectives, but care-focused dilemmas were more likely to be generated by women and justice-focused dilemmas by men. Others, however, failed to find sex differences in reasoning about real-life moral conflicts (e.g., Ford & Lowery, 1986; Walker, de Vries, & Trevethan, 1987), and there is little evidence that moral orientations are used consistently within or between dilemmas (Jaffee & Hyde, 2000; Walker, 2006).

In their comprehensive meta analysis of 113 studies, Jaffee and Hyde (2000) found small, but significant sex differences, both in care orientation (favoring females, d = -.28) and in justice orientation (favoring males, d = .19). Furthermore, moderator analyses showed that the magnitudes of the effect size for both care and justice reasoning were greater for self-generated real-life dilemmas compared with standardized dilemmas. One possible reason for this is that regardless of age, education, occupation or marital status, women have consistently been observed to generate more personal or relational real-life dilemmas (involving an ongoing, significant relationship) than men, whereas men generate more impersonal or non-relational ones (involving relative strangers or an issue primarily intrinsic to self) than women (e.g., Pratt, Diessner, Hunsberger, Pancer, & Savoy, 1991; Pratt, Golding, Hunter, & Sampson, 1988; Skoe & Diessner, 1994; Skoe & Gooden, 1993; Skoe, Cumberland, Eisenberg, Hansen, & Perry, 2002; Skoe, Eisenberg, & Neset, 2012; Walker et al., 1987). In line with Gilligan's theory, this indicates (at least indirectly) that women prefer a care orientation because such personal or relational real-life dilemmas tend to evoke more care-based moral judgments than other types of dilemma for both sexes. Conversely, both men and women tend to use justice more than care reasoning when discussing an impersonal or nonrelational dilemma. Although this indicate that nature or type of dilemma can predict moral orientation better than sex, as Walker (e.g., 2006) argued, overall women generate more relational real-life dilemmas than men, which means that women actually show more care responses than men (Skoe, 1998; Turiel, 1998). The trend for women to report more personal or relational real-life dilemmas than men has been observed already in early adolescence (Meyers, 2001; Skoe & Gooden, 1993), as well as in late adulthood (Skoe, Pratt, Matthews, & Curror, 1996). This sex difference seems to remain rather constant across time and cultures studied so far.

Moreover, women have been found to view a variety of dilemmas (both real life and hypothetical) as involving more moral concerns and as more difficult to resolve than do men (e.g., Skoe et al., 2002, Skoe et al., 2012; Wark & Krebs, 1997, 2000). Women also generate more prosocial dilemmas (involving reacting to others' needs) and less antisocial ones (involving reacting to temptations and transgressions) than do men (Juujärvi, 2005; Wark & Krebs, 1996). Hence, there is empirical evidence that women and men differ in terms of how they experience and evaluate moral conflict situations, somewhat as Gilligan had suggested.

Regardless of such specifics, by linking care-related reasoning with sex, Gilligan (e.g., 1982) has drawn attention to the potential role of emotional responses such as sympathy and other empathy-related feelings in moral thinking. Indeed, the type of dilemma that is used to assess moral reasoning may affect not only the type of reasoning used and the difficulty in dealing with the conflict, but also the emotions evoked in regard to the moral conflict. Skoe, Eisenberg, and Cumberland (2002), for instance, found that emotions were significantly related to how important and difficult people considered their moral dilemmas as well as to care and justice orientation responses in resolving the conflicts. More specifically, feelings of turmoil and upset were positively related to people's perceptions of the importance/difficulty of both real-life and hypothetical moral dilemmas. Furthermore, higher levels of angry, frustrated feelings as well as sympathy were associated with more care reasoning in the participants' everyday (real-life) moral dilemmas, but not in the standardized (hypothetical) dilemmas. Notably, sympathy and anger/frustration were negatively related to justice orientation scores on the real-life dilemmas. Largely, this pattern of findings is consistent with the view that a justice orientation involves a focus on rational, impartial rules, principles and individual rights - and therefore is likely influenced more by cognitive than emotional processes. Understandably, compared to the non-relational dilemmas, the relational ones evoked higher levels of upset, anger and sympathy. Individuals likely become more emotionally engaged in conflicts involving persons with whom they have close, long-term relationships than in interactions with strangers or in conflicts concerning mainly intrapersonal issues. Strong emotional reactions may be a sign of caring or investment in the actual relationship. Across all dilemmas women scored higher than men on upset and anger (but not on remorse-related feelings). Compared to men, women scored higher on care reasoning both on the real-life and hypothetical dilemmas. Women also reported more relational dilemmas which perhaps partly can account for their higher care reasoning scores on the real-life dilemmas. Walker (e.g., 2006) has argued that males and females do not differ in basic moral orientation but rather in the type of everyday conflicts they encounter and report. Still, the same pattern of sex differences was observed on the hypothetical dilemmas in this study. Clearly, this sex difference cannot be accounted for by dilemma content effects, and this finding is thus more clearly in line with Gilligan's original theoretical argument for more general orientation differences.

Since the sample was limited to North American students, this study was recently replicated in Norway (Skoe et al., 2012). Comparing findings in the United States with those in Norway, national similarities as well as differences were found. For example, similar patterns of results regarding emotions predicting the importance/difficulty of the dilemmas and care reasoning were observed, as well as similar sex differences in care reasoning and emotional reaction levels. Given the long-standing rank of Sweden and Norway as the two highest among all countries evaluated on gender equality by Hofstede (1984, 2001), the latter finding is perhaps rather surprising. The United States was ranked much lower (nr. 27). However, despite an active governmental policy of equal opportunities for women and men over many years in Norway, there are today still strong and traditional sex differences in occupational preferences; more women (about 80%) than men chose to study and work within the helping professions (e.g., nursing, teaching, social work), and more men (about 70%) than women chose technical (e.g., engineering, data processing) or economy-related professions (Hirsch et al., 2010). Paradoxically, then, in the country with the highest rating (after Sweden) on gender quality, there is a strongly sex-divided work market, unequal pay in equal positions and traditional career choices for men and women.

Furthermore, in the Skoe et al. (2012) study with Norwegian young adult students (a sample in which one would expect the least sex differences), compared to men, across all dilemmas (real-life as well as hypothetical) women scored significantly higher on several emotions such as upset, empathic anger, and sympathy. On the real-life dilemmas (but not the hypothetical), women also scored higher than did men on remorse. Thus, congruent with some stereotypes regarding emotionality, Norwegian women (like their American counterparts) seemed overall to be more emotionally engaged in the moral dilemmas than did the Norwegian men. Furthermore, women viewed the moral dilemmas as more difficult and scored higher on a care orientation in resolving them. As in the American sample (Skoe et al., 2002), Norwegian women also generated more personal or relational real-life dilemmas than did men, and men generated more nonrelational ones than did women. The apparent gap between politics and reality suggests that social factors such as equal opportunities may not eliminate certain psychological differences or preferences between men and women, even among well-educated young people, at least so far.

The national similarities and differences observed by Skoe et al. (2012) underscore the importance of cross cultural studies. Certainly, social contextual factors such as culture can influence the moral orientation of men and women through affecting the interpretation of- and priority given to care and justice relative to competing moral as well as nonmoral concerns (Carlo, Koller, Eisenberg, Da Silva, & Frohlich, 1996; Miller, 2006). Values and socialization emphases or practices may vary across time and culture. Hence, as Miller noted, it is a major challenge for work on morality to consider culture as well as context as it explores both common and culturally variable dimensions of moral outlooks.

Critiques of Gilligan's Theory

Gilligan has received ample criticism for her theory regarding the ethics of care and justice. To give some examples, she has been accused of oversimplifying Kohlbergian moral reasoning in her description of the justice orientation in that her description comes closest to the rather rigid law-and-order reasoning of Kohlberg's Stage 4. Critics have pointed out that Gilligan ignores the contention that justice and individual rights also exist in the context of social responsibilities and obligations; hence, at the higher stages of moral justice reasoning, individuals will follow rules and laws only if they benefit the common good (Jaffee & Hyde, 2000). Kohlberg and colleagues also have suggested that the care orientation is unnecessary or insufficient as a distinct mode of moral reasoning because Kohlberg's cognitive-developmental framework encompasses both care and justice; considerations of care, relationship and interpersonal trust are represented as norms and elements at each stage in Kohlberg's scoring scheme (Jaffee & Hyde, 2000). Another ardent critic, Walker (e.g., 2006) in his many studies (including some meta-analyses) has concluded that there is no meaningful relation between sex and Kohlberg's moral stage and little evidence for Gilligan's claim that his model undervalues the ethic of care, categorizing such reasoning at lower justice stages.

Shortly before his untimely death, Kohlberg (1986) wrote a chapter as a response to some of the critiques of his theory. Although arguing that cognitive moral judgment is the only factor that makes behavior moral, he seemed open to the idea that there is more to morality than his justice stage theory. Referring to Turiel's work on convention and Gilligan's on care and response, for example, Kohlberg stated that "Both of these researchers have contrasted their constructs with the justice construct in order to enlarge the social cognitive domain rather than rejecting the distinctive definition of the justice domain" (p. 500). Hence, rather than rejecting Gilligan's work, Kohlberg seems to think that her as well as others' research enlarged the social cognitive domain, and should exist alongside his justice domain (Jorgensen, 2006).

Critics have also complained that too little work has been done to characterize or validate the existence of Gilligan's proposed care and justice orientations other than to demonstrate that these two modes of moral reasoning are present in individuals' responses to moral dilemmas (e.g., Jaffee & Hyde, 2000; Walker, 2006.). Consequently, it is unclear whether moral orientations are used consistently across situations and over time or how they relate to each other or to moral actions. There is minimal evidence that moral orientations are used consistently between or within dilemmas, even when using Gilligan's preferred paradigm of real-life moral dilemmas. Walker has stated that many individuals use a mix of both orientations, with no clear focus or preference. As such, he further has argued, the term *orientation* seems unwarranted. Nevertheless, although it appears that most people can use both moral modes, overall women use somewhat more care reasoning and men more justice reasoning (e.g., Jaffee & Hyde, 2000; Skoe et al., 2002).

Gilligan (1982) has advanced the possibility that moral maturity entails a greater understanding or integration of the care and the justice perspectives. However, it has been noted that her conceptualizations offer few guidelines as to when one moral perspective represents a more adequate basis for moral action (Jaffee & Hyde, 2000), and that it is unclear how and at what level an integration of the two moral orientations might occur (Walker, 2006).

Critics (especially quantitative researchers) have highlighted the inaccessibility and subjectivity of the primarily qualitative coding systems developed within the Gilligan group (e.g., the *Reading Guide*, Brown, Tappan, Gilligan, Miller, & Argyris, 1989), precluding their widespread adoption by other researchers. Moreover, as noted by Jaffee and Hyde (2000), researchers have rarely agreed on how Gilligan's care and justice orientations should be defined or measured. Walker (2006) has criticized Gilligan for compounding this problem by her relative lack of interest or attention to measurement matters. Much of the debate and discrepancy between the Gilligan group and various quantitative critics, however, can be traced to the fact that they argue from different epistemological frameworks (Jaffee & Hyde, 2000).

Further questions have been raised by various researchers regarding Gilligan's theory on the developmental origin of the two moral orientations. For example, the notion that attachment and inequality are strongly related to sex has been challenged (Turiel, 1998; Walker, 2006), as has her exclusive focus on parents and the child's sense of identification with each parent. The child's relationships with siblings, peers and other adults may also play an important role for moral development. Walker (2006) pointed out that Gilligan's argument that the orientations arise in the context of gendered parent-child relationships ignores the role played by social, political, and economic structures in creating and maintaining the orientations as sex related as well as the role of culture.

Regarding the role of culture, in a series of studies Miller (e.g., 2006) observed that Indian respondents, as compared with U.S. respondents, show a greater tendency to see meeting the needs of others in close relationships as a matter of *moral duty* rather than of *personal choice*. Importantly, however, individuals' responses varied depending on the contextual factors being manipulated; cross-cultural commonalities as well as differences were found. For example, even U.S. respondents considered helping as obligatory in cases involving extreme need. Generally, the pattern of results among U.S. respondents, best described as an "individually oriented" morality of caring, was congruent with Gilligan's theory. However, the pattern of results observed in India, best described as a "duty-based" morality of caring, was not well captured by Gilligan's morality of caring framework, according to Miller (2006). Hence, she concluded that there are multiple forms rather than only one form of the morality of caring. Further work on the generalizability of the ethic of care theory across cultures, ethnicities and religions is required.

Developmental Levels of Care Reasoning

The extensive focus on sex differences in moral orientation has tended to obscure another important implication of Gilligan's (1982) original theory. In addition to defining care as a separate moral orientation, she also has outlined a developmental sequence of moral perspectives based on an ethic of care, just as Kohlberg has outlined a sequence based on an ethic of justice. On the basis of her 1-year follow up study of 21 women, diverse in age, ethnic background, and socioeconomic status (the *Abortion Decision Study*), Gilligan outlined a developmental continuum in their care orientation consisting of three main levels with two intermediary transition points. The first level is characterized by a focus on one's own needs, the second level by self-sacrifice and focus on the needs of others, and the third level by balanced care for self and others. Gilligan has since then abandoned a stage model of human development, focusing instead on more interpretive readings of narratives regarding justice, care and self-in-relation (e.g., Gilligan, Brown, & Rogers, 1990). As noted by Walker (2006), one reason for this retreat was her observation that the developmental sequence did not reflect the moral experiences of girls, given that the initial levels had been rooted in the reasoning of women considering whether to undergo an abortion. Another, more ideological reason was her increasing discomfort with certain concepts of developmental psychology, such as hard stages (e.g., those of Freud, Piaget, & Kohlberg) and her preference for describing these moral orientations using literary or musical analogies (Gilligan et al., 1990). In a recent interview (Jorgensen, 2006, p. 186), Gilligan said:

> In *In a different voice* I had stages. I was still bound to that paradigm. I have never written about stages since then ... my thinking about development is closer to Erikson's thinking.... That at different points in life you have an individually different ... psychological capacities was different, biological and physiological experiences... an adolescent has access to a range of emotions and a capacity to think beyond their own experience ... that the younger child doesn't have. Now, at each of these stages there is a different kind of encounter between the person and the society or culture. But I'm very much with Erikson, I mean, a statement of Erikson's that I took with me was, you can't take a life out of history. You can't talk about development apart from culture and history. And you could see all of my work as, what happens when you put a woman's life, or women's lives, into a history that hasn't carried those lives, and how it changes.... It affects the lives when you have no resonance coming back that reflects your experience. But it also changes history at the point that those voices become part of the conversation. And then I'd say, not only women, but also people of colour, people of all those cultures that we call, quote, different, and people of all those sexualities that we call different. And it suddenly became very clear, it certainly became very clear to me, that what was being called development, was a very particular slice through ... you know ... development. And that this was being held up as the ideal.

Skoe's Model

Despite Gilligan's abandonment of her developmental stages, the issue of developmental progression in the care ethic is still of empirical and theoretical interest to developmental researchers. In a series of studies, I have explored Gilligan's suggestions of developmental trends in the growth of care-oriented moral thought in both men and women. In my PhD dissertation (Skoe, 1987), I constructed and partially validated the *Ethic of Care Interview* (ECI). This instrument appears to be the first and, to my knowledge, only attempt at operationalizing Gilligan's (1982) early theory regarding developmental stages of the care ethic. The ECI provides a tool with which to answer questions about the relevance and usefulness of a care-based approach to moral reasoning in development.

THE ETHIC OF CARE INTERVIEW (ECI)

The purpose of the ECI is to attempt to categorize individuals' thinking in one of the Ethic of Care levels based on their responses to four moral dilemmas. Following Gilligan (1982), each level represents a different mode of resolving conflicts in human relationships and a different apprehension of the central concept that self and other are interdependent. Developmentally, the five levels described below involve a progressively more complex understanding of human relationships and an increasing differentiation of self and other.

The ECI consists of four dilemmas administered individually in a semistructured interview format. In addition to a real-life conflict generated by the participant, three standard interpersonal dilemmas are presented that involve conflicts about (a) unplanned pregnancy, (b) marital fidelity, and (c) care for a parent (see Appendix). Following the theories of Gilligan (1982) and Haan (1975), these dilemmas are used because they represent relatively frequently occurring interpersonal situations where helping others could be at the price of hurting oneself. The interviews are audio-recorded and take about 30 minutes to administer. They are scored according to the Ethic of Care Interview Manual (Skoe, 1993), which contains descriptions consistent with those outlined by Gilligan (1982) and sample responses for five care levels. The following are brief descriptions of the ECI levels and sample responses to the Betty/Erik dilemma (see Appendix) about an unhappy marriage to a recalcitrant spouse and the possibility of an emotionally satisfying extramarital relationship:

At *Level 1,* survival (caring for self), the lowest level in the ECI sequence, individuals think about relational issues in a self-protective, pragmatic way, neglecting the needs or feelings of others. The aims are primarily to ensure one's own happiness and to avoid being hurt or suffering. There are little, if any, considerations of abstract ethical principles or values.

> I don't think he should keep having an affair on his wife because that is going to end up not going in a positive direction. (*Why shouldn't he have an affair?*) Either his mistress is going to want him to leave his wife or his wife is going to find out. He is just going to get himself into more problems ... I think life is too short to stay in an unhappy situation. There are too many other opportunities to be happy. (*Why is it important to be happy?*) We are only here for about 80 years or so, we may as well make the best of it.

Level 1.5 concerns transition from self-care (survival) to a sense of responsibility. Concepts of selfishness and responsibility first appear. Caring for the self to ensure survival is criticized as selfish. Although aware of the needs of others, self-interest in relationships still is favored.

> There's actually three angles you can take it from. The first one would be Erik's happiness. If he's unsatisfied, he should do it. But from a legal/financial standpoint he shouldn't do it because he'd get screwed in the end, just like Derek would, and he'd get into that dilemma where he would lose his kids and Betty would divorce him; he'd lose a lot of money, Carol might leave.... Religiously, I don't know, slash morally, I guess, he shouldn't do it, just because he's married.... It would be very selfish. If you're unhappy try to fix the situation. If not, get a divorce quickly.

At *Level 2,* (caring for others), individuals are able to reason over the issues in terms of responsibility and care for others to the exclusion of the needs of self. Being a good person is equated with self-sacrificial concern for others, and right is externally defined, often by the parents, church, or society. There is a strong need for security. Being accepted or liked by other people is so important that others may be helped and protected, even at the expense of self-assertion.

> I don't believe in divorces or extramarital flings. She could try other ways to make her husband realize that she wants a bit more out of the marriage, possibly volunteer work or take a part-time job. The kids are old enough to be left alone some of the time.... She has been married a long time. She should try a bit harder to get through to her husband. She has children; divorce is hard on children. I believe in marriage and staying together. Marriage is a commitment, you should stay married.

Level 2.5 concerns transition to a reflective care perspective, marked by a shift in concern from goodness to truth and personal honesty in relationships. In comparison to the more "black-and-white" worldview of the previous level, complexities and nuances are expressed. The goodness or rightness of protecting other people at one's own expense is questioned.

> Communication doesn't seem to be too good between her and her husband. Her happiness is important because it affects the way you raise your children. If you're not happy in a situation, I think you should resolve it. Maybe she should tell her husband that she likes someone else now, or, I guess, divorce or something like that. Whichever way she feels she is more confident about herself.... I think it has a big influence on the kids. Divorce would as well. But if you weigh out the two, an unhappy marriage could be worse for the kids. If he is not going to listen, obviously she does

> not have a good relationship. You can't have a family if you can't communicate to each other. I think it is best that she get out of it then, put herself into a family where she is more settled and relaxed and the communication is better.

Finally, at *Level 3,* individuals fully realize the ethic of care (caring for both self and others). The needs and welfare of others as well as self are encompassed in a more balanced approach to reasoning about relationships. The tension between selfishness and responsibility is resolved through a new understanding of human interdependence. The insight now arises that by caring for others, you care for yourself, and vice versa. Thus, concern is expressed for everyone impacted in the situation, and attempts are made to minimize hurt or harm to all parties.

> I think that he should seek counseling personally and possibly try and get his wife in some type of counseling as well. I think in this relationship there is more at stake, as they have two children which is a big concern. I don't have children, but I assume that I will have a very strong bond with my children and I would not want to do anything to hurt that. So, my advice would be to seek professional help from people who are experienced in dealing with situations like these on a daily basis.... If that didn't work, I would seriously consider divorce if the situation were bad enough. I couldn't live in a miserable situation like that for an extended length of time because I feel that it would just deteriorate to arguing all the time or just a cold indifference, and I don't think either situation is good or beneficial for either the wife or the husband or the children.

To avoid biasing real-life choice by providing an example beforehand, the real-life dilemma is elicited first in various ways: "Have you ever been in a situation where you were not sure what was the right thing to do?" "Have you ever had a moral conflict?" "Could you describe a moral conflict?" Adapted from the work of Gilligan (1982), these questions eliciting a dilemma are then followed by a set of six probe questions: "Could you describe the situation?" "What were the conflicts for you in that situation?" "In thinking about what to do, what did you consider?" "What did you do?" "Did you think it was the right thing to do?" and "How do you know?" The standardized dilemmas are read aloud to the participants while they read along. Probes such as "What do you think Betty/Erik should do?" and "What would you do if you were in the same situation? Why?" are used to assess dilemma reasoning.

The ECI can be scored according to total score across the four dilemmas, yielding a potential range of 4.00-12.00 for any single participant, or according to level, yielding five discrete levels. The participant is given a level score for each dilemma. Quarter-level scores (e.g., 1.75, 2.25) can be assigned on any given dilemma when the response seems to fall between two levels, but should be used sparingly. If the person does not generate a real-life dilemma, the mean score for the other three dilemmas may be used in place of a real-life score. The total score is the sum of the ratings for the four dilemmas. Overall level scores on the ECI are determined by dividing the total scores by four and then rounding to the nearest of the .5 levels (e.g., 1.15 = Level 1; 2.45 = Level 2.5; 2.80 = Level 3). If a person's overall level score falls exactly between two levels (e.g., 2.25, 1.75), a second rater independently scores the person at one of the two adjacent levels.

With regard to inter-rater reliability, correlations between raters generally have ranged from .76 to .95 (Cohen's Kappa .63 – 1.00). Internal consistency, assessed via intercorrelations of scores on the four dilemmas, has generally ranged from .73 to .92, and the dilemma-total score correlations from .82 to .97. Cronbach's alphas of .94-.97 also have been calculated (Skoe, 1998). Thus, the ECI can be scored with a fair degree of inter-rater reliability and internal consistency. The concurrent and construct validity of the ECI will be discussed below.

Empirical Studies With the ECI

In the initial PhD study of 86 Canadian university women, 17-26 years of age (Skoe, 1987; Skoe & Marcia, 1991), the ECI was designed to examine care levels following Gilligan's (1982) theory. Based upon a proposed reciprocal linkage between moral development and identity (e.g., Kohlberg & Gilligan, 1972; Marcia, 1980), it was hypothesized that this new measure of care-based moral reasoning would be positively related to ego identity and to justice-based reasoning. In support of these expectations, the ECI was found to be positively related to age and ego identity development (Marcia, Waterman, Matteson, Archer, & Orlofsky, 1993), as well as to a written Kohlbergian justice measure, the *Sociomoral Reflection Measure* (SRM, Gibbs & Widaman, 1982). Furthermore, the ECI was more closely related to identity (r = .86) than was the Kohlbergian test (r = .37). What these findings demonstrated is that women's identity development and the development of women's care-based moral reasoning are closely related. Hence, they furnished some support for Gilligan's (1982) theory that a morality of care has relevance for women's personality development and that women's conceptions of self and morality are intricately linked.

Because the above study was restricted to women, however, it could not address potential sex differences or whether care-based moral reasoning is more applicable to women than to men, as Gilligan (e.g., 1982) has suggested. In addition, the finding that the ECI was more strongly related to identity than was the Kohlbergian measure may have been confounded because the ECI and identity were both assessed in interviews, whereas the SRM was a paper and pencil test. Therefore, a subsequent study was conducted with men as well as women (Skoe & Diessner, 1994), examining the relations among ego identity, care-based and justice-based moral reasoning with use of Kohlberg's *Moral Judgment Interview* (MJI; Colby & Kohlberg, 1987). The participants were 58 men and 76 women, mainly university students (91%) and some high school students in the United States, 16-30 years of age (M = 21, SD = 3). This extended study showed that the ECI was positively related to age, and strongly related both to ego identity (especially) and to justice-based moral development for men as well as women. The positive relationship between the ECI and Kohlberg's MJI has been replicated in several other studies (e.g., Juujärvi, 2003; Skoe et al., 1996).

There were no significant sex differences on the identity, justice or care measures themselves. Although these results indicated that sex differences may not be as pronounced as proposed by Gilligan (e.g., 1982), at least not when men and women are directed to focus on interpersonal dilemmas, further analyses suggested the care ethic still may operate differentially in men and women in important ways. For example, the partial correlation controlling for age between the ECI and identity was significantly higher than the correlation between the MJI and identity for women, but not for men (for further details, see Skoe & Diessner, 1994). Thus, the ethic of care may be a more central component of ego identity for women than for men. Replicating the above findings for women (Skoe, 1987; Skoe & Marcia, 1991), care-based moral development was more highly related to identity than was justice-based moral development. Furthermore, the extended study demonstrated that this differential relationship holds even when all three variables are measured by interview, precluding the alternative interpretation of common method variance for these effects. These results are consistent with Gilligan's (1982) claim that women's conceptions of self and morality are closely linked and that the care ethic has special relevance for women's personality development. Moreover, more women than men reported personal real-life dilemmas, whereas more men than women reported impersonal ones. The care ethic may influence women's everyday life experiences, memories and thought more than men's, perhaps due to culture, socialization, norms and values in the male peer group, or activity preferences.

Further construct validity was assessed by relating the ECI to ego development. Conceptually, morality has been considered an aspect of ego development (e.g., Blasi, 1998; Gilligan, 1982; Kohlberg, 1984; Loevinger, 1979). In Loevinger's view, ego is that aspect of personality that establishes a basic unity by constructing the meanings one gives to oneself, to other people and to the social world. Her sentence completion test measures sequential stages in the growth of this broad construction of meaning. The link between ego development and justice reasoning has been reasonably well researched (e.g., Snarey, 1998), but little attention has been devoted to the relationship between ego growth and the ethic of care. Furthermore, since relations among personality aspects and morality seldom have been studied outside North America, it is unclear whether the patterns of relations found in the United States can be generalized to other groups. Hence, Skoe and Lippe (2002) conducted a study in Norway, examining the relations among ego development and justice and care ethic reasoning levels in 144 Norwegian university students (equal number of men and women), 15 to 48 years old. The aims of this study were threefold: (a) to examine the relationship between ego and moral development in a non-American sample; (b) to look at the differential association between ego development and that of the justice and care ethics; and (c) to control for variations in age, sex, education and verbal intelligence.

As predicted on the basis of theory and previous research (e.g., Kohlberg, 1984; Loevinger, 1979; Skoe, 1998; Skoe & Diessner, 1994), both care as measured by the ECI and justice as measured by the *Defining Issues Test* (DIT, Rest, 1979) were positively related to ego development as measured by Loevinger's sentence completion test (Hy & Loevinger, 1996). Furthermore, the correlation between ECI total scores and ego development, $r(144) = .58, p < .0001$, was significantly higher than the one between DIT P scores and ego development, $r(141) = .20, p < .02, t(138) = 4.38, p < .0001$. Sex was not significantly related to any of the measures and was therefore dropped in subsequent analyses. When age, education and verbal intelligence were controlled, the relation between ego development and ECI remained significant, $r(136) = .51, p < .0001$, but the relations between ego development and the DIT, $r(136) = .13$, *ns*, and between the ECI and the DIT, $r(136) = .13$, *ns*, were not. In this Norwegian study, there were no significant sex differences in the correlation between ego development and the ECI. The link between care reasoning development and ego growth was strong for both men and women.

The ECI's low positive relationship to verbal intelligence ($r = .34$) seems reasonable since it is a verbal test assessing complex reasoning about care for self and others. The results also showed that the ECI is conceptually distinct from verbal intelligence. With verbal ability partialed out, the variance shared between the ECI and ego development remained substantial. The DIT, however, did not relate significantly to ego development or to care reasoning when the effect of verbal intelligence was controlled. These findings suggested that the weak positive relationships between the DIT and ego development, as well as between the DIT and ECI are reduced to their common overlap with verbal ability which has been called "the most salient marker of general intelligence" (Sanders, Lubinski, & Benbow, 1995, p. 502). This is not the case for the relationship between the ECI and ego development. Ego and care development seem to have more in common with each other than they have with justice development, perhaps especially at the higher stages where both ego and care developments involve greater ability to integrate respect for personal autonomy with responsibility, compassion and intimacy in relationships. In this way, ego growth and care development may be seen as mutually enhancing.

Overall, research with the ECI has supported the relevance and usefulness of a care-based approach to moral reasoning. A series of studies has shown that balanced care for the needs of self and others seems to develop gradually across childhood into young adulthood, somewhat paralleling the developmental trends in justice reasoning (e.g., Pratt, Skoe, & Arnold, 2004; Skoe & Diessner, 1994; Skoe & Lippe, 2002). The pattern of results indicates that variations in care reasoning levels have implications for personal and social adaptation across the life cycle for both men and women. The sequence of ECI levels is, for example, positively related, not only to identity, ego growth and justice reasoning, as demonstrated in the studies above, but also to empathic perspective-taking (Skoe, 2010), androgyny (Skoe, 1995; Sochting, Skoe, & Marcia, 1994), cognitive complexity, perceived social support, and physical health in maturity (Skoe et al., 1996). Furthermore, care levels were negatively related to personal distress (Skoe, 2010) and authoritarianism (Skoe et al., 1996). Hence, people higher in the ethic of care appear also to have a stronger sense of self and social awareness, a greater tolerance for ambiguity and for people with problems, and a greater ability or willingness to see the world from others' viewpoint.

Moreover, higher ECI levels of reasoning are associated with prosocial behavior (Pratt et al., 2004; Skoe, 1998), such as greater volunteer participation in community activities (e.g., helping the elderly, visiting those in hospitals, and charity donations). In comparison, a group of adult forensic psychiatric patients, all of whom had committed acts of serious violence (Adshead, Brown, Skoe, Glover, & Nicholson, 2008), almost uniformly scored at the lowest ECI levels (survival, caring for the self). Given the positive relationships observed between sophistication in ECI care reasoning and personal as well as psychosocial growth, the ability to care *both* for oneself and others seems to be a central component of what is called maturity or wisdom (Skoe, 2008).

The evidence for average sex differences in levels on the ECI has been rather intricate. No differences have been found between males and females in average levels of care reasoning during adolescence and young adulthood (e.g., Skoe, 1998; Skoe, 2010), with the exception of one finding of greater sophistication among girls in early adolescence (Skoe & Gooden, 1993, but see Skoe et al., 1999). In later adulthood, however, women have been observed to score higher than men on the ECI (Skoe et al., 1996), though these differences might also be evidence for a cohort effect, since the design in this study could not separate age and year of birth. Results for a meta-analysis on the ECI (covering seven independent samples) suggested a small to moderate sex difference (favoring women) that seemed larger among middle-aged and older adults. However, moderator analyses for age differences could not be conducted on such a small sample of studies (Jaffee & Hyde, 2000); thus, these results should be viewed with caution.

Relatively few people, about 15% (Skoe, 1998), score at the highest ECI level (balanced care for others and self). An important question then arises: what kind of mechanisms or factors may facilitate change and growth in care-based moral thought? A Canadian longitudinal study (Pratt et al., 2004) examined patterns of development in the ECI over the period from age 16 to age 20. Findings showed no sex differences, but a significant gain in level of care reasoning over time. Although the increases over the 4 years were significant, they were modest in nature. Nonetheless, such modest gains are typical of late adolescents for the Kohlbergian justice tests as well (e.g., Walker, 1989). Hence, the results suggested that the ECI is developmental in nature during the middle to late adolescent period. Furthermore, parenting factors when the children were age 16, such as parents' emphasis on caring as a goal in family stories and the use of more authoritative and autonomy-encouraging child-rearing practices, were associated with higher levels of care reasoning in adolescents at age 20.

In addition to family styles and relationships, there is evidence that certain types of education may play a significant role in care development. As part of her PhD dissertation, Juujärvi (2003, 2006) investigated changes in ECI levels over a 2-year period among practical nursing, social work and law enforcement students in Finland. Perhaps not surprisingly, the first groups both progressed significantly in care reasoning, but not the latter one. Furthermore, at the beginning of the students' education, there was no significant relation between scores on the ECI and emotional empathy. After two years of studying, however, participants (both men and women) at ECI Level 3 scored higher on empathy than did those at the other levels (2.5, 2 and 1.5). Thus, education might be an important intervening factor, as Juujärvi (2003) has suggested. In addition to family relations and education, other factors that should be considered are cognitive as well as emotional development, social opportunities, period in life, historical cohort, cultural background, major life events, faith and religious experience (Skoe, 2008, in press). Further work, such as cross cultural longitudinal studies across the lifespan, is needed to establish whether individuals progress sequentially through the ECI levels.

Summary and Conclusion

In sum, the use and application of Gilligan's theory in research have yielded many new insights in the field of morality. Although parts of her theory have been refuted, other parts have been supported. Generally, Gilligan's controversial claim of sex differences in morality seems correct more in terms of emotional than in reasoning capacities, at least in young adulthood, when this has been studied most extensively. There are few differences between men and women in competence or abilities with a strong sociocognitive basis, such as stages of moral reasoning and empathic perspective taking; but there are more differences between men and women in some capacities with a strong emotional basis, such as sympathy, empathic distress and spontaneous care-oriented responses in moral conflict situations (e.g., Eisenberg, Cumberland, Guthrie, Murphy, & Shepard, 2005; Skoe, Eisenberg, & Cumberland, 2002). It is unclear whether these rather persistent patterns of sex differences are due to socialisation in the home or in schools, norms, values and expectations in the peer groups of men and women, or due to other factors (e.g., definition or measurement). Because of differences in socialisation, social roles and relational experiences, early in life women may learn to focus more than men on others' needs and wishes. Research has indicated that sex differences in care components appear before school age. As an example, in a recent study of 6-year-old kindergarten children, girls showed more sympathy and moral motivation; furthermore, mothers and teachers rated girls higher than boys on prosocial behavior (Malti, Gummerum, Keller, & Buchmann, 2009).

In any case, the evidence on sex differences in moral reasoning is contentious for good reasons. Especially in late adolescence and young adulthood (which are the age groups most frequently studied) sex differences seem to be complex and subtle. Rather than showing up as simple main effects on standardized measures, sex differences have been observed mainly in the relations among standardized tests, and in the content or nature of participants' spontaneously reported, self-chosen real-life conflicts. These findings may reflect the possibly important distinction between what people *can* do (competence) when it is required of them and what they *will* do (preference) on their own initiative. By design, Kohlberg's measure pulls for justice reasoning, pitting social rules and laws against human needs, and the ECI pulls for care reasoning, pitting the needs of others against those of oneself (Skoe & Diessner, 1994).

Despite considerable critical comments and mixed support for her theory, Gilligan also has received some proper praise for many positive contributions. She has been credited with extending the scope of the moral domain to include a moral orientation of care as well as a moral orientation of justice. Although Gilligan (1982) argued that these two moral orientations were sex related, she was not asserting that girls and women always reason in terms of caring and never give weight to justice issues. Rather, her point was to identify a qualitatively distinct approach to moral reasoning that was not at that time represented in psychological theory, with its exclusive focus on the justice ethic (Miller, 2006). Today, it is generally acknowledged that Gilligan's theorizing has augmented our understanding of moral psychology with her emphasis on care, response, human interconnection, and relationships. In contrast, Kohlberg's approach emphasizes cognitive reasoning as being the essence of morality, excluding serious consideration of other aspects of moral functioning (Walker, 2006). Importantly, Gilligan has highlighted the role that sex, emotion, context and type of content or dilemma (real-life versus hypothetical) may play in responding to moral dilemmas. With her reliance on personally experienced, real-life dilemmas, she has introduced a new methodology to assess moral reasoning, an approach that has generated numerous studies and new insights (Jaffee & Hyde, 2000; Walker, 2006). Certainly, Gilligan has successfully underscored the need to include and represent more carefully the lived experience of women in psychological theories and research.

Furthermore, my research program has provided some empirical evidence for the validity of Gilligan's suggested developmental levels in the care ethic (e.g., Skoe, 1998, 2008, in press). Findings with the ECI indicate that sophistication in care reasoning, or balanced care for self and others, may be an aspect of positive adaptation across the lifespan. Considering the persistence and even perhaps increase in violence worldwide, it seems that moral education, including both the care and justice ethics, deserves a more prominent place in our societies. Teaching and training young people to include both self and others in the compass of care, and to practice justice as well as mercy, should serve the future well. Therefore, the first obligation of schools is to make care manifest in their structure, relationships and curriculum, as argued by Noddings (2002). In schools as well as in higher education the development of the person as a whole human being should be emphasized—

not only factual or intellectual knowledge but also sociomoral and spiritual growth. For students living in a violent world, the search for meaning is especially important. Engaging in such a search is a sign of caring for one's self, and part of learning to care for self is "a concomitant learning to care for others" (Nodding, 2002, p. 35). Similarly, Kohlberg (1970) stated that we must find meaning in our own lives before we can find it in helping others. Contemplating a metaphoric Stage 7, he said that to answer the question of "why be moral is to tell you the meaning of life, to give you faith" (p. 1). The essence of Stage 7 is "the sense of being a part of the whole of life and the adoption of a cosmic, as opposed to a universal humanistic (Stage 6) perspective" (Kohlberg & Ryncarz, 1990, p. 192). Perhaps faith and meaning also are an answer to another important question—why care? Finding meaning in life may be a key to gaining insight into human interconnection and to developing the ability to take care of *both* self and others.

APPENDIX: THE ETHIC OF CARE INTERVIEW

THE RESEARCHER GENERATED DILEMMAS

The specific researcher generated dilemmas for *females* are as follows:

THE LISA DILEMMA

Lisa is a successful teacher in her late 20s who has always supported herself. Her life has been centered on her work and she has been offered a permanent position for next year. Recently she has been involved in an intense love affair with a married man and now finds that she is pregnant.

What do you think Lisa should do? Why?

THE BETTY DILEMMA

Betty, in her late 30s, has been married to Erik for several years. They have two children, 8 and 10 years old. Throughout the marriage Betty has been at home, looking after the house and the children. For the last few years Betty has felt increasingly unhappy in the marriage relationship. She finds her husband demanding, self-centered, and insensitive as well as uninterested in her needs and feelings. Betty has several times tried to communicate her unhappiness and frustration to her husband, but he continually ignores and rejects her attempts. Betty has become very attracted to another man, Steven, a single teacher. Recently, Steven has asked Betty for a more intimate, committed relationship.

What do you think Betty should do? Why?

THE KRISTINE DILEMMA

Kristine, a 26-year-old woman, has decided to live on her own after having shared an apartment with a girlfriend for the last 3 years. She finds that she is much happier living alone as she now has more privacy and independence and gets more work and studying done. One day her mother, whom she has not seen for a long while as they do not get along too well, arrives at the doorstop with two large suitcases, saying that she is lonely and wants to live with Kristine.

What do you think Kristine should do? Why?

The specific researcher generated dilemmas for *males* are as follows:

THE DEREK DILEMMA

Derek is a married, successful teacher in his late 20s. His life has been centered on his work and he has been offered a permanent position for next year. Recently, he has been involved in an intense love affair with a single woman who has just told him that she is pregnant and that it is his child.

What do you think Derek should do? Why?

THE ERIK DILEMMA

Erik, in his late 30s, has been married to Betty for several years. They have two children, 8 and 10 years old. Throughout the marriage Betty has been at home, looking after the house and the children. For the last few years Erik has felt increasingly unhappy in the marriage relationship. He finds his wife demanding, self-centered, and insensitive as well as uninterested in his needs and feelings. Erik has several times tried to communicate his unhappiness and frustration to his wife, but she continually ignores and rejects his attempts. Erik has become very attracted to another woman, Carol, a single teacher. Recently, Carol has asked Erik for a more intimate, committed relationship.

What do you think Erik should do? Why?

THE CHRIS DILEMMA

Chris, a 26-year-old man, has decided to live on his own after having shared an apartment with a friend for the last 3 years. He finds that he is much happier living alone as he now has more privacy and independence and gets more work and studying done. One day his father, whom he has not seen for a long while as they do not get along too well, arrives at the doorstop with two large suitcases, saying that he is lonely and wants to live with Chris.

What do you think Chris should do? Why?

REFERENCES

Adshead, G., Brown, C., Skoe, E. E., Glover, J., & Nicholson, S. (2008). Studying moral reasoning in forensic psychiatric patients. In G. Widdershoven, J. McMillan, T. Hope, & L. van der Scheer (Eds.), *Empirical ethics in psychiatry* (pp. 211-230). New York, NY: Oxford University Press.

Blasi, A. (1998). Loevinger's theory of ego development and its relationship to the cognitive-developmental approach. In P. Michiel Westenberg, A. Blasi, & L. D. Cohn (Eds.), *Personality development: Theoretical, empirical, and clinical investigations of Loevinger's conception of ego development* (pp. 13-25). London, England: Erlbaum.

Brown, L. M., Tappan, M. B., Gilligan, C., Miller, B. A., & Argyris, D. E. (1989). Reading for self and moral voice: A method for interpreting narratives of real-life moral conflict and choice. In M. J. Packer & R. B. Addison (Eds.), *Entering the circle: Hermeneutic investigations in psychology* (pp. 141-164). Albany, NY: State University of New York Press.

Brown, L., Tappan, M., & Gilligan, C. (1995). Listening to different voices. In W. M. Kurtines & J. L. Gewirtz (Eds.), *Moral development: An introduction* (pp. 311-335). Boston, MA: Allyn & Bacon.

Carlo, G., Koller, S. H., Eisenberg, N., Da Silva, M. S., & Frohlich, C. B. (1996). A cross-national study on the relations among prosocial moral reasoning, gender role orientations, and prosocial behaviors. *Developmental Psychology, 32(2)*, 231-240.

Chodorow, N. (1978). *The reproduction of mothering.* Berkeley, CA: University of California Press.

Colby, A., & Kohlberg, L. (Eds.). (1987). *The measurement of moral judgment.* New York, NY: Cambridge University Press.

Eisenberg, N., Cumberland, A., Guthrie, I. K., Murphy, B. C., & Shepard, S. A. (2005). Age changes in prosocial responding and moral reasoning in adolescence and early adulthood. *Journal of Research on Adolescence, 15*(3), 235-260.

Ford, M. R., & Lowery, C. R. (1986). Gender differences in moral reasoning: A comparison of the use of justice and care orientations. *Journal of Personality and Social Psychology, 50*, 777-783.

Gibbs, J. E., & Widaman, K. F. (1982). *Social intelligence: Measuring the development of sociomoral reflection.* Englewood Cliffs, NJ: Prentice-Hall.

Gilligan, C. (1982). *In a different voice: Psychological theory and women's development.* Cambridge, MA: Harvard University Press.

Gilligan, C., & Attanucci, J. (1988). Two moral orientations: Gender differences and similarities. *Merrill-Palmer Quarterly, 34*, 223-237.

Gilligan, C., Brown, L. M., & Rogers, A. (1990). Psyche embedded: A place for body, relationships, and culture in personality theory. In A. I. Rabin, R. A. Zucker, R. A. Emmons, & S. Frank (Eds.), *Studying persons and lives* (pp. 86-147). New York, NY: Springer.

Haan, N. (1975). Hypothetical and actual moral reasoning in a situation of civil disobedience. *Journal of Personality and Social Psychology, 32*, 255-270.

Hirsch, A. A., Flatebø, G., Modig, I., Sandnes, T., Aalandslid, V., Thorsen, L. R., & Stene, R. J. (2010). *Dette er Kari og Ola: Kvinner og menn i Norge* [This is Kari and Ola: Women and Men in Norway]. Oslo, Norway: Statistisk Sentralbyrå.

Hofstede, G. (1984). *Culture's consequences: International differences in work-related values.* Beverly Hills, CA: SAGE.

Hofstede, G. (2001). *Culture's consequences: Comparing values, behaviors, institutions, and organization across nations.* Thousand Oaks, CA: SAGE.

Hy, L. X., & Loevinger, J. (1996). *Measuring ego development.* Mahwah, NJ: Erlbaum.

Jaffee, S., & Hyde, J. S. (2000). Gender differences in moral orientation: A meta-analysis. *Psychological Bulletin, 126*(5), 703-726.

Jorgensen, G. (2006). Kohlberg and Gilligan: Duet or duel? *Journal of Moral Education, 35(2)*, 179-196.

Josselson, R. L. (1987). *Finding herself: Pathways to identity development in women.* San Francisco, CA: Jossey-Bass.

Juujärvi, S. (2003). *The ethic of care and its development. A longitudinal study among practical nursing, bachelor-degree social work and law enforcement students* (Unpublished doctoral dissertation). University of Helsinki, Finland.

Juujärvi, S. (2005). The ethic of care and its development. Care and justice in real-life moral reasoning. *Journal of Adult Development, 12*(4), 199-210.

Juujärvi, S. (2006). The ethic of care development. A longitudinal study of moral reasoning among practical-nursing, social-work and law-enforcement students. *Scandinavian Journal of Psychology, 47*, 193-202.

Kohlberg, L. (December, 1970). *The Ethical Life, the Contemplative Life and Ultimate Religion—Notes Toward Stage 7—Social Sciences 154 lecture* (Unpublished manuscript). Pusey Archives, Harvard University. (HUGFP 130.54, Box 3, "Notes Toward Stage 7").

Kohlberg, L. (1984). *The psychology of moral development.* San Francisco, CA: Harper & Row.

Kohlberg, L. (1986). A current statement on some theoretical issues. In S. Modgil & C. Modgil (Eds.), *Lawrence Kohlberg: consensus and controversy* (pp.485-546). Philadelphia, PA: The Falmer Press.

Kohlberg, L., & Gilligan, C. (1972). The adolescent as a philosopher: the discovery of the self in a postconventional world. In J. Kagan & R. Coles (Eds.), *12 to 16: Early adolescence* (pp. 144-180). New York, NY: Norton.

Kohlberg, L., & Ryncarz, R. A. (1990). Beyond Justice Reasoning: Moral Development and Consideration of a Seventh Stage. In C. N. Alexander & E. J. Langer (Eds.), *Higher stages of human development* (pp. 191-207). New York, NY: Oxford University Press.

Loevinger, J. (1979). Construct validity of the sentence completion test of ego development. *Applied Psychological Measurement, 3*, 281-311.

Lyons, N. (1983). Two perspectives: on self, relationships, and morality. *Harvard Educational Review, 53*, 25-145.

Malti, T., Gummerum, M., Keller, M., & Buchmann, M. (2009) Children's moral motivation, sympathy, and prosocial behaviour. *Child Development, 80*(2), 442-460.

Marcia, J. E. (1980). Identity in adolescence. In J. Adelson (Ed.), *Handbook of adolescent psychology* (pp. 159-187). New York, NY: Wiley.

Marcia, J. E., Waterman, A. S., Matteson, D. R., Archer, S. L., & Orlofsky, J. L. (1993). *Ego identity: A handbook for psychosocial research.* New York, NY: Springer–Verlag.

Meyers, C. S. (2001, October). *Care-based reasoning of early adolescents: Its relationship with sex differences, feminine gender role identity, and teacher-perceived cooperation.* Paper presented at the Association for Moral Education Conference. Vancouver, B.C. Canada.

Miller, J. G. (2006). Insights into moral development from cultural psychology. In M. Killen & J. Smetana (Eds.), *Handbook of moral development* (pp. 375-393). Mahwah, NJ: Erlbaum.

Noddings, N. (1984). *Caring: A feminine approach to ethics and moral education.* Berkeley, CA: University of California Press.

Noddings, N. (2002). *Educating moral people. A caring alternative to character education.* New York, NY: Teachers College Press.

Pratt, M. W., Diessner, R., Hunsberger, B., Pancer, S. M., & Savoy, K. (1991). Four pathways in the analysis of adult development and aging: Comparing analyses of reasoning about personal-life dilemmas. *Psychology and Aging, 6,* 666-675.

Pratt, M. W., Golding, G., Hunter, W., & Sampson, R. (1988). Sex differences in adult moral orientations. *Journal of Personality, 56,* 373-391.

Pratt, M. W., Skoe, E. E., & Arnold, M. L. (2004). Care reasoning development and family socialization patterns in later adolescence: A longitudinal analysis. *International Journal of Behavioral Development,* 28(2), 139-147.

Rest, J. R. (1979). *Development in judging moral issues.* Minneapolis, MN: University of Minnesota.

Sanders, C. E., Lubinski, D., & Benbow, C. P. (1995). Does the Defining Issues Test measure psychological phenomena distinct from verbal ability?: An examination of Lykken's Query. *Journal of Personality and Social Psychology, 69,* 498-504.

Skoe, E. E. (1987). The development and partial validation of a care-based measure of moral development. *Dissertation Abstracts International, 50*(04-B), p. 1657.

Skoe, E. E. (1993). *The ethic of care interview manual.* Unpublished manuscript available from the author upon request. University of Oslo, Oslo, Norway.

Skoe, E. E. (1995). Sex role orientation and its relationship to the development of identity and moral thought. *Scandinavian Journal of Psychology, 36,* 235-245.

Skoe, E. E. A. (1998). The ethic of care: Issues in moral development. In E. E. Aspaas Skoe & A. L. von der Lippe (Eds.), *Personality development in adolescence: A cross national and life span perspective* (pp. 143-171). London: Routledge.

Skoe, E. E. (2008). Care, inventory of (Ethic of Care Interview). In F. Clark Power, R. J. Nuzzi, D. Narvaez, D. Lapsley, & T. C. Hunt (Eds.), *Moral Education. A Handbook. Vol. 1: A-L* (pp. 57-58). Westport, CT: Praeger.

Skoe, E. E. A. (2010). The relationship between empathy-related constructs and care-based moral development in young adulthood. *Journal of Moral Education, 39(2),* 191-211.

Skoe, E. E. A. (in press). Measuring care-based moral development: The Ethic of Care Interview. *Journal of Adult Development.*

Skoe, E. E. A., Cumberland, A., Eisenberg, N., Hansen, K., & Perry, J. (2002). The influences of sex and gender-role identity on moral cognition and prosocial personality traits. *Sex Roles, 46*(9-10), 295-309.

Skoe, E. E., & Diessner, R. (1994). Ethic of care, justice, identity and gender: An extension and replication. *Merrill-Palmer Quarterly, 40,* 102-119.

Skoe, E. E. A., Eisenberg, N., & Cumberland, A. (2002). The role of reported emotion in real-life and hypothetical moral dilemmas. *Personality and Social Psychology Bulletin, 28,* 962-973.

Skoe, E. E. A., Eisenberg, N., & Neset, S. (2012). *A cross-national comparison on the role of reported emotion in real-life and hypothetical moral dilemmas in young adulthood.* Manuscript submitted for publication.

Skoe, E. E., & Gooden, A. (1993). Ethic of care and real-life moral dilemma content in early adolescents. *Journal of Early Adolescence, 13(2),* 154-167.

Skoe, E. E. A., Hansen, K. L., Mørch, W. T., Bakke, I., Hoffmann, T., Larsen, B., & Aasheim, M. (1999). Care-based moral reasoning in Norwegian and Canadian early adolescents: A cross national comparison. *Journal of Early Adolescence, 19,* 280-291.

Skoe, E. E., & Lippe, A. L. von der. (2002). Ego development and the ethics of care and justice: The relations among them revisited. *Journal of Personality, 70,* 485-507.

Skoe, E. E., & Marcia, J. E. (1991). A care-based measure of morality and its relation to ego identity. *Merrill-Palmer Quarterly, 37*(2), 289-304.

Skoe, E. E., Pratt, M. W., Matthews, M., & Curror, S. E. (1996). The Ethic of Care: Stability over time, gender differences and correlates in mid to late adulthood. *Psychology and Aging, 11,* 280-293.

Snarey, J. (1998). Ego development and the ethical voices of justice and care: An Eriksonian interpretation. In P. M. Westenberg, A. Blasi, & L. Cohn (Eds.), *Personality development: Theoretical, empirical, and clinical investigations* (pp. 163-180). London: Erlbaum.

Sochting, I., Skoe, E. E., & Marcia, J. E. (1994). Care-oriented moral reasoning and prosocial behavior: A question of gender or sex role orientation. *Sex Roles, 31,* 131-147.

Turiel, E. (1998). The development of morality. In W. Damon (Ed.), *Handbook of child psychology* (5th ed., Vol. 3, pp. 863-932). New York, NY: Wiley.

Walker, L. J. (1984). Sex differences in the development of moral reasoning: A critical review. *Child Development, 55,* 677-691.

Walker, L. J. (1989). A longitudinal study of moral reasoning. *Child Development, 60,* 157-166.

Walker, L. J. (2006). Gender and morality. In M. Killen & J. Smetana (Eds.), *Handbook of moral development* (pp. 93-115). Mahwah, NJ: Erlbaum.

Walker, L. J., de Vries B., & Trevethan, S. D. (1987). Moral stages and moral orientations in real-life and hypothetical dilemmas. *Child Development, 58,* 842-858.

Wark, G. R., & Krebs, D. L. (1996). Gender and dilemma differences in real-life moral judgment. *Developmental Psychology, 32,* 220-230.

Wark, G. R., & Krebs, D. L. (1997). Sources of variation in moral judgment: Toward a model of real-life morality. *Journal of Adult Development, 4,* 163-178.

Wark, G. R., & Krebs, D. L. (2000). The construction of moral dilemmas in everyday life. *Journal of Moral Education, 29*(1), 5-21.

Zahn-Waxler, C., Cole., P. M., & Barrett, K. C. (1991). Guilt and empathy: Sex differences and implications for the development of depression. In J. Garber & K. A. Doge (Eds.), *The development of emotion regulation and dysregulation* (pp. 243-272). New York, NY: Cambridge University Press.

Author Contact Information: Eva E. A. Skoe, PhD, Department of Psychology, University of Oslo, P. O. Box 1094 Blindern, N-0317 Oslo, Norway. Phone: +47 22 84 50 00. E-mail: eva.skoe@psykologi.uio.no

CHAPTER 52

Making a Moral Decision

A Proposition for an Integrated Model of Cognition, Emotion, and Social Interaction

Lily Dyson
Simon Fraser University

Paul Crawford and Sonya Frey
University of Victoria

Sarah Dykstra
University of British Columbia

This chapter will address the moral decision-making processes that lead to moral behaviors and actions in adolescents and children. An integrated model of cognition, emotions, and social interaction is proposed which may be applied to elucidate the developmental processes that contribute to moral judgment. The chapter will begin with a review of major theories of moral development, focusing on the cognitive-structural models of Piaget and Kohlberg, the affective model of Hoffman, and theories associated with socialization. The review will be followed by a proposed theoretical model that outlines the processes involved in making a moral decision. The model integrates cognitive, affective, and social interaction domains. Finally, the chapter will present empirical research to preliminarily validate and support the proposed model.

MORALITY

Over the course of the past century, various definitions of morality have been presented. Morality is typically defined as "a practical, directive mode of discourse functioning to guide conduct and alter behavior" (Nielsen, 1963, p. 91). Turiel (1983) defined the moral domain as the "prescriptive judgments of justice, rights, and welfare pertaining to how people ought to relate to each other" (p. 3). Haidt (2001) conceptualized morality as the positive and negative evaluations of the "actions or characters of a person that are made with respect to a set of virtues held to be obligatory by a culture or subculture" (p. 817). In spite of varying definitions regarding the concept of morality (Whiteley, 1970), there is a certain consensus regarding the central axiom that characterizes morality: in general, it is thought to revolve around the protection of individuals (Haidt & Graham, 2007). According to these authors, justice and care both matter only insofar as they protect individuals.

As Sprigge (1970) observed, "moral issues are everyone's concern" (p. 145). Children encounter moral issues within their families from very early in their lives (Dunn, 2006). Morality is central to human interactions and individuals are frequently faced with situations which involve morality. The issue of morality arises in many of these instances where a decision has to be made between conflicting circumstances. The process of making a moral decision or moral judgment is thus

The Handbook of Educational Theories, pp. 629–642

set in motion. An interest of social significance emerges then: "how individuals come to manage the inevitable conflict between personal needs and social obligation" (Hoffman, 1983, p. 236). In this regard, a specific question is: How do individuals come to make a moral judgment or moral decision? This question constitutes the primary focus of this chapter.

MORAL JUDGMENT AND MORAL DECISION MAKING

Stein and Nemeroff (as cited in Haidt, 2001) define *moral judgments* as "evaluations (good vs. bad) of the actions or character of a person that are made with respect to a set of virtues held to be obligatory by a culture or subculture" (p. 817). In the literature, the term "moral judgment" is commonly used interchangeably with the term "moral reasoning." Based on Galotti (1989), Haidt defines *moral reasoning* as "conscious mental activity that consists of transforming given information about people in order to reach a moral judgment" (p. 818). Further drawn from Bargh (1994), Haidt adds that, "To say that moral reasoning is a conscious process means that the process is intentional, effortful, and controllable and that the reasoner is aware that it is going on" (p. 818). According to Schlaefli, Rest, and Thoma (1985), *moral judgment* concerns "how people define one or another course of action in a situation as morally right" (p. 319). Narvaez, Getz, Rest, and Thoma (1999) have expanded the concept of moral judgment by using the term *moral thinking* to refer to "people's judgments about right and wrong and the rationale behind such thinking" (p. 478). For Narvaez and associates, moral thinking is meant to encompass a broader spectrum of meaning than moral judgment in that *moral judgment* refers more narrowly to the cognitive construction of basic epistemological categories (e.g., justice, duty, legitimate authorities, and rights). By contrast, *moral thinking* refers to an individual's views on such issues as abortion, the rights of homosexual individuals, the presence of religion in public schools, women's roles, and euthanasia. These theoretical perspectives collectively suggest that moral judgment and moral reasoning, as well as moral thinking, primarily involve the evaluation of just and unjust and right and wrong based on a set of criteria established by a society, culture or subculture. Moreover, moral reasoning or moral judgment is a conscious, controllable, and intentional process. As seen, these three terms, *moral reasoning, moral judgment,* and *moral thinking,* have been referred by theorists and researchers to similar characteristics and, therefore, are used interchangeably in the present chapter.

THEORIES OF MORAL DEVELOPMENT AND JUDGMENT

COGNITIVE-STRUCTURAL THEORY—PIAGET

Numerous theories have been developed to explain moral judgment or moral reasoning. Leading the modern theories is Piaget's. Drawing from his epistemological study of children's mathematical and scientific reasoning, Piaget (1932/1965) explored how children come to understand and respect rules (Lapsley, 2006). As with his study of mathematical and scientific reasoning, he perceived moral judgment to be governed by both biological and developmental processes. Such a developmental trend also has a sociogenetic and psychological basis. For Piaget, moral judgment is thus based on the structure and organization of the cognitive system that unfolds as determined by the genetic and developmental predisposition within certain sociopsychological constraints. The transformation of moral judgment proceeds in stages.

Piaget's (1932/1965) main research method involved a set of questions concerning rules. These questions were presented to children as they played a formal game with a shared set of rules or as they encountered certain moral dilemmas in the game. Children were asked such questions as: "What are the rules?", "Can new rules be invented?", and "Where do rules come from?" Children were also asked to judge the rightness and wrongness of a central character in a scenario who had committed a transgression. They were also presented with the various intentions which had precipitated this transgression as well as the consequences of the act. The children's responses led Piaget to propose two stages of moral development which highlight the progression from an egocentric confusion of subjective and objective consequences to a more rational understanding. In Stage 1 ("moral realism" or "heteronomy"), moral conduct is determined by the consequences of an act. Here morality is judged by objective consequences and thus is based on the actor's intentions. Moral thinking then is dominated by subjectivity, egocentrism, and realism. Justice is further seen by the child as being immanent. In Stage 2 ("autonomy"), moral reasoning is driven by the desire for equality and mutual respect. Piaget conceived rational moral development to be a movement away from external, heteronomous impositions to a morality characterized by autonomy, mutual respect, and democratic cooperation (Lapsley, 2006).

COGNITIVE-STRUCTURAL THEORY—KOHLBERG

Lawrence Kohlberg (1981) expanded upon Piaget's cognitive-structural conceptualization of moral development. Turiel (2006) summarizes two fundamental propositions of Kohlberg's model of morality. One proposition hypothesizes that "human moral functioning involves thinking, along with emotions, of a systematic kind about matters of right and wrong in social relationships" (p. 9). Central to moral functioning is how people conceptualize issues of right and wrong based on their understanding of justice, fairness, and the welfare of other people. The second proposition contends that moral understanding begins to be formed in systematic ways during childhood. Moreover, rather than merely acquiring moral values from their parents, teachers or other agents of socialization, children also construct their perceptions of morality (Nucci, 2006). Kohlberg argued that the individual—rather than the society—determines what is right from wrong by interpreting social and moral situations and in turn making moral judgments (Rest, 1994). Extending Piaget's model of cognitive-structural stages, Kohlberg (1981) proposed that moral development was the progressive elaboration of sociomoral reasoning through various stages. He applied the Moral Judgment Interview as a semistructured discussion to measure how individuals evaluate moral problems. The focus of the interview is a set of dilemmas that put obedience to authority in direct conflict with helping a person in need. The standard question is: "Should a man steal an over-priced drug that he cannot obtain legally in order to save his wife?" Through the interviewees' responses, Kohlberg identified at what level of moral development each individual resided. Three distinct levels of moral development were derived: (a) the preconventional level, (b) the conventional level, and (c) the postconventional level. Each echelon consisted of two stages, resulting in six defined stages of moral development (Kohlberg, 1963/2008).

Most children under the age of ten first explore morality at the preconventional level (Gibbs, Kohlberg, Colby, & Speicher-Dubin, 1976). At the preconventional level, the first stage is termed, "the punishment and obedience orientation," and focuses on a child's avoidance of punishment. At this stage, decisions are based on whether or not punishment will follow. Stage 2, "the instrumental purpose orientation," builds upon this avoidance of punishment but further seeks to find behaviors that will result in rewards or positive outcomes for personal needs (Kohlberg, 1981). The concept of reciprocity is explored but is understood as equal exchange of benefits. Furthermore, an understanding of the norms and conventions of a specific culture are explored (Colby et al., 1983).

In the conventional level of moral development, broader issues of morality are addressed. Individuals start to evaluate their actions based on whether they will yield approval or disapproval among their in-group. In Stage 3, "the interpersonal concordance orientation," the individual seeks to follow social norms and rules as a means of avoiding group disapproval. In short, one endeavors to be liked by and approved of by others in his or her social group. This stage is followed by "the social-order maintaining orientation" (Stage 4), which addresses the need to obey authority so that one will be accepted as a member of a group. A democratic society operates at this level. Authority figures are chosen to uphold justice and are respected by the group; harmony is achieved within the group by conforming to the cultural norms and rules which are in turn enforced by individuals in positions of authority (Kohlberg, 1981).

At the cusp of adulthood, individuals will, for the most part, function at the conventional level of moral development which composes of two stages (Stage 5 and 6). However, this level is seldom exemplified by all members of a population (Kohlberg, 1981). In Stage 5 ("the social contract orientation"), individuals regard laws and rules as tools for maintaining social order and furthering human well-being. They believe in fair procedures for interpreting and changing the law. When laws are consistent with individual rights and the interest of the majority of the society, they are followed because they are social contract and because they will bring about more good for people than if they did not exist (Berk, 2004).

The final stage (Stage 6) of the conventional level of moral development is known as 'the morality of individual principles of conscience" stage, in which the individual defines right and wrong according to self-chosen ethical principles. The universal principles regarding justice are regarded as the best outcome for all members of a society (Kohlberg, 1963/2008). One's commitment to such universal principles is thus of greater importance than one's own welfare (Kohlberg, 1981). Above all, the principle that all humans are equal must be upheld in every moral dilemma. Few individuals have exhibited consistent moral judgments at this level of moral reasoning. Because it is rarely displayed in the general population, Kohlberg has classified this stage as being merely theoretical (Gibbs et al., 1976).

Validation and Critique of Cognitive-Structural Theory

Studies have confirmed the various stages of moral reasoning and the way in which individuals progress through them (e.g., Boom, Brugman, & van der Heijden, 2001). There has also been cross-cultural validation of stage progression in countries such as India, Turkey, Japan, and Finland (Bukatko, 2008). However, the proposition that the higher level of reasoning applies only to older children (i.e., age 10 years and above) has been challenged. Preschool children, for example, were found capable of recognizing that actions which produced psychologically harmful behavior were just as unacceptable as those which caused physical hurt (Helwig, Zelazo, & Wilson, 2001). Snarey's (1985) review of 45 studies of moral development found that Kohlberg's early measures favored urban societies and middle-class populations. While Stages 1 to 4 were found to have universal validity, Stages 5 and 6 were extremely uncommon in all populations, and were found almost never to occur in folk and traditional societies.

A major criticism of Kohlberg's theory is its failure to explain different modes of moral reasoning in individuals and in different cultural groups (Bukatko, 2008; Teo, Becker, & Edelstein, 1995). Kohlberg's hypothetical dilemmas, which require a choice between rules/laws and the needs of individuals to bring about justice, also do not allow expression of such modes as happiness or the valuing of modesty and humility (Lee, Cameron, Xu, Fu, & Board, 1997). Moreover, there is a general lack of consistency between moral reasoning and behavior when defined according to Kohlberg's stages (Colby & Damon, 1992; Nucci, 2006). The cognitive-structural perspective that attributes moral decision making to a single cognitive structure and principled moral judgment has been replaced by a conceptualization of moral and social reasoning that are more heterogeneous and multifaceted (Nucci, 2006). Other perspectives of morality and moral judgment have also been offered as additions or contrasts. Pertinent to the present thesis is the concept of empathy and the socialization perspectives.

The Affective Face of Moral Development: Prosocial Reasoning and Empathy

Among the most prominent approaches contrasting cognitive-structural models are those focusing on prosocial reasoning and empathy. Eisenberg (1986) used a similar approach to Kohlberg's by employing a hypothetical dilemma to investigate moral reasoning in terms of the values underlying prosocial behavior. She found five stages of prosocial reasoning upon which moral thinking is based: (a) self-focused consequences (hedonism), (b) the specific needs of another person, (c) gaining the approval of others, (d) an empathic awareness of others, and (e) strongly internalized values such as maintaining self-respect and believing in the dignity and rights of others. Eisenberg, although introducing an affect component to the explanation of moral reasoning, is similar to Kohlberg in identifying the individualistic reasoning process as the major activity involved in making moral decisions. Hoffman presents a contrasting theory to the cognitive-structural perspective with a more concentrated focus on the affective dimension. He posited that "empathetic affect and related emotions [served as] the basis for moral motivation" (Gibbs, 1991, p. 183).

Martin Hoffman (2001) has focused his research on how and why people care for another human being, and how the sentiment of empathy relates to morality. Empathy is formally defined as "an affective response more appropriate to another's situation than one's own" (p. 4). In essence, it is the ability to share the emotional experience of another individual. Hoffman argues that moral judgment arises in scenarios that pose a conflict between one's personal self-interest and one's social obligations. According to Hoffman (1991), because empathic affects reliably dispose people to act on behalf of others, empathetic affects must constitute an important type of moral motive. Unlike Kohlberg and Piaget, Hoffman places less of an emphasis on developmental stages. Instead, he stresses that empathy develops continuously through social interactions and personal growth (Hoffman, 2001). This position is supported by research with male delinquents, which found that empathy can be a taught characteristic (Jolliffe & Farrington, 2004; Spiro, 1992).

Hoffman (2001) suggests that because empathy is congruent with caring and most just principles, it can therefore be assimilated with caring and justice principles. The result of this assimilation is that the justice principles are charged with empathetic affect which in turn benefits both empathy and the justice principles by themselves. The principle of caring refers to an "abstraction, a moral imperative, a fundamental value, a philosophical idea … [which says that] … we must always consider others" (p. 225). According to Hoffman, empathizing with a victim may lead to affirming the caring principle and using this principle as a premise for judging laws that violate or support it. Hoffman further suggests that the relationship between empathy and justice can manifest in several ways. For example, while empathy may not make a structural contribution to justice, it may provide the motive to rectify instances of violation of justice done to others. Empathy may also make a direct substantive contribution to justice based on need and effort. The integration or bonding of empathy and moral principles benefits both in that when a moral principle charged with empathetic affect is activated, it has the stabilizing effect of heightening or lowering the intensity of the observer's empathetic affect. Reciprocally, empathy may transform moral cognition into prosocial cognition that is charged with empathetic affect. Hoffman thus proposes that empathy and moral principles are related to prosocial action in three different ways: (a) empathy relates to prosocial action; (b) upholding a prosocial moral principle relates to prosocial action; and (c) empathy combined with moral principles relates to prosocial action to a greater degree than either alone.

Hoffman (2001) argues that "most moral dilemmas in life arouse empathy because they involve victims, seen or unseen, present or future. Empathy activates moral principles, and either directly or through these principles, influences moral judgment and reasoning" (p. 247). Hoffman classifies morality into 4 categories: (a) an internal moral orientation, (b) guilt intensity, (c) resistance to temptation, and (d) confession and acceptance of blame. Despite his de-emphasis of developmental stages, Hoffman nevertheless proposes four stages in the development of empathetic affects that consist of: (a) global empathy, as characterized by behaviors that match another's strong emotion; (b) egocentric empathy, as characterized by the understanding of another's experience as it relates to one's own; (c) empathy for another's feelings; and (d) empathy for another's life condition as characterized by the ability to experience empathic concern that extends to the general life experience of others. These stages suggest that as the child matures, empathetic responses are "guided less and less by just the immediate, observed emotions and much more by [his] inferences or deductions about the other person's feelings" (Bee, 1989, p. 438). This means that a developmental increase in the cognitive awareness and use of moral principles contribute substantially to the impact of empathic affect on the process of making moral decisions. Thus, "although empathy plays a primary role, cognition also plays an important role in Hoffman's theory of morality" (Gibbs, 1991, p. 204).

According to Hoffman (2001), through cognitive mechanisms, such as social appraisal and perspective taking, children develop a sense of empathy. Much of this learning is dependent on strong role models, such as parents, who teach and reinforce empathetic responses. For example, a child's age, combined with parental factors (such as a parent's emotional empathy and emotional expressiveness) account for 32% of the variance in a child's emotional development which, when supplemented by the social perspective taking, strongly influences empathy (Strayer & Roberts, 2004). Frequent parental use of power assertion, such as punishment and the withholding of love, can have a significantly negative impact on the child's prosocial moral development. For example, parents will often withdraw love in response to a child's anger response – a strategy which can have negative effects on a child's self-esteem (Hoffman, 1970b).

SOCIALIZATION FRAMEWORK—SOCIAL INTERACTION PERSPECTIVE

Still another theoretical framework attempting to explain moral development is that of socialization. Partly inherited from Freud (1930/1955), a socialization-oriented framework focuses on the behavioral and emotional manifestations of conscience and on the internalization of societal values as the individual's own values (Grusec, 1991). Socialization refers to the process "by which individuals acquire a set of standards, values, attitudes, beliefs, and behaviors that they accept as their own and that are based on or derived from the standards of one or more groups of which they are a member" (p. 244). The socialization process is facilitated or aided by parents, teachers, peers, siblings, the media, and other members in society. Beginning with a focus on discipline strategies, socialization theorists contend that discipline is the primary context in which the socialization of morality occurs (Grusec, 1991). In this sense, parents serve as the central orchestrators of children's socialization. Parents contribute to those aspects of socialization that are related to moral development through such processes as: identification and observational learning, parental responsiveness to and compliance with the wishes of their children, and discussion of moral issues outside the bounds of specific conflicts. Socialization theories, as presented by such researchers as Sears, Maccoby, and Levin (1957), and Bandura (1977), treat social behaviors, including morality, as a single class of behaviors and assume the development of these behaviors as being governed by the same psychological mechanisms (Grusec, 2006). However, such perspectives have been challenged (Bugental, 2000) and other perspectives of socialization have arisen. One such a perspective is that of social interaction.

It is commonly recognized that family interaction is an important contributor to the development of morality (Dunn, 2006). Various approaches within the socialization framework have thus charted the relationship between family relationships and moral development. The sociocognitive approach views the development of social and emotional understanding as a key element of the development of moral reasoning and judgment (Arsenio, Gold, & Adams, 2006; Turiel, 2002). Here, family interaction is thought to influence the development of social understanding and hence the development of moral reasoning and judgment. Another socialization approach emphasizes the development of self and the growth of conscience in moral development (Hinde, 2002). This approach focuses on family discipline and children's response to parent-child conflict. Still another socialization approach analyzes prosocial behavior in terms of linking family experience to children's caring behavior (Eisenberg & Fabes, 1998). These approaches, each or together, are embodied in a social interaction perspective which centers on the parent-child relationship as constituting the primary influence on children's moral development. This parent-child social interaction perspective, also referred to as the family interaction framework (Dunn, 2006), considers the parent-child relationship—rather than parenting alone—as key to children's development of morality. According to this perspective, reciprocity and the motivating power of relationships serve as the main factor that contributes to the development of social understanding (Dunn, 2006). The perspective further considers that moral understanding and reasoning consist of both cognition and emotions.

According to the parent-child interaction perspective, through their interactions within the context of the family, children cultivate their understanding of others' psychological states and feelings. Children also learn that they can alter other individuals' psychological states, thus indicating their understanding of how their actions can affect another individual's emotional state. They learn that they can do this, for example, not only by comforting, but also by teasing, and thus exacerbating the distress of those whom they taunt (Dunn, 2006; Reddy, 1991). As children grow older, they can discuss the feeling states and psychological conditions of both self and others in terms of the causes and connections between inner states and actions (Bartsch & Wellman, 1995; Dunn, 2006). Within the family, children also comprehend the idea of responsibility—they understand that individuals are accountable to others for certain prohibited actions such as causing harm to others or breaching standards of acceptable behavior. Dunn further suggests that the bases of children's excuses and justifications, as well as their jokes, include not only the unique practices of their family but also some of the key principles as espoused by the wider culture outside of the context of their family. The child-parent interaction approach also adds that the emotions of guilt and fear experienced by children when they fail to follow the standards set by their parents are crucial to moral development. Family discussion of emotion in conflict is related to early conscience development and prosocial conceptions of relationships (Laible & Thompson, 2000). Moreover, children's understanding of moral behavior derives primarily from parents' socialization approaches and their internalization of social norms leads them to experience their moral behavior as self-generated. How parents respond to various breaches of acceptable behavior thus has a profound effect that contributes to the development of individual differences in moral sensibility, judgment, and moral behavior.

A family interaction approach also observes that moral development does not always proceed smoothly but that empathetic behavior and understanding of moral transgressions, as displayed by children, may vary according to context (Dunn, 2006). Whereas the affective domain of family relationship provides a powerful motivation for children to understand moral issues and conventional rules, the tension between children's self-interest and their family relationships contributes to children's growing understanding of what constitutes acceptable and unacceptable behavior. According to Dunn, children are also motivated to understand the moral and social rules of their cultures. Furthermore, the effect of family interaction is reciprocal; as the parent affects the child, so does the child affect the parent. Family interaction may therefore contribute in many important ways to children's moral development.

A Proposed Integrated Model of Moral Judgment: A Convergence of Cognition, Emotions, and Social Interaction

The Theoretical Model

Many theoretical models thus exist to explain the moral development of children. Theories have been developed which seek to supplement or revise the cognitive-structural models pioneered by Piaget and Kohlberg. According to cognitive-structural theories, the basis of morality development is thought or cognition. In contrast, Eisenberg and Hoffman have presented an affective base of moral development which focuses on empathy. Both Kohlberg and Hoffman each thus focuses on one aspect of moral development and views it being associated with either thought or emotion. The advent of the family interaction perspective integrates both thought and emotion as the foundation of moral development and regards it as advancing through the mediation of parent-child interaction. This latter perspective would appear to more comprehensively explain moral development in children and adolescents and, indeed, support for the tenability of such a perspective exists.

Primary support for an integration of thought and emotion as the basis for moral development has derived from the theorists themselves. Interestingly, although Piaget was a cognitive-structural theorist, emotions did in fact find an important place in his understanding of moral reasoning and its development. The emotions that he highlighted were affection, sympathy, compassion, and respect. According to Piaget (1932/1965), a mixture of the inborn or very early emerging emotions of fear, affection, and sympathy, along with vindictiveness and compassion, provides the foundation for the development of morality (Turiel, 2006). However, Piaget (1932) also believed that instinctive tendencies, although a necessity, are not a sufficient condition for the formation of morality. He elaborated that

> the child's behavior towards persons shows signs from the first of those sympathetic tendencies and affective reactions in which one can easily see the raw material of all subsequent moral behavior. But an intelligent act can only be regarded as logical and a good-hearted impulse moral from the moment that certain norms impress a given structure and rules of equilibrium upon this material. (p. 405)

According to Turiel, Piaget also viewed the multiplicity of experiences, including relations with adults and peers, to influence moral development. Furthermore, Piaget advocated certain systems of relations which included not only reciprocal social interactions but also relations between thought, emotion, and actions. Supporting a cognitive, social, and emotional base of moral judgment, Turiel concluded that "humans are reasoning beings, with emotional commitments and flexibility of thought" (p. 30).

Hoffman's model of the stages of empathy also suggests that a developmental increase in the cognitive awareness and use of moral principles contribute substantially to the impact of empathic affects on the process of making moral decisions. Thus, "although empathy plays a primary role, cognition also plays an important role in Hoffman's theory of morality" (Gibbs, 1991, p. 204). Gibbs further notes, "Kohlberg was, and Hoffman is, open to the possibility of theoretical integration" (p. 209). Gibbs, however, concluded that the most broadly encompassing position is the Piagetian view which maintains that "affect and cognition are inseparable; if anything is 'primacy,' it is not 'affect' or 'cognition' but the dynamic organizations of experience" (p. 209).

The integration of thought, emotions, and social interaction as a mediating force for the development of moral reasoning is especially operationalized by the family interaction perspective. This perspective advances the theory that moral reasoning and understanding, which entail both emotion and cognition, are fostered in the social interaction which takes place mainly within the family but perhaps outside the family as well (Dunn, 2006). Together, the notion of morality as the co-occurrence of thought and emotion which is further mediated by social interaction would appear to more completely explicate the nature of moral reasoning and moral judgment. Such a notion can be validated and is illustrated by contemporary research.

VALIDATION OF THE INTEGRATED MODEL OF MORAL JUDGMENT: RESEARCH STUDIES

Three studies conducted by two of the authors offer preliminary validation of the proposed integrated model of moral judgment. These studies were carried out with different age groups, early childhood, middle childhood, and adolescence, with each age period demonstrating some aspects of an integrated model of moral judgment and moral behavior. The studies are summarized in the following sections.

STUDY 1: "HOW DO ADOLESCENTS DETERMINE THE RIGHT THINGS TO DO?" (CRAWFORD, 1995)

This study was conducted by Crawford (1995) and partially reanalyzed by Dyson for this report. Adolescence is a time when changes take place along many child development dimensions: Physical, cognitive, social, and emotional. Along with the changes, adolescents also advance in moral development. At the same time, they may also have to "contend with the contradictions between the moral concepts they have accepted and experiences outside their family and neighborhood" (Santrock, 1993, p. 437). As a result, adolescents may "question their former beliefs, and in the process, develop their own moral system" (p. 437). According to Kohlberg (1976), most adolescents are functioning at the conventional level of morality. At this level, adolescents may function at Stage 3 which is dominated by mutual interpersonal expectations, relationships and conformity. Adolescents functioning at Stage 4 are concerned with societal order and rules and obey their conscience and law. Kohlberg's stages have been generated from hypothetical dilemmas as reviewed earlier. Yet, "morality is not a subject: it is life put to the test in dozens of moments ... it's life affecting the views of people every day" (P. Tillich, as cited in Coles, 1986, p. 16). There is thus a need for information on morality derived from real-life experience and the meanings attached to it. What do adolescents have to say about how they make moral decisions in the context of everyday life experience? The answers were to be revealed in this study.

The study participants included 15 grade 10 adolescents (12 female and 3 male) who lived in a semirural area on the west coast of Canada. The school enrolled an ethnically diverse population of approximately 1,000 students, with 25% being of Aboriginal status. The volunteer participants were interviewed twice, and were also observed in their classrooms. The purpose of the observation was to understand the classroom contexts so as to help validate and interpret the interview data where appropriate. The interview questions related to the present report were: (a) how does choosing the right thing to do fit into your day-to-day life; (b) what are the major influences on the way you determine what's right; and (c) where do the values that influence you come from? Subquestions were included in order to elicit more focused details. The data were coded and categorized into major themes, using the constant comparison method of Strauss and Corbian (1990).

While the result found themes that included the preliminary phase (which prepared the participants to engage in moral activities), only those that apply to the actual phase of moral activities and that pertain to the present topic are presented. The results centered on moral decision making in terms of the process involved and the influencing factors. The major themes consisted of the following, with the fictitious name of the participant at the end of each quote.

Feeling Empathetic

Despite the fact that the interview questions focused on morality, the theme of empathy prevailed among the adolescents. Moral behavior and activities were generated by the participants' own ordinary experience, with the primary moral activity being empathy. Empathetic reactions were aroused in circumstances involving others in general or in specific situations involving the participants' own family members or relatives. Empathy was elicited by knowing and caring about another person but was also experienced when reflecting on one's own life. For example, an adolescent girl exhibited empathy which was rooted in her personal experience of having a brother with a disability. The empathy in turn generalized to other individuals:

> Lots of things I learn about how to help him [brother with disabilities] influences me on how to help other kids ... 'cause I know when I see kids in the hall getting picked on, just because they're little, it really gets to me because I can just picture my brother being in the same situation.... It really upsets me when people pick on him.... I know when I see kids in the hall getting picked on, I don't know what it is, it's just a feeling I get in my stomach; I guess 'cause I see my brother's pain lots of days when he comes home.... It gives me a lot of strength 'cause ... every day I learn something new with him, and ... I think it makes me stronger to deal with other people. (Alexis)

Another boy, in explaining his moral reasoning, recounted how he would help someone in a situation that involved personal sacrifice:

> Well, I think it would be out of love. You know just, certain ... well, just general love, right? Maybe I should break it down, love as in caring ... just understanding and caring ... probably, would be that ... you just understand their circumstances, and you relate to them, and probably help them out ... yah, understanding the circumstances they've gone through probably because you've gone through them as well. (Charles)

Conscience as a Moral Judge and in Interaction With Emotion

In making a moral decision and being engaged in moral activities, adolescents assigned conscience a governing role. Conscience served two functions: as a means of knowing and as a means of evaluating information. Conscience provided knowledge about right and wrong (e.g., "it's something that [one] knows") and it also served as a motive for behavior (e.g., "[it's] something you have to deal with ... you gotta decide what you wanna do"). Conscience was at times experienced as an internal struggle involving actions that had already been classified in moral terms. An adolescent revealed her struggle:

> Everyone has a conscience. I think that ... it plays a big part in decision-making, you know. I guess I'm not really sure what a conscience is but my feeling of it is that, you know, it's kind of a voice inside, a voice that kinda fights the good stuff and then the bad stuff, you know, what you will get out of it and what you will lose or stuff.... But then, I don't know, sometimes.... I guess I maybe happen to ... [have] ignored mine, maybe and, I didn't listen to it. And that's probably what caused me to not think about the consequences, because the voice inside my head kind a disappeared for awhile. (Allie)

Conscience was also experienced among the participants as an internal dialogue between cognitive and emotive states. Conscience provides the information and evaluation for right and wrong and this may also interact with emotions. For example, adolescents spoke of the interaction between conscience, thought, and emotion:

> Conscience: I think that's ... just ... it's [conscience] just telling you what's right and wrong ... just the way we ... [it's] kind of a discussion in our mind, a sense, just saying.... "Ah, if you do this, these are the consequences but this is what we'll get out of it; if you do this, you know, you may get this out of it but you'll be able to do this." (Charles)

> The way you think is here, and the way you feel is here, and your conscience is sort of in the middle and, it's sort of just, like it balances your decision that you made, kind of and ... it just, whenever you think a decision, you really feel the right one and the wrong one ... well for me anyways, I'm like ... I just decide which one I feel best in. (Winnie)

Values as Mediated By the Context

Acquired values were firmly established and accepted as standards for personal conduct which were to be abided by. However, these values might still be open to interpretation according to the specific circumstances. Simply ascribing to certain values was not as important for the participants as how they applied these values within the context of their daily activities. For the adolescents, the daily, practical applications began with differentiating actions in terms of right and wrong which, nevertheless, might be adjusted according to the specific circumstances. As one adolescent observed:

> Well, I interpret as don't lie meaning don't lie, don't tell a white lie, don't bend the truth. I try to tell the truth all the time ... even in circumstances where it may not suit my best interests to tell the full truth, I still try to tell the truth.... My values are the same. There could be some way in interpreting them ... may be different ... I don't know. Like there could be a ... circumstance where somebody has taken something from me, say, and I know it's not his, it's mine, and then he has it. Would I consider it stealing to go and take it back?.... So, there the moral may, or the value, may be ... two different lights to look at it. (Perrin)

The influence of the context on a moral valuation and hence on a moral act was also expressed by other participants who, when asked about their value-related decisions, typically responded with the words "well, it depends"

Family Influence on Value Judgment

Distinguishing values began within the individual and involved cognitive and emotional processes. The processes, however, were often influenced by the family. The adolescents revealed their inner moral decision-making processes as they were mediated by their families. The effects of the family, however, also rested on what the specific circumstances were and how the adolescents individually interpreted their family experiences. One effect was associated with learning how their behavior impacted the welfare of others. Another effect would be cultivating the ability to assess what is right and wrong, an ability which would in turn lead to independent decision making. Parents also offered support and served as consultants for adolescents when they were confronted with moral issues. The adolescents drew support and consultation from both their mothers and their fathers, depending on the nature of the issue; emotional issues were brought to the mother whereas intellectual problems were presented to the father. The adolescents also modeled their parents and, in some cases, their grandparents. Some adolescents recounted:

> I remember we got caught for stealing in grade 7, and I, like, felt really—at first I didn't really care what I was doing. I didn't care, "Oh, who cares." I mean it didn't really bother me at all.... And then, like after we got caught, my mom was like totally laying a guilt trip on me. Like she's saying, "Oh, well, that raises the prices for everybody." And, 'cause I guess I only thought of myself, I didn't think, I didn't think of, about like what other people would think, or how they'd feel if their candy got stolen. So now I'm like, I think about how, how I would feel if that happened to me. (Janice)

> My mom.... Now that we're closer and we talk about a lot more things, you know, she tells me of her experiences and ... I listen to her and ... I just, even like, with my older cousin too, 'cause she's, she's kinda been in my position so she can tell me and she can help me out ... she doesn't make decisions for me, but she gives me her advice about what's right. (Allie)

> My mom often helps me with things. She always says, "you'll always have to make decisions in your life and you should make this decision by yourself"; and then I'll come to her, like, I can't decide what to do, so she'll help me ... she's always really supportive and always guides me in the right direction of where I should be going. (Alexis)

> I go to either parents for different help. If I'm usually having an emotional problem it'll usually be my mom.... She deals emotionally. My dad is more intellectually, he likes to assess the problem and solve it—doesn't want to deal with the feelings that go with it ... Where my mom likes to feel "why do you feel that way ... what could be making you feel like this" ... sort of idea. So I go to either for different help. (Perrin)

Influence of Other Social Interactions

Friends and peers also exerted an impact on adolescents' moral values. Friends provided support and advice about their decisions and shared experiences of personal concern. Peers might also apply peer pressure to influence an adolescent's moral choice. However, ultimately, the individuals themselves made the decision about their moral acts and judgment, primarily dictated by their conscience. Participants observed the following:

> Most people rely on their friends, and like, if their friends are doing something, they'll want to do it too, because their friends are doing it. But, it's not actually, if you don't feel comfortable doing anything, then you won't do it.... Like you rely on your friend's opinion and you rely on your friends to help you to make decisions but, in the end, it's just what you feel comfortable with. But they give you the suggestions or help you, or they tell you to do something but you don't have to do it. (Terry)

> I mean, if you have a lot of people pressuring you, sometimes you are gonna give in. I mean, if some of your friends are telling you to, to smoke pot or something, sometimes you're gonna give in, just because everybody else is doing it, you feel ... left out. But I personally ... don't make that a big, big issue with my friends. Like my friends ... know the way I am and

> they don't make a big issue out of forcing me to do things I don't wanna do. And I mean, if I don't wanna do something, I'm not going to do it. And if I do it, my conscience just, I have a huge conscience, it just nags at me ... until I do something to make it better. (Janice)

Friends also provided mutual influence—thus helping the individual to make a conscious decision. Disagreement with friends also offered an occasion for learning about others' perspective and hence expanded adolescents' moral thinking. A decision was often made rationally through discussion with friends and logical reasoning by the adolescents themselves. As two adolescents reported:

> I also have friends who are an influence. I have a close friend who's also a Christian and he influences my decisions sometimes. Where I may wanna do something like, oh ... I don't know, let me think. Say, there's one time we were after ... a rowing party, and we all wanted to go out ... to town, you know, just go to town and goof around, and it was quite late and we were tired from rowing that day, and I thought, "Yah, let's go for it." But then my friend says, "Maybe this isn't a safe thing to do; you don't know, you're, you're all wound up and we're tired, maybe we should just go home and play a game or something." And, I, I reflected on it and I thought, "That's probably the better idea." And then there are circumstances when, we want to go to a show, and ... I'm very strict about what I like to see. I don't wanna see anything that will influence me. He's not quite that way, so sometimes I will influence him not to go to these, these shows. It will work both ways. (Perrin)

> I do have some friends ... we agree on some of the same things but we don't on other things. And ... we try and avoid the subjects as much as possible so we don't get in arguments or anything. We're always willing to hear each other's side of it so it's not really ... it's not really one-sided and that you should believe this.... You learn a lot more.... Well, you understand the way other people think better. Like their values ... are different from yours so, the things they believe ... are probably different from yours too and so ... it really expands on ... like, yah, expands on everything. (Alexis)

The results support certain characteristics of adolescents' moral development as proposed by Kohlberg. These characteristics include interpersonal expectations, relationships, and conscience. However, the results especially indicate that in making a moral decision and engaging in moral reasoning, adolescents experience and enlist all psychological and social resources (i.e., empathy, conscience, cognition, parents, and peers) while at the same time taking into consideration the social contexts. Their decisions and reasoning thus incorporate emotions, thought, and social interaction with their families and peers.

Study 2: Kindergarten Children's Understanding About and Attitudes Toward Peers With Disabilities (Dyson, 2005)

This study investigated young children's understanding of disabilities and their attitudes toward individuals with disabilities. Attitudes have been defined as cognitive schema or ideas characterizing either groups or individuals that may incorporate some degree of positive or negative evaluation (Eagly & Chaiken, 1993). Negative attitudes demonstrated by children towards their peers with disabilities have commonly been reported (e.g., Favazza, Phillipsen, & Kumar, 2000). Researchers have therefore stressed that an understanding of children's knowledge and attitudes toward disabilities is essential to the acceptance of children with disabilities (Hazzard, 1983) and to developing educational interventions to cultivate positive attitudes toward individuals with disabilities (Diamond, 1993).

Of the present interest is whether children's attitudes toward people with disabilities are related to their moral behavior and reasoning. This question is examined presently based on the study (Dyson, 2005). The study included a sample of 77 kindergarten children attending schools in middle-class neighborhoods in a midsize, west-coast metropolitan city in Canada. The children were interviewed with a revised instrument, *The Primary Student Survey of Handicapped Persons (PSSHP)* (Esposito & Peach, 1983). This qualitative questionnaire measures children's awareness about and sensitivity toward disabilities and their attitudes toward persons with disabilities. One of the questions asked: "Do you like people who have special needs or disabilities? Why or why not?"

The results found that the overwhelming majority of children answered affirmatively. Only a small proportion (17%) answered negatively, were ambivalent, or did not answer at all. Children gave reasons for their positive attitudes which were generally associated with the good character of persons with disabilities ("They're nice," and "they still are nice"; "they can still play"). Children especially used altruistic and empathetic reasons to justify their fondness and support for people with disabilities. Among such reasons were:

- Yes, because I can help them.
- Yes, because they need help; people can take care of them, and it's nice to do that.
- Yes, because I love them.
- Yes, because you should be nice to them so they get to know you better.

A sense of reciprocity was also mentioned as reasons for liking individuals with disabilities as illustrated by the children's answers: "they help me and I help them"; "they like me and I like them," and "they always play with me." Only two children gave reasons for not liking individuals with disabilities. The reasons provided were associated with the unique nature and special needs of people with disabilities ("They're different" and "I'm tired of helping them"). These results suggest that children as young as the kindergarten age were incorporating both cognitive and affective faculties to determine their attitudes, and, to some extent, were demonstrating their moral decisions. Through their action and reasoning, young children were demonstrating their desire to be prosocial and to be empathetic, as well as their belief in the reciprocity of friendship, and possibly morality.

Study 3: Attitudes of Children Toward People With Disabilities (Dyson, 2010)

The relationship between cognitive and affective domains involved in the attitudes toward individuals with disabilities was the subject of further validation. One factor that may affect empathy and acceptance of others is contact. Contact has been found to be a social factor affecting individuals' attitudes towards disability. For example, preschool children who had more interaction with peers with disabilities demonstrated more positive attitudes towards them (Diamond, 2001). Meanwhile, empathy is thought to involve two elements: apprehending another person's emotional state or condition and matching that emotional state oneself (Bee, 2000). Denham (1986) found that preschool children's prosocial behavior is related to their understanding of others' emotions. A relationship between empathy and moral behavior—as it relates to the acceptance of individuals with disabilities—would thus likely exist. Such a possibility was tested in this study.

The study included a sample of 2,598 children (1,329 males and 1,269 females), grades 4 to 7, who were attending schools located in both low-income and middle-income neighborhoods in a metropolitan city located on the west coast of Canada. Children were administered two quantitative measures: *An Index of Empathy for Children and Adolescents* (Bryant, 1982), which assesses empathy, and the modified *Chedoke-McMaster Attitudes towards Children with Handicaps Scale* (CATCH) (Rosenbaum, Armstrong, & King, 1986), which evaluates attitudes toward people with disabilities. CATCH contains 3 factors: (A) affective, (B) cognitive, and (C) behavioral. Bryant (1982) defines empathy as a "vicarious emotional response to the perceived emotional experiences of others" (p. 414).

As expected, the results found that those children who had more contact with persons with disabilities had higher scores on all measures assessing interaction with or friendship with children with disabilities. There was also a positive relationship between empathy and attitudes toward individuals with disabilities, with the total empathy score ($p < .0001$) being correlated with two of the CATCH factors: Affective ($p < .0001$) and Cognitive ($p < .0001$). The more empathic a child was, the more positive his/her attitudes towards individuals with disabilities, especially in regard to the affective and cognitive domains of these attitudes. The attitudes, which may be considered as one form of moral behavior, were thus influenced by such factors as the affective factor of empathy and the social factor of contact or exposure to an individual with disabilities.

The three studies conducted with a range of age groups (i.e., adolescence, middle childhood, and early childhood), similarly demonstrated the association between thought, emotions, and social interaction in determining children's and adolescents' moral reasoning, moral behavior, and attitudes towards individuals with disabilities. Together, the results preliminarily support the contention that cognition, affect, and social interaction are coalesced to determine children's moral reasoning and moral behavior. Such integration is consistent with the major theoretical perspectives: Piaget's (1932/1965) hypothesis that both the emotional and affective base of intelligence contributes to moral judgment; Hoffman's (2001) contention that empathy serves as a precursor to prosocial behavior, and Dunn's (2006) focus that family interaction provides a context of moral development. The present studies added other social factors which would also contribute to the development of moral reasoning and moral behavior in children. Such factors would be peers.

Practical Issues Regarding the Integrated Model of Moral Judgment

Aspects Particular to the Proposed Theory

The proposed integrated model of moral judgment would provide a more comprehensive and clear analysis and understanding of the processes and components involved in moral development—especially as it relates to making a moral judgment or being engaged in moral acts. The model would also serve to integrate theories of moral development which presently appear fragmented. The proposed integrated model of moral judgment possesses particular merits, which include the following:

1. It embodies the concepts of the major theories of moral development.

2. It identifies and integrates cognitive, affective, and social forces that influence the making of a moral decision and judgment.
3. It is not only supported by major theoretical perspectives—as presented by Piaget, Kohlberg, Hoffman, and Dunn—but it is also preliminarily validated by empirical research.
4. It clearly outlines the components involved (which include cognitive, affective, and social domains) and, hence, more concretely provides the operational definition, sources and influences for moral development. This in turn allows for the systematic analysis of moral judgment.
5. It provides a more comprehensive and thorough model and will thus facilitate research which will yield results of greater scientific quality.
6. The model would also have clinical utility for identifying the source of difficulty in deviant moral cases.

Use and Application of the Theory

The proposed model will have broader applications to practice and research as it will elucidate the influence of three major domains of human development (cognitive, affective and social) on moral development. Practical applications to education may begin with the specification of individual components such as cognition, emotion, and social interaction that drive moral judgment. Such specification can then guide the designing of a program of moral education. The proposed model may also lead research to identify, through statistical methods, the individual and combined contributions to the development of moral judgment of such components as thought, affect, and social interaction. These components may also provide a base for the development of instruments that can be employed for both quantitative and qualitative studies.

Critiques of the Theory

Despite its theoretical merits and preliminary validity, the proposed model of moral judgment has certain weaknesses—as commonly associated with a new theory. These include the following:

1. The model is a proposition and has yet to stand the test of repeated validation.
2. The model may be considered to be more complicated than the traditional and established theories (e.g., Kohlberg, Piaget, Hoffman). The interpretation and analysis of moral development may thus be complex.
3. A cross-cultural validation of the proposed model has yet to be carried out.

Instruments Associated With the Theory

Both qualitative and quantitative tools have been developed which have been applied to the studies leading to the development of the proposed model. These include the following instruments:

1. An interview protocol as outlined earlier has been applied to the qualitative study that focuses on adolescents' moral decision-making processes.
2. An existing interview tool exploring young children's empathy and attitudes toward others with disabilities which is *The Primary Student Survey of Handicapped Persons* (PSSHP) (Esposito & Peach, 1983).
3. An existing questionnaire which examines elementary school children's understanding and attitudes toward disabilities (*Chedoke-McMaster Attitudes towards Children With Handicaps Scale*) (Rosenbaum et al., 1986)
4. An existing quantitative measure of empathy such as *An Index of Empathy for Children and Adolescents* (Bryant, 1982).

The above two scales have been jointly applied to examine the relationship between empathy and prosocial behavior as it applies to children's attitudes toward individuals with disabilities (Dyson, 2010).

Conclusion

This chapter proposes an integrated model of moral judgment and reasoning which incorporates cognition, emotions, and social interaction. The proposed model shows a potential to more adequately and comprehensively explicate moral judgment and reasoning in children than existing theories. The proposed model is drawn from the theoretical foundations of Kohlberg, Piaget, and Hoffman, as well as from the social interaction perspective. Moreover, support for an integration of emotion and thought as the basis for moral judgment has been indicated by theorists themselves such as Piaget, Hoffman, and Dunn. The empirical validation has preliminarily been made by the studies reported in this chapter. However, as a new proposition, the model contains weaknesses and has yet to be validated by further empirical data. Cross-cultural validation of the model would add to its generalizability. Nevertheless, the proposed model has initial utility for education, research, and further theory development. Researchers are therefore encouraged to test and refine the proposed model.

AUTHOR NOTE

The research studies in this report conducted by Dr. Lily Dyson were supported by the Social Sciences and Humanities Research Council of Canada and Health Canada (National Health Research and Development Promotion Program).

REFERENCES

Arsenio, W. F., Gold, J., & Adams, E. (2006). Children's conceptions and displays of moral emotions. In M. Killen & J. Smetana (Eds.), *Handbook of moral development* (pp. 581-609). Mahwah, NJ: Lawrence Erlbaum.

Bandura, A. (1977). *Social learning theory.* Englewood Cliffs, NJ: Prentice-Hall.

Bargh, J. (1994). The four horsemen of automaticity: Awareness, efficiency, intention, and control in social cognition. In J. R. S. Wyer & T. K. Srull (Eds.), *Handbook of social cognition* (2nd ed., pp. 1-40). Hillsdale, NJ: Erlbaum.

Bartsch, K,. & Wellman, H. M. (1995). *Children talk about the mind.* Oxford, England: Oxford University Press.

Bee, H. (1989). *The developing child.* New York, NY: Harper & Row.

Bee, H. (2000). *The developing child* (9th ed.). Needham Heights, MA: Allyn & Bacon.

Berk, L. E. (2004). *Development through the lifespan* (3rd ed.). Boston, MA: Allyn & Bacon.

Boom, J., Brugman, D., & van der Heijden, P. G. M. (2001). Hierarchical structure of moral stages assessed by a sorting task. *Child Development, 72,* 535-548. doi:10.1111/1467-8624.00295.

Bryant, B. K (1982). An index of empathy for children and adolescents. *Child Development, 53,* 413-425. doi:10.1111/1467-8624.ep8588354.

Bugental, D. B. (2000). Acquisition of the algorithms of social life: A domain-based approach. *Psychological Bulletin, 126,* 187-219. doi:10.1037/0033-2909.126.2.187.

Bukatko, D. (2008). *Child and adolescent development - A chronological approach.* Boston: Houghton Mifflin.

Colby, A., & Damon, W. (1992). *Some do care: Contemporary lives of moral commitment.* New York, NY: Free Press.

Colby, A., Kohlberg, L., Gibbs, J., Lieberman, M., Fischer, K., & Saltzstein, H. (1983). A longitudinal study of moral judgment. *Monographs of the Society for Research in Child Development, 48,* 1-124. Retrieved from http://www.jstor.org/stable/1165935

Coles, R. (1986). *The moral life of children.* Boston, MA: Houghton Mifflin.

Crawford, P. (1995). *How do adolescents determine the right things to do? A cultural ecological exploration of making moral decisions in the lives of fifteen grade ten students* (Unpublished MA thesis). Victoria, B. C., Canada: University of Victoria.

Denham, S. (1986). Social cognition, prosocial behavior and emotion in preschoolers: Contextual validation. *Child Development, 57,* 194-201.

Diamond, K. E. (1993). Preschool children's concepts of disability in their peers. *Early Education and Development, 4,* 124-129.

Diamond, K. (2001). Relationships among young children's Ideas, emotional understanding, and social contact with classmates with disabilities. *Topics in Early Childhood Special Education, 21,* 104-114. doi:10.1177/027112140102100204

Dunn, J. (2006). Early moral development and social interaction in the family. In M. Killen & J. Smetana (Eds.), *Handbook of moral development* (pp. 331-350). Mahwah, NJ: Lawrence Erlbaum.

Dyson, L. (2005). Kindergarten children's understanding about and attitudes toward people with disabilities. *Topics in Early Childhood Special Education, 25,* 95-105. doi:10.1177/02711214050250020601

Dyson, L. (2010, April). *Factors influencing the attitudes of children toward people with disabilities.* Poster session presented at the American Educational Research Association Annual International Conference, Denver, CO.

Eagly, A. H., & Chaiken, S. (1993). *The psychology of attitudes.* Orlando, FL: Harcourt Brace Jovanovich College.

Eisenberg, N. (1986). *Altruistic emotion, cognition, and behavior.* Hillsdale, NJ: Lawrence Erlbaum Associates.

Eisenberg, N., & Fabes, R. (1998). Prosocial development. In W. Damon (Ed.) *Handbook of child psychology* (Vol.3, pp. 701-778). New York, NY: Wiley.

Esposito, B. G., & Peach, W. (1983). Changing attitudes of preschool children toward handicapped persons. *Exceptional Children, 46,* 504-514. Retrieved from ERIC database. (EJ276469)

Favazza, P., Phillipsen, L., & Kumar, P. (2000). Measuring and promoting acceptance of young children with disabilities. *Exceptional Children, 66,* 491-508.

Freud, S. (1930/1950). *Civilization and its discontents.* London: Hogarth Press.

Galotti, K. M. (1989). Approaches to studying formal and everyday reasoning. *Psychological Bulletin, 105,* 331-351. doi:10.1037/0033-2909.105.3.331

Gibbs, J. C. (1991). Toward an integration of Kohlberg's and Hoffman's theories of morality. In W. M. Kurtines, & J. L. Gewirtz (Eds.), *Handbook of moral behavior and development,* (Vol, 1, pp. 183-222). Hillsdale, NJ: Erlbaum.

Gibbs, J., Kohlberg, L., Colby, A., & Speicher-Dubin, B. (1976). The domain and development of moral judgment: A theory and a method of assessment. In Meyer J. R. (Ed.), *Reflections on values education* (pp. 19-46). Waterloo, Ontario, Canada: Wilfrid Laurier University Press.

Grusec, J. E. (1991). Socializing concern for others in the home. *Developmental Psychology, 27,* 338-342. doi:10.1037/0012-1649.27.2.338

Haidt, J. (2001). The emotional dog and its rational tail: A social intuitionist approach to moral judgment. *Psychological Review, 108,* 814-834. doi:10.1037/0033-295X.108.4.814

Haidt, J. & Graham, J. (2007). When morality opposes justice: Conservatives have moral intuitions that liberals may not recognize. *Social Justice Research, 20,* 98-116. doi:10.1007/s11211-007-0034-z.

Hazzard, A. (1983). Children's experience with, knowledge of, and attitude toward disabled persons. *The Journal of Special Education, 17,* 131-139. doi:10.1177/002246698301700204.

Helwig, C. C., Zelazo, P. D., & Wilson, M. (2001). Children's judgments of psychological harm in normal and noncanonical situations. *Child Development, 72,* 66-81.

Hinde, R. A. (2002). *Why good is good: The source of morality.* New York, NY: Wiley.

Hoffman, M. L. (1970b). Conscience, personality, and socialization techniques. *Human Development, 13,* 90-126.

Hoffman, M. L. (1983). Affective and cognitive processes in moral internalization. In E. T. Higgins, D. Ruble, & W. Hartup (Eds.), *Social cognition and social development: A sociocultural perspective* (pp. 236-274). Cambridge, MA: Cambridge University Press.

Hoffman, M. (1991). Toward an integration of Kohlberg's and Hoffman's moral development theories: Commentary. *Human Development, 34,* 105-110. doi:10.1159/000277037.

Hoffman, M. L. (2001). *Empathy and moral development: Implications for caring and justice.* Cambridge, England: Cambridge University Press.

Jolliffe, D., & Farrington, D. (2004). Empathy and offending: A systematic review and meta-analysis. *Aggression and Violent Behavior, 9,* 441-476. doi:10.1016/j.avb.2003.03.001.

Kohlberg, L. (1976). Moral stages and moralization: The cognitive-developmental approach. In T. Lickona (Ed.), *Moral development and behavior: Theory, research, and social issues* (pp. 31-53). New York, NY: Holt, Rinehart, & Winston.

Kohlberg, L. (Ed.). (1981). *Essays on moral development.* New York, NY: Harper and Row.

Kohlberg, L. (2008). The development of children's orientations toward a moral order: I. Sequence in the development of moral thought. *Human Development, 51,* 8-20. doi:10.1159/000112530. (Reprinted from *Vita Humana,* 6, 6-33, 1963).

Laible, D., & Thompson, R. (2000). Mother–child discourse, attachment security, shared positive affect, and early conscience development. *Child Development, 71,* 1424-1440. doi:10.1111/1467-8624.00237.

Lapsley, D. K. (2006). Moral stage theory. In M. Killen & J. Smetana (Eds.), *Handbook of moral development* (pp. 37-66). Mahwah, NJ: Lawrence Erlbaum.

Lee, K., Cameron, C. A., Xu, F., Fu, G., & Board, J. (1997). Chinese and Canadian children's evaluations of lying and truth telling: Similarities and differences in the context of pro- and antisocial behavior. *Child Development, 68,* 924-934. doi:10.1111/j.1467-8624.1997.tb01971.x

Narvaez, D., Getz, I., Rest, J., & Thoma, S. (1999). *Individual moral judgment and cultural ideologies. Developmental Psychology, 35,* 478-488. doi:10.1037/0012-1649.35.2.478.

Nielsen, K. (1963). Wanton reason. *Philosophical Studies, 12,* 82-91.

Nucci, L. (2006). Education for moral development. In M. Killen & J. Smetana (Eds.), *Handbook of moral development* (pp. 257-681). Mahwah, NJ: Lawrence Erlbaum.

Piaget, J. (1932/1965). *The moral judgment of the child.* New York, NY: The Free Press.

Reddy, V. (1991). Playing with others' expectations: Teasing and mucking about in the first year. In A. Whiten (Ed.), *Natural theories of mind.* Oxford, England: Blackwell.

Rest, J. (1994). Background: Theory and research. In J. R. Rest & D. Narvaez (Eds.), *Moral development and professions: Psychology and applied ethics* (pp. 1-26). Hillsdale, NJ: Erlbaum.

Rosenbaum, P. L., Armstrong, R. W., & King, S. M. (1986). Children's attitudes toward disabled peers: A self-report measure. *Journal of Pediatric Psychology, 11,* 517-530.

Santrock, J. W. (1993). *Adolescence: An introduction.* Madison, WI: WCB Brown & Benchmark.

Schlaefli, A., Rest, J. R., & Thoma, S. J. (1985). Does moral education improve moral judgment? A meta-analysis of intervention studies using the defining issues test. *Review of Educational Research, 55,* 319-352.

Sears, R. R., Maccoby, E. E., & Levin, H. (1957). *Patterns of child rearing.* Evanston, IL: Row Peterson.

Snarey, J. (1985). Cross-cultural universality of social-moral development: A critical review of Kohlbergian research. *Psychological Bulletin, 97,* 202-232. doi:10.1037/0033-2909.97.2.202

Spiro, H. (1992). What is empathy and can it be taught? *Annals of Internal Medicine, 116,* 843-846.

Sprigge, T. L. S. (1970). Definition of moral judgment. In G. Wallace & A. D. M. Walker (Eds.), *The definition of morality* (pp. 119-145). London: Methuen.

Strauss, A., & Corbin, J. (1990). *Basics of qualitative research: Grounded theory procedures and techniques.* Newbury Park, CA: SAGE.

Strayer, J., & Roberts, W. (2004). Children's anger, emotional expressiveness, and empathy: Relations with parents' empathy, emotional expressiveness, and parenting practices. *Social Development, 13,* 229-254. doi:10.1111/j.1467-9507.2004.000265.x.

Teo, T., Becker, G., & Edelstein, W. (1995). Variability in structured wholeness: Context factors in L. Kohlberg's data on the development of moral judgment. *Merrill-Palmer Quarterly, 41,* 381-395.

Turiel, E. (1983). *The development of social knowledge: Morality and convention.* Cambridge, England: Cambridge University Press.

Turiel, E. (2002). *The culture of morality.* Cambridge, England: Cambridge University.

Turiel, E. (2006). Thought, emotions, and social interactional processes in moral development. In M. Killen & J. Smetana (Eds.), *Handbook of moral development* (pp. 7-35). Mahwah, NJ: Lawrence Erlbaum.

Whiteley, C. H. (1970). On defining "moral". In G. Wallace & A. D. M. Walker (Eds.), *The definition of morality* (pp. 21-25). London: Methuen

Author Contact Information: Lily Dyson, PhD, Faculty of Education, Simon Fraser University Burnaby, B.C., Canada 8888 University Dr. Burnaby, BC V5A 1S6 Canada. Phone: 250-721-1653. E-mail: ldyson@uvic.ca or ldyson@sfu.ca

CHAPTER 53

Moral Development Theory

Neo-Kohlbergian Theory

Heather S. Mechler
Bucknell University

Stephen J. Thoma
The University of Alabama

KOHLBERG'S THEORY

When Lawrence Kohlberg proposed his theory of moral judgment development, he was attempting to provide a cognitive-developmental structure for a phenomenon that had previously been described in primarily social terms. Previous notions of morality focused on societal norms, so that any action or decision could be deemed moral so long as it conformed to a particular set of conventions held by the group (Lapsley, 1996). However, this understanding of morality troubled Kohlberg, as it would have theoretically justified Nazi atrocities and other behaviors that were arguably wrong but congruent with the social norms of a time and place. His theory of moral judgment development outlined a series of stages through which a person would pass over time with development that culminated in the highest stage, which was considered the most developmentally adaptive, and therefore good, regardless of culture, location, or era (Kohlberg, 1969; Lapsley, 1996).

Kohlberg's theory sought to describe the ways in which the underlying thought processes of morality changed with increased cognitive capacity and other developmental gains. This developmental progression was divided into three levels and six stages that described increasingly broad scopes of consideration that factored in to moral decision making. The first level, *Preconventional*, corresponded to a self-focused morality in which the individual made moral judgments. The second, *Conventional*, described a norms-centered morality in which moral judgment relied on legal and social norms. The final (and highest) level of moral judgment development was *Postconventional*, in which the individual formed moral judgments based on universal principles of justice that transcended both personal claims and the dictates of law and culture. Each level contained two stages, the first representing the beginnings of a level, and the second a more sophisticated manifestation of that type of moral reasoning. Kohlberg developed these levels and stages from a series of interviews in which he told respondents a moral dilemma story and then asked them what the protagonist should do and why. Kohlberg claimed that these probing questions allowed the researcher to access the underlying thought processes of these decisions.

CRITICISM OF KOHLBERG'S THEORY

The fact that Kohlberg's theory of moral judgment development used an interview method of assessment that then assigned a specific hard developmental stage to the interviewee elicited critiques from some who felt that the interview method was an inefficient means of gathering data and would limit the extent to which researchers could adequately measure moral judgment development. The interviewee was expected to produce an articulation of his or her moral judgment, but some were uncomfortable with the assumption that the interviewee would be able to articulate his or her

The Handbook of Educational Theories, pp. 643–651

thoughts in a way that the interviewer could correctly interpret. Further, this method was subject to the interviewer's interpretation and the participant's ability to fully articulate his thoughts. The reliance on purely verbal data and subjective interpretation led some to question the utility and validity of Kohlberg's method. Some felt that the fixed developmental stages did not reflect actual developmental trajectories and neglected to consider within-person variation in moral judgment. Kohlberg's definition of postconventional thinking centered on Rawls's notion of justice-based reasoning, which lent a Western philosophical bias to the theory, and neglected other types of postconventional moral reasoning found in moral philosophy (Rest, Narvaez, Bebeau, & Thoma, 1999).

Neo-Kohlbergian Theory

The neo-Kohlbergian approach to the study of moral judgment development improves on Kohlberg's earlier theory with its more complex stage model that reflects gradual development and does not privilege justice-based moral reasoning in its definition of the highest forms of moral reasoning. Further, the neo-Kohlbergian approach defines postconventional thinking more broadly than Kohlberg by considering many philosophical bases for shared ideals. The measurement of moral judgment development in this approach is more efficient, less prone to interviewer subjectivity, and is not contingent on the ability to spontaneously produce verbal descriptions of the moral thought process.

A functional developmental theory must simultaneously explain both the universals in the human condition and the vast array of differences between and within individuals. In the neo-Kohlbergian theory of moral judgment development, the order of developmental progression is the same in all people, although not everyone will necessarily attain the most sophisticated type of moral reasoning. The neo-Kohlbergian approach uses schemas as opposed to hard stages to both reflect more realistic developmental trajectories and account for within-person variation.

The neo-Kohlbergian approach describes moral judgment development according to three types of reasoning, or schemas: Personal Interest, Maintaining Norms, and Postconventional. Personal Interest reasoning involves making moral judgments that prioritize the satisfaction of personal claims to the detriment of others' rights and needs. A person who uses the Maintaining Norms schema relies on social and legal norms to determine the best outcome in a moral dilemma. Postconventional reasoning is based on the notion that society is organized according to a set of negotiable shared ideals.

Postconventional Moral Reasoning

Rest, Narvaez, Bebeau, et al. (1999) defined postconventional reasoning according to four elements: primacy of moral criteria, appeal to an ideal, sharable ideals, and full reciprocity. The first, primacy of moral criteria, defines morality as existing apart from existing social, legal, or religious norms. In Maintaining Norms reasoning, something is inherently moral by virtue of its conformity to group expectations. Postconventional reasoning, however, transcends convention and views rules as means to a moral ends, and therefore negotiable. The second element, appeal to an ideal, proposes the adoption of an overarching theme within which all moral decisions and negotiations should be made. Promotion of the common good, guaranteed minimum rights for all, and mandatory fair treatment are some ideals upon which a society can organize. The third element of Postconventional reasoning states that any ideal must be subject to scrutiny and justified by those who hold it. This does not preclude an existing legal or religious norm from qualifying as a Postconventional ideal, but these ideals are also bound by tests of logic, rational critique, and rules of evidence. The fourth element, full reciprocity, affirms that all persons are subject to rules, but that these rules must also benefit all people equally.

Schemas in Neo-Kohlbergian Theory

Neo-Kohlbergian theory departs from the Kohlberg tradition in that it focuses on schema preferences rather than hard developmental stages. The Personal Interest, Maintaining Norms, and Postconventional schemas loosely correspond with Kohlberg's three levels of moral judgment development (preconventional, conventional, and postconventional, respectively). The emphasis on schemas allows researchers to assess not only what type(s) of reasoning an individual uses, but also to what extent a person relies on each moral developmental schema (Rest, Narvaez, Bebeau, et al., 1999).

Development generally follows a complex model in which the more advanced schemas gradually become more central in the decision-making process. At any given time multiple schemas make be a part of an individual's decision-making repertoire. This notion of shifting preferences across development can be contrasted to Kohlberg's model that described development as fitting a stair step model; therefore, assessing schema preference rather than stages would better reflect this gradual progression from Personal Interest to Maintaining Norms to Postconventional reasoning. As an individual moves from one schema to the next, the lower schema gradually declines in use as the individual's reasoning becomes more sophisticated with the adoption of higher developmental schemas (Rest, Narvaez, Bebeau, et al., 1999) (see Figure 53.1).

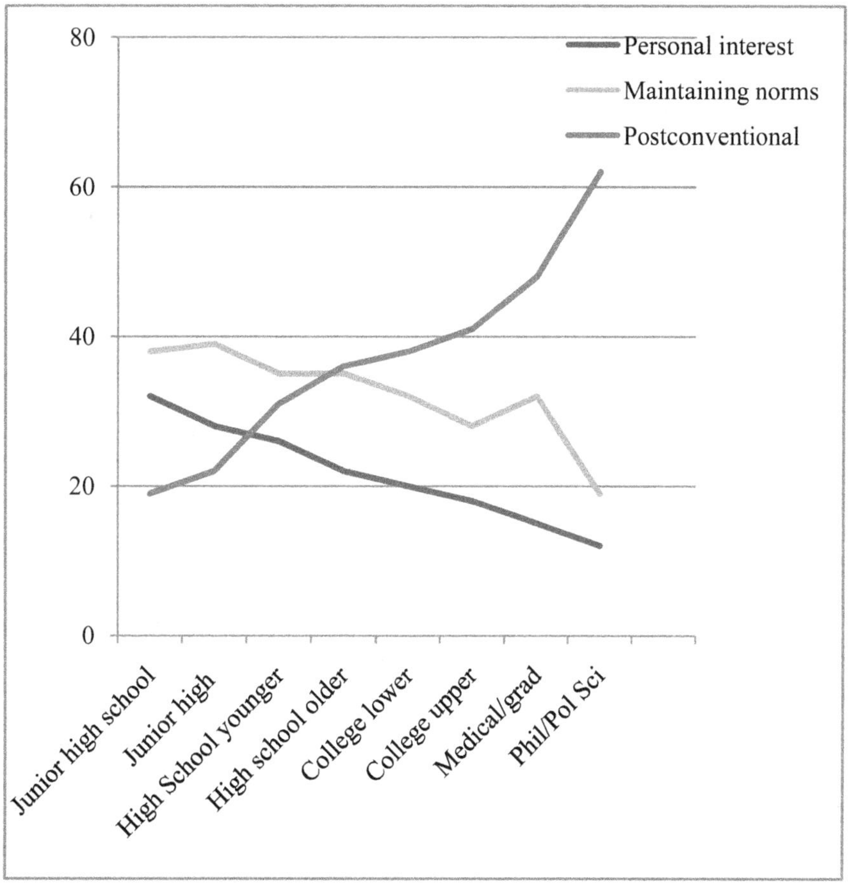

Source: Adapted from Thoma and Bebeau (2003).

Figure 53.1. Schema scores by level of education.

In the neo-Kohlbergian perspective, the measurement of moral judgment reflects schema preference rather than conformance to a specific developmental stage. This allows for a less rigid form of measurement in which the participant must first recognize the postconventional schema as developmentally superior and then show a preference for it over other schemas. Additionally, the ability to measure moral judgment development by assessing recognition and preference makes the assessment process less subjective and not contingent on expressive abilities.

Measurement

The measurement of moral judgment development in neo-Kohlbergian theory relies on the Defining Issues Test (DIT) and its more recent version, the DIT-2. The DIT was developed in response to critiques of Kohlberg's theory and measurement methods, in particular the use of hard developmental stages and the inefficient, somewhat subjective means of data collection. Rest and his colleagues created the original version of the DIT in the early 1970s to address these concerns (Rest, Cooper, Coder, Masanz, & Anderson, 1974). In the DIT, participants read six moral dilemma stories, decide the optimal outcome for each story (should do, should not do, can't decide), and then consider 12 statements that could justify the selected outcome in each dilemma. Participants then rate each of these statements according to their importance, and then are asked to list in rank order the four most important justification statements. Within each set of 12 statements are an equal number of statements designed to assess moral reasoning using the Personal Interest, Maintaining Norms, and Postconventional schemas. The rating and ranking response patterns for statements pertaining to each schema determines the individual's schema scores. The DIT and DIT-2 are intended to be schema activation measures in which a person must possess a schema in order for its corresponding items to make sense. The schema that an individual recognizes and prioritizes is said to be that person's dominant schema (Narvaez & Bock, 2002; Rest, Narvaez, Thoma, & Bebeau, 1999).

When comparing the moral developmental schemas to Kohlberg's stages, the Personal Interest schema is consistent with Kohlberg's Stages 2 and 3, the Maintaining Norms schema represents Stage 4, and the Postconventional schema parallels Stages 5 and 6. These schema-stage relationships were determined by the factor loadings from a factor analysis of a large data set of DIT research (N > 45,000). This analysis revealed that the Postconventional factor loaded on items representing Stages 5 and 6, the Maintaining Norms factor loaded on Stage 4 items, and the Personal Interest factor loaded on Stages 2 and 3 items. This last factor loading is of interest because Stage 3 typically corresponds to the conventional (or Maintaining Norms) level in the Kohlberg system. However, Rest and his colleagues note that individuals who take the DIT are often adults, and therefore have moved beyond Stages 2 and 3 reasoning (Rest, Narvaez, Bebeau, et al., 1999).

The DIT-2

The updated version of the DIT, the DIT-2, contains new dilemmas and five stories. Rest and his colleagues reduced the number of stories to decrease the amount of time necessary to complete the measure and to eliminate a dilemma story that was identified as having the weakest psychometric properties. The DIT-2 also contains reliability checks that purge the data of unreliable participants and spurious response sets. In addition, some new indices that more thoroughly describe moral judgment development have emerged over the past 4 decades. Most notable of these changes was the development of a new summary index of the DIT, the N2 score. The interest in a new summary score was prompted by concerns that the Postconventional score (P score) was an inadequate primarily summary index of the DIT since it did not utilize all of the information available from the measure. These critics wondered whether a more comprehensive index was warranted that could incorporate preference for lower types of moral reasoning (Rest, Narvaez, Bebeau, et al., 1999). To highlight this concern, it is helpful to note that individuals with P scores only slightly higher than their Maintaining Norms and Personal Interest scores would be considered as developed as a person with a similar P score but lower Maintaining Norms and Personal Interest scores. However, one might argue that there is a developmental difference between someone who is not distinguishing among the three schemas and someone who makes a clear distinction. To address this concern, Rest and his colleagues established the N2 index, which accounts for preference of higher levels of moral reasoning and rejection of lower levels of reasoning. DIT and DIT-2 research now primarily uses the N2 index as a descriptor of moral judgment development, although the individual moral schemas scores are also reported and used in various types of analyses (Rest, Thoma, Narvaez, & Bebeau, 1997).

Other Indexes

Other scores that have emerged from decades of DIT research are the Utilizer score, Religious Orthodoxy, Type Indicator, and Consolidation/Transition. The Utilizer score was designed to predict the likelihood of moral action consistent with one's moral reasoning. Higher Utilizer scores correspond with a greater probability that a person will engage in an action informed by his or her moral judgment. The Religious Orthodoxy score is a proxy measure of religious orthodoxy that has reliably corresponded with other independent measures of religious orthodoxy. This score derives from a response to the statement, "Should only God decide when a person's life should end?" from the fourth dilemma story, in which a doctor must decide whether to give a potentially fatal dose of medicine to a terminally ill patient who has requested it (Thoma, 2006).

Type scores provide a description of moral judgment development that combines schema and consolidation/transition data. These scores range from 1 to 7 and indicate not only which schema an individual prefers, but also whether that person is consolidated on, transitioning out of, or transitioning into a schema. Type 1 represents consolidation on Personal Interest reasoning, Type 2 is transitioning out of the Personal Interest schema, Type 3 is transitioning into Maintaining Norms reasoning, Type 4 is consolidation on Maintaining Norms, Type 5 is transitioning out of Maintaining Norms, Type 6 is transitioning into Postconventional reasoning, and Type 7 represents consolidation on the Postconventional schema. Similar to Type scores, Consolidation/Transition specifies whether an individual is consolidated on or transitioning between any of the three moral developmental schemas. Accordingly, Types 1, 4, and 7 correspond to consolidation; and Types 2, 3, 5, and 6 correspond to transition (Rest, Narvaez, Bebeau, et al., 1999) (see Figure 53.2).

Reliability of the DIT and DIT-2

The DIT and DIT-2 have been administered as both paper-and-pencil measures and online versions, and both have similar levels of reliability and internal consistency (Thoma & Bebeau, 2010). The DIT P score has a Cronbach's alpha of .78, and the N2 index has a Cronbach's alpha of .83. The DIT-2 P score has a Cronbach's alpha of .74 and a .81 for the DIT-2 N2 index. Test-retest reliability has been in the upper .70s to low .80s for both measures (Rest, Narvaez, Bebeau, et al., 1999).

Validity of the DIT and DIT-2

Rest, Narvaez, Bebeau, et al. provide six validity criteria to support the DIT as a measure of the neo-Kohlbergian theory. These six validity criteria are rooted in decades of research with thousands of partic-

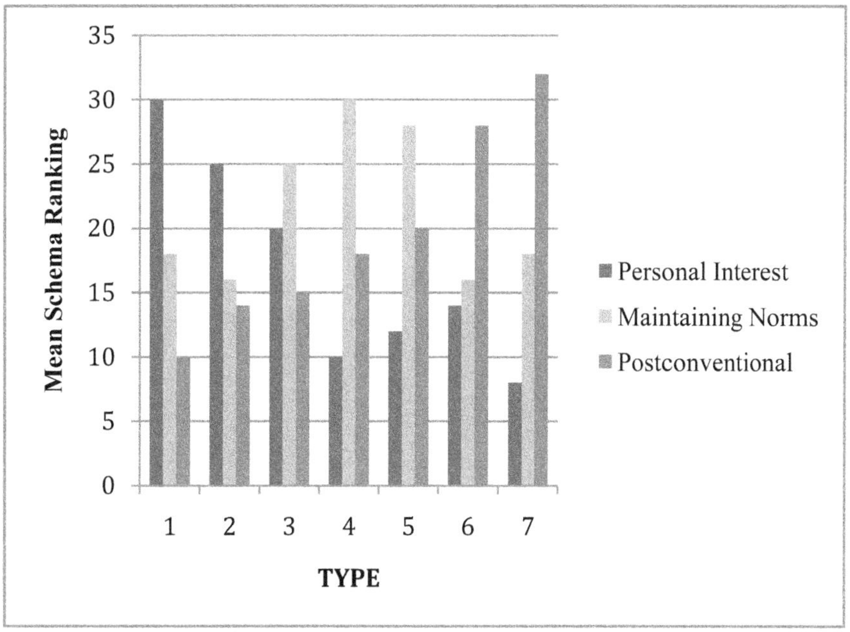

Source: Adapted from Thoma (2006).

Figure 53.2. Mean DIT item ratings by type score.

ipants. The first criterion, *differentiation of experts from nonexperts*, states that people who regularly consider and deliberate on moral dilemmas (for example, philosophers and judges) will have more developed moral judgment than people who are not well versed in reasoning about moral problems. Accounting for all other factors, level of education has been shown to be the strongest predictor of postconventional reasoning. The second, *upward movement in longitudinal study*, asserts that an individual's moral judgment development will become more sophisticated over time. A developmental measure or theory that posits to describe an invariant sequence of development must show that there is a consistent upward trend in development with no retrogression. The third validity criterion is *sensitivity to moral education interventions*. In a number of studies, people who participated in moral dilemma discussions or other types of moral education programs showed meaningful gains in postconventional moral reasoning. The fourth, *developmental hierarchy*, shows that the measurement of moral judgment development should correspond with the measurement of other constructs such as moral comprehension, cognitive capacity, and other types of developmental measures. The fifth validity criterion, *correlations with prosocial behaviors*, was developed from research that examined the relationship between neo-Kohlbergian measures of moral judgment development and altruistic behaviors, whistle blowing, and cheating. The sixth and final validity criterion states that measures of moral judgment development should predict (but not be reducible to) political choices and attitudes. A number of research studies have shown that moral judgment development relates to civil liberties beliefs, candidate preference, and measures of political tolerance (Rest, Narvaez, Bebeau, et al., 1999).

These validity criteria apply to the measurement of moral judgment development within any kind of demographic or cultural group. However, all three moral developmental schemas are not always represented in all groups. Within some environments, such as prisons, the use of Postconventional reason may be not only maladaptive but also personally hazardous. Additionally, people within cultures that prioritize group solidarity over individuality may discard Personal Interest reasoning at an earlier age but use very little Postconventional reasoning as an adult in service of maintaining interpersonal harmony and cultural norms (Snarey, 1985).

Generalizability of the Theory

Meta-analyses of decades of data have shown that there are no discernible differences in moral judgment development between genders, despite earlier claims that Kohlberg's theory neglected the care orientation of moral judgment, thereby casting women as morally inferior (Gilligan, 1982). In one overview of DIT research, women appeared to have a slight edge over men in measures of Postconventional reasoning that could likely be attributed to women's higher levels of verbal ability (Thoma, 1986). When examining differences by ethnicity, there are generally no differences in moral judgment development between ethnic groups. In a nationwide sample, there have been noted ethnic differences (particularly between African Americans and Caucasians in the South), but the effects of religious orthodoxy can account for these differences (Thoma & Mechler, 2010).

Applications of the DIT

Much of the research on the neo-Kohlbergian approach has focused on college-age populations, as this time marks a period of large gains in moral judgment development (King & Mayhew, 2002; Pascarella and Terenzini, 2005). These reviews note that institutions of higher education have an overarching goal to develop their students into thoughtful citizens who will contribute meaningfully to society, and therefore are interested in tracking moral development trajectories in their students from freshman year through graduation. In earlier research, college students showed a significant gain in moral judgment development indices (as much as 6-10% over the span of 4 years); however, recent studies have shown that college students' moral development trajectories suggest less growth in postconventional reasoning (Rest, 1988; Mechler & Bourke, 2010). The level of moral judgment development once found in college seniors is now exhibited in graduate and professional school students. While the reasons for this phenomenon are not yet known, some attribute this deferral to generational shifts in development and social interactions (Twenge, Konrath, Foster, Campbell, & Bushman, 2008).

There have been many DIT studies with professional school populations (law, medical, dental) to assess the effectiveness of ethics curricula and the relationship between moral judgment development and other indicators of moral functioning. DIT and DIT-2 research has also been used in research involving businesses, religious groups, athletic teams, public administration, and military samples, and has been used with participants ranging from early adolescence to old age (Fraedrich, Thorne, & Farrell, 1994; Narvaez, Getz, Rest, & Thoma, 1999; Rest & Narvaez, 1994; Stewart, Sprinthall, & Shafer, 2001).

Critiques of the Neo-Kohlbergian Approach

One of the most significant critiques of the neo-Kohlbergian approach has centered on its assessment method. Beginning with their 1983 article, Emler, Renwick, and Malone argued that the DIT was actually a measure of political ideology rather than a developmental measure. They based their claim on research in which participants were asked to take the DIT as usual and then retake it as if they were either radicals or conservatives. The differences between administrations, particularly for conservatives who answered as radicals, prompted Emler and his colleagues to conclude that the DIT conflated liberal political ideology with Postconventional reasoning, thereby measuring political preference rather than moral judgment development (Emler, Renwick, & Malone, 1983). A subsequent study showed that political ideology actually accounted for very little of the variance in moral judgment development and that the results from Emler et al.'s study were not legitimate because they manipulated the test in a way that invalidated the outcomes. An exploration of trends in rating data revealed that the two scores were not independent, thereby allowing for both Postconventional and Maintaining Norms reasoning simultaneously within participants (Barnett, Evens & Rest, 1995). Emler and his colleagues later argued that the P score and the Maintaining Norms score were mutually exclusive, and that the DIT was an ipsative measure that inevitably forced conservatives to pick Stage 4 items and liberals to select Postconventional items (Emler, Palmer-Canton, & St. James, 1998). This claim was unfounded, however, as Emler focused on DIT ranking data to the exclusion of item rating data (Thoma, Barnett, Rest, & Narvaez, 1999). Emler continues to investigate the relationship between moral development and political ideology by examining the role of identity (Bynner, Romney, & Emler, 2003; Emler, 2002).

Another critique of neo-Kohlbergian theory and the Defining Issues Test was that it was actually a measure of verbal and intellectual ability rather than moral comprehension. Sanders, Lubinski, and Benbow (1995) argued that the DIT measured verbal ability rather than moral judgment development, given that the DIT showed moderate correlation with measures of cognitive ability. Sanders et al.'s study compared DIT indices with various cognitive, personality, and social-environmental measures and found that when accounting for verbal ability, the relationship between DIT P-scores and these measures became statistically nonsignificant. However, a number of studies have shown that after accounting for the effects of verbal and intellectual aptitude, the DIT still correlates with moral comprehension at a highly significant level (Crowson, Debacker, & Thoma, 2007; Thoma et al., 1999; Thoma, Narvaez, Rest, & Derryberry, 1999). These studies have shown that verbal ability does not account for moral judgment development trends in the DIT validity criteria, meaning that the DIT is a reliable measure of moral judgment development that cannot be reduced to other variables.

Uses of the DIT in Research

Over the past 40 years, the Defining Issues Test has been used to explore the links between moral judgment development and many constructs. One of the most common types of studies has focused on the relationship between moral judgment development and political choices. Neo-Kohlbergian theory proposes that these two processes are interrelated because they both rely on macromoral reasoning that determine an individual's beliefs on how a society should function (Narvaez et al., 1999).

Beginning with the 1976 elections, there have been a series of election-year studies that compare voter trends with DIT (and DIT-2) scores. The purpose of these studies is to examine the relationship between moral judgment development and political candidate preference, stances on campaign issues, and general political ideology. These data have consistently yielded a curvilinear pattern with liberals at the top and bottom of the developmental spectrum and conservatives in the middle (Thoma, 1993). More recently, there have also been a number of studies that examined the relationship between moral judgment development and political beliefs that extend beyond the liberal-conservative dichotomy. A study by Crowson and his colleagues (2007) assessed the relationship between moral judgment development and post-9/11 attitudes such as civil liberties beliefs, support for President George W. Bush, and political self-identification. They designed this study to further challenge the assertion by Emler and colleagues that the DIT was a measure of political affiliation. In addition, the authors also tested the assertion that the DIT was a measure of intellectual ability by comparing DIT scores with scores on the American College Test (ACT). The data revealed that the DIT showed no significant relationship to self-identified political conservatism and that moral judgment development was negatively related to the endorsement of civil liberties restrictions. As expected, political conservatism was significantly correlated with the endorsement of restrictions on civil liberties and support for President Bush. Overall, the data showed that DIT scores had unique qualities as a predictor variable in predicting civil rights attitudes that distinguished it from both political ideology and intellectual ability. The authors noted that this study demonstrated the ways in which moral reasoning applies to quotidian concerns such as public policy and voter decisions (Crowson, DeBacker, & Thoma, 2007).

Another study by Crowson, Thoma and Hestevold (2005) examined the role of right-wing authoritarianism (RWA) in the relationship between moral judgment development and political conservatism. Additionally, the study included measures of need for cognition and need for closure to evaluate the link between RWA and epistemological naïveté. The authors hypothesized that RWA would be inversely related to DIT N2 scores and would moderate the relationship between political conservatism and cognitive inflexibility. This would theoretically explain the adoption of politically conservative beliefs for principled ideological reasons rather than nonideological cognitive motivation.

When accounting for the effects of RWA, the correlations between cognitive rigidity and political conservatism became nonsignificant. Maintaining Norms reasoning was unrelated to political conservatism, but significantly correlated with RWA. Interestingly, the relationship between conservatism and Postconventional reasoning became positive and significant when RWA was partialed out. This suggested that cognitive rather than ideological constructs relate more significantly to moral judgment development, which further challenged the contention that the DIT is an ideological measure (Crowson, et al., 2005).

The most recent iteration of DIT election-year studies included affective manipulation to address recent claims that moral judgment is a primarily affective process (Haidt, 2001). Haidt's Social Intuitionist Model has spawned criticism based on its broad assertion that moral judgments occur on an affective basis and neglect of developmental differences (Pizarro & Bloom, 2003; Saltzstein & Kasachkoff, 2004). In this study, four experimental conditions were set up within the section on political choices and affiliation to examine the effects of affective arousal on political choice patterns. These conditions consisted of one control condition, one neutral photograph condition of the 2008 U.S. presidential candidates, and two affectively charged photograph conditions in which the candidates were depicted in either a positive or negative manner. In addition to the political choice measures and the DIT-2, the study also included measures of RWA, dogmatism, and Competitive Jungle Worldview to examine the cognitive and epistemological aspects of moral judgment development and political decision making.

The data showed that affective responses to candidate pictures differed according to moral judgment development, with higher DIT-2 N2 scores corresponding to lower levels of affective arousal. In addition, moral stage consolidation/transition was found to influence the extent of affective arousal, although this effect was stronger in conservatives than liberals. Conservatives in the affectively charged photograph conditions selected more extreme political choices than conservatives in the neutral and experimental conditions or liberals in any of the conditions.

Another noteworthy finding from this study concerns the relationship between dogmatism, affective arousal, moral judgment development, and political affiliation. Regression analyses revealed that as liberals' DIT-2 N2 scores increase, their dogmatism scores decrease, while their levels of affective arousal remained low and constant. An increase in conservatives' N2 scores spurred a decrease in affective arousal, while dogmatism scores remained high and constant. This suggests that the same processes that guide political choices and ideological affiliations may also influence the underlying processes of moral judgment. These findings also indicate that moral judgment is a primarily cognitive process that relies less on affective priming with developmental progression, which challenges Haidt's primarily affective model of moral judgment (Mechler, 2010).

CONCLUSION

Neo-Kohlbergian theory is rooted in the Kohlbergian tradition but has extended beyond the scope of Kohlberg's theory through decades of research and refinement. In summary, the neo-Kohlbergian approach more adequately describes moral judgment development using a complex stage theory; emphasizes schema preference in lieu of hard developmental stages; assesses moral judgment development using a less subjective and more efficient method; uses schema activation rather than production in measurement; uses a more inclusive definition of postconventional moral reasoning; and provides a set of validity criteria by which the DIT and other measures of moral judgment development may be evaluated. The DIT has been shown over time to be a valid and reliable measure of moral judgment development, and its efficient method of assessment allows for large scale and longitudinal studies that help us better understand the development of moral reasoning in many settings.

Despite nearly 40 years of DIT research, there are still many questions to be explored. Recent discussion of the role of affect in moral functioning has opened the door to investigations of the relationship between affect and moral judgment development. As political dispositions shift over time, there will be an abundance of opportunities to continue to examine political ideology in moral developmental contexts. Educational institutions at all levels have a vested interest in promoting moral development to shape students who will become productive and ethical citizens and professionals. The DIT will continue to be beneficial to educators who wish to assess character development programs and predict future behaviors. In all of these and other studies, neo-Kohlbergian theory should continue to provide researchers with a solid theoretical framework upon which to base their research and a proven and reliable means of assessing moral judgment development.

REFERENCES

Barnett, R., Evens, J., & Rest, J. (1995). Faking moral judgment on the Defining Issues Test. *British Journal of Social Psychology, 34*, 267-278.

Bynner, J., Romney, D., & Emler, N. (2003). Dimensions of political and related facets of identity in late adolescence. *Journal of Youth Studies, 6*, 319-335.

Crowson, H. M., DeBacker, T. K., & Thoma, S. J. (2007). Are DIT scores empirically distinct from measures of political identification and intellectual ability? A test using post-9/11 data. *British Journal of Developmental Psychology, 25*, 197-211.

Crowson, H. M., Thoma, S. J., & Hestevold, N. (2005). Is political conservatism synonymous with authoritarianism? *The Journal of Social Psychology, 145*(5), 571-592.

Emler, N. (2002). Morality and political orientations: An analysis of their relationship. *European Review of Social Psychology, 13*, 259-291.

Emler, N., Palmer-Canton, E., & St. James, A. (1998). Politics, moral reasoning and the Defining Issues Test: A reply to Barnett et al. (1995). *British Journal of Social Psychology, 37*, 457-476.

Emler, N., Renwick, S., & Malone, B. (1983). The relationship between moral reasoning and political orientation. *Journal of Personality and Social Psychology, 45*, 1073-1080.

Fraedrich, J., Thorne, D. M., & Farrell, O. C. (1994). Assessing the application of cognitive moral development theory to business ethics. *Journal of Business Ethics, 13*(10), 829-838.

Gilligan, C. (1982). *In a difference voice: Psychological theory and women's development.* Cambridge, MA: Harvard University Press.

Haidt, J. (2001). The emotional dog and its rational tail: A social intuitionist approach to moral judgment. *Psychological Review, 108*, 814-834.

King, P. M., & Mayhew, M. J. (2002). Moral judgement development in higher education: Insights from the Defining Issues Test. *Journal of Moral Education, 31*, 247-270.

Kohlberg, L. (1969). Stage and sequence: The cognitive-developmental approach to socialization. In D. Goslin (Ed.), *Handbook of socialization theory and research* (pp. 347-480). Chicago, IL: Rand McNally.

Lapsley, D. (1996). *Moral psychology.* Boulder, CO: Westview.

Mechler, H. S. (2010). *Does affect explain the relationship between moral judgment development and political choices?* (Unpublished doctoral dissertation). The University of Alabama. Tuscaloosa, AL.

Mechler, H. S., & Bourke, B. D. (2010). *Millennial college students and moral judgment: Generational differences in moral development indices.* Manuscript submitted for publication.

Narvaez, D., & Bock, T. (2002). Moral schemas and tacit judgement or how the Defining Issues Test is supported by cognitive science. *Journal of Moral Education, 31*(3), 297-314.

Narvaez, D., Getz, I., Rest, J., & Thoma, S. (1999). Individual moral judgment and cultural ideologies. *Developmental Psychology, 35*, 478-488.

Pascarella, E. T., & Terenzini, P. T. (2005). *How college affects students: Vol. 2. A third decade of research.* San Francisco, CA: Jossey-Bass.

Pizarro, D. A., & Bloom, P. (2003). The intelligence of the moral intuitions: Comment on Haidt (2001). *Psychological Review, 110*(1), 193-196.

Rest, J. R. (1988). Why does college promote development in moral judgement? *Journal of Moral Education, 3,* 183-194.

Rest, J., Cooper, D., Coder, R., Masanz, J., & Anderson, D. (1974). Judging the important issues in moral dilemmas: An objective measure of development. *Developmental Psychology, 10*(4), 491-501.

Rest, J., & Narvaez, D. (Eds.). (1994). *Moral development in the professions: Psychology and applied ethics.* Hillsdale, NJ: Erlbaum.

Rest, J., Narvaez, D., Bebeau, M., & Thoma, S. J. (1999). *Postconventional moral thinking.* Mahwah, NJ: Erlbaum.

Rest, J., Narvaez, D., Thoma, S., & Bebeau, M. (1999). DIT2: Indexing and testing a revised instrument of moral judgment. *Journal of Educational Psychology, 91,* 644-659.

Rest, J., Thoma, S., Narvaez, D., & Bebeau, M. (1997). Alchemy and beyond: Indexing the Defining Issues Test. *Journal of Educational Psychology, 89*(3), 498-507.

Saltzstein, H. D., & Kasachkoff, T. (2004). Haidt's moral intuitionist theory: A psychological and philosophical critique. *Review of General Psychology, 8*(4), 273-282.

Sanders, C. E., Lubinski, D., & Benbow, C. P. (1995). Does the Defining Issues Test measure psychological phenomena distinct from verbal ability? An examination of Lykken's query. *Journal of Personality and Social Psychology, 69*(3), 498-504.

Snarey, J. R. (1985). Cross-cultural universality of social-moral development: A critical review of Kohlbergian research. *Psychological Bulletin, 97*(2), 202-232.

Stewart, D. W., Sprinthall, N. W., & Shafer, D. M. (2001). Moral development in public administration. In T. L. Cooper (Ed.), *Handbook of administrative ethics* (pp. 457-480). New York, NY: Dekker.

Thoma, S. (1986). Estimating gender differences in the comprehension and preference of moral issues. *Developmental Review, 6*(2), 165-180.

Thoma, S. (1993). The relationship between political preference and moral judgment development in late adolescence. *Merrill-Palmer Quarterly, 39,* 359-374.

Thoma, S., Barnett, R., Rest, J., & Narvaez, D. (1999). What does the DIT measure? *The British Journal of Social Psychology, 38,* 103-111.

Thoma, S., & Bebeau, M. (2010). *Guide for the DIT-2* (Unpublished manuscript). Available from the Center for the Study of Ethical Development.

Thoma, S. J. (2006). Research on the Defining Issues Test. In M. Killen & J. Smetana (Eds.), *Handbook of moral development* (pp. 67-91). Mahwah, NJ: Erlbaum.

Thoma, S. J., & Mechler, H. S. (2010, May). *Investigating the link between moral judgment development and political choices: Evidence from 30 years of DIT research.* Paper presented at the annual meeting of the American Educational Research Association, Denver, CO.

Thoma, S. J., Narvaez, D., Rest, J., & Derryberry, W. P. (1999). Does moral judgment development reduce to political attitudes or verbal ability? Evidence using the Defining Issues Test. *Educational Psychology Review, 11*(4), 325-341.

Twenge, J. M., Konrath, S., Foster, J. D., Campbell, W. K., & Bushman, B. J. (2008). Egos inflating over time: A cross-temporal meta-analysis of the narcissistic personality inventory. *Journal of Personality, 76,* 875-901.

Author Contact Information: Heather S. Mechler, PhD, Bucknell University, Department of Education, 1 Dent Drive, Lewisburg, PA 17837. Telephone: 570-577-1829. E-mail: hsmechler@gmail.com

CHAPTER 54

Playful Activity and Thought as the Medium for Moral Development

Implications for Moral Education

Doris Bergen and Darrel Davis
Miami University

Themes related to moral development and moral education have been proposed over many centuries by Western theorists (e.g., Plato, Rousseau, Calvin) and often these themes had playful, or at least imaginative aspects (Plato's cave, Rousseau's free spirit, Calvin's Biblical origin story). Themes related to morality in other cultures have also been pervasive and these theories have often drawn on imaginative spirits (e.g., Zeus, Athena, Raven, Coyote) or on childhood playful repetition of adult behaviors to instill moral education (e.g., Confucius, Puritans). During the early half of the 20th century, theorists who were prominent primarily for other aspects of their theoretical writings, such as Sigmund Freud, Anna Freud, Jean Piaget, Erik Erikson, and Lev Vygotsky, also looked at aspects of moral development through the lens of playful activity. For example, they discussed the moral-emotional meanings of pretense and block play (Erikson, 1977), the influence of games with rules on moral reasoning (Piaget, 1965), the creation of guilt and shame through imagined wish-fulfilling plots (S. Freud, 1938), expressions of inappropriate thoughts and behaviors through joking (S. Freud, 1960), playful demonstration of painful moral-emotional themes as part of a healing process (A. Freud, 1989), and practice of self-regulation behavior in sociodramatic play (Vygotsky, 1967). Through these aspects of their work they suggested that playful actions and imaginative thoughts often address moral issues, promote moral behaviors, and enhance moral emotions and thus can contribute to understanding of moral development, definitions of morality, sources of moral capacities, and suggestions for moral education.

The latter half of the twentieth century and the early part of the twenty-first century have produced a number of theorists and researchers who have enriched understanding of moral reasoning (e.g., Kohlberg, Turiel), moral emotions (e.g., Eisenberg, Damon), and moral behaviors (e.g., Bandura, Pelligrini). They often conducted their research in playful settings but usually did not speculate directly on the role that playful activity and thought may have in influencing such moral development. This chapter elaborates on a theoretical perspective that emphasizes how moral development may be affected by playful experiences in important ways. It draws on Plato's view that playful activity (Paidia) results in determining basic habits of character (Paideia) (see Morris, 1998). Our goal is to describe how a playful theory of moral development may promote integration of the three major moral dimensions that often have been studied separately by others: moral emotion, moral behavior, and moral reasoning. In addition, the potential influence of playful opportunities for moral development in varied cultural mileus and in present-day culture is discussed. We suggest that the increased opportunities both for direct and virtual playful activity and thought in present-day culture

The Handbook of Educational Theories, pp. 653–666

may be affecting development of these moral dimensions in new ways.

Basic Statement of the Paidia Theory of Moral Development

The basic premise of the theory is that engaging in playful activity and thought influences how moral emotions, behavior, and reasoning are constructed and expressed both in childhood and in later years. It borrows an assumption from constructivist theory (e.g., Piaget, 1964), in that the functions underlying moral development are considered invariant while the structures change with age as they are constructed and reconstructed during playful experiences. Six other assumptions of the theory are: (a) through playful activity and thought moral development can proceed to higher and more complex levels; (b) the types of playful activity and thought in which one engages differentially influence both the direction and the strength of moral emotions, behavior, and reasoning; (c) individuals are complex, dynamic systems that self-organize their experiences; (d) the direction and richness of moral development is affected by both the immediate culture of family and community and the broader societal culture; (e) the dynamic interactions that occur between moral reasoning and moral emotional experience affect how moral behavior is exhibited in that culture, (f) imagining moral or immoral emotion or action is as *salient* as performing such actions, but the consequences of moral behavior are not as evident in playful thought as they are in playful action.

Functions of the Theory

Functions are the processes that occur throughout life and that shape moral development. They include the following:

- *Embodiment*: the player is not engaged in surface activity only but rather, actions and beliefs about moral issues are embodied within the playful context. That is, they become an integral part of the player's psyche. Embodied cognition ties the brain circuits responsible for abstract cognition to circuits that analyze and process sensory information (Isanski & West, 2010).
- *Practice*: the opportunity for practice within a low-risk environment is facilitative. Opportunities to practice emotions such as empathy, behaviors such as sharing and reasoning regarding issues such as fairness are tested using the available cultural tools.
- *Dialectic interactions*: many forms of experience are involved and interact during play with moral issues. They are in constant interplay and influenced by cultural issues.
- *Dynamic*: the features of nonlinear dynamic experience are present in playful activity and thought. Self-organization, control parameters, plasticity, phase transitions, self similarity, and sensitive dependence on initial conditions are involved. Thus, play is not a linear venue with predictability of outcome but rather a dynamic interactive experience.
- *Choice driven*: play involves constant morally salient choices of when, what, and how to play, as well as who to play with and how to resolve value conflicts.
- *Core/surface driven*: players bring with them their deepest values as well as their more fluid less established values. They test out both types during playful activity and thought.
- *Bounded/unbounded*: Some types of play involve adhering to boundaries while others involve imagining boundlessness or creation of new types of boundaries. Each has moral consequences that must be faced if play is to continue.

Structures of the Theory

Structures are the cognitive schema/brain connections that are constructed through playful functioning. These moral structural elements change as playful functioning occurs within cultural contexts. The structural changes occur in three areas: emotions, behaviors, and reasoning, as follows:

- *Moral emotions*: (a) feeling moral emotional "as ifs" in playful low risk situations helps those emotions to be recognized and labeled as good/bad cognitively and behaviorally; (b) observing how one's prosocial emotions may affect actions of and consequences for others during play fosters embodied knowledge of social justice and care issues; (c) confronting emotional effects of one's unfair or shameful actions during play provides an evaluative structure that signals when such actions are contemplated later; (d) emotion narratives are present with scripts that change as emotions change.
- *Moral behavior*: (a) behavior choices between "good" and "bad" behaviors (or potential behaviors) are practiced during playful activity and thought; (b) imagining behavioral consequences in playful thought can create the ability to imagine consequences of later positive and negative moral actions; (c) fitting actions to appropriate rules in play results in "habits of mind" that may support socially sanctioned rule governed behaviors, (d) negotiating appropriate rules of action and thought in play with others fosters understanding of social justice.
- *Moral reasoning*: (a) mentally taking apart and putting together possible emotions and potential

actions results in a personal construction/reconstruction of moral reasoning structures; (b) understanding principles of fairness and caring and other moral dimensions through imagining ways to solve moral dilemmas supports development of such moral reasoning; (c) observing the effects of decisions based on moral reasoning in playful setting promotes higher order thinking about moral issues.

DEFINITIONS OF MORALITY

Most theorists have focused on one of three major dimensions of morality; either on moral emotions, moral behavior, or moral reasoning rather than emphasizing all of these aspects. For example, Erikson and the Freuds were concerned most with the internal emotions such as guilt and shame generated in play or elaborated in imaginative thought, Vygotsky with social behaviors such as self-regulation that children could learn to control during play, and Piaget with advances in reasoning about moral dilemmas generated during marble game play with peers. Since all three of these components comprise morality, however, they are all considered as essential aspects of the playful theory of moral development. Recently, moral development also has been characterized as a dynamic system, in which, rather than having invariant stages, moral development is "highly variable, dynamic and often nonlinear." Children are viewed as self-organizing systems and thus their moral development "is dynamic and emergent from the predilection to value" (Kim & Sankey, 2008, p. 283).

For young children, moral *emotions* such as empathy, sympathy, guilt, shame, and caring, while engendered through many types of social interaction, are particularly practiced in playful activity and thought. By imagining the feelings of others in pretense and facing consequences of behaviors in play with peers, young children fine-tune their moral emotion sensibilities. This extends to older children who use games and other advanced play venues to test out the emotions that are appropriate in various situations and learn ways to express or repress moral emotions. Children and adults also experience ways to control or express moral emotions through media such as virtual games, television, and internet sites that call upon playful and imaginative actions and responses and require evaluating the consequences (or lack of consequences) of acting on their moral emotions generated in these venues. For example, a television news story or newspaper article about someone similar to oneself may elicit emotions that are congruent with those that would be generated in a real life situation.

Moral *behaviors*, while often rule bound and controlled for young children by adults, are also practiced in their play. Behaviors such as sharing, comforting, defending the weak, or fighting the evil ones are often the substance of play pretend roles, virtual games, and other imaginary venues. Older children's game play, in which they grapple with issues such as honesty, fairness, and altruism give many opportunities for the practice of moral behaviors and, because of the desire to keep the game going, often provide the incentive for behavior that may be more caring or fair. For all ages, viewing imaginative plots and imagining consequences for oneself can often promote moral behaviors toward others and these thoughts, which also affect moral emotions, may lead to demonstrations of new moral behaviors. As William James (1906) asserted long ago, much of education involves creating "habits of mind;" that is, the act of organizing acquired habits of conduct and behavior that influence lifelong performance. For example, learning that cheating is not fair in a game and practicing honesty in game play may affect behavior in other situations where cheating may be tempting.

Moral *reasoning* also is evident in young children's play, as the many arguments children commonly have about fairness in distribution of resources and other justice-related issues demonstrate. Although young children may not have higher order types of reasoning, attempts at reasoning about such issues occur during their play and the discussion of real moral dilemmas become much more elaborated when games with rules are played. Many virtual games played by older children and adolescents also have moral reasoning dimensions and require imagining consequences of moral reasoning decisions. Actions requiring moral decision making occur both in real life and in virtual pretense settings, especially when there are consequences related to issues of fair distribution of resources. For older children and adults, simulation activities also often provide opportunities for making decisions based on moral reasoning and seeing the resulting consequences in a "safe" environment. For example, even adults have found that simulations, such as the Barnga simulation (Thiagarajan, 1994), about promoting acceptance of diversity that force groups to start with different levels of financial and social resources are often effective in changing perceptions about the fairness of society toward the distribution of resources for certain groups.

PLAYFUL ACTIVITY AND THOUGHT AS A MORAL DEVELOPMENT MEDIUM

The question remains, however, as to why playful activity and thought should provide such fertile ground for moral development. The answer is not trivial, but it may lay in the inherent qualities present in playful activity and thought. There are many aspects of play that suggest it can serve as a medium for development, a few of which are reviewed here (see Bergen, 1998, 2001, for detailed discussion). Four definitions of the term "medium" may give particular insights into why moral development may be enhanced by playful activity and thought. They are as follows (see Merriam-Webster online):

- A medium is an environment in which an organism can function and flourish (moral emotions and reasoning can flourish in such an environment)
- A medium is a means of transmitting a force or producing an effect (various versions of moral behavior can be enacted and the effects observed in a safe environment)
- A medium is a channel or system of communication, information, or entertainment (moral reasoning can be discussed and opinions shared with others and moral emotion can be enriched and enjoyed in such an environment)
- A medium is a surrounding or enveloping substance (the protective nature of a playful world allows risk taking and testing of moral possibilities within relative safety)

Playful activity has been defined in many ways but the definition usually contains these elements: (a) motivated by the satisfaction embedded in the activity itself, (b) concerned more with the activity than with reaching goals, (c) primarily controlled by the players not by others, (d) supplied with meaning by the players, and (e) nonliteral and dynamic (Fromberg, 2006; Spodek & Saracho, 1998). The nonlinear, dynamic qualities of play include plasticity (continuing capacity for change and renewal), self organization (patterns emerge from chaotic states), control parameters (invariant rules are underlying), phase transitions (movement to newer and higher levels), sensitive dependence on initial conditions (small differences can affect outcomes differentially), and self-similarity (patterns are repeated at different levels of scale) (see Fromberg, 2006; Guastello, 1997; Vanderven, 2006). Playful activity exists only when an individual is motivated to engage in it, fosters a sense of internal control by the player, and allows the player to develop a sense of internal reality (Neumann, 1971). Playfulness embodies spontaneity of thought, action, and real or imagined social interaction, and usually incorporates emotions such as joy and humor (Barnett & Kleiber, 1984).

Playful thought has qualities similar to those of playful activity but the motivations and actions are not observable unless deliberately communicated. They are known only to the player and are controlled by the player, and they are unconstrained by physical limitations of environments. Thus, they exist as meaningful, nonliteral, and dynamic elements within the player's mind. The dynamic qualities of playful thought also include phase transitions between reality and pretense, openness to new energy sources (e.g., new play materials or media stimuli) and self-similar recursive patterns (Bergen, 2011). Playful thought often accompanies playful activity and playful activity often generates playful thought. According to Singer and Singer, the elements of playful thought, which they call "fantasy" or "imagination" are the "most powerful components of human experience" (D. G. Singer & Singer, 2006, p. 371). The Singers assert that such fantasy enables children to "enter the fascinating realm of possibility" (p. 377). They have found that imagination has a major role in helping children learn self-control and even reduce their aggressive behaviors (D. G. Singer & Singer, 1990; J. L. Singer & Singer, 1981).

It is clear that playful activity and thought can promote moral development because the very nature of playfulness allows risk taking, experimenting with roles and ideas, going beyond the bounds of permitted real-world behaviors, entertaining unusual possibilities, and hypothesizing consequences of imagined actions. Through playful activity and thought, individuals experience imagined lives that can influence morally responsible "habits of mind" (James, 1906). Playful activity and thought provide a medium for addressing moral emotions, moral behaviors, and moral reasoning issues while avoiding debilitating "real-world" consequences of those actions. While these phenomena are especially evident during childhood, they continue to be important influences during adolescence and adulthood, especially in present-day society, which has expanded opportunities for playful activity and thought for adults as well.

Original Development of and Interactions of the Theory

While there are a number of other early theorists who also addressed the role of playful activity and thought in promoting moral development (e.g., George Herbert Mead), there are five twentieth century theorists who discussed this possibility in enough depth to form the base for the playful theory of moral development. They include Sigmund Freud on Oedipal imagination and playful humor generation, Anna Freud on play as children's means of making sense of moral issues, Jean Piaget on the role of games with rules in promoting moral development, Erik Erikson on the role of pretense and block construction in learning appropriate expression and management of emotion, and Lev Vygotsky on the role of imagination and sociodramatic play in the process of gaining behavioral self-regulation.

View of Sigmund Freud

Sigmund Freud did not have an elaborated view of children's play; however, he did discuss how a child at play "behaves like an imaginative writer, in that he creates a world of his own or, more truly, he rearranges the things of his world and orders it in a new way ... the opposite of play is not serious occupation but—reality" (1917/1956, p. 123). Freud also located a number of his ideas about emotional development within the context of child play and imaginative (i.e., playful) thought processes. For example, he asserted that the moral emotions of shame and guilt were directly related to suppression of the wish-fulfillment imaginary stories 4-6-year-old children entertained about marrying their opposite sex parent and disposing of their same sex parent (i.e., Oedipus and Electra complexes) (S. Freud, 1938). He called the imaginary enforcer that promoted suppression of such bad thoughts the *superego*, which creates an "ego ideal" that represents higher aspirations and is the source of self-judgment and moral censorship.

Imaginative thought in adults was also addressed by S. Freud in a number of ways. He believed that the child's playful activity was transformed into adult playful thought and wrote, "So when the human being grows up and ceases to play he only gives up the connections with real objects, instead of playing he then begins to create fantasy" (1917/1956, p. 124). According to Erikson (1972), S. Freud "invented a method of playful communication called *free association* which has taught man [*sic*] ... to play back and forth between what is most conscious to him and what has remained unverbalized or has become repressed. And he has taught man [*sic*] to give freer play to fantasies and impulses" (p. 163). In Erikson's view, although Freud did not make all of these ideas morally explicit, they had an underlying moral dimension, since Freud "took morality for granted" (Erikson, p. 162). That is, he believed there was a moral dimension even in "lighter" aspects of life.

S. Freud (1960) provided examples in his book, *Jokes and Their Relation to the Unconscious*, which discussed the meanings behind the "playful" quality of joking. He described how children's playful activity is often the earliest form of humor expression, marked by exuberance and nonsensical qualities. Their playful humor then becomes jesting, which has humorous meaning but no underlying intent to harm or shame others. Freud then discussed joking, which becomes a major form of playful thought in later childhood and adulthood, and he asserted that "the pleasure in a joke is derived from play with words or from the liberation of nonsense" (p. 160). He noted that joking is a socially acceptable means of expressing tendacious (hurtful) thoughts that could shock or harm others. One type of joke "overcomes the inhibitions of shame and respectability by means of the bonus of pleasure which it offers" while another type "shatters respect for institutions and truths ... (and) ... endeavors to push the criticism out of sight" (p. 163). He suggested that such jokes "make it possible for their hearers to enjoy aggressiveness in the form of insults" and also "make it possible for him [*sic*: the jokester] to produce them" (p. 164). Joking thus has two dimensions: a tendacious (hurtful) and a nontendacious (thoughtful) aspect. According to Martin (1998), Freud reserved the word "humor" for times when a person was attempting to cope with difficult situations while not being overwhelmed by negative emotions. In sum, there are many indications that Freud saw a role for playful actions and thoughts both in the development and the expression of moral emotions.

Views of Anna Freud

Although Freud mentioned children's play, he gave cursory attention to play experiences as a source of children's moral growth; thus, it remained for Freud's daughter Anna to make play a major therapeutic resource for children who had faced trauma that affected their lives (A. Freud 1989; A. Freud & Burlington, 1943). Anna Freud's work was primarily with children who had experienced the trauma of war and parental separation and she found that a therapeutic play environment was the most likely one to elicit their emotions regarding their traumatic stress and to help them deal with and manage such emotions. In a chapter using Freudian terminology to discuss child analysis as a way to study children's developmental growth over time she states,

> While adopting the reality principle, he [*sic*] (the child) develops a whole secret domain of imagination and fantasy, free of interference by external demands. While learning to work in obedience to ego and environmental pressure, he [*sic*] (the child) invents hobbies to replace the pleasure formerly gained from play. (A. Freud, 1989)

Although Anna Freud did not use terms such as empathy or justice, she clearly saw that learning to master ego (reality) and superego (morality) demands were promoted by early play and fantasy experiences and by other imaginative activities at later ages.

Views of Erik Erikson

Erikson initially worked with Anna Freud and thus he gained an enormous respect for the power of play in children's lives. He described in detail how children use their play (both pretense and construction) as a major way to gain control over their emotions and have feelings of power over their life events. By taking on the roles of more powerful people (and media characters), young children feel the emotions of those roles and also learn to use those emotions responsibly. Erikson discussed how children's creations of small block construction "worlds" in which they rule allows them to deal with emotional and behavioral dilemmas they have encountered in "real" life that may have caused them to feel guilt, anger, shame, and powerlessness. Such play is empowering and ultimately leads to moral growth. In what Erikson termed the play age (3-6), he stated,

> the "Oedipal" stage results not only in the oppressive establishment of a moral sense restricting the horizon of the permissible; it also sets the direction toward the possible and the tangible, which permits the dreams of early childhood to be attached to the goals of an active adult life. (1963, p. 20)

As his theory developed, Erikson expanded his viewpoint and began to discuss how play-based rituals actually perform a role throughout life and are closely linked to many aspects of moral development. He made these ideas explicit in his book, *Toys and Reason* (1977), in which he discussed the process by which childhood play can become the dynamic force behind adult principled actions and creative achievements. He stated, "The growing child's play (and that is what a long childhood is for) is the training ground for the experience of a leeway of imaginative choices within an existence governed and guided by roles and visions" (p. 78). Erikson suggested that playful activity is later transformed into ritualizations (e.g., weddings, parades) that govern much of adult life and he remarked on the paradoxical quality of most rituals because they are playful yet formalized, familiar yet surprising, and affirming yet ambivalent. Rituals often involve discriminating between right and wrong or lawful and unlawful acts and thus Erikson says, "there is no ritual … which does not imply a severe discrimination between the sanctioned and the out-of-bounds" (p. 92). He believed that adults carry their heritage of childhood within them and stated, "in order to be truly adult, he [*sic*] must on each level renew some of the playfulness of childhood and some of the sportiveness of the young … [and] … remain playful in the center of his concerns … to renew and increase the leeway and scope of his [*sic*] and his fellow man's activities" (Erikson, 1972, p. 158).

Views of Jean Piaget

Piaget is better known for his work on logical mathematical reasoning than for his ideas about how playful games with rules can affect the development of reasoning about moral issues. However, one of his earliest books, *The Moral Judgment of the Child* (1948/1965), was based on his study of boys' marble game play and on interviews with children concerning their reasoning about the imaginary moral dilemmas that he provided. From his interviews he concluded that young children are more likely to think an action that results in bad consequences is morally worse than an act arising from bad intentions and belief that rules handed down by authority figures are fixed and unmodifiable (heteronomous/moral realism). At later ages, however, through their interactions in game play with other children, they realize that rules are not rigid but can be modified, and they judge acts more by their intentions rather than by their consequences. By age 12, children can differentiate their values from those of others and have developed internalized rules based on mutual agreements (autonomous/moral cooperation). Piaget's interest in morality was focused on the development of ability to reason about moral issues rather than as a behavioral repertoire of arbitrary rules given by authority figures. He believed that peer play in games such as marbles fosters children's movement to higher moral stages because when children resolve cognitive disequilibrium related to issues of fairness and equity in peer play interactions, they are able to progress to higher levels of moral development. Thus, Piaget saw play as the medium through which moral reasoning flourished.

Although Piaget did not discuss playful activity or thought in adults, he did point out that at any age creative and innovative thought relies on openness to possibilities. In a book written late in his career entitled *Possibility and Necessity* (1987), he states, "any idea or action that gets realized must have existed previously as a possibility, and a possibility, once conceived, will generally breed other possibilities … (which are, however) … not observable, resulting as they do from subjects' active constructions" (p. 3). Piaget saw the generation of possibilities as developing with age, expanding from a narrow and concrete set in childhood to abstract and infinite in adulthood. Although his primary focus was on logical mathematical cognition, he saw moral reasoning as a cognitive process and thus his view of openness to entertaining possibilities can also apply to the moral realm. The moral dilemmas investigated by Kohlberg (1987) were built upon Piaget's earlier work which asked children to reason about moral dilemmas (i.e., imagining "good" and "bad" possibilities of action in problematic situations). Moral dilemmas are examples of a way to use playful thought to enhance moral reasoning.

Views of Lev Vygotsky

Vygotsky agreed with Piaget that knowledge is constructed by each person but he saw the role of the cultural context as vital in determining the substance of such constructions; that is, he asserted that knowledge is socially constructed (coconstructed). Building on Marxist thought, he saw development as a progression of dialectical conflicts and resolutions, with the resolutions then building the knowledge base. From his study of children's block play he outlined basic stages of problem solving and from his study of early language he noted the role of language in accompanying play as a factor in the internalization of thought. Vygotsky (1967) was interested in how play that has imaginary situations, defined roles, and implicit rules, and that is accompanied by language, can foster qualities related to rules of moral behaviors. Although he did not label these qualities as moral behaviors, he stressed that gaining the ability to control ones' actions within a limited set of behaviors (e.g., to stay in one's assigned pretend role and follow its rules), to negotiate and renegotiate roles and rules as the "script" changes, and to create fantasy worlds that may have objects that do not exist in reality and act "as if" they do, were all elements leading to "self-regulation." He was especially interested in the development of children's ability to plan, monitor, and reflect on their own behavior (Elkonin, 1978). Vygotsky suggested that self-regulation is primarily fostered in sociodramatic play because such successful collaborative thematic play requires a great deal of planning and coordinating of each players' actions with other players, as well as monitoring whether all players are exhibiting the appropriate behaviors (Bordrova & Leong, 2006).

Vygotsky stated

> there is no such thing as play without rules. The imaginary situation of any form of play already contains rules of behavior, although it may not be a game with formulated rules laid down in advance. The child imagines himself to be the mother and the doll to be the child, so he must obey the rules of maternal behavior. (pp. 1978, p. 74)

He asserted, "In play thought is separated from objects and action arises from ideas rather than from things … action according to rules begins to be determined by ideas and not by objects themselves (p. 97). As children grow older and their language becomes internalized private speech, these abilities continue to develop until individuals achieve "the mastery of one's own behavior with the assistance of symbolic stimuli (Vygotsky & Luria, 1994 p. 135). Although much imaginative play occurs in the company of other people, it can also occur when a child is alone. In this situation, the child develops the scripts, builds the settings, and gives all characters voice. Older children often do this with small scale objects and create their own "worlds." Vygotsky called this "director's play" (Bodrova & Leong, 2006). Many types of virtual play that are prominent today have this quality when the player directs the actions and experiences the emotions of virtual characters. In a survey of recipients of the MacArthur Foundation "Genius" awards, the Root-Bernsteins (1999) found that many of the adult recipients reported that as children they had engaged in "worldplay," which involves extended periods of creating imaginary "worlds" with scripted events, dynamic actions, and detailed settings (and some reported still engaging in imagining such worlds!).

Validation of the Theory

A number of more recent theorists have addressed issues of moral development within playful activity and thought contexts, often emphasizing either emotions, behavior, or reasoning. These examples show that playful activity and thought have been useful environments for research observations that suggest a variety of ways such experiences contribute to moral development. For example, Eisenberg (Eisenberg, 2000; Eisenberg & Hand, 1979) discussed the relationship between moral emotions and moral behavior and the potential linkage of these two in peer interactions that occur in early childhood play. Her longitudinal study of the relationship of early sharing behaviors and later adult moral actions show the existence of this relationship that lasts into adulthood (Eisenberg et al., 2002).

Damon has described how sociomoral development is coconstructed, stating that "Morality is a fundamental, natural, and important part of children's lives from the time of their first relationships" (Damon, 1988, p.1). In his studies of children's sharing of unequal numbers of toys and other resources, he demonstrated how young children are concerned about issues of morality and try to solve them within their level of understanding. He outlined a set of moral characteristics emotions (empathy, shame, guilt, distributive justice, respect for rules, and reciprocity) and described how these gain increasing depth at later ages. Although he did not outline a playful theory of moral development, he did give examples of how many of these characteristics are practiced in playful, active settings. He also designed a program for adolescents involving activities that promote taking responsibility and evaluating the moral meaning of their choices (Damon, 1997).

Bandura (Bandura, Ross, & Ross, 1963), in a classic study that focused on one behavioral aspect of moral development (i.e., aggression), gave evidence of how simply witnessing models of aggression during play with a toy can influence the magnitude of aggressive behavior that is later exhibited by children. In his work on the development of self-efficacy (Bandura, 1997) he described the early childhood period as the time for gaining "self-appraisal skills," which are fostered both by direct experiences and social comparisons, in which children monitor and compare their behavior to that of peers. Self-appraisal is often evident during both pretense and game play and is a factor in developing self-control.

Pelligrini (2002, 2009), who has studied rough and tumble playground play extensively, has described how such play is important in helping children learn to encode, decode, and regulate emotions; this ability is "an important dimension of social skill" (2009, p. 104). He views this type of play as especially important for boys and it differs from aggression because the players have "reciprocal role-taking and self-handicapping" (p. 99). That is, the player with more skill alternates roles with the less skilled player so that the play is enjoyable to both. This is a behavioral demonstration of the concept of "fair play." He and colleague Bjorkland have also outlined dimensions of object and fantasy play that can affect social learning related to moral development (Pelligrini & Bjorkland, 2004).

As stated earlier, playful thought is an essential part of Kohlberg's (1987) use of moral dilemmas and his suggestions that moral reasoning grows through hearing the reasoning of slightly older peers supports the peer interaction element of playful thought. Moral dilemmas are clear examples of such playful thought because they open the participants' thinking to consideration of many possibilities that, if selected through imaginative discussion, are without serious consequences. Kohlberg did not connect his use of moral dilemmas to playful thought directly but he did devise a series of filmed "stories" for elementary aged children that could be used by teachers, suggesting that by discussing the imagined consequences of various action solutions, moral reasoning could be enhanced.

Turiel (1983, 2002) has explored differences in children's ability to discriminate among personal choices (individual preferences that have no moral consequences), social conventions (rules of social groups that members of that group uphold) and moral imperatives (universal values across groups and cultures.) Some of his research has been conducted during recess times at schools. He has observed that during playground activities, even quite young children distinguish between moral imperatives (e.g., not cheating at games) and social conventions (e.g., standing in line without talking). They react much more strongly to violations of moral imperatives and do not believe such imperatives can be easily changed, although they know social conventions can change if the group decides to change them.

Generalizability of the Theory Across Cultures

A question that remains is whether playful activity and thought are more or less important in fostering moral development for particular cultural groups and whether changes in playful activity and thought opportunities in present-day cultures are affecting moral development. Culture is an important issue that must be considered if an honest examination of playful activity and thought is to be attempted, and this is especially true if the examination is done within the context of moral development. The relationships among culture, playful activity and thought, and moral development are complex and nonlinear. Characterizations of these relationships range from "influences" to "causes" where the former does not go far enough to provide a useful framework, and the latter goes too far and trivializes the intricacies of the relationships. Early perspectives valued the importance and contribution of play, with theorists such as Huizinga (1970) viewing play as anterior to culture in both a temporal and a significance sense. Later perspectives have embraced the role of culture although not at the expense of play. Critiques such as Nagel's (1998) not only emphasized the purposefulness of play by rejecting the "purposeless, disinterested modernist idealism" perspective (Nagel, 1998, p. 27), but also suggested that the 1950's German culture and context may have influenced Huizinga's puritan perception of play. Göncü, Tuermer, Jain and Johnson (1999) extended the critiques of early perspectives, for example the Western bias, and challenged core assumptions that play is "a universal activity" (p. 149). Göncü et al. argued, instead, that play is an "interpretive cultural activity" requiring caution when examining one culture via the lens of another. Thus, culture is significant. It influences and shapes individuals both overtly and covertly via the tools it possesses. For example, a culture's ability to define the terms of a discourse significantly affects all products of that conversation (Muthivhi, 2010). To a large extent, a culture can apply boundaries to the internal conversation, affecting both the individuals within the culture and the external viewers and their perceptions.

Playful activity and thought are not exempt from cultural influences; in fact, play provides an excellent medium to examine culture's effect on moral emotions, behavior, and reasoning (see Ramsey, 2006; Roopnarine & Krishnakumar, 2006). Cross cultural studies looking at different aspects of playful activity and thought have shown differences across cultures, while providing the cultural contexts through which the differences arise and are maintained. For example, Nwokah and Ikekeonwu (1998) found cultural differences in play between American and Nigerian children in terms of punishment for losers of games. Nigerian games had higher degrees of physical penalties than American games and more instances of sanctioned rough play. Taylor, Rogers, and Kaiser (1999) suggested that American preschoolers were more playful than their Japanese counterparts. While both Nwokah and Ikekeonwu

(1998) and Taylor et al. found differences, both studies acknowledged the contributions of a culture's perspective on the group versus the individual. In this case, the Nigerian and Japanese cultures placed more emphasis on the group or collective while the American placed more emphasis on the individual. The pattern of differences is also visible via the emotions such as shame and guilt. For example, comparisons between eastern and western cultures demonstrate how shame and guilt are used to varying degrees either to teach or to maintain desired behaviors (Bedford & Hwang 2003; Slonim, 1991). Gaskins and Miller (2009) also focused on emotions. Their examination of Mayan and European-American children demonstrated how cultural differences mediated the roles of emotion in pretend play, affecting both the quantity and intensity of these roles. They showed "how the role of emotion is one of the complex ways in which pretend play is constructed out of cultural values and practices" (p. 17). The impact of culture is not only expressed across cultures, but similar results are reported within cultures and subcultures. Tudge, Lee, and Putnam (1998) found differences described as "a function both of social class and gender" (p. 88) within the American and Korean middle and working class cultures in terms of the amount and type of observed play.

The relationship among culture and playful activity and thought provides an opportunity and context to examine the issue of moral development. Cultures often determine the types of playful activity and thought that are allowed and the resources available for play, and the cultural medium also affects how moral emotions, behavior, and reasoning may develop. This perspective is supported by Haste and Abrahams (2008) who argued that culture provides the tools that frame moral development. Her model views moral development as occurring within a sociocultural context that is mediated by the particular tools that a culture possesses; for example, language and customs. Larson and Verma (1999) highlighted how time spent playing was influenced by both the cultural and physical realities present within communities. The Nwokah and Ikekeonwu (1998) and Taylor et al. (1999) studies both showed how cultural tools, in this case the perception of the collective versus the individual, can inform the differences in the way play is performed. Thus, playful activity and thought help individuals make sense of their world and the social interactions of their world, and it allows practice of the rules and values of the culture in a low risk manner. Play is a tool the culture uses to promote the moral aspects that are valued by the culture. Thus, play is woven into cultural contexts and subsequently differentially affects moral development.

Potential Effects of the Worldwide, Technology-Driven Culture

Culture is always in a state of flux but in the past the sources of change were rarely obvious. However, concepts such as play and morality provided feedback to the culture and thus shaped new cultural tools which were in turn used to redefine the concepts. Currently, a worldwide, technology-driven culture may be shaping both play and morality. For example, television, the internet, and augmented toys are providing new materials for play, and the introduction of such technology is influencing the way both children and adults engage in playful activity and thought. These changes may provide the catalyst for a cultural redefinition of the activity, reenvisioning of cultural tools, and consequently a dynamic change in the development of moral emotion, behavior, or reasoning.

Potential Uses and Application of the Theory

The cultural milieu for playful activity and thought has traditionally been composed of face-to-face institutions (e.g., family events, school playgrounds, outdoor games), in which the consequences of expressing particular moral emotions, behavior, or reasoning are immediate and embodied. This is now changing to involve a virtual culture in which constraints on the moral dimensions and consequences of action are more diffuse and blunted. The presence of new technological venues for playful activity and thought changes the physical realities present in the culture and forces new definitions and tool use. These new tools may redefine concepts such "morals." Families may adopt the tools and guide children's use of such tools in their play. Most importantly, the nature of the new "play world" is likely to affect playful activity and thought and thus, moral development. Even young children are being exposed to technology-enhanced play materials (i.e., augmented toys) that have the potential to change the dynamics of play. These toys are enhanced with computer chips that enable the toy to "talk" and "act" and thus direct the child's play actions instead of the child directing the toy's actions (Bergen, 2001). The implications of such play on empathy development, sharing behaviors, or reasoning about moral actions is as yet unexplored. However, the potential impact of television on children's play and moral development has been of concern for many years (Levin, 2006). Older children's play has been greatly affected by access to video games and internet play (Funk, 2005; Kafai, 2006).

Technology, particularly as exemplified by the internet and other virtual media, may have an intense effect on moral development because, the "culture" is defined by the virtual "people" in the technological environment. These media differ from earlier media such as television and radio. Their size and scope are significant and the participatory nature of the newer media may greatly influence the perceptions of the user. During playful activity and imaginative thought with these media, moral emotions, behaviors, and reasoning values differing from those of the home culture may be transferred more easily because individuals feel that they are members of the virtual community. Thus, the message is inseparable from the messenger because individuals may feel they know the messenger even though in many cases the messenger is either anonymous or is an inauthentic persona created for use in the venue. The interaction in this case is paramount because as individuals interact, they form a community and a culture evolves. Although technology accommodates and encourages this interaction and affords the easy formation of communities/cultures via, for example, chat rooms or blogs, or more feature rich portals such as Facebook and MySpace, the culture and survival of the community remains at risk if individuals within the community are simply inauthentic personas. This technological reality introduces a potential disconnect between action and consequence where a messenger is free to create or distribute messages independent of consequences that may be associated with the actions. Although this reality can produce both positive and negative outcomes, it does represent a new fundamental possibility in which technology is changing the way playful activity and thought are expressed and consequently forcing a reenvisioning of culture tools.

Potential Critiques of the Theory

Critiques extend, naturally, from dilemmas that exist with the scholarship of play. For example, Goncu et al. (1999) have questioned the common assumption that children need play for optimal development. Although they viewed play as a valuable activity in its own right, not limited to the development that it promotes, they argued that the implicit acceptance of the assumption focused play research specifically along the lines of children's development, ignoring other areas that may be just as important. Sutton-Smith (2004) has expressed concern not only regarding the development bias in play inquiry, but also in the theoretical foundations of the area. His concerns are evident when he commented "There has never been a consensus about the theoretical meaning of play, so it has become a veritable Rorschach inkblot in modern social science" (p. ix). This concern challenges the identity of play theory and by extension the ideas that use play theory as support for its role in moral development.

Critiques also may come from those who advocate teaching morality through character education in schools (see Lickona, 1991). Lickona suggests that achieving character education is fostered by the moral leadership of adults in authority (e.g. principals), schoolwide discipline and sense of community, a moral atmosphere, and time and attention given to moral concerns (p. 325). The proponents of this approach (e.g., Elkind & Sweet, 2004; Josephson & Hanson, 1998) typically advise direct attempts to teach moral behaviors. For example, they may suggest using character education slogans and posters (e.g., Honesty; Respect; Caring), and students are asked to practice this behavior in school during a certain time period. The moral behaviors are taught directly by teachers and other staff and there may be some types of reward for classes that most exhibit the behavior. Although advocates of character education occasionally use role-playing to help children practice the behaviors, they rarely suggest including imaginative or child-initiated playful elements in their moral education approach.

Instruments Associated With or Needed for Research on the Theory

Observational methods, clinical experiments, and interviews/surveys have all been used to study playful activity and thought. For example, the observational schemes of Lowe and Costello (1976), Rubin (2001), and Rice, Sell, and Hadley (1990) have been used extensively in researching play. Moral behavior development has been studied through a variety of methodologies (e.g., Bandura, Ross, & Ross, 1963), and moral development studies have incorporated the recording of responses during discussion of moral dilemmas that have incorporated playful thought (e.g., Kohlberg, 1987). Research reports focused on either of these two areas have often suggested a connection between them, but it is only rarely that research instruments specifically targeted moral issues exhibited during playful activity and thought. One example of research that included both play and moral development issues is that of DeVries (2006) who used children's game play to observe their moral reasoning. While DeVries provides some support for the Paidia theory, in order to find additional evidence supporting or questioning the theory, a greater variety of focused instruments are needed.

Examples of Research Exemplifying This Theoretical Framework

As noted earlier, a number of present-day theorists have shown in their research on moral development that moral emotions, behavior, and reasoning are exemplified in playground, classroom, and home playful activity and thought (e.g., Eisenberg, Turiel, Pelligrini). Research on exposure to videos of aggression in play (Bandura) and to playful thought (e.g. Kohlberg's and Damon's moral dilemmas) all give support to the Paidia theoretical framework. In a recent study of the moral dimensions of a young child's pretense, which involved acting out many violent roles, Edmiston argues that when young children play out mythic roles of good and evil, it helps them learn the moral dimensions of their own behavior. He says, "Pretend play makes visible what in everyday life might be considered only appropriate as inner thoughts or narrated events ... children can say and do what would never happen in everyday life" (2008, p, 118), and he views such play as a medium for moral development. Studies of play in various cultural milieus also have suggested it has a role in differentially shaping moral emotions, behavior, and reasoning (e.g., Gaskin & Miller; Nwokah).

Other recent studies of older children's play in the "technology culture" suggest, however, that the "effectance" link between playful activity and thought and moral emotions, behavior, and reasoning may develop differently when play is in the virtual world. For example, a meta-analysis study by Konrath, O'Brien, and Hsing (2010) found that college students do not have as much empathy as they used to, and they speculate "that one likely contributor to declining empathy is the rising prominence of personal technology and media use in everyday life" (p. 9). They suggest that intense media use may have "negative interpersonal effects—such as leading people to care more about themselves and to interact less with real others" (p. 10). In an analysis of the effects of video games, Gentile and Gentile (2008) stated that the moral development goals schools try to teach, such as sharing, tolerance, and peaceful ways to resolve conflicts "compete with the popular media, and especially video games, in which such values as competition, aggression, acquisitiveness, lust, gender bias, pride, and winning at all costs through whatever means are often vividly portrayed and celebrated" (p. 137). Violence exposure in real life from video games, television, movies, and the internet also may result in desensitization (Funk, 2005.) In a study of high school internet users Mishna, Cook, Gadalla, Daciuk, and Solomon (2010) found that half of participants stated that they had been bullied online and one third admitted to bullying others online.

Although current research primarily focuses on the negative aspects of technology, especially in reference to video games, not all results justify the "moral panic" that seems to accompany new or emerging technologies. While there are countless faith-based games that overtly attempt to teach morals, Sicart (2009) focused on mainstream games and showed that a game could go beyond the binary of good versus evil, and force moral reflection on the part of the player. His reflection on his experience "I felt that a computer game was challenging me as a moral being, showing me new ways of understanding games as well as my presence and actions as a player" (p. 2), exemplified the positive contributions that are possible given well-designed games. Positive possibilities also exist in other technology areas. Herzog and Golden (2009) used social networking sites to investigate moral emotions and social activism with respect to animal rights, and Bradley (2005) showed that in addition to the possibility of negative effects, online social networks have the potential to empower youths, positively affecting moral development. She argued that the internet "frees young people from adult control and forces them into conflict and disequilibrium as they interact with others online. It is out of that disequilibrium that moral development takes place" (p. 74.).

Summary

In this chapter we have suggested that there are good theoretical reasons for seeing playful activity and thought as important facilitators of moral emotion, behavior, and reasoning. The processes involved in play allow practice on such dimensions, observation of effects of moral and immoral actions, and understanding of the morally involved reasons for behavior. These processes are influenced by the culture tools available to the individual. Cultural realities, for example technology, may serve as mediators, changing how play is performed and affecting both moral development and to an extent, the culture itself. The chapter also suggests that the types of playful activity and thought in which children engage may facilitate different aspects of emotion and reasoning and thus result in different types of behavior. Because of the dynamic system qualities of human development, all of these play experiences will influence moral development in some way.

The implications of this theory for moral education arise from the evidence showing that when children engage in playful activities and in imaginative playful thought, the moral emotions, behavior, and reasoning that emerge and are practiced can be influential in focusing the direction of their moral development. Thus, it suggests that didactic methods of promoting moral development may be less effective than playful methods that engage students in imagining the moral impact of their emotions, behavior, and reasoning that occur in such activity. In particular, the emerging technological culture can be an important educational factor in determining the direction and quality of moral development. Moral education may be influenced both positively and negatively by these new cultural influences on playful activity and thought. Further research on the role of playful activity and thought in moral development is recommended, especially in relation to the changing technologically influenced culture of the present day.

REFERENCES

Bandura, A., (1997) *Self-efficacy: The exercise of control.* New York, NY: W. H. Freeman

Bandura, A., Ross, D., & Ross, S. A. (1963). Imitation of film-mediated aggressive models. *Journal of Abnormal and Social Psychology, 66*, 3-9, 11.

Barnett, L., & Kleiber, D. A. (1984). Playfulness and the early play environment. *Journal of Genetic Psychology, 144*(2), 153-164.

Bedford, O., & Hwang, K. (2003). Guilt and shame in Chinese culture: A cross-cultural framework from the perspective of morality and identity. *Journal for the Theory of Social Behaviour, 33*(2), 127-144. doi:10.1111/1468-5914.00210

Bergen, D. (Ed.) (1998). *Readings from play as a medium for learning and development.* Olney, MD: Association for Childhood Education International.

Bergen, D. (2001). Technology in the classroom: Learning in the robotic world: Active or reactive? *Childhood Education, 8 8*(2), 249-250.

Bergen, D. (2012). Play, technology toy affordances, and brain development: Considering research and policy issues. In S. Waite-Stupiansky & L. Cohen (Eds.), *Play: A polyphony of research, theories and issue* (Vol. 12, pp. 163-174). Lanham, MD: University Press of America.

Bordova E., & Leong, D. J. (2006). Adult influences on play: The Vygotskian approach. In D. P. Fromberg & D. Bergen (Eds.), *Play from birth to twelve: Contexts, perspectives, and meanings* (2nd ed., pp. 167-172). New York, NY: Routledge.

Bradley, K. (2005). Internet lives: Social context and moral domain in adolescent development. *New Directions for Youth Development, 108*, 57-76.

Damon, W. (1988). *The moral child: Nurturing children's natural moral growth.* New York, NY: Free Press.

Damon, W. (1997). *The youth charter: How communities can work together to raise standards for all children.* New York, NY: Free Press.

Edmiston, B. (2008). *Forming ethical identities in early childhood play.* New York, NY: Routledge.

Eisenberg, N. (2000) Emotion, regulation, and moral development. *Annual Review of Psychology, 51*, 665-697.

Eisenberg, N., Guthrie, I. K., Cumberland, A., Murphey, B. C. Shepard, S,A., Zhou, Q., & Carlo, S. M. (2002). Prosocial development in early adulthood: A longitudinal study. *Journal of Personality and Social Psychology, 82*(6), 993-1006.

Eisenberg, N., & Hand, M. (1979). The relationship of preschoolers' reasoning about prosocial moral conflicts to prosocial behavior. *Child Development, 50*, 356-363.

Elkind, D. H., & Sweet, F. (2004). How to do character education. *Today's Schools.* Retrieved from http://www.goodcharacter.com/Article_4.html

Elkonin, D. (1978). *Psikhologija igry* [The psychology of play]. Moscow, Russia: Pedagogika.

Erikson, E. H. (1963). *Childhood and society* (2nd ed.) New York, NY: Norton.

Erikson, E. H. (1972). Play and actuality. In M. W. Piers (Ed.), *Play and development* (pp. 127-163) New York, NY: Norton.

Erikson, E. H. (1977). *Toys and reason.* Toronto, Ontario, Canada: G. J. McLeod.

Fromberg, D. P. (2006). Play's pathway to meaning: A dynamic theory of play. In D. P. Fromberg & D. Bergen (Eds.). *Play from birth to twelve: Contexts, perspectives, and meanings* (2nd ed., pp. 159-166). New York, NY: Routledge.

Freud, A. (1989) Child analysis as the study of mental growth (normal and abnormal). In S. I. Greenspan & G. H. Pollock (Eds.) *The course of life: Vol. 1. Infancy* (pp.1-14). Madison, CT: International Universities Press.

Freud, A., & Burlington, D. T. (1943). *War and children.* New York, NY: Medical War Books.

Freud, S. (1956). *Delusion and dream.* Boston, MA: Beacon Press. (Original work published 1917)

Freud, S. (1938). *The basic writings of Sigmund Freud* (A. A. Brill, Trans.) New York, NY: Random House.

Freud, S. (1960). *Jokes and their relation to the unconscious.* London, England: Routledge and Paul.

Funk, J. B. (2005). Children's exposure to violent video games and desensitization to violence. *Child and Adolescence Psychiatric Clinics of North America, 14*(3), 387-404.

Gaskins, S., & Miller, P. J. (2009). The cultural roles of emotions in pretend play. In C. D. Clark (Ed.), *Play & culture studies: Vol. 9. Transactions at play* (pp. 5-21). Lanham, MD: University Press of America.

Gentile, D. A., & Gentile, J. R. (2008). Violent video games as exemplary teachers: A conceptual analysis. *Journal of Youth Adolescence, 17*, 127-141.

Guastello, S. (1997). Science evolves: An introduction to nonlinear dynamics, psychology, and life sciences. *Nonlinear Dynamics, Psychology, and Life Sciences, 1*(1), 1-6.

Göncü, A., Tuermer, U., Jain, J., & Johnson, D. (1999). Children's play as cultural activity. In A. Göncü (Ed.), *Children's engagement in the world: Sociocultural perspectives* (pp. 148-70). Cambridge, England: Cambridge University Press.

Haste, H., & Abrahams, S. (2008). Morality, culture and the dialogic self: Taking cultural pluralism seriously. *Journal of Moral Education, 37*(3), 377–394.

Herzog, H. A., & Golden, L. L. (2009). *Moral emotions and social activism: The case of animal rights. Journal of Social Issues, 65*(3), 485-498. doi:10.1111/j.1540-4560.2009.01610.x

Huizinga, J. (1970). *Homo Ludens: A study of the play element in culture.* New York, NY: Harper and Row.

Isanski, B., & West, C. (2010). The body of knowledge: Understanding embodied cognition. *APS Observer, 23*(1), 14-18.

James, W. (1906). *Talks to teachers on psychology: And to students on some of life's ideals.* New York, NY: Henry Holt.

Kafai, Y. B. (2006). Play and technology: Revised realities and potential perspectives. In D. P. Fromberg & D. Bergen

(Eds.). *Play from birth to twelve: Contexts, perspectives, and meanings* (2nd ed., pp. 207-214). New York, NY: Routledge.

Kim, M., & Sankey, D. (2008). Towards a dynamic systems approach to moral development and moral education: A response to the JME [Special issue]. *Journal of Moral Education, 38*(3), 283-298.

Kohlberg, L. (1987). *The philosophy of moral development: Moral stages and the idea of justice*. New York, NY: Longman.

Konrath, S. H., O'Brien, E. H., & Hsing, C. (2010). Changes in dispositional empathy in American college students over time: A meta-analysis. *Personality and Social Psychology Review, 20*(10), 1-19.

Larson, R. W., & Verma, S. (1999). How children and adolescents spend time across the world: Work, play, and developmental opportunities. *Psychological Bulletin, 125*(6), 701-736.

Levin, D. (2006). Play and violence: Understanding and responding effectively. In D. P. Fromberg & D. Bergen (Eds.). *Play from birth to twelve: Contexts, perspectives, and meanings* (2nd ed., pp. 395-404). New York, NY: Routledge.

Lickona, T. (1991). *Educating for character: How our schools can teach respect and responsibility*. New York, NY: Bantam Books.

Lowe, M., & Costello, A. J. (1976). *A manual for the symbolic play test*. London, England: NFER.

Martin, R. (1998). Approaches to the sense of humor: A historical review. In W. Ruch (Ed.) *The sense of humor: Explorations of a personality characteristic* (pp. 15-60). Berlin, Germany: Mouton de Gruyter.

Merriam-Webster Online Dictionary. (2010). Medium. Retrieved from http://www.merriam-webster.com /dictionary/medium

Muthivhi, A. E. (2010). Piaget, Vygotsky, and the cultural development of the notions of possibility and necessity: An experimental study among rural South African learners. *South African Journal of Psychology, 40*(2), 139-148.

Mishna, F., Cook, C., Gadalla, Daciuk, J., & Solomon, S. (2010). *American Journal of Orthopsychiatry, 80*(3), 362-374.

Morris, S. R. (1998). No learning by coercion: Paidia and Paideia in Platonic philosophy. In D. P. Fromberg & D. Bergen (Eds.), *Play from birth to twelve and beyond: Contexts, perspectives, and meanings* (pp. 109-118). New York, NY: Garland.

Nagel, M. (1998). Play in culture and the jargon of primordiality: A critique of Homo Ludens. In M. C. Duncan, G. Chick, & A. Aycock (Eds.), *Play & culture studies: Vol. 1: Diversions and divergences in fields of play* (Vol. 1, pp. 19-30). Greenwich, CT: Ablex.

Neumann, E. A. (1971). *The elements of play*. New York, NY: MSS Information Corp.

Nwokah, E. E., & Ikekeonwu, C. (1998). A sociocultural comparison of Nigerian and American children's games. In M. C. Duncan, G. Chick, & A. Aycock (Eds.), *Play & culture studies: Vol. 1: Diversions and divergences in fields of play* (pp. 59-76). Greenwich, CT: Ablex.

Pelligrini, A. D. (2002). The development and possible functions of rough-and-tumble play. In C. H. Hart & P. K. Smith (Eds.), *Handbook of social development* (pp. 438-454). Oxford, England: Blackwell.

Pelligrini, A. D. (2009). *The role of play in human development*. New York, NY: Oxford University Press.

Pelligrini, A. D. & Bjorkland, D. F. (2004). The ontogeny and phylogeny of children's object and fantasy play. *Human Nature, 15*, 23-43.

Piaget, J. (1964). Cognitive development in children. *Journal of Research in Science Teaching, 2*, 176-186.

Piaget, J. (1965). *The moral judgement of the child*. New York, NY: Norton. (Original work published 1948)

Piaget, J. (1987). *Possibility and necessity: The role of possibility in cognitive development* (Vol. 1, H. Feider, Trans.). Minneapolis, MN: University of Minneapolis Press.

Ramsey, P. (2006). Influences of race, culture, social class, and gender: Diversity and play. In D. P. Fromberg & D. Bergen (Eds.), *Play from birth to twelve: Contexts, perspectives, and meanings* (2nd ed., pp. 261-274). New York, NY: Routledge.

Rice, M. L., Sell, M. A., & Hadley, P. A. (1990). The social interactive coding system (SICS). *Language, Speech, and Hearing Service in Schools, 21*, 2-14.

Roopnarine, J. I., & Krishnakumar, A. (2006). Parent-child and child-child play in diverse cultural contexts. In D. P. Fromberg & D. Bergen (Eds.). *Play from birth to twelve: Contexts, perspectives, and meanings* (2nd ed., pp. 275-288). New York, NY: Routledge.

Root-Bernstein, R., & Root-Bernstein, M. (1999). *Sparks of genius: The 13 thinking tools of the world's most creative people*. New York, NY: Mariner Books.

Rubin, K. H. (2001). *The play observation scale (POS)*. College Park, MD: University of Maryland.

Sicart, M. (2009). *The ethics of computer games*. Cambridge, MA: MIT Press.

Singer, D. G., & Singer, J. L. (1990) *The house of make-believe: Children's play and the developing imagination*. Cambridge, MA: Harvard University Press.

Singer, D. G., & Singer, J. L. (2006). Fantasy and imagination. In D. P. Fromberg & D. Bergen (Eds.), *Play from birth to twelve: Contexts, perspectives, and meanings* (2nd ed., pp. 371-378). New York, NY: Routledge.

Singer, J. L., & Singer, D. G., (1981). *Television, imagination and aggression: A study of preschoolers*. Hillsdale, NJ: Erlbaum.

Slonim, M. B. (1991). *Children, culture and ethnicity: Evaluating and understanding the impact*. New York, NY: Garland.

Spodek, B., & Saracho, O. N. (1998). *The challenge of educational play*. In D. Bergen (Ed.), *Readings from play as a medium for learning and development* (pp. 11-28). Olney, MD: ACEI.

Josephson, M., & Hanson, W. (Eds.). (1998). *The power of character*. San Francisco, CA: Jossey Bass.

Sutton-Smith, B. (2004). Foreword. In J. H. Goldstein, D. Buckingham, & G. Brougère (Eds.), *Toys, games, and media* (pp. vii-x). Mahwah, NJ: Erlbaum.

Taylor, S. I., Rogers, C. S., & Kaiser, J. (1999). A comparison of playfulness among Japanese and American children. In S. Reifel (Ed.), *Play & culture studies: Vol. 2. Play contexts revisited* (pp. 143-150). Stamford, CT: Ablex.

Thiagarajan, S. (1994). *Barnga, a simulation game on cultural clashes*. Yarmouth, ME: Intercultural Press.

Tudge, J., Lee, S., & Putnam, S. (1998). Young children's play in socio-cultural context: South Korea and the United States. In M. C. Duncan, G. Chick, & A. Aycock (Eds.), *Play & culture studies: Vol. 1. Diversions and divergences in fields of play* (pp. 77-90). Greenwich, CT: Ablex.

Turiel, E. (1983). *The development of social knowledge*. Cambridge, MA: Cambridge University Press.

Turiel, E. (2002) *The culture of morality: Social development, context, and conflict.* Cambridge, MA: Cambridge University Press.

Vanderven, K. (2006). Attaining the Protean self in a rapidly changing world: Understanding chaos through play. In D. P. Fromberg & D. Bergen (Eds.), *Play from birth to twelve: Contexts, perspectives, and meanings* (2nd ed., pp. 405-406). New York, NY: Routledge.

Vygotsky, L. S. (1967). Play and its role in the mental development of the child. *Soviet Psychology, 5,* 6-18.

Vygotsky, L. S. (1978). *Mind and society: The development of higher mental processes.* Cambridge, MA: Harvard University Press.

Vygotsky, L. S., & Luria, A. R. (1994). Tool and symbol in child development. In R. van der Veer & J. Valsiner (Eds.), *The Vygotsky reader* (pp. 99-174). Cambridge, MA: Blackwell.

Author Contact Information: Doris Bergen, PhD, Miami University, Oxford, Ohio, 45056, 201 McGuffey Hall, Department of Educational Psychology. Telephone: 513-529-6622. E-mail: bergend@muohio.edu

CHAPTER 55

The Innocence of Experience Theory

Young Adolescent Encounters and Life-Long Moral Development

David L. Hough
Missouri State University

"Pre-teen," "preadolescent," "tweenager," "inbetweenager," "transescent," and "early adolescent" are all cognomens that have been used to try to label children ranging between 10 and 15 years of age. Perhaps the most widely used and appropriate term is now "young adolescent," and it denotes a separate developmental stage of human growth and development that bridges the span between childhood and adolescence. This period of time is marked by rapid changes in physical, intellectual, psycho-social, emotional, and moral development—leading many to characterize it as "The Wonder Years," a term used in the 1980s for a television show by the same name.

Middle grades teachers who educate them, scholars who study them, and parents who struggle to understand them, generally agree that young adolescents are delightfully challenging to reach and that one approach for helping all parties "cope" with this developmental stage is to simply celebrate their world of first encounters and experiences. Young adolescents prefer to be acknowledged in positive ways and refer to their growth and development stage as one that is "separate" rather than "unique." This may actually work to the advantage of teachers, parents, and others who strive to promote and inculcate appropriate behaviors. Central to these efforts is the fact that young adolescents naturally begin to encounter a growing number of "adult" experiences that may, in part, shape their sense of morality with influences and behaviors that can become common for them throughout the rest of their lives.

Often leaping from the world of innocence into the world of experience with no Holden Caufield to catch them, young adolescents encounter moral dilemmas that may account for who they become many years later. Who we are today may be, in large part, a function of what we experienced as a young adolescent. Moreover, what those experiences were and how we reacted and adapted to them may have influenced future rationalizations regarding our sense of right and wrong. And because the young adolescent stage of development is marked, in part, by a movement away from the innocence of childhood into a world of first adult-like experiences, most individuals begin to form a sense of moral reasoning from a rather naïve perspective, lacking a "bank" of prior experiences on which to reflect. I call this phenomenon the innocence of experience theory.

GOALS OF THE INNOCENCE OF EXPERIENCE THEORY

The primary goal of delineating the innocence of experience theory is to demonstrate how young adolescent experiences, specifically those of a more "adult" nature and most often encountered for the first time can sometimes shape our sense of morality for many years to

The Handbook of Educational Theories, pp. 667–677

come, perhaps throughout an entire life span. As will be demonstrated subsequently, adults commonly attribute life-long behaviors to influences they encountered during their early adolescence (a.k.a. young adolescence) and adolescent years. In addition, many human beings experience life-long morality development that can be linked to young adolescent physical, psycho-social, emotional, and cognitive/intellectual experiences. These linkages make it necessary to examine the interconnected nature of these domains and to explore how those connections influence, directly or indirectly, subsequent behaviors both in immediate and future situations. Ergo, some sense of adult morality and the behaviors associated with one's perspective of them may be a function of prior encounters during young adolescence.

While researchers have long known that young adolescence is marked by many rapid changes, less attention has been given to how individuals adapt to and from beliefs and behaviors from those experiences during the so-called "wonder years." Moreover, little discussion has focused on the impact of innocent responses to adult situations that are sometimes inappropriately and prematurely encountered by young adolescents. Therefore, an underlying goal of the innocence of experience theory is to further discussion and study of the premises contained herein. In this way, others may become compelled to design studies to explore the theory more fully and deeply in an effort to augment, further define, substantiate, or repudiate the theory's major principles and conclusions.

Finally, because the ideas, premises, principles, and conclusions presented in this chapter are exploratory rather than confirmatory, the development and presentation of a new theory as put forth required a new label; hence, I have chosen to name it the innocence of experience theory. In so doing, perhaps this new sub-category to theories of moral development will emerge as a focal point leading to future refinement and/or development of other theories. For now, however, the innocence of experience theory is needed both to frame descriptions and offer explanations for life encounters that may influence moral beliefs and behaviors not only during a critical time in human development but also throughout a life time of adaptation.

Assumptions and Peculiarities of the Innocence of Experience Theory

Is it true that who we are today is in some part, be it large or small, are a function of what we encountered and how we came to manage and view those encounters during young adolescence? A major assumption of the innocence of experience theory is that young adolescents do, indeed, move from some type of sheltered, protected childhood state or condition into a more adult world of experiences sometime between the ages of 10 and 15 years. In addition, it is assumed that during this same age-span of human growth and development, young adolescents do change very rapidly, making their experiences more of a matter of degree than kind. That is, one is asked to assume that all human beings encounter similar individual and group situations throughout life but that young adolescents who encounter these same experiences do so while also encountering additional changes, again, physically, psycho-socially, emotionally, and cognitively/intellectually at a more sudden and rapid rate and to a greater degree than during any other time in human growth and development outside of infancy. It is further assumed that these changes are interconnected with moral development that is also changing rapidly during young adolescence and that the myriad combinations of the former domains are inextricably interwoven into the complex development of the latter, that is, moral domain.

A body of scientific evidence encompassing many decades since the 1950s supports the notion that young adolescence should be recognized as a separate developmental stage of human growth (Thornburg, 1986). Young adolescent physical developmental changes include increased body weight, height, internal organ growth, increased skeletal systems, and muscular changes. In his book, *Growth at Adolescence*, for example, Tanner (1962) documents such phenomena in so-called early and late "maturers," and details trends relating to earlier onset of puberty, and trends indicating larger body size for children aged 10 to 14 along with development of both primary and secondary sex characteristics. Little is known about the reasons for more dramatic changes in young adolescent physical growth over the past 100 years, but much has been theorized about its relationship to and impact on the other domains of growth and development.

It was Tanner's (1962) research that formed the basis for much theory development beginning in the mid to late 1960s regarding the relationship of physical growth to moral development. Because young adolescents were found to be maturing earlier and faster, it has been theorized that these rapid growth spurts impact moral development (Fabes, Jupanoff, Carlo, & Laible, 1999). Both female and male young adolescents experience growth spurts; however, for girls this physical spurt peaks earlier than for boys. Girls' physical changes are rapid and dramatic and, on average, peak at or about age 12. Boys' physical changes are also rapid and dramatic and, on average, peak at or about age 14. For both genders, these growth spurts may begin and/or end earlier or later; however, these sudden physical changes are the second most dramatic in all of human experience; only infancy (birth to age 2) is greater.

Again, these physical changes may also influence changes in young adolescent moral development, be it hormonal in nature or simply the fact that many are beginning to develop physical features that make them look more adult than childlike. The combination of changes in hormones and developing sexual characteristics that make young adolescents look more like adults and less like children enable them actually to do more things and also cause others to view them differently, i.e., more as adults. Because young adolescents' developing physical strength allows them to engage in more strenuous activities than in childhood, adults may come to treat them more as adults, even if they lack adult psycho-social and emotional skills. In addition, young adolescents become more sexually aware and begin to develop sexual hormones and features associated with more adult-like characteristics that lead them to develop more interest in sexual activities (Fabes et al., 1999). As they gain more interest in and exposure to sexual situations, they also develop new relationships and interests in romantic feelings, leading to new desires to find "partners." Complicated first experiences nurtured by changes such as these engage young adolescents in moral reasoning processes that accompany a complicated set of interconnected physical, psycho-social, and emotional developmental changes.

Unfortunately, some research has demonstrated how physical changes such as those just described can complicate moral development in negative ways. If some emotions caused by hormonal changes lead to negative perceptions regarding physical changes experienced by young adolescents, then aggressive behaviors, embarrassment, and anxieties may lead to inappropriate moral decisions (Fabes et al., 1999). This phenomenon is seldom seen in reverse, as evidenced by a dearth in research to examine the likelihood that adolescent physical changes can impact moral development in positive ways. Whether or not physical changes that young adolescents view as positive can be linked to decreases in anxiety and appropriate moral decisions remains to be determined.

A subcategory of physical growth that has been examined in young adolescents is brain development research. Since the 1960s much data from neurological science indicate that young adolescent brains may experience internal growth spurts and plateaus and that dendrite connections may be associated with these developmental patterns. Strauch (2003) notes that while the young adolescent brain may not be growing in size as much as some had thought in the past, internal changes may be related to sudden impulses and oscillating judgments. Mental processes cannot be overlooked as young adolescents often times develop insecurities when they observe their bodies changing in ways they may not understand, and their observations may be complicated when they make comparisons to peers and/or idealized images (Alonso et al., 2005). As in other areas of physical growth and development, however, research has yet to examine whether or not connections can be made between moral development and brain growth patterns. Even so, it remains an issue of debate and should be examined in the future to determine whether or not such linkages exist. Only then could its impact be related to the theory articulated herein.

Socially, young adolescents are leaving the world of childhood where they may have had one best friend or a few best friends and now begin to enter a world of adult-like experiences where they develop new friendships and form social groups, both positive and negative. Some develop group identities by adopting specific behaviors, language systems, and dress codes. Middle schools are commonly seen as places where students form cliques and identify with others who share their likes, dislikes, habits, and hobbies. They are often seen "running in packs" and displaying behaviors, perhaps, they would not otherwise display. Too often, unfortunately, groups of young adolescents who are beginning to look older than they act are left unsupervised by parents, teachers, or other adults whether at an arcade on a Saturday afternoon or on school grounds before or after school, between classes, during lunch, and at events. These latter occurrences at school are often referred to as the so-called "hidden curriculum," that is, all those things students learn from one another at school settings that are not necessarily intentional teachings or experiences. The hidden curriculum phenomenon can be seen in middle schools when students emerge as leaders within subgroups and cliques and then influence their group of followers. As these social mores play themselves out, young adolescents are placed into situations that require them to make decisions such as whether or not to participate, "join" the group, or any other way(s) become associated with whatever activities may be involved. Moral dilemmas often present themselves, and young adolescents must determine what they believe to be prudent decisions based on situational involvement. And such dilemmas are no longer "in person" encounters. Social networking has become a major component of young adolescent lives. A National School Boards Association study in 2007 found that 96% of teenagers with Internet access have used some type of social networking technology and 71% use social networking on a weekly basis. This relatively new avenue to social interactions, engagement, and behaviors may also impact moral development and may have important long-term effects. Unfortunately, and as is the case in too many other facets of young adolescent experiences, the extent of social networking's relationship to moral development has yet to be fully researched. Again, this leaves linkages between the two a matter of conjecture rather than science and further supports the need for future theory development to compel inquiry. At present, it is reasonable to assume that social networking among young adolescents may impact their moral development, again, for better or worse. Clearly, however, the sudden and growing involvement in social networking presents yet another avenue for interactions that are contribute to moral development, even though those contributions have yet to be fully studied.

Young adolescents experience a wide range of emotional instabilities related to the dramatic physical changes just discussed. Powell (2005) explains that many of these emotions impact the well-being of students, from enhanced social anxiety, to severe outbursts of frustration. Powell is quick to point out, however, that not all young adolescent emotions are negative. In fact, students in this age range often demonstrate "optimism and excitement" towards the future. Zeman (1998) observed that young adolescents have already developed "scripts" with regard to the way people react to a wide range of emotional displays. She notes that young adolescents are fully aware of how others will react when they display inappropriate behaviors and make public displays such as using profanity loudly in public places. Some choose to make obscene gestures among peers, and it is not uncommon for them to congregate as a group ("pack-like") on a Friday or Saturday night at the local shopping mall. Understanding that young adolescents are, in fact, generally aware that certain behaviors are inappropriate is key to understanding that they sometimes choose to exhibit these behaviors to elicit "shock" among others, notably adults who would disapprove. Adults can control these young adolescent "scripts" by modeling appropriate behaviors and by addressing inappropriate ones in whatever setting they occur. The effect of adult modeling or the lack thereof as well as the effect of adult supervision versus the lack of oversight need to be taken into consideration as one examines their impact on young adolescent moral development. In so doing, one should not overlook or underestimate the degree to which adult interventions influence moral development processes and their long-term ramifications.

Young adolescents may not always accurately predict how others will react in a given setting when a specific behavior is displayed. An emotion displayed in a given way in one setting in front of a specific group designed to elicit an expected response may very well lead to an altogether different reaction when displayed in front of a different group in a different setting. When young adolescent emotional development is viewed from this framework, it can help explain how young adolescents are in a state of "emotional identity crisis." "Scripts" can help explain why adolescents will sometimes confide in peers rather than with parents, teachers, or other adults—even if these adults are significant in their lives. Young adolescents, then, are often more apt to confide in those whose reactions can be controlled or readily expected or anticipated rather than in those whose reactions may not be as easily understood. Again, the role emotional responses play in moral development among young adolescents needs consideration in relationship to all other domains of human growth and development.

In addition to their efforts to regulate their emotions (as well as others), young adolescents also experience changes in how they view the environment and society around them. These views often begin to reflect adult perspectives that, at times, might appear to be sophisticated. Even so, young adolescents' emotions are in a transitional state, so these seemingly sophisticated anxieties or concerns for the world around them more often than not give way to other, more important issues, such as personal appearance, cliques, popularized slogans, and popularity in general. This transitional state of mind and emotions commonly leads to alienation from the world of childhood and home environments. Stress management and the regulation of emotions are an integral part of puberty and prepuberty, contributing to one's view of "self" and the development of moral principles that may become more internalized than incipient.

While dealing with myriad emotionally challenging situations, many of which are first experiences of a more "adult" nature, young adolescents seemingly have layer upon layer of convoluting circumstances that add to the situation, such as the change from elementary to junior high or middle school where a world of "firsts" awaits: bells, lockers, showers, different teachers (often a male teacher for the first time), social gatherings such as dances, courtships, "hard" classes, multiple large, heavy textbooks, homework that cannot be completed by parents, tryouts for sports teams and cheerleading, and so on. First encounters such as these can lead to stress and anxiety at the very time young adolescents are developing a more structured, intense sense of morality. While all humans manage stress and sometimes face multiple tasks that appear overwhelming, and while young adolescents are not immune to these situations, the situations may appear to be very different to them with regard to the degree to which such circumstances are viewed as well as how the cope. Overlaying multiple tasks, often disjointed or seemingly so, with multiple rapid environmental changes at a time when the human biological being is undergoing sudden, rapid physiological and psychological changes inevitably create moral dilemmas that have to be faced and negotiated. The relationship of such situations on young adolescent moral development and its long-term effects should not be excluded from any theory of moral development. In fact, more research is needed to determine the degree to which immediate and life-long behaviors might be associated with the types of situations that can be linked to specific outcomes in terms of moral reasoning and actions taken as a result of these experiences.

While many theories exist regarding intellectual or cognitive development, the most widely accepted and utilized in education, perhaps, is the work of Jean Piaget. Piaget's (1932) four distinct stages of human cognitive development, that is, the ability of one to organize and process information around concepts or categories leading to increasingly more sophisticated rational functions, can be identified and attributed to all human beings, naturally have application to young adolescent moral development theory. Because many young people 10 to 14 years of age are beginning to move from concrete to formal operations, a number of challenging considerations face them. First, not all young adolescents begin "dabbling" in formal operations at the same time. For some, this stage may begin at age 11 or even a bit earlier while for others even at age 14 or 15 or beyond, formal operations are not yet being solidified. In fact, it has been estimated that as many as 15% of adults beyond age 20 are not "formal" thinkers. Second, the switch from one stage of cognitive development to another is a gradual process, not an immediate one. This means that all humans move toward higher levels of thinking, reasoning, and information processing incrementally over time; and it is not always readily apparent where any one person is on such a scale or continuum. Third, the process may be gender-specific. That is, some researchers have found that girls develop not only physically but cognitively at earlier ages than do boys, even given the rather vast range of development among both genders. Fourth, any "in-between" development or transition between one stage and another often leads to "faulty" or confused generalizations or conclusions as the human mind moves from one mode of thinking into another. That is, when young adolescents begin moving from concrete to formal operations, they necessarily face cognitive transitional issues that lead to sometime spurious logic (Elkind, 1986).

Noted psychologist David Elkind has identified several different types of faulty reasoning behaviors often displayed by young adolescents that he attributes to the movement across concrete to formal operations. "Pseudo stupidity," for example is one term Elkind uses to describe a situation in which a young adolescent "dabbling" in formal operations but obviously not quite there can reach a conclusion that may appear to be "stupid" when, in fact, it is just faulty reasoning; ergo, pseudo—stupid. Another one of Elkind's terms, "apparent hypocrisy," describes situations in which young adolescents' actions are not consistent with their expressed thoughts (Elkind, 1986). The connection Elkind has drawn between cognitive development and social behavior has given rise to a more complex mixture of interconnectedness that calls for further examination between and among physical, psycho-social, emotional, and intellectual/cognitive development and their relationship to and impact on moral development. Young adolescents may arrive at seemingly contradictory conclusions and/or those that appear to be "hypocritical." Arriving at faulty conclusions from syllogistic reasoning approaches is not peculiar to young adolescents; however, the process of doing so may be more problematic due to changing cognitive processes. Given this, the development of moral reasoning may also be compromised. That is, if young adolescents begin experiencing transitional difficulties with cognitive processes, it not a leap of thought to consider the possibility that they may also begin experiencing difficulties with moral reasoning. Even so, this developmental stage may provide an important opportunity to actively address moral reasoning approaches and study situations that call for understanding, compassion, and appropriate thought processes that lead to positive outcomes. While couched as "situational ethics" in the past, perhaps a more effective approach would be the study of what might be labeled "metacognition ethics." That is, exploring how we come to derive moral understandings in different settings and under different conditions may hold promise as a technique for helping young adolescents develop their own sense of morality. Whether or not one approach is more effective than another does not change the assumptions that young adolescent cognitive development is necessarily and naturally related to their moral development. One's reasoning capacity in one domain is most likely associated with similar capacities in other domains.

In sum, the major assumptions of the innocence of experience theory peculiar to young adolescence are those that focus on relationships between and among the physical, psycho-social, emotional, and cognitive domains of human growth and development as they impact moral development. Further, the growing number of adult-like experiences young adolescents encounter while still relatively innocent in terms of past associations contribute to their sense of moral development. Because these experiences are often many, sudden, and novel, young adolescents may choose to rely on others for guidance as they further fashion their own sense of morality. Finally, it is assumed that long term, perhaps life-long, influences can be formed at this stage of human growth and development. That is not to say that these cannot or might not change, but that they are inextricably interwoven into the fabric of moral reasoning processes that contribute to the formation of morality throughout one's life span.

Original Development of the Innocence of Experience Theory

Background

Interconnected associations between and among the physical, psycho-social, emotional, and cognitive/intellectual domains as they influence the moral domain as discussed above undergird the innocence of experience theory. In addition, I relied on Kohlberg's (1958, 1981) theory of moral development to help explain how the innocence of experience theory manifests itself throughout his six stages, not by focusing on and analyzing each stage but by conceptualizing them as a continuum. While this does not necessarily follow Kohlberg's process as he theorized outcomes, it does provide a more unified, organic approach from which participants used to provide data for theory development could respond.

The interconnected nature of one's physical, psycho-social, emotional, intellectual/cognitive, and moral development was hypothesized to be evident in young adolescents ages 10 to 15. The myriad changes mentioned in the previous sections occur not at separate intervals at different times, but most often simultaneously and at a rapid pace. A basic tenant in the development of the innocence of experience theory is that it is reasonable to assume all five domains of development influence one another and in a variety of combinations. Factoring out the moral development domain and using it conceptually as a dependent variable allows us to examine the other four both separately and in concert as they independently and collectively contribute to the development of the moral domain.

A closer examination of the six stages of Kohlberg's theory of moral development will reveal how elements of each stage can often be found in young adolescent development as reflected upon by older adults. In sum, Kohlberg provides a framework (Kohlberg, Levine, & Hewer, 1983) for discussion around which adults can reflect on prior experiences encountered (most usually) for the first time during young adolescence. In this way, the innocence of experience theory is developed holistically, rather than along a progression. While the impact of this process may not be fully realized until later in life, its immediate understanding can have immediate application and influence over young adolescent decisions and behaviors. These decisions and behaviors, then, can be related to subsequent moral reasoning throughout adulthood. Finally, it is theorized that the coping mechanism used by young adolescents to balance the many adult-like experiences encountered from age 10 to 15 from a more innocent, naïve, childlike perspective can have long-term, perhaps lifelong implications.

Framework for Innocence of Experience Theory Development

Even while struggling with self identities, most young adolescents have been found to begin the process of defining themselves in ways that represent a strong sense of incipient moral development. Hart and Fegley (1995), for example, found that even prior to emergent self identity among adolescents, prosocial behaviors and attitudes begin to manifest themselves. When one applies the notion of interconnected human domains as discussed previously, it is reasonable to assume, then, that young adolescents are at a pivotal point in the development of moral reasoning. Blasi's (1993) examination of identity and the moral self lends credence to this assumption. His research on sense of self demonstrates a grounding in and association with motivation to develop moral responsibility prior to adulthood. Moreover, these associations, while absent in younger children, begin to be fashioned and solidified sometime near the age of 12. This has led many to conclude that children have the capacity to develop their sense of self and moral reasoning during their young adolescent years. This can occur in the absence of moral concerns for identified and well thought-out outcomes, possibly explained by a lack of experiences on and from which to drawn. Encountering moral dilemmas without a background or understanding of potential effects can result in one's naïve being invoked to address situations.

In addition to sense of self and moral comprehension, young adolescents have been found to conceptualize and construct ideals related to a sense of what type of person they would like to become both in immediate applications and in future settings. Later research by Power, Power, and LaVoi (2005) found that students enrolled in college classes who were more active in community or civic groups, organizations, and activities were also more likely to include higher level moral characteristics in descriptions of their ideal selves. Thus, the link between sense of self and sense of morality can be established.

While a number of sequential, moral development stages and levels have been theorized, developed, and described; Kohlberg's six stages as presented in Crain (2005) were chosen for the purpose of developing the innocence of experience theory. In brief, these consist of the following: (a) obedience and punishment, (b) individualism and exchange, (c) good interpersonal relationships, (d) maintaining the social order, (e) social contract and individual rights, and (f) universal principles. In addition, Havighurst's (1972) developmental tasks were examined in an effort to bridge the gap between childhood and adulthood tasks by identifying those that might better be associated with young adolescence.

Methods of Data Collection for Theory Development

Between June 2007 and August 2010, the researcher conducted a series of nine separate focus group interviews with 7 to 12 individuals in each, [(n = 83) total participants] ranging in age from 26 to 67, with a mean of 36 years of age. Participants were college students enrolled in a graduate-level curriculum theory course. Fifty-one participants were female, and 32 were male. While 59 participants had some experience teaching, 45 of these had only limited classroom experience as practicum students or were in their first or second year of teaching. Twelve students had teaching experience with middle grades students.

Each focus group interview was tape-recorded and lasted approximately 50 minutes. Eight topical issues were presented, each allowing for some supporting/follow-up questions. The eight issues presented were: (1) When did you first experience some type of "failure" that caused you to closely examine the ethics of the experience? (2) When did you first begin to question parents', teachers', and/or other adults' actions based on a sense of "right" and "wrong?" (3) When did you first begin to examine what type of person you were/are and wanted to become? (4) When did you first begin carefully considering "good" versus "evil" traits? (5) When did you first begin making decisions based on what you considered to be the "right" thing to do regardless of peer pressure or other "outside" influences? (6) Who or what do you believe has had the greatest influence on your moral development? (7) During what time period of your life, to date, can you attribute the greatest impact on your sense of "right" and "wrong" and your choice to pursue one over another? (8) At which of Kohlberg's six stages do you see yourself today [all six listed on a flip chart and explained by the facilitator]? Why? And at which of the six do you believe you exhibited by the end of eighth grade? Why?

Findings Leading to the Innocence of Experience Theory

While data collected from these focus groups reveal a wide range of influences that had occurred over different periods of time throughout participants' lives, the following findings were viewed as the most salient and supportive of the innocence of experience theory: (a) by about Grade 7 or 8, most individuals had experienced a number of "adult-like" situations that caused them to question themselves, their families, teachers, and other adults; (b) most had experienced a type of failure such as being "cut" from a team tryout, making an "F" on an assignment in an academic class, or being intentionally excluded from a group that led them to examine critically the ethics of the situation by Grade 8; (c) a sense of "good" versus "evil" and/or "right" versus "wrong" while encountered at earlier ages became strong factors in decision making by Grade 6; (d) many current situational ethics and moral dilemmas can be compared to those experienced for the first time during the middle school years; (e) many first adult experiences with things such as profane language, sexual encounters, experimentation with drugs, and involvement in crime were encountered in middle schools between grades six and eight; (f) *"social contract and individual rights"* was identified by 85% of participants as the stage at which they currently found themselves; of these, 80% believed they were developing traits and characteristics associated with this same stage by eighth grade.

Articulating the Innocence of Experience Theory

Much can be made of the above findings; however, for the purposes of theory development, the focus here is on how the adult focus group participants reflected on those experiences years after they had occurred. Approximately 85% of the adults studied noted that their "adult" experiences were first encountered during the middle school years when they were naïve and most often ill-prepared to deal with many of those situations for lack of knowledge and/or understanding. Even so, by the end of middle school, over 70% noted they had developed coping mechanisms and moral reasoning processes that they, in part, still use today. These coping mechanisms and reasoning processes range from situational abstinence and/or disassociation to passive-aggressive behaviors to engagement in proactive measures as a result of compulsion to "do the right thing" in and of itself for no reward or recognition. In addition, a number of attitudinal mannerisms were expressed by participants who indicated that "whether for better or worse," many of these traits are still with them today, in adulthood. Some of these traits included ignoring inappropriate behaviors from others if deemed too inconsequential to warrant attention, behaving in particular ways in specified situations as a matter of decorum, and providing information as a matter of principle, rather than as a requirement or order from a person in authority. Approximately 88% of all focus group participants expressed the belief that they had begun to develop these traits most intentionally during young adolescence.

At the risk of overstating the obvious, then, it became logical to assume that young adolescence was a critical time for moral development. It is not only a time of "firsts" in terms of physical, psycho-social, emotional, and intellectual/cognitive development as supported by prior research, but it is also a time of "firsts" for encountering adult situations and forging a sense of moral reasoning and understanding. Innocent, naïve, unprepared young adolescents do, in fact, experience a number of moral dilemmas and do begin to develop coping mechanisms as well as moral reasoning and understanding. While situations change, and young adolescents become adolescents and then adults, many cite their middle school years as a pivotal point in the development of their sense of morality. Moreover, many adults express concern that their first encounters with many adult situations occurred when they were innocent and naïve in terms of knowing how to respond or cope. Finally, it must be noted that the majority of adult participants agreed that who they perceive themselves to be today is due in no small part to what they encountered and how they managed first-time adult situations during their middle school years.

In terms of Kohlberg's six well anthologized stages of moral development, regardless of how adults currently perceive themselves, an overwhelming majority 88%, also perceived themselves developing moral reasoning skills associated with whatever stage they currently view themselves sometime before the end of eighth grade. Hence, the innocence of experience theory is developed, not only to describe but to explain who we are today and how we came to develop our sense of morality. While schools, church, family, and community factors naturally influence moral development, it may very well be that the stage of human growth and development we now call young adolescence is in large part responsible for our current stage of moral development. In sum, we now are who we once were becoming and sought to achieve. And we once were innocently trying to make sense out of any number of experiences encountered for the first time during young adolescence.

The latter phenomenon just mentioned deserves more scrutiny. If as adults we now believe that our young adolescent naiveté obfuscated our ability to make sense out of the adult experiences we had during our middle school years, one is left to ponder whether it would have been better to have remained "sheltered" or to have been "forewarned and prepared." In other words, is it better to be quarantined from potential harmful contact or to be vaccinated to build up immunities? When presented with this dichotomy, the 83 adult focus group participants were split. Roughly one half believed that keeping young adolescents away from potentially harmful adult situations was preferable. The other half believed that young adolescents should have limited, supervised exposure to adult situations so long as they would not be unintentionally harmed. Either way, participants generally agreed that the goal was to help young adolescents develop positive behaviors, traits, and approaches to the development of moral judgments and actions. Moreover, participants generally agreed that doing so would have lasting, life-long effects. Again, much of this reasoning is predicated on the notion that who adults are today is in part related to what they encountered and how they managed those encounters during the middle school years. And while this can most certainly be true at any stage of human growth and development, in terms of moral development, the innocence of experience theory supports the position that young adolescence is, perhaps, the most critical stage at which adult encounters influence subsequent adaptations that may persist throughout a life time. In sum, it is fair to say that critical incidents that occur during young adolescence serve as imprints for functioning adults.

Cross-Cultural Generalizations of the Innocence of Experience Theory

Cultural considerations for the innocence of experience theory need to be considered, studied, and examined more fully. It is reasonable to assume that individuals living in cultures where adult situations are experienced by greater numbers of children prior to young adolescence might very well differ from individuals living in cultures where adult situations are experienced most frequently postyoung adolescence. Such "cultures" could range from so-called "third world" primitive societies to those that are more "closed" such as Amish, Mennonite, and private, parochial, and "home schooling" groups. Data from the 83 focus group participants used to develop the innocence of experience theory indicate that societal/cultural differences such as these may impact moral development. Roughly 20% (n = 16) of the adult focus group participants fell into this latter category. That is, they identified themselves as living in environments that "forced" young adolescents to take on adult responsibilities prior to age 15. These adult responsibilities included such things as cooking daily for an entire family, serving as the primary caregiven for a sibling under the age of six, earning income outside the home to contribute to family income, and providing one's own transportation to school, work, the grocery store and other necessary places within the community. These same individuals expressed a belief that their sense of moral development was formed during early childhood and was not influenced dramatically again until much later in life, most often after age 18 or 21.

Because myriad cultures exist, it is impractical to generalize from these data at this point. However, one could hypothesize that regardless of culture, some adult-like experiences encountered at whatever impressionable age, may in fact, contribute substantially to moral development. In this way, the innocence of experience theory might hold as a more general construct than is presented herein. That is, while young adolescence has been found in this work to be the pivotal stage of human growth and development where adult experiences are encountered and managed by individuals in a state of "innocence," relatively speaking, other cultures may provide earlier or later developmental stages where this phenomenon occurs. Again, either way, the application of the innocence of experience theory can be made.

Applications of the Innocence of Experience Theory

Applications of the innocence of experience theory are many and far reaching. Parent, teachers, and other adults who interact with young adolescents need to reassure them that the changes they observe in themselves and others during this stage of human growth and development are necessary, expected, and normal. Because gender differences exist and numerous studies have found that girls' sense of security, self-efficacy, and future aspirations often decline during the middle school years, special care, understanding, and reassurance need to be given them. A greater emphasis on inclusion and less emphasis on competition should be stressed to help develop a sense of fairness and participation that could more positively impact their developing sense of morality. Safe boundaries throughout schools and communities should be established and continually reinforced. Parents, teachers, and community members should make it a priority to discuss moral issues with middle school students. Physical, emotional, psycho-social, and cognitive engagement in proactive, prosocial environments should be carefully supervised by caring, informed adults who are positive role models. Parents, teachers, caregivers and other adult role models should exercise understanding and patience while encouraging young adolescents to begin developing positive moral traits and understanding. Many believe that the "adult" approach should be one that "celebrates" young adolescence as a stage of human growth and development that can shape one's future as well as one's character. Rather than struggling to cope with young adolescence, parents and other adults should seize opportunities both to guard against innocent, yet unhealthy life choices and to promote active, positive strategies for handling adult situations.

Adult role models and mentors should become engaged in all facets of young adolescent lives rather than separating themselves from awkward or confusing situations. Teachers in particular have myriad opportunities to capitalize on social aspects of young adolescent lives that can support learning and moral development. Ryan and Patrick (2001), for example, identified the following dimensions of social learning in the middle grades associated with fewer disruptive behaviors and off-task incidents: (a) student beliefs that teachers cared about young adolescents as persons and supported them as learners, (b) teacher encouragement for students to interact with one another in class in appropriate, acceptable ways, (c) classroom climates and cultures that fostered mutual respect and social harmony among students as well as between students and teachers. A fourth dimension, teacher-created "rivalries" in classrooms encouraging students to compete with one another, was found to negatively impact teaching and learning. In fact, the implications of social learning environments to the development of one's sense of morality may be inextricably interwoven. Again, Ryan and Patrick (2001) found that classroom competitions (whether intentional or not) on the part of teachers or students are counterproductive, resulting in middle grades students becoming less likely to engage in academic tasks. Evidently, comparing one student's performance to others as an indicator of ability is NOT an effective middle grades teaching approach and not one that promotes positive moral development. Middle grades students ARE more likely to be engaged and motivated when they feel as if their teachers are supportive and care about them. This, in turn, encourages young adolescent learners to interact with classmates in more appropriate ways en route to completing academic assignments. This culture or social order of mutual respect and harmony is most often found in middle grades classrooms that do not foster competition between and among students, and it may very well be of value to one's sense of moral development.

Helping young adolescents understand and deal with stress may also be connected to one's moral development. Prioritizing calamities is essential for all human beings, and understanding which stressors are serious issues and which are not is essential, especially for young adolescents most often encountering such situations for the first time. Physical activity remains one of the best stress reducers and holds promise as a technique for the development of prosocial morals, as well. Adults are challenged to create and provide environments to help every young adolescent feel safe, of value, and successful. Doing so may contribute to positive moral development traits, as well.

Critiquing the Innocence of Experience Theory

The goal of the innocence of experience theory is to provide a framework for understanding how young adolescence impacts our sense of moral development, not only during an awkward stage of first encounters, but throughout a life-span, as well. As such, subsequent moral traits and behaviors throughout adulthood are in part a function of the manner in which we adjusted to and made sense out of adult situations we encountered in our middle school years. During this young adolescent stage of rapid human growth and development, our relatively "innocent" state of being is impacted by physical, emotional, psycho-social, and cognitive/intellectual changes that influence our moral development. And while it is reasonable to assume that we continually modify our sense of morality throughout our lifetimes, it is sobering to contemplate how encounters with and management of adult situations during young adolescence may have effected who we later become and aspire to be at some later stage in life.

Such a theory begs a number of issues. Can we influence the impact of the innocence of experience theory by exuding more control over individual and group interactions during young adolescence? If so, which adults are in the best position for making positive contributions to the shaping of this type of moral development? Should the approach be one of isolationism or inoculation? Is it possible to "script" ways in which "innocent" beings can and should deal with adult "experiences"? Is the innocence of experience theory a phenomenon or merely a description of the obvious?

A number of theories exist concerning relationships between levels of moral development and cognitive development that span life cycles. Some suggest a distinct difference in how young adolescent males and females function morally, and general reasonableness has been considered a learned trait. For example, when Lawrence Kohlberg observed children, young adolescents, and others during stages of cognitive development, he found them to exhibit specific stages of morality. His levels of preconventional morality, conventional morality, and postconventional morality posit a graduation from ego centric thoughts and behaviors to being a positive member of society, to believing strongly enough in a cause to pay an ultimate sacrifice to accomplish it. The innocence of experience theory does not attempt to build upon or challenge others' theories, such as Kohlberg's. Rather, it is offered as a value-added approach for understanding how levels and/or stages are connected to several other developmental stages, (again, physical, emotional, psycho-social, and cognitive) in interconnected ways. In this way, other theories that support one-to-one relationships are encouraged to consider a broader, more interconnected phenomenon that spans virtually all types of human growth and development.

In addition, the interconnected associations mentioned above as well as throughout this chapter are examined within the context of a single developmental stage, that is, young adolescence. This is because my data suggest that it is during that stage of human growth and development more than at any other, that moral development is impacted most dramatically. In his review of the literature on this issue (Hart, 2005) found that "moral character is given some shape in adolescence" and by "understanding and eventually controlling the influences acting on the adolescent, adult moral character can be set on the correct path" (p. 225).

The innocence of experience theory does not attempt to examine differences between young adolescent females and males, even though a body of evidence exists to suggest that the former may be impacted to greater degrees than the later during middle school years. Some researchers have found that females demonstrate more emotional and spiritual sensitivity in their thoughts on scientific dilemmas and may use more empathy and role playing than males of the same age. Females may be less likely than males to think about dilemmas from a personal perspective, and males may tend to use more logic than emotion as compared to females when presented with the same opportunities to assess given situations (Tirri & Pehkonen, 2002). The innocence of experience theory needs to undergo further investigation to examine how young adolescents develop differently and how gender may influence situational activities related to moral development during young adolescence.

Even though further examination of some aspects of the theory as mentioned above need to be undertaken, the phenomenon described herein as innocence of experience provides a strong foundation upon which further future theory development can take place. Replication and further research could lend credence to, challenge, and/or contribute to refinement of the theory. Taken in sum, however, support for the concept of moral development as having firm roots in our young adolescent experiences provides a focus for study and further theory development. Occurring during a period of rapid growth and development in other aspects of the human experience, moral development that is shaped during ages 10 to 15 can provide insight into the complex set of circumstances that contribute to the shaping of one's character later in life. If the innocence of experience theory holds true as a valid phenomenon describing how our initial, naïve reactions and adaptations to adult-like situations and encounters help shape our sense of moral development, then we must all seek to understand better the conditions associated with its impact on life-long behaviors, attitudes, and beliefs.

REFERENCES

Alonso, A., & Rodriguez, R. (2005). Eating disorders: Prevalence and risk profile among secondary students. *Social Psychiatry Psychiatric Epidemiology, 40,* 980-987.

Blasi, A. (1993). The development of identity: Some implications for moral functioning. In G. G. Noam & T. E. Wren (Eds.), *The moral self* (pp. 99-122). Cambridge, MA: MIT Press.

Crain, W. C. (1985). Kohlberg's stages of moral development. *Theories of development*. New York, NY: Prentice-Hall.

Elkind, D. (1986). Understanding the young adolescent. *Adolescence, 13*(49), 128-134.

Fabes, R. A., Kupanoff, K., Carlo, G., & Laible, D. (1999). Early adolescence and prosocial/moral behavior I: The role of individual processes. *Journal of Early Adolescence, 19*(1), 5-16.

Hart, D. (2005). Moral development in adolescence. *Journal of Research on Adolescence, 15*(3), 223-233.

Hart, D., & Fegley, S. (1995). Prosocial behavior and caring in adolescence: Relations to self-understanding and social judgment. *Child Development, 66*, 1346-1359.

Havighurst, R. J. (1972). *Developmental tasks and education.* New York, NY: David McKay.

Kohlberg, L. (1958). The development of modes of thinking and choices in years 10 to 16 (Published dissertation). University of Chicago, IL.

Kohlberg, L. (1981). *Essays on moral development, Vol. I: The philosophy of moral development.* San Francisco, CA: Harper & Row.

Kohlberg, L., Levine, C., & Hewer, A. (1983). *Moral stages: A current formulation and a response to critics.* Basel, NY: Karger.

Piaget, J. (1932). *The moral judgment of the child.* London, England: Kegan Paul, Trench, Trubner and Co.

Powell, S.D. (2005). Emotional development in middle school. *Education.com.* Retrieved from http://www.education.com/reference/article/emotional-development-middle-school/?page=3

Power, F. C., Power, A. M. R., & LaVois, N. (2005, April). *Engaged democratic citizenship and moral and civic identity.* Paper presented at the annual meeting of the American Educational Research Association, Montreal, Quebec.

Ryan, A. M., & Patrick, H. (2001). The classroom social environment and changes in adolescents' motivation and engagement during middle school. *American Educational Research Journal 38*(2), 437-460.

Strauch, B. (2003). *The primal teen.* New York, NY: Doubleday.

Tanner, J.M. (1962). *Growth at adolescence* (2nd ed.). London: University of London Press.

Thornburg, H. (1986). The counselors impact on middle-grades students. *The School Counselor, 33*(3), 170-77.

Tirri, K., & Pehkonen, L. (2002). The moral reasoning and scientific argumentation of gifted adolescents. *The Journal of Secondary Gifted Education, 13*(3), 120-129.

Zeman, J. (1998) *Emotional development. Encyclopedia of childhood and adolescence.* Retrieved from http://findarticles.com/p/articles/mi_g2602/is_0002/ai_2602000223/

Author Contact Information: David L. Hough, PhD, Missouri State University, Springfield, Missouri, 5882 N. Farm Road, 183 Springfield, MO 65803. Phone: 417-576-4468. E-mail: DavidHough@missouristate.edu

Section 8: Classroom Management Theory

INTRODUCTION

SECTION EDITORS
Patricia Williams
Sam Houston State University

Sandra Harris and Vicky Farrow
Lamar University

Begin class on time, use appropriate seating arrangements, reward students for good behavior, know students on a personal level—Isn't it enough to follow the laundry list of worthwhile tips that crowd education textbooks if teachers want to manage their classes and have few discipline headaches? No. Without a deep understanding of the "why"—the theory behind what they are doing—teachers typically don't grasp why particular practices are essential in maintaining a well-managed classroom or gym.

How much do teachers know about major theorists and how important is it that they have a theoretical construct that guides them in making management decisions and handling discipline issues? When Clement (2002) questioned 48 cooperating teachers, she discovered that only one half of them could name an author or theorist in classroom management. However in Veenman's 1984 meta-analysis research concerning perceived beginning teacher problems, discipline ranked as the number one problem facing neophytes. Marzano supports that conclusion in his analysis of over 100 separate reports on effective schools. His study emphasizes that classroom management is an essential component for effective teaching (Hardin, 2008). Mixon's chapter, "Marzano's Evidenced-Based Practices in Classroom Management," focuses on four management factors that move theory into practice, and he explains how significant these components are. Others, such as Callahan, Clark, and Kellough (2002), reached similar assumptions. They believe that "classroom management is perhaps the single most important factor influencing student learning" (2002, p. 161).

Well, if it's that critical to understand classroom management, what should teachers read? When Clement (2010) did an online Google search for classroom management, she found more than 5 million hits and an Amazon.com search provided 11,000+ books, so there is a proliferation of materials. In this section, we narrowed the field to five renowned theorists who have influenced countless others and shaped classroom management practices—Robert Marzano, Burrhus Frederic (better known as B. F.) Skinner, William Glasser, Alfie Kohn, and Haim Ginott. Do these psychologists, psychiatrists, and researchers agree on what works best? Absolutely not. Glasser, the father of reality therapy and control theory, disagrees vehemently with Skinner's ideas about stimulus-response. For instance, Skinner would state that if a child touched a hot stove and was burned, he would not do it again. Behaviorists have argued that we, as teachers, should apply this concept to the classroom. If the student is rewarded with praise or a tangible item, such as a sticker or fun activity, the behavior is likely to be repeated. If the child is reprimanded, the behavior will probably cease. Peck's chapter, "Freedom Through Control," provides insight into such controversial issues as shaping behavior and the perceived benefits.

Glasser, viewing human behavior through a psychiatrist's eyes, thinks that we have individualized picture albums in our heads of what we consider rewarding. While one child may love a sticker, another may throw it in the trash. He, similar to Maslow, thinks that we need to help fulfill our students' needs for power, freedom, and fun. During presentations, Glasser often asks

The Handbook of Educational Theories, pp. 679–680

high school students if they enjoy school and what causes them to be there. Answers typically focus on extracurricular activities rather than academic classes (Williams, Alley, & Henson1999). By giving students what they desire, such as more power and freedom, he asserts that they will find classes more appealing and want, rather than be required, to attend. In Cassell and Nelson's chapter, "Control, Choice and the Fulfillment of Fundamental Human Needs," they examine Glasser's humanistic vision of students making choices and controlling their lives.

Kohn agrees with Glasser about behaviorist theory. In the 2010 Gallup Poll findings, he commented that the people polled say, "no to threatening (to close schools) and to bribing (kids with money), which together define the carrot-and-stick approach favored by economists and behaviorists who run the show. If contemporary 'school reform' is a stool, that's one of the three legs gone" (Kohn, 2010a, p. 18). Bribes, as he calls tokens, stickers, and even praise, "give students no reason to act responsibly when there is no longer a goody to be gained by doing so" (Kohn, 2010b). As noted in Guillaume's chapter, "Beyond Compliance and Control," creating a caring environment makes more sense to Kohn than offering students another candy for complying with the teacher's wishes.

In his book, *Schools Without Failure*, Glasser asserts that "To begin to be successful, children must receive at school what they lack [at home]: a good relationship with other people, both children and adults" (Glasser, 1969, p. 19). Ginott, who spent much of his life conducting parental group and individual psychotherapy sessions, emphasizes the home environment too and "set forth basic principles to guide parents in living with children in mutual respect and dignity" (Ginott, 1965, p. 12). He also offers several controversial ideas, including that "parents' attitudes should convey that homework is *strictly* the responsibility of the child and his teacher" (Ginott, p. 77). He even states that parents should neither nag children nor supervise their homework (Ginott, 1965). Whether or not teachers agree with his assertions regarding homework, it is helpful to understand his ideas and to discuss with colleagues the pros and cons of following his advice. For a more in depth understanding, read Yates and Holloman's chapter, "Haim Ginott—Congruent Communication."

No theory will work perfectly at all times. However, we hope these brief snippets into the theorists' views intrigue teachers to learn more about them. It is crucial to understand a multitude of theories, and use the concepts to make prudent choices based on the needs of those involved and the situation. As teachers, we must ask ourselves what we should do using sound, best-practice principles that have a foundation in solid theoretical constructs. The theories help us answer the crucial "why" question. Why should I handle XYZ that way? Now, let's look at these five major classroom management theorists and delve into how we can use their ideas.

REFERENCES

Callahan, J. F., Clark, L. H., & Kellough, R. D. (2002). *Teaching in the middle and secondary schools* (7th ed.). Upper Saddle River, NJ: Merrill Prentice Hall.

Clement, M. C. (2002). What cooperating teachers are teaching student teachers about classroom management. *The Teacher Educator*, 38(1), 47-62.

Clement, M. C. (2010). Preparing teachers for classroom management: The teacher educator's role. *The Delta Kappa Gamma Bulletin*, 77(1), 41-44.

Ginott, H. G. (1965). *Between parent and child: New solutions to old problems*. New York, NY: Macmillan.

Glasser W. (1969). *Schools without failure*. New York, NY: Harper & Row.

Hardin, C. J. (2008). *Effective classroom management: Models and strategies for today's classrooms* (2nd ed.). Upper Saddle River, NJ: Pearson.

Kohn, A. (2010a). On bribing students to learn: Second thoughts about A's, praise, stickers, and contests. Retrieved from http://www.alfiekohn.org/topics/topics_e4.htm

Kohn, A. (2010b). 'No' to threats and bribes. *Phi Delta Kappan*, *92*(1), 18.

Veenman, S. (1984). Perceived problems of beginning teachers. *Review of Educational Research*, *54*(2), 143-178.

Williams, P. A., Alley, R. D., & Henson, K. T. (1999). *Managing secondary classrooms: Principles, and strategies for effective management and instruction*. Boston, MA: Allyn & Bacon.

Author Contact Information: Sandra Harris, PhD, Professor, Director, Center for Doctoral Studies in Educational Leadership, Lamar University, P.O. Box 10034, Beaumont, Texas 77710. Telephone: 409-880-8676. E-mail: drsandy@flash.net; Sandra.harris@lamar.edu

CHAPTER 56

Marzano's Evidence-Based Practices in Classroom Management

Four Management Factors for Moving Theory to Practice

Jason R. Mixon
Lamar University

"Research not only supports the importance of classroom management, but it also sheds light on the dynamics of classroom management."

—Marzano (2003, p. 6)

"The single most influential component of an effective school is the individual teachers within the school."

—Marzano (2003, p.8)

Research is replete with theories of classroom management techniques and processes that formulate the teaching objectives for many teacher preparation programs across the nation. These aspiring teachers are instructed and trained in such intricate operational components of Skinner's human behavioral theory, Ginott's congruent communication theory, Kohn's control theory, and Glasser's choice theory as evidenced in the previous chapters. More important than the knowledge of the theories and training is when these teachers instruct in the numerous classrooms in our nation and initiate a transfer of classroom management theories (knowledge/training) into classroom management *practices.* Teachers should be educated and sustained in implementing classroom management practices that will be successful and that is practices that are supported by evidence (Simonsen, Fairbanks, Briesch, Myers, & Sugai, 2008). Understanding the theories will grow the teacher in becoming more knowledgeable about a specific topic, while the practices will educate the teacher in becoming more effective in managing the classroom. How does a teacher move from theory to practice? This chapter examines succinctly that process by reviewing Robert Marzano's evidence-based practices in classroom management. Much of the content from this chapter is derived from his book *Classroom Management That Works* (2003).

DESCRIPTION OF MARZANO'S THEORY

Is it evidence-based practices in classroom management or is it evidence-based theories in classroom management? This question invites much debate with reference to practice and theory as they are often considered equivalent in many research arenas; however, when the two terms are operationalized for research application, evidence depicts that the words are diverse in application and meaning (MacKinnon & Scarf-Seatter, 1997). Research exemplifies that the term theory is a synonym for such words as hypothesis, speculation, possibility, guess, conjecture and a philosophical explanation. Contrary to theory, research also shows that practice is a synonym for such terms as usage, utilization, employed, exercising, exertion and

The Handbook of Educational Theories, pp. 681–689

praxis. More concretely, evidence-based practices favor empirical knowledge and have gained prominence over more theoretical approaches as they apply to classroom management in our public schools (Valdez, 2010). With an extensive list of classroom management theories such as Skinner's Behavior Modifications, Canter's Assertive Discipline, Dreikur's Logical Consequences, Berne and Harris' Transactional Analysis, Gordon's Teacher Effectiveness Training, Glasser's Choice Theory, and Gathercoal's Judicious Discipline, to name a few, being utilized in a myriad of classrooms, what evidence has been accumulated via actual classroom practices that any of these theories actually work?

Valdez (2010) highlighted that these often interchanged words are dissimilar in application and meaning, yet they are supportive of each other in scientific research. He explained the major division in meaning is more historical in that theoretical evidence in based in rationalism while practices are based in empiricism. Evidence-based practices are a combination of science and experience and is the proof supporting a theory (Helmenstine, 2010). Practice and theory are not interchangeable; they are supportive in nature. Kerr and Nelson (2010) explained that evidence-based practices must meet the following criteria: (a) the use of a sound experimental or evaluation design and appropriate analytical procedures, (b) empirical validation of effects, (c) clear implementation procedures, (d) the replication of outcomes across implementation sites, and (e) evidence of sustainability.

The movement for evidence-based practices gained heavy momentum in the 1970's and most recently by the "meta-study" of Robert Marzano (2003). Marzano's evidence-based classroom management practices was a meta-analysis that included over 100 reports and 134 rigorous experiments designed to find out which classroom management practices work best. Petty (2006) noted that such studies of studies are the paramount supplier of evidence for classroom management practices that work because all reliable findings are integrated. Marzano's work catapulted the importance of universal classroom management practices in the classrooms via evidence above the often unfounded theoretical speculation (rationalism) of what might work to the practices of what has been proven to work (empiricism).

Original Development of Marzano's Evidence-Based Practices in Classroom Management

Humble beginnings as a teacher in New York City and Seattle, Washington public schools, Robert Marzano dedicated his professional life to developing improved classrooms for all teachers and students. These foundational experiences in the classroom enabled Marzano to experience success and research on best practices in the classroom that encompassed his entire career. After receiving his doctorate in Curriculum and Instruction from the University of Washington-Seattle in 1974, he began his professorate endeavors for the next 8 years at the University of Washington-Seattle and the University of Colorado-Denver.

Robert Marzano's research interests developed during his tenure at the universities and matured into an extensive 27 year career in research at the Mid-Continent Research for Education and Learning (McREL). While at the McREL Institute, Marzano has served as Director of Research, Deputy Director of Training and Development, Vice President, Senior Fellow, and most recently as Senior Scholar. This extensive career in research was the underpinning for his evidence-based practices approach utilized in over 150 articles, 20 books, numerous book chapters, and more than 100 curriculum guides for teachers and students.

Marzano's publications entitled, *Classroom Instruction that Works: Research-based Strategies for Increasing Student Achievement* (2001), *What Works in Schools: Translating Research into Action* (2003), and *Classroom Management that Works: Research-based Strategies for Every Teacher* (2003) reveal a consistency in providing strategies that are research based, that extend theory into practice, and summarize the best practices available. An evolution of evidence-based practices occurred for Dr. Robert Marzano through extensive research over a long career with an intense focus on discovering the practices that work and not getting mired in the theory enveloping the practices.

Description of Marzano's Evidence-Based Classroom Management Practice

The research technique of a meta-analysis utilized by Robert Marzano in *Classroom Management that Works* gave merit to the many studies previously conducted on classroom management theories. Gall, Gall and Borg (2003) defined a meta-analysis as a technique that can be used to investigate for trends in a set of quantitative research studies. Marzano (2003) explored for these trends by combining the findings from over 100 studies and four themes or trends emerged as factors in improving classroom management. The four management factors are: (a) rules and procedures, (b) disciplinary interventions, (c) teacher-student relationships, and (d) mental set. Each management factor will be discussed individually, although their function is interdependent. The findings are the synopsis of the meta-analysis conducted on numerous classroom management practices utilized by teachers in classrooms over the past 30 years.

Rules and Procedure

According to Marzano (2003), "the most obvious aspect of effective classroom management involves the design and implementation of classroom rules and procedures" (p. 13). He elaborated that although the terms rules and procedures are used interchangeably, there are some important differences between the two. According to Evertson, Emmer, Worsham (2003), a rule highlights expectations or standards, while a procedure communicates expectations for explicit behaviors. Although rules and procedures vary from teacher to teacher and classroom to classroom, Marzano was able to confidently examine the effect of designing and implementing rules and procedures in the classroom as it relates to classroom management. A rule could be exemplified as: Bring all materials to class. In comparison, a procedure could be exemplified as: Work must be completed prior to the bell sounding and all work must be turned in to the teacher.

By reviewing over 630 subjects in 10 different studies, he was able to determine that when teachers place a keen emphasis on design and implementation of rules and procedures in the classroom, a 28% decrease in classroom disruptions will occur. Corroborating this finding, Simonsen et al. (2008) highlighted five steps to incorporating evidence-based practices in classroom management with the first step being, maximizing structure in the classroom through the development of predictable routines and the design of the environment. This step alone can greatly decrease the disruptions because expectations are clear and reasonable.

Marzano's (2003) meta-analysis produced the following general categories regarding rules and procedures for teachers to follow in order to improve overall classroom management:

- general expectations for behavior;
- beginning and ending the day or the period;
- transitions and interruptions;
- materials and equipment;
- group work; and
- seatwork and teacher-led activities (p. 18).

Although it is not imperative that rules and procedures are developed for each of these general categories (Emmer, Evertson, & Worsham, 2003; Marzano, 2003; Simonsen et al., 2008), it is recommended that five to eight rules and procedures are carefully selected for the classroom from these topics. Time needs to be spent on instruction and not on the enforcement of too many rules and procedures.

A second component of findings from the meta-analysis was the involvement of students in the design of the rules and procedures. Marzano (2003) noted that it is constructive to have a classroom dialogue about applicable rules and procedures for each of the general categories aforementioned. Several common methods of seeking student involvement are classroom meetings designed to discuss rules and procedures, groups developing rules and presenting to the class, and collaboration between several classes to develop the rules and procedures for a team. Student involvement creates buy-in from the class and students are more apt to follow the rules and procedures because they played a role in developing them. In support of this finding, Petty (2006) explained that classrooms become much more orderly when rules are stated, or negotiated, discussed and fully justified with the students. This incorporation of student-teacher planning creates an environment that is supportive in nature versus punitive.

The first classroom management factor produced from Marzano's extensive meta-analysis was the importance of rules and procedures in improving classroom practices. Developing rules and procedures for the day-to-day operations of the class are vital and even more essential was the student involvement necessary to decrease discipline issues. The second classroom management factor addressed discipline interventions used in the classroom.

Disciplinary Interventions

According to Cotton (1990), about 50% of all time spent in the classroom by a teacher is directed toward correcting students who are misbehaving. Obviously, it is imperative that teachers are educated in various intervention practices that have shown to decrease discipline occurrences in the classroom so more focus can be placed on instruction. Marzano (2003) stated, "that effective discipline is a combination of effective management at the school level and effective management at the classroom level" (p. 27). His meta-analysis study for disciplinary interventions expanded the work of Stage and Quiroz (1997) and focused on five types of discipline interventions that included both negative and positive consequences. The five types of disciplinary interventions explained by Marzano (2003) are: (a) teacher reaction, (b) tangible recognition, (c) direct cost, (d) group contingency, and (e) home contingency. He also reviewed these interventions at various grade levels and when teachers implement the aforementioned disciplinary interventions in their classroom, a substantial decrease in discipline incidences occurred of between 25% (High School) and 35% (Primary). All five interventions produce a substantial decrease in discipline disruptions; however, two interventions illicit a

34% decrease in discipline disruptions, *teacher reaction* and *group contingency,* and they will be examined individually.

Teacher Reaction

All teachers experience problems with student behavior, it is just that some teachers are better at dealing with it than others (Petty, 2006). Marzano defined teacher reaction as, "the verbal and physical behaviors of teachers that indicate to students that their behavior is appropriate or inappropriate" (p. 29). His comment suggested that it is just as important to address the appropriate behavior as it is inappropriate behavior and research validates this statement. This reinforcement of acceptable behavior increases the likelihood that the student will continue the behavior, and it is important for teachers to provide negative consequences for inappropriate behavior to subside. His meta-analysis supported the findings of Emmer, Evertson, and Worsham (2003), with such teacher reactions as:

- making eye contact with the students and using your proximity to the student to increase students level of concern;
- use of a physical symbol to indicate inappropriate behavior;
- verbal reminders for not following directions;
- state desired behaviors for students that are off task or not following directions;
- use more forceful interventions and tell the student directly to stop behavior.

This is not an all inclusive list of teacher reactions that increase desired behaviors and decrease undesired behaviors; however, when used in cohort with the other four interventions a well disciplined classroom develops. Teachers often are dealing with not only individuals who are acting out but also certain groups of students not following protocol. A teacher intervention that also exhibited a 34% decrease in discipline disruptions similar to teacher reactions was group contingency.

Group Contingency

Marzano (2003) defined group contingency strategies as those in which a specific group of students must obtain a certain level of appropriate behavior. An example of group contingency would be a reward for the entire class if a certain behavior is accomplished throughout the period (i.e. raising hands before speaking, being quiet during instruction, and not getting out of their seat without permission). When these appropriate behaviors are completed, the teacher can reward the group of students with awards such as a field trip, go outside and work, watch a DVD that fits the lesson, or an extended lunch period. He goes on to illustrate that there are two forms of group contingency, interdependent and dependent, and that one needs to be cautious when utilizing the dependent group contingency intervention. Interdependent group contingency is defined as, "a technique that requires every student in the group to meet the behavioral criterion for the group to earn credit" (p. 38). In contrast to interdependency and one that should be used with caution is the dependent group contingency which is, "a technique that requires a specific individual or a specific set of individuals in the group to meet the behavioral criterion for the group to earn credit" (p. 38). Caution is designated here because embarrassing students or singling students out is frowned upon by teachers. Both techniques have been proven to decrease discipline disruptions in the classroom when used appropriately (Litow & Pumroy, 1975).

Marzano (2003) concluded:

> The guiding principle for disciplinary interventions is that they should include a healthy balance between negative consequences for inappropriate behavior and positive consequences for appropriate behavior … teacher reaction, group contingency, tangible recognition, direct costs, and home contingency are specific interventions that establish behavioral limits and allows you to keep track of student behavior efficiently and unobtrusively. (p. 40)

The second classroom management factor produced from Marzano's extensive meta-analysis was the importance of discipline interventions in improving classroom practices. Developing discipline interventions for the day-to-day operations of the class are extremely important and mandatory to decreasing discipline disruptions. The third classroom management factor addressed teacher-student relationships used in the classroom.

Teacher-Student Relationships

Dr. Comer stated that "no significant learning can occur without a significant relationship." Marzano (2003) transferred this statement from learning into discipline with, "if a teacher has a good relationship with students, then students more readily accept the rules and procedures and the disciplinary actions that follow their violations" (p. 41). Obviously, positive relationships are pivotal for teachers to develop as it applies to learning and discipline in general.

The third classroom management factor that improves discipline in the classroom is teacher-student relationships. Sheets and Gay (1996) reported that a large portion of discipline problems could have been avoided and usually developed because there was a breakdown in teacher-student relationships. Marzano, in *Classroom Management that Works,* capsuled from several studies and over 1,000 participants that when teachers use specific techniques to establish strong teacher-student relationships, a 31% decrease in discipline disruptions occur. Extending the work of Wubbels, Brekelmans, van Tartwijk, and Admiral (1999), Marzano addressed the two dimensions of *dominance* versus *submission* and *cooperation* versus *opposition* in the classroom.

From his meta-analysis, Marzano (2003) concluded several action steps to address dominance and cooperation. He stated, "the core of effective teacher-student relationships is a healthy balance between dominance and cooperation" (p. 49). If a teacher has established clear rules and procedures in the classroom and also developed positive and negative consequences in the classroom, dominance by the teacher has been established. Exhibiting assertive behavior and establishing clear learning goals are two ways that Marzano found successful in decreasing discipline disruptions in the classroom. Emmer, Evertson, and Worsham (2003) defined assertive behavior as, "the ability to stand up for one's legitimate rights in ways that make it less likely that others will ignore or circumvent them" (p. 146). They also highlighted three examples of specific dominant teacher behavior that decreased discipline disruptions in the classroom such as the use of assertive body language, use of appropriate tone of voice, and persisting until the appropriate behavior is displayed.

Marzano also identified the use of specific behaviors that communicate the appropriate level of cooperation in the classroom. By providing flexible learning goals, taking a personal interest in students, using equitable and positive classroom behaviors, and responding appropriately to students' incorrect responses, teachers are able to communicate the appropriate level of cooperation in the class.

The third classroom management factor produced from Marzano's extensive meta-analysis was the importance of teacher-student relationships in decreasing discipline disruptions in the classroom. By balancing dominance and cooperation, teachers are able to better manage their classrooms because of improved relationships. The fourth classroom management factor addressed the mental state used by the teacher in the classroom.

Mental Set

Extending his management factors even more, Marzano noted that effective classroom managers approach discipline with a specific mental set. He noted in *Classroom Management that Works,* "the mental set necessary for effective classroom management requires teachers to cultivate a mindful stance relative to their withitness and emotional objectivity" (p. 66). The term "withitness" was coined by Jacob Kounin (1983), who is considered to be one of the foundational researchers on classroom management. Classroom management is unrelated to how you manage misbehavior, he emphasized that effective classroom management was in the disposition of the teacher and how quickly they responded and intervened to the behavior. This withitness, explained by Brophy (1996) is sometimes referred to as "being aware of what is happening in all parts of the classroom by continuously scanning the classroom, even when working with small groups or individuals" (p. 11). Often students wonder if teachers utilizing withitness have eyes in the back of their head because nothing goes unnoticed in the classroom. Marzano found in over 400 subjects that having withitness will decrease disruptions in a classroom by 42%. Three concrete actions to enhance your withitness emerged during Marzano's research and the actions are to react immediately, forecast problems, and observe a master teacher.

Emotional objectivity, as coined by Nelson, Martella, and Galand (1998), allows the teacher to address discipline issues in the classroom in an unemotional, matter-of-fact manner even though you might be experiencing strong emotions. Without emotional objectivity, teachers run the risk of undermining the entire classroom management system (Brophy & Everston, 1976). Teachers can forge relationships that are professional and trustworthy to improve classroom management. Marzano supported these findings in his meta-analysis with a 26% decrease in the number of discipline disruptions for those teachers who exhibited emotional objectivity. Three concrete actions that enhance your emotional objectivity were found in his research and the actions are evidenced by looking for reasons why, monitoring your own thoughts, and taking care of yourself.

The four classroom management factors produced from Marzano's extensive meta-analysis included rules and procedures, disciplinary interventions, teacher-student relationships, and mental state. Although each of the management factors was presented individually, they work in an interdependency design for effective classroom management to occur. Decades of research supports these evidence based practices, and "equipped with this knowledge and understanding, schools and classroom teachers can educate students in a safe, orderly, and respectful environment" (Marzano, 2003, p. 115).

Validation of Marzano's Evidence-Based Practices in Classroom Management

The validation of Robert Marzano's Evidence-Based Practices can be found in the strength of the effect size in his meta-analysis findings and the implementation of these practices in thousands of classrooms across the nation. Gall, Gall, and Borg (2003) describe the effect size as an estimate of the magnitude of difference, a relationship, or other effect in the population represented by the sample. These authors noted that the effect size is a metric that illustrates for you how much of a difference in behavior you can expect between teachers that effectively employ a given practice of classroom management and teachers that do not employ this strategy. Gall, Gall, and Borg (2003) also proposed that the meta-analysis technique has three advantages that validate this research: (a) it focuses on a level of difference between a control group and an experimental group; (b) the effect size measurement can be applied to any statistic and any measure, and (c) allows the researcher to determine whether certain features of the study affected the findings that were obtained. Marzano strategically chose research studies that "set the stage for research and practice in classroom management" (p. 6) and "selected a methodology not previously employed with the classroom management literature" (p. 7).

Marzano employed a meta-analysis research technique and only reported those practices that exemplified the highest average effect size. Many classroom management practices were scrutinized with four classroom management practices obtaining the highest average effect size. Marzano (2003) stated, "one of the benefits of using the effect size metric is that we can translate it into a percentile change relative to the average number of disruptions that occur in a classroom" (p. 8). True validation of his "theory" can be found in his findings with effect sizes ranging from –1.294 to –.763. The four classroom management practices of rules and procedures, disciplinary interventions, teacher-student relationships, and mental set range in percentile decreases in classroom discipline disruptions from 28% to 40%. The importance of these findings was twofold with a validation of sound classroom management practices as well as implementation practices that teachers can begin to exploit immediately.

Over the last 8 years, Marzano's Evidence-Based Practices in Classroom Management influenced many alterations to classroom processes and procedures in such contemporary topics as Response to Intervention (Kukic, 2010), Sheltered Instruction Observation Protocol Model (Himmel, Short, Richards & Echevarria, 2009), differentiated instruction (Tokuhama-Espinosa, 2009), and English language learners (Barrera, Shyyan, Lui, & Thurlow, 2008) to name a few areas. His evidence-based practices have been applied in numerous schools throughout the nation with improved results in many areas as mentioned. True validation is in the results and schools are seeing dramatic changes in their teachers as the four classroom management practices are being implemented.

Generalizability and Application of Evidence-Based Practices in Classroom Management

Dr. Robert Marzano plunged into a new research methodology that had not previously been employed very often for classroom teachers. There had been numerous individual studies (i.e. single subject, or whole class design) on classroom management practices and what works and does not work. Serving as a pathfinder in meta-analysis research, he combined over 100 studies that embraced the macro concept of examining all facets of school populations (i.e. primary, elementary, secondary, urban, rural, and suburban). The closest methodology similar to Marzano's work was the quasi macro work of Wang, Haertel, and Walberg in 1993. These researchers examined the findings from three studies and established that classroom management is pivotal to the success of student achievement and can be generalized to all classrooms. The success of the findings by these researchers sparked a move from micro examination of classroom management practices in isolation to a more holistic macro examination with companion studies.

Mertler and Charles (2008) defined generalizability as the findings from a researchers study can be applied to other individuals and other settings. In conceptualizing the numerous studies that Marzano selected for inclusion in his meta-analysis, close attention was initiated in the origin to include differentiated samples and populations. Mertler and Charles (2008) asserts that a "close correspondence between sample and population is assumed when participants are randomly selected from the larger population" (p. 14). These authors stress that random sampling is the best way to obtain a representative sample. Thus, the findings from Marzano's work can be generalized across cultures, ethnicities, and genders as all of the descriptors were present in the 100 studies previously conducted over the past 30 years. As Bogdan and Biklen (2003) introduced the question, do the findings of Marzano's study hold up beyond the specific subjects and the locale that are involved? The answer can be found in the application of his best practices in a multitude of classrooms throughout the nation.

Marzano directly engaged his efforts in applying his best practices to classrooms with the intention of improving classroom management practices based on educational research. Wong and Wong (1998) exclaimed that classroom management practices are the most important aspect of student learning. Many school districts, campuses, organizations and teachers applied Marzano's classroom management practices and have found measurable success in implementation. Success as measured in Marzano's perspective is a well mannered, manageable, organized classroom that allows for learning to occur. A few studies such as (Owens et al., 2006), and (Thornberg, 2008), highlighted the measurable successes in implementation with decreased discipline referrals, more structured classrooms and an increase in teacher efficacy. Many school districts are utilizing Marazno's work for professional development, goal setting, and for teachers who are in need of assistance in classroom management. The generalizabilty and application of Marzano's four classroom management practices are evidenced in the abundant use of his practices to support "a major gap that appears to be in the lack of teacher understanding and use of theoretical perspectives in classroom discipline management" (Irons & Allen, 2006, p. 1).

Critiques of Marzano's Evidence-Based Practices Classroom Management

Some educators and researchers are critical of the work of Robert Marzano because the evidence-based practices classroom management is more practice oriented than it is theoretical in nature and there are problems with the research design (Becker, 2009; Kohn, 2006). These practices are cultivated through a meta-analysis research approach that contains some limitations or critiques in methodology. Shuttleworth (2009) noted that there are several disadvantages of using meta-analysis methodology in education. The disadvantages are the potential for publication bias and skewed data. The data must be able to be compared across various research programs to allow for a strong statistical analysis, the researcher not utilizing preselected studies to ensure quality, and the researcher not striking a balance in research studies to ensure that the sample size is statistically relevant. Marzano (2003) counters this disadvantage with, "by combining the results of many studies, we can say with far more certainty than we can with a single study that certain strategies work or do not work" (p. 7). As with any research method, there are advantages and disadvantages that must be accounted for in the origin of the study.

The findings of Marzano's Evidence-Based Practices in classroom management (i.e., rules and procedures, disciplinary interventions, teacher-student relationships, and mental state) can be scrutinized through the lens of behavioralism associated in the findings of his practices. Strong critiques of Marzano's work can be found from the cognitive and humanist orientation as key assumptions from a cognitive view depict, "that the memory system is an active organized processor of information and that prior knowledge plays an important role in the learning" (Gredler, 1997, p. 144). These thoughts rival the behavioralist components of Marzano's work. His findings from his meta-analysis, (i.e. rules and procedures, disciplinary interventions, teacher-student relationships, and mental set) arguable have some critical attributes associated with behaviorism in each of the findings. The teacher initiates language and verbal behavior in the management practices for all four and Driscoll (2004) verifies that behavioralism has a long-standing significance in language, with the verbal behavior of children being shaped through reinforcement as inappropriate behaviors are extinguished. Merriam, Caffarella, and Baumgartner (2007) supported this statement in describing that the teacher's role is to create an environment that increases desired behaviors toward meeting the classroom discipline goals and to halt the undesired behaviors. Also, Grippen and Peters (1984) stated that behavioralism is founded in operant conditioning which means "reinforcing what you want the individual to do again; ignoring what you want the individual to stop doing" (p. 65). Expanding the concepts of these authors, dissecting rules and procedures, disciplinary interventions, teacher-student relationships, and the mental states of teachers can be criticized by several orientations of learning. Cognitivist, humanist, social cognitivist, and constructivist orientations examine classroom management from an internal perspective as opposed to the behavioralist external influences. These orientations of learning arguably play a role in each of the four classroom management practices and warrant more examination in the implementation of these practices for the classroom.

Conclusion

The four management practices of Robert Marzano augment the discipline environment for all classrooms. His work offers realistic, doable, and sensible classroom management strategies that can be implemented by the veteran teacher or the teacher just embarking on his/her educational career. Marzano's strategies are not presented as being successful in a vacuum as many other factors are at hand and must be addressed for true change is to occur. He believed that classroom management exists in a much larger context with the schoolwide management policies also playing a very important role.

The question posed at the beginning of the chapter referenced how a teacher moves classroom discipline management theories to classroom discipline management practices. The findings from Marzano's study reveal that practices are a combination of many elements of science and the experience is the proof that supports a theory. The experiences provided in *Classroom Management that Works* infer that every teacher and every school in the country can readily achieve effective classroom management through the implementation of Marzano's practices, thus bridging the gap between theory and practice.

REFERENCES

Barrera, M., Shyyan, V., Liu, K., & Thurlow, M. (2008). *Delphi study of instructional strategies for English language learners with disabilities: Recommendations from educators nationwide* (ELL with Disabilities Report 21). Minneapolis, MN: University of Minnesota, National Center on Educational Outcomes.

Becker, J. (2009). *Peer-review of Marzano's IWB study, Part IV.* Retrieved from http://edinsanity.com/2009/06/07/marzano_part5/

Bogdan, R., & Biklen, S. K. (2003). *Qualitative research for education: An introduction to theories and methods.* Boston, MA: Allyn & Bacon.

Brophy, J. E. (1996). *Teaching problem students.* New York, NY: Guilford.

Brophy, J. E., & Evertson, C. M. (1976). *Learning from teaching: A developmental perspective.* Boston, MA: Allyn & Bacon.

Cotton, K. (1990). *School improvement series. Close-up #9: Schoolwide and classroom discipline.* Portland, OR: Northwest Regional Educational Laboratory.

Driscoll, M. P. (2004). *Psychology of learning for instruction* (3rd ed.). Boston, MA: Allyn & Bacon.

Emmer, E. T., Evertson, C. M., & Worsham, M. E. (2003). *Classroom management for secondary teachers* (6th ed.). Boston, MA: Allyn & Bacon.

Evertson, C. M., Emmer, E. T., & Worsham, M. E. (2003). *Classroom management for elementary teachers* (6th ed.). Boston, MA: Allyn & Bacon.

Gall, M. D., Gall, J. P., & Borg, W. R. (2003). *Educational research: An introduction.* (7th ed.). Boston, MA: Pearson, Allyn & Bacon.

Gredler, M. E. (1997). *Learning and instruction: Theory into practice* (3rd ed.). Englewood Cliffs, NJ: Prentice Hall.

Grippin, P., & Peters, S. (1984). *Learning theories and learning outcomes.* Lanham, MD: University Press of America.

Hemelstine, A. M. (2010). Scientific hypothesis, theory, law definitions. Retrieved from http://chemistry.about.com/od/chemistry/ol/a/lawtheory.htm

Himmel, J., Short, D.J., Richards, C., & Echevarria, J., (May, 2009). Using the SIOP model to improve the middle school science instruction. Center for Research on the Educational Achievement and Teaching of English Language Learners (CREATE) Brief. Retrieved from http://www/cal.org/create/resources/pubs/siopscience.html

Irons, E. J., & Allen, D. (2006). A theoretical discipline management foundation: The missing link in secondary teachers' practice and preparation. Retrieved from http://tcpea.org/slr/2006/irons.pdf

Kerr, M. M., & Nelson, C. M. (2010). *Strategies for addressing behavior problems in the classroom.* (6th ed.). Princeton, NC: Merrill.

Kohn, A. (2006). Abusing research: The study of homework and other examples. *Phi Delta Kappan, 88*(1), 8-22.

Kounin, J. S. (1983). *Classrooms: Individual or behavior settings? Micrographs in teaching and learning* (General Series No. 1). Bloomington, IN: Indiana University, School of Education. (ERIC Document Reproduction Service No. 240 070)

Kukic, S. J. (2010). *RtI: Leadership that works.* Frederick, CO: Sopris West Educational Services.

Litow, L., & Pumroy, D. K. (1975). A brief review of classroom group-oriented contingencies. *Journal of Abnormal Child Psychology, 2*, 143-148.

MacKinnon, A., & Scarff-Seatter, C. (1997). Constructivism: Contradictions and confusion in teacher education. In V. Richardson (Ed.), *Constructivist teacher education: Building new understandings* (pp. 41-55). Washington, DC: Falmer Press.

Marzano, R. J. (2001). *Classroom instruction that works: Research-based strategies for increasing student achievement.* Alexandria, VA: Association of Supervision and Curriculum Development.

Marzano, R. J. (2003). *What works in schools: Translating research into action.* Alexandria, VA: Association of Supervision and Curriculum Development.

Merriam, S. B., Caffarella, R. S., & Baumgartner, L. M., (2007). *Learning in adulthood: A comprehensive guide.* San Francisco, CA: Josey-Bass.

Mertler, C. A., & Charles, C. M. (2008). *Introduction to educational research* (6th ed.). Boston, MA: Allyn & Bacon.

Nelson, J. R., Martella, R., & Galand, B. (1998). The effects of teaching school expectations and establishing a consistent consequence on formal office disciplinary actions. *Journal of Emotional and Behavioral Disorders, 4*(3), 153-161.

Owens, W. A., Kaplan, L. S., Nunnery, J., Marzano, R., Myran, S., & Blackburn, D. (2006). Teacher quality and troops to teachers: A national study with implications for principals. *NASSP Bulletin, 90*(2), 102-131.

Petty, G. (2006). *Evidence based teaching: A practical approach.* Gloucestershire, England: Nelson Thornes.

Sheets, R. H., & Gay, G. (1996). Student perceptions of disciplinary conflict in ethnically diverse classrooms. *NASSP Bulletin, 580*(80), 84-93.

Shuttleworth, M. (2009). Meta-analysis. Retrieved from http://www.experimentresources.com/meta-analysis.html

Simonsen, B., Fairbanks, S., Briesch, A., Myers, D., & Sugai, G. (2008). Evidence-based practices in classroom management: Considerations for research to practice. *Education and Treatment of Children, 31*(3), 351-380.

Stage, S. A., & Quiroz, D. R. (1997). A meta-analysis of interventions to decrease disruptive classroom behavior in public education settings. *School Psychology Review, 26*(3), 333-368.

Thronberg, R. (2008). The lack of professional knowledge in values education. *Teaching And Teacher Education, 24*(7), 1791-1798.

Tokuhama-Espinosa, T. (2009). *The new science of teaching and learning: Using the best of mind, brain, and education science in the classroom.* New York, NY: Teacher College Press.

Valdez, A. (2010). Difference between theory guided practice and evidence based practices. Retrieved from http://www.ehow.com/about_6646089_difference-practice-evidence-based-practice.html

Wang, M. C., Haertel, G. D., & Walberg, H. J. (1993). Toward a knowledge base for school Learning. *Review of Educational Research, 63*(3), 249-294.

Wong, H. K,. & Wong, R. T. (1998). *The first days of school.* Mountain View, CA: H. K. Wong Publications.

Wubbels, T., Brekelmans, M., van Tartwijk, J., & Admiral, W. (1999). Interspersonal relationships between teachers and students in the classroom. In H. C. Waxman & H. J. Walberg (Eds.), *New directions for teaching practice and research* (pp. 151-170). Berkeley, CA: McCutchan.

Author Contact Information: Jason R. Mixon, EdD, Assistant Dean of Academic Partnerships and Outreach College of Education and Human Development, Lamar University, 1400 Martin Luther King Blvd., Beaumont, Texas 77710. Telephone: 409-880-7362. E-mail: jason.mixon@lamar.edu

CHAPTER 57

Freedom Through Control

B. F. Skinner and Classroom Management Theory

Craig Peck
The University of North Carolina at Greensboro

"The natural, logical outcome of the struggle for personal freedom in education is that the teacher should improve his control of the student rather than abandon it."

—B. F. Skinner (1973, p. 16)

"Skinner could be described as a man who conducted most of his experiments on rodents and pigeons and wrote most of his books about people."

—Alfie Kohn (1993, p. 6)

In his rise to prominence in the latter half of the twentieth century, the American research psychologist Burrhus Frederic (B. F.) Skinner achieved great fame that simultaneously depended upon and complicated his scientific contributions. Skinner helped inspire pioneering human behavioral theories and is often viewed as a pivotal figure in the study of human psychology. The fact, however, that Skinner derived his ideas from research studies intended to induce and record the modification of voluntary behavior in animals gained him sustained notoriety and, in some quarters, enduring criticism and derision. Today, he is perhaps as well-known for the device dubbed the "Skinner box" (a confined, lever-based, food-reward system for inducing changes in a subject's behavior) used in his animal experiments as any theories he produced (Bjork, 1993; Rutherford, 2009).

B. F. Skinner's writings for popular publication also tended to spark debate. Hoping to share what he considered an important innovation, Skinner (1945/1972) wrote a *Ladies Home Journal* article explaining the virtues of his self-designed, climate-controlled, mechanical crib that he created especially for his young daughter. The accompanying photo showed the baby behind a clear window in a tall, rectangular structure; she was smiling as she stood and played with a toy suspended from the structure's roof. In the text, Skinner mentioned the device offered benefits such as "freedom from clothes" other than diapers, a stimulating environment that made "the waking hours ... active and happy ones", and "contribution to the baby's good health" (p. 570). He noted, "neighborhood children troop in to see her, but they see her through glass and keep their school-age diseases to themselves" (p. 571). A reader backlash ensued after publication, and was helped along by the *Ladies Home Journal* editors' decision to title the article "Baby in a Box" (Bjork, 1993; Rutherford, 2009). In addition, one of Skinner's most enduring written works was not a scientific tract, but a fictional Utopian novel that described how a centrally planned, behaviorism-centered small community called "Walden II" instituted a system of social controls to provide its residents a safe and happy alternative to chaotic modern city life (Skinner, 1976).

No matter the publicity or controversy that his scientific and public work generated, Skinner consistently exhibited attention to human education, especially in the latter half of his career. As a behaviorist, Skinner asserted that humans, much like any living organism, were guided by their responses to external stimuli, and his educational philosophies reflected this scientific construct. Toward instructional delivery, Skinner advocated for self-managed instruction through approaches such as his "teaching machine" that provided the learner with structured activities and quick recognition (Skinner, 1986). Toward classroom management, Skinner argued that teachers must assert control over their environment and utilize rewards in order to establish the conditions necessary to generate proper student

The Handbook of Educational Theories, pp. 691–698

behavior (Skinner, 1969). Though criticized by theorists such as Kohn (1993, 2006, 2010), Skinner's classroom management ideas continue to resonate in popular, contemporary student behavior products such as *Assertive Discipline* (Canter, 2010) and *Positive Behavior Supports* (Wheeler & Richey, 2010).

This chapter explores B. F. Skinner's theories regarding classroom management in relation to his broader scientific work, and how those theories have influenced schools and other educational thinkers. For Skinner, effective classroom management presented an essential antidote to what he considered the debilitating, unstructured educational activity such as "free schools" that emerged in the late 1960s. He advocated instead that teachers apply conditions of positive reinforcement in order to help students "be successful in their work," "get on well with their fellows," and "enjoy what they will do" so that, as a result, they would "feel free and happy" (Skinner, 1973, p. 13). For Skinner, student freedom came only through effective classroom control, much as he believed human freedom came only through effective social control.

Presentation and Analysis: Description of the Specific Theory

At its most basic and using his terminology, Skinner's approach to classroom management involved "operant conditioning" (modification of behavior) through the application of "contingencies" (circumstances or conditions) of "reinforcement" (consequences or rewards). Stated in educational terms, Skinner endorsed a teacher's use of quick rewards (known as "positive reinforcements") as a means to change student behavior. Skinner disapproved of the use of admonishments and physical punishment (known as "negative reinforcements"); he contended that these approaches would only encourage undesirable student behavior such as truancy. He considered it essential that teachers retain effective control over the classroom in order to create optimal conditions to establish the behaviors necessary to enable student learning.

Skinner's conception of classroom management drew directly from his work in applying his experimentally-derived organism behavior theories to understand human actions. Though it is important to note that Skinner never conducted experiments on human subjects, in *Science and Human Behavior* (1953) he contended that "what a man does is the result of specifiable conditions and that once these conditions have been discovered, we can anticipate and to some extent determine his actions" (p. 6). In this work, he also defined some of the concepts and terms that became central to his classroom management theories. In explaining how he used food as the reward that would induce behavior change in the animal subjects, for example, he wrote,

> In the pigeon experiment, then, food is the *reinforcer* and presenting food when a response is emitted is the *reinforcement*. The *operant* is defined by the property upon which reinforcement is contingent–the height to which the head must be raised. The change in frequency with which the head is lifted to this height is the process of *operant conditioning* [italics in original]. (pp. 66-67)

Paraphrasing Skinner's language in applying his theories to a classroom setting, a reward such as verbal praise is the *reinforcer* and offering verbal praise to a student response is the *reinforcement*. A student's behavior (or "operant") is defined as something such as appropriate participation (as opposed to calling out or talking over the teacher) during a lesson. The change in frequency with which the student participates appropriately can be called *operant conditioning*.

Importantly, Skinner (1969) contended that teachers, whom he described as acting as "the governor of a community," have the primary role in arranging the circumstances necessary to enable good student behavior (p. 96). To do so, they must practice effective "contingency management in the classroom." He explained, "Certain kinds of consequences called reinforcers (among them the things the layman calls rewards) are made contingent upon what an organism is doing and upon what circumstances under which it is doing it" (p. 94). For Skinner (1973), the speed with which students received the reinforcers was of greater import than the specific type of reinforcer in making them effective. He mentioned verbal praise and also "tokens" (e.g. check marks, green tickets, or other symbols) "that can be made clearly contingent upon behavior" as potentially useful approaches (p. 15). Prevailing classroom practices from a student receiving a gold star for fine conduct, to a student earning positive citizen points toward products like school sweatshirts at the school store, to the simple act of a teacher praising a previously recalcitrant student who has made a good behavior choice are all modern-day disciplinary techniques Skinner might have considered constructive.

Skinner was skeptical about traditional punishments, including such approaches as teacher verbal admonishments, detention, and corporal punishment. In his view, punishment tended not to generate positive behavior and could, in fact, serve merely as a negative reinforcer. Skinner (1968) explained, "When we punish a student who displeases us, we do not specify pleasing behavior" (p. 187). Skinner accepted that some form of punishment, especially verbal, was perhaps inevitable and could be made somewhat effective if coupled with inducements intended to help guide the child toward proper future behavior. However, he emphasized the deleterious effects of a modern education system that, as he saw it, relied almost exclusively on punishment as means to correct student behavior. Skinner (1969) noted, "Violent or not, punitive methods have serious consequences, among them truancy, apathy, resentment, vandalism, and ultimately anti-intellectualism which includes an unwillingness to support education" (p. 93). While Skinner believed that the current "system in which students study primarily to avoid the consequences of not studying is neither humane nor very productive," he also believed managing classrooms through contingencies of reinforcement could serve as an antidote (Skinner, 1973, p. 14).

Skinner was aware that educators may not exhibit initial enthusiasm for his theories. He acknowledged that "behavioral objects remove much of the mystery from education, and teachers may feel demeaned when their task is reduced to less awesome dimensions." Nonetheless, Skinner (1969) believed that "the loss [of the mystery of teaching] is more than offset by a greater sense of achievement" (p. 95). In the end, Skinner intended his approach to "contingency management in the classroom" to serve as a catalyst not only for better schools, but for better communities. He contended, "in the long run education must take its place as the method of choice in all forms of social control," adding, "the sooner we find effective means of social control, the sooner we shall produce a culture in which man's potential is realized" (p. 100).

The Original Development of the Theory

Long before B.F. Skinner articulated his classroom management theories, he gained worldwide renown and, in some cases, sustained acrimony for his pioneering research into the behaviors of animals such as rats and pigeons. In his laboratory work, he joined theorists including Watson and Pavlov in establishing the theoretical and experimental basis for scientific behaviorism, which contended that organism actions can be understood as responses to external stimuli. As Skinner moved from experimental work on animal behavior generally to theoretical work about human behavior specifically, he began to examine humans, including a short analysis of the behavior control factors latent in their educational institutions (Skinner, 1953). By the mid-1950s, Skinner had begun working on a "teaching machine" that provided quick, positive feedback to correct student responses and a means for adjusting academic pace to an individual student's particular needs. Skinner helped market his product extensively into the 1960s. Nonetheless, much like computers in the classroom today, the teaching machines never achieved Skinner's hopes for widespread adoption nor did they fulfill his expectations for revolutionary change in education (Bjork, 1993; Cuban, 2001; Rutherford, 2009).

Despite the checkered success of the teaching machines, by the 1960s education had become a prominent concern for Skinner, as evidenced by his 1968 publication of *The Technology of Teaching*. This collection of essays, taken as a whole, offered the psychologist's most expansive declaration of educational principles. In the text, he covered a host of topics, ranging from student motivation to teacher failure, but more importantly he argued that education must function, ultimately, as a system, or "technology," for conditioning and controlling students for their betterment. Over the next several years, Skinner (1969) elaborated more specifically on his classroom management theories in popularly distributed educational journals, and in one case he defended deriving his theories from his experimental work with animals. He explained, the

> fact that much of the early work involved the behavior of lower animals such as rats and pigeons has often been held against it. But man is an animal, although an extraordinarily complex one, and shares many basic behavioral processes with other species. (p. 94)

He also critiqued those who accepted "the belief that men have a natural curiosity or love of learning, or that they naturally want to learn." He explained,

> We do not say that about a pigeon; we say only that under the conditions we have arranged, a pigeon learns. We should say the same thing about human students. Given the right conditions men will learn—not because they want to, but because, as the result of the genetic endowment of the species, contingencies bring about changes in behavior. (p. 96)

In 1971, Skinner caused a firestorm of public controversy when he published *Beyond Freedom and Dignity*, which argued essentially that human free will is an illusion and humans would be better off in a tightly structured society established according to a technology of behavior (Rutherford, 2009; Skinner, 1971). By 1973, Skinner argued that effective, positive measures for control, as represented in his approach to contingency management in the classroom, were a necessary condition for developing "free and happy students" and a "better way of life" (p. 16).

Validation of the Theory

Since Skinner did not conduct experiments on people, he never personally validated his classroom management theories. Nonetheless, his ideas would come to influence a host of contemporary and future scientists who investigated his theories in both experimental and applied settings. Toward experimental settings, in the

1950s the behavioral psychologist Sidney Bijou established a mobile laboratory for experiments regarding pre-school child behavior that he could move from school to school to increase the number of children studied. In a letter to Skinner, a colleague of Bijou characterized it as a "Skinner-box for little kids" (Rutherford, 2009, p. 56). By the late 1960s, Skinner-influenced classroom management approaches had become more commonplace in education. Researchers, for instance, investigated a "good behavior game" as a means for altering an individual disruptive student's behavior through "group consequences" (i.e., applying a reward or punishment for one single student's behavior to all the members of a group) (Barrish, Saunders, & Wolf, 1969). In addition, two researchers/practitioners provided a revised edition of "manual of procedure for classroom teachers" regarding "modifying classroom behavior" that cited Skinner and explained basic concepts such as positive and negative reinforcement (Buckley & Walker, 1978).

Generalizability of the Theory Across Cultures, Ethnicities, and Genders

Skinner, it has been argued, provided attention to diversity by developing systems such as programmed instruction and teaching machines that were intended to meet the varied needs of individual learners (Richelle, 1993). In conceptualizing his theories of classroom management, however, Skinner provided scant attention to matters such as differences among human cultures, ethnicities, and genders. Instead, Skinner wrote about students and teachers in a generalized, nondistinguishing sense. One might speculate that for Skinner, who believed that animal species from pigeons to people behaved as they did for a similar set of reasons, characteristics of diversity within the human population held little importance.

Curiously, Skinner used examples drawn from highly distinctive human populations to augment his broader points regarding the efficacy of using classroom contingency management for all human students. In a lecture paper published in the journal *Education*, for instance, Skinner (1969) referenced a study on "token economies" (i.e., a *de facto* currency system in which subjects, based upon good conduct, receive tokens like check marks or stars that can be exchanged for desirable goods) in a mental hospital as an example of how behavioral theories "have been put to work in practical ways" on "human subjects." He explained that the research demonstrated, "how a hospital for psychotics can be converted into a community in which patients care for themselves and their possessions, avoid trouble with their associates, and (within the limits imposed by their illness) enjoy life" (p. 95). In the same text, he advocated using "tokens" as a form of "money in the classroom" that could serve as a reinforcer for good student behavior (p. 97).

In the widely distributed *Phi Delta Kappan*, Skinner (1973) characterized the "hippie culture" as providing testimony to the destructive harm that the current, noncontingent educational system had on students. He wrote,

> The members of that culture do not accept responsibility for their own lives; they sponge on the contributions of those who have not yet been made free and happy—who have gone to medical school and become doctors, or who have become the farmers who raise the food or the workers who produce the goods they consume. (p. 14)

Though Skinner acknowledged that the group represented an "extreme" and that his comments were "no doubt overstatements," he emphasized that hippies offered "a trend in a well-defined direction" and were "symptomatic of a more general problem" (p. 14).

In the end, Skinner's use of mental hospital residents and hippie culture participants as representative examples of the human population may help suggest his unconcern for issues of human diversity. These instances may also have hinted at an underlying motive of his general approach: contingency management in the classroom could serve as a means for remediating nonconformists through the application of appropriate controls, thereby ensuring greater classroom and social cohesion.

The Use and Application of the Theory

Though Skinner did not engage directly in efforts to apply his theories to schools, he proved influential in helping university researchers and K-12 reformers develop new classroom management approaches that became popular and pervasive in the 1960s and 1970s. For instance, Harris (1972) provided a general overview of classroom behavior modification approaches as well as several related journal articles and studies. By the late 1970s, an annotated bibliography described hundreds of studies that examined efforts to apply behavior modification in educational settings ranging from preschool to elementary to high school, and in "normal" and "special education settings." Specific study topics included such Skinner-related techniques as operant conditioning, reinforcement, and token economies (Benson, 1979).

In terms of reformers, Skinner proved particularly influential in the genesis of wide-scale classroom management approaches that emphasize establishing the conditions necessary for students to behave appropriately. For instance, early versions of Canter's "Assertive Discipline" provided an approach that linked evolutionarily to Skinner. Canter and Canter (1976) argued in the first edition of *Assertive Discipline* that "*distorted* [sic] and misinterpreted" ideas from psychologists like "Skinner (Behavior Modification)" had negatively affected the ability of teachers to engage in the type of firm yet fair classroom disciplinary interventions (especially verbal) necessary to maintain a proper learning environment (p. 4). Canter and Canter encouraged direct, nonhostile statements that would make expected behaviors clear and explicit, and promoted positive reinforcement through verbal praise. They also directly echoed Skinner's concern for establishing an effective classroom environment by entitling the book's first chapter "Power to the Teacher" (Canter & Canter, 1976). Contemporary scholars have explained that modifications of the Assertive Discipline program over time have placed less prominence on teacher-orchestrated contingency management strategies (Brophy, 2006; Tauber, 2007). Nonetheless, in the fourth edition of *Assertive Discipline*, Canter (2010) maintained a Skinnerian connection by providing significant attention to "positive support strategies" such as "verbal recognition," "behavior awards," and "points on the board" (pp. 27-29).

In other popular contemporary programs, there are clear signs of Skinnerian influence. Positive behavior supports (PBS) applies behavioral intervention strategies to individual students, most often those with developmental disabilities or behavior disorders. Wheeler and Richey (2010) explained, "PBS is founded in the learning, behavioral theory, and research of B.F. Skinner and others," and that the overarching "goal" for the program in practice "should be to better use PBS to support persons with disabilities in experiencing a rich lifestyle, as evidenced by the enhanced quality of their lives as individuals and within their families and by their improved abilities and opportunities for self-determination" (p. 60). While PBS has targeted students with disabilities primarily, the program has also been applied to the "general student population" through "establishing school policies that promoted a sense of community for the students with the intent of improving school climate, such as school-wide incentives for appropriate conduct and behavior" (p. 29). Wheeler and Richey (2010) provided several "classes" of reinforcers that can be employed in a PBS system, including "edibles" (i.e. "food and drink preferences"), "activity" (e.g. "computer games, reading a book"), and "tangibles" (e.g. "backpacks, notebooks, pencils") (p. 281-282). In the end, the authors considered PBS

> an outgrowth of applied behavior analysis relying on the use of person-centered interventions that depend on the use of positive approaches to engineer environments, teach alternative behaviors, and employ meaningful consequences to enhance the quality of life for the individual. (p. 22)

Other prominent programs appear to have elements in line with Skinner's classroom management theories. Offering a blended disciplinary approach that combines best practice findings from over 100 classroom management studies, Marzano, Marzano, and Pickering (2003), in their *Classroom Management That Works*, described action steps such as "acknowledge and reinforce acceptable behavior" and "establish an appropriate level of dominance in the classroom" that hearken to the very fundamentals of Skinner's contingency management in the classroom (pp. 35, 49). The renowned Knowledge Is Power Program (KIPP) network of charter schools relies on a disciplinary system that has Skinner-like elements, such as their schools' use of a weekly "paycheck" system intended to reward good student behavior (Matthews, 2009). As a related story in *Time* magazine explained, "KIPP students get paid for actions they can control—getting to school on time, and having a positive attitude—with 'money' they can redeem for supplies at the school store." Suggesting a Skinnerian concern with rapidity of rewards, the article noted, "Recognition, like punishment, works best if it happens quickly. So KIPP schools pay their kids every week" (Ripley, 2010, p. 8). Perhaps indicative of the close affinity of programs and professionals influenced by Skinner's ideas, Dave Levin, KIPP cofounder, and Robert J. Marzano, author of *Classroom Management That Works*, were both recognized as reviewers for the fourth edition of *Assertive Discipline* (Canter, 2010, p. v).

Critiques of the Theory

B.F. Skinner had no shortage of critics, whether in regard to his psychological theories generally or his educational views specifically. In the late 1950s, for instance, linguist Noam Chomsky criticized Skinner's work that contended human speech resulted from behavioral responses, rather than deep, complex cognitive processes. As Skinner marketed his teaching machines in the 1960s, opinion makers expressed concerns that the introduction of the devices as a principal means of instructional delivery would harm the basic humanist ethos in schools. Chomsky and many others provided even more intense criticism in regard to Skinner's argument in the 1970s that, essentially, humans would benefit from admitting that there was no free will and establishing proper social controls essential for human happiness. An evolutionary descendent of Skinner's original theories, behavior modification, also generated significant backlash in the 1970s over issues such as whether patients, prisoners, and students who underwent experimental interventions should have the right to refuse such treatment (Bjork, 1993; Rutherford, 2009; Toates, 2009). In other words, the question became: did behavior modification simply constitute psychological manipulation?

Skinner's attention to reinforcement (or rewards) as a behavior modification strategy also received scrutiny. Lepper and Greene (1978) provided multiple university researchers with a forum to examine the "hidden costs of reward." Toward education, Alfie Kohn, an advocate for a strong humanist approach, proved diametrically opposed to the behaviorist Skinner in regard to classroom management theories. Whereas Skinner considered quick, desirable-behavior reinforcers an essential, necessary element in an effectively managed classroom, Kohn argued that reinforcers such as praise had deleterious effects on students by elevating compliance as the grandest goal in schools. Kohn held further that external rewards inhibited the development of intrinsic motivation, which he considered the lynchpin to sustaining students' long term educational interest and growth (Kohn, 1993; Kohn, 2006; Kohn, 2010; Tauber, 2007).

Indicative of the fierce feelings that Skinner's theories could provoke in those apparently repelled by their substance and implications, Kohn's (1993) seminal *Punished by Rewards* employed a tone that vacillated between disbelief and mockery in regard to the behavioral theorist. The first chapter of the work was titled "Skinner-Boxed," and in it Kohn used Skinner's theories, statements, and life anecdotes as a means to undermine him. Kohn wrote, "Skinnerians are not only interested in figuring out how rewards work; they are apt to argue that virtually everything we do—indeed who we are—can be explained in terms of the principle of reinforcement" (p. 6). Kohn quoted Skinner referring to himself as "a nonperson," and acknowledging in another instance that a book he wrote "naturally came out of my behavior and not because of anything called a 'me' or an 'I'" (p. 7). Though Kohn spent the remainder of his book providing theoretical and practical evidence in support of his educational, philosophical, and moral arguments for intrinsic motivation in education, a good part of the text's persuasive power lies in the author's early rhetorical indictment of Skinner. The opening chapter provides a lasting message to readers: following practices such as classroom rewards is to follow the beliefs of a man with dangerous, damaging views about people.

Kohn has not been alone in critically evaluating Skinner and behaviorism, and the effects of both on classroom management. Freiberg (1999) explored ways to move beyond standard applications of behaviorist approaches evidenced in Skinner-influenced programs such as Assertive Discipline. Tauber (2007) presented a classroom management continuum in which he designated Skinner as the behaviorist end point on a scale that ran to another end point of humanist, which Carl Rogers occupied. Other theorists whom Tauber clustered near the humanist end point, such as William Glasser and Thomas Gordon, suggest further alternatives to a Skinner-like behaviorist approach. Charles (2008) credited Skinner with inspiring the development of behavior modification. Though the author offered no sources to support the following ideas, she also contended that today at the "primary grade" level "behavior modification is not used so much for discipline as for encouraging and strengthening learning" and that it had come to be considered "unsuitable" above "the primary grades." The author speculated that instructors "found that it is simply easier to teach students how to behave desirably and show them how they should *not* [sic] behave" (p. 58). In a previous edition, Charles (2005) took a clear, Kohn-esque swipe at Skinner by closing the same section with the sentence, "[Students] don't have to learn [good behavior] through lengthy nonverbal and nonimitative processes as do pigeons and rats" (p. 25).

PARTICULAR STUDIES EXEMPLIFYING SKINNER'S THEORIES

Research studies conducted over the last four decades help demonstrate how scholars have utilized, in their conceptual frameworks, the classroom management theories that Skinner theorized and helped influence. Hall, Panyan, Rabon, and Broden (1968), for example, adopted a Skinnerian lens by focusing concretely on providing beginning teachers with the "reinforcement procedures" necessary to "improve classroom control" (p. 315). The study population (three new instructors unfamiliar with contingency management theory) had significant issues with classroom discipline. The researchers used a timed-interval recording system that measured student behavior (on-task or off-task) and teacher verbal interventions (positive or negative). After providing each participating teacher with coaching regarding successful positive reinforcement techniques, the researchers found that teachers' use of the reinforcers of "attention, a classroom game, and access to a between-period break" generated increased rates of study and decreased rates of disruption in all three classrooms. They concluded that "the beginning teacher who otherwise may have been doomed to failure" could "learn to manage his classroom through systematic use of the reinforcing contingencies available to him" (p. 321).

Winett and Winkler (1972) offered an early assessment of classroom uses of behavior modification by reviewing works published in *Journal of Applied Behavior Analysis*. Focusing their investigation on research projects conducted in "relatively normal classrooms," they sought to determine, "the kinds of target behaviors that were either reinforced or in various ways proscribed" (p. 500). They found that every study they examined but one characterized silence and obedience as the most appropriate classroom behaviors, and that, in effect, behavior modification had become a means for preserving rather than challenging the notion of schools as controlling institutions. Though B. F. Skinner may have in fact welcomed such findings as evidence that classroom operant conditioning could provide a means of effective social management, Winsett and Winkler made their own disappointment plain in the title they provided: "Current Behavior Modification in the Classroom: Be Still, Be Quiet, Be Docile." Nonetheless, they ended their article by contending their firm hope that behavior modification could "investigate and implement social change" (p. 503).

Pfiffner, Rosen, and O'Leary (1985) conducted a study that intended to test the "efficacy of an all-positive approach to classroom management," and their findings seemed to cast doubt on Skinner's advocacy for positive reinforcement as the central strategy for effective management (p. 257). The authors' first sentence established a clear connection to Skinner: "Spurred by Skinner's message of the 1950s, the behavioral Zeitgeist championed the view that a positively managed environment was possible, superior, and a goal to be aimed for" (p. 257). In their literature review, the authors described how previous studies had found that relying solely on positive reinforcement rarely worked, and the absence of negative reinforcements could cause significant classroom disruption. The authors' own rigorously-designed study employed the use of a one-way mirror for observation and a timed-interval recording process to examine the behavior of eight pupils in a special education classroom. Two trained study researchers recorded student behavior and one observer recorded teacher behavior according to ten second intervals during one hour of instruction. During the study period of over 45 days, the teacher delivered a varied verbal reinforcement approach (e.g. from "positives alone" for several days to "positives and negatives" over several other days). The researchers found that "behavior problem children cannot be successfully managed in an all-positive environment ... when praise is the primary form of positive feedback." They emphasized that the finding "does not hold when a powerful and individualized incentive system is used" (p. 260). In their conclusion, though, they speculated that such an all-encompassing intervention approach may require highly intensive teacher work, significant tangible rewards, and previously successful attempts at establishing student behavior through positive and negative reinforcers.

As Toates (2009) notes, contemporary researchers and educators continue to use Skinner's classroom management theories as conceptual guides. For instance, Swinson and Knight (2007) investigated the patterns and effects of teacher positive and negative verbal feedback on student behavior. The researchers specifically included in their study children whom a school's faculty described as challenging in terms of behavior, and they recorded how their teachers interacted with them in comparison to other classmates. The study found that teachers tended to provide positive comments toward academic work, but less frequently toward behavior, and that the approaches helped the academic engagement of the students originally deemed disruptive. Toward teachers' delivery of positive feedback in general, Snowman, McCown, and Biehler (2009) cited a 1984 Goodlad study that examined over 1000 teachers and 17,000 students, and determined that instructors' "praise of student work occurred about 2 percent of the observed time in the primary grades and about 1 percent of the time in high school" (p. 238).

Conclusion

In theorizing a system of contingency management in the classroom, B.F. Skinner proved influential. On the one hand, his ideas served and continue to serve as a starting point for researchers and practitioners who have applied and studied the use of tokens, games, praise, and other immediate, positive reinforcements in the pursuit of better student behavior. On the other hand, Skinner, whose organism behavior theories were grounded most firmly in experiments on animals, has served as a continuing foil for those who desire a more humanistic approach to classroom discipline. A straightforward way to consider the lasting impact of Skinner and his ideas is to visit a contemporary K-12 school. When a student receives verbal praise, a green ticket, or other quick reward for good behavior from a teacher, an observer may consider the role that B. F. Skinner played in helping generate widespread use and acceptance of that type of behavior reinforcement. Observers also might ask themselves: Is that verbal praise, green ticket, or other reward simply a reward? Or is it a means to make a young human organism feel free and happy, while they are becoming subject to greater external control in the service of the greater social good?

References

Barrish, H. H., Saunders, M., & Wolf, M.M. (1969). Good behavior game: Effects of individual contingencies for group consequences on disruptive behavior in a classroom. *Journal of Applied Behavior Analysis, 2*(2), 119-124.

Benson, H. B. (1979). *Behavior modification and the child: An annotated bibliography.* Westport, CT: Glenwood Press.

Bjork, D.W. (1993). *B. F. Skinner: A life.* New York, NY: Basic Books.

Brophy, J. (2006). History of research on classroom management. In C. M. Everston & C. S. Weinstein (Eds.), *Handbook of classroom management* (pp. 17-43). Mahwah, NJ: Erlbaum.

Buckley, N. K., & Walker, H. M. (1978). *Modifying classroom behavior: A manual of procedure for classroom teachers.* Champaign, IL: Research Press.

Canter, L., & Canter M. (1976). *Assertive discipline: A take charge approach for today's educator.* Santa Monica, CA: Canter and Associates.

Canter, L. (2010). *Assertive discipline: Positive behavior management for today's classroom* (4th ed.). Bloomington, IN: Solution Tree Press.

Charles, C. M. (2005). *Building classroom discipline* (8th ed.). Boston, MA: Allyn & Bacon.

Charles, C. M. (2008). *Building classroom discipline* (9th ed.). Boston, MA: Pearson, Allyn & Bacon.

Cuban, L. (2001). *Oversold and underused: Computers in the classroom.* Cambridge, MA: Harvard University Press.

Freiberg, H. J. (Ed.). (1999). *Beyond behaviorism: Changing the classroom management paradigm.* Boston, MA: Allyn & Bacon.

Hall, R.V., Panyan, M., Rabon, D., & Broden, M. (1968). Instructing beginning teachers in reinforcement procedures which improve classroom control. *Journal of Applied Behavior Analysis, (1)*4, 315-322.

Harris, M. B. (1972). *Classroom uses of behavior modification.* Columbus, OH: Charles E. Merrill.

Kohn, A. (1993). *Punished by rewards: The trouble with gold stars, incentive plans, A's, praise, and other bribes.* Boston, MA: Houghton Mifflin.

Kohn, A. (2006). *The homework myth: Why our kids get too much of a bad thing.* Cambridge, MA: Da Capo Life Long.

Kohn, A. (2010). No to threats and bribes. *Phi Delta Kappan, 91*(9), 18.

Lepper, M. R., & Greene, D. (1978). *The hidden costs of reward: New perspectives on the psychology of human motivation.* Hillsdale, NJ: Erlbaum.

Marzano, R. J., Marzano, J. S., & Pickering, D. J. (2003). *Classroom management that works: research-based strategies for every teacher.* Alexandria, VA: ASCD.

Matthews, J. (2009). *Work hard. Be nice: How two inspired teachers created the most promising schools in America.* Chapel Hill, NC: Algonquin Books.

Pfiffner, L. J., Rosen, L. A., & O'Leary, S. G. (1985). The efficacy of an all-positive approach to classroom practice. *Journal of Applied Behavior Analysis, 18*(3), 257-261.

Richelle, M. N. (1993). *B.F. Skinner: A reappraisal.* Hove, England: Erlbaum.

Ripley, A. (2010, April 8). Should kids be bribed to do well in school? *Time,* 1-9. Retrieved from http://www.time.com/time/nation/article/0,8599,1978589,00.html

Rutherford, A. (2009). *Beyond the box: B.F. Skinner's technology of behavior from laboratory to life, 1950s–1970s.* Toronto, Canada: University of Toronto Press.

Skinner, B. F. (1945, October). Baby in a box. *Ladies Home Journal, 62.* (Reprinted in Skinner, B. F. (1972). *Cumulative record: A selection of papers* (3rd ed.). New York, NY: Appleton-Century-Crofts, Educational Division, Meredith Corporation, 567-573).

Skinner, B. F. (1953). *Science and human behavior.* New York, NY: Macmillan.

Skinner, B. F. (1968). *The technology of teaching.* Englewood Cliffs, NJ: Prentice-Hall.

Skinner, B. F. (1969). Contingency management in the classroom. *Education, 90*(2), 93-102.

Skinner, B. F. (1971). *Beyond freedom and dignity.* New York, NY: Alfred A. Knopf.

Skinner, B. F. (1973). The free and happy student. *Phi Delta Kappan, 55*(1), 13-16.

Skinner, B. F. (1976). *Walden Two.* New York, NY: Macmillan.

Skinner, B. F. (1986). Program instruction revisited. *Phi Delta Kappan, 68*(2), 103-111.

Snowman, J., McCown, R., & Biehler, R. (2009). *Psychology applied to teaching* (12th ed.). Boston, MA: Houghton Mifflin.

Swinson, J., & Knight, R. (2007). Teacher verbal feedback directed towards secondary pupils with challenging behavior and its relationship to their behavior. *Educational Psychology in Practice, 23*(3), 241-255.

Tauber, R. T. (2007). *Classroom management: Sound theory & effective practice* (4th ed.). Westport, CT: Praeger.

Toates, F. (2009). *Burrhus F. Skinner: The shaping of behaviour.* London, England: Palgrave Macmillan.

Wheeler, J. J., & Richey, D. D. (2010). *Behavior management: Principles and practices of positive behavior supports* (2nd ed.). Boston, MA: Pearson.

Winettt, R. A., & Winkler, R. C. (1972). Current behavior modification in the classroom: Be still, be quiet, be docile. *Journal of Applied Behavior Analysis, 5*(4), 499-504.

Author Contact Information: Craig Peck, PhD, assistant professor, Department of Educational Leadership & Cultural Foundations School of Education, The University of North Carolina at Greensboro, 350 SOEB, 1300 Spring Garden Street Greensboro, NC 27402. Phone: 336-334-9877. E-mail: c_peck @uncg.edu

CHAPTER 58

Control, Choice, and the Fulfillment of Fundamental Human Needs

William Glasser's Humanistic Vision of Individual, Classroom, and Schoolwide Positive Behavioral Support

John A. Cassell and Thomas Nelson
University of the Pacific

From the broadest perspective, Glasser's work in the general field of K-12 student behavior and discipline must be viewed as located along a spectrum of work done over many years by numerous practitioners and scholars. In some quarters, this area of practice and research has been called "group management techniques" (Brophy, 1982). One broad approach to this field has emphasized group relationships and has studied academic group work as a mechanism for preemptively addressing classroom behavioral issues. Another approach has centered on behavioral modification and has undergone a shift in emphasis over the years. Earlier forms of this approach emphasized shaping the behavior of individuals through material reinforcements. Later forms were developed with the behavior of whole groups in mind (i.e., classes of students) and moved away from the idea of eliminating misconduct in favor of rewarding good academic performance. This resulted in a shift away from controlling behavior through the use of external stimuli and toward teaching individuals to control themselves (Brophy, 1982).

William Glasser entered this evolving landscape from another direction. His background was rooted in individual psychiatric counseling and therapy. As his work progressed through the years, he came to stand on ground between the two overarching disciplinary trends presented above; he occupied a niche between operative group dynamics and classic formulations of behavioral modification. Glasser was part of a group of counselors and psychotherapists who developed practical methodologies for dealing with young people presenting chronic personal or behavioral problems. Earlier forms of this broad approach stressed classic psychoanalytical or other "depth" investigations and interpretations of behavior and employed treatment through methods such as free association. Later forms shifted emphasis from the realm of unconscious motivations and past points of origin for problematic behavior to overt behaviors rooted in present conditions. This resulted in a movement from long-term general treatment to briefer crisis intervention and management strategies. At risk and disturbed students were no longer viewed as "sick," but were now considered as in need of information or insight which would allow them to better understand themselves and achieve better control over their emotions and behaviors.

The Handbook of Educational Theories, pp. 699–713

The Origins and Development of Glasser's Theoretical Models

Glasser himself found the origins for his particular point of view in his foundational work (1956-1967) among delinquent adolescent girls at the Ventura School for Girls, a juvenile prison facility in Ventura California (Glasser, 1978). Glasser came to believe that the girls could benefit from their experience at the school if they were well cared for and were given a chance to learn that they were willing and/or incentivized to accept. He learned that these girls were willing to follow rules if they felt cared for and were not exposed to failure in their studies. When he began his work in the public schools in 1961 he operated from basic premises developed during his work in Ventura. That is, the only truly effective way to solve discipline problems in school and the lack of learning associated with them was to make school a place where students were cared for, and students are not allowed to fail. This represented a rather bold departure from conventional thinking and practice.

Although some view Glasser's work before the middle 1980s as very different in tone and substance from his work after that point in time, the development of his thinking involves not so much a fundamental change in direction as the ongoing assembly of an increasingly complex latticework of tiered concepts and interlocking ideas (Charles, 1989; 2010). From the time of his work in Ventura, Glasser was interested in *both* individual behavior *and* the situational conditions in which the behavior unfolded, and possible causative points of interplay between the two. The concept of "reality therapy" emerged within the context of his experiences in Ventura. It began as a technique in psychiatric counseling and evolved over time into a multifaceted strategy for providing individual, classroom and school site positive behavioral support. In this effort, Glasser's approach to student behavior and discipline shared the fundamental points of emphasis found in Dreikurs, Morse, Good and Brophy, and Gordon: respect for the individual student and their unique identities; tolerance for individual differences; willingness to try to understand and help students with their special needs and problems; use of persuasion and instruction rather than the assertion of power; and the broad application of humanistic values. But this school of thought also advanced the position that students had responsibilities as well as rights and that an individual's behaviors and actions have consequences when they represent a failure to honor responsibilities one owes to themselves and/or others (Brophy, 1982).

Reality therapy assumed that there are two vital human needs: the need for relatedness (that is, to love and be loved) and the need for respect (to feel worthwhile to oneself and to others). Glasser proposed that persons suffering from psychic stress were experiencing difficulties in fulfilling these core needs. He further proposed that an inability to fulfill needs, and many related personal problems, can be traced back to a lack of supportive and productive emotional relationships with other persons on whom we can depend. In addition, Glasser stated that the ability to fulfill our basic needs can be made more difficult if we fail to understand and address the reality in which we live in the present moment. He believed that people must learn to squarely face reality and be shown how to fulfill their needs within that reality.

The general outline of reality therapy included the following basic principles: focus on the present and on what can be done in the here and now to address problems; avoid criticism and blame; be nonjudgmental and noncoercive, assess one's own actions from the standpoint of results; avoid making excuses for one's actions; remain focused on the source of the problem, disconnectedness. In creating this formulation for psychiatric counseling, Glasser stressed responsibility over insight, emphasized present behavior over influences from the past and gave greater weight to moral and ethical issues in evaluating behavior (Charles, 2010; Frazier & Laura, 1972; Rich, 1979).

The concept of reality therapy developed in relation to Glasser's work in psychiatric counseling evolved over time to become the foundation for the choice-based theories of human behavior and, eventually, school structure and organization he developed later in his career (and that are discussed below). In the course of this intellectual journey, Glasser changed his conception of the array of basic human needs, elaborated further on issues related to the original concept of reality therapy and introduced new ideas related to student failure, behavior as conscious choice and student participation and reflection as he applied his thinking to the environment of public education (Charles, 2010).

The basic premise of the approach to student behavior, and the disciplinary issues associated with it that emerged from reality therapy represented a departure from the traditional psychoanalytical emphasis on working to uncover situations and events from one's past that have contributed to problematic behaviors (i.e., classic Freudian psychoanalysis). Instead, Glasser emphasized working in the context of the present and tied treatment of behavioral issues to the reality of the current situation in which persons find themselves. He came to believe that it is what a person does in the here and now that matters and that the present reality of a person's situation and condition is the proper focus of psychoanalysis and, as his thinking developed, behavioral issues in school settings (Charles, 1989, 2010).

Glasser's work with reality therapy led him to conceive of individuals' behaviors as a matter of choice.

Positive and productive behavior results from the making of positive and productive choices oriented toward the betterment of one's situation. Negative and destructive behavior results from making negative and personally destructive choices. However, Glasser posited that in neither case is an individual's decision making necessarily contrary to the person's perceived internal logic. In fact, he asserted that a person's choices relative to their behaviors are the results of human beings constantly attempting to fulfill basic needs associated with the immutable nature of the species. Glasser believed that humans have rational minds and are capable of making rational choices. In line with this general position, as he moved into his career in public schools, he based his early work in positive behavior support on the idea that students can understand what acceptable behavior in school is and that they can choose to adopt these forms of behavior in the situational context of school. As he extended the core ideas of reality therapy into his work in public schools, Glasser came to believe that the crux of the matter was in school staff helping students make better choices about their behavior in school. Students must be turned away from seeking to fulfill basic human needs through destructive behaviors that achieved needs-related goals in the short term (Charles, 1989; 2010; Glasser, 1978).

Glasser came to believe that the responsibility for an individual's behavior resides squarely with that individual, and there is no utility in seeking to blame others for one's behavioral patterns. Hence, he insisted that teachers never excuse the bad behavior of students. Low socioeconomic status, bad family or home situations, racial and ethnic identity—none of this can be used as an excuse for unacceptable behavior. Students cannot be exempted from their responsibility to behave in a situationally appropriate way. Glasser advanced the idea that people are capable of being successful in any given environment and can be successful in one while failing or having challenges in another (Glasser, 1978).

New Applications of Reality Therapy and Control Theory to the Venue of Public Education

Based on what he saw at the Ventura School for Girls, Glasser posited the concept that many children can find in schools what they may not be able to find in the other settings of their lives. During the 1960s and 1970s he advanced the idea that for some students, school was the only place they had an opportunity to associate with quality adults who genuinely cared about them and their welfare. Part of this caring was working with students to assist them in making better choices in support of more advantageous and productive forms of behavior. In service of this effort, Glasser developed an operative framework for bringing his concept of behavioral self-control into the practice of professional educators. The basic features of this framework are as follows:

a. stress student responsibility;
b. Establish rules that lead to success;
c. Accept no excuses;
d. Call for value judgments as part of behavior remediation;
e. Suggest suitable alternatives;
f. Invoke reasonable consequences;
g. Be persistent; and
h. carry out continual review (Charles, 1989, pp. 121-125; 2010, p. 148).

Based upon these broad features, Glasser developed a corrective behavioral intervention program that he called the "10 steps to good discipline." He described this intervention protocol as a constructive and nonpunitive, but no nonsense, approach to student misbehavior (Brophy, 1982). The 10 steps in this protocol are as follows:

1. Select a student for concentrated attention and list typical reactions to the student's disruptive behavior.
2. Analyze the list to see what techniques do and do not work and resolve not to repeat the ones that do not work.
3. Improve personal relationships with the student by providing extra encouragement, asking the student to perform special errands, showing concern, implying that things will improve, etc.
4. If the problem behavior continues, focus the student's attention on the disruptive behavior by requiring the student to describe what he or she has been doing, "what are you doing?" "I saw you doing ..."—continue until the student describes the behavior accurately and then request that he or she stop it.
5. If the behavior persists, call for a short conference–again, have the student describe the behavior and state whether or not it is against the rules or recognized expectations. Ask the student what he or she should be doing instead and what his or her current behavior is accomplishing *for* him or her.
6. If the behavior continues to persist, call another conference and this time work with the student to develop a negotiated plan designed to address the problem behavior. The plan should be more than a simple agreement to stop misbehaving—it should include the student's commitment to positive

actions designed to eliminate the problem. However, it should cover a relatively short period of time and be scaled in such a way as to present the student with a high probability of success. The plan should help the student fulfill his or her needs in a productive and healthy way. The student should be asked questions such as "what can we do to ensure that this does not happen again?"

7. If the student behavior continues, isolate the student or use time-out procedures. During these periods of isolation, the student should be asked if he or she wants to continue experiencing the negative consequences associated with his or her behavior. If the answer is no, then he or she will be charged with devising his or her own plan to ensure the following of the rules in the future. Isolation will continue until the student has devised this plan, gotten it approved by the teacher and made a personal commitment to follow it (Glasser recommends this approach for elementary students, in situations involving secondary students he recommends moving on to Step 8).
8. If this does not work, the next step is in-school suspension. Now the student must deal with the principal or someone other than the teacher, but this other person will repeat earlier steps in sequence and press the student to develop a new plan. It is made clear at this point that the student will either return to class and follow reasonable rules in effect there, or continue to be isolated outside of class.
9. If the student remains out of control or in in-school suspension, their parents are called to take them home for the day, and the process is repeated starting the next day.
10. Students who continue to not respond to the previous steps should be removed from school and referred to another agency (pp. 43-44).

The key underlying Glasser's protocol was the idea that teachers and school officials had to develop responses to student misbehavior that forced the student to take the ultimate responsibility for his/her choices and behaviors. The response must set up a clear relationship between student actions and the consequences of those actions and a continuing focus on this relationship had to be maintained in dealing with the misbehaving student. School staff must refuse to accept any excuse for the student's behavior—the student must not be allowed to deflect the responsibility for their actions in some other direction (Brophy, 1982; Glasser, 1965; Savage & Savage, 2010).

Glasser insisted that students be confronted with the connection between their actions and the consequences associated with them. They should be asked questions, such as "what happens when people do that?" Students must be made to understand that their behavior is a matter of choice and that consequences result from these choices. In addition, students must be called upon to make value judgments about the behavior in which they are engaged. Students should be asked if they want to continue to experience the negative consequences of their actions—they should be asked the question "how are these actions helping you?"

The Bridge Between Intervention and Prevention in the Application of Glasser's Theoretical Framework

Certainly, Glasser's background in psychotherapy led him to recognize the utility of corrective intervention and this informed his thinking during the 1950s, 1960s and 1970s. However, as noted above, he also attached importance to the situational context in which individual behaviors emerged. His work at the Ventura School for Girls left him with a deep-seated belief in the power of school environments to impact the behavior of students. Based on his experience in Ventura, Glasser firmly believed that if educators in the school environment truly cared for students and supported them sufficiently to avoid school failure, then even very problematic behaviors could be controlled and habitually misbehaving students could find reasons to obey school rules. Again, behavior and the choices upon which they are based are rooted in deeply embedded chains of logic and rational thought processes tied to the constantly continuing effort of all persons to secure the fulfillment of basic needs that go to the inner-most recesses of their innate humanity.

Glasser never abandoned the concept of individualized corrective intervention as part of a behavior management process in schools. However, as time went on he developed a more elaborate conception of generalized preventative discipline tied closely to the form and substance of the school environment (Charles, 1989; 2010). As early as the late 1970s, Glasser had begun to cast a somewhat less optimistic light on the nature of the public school environment, particularly with regard to the environment of secondary public school. He came to the position that disorder anywhere is essentially the same phenomenon and that anyone has the capacity to break rules and misbehave under certain circumstances. School is no different in this regard and Glasser came to see the public school environment as one that presented circumstances that supported the existence of negative behavioral patterns among the students in attendance (Glasser, 1978). He came to believe that students who do poorly academically and behave badly in school are often not getting anything out of the school experience—either inside or outside the classroom per se. They have little stake in the school environment. They come to school and do whatever makes them feel good in the moment, even if the behavior is personally destructive in the long term. They make minimal positive contributions in school, and are generally centered entirely on themselves and have little interest in the rules of school. Consistent with exhibiting little interest in school, these students gravitate toward the sporadic pleasure that misbehaving gives them and are largely detached from the punitive consequences schools put in place in an attempt to ensure a stable operational environment (Glasser, 1978). He came to the conclusion that the only real answer to school discipline problems is to offer students more of a stake, a greater sense of ownership in the environment and context of public schools and classrooms. Again, based on his experience in Ventura and his earlier work with reality therapy, Glasser advanced that the means to do this lay in creating school environments in which students felt cared for and were free of the grindingly destructive fear of failure.

This became the basis for the "schools without failure program" Glasser pioneered in an effort to give students a meaningful stake in school. He firmly believed that any such program designed to help students must also support faculty and teach them techniques to work more successfully with their students. This necessarily had powerful pedagogical and curricular implications (Glasser, 1978). He saw a major issue in destructive patterns in which students could become trapped in the course of working in school. If children who come to school do not learn as expected by others, Glasser observed that they can become labeled as failures and, as a result, receive less care from the adults in school upon whom they depend for care and support—vital elements in the fulfillment of basic and powerful needs in all human beings. They, therefore, lose support and recognition on which they depend and may very well stop working and even trying to perform in their academic work. It was in this enervating cycle that Glasser found the origin point of much of the routine disengagement and misbehavior in school. Over time the situation can become more critical as the student feels trapped in a situation with no acceptance and no recognition except for what they can gain through impulsive and unacceptable behavior.

By the close of the 1970s, Glasser came to the conclusion that if positive student behavior was to be made the norm in schools and discipline problems were to be effectively dealt with, individualized corrective intervention strategies would need to be augmented by proactive steps designed to ensure that students are offered more opportunities for acceptance and meaningful academic support. The foundational tool he developed for this purpose was the class meeting which came to be known as "Glasser Circles." In the classroom meeting, as conceived by Glasser, the teacher would on a daily basis gather the class into a circle configuration and engage them in interesting, intellectually enjoyable discussions. The desired effect here was to stimulate students into thinking that they are, at the very least, a meaningful part of the class (Glasser, 1978). He turned to this as a time-effective and powerful technique for getting students to believe that they are accepted and cared for by visibly engaged adults and student colleagues.

At the same time, Glasser warned that schools would need to take proactive measures to limit rates of academic failure and disaffection among students if they were to avoid endemic discipline problems and unacceptable behavioral patterns. He saw the failure to read adequately as the prime issue in academic failure generally and urged schools to support students by providing more interesting and engaging reading materials as well as opportunities to verbally contribute to learning activities in class in meaningful ways. He advocated for the use of Glasser circles for this purpose. Glasser also urged schools to abandon the traditional concept of the "progress curve" in moving students through academic work. He rejected the notion of classrooms as cognitively homogenous entities and stressed the proposition that they are, in fact, highly heterogeneous environments in which all students learn at different rates and need to be academically supported by recognizing their progress and celebrating their successes. Students, he said, must be reassured that they will not fail, no matter how long it takes for them to progress to higher levels of understanding (Glasser, 1978).

He recognized that though creating more accommodative school environments would not work for every student, his corrective intervention protocol would continue to have a place in the positive behavioral support systems of public school. However, he increasingly stressed that the stepped withdrawal of privileges and behavioral confrontation strategies described above would be meaningless in aversive school environments that provide students with little meaningful stake in the school. Changes in the school environment designed to increase acceptance and the chances for academic success must therefore precede the implementation of his 10-step protocol if student misbehavior was to be dealt with in a truly effective manner. Hence, generalized preventative environmental measures came to be viewed by Glasser as a precondition to the meaningful implementation of individualized corrective behavioral interventions (Glasser, 1978; 1990).

Questions of Quality, Control and Choice: Bosses, Leaders and the Fulfillment of Fundamental Human Needs

Glasser's conception regarding the connection points between corrective and preventative behavioral management techniques entered a new stage of development with the publication of his 1985 book *Control Theory in the Classroom* and the evolving concept of the "quality school." Of key importance to this stage of his thinking on student behavior and disciplinary measures in school was the question of quality work in schools and student satisfaction with their work in school and the environment with which they are presented in public school. This line of inquiry led Glasser to new and more sophisticated assertions relative to student behavior, disciplinary challenges and the fulfillment of basic human needs (Glasser, 1985, 1990).

During this phase of his career, Glasser gravitated toward management models in operation in corporate America and the management philosophy of W. Edwards Deming who specialized in teaching business executives how to manage so that virtually all workers do high quality work. Glasser argued that this line of thinking had great utility in the management of public schools and could be brought into public schools undistorted and intact (Glasser, 1990). The conceptual framework for the implementation of Deming's ideas on management in the setting of public school was a further evolution in Glasser's thinking on student behavior and discipline that he dubbed "control theory". Glasser increasingly turned his attention toward the relationship between basic and compelling human needs and core factors associated with human motivation. He posited that his control theory explains both why and how we behave better than any other existing theoretical framework and that it clearly explains why Deming's ideas, when used correctly, work so well and how they can be transferred into the operational dynamic of public education to address problematic student behavior and disciplinary challenges.

Glasser seized on one of Deming's core propositions, namely, that workers (students being the workers in public school as well as the product produced by public school) will not work hard unless they believe that there is quality in what they are asked to do. Working hard in and of itself will not satisfy basic human needs critical to school students, such as the need for personal empowerment, if they are engaged in what they believe to be a low-quality task (i.e., a task with unimportant and/or irrelevant outcomes or impacts). Very few people (including school students) will rise to the effort to produce high quality work if they believe that there is no real quality in what they are asked to do (Glasser, 1985, 1990). The feeling of being trapped in low-quality work routines can lead to disaffection and dissatisfaction which, in turn, can lay the foundation for student boredom, disengagement and misbehavior as they look for ways to satisfy their needs outside the scope of officially sanctioned school work and activities.

Control theory holds that no one can make anyone do anything. The job and hallmark of a truly effective manager is to manage in a way that makes it easy for workers to see the connection between what they are asked to do and what they believe is worth doing (Glasser, 1990). Glasser believes that the main complaint of students in American secondary schools is not that their school work is too hard, but that it is too boring, and he feels that this complaint is entirely valid. Here "boring" means that the student cannot connect what they are asked to do to a real form of usefulness in their actual lives. For work to not be boring it must be somehow satisfying to and for the worker. It must be meaningful in a felt way. Hence, effective teachers, as in the case of any effective manager, are effective because they ask students to do things that are satisfying and self-affirming. Glasser asserts that the traditional coercive practices designed to ensure academic performance outlined in *A Nation at Risk* (and later, No Child Left Behind) have the opposite effect because, ultimately, nothing of any real intellectual quality can be measured by machine scored standardized tests (Glasser, 1990).

What Glasser calls for is a new managerial paradigm for public education that mirrors that which has been used successfully in large American corporations for several decades and is outlined in the work of W. Edwards Deming. He calls for the abandonment of the traditional form of management of students and school sites historically used in American public schools based upon a stimulus/response theoretical foundation and tethered the use of reward/ punishment coercive and adversarial practices ("boss" management). Glasser states that the simple fact is that people will not work hard for a person they view as an adversary. Children are boss managed in school from the beginning. As early as first grade, the child who does not do what the teacher says, or does not work in the way the teacher demands, is apt to be boss managed and subjected to coercive management methods. A child knows when he is being coerced and, as soon as this begins, the student's main agenda reverts to resistance and the personal power struggle between student and teacher is under way. Education can be largely forgotten and discipline moves front and center. The student learns less and resists more. As a result, the student and teacher are caught in a perpetual power struggle. Boss management, then, limits the amount of learning that can occur in the classroom and exacerbates discipline problems and student misbehavior as students rebel against coercive management practices, which in turn leads to ever-escalating levels of coercion (Glasser, 1985, 1990).

Glasser advocates for the use of what he calls "lead" management as an alternative to the coercive and counterproductive boss management model. Lead management, in contrast, uses persuasion and problem solving processes. The system of work is organized so that workers (i.e., students) see that it is to their benefit to produce high quality work and engage in positive and productive behavior. The lead manager adopts four basic management principles to make this happen:

1. They engage the workers in discussions of the quality of the work to be done, and consider workers' input.
2. They model the job so that workers can see exactly what the manager thinks is the best way to do the work.
3. They ask workers to evaluate their own work for quality and they will listen to what workers tell them about what constitutes quality in doing the work.
4. They act as facilitators—showing the worker what is being done to support their efforts and actually do things to actively support workers in producing high quality work (Glasser, 1990, p. 431).

Glasser contends that these features of lead management, drawn from the work of Deming, can be successfully used in the classroom and the wider school environment. So, students should be encouraged to evaluate their own work and keep their own records on their work in order to track their progress. This supports their realization that they can do high quality work and this can, in turn, lead to truly intrinsic motivation and self-actuated academic progress. Glasser contends that there should be no coercion involved in this approach and if all this happens, there should be virtually no discipline problems.

Although Glasser disagreed with the basic tenet of boss management, that is, our behaviors originate in response to stimuli external to ourselves (i.e., the withdrawal of aversive stimuli or the introduction of positive stimuli), he believed that the environment(s) in which we live and work have an impact on what we do. However, he felt that this should be understood from the standpoint of our taking in and analyzing information from the external environment around us—a process that is, ultimately, under our own control. We take in and analyze information drawn from the environment in ways that make sense for and to us—how we choose to react to the information is up to us. Information from the teacher is important, but the students make the final judgment about how important that information is to them. The more important they think it is, the more they will do what they are asked. The difference between boss and lead managers lies in the information each gives to the workers or students. The boss manager's message on work to be done is coercive and is based on reward and/or punishment. Lead managers avoid coercive language—they try to give workers the kind of information that will persuade them to do as directed because it is as much to the worker's benefit as it is to the manager's (Glasser, 1990).

The ideas underlying control theory are of critical importance in all this in that they inform managers regarding what we as human beings are always looking for—the fulfillment of basic needs deeply embedded in our human DNA. Lead managers combine what we are all looking for and need with what they are asking us to do. They know that we are always motivated by the basic needs of our species and, therefore, the alignment of tasks with needs forms a vital connection in support of personal satisfaction and motivation. Control theory (and the later version that emerged in the mid 1990s which Glasser renamed choice theory) proposed that all human beings (including workers and students) are born with a number of basic needs. Glasser revised the needs concept he had developed earlier as part of reality therapy. He now identified five such needs: survival, love, power (not the power over others as much as power over one's own situation in life—self-empowerment), fun and freedom (the freedom to make decisions and choices about one's behavior and life course). When control theory gave way to choice theory, survival and love were collapsed into the single concept of "belonging" (Glasser, 1996). In line with his earlier thinking, Glasser contends that throughout our lives, we are compelled to attempt to live in a way that best satisfies these needs. Control theory was a descriptive term in that humans try to control their behavior so that what they choose to do is the most need-satisfying course of action that can be done at any given point in time (Glasser, 1990, 1996).

This brings us back to the concept of quality work in school. Deming found, and Glasser agreed, that workers/students will not work hard if they do not see quality in what they are asked to do. Most students in school do not see the quality or value in the work they are asked to do in school. Hence, there is little motivation to do the work, there is little satisfaction in doing the work and little importance is attached to it. Glasser felt that students, therefore, will turn to other activities they find more satisfying, including misbehavior. He asserted that when students say they hate school, they mean that they hate being asked to work hard on something that does not fulfill their needs that offers little personal meaning. Boring low quality academic tasks in support of machine graded standardized exams are just that sort of work. The goals of administrators and teachers under the current reform regime is not oriented toward quality but, rather, is focused on low quality or nonquality work—such as, getting scores up, getting the dropout rate down, getting more students pushed through the schooling process, regardless of how unsatisfactorily.

Glasser contended that doing high quality work tends to make people feel good and, therefore, they naturally come to the conclusion that this type of work is worth doing. But the sort of self-evaluation this awareness is based on tends not to happen under boss management. In this situation, workers spend too much time evaluating the boss to effectively evaluate themselves and their work. When workers and students are coerced, they waste time and effort evaluating the coercers and trying to outwit or evade them and this process reduces the level of quality in the workplace, the level of needs satisfaction among workers and the chances that in school students will turn to opting out and misbehaving in order to satisfy their needs.

Glasser believed that schools must move beyond quality being defined as doing well on what the teachers give students to do. They must, rather, move toward students setting their own standards for quality and working with teachers in the learning process and not just under them. As Deming pointed out, given the right tools, workers can create better products than boss managers can even envision. This is what Glasser felt lead management had been shown to accomplish in schools—make quality contagious and self-perpetuating (Glasser, 1990). The crux of the matter, then, settled on Glasser's assertion that if students are to work and behave properly, they must believe that if they do some work, they will be able to satisfy their needs enough so that it makes sense to keep working. So, he gave much more emphasis than previously to the school's role in meeting basic student needs, and this represents a prime factor in discipline and work output. Therefore, by the end of the 1990s, Glasser's work can be viewed from the standpoint of two overarching and intertwining themes that operate as foundational premises: (a) schools must provide a classroom and wider school environment and curriculum that meets students' basic needs for belonging, power, fun and freedom as a means of motivating students and reducing misbehavior; and (b) school staff must work to help students make good behavioral choices that lead ultimately to personal success. It should be noted that critical to the implementation of Glasser's concept of systemic positive behavioral support is the foundational premise that the individual controls their own behavior and that behavior is, in point of fact, a choice made by that individual. It is a choice they themselves can modify and redirect upon reflection and evaluation of the impact it has on their ability to fulfill basic needs.

Curriculum, Pedagogy and the Quality School Environment: The Role of Critical Thinking, Skill Augmentation, and Cooperative Group Work

In the most mature form of his thinking, Glasser considered both curriculum and pedagogy in conceiving what a school environment that provided for the fulfillment of student needs through the provision of opportunities to be cared for, academically supported and exposed to high quality work should look like. Glasser posited that, absent compelling, relevant curriculum and inclusive, participatory pedagogy, lead management style was, in and of itself, incapable of creating a "quality school". He observed that many students, including many good students, felt that the curriculum being used in schools was not worth the effort and time required to learn it—it did not constitute meaningful, high quality work (Glasser, 1992). Students did not feel that there was any need to work hard on curriculum focused on the memorization of disparate bits of information and data that had no meaningful use in their real lives beyond the classroom. They felt that this was "throwaway" information and that work to memorize it was nothing more than "busy work". Glasser referred to this type of school work as nonsense and believed that it contributed to student misbehavior and discipline problems by forcing students to look to behaviors outside of sanctioned academic activities in their search for needs fulfillment.

He advanced the idea that people and not curricula are the outcomes envisioned by educators and, therefore, the concentration on wide and shallow content-based curricula driven by pacing guides was counterproductive. In Glasser's view, in order to be satisfying and impactful, curricula should concentrate not on memorization of "factoids", but on the acquisition of valuable skills genuinely useful to people in living their lives, both at the time of their acquisition and in their future lives and endeavors (Glasser, 1992). Information and data should not be approached from the standpoint of what it is, but from the standpoint of where, why and when it should be used. Glasser applied the ideas of W. Edwards Deming in this regard in stating that students should be introduced to information in order to make use of it to create and transfer knowledge in an effort to develop and hone useful skills which serve to empower them and support their personal growth (and in so doing, fulfill basic needs for freedom, fun, acceptance and power).

Glasser went on to describe the pedagogical practices he believed should be used to deliver the form of curriculum described above. Once again, he was interested in what sort of instructional practice and classroom organization would serve the purpose of engaging students and satisfying their most basic needs to the extent necessary to ensure that they would invest in the process and substance of schooling and avoid the temptation to make inappropriate choices relative to behavior at school. Glasser posited that the institution of school operated under the self-defeating assumption that our deeply embedded genetically coded needs as human beings somehow "turn off" upon entering a classroom door. As he put it, "Students are taught as if they were supposed to suspend this need, put it into abeyance, sit still and pay attention to what is being taught and not to each other" (Brandt, 1988, p. 39). He firmly asserted that teachers must find ways in class for students to have the chance to associate with others in a friendly fashion and to do so as a planned part of instruction. In interviewing students about where in school they found needs fulfillment, Glasser discovered that extracurricular activities provided powerful venues for addressing some of the most compelling psychological needs felt by school students.

Student stories about how they felt being a part of the group dynamics inherent in activities such as the school band, the yearbook, drama clubs, and organized athletics made a powerful impression on Glasser and led him to the realization that it was the operative qualities of these group dynamics which held the key to pedagogy in support of human needs fulfillment. He came to attach particular significance to the role these activities played in the fulfillment of the human need for power—the compelling urge in every human being to be recognized as someone who matters, someone who is listened to, someone who makes a difference. Glasser asserted that the frustration of the need for power, even more than the need for belonging, lay at the core of behavioral difficulties in school (Brandt, 1988; Gough, 1987). People who are not able to say "I'm at least a little important" with regard to a situation in which they are involved will not, he believed, work hard to preserve and/or improve upon the structure of that situation. Frustration relative to this very basic form of self-esteem will result in compensatory behavior in an effort to gain some form of attention and interest from others. Some of this behavior can easily slide into antisocial and even personally destructive practices that diminish the quality of the school environment for everyone. Glasser observed that most people satisfied the need for power, and many other core human needs, through working in teams with people they respect and care for (Brandt, 1988; Gough, 1987). He noted that a well-functioning family is just such a team and that the extracurricular activities in which students found needs fulfillment (including the need for power) all involved the group dynamics of teams.

Glasser came to the conclusion that cooperative group learning was the most efficacious instructional dynamic relative to meeting students' needs for belonging, power, freedom and fun. It provided a powerful platform for bringing the group dynamics of needs-fulfilling team-based extracurricular activities into the classroom as a formally structured context for learning. Belonging was addressed through becoming a valued member of a group (sometimes referred to by Glasser as "learning teams") in which people care for one another; power was addressed by the provision of the opportunity to be heard in a meaningful context by others; contribute ideas and influence others; freedom was addressed by being given opportunities to make decisions as groups and within groups working independently on academic projects; and fun was addressed through being able to talk, socialize and work directly with peers as opposed to simply acting as passive receptors working largely in isolation from classmates (Charles, 1989).

Glasser relied heavily on the work of David and Roger Johnson, Robert Slavin, and Spencer Kagan in considering the specific form of cooperative group most useful in the fulfillment of key human needs and most efficient in delivering the type of curriculum discussed above (Brandt, 1988; Gough, 1987; Johnson, Johnson, Holubee, & Roy, 1984). The vision of cooperative group work put forth by the Johnson's was based on small groups of students working together to complete instructional activities in the form of project work. The groups are made of no fewer than two people and no more than six, with groups of four being the preference of most teachers using this instructional approach. The process of cooperative group work advocated by Glasser and designed by the Johnson's included four elements thought to be essential for genuinely cooperative learning to occur:

1. Positive interdependence—students must be dependent upon each other in the completion of the learning activities and this dependency is built into the group tasks through the use of students performing different roles in the group work so that the project task cannot be completed without the contributions of each member.
2. Face-to-face interaction—students must be able to interact with each other and exchange information freely.
3. Individual accountability—each member is held individually accountable for learning the material or skills being covered in the group work. Further, each group will include a mix of abilities, intelligences and learning styles and preferences so as to support students learning from each other as well as providing mutual assistance.

4. Use of interpersonal and small-group skills—students must be put in situations that demand the development and use of social skills to complete tasks. This includes communication skills and conflict management and resolution. Groups are given time and procedures for analyzing the overall effectiveness of their group interaction and the quality of their work product (Charles, 1989, pp. 144-145).

In this setting, the teacher becomes a consultant and facilitator as the locus for learning shifts from a teacher-centric to a student-centric model. The teacher moves about the room from team to team encouraging, helping, inquiring and prodding (Brandt, 1988). However, Glasser was quick to point out that the nature of schoolwork must change if learning teams are to be successful academically. The assignments in this setting could not be traditional "fill in the blank" or "find *the* right answer" sort of exercises. This type of work can (and typically will) be done by one person in the group and copied by the others. True group projects are open-ended and invite people to work together by being structured so as to require the effort and input of more than one person and more than skill set.

The teacher will select team members so as to create a mix of academic levels and learning styles in support of wider involvement and participation. The learning team environment is one in which no one student can monopolize the learning process because the nature of both the team and task structure is such that no one student can or would want to do so (Brandt, 1988; Gough, 1987). A good team assignment causes students to actively want to work together because they perceive that together they can accomplish more and do it better than they can work independently. In this way, pedagogical practice can actively support school environments designed around lead management, needs fulfillment and positive behavioral support. It is pedagogical practice that leads students toward making positive and productive choices with regard to their behavior in school.

High Praise, Skepticism and Open Questions: Reactions to Glasser's Theoretical Propositions and Recommendations for Practice

As influential as Glasser's work has been relative to both scholarly and practice-based inquiry into behavior, discipline and learning in public school, it has not suffered from a lack of healthy skepticism and critical caution with regard to some of its assertions and recommendations. Brophy (1982) and Welch and Dolly (1980) are among those who point out that Glasser's ideas and proposals for practice have not been subjected to a great deal of systematic study or programmatic research. White (2005) echoes this concern in his review of *Warning: Psychiatry can be Hazardous to Your Mental Heath* by pointing out that Glasser does not include therein a set of randomized clinical trials demonstrating the success of his various theoretical propositions. This cautionary observation is compounded by the fact that much of what one reads in the literature regarding the impact of Glasser's ideas in real school settings is anecdotal and some of it is provided by Glasser himself. In 1977, at the annual meeting of the American Association of School Administrators, Glasser presented survey data gathered from 24 schools around the country that were taking part in his *Schools Without Failure* behavior management program. Not altogether surprisingly, the survey data were very positive with regard to dropping rates of disciplinary referrals, reductions in levels of school violence, and increases in positive affective teacher and student behavior (Glasser, 1977).

There are a number of "one off" anecdotal reports of positive outcomes at individual school sites. Melanie Fox Harris and R. Carl Harris (1992) provide one such report for a rural elementary school in central Utah. Their article is typical of this vein within the literature dedicated to discussions of Glasser's ideas. They report on the process and positive outcomes associated with the implementation of Glasser recommendations such as multistage grouping, self-evaluation for assessment, the use of student work portfolios in the replacement of letter grades, and the implementation of a system the authors refer to as "democratic discipline" (i.e., cooperative solutions to behavioral problems in a lead management atmosphere of shared power which leverages the multistep behavioral management process outlined in Glasser's reality therapy). Harris and Harris report that these schoolwide program elements resulted in demonstrable behavioral and academic improvements across the school population. In his presentation before the American Educational Research Association Annual Meeting, Bruce Keepes (1973) provides a more formal and serious version of this "testimonial" approach in his observation-rich case study describing the formal application of Glasser's *Schools without Failure* program to one elementary school used as an experimental site within the Palo Alto Unified School District in the San Francisco Bay Area. Keepes tracks a number of positive outcomes at the school which he attributes to the implementation of Glasser's recommendations for structuring school environments: more positive and genuinely personal teacher-student relationships; an emphasis upon individualized instruction oriented to the actual academic and personal needs of students; a more equitable and democratic problem-solving orientation toward discipline; increase in cooperative student-student relationships in instructional settings; less social competitiveness in the classroom; and a marked increase in joint effort within the classroom and across the school site as a whole.

With regard to empirical research generally, both qualitative and quantitative, studies of Glasser's theories in action have yielded mixed results over the last 30 years. Shearn and Randolph (1978) note in a review of the literature back to 1970 that several quasi-experimental studies appear to support the use of choice-based reality therapy techniques for a number of different types of students with regard to self-concept, on-task behavior and self-responsibility. However, they also found a number of other such studies where statistical analysis of variance did not support the use of reality therapy for these purposes. In addition, Shearn and Randolph found troubling design flaws in some of the studies which supported the use of Glasser's techniques (e.g., lack of treatment controls for "placebo effect" and overly transparent placebo treatments in the control groups).

Shearn and Randolph's own quasi-experimental study (1978) which sought to fill the design gaps in previous research found no statistically significant differences in self-concept and on-task behavior between experimental classrooms subjected to reality therapy based instructional dynamics and placebo control classrooms which were subjected to another instructional dynamic also presented as an instructional treatment. The study did not support the use of reality therapy methods in the classroom.

The 1974 study by Josephine Fletcher is another example in this vein. She investigated the impact of Glasser's class meeting technique, sometimes referred to as "Glasser Circles," relative to levels of student motivation and self-concept. She applied an experimental research design in the form of an analysis of pre- and posttreatment scores on the SCAMIN Self-Concept and Motivation Inventory for experimental and control subject groups. Experimental groups experienced a treatment in the form of the utilization of Glasser Circles as part of the instructional routine and control groups did not receive the treatment. Fletcher found that Glasser's discussion techniques resulted in only a minimal degree of increase in motivation for students in the primary grades where counselors led such discussions over the period of a school semester. She found a greater degree of increase in self concept among students at the same grade level where discussions are led by classroom instructors. Fletcher concluded that more data would be needed to make a reliable determination as to the efficacy of these methods and recommended that the use of Glasser Circles be studied over a longer period of time.

Masters and Laverty (1974) report mixed results in their review of the relevant literature in which they concentrate, to some extent, on longitudinal studies investigating schools implementing Glasser's *Schools Without Failure* program. They present a number of studies that report mixed effects of Glasser's program with teacher attitudes and behaviors showing more change than that of students. Their own quasi-experimental study (1974) generally runs in line with these findings with differences between experimental and control schools revealing little in the way of patterns regarding positive results for the Glasser methods. In some categories of investigation (e.g., student academic achievement), traditional control schools actually performed better than the experimental Glasser schools for certain subjects at certain grade levels. Similarly, differences in student attitudes toward school and school work were uneven between the experimental and control schools. Interestingly, some data does emerge from these studies indicating that schools further along in the program implementation timeline may show more positive results in more research categories than schools in their first year of implementation.

Frances Welch and John Dolly (1980) studied the impact of in-service teacher training in Glasser's Reality Therapy and class meeting techniques on teacher affective behaviors, student on-task behaviors, discipline referrals and student absences. The authors observed 24-hours of teacher training conducted in several different training contexts and using multiple training techniques and structures. The researchers used the Teacher Observation Scale to assess teacher behaviors. The scale measures ten teacher affective behaviors. Student behavior was analyzed using the Student Observation Scale of Overt On-Task Behaviors which measures four student behavior types. School principals provided the data on student absences and discipline referrals. Data were collected during the 3 weeks immediately preceding training and the 3 weeks immediately following the training. The research results show no significant changes in teacher and student behavior as a result of the in-service training in Glasser's techniques. However, the researchers here note that the length of training observed was less than is often the case with Glasser's techniques. Also, they point out that the instruments selected were not designed to measure changes in variables such as classroom climate or student and teacher self-concept. Nonetheless, the results raise questions as the true effect of Glasser's techniques in actual instructional settings.

Some have identified what they believe to be more foundational concerns with Glasser's ideas than the implementation issues raised by the sort of research studies discussed above. Rich (1979) feels that Glasser's conception of the role of present reality in the process of behavioral adjustment is problematic. He asserts that Glasser glosses over complex issues regarding the nature of reality and how it actually relates to human behavior and ponders whether one can really say that because a person is seen by some as acting responsibly they are "in touch with reality." This begs the question of how objective reality—as a core concept—really is. Whose reality is used as the baseline for assessing a person's orientation toward their behavior? Does everyone perceive the same reality when they look at the world around them?

Additionally, Rich points out that the value judgment element in Glasser's approach to behavioral self-reflection requires judging maladjustment and misbehavior in what are essentially moral terms. Rich asks whether this is ethically acceptable and even if it is, is it therapeutically and/or pedagogically sound? He also raises questions regarding the needs deficiency nature of Glasser's overall model for positive behavior support. The issue here is what Glasser calls basic needs. What is the relationship between "basic" needs and "derived" needs? Rich proposes that needs operate to fulfill objectives and that, in reality, a need is only meaningfully recognized as such if it fulfills an objective which is desirable from the standpoint of sociocultural value systems. In focusing on a concept of biologically rooted genetic core needs, Glasser is not only inconsistent with his objection to the notion of mental illness as a biological manifestation, but also glosses over objectives defined by life circumstances of actual persons functioning in the world which give felt human needs their power to influence behavior.

In addition, Rich points out that those psychologists who employ needs approaches to explain human behavior often disagree about what constitutes a "basic" need. As an example, Maslow's hierarchy of needs markedly differs from Glasser's approach. Beyond this, some psychologists disagree that a deficiency in affection or love from another significant person or group of persons will inevitably lead to the type of psychic stress / emotional illness Glasser describes (Ellis, 1962).

Funnell's ethnographic study (2009) carries on in this same vein by noting fundamental issues related to the very core of Glasser's theoretical framework. Funnell places Glasser's work within a broad tradition of rational choice approaches to behavioral management wherein the focus is placed on modification of personal choices relative to behavioral decisions as a strategy for maintaining discipline and order in institutional settings such as psychiatric hospitals and schools. Funnell's field research led him to the conclusion that such an approach is "over psychologized" in that it overemphasizes a detached focus on singular individuals' decision/choice processes in analyzing behavioral patterns while not paying enough attention to the social dynamics associated with human behavior in institutional settings. This can be seen from the standpoint of both the internal social systems of institutions (i.e., the nature of the interaction patterns between and among members of the institutions) and the sociocultural dynamics outside of the institution that impact the relational patterns within it.

In the case of schools specifically, Funnell posits that classroom disorder is, in fact, a social dynamic which has been mistakenly isolated within psychologically based methodologies associated with student self-reflection and rational choice. Funnell's field observations give some evidence that this approach can lead to unworkable behavior management strategies and place professional staff in ambivalent positions bordering on loss of professional status by way of diminished positional authority and respect (Funnell, 2009). Funnell observes that Glasser's multistep behavior repair cycle can draw the teacher into exchanges with students that can turn into competition for control within the interactive system of the classroom. A failure to understand those dynamics and understand what forms of interaction are present in the institutional environment will lead to the failure of repair protocols of the sort advocated by Glasser. Such approaches cannot be undertaken in an operational vacuum separated from the sociocultural dynamics of the situation. Funnel posits that a failure to take into account how classroom interaction is ordered and structured, how the formal institutional order can come into competition with the informal student order and the institutional effects of student disengagement from learning (student academic biographies and histories) can result in Glasser's protocols actually serving to increase disorder and misbehavior as the teacher can be put in the position of trying and failing to engage a person in a dialogue based on approved set procedures designed to achieve a common purpose. Funnell observed that if the social and cultural determinants of the student's behavioral decisions and the interaction dynamics of the classroom are not fully understood and factored into the process, Glasser's repair cycle protocol can fail and make matters markedly worse (Funnell, 2009).

This relates directly to the question Rich raises with regard to the nature of human needs and the extent to which they can be understood from a purely internalized psychological perspective as opposed to a social, cultural and economic perspective. We are led to ask, then, whether core human behaviors are driven by genetically encoded biologically defined needs or by socioculturally and economically encoded preferences that guide decisions based on culturally understood objectives, or whether, in fact, both forces operate concomitantly with their interaction defining the course of behavioral decisions. The answer to this question has great import for the degree to which psychological and/or sociological approaches are employed in the design of positive behavioral support systems in schools.

On a more micro level, criticism has emerged over the years regarding Glasser's opposition to the use of social competition in the classroom, something he sees as an integral part of the traditional reliance of educators on stimulus/response extrinsic motivational theory, the "boss" management approach and the creation of a "failure identity" in public schools which can result in conditions rife with behavioral and discipline problems. Nonetheless, competition is seen by many as a necessary motivational lever that has important "real world" implications for school students in that dealing with it effectively is seen by some as a life skill that people need as they engage the wider world of work and social interaction beyond the classroom (Blair, 1999). It is important to note there that Glasser does see a role for certain forms of what he perceives to be healthy competition within the framework of Slavinesque competitive team group work (Gough, 1987).

Funnell (2009) and White (2005) both raise the issue of "quo bene" with regard to the publishing and consulting industry that has grown up around rational choice behavioral management approaches. This "cottage industry" is part self-help and part academic and William Glasser sits at the center of it. White states that *The William Glasser Institute* promotes Glasser's ideas in an openly commercial way and that Glasser has gone into the business of promoting the dissemination of choice theory for profit. In White's view this has led Glasser to become extreme in his support for rational choice methodologies and to advocate self-help remedies over formal psychiatric treatment in an overly aggressive way.

Finally, in line with Funnell's statements on the possible role of sociological systems analysis in classroom behavior optimization, it must be pointed out that Glasser's approach to the use of cooperative learning techniques in the classroom, as a mechanism through which student needs can be fulfilled, may be a bit naïve and incomplete with regard to the factors he considered in making his recommendations in this area. Although cooperative learning offers advantages relative to addressing the complications inherent in dealing with the learning needs of diverse student populations, it does not necessarily deal with the issue of status differentiation in the classroom, and this issue can pose tremendous difficulties for affecting the sort of needs fulfillment in which Glasser is interested. Classrooms are not unlike other forms of close association of people in a formal and structured setting. There is some form of "pecking order." Cohen (1986) defines "status" as "agreed upon social ranking where everyone feels it is better to have a high rank than a low rank." Students in school will use "status ordering" to arrange themselves into preference ranks within a group (Cohen, 1986). In the school setting, status is linked to expectations of competence, task activity and personal influence. High status students are seen as more competent. This status and the associated competency expectation translates into the student being more active in academic tasks and exerting more influence on the work of any group of which they are a part. Students assign status on the basis of perceived academic abilities and will do so even in cases were the skill in question is not applicable—if the skill is one viewed by students as being an indicator of overall intelligence (e.g., reading ability) (Cohen, 1994; Cohen, Lotan, Scarloss, & Arellano, 1999). On the other hand, students not seen as being competent by their peers will have a low status and will be less active and less influential in the conduct of group work.

In addition, beyond the realm of the academic, we are all socialized to value certain physical and sociocultural characteristics over others (e.g., high socioeconomic status, White skin, male gender, outgoing personalities and social popularity with peers). Students will tend to assign high status to peers who possess these characteristics and lower status to students who do not. Hence, some status characteristics are diffuse and based on general social distinctions and some are specific, based on perceived ability related to a given task or areas of overall intelligence seen as applicable to a given task (Cohen et al., 1999).

Because of the socialization processes outlined above, students come to tasks in the classroom—including those contained within cooperative group work—with differential status levels and these fundamentally affect the way in which students interact with the group and participate in the tasks. "Students who lack traditional academic skills or proficiency in the language of instruction, or who are social isolates, are often perceived as low status students. They barely participate, are often ignored, and frequently are not given a share of the materials or a turn at the activity" (Cohen et al., 1999, p. 84). They are excluded from the group interactions and are denied equity of treatment and opportunity within group dynamics. They are often denied the opportunity to enter into equitable relations with other group members (Cohen et al., 1999). If this status ordering mechanism is left unmonitored and uncontrolled, cooperative learning has the potential to reinforce very real and serious educational and social problems and can make it almost impossible for low status students to fulfill important needs for belonging and personal empowerment. If left unresolved, status issues in cooperative learning groups can work to exacerbate the very issues about which Glasser is so concerned and result in the damaging of students' self-concepts, leaving them frustrated and open to counterproductive behavioral patterns. Direct and structural status remediation by the teacher is a necessary component of cooperative group work and should have been considered by Glasser in making his recommendations in this regard (see Rosenholtz, 1985; Tammivaara, 1982).

Legacies and Reflections: Theories in Perspective

Despite these critiques of, and open questions regarding, Glasser's work, the breadth of its influence is undeniable. Glasser's control/choice theory and reality therapy have been used to establish a process that speech/language pathologists can employ in managing and implementing instructional transition services (Easterbrooks & Miller, 1996). These two theoretical propositions have been employed by crisis counselors in public education (Palmatier, 1998). His core ideas have been used in the development of instruments for the assessment of human behavioral components such as the Hutchins Behavior Inventory. Glasser's conception of the most basic of human needs underlying control/choice theory has even been used as an operational framework for completing functional assessments of behavior under the Individuals with Disabilities Education Act (Mishler & Cherry, 1999). In addition, one can see the theoretical and practical balance between corrective individual treatment intervention and preventative environmental restructuring that Glasser worked to effect in his research and practice in schoolwide positive behavior support programs so popular with educational administrators at present.

Through his entire career, Glasser was, penultimately, a psychiatrist and a humanist. As Roger Zeeman has noted (2006), Glasser strove to "seek, find, encourage and applaud development of the most positive characteristics in people" (p. 47). He sought out a different approach to working with people that created the basis for raising self-esteem and personal empowerment. True to his roots as a counselor and therapist, he viewed education as a developmental process of change in which the person acquires new identities through self-reflection and personal growth. In the final analysis, he viewed schools as environments which must be dedicated to the recognition of the worth and dignity, rights and needs of every person. Part of this recognition was the idea that with rights come responsibilities to oneself and to others. So, in the end, human behavior and the responsibilities associated with it are social constructs—they are measures by which we gauge the depth of our humanity and the quality of our relationships with others.

References

Blair, K. D. (1999). Transmission versus transformation: A qualitative case study and critique of the Glasser quality school model. *Journal for a Just and Caring Education, 5*(3), 298-317.

Brandt, R. (1988). On students' needs and team learning: A conversation with William Glasser. *Educational Leadership, 45*(6), 38-45.

Brophy, J. (1982). Supplemental group management techniques. In D. L. Duke (Ed.), *Helping teachers manage classrooms.* Alexandria, VA: Association for Supervision and Curriculum Development.

Charles, C. M. (1989). *Building classroom discipline* (3rd ed.). New York, NY: Longman.

Charles, C. M. (2010). *Building classroom discipline* (10th ed.). New York, NY: Pearson.

Cohen, E.G. (1986). *Designing groupwork: Strategies for the heterogeneous classroom.* New York, NY: Teachers' College Press.

Cohen, E. G. (1994). Restructuring the classroom: Conditions for productive small groups. *Review of Educational Research, 64* (1), 1-35.

Cohen, E. G., Lotan, R. A., Scarloss, B. A., & Arellano, A. R. (1999). Complex instruction: Equity in cooperative learning classrooms. *Theory into Practice, 38*(2), 80-86.

Easterbrooks, S. R., & Miller, D. L. (1996). Expanding the role of speech-language pathologists in instructional transition via Glasser's choice theory. *Journal of Children's Communication Development, 18*(2), 73-81.

Ellis, A. (1962). *Reason and emotion in psychotherapy.* New York, NY: Lyle Stuart.

Fletcher, M. J. (1974). *Glasser's discussions in elementary school.* Washington, DC: U.S. Department of Health, Education and Welfare, National Institute of Education. (ERIC Document Reproduction Service No. ED113621)

Frazier, S. L., & Laura, R. S. (1972). Reality therapy: A critical examination. *Pastoral Psychology, 23*(220), 39-49.

Funnell, R. (2009). Struggles for order and control of school behaviour: A sketch for a social psychology. *Social Psychology of Education: An International Journal, 12*(4), 481-499.

Glasser, W. (1965). *Reality therapy: A new approach to psychiatry.* New York, NY: Harper & Row.

Glasser, W. (1977, February). *Schools without failure–1977, Glasser's approach to discipline–Realistic and working.* Paper presented at the annual meeting of the American Association of School Administrators, Las Vegas, NV. (ERIC Document Reproduction Service No. ED137958)

Glasser, W. (1978). Disorders in our schools: Causes and remedies. *Phi Delta Kappan, 59*(1), 331-333.

Glasser, W. (1985). *Control theory in the classroom.* New York, NY: Perennial Library.

Glasser, W. (1990). The quality school. *Phi Delta Kappan, 71*(6), 424-435.

Glasser, W. (1992). The quality school curriculum. *Phi Delta Kappan, 73*(9), 690-694.

Glasser, W. (1996). Then and now: The theory of choice. *Learning, 25*(3), 20-22.

Gough, P. B. (1987). The key to improving schools: An interview with William Glasser. *Phi Delta Kappan, 68*(9), 656-652.

Harris, M. F., & Harris, R. C. (1992). Glasser comes to a rural school. *Educational Leadership, 50*(3), 18-21.

Johnson, D., Johnson, R., Holubee, E., & Roy, P. (1984). *Circles of learning: Cooperation in the classroom.* Alexandria, VA: Association for Supervision and Curriculum Development.

Keepes, B. D. (1973, March). *A school without failure: A description of the Glasser approach in the Palo Alto Unified School District.* Paper presented at the American Educational Research Association annual meeting, New Orleans, LA. (ERIC Document Reproduction Service No. ED081062).

Masters, J. R., & Laverty, G. E. (1974). *The effects of a school without failure program upon classroom interaction patterns, pupil achievement and teacher, pupil and parent attitudes (Summary report of first year of program).* Washington, DC: U.S. Department of Health, Education and Welfare, Office of Education, National Center for Educational Research and Development, Region III.

Mishler, J. A., & Cherry, S. (1999, March). Correlating Glasser's choice theory to the behavioral requirements of IDEA 97. In *Rural Special Education for the New Millennium, Conference Proceedings of the American Council on Rural Special Education.* (ERIC Document Reproduction Service No. ED429741).

Palmatier, L. L. (Ed.). (2000). *Crisis counseling for a quality school community: Applying William Glasser's choice therapy.* Bristol, PA: Accelerated Development, Taylor and Frances Group.

Rich, M. J. (1979). Glasser and Kohl: How effective are their strategies to discipline? *NASSP Bulletin, 63*(428), 19-26.

Rosenholtz, S. J. (1985). Modifying status expectations in the traditional classroom. In J. Berger & M. Zelditch, Jr. (Eds.), *Status, rewards, and influence* (pp. 445-470). San Francisco, CA: Jossey-Bass.

Savage, T. V., & Savage, M, K, (2010). *Successful classroom management and discipline: Teaching self-control and responsibility.* Thousand Oaks, CA: SAGE.

Shearn, D. F., & Randolph, D. L. (1978). Effects of reality therapy methods applied in the classroom. *Psychology in the Schools, 15*(1), 79-82.

Tammivaara, J. (1982). The effects of task structure on beliefs about competence and participation in small groups. *Sociology of Education, 55*, 212-222.

Welch, F. C., & Dolly, J. P. (1980). A systematic evaluation of Glasser's techniques. *Psychology in the Schools, 17*(3), 385-389.

White, C. (2005). Warning: Psychiatry can be hazardous to your mental health. *Primary Care Companion Journal of Clinical Psychiatry, 7*(2), 76.

Zeeman, R. D. (2006). Glasser's choice theory and Purkey's invitational education—Allied approaches to counseling and schooling. *Journal of Invitational Theory and Practice, 12*, 46-51.

Author Contact Information: John A. Cassell, MLS, MA, doctoral candidate, University of the Pacific, Benerd School of Education, 3601 Pacific Ave., Stockton, CA 95211. Telephone: 209-946-3253. E-mail: j_cassell@u.pacific.edu

CHAPTER 59

Beyond Compliance and Control

Creating Caring Classrooms—Alfie Kohn's Alternative to Discipline and Management

Andrea M. Guillaume
California State University

An outspoken critic of many U.S. schooling practices, Alfie Kohn offers his approach to working with students as "a modest effort to overthrow the entire field of classroom management" (Kohn, 2006a, p. 138). He implores educators to examine the assumptions, intents, methods, and effects of conventional discipline programs and practices, reasoning that such an examination inevitably leads to the conclusion that schools focus on compliance and control rather than on autonomy, care, or community. Kohn provides a framework—a "practical alternative" to management and discipline—for teachers to transform their practice.

Trained in the social sciences, Alfie Kohn is a prodigious writer who addresses a wide array of topics. His works range from psychology to business management. In his many writings in public education, Kohn criticizes deeply entrenched traditions such as academic standards, competition, and homework. Although he has classroom teaching experience, Kohn laments that his classroom experience serves as the "basis for a lesson not in pedagogy but in humility" (Kohn, 1998, p. ix). Instead, Kohn formed his approach to management and discipline through wide reading, research, and observation of excellent teachers (Kohn, 1998).

This chapter explores Kohn's theory, discusses its development, examines its generalizability, reflects on critics of its components, and investigates some empirical studies that employ it. Although this chapter addresses many of Kohn's works (given in the reference list, also highlighted on Kohn's homepage at http://www.alfiekohn.org), it focuses particularly on the two that most closely relate to his theory of discipline and management: *Beyond Discipline: From Compliance to Community* (the 10th anniversary edition; 2006a) and *Unconditional Parenting: Moving from Rewards and Punishments to Love and Reason* (2005a).

BEYOND DISCIPLINE: THE THEORY

At the core of Kohn's theory is the notion that schools pursue the mistaken goal of managing students' outward behavior to ensure compliance rather than helping students develop into moral beings capable of acting of their own accord on behalf of others. This section explores Kohn's theory in six subsections that include its overall questioning approach and its major components.

A QUESTIONING APPROACH

Kohn's framework for working with children is driven by a reflective, questioning stance: Teachers individually and as a community must continually ask meaningful, radical ("of the root;" Kohn, 1998) questions. Such questions address both *what is* and *what should be.* Kohn's (2006a) central questions, roughly sequenced and with his responses, include the following:

1. What do children need? How can we meet those needs? Kohn offers these two questions as the force that should drive our decision making in schools. They are very different questions than the question

The Handbook of Educational Theories, pp. 715–723

that seems paramount to conventional discipline programs, namely, "How can we get children to do what we want?" Focusing on the latter question inspires students' temporary, perhaps mindless compliance, but it is unlikely to help us reach our long-term goals for student development.

2. What are our long-term goals for children? Kohn (1991a), like many, holds fast to the aspiration that schools should help students become good people. When Kohn asks parents and teachers what they hope their students and children will be—and be like—they answer with terms like independent, happy, productive, thoughtful, and inquisitive (Kohn, 2005a, 2006a). A subsequent related question then arises:
3. How well do our current structures and practices support attainment of these long-term goals? Kohn holds that typical classroom practices that employ power to effect conformity and compliance—practices like rewards and punishments—run counter to our long-term goals (Kohn, 1993a). Children become independent, moral individuals by reasoning through their actions rather than by being manipulated into behavior. In fact, according to Kohn, "The more we 'manage' students' behavior and try to make them do what we say, the more difficult it is for them to become morally sophisticated people who think for themselves and care about others" (2006a, p. 62). Thus, Kohn is a vocal opponent of behavior modification approaches and other techniques that purely aim to change the ways students act.
4. What are the inherent views of human nature? Each teacher and every discipline program holds a view of human nature, a view that is often implicit and that is accompanied by assumptions about how people will predictably act. Kohn concludes that most discipline programs are based on pessimistic views of children, views that regard humans as power hungry, aggressive, and self-centered. Without strict teacher control, chaos reigns, according to such views. Kohn further suggests that students' behavior can be predicted based on their teachers' view of human nature (if a teacher expects a child to behave selfishly, the child probably will, thus creating a vicious cycle of negative expectations and self-fulfilled prophesies). In *The Brighter Side of Human Nature*, Kohn (1990) explores evidence from many fields to suggest, instead, that humans—even very young ones—are just as likely to behave altruistically as they are to behave selfishly. Examining inherent views of human nature, then, can help educators to discern the motives and methods of discipline practices, and holding optimistic views of human nature is more likely, according to Kohn, to produce effective principles for classroom practice.
5. How do we view disturbances? In conventional classroom practice where compliance and conformity are the goal, disturbances caused by students are typically deemed "misbehavior" and thus demand correction. Similarly, minimization of conflict—a threat to order—is a conventional goal. Kohn argues, instead, that disturbances should be viewed as problems to be solved together by members of a thoughtful community. And, indeed, reasoning through dilemmas and conflicts spurs moral development (Kohn, 2006a). Rather than pursuing the false goals of control and minimization of conflict, in *Punished by Rewards* (1993a), Kohn recommends that teachers and students use the 3 Cs to solve problems: Consider the *content* at issue, *collaborate* for solution, and allow for student *choice.* In considering *content*, we ask what students are being asked to learn or do and determine whether that content is in fact desirable. In *collaborating*, we consult with children—to the extent that their development allows—in order to consider motives and make plans to address the problematic situation. In encouraging *choice*, we provide authentic opportunities for students to exercise autonomy as they solve issues together. Using the 3 Cs turns what some may view as "problems" into opportunities to further students' emotional development.
6. How does the current context contribute to students' actions? Kohn (2006a) argues that, in their quest for conformity, many discipline theorists and programs "blame the kids" when students fail to comply with classroom demands. One example of a "blame the kids" approach is Dreikurs's (1968) formulation of four mistaken goals. According to Dreikurs, if teachers can discover students' mistaken goals (i.e., attention seeking, power, revenge, and display of inadequacy), the teachers can make informed choices about how to address misbehavior. Kohn criticizes this formulation because it assumes a dim view of students and does little to consider the context in which behavior occurs. Another "blame the kids" approach, in Kohn's view, is the Canter's (1992, 2009) popular Assertive Discipline. Assertive Discipline emphasizes a 'no questions asked' demand for compliance. A more recent example of "blaming the kids" is the cry for students to come to school "ready to learn" (Kohn, 2010). "Blame the kid" approaches assume the worst about students (for instance, kids are not ready to learn rather than assuming that schools should be made ready for kids) and fail to consider any explanations for behavior that are external to the student.

Kohn argues that, to conduct more successful and productive analyses of disturbances, teachers must thoughtfully consider many facets of the classroom and schooling environment, reasoning that students' actions usually constitute a reasonable response to the environment and demands at hand. In a variety of his works, Kohn poses the following questions as sparks to fuel educators' development of humane approaches and responses to disturbances.

What Does It Mean To Be Well Educated?

In *The Schools Our Children Deserve,* Kohn (1999) demonstrates that is difficult to collectively develop a single good answer to this question; instead we have many bad answers. Kohn's own vision of education and schooling "is defined by a concern for both the fulfillment of each child and the creation of a more democratic society" (p. 120). To the extent that the educational community does not consider its communal vision for education, it is likely to continue to pursue insufficient aims using unsatisfactory means.

What Are We Asking the Students To Do, And Why?

Both for day-to-day events and issues at the international level, students' failure to comply with classroom tasks may be related to the inherent unworthiness of the tasks themselves. In a number of sources including *What Does It Mean to Be Well Educated?* (Kohn, 2004a; O'Neil & Tell, 1999) Kohn argues that the standards-based curriculum with its emphasis on isolated then sequenced facts taught through the transmission model of instruction provides low-quality teaching that holds little interest or meaning for students and cannot meet the needs of children in a variety of contexts. Kohn supports instead learning activities that are driven by students' questions and that include rich opportunities for decision making. The U.S. practices of plentiful and routine homework should give similar cause for question (Kohn, 1996), as should our overreliance on the measurement of learning through standardized testing (Kohn, 2000). In the face of students' lack of interest in school activities, structures, and procedures, then, Kohn admonishes us to examine the quality of the tasks we propose.

How Do Our Classrooms Feel, and How Do We Want Them to Feel?

By raising these questions, educators can consider classroom life from the students' perspective and take responsibility for the many factors of classroom life that they can in fact change.

Is It a "'Doing-to' Or 'Doing-With' Students" Strategy?

In contrast to traditional classrooms where students have little say over their days or destinies, Kohn urges educators to involve students to the full extent possible in making choices about how to set up and maintain the classroom environment, about what and how they learn, and about how problems are to be solved. Students become independent only through plentiful practice of making meaningful decisions, and students who have no voice in the classroom quickly disengage (Kohn, 1993b).

Who Benefits?

As educators plan their discipline and management approach and as they respond to disturbances, Kohn encourages them to ask who benefits by the proposed strategy or approach. He reminds us that students' needs—not teachers' preferences—should be the criteria by which we make our decisions. For example, although the practice of "time out" (teacher-imposed isolation from the group) can meet the teacher's immediate preference for quiet through the removal of a student behaving obnoxiously, "time out" does little to support the student's academic or social learning and might cause other detrimental outcomes.

Thus, these and other questions pertaining to the classroom context need to be examined as we choose our discipline course. In order to respond effectively to students' behavior, we must consider the context in which it occurs. According to Kohn (2006a), "An authentic response to the behavior calls upon us to examine the whole of that context and consider changing it" (p. 21). At its core, then, Kohn's approach requires educators to pursue an ongoing, reflective examination of classroom practices and, importantly, to consider changing those practices when they fail to meet students' needs or when they run counter to our vision of who we want students to become.

An Emphasis on Authentic, Trusting Relationships

Although every relationship among classroom participants matters in Kohn's view, a central relationship is the one between teacher and student. In order to form trusting, respectful relationships, teachers must re-envision their roles in significant ways. Rather than serving as the unquestioned authority, they must act as partners in the educational enterprise. They must be real people (fragile and imperfect) who focus on building authentic connections with and among their students. They must view their students as having valuable perspectives and opinions, and they must regularly seek out those perspectives. Teachers must actively communicate their faith in students as people who can, with support, make moral, responsible, caring choices.

Warm and secure relationships between adult and child do not rely on displays of power. Typical schooling practices such as coercion, praise, rewards, and punishments thus have no place in Kohn's classrooms or schools. Kohn writes frequently about the perils of punishments and rewards; a recent example is Kohn's opposition to the "carrot and stick" approach employed by the No Child Left Behind Act (Kohn, 2010). At the classroom level, among their many negative effects, practices based on punishment and rewards warp the adult/child relationship; a relationship that should be based on care, concern, and cooperation becomes one that requires the adult to act as a feared enforcer or as "a goody dispenser on legs" (Kohn, 2006a, p. 36).

Rather than doing things *to* students, teachers in authentic relationships with students do things *with* them. They provide structure and support while minimizing the use of control. They model, guide, provide reasons, and communicate their unconditional love and acceptance for children (Kohn, 2005a, 2006a, 2009). They value the students unconditionally for who they are rather than what they do (Kohn, 2005b).

> [Unconditional teachers] … are not afraid to be themselves with students—to act like real human beings rather than crisply controlling authority figures. Their classrooms have an appealing informality about them. They may bring in occasional treats for all their students for no particular reason. They may write notes to students, have lunch with them, respond from the heart to their journal entries. Such teachers listen carefully to what kids say and remember details about their lives: "Hey, Joanie. You said on Friday that your mom might take you to the fair over the weekend. Did you go? Was it fun?" (p. 23)

And when unconditional teachers respond to troublesome behavior, they do so in ways that demonstrate their steady concern for students, regardless of the students' behavior. Kohn illustrates with an example of a teacher who responded to a challenging student as follows:

> You know what? I really, really like you. You can keep doing all this stuff and it's not going to change my mind. It seems to me that you are trying to get me to dislike you, but it's not going to work. I'm not ever going to do that. (Watson, 2003, p. 2, as cited in Kohn, 2005b)

In fact, unconditional teachers—teachers in authentic relationships—act on the understanding that more challenging the students, the more important it is that teachers forge connections with them and that they persevere with caring and trust.

Letting Go of Control

If we hold as important the long-term goals of students' autonomy and ethical, social, and moral development, we face a basic conflict, says Kohn, between those goals and two other things: Our short-term classroom goals of compliance obedience, and our methods of bringing about our short-term goals. Compliance and obedience run counter to autonomy, and when students concern themselves with complying with the dictates of others, they necessarily have less opportunity to develop their own principles for ethical and caring behavior. The problem with controlling behavior is twofold. First, it addresses only surface-level, explicit behavior; it does not address students' perspectives or motivations. Second, it does nothing to help students develop into autonomous, good, caring, ethical, responsible people (Kohn, 2006a). It is therefore critical in Kohn's theory that teachers abandon the goal of student control.

Letting go of the goal of control entails discarding the prevalent classroom methods used to establish that control: coercion, punishment, and rewards. Through coercion, schools simply force students to do as they say. We might ban certain items at school, or compel students to wear uniforms. Through punishment, schools attempt to change students' future behavior by providing an aversive intervention. We might use detention, suspension, and expulsion, for example. Through rewards, schools attempt to influence behavior by providing a response seen by the student as pleasant. We might provide public praise, gold stars, or pizza as an incentive for reading.

Coercion, rewards, and punishment can be effective at gaining short-term compliance, but, holds Kohn (1993a), they fail in every other respect. They do little to teach students to be good people or to consider the effects of their actions on others; in fact these techniques most often produce results that are counter to our long-term goals. They encourage students to form self-centered perspectives where they make decisions based on perceived benefit for self and remain thoughtlessly dependent on others.

More recent discipline programs claim to support students' emotional and social development in democratic settings; however, they employ the traditional "do things to students" tactics: They continue an emphasis on reward, and they repackage coercion and punishment through techniques like Time Out and "choices." Punishment is thinly disguised as "consequences." Such techniques still insist upon compliance as dictated by the teacher by attempting to change student behavior by manipulating what happens to students (Kohn 2006a).

Abandoning Behavior: Constructing Moral Reasoning

Abandoning our attempts to control students aids us in casting aside our emphasis on students' behavior so that we can focus instead upon the process of making "moral meaning" (Kohn, 2006a). Kohn contends that, just as children construct academic concepts, they construct ethical principles. Teachers must actively include students in the process of developing and justifying ethical principles, remaining present from the start and providing structure and support for students' efforts. They must use a democratic approach that focuses not solely on behavior but on action (behavior plus underlying reasons) in order to assist students in developing morality.

In Kohn's (2006b) words, teachers must look *through* a given action to understand the motives that drove it and to help shape future actions. For example, an observer views the same behavior in two different lunchrooms: One student shares his lunch with a peer who does not have lunch. The same act might mean very different things, things that are not outwardly observable. One sharer, for example, may have been hoping the teacher would see him sharing and thus praise his generosity. The other sharer may have had no interest in the teacher's opinion and instead simply may have been concerned that his peer would go hungry. In order to help the students derive moral meaning from the lunch-sharing act, the teacher should avoid praise ("I'm so proud of you when you share!") and instead focus on the effects of the act on the lunch recipient ("Boy, would you look at Jaime's face! He is one happy guy now that he has enough to eat, isn't he?" [p. 70]). Central to helping students derive principles for ethical behavior is the effort to overcome our preoccupation with external behaviors, specific behaviorist rules, and the goal of quashing any conflict. Choice is also central.

Choice

Students develop moral meaning—the ability to make choices—by making choices, not by following directions. Classrooms that invite real choice "bring the kids in on it" for decisions related to what and how to learn and for planning issues and issues related to how to treat each other. Choice elicits compliance, but more importantly, it encourages students to become self-directed, and (most importantly) it encourages students to become autonomous problem solvers. Each day in the classroom should engage students in the community of democratic decision making: "Students should not only be trained to live in a democracy when they grow up; they should have the chance to live in one today" (Kohn, 1993b, p. 12).

Community

The context within which students make choices and decisions is a community, wherein students and teacher feel safe, respected, and cared for (Kohn, 2004b). They think in the plural: we. A community is not the same as a collective, wherein there is an emphasis on coercion, conformity, and a lack of true commonalities. Many schooling practices, such as ability grouping and competition, work to destroy community (Kohn, 1986). True community requires time to develop, a relatively small number of participants, and a teacher who is a true member of the larger school community. Strategies for building and maintaining community focus on relationship building and activities to work together toward common ends—including academic goals.

In the community, teachers and students work together to solve problems. Kohn (2006a) gives 10 suggestions for teachers who work on solving problems with their students—and help students develop skills for future problem solution:

1. Work from the strengths of the existing relationship.
2. Teach skills for problem solving: Listening, calming selves, generating alternatives.
3. Adult needs to diagnose what happened and why.
4. Question our own practices.
5. Maximize student involvement: Talk less, ask more.
6. Help kids construct authentic solutions.
7. Help child think about making restitution or reparations.
8. Check back later.
9. Use flexibility about logistics and substance.
10. Minimize punitive impact.

Classroom meetings, in Kohn's vision, present the best forum for democratic decision making and community building. Classroom meetings meet several purposes:

- Sharing: Participants take pleasure in others' experiences and contributions.
- Deciding: Participants make decisions about simple things (such as the room arrangement) and sophisticated ones (such as the class's social action project).
- Planning: Participants decide how to bring about classroom goals and events.
- Reflecting: Participants tackle questions such as, "What kind of place should the classroom be?"

Kohn cautions against "meetings" that are highly controlled by the teacher and that consequently limit students' opportunities to select and solve important issues. True meetings should be student directed. He also cautions against ritualizing the classroom meeting, arguing that the democratic, community-centered approach pursued in the classroom meeting should be pervasive throughout the day. In sum, meetings and a democratic approach place "community" at the center of classroom life; through their communities, teachers and students together pursue meaningful choices, and make decisions through consensus. They welcome conflict and struggles as opportunities to grow.

The Development of Kohn's Approach

Kohn is very much a current theorist. Born in Florida in 1957, Alfie Kohn was educated at Brown University and at the University of Chicago, where he earned a master's degree in the social sciences. He taught at the high school and college levels. He has written a dozen books and scores of articles, many centering on educational issues such as standardized testing, homework, and the purpose and practices of schooling. He is an independent scholar, not currently associated with a university or other institution. Notably, Kohn is cautious about sharing biographical information. On his website, Kohn notes that he would rather readers focus on the quality of his ideas as they stand rather than filtering those ideas through a biographical lens (Kohn, n.d.).

The approach Kohn explicates in *Beyond Discipline* is a remarkably consistent one, drawing from many fields and from Kohn's own earlier works. Early influences on Kohn's work include Dewey with his progressive approach to education and Piaget with his emphasis on the construction of meaning (Kohn, 2006a). We see Dewey's influence, for example, in Kohn's emphasis on a progressive, meaning-centered curriculum—one organized around problems, projects, and questions—rather than one organized by discrete and sequenced outcomes (Kohn, 1999, 2004a). We see Piaget's constructivist influence in Kohn's emphasis on the construction of moral reasoning, or in Kohn's words, the making of moral meaning (Kohn 2006a).

Although he was educated in the social sciences, Kohn's interests and writings began to pull him toward education in the 1980s (Kohn, 1998), where he rails "against a lot of what goes on in schools chiefly because those practices threaten to eclipse the values I affirm" (p. xii). His *No Contest: The Case against Competition* (Kohn, 1986) led Kohn to alternatives to competition (cooperative learning), which led to his interest in collaboration (cooperation without extrinsic reinforcers) and the processes by which people learn (constructivism). From there, Kohn studied the deleterious effects of extrinsic reinforcers on learning and a number of other outcomes. Examination of reinforcers led Kohn to an investigation of human nature and influenced his optimistic view of our species. In terms of management and discipline, this trajectory led Kohn to practices that encourage children to become compassionate, caring people. Thus, despite the fact that Kohn (1998) claims never to have had a focused scholarly agenda and instead pursued the questions of interest at the time, his approach to management and discipline reflects his far-ranging exploration of human nature, motivation, and relationships in a manner with tight logical consistency.

Validation

To this point, Kohn (2006) has not conducted primary research. Nor do there seem to exist studies by other researchers attempting to validate Kohn's approach. This perhaps is a result of the fact that Kohn offers not "yet another discipline plan to be placed alongside those that are already out there" (p. xiii), nor a recipe, nor a set of techniques for gaining student compliance. Additionally, Kohn states that his aim has not been to develop an approach that can be tested as much as it is to synthesize already tested ideas (A. Kohn, personal communication, January 11, 2011). He cites, for instance, studies that support the building of community, the importance of autonomy, and the perils of rewards and punishments. Kohn's contribution is primarily its sharp reaction to existing theories and approaches and its consideration of greater possibilities.

Kohn (1991a, 2006a) admits a deep appreciation of the work done through the Child Development Project, a systematic, school-wide attempt at prosocial education. Though not based on Kohn's work, the Project put into place many of the tenets central to Kohn's approach such as an emphasis on warm and caring teacher/student relationships, the development of democratic communities, the use of classroom meetings, and the rejection of rewards and punishments. Now modified and deemed the Caring School Community, the project has demonstrated positive effects on some aspects of student behavior (such as spontaneous pro-social behavior and helping behavior). Effects on students' values and academic performance appear positive—particularly in high-implementation sites—but less certain (Battistich, Schaps, Watson, Solomon & Lewis, 2000; Institute of Education Sciences, 2007; Solomon, Battistich, Watson, Schaps, & Lewis, 2000).

Generalizability of Kohn's Approach across Cultures, Ethnicities, and Classes

Although there appear not to be studies of the generalizability of Kohn's approach, Kohn explores the generalizability of components of his approach through scholarly analysis of studies from a number of fields and around the world, and he addresses the question philosophically as well. In his appendix to *Unconditional Parenting*, Kohn (2005a) admits the possibility that any description or analysis of human behavior runs the risk of not being universal, and he notes that his approach is necessarily colored by his race, class, and nationality. He then explores the empirical evidence supporting a number of tenets of his approach including coercive and controlling methods, methods that focus more on autonomy, and the use of corporal punishment. Despite the difficulty of drawing conclusions from such evidence, Kohn does find support for practices that deemphasize coercion and cites studies that indicate that, regardless of class, culture, or country, approaches that focus on punishment tend to have on negative results on children. Beyond the empirical evidence, Kohn asks the compelling philosophical question, "Can we declare that some things are just wrong and it's the attempt to *silence* judgment that's more offensive?" (p. 216). Kohn thus advocates the use of his approach for children in a variety of settings, arguing that it's precisely the students who grow up in difficult settings who might most benefit from a humane, caring approach that emphasizes unconditional love and respect.

Critiques of Kohn's Approach

Kohn's writings draw plentiful praise and caustic criticisms. Criticisms are often quite heated (e.g., Rochester, 1998), and Kohn seems to welcome lively debate, often sparking discussions in the literature himself. Authors trade aspersions regarding the soundness of each other's logic, the accuracy of their facts, and their selection or interpretation of the research. Prevalent criticisms and conversations related most closely to Kohn's approach to management and discipline include his denouncement of competition (questioned by Shields & Bredemeier, 2010) and, more frequently, his disparagement of extrinsic reinforcers.

Criticisms and conversations regarding extrinsic reinforcers cover a number of fronts. Strain and Joseph (2004) criticize Kohn's (2001) plea that educators curb the use of praise with young children. Kohn (1991b) and Slavin (1991) debate the necessity and effectiveness of using group rewards in cooperative learning, and even Child Development Project staff joins that discussion (Schaps & Lewis, 1991). A similar debate rages between Kohn (1996) and Cameron and Pierce (1996) regarding the latter's meta analysis of the effects of rewards on intrinsic motivation. One likely conclusion regarding criticisms of Kohn's work is that, with the strong stance he takes, as long as he continues to write, he will continue to draw—and return—fire.

Studies Employing or Investigating Kohn's Approach

Despite the fact that Kohn writes prolifically and is widely cited (Google Scholar counts citations of *Beyond Discipline* alone at greater than 300), I find few studies that employ or investigate Kohn's approach as a whole. Perhaps the reason we see few studies that explore "the Kohn approach" is that Kohn himself does not view his approach as constituting an intact model for classroom management and discipline; rather he sees it as an alternative to set models.

Much research does, however, examine individual components or strategies that Kohn advocates. For example, Marzano, Marzano, and Pickering (2003), in reviewing research on classroom management, found that student-teacher relationships contribute to successful classrooms. As another example, Brophy's (1981) review of research on teacher praise found that praise is used with little credibility; Brophy consequently recommended the infrequent use of classroom praise. Finally, the research on cooperative learning (e.g., Marzano, Pickering, & Pollock, 2001) demonstrates a clear positive effect on student achievement and other outcomes.

One empirical study that does directly employ Kohn's approach is Bentley-Palmer's (2005) master's thesis, *A Generation of Puppets: External Motivation, a Classroom Dilemma*. Intrigued by a Kohn lecture on the potential damages of extrinsic motivators, Bentley-Palmer inquired into the use of extrinsic motivators in four middle school classrooms. Using observation, interview, and paper/pencil surveys, the author gathered the perspectives of students, teachers, and the administrator. Bentley-Palmer found plentiful evidence of the existence of punishments and rewards and concluded that rewards served a number of mis-educative purposes such as limiting students' choices, rupturing relationships, ignoring reason, and discouraging risk taking. Finally, Bentley-Palmer concluded that the use of punishment and rewards tended to concentrate power in the hands of the teachers and the administrator and hold it far from the students' reach.

Although their purpose was different—to review the literature rather than to test ideas through primary research—Marzano, Marzano, and Pickering (2003) also addressed Kohn's work. Specifically, they examined research related to discipline interventions (namely, praise, punishment, and lack of intervention). They conclude that Kohn's distrust of disciplinary interventions is not supported by the research, stating that punishment and reinforcement together result in decreases in disruptive classroom behavior equal to 33 percentile points.

However, Marzano et al.'s (2003) conclusions regarding Kohn's work are ill founded for two reasons. First, Kohn does not—as suggested by Marzano—advocate a "do nothing" approach to helping students behave. He instead advocates a very active approach that focuses on structure, modeling, gentle guidance, and reasoning in order for teachers and students to address problems together. Second, Kohn himself agrees that praise and punishment can indeed be effective for changing students' behavior. Change in behavior is precisely the variable demonstrated in Marzano et al.'s work. However, Kohn, with his critical approach to classroom discipline, would have us question the appropriateness and feasibility of using praise and punishment to achieve our ultimate goal of helping students become ethical people. In sum, there is research to support many of the individual practices Kohn advocates, though few studies explore the use of Kohn's approach as a whole. Kohn's interests in the inner lives of children, in their long-term growth, in their moral reasoning, and in their work as members of democratic communities perhaps lend themselves less well to empirical study than do approaches that focus on easily operationalized and measured external behaviors.

Conclusion

In the afterword to the 10th anniversary edition of *Beyond Discipline*, Kohn (2006a) reminds the reader that

> The moral is that we need to focus on the bigger issues: the counterproductive effects of all rewards and punishments, the importance of staying focused on our long-term goals for students, the value of supporting kids' autonomy rather than looking for cleverer ways to control them, and the urgency of attending to reasons and motives instead of just looking at behavior. (p. 140)

Perhaps Kohn's most valuable contribution to our thought and practice is that his approach causes us to question classroom life as usual and imagine more autonomous and empathetic lives for our children. He provides a set of questions that can continually guide us as we interact with the youth who will inherit our world.

Acknowledgment

The author appreciates Mr. Kohn's timely and helpful conversation regarding culturally relevant classroom discipline and for his review of this chapter.

References

Battistich, V., Schaps, E., Watson, M., Solomon, D., & Lewis, C. (2000). Effects of the Child Development Project on students' drug use and other problem behaviors. *The Journal of Primary Prevention, 21*(1), 75-99.

Bentley-Palmer, S. (2005). *A generation of puppets: External motivation, a classroom dilemma*. Unpublished master's thesis. Pacific Lutheran University, Tacoma, WA.

Brophy, J. (1981). Teacher praise: A functional analysis. *Review of Educational Research, 51*(1), 5-32.

Cameron, J., & Pierce, W. D. (1996). The debate about rewards and intrinsic motivation: Protests and accusations do not alter the results. *Review of Educational Research*, 66, 39-51.

Canter, L., & Canter, M. (1992). *Lee Canter's assertive discipline: Positive behavior management for today's classroom*. Santa Monica, CA: Lee Canter & Associates.

Canter, L., & Canter, M. (2009). *Assertive discipline: Positive behavior management for today's classroom*. Bloomington, IN: Solution Tree.

Dreikurs, R. (1968). *Educational psychology in the classroom* (2nd ed.). New York, NY: Harper & Row.

Institute of Education Sciences. (2007). What Works Clearinghouse: Caring School Community (formerly Child Development Project). Retrieved from http://ies.ed.gov/ncee/wwc/pdf/WWC_Caring_School_042307.pdf

Kohn, A. (n.d.). *Alfie Kohn*. Retrieved from www.alfiekohn.org

Kohn, A. (1986). *No contest: The case against competition*. Boston, MA: Houghton Mifflin.

Kohn, A. (1990). *The brighter side of human nature: Altruism and empathy in everyday life.* New York, NY: Basic Books.

Kohn, A. (1991a). Caring kids: The role of the schools. *The Phi Delta Kappan, 72*, 496-506.

Kohn, A. (1991b). Don't spoil the promise of cooperative learning. *Educational Leadership, 48*(5), 93-94.

Kohn, A. (1993a). *Punished by rewards: The trouble with gold stars, incentive plans, A's, praise, and other bribes*. Boston, MA: Houghton Mifflin.

Kohn, A. (1993b). Choices for children: Why and how to let students decide. *Phi Delta Kappan, 75*(1), 8-18.

Kohn, A. (1996). By all available means: Cameron and Pierce's defense of extrinsic motivators. *Review of Educational Research, 66*(1), 1-4.

Kohn, A. (1998). *What to look for in a classroom … and other essays*. San Francisco, CA: Jossey-Bass.

Kohn, A. (1999). *The schools our children deserve: Moving beyond traditional classrooms and "tougher standards."* Boston, MA: Houghton Mifflin.

Kohn, A. (2000, September 27). Standardized testing and its victims. *Education Week, 20*(4), 60-63.

Kohn, A. (2001). Five reasons to stop saying, "good job!" *Young Children, 56*(5), 24-30.

Kohn, A. (2004a). *What does it mean to be well educated? And other essays on standards, grading, and other follies*. Boston, MA: Beacon Press.

Kohn, A. (2004b). Rebuilding school culture to make schools safer. *Education Digest, 70*(3), 23-30.

Kohn, A. (2005a). *Unconditional parenting: Moving from rewards and punishments to love and reason*. New York, NY: Atria Books.

Kohn, A. (2005b). Unconditional teaching. *Educational Leadership, 63*(1), 20-24.

Kohn, A. (2006a). *Beyond discipline: From compliance to community* (10th anniversary ed.). Alexandria, VA: ASCD.

Kohn, A. (2006b). *The homework myth: Why our kids get too much of a bad thing.* Cambridge, MA: Da Capo Life Long.

Kohn, A. (September 5, 2009). When a parent's "I love you" means "do as I say." *New York Times*, p. D5.

Kohn, A. (2010). "No" to threats and bribes. *Phi Delta Kappan, 92*(1), 18.

Kohn, A. (2010, November 18). "Ready to learn" equals easier to educate. *Huffington Post.* Retrieved from http://www.huffingtonpost.com/alfie-kohn/ready-to-learn-easier-to-_b_785362.html

Marzano, R. J., Marzano, J. S., & Pickering, D. J. (2003). *Classroom management that works: Research-based strategies for every teacher.* Alexandria, VA: Association for Supervision and Curriculum Development.

Marzano, R. J., Pickering, D. J., & Pollock, J. E. (2001). Classroom *instruction that works: Research based strategies for increasing student achievement.* Alexandria, VA: Association for Supervision and Curriculum Development.

O'Neil, J., & Tell, C. (1999). Why students lose when "tougher standards" win: A conversation with Alfie Kohn. *Educational Leadership, 57*(1), 18-22.

Rochester, J. M. (1998). What's it all about, Alfie? A parent/educator's response to Alfie Kohn. *The Phi Delta Kappan, 80*, 165-169.

Schaps, E., & Lewis, C. (1991). Extrinsic rewards are education's past, not its future. *Educational Leadership, 48*(7), 81.

Shields, D., & Bredemeier, B. (2010). Competition: Was Kohn right? *Phi Delta Kappan, 91*(5), 62-67.

Slavin, R. (1991). Group rewards make groupwork work. *Educational Leadership, 48*(5), 89-91.

Solomon, D., Battistich, V., Watson, M., Schaps, E., & Lewis, C. (2000). A six-district study of educational change: Direct and mediated effects of the Child Development Project. *Social Psychology of Education, 4*, 3–51.

Strain, P. S., & Joseph, G. E. (2004). A not so good job with "good job": A response to Kohn 2001. *Journal of Positive Behavior Interventions, 6*(1), 55-59.

Watson, M. (2003), *Learning to trust: Transforming difficult elementary classrooms through developmental discipline.* San Francisco, CA: Jossey-Bass.

Author Contact Information: **Andrea M. Guillaume**, PhD, professor of elementary and bilingual education, California State University, Fullerton Fullerton California, 92834. Phone: 657-278-3237. E-mail: aguillaume@fullerton.edu

CHAPTER 60

Haim Ginott-Congruent Communication

Peggy H. Yates and Hal Holloman
East Carolina University

"I have come to a frightening conclusion. I am the decisive element in the classroom. It is my personal approach that creates the climate. It is my daily mood that makes the weather. As a teacher I possess tremendous power to make a child's life miserable or joyous. I can be a tool of torture or an instrument of inspiration. I can humiliate or humor, hurt or heal. In all situations it is my response that decides whether a crisis will be escalated or deescalated, and a child humanized or dehumanize."
—Ginott (1972, pp. 15-16).

Cloudy with a chance of sarcasm. Sunny with the highest expectations. A teacher's words and actions make all of the difference in the classroom. Haim Ginott challenges us to a standard of professional practice that is decisively *affective* and significantly *effective*. This chapter presents the highlights of Haim Ginott's theory of classroom management. Much of the content in this chapter comes from his book *Teacher and Child* (1972) along with information from *Building Classroom Discipline* by C.M. Charles (2008, 2010). Throughout *Teacher and Child*, Ginott explains his theories of classroom management eloquently and concretely. His major focus centers on the vital role communication plays in teaching, student learning, student behavior and classroom management. While Ginott contends that this language phenomenon makes a lasting impact on students, Charles (2008) asserts that it creates the personal and caring *tone that prevails in classroom discipline theory today.*

THE ORIGINAL DEVELOPMENT OF AND INTERACTIONS OF GINOTT'S THEORY

Early in his career, while working as an elementary classroom teacher in Israel, Haim Ginott began to feel he was not sufficiently prepared to deal with "live" children. These experiences "left him with an appreciation of the problems that confront the well intentioned adults who interact with children" (Gottman, Katz, & Hooven, 1997, p. xiii). Subsequently, these feelings prompted him to pursue additional education, and he earned his doctorate in clinical psychology from Columbia University in 1952. As a graduate student assistant to Virginia Axline, who had been a student of Carl Rogers, Ginott learned Rogers' techniques of "how to communicate empathy by acknowledging and reflecting feelings." He successfully used and shared these strategies as a child therapist and parent educator (p. xiii).

As Chief Psychologist at the Guidance Clinic in Jacksonville, Florida, Ginott worked with troubled children and refined his use of both compassion and boundary setting. During the 1960s and 70s, Haim Ginott's theories of congruent communication gained substantial interest. While he never synthesized the major tenets of his theory into a solid workable management model, many others have taken his ideas and developed their own (Charles, 2008; Gottman et al., 1997; Manning & Bucher, 2001; & Roebuck, 2002).

Ginott's book, *Between Parent and Child* (1965), introduced many parents to strategies that helped them set boundaries with compassion. These strategies were again promoted in Ginott's book, *Between Parent and Teenager,* which was written in 1967. Several years later, Ginott's book, *Teacher and Child* (1972), drew parallels between those parent-child relationships and the relationship between teachers and their students.

The Handbook of Educational Theories, pp. 725–733

Description of Ginott's Theory With Goals, Assumptions, and Aspects Particular to the Theory

In his book, *Teacher and Child* (1972), Ginott shares enlightening examples of positive and effective communication encounters with students. He advocates that teachers must create and sustain the emotional climate for learning by providing both an affective as well as an effective education for their students. He also believes that true discipline is self-discipline—and it occurs one conversation at a time—with small victories with the student. Ginott's theory of classroom management includes vital principles that serve as a guide for teachers.

1. Communication is powerful—the way teachers talk with and to students makes all the difference. Teachers must use congruent communication with sane messages—messages that address the situation at hand rather than the character or past mistakes of a student. Ginott believed that there were no unacceptable children—only unacceptable behaviors. "A teacher's response has crucial consequences. It creates a climate of compliance or defiance, a mood of contentment or contention, a desire to make amends or to take revenge. It affects the child's conduct and character for better or for worse" (Ginott, 1972, pp. 38-39).
2. Learning always takes place in the 'present tense' and is therefore intensely personal to students. When encountering student behavior issues, teachers must address each issue in the here and now—prejudgments about students should not enter into the picture. It is critical for teachers to remember that every student requires and deserves individual personal attention. Ginott illustrates this idea with the following poignant story.

> A teacher distributed new books to her class. The supply ran out before Paul Z., age nine, got his book. He melted into tears. "I am always the last one to get anything," he protested. "Because my name starts with a Z, I get zero. I hate my name. I hate school. I hate everybody." Paul's teacher wondered how to be of immediate help. She wrote him a note
>
> Dear Paul,
>
> I know how sad you must feel. You waited for your new book eagerly, and suddenly—such a disappointment. Everyone got a book except you. I personally am going to see to it that you receive your new book. Paul calmed down, comforted by his teacher's warm words. He will long remember this kind moment (pp. 40-41).

3. Teachers should promote and model self-discipline in their classrooms. When students misbehave Ginott advises teachers to stop the misbehavior using laconic language—language that is brief and to the point—and then teach the student the correct way to behave. While promoting and modeling self-discipline teachers must avoid demonstrating the behaviors they are attempting to eliminate. The process of learning and practicing self-discipline begins with a change in student attitude and is sustained with repeated practice. Self-discipline in students does not occur instantaneously.

Throughout his book, Ginott weaves a picture of teachers at their best. He shares stories of teachers who connect, relate, empathize and guide students with congruent communication—a language that respects students' feelings and the situations they are encountering. When minor misbehaviors occur in classrooms the best teachers do not pry into the causes. They respond with understanding, sympathy, maturity, consolation, and validation of students' feelings and fears. All misbehaviors are addressed without a preoccupation of a student's past history or the thought of his/her distant future—the best teachers deal with the present—the here and now of a situation.

According to Ginott the best teachers do not preach, moralize, impose guilt or demand promises from their students. Thomas Gordon agrees. In his best-selling book, *Teacher Effectiveness Training* (1974) he outlines communication roadblocks that create a strain on teacher-student relationships. One major roadblock is called moralizing, preaching, giving "shoulds" and "oughts". These types of put-down messages most often begin with "You" and convey to students an outside force of power or authority over them (Williams, Alley & Henson, 1999). Moralistic messages communicate to students that the teacher does not trust them, and that they will need to accept what others consider correct behavior. An example of a moralistic message would be "You ought to do the right thing, tell the assistant principal what you know" (Gordon, 1974, p. 81). These moralistic or preaching messages cause students to feel guilty and make students feel they are bad. "You shouldn't do things that are going to bring shame on you and the school" (Gordon, 1974, p. 81).

Ginott also tells his readers that the best teachers prevent a "punitive" classroom culture and treat their students as social equals by inwardly believing and outwardly recognizing them as individuals capable of making good decisions. Conferring dignity on students is of utmost importance to the best teachers. When student problems occur the best teachers empathically describe the situation to the student and then indicate what needs to be done to solve the problem. Finally the best teachers have a hidden skill they rely upon—the practice of asking themselves, "How can I be most helpful to my students right now?" Many classroom misbehaviors and difficulties can be prevented when teachers make use of this skill. Finally, teachers who represent the best of the best do not dictate to students or boss them around—which are acts that demean students and provoke resistance—but rather, invite student cooperation.

Congruent Communication

Teacher language—the manner in which teachers communicate and respond to students—dominates the theories of Haim Ginott. Effective teachers improve life in their classrooms by first examining how they communicate with students. They realize the vital importance of communication and how it affects their students in either a good or a bad way. They know that the difference between an accepting response and a rejecting response can be critical and in some cases fatal to students. Ginott (1972) writes, "Teachers who want to improve relations with children need to unlearn their habitual language of rejection and acquire a new language of acceptance. To reach a child's mind a teacher must capture his heart. Only if a child feels right can he think right" (p. 81). In Capturing Kid's Hearts, Flip Flippen (2010) outlines a training model for nurturing strong relationship between educators and students that are built on trust. He asserts, "If you have a child's heart, you have his head." He acknowledges that creating these relationships in our current environment is a tremendous challenge; however, he believes that "truly remarkable outcomes are possible in a classroom where trust, respect, and caring relationships flourish" (Flippen Education, 2010).

When adults communicate with children, their language reveals how they feel about them. In other words adult language affects the self-esteem and self-worth of children. Consider this quote, "To a large extent, their (adults') language determines his (a child's) destiny" (Ginott, 1972, p. 82). Therefore, teachers must use congruent communication. Congruent communication is in harmony with students' feelings in respect to themselves and their situations. When teachers use congruent communication they convey sane messages—messages that address the situation at hand rather than the character or past mistakes of a student. Children deserve sane messages, and teachers must eliminate the insanities that hide within their language. Insane messages convey feelings of distrust for students' perceptions, disown students' feelings, and make students doubt their own worth. The difference between effective and ineffective communication rests in addressing oneself to a child's situation rather than judging his character and personality. Speaking from his role as a child therapist, Ginott believed that caring communication could drive sick children to sanity (Gottman et al., 1997, p. xi). Therefore, the principles and practices of congruent communication must be shared and used by parents and teachers to establish and maintain positive relationships with children.

Consider this example of addressing the situation rather than the student's character.

> A child spilled paint. Addressing himself to the situation, Teacher A said, "Oh, I see the paint spilled. We need water and a rag." Addressing himself to the child's character, Teacher B said, "You are so clumsy. Why are you so careless?" (Ginott, 1972, p. 83)

Congruent communication has the power to impact and change education. When teachers practice congruent communication their language demonstrates understanding and reveals an awareness of students' feelings. No longer does their language include shame or blame, insults or intimidation. Their language becomes constructive rather than destructive. Congruent communication is an accomplishment that takes effort, practice and self-discipline.

Validation of the Theory

Over the last 30 years, Ginott's theory of congruent communication has influenced the work of many researchers and scholars across various fields of study (Berne, 1964; Faber & Mazlish, 1982; Goleman, 1995; Gordon, 1974; Gottman & Declaire, 1997; Holloman & Yates, 2010). Although his theory of congruent communication was never formalized into a model that allowed for scientific validation, researchers (Gottman & Declaire, 1997; Warner, 1984) have worked to develop observational measures based on his theories. Gottman and Declaire (1998) state, "Ginott's theories had never been proven using empirically sound, scientific methods. But . . . I can provide the first quantifiable evidence to suggest that Ginott's ideas were essentially correct. Empathy not only matters; it is the foundation of effective parenting" (p. 35). John Gottman and Joan Declaire's work with emotional intelligence and their book, *Raising an Emotionally Intelligent Child: The Heart of Parenting* has strong influences from Ginott's theories. Ginott's ideas had such a profound influence on Gottman, Katz, and Hooven (1999) they dedicated their book, *Meta-emotion: How Families Communicate Emotionally,* to him. Furthermore, Faber and Mazlish's (1982) book *How to Talk so Kids Will Listen and Listen so Kids Will Talk,* is based on lessons learned from Ginott as Faber and Mazlish were his students. As previously mentioned, Gordon's best-selling Teacher Effectiveness Training Resources are closely aligned with Ginott's theories and reinforce the importance of revisiting our language of practice in working with students. The

Transactional Analysis Method, presented by Eric Berne, in his book, *Games People Play* (1964) runs parallel with Ginott's theories related to effective and ineffective modes of communication. Berne and Ginott encourage adults (i.e. parents and teachers) to communicate messages to children that set clear boundaries with positive and caring methods.

Generalizability of the Theory Across Cultures, Ethnicities, and Genders

In the ever increasing diversity that permeates our schools of today, Ginott's theories of classroom management address this issue and promote the use of congruent communication among all cultures, ethnicities and genders. His theories encourage the development of positive student perceptions that all students need regardless of their cultural background, ethnic heritage or gender. Ginott's theory of congruent communication has a universal quality and acknowledges that all children, from all cultures, have the right to a learning environment that promotes both cognitive and psychosocial success (Manning & Bucher, 2001).

The Use and Application of Ginott's Theory

Improving Behavior in the Classroom With Best Practice Language

In their book *What Do You Say When...? Best Practice Language for Improving Student Behavior,* authors Holloman and Yates (2010) recognize and extend the tenets of Ginott's theory of congruent communication. Their research revisits teacher language as a key element of our professional practice and strongly supports Ginott's ideas related to how each teacher sets the mood and "the weather" in the classroom every day. During their research Holloman and Yates uncovered a powerful style of language while interviewing exemplary teacher leaders who were recognized by their peers as experts in demonstrating promising and consistent outcomes in the area of classroom management. Holloman and Yates call this language Best Practice Language (BPL), and define it as one's professional language of practice that resonates with others, influences others and produces promising and consistent outcomes.

Former Nebraska Teacher of the Year, Duane Obermier is an example of the exemplary teacher leader who uses Best Practice Language. He states, "I firmly believe in treating students like fellow human beings who have feelings just like I do. They don't appreciate being embarrassed, humiliated, or confronted with problems in front of their peers. But they do respond to kindness, encouragement, a friendly tease, and a smile. I try to teach manners in the classroom by being mannerly. "John, I never interrupt you when you are speaking. Please don't interrupt me" (Williams et al., 1999, p. 63).

In their book Holloman and Yates (2010) present eleven classroom management scenario chapters ranging from "What do you say on the first day of school" to "What do you say to prevent, diffuse and resolve student conflict" to "What do you say to encourage and promote a culture of positive student behavior?" Within these chapters the authors share their theoretical perspective concerning classroom management as well as powerful BPL examples teachers can use to address each classroom management issue. In addition they offer their research-based *Best Practice Language Framework for Improving Student Behavior* with its 11 BPL Word Categories that represent a powerful combination of BPL (see Table 60.1).

The BPL Framework serves as a significant starting point for revisiting one's professional language and provides teachers a reflective model for turning their language of practice into Best Practice Language. The BPL Word Categories within the framework and the outlined goals are clearly aligned with Ginott's classroom management philosophy and the tenets of his theory. Their BPL aligns itself to Ginott's congruent communication. Holloman and Yates (2010) believe when teachers use Best Practice Language from a variety of the BPL categories, they are modeling a high standard of professionalism. Such exemplary professionalism encourages the use of caring, constructive language and promotes a school culture of congruent communication.

Classroom Management and Best Practice Language—Ginott Style

> In discipline whatever generates hate must be avoided. Whatever creates self-esteem is to be fostered.
>
> Good discipline is a series of little victories in which a teacher, through small decencies, reaches a child's heart.
>
> —Ginott (1972, p. 148)

Below are 10 helpful and practical suggestions for creating positive and effective classroom management—Ginott style. Each suggestion is clearly aligned to a BPL category from the *Best Practice Language Framework for Improving Student Behavior*

1. Always be ready to ask yourself—How can I be most helpful to my students right now? Teachers have a hidden asset at their disposal—the opportunity to ask themselves how they can be of help to their students. When this skill is learned and prac-

ticed innumerable student behavior issues can be averted (see Table 60.1, words of understanding).

> Example: Ada, age fourteen, found it difficult to understand algebra. She felt ashamed, too shy to ask for help. The teacher noticed her reticence and offered assistance discreetly and graciously: He said, "Ada, algebra is a very difficult subject. You have to use symbolic solutions. You have to substitute numbers for figures and remember to change the signs when a number is moved from one side of the equation to the other. You may need help with algebra. Ask me when the occasion demands." (Ginott, 1972, p. 41)

2. Do not label students—labeling is disabling. When teachers label students they embarrass students. Even more devastating is the probability that students will live up to the negative label and become what it implies. When teachers make doom predictions about students' futures, they are creating psychological fissures in the lives of children. This practice results in disaster. An effective teacher speaks with students as if they are guests—with respect and care not with disrespect and labels (see Table 60.1, words of hope).

> Example: Simon, age fourteen, was late for school. His teacher said, "What's your excuse this time?" Simon told his story. The teacher answered, "I don't believe a word you said. I know why you are late: You are too lazy to get up on time. I still remember your brother; he too suffered from congenital indolence. If you don't shape up, you know where you'll end up." Instead the teacher should have said, "I don't like to stop and start in the middle of a lesson. Disruptions are annoying." (Ginott, 1972, pp. 99-100)

3. Avoid asking rhetorical "why" questions when discussing behavior. "Why" questions make students feel guilty and defensive. Most students believe "why" stands for a teacher's disapproval, displeasure, criticism or disappointment in them. To some students asking "why" stirs up memories of past blame or shame (see Table 60.1, words of understanding).

> Example: A wise teacher avoids harmful questions (like why). A child said: "I am not prepared for the test." The teacher resisted the temptation to ask why not. He knew that such a question would only provoke excuses, half-truths, and defensive lies. The teacher said, "We have a problem. What's the solution? What are your options?" This nondramatic response has an indelible impact. It conveys respect, safeguards autonomy and leaves with the child the responsibility for his life. (Ginott, 1972, p. 107)

4. No sarcasm or punishment. Sarcasm is almost always dangerous. Teachers should not use sarcasm when communicating with students. Thomas Gordon (1974) includes sarcasm as a major roadblock to communication. He warns teachers to avoid the use of sarcasm. Students want to be treated respectfully and need to be heard. When teachers use sarcasm they inadvertently train their students to go elsewhere to look for solutions to their problems. Sadly, students write these teachers off and do not regard them as persons with whom they would want a relationship (p. 89).

> Example: Andy, age ten, was at the blackboard, trying, unsuccessfully, to explain a problem in multiplication. The teacher said, "Whenever you open your mouth you subtract from the sum of human knowledge." The class roared. Andy stood in stony silence. The teacher asked another boy to solve the problem and told Andy to listen with both ears. Chances are that Andy did not listen even with one ear.... Andy had learned to escape adults' attacks by blocking out their words. (Ginott, 1972, p. 64)

Punishment should never be used. According to Ginott the quintessence of discipline is discovering alternatives to punishment. Punishment results in resentment, bitterness and sometimes vengefulness. It does not make students want to improve, and it does not deter misbehavior (see Table 60.1, words of grace).

> Example: One high school student related, "Our teacher gave us a long sermon on integrity. I listened and laughed inside. She herself teaches us dishonesty and doesn't know it. I was late to school once because I overslept. She said, "That is not a good excuse,' and she punished me. I got the message. The next time I was late I made up a more convincing story." (Ginott, 1972, p. 151)

5. Respect students' privacy. Teachers should never pry when students don't want to discuss personal matters. It's a sign of courtesy and good taste to remain at a distance and wait for an invitation or permission to intervene in personal issues with a student. However, students should be made aware that teachers are available if they want to talk (see Table 60.1, words of relationship).

> Example: This incident was related by a third-grade teacher: "On lunch day, whenever a child approached me crying, I consoled him instead of prying into etiology. The tears would cease. A changed look would appear on the child's face, as if saying: 'You understand. Thank you!" (Ginott, 1972, p. 47)

Table 60.1. Best Practice Language Framework for Improving Student Behavior in the Classroom and Beyond

Instead of	Use	To	So That Students
Permitting students to be irresponsible	Words of accountability	Hold them accountable all along the way	Reach personal accountability
Unintentionally allowing students to become discouraged	Words of encouragement	Rally students with the courage to overcome challenges, obstacles, barriers, failures, defeats, fears, apathy, et cetera	Live a better way; To be all they can be
Harboring ill feelings like unforgiveness and blame	Words of grace	Separate the student from the behavior, forgive their past mistakes and give them another chance to get it right	Experience and practice the power of forgiveness and second chances
Hoping that students find their way	Words of guidance	Help students find a path to success and appropriate behavior	Practice self-management
Unintentionally discouraging and limiting students with low expectations	Words of high expectations	Help students envision and pursue their best	Achieve their full potential
Survival for today	Words of hope	Inspire a vision of a better tomorrow	Hope for and work for a better tomorrow
Speaking only to the minds of our students	Words of love	Touch their hearts and demonstrate love and care unconditionally	Experience and practice the selfless power and purpose of putting others first
Focusing only on the course content	Words of relationship	Establish a caring and positive connection with each student	Develop positive lifelong relationships with others
Allowing a climate of disrespect in your classroom	Words of respect	Demonstrate a mutual admiration for one another	Model respect for self and others
Making assumptions based upon your perspective	Words of understanding	Discover the student's perspective	Experience and practice empathy for others
It's my way or the highway	Words of unity	Nurture a culture of collaboration and teamwork in your classroom	Practice transformational teamwork through collaboration, agreement and cooperation

Source: Holloman and Yates (2010). Reproduced with permission.

6. Promote and model self-discipline/genuine discipline. Teachers must demonstrate self-discipline and good manners at all times. They must live by the law of compassion and never enter into a power struggle with misbehaving students. When confronted with students who misbehave or who challenge them, effective teachers choose their words wisely, select their actions with care and never seek private vendettas against them. As teachers seek to promote self-discipline they must be careful not to display the behaviors they are trying to eradicate (see Table 60.1, words of grace).

   Example: A teacher was about to give his first lesson in a school for delinquent boys. He was very apprehensive. Success and failure hinged on this first meeting. As the teacher walked briskly to his desk, he stumbled and fell. The class roared in hilarious laughter. The teacher rose slowly, straightened up, and said, "This is my first lesson to you: A person can fall flat on his face and still rise up again." Silence descended. Then came applause. The message was received. (Ginott, 1972, p. 147)

7. Invite cooperation from your students. When children are dependent on adults this dependency gives rise to hostility. To minimize hostility effective teachers provide students with opportunities to experience independence and autonomy. For example, independence can be increased by granting students a voice and a choice in matters that affect their existence in the classroom. Effective teachers do not dole out orders or commands—they invite students to cooperate and experience self-reliance. Allowing students to make self-inferred decisions reduces both their defiance and resistance. When students misbehave teachers also invite student cooperation by calmly describing the situation and clearly indicating what needs to be done (see Table 60.1, words of guidance).

   Example: It started to snow. The children ran to the window and began to scream and cheer. I offered them a choice: "You can watch the snow in silence. You can go back to your work. You decide." The noise died instantly. The children watched the snow in delightful calm. (Ginott, 1972, p. 91)

8. Confer dignity on students. Students deserve and should be offered the same respect and dignity that teachers expect. When teachers treat students as social equals and recognize them as individuals who are qualified to make decisions on their own they confer dignity on them (see Table 60.1, words of respect).

   Example: Susan, age twelve, volunteered to assist in cataloguing the books in the school library during the weekend. On Saturday she realized that she was swamped with homework. She regretted her promise, and felt disgruntled and depressed. When she arrived at the library that morning, she was full of tears. Her teacher listened to her story with attentive silence. Then she said, "Feeling so disheartened, you still came to work. That's discipline. That's character. That's integrity." The teacher's words brought an instant balm to Susan. She felt like a heroine, a remarkable person, a responsible individual. (Ginott, 1972, p. 52)

9. Use "I" messages rather than "You" messages. "I" messages allow teachers to describe exactly what they see, share exactly what they feel, and impart their exact expectations. Williams, Alley and Henson (1999) define an "I" message by describing its three components. First most "I" messages begin with 'when' as the teacher explains to the students the specific type of issue/misbehavior that is bothering him/her. The second part of the "I" message describes the effect that the issue/misbehavior is making on him/her in a nonjudgmental way. The last component of the "I" message states the teacher's feeling due to the issue that is happening. For example, "When I'm interrupted while I'm giving directions, I have a difficult time making the directions clear and then I become very frustrated" (p. 67).
   According to Ginott using "I" messages ensures that the teacher addresses the problem at hand not the person or his character. For example, using statements like 'I am appalled—I am annoyed—or I am angry' represent "I" messages and are much more effective than saying to students 'You are a pest—Look what you have done—Who do you think you are?' When teachers become angry they should share their feelings without using humiliating and harmful language. "I" messages focus on sharing how a teacher feels and what he/she expects to happen without blame and humiliation (see Table 60.1, words of high expectation).

   Example: When Mr. Hunt, the fourth-grade teacher, saw his classroom in disarray, he said, "I see books scattered all over the floor. I am displeased and angry. Books do not belong on the floor. They belong in your desks." The teacher deliberately avoided insult, "You are such slobs! You mess up everything in this class. You are so irresponsible." (Ginott, 1972, p. 86)

10. Use appreciative praise rather than evaluative praise. Most teachers are surprised with Ginott's belief concerning the use of praise in the classroom. Ginott contends that evaluative praise is worse than no praise at all and should not be used. Evaluative praise comments on a student's character or talent rather than his effort. It tends to create student anxiety and increased dependency. It does not lead to self-reliance, self-direction or self-control because these characteristics require freedom from judgment from an outside source. Examples of evaluative praise include, "You are being such a good boy by raising your hand" or "You are doing great."
   Appreciative praise recognizes and shows appreciation for a student's effort, improvement or accomplishment. For example, "I can almost feel the waves hitting that boat in your painting" or "Your work today shows me that you understand what we learned yesterday."

   Example: Phyllis, age ten, wrote a poem describing her reaction to the first snow of the season. The teacher said, "Your poem reflected my own feelings; I was delighted to see my winter thoughts put into such poetic phrases." A smile crossed the little poet's face. She turned to her friend and said, "Mrs. A. really likes my poem. She thinks I am terrific." (Ginott, 1972, p. 127)

   This example exemplifies the power of appreciative praise and how this teacher's words of recognition and personal connection enabled the student to make her own inferences concerning her work (see Table 60.1, words of encouragement).

Critiques and Instruments Associated With Ginott's Theory

Although Ginott began his career as an elementary teacher in Israel in 1947 before immigrating to the United States, some educators have expressed concern that Ginott did not work extensively as a classroom teacher. His theories are more "theoretical" and less practical and are not based on real experiences. However, Ginott's experiences in counseling at-risk students as a clinical psychologist provided insight into what children want and need to hear from the adults in their world. Other educators argue that Ginott does not provide a specific list of rules for teachers to follow in the classroom. They also contend that he does not have specific "how to" examples for extremely bad behaviors. Many educators have accepted Ginott's theory of congruent communication because it promotes a bridge between being completely firm and being completely compassionate. Many teachers want to be caring, but they also want to hold students accountable for their behaviors.

Researchers have used Ginott's techniques to develop tools for observing and measuring parent-child interactions—specifically limit setting skills (Warner, 1984). Warner found that Ginott's limit setting behaviors are observable which suggests that other instruments could be developed to observe and measure teacher-student interactions.

Gottman, Katz and Hooven's (1997) research on meta-emotion are greatly influenced by the ideas of Ginott. In fact, the researchers state, "Ginott's work plays a central role in our book because we think that our results on meta-emotion represent the first prospective longitudinal data to suggest that Ginott's ideas were essentially correct (pp. 18-19).

In their article *Revisiting Ginott's Congruent Communication after Thirty Years*, Manning and Bucher (2001) discuss the basic tenets of Ginott's theory. They describe the type of teacher who would feel comfortable and successful following Ginott's theory. This teacher is one who strives to promote cooperation with students and encourages harmony while avoiding autocratic behaviors. The authors share practical ideas of how to apply Ginott's theory in one's classroom along with poignant stories that demonstrate and describe the principles of Ginott's beliefs concerning teacher/student communication, relationships and successful classroom management. By describing a modern day diversity perspective of his theory, they offer an explanation of how Ginott's theories reach all cultures within the classroom. They explain that students no matter what their cultural background require and should possess positive perceptions of both their culture and themselves. As schools become increasingly diverse, Ginott's theories of congruent communication are better suited to address any number of student differences and do not risk making students of any culture feel uncomfortable (p. 217).

Dave Brown (2005) elaborates on the significance of congruent communication in the middle school by delineating five ways teachers can communicate congruently with young adolescents: (1) Use active listening techniques that include such things as frequent eye contact and being certain not to interrupt students while they are speaking. (2) Exhibit proper body language and facial expressions that align with verbal messages. (3) Avoid traditional roadblocks to effective communication with middle school students. (4) Respond to students' feelings of frustration and anxiety with empathy. (5) Use culturally responsive communication with students. This article revisits and extends Ginott's theory of congruent communication by providing specific strategies for connecting with students through careful verbal and nonverbal messages.

As previously mentioned, research conducted by Holloman and Yates (2010) resulted in the Best Practice Language Framework for Improving Student Behavior (see Table 60.1). The framework offers 11 BPL Word Categories that represent a powerful combination of teacher language and is clearly aligned with Ginott's classroom management philosophy and the tenets of his congruent communication theory. Much like Ginott's challenge to teachers, the BPL Framework for Improving Student Behavior serves as a significant starting point for revisiting our professional language and provides teachers a reflective model for turning their Language of Practice into Best Practice Language.

CONCLUSION

Ginott challenges every educator to revisit their language of practice. His works offer concrete language examples of "what to say when" and his book should be in every teacher's library. Ginott realized that his theory would not produce instantaneous results; however, through genuine repetition. He believed his suggestions would lead students to true discipline which is self-discipline. Occurring one conversation at a time, Ginott's tenets can take effect and produce life-changing results.

REFERENCES

Berne, E. (1964). *Games people play: The psychology of human relationships.* New York, NY: Random House

Brown, D. F. (2005). The significance of congruent communication in effective classroom management. *The Clearing House: A Journal of Educational Strategies, Issues and Ideas, 79*(1), 12-15.

Charles, C. M. (2008). *Building classroom discipline.* Boston, MA: Pearson.

Charles, C. M. (2011). *Building classroom discipline.* Boston, MA: Pearson.

Faber, A., & Mazlish, E. (1982). *How to talk so kids will listen and listen so kids will talk.* New York, NY: Avon Books.

Flip Flippen. (2010). Retrieved from http://www.flippengroup.com/education/ckh.html

Ginott, H. G. (1965). *Between parent and child.* New York, NY: Macmillan.

Ginott, H. G. (1967). *Between parent and teenager.* New York, NY: Macmillan.

Ginott, H. G. (1972). *Teacher and child.* New York, NY: Macmillan.

Gordon, T. (1974). *Teacher effectiveness training.* New York, NY: Three Rivers Press.

Goleman, D. (1995). *Emotional intelligence.* New York, NY: Bantam Books.

Gottman, J., & Declaire, J. (1997). *Raising an emotionally intelligent child: The heart of parenting.* New York, NY: Simon & Schuster.

Gottman, J. M., Katz, L. F., & Hooven, C. (1997) *Meta-emotion: How families communicate emotionally.* Mahwah, NJ: Erlbaum.

Holloman, H., & Yates, P. H. (2010). *What do you say when …? Best practice language for improving student behavior.* Larchmont, NY: Eye on Education.

Manning, M. L., & Bucher, K. T. (2001). Revising Ginott's congruent communication after thirty years. *The Clearing House, 74*(4), 215-18.

Roebuck, E. (2002). Beat the drum lightly: Reflections on Ginott. *Music Educators Journal, 88*(5), 40-44.

Warner, D. J. (1984). *A measure of parents' limit setting skills* (Doctoral dissertation). East Carolina University, Greenville, NC. Retrieved from http://www.ecu.edu

Williams, P. A., Alley, R. D., & Henson, K. T. (1999). *Managing secondary classrooms: Principles and strategies for effective management and instruction.* Boston, MA: Allyn & Bacon.

Author Contact Information: **Peggy H. Yates**, PhD, East Carolina University, Department of Curriculum and Instruction, 119 Speight Building, Greenville, NC 27858.Telephone: 252-737-2109. E-mail: yatesp@ecu.edu

Section 9: Assessment Theory

INTRODUCTION

SECTION EDITORS
Samuel O. Ortiz and Dawn P. Flanagan
St. John's University

The application of assessment theories in education has a long and storied history. Indeed, the relationship between educator's desires to evaluate student success and attempts to measure that success dates to the very advent of the field of psychometrics when Alfred Binet was commissioned to identify the lowest performing students in school so that they might benefit from additional or specialized academic intervention (Gould, 1994; Wasserman & Tulsky, 2005). It was in the service of this endeavor that Binet, and later with his colleague, Theodore Simon, developed the first practical, systematic mental test designed specifically to assess and evaluate the learning and capabilities of students at various grades. Binet effectively married a theoretical model of assessment (measurement of mental abilities by requiring individual demonstration of specific academic skill or expression of acquired knowledge under rather controlled circumstances) to an applied educational goal—evaluation of and improvement in student learning (Urbina, 2004). Although Binet's scale was later transformed by U.S. psychologists into the IQ tests we know well today, this example illustrates perhaps the first venture into the application of theoretical model of assessment in the educational realm (Gould, 1994; Urbina, 2004; Wasserman & Tulsky, 2005).

The U.S. public school system has seen immense growth since the early twentieth century and today, more and more students are entering schools than ever before (Rothstein, 1998). Whether spurred by legislation regarding compulsory attendance or economic factors related to technological demands in the workplace, public education has grown significantly in the past century and along with it, the expected and necessary minimum educational standards for entry into the workforce have also increased steadily. Whatever the reasons for this incredible expansion, education has become an integral part of the fabric of our modern society and an extremely important issue in assessing the health of the union from local governance all the way to the federal level. But with such a spot light comes a more critical eye and recent trends in assessing education on the whole has led to widespread practices ranging from evaluation of statewide improvement in student achievement, or school performance via their own "report cards," or even individual teacher effectiveness in promoting student learning and success. For some time now, there appears to have emerged a sense in the psyche of the country regarding a growing discontent at the performance of our nation's schools and more so at the outcomes, many of which are revealing disparities that belie equal opportunity (Darder, 1991). The idea that our schools are not performing up to expected standards has been based on data generated largely on the basis of various assessment models and methods. The goal in each case, of course, has been to identify whether or not performance (by state, district, school, or even teacher) is actually up to standards and if not, what might be done regarding efforts toward improvement (Schultz et al., 2011). As such, education, or as the current catch phrase has it, "educational reform," has become a political mainstay in the United States and no politician can survive election or reelection without having a clear plan for what to do to improve our nation's schools and resolve the problems and disparities that are not acceptable.

From the largest scale (national and state) to the smallest (schools and classrooms), all efforts to evaluate academic outcomes and performance have relied upon one or another theoretical assessment models. Such activities have adopted notions regarding improvement that revolve around accountability which is perhaps best exemplified by recent legislation (i.e., No Child Left Behind, also known as the Elementary and

The Handbook of Educational Theories, pp. 735–737

Secondary Education Act) where funding has been tied specifically to measurable improvements in performance and penalties leveled for lack thereof. The "trickle down" effect of measurable standards for accountability has put a significant amount of pressure on educators and administrators at all levels to demonstrate that what they are doing to instruct, intervene with, and improve the academic attainment of all students, has in fact been successful. To that end, assessment models continue to be implemented in education for a variety of different intents and purposes.

The focus of this section is, of course, on assessment theories and specifically their relevance and application in the educational setting. Assessment theories in education are those that provide a broad framework for understanding how children learn and how we might be able to gauge their learning in school. The focus of assessment may be at the individual level but it can also operate at the group level, particularly when there is an interest in populations who share certain important demographic characteristics (e.g., socioeconomic status, children with disabilities, urban vs. suburban schools, English language learners, etc.). Whether centered on large or small scale questions, such theories are invariably based largely on broader theories of general cognition and learning. That is, how one sets out to evaluate a skill, knowledge base, process, or ability will depend largely on the theory that underlies the assessor's beliefs regarding the nature of those abilities and how they develop or are learned. Thus, theories of assessment in education tend to be based on various models of learning and development where each spells out its own methods and procedures regarding measurement and evaluation (Salvia, Ysseldyke, & Bolt, 2010). In addition to structural and foundational differences, assessment models also tend to vary in terms of their purpose and intent. For example, psychometric theory guides norm-referenced cognitive testing methods which provide information regarding how an individual compares on a range of abilities or knowledge bases relative to other children of the same age or grade. Such information reveals important developmental information relative to the general population but by itself does not necessarily address questions regarding what specifically the individual has actually mastered or not mastered within the academic curriculum. Conversely, the main purpose of criterion-referenced assessment is to reveal what an individual can do or what they know and how accurately they can do it or recall it. Yet, such data may not reveal sufficient information regarding whether the individual is comparable to, ahead of, or behind their age or grade peers in terms of academic skills mastery or knowledge acquisition (Salvia et al., 2010).

This section provides chapters grouped into the three major models of learning and development. The first assessment model is psychometric theory and is perhaps the most influential and certainly the one with the longest history as described previously. Under this model, Willis, Dumont, and Kaufman discuss the application of individual, norm-referenced standardized tests (both cognitive and academic) in the educational setting. It should be noted that although the focus is primarily on individual assessment, the principles that are discussed in the chapter and which govern the structure of this assessment model apply equally well to large groups. In fact, it was the efforts of a group of eminent psychologists during WWI that established the first practical methods for mass mental testing and set a precedent for the development and application of instruments that could be delivered to large numbers of examinees simultaneously, including the Army Mental Tests and later the very SAT itself (Brigham, 1923; Yerkes, 1921).

The second assessment model is based on information processing theory—a framework that has served as the primary foundation for developments and advances in neuropsychology. The first chapter in this group by Schneider, Parker, Crevier-Quintin, Kubas, and Hale provides a discussion on the most significant figure in neuropsychology, Luria, and discusses the major components of the Lurian neuropsychological framework as well as some of the issues regarding its translation into educational practice. The second chapter in this group by Miller provides a further extension of Lurian theory into the practice of applied school psychology to form a theoretical framework known as the school neuropsychology model. The purpose and intent of the school neuropsychology model includes facilitation of clinical interpretation, strengthening the linkage between assessment and evidence-based interventions, and providing a common frame of reference for evaluating the effects of neurodevelopmental disorders on neurocognitive processes related to school learning and academic functioning. The third chapter in this group by Schneider and McGrew represents an attempt to integrate information processing and psychometric theory. That is, the focus becomes one that is centered on both how learning occurs (information processing theory) and how individuals differ in terms of what they have learned (psychometric theory). The primary goal and intent of cognitive performance models is to enhance the work of educators by providing them with the ability to generate information that describes individual cognitive strengths and weaknesses in highly informative detail which also reveals a logical path for addressing or remediating academic deficiencies.

The third assessment theory group is based primarily on learning models and are perhaps the most familiar type of assessments to educators. Learning theories can vary widely but share some common features, notably a focus on individual progress as well as direct and discrete skills instruction followed closely by evaluation to assess progress—sometimes referred to as a "teach, test, teach" approach. The first chapter in this group by Shinn, describes the application of learning theory within a curriculum-based measurement approach. This approach reflects an emphasis on learning and direct instruction by measuring academic achievement and progress by using the very same instructional materials and content with which students are taught. In a similar vein, the purpose and intent of curriculum-based measurement is to provide data that can be used to evaluate the effects of instructional interventions on individual students rather than a group of students. The other chapter in this group by Robinson-Zanartu employs learning theory related to cognitive modifiability which is most often operationalized via an approach known as dynamic assessment. Much like curriculum-based measurement, dynamic assessment can be conducted using the materials from the curriculum but it is not necessarily limited to them. The purpose and intent of dynamic assessment is to first ensure that all the essential elements necessary for successful learning are in place, evaluate the individual's cognitive structures related to learning, directly teach those structures that are not being utilized, mediate the learning process, and evaluate success as well as the ability to generalize the learning.

Assessment theories have long been relied upon for a variety of educational purposes and they remain central to present efforts regarding educational reform and school improvement initiatives. Which theories are applied and when are questions answered primarily by the purpose and intent of the assessment. In education we may wish to examine the level of academic skills or knowledge for all sixth graders in the United States. Or we may wish to know whether the mathematics skills of a particular student are comparable to that of other students in the same district only. Or we may wish to assess whether the lack of academic progress for an individual or small group of individuals is due to ineffective instruction or possibly a learning disorder. All of these and many more of the myriad questions raised everyday with respect to evaluating the education of our nation's children can be addressed in one way or another through careful analysis and deliberate selection of an appropriate assessment theory.

References

Brigham, C. C. (1923). *A study of American intelligence*. Princeton, NJ: Princeton University.

Darder, A. (1991). *Culture and power in the classroom: A critical foundation for bicultural education*. New York, NY: Bergin & Garvey.

Gould, S. J. (1994). *The mismeasure of man*. New York, NY: W.W. Norton.

Rothstein, R. (1998). *The way we were? The myths and realities of America's student achievement*. New York, Ny: The Century Foundation Press.

Salvia, J., Ysseldyke, J., & Bolt, S. (2010). *Assessment in special and inclusive education* (11th ed.). New York, NY: Wadsworth, Cengage Learning.

Schultz, P. W., Hernandez, P. R., Woodcock, A., Estrada, M., Chance, R. C., Aguilar, M. & Serpe, R. T. (2011). Patching the pipeline: Reducing educational disparities in the sciences through minority training programs. *Educational Evaluation and Policy Analysis, 33*(1), 95-114.

Urbina, S. (2004). *Essentials of psychological testing*. Hoboken, NJ: Wiley.

Wasserman, J. D., & Tulsky, D. S. (2005). A history of intelligence assessment. In D. P. Flanagan & P. L. Harrison (Eds.), *Contemporary intellectual assessment: Theories, tests and issues* (2nd ed., pp. 3-22). New York, NY: Guilford Press.

Yerkes, R. M. (1921). Psychological examining in the United States Army. *Memoirs of the National Academy of Sciences, 15*, 1-890.

Author Contact Information: Samuel O. Ortiz, PhD, Department of Psychology, St. John's University, Jamaica, NY 11439. Telephone: 718-990-5926. E-mail: ortizs@stjohns.edu

CHAPTER 61

Individual Norm-Referenced Standardized Assessment

Cognitive and Academic

John O. Willis
Rivier College

Ron Dumont
Fairleigh Dickinson University

Alan S. Kaufman
Yale University School of Medicine

One of the more prominent, and perhaps most influential, traditions in assessment is psychometrics. Psychometrics is the field of study concerned with the theory and technique of psychological measurement, which includes the measurement of knowledge, abilities, attitudes, personality traits, and academic skills. The field is primarily concerned with the construction and validation of measurement instruments, such as questionnaires, tests, and personality assessments.

Although a general distinction is usually made between tests of ability/aptitude (intelligence tests) and tests of achievement (academic proficiency), both of these domains typically utilize the theoretical bases of psychometric theory, which recognizes the importance of reliability, validity, acceptable norming samples, and standard procedures for administration, scoring, and interpretation.

This chapter will examine the principles of the psychometric approach as they apply to individualized, norm-referenced standardized assessment. Examples used will come primarily from the field of cognitive assessment, although the general principles apply to most psychological and educational measures.

Psychometric Theory: Individual Norm-Referenced Standardized Assessment

Psychometric theory for individual, norm-referenced, standardized assessment rests on several essential foundations.

Foundations of Psychometric Theory

- Persons possess, and differ in, certain abilities, such as vocabulary, visual-motor speed, and reading comprehension.
- These individual abilities are manifested in—and can be inferred from—overt behaviors, such as defining words, answering factual questions, solving puzzles, rapidly copying rows of symbols with a pencil, and correctly filling in missing words removed from a reading passage.
- Tests can be constructed to measure performance on a relatively small sample of the overt behaviors, such as a list of words to be defined, a list of questions or

The Handbook of Educational Theories, pp. 739–749

set of puzzles, a page with rows of symbols to be copied, or a set of reading passages with every fifth word blanked out.

- The test can be "standardized" with a standard set of instructions that includes the precise items, particular wording of instructions and other aspects of test administration, and rules for scoring responses to the test items (such as pass/fail, different point values for various possible responses, or scores based on the time required to complete the task correctly).
- The strength of the underlying ability can be estimated from performance on the test.
- Test performance can be summarized by *a score* on the test, such as the number of items completed correctly or points earned according to the standardized scoring rules.
- A standardized test can be *normed* by administering it to a representative *sample* of people and using those persons' scores as a yardstick for assessing the performance of other persons who take the test.
- The *reliability* of the test can be determined by various statistical means, such as (a) repeating the test and seeing how close the two scores are to each other, (b) comparing scores on two or more equivalent, alternate forms of the test, and (c) comparing performance on one part of the test with performance on another part of the test.
- The *validity* of the test can be determined by other statistical means, such as comparing test scores to other estimates of the same ability. For example, individuals' scores on an intelligence test could be compared to their scores on another intelligence test, to their academic marks in school, to their highest level of educational attainment, to their vocational success, or to some other measure presumed to reflect "intelligence."

The Original Development and Iterations of Psychometric Theory

Although we might think of assessment as a modern-day creation, it actually has its roots dating back more than 4,000 years (Kaufman, 2009). The Emperor of China, around 2200 B.C., reportedly gave triennial proficiency tests to his officials, a practice that continued for quite some time. About a thousand years later, at the start of the Chan dynasty, formal ability tests were required for candidates for office—a policy that might appeal to some voters today. There is even a biblical reference to mental examinations (Judges 12:46), a one-item test given by the Gileadites to identify the fleeing Ephraimites hiding among them ("Pronounce the word 'shibboleth'") (Wainer, 1990). Never have the results of a test had harsher consequences than the biblical exam. The bodies of the 42,000 who mispronounced the word and flunked the test decorated the Jordan River (Wainer, 1990). Today, the Americans with Disabilities Act would have prevented the application of this test to persons with speech articulation disorders.

Much of the early theoretical and applied work in psychometrics was undertaken in an attempt to measure intelligence. Sir Francis Galton, often referred to as the father of psychometrics, devised and included mental tests among his anthropometric (measurement of persons) measures. Galton, a half cousin to Charles Darwin, earned awards for his explorations of southern Africa, invented instruments for charting the weather, and translated his half cousin's ideas about evolution into the study of genetics and mental measurements (Cohen & Swerdlik, 1999). He became the first scientist to actively study individual differences in the ordinary man, not just the tail ends of the normal curve. He developed mental tests that were a series of objective measurements of such sensory abilities as keenness of sight, color discrimination, and pitch discrimination; sensory-motor abilities such as reaction time and steadiness of hand; and motor abilities including strength of squeeze and strength of pull (Cohen & Swerdlik, 1999). Galton's tests were scientific, objective, reliable, consistent, accurate, and accepted. And, because he said so, they were valid measures of intellectual ability.

Interestingly, the origin of psychometrics also has connections to the related field of psychophysics. Besides Galton, two early pioneers of psychometrics, James McKeen Cattell and Charles Spearman, obtained doctorates in the Leipzig Psychophysics Laboratory under Wilhelm Wundt.

James Cattell, who coined the term "mental test," established a Galtonlike mental test laboratory in 1890 at the University of Pennsylvania. Cattell (1890) moved his laboratory to Columbia University in New York City the next year, and IQ testing in the United States was born. Following Galton's approach, Cattell developed 50 tests of sensory capacity, discrimination, and reaction time; his goal was to select superior individuals for responsible positions.

Spearman (1904, 1927) is known as the father of classical test theory, which treats a measurement (e.g., a numerical score on a test item or on a whole test composed of various items) as consisting of a "true score" plus an "error" component. Spearman's best known and most widely used contribution to statistical methods is the rank-order coefficient of correlation that bears his name, although he was also instrumental in the development of modern factor-analytic methods.

Alfred Binet and his colleagues (Binet & Henri, 1896; Binet & Simon, 1905, 1916/1980) moved intelligence assessment from psychophysics to oral questions, puzzles, and skills that we would today recognize as components of modern-day intelligence tests. Lewis Terman (1916; Terman & Merrill, 1937, 1960) translated the Binet-Simon scale into English, substantially revised and adapted it for an American population, normed his Stanford-Binet scale on a sample of examinees, and introduced the statistical IQ score (the ratio of mental age to chronological age). David Wechsler (1939) applied to his individual intelligence test (the Wechsler-Bellevue Intelligence scale) two concepts that had been used for group tests: subtests with separate scores to be summed to derive the total score and IQ and subtest scores expressed as standard scores, based on their means and standard deviations, a significant improvement over Terman's ratio.

The history and development of the theories and practice of intelligence testing are discussed in Kaufman (2009) and Sattler (2008, Ch. 7-8).

Two Branches of Psychometric Theory

Modern psychometric theory has two main branches. Classical test theory, mentioned above, has been developed to considerable levels of sophistication. Lord and Novick (1968) offer a detailed and highly technical explanation of classical test theory. Although the newer item response theory (IRT) is increasingly used as the basis for test development and standardization, many test manuals and practicing psychologists still apply classical test theory to interpretation of tests and scores.

The more recent development that has come to dominate construction of current tests—IRT (e.g., Rasch, 1960; Woodcock & Dahl, 1971; Wright & Stone, 1979)—allows both the difficulty levels of test items and the ability levels of examinees to be measured on the same scale. This joint scale allows us to predict the likelihood of success of any examinee of known ability on any item of known difficulty. It permits not only the traditional scores from classical test theory (percentile ranks, standard scores, and age- or grade-equivalent scores), but also statements of an examinee's probable proficiency at age-appropriate or grade-level tasks. IRT also permits adaptive testing so that the examinee can take only a relatively small number of items clustered around that examinee's ability level. A score can be calculated from that small number of items, rather than from a large number of items including many that are too easy or too difficult for the examinee. One application has been the development of computerized tests, on which the next item is selected on the basis of the examinee's response to the current item, so that the difficulty level is constantly adjusted to center around the examinee's ability level on the task (Wainer, 1990). IRT also permits calculation of separate reliabilities and standard errors of measurements for different groups of test items within a scale and even recalculation of a normative score omitting a test item that was spoiled or that was inappropriate for the examinee. Alan Birnbaum (1968) contributed an early discussion of this theory to Lord and Novick's (1968) text. Embretson and Reise (2000) offer an accessible, more recent discussion. Colin Elliott (2007, pp. 265-272) provides a clear and concise overview of the theory.

Key Concepts in Psychometrics

Standardized Assessment

A *standardized test* is a test that is administered and scored in a consistent, or "standard," manner developed and prescribed by the test authors. Standardized tests are designed in such a way that the questions, conditions for administering, scoring procedures, and interpretations are consistent and are administered and scored in a predetermined, standard manner. Any test in which the same procedures are given in the same manner to all test takers may be considered a standardized test. The establishment of such a controlled assessment situation adds to the development of psychometrically sound results and thus, ideally, more valid and reliable interpretations of those results. Whenever examiners administer tests, whether group or individual, they must use exactly the same words with each person or group tested to maintain *standardized* procedures. Our favorite set of test directions comes from the Army Alpha test ("E." refers to the examiner):

> In giving the following directions E. should speak rather slowly, distinctly, and with proper emphasis. *He should expect and demand perfect order and prompt response to commands.*
>
> When everything is ready E. proceeds as follows: "Attention! The purpose of this examination is to see how well you can remember, think, and carry out what you are told to do. We are not looking for crazy people. The aim is to help find out what you are best fitted to do in the Army. The grade you make in this examination will be put on your qualification card and will also go to your company commander." (Yoakum & Yerkes, 1920, p. 53)

Examiners using standardized procedures must not alter the administration of tests in any way. This typically requires them to be vigilant with regard to basal and ceiling rules; to the specific test and item instructions; and to adhere to any and all time limits, timed presentations, and timed delays. Examiners must also avoid any ad libbing, coaching, helping, or teaching, except as instructed by the test procedures. For students with severe and low-incidence disabilities, examiner should consciously adopt appropriate tests rather than adapt inappropriate ones. If modifications of materials or instructions ("testing the limits") have been used, the report should contain clear statements about what was done, why it was done, and how it was done. It is the examiner's responsibility to make absolutely certain that results of limits-testing cannot possibly be confused with valid scores. If examiners do choose to test the limits, they should ensure that it will not influence later items, e.g., by providing extra practice.

Sampling of Behavior

The overall goal of the standardized assessment is to obtain a sampling of the specific behavior or construct we desire to assess and evaluate. It would, for example, be impossible to include all of the quarter million or so English words in a vocabulary test, so we must make do with a sample of representative words that will allow us to estimate an individual's knowledge of words. [Confusingly, we construct a test with a small "sample" of all possible items and administer it to a "sample" of persons representing the total population for which we want to construct norms.]

Models of Cognitive Abilities

The behaviors or constructs to be assessed are formulated first by theory (or, unfortunately, sometimes by armchair assumption). Using the psychometric approach, models of assessment based upon the various theories are created.

Many researchers, following the lead of Spearman (1904, 1927), focus on the measurement of general or global intelligence ("psychometric *g*"). Others, in the tradition of L. L. Thurstone (1926, 1931, 1938) and Raymond Cattell (1941, 1963, 1987), emphasize the separate contributions of various cognitive abilities, such as verbal ability, fluid reasoning, or spatial ability. The debate between the two camps continues unabated, for example, Carroll (1993, 1997/2005), Horn and Blankson (2005), Sternberg and Grigorenko (2002). Both the *g* and separate ability systems, however, fit within psychometric theory.

The myriad theories of cognitive abilities have resulted in numerous models for assessment. For example, Guilford (1967) defined intelligence in terms of three dimensions: (a) the mental operations used, (b) the content of the problem, and (c) the products (how the stimuli are organized, such as Units and Systems). Based on these three dimensions, any mental task could be categorized into one or more of 120 different cells (implying that there are 120 types of intelligence, i.e., 5 operations × 4 contents × 6 products). Guilford's structure of the intellect model turned out not to be the theory that would turn IQ testing into a theory-based profession. One hundred twenty abilities were just too many, but Guilford (1988) kept refining the theory, adding to its complexity.

In the 1980s, as Guilford's structure of the intellect theory was going out of favor, two important things occurred: (1) neurological theories of mental processing—notably Sperry's (1968) ideas about cerebral specialization and Luria's (1966, 1973) notions of successive and simultaneous processing—formed the basis of a clinical test of intelligence, the Kaufman Assessment Battery for Children (K-ABC; Kaufman & Kaufman, 1983); and (2) Horn's (1985) expansion of Cattell's (1941, 1963) *Gf-Gc* (fluid and crystallized abilities) theory to include additional broad abilities, such as short-term memory (*Gsm*), visualization (*Gv*), and processing speed (*Gs*)—and its subsequent merger with Carroll's (1993) model to form CHC (which stands for Cattell, Horn, Carroll) theory—zoomed in popularity and soon formed the solid foundation for several IQ tests, most notably the Woodcock-Johnson—Revised (WJ-R; Woodcock & Johnson, 1989) and its sequel, the WJ III (Woodcock, McGrew, & Mather, 2001). Ironically, Carroll (1997/2005) firmly maintained that the many separate abilities he identified (which were remarkably similar to those found by Cattell and Horn) were components of a higher order general ability (*g*), while Horn persisted in rejecting the reality of this single, overarching factor. CHC theory has been used in the development, or at least acknowledged in the manuals of a great many tests. The second edition of the Kaufman Assessment Battery for Children (KABC-II, Kaufman & Kaufman, 2004a) is designed for interpretation by both Luria and CHC theories. Dawn Flanagan, Kevin McGrew, Samuel Ortiz, Vincent Alfonso, Jennifer Mascolo, and colleagues have developed the cross-battery approach to apply CHC theory to the selection and interpretation of tests (e.g., Flanagan, Ortiz, & Alfonso, 2007; Flanagan, Ortiz, Alfonso, & Mascolo, 2006; and McGrew & Flanagan, 1998).

Many other models of cognitive abilities have been developed and used for the development of tests. Jack Naglieri, J. P. Das, and colleagues (e.g., Das, Kirby, & Jarman, 1979; Naglieri & Das, 2002; 2005) developed the planning, attention, simultaneous, successive (PASS) theory of intelligence based on the work of Russian psychologist A. R. Luria (1966, 1973, 1980) and based the Cognitive Assessment System (Naglieri & Das, 1997) on this theory. Luria posited three functional units or "blocks": arousal and attention (the attention in PASS), representing Luria's Block 1; taking in, processing, and storing information (the simultaneous and successive processes in PASS), or Block 2 coding processes; and synthesizing information and regulating behavior (the planning in PASS), which are the executive functions associated with Block 3. The simultaneous and sequential scales of the K-ABC (Kaufman & Kaufman, 1983) and simultaneous/Gv, sequential/Gsm, and planning/Gf scales of the KABC-II (Kaufman &

Kaufman, 2004a) are based on the same theoretical framework.

Robert Sternberg's triarchic theory (Sternberg, 1985, 2005) includes analytical, creative, and practical abilities. Sternberg (2005) states: "successful intelligence is (1) the use of an integrated set of abilities needed to attain success in life, however an individual defines it, within his or her sociocultural context. People are successfully intelligent by virtue of (2) recognizing their strengths and making the most of them, at the same time that they recognize their weaknesses and find ways to correct or compensate for them. Successfully intelligent people (3) adapt to, shape, and select environments through (4) finding a balance in their use of analytical, creative, and practical abilities (Sternberg, 1997, 1999)" (p. 104).

Reliability and Validity

A reliable measure is one that measures a construct consistently across time, individuals, and situations. A valid measure is one that measures what it is intended to measure. A measure may be reliable without being valid. However, reliability is necessary, although not sufficient, for validity.

As Kaufman (2009) notes, hopefully tests predict pretty well, but not with pinpoint accuracy, not in isolation, and not 10 years down the road. IQ tests can sometimes yield high scores for people who act dumb (e.g., Sternberg, 2002), and no one seems to deny that. For example, as reported in *The Book of Lists #3* (Wallace, Wallechinsky, & Wallace, 1983, p. 409), a 29-year-old Florida woman named Tina had an IQ of 189. She became obsessed that she was dying from stomach cancer, the illness that killed her mother, and vowed to cleanse her body. Her method: eating no food for days at a time, but drinking as much as four gallons of water a day. The result: Tina actually drowned herself from the inside out, overwhelming her kidneys and lungs with fluid. Not too bright for a genius. All tests have errors of measurement, even the most accurate and reliable tests, and different tests yield different score results for the same person; so do different examiners, and so do different scales within the same test.

The amount of measurement error in a test is called its *standard error of measurement* (SEm) expressed as a certain number of test-score points. For example, most good IQ tests have SEm's of about 3 points. Translation: The odds are about 2 out of 3 that the person's IQ on the test is within 3 points of his or her "true" IQ. True IQ, a figment of a statistician's imagination, is the average IQ a person would earn if given the same exact test over and over and over without fatigue, boredom, learning from practice, or growing dislike of examiners. It may be a figment, but it is valuable. If a person could be tested thousands of times the person's test scores would form a normal curve. The mean of that normal distribution of scores is the person's *true score*. The standard deviation is the *standard error of measurement* (*SEm*).

The evaluator must be aware of, understand, and take into account the standard error of measurement. This psychometric value allows the examiner to report test results at specific confidence intervals (e.g., 90%, 95%). It is also important to note that the psychometric properties of the SEm do not include errors and problems with test administration and conditions.

The psychometric approach also requires that examiners pay close attention to a test's validity. Examiners must appreciate the implications of test validity, weighing such questions as: are the tests valid and for what purposes?; for what groups?; how were the validity data obtained?; how large were the samples?; and are there validity data presented applicable to the individual being tested? A test might be valid for one purpose and utterly invalid for another.

Norming

In psychometric theory, once a measurement of some behavior (i.e., test performance) is obtained, it is evaluated relative to other individuals of the same age, grade, gender, and so forth. Before any score results can be assigned, we must find out how well large groups of people perform on the questions and novel problems included in the test. These groups are called *standardization* samples or *norms* groups. But they cannot be made up of just any people. In order to be useful, the norming sample should be not only sufficiently large but also appropriately stratified and randomized.

To give accurate results, the test must be normed on a *sample* that is truly representative of the *population* it is intended to reflect, such as all school children in the United States, all persons in specified age groups in Canada, all currently employed police officers in New York City, or all high school seniors applying to college in the United States and Canada. Like an opinion poll, a test will give trustworthy results only to the extent that the sample assessed is truly a microcosm of the intended population.

The size of the sample can vary depending upon the construct being assessed and the population with which you care to use the results. If one were creating or using a test that was designed to measure 5-year-olds' prereading abilities, a norming sample of 10 children might seem very limited while a sample of 2,000 would be excessively large. Taking care to provide a sample of appropriate size and demographic characteristics will help to ensure that the test results are both stable and representative of the particular population. A general rule of thumb is that the sample should contain a minimum of 100 people for each group being assessed (e.g., age, grade). Because in younger children certain skills typically develop at a rapid pace, many tests separate norms by age groups that might begin with 6-month increments (e.g., an age group for 3-year-olds followed by an age group for 3½-year-olds), and then use 1-year increments (age 9, age 10), and graduate to broader intervals when development has slowed down (ages 18-19 or 20-24). Some tests have several thousand people in the norming sample (e.g., the KABC-II, designed for children 3 to 18 years, has a norming sample of 3,025 children) while others have even larger samples (e.g., the WJ III, designed for people ages 2 to 90+, has a norming sample of more than 8,000). In contrast, the original published norms for the Boston Naming test, a test often used by speech and language professionals as well as neuropsychologists, had a published norming sample, at age 18 of 1! The joke heard was that persons' name was Norm, and so it was deemed adequate.

Besides the size of the sample, we must also be concerned about the representativeness of the sample (Kaufman, 2009).

If you want to know how well a 9-year-old does on a particular task, you must compare the number of questions answered correctly to the number gotten right by other 9-year-olds. But not just any 9-year-olds. If all the children in the age 9 norms group had parents with MD and PhD degrees, she would be unfairly penalized. The norms would be too "steep" because the reference group would have set the bar for "average performance" too high. However, if all the 9-year-olds in the sample were the children of parents who dropped out of elementary school, then the norms would be biased in the opposite direction—too easy or "soft." To avoid built-in bias, the sample must be *representative* of children age 9 living in the United States. The principle is: To determine how well or poorly a person does on the tasks presented in a test, a person's performance must be compared to the performance of *representative* groups of children, adolescents, or adults the same approximate age (or in some cases the same grade) as the person tested. Similarly, a political opinion poll conducted among the listening audience of an extreme left- or right-wing talk show or only in the urban Southwest or only in the rural Northeast would not accurately reflect the opinions of the entire nation.

From the psychometric theory's viewpoint, norming samples demonstrate representativeness when they have sufficiently addressed the stratification variables of gender; geographic region; racial and ethnic group; disability; income and educational level; other germane variables and the interactions of these variables (so, for example, all the high income, rural, African American females do not live in the Midwest).

The method for obtaining such samples is simple, at least conceptually. In practice, it is time consuming and expensive (Kaufman, 2009). First, test makers must study the U.S. Census data on key variables like gender, ethnicity, socioeconomic status, geographic region, and community size to determine the proportions that characterize the United States. Then they must select the standardization sample for their tests to match the census proportions. For example, when the Kaufmans normed the KABC-II in 2004, the distribution of children ages 3-18 years living in the four geographic regions of the United States was as follows, according to the March 2001 *Current Population Survey*: 19.2% in the Northeast, 22.1% in the North Central region, 34.7% in the South, and 24.1% in the West (Kaufman & Kaufman, 2004a, Table 7.5). To be representative, their IQ test's standardization sample for children and adolescents needed to match the regional percents of the United States as a whole for all of the variables (ethnic groups, socioeconomic status categories, geographic regions, and so forth).

For his original IQ test, David Wechsler (1939) tested nearly 2,000 children, adolescents, and adults in Coney Island, Brooklyn, New York. The sample did not represent the whole country, and it was far too urban. But it was still quite good because Wechsler knew from his own research that socioeconomic status was the key to getting a good "norms" sample. If you want to find out how well Americans aged 7 to 70 do on an IQ test, then test people at each age who form a "mini-U. S." sample on variables like education and occupation. If the U.S. Census in the 1930s says that 5% of adults in the United States. were college graduates, then make sure that 5% of the adults tested in the norms sample graduated from college. But when the Census called for farmers, farm managers, or farm laborers to be included in the norms group, Wechsler could not find any farmers in Brooklyn. So he tested barbers. He had done some research, and found that barbers and farmers performed about the same, on average, on his Wechsler-Bellevue test. His sample may have had too many barbers, too many people who were raised on Nathan's hotdogs and fries in Coney Island, and not enough Midwesterners. But for the 1930s, his methods were darned clever (Kaufman, 2009).

And just because a test is published, this is not a guarantee that the norms are adequate or representative for use. According to Boll (1981), the original norms for the Halstead-Reitan, a popular test used by neuropsychologists, were based on a tiny and inadequate sample of 21 men and 8 women. Ten of the subjects were servicemen who happened to be available for testing because of what was described as "minor" psychiatric problems; another was awaiting sentencing for a capital crime (in the state at that time it could have been either life imprisonment or execution. Halstead notes that the subject appeared "anxious"). Four were awaiting lobotomies because of behavior threatening their own lives and/or those of others; two sets of scores were made by one subject, a young man, since he was still waiting at the hospital after 2 months and so took the test again. This is the group whose test performance defined the unimpaired range for the cutting scores in the original version of the test!

The psychometric approach to individualized testing also provides basic, general theoretical notions to guide and permit interpretation of cognitive or academic abilities. Today's standards—which are guided by cognitive theories and neuropsychologically based approaches, aid greatly in the empirical interpretation of the test's results.

Test Scores

Test scores are typically expressed in three ways.

- First, examinees can be placed in rank order from lowest to highest. This ranking can be expressed as a percentage so, for example, a "percentile rank" of 32 would mean that the examinee scored higher than 32% of the norming sample and lower than the other 68%.
- Second, we can find the mean (arithmetic average) and standard deviation (a measure of variability) for the distribution of scores from the norming sample and then express the score in terms of how many standard deviation units it falls from the mean. These scores are called *z scores*. A *z* score of 0.00 would be precisely average. A *z* score of +1.00 would be one standard deviation above the mean. A *z* score of –1.00 would be one standard deviation below the mean. Authors of various tests have assigned different values to the mean and standard deviation, producing different systems of "standard scores." For example, with a mean and standard deviation set, respectively, at 100 and 15 (a very common choice popularized by the Wechsler-Bellevue Intelligence Scale, a score one standard deviation above the mean would be 115 and a score one standard deviation below the mean would be 85).
- Third, we can state the average age or the average school grade placement of all the norming sample examinees who passed the same number of items as the present examinee. This score, called a "mental age," "age-equivalent score," or "grade-equivalent score," is not a very useful score. It does not mean the examinee is functioning like the typical person of that age or grade. It becomes meaningless after the teenage years. The scores are not equal units, so they cannot be added, subtract, multiplied, or divided. One of Wechsler's (1939) key contributions when he published the Wechsler-Bellevue was to use standard scores, a far superior choice to the mental ages used by the Stanford-Binet, the most popular IQ test of that era (Kaufman, in press).

Validation of Psychometric Theory

With very few exceptions, modern individually administered tests of intelligence and academic achievement are based on classical test theory, IRT, or a combination of the two. Each time a new test or a new edition of a older test is released, the publishers perform validation studies to compare the new test to other tests intended to measure similar abilities; to any previous edition of the new test; to tests of abilities intended to be predicted by the new test (e.g., validating an IQ test by its correlation with tests of academic achievement); and sometimes with other nontest measures, such as school grades, teacher reports, and diagnoses of medical and psychological disabilities. Tests are also validated by studies of their "factor structure." All component subtests should correlate to some extent with the total score. They should have high correlations with scores of cohesive subscales of which they are parts, and they should have lower correlations with subscales in which they are not included. For example, in an IQ test with verbal comprehension and perceptual reasoning subscales, each verbal comprehension subtest should have higher correlations with the total verbal comprehension score and with other verbal comprehension subtests than with the total perceptual reasoning score and the perceptual reasoning subtests. All subtests should have at least moderately high correlations with the total score for the entire IQ test. [The process and mathematics are more complicated than this simplified note. See Keith (1997) for a clear and helpful explanation.] Such studies can be found in the technical manuals of the tests. Just a few examples of manuals for tests of intelligence and academic achievement include the Differential Ability Scales, Second Edition (Elliott, 2007), Kaufman Assessment Battery for Children, Second Edition (Kaufman & Kaufman, 2004a), Kaufman Test of Educational Achievement, Second Edition (Kaufman & Kaufman, 2004b), Reynolds Intellectual Assessment Scales (Reynolds & Kamphaus, 2003), Stanford-Binet Intelligence Scales, Fifth Edition (Roid, 2003), Wechsler Intelligence Scale for Children, Fourth Edition (Wechsler, 2003), and Woodcock-Johnson III (McGrew & Woodcock, 2001).

These and independent validation studies are summarized and evaluated in many authoritative texts such as Jerome Sattler's *Assessment of Children* (5th ed.) (Sattler, 2008), *The Cambridge Handbook of Intelligence* (Sternberg & Kaufman, 2011), *Contemporary Intellectual Assessment* (3rd ed.) (Flanagan & Harrison, 2012), the *Achievement Test Desk Reference* (2nd ed.) (Flanagan et al., 2006), *The Handbook of School Psychology* (4th ed.) (Gutkin & Reynolds, 2008), and the *Encyclopedia of*

Special Education 4th Edition (Reynolds, Vannest, & Fletcher-Janzen, in press).

Many studies have examined in detail the relationships between tests of cognitive ability and tests of academic achievement (e.g., Evans, Floyd, McGrew, & Leforgee, 2002; Floyd, Evans, & McGrew, 2003; Hale et al., 2008; Hale, Fiorello, Kavanagh, Hoeppner, & Gaitherer, 2001; Hammill, 2004). There is considerable controversy about whether measures of specific cognitive abilities may be better predictors than total IQ scores of some aspects of academic achievement, but it is clear that there is a strong relationship between IQ and achievement tests.

Generalizability of Psychometric Theory Across Cultures

Ethnicity, Genders, and Critiques of the Theory

Psychometric theory itself is fairly neutral. Cultural and other concerns arise before and beyond the actual theory. Psychometric theory would, for example, be pointless in a setting in which people rejected the validity or appropriateness of measuring human abilities and comparing individuals to each other. At the other end, many concrete applications of psychometric theory are highly specific to certain demographic groups. Obviously, a test with instructions and items written in English would not be appropriate to persons who did not speak English as a first language. Simply translating the test would invalidate the standardization and norms; it would have to be reconstructed and renormed in the other language.

Many tests (and IQ and scholastic aptitude tests in particular) have been savagely criticized as biased against various groups (e.g., Jacoby & Glauberman, 1995) and equally strongly defended (e.g., Herrnstein & Murray, 1994). For the most part, the controversy has involved the application of tests and testing programs, not the underlying psychometric theory, although the idea that human abilities are generally more or less normally distributed has occasionally been disputed (see, for example, Goertzel & Fashing, 1981).

For example, Dr. Robert Williams, a leading spokesperson against IQ tests in the 1970s when anti-IQ sentiments were rampant, accused tests of "silently mugging" the African American community and of committing "Black intellectual genocide" (Williams, 1974a, 1974b).

In *The Mismeasure of Man,* the paleontologist Stephen Jay Gould (1981) condemned the history of racial, ethnic, gender, cultural, and socioeconomic bias in the application of intelligence tests. Although many of Gould's observations were all too accurate and his opinions found an appreciative audience, some of his information and many of his conclusions were disputed by critics (e.g., Jensen, 1982; Lewis et al., 2011).

Minimizing bias in assessment has been the subject of a great deal of interest and research (e.g., Helms, 1997; Jensen, 1980; Neisser, 1998; Office for Civil Rights, 2000; Ortiz & Dynda, 2005; Ortiz & Ochoa, 2005). The two major concerns have been (a) the question of whether a test or a class of tests gives consistently lower scores to a particular group of people, and (b) whether an ability test predicts outcomes (such as academic achievement or scholastic or vocational success) less validly for one group than for another. Again, these are concerns about specific tests and testing programs rather than about psychometric theory.

Many critics maintain that IQ tests overlook important cognitive abilities. Sternberg's (1985, 2005) Triarchic Theory, mentioned above, emphasizes some components of "successful intelligence" (creativity, practical intelligence) that are not tapped by traditional IQ tests. Keith Stanovich joins Sternberg in emphasizing rationality. Stanovich (2009) says that rationality is "*What Intelligence Tests Miss.*" Howard Gardner (1983/1993) has posited a number of "intelligences" such as musical and bodily-kinesthetic intelligences that go far beyond the abilities measured by traditional IQ tests.

Use and Application of Psychometric Theory

Test scores based on psychometric theory have many purposes and applications. Some examples follow.

- use in diagnosis of disabilities;
- evaluation of baseline skills or functioning;
- informing educational programming and intervention efforts; and
- selection of applicants for schools, programs, and jobs.

Representative Studies

Assessment of intellectual abilities and academic achievement has grown into a big business over the past 100 years. There have been thousands of studies of these tests over that century. As mentioned above, many of the most important studies are discussed in sources such as Flanagan and Harrison (2012), Flanagan et al. (2006), Gutkin and Reynolds (2008), Sattler (2008), and Sternberg and Kaufman (2011).

REFERENCES

Binet, A., & Henri, V. (1896). La psychologie individuelle [Individual psychology]. *L'Annee Psychologique, 2*, 411-465.

Binet, A., & Simon, T. (1905). Methodes nouvelles pour le diagnostic du niveau intellectual des anormaux [New methods for the diagnosis of intelligence levels of the abnormal]. *L'Annee Psychologique, 11*(S), 191-244.

Binet, A., & Simon, T. (1980). *The development of intelligence in children* (E. S. Kite, Trans.). Nashville, TN: Williams (Original work published 1916)

Birnbaum, A. (1968). Part 5: Some latent trait models and their use in inferring an examinee's ability. In F. M. Lord & M. R. Novick (Eds.), *Statistical theories of mental test scores* (pp. 395-479). Reading, MA: Addison-Wesley.

Boll, T. J. (1981). The Halstead-Reitan Neuropsychological Battery. In S. B. Filskov & T. J. Boll (Eds.), *Handbook of clinical neuropsychology* (Vol. 1, pp. 577–608). New York, NY: Wiley.

Carroll, J. B. (1993). *Human cognitive abilities: A survey of factor-analytic studies.* New York, NY: Cambridge University Press.

Carroll, J. B. (2005). The three-stratum theory of cognitive abilities. In D. P. Flanagan, & P. L. Harrison (Eds.), *Contemporary intellectual assessment: Theories, tests, and issues* (2nd ed., pp. 41-68). New York, NY: Guilford Press. (Original work published 1997)

Cattell, J. M. (1890). Mental tests and measurement. *Mind, 15*, 373-381.

Cattell, R. B. (1941). Some theoretical issues in adult intelligence testing. *Psychological Bulletin, 38*, 592.

Cattell, R. B. (1963). Theory of fluid and crystallized intelligence: A critical experiment. *Journal of Educational Psychology, 54*, 1-22.

Cattell, R. B. (1987). *Intelligence: Its structure, growth and action.* Amsterdam, The Netherlands: North-Holland.

Cohen, R. J., & Swerdlik, M. E. (1999). *Psychological testing and assessment* (4th ed.). Mountain View, CA: Mayfield.

Das, J. P., Kirby, J. R., & Jarman, R. F. (1979). *Simultaneous and successive cognitive processes.* New York, NY: Academic Press.

Elliott, C. D. (2007). *Differential Ability Scales 2nd edition introductory and technical handbook.* San Antonio, TX: The Psychological Corporation.

Embretson, S. E., & Reise, S. P. (2000). *Item response theory for psychologists.* Mahwah, NJ: Erlbaum.

Evans, J. J., Floyd, R. G., McGrew, K. S., & Leforgee, M. H. (2002). The relations between measures of Cattell-Horn-Carroll (CHC) cognitive abilities and reading achievement during childhood and adolescence. School *Psychology Review, 31*(2), 246-262.

Flanagan, D. P., & Harrison, P. L. (Eds.) (2012). *Contemporary intellectual assessment, third edition: Theories, tests, and issues.* New York, NY: The Guilford Press.

Flanagan, D. P., Ortiz, S. O., & Alfonso, V. (2007). *Essentials of cross-battery assessment* (2nd ed.). Hoboken, NJ: Wiley.

Flanagan, D. P., Ortiz, S. O., Alfonso, V. & Mascolo, J. T. (2006). *Achievement test desk reference (ATDR-II): A guide to learning disability identification* (2nd ed.). Hoboken, NJ: Wiley.

Floyd, R. G., Evans, J. J., & McGrew, K. S. (2003). Relations between measures of Cattell-Horn-Carroll (CHC) cognitive abilities and mathematics achievement across the school-age years. *Psychology in the Schools, 60*(2), 155-171.

Gardner, H. (1993) *Frames of Mind: The theory of multiple intelligences,* New York, NY: Basic Books. (Original work published 1983)

Goertzel, T., & Fashing, J. (1981). Myth of the normal curve: a theoretical critique and examination of its role in teaching and research. *Humanity and Society 5*, 14-31.

Gould, S. J. (1981). *The mismeasure of man: A carefully researched and shrewdly argued polemic against the abuses of testing, especially IQ testing.* New York, NY: Norton.

Guilford, J. P. (1967). *The nature of human intelligence.* New York, NY: McGraw-Hill.

Guilford, J. P. (1988). Some changes in the structure-of-intellect model. *Educational and Psychological Measurement, 48*, 1-4.

Gutkin, T. B, & Reynolds, C. R. (2008). *The handbook of school psychology* (4th ed.). Hoboken, NJ: Wiley.

Hale, J. B, Fiorello, C. A., Dumont, R., Willis, J. O., Rackley, C., & Elliott, C. (2008). Differential Ability Scales-Second Edition (neuro)psychological predictors of math performance for typical children and children with math disabilities. *Psychology in the Schools, 45*(9), 838-858.

Hale, J. B., Fiorello, C. A., Kavanagh, J. A., Hoeppner, J. B., & Gaitherer, R. A. (2001). WISC-III predictors of academic achievement for children with learning disabilities: Are global and factor scores comparable? *School Psychology Quarterly, 16*(1), 31- 35.

Hammill, D. D. (2004). What we know about correlates of reading. *Exceptional Children, 70*(4), 453-469.

Helms, J. E. (1997). The triple quandary of race, culture, and social class in standardized cognitive ability testing. In D. P. Flanagan, J. L. Genshaft, & P. L. Harrison (Eds.), *Contemporary intellectual assessment: Theories, tests, and issues* (pp. 517-532). New York, NY: Guilford Press.

Herrnstein, R. J., & Murray, C. (1994). *The bell curve: Intelligence and class structure in American life.* New York, NY: Simon & Schuster (Free Press Paperbacks).

Horn, J. L., & Blankson, N. (2005). Foundation for better understanding of cognitive Abilities. In D. P. Flanagan & P. L. Harrison (Eds.), *Contemporary intellectual assessment: Theories, tests, and issues* (2nd ed., pp. 41-68). New York, NY: Guilford Press.

Jacoby, R., & Glauberman, N. (Eds.). (1995). *The bell curve debate.* New York, NY: Times Books (Random House).

Jensen, A. R. (1980). *Bias in mental testing.* London, England: Methuen.

Jensen, A. R. (1982). The debunking of scientific fossils and straw persons. *Contemporary Education Review, 1*(2), 121-135.

Kaufman, A. S. (2009). *IQ testing 101.* New York, NY: Springer.

Kaufman, A. S. (in press). Biography of David Wechsler. In F. Volkmar (Ed.), *Encyclopedia of autistic spectrum disorders.* New York, NY: Springer.

Kaufman, A. S., & Kaufman, N. L. (1983). *K-ABC interpretive manual.* Circle Pines, MN: American Guidance Service.

Kaufman, A. S., & Kaufman, N. L. (2004a). *Kaufman Assessment Battery for Children—Second Edition manual.* Circle Pines, MN: American Guidance Service.

Kaufman, A. S., & Kaufman, N. L. (2004b). *Kaufman Test of Educational Achievement Second edition manual.* Circle Pines, MN: American Guidance Service.

Lewis, J. E., DeGusta, D., Meyer, M. R., Monge, J. M., Mann, A. E., & Holloway, R. L. (2011). The mismeasure of science: Stephen Jay Gould versus Samuel George Morton on skulls and bias. *PLoS Biology, 9*(6), e1001071.

Keith, T. Z. (1997). Using confirmatory factor analysis to aid in understanding the constructs measured by intelligence tests. In D. P. Flanagan, J. L. Genshaft, & P. L. Harrison (Eds.), *Contemporary Intellectual assessment: Theories, tests, and issues* (pp. 373-402). New York, NY: Guilford Press.

Lord, F. M., & Novick, M. R. (1968). *Statistical theories of mental test scores with contributions by A. Birnbaum.* Reading, MA: Addison-Wesley.

Luria, A. R. (1966). *Higher cortical functions in man.* New York, NY: Basic Books.

Luria, A. R. (1973). *The working brain: An introduction to neuropsychology.* London, England: Penguin Books.

Luria, A. R. (1980). *Higher cortical functions in man* (2nd ed.). New York, NY: Basic Books.

McGrew, K. S., & Flanagan, D. P. (1998). *The intelligence test desk reference (ITDR): Gf-Gc cross-battery assessment.* Boston, MA: Allyn & Bacon.

McGrew, K. S., & Woodcock, R. W. (2001). Technical manual. *Woodcock-Johnson III.* Itasca, IL: Riverside.

Naglieri, J. A, & Das, J. P. (1997). *Cognitive Assessment System administration and scoring manual.* Itasca, IL: Riverside.

Naglieri, J. A, & Das, J. P. (2002). Practical implications of general intelligence and PASS cognitive processes. In R. J. Sternberg & E. L. Grigorenko (Eds.), *The general factor of intelligence: How general is it?* (pp. 855-884). New York, NY: Erlbaum.

Naglieri, J. A, & Das, J. P. (2005). Planning, attention, simultaneous, successive (PASS) theory. In D. P. Flanagan & P. L. Harrison (Eds.), *Contemporary intellectual assessment: Theories, tests and issues* (2nd ed., pp. 120-135). New York, NY: Guilford.

Neisser, U. (Ed.) (1998). *The rising curve: Long-term gains in IQ and related measures.* Washington, DC: American Psychological Association.

Office for Civil Rights. (2000). *The use of tests when making high-stakes decisions for students: A resource guide for educators and policymakers.* Retrieved from http://www2.ed.gov/offices/OCR/archives/pdf/TestingResource.pdf

Ortiz, S. O., & Dynda, A. M. (2005). Use of intelligence tests with culturally and linguistically diverse populations. In D. P. Flanagan & P. L. Harrison (Eds.), *Contemporary intellectual assessment: Theories, tests, and issues* (2nd ed., pp. 545-556). New York, NY: Guilford Press.

Ortiz, S. O., & Ochoa, S. H. (2005). Advances in cognitive assessment of culturally and linguistically diverse individuals. In D. P. Flanagan & P. L. Harrison (Eds.), *Contemporary intellectual assessment: Theories, tests, and issues* (2nd ed., pp. 234-250). New York, NY: Guilford Press.

Rasch, G. (1960). *Probabilistic models for some intelligence and attainment tests.* Copenhagen, Denmark: Danish Institute for Educational Research.

Reynolds, C. R. & Fletcher-Janzen, E. (Eds.) (in press). *Encyclopedia of special education* (4th ed). New York, NY: Wiley.

Reynolds, C. R., & Kamphaus, R. W. (2003). *Reynolds Intellectual Assessment Scales and the Reynolds Intellectual Screening professional manual.* Lutz, FL: Psychological Assessment Resources.

Roid, G. H. (2003). *Stanford-Binet Intelligence scales, Fifth Edition technical manual.* Itasca, IL: Riverside.

Sattler, J. M. (2008). *Assessment of children: Cognitive foundations* (5th ed.) San Diego, CA: Author.

Spearman, C. E. (1904). "General intelligence," objectively determined and measured. *American Journal of Psychology, 15,* 201-293.

Spearman, C. E. (1927). *The abilities of man: Their nature and measurement.* New York, NY: Macmillan.

Sperry, R. W. (1968). Hemisphere deconnection and unity in conscious awareness. *American Psychologist, 23,* 723-733.

Stanovich, K. E. (2009). *What intelligence tests miss: The psychology of rational thought.* New Haven, CT: Yale University Press.

Sternberg, R. J. (1985). *Beyond IQ: A triarchic theory of human intelligence.* New York, NY: Cambridge University Press.

Sternberg, R. J. (Ed.) (2002). *Why smart people can be so stupid.* New Haven, CT: Yale University Press.

Sternberg, R. J. (2005). *The triarchic theory of successful intelligence.* In D. P. Flanagan & P. L. Harrison (Eds.), *Contemporary intellectual assessment: Theories, tests and issues* (2nd ed., pp. 103-119). New York, NY: Guilford.

Sternberg, R. J., & Grigorenko, E. L. (Eds.). (2002). *The general factor of intelligence: How general is it?* New York, NY: Erlbaum.

Sternberg, R. J., & Kaufman, S. B. (Eds.). (2011). *The Cambridge handbook of intelligence.* New York, NY: Cambridge University Press.

Terman, L. M. (1916). *The measurement of intelligence.* Boston, MA: Houghton-Mifflin.

Terman, L. M., & Merrill, M. A. (1937). *Measuring intelligence: A guide to the administration of the new revised Stanford-Binet Tests of Intelligence.* Boston, MA: Houghton Mifflin.

Terman, L. M., & Merrill, M. A. (1960). *Stanford-Binet Intelligence scale: Manual, Form L-M.* Boston, MA: Houghton Mifflin.

Thurstone, L. L. (1926). A method for scaling psychological and educational tests. *Journal of Educational Psychology, 16,* 433-451.

Thurstone, L. L. (1931). Multiple factor analysis. *Psychological Review, 38,* 406-427.

Thurstone, L. L. (1938). Primary mental abilities. *Psychometric Monographs, 1,* i-ix, 1-121.

Vannest, K., Reynolds, C. R., & Fletcher-Janzen, E. (Eds.) (in preparation). *Encyclopedia of Special Education* (Vol. 3). Hoboken, NJ: Wiley.

Wainer, H. (1990). *Computerized adaptive testing: A primer.* Hillsdale, NJ: Erlbaum.

Wallace, A., Wallechinsky, D., & Wallace, I. (1983). *The book of lists # 3.* New York, NY: Bantam Books.

Wechsler, D. (1939). *The measurement of adult intelligence.* Baltimore, MD: Williams & Wilkins.

Wechsler, D. (2003). *WISC-IV technical and interpretive manual.* San Antonio, TX: Pearson.

Williams, R. L. (1974a). From dehumanization to black intellectual genocide: A rejoinder. In G. J. Williams & S. Gordon (Eds.), *Clinical child psychology* (pp. 320–323). New York, NY: Behavioral Publications.

Williams, R. L. (1974b). Scientific racism and IQ: The silent mugging of the Black community. *Psychology Today, 7,* 32-34, 37-38, 41, 101.

Woodcock, R. W., & Dahl, M. N. (1971). *A common scale for the measurement of person ability and test item difficulty* (AGS Paper No. 10). Circle Pines, MN: American Guidance Service.

Woodcock, R. W., & Johnson, M. B. (1989). *Woodcock-Johnson Psychoeducational Battery* (Rev. ed). Itasca, IL: Riverside.

Woodcock, R. W., McGrew, K. S., & Mather, N. (2001). *Woodcock-Johnson III.* Itasca, IL: Riverside.

Wright, B. D., & Stone, M. H. (1979). *Best test design: Rasch measurement.* Chicago, IL: MESA Press.

Yoakum, C. S., & Yerkes, R. M. (Eds.). (1920). *Army mental tests.* New York, NY: Henry Holt.

Author Contact Information: John O. Willis, Rivier College, 419 Sand Hill Road, Peterborough, NH 03458-1616. Telephone: 603-924-0993. E-mail: jwillis@rivier.edu

CHAPTER 62

Luria and Learning

How Neuropsychological Theory Translates Into Educational Practice

Andrea N. Schneider, Daniel J. Parker, Emilie Crevier-Quintin, Hanna A. Kubas, and James B. Hale
University of Victoria

Rooted in the philosophical writings of structuralists like Rene Descartes and functionalists like John Locke, the field of psychology turned to measurement to answer long-held observations and beliefs about constructs such as intelligence and personality as early as the 1800s. It was believed that psychological constructs such as sensation, perception, or affect could be quantified and measured with mathematical precision. With the advent of Galton's psychometrics, Terman's intelligence quotient, and Spearman's factor analyses revealing *g*, Western psychology increasingly used nomothetic and quantitative approaches to understand the human experience. As we will argue here, this measurement obsession has undermined the utility of psychological assessment, and assumptions underlying psychological test interpretation need to be reconsidered, or even deconstructed altogether.

As psychological practice evolved, the underlying abilities and skills that comprise the *g* factor were modified, refined, generalized, and ultimately challenged, but it was quantitative psychology that dominated Western psychology for the next 100 years. Until recent times, few challenged this dominant orientation. However, with the advent of brain imaging technology a new ideology and theoretically sound approach to psychological assessment has emerged. This process-oriented approach, while new to Western psychology, was the mainstay of Eastern neuropsychology nearly 50 years ago, with the iconic A. R. Luria prophetically extolling how interpretation of psychological processes, not overt or measurable outcomes, was the key to understanding human brain-behavior relationships.

While *g* is often interpreted as general mental energy or ability, Spearman correctly noted that it was merely a mathematical not a psychological phenomenon. Unfortunately, this quantitative approach is not sensitive to the underlying psychological processes and patterns of performance that have clinical utility (Luria, 1973). Many tasks used to assess global "ability" share little variance among them in the prediction of meaningful outcomes, and are contaminated by prior experience and education (i.e., achievement), so are in part dependent on individual prior learning experiences, sociocultural expectations, and acquired knowledge.

Normative data required for nomothetic interpretation of intelligence measures requires collapsing potentially meaningful individual differences into large heterogeneous samples. Assuming universality rather than individuality of cognitive function, these interpretive approaches persist despite empirical findings attesting to substantial (80-85% of sample) cognitive variability within these large populations, which undermines the predictive validity of global scores (Hale, Fiorello, Kavanagh, Holdnack, & Aloe, 2007). Nomothetic approaches can help determine only if a problem exists—they do little to inform diagnosis or intervention. In other words, nomothetic interpretation approaches may have sensitivity for detecting the existence of a problem sounds better than for detecting a problem exists, but they lack specificity for diagnosis

The Handbook of Educational Theories, pp. 751–759

and intervention. Thus, nomothetic assessment approaches to intellectual test interpretation do little to inform educational instruction—they do not tell teachers what to teach, or how to teach, struggling learners in the classroom (Fuchs, Hale, & Kearns, 2011).

Unlike Spearman's global approach which focuses on a child's *level* of performance, idiographic interpretation approaches championed by A. R. Luria focus on *patterns* of processing strengths and weaknesses from a neuropsychological perspective. Fostered by advances in neuroimaging, idiographic assessment advocates note that interpretive accuracy can only come from inferences regarding *psychological processes* that have greater specificity than stimulus *input* and response *output* traditionally recognized by nomethically-driven psychometric approaches to interpretation. When assessing children who manifest atypical behavior and cognition, it is crucial to examine the unique processing demands that explain performance variations demonstrated across different measures (Fiorello, Hale, Snyder, & Teodori, 2008; Hale, Wycoff, & Fiorello, 2010).

As any teacher knows, there are multiple ways to approach any given cognitive or academic task, leading to tremendous variability in interpretive outcomes across children. When looking at a "problematic" subtest score, practitioners must not only focus on the affected cognitive processes, but they must also examine processes allowing compensation for these deficits, a finding now regularly supported by neuroimaging studies of children with disabilities (Fiorello, Hale, Decker, & Coleman, 2009). As A. R. Luria (1973) suggests, considering *how* a child approaches a task, and adapts to task demands within and across measures, we need to think about *dynamic* interpretation of a child's unique cognitive processing *states* within a developmental context, and not make the mistake of thinking we are measuring static underlying *traits* that will remain stable. This is why repeated measurement across time is essential practice when conducting psychological evaluations, to ensure accurate interpretation of both psychological process and product. This deconstruction of traditional nomothetic, quantitative approaches to test interpretation is critical if our results are to have diagnostic specificity and treatment validity for children struggling in classrooms.

SPECIFIC LEARNING DISABILITIES: RETHINKING PARADIGMS AND THE "THIRD METHOD"

Vague educational definitions of childhood disorders such as specific learning disabilities (SLD) essentially require practitioners to make dichotomous level of performance interpretations of data (e.g., disabled/nondisabled). This explains why psychologists' roles have traditionally focused on identification purposes, and their assessments do little to inform intervention. Not only does this ineffectual practice undermine practitioner efforts at idiographic interpretation of assessment results, it also leads to vague classification categories that lack specificity for diagnosis and intervention.

The dramatic increase in SLD prevalence in the last quarter century is thought to be partially due to great variability in SLD definition and identification practices (Hale, Wycoff, & Fiorello, 2010). The ability-achievement discrepancy model has been the dominant method for legally classifying children as having a SLD for over 30 years. A growing body of evidence suggests that the discrepancy model is neither a useful nor valid tool in SLD identification (Fletcher et al., 2002; Hale, Wycoff, & Fiorello, 2010). Applying a uniform discrepancy approach to all children struggling in school fails to account for developmental differences in cognition and achievement, and does little to discriminate between children with SLD and low achievement. Using global intellectual/cognitive scores for discrepancy criteria essentially ignores the profile variability inherent in children with SLD. Not only does this variability potentially explain the *processing deficit* that is causing the SLD, but it also explains why subtests account for more achievement variance than factor scores, with the least amount of variance explained by global IQ (Hale, Flanagan, & Naglieri, 2008; Hale, Wycoff, & Fiorello, 2010). Thus, the ability-achievement discrepancy model fails to provide a direct link between eligibility criteria, assessment results, and subsequent individualized interventions, resulting in lifelong achievement deficits with minimal documented improvement (Hale, Wycoff, & Fiorello, 2010).

An alternative model for identifying and serving children with learning problems, called response-to-intervention or instruction (RTI) views learning problems as socially-constructed phenomena external to the child (Ysseldyke, 2009). Rather than focusing on summative intelligence test scores for identification of SLD, RTI adopts a more outcome-based approach, executed through ongoing formative assessments of academic achievement and regular progress monitoring of response. The RTI approach suggests that struggling students who are unresponsive to empirically validated interventions should be considered eligible for special education services under the SLD category (Burns & Vanderheyden, 2006). Although RTI is useful in providing early intervention services in an attempt to prevent disability, determining reliable responsiveness has not been achieved (e.g., Barth et al., 2008; Brown-Waesche, Schatschneider, Maner, Ahmed, & Wagner, 2011; Fuchs, Fuchs, & Compton, 2004; Speece, 2005) because there is no *true positive* in an RTI model—you do not know what the child has, only that they didn't respond (Hale, Wycoff, & Fiorello, 2010). Therefore, inferring SLD from a failure to respond to intervention is not a clinically or scientifically valid method for identification (Hale, Wycoff, & Fiorello, 2010).

More individualized and comprehensive evaluations using cognitive and neuropsychological measures should be taken for children who do not improve with RTI, according to both the Individuals with Disabilities Education Act (IDEA) and U.S. Supreme Court rulings (Dixon, Eusebio, Turton, Wright, & Hale, 2011). This will ensure accurate differential diagnosis of SLD, and ultimately information to help educators develop more effective classroom interventions (Hale et al., 2008; Hale, Wycoff, & Fiorello, 2010). Reflecting this growing concern for using discrepancy and RTI for SLD identification, a panel of 58 experts in education, psychology, medicine, and law commissioned by the Learning Disabilities Association of America produced a white paper that affirmed that children with SLD have a disorder in the *basic psychological processes* that adversely affects academic achievement. Comprehensive evaluations using cognitive and neuropsychological measures are necessary to identify these processes and guide academic intervention (Hale, Alfonso, et al. 2010).

Given the limitations of the traditional ability-achievement discrepancy and RTI models for SLD identification, the Office of Special Education and Rehabilitative Services (OSERS) incorporated what has been called the "third method" or "processing strengths and weaknesses" approach for determining SLD in their final IDEA regulations (Hale, Wycoff, & Fiorello, 2010). Unlike discrepancy and RTI models, the third method approach addresses regulatory and statutory SLD identification requirements through identification of academic achievement deficits associated with cognitive and/or neuropsychological processing patterns (Hale, Flanagan, & Naglieri, 2008; Hale, Alfonso, et al., 2010a). To adopt a third method approach practitioners must understand *psychological processes*. However, to understand psychological processes, we argue here that neuropsychological theory and practices provide the foundation for interpretation, with arguments based primarily based on the works of A. R. Luria (1973), E. Goldberg (2001), and J. B. Hale and C. A. Fiorello (2004).

School Neuropsychology in Assessment and Intervention

Nomothetic approaches to interpretation are limited because most children have cognitive processing strengths and weaknesses, suggesting cognitive diversity is the norm rather than the exception, and that profile variability in and of itself is not diagnostic (Hale Fiorello, Kavanagh, Holdnack, & Aloe, 2007). However, some children with variable test profiles have disabilities requiring individualized intervention. While psychometric theories such as Cattell-Horn-Carroll theory provide a strong foundation for understanding the cognitive processing components involved in learning and identification of SLD (see Flanagan, Fiorello, & Ortiz, 2010). A neuropsychological approach recognizes and investigates individual differences found on subcomponent measures, and is thus an essential part of assessment in children (Fiorello et al., 2008; Hale, Wycoff, & Fiorello, 2010).

Neuropsychological approaches to interpretation examine the relationship between the brain and behavior from an idiographic perspective in a data-driven, empirically-supported, and clinically sensitive manner. Unlike psychometric approaches, the focus is on the child's unique processing characteristics inferred from patterns of performance within and across cognitive and neuropsychological tests. This approach not only identifies whether there is a problem (i.e., sensitivity), but it also promotes *specificity* for differential diagnosis. Not only does this help recognize the unique characteristics of identified children, but it also fosters teacher insight into individual differences among children and provides useful information to guide targeted interventions for affected children.

Neuropsychological Approaches to Cognitive Processing

Considered by many to be the founder of modern neuropsychology, A. R. Luria provided the foundation for conceptualizing the processes underlying cognitive strengths and weaknesses. Luria (1973) argued in his three Laws of Functional Organization that:

1. The brain is hierarchically organized from basic input (primary cortical) areas to increasingly complex regions (secondary and tertiary cortical) areas, with the tertiary areas being most complex;
2. The specificity of neural tissue diminishes from simple input in the basic zones (very specific and one mode of processing) to increasingly complex integration of information in the tertiary zones (not specific and multimodal processing);
3. The lateralization (left/right hemisphere) of specific processing demands becomes increasingly differentiated as one goes up the hierarchy, from basic and specific cell functions to complex hemisphere-specific systems.

Luria proposed the brain be conceptually separated into three different functional units. The first unit, composed of reticular and other subcortical structures, regulates states of cortical alertness, and allows the brain to be ready to process incoming information and act on the environment. The second unit receives, stores, and analyzes information, and includes the posterior occipital, parietal, and temporal areas which process visual, somatosensory, and auditory information respectively. Information is interpreted in the second unit in the occipital-temporal-parietal convergence zone. Aptly named the *zones of overlapping*, information from different sensory modalities is integrated here, allowing the highest levels of understanding to take place. Luria's third functional unit acts upon information, governs all brain activity, and monitors higher-level mental functions. This *superstructure* unit involves the anterior frontal cortex and supporting structures (e.g. frontal-subcortical circuits), where top-down executive control of all brain functions takes place.

Building upon Luria's theories, Hale and Fiorello (2004) provided the cognitive hypothesis testing model (CHT) by using neuropsychological theory to guide interpretation of cognitive and neuropsychological test results. Expanded upon by Hale et al. (2009), this model posits three *axes* of clinical interpretation to aid in the integration of cognitive and neuropsychological data for both assessment and intervention purposes (see Figure 62.1). They are called "axes" of interpretation because they are interrelated systems that influence each other. As Goldberg (2001) notes, it is not important to localize function, but instead think of a continuum or gradiential approach for interpretation. The question therefore is not an either it is this structure or that structure, but instead it is *how much* one structure involved over another.

The *posterior-anterior axis* receives, analyzes and stores information in the posterior of the brain, and then acts on this information using the prefrontal and motor regions. Incoming information is integrated in the highly interconnected association cortex (Luria's *zones of overlapping*) where the highest forms of comprehension take place. Information is forwarded to the anterior prefrontal brain regions (Luria's *superstructure*) where it is coordinated, managed, and used to inform action. A useful and typical pattern is the finding that most SLDs are related to the second functional unit (i.e., zones of overlapping), while most psychopathologies are related to the third functional unit (i.e., superstructure).

The *left-right axis* represents the functions of the left and right hemispheres. The traditional dichotomy of hemispheric specialization in differentiated forms of processing has been reevaluated in the presence of neuroimaging studies that establish the intricacies of hemispheric divisions of labor (Tulving, Kapurt, Craik, Moscovitch, & Houle, 1994). Old ways of conceptualizing hemispheric function (e.g., left-verbal, right-nonverbal) have been replaced with current conceptualizations, where hemispheric asymmetries appear to be process specific, not stimulus specific (Reynolds, Kamphaus, Rosenthal, & Hiemenz, 1997). The currently accepted division establishes the right hemisphere as being involved in novel, discordant, divergent, global forms of processing, resulting in fluid abilities for novel problem solving and new learning, while the left hemisphere processes routinized, concordant, convergent, detailed, and specific information resulting in crystallized knowledge (Goldberg, 2001; Hale & Fiorello, 2004). For instance, the left hemisphere specializes in common, straightforward, explicit language, while the right is called upon for implicit language, such as indirect meanings, metaphors, humor, idioms, and sarcasm (Bryan & Hale, 2001).

The *superior-inferior axis* of interpretation allows practitioners to interpret top (prefrontal) and bottom (subcortical) structure-function relationships. This axis is critical for regulation of brain function, with superior structures important for executive regulation and supervision of ongoing brain activity, and inferior structure important for executive efficiency and precision of action. Most of our psychopathologies are related to this axis, with neuroimaging evidence supporting poor superior-inferior functioning in disorders such as ADHD, depression, anxiety, and autism. However, some children with SLD can have problems with the axis, including reading, math, and writing subtypes, so the earlier dichotomy suggested—that the zones of overlapping are the source of SLD and the executive superstructure was responsible for psychopathology was an oversimplification requiring more careful examination here, and in clinical practice.

Table 62.1 presents the various neuropsychological constructs associated with academic domains. Clearly, competence in reading, math, and writing require multiple brain structures and functions. A careful examination of the neuropsychology of these disorders, based on results of both neuropsychological test and neuroimaging studies (see Berninger & Richards, 2002; Fiorello et al., 2009; Hale & Fiorello, 2004; Hale et al., 2009), suggests dysfunction in one or more of the three axes can explain the type of SLD or other disorder a child is experiencing, and whether comorbid conditions can be explained by this dysfunction. For instance, poor working memory due to prefrontal dysfunction in depression can lead to reading comprehension problems. However, it is important to recognize that these psychological processes are interrelated, so pinpointing the exact cause for a SLD or other disorder requires a systemic approach and careful analyses of the cognitive, neuropsychological, academic, and behavioral test data. It is only through careful CHT analyses that the child's pattern of performance, and associated characteristics, can be revealed.

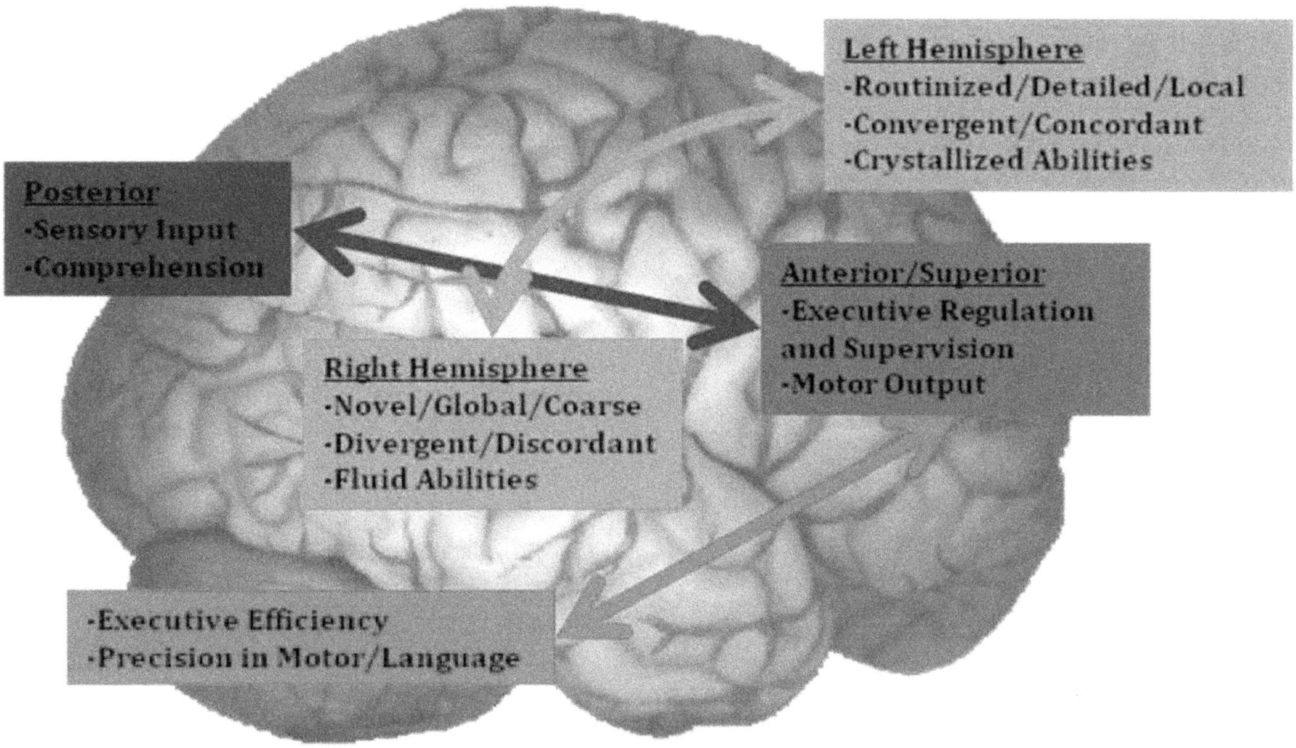

Figure 62.1. The Hale and Fiorelllo three axes approach to neuropsychological interpretation.

Table 62.1. Major Cortical Brain Regions Typically Associated With Academic Competence

Brain Region	Word Reading, Fluency, Comprehension	Mathematics Calculation and Word Problems	Written Expression and Spelling
Occipital striate—extrastriate	Orthography	Orthography	Orthography Visualization
Superior temporal	Phonology	Phonology	Phonology
Inferior temporal	Sight words Rapid naming Fluency	Sight words (reading word problems)	Sight word generation
Middle temporal	Lexical-semantic knowledge	Math fact knowledge Algorithm knowledge	Lexical-semantic for idea generation
Wernicke's area	Comprehension	Comprehension	Comprehension
Somatosensory parietal		Touch for writing Kinesthetic feedback	Touch for writing Kinesthetic feedback
Parietal zones of overlapping	Alphabetric principle (sound-symbol) Letter orientation	Number-quantity association Spatial alignment	Alphabetic principle (sound-symbol) Letter orientation
Dorsolateral	Working memory Encoding/retrieval	Working memory Encoding/retrieval Sequential processing Problem solving Fluid reasoning	Planning Organization Retrieval Ideational flexibility Evaluation Revision
Cingulate	Rapid naming Fluency	Math fact automaticity	Integration of process and knowledge
Broca's area/Exner's area	Oral expression Articulation Grammar/syntax	Oral expression Grammar/syntax (word problems)	Written expression Grammar/syntax
Occulomotor	Visual tracking	Visual tracking	Visual tracking Visual proofing
Motor		Praxis for handwriting	Praxis for handwriting

Hemispheric Functions and Academic Achievement

When acquiring a new academic skill, the frontal lobes and right hemisphere are highly involved, with executive functions working with right hemisphere functions to determine what is novel and what is known about a given academic task. The goal during learning acquisition is to shift the novel content from right frontal to left posterior regions for proficient performance, consistent with neuroimaging findings of novices and experts (Goldberg, 2001; Hale & Fiorello, 2004). As subject matter becomes well-known, the majority of processing shifts to the left hemisphere for long-term storage of automatized information and skills. When these automatized skills are later recruited to respond in a setting similar to the initial learning environment, the frontal lobes again become involved in conjunction with the left hemisphere, allowing for the utilization of learned material (e.g., retrieval of information from long-term memory). Finally, when one must think flexibly and adaptively to extend previous knowledge to novel situations or incorporate new knowledge into existing schemas, the right hemisphere once again becomes involved. This activation occurs under the direction of the frontal lobes, allowing one to capitalize on prior knowledge and learned skills. Overall, academic competency requires good executive skills and hemispheric cooperation to allow for seamless and efficient learning and application of knowledge (Hale et al., 2008).

For example, as is the case in early stages of learning any novel task, the right hemisphere is activated when children are learning the sound-symbol associations necessary for word reading. As a child starts to master these associations, activity becomes more dominant in the left hemisphere where routinized behaviors are processed (Goldberg, 2001; Shaywitz, 2003; Temple, 2003). Children who have trouble creating these associations rely heavily on right hemisphere processing for holistic and novel processing of stimuli (Ramus, 2004). Reading in these children is less automatized, thus they show substantial trouble with automatic word recognition. They also use Broca's area to help with word attack skills through articulatory mechanisms. As reading becomes more efficient (e.g., left hemisphere predominance), fMRI activation in the right hemisphere and Broca's area declines (e.g., Simos et al., 2007).

This pattern is found because the left hemisphere is a specialist in processing of automatic, routinized information (Goldberg, 2001; Bryan & Hale, 2001), making it especially good at achievement or crystallized abilities. The left hemisphere shows activation when proficient readers perform routinized tasks like remembering word meanings or recalling the sound associated with a written symbol (letters). Children with reading disabilities do not show the activation of the left posterior hemisphere typical of proficient readers (Temple, 2003; Shaywitz et al., 2004). Indeed, the left hemisphere is vitally involved in many aspects of reading, including decoding, word recognition, lexical-semantic processing, and receptive and expressive language (Daelaar, Veltman, Rombouts, Raaijmakers, & Jonker, 2003; Fiorello et al., 2006; Hale et al., 2008;). However, it is imperative to remember that reading tasks involve both hemispheres, to varying degrees. While the left hemisphere is more likely to be involved in reading that engages well-known, uncomplicated syntax and familiar language, the right hemisphere becomes involved when content becomes difficult, novel, or ambiguous (Bryan & Hale, 2001; Fiorello et al., 2009; Hale & Fiorello, 2004).

INTEGRATING NEUROPSYCHOLOGICAL PRINCIPLES IN CURRENT ASSESSMENT AND INTERVENTION PRACTICES

As discussed earlier, the best of both worlds for assessment and intervention rests in individualized assessment and intervention using a variety of data sources, and both nomothetic and idiographic interpretation of the data. With a nuanced appreciation of brain-behavior relationships, both on standardized norm-referenced tests and classroom performance, practitioners will have skill at making assessment results meaningful for intervention, especially if they adopt a Cognitive Hypothesis Testing approach. If a balanced practice approach is adopted (see Hale, 2006), RTI can be combined with comprehensive evaluation for nonresponders. The lack of response in RTI only identifies those in need of individualized neuropsychological assessment; it is the neuropsychological evaluation that determines the specific type of disorder interfering with academic achievement and/or behavior. This combined approach allows practitioners to manage a large number of children with academic difficulty, while providing individualized assessment and intervention when needed for nonresponders. Identifying the pattern of processing through neuropsychological assessment not only makes empirical sense, it also addresses the fact that children's academic difficulties may stem from specific developmental deficits, rather than developmental delays (Hale, Alfonso, et al., 2010a).

Using a cognitive/neuropsychological strengths and weaknesses processing approach through individualized comprehensive evaluation ensures only true positives for a disorder will be identified, and embraces the well-established link between cognitive processing and academic achievement. For example, to accurately identify a SLD, processing weaknesses should be associated with achievement deficits, and these difficulties should be found in the presence of processing strengths for children to meet the statutory and regulatory criteria for this disorder (Berninger & Richards, 2002; Decker, 2008; Dixon et al., 2011; Flanagan et al., 2010; Fiorello et al., 2006; Hale, Kaufman, Naglieri, & Kavale, 2006; Hale Alfonso, et al., 2010; Hale, Wycoff, & Fiorello, 2010; Mather & Gregg, 2006; Semrud-Clikeman, 2005; Wodrich, Spencer, & Daley, 2006).

Hale and Fiorello's (2004) concordance-discordance model (C-DM) offers a SLD identification method grounded in neuropsychology that follows the principles of CHT. Individual assessments are conducted with standardized cognitive and achievement measures to establish the presence of: a cognitive strength(s), a cognitive weakness(es), and an achievement deficit(s) (Hale & Fiorello, 2004). The null hypothesis that there is no cognitive processing weakness associated with the achievement deficit, or that there are no cognitive strengths relative to the cognitive weaknesses, is tested using the relatively straight forward standard error of difference formula (SED; Anastasi & Urbina, 1997) with practitioners determining whether to use 95% or 99% confidence in decision making. When combined with RTI, the C-DM approach to identifying cognitive weaknesses in the presence of cognitive integrities results in fewer children identified with SLD (Hale, Wycoff, & Fiorello, 2010). This C-DM approach has been adopted in modern achievement measures such as the WIAT-III, where it is termed a processing strengths and weaknesses model. To implement a C-DM method for identifying SLD, please see the step-by-step process in Hale, Wycoff, and Fiorello (2010).

Idiographic analysis of cognitive and neuropsychological assessment data not only leads to more accurate diagnostic decision making, but it can be used to inform intervention as well (e.g., Dixon et al., 2011; Fiorello et al., 2009; Hale, Alonso, et al., 2010; Hale, Wycoff, 7 Fiorello, 2010; Miller & Hale, 2008). CHT intervention methods are supported by recent neuroimaging and neuropsychological research showing that children with SLD and other psychopathologies use different brain areas than typical children to complete cognitive and academic tasks (Berninger & Richards, 2002; Hale et al., 2008; Simos et al., 2007). Interestingly, children who respond to intervention display normalization of brain function on neuropsychological and neuroimaging measures (Berninger & Richards, 2002; Coch, Dawson, & Fischer, 2007; Simos et al., 2007). It is only a matter of time before these technologies become prevalent and cost effective, and we will one day be using neuroimaging to determine RTI.

CONCLUSION

The cognitive processes underlying academic skills such as reading, mathematics, and writing are complex, and intertwined with psychosocial functioning. Thus, reductionistic approaches to assessment, instruction, and intervention often prove unsuccessful for young learners who do not respond to intervention. Assessment models must be sensitive and specific enough to account for the diversity of processing assets and deficits that lead to academic achievement and psychosocial problems within the context of normative levels of achievement for any given developmental stage. When standard instructional techniques are unsuccessful in helping struggling learners, differentiated and individualized instruction should take place, informed by neuropsychological theories and practices. In this chapter we propose that combining current preventative models (e.g., RTI) with comprehensive evaluation of cognitive and neuropsychological processes will meet the academic and behavioral needs of all children. As Bandura's (1978) reciprocal determinism model told us long ago, effective practice requires an understanding of cognition, behavior, and environmental interactions. As neuropsychological theory, research, and practices have emerged to affirm the value of A. R. Luria's (1973) seminal idiographic position, they are now being incorporated into classroom instruction and intervention, which we believe represents the future of education.

REFERENCES

Anastasi A., & Urbina, S. (1997). *Psychological testing.* Upper Saddle River, NY: Prentice-Hall International.

Bandura, A. (1978). The self system in reciprocal determinism. *American Psychologist, 33,* 344-358.

Barth, A. E., Stuebing, K. K., Anthony, J. L., Denton, C. A., Mathes, P. G., Fletcher, J. M., & Francis, D.J . (2008). Agreement among response to intervention criteria for identifying responder status. *Learning and Individual Differences, 18*(3), 296-307.

Berninger V., & Richards T. L. (2002). *Brain literacy for educators and psychologists.* Boston, MA: Academic Press.

Brown Waesche, J. S., Schatschneider, C., Maner, J. K., Ahmed, Y., & Wagner, R. K. (2011). Examining agreement and longitudinal stability among traditional and RTI-based definitions of disability using the affected-status agreement statistic. *Journal of Learning Disabilities, 44*(3), 296-307.

Bryan, K. L., & Hale, J. B. (2001). Differential effects of left and right cerebral vascular accidents on language competency. *Journal of the International Neuropsychological Society, 7,* 655-664.

Burns, M. K., & VanDerHeyden, A. M. (2006). Using response to intervention to assess learning disabilities: Introduction to the special series. *Assessment for Effective Intervention, 32*(1), 3-5.

Coch, D., Dawson, G., & Fischer, K. (2007). *Human behavior learning and the developing brain.* New York, NY: The Guilford Press.

Daelaar, S. M., Veltman, D. J., Rombouts, S. A. R. B., Raaijmakers, J. G. W., & Jonker, C. (2003). Neuroanatomical correlates of episodic encoding and retrieval in young and elderly subjects. *Brain, 126,* 43-56.

Decker, S. L. (2008). School neuropsychology consultation in neurodevelopmental disorders. *Psychology in the Schools,* 45(9), 799-811. doi:10.1002/pits.20327

Dixon, S. G., Eusebio, E. C., Turton, W. J., Wright, P. W. D., & Hale, J. B. (2011). *Forest Grove School District v. T.A. Supreme Court Case*: Implications for school psychology practice. *Journal of School Psychoeducational Assessment, 29*(2), 103-113.

Fiorello, C. A., Hale, J. B., Decker, S. L., & Coleman, S. (2009). Neuropsychology in school psychology. In E. Garcia-Vazquez, T. D. Crespi, & C. A, Riccio (Eds.), *Handbook of education, training and supervision of school psychologists in school and community* (Vol. 1, pp. 213-232). New York, NY: Taylor & Francis.

Fiorello, C. A., Hale, J. B., Holdnack, J. A., Kavanagh, J. A., Terrell, J., & Long, L. (2007). Interpreting intelligence test results for children with disabilities: Is global intelligence relevant? Applied *Neuropsychology, 14,* 2-12.

Fiorello, C. A., Hale, J. B., & Snyder, L. E. (2006). Cognitive hypothesis testing and response to intervention for children with reading problems. *Psychology in the Schools, 43*(8), 835-853.

Fiorello, C. A., Hale, J. B., Snyder, L. E., & Teodori, A. (2008). Validating individual differences through examination of converging psychometric and neuropsychological models of cognitive functioning. In S. K. Thurman, & C. A. Fiorello (Eds.) *Applied Cognitive Research in K-3 Classrooms* (pp. 151-185). New York, NY: Routledge.

Flanagan, D. P., Fiorello, C. A., & Ortiz, S. O. (2010). Enhancing practice through application of Cattell-Horn-Carroll theory and research: A "third method" approach to specific learning disability identification. *Psychology in the Schools, 47,* 739-760.

Fletcher, J. M., Foorman, B. R., Boudousquie, A., Barnes, M. A., Schatschneider, C., & Francis, D. J. (2002). Assessment of reading and learning disabilities: A research-based intervention-oriented approach. *Journal of School Psychology, 40*(1), 27-63. doi:10.1016/S0022-4405(01)00093-0

Fuchs, D. F., Fuchs, L. S., & Compton, D. L. (2004). Identifying reading disabilities by responsiveness-to-instruction: Specifying measures and criteria. *Learning Disability Quarterly, 7*(4), 216-227.

Fuchs, D., Hale, J. B., & Kearns, D. (2011). Cognitive and neuropsychological assessment data that inform educational intervention: An introduction to the special issue and critical analysis. *Journal of Learning Disabilities, 44,* 99-104.

Goldberg, E. (2001). *The executive brain: Frontal lobes and the civilized mind.* New York, NY: Oxford University Press.

Hale, J.B. (2006). Implementing IDEA 2004 with a three-tier model that includes response to intervention and cognitive assessment methods. *School Psychology Forum: Research in Practice, 1*(1), 16-27.

Hale, J., Alfonso, V., Berninger, V., Bracken, B., Christo, C., Clark, E., … Yalof, J. (2010). Critical Issues in response-to-intervention, comprehensive evaluation, and specific learning disabilities identification and intervention: An expert white paper consensus. *Learning Disability Quarterly, 33,* 223-236.

Hale, J. B., Fiorello, C. A., Miller, J. A., Wenrich, K., Toedori, A. M., & Henzel, J. (2008). WISC-IV assessment and intervention strategies for children with specific learning disabilities. In A. Prifitera, D. H. Saklofske, & L. G. Weiss (Eds.), *WISC-IV Clinical Assessment and Intervention* (2nd ed., pp. 109-171). New York:, NY: Elsevier.

Hale, J. B., & Fiorello, C. A. (2004). *School neuropsychology: A practitioner's handbook.* New York, NY: Guilford Press.

Hale, J. B., Fiorello, C. A., Kavanagh, J. A., Holdnack, J. A., & Aloe, A. M. (2007). Is the demise of IQ interpretation justified? A response to special issue authors. *Applied Neuropsychology, 14,* 37-51.

Hale, J. B., Flanagan, D. P., & Naglieri, J. A. (2008). Alternative research-based methods for IDEA (2004) identification of children with specific learning disabilities. *Communiqué, 36*(8), 1, 14-17.

Hale, J. B., Kaufman, A., Naglieri, J. A., & Kavale, K. A. (2006). Implementation of IDEA: Integrating response to intervention and cognitive assessment methods. *Psychology in the Schools, 43*(7), 753-770. doi:10.1002/pits.20186

Hale, J. B., Reddy, L. A., Wilcox, G., McLaughlin, A., Hain, L., Stern, A., … Eusebio, E. (2009). Assessment and intervention for children with ADHD and other frontal-striatal circuit disorders. In D. C. Miller (Ed.), *Best practices in school neuropsychology: Guidelines for effective practice, assessment and evidence-based interventions* (pp. 225-279). Hoboken, NJ: John Wiley & Sons.

Hale, J. B., Wycoff, K. L., & Fiorello, C. A. (2010). RTI and cognitive hypothesis testing for identification and intervention of specific learning disabilities: The best of both worlds. In D. P. Flanagan, & V. Alfonso (Eds.), *Essentials of Specific Learning Disability Assessment* (pp. 173-201). Hoboken, NJ: Wiley.

Luria, A. R. (1973). *The working brain.* New York, NY: Basic Books.

Mather, N., & Gregg, N. (2006). Specific learning disabilities: Clarifying, not eliminating, a construct. *Professional Psychology: Research and Practice, 37*(1), 99-106. doi:10.1037/0735-7028.37.1.99

Miller, D. C., & Hale, J. B. (2008). Neuropsychological applications of the WISC-IV and WISC-IV Integrated. In A. Prifitera, D. H. Saklofske, & L. G. Weiss (Eds.), *WISC-IV clinical assessment and intervention* (2nd ed., pp. 445-495). New York, NY: Elsevier Science.

Ramus, F. (2004). The neural basis of reading acquisition. In M.S. Gazzaniga (Ed.), *The cognitive neurosciences* (3rd ed., pp. 815-824). Cambridge, MA: MIT Press.

Reynolds, C. R., Kamphaus, R. W., Rosenthal, B. L., & Hiemenz, J. R. (1997). Applications of the Kaufman Assessment Battery for Children (K-ABC) in neuropsychological assessment. In *Handbook of clinical child neuropsychology* (2nd ed., pp. 252-269). New York, NY: Plenum.

Semrud-Clikeman, M. (2005). Neuropsychological aspects for evaluating learning disabilities. *Journal of learning Disabilities, 38,* 563-568.

Shaywitz, S. E. (2003). *Overcoming dyslexia: A new and complete science-based program for reading problems at any level.* New York, NY: Alfred A. Knopf.

Shaywitz, B. A., Shaywitz, S. E., Blachman, B. A., Pugh, K. R., Fullbright, R. K., Skudlarski, P., … Gore, J. C. (2004). Development of left occipitotemporal systems for skilled reading in children after a phonologically-based intervention. *Biological Psychiatry, 55*(9), 926-933.

Simos, P. G., Fletcher, J. M., Sarkari, S., Billingsley, R. L., Denton, C., & Papnicolaou, A. C. (2007). Altering the brain circuits through intervention: A magnetic source imaging study. *Neurospsychology, 21*(4), 485-486. doi:10.1037/0894-4105.21.4.485

Simos, P. G., Fletcher, J. M., Sarkari, S., Billingsley, R. L., Francis, D. J., Castillo, E. M., ... Papanicolaou, A. C. (2005). Early development of neurophysiological processes involved in normal reading and reading disability: A magnetic source imaging study. *Neuropsychology, 19*(6), 787-798. doi:10.1037/0894-4105.19.6.787

Speece, D. L. (2005). Hitting the moving target known as reading development: Some thoughts on screening children for secondary interventions. *Journal of Learning Disabilities, 38*(6), 487-493.

Temple, E. (2003). Changes in brain function in children with dyslexia after training. *Phonics Bulletin, The International Reading and Special Report, 1.*

Tulving, E., Kapurt, S., Craik, F. I. M., Moscovitch, M., & Houle, S. (1994). Hemispheric encoding/retrieval asymmetry in episodic memory: Positron emission tomography findings. *Proceedings of the National Academy of Sciences of the United States of America, 91*, 2016-2020.

Ysseldyke, J. E. (2009). When politics trumps science: Generalizations from a career of research on assessment. *Communique, 38*(4), 14-16.

Wodrich, D. L., Spencer, M. L., & Daley, K. B. (2006). Combining RTI and psychoeducational assessment: What we must to do otherwise. *Psychology in the Schools, 43*, 797-806.

Author Contact Information: Andrea Schneider, Department of Psychology, P. O. Box 3050, University of Victoria, Victoria, British Columbia, Canada, V8W 3P5.

CHAPTER 63

School Neuropsychology Conceptual Model

Daniel C. Miller
Texas Woman's University

Miller (2007, 2010) introduced the school neuropsychological conceptual model (SNP model) as a way of organizing school-age, cross-battery assessment data based upon the underlying principle neuropsychological constructs being measured. The purposes of the SNP model are: (a) to facilitate clinical interpretation by providing an organizational framework for the assessment data; (b) to strengthen the linkage between assessment and evidence-based interventions; and (c) to provide a common frame of reference for evaluating the effects of neurodevelopmental disorders on neurocognitive processes. The complete SNP model includes the integration of academic achievement and social-emotional functioning with the major neuropsychological assessment components (see Miller, 2007, 2010; Miller & Maricle, 2012); however, the focus of this narrative will only be on the neurocognitive portions.

The SNP model (see Table 63.1) is divided into seven broad classifications representing basic neurocognitive functions and processes, including: sensorimotor functions, attentional processes, visual-spatial processes, language functions, learning and memory, executive functions, and speed and efficiency of cognitive processing. Within the SNP model, all of these broad classifications except for speed and efficiency of cognitive processing are further subdivided into what are being referred to as second order classifications. As an example, sensorimotor tasks (broad classification) can be further subdivided into the second order classifications of lateral preference, sensory functions, gross motor functions, and fine motor functions. These second order classifications can be further subdivided into third order classifications. As an example, the second order classification of sensory functions can be further subdivided into the third order classifications of visual acuity, auditory perception, kinesthetic perception, olfactory perception, and tactile sensation and perception. See Table 63.1 for the full delineation of the broad classifications broken down by second and third order classifications.

Original Development and Iterations of the Model

The school neuropsychology conceptual model was introduced in *Essentials of School Neuropsychological Assessment* (Miller, 2007). Early iterations of the model stem from neuropsychological assessment classes taught since 1990 at Texas Woman's University as part of the Doctoral School Psychology Program. The SNP model represents a synthesis of several theoretical and clinical approaches including: Lurian theory (Luria, 1966, 1973), a process-oriented approach to assessment (Milberg, Hebben, & Kaplan, 2009), neuropsychological theories (e.g., Mirsky's [1996] theory of attention), the cross-battery assessment approach (Flanagan, Ortiz, & Alfonso, 2007), and Cattell-Horn-Carroll (CHC) theory (McGrew, 2005). Since, 2007, the SNP model has evolved as a result of extensive usage in the field with clinical cases (see Miller, 2010; and Miller & Maricle, 2012, for the more recent iterations of the model).

In the initial development of the SNP model, CHC theory and cross-battery assessment were used to classify the subtests from the major tests of cognitive abilities into broad classifications. However, these theoretical models did not adequately address other important neurocognitive processes such as sensorimotor functions, attentional processes, working memory, and executive functions. Therefore, the SNP model integrated additional neuropsychological theories such as Mirsky's (1996) theory of attention and Baddeley

The Handbook of Educational Theories, pp. 761–766

Table 63.1. School Neuropsychology Conceptual Model

Broad Classifications	*Second Order Classifications*	*Third Order Classifications*
Sensorimotor functions	• Lateral preference	
	• Sensory functions	• Visual acuity • Auditory perception • Kinesthetic perception • Olfactory perception • Tactile sensation and perception
	• Gross motor functions	• Balance • Coordination
	• Fine motor functions	• Coordinated finger/hand movements • Psychomotor speed • Visual-motor copying skills
Attentional processes	• Selective/focused attention	• Auditory selective/focused attention • Visual selective/focused attention
	• Sustained attention	• Auditory sustained attention • Visual sustained attention • Auditory and visual sustained attention
	• Shifting attention	• Verbal shifting attention • Visual shifting attention • Verbal and visual shifting attention
	• Attentional capacity	• Memory for numbers, letters, or visual sequences • Memory for words and sentences • Memory for stories
Visuospatial processes	• Visual spatial perception	• Visual discrimination and spatial localization • Visual-motor constructions
	• Visual spatial reasoning	• Recognizing spatial configurations • Visual gestalt closure • Visuospatial analyses with and without mental rotations
	• Visual scanning/ tracking	• Direct measures • Indirect measures
Language functions	• Sound discrimination	
	• Auditory processing	
	• Oral expression	• Oral motor production • Vocabulary knowledge • Verbal fluency (rapid automatic naming)
	• Receptive language	• Receptive language with verbal response • Receptive language with nonverbal motor response
Learning and memory	• Rate of learning	• Verbal learning • Visual learning • Paired associative learning
	• Immediate verbal memory	• Letter recall (no contextual cues) • Number recall (no contextual cues) • Word recall (no contextual cues) • Sentence recall (contextual cues) • Story recall (contextual cues)
	• Delayed verbal memory	• Recall with contextual cues • Recall without contextual cues • Verbal recognition
	• Immediate visual memory	• Abstract designs, spatial locations, or visual sequences with motor response (no contextual cues) • Faces, objects, or pictures with verbal or pointing response (no contextual cues) • Visual digit span with verbal response (no contextual cues) • Picture or symbolic (with context)

(Table continues on next page)

Table 63.1. Continued

Broad Classifications	*Second Order Classifications*	*Third Order Classifications*
	• Delayed visual memory	• Recall without contextual cues • Recall with contextual cues • Visual recognition
	• Verbal-visual associative learning and recall	• Verbal-visual associative learning • Verbal-visual associative delayed recall
	• Working memory	• Verbal working memory • Visual working memory
	• Semantic memory	•
Executive Functions	• Concept recognition and generation	• Concept recognition • Concept generation
	• Problem solving, fluid reasoning, and planning	• Verbal problem solving, fluid reasoning, and planning • Visual problem solving, fluid reasoning, and planning
	• Response inhibition	• Verbal response inhibition • Motoric response inhibition
	• Retrieval fluency	• Verbal retrieval fluency • Nonverbal retrieval fluency
Speed and Efficiency of Cognitive Processing	• Speed efficiency • Speed efficiency and accuracy	

and Hitch's (1974) theory of working memory (Baddeley, 2003). The SNP Model is also heavily influenced by Kaplan's process-oriented approach (Milberg et al., 2009), which resulted in the inclusion of qualitative, as well as, quantitative assessment data. Recognizing what strategies individuals employ during performance on any given task is just as important, if not more, than the test score itself. This principle is inherent to the SNP Model.

Finally, the SNP model follows a Lurian approach in which an individual's neurocognitive strengths and weakness are systematically determined by varying the input, processing, and output demands across a variety of tasks (see Hale & Fiorello, 2004 for a discussion of what is called conducting demand characteristics analyses). As an example, it is not sufficient to say a child has an attentional processing problem and leave it at that broad diagnostic level. The SNP model emphasizes the need to further define the type of attentional deficit(s) the child may be experiencing such as a shifting, sustained, or selective attention deficit. Narrowing down to greater neurocognitive processing specificity in assessment for each of the broad SNP classifications will lead to more refined prescriptive remediations, accommodations, and interventions.

Once the classification schema for the SNP model was created, individual tests from the major instruments used in the assessment of pediatric cognition, academic achievement, neuropsychological functioning, attention, learning and memory were classified into the SNP model using a variety of techniques. Published correlational and factorial data were used to group tests together that were shown to measure similar neuropsychological processes or functions. When such data were not available, tests were classified into the SNP Model based on what the authors reported the tests were designed to measure.

Validation of the Model

The neuropsychological constructs posited by the SNP model are widely accepted in the neuropsychological and cognitive literature. The measures being utilized in the SNP model have been validated and are widely accepted to be adequate measures of their respective neurocognitive constructs. What makes the SNP model unique is the cross-battery integration of neurocognitive constructs. The validation of the SNP model as delineated is what is beginning to be validated.

In a series of initial unpublished studies, data were drawn from an archival sample of 956 mixed clinical case studies conducted by students in the KIDS, Inc.'s (2010) School Neuropsychology Post-Graduate Certification Program. Cross-battery data from the *Woodcock Johnson III Tests of Cognitive Abilities* (WJIII-COG: Woodcock, McGrew, & Mather, 2007), *Wechsler Intelligence Scale for Children—Fourth Edition Integrated* (Wechsler et al., 2004), NEPSY/NEPSY-II (Korkman, Kirk, & Kemp, 1998, 2007), *Delis Kaplan Executive Function System* (D-KEFS: Delis, Kaplan, & Kramer, 2001), *Test of Everyday Attention for Children* (TEA-Ch: Manly, Robertson, Anderson, & Nimmo-Smith, 1999), *Comprehensive Test of Phonological Processing* (CTOPP: Wagner, Torgensen, & Rashotte, 1999), *Test of Memory and Learning—Second Edition* (TOMAL-2: Reynolds & Voress, 2007), and the *Wide Range Assessment of Memory and Learning—Second Edition* (WRAML2: Sheslow & Adams, 2003) were initially classified into the SNP model based on the procedures previously outlined.

Separate exploratory factor analyses were conducted on the cross-battery of tests classified into each of the broad SNP classifications. The purpose of these analyses was to determine the validity of the second order classifications within the SNP model. Please note that due to the limits of the data sets analyzed in the factor analyses, that not all second order classifications could be validated; therefore, some the second order classifications in the SNP model as presented in Table 63.1 remain to be validated.

The factor analysis of the second order classifications of sensorimotor functions (Phillips, Fournier, Miller, & Maricle, 2011) revealed a three factor solution: visual motor copying skills, coordinated hand/finger movements, and psychomotor speed. In these analyses, no measures of lateral preference were included so this second order sensorimotor function could not yet be validated.

Within the attentional processing broad classification, the factor analyses supported the second order classifications of selective/focused, sustained, and shifting attention, but did not support a separate factor for divided attention (Miller, Bradford, & Maricle, 2011). In these analyses, no measures of attentional capacity were included so this second order attentional process could not yet be validated. The factor analyses of the visual-spatial processes did not support the visual perception with motor and without motor response dichotomy as second order classifications, but rather supported two factors related to visual-spatial perception and visual-spatial reasoning (Canas, Sevadjian, Miller, & Maricle, 2011). In these analyses, no measures of visual scanning/tracking were included so this second order visual-spatial process could not yet be validated.

The factor analysis of second order classifications of language functions (Rowden, Cioffi, Miller, & Maricle, 2011) generally supported a three factor solution: phonological/auditory processing, oral expression, and receptive language. However, the tests thought to measure phonological/auditory processing subdivided into broader language constructs. For example, the WJIII-COG Incomplete Words and Sound Blending formed a factor reflecting higher order auditory analysis/synthesis. In terms of oral expression, not all tests designed to measure verbal fluency loaded together. The factor analyses yielded three separate factors related to verbal fluency, based on differences in the format of the test. The receptive language tests generally held together into one factor.

The factor analysis of the second order classifications of memory (Cioffi, Rowden, Miller, & Maricle, 2011) did not support the predicted factor structure consisting of immediate memory, delayed memory, associative memory, and working memory. Many of the factors obtained were specific to the test batteries they came from. For example, immediate memory tests from the TOMAL2 and WRAML2, loaded on two separate factors. Additional analyses need to be performed to better clarify the factor structure of the memory tests from across various instruments.

The factor analysis of the second order classifications of executive functions (Sevadjian, Canas, Miller, & Maricle, 2011) generally supported the factors of concept recognition/generation, problem solving, fluid reasoning, and planning, response inhibition, and retrieval fluency. Some of the tests designed to measure constructs such as problem solving or fluid reasoning separated into two or more factors based on modality (verbal or visual).

The factor analysis of the speed and efficiency of cognitive processing tests (Fournier, Phillips, Miller, & Maricle, 2011) yielded a two factor solution. The processing speed tests from the WISC-IV/WISC-IV Integrated and the WJIII-COG separated into two distinct factors. As a result of these preliminary factor analytic studies, several changes were made in the SNP Model from previous versions (Miller, 2007, 2010; Miller & Maricle, 2012), and are reflected in Table 63.1.

The Use and Application of the Model

Traditional psychoeducational reports frequently present test results from the first instrument, then the second, third, and so on with little deference given to the common underlying neuropsychological constructs being measured. Rather than reporting test scores in a linear fashion, the SNP model reports test scores in a more integrative fashion. If a practitioner followed the SNP Model, the school neuropsychological assessment report would report the test results according to the broad classifications, rather than being test battery dependent.

The goal of any formalized assessment of a child's potential learning problems should be to gain greater insight into the student's strengths and weaknesses and to provide linkage to evidence-based prescriptive interventions. Too often school districts try a "one size fits all" approach to teaching without acknowledging each individual learner's neurocognitive strengths and weaknesses. A major goal of the SNP model is to provide clinicians with a framework for generating and testing hypotheses about a student's learning profile in order to use that information gleaned from assessment to provide more efficient and effective interventions.

From a clinical research standpoint, the SNP model is helpful in providing a common "lens" to examine the unique and shared neurocognitive profiles of neurodevelopmental disorders. For example, what are the neurocognitive strengths and weakness of children diagnosed with autism and how is that pattern of processing different from children identified with attention deficit hyperactivity disorder. See Miller (2010) for examples of how the SNP model is applied to common neurodevelopmental disorders.

Critiques of the Model

The primary intended purpose of the SNP model is to provide clinicians with a framework for clinical interpretation of cross-battery neuropsychological assessment data. There are several inherent cautions that clinicians must keep in mind when interpreting cross-battery data. First, just because two authors claim to be measuring the same cognitive process, there can be statistically significant differences between those two measures due to differences in the standardization samples used in the norming process of each test and the psychometric characteristics (e.g., reliability) of the two measures. A second consideration is the demand characteristics of tasks. As an example, two tasks can be designed to measure working memory but one used digits recalled backwards and another requires letters recalled backwards. The differences in how test stimuli are presented and what cognitive processes are employed to solve the tasks will ultimately affect performance. Therefore, tests designed to measure the same neurocognitive construct are not always interchangeable. The processing speed measures from the WJ III COG and the WISC-IV are classic examples, as presented in the previous section.

A third consideration is the unique variance that each individual brings to the assessment process. Two tests may be designed to measure the same cognitive process but the individual may approach each task using a different strategy based on the input and output demands of the task and as a result yields differing results. The SNP Model does not replace clinical judgment by the clinician. It is hoped that the SNP model will help facilitate better informed clinical judgments based on the analyses of individual strengths and weaknesses within a processing approach to assessment.

Research Related to the Model

Avirett (2011) examined the underlying factor structure of executive functions tests from the WJIII-COG (Woodcock et al., 2001), the *NEPSY* (Korkman et al., 1998), and the D-KEFS (Delis et al., 2001), and their fit with three theories of executive functioning. The three theories that were analyzed included the Anderson, Levin, and Jacob (2002) model of executive functioning, the Cattell-Horn-Carroll theory of cognitive abilities (McGrew, 2005), and the conceptual model for school neuropsychological assessment (Miller, 2007, 2010). The level of fit between executive functioning models and the sample data was depicted using structural equation modeling and analyzed using confirmatory factor analysis. The SNP model indicated the best fit with sample data.

Mortimer (2011) conducted a similar study by examining the underlying factor structure of the tests designed to measure aspects of attention from the WJ III COG (Woodcock et al., 2007), the *NEPSY* (Korkman et al., 1998), and the D-KEFS (Delis et al., 2001), and their fit with four theories of attention. The four theories analyzed were Mirsky's (1996) model of attention, CHC theory (McGrew, 2005), the SNP model (Miller, 2007, 2010), and a model which examines tasks based on the sensory input demands (auditory or visual) of the attention tasks. Relationships between the theories and attention subtests were examined using structural equation modeling and analyzed using confirmatory factor analysis. A simple two factor model, either visual attention or auditory attention was the best fit with the sample data. Unfortunately this study did not include data from the TEA-Ch (Manly et al., 1999), which is based on Mirsky's (1996) model of attention, and serves as the theoretical foundation for the attentional processing classifications within the SNP Model. Inclusion of the TEA-Ch data in the analysis might have altered the outcome of the factor analysis. As it stands the results of Mortimer's study suggests that the attentional measures from the WJIII-COG, NEPSY, and D-KEFS do not seem to have an underlying and unifying theory.

References

Anderson, V., Levin, H. S., & Jacobs, R. (2002). Executive functioning after frontal lobe injury: A developmental perspective. In D. T. Stuss & R.T. Knight (Eds.), *Principles of frontal lobe function* (pp. 504-527). New York, NY: Oxford University Press.

Avirett, E. K. (2011). *Validity of executive functioning tasks across the WJ III COG, NEPSY, and D-KEFS in a clinical population of children: applicability to three neurocognitive theories.* (Doctoral dissertation). Texas Woman's University, Denton, TX.

Baddeley, A. (2003). Working memory: Looking back and looking forward. *Nature Reviews Neuroscience, 4*, 829-839.

Baddeley, A., & Hitch, G. J. (1974). Working memory. In G. H. Bower (Ed.), *The psychology of learning and motivation: Advances in research and theory* (Vol. 8, pp. 47-89). New York, NY: Academic Press.

Canas, A. M., Sevadjian, C. P., Miller, D. C., & Maricle, D. E. (2011, July). *Validation of visual spatial classifications within the school neuropsychological conceptual model using exploratory factor analysis in a mixed clinical group sample.* Poster session presented at the School Neuropsychology Summer Institute, Grapevine, TX.

Cioffi, P., Rowden, A., Miller, D. C., & Maricle, D. E. (2011, July). *Validation of memory processing classifications within the school neuropsychological conceptual model using exploratory factor analysis in a mixed clinical group sample.* Poster session presented at the School Neuropsychology Summer Institute, Grapevine, TX.

Delis, D. C., Kaplan, E., & Kramer, J. (2001). *Delis Kaplan executive function system.* San Antonio, TX: The Psychological Corporation.

Flanagan, D. P., Ortiz, S. O., & Alfonso, V. C. (2007). *Essentials of cross-battery assessment*—(2nd ed.) Hoboken, NJ: Wiley.

Fournier, A., Phillips, J, Miller, D. C., & Maricle, D. E. (2011, July). *Validation of processing speed within the school neuropsychological conceptual model and neuropsychological processing concerns checklist using exploratory factor analysis and pearson product-moment correlations.* Poster session presented at the School Neuropsychology Summer Institute, Grapevine, TX.

Hale, J. B., & Fiorello, C. A. (2004). *School neuropsychology: A practitioner's handbook.* New York, NY: Guilford Press.

Manly, T., Robertson, I. H., Anderson, V., & Nimmo-Smith, I. (1999). *Test of Everyday Attention for Children (TEA-Ch)* manual. San Antonio, TX: Harcourt Assessment.

KIDS, Inc. (2010). [Archival data from case studies collected as part of requirements for the School Neuropsychology Post-Graduate Certification Program—2007-2010]. Unpublished raw data. Hickory Creek, TX.

Korkman, M., Kirk, U., & Kemp, S. (1998). *NEPSY: A Developmental Neuropsychological Assessment.* San Antonio, TX: The Psychological Corporation.

Korkman, M., Kirk, U., & Kemp, S. (2007). *NEPSY II: A developmental neuropsychological assessment: Administration Manual.* San Antonio, TX: The Psychological Corporation.

Luria, A. R. (1966). *The working brain: An introduction to neuropsychology.* New York, NY: Basic Books.

Luria, A. R., (1973). *Higher cortical functions in man* (2nd ed.). New York, NY: Basic Books.

McGrew, K. (2005). The Cattell-Horn-Carroll theory of cognitive abilities: past, present, and future. In D. P. Flanagan, J. L. Genshaft, & P. L. Harrison (Eds.), *Contemporary intellectual assessment: Theories, tests, and issues* (pp. 151-179). New York, NY: Guilford.

Milberg, W. P, Hebben, N. A, Kaplan, E. (2009). The Boston process approach to neuropsychological assessment. In I. Grant & K. Adams (Eds.), *Neuropsychological assessment of neuropsychiatric disorders* (3rd ed., pp. 42-65). New York, NY: Oxford University Press.

Miller, D. C. (2007). *Essentials of school neuropsychological assessment.* Hoboken, NJ: Wiley.

Miller, D. C. (2010). School neuropsychological assessment and intervention. In D. C. Miller (Ed.), *Best practices in school neuropsychology: Guidelines for effective practice, assessment, and evidence-based intervention* (pp. 81-100). Hoboken, NJ: Wiley.

Miller, D. C., Bradford, J., & Maricle, D. E. (2011, July). *Validation of attentional processing classifications within the school neuropsychological conceptual model using exploratory factor analysis in a mixed clinical group sample.* Poster session presented at the School Neuropsychology Summer Institute, Grapevine, TX.

Miller, D. C., & Maricle, D. (2012). The emergence of neuropsychological constructs into tests of intelligence. In D. P. Flanagan & Patti L. Harrison (Eds.), *Contemporary intellectual assessment* (3rd ed.) New York, NY: The Guilford Press.

Mirsky, A. F. (1996). Disorders of attention: A neuropsychological perspective. In G. R., Lyon & N. A. Krasnegor (Eds.), *Attention, memory, and executive function* (pp. 71-95). Baltimore, MD: Paul H. Brookes.

Mortimer, J. E. (2011). *Examining the concurrent validity of visual and auditory attention tasks of the D-KEFS, NEPSY, and WJ III COG using structural equation modeling* (Doctoral dissertation). Texas Woman's University, Denton, TX.

Phillips, J., Fournier, A., Miller, D. C., & Maricle, D. E. (2011, July). *Validation of sensory motor classifications within the school neuropsychological conceptual model using exploratory factor analysis in a mixed clinical group sample.* Poster session presented at the School Neuropsychology Summer Institute, Grapevine, TX.

Reynolds, C. R., & Voress, J. K. (2007). *Test of memory and learning* (2nd ed.). Austin, TX: Pro-Ed.

Rowden, A. S., Cioffi, P., Miller, D. C., & Maricle, D. E. (2011, July). *Validation of language classifications within the school neuropsychological conceptual model using exploratory factor analysis in a mixed clinical group sample.* Poster session presented at the School Neuropsychology Summer Institute, Grapevine, TX.

Sevadjian, C. P., Canas, A. M., Miller, D. C., & Maricle, D. E. (2011, July). *Validation of executive functions classifications within the school neuropsychological conceptual model using exploratory factor analysis in a mixed clinical group sample.* Poster session presented at the School Neuropsychology Summer Institute, Grapevine, TX.

Sheslow, D., & Adams, W. (2003). *Wide range assessment of memory and learning* (2nd ed.). Wilmington, DE: Wide Range.

Wagner, R., Torgensen, J., & Rashotte, C. (1999). *Comprehensive Test of Phonological Processing.* Minneapolis, MN: Pearson, Assessments.

Wechsler, D., Kaplan, E., Fein, D., Morris, E., Kramer, J. H., Maerlender, A., & Delis, D. C. (2004). *The Wechsler Intelligence Scale for Children—Integrated technical and interpretative manual* (4th ed.). San Antonio, TX: Harcourt Assessment, Inc.

Woodcock, R. W., McGrew, K. S., & Mather, N. (2007). *Woodcock Johnson-III Tests of Cognitive Abilities.* Itasca, IL: Riverside.

Author Contact Information: Daniel C. Miller, PhD, Texas Woman's University, Department of Psychology and Philosophy, P.O. Box 425470, Denton, TX 76204.

CHAPTER 64

Individual Differences in the Ability to Process Information

W. Joel Schneider
Illinois State University

Kevin S. McGrew
The Institute of Applied Psychometrics

Cognitive performance models attempt to integrate the findings of two grand traditions of scientific psychology: the experimental study of information processing and the measurement of individual differences in cognitive abilities. One tradition is concerned with how the mind typically works while the other describes how minds differ. To use a statistical metaphor and only a mild exaggeration, one is about the mean, the other the standard deviation. One tradition draws mostly from experimental findings from academic labs whereas the other draws primarily from population-wide psychometric studies of cognitive abilities thought to be important for success in academic, occupational, and other life settings.

Information processing theories describe the interplay of perception, attention, memory, and reasoning as people learn information and solve problems. Although information processing theorists do care about the brain, their emphasis is less on brain function location and more how the brain processes information during the learning and problem-solving process. Information processing theorists acknowledge the fact that not all people process information equally well or even in the same way. However, the emphasis is less on understanding the unique challenges of individuals and more on understanding what we have in common, the species-typical functions of the mind.

In contrast, cognitive ability theorists focus on identifying meaningful differences in people's measured discrete abilities. Whereas information processing theorists describe *how* different kinds of cognitive functions work, cognitive ability researchers measure *how well* those functions work in an individual. Cognitive ability researchers focus on establishing empirical relations between specific cognitive abilities and important life outcomes such as academic and occupational success. In general, cognitive ability theorists do not necessarily need to understand how problems are solved as they are mainly concerned about whether a person can solve it, and how individuals differ in their relative proficiency. By analogy, although a racecar driver might be interested how engineer describes how a particular car works, the driver's primary concern is knowing how well the car performs under various conditions during a race.

Cognitive performance models are attempts to integrate findings from both traditions in cognitive psychology. The goal is to assist educators, clinicians, and caregivers in providing their clients with (a) a rich informative understanding of their cognitive strengths and weaknesses and (b) a realistic and practical plan for overcoming their academic and occupational difficulties. This is not always easy as the development of cognitive performance models are still in their infancy. This introduction to cognitive performance models provides a broad overview of the main features of cognitive performance models. Space does not allow a detailed comparison of different models. A more thorough review can be found in Hunt (2011) and Floyd and Kranzler (2012).

The Handbook of Educational Theories, pp. 767–782

Information Processing

To process something is to alter it so it becomes more useful. A carrot is not useful until your digestive system breaks it down to usable components and discards what is not useful. Likewise, the raw information your senses gather is not useful to you until your brain breaks it down into elementary parts and then reassembles it in ways that make it understandable and usable. That is, *perception* is when the brain makes sense of sensation. Much of what occurs in perception is automatic and occurs without your conscious knowledge. When you are aware of what your brain is perceiving, it is called *consciousness*. The processes that govern which perceptions arise in consciousness are called *attention*. Sometimes important information comes to our attention but we do not need it immediately. Storing and retrieving information for later use is called *memory*. Combining information in memory in ways that solve new problems is called *reasoning*. Information processing theories attempt to explain how information is perceived, attended to, stored in memory, retrieved from memory, and reasoned with to solve problems.

Sensation and the Problem of too Much Information

Much of what information processing theories need to explain is the fact that our senses gather much more information than we can perceive at one time. From the myriad of information our brain perceives at any moment, only a fraction can be the focus of attention. That is, at every moment your senses are relaying to your brain an extraordinary amount of information about the external world. Some of this sensory information is selected for processing to see if it might be useful. Most perceived information is not particularly useful and is forgotten almost immediately as it is not attended to consciously. For example, as you read this chapter, you are unlikely to have noticed the sensation of the fabric of your shirt on your shoulder, the sound of your own breathing, the particular shade of white used for the paper in this book, or the smell of the room. Even when you are not eating, messages about the taste of your own saliva are continuously being sent to your brain. Fortunately, we are able to ignore these signals until more interesting and informative events occur.

Your brain, whether you are aware of it or not, is constantly monitoring sensory information for changes that might be important. When a sensation on your brain's watch list is detected (e.g., the smell of toxic fumes, a sharp pain of an injury, the cry of a distressed child, the sight of large objects rushing towards you), the focus of your attention is drawn to it immediately and automatically. When conversing in a crowded room, you typically ignore all other conversations. However, if anyone in the room says your name, even in passing, you often hear it and orient to that person (for obvious reasons, this observation is known as the "Cocktail Party Effect."). Thus, even the sound of your own name is on your brain's watch list.

Perception With Feature Detectors

Your brain adopts a divide-and conquer-strategy as it is bombarded with a constant stream of information. If you ever had an instructor assign more reading than one person could possibly cover in the time provided, you may have deployed a strategy with a group of students in the class. Each group member would read part of the assigned reading and then summarize it for the rest of the group. This works well unless there are weak links in specific group members' summaries. This group strategy can backfire if the exam requires you to integrate information across all readings. The brain has similar integration problems.

The brain takes raw sensory information and different specialized groups of neurons called *feature detectors* respond to different characteristics of the information (Treisman, 1998). For example, when you see the capital letter "A", one feature detector says, "Somewhere (and I have no idea where, that is another detector's job!) there is a horizontal line." Another detector, the 70° line detector, says, "I detect a line at an orientation of 70°." The 110° line detector also reports that there is a line at a 110° angle. The other line detectors that are responsible for detecting lines at different orientations (e.g., 10°, 20°, 30°, ... 160°, 170°) all say "I have nothing to report." Other detectors are insensitive to the orientation of the lines but instead report when lines are joined at certain angles. In this case, the top of the A makes the 50° angle detector report the presence of a 50° angle. Other detectors that are insensitive to the orientations and angles of the lines specify where the lines are in the visual field. Other detectors report on the presence or absence of other visual features such as curves, colors, textures, and movement.

Much of the perceptual information the brain constantly processes remains unconnected until a stimulus becomes the object of focus in attention (Treisman, 1998). That is, the legions of feature detectors do not talk among themselves much (although some talk to higher-order detectors that detect complex features). However, at the moment of consciousness, the various features of the object are recognized as belonging to the same object. The combination of features is compared with templates stored in long-term memory and if a match is found the object is recognized, in this case as the letter "A."

Feature detectors are not entirely passive. They respond to experience and adapt to frequently encountered patterns. They also can be primed to respond to expected stimuli. That is, the brain is constantly forecasting what is likely to happen in the next few seconds and attempts to match incoming stimuli with expectations (Hawkins, 2004). Information that is very discrepant with expectations tends to capture one's attention.

Attention

Attention is often controlled by automatic processes but it is also deployed flexibly in goal-directed behavior. Much of what is perceived is in line with expectations and triggers well-rehearsed action schemas (Norman & Shallice, 1980). For example, most people can drive to work without thinking very much about what they are doing and few attentional resources are consumed while driving familiar routes. Many of us have had the experience of intending to drive somewhere else on the weekend but find that we have instead driven "on autopilot" and taken a wrong turn or two as if we were driving to work. However, sometimes, in the middle of performing a well-rehearsed action sequence, something unanticipated occurs and we immediately orient to this new event or stimulus. For example, if while driving to work in the usual way, a pedestrian steps into the street heedless of oncoming traffic, we immediately focus and taken action to avoid hitting the person. This orienting response is made possible by the fact that the brain is automatically feeding predictions (typically only milliseconds in the future) to the perceptual systems and "primes" them to perceive particular stimuli. These predictions are typically accurate within a reasonable range. For example, when a friend turns her head towards us, the perceptual system anticipates what her face is going to look like and is typically not surprised. However, if her lips have fluorescent green lipstick (and this friend is not typically adventurous with her makeup), the perception of the color violates our expectations and causes an automatic orienting response. We cannot help but notice the unusual color. However, if the color of her lipstick is within the normal range for that friend, we are unlikely to notice it at all. Although students' attention is naturally captured by innumerable distractions (e.g., the sound of their peers' off-task merriment), good students learn to disengage their attention from task irrelevant distractions and tune them out in order to complete their coursework. Much of what we label "attention" is concerned with the checking our natural impulses to attend to inherently interesting things (competition, social drama, romance, danger, and so forth) and directing our attention toward less interesting things that have a larger long-term payoff (homework, performing the duties of one's job, minding children, and so forth). This function of attention is often called *inhibition*, as the purpose is to inhibit responding to task irrelevant information that may capture or hijack our attention.

The ability to consciously direct the focus of attention in the service of short- and long-term goals has been given many names. We prefer the term *attentional control* but near synonyms include cognitive control, executive control, effortful control, controlled executive attention, executive functions, and central executive functioning, among many others (it seems like almost every combination and permutation of *executive, control, attention,* and *function* has been used by one scholar or another). It is likely that there is not just one attentional control mechanism but several interrelated attentional control mechanisms.

The ability to monitor multiple streams of information simultaneously is typically called *divided attention* (e.g., conversing while driving). The ability to focus attention to one stream of information and ignore competing signals is called *selective attention* (e.g., listening to a teacher while other students are giggling). *Attentional fluency* has to do with the speed, smoothness, and ease with which one is able to engage and disengage the focus of attention without mental lapses while performing a series of simple tasks (e.g., performing a series of easy calculations) or alternating between tasks (e.g., taking notes while listening to a lecture). This is also referred to as task-switching ability, alternating attention, cognitive fluency, mental agility, and a host of other similar terms.

Sustained attention is a kind of mental stamina, the ability to control and focus attention over long periods of time. One kind of sustained attention, *vigilance,* is the ability to monitor an uninteresting stimulus over long periods of time without lapses (e.g., watching the output of a factor assembly line to detect quality control problems). A vigilant person can resist boredom and stay alert. *Concentration* typically refers to a different kind of sustained attention, the ability to engage in difficult, attention-demanding tasks for a long time without lapses (e.g., playing in chess tournaments).

It is likely that some people are better at these various types of kinds of attention than others. However, it is also clear that most complex activities (such as reading Shakespeare and writing geometry proofs) require that attentional control processes act in concert with each other. A person's excellent selective attention abilities are of little help if the person cannot sustain attention long enough to master a new skill. Thus, it is typically a person's overall synchronized attentional abilities that determine success in complex domains.

The Limits of Attention

It is impossible to attend to many things simultaneously. Attention can be compared to a zoom lens or an adjustable spotlight (Eriksen & St James, 1986). When the light is narrowly focused, a small area is brightly illuminated. When the light is dispersed, a wide area is illuminated but not as brightly. Most spotlights can provide a compromise between these extremes by illuminating a moderately sized area but the center is more brightly illuminated than the periphery. If we wish to simultaneously illuminate two areas brightly, we can move the spotlight back and forth quickly. So it is with attention.

Consider the task demands air traffic controllers face as they guide airplanes safely to their destinations. They can focus their attention very narrowly on a single plane to insure accurate awareness of the position of the specific plane. This accuracy, of course, comes at the expense of awareness of other planes in the immediate vicinity. Air traffic controllers can attempt to be aware of all of the planes concurrently but this grand view comes at the expense of accurate awareness for any particular plane. What they cannot do is be fully aware of all planes concurrently and be completely accurate with regard to any individual plane. Therefore, they compromise by quickly switching their awareness back and forth between planes. They can also quickly zoom their attention in and out between a narrow focus on one plane and a broader view of all the planes.

Our ability to focus attention is extremely fragile. Almost any brain injury affects attention. Although Attention-Deficit/Hyperactivity Disorder is the only mental disorder to have the word "attention" in its name, almost all of the major mental disorders (e.g., mood disorders, anxiety disorders, psychotic disorders, dissociative disorders) involve attention deficits of one kind or another. Even moment to moment, our ability to pay attention fluctuates considerably. Contrast this with the ability to hear. Tired or energized, sick or healthy, hungry or well fed, distressed or content, intoxicated or sober, our ability to hear remains fairly consistent. On the other hand, when we are even a little bit tired, sick, hungry, distressed, or intoxicated, our ability to concentrate is much reduced.

MEMORY

The process of storing and retrieving information is not the same for all types of information (e.g., visual/spatial versus acoustic/verbal). Cognitive psychologists have developed numerous fine-grained distinctions when discussing the various types of memory. In this discussion we will highlight the distinction between short-term memory and long-term memory. Because short-term memory has a special relationship with the active processes of attention, it is often referred to as *working memory* (Baddeley, 1986).

Working Memory

Descriptions of working memory often invoke a metaphor of a temporary storage space for information. Although no metaphor is perfect, this one is misleading because it suggests that the information just sits there, inert. A more helpful comparison is that working memory is similar to the RAM in your computer (in that it is a form of memory that is held temporarily in a state that can be manipulated very quickly). However, if you are not a computer geek, that metaphor might be confusing. In many ways, a more illuminating (if likely less accurate) comparison is that working memory is like the screen on your computer. It displays a very limited amount of information at a time, and counter-intuitively, this is what makes it so useful. If all the gigabytes of data on your computer could be displayed simultaneously on the screen, it would be impossible to sort through it all to select the specific bits of information relevant to your current task. What makes the screen so useful is that it is updated constantly to display relevant information only. However, it is not just a dumb display. The screen is a point of contact between you and the computer. Via the graphical user interface, you manipulate images on the screen to control the computer to do what you want to accomplish your task. On the screen you combine and manipulate information.

Working memory is like an active updatable screen for your conscious awareness. By controlling the focus of your attention, you can activate relevant long-term memories, compare them to incoming sensory perceptions, and manipulate information internally to make it more useful. A classic example of this is performing arithmetic in your head, such as multiplying 9 by 14. You probably do not have the product of 9 and 14 stored in long-term memory. However, you most likely do have basic math facts stored in memory and the procedure of multiplying large numbers in memory. If you were to solve this problem in your head, it might go like this:

> Activate (i.e., retrieve) memory of the procedure for multiplying large numbers
>
> Recall the first step: Multiply the units digits
>
> Implement: $9 \times 4 = 36$
>
> Recall the next step: Multiple the bottom number's units by the top number's tens digit
>
> Implement: $9 \times 1 = 9$
>
> Recall the next step: Place the results of the second step under the results of the first step and shift the result one digit to the left.

Implement: $\begin{array}{r}36\\9\end{array}$

Recall the next step: Add the columns of numbers, starting at the left.

Implement: $\begin{array}{r}36\\+9\\\hline 126\end{array}$

Notice that once the answer of 126 is found, you no longer need to remember the intermediate steps (e.g., 9 × 4 = 36). Once it is deemed unnecessary, this information can be forgotten or dumped from your memory. Information in working memory is very vulnerable to interference. Unless constantly maintained via conscious rehearsal, the information is likely to be forgotten with 10 to 30 seconds. If new information captures attention, the previous contents of working memory are likely to be forgotten much more quickly. If the memory is kept active long enough or if it is processed deeply or vividly, it is possible that it will stored in more robust coding system. That is, it will enter long-term memory.

Long-Term Memory

Whereas working memory holds recently activated information for a matter of mere seconds, long-term memory lasts for minutes, hours, days, weeks, years, or even a lifetime. There are many different kinds of long-term memory. *Explicit memory* (or *declarative memory*) can be articulated verbally. Two types are explicit memory are *episodic memory,* the memory of particular events (e.g., your first kiss) and *semantic memory,* the memory of particular facts (e.g., that Antarctica is an icy continent that surrounds the South Pole). Implicit memory is difficult to articulate verbally but is expressed indirectly via behavior. Two types of implicit memory are conditioned responses (e.g., after recently being bitten by a dog, you feel jumpy at the sight of any dog, even one that is calm, far away, and on a leash) and *procedural memory,* the memory of how to implement a sequence of motor actions skillfully (e.g., riding a bicycle). *Retrospective memory* is about past events whereas *prospective memory* is about remembering to implement plans in the future (e.g., go to the dentist at 2 P.M. today).

Information in long-term memory is processed in various stages. Information is encoded by perceptual functions of the brain. Different aspects of an object are bound together and elaborated upon when attended to in consciousness. The object is compared and contrasted with previously encountered objects stored in memory. The memory of the object is abstracted and consolidated (the essential features are analyzed and stored in a durable code that can be retrieved later). When needed, the memory of the object can be retrieved. This process is not like the playback of a video. Rather, the various features of the object have been stored separately and must be reassembled in working memory. Thus, remembering is an act of reconstruction rather than an act of reproduction. Of course, memory errors can occur at any of these stages.

Individual Differences in Cognitive Abilities

People have always known that not everyone has the same level or pattern of cognitive abilities. When psychologists conducted the first scientific studies of cognitive abilities, one of the first nonobvious findings to emerge was that all cognitive abilities were positively correlated. That is, if we know some of an individual's cognitive abilities, we can forecast the unmeasured abilities with better-than-chance accuracy. If a person has an excellent vocabulary and good logical reasoning, it is likely that the person also has above average spatial reasoning, is more creative than average, and has a faster reaction time than average. Some of these predictions might turn out to be false but such predictions will turn out to be correct more often than not. Some interpret the finding that cognitive abilities are positively correlated as evidence that there is something called *general intelligence*.

IQ tests are designed to measure general intelligence. They test a wide variety of cognitive abilities and then average the scores to estimate what the tests measure in common (i.e., general intelligence). A person with high general intelligence is likely to perform above average on most cognitively demanding activities. A person with low general intelligence is likely to have difficulty in general in almost any domain requiring learning, judgment, or reasoning.

Not all researchers believe that general intelligence is a helpful explanation for the positive correlations in ability. The issue is hotly debated and the evidence for either side of the debate is less than compelling. The point of agreement, however, is that general intelligence is not the only ability that exists and it is not the only ability that matters.

All researchers accept that cognitive abilities tend to be positively correlated. They also know that some cognitive abilities are more correlated than others. That is, certain cognitive abilities tend to cluster together in meaningful ways. For example, if a person has difficulty with language comprehension, a prediction that the person also has deficits in general knowledge (i.e., knows few facts that his or her culture deems important) is more likely to be accurate than the prediction that the person has difficulty concentrating. Clusters of highly similarly and correlated specific abilities are often called *broad abilities*.

Many lists of broad abilities have been proposed by psychologists over the last century. In the last 20 years, researchers have come to a tentative consensus about the broad abilities that must be included in any successful theory of cognitive abilities. The field is not unanimous but it is now more unified than it has ever been in the past. The unification occurred when Carroll (1993) produced a convincing demonstration that one of the many competing models of cognitive abilities was largely correct, the Horn-Cattell model. Carroll's demonstration was accomplished by re-analyzing hundreds of datasets that measured the relations between various cognitive abilities. The datasets he analyzed were collected over the span of many decades and consisted of all of the relevant studies Carroll could identify at that time. Carroll made a number of modifications to the Horn-Cattell model. Some of these were minor but a major difference is that Carroll believed that general intelligence is a real ability whereas Horn and Cattell believed that it was an unnecessary concept and that there were better explanations of the positive correlations between cognitive abilities. Despite their difference of opinion, Horn and Carroll agreed to have their two theories yoked together under a common framework. The integration, accomplished primarily by McGrew (1997, 2005, 2009), is known as the Cattell-Horn-Carroll theory of cognitive abilities (CHC theory). The most recent summary of CHC theory is that by Schneider and McGrew (2012).

Cattell's Gf-Gc Theory

After conducting many studies on general intelligence and reading many more studies conducted by others, Raymond Cattell (1943) noticed an interesting pattern of results. Certain abilities tended to be affected by brain injuries more than others. These abilities were also the ones most likely to decline in old age. Furthermore, these abilities tended to be measured by tests that required reasoning and did not require much previously learned knowledge. Indeed, some of them were useful for measuring cognitive abilities in cross-cultural research.

Knowledge tests measure skills and information that are highly valued by one's culture. For this reason, they are not useful for cross-cultural research. Cattell noticed that such knowledge tended to remain relatively intact after brain injuries and did not decline much as people age.

Cattell hypothesized that the reason for these findings was that there was not one general intelligence but two general intelligences: fluid intelligence and crystallized intelligence. Fluid intelligence was thought to represent the natural raw talent and overall biological integrity of the brain. Crystallized intelligence was hypothesized to be acquired via investment of fluid intelligence during the learning process. The abbreviations for these abilities (Gf and Gc, respectively) reflect that they are general abilities. That is, they are not tied to any particular sensory system, academic subject, or occupational skill. They influence a very wide set of skills.

Fluid Intelligence (Gf)

Fluid intelligence is the ability to solve unfamiliar problems using logical reasoning. It requires the effortful control of attention to understand what the problem is and to work toward a logically sound answer. People with high fluid intelligence are able to figure out solutions to problems with very little instruction. Once they have found a good solution to a problem, they are able to see how it might apply to other similar problems. People with low fluid intelligence typically need hands-on, structured instruction to solve unfamiliar problems. Once they have mastered a certain skill or solution to a problem, they may have trouble seeing how it might apply in other situations. That is, their newfound knowledge does not generalize easily to other situations.

Fluid intelligence appears to have a special relationship with working memory capacity. Working memory is the site where difficult problems are solved for the first time. It is possible to have high fluid intelligence with only middling working memory capacity and it is possible to have low fluid intelligence with excellent working memory capacity. However, people with excellent short-term memory capacity and good control of their attention seem appear to have a significant advantage in solving novel problems.

Crystallized Intelligence (Gc)

Crystallized intelligence is acquired knowledge. When people solve important problems for the first time, they typically remember how they did it. The second time the problem is encountered , the solution is retrieved from memory rather than recreated anew using fluid intelligence. However, much of what constitutes crystallized intelligence is not the memory of solutions we personally have generated but the acquisition of the cumulative wisdom of those who have gone before us. That is, we are the intellectual heirs of all of the savants and geniuses throughout history. What they achieved with fluid intelligence adds to our crystallized intelligence. This is why even an average engineer can design machines that would have astounded Galileo, or even Newton. It is why ordinary high school students can use algebra to solve problems that baffled the great Greek mathematicians (who, for lack of a place-holding zero, could multiply large numbers only very clumsily).

Crystallized intelligence, broadly speaking, consists of one's understanding of the richness and complexity of one's native language and the general knowledge that members of one's culture consider important. Of all the broad abilities, crystallized intelligence is by far the best single predictor of academic and occupational success. A person with a rich vocabulary can communicate more clearly and precisely than a person with an impoverished vocabulary. A person with a nuanced understanding of language can understand and communicate complex and subtle ideas better than a person with only a rudimentary grasp of language. Each bit of knowledge can be considered a tool for solving new problems. Each fact learned enriches the interconnected network of associations in a person's memory. Even seemingly useless knowledge often has hidden virtues. For example, few adults know who Gaius and Tiberius Gracchus were (Don't feel bad if you do not!). However, people who know the story of how they tried and failed to reform the Roman Republic are probably able to understand local and national politics far better than equally bright people who do not. It is not the case that ignorance of the Gracchi brothers dooms anyone to folly. It is the case that a well-articulated story from history can serve as a template for understanding similar events in the present.

Horn's Expansion of Gf-Gc Theory

Cattell's student and collaborator, John Horn, conducted the first direct test of his mentor's theory. Horn's (1965) dissertation confirmed some of Cattell's ideas about fluid and crystallized intelligence, but it also suggested that the theory needed elaboration. Over the course of his career, Horn refined Gf-Gc theory several times, sometimes in collaboration with Cattell, sometimes not, and sometimes with other cognitive ability scholars (Cattell, 1987; Horn & Blankson, 2005; Horn & Cattell, 1966). In honor of the original theory, the model retained the name of Gf and Gc, but it identified a number of other broad abilities that Horn believed were just as important as Gf and Gc. Horn and Cattell identified abilities that were linked to specific perceptual systems. Although these abilities are not as broad as Gf and Gc, they are still very broad and thus are abbreviated with G, which stands for "general." They also distinguished between various memory-related abilities and abilities linked to the speed of information processing. In this discussion, the names and abbreviations are from modern CHC theory (see Schneider & McGrew, 2012) instead of the slightly different terms and abbreviations used by Horn.

Domain-Specific Abilities

Visual-Spatial Ability (Gv)

General visual-spatial ability consists of many different specific perceptual capabilities that are similar in that they all deal with complex processing of visual information (although touch and hearing sometimes play a role in visualizing objects and locating them in space). Rather, visual-spatial ability is not visual acuity—people with impaired vision often have excellent visual-spatial skills. Visual-spatial ability has to do with perceiving complex visual patterns, visualizing objects as they might appear from different angles, and being aware of where things are located in space, including oneself. Visual-spatial ability is in the "minds eye."

People with high levels of Gv are able to use their visual imagination to see more than what is before them. If they see part of an object, they imagine what the rest of it looks like. If they see it from one angle, they imagine how it would look from another, mentally rotating it in space. If they see a tool, they generate a moving image to simulate its operation. If they see a complex image, they mentally break it down to smaller, more basic parts (lines, angles, curves, basic 2D and 3D shapes such as triangles, rectangles, ellipses, spheres, cubes, and cylinders) and then mentally reassemble the parts to form a three-dimensional internal mental model. Their mental models are accurate which allows them to answer "what-if" questions (What if this stick is used like a lever to pry this stuck drawer loose? Will it pry the struck drawer loose or will it break the stick? Will it damage the drawer?). These mental simulations (movies in the mind's eye) allow people to experiment with various courses of action rapidly and inexpensively in mental space so that fewer trial-and-error solutions need be attempted in physical space and time.

People with low levels of Gv, are less able to perform mental simulations in working memory and thus have difficulty knowing how something will look until it is physically moved. While working with objects, they must rely more on trial-and-error problem-solving methods. While navigating, they must rely on memory of landmarks instead of using a mental map of their location in space.

Auditory Processing (Ga)

Auditory processing is the ability to make use of nonverbal information in sound. It is the ability to distinguish between sounds by their volume, pitch, and tonal quality. It is the ability to hear the melody in music and the rise and fall of pitch in ordinary language. It is the ability to hear the difference between phonemes in speech (e.g., hearing the difference between "pat" and "bat"). Although auditory processing is a precursor ability for oral language comprehension, it is not language comprehension itself (that is Gc). It is not sensory acuity, either. As vision is to visualization, hearing is to auditory processing. Auditory processing is what the brain does with sound after it has been detected, sometimes long after it has been heard. Thus even people who have suffered hearing loss, like Beethoven at the end of his life, can use their Ga abilities to simulate new sounds in their heads.

People with high Ga, if they like music, have a richer appreciation of the sounds in music because their perception of sound is more nuanced. They hear variations in volume, pitch, rhythm, and sound texture that people with low Ga cannot distinguish. People with high Ga have an advantage in learning foreign languages because they can hear subtle variations in phonemes (units of speech sounds) that differ across languages. People with low Ga abilities have difficulty pronouncing words with anything other than the phonemes from their native language. The ability to hear individual speech sounds distinctly gives people with high Ga an edge in learning to read alphabetic writing systems. People with low Ga are at risk of developing phonological dyslexia because it is hard for them to understand how individual letters correspond to individual phonemes, especially in long words. This puts them at a disadvantage in sounding out unfamiliar words.

Other Abilities Related to Specific Sensory Modalities and Motor Functions

It is likely that something analogous to Gv and Ga exists for each of the major senses. We know very little about these abilities because they are difficult to measure and few researchers have devoted sustained efforts to understand them.

Haptic processing (Gh) refers to higher-order cognitive related to touch (e.g., visualizing and naming objects by touch alone). Kinesthetic processing (Gk) refers to higher-order cognition related to proprioception (awareness of limb position and movement). Presumably this is what dancers and athletes use to employ to achieve artistry in their profession. It may be what people use to imitate the movements of others accurately. It may also refer to what is known as dynamic touch (Turvey, 1996), which is the ability to infer characteristic of objects by moving them (e.g., hefting a hammer before using it) and hitting them (e.g., tapping a piñata with a bat before swinging at it). Olfactory processing (Go) has to do with higher-order cognition related to smell (e.g, being about to identify plants, food, and other objects from odors, knowing when fruit is ripe or rotten from smell, even the ability to diagnose certain medical conditions from particular odors). Gustatory processing (Gg?) would be higher-order cognition related to taste and presumably would be analogous to olfactory processing.

Analogous to domain-specific abilities related to perception, there may be higher-order cognitive abilities related to motor functions. Psychomotor abilities (Gp) would include conscious control of muscle movement (e.g., aiming a ball at a target, playing the piano), the conscious control of body movement to maintain balance, and other movements that require higher order cognition.

Memory-Related Abilities

There are many different kinds of memory but the primary distinction in CHC theory is between short and long-term memory.

Short-Term Memory (Gsm)

The working memory system encompasses temporary storage and manipulation of information via attentional control (Unsworth & Engle, 2007). In terms of individual differences, it is possible to measure two distinct abilities. First, people differ in how much information they can store in working memory if few demands on attention are made. The classic measures of this ability are memory span tests in which people must repeat back increasingly long sequences of random numbers, letters, or words. Working memory capacity has to do with how well people can maintain information in working memory if they must simultaneously deploy attentional resources to manipulate information. For example, if a string of letters is presented in random order, having to repeat them back in alphabetical order requires more attentional resources than repeating the letters back in the same order as they are heard. The letters must be maintained in memory, usually by subvocal rehearsal (saying them over and over in one's head), and at the same time attentional resources are used to sort the letters.

People with high Gsm are able to engage in multistep problem-solving without getting lost in the process and making careless errors. They are able control the focus of attention adaptively and flexibly, depending on the needs of the moment. People with low Gsm are likely to make careless errors when performing attention demanding tasks. They are highly vulnerable to distraction because once there is a small lapse of attention, the information they were using in working memory is likely to be lost. This weakness results in difficulties in planning, implementing planned actions, and following through on plans until they are completed successfully. Sometimes people with low Gsm find planning effortful and unpleasant. The payoff for planning is lessened because their plans are less likely to be carried out successfully. Thus, people with low

Gsm often prefer to "take life as it comes" and live spontaneously. Of course, other factors unrelated to Gsm, such as personality preferences, can play an even larger role in influencing how much a person prefers to plan.

Long-Term Memory

An important distinction in long-term memory abilities is between the ability to learn efficiently and the ability to retrieve information fluently from long-term memory. People who can learn efficiently can associate new information with previously acquired knowledge. One of the most important ways in which they learn more efficiently is that they tend to remember the gist of things (i.e., distinguish between essential and nonessential details). Doing so requires some combination of fluid and crystallized knowledge. This is why people who reason well and who have broad knowledge tend to learn new information more efficiently. They see the logical connections between the new information and what they already know. The greater the number of connections, the more likely the new information will be retained permanently and used in the future. People who can retrieve memories fluently tend to speak fluently and often read fluently. A type of retrieval fluency called *divergent production* (being able to generate many responses to a prompt such as "name as many kinds of sports as you can" or "come up with as many ways as you can to use a pencil") appears to be an important component of creativity (Kaufman, Kaufman, & Lichtenberger, 2011). Deficits in a fluency ability called *naming fluency* (the ability to identify well known objects quickly and easily) are associated with reading comprehension problems (Neuhaus, Foorman, Francis, & Carlson, 2001), in part because the act of reading involves "naming" (identifying) printed words.

General Cognitive Speed

Before cognitive ability research was conducted on the speed at which people could perform various tasks, it was not entirely clear whether speediness would emerge as an ability distinct from other kinds of abilities. For example, it is possible that people who reason well also reason quickly and that the speed is irrelevant. It was also not obvious whether there would be a single mental speed ability, several speed abilities, or one speed ability for each kind of task. Research has suggested that there are at least three cognitive speed factors and a one psychomotor speed factor. The speed/fluency of memory retrieval has already been described. The psychomotor speed factor is the speed at which people can perform fine motor tasks (e.g., press a button quickly, articulate word sounds quickly, move a limb quickly). The remaining two speed factors appear at first glance to be very much alike. However, they have very low correlations with each other, suggesting that they represent very different aspects of mental speed.

Reaction and Decision Time (Gt)

Tasks in which this ability is measured are among the simplest tests ever devised. For example, in one test, a person is given a box with two buttons. Whenever one of the buttons lights up, the person hits the button as quickly as possible. In another test, a two lines flash briefly on the computer screen. One line is clearly longer than the other one. The person indicates which line is longer. The task is repeated many times. The duration of the display becomes shorter and shorter until the person can no longer tell which line is the longer of the two (i.e., the person's accuracy is at chance levels). These kinds of tests are so simple that they are called *elementary cognitive tasks*. They are used by researchers working to discover the essential cognitive roots of intelligence. The working hypothesis of this research is that the essence of general intelligence will be understood by breaking complex tasks down into very simple steps and measuring the millisecond speed of these simple perceptions and decisions. Research has reported that the correlations of such simple elementary cognitive tasks with IQ tests is surprisingly high (around 0.4). This suggests that a significant portion of what causes differences in overall intellectual ability is due to the speed at which basic perceptual processes executed. Although a correlation of 0.40 is meaningfully large, it must be put in proper context. This means that approximately 16% (.40 squared; the coefficient of determination) of general intelligence is related to performance on Gt tasks. Clearly this means that Gt abilities do not provide the whole explanation of intelligence, however intriguing the findings in this area of research.

People with fast reaction and decision times and perception speeds are better able to perform complex tasks such as flying fighter planes. Note that people who perform well on decision speed tests are not necessarily hasty people who make rash decisions. They perceive and respond to events and stimuli quickly when that is the required task demand. When making important decisions, they are no more likely to rush into risky investments or ill-advised marriages than anybody else.

Processing Speed (Gs)

This broad ability is measured by tasks in which a person performs a very simple task repeatedly (e.g., underlining all of the 3s on a paper full of single digit numbers). Such tasks are so simple that almost anyone can complete them without error if they were given unlimited time to complete the task. It might seem that such tasks are just like the tasks described in the Gt section. However, there is an important difference. In the Gt tasks, each stimulus is presented one-at-a-time and the experimenter controls the rate of presentation. In Gs tasks, the stimuli are presented all at once on a screen or a piece of paper. The evaluee then sets his or her own sustained pace in completing the items. In the Gt tasks, the role of attentional control is minimized, although the evaluee must remain reasonably vigilant. To minimize differences in vigilance, a cue, such as a cross in the center of the screen, flashes so that an evaluee with a meandering mind will re-orient to the task before the next item appears. In Gs tasks, there are no such safeguards. People with problems of attentional fluency will attempt to perform the simple tasks quickly but their speed will be uneven, proceeding in fits and starts. What happens is that certain items briefly "capture" their attention and then it is difficult to move on to the next item smoothly. Thus, the name "processing speed" may be a bit of a misnomer, suggesting too broad a construct. It is not the speed of all types of processing. It is the speed and fluency with which a person can perform a self-paced, attention-demanding task.

People who perform well in Gs tasks tend to be able to learn tasks well and can "automatize" them so that they can be performed without consuming attentional resources. For example, when people first learn to drive a car, it requires all of their attention to operate the vehicle safely. After a few weeks of driving, they can drive long distances without being mentally fatigued by the activity. They can even converse with other people in the car without appreciably increasing the risk of accidents. For people with high Gs, this automatization process seems to occur more rapidly and more thoroughly.

Processing speed (Gs) is the ability that declines the most with age and decreases the most after almost any kind of brain injury. It is for this reason that neuropsychologists use processing speed tests to screen for the effects of possible brain injuries. Gs is also extremely sensitive to minor fluctuations in alertness and sobriety. Most people are fairly consistent in their performance on these tests, but some people are extremely variable. Sometimes people with below normal processing speed deficits can, on a particularly good day, perform at an average level. For this reason, it is a good idea to measure this ability in several ways across different days to make sure that an accurate estimate of the individual's Gs ability is obtained.

Other Kinds of Acquired Knowledge (Gkn, Grw, and Gq)

For Horn and Cattell (1966), crystallized intelligence originally encompassed all acquired knowledge. Later in their careers, however, they independently had misgivings about the unitary nature of Gc (Cattell, 1987; Horn & Blankson, 2005). There seems to be something different about general knowledge (measured by Gc tests) and knowledge that can only come from deep involvement with a subject matter. In particular, experts in a subject seem to be able to maintain huge amounts of information in working memory as they solve problems related to their field of expertise. When faced with problems outside their area of mastery, experts no longer are able to perform extraordinary feats of memory. For this reason, CHC theory distinguishes between general knowledge, Gc, and domain-specific or specialized knowledge, Gkn.

Two additional kinds of acquired knowledge are so important that they are named separately. They are reading/writing ability (Grw) and quantitative ability (Gq). These refer to specific skills of reading decoding, spelling, calculations procedures and other low-level academic skills. When a student performs complex academic tasks such as writing an essay, Grw skills are used, but also general knowledge (Gc) is employed and, if the essays involves reasoning that is novel to the student, fluid reasoning (Gf).

A Cognitive Performance Model Applied to Individuals

The mind is certainly more complex than can be captured via any single proposed cognitive performance model. However, it is better to start with a simple model that approximates the truth than to have no model at all and flounder in uncertainty. Here, in Figure 64.1, we present a variation of a model that we proposed in Schneider and McGrew (2011). Both models draw heavily from cognitive processing models proposed by Woodcock (1993) and Kyllonen (2002) but differ from both those models in that our models are more detailed and more closely aligned with developments in CHC Theory. The major difference between this model and the Schneider and McGrew (2011) model is how working memory is conceptualized. Many researchers represent working memory as a gateway from perception to long-term memory (e.g., Baddeley, 1986). However, many researchers are reporting findings that suggest that perceptual systems interact directly with long-term memory and that working memory is simply the activated portion of long-term memory (e.g., Cowan, 1995). It will likely be a long time before this debate is settled conclusively. Fortunately, in

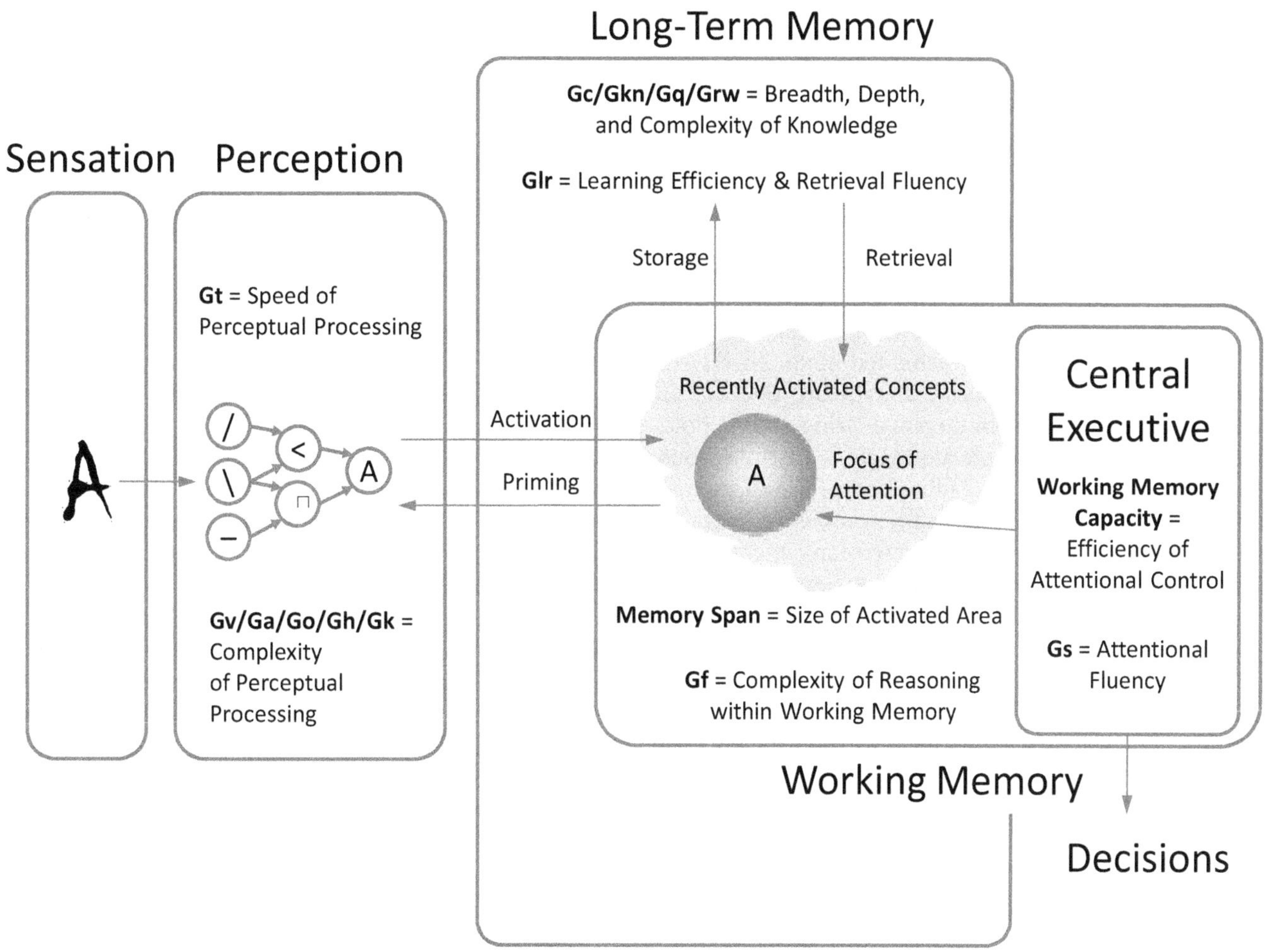

Figure 64.1 Cognitive performance model with CHC abilities as parameters of information processing.

terms of predicting the performance of individuals, this difference may not matter that much.

Performance Parameters of Sensation and Perception

In the cognitive performance model in Figure 64.1, sensations are perceived by their respective sensory organs and then processed by different perceptual systems. People vary not only in their sensory acuity, but also in the speed of perception (Gt, and possibly Gs). Some people are able to extract much more detailed and complex information from their perceptions and these differences are often driven by domain-specific abilities such as Gv, visual-spatial ability. Of course, experience alters how much a person can take in all at once. Any videogame novice is daunted by observing how much experienced gamers can simultaneously process on screens that seem to be, at first, scenes of blooming, buzzing confusion. However, after deep immersion in the game, the novice is no longer confused. However, some individuals are better at processing complex sensory information than others and these differences persist even after extensive practice and training.

In the domain of reading, the higher-order perceptual skills associated with sound (auditory processing ability) have a special relationship with the ability to use phonics skills to sound out unfamiliar words (Gathercole, 2006). Skilled readers do not usually sound out familiar words; they simply retrieve the word's sounds and meaning directly from memory. For very skilled readers, this process occurs automatically; skilled readers can't help reading words they see. However, when encountering unfamiliar words, even skilled readers sound them out. For people with poor auditory processing ability, the process of mapping sounds to letters is effortful and error-prone. Thus, when learning to read, a child with low Ga must rely heavily on rote memory to recognize words. If a child is unable to do so, the child's reading problems may become serious enough to warrant a diagnosis of *phonological dyslexia* (word reading problems caused primarily by the inability to hear speech sounds distinctly).

Performance Parameters of Working Memory

Different cognitive ability factors are associated with different aspects of attention and attentional control. Within the Short-Term Memory (Gsm) factor, a person's memory span is a measure of how much information a person can maintain in an activated state. In Figure 64.1, memory span is associated with the size of the activated area of long term memory. Being able to hold more information in an activated state is advantageous in complex tasks such as reading comprehension, text composition, and applied math problems because information can be combined in working memory in ways that facilitate comprehension and problem-solving.

More complex measures of Gsm (ones that require simultaneous storage and processing of information) measure not only how much information can be maintained in an activated state but also the efficiency of attentional control (i.e., divided attention, selective attention, and concentration). Measures of processing speed (Gs) are measures of attentional fluency, speed at which attention can be accurately and smoothly directed to tasks as they are completed. No test, however, is a pure measure of any ability. Tests measuring Gs are influenced by many other abilities as well.

If your reading decoding skills are very poor, sounding out the words is likely to consume almost all of your available attentional resources. That is, the size of the activated area in working memory shrinks and it becomes much harder to understand what your read because most texts require that you hold information in mind across sentences and paragraphs to make connections, particularly understanding complex aspects of language such as irony and humor.

If your decoding skills are good but your working memory capacity is poor, the risk of developing reading comprehension problems increases. Working memory capacity has a strong connection with vocabulary acquisition during reading. Some words occur only in high-level text and most of us learn them by inference rather than by looking them up in a dictionary. That is, looked up words are hard to remember but words that are embedded in the context a narrative are easier to recall and use correctly. Inferring the meaning of an unfamiliar word in context often requires that the preceding sentence or two is held in mind. Sometimes the meaning of an unfamiliar word (e.g., "decadence") can only be inferred after reading the sentence after the one in which it occurred (e.g., "The corporate sponsors of the party at the conference spared no expense to impress the academic researchers. Overwhelmed, the shy professor could not allow himself to be at ease in the midst of so much decadence. Watching his colleagues partaking of and enjoying the indulgences a little too much, he sneered 'First comes wealth, then comfort, then weakness, decay, and corruption.'"). To guess that decadence is related to the corrupting influence of too much luxury and comfort, the preceding sentences need to be maintained in memory while the last sentence is processed and interpreted. Then the inference is made by combining the information in all three sentences. Skilled readers, of course, look backward and reread sentences they do not quite understand. However, this is an effortful process. People with high working memory seem to be able to infer more meaning from of text with less effort (Calvo, 2005).

One way to conceptualize measures of fluid intelligence (Gf) is that they represent the complexity of mental representations that a person can assemble for the first time in working memory. For people with high Gf abilities, complex ideas with multiple parts can be held in working memory, analyzed (broken down), synthesized (integrated with other ideas), and evaluated (judging the relevance and the implications of the ideas to new situations). People with low Gf have find complex ideas particularly hard to understand unless they are broken down into simple parts so that they can be mastered independently. Only then can the parts be integrated to a coherent whole, typically with the assistance and guidance of a gifted teacher.

Performance Parameters of Long-Term Memory

The speed and ease with which new information is stored in long-term memory is measured by tests associated with the Long-term Storage and Retrieval (Glr) ability factor. To estimate how easily a person learns, we present the evaluee with information (sometimes all at once, sometimes in a structured sequence) and then test the person's recall of the material. In most tests, the new information is presented and recalled many times, often with delays in between so that we are measuring long-term memory processes rather than working memory processes.

Sometimes people have learned information but they cannot recall it easily. The way that we distinguish between a person's ability to learn and the person's ability to recall is to give memory tests in two different formats: one in which the person has to recall the information with no cues and one which the person has to recognize whether or not the information was presented previously. Recognizing information is much easier than recalling it. This is why a multiple-choice test is much easier than a free recall test that asks the same question. For example, could you recall the capital of Poland? If not, could you identify it from among these European capitals? Athens Berlin Lisbon London Madrid Moscow Oslo Paris Rome Warsaw Vienna. A person with memory retrieval problems often performs reasonably well on multiple choice tests but has difficulty with free recall formats, even more so than most people.

The act of reading is the act of retrieving from memory the meaning of a series of words and then assembling those ideas into a coherent whole. A reader with slow retrieval fluency may find reading too effortful to be enjoyable. If word retrieval takes too long, attention starts to wander and it is difficult to extract meaning, much less enjoyment from the text. Something similar happens with solving complex problems in mathematics. If a person cannot retrieve basic math facts fluently ($8 + 6$, 7×9, $15 - 6$, etc.), during the time that a person has to recall (or calculate) the basic math fact, attention has time to wander and the person can become lost in the larger math problem. Thus, poor retrieval fluency disrupts the flow of reasoning and problem-solving, consuming attentional resources and increasing the likelihood of careless errors.

The contents of long-term memory are measured with tests of crystallized intelligence (or specialized knowledge tests). After basic reading decoding skills have been mastered, a primary determinant of reading comprehension is the breath, depth, and complexity of knowledge a person has already acquired. Most writers assume that the reader knows a lot of information and leaves the reader to read between the lines. Without the requisite vocabulary, language comprehension skills, and general knowledge, many kinds of text are very difficult to understand.

An Example of Qualitatively Applying a Cognitive Performance Model

In Figure 64.1, a stimulus that is shaped like the letter A is perceived and is currently at the center of attention. In order to recognize it, you need reasonable visual acuity (corrected with glasses, if need be). If there is sufficient visual acuity, your feature detectors must be unimpaired and must work efficiently. The results of the simple feature detectors are fed to complex feature detectors and those results are mapped onto schemas stored in long-term memory. In this case, the letter A is recognized.

Suppose you are reading a novel and this letter A is the first letter of the name of a new character: "Dr. Amuchástegui." The novelty of the name captures your attention. You might decide to phonetically sound out the name and this will require focused attention. If you decide you want to remember the name, you might repeat it a few times. To make the name stick in memory, you might visualize what Dr. Amuchástegui might look like as you repeat the name aloud. The success of this attempt to remember the name will depend on many factors, some of which are not included in the model (e.g., your motivation to remember, your experience with Basque surnames, your level of mental fatigue, and many others). However, if you have good auditory processing (Ga) and have specialized knowledge (Gkn) of how to sound out Spanish words, you are likely to succeed in sounding out the name correctly. If your learning abilities (Glr) are efficient, the name is likely to be stored in long-term memory. If your memory span is reasonably large, you'll be able to recall and integrate the details surrounding this character and the memory is likely to be more vivid than it otherwise would have been. This is particularly true if your memory representation of the events in the novel is extremely rich, nuanced, and interconnected. Later, if you run into a friend who is also reading the book, initiating a conversation about the book might trigger the memory of the unusual name and you are likely to remember it.

If, on the other hand, the book is assigned reading and you are not a skilled decoder (low Grw), the name may look like gibberish ("Dr. Amhgtigiu"). If your auditory processing ability (Ga) is low, you may never have mastered the art of phonetic decoding and you might not even try to remember the name. You might remember the character simply as "That doctor with the weird name that started with an A or something." Without a verbal label on which to link the character's unique attributes, you are less likely to remember what he did in the story, especially if the story is filled with other characters with unusual names.

Future Developments in Cognitive Performance Models

In the discussion of reading and the cognitive performance model above, we have taken a narrative, non-quantitative approach. However, it is possible to measure a child's relevant cognitive abilities and use sophisticated statistical methods to obtain an empirically-based prediction of which kinds of academic problems the child will face. If the child's academic weaknesses are already known, it is possible to use a cognitive performance model to estimate how much improvement in complex academic skills (e.g., reading comprehension and applied math problem-solving) would result from the remediation of cognitive deficits (e.g., attention deficits) or deficits in simple academic skills (e.g., word decoding or math fact fluency).

Recently Schneider (2010) developed methods and software that allows clinicians to create their own cognitive performance models and apply them to individuals. This program, the Compositator is available for free from the Woodcock-Muñoz Foundation to users of the Woodcock-Johnson III, Normative Update (Woodcock, McGrew, Schrank, & Mather, 2007), a comprehensive battery of tests of cognitive abilities and academic skills. It is likely that a more general version of the software will be developed for users of other measures of cognitive and academic abilities at some point in the future.

In Figure 64.2, the Compositator was used to create a very simple cognitive performance model that predicts that mathematics reasoning is a function of fluid reasoning, short-term memory, and basic math skills. It is unlikely that a well-developed model would be this simple. This model is only for purposes of illustration.

The model's predictions were applied to an individual who struggles with math calculation and applied math problems that require quantitative reasoning. The lines and numbers represent a statistical procedure called path analysis. A path analysis is a set of multiple regression equations that use some variables to predict other variables. The numbers and lines may look like visual gobbledygook but they represent a precise set of predictions about what is likely to happen if any one of the student's cognitive or academic abilities were to change. For example, this cognitive performance model predicts that if the student's weaknesses in short-term memory (and the attentional control deficits associated with those weaknesses) were remediated, the student's math calculation and math reasoning skills are expected to rise as well. Figure 64.3 shows how much, if the model in Figure 64.2 is correct, the student's math skills would improve if the short-term memory problems were remediated to the average range (the gray area in the middle). Predictions are not expected to be perfectly accurate and the model gives an estimate of the likely range of scores that might occur if the remediation of short-term memory were to be achieved. The improvements are not expected to happen instantly and it is not expected to occur if the new math skills are not explicitly taught. However, the model does provide parents, teachers, and clinicians some direction about what to do and some hope that the remediation efforts could pay off. Such predictions, of course, are only likely to be accurate if the model upon which it is based is valid. An inaccurate cognitive performance model will result in predictions that are unlikely to come true. Thus, the clinician creating the cognitive performance model must base it on solid science.

Future research will need to be conducted to see if the use of such cognitive performance models results in better outcomes for students. For now, the use of cognitive performance models applied to individuals in this manner is experimental. It is hoped that better methods and practical tools for clinicians will inspire researchers to develop better and more sophisticated cognitive performance models that will be truly useful for struggling children.

REFERENCES

Baddeley, A. (1986). *Working memory.* New York, NY: Clarendon Press/Oxford University Press.

Calvo M. G. (2005). Relative contribution of vocabulary knowledge and working memory span to elaborative

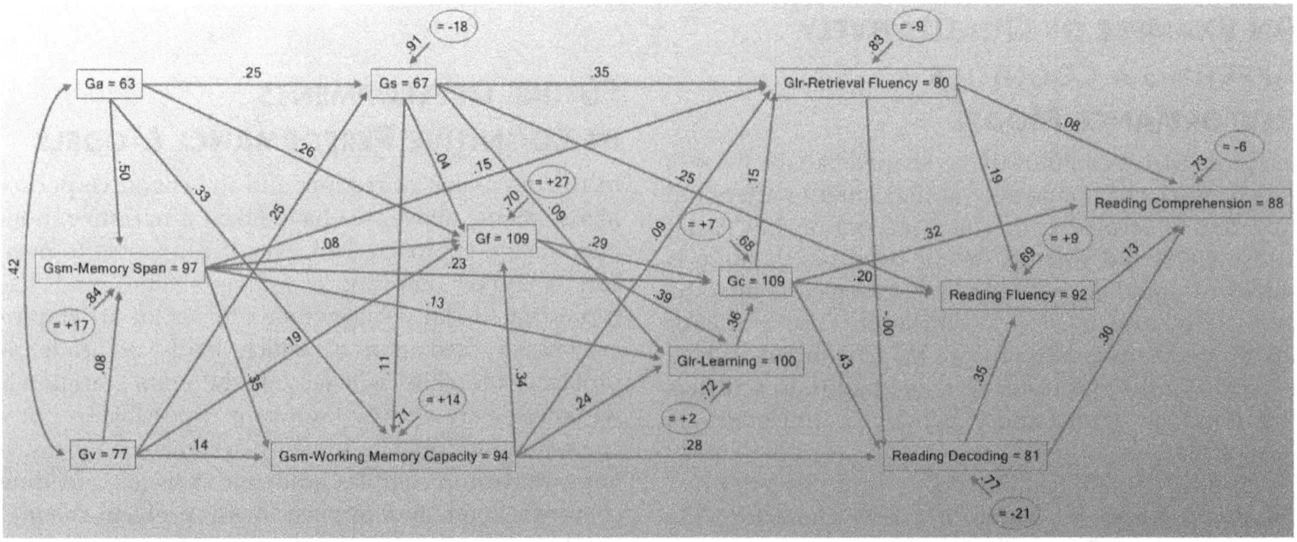

Figure 64.2. Path analysis applied to an individual with average fluid reasoning but with difficulties in short-term memory, math calculation skills and math reasoning.

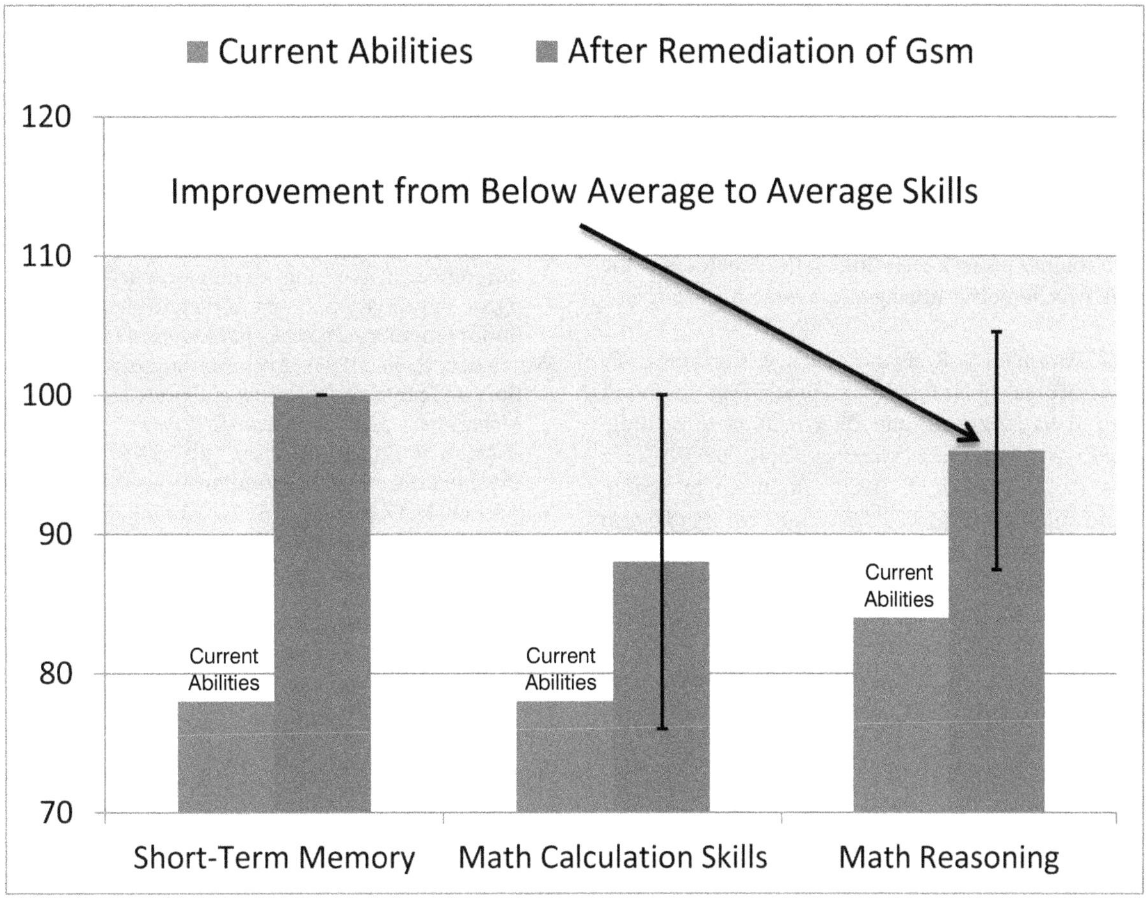

Figure 64.3. A forecast based on the model in Figure 64.2 of the likely improvement in an individual student's math skills if the student's short-term memory deficits could be remediated.

inferences in reading. *Learning and Individual Differences, 15,* 53-65.

Carroll, J. B. (1993). *Human cognitive abilities: A survey of factor-analytic studies*. New York, NY: Cambridge University Press.

Cattell, R. B. (1943). The measurement of adult intelligence. *Psychological Bulletin, 40,* 153-193.

Cattell, R. B. (1987). *Intelligence: Its structure, growth, and action.* New York, NY: Elsevier.

Cowan, N. (1995). *Attention and memory: An integrated framework* (Oxford Psychology Series, No. 26). New York, NY: Oxford University Press.

Eriksen, C., & St James, J. (1986). Visual attention within and around the field of focal attention: A zoom lens model. *Perception & Psychophysics, 40*(4), 225-240.

Floyd, R. G., & Kranzler, J. H. (2012). Processing approaches to interpretation of information from cognitive ability tests: A critical review. In D. P. Flanagan & P. Harrison (Eds.), *Contemporary intellectual assessment: Theories, tests, and issues* (3rd ed., pp. 497-523). New York, NY: Guilford Press.

Gathercole, S. E. (2006). Keynote article: Nonword repetition and word learning: The nature of the relationship. *Applied Psycholinguistics, 27,* 513-543.

Hawkins, J., & Blakeslee, S. (2004). *On intelligence.* New York, NY: Times Books.

Horn, J. L. (1965). *Fluid and crystallized intelligence: A factor analytic study of the structure among primary mental abilities* (Unpublished doctoral dissertation). University of Illinois, Champaign, IL.

Horn, J. L., & Blankson, N. (2005). Foundations for better understanding of cognitive abilities. In D. Flanagan & P. Harrison (Eds.), *Contemporary intellectual assessment: Theories, tests, and issues* (2nd ed., pp. 41-68). New York, NY: Guilford Press.

Horn, J. L., & Cattell, R. B. (1966). Refinement and test of the theory of fluid and crystallized intelligence. *Journal of Educational Psychology, 57,* 253-270.

Hunt, E. (2011). *Human intelligence.* New York, NY: Cambridge University Press.

Kaufman, J. C., Kaufman, S. B., & Lichtenberger, E. O. (2011). Finding creative potential on intelligence tests via divergent production. *Canadian Journal of School Psychology, 26*(2), 83-106.

Kyllonen, P. C. (2002). Knowledge, speed strategies, or working memory capacity? A systems perspective. In R. J. Sternberg & E. L. Grigorenko (Eds.), *The general factor of intelligence: How general is it?* (pp. 415-465). Mahwah, NJ: Erlbaum.

McGrew, K. S. (1997). Analysis of the major intelligence batteries according to a proposed comprehensive Gf-Gc framework. In D. P. Flanagan, J. L. Genshaft, & P. L. Harrison (Eds.), *Contemporary intellectual assessment* (pp. 151–179). New York, NY: Guilford Press.

McGrew, K. S. (2005). The Cattell–Horn–Carroll theory of cognitive abilities. In D. P. Flanagan & P. L. Harrison (Eds.), Contemporary intellectual assessment (2nd ed., pp. 136-181). New York, NY: Guilford Press.

McGrew, K. S. (2009). Editorial: CHC theory and the human cognitive abilities project: Standing on the shoulders of the giants of psychometric intelligence research. *Intelligence, 37,* 1–10.

Neuhaus, G., Foorman, B. R., Francis, D. J., & Carlson, C. D. (2001). Measures of information processing in rapid automatized naming (ran) and their relation to reading. *Journal of Experimental Child Psychology, 78*(4), 359-373.

Norman, D. A., & Shallice, T. (1980). Attention to action: Willed and automatic control of behavior. *Center for Human Information Processing Technical Report* No. 99.

Schneider, W. J. (2010). *The Compositator 1.0.* WMF Press.

Schneider, W. J., & McGrew, K. S. (2012). The Cattell-Horn-Carroll model of intelligence. In D. Flanagan & P. Harrison (Eds.), *Contemporary intellectual assessment: Theories, tests, and issues* (3rd ed., pp. 99-144). New York: Guilford.

Spearman, C. (1904). "General intelligence," objectively determined and measured. *American Journal of Psychology, 15,* 201-293.

Treisman, A. (1998)Feature binding, attention and object perception. *Philosophical Transactions of the Royal Society, Series B, 353,* 1295-1306.

Turvey, M. T. (1996). Dynamic touch. *American Psychologist, 51,* 1134-1152.

Unsworth, N., & Engle, R. W. (2007). The nature of individual differences in working memory capacity: Active maintenance in primary memory and controlled search from secondary memory. *Psychological Review, 114,* 104–132.

Woodcock, R. W. (1993). An information processing view of the Gf-Gc theory. In *Journal of Psychoeducational Assessment Monograph Series: Woodcock-Johnson Psycho-Educational Assessment Battery—Revised* (pp. 80-102). Cordova, TN: Psychoeducational Corporation.

Woodcock, R. W., McGrew, K. S., Schrank, F. A., & Mather, N. (2007). *Woodcock-Johnson III normative update.* Rolling Meadows, IL: Riverside.

Author Contact Information: W. Joel Schneider, PhD, Department of Psychology, Illinois State University, Normal, IL 61790-4620. E-mail: wjschne@ilstu.edu

CHAPTER 65

Curriculum-Based Measurement

Mark R. Shinn
National Louis University

Out of clutter, fnd simplicity.

—*Albert Einstein*

Curriculum-Based Measurement (CBM) is a "family" of assessment instruments that are designed first and foremost to assess student progress in the area of basic skills, reading, early literacy, mathematics, early numeracy, and written expression, including spelling. CBM is by far the most commonly used form of curriculum-based assessment, which was derived from the theory that student achievement is best assessed using the instructional materials with which students are taught (Tucker, 1985). That is, for curriculum-based assessment, content validity is its defining, if not sole, feature. CBM's defining features much more than content valid tests. Although content validity originally was one of CBM's defining features, and research knowledge was accumulated, its importance was greatly diminished. Instead, CBM's defining features emphasize the use of *standardized* tests that are: (a) short, usually less than 5-10 minutes; (b) authentic, emphasizing production-type responses; (c) easy to administer and score; (d) psychometrically sound, especially with respect to construct validity; (e) sensitive to differences among individuals or within individuals over time, and (f) administered frequently over time to judge individual student growth.

The Einstein quote at the beginning of the chapter symbolizes what CBM is intended to do and the quote does so at multiple levels. A foundational principle of CBM is that close attention must be paid to the effects of intervention/instruction on the individual student rather than a group of students (Deno, 1991). The premise is that because no intervention works with every student and, in fact, because even poorly designed intervention may be effective with some students, progress must be monitored to ensure intervention outcome certainty. Failure to monitor progress can produce "clutter," schools not knowing what interventions work with which students, meaning that ineffective programs may be used with too many students for too long a period of time.

The second interpretation of the Einstein quote represents the tie of CBM to the underlying idea of General Outcome Measurement (GOM), one of two methods for monitoring student progress. The other method is Mastery Monitoring (Fuchs & Deno, 1991). GOM is predicated on the empirical identification of a single outcome indicator representative of a socially important construct. In other disciplines, the use of GOM is routine. For example, the Dow Jones Industrial Index is used to judge progress of a very complex economy. Blood pressure is used to judge health status and often response to intervention for medicine.

With respect to education, the socially important construct of reading consists of a variety of skills that can be taught and tested. In Mastery Monitoring, each skill would be tested after it is taught. GOM is quite different. Out of all the potential reading skills (i.e., the clutter), GOM seeks the identification of a single outcome that is validated as an *indicator* or correlate of the construct. In reading, having students read aloud for a standard period of time (e.g., 1 minute) and counting the number of words read correctly is a validated general outcome measure (Fuchs, Fuchs, & Maxwell, 1988; Miura Wayman, Wallace, Ives Wiley, Ticha, & Espin, 2007; Shinn, Good, Knutson, Tilly, & Collins, 1992).

The research base for CBM is impressive. As summarized by Jenkins and Fuchs (in press), a 2004 synthesis by the US Department of Education's Research Insti-

The Handbook of Educational Theories, pp. 783–791

tute on Progress Monitoring identified "585 CBM research reports, 307 of which were published in journals (121 were unpublished documents; 131 were dissertations; 26 were unclassified). Among the 307 publications, 141 reported empirical studies addressing questions of technical adequacy, instructional utility, and the logistics of implementation in reading, writing, spelling, and math."

The practice base for CBM is equally impressive. As part of its funded mission to support implementation of Response to Intervention (RtI), the US Department of Education's National Center on Response to Intervention Center reviews assessment instruments for use in progress monitoring and screening. The majority of tests reviewed favorably for use in RtI are members of the CBM family. Each year, millions of students are tested with CBM through test publishers like DIBELS, AIMSweb, Yearly Progress Pro, or Easy CBM.

Original Development

CBM of 2011 is a product of 50 years of research and practice beginning in the late 1960s with roots in social justice with (a) international efforts to bring psychological science to education and (b) provision of protection and services for students with disabilities. In the mid to late 1960s, psychologists in large numbers were beginning to translate its basic science, the experimental analysis of behavior to education through applied behavior analysis (Baer, Wolf, & Risley, 1968). Key among these efforts was the use of direct, low-inference data that were graphed over time for individuals to allow judgments about what treatments or interventions worked. The first efforts were tied to maladaptive social behaviors (e.g., biting, self-destruction behavior) or classroom behavior that was indirectly related to academic achievement (Becker, 1971). Other psychologists quickly began to generalize the experimental analysis of behavior concepts directly to academics and especially to assessment through the development of *Precision Teaching* (Lindsley, 1964; Lovitt, Schaff, & Sayre, 1970; White, 1971). It is easy to see the influence of *Precision Teaching* on CBM. Its measures were short, authentic, and administered frequently, typically daily, to assess student progress and judge intervention effectiveness.

In 1971, Stanley Deno, the principal theorist of what became CBM, began his work as part of supervision efforts with special education teachers in Minneapolis Public Schools while at the University of Minnesota. Among his goals was to ensure teachers knew the effects of their instruction. He taught skills like graphing, direct measurement, and elements of *Precision Teaching*. However, his scientific training, especially measurement, drove him ponder other features of good assessment, including standardization and sound psychometrics, such as construct validity in addition to content validity.

Concurrent with efforts to bring basic psychological science to education was a national effort to provide protection and services to students with disabilities. As a result of repeated instances of abuses with a strong emphasis on lack of special education progress in court cases, the *Educational Act for Children with Handicaps Act* (1975) was passed. Chief among the remedies for children with disabilities was the Individualized Educational Plan (IEP) that required teams, including parents, to write observable and measurable goals that would be used to monitor progress and judge the effectiveness for special education for individual students. It was clear at that time that there was no validated assessment technology to write IEP goals and monitor progress. Fortunately, *Educational Act for Children with Handicaps Act* was followed by an extensive, large-scale program of federally funded special education research authorizing five research universities to address implementation concerns, including IEP goals and progress monitoring (Ysseldyke, Thurlow, & Shinn 1978).

Having recently completed a monograph for the Council for Exceptional Children, *Data-Based Program Modification*, (Deno & Mirkin, 1977) summarizing his work in Minneapolis Schools and establishing the philosophical and practice underpinnings for the data system that became CBM, Deno became coprincipal investigator at the University of Minnesota Institute for Research on Learning Disabilities (IRLD) with the charge of developing and validating a technology for writing IEP goals and monitoring progress for students with disabilities. With his colleague Phyllis Mirkin and a cadre of graduate students, including Lynn Fuchs, Doug Marston, Mark Shinn, Jerry Tindal, and Caren Wesson, extensive validation and implementation efforts were begun in the areas of reading and written expression, including spelling, and less successfully, social behavior. Mathematics was not a funded priority in the original research. For an extensive history of the research on CBM from a historical perspective, see Jenkins (in press).

Validation of the Theory

Research activities began in 1978 and continue to this day. As part of the IRLD research rational and empirical test construction methods were employed. With another colleague, Joseph Jenkins, Deno and Mirkin (1979) created a set of rationally designed test criteria that were published in a peer-reviewed journal. The measures had to be:

1. Relevant, with an emphasis on content validity.
2. Sensitive to improvement such that the scale would "move" when student learning occurred.

3. Flexible, meaning that the measure had to assess more than a single and specific learning objective.
4. Repeatedly administrable, being capable of being given to a student more than just once, but many times, meaning multiple alternate forms and meaning time efficient so that loss of valuable instructional time would be minimized.
5. Easily administrable, meaning that the test(s) had to be easy to give, without extensive training, easy to score, and easy to interpret.

Graduate students were assigned to review the literature and identify a number of potential reading, written expression, and social behavior measures that might meet these criteria with the intent that these "candidates" would be compared empirically with respect to psychometric attributes of reliability and validity. In the area of reading, a number of candidates were identified, including the type of oral passage reading represented in Informal Reading Inventories, but also reading word lists, only selected words in a passage, and others such as silent reading measures like cloze and maze. In addition to a variety potential candidate measures, a variety of candidate administration times ranging from 30 seconds to 10 minutes were also identified to address the criteria of repeatedly and easily administrable.

Because of the early research emphasis on the relevant criterion, most, but not all the measures were developed from specific curricula. In reading then, reading passages or word lists were derived from commonly used reading basal series such as *Ginn, Scott-Foresman,* etc. However, to improve psychometrics content validity was necessary, but not sufficient. A series of studies was conducted examining reliability, including alternate form, and test-retest, and a variety of construct validity issues, including, but but not limited to concurrent and predictive validity.

Results were published in a series of IRLD research reports (Deno, Marston, Mirkin, Lowry, Sindelar, & Jenkins, 1982) and refereed journals, the first of which was published in 1982 (Deno, Mirkin, & Chiang, 1982). After 5 years of research, although a number of the measures that were investigated met conventional psychometric standards for reliability and validity, the following basic CBM tests had both a strong psychometrics *and* met Jenkins, et al. (1979) design features for use in frequent progress monitoring:

In reading, counting the number of words read correctly from a basal reading series passage in 1 minute was useful for general reading skill.

In spelling, counting the number of correct letter sequences from an orally presented list of spelling series' words in 2 minutes was useful for spelling.

In written expression, counting the number of total words written or correct writing sequences from an orally presented story starter in 3 minutes was useful for general written expression skills.

MATURING RESEARCH AND ITERATIONS

In 2004, the most prolific researcher on CBM Lynn Fuchs (2004), described the history of CBM research and laid out a schemata for a program of research detailing expectations and accomplishments for each of three phases, (a) Stage 1, technical features of a static score, (b) Stage 2 technical features of slope (i.e., repeated data over time), and (c) Stage 3, instructional utility and how the information informs instruction and impacts student achievement. Over 35 years, the bulk of the research has addressed Stages 1 and 3. Considerable information is known about the technical properties of CBM tests at a single point in time. See for example, the special issue of *The Journal of Special Education* devoted to a synthesis of the CBM research (Wallace, Espin, McMaster, Deno, & Foegen, 2007).

A considerable amount also is known regarding Stage 3 research. The original intent of the CBM research plan was to develop and validate technology that was useful to monitor basic skills progress in reading, written expression, and social behavior for students with disabilities. The purpose was the development and use of graphed data that allowed judgments of student progress toward annual IEP goals such as shown in Figure 65.1. An IEP goal would be written by the special education team and progress would be measured regularly and frequently (i.e., 1-2 times per week) on a randomly sampled CBM test from a specified domain (e.g., Grade 2 reading passages).

The solid line in each graph represents the *expected* rate of improvement (ROI) reflected in the IEP annual goal that would reduce the achievement gap for students with IEP goals. The dashed line represents the *actual* ROI. In the first graph, the student's ROI greatly exceeds the IEP goal ROI. A team could conclude the intervention is effective, and in fact, a case would be made to *raise* the IEP goal. In the second graph, the student's ROI is significantly below the IEP ROI. In this instance, commensurate with Individuals with Disabilities Education Act of 1997 and Individuals with Disabilities Education Act of 2004, the special education team would revise the IEP and the intervention plan to address this lack of expected progress.

By 1984, the first published study (Fuchs, Deno, & Mirkin, 1984) appeared documenting the achievement effects of CBM when used formatively. Subsequent studies and reviews reported by Fuchs and Fuchs (1986, 2004), reported effect sizes of .5 and greater with students with disabilities when CBM is used to write individualized goals and monitor progress with students with disabilities. Instructional utility with effect sizes around 1.0 is increased with combined with deci-

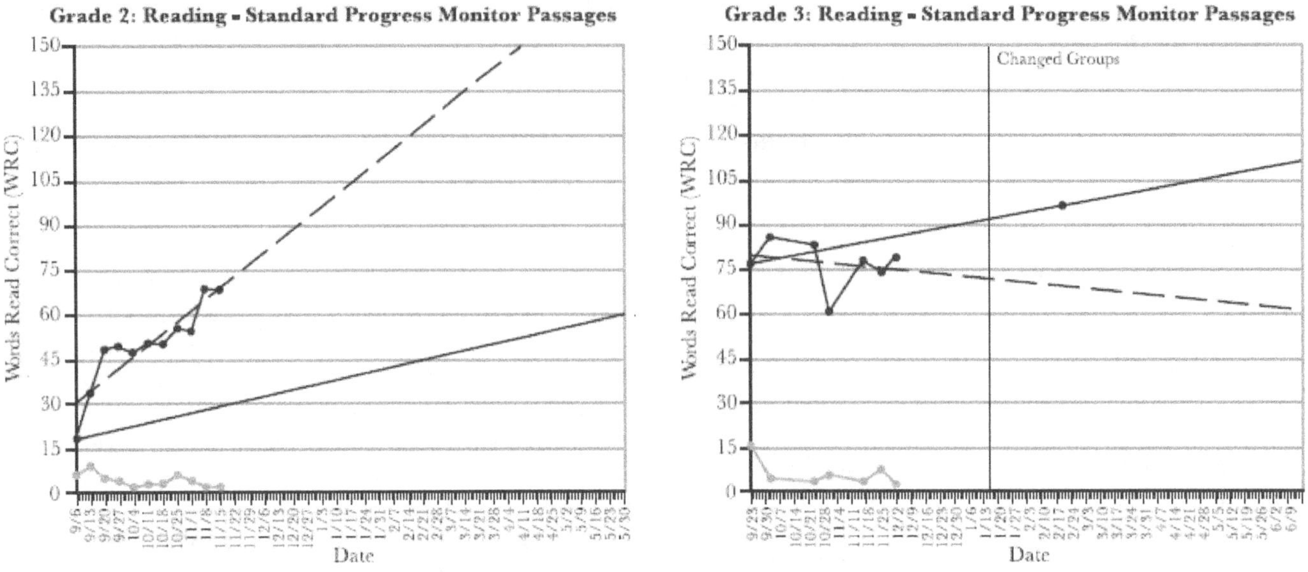

Source: Shinn (2008).

Figure 65.1 An illustration of two students' progress toward IEP goals using CBM.

sion rules (Fuchs, 1988; Fuchs, Fuchs, Hamlett, & Ferguson, 1992). Most recently, Hattie's review of over 800 meta-analyses (Hattie, 2009) had this type of formative evaluation ranked third overall and number one in terms of teacher practices that improve achievement.

Despite the early emphasis on progress monitoring and assessing from specific curriculum, iterations on the original theory were quickly undertaken, including (a) the importance of curriculum to CBM, (b) use of CBM for other assessment decisions (e.g., screening), (c) development of CBM in other academic areas (e.g., early literacy, mathematics), and (d) use of CBM with other populations (e.g., English learners, general education students), and other cultures (e.g., Spanish, Taiwanese, Korean).

Role of the Curriculum

As noted earlier, originally CBM tests were developed from the specific curriculum used in a community's general education classrooms. However, this curriculum-specific approach, although defensible, was pragmatically challenging given curriculum differences within and across schools and across time. In every sense, schools were making their own CBM test materials. More importantly, this curriculum-specific approach generated test probes that were variable in difficulty due to the considerable variability in passage-to-passage difficulties within basal reading series. Compounding the problem was the sizable numbers of schools were not using basal reading or other curriculum programs. A foundational research question became "how important is the curriculum in CBM? Subsequent research showed that the creation of standard, curriculum independent test materials worked better than curriculum specific tests. Alternate form reliability was improved with no loss in validity of progress decisions (Fuchs & Deno, 1992; Hintze & Shapiro, 1997; Hintze, Shapiro, & Lutz, 1994). Progress monitoring logistics were improved as well. By 1999, the original design features that defined a test as CBM were modified by Fuchs and Fuchs (1999) to include: (a) technical adequacy, an explicit revision valuing more than content validity as a standard; (b) capacity to model growth, to draw attention to utility or all students and across years rather than within a year; (c) treatment sensitivity, a restatement of the original feature; (4) instructionally eclectic, explicitly rejecting ties to specific curriculum, and, (5) feasibility, a more compact statement of efficiency and efficacy.

Use in Other Assessment Decisions

Contemporary assessment emphasizes four major types of decisions, screening, diagnosis and intervention planning, progress monitoring, and program evaluation. The early research on the validity of short, general basic skill achievement tests for use in progress monitoring also had theoretical and practical implications for more than progress monitoring. Deno and Mirkin (1977) for example, detailed the importance of defining problems as a discrepancy between what was expected and what was occurring in a particular situation. In other words, achievement problems may be best identified by comparing a student of concern to other students in their own community. This theory was tested by Shinn's 1981 IRLD doctoral dissertation (Shinn, Ysseldyke, Deno, & Tindal, 1986) and a program of school-based research comparing students identified with specific learning disabilities with low-achieving and typically achieving general education students. CBM was shown to accurately discriminate among the groups with about 1 standard deviation difference between specific learning disabilities and low-achieving students, and 1 standard deviation difference between low-achieving and general education students (Shinn, 2007; Shinn & Marston, 1985; Shinn, Tindal, Spira, & Marston, 1987; Shinn, Tindal, & Stein, 1988). This research had significant implications for practice, especially in a response to intervention model.

CBM in Other Academic Areas

Although the original program of CBM research resulted in three major general outcome measures in reading, spelling, and written expression, validation of other CBM measures has occurred. The most visible addition to members of the CBM "family" is the *Dynamic Indicators of Basic Early Literacy Skills* (DIBELS; Kaminski & Good, 1996; Kaminski & Good, 1998). DIBELS was developed as a downward extension of CBM to early literacy to help solve the problem of waiting for reading–curriculum based measurement (R-CBM) to be sensitive to between and within student reading differences. DIBELS initially consisted of a set of early literacy tests of Initial Sound Fluency, Phonemic Segmentation Fluency, and Nonsense Word Fluency. It was later expanded to include Letter Naming Fluency, a R-CBM task, and other measures of vocabulary and comprehension. Recent research has identified what is likely the best kindergarten screening and progress monitoring, Letter Sounds, a 1 minute CBM test that requires young children to say the sound of visually presented letters.

In reading, additional research has been conducted with a 3-5 minute silent reading test, Maze, that also can serve as a measure of general reading ability (Fuchs & Fuchs, 1992; Parker, Hasbrouck, & Tindal, 1992). The primary advantage of maze is for reading screening of older students because it can be group and/or computer administered.

Outside of reading, the academic area with the strongest research support is mathematics. Although it was not in the original research objectives, it quickly attained prominence through the research efforts of Lynn and Doug Fuchs. Stage 1 and 3 research data have been obtained for mathematics computation, and mathematics application and problem solving, and algebra (Foegen, Jiban, & Deno, 2007; Foegen, Olson, & Impecoven-Lind, 2008; Fuchs, Fuchs, Hamlett, Thompson, Roberts, & Kupek, 1994; Fuchs, Fuchs, Karns, Hamlett, & Katzaroff, 1999; Thurber & Shinn, 2002). Stage 1 research information also is available on early numeracy for kindergarten and beginning first graders (Clarke & Shinn, 2004; Methe, 2008)

Other Languages and Cultures

Very early in CBM progress monitoring and screening implementation, school-based efforts included english learners. For example, CBM was the cornerstone tool for educational decision making in St. Paul, MN schools in 1980. More than 3,000 children had recently arrived from Southeast Asia and the district had an additional 4,000 students whose language at home was Spanish (Robinson, Robinson, & Blatchley, in press). Research efforts followed very quickly first with Spanish-speaking students (Baker & Good, 1995). And later expanding to a number of other countries, including Korea (Kim, in press) where CBM is integrated into the national *Basic Academic Skills Assessment* and as of 2010, more than 70 empirical research articles on Korean use have been identified, and Greece (Kendeou & Papadopoulos, in press). According to (Linan-Thompson, in press), the United Nations Educational, Scientific and Cultural Organization initiative developed and is using the *Early Grade Reading Assessment*, which uses of CBM in developing countries as a means to respond to United Nations Educational, Scientific and Cultural Organization's literacy activities.

Use and Application of the Theory

CBM has achieved prominence as an essential tool in a RtI model (Fuchs & Vaughn, 2005; Shinn, 2010) with important roles in data-based decision making. The most obvious use of CBM in RtI is as a tool for progress monitoring to judge response to intervention. When RtI is used as part of special education eligibility, CBM is used to determine whether a student's response to an intensive intervention is sufficient or, lacking same, may require a special education intervention to reduce the achievement gap. This is the second part of what is referred to as the *dual discrepancy* (Speece, Pericola Case, & Eddy Molloy, 2003). Additionally, CBM is often used to assess the achievement or performance discrepancy, defined as determining whether an individual student's level of achievement is significantly discrepant from peers. This process is also part of the dual discrepancy. CBM is used in RtI when special education decisions are made because it is scientifically based, meeting the psychometric standards required for decision making by Individuals with Disabilities Education Act of 2004, and as noted earlier, has been reviewed favorably by the National RTI Center.

However, RtI is much more than special education eligibility (Burdette, 2007). Contemporary RtI perspectives are focused instead on a model of multi tiered services and supports, featuring data-based decision making where progressively more intensive evidence-based interventions are provided to any student who is not progressing. Furthermore, these more intensive interventions are provided early (i.e., as soon as possible) to reduce the likelihood of long-term failure. CBM is used routinely in multi tiered services and supports as a basic skills screening tool because it is time efficient, accurate, and inexpensive. Importantly, the screening use is combined with a progress monitoring component in a Benchmark approach (Shinn, 2010).

An example of Benchmarking is shown in Figure 65.2. In this example, the small circle represents a second-grade student, Arianna's R-CBM scores on Grade 2 reading passages when she was tested along with all the other second graders in the Fall, Winter, and Spring of the school year.

Arianna's Fall Benchmark score of 25 words read correctly (WRC) placed her below the 25th percentile and these screening results were used by the grade-level team to identify her for a Tier 2 intervention, which began shortly after screening. Her CBM scores from the Winter and Spring Benchmark data grew dramatically and provide convincing evidence that she was progressing and reducing the achievement gap from peers. CBM is also used frequently for monitoring progress for students who receive Tier 2 intervention once per month to weekly and for students who receive Tier 3 intervention weekly.

Critiques of the Theory

Of the three phases of CBM program of research described by Fuchs (2004), nearly all of the critiques center around Stage 1, the technical features of a static score, and in particular around the construct of CBM reading (i.e., R-CBM) and DIBELS. For many practitioners, issues of face validity for R-CBM's 1-minute oral reading test and statements about reading comprehension create a lack of confidence in the measure. Some teachers report students who read "fluently," but who don't understand what they read, despite empirical evidence of the high correlation between R-CBM and other measures of comprehension (e.g., L.S. Fuchs et al., 1988; Shinn et al., 1992) and studies disconfirming the lack of association (Hamilton & Shinn, 2003). For others, the reading and early literacy measures, espe-

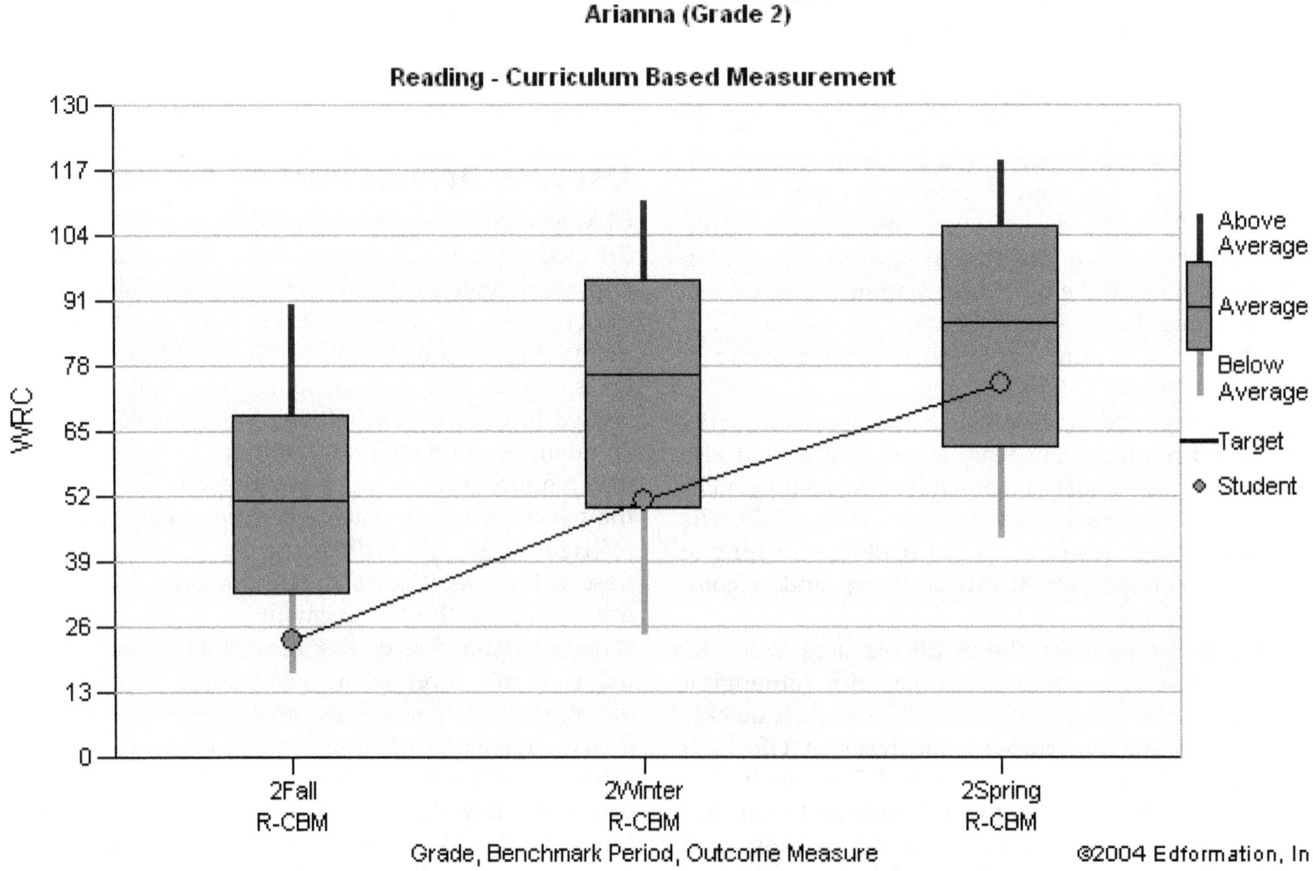

Figure 65.2 *An example of a benchmark assessment where information is used for screening, early intervention, and progress monitoring*

cially those tests associated with DIBELS, are criticized as being reductionist, inauthentic, (Goodman, 2006) and focused on speed versus quality and understanding (Riedel, 2007; Samuels, 2007). Unfortunately, these critiques are not empirical, but seem to be ones of differences in reading, and especially reading assessment philosophy.

More recently, critiques have focused Stage 2 questions or technical features of slope (i.e., repeated data over time) with important questions as to variability in improvement estimates over time (Ardoin & Christ, 2009; Christ, 2006; Christ & Silberglitt, 2007) in efforts to enable more accurate progress decisions and judgments about reading intervention success.

Representative Studies

With over 250 published articles in refereed journals, it is challenging to select representative studies so a few that sample across the three programs of research are presented. For Stage 1 research on the technical properties of the static measure, two articles are cited frequently. The first, Fuchs, Fuchs, and Maxwell (1988), compared R-CBM with other researcher constructed reading comprehension measures (e.g., oral and written recall, cloze, and a number of subtests from the Stanford Achievement Test external measures (e.g., Word Study Skills, Reading Comprehension). Subjects were 70 middle school or junior high students identified with mild disabilities. Results showed that R-CBM correlated highest with Stanford Achievement Test Reading Comprehension ($r = .91$) and was related more highly than the other measures.

A second commonly cited Stage 1 research study was conducted by Shinn, Good, Knutson, Tilly, and Collins (1992). This study was a test of developmental reading assessment models with 114 Grade 3 and 124 Grade 5 students who were given a number of reading tests, including R-CBM, phonetically regular words, nonsense words, and the Stanford Diagnostic Reading Comprehension subtest. Obtained results for each grade were compared to a priori theoretical models. The study demonstrated that R-CBM was a robust measure of general reading ability that correlated directly and indirectly with measures of reading comprehension.

A representative study of Stage 2 investigations of the characteristics of slope was conducted by Ardoin and Christ (2009). In this study, 68 Grade 2 and 3 students were progress monitored using different R-CBM materials (e.g., FAIP-R, AIMSweb, DIBELS) and estimates of growth were compared with respect to measurement error. Results showed that different publishers' reading passages would result in different estimates of skill level and there were marked differences in the reliability of slope over time.

A representative study of Stage 3, use of CBM in decision making and effects on achievement was the first experimental study published in 1984 (Fuchs et al., 1984). These researchers investigated the effects of CBM progress monitoring with 39 New York City special education teachers, each with three to four students, randomly assigned to progress monitoring group where CBM was used to write individualized goals and adjust instruction based on growth or a control group which employed standard, but unsystematic progress practices. Results showed significant gains in student achievement on the Stanford Diagnostic Reading Test and students' own awareness of their own achievement.

Summary

Curriculum-Based Measurement is a type of assessment characterized by short, standardized tests typically administered over time for purposes of progress monitoring, but also as short screeners in the areas of basic skills. A considerable body of knowledge has emerged regarding their technical adequacy through Stage 1 and 2 programmatic research and Stage 3 use in decision making and gains in student achievement. With over 35 years of accumulated research, CBM in its various forms is used with very young children and students with basic skills challenges through high school. It remains a set of assessment tools that continue to be studied and expanded to different decisions, academic areas, and student populations.

References

Ardoin, S. P., & Christ, T. J. (2009). Curriculum-based measurement of oral reading: Standard errors associated with progress monitoring outcomes from DIBELS, AIMSweb, and an experimental passage set. *School Psychology Review, 38*, 266-283.

Baer, D. M., Wolf, M., & Risley, T. R. (1968). Some current dimensions of applied behavior analysis. *Journal of Applied Behavior Analysis, 1*, 91-97.

Baker, S. K., & Good, R. H. (1995). Curriculum-based measurement of English reading with bilingual Hispanic students: A validation study with second-grade students. *School Psychology Review, 24*, 561-578.

Becker, W. C. (Ed.). (1971). *An empirical basis for change in education*. Chicago, IL: SRA.

Burdette, P. (2007). *Response to intervention as it relates to early intervention services*. Washington, DC: Project Forum at National Association of State Directors of Special Education.

Christ, T. J. (2006). Short-term estimates of growth using curriculum-based measurement of oral reading fluency: Estimating standard error of the slope to construct confidence intervals. *School Psychology Review, 35*, 128-133.

Christ, T. J., & Silberglitt, B. (2007). Estimates of the standard error of measurement for curriculum-based measures of oral reading fluency. *School Psychology Review, 36*, 130-146.

Clarke, B., & Shinn, M. R. (2004). The identification, development, and investigation of early mathematics curriculum-based measurement. *School Psychology Review, 33*, 234-248.

Deno, S. L. (1991). Individual differences and individual difference: The essential difference of special education. *The Journal of Special Education, 24*, 160-173.

Deno, S. L., Marston, D., Mirkin, P. K., Lowry, L., Sindelar, P., & Jenkins, J. (1982). *The use of standard tasks to measure achievement in reading, spelling, and written expression: A normative and developmental study.* Minneapolis, MN: University of Minnesota Institute for Research on Learning Disabilities.

Deno, S. L., & Mirkin, P. (1977). *Data-based program modification: A manual.* Reston, VA: Council for Exceptional Children.

Deno, S. L., Mirkin, P., & Chiang, B. (1982). Identifying valid measures of reading. *Exceptional Children, 49*, 36-45.

Foegen, A., Jiban, C., & Deno, S. L. (2007). Progress monitoring measures in mathematics: A review of the literature. *The Journal of Special Education, 41*, 121-139.

Foegen, A., Olson, J. R., & Impecoven-Lind, L. (2008). Developing progress monitoring measures for secondary mathematics: An illustration in algebra. *Assessment for Effective Intervention, 33*, 240-249.

Fuchs, L. S. (1988). Effects of computer-managed instruction on teachers' implementation on systematic monitoring programs and student achievement. *Journal of Educational Research, 81*, 294-304.

Fuchs, L. S. (2004). The past, present, and future of curriculum-based measurement research. *School Psychology Review, 33*, 188-192.

Fuchs, L. S., & Deno, S. L. (1991). Paradigmatic distinctions between instructionally relevant measurement models. *Exceptional Children, 57*, 488-500.

Fuchs, L. S., & Deno, S. L. (1992). Effects of curriculum within curriculum-based measurement. *Exceptional Children, 58*, 232-243.

Fuchs, L. S., Deno, S. L., & Mirkin, P. (1984). The effects of frequent curriculum based measurement and evaluation on pedagogy, student achievement and student awareness of learning. *American Educational Research Journal, 21*, 449-460.

Fuchs, L. S., & Fuchs, D. (1986). Effects of systematic formative evaluation on student achievement: A meta-analysis. *Exceptional Children, 53*, 199-208.

Fuchs, L. S., & Fuchs, D. (1992). Identifying a measure for monitoring student reading progress. *School Psychology Review, 21*, 45-58.

Fuchs, L. S., & Fuchs, D. (1999). Monitoring student progress toward the development of reading competence: A review of three forms of classroom-based assessment. *School Psychology Review, 28*, 659-671.

Fuchs, L. S., & Fuchs, D. (2004). *What is scientifically based research on progress monitoring?* Washington, DC: National Center on Progress Monitoring, American Institute for Research, Office of Special Education Programs.

Fuchs, L. S., Fuchs, D., Hamlett, C. L., & Ferguson, C. (1992). Effects of expert system consultation within curriculum-based measurement, using a reading maze task. *Exceptional Children, 58*, 436-450.

Fuchs, L. S., Fuchs, D., Hamlett, C. L., Thompson, A., Roberts, P. H., & Kupek, P. (1994). Technical features of a mathematics concepts and applications curriculum-based measurement system. *Diagnostique, 19*, 23-49.

Fuchs, L. S., Fuchs, D., Karns, K., Hamlett, C. L., & Katzaroff, M. (1999). Mathematics performance assessment in the classroom: Effects on teacher planning and student problem solving. *American Educational Research Journal, 36*, 609-646.

Fuchs, L. S., Fuchs, D., & Maxwell, L. (1988). The validity of informal reading comprehension measures. *Remedial and Special Education, 9*, 20-28.

Fuchs, L. S., & Vaughn, S. R. (2005, Spring). Response to intervention as a framework for the identification of learning disabilities. *Forum for Trainers of School Psychologists*, 12-19.

Goodman, K. S. (2006). *The truth about DIBELS: What it is. What it does.* Portsmouth, NH: Heinemann.

Hamilton, C., & Shinn, M. R. (2003). Characteristics of word callers: An investigation of the accuracy of teachers' judgments of reading comprehension and oral reading skills. *School Psychology Review, 32*, 228-240.

Hattie, J. (2009). *Visible learning: A synthesis of over 800 meta-analyses relating to achievement.* New York, NY: Routledge.

Hintze, J. M., & Shapiro, E. S. (1997). Curriculum-based measurement and literature-based reading: Is curriculum-based measurement meeting the needs of changing reading curricula? *Journal of School Psychology, 35*, 351-375.

Hintze, J. M., Shapiro, E. S., & Lutz, J. G. (1994). The effects of curriculum on the sensitivity of curriculum-based measurement of reading. *The Journal of Special Education, 28*, 188-202.

Jenkins, J. R., Deno, S. L., & Mirkin, P. K. (1979). Measuring pupil progress toward the least restrictive environment. *Learning Disability Quarterly, 2*, 81-92.

Jenkins, J. R., & Fuchs, L. S. (in press). Curriculum-based measurement: The paradigm, history, and legacy. In K. L. M. C. Espin, S. Rose, & M. M. Wayman (Ed.), *Measure of success.* Minneapolis, MN: University of Minnesota Press.

Kaminski, R. A., & Good, R. H., III. (1998). Assessing early literacy skills in a problem-solving model: Dynamic indicators of basic skills. In M. R. Shinn (Ed.), *Advanced applications of curriculum-based measurement* (pp. 113-142). New York, NY: Guilford.

Kaminski, R. A., & Good, R. H. (1996). Toward a technology of assessing basic early literacy skills. *School Psychology Review, 25*, 215-227.

Kendeou, P., & Papadopoulos, T. C. (in press). The use of CBM maze in Greek: A closer look at what it measures. In K. L. M. C. Espin, S. Rose, & M. M. Wayman (Ed.), *Measure of success.* Minneapolis, MN: University of Minnesota Press.

Kim, D. (in press). Current status of curriculum-based measurement in Korea. In K. L. M. C. Espin, S. Rose, & M. M. Wayman (Ed.), *Measure of success.* Minneapolis, MN: University of Minnesota Press.

Linan-Thompson, S. (in press). Expanding the use of CBM here, there, everywhere: A look at Nicaragua. In K. L. M. C. Espin, S. Rose, & M. M. Wayman (Ed.), *Measure of success.* Minneapolis, MN: University of Minnesota Press.

Lindsley, O. R. (1964). Direct measurement and prosthesis of retarded behavior. *Journal of Education, 147*, 47-49.

Lovitt, T. C., Schaff, M. E., & Sayre, E. (1970). The use of direct and continuous measurement to evaluate reading materials and pupil performance. *Focus on Exceptional Children, 2*, 1-11.

Methe, S. A., Hintze, J. M., & Floyd, R. G. (2008). Validation and decision accuracy of early numeracy skill indicators. *School Psychology Review, 37*, 359-373.

Miura Wayman, M., Wallace, T., Ives Wiley, H., Ticha, R., & Espin, C. (2007). Literature synthesis on curriculum-based measurement in reading. *The Journal of Special Education, 41*, 85-120.

Parker, R., Hasbrouck, J. E., & Tindal, G. (1992). The maze as a classroom-based measure: Construction methods, reliability, and validity. *The Journal of Special Education, 26*, 195-218.

Riedel, B. W. (2007). The relation between DIBELS, reading comprehension, and vocabulary in urban first-grade students. *Reading Research Quarterly, 42*, 546-567.

Robinson, S. L., Robinson, M. J., & Blatchley, L. A. (in press). Curriculum-based measurement and English language learners: District-wide academic norms for special education eligibility. In K. L. M. C. Espin, S. Rose, & M. M. Wayman (Ed.), *Measure of success*. Minneapolis, MN: University of Minnesota Press.

Samuels, S. J. (2007). The DIBELS tests: Is speed of barking at print what we mean by reading fluency? *Reading Research Quarterly, 42*, 563-566.

Shinn, M. R. (2007). Identifying students at risk, monitoring performance, and determining eligibility within RTI: Research on educational need and benefit from academic intervention. *School Psychology Review, 36*, 601-617.

Shinn, M. R. (2008). Best practices in curriculum-based measurement and its use in a problem-solving model. In A. Thomas & J. Grimes (Eds.), *Best practices in school psychology V* (pp. 243-262). Bethesda, MD: National Association of School Psychologists.

Shinn, M. R. (2010). Building a scientifically based data system for progress monitoring and universal screening across three tiers including RTI using curriculum-based measurement. In M. R. Shinn & H. M. Walker (Eds.), *Interventions for achievement and behavior problems in a three-tier model, including RTI* (pp. 259-293). Bethesda, MD: National Association of School Psychologists.

Shinn, M. R., Good, R. H., Knutson, N., Tilly, W. D., & Collins, V. (1992). Curriculum-based reading fluency: A confirmatory analysis of its relation to reading. *School Psychology Review, 21*, 458-478.

Shinn, M. R., & Marston, D. (1985). Differentiating mildly handicapped, low-achieving and regular education students: A curriculum-based approach. *Remedial and Special Education, 6*, 31-45.

Shinn, M. R., Tindal, G., Spira, D., & Marston, D. (1987). Practice of learning disabilities as social policy. *Learning Disability Quarterly, 10*, 17-28.

Shinn, M. R., Tindal, G., & Stein, S. (1988). Curriculum-based assessment and the identification of mildly handicapped students: A research review. *Professional School Psychology, 3*, 69-85.

Shinn, M. R., Ysseldyke, J., Deno, S. L., & Tindal, G. (1986). A comparison of differences between students labeled learning disabled and low achieving on measures of classroom performance. *Journal of Learning Disabilities, 19*, 545-552.

Speece, D. L., Pericola Case, L., & Eddy Molloy, D. (2003). Responsiveness to general education instruction as the first gate to learning disabilities identification. *Learning Disabilities Research & Practice, 18*, 147-156.

Thurber, R. S., & Shinn, M. R. (2002). What is measured in mathematics tests? Construct validity of Curriculum-Based mathematics measures. *School Psychology Review, 31*, 498-513.

Tucker, J. (1985). Curriculum-based assessment: An introduction. *Exceptional Children, 52*, 199-204.

Wallace, T., Espin, C. A., McMaster, K., Deno, S. L., & Foegen, A. (2007). CBM progress monitoring within a standards-based system: Introduction to the special series. *The Journal of Special Education, 41*, 66-67.

White, O. (1971). *A pragmatic approach to the description of progress in the single case* (Unpublished doctoral dissertation). University of Oregon, Eugene, OR.

Ysseldyke, J., Shinn, M. R., & Thurlow, M. (1978). The University of Minnesota Institute for Research on Learning Disabilities. *Learning Disability Quarterly, 1*, 75-77.

Author Contact Information: Mark R. Shinn, PhD, National Louis University. Phone: (847) 275-7200. E-mail: markshinn@me.com

CHAPTER 66

Dynamic Assessment

An Intervention-Based Approach

Carol Robinson-Zañartu
San Diego State University

Although a variety of approaches to dynamic assessment exist, three assumptions underlie virtually all of them: (a) that human cognition is an open system; (b) that it is modifiable through interactions with key others; and (c) that those interactions provide a form of intervention. Thus, dynamic assessment seeks to produce change rather than to measure a stable trait or set of traits. It makes deliberate use of examiner-examinee relationships rather than seeking to limit them. Finally, dynamic assessment embeds intervention within the assessment, observing the effects of intervention, rather than observing unaided responses in an environment of strict standardization (Lidz & Elliott, 2000). Additionally, the issue of cultural "fairness" has been central to most forms of dynamic assessment, and treated differently across the range of dynamic assessment models. The complex question of differentiating cultural difference from disability was the subject of much of Feuerstein's early research with dynamic assessment (Feuerstein, Rand, & Hoffman, 1979), and has continued to be a focus of the work in both clinical and school settings (cf. Budoff, 1987; Green, McIntosh, Cook-Morales, & Robinson-Zañartu, 2005; Hessels, 2000; Lidz & Peña, 2009; Peña et al., 2006).

Although two theories are considered by most to be foundational for dynamic assessment, and hold many parallels, a range of models of dynamic assessment that have emerged from those foundations have taken quite unique directions. Reschly and Robinson-Zañartu (2000) described this range of models as a continuum. On one end of that continuum, psychometric models adhere to varying amounts of standardization and thus lend themselves to psychometric analysis. On the other end, assessors working from more clinical or interactionist models use subject responses to guide examiner questions, examples, or probes; thus, examiner prompts are not standardized, and vary based on the individual dynamics of each examinee. In this chapter, both the theoretical grounding and the diversity of models that have emerged are discussed.

HISTORICAL AND THEORETICAL FOUNDATIONS

Long before the term dynamic assessment came into use, we find accounts of theorists considering the nature of cognition or intelligence as modifiable, rather than fixed, or relatively fixed. Itard's account of the "Wild Boy of Aveyron" in which he proposed that environmental enrichment could compensate for developmental delays may be the earliest (Robinson-Zañartu & Carlson, 2013). A century later, Binet proposed that attention, memory, judgment and intelligence could be enhanced with a methodological approach involving practice (Dweck, 2006). During the early part of the twentieth century, a number of psychologists explored the idea of examining learning during the learning process, as opposed to using a static one-time measure. However, it is the theoretical work of Lev Vygotsky (1962, 1978) and Feuerstein (Feuerstein, Rand, & Hoffman, 1979) that are most commonly associated with dynamic assessment.

Theoretically, dynamic assessment is broadly centered in Vygotskian notions of cognitive development as mediated through sociocultural influences. Vygotsky's (1962, 1978) social interactionist model proposed that cognitive change was culturally contextual-

The Handbook of Educational Theories, pp. 793–799

ized and could be fostered; that is, that children acquire verbal tools and other higher order thinking through mediation from adults for the purpose of mastery of the culture (Karpov, 2003). In Vygotsky's view, adults and more capable peers supply psychological tools (e.g., language; concepts), which then mediate the higher order thinking. Furthermore, during the process of learning, children would exhibit not only a level of independent development, reflecting what they could achieve alone, but also a level of potential development "as determined through problem solving under adult guidance or in collaboration with more capable peers" (Vygotsky, 1978, p. 86). He called the difference between the two the zone of proximal development (ZPD). This ZPD was not conceptualized as a fixed zone of capability; rather, as able to be observed as "constantly changing with the learner's increasing independent competence" (Bransford, Brown, & Cocking, 2000, p. 81). In keeping with this theory, Vygotsky believed that assessment should go beyond symptoms and present status, and should assume deliberate interaction with a significant adult, thereby trying to predict the child's course of development, or potential to learn. His work to stimulate development and to modify children's learning ability is considered seminal in the dynamic assessment history. Vygotsky's work was promoted outside the Soviet Union by his colleague Luria, who, as early at 1961, proposed rejecting static assessment of independent performance in favor of comparing independent success with that achieved with the help of an adult (Luria, 1961). Vygotsky's work influenced remarkable scholars in development and education (cf. Cole; Rogoff), and decades of work in dynamic assessment, from Budoff (1987) to Campione and Brown (1987), Guthke (1992), and Poehner (2008).

In the early 1970s, Israeli psychologist Reuven Feuerstein began to publish his theoretical position and clinical findings on the need to depart from static measures of intellectual potential, and to measure the potential for change, or potential to be modified by learning. He was clear that this should occur by attempting "to modify the examinee in some way, while measuring the extent of the change, and the means by which this was attained" (Feuerstein, Rand, & Hoffman, 1979, p. 43). With the publication of *The Dynamic Assessment of Retarded Performers,* he articulated his theory of structural cognitive modifiability as well as his methods and procedures of dynamic assessment. Feuerstein acknowledged the influences of several other researchers who shared or had influenced his perspectives on the need for a dynamic rather than static measure. For instance, André Rey had been Feuerstein's mentor, and as early as 1934 had observed that the goal of assessment should be the potential for modifiability. Wesman wrote specifically about individual variability in the levels of modifiability and the levels of stimulus to promote modifiability.

Some of Feuerstein's theoretical premises paralleled those of Vygotsky. He saw the intergenerational transmission of culture as central to a child's learning to learn; thus, the sociocultural context provided the interactions with which learning emerged. According to Feuerstein, it was within cultural contexts of intergenerational transmission of the culture that the individual would learn key cognitive functions essential to the input, elaboration and output of relevant content. The richness of the sociocultural context and natural propensity for intergenerational cultural transmission gave the content affective and motivational value and support. It was his premise that when a child was deprived from this rich learning due to poverty, war, or other traumas, that learning how to learn suffered. He called this condition cultural deprivation, meaning deprivation from one's own culture and from the cognitive processes that come with that transmission. In fact, he had seen this occur repeatedly in Israel after World War II, with the influx of a tremendous number of children who had been survivors of war. Many of these children's parents, fighting for survival or in fact not surviving, had not been able to engage with them in regular intergenerational transmission of their own cultures. In his clinical work with the children, Feuerstein saw their ability to learn those cognitive functions emerge using intense and deliberate "mediating" interactions with an adult.

Feuerstein listed and described specific cognitive functions in each of three "phases of the mental act," which he called input, elaboration and output. In addition, he described the characteristics of adult interactions, called mediation, which helped the child develop those functions. His theory of structural cognitive modifiability premised that the human organism is an open system, and therefore modifiable by others. Thus, for an individual "deprived of their own culture," it would be possible for another adult or more capable person to "stand in" and provide mediation, helping the individual develop and habituate new cognitive functions, and thus enhanced functioning. Feuerstein's dynamic assessment was designed "to search for the modifiability of these [deficient] cognitive functions and concomitantly to look for strategies and modalities for the most efficient and economical way to overcome the barriers imposed by these differences" (Feuerstein et al., 1979, p. 125).

His Learning Propensity [formerly Potential] Assessment Device, or LPAD, provided assessment tools designed to help the mediator elicit engagement in those cognitive functions on a number of tasks. The learners' response to that mediation would then provide a way to differentiate children whose learning had been interrupted or insufficiently mediated, but could be re-initiated, mediated and modified. He contrasted this with individuals operating in culturally unfamiliar environments, who had been well mediated in their own cultures, but who might be temporarily functioning below expected levels in new environments because they had not yet had the time to fully adjust.

Feuerstein's models and work continue around the world, from South Africa to Canada, Chile to Singapore. Many researchers and practitioners who have gone on to create new programs or models were initially grounded in Feuerstein's ideas and approaches. For example, Haywood created his Cognitive Curriculum for Young Children; Tzuriel developed his Dynamic Cognitive System for Young Children; Jensen went on to establish his Mindladder Model and dynamic assessment tools; Lidz developed a number of instruments and authored numerous books.

Variations on a Theme: The Continuum of Models of Dynamic Assessment

Virtually all forms of dynamic assessment assume the potential for modifiability, and that through deliberately using the examiner-examinee relationship, one can measure change. In some models, measuring that change is done to classify students as able to learn in general settings; in other models, describing the response to intervention, or change, serves as a base for intervention planning. Seen as two endpoints of a continuum, the models have been classified as either clinical or psychometric.

Those working from clinical approaches work from the assumptions found within Feuerstein's theories, although often not from his direct model or tools. For instance, they assume individuals use a set of cognitive functions or thinking and learning skills to engage with, process and communicate information, or to construct knowledge. Their mediating examiner-examinee interactions are characterized by intentionality, reciprocity with the subject, infusion of meaning into the task and into the use of new cognitive functions, deliberate support for developing self-regulating behavior, developing internal locus of control and self-efficacy, and transfer of their skills using cognitive functions across tasks and venues. Thus, examiner prompts are not standardized, and vary based on the individual dynamics of each examinee. Subject responses guide examiner questions, examples, or probes. Examples of such models include Tzuriel's (2000) Dynamic Assessment of Young Children, and Jensen's (2000) theory of mediated constructivism and mindladder dynamic assessment tools.

However, a number of other dynamic assessment approaches do not assume that dynamic assessment should attempt to fundamentally modify cognition. Classified as the more psychometrically oriented, this group of dynamic assessment practices assumes that providing some intervention in the midst of assessment, ranging from graduated prompts to explicit instruction, will provide a measure of learning potential. Usually a test-train-retest paradigm is employed. For example, Budoff and colleagues (1987) developed their learning potential assessment to identify gainers from nongainers, hoping to ameliorate what he saw as inappropriate placement decisions for low income and minority youth in special education. He used tests such as the Ravens Progressive Matrices and Kohs Blocks to establish baselines, familiarize examinees with the task demands, and then teach learning strategies. Standardization was described as approximate, since his interventions varied across examinees. He found that for his nongainers, the pretest accurately predicted their outcomes; however, for his "gainers" the LPA was a more accurate predictor.

Brown and Campione (1986) developed a model heavily influenced by Vygotsky. Their premise was that children move from cognitive dependence to independence with assistance from adults. That assistance would begin as child observation and the guiding questions of adults, which would gradually give way to an internalized self-questioning and self-regulation. It was that "transfer of control" (p. 83) that their dynamic assessment system sought to capture. To do this, they focused on processes underlying performance and specific domains, and they used standardized hints and questions to support the child's learning the task. Estimates of potential were based on the type and number of hints about how to approach the task needed by the child, using measures of the amount of aid and the degree to which transfer could be demonstrated.

Issues of Validity

Individual researchers have examined validity issues within their particular models; however, because this chapter deals with the spectrum of models, two meta-analytic studies that address the robustness of findings across dynamic assessment methodologies will be discussed.

Swanson and Lussier (2001) conducted a study employing meta-analysis techniques, which synthesized the literature around two questions comparing dynamic with static forms of assessment: first, whether dynamic assessment modified group differences in ability on different dependent variables and provided a better estimate of ability; and second, whether effect sizes related to dynamic assessment were products of research design, treatment intensity and type of instruction. They framed validity in terms of usefulness. Inclusion criteria required that the dynamic assessment method used a pretest-train-posttest paradigm. Their search for articles included an expanded PSYINFO database and two articles reviewing the literature. Their sample size, 5,104, was drawn from 30 articles that met criteria for inclusion, and was unevenly distributed across average achievers, underachieving hearing impaired and those who had been qualified for special services with learning disabilities or educable mental retardation. Three dynamic assessment models were represented: testing-the-limits, mediated training employing coaching, and structured strategy training and feedback (scaffolding). Two types of dependent variables were included: verbal (story recall, rhyming, phrase recall, Peabody Picture Vocabulary Test) and visual-spatial (visual matrix, Raven Matrices). Results indicated an overall effect size of 0.70, indicating dynamic assessment resulting in substantial improvement on dependent variables. Studies involving verbal elaboration or mediation produced the highest effect sizes. No ability group variables were shown to yield different effect sizes, which Swanson and Lussier interpreted as an indication that performance changes resulting from dynamic assessment reflect abilities independent of those measured by static or more conventional measures.

Cafferty, Fuchs, and Fuchs (2008) conducted a second meta-analysis. They focused on the validity of dynamic assessment for predicting future achievement. Their search included articles from ERIC, PSYCINFO, and ECER, using key phrases *dynamic assessment* or *interactive assessment* or *learning potential* or *mediated assessment*, and an expanded search including the terms *mediated learning* and *predictive validity.* In addition, they searched the articles referred to in the Swanson and Lussier study, in a special issue of *The Journal of Special Education* on the topic, and a literature review by Grigorenko and Sternberg. Twenty-four articles met their selection criteria: (a) publication in English; (b) participants enrolled in preschool through high school; (c) participants who were either average achieving, at-risk due to cultural or economic factors, identified high-incidence disabilities, or second-language learners and (d) articles reporting data used to determine predictive validity. They analyzed data on four dimensions: (a) correlations between traditional testing, dynamic assessment and achievement; (b) the type of feedback used in the studies (contingent vs. noncontingent); (c) predictive validity of dynamic assessment by type of student; and (d) predictive relationships between dynamic assessment and different achievement criteria. Caffrey et al. (2008) summarized their findings:

> When feedback is noncontingent, predictive validity is higher for dynamic assessment approaches than for traditional assessment. It is also higher for students with disabilities than normal achieving but at-risk students. Finally, it is higher when the achievement criteria are assessed with criterion referenced tests as opposed to norm-referenced or teacher judgment. (p. 254)

Critiques of Dynamic Assessment

Because of the range of models of dynamic assessment, no one set of tools, tasks or procedures can be assumed to comprise it. For the clinical types of dynamic assessment models, in which examiners deliberately use the cues from examinees rather than a manual to create prompts, lack of standardization is criticized. Critics argue that reliability is compromised. On the other end of the continuum from the clinical models, some types of dynamic assessment are designed for psychometric integrity, and reliability is strong. For instance, Hessels (2000) reports that for his Learning Potential Test for Ethnic Minorities (LEM), designed to assess immigrant children in the Netherlands, Cronbach's alpha varies from 0.88 to 0.92 across respective age and nationality groups (Turkish, Moroccan, and Danish). However, the examiner does no mediation, no pretest or specific training phase. He provides limited and concrete hints when examinees falter.

Four other critiques, framed as barriers to the use of dynamic assessment, were raised by Sternberg (2000; Sternberg & Grigorenko, 2002). First, due to its uniqueness, inertia keeps psychologists from learning it. Second, because it can be complicated to learn and administer, the complexity has become a second barrier. Related to this, usually special training is required to learn dynamic assessment; thus, time and availability of training can be barriers. Finally, depending on the type of model used, the psychometrics can be complicated and some types of dynamic assessment, as has been discussed, are subject to clinical interpretation.

Use of Dynamic Assessment in Schools

Most often it has been school psychologists or speech and language pathologists who have used dynamic assessment in school settings. Their purposes have been either to predict future success or to create interventions. In the last decade, more research and practice are emerging with increased attention to the role of interventionists, and to response to intervention (RtI) models. A few of these school-based uses of dynamic assessment, across clinical and psychometric models, will be briefly explained.

Speech and language pathologists (SLP) may have been the professionals in schools to use dynamic assessment most widely to date. Because they must develop and deliver interventions, dynamic assessment has been seen as a method to use assessment to directly inform those interventions. For instance, some

SLPs have used successive cuing approaches to determine ability beyond what they get from static tests. Others have used mediation approaches to differentiate difference and disorder, and found metacognitive skill and flexibility in children to be highly predictive of language ability. Lidz and Peña (2009) discuss several examples of how test-teach-test strategies have helped either identify or differentiate children with and without language impairments:

> Roseberry and Connell [1991] ... found that children from culturally diverse backgrounds with and without language impairment learned an invented morpheme rule at different rates. This differential learning rate allowed the authors to classify the two groups with better sensitivity and specificity. Similarly, Jacobs [2001] found that the addition of a learning component to her computerized preschool language screening enhanced the information available to her linguistically diverse preschoolers from low socioeconomic backgrounds. (p. 123)

For many forms of dynamic assessment, intervention is embedded. The student's response to that intervention should be helpful to teachers or specialists. Most response to intervention (RTI) models use three tiers of intervention: the first, a whole school approach to effective teaching; the second a targeted intervention with a smaller group, and the third often consideration for special education placement and intervention. Fuchs et al. (2008) suggest that dynamic assessment might help with early identification of students who will ultimately prove unresponsive to preventive efforts at Tier 1, and thus receive support earlier. To study this premise, they randomly sampled 150 third graders for participation, and blocked within instruction condition and three strata. Ethnicity was distributed across Africa-American (48%), Euro-American (42%), Hispanic (8%) and other (2%). Half the group received conventional math problem-solving instruction while the other half received a validated schema-broadening math problem solving instruction. In October they administered a test-teach-test form of dynamic assessment in which they use graduated prompts and instructional scaffolding until the student reaches criterion. The intervention was an unrelated academic task, in this case algebra instruction. With multiple measures pre and post, they examined the difference in unassisted pre- and posttests, as well as the number of scaffolds required. In March, five tests of word-problem skill were administered. They found this form of dynamic assessment to be helpful in differentiating students who would later have difficulty with reading or math, and they suggest that dynamic assessment could play an important role in the arena of prediction of future learning. They point out that if dynamic assessment were to provide this earlier identification, then up to 30 weeks of additional failure, found in more conventional RTI models, could be avoided.

In a contrasting approach to using dynamic assessment to support response to intervention models, Robinson-Zañartu and colleagues (2012) have used clinical dynamic assessment to isolate cognitive skills and accompanying mediations found to produce changed performance during dynamic assessment, and pair those with academic interventions for children not responding to academic intervention alone at Tiers 2 and 3 (Robinson-Zañartu & Carlson, 2013). She calls this response to mediated intervention (RTMI). Rather than intervene with an unrelated task for the purpose of prediction, RTMI intervenes with a set of critical thinking and metacognitive skills paired with the actual area of academic difficulty. Dynamic assessment interactions are considered trial interventions, and based on their outcomes, the more formal intervention is designed to support transfer into the area of academic challenge, so that the student gains new skills both cognitively and academically. Baseline data are collected prior to dynamic assessment in the areas of academic or academically related behavioral target (e.g., time on task; reading comprehension; math calculation or problem solving). Progress is monitored for fidelity and data collected following the 6-week intervention measure the change in the academic target area. Pilot data with students from grades three to eight, across ethnicity and subject areas, are extremely promising. RTMI is designed to exist side by side with behavioral and academic RTI models, augmenting both Tier 2 and Tier 3 interventions.

Two single case studies illustrate. In the first, a third grade Latino male was referred for math performance problems. Dynamic assessment demonstrated his responsiveness to mediation of four thinking skills which resulted in improved performance on dynamic and authentic tasks: Gathering and using multiple sources of information, goal setting, planning and finding connections and relationships. A 6-week intervention was designed in which evidence-based math interventions paired with mediation of the four identified thinking skills focused on recalling and applying basic addition and subtraction facts, increasing automaticity of multiplication facts, and using regrouping for borrowing. Outcomes demonstrated increased performance on correct math facts (33% to 87%), knowledge of multiplication facts (23% to 60%), and problem solving in subtraction with regrouping (0 to 50%). In a second case, a third grade Euro-American girl was referred for difficulties with subtraction. Four thinking skills supported her changed performance during dynamic assessment: gathering data with precision and accuracy, using multiple sources of information; enhanced use of accurate labels, words and concepts; and using feedback for self-regulation. Intervention goals included development of thinking skills, understanding the purpose for these skills, and transfer of the skills into math. An error analysis determined specific academic skills and concepts of focus; that is, bases of ten, regrouping, and attending to details within word problems. Multiple activities were designed to build conceptual understanding. Meditated interactions paired with instructional strategies were used to help her develop the four thinking skills, which were then transferred into the academic tasks. Baseline and outcomes data demonstrated increased accuracy from 60% to 100% in subtraction without regrouping, and from 0% to 80% in both subtraction with regrouping and subtraction word problems.

CONCLUSION

Dynamic assessment is not one method, set of assessment tools, or even one theory. Rather, it is a system of thought which considers the nature of thinking and learning as a dynamic or modifiable set of interrelated skills rather than as a fixed set of measurable traits. It holds that the human organism and cognitive system is open to change with the intentional intervention of an adult or more knowledgeable peer, and that the response of the individual to that intervention can be linked with meaningful outcomes for them. Vygotsky and Feuerstein, both considered foundational theorists behind dynamic assessment, attached strong meaning to the sociocultural contexts underlying the development of thinking. Both had serious misgivings about the usefulness of static assessment techniques. Yet the methods of dynamic assessment that have emerged from these beginnings split into two camps, the psychometric and the clinical. Some consider cultural grounding as central to their models; others ignore it and focus on the issue of production of change. Some use dynamic assessment for its value as a predictor; others see it as a tool to inform intervention. Each has important contributions to make. Applications of dynamic assessment have ranged from working with adult clients with brain injury or schizophrenia to developing interventions for school-aged children and youth. Practitioners and researchers are found across continents from North America to Africa, Europe, Asia, South America, and Australia. Dynamic assessment represents an evolving set of theories and practices.

REFERENCES

Bransford, J. D., Brown, A. L., & Cocking, R. R. (Eds.). (2000). *How people learn: Brain, mind, experience, and school.* Washington, DC: National Academy Press.

Brown, A., & Campione, J. (1986). Psychological theory and the study of learning disabilities. *American Psychologist, 41*(10), 1059-1068. doi:10.1037/0003-066X.41.10.1059

Budoff, M. (1987). Measures for assessing learning potential. In C. S. Lidz (Ed.), *Dynamic assessment: An interactional approach to evaluating learning potential* (pp. 52-81). New York, NY: Guilford.

Caffrey, E., Fuchs D., & Fuchs, L. (2008). The predictive validity of dynamic assessment: A review. *Journal of Special Education, 41*, 254-270.

Campione, J. C., & Brown, A. L. (1987). Linking dynamic assessment with school achievement. In C. S. Lidz (Ed.), *Dynamic assessment: An interactional approach to evaluating learning potential* (pp. 82-115). New York, NY: Guilford Press.

Cole, M., Gay, J., Glick, J .A., & Sharp, D. (1971). *The cultural context of learning and thinking*. New York, NY: Basic Books.

Dweck, C. (2006). *Mindset: The new psychology of success*. New York, NY: Random House.

Feuerstein, R., Rand, Y., & Hoffman, M. (1979). *The dynamic assessment of retarded performers*. Baltimore, MD: University Park Press.

Fuchs, L. S., Compton, D. L., Fuchs, D., Hollenbeck, K. N., Craddock, C. F. & Hamlett, C. L. (2008). Dynamic assessment of algebraic learning in predicting their graders' development of mathematical problem solving. *Journal of Educational Psychology, 100,* 829-850. doi:10.1037/a0012657

Green, T. D., McIntosh, A. S., Cook-Morales, V. J. & Robinson-Zañartu, C. (2005). From old schools to tomorrow's schools: Psychoeducational assessment of African American Students. *Remedial and Special Education, 26*, 82-92. doi:10.1177/07419325050260020301

Guthke, J. (1992). Learning tests: The concept, main research findings, problems and trends. In J. Carlson (Ed.), *Advances in cognition and educational practice* (Vol. 1, pp. 213-235). Greenwich, CT: JAI Press.

Hessels, M. G. (2000). The learning potential test for ethnic minorities (LEM). In C. S. Lidz & J. G. Elliott (Eds.), *Dynamic assessment: Prevailing models and applications* (pp. 109-131). New York, NY: JAI.

Jacobs, E. L. (2001). The effects of adding dynamic assessment components to a computerized preschool language screening test. *Communicative Disorders Quarterly, 22*, 217-226.

Jensen, M. R. (2000). The Mindladder Model: Using dynamic assessment to help students learn to assemble and use knowledge. In C. S. Lidz & J. G. Elliott (Eds.), *Dynamic assessment: Prevailing models and applications* (pp. 187-228). New York, NY: JAI.

Karpov, Y. (2003). Vygotsky's concept of mediation. *Journal of Cognitive Education and Psychology* [online], *3*, 46-53. Retrieved from www.iace.coged.org

Lidz, C. S. & Elliott, J. G. (Eds.). (2000). Dynamic assessment: Prevailing models and applications. In J. S. Carlson (Series Ed.), *Advances in cognition and educational practice.* New York, NY: Elsevier.

Lidz, C. S., & Peña, E. D. (2009). Response to intervention and dynamic assessment: Do we just appear to be speaking the same language? *Seminars in Speech and Language, 30*, 121-133. doi:10.1055/s-0029-1215719

Luria, A. R. (1961). *The role of speech in the regulation of normal and abnormal behavior.* New York, NY: Liveright.

Peña, E. D., Gillam, R., Malek, M., Ruiz-Felter, R., Resendiz, M., Fiestas, C., & Sabel, T. (2006). Dynamic assessment of children from culturally diverse backgrounds: Applications to narrative assessment. *Journal of Speech, Language, Hearing Research., 49,* 1037-1057. Retrieved from http://jslhr.asha.org/

Poehner, M. E. (2008). *Dynamic assessment: A Vygotskian approach to understanding and promoting L2 development.* New York, NY: Springer.

Reschly, D. J., & Robinson-Zañartu, C. A. (2000). Aptitude tests in educational classification and placement. In G. Goldstein & M. Hersen (Eds.), *Handbook of psychological assessment* (3rd ed., pp. 183-201). Oxford, England: Pergamon.

Robinson-Zañartu, C., Barba, Y., Cardosa, N. & Rachel, M. (2012, February). *Response to mediated intervention (RTMI): Three case studies.* Paper presented at the annual meting of the National Association of School Psychologists, Philadelphia, PA.

Robinson-Zañartu, C. & Carlson, J. (2013). Dynamic assessment. In K. F. Geisinger (Ed.), *APA handbook of testing and assessment in psychology.* Washington, DC: American Psychological Association.

Rogoff, B. (2003). *The cultural nature of human development.* New York, NY: Oxford University Press

Roseberry, C. A., & Connell, P. J. (1991). The use of an invented language rule in the differentiation of normal and language-impaired Spanish-speaking children. *Journal of Speech Language and Hearing Research, 34,* 596-603.

Sternberg, R. J. (2000). Prologue. In C. S. Lidz & J. G. Elliott (Eds.), *Dynamic assessment: Prevailing models and applications* (pp. xiii-xv). New York, NY: Elsevier Science.

Sternberg, R. J., & Grigorenko, E. L. (2002). *Dynamic testing.* New York, NY: Cambridge.

Swanson, H. L., & Lussier, C. (2001). A selective synthesis of the experimental literature on dynamic assessment. *Review of Educational Research,* 71, 321-363.

Tzuriel, D. (2000). Dynamic assessment of young children: Educational and intervention perspectives. *Educational Psychology Review, 12,* 385-435. doi:10.1023/A:1009032414088

Vygotsky, L. S. (1962). *Thought and language.* Cambridge, MA: MIT Press. doi:10.1037/11193-000

Vygotsky, L. S. (1978). *Mind in society: The development of higher psychological processes.* Cambridge, MA: Harvard.

Author Contact Information: Carol Robinson-Zañartu, Department of Counseling and School Psychology, San Diego State University, San Diego, CA 92128. E-mail: crobinsn@mail.sdsu.edu

Section 10: Organizational Theory

INTRODUCTION

SECTION EDITOR
Fred C. Lunenburg
Sam Houston State University

Organizational theory is not a single theory. Instead, it is an interdisciplinary (or multidisciplinary) community of many approaches to organization analysis (Gortner, Nichols, & Ball, 2007). Most social science disciplines contribute to organizational theory. The predominant areas are anthropology, sociology, psychology, social psychology, economics, and political science (Robbins & Judge, 2011). These disciplines have contributed behavioral studies on such topics as leadership, motivation, organizational structure, decision making, organizational culture, change, and policy analysis, to name only a few. Theorists and practitioners look to these disciplines for answers to critical everyday questions; and the disciplines, in turn, provide new concepts and models that create new approaches to our understanding of how organizations function (Eriksson-Zetterquist, 2012).

This variety of disciplines contributes to the richness and complexity of theory and some fundamental assumptions about the nature of organizations and the purposes of organizational theory. For some scholars and practitioners, the purpose of theory is to explain phenomena; for others, its purpose is to provide guidelines for the selection of effective leadership styles or best practices (Albers Mohrman, 2012). As such, organizational theory makes an important and useful contribution to our understanding of the dimensions of organizational life in schools (Lunenburg & Ornstein, 2012).

James Vornberg introduces the section on organizational theory with his chapter, entitled "Systems Theory." A system can be defined as an interrelated set of elements functioning as an operating unit. Systems theory has had an important role in much of theoretical and operational applications within the natural sciences and social sciences, as well as the field of management. In these three areas, the use of systems as a basis of theory and application differs to some degree. Vornberg's discussion focuses primarily on the social sciences and management fields. He traces the history of systems theory and makes application to educational organizations and leadership.

In the chapter following, "Complexity Theory," Timothy Jones examines complexity theory in educational organizations. Complexity theory was born in the 1960s as a natural byproduct of systems theory and the study of systems and cybernetics. Where systems theory explains the world as a vast interconnected system made up of many parts, complexity theory attempts to explain the phenomenon associated with the relationship and interconnectedness of those parts with each other and with the system itself. Although systems theory and cybernetics were born in the field of mathematics and physics (quantum mechanics), the late twentieth century and early twenty-first century have found complexity theory equally applicable to both physical and social systems. This progression of thought and the exploration of how multiple systems network into larger systems are today characterized by the term *new sciences*. It is this theoretical underpinning and an emerging postmodern understanding of the new sciences that have given way to what the field of organizational behavior regards as the learning community. Learning communities, as a model of organizational development, permeate education particularly in the public school setting.

Lyse Langlois provides a perspective on ethical theory. Interestingly enough, the focus on ethics within the field of school management was not the result of reactions to scandals, corruption, and conflicts of interest that marred the business world. Misconduct in business drove ethics to the forefront, creating a new field of study: business ethics. However, this scenario did not take place in the same manner in school adminis-

The Handbook of Educational Theories, pp. 801–803

tration. Instead, ongoing questioning was prevalent in this field of study, whether in the field itself or in the areas of school dropout and lack of leadership. This process paved the way for school management ethics. In her chapter entitled, "Ethical Sensitivity Unfolding in Educational Settings," she provides background information on how ethics were introduced in the field of school administration and then presents two emerging trends in Canada. Next, she makes connections between her views on ethics and applied ethics to argue in favor of a major concept in ethics: ethical sensitivity. In light of this context, she suggests furthering this ongoing development jointly with educational leaders by showing that ethical sensitivity is a potential driver of social change.

Martha McCarthy addresses the topic of jurisprudence in her chapter, "Legal Theory and Research," because the law provides the framework for everything that transpires in schools. *Black's Law Dictionary* defines "theory of law" as the "legal premise or set of principles on which a case rests" (Garner, 2009, p. 1616), which narrowly confines legal theory to court cases. Freeman (2008) similarly has opined that much of what is considered legal theory has focused on the "inner workings of the judicial system" (p. 18). But Freeman (1998) also has referred to "high theory" as "general questions about the nature and functions of law, the concept of a legal system, the relationship between law and morality, the differences between law and other types of social control, and other central aspects of legal discourse" (p. vi), which is a somewhat broader view of legal theory and the one she discusses in her chapter.

Given the importance of theory in understanding the nature of organizations, researchers devote attention to studying new and insightful perspectives. Fred C. Lunenburg provides a discussion of five contemporary perspectives of recent interest in his chapter, entitled "Other Contemporary Organizational Theories." The five contemporary theories Lunenburg discusses include: the leader-member exchange theory, reciprocal influence theory, substitutes for leadership theory, total quality management, and transformational leadership. The latter theory, currently the most popular management approach, is discussed in-depth, using Bernard Bass's framework with two first-time, large-scale education samples.

Arthur Shapiro examines organizational theory in light of constructivist thinking in his chapter, entitled "Organizational Theory in Light of Constructivist Thinking." To achieve this, he discusses the philosophic roots of and nature of constructivism and applies constructivist philosophy, theory, and practice to analyze organizational theory/functioning and operations, particularly as they apply to educational organizations. According to Shapiro, many scholars have contributed to the development of constructivist thought, including Rene Descartes, Immanuel Kant, Jacques Rousseau, Johann Pestalozzi, John Dewey, Jerome Bruner, Jean Piaget, Lev Vygotsky, Paulo Freire, and Howard Gardner. Constructivist theories assert that people are not recorders of information, but builders of knowledge structures.

Fenwick English provides a perspective on postmodernism in his chapter, entitled "Postmodernism—(The Antitheory)." Postmodernism has been a recognizable part of the philosophical lexicon since the 1960s. Its influence in educational administration has been growing steadily, mainly due to some of its concepts and ideas that have been used by critical theorists and by advocates for particular groups. Examples include the examination of language as a vehicle for silencing, and the use of power for the control of social institutions to maintain privilege and disadvantage others. Work on racial/ethnic and gender issues is a related area. English discusses the implications of postmodernism for theory development; postmodern tools of analysis (deconstruction, genealogical analysis, and a search for trace); and what postmodernism offers researchers and practitioners.

Using a postmodernist approach, William Kritsonis discusses how he envisions using six realms of meaning, derived from "Ways of Knowing through the Realms of Meaning," to teach higher-level thinking skills to low-income students. He defines the six realms of meaning as follows. The first realm of meaning is *symbolics* and encompasses ordinary language, mathematics, and nondiscursive, subjective symbolic forms. The second realm of meaning is *empirics*. The subjects of psychology, biology, physical science, and the social sciences are all included in this realm of study. The third realm of meaning focuses on *esthetics*. Understanding *esthetics* allows us to see and understand our world through the avenues of literature, movement, the visual arts, and music. *Synnoetics*, the fourth realm, centralizes its focus on our personal knowledge. The fifth realm is about *ethics* and how moral knowledge affects the quality and characteristics of our life on a day to day basis. The sixth realm of meaning is *synoptics*. Synoptics takes an in-depth view of history, religion, and philosophy, and provides the opportunity to study these disciplines in the light of their relationship to other disciplines and their contributions to the realms of meaning included in a disciplined and familial approach.

REFERENCES

Albers Mohrman, S (2012). *Useful research: Advancing theory and practice.* San Francisco, CA: Berrett-Koehler.

Eriksson-Zetterquist, U. (2012). *Introduction to organization theory.* New York, NY: Oxford University Press.

Freeman, M. D. A. (2008). *Lloyd's introduction to jurisprudence.* London, England: Sweet & Maxwell.

Garner, B. A. (Ed.) (2009). *Black's law dictionary* (9th ed). St. Paul, MN: Thompson/West.

Gortner, H. F., Nichols, K. L., & Ball, C. (2007). *Organization theory* (3rd ed.). Belmont, CA: Wadsworth Cengage Learning.

Lunenburg, F. C., & Ornstein, A. O. (2012). Educational *administration: Concepts and practices* (6th ed.). Belmont, CA: Cengage/Wadsworth.

Robbins, S. P., & Judge, T. A. (2011). *Organizational behavior* (14th ed.). Upper Saddle River, NJ: Prentice Hall.

Author Contact Information: Fred C. Lunenburg, PhD, Merchant Professor of Education, Sam Houston State University, 1908 Bobby K. Marks Drive, Box 2119, Huntsville, TX 77341-2119. Telephone: 939-294-3838. E-mail: edu_fcl@shsu.edu

CHAPTER 67

Systems Theory

James A. Vornberg
Texas A&M University-Commerce

In 1963 Edward Lorenz, an MIT professor in meteorology, discussed an idea at the New York Academy of Science meeting that a butterfly could flap its wings on one side of the earth and move molecules of air that would move other molecules of air and eventually were capable of changing the weather and perhaps even start a hurricane on the other side of the world (Lorenz, 1972). This possibility became known as the "butterfly effect" and although it was first considered preposterous, it was determined 30 years later to be a viable and accurate condition or force that has been elevated to the level of a "law" by physicists; this effect is now know as The Law of Sensitive Dependence Upon Initial Conditions. Although this idea was originally conceived in the physical sciences, this principle "has also been applied to human society. Tiny changes in one person's state of mind can, on occasions, lead to major changes in society as a whole" (Russell, 2005).

The "butterfly effect" phenomenon was possible to imagine due to an idea which had been present in scientific thinking for many years; however, its existence was not recognized formally until the mid-twentieth century. This idea has become known as "systems theory."

What Is a System?

Each thing and everything can be viewed as a system. A system is organized of components that come together to make a unique structure of mass and energy. This organized mass has properties that are not present when the components are not present and functioning as they are. So every plant, animal, and inanimate object exists as a system. If a component were removed from the presence of the other components, the system would be different, although still a system. So people as individuals, as organizations, as societies can be viewed as systems. Of course when these systems are in close contact or appropriate or inappropriate contact they might become part of a larger system. The various components that make up a system can change and therefore the system itself changes as each of the parts of a system help to make the system what it is, how it operates, and how it changes. The individual people are also made up of systems that are continually changing as a result of growth, contact, and interaction with other systems.

History

In general, the function of systems has actually been used for many years as natural scientists and social scientists have worked to understand problems and what makes things occur the way in which they do. Systems theory also serves to extend a link between many separate disciplines in understanding how these can impact each other.

There is evidence that the concept of systems extends back even into past centuries but the originator of the theory of systems concept is generally acknowledged to be credited to Ludwig von Bertalanffy, a biologist. Von Bertalanffy is often credited with being the scientist that originated in presentations about systems biology (1937) and writing on general systems theory in the *British Journal for the Philosophy of Science* in 1950. There are numerous other writers that used some of the terms and ideas over a long period of time; however, Bertalanffy used the term "system" to outline principles which were common to systems in general. As a result he is often considered the initiator of general systems theory. He integrated the ideas of the general systems theory using biological systems as a means to understand the world at large. Thus the biological metaphor was a disguise in which general systems theory initially developed (Morgan, 1997).

The Handbook of Educational Theories, pp. 805–813

As one of the early "thinkers" in the field of organizational studies, Alexander Bogdanov developed tectology, a theory developed around the model and design for human organizations. Tectology is considered a precursor to general systems theory. Kurt Lewin was also a contributor in developing a perspective within organization theory known as "systems of ideology." More recently in education Griffiths (1964), Senge (1990) and Morgan (1997) incorporated the systems concepts into their theoretical constructs and their application to the leadership field.

SYSTEMS THEORY

Systems theory has had an important role in much of theoretical and operational applications within the natural sciences and social sciences, as well as the field of management. In these three areas the use of systems as a basis of theory and application differs to some degree; this discussion will focus primarily on the social sciences and management fields.

A system is a structure of mass and energy which is organized but yet it is more than just a collection of parts (referred to as elements). A system has properties that are built from the elements interacting with one another that make the entire system more than just the sum of its elements. A *system* consists of interrelated parts that work together or in some fashion and impact each other in a *process* that produces what are usually referred to as *outputs*. The parts are usually referred to as *elements* that make up the system. The elements have *characteristics* that can be perceived and measured. The effect of the elements on one another result in outputs that are produced by the system. *Relationships* are the associations that occur between the elements (Pidwimy, 2009).

Actually each system is likely a *subsystem* for a broader system that takes in numerous subsystems as elements. It would be possible to break down most or all systems into smaller and smaller subsystems until they reach the level of being classified as a cell or molecule. "All systems except the smallest have subsystems, and all but the largest have suprasystems, which are their environments" (Griffiths, 1964, p. 116). When various elements are combined together these are considered inputs to the system. The interaction of elements or *inputs* to the system occurs in what is known as a *process*. The process can be uncontrolled or it can be controlled in some respects as the result of planning such as one might find within an organization or its operations. In either case, uncontrolled or controlled, *outputs* result from the process. Where the output results in a desired effect, the result may be caused through planning and application which control the ultimate output.

Typically the basic system and its major parts are described in Figure 67.1. Systems have been classified in different ways. One of the important characteristics of a system is that of boundaries. The *boundaries* of a system set some of the parameters of what is inside and what is outside the system; it separates the environment from the actual system. In considering problems that are at issue, the boundary is certainly a function of that consideration (Sauter, 2008). Examples of system boundaries in education would include the school building as a unit of the district. Others would include a single classroom, the central office or the school district as a whole (Hoy & Miskel, 1982). Still others could include the state education system whose boundaries would include all the policies, laws and state level decision makers in public education. The boundaries are important in defining the classifications which include: (a) Isolated system: One that has no interactions outside the boundary of the system itself. Isolated systems are present in laboratory situations where the elements are isolated and controlled within the system; (b) Closed system: One in which energy but not matter is transferred across the boundary of the system. Closed systems are *entropic*, meaning that they tend to deteriorate and run down; (c) Open system: One in which

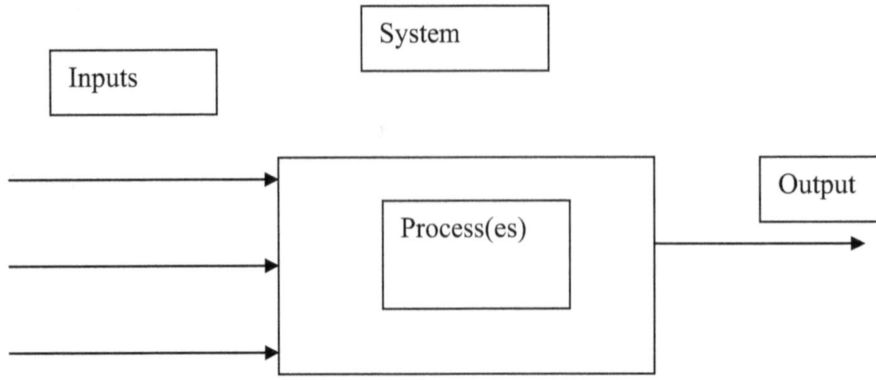

Figure 67.1. The basic system and its major parts.

both matter and energy are transferred into the surrounding environment in the output. Each open system is the part of a greater system and the effect or outputs of each system impacts or has an influence or possible influence on other open systems within the environment. This exchange with the environment is important or critical as it becomes the life of the living system since there is a continuous cycle of input, internal transformation, output and feedback that each element of experience influences the next. Therefore there is a state of interaction and interdependence within open systems. This becomes self regulating within an open system and this ability to maintain a steady state is referred to as the concept of homeostasis (Morgan, 1997, p. 40).

Social sciences, including education and business, are open systems which take in resources from the environment and after a process occurs within the system, outputs are produced. When examining an open system such as an educational system to understand the process, it is important to consider that the environment made up of other systems such as governmental structure and relationships as well as to observe and sort out the direct inputs to the system itself, which could include students, teachers and the setting. Many educational systems have "permeable boundaries which permit an exchange with their environments. Thus it becomes a bit arbitrary and risky to draw tight boundaries around problems and/or new opportunities and to constrain or limit input" (Paolucci-Whitcomb, Bright, & Carlson, 1991, p. 305).

In visualizing the relationship of elements on the entire system or other elements (variables) in the system the use of links and loops are often used. *Links* are indicated by the use of arrows which trace the influence of one element upon another. *Loops* are diagramed with trails of arrows that follow the impact or influence of elements or variables on one another until they ultimately build or deteriorate the ultimate output of the system. As the loop continues in the process it tends to generate exponential growth or the collapse of the system. These loops are referred to as reinforcing loops in that they continue the growth of whatever direction the output continues in. Balanced loops, on the other hand, depict the condition where the elements continue to adjust to a level that offers more stability to the system (Goodman, Kemeny, & Roberts, 1994).

In the accountability efforts of today's schools and instructional program a typical feedback loop might look as in Figure 67.2.

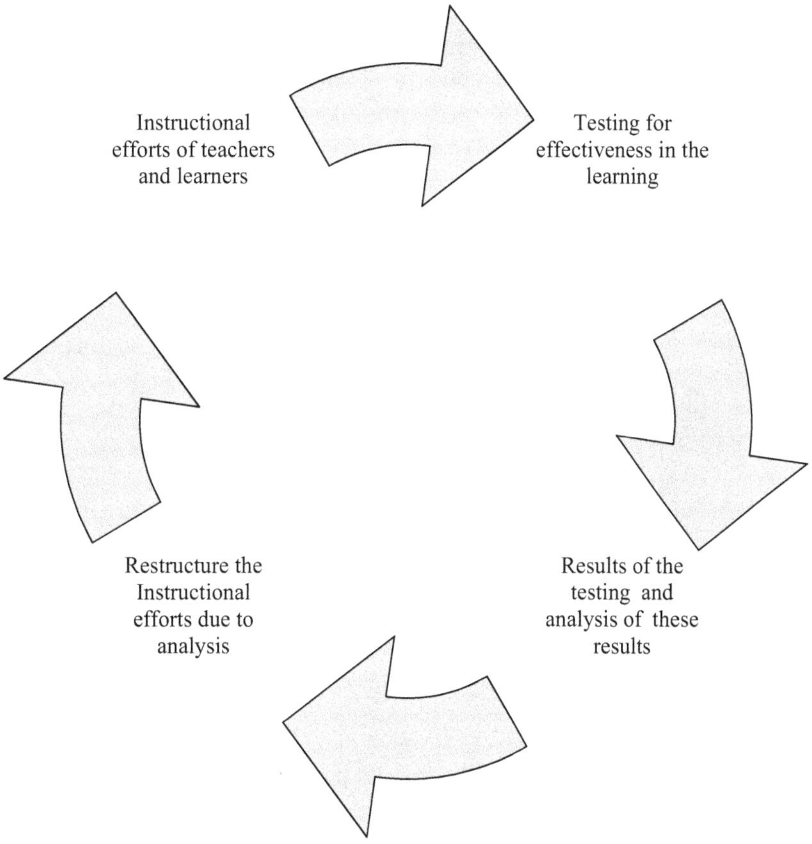

Figure 67.2. Feedback loop.

In addition to systems as a theory, "systems approach" is a term often used which plays a major role in most administrative or management procedures that organizations use to achieve their goals or outputs. "The systems approach suggests a view of the school as a network of interrelated subsystems, each charged with accomplishing part of the overall task of converting inputs into desired outputs" (Knezevich, 1975, p. 167).

Griffiths (1964) discussed open systems in the now classic yearbook of the National Society for the Study of Education. He noted that open systems:

- Exchange energy and information with their environment; they have inputs and outputs.
- Tend to maintain themselves in steady states; they are characterized by a constant ratio being maintained among components of the system.
- Are self-regulating; they may be disturbed, but once the disturbance ceases it returns its normal characteristics.
- Display equifinality; identical results may be obtained from different initial conditions.
- Maintain their steady states, in part, through the dynamic interplay of subsystems operating as functional processes; parts of the system function without persistent conflicts that can be neither resolved nor regulated.
- Maintain steady states, in part, through feedback processes which feeds back to adjust input and affect succeeding outputs; they adjust future conduct by past performance.
- Display progressive segregation by dividing into a hierarchical order of subordinate systems which also gain a certain degree of independence to each other (Griffiths, 1964, pp. 116-117).

Thus the open system includes feedback to the inputs of the system and may be diagramed as in Figure 67.3.

General systems theory consists of concepts that apply to all systems. The use of the ideas or concepts which make up the theoretical basis of systems is so natural to those who work with problems, simple or complex, that many individuals never recognize or stop to consider that they are applying the ideas of system theory as they work through their experience. Systems theory is logical in most individual's thinking consequently the term "systems thinking" is used to describe this method of solving problems or issues that exist in all types of fields of knowledge. Some basic concepts of systems theory include:

- A system contains a structure of organized components of similar and/or different types.
- No system exists in isolation. A system interfaces with other systems that may be of a similar or different type.
- The functioning of a system affects multiple other systems and is effected by multiple other systems.
- With the possible exception of the universe and the smallest component of energy or matter, all systems are components of larger systems and are composed of smaller systems.

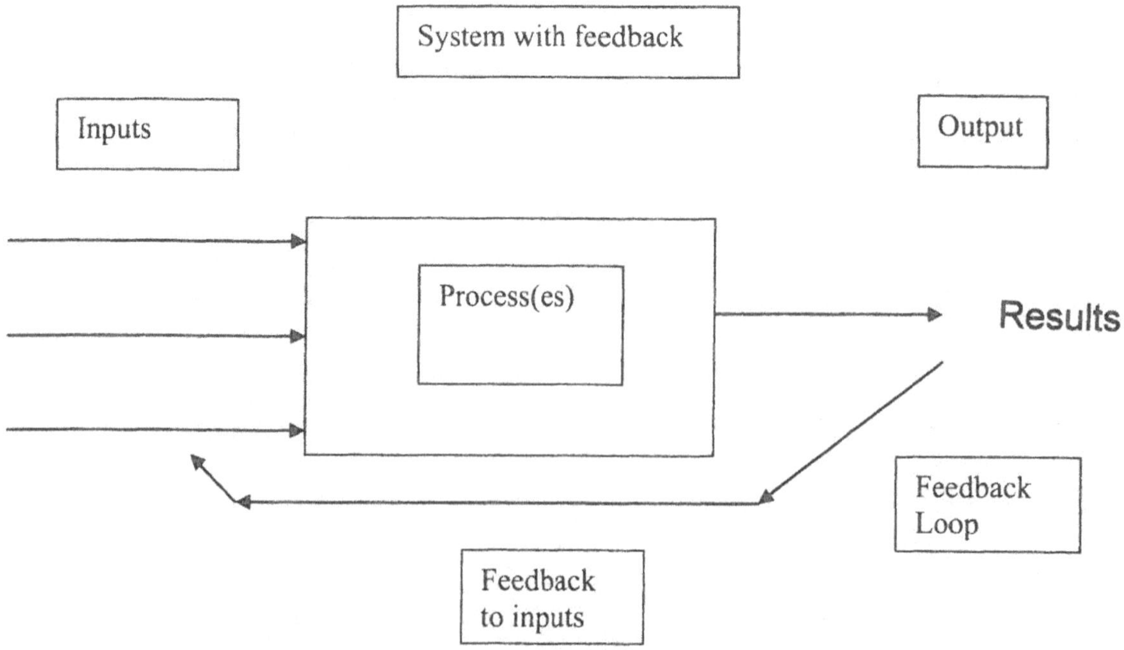

Figure 67.3. Model of open system with feedback.

- The constant interaction between systems results in a constant state of change.
- When a system remains stable while there are changes in other systems, it is in a state of balance. Balance is a fundamental concept in nature.
- Time is a significant dimension and different effects occur over time.
- A system exerts a feed-forward effect upon a second system. This effect may be stimulatory (positive) or inhibitory (negative). The second system may then exert a feedback effect on the first system, which may be either stimulatory or inhibitory. Stimulatory feedback may increase the initial effect, while inhibitory feedback may decrease the inhibiting effect.
- Modulation occurs when the feedback or feed-forward is a complex combination of different positive and negative effects (Mental Health and Illness, 2010).

> Some propositions which impact organization change have been attributed to how systems are impacted (Griffiths, 1964, pp. 117-118):

- The major impetus for change in organizations is from the outside.
- Change within the organization is more probable if the successor to the chief administrator is from outside the organization rather than from inside.
- When change does occur it tends to come from the top of the organization rather than from the bottom up.
- The more hierarchical the structure of an organization, the less possibility of change within the organization.
- The more functional the dynamic interplay of the subsystems within an organization, the less possibility of change occurring within the organization.
- "Living systems respond to continuously increasing stress first by a lag in response, then by an over-compensatory response, and finally by catastrophic collapse of the system" (Miller, 1955, p. 527).

Hern (1958) summarized the properties of open or organismic systems when he wrote:

> There is a dynamic interplay among the essential functional sub-processes or sub-systems in the organismic system which enables it to maintain itself in a homeostatic steady state. Assuming a sufficient input of materials from its environment, the organism develops toward a characteristic state despite initial conditions (equifinality). All of this is accomplished through an automatic self-regulatory process. (p. 48)

APPLICATION

SYSTEMS THINKING

The use of systems theory in the process of solving problems, making plans, and understanding the working components of organizations is generally referred to as "systems thinking." It differs from traditional analysis which tends to separate all the parts in the process of analyzing them. This thinking has opened a wide world that helps leaders, planners, and researchers to better achieve goals within their domains and also within the broader organization perspectives in which they participate. Using such thinking lets one see not only their domain but also see the big picture of all the other systems and subsystems that impact their component system so they can understand the pressures, problems, and relationships that serve to help or inhibit their efforts to achieve success. Realizing the overall structure of how the sub systems interact and the impact of larger systems influencing the system of focus can help identify issues and problems, patterns which exist and cycles that repeat themselves within the such a system. Senge (1990) made systems thinking the first of his five disciplines that he named the new "component technologies" which would converge to innovate learning organizations (p. 6).

The process of systems thinking usually involves several steps on the part of the manager or investigator. The first of these is "systems analysis." Because systems develop from a wide spectrum of natural and man made interactions, it become necessary to examine the existing system and determine as many of the forces that are being exerted on the system and understand the inputs to the system. (The term systems analysis is somewhat of a problem for explaining systems, as systems are studied in total to understand how they work, rather than dissecting them into parts; yet a systems analyst does a dissection of these components when attempting to develop a program to create a system for a computer.) From this analysis the investigator can attempt to determine which inputs and/or forces are important and which ones are present but of lesser or no importance. From that point "systems planning" would occur in order to change the system by controlling the inputs and other pressures so the system produces the desired outputs. This phase is often referred to as "systems design." As those outputs are further examined for positive changes as a result of the implemented plans feedback to the processes continues to be developed. In some cases this means changing inputs to tweak the results; in other cases it may mean adjusting the management applications within the process to change the outputs. This third phase is frequently referred to as "systems management" (Hostrop, 1973). It involves the use of the feedback loop to make contin-

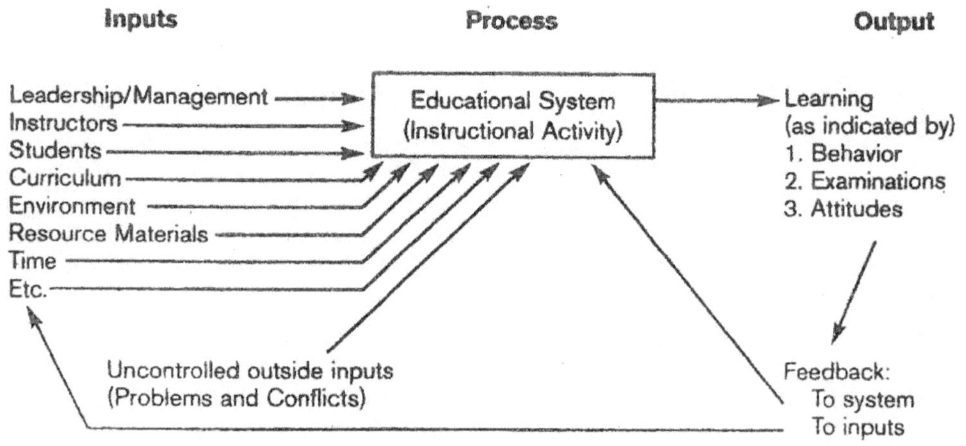

Source: Adapted from Vornberg (2010, p. 117).

Figure 67.4. System model of education.

ual changes in managing and adjusting the elements to better impact results based on the goals which the design is structured to attain. When the issues are solved using the systems thinking process, the design may be expanded to create wider achievement of these goals in a larger setting. This is sometimes referred to as "systems engineering."

Vornberg (2010) has depicted the systems model for education as in Figure 67.4.

Social Systems

Within the field of education systems theory plays a major role in understanding how schools as social systems function. Some of the assumptions gleaned by Hoy and Miskel (1982, pp. 56-58) include:

- Schools as social systems are goal-oriented and may have a multiplicity of goals but the central one is preparation of its students for adult roles.
- Social systems are peopled, and these individuals act in roles as students, teachers, administrators, and others.
- Social systems are normative with individual role expectations for the role structure and prescribed behavior.
- Sanctions exist in social systems with norms being enforced with rewards and punishments. Informal sanctions also exist such as ostracism.
- Schools are generally open systems that operate in an environment that include exchanges. They are affected by the values of the community, by politics, and outside forces.

One of the most identified school social systems models was developed by Getzel and Guba (1957) that has become somewhat of a classic. This model points out two major subsystems that may conflict or support each other: the institution and the individual (see Figure 67.5).

As this school system model was discussed and examined over time additional subsystems were added to recognize that the informal work groups that were within the school were having additional internal influences on the system and thus a third line of influence was added to include work groups, their informal organization and the norms which developed has their behavioral effect out the outputs of the system (Abbott, 1965). See Figure 67.6.

The Research Process

As one understands the systems theory paradigm, it becomes clearer that systems theory is an underlying assumption in much of research that is being conducted. So this theory is basic in understanding the structure of almost everything and as a result most experiments that are conducted are dependent on this systems idea.

In the last 35 years, although slowly at first, the use of qualitative research has made its way into the research arena as it impacts design and techniques as valued in the fields of both education and social sciences. This has been a slow process; however, visualizing what is often referred to as "the research wheel" can assist students and researchers alike in understanding the impact of this newer phenomena in making progress in understanding reality—and the process of better developing theories that lead us to insights in the social sciences. The wheel (as depicted in Figure 67.7) is actually another example of a loop in the systems process. (Johnson & Christenson, 2008, p. 20)

Research is all about testing theories using quantitative designs that allow the researcher to determine results. This is done by developing hypotheses or pre-

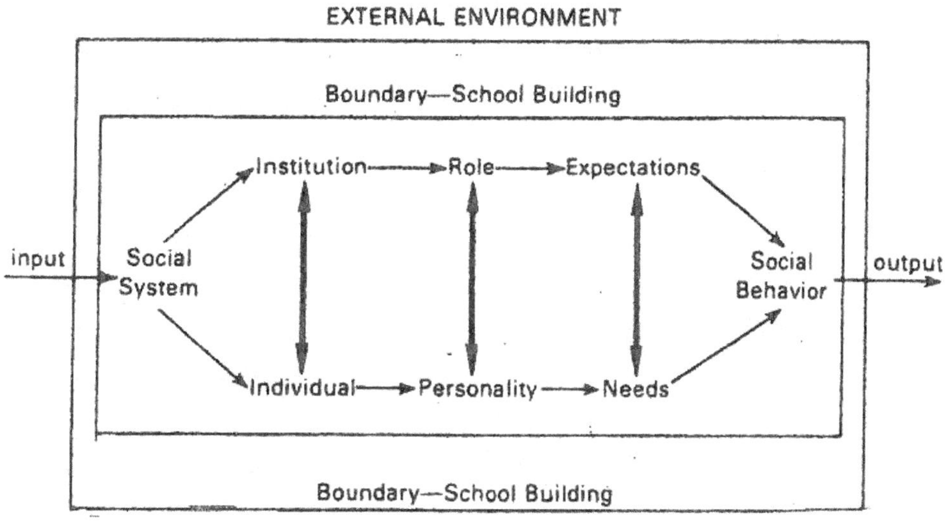

Source: Adapted from Getzel and Guba (1957, p. 429).

Figure 67.5. Subsystems of the Getzels-Guba Systems Model.

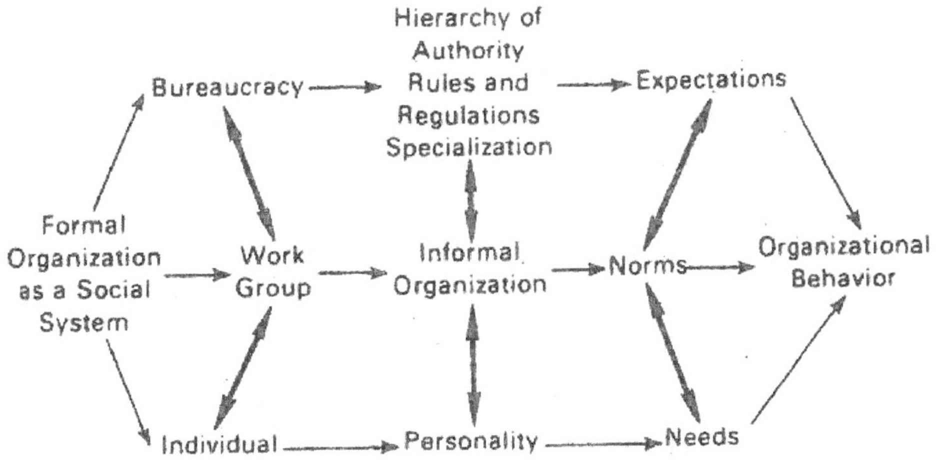

Figure 67.6. Reformulated elements for a social systems model of schools.

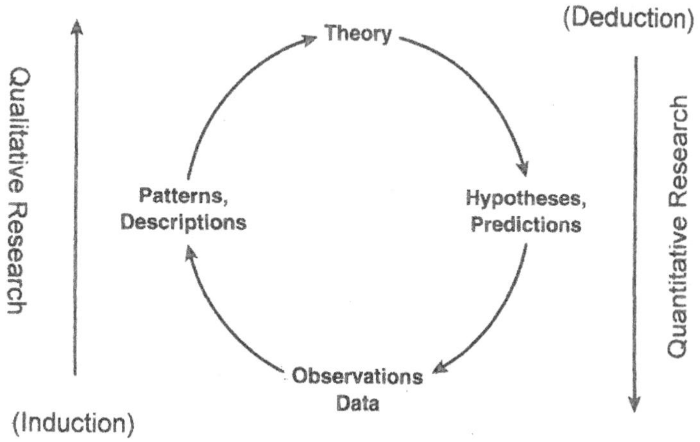

Source: Adapted from Johnson and Christensen (2008).

Figure 67.7. Research wheel as illustration of systems loop.

dictions and testing to see if they hold up under scrutiny of measurement in a confirmatory experiment—done usually with quantitative means. This is accomplished by using deductive reasoning. But prior to the theory being developed that is tested, qualitative research is oftentimes used to determine patterns and descriptions that then help researchers or practitioners develop new theories or ideas that explain what might be happening. Once the new theory is structured using inductive reasoning from observations and classification schemes that help to enable insightful thinking, then experiments can be developed and the new theory tested. So the wheel depicted in Figure 67.7 is actually a systems loop which helps scientists understand the process that allows better theory to be developed and then tested to confirm or reject the theory. When rejection is indicated, then the process starts over by making additional observations and developing new or altered theory that can be tested in another round of the research process.

Research Technique

The systems thinking process helps the student or researcher to envision the situation of how predictor (independent) variables will impact or predict a criterion (dependent) variable. The use of multiple regression in its several forms will allow the researcher to determine this by collecting specific data on the variables involved. Included in this family of techniques is simultaneous multiple regression, hierarchical multiple regression and stepwise multiple regression. Hierarchical multiple regression can identify how much variance can be attributed to the predictor variables. If the criterion variable is a categorical one, discriminate analysis and logistic regression may be used. Should there be a large number of dependent variables which need to be reduced to a smaller number of factors, factor analysis is the statistical techniques that is employed (see Gilner & Morgan, 2000, p. 294, for more information).

Summary

This explanation of systems began with the Butterfly Effect and how a small difference could impact happenings in another part of the planet. Such an effect was difficult for investigators and theorists to imagine being valid. However, as time and understanding of effects were better understood, the concept of systems continues to be one that has withstood the test of time and additional theory building.

Systems theory is an important mechanism to help one to understand what causes things to be the way that they are or why they change. As a concept, the systems idea has been used for many years to understand phenomena, yet general systems theory is considered to have a rather recent establishment. In today's environment, systems theory or systems thinking plays a major role in the way that organizations work, that education occurs, or how living things react or change to their environment. To appreciate and understand general systems theory and its many ramifications, is to be living in the present and to understand how much all of life is dependent on everything in the universe.

References

Abbott, M. G. (1965). Intervening variables in organizational behavior. *Educational Administration Quarterly, 1*, 1-13.

Getzels, J. W., & Guba, E. G. (1957). Social behavior and the administrative process. *School Review, 65*, 423-441.

Gilner, J. A., & Morgan, G. A. (2000). *Research methods in applied settings: An integrated approach to design and analysis*. Mahwah, NJ: Erlbaum .

Goodman, M., Kemeny, J., & Roberts, C. (1994). The language of systems thinking: "Links" and "loops." In K. Senge, R. B. Roberts, & B. J. Smith (Eds.), *The fifth discipline fieldbook* (pp. 113-148). New York, NY: Doubleday.

Griffiths, D. E. (1964). The nature and meaning of theory. In *Behavioral science and educational administration* (Yearbook of National Society for the Study of Education, Part II). Chicago, IL: The University of Chicago Press.

Hern, G. (1958). *Theory building in social work*. Toronto, Ontario, Canada: University of Toronto Press.

Hostrop, R. W. (1973). *Managing education for results*. Homewood, IL: ETC.

Hoy, W. K., & Miskel, C. G. (1982). *Educational administration Theory, research and practice* (2nd ed). New York, NY: Random House.

Johnson, B., & Christensen, L. (2008). *Educational research quantitative, qualitative and mixed approaches* (3rd ed.) Los Angeles, CA: SAGE.

Knezevich, S. J. (1975). *Administration of public education*. New York, NY: Harper & Row.

Lorenz, E. N. (1972, December). *Predictability: Does the flap of a butterfly's wings in brazil set off a Tornado in Texas?* Paper delivered at American Association for the Advancement of Science, Washington, DC.

Mental Health and Illness. (2010) Systems theory. Retrieved from http://www.mentalhealthandillness.com/systemstheory.html on 2/17/2010

Miller, J. G. (1955). Toward a theory for the behavioral sciences. *American Psychologist, 10*(9), 513-532.

Morgan, G. (1997). *Images of organization*. Los Angeles, CA: SAGE.

Paolucci-Whitcomb, P., Bright, W. E., & Carlson, R. V. (1991) Interactive leadership: Processes for improving planning. In R. V. Carlson & G. Awkerman (Eds.), *Educational planning Concepts, strategies, and practices* (pp. 295-312). New York, NY: Longman.

Pidwirny, M. (2009). *Definitions of systems and models: Fundamentals of physical geography* (2nd ed.). Retrieved from http://physicalgeography.net/fundamentals/4b.html

Russell, P. (2005). *Spirit of now*. Retrieved from www.peterrussell.com/SP/Butterfly.php

Sauter, V. L. (2008). *Systems theory.* Retrieved from http://www.umsl.edu/~sauterv/analysis/intro/system.htm

Senge, P. M. (1990). *The fifth discipline.* New York, NY: Doubleday.

von Bertalanffy, L. (1950). An outline of general systems theory. *British Journal for the Philosophy of Science, 2,* 134-165.

Vornberg, J. A. (2010). Systemic approach to educational accountability: Balancing national and state standards, programs and procedures. In J. A. Vornberg (Ed.), *Texas public school organization and administration.* Dubuque, IA: Kendall Hunt.

Author Contact Information: James A. Vornberg, PhD, professor emeritus of the College of Education and Human Services, Texas A&M University—Commerce, P.O. Box 3011, Ed. Leadership Commerce, TX 75429. Phone: 903-886-5520. E-mail: James.Vornberg@tamuc.edu

CHAPTER 68

Complexity Theory

Timothy B. Jones
Sam Houston State University

> [We discuss] the changes in our collective philosophy as the new sciences, systems thinking, and comparable developments in other fields come to replace a Newtonian frame of reference. We introduce the new paradigm from the perspective of several new developments, the core of which is *complexity theory*. We explore ways in which complex adaptive systems self-organize. We suggest that the central issue with education is that, although the system is becoming more dynamical and is moving toward the edge of possibility, the fundamental ideas and purposes of traditional approaches to education still inhibit the appropriate type of change and adaption. The new paradigm requires a new type of person. The key to the emergence of that person—the possible human—is to better understand what human potential means in terms of brain research and other developments, and then to teach to actualize that potential. (R. N. Caine & Caine, 1997, p. ix)

With the emergence of the atomic age, scientist since the early twentieth century were forced to call into question the very basic understandings that date back to Descartes and Newton (Capra, 1984). This Cartesian and Newtonian thinking, overwhelmingly mechanistic and linear, was highly limited in grappling with and understanding atomic energy and theory which was far more dynamic. It was these limitations that gave scientist an opportunity to construct new forms, language, and concepts that began to account for that phenomenon.

Complexity theory was born in the 1960s as a natural byproduct of systems theory and the study of systems or cybernetics. Where systems theory explains the world as a vast interconnected system made up of many parts, complexity theory attempts to explain the phenomenon associated with the relationship and interconnectedness of those parts with each other and with the system itself. It is a dynamic theory as opposed to traditional mechanistic theory. Although systems theory and cybernetics were born in the field of mathematics and physics (quantum mechanics), the late twentieth century and early twenty-first century have found complexity theory equally applicable to both physical and social systems. This progression of thought and the exploration of how multiple systems network into larger systems are today characterized by the term *new sciences*. It is this theoretical underpinning and an emerging postmodern understanding of the new sciences that have given way to what the field of organizational behavior regards as the learning community. Learning communities, as a model of organizational development, permeate education particularly in the public school arena.

In this chapter, we will understand complexity theory in the educational context of the learning community by exploring self-organization of living things and a brief introduction into brain research. Self-organization explains the interconnectedness of living that is the foundation of complexity theory and brain research provides physiological support for how human beings benefit from such complex interconnectedness by naturally learning, adapting, and growing. A learning community is a system that learns and grows (adapts and changes) from a natural process known as self-organization. Complexity theory explains how individual living things are interconnected, through self-organization, within the larger complex adaptive system that we understand through systems theory.

Self-Organization

Capra (1984, 1997) and Byars and Capra (1990) explained the self-organization of living things as the very essence of life by characterizing three distinct

The Handbook of Educational Theories, pp. 815–819

attributes: *self-maintaining, self-renewing and self-transcending.*

SELF-MAINTAINING

Although dependent on their environment, living things are not determined by their environment as evidenced by naturally maintaining themselves. Animals, including human beings for example, have a natural sense of urgency when threatened that continues until the threat is neutralized or alleviated. The more sophisticated the animal, the more options and tools available. The body of living organisms regulates the supply of a variety of things such as vitamins, hormones, and oxygen as the body increases or decreases the demand for the same. Plants self-maintain in their search for light and water that result in growth toward those resources (foliage for light and roots for water) in order to insure an adequate supply.

SELF-RENEWING

Living things constantly renew themselves. For example, a body of a blood donor will replace the blood taken from the body in less than 8 weeks. That same body replenished most of the cells of the pancreas in less than 24 hours. The most obvious example of self-renewing may be in the loss of thousands of skin cells every minute, yet we never lose our generally same appearance as our bodies replace those cells and maintain a similar pattern of organization. A lizard losing its tail will grow a new one in order to continue to store necessary fat and other nutrients. The lizards' built-in tourniquet in the base of the tail is designed to easily constrict to prevent significant blood loss until the tail replaces itself with new growth. This cycle will only occur two or three times as if the lizard remembers losing it before and as part of self-maintenance determines it is unneeded or undesirable.

SELF-TRANSCENDING

Finally, and perhaps most interestingly, living things self-transcend. Living things have an inherent tendency to adapt and change as needed. In the process of adapting, changing, or transcending, living things become very creative (in order to deal or cope with the adaptation or change) which then fuels new forms and ideas. The human brain, for example, naturally conceptualizes and analyzes anything it encounters or contemplates. Self-transcendence is what makes humans constant and natural learners; learning that can only be turned off when the body ceases to function or dies. Further, its activity is enhanced by novelty and curiosity and thus intrinsically motivated making the transcendence natural and unavoidable. In education, students may not be motivated to learn a particular lesson on a particular day, but that does not mean they are not motivated to learn. Learning is transcendence and thus is as natural as eating or breathing. As R. N. Caine and G. Caine suggested in the opening passage to this chapter, to foster the emergence of the possible human or to teach to the individual learner's potential (thus learner centered), educators must understand how learning (transcending) naturally occurs and embrace methods and strategies to support that learning.

Self-organization, living things naturally existing, adapting and changing, creates a rippling and displacing effect (also known as turbulence) within and to the system in which it exists. In other words, one person's self-organization forces the self-organization of other living things in the system which, in turn, displaces back on the first person. In the quantum world (the concept was developed by a mathematician) that displacement is called *chaos* because it involves so much complicated information as opposed to a misunderstood definition of being devoid of order. Hence, the living system that we know as the universe is full of constant displacement and chaos making life itself interconnected. In education the concept has also benefitted with the advent of brain research. In the "brain world," displacement and chaos are called disequilibrium.

DISEQUILIBRIUM

A critical component of the new sciences and complexity is how we deal with chaos or disequilibrium. Merriam-Webster Dictionary (n.d.) defines equilibrium as "a state of intellectual or emotional balance" and "a state of adjustment between opposing or divergent influences or elements." Their definition further stated that equilibrium is:

> a state of balance between opposing forces or actions that is either static (as in a body acted on by forces whose resultant is zero) or dynamic (as in a reversible chemical reaction when the rates of reaction in both directions are equal).

The operative in understanding disequilibrium is understanding that *the state* of equilibrium or *the rates* of equal reaction are temporary and hence our world is typically in a state of disequalibrium rather than a state of equilibrium. Complexity theory suggests that as we self-transcend, we naturally adapt to the chaos or disequilibrium in the complex adaptive system in which we live. Our natural adaptation to that disequilibrium comes from creativity. The more chaotic the circumstance, the greater the need for adaptation and thus the greater the creativity needed to fuel that adaptation. Creativity, therefore, is our natural response to life and the constant disequilibrium in which we live.

THE BRAIN AND DISEQUILIBRIUM

Disequilibrium, chaos, turbulence, and self-organization--it is no wonder the world is such a dynamic and messy place. Such a place must be difficult on the living things within the system, particularly for humans. Actually, that simply is not the case. With the advent of brain research, neuroscientists have learned a great deal about the brain over the past 40 years. R. N. Caine and Caine (1997) documented 12 brain/mind principles of note for educators that have been constructed from these developments:

1. The brain is a complex adaptive system.
2. The brain is social.
3. The search for meaning is innate.
4. The search for meaning occurs through patterning.
5. Emotions are critical to patterning.
6. Every brain simultaneously perceives parts and wholes.
7. Learning involves both focused attention and peripheral perception.
8. Learning always involves conscious and unconscious processes.
9. We have at least two ways of organizing memory.
10. Learning is developmental.
11. Complex learning is enhanced by challenge and inhibited by threat.
12. Every brain is uniquely organized (pp. 104-108).

G. Caine and Caine (2001) further described the brain as a complex adaptive system by adding that "body, mind and brain are one dynamic unity" (p. 99). Principle 10 indicates that since learning is developmental that it must be constant and natural and thus cannot be turned off or on. This also indicates that learning (perceived as relevant) is a natural part of life and something the body does naturally which suggests intrinsically motivated like breathing for example. Learners are intrinsically motivated to learn anything that is deemed relevant or needed.

To the contrary, it would seem that the brain is perfectly suited to naturally deal with a world or system of disequilibrium, chaos, and mess as indicated in Principle 1, 7, and 8. So true, that it seems clear the only way for the brain to be fully utilized is for it to be in a state of disequilibrium as it is maximized when dealing with multiple things simultaneously including taking things apart and reassembling them. To over simplify a concept is to remove the need for the brain to process that concept or eliminate the need to figure out how it fits with prior learning. Figuring it out includes cognitive conflict which is what the brain does in processing new information that it seeks to transfer to long-term memory. Until the conflicts are resolved, the brain will not locate the correct place for permanently storing the information. Without that resolution, the brain will perceive the information as unneeded and discard it with lightning fast precision. Thus, the disequilibrium is absolutely necessary in many ways for learning to occur.

So true in fact, a brain that achieves equilibrium does not internally need to process, create, or construct but rather has reached a state of calm and no need. This phenomenon actually reduces brain activity. However, such equilibrium or state of calm, because of the dynamics of the complex adaptive system, physiologically never arrives until seemingly when the living thing dies. Death is the ultimate state of equilibrium in the quantum or complex world. Hence, although human beings often strive to achieve a state of equilibrium, to the brain that equilibrium never really happens. The complexity of the interconnections always provides some turbulence to the system and all living things within the system. Rather, the brain is constantly poised to deal with the next dose of chaos or turbulence that is sure to come as other living things self-organize around it. Once it does, the brain naturally becomes very creative in dealing with that mess as it made adaptations and constructed new forms and ideas necessary to transcend and self-organize as well. It takes the chaos, the turbulence, or the mess that is life to spur the brain into that creative stance. Self-transcendence, and thus new learning, depends on creativity.

This is not to say that the more disequilibrium the better. In fact we have learned that ideally the brain needs a combination of stability and disequilibrium for total despair can lead to downshifting of the brain (R. N. Caine, Caine, & Crowell, 1999). Likewise, a legitimate threat of health, safety or survival can hijack the brain to focus solely on that threat. So while disequilibrium is natural and a necessary part of self-transcendence, basic needs such as survival and safety must provide some degree of stability in order to avoid downshifting or for the brain devoting all of its resources to a threat or concern needing a higher priority. Complexity theory allows for this reality as complex systems can be dynamic and also be stable. Optimally, disequilibrium that exists in a safe or threat-free environment for the brain results in a state called relaxed alertness (R. N. Caine et al., 1999). Relaxed alertness is particularly optimal in learners in an educational setting.

COMPLEXITY THEORY IN EDUCATION

Evidence of the use of complexity theory in education is sizable. First, complexity theory is part of the theoretical underpinnings of learning communities because of the importance of the interconnections and relationships within the organization. The learning community is a complex adaptive system made up of living things that self-organize. Again, these interconnections and relationships are complexity theory at work. Learning communities rely on a constant supply of new information that becomes the driving force of learning, change, and thus adaptation of individual members of the organization. Change, in a learning community, occurs when the individuals within the learning community change not when change is externally imposed on the organization. Leaders infuse new information and ideas into the learning community to generate displacement with the status quo. This displacement brings about creativity which provides the learning community new opportunities for adaptation and growth.

Teachers in a learning community, for example, construct and create instructional models and methods based on new information introduced into the organization. Senge (1994, 2000; Senge et al., 1999) and Wheatley (2006) characterized the adaption as natural in this setting, because the adaptation came from the individuals within the organization instead of being stipulated in a more traditional top down way. In other words, because of the influence of new information and the use of that information by others in the organization, the individual adapted through self-transcendence and thus the adaption occurred naturally instead of being forced upon them externally. Individuals within the learning community learn by doing it themselves.

Like the brain, learning communities while dynamic also need enough stability to achieve a relaxed alertness in order to avoid downshifting (G. Caine & Caine, 2010). Dufour, Dufour, Eaker, and Many (2010), Schlechty (2004, 2009) and others have worked extensively with schools on building this organizational strategy with the objective of improving student performance. They document, that schools are probably as good as they can be without our changing our paradigm and returning to what all humans do naturally.

Moreover, the same idea applied to schools has been applied to learning in the individual classroom given the students in the classroom are also members of the learning community. In addition to Dufour et al. (2010) and Schlechty (2004, 2009) cited above, Caine and Caine (R. N. Caine & Caine, 1997; R. N. Caine & Caine, 2011; G. Caine & Caine, 2001, 2010) and Jensen (2006, 2008) have worked with teachers and schools all over the world in creating brain/mind and brain enriched classrooms. Wiggins and McTighe (2005, 2007) have authored books on how learners understand and process information as well as how that needs to impact schooling which further supports complexity theory. Students too can learn (transcend and adapt) naturally if given the opportunity to do so. Instead of simply reciting back what is taught, learners learning in a brain compatible way construct new and individually relevant meaning through higher order and critical thinking.

Brain enriched instructional environments and brain/mind instructional methods are critical for schools to teach to individual student potential as opposed to teaching students to a minimum state standard. Self-organization is the epitome of being learner-centered and thus is teaching to the individual potential of the learner. Equally beneficial, the result is a far greater likelihood of the new knowledge and information being deposited into the learners' long-term memory because the learning is self-directed, relevant and naturally attained. The construction of meaning, grounded in constructivist theory and covered elsewhere in this text, further supports this environment for learning as well as provides a method for putting it into operation within the school.

Conclusion

While the multitude of uses of complexity theory in education may seem somewhat recent, systems theory and thus complexity theory are not so recent. Progressive educators, however, including John Dewey a century ago, advanced many ideas during those early systems days and even before that are consistent with complexity theory today and finally being utilized in education (Jones, 2009). To continue this next critical step in the evolution of educational thought will require educators to leave the comfort zone of our Cartesian and Newtonian perspective. Our understanding of complexity can help find that path and provide a new paradigm for education for the next millennium, just as the thought of Descartes and Newton provided us in the previous one.

References

Byars, F., & Capra, F. (1990) *Mindwalk: A film for passionate thinkers.* Hollywood, CA: Paramount Pictures.

Caine, R. N., & Caine, G. (1997). *Education on the edge of possibility.* Alexandria, VA: Association for Supervision and Curriculum Development.

Caine, R. N., & Caine, G. (2011). *Natural learning for a connected world: Education, technology, and the human brain.* New York, NY: Teachers College Press.

Caine, G., Caine, R. N., & Crowell, S. (1999). *Mindshifts: A brain compatible process for professional development and the renewal of education.* Tucson, AZ: Zephyr Press.

Caine, G., & Caine, R. N. (2001). *The brain, education, and the competitive edge.* Lanham, MD: Scarecrow Education.

Caine, G., & Caine, R. N. (2010). *Strengthening and enriching your professional learning community: The art of learning together.* Alexandria, VA: Association for Supervision and Curriculum Development.

Capra, F. (1984). *The turning point: Science, society and the rising culture.* New York, NY: Bantam Books.

Capra, F. (1997). *The web of life: A new scientific understanding of living systems*. New York, NY: Anchor Books.

DuFour, R., Dufour, R., Eaker, R., & Many, T. (2010). *Learning by doing: A handbook for professional learning communities at work*. Bloomington, IN: Solution-Tree.

Jensen, E. (2006). *Enriching the brain: How to maximize every learners potential*. San Francisco, CA: Jossey-Bass.

Jenson, E. (2008). *Enriching the brain: How to maximize every learner's potential*. San Francisco, CA: Jossey-Bass.

Jones, T. (2009). John Dewey: Still ahead of his time. In P. Jenlink (Ed.) *Democracy and education revisited: Contemporary discourses for democratic education and leadership* (pp. 137-154). New York, NY: Roman & Littlefield.

Merriam-Webster. (n.d.). Equilibrium. Retrieved from http://www.merriam-webster.com/dictionary/equilibrium?show=0&t=1294170292

Schlechty, P. C. (2004). *Shaking up the schoolhouse: How to support and sustain educational innovation*. Indianapolis, IN: Jossey-Bass.

Schlechty, P. C. (2009). *Leading for learning: How to transform schools into learning organizations*. Indianapolis, IN: Jossey-Bass.

Senge, P. (1994). *The fifth discipline: The art and practice of the learning organization*. New York, NY: Doubleday.

Senge, P. (2000). *Schools that learn*. New York, NY: Doubleday.

Senge, P., Kleiner, A., Roberts, C., Roth, G., Ross, R. & Smith, B. (1999). *The dance of change: The challenges of sustaining momentum in learning organizations*. New York, NY: Doubleday.

Wheatley, M.J. (2006). *Leadership in the new science: Learning about organization from an orderly universe*. San Francisco, CA: Berrett-Koehler.

Wiggins, G., & McTighe, J. (2005). *Understanding by design*. Alexandria, VA: Association for Supervision and Curriculum Development.

Wiggins, G., & McTighe, J. (2007). *Schooling by design: Mission, action, and achievement*. Alexandria, VA: Association for Supervision and Curriculum Development.

Author Contact Information: Timothy B. Jones, EdD, Associate Professor of Educational Law and Policy, Department of Educational Leadership and Counseling, Sam Houston State University, Huntsville, TX

CHAPTER 69

Ethical Sensitivity Unfolding in Educational Settings

Lyse Langlois
Laval University

The concept of leadership emerged in the early twentieth century in the wake of the industrial revolution that influenced the organization of work. This continues to arouse great interest in academic circles. Studies on leadership in education are numerous and increasingly diversified. The concept still sparks debate and many still attempt to define it to gain a better understanding of its most fundamental characteristics, all the while encouraging commitment to major organizational and social change.

Running an organization has become increasingly difficult. Clearly, leadership is lacking and there are many challenges to be faced. The actual context has become more complex: stiffer economic competitiveness, increased productivity through technological progress and higher levels of stress at work—not to mention the rising level of organizational dysfunction entailing major adjustments—are just but a few of the symptoms observed. Could a different method of running an organization be one of the solutions? The emergence of new management approaches and leadership abilities based on keen insight within organizations is an avenue not to be underestimated for sustainable change to take place. But what are those new abilities?

In this chapter, we will first provide background information on how ethics were introduced in the field of school administration and then present two emerging trends in Canada. Next, we will make connections between our views on ethics and applied ethics to argue in favor of a major concept in ethics: ethical sensitivity. In light of this context, we suggest furthering this ongoing development jointly with educational leaders by showing that ethical sensitivity is a potential driver of social change.

THE EMERGENCE OF ETHICS IN SCHOOL ADMINISTRATION

Interestingly enough, the focus on ethics within the field of school management was not the result of reactions to scandals, corruption and conflicts of interest that marred the business world. Misconduct in business drove ethics to the forefront, creating a new field of study: business ethics. However, this scenario did not take place in the same manner in school administration. Instead, ongoing questioning was prevalent in this field of study, whether in the field itself or in the areas of school dropout and lack of leadership. This process paved the way for school management ethics. For the purpose of this discussion, we will briefly look into the three primary turning points that allowed ethics to gradually make their way into the field of school administration.

SEEKING IDENTITY

In 1974, Greenfield cautioned academic circles against imitating business management and recommended that they consider school management in its specific setting. For Greenfield, it was important to recognize the particular context from which school management was to draw its unique identity. Greenfield came to perceive the purposes of school management as different from business management. Griffiths (1979), Hodgkinson (1978), Bates (1983), Foster (1980) and Gronn (1978) later shared his views. Bates, Hodgkinson and Foster highlighted anomalies to be considered as ever irreconcilable paradigms, such as the exclusion of values from facts. Foster believed that moral, ethical and justice issues were never integral

The Handbook of Educational Theories, pp. 821–839

parts of the field of school administration at the onset, in spite of being central to education. Through this initial thinking process, ethics were repositioned at the core of research by providing new avenues to explore the place of values and inter-subjectivity.

The Place of Ethics at the Core Of Leadership

Beck and Murphy (1994), Sergiovanni (1992) and Starratt (1991) marked the 1990s with their work and insight. Their theoretical contribution on ethical or moral leadership and the place of ethics in the field of school administration was eventually felt in the early millennium and influenced several researchers, leading to empirical studies on the subject. Their views also served to redefine educational purposes from an ethical perspective while consolidating the educational identity of school management. Strike, Haller, and Soltis (1998, 2005) contributed to the thought process by formalizing a code of conduct for school managers to ensure a measure of balance between the managerial and interpersonal aspects of their work. During that time, more specific work was also conducted with regard to the place of values in school management (Begley, 1999; Fullan, 2003; Gregory, 2009; Leithwood, 1999; Johansson & Bredeson, 1999) and ethical challenge in leadership (Cuilla, 2004; Johnson, 2007, 2009; Starratt, 2004).

Research on Ethical Decision Making

Research on decision making is another key aspect through which the dire need in training in this respect was demonstrated (Cooper, 1998; Kidder, 2009; Langlois, 2004; Nash, 1989; Shapiro & Stefkovich, 2001). This study helped to raise the awareness of educational leaders regarding the ethical dimensions of the decision-making process. It is also through ethical decision making that the concepts of dilemma and ethical issues were brought to the forefront. This work eventually led to training programs that helped improve school management by better preparing educational leaders. Still today, several theories add to this effort; in the future, the field itself and the profession of school manager will benefit from these contributions.

We highlighted what we consider to be the three key stages that demonstrate the inclusion of ethics in the field of school administration, a process built on the distinct identity of ethics. We then positioned this process in relation to leadership to better focus on an important activity in management: ethical decision making.

In Canada, the same path was followed closely. However for ethics, the end of the first decade of the new millennium was marked by a form of institutionalization within organizations, taking shape from the following two models: *values-based approach* (Stansbury & Barry, 2007) and *compliance program*—(Weaver & Trevino, 1999). These two proposals were strongly influenced by the Organisation for Economic Co-operation and Development (OECD),[1] which recommended that public organizations establish an ethical infrastructure. The two approaches currently coexist within several Canadian departments and Quebec ministries. The compliance model is more prevalent within the federal government, while two models are emerging within the Quebec provincial government. To date, some educational institutions have institutionalized ethics within their structure. In Quebec, for the most part, stakeholders seem to prefer the value-based model. The process is still in its initial stages, but progress has been ongoing since 2005.

In the first part of this chapter, we briefly reviewed the main turning points positioning ethics within the field of school administration. It is through empirical research that ethics emerged in this field of activity and that a conceptual vocabulary was established as an integral part of knowledge specific to school administrations. But what does the polysemic concept of ethics actually mean? How is it defined?

Èthos, Ethics: A New Dwelling of the Mind

It is interesting to note that the primary meaning of the Greek term Èthos is "habitat." To this word the meaning of *individual character* is added, which refers to how a person inhabits the world. The last characteristic of the word Èthos is that of morals, which refers to how people behave in a given society in a given era. This term should not be viewed exclusively from a descriptive perspective. For instance, the morals and customs of the Inuit in Nunavut, Canada may be documented in anthropological terms by merely describing how they behave. However, another possible analysis is to seek how to best behave; the issue of moral judgment is raised in that very instance. There is a risk of falling into the trap of making a distinction between appropriate and inappropriate conduct and attempting to impose this vision on others. Instead, a reflective approach to ethics is proposed here seeking to identify the bases on which some kinds of conduct are better than others. As highlighted by Roger Pol Droit (2009), conduct fostering positive values should be distinguished from immoral or antimoral conduct that entails risks to the self and others or generates destructive values. Therefore, ethics concerns values indistinctly and, above all, what is good or bad. Ethics fosters a thought process on the bases of these two distinctions and question how fundamental rules are to be distinguished and applied. Along the same line of Fuch's (1995) views, ethics address how to behave properly. Nowadays, ethics take their meaning in areas where standards and rules of conduct are to be established, invented and forged through a reflection process ideally conducted collectively.

A Thinking Process Building on Cooperation

The publishing of J. Fletcher's book titled *Situations Ethics: The New Morality* (1966) marked a turning point in the field of ethics. Fletcher suggested basing moral reasoning on the decision-making process rather than moral obligation. To some extent, this position marked the development of applied ethics, promoting a different kind of reasoning that focuses more particularly on the decision-making process. By placing more emphasis on the decision-making process instead of moral obligation, a certain form of moral deliberation was promoted, paving the way for applied ethics.

Fletcher's (1966) proposal is of major importance. We qualify it as a paradigmatic change. According to Legault (2002), it "is not a simple reversal of analysis from the moral agent's point of view. It is the transformation of moral decision with a legitimacy based on value instead of duty" (p. 14, author translation). Hence, Fletcher breaks away from what was exclusively considered as ethical at the time: deontological reasoning. The author does not necessarily reject that type of reasoning, but considers it as a guide to shed light on action not solely in terms of obligation: "To repeat the term used above, principles or maxims or general rules are illuminators. But they are not directors" (p. 31). Judgment is exercised not exclusively in terms of duty but in terms of autonomy, involving the reflective ability of individuals to establish their conduct based on norms as well as values.

Ethics Applied to Daily Life

Reflection on values, standards and rules with a view to exercise responsible, independent judgment is based on social and historical conditions from which emerges the need for ethics known as "applied ethics." Two positions emerged with regard to applied ethics. The first, supported by a large majority of researchers, was proposed by Childress (1986), an influential philosopher:

> The terms "applied ethics" and "practical ethics" are used interchangeably to indicate the application of ethics to special arenas of human activity, such as business, politics and medicine, and to particular problems, such as abortions. (p. x)

Childress identified applied ethics as the application of ethical theories to human activities. Therefore, applied ethics is the bidirectional movement between theory and practice, experience and reflection, intuition and principle (Beauchamp, 2003; Winkler & Coombs, 1993).

The second position is much more nuanced. Applied ethics are viewed as an art or science allowing reflection on ethical dilemmas and issues experienced in the workplace. This position is viewed as a practice that guides judgment to make better decisions or, as Michela Marzano (2008) affirms, a theorization of sound ethical practices and issues. However, according to this author, applied ethics do not consist of applying "pre-established moral theories to different objects" (p. 4, author translation). It is more appropriate to consider applied ethics as a practice involving theoretical development based on issues raised by various social practices. For this reason, understanding the context in which issues arise is essential, *a fortiori* when it comes to "proposing agreements on strategies to implement recognized by a maximum of people" (p. 5).

Understanding the context involves language, dialogue and deliberation to inform, help understand and provide better guidance in decision making. In as much as applied ethics is an educational practice providing guidance and support to judgment, it is also a political practice because it underlies the concern for others in this reflective process. It is also a philosophical practice because it involves critique and taking the time needed to reflect. Applied ethics features these triple-end purposes.

Illustration of Ethical Questioning

The following section illustrates the concept of applied ethics and constitutes an ethical reflection in action. By illustrating this key concept, we wish to highlight ethical sensitivity as opening the door to the development of ethics on a daily basis.

Frame 1: Everyday Ethical Interrogations

A team of high school principals engaged discussions about violence and bullying apparently prevalent in their schools. They attempted to understand underlying causes and their occurrences and identify the means to reduce and/or prevent them.

At the onset of an ethical reflection process, the team had to agree on the very definition of violence (what relates to the concept and what does not fall under it) to assess the perceived phenomenon against what is "appropriate conduct" for the purpose of identifying the phenomenon adequately and introducing guidance measures for conduct deemed as violent. Determining what the team considered as "appropriate" could not be established without clarifying the convictions, values and mission promoted by the schools in order to

> learn to live together. This ethical reflection process may result in a policy or the development of violence-specific rules. If such were the case, the team should assess the relevance of sanctions to be applied (positive/negative), their gradation (warning, note in the student's school record, suspension, expulsion) and the measures to be implemented, including meeting with the person in charge or the school psychologist and a mediation process; in short, measures to be taken to reduce the phenomenon of violence.

Frame 1 shows that addressing ethics applied on a daily basis is much more than merely settling for commendable intentions and the sole desire to do something. As Canto-Sperber (2001) stated, "no one has a monopoly on ethical reflection," and everyone is prompted to use and develop this skill "Underlying the term ethics is an intellectual process often requiring specific knowledge, reasoning methods and procedures for which there are no ready-made solutions" (p. 87, author translation). According to Canto-Sperber, the issue lies in the prevailing loss of meaning in society. Undoubtedly, answers are no longer unique. It is now a matter of plurality of criteria and a breakdown of sorts in values and ways to appreciate what is distinguished as appropriate and fair from what is inappropriate and unfair. In our opinion, therein lies the real challenge of ethics at work. As illustrated previously in Frame 1, a collective reflection process should be initiated and we should confer with others to establish new bearings. The challenge will be to propose solutions that will give rise to consensus or agreement deemed acceptable by everyone. The current purpose of ethics, as proposed here, is to organize learning to live together in order for acceptable agreement to be reached. Learning to live together is organized based on the following questions:

- On what grounds are we to take this decision?
- What values will serve as bearings?
- What criteria are to be met?

As can be observed, ethical reflection is not a mere mechanism used to apply rules. It invites us to reflect and exercise professional judgment in order to consider what justifies the rules and laws that we enforce, what underlies our actions and the reasons to legitimize our choices in a relation between "us and the others". Hence, we believe that ethics postulates a concern for others.

CONCERN FOR OTHERS: AWARENESS OF ETHICAL SENSITIVITY

In education, concern for others is often the central point of actions taken by educational stakeholders. They act for the good of students by proposing special educational support services, because they are concerned with their students' intellectual and social development. However, such concern for others involves a reflection process, will (volition) and a critical mind. The fact of being concerned for others enables us to be aware of their needs, vulnerabilities and possibilities; in other words, we are sensitive to and aware of what others are experiencing and the context.

Barbier (1997) defines sensitivity as "the extended form of the sense of re-linking: a general empathy for every living being. There is a fundamental feeling at the heart of this sensitivity that I refer to as 'love' or 'compassion'" (p. 288, author translation). Barbier also proposed a typology of sensitivity rooted in the issue of the real, the good and the beautiful that begins as ecological sensitivity and evolves into aesthetic sensitivity as follows:

> Through "ecological" sensitivity, we are able to feel concerned and involved about the balance of life on earth through facts, events and situations that affect it. This sensitivity addresses the issue of truth.
>
> Ecological sensitivity leads to ethical sensitivity. Through the sense of re-linking, we open ourselves to the sense of goodness. We find "good" what we can link to life in its interactive entirety. This sense of ethics may cause us to adopt contentious and distressful conduct, in conflict with prevailing "morals." It provides an answer to the philosopher who asks at "What is the Good?"
>
> Ethical sensitivity leads to aesthetic sensitivity. We find "beautiful" what we find "good" in the sense previously defined. Artists and philosophers are not mistaken in stating that the actions of some beings betray "inner beauty".... From the sense of ethics, the sense of aesthetics thus reveals itself: the "acts of joy" so eloquently referred to by Robert Misrahi lead us to recognize the beauty of life in keeping with more democracy. (pp. 290-291, author translation)

ETHICAL SENSITIVITY

Sensitivity addressed here concerns ethical sensitivity more particularly. We propose a definition of this sensitivity as follows: ethical sensitivity first emerges from a connection to the self and a quest for meaning to, in turn, connects with others in a process of relinking to them. It is a permanent vigilance of sorts, as opposed to obscurantism and absolute ideologies and certainties likely to interfere with judgment and reality. Through ethical sensitivity, we are touched by situations and events involving ethical issues of concern to us as we question them to situate ourselves authentically and critically in context against dogmatism and certainties. In other words, ethical sensitivity constitutes openness to ethical reflection and to an ongoing connection with the self and others.

When it reveals itself either through family education, a specific learning experience or personal life experiences, ethical sensitivity fosters human development. Awareness of ethical sensitivity can be raised; hence, it can be taught in every sense of the word. It is, so to speak, a potential that is developed through contact with others and debates on ethical issues. However, some conditions are essential to heighten our awareness of ethical sensitivity and become more active participants in life around us while raising our consciousness.

During our research work, we recognized the importance of ethical sensitivity as a major driver of reflection and ethical decision-making. The challenge that we set for ourselves was to determine if it were possible to develop ethical sensitivity. Frame 2 summarizes a research project conducted between 2005 and 2008 with school administrators in Ontario and Quebec. One of the main goals of this project was to raise participants' ethical sensitivity and better guide their ethical reflection process.

Frame 2: Ethical Sensitivity

We developed a training program called TERA—trajectory, ethics, responsibility, and authenticity, based on a process of knowledge, volition, and action (Langlois & Lapointe, 2010) and rooted in a reflective, action-training approach to professional development (see Figure 69.1).

The first dimension of the TERA model is knowledge. During this program, this dimension served to raise administrators' awareness of ethical sensitivity based on the three specific and interdependent dimensions of ethics: justice, critique, and care (Starratt, 1991).

To guide such ethical sensitivity properly, it was important for individuals to understand their own ethical profiles. To achieve this, a questionnaire was administered to assess the presence of these three ethical dimensions in their work role. The questionnaire was administered before and after the TERA training.

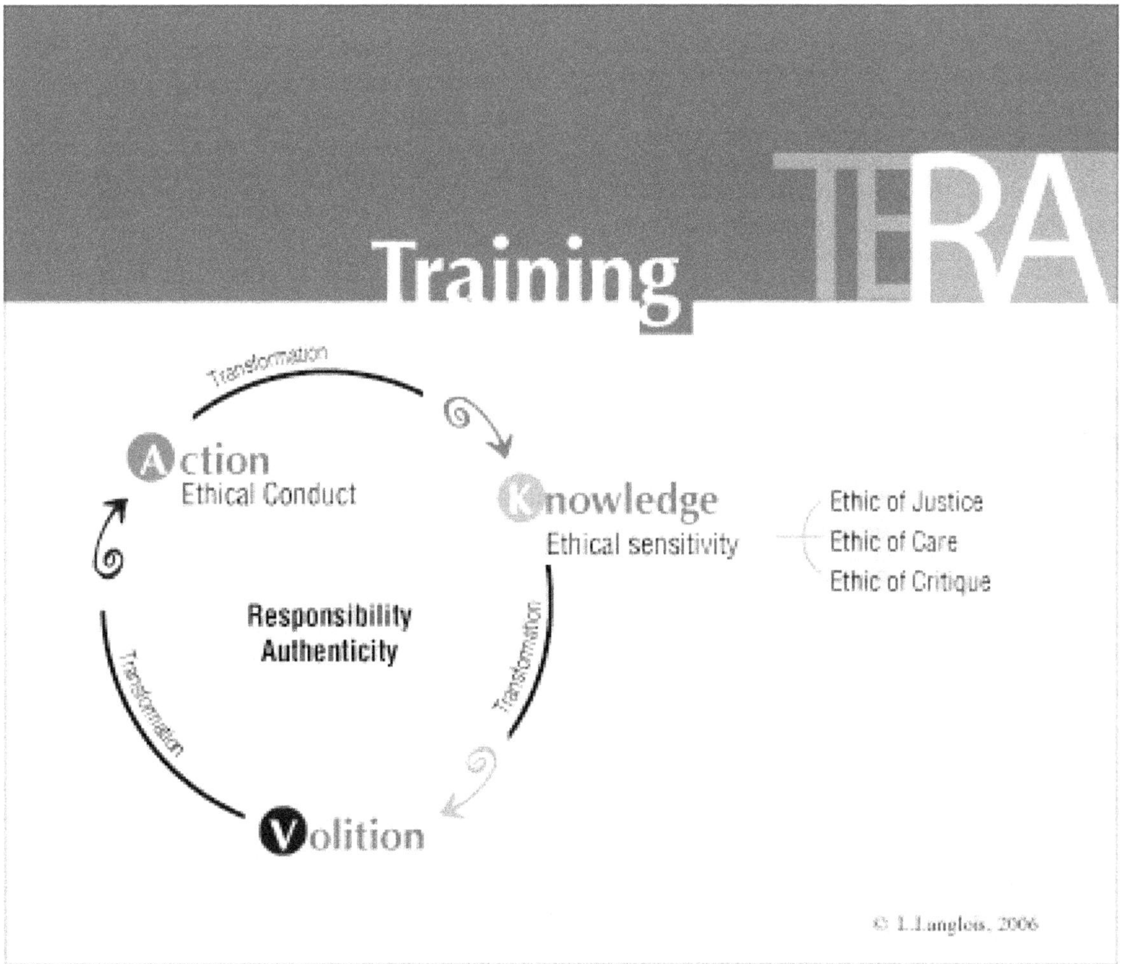

Figure 69.1. TERA training.

Results obtained for the ethical profiles represented a turning point for the administrators in terms of the ethical strengths they possessed and the ethical aspects seemingly lacking in their profiles.

From the outset, we determined that the administrators were better able to identify ethical sensitivity by understanding their own profiles and combining it with training on reflection and ethical decision making. Most of them viewed this training experience as an important discovery and, for the first time, they felt they had the words to properly justify their ethical reflection process. They were in a better position to justify their decisions.

Through a more in-depth analysis of each profile, we found that some administrators' ethical sensitivity appeared to be well developed. We also found that those individuals already aware of ethical sensitivity had a more highly developed over all ethical dimensions than the other participants. Hence, we found that a specific ethical dimension played a determining role and was a significant contributor to the development of ethical sensitivity: the ethics of critique, as identified by Starratt and quite similarly described in Paulo Freire's work (Langlois & LaPointe, 2010).

At the end of the TERA training program, we analyzed the posttraining results. The administrators had become more aware of their reflection process, the impact of their decisions on themselves and others and the primary ethical issues raised when complex decisions are to be made. Those exhibiting sensitivity integrating the three ethical dimensions were able to apply ethical skills at work harmoniously.

Developing Ethical Reflection by Implementing an Ethics Training Program

The TERA model is part of the shift proposed by Fletcher whereby deliberation and dialogue are key elements of ethical reflection. Ethical sensitivity with regard to Starratt's (1991) three dimensions (critique, justice, and care) highlights the values to be promoted that supplant obligation in the decision-making process. Decision making is constructed as a process through which moral agents exercise autonomy and their ability to provide themselves with their own rules of conduct in order to exercise full professional judgment. The choice of value must be justified based on other values and norms that preclude acceptable and responsible decision making for the time being. Through this position, critique could lead to a certain form of relativism. To prevent this, it is important to root the arising situation in its context. Therefore, the "context" and specificity of the "situation" can counter all forms of relativism. However, ethical sensitivity is an essential pre-requisite to the analysis of the situation.

Ethical sensitivity requires specific guidance likely provided through a systematic training program based on self-knowledge in terms of ethical reasoning then extending to external analysis. In other words, ethical sensitivity is a disposition developed in a process where individuals are invited to construct their own moral autonomy. Individuals are responsible for developing their own ethical sensitivity before feeling confident in justifying their actions as morally responsible individuals. However, it should be highlighted that the dimension of critique remains the main trigger of ethical sensitivity through which individuals can avoid the impasse of a mechanism that opposes indifference and dogmatism by reintegrating a new way of thinking and acting in solidarity. According to Professors Kegan and Lahey (2010) of Harvard University, workplace requirements do not necessarily involve the introduction of new skills; instead, reaching a new threshold of awareness or changing how we give meaning to the world and behave in it is most important.

Conclusion

Implementing ethics training programs is instrumental to the development of ethical sensitivity in the workplace. Heightening ethical sensitivity helps to gain a better understanding of the need to make choices, apply them in professional practices and make changes needed to improve educational settings. However, clearly far too few courses on ethical sensitivity are offered at faculties of education, more particularly at leadership and school management departments. We believe that this concept paves the way to changing practices and organizations. One of our research projects (Langlois & Lapointe, 2010) [2] demonstrated the fact that ethical sensitivity correlates to the ethics of critique significantly. This correlation emphasizes the importance of the aspect of critique in raising awareness of ethical sensitivity and driving ability.

Implementing training programs and institutionalizing ethics in the workplace requires a great deal of time and a long-term vision. The culture of urgency blithely marring our relationships and organizations is a major challenge that sometimes distracts us from the essential. Reaction in urgent situations has not only become the norm, but also a response to economic hyper-competitiveness. It impedes on our interactions with others and reveals itself as a form of competence to some people. Nowadays, we have less time to reflect on the consequences of our decisions. We have even less time to cultivate our social relations and have a better perception of our actions by considering end-purposes carefully. Immediate hyperreactivity has become a natural operating mode whose effects on the organization of work we have barely started to observe, as opposed to ethical sensitivity. We value action as an antidote to uncertainty. Ethics achieved through the development of ethical sensitivity involves taking the time to reflect. School managers are invited to do so by remaining connected with this sensitivity in order to prevent all these strains from shrouding our collective conscience.

NOTES

1. "Ethical infrastructure" refers to all the institutions, systems and mechanisms dedicated as a whole to the promotion of ethics and the prevention of corruption in public administration (OECD, 2005, p. 20).

2. We developed a quantitative questionnaire to measure the three ethical dimensions: Ethical Leadership Questionnaire (ELQ).

REFERENCES

Barbier, R. (1997). *L'Approche Transversale, l'écoute sensible en sciences humaines,* Paris, France: Anthropos (Economica).

Bates, R. (1983). Educational administration and the management of knowledge. Geelong, Victoria, Australia: Deakin University Press.

Beauchamp T. L. (2003). The nature of applied ethics. In R. G. Frey & G. H. Wellman (Eds.), *A companion to applied ethics* (pp. 1-16). Oxford, England: Blackwell.

Beck, L., & Murphy, J. (1994). *Ethics in educational leadership programs.* Thousand Oaks, CA: Corwin Press.

Begley, P. (Ed.). (1999). Practitioner and organizational perspectives on values. In *Administration, values and educational leadership.* Albany, NY: State University of New York Press.

Canto-Sperber, M. (2001). *L'inquiétude morale et la vie humaine.* Paris, France: Presses Universitaires de France.

Cooper, T. (1998). *The responsible administrator* (4th ed.). San Francisco, CA: Jossey-Bass.

Childress, J. (1986). Applied ethics. In J. Macquarrie & J. Childress (Eds.), *A new dictionary of Christian ethics.* London, England: The Westminster Press.

Cuilla, J. B. (2004). *Ethics, the heart of leadership* (2nd ed.). Westport, CT: Praeger.

Fletcher, J. (1966). *Situation ethics: The new morality.* Philadelphia, PA: The Westminster Press.

Foster, W. (1980). The changing administrator: Developing managerial praxis. *Educational Theory, 30*(1), 11-23.

Fuch, E. (1995). *Comment faire pour bien faire? Introduction à l'éthique.* Genève, Switzerland: Labor et Fides.

Fullan, M. (2003). *The moral imperative of school leadership.* Thousand Oaks, CA: Corwin Press.

Greenfield, T. B. (1974, July). *Theory in the study of organizations and administrative structures: A new perspective.* Paper presented at the annual meeting of the International Intervisitation Programme on Educational Administration, Bristol, England.

Griffiths, D. E. (1979). Intellectual turmoil in educational administration. *Educational Administration Quarterly, 15*(3), 43-65.

Gregory, R. (2009). Dimensions of educational leadership: Cultural, ethical and moral. *School Leadership Review, 4*(2), 3-21.

Hodgkinson, C. (1978). *The philosophy of leadership.* Oxford, England: Blackwell.

Johnson, C. (2007). *Ethics in the workplace.* Thousand Oaks: SAGE.

Johnson, C. (2009). *Meeting the ethical challenges of leadership: Casting light or shadow.* Thousand Oaks, CA: SAGE.

Johansson, O., & Bredeson, P. (1999). Value orchestration by the policy community for the learning community: Reality or myth. In P. Begley (Ed.), *Administration, values and educational leadership* (pp. 51-72). Albany, NY: State University of New York Press.

Kegan, R., & Lahey, L. L. (2010). *Immunity to change: How to overcome it and unlock the potential in yourself and your organization.* Boston, MA: Harvard Business School.

Kidder, R. (2009). *The ethics recession.* Rockland, ME: Institute for Global Ethics.

Kidder, R. (2009). *How good people make tough choices: Resolving the dilemmas of ethical living* (Rev. ed.). New York, NY: Harper Collins.

Langlois, L. (2004). Responding ethically: Complex decision-making by school district superintendent. *International Studies Educational Administration Management, 32*(2), 78-93.

Langlois, L. & Lapointe, C. (2010) Can ethics be learned? Results from a three-year action-research project. *Journal of Educational Administration, 48*(1),147-163.

Lapoint, C., & Gaudet, J.-D. (2002). L'équité en éducation et en pédagogie actualisante. *Éducation et Francophonie, 30*(2). Retrieved from http://www.acelf.ca/c/revue/resume.php?id=66

Legault, G. (2002). La médiation et l'éthique appliquée en réponse aux limites du droit. Communication présentée au 70e congrès de l'ACFAS 2001, Les transformations du droit et la théorie normative du droit, Montréal, Québec.

Leithwood, K. (1999). An organizational perspective on values for leaders of future schools. In P. Begley (Ed.), *Administration, values and educational leadership* (pp. 25-50). Albany, NY: State University of New York Press.

Marzano, M. (2008). *L'éthique appliquée.* Paris, France: PUF.

Nash, L. (1989). Ethics without a sermon. In K. R. Andrews (Ed.), *Ethics in practice: Managing the moral corporation* (pp. 243-257). Boston, MA: Harvard Business School Reform.

Pol Droit, R. (2009). *Les héros de la sagesse.* Paris, France: Éditeur Plon.

Starratt, R. J. (1991). Building an ethical school: A theory for practice in educational leadership. *Educational Administration Quarterly, 27*(2) 185-202.

Starratt, R. J. (2004), *Ethical leadership.* San Francisco, CA: Jossey-Bass.

Sergiovanni, T. (1992). *Moral leadership.* San Francisco, CA: Jossey-Bass.

Strike, K. A., Haller, E. J., & Soltis, J. F. (1998). *The ethics of school administration* (2rd ed.). New York, NY: Teachers College Press.

Strike, K., Haller, E., & Soltis, J. (2005). *The ethics of school administration* (3rd ed.) New York, NY: Teachers College Press.

Shapiro, J. P., & Stefkovich, J. A. (2001). *Ethical leadership and decision making in education: Applying theoretical perspectives to complex dilemmas.* Mahwah, NJ: Erlbaum Associates.

Stansbury, J., & Barry, B. (2007). Ethics programs and the paradox of control. *Business Ethics Quarterly, 17*(2), 239-261.

Winkler, E. R., & Coombs, J. R. (1993). *Applied ethics: A reader.* Oxford, England: Blackwell.

Author Contact Information: Lyse Langlois, PhD, Department of Industrial Relations, Laval University, Sainte-Foy, Quebec City, Canada. Telephone: 418-656-2131, ext. 3483.

CHAPTER 70

Legal Theory and Research

Martha McCarthy
Indiana University

Theory is a term often applied to efforts in the natural and social sciences to describe occurrences in our environment to assist in better understanding the past and forecasting the future. In the context of educational inquiry, Kerlinger (1986) has defined theory as "a set of interrelated constructs, definitions, and propositions that presents a systematic view of phenomena by specifying relations among variables, with the purpose of explaining and predicting phenomenon" (p. 9). One might wonder why a chapter on the law is appearing in a *Handbook of Educational Theories* and whether such a chapter is suited for a section on organizational theories. There is even debate over whether there *is* or *should be* legal theory because sometimes what is identified as legal theory actually is a more general theory from other areas, such as political or social theory (Bix, 1999). The law undoubtedly differs from other topics in this section and indeed in this book, but including a brief discussion of jurisprudence in this volume on education theories seems appropriate because the law provides the framework for everything that transpires in schools.

Black's Law Dictionary defines *theory of law* as the "legal premise or set of principles on which a case rests" (Garner, 2009, p. 1616), which narrowly confines legal theory to court cases. Freeman (2008) similarly has opined that much of what is considered legal theory has focused on the "inner workings of the judicial system" (p.18). But Freeman (1998) also has referred to *high theory* as "general questions about the nature and functions of law, the concept of a legal system, the relationship between law and morality, the differences between law and other types of social control, and other central aspects of legal discourse" (p. vi), which is a somewhat broader view of legal theory and the one used here.

This chapter is divided into four sections. The first two sections provide an overview of the law in the United States and selected theoretical schools of thought on the nature of jurisprudence. Because epistemological questions may seem somewhat removed from legal and educational practice, the last two sections focus on conducting legal research and the need for educators to understand the law and the values undergirding it. The organization of this chapter no doubt differs from others in this volume, given the unique features of legal theory and scholarship affecting schools compared to traditional educational theories and research.

Overview of the Law in the United States

One definition of *law* is "the regime that orders human activities and relations through systematic application of the force of politically organized society or through social pressure, backed by force, in such a society" (Garner, 2009, p. 962). All institutions and organizations reach some type of consensus regarding how they will function in terms of rules and principles in order to operate efficiently. Such rules and principles "embody social objectives and policy choices" and are purposive instruments (Freeman, 2008, p. 1534). In fact, in an ordered society, everything takes place within a legal environment (Carter, 1987), and the law provides a structure to express public values (McCarthy, 2010). The law assumes some duty to obey and consequences for noncompliance.

The law in the United States is generally viewed as the aggregate of constitutional mandates, legislation, agency rules, and judicial interpretations of these provisions. An overview of these sources of law and tensions among them provides a context for the subsequent discussion of theoretical perspectives on central questions pertaining to the nature of law.

The Handbook of Educational Theories, pp. 829–831

The American common law tradition originated in English common law in the Middle Ages, and it derives authority from court decisions affirming usages and customs and reflects respect for judicial precedent and fundamental human rights (Sellers, 2006). According to Bix (1999), common law reasoning involved "the incremental development of the law" by judges through rendering decisions consistent with earlier rulings by a higher court (p. 133).

The U.S. Constitution is the supreme law of the land in our nation, and laws and regulations made at any level must be consistent with this document. It was settled in 1803 in *Marbury v. Madison* that the U.S. Supreme Court has the final word in interpreting the Federal Constitution, and the court's interpretations can be overridden *only* by a constitutional amendment. The framers of the U.S. Constitution established an amendment process that makes it very difficult to change constitutional provisions. Under Article V of the U.S. Constitution, amendments must be proposed by a two-thirds vote of each house of Congress (or by a special convention called by Congress on the request of two thirds of the state legislatures) and ratified by three fourths of the states. Since the U.S. Constitution was written almost 225 years ago, only 27 amendments have been adopted, and 10 of these were in the original Bill of Rights.

Individual state constitutions address a number of issues that the U.S. Constitution reserves to the states or to the people via the Tenth Amendment. For example, the Federal Constitution is silent regarding education, but every state places a duty on the respective state legislative body to provide for a thorough and efficient, adequate, or uniform system of education that will be provided free for children between specified ages. All states also make school attendance mandatory between certain ages and place penalties on parents or guardians for not complying with such compulsory attendance mandates (Cambron-McCabe, McCarthy, & Thomas, 2009). Before the state-created right to an education can be denied for even a short period of time, a student must be given notice of the reasons and a fair opportunity to refute them (*Goss v. Lopez,* 1975).

In addition to federal and state constitutional provisions, state and federal laws and regulations are significant sources of law in our nation. The legislative history of statutory provisions can be very helpful in assessing the meaning of laws; an analysis of the deliberations when a given measure was introduced can often clarify what the lawmakers intended in enacting the provision.

Case law emanating from court decisions is an extremely important source of legal authority because courts often are called upon to interpret what constitutional and statutory provisions mean. Although courts do not initiate laws as legislative bodies do, they certainly influence the law by exercising their interpretive powers. Sellers (2006) has observed that "common-law customs, state and federal constitutions, and the enactments of legislatures all establish broad principles and general rules that are worked out in detail by courts in deciding actual cases and controversies brought by litigants whose real interests are at stake" (p. 68). Judicial decisions are expected to be made rationally based on established principles. Adjudication according to rules and standards precludes ad hoc decision making, but there will always be legal conflicts and room for interpretation of legal mandates (Freeman, 2008).

The Supreme Court has established rules of judicial review for federal courts to follow. One rule is that the judiciary will render opinions only on claims initiated by parties with standing to sue. This usually means that the party bringing the suit has been harmed by the challenged policy or practice (*Frothingham v. Mellon,* 1923). Another rule is adherence to precedent in cases already decided, which will be explored in more detail later in this chapter. In interpreting the U.S. Constitution, the Supreme Court considers the document's historical context, but ultimately the Supreme Court decides what the Constitution means. This is daunting when some case outcomes that expand or contract personal and political rights are determined by the vote of a single justice. And, as described below, the Supreme Court's constitutional interpretations can change over time.

If the Supreme Court rules that a state law or policy, such as those requiring school segregation on the basis of race, conflicts with the U.S. Constitution or federal civil rights laws (*Brown v. Board of Education,* 1954), all states must eliminate such laws, and a national precedent is established. If, instead, the Supreme Court finds that a challenged state law satisfies the U.S. Constitution, this does not mean that states *must* engage in the practice. Indeed, such a ruling nurtures diverse standards across states and encourages state legal activity. To illustrate, only one state restricted by law the use of corporal punishment in public schools at the time the Supreme Court rejected a constitutional challenge to the use of this disciplinary technique under the Eighth or Fourteenth Amendments (*Ingraham v. Wright,* 1977). Since then, more than half of the states have banned this disciplinary technique from public schools by state law, and many school boards prohibit its use in the absence of a state statutory bar (Cambron-McCabe et al., 2009). Also, after the Supreme Court ruled that state school funding systems that produce fiscal inequities across school districts do not abridge the Equal Protection Clause of the Fourteenth Amendment (*San Antonio Independent School District v. Rodriguez,* 1973), a number of state courts subsequently have invalidated school funding schemes under state law, and most states have revised their school finance systems in an effort to make them more equitable (see Sergiovanni, Kelleher, McCarthy, & Fowler, 2009).

Checks, Balances, and Tensions

The legal system in the United States is characterized by checks and balances. Congress makes laws that are carried out by the executive branch, and the judicial branch uses its interpretive powers to resolve conflicts over interpretations of laws, administrative rules, and constitutional provisions. The president nominates federal judges who must be confirmed by the Senate, and the Supreme Court ultimately can resolve whether congressional acts satisfy the U.S. Constitution. Across the branches, only federal judges are appointed for life. The President can be elected for two terms, and federal and state legislators are elected at regular intervals as are some state judges.

Despite this system of checks and balances, several tensions exist in our nation's legal system. For example, the tension between majority rule and the protection of minority rights is often contentious. The Bill of Rights safeguards in part basic individual liberties from the will of the majority, even though the notion of majority rule is also highly valued. Without the constitutional protection of minority rights, each community could impose the prevailing beliefs on its citizenry. For example, the community could decide if public schools would be segregated by race, ethnicity, or sex and whether prayers of the dominant sect would be said in school activities.

Another related tension exists between protecting individual liberties and promoting the general welfare of the citizenry. For example, in public schools this tension is seen in vaccination requirements as a prerequisite to school attendance, which have been upheld over parental objections because of legitimate health concerns for the citizenry (*Zucht v. King*, 1922). In contrast, when balancing individual and general welfare interests, the Supreme Court found no overriding public interest to justify compelling Amish students to attend school beyond eighth grade (*Wisconsin v. Yoder*, 1972). The court concluded that the state's general welfare interest in having an educated citizenry could be met by requiring school attendance through eighth grade, so an additional 2 years of schooling until age 16 could not be required for Amish youth who were returning to their agrarian communities where they would receive vocational training. Also, students have a right to be excused from saying the Pledge of Allegiance in public schools if this observance conflicts with their religious or philosophical beliefs; the school's interest in promoting patriotism for the general welfare is overridden by the individual's First Amendment rights (*West Virginia State Board of Education v. Barnette*, 1943).

At times, the appropriate balance between individual and general welfare interests is not clear, and if the Supreme Court has not addressed the topic, lower courts may issue a range of opinions. For example, public school students have asserted a free speech right to condemn homosexuality based on their religious beliefs, whereas school authorities have argued that they are obligated to curtail such expression to protect other students and the educational environment. Some courts have upheld students' First Amendment right to express these views (see *Nuxoll v. Indian Prairie School District*, 2008), whereas others have upheld the schools in curtailing such hurtful expression (see *Harper v. Poway Unified School District*, 2006).

There also are tensions across the federal, state, and even local levels of government, given the complicated intergovernmental relationships (McCarthy, 2009). If state laws conflict with federal civil rights laws or constitutional mandates, the federal mandates would normally prevail. However, a state constitutional or statutory provision that conflicts with a federal funding law would not necessarily be invalid; the state could forgo the federal funds if its laws preclude it from complying with the funding requirements. Often the judiciary has to address such conflicts between state and federal statutory and constitutional provisions.

There are others tensions among the three governmental branches *within* a given level. An act of Congress may conflict with the regulations adopted by a federal administrative agency to implement the act. Similarly, a federal court may misinterpret congressional intent in reviewing a challenged law. Statutes are much easier to change than are constitutional provisions, so Congress can clarify the correct meaning of its act if either the administrative agency or the judiciary has misinterpreted the law's meaning. This has happened numerous times. To illustrate, after the Supreme Court ruled that discrimination based on pregnancy is not covered by Title VII of the Civil Rights Act of 1964 (*General Electric Company v. Gilbert*, 1976), Congress responded by enacting the Pregnancy Discrimination Act in 1978, amending Title VII to make explicit that employers may not discriminate against employees based on pregnancy, childbirth, or related medical conditions (Cambron-McCabe et al., 2009). Of course, as noted, if the Supreme Court rules that a given law abridges the U.S. Constitution, this can be overridden only by adopting a constitutional amendment.

The Evolving Law

A widely held view is that the law is objective, perhaps in part to encourage citizens to respect the law and to discourage legislators and judges from acting on whims of the majority. But laws and judicial interpretations of constitutional guarantees are not impersonal or static. Laws change to mirror changes in societal sentiments, and courts are continually rendering decisions that reinterpret constitutional and statutory provisions. There is some sentiment that laws are governed more by politics than precedent in our country (Gee, 2009). In addition to using the legislative process to change laws, boycotts and other forms of civil disobedience have resulted in some laws being changed in our nation. Moreover, courts do not operate in a vacuum; they consider history and tradition in giving meaning to constitutional provisions (Sellers, 2006).

Notwithstanding the pretense that the law is transparent and clear, legal rules often may be ambiguous. Edward Levi (1948) in his seminal article on legal reasoning observed that "legal rules are never clear, and, if a rule had to be clear before it could be imposed, society would be impossible" (p. 501). Words can be subject to multiple interpretations, and the citizenry and courts become involved in resolving these ambiguities. Judge Jerome Frank (1930/1970) observed that it is a myth to consider the law as fixed instead of fluid. He also noted that the law always will entail uncertainties because it "deals with human relations in their most complicated aspects" (pp. 5-6).

THE RANGE OF THEORETICAL PERSPECTIVES

Often those writing about the meaning of law use the terms *philosophy of law, jurisprudence,* and *legal theory* interchangeably. There is not one overarching legal theory; different theories of law and variations of these theories have been proposed over time. Legal thought started receiving attention in the United States in the latter 1800s, and since then, there have been debates between formalists and realists, between positivists and pragmatists, and within the various theoretical schools of thought. It is beyond the scope of this chapter to address all the strands of these various positions and how some of these theoretical perspectives blend into one another. Legal scholars espouse different views as to what each perspective entails, how it differs from other theoretical positions, and how discreet and significant each perspective is in influencing current legal thinking (see Bix, 1999; Freeman, 1998, 2008). Instead of attempting to assess the theoretical debates, this section will simply provide a very brief overview of selected theoretical perspectives that depict the range in thought among philosophers of law regarding central questions about the nature of law and legal systems. It must be kept in mind that this section addresses only selected theoretical movements, these perspectives are far more complex than might be suggested here, and several are not one position but actually a continuum of perspectives.

SELECTED SCHOOLS OF THOUGHT

Natural law theory dates back to the work of the theologian and philosopher, St. Thomas Aquinas (1225-1274), and subsequently, William Blackstone (1723-1780) elaborated on this position. Naturalists believe that there are eternal principles of justice and morality derived from theology, moral philosophy, or other sources that existed before the establishment of government, and that these principles inform the law (Prest, 2008). Under this theory, there is a necessary relationship between law and morality, and while government rules and regulations are a legitimate source of law, such enactments are based on these eternal principles. A modern approach to natural law focuses more narrowly on the proper understanding of law as a social institution or a social practice to distinguish it from positivist schools of thought discussed below (Bix, 1999).

Legal positivism is based on the assertion that "the proper description of law is a worthy objective, and a task that needs to be kept separate form moral judgments" (Bix, 1999, p. 31). This theoretical perspective began with the work of Jeremy Bentham (1748-1832), who distinguished the appropriate task of explaining what the law is from criticizing the law and suggesting what the law *should be*. Bentham was opposed to the concept of natural law and natural rights (Bowring, 1962). Positivism also was greatly influenced by the work of John Austin (1790-1859), who argued that the law is conceptually separate from moral and ethical values. He viewed the law as commands from an entity with authority (i.e., the government), which is supported by the threat of sanctions for noncompliance (Austin, 1832/1998). Hans Kelsen (1881-1973) also is classified as a positivist who viewed the law as a science and described the legal process as a hierarchy of norms. He is most remembered for what he called a *pure theory of law,* describing law as logical within itself and not dependent on values external to the law (Kelsen, 1967/2002).

According to legal positivists, the only legitimate sources of law are rules and principles that have been established by the government—a legislative or administrative body or a court. Positivists contend that such rules and principles are appropriately considered laws, whereas religious and moral beliefs convey goals and aspirations; only the former should be considered by judges in deciding cases. Legal positivists attempt to place the study of law on a scientific foundation free from biases and "should be" questions. Some adherents have moved legal positivism from merely analyzing the law and empirically understanding the actions that occur to looking at the "meaning those actions have" for the participants or institutions being investigated (Bix, 1999, p. 33). H.L.A. Hart (1907-1992) refined positivist notions distinguishing primary legal rules that govern conduct and secondary legal rules governing procedural methods by which primary rules are enforced (Hart, 1964). At the close of the twentieth century, it was apparent that "even in an age when many jurisprudential flowers bloom, the positivism of Austin and Bentham, like a hardy perennial, remains deeply embedded within the garden of legal theory" (Freeman, 1998, p. v).

Different opinions have been offered as to whether *legal formalism*, which reached its heyday during the first third of the twentieth century, is a positivist view. Formalism is marked by "a reverence for the role of logic and mathematics and a priori reasoning as applied to philosophy, economics and jurisprudence" (Freeman, 2008, p. 985). Formalism, which also is referred to as conceptualism, treats law as a science. Formalists rely on inductive reasoning to settle legal disputes in that the analysis starts with specific rules, and broader legal principles are inferred from these rules. This approach is contrasted with deductive reasoning that involves applying general principles to the facts of a case to produce a specific rule. In essence, formalists contend that the law has rules that are meaningful and can be applied to resolve disputes (Solum, 2006). Formalism may be experiencing a resurgence in popularity, with self-professed current *neoformalists* criticizing the judicial discretion in rendering some controversial decisions such as *Roe v. Wade* (1973) that recognized a woman's constitutional privacy right to have an abortion. Neoformalists assert that there should be certainty and predictability in principled judicial decisions (Solum, 2006).

Ronald Dworkin, a major legal theorist of the twentieth century, has criticized legal positivism and developed an alternative perspective referred to as an *interpretive theory of the law* (Dworkin, 1977). Dworkin contends that legal practice is an exercise in interpretation and is deeply political; moreover, judges impose their own views in rendering decisions. Dworkin promotes a moral reading of the U.S. Constitution, and his view of law as "integrity" is among the most influential current perspectives on law. He argues that legal propositions are valid if they follow from principles of justice, fairness, and procedural due process (Dworkin, 1986). He treats integrity in litigation and legislation as being inherently valuable (Crowe, 2007). According to Dworkin, integrity as a legislative principle requires lawmakers to make morally coherent laws, and judges are expected to enforce these coherent principles. Dworkin's early work is associated with the "right answer thesis" that there is a unique and best answer to all or almost all legal questions (Bix, 1999, p. 87).

Justice Oliver Wendell Holmes (1841-1935) is associated with the school of thought referred to as *legal realism*, which emphasizes that "the life of the law has not been logic; it has been experience" (Holmes, 1881, p. 1). Realists assert that the law is not a science in which deductive reasoning can be used to determine all case outcomes. Instead, they contend that judges balance interests of the parties involved and come to a conclusion that is based on the political and psychological biases of the judge, which neoformalists criticize, as noted above (Solum, 2006). Jerome Frank (1889-1957) actually coined the term legal realism, and he argued that the law is not predictable and that a judge's decision can be influenced by many things affecting the judge's attitude and state of mind (Frank, 1930/1970). According to realists, judges set a goal they hope to achieve in resolving a particular legal dispute, so judicial decisions are not objective; judges create law through exercising their discretion, which is guided by political and moral values (Bix, 19991; Freeman, 2008).

Realists advocate interdisciplinary, particularly anthropological and sociological, approaches to the study of law, and they were the first lawyers to engage in empirical research focusing on laws and legal institutions (Freeman, 2008). There is some sentiment that "legal realism has fundamentally altered our conceptions of legal reasoning and of the relationship between law and society" (Singer, 1988, p. 467). Horowitz (1992) has opined that the value of legal realism is "its challenge to the orthodox claim that legal thought was separate and autonomous from moral and political discourse" (p. 193). *Legal instrumentalists* are associated with the realist movement and would concur that legal rules should be interpreted in light of their social purposes (Solum, 2006). The concept that judges apply their biases and not simply the law in reaching decisions has been picked up more recently by the critical legal studies movement that has criticized the judiciary for rendering decisions based on prejudices.

Recent theoretical perspectives have introduced into legal dialogue the relativity of truth and the notion that reality and identity are socially constructed (Bix, 1999). The *critical legal studies* movement began in the late 1970s and extended the more radical features of American legal realism including the belief that law is political and reflects ideological biases (Bix, 1999; Freeman, 2008). The critical legal studies theorists noted that seemingly neutral rules actually advantage the powerful and emphasized that rules could have developed in very different ways (Olsen, 1998).

Both *feminist legal theory* and *critical race theory* emanated from the belief that "the law reflects the perspective of and the values of White males and the resulting effects on citizens and on members of the legal profession who are not White males" (Bix, 1999, p. 207). Feminist legal theory was an outgrowth of the women's movement and critical legal studies. Feminist legal theorists challenge the positivist empirical tradition and assert that purportedly objective theory and practice have been distorted toward the interests of men

(Freeman, 2008; Olsen, 1998). They contend that there are intrinsic differences between men and women and that society and law are organized around male standards and norms. Feminist legal theorists argue that since the hierarchies created by law and legal institutions favor men and do not recognize the contributions and circumstances of women, society and law should be reformed to remove these biases (Bix, 1999).

Critical race theory developed as an offshoot of critical legal studies or perhaps even earlier to address what the civil rights movement had not accomplished. Some associate the beginning of this scholarly movement with the writing of civil rights lawyer Derrick Bell in the early 1970s (Delgado & Stefancic, 1998). Critical race theorists argue that racism is pervasive in the legal system and society and that individuals from minority groups have distinctive views and experiences that are not properly recognized or fully considered in mainstream discussions of the law.

These various perspectives on the nature of law and sources of legal authority differ as to whether there are eternal principles of justice, law is a science, law must be enacted by the government, law is inherently political, the purpose of law should be to emancipate oppressed groups, and other philosophical points. Nonetheless, as discussed below, there are certain core elements of the law that are recognized by most legal theorists.

Selected Elements of Jurisprudence

Most of the theoretical schools of thought recognize at least to some extent several common concepts that are fundamental to our system of law. These concepts underlie the practical doctrinal principles addressed in the first section of this chapter, and they also are embodied in the theoretical perspectives that seek to explain the doctrinal system. Four of these elements are briefly addressed below: justice, individual rights, precedent, and sanctions.

Justice

Black's Law Dictionary defines "justice" as "the fair and proper administration of laws" (Garner, 2009, p. 942). Justice can be viewed from a number of vantage points. To illustrate, it can be considered corrective in dealing with rights and wrongs. Victims of crimes are often said to receive justice when the offenders are punished. Justice also can be looked at from the standpoint of distributing goods to individuals, such as liberties or wealth; it is considered just to treat equals equitably and to compensate those with disadvantages, which may mean unequal treatment is needed to be just (Freeman, 2008). And justice can be viewed from a political perspective in terms of ensuring procedural fairness for all. Also, it can be considered from the vantage point of social justice, emphasizing the conformance to moral principles, such as the principle that all people are created equal (Garner, 2009).

Modern legal theorists in the United States have been influenced in their views of justice by the historical writings of Thomas Hobbes (1588-1679), Jean-Jacques Rousseau (1712-1778), and particularly John Locke (1632-1704) and their perspectives regarding the social contract theory (see Freeman, 2008; Bix, 1999). American law has incorporated the social contract notion that the government has authority that is limited to the powers the citizens agree to delegate to it.

Social contract theory influenced John Rawls (1921-2002), who wrote *A Theory of Justice*, which has had a seminal impact on political theory in our nation. In this volume, Rawls (1972) asserted that "justice is the first virtue of social institutions, as truth is of systems of thought" (p. 3). He developed a theory of fairness, which has two basic elements—the equal liberty principle and the difference principle. According to Rawls, every person has the same rights to basic liberties, and social and economic inequalities should be addressed by making positions and opportunities available to all equally with the exception that greater benefits should be provided to the least advantaged in society. Rawls contends that "justice is the structural rule of society, within which people who (inevitably) have different sets of values and goals in life, can coexist, cooperate, and, to some extent, compete" (Bix, 1999, p. 97). Rawls uses the hypothetical *original position* in which everyone decides what is just from a position of ignorance about their own personal circumstances to ensure principles of fairness.

Precedent

An important theoretical underpinning of legal theory and research is the reliance on precedent. Judicial rulings create precedent by which lower courts in the jurisdiction must abide. Decisions in other jurisdictions may be cited but they are not controlling when judges consider a specific case. The term *stare decisis* means to stand by what has already been decided when confronted with similar factual situations (Solum, 2006). Freeman (2008) has asserted that "in almost any form of organization, precedents have to be established as guides to future conduct, and this applies not merely to legal systems but to all rule- or norm-creating bodies, whether clubs, government departments, schools, business firms, or churches" (p. 1536). Sellers (2006) has observed that the notion of precedent in American legal consciousness reflects the view that judicial rulings must be respected as the law.

Despite the deep respect for *stare decisis*, at times the Supreme Court has overturned its own precedent as it did in 1954 when in it struck down the "separate but equal" doctrine that had been the court's precedent for more than 50 years (*Brown v. Board of Education*, 1954). Within a much shorter span of time, the Supreme Court overturned its 1940 precedent allowing public schools to compel students to recite the Pledge of Allegiance (*Minersville School District v. Gobitis*, 1940). Only 3 years later, the court rejected this interpretation of First Amendment guarantees, holding that public schools are precluded from forcing students to recite the Pledge if it conflicts with their religious or philosophical beliefs (*West Virginia State Board of Education v. Barnette*, 1943).

Notwithstanding these exceptions, the Supreme Court is very reluctant to overrule its prior opinions. Instead of overturning precedent, more often the court will carve out exceptions to its earlier rulings or perhaps will reinterpret what a precedent means. For example, in *Hazelwood School District v. Kuhlmeier* (1988), the Supreme Court did not overturn *Tinker v. Des Moines Independent School District* (1969). In *Tinker*, the court held that private student expression in public schools cannot be curtailed or be the basis for punishment unless it threatens a material or substantial disruption or interferes with the rights of others. Maintaining this precedent, in *Hazelwood*, the court restricted *Tinker's* application by ruling that student expression representing the school is not constitutionally protected, so *Tinker* does not apply. The *Tinker* precedent was thus preserved, but its application was narrowed.

The court also can avoid directly overturning precedent by more narrowly or broadly interpreting a specific constitutional provision. To illustrate, the court in *Roe v. Wade* (1973) expanded the individual's constitutionally protected liberty rights under the Due Process Clause of the Fourteenth Amendment to include a woman's right to have an abortion. This decision established a new constitutional right without overturning any prior ruling. In *San Antonio Independent School District v. Rodriguez* (1973), four members of the Supreme Court wanted to expand constitutionally protected liberty rights to include the implied right to an education because an education is necessary for individuals to fully exercise other constitutional freedoms even though education is not an enumerated constitutional right. But five members of the court disagreed, reasoning that since education is not explicitly mentioned in the U.S. Constitution, it should not be considered a constitutionally protected right. If one more justice had agreed that education is an implied fundamental right under the Federal Constitution, all challenged educational policies and practices subsequently would have been subjected to strict judicial scrutiny.

Individual Rights

Individual rights can be viewed from a number of perspectives. Rights asserted to spring from natural law include life, liberty, and privacy. Rights referred to as civil rights belong to every individual by virtue of citizenship and in our nation would include the personal freedoms in the U.S. Constitution. Political rights entail the right to participate in establishing or administering the government, which would include the right to vote and to petition the government (Garner, 2009). Rights usually impose obligations on others to respect the rights.

Individual rights can be guaranteed by state and/or federal constitutions, state and/or federal laws, administrative regulations, and court decisions interpreting these provisions. The personal rights guaranteed and protected by the U.S. Constitution, such as freedom of speech and protection against arbitrary governmental searches, place constraints on governmental action so are sometimes called negative rights. Several states would not ratify the Constitution until the Bill of Rights became part of the Constitution. The United States differs from some other countries in its reverence for individual rights. Some rights apply to individuals because of their group membership. For example, the Nineteenth Amendment to the U.S. Constitution gave women as a group the right to vote in our nation.

States may recognize more extensive liberty interests than those protected by the U.S. Constitution. To illustrate, some state constitutions have explicit provisions guaranteeing equal rights for women and men, but such an Equal Rights Amendment has not been adopted as part of the Federal Constitution. Also, some states by law prohibit use of corporal punishment in public schools, but such a prohibition is not included in the Federal Constitution or federal civil rights laws. The Supreme Court has recognized that states can go beyond federal constitutional minimums in protecting individual rights, but they cannot take away a right guaranteed by the U.S. Constitution. A state, for example, cannot decide to have segregated public schools because state-mandated school segregation abridges the Fourteenth Amendment (Cambron-McCabe et al., 2009).

Many court cases have been generated by conflicts over the scope of citizens' free speech rights, religious liberties, privacy rights, and other personal freedoms (see Alexander & Alexander, 2009; Russo, 2009). At times, individual rights may appear to conflict with each other. For example, a public school student may assert a free speech right to express private religious views at school, but school authorities may contend that the Establishment Clause precludes such religious expression under the auspices of the school. In such instances, federal courts usually are called on to resolve the conflict and decide which constitutional rights prevail in a given situation (Russo, 2009). And of course, protected rights are not without limits. Freedom of speech is perhaps the most preciously guarded individual right in our nation, but expression rights can be constrained under certain circumstances. Accordingly, constraints can be placed on public school teachers' expression rights while in school or when making comments pursuant to their job responsibilities (see *Garcetti v. Ceballos*, 2006). Also, students cannot express views that advocate unlawful behavior (see *Morse v. Frederick*, 2007).

Sanctions

A basic legal principle is that consequences are attached to violations of the law. In short, when society adopts a rule, offenders can be punished. Such sanctions for violations are expected to be clear to those who are faced with punishment for possible infractions. Schwartz and Orleans (1967) have asserted that sanctions "constitute the core, if not the defining characteristic, of the legal order" (p. 274).

Many theories have been offered to justify punishments. Sanctions can be imposed to deter future violations of the law or to emphasize that certain behaviors are condemned by society. Sanctions also can be used as retribution, in effect to compensate the victim for the harm suffered by punishing those who inflicted the harm. A monetary sanction in this regard might be viewed as restitution by making the victim whole again. Additional punitive damages can be assessed against the one who inflicted the harm for particularly egregious or wanton behavior (Garner, 2009). Some consider punishment as having value in itself by punishing wrongdoers, with more serious crimes receiving more severe sanctions (Bix, 1999). And punishments may be designed to keep certain offenders away from society because of the threat of harm they pose.

Punishments for breaking the law can include minor penalties, such as fines, community service, or probation. Although rehabilitation is preferred to incarceration, for serious crimes, individuals may give up their freedom under house arrest or incarceration in jail. For the most heinous crimes committed by individuals who are considered a threat to society, the offenders can face the death penalty in the majority of states. The death penalty in general is not considered cruel and unusual punishment under the Eighth Amendment to the Federal Constitution (*Gregg v. Georgia*, 1976).

The law often seems to be viewed by citizens primarily from the vantage point of penalties imposed for noncompliance rather than from the perspective that the law can serve as a guide to appropriate action. This perhaps perpetuates the erroneous attitude that the law is merely a negative force, creating externally imposed constraints on behavior, rather than guides to appropriate action.

Conducting Legal Research

The various philosophical schools of thought can influence the type of legal research that is conducted and are deeply imbedded in the study of the nature of law. However, the theoretical positions are not as apparent in most legal research, which has a more practical orientation. The majority of legal research is not philosophical, but focuses more on the application of legal standards and principles in a given substantive domain than on questions pertaining to the nature of law. Most legal research is intended to provide analyses that support legal decision-making in a range of contexts and inform policymakers and practitioners (Mersky & Dunn, 2002). Accordingly, legal research usually is designed to assist in understanding past practices and in predicting legal outcomes in the future.

Some legal research involves gathering and analyzing statistical data, such as studies of the voting behavior of justices, comparisons of case outcomes, or surveys of constituencies regarding their knowledge of or attitudes toward the law (McCarthy, 2010). However, quantitative studies are not the dominant type of legal research. More often, legal scholarship entails doctrinal legal scholarship (Hollander, 2007) that relies on legal logic or reasoning by example (Levi, 1948). Often, the intent of legal research is to build an argument that a particular judicial decision was wrongly decided, to support the constitutionality of a legislative act, to predict how courts should rule on a specific issue in light of judicial precedent in related areas, or to test a hypothesis regarding the legal principles governing a question that has not yet been addressed by the courts. Applying legal logic or reasoning, a researcher relies on precedent and analogy in asking questions and framing logical arguments to interpret case law, statutes, and constitutional provisions.

The legal researcher must examine all evidence, including evidence that may refute the hypothesis or argument being advanced. There are primary and secondary sources of legal authority. Primary sources include court opinions, constitutional provisions, laws, and administrative rules, and they are usually "mandatory" or "binding" in that they must be followed (Mersky & Dunn, 2002; Sloan, 2006). Secondary sources include encyclopedias, treatises, periodicals, and other research and analysis that can be cited to build a legal argument but are not binding on courts.

There are similarities between legal research and historical research. Both often start with a hypothesis, and evidence is gathered to substantiate or refute the hypothesis. Like historical research, legal analysts often synthesize trends in the law and develop arguments and draw conclusions based on these trends. By synthesizing the evolution of the law in a specific area, current issues can be illuminated. Like historical research, legal research also may include criticism or may build an argument that a particular court decision was wrongly decided or that a specific law conflicts with constitutional interpretations. Legal research, similar to historical research, can employ quantitative and qualitative techniques in gathering and analyzing data, even though qualitative approaches are dominant (McConville & Chui, 2007).

Unlike some types of legal scholarship, the legal researcher who is exploring school issues must often consult the relevant education literature on the topic under investigation. To illustrate, if conducting legal research on the collision of student expression rights and public school antiharassment provisions, it is important to consider social science research on the impact of hurtful student expression on classmates in terms of their school performance and psychological wellbeing (see Savin-Williams, 1994; Smalls, White, Chavous, & Sellers, 2007; Williams, Connolly, Pepler, & Craig, 2005). The education and social science literatures can influence case outcomes. The most notable example, of course, was the landmark Supreme Court decision, *Brown v. Board of Education* (1954); the court relied on the now famous social science "doll" studies by Kenneth Clark indicating that state-mandated segregation imposed a sense of inferiority on Black children. Some legal scholars would like for legal research to be autonomous, "standing alone and separate from other spheres of knowledge," but legal research increasingly is interdisciplinary in scope (Hollander, 2007, p. 774).

WHY EDUCATORS SHOULD UNDERSTAND AND EMBRACE THE LAW

It cannot be disputed that from the mid-twentieth century through the 1980s, public schools became increasingly legalized (Fischer, 1989). Starting with the *Brown* desegregation decision in 1954, federal courts became more assertive in applying constitutional guarantees to a range of school controversies, and legislatures increasingly regulated various aspects of the educational enterprise (Wise, 1979). It was not a coincidence that the Education Law Association (formerly the National Organization on Legal Problems of Education) was launched in 1954 by a group of forward thinking educators and attorneys who anticipated that *Brown* marked the beginning of a new era in applying federal constitutional provisions in schools. During the 1970s, more legal challenges were initiated involving schools than in the prior 7 decades combined (Zirkel & Richardson, 1989). Even though the number of school cases has leveled off since the latter 1980s (with the exception of cases dealing with children with disabilities), the United States still has far more school litigation than any other nation.

Because of the prevalence of legal activity involving schools, many educators perceive the law as limiting their professional autonomy. They think the law consists of external rules and mandates that they should know or at least know how to locate (Bull & McCarthy, 1995). Under this passive and narrow view of the law, educators do not feel ownership of the law or believe that they can have any impact in changing the legal requirements. Rather than considering the law in our nation as a concrete set of rules to be learned, it is preferable to consider the law as many sets of delicately balanced interests and processes designed to advance order, democracy, and freedom (McCarthy, 2010).

Understanding various perspectives on the nature of the law can inform educators, students, and others involved in the school community regarding the role of law in society generally and in schools more specifically. Such understanding also can illuminate the sources of their rights and responsibilities. There certainly are practical reasons for teachers and school leaders to be knowledgeable of legal research on a range of topics from negligence for student injuries to employees' private conduct. Such knowledge can assist educators in complying with the law and identifying areas of potential legal vulnerability. Understanding the law can assist policymakers and practitioners in making informed choices among alternative courses of action (McCarthy, 2010).

Perhaps more importantly, however, a legal perspective can have an impact on how educators perform their jobs so that their daily decisions are more equitable and fair, particularly in areas where the status of the law is ambiguous. Understanding the values that form the basis of law in our society, such as equity, justice, liberty, and privacy, is probably more important than knowing the legal mandates themselves. If educators internalize the concept of fundamental fairness, for example, this can guide their daily actions as well as enhance their understanding of procedural requirements that may be legally required.

Educators who view the law as setting externally imposed boundaries are more likely to overreact to legal provisions. For example, all states have adopted provisions requiring educators to report their suspicions of child abuse (Cambron-McCabe et al., 2009). Fearing that teachers may be accused of being abusers, some school districts have enacted policies prohibiting any physical contact between staff members and students. Thus, a kindergarten teacher could not comfort a child who has fallen down by putting an arm around the student. Educational policy makers and practitioners also have overreacted to the provisions of the

Family Educational Rights and Privacy Act of 1974 (FERPA) by removing pertinent information from students' permanent records because of concerns that parents may challenge the content of their children's records. In reality, very few sanctions have been imposed on school districts under FERPA, but material that might be helpful in instructing specific children often has been removed in anticipation of sanctions. Sadly, the law too often is viewed as something to be feared rather than embraced. And educators who fear the law are more likely to ignore it, which can also be as damaging.

Educators who have a thorough grasp of the law are able to model democratic ideals in their classrooms and create instructional opportunities that help students appreciate the basic values undergirding the law in our nation. Indeed, educators who understand the law also are more likely to infuse a legal perspective throughout the instructional program. This can increase their students' knowledge and appreciation of the law and its underlying assumptions and obligations, which should help them become better informed and contributing citizens.

REFERENCES

Alexander, K., & Alexander, M.D. (2009). *American public school law* (7th ed.). Belmont, CA: Wadsworth.

Austin, J. (1998). *The province of jurisprudence determined.* Indianapolis, IN: Hackett. (Original work published 1832)

Bowring, J. (Ed.). (1962). *The works of Jeremy Bentham.* New York, NY: Elibron Classics.

Bix, B. (1999). *Jurisprudence: Theory and context.* London, England: Sweet & Maxwell.

Brown v. Board of Education, 347 U.S. 483 (1954).

Bull. B., & McCarthy. M. (1995). Reflections on the knowledge base in law and ethics for educational leaders, *Educational Administration Quarterly, 31,* 613-631.

Carter, L. H. (1987). *Reason in law.* Glenview, IL: Scott-Foresman.

Cambron-McCabe, N., McCarthy, M., & Thomas, S. (2009). *Legal rights of teachers and students* (2nd ed.). Boston, MA: Allyn & Bacon.

Crowe, J. (2007). Dworkin on the value of integrity. *Deakin Law Review, 12,* 167-180.

Delgado, R., & Stefancic, J., (1998). Critical race theory: Past, present, and future. In M. D. A. Freeman (Ed.), *Legal theory at the end of the millennium* (pp. 467-92). Oxford, England: Oxford University.

Dworkin, R. (1977): *Taking rights seriously.* London, England: Duckworth.

Dworkin, R. (1986). *Law's empire.* Cambridge, MA: Belknap.

Family Educational Rights and Privacy Act of 1974, 20 U.S.C. § 1232g (2010).

Fischer, L. (1989). When courts play school board. *Education Law Reporter, 51,* 693-709.

Frank, J. (1970). *Law and the modern man.* Gloucester, MA: Peter Smith. (Original work published 1930).

Freeman, M. D. A. (Ed.) (1998). *Legal theory at the end of the millennium.* Oxford, England: Oxford University.

Freeman, M. D. A. (2008). *Lloyd's introduction to jurisprudence.* London, England: Sweet & Maxwell.

Frothingham v. Mellon, 262 U.S. 447 (1923).

Garcetti v. Ceballos, 547 U.S. 410 (2006).

Garner, B. A. (Ed.) (2009). *Black's law dictionary* (9th ed). St. Paul, MN: Thompson/West.

Gee, K. (2009). Establishing a constitutional standard that protects public school teacher classroom expression. *Journal of Law and Education, 38,* 409-454.

General Electric Company v. Gilbert, 429 U.S. 125 (1976).

Goss v. Lopez, 419 U.S. 565 (1975).

Gregg v. Georgia, 428 U.S. 153 (1976).

Harper v. Poway Unified School District, 445 F.3d 116 (9th Cir. 2006), vacated and remanded, 549 U.S. 1262 (2007), on remand, 545 F. Supp. 2d 1072 (S.D. Cal. 2007).

Hart, H. L. A. (1964). *The concept of law.* Oxford, England: Clarendon.

Hazelwood School District v. Kuhlmeier, 484 U.S. 260 (1988).

Hollander, D. A. (2007). Interdisciplinary legal scholarship: What can we learn from Princeton's long-standing tradition? *Law Library Journal, 99,* 771-790.

Holmes, O. W. (1881). *The common law.* Boston, MA: Little Brown, and Co.

Horowitz, M. (1992). *The transformation of American law 1870-1960.*Oxford, England: Oxford University.

Ingraham v. Wright, 430 U.S. 651 (1977).

Kelsen, H. (2002). *Pure theory of law* (M. Knight, Trans.). Union, NJ: Lawbook Exchange. (Original work published 1967)

Kerlinger, F. N. (1986). *Foundations of behavioral research* (3rd ed.). New York, NY: Holt, Rinehart & Winston.

Levi, E. H. (1948). An introduction to legal reasoning. *The University of Chicago Law Review, 15,* 501-574.

Marbury v. Madison, 5 U.S. 137 (1803).

McCarthy, M. (2009). Research on actors and institutions involved in education policy: Themes, tensions, and topics to explore. In G. Sykes, B. Schneider, & D. N. Plank (Eds.), *Handbook of education policy research* (pp. 842-847). New York, NY: Routledge.

McCarthy, M. (2010). Legal research: Tensions involving student expression rights. In W. K. Hoy & M. Dipaola (Eds.), *Analyzing school contexts* (pp. 229-53). Charlotte, NC: Information Age.

McConville, M., & Chui, W.H. (2007). *Research methods for law.* Edinburgh, Scotland: Edinburgh University.

Mersky, R., & Dunn, D. (2002). *Fundamentals of legal research* (8th ed.). New York, NY: Foundation.

Minersville School District v. Gobitis, 310 U.S. 586 (1940).

Morse v. Frederick, 551 U.S. 393 (2007).

Nuxoll v. Indian Prairie School District, 523 F.3d 668 (7th Cir. 2008).

Olsen, F. E. (1998). Some jurisprudential foundations of critical legal studies and feminist legal theory. In M. D. A. Freeman (Ed.), *Legal theory at the end of the millennium* (pp. 533-552). Oxford, England: Oxford University.

Prest, W. (2008). *William Blackstone: Law and letters in the eighteenth century.* Oxford, England: Oxford University.

Rawls, J. (1972). *A theory of justice.* Cambridge, MA: Harvard University.

Roe v. Wade, 410 U.S. 959 (1973).

Russo, C. (2009). *Reutter's the law of public education.* New York, NY: Foundation.

San Antonio Independent School District v. Rodriguez, 411 U.S. 1 (1973).

Savin-Williams, R. (1994). Verbal and physical abuse as stressors in the lives of lesbian, gay male, and bisexual youths: Associations with school problems, running away, substance abuse, prostitution, and suicide. *Journal of Consulting and Clinical Psychology, 62,* 261-269.

Schwartz, R., & Orleans, S. (1967). On legal sanctions. *University of Chicago Law Review, 34,* 274-300.

Sellers, M.N. (2006). Legal history and legal theory: The doctrine of precedent in the United States of America. *American Journal of Comparative Law, 54,* 67-88.

Sergiovanni, T., Kelleher, P., McCarthy, M., & Fowler, F. (2009). *Educational governance and administration* (6th ed.). Boston, MA: Allyn & Bacon.

Singer, J. (1988). Legal realism now. *California Law Review, 76,* 465-505.

Sloan, A. (2006). *Basic legal research: Tools and strategies* (3rd ed.). New York, NY: Aspen.

Smalls, C., White, R., Chavous, T., & Sellers, R. (2007). Racial/ideological beliefs and racial discrimination experiences as predictors of academic engagement among African American adolescents. *Black Psychology, 33,* 299-330.

Solum, L. (2006). The Supreme Court in bondage: Constitutional stare decisis, legal formalism, and the future of unenumerated rights, *University of Pennsylvania Journal of Constitutional Law, 9,* 155-208.

Tinker v. Des Moines Independent School District, 393 U.S. 503 (1969).

Title VII, Civil Rights Act of 1964, 42 U.S.C. § 2000e *et seq.* (2010).

West Virginia State Board of Education v. Barnette, 319 U.S. 624 (1943).

Williams, T., Connolly, J., Pepler, D., & Craig, W. (2005). Peer victimization, social support, and psychosocial adjustment of sexual minority adolescents. *Journal of Youth and Adolescence, 34,* 471-482.

Wisconsin v. Yoder, 406 U.S. 205 (1972).

Wise, A. E. (1979). *Legislated learning: The bureaucratization of the American classroom.* Berkeley, CA: University of California.

Zirkel, P., & Richardson, S. (1989). The "explosion" in education litigation. *Education Law Reporter, 53,* 767-768.

Zucht v. King, 260 U.S. 174 (1922).

Author Contact Information, Martha McCarthy, PhD, President's Professor, Loyola Marymount University, Los Angeles, and Indiana University, Bloomington, IN. Telephone: 310-338-5280. E-mail: Mmccar26@lmu.edu

CHAPTER 71

Other Contemporary Organizational Theories

Fred C. Lunenburg
Sam Houston State University

Given the importance of theory in understanding the nature of organizations, researchers devote attention to studying new and insightful perspectives. Five contemporary perspectives of recent interest are the leader-member exchange theory, reciprocal influence theory, substitutes for leadership theory, total quality management, and transformational leadership. Let's examine these theories in more detail.

LEADER-MEMBER EXCHANGE THEORY

Many organization theories assume that the superior behaves in essentially the same manner toward all members of his or her work group. In fact, however, leaders often act very differently toward different subordinates, and develop contrasting kinds of relationships with them. This perspective on the leadership process is provided by the *leader-member exchange theory* (LMX) (Graen & Uhl-Bien, 1995).

The LMX theory focuses on a dyad, that is, the relationship between a leader and each subordinate considered independently, rather than on the relationship between the superior and the group. Each linkage, or relationship, is likely to differ in quality. Thus, the same administrator may have poor interpersonal relations with some subordinates and open and trusting relations with others. The relationships within these pairings, or dyads, may be of a predominantly in-group or out-group nature.

A leader initiates either an in-group or an out-group exchange with a member of the organization early in the life of the dyadic relationship. Members of the in-group are invited to participate in decision making and are given added responsibility. The leader allows these members some latitude in their roles; in effect, the leader and key subordinates negotiate the latter's responsibilities in a noncontractual exchange relationship. In essence, an in-group member is elevated to the unofficial role of "trusted lieutenant." In-group members, in many respects, enjoy the benefits of job latitude (influence in decision making, open communications, and confidence in and consideration for the member). The subordinate typically reciprocates with greater than required expenditures of time and effort, the assumption of greater responsibility, and commitment to the success of the organization (Eden, 1992; Liden, Erdogan, Wayne, & Sparrowe, 2006).

In contrast, members of the out-group are supervised within the narrow limits of their formal employment contract. Authority is legitimated by the implicit contract between the member and the organization. The leader will provide support, consideration, and assistance mandated by duty but will not go beyond such limits. In effect, the leader is practicing a contractual exchange with such members; they are "hired hands," who are being influenced by legitimate authority rather than true leadership. In return, out-group members will do what they have to do and little beyond that.

IMPLICATIONS FOR PRACTICE

An important implication of the leader-member exchange theory is that the quality of the relationship between the leader and each group member has important job consequences. Specifically, the research supporting the LMX theory indicates that subordinates with in-group status with their leaders will have higher productivity and job satisfaction, improved motivation, and

The Handbook of Educational Theories, pp. 841–854

engage in more citizenship behaviors at work (Chen, Lam, & Zhong, 2007; Gerstner & Day, 1997; Ilies, Nahrgang, & Morgeson, 2007). Leaders invest more resources in those they expect to perform well (i.e., those they have designated as in-group members); and they treat them differently than they do out-group members. Therefore, it is suggested that school administrators develop high-quality relationships with as many subordinates as possible. They should have as large an in-group and as small an out-group as possible.

Reciprocal Influence Theory

Most theories of organization share one underlying assumption: Leader behavior affects subordinate behavior. Particularly in correlation studies, any association between leader behavior and group effectiveness has been interpreted as measuring the impact of the leader's action on subordinate satisfaction, motivation, or performance (Bennis & Nanus, 2007; Dumdum, Lowe, Avolio, 2002; Judge & Piccolo, 2004; Yukl, 2010). More recently, however, it has been recognized that in any complex organization the flow of influence or authority is not unilateral and downward—from leader to subordinate—but also upward from subordinate to leader. According to *reciprocal influence theory* certain leader behaviors cause subordinate behaviors, and certain acts of subordinates (for example, low performance) can cause the leader to modify behavior (Starke, 2001).

The reciprocal influence theory is a reality in most organizations. For example, consider the principal of a school who is dedicated to the mission of improving student achievement scores in the building. How is the principal's behavior influenced by subordinates? One obvious response is that the leader will closely supervise teachers who are not performing well and will loosely supervise others who are fulfilling their mission of improving instruction. Thus, by their performance, subordinates are influencing the leader (Lunenburg & Irby, 2006). As another example, consider a university dean who has a tenured professor who is very hot tempered. Although the dean has authority over this faculty member and can order the individual to perform many job-related activities, the dean may be fearful of the subordinate's temper and will modify her leadership style to accommodate this individual. In this case, the professor is probably exerting more influence on the university dean than the leader is influencing the subordinate.

Implications for Practice

Several studies support the notion of reciprocal influence between leaders and subordinates. The results to date suggest the following:

1. Leader consideration or employee-centered behavior and leader positive reinforcement both can lead to employee job satisfaction.
2. High initiating structure or production-centered leadership sometimes leads to lower employee job satisfaction.
3. Low-performing subordinates tend to cause leaders to use more initiating structure/production-centered leadership and punitive reward behavior (that is, punishment).
4. High leader positive reward behavior tends to lead to improved subordinate performance. However, few studies have shown any direct evidence that leader initiating structure or leader consideration causes increases or decreases in subordinate performance. These findings emphasize the importance of rewards as an influence factor in determining subordinate behavior (Szilagi, 2010).

In short, it is realistic to view organizations as places where leaders and subordinates interact in a complex way, each exerting reciprocal influence on the other. Research efforts examining the reciprocal influence process will continue to be of interest to school administrators and researchers and will be used to emphasize the dynamics of leadership in organizations.

Substitutes for Leadership

The concept of substitutes for leadership has evolved in response to dissatisfaction with the progress of organizational theory in explaining the effects of leader behavior on performance outcomes. Research studies demonstrate that, in many situations, leadership may be unimportant or redundant. Certain subordinate, task, and organizational factors can act as *substitutes for leadership* or neutralize the leader's influence on subordinates (Hovell & Dorfman, 1986; Kerr & Jermier, 1978). Table 71.1 lists some possible leadership substitutes and neutralizers for supportive/relationship leadership and instrumental/task leadership.

As shown in Table 71.1, subordinate experience, ability, and training may substitute for instrumental leadership. For example, professionals such as teachers may have so much experience, ability, and training that they do not need instrumental leadership to perform well and be satisfied. Such leadership acts would be redundant and might be resented, and could even lead to reduced performance. Similarly, subordinates who have a strong professional orientation (like teachers) might not require instrumental or supportive leadership. When subordinates do not desire the rewards a leader can provide, this would neutralize almost any behavior on the part of the leader.

Certain types of work (for example, teaching) are highly structured and automatically provide feedback

Table 71.1. Substitutes and Neutralizers for Supportive and Instrumental Leadership

Factor	Supportive Leadership*	Instrumental Leadership*
Subordinate Characteristics		
1. Experience, ability, training	Substitute	Substitute
2. "Professional" orientation		Substitute
3. Indifference toward organizational rewards	Neutralizer	Neutralizer
Task Characteristics		
1. Structured, routine task		Substitute
2. Task feedback		Substitute
3. Intrinsically satisfying task	Substitute	
Organizational Characteristics		
1. Cohesive work group	Substitute	Substitute
2. Leader lacks position power	Neutralizer	Neutralizer
3. Formalization of goals and plans		Substitute
4. Rigid rules and procedures		Neutralizer
5. Physical distance between leader and subordinates	Neutralizer	Neutralizer

Source: Yukl (2010, p. 237) Reprinted by permission of Prentice Hall.
Note: *Supportive and instrumental leadership are analogous to leader consideration and leader initiating structuring.

(through students' oral and written responses) and, therefore, substitute for instrumental leadership. Furthermore, when the task is intrinsically satisfying (like teaching), there will be little need for supportive behavior on the part of the leader to make up for poor organizational design. Finally, when the organization is structured in a way that makes clear the paths to goals—for example, through plans, rules, policies, and standard operating procedures—such structure reduces the need for instrumental leadership. This is particularly apparent in sociotechnical and autonomous work groups found in schools. Sometimes a strong union has the same effect, if it has a collective bargaining agreement that severely constrains the administrator's position power (Lunenburg, 2000).

Implications for Practice

It appears that leadership matters most when substitutes are not present in subordinates' skills, task design, or the organization's structure. When substitutes are present, the impact of leadership is neutralized.

Total Quality Management

The Japanese transformed their economy and industry through a visionary management technique called *total quality management* (TQM). School administrators are finding that TQM principles can provide the formula for improving America's schools.

TQM is a systematic approach to education reform based on the philosophy of W. Edwards Deming (1988, 2000). Deming's work is not merely about productivity and quality control; it is a broad vision on the nature of organizations and how organizations should be changed.

When educators look at TQM principles, they assume that the model applies only to profit-making organizations. Actually, TQM applies as well to corporations, service organizations, universities, and elementary and secondary schools.

Indeed, the concepts formulated by TQM founder, Deming, have proved so powerful that educators want to apply TQM to schools. Deming's philosophy provides a framework that can integrate many positive developments in education, such as team-teaching, site-based management, cooperative learning, and outcomes-based education.

The problem is that words like *learning* and *curriculum* are not found in Deming's 14 principles. Some of Deming's terminology needs to be translated to schools as well. For example, superintendents and principals can be considered *management*. Teachers are *employers* or *managers* of students. Students are *employees*, and the knowledge they acquire is the *product*. Parents and society are the *customers*. With these translations made, we can see many applications to schools.

Deming's 14 TQM Principles Applied to Schools

Deming's 14 principles are based on the assumption that people want to do their best and that it is management's job to enable them to do so by constantly improving the *system* in which they work. The framework for transforming schools using Deming's 14 principles follows.

1. Create constancy of purpose for improvement of product and service. For schools, the purpose of the system must be clear and shared by all stakeholders—school board members, administrators, teachers, support staff, parents, community, and students. Customer needs must be the focus in establishing educational aims. The aims of the system must be to improve the quality of education for all students.

2. Adopt the new philosophy. Implementation of Deming's second principle requires a rethinking of the school's mission and priorities, with everyone in agreement on them. Existing methods, materials, and environments may be replaced by new teaching and learning strategies where success of every student is the goal. Individual differences among students are addressed. Ultimately, what may be required is a total transformation of the American system of education as we know it.

3. Cease dependence on inspection to achieve quality. The field of education has recently entered an era that many American corporations have abandoned: inspection at the end of the line (Bonstingl, 2001). In industry this was called "product inspection." According to Deming, it always costs more to fix a problem than to prevent one. Reliance on remediation can be avoided if proper intervention occurs during instruction. Examples of preventive approaches in schools include Slavin and Madden's (2009) "success for all schools," James Comer's (2000, 2006) "school development program," Henry Levin's (1986) "accelerated schools," Joyce Epstein's (2010) "parent involvement strategies," Cara Shores' (2009) "RTI process," and the more traditional, long-standing intervention approaches: Head Start, Follow Through, preschool programs, and other early interventions (Lunenburg, 2011). These intervention strategies can help students avoid learning problems later.

4. End the practice of awarding business on the basis of price alone. The lowest bid is rarely the most cost-efficient. Schools need to move toward a single supplier for any one time and develop long-term relationships of loyalty and trust with that supplier.

5. Improve constantly and forever every activity in the organization, to improve quality and productivity. The focus of improvement efforts in education, under Deming's approach, are on teaching and learning processes. Based on the latest research findings, the best strategies must be attempted, evaluated, and refined as needed. And, consistent with learning style theories (Dunn & Dunn, 1992; Dunn, Dunn, & Perrin, 1994), Howard Gardner's (1993) multiple intelligences, and Henry Levin's (1986) accelerated schools for at-risk students, educators must redesign the system to provide for a broad range of people—handicapped, learning disabled, at-risk, special needs students—and find ways to make them all successful in school. This means requiring universal standards of achievement for all students before permitting them to move to the next level. Such provisions are stipulated in the No Child Left Behind Act.

6. Institute training on the job. Training for educators is needed in three areas. First, there must be training in the new teaching and learning processes that are developed. Second, training must be provided in the use of new assessment strategies (Popham, 2010a, 2010b). Third, there must be training in the principles of the new management system. For schools, this means providing continuous professional development activities for all school administrators, teachers, and support staff.

7. Institute leadership. Deming's seventh principle resembles Peter Senge's (2006) systems thinking. According to both Senge and Deming, improvement of a stable system comes from altering the system itself, and this is primarily the job of management and not those who work within the system. Deming asserts that the primary task of leadership is to narrow the amount of variation within the system, bringing everyone toward the goal of perfection. In schools this means bringing everyone toward the goal of learning for *all*. It means removing achievement gaps for all population groups—a movement toward excellence and equity. Numerous books have been devoted to this pursuit recently, such as Linda Darling-Hammond's (2010) *The Flat World and Education*, Tyrone Howard's (2011) *Why Race and Culture Matter in Schools: Closing the Achievement Gap in America's Classrooms*, Rod Paige's (2011) *The Black-White Achievement Gap: Why Closing the Gap is the Greatest Civil Rights Issue of Our Time*, and Alan Blankstein's (2010) *Failure is not an Option: Six Principles for Making Student Success the ONLY Option*.

8. Drive out fear. A basic assumption of TQM is that people want to do their best. The focus of improvement efforts then must be on the processes and on the outcomes, not on trying to blame individuals for failures. If quality is absent, the fault is in the system, says Deming. It is management's job to enable people to do their best by constantly improving the system in which they work. Fear creates an insurmountable barrier to improvement of any system. In schools, faculty and staff are often afraid to point out problems, because they fear they may be blamed. School leaders at all levels need to communicate that staff suggestions are valued and rewarded.

9. Break down barriers among staff areas. Deming's ninth principle is somewhat related to the first principle: Create constancy of purpose for improvement of product and service. In the classroom, this principle applies to interdisciplinary instruction, team teaching, writing across the curriculum, and transfer of learning. Collaboration needs to exist among members of the learning organization so that total quality can be maximized. In schools, total quality means promoting learning for all. It is the essence of initiating and maintaining a professional learning community (DuFour & Eaker, 1998; DuFour, DuFour, & Eaker, 2008).

10. Eliminate slogans, exhortations, and targets that demand zero defects and new levels of productivity. Implicit in most slogans, exhortations, and targets is the supposition that staff could do better if they tried harder. This offends rather than inspires the team. It creates adversarial relationships because the many causes of low quality and low productivity in schools are due to the system and not the staff. The system itself may need to be changed. I am not in total agreement with Deming's 10th principle. Deming's assertion may be true for business organizations, but educators tend to use a lot of slogans as a general practice. Typical slogans used by educators are "Keep the main thing, the main thing." This slogan refers to keeping *students* the focus of all discussions. Another slogan that most teachers adopt is "All children can learn." Slogans, such as these serve as targets in school organizations.

11. Eliminate numerical quotas for the staff and goals for management. There are many practices in education that constrain our ability to tap intrinsic motivation and falsely assume the benefits of extrinsic rewards. They include rigorous and systematic teacher evaluation systems, merit pay, management by objectives, grades, and quantitative goals and quotas. These Deming refers to as forces of destruction. Such approaches are counterproductive for several reasons: setting goals leads to marginal performance; merit pay destroys teamwork; and appraisal of individual performance nourishes fear and increases variability in desired performance.

12. Remove barriers that rob people of pride in their work. Remove the barriers that rob people in leadership of their right to pride in their work. Most people want to do a good job. Effective communication and the elimination of "demotivators"—such as lack of involvement, poor information, the annual or merit rating, and supervisors who do not care—are critical.

13. Institute a vigorous program of education and retraining for everyone. School administrators and staff members must be retrained in new methods of school based management, including group dynamics, consensus building, and collaborative styles of decision making. All stakeholders on the school's team must realize that improvements in student achievement will create higher levels of responsibility, not less responsibility.

14. Put everyone in the organization to work to accomplish the transformation. The school board and superintendent must have a clear plan of action to carry out the quality mission. The quality mission must be internalized by all members of the school organization (school board members, administrators, teachers, support staff, students, parents, community). The transformation is everybody's job (Deming, 1988, pp. 23-24).

Implications for Practice

The concepts formulated by TQM founder, W. Edwards Deming, have been suggested as a basis for achieving excellence in schools. It is based on the assumption that people want to do their best and that it is management's job to enable them to do so by constantly improving the *system* in which they work. It requires teamwork, training, and extensive collection and analysis of data. It is an opportunity to conceptualize a systematic change for school districts and schools.

Transformational Leadership

Building on the work of James McGregor Burns (1978), Bernard Bass (1985) has developed an approach that focuses on both transformational and transactional leadership. Recent research has focused on differentiating transformational leaders from transactional leaders (Bass, Avolio, Jung, & Berson, 2003; Dumdum, Lowe, & Avolio, 2002; Judge & Piccolo, 2004). The more traditional *transactional leadership* involves leader-follower exchanges necessary for achieving agreed upon performance goals between leaders and followers. These exchanges involve four dimensions: contingent reward, management by exception (active), management by exception (passive), and laissez-faire (Bass & Riggio, 2006).

- *Contingent reward:* contracts the exchange of rewards for effort; promises rewards for good performance; recognizes accomplishments.
- *Management by Exception (active):* watches for deviations from rules and standards; takes corrective action.
- *Management by exception (passive):* intervenes only if standards are not met.
- *Laissez-faire:* abdicates responsibilities; avoids making decisions.

Transformational leadership is based on leaders' shifting the values, beliefs, and needs of their followers in three important ways (a) increasing followers awareness of the importance of their tasks and the importance of performing them well; (b) making followers aware of their needs for personal growth, development, and accomplishment; and (c) inspiring followers to transcend their own self-interests for the good of the organization (Bass, 2010).

Transformational leadership has four dimensions: idealized influence, inspirational motivation, intellectual stimulation, and individualized consideration. These four dimensions are often called "the Four Is" (Bass & Riggio, 2006).

- *Idealized influence*: involves behaving in ways that earn the admiration, trust, and respect of followers, causing followers to want to identify with and emulate the leader. Idealized influence is synonymous with *charisma*. For example, Steve Jobs, who founded Apple Computer, showed idealized influence by emphasizing the importance of creating the Macintosh as a radical new computer. He has since followed up with products like the iPod and iPad.
- *Inspirational motivation*: involves behaving in ways that foster enthusiasm for and commitment to a shared vision of the future. Frequently, that vision is transmitted through the use of symbols to focus efforts. As an example, in the movie *Patton*, George C. Scott stood on a stage in front of his troops with a wall-sized American flag in the background and ivory-handled revolvers in holsters at his sides.
- *Intellectual stimulation*: involves behaving in ways that challenge followers to be innovative and creative by questioning assumptions and reframing old situations in new ways. For example, your boss encourages you to "think out of the box," that is, to look at a difficult problem in a new way.
- *Individualized consideration*: involves behaving in ways that help followers achieve their potential through coaching, professional development, and mentoring. For example, your boss stops by your office and makes comments which reinforce your feeling of personal worth and importance in the organization.

The full range of leadership model (transactional and transformational leadership) is depicted in Figure 71.1. As shown in Figure 71.1, laissez-faire is the least effective of the leader behaviors. Leaders using this style are rarely viewed as effective. Management by exception (active or passive) is slightly better than laissez-faire, but it is still considered ineffective leadership. Leaders who practice management by exception leadership either search for deviations from standards and take corrective action or tend to intervene only when there is a problem, which is usually too late. Contingent reward leadership can be an effective style of leadership. The leader attains follower agreement on what needs to be accomplished using promised or actual rewards in exchange for actual performance. Leaders are generally most effective when they regularly use each of the four transformational leadership behaviors: idealized influence, inspirational motivation, intellectual stimulation, and individualized consideration (Bass & Riggio, 2006).

How Transformational Leadership Works

A great deal of research has been done to explain how transformational leadership works. Generally four elements emerge: creativity, goals, vision, and commitment.

Creativity. Transformational leaders are more effective because they are more creative themselves. They are also more effective because they encourage their followers to be more creative as well (Jung, 2001; Jung, Chow, & Wu, 2003). Transformational leaders are proactive rather than reactive; creative rather than compliant; and audacious rather than adherent (Bulach, Lunenburg, & Potter, 2011).

Goals. Goals are another key element in how transformational leadership works. Followers of transformational leaders are more likely to pursue ambitious goals, understand and agree with the formal goals of the organization, and believe that the goals they are pursuing will lead to their own self-fulfillment (Berson & Avolio, 2004).

Vision. Transformational leaders create a strategic vision that energizes and unifies followers (Bennis & Nanus, 2007; Quinn, 2004). They communicate the vision with emotional appeal that captivates followers and other stakeholders (Rafferty & Griffin, 2004). Not only do transformational leaders communicate a vision, they also model the vision. In other words, they "walk the talk" by doing things that enact the vision (Simons, 2002). For example, leaders in higher education (deans, associate deans, department heads) walk the talk by doing research, acquiring grants, and publishing extensively in the research and professional literature alongside faculty members they lead.

Commitment. Making a vision a reality requires followers' commitment. Transformational leaders build commitment to the vision through enthusiasm for every project they tackle; by being persistent in their follow-through on all projects; and by involving followers in the creation of the vision (Dvir, Taly, Kass, & Shamir, 2004).

Transformational leadership is currently the most popular organizational theory and leadership approach. The evidence supporting transformational leadership is impressive. Transformational leadership has been supported in various occupations (for example, school superintendents, school principals, college presidents, naval commanders, military cadets, ministers, shop stewards, sales personnel, and school teachers) and at various job levels. Most of the research on transformational leadership to date has relied on Bass and Avolio's (1997) Multifactor Leadership Questionnaire (MLQ).

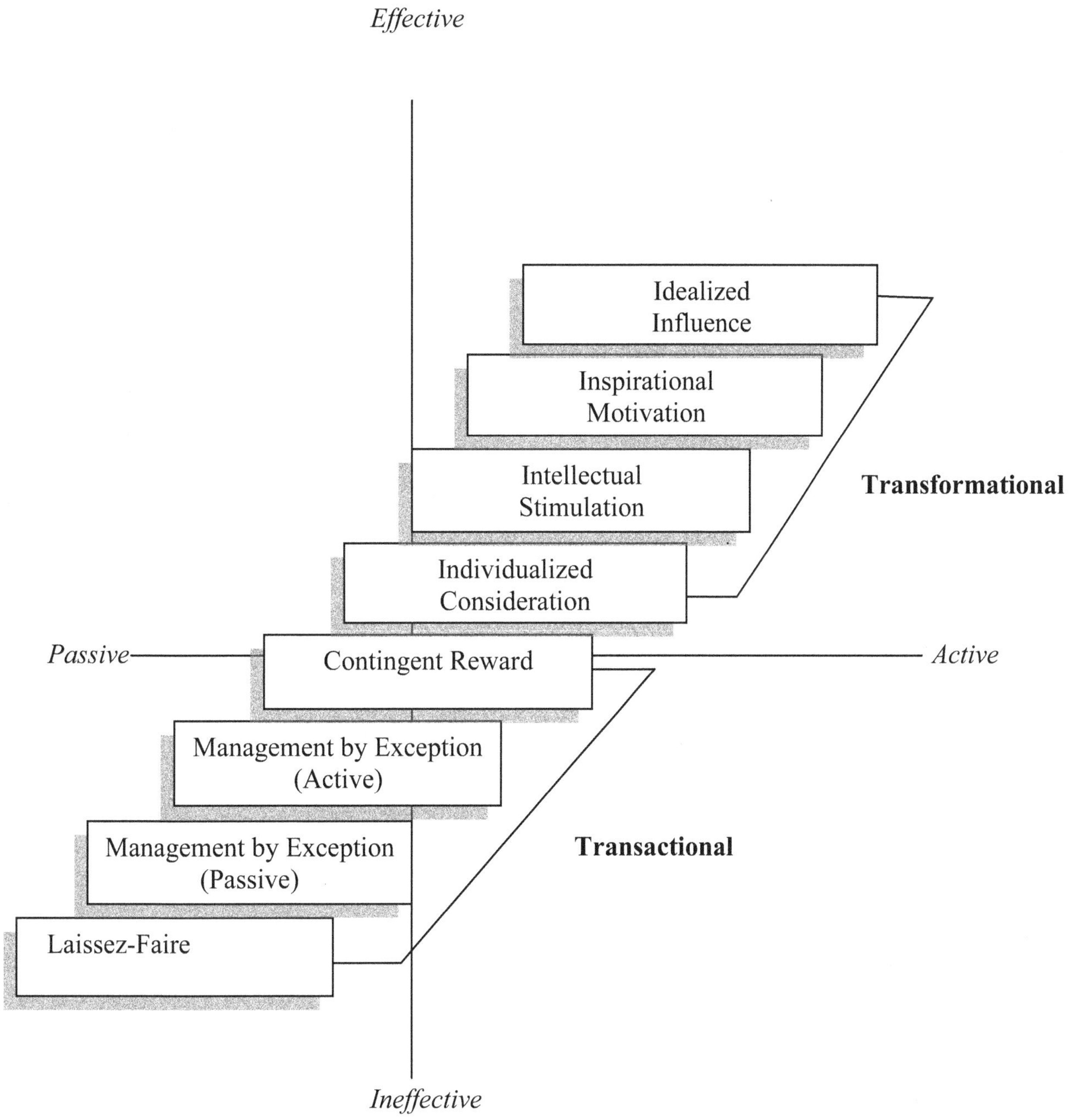

Figure 71.1. Full-range leadership model.

MLQ: Some Research Findings

Bass, Avolio, and their associates (see, e.g., Avolio & Howell, 1992; Bass, 1985, 2010; Bass & Avilio, 1990, 1994; Hater & Bass, 1988; Seltzer & Bass, 1990) found support for the predictive validity of the MLQ. They found significant relationships between transformational leadership and followers' satisfaction with the leader and leader effectiveness. However, there have been some criticisms concerning the measurement adequacy of the MLQ. Bycio, Hackett, and Allen (1995) questioned the validity of the factor structure of the MLQ. Yukl (2010) stated that some of the items of the MLQ measure leader attributes, not leader behaviors. Furthermore, Yukl pointed out some limitations of the research used in developing the MLQ. Sashkin and Burke (1990) stated that the MLQ does not incorporate key components of transformational leadership.

There have been a few studies conducted to assess the factor structure of the MLQ. Bycio et al. (1995) examined a five-factor model that included idealized influence (II or charisma), individualized consideration (IC), intellectual stimulation (IS), and two transactional leadership factors: contingent reward and passive management by exception. They found weak support for the five-factor model. Correlations among the transformational and transactional dimensions were high (0.81 to 0.91). Tepper and Percy (1994) conducted a series of confirmatory factor analyses using an eight-factor model: the "Four Is" (idealized influence, inspirational motivation, intellectual stimulation, and individualized consideration) and four dimensions of transactional leadership (two contingent reward factors and active and passive management-by-exception). The best fitting model consisted of four factors. Idealized influence (II) and inspirational motivation (IM) loaded on a single factor; individualized consideration (IC), intellectual stimulation (IS), and contingent reward each loaded on their own factor. Yammarino and Dubinsky (1994) conducted a principal components factor analysis of the Four Is. They found very high loadings on a single transformational leadership factor and high correlations among the four dimensions (0.70 to 0).

The studies by Bycio et al. (1995), Tepper and Percy (1994), and Yammarino and Dubinsky (1994) support the measurement concerns with the MLQ, especially with the idealized influence (charisma) dimension. However, these three findings should be interpreted with caution. All three studies used earlier versions of the MLQ. Furthermore, neither study considered the theoretical implications of the findings. Therefore, a more rigorous assessment of a more recent version of the MLQ was justified. In many subsequent studies, the full range leadership scale was used.

Three meta-analyses produced more positive findings regarding Bass and Avolio's Four Is. The first meta-analysis of 49 studies indicated that transformational leadership was positively associated with measures of leadership effectiveness and followers' job satisfaction (Dumdum et al., 2002). A second meta-analysis of 87 studies indicated that transformational leadership was positively related to leader effectiveness ratings, group or organizational performance, and followers' job satisfaction and motivation (Judge & Piccolo, 2004). A third meta-analysis of 39 studies revealed that the transformational leadership dimensions of inspirational motivation, individualized consideration, and intellectual stimulation were related to leadership effectiveness in most studies, as well as idealized influence when an organization was in crisis. Moreover, except for the contingent reward dimension, the transactional leadership styles did not result in leadership effectiveness ratings (Lowe, Kroeck, & Sivasubramaniam, 1996). However, until recently, no studies have used the MLQ in school organizations.

MLQ IN SCHOOL ORGANIZATIONS

Three studies in school organizations were conducted to explore the measurement adequacy and factor structure of the MLQ, and to provide guidance for future scale development and refinement (Lunenburg, Thompson, & Pagani, 2010). In Study 1 (Thompson & Lunenburg, 1998), a content adequacy assessment (see Schriesheim, Powers, Scandura, Gardiner, & Lankua, 1993) of the transformational leadership items was conducted. In Study 2 (Thompson & Lunenburg, 2003) and in Study 3 (Pagani & Lunenburg, 2003), a series of confirmatory factor analyses, internal consistency estimates, and correlations were conducted on a revised set of transformational leadership items, using large samples of superintendents, principals, and teachers.

Study 1: Sample, Procedure, and Measure. A content adequacy assessment (Schriesheim et al., 1993) was conducted to examine the extent to which the transformational leadership items adequately represent the respective leadership dimensions. The sample consisted of 64 graduate educational administration students at a public Midwestern university. The researchers administered questionnaires during regular class hours. Completion of the questionnaires took approximately 20 minutes. Verbal instructions, as well as written instructions, were provided prior to administration of the instrument. Responses were anonymous.

Respondents in the current study rated each of the 39 transformational leadership items from the MLQ Form V (Bass & Avolio, 1990) on the extent to which they believed the items were consistent with each of the four dimensions of transformational leadership. Response choices ranged from one (not at all) to five (completely). The definition of one of the four transformational leadership dimensions was presented at the top of each page of the questionnaire followed by a listing of all transformational leadership items. To control for response bias that may occur from order effects, four versions of the questionnaire were administered, each with the definitions presented in a different order. Extreme care was taken to ensure that the definitions were consistent with Bass and Avolio's (1994) conceptualization of the four transformational leadership dimensions. Table 71.2 presents the definitions used for this assessment.

Analyses. To identify those items that were appropriately categorized, an analysis of variance procedure was employed. First, the mean score for each item on each of the four transformational leadership scales was conducted for each item across the four definitions to identify those items that were evaluated appropriately (i.e. statistically significantly higher on the appropriate definition utilizing *t* tests; $p < 0.05$). Although the sample size ($n = 64$) was relatively small, it was felt the sample was quite adequate for assessing the practical significant differences between the means. A larger sample would have produced smaller statistically significant differences that may be less consequential.

Table 71.2. Definitions of Transformational Leadership Dimensions

Idealized influence: Transformational leaders behave in ways that result in their being a role model for their followers. The leaders are admired, respected, and trusted. Followers identify with the leaders and want to emulate them. Among the things the leader does to earn this credit is considering the needs of others over his or her own personal needs. The leader shares the risk with followers and is consistent rather than arbitrary. He or she can be counted on to do the right thing, demonstrating high standards of ethical and moral conduct. He or she avoids using power for personal gain and only when needed.

Inspirational motivation: Transformational leaders behave in ways that motivate and inspire those around them by providing meaning and challenge to their followers' work. Team spirit is aroused. Enthusiasm and optimism are displayed. The leader gets followers involved in envisioning attractive future states. The leader creates clearly communicated expectations that followers want to meet and also demonstrates commitment to goals and shared vision.

Intellectual stimulation: Transformational leaders stimulate their followers' efforts to be innovative and creative by questioning assumptions, reframing problems, and approaching old situations in new ways. Creativity is encouraged. There is no public criticism of individual member's mistakes. New ideas and creative problem solutions are solicited from followers, who are included in the process of addressing problems and finding solutions. Followers are encouraged to try new approaches, and their ideas are not criticized because they differ from the leader's ideas.

Individualized consideration: Transformational leaders pay special attention to each individual's needs for achievement and growth by acting as coach or mentor. Followers and colleagues are developed to successively higher levels of potential. The individually considerate leader listens effectively. The leader delegates tasks as a means of developing followers. Delegated tasks are monitored to see if followers need additional direction or support and to assess progress; ideally, followers do not feel they are being checked.

Results. The results from the content adequacy analysis revealed that 24 of the 39 items were classified correctly. These results provided some support for the Four Is, as four idealized influence items, four inspirational motivation items, eight intellectual stimulation items, and eight individualized consideration items were judged to reflect the proposed leadership dimension. Table 71.3 presents the mean ratings for all items.

Studies 2 and 3: Sample, Procedure, and Measure. The sample for Study 2 consisted of 175 superintendents and 425 principals (Thompson & Lunenburg, 2003). The sample for study 3 included 237 principals and 711 teachers (Pagani & Lunenburg, 2003). In Study 2, each superintendent and three subordinates (principals) completed the MLQ Form V. In Study 3, each principal and three subordinates (teachers) completed Form V of the MLQ. The authors administered questionnaires to respondents by mail. Of the usable questionnaires (65%) were returned. There were no significant mean differences among the three subsamples on any of the variables used in this study. Therefore, all analyses were based on a total sample of 1,062 cases. All participants responded on a voluntary basis and were assured that responses would remain confidential.

The 39 items that comprise the transformational leadership measures of the MLQ were administered to all respondents. However, only the reduced set of items from Study 1 (24 items) was retained for further analysis.

Analyses. First, a confirmatory factor analysis of the 24 items was conducted using LISREL 8.03 (Joreskog & Sorbom, 1993). Internal consistency reliabilities (Cronbach's α) were then computed for each of the revised factors. Finally, correlations among the revised scales were computed to examine the relationships among the dimensions.

Results. Results from a confirmatory factor analysis of the revised scales supported a three-factor model. Using the sample variance-covariance matrix as input and a maximum likelihood solution, the overall chi-square was statistically significant ($\chi^2 = 164.00$; $p < 0.01$). The goodness of fit index was .93, the normed fit index was 0.95, and the root mean square residual for the predicted minus observed correlation matrices was 0.07. Although the chi-square was statistically significant, this finding was not considered problematic, as this statistic is particularly sensitive to sample size (see Bollen, 1989). Moreover, all other indices provided convincing support for a three-factor model.

Descriptive statistics, internal consistency reliability estimates, and correlations among the revised transformational leadership scales are listed in Table 71.4. The internal consistency estimates were adequate (0.82 to 0.87), and the correlations among the revised transformational leadership scales were substantially lower than those found in previous research.

Discussion. The three factors supported by the confirmatory factor analyses in Study 2 and Study 3 appear to be consistent with three of the "Four Is" proposed by Bass. However, a close inspection of the items revealed a narrower behavioral operationalization of transformational leadership, suggesting the MLQ dimensions are too broadly defined as shown in Table 71.5.

A deemphasis on the importance of idealized influence (charisma) in stable school organizations as a component of transformational leadership seems appropriate, with a focus, instead, on specific, identifiable leadership behaviors. The idealized influence dimension was derived from the study of charismatic leadership, characterized by extraordinary leaders who

Table 71.3. Mean Ratings
From Content Adequacy Assessment for Study 1

ITEM	II	IM	IS	IC
II1	**3.99**	3.90	2.84	3.16
IM1	**3.98**	**4.39**	3.29	3.66
IS1	**2.99**	3.09	**4.69**	3.03
IC1	3.30	2.84	3.84	**4.67**
II2	3.90	4.39	3.29	3.50
IM2	3.01	4.34	4.36	3.14
IS2	2.84	2.80	**4.59**	3.01
IC2	3.51	3.08	3.73	**4.59**
II3	3.91	4.27	3.02	3.79
IM3	3.53	**4.68**	3.22	3.40
IS3	2.90	3.03	**5.06**	3.45
IC3	3.43	2.51	3.02	**4.78**
II4	**4.78**	2.81	2.60	3.01
IM4	3.70	**4.64**	3.30	3.91
IS4	2.51	2.72	**4.69**	2.81
IC4	3.30	2.81	3.21	**4.84**
II5	4.40	4.03	2.82	3.12
IM5	3.99	4.03	3.82	4.43
IS5	2.91	2.68	**4.69**	3.06
IC5	3.1	3.05	3.22	**4.87**
II6	**3.98**	3.01	2.37	2.62
IM6	3.20	3.09	2.34	3.76
IS6	2.81	3.03	**4.69**	3.31
IC6	3.60	2.91	3.43	**4.79**
II7	3.56	4.27	2.99	3.26
IM7	3.54	**4.59**	3.21	3.36
IS7	3.24	3.22	4.67	**4.43**
IC7	3.29	3.09	3.46	3.52
II8	3.56	3.37	2.69	3.02
IM8	3.01	3.41	2.64	3.23
II9	3.38	4.76	2.66	3.11
IM9	3.44	**4.98**	3.01	2.65
IS9	2.78	2.91	**4.89**	3.35
IC8	3.42	2.66	3.70	**4.93**
II10	**4.53**	3.63	3.01	3.27
IM10	4.21	3.87	2.98	3.06
IS9	2.76	2.63	**4.96**	3.01
IC9	3.36	2.96	2.86	**4.58**
IS10	3.37	3.12	3.09	3.01

Table 71.4. Means, *SD*, Internal Consistency Reliability Estimates, and Correlations Among Revised MLQ Scales

Mean	*SD*	α	1	2	3	4	5
IM	2.27	1.11	0.87				
IS	2.17	0.93	0.81	0.66			
IC	1.74	1.15	0.86	0.66	0.69		

Note: Correlations 0.26 and above are significant at $p < 0.01$; IM = inspirational motivation; IS = intellectual stimulation; IC = individualized consideration.

emerge during a crisis or major change (Yukl, 2010). It has been highly correlated with the inspirational motivation dimension (see, e.g., Hinkin & Tracy, 1999; Yammarino & Dubinski, 1994).

Despite the shortcomings of the MLQ, it appears that Bass and his colleagues have identified several leader behaviors that appear to be components of transformational leadership. A confirmatory factor

Table 71.5. Questionnaire Items From the Multifactor Leadership Questionnaire

Idealized influence
1. Talks to us about his/her most important values and beliefs
5. Emphasizes the importance of being committed to our beliefs
9. Specifies the importance of having a strong sense of purpose
25. Clarifies the central purpose underlying our actions
29. Talks about how trusted each other can help us to overcome our difficulties
31. Emphasizes the importance of having a collective sense of mission
17. *Displays conviction in his/her ideals, beliefs, and values*
13. *Considers the moral and ethical consequences of his/her actions*
21. *Takes a stand on difficult issues*
35. *Behaves in ways that are consistent with his/her expressed values*

Inspirational motivation
1. Sets high standards
6. Envisions exciting new possibilities
18. Provides continuous encouragement
22. Focuses my attention on "what it takes" to be successful
30. Makes me aware of essential work-related issues
36. Shows determination to accomplish what he/she sets out to do
14. *Expresses his/her confidence that we will achieve our goals*
10. *Talks optimistically about the future*
26. *Talks enthusiastically about what needs to be accomplished*
32. *Articulates a compelling vision of the future*

Intellectual stimulation
27. Encourages me to express my ideas and opinions
39. Encourages addressing problems by using reasoning and evidence, rather than unsupported opinion
15. *Questions the traditional ways of doing things*
3. *Emphasizes the value of questioning assumptions*
7. *Reexamines critical assumptions to question whether they are appropriate*
11. *Encourages us to rethink ideas, which had never been questions*
19. *Seeks differing perspectives when solving problems*
23. *Suggest new ways to look at problems from different angles*
33. *Gets me to look at problems from different angles*
37. *Encourages nontraditional thinking to deal with traditional problems*

Individualized consideration
28. Teaches me how to identify the needs and capabilities of others
4. *Treats me as an individual rather than just a member of a group*
16. *Focuses me on developing my strengths*
24. *Treats each of us as individuals with different needs, abilities, and aspirations*
34. *Promotes self-development*
38. *Gives personal attention to members who seem neglected*
8. *Listens attentively to my concerns*
12. *Provides useful advice for my development*
20. *Spends time teaching and coaching me*

Note: Number denotes item number on questionnaire. Items in italics were retained as a result of content validity analysis.

analysis of the MLQ using data from the aforementioned public school studies (n = 693) supported a three-factor model of transformational leadership (Lunenburg et al., 2010). The three factors supported by the confirmatory factor analysis appear to be consistent with three of the "Four Is" proposed by Bass. The first dimension, "intellectual stimulation," might be more appropriately defined as nontraditional approaches to problems. The second dimension, "individualized consideration," may be better thought of as individualized development. Dimension three, "inspirational motivation," might be better described as articulating a future orientation.

Implications for Practice

There are several important implications that can be derived from the studies of transformational leadership. Previous research has found transformational leadership to be positively related to leader effectiveness ratings, group or organizational performance, and follower job satisfaction and motivation (Bennis & Nanus, 2007; Dumdum et al., 2002; Judge & Piccolo, 2004; Yukl, 2010). However, idealized influence, or charisma, may not be relevant for leaders in stable public school environments.

Some researchers have begun to explore the idea that idealized influence, or charisma, may be more appropriate in some situations than in others (Egri & Herman, 2000; Pawar & Eastman, 1997). For instance, idealized influence is probably more appropriate when organizations are in crisis and need to adapt than when environmental conditions are stable; that is, when dissatisfaction is high and value congruence and unquestioned obedience are needed to ensure organizational survival (Bulach et al., 2011; Hinken & Tracey, 1999). This line of thinking is consistent with several contingency theories of leadership proposing that individuals must modify their behavior to fit the situation or find a situation that fits their leadership style (e.g., Evans, 1970; Fiedler, 1967; House, 1971; Irby, Brown, Duffy, & Trautman, 2002). Clearly, studying transformational leadership in turbulent environments might lead to a better understanding of idealized influence, or charisma, as implied also by the studies of Bycio et al. (1995) and Keller (1992).

However, the other three dimensions of transformational leadership (inspirational motivation, intellectual stimulation, and individualized consideration) may be very important in achieving leader effectiveness. This approach would be in agreement with Bennis and Nanus (2007), who studied 90 innovative leaders in industry and the public sector and found that articulating a vision of the future; emphasis on organizational and individual learning; and the development of commitment and trust were factors that characterized transformational leaders. These results are consistent with the three public school studies reported earlier. Similarly, Yukl (2010) describes transformational leadership as influencing major changes in organization members and building commitment for the organization's goals. Thus, educational leaders should communicate a sense of where the organization is going, develop the skills and abilities of followers, and encourage innovative problem solving.

CONCLUSION

In the broadest sense, the usefulness of organization theory in the field is its search for a conceptual formula that can open the secrets of successful organizations. It is an attempt to create organizations with sensitivity to internal and external changes; best management styles or practices; increased capacity for organizational learning; greater opportunities for the individual growth and fulfillment of its members; and ultimately organization success (Senge, 2006, 2011). In this chapter, I examined five contemporary organizational theories of recent vintage: leader-member exchange theory, reciprocal influence theory, substitutes for leadership theory, total quality management, and transformational leadership.

REFERENCES

Avolio, B. J., & Howell, J. M. (1992). The impact of leader behavior and leader-follower personality match on satisfaction and unit performance. In K. E. Clark, M. B. Clark, & D. R. Campbell (Eds.). *Impact of leadership* (pp. 227-256). Greensboro, NC: The Center for Creative Leadership.

Bass, B. M. (1985). *Leadership and performance beyond expectations*. New York, NY: Free Press.

Bass, B. M. (2010). *Bass and Stogdill's handbook of leadership: Theory, research, and managerial applications* (5th ed.). New York, NY: Simon & Schuster.

Bass, B. M., & Avolio, B. J. (1990). *Multifactor leadership questionnaire*. Palo Alto, CA: Consulting Psychologist Press.

Bass, B. M., & Avolio, B. J. (1994). *Improving organizational effectiveness through transformational leadership*. Thousand Oaks, CA: SAGE.

Bass, B. M., & Avolio, B. J. (1997). *Full range leadership development: Manual for the multifactor leadership questionnaire*. Palo Alto, CA: Mindgarden.

Bass, B. M., Avolio, B. J., Jung, D. I., & Berson, Y. (2003). Predicting unit performance by assessing transformational and transactional leadership. *Journal of Applied Psychology, 88*, 207-218.

Bass, B. M., & Riggio, R. E. (2006). *Transformational Leadership* (2nd ed.). Mahwah, NJ: Erlbaum.

Bennis, W., & Nanus, B. (2007). *Leaders: The strategies for taking charge*. New York, NY: HarperCollins.

Berson, Y., & Avolio, B. J. (2004). Transformational leadership and the dissemination of organizational goals: A case study of a telecommunications firm. *Leadership Quarterly, 15*, 625-646.

Blankstein, A. M. (2010). *Failure is not an option: Six principles for making student success the ONLY option*. Thousand Oaks, CA: Corwin Press.

Bollen, K. A. (1989). *Structural equations with latent variables*. New York, NY: Wiley.

Bonstingl, J. J. (2001). *Schools of quality* (3rd ed.). Thousand Oaks, CA: Corwin Press.

Bulach, C., Lunenburg, F. C., & Potter, L. (2011). *Creating a culture for high-performing Schools: A comprehensive approach to school reform* (2nd ed.). Lanham, MD: Rowman & Littlefield.

Burns, J. M. (1978). *Leadership*. New York, NY: Harper & Row.

Bycio, P., Hackett, R. D., & Allen, J. S. (1995). Further assessments of Bass's (1985) conceptualization of transactional and transformational leadership. *Journal of Applied Psychology, 80*, 468-478.

Chen, Z., Lam, W., & Zhong, J.A. (2007). Leader-member exchange and member performance: A look at individual-level negative feedback- seeking behaviors and team-level empowerment culture. *Journal of Applied Psychology, 92*, 202-212.

Comer, J. P. (2000). *Child by child: The Comer process for change in education*. New York, NY: Teachers College Press.

Comer, J. P. (2006). *Leave no child behind: Preparing today's youth for tomorrow's world*. New Haven, CT: Yale University Press.

Darling-Hammond, L. (2010). *The flat world and education: How America's commitment to equity will determine our future*. New York, NY: Teachers College Press.

Deming, W. E. (1988). *Out of the crisis*. Cambridge, MA: MIT Press.

Deming, W. E. (2000). *Out of the crisis* (Rev. ed.). Cambridge, MA: MIT Press.

DuFour, R., & Eaker, R. (1998). *Professional learning communities at work: Best practices for enhancing student achievement.* Bloomington, IN: Solution Tree.

DuFour, R., DuFour, R., & Eaker, R. (2008). *Revisiting professional learning communities at work: New insights for improving schools.* Bloomington, IN: Solution Tree.

Dumdum, U. R., Lowe, K. B., & Avolio, B. J. (2002). A meta-analysis of transformational and transactional leadership correlates of effectiveness and satisfaction: An update and extension. In B. J. Avolio & F. J. Yammarino (Eds.). *Transactional and charismatic leadership: The road ahead* (pp. 35-66). New York, NY: JAI Press.

Dunn, R., & Dunn, K. (1992). *Teaching students through their individual learning styles: Practical approaches for grades 3-12* (2 vols.). Needham Heights, MA: Allyn & Bacon.

Dunn, R., Dunn, K., & Perrin, J. (1994). *Teaching young children through their individual learning styles: Practical approaches for Grades K-2.* Needham Heights, MA: Allyn & Bacon.

Dvir, T., Taly, N., Kass, N., & Shamir, B. (2004). The emotional band: Vision and organizational commitment among high-tech employees. *Journal of Organizational Change Management, 17,* 127-143.

Eden, D. (1992). Leadership and expectations: Pygmalion effects and other self-fulfilling prophesies in organizations. *Leadership Quarterly, 3*(4), 271-305.

Egri, C. P., & Herman, S. (2000). Leadership in the North American environmental sector: Values, leadership styles, and contexts of environmental leaders and their organizations. *Academy of Management Journal, 43,* 571-604.

Epstein, J. L. (2010). *School, family, and community partnerships: Preparing educators and improving schools* (2nd ed.). Boulder, CO: Westview Press.

Evans, M. G. (1970). The effects of supervisory behavior on the path-goal relationship. *Organizational Behavior and Human Performance, 5,* 227-298.

Fiedler, F. (1967). *A theory of leadership effectiveness.* New York, NY: McGraw-Hill.

Gardner, H. (1993). *Frames of mind: The theory of multiple intelligences.* New York, NY: Basic Books.

Gerstner, C. R., & Day, D. V. (1997). Meta-analytic review of leader-member exchange theory: Correlates and construct issues. *Journal of Applied Psychology, 82*(6), 827-844.

Graen, G. B., & Uhl-Bien, M. (1995). Relationship-based approach to leadership: Development of leadership leader-member exchange (LMX) theory over 25 years: Applying a multi-level multi-domain perspective. *Leadership Quarterly, 6,* 219-247.

Hater, J. J., & Bass, B. (1988). Superiors' evaluations and subordinates' perceptions of transformational and transactional leadership. *Journal of Applied Psychology, 73,* 695-702.

Hinken, T. R., & Tracey, B. T. (1999). The relevance of charisma for transformational leadership in stable organizations. *Journal of Organizational Change Management, 12,* 105-119.

House, R. J. (1971). A path-goal theory of leadership effectiveness. *Administrative Science Quarterly, 16,* 321-339.

Howard, T. G. (2011). *Why race and culture matter in schools: Closing the achievement gap in America's classrooms.* New York, NY: Teachers College Press.

Hovell, J. P., & Dorfman, P.W. (1986). Leadership and substitutes for leadership among professional and nonprofessional workers. *Journal of Applied Behavioral Science, 22,* 29-46.

Ilies, R., Nahrgang, J. D., & Morgeson, F. P. (2007). Leader–member exchange and citizenship behaviors: a meta-analysis. *Journal of Applied Psychology, 92,* 269-277.

Irby, B. J., Brown, G., Duffy, J. A., & Trautman, D. (2002). The synergistic leadership theory. *Journal of Educational Administration, 40,* 304-322.

Joreskog, K. G., & Sorbom, D. (1993). *LISREL 8.03.* Morrisville, IN: Scientific Software.

Judge, T. A., & Piccolo, R. F. (2004). Transformational and transactional leadership: A meta-analytic test of their relative validity. *Journal of Applied Psychology, 89,* 755-768.

Jung, D. I. (2001). Transformational and transactional leadership and their effects on creativity in groups. *Creativity Research Journal, 13,* 185-195.

Jung, D. I., Chow, C., & Wu, A. (2003). The role of transformational leadership in enhancing innovation: Hypotheses and some preliminary findings. *Leadership Quarterly, 14,* 525-544.

Keller, R. T. (1992). Transformational leadership and the performance of research and development project groups. *Journal of Management, 18,* 489-501.

Kerr, S., & Jermier, J.M. (1978). Substitutes for leadership: Their meaning and measurement. *Organizational Behavior and Human Performance, 22,* 375-403.

Levin, H. M. (1986). *Accelerated schools for at-risk students* (CPRHE Research report RR-010). New Brunswick, NJ: Rutgers University, Center for Policy Research in Education.

Liden, R. C., Erdogan, B., Wayne, S. J., & Sparrowe, R. T. (2006). Leader-member exchange, differentiation, and task interdependence: Implications for individual and group performance. *Journal of Organizational Behavior, 27*(6), 723-746.

Lowe, K. B., Kroeck, K. G., & Sivasubramaniam, N. (1996). Effectiveness correlates of transformational and transactional leadership: A meta-analytic review of the MLQ literature. *Leadership Quarterly, 7,* 385-425.

Lunenburg, F. C. (2000). Collective bargaining in the public schools: Issues, tactics, and new strategies. *Journal of Collective Negotiations, 29*(4), 259-272.

Lunenburg, F. C. (2011). Early childhood education: Implications for school readiness. *Schooling, 2*(1), 1-8.

Lunenburg, F. C., & Irby, B. J. (2006). *The principalship: Vision to action.* Belmont, CA: Wadsworth Cengage Learning.

Lunenburg, F. C., Thompson, B., & Pagani, D. (2010, May). *Transformational leadership: Factor structure of the MLQ in public school organizations.* Paper presented at the annual meeting of the American Educational Research Association, Denver, CO.

Pagani, D., & Lunenburg, F. C. (2003, April). *Principals' transformational leadership styles, school accountability ratings, and school district financial and demographic factors.* Paper presented at the annual meeting of the American Educational Research Association, Chicago, IL.

Paige, R. (2011). *The Black-White achievement gap: Why closing it is the greatest civil rights issue of our time.* New York, NY: Amacom.

Pawar, B. S., & Eastman, K. K. (1997). The nature and implications of contextual influences on transformational leadership: A conceptual examination. *Academy of Management Review, 22*, 80-109.

Popham, W. J. (2010a). *Educational assessment: What school leaders need to understand*. Thousand Oaks, CA: Corwin Press.

Popham, W. J. (2010b). *Classroom assessment: What teachers need to know.* Upper Saddle River, Nj: Prentice Hall.

Quinn, R. E. (2004). *Building the bridge as you walk on it: A guide for leading change.* San Francisco, CA: Jossey-Bass.

Rafferty, A. E., & Griffin, M. A. (2004). Dimensions of transformational leadership: Conceptual and empirical extensions. *Leadership Quarterly, 15*, 329-354.

Sashkin, M., & Burke, W. W. (1990). Understanding and assessing organizational leadership. In K. E. Clark & M. B. Clark (Eds.), *Measures of leadership* (pp. 227-256). West Orange, NJ: Leadership Library of America.

Schriessheim, C. C., Powers, K. J., Scandura, T. A., Gardiner, C. C., & Lankua, M. J. (1993). Improving construct measurement in management research: Comments and a quantitative approach for assessing the theoretical adequacy of paper-and-pencil survey-type instruments. *Journal of Management, 19*, 385-417.

Seltzer, J., & Bass, B. M. (1990). Transformational leadership: Beyond initiation and structure. *Journal of Management, 16*, 693-704.

Senge, P. (2006). *The fifth discipline: The art and practice of the learning organization* (Rev. ed.). New York, NY: Doubleday.

Senge, P. (2011). *Schools that learn: A fifth discipline fieldbook for educators, parents, and everyone who cares about education.* New York, NY: Knopf Doubleday.

Shores, C. (2009). *A comprehensive RTI model: Integrating behavioral and academic interventions.* Thousand Oaks, CA: Corwin Press.

Simons, T. (2002). Behavioral integrity: The perceived alignment between managers' words and deeds as a research focus. *Organization Science, 13*, 18-35.

Slavin, R. E., & Madden, N. A. (2009). *2 million children: Success for all*. Thousand Oaks, CA: Corwin.

Starke, F. A. (2001). *Management: leading people and organizations in the 21st century.* Upper Saddle River, NJ: Prentice Hall.

Szilagi, A. D. (2010) *Management and performance*. Upper Saddle River, NJ: Addison-Wesley.

Tepper, B. T., & Percy, P. M. (1994). Structural validity of the Multifactor Leadership Questionnaire. *Educational and Psychological Measurement, 59*, 734-744.

Thompson, B., & Lunenburg, F. C. (1998, April). *A content adequacy assessment of transformational leadership items on the MLQ*. Paper presented at the annual meeting of the American Educational Research Association, San Diego, CA.

Thompson, B., & Lunenburg, F. C. (2003, April). *Superintendents' transformational leadership styles, school accountability ratings, and school district financial and demographic factors.* Paper presented at the annual meeting of the American Educational Research Association, Chicago, IL.

Yammarino, F. J., & Dubinsky, A. J. (1994). Transformational leadership theory: using levels of analysis to determine boundary conditions. *Personnel Psychology, 47*, 787-811.

Yukl, G. A. (2010). *Leadership in organizations* (4th ed.). Upper Saddle River, NJ: Prentice Hall.

Author Contact Information: Fred C. Lunenburg, PhD, Merchant Professor of Education, Sam Houston State University, 1908 Bobby K. Marks Drive, Box 2119, Huntsville, TX 77341-2119. Telephone: 939-294-3838. E-mail: edu_fcl@shsu.edu

CHAPTER 72

Organizational Theory in Light of Constructivist Thinking

Arthur Shapiro and Steve Permuth
University of South Florida

We do not see things as they are;
We see things as we are.

—The Talmud

The twenty-first century will mature into a constructivist's view of the value derived from learning from humanities' twentieth century mistakes.

—John "Jack" Hunt, *Educator*

The behavior of an organization often can be predicted by assuming it to be controlled by a cabal of its enemies.

— Robert Conquest's Law

The purpose of this chapter is to hold constructivist theory and practice aloft as a prism to shed light on the role of organizational theory in analyzing and evaluating the functioning and operations of organizations. To achieve this, the chapter, like Gaul, is divided into three parts. The first two briefly deal with the philosophic roots of and the nature of constructivism. The third applies constructivist philosophy, theory, and practice to analyze organizational theory/functioning and operations, particularly as they apply to educational organizations.

The Roots of Constructivism: A Quick Peek

Although the actual use of the word constructivism is relatively recent, constructivist thinking was first articulated by Bishop Nicole D'Oresme in 1377. "In his musical aesthetics, Oresme formulated a modern subjective 'theory of perception', which was not the perception of objective beauty of God's creation, but the constructive process of perception, which causes the perception of beauty or ugliness in the senses. Therefore, we can see that every individual perceives another 'world'" (Taschow, 2003). Four hundred years later, this followed by eighteenth century Immanuel Kant. As philosopher D. C. Phillips (2000, p. 8) noted, Kant "argued that certain aspects of our knowledge of the physical universe (time and space, for example) were the products of our own cognitive apparatus—we 'construct' the universe to have certain properties, or, rather, our faculty of understanding imposes those temporal and spatial properties on our experience."

Descarte (1637) claimed that he shed all of his beliefs and started with, "I think, therefore, I am." Rousseau (1762) and Pestalozzi (Biber, 1831) believed that students learn through their senses, therefore contributing to developing constructivist thought. In the twentieth century, Piaget (1954) asserted that the child constructs his own reality (which often differs substantially from that of the adult world) as witnessed by the title of his empirically based book, *The Construction of Reality in the Child.* Although not using the word constructivism, Dewey, Bruner, Freire, and Vygotsky are cited by Marlow and Page (1998, pp. 13-19) as major contributors to developing constructivist thought. George Herbert Mead (Dewey's colleague at the University of Chicago and founder of the school of Symbolic Interactionism in social psychology), and Gardner contributed to the development of constructivist thought.

The Nature of Constructivist Thinking

Phillips (2000, pp. 6-7), commissioned by the National Society for the Study of Education to edit a book con-

The Handbook of Educational Theories, pp. 855–869

cerning opinions on constructivism in education, noted "constructivism" refers to at least two quite different concepts. In the first concept, "constructivism" embodies a thesis about the disciplines or bodies of knowledge that have been built up during the course of human history. In the second case, constructivism refers to a set of views about how individuals learn (and about how those who help them learn ought to teach).

It is best to begin by dealing with aspects of constructivism's view concerning how people learn. In Part 3 of the paper, constructivist theory and practice will be used to analyze key bodies of knowledge regarding organizations. Phillips notes that constructivist thinking about how people learn has led to two strands, psychological constructivism and social constructivism. This chapter briefly focuses first on psychological constructivism.

Psychological Constructivism: Moderate and Radical

Psychological constructivism concerns itself with psychological understandings of the individual. That is, it deals with how individuals learn, how people develop their knowledge, their perceptions, their concepts and attitudes. Phillips notes:

> Roughly, this … type of constructivist view is that learners actively construct their own ("internal," as some would say) sets of meaning or understandings; knowledge is not a mere copy of the external world, nor is knowledge acquired by passive absorption or by simple transference from one person (a teacher) to another (a learner or knower). In sum, knowledge is *made*, not *acquired*. (2000, p. 7)

Succinctly, each of us builds our perceptions, our understandings of new concepts, ideas, symbols, facts, and attitudes based on our existing bodies of knowledge and attitudes, in essence, through the prisms of our backgrounds and experience. Further support is in sociologists Berger and Luckman's *The Social Construction of Reality* (1966) asserting that people construct their own realities within and in accord with the society and culture in which they are raised. People's construction of their realities is culturally based upon such factors as age, gender, socioeconomic class, subculture, rural, urban, or suburban background, and their experiences. Consequently, people develop varying perceptions, views, expectations of such fundamentals as their families, people, money, education and school, work, politics, religion, art, sports, and other cultural components as they develop different experiences with these and other phenomena. Thus, each of us perceives the world differently based upon all these factors. One might conjecture that this does not apply to twins, but does it? My wife, who is an older twin, can recognize 9 out of 10 times which twin is older since their behaviors are significant symbols to her. Her younger twin does not perceive that as significant, so is virtually unaware of behaviors onto which her older sister keys.

Radical psychological constructivist thought is best analyzed by von Glasersfeld (1998, p. 1) who asserts that his understanding of the concept of blue may differ from my understanding which he notes "is a profoundly shocking view." Phillips and von Glasersfeld are both stating that

> we cannot be certain that any two individuals will construct the same understandings; even if they use the same linguistic formulations to express what they have learned, their deep understandings might be quite different. (Phillips 2000, p. 7)

This viewpoint is correct since no one can share the experiences and perceive the same things similarly. However, von Glasersfeld misses the key processes that make us human, that make us become social animals, i.e., the great power of culture and its underpinning vehicle of language, which itself is a socially constructed phenomenon. Mead (1934) pointed out that the human mind, the self we all form, and our society are all socially formed.

Social Constructivism: Moderate and Radical

This second form of constructivism is central to this analysis as it deals with organizations, which sociologists perceive as socially constructed, shared realities. Phillips identifies this second form of constructivism stating that it

> embodies a thesis about the disciplines or bodies of knowledge that have been built up during the course of human history. I have described this thesis as, roughly, that these disciplines (or public bodies of knowledge) are human constructs, and that the form that knowledge has taken in these fields has been determined by such things as politics, ideologies, values, the exertion of power and preservation of status, religious beliefs, and economic self-interest. This thesis denies that the disciplines are objective reflections of an "external world." (2000, p. 6)

Moderate social constructivism holds that the *social world* is socially constructed, as Berger and Luckman's (1966) title, *The Social Construction of Reality*, implies. For example, a high school's customs and rituals, such as homecoming queens, cheerleaders, football games, did not exist 150 years ago. National Board certification and the National Merit program comprise recent social constructs, as does the emergence of day care.

Radical social constructivists push the envelope very hard. Their "strong program in the sociology of knowledge" believes

> That the form that knowledge takes in a discipline can be *fully explained*, or *entirely accounted for*, in sociological terms. That is, ... what is taken to be knowledge is any field has been determined by sociological forces including the influence of ideologies, religion, human interests, group dynamics, and so forth ... this group of thinkers wishes to deny that so-called knowledge is in any sense a reflection or copy of that "external reality" that the community in question is investigating. (Phillips, 2000, pp. 8-9)

While this chapter will not deal with this form of constructivism, which has led to the "science wars," but rather with moderate social constructivism, it is worthwhile to note Phillips' point that the major concepts of the sciences did not drop from heaven like manna. They were and are developed:

> It should be clear that the concepts we use, whether in everyday or in the scholarly disciplines, did not descend—fully formed—out of the blue. There was a time when the concepts of "energy" or "mass" or "molecule" or "psychosis" or "working class" did not exist; and the halting and interactive process can be traced by which these concepts and the very things or categories themselves were developed. (2000, p. 88)

Applying Constructivist Thinking to Organizational Theory/ Functioning Operations

Sociologists perceive organizations as *socially created, shared realities*, since humans construct organizations to achieve certain purposes.

Characteristics of Behavior in Constructivist Organizations as Criteria for Evaluating Organizational Theories

Interestingly, when a graduate class in Educational Leadership was asked to describe characteristics and behavior in constructivist organizations, they cited Maslow's hierarchy of needs as starting points, as did Shapiro (1995, 1996, 2000). Other sources include:

- A structured environment with extensive use of groups (Maslow's, 1954, third level of social needs; Shapiro, 1996, 2000);
- Respect/acceptance (Maslow's fourth level, esteem needs), authentic relationships (Hills, 1975; Poplin & Weeres, 1993);
- Safety (Maslow's second level, safety needs);
- Focus on the construction of meaning (Lambert, Collay, Dietz, Kent, & Richert, 1996; Mead, 1934), that is, sensemaking, fundamental to establishing meaning and a culture in any organization;
- Establish a trusting environment (Bryk & Schneider, 2002; Lambert et al., 1996);
- Create a culture which is people centered, caring, valuing all people (Shapiro, 1996, 2000); reaches everyone where they are (Dewey, 1938);
- Establish a community (Lambert et al., 1996), establish a learning community (Lambert et al., 1996; Senge, 1990);
- Empowerment (Isaacson, 2004; Macy, 1994-1995), involving people in a significant enterprise that has meaning (Bass, 1985);
- Multiply roles to increase involvement (Thelen, 1949); and
- Bottom-up decision making

This next section deals with a number of major formulations concerning organizational theory, functioning, and operations against which constructivist criteria can be applied. It starts with Barnard's fundamental contributions (1938), social systems theory (Parsons & Shills, 1951) and several formulations of leadership including synergistic leadership (Irby, Brown, Duffy, & Trautman, 2002), and constructivist leadership (Lambert et al., 1995; Lambert et al. 1996; Shapiro, 2003, 2008). Taylorism (F.W. Taylor, 1911), Theory X, Y (McGregor, 1960), and Z (Ouchi, 1981) will be analyzed, as will the Ohio State Studies (Stogdill & Coons, 1957) and the Managerial Grid (Blake & Mouton, 1985). The tripartite theory of organizational change and succession by Wilson, Byar, Shapiro, and Schell (1969) will be analyzed in the section of leadership, although it is an organizational theory since it also includes a theory which predicts leadership succession and change. Servant leadership (Greenleaf, 1977), transformational leadership (Burns, 1978), and others will follow. Next analyzed are Morgan's (1977) images of organizations including the fundamental social science construct of culture, with Lewin's (1952) and Deming's (1982) contributions to the theory and practice of change and decision making. Next are Mintzberg's (1979) contributions to organizational thinking, particularly his logo, then roles, role expectations, role conflict, the Getzels-Guba (1957) idiographic and nomothetic model, and Weick's (1976, March) notion of organizations as loosely or tightly coupled. Additionally, in view of the pervasive, widespread, almost unconscious impact of behaviorist thinking such as Taylorism (F.W. Taylor, 1911) today, the theory and consequences will be utilized to compare and contrast its thinking with constructivist thinking. No analysis of organizations makes sense without dealing with such eternal verities as trust (Bryk & Schneider, 2002), and power, authority and influence (Weber, 1946; Bierstedt, 1950). Last, critical theory will be mentioned.

Barnard

Barnard, the chief economic officer of Bell Labs, is widely perceived as the father of administration. In *Functions of the Executive* (1938), he structured three interlocking essential functions of any executive, the first to facilitate creating a common purpose. The second is to facilitate creating a system of communications as direct as possible to enable development of a common purpose. Third is to facilitate creating a system of cooperation to achieve the common purpose. All are essential to the health and effective functioning of any organization, since without shared purposes, organizations experience great difficulties achieving them (somewhat of an understatement). Barnard also changed the way we look at organizations from viewing an organization as its structure, that is, literally its table of organization, to the informal social systems which protect the individual from the organization and which are key to its achieving its common purpose, its effective communications and its system of cooperation. These formulations are bottom-up. Without a system of cooperation and a system of communication, it is impossible to create a common purpose to which people can be loyal and cooperate to achieve it (or them), a constructivist phenomenon. Barnard's recognition of small groups/social systems as the basis of functioning of any organization is a fundamental insight to constructivist thought since it establishes the vital role of social systems in every culture and society. This is the key to establishing a community, which rests on trust, another key constructivist criterion. This understanding of Barnard also values the individual. Underlying Barnard is respect for individuals and empowering them.

Barnard also was quite insistent that administrators operate in a climate of morality, an interesting caveat these days when many subordinates tend to be suspicious of top level administrators' loyalty to troops on the bottom, and constructivist in that respect, acceptance and authentic relationships are involved.

Systems Theory and Social Systems Theory

Manifestly, organizations are systems, defined as a set of interrelated elements that function as a unit for a specific purpose or purposes (Lunenburg & Ornstein, 2008). Systems theory treats organizations and other systems as a gestalt, perceiving their elements as interrelated, useful in understanding them as wholes. Social systems, usually perceived as dealing with people, consist of two or more people in meaningful interaction, (Parsons & Shills, 1951) comprise the basic human unit, the basic unit of all organizations, a key social science concept. All organizations are composed of a series of small groups of people who hang together, who develop alliances with each other. That is, the social system is the fundamental unit of structure in all organizations (Barnard, 1938; Parsons & Shills, 1951). Observing social systems is a key requirement for people to operate effectively in organizations, as it tells us who has relationships with each other, who has power and influence and authority, to whom to go to get things done. The astute leader quickly learns which people will want to and/or be able to work together, and which people to avoid at all costs in working together, as well as who trusts whom.

The number of social systems in organizations almost boggles the mind. In a small social system of 5 people, we find 10 dyads (2s), 6 triads (3s), 5 social systems of 4s, and a fifth consisting of the entire social system. This totals 22 different social systems, merely in a single small group of five people. If a school has a staff of 35 or 40 people, let alone one with a hundred or more, the number of social systems is huge. But, we are pretty astute in that we can usually pick out key social systems in an organization or faculty and learn which to approach to get different things done. And, as Barnard (1938) cogently put it, social systems act to protect individuals from the organization. Easton (1965) noted that virtually all organizations develop relationships and interact with other organization: they are open. Except for closed cloistered communities, this applies to all organizational entities.

The social system construct fits like a glove into constructivist thought. It *is* the group, and much of the other criteria listed above apply. We cannot have social systems without people in them respecting and accepting each other, without people feeling safe with and trusting each other, or the system falls apart. Social systems create their own subculture (gangs identify fellow gang members, such as by wearing a defined color). Social systems empower each other and often the entire group. Social systems which we respect and turn to for guidance are termed reference groups. Everyone develops reference groups to whom we refer for approval and guidance, asking such questions as what they would do in certain situations.

Leadership

The Synergistic Theory of Leadership

While entire rooms could be filled with books on leadership, fewer than a dozen or so theories have been developed in the three millennia people in the West have focused on the construct. Only two theories have been developed in the last 3 decades, both in this century, and both clearly constructivist. The Synergistic theory of leadership (Irby, Brown, Duffy, & Trautman, 2002) uses four factors as its basis: leadership behavior, organizational structure, external forces and attitudes, beliefs, and values. This is the first leadership theory to include the feminine voice in its development and language, a phenomenon missing from virtually all other leadership theories. Another key element is that of social justice. As such, it is thoroughly constructivist by insisting on involvement of all and, therefore, respect, acceptance and valuing all, on authentic and trusting relationships, on bottom-up decision making, on developing a person-centered culture, among other constructivist elements.

Constructivist Leadership

The elements of a theory of constructivist leadership were first articulated by Lambert et al. (Lambert et al. 1995; Lambert et al. 1996), followed by a comprehensive theory developed by Shapiro (2002, 2008). One clear aspect of this theory is its heavy involvement of everyone as much as possible in decision making due to its respect for everyone and its abhorrence of hierarchies. Isaacson's (2004) study of developing a constructivist school assisted by Shapiro as consultant, elicited several themes that underlie the theory, including building a constructivist philosophy as its base, a theme of change, three themes of leadership as applied to education including supporting teachers, feeling appreciated and providing a professional work environment. Teachers as leaders was a major theme which included collaboration (shades of Barnard), trust building, and taking leadership roles. The last factor, quite unexpected, was teachers' affect in which teachers loved being in the school, felt they were a family. This theory, like the Synergistic Theory, obviously respects everyone, supports their ability and their autonomy, vital for many people, and abhors hierarchies. It also includes criteria cited as constructivist thinking characteristics, such as developing a trusting community.

Taylor's Scientific Management, Theory X and Y, Theory Z

Some leadership theories are antithetical to constructivism, such as Taylorism (F.W. Taylor, 1911) and Theory X (McGregor, 1960), since both believe the faulty assumption that workers dislike work and, therefore, have to be controlled and directed since only leaders know best, although Taylor was an early and strong advocate for Labor. McGregor's theory Y is based on trusting subordinates, including their involvement, because work is considered as natural as play, that people accept and seek responsibility. It supports empowerment of subordinates. The theory addresses itself more to the individual in contrast to Ouchi's theory Z (1981), which focuses on the organization's culture, particularly concerning issues of trust, intimacy of interpersonal relationships, shared control and decision making, and cooperation. These theories clearly are based on constructivist principles and criteria, although they manifestly involve acceptance of the hierarchical structure. Theory Z crosses across cultures into the art of Japanese management (obviously helped by management guru W. Edwards Deming).

The Ohio State Studies and the Managerial Grid

The Ohio State studies (Stogdill & Coons, 1957) led to the Leader Behavior Description Questionnaire, which stimulated huge numbers of empirical studies. From factor analysis two dimensions were discovered: Initiating structure and consideration of subordinates. The first referred to a leader establishing channels of communication, performance goals, evaluating group performance. The second refers to the leader's ability to establish concern for employees, support, trust, be friendly and approachable, in short, a close psychological atmosphere with subordinates. While the first dimension may appear to differ from a constructivist environment, constructivism does have structure which includes establishing a structure to facilitate wide use of groups. Consideration reeks of constructivist thinking and behavior.

The Managerial Grid (Blake & Mouton, 1985) also generated substantial numbers of studies. They developed a grid with two dimensions, concern for production and concern for people, similar to the Ohio State studies. The format generated five leadership styles, from impoverished (low on both dimensions), country club (high only on concern), team management (high on both task and person), authority-obedience (high only on task), and organization man management (middle on both dimensions). Obviously, dimensions focusing on concern for people would fit into a constructivist mindset, yet constructivism also respects structure, but not structure for control, the authority-obedience style.

Situational Leadership

Reddin (1971) developed a leadership model with an effectiveness dimension added to the Ohio State model of task and person dimensions, which focused on situational demands. This led to generating four effective and four ineffective leadership styles. Interestingly, one can make a case for two of the effective styles (developer and executive) and possibly two of the ineffective styles (missionary and compromiser) as somewhat constructivist since they pay attention to consideration, respect, developing a culture of trust and being people centered.

The Tripartite Theory of Organizational Succession and Change

Another theory of organization, the tri-partite theory of organizational succession and change (Wilson et al., 1969; Shapiro, 1995, 2009) is not only a predictive theory of three cycles or phases of organizational change, but also a theory of leadership, the rationale for placing it in this section. The tripartite is also a theory of organizational entropy, entropy in the physical universe meaning that every physical system runs down, from a clock to your auto to plumbing to a solar system. Similarly, the theory predicts that organizations inevitably cycle through three phases, and that each of the three stages of the organization's career is characterized by a markedly different style of leadership, the first having a charismatic leader who expresses the ideas and hopes of the organization, a person-oriented stage due to the loyalty of the troops to the leader. The organization is dynamic, forward looking, with many creative ideas emerging out of the woodwork as people become excited by possibilities of doing something significant. The place becomes a beehive of action, with numerous initiatives, often uncoordinated, developing. People are excited, energized, creative. Examples abound: Lee Iacocca in industry; Presidents Kennedy, Clinton, and Obama, Sarah Palin, Martin Luther King, Winston Churchill, Hitler; Generals Robert E. Lee, Eisenhower, and MacArthur; John Dewey, Ted Sizer, and Robert Maynard Hutchens of the University of Chicago in education; in religion Christ, Buddha, Moses, Martin Luther, Joan of Arc, Jim Jones of Kool-Aid fame.

Usually, a charismatic leader moves on to other organizations who want the dynamic excitement and elevated hopes they see in the leader's organization. Or, sometimes he/she gets shot out of the saddle. Because the charismatic leader's tenure is short, supporters want to retain some ideas they felt were important and look to a planner to follow. Planners come in many forms, as do their plans. In education a plan could be decentralized small learning communities, a middle school, building professional learning communities, team teaching models, top-down state assessment testing models, state and national standards, reading programs, charter schools. Since people become loyal to the plans, and become plan-oriented, this phase and the plans tend to last longer than the person-oriented phase. Planners were and are Lyndon Johnson, Hillary Clinton, Obama's Chief of Staff Emanuel Rahm; Generals Omar Bradley in World War II (Eisenhower's planner), MacArthur and Petraeus; Hutchens, who developed survey courses and the Great Books curriculum for the College of the University of Chicago; Bill Gates, Ben Bernanke (the Federal Reserve chairman), among others.

However, plans unravel as people develop procedures to accomplish the plan, role descriptions to guide new and old hires, and day-to-day, bit-by-bit incremental procedures developed to run the organization. After 3 years or so, the plan becomes more of the "good old days" mentality as it loses its hold on the imagination as new people enter and really do not understand nor share the goals—their loyalty, once fierce, diminishes. The organization drifts from holding the plan aloft to guide decisions and behavior so it slowly loses that touchstone function to guide actions. Eventually, the planner leaves. And, the organization becomes headed by a person whose main thrust is stabilizing things—in short, a bureaucrat who relies on red tape, rules, regulations. The organization becomes backward looking; loyalty to the person and plan becomes replaced by loyalty to the position, not the leader, since he or she is hardly charismatic or inspiring. Position-orientation is this stage. Examples of bureaucrats? George H. W. Bush, who noted that he dealt with things in his in-box and placed the results in the out-box, Gerald Ford, this is usually a Theory X person, and, unfortunately, this is a relatively long-lasting stage of an organization's career. The organization becomes backward looking, resistant to change, loaded with rules and regulations inhibiting creativity and enterprise. It is defensive, immobilized, headed by tinkerers, often more interested in power and control.

Once in a blue moon an organization is able to recruit a *synergist*, a combination of a charismatic leader *and* a planner, who can take the organization to new heights. Synergists are highly useful in breaking an organization out of the doldrums into which it has found itself under a position-oriented leader. Examples include some formerly mentioned, such as Generals Robert E. Lee and MacArthur, Barack Obama, Mahatma Ghandi and Lyndon Johnson, Robert Maynard Hutchins, Dewey, Iacocca, Martin Luther King. Since synergists are rare, synergistic staffing may be a solution, if a charismatic and a planner can function maturely to work cooperatively together. The organization is constructivist in its person-orientation and in the early stages of its plan-orientation career, when it is heavily focused on meeting people's needs. And, certainly, the synergist's presence can be a constructivist experience if he or she is not a control freak, a micromanager or a dictator. The organization is bottom-up in decision making in these two stages, respects people and their talent, trust becomes a strong element, as do characteristics of a constructivist organization, such as empowerment. These two phases generate considerable excitement and elevated morale.

SERVANT LEADERSHIP

Greenleaf's (1977) servant leadership treats the leader as servant, certainly a contrarian point of view to those who see leadership as a base to use and to exert their power. Greenleaf asks if a chief purpose of servant leadership is "do those served grow as persons; do they while being served, become healthier, wiser, freer, more autonomous, more likely themselves to become servants?" (1977, p. 13). A vision is crucial, which he calls an "overarching purpose," as is self-searching, self-understanding, self-examination. Southwestern Airlines is a prominent example. That this a constructivist form of leadership is manifest, with its respect and acceptance of people, its emphasis on authentic relationships, empowerment, self-understanding, establishing an environment of trust, plus facilitating people's growth.

TRANSACTIONAL AND TRANSFORMATIONAL LEADERSHIP

Transformational leadership (Bass, 1985; Burns, 1978) is contrasted with transactional leadership. The latter is supportive, works within organizational boundaries and limits, but lacks the dynamism of transformational leaders who actually transform their organizations into different, productive enterprises, harkening somewhat to the leadership of the charismatic synergist discussed in the tripartite theory. This leadership tends to motivate subordinates (a) to new levels of consciousness about achieving results; (b) stimulating subordinates to "transcend their own self-interest in favor of the team, organization, or larger polity; and (c) raising followers' need levels to the higher order needs" (Lunenburg & Ornstein, 2008, p. 151). Examples include Henry Ford who developed the assembly line, Bill Gates, Robert McNamara, Robert Maynard Hutchins, Franklyn Delano Roosevelt, and others who changed their organizations significantly. That the theory is constructivist is certainly valid (although it permits hierarchy), inasmuch as it respects people, it must establish a trusting environment, and it obviously creates a productive culture that meets needs of being involved in a significant enterprise, thus empowering people.

MORGAN'S (1977) *IMAGES OF ORGANIZATIONS*

Morgan considers metaphors as "ways of thinking, ways of seeing," providing a tool to understand our and others' models of perceiving (usually unconsciously) the organizational world around us. Such perceptions, since they are likely unconscious, usually tend to drive our behavior. Professor Harold Dunkel at the University of Chicago changed his focus from "assumptions" in his philosophy course to "starting points" providing the following semihumorous examples. If the curtains catch fire in a room, asking "How can I get out of here?" leads to the exits. If the question becomes, "How can I stop this fire?" one pulls the curtains down and stamps them out. The joke is that social workers will ask "How can we get consensus on this?", and will call a meeting.

Organizational metaphors drive our beliefs, and, thus, behavior. Morgan lists the following as relevant:

- a machine;
- an organism;
- a culture and symbolism;
- a political system;
- a self-learning system, that is, a learning organization (Senge, 1990);
- involved in change;
- an instrument of domination—or, a psychic prison (you know, an abusive marriage);
- a social sorting mechanism;
- a refuge; and
- a family (my wife added this).

Some of these are fairly easy to illustrate.

The Organization as a Machine (Obviously Implying a Bureaucracy)

When we read F. W. Taylor (1911) or go into McDonalds or Walmart, we are in machine heaven. Taylor actually told workers, "You are not supposed to think. There are other people paid to think around here." Workers were considered literally a pair of hands to do what they were told to do. In Taylor's time, people thought that organizations were like clocks, like machines. He simplified jobs so that workers were:

- cheap;
- easy to train;
- easy to supervise;
- easy to replace; and
- easy to standardize.

This describes not only Walmart, but the fast food industry, which for years, has been run by teenagers. And this is quite behaviorist, that is, similar to Pavlov's stimulus-response theory of human motivation and behavior in that all people, dogs, and pigeons supposedly will respond the same way to the same stimulus. In education, this approach has led and is leading to calls for national standards, national testing, teaching to the tests, direct instruction, scripted instruction to take the art of teaching out of the hands of teachers. So, Taylorism is alive and well one full century after he published *The Principles Scientific Management in* 1911. But, its control and disrespect comprise the antithesis of constructivist thinking and beliefs. Actually, the actual term, the "clockwork universe" construct appeared in 1377 by Bishop Nicole D'Oresme (Rifkin, 1989). Indeed, the organization as a machine comprises the essence of the construct of bureaucracy, as Weber (1946) portrayed it with its division of labor, impersonal orientation, hierarchy of authority, rules and regulations and career orientation. Schools, however, are professional bureaucracies with widespread technical knowledge and expertise, norms of service, colleague-oriented reference groups and self-imposed control structures, all of which combine to generate a more professional set of norms and differing types of conflict among the professional staff and administration (Orlosky, McCleary, Shapiro, & Webb, 1984).

The Organization as an Organism

At the other end of the continuum describing organizations as machines is the image of them as organisms. Usually, we perceive an organism as a physical, living, growing, changing entity, but it would be difficult to describe organizations in those terms. Organizations are human constructs, socially constructed realities, not physical living entities, so that this image is not quite accurate. Physical organisms can become extinct, as can organizations, but organizations can adapt more quickly to major environmental changes, so may be able to avoid extinction. This metaphor is closer to constructivist criteria such as trust, respect, developing a culture, empowerment, and the like—if it adopts those values.

The Organization as a Culture—And Symbolism

Every organization develops a culture from a family to a business to a Marine Corps company to a bank to a kindergarten class to a high school. And, in the course of their existence, their culture differs from that of other groups, sometimes modestly, sometimes greatly. Banks and Marines usually do not have afternoon naps, cookies and milk as norms.

The culture metaphor, a fundamental construct of the social sciences, provides sharp insights into how organizations work and can flourish, inasmuch as a culture consists of the common understandings, feelings, perceptions and values that people develop and learn in connection with social living (Kroeber & Kluckholm, 1952; Linton, 1955). A shorter definition might be that a culture consists of patterns of shared, learned behavior. Since organizations are created, socially constructed, shared realities, they develop a culture which consists of shared language, symbols, beliefs, and norms that people generate as we interact. Organizations develop a culture, but they also are a great deal more, such as climates as well as political systems. Owens (1998, p.165) notes that "culture refers to the behavioral patterns, assumptions, and beliefs of an organization, whereas *climate* refers to perceptions of persons in the organization that reflect those norms, assumptions, and beliefs."

Symbolism refers to the meanings we attribute to objects (a statue of Christ, a flag), actions (scoring a run), people (the president, a homeless person), artifacts (a city, a pencil), ideas (democracy), other cultures and subcultures (the Swiss, tacos). Virtually all objects, actions, and concepts develop meanings.

Does constructivist thought apply to this image of an organization? Since organizations can range from libertarian, even anarchic (witness some definitions of universities) to highly despotic, some principles of constructivism apply and some do not, depending upon the nature of the organization. But, the complexities of organizations are sometimes overlooked, as one colleague who transferred from principal of a highly successful constructivist elementary school to a graduate educational leadership program, noted this past weekend. "It has taken me 3 years to finally grasp the culture of this college, and I'm still not sure of all of it" (L. S. Isaacson, personal communication, March 1, 2010).

Schools as Political Systems—In Short, Battlefields

Almost anyone in a culture can look around an organization and can spot people who have more power, authority and influence than others. In a recent class, a new teacher noted that her principal assigned high achieving students to her favorite teachers, mediocre students to teachers who were not on her favorites list, and lower socioeconomic class and difficult students to teachers she either did not like or persecuted. The principal's buddies constantly were rewarded with "goodies." So, a new teacher found out the hard way that some people developed more power, authority and influence than she and that she got very few "goodies" as she served her internship and learning to acquiesce or to curry favor with the head tyrant.

Political systems often serve as arenas allocating resources to varying social systems (remember, two or more people in meaningful interaction). They provide arenas for conflicting interests and power, for accommodation and decision making, as well as providing systems to manage conflict. Since conflict is normal in almost any organization (including families), let alone complex organizations, some have developed internal mechanisms, such as grievance procedures and structures, to try to handle such conflict attempting to depersonalize the situation(s).

Schools as Self-Learning Systems—And Senge's Learning Organization

Metaphors can sharpen or blur reality—this metaphor does the latter. Sharp people in schools or businesses can establish structures to improve their practices (small learning communities, professional learning communities curriculum generating structures [Shapiro, 2009]), but the organization can hardly be considered as a learning system. It's the people in the organization who learn or, hopefully, remember. Thomas Ricks (2009), in discussing the strategies followed by the American armies in Iraq in this decade points to the fact that the counterinsurgency lessons learned in Vietnam were forgotten by the generals, which has proved very costly. Note it was generals and politicians who forgot, not the organization. Actually, the culture of the organization can remember, but this did not happen. This supports the tripartite theory analyzed earlier which predicts that organizations, being entropic, lose their way and become highly ineffective.

The problem becomes how to keep an organization in its two creative phases, and precious little literature focuses on that difficult process. The literature on internal structures to keep an organization in a productive phase of its career is virtually nonexistent, except for a notable exception. Scottish physicist James Clark Maxwell whimsically suggested a demon, called *Maxwell's Demon*, to break the second law of thermodynamics by permitting faster moving molecules to move into a second chamber to equalize both chambers, an early, tongue-in-cheek, attempt to break the virtually inevitable entropic decay of systems. Actually, in organizations, this means encouraging the development of "hot" ideas (Morton, 1971).

Actually, Shapiro (1995, 2003, 2009) developed such a structure, a curriculum steering committee task force, to attempt to maintain a school system in its productive phases by injecting controlled change into it, thus *generating controlled change as a routine*, that is, organizing for continuous improvement by selecting the "hot" ideas. Brown (2006) conducted a study of a school which had changed into a constructivist model to determine its success in avoiding entropic forces, and found that the school had, indeed, been able to retain its constructivist model, but did need in-service to ensure that teachers understood the rationale underlying constructivist practices.

Senge's (1990) learning organization is considered an ideal-type model, although it is "very difficult to identify real life examples…", and whose theoretical underpinning is underpowered (Smith, 2001). Garvin (2000, p. 9) noted that "a clear definition of the learning organization has proved to be elusive." Senge and colleagues have extended the concept to schooling (2000), where it has received attention. The trouble with an ideal-type model may be the difficulty of locating it in the complex world of reality, as noted above. "It might well be that the concept is being oversold as a near-universal remedy for a wide variety of organizational problems" (Kuchinke, 1995 , quoted in Kerka, 1995).

Organizations as Involved in Change (And, Lewin, Deming, and a Fillip of Decision Making)

Most people living in organizations in Western civilization become uncomfortable with the notion that organizations will inevitably lose their edge, their purpose, and will drift mindlessly, as the tripartite theory predicts. We tend to want stability in the face of change, most of us being uncomfortable with the ying-yang tensions between stability and change. However, another way of looking at change is that *it represents opportunity*, opportunity to accomplish key goals that were difficult to reach when the organization was, or is, stable and rejects change. The curriculum task force structure just mentioned is a structure designed to inject controlled change into a system, a constructivist strategy. This image can be constructivist or not, depending upon the approach. Lewin (1952) developed the granddaddy of change strategies with his unfreeze—move to a new level—and refreeze model, and his force-field analysis to determine the forces pressing for and resisting change in order to be successful. Similarly, his experiments discovering that individuals are more likely to follow through on change if they agree to that behavior publicly in a group, essentially challenges the American proclivity to see life as an individual deciding or not to make a change. Lewin's experiments pointed out the essential value of the group as the medium for effective change. Deming's (1982) great contribution is to point out that effective change to generate quality as a strategy must be the continual priority of everyone in the organization, or it will not occur. *Organizations as instruments of domination —or, psychic prisons (like some bad marriages or jobs)* In a recent class, I asked if anyone had been divorced. Several hands went up. Then, I asked if they felt that their marriage was a psychic prison. Dead silence ensued; then a couple of people nodded.

Any organization can become a psychic prison—even schools. In Florida, third graders who fail the state's No Child Left Behind knockoff, the Florida Comprehensive Assessment Test, are retained. In 2003, over 26,398 were held back and the following year 10,000 were retained a second time because they could not pass the state mandated test (Florida legislators passed a law mandating retention for kids who could not pass the Florida Comprehensive Assessment Test a second time). How many third graders feel their school is toxic for them under these circumstances? And, over 12,000 seniors who did not pass their graduation test also were unable to graduate. Research indicates that one such failure generates a 65% dropout result (Roderick, 1994) and two leads to 90% dropping out (Mann, 1987). Perhaps many of the high schoolers who have given up feel they are in a no-win setting in an inhospitable school, and just stop working, which may comprise a rational accommodation for them (but not to teachers and administrators who want them to work to pull the school's testing averages up).

At times, adults may feel that they have no option but to stay in an organization which is toxic. Often, this may be abused women who see no alternative to their circumstances. Or, people holding a job during a recession where they see few or no opportunities to move, or, believe that they cannot sell a house in a poor housing market. If an organization is a psychic prison it is diametrically opposed to constructivist beliefs.

Schools as Social Sorting Mechanisms

Most kids learn quickly in schools where they stand in our society, as do Japanese snow monkeys in their society. When I asked my high school daughter about the social structure of her high school, she responded, "Well, there are the beautiful people who only talk to themselves. Then, there are the preppies, the geeks (the Bill Gateses), the jocks, three groups of kids … (she described as rejectees), [and] the underclass." The yearbook confirms these intuitions in that the most popular kids are in numerous activities pictures, while underclass kids may only have a class photo.

Brantlinger (1995) and Kozol (1991) point to the social sorting function of the schools, which often starts early in grouping and tracking processes schools use (Oakes, 1995). How do kids respond to this? Usually, they feel humiliated being in classes or tracks considered for slow students. Internal structures also perform this function, such as membership in the National Honor Society, International Baccalaureate programs, arts and science magnets, which tend to attract upper middle class students. Many private schools perform this function, such as the Briarcrest Christian School in the film, the *Blind Side* (Lewis, 2006, 2009). The accountability movement we presently swim in has generated a huge profitable testing movement which supports the social sorting function of schools. (Other nations use testing to track kids into different high schools, such as academic, vocational, and the like). Constructivist thinking is critical of this social sorting model and is in harmony with Calvin Taylor (1968,), who perceived that humans have a variety of families of talents, and that schools should recognize them and utilize them to develop human potential. His families of talents include academic, planning, communicating, artistic, physical, decision making, and others.

Organizations, Particularly Schools, as a Refuge

A school may provide a haven from an abusive family. As for schools, since more than 20% of our students are in poverty, a school may provide them breakfast and lunch. Schools often provide positive role models for children, caring teachers with whom kids can identify. Virtually every child, every adult has teachers for whom they feel great affection.

In virtually every class I teach, people report on children who are homeless, whom they have befriended; a teen who sleeps in a baseball dugout and then comes to school daily; a teen who sleeps under a portable, who hides this, and comes to school and graduates; a teen who moves out and then takes care of his or her siblings, often for several years. Schools can meet students' needs, particularly visible if Maslow's (1954) hierarchy of needs is used. Level one, physiological needs, are referenced above with food provided. Safety needs are met if kids feel safe in schools. Certainly, social needs are met, and so can esteem need when students feel some teachers care for them. Schools may also function as a haven for adults if they can meet their needs.

The Family as an Organization

It is—and is as subject to the various images as any organization, and constructivist components as any, from a hell on earth to a nirvana.

Mintzberg's Insightful Logo—Predicting Pulls From the Five Parts of the Organization

Mintzberg's (1979) logo provides prescient predictions regarding how various parts of complex organizations tend to behave. His logo has five parts:

- The strategic apex—those who run things: Their pull is to centralize to maximize their power and control by controlling decision making;
- The middle line—in schools, the principals, in business the regional and district managers: Their goal is to Balkanize the organization to maximize their autonomy;
- The operating core—the teachers; in hospitals, the nurses and orderlies: their goal is to improve their position and treatment by becoming increasingly professional. The National Board for Professional Teachers Standards certifies teachers' professional expertise. The Nurse Practitioner provides the same prestige to counter physicians' power;
- The technostructure—the technocrats, such as the computer mavens who want to standardize everything. In schools they push for such practices as the same report card for all middle and elementary schools making it difficult to develop different programs; and
- The support staff—the secretarial and custodial staffs: Their focus is on people collaborating, usually a very sensible strategy for the rest of us to ensure getting our work done.

Constructivist thinking, of course, has to deal with organizational dynamics. Obviously, Mintzberg has provided a strong analysis of the pulling and hauling in which people and social systems in the various parts of the organization engage. Since this is predictive, it provides an important base of knowledge with which individuals and social systems may strategize thoughtfully. Constructivist thinking can be used to develop more humanistic options.

Structure, Roles, Role Expectations, Role Conflict, and the Getzels-Guba Idiographic and Nomothetic Model of Organizational Behavior

All organizations develop a structure, composed of positions. A local store will have a manager, clerks, a computer expert, customers, and other positions. A school will have a principal, secretary, teachers, reading specialists (if an elementary school), students, and so on. High schools develop structure in the form of positions among students, such as class president, Honor Society members, athletic and academic teams, clubs, and many more.

Another fundamental concept in organizational theory is that of roles, role expectations, and role conflict. All organizations create roles, defined as a series of expectations for a position, any position (Gross, Mason, & McEachern, 1966). People may develop different expectations for each position. For example, one may perceive himself or herself as a principal in the role of a custodian, merely maintaining the organization. Another option consists of generating content innovation and making modest changes in roles, norms, expectations and beliefs. At the other end of this spectrum is role innovation in which the principal may redefine the role by changing its purpose and focus which can lead to major institutional changes (VanMaanen & Schein, 1979). In this last role definition, "a genuine attempt is made by the role holder to redefine the ends for which the role functions" (p. 229).

Getzels and Guba (1957) developed their model to understand and to predict how people and social systems in organizations behave, particularly focusing on conflicts among role expectations. The model comprises two dimensions, the nomothetic comprising the roles and role expectations of the institution to achieve its purposes. The second dimension, the idiographic, consists of the dimensions of the individual, his/her personality and need dispositions. The model predicts conflicts that can and do occur in any individual and in any organization within both our personal and professional roles, role conflicts, personality conflicts and role-personality conflicts. An example of the last may be illustrated by a principal wishing to be caring, but having to evaluate a teacher doing a poor job. Enabling behavior similarly illustrates conflicting role expectations since one wants to be nourishing, yet supporting harmful behavior is usually not an aim of most. The model was later amended by adding a cultural component to the organizational side and an organism/constitution to the idiographic dimension. Constructivism may focus more on the idiographic dimension.

Weick—The School as a Loosely Coupled Organization

Weick (1976) introduced the idea that some organizations are loosely coupled contrasting with some that are more tightly coupled. Schools tend to be in the category of loosely coupled, since teachers and principals tend to have a considerable degree of professional autonomy, although the recent emergence of a national drive for accountability seems to be reducing this zone. Obviously, constructivist thinking implies the greatest autonomy and freedom of professional function possible.

Behaviorism, No Child Left Behind (NCLB) and the Scientific Management of Taylorism

Shockingly to some, the behaviorism of Pavlov and Skinner, thought to be long dead and abandoned, is alive and perhaps gaining strength in the top-down, one-size-fits-all prescriptions of No Child Left Behind, essentially a politically concocted and politically motivated coercive "reform" for American education whose drivers mandate accountability through testing and free markets through privatization, choice and charter schools (Ravitch, 2010), which Ravitch recently noted is structured to undermine and to privatize public education. Behaviorism, championed by Pavlov (1927/1960), Watson (1919) and Skinner (1938), focuses only on measureable, observable behavior, resulting in considering only conditioning and stimulus response as drivers of human behavior. Taylorism reeks of behaviorism, as does No Child Left Behind, which has instituted testing as a sanction and the market remedy of choice as a remedy. Alas, for the behaviorist, the sanctions of testing are being gamed and choice makes no difference (Ravitch, 2010)—and another behaviorist approach collapses from the reality that people interpret, make meanings from social phenomena with even the staunchest conservative supporters beginning to peel away. Thus, how individuals think, how they make meaning, interact with others, is not important. In the behaviorist world, constructivist philosophy and theory are ignored.

Social Trust

A seminal 10-year study by Bryk and Schneider (2002) of effective and ineffective elementary schools focused on the impact of relational trust on student achievement. Relational trust is based on social respect and interpersonal regard for others. When high levels of relational trust are present, schools have a one in two chance of improving academic achievement in mathematics and reading. With low levels of such trust, schools have a one in seven probability (14%), in short, "virtually no chance of showing improvement in either math or reading" (Gewertz, 2002). In addition, small school size was found crucial in that building trusting relationships is considerably easier in small schools (Shapiro, 2009).

The Poplin and Weeres study titled *Voices From the Inside* (1993) cited in Lambert et al. (1996), noted the "deep absence of authentic relationships in the schools. Often community members do not feel 'trusted, given responsibility, spoken to honestly and warmly, and treated with dignity and respect' " (p. 28). In view of the considerable top-down pressure being exerted by the U.S. accountability driver, No Child Left Behind, the focus is on results rather than on such humanistic basics as respect. And, of course, while trust comprises a fundamental component of constructivist thought and practice, it seems to be glaringly absent from the bureaucratic drive to ratchet up test scores.

Power, Authority, and Influence

Any article dealing with organizations must address issues of power, authority, and influence. The question becomes what literature to cite. In this study, Barnard (1938), Weber (1946) and sociologist Robert Bierstedt (1950) form the basis of thinking. Barnard, considered the father of administrative thought, postulated four conditions for authority to exist in organizations.

1. The communication must be understood by subordinates.
2. The communication must be consistent with the subordinate's perceptions of the purposes of the organization.
3. Subordinates have to perceive the communication as consistent with their own purposes.
4. Subordinates have to be able to carry out the communication both physically and mentally.

Barnard now has transformed our previous thinking about the nature of authority into a theory and practice of communication, an enormous shift from the widespread belief that authority and power are derived from above. Barnard's paradigm shift is that authority exists because a subordinate *accepts a communication* because he or she *perceives it* as coming from a superior and *accepts it* because the superior has *the right* to make decisions. Thus, power and authority exist *because people believe it exists*. If they do not accept it, leadership usually is finished, often exemplified by an incident of high drama, such as when very unpopular officers in Viet Nam were fragged (murdered) by their own troops.

Weber, a late nineteenth–early twentieth century sociologist, parsed the relationships among power, authority and influence. First, was *influence* upon others' behavior, which he split into voluntary and involuntary compliance. The latter rests on power, forced compliance. Power rests on threats, actual use of force, or manipulation of social and/or economic conditions. On the other hand, authority and influence are based on voluntary compliance. Authority is willingly obeyed because people perceive it as coming from a superior's position, therefore treating the authority as legitimate. As a consequence, we do not search for alternative options to any communication. Weber perceives persuasion as key in involuntary compliance, inasmuch as it emerges from the superior's charisma, cogency of arguments, or prestige. For Weber, it pays to be a reference person.

Bierstedt focused on social power. That is, like this paper, he perceived organizations as *socially constructed realities*, as *social entities*. In the process of forming organizations, positions, roles and role expectations are created. And some positions have more power and authority than others. Bierstedt (1950) developed the following formulation:

- Power is institutionalized authority.
- Authority, in turn, rests on the capacity to apply sanctions.
- Sanctions are stored force.

As Bierstedt perceives social power, it rests upon one's *capacity* ultimately to use force. Bierstedt has neatly summed up the limits of using power—if we use it and it fails—we no longer have it—nor influence. Power, therefore, consists of *the capacity to use force*. Power, therefore, *is potential*. It consists of *stored force*, the ability to use force. This explains why militaries are so reluctant to use force. If it fails, their power and influence are kaput.

Myths About Power

Macy (1994-1995), cited by Lambert et al. (1996), listed myths about power:

- Power is a scarce commodity—only some people have it.
- Power and influence are vested only in positioned leaders.
- For me to have power, I have to reduce yours (because power is limited in organizations).

- Power is forcing one's will on another and reducing choices for others.
- Building defenses makes us powerful.
- Having power gives me the ability to legislate meaning and fix identity.

Hopefully, this analysis has demolished such myths. Inside and outside of any organization are power structures, which must be taken into account by all members. As for the relationship of constructivism to the phenomena of power, authority and influence, it is complicated. Clearly, constructivist thinking is impatient with hierarchies, and would rather proceed with influence rather than with authority and power. Robert Maynard Hutchins, president of the University of Chicago, who developed the Great Books curriculum, noted that he proceeded only through influence, not authority, a criterion of a constructivist organization.

Critical Theory

Please see the section on curriculum in this handbook.

Conclusions

This chapter has evaluated the main tenets of organizational theory, operations and functioning in light of constructivist thinking by first delineating the philosophical roots of the nature of constructivist philosophy, theory and practice, as well as its psychological and sociological branches. It then summarized the major keys of organizational theory and applied constructivist thinking to each. Keys included Barnard's seminal thinking about the functions of executives and his formulations of power. Next, social systems theory, major leadership theories, images of organizations, Lewin's formulations regarding social change, Mintzberg's contributions, Getzels and Guba's nomothetic-idiographic model, trust, power and authority, and finally, behaviorist thinking were analyzed in the light of constructivism.

The education profession has been moving toward more democratic, humanistic practices. Clearly, this analysis utilizes constructivist thinking to clarify which theories approach such values—and which do not—criteria useful to add precision in selecting, analyzing, and predicting which theories to utilize in one's professional practice.

References

Barnard, C. I. (1938). *The functions of the executive*. Cambridge, MA: Harvard University Press.

Bass, B. M. (1985). *Leadership and performance*. New York, NY: Free Press.

Berger, P. L., & Luckman, T. (1966). *The social construction of reality*. Garden City, NY: Doubleday.

Biber, G. E. (1831). *Henry Pestalozzi and his plan of education*. London, England: John Souter.

Bierstedt, R. (1950). An analysis of social power. *American Sociological Review, 15*, 730-738.

Blake, R. R., & Mouton, J. S. (1985). *The managerial grid III*. Houston, TX: Gulf.

Brantlinger, E. (1995). *Social class in school: Students' perspectives*. Bloomington, IN: Phi Delta Kappa, Center for Education, Development, and Research.

Brown, J. C. (2006). *A case study of a school implementing a constructivist philosophy* (Unpublished doctoral dissertation) University of South Florida.

Bryk, A., & Schneider, B. (2002). *Trust in schools: A core resource for improvement*. New York, NY: Russell Sage Foundation.

Burns, J. M. (1978). *Leadership*. New York, NY: Harper & Row.

Deming, W. E. (1982). *Quality, productivity, and competitive position*. Cambridge, MA: Massachusetts Institute of Technology, Center for Advanced Engineering Study.

Descarte, R. (1637). *Discourse on method*. Leiden, The Netherlands: Ian Maire.

Dewey, J. (1938). *Experience and education*. New York, NY: Macmillan.

Easton, D. (1965). *A framework for the analysis of political systems*. Upper Saddle River, NJ: Prentice-Hall.

Garvin, D. A. (2000). *Learning in action: A guide to putting the learning organization to work*. Boston, MA: Harvard Business School Press.

Getzels, J. W., & Guba, E. G. (1957, Winter). Social behavior and administrative process. *School Review, 65*, 429.

Gewertz, C. (2002, October 16). Trusting school community linked to student gains. *Education Week on the Web*. Retrieved from http://www.edweek.com/ew/ewstory, cfm?slug=07trust.h22

Greenleaf, R. (1977). *Servant leadership: A journey in the nature of legitimate power and greatness*. New York, NY: Paulist.

Gross, N., Mason, W. S., & McEachern, A. W. (1966). *Explorations in role analysis: Studies of the school superintendency role*. New York, NY: Wiley.

Hills, J. (1975). Preparation for the principalship: Some recommendations from the field. Midwest Administration Center, University of Chicago. *Administrator's Notebook, 23*(9), 1-4.

Irby, B. J., Brown, G., Dufy, J. A., & Trautman, D. (2002). The synergist leadership theory. *Journal of Educational Administration, 40*, 304-322.

Isaacson, L. S. (2004). *Teachers' perceptions of constructivism as an organizational change model: A case study* (Doctoral dissertation). University of South Florida.

Kerka, S. (1995). The learning organization: Myths and realities. *Eric Clearing House*. Retrieved from http://www.cete.org/acve/docgen.asp?tbl=archive&ID=Ao28

Kozol, J. (1991). *Savage inequalities: Children in America's schools*. New York, NY: Crown.

Kroeber, A., & Kluckholm, C. (1952). *Culture: A critical review of concepts and definitions*. Cambridge, MA: Harvard University Press.

Lambert, L., Collay, M., Dietz, M. E., Kent, K., & Richert, A. E. (1996). *Who will save our schools?* Thousand Oaks, CA: Corwin.

Lambert, L., Walker, D., Zimmerman, D. P., Cooper, J. E., Lambert, M. D., Gardner, M. E., & Ford-Slack, P. J. (1995). *The constructivist leader.* New York, NY: Teachers College Press.

Lewin, K. (1952). Group decision and social change. In T. M. Newcomb & E. L. Hartley (Eds.) *Readings in social psychology.* New York, NY: Holt.

Lewis, M. (2009). *The blind side.* New York, NY: W. W. Norton. (Original work published 2006)

Linton, R. (1955). *The tree of culture.* New York, NY: Vintage.

Lunenberg, F. C., & Ornstein, A. C. (2008). *Educational administration: Concepts and practices.* Belmont, CA: Wadsworth.

Macy, J. (1994-1995, Winter). Viewpoints. *Noetic Sciences Bulletin,* p. 2.

Mann, D. (1987). Can we help dropouts? Thinking about the undoable. In G. Natriello (Ed.), *School dropouts: Patterns and Policies.* New York, NY: Teachers College Press.

Marlow, B. A., & Page, M. L. (1998). *Creating and sustaining the constructivist classroom.* Thousand Oaks, CA: Corwin.

Maslow, A. H. (1954). *Motivation and personality.* New York, NY: Harper & Row.

McGregor, D. (1960). *The human side of enterprise.* New York, NY: McGraw-Hill

Mead, G. H. (1934). *Mind, self, and society: From the standpoint of a social behaviorist.* Chicago, IL: University of Chicago Press.

Mintzberg, H. (1979). *The structuring of organizations.* Englewood Cliffs, NJ: Prentice-Hall.

Morgan, C. (1977). *Images of organizations.* Thousand Oaks, CA: SAGE.

Morton, J. A. (1971). *Organizing for innovation.* New York, NY: McGraw-Hill.

Oakes, J. (1995). *Keeping track: How schools structure inequality.* New Haven, CT: Yale University Press.

Orlosky, D. E., McCleary, L. E., Shapiro, A., & Webb, L. D. (1984). *Educational administration today.* Columbus, OH: Merrill.

Ouchi, W. G. (1981). Type Z: *How American business can meet the Japanese challenge.* Reading, MA: Addison-Wesley.

Owens, R. (1998). *Organizational behavior in education* (6th ed.). Boston, MA: Allyn & Bacon.

Parsons, T., & Shils, E. A. (Eds.). (1951). *Toward a general theory of action: Theoretical foundations for the social sciences.* Cambridge, MA: Harvard University Press.

Pavlov, I. P. (1960). *Conditioned reflexes.* New York, NY: Dover. (Original work published 1927, G. V. Anrelk, Trans.)

Phillips, D. C. (Ed). (2000). Constructivism in education: Opinions and second opinions on controversial issues. In *Ninety-ninth yearbook of the Society for the Study of Education, Part I.* Chicago, University of Chicago Press.

Piaget, J. (1954). *The construction of reality in the child.* New York, NY: Basic Books.

Poplin, M., & Weeres, J. (1993). *Voices from the inside.* Claremont, CA: Institute for Education in Transformation of the Claremont Graduate School.

Ravitch, D. (2010). *The death and life of the great American school system: How testing and choice are undermining education.* New York, NY: Basic Books.

Reddin, W. J. (1971). *Effective management by objectives: The 3-D method of MBO.* New York, NY: McGraw-Hill.

Ricks, T. E. (2009). *The gamble: General Petraeus and the American military adventure in Iraq.* New York, NY: Penguin.

Rifkin, J. (1989). *Time wars.* New York, NY: Simon & Schuster.

Roderick, M. (1994). Grade retention and school dropout: Investigating the association. *American Educational Research Journal, 31,* 729-59.

Rousseau, J. J. (1762). *The social contract, or principles of political right.* Amsterdam, The Netherlands: Marc Michelle Rey.

Senge, P. M. (1990). *The fifth discipline: The art and practice of the learning organization.* New York, NY: Doubleday.

Senge, P. M., Camron-McCabe, N., Lucas, T., Smith, B., Dutton, J., & Kleiner, A. (2000) *Schools that learn: A fifth discipline fieldbook for educators, parents, and everyone who cares about education.* New York, NY: Doubleday.

Shapiro, A. (1995). *Curriculum and schooling: A practitioner's guide.* Palm Springs, CA: ETC.

Shapiro, A. (1996). Creating the culture of constructivist classrooms in public and private schools. In *Global-local articulations.* The Society for Applied Anthropology (SfAA), 1996 Annual International Meeting, Baltimore, MD.

Shapiro, A. (2000, May). Creating the culture for a constructive classroom and team. *Wingspan, 13*(1), 5-8.

Shapiro, A. (2002). *Leadership for constructivist schools.* Lanham, MD: Scarecrow.

Shapiro, A. (2003). *Case studies in constructivist leadership and teaching.* Lanham, MD: Scarecrow.

Shapiro, A. (2008). *The effective constructivist leader: A guide to the successful practices.* Lanham, MD: Rowman & Littlefield.

Shapiro, A. (2009). *Making large schools work: The advantages of small schools.* Lanham, MD: Rowman & Littlefield.

Skinner, B. F (1938). *The behavior of organisms: An experimental analysis.* New York, NY: Appleton-Century.

Smith, M. (2001). The learning organization. *The encyclopedia of informal education.* Retrieved from http://www.infed.org/biblio/learning-organization.htm

Stodgill, R. F., & Coons, A. E. (1957). *Leader behavior: Its description and measurement.* Columbus, OH: Bureau of Business Research, Ohio State University.

Taschow, U. (2003). *Nicole Oresme und der fruhling der moderne.* Retrieved from http://www.nicole-oresme.com/seiten/oresme-biography.html

Taylor, C. W. (1968, February). Nearly all students are talented—Let's reach them. *Utah Parent Teacher,* pp. 9-10.

Taylor, F. W. (1911). *The principles of scientific management.* New York, NY: Harper & Row.

Thelen, H. A. (1949, March). Group dynamics in instruction. The principle of least group size. *School Review,* pp. 139-148.

VanMaanen, J., & Schein, E. H. (1979). *Organizational careers: Some new perspectives.* London, England: Wiley and Sons.

von Glasersfeld, E. (1998). Why constructivism must be radical. In M. Larochelle, N. Bednarz, & J. Garrison (Eds.), *Constructivism and education.* Cambridge, England: Cambridge University Press.

Watson, J. B. (1919). *Psychology from the standpoint of a behaviorist.* New York, NY: Lippincott.

Weber, M. (1946). *From Max Weber: Essays in sociology* (H. H. Gerth & C. W. Mills, Eds.). New York, NY: Oxford University Press.

Weick, K. (1976, March). Educational organizations as loosely coupled systems. *Administrative Science Quarterly, 21,*1-19.

Wilson, C., Byars, T. M., Shapiro, A. S., & Schell, S. H. (1969). *Sociology of supervision. An approach toward comprehensive planning in education.* Boston, MA: Allyn & Bacon.

Author Contact Information: **Arthur Shapiro**, PhD, College of Education, University of South Florida, Tampa, FL 33620. Preferred mailing address: 35536 Wickingham Court, Zephyrhills, FL 335410. Telephone: 813-780-9049. E-mail: ashapiro@tampabay.rr.com

CHAPTER 73

Postmodernism—(The Antitheory)

Fenwick English
University of North Carolina at Chapel Hill

Postmodernism is not a theory but an *antitheory*. By an antitheory is meant that it does not have a specified content, format, propositions or properties. It is not a frame or a set of tenets to be tested. Postmodernists reject claims that there is a *totality* independent of human language and culture, and that includes science and all scientific claims asserting the existence of such a totality. Because of the unique nature of postmodernism many modernists dismiss it as standing for nothing, the epitome of total relativism. The image of a jellyfish comes to mind which is not entirely inappropriate for while a jellyfish has no form, it can also leave a nasty sting if provoked. This is the case with postmodernism.

So what is postmodernism? Definitions are hard to come by as well as its emergence. Woods (1999) offers this comment:

> The origins of postmodernism appear to be completely confused and underdetermined; And perhaps appropriately so, since postmodernism denies the idea of knowable origins. Postmodernism has acquired a semantic instability or a shifting meaning that shadows and echoes its notes of indeterminacy and insecurity. (p. 3)

Ward (2003) has found references to postmodernism which date to the 1870s when an English artist named John Watkins Chapman "used it to describe painting which he saw as more advanced than that of French Impressionist painters like Claude Monet or Auguste Renoir" (p. 7). The modern age is generally described as originating with Rene Descartes (1596-1650) and proceeds into the contemporary times. The field of educational administration is thoroughly steeped in modernism, especially its perspectives on what constitutes acceptable or "good" research (National Research Council, 2002). The metaphors of modernism are those of "progress, optimism, rationality, the search for absolute knowledge in science, technology, society, and politics [and] the idea that gaining knowledge of the true self was the foundation for all other knowledge" (Ward, 2003, p. 9). Postmodernists are more concerned with

> an erosion of conventional distinctions between high and low culture; fascination with how our lives seem increasingly dominated by visual media; a questioning of ideas about meaning and communication, and about how signs refer to the world; a sense that definitions of human identity are changing…; [and] skepticism about the stories we tell to explain "the human race," and about the idea of progress. (p. 11)

In this chapter postmodernism is defined as a stance, an attitude which employs distinctive methods of analysis which have a history in literary criticism, semiotics, and linguistics. Among the most powerful is that of *deconstruction*, which means a "taking apart," not only of the content of any specific message or text, but a search for the unsaid, the so-called "structured silences" which are contained in all texts, including that of science and its methods for as Usher and Edwards (1994) note, "we construct our world through discourse and practice and that therefore, with a different discourse and a difference set of practices, things could be otherwise" (p. 28). This difference is sometimes called "the other" and is often the silent opposite in a binary term as for example using the term "truth" to describe a perspective. The opposite term "false" is in use even if it is only silent because to say something is true makes

The Handbook of Educational Theories, pp. 871–876

no sense without its opposite being present at the same time.

Postmodernism is about exposing the silent "otherness" in choices of terms, concepts and theories. Postmodernists reject what they call "grand theory" or "metanarratives" because as McGowan (1991) indicates, "the finiteness of a context is never secured or simple, there is an indefinite opening of every context, an essential nontotalization" (p. 111).

Most theories are examples of efforts to totalize or freeze reality in some way so as to fit a theoretical explanation to it. In his early work in pushing educational administration to become more theoretical and scientific, Griffiths (1959) noted that "It is the aim of science to accomplish three things concerning its subject matter: description, explanation, and prediction" (p. 22). Griffiths then asserted that accurate predictions can be made if "scientific inquiry is regulated by certain criteria" (p. 22). These were objectivity, reliability, operational definitions, coherence or systematic structure and comprehensives. Behind this image of constructing a science of educational administration was the metaphor of the tree, a symbol of what would become "foundational" (i.e., root systems) which would support a trunk (the conceptual system) and that this would support branches and leaves (concepts and facts). Deleuze and Guattari (1987) called this metaphor "arborescent" and it supports a "totalizing, hierarchical narrative" (a metanarrative). Deleuze and Guattari called an alternative perspective "rhizomatic" which would be characterized by "non-hierarchical systems of deterritorialized lines that connect with others lines in random, unregulated relationships" (Best & Kellner, 1991, p. 99).

Postmodern perspectives directly refute the primary assertions of science regarding the nature of reality. To the modernist claim that there is only one reality "out there," the postmodern position is that "it rejects the doctrine of the unity of reason. It refuses to conceive of humanity as a unitary subject striving towards the goal of perfect coherence" (Lovibond, 1989, p. 6). Supporting this perspective about the goal of "perfect coherence" is that science is simply a language game and is dependent on the "notion of linguistic consensus which is arbitrarily fixed unscientifically. There can be no independent verification of truth" (Usher & Edwards, 1996, p. 157). The postmodern position is that there are multiple views of reality and that reality is a mental construct and "in there" more than anything else (Clark, 1985, p. 76).

Another modernist claim regarding the supremacy of science is that the knower and the known are separable. This premise eliminates subjectivism and permits objectivity, the very first criterion on Griffiths (1959) list of the nature of a theory (p. 22). The separation of the knower from the known also makes the use of binaries such as true/false, fact/nonfact, science/nonscience possible. The postmodern position on the claim of the separation of the knower from the known is that it is an act of faith since it is unprovable. Observation is not a netural act. Rather it is a theoretical and value laden act.

Modernists also proffer that "truth" is "discovered" and is therefore context free. In fact, quantitative analysis is all about generalizing from a form of inquiry that aims to neutralize or "control" the vagaries of context. The postmodern perspective is that everything is context. The great military historian of leadership, John Keegan (1987), criticized the modernist claim regarding the aim of social science to discover context free generalization when he said, "and, as with all social science, [they, the social scientists] condemn those who practice them to the agony of making universal and general what is stubbornly local and particular" (p. 1). The postmodern position is that "truth" is constructed and not "discovered." Furthermore, using linguistics as a platform for examination, postmodernists proffer that truth is relational and contained within a structure of signs and symbols. It is therefore not waiting to be revealed. It does not preexist and it is not independent of language. If anything, truth is circular and is embedded in itself. Karl Popper (1968) observed that most theories contain their own truth and are unable to predict any situation which involves their own rejection (p. 67). McGowan (1991) similarly commented:

> Western reason is not transparent to itself, as it loves to believe, but actually founds itself on a constitutive blind spot; its willful refusal to recognize the others that it dominates. This dominated other (in a master-slave dialectic) is both within the system and invisible. (p. 102)

The function of theory, according to modernists, is that it is the touchstone upon which a "science of administration" can be founded (Griffiths, 1959, p. 45; Immegart, 1969, p. 217) and upon which a knowledge base can be constructed (Culbertson, 1988). Yet as postmodernists point out, science cannot be an arbiter for the truth, because it is simply one kind of tradition among many. Among the heaviest tradition in science is that of the so-called "scientific method" which is believed will lead to the truth. The problem with the "scientific method" is that it has almost nothing to do with real scientific discoveries. Paul Feyerabend (1993) pointed out that Galileo did not follow the "scientific method" in his groundbreaking insights, nor could he produce any data or even a theory to support his claims. And Gerald Geison (1995) similarly observed that Louis Pasteur failed to follow the "scientific method" in conducting his precedential scientific work on rabies. When this was exposed in Geison's book, Max Perutz (1996), a Nobel Prize winning chemist, defended Pasteur by saying, "scientists rarely follow any of the scientific methods that philosophers have prescribed for them" (p. 69). Other critical perspectives on this important point indicate that true scientific discovery rarely follows any rules. This was certainly the case in the creation of modern medicine (see LeFanu, 1999) as an applied field. The reason is that as Edward DeBono (1972) has explained is that logical foresight rarely, if ever, leads to a creative solution to a problem or dilemma. However, to be judged meaningful, a creative idea has to be logical in hindsight. So while there can be no way or predicting a true breakthrough via theoretical logic, a breakthrough has to be seen has logical after it is "discovered." This phenomenon masks the true nature of discovery.

On-the-other-hand, the usual sort of exercise undertaken in most research follows what Feyerabend (1993) has called "the logic of justification" (p. 147). This foray must stand the test of theoretical speculation and testing, but it rarely leads to new discoveries.

Implications of Postmodernism for Theory Development

Postmodernism is antitheory only to the extent that a theory or narrative is elevated to a singular truth, that is, a *metanarrative.* This claim to exclusivity is stoutly resisted by postmodernists who see such a stance as a retreat into power politics because such a position cannot be defended any other way. Feyerabend (1999) wrote a small essay called "Theses on Anarchism" in 1973. He eschewed science because in his view science had become big business in the twentieth-century, and that "its theories as well as its factual statements are *hypotheses* which often are not just locally incorrect but entirely false, making assertions about things that never existed" (p. 114). In short, science could not be trusted. The solution was to embrace *epistemological anarchism* which is neither skepticism nor political anarchism. Here is Feyerabend's definition of an epistemological anarchist:

> There is no view, however "absurd: or "immoral" he refuses to consider or to act upon, and no method he regards as indispensable. The only thing he opposes positively and absolutely are universal standards, universal laws, universal ideas such as "Truth," "Justice," "Honesty," "Reason," and the behavior they engender, though he does not deny that it is often good policy to act as if such laws (such standards, such ideas) existed and as if he believed in them. (p. 115)

If theories in use advance a perspective that enslave humans or make them dependent or deny them dignity they must be resisted. It must be remembered that the Nazis used the scientific thinking of the times to build the gas chambers and exterminate the unfit as the science of the times via eugenics had propounded. Even in America in the twenty-first century some state health agencies are still apologizing for the use of sterilization of the unfit pursued in the last century. Feyerabend (1999) advises, "People and nature are very whimsical entities which cannot be conquered and understood if one decides to restrict oneself in advance" (p. 116). And so it is with theoretical development. Theories must be understood to be partial explanations and not totalities. And since all theories are embedded in existing power hierarchies, they have to be examined with great skepticism about whose interests are being advanced when they are tested, when the results are presented, and the ultimate meaning attached to the implications of any empirical outcomes. There are no neutral places in society. No places where vested interests are not at work. Theories are one kind of narrative. They benefit some in society and hinder or marginalize others. Scientific theories are not an antidote in this regard. Science is simply one kind of narrative. Poetry is another and the whole application of aesthetics in leadership another (see English, 2008). Perhaps the most pungent definition of postmodernism was proffered by Lyotard, 1997) who defined it as "an incredulity toward metanarratives" (p. xxiv). And the idea that only scientific theories are viable to understand leadership was vitiated by S. L. A. Marshall (1966) who wrote about effective military leadership:

> The chronicles of effective military leadership date back to Gideon and his band. Therefore any notion that it is impossible for an officer to make the best use of his men unless he is armed with all available research data and can talk the language of the philosopher and modern social scientist is little more than a twentieth- century conceit. (p. 253)

Postmodern Tools of Analysis

The postmodernist has three analytical tools which are very powerful in the arsenal of critique. They are de-construction, genealogy, and a search for the *trace*, though it could be argued that both genealogical analysis involves the search for a trace and both of these are examples of deconstruction.

Deconstruction

Deconstruction is simply a double reading of a text (see Critchley, 1992). The first reading is merely how any passage or text would be read by the majority of readers. The second reading is a critical analysis of the deeper meanings of the text by what is not there, that is, elements which are missing called *silences* as well as how a line of argument is constructed using binaries and logic. Logic is a peculiar form of linguistic grammar and both the logic and the grammar can be deconstructed, that is, taken apart or stripped down. Reading a text for what is not present exposes what the text author did not think important enough to mention or deliberately withheld in the framing of a line of argument. Reaching into a text and recovering the "unthought" or "unspoken" is often a way to show the hidden biases or prejudices in a text. It is not unique to postmodern thinkers, but it is a major way to strip down and erase a line of thought expressed in words which contradict the one that is spoken. Postmodern analysts use deconstruction to strip down metanarratives and among them current theories in use. For example, if some theories profess that everything must be observed to be considered true then the premise itself cannot be established as true because it ca not be observed. It is an article of faith. This is one way postmodernists attack empiricism.

Genealogical Analyses

Genealogical analyses consist of recovering what is lost in the past as a new theoretical position is adopted. For example, English (2002a) illustrated how educational administration was "turned" when it adopted a new metanarrative in 1957 when 50 professors from leading universities met at the University of Chicago and initiated the "theory movement" in the field. Foucault's (1972) notion of a field of memory, a field of concomitance and a field of presence apply here. A field of memory consists of statements which are no longer considered true. A field of concomitance are statements from other fields which are considered true and can be transferred. And a field of presence are statements which are acknowledged to be truthful and resonant. The "theory movement" changed from that point on what could be considered true in educational administration. From 1957 on educational administration had to be become a "science" and lost in the translation were the great works of leadership which had been honored in the past such as Plutarch, Suetonius, Machiavelli, Shakespeare, and Carlyle. These literary and artistic sources were junked because they were not "science" (English, 2002a). The "art" of leadership was erased by one interpretation of the "science" of leadership. One of the major consequences of this shift was the erasure of morality and ethics in educational decision making. What is moral is not any question science can answer. Jacob Heilbrunn (1996) summarized this dilemma as follows:

> The mystery of leadership touches on some of the more vexing philosophical questions about human existence, which theorists ignore only at the risk of ultimate irrelevance … to grow as a discipline, it [the study of leadership] may discover that the most important things about leadership lie far beyond the capabilities of science to analyze. (p. 11)

Paul Johnson (1996) echoed these sentiments when he said:

> Leadership is a moral issue. As such it requires that we make use of the methods and conceptual tools that have always been the special concern of the humanities in general, and philosophy in particular. We need to develop a philosophy of leadership which sets moral theory at the center of things. (p. 41)

Postmodernism resurfaces claims of the "science" of educational administration and exposes them as simply a consensus of opinion rather than any sort of "discovery" of a permanent or enduring *truth*. The postmodern attitude is that there are many *truths*. The imposition of one is simply an exercise in political power of those in control of a professional field.

A Search for the Trace

A search for the trace involves taking a concept or an idea and tracking it back to the original use. It is well known that ideas and concepts often jump fields. The postmodern position is that there is "no unmodified zero point, no pure origin of all modifications" (Evans, 1991, p. 125). For example, Sulloway (1979) showed that Freud's basic concepts of psychoanalytic theory were borrowed from Darwin, something which he took great pains to erase (p. 498). A similar exposition was completed on the work of best-selling management guru Stephen Covey (1990) by English (2002c) who showed that by using the postmodern "trace" it was possible to directly link Covey's "habits" to the tenets of the Church of Jesus Christ of Latter Day Saints, that is, the "Mormons." English (2002c) showed that by using what he termed "stealth metaphysics" Covey used "habits" to mean "correct principles" and that this phrase was used by the Mormon prophet Joseph Smith who said, "We teach them correct principles and they govern themselves" (Bitton, 1994, p. 329). In fact, Covey (1990) himself said in *7 Habits*, "I believe that correct principles are natural laws, and that God, the Creator and Father of us all, is the source of them" (p. 164).

English (2002c) concluded that, "The *7 Habits* are a gift of prophecy. If one does not accept them, based as they are on a foundation of fundamental truth defined by revelation, the rejection becomes the basis of damnation" (p. 12). Trace analysis further shows that the Mormon belief of a three-tiered heaven and the necessity of doing work to attain salvation define Covey's concept of "effectiveness." In all of *7 Habits* Covey never reveals the true sources of his "correct principles," his use of binaries to define effectiveness straight from *The Book of Mormon* and from the writings and speeches of Joseph Smith, the prophet and founder of the Mormon faith. One can only speculate why Covey was not forthcoming about his sources, but chose instead to cover his religion with the veneer of social science.

Postmodernism has developed a formidable sting via forms of textual analysis. While they are not unique to postmodernism per se, they have become the standard arsenal of works of critique within the postmodern tradition employed against prevailing metanarratives, especially those which rest on claims of inerrancy of content (as in revelation and opinion) or on inerrancy of method (as in science).

What Does Postmodernism Offer Researchers and Practitioners?

Since postmodernism is not a doctrine, a tenet, a philosophy or even a theory, why is it important in approaching theoretical development in education? The answer is that it should make us cautious about advancing any theory as universal, good for all times and places; in short, making a theory into dogma, or in preventing any theory from being challenged or immune from deep questioning. It also ought to remind us that context free generalizations are not only likely to produce error, but lead to distortions in practice. The importance of culture, language and symbols always configure practice in idiosyncratic ways that are erased when context is marginalized in theoretical developments and subsequent research based on those developments (see English, 2003).

While postmodernism is antitheory in content, it is not antitheory qua theory. It is only when theory becomes a metanarrative, beyond serious questioning that the postmodernist objects. Postmodernism then is a form of critique, not only of theories but the practices based on them as well. It ought to keep theorists a little more humble and open to dissent when they know their work can be deconstructed and unraveled with postmodern criticism. Some jellyfish!

References

Best, S., & Kellner, D. (1991). *Postmodern theories.* New York, NY: The Guilford Press.

Bitton, D. (1994). *Historical dictionary of Mormonism.* Metuchen, NJ: Scarecrow Press.

Clark, D. (1985). Emerging paradigms in organizational theory and research. In Y. S. Lincoln (Ed.), *Organizational theory and inquiry* (pp. 43-78). Beverly Hills, CA: SAGE.

Covey, S. (1990). *The 7 habits of highly effective people: Restoring the character ethic.* New York, NY: Simon & Schuster.

Critchley, S. (1992). *The ethics of deconstruction.* Oxford, England: Blackwell.

Culbertson, J. (1988). A century's quest for a knowledge base. In N. J. Boyan (Ed.), *Handbook of research on educational administration* (pp. 3-26). New York, NY: Longman.

DeBono, E. (1972). *Po: Beyond yes and no.* New York, NY: Penguin Books.

Deleuze, G., & Guattari, F. (1987). *A thousand plateaus.* Minneapolis, MN: University of Minnesota Press.

English, F. (2003). *The postmodern challenge to the theory and practice of educational administration.* Springfield, IL: Charles C. Thomas.

English, F. (2002a). The fateful turn: Understanding the discursive practice of educational administration. In G. Perreault & F. Lunenburg (Eds.) *The changing world of school administration* (pp. 44-59) Lanham, MD: The Scarecrow Press.

English, F. (2002c, January). The penetration of educational leadership texts by revelation and prophecy: The case of Stephen R. Covey, *Journal of School Leadership, 12*(1), 4-22.

English, F. (2008). *Anatomy of professional practice: Promising research perspectives on educational leadership.* Lanham, MD: Rowman and Littlefield Education.

Evans, J. (1991). *Strategies of deconstruction.* Minneapolis, MN: University of Minnesota Press.

Feyerabend, P. (1993). *Against method.* New York, NY: Verso.

Feyerabend, P. (1999). Theses on anarchism. In M. Motterlini (Ed.) *For and against method* (pp. 113-118). Chicago, IL: University of Chicago Press.

Foucault, M. (1972). *The archaeology of knowledge and the discourse on language.* New York, NY: Pantheon Books.

Geison, G. (1995). *The private science of Louis Pasteur.* Princeton, NJ: Princeton University Press.

Griffiths, D. (1959). *Administrative theory.* New York, NY: Teachers College, Columbia University.

Heilbrunn, J. (1996). Can leadership be studied? In P. Temes (Ed.) *Teaching leadership: Essays in theory and Practice* (pp. 1-12). New York, NY: Peter Lang.

Immegart, G. (1969). Systems theory and taxonomic inquiry into organizational behavior in education. In D. Griffiths (Ed.) *Developing taxonomies of organizational behavior in educational administration* (pp. 675-238). Chicago, IL: Rand McNally.

Johnson, P. (1996). Antipodes: Plato, Nietzsche, and the moral dimension of leadership. In P. Temes (Ed.), *Teaching leadership: Essays in theory and practice* (pp. 83-104). New York, NY: Peter Lang.

Keegan, J. (1987). *The mask of command.* New York, NY: Elisabeth Sifton Books.

LeFanu, J. (1999). *The rise and fall of modern medicine.* New York, NY: Carroll & Graf.

Lovibond, S. (1989). Feminism and postmodernism. *New Left Review, 178*, 6.

Lyotard, J. (1997). *The postmodern condition: A report on knowledge.* Minneapolis, MN: University of Minnesota Press.

Marshall, S. (1966). *The officer as leader.* Harrisburg, PA: Stockpole Books.

McGowan, J. (1991). *Postmodernism and its critics.* Ithaca, NY: Cornell University Press.

National Research Council (2002). *Scientific research in education.* R. Shavelson & L. Towne (Eds.), Washington, DC: National Academy Press.

Perutz, M. (1996). *Pasteur and the culture wars: An exchange. New York Review of Books, 43*(6), 69.

Popper, K. (1968). *The logic of scientific discovery.* New York, NY: Harper & Row.

Sulloway, F. (1979). *Freud: Biologist of the mind.* New York, NY: Basic Books.

Usher, R., & Edwards, R. (1994). *Postmodernism and education.* London: Routledge.

Ward, G. (2003). *Postmodernism.* London, England: Hodder & Stoughton.

Woods, T. (1999). *Beginning postmodernism.* Manchester, England: Manchester University Press.

Author Contact Information: **Fenwick W. English,** R. Wendell Eaves Senior Distinguished Professor of Educational Leadership School of Education, 121 Peabody Hall, University of North Carolina at Chapel Hill, Chapel Hill, North Carolina 27599-3500. Phone: 919-451-1493. E-mail: fenglish@attglobal.net

CHAPTER 74

Ways of Knowing Through the Realms of Meaning

A Postmodernist Approach to Teaching Low-Income Students

William Allan Kritsonis Prairie View A&M University

To successfully begin a program that will meet the needs of all students in today's educational classroom environment, it is necessary to develop a curriculum that will challenge and inspire students to seek excellence in their academic endeavors. My book, the *Ways of Knowing Through the Realms of Meaning* (Kritsonis, 2007), provides powerful insights on how to effectively address the learning and educational needs of all students in the general education classroom.

The purpose of this chapter is to demonstrate how to integrate the *Ways of Knowing Through the Realms of Meaning* into an educational philosophy in higher level curriculum studies in order to help at-risk students succeed and flourish, not only in their academic pursuits, but also in their life goals and future career aspirations.

REALMS OF MEANING: THE HEURISTICS APPROACH

"The object of general education is to lead to the fulfillment of human life through the enlargement and deepening of meaning" (Kritsonis, 2007, p. 3). To be efficient and purposeful in planning a curriculum, educators must ensure that they have a well-developed curriculum that gives students the opportunity to learn heuristically, and to apply their new knowledge to the world around them in which they live. As our world seemingly becomes more impersonal and therefore meaningless in many of its pursuits, it is important to help ground our students in meaningful study that will increase their ability to effectively interact with their world and environment in order to achieve the highest possible level of meaning and fulfillment.

The foundation of all educational instruction should be focused on student learning and achievement. "Today the focus on education at all levels and for students of all abilities is increasingly upon excellence and adequacy of knowledge" (Kritsonis, 2007, p. vii). The No Child Left Behind Act mandates educational administrators and teachers provide a meaningful education and academic success rate among all students, regardless of their innate inclination toward academic achievement and success.

A CHALLENGE TO EDUCATORS: DESIGNING AND IMPLEMENTING AN EFFECTIVE CURRICULUM

In an age where simplistic thinking and "fill-in-the-blank" tests rob our students of the opportunity to be creative problem solvers and thinkers, *Ways of Knowing Through the Realms of Meaning*, can be utilized as an effective tool for learning and provide an effective philosophical basis for all classroom learning and meaning.

It is therefore incumbent upon educators to provide a thorough and complete education to the students who are entrusted in their educational care. Curriculum selection should be based on the highest good for all students, regardless of their ability level. Making a decision on what to present to the students in the form of a curriculum is one of the most challenging decisions facing administrators and teachers today.

An unprecedented amount of knowledge is available to anyone who is literate and able to read and understand vast amounts of material. Educators must judiciously choose what materials should be taught and read in the classroom. "The first principle for the selection of the material for instruction is that all of it should be drawn from the organized scholarly disciplines" (Kritsonis, 2007, p. 661). Utilizing the philosophy of *Ways of Knowing Through the Realms of Meaning* gives an organized structure of the components that should be included in an organized and dynamic curriculum.

The fundamental patterns of meaning can be organized into six realms of meaning. The first realm of meaning is *symbolics* and encompasses ordinary language, mathematics, and nondiscursive, subjective symbolic forms. The second realm of meaning is *empirics*. The subjects of psychology, biology, physical science, and the social sciences are all included in this realm of study. The third realm of meaning focuses on *esthetics*. Understanding esthetics allows us to see and understand our world through the avenues of literature, movement, the visual arts, and music. *Synnoetics*, the fourth realm, centralizes its focus on our personal knowledge. The fifth realm is about *ethics* and how moral knowledge affects the quality and characteristics of our life on a day to day basis. The sixth realm of meaning is *synoptics*. Synoptics takes an in-depth view of history, religion, and philosophy, and provides the opportunity to study these disciplines in the light of their relationship to other disciplines and their contributions to the realms of meaning included in a disciplined and familial approach.

The Art and Mastery of Teaching Shakespeare

> Shakespeare is hard. Even seasoned scholars differ on subjects ranging from the meaning of individual words to the implications of entire plays. (Rosenblum, 2005, p. xiii).

However, students who struggle in their general academic classrooms can be taught to read and understand Shakespeare. Utilizing the book, *Ways of Knowing Through the Realms of Meaning*, teachers can develop curriculum models that will address how to engage at-risk students in learning and in meaningful conversation and communication regarding the study of William Shakespeare and his timeless, poetic and thematic writing style.

The Six Realms of Meaning and the Teaching of Shakespeare

Just as there is order and purpose in the universe, there must be order and meaning in learning. "Six fundamental patterns of meaning emerge from the analysis of the possible distinctive modes of human understanding" (Kritsonis, 2007, p. 11). Teaching students to understand and seek out knowledge through the application of utilizing and understanding a subject matter in an organized and sequential manner can allow students to be successful who otherwise were not succeeding and are at-risk of academic failure.

The study of Shakespeare lends itself to the development and implementation of a curriculum guide and study based on the six realms of meaning. Each pattern represents a form of human understanding and knowledge that can be taught and illustrated utilizing the writings of William Shakespeare.

Symbolics: The First Realm of Meaning

"The first realm, symbolics, comprises ordinary language, mathematics, and various types of nondiscursive symbolic forms such as gestures, rituals, rhythmic patterns, and the like" (Kritsonis, 2007, p. 11). Discursive symbolics refer to how speech is utilized in ordinary communication. "Nondiscursive symbolic forms are used in all the arts and for the expression of feelings, values, commitments, and insights in the domains of personal knowledge, metaphysics, and religion" (Kritsonis, 2007, p. 151). By utilizing symbolics in our interpretation of Shakespeare, we can provide an ordered system of learning that will enhance a student's knowledge and understanding of William Shakespeare and his literary accomplishments through the written word.

Discursive Symbolic Forms

The obvious feature of all literature is that it is composed of language that is intended to communicate meanings and ideas to those who read and study its content. In Shakespeare, language played an integral part in understanding its relevant meaning and application. As the English language emerged from its classical roots, new words were added to accommodate the new learning and understanding of the sixteenth century scholar. Shakespeare himself helped to add many words to our English language.

"Demonstrations of Shakespeare's verbal inventiveness are based in part on his so-called neologisms, or words first recorded in his works and therefore possibly invented by him" (Rosenblum, 2005, p. 91). Today's student can understand how new vocabulary can emerge. New words that have emerged over the last few decades include Internet, computer, cell phone, and computer disc. When students understand how modern language has evolved into our present day vernacular, comparing Shakespeare's own inventive words can add meaning and understanding to the discursive symbolic meaning found in Shakespeare's writing.

Seeing Shakespeare's writing as a canvas of creativity can inspire students to seek deeper meaning in their studies and academic disciplines. "Some words that we think of as part of the general vocabulary of English made their first appearance (or at least their first appearance) in Shakespeare's works" (Rosenblum, 2005, p. 91). Words credited to Shakespeare's creativity include "assassination, fretful, laughable, duteous, dwindle, domineer, and amazement" (Rosenblum, 2005, p. 91).

Nondiscursive Symbolic Forms

Symbolics not only focuses on the discursive concepts and applications of ordinary language, but also provides an opportunity for expression through the use of nondiscursive symbolic forms. Types of nondiscursive symbolic forms include the use of signals, bodily gestures, and facial expressions. In Shakespeare, the stage positioning and bodily gestures of the actors aided the audience in understanding the thoughts and feelings of the actors not known by other characters in the play. For example, bodily gestures in the form of "asides" were powerful tools of communication in Shakespeare's theatrical writings and prose.

In today's society, students have the opportunity to see and understand the thoughts and feelings of characters in moments translated outside of the main action of the play. Many movies today aimed at the teenage audience will use "asides" by the main characters in order to add depth and psychological meaning to their product.

A technique to connect nondiscursive learning methods to student's overall learning achievement and mastery would be to divide the students in groups and brainstorm movie names that utilize this dramatic and literary symbolic tool of asides. When students see that Shakespeare utilized symbolic tools to help create meaning and understanding, they will be better able to identify and understand Shakespeare's deeper meanings and intonations in his writings.

Dreams

"It is important for an educator to realize that everyone dreams, including the teacher. In order for students to have genuine interest in a subject, it must appeal to their imagination, not to the teachers" (Kritsonis, 2007, p. 754). In a *Midsummer Nights Dream,* dreams are used to describe bizarre happenings that had to do with fairies. This nondiscursive symbolic form is another way to add meaning and clarity to student's global understanding of Shakespeare's plays. Students can connect with times they may have dreamed themselves and what these dreams have meant to their own personal lives and understandings.

Empirics: The Second Realm of Meaning

Kritsonis (2007) explains the second realm of meaning.

> Empirics includes the sciences of the physical world, of living things, and of man. These sciences provide factual descriptions, generations, and theoretical formulations and explanations that are based upon observation and experimentation in the world of matter, life, mind, and society. (p.12)

Psychology and the social sciences are also important parts of the *empiric* philosophy and second realm of meaning. In the psychological realm, Freud's interpretation of Shakespeare opened new opportunities for study and reflection. According to Dunton-Downer and Riding,

> Freud focuses on Hamlet's supposed Oedipal complex. His approach freed scholars and critics to study Shakespeare and his characters through an ever imaginable prism from Marxism to feminism. Indeed, in recent decades, near-scientific analysis has come to dominate academia's view of Shakespeare. (2004, p. 37)

At-risk students can be challenged to see the correlation between political science, psychology, and science in their study of Shakespeare. As the students began to emerge to a new level of academic achievement, they will see that all learning is connected. Creative teachers can utilize hands-on activities and group discussion and interaction to reinforce the ideas that the world of Shakespeare was multifaceted and worthy to be studied and understood.

Included in the realm of empirics is the area of the social sciences. "Social science deals with the world of culture and society, a world of which human beings are themselves the architects" (Kritsonis, 2007, p. 245). Sociology studies people, their needs and values, and their family structures and how individuals can relate to themselves, their families, and the world at large. When studying sociology, it is important to note that "the chief aim of sociology is to provide an array of relatively precise descriptive and explanatory categories for understanding the exceedingly diverse and complicated phenomena of social behavior" (Kritsonis, 2007, p. 246).

Students today live in a world where wealth is not always distributed evenly or fairly. Many of our students in today's classroom are considered middle class. Open discourses on what it is like to be a member of a particular class can help students further enjoy and gain a better understanding of the multilayered characterization of Shakespeare's literary figures.

Esthetics: The Third Realm of Meaning

Most every student in today's educational community can identify with art, music, and dance. "In the *esthetic* realm the functional curriculum makes use of the arts as means of self-expression, affording psychological release and better integration of vital energies" (Kritsonis, 2007, p. 765).

The third realm of meaning, esthetics, has much to offer in the realm of communicating to today's teenage population. Kritsonis (2007) states that

> Esthetics contains the various arts, such as music, the visual arts, the arts of movement, and literature. Meanings in this realm are concerned with the contemplative perception of particular significant things as unique objectifications of ideated subjectivities. (p. 2)

Shakespeare is filled with beautiful and artistic metaphors, symbolic images, and graceful forms of artistic literary renditions. Kritsonis (2007) says:

> Of all the arts, probably the most widely influential in the communication of meaning are the arts of literature. Since language is a highly developed means of expression for purposes of general communication, the literary artist has the advantage of employing a commonly accepted and widely understood medium. (p. 363)

Many students, who do not excel academically, are dramatically gifted in other areas. Therefore, by highlighting the connection of art, movement, and literature found in Shakespeare, students are given another avenue of expression and opportunity for success by learning and applying their own artistic talents to classroom learning objectives and goals.

Pageantry and staging became an important part of in the performance of Shakespeare's plays. Roseblum (2005) states:

> From the 1850s to World War I, Charles Kean, Henry Irving, and Herbert Beerhom Tree produced Henry VIII in a manner of extravagant opulence that had not been known before and would not be attempted afterwards. They spent lavishly on realistic sets and costumes. (p. 298)

This beauty and pageantry "was by far the most ambitious presentation as to splendor of background and pageantry" (Rosenblum, 2005, p. 299). Pageantry and beauty used in Shakespeare's plays is another example how understanding the applying of the third realm of meaning, *esthetics*, can be used to enhance student learning and appreciation of Shakespeare drama and theatrical productions.

The Visual Arts

"A new art form was created in the [eighteenth] century known as bardolatry symbolizing its connection with the "Bard." Artists such as Henry Fuseli, William Blak, and later, John Everett Millais, helped to enshrine Shakespeare as England's great poet" (Dunton-Downer & Riding, 2004, p. 472). These artists reproduced prints that depicted characters and scenes in Shakespeare's most famous plays. The trend continued throughout the nineteenth century. "French Romantics like Delacroix, Classeriau, and Moreau were also depicting key moments from Shakespeare plays. By the end of the nineteenth century, the fashion for Shakespeare in art had run its course" (Dunton-Downer & Riding 2004, p. 472).

Artistic beauty can also be seen in the writings of Shakespeare through the descriptive use of words to describe natural beauty and metaphorical comparisons. Artists have long provided their constituents with beautiful, naturalistic pictures and paintings of nature and her surroundings. Artistic imagery is pronounced in *Romeo and Juliet* when Juliet is overheard musing about the fair young man that she has met. "That which we call a rose by any other name would smell as sweet" (Act II, Scene II).

Many students feel that they are not capable of understanding higher order, cognitive thinking material and texts. They therefore give up and sometimes refuse to cooperate with administrators, teachers and school officials. However, when students began to explore the six realms of meaning and find that they can achieve meaning and significance in their learning, they become motivated and inspired to try harder in their classrooms and to worker harder for academic success.

Music and the Arts

Shakespeare was also influential in the area of musical composition and performance. Plays such as *A Midsummer Night's Dream* have inspired musical composers and artistic choreographers for hundreds of years. "Purcell's 1692 *Fairy Queen*, was based on *A Midsummer Night's Dream*" (Dunton-Downer & Riding, 2004, p.

207). Numerous movies and Broadway plays have derived their inspiration and story lines from Shakespeare's writing. "*The Comedy of Errors* gave Richard Rodgers and Lorenz Hart their story for *The Boys from Syracuse* in 1938, while a decade later Cole Porter borrowed from *The Taming of the Shrew* to write the musical *Kiss Me Kate*" (Dunton-Downer & Riding, 2004, p. 207). With such a rich heritage of modern theatrical plays, musicals, operas, and modern-day themed movies, connecting the curriculum with students' everyday world will be easier, making students learning more significant and long lasting.

The Art of Movement

Movement is another form of esthetic symbolic communication. Shakespeare's romantic and philosophical play about young love has been immortalized through "Prokofiev's ballet *Romeo and Juliet*" (Dunton-Downer & Riding, 2004, p. 473). Teenagers will be able to relate to the communication of meaning through dance.

Literature, Shakespeare and the Fairy Tale

Ways of Knowing Through the Realms of Meaning encourages the creative use of all genres of literature to create meaning and understanding in a subject matter. One symbolic tool used to create meaning is the fairy tale. Fairy tales are rich in imagery and can communicate life lessons in creative and visionary manners.

The story of *King Lear* lends itself to connecting it to the fairy tale genre. If one compares the story of Cinderella with the story of *King Lear* one can find relationships that may not have been seen or enjoyed by the student learners in previous studies.

In the story of *Cinderella*, there was a beautiful young girl everyone called Cinderella. She was treated as a stepchild and was not loved by her stepmother and stepsisters, who were evil and cruel, and therefore not very beautiful. All is not lost for Cinderella. A handsome prince is charmed by her beauty. He falls in love with her, they are married and they live happily ever after.

In another kingdom, there was a king who was near death. He had a deep love for his three daughters and believed that they loved him, too. Two of his daughters, unknown to him at the beginning, were very evil, and did not really love their father. They professed their love for their father and were given great portions of land as an inheritance. When the third daughter was asked to express her love for her father, she could not find the words. Although she loved her father deeply, she could not express herself except to say "my love's more richer than my tongue" (Act I, Scene I).

At the end of the story, the King saw the treachery of his two daughters who professed a love they did not possess. His remorse was penned by William Shakespeare in these words, "How sharper than a serpent's tooth it is to have a thankless child" (Act I, Scene IV). He realizes that the one true daughter, who has by this time married to the King of France, is the only daughter who truly loved him.

The Fourth Realm of Meaning: Synnoetics

High school students are in a transitional time period in their lives. Personal relationships become more important to the teenager's everyday life. High school students are emerging into young adulthood. Emotions and relationships are extremely important during this time period.

According to Gajowski (2004),

> Shakespeare places as great a value on the sanctity of personal relations in the History Plays as in the tragedies, because he intuits that order depends, not on concepts of hierarchy and degree, but on the fabric of personal and social relationships which is woven by ties of marriage, kinship, and friendship, by communal interests of loyalty and truest. (p. 20)

The synnoetic realm of meaning is structured in order to show general education curriculum how relationships, feelings, and emotions are reflected in learning, literature, and the general education curriculum. "The fourth realm, *synnoetics*, embraces what Michael Polanyl calls "personal knowledge" and Martin Buber the "I-Thou" relation" (Kritsonis, 2007, p. 12).

Relationships are key to understanding Shakespeare. The "I-Thou" relationship affects your thoughts, feelings, and relationships with another person. The "I-It" relationship analyzes how you are able to relate with the objects that enshrine your personal lifestyle and philosophy. In *Romeo and Juliet*, the "I-Thou" relationship is seen countless times. In Act II, Scene II, Romeo laments, "It is the east, and Juliet is the sun."

A primary goal of the study of *synnoetics* is to learn about one's self and his or reaction to everyday life scenarios and happenings. In one of Shakespeare's most notable quotations, Hamlet decries to himself, "to be, or not to be: that is the question" (Scene I, Act III). Hamlet, in a period of self-reflection, begins to mediate on what he sees in himself. He reflects on everything his soul and spirit feels in "his mind's eye" (Act I, Scene II). The universal need to know one's self and to be true to that self is a universal principal of survival for mankind.

> For most people, literature is more influential than any other cultural resource for growth in personal knowledge. Drama, poetry, the novel, and biography exert profound effects on the consciousness of human relatedness. (Kritsonis, 2007, p. 426)

Shakespeare's writings are filled with the psychoanalytical personality descriptions and nuances of individual characters that are portrayed in such a way as to make them viable figures to understand and to mirror and compare our own reactions to life challenges and unexpected tragedies and grief.

Synnoetics allows for character exploration by assessing one's knowledge of himself and his environment. Kritsonis (2007) states,

> In Shakespeare's *King Lear,* one can see by means of the various characters, the revelation of personality running the gamut from nobility to foolishness, modesty to arrogance, generosity to greed, loyalty to treachery, compassion to cruelty, love to hate, and honesty to deceitfulness. (p. 428)

Because Shakespeare is a pronounced and influential dramatist, studying his plays and characters can give insight into personal meaning and existence.

Students taught that there is room for personal meaning and reflection in literature will be more apt to study and apply the literary concepts to their own lives when they know that what they are reading has meaning and purpose that can directly relate to their daily existence and lifestyle.

Shakespeare is a literary giant in terms of his penned contributions to the field of exceptional drama and written discourse. Shakespeare is responsible for significant plays that run the gamut of classification from tragic drama, stimulating historical plays, amusing and entertaining comedies, as well as heart wrenching romantic stories about love, sacrifice, and commitment, such as found in the story of *Romeo and Juliet.*

Utilizing Shakespeare and the *Ways of Knowing Through the Realms of Meaning* will help high school students to better analyze characters and situations in order to make better decisions in their own personal life. A teacher can use the story of *King Lear* to discuss how greed can affect family relationships. Inner feelings about love and relationships can find a fertile soil for discussion in the love story of *Romeo and Juliet.* High school students have mostly learned by this time that there is evil and good in the world in which we live. Literature gives at-risk and low performing students the opportunity to see that their inner feelings and ambitions are not significantly different from characters they read about in their literature studies.

The Fifth Realm of Meaning: Ethics

The fifth realm of meaning, ethics, has to do with moral conduct and knowledge based on morality. Understanding morality and applying ethics to our everyday experiences provides insight into our decision making processes. "The realm of ethics, then, is right action. The central concept in this domain is obligation or what ought to be done" (Kritsonis, 2007, p. 452).

In Shakespeare's *Macbeth,* there are moral decisions made by Macbeth and his wife, Lady Macbeth, that corrupt the human nature and allow evil consequences to abound. "It is said that every person is endowed with a native intuition of the right which, if he attend to it and obeys it, will enable him to know right from wrong" (Kritsonis, 2007, p. 441). Disobeying one's conscience can lead to guilt and despair. Macbeth succumbed to murder. Guilt and remorse came quickly. According to Kritsonis (2007),

> Authentic moral meanings are reestablished only when the extraordinary mystery of unconditional obligation is recognized and when the secret inward claim of conscience is reinforced by the consideration of moral dilemmas where the easy justification of prudence and custom do suffice. (p. 766)

Morality and the study of right and wrong are critical themes worthy of study in our society. Students who learn to make sound decisions based on their own logic and reasoning skills will have a deeper understanding of how their moral decisions affect their own personal lives and the society in which they live.

The Sixth Realm of Meaning: Synoptics

The sixth realm of meaning is synoptics. Synoptics "comprises meanings having an integrative function, uniting meanings from all the realms into a unified perspective, that is providing a "single vision" or "synopsis" of meanings. The chief synoptic disciplines are history, religion, and philosophy" (Kritsonis, 2007, p. 479).

History

Shakespeare used his plays to influence and fortify public opinion on political events taking place on the world stage. At-risk and low performing high school students will benefit from the study of Shakespeare's historical dramas because they will gain historical knowledge coupled with the ability to make literary interpretations of Shakespeare's meanings utilizing the framework of the *Ways of Knowing Through the Realms of Meaning*. According to Rosenblum (2005),

> Shakespeare's primary concerns in *Henry VIII* lie in the uses and abuses of power in relation to justice, injustice, conscience, and truth, and not so much the legitimacy of the monarch's authority that he had explored in the history plays covering the reigns from King John to Richard III. (p. 294)

Shakespeare's plays bore some resemblance to historical correctness. However, Shakespeare did use literary license at times to rearrange chronological orders and to define characters in a way that would fit his story line rather than history's exacting standards for accuracy. Shakespeare's digression from historical fact is evidenced in the Henry IV plays. Rosenblum (2005) further explains,

> Shakespeare makes three important alterations to historical characters: Falstaff, Henry IV, and Hotspur. Supposing Falstaff to have been based originally, for whatever reason, on Sir John Oldcastle, Shakespeare changes the age of this character. Oldcastle died at the age of 35, yet Shakespeare presents Falstaff as being much older (p. 235).

At-risk students benefit from reading Shakespeare by understanding that Shakesperian literature is multifaceted. Shakespearian studies allow a student's knowledge and understanding of the curriculum to be enhanced to a degree that the student recognizes the significance of his learning and the reason for his or her commitment to the discipline and acquisition of meaning and knowledge.

Shakespeare's knowledge of history gives him an added advantage to incorporate historical events with literary excellence. Students who study Shakespeare's history plays will find that they are immersed in studies that cross the line of the academic disciplines. While Shakespeare is studied in English classes, his work is equally important to those who study world history.

Religion

According to Noble (1935),

> Opinion has differed somewhat sharply as to the extent of Shakespeare's Biblical knowledge. Some have maintained that he knew much, others that such acquaintance with the Bible as he exhibited was no more than might be expected from an intelligent listener in an age when Biblical subjects were much discussed. (p.18)

However, "much of the greatest music, painting, and architecture has been inspired by religious faith and has served to inspire others to a similar devotion" (Kritsonis, 2007, p. 504).

Biblical allusions are pronounced in Shakespeare's writings. "Allusion is made in *King John* to the sun standing still, without mentioning Joshua. Five times, most notably by Cleopatra, reference is made to the reply by the Shunamite woman to Elisha's inquiry as to her dead child's health" (Noble, 1935, p. 21). It is clear that Shakespeare's reflections and knowledge of the Christian Bible were influential in his writings. Scripture referential usages in Shakespeare enriched the overall language and depth of meaning of his writings.

In the story of *Macbeth*, Lady Macbeth tries to rid herself of guilt and responsibility. "A little water clears us of this deed" (Act II, Scene II). This incident of cleansing and purification can be seen when Pilate washed his hands to symbolize his relinquishment of responsibility from the crime of sentencing Jesus to death.

Philosophy

All levels of human experience fall within the realm of philosophy. Philosophy challenges the individual to develop and "construct a synoptic view of the entire range of expressible human experiences, insofar as they can be interpreted within the categories of rational discourse" (Kritsonis, 2007, p. 535). Analyzing and interpreting philosophical viewpoints requires a higher level of thinking than is generally displayed by at-risk and lower performing students in the high school academic arena. Teaching students through *Ways of Knowing Through the Realms of Meaning* can clarify and enhance a student's ability to gain a deeper understanding and knowledge of the subject matter.

There are three main components of interpreting philosophy: analysis, evaluation, and synthesis. Utilizing the *Ways of Knowing Through the Realms of Meaning*, students can be taught to analyze a selection of reading material, evaluate the material based on their experiences, and then apply their new learning to their own daily life experiences and life goals.

Well-known famous quotes from Shakespeare exhibit how philosophical ideas can be translated into the human psyche. Philosophical inquiries allow the student of philosophy to think deeply and develop life goals and edicts that can help the student to exhibit sound judgment and make wise decisions.

Jewels of wisdom and expression are replete in Shakespeare's writings. Famous quotes with philosophical meanings and intent from Shakespeare's play, *As You Like It* include "The fool doth think he is wise, but the wise man knows himself to be a fool" (Act V, Scene I). Deeper reasonings and philosophical understandings can also be found in the play *Julius Caesar*, "Men at some time are masters of their fates: The fault, dear Brutus, is not in our stars, but in ourselves, that we are underlings" (Act I, Scene II).

The Value of Utilizing Ways of Knowing Through the Realms of Meaning

"Disciplined understanding leads to further insight; undisciplined thought does not" (Kritsonis, 2007, p. 665). *Ways of Knowing Through the Realms of Meaning* offers a framework for curriculum study that adds meaning and direction to the study and mastery level of a given subject area. Teaching students to critically view their world is an important part of the total education process. Kritsonis (2007) defines the complete person. He says,

> A complete person should be skilled in the use of speech, symbol, and gesture (symbolics), factually well-informed (empirics), capable of creating and appreciating others (synnoetics), able to make wise decisions and judge between right and wrong (ethics), and possessed of an integral outlook (synoptics). (p. 15)

These realms of meaning will prove to be an affective component of a strong and vibrant curriculum for the at-risk and underachieving high school student.

CONCLUSION

A productive society is a literate society. Today's student must engage in higher level cognitive thinking in order to be able to successfully live and compete in today's technologically advanced society. It is incumbent for a society to prepare future generations to think creatively, apply knowledge responsibly, and to teach students the importance of critical thinking utilizing the philosophies based on the *Ways of Knowing Through the Realms of Meaning*.

In order to ensure that our citizenry is prepared to meet the challenges of the future, educators must provide an avenue of learning that is conducive to the challenges of the twenty-first century. The philosophical basis for *Ways of Knowing Through the Realms of Meaning* provides a framework for a creative, structured approach to education.

"Knowledge can be derived from a variety of sources. However, knowledge has permanent value leading to greater meaning and greater understanding when drawn from the fundamental disciplines as exemplified in the realms of meaning" (Kritsonis, 2007, p. 716). Now teacher's can utilize the philosophy outlined in *Ways of Knowing Through the Realms of Meaning* to structure learning so that the classroom educational goals will be met and students will be engaged in active and creative learning.

The final outcome of education should be a populace of educated, well-versed students who are able to read, analyze, and synthesize meaning in the daily construct of their life existence. "Knowledge can be derived from a variety of sources. However, knowledge has permanent value leading to greater meaning and greater understanding when drawn from the fundamental disciplines as exemplified in the realms of meaning" (Kritsonis, 2007, p. ix).

The students in our classroom are filled of potential. Unleashing the potential within the student is the educator's greatest challenge in this new century of explosive knowledge and discovery. "A revolution of quantity has taken place, demanding a wholly different orientation to learning" (Kritsonis, 2007, p. 648). This knowledge explosion has been accelerated with significant advances in technology. Incorporating technology into the classroom can greatly increase the learning capabilities of all students, especially those considered "at risk" in today's high school classroom. Utilizing the structure found my book the *Ways of Knowing Through the Realms of Meaning*, students can research new material for study in an organized and easy to understand format.

As school leaders seek to make decisions on what to teach in the curriculum, "the curriculum designer must spend more time narrowing down what material to teach than looking for material to teach" (Kritsonis, 2007, p. 644). This poses a particular dilemma for educators who seek to find a way to teach students who are already struggling to be academically successful. "When a person is faced with a huge mass of bewildering material that he cannot master his frustration begets a feeling of hopelessness and despair" (Kritsonis, 2007, p. 642).

To turn academic frustration into academic achievement, utilizing the concepts of *Ways of Knowing Through the Realms of Meaning* can provide a structure for academic achievement and success in the classroom. Teaching Shakespeare using the structure of the *Ways of Knowing Through the Realms of Meaning* can significantly increase academic achievement, even for at-risk students.

The future will go to those who are prepared. By uniting the curriculum Through the structure found in the *Ways of Knowing Through the Realms of Meaning*, "the educator can seize the opportunity to battle such areas as fragmentation, surfeit, and transience of knowledge, by showing what kinds of knowledge are required for full understanding" (Kritsonis, 2007, p. 74). Students can be inspired to gather knowledge from classic literature and to apply their new knowledge to the overall purpose and meaning of their education.

Shakespeare studies, cloaked with the philosophy and curriculum structure of the *Ways of Knowing Through the Realms of Meaning*, can be mastered successfully by at-risk students. Students can be creatively challenged to learn using this structure. Teachers can be inspired to apply new heuristic methods of teaching to their curriculum. In the end, great teachers will keep in mind that "students do not fantasize about what they already have. The successful teacher will take them where they have not been" (Kritsonis, 2007, p. 762).

REFERENCES

Dunton-Downer, L. & Riding, A. (2004). *Essential Shakespeare handbook*. New York, NY: DK.

Gajowski, E. (2004). *Re-visions of America.* Newark, NJ: University of Delaware Press.

Kritsonis, W. A. (2007). *Ways of knowing Through the realms of meaning.* Houston, TX: National Forum Journals.

Noble, R. (1935). *Shakespeare's biblical knowledge.* New York, NY: Macmillan.

Rosenblum, J. (2005). *Shakespeare: A comprehensive guide for students.* Westport, CT: Greenwood Press.

Author Contact Information: William Allan Kritsonis, PhD, Whitlowe R. Green College of Education, Delco 233, Prairie View A&M University/The Texas A&M University System, Box 519, Prairie View, TX 77446. Telephone: 936-261-3530. E-mail: wakritsonis@pvamu.edu

Section 11: Leadership and Management Theory

INTRODUCTION

SECTION EDITOR

Fenwick W. English

University of North Carolina at Chapel Hill

Managerial theory or perhaps more accurately managerial concepts have a long history of influence in educational administration and leadership (Callahan, 1962; Culbertson, 1988). One of the very earliest texts in school administration set forth tenets which still resonate in the accountability movement in the twenty-first century.

> Good management begins with economy. The management of a school, as of any other enterprise, has for its prime purpose the securing of the largest possible returns for the expenditure involved. Money paid for schools and the yet more valuable time of children are the investments entrusted by the public to the hands of teachers. Results, in the form of practical efficiency, mental power, character, and that intangible product called culture, are the returns demanded. (Bennett, 1917, p. 2)

Furthermore, even at this very early time, Bennett stressed the need for "demonstrable results" by intoning:

> The time has come when *results should be of a more demonstrable and largely measurable sort.* Merely spending so many hours a year in "completing" time-hallowed "courses" in traditional "subjects" can no longer be accepted without challenge as adequate proof of efficiency. Nor should a school or system be measured by tests of its own devising. To encourage investment the net profits of an industry should be measurable directly by the investors. (p. 2, emphasis in original)

Much of the reform rhetoric of the early twenty-first is replete with calls for efficiency and results based on standardized test data (Ravitch, 2010). Many of the reformers come from private sector management and believe that the application of proven business techniques represent the savior of public school administration (Gerstner, 2008; Riley, 2009). Managerial theory is itself an eclectic hodgepodge from a variety of disciplines. And in the classic sense it isn't even a theory in that most approaches to management are not about testing hypotheses as Griffiths (1959) once advocated, but rather about fidelity to set of precepts or principles upon which the practice of management or administration is then based. So theory as it is used in this section assumes the broadest and most inclusive focus, that is, a narrative regarding the conduct of educational organizations of which only some may be possible to empirically test in the classic notion of positivistic theory formulation (English, 1994). To be useful to advance the field it must be possible to formulate notions of practice that are conceived as art forms as opposed to classical behaviorist theory (English, 2008; English & Papa, 2010). In short, for educational administration and leadership to advance, science must be blended with art to capture the dimensions of values and morality that are integral parts of creating a more ethical and equitable society (English, 2008). The chapters in this section reflect that purpose. Here now is a chapter by chapter review.

GENERAL MANAGEMENT THEORY

The opening chapter in this section by Thu Suong Thi Nguyen of Indiana University-Indianapolis and Gary Crow of Indiana University in Bloomington provides a good historical background of what has been termed "classical management theory" in educational administration. For anyone who wants to understand the continuing influence of Taylorism (the "scientific management" of Frederick Taylor) in the accountability movement, this chapter frames out the issues very well.

Scientific management is far from dead, it keeps on being reinvented decade after decade.

The Handbook of Educational Theories, pp. 887–890

TRAIT THEORY

Professor Kathleen Brown of the University of North Carolina at Chapel Hill discusses the creation of trait theory as the culmination of one of the first notions of leadership and the oldest actual theory of leadership. The precept that leaders are born and not made rests on the idea that leadership is anchored to innate, internal traits that some people have and others do not. Such ideas are still popular in the literature, having originated in such classics as Plutarch's *Lives* and Plato's *Republic.* Brown asserts that leadership theories have revived the trait approach because of new research on heritability and genes. She also reviews recent critiques of it. This is a completely refocused vision of the origination and impact of the trait theory of leadership.

DISCOURSE THEORY

Professor Autumn Cyprés of the University of Tennessee at Knoxville indicates that discourse theory, semiotic studies and sociolinguistics have had a profound impact on notions concerning leadership studies, especially through the work of the post-structuralists as Foucault, Derrida and Barthes. Behind the work of these theorists is the aim of deconstructing traditional perspectives regarding the nature of reality and truth. Of particular concern is the concentration on power and the politics of words and their meaning. It is generally accepted that leaders tell stories and discourse theory seeks to understand the difference between "ordinary" narratives and how they are part of constructing political hegemony, especially in the case of school leaders.

BUREAUCRATIC THEORY

Professor Eugenie Samier of the British University of Dubai, a Canadian scholar on Max Weber, reviews the myths, models and critiques around bureaucratic theory. Samier has read Weber in the original German and is acknowledged as an international expert on Weber. She differentiates between bureaucratic organizations and the analytic theory of bureaucracy in interpretive and critical studies. Finally, Samier reviews the major critiques of bureaucratic theory in both public administration and educational administration.

CONTINGENCY MANAGEMENT AND SITUATIONAL LEADERSHIP THEORIES

Professor Joann Danelo Barbour of Texas Woman's University presents contingency management and situational leadership as two sides of the same coin embedded in open systems theory. Barbour indicates why leaders or managers who may be successful in one setting may fail in other settings. She differentiates between contingency management theories and situational theorists as it pertains to leader capability and other contextual variables, but acknowledges that the major strength behind both is that they move the thinking of the field beyond the "one best type of leader" notion of the trait theorists and the early behaviorists.

CRITICAL RACE THEORY

Floyd D. Beachum, Bennett Professor of urban school leadership at Lehigh University in Pennsylvania, explains how critical race theory (CRT) provides a unique way to examine race and racism in American society. CRT is an offshoot of critical legal studies and critical pedagogy. Beachum denotes the major tenets of critical race theory which includes counter-story telling, the permanence of racism, whiteness as property, interest convergence and a general critique of liberalism. CRT places value on qualitative data sources and the importance of recognizing the perspectives of the voices and viewpoints of communities of color.

RATIONAL CHOICE THEORY

The predominance of economics and economic analyses as embodied in rational choice theory (RCT) in educational administration and leadership is highlighted in this chapter by Ric Brown, a former provost in the California State University system, and Rosemary Papa, the Del and Jewell Lewis Endowed Chair at Northern University in Flagstaff, Arizona. They trace the origin of the theory to Frederick Taylor's scientific management and the theories of Mary Parker Follett and later Herbert Simon's concept of *satisficing.* RCT is also influenced by Weberian bureaucratic theory. RCT places a premium emphasis on the creation of organizational goals, roles and technology. There are many variations of RCT and the chapter closes with how the theory has been criticized, including the notion that not all administrative actions are rational.

THEORY OF DEMOCRATIC ADMINISTRATION

Lisa A.W. Kensler of Auburn University and Jeffrey S. Brooks of the University of Missouri-Columbia review the intersection of democracy and school administration, beginning with the concept of democracy in education as advanced by John Dewey. They also review the assumptions of democracy which include the idea that humanity is perfectible and that every person is worthy of participation and should be treated with dignity, as well as the tenet that gains should be shared by all in an organizational (school setting).

Theory of Aesthetics and Administration

A second chapter by Eugenie Samier of the British University of Dubai is centered on the aesthetics of leadership. She points out that while aesthetics is rarely explicitly discussed, it is usually implicitly present and frequently referred to metaphorically in leadership studies because it helps identify and analyze the expressive qualities of leaders. In addition it has value in assessing creativity and innovation and styles of performance and communication. It is only through aesthetics that the disciplines informing leadership can be integrated between the humanities and the social sciences.

Bourdieu's Theory of Misconnaissance or Misrecognition by Educational Leaders

Senior Lecturer Cheryl L. Bolton of Staffordshire University in the United Kingdom explains how the French philosopher and sociologist Pierre Bourdieu's theory of misrecognition explains why even with the express intent of changing schooling practices there is little actual change. The reason is that the reformers fail to take into account their own self-interests in proposing innovation and changes. She also explores the idea that change agents exist within fields of influence in which they compete with one another and other agencies for legitimacy. Educational leaders are one such group within the larger educational field and their ideas of change or reform advance their own power and authority to continue controlling and enhancing their own position within contested social fields. The chapter closes with several critiques of the theory of misrecognition based on empirical investigations in several countries.

Mentoring Theories for Educational Practitioners

Professor Carol A. Mullen of the University of North Carolina at Greensboro explores the many types of mentoring theories in use including collaborative mentoring, mosaic mentoring, multiple-level comentoring and synergistic leadership. The historical roots of mentoring are cited in the creation of apprenticeship learning which later morphed into craft guilds. Today mentoring can consist of short-term, needs-based training or in forms of peer coaching. True mentoring, however, is more steeped in theory than either coaching or forms of professional induction experiences. The chapter includes descriptions of specific alternative mentoring theories.

Kitsch Leadership Models: A Critique or "Who Moved My Theory?"

Professor Rosemary Papa and Ric Brown team up with Daniel L. Kain, Vice Provost of Academic Personnel at Northern Arizona University, to critique pseudo theory as embodied in Eugenie Samier's (2005) notion of "kitsch leadership." This leadership model is best exemplified in many of the simplistic ideas of leadership as represented in some of the best selling paperback books about leadership which promise easy answers to complex problems replete with happy endings. Such works are usually *atheoretical* and consist of common platitudes which are passed off as theory.

Critical Feminist Theory

Professors Michelle D. Young of the University of Virginia and Catherine Marshall at the University of North Carolina at Chapel Hill examine a broad range of feminist criticism in sociopolitical contexts which has lead to the evolution of critical feminist theory or CFT. They address the need for identifying the forces which have led to the construction of gender and exposed gendered power relationships in employment, families, religions, schools, businesses and politics. A pursuit of these questions illustrates how governments provide legitimacy for patriarchal institutions and reify gender domination in policy and practice. Young and Marshall's concept of critical feminist theory builds on critical theory's focus on issues of power and privilege and the way social systems are constituted to embody these power relations around gender. They also explore the question of whether critical feminist theory does indeed represent all women or does not recognize, lesbian-gay-bisexual-transgendered-queer members as well. Finally, this chapter identifies hegemonic realities and illustrates how women and men can help people with agency resist oppression and assist them in the struggle to challenge the assumptions that dominate programs and even research methods in our field.

The Synergistic Leadership Theory: An Inclusive Theory in the Twenty-First Century

The last chapter in this section, authored by Drs. Beverly Irby, Genevieve Brown, and LingLing Yang, presents the first leadership theory, the synergistic leadership theory (SLT), published in the twenty-first century, appearing in the *Journal of Educational Administration* in 2002. The SLT is an inclusive theory which was developed purposefully to include the voices and experiences of female leaders. Additionally, there are several validation studies which have tested the theory related to (a) both male and female leaders, (b) various levels of administrative positions, and (c) differing ethnicities and cultures.

REFERENCES

Bennett, H. (1917). *School efficiency: A manual of modern school management.* Boston, MA: Ginn and Company.

Callahan, R. (1962). *Education and the cult of efficiency.* Chicago, IL: University of Chicago Press.

Culbertson, J. (1988). A century's quest for a knowledge base. In N.J. Boyan (Ed.). *Handbook of research on educational administration* (pp. 3-26). New York, NY: Longman.

English, F. (1994). *Theory in educational administration.* New York, NY: Harper Collins.

English, F. (2008). *Anatomy of professional practice: Promising research perspectives on educational leadership.* Lanham, MD: Rowman & Littlefield Education.

English, F., & Papa, R. (2010). *Restoring human agency to educational administration: Status and strategies.* Lancaster, PA: Pro-Active.

Gerstner, L. (2008, December 1). Lessons from 40 years of education reform. *The Wall Street Journal,* p. A23.

Griffiths, D. (1959). *Administrative theory.* New York, NY: Appleton-Century-Crofts.

Ravitch, D. (2010). *The death and life of the great American school system.* New York, NY: Basic Books.

Riley, N. (2009, August 29). We're in the venture philanthrophy business. *The Wall Street Journal,* p. 11.

Samier, E. (2005). Toward public administration as a humanities discipline: A humanistic manifesto. *Halduskultuur: Administrative Culture, 6,* 6-59.

Author Contact Information: Fenwick W. English, PhD, 121B Peabody Hall, University of North Carolina Chapel Hill, North Carolina. Phone: 919-843-4572. E-mail: fenglish@attglobal.net

CHAPTER 75

Classical Management Theory

Thu Suong Thi Nguyen and Gary M. Crow
Indiana University-IUPUI, Indianapolis, IN

The descriptor "theory" assigned Classical Management Theory is something of a misnomer serving to perpetuate what is in effect a set of normative principles. Grounded in notions of technical rationality, these principles presume to enhance the efficiency of organizations through systematization, standardization, and scientific investigation. Unmerited moniker notwithstanding, the legacy of classical management theory—or scientific management to which it will be referred hereafter—cannot be understated. This chapter provides a description of the goals and assumptions particular to scientific management, a discussion of its development and legacy; a review of the validity and generalizability of the model; uses and applications of the model; and suggests critiques of the model.

The goals and assumptions undergirding Scientific Management can be traced to the early work of Frederick Winslow Taylor (1911). In his *Principles of Scientific Management*, Taylor delineated 13 principles of management[1] meant to advance and inform the work of industrial engineers at the turn of the century. Administration of organizations through these principles facilitated goals of efficiency and economy through maximization of output production with minimization of inputs.

Taylor's (1911) conception of scientific management assumes a technical rational view of individuals and organizations. That is, the worker was viewed as wanting "beyond anything else high wages, and what employers want from their workmen most of all is a low labor cost of manufacture" (p. 22). Thus, organizational structures could be designed to capitalize on the self-interest of individuals—a "specially designed system of compensation would help bring employee contributions into alignment with organizational interests" (Ogawa, Crowson, & Goldring, 1999, p. 280). The resulting division of labor became one mechanism through which workplace tasks could be systematized and standardized with managers and consultants taking up scientific investigation toward these ends. In short, it was assumed administrative work could be reduced to a set of technical propositions which when applied to organizations would enhance efficiency (Fayol, 2005; Gulick & Urwick, 1969).

In his analysis of Taylorism, Littler (1978) examined three dimensions of the management model including: (a) divisions of labor; (b) structures of control over task performance; and (c) implicit employment relationships. The first of these dimensions, divisions of labor, were based on five principles constituting a "dynamic of deskilling." These principles include: (a) a general principle of maximum fragmentation promoting limitations of individual jobs to a single task; (b) separation of planning and doing; (c) suppression of worker's activities and involvement in the preparation and organization of his/her own work; (d) minimization of skill requirements and job-learning time; and (e) material handling reduced to a minimum.

The second dimension of Taylor's scientific management—structure of control over task performance—is characterized by standardization. Taylor (1967) described standardization as follows:

> The work of every workman is fully planned out by the management at least one day in advance, and each man receives in most cases complete written instructions, describing in detail the task which he is to accomplish, as well as the means to be used in doing the work.... This task specifies not only what is to be done but how it is to be done and the exact time allowed for doing it. (p. 39)

The structure of control was also characterized by what Taylor termed *functional organization*. That is, not only were workers to be subdivided and deskilled, but managers too were functionally organized into a division of

The Handbook of Educational Theories, pp. 891–896

management paralleling the division of labor. Monitoring systems became central to Taylor's structure of control. As supervisory abilities diminished due to the growth of large complex organizations with increased physical separation, demand for monitoring from a distance through performance documentation grew.

Finally, Taylor's incentive payment scheme implied a particular employment relationship. Beyond a means of control over task performance, reproduction of "the bifurcation of the organization into the rulers and the ruled" (Foster, 1986, p. 190), is perpetuated in the "atomization of the workforce" instituted through worker self-interest. This move within the science of administration pointed toward a method of *system* integration and reaffirmed Taylor's apparent disregard for *social* integration.

ORIGINAL DEVELOPMENT AND LEGACY

At the turn of the century and into the 1930s, Taylor's scientific management as a method of labor discipline and plant organization to improve efficiency and expand production through maximization of output to input ratios and benefits to cost were well-received in the United States. Dramatically increased productivity in the business sector evidenced the success of scientific management which was soon championed by the so called "administrative progressives" (Tyack, 1974) in education. Franklin Bobbitt at the University of Chicago and Ellwood Cubberley, Dean of Education at Stanford, among others endorsed the application of Taylor's management principles arguing systematization, standardization, and scientific investigation to enhance productivity and efficiency would benefit schools.

Beginning in the late 1920s research projects including the Hawthorne Experiments of Western Electric Company attempted to extend Taylor's work through investigation of industrial conditions. However, this work "essentially put the Taylorism movement into perspective by arguing that a simple economic approach to work was inadequate, even misguided, in terms of human psychology" (Foster, 1986, pp. 40-41). This marked the beginning of empirical work elaborating on Mary Parker Follett's conceptions of coordination and the resulting human relations movement in administrative theory. As discussed elsewhere in this volume, the human relations movement entered human subjectivity and values into the educational management discourse with an emphasis on informal organization and cultural systems.

The rise of science in educational administration during the 1950s resulted in a movement to replace naïve empiricism with rigorous theorizing. Thirty years later, Willower deciphered a number of trends in research on educational administration including a decided "turn towards philosophy and especially towards epistemological questions" (as cited in Evers & Lakomski, 1996, p. 16). This is demonstrated in Foster's (1986) text *Paradigms and Promises: New Approaches to Educational Administration* that explored epistemological assumptions guiding multiple perspectives of administration. However, Taylor and Fayol's legacy of scientific management in educational administration persists.

Although some might argue Taylorism is dead in the United States, that such an approach to the management of individuals and organizations is no longer feasible in this more complex society dependent on knowledge and information workers rather than factory line workers, our reading of the literature suggests Taylorism is not dead. Through examination of performance indicators, Helsby and Saunders (1993) asserted that Taylorism remains easily identifiable in large-scale social and educational programs. They suggest these manifest in the

> recurrent pattern of centrally devised and standardized programmes, divided into manageable units, aimed at particular target groups, implemented by teacher/ workers, who had not been involved in the planning of the programme, constantly monitored by outsiders concerned with efficiency, and finally judged by "consumers" rather than by "workers." (p. 61)

More recently, Maurice Holt (2001) delineated four "regrettable respects" by which Taylorism persists in education including: (a) separation between educational administration and curriculum planning; (b) a fostering of the teachers viewed as "mere functionaries on the receiving end of curriculum schemes devised elsewhere" (p. 147); (c) an emphasis on outcomes rather than inputs; and (d) a "mania for numerical results" leading to an overly heavy reliance on tests, assessments, audits, and appraisals. Hoy and Miskel (2001) too argue that while Taylorism may be "intellectually out of fashion ... few deny its lasting impact on American society" (p. 12). They describe the lasting effects in contemporary rational systems as embedded in the stress on "goal specificity and formalization because these elements make important contributions to the rationality and efficiency of organizations" (p. 12).

The scientific management envisioned by Taylor and the administrative progressives appears to have undergone a revival. Pollitt (1990) characterized this revival as "more tightly focused, financially disciplined, performance-conscious management" (p. 112). Dubbed neo-Taylorism in British and American managerial reforms of the 1970s and 1980s, neo-Tayloristic means of restructuring and managing schools are constituted in the dynamic deskilling and reskilling of teachers as "'classroom managers' or as supervisors of a predetermined classroom production process" (Carlson, 1986,

p. 22). Further, Ball's (1993, 1994, 2003) "new managerialism" highlights the "installation of the new culture of competitive performativity involves the use of a combination of devolution [site-based management], targets and incentives to bring about new forms of sociality and new institutional forms" (Ball, 2003, p. 219). Taylorism's uniform practices and operating procedures, monitoring systems to enhance performance comparisons, and the stabilization of performance efforts through incentive schemes to ensure calculability and predictability within organizations (Helsby & Saunders, 1993) are augmented with this intensification of scientific management. Specific illustrations of the contemporary uses of scientific management are presented under "Uses and Applications" in this chapter.

VALIDITY OF CLASSICAL MANAGEMENT THEORY

Described as "naïve empiricism" by Evers and Lakomski (1996), mere proverbs by Simon, and "scientism" or "pseudoscience" by English (1994), the validity of scientific management as a theory of administration has been in doubt for no less than eight decades. In his sharp critique, Simon questioned the validity of the "theory" as a set of propositions implying a testable relationship confirming correspondence between theory and observation. He observed, a theory so simply and unambiguously stated ought easily be submitted to empirical test. Taking propositions set forth by Taylor, Simon (1946) illustrated how "for almost every principle one can find an equally plausible and acceptable contradictory principle" (p. 53). Since this time, it is widely acknowledged that scientific management is best understood as a set of normative precepts rather than a "theory" of management.

USES AND APPLICATIONS

As we emphasized previously, the legacy of scientific management has not ended. To illustrate the continuing legacy, in this discussion of the uses and applications of scientific management we present three examples from contemporary educational reform: standardization of teaching, leadership development and turnaround schools. First, few would argue that teaching is less standardized than in the past. For the first time in U.S. history there is a serious and probable move to develop national core standards for all schools. In addition, states and districts have established benchmarks for what teachers must teach and students should learn at different grade levels and periods of the school year. Moreover, with the advent of No Child Left Behind, performance testing and its associated stakes have intensified. This standardization of teaching reflects at least four scientific management principles: (a) the structure of control over task performance; (b) separation of planning and doing; (c) an exclusive focus on the measureable; and (d) an emphasis on performance testing. As Holt (2001) concludes teachers have become "mere functionaries" who are implementing standards, benchmarks, and curriculum created more frequently by noneducators. Numerous reports conclude that there is a narrowing of the curriculum in most U.S. districts to those areas—primarily literacy and numeracy—which are more easily measured. Hargreaves (2004) points out that this standardization of teaching diminishes the creativity and ingenuity necessary in a knowledge society. Even the historian Diane Ravitch (2010) faults the extreme use of testing in public schools in the United States.

A second illustration from contemporary educational reform, which reflects an application of scientific management principles, relates to school leadership development. The preparation of educational leaders, particularly principals, has taken a decided turn toward the acquisition of technical skills. While most experts on leadership development do not deny the importance of skills such as data use and teacher observation, the current lack of emphasis on values, beliefs, and identities reflects an international pattern toward a more technocratic view of leadership development. Leicht and Fennel (2001) describe a trend from a professional orientation to work to a more technocratic and managerial orientation to work. Gronn (2003), contemplating the same trend, refers to this as a move toward "designer leadership," in which leadership development programs become focused on teaching for the test. In fact a host of new providers of leadership development has arisen in the last few years to emphasize skill-based and rapid-entry preparation. One example of this trend is the set of 92 competencies identified by the state of Florida, required of all principal preparation programs in the state, and measured on the Florida educational leadership exam for principal certification. These competencies reflect areas of the job that are easily measured, rather than larger issues of values, beliefs, creativity and identity. This technocratic trend in leadership development reflects several principles of scientific management, including a focus on the measurable, an emphasis on fragmentation and minimalization of skill requirements, and minimalization of job learning time. Lumby and English (2009) assess the trend as the trivialization and miniaturization of leadership. Crow (2009) and Scribner and Crow (2010) note the way professional identity is currently ignored in leadership development with its attendant emphasis on values and beliefs.

The final illustration of the use and application of scientific management in contemporary educational reform relates to turnaround schools. The U.S.

Department of Education has identified four acceptable models for school turnaround (and the funding of these projects) which emphasize firing the principal and half of the teaching staff or turning over the school to a management organization (http://www.ed.gov/blog/2010/03/whats-possible-turning-around-americas-lowest-achieving-schools). Again the focus of these models tends to be more managerial with the emphasis on a reduced set of skills. These models and approaches also reflect scientific management principles, including the minimalization of skill requirements, the separation of planning and doing, and the structure of control over task performance. Schools, which have the misfortune of being categorized as needing intervention or as turnaround schools, risk being taken over by the state and having a substantial number of their activities, policies and programs in the school controlled and mandated by outside agencies. As we note above, scientific management, far from being a theory which can be tested, is a set of normative principles. Nowhere is this more obvious than in the case of turnaround schools. The U.S. Department of Education acceptable models for funding interventions in turnaround schools have no research evidence that validates these models. Rather they constitute normative principles, largely from the business management literature, that reflect little understanding of school organizations. For example, the Malen, Croninger, Muncey, and Redmond-Jones (2002) study of reconstituted schools demonstrated no improvement in student performance.

Critique of Method

In the mid-twentieth century, Simon (1946) remarked regarding scientific management qua administrative principles,

> If it [putting the principles to use] is a matter of rationalizing behavior that has already taken place or justifying action that has already been decided upon, proverbs are ideal.... But when one seeks to use proverbs as the basis of a scientific theory, the situation is less happy. (p. 53)

More recently, Owens and Shakeshaft's (1992) analysis of rational bureaucratic forms of administrative theory suggests that these "have largely proven to be sterile and to have little application to administrative practice in the 'real world'"(p. 4). Yet, more than a century after its conception, we seem to continue battling a legacy of Tayloristic principles adopted by educational administrators. Answering their own pondering over scientific management and "why a science that does not work is still hailed as science," Greenfield and Ribbins suggest that such a science "offers a world in which there are answers to all problems" (p. 251).

Described as a pseudoscience or scientism (English, 1994), scientific management was critiqued as mimicking science and borrowing on the "legitimacy" of positivist approaches to research while actually pursuing a naïve empiricism. English asserts,

> scientific management and its offshoots are not based on a theoretical framework that courts refutation since there is no theory that is really being tested in its application. It is, rather, an *ideology* encapsulated as a *method*. (p. 118)

To provide a critique of scientific management as method, we draw on Bush's (2003) typology of theories rooted in rational functionalist conceptions of educational administration—including scientific management—as "formal models." According to Bush, these models of leadership and management are marked by seven commonalities. These commonalities include: (a) a tendency to treat organizations as systems where subunits are clearly linked together; (b) an emphasis on the formal structures of the organization; (c) a hierarchical ordering of those formal structures; (d) a view of organizations as goal seeking whose members accept and pursue the organizational purposes; (e) an assumption that administrative decisions are made through rational processes; (f) authority is a function of official position; and (g) an emphasis on accountability to the sponsoring body. Formal models include structural models, systems models, bureaucratic models, rational models, and hierarchical models. As Bush notes, limitations of these types of leadership models have been described and explored; however, they continue to play central roles in the way schools are conceived and lived.

Formal models of educational leadership or management presume organizational goals are clear and widely accepted. However, goals may in fact be difficult to ascertain. This difficulty often arises as a function of overly vague and general goals, a multiplicity of goals competing for resources, multiple goals derived from individuals and groups in addition to formal leaders. The difficulty of deciphering goals may also be compounded when formal objectives have little operational relevance. Further, goal attainment may be difficult to judge particularly in educational contexts where goals are often difficult to measure.

The presumption of rational decision making processes excludes the possibility of alternative modes and means by which decisions are made. As others have noted, the design principle of scientific management predicated on technical rationality does not account for the complexity of human relations, values and ethics (Greenfield, 1973, 1991).

Formal models often center the organization (structures and goals) and underestimate the role and contributions of individuals. Moreover, organizations are conceived as separate and independent of the individuals comprising them. Thomas Greenfield's (1973, 1991) critique challenged such a conception of organizations and treatment of individuals as passive and whose energies can be channeled effortlessly by the structures and objectives of the organization. Rather, he asserted the centrality of human subjectivity in the social construction of organizations.

Formal models of administration and managerial approaches to leadership invest authority in formal positions and roles. This narrowly drawn understanding of the way power operates within and across organizations neglects other forms of authority (expert, moral, etc.) as well as underappreciates alternative notions of power.

Finally, formal models of leadership often assume stable environments. As Bush (2003) notes, rationality models require a degree of stability and predictability. However, rarely are school organizations and contexts stable and fixed. Rather, the flux of individual interactions and relations, permeability of organizational boundaries, and macrolevel forces (social, political, economic) to which organizations are subject play into the (un)predictability and (in)stability of schools.

Epistemological Critique

Foster asserted classical management models—of which he included Tayloristic models of management, human relations models, and systems models—inform contemporary versions of functionalist theories of administration. "Positivistic, objectivistic, and supposed neutrality" were among descriptors he used to elaborate on these functionalist models where the social world is viewed as objective, real and apprehendable; scientists are able to record and accumulate facts about the social world; all things have a function and serve some ultimate interest; and the model does not challenge the existing social order. That is, a positivist naïve realism assumes a unitary reality that is apprehendable through our increasingly refined and sophisticated measures. It is through "objective" measures that organizations are interrogated and subsequently better designed and socially engineered toward greater productivity. Through use of these objective measures, neutrality is preserved.

However, as Foster (1986) suggested, "it could reasonably be argued that the human relations movement and the contemporary focus on administrative decision making have progressively and systematically reinforced Taylorism's basic accomplishment: the concentration of control in the hands of management" (p. 42). Noted above is the centrality of organizational goal attainment in functionalist models of management, combined with the presumed rational processes of decision making the "purposive-rational conception of action becomes an administration of means and *forecloses discussion of ultimate goals and values*" (p. 79, emphasis added). Further, the naturalization of hierarchical structures and authority tied to formal roles obscures how the social (dis)integration of organizations is made (im)possible. Critical management studies scholars contest and attempt to expose the consequences of such naturalized accounts of management. Yet, the obfuscation of asymmetrical power relations through technical rationalist accounts of management seems to persist. To counter this, Foster argues the need in research on educational administration for a critical context—a context that "requires a foundation in critical social theory, an analysis of the production and reproduction of culture, and an orientation to leadership and change" (p. 190).

Note

1. These would be later condensed into five principles in the mid-1960s in Raymond Callahan's (1962) important study, *Education and the Cult of Efficiency.*

References

Ball, S. J. (1993). Education policy, power relations and teacher's work. *British Journal of Educational Studies, 41*(2), 106-121.

Ball, S. J. (1994). *Education reform: A critical and post-structural approach.* Philadelphia, PA: Open University Press.

Ball, S. J. (2003). The teacher's soul and the terrors of performativity. *Journal of education policy, 18*(2), 215-228.

Bush, T. (2003). *Theories of educational leadership and management* (3rd ed.). Los Angeles, CA: SAGE.

Callahan, R. (1962). *Education and the cult of efficiency: A study of social forces that have shaped the administration of the public schools.* Chicago, IL: University of Chicago Press.

Carlson, D. (1986). Teachers, class culture, and the politics of schooling. *Interchange, 17*(4), 17-36.

Crow, G. M. (2009). The development of school leaders' professional identities: Challenges and implications for interprofessional practice. In J. Forbes & C. Watson (Eds.), *Research into professional identities: Theorizing social and institutional identities.* Aberdeen, Scotland: School of Education, University of Aberdeen.

English, F. W. (1994). *Theory in educational administration.* New York, NY: HarperCollins.

Evers, C. W., & Lakomski, G. (1996). *Exploring educational administration: Coherentist applications and critical debates.* New York, NY: Pergamon Elsevier Science.

Fayol, H. (2005). General principles of management. In J. M. Shafritz, J. S. Ott, & Y. S. Jang (Eds.), *Classics of organization theory* (6th ed., pp. 48-60). Belmont, CA: Thomas Wadsworth.

Foster, W. (1986). *Paradigms and promises: New approaches to educational administration.* Amherst, NY: Prometheus Books.

Greenfield, T. B. (1973). Organisations as social inventions: Rethinking assumptions about change. *Journal of Applied Behavioural Science, 9*(5), 551-574.

Greenfield, T. B. (1991). Re-forming and re-valuing educational administration: Whence and when cometh the Phoenix? *Educational Management and Administration, 19*(4), 200-217.

Greenfield, T., & Ribbins, P. (Eds.). (1993). *Greenfield on educational administration: Towards a humane science.* New Fetter Lane, London, England: Routledge Press.

Gronn, P. (2003). *The new work of educational leaders. Changing leadership practice in an era of school reform.* London, England: Paul Chapman.

Gulick, L. H., & Urwick, L. F. (1969). *Papers on the science of administration.* New York, NY: A. M. Kelley.

Hargreaves, A. (2004). *Teaching in the knowledge society. Education in the age of insecurity.* New York, NY: Teachers College Press.

Helsby, G., & Saunders, M. (1993). Taylorism, Tylerism and performance indicators: Defending the indefensible? *Educational Studies, 19*(1), 55-76.

Holt, M. (2001). The comprehensive high school in the United States: A view from Europe and the United Kingdom. *Journal of Curriculum and Supervision, 16*(2), 137-161.

Hoy, W. K., & Miskel, C. G. (2001). *Educational administration: Theory, research, and practice* (6th ed.). Boston, MA: McGraw-Hill.

Leicht, K. T., & Fennell, M. L. (2001). *Professional work. A sociological approach.* Oxford, England: Blackwell.

Leithwood, K., & Duke, D. L. (1999). A century's quest to understand school leadership. In J. Murphy & K. Seashore-Louis (Eds.), *Handbook of research on educational administration* (2nd ed., pp. 45-72). San Francisco, CA: Jossey-Bass.

Littler, C. R. (1978). Understanding Taylorism. *The British Journal of Sociology, 29*(2), 185-202.

Lumby, J., & English, F. (2009). From simplicism to complexity in leadership identity and preparation: Exploring the lineage and dark secrets. *International Journal of Leadership in Education, 12*(2), 95-114.

Malen, B., Croninger, R., Muncey, D., & Redmond-Jones, D. (2002). Reconstituting schools: "Testing" the "theory in action." *Educational Evaluation and Policy Analysis, 24*(2), 113-132.

Ogawa, R. T., Crowson, R. L., & Goldring, E. B. (1999). Enduring dilemmas of school organization. In J. Murphy & K. Seashore Louis (Eds.), *Handbook of research on educational administration* (2nd ed., pp. 277-296). San Francisco, CA: Jossey-Bass.

Owens, R., & Shakeshaft, C. (1992). The new 'revolution' in administrative theory. *Journal of Educational Management, 30*(9), 4-17.

Pollitt, C. (1990). *Managerialism and the public services: The Anglo-American experience.* Cambridge, MA: Basil Blackwell.

Ravitch, D. (2010). *The death and life of the great American school system: How testing and choice are undermining education.* New York, NY: Basic Books.

Scribner, S. P., & Crow, G. M. (2010, May). *Employing professional identities: Case study of a high school principal in a reform setting.* Paper presented at University of Southampton, Southampton, England.

Simon, H. A. (1946). The proverbs of administration. *Public Administration Review, 6*(1), 53-67.

Taylor, F. W. (1911). *The principles of scientific management.* New York, NY: Harper & Brothers.

Taylor, F. W. (1967). *The principles of scientific management.* New York, NY: Norton.

Tyack, D. (1974). *The one best system: A history of American urban education.* Cambridge, MA: Harvard University Press.

Author Contact Information: Thu Suong Thi Nguyen, PhD, Assistant Professor of Educational Leadership and Policy Studies, School of Education, 902 West New York Street, Indiana University, Indianapolis, Indiana 46201. Phone: 317-274-7318. E-mail: nguyen20@iupui.edu

CHAPTER 76

Trait Theory

Kathleen M. Brown
University of North Carolina–Chapel Hill

INTRODUCTION

Trait theory of leadership is the culmination of one of the first systematic, scientific studies of leadership. It is a range of leadership theories that assume that people are born with, or display, certain inherited qualities and traits that make them better suited for leadership. Trait theory often identifies and describes key personality or behavioral characteristics shared by successful leaders. It suggests that you can identify a potential leader by examining the personality traits of the person and matching them to the characteristics that effective leaders possess. It also suggests if a person possesses the correct combination of traits he or she will be able to take the lead in different situations. Assuming that leaders are born, not made, trait theory often asks: What are the common traits underlying all great leaders?

Trait theory of leadership developed from the belief that ability arises from innate, internal traits that some have and some do not. Through this approach critical leadership traits can be isolated and people with such traits can then be recruited, selected, and inducted into leadership positions. Early scholars taking the trait approach attempted to identify physiological (appearance, height, and weight), demographic (age, birth order, education, and socioeconomic status), personality (self-confidence and aggressiveness), intellectual (intelligence, decisiveness, judgment, and knowledge), task-related (achievement drive, initiative, and persistence), and social characteristics (child-rearing practices, sociability, and cooperativeness) with leader emergence and leader effectiveness. They focused on "what" an effective leader is, not necessarily on "how" to lead effectively.

Although the lists of traits or qualities associated with leadership tend to be very long, exist in abundance, and continue to be produced, initial conclusions from early research indicated that there were no universal traits that consistently separated effective leaders from other individuals. Even though some traits were found in a considerable number of studies, the results were generally inconclusive. Some leaders might possess certain traits but the absence of them did not necessarily mean that the person was not a leader. In an important review of the leadership literature published in 1948, Stogdill concluded that the existing research at the time had not demonstrated the utility of the trait approach. In other words, he found that there was no single set of *universal* traits that is predictive of leadership. As a result, questions remained. Can people learn to become effective leaders? Is leadership an art or a science? Are these two mutually exclusive alternatives? Over time, recognition grew that traits can generally be affected by inheritance, learning, and environmental factors. Although initial research suggested that traits are not reliable predictors of who will emerge into leadership roles (Mann, 1959; Stogdill, 1948), other reviews have shown that traits influence our perceptions of whether someone is a leader (Lord, De Vader, & Alliger, 1986). More recent research on twins separated at birth along with new sciences such as behavioral genetics also found that far more is inherited than was previously supposed.

DEVELOPMENT

EARLY DEVELOPMENT

The idea that leadership is based on individual attributes, coupled with the search for those characteristics or traits, has been ongoing for centuries. From Plato's *Republic* to Plutarch's *Lives*, history's greatest philosophical writers have explored what qualities distinguish an individual as a leader. Underlying this search

The Handbook of Educational Theories, pp. 897–901

was the early recognition of the importance of leadership and the assumption that leadership is rooted in the characteristics that certain individuals possess. Aristotle himself declared that from the hour of birth, some are marked out for subjection, others for rule. This philosophy continued for more than 2,000 years. For example, in 1841, in *Heroes and Hero Worship*, Carlisle identified the talents, skills, and physical characteristics of men who rose to power. Likewise, in 1869, in *Hereditary Genius*, Galton examined leadership qualities in the families of powerful men and concluded that leadership was inherited and that leaders were born, not developed. All of these notable writings provided the foundation for leadership as rooted in the characteristics of the leader. Decades of further research followed.

The actual terminology "trait theory of leadership" can be traced back to the 1920s. It developed from the Great Man theory of history as researchers tried for 50 years to identify specific inherited characteristics and skills that differentiated leaders from followers. According to B. M. Bass (1990), early in the twentieth century leaders were generally regarded as superior individuals who, due to fortunate inheritance and/or social circumstances, possessed qualities and abilities that differentiated them from people in general. During the 1920s and 1930s, theorists compiled lists of traits but these were often contradictory and no single trait was consistently identified with good leadership. The research was pioneered by Binet and Simon and reached somewhat of a climax in 1948 when Stogdill completed a comprehensive review of the literature. By synthesizing more than 124 studies of the trait approach completed between 1904 and 1948 he identified the following five general categories of traits that were positively associated with leadership:

- capacity—intelligence, alertness, verbal facility, originality, judgment;
- achievement—scholarship, knowledge, athletic accomplishments;
- responsibility—dependability, initiative, persistence, aggressiveness, self-confidence, desire to excel;
- participation—activity, sociability, cooperation, adaptability, humor; and
- status—socioeconomic position, popularity.

By the early 1950s, Stogdill concluded that initial searches proved remarkably unsuccessful and that the trait approach had actually yielded negligible results. Mann's (1959) review of 125 leadership studies generated 750 findings about the personality traits of leaders and produced similar conclusions. Both men suggested that persons who are leaders in one situation may not necessarily be leaders in other situations. Early attempts to isolate specific individual traits led to the conclusion that no single characteristic can distinguish leaders from nonleaders.

Early Critiques

As trait theory continued to develop, criticism became more widespread against it, especially since each study tended to identify a different set of traits associated with leadership. For example, in one summary of over 100 studies, Carlisle (1973) concluded that only 5% of the traits were found in four or more studies. Another criticism claimed that the trait theorists were focusing too much on inherited versus learned traits and not enough on situational factors. Since most trait type models disregarded interaction effects, it was difficult to establish cause and effect. Stogdill (1948) himself came to this conclusion:

> A person does not become a leader by virtue of the possession of some combination of traits, but the pattern of personal characteristics of the leader must bear some relevant relationship to the characteristics, activities, and goals of the followers. Thus, leadership must be conceived in terms of the interaction of variables that are in constant flux. (p. 64)

As researchers continued to question the driving force behind leadership, critics of the trait theory approach led leadership research into situational and behavioral studies. Instead of viewing leaders as born, researchers began to believe leaders could be developed or made. Subsequently, leadership was no longer characterized as an enduring individual trait, as situational approaches posited that individuals can be effective in certain situations, but not others. As a result, the focus of leadership research shifted away from leader traits to leader behaviors. The premise behind this line of research was that the behaviors exhibited by leaders were more important than their physical, mental, or emotional traits. The situational leadership approach dominated much of the leadership theory and research for the next few decades.

Several problems with early trait research help explain the perceived lack of significant findings. First, trait theory is complex and measurement theory at the time was not highly sophisticated. Little was known about the psychometric properties of the measures used to operationalize traits. As a result, different studies used different measures to assess the same construct, which made it very difficult to replicate findings. Traits, amongst other things, are hard to measure—they change over time. How, for example, does one measure traits such as honesty, integrity, loyalty, or diligence? Likewise, there is bound to be some subjective judgment in determining who is regarded as a "good" or "successful" leader. There is also disagreement over which traits are the most important for effective leaders. Additionally, early trait research was largely atheoretical, offering no explanations for the proposed relationship between individual characteristics and leadership. Finally, early trait research did not consider the impact of situational variables that might moderate the relationship between leader traits and measures of leader effectiveness. As a result of the lack of consistent findings linking individual traits to leadership effectiveness, empirical studies of leader traits were largely abandoned in the 1950s.

RECENT DEVELOPMENTS

Fortunately, after a period where it was almost discarded, more recent research indicates that trait theory is important for understanding *effective leadership*. Because situational research tended to focus too much on the situation and not enough on character traits, balance was needed and trait theory was revived. By the 1970s, Stodgill's (1974) second generation of studies produced a more consistent set of traits. After reviewing another 163 new trait studies conducted between 1949 and 1970, he developed the following list of traits and skills critical to leaders.

New research methods and a greater variety of statistical measurement procedures, including projective tests, were developed after these influential reviews, ultimately reestablishing the trait theory as a viable approach to the study of leadership. Improvements in the use of round robin research design methodology allowed researchers to conclude that individuals can and do emerge as leaders across a variety of situations and tasks. Additionally, during the 1980s, statistical advances allowed researchers to conduct meta-analyses, in which they could quantitatively (rather than just qualitatively) analyze and summarize findings and results from a wide array of studies. This process allowed trait theorists to create a much more comprehensive and parsimonious picture of previous leadership research. By using these new methods, Northouse (2004) and other leadership researchers revealed that significant relationships do in fact exist between leadership and such individual traits as intelligence, adjustment, extraversion, conscientiousness, openness to experience, and general self-efficacy.

Some of these timeless and universal characteristics are also found in psychologists' Big Five personality traits. Beginning in the early 1990s the Big Five were examined in the workplace and the well known traits of introversion/extroversion, openness to experience, conscientiousness, agreeableness, and emotional stability were found. In 2003, Sashkin and Sashkin compared the Big Five with McCall and Lombardo's (1983) four primary traits of success or derailment (i.e., emotional stability and composure, admitting error, good interpersonal skills, and intellectual breadth) and concluded that "the obvious parallels suggest that while leadership may not be the result of having and applying certain traits, failure in leadership may well be attributable at least partly to the lack of key traits" (pp. 27-28). Chamorro-Premuzic (2007) came to a similar conclusion when he wrote that "stable individual differences (i.e., traits) do predict who becomes, stays, and derails a leader.... Great leaders tend to be bright, open to experience, conscientious, extraverted, and stable" (p. 152).

Through these and many other research studies conducted in the last part of the twentieth century, a set of core traits of successful leaders have been identified such as intelligence, determination, integrity, sociability, and self confidence (Northouse, 2004). Successful leaders definitely have interests, abilities, and personality traits that are different from less effective leaders. While these traits are not exclusively responsible in identifying whether a person will be a successful leader or not, they are perceived as preconditions that endow people with leadership potential. Even so, when examining leadership more in depth, things such as what leaders do, what they say, and how they influence

Table 76.1. Critical Leadership Traits and Skills

Traits	Skills
• Adaptable to situations	• Clever (intelligent)
• Alert to social environment	• Conceptually skilled
• Ambitious and achievement-orientated	• Creative
• Assertive	• Diplomatic and tactful
• Cooperative	• Fluent in speaking
• Decisive	• Knowledgeable about group task
• Dependable	• Organized (administrative ability)
• Dominant (desire to influence others)	• Persuasive
• Energetic (high activity level)	• Socially skilled
• Persistent	
• Self-confident	
• Tolerant of stress	
• Willing to assume responsibility	

people become much more important from a behavioral perspective than what traits they possess. More recently people have tried looking at what combinations of traits might be good for a particular situation. It appears possible to link clusters of personality traits to success in different situations, as Stogdill has subsequently suggested. However, it remains an inexact science!

A further reason why leadership theory has revived the trait approach is because of the current scientific research in heritability and genes. With these new studies leadership theorists are now balancing the importance of situation with traits. According to R. Bass (2008), "Leaders may be born as well as made, as we can see if we examine research of the past 30 years on genes, heritability, and leadership. Leadership theory and research from 1975 to 2005 have turned us back again to considering the importance of traits" (p. 104). Research in cotwin studies (i.e., the study of fraternal and identical twins), has shown a direct linkage of genetics and leadership. R. Bass continues, "Not only are we able to present numerous studies showing the effects of genes on personality traits found to be predictive of leadership; there are also investigations that have directly connected genetics to leadership." For example, in 2006, Avery, Rotundo, Johnson, Zhang, and McGue obtained data from the Minnesota Twin Registry to compare 238 identical twins (each pair genetically the same) with188 fraternal twins (each pair with 50% in common in genetic background). They found that 30% of the variance in emergence as leaders was attributable to genetics (R. Bass, 2008, p. 105). With the current research on genetics and the development of the Big Five leadership theorists are reconsidering whether leadership is a consequence of nature or nurture. Although situation and behavior remains important, evidence suggests that nature has a great role in all leaders. In conclusion, the evidence supports the conclusion that the possession of certain traits increases the likelihood that a leader will be effective (Yukl, 2002), but it does not represent a return to the original trait assumption that "leaders are born, not made."

Recent Critiques

Not surprisingly, one major limit of trait theory is that it is impossible to see how traits such as intelligence and determination can bring about influence in other people's motivation and performance (Maurik, 2001). In other words, how do stable leader attributes account for the behavioral diversity necessary for effective leadership? Also, while the trait theory of leadership has certainly regained popularity, its reemergence has not been accompanied by a corresponding increase in sophisticated conceptual frameworks. Specifically, Zaccaro (2007) noted that trait theories still:

1. focus on a small set of individual attributes such as Big Five personality traits, to the neglect of cognitive abilities, motives, values, social skills, expertise, and problem-solving skills.;
2. fail to consider patterns or integrations of multiple attributes; and
3. do not distinguish between those leader attributes that are generally not malleable over time and those that are shaped by, and bound to, situational influences.

Validity, Generalizability, and Use

The power of the trait approach to leadership has been tested and found credible through centuries of research, question, critic, and debate. As the oldest theory of leadership, it has withstood the test of time, revealing that nature as well as nurture is important in today's world of leaders. Even though it had a few earlier battles and a period of decline, trait theory has now become the associate of situational leadership through its reemergence with the Big Five and the study of heritability and genetics. Industrial psychologists interested in improving managerial selection continue to conduct trait research. The emphasis has shifted from comparison of leaders and nonleaders to the relation of leader traits to leader effectiveness, from predicting who will become leaders to predicting who will be more effective. As such, the trait theory gives constructive information about leadership. It can be applied by people at all levels in all types of organizations. From a practical standpoint, Northouse (2004) describes how individuals can assess their strengths and weaknesses and then take actions to develop their leadership abilities. Likewise, school organizations seeking to identify individuals with particular traits and skills who will fit within and help lead their organizations, can use trait theory to do so.

References

Avery, R. D., Rotundo, M., Johnson, W., Zhang, Z., & McGue, M. (2006). The determinants of leadership role occupancy: Genetic and personality factors. *The Leadership Quarterly, 17*(1), 1-20.

Bass, B. M. (1990). *Bass & Stodgill's handbook of leadership: Theory, research, and managerial applications* (3rd ed.). New York, NY: Free Press.

Bass, R. (2008). *The Bass handbook of leadership: Theory, research, and managerial application* (4th ed.). New York, NY: Simon and Schuster.

Carlisle, H.M. (1973). *Situational management a contingency approach to leadership.* New York, NY: AMACOM.

Chamorro-Premuzic, T. (2007). *Personality and individual differences.* Grand Rapids, MI: Blackwell.

Galton, F. (1969). Hereditary genius: An inquiry into its laws and consequences. London, England: MacMillan.

Lord, R. G., De Vader, C. L., & Alliger, G. M. (1986). A meta-analysis of the relation between personality traits and leadership perceptions: An application of validity generalization procedures. *Journal of Applied Psychology, 8*(1), 407.

Mann, R. D. (1959). A Review of the relationship between personality and performance in small groups. *Psychological Bulletin, 7*(3), 241-270.

Maurik, J. V. (2001). *Writers on leadership.* London, England: Penguin.

McCall, M. W., & Lombardo, M. M. (1983). *Off the track: Why and how successful executives get derailed.* Greensboro, NC: Center for Creative Leadership.

Northouse, P. G. (2004). *Leadership: Theory and practice* (3rd ed.). London, England: SAGE.

Sashkin, M., & Sashkin, M. (2003). *Leadership that matters.* San Francisco, CA: Berrett-Koehler.

Stogdill, R. M. (1948). Personal factors associated with leadership: A survey of the literature. *Journal of Applied Psychology, 25*(1), 35-71.

Stogdill, R. M. (1974). *Handbook of leadership: A survey of the literature.* New York, NY: Free Press.

Yukl, G. (2002). *Leadership in organizations*, Delhi, India: Pearson Education.

Zaccaro, S. J. (2007). Trait-based perspective. *American Psychology, 62*(1), 7-16.

Author Contact Information: Kathleen M. Brown, EdD, Professor and Chair of Educational Leadership, UNC-CH School of Education, CB# 3500, 120 Peabody Hall, Chapel Hill, NC 27599. Phone: 919-966-1354. E-mail: BrownK@email.unc.edu

CHAPTER 77

Discourse Theories and School Leadership

Autumn K. Cyprés
The University of Tennessee

General understandings of the term *discourse* refer to a vast umbrella that in its simplest form, is best described as written or spoken communication. In the social sciences, discourse is used to refer to a formalized way of thinking through the social strictures and spaces created by words, phrases, and interactions. Thus, discourse is understood as a kind of social action with the idea that language mostly works as a vehicle to construct reality. Ultimately, what discourse does is construct and deconstruct objects, relationships, and political frameworks.

Roots, Assumptions, and Aspects of Discourse Theories

Specific lines of inquiry within the realm of discourse research include discourse studies (also known as discourse analysis, semiotic studies, and sociolinguistics.

Discourse Studies

Also known as discourse analysis, discourse studies is a general term for a myriad of approaches used to analyze written, spoken, or signed language. The particular bits of this analysis include the study of interaction between the sender of a message and the receiver of said message. The message can be delivered via writing, conversation, and speech acts. It is a field of inquiry used in a variety of social science disciplines that include sociology, anthropology social work, psychology, and communication studies (Gee, 1999).

Semiotic Studies

Semiotic studies, or semiotics, is the study of signs, symbols and communication and is typically understood to have three main branches within the discipline: (a) semantics (the relationship between signs and the things in which they refer to); (b) syntactics (the study of the rules that determine how words are combined to form phrases and sentences), and (c) pragmatics (the study of the psychological and sociological phenomena which occur in functioning of signs (Derrida, 1981).

Sociolinguistics

Sociolinguistics is the study of the effect of the aspects of society on the way language is used and the effect of society on the language itself. Sociolinguistics is different than discourse analysis in that it considers the relationship between society and language; thus the lens is a broader one than that of discourse analysis. Sociolinguists considers how language differs between groups of people (known as speech communities) in terms of frameworks of identity (gender, sexual identity, race, religion, and (dis)ability) and socioeconomic class (Bernstein, 1971).

Germinal discussions of a theory of discourse include John Locke's (1823/1963) reference to "the doctrine of signs" used by humanity as a way to learn via experience, and Saussure's passionate argument that the study of language and signs rightfully should be understood within the social sciences (Chandler, 2007).

Modern extensions of discourse theory are best identified through the work of the poststructuralists. Poststructuralism as a movement began in Paris in the mid twentieth century and encompasses the intellectual developments of French and continental philosophers such as Foucault (1975, 1980, 1983), Derrida (1982), and Barthes (1968). The prefix "post" refers to the movement's rejection of structuralism, or the idea

The Handbook of Educational Theories, pp. 903–907

of an independent and superior signifier that asserts knowledge of absolute reality and truth (Capper, 1999; Cherryholmes, 1988; Foucault, 1983; Scheurich, 1997). One of the aims of poststructuralism is to deconstruct such traditional points of view regarding reality and truth. In other words, poststructuralism views the realities of underlying structures (such as discourse) as culturally conditioned, ongoing interpretations, filled with biases and glaring omissions. At the heart of poststructuralism (and thus modern discourse theory) is the concern with deconstructing the power relationships embedded in the texts and discourse practices that shape our social relationships and status. In this context, discourse and discursive practices include the different ways in which we integrate language with the communicative tools of nonlanguage such as symbols and nonverbal behavior in an effort to give meaning to the world (Blumer, 1969; Gee, 1996).

It is important for the reader not to conflate post structuralism with post modernism. Pillow (2003) buttressed this argument when she mentioned that post modernism and post structuralism are commonly conflated, resulting in the homogenization of the terms in the minds of some scholars. This chapter is built upon a foundation of post structuralism because it is dedicated to the power and political constraints of words and their use. Unlike post structuralists, post modernists rely on a much broader lens in their analyses of events and realities. Finally this chapter recognizes that while a feminist lens is most often used in parallel with post structuralist thought, it is important to note that this effort does not conflate post structuralism with a feminist stance regarding language and discourse.

Big D and Little d Discourse

Studies in discourse have revealed major theories in the last several decades that include the coconstruction of reality through language and discursive interaction (Gergen, 1999); the marginalization of groups and people through discursive frameworks (Butler, 1997; Cherryholmes, 1998), and the explanation of face-to-face interactions and identity negotiation (Friere, 1970; Goffman, 1959, 1961, 1963, 1967).

One of the most significant branches of modern discourse theory is the concept of "Big D" and "Little d" discourse (Gee, 1996, p. 14). Gee (1996) drew on the work of Foucault (1975, 1980 and Derrida (1976), to specify understandings of the nexus between large discursive practices and everyday discursive interactions. Big D discourse, which is represented in writing as *D/discourse* refers to the many ways of acting and being in the world. It is a set of communicative constellations and talk patterns consisting of language working in concert with one, many, or all the following: feelings, bodies, nonlinguistic symbols, objects, clothes, interaction, action, technologies, geography, time, tools, symbols, verbal and non verbal expressions, and people (Gee, 1996). D/discourse contours social practices by creating particular kinds of subjectivity in which human beings are managed and given certain forms which are viewed as self evident, rational, normal, or irrational and abnormal (Alvesson & Karreman, 2000; Derrida, 1982; Foucault, 1980; Gramsci, 1971). Little d discourse which is represented in writing as *d/discourse*, centers on the pragmatics of language in use in everyday exchanges between people. It refers to the flotsam and jetsam of language bits and grammatical resources that make up greetings, questions, discussions, and the distribution of information. Ultimately, D/discourse and d/discourse merge together to form constellations that frame the reality of our existence. More importantly, D/discourse contours d/discourse as people reference via talk in their everyday lives the D/discourse messages they have encountered via the media and other sources.

Doing "Being Ordinary" and the Everydayness of Story Telling

Another significant notion related to d/discourse is based on the work of Harvey Sacks (1985). He argued that we often confuse the everydayness of our lives as mundane, ordinary, and of little import. When we peel away our conditioned biases regarding what is mundane, we see that the one of the most taken for granted exercises, storytelling, are actually the nexus of d/discourse and D/discourse. We tell stories to construct or reconstruct the interstices of identity and relationships within our lives. Sacks (1985), one of the fathers of discourse analysis, explained the importance of story telling in relation to lived experiences when he noted:

> It seems fair to suppose that there is a time when kids do "kissing and telling" that they are doing the kissing and happen to do the telling, or that they want to do the kissing and happen to do the telling. But that a way to get them to like the kissing is via the fact that they like the telling. (Sacks, 1985, p. 417)

The telling of a story constructs new realities and confirms the relationship (or lack of relationship) between events, groups, and people. Sacks also noted that ironically, within the telling of a story we often do not allow ourselves the luxury of doing anything but "being ordinary" in terms of blurring or masking details deemed as irrelevant. Sacks further argued that we do "being ordinary" as a natural extension of being human (1985). When we do being ordinary we blur the details that make a story something more than an ordinary or mundane account. That is not to say that a story can not have interesting or exciting elements to it. Rather, we tend to do being ordinary because we do not believe that we are entitled to claiming things extraordinary for ourselves. These extraordinary things that are mundane are reserved for literature, painting, and other forms of art that are created by those very few who are deemed as extraordinary by society. To illustrate this, consider the works of Tolstoy who is famous for constructing for his readers within the context of his books not only the completeness of his characters but the texture of the curtains in the room that his characters occupy (Tolstoy, 1869/2008). Or Sir Frederick Leighton's pre-Raphaelite painting, *Flaming June;* which depicts a red headed woman curled up on a bench in slumber. The viewer is privy to the folds in the woman's orange dress, the curvature of her hip and the angle of her foot. Considered one of the great masterworks of the Pre-Raphaelite period, this painting depicts an ordinary moment: that of sleep.

Let us begin again in our discussion of doing *being ordinary* by utilizing Tolstoy and Leighton as context and consider the following example of doing being ordinary within the telling of a story.[1] Howard and Dominique separately recounted what happened when they spent the day together exploring the Smoky Mountains of eastern Tennessee. Howard said whilst playing poker with his friends, "She saw a bear, the butterflies followed her around, and we had dinner at The Peddler steakhouse." Dominique said to her sister in a phone conversation, "We drove around in his Jeep, took some photographs at a creek; I saw a bear, and butterflies followed us around. And oh yeah, dinner was great."

Both Howard and Dominique were doing being ordinary because they left out of their stories details deemed as not worthy of the telling. They were doing being ordinary because they did not mention in their stories an interpretation of the sound of the water cascading down the creek, a description of the play of light in cocktail glasses at dinner, an analysis of the timbre of each other's laugh, or a description of air that rushed through the windows of the Jeep during the evening's drive home. While these aspects of the day may be ensconced in the minds of both Howard and Dominique, society has conditioned us to understand that they are not worth sharing via the story because we regularly sift through scenes in our life for their storyable possibilities. The telling of a story is not like the construction of a novel or a painting, which is deemed as something the extraordinary do and thus beyond the scope of our daily lives. In sum, doing being ordinary essentially means that "the business of life is to see and report the usual aspects of any possibly usual scene" (Sacks, 1985, p. 416). Thus, bears and butterflies find their way into a story rather than light bouncing off of ice in a gimlet cocktail.

The sobering gravitas of doing being ordinary and storytelling becomes more evident when we consider something other than the retelling of a date in the woods. We see the potentiality for sinister politics more clearly when we consider the intersections between storytelling (a mode of d/discourse) and the formidable politics of hegemony.

D/Discourse and Hegemony

Like the constellations in the evening sky, the reality formed by D/discourse and d/discourse is fluid, ever-present, and unstable. The metaphor of stargazing is useful for understanding how discourse shapes our lives because when you look up at the stars, at first blush you are not really aware of the fluidity of the constellations that are looming above you. You are aware that there are certain constellations that serve as touchstones for understanding how the sky is constructed, for understanding its reality. But when you take a telescope and look deeper, closer, you see the flotsam and jetsam of the universe and how precarious the stars are. The same can be said for discourse, language, and its relationship to power. Understanding this relationship is vital to school leaders and those who prepare them as leadership actions are framed with both kinds of discourse and the concept of hegemony that we see as integral to the shape of discursive constellations.

This discussion discusses hegemony in a *Gramscian* sense to explain how social groups maintain their dominance over other groups in a society through manufacturing consent via D/discourse rather than relying on coercion (Gramsci, 1971). Hegemonic leadership in a society is commonly achieved when a powerful, but minority, social class is able to construct an alliance with other social groups, in order to achieve ideological dominance. This is inevitably a complex and frequently contested process but it is at least in part achieved by taking core concerns expressed by those in subordinate groups, and reframing them in terms that connect them with the dominant ideology. Hence those in subordinate groups are persuaded to accept, adopt, and internalize the dominant group's definition of what is normal or common sense (Cherryholmes, 1988). Thus hegemony is a kind of macro political structure in which one group maintains its social privilege over other groups through a kind of veiled oppression created via common sense stories dispersed in the media and school curriculum which are used to inculcate and maintain this viewpoint and the power of the dominant class (Apple, 2001; Derrida, 1982; Foucault, 1980). These common sense D/discourses form constellations that marginalize some people and privilege others. People who are the victims of hegemony self-regulate their behavior because they believe and internalize the stories they have been told about what is good, bad, or normal.

For example, it was a common story in the mid twentieth century in the United States that appropriate goals for women should center on rearing children and creating a lovely home rather than building a career. A good wife was one that had dinner ready for her husband upon his return from a long work day and who kept a tidy home. Thus many women aspired to be good wives and eschewed goals in the professional fields of medicine, law, et cetera. Another example specific to schools are the stories that supported segregation in schools before the 1954 U.S. Supreme Court decision in the case of *Brown v. Board of Education of Topeka.*[2]

Discourse Theories and Research on School Leadership

The strictures and spaces between discourse theories and school leadership can be understood through both macro- and micropolitics. In the context of this discussion, macropolitics is defined as residing within the arena of D/Discourse. It is the stuff of policy and globalization, and of the forces that shape how nation-states and cultures understand the purpose of school in society. Harvey (2005) alludes to the relationship between D/discourse and hegemony this way:

> For any one way of thought to become dominant, a mechanism must be advanced which speaks to our values, our desires, our instincts, and the possibilities inherent in the world we understand. If successful, this mechanism becomes so embedded in our consciousness that it is understood as common sense, and thus not open for question. (p. 4)

The simplest way to understand what D/discourse does in terms of school leadership is to understand that hegemonic D/discourses exist as a kind of common sense in societies in terms what the purpose of school is and how its efficacy is evaluated. Critical examinations of discourse and policy by researchers such as Apple (2001), Giroux (1981), Kinchloe (2008), and Spring (2004), have revealed that while the common sense in D/discourses around the world is centered on rhetoric about leaving no child behind, in truth schools sift and sort students on the basis of their ability which is taken into consideration apart from economic and social factors that contribute to academic success.

Furthermore, the D/discourses of what is acceptable or normal in terms of human behavior is a central factor of how schools around the world tend to sift, sort, and marginalize students in terms of frameworks of identity that include gender, ethnicity, religion, sexual identity, and (dis)abilty (Lugg, 2003, 2006,). Examples of such efforts can be found in the panoply of critical race literature and feminist literature (hooks, 1991; Lakoff, 2004; Marshall & Gerstl-Pepin, 2005).

Research within the field educational administration can claim several noteworthy efforts that utilize difference discourse theories, particularly since the 1980s in which the international and national conversations about school and school leadership focused on issues of equity, power, identity, and social justice. Arguably, Foucault (1975, 1980), and Gramsci (1971) are the most cited scholars in works of this kind. In terms of methodology and approaches to the research of leadership and difference, one can also argue that scholarly work in the field under the umbrella of social justice has utilized the personal narrative and dialogic/discursive constructs (Shields & Edwards, 2005) such as storytelling and doing being ordinary to explain the differences in identity frameworks and their relationship to the school experience (hooks, 1991; Kumanshiro, 2004; Lyman, Ashby, & Tripses, 2005; Shakeshaft, 1999; Tooms & Boske, 2010; Waite, Nelson, & Guajardo, 2008).

In conclusion it must be said that educational leaders and academics who prepare educational leaders can benefit greatly from recognizing and seeking connections between discourse theories and the work of school leadership because such nexus points illustrate how schools function in society and moreover how they can be changed through consistent attention to the ordinary exchanges and interactions between stakeholders that are, as demonstrated earlier, anything but mundane.

Discourse analysis is important to principals in particular because the work of leading a school is rooted in the everydayness of interaction. Principals build trust and lead through doing being ordinary through recognizing what is ordinary and what is extraordinary in the everydayness of their job. Principals, like other school leaders, improve the quality of their schools by listening to and telling stories, and through developing and promoting a vision that colleagues and community members can understand, support, and ultimately articulate. And in order to develop a vision, one must understand their world and their role in it. Hence the necessity of recognizing D/discourse and d/discourse as tools to empower authentic leadership.

Notes

1. While the events are accurate, and the recounting of them are accurate; the storytellers' names have been changed to ensure anonymity.
2. *Brown v. Board of Education of Topeka* was a landmark decision by the U.S. Supreme Court that declared laws which established separate public schools for Black and White students and denied Black children equal educational opportunities as unconstitutional. The unanimous decision by the Warren Court overturned the *Plessy v. Ferguson* decision of 1896, which permitted segregation. As a result, de jure racial segregation was ruled in violation of the Equal Rights Protection Clause of the Fourteenth Amendment of the United States Constitution.

REFERENCES

Alvesson, M., & Karreman, D. (2000). Varieties of discourse: On the study of organizations through discourse analysis. *Human Relations, 53*(9), 1125-1149.

Apple, M. (2001). *Educating the "right" way: Markets, standards, God, and inequality.* New York, NY: Routledge.

Barthes, R. (1968). *Elements of semiology.* New York, NY: Hill and Wang.

Bernstein, B. (1971). *Theoretical studies toward sociology of language.* London, England: Shoken Books.

Blumer, H. (1969). *Symbolic Interactionism: Perspective and method.* Englewood Cliffs, NJ: Prentice-Hall.

Butler, J. (1997). *Excitable speech: A politics of the performative.* New York, NY: Routledge.

Capper, C. A. (1999). (Homo)sexualities, organizations, and administration; Possibilities for in(queery). *Educational Researcher, 28*(5), 4-11.

Cherryholmes, C. (1988). *Power and criticism: Post-structural investigations in education.* NY: Teachers College Press.

Chandler, D. (2007). *Semiotics: The basics.* London, England: Routledge.

Derrida, J. (1976). *Of grammatology.* Baltimore, MD: The Johns Hopkins University Press.

Derrida, J. (1981). *Positions.* London, England: Althone Press.

Foucault, M. (1975). *Discipline and punish: The birth of a prison.* New York, NY: Vintage Books.

Foucault, M. (1980). *Power/knowledge: Selected interviews and other writings, 1972-1977.* New York, NY: Pantheon Books.

Foucault, M. (1983). *This is not a pipe* (J. Harkness, Trans.). Berkley, CA: University of California Press.

Freire, P. (1970). *Pedagogy of the oppressed.* New York, NY: Continuum.

Gee, J. P. (1996). *Social linguistics and literacies.* New York, NY: Routledge.

Gee, J. P. (1999). *An introduction to discourse analysis: Theory and practice.* New York, NY: Routledge.

Gergen, K. (1999). *An invitation to social construction.* Thousand Oaks, CA: SAGE.

Giroux, H. (1981). *Ideology, culture, and the process of schooling.* Philadelphia, PA: Temple University Press.

Goffman, E. (1959). *The presentation of self in everyday life.* Garden City, NY: Anchor/Doubleday.

Goffman, E. (1961). *Asylums: Essays on the social situation of mental patients and other inmates.* Garden City, NY: Anchor/ Doubleday.

Goffman, E. (1963). *Stigma: Notes on the management of spoiled identity.* New York, NY: Simon & Schuster

Goffman, E. (1967). *Interaction ritual: Essays on face to face behavior.* Garden City, NY: Anchor/Doubleday.

Gramsci, A. (1971) *Selections from the prison notebooks.* London, England: Lawrence and Wishart.

Harvey, D. (2005). *A brief history of neoliberalism.* Oxford, England: Oxford University Press.

hooks, b. (1991). *Yearning, race, gender and cultural politics.* Boston, MA: South End Press.

Locke, J. (1823). *The works of John Locke, a new edition, corrected in ten volumes, Volume 3.* (Facsimile reprint by Sceintia, London, 1963)

Kinchloe, J. (2008). *Critical pedagogy.* New York, NY: Peter Lang.

Kumashiro, K. K. (2004). *Against common sense: Teaching and learning toward social justice.* New York, NY: Routledge-Falmer.

Lakoff, R. (2004). *Language and woman's place: Text and commentaries.* New York, NY: Oxford Press.

Lugg, C. A. (2003). Sissies, faggots, lezzies, and dykes: Gender, sexual orientation, and a new politics of education? *Educational Administration Quarterly, 39*(1), 95-134.

Lugg, C. A. (2006) Thinking about sodomy: Public schools, legal panopticons, and queers. *Educational Policy,* 20(1), 35-58.

Lyman, L., Ashby, D., & Tripses, J. (2005). *Leaders who dare: Pushing the boundaries.* Lanham, MA: Roman & Littlefield.

Marshall, C., & Gerstl-Pepin, C. (2005). *Reframing educational politics for social justice.* Boston, MA: Allyn & Bacon.

Pillow, W. S. (2003). Confessions, catharsis, or cure? Rethinking the uses of reflexivity as methodological power in qualitative research. *The International Journal of Qualitative Research in Education, 16*(2), 175-196.

Sacks, H. (1985). On doing being ordinary. In J. M. Atkinson & J. Heritage (Eds.), *Structures of social action: Studies in conversation analysis* (pp. 413-429). New York, NY: Preager.

Scheurich, J. (1997). *Research method in the postmodern.* London, England: The Falmer Press.

Shakeshaft, C. (1999). The struggle to create a more gender-inclusive profession. In J. Murphy & K. S. Louis (Eds.), *Handbook on research in educational administration* (2nd ed., pp. 99-118). San Francisco, CA: Jossey-Bass.

Shields, C. M., & Edwards, M. M. (2005). *Dialog is just not talk: A new ground for educational leadership.* New York, NY: Peter Lang.

Spring, J. (2004). *Conflict of interest: The politics of American education.* New York, NY: McGraw Hill.

Tolstoy, L. (2008). *War and peace.* London, England: Vintage Classics. (Original work published 1869)

Tooms, A. (2007). The right kind of queer: Fit and the politics of school leadership. *Journal of School Leadership, 17*(5), 601-630.

Tooms, A. K., & Boske, C. (Eds.) (2010). *Bridge leadership: Connecting educational leadership and social justice to improve schools.* Greenwich, CT: Information Age.

Waite, D., Nelson, S. W., & Guajardo, M. (2008). Teaching and leadership for social justice and social responsibility: Home is where the struggle starts. *Journal of Educational Administration and Foundations.*

Author Contact Information: Autumn K. Cyprés, EdD, Professor, Director of The Center for Educational Leadership, The University of Tennessee, 303 Bailey Education Complex, Knoxville, Tennessee 37966. Telephone: 865-974 4559. E-mail: atooms@utk.edu

CHAPTER 78

Bureaucratic Theory

Myths, Theories, Models, Critiques

Eugenie A. Samier
The British University in Dubai

Bureaucracies are not new, and, in the modern world, are ubiquitous. Empirically, they are old, found in ancient societies such as China and Egypt that had need of a large and coordinated workforce (Wittfogel, 1957), with elements carried up through the last few centuries in various empires in the west and through the Caliphate and Ottoman empires in the Arab and Muslim worlds, through the Vatican to modern bureaucracies. A centralized bureaucracy began to form in eleventh century C.E. France, from which Prussia later developed its well known bureaucracy upon which Japan based its. An exam based meritocracy was first established on a large scale in the Chinese mandarin tradition, adopted by the British India Company, and then influencing U.K. meritocracy, and spreading then through Canada, the United States, Australia, and so on. Bureaucracies, therefore, are also a world historical phenomenon with complex causal relations spread across empires, colonial systems, and nations. Its development in Europe was originally seen in positive terms, associated with liberal democracy, elevating the social status and power of the bourgeoisie to cure the problem of corruption through patronage by introducing a merit system of qualification and to release the crown from strong influence by the nobility. The formation of the modern Western bureaucracy therefore accompanied and provided a causal condition for democracy, and demands for a well-educated cadre heavily influencing educational systems that conferred the knowledge and privileges of an educated professional class. The history of bureaucracy is very different from how it is usually characterized in the educational administration field.

THE MULTIDIMENSIONAL NATURE AND SCOPE OF BUREAUCRACY THEORY

Bureaucratic theory in educational administration comes predominantly from public administration and private sector style management studies, themselves derivative disciplines based on a number of core disciplines, such as political science, sociology, economics, psychology, anthropology, philosophy, and arts critiques (e.g., literary critiques of bureaucrats) (see Kettl & Milward, 1996). It also derives from a number of other area studies like state/government theory, organization studies (itself broadly composed of behavior, micro politics, culture, aesthetics), motivation theory, professionalism and professional identity, value theory, and institutional theory making it an inter- and multidisciplinary field. Generally, the theories and models are drawn from these sources and applied to educational systems and organization. The only original contribution to date from education that has been made to bureaucratic theory is Weick's (1976) concept of "loose-coupling."

The term "bureaucracy" means many different things. Its conception varies considerably depending upon whether one is referring to actual organizations that are bureaucratic in character, an analytic theory of bureaucracy for interpretive and critical use as Weber developed, an attitude that is captured in the notion of mentality such as "bureaucrat" (Aberbach, Putnam, & Rockman, 1981), variously regarded as "technocrat," "fonctionnaire" (functionary in the French) (Howton, 1969), or "apparatchik" (in the Russian), or a set of malpractices as in "bureaupathology" taking a multitude of forms. And there are probably many others. On an

The Handbook of Educational Theories, pp. 909–915

empirical level, it may be a way of administering that connotes ratio-pragmatic practices, as in the general Anglo-American form, or a set of legal-administrative practices in the legalistic-bureaucratic traditions of Germany and France, a command system of authority in the former Soviet world, the scribal bureaucracy of the Ottoman Empire, or the scholar-administrators of the traditional mandarinate in China. There are, therefore, three types of theory and associated models: an empirical-historical varying by society and culture, analytic (ideal type) for comparative world historical-sociology, and normative (good practices), each with a different purpose.

Generally, bureaucracy studies are considered a social science in the English-speaking world, associated most frequently with organizational structure, administrative functions, management techniques and economic modeling informed primarily by rationalism derived from modern economics, analytic philosophy, systems analysis, and behavioral and cognitive science. Bureaucratic studies from this perspective break down taxonomically by subset into the structural and functional domains of bureaucratic style organizations that form the conventional basis of graduate programs and research: organizational behavior, public policy process (formulation, analysis, implementation, evaluation), planning (strategic), personnel or human resources management, finance and budgeting, accountability and responsibilities, information systems, intergovernmental relations, municipal and regional, administrative law, and comparative international administration. Many educational administration texts follow this functionalist and structural approach to varying degrees of positivism, for example Bezeau (1989), Giles and Proudfoot (1994), Guthrie and Reed (1991), Hoy and Miskel (1987), Kimbrough (1988), and Sergiovanni (2009).

Some of the general critiques of this approach indicating the limitations of a predominantly descriptive, positivist, and social science view are the following: (1) values of hierarchy, control, and power are implicit, if not explicit; (2) a hidden agenda of conformity permeates the literature and training programs, reducing effective critique; and (3) historical and cross-cultural comparison is scant since value analysis and historical and anthropological theories and research methods are required for this kind of research (see, e.g., English, 1994; Samier, 2005; Smyth, 1989).

Since the 1980s, consequently, a contrary interpretive and critical tradition has emerged, including a number of more fundamental critiques of the nature and purpose of public sector bureaucracies that focus on problematic experiential, social, and political aspects. This includes the abuse of authority and administrative evil, the development of a professional identity, cultural and historical studies including problems of colonization, explorations of ideologies and doctrines of administration, problems of modernity, technical rationality and the fate of liberalism, theories of leadership and governance, and the incompatibility of democracy and bureaucracy. Drawing on a broader range of disciplines, including philosophy, cultural studies, humanistic psychology, and critical historiography, scholars have introduced a wide variety of critiques: critical theory, postmodernism, hermeneutics, phenomenology, the feminist critique, decolonization, ethics, and aesthetic analysis (Samier, 2005).

The Evolution and Development of Bureaucratic Theory

To some, public administration and educational administration are regarded as almost synonymous with bureaucracy, although other forms of administrative traditions have existed and still do in countries where traditionalism is a dominant institutional feature or where strong charismatic authority has established itself (see Weber, 1968). However, "bureaucracy" represents only one form of administration, that emphasizing modernist principles of rationality. However, the critique of theory in bureaucracy reflects much of the modern anxiety about public administration lacking a sufficient theoretical foundation equivalent to that in core disciplines. This issue has appeared a number of times: first raised by Waldo (1968), followed by Ostrom (1973), who regarded it as too closely tied to public choice theory and preoccupied with efficiency; LaPorte (1971) contending that it existed in a state of antique maladapted analytical models and normative aridity; Golembiewski (1977), who claimed that the field was in drift, in intellectual crisis, and in need of a new perspective; and Caiden (1971), who critiqued its "theoryless" state.

In spite of these contentions, the notion of "bureaucracy" in empirical or analytic form is shaped by a long history of political philosophy including Aristotle, Kant, Hobbes, Locke, Hegel, and Rousseau, all of whom contributed heavily to our ideas of government. Based partially on this philosophical foundation, social theory of Comte, Marx, Weber, Simmel, Michels, and Habermas have contributed to an understanding of bureaucratic organization. One neglected area of theory has been that of women philosophers who examined the rationale for state structures and their values (particularly moral) implications: Madame de Staël, Rosa Luxemburg, Hannah Arendt, Simone Weil (see Grey, 1996), Susanne Langer, and Martha Nussbaum (see Hodgkinson, 1996).

The earliest modern tradition affecting an understanding of bureaucracy is scientific management, in part shaped by Wilson's (1887) introduction of the politics-administration dichotomy. The most important influences here are Taylor's (1911) highly mechanized model emphasizing time and motion studies, greatly affecting educational management (Callahan, 1962), and Simon (1947) on rational decision making. Subsequent writers have emphasized the effect of rational authority on organizational structure (Meyer, 1972). This approach also misrepresented Weber's (1968) analytic bureaucracy type, treating it as either an empirical or normative model. Hodgkinson (1978) and Greenfield (1986) were among the first in educational administration to fundamentally question the scientific paradigm, followed shortly thereafter by such authors as Smyth (1989), and a host of others throughout the late 1980s and 1990s and into the present (see below).

The political critique includes a number of issues, from the relationship between political regime and bureaucracy to micropolitics of the bureaucratic organization. One area of that has long been developed is the uneasy relationship between democracy and bureaucracy, found in Etzioni-Halevy (1983) examining the dilemmas each poses for the other, and Richardson (2003), who questions the relative power of bureaucracies that have captured the policy process, an argument pursued by Chapman (1990) in education. Other critiques of bureaucratic elite politics include the power of senior bureaucrats in relation to the political regime, explored by Strauss (1961), Peters (1978), and particularly Wildavsky's (1979) *Speaking Truth to Power.* In educational administration, the micropolitical has been explored as a more realistic treatment of educational bureaucracies (e.g., Ball, 1987). Postmodern critiques, focusing on power, particularly the insights of Foucault (1980), have been adopted widely in educational administration supplanting a "modernist" approach exemplified by Nyberg (1981).

Economics has played a stronger role in the last thirty years internationally, especially as a founding discipline for the New Public Management (NPM) neoliberal administrative ideology, through rational choice theory, economic institutionalism theory, corporate culture doctrine, scientific management, and the importation of business management in the public sector essentially opening the public sector to market principles and forces (see Gewirtz, Ball, & Bowe, 1995; Samier, 2001). Its emphasis is on the elimination of waste and the measure of work outputs as a precondition for control (Savoie, 1994), led intellectually by conservative economists William Niskanen, Friedrich Hayek, and Milton Friedman.

Interestingly, despite a large international literature on the NPM, very little of it has been used in educational administration. This new managerialism, though, has spawned a number of subliteratures that have directly affected educational administration: its promise to "debureaucratize" the public sector (e.g., Barzelay, 1992; Osborne & Gaebler, 1992); a popularity in leadership training (e.g., Maccoby, 1981; Tichy & Devanna, 1986); and a functionalist use of organizational culture (e.g., Deal & Kennedy, 1982; Schein, 1985). Many educational administration texts reflected these new views: debureaucratization in Lawton, Freedman, and Robertson (1995), leadership in education in Cunningham (2003), Hodgkinson (1978), and Maxcy (1991), and culture of educational organizations in Walker and Dimmock (2002). The most popular texts in the new managerialism have been critiqued by a number of writers who have regarded them as superficial and lacking in scholarly rigour and uncritically accepted too often in educational administration, such as Covey (1989), Peters and Waterman (1982), and Senge (1990) (see English, 2008; Mickelthwait & Wooldridge, 1996). The economic has also been used to examine the internal relationships and bureaucratic conduct, as composed of competition and exchange relationships (Breton & Wintrobe, 1982; Lubiensky, 2003).

Sociology is a major informing discipline of bureaucratic studies, initially developed by Weber, in the sociological introduction to *Economy and Society* (1968), where the process of bureaucratization was emphasized over reified notions of social structures independent of human value orientations and social action, and bureaucratization was taken to have negative characteristics leading modernized societies into "disenchantment" and the "iron cage." This approach has been used by Torstendahl (1991) in his studies of bureaucratized organizations, and explored to its logical end by Jacoby (1973). Bureaucratic organizations sociologically are those in which legal-rational values are dominant, informing the style of authority, practices and structures (Crozier, 1964; Meyer, 1972), an effect Mueller (1984) has traced through its effect on education.

Cultural analysis from organization studies (see Smircich, 1983) has had a strong impact on theories of bureaucracy, and more recently the related field of aesthetic analysis (e.g., English, 2008; Samier & Bates, 2006; Strati, 1999), that examine bureaucratic features as creative social constructions. Related to culture and aesthetics is the study of bureaucratic mentality and personality, a field well-established in bureaucracy studies for decades, particularly of the senior bureaucrats, or "mandarins," in the British Commonwealth tradition (e.g., Campbell & Szablowski, 1979; Hennessy, 1989), and carried through biographical and historical studies (e.g., English, 2008; Fitzgerald & Gunter, 2009; Ribbins, 2006).

Psychological studies of personality and character began with the human relations or organizational humanism school, like Mayo (1933), Barnard (1938), Argyris (1957), Selznick (1957), and McGregor (1960); however, the emphasis was still tied to managerial control and organizational imperatives. At the same time, psychoanalytic studies was another mode of investigating the effects of bureaucratic organization and the influence of neurotic individuals, with authors like Horney (1950), carried into contemporary literature with Diamond (1990), Zaleznik (1990), and Kets de Vries (2006).

Research Traditions

Generally, research on bureaucracy and bureaucratic characteristics has been carried out through positivistic research methods emphasizing quantification and description: experimental methods, statistical analyses, and descriptive case studies (e.g., Hoy & Miskel, 1987). These are aimed at a functionalist purpose in improving managerialism, creating a corporate culture, putting into place more effective performance appraisal and accountability systems, and establishing more efficient practices. For the educational sector this has included the application of quality management, systems analysis, and social science techniques that are grounded in positivism, renewed by such collections as Mitchell's (2006) that attempts to reconcile "science" with moral values and political ends.

Alternative approaches have been developing since Weber's initial interpretive comparative historical-sociological studies (although his writings have mostly been misinterpreted in English), emphasizing critical and interpretive approaches (see Ball, 1994; English, 2005), such as historiography, ethnography, hermeneutics (Balfour & Mesaros, 1994; Hummel, 1991), critical theory (Denhardt, 1984; Forester, 1981) used also in feminist and minority studies, phenomenology (Brown, 1978; Forester, 1990; Harmon, 1990), and discourse and narrative analysis (Farmer, 1995). The aim of these perspectives is to address such problems as hegemonic systems, overly rational decision making, capitalism and the commercialization of the public sector, while exploring the cultural life of bureaucratized organizations, examining the role of language and culture in supporting the hierarchy of power, systems of meaning, and the critique of bureaucratic mentality and ideologies (see Evers & Lakomski, 1991). The study of bureaucracy in education, as in other public sector studies, is also well represented by case study analysis, seen in Hanson (2003) and Pusey (1976).

Major Critiques

The critique of bureaucracy began with one of its most virulent critics, Max Weber (1930), who saw that the emphasis on legal-rational values and thinking would create people and organizations that would lose connection with other values, such as affect, tradition, and higher order values, leading to disenchantment and an iron cage of modernity (bureaucratization). Similarly problems were identified in Michels' (1962) notion of the iron law of oligarchy where the bureaucratic elite will pursue its own interests at the expense of those dependent upon them, see in Mieczkowski's (1995) *The Rot at the Top*.

Marxist and neo-Marxist critiques are common in the antibureaucracy movement connecting the harnessing of education to capitalism. One of the most famous is Bowles and Gintis's (1976) *Schooling in Capitalist America*, followed by a number of educational administration authors adopting a neo-Marxist and critical theory perspective such as those in Smyth's (1989) *Critical Perspectives on Educational Leadership*, Katz (1971) critiquing the role of bureaucracy in maintaining class structure, and many others like Apple (1982) and Giroux and McLaren (1989) who critique the role bureaucracy plays in maintaining capitalism. More recent critiques derived in part from Marxist theory are those drawing on Bourdieu and Habermas, like those from feminism, many of which applied neo-Marxist analysis to the rights of women and minorities for social justice (e.g., & Kenway, 1993; Ferguson, 1984; McElroy, 1986).

The critical literature on the NPM is now extensive, reviewing both its evolution and failures, and particularly the role of "bureaucrat bashing" and "mandarin" resistance that characterize its development (e.g., Aucoin, 1995; Campbell & Wilson, 1995; Savoie, 1994). The most recent critique of bureaucratic elements in education is that aimed at the new public management for its role in transforming education into private enterprise, and its subjection to the military-industrial complex in more systematic way than ever before (Giroux, 2007). A related economic phenomenon is globalization, which has subjected many parts of the public sector, including education, to global market forces (e.g., Bottery, 2004; Shields & Evans, 1998). There are many in the educational administration field who have critiqued this movement, aimed mostly at identifying the damaging effects, through its commodification of educational systems (e.g., Ball, 2006; Bates, 1985; Priest & St John, 2006; Slaughter & Leslie, 1997; Smyth, 1993).

Studies in the Bureaucracy of Education

There have been many studies of bureaucratic elites, two of the most notable of which are Aberbach, Putnam, and Rockman (1981), Fleischer (1986), and Page and Wright (1999). Similar studies in education are Ringer's (1990) and Nitta's (2008) study of the educational bureaucratic elite, and Hartmann (2007) who examines the role education, particularly elite schools play in shaping a national bureaucratic elite.

Other studies examine the role of bureaucratic politics and the relationship with government, such as Rogers' (1968) early critical study of bureaucratic politics and its detrimental effect on New York City schools and Corwin's (1983) examination of two federal programs in U.S. education, adopting a biographical metaphor to explore the relationships between the educational system and federal government, at a time when the new public management was coming into force, and entrepreneurialism was introduced drawing from private sector management practices. A number of departures from the bureaucratic have been attempted in restructuring and reforms, such as the self-managed school (Smyth, 1993) and Larson and Ovando's (2000) study of equity and multiculturalism in the bureaucratic environment of education, where bureaucratic features themselves inhibit and obstruct the pursuit of social justice.

REFERENCES

Aberbach, J., Putnam, R. & Rockman, B. (1981). *Bureaucrats and politicians in western democracies.* Cambridge, MA: Harvard University Press.

Apple, M. (Ed.). (1982). *Cultural and economic reproduction in education.* London: Routledge & Kegan Paul.

Argyris, C. (1957). *Personality and organization.* New York, NY: Harper & Row.

Aucoin, P. (1995). *The new public management.* Montreal, Canada: The Institute for Research on Public Policy.

Balfour, D., & Mesaros, W. (1994). Connecting the local narratives: Public administration as a hermeneutic science. *Public Administration Review,* 54(6), 559-564.

Ball, S. (1987). *The micro-politics of the school.* London: Methuen.

Ball, S. (1994). *Education reform: A critical and post structural approach.* Buckingham, England: Open University Press.

Ball, S. (2006). *Education policy and social class.* Abingdon, Oxfordshire, England: Routledge.

Barnard, C. (1938). *The functions of the executive.* Cambridge, Ma: Harvard University Press.

Barzelay, M. (1992). *Breaking through bureaucracy.* Berkeley, CA: University of California Press.

Bates, R. (1985). *Liberalism, Marxism and the struggle for the state.* Waurn Ponds, Geelong, Victoria, Australia: Deakin University Press.

Bezeau, L. (1989). *Educational administration for Canadian teachers.* Toronto, Canada: Copp Clark Pitman.

Blackmore, J., & Kenway, J. (Eds.). (1993). *Gender matters in educational administration and policy.* Bristol, PA: Falmer.

Bottery, M. (2004). *The challenges of educational leadership.* London: Paul Chapman.

Bowles, S., & Gintis, H. (1976). *Schooling in capitalist America.* London: Routledge & Kegan Paul.

Breton, A., & Wintrobe, R. (1982). *The logic of bureaucratic conduct.* Cambridge, England: Cambridge University Press.

Brown, R. (1978). Bureaucracy as praxis. *Administrative Science Quarterly, 23*(3), 365-382.

Caiden, G. (1971). *The dynamics of public administration.* Hinsdale, IL: Dryden Press.

Callahan, R. (1962). *Education and the cult of efficiency.* Chicago, IL: University of Chicago Press.

Campbell, C., & Szablowski, G. (1979). *The Superbureaucrats.* Toronto, Canada: Macmillan.

Campbell, C., & Wilson, G. (1995). *The end of Whitehall.* Oxford, England: Blackwell.

Chapman, J. (1990). *Democracy and bureaucracy.* London: Falmer Press.

Corwin, R. (1983). *The entrepreneurial bureaucracy.* Greenwich, CN: JAI Press.

Covey, S. (1989). *The seven habits of highly effective people.* New York, NY: Simon & Schuster.

Crozier, M. (1964). *The bureaucratic phenomenon.* London, England: Tavistock.

Cunningham, W., & Cordeiro, P. (2003). *Educational leadership.* Boston, MA: Allyn & Bacon.

Deal, T., & Kennedy, A. (1982). *Corporate cultures.* Reading, MA: Addison-Wesley.

Denhardt, R. (1984). *Theories of public organization.* Monterey, CA: Brooks/Cole.

Diamond, M. (1990). Psychoanalytic phenomenology and organizational analysis. *Public Administration Quarterly, 14*(1), 32-42.

English, F. (1994). *Theory in educational administration.* New York, NY: HarperCollins.

English, F. (Ed.) (2005). *The Sage handbook of educational leadership.* Thousand Oaks, CA: SAGE.

English, F. (2008). *The art of educational leadership.* Los Angeles, CA: SAGE.

Etzioni-Halevy, E. (1983). *Bureaucracy and democracy* (2nd ed.) London: Routledge & Kegan Paul.

Evers, C., & Lakomski, G. (1991). *Knowing educational administration.* Oxford, England: Pergamon.

Farmer, D. (1995) *The language of public administration.* Tuscaloosa, AL: University of Alabama Press.

Ferguson, K. (1984). *The feminist case against bureaucracy.* Philadelphia, PA: Temple University Press.

Fitzgerald, T., & Gunter, H. (Eds.). (2009). *Educational administration and history.* London: Routledge.

Foucault, M. (1980). *Power/knowledge.* New York, NY: Pantheon.

Fleischer, C. (1986). *Bureaucrat and intellectual in the Ottoman Empire.* Princeton, NJ: Princeton University Press.

Forester, J. (1981). Questioning and organizing attention. *Administration and Society, 13,* 161-207.

Forester, J. (1990). No planning or administration without phenomenology? *Public Administration Quarterly, 14*(1), 56-65.

Gewirtz, S., Ball, S. & Bowe, R. (1995) *Markets, choice, and equity in education.* Philadelphia, PA: Open University Press.

Giles, T. & Proudfoot, A. (1994) *Educational administration in Canada* (5th ed.). Calgary, AB, Canada: Detselig.

Giroux, H. (2007). *The university in chains.* London: Paradigm.

Giroux, H., & McLaren, P. (Eds.). (1989). *Critical pedagogy, the state, and cultural struggle.* Albany, NY: SUNY Press.

Golembiewski, R. (1977). *Public administration as a developing discipline*. New York, NY: Marcel Dekker.
Greenfield, T. (1986). The decline and fall of science in educational administration. *Interchange, 17*(2), 57-80.
Grey, C. (1996). Towards a critique of managerialism: The contribution of Simone Weil. *Journal of Management Studies, 33*(5), 591-612.
Guthrie, J., & Reed, R. (1991). *Educational administration and policy*. Englewood Cliffs, NJ: Prentice-Hall.
Hanson, E. (2003). *Educational administration and organizational behavior* (5th ed.). Boston, MA: Allyn & Bacon.
Hartmann, M. (2007). *The sociology of elites*. Abingdon, Oxfordshire, England: Routledge.
Harmon, M. (1990). Applied phenomenology and organization. *Public Administration Quarterly, 14*(1), 10-17.
Hennessy, P. (1989). *Whitehall*. London: Fontana.
Hodgkinson, C. (1978). *Towards a philosophy of administration*. Oxford, England: Blackwell.
Hodgkinson, C. (1996) *Administration philosophy*. Oxford, England: Pergamon.
Horney, K. (1950) *Neurosis and human growth*. New York, NY: W. W. Norton.
Howton, F. (1969). *Functionaries*. Chicago, IL: Quadrangle Books.
Hoy, W., & Miskel, C. (1987). *Educational administration* (3rd ed.). New York, NY: Random House.
Hummel, R. (1991). Stories managers tell: Why they are as valid as science. *Public Administration Review, 51*(1), 31-41.
Jacoby, H. (1973). *The bureaucratization of the world*. Berkeley, CA: University of California Press.
Katz, M. (1971). *Class, bureaucracy and schools*. Santa Barbara, CA: Praeger.
Kettl, D., & Milward, H. (1996). *The state of public management*. Baltimore, MD: John Hopkins University Press.
Kets de Vries, M. (2006). *The leadership mystique* (2nd ed.). London: Prentice-Hall.
Kimbrough, R. (1988). *Educational administration* (3rd ed.). New York, NY: Macmillan.
LaPorte, T. (1971). The recovery of relevance in the study of public organization. In F. Marini (Ed.), *Toward a new public administration* (pp. 17-47). San Francisco, CA: Chandler.
Larson, C. & Ovando, C. (2000). *The color of bureaucracy*. Belmont, CA: Wadsworth.
Lawton, S., Freedman, J., & Robertson, H.-J. (1995). *Busting Bureaucracy to reclaim our schools*. Montreal, QC, Canada: McGill-Queen's University Press.
Lubiensky, C. (2003). Innovation in education markets. *American Educational Research Journal, 40*(2), 395-443.
Maccoby, M. (1981). *The leader*. New York, NY: Simon & Schuster.
Maxcy, S. (1991). *Educational leadership*. New York, NY: Bergin & Garvey.
Mayo, E (1933). *The human problems of an industrial civilization*. New York, NY: Macmillan.
McElroy, W. (Ed.) (1986). *Freedom, feminism and the state*. Washington, DC: Cato Institute.
McGregor, D. (1960). *The human side of enterprise*. New York, NY: McGraw-Hill.
Meyer, M. (1972). *Bureaucratic structure and authority*. New York, NY: Harper & Row.
Michels, R. (1962). *Political parties*. New York, NY: Free Press.
Mickelthwait, J., & Wooldridge, A. (1996). *The witch doctors*. London: Heinemann.
Mieczkowski, B. (1995). *The rot at the top*. Lanham, MD: University Press of America.
Mitchell, D. (Ed.). (2006). *New foundations for knowledge in educational administration, policy, and politics*. Mahwah, NJ: Lawrence Erlbaum Associates.
Mueller, H.-E. (1984). *Bureaucracy, education, and monopoly*. Berkeley, CA: University of California Press.
Nitta, K. (2008). *The politics of structural educational reform*. Abingdon, Oxfordshire, England: Routledge.
Nyberg, D. (1981) *Power over power*. Ithaca, NY: Cornell University Press.
Osborne, D., & Gaebler, T. (1992). *Reinventing government*. Reading, MA: Addison-Wesley.
Ostrom, V. (1973). *The intellectual crisis in American public administration*. Tuscaloosa, AL: University of Alabama Press.
Page, E., & Wright, V. (1999). *Bureaucratic elites in western European states*. Oxford, England: Oxford University Press.
Peters, B. (1978). *The politics of bureaucracy*. New York, NY: Longman.
Peters, T. & Waterman, R. (1982). *In search of excellence*. New York, NY: Harper & Row.
Priest, D., & St John, E. (Ed.). (2006). *Privatization and public universities*. Bloomington IN: University of Indiana Press.
Pusey, M. (1976). *Dynamics of bureaucracy*. New York, NY: John Wiley.
Ribbins, P. (Ed.) (2006). *Journal of Educational Administration and History. History and the Study of Administration and Leadership in Education* (Special issue).
Richardson, H. (2003). *Democratic autonomy*. Oxford, England: Oxford University Press.
Ringer, F. (1990). *The decline of the German mandarins* (2nd ed.) Hanover, NH: University Press of New England.
Rogers, D. (1968). *110 Livingston Street*. New York, NY: Random House.
Samier, E. A. (2001). Demandarinisation in the new public management. In E. Hanke & W. Mommsen (Eds.), *Max Webers herrschaftssoziologie: studien zu entstehung und wirkung* (pp. 235-263). Tübingen, Germany: Mohr/Siebeck.
Samier, E. A. (2005). Toward public administration as a humanities discipline. *Halduskultuur, 6*, 6-59. (Reprinted in F. English (Ed.) *Educational leadership and administration*, SAGE, 2009.)
Samier, E. A., & Bates, R. (2006). *Aesthetic dimensions of educational administration and leadership*. Milton Keyes, England: Routledge.
Savoie, D. (1994). *Thatcher, Reagan, Mulroney*. Pittsburgh, PA: University of Pittsburgh Press.
Schein, E. (1985). *Organizational culture and leadership*. San Francisco, CA: Jossey-Bass.
Selznick, P. (1957). *Leadership in administration*. New York, NY: Harper & Row.
Senge, P. (1990). *The fifth discipline*. New York, NY: Doubleday.
Sergiovanni, T. (2009). *Educational governance and administration* (6th ed.). Boston, MA: Pearson Allyn.
Shields, J. & Evans, B. (1998). *Shrinking the state*. Halifax, British Columbia, Canada: Fernwood.
Simon, H. (1947). *Administrative behavior*. New York, NY: Macmillan.

Slaughter, S., & Leslie, L. (1997) *Academic capitalism*. Baltimore, MA: Johns Hopkins University Press.

Smircich, L. (1983). Concepts of culture and organizational analysis. *Administrative Science Quarterly, 28*, 339-358.

Smyth, J. (Ed.). (1989). *Critical perspectives on educational leadership*. London: Falmer.

Smyth, J. (Ed.). (1993). *A socially critical view of the self-managing school*. London: Falmer.

Strati, A. (1999). *Organization and aesthetics*. London: SAGE.

Strauss, E. (1961). *The ruling servants*. New York, NY: Praeger.

Taylor, F. W. (1911). *The principles of scientific management*. New York, NY: Harper & Brothers.

Tichy, N., & Devanna, M. (1986). *The transformational leader*. New York, NY: Wiley.

Torstendahl, R. (1991). *Bureaucratization in northwestern Europe*. London: Routledge.

Waldo, D. (1968). Scope of the theory of public administration (pp. 1-26). In J. Charlesworth (Ed.), *Theory and practice of public administration*. Philadelphia, PA: American Academy of Political and Social Science.

Walker, A., & Dimmock, C. (Eds.). (2002). *School leadership and administration*. New York, NY: RoutledgeFalmer.

Weber, M. (1930). *The protestant ethic and the spirit of capitalism*. London: Unwin Hyman.

Weber, M. (1968). *Economy and society*. Berkeley, CA: University of California Press.

Weick, K. (1976). Educational organizations as loosely coupled systems. *Administrative Science Quarterly, 21*(1), 1-19.

Wildavsky, A. (1979) *Speaking truth to power*. New York, NY: Little Brown.

Wilson, W. (1887). The study of public administration. *Political Science Quarterly, 2*, 481-507.

Wittfogel, K. (1957). *Oriental despotism: A comparative study of total power*. New Haven, CT: Yale University Press.

Zaleznik, A. (1990) *Executive's guide to motivating people*. Chicago, Il: Bonus.

Author Contact Information: Eugenie A. Samier, Faculty of Education, The British University in Dubai, Dubai, United Arab Emirates. Phone: 971.(0)55.96.44.295. E-mail: Eugenie.samier@buid.ac.ae

CHAPTER 79

Contingency Management and Situational Leadership Theories

JoAnn Danelo Barbour
Texas Woman's University

Contingency management and situational leadership are two sides of the coin of belief that there is no one best way of managing or leading, the twin concepts I will address in this chapter. Sometimes there is overlap in use and meaning; sometimes the concepts veer in meaning or use. I will discuss the conceptual overlaps and differences as I describe the theories and discuss their original development, iterations, and uses and applications of the theories. I conclude with a discussion of the strengths of the theories and comments from critics of the theories.

From a somewhat evolutionary standpoint, management and leadership theorists wanted to expand beyond the early great man and trait theories and early behavioral theories. They wanted to address the criticism in management and leadership studies that did not take into account the contexts or situations in which managers and leaders make decisions. Contingency and situational theorists attempt to discuss management and leadership from both organizational and behavioral perspectives.

Embedded in open systems theory, both contingency and situational theories are influential in management and leadership theory development. In open systems theory, organizations are capable of self-maintenance based on environmental input or interaction, essential for open system functioning. From an organizational perspective within systems theory, contingency and situational theorists view administrative and leadership processes and choices as a condition of the particular character or nature of the organization itself, the environment of the organization at a given point in time, the nature of the key decision makers, and the specific task or tasks the organization seeks to accomplish within a particular timeframe.

DESCRIPTION

In coining the term, *contingency theory*, Lawrence and Lorsch (1967) argued that different environments place differing requirements on organizations, and, accordingly, on the leaders of those organizations (Scott, 1987). Consequently, theorists from a perspective grounded in behavioral theory contend that there is no one best way of leading or decision making, that a leadership style that is effective in some situations may not be successful in others. A major assumption, therefore, of contingency management and situational leadership is that one's ability to manage or lead is dependent upon or influenced by various situational factors, including the leader's preferred style and the capabilities and behaviors of organizational members (traditionally noted in the literature as followers), as well as other variables.

There are two conclusions one can draw based on this assumption. First, leaders and managers who may be effective at one place and time may become unsuccessful either when transplanted to another situation or when the factors around them change. Additionally, because manager and leader behavioral expectations will vary depending on the situations, managers and leaders will be more or less successful depending on their ability to change behaviors based on situational factors. A second conclusion, therefore, is that success

The Handbook of Educational Theories, pp. 917–921

as a leader or manager may depend upon one's ability to adapt and change one's behaviors as requirements and needs of situations change. As the theories evolved, they were characterized by two orienting sets of behaviors, one toward the task (initiating structure, concern for production) and one set toward interpersonal relations (consideration, concern for people).

As contingency theorists view organizational and management processes and choices as dependent upon a set of variables (nature of the organization, environment at a point in time, nature of key decision makers, and specific tasks to be accomplished), similarly, the major premise of situational leadership is that the best action of the leader depends on a range of situational factors. An effective leader does not fall into a single preferred style of decision making. Factors that affect situational decisions include motivation and capability of followers, factors that, in turn, are affected by particular issues, features or dynamic within the situational context, including the relationship between followers and the leader. One's perception of oneself, of the follower, of the tasks, and of the situation will often affect what a leader does rather than the truth or reality of the situation.

Development and Iterations of Contingency and Situational Theories

Although both contingency management and situational leadership theorists hold the assumption that there is no simple one right way to manage or lead, there are differences in the theories. Contingency theorists take a broader view that includes contingent factors about leader capability and other variables within the situation, whereas situational theorists tend to focus more on the behaviors that the leader should adopt when encountering factors within a given context or situation, for example follower behavior, environmental issues, or political concerns.

Situational and contingency theorists stress several key concepts. There is no universal or one best way to lead. There are, however, some universal principles of leadership that fit all situations. Organizationally, the design and its subsystems must be a fit for the leader; the organization, its subsystems and leader must have a proper fit with the environment; and each situation within the organizational environment is unique and therefore must be studied and treated as unique. The success of the leader is a function of various organizational contingencies in the form of subordinate, task, and/ or group variables.

Because the effectiveness of a given pattern of leader behavior is contingent upon the demands imposed by the situation, the leader's style is, of necessity, highly variable. For an individual leader, situational theorists assume that leadership is changeable and should be variable for different situations; thus, leaders use different styles of leadership appropriate to the needs created by different organizational situations. Tannenbaum and Schmidt (1973) suggest three elements produce a leader's action: factors or forces in the situation, capabilities or forces in the followers, and capabilities or forces in the leader. These elements are parts of four classic and frequently cited management and leadership contingency and situational models, which I will discuss next. The contingency model of leadership effectiveness and cognitive resource theory focuses on the leader's internal state and traits (Fiedler, 1967, 1972, 1973, 1974). Others focus on the leader's perceived behaviors, such as path-goal theory (House & Mitchell, 1974, 1997; and Tannenbaum & Schmidt, 1973), situational leadership theory (Hersey & Blanchard, 1974, 1993), and the normative decision making model (Vroom & Jago, 1988; and Vroom & Yetton, 1973).

Generally considered the father of leadership contingency theory, Fred Fiedler (1967, 1972, 1973, 1974) veered from traditional trait and behavioral models with his assertion that three organizational contingencies determine appropriate manager or leader behavior. These organizational contingencies include leader-member relations (the degree to which a leader is accepted and supported by group members), task structure (the extent to which tasks are structured and defined with clear goals and procedures), and leader positional power (the ability of a leader to control subordinates through reward and punishment). Fiedler argued that combinations of the three contingencies create favorable or unfavorable conditions for leadership, that is, situations in which the leader can exert influence over the group. High levels of leader-member relations, task structure and positional power provide the most favorable situation to exert influence over others; low levels of the three contingencies provide the least favorable leadership situation to exert influence. Fiedler determined that a task-oriented style is more effective in situations wherein the leader has very much or very little influence; a relationship-oriented leader is more effective in situations only moderately favorable to influence. Fiedler concluded that the organization should match up a particular manager or leader and style to the demands of the situation, or alter the variables within the situation, that is, the power that goes with the leadership position, so that the situation becomes more conducive to one's style of influence. In other words, it may be easier for leaders to change a situation to achieve effectiveness, rather than change leadership style.

Variations to Fiedler's model include two examples of path-goal theory: those of House and Mitchell (1977,

1994) and Tannenbaum and Schmidt (1973). Influenced by expectancy theories of motivation, House and Mitchell developed the path-goal contingency model, asserting that the leader's behavior is acceptable to subordinates insofar as they view the leader's behavior as a source of immediate or future satisfaction. The leader is to observe and understand the situation and choose appropriate leadership styles and actions (paths) depending upon goals of subordinates and leader. The responsibilities of the leader, to offer rewards for achievement of performance goals, to clarify paths towards these goals, and to remove obstacles, are accomplished by adopting certain leadership styles according to the situation. The leader styles will be directive, supportive, participative, and achievement-oriented, depending on subordinate needs and abilities. Leadership behaviors are matched along a continuum of subordinate and environmental characteristics, from structured to unstructured situations; thus, if group members have a high need for motivation, directive leadership is provided, specific advice is given and ground rules are established to provide structure. If members have a low need for motivation, achievement-oriented leadership is provided and challenging goals are set with high performance encouraged while showing confidence in members' ability, a more unstructured situation.

Effective leaders adjust their leadership to fit these contingencies of group and environment and to motivate subordinates. To the House and Mitchell model, Tannenbaum and Schmidt (1973) add a range of behavioral patterns available to a manager or leader, from authoritarian (task-oriented) leadership to democratic (relationship-oriented) leadership. Leader action choices are connected to the degree of authority used by the leader and the amount of freedom available to the subordinates. Action choices begin on the left of the continuum with a high degree of control; the action choice on the farthest right of the continuum is a leader who delegates authority. Tannenbaum and Schmidt believe a leader should be flexible and adapt the leadership style to the situation.

Hersey and Blanchard (1974, 1993) developed the Situational Leadership Grid that contains two dimensions of leadership: task behavior and relationship behavior. More specifically, the effectiveness of four leadership behaviors (telling, selling, participating, and delegating) depends on whether the behaviors complement the subordinates' maturity. Hersey and Blanchard proposed that one's leadership style should be matched to the maturity of the subordinates' psychological maturity (willingness, self-confidence, motivation, and readiness to accept responsibility) and task maturity (education, skills, ability, technical knowledge, and experience). As the subordinate maturity increases, leaders should be more relationship-motivated than task-motivated. Leadership will vary with the situation and the leader may delegate to, participate with, sell ideas to, or tell subordinates what to do. Although the theory has a measure, the leadership effectiveness and adaptability description, to assess the leader's style, "many of the empirical studies on this model seem to use the Leader Behavior Description Questionnaire in measuring the leader's behaviors" (Ayman, 2004, p. 162).

Vroom and Yetton (1973) and Vroom and Jago (1988) developed a contingency model focused on the leader's decision strategy, a normative model that emphasizes leader behavior from authoritative to participative. With this model, the effectiveness of a decision depends upon a number of situational variables: (a) the importance of the decision quality and acceptance of the decision; (b) the amount of relevant information possessed by the leader and subordinates; (c) the likelihood that subordinates will accept an autocratic decision or collaborate in trying to make a good participative decision, and (d) the amount of disagreement among subordinates with respect to their preferred alternatives. The Vroom-Yetton leadership model (1973) includes the selection of one of five leadership styles for making a decision: (a) Autocratic 1 when the problem is solved using information already available; (b) Autocratic 2 when additional information is obtained from the group before the leader makes decision; (c) Consultative 1 when the leader discusses the problem with subordinates individually before making a decision; (d) Consultative 2 when the problem is discussed with the group before deciding, and (e) Group 2 when the group makes the decision with the leader simply acting as facilitator. The leadership style is chosen by progressing through seven questions at various nodes along the decision tree. Vroom and Yetton suggest that the overall effectiveness of a decision depends on two intervening variables: (a) decision quality--the objective aspects of the decision that affect group performance regardless of any effects mediated by decision acceptance, and (b) decision acceptance by followers--the degree of follower commitment in implementing a decision effectively. They maintain that both decision quality and acceptance are affected by follower participation during decision making.

CONCLUSIONS

One major strength in the contingency and situational models is that these scholars moved thinking beyond the *one best type of leader* assumption of the trait theorists and the *one best way to lead* model of the early behaviorists. The contingency and situational theorists began to conceptualize management and leadership theory within an organizational framework; thus, leader or manager style had to be discussed within an organizational context that includes the workers within the organization. Critics suggest, however, that contingency and situational theorists are limited in their conceptualization of leadership and the empirical strength to support the various arguments. While scholars might agree that the most effective leaders are those who are both task oriented and people oriented (that is, high-high leaders), the empirical research based on questionnaires, according to Yukl (1998), seems to provide limited support for the universal proposition that high-high leaders are more effective, and few studies have directly investigated whether the two types of leader behavior interact in a mutually facilitative way. In contrast, "The descriptive research from critical incidents and interviews strongly suggests that to be effective a leader must be able to guide and facilitate the work to accomplish task objectives while at the same time maintaining cooperative relationships and teamwork" (Yukl, 1998, p. 64).

Within an organizational context, contingency and situational theorists pay little attention to the structure of the organization—neither that over which the managers have control nor structural components to which managers have little control. These theorists oversimplify the options available to leaders and managers as well as the range of situations that they encounter. They pay little attention to cultural and symbolic aspects of the organization and the values of those who collectively lead, manage, and work within the organization; and pay no consideration to politics and the political climate within the organization and in the larger context outside and tangential to the organization (Blake & Mouton, 1969, 1985; Bolman & Deal, 2009; Hofstede, 1984; Morgan, 1997; and Schein, 1992). Additionally, they tend to overlook contextual factors such as hierarchical level, national culture, or leader-follower gender (Antonakis, Avolio, & Sivasubramaniam, 2003), and issues of paradoxical behavioral complexity (Denison, Hooijberg, & Quinn, 1995).

Effective leaders respond to situations by changing behaviors, by being perceived as behaving differently, or by choosing and then managing the situation (Ayman, 2004). Theoretically, contingency and situational approaches to management and leadership work because they are based on a person-to-situation fit concept. As a set of theories, contingency and situational theories are evolutionary. They help bridge a gap between trait theorists and the early behaviorists. The interactions of all organizational factors are very complex, however, and unpredictable; and, since circumstances do not stay fixed for long, a constant renegotiating of leadership behaviors and styles would have to occur.

REFERENCES

Antonakis, J., Avolio, B. J., & Sivasubramaniam, N. (2003). Context and leadership: An examination of the nine-factor full-range leadership theory using multifactor leadership questionnaire (MLQ Form 5X). *Leadership Quarterly, 14*, 261-295.

Ayman, R. (2004). Situational and contingency approaches to leadership. In J. Antonakis, A. T. Cianciolo, & R. J. Sternberg (Eds.), *The nature of leadership* (pp. 148-170). Thousand Oaks, CA: SAGE.

Blake, R., & Mouton, J. S. (1969). *Building a dynamic corporation through grid organizational development.* Reading, MA: Addison-Wesley.

Blake, R., & Mouton, J. S. (1985). *Managerial grid III.* Houston, TX: Gulf.

Bolman, L. G., & Deal, T. E. (2009). *Reframing organizations: Artistry, choice and leadership* (4th ed.). San Francisco, CA: Jossey-Bass.

Denison, D. R., Hooijberg, R., & Quinn, R. E. (1995). Paradox and performance: Toward a theory of behavioral complexity in managerial leadership. *Organization Science, 6*(5), 524-540.

Fiedler, F. E. (1967). *A theory of leadership effectiveness.* New York, NY: McGraw-Hill.

Fiedler, F. E. (1972). The effects of leadership training and experience: A contingency model interpretation. *Administrative Science Quarterly, 17*(4), 453-470.

Fiedler, F. E. (1973). The contingency theory and the dynamics of leadership process. *Advances in Experimental Social Psychology, 11*, 60-112.

Fiedler, F. E. (1974). The contingency model: New directions for leadership utilization. *Journal of Contemporary Business, 3*, 65-79.

Hersey, P., & Blanchard, K. H. (1974). So you want to know your leadership style? *Training and Development Journal, 2*, 1-15.

Hersey, P., & Blanchard, K. H. (1993). *Management of organizational behavior: Utilizing human resources* (6th ed.). Englewood Cliffs, NJ: Prentice Hall.

Hofstede, G. (1984). *Culture's consequences: International differences in work-related values.* Newbury Park, CA: SAGE.

House, R. J., & Mitchell, T. R. (1974). A path-goal theory of leader effectiveness. *Journal of Contemporary Business, 3*, 81-97.

House, R. J., & Mitchell, T. R. (1997). Path-goal theory of leadership. In R. P. Vecchio (Ed.), *Leadership: Understanding the dynamics of power and influence in organizations* (pp. 259-273). Notre Dame, IN: Notre Dame University Press.

Lawrence, P. R., & Lorsch, J. W. (1967). *Organization and environment: Managing differentiation and integration.* Boston, MA: Harvard University Graduate School of Business Administration.

Morgan, G. (1997). *Images of organization* (2nd ed.). Thousand Oaks, CA: SAGE.

Schein, E. H. (2004). *Organizational culture and leadership* (3rd ed.) San Francisco, CA: Jossey-Bass.

Scott, W. R. (1987). *Organizations: Rational, natural, and open systems* (2nd ed.). Englewood Cliffs, NJ: Prentice-Hall.

Tannenbaum, R., & Schmidt, W. H. (1973). How to choose a leadership pattern. *Harvard Business Review, 51*(3), 162-175, 178-180.

Vroom, V. H., & Jago, A. G. (1988). *The new leadership: Managing participation in organizations*. Englewood Cliffs, NJ: Prentice Hall

Vroom, V. H., & Yetton, P. W. (1973). *Leadership and decision making*. Pittsburgh, PA: University of Pittsburgh Press.

Yukl, G. (1998). *Leadership in organizations* (4th ed.) Upper Saddle River, NJ: Prentice-Hall.

Author Contact Information: JoAnn Danelo Barbour, PhD, Professor of Education Administration and Leadership, College of Professional Education, Texas Woman's University, Denton, Texas 76204. Telephone: 940-898-2248. E-mail: jbarbour@twu.edu

CHAPTER 80

Critical Race Theory and Educational Leadership

Floyd D. Beachum
Lehigh University

Critical race theory (CRT) is a framework that attempts to provide unique ways to examine, analyze, and explain the roles, rules, and recognition of race and racism in society. It has its origins in law as a response to critical legal studies (CLS). Critical race theory views racism as a natural aspect of everyday life in the United States, thus permeating everything from academic disciplines to legal decisions to the modern workplace. Derrick Bell (1995a), one of CRT's founders, described it as "a body of legal scholarship … a majority of whose members are both existentially people of color and ideologically committed to the struggle against racism, particularly as institutionalized in and by law" (p. 888). This chapter will examine the origins and development of CRT, its use and application, validation, and critiques of the framework.

Although CRT traces its origins to legal studies, it has found a theoretical home in disciplines such as education, political science, and a broad range of ethnic studies. Critical race theory has also informed movements to explore additional frameworks such as: critical race feminism (CRF), Latino critical race studies (LatCrit), Asian American critical race studies (AsianCrit), and American Indian critical race studies. All of these deal with applying a more critical stance against dominant ideologies and placing the concerns and experiences of these various groups in the center of the discussion as opposed to the periphery. Though very distinct, critical race theory overlaps and diverges from other approaches such as critical pedagogy.

CRITICAL THEORY AND CRITICAL RACE THEORY

Critical race theory can be viewed under the larger umbrella of critical theory. According to Sims and Van Loon (2002) critical theory can be described as

> an amalgam of philosophical and social-scientific techniques (often making extensive use of statistical questionnaires in its inquiries) that had wide-ranging applications. Established as a research institute at the University of Frankfurt in the early 1920s, the School fled from Germany on the Nazi takeover in 1933 and subsequently relocated in New York (retuning to Frankfurt after the Second World War). (p. 39)

Part of this tradition is an approach called critical pedagogy, first used by Henry Giroux in his 1983 work, *Theory and Resistance in Education*. In education, critical pedagogy has been articulated as a way for educators to pose critique, construct a language to address oppression, and work for change in schools and society. "Critical pedagogy calls for educators to be agents working for social change and equity in schools and communities" (Parker & Stovall, 2004, p. 168). While this is a hopeful direction for education, the theoretical analysis, many times, juxtaposes those who argue for a postcritical pedagogy with others who are deeply steeped in a class-based analysis (Wright, 2002). Unfortunately, this debate marginalizes issues of race and racism. This was even evident in the Frankfurt School as "its principal male theorists, to its mostly female critics, the figures involved in the discourse have been white" (Parker & Stovall, 2004, p. 173). Thus, even with critical approaches that question everything from wealth distribution to change in schools, they still can fall short of an analysis that deeply interrogates the ubiquitous, insidious, and covert nature of modern racism in U.S. society. In addition, many of these approaches did not reflect the stories, interpretations, and theoretical insight of people of color. Therefore, what was needed was a framework that did provide a way to analyze racism and include the voice of people of color, those who were most impacted by racism's results. What emerged was critical race theory.

The Handbook of Educational Theories, pp. 923–928

Origins of Critical Race Theory

Critical race theory was born out of critical legal studies (CLS). CLS is a line of inquiry that asserts that power and interests trump precedent (and principles) with regard to legal judgments. CLS still did not address issues of inequality, oppression, and racism. West (1993) argued:

> critical legal theorists fundamentally question the dominant liberal paradigms prevalent and pervasive in American culture and society. This thorough questioning is not primarily a constructive attempt to put forward a conception of a new legal and social order. Rather, it is a pronounced disclosure of inconsistencies, incoherencies, silences, and blindness of legal formalists, legal positivists, and legal realists in the liberal tradition. Critical legal studies is more a concerted attack and assault on the legitimacy and authority of pedagogical strategies in law school than a comprehensive announcement of what a credible and realizable new society and legal system would look like. (p. 196)

Therefore, some supporters of CLS began to break away and form what became known as critical race theory. These supporters became CRT founders; they included: Derrick Bell, Kimberle Crenshaw, Richard Delgado, Alan Freeman, and Mari Matusda. According to Ladson-Billings (2009), "CLS scholars critiqued mainstream legal ideology for its portrayal of U. S. society as a meritocracy but failed to include racism in its critique. Thus, CRT became a logical outgrowth of the discontent of legal scholars of color" (p. 21). Although it has its beginnings in the field of law, CRT eventually spread to education.

CRT's usefulness and utility was not only confined to the legal arena. Educational scholars began to see meaningful applications of CRT to the racial obstacles so prevalent in the U.S. educational system. Ladson-Billings and Tate challenged educational scholars in 1995 to engage in a more complex, systemic, and nuanced view of race at the annual meeting of the American Educational Research Association. Their work was materialized in an article that same year titled, "Toward a Critical Race Theory of Education," which appeared in *Teachers College Record*. This article introduced and explained CRT and its educational applications as well as encouraged scholars in education to look towards other fields (e.g., law) in order to provide a deeper analysis of race and inequality in education (Zamudio, Russell, Rios, & Bridgeman, 2011). As CRT further develops and delves deeper into its analysis of educational issues, it still has much to gain from its legal beginnings. Dixon and Rousseau (2005) wrote:

> Thus, while CRT in education must necessarily grow and develop to become its own entity, we would argue that there is still much support and needed nourishment yet to be gained from the legal roots of CRT. In this way, the direction forward with respect to CRT in education requires, in some sense, a return back to the place we started. (p. 24)

In this manner, while CRT expands its analytic capabilities into education, it still benefits from the lessons of its legal origins. CRT then has contemporary relevance to immediate issues in education while still being linked to a legal heritage that not only forms a firm foundation, but continues to benefit as the education movement grows.

Major Tenets of Critical Race Theory

In order to better understand critical race theory, one needs to be aware of the major tenets or themes upon which the theory rests. There are at least six major themes that define CRT.

1. Racism is a permanent aspect of American life.
2. Skepticism towards legal-based claims of "neutrality, objectivity, colorblindness, and meritocracy."
3. The challenging of historical and support of contextual/historical analyses.
4. The recognition and importance of the voice and stories of people of color.
5. The emphasis on interdisciplinary approaches.
6. The dismantling of racial oppression as well as the elimination of oppression in all of its forms (Matsuda, Lawrence, Delgado, & Crenshaw, 1993, p. 6).

Though the original intent was for legal analysis, these themes proved to be a useful tool for educational analyses as well. In its educational application, some of the major tenets include: counterstorytelling, the permanence of racism, Whiteness as property, interest convergence, and critique of liberalism (DeCuir & Dixson, 2004). The following explanation details how these tenets are defined, used, and applied. Counterstorytelling or counternarrative stresses the importance of people of color telling their own stories. Their experiential knowledge is highly valued as opposed to being pushed to the margins. DeCuir and Dixon agree, "The use of counter stories allows for the challenging of privileged discourses, the discourses of the majority, therefore, serving as a means for giving voice to marginalized groups" (p. 27). These stories not only build voice, but also communal bonds and solidarity (Delgado, 1989). The emphasis on voice also helps people of color makes sense of and construct reality within a social constructivist framework (Bergerson, 2003). The narrative aspect of CRT also has the ability to inform research methodology and analyses as well as epistemology. A more controversial tenet of CRT is the permanence of racism. "This notion asserts that racism is a consistent, persistent, and pervasive component of American social life" (Beachum, Dentith, McCray, & Boyle, 2008, p. 207). Since the eradication of overt manifestations of racism (i.e., Jim Crow laws and overtly racist behaviors), many Americans now believe that racism is a thing of the past. CRT asserts the idea that the racism of today is more covert and complex. The "permanence of racism suggests that racist hierarchical structures govern all political, economic, and social domains" (DeCuir & Dixon, 2004, p. 27). In K-12 schools it is evident in the many microaggressions (racial incidents and comments) that students (and adults) face on a daily basis (Tatum, 1997). It is also expressed in teacher attitudes that devalue or undervalue the contributions, intelligence, and culture of students of color and their communities (Kailin, 2002; Perry, 2003). In addition, it appears in deficit views and unreflective teaching practices that work against students of color (Villegas & Lucas, 2002). Furthermore, it is evidenced in the resegregation of many schools, students of color being placed into lower academic tracks, school funding disparities, and the overrepresentation of students of color (especially African American males) in special education (Irvine, 2003; Morris, 2009; Obiakor, 2001; Tatum, 2007). In all of these examples, race plays a factor in such a way that supports White control while many times sacrificing the educational aspirations of people of color.

Another major tenet of CRT is the notion of Whiteness as property. Zamundio et al. (2011) provided acute insight when they wrote,

> In all things political and economic, whiteness was treated as a political right in the same way as liberal political economy treats the ownership of property as a right, an inalienable right. In fact, whiteness was constructed as a precondition to claiming the rights of a liberal society. Thus, race became an objective fact: a social construct was treated as a biological and natural difference. (p. 33)

In this tenet, Whiteness operates as a property interest. This includes the right to possession, use, and disposition. In addition, this also includes the right to transfer and right to exclude (DeCuir & Dixon, 2004). In K-12 education this means that Whites typically enjoy the rights to an effective and rigors curriculum and high-quality, certified teachers. They also are frequently found in honors classes and disciplined less and less harshly than their peers of color (Ladson-Billings & Tate, 1995; Skiba & Knesting, 2001). Although some students of color also benefit from the current structure of American schooling, White students benefit more and in greater numbers. DeCuir and Dixon (2004) explained,

> Thus, through the myriad policies and practices that restrict the access of students of color to high-quality curricula, and to safe and well-equipped schools, school districts have served to reify this notion of Whiteness as property whereby the rights to possession, use and enjoyment, and disposition, have been enjoyed almost exclusively by Whites. (p. 28)

Therefore, numerous educational benefits are viewed as the norm for Whites. Those in control also have the power to exclude, thus policies and practices reinforce a structure of dominance whereby majorities of Whites can reap the benefits of education, while at the same time excluding large numbers of people of color (Zamudio et al., 2011). Interest convergence is a tenet of CRT that basically exemplifies White self-interest. In other words, CRT dictates that much of the racial progress that we have seen over the years has only occurred when it also benefits Whites. According to Bell (1995b), "the interest of blacks in achieving racial equality will be accommodated only when in converges with the interests of whites" (p. 22). In fact, racial progress in the U.S. does not seem to advance in a linear pattern towards a more socially just society. The actual trajectory is more cyclical, with episodes of progress and eras of digression. An example of interest convergence would include *Brown v. Board*. Zamudio et al. (2011) asserted,

> The landmark civil rights policies of the 1960s were necessary to quell the growing discontent among urban people of color who were ready to fight back by any means necessary. The development of anti-war, feminist, new left, and Civil Rights movements threatened the hegemony of white elites in society. Civil rights policy worked to quell the more radical segments of these movements, and to secure the dominance of those in power. (p. 35)

Interest convergence can be masked in noble intentions or ethical insight, but it is actually rooted in self-interest. Lastly, CRT encourages a critique of liberalism. This critique is summarized by "the notion of colorblindness, the neutrality of the law, and incremental change" (DeCuir & Dixon, 2004, p. 29). It is important to note that the use of the term liberalism here is not synonymous with the specific political identification used so much in contemporary political discourse. In this case, "both liberals and conservatives often support the principles of liberalism underlying modern capitalist democracies" (Zamudio et al. 2011, p. 15). In this case liberalism supports broader notions of freedom, equality, meritocracy, and individual rights. These ideas are very attractive to most Americans. The problem with liberalism is that it "presents society as a meritocracy where individual actors compete on a level playing field.... Liberalism's emphasis on individual rights precludes any consideration of special protections under the law for minority groups (p. 16). This view undergirds liberal education policies that permeate American education. This perspective encompasses notions of colorblindness, neutrality of the law, and incremental change. Colorblindness assumes that everyone will enjoy equal treatment under the law and in society. Neutrality of the law asserts that laws and educational policy are not racially influenced in their enforcement and the ones that are currently on the books (e.g., Civil Rights Act of 1964) are sufficient in addressing inequality. Incremental change reinforces that idea that the rate and pace of change in society is slow. CRT rejects colorblind notions, advocating that

> colorblindness does not take into account the persistence and permanence of racism and tends to ignore or diminish the effects of racism that have resulted in great inequities in all aspects of everyday life for people of color in the United States. (Beachum et al., 2008, p. 205)

CRT disagrees with all of these ideas contending that the laws that govern us and educational policies are not necessarily neutral, they depend on who gets to judge and who writes the policy. Incremental change advances the idea that the gains of oppressed groups happen slowly. CRT advocates also reject this notion. DeCuir and Dixon (2004) wrote, "Under the notion of incremental change, gains for marginalized groups must come at a slow pace that is palatable for those in power" (p. 29).

The validation of critical race theory could be ambiguous at best. According to traditional standards, many may reject CRT under the guise of it being too subjective or not empirical enough. CRT supporters would probably respond by questioning who gets to validate CRT? And if validation rests in the hands of individuals who are biased against CRT for its claims and content, then validation is problematic. They may go further stating that CRT explicitly supports people of color's voice and validation should come from them and not from people who have no interest or understanding for CRT. This is not to say that Whites cannot benefit from CRT. Bergerson (2003) advanced the idea that

> white scholars must join the fight to legitimize research that utilizes alternative methods such as CRT, that comes from the lived experiences of individuals who have traditionally been marginalized and considered unimportant to scholarship, and grows from the passion of doing research to effect changes that will benefit people of color. (p. 60)

The Intersection of Critical Race Theory and Educational Leadership

Critical race theory could be useful in analyzing educational leadership. The framework for the establishment, maintenance, and management of American schools was largely based on factory models. Educational leadership "has borrowed idioms and syntax from economics and the business world all in an effort to legitimate itself as a valid field" (Dantley, 2002, p. 336). In this process it has inculcated educational leaders into an ideology of objectivity, neutrality, technical efficiency, and an uncritical belief in meritocracy (Beachum et al., 2008; English, 2008). A CRT analysis of this kind of educational leadership would take issue with these notions. While administrators in schools surely have to be objective at times, it is not possible to be totally objective at all times. And many times when administrators claim to be objective, they can subtly make decisions that work against students of color (Dantley, 2003). Similarly, many educational leaders make the faulty assumption that the law and school policies are neutral, but this perspective is countered by CRT advocates who point to policies like zero tolerance and special education referrals which both target students of color (McCray & Beachum, 2006; Obiakor, 2001). Although the laws and policies seem race-neutral, the enforcement is race conscious. Technical efficiency alludes to administrator's overreliance on science, predictability, and control. This is undergirded by a strong belief in quantitative data, empiricism, and rationality. The CRT response would not totally reject all of these notions, but would interject the permanence of race because science and data can be used to avoid or mask race-related issues. Furthermore, the CRT position with regard to educational leadership also places value on qualitative data sources and the importance of the voices and viewpoints of communities of color. When educational leaders position themselves as rigid bureaucrats, who emphasize empiricism over understanding their students' communities, the voice and concerns of these students can get lost (Morris, 2009; Theoharis, 2009). Many educational leaders also embrace an uncritical belief in meritocracy, the belief that if you work hard you can overcome almost any obstacle and be successful. While part of this notion is true, CRT advocates would add additional layers of complexity. In K-12 schooling, students come from different racial and economic backgrounds. In essence, the playing field is not level. Students from more stable communities, with more wealth and resources frequently find it easier to successfully navigate through the educational system. While students from more challenging backgrounds who do not have as many resources and may not come from the safest or most stable community has to work much harder to be successful. In addition, while many laws and initiatives have allowed greater access into schools, jobs, and so on, for women and people of color, in many cases access does not equal opportunity. Thus, when students of color enter White-dominated schools, they frequently have the additional burden of dealing with different forms of racism in addition to their academic responsibilities. Bergerson (2003) indicated that "although merit is an espoused American value, it operates under the burden of racism, which limits its applicability to people of color" (p. 54). Although educational leadership has been influenced by other fields and has adopted other models, it can benefit from the additional insight provided by CRT. The tenets of CRT could be powerful tools for educational leaders as they create and enforce policy, work with teachers and influence curriculum, and interact with students and diverse communities.

Criticisms of Critical Race Theory

Critical race theory has its criticisms. First, is the idea that critical race theory does not measure up to traditional standards of academic rigor because of its emphasis on nontraditional approaches like narratives and storytelling. Another criticism is that CRT fails to properly address the impact of capitalism and the rigidity of social class stratification. According to Darder and Torres (2003), "in much of the work on African American, Latino, Native American, and Asian populations, an analysis of class and a critique of capitalism is conspicuously absent" (p. 247). Similarly, Parker and Stovall (2004) indicated that "post-Marxist critics of CRT in particular have forcefully argued that it fails to provide a systemic analysis of global capitalism and its effect on communities" (p. 168). Still yet another critique of CRT is that it does not offer comprehensive solutions for the problems it unearths (Brooks, 2009). Thus, it is heavy on interrogation, investigation, and critical analysis, yet light on practicality and providing a roadmap or vision for moving from theory to practice.

Critical Race Theory in Educational Leadership Research

Critical race theory can benefit educational researchers and practitioners. With regard to research, Parker (1998) wrote, "the use of narrative in critical race theory adds to the dimension and purpose of qualitative inquiry and ethnographic research in education" (p. 50). Critical race theory's tenets can also be used in the analysis of qualitative data (Beachum et al., 2008; Lynn, 2002). In educational leadership, CRT is finding more utility as a tool for research in educational leadership (see Aleman, 2007; Horsford, 2009; Lopez, 2003; McCray, Wright, & Beachum, 2007).

Ultimately, CRT can be an effective tool for conducting educational research and analyzing educational practice. It was born out of a theoretical need by scholars of color to provide acute racial insight. It acknowledges the past and emphasizes context, interdisciplinary approaches, and intersectionality (Dantley, Beachum, & McCray, 2008) as it offers major tenets that illuminate, analyze, and encourage transformation in education and society. Zamudio et al. (2011) summarized CRT well when they wrote:

> CRT offers a framework that goes beyond understanding racialized structures. It also insists that we continue to work towards a more just system of education. As educators and students, we are well aware of the transformative power of ideas. It is our hope that educators and students consider CRT a call to action, a call to participate in a movement for an emancipatory education. (p. 165)

References

Aleman, E. (2007). Situating Texas school finance policy in a CRT framework: How "substantially equal" yields racial inequity. *Educational Administration Quarterly, 43*(5) 525-558.

Beachum, F. D., Dentith, A., & McCray, C. R., & Boyle, T. (2008). Havens of hope or the killing fields: The paradox of leadership, pedagogy, and relationships in an urban middle school. *Urban Education, 43*(2), 189-215.

Bell, D. A. (1995a). Who's afraid of critical race theory? *University of Illinois Law Review*, 893-910.

Bell, D. A. (1995b). *Brown v. Board of Education* and the interest convergence dilemma. In K. Crenshaw, N. Gotanda, G. Peller, & K. Thomas (Eds.), *Critical race theory: The key writings that formed the movement* (pp. 20-29). New York, NY: The New Press.

Bergerson, A. A. (2003). Critical race theory and white racism: Is there room for white scholars in fighting racism in education? *Qualitative Studies in Education, 16*(1), 51-63.

Brooks, R. L. (2009). *Racial justice in the age of Obama*. Princeton, NJ: Princeton University Press.

Dantley, M. (2002). Uprooting and replacing positivism, the melting pot, multiculturalism, and other impotent notions in educational leadership through an African American perspective. *Education and Urban Society, 34*, 334-352.

Dantley, M., Beachum, F. D., & McCray (2008). Exploring the intersectionality of multiple centers within notions of social justice. *Journal of School Leadership, 18*(2), 124-133.

Darder, A., & Torres, R. D. (2003). Shattering the "race" lens: Toward a critical theory of racism. In A. Darder, M. Baltodano, & R. D. Torres (Eds.), *The critical pedagogy reader* (pp. 245-261). New York, NY: Routledge.

DeCuir, J. T., & Dixson, A. D. (2004). "So when it comes out, they aren't that surprised that it is there": Using critical race theory as a tool of analysis of race and racism in education. *Educational Researcher, 33*(5), 26-31.

Delgado, R. (1989). Storytelling for oppositionist and others: A plea for narrative. *Michigan Law Review, 87*(8), 2411-2441.

Dixon, A. D., & Rousseau, C. K. (2005). And we are still not saved: Critical race theory in education ten years later. *Race, Ethnicity, and Education, 8*(1), 7-27.

English, F. W. (2008). *The art of educational leadership: Balancing performance and accountability*. Thousand Oaks, CA: SAGE.

Giroux, H. (1983). *Theory and resistance in education: A pedagogy for the opposition*. South Hadley, MA: Bergin & Garvey.

Horsford, S. D. (2009). From Negro student to Black superintendent: Counternarratives on segregation and desegregation. *Journal of Negro Education, 78*(2), 172-178.

Irvine, J. J. (2003). *Educating teachers for diversity: Seeing with a cultural eye*. New York, NY: Teachers College Press.

Kailin, J. (2002). *Antiracist education: From theory to practice*. New York, NY: Rowan & Littlefield.

Ladson-Billings, G. (2009). Just what is critical race theory and what's it doing in a nice field like education? In E. Taylor, D. Gilborn, & G. Ladson-Billings (Eds.), *Foundations of critical race theory in education* (pp. 17-36). New York, NY: Routledge.

Ladson-Billings, G., & Tate, W. (1995). Toward a critical race theory of education. *Teachers College Record, 97*(1), 47-68.

Lopez, G. R. (2003). The (racially neutral) politics of education: A critical race theory perspective. *Educational Administration Quarterly, 39*(1), 68-94.

Lynn, M. (2002). Critical race theory and the perspectives of Black men teachers in the Los Angeles public schools. *Equity and Excellence in Education, 35*(2), 119-130.

Matsuda, M., Lawrence, C., Delgado, R., & Crenshaw, K. (Eds.). (1993). *Words that wound: Critical race theory, assaultive speech and the first amendment*. Boulder, CO: West view Press.

McCray, C. R., & Beachum, F. D. (2006). A critique of zero tolerance policies: An issue of justice and caring. *Values and Ethics in Educational Administration, 5*(1), 1-8. Retrieved from http://www.ed.psu.edu/UCEACSLE/VEEA/VEEA_Vol5Num1.pdf

McCray, C. R., Wright, J. V., & Beachum, F. D. (2007). Beyond Brown: Examining the perplexing plight of African American principals. *Journal of Instructional Psychology, 34*, 247-255.

Morris, J. E. (2009). *Troubling the waters: Fulfilling the promise of quality public schooling for Black children*. New York, NY: Teachers College Press.

Obiakor, F. E. (2001). *It even happens in "good" schools: Responding to cultural diversity in today's classrooms*. Thousand Oaks, CA: Corwin Press.

Parker, L. (1998). "Race is race ain't": An exploration of the utility of critical race theory in qualitative research in education. *International Journal of Qualitative Studies in Education, 11*(1), 43-55.

Parker, L., & Stovall, D. O. (2004). Actions following words: Critical race theory connects to critical pedagogy. *Educational Philosophy and Theory, 36*(2), 167-182.

Perry, T. (2003). Up from the parched earth: Toward a theory of African-American achievement. In T. Perry, C. Steel, & A. G. Hilliard (Eds.), *Young gifted and Black: Promoting high achievement among African-American students* (pp. 1-108). Boston, MA: Beacon.

Sim, S., & Van Loon, B. (2002). *Introducing critical theory*. Lanham, MD: Totem Books.

Skiba, R. J., & Knesting, K. (2001). Zero tolerance, zero evidence: An analysis of school disciplinary practice. *New Directions for Youth Development, 92*, 17-43.

Tatum, B. D. (1997). *Why are all the Black kids sitting together in the cafeteria? And other conversations about race*. New York, NY: Basic Books.

Tatum, B. D. (2007). *Can we talk about race? And other conversations in an era of school resegregation*. Boston, MA: Beacon Press.

Theoharis, G. (2009). *The school leaders our children deserve: Seven keys to equity, social justice, and school reform*. New York, NY: Teachers College Press.

Villegas, A. M., & Lucas, T. (2002). *Educating culturally responsive teachers: A coherent approach*. Albany, NY: State University of New York Press.

Wright, H. (2002, April). *Homes don't play posties, homes don't play neos: Black ambivalent elaboration and the end(s) of critical pedagogy*. Symposium presentation at the annual meeting of the American Educational Research Association. New Orleans, LA.

West, C. (1993). *Keeping faith*. New York, NY: Routledge.

Zamudio, M. M., Russell, C., Rios, F. A., & Bridgeman, J. L. (2011). *Critical race theory matters: Education and ideology*. New York, NY: Routledge.

Author Contact Information: Floyd D. Beachum, EdD, Bennett Professor of Urban School Leadership, Program Director Educational Leadership Program, Iacocca Hall Lehigh University, 111 Research Drive Bethlehem, PA 18015. Phone: (610) 758-5955. E-mail: fdb209@lehigh.edu

CHAPTER 81

Rational Choice Theories in Education Administration

Ric Brown and Rosemary Papa
Northern Arizona University

What are rational models in education administration? Generally, these models describe a "scientific" approach (Kowalski, 2003) to making decisions and they reflect some of the following tenets: (a) Administrators can and will be rational when making decisions; (b) Administrators can and will be unbiased when making decisions; and, (c) Administrators can identify and evaluate alternative solutions, making it possible for them to select the most appropriate decision.

Silver (1983) noted that rationality refers to the goal directedness of the organization. Each activity undertaken by the organization is explicitly related to organizational goals; this goal directedness provides the rationale for action and the idea that an action is best or the most positive is then invoked to support the rationality of a particular action.

In the context of leadership and administration rationality has a unique interpretation that leads to models of decision making, cognitive thought processes to be learned, and skills that can lead to crafted practices. What follows then is an in depth look at the so called rational theories, where they began, their application to education administration, the psychological, sociological and economic relationships, critiques and recent uses of the theory for research purposes.

Origin of the Theory

The historical underpinnings (Covrig, 2006) began over 100 years ago. From the tenets of Taylorism scientific management in the early years of twentieth century followed by the depression era Mary Parker Follett and her introduction of the social dynamic aspects of management, to Herbert Simon's concept of satisficing in the 1950s. He argued that in order to make objectively rational decisions, an individual must: view alternative decision possibilities before making a decision, consider the consequences of each choice, and assign a value to each alternative and select the best.

In the 1960s Weber wrote of another perspective he called the theory of bureaucracy. In this model:

- organizations based on legal authority (bureaucracies) are more efficient and more rational than those based on charismatic authority or those based on traditional authority;
- The more nearly an organization approximates a pure bureaucracy, the more efficient and rational the organization is; and,
- The presence of any one characteristic of bureaucracy in an organization increases the likelihood that other characteristics of bureaucracy will be present in that organization (Silver, 1983, pp. 78-79).

Chin and Benne in 1969 (in Hall & Hord, 2001) wrote about two theories. The first theory, the rational empirical approach to change suggested that a good program or process provided to good people would find its way into their practice. The salience here is a good program and good people. The second theory, the power coercive approach maintained that a good program or policy delivered to good people through a power or authoritarian figure would ensure change in practice. The key here is power and its influence.

Karl Weick (1976) framed a programmatic approach to analyze complex organizations. Weick felt it is conceivable that preoccupation with rationalized, efficient, coordinated structures kept many practitioners, as well as researchers, from finding some of the attractive and

The Handbook of Educational Theories, pp. 929–934

unexpected outcomes of less rationalized and less tightly related groups of events. His nuanced rationality focused on loosely coupled systems in organization theory development.

Validation: Rational Models and Education Administration

What holds all of these approaches of rationality together is their focus on "rational." In its most literal sense rational refers not only to the selection of goals but to their implementation as well as their technical and functional rationality that structures work activity with emphasis upon information, efficiency, optimization, implementation, and design (Covrig, 2006).

To more fully understand the application of rational models to education administration, one must first explore the general notion of a theory. Kimbrough and Nunnery (1983) suggested that a theory of education administration is a collection of concepts or principles that define and give directions to a leader of a school or district. It is likely that such a would include concepts relating to the nature of individual and group life, the major components of American democracy, the purposes of education, the nature of the administrative process, and functions of administration. This definition implies that theory should encompass both what is and what ought to be and would include values.

There are those who would argue that value statements cannot be expressed in factual terms and therefore cannot be tested empirically. A far more restrictive definition has been offered by Feigl (Kimbrough & Nunnery, 1983) who proposed that, "a theory as a set of assumptions from which can be derived by purely logico-mathematical procedures a larger set of empirical laws" (p. 241). This reflects a philosophical leaning to positivism.

Bolman and Deal (1991) stated that rational systems theorists "emphasize organizational goals, roles, and technology, and they look for ways to develop structures that best fit organizational purposes and environmental demands" (p. 9). Sergiovanni (1990) further suggested that the standard dictionary definition of 'rational' includes sensible, showing reason, not foolish or silly and he feels is a good definition to apply to school-management and leadership policies. For him, the key word in this definition is *showing*; a school-management and leadership policy must be judged rational or not based on demonstrated evidence. "Too often, however, rationality is determined on the basis of how a policy sounds or appears and not on whether it fits the real world or works in that world" (p. 48).

Sergiovanni continues by noting that theories of school management and leadership are based on different images of human rationality. When a school leader chooses a theory from which to practice, a particular image of rationality is assumed whether or not it fits the real world. A better fit between theory and practice will occur by starting the other way around. Choose the image of rationality that fits the real world first and then find a theory that fits that image of rationality. Sergiovanni (1990) referred to Shulman (p. 49) who provided three images of human rationality each described briefly below. All three are true to a certain extent but some are truer than others. It makes a difference which of the three or which combination of the three provides the strategic basis of ones' leadership practice:

1. Humans are rational.
2. Humans re limited in their rationality; they can make sense of only a small piece of the world at a time and they strive to act reasonably with respect to their limited grasp of facts and alternatives.
3. Humans are rational only when acting together; since individual reason is so limited, men and women find opportunities to work jointly on important problems, achieving through joint effort what individual reason and capacity could never accomplish. If you want them to change, develop ways in which they can engage in the change process jointly with peers (Sergiovanni, 1990, pp. 49-50).

Van Geel (1995) suggested that rational choice theory has problems, but provides a way to address the problems. For example, he said that his model sheds light on school politics, for example, by predicting such things as union strikes, and school board decisions. In addition, rational choice theories promise to highlight bureaucratic politics and organization dynamics.

> Thus, rational choice theory should be able to explain the reasons why school administrators decide or decide not to bring dismissal proceedings against incompetent teachers, why school administrators seem unable or unwilling to actively supervise to achieve educational productivity, and why there is a tendency for school personnel to form "treaties" and establish peaceful but unproductive relationships. (Van Geel, 1995, p. 254)

Abrahamsson (1993) believed that a "feasible starting point in the study of organizations is the assumption that organizations are instruments for representing interests, and that they are best regarded as expressions of rationality" (p. 29).

Psychological, Sociological and Economic Applications and Generalizability

Because rational models touch upon aspects of individuals and organizations, there are psychological, sociological and economical implications. For example, Kowalski (2003) noted that leadership is influencing people to seek of a common goal and also of influencing people to strive for group objectives.

PSYCHOLOGICAL

Cohen and March (1974) began the psychological discussion by noting the concepts of choice and rationality. However, they argue that the concept of choice has problems concerning aspects of free will and the "doubts of psychological behaviorism and by the claims of historical, economic, social and demographic determinism" (p. 216). However, the idea that humans make choices has become an important component of Western civilization and professed by almost all theories of social policy making. The major tenets are that "human beings make choices ... choices are properly made by evaluating alternatives in terms of goals and on the basis of information currently available. The alternative that is most attractive in terms of the goals is chosen" (p. 216).

Cohen and March (1974) continue the theme by noting "The first idea is the preexistence of purpose" (p. 217). The professional literature is replete with notions of values, needs, wants, goods, aspirations, et cetera.

> All of these reflect a strong tendency to believe that a useful interpretation of human behavior involves defining a set of objectives that (1) are prior attributes of the system and (2) make the observed behavior in some sense intelligent vis-a-vis those objectives. (p. 217)

A second idea is individuals will be reliable with respect to their behavior. And, the third idea is that by defining procedures of what is the correct behavior by relating consequences systematically to objectives is rational. By placing primary emphasis on rational techniques, they reject any processes of intuition or processes of tradition and faith. "Both within the theory and within the culture we insist on the ethic of rationality. We justify individual and organizational action in terms of an analysis of means and ends" (Cohen & March, 1974, p. 218). Thus, decision making assumes prior existence of a set of consistent goal and that the goals are acted on by choosing alternatives based on available information. Educational leadership and policy emphasizes goal setting, evaluation and accountability (Cohen & March).

This perspective ties strongly to the pyschological construct of attribution theory. As well, Kowalski (2003) invokes the locus of control dimension. Silver (1983) wondered why people behave as they do. Have they been conditioned to respond automatically to certain stimuli, or are they sublimating impulses for self-gratification? Are they affected by an external force, or do they seek to attain particular objectives? Are they driven by needs, or do other people compel them? These questions are answered partially by Brown (1990) and Brown and Marcoulides (1996) who identify the existence in some individuals of an internal locus of control. The locus suggests that these individuals have expectations that events in the realm are contingent upon *their* behavior as opposed to the behavior of others, luck or chance. Thus, rational decisions are made based on expectations that they have the background and ability necessary to implement actions.

Stogdill (1974, in Hanson, 1991) argued that isolated traits have minimal diagnostic or predictive significance. In clusters or combinations, they interact in a way advantageous to the individual seeking leadership responsibilities. He identified the six clusters of traits as:

1. capacity (intelligence, alertness, verbal facility, originality, judgment);
2. achievement (scholarship, knowledge, athletic accomplishment;
3. responsibility (dependability, initiative, persistence, aggressiveness, self-confidence, desire to excel;
4. participation (activity, social ability, cooperation, adaptability, humor;
5. status (socioeconomic, popularity; and,
6. situation (mental level, status, skills, needs & interests of followers, objectives to be achieved (Hanson, 1991, pp. 181-183).

The last trait noted above, *situation*, makes clear leadership is actually a combination of specific personal attributes fulfilling leadership needs that arise in specific situations. Stogdill wrote:

> Strong evidence indicates the different leadership skills and traits are required in different situations. The behaviors and traits that enable a mobster to gain and maintain control over a gang are not the same as those enabling a religious leader to gain and maintain a large following. Yet certain general qualities –such as courage, fortitude, and conviction—appear to characterize both. (Hanson, 1991, p. 182)

Other difficulties associated with trait approaches to leadership can be contradictory with the role of the individual and interaction within the group are ignored.

SOCIOLOGICAL

Brown, Noble, and Papa (2009) noted the culturally bound nature of an organization and that success of an administrator is dependent on that recognition. Thus, as with other sociological perspectives, there are many variations of rational theory. Each tends to differ from other sociological perspectives in two ways.

First, it begins from the viewpoint of the individual, rather than from several individuals interacting together, from social situations, or from groups. The emphasis on the individual and his or her interest is always a starting point for any theory of rational choice. Different theorists of rational choice may make somewhat different assumptions about the individual and proceed in different ways from the individual to larger social groupings and systems, but each begins with the individual as the basic unit of the theory. Secondly, the theory continues with assumptions about the individual and the relationship among individuals, and from these builds models of social action and interaction that describe and explain the complexities of larger groups, systems and whole societies (Sociology 319, 2000, p. 1).

Again, Brown and Marcoulides (1996) and Brown (1990) utilizing attribution theory suggest that some individuals possess an external social locus of control and have the expectation that events are contingent upon events and others in their environment. In this regard, decisions may be based on traditions, or expectations that others are responsible for events.

ECONOMIC

Van Geel (1995) promoted the idea that "rational choice theorists attempt to make sense of the complexity of human inaction by starting with a few simple but powerful assumptions, or axioms, about human motives and behaviors" (p. 238). He argues that the most well developed of the rational choice theories is economics.

Silver (1983) found that efficiency refers to the cost-effectiveness of the organization, where cost is the expenditure of organizational resources, and effectiveness is the organizations attainment of its goal.

> In education a school district's efficiency would be a function of that district's per pupil expenditure in relation to the students' educational attainments ... rules and regulations ensure that personnel are available to perform the required tasks as needed ... or that will impede the performance of goal-related tasks. (p. 77)

> For example, the specialization of tasks enhances impersonality: decisions based on expertise in task performance rather than whim. (p. 78)

CRITIQUES OF THE THEORY

There are a number of weaknesses of rational choice theory that include:

1. Problems associated with inadequate information and uncertainty, the difficulty to make rational decisions and possible reliance on other ways to make decisions.
2. Human social action and interaction are complex and many other theories may be better.
3. Theorists of RC argue that macro level structures and institutions can be explained from the models of individual social action. But, problems from individual to societal levels have the same difficulties in well developed economic models.
4. Norms and habits may guide must action and once rooted people may not question them but use them to pursue meaningful social action.
5. Are all actions rational? Some argue this. By including all, actions that are nonrational or irrational become part of the model. By including all, it is not clear how the standards of what is rational and what is not are constructed (Sociology 319, 2000, p. 13).

Other scholars have expanded on the limitations of rational choice theory and leadership. Kowalski (2003) noted that some researchers feel that rationality requires a choice among a complete set of with only a limited set of solutions and consequences present; the political nature of schools and their contextual variables may limit rationality and objectivity; and, administrators often do not have complete information or a complete list of solutions, or unbiased predilections. Thus, decisions in school districts may be made with mixed motives, ambiguous strategies, and/or limited information. These characteristics often lessen the potential effectiveness of rational models.

Rationalistic theory is often criticized (Abrahamsson, 1993) as being limited to the individual's thought processes. "The critics say that this makes rationalistic theory subjective and poorly suited to tackling the processes and circumstances that occur in the actors' environment" (p. 32).

The limits to rationality are most evident because leaders within organizations make decisions and initiate action within a limited perspective of reality. "If an organization were to function in a truly rational fashion, it would have to consider all the possible alternatives of a decision and select the one that would maximize (over all other possible alternatives) the desired end" (Hanson, 1991, p. 33). Thus, precise evaluation is limited.

Without precision, piece meal decision making occurs. Ideal decisions are not made hence RCT morphed into what some consider *bounded rational models* (Kowalski, 2003). Bounded rational models reflect recognition of the following conditions:

- complete information is not typically available to the decision maker;

- decisions are usually made in the context of conflicting values and interests; Bias rarely can be eliminated; and
- administrators often make decisions by selecting the first available satisfactory course of action rather than endlessly pursuing the ideal course of action (p. 211).

THEORETICAL RESEARCH

A review of dissertations on ProQuest (2010) show that few recent studies focused on rational choice theory. One study done in *Educational Leadership* (Keith, 1991) focused on ethics, ethical decision making and rationality as one of ten definitions used to address leader expressions. A more recent dissertation (Flaming, 2007) studied leader risk decision making in a complex organization. This study proposes a new decision making model, "which extends the insights of prominent decision making models including the rational … and qualifies claims made by bounded rationality theory" (p. 1). Two other dissertations from the areas of public administration and information systems (Baxter, 2005; Warfield, 1990) used RCT as a way to study collaborative decision making and competing values and organizational theory.

Finally, a review of the most common test measurements reviewed through the Buros Institute (2010) lists a well known indicator, the Myers-Briggs Type Indicator (Briggs, Myers, McCaulley, Quenk, & Hammer, n.d.). Buros Institute defines the purpose of this measurement test is for "the identification of basic preferences on each of the four dichotomies specified or implicit in Jung's theory" and "the identification and description of the 16 personality types that result from interactions among the preferences" (p. 1). A further review of the Buros Institute website reveals that subject matter testing for high school students, the ACT and SAT tests, et cetera, are ready use examples of rational choice theories.

CONCLUSION

Today, rational choice theory offers opportunities for management and leadership research especially, focused on curricular outcomes. Scientific approaches found in rational choice theory from a psychological, sociological and economic perspective were presented in this chapter for the education leader to understand their role in decision making within their educational setting.

REFERENCES

Abrahamsson, B. (1993). *Why organizations?: How and why people organize.* Newbury Park, CA: SAGE.

Baxter, F. M. (2005). *Organizational leadership and management in interorganizational partnerships: Varieties of networking in the era of new governance.* Retrieved from http://libproxy.nau.edu:2079/pqdweb?index=1&sid=5&srchmode=2&vinst=PROD&fmt=2&startpage=-1&clientid=15474&vname=PQD&RQT=309&did=1176532521&scaling=FULL&ts=1285005401&vtype=PQD&rqt=309&TS=1285005555&clientId=15474&cc=1&TS=1285005555

Bolman, L. G. & Deal, T. E. (1991). *Reframing organizations: Artistry, choice and leadership.* San Francisco, CA: Jossey-Bass.

Briggs, K. C., Myers, I. B., McCaulley, M. H., Quenk, N. L. & Hammer, A. L. (n.d.). *Myers-Briggs type indicator, form m.* Retrieved from http://buros.unl.edu/buros/jsp/results.jsp

Brown, R., Noble, P., & Papa, R. (2009). *So you want to be a higher education academic administrator. Avoid crossing to the dark side.* Lancaster, PA. Proactive Publications.

Brown, R. (1990). The construct and concurrent validity of the social dimension of the Brown locus of control scale. *Educational and Psychological Measurement, 50,* 337-382.

Brown, R., & Marcoulides, G. (1996). A cross-cultural comparison of the Brown locus of control scale. *Educational and Psychological Measurement, 56,* 5, 858-863.

Buros Institute. (2010). Buros institute of mental measurements: Tests online. Retrieved from http://buros.unl.edu/buros/jsp/results.jsp

Cohen, M. D., & March, J. G. (1974). *Leadership and ambiguity: The American college president.* New York, NY: McGraw-Hill.

Covrig, D. M. (2006). Rational organizational theory. In F. English (Ed.), *Encyclopedia of educational leadership* (2nd ed.). Thousand Oaks, CA: SAGE.

Flaming, S. C. (2007). *Leadership of risk decision making in a complex, technology organization: The deliberative decision making model.* Retrieved from http://libproxy.nau.edu:2079/pqdweb?index=0&sid=5&srchmode=2&vinst=PROD&fmt=2&startpage=-1&clientid=15474&vname=PQD&RQT=309&did=1417809661&scaling=FULL&ts=1285005401&vtype=PQD&rqt=309&TS=1285005455&clientId=15474&cc=1&TS=1285005455

Hall, G. E., & Hord, S. M. (2001). *Implementing change: Patterns, principles and potholes.* Boston, MA: Allyn & Bacon.

Hanson, E. M. (1991). *Educational administration and organizational behavior* (3rd ed.). Boston, MA: Allyn & Bacon.

Keith, W. D. (1991). *Ethical choices: The nature of ethical decision-making in educational leadership.* Retrieved from http://libproxy.nau.edu:2079/pqdweb?index=0&did=745956481&SrchMode=1&sid=3&Fmt=2&VInst=PROD&VType=PQD&RQT=309&VName=PQD&TS=1285004978&clientId=15474

Kimbrough, R. B., & Nunnery, M. Y. (1983). *Educational administration* (2nd ed.). New York, NY: Macmillan.

Kowalski, T. J. (2003). *Contemporary school administration: An introduction* (2nd ed.). Boston, MA: Pearson Education.

ProQuest. (2010). *NAU dissertations & theses: Full text (ProQuest).* Retrieved from http://library.nau.edu/cf/info/rec-display.cfm?resource_id=41

Sergiovanni, T. J. (1990). *Value-added leadership: How to get extraordinary performance in schools.* San Diego, CA: Harcourt Brace Jovanovich.

Silver, P. F. (1983). *Educational administration: Theoretical perspectives on practice and research.* New York, NY: Harper & Row.

Sociology 319. (2000, February, 8-10). *Rational choice theory (RCT).* Retrieved from http://uregina.ca/gingrich/f1000.htm

Van Geel, T. (1995). The preparation of educational leadership and rational choice theory. In R. Donmoyer, M. Imber, & J. J. Scheurich (Eds.), *The knowledge base in educational administration: Multiple perspectives* (pp. 238-258). New York, NY: The State University of New York Press.

Warfield, A. L. (1990). *The team member workbench: A case study of an innovative information system at Domino's pizza distribution.* Retrieved from http://libproxy.nau.edu:2079/pqdweb?index=3&sid=5&srchmode=2&vinst=PROD&fmt=2&startpage=-1&clientid=15474&vname=PQD&RQT=309&did=744116871&scaling=FULL&ts=1285005401&vtype=PQD&rqt=309&TS=1285005706&clientId=15474&cc=1&TS=1285005706

Weick, K. E. (1976). Educational organizations as loosely coupled systems. *Administrative Science Quarterly, 21,* 1-19.

Author Contact Information: Dr. Ric Brown, Adjunct Faculty, Northern Arizona University, PO Box 5774, Flagstaff, Arizona 86011-5774. Telephone: 916-606-8025. E-mail: ric.brown@nau.edu

CHAPTER 82

Democratic Administration

Lisa A. W. Kensler
Auburn University

Jeffrey S. Brooks
Iowa State University

This chapter examines the intersection of democracy and school administration. In the United States, Dewey receives credit for inspiring the direct application of democratic ideals to education with his 1916 publication, *Democracy and Education: An Introduction to the Philosophy of Education.* Approximately 20 years later he clearly articulated a call for the practice of "cooperative inquiry and experimentation in this field of democratic administration of our schools" (Dewey, 1937, p. 462). Dewey's extensive philosophical works provided foundational ideas upon which educational leaders in the early twentieth century built. Campbell, Fleming, Newell, and Bennion (1987), in their history of educational administration in the United States cited Fleming's dissertation as evidence that

> democratic administration was not based on empirical research that tested theoretical propositions about human behavior in work groups; rather it was principally a "home grown" philosophy of school management that drew its strength from the ideas of educational reformers and was founded on a loosely integrated set of beliefs about democratic rights, individual welfare, and the need for cooperation in human enterprise. (Fleming, 1982, pp. 53-202, as cited in Campbell et al. 1987, p. 50)

Democratic school administration, it seems, developed first from individuals' striving to put into practice the ideals of democracy for the perpetuation of democracy—reflecting the belief that children might best learn how to participate and contribute to a democracy in more democratically operated schools. From these early days of experimentation and exploration in school administration, the field has evolved and changed in response to internal and external influences and with it the intersection of democracy and school administration has taken different forms and different labels. Although, educational administration is an "applied field" and "does not draw on a single body of literature nor use a single set of scholarly tools" (Campbell et al., 1987, p. 5), this chapter will introduce the reader to the evolution of ideas, theory, and practice related to democratic school administration.

Democracy and Administration: Foundational Assumptions and Goals

Democratic school administration is the intersection of democracy and administration in schools. We will begin the chapter with a look at the foundational assumptions and goals of democracy and administration separately and then at their integration in the educational literature. In essence, if one digs deeply enough, the fundamental assumptions of any social process, are assumptions about humanity. What does one believe about people? McGregor (1960) presented a classic and stark distinction between two views of people underlying administration, management, and leadership theory. Theory X captured the view of people as basically lazy, unreliable, and in need of tight supervision and control; the threat of punishment served as a primary motivating strategy. Theory Y suggested the opposite, that people inherently desire to participate and contribute to the success of endeavors for which they are working and they have the capacity to do so, if

The Handbook of Educational Theories, pp. 935–944

organizations engage them appropriately. (For a thorough discussion of Theories X and Y in the context of organizational democracy, see Cloke and Goldsmith (2002). Keep Theory X and Y in mind as we examine the assumptions of democracy and administration in more detail.

Scholars in educational leadership have rarely, if ever, clearly and explicitly stated assumptions they understand as inherent to democracy. Merriam (1938), a political scientist, explicitly articulated five assumptions of democracy that Kensler (2010) has discussed more thoroughly in previous work related to educational leadership. To summarize here, Merriam's five assumptions of democracy included:

1. the constant drive toward the perfectibility of humanity;
2. the essential dignity of each individual;
3. each individual is worthy of participation;
4. progress through consent rather than violence; and
5. gains should be shared.

As an integrated system of assumptions, the primary goal of democracy is the perfectibility of humanity; this nonviolent process of perfectibility assumes that each individual has essential dignity, is worthy of participation in the effort, and ought to share in the gains resulting from the effort. These assumptions, reflecting theory Y more than theory X, certainly appear consistent with discussions of democracy in education, however, the extent to which individuals and groups explicitly hold, interpret, and enact these assumptions has varied and will no doubt continue to vary dramatically (For a thorough discussion of different meanings of democracy and democratic leadership in education, see Woods, 2005). As Dewey (1916, 1937) and others have also emphasized, democracy is processual in nature (Apple & Beane, 1995; Furman & Starratt, 2002). The ultimate goal—the perfectibility of humanity via an inclusive, respectful and nonviolent process—may be an unreachable ideal; however, striving for the democratic ideal suggests a moral purpose underlying the pursuit that may provide a motivating force for advocates of such practice in schools (Murphy, 2002; Sergiovanni, 1996, 2005).

Turning now to administration, Campbell et al. (1987) described the field of educational administration as comprising scholarship, practice, and preparation, with roots in the early 1900s when schools were growing rapidly and taking form in the factory's image. During this time of rapid industrialization in the United States, foundational thinkers in educational administration believed,

> schooling was too important to be left to teacher-managers. Leadership and control ... must be centralized and placed in the hands of those who had specific training, skills, and vision to advance societal purposes. This was no job for the amateur. The reformers of this era sought educational salvation through centralized, rational control. (Campbell et al., 1987, p. 8)

The primary influences on these early scholars in educational administration included Taylor's principles of scientific management, first published in 1911 (Taylor, 2001). Scientific management or Taylorism sought to increase efficient productivity through scientific analysis of work duties and administrative control. This model of administration established the school leader as the supervisor and manager of all school related activities. Since the teachers could not be trusted with the management of the school, the administrator had to take control by communicating expectations, supervising activities, and making decisions in favor of increasing productivity. The process of administrating a school was clearly assumed to be in the domain of the positional leader or administrator and trusting organizational members to know and practice without close administrative supervision was unheard of. Theory X in action.

The integration of democracy and administration, then, is the realignment of fundamental assumptions about people and their motivations and capacities from those grounded in scientific management and Theory X to those grounded in the ideals of democracy and Theory Y. Democratic administration integrates the ideals and processes of democracy with administration of organizational systems and processes. Prior to World War I, the primary purpose of public schooling, for many, was to "serve societal ends" (Campbell et al., 1987) by preparing the work force needed for the growing economy. For this purpose, assumptions consistent with those of the industrialization movement seemed expected. Following World War I, Dewey's early calls for a broader educational purpose, serving the ideals of democracy, resonated with many more educators and warranted fundamental assumptions more consistent with the assumptions of democracy. Democratic school administration thus grew to take on a more prominent role in educational administrative theory and practice.

ORIGINS AND EVOLUTION OF DEMOCRATIC ADMINISTRATION

As mentioned in the introduction, democratic school administration has been, in many ways, a homegrown field that scholars and practitioners have cocreated (Fleming, 1982). One of the earliest educational leaders who translated Dewey's philosophy of democratic education and administration into practice was his contemporary and colleague, Ella Flagg Young (Webb & McCarthy, 1998). Webb and McCarthy reminded the field of Young's pioneering work—the first woman superintendent of an urban school system, the first woman president of the National Education Association, and a professor of education with Dewey at the University of Chicago (p. 223)—and highlighted her role in laying the groundwork for the field of democratic school administration that grew rapidly in the 1930s, over 10 years after her death in 1918.

Converging forces after World War I provided momentum behind the movement democratizing school administration. One force was the deepening awareness of the role schools could play in nurturing and sustaining democracy and the other was a growing set of empirical and philosophical writings from scholars in the fledgling field of human relations that suggested more democratic forms of leadership actually elicited higher productivity from workers than the more authoritarian forms of leadership (Campbell et al., 1987). Findings from Lewin and his colleagues (Lewin & Lippitt, 1938; Lewin, Lippitt, & White, 1939) as well as the Hawthorne studies (Mayo, 1933) and others indicated that people worked more effectively and efficiently within the context of positive human relationships. Mary Parker Follett's writings provided a strong foundation for the human relations field with "the accomplishments of her 65 years [1868-1933] mark[ing] this New England thinker and doer as one of our most outstanding theorists about democracy and social organization" (Tonn, 2003, p. 3). Philosophical calls for democratic schools found increasing empirical support from another growing field of study.

In 1943, Koopman, Miel, and Misner, published a "comprehensive statement of the philosophy of democratic administration with a practical set of techniques for introducing and carrying out a local school program" (p. xiv). Although there were other educational administration books and resources at the time that also promoted democratic approaches, the Koopman et al. book was the "bell ringer" (Glass, 2004, p. 133) of the group in its clarity about the purpose of schools to serve the country's democracy through the democratization of schools:

> Can the education function be so conceived and so administered that it will not only conserve but continuously improve the democratic way of life? To contribute effectively to the larger purposes of democracy, the school itself must first become a contagious illustration of and a laboratory for the highest possible level of democratic living. The forthright democratization of the educational process thus becomes a pressing social responsibility of educational administration. (Koopman et al., 1943, p. 1)

Koopman et al. continued on with an explicit acknowledgement that enacting democracy in schools "must depend upon an emergent idealism based on the methodology of experimentalism" (1943, p. 1). The practice of democratic administration was grounded in the understanding that striving to live the ideal of democracy was going to be a constant evolution of trial and error, a constant interplay among political, cultural, and educational forces.

Many of today's best educational practices are evident in Koopman et al.'s (1943) text, *Democracy in School Administration*. They discussed and promoted "clarity of purpose and the elimination of traditional procedures" (p. 70), an emphasis on "group purposing, planning, and evaluating" (p. 66), continuous improvement as the result of group learning (pp. 112, 116-117), teacher leadership throughout the school (p. 133), the use of "evidence of a scientific nature which indicates the desirability of educational change" (p. 174), teacher evaluation focused on "bettering the conditions that surround learning" (p. 53), broad authentic student participation in those aspects of school governance that affects them directly (p. 225), and the engagement of the community beyond the school walls (p. 307). Recommendations in books and articles following this early volume on the democratic administration of schools have maintained remarkable consistency with the core recommendations of Koopman et al. (Apple & Beane, 1995; Josheph Blase & Blase, 2001; Joseph Blase, Blase, Anderson, & Dungan, 1995; Chaltain, 2009; Glickman, 1993).

Since the height of interest in democratic administration in the 1940s and 1950s, the use of the term has nearly disappeared from the educational leadership literature. However, concepts related to and supportive of democratic administration continue to be prominent in the literature, including democratic leadership (Woods, 2005), democratic community (Furman & Starratt, 2002; Murphy, 2002), site-based management (Leithwood & Menzies, 1998), shared decision making (Hallinger & Richardson, 1988), teacher leadership (York-Barr & Duke, 2004), constructivist leadership (Lambert et al., 2002), student voice (Mitra, 2008; Mitra & Gross, 2009; Noyes, 2005), and distributed leadership (Woods, 2004; Woods & Gronn, 2009). Campbell et al. (1987, p. 60) explained that an increased interest in the functions of school leadership rather than "loftier notions" of purpose and idealism explained this shift away from a focus on democracy in schools after the 1950s. One of the challenges in the field has been what seems to be an "either-or" mentality (Hoy, 1978); either we rely on empirical evidence via a positivistic model and aim to remain ideologically neutral or we embrace the moral purpose of education in a democracy and find ourselves in the realm of advocacy and philosophy. It may be time to embrace a "both-and" mentality; recognizing that both empirical evidence and moral purpose converge to support calls for schools *as* democracies and schools *for* democracy (Allen & Glickman, 1998; Glickman, 1993; O'Hair & Reitzug, 1997). In other words, there are both strong ideological arguments for democratizing schools and there is a broad range of empirical support for practices in schools that reflect democratic assumptions and principles, even if not always presented under the democracy label. The following section will present some of this empirical support.

EMPIRICAL VALIDATION OF DEMOCRATIC ADMINISTRATION

Democratic school administration, although never permeating public education practice in the United States, has maintained a consistent presence in educational administration and leadership literature in some form (Apple & Beane, 1995; Chaltain, 2009; Furman & Starratt, 2002; Koopman et al., 1943; Murphy, 2002). However, evidence of empirical validation of a distinct theory of democratic administration remains scant. The diffuse nature of theory and little theory validation in the field of educational administration has characterized the field since the beginning of formal inquiry (Greenfield, 2005; Hoy, 1996; Oplatka, 2009; Willower, 1980). This lack of a clear theory of democratic administration with a supporting line of evidence makes the question of empirical validation challenging to answer. Adding to the challenge is the gradual shift in terminology from the study of democratic administration (Dewey, 1937; Koopman et al., 1943) to democratic leadership (Joseph Blase et al., 1995; Woods, 2005) and to democratic community (Furman & Starratt, 2002; Kensler, Caskie, Barber, & White, 2009), as well as the many related concepts mentioned earlier, including site-based management, shared decision making, distributed leadership, and teacher leadership. For example, although never mentioning democracy, democratic administration, or democratic leadership, Bridges (1967) presented a thorough synthesis of the empirical support for shared decision making and presented a model for the school principal that aligns closely with Koopman et al.'s (1943) recommendations for democratic school administration, published nearly 20 years prior. As Oplatka (2009) made clear, "the field is typically embedded with debates over similar ideas, assumptions, and insights about EA [educational administration]" (p. 26).

With the recognition that empirical support for practices consistent with democratic administration exists under additional labels, there are studies of democratic administration, democratic leadership, and democratic community that have demonstrated strong relationships with positive school outcomes. Democratic administration has been associated with higher morale of administrators (Barry & Lonsdale, 1956), more effective curriculum change (Jackson, 1957), and successful school district reorganization (Strolle, 1956). Democratic leadership has been associated with increased teacher engagement, motivation, morale, leadership, work effort, and collaboration (Joseph Blase & Blase, 2001; Joseph Blase et al., 1995), and increased focus on instructional improvements and principal reflection (Jo Blase & Blase, 1999). The study of democratic community has found increased teacher engagement, student voice and participation, and a clearer focus on student needs (Williams, Cate, & O'Hair, 2009), improved student learning and achievement (Cate, Vaughn, & O'Hair, 2006), and higher reports of faculty trust and teachers' continuous and team learning (Kensler et al., 2009).

DEMOCRATIC ADMINISTRATION BEYOND THE UNITED STATES

"Democracy is not a single definable entity but the broad term for a set of political processes toward the ends of justice, prosperity, and peace" (Davies, 1999, p. 128); the ways people around the world conceptualize, interpret, and enact democracy both politically and within educational institutions differ (Davies, 1999; Louis, 2003). However, scholars have presented findings that suggest core values of democracy are relevant and valuable to the global community.

> We argue that "democracy" is not an endpoint, a Western imposition or an ideal state, but a term for a *process*—and for us the only process which can enable schools and their participants effectively to debate and meet the international challenges which the twenty-first century will generate. (Harber & Davies, 1998, p. 5)

Amartya (1999) lent further support for the possibility that democracy provides a universal value,

> While democracy is not yet universally practiced, nor indeed uniformly accepted, in the general climate of world opinion, democratic governance has now achieved the status of being taken to be generally right (p. 5).... I would argue that universal consent is not required for something to be a universal value. Rather, the claim of a universal value is that people anywhere may have reason to see it as valuable. (p. 12)

According to Sorensen (2010), between 1974 and 2007 the number of democratic regimes around the world increased from 40 to 90 countries (Sorensen provided a detailed discussion of a process for defining and indentifying democratic regimes; space does not allow for a summary here). Democracy, even if only in early emergent forms, now has a presence on every continent, having appeared in Southern Europe, Latin and Central America, Eastern Europe, Africa, the old Soviet Union, and across Asia (Haynes, 1997; Sorensen,

2010). Since "a large number of countries remain in the gray area between being outright authoritarian and fully democratic" (Sorensen, 2010, p. 441), some scholars have provided empirical evidence for the critical role education in general (Glaeser, Ponzetto, & Shielfer, 2007; Haynes, 1997) and democratic education in particular (Harber & Davies, 1998; Harber & Meighan, 1989) have played in developing citizen capacity to engage, grow and sustain political democracy. In some cases (e.g. Botswana, South Africa, and Cyprus), emerging democracies have developed policies that call for the democratization of schools, reflecting the belief that students will best learn how to engage and sustain political democracies if they first have the opportunity to do so in school (Davies, 2002; Monyatsi, 2005; Osler & Starkey, 2006; Pashiardis, 2004). As we have already described for the United States, the international study of democracy and schools is also complex and extensive, especially related to developed Western countries such as England and Australia.

Davies (1999) provided an eight-point framework for comparing the extent to which educational systems in different countries interpret and enact democracy. The framework (pp. 131-134) includes the following: (a) *basic values* (The who, what, where, when, and why of identifying and communicating the values associated with practicing democracy.); (b) *rights* (What are the rights of individuals? Does everyone, including students, have equal rights?); (c) *system structures* (To what extent are there formal avenues for broad participation within different system levels?); (d) *structures within schools* (How is democracy conceived and enacted in schools? Where does the school exist along the spectrum from purely majority vote/rule to a broader and deeper practice of democracy?); (e) *learning content* (The who, what, when, where, how, and why of curriculum development and implementation as it relates to democracy.); (f) *balance* (How are freedom and constraint balanced in schools and educational systems?); (g) *training* (To what extent are teachers and administrators provided the opportunity to learn about and deepen their understanding of democracy?); (h) *outcomes* (What purpose do schools serve? Are these purposes consistent with equity and justice?). The framework is a useful tool for conceptualizing and comparing the practice of democracy across different countries and cultures.

Use and Application of Democratic School Administration: Discrete Levels in a Nested System

Studies that use and apply theories of democratic school administration, and those theories closely related to its principles, have examined various levels of education. In general, research tends to emphasize a single level of education such as the classroom, school, school district or school community. These studies tend also to concentrate on the practice of democracy among students or among teachers and administrators. However, taken as a whole, the use and application of democratic school administration theories can be conceived as a nested system that includes multiple levels of education, each of which exerts some influence on the others. Although there are outlier studies, we focus on four levels of schooling that have received the most attention: classrooms; schools and school districts; local/state/provincial communities, and; the national level. We also suggest that it will become increasingly important for scholars to consider the international and global levels in order to develop a more holistic perspective on the way they apply democratic school administration theories.

Democratic Processes in Classrooms

For many students, their day-to-day experience with democratic processes in schools takes place in their classrooms (Reynolds, 1940). These experiences consist both of learning *about* democracy and learning *from* democracy, as they observe and practice it in schools:

> in order to respond to both students and the democratic culture, schools must become participatory communities where students, parents, and administrators work together and share decision making. Therefore, students must be assisted in practicing democracy while they learn about it in schools. Schools need to walk the talk of democracy, instead of promoting do as we say, not as we do. (Wallin, 2003, p. 57)

Of course, democracy can take many forms in the classroom. Research on democratic decision making in classrooms has focused on many of the important and daily tasks of teaching, and has examined the ways that teachers structure the various tasks they design for students, the ways they receive or refuse input from students, and on the ways that students learn and practice democratic values and citizenship (Westheimer & Kahne, 2004). In terms of content, these studies consider topics such as democratic classroom management (Copeland, 1987), democratic instructional and assessment strategies (Kohn, 1992), democratic professional and moral imperatives (Goodlad, Soder, & Sirotnik, 1993), social dimensions of democratic classrooms (DeMarrais & LeCompte, 1992; McLaren, 1989), and psychological and political ramifications of democratic decision making (Green, 1999).

Democratic Administration in Schools and School Districts

School and district-level research evoking democratic school administration-related themes has centered on various aspects of sharing governance, including multiple stakeholders in school and school district decision making, and the nature and function of school boards as a representative democratic structure (Feurstein, 2004; Koopman et al., 1943; Noddings, 1999). At the school level, there has been particular interest in examining schools through theoretical perspectives such as democratic communities (Furman & Starratt, 2002), distributed leadership (Spillane, Halverson, & Diamond, 2001), and teacher leadership (Brooks, Scribner, & Eferakorho, 2003).

Democratic administration in Local/State/Provincial Communities

Some research has investigated the various ways that local communities, states and provinces' governance processes influence educational systems. This impacts the manner and degree to which schools are funded, governed, and legislated (Carnoy & Levin, 1985). In a federal system such as the United States, this level of schooling is an especially important component of the democratic system as states interpret national educational policy. This, in turn, means that states—and particularly their legislatures and educational departments—serve an intermediary role between local and national educational bodies and also develop unique sets of education-related legislation that constrains and facilitates the practice of democracy at state and local levels (Chubb & Moe, 1999).

National Democratic Administration of Schools and International Democratic Administration in Education

At the national level, the manner in which nations develop and implement educational policy is often a form of democratic negotiation and representative participation (Apter, 1977). The practice and results of this process in turn have tremendous influence on state, province and local educational systems. Further, it is important to note that engagement at the national level is no longer sufficient, and that students must be educated as engaged global citizens who can negotiate cultural and global democracy:

> As citizens of the global community, students also must develop a deep understanding of the need to take action and make decisions to help solve the world's difficult problems. They need to participate in ways that will enhance democracy and promote equality and social justice in their cultural communities, nations, and regions, and in the world. (Banks, 2007, pp. 134-135)

Moreover, as Brooks and Normore (2010) noted, it is important that educators understand that their actions not only take place within a larger context, but actually within a nested system wherein each level of education influences those above and below (Figure 82.1).

Davies (2002) further pointed out that

> one cannot be prescriptive about where to start, whether at governmental level to set a framework or at classroom level to demonstrate a possibility. While there are ethical dilemmas that have surfaced about outside intervention and "transfers" of democracy or democratic research methods, my view is that democracy is important enough to take the risks and start the engagement—as long as the dialogue remains open. (pp. 264-265)

Critiques of Democratic Administration

Like any theory, democratic school administration emphasizes certain constructs while minimizing others. Thus, it is important to address certain criticisms leveled at the theory. The social contract critique: Does democratic administration promote or stifle individualism?

One of the primary difficulties with democracies in general, and democratic administration in particular concerns the role and relationship of individualism in relation to the collective. Teacher autonomy is alternately hailed as a sacred, powerful, and meaningful institution that protects teachers as qualified professionals, and derided as a license for pedagogical irresponsibility that undermines the effectiveness and quality of students' educational experiences (Green, 1999). In the twenty-first century, the stakes of this debate have been raised due to the proliferation of high-stakes educational policy and legislation—whereby individual teachers, educational leaders, and even entire teaching staffs are fired en bloc based on student performance on statewide standardized tests (Dorn, 1998). Increasingly, unchecked teacher autonomy and lack of professionalism are made the scapegoat for these "failures" (Hargreaves, 1993; Watson & Supovitz, 2001). As this new-millennium statistical accountability movement (Dorn, 1998) gains momentum, both in legislation and among many education theorists and funders, teacher autonomy, and by extension democracy in schools, is under scrutiny and changing as never before. The very nature of the relationship between teachers and their students, colleagues, administrators and external stakeholders are exposed by data and mediated by accountability mechanisms in an unprecedented manner.

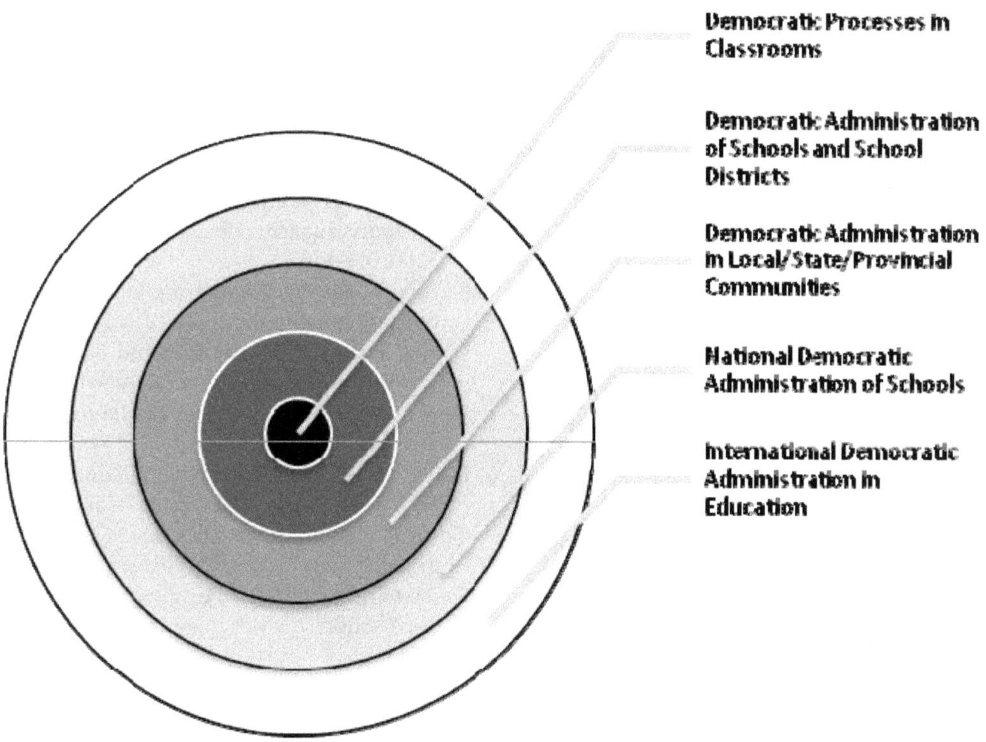

Figure 82.1. Levels of schooling as a nested system.

The Restructuring Critique: Can Authority and Decision Making Be Redistributed in a Rigid Hierarchical System?

The manner in which authority is distributed, shared, constrained and facilitated throughout a school or school system is due in large part to the nature of administrative practice throughout the system. While there are many approaches to school administration, democratic administration has an appeal in that it

> has a basic commitment toward individuals and the enhancement of their opportunities, it also recognizes and provides for such individual opportunities to take place in organizations designed to offset the authoritarian proclivities typically associated with government bureaucracies. Simply, the pursuit of human aspirations occurs through the design of multiple organizational arrangements characterized by fragmentation and the overlap of authority. (Davis, 1990, p. 390)

Establishing and sustaining a political system that coordinates this necessary fragmentation is part of the function of administration. Importantly, democratic school administration differs from theoretical approaches such as shared governance, professional bureaucracies, and distributed leadership in that it is not value-free and instead promotes transparency and inclusion (Furman & Starratt, 1999).

Exemplary Studies of Democratic Administration

Much of the research on democratic school administration is conceptual, however an increasing number of empirical studies have appeared as studies of leadership and democratic community or as democratic leadership. Among noteworthy conceptual articles, Webb and McCarthy's (1998) article "Ella Flagg Young: Pioneer of democratic school administration" bears special mention. This article documented Young's life and teaches important lessons regarding both the emancipation of women leaders and the practice of transparent democratic administration. Koopman et al.'s (1943) book *Democracy in school administration* was a landmark publication in the field that helped establish the conceptual foundation of our contemporary understanding of democratic school administration and Woods' (2005) *Democratic leadership in education* did much to update and put that work in modern context. Also, Louis' (2003) *Democratic schools, democratic communities: Reflections in an international context* explored and considered international implications of democracy in multiple contexts.

Among empirical research on democratic school administration-related issues, several articles are noteworthy. Kensler et al.'s (2009) *The ecology of democratic learning communities: Faculty trust and continuous learning in public middle schools* investigated the relationships between democratic community, faculty trust, and continuous and team learning. The researchers found that faculty trust mediated the relationship between democratic community and continuous and team learning. Mitra and Gross' (2009) article, *Increasing student voice in high school reform: Building partnerships, improving outcomes* drew on data from both the United States and Australia to understand the ways that students participate in school processes.

REFERENCES

Allen, L., & Glickman, C. D. (1998). Restructuring and renewal: Capturing the power of democracy. In A. Hargreaves, A. Lieberman, M. Fullan, & D. Hopkins (Eds.), *International handbook of educational change* (pp. 505-528). Boston, MA: Kluwer Academic.

Apter, D. E. (1977). Political life and cultural pluralism. In M. M. Tumin & W. Plotch (Eds.), *Pluralism in a democratic society* (pp. 58-91). New York, NY: Praeger.

Amartya, S. (1999). Democracy as a universal value. *Journal of Democracy, 10*(3), 3-17.

Apple, M. W., & Beane, J. A. (Eds.). (1995). *Democratic schools.* Alexandria, VA: Association for Supervision and Curriculum Development.

Banks, J. A. (2007). Diversity, group identity, and citizenship education in a global age. *Educational Researcher, 37*(3), 129–139.

Barry, F. S., & Lonsdale, R. C. (1956). School administration staffing practices: Influences upon administrative morale. *School Executive, 76*, 76-78.

Blase, J., & Blase, J. (1999). Implementation of shared governance for instructional improvement: principals' perspectives. *Journal of Educational Administration, 37*(5), 476-500.

Blase, J., & Blase, J. (2001). *Empowering teachers: What successful principals do* (2nd ed.). Thousand Oaks, CA: Corwin Press.

Blase, J., Blase, J., Anderson, G. L., & Dungan, S. (1995). *Democratic principals in action: Eight pioneers.* Thousand Oaks, CA: Corwin Press.

Bridges, E. M. (1967). A model for shared decision making in the school principalship. *Educational Administration Quarterly, 3*, 49-61.

Brooks, J. S., Scribner, J. P., & Eferakorho, J. (2004). Teacher leadership in the context of whole school reform. *Journal of School Leadership, (14)*3, 242-265.

Campbell, R. F., Fleming, T., Newell, L. J., & Bennion, J. W. (1987). *A history of thought and practice in educational administration.* New York, NY: Teachers College Press.

Carnoy, M., & Levin, H. (1985). *Schooling and work in the democratic state.* Stanford, CA: Stanford University Press.

Cate, J. M., Vaughn, A., & O'Hair, M. J. (2006). A seventeen-year case study of an elementary school's journey: From traditional school to learning community to democratic school community. *Journal of School Leadership, 16*, 86-111.

Chaltain, S. (2009). *American schools: The art of creating a democratic learning community.* New York, NY: Rowman & Littlefield Education.

Chubb, J., & Moe, T. (1990). *Politics, markets, and America's schools.* Washington, DC: Brookings Institute.

Cloke, K., & Goldsmith, J. (2002). *The end of management and the rise of organizational democracy.* San Francisco, CA: Jossey-Bass.

Copeland, W. D. (1987). Classroom management and student teachers' cognitive abilities: A relationship. *American Educational Research Journal, 24*,(2), 219-236.

Davis, C. R. (1990). Public organizational existence: A critique of individualism in democratic administration. *Polity, 22*(3), 397-418.

Davies, L. (1999). Comparing definitions of democracy in education. *Compare, 29*(2), 127-140.

Davies, L. (2002). Possibilities and limits for democratisation in education. *Comparative Education, 38*(3), 251-266.

Dewey, J. (1916). *Democracy and education.* New York, NY: The Free Press.

Dewey, J. (1937). Democracy and educational administration. *School and Society, 45*(1162), 457-462.

Dorn, S. (1998). The political legacy of school accountability systems. *Education Policy Analysis Archives, 6*(1), 1-33.

Feuerstein, A. (2002). Elections, voting, and democracy in local school district governance. *Educational Policy, 16*(1), 15.

Fleming, T. (1982). *Management by consensus: Democratic administration and human relations, 1929-1954* (Unpublished PhD dissertation). University of Oregon.

Furman, G. C., & Starratt, R. J. (2002). Leadership for democratic community in schools. In J. Murphy (Ed.), *The educational leadership challenge: redefining leadership for the 21st century.* Chicago, IL: The University of Chicago Press.

Giroux, H. A., & McLaren, P. (1989). *Critical pedagogy, the state, and cultural struggle.* Albany, NY: State University of New York Press.

Glaeser, E. L., Ponzetto, G. A. M., & Shielfer, A. (2007). Why does democracy need education? *Journal of Economic Growth, 12*, 77-99.

Glass, T. E. (2004). *The history of educational administration viewed through its textbooks.* Lanham, MD: Rowman & Littlefield.

Glickman, C. D. (1993). *Renewing America's schools.* San Francisco, CA: Jossey-Bass.

Goodlad, J. I., Soder, R., & Sirotnik, K. A. (1993). *The moral dimensions of teaching.* San Francisco, CA: Jossey-Bass.

Green, J. M. (1999). *Deep democracy: Community, diversity, and transformation.* Oxford, England: Rowman & Littlefield.

Greenfield, W. D., Jr. (2005). Postscript: Where have we been? *Journal of Educational Administration, 43*(1), 121-126.

Hallinger, P., & Richardson, D. (1988, April). *Models of shared leadership: Evolving structures and relationships.* Paper presented at the annual meeting of the American Educational Research Association, New Orleans, LA.

Harber, C., & Davies, L. (1998). *School management and effectiveness in developing countries: The post-bureaucratic school.* London, England: Continuum.

Harber, C., & Meighan, R. (1989). *The democratic school: Educational management and the practice of democracy.* Ticknall, England: Education Now.

Hargreaves, A. (1993). Individualism and individuality: Reinterpreting the teacher culture. In J. W. Little & M. W. McLaughlin (Eds.), *Teachers' work: Individuals, colleagues, and contexts* (pp. 51-76). New York, NY: Teachers College Press.

Haynes, J. (1997). *Democracy and civil society in the third world.* Malden, MA: Blackwell.

Hoy, W. K. (1978). Scientific research in educational administration. *Educational Administration Quarterly, 14*(3), 1-12.

Hoy, W. K. (1996). Science and theory in the practice of educational administration: A pragmatic perspective. *Educational Administration Quarterly, 32*(3), 366-378.

Jackson, D. M. (1957). Administrative procedure in curriculum revision. *Administrator's Notebook, 5*, 1-4.

Kensler, L. A. W. (2010). Designing democratic community for social justice. *International Journal of Urban Educational Leadership, 4*(1), 1-21.

Kensler, L. A. W., Caskie, G. I. L., Barber, M. E., & White, G. P. (2009). The ecology of democratic learning communities: Faculty trust and continuous learning in public middle schools. *Journal of School Leadership, 19*(6), 697-734.

Kohn, A. (1992). Resistance to cooperative learning: Making sense of its deletion and dilution. *Journal of Education, 174*(2), 38-56.

Koopman, G. R., Miel, A., & Minsner, P. J. (1943). *Democracy in school administration.* New York, NY: D. Appleton-Century Company.

Lambert, L., Walker, D., Zimmerman, D.P., Cooper, J. E., Lambert, M. D., Gardner, M. E., & Szabo, M. (2002). *The constructivist leader.* New York, NY: Teachers College Press.

LeCompte, M. D., & deMarrais, K. B. (1992). The disempowering of empowerment: Out of the revolution and into the classroom. *Educational Foundations, 6*(3), 5-31.

Leithwood, K., & Menzies, T. (1998). A review of research concerning the implementation of site-based management. *School Effectiveness and School Improvement, 9*(3), 233-285.

Lewin, K., & Lippitt, R. (1938). An experimental approach to the study of autocracy and democracy: A preliminary note. *Sociometry, 1*(3/4), 292-300.

Lewin, K., Lippitt, R., & White, R. (1939). Patterns of aggressive behavior in experimentally created social climates. *Journal of Social Psychology, 10*, 271-299.

Louis, K. S. (2003). Democratic schools, democratic communities: Reflections in an international context. *Leadership and Policy in Schools, 2*(2), 93-108.

Mayo, E. (1933). *The human problems of an industrial civilization.* New York, NY: Macmillan.

McGregor, D. M. (1960). *The human side of enterprise.* New York, NY: McGraw Hill.

Merriam, C. E. (1938). The assumptions of democracy. *Political Science Quarterly, 53*(3), 328-349.

Mitra, D. L. (2008). *Student voice in school reform: Building youth-adult partnerships that strengthen schools and empower youth.* Albany, NY: State University of New York Press.

Mitra, D. L., & Gross, S. J. (2009). Increasing student voice in high school reform: Building partnerships, improving outcomes. *Educational Management Administration & Leadership, 37*(4), 522-543.

Monyatsi, P. P. (2005). Transforming schools into democratic organisations: The case of the secondary schools management development project in Botswana. *International Education Journal, 6*(3), 354-366.

Murphy, J. (2002). Reculturing the profession of educational leadership: new blueprints. *Educational Administration Quarterly, 38*(2), 176-191.

Noddings, N. (1999). Renewing democracy in schools. *Phi Delta Kappan, (80)8*, 579-583.

Noyes, A. (2005). Pupil voice: purpose, power and the possibilities for democratic schooling. *British Educational Research Journal, 31*(4), 533-540.

O'Hair, M. J., & Reitzug, U. C. (1997). Restructuring schools for democracy: Principal's perspectives. *Journal of School Leadership, 7*, 266-286.

Oplatka, I. (2009). The field of educational administration. *Educational Administration Quarterly, 47*(1), 8-35.

Osler, A., & Starkey, H. (2006). Education for democratic citizenship: A review of research, policy and practice 1995-2005. *Research Papers in Education, 21*(4), 433-466.

Pashiardis, P. (2004). Democracy and leadership in the educational system of Cyprus. *Journal of Educational Administration, 42*(6), 656-668.

Reynolds, R. G. (1940, February). Democracy in the Classroom. *Teachers College Record, XLI*, 427-436.

Sergiovanni, T. J. (1996). *Leadership for the schoolhouse.* San Francisco, CA: Jossey-Bass.

Sergiovanni, T. J. (2005). *Strengthening the heartbeat.* San Francisco, CA: Jossey-Bass.

Sorensen, G. (2010). Democracy and democratization. In K. T. Leicht & J. C. Jenkins (Eds.), *Handbook of politics: State and society in global perspective* (pp. 441-458). New York, NY: Springer.

Spillane, J., Halverson, R., & Diamond, J. B. (2001). Investigating school leadership practice: A distributed perspective. *Educational Researcher, 30*(3), 23–28.

Strolle, R. (1956). Educating citizens for reorganization. *Nation's Schools, 58*, 48-49.

Taylor, F. W. (2001). The principles of scientific management. In J. M. Shafritz & J. S. Ott (Eds.), *Classics of organization theory* (5th ed., pp. 61-72). Belmont, CA: Thompson Learning.

Tonn, J. C. (2003). *Mary P. Follett: Creating democracy, transforming management.* New Haven, CT: Yale University Press.

Wallin, D. (2003). Student leadership and democratic schools. *NASSP Bulletin, 87*(636), 55-78.

Watson, S., & Supovitz, J. (2001, August 26). Autonomy and accountability in the context of standards-based reform. *Education Policy Analysis Archives, 9*(32). Retrieved from http://epaa.asu.edu/epaa/v9n32.html

Webb, L. D., & McCarthy, M. M. (1998). Ella Flagg Young: Pioneer of democratic school administration. *Educational Administration Quarterly, 34*(2), 223-242.

Westheimer, J. & Kahne, J. (2004). What kind of citizen? The politics of educating for democracy. *American Educational Research Journal, 41*(2), 237-269.

Williams, L. A., Cate, J., & O'Hair, M. J. (2009). The boundary-spanning role of democratic learning communities. *Educational Management Administration & Leadership, 37*(4), 452-472.

Willower, D. J. (1980). Contemporary issues in theory in educational administration. *Educational Administration Quarterly, 16*(3), 1-25.

Woods, P. A. (2004). Democratic leadership: drawing distinctions with distributed leadership. *International Journal of Leadership in Education, 7*(1), 3-26.

Woods, P. A. (2005). *Democratic leadership in education.* Thousand Oaks, CA: SAGE.

Woods, P. A., & Gronn, P. (2009). Nurturing democracy. *Educational Management Administration & Leadership, 37*(4), 430-451.

York-Barr, J., & Duke, K. (2004). What do we know about teacher leadership? Findings from two decades of scholarship. *Review of Educational Research, 74*(3), 255-316.

Author Contact Information: Lisa A. W. Kensler, Assistant Professor of Educational Leadership, College of Education, 4002 Haley Center, Auburn University, Auburn, AL 36832. Phone: 334-844-3020. E-mail: lisakensler@auburn.edu

CHAPTER 83

The Aesthetics of Leadership and Administration

Eugenie A. Samier
The British University in Dubai

While aesthetics is rarely discussed in educational administration and leadership, it is a foundation to much of what we consider activity in this field. It is implicitly present, and frequently referred to metaphorically, suggesting that aesthetics plays some role in how we conceptualize and carry out these roles. Since aesthetics is not usually grasped through positivist theories or research, it remains liminal as an informing foundation, emerging only in the 1990s in the organization aesthetics movement. Many public administration classics allude to an underlying aesthetic, however, without explicitly developing it, such as Barnard's *Functions of the Executive* (1938), Banks and Hislop's *The Art of Administration* (1961), and Wildavsky's *Speaking Truth to Power: The Art and Craft of Policy Analysis* (1979). The frequency of such titles occasioned a published bibliography by Georgi in 1970. The notion of art has persisted in more recent authors like Hodgkinson's *Educational Leadership: The Moral Art* (1991), Lynn's *Public Management as Art, Science, and Profession* (1996), Samier and Bates's *Aesthetic Dimensions of Educational Administration and Leadership* (2006), and English's *The Art of Educational Leadership* (2008).

Early works generally use art metaphorically, focusing on craft discipline, recognizing intuition, and other subsidiary aspects of artistic production. The craft approach has been promoted by Blumberg (1989), Deal and Peterson (1994), and Goodsell (1992), who regard organizations as designed and created like an artifact. The limitation here lies in the distinction between craft and creation, artisan and artist, where the former is a pragmatic or utilitarian means-oriented practice and the latter nonutilitarian, its value intrinsic, enriching the quality of life. From a humanistic perspective, administration and leadership require both for a meaningfully grounded professional practice and critique. Some authors (e.g., English, 2008; Samier & Bates, 2006; Sköldberg, 2002) explicitly recommend that administrators draw from the arts in supplementing skills and knowledge, however, they do not develop an underlying, foundational or grounding aesthetic for administration per se.

But what is aesthetics, and how can administration and leadership be aesthetically grounded? How does aesthetics relate to the many constructs that make up the field, such as organizations, social relations, authority, power, and decision making? Essentially, aesthetics is the study of form and our perceptive abilities as they relate to creating structured thought and action, in the conceptual, physical and cultural and sociopolitical environments. In this sense, then, our conceptualizations, principles and standards, our interpersonal and organizational social constructions upon which leadership and administration are built, and how we manipulate the material environment in which they reside are aesthetic activities. The analysis of this is leadership and administrative aesthetic theory, applying as much to how we structure and embody our roles, responsibilities, functions, programs, and organizational designs as it does to the creative principles underlying knowledge and ethics.

Aesthetic theory is necessary to intellectual approaches, in designing analytical models, taxonomies, and maps of the field. It also has theoretical importance to identifying and analyzing expressive qualities. As the rapidly expanding application of aesthetic analysis to organizations indicates, it also has practical value in creativity and innovation, and styles of performance and communication—the embodiment in social relations of ideals, values, and emotions.

The Handbook of Educational Theories, pp. 945–952

Without aesthetics, there is an inadequate explanation and understanding of the ways in which leadership and administration form and change, as well as a multitude of critical and conceptual possibilities in exploring the material and nonmaterial worlds of social relations. Adopting an aesthetic perspective also allows for a clearer integration of disciplines, integrating the humanities and social sciences.

The argument for aesthetics has appeared in a number of sources. Aspiring to truth requires, for Guillet de Montoux (2000), aesthetic power—the imagination necessary in synthesizing observations into knowledge in the sciences, through organizing properties that transport "us from our private individuality into a space of public human community" (p. 36). Smircich's (1983) root metaphor approach defines organizations symbolically through their aesthetic activities: images and symbols, and styles of behavior to produce organizational artifacts such as rituals, legends, and ceremonies. From this perspective, organizations are constructed through aesthetic means and take aesthetic form. Expressed in terms that apply more directly to leadership's visionary character, it is the aesthetic capacity that allows us to perceive, construct forms, and harness imagination—it is the stuff out of which we think, reflect, critique, and form judgments; it serves as the foundation for knowledge (Samier, 2006a). For Alvesson and Berg (1992) "symbols are ... instruments to create order and clarity out of chaos" (p. 85) in research and writing, that is, knowledge construction.

Origins and Development of Social Aesthetic

The origins of aesthetic analysis are found in the writings of Plato and Aristotle as it informed their critiques of governmental and administrative practice, and carried up through various traditions, such as German Idealism in the Enlightenment and Romantic periods, such as Baumgarten, Kant, Schiller, Hegel, and Schopenhauer, for which the aesthetic is integral to creative cognitive processes leading to insight, intellectual freedom, and concept formation producing social reality (see Samier, 2006a). As Hofstadter (1965) demonstrates, this central role of the aesthetic was adopted by post-idealist thinkers in social and political philosophy such as hermeneutics, phenomenology and critical theory, including the writings of Nietzsche, Dilthey, Simmel, Maritain, Weber, Whitehead, Dewey, Heidegger, and Habermas. Art provides the means by which the three functions of symbolism, expression, and meaning are integrated (Hofstadter, 1965), for social import derived from the expressive theories of art by Croce, Cassirer, Collingwood, and Langer. It's evident in Arendt's aesthetico-moral examination of politics and the evils that arise: it is through aesthetics that we find pleasure in the "density" of experiencing human particularity and plurality producing a sense of the tragic—the ability to apprehend "encroachments, hostilities, tensions, and provocations" from which moral political action ensues rather than to slip into the a de-aestheticized "oblivion and inattentiveness" produced through forms of power, or domination (Curtis, 1999, p. 126). It is from this heritage that Morgan (1986), draws in *Images of Organization* where experience is mediated through images of form.

During the 1990s, a number of organization theorists pursued an aesthetic analysis, largely derived from anthropology and cultural studies for which aesthetics formed the basis for social interaction, communication, political systems, and ethical rules in societies. It also originates in symbolic interactionism where imagination and creativity as they are expressed through symbols, narrative, and performance are regarded as foundational principles in the construction of the self, social roles, and organizations (Blumer, 1969; Collins, 1994; Cooley, 1964; Goffman, 1959, 1974; Mead, 1934; Turner, 1988). This has led to numerous conferences such as the series on the "Art of Management and Organization" in London (2002), Paris (2004), and Krakow (2006). Aesthetics warranted a chapter in the *Handbook of Organization Studies* (Gagliardi, 1996), and has been the focus of a number of major journal special issues (e.g., *Human Relations*, 2002; *Organizational Science*, 1998). In 2006, the journal *Aesthesis* was launched to explore the potential of art and aesthetics in management through empirical and theoretical studies.

The evolution of aesthetic studies has grown from a predominantly functionalist perspective in the 1970s and 1980s when aesthetics was appreciated in its symbolic and representational form serving conventional administrative goals (what Gagliardi [1996] calls the "corporate view"), to an independent analysis derived from aesthetic theory which ontologically underpins organizational life. In this last sense, organization, administration, and leadership are aesthetic constructions - the means by which interpersonal relationships and organizations take form. A significant number of authors have explored aesthetics as a foundational discipline (e.g., Harding, 2001; Linstead & Höpfl, 2000; Ramirez, 1991; Strati, 1990, 1992, 1999; Strati & Montoux, 2002; White, 1996) to interpret, critique and understand the physical environment, narratives that structure experience, sources of role construction and authority, the establishment and conveying of values, and qualities of social structure such as power and hierarchy that create administrative and leadership worlds.

Aesthetics and Research

Qualitative research has often been described as an artistic process. Denzin and Lincoln (2000) liken it to *bricolage*, "a maker of quilts, or, as in filmmaking, a person who assembles images into montages" (pp. 4-5). Palys (1997) describes several artistic features: the aesthetic appeal of well-designed questionnaires; dramaturgy that emphasizes interview roles; the role of storytelling for research subjects; researcher's notes using plot and characterization; and the use of literary devices as abstraction to produce understanding and maintain creativity. The aesthetic perspective is emphasized by Wolcott (1995) who regards a field researcher as "ethnographer-as-artist" and "ethnographer-as-craftsperson." Cultural ethnography has long been seen by Clifford (1986a) as having literary qualities like "metaphor, figuration, narrative," allegory providing its interpretive construction of knowledge (pp. 3-4) and as "a performance emplotted by powerful stories" lending immediacy and constituting the "conditions of its meaningfulness" (Clifford, 1986b, pp. 98-9). Fischer (1986) even regards ironic humor as particularly apt in conveying the complexities of social life, since it can expose or subvert "oppressive hegemonic ideologies" and give depth or expanded "resonance" to "techniques of transference, talk-stories, multiple voices or perspectives" (p. 224).

Not only does research use many data analysis procedures requiring aesthetic abilities like representing, visualizing, describing, classifying, and interpreting, but an appreciation of narrative storytelling such as consideration of audience, encoding (interpreting symbols and metaphors), the use of quotations (akin to dialogue), and authorial representation presented through rhetorical structures (Creswell, 1998; Glesne & Peshkin, 1992; Van Maanen, 1988). Czarniawska (2002) claims that narrative is important to research in four ways: written in story form; collecting stories; conceptualizes organizing as story making; and reflecting "on organization theory as a literary endeavor" (p. 72). In particular, she traces the influence of Barthes (1977) on a number of authors in disciplines relevant to the role of narrative in leadership studies focused on the construction of social reality: MacIntyre (1981) and Rorty (1991) in philosophy, White (1987) in history, Mandler (1984) in psychology, Fisher (1987) in political science, Brown (1987) in sociology, and Geertz (1980) in anthropology. Kvale (1996) regards research as consisting of many aesthetic aspects including narrative qualities (p. 29), "an aesthetic sensibility," creative ability, sensitivity to qualitative distinctions comparable to that of the artist, the art critic's "ability to communicate new perspectives and to evaluate the quality of a work of art," and the narrative qualities of storytelling (p. 106).

Using Aesthetic Analysis

Aesthetic analysis has been applied to a broad range of social constructions and phenomena, aimed primarily at interpretation and critique that informs understanding in the *verstehen* tradition. This has varied from studies in creative social action resulting in organizational structure, culture, politics and change to the interpretation of aesthetic sources in illuminating the human condition in leadership and administration—examining the many ways in which aesthetics shapes the world and mentality, responsibilities and activities of leader and administrator actors. This includes the creation of ideas and ideals, their embodied expressions and influence on interpersonal relationships, and the organizational environment that carry judgment, decision making, and policy formation. Using aesthetic analysis requires an interdisciplinary approach that synthesizes the social sciences and humanities, and the full range of expressive forms.

The capacity to envision new values, structures and practices, and reshape organizational cultures and interaction styles is central to many leadership theories such as transforming (Burns, 1978) and transformational leadership (Bass, 1990), and charisma (Conger & Kanungo, 1998), where the complex nature of creativity is assumed. Sternberg (2005) demonstrates that many aspects of creativity run counter to current accountability regimes: independent judgment, idiosyncratic defining of problems, experiencing failure and uncertainty, and evolving in ways that fixed measures do not apply (pp. 30-31). Kets de Vries (2009) presents much the same view: creative people do not fit well into usual organizational frameworks, requiring greater organizational "space," nurturing, and special treatment (p. 196), they are "disorderly, unorthodox and unconventional, and their playful, intuitive methods can wreak havoc in a by-the-book organization" (p. 227). It also has destructive potential, what Cropley, Kaufman, and Cropley (2008) call "malevolent creativity", "deliberately planned to damage others" (p. 106). One source of creativity that has not been previously examined is the avant-garde, an aesthetico-political movement that provides insight into societal change, however, this tradition also runs into the same problems identified by Sternberg and Kets de Vries (Samier, 2012).

Administration and leadership express themselves creatively in three basic forms: the architectural and artefactual, the performative or theatrical, and the literary (see Samier, 2006b). In addition to drawing from the arts to analyze professional activity, some also argue for the use of aesthetic sources in research, training, and education such as literature and cinema—all of which provide a means for critiquing administrative and leadership expression and the reinforcement of culture, ideology, politics, and power structures.

Architectural analysis has been explored by a number of writers, demonstrating how the manipulation of physical reality through architectural design and positioning of buildings establishes and maintains power and authority (Dutton & Grant, 1991; Guillén, 1997; Klein & Diket, 1999; Spotts, 2003). Interiors are just as important: part of our aesthetic environment is composed of furnishings and decorative objects—all expressions of value, power, status, and privilege carried in the relative form and quality of crafting and materials that distinguish the offices of those in the "corridors of power." The significance of office artefacts has been pursued by Strati (1990, 1992, 1996) who examines the relationship between everyday objects and conceptions of individualism, democratization, authority, and leadership. Myerson and Ross (2003) offer an aesthetic theory for differentiating twentieth century offices that were "architectural containers" expressing "management efficiency theory, systemic modern design and bulky, tethered technology" (p. 8), from four styles of team-based, knowledge-driven, and community-oriented contemporary "creative offices": narrative, which tells "a story about a company and its brands"; nodal, which is "imaginative new offices that provide a fixed point in an increasingly virtual world" offering "places where people interact"; neighborly, that supports conversation, social contact, and teamwork; and nomadic, which is not in a fixed place, or in a conventional office building (pp. 9-10). Architecture and artifacts can also be viewed as symptomatic of more destructive phenomena like narcissism where the inanimate environment is manipulated to express the grandiosity and egocentrism of leaders or administrators (Samier & Atkins, 2009).

The performative includes verbal and nonverbal interactive expression and the narrative and poetic qualities that structure presentation—the rituals and ceremonies of everyday life, in positive or constructive, punitive or abusive and exploitative or repressive forms. It provides the medium for enacting role and identity from which organization derives (Light & Smith, 2005). This view is adopted also by Kets de Vries (2009) for whom leadership expression is not only conscious, but unconscious and intuitive, employing "speeches, ceremonials, and rituals," as well as the manipulation of media through "propaganda techniques" (p. 136). The performative view has been proposed by a number of authors, such as Maxcy (1995), Meyer (2001), and Starratt (1993). The "theatre of leadership" (English, 1994, p. 146) carries not only the ritual and ceremonies of everyday life, but also creates and reinforces moral, social, and political values and practices. This performative art, for English (2008), consists of a construction of self, assuming a role, expressed through various types of narratives (stories and myths), "symbols, customs, and linguistic traditions" using verbal and nonverbal communication (p. 143), and is "anchored in the essential core of every leader's deeply held beliefs" (p. 53). Drawing upon the performance arts, one can identify corresponding constructions in the social world: the casting of actors in roles, proximity to audience, elevation in the audience's visual plane, posture, lighting, background sounds or absence of sounds, off-stage action (the behind closed doors politics), staging arrangements, scripts, and suspension of disbelief (Samier, 2005).

The use of literary sources in illuminating leadership and administrative practices has been established for almost a century (Waldo, 1968; Wolfe, 1924). Many authors since have drawn upon literature for theoretical and teaching purposes: Adams and Pugh (1994), Brieschke (1993), Carroll and Gailey (1992), Cohen (1998), Czarniawska-Joerges and Monthoux (1994), Gormley (2001), Howe (2002), McDaniel (1978), and Marini (1992). They have argued that aesthetic sources like literary works provide an emotional stimulation or release, a sympathetic identification through ego ideal, cautionary morality tales of characters trapped in organizational politics or experiencing frustration with bureaucratic excess, and a moral education by portraying intention, motive, will, their consequences and dilemmas, the conflict of good and evil, the commingling of rational and irrational, the noble and petty, and high achievement and tragedy. Literature, because of its narrative and descriptive character can capture subtle and intangible and dilemma-ridden experiences that issue from the emotional, spiritual, and visceral, making connections across the life of a character from early childhood through professional career, and the emotional states including fear, ennui, despair, powerlessness, and isolation (Samier, 2005).

Townsend (1991) examined verbal expression, or bureaucratic poetics, through which "human agency is reflected" by structuring the policy process in "modes" or "frames" of argumentation: "method-centered, intuitive, ethical, causal, motivational, parallel case or comparative, and authoritative" (p. 45). Organizations are also formed, sustained, and changed through myths that provide meaning, explanation, and legitimation as well as furnishing values, scripts, and modes of interaction. Midgley (2004) argues that myths are "imaginative patterns, networks of powerful symbols that suggest particular ways of interpreting the world" (p. 1), central to our conceptions of the state, of society, and legitimate roles within them. Currently, under the regime of new public management, *homo economicus* is one of the most powerful, along with myths of service, impartiality, efficiency, teamwork, consensus, accountability (Samier, 1997), and the romanticist heroic myth in conceptions of success and achievement (Samier, 2009). Literature also provides an interpretive and critical research method (Czarniawska, 2002), combining the disciplines of historiography, language analysis, and literary criticism in a thematic critique that allows one to construct analytic categories for use comparatively across national or international traditions. Major categories consist of: organizational structure and purpose (Kafka, *The Trial*); administrative culture (Roth, *Radetzsky March*); administrative power and politics (Havel, *The Garden Party*); personality, character and identity formation (Gogol, "The Overcoat"); and bureaucratic poetics (Havel, "The Memorandum") (Samier, 2005). These features are seen in Gogol's stories about functionaries in which alienation, dehumanization, a moral vacuum, and deceit produce many bureaupathologies (Samier & Lumby, 2010).

The biographical is a quasi-historical and quasi-literary field that takes a more holistic view of the influences in making one a leader or administrator, consisting of biographies, memoirs, correspondence, journals, diaries, and so on, emphasized in one of the classic texts in the field, Burns' *Leadership* (1978). The rationales often provided are that such sources provide detailed case histories, evidence of leadership attributes, analytical "balance sheets" on strategies and approaches, evidence through comparative analysis about factors involved in career paths such as gender, class, and race. They have an inspirational purpose through role modeling and provide cases for qualitative generalizations and detailed information by which theories can be tested (see English, 1994, 1995, 2006; Gronn & Ribbins, 1996; Ribbins, 2003). To these one can add more realistic and detailed information about the relationships of administrators and politicians, the media, and the public in addition to organizational culture and politics, the role that personality, character and mentality plays, the effects of ideology, and the importance of early formative experiences. A common form of such work is found in portraiture, advocated by several as a primary medium for understanding professional practice (Hackmann, 2002; Lawrence-Lightfoot & Hoffmann Davis, 1997).

Aesthetic Critiques

Political studies have drawn upon aesthetics for some time in analyzing a variety of phenomena: the relationship between theater and politics (Borreca, 1993; Friedland, 2002) and the affinity of political ideologies for harnessing and distorting the arts (e.g., Michaud, 2004). The dangerous side of creativity is evident in politics through the close relationship between aesthetics and fascism, particularly the role of the arts in creating ideology (Hamilton, 1971; Kaplan, 1986; Witt, 2001). This analysis can be extended to administrative and leadership ideologies, the structuring of power, hierarchy, and authority including the marginalization of women, minorities, and the disabled.

The kitsch critique, as a form of aesthetic judgment applied to leadership and policy, first appeared in Lugg's (1984) *Kitsch: From Education to Public Policy.* Subsequently, Samier (2008) has presented a theory of *kitischification*, consisting of the origins of kitsch, the qualities of the kitsch artifact as well as considerations of motivations of the kitsch producer and of the kitsch consumer as they apply to educational scholarship, theories, models and practices, particularly in advancing ideology, compromising ethics and academic quality. English (2008) has effectively used a kitsch critique of over 40 influential "guru" type leadership books, demonstrating how misleading they are in their "dumbing down" of leadership, by using faked data to support oversimplified illustrations, neglect conflict and complexities, promote social Darwinism, or simply provide no supporting evidence at all.

One theme that has run through cultural and micropolitical studies on educational leadership and administration is the covert. It is essentially practiced through what de Grazia (1989) calls "the rhetoric of imposture," a mask through which the leader presents qualities that are not inherent to the person, but which are effective on followers, a concept drawn from Machiavelli's *The Prince*. Aesthetics is the essence of covert activity, constructing a deception through which one organizes resistance, acquires information, or disseminates disinformation (Samier, 2007).

Illustrative Studies

An aesthetic approach in administration has recently been explored by a few authors. Pekonen's (2007) study of concept formation and its effect on the choices we make in government and politics examined the two key concepts of government, "ruling" and "governing" and the notions of obedience, authority, appropriate action, the "good" and morality embedded in them, as metaphors through an aesthetic approach originating in Plato, Hobbes, Nietzsche and Heidegger. Harris (2008) explains how aesthetic awareness in teaching creates in students a heightened awareness of self and one's perspective on others, and how this can provide a deepened and more critical social action towards social justice. Ahonen (2008) draws on psychoanalytic aesthetics as a form of analysis that can uncover deep motivations and creativity directed towards neurotic dispositions underlying university politics, decision-making, and policy. Ellenius (1998) extends the aesthetic analysis of political power through the various ways in which it is visualized and the symbols and metaphors of power rhetoric, including the icons, portraits, installation ceremonies, and processions used for propaganda and legitimation purposes. Mykkanen's (2007) application of aesthetics to politics exemplifies this relationship: he explores image-creation in television advertising as a construction and presentation of the political self, drawing in part from Goffman and Welsch's aesthetic analysis.

REFERENCES

Adams, E., & Pugh, D. (1994). The humanities and professional studies: Adding people to policy. *College Teaching, 42*(2), 63-65.

Ahonen, P. (2008). Psychoanalytic aesthetics, *Journal of Educational Administration and Foundations, 19*(1), 19-54.

Alvesson, M., & Berg, P. O. (1992). *Corporate culture and organizational symbolism: An overview.* Berlin, Germany: Walter de Gruyter.

Banks, A., & Hislop, J. (1961). *The art of administration.* London: University Tutorial Press.

Barnard, C. (1938). *The functions of the executive.* Cambridge, MA: Harvard University Press.

Barthes, R. (1977). *Image-music-text.* New York, NY: Hill & Wang.

Bass, B. (1990). From transactional to transformational leadership: Learning to share the vision. *Organizational Dynamics, 18*(3), 19-31.

Blumberg, A. (1989). *School administration as a craft: Foundations of practice.* Boston, MA: Allyn & Bacon.

Blumer, H. (1969). *Symbolic interactionism.* Englewood Cliffs, NY: Prentice-Hall.

Borreca, A. (1993). Political dramaturgy: A dramaturg's (re)view, *The Drama Review, 37*(2), 56-79.

Brieschke, P. A. (1993). Interpreting ourselves: Administrators in modern fiction. *Theory into Practice, 32*(4), 228-235.

Brown, R. (1987). *Society as text: Essays on rhetoric, reason, and reality.* Chicago, IL: University of Chicago Press.

Burns, J. M. (1978). *Leadership.* New York, NY: Harper & Row.

Carroll, V., & Gailey, J. (1992). Using literature to teach about bureaucratic structure, *College Teaching, 40*(1), 24-26.

Clifford, J. (1986a). Introduction: Partial truths. In J. Clifford & G. Marcus (Eds.), *Writing culture: The poetics and politics of ethnography* (pp. 1-26). Berkeley, CA: University of California Press.

Clifford, J. (1986b). On ethnographic allegory. In J. Clifford & G. Marcus (Eds.), *Writing culture: The poetics and politics of ethnography* (pp. 98-121). Berkeley, CA: University of California Press.

Cohen, C. (1998). Using narrative fiction within management education, *Management Learning, 29*(2), 165-181.

Collins, R. (1994). *Four sociological traditions.* New York, NY: Oxford University Press.

Conger, J., & Kanungo, R. (1998). *Charismatic leadership in organizations.* Thousand Oaks, CA: SAGE.

Cooley, C. (1964). *Human nature and the social order.* New York, NY: Schocken.

Creswell, J. (1998). *Qualitative inquiry and research design: Choosing among five traditions.* Thousand Oaks, CA: SAGE.

Cropley, D., Kaufman, J., & Cropley, A. (2008). Malevolent creativity: A functional model of creativity in terrorism and crime, *Creativity Research Journal, 20*(2), 105-115.

Curtis, K. (1999). *Our sense of the real: Aesthetic experience and arendtian politics.* Ithaca, NY: Cornell University Press.

Czarniawska, B. (2002). Narrative, interviews, and organizations. In J. Gubrium & J. Holstein (Eds.), *Handbook of interview research: Context & method* (pp. 799-750). Thousand Oaks, CA: SAGE.

Czarniawska-Joerges, B., & Guillet de Monthoux, P. (1994). *Good novels, better management: Reading organizational realities.* Chur, Switzerland: Harwood Academic Press.

Deal, T., & Peterson, K. (1994). *The leadership paradox: Balancing logic and artistry in schools.* San Francisco, CA: Jossey-Bass.

de Grazia, S. (1989). *Machiavelli in hell.* Princeton, NJ: Princeton University Press.

Denzin, N., & Lincoln, Y. (2000). Introduction: The discipline and practice of qualitative research. In *Handbook of qualitative research* (2nd ed., pp. 1-36). Thousand Oaks, CA: SAGE.

Dutton, T., & Grant, B. (1991). Campus design and critical pedagogy, *Academe, 77*(4), 37-43.

Ellenius, A. (1998). Introduction: Visual representations of the state as propaganda and legitimation. In *Iconography, propaganda, and legitimation* (pp. 1-7). Oxford, England: Clarendon Press.

English, F. W. (1994). *Theory in educational administration.* New York, NY: HarperCollins.

English, F. W. (1995). Toward a reconsideration of biography and other forms of life writing as a focus for teaching educational administration, *Educational Administration Quarterly, 31*(2), 203-223.

English, F. W. (2006). Understanding leadership in education: Life writing and its possibilities, *Journal of Educational Administration and History,* 38(2), 141-154.

English, F. W. (2008). *The art of educational leadership: Balancing performance and accountability.* Los Angeles, CA: SAGE.

Fischer, M. (1986). Ethnicity and the post-modern arts of memory. In J. Clifford & G. Marcus (Eds.), *Writing culture: The poetics and politics of ethnography* (pp. 194-233). Berkeley, CA: University of California Press.

Fisher, W. (1987). *Human communication as narration: Toward a philosophy of reason, value, and action.* Columbia, SC: University of South Carolina Press.

Friedland, P. (2002). *Political actors: Representative bodies & theatricality in the age of the French revolution.* Ithaca, NY: Cornell University Press.

Gagliardi, P. (1996). Exploring the aesthetic side of organizational life. In S. Clegg, C. Hardy, & W. Nord (Eds.), *Handbook of organization studies* (pp. 565-580). London: SAGE.

Geertz, C. (1980). Blurred genres: The refiguration of social thought, *American Scholar,* 29(2), 165-179.

Georgi, C. (1970). *The arts and the art of administration: A selected bibliography.* Los Angeles, CA: University of California, Graduate School of Business Administration.

Glesne, C., & Peshkin, A. (1992). *Becoming qualitative researchers: An introduction.* White Plains, NY: Longman.

Goffman, E. (1959). *The presentation of self in everyday life.* Garden City, NY: Doubleday.

Goffman, E. (1974). *Frame analysis.* New York, NY: Harper.

Goodsell, C. (1992). The public administrator as artisan, *Public Administration Review, 52*(3), 246-253.

Gormley, W. (2001). Moralists, pragmatists, and rogues: Bureaucrats in modern mysteries. *Public Administration Review, 61*(2), 184-193.

Gronn, P., & Ribbins, P. (1996). Leaders in context: Postpositivist approaches to understanding educational leadership, *Educational Administration Quarterly, 32*(3), 452-473.

Guillén, M. (1997). Scientific management's lost aesthetic: Architecture, organization, and the taylorized beauty of the mechanical. *Administrative Science Quarterly, 42*(4), 682-715.

Guillet de Monthoux, P. (2000). The art management of aesthetic organizing. In S. Linstead & H. Höpfl (Eds.), *The aesthetics of organization* (pp. 35-60). London: SAGE.

Hackmann, D. (2002). Using portraiture in educational leadership research. *International Journal of Leadership in Education, 5*(1), 51-60.

Hamilton, A. (1971). *The appeal of fascism, 1919-1945: A study of intellectuals and fascism.* New York, NY: Macmillan.

Harding, N. (2001). Aesthetics of organizations. *Journal of Management in Medicine, 15*(4), 323-329.

Harris, C. (2008). Exploring dimensions of critical awareness through aesthetic experience, *Journal of Educational Administration and Foundations, 19*(1), 55-80.

Hodgkinson, C. (1991). *Educational leadership: The moral art.* Albany, NY: SUNY Press.

Hofstadter, A. (1965). *Truth and art.* New York, NY: Columbia University.

Howe, L. (2002). Mourning administrative generosity in a postgenerous time: Lessons from Wallace Shawn's "The Designated Mourner." *Administration & Society, 33*(6), 583-609.

Kaplan, A. Y. (1986). *Reproductions of banality: Fascism, literature, and French intellectual life.* Minneapolis, MN: University of Minnesota Press.

Kets de Vries, M. (2009). *Reflections on character and leadership.* San Francisco: Jossey-Bass.

Klein, S., & Diket, R. (1999). Creating artful leadership, *Leadership in Education, 2*(1), 23-30.

Kvale, S. (1996). *Interviews: An introduction to qualitative research interviewing.* Thousand Oaks, CA: SAGE.

Lawrence-Lightfoot, S., & Hoffmann Davis, J. (1997). *The art and science of portraiture.* San Francisco, CA: Jossey-Bass.

Light, A., & Smith, J. (Eds.). (2005). *The aesthetics of everyday life.* New York, NY: Columbia University Press.

Linstead, S., & Höpfl, H. (Eds.). (2000). *The aesthetics of organization.* London: SAGE.

Lugg, C. (1984) *Kitsch: From education to public policy.* London: Harwood.

Lynn, L. (1996). *Public management as art, science, and profession.* Chatham, NJ: Chatham House.

MacIntyre, A. (1981). *After virtue.* London, England: Duckworth.

Mandler, J. (1984). *Stories, scripts and scenes: Aspects of schema theory.* London, England: Erlbaum.

Marini, F. (1992). The uses of literature in the exploration of public administration ethics: The example of "Antigone." *Public Administration Review, 52*(5), 420-426.

Maxcy, S. (1995). *Democracy, chaos, and the new school order.* Thousand Oaks, CA: Corwin.

McDaniel, T. (1978). The search for the administrative novel, *Public Administration Review, 38*(6), 545-549.

Mead, G. H. (1934). *Mind, self, and society.* Chicago, IL: University of Chicago Press.

Meyer, M. (2001). Reflective leadership training in practice using theatre as representation. *International Journal of Leadership in Education, 4*(2), 149-169.

Michaud, E. (2004). *The cult of art in Nazi German.* Stanford, CA: Stanford University Press.

Midgley, M. (1984). *Wickedness: A philosophical essay.* London: Routledge & Kegan Paul.

Midgley, M. (2004). *The myths we live by.* London, England: Routledge.

Morgan, G. (1986). *Images of organization.* Newbury Park, CA: SAGE.

Myerson, J., & Ross, P. (2003). *The 21st century office.* London: Laurence King.

Mykkanen, J. (2007). The aestheticisation of politics: The presentation of self in Finnish political advertising. *Halduskultuur, 4,* 84-100.

Palys, T. (1997). *Research decisions: Quantitative and qualitative Perspectives* (2nd ed.). Toronto, ON, Canada: Harcourt Brace.

Pekonen, K. (2007). Aesthetic tension between politics and government. *Halduskultuur, 4,* 70-83.

Ramirez, R. (1991). *The beauty of social organization.* Munich, Germany: Accedo.

Ribbins, P. (2003). Biography and the study of school leader careers: Towards a humanistic approach. In M. Brundrett, N. Burton, & R. Smith (Eds.), *Leadership in education* (pp. 55-73). London: SAGE.

Rorty, R. (1991). *Objectivity, relativism and trust: Philosophical papers* (Vol. 1). New York, NY: Cambridge University Press.

Samier, E. A. (1997). Administrative ritual and ceremony: Social aesthetics, myth and language use in the rituals of everyday organizational life. *Educational Management Administration & Leadership, 25*(4), 417-436.

Samier, E. A. (2005). Toward public administration as a humanities discipline: A humanistic manifesto. *Halduskultuur, 6,* 6-59.

Samier, E. A. (2006a). Imagination, taste, the sublime, and genius in administration: A kantian critique of organizational aesthetics. In E. A. Samier & R. J. Bates (Eds.), *Aesthetic dimensions of educational administration and leadership* (pp. 21-33). Abingdon, Oxfordshire, England: Routledge.

Samier, E. A. (2006b). The aesthetics of charisma: architectural, theatrical, and literary dimensions. In E. A. Samier & R. J. Bates (Eds.), *Aesthetic dimensions of educational administration and leadership* (pp. 161-174). Abingdon, Oxfordshire, England: Routledge.

Samier, E. A. (2007, November). *Administrative secrecy and tradecraft: On the covert side of educational life.* Paper presented at the University Council for Educational Administration annual conference, Alexandria, Virginia.

Samier, E. A. (2008). On the kitschification of educational administration: An aesthetic critique of theory and practice in the field. *International Studies in Educational Administration, 36*(3), 3-18.

Samier, E. A. (2009). The romantic philosophy of mind: The elevation of emotion to the (anti-)heroic ideal. In E. A. Samier & M. Schmidt (Eds.), *Emotional dimensions of educational administration and leadership* (pp. 21-30). London: Routledge.

Samier, E. A. (2012). Pursuing the administrative avant-garde: An aesthetic critique of change in educational Systems. *Critical Studies in Education, 53*(1), 47-58.

Samier, E. A., & Atkins, T. (2009). Psychopathy in educational leadership: The problem of narcissists in positions of power. In E. A. Samier & M. Schmidt (Eds.), *Emotional dimensions of educational administration and leadership* (pp. 212-223). Milton Keyes, England: Routledge.

Samier, E. A., & Bates, R. (Eds.). (2006). *Aesthetic dimensions of educational administration and leadership*. Abingdon, Oxfordshire, England: Routledge.

Samier, E. A., & Lumby, J. (2010). Alienation, servility, and amorality: Relating Gogol's portrayal of bureaupathology to an accountability era, *Educational Management, Administration and Leadership, 38*(3), 360-373.

Sköldberg, K. (2002). *The poetic logic of administration: Style and changes of style in the art of organizing*. London: Routledge.

Smircich, L. (1983). Concepts of culture and organizational analysis, *Administrative Science Quarterly, 28*, 339-358.

Spotts, F. (2003). *Hitler and the power of aesthetics*. Woodstock, NY: Overlook Press.

Starratt, R. (1993). *The drama of leadership*. Abingdon, Oxfordshire, England: Routledge Falmer.

Sternberg, R. (2005). WICS: a model of leadership. *Psychologist-Manager Journal, 8*(1), 29-43.

Strati, A. (1990). Aesthetics and organizational skill. In B. Turner (Ed.), *Organisational symbolism* (pp. 207-222). Berlin, Germany: de Gruyter.

Strati, A. (1992). Aesthetic understanding of organizational life, *Academy of Management Review, 17*(3), 568-581.

Strati, A. (1996). Organizations viewed through the lens of aesthetics. *Organization, 3*(2), 209-218.

Strati, A. (1999). *Organization and aesthetics*. London: SAGE.

Strati, A., & Guillet de Montoux, P. (2002). Introduction, *Human Relations, 55*(7), 755-766.

Townsend, R. (1991). Policy administration as rhetoric: One leader and his arguments. In K. Leithwood & D. Musella (Eds.), *Understanding school system administration: Studies of the contemporary chief education officer* (pp. 42-77). London: Falmer.

Turner, J. (1988). *A theory of social interaction*. Stanford, CA: Stanford University Press.

Van Maanen, J. (1988). *Tales of the field: On writing ethnography*. Chicago, IL: University of Chicago Press.

Waldo, D. (1968). *The novelist on organization and administration: An inquiry into the relationship between the two worlds*. Berkeley, CA: Institute of Governmental Studies.

White, D. (1996). "It's working beautifully!" Philosophical reflections on aesthetics and organization theory. *Organization, 3*(2), 195-208.

White, H. (1987). *The content of the form: Narrative discourse and historical representation*. Baltimore, MD: Johns Hopkins University Press.

Wildavsky, A. (1979). *Speaking truth to power: The art and craft of policy analysis*. Boston, MA: Little, Brown.

Witt, M. (2001). *The search for modern tragedy: Aesthetic fascism in Italy and France*. Ithaca, NY: Cornell University Press.

Wolcott, H. (1995). *The art of fieldwork*. Walnut Creek, CA: AltaMira Press.

Wolfe, H. (1924). Some public servants in fiction. *Public Administration, 2*, 39-57.

Author Contact Information: **Eugenie A. Samier**, Faculty of Education, The British University in Dubai, Dubai, United Arab Emirates. Phone: 971.(0)55.96.44.295. E-mail: Eugenie.samier@buid.ac.ae

CHAPTER 84

Bourdieu's Theory of Misconnaissance or Misrecognition by Educational Leaders

Cheryl L. Bolton
Staffordshire University

Misrecognition is a concept devised by influential philosopher and sociologist Pierre Bourdieu (1930-2002). In introducing the notion of misrecognition and of ways of which it might be manifested, it is important to note that Bourdieu developed a number of differing concepts that were all interconnected to form his sociological perspectives. He created his own vocabulary of terms in order to distinguish these concepts but did not necessarily intend them to be used in isolation as each had an impact on the others. Some of these concepts will be briefly outlined in this chapter but only as they relate to misrecognition.

Misrecognition or *meconnaissance* refers to a "denial of the economic and political interests present in a set of practices" (Swartz, 1997, p. 89). This stems from what Bourdieu termed as symbolic power which in effect is a legitimizing power in that it legitimizes the existing power and economic relations in such a way that these structures are accepted by both the dominant and dominated parties alike. Misrecognition assists in this process as it disguises the fact that all actions have an underlying element of self-interest even though they may be enacted in such a way as to appear disinterested, or that they are not being pursued with intent. In this way it contributes to maintaining and reproducing the ongoing nature of the existing social structures with their inherent distinctions and hierarchies.

Bourdieu (2008) criticizes some agents who provide explanations of their own practice which "conceals, even from their own eyes, the true nature of their practical mastery, that is, that is *learned ignorance*, a mode of practical knowledge not comprising knowledge of its own principles" (p. 19). The result is that the agents as speakers mislead themselves and this is a form of misrecognition. "Such agents fail to be sufficiently critical of their own stake in pursuing goals within their power and control" (Cicourel, 1993, p. 102). When those agents with power employ it on a day-to-day basis, it "is seldom exercised as overt physical force; instead, it is transmuted into a symbolic form, and thereby endowed with a kind of legitimacy that it would not otherwise have" (Thompson, 1991, p. 23). Symbolic power is thus legitimated and even in the eyes of those who are least likely to benefit from its application see it as legitimate and "fail to see that ... [it] ... is, after all, an arbitrary social construction which serves the interests of some groups more than others" (Thompson, 1991, p. 23).

The theory of misrecognition is part of Bourdieu's larger sociological perspective regarding how groups and special interests maintain themselves over periods of time. Bourdieu's lens includes the concept of *habitus* by which he meant "a property of social agents (whether individuals, groups or institutions) that comprise a 'structured and structuring structure'" (Maton, 2009, p. 51). It also refers to "a way in which individuals 'become themselves'—develop attitudes and dispositions—and, on the other hand, the ways in which those

The Handbook of Educational Theories, pp. 953–957

individuals engage in practices" (Webb, Schirato, & Danaher (2002, p. xii).

Swartz (1997) indicates that "Bourdieu's approach to understanding the relationship between actors and structures builds on one key idea: that objective structures have subjective consequences is not incompatible with the view that the social world is constructed by individual actors" (p. 97). Swartz (1997) also notes that "Habitus tends to shape individual actions so that existing opportunity structures are perpetuated" (p. 103). In the context of this paper habitus refers to the ways in which agency and institutional authors think about themselves and their work.

Bourdieu also believed that, "All activities (including the production of knowledge) are informed by the notion of self-interest to some extent and can be contextualized with regard to the various fields in which those activities take place, and the agent's place within that field" (Webb, Schirato and Danaher 2002, p. 12).

The notion of *field* is related to that of habitus. A *field* is a social space comprised of various agents who vie for influence. They are competitive places where actors and groups compete for power by composing and imposing "their meaning on language'" (Webb, Schirato, & Danaher, 2002, p. 13). Thus, it would be a mistake to conclude that simply because people may share a common field that they will also share common interests or hold the same levels of power and influence. Neither are fields isolated but will exert influence on each other.

The means by which interests are organized and enacted are through what Bourdieu termed *pedagogic authority* which effectively is the face of a pedagogic action or the legitimization of the action. This pedagogic action is in turn achieved via pedagogic work meaning the training which implements the pedagogic action via for example, curriculum and teaching. "The arbitrary power which makes imposition possible is never seen in its full truth" (Bourdieu & Passeron, 2000, p. 11). This imposition constitutes a form of *symbolic violence* because it involves the definition of the linguistic expressions as symbols. Such symbols comprise *the cultural arbitrary.* For purposes of this analyses Bourdieu and Passeron, (2000) state:

> In any given social formation, the agencies which objectively lay claim to the legitimate exercise of a power of symbolic imposition and, in so doing, tend to claim the monopoly on legitimacy, necessarily enter into relations of competition, i.e, power relations and symbolic relations whose structure expresses in its own logic the state of the balance of power between the groups or classes. (p. 18)

Bourdieu and Passeron (2000) indicate that competition "sociologically necessary because legitimacy is indivisible: there is no agency to legitimate the legitimacy-giving agencies because claims to legitimacy derive their relative strength ... from the strength of the groups or classes whose material and symbolic interests they directly or indirectly express" (p. 18).

An Applied Example of Misrecognition

For the purposes of this chapter examples of misrecognition have been given from official government or agency documents concerning the teaching cadre in the English further education (FE) system. It should not be assumed that these documents have been singled out as being unique or even unusual examples of misrecognition, only that they provide an illustration of it. The Bourdieusian lens assumes that the production of such documents were: (a) expressions of self-interest of the agency or institution in the larger field to expand its influence, power and legitimacy; (b) misrecognition in which agents and/or agencies do not question their own presuppositions or assumptions assuming them to be "the natural order of things" (Webb, Schirato, & Danaher, 2002, p. 25). These are reflective of the status quo in any given social field. In the words of Bourdieu and Passeron (2000):

> In any given social formation, legitimate culture, i.e., the culture endowed with the dominant legitimacy, is nothing other than the dominant cultural arbitrary insofar as it is misrecognized in its objective truth as a cultural arbitrary and as the dominant cultural arbitrary. (p. 23)

The documents referred to illustrate expressions of establishing legitimacy in the English further education field. Legitimacy refers to the bestowal of lawfulness and authenticity to the construction and use of arbitrary social power to define an agent or agency in its own self-interests as best for everyone by concealing its arbitrariness as objective rather than subjective and by hiding or failing to recognise those self-interests as arbitrary. It is the function of educational institutions to confer legitimacy on the use of certain forms of cultural and social capital, and thus to establish the embodied forms of cultural capital contained in them as a "legitimating discourse which 'under cover of formal equality—between the qualifications people obtain and the cultural capital they have inherited—in other words, through the legitimacy it confers on the transmission of this form of heritage'" (Bourdieu, 2008, p. 19). The use of specific language and the symbolism which it contains by "the group which authorizes and invests it with authority" (p. 21) establishes "the dividing line between the thinkable and the unthinkable" (Bourdieu, 2008, p. 21) and thereby maintains its own position in the larger social order.

These documents present a range of purposes that include the definition of specific terms, of specifying institutional direction, announcing planned and proposed changes and establishing the rationale for all sorts of actual or desired alterations. They serve to reinforce the position of the various agencies and institutions peculiar to FE and to advance their leverage and legitimacy within the FE field. Utilizing this Bourdieusian lens some of the documents do indeed appear as undisguised attempts to increase the importance of the issuing agents to expand their legitimacy and influence. The following are illustrative examples taken from these documents.

Example #1

This example draws on *"Further Education: Raising Skills, Improving Life Chances"* (Department for Education and Skills, 2006). This document sets out the government drivers for reforming further education. It stipulates two urgent requirements as being first, the transformation of the life chances of young people and second, a transformation of the skills of the workforce. It states that:

> We will develop a new national strategy for raising the quality of teaching and learning in further education, with robust intervention to tackle failing and mediocre provision, combined with more autonomy for the excellent. We will invest more in recruiting and training the best staff, with a stronger flow of business expertise coming into the sector and more college staff helped to gain workplace experience. (p. 2)

The language suggests a collaborative approach by using the term "we." However, the power for "robust intervention" is not collaborative. Neither is the definition of "excellent," "best," "mediocre," or "failing" collaborative. Rather they imply one set of values being imposed on the other agents/actors in the field. The power to discipline is the power to deal with real and potential rivals and to enhance the status of the issuing agency and advance its language as the most legitimate. This is a form of misrecognition because the use of "we" hides the actual unilateral actions to be taken.

Example #2

This example is taken from a government Cabinet Office report titled *Excellence and Fairness (Cabinet Office, 2008).* While this report does not specifically refer to the FE system, it is concerned with the public sector as a whole and as such incorporates FE. It defines a "new professionalism" as "maintaining high standards of service and performance, and strengthening user choices and voice, but at the same time providing space for the best professionals to manage and run their own services" (p. 17). Further statements from this report include:

> Professionals should no longer simply be accountable to their managers or to government. Nor should services return to a time in which autonomous professionals were essentially accountable to themselves. (p. 15)

> In addition to greater citizen empowerment, we must unleash a new professionalism in our public services. We know that real excellence depends upon liberating the imagination, creativity and commitment of the public service workforce. (p. 4)

There are several apparent contradictions contained in these quotations from the *Cabinet Office* (2008). For instance, how can something be unleashed when it is already confined within a given social structure and such strict controls? Similarly, what is meant by liberation? If accountability is for everyone and dependent on the existing role structure, how can an entire structure be liberated? The structure defines the system itself. When roles are relational, how can one role be accountable without the others? It is difficult to view these apparent reforms as an example of true reform, but more as examples of misrecognition where the rhetoric of change is employed to retain the present "structured structure."

Example #3

This example comes from an earlier government report, namely *Success for All: Reforming Further Education and Training—Our Vision for the Future* (Department for Education and Skills, 2002). This was an important document in setting targets for the training of teachers working within the FE sector and of setting the required qualification framework.

> The reforms will lead to a new relationship between the Learning and Skills Council and providers based on partnership and trust, underpinned by clear accountability. This change will be a shared challenge. It will require greater openness and a close collaborative working relationship. The Learning and Skills Council will be discussing with key partners, including the representative bodies of its providers, how this new relationship can be achieved together. (pp. 13-14)

Under a Bourdieusian lens, the statement appears to recognize that there are other agents in this social space by referencing "key partners," but it does so in a collaborative way as if assuming all agents share common interests and goals. However, since any professional field is a social space containing various agents and bodies competing for leverage and legitimacy, calls for "clear accountability" by one agent in such a field, especially a government agent, is not an invitation but a command. The definitions of linguistic terms contained in this document represents an example of Bourdieu's "cultural arbitrary" being imposed and is also an example of "symbolic violence."

The statements analyzed through the Bourdieusian lens do indeed reveal many of his key premises regarding pedagogic authority and pedagogic work derived from that authority. The statements are deeply reflective of the current social and economic order. No change advocated by the agencies or agents issuing the reviewed documents will disestablish or undermine that agent's or agency's place within their field. Nearly all will be enhanced and advanced if the agenda advocated is implemented. While the relative positions of the agents or agencies within the overall structure may be altered if the subordinate actors or agents accept the reforms advocated, the overall field will still contain the fundamental structure in which the actors or agents are embedded. The concept of social justice so often mentioned in these documents must therefore "fit into" the existing socioeconomic field and therefore cannot mean or signify any fundamental changes of power within it. If there is a change in the power relations it will flow to the agency or agent issuing the document. The documents do reveal that the actions and definitions of them will be "best" for everyone if followed. By employing collaborative words and linking the proposed actions to "fairness" and "social justice" the arbitrariness of the proposed actions are hidden. This is a form of misrecognition.

CRITIQUES OF THE THEORY

Because misrecognition, according to Bourdieu, "is a legitimating power that elicits the consent of *both* the dominant and the dominated" (Swartz, 1997, p. 89), critiques of the theory turn on how a person within a field comes to recognize that he/she misrecognizes his/her position within it. LiPuma (1993) notes that "apprehending another's position turns on one's own position and position taking in that field" (p. 23). Exactly how a person would be able to step outside this relational field is never really articulated by Bourdieu. Is misrecognition simply a quest for more status within a competing field, or is a distinct and nonrelational awareness outside of a field? Another sticky issue is that of the exercise of symbolic power which according to Bourdieu is often misrecognized. But what exactly is misrecognized? Is it the application of symbolic power or is it the fact that such power is often embedded in the relations within a social structure. LiPuma (1993) observes, "What is unspecified is why symbols should be able to generate such power" (p. 20).

There are an emerging series of empirical studies in many nations testing Bourdieu's ideas regarding symbolic power. For example, Hjelbrekke and Korsnes (2009) examined data from 1,710 persons taking a leadership survey in Norway who occupied formal, leading positions in ten central areas in that country and found that there were configurations of elite positions which could be objectified "in terms of a field power" (p. 36). While they did not test forms of misrecognition, the establishment of relational fields of power was an important step in validating Bourdieu's platform premises.

Similarly Bourdieu's work in education, specifically his concepts regarding cultural and social capital in Cyprus and Greece impact parental educational and occupational choices. Vryonides (2009) found that "different forms of capital (material and nonmonetary) acquire specific value within particular social contexts and fields and have the potential to produce substantially different profits for their owners" (p. 140). Specifically, middle class parents are able to use forms of social and cultural capital to advance their interests over those in lower classes because their interests "escape observation and control, obscured perhaps by their complexity, they effectively transmit and reproduce power and privilege" (p. 140). This is a form of misrecognition.

Bourdieu's theory of misrecognition is an important feature of his overall social analysis as to why dominant groups remain dominant in every culture. It takes the assent of the dominated as well as the will of the group in power to continue their power. However, the form of domination must remain hidden behind forms of symbolic power to be effective.

REFERENCES

Bourdieu, P. (2008). *Outline of a theory of practice* (R. Nice, Trans.). Cambridge, England: Cambridge University Press.

Bourdieu, P., & Passeron, J. C. (2000). *Reproduction in education, society and culture* (2nd ed., R. Nice, Trans.). London, England: SAGE.

Cabinet Office. (2008). *Excellence and fairness: achieving world class public services.* London, England: Author.

Cicourel, A. (1993). *Aspects of structural and processual theories of knowledge.* In C. Calhoun, E. LiPuma, & M. Postone (Eds.) *Bourdieu: Critical perspectives* (pp. 89-115). Chicago, IL: University of Chicago Press.

Department for Education and Skills. (2002). *Success for all: Reforming further education and training: Our vision for the future.* London, England: Author.

Department for Education and Skills. (2006). *Further education: Raising skills, improving life chances.* London, England: Author.

Hjellbrekke, J., & Korsnes, O. (2009). Quantifying the field of power in Norway. In K. Robson & C. Sanders (Eds.), . *Quantifying theory: Pierre Bourdieu* (pp. 31-46). New York, NY: Springer.

LiPuma, E. (1993). Culture and the concept of culture in a theory of practice. In C. Calhoun, E. LiPuma, & M. Postone

(Eds.), *Culture in a theory of practice* (pp. 14-34). Chicago, IL: University of Chicago Press.

Maton, K. (2009) *Habitus*. In M. Grenfell (Ed.), *Pierre Bourdieu: Key concepts* (pp. 49-66). Durham, England: Acumen.

Swartz, D. (1997) *Culture & power: The sociology of Pierre Bourdieu*, Chicago, IL: University of Chicago Press.

Thompson, J. B. (1991). Introduction. In P. Bourdieu (Ed.), *Language and symbolic power.* Cambridge, MA: Harvard University Press.

Vryonides, M. (2009). Applying Bourdieu's concepts of social and cultural capital in educational research in Greece and Cyprus. In K. Robson & C. Sanders (Eds.), *Quantifying theory: Pierre Bourdieu* (pp. 129-140). New York, NY: Springer.

Webb, J., Schirato, T., & Danaher, G. (2002). *Understanding Bourdieu.* London, England: SAGE.

Author Contact Information: Cheryl L. Bolton, Institute of Education Policy Review, Staffordshire University, Stoke-on-Trent, United Kingdom, ST4 2DF. Telephone: 011-44-178-229-4413. E-mail: c.bolton@staffs.ac.uk

CHAPTER 85

Mentoring Theories for Educational Practitioners

Carol A. Mullen
The University of North Carolina at Greensboro

Alternative mentoring is a countercultural theory and practice. While focus is on alternative mentoring theories herein, traditional mentoring theories are included because of the dominant role they assume in educational discourse. Mentoring change theorist Darwin (2000) believed this imbalance can be redressed by perpetuating awareness of alternative mentoring for the purpose of changing educational relationships and cultures. Alternative mentoring theories include collaborative mentoring or comentoring, mosaic mentoring, multilevel comentoring, and synergistic leadership. Traditional mentoring theories are exemplified by technical (or functionalist) mentoring in such pervasive forms as apprenticeships and systems thinking. As will be seen, while alternative and traditional mentoring theories can be treated separately, they blur and even overlap. The frame of reference for this discussion is public schooling and education.

General Description of Mentoring Theories

Mentoring is construed as a personal relationship, an educational process, and a systemic reform strategy that builds the capacity of people and organizations across different educational contexts (Mullen, 2009). This form of educational learning occurs on a voluntary basis, connecting people with the values, attitudes, understandings, and skills that characterize educational practice as learning. The idea is that mentoring has a ripple effect where mentors not only help their mentees over the long haul but also commit to having a *multiplying investment* in the lives of others (Moerer-Urdahl & Creswell, 2004).

Traditional mentoring theory posits that mentoring is a learning activity passed down from one generation to another. Educators carry out this work of development on a one-to-one basis in what is known as dyads. Mentors who are veteran teachers and school principals, for example, shoulder the work of nurturing, advising, befriending, and instructing, and they serve as advocates, advisors, and promoters. In this picture, seasoned school practitioners shape how interns, beginning teachers, and other novices learn through initial and ongoing professional development (Portner, 2002).

From a broad perspective, alternative and traditional theories alike have relevance to the mentoring of education practitioners, whether teachers or administrators, preservice or inservice, and the mentoring they in turn do. Synergistic leadership (defined later) can be adapted to this broader framework of mentoring to communicate the idea that each theory and subtheory is itself a philosophical framework for describing interactions and dynamics, leadership behaviors, external and internal forces, organizational structure, and cultural change. Each of the alternative models identified (e.g., comentoring) reflects an articulated theory unto itself that overlaps in the fundamental principles espoused. The spectrum of traditional and alternative theories of mentoring is influential in the interpersonal areas of learning, socialization, and professional development, and in the organizational functions of leadership, management, and preparation. Adult learning principles inform these theories and models (Hansman, 2003), as do systems thinking (Lick, 1999) and instrumental thinking (Cain, 2007).

The Handbook of Educational Theories, pp. 959–968

Historical Roots of Mentoring and Conventions

Traditional mentoring theories are technical/functionalist in form and they are fostered by apprenticeship learning and systems thinking. The root of mentor is *men*, which means to counsel, and protégé (currently *mentee*) refers to the need for mentors to protect. Apprenticeship in the Middle Ages occurred through the trades with master tradesmen that mostly benefitted males in such occupations as tailors. Craft guilds and town governments formed, replacing the older apprenticeship model. In modern times, apprenticeships continue as a required career step, especially in Germany. Alternative expressions of the traditional apprenticeship include the whole-community apprenticeship endeavor undertaken in Britain for preservice teachers specializing in music (Cain, 2007).

The historical and originating antecedents of mentoring set the stage for the countercultural thrust of alternative conceptions. Mentoring theory has its roots in a range of disciplines, primarily social psychology, learning theory, adult theory, organizational development, and systems thinking. Mentorship historically involves training youth or adults in skills building and knowledge acquisition, both inside and outside education (Merriam, 1983). Professionals in schools, universities, and other organizations enact *technical mentoring*—a needs-based, short-term solution involving the transfer of know-how to apprentices within advising and training contexts (Darwin, 2000; Mullen, 2005). Examples within the academic disciplines and professional domains include scientific management, technical efficiency, bureaucratic leadership, and skills-based learning—what English (2003) quipped "management-speak." An example might be David Kolb's theory of experiential learning that some mentoring researchers have adapted as an instrumental framework to characterize the learning style of mentors and mentees (see, e.g., Cain, 2007). Thus, mentoring theories are not just informed by but enveloped within developmental theories that make assumptions about how people learn.

Mentoring gets confused with peer coaching and they are unfortunately becoming blurred and even viewed as interchangeable. Mentoring, like *peer coaching*, is a nonjudgmental and nonevaluative approach to professional development—some theorists think of peer coaching as a type of mentoring whereas others see the exact reverse—mentoring as a type of coaching. Since it is amenable to quick results, skills development, and instrumental learning, peer coaching has become more popular than mentoring (Becker, 2010). This treatment of professional learning has a managerial quality—it is framed by short-term goals and a one-way emphasis on the coach (e.g., veteran teacher) giving feedback to the coachee (e.g., preservice teacher) (Megginson & Clutterbuck, 2005). Observations of performance are combined with practical work, such as lesson development. Coaching has been recently formulated as more than a structured apprenticeship guided by best practices of learning—that is, as a reform strategy that socializes newcomers into the profession (Cox, Bachkirova, & Clutterbuck, 2010). English's (2003) critique of *best practice* draws attention to the suspicious way this concept is used to package knowledge and in such reified forms as educational standards. Mentoring theorists tend to prefer the notion of promising practice over best practice.

As another distinguishing point of reference, mentoring and induction, while also treated as interchangeable concepts, vary in their relationship as well. Some researchers (e.g., Wong, 2004) see mentoring (and coaching) as elements of induction theories and components of induction programs. Along these lines, site-based induction programs deemed effective incorporate the mentoring of new teachers in a "highly organized and comprehensive staff development process" for 2 to 5 years (Wong, p. 107). Overall, induction, like coaching, is a one-way learning process that focuses on the mastery of content and on the expected outcomes of the coachee's development (Portner, 2002).

Mentoring, however, is more theory-steeped than coaching and induction. Whether traditional or progressive in form, the relationship is longer term and sustained, and the learning relationship intrinsically focused, with feedback geared toward self-learning. In its alternative forms, mentoring is a developmental theory that promotes growth of the mentee as a whole person or transformation of a community; the growth patterns are not unidirectional or limited to one-way development in that mentees and mentors alike are situated as learner and comentor, and sometimes as change agent.

Alternative Mentoring Theories

Alternative mentoring theories are steeped in a critique of traditional mentoring relationships as developmentally limited and noninclusive of diverse and female populations. Traditional mentoring theories make assumptions about learning, about males learning from other males, and about the privilege and success of White males. Mentoring that embeds a biased class structure facilitates for some people only the psychosocial and career benefits of mentoring (Darwin, 2000; Mullen, 2005). Mentoring feminists have critiqued the implicit tenets of this age-old theory of learning to expose connotations of paternalism, dependency, privilege, and exclusion in learning relationships. Alternative theories thus present a break away mindset from defunct hierarchical systems, relationship power imbalances, and exploitative arrangements involving vulnerable individuals and groups.

Democratic theories have emerged out of adult learning and feminist epistemologies that wrestle with new worldviews which promote radical humanist conceptions of relationships and systems. These epistemologies underscore (a) the need for collaborative and cross-cultural learning partnerships that are mutual and egalitarian and less role-defined and (b) the necessity for learning organizations to shed outdated systems in favor of interdependence, inclusiveness, and openness at all institutional levels (Hansman, 2003; Johnson-Bailey & Cervero, 2004).

Contrasting with functionist mentoring approaches, alternative mentoring is nonauthoritative and progressive. Called for is a vision of a world in which organizing principles are adopted that foster holistic development, cultural engagement, and institutional change. Mentoring as an equalizing force requires a commitment to ethical agendas centered on power, virtue, and circumstance in all projects (Easterly, 2008; Hansman, 2003). Intentional mentors promote the dynamics of critical care, and they foster satisfying but challenging learning environments through promising practices of learning (Galbraith, 2003). Alternative learning contexts include cohort learning, cross-cultural mentoring, inquiry/writing groups, learning communities, mentor-based programs, peer coaching, professional activism, staff development, and e-mentoring (Mullen, 2005). Mentors use such conduits to remedy the drawbacks of archaic notions of the educational relationship, support quality in student learning and success, confront biases and assumptions, and vigorously problem solve within changing organizations.

Ideologies of alternative mentoring include collaboration, comentorship, democratic learning, and shared leadership. Democratic learning can be a formal or an informal experience of mentoring wherein the team helps all members develop the desired knowledge and/or skills toward a common vision. Members participate in democratic forms of learning through team building, setting such goals as identifying and resolving conflict. Shared leadership and collaborative decision making are facilitated by a team that functions democratically or by a leader who distributes power and authority (Mullen, 2005).

Institutional leaders who mentor in nontraditional ways strive to make a difference and concurrently learn from others (e.g., comentorship). They mentor beyond the demands of their position, seeking to enhance the education of mentees outside the supervisory or advisory context. In fact, psychologists describe mentorship as a superordinate function *above and beyond* teaching and instruction. (Pivotal studies from the 1980s and 1990s are summarized in Clark, Harden, & Johnson, 2000.) Alternative mentors take risks, experiment with ideas, and exert influence in guiding others. They also confront forces and dynamics within workplaces that can adversely affect mentees and programs. Mentors exhibit transparency in their performance feedback and they seek self-improvement and understanding of how their ideologies, values, and allegiances influence people and contexts. Alternative mentors who are social justice advocates commit to changing archaic structures and policies that keep systems closed off from disenfranchised groups (Darwin, 2000). Such mentors and mentoring researchers have proactively integrated diversity in what they envision as transformative cultural work (Johnson-Bailey & Cervero, 2004; Mullen & Tuten, 2010).

Specific Alternative Mentoring Theories

Next, several influential alternative mentoring theories are briefly described.

Collaborative Mentoring Theory

Also known as relationship comentoring, collaborative mentoring is a proactive force that unites individuals or groups in a reciprocal, mutual exchange and dynamic context for learning. This theory is founded upon feminist postmodern values that are aligned with a transcendence of status and power differences and diversity that incorporates women and minorities in networks (Bona, Rinehart, & Volbrecht, 1995). A goal is to mobilize social equality among individuals of various statuses and ability levels, enabling productive synergy and solidarity (Mullen, 2000).

Collaborative mentoring is a key element in the creation of think tanks, such as mentoring mosaics and cross-cultural mentorships, propelled by vision, commitment, discipline, and synergy (Davis, 2008; Easterly, 2008; Johnson-Bailey & Cervero, 2002). The comentoring theory is founded within dyadic mentoring relationships and mentoring mosaics and used as a model for engaging adult learners. Comentors model power sharing, turn taking, coleading, dialogue, constructive feedback, collegiality, transparency, and authenticity in learning. As reciprocal learners, mentors may function as adult educators and mentees as adult learners within the mentoring dyad or group (Cohen, 2002; Mullen, 2005). Because comentors who make a difference have deep personal cultural influence, they have outward impact on their institutions.

Mentoring Mosaic Theory

A significant alternative conception of mentoring is Kram's (1985/1988) relationship constellation, also known as a mentoring mosaic (Tharp & Gallimore, 1995/1988). Even though the concept of network mentoring was articulated more than 25 years ago, it is only more recently impacting educational studies. The mentoring mosaic theory posits that peer interaction is based on shared interests and that members tap each others' strengths and qualities. Members who are primary mentors (e.g., instructional leaders) and secondary mentors interchange roles as mentors and mentees, sponsoring the learning of all through a synergistic, flexible structure. This kind of network is indispensable for cultivating peer mentors, compensating for the dissatisfactions of traditional mentoring, and facilitating team projects (Mullen, 2005). Indeed, if mentoring is defined more as a learning process than an activity performed by an individual, then teams that extend to professional (and virtual) learning communities can simultaneously engage in nurturing, advising, befriending, and instructing. Within such networks, people serve as subject specialists, counselors, advocates, and so forth. The camaraderie, interdependence, identity formation, and ownership that this model supports places value on *how* learning and mastery are achieved, not just what is learned (Galbraith, 2003).

Multilevel Comentoring Theory

Multilevel comentoring theory underscores the importance of facilitating comentoring at the various levels of an organization via school-based focus teams, study groups, and leadership (Lick, 1999, 2000). The idea is that serious research and inquiry aimed at reform initiates a mentoring process that is not limited to classrooms or certain groups. The belief is that entire social cultural systems must be deliberately reshaped and teacher resistance to change transformed so that all students can succeed.

This theory presents a view of collaborative mentoring as a key to building a climate of interdependence, commitment, and empowerment, as well as participative leadership and involvement. Principals, teachers, and staff decide what changes are necessary and they spearhead and monitor them with the goal of creating "synergistic comentoring" that activates change vertically and horizonally. Systems thinking, change management, instrumental methods, and comentoring techniques are all embedded functions. Entire systems are the target of change, meaning that the reforms can be sponsored or initiated by outsiders (e.g., school boards). Ownership of the change process is accentuated through stakeholder buy-in and planned transitions. Design scripts adapted from change management theorists, classically Peter Senge, guide this mentoring theory.

Synergistic Leadership Theory

Synergistic leadership theory, while not identified as a type of mentoring theory *per se*, can be interpreted as such—it offers a holistic alternative to traditional mentoring. This theory is framed around feminist, postmodern interpretations of public schooling and administrator preparation for which male-based theories do not accommodate feminine-aligned values and approaches, such as collaborative types of relationships and diversity in community building (Ardovini, Trautman, Brown, & Irby, 2010; Irby, Brown, Duffy, & Trautman, 2002). Traditional leadership theories, Irby et al. (2002) argue, do not even recognize the changing reality that most individuals in university-based leadership preparation programs are female (and increasingly culturally diverse). The synergistic leadership theory presents a proactive process for leading change through the integration of four factors that leaders should strive to incorporate in a dynamic way: "leadership behavior, organizational structure, external forces, and attitudes, beliefs, and values" (Irby et al., p. 312; see also Ardovini et al., 2010). Arguably, as a type of alternative mentoring theory, synergistic leadership enhances the relevancy of collaborative and multilevel mentoring through an overarching but situated view of "the feminist organization." In this worldview, the politically engaged workplace is one in which leadership, decision making, and power are shared experiences for all cultures.

Validation and Generalizability of Mentoring Theory

New theories require validation and at least some degree of generalizability in order to be taken seriously. What follows are some results for the alternative theories already presented. In addition, particular studies exemplifying particular theories are included.

Collaborative Mentoring Results

The collaborative mentoring theory has been validated through case studies ranging from schools to universities to partnerships, and within educational leadership and teacher education programs (Cannon, 2003; Mullen & Lick, 1999; Saltiel, 1998). Researchers have shown collaborative mentoring to be a vital form of professional partnership in the context of professors and teachers being paired within codirectional mentoring processes (Lick, 2000; Mullen, 2000). Action research study of classrooms and schools has been mutually conducted, and mentoring duties and processes equally shared. For example, in Florida, a peer assessment of a school–university team's shared inquiry into purposeful collaboration as the Partnership Support Group concluded that the collective experience had mostly proven successful. Areas of strength included shared leadership, appreciative understanding, and structured inquiry; areas needing further support and development were conflicting responsibilities, uneven commitment, and variation in writing skill (Mullen, 1999). Research on collaborative mentoring needs to become sustained as well as multidisciplinary and international.

In a school in France, an intern and cooperating teacher participated in a learning relationship that was designed to bring collaborative mentoring to life. Researchers, Chaliès, Bertone, Flavier, and Durand (2008), validated the collaborative mentoring model based on their review of a sequence of comentoring that involved copreparation, coteaching, and coevaluation. The preservice teacher was able to learn through teaching incidents that were analyzed vis-a-vis her learning partnership, in turn deepening her repertoire for recognizing and dealing with classroom challenges. The cooperating teacher shared insights into situations involving students' difficulties in learning, which in turn contributed to the intern's deeper understanding of how students learn. Contrasting the learning gains of this intern with research based on traditional preservice programs, the researchers concluded that she had learned important pedagogical content about student learning that would not otherwise have been modeled or internalized.

Mentoring Mosaic Results

Group approaches to comentoring have proven indispensible for structuring activity settings that enable organizations to change and practitioners to be professionally prepared (Tharp & Gallimore, 1995/1988). Prospective and practicing teachers, leaders, and staff have participated in sociocultural learning environments designed to foster and sustain mentoring mosaics. Tharp and Gallimore's mentoring mosaic theory was founded upon John Dewey's notion of activity settings as crucial for students' experiential growth and Lev Vygotsky's social-psychological theories of learning and instruction.

The mosaic learning innovation had discernible impact: In a decade-long intervention that ended in 1983 and that spanned three U.S. states, 3,000 students, representing many diverse cultures and languages, participated in the Kamehameha Early Education Project. The mosaic innovation, an interdisciplinary public school literacy program, fostered the opportunity for teachers to create and study meaningful contexts that drive instruction. Teacher–student instructional conversation and role modeling assisted at-risk ethnic children (e.g., native Hawaiians) with new learning. The activity setting contained independent stations (e.g., listening-skills center) designed to harness peer learning among young apprentices. Results indicate that cognitive thought and language development dramatically improved as students took part in structured learning activities with teachers and peers. Also, the classroom teachers learned how to better engage student learning through the "assisted performance" they received.

The Kamehameha Early Education Project program inspired school efforts with other marginalized ethnic groups, including Latino Americans in Los Angeles and Native Americans in Arizona (Tharp & Gallimore, 1995/1988) and a school project in Israel (Almog & Hertz-Lazarowitz, 1999).

In the Israeli context, a peer learning community program was designed to empower teachers to become change agents aided by advanced technologies and interdisciplinary curricula. For this sociocultural learning activity that occurred for 12 group sessions, the participants developed collaborative working teams and broke past their individual isolation. They then experimented with transferring the new cognitive learning and mentoring skills to their own classrooms and schools (Almog & Hertz-Lazarowitz, 1999).

Mentoring needs, abilities, and resources are essential to sociocultural mentoring activity. These components, most effective when integrated, have been used to identify aspects of mentoring that best nurture mentees at a particular time. For example, the issue of mentor pairing with respect to similarities in gender, ethnicity, age, and discipline (Wilson, Pereira, & Valentine, 2002) has diminished when groups have been configured to reflect diversity. Some ethnic minority students may feel that ethnic mentors would be ideal but have nonetheless drawn strength from diversified activity settings and peer mentors. Female students, who are thought to generally prefer female mentors because of the perceived opening for personal contact (Wilson et al., 2002), have made learning and social gains from mixed-gender groups led by male mentors. Peer mentoring within mosaics has promoted positive synergy, the exchanging of ideas and experience, critical self-awareness, knowledge about international work, and enhanced social skills and leadership capacity (Bona et al., 1995; Kram & Higgins, 2008; Mullen & Tuten, 2010).

Proliferating examples of the mosaic mentoring model are an outgrowth of critical democratic frameworks. Dynamic mentoring mosaics have enabled culturally ethnic students, female students, and immigrant students to generate new ways of working, creating cultures of collaboration to do so. A longitudinal example is that of the higher education mosaic self-named Writers in Training. Studied for the 7 years it existed, this informal mentoring cohort brought together an ethnically diverse group of female and male school practitioners to undertake the dissertation process as a group. The cohort sponsored critical thinking, quality writing, and peer mentoring; it was continually adapted to build strength, confront challenges, and diversity its membership. Data were analyzed through audiotaped conversations with 20 members from the group sessions and with individual interviewees. It was found that members had developed confidence about applying inquiry-based ways of thinking to their leadership topics, becoming scholar practitioners, and experiencing social belonging (Mullen & Tuten, 2010).

Multilevel Comentoring Results

Multilevel comentoring outcomes have resulted from whole-faculty study group interventions. This site-based model is a type of professional learning community that has been implemented in hundreds of public schools across North America (Clauset, Lick, & Murphy, 2008). The school practitioners involved have studied relevant research and teaching strategies for making decisions on how to best impact student achievement. Systems-level study groups are built upon teacher participation in learning communities and they manifest in such forms as multiage teams, teacher-led, student learning communities, faculty study groups, learning teams, grade-level teams, and specialist teams (e.g., reading).

Curricular innovations and assessments as well as standards-driven test results provide the focus of teacher study groups. Areas of work pursued within them include identifying student needs based on data results, addressing deficiencies in learning, and generating pedagogical solutions (Clauset et al., 2008; Hutinger & Mullen, 2007). Richardson (2007) reported that teacher teams in a secondary school in Michigan identified outcomes for courses, created common assessments, and monitored student progress. Curricular outcomes were calculated by observing the impact of instructional strategies on student learning. Teacher groups have introduced change by integrating effective practices into school programs to positively affect student learning.

Other researchers who have studied effective practices in teacher professional development affirmed that participation in faculty study groups affords teachers an opportunity to focus on student needs and school improvement goals in a supportive context (Tallerico, 2005). Analysis of student data has, for example, led to the teaching of higher order thinking skills. Administrators, teachers, and counselors have all committed to principles that guide study groups: students come first, everyone participates, leadership is shared, responsibility is equal, and work is public (Clauset et al., 2008).

An elementary school site in Florida undergoing mandated whole-school mentoring change served as a case study. It was found that at the completion of the school year more than 90% of teachers (61 in total) involved in the study group structure felt confident about assisting their colleagues in analyzing student data and improving instruction (Hutinger & Mullen, 2007). Additionally, the majority reported, through an original survey instrument—focused on the teachers' perceptions and knowledge of study groups and anticipated advantages and disadvantages of faculty involvement—that the group process benefited their professional development. Although the teachers reported positive outcomes overall, their initial feedback suggested emotional variance and varying degrees of receptivity due to the perceived resistance on the part of some colleagues and insufficient time to complete other tasks. Such cautionary messages qualify the assertion that multilevel mentoring interventions can be wholly positive.

Synergistic Leadership Results

Studies of synergistic leadership have produced encouraging results. Interaction has proven positive among the crucial factors of "leadership behaviour, organizational structures, external forces, and values, beliefs, and attitudes" (e.g., Schlosberg, Irby, Brown, & Yang, 2010, part 2, p. 12; also, Irby et al., 2002; Trautman, 2000). Promoting understanding of non-American cultures, disenfranchised populations, and feminine leadership is an intentional outcome of this model. For example, a case study methodology was used to develop understanding of a private school in an impoverished part of Mexico. Its leaders were committed to serving highly at-risk student populations as a fundamental part of their social justice mission (Schlosberg, et al.). Two school leaders, school staff, and community members participated through such means as interviews, focus groups, and observation. Results underscored the importance for leaders in balancing the four leadership factors as they facilitate change that is holistic and inclusive. On a practical level, the school's leaders served as "positive influencers" (p. 11) whose behaviors, such as servant leadership, were aligned with their values, such as citizenship. Their work was supported by an organizational structure they kept flexible.

Another example of this model in action is Trautman's (2000) dissertation that validated this synergistic leadership framework. Using the Organizational and Leadership Effectiveness Inventory (self-report instrument) validated by Irby, Brown, and Duffy (2000) as a measure of the synergistic leadership theory, Trautman analyzed qualitative and quantitative data collected from 243 school and district leaders. It was confirmed that (1) this leadership theory is inclusive of a range of male and female leadership behaviors and of females at different levels of administration, and (2) some female leaders experience leadership behaviors differently than males; for example, they may fear being perceived as aggressive when introducing change through collaborative culture building.

Critiques of Mentoring Theories

Alternative mentoring theories are not simply divorced from traditional mentoring, as suggested by the variance among those theories presented. Some are, in fact, predicated upon technical forms of mentoring, such as the apprenticeship model, while others are influenced by mandated mentoring models. The postmodern perspective does not support the perpetuation of binaries, such as traditional mentoring is bad and alternative mentoring is good; rather, postmodernist theory argues for coexistences and continuities to be accepted in educational discourse (English, 2003; Irby et al., 2002). However, this is not to imply that unquestioned assumptions that guide administrative management and leadership theories, including mentoring theories, should fester undetected. Given that comentoring theory was birthed out of a critique of traditional mentoring, it functions intentionally as a catalyst for changing traditional practices, hierarchical systems, and homogeneous cultures (Bona et al., 1995; Easterly, 2008).

Political agendas are a driving element within all or most alternative mentoring theories. As postmodern feminists have argued, because career advancement is a protected "investment," educators who are selected as mentors "represent dominant cultural values" (Hansman, 2003, p. 103). Hence, intentional mentors seek to diversify school systems by eliminating constrictive access and critiquing the replication of organizational values. Thus, it is a concern that "technical rationality" serves as the "foundational epistemology" upon which faith-based, nonempirical performances of knowledge are produced (English, 2003, p. 122). From a postmodern perspective, multilevel mentoring reforms resemble a management makeover for schools in which educators are situated as overloaded workers. That is, educators, even when envisioned democratically as change agents, do even more labor within the same work day without additional compensation. A school's transformative processes and outcomes can occur, then, at the cost of exploiting practitioners. In reality, alternative theorists are hybrid borrowers of different frameworks. As another example, some collaborative mentors initiate the apprenticeship of culturally diverse and female leaders and have at their core the double helix of shared power and systems thinking. Perhaps mentoring in contemporary times is less a concept of comentoring than a kind of process model for the implementation of collaborative (and systems) concepts (Cannon, 2003).

Technical mentoring circumvents "why" and "what if" questions, the spectrum of sociocultural and political issues, and especially the regulatory dimensions of its own making (Mullen, 2005). While ideologically restrictive, many would counter that technical mentoring is useful and necessary for the support it gives within practical apprenticeships and in skills building contexts. Human interaction, positive engagement, and fair treatment can be honored in this context. Hence, one cannot assume that technical mentoring has absolutely no educational value or that it cannot function synergistically with alternative forms. On the other hand, critics (Darwin, 2000; Freire, 1997; Hansman, 2003) believe that the power and authority, and the efficiency and competitive values implicit in technical mentoring undermine the capacity for democratic mentoring at human and organizational levels, and so should not be tolerated.

Finally, mandatory mentoring, an oxymoron, signals the presence of a hidden curriculum where teachers are *required* to mentor and make documented gains (Mullen, 2005). While the mentoring of beginning teachers and principals is a reform strategy, it is increasingly being mandated by U.S. states. New teacher mentoring thus resembles more of a technical, evaluative activity than a process for fostering professional cultures of collaboration. Mandated mentoring in public schools has mixed reactions from teachers for whom emotional issues and practical constraints are unresolved tensions and even barriers to change (Hutinger & Mullen, 2007). Entire schools are subjected to change-based mentoring processes that strip away the voluntary nature of this act. A primary motivation for this change seems to be the push from governmental authorities to reduce the high teacher attrition that plagues schools. While the heightened expectations could catapult the performance of veteran teachers and improve organizational efforts, accountability expectations may confound the very integrity and spirit associated with mentoring. To what extent mentoring relationships, which are personal and cultural in nature, can be successfully formalized (in reality, regulated) depends on many variables. Mentoring practice does not always reach its ideals—moreover, organizations typically treat it as an *add-on* responsibility.

Arguably, the adaptation of mentoring as a policy mechanism has turned this educational learning process into an achievement measure for schools. Changes in American law have established an even closer fit for schools with systems thinking and accountability in meeting student achievement goals. Mentoring is infused with leading, teaching, and supervising, and, notably, teacher evaluation. Because mentoring summons notions of civic virtue and goodness, it is useful as a political tool. Rhetorically exploited, mentoring concepts (e.g., instructional mentorship, mentor teacher, mentoring for success) have been co-opted and aligned with national standards. As one effect, policymaking has advanced technical forms of mentoring in a contemporary guise. Goals and processes of management (e.g., monitoring quality, managing conflict, accountability safeguards) have been resurrected as a source of empowerment (e.g., learning environments, relationship sensitivity, cross-cultural mentoring). Within education, technical mentoring scaffolds (processes and systems) have magnetic appeal.

Conclusion

The alternative mentoring theories described in this essay would benefit from further explication along with the mentoring policy context governing the work of schools. Because mandated mentoring undergirds their professional contexts, educational practitioners will find it necessary to process the disparate messages of their own higher calling and from governments. However, clearly mentoring programs and processes are needed for effectively attracting, retaining, and advancing new professionals, including principals, in schools. Mentoring programs and interventions of other kinds enable educational practitioners to see the translation of educational theory in daily practice (Daresh, 2004). Through this process, school leaders can become that much more aware of the need to monitor and change dynamics of power and oppression that can occur in their buildings. Finally, as more educators come to understand mentoring theory, put into practice its desirable tenets, and make the effort to report outcomes, educators should see their organizations change for the better across the relationship–systems continuum.

References

Almog, T., & Hertz-Lazarowitz, R. (1999). Teachers as peer learners: Professional development in an advanced computer learning environment. In A. M. O'Donnell & A. King (Eds.), *Cognitive perspectives on peer learning* (pp. 285-311). Mahwah, NJ: Erlbaum.

Ardovini, J., Trautman, H. D., Brown, G., & Irby, B. (2010). Including female leadership experiences and behaviors: A qualitative validation of synergistic leadership theory. *International Leadership Journal, 2*(3/4), 22-52. Retrieved from http://www.tesc.edu/files/ILJ_Spring_2010_final.pdf

Becker, J. M. (2010). *Peer coaching for improvement of teaching and learning*. Retrieved from http://www.teachnet.org/TNPI/research/growth/ becker.htm

Bona, M. J., Rinehart, J., & Volbrecht, R. M. (1995). Show me how to do like you: Co-mentoring as feminist pedagogy. *Feminist Teacher, 9*(3), 116-124.

Cain, T. (2007). Mentoring trainee music teachers: Beyond apprenticeship or reflection. *British Journal of Music Education, 24*, 281-294.

Cannon, D. A. (2003). *Mentoring: A study of processes and relationships in a collaborative curriculum reform research project* (Unpublished dissertation). The Ohio State University, Columbus, Ohio.

Chaliès, S., Bertone, S., Flavier, E., & Durand, M. (2008). Effects of collaborative mentoring on the articulation of training and classroom situations: A case study in the French school system. *Teaching and Teacher Education, 24*(3), 550-563.

Clark, R. A., Harden, S. L., & Johnson, W. B. (2000). Mentor relationships in clinical psychology doctoral training: Results of a national survey. *Teaching of Psychology, 27*(4), 262-268.

Clauset, K. H., Lick, D. W., & Murphy, C. U. (Eds.). (2008). *Schoolwide action research for professional learning communities: Improving student learning through the whole-faculty study groups approach*. Thousand Oaks, CA: Corwin.

Cohen, N. H. (2002). The journey of the Principles of Adult Mentoring Inventory. *Adult Learning, 14*(1), 4-7.

Cox, E., Bachkirova, T., & Clutterbuck, D. A. (2010). *The complete handbook of coaching*. Thousand Oaks, CA: SAGE.

Daresh, J. C. (2004). Mentoring school leaders: Professional promise or predictable problems? *Educational Administration Quarterly, 40*(4), 495-517.

Darwin, A. (2000). Critical reflections on mentoring in work settings. *Adult Education Quarterly, 50*(3), 197-211.

Davis, D. J. (2008). The mentorship of a sharecropper's daughter: Being young, gifted, and Black in academe. In C. A. Mullen (Ed.), *The handbook of formal mentoring in higher education: A case study approach* (pp. 73-83). Norwood, MA: Christopher-Gordon.

Easterly, D. (2008). Women's ways of collaboration: A case study in proposal development. *Journal of Research Administration, 39*(1), 48-57.

English, F. W. (2003). *The postmodern challenge to the theory and practice of educational administration*. Springfield, IL: Charles C. Thomas.

Freire, P., with Fraser, J. W., Macedo, D., McKinnon, T., & Stokes, W. T. (Eds.). (1997). *Mentoring the mentor: A critical dialogue with Paulo Freire*. New York, NY: Peter Lang.

Galbraith, M. W. (2003). The adult education professor as mentor: A means to enhance teaching and learning. *Perspectives: The New York Journal of Adult Learning, 1* (1), 9-20.

Hansman, C. A. (2003). Power and learning in mentoring relationships. In R. Cervero, B. Courtenay, & M. Hixson (Eds.), *Global perspectives: Volume III* (pp. 102-122). Athens, GA: University of Georgia. Retrieved from http://www.coe.uga.edu/hsp/pdf/year3/hansman.pdf

Hutinger, J. L., & Mullen, C. A. (2007). Supporting teacher leadership: Mixed perceptions of mandated faculty study groups. In S. Donahoo & R. C. Hunter (Eds.), *Teaching leaders to lead teachers: Educational administration in the era of constant crisis, 10* (pp. 261-283). Oxford, United Kingdom: Elsevier (JAI Press).

Irby, B. J., Brown, G., & Duffy J. A. (2000). *Organizational and leadership effectiveness inventory.* Huntsville, TX: Sam Houston Press.

Irby, B. J., Brown, G., Duffy J. A., & Trautman, D. (2002). The synergistic leadership theory. *Journal of Educational Administration, 40*(4), 304-322.

Johnson-Bailey, J., & Cervero, R. M. (2002). Cross-cultural mentoring as a context for learning. *New Directions for Adult and Continuing Education, 96*, 15-26.

Kram, K. E. (1988). *Mentoring at work: Developmental relationships in organizational life*. Lanham, MD: University Press of America. (Original work published 1985)

Kram, K. E., & Higgins, M. C. (2008, September 22). A new approach to mentoring. *The Wall Street Journal*, R10-R11.

Lick, D. W. (1999). Multiple level comentoring: Moving toward a learning organization. In C. A. Mullen & D. W. Lick (Eds.), *New directions in mentoring: Creating a culture of synergy* (pp. 202-212). London, England: Falmer.

Lick, D. W. (2000). Whole-faculty study groups: Facilitating mentoring for school-wide change. *Theory Into Practice, 39*(1), 43-49.

Megginson, D., & Clutterbuck, D. (2005). *Techniques for coaching and mentoring*. New York, NY: Butterworth-Heinemann.

Merriam, S. B. (1983). Mentors and protégés: A critical review of the literature. *Adult Education Quarterly, 33*, 161-173.

Moerer-Urdahl, T., & Creswell, J. (2004). Using transcendental phenomenology to explore the "ripple effect" in a leadership mentorship program. *International Journal of Qualitative Methods, 3*(2), 1-28.

Mullen, C. A. (1999). Epilogue. In C. A. Mullen & D. W. Lick (Eds.), *New directions in mentoring: Creating a culture of synergy* (pp. 242-247). London, England: Falmer.

Mullen, C. A. (2000). Constructing co-mentoring partnerships: Walkways we must travel. *Theory Into Practice, 39*(1), 4-11.

Mullen, C. A. (2005). *The mentorship primer*. New York, NY: Peter Lang.

Mullen, C. A. (Ed.). (2009). *The handbook of leadership and professional learning communities*. New York, NY: Palgrave Macmillan.

Mullen, C. A., & Lick, D. W. (Eds.). (1999). *New directions in mentoring: Creating a culture of synergy*. London, England: Falmer.

Mullen, C. A., & Tuten, E. M. (2010). Doctoral cohort mentoring: Interdependence, collaborative learning, and cultural change. *Scholar-Practitioner Quarterly, 4*(1), 11-32.

Portner, H. (2002). *Being mentored: A guide for protégés*. Thousand Oaks, CA: SAGE.

Richardson, J. (2007). Dynamic groups: Teachers harness the power of professional learning communities. *The Learning Principal, 2*(6), 1, 6-7.

Saltiel, I. (1998). Defining collaborative partnerships. *New Directions for Adult and Continuing Education, 79*, 5-11.

Schlosberg, T., Irby, B., Brown, G., & Yang, L. (2010). A case study of Mexican educational leaders viewed through the lens of the synergistic leadership theory. *International Journal of Educational Leadership, 5*(1), 1-18 (part 1); 1-14 (part 2). Retrieved September 8, 2010, from http://ijelp.expressacademic.org.

Tallerico, M. (2005). *Supporting and sustaining teachers' professional development: A principal's guide*. Thousand Oaks, CA: Corwin.

Tharp, R. G., & Gallimore, R. G. (1995). *Rousing minds to life: Teaching, learning, and schooling in social context*. New York, NY: Cambridge University Press. (Original work published 1988)

Trautman, H. D. (2000). *A validation of the synergistic leadership theory: A gender-inclusive leadership theory*. ProQuest Dissertations and Theses. Retrieved from https://ezproxy.shsu.edu/login?url=http://search.proquest.com/docview/250729673?accountid=7065. (250729673)

Wilson, P. P., Pereira, A., & Valentine, D. (2002). Perceptions of new social work faculty about mentoring experiences. *Journal of Social Work Education, 38*(2), 317-333.

Wong, H. K. (2004). Producing educational leaders through induction programs. *Kappa Delta Pi Record*, 106-111. Retrieved from http://www.newteacher.com/pdf/Producing_Educational_Leaders.pdf

---

Author Contact Information: Carol A. Mullen, PhD, Department Chair and Professor, Department of Educational Leadership & Cultural Foundations, School of Education, The University of North Carolina at Greensboro, 239B Curry Building, 1109 Spring Garden Street, Greensboro, NC 27402. E-mail: camullen@uncg.edu

CHAPTER 86

Who Moved My Theory?

A Kitsch Exploration of Kitsch Leadership Texts

Rosemary Papa, Daniel L. Kain, and Ric Brown
Northern Arizona University

As far as we know, there is not yet a school leader text called *The Garden Gnome Guide to Leadership*, but such a work might represent the most self-conscious kitsch approach to educational leadership. And it would probably sell: the gnome leader *never loses his focus*; the gnome leader *anchors the system*; the gnome leader *doesn't change when the storms arrive*.... Traditionally, *kitsch* refers to "low-brow" or popular art, something that appeals to a broad audience of people of unrefined tastes versus the kind of art that impresses the critic. The classic contemporary example of kitsch is the garden gnome one finds in so many yards—beloved, despite its kitschiness. So what is "kitsch" leadership theory? Is "kitsch," as some would argue (Kulka, 1996) in the eyes of the beholders? One person's pet theory is another person's kitsch.[1] Or is the notion of kitsch leadership something we might agree on more broadly? However we come to understand the concept, clearly there are leadership perspectives that draw more on the personal charisma and writing charms of their originators than on empirical research. This chapter explores the idea of kitsch leadership (see Samier, 2005), with a nod to kitsch methodology. English and Papa (2010) describe *kitsch* texts as works that encourage leaders to study and use simple bromides to address complex issues, and there are numerous authors (e.g., Ken Blanchard & Hodges, 2005; Jim Collins, 2001; Stephen Covey, 1989; Spencer Johnson, 1998) providing textbooks for leadership courses.

Whatever else they are, these "popular" leadership perspectives are indeed *popular*. Consider the enormous success (15 editions!) of *All I Really Need to Know I Learned in Kindergarten* (Fulghum, 1989/2003), *Who Moved My Cheese* (Johnson, 1998), or any of the sports hero/political guru/business maven leadership books so commonly found on school leaders' bookshelves. What explains the presence of toy hedgehogs in plastic buses (Collins, 2001) and stuffed fish (Lundin, Paul, & Christensen, 2000) proudly displayed on the desks of educational leaders if not a combination of popularity and perceived effectiveness?

There are, as this volume makes clear, a number of traditions or schools of leadership theory. For example, one encounters the *leadership traits* theoretical perspective, the *leadership state* theoretical perspective, the *great man leadership* perspective, the *situational leadership* perspective, and so on. Following English and Papa (2010), we distinguish kitsch theories as leadership guidance provided without an empirical research base tied to a theoretical perspective. Thus, for example, the personal reflections of an accomplished leader would qualify as theoretical kitsch. This is not to say that the perspective is not insightful, helpful or engaging. School leaders can learn from the experience of the National Basketball Association Lakers' coach Phil Jackson (Jackson & Delehanty, 1995) or the retail acumen of a Sam Walton (Walton & Huey, 1992), but the detachment from empirical research informed by a theoretical perspective moves this type of work into kitsch.

We are not arguing that every leadership piece must explicitly tie to accepted theories—such a position would stifle discovery. However, even powerful analogies for leadership can draw on research-based theoretical perspectives (e.g., Kain, 1997).

Going further, is leadership best learned through metaphors, bromides, parables, and similar gems of wisdom? Many textbooks in the areas of leadership management or ethics and values give rise to this

The Handbook of Educational Theories, pp. 969–973

notion that the skills leaders need can be readily learned "replete with happy endings" (English & Papa, 2010, p. 39).

One special case worth considering is what might be seen as a "cross-over" perspective. Some leadership texts invoke the techniques of empirical research, the charisma of popular writing, and the power of pithy heuristics. For example, Buckingham and Coffman (1999) create a user-friendly framework of a dozen guiding questions to enhance management, drawing on interviews of 1 million employees and 80,000 managers. Collins's (2001) metaphor-based framework derives from an extensive and carefully documented research process, involving documentary analysis, financial analysis, and interviews. These examples demonstrate that there can be empirical research undergirding what are essentially a-theoretical leadership texts.

Theories: Scientific and Pseudo

Leaders practice what they know. Cognition and action provide the beginnings and endings through stories or narratives. "Stories provide the fabric for both leaders and followers to come together. Stories also contribute meaning and hence value to human activities. The academic name given to stories is *theories*" (English & Papa, 2010, p. vii). However, while theory may start as a story, it is only a beginning that then engages research to test the theory's reliability over time and its validity as to context. Theoretical perspectives of leadership from business, management, psychology, psychiatry and religion have, since Aristotle, given meaning or value to one's actions. Further,

> we argue that practice in not improved by consolidating what is known, but engaging in a pursuit of the unknown. It is only through improved and different research that we can accomplish the ambitious objective of being successful with all students in our schools. (English & Papa, 2010, p. vii)

One problem in educational leadership may be the lack of agreement as to what constitutes theory. Kimbrough and Nunnery (1983) suggested that such variation in definition was not unusual given the varying philosophical perspectives in the field. A scientific definition given by Hall and Lindzey (1978) states, "a theory consists of a set of related assumptions concerning the relevant empirical phenomena and empirical definitions to permit the user to move from the abstract theory to empirical observations" (pp. 12-13). Kerlinger (1973) saw a theory as a set of interrelated constructs that demonstrated the relationship among variables with the purpose of explaining and predicting behavior.

Conversely, some see theory much more broadly; for example, Kimbrough and Nunnery (1983) declare that "any abstraction developed to understand 'what is' can be called a theory" (p. 240). As well, they state that theory has no common rules. And, although Silver (1983) defines *empirical* theory (emphasis ours), her definition admits that it "does not sound very scientific" and that formal definitions are "dry ... robbing theory of it beauty, its emotional significance, its importance in everyday life. A theory is a distinctive way of perceiving reality" (p. 4).

Is it any wonder that the field of education leadership has such a range of views: from very well-defined scientific theories, such a rational choice theory, to ambiguous theories relying on relationships with the divine? Our point is that if the field is to have relevance and ultimately lead to improved success of our schools, then what we call *theory* and what we pass on to those who will lead in the future cannot be a concatenation of individuals' perceptions of reality. And while schools and universities are complex organizations not easily subject to empirical research, in our view, we must attempt to provide theories that are closer to Kerlinger's (1973) view.

The range of what we view as a-theoretical perspectives is broad: from spiritual guides to clever analogies. One a-theoretical perspective is that of spiritual or moral guidance (homilies of a sort), for example those found in Judeo-Christian and other various religions. They reflect skepticism to scientific theory development and instead offer pseudo-theoretical perspectives. Even the political landscape of the neoconservative would be included in this landscape.

For example, former President George W. Bush (Schuman, 2005) asked schools to teach *intelligent design theory* alongside evolution theory, as he asserted that an intelligent design agent helped shape the origins and history of the earth and life. This spiritual sense of a higher being lends itself to parables used in leadership texts (such as Stephen Covey, 1989; Spencer Johnson, 1998, etc.) following the life of a man named Jesus. These pseudo theories seem to fit every situation. For example, *The Spiritual Dimension of Leadership* (Houston & Sokolow, 2006) is a candidate. Another, *Leadership by the Book* (Blanchard, Hybels, & Hodges, 1999) is written using parables to tell the story of a professor and a minister who school a young professional in management skills and ethics. Citing Jesus as a source for practical lessons in effective leadership, the authors explore the concept of "servant leadership" and offer simple strategies for bringing vision and values to any organization. Individuals learn how to:

- achieve goals without sacrificing character or faith;
- inspire and sustain commitment and others to give their best;

- build teamwork and celebrate successes; and
- find personal passion and meaning in work. (p. 1)

Other book titles of note include: *Servant Leadership* and *Lead Like Jesus: Lessons For Everyone From the Greatest Leadership Role Model of All Time* and *Servant Leadership* (Blanchard & Hodges, 2003, 2005).

A second a-theoretical perspective is that of building leadership skills through the use of metaphors, allegories, analogies, parables, and so on. Each of the preceding is a form of representation that attempts to assist in explanation, but not the explanations themselves. Metaphors and the others are the modes of delivery, NOT the concepts or constructs. When we merely use the metaphor as the concept, we may miss the underlying meaning. The complexity of the concept is diminished by the metaphor.

Are metaphors and similar tools important to leaders? Theorists such as Lakoff and Johnson (1980) believe metaphors are used to describe personal meaning within contexts. These meanings can transform two things that are not alike into a common more important meaning. For example, "never carry the wood when they are burning you at the stake" is a powerful leadership metaphor that means "don't help those that are trying to get you fired!" Delving deeper into the construct uncovers the principles of understanding the political environment and the members that inhabit it. Metaphors and similar statements can serve a vital role to help in understanding complex topics. However, they must not stand alone as a substitute for theory.

A third school of a-theoretical works includes collections of common platitudes that have found their way into leadership textbooks as guidance for leaders. The popular leadership management book *Cowboy Ethics* (Owen, 2004), feeds our need for simple slogans framed around the American cowboy icon, who provides common guidance to those within an organization. The commonsense guides include: "live each day with courage" (p. 24); "take pride in your work" (p. 30); "always finish what you start" (p. 34); "ride for the brand" (p. 50); "talk less and say more" (p. 54); "know where to draw the line" (p. 62); and remember that "some things aren't for sale" (p. 62). "Just because something isn't illegal doesn't mean it's right ... boundaries needed to get along were set by shared standards of right and wrong ... good as fences because everyone knew where they were" (p. 62). While these slogans are well suited for coffee mugs and do offer common sense approaches to everyday programs, the accumulation of slogans is NOT theory.

Finally, often an individual who has been in a leadership position writes a book, or has a book written, concerning experiences in that position. Often, these works are not simply biographies or autobiographies, but collected anecdotes that offer leadership training based on the experiences of the famous (see, e.g., Harari, 2003; Iacocca, 2007; Krames, 2005; Vandemark & McNamara, 1996). Particularly irksome are the all too common apologies for transgressions or mistakes made during the tenure in the position. Perhaps some theory-based leadership training, rather than simple trial and error experience, would have assisted in avoiding the mistake in the first place.

When Kitsch Supplants Theory

As in the case of other professions (e.g., medicine, psychology, business), the field of educational leadership has books based on metaphors or broad pronouncements that attempt to portray leadership as simple, step-by-step approaches that unravel complex situations. The goal of this section is not to deride such books, but only to point out their inherent weaknesses as guidelines for leadership development. If you can manage in a minute or lead a changing school environment by following the cheese, who are we to argue?

As an example, *The One Minute Manager* (Blanchard & Johnson, 1983) offers a truism that, "people who feel good about themselves produce good results" (p. 19). It is given as the rationale for positive reinforcement by managers—but in a minute! While this statement may look good on a plaque on a desk or surrounding a picture frame of the family, does it define an effective management tool? As a leader, is one of your guiding principles to make even poor managers feel good about themselves (thus magically developing the skills to do the job better)? Or, should your principles really revolve around professional development (Brown, Noble, & Papa, 2009) that gives individuals the necessary background for their particular tasks and consequently feel better about themselves and their work? We have all experienced good ol' boy/girl principals, superintendents or deans who make us feel good, but are they effective leaders in a complex situation? What guiding principles from metaphors and bromides can assist with budget reductions, personnel problems, and organization issues? What would be more effective to study: a tested theory or a book of metaphors?

A second example comes from the book *Who Moved My Cheese* (Johnson, 1998). There's a scene where the mice discover the cheese is no longer where they expect it to be (p. 35). One of the points seems to be that some keep doing the same thing over and over even if things are changing. While the story is provocative, beyond the scene is the reality of the totality of change and the scientific theories and case studies regarding organizational change, monitoring change, redesigning, rethinking and sustaining momentum (Senge et al., 1999).

As a new administrator, one of the co-authors had a boss who had the staff spend one-half hour at our biweekly meeting discussing *Who Moved My Cheese* and applying it to the problems we faced. While we all made good faith efforts to apply the story, it became clear that there was little or no value in the metaphor itself and that a deeper understanding of change theory for leadership development would have been more effective.

Yet another example can be found in *The Spiritual Dimension of Leadership* (Houston & Sokolow, 2006), which gives eight key principles as guides to lead more effectively. Spirituality is defined as a relationship with the divine. And while, the eight principles are logical, the evidence that one will become more enlightened, or that becoming more enlightened means being more effective, is lacking. And, what if one does not have the prerequisite divine relationship?

Sometimes the lack of scientific support is not just a feature of the kitsch texts, but rejection of science is a goal! In *Value-Added Leadership,* Sergiovanni (1990), "takes comfort" (p. xi) that James (1892) "gradually weeded out the former (analytical technicality) and left the latter unreduced (concrete practical application)" (p. xii). Continuing, Sergiovanni broadly states, without any of those analytical technicality weeds, that value added leadership can get the results we want in a jigsaw world (p. 51).

Thus, the quirkiness of pseudo leadership theory use! Take the test below. There are 10 titles listed. Can you distinguish between those which are real books on the market and those we made up? In our view, they all fit the definition of quirky and reality is rather indistinguishable from fantasy. The answers are at the end of the article.

1. Who Cut the Cheese? Making Budget Reductions Humane.
2. Leadership Secrets of Attila the Hun.
3. Leadership Secrets of Santa Clause.
4. Drive through Leadership: Making a Difference on the Run.
5. The Leadership Genius of George W. Bush.
6. Maid Service Leadership: Cleaning Up the Mess That Others Make.
7. Why Is My Head Where the Sun Doesn't Shine? How Missing Critical Signs Affects Leadership Decision Making.
8. Leadership by Flash Card: Simple Rules for Daily Leadership Tasks.
9. Organic Leadership: Leading Naturally Right Where You Are.
10. A Whack on the Side of the Head: How You Can Be More Creative.

What Do We Make of These?

So what is the harm in simplistic solutions that on their face seem to be the answer to complex problems? The answer is in the very question. Schools and universities (and indeed businesses) are complex, thus their leadership and administration are complex. Simple solutions, often proffered as bromides may delude us into fixes or approaches that are certainly not sustainable at best and may be harmful at worst. If the focus is on the metaphors and/or broad pronouncements then the underlying theory (with all its nuances) may be lost.

The question is whether educational leadership is theory based or craft knowledge? Or, perhaps it is a healthy combination of both. *Practice of Theory to Theory of Practice: The Prime Directive* (Papa, 2004) is an excellent description of what the field might best look like.

In his extensive criticism of school leadership programs, Levine (2005) argued that one key problem with the preparation of leaders was the atheoretical nature of much of the background preparation leaders experience. Without endorsing the Levine critique, we would argue that leadership exclusively by bromides does not serve the profession well. So the dilemma becomes how to extract useful perspectives from this kitsch literature without undermining the basic credibility of an academic area.

Perhaps we ought to do some weeding as Sergiovanni (1990) suggests. However, rather than ridding ourselves of those analytical technicalities, perhaps we can prune (to continue the metaphor) the theories to be more applied and plant more practical application that is more theory based and not simply unwanted volunteers that blow into our garden.

Slogans, heuristics, and metaphors all may have a role in leadership just as a simple mission statement posted throughout a school district can provide focus, and such slogans may serve well to create a culture in the district, college, or university. However, they must not be a substitute for the substance beyond the statement. When using the above, constant attention must be paid to the underlying theory. When one of your principals uses a racial slur, you as superintendent, saying "the buck stops here" is not an explanation for a lack of leadership with regard to staff training in understanding ethical leadership theory.

With apologies to Stephen Covey (1989), we offer five random catchphrases for making the most of kitsch leadership:

- Random catchphrase one: *Even a blind squirrel finds a nut from time to time.* What can I use in this perspective to improve my leadership effectiveness?
- Random catchphrase two: *Who's your daddy?* Develop the habit of questioning the research base behind the bromides.
- Random catchphrase three: *Rhizomes rule because they are connected.* How can I connect this to the tested theories in my academic preparation?

- Random catchphrase four: *Shocking someone else can leave your fingers tingling.* Consider whether the value added of a disruptive metaphor or perspective serves your purposes or undercuts your credibility.
- Random catchphrase five: *Use it and lose it.* You may find a practical use for a concept like hedgehogs or a servant-leadership perspective, but you will want to consider the wisdom of referring to your faculty members as hedgehogs, your boss as the lead goose, and yourself as Jesus.

[Test answers—real books are 2, 3, 5, 9 and 10—the others are yet to be written]!

NOTE

1. Kulka focuses on art as kitsch, but points out that the relevant features are sociohistorical or anthropological rather than any fixed or intrinsic characteristics in art. The principle seems applicable to our argument about kitsch in leadership theory.

REFERENCES

Blanchard, K., & Hodges, P. (2003). *Servant leadership.* Nashville, TN: Thomas Nelson.

Blanchard, K., & Hodges, P. (2005). *Lead like Jesus: Lessons for everyone from the greatest leadership role model of all time.* Nashville, TN: Thomas Nelson.

Blanchard, K., Hybels, B., & Hodges, P. (1999). *Leadership by the book: Tools to transform your workplace.* New York, NY: William Morrow. Retrieved from http://206.18.166.7/adbl/site/products/ProductDetail.jsp?BV_SessionID=@@@@0975387428.1275416713@@@@&BV_EngineID=cccgadekiheegfkcefecekjdffidflj.0&productID=BK_RAND_000948

Blanchard, K., & Johnson, S. (1983). *The one minute manager.* New York, NY: Berkeley Books.

Brown, R., Noble, P., & Papa, R. (2009). *So you want to be an academic administrator. Avoid crossing to the dark side.* Lancaster, PA: Proactive.

Buckingham, M., & Coffman, C. (1999). *First, break all the rules: What the world's greatest managers do differently.* New York, NY: Simon & Schuster.

Collins, J. (2001). *Good to great: Why some companies make the leap … and others don't.* New York, NY: HarperCollins.

Covey, S. R. (1989). *The 7 habits of highly effective people: Powerful lessons in personal change.* New York, NY: Free Press.

English, F., & Papa, R. (2010). *Restoring human agency to educational administration: Status and strategies.* Lancaster, PA: ProActive.

Fulghum, R. (2003). *All I really need to know I learned in kindergarten.* New York, NY: Ballantine. (Original work published 1989)

Hall, C. S., & Lindzey, G. (1978). *Theories of personality* (3rd ed.). New York, NY: Wiley.

Harari, O. (2003). *Leadership secrets of Colin Powell.* Princeton, NJ: McGraw-Hill.

Houston, P. D., & Sokolow, S. L. (2006). *The spiritual dimension of leadership.* Thousand Oaks, CA: Corwin Press.

Iacocca, L. (2007). *Where have all the leaders gone?* New York, NY: Pocket Books.

Jackson, P., & Delehanty, H. (1995). *Sacred hoops: Spiritual lessons of a hardwood warrior.* New York, NY: Hyperion.

James, W. (1892). *Talks to teachers on psychology and to students on some of life's ideals.* Mineola, NY: Dover Books

Johnson, S. (1998). *Who moved my cheese.* New York, NY: G. P. Putman's Sons.

Kain, D. L. (1997). Misplaced camels, crowded captains, and achieving greatness: Leadership of interdisciplinary teams. In T. Dickinson & T. Erb (Eds.), *We gain more than we give: Teaming in middle schools* (pp. 403-424). Columbus, OH: National Middle School Association.

Kerlinger, F. N. (1973). *Foundations of behavioral research* (2nd ed.). New York, NY: Holt.

Kimbrough, R. B., & Nunnery, M. Y. (1983). *Educational administration.* New York, NY: MacMillan.

Kulka, T. (1996). *Kitsch and art.* University Park, PA: Pennsylvania State University.

Krames, J. A. (2005). *Jack Welch on the 4 Es of leadership.* Princeton, NJ: McGraw-Hill.

Lakoff, G., & Johnson, M. (1980). *Metaphors we live by.* Chicago, IL: University of Chicago Press.

Levine, A. (2005). *Educating school leaders.* Washington, DC: The Education Schools Project.

Lundin, S. C., Paul, H., & Christensen, J. (2000). *Fish: A remarkable way to boost morale and improve results.* New York, NY: Hyperion.

Owen, J. P. (2004). *Cowboy ethics: What wall street can learn from the code of the west.* Ketchum, ID: Stoecklin.

Papa, R. (2004). Practice of theory to theory of practice: The prime directive. In *The Eighth Yearbook of the National Council of Professors of Educational Administration.* Lancaster, England: Economic Publishing.

Samier, E. (2005). Toward public administration as a humanities discipline: A humanistic manifesto. *Halduskultuur: Administrative Culture, 6,* 6-59.

Schuman, J. (2005, August 12). Schools should teach intelligent design theory, Bush says. *The Chronicle of Higher Education, Archives,* p. 1.

Senge, P., Kleiner, A., Roberts, Ross, R., Roth, G. & Smith, B. (1999). *The dance of change.* New York, NY: Doubleday.

Sergiovanni, T. J. (1990). *Value-added leadership.* New York, NY: Harcourt, Brace, Jovanovich.

Silver, P. (1983). *Educational administration: Theoretical perspectives on practice and research.* New York, NY: Harper & Row.

Vandemark, B., & McNamara, Robert S. (1996). *In retrospect, the tragedy and lessons of Vietnam.* New York, NY: Vintage Books.

Walton, S., & Huey, J. (1992). *Sam Walton: My story, made in America.* New York, NY: Bantam.

Author Content Information: Dr. Rosemary Papa, Del and Jewell Lewis Endowed Chair, Learning Centered Leadership, Northern Arizona University, PO Box 5774, Flagstaff, Arizona 86011-5774. Phone: 916-832-13. E-mail: rosemary.papa@nau.edu

CHAPTER 87

Critical Feminist Theory

Michelle D. Young
University of Texas at Austin

Catherine Marshall
University of North Carolina at Chapel Hill

Over the last few decades, feminists have challenged fundamental understandings of the way we think about and research, women, men and social-political contexts. They have offered a perspective and research strategies that consider women from the perspective of their own experiences, that emphasize identification, trust, empathy, and relationships, and that has as one of its primary goals providing "women explanations of social phenomena that they want and need" (Harding, 1987, p. 8). In doing so, it has produced radical reexaminations of assumptions and reconstructions of previously accepted interpretations across a broad range of disciplines. Within this chapter we discuss the development of feminist theories, and attempt to disentangle some of the issues concerning generalizability, validity and method regarding feminist critical theory. Subsequently, we turn our attention to how the theory has been used within educational research and then address some of the most common and robust critiques of this perspective.

Definitions and Origins of Feminist and Critical Feminist Theories

Derrida (1974) asserted the impossibility of identifying a definitive origin for any theory. Reinharz (1992) affirms this adding that we should talk about the plural—"feminisms." Viewing feminist research in this manner emphasizes that "rather than there being a 'woman's way of knowing' or a 'feminist way of doing research,' there are women's ways of knowing" (Reinharz, 1992, p. 4) and multiple ways of studying and carrying out research on the conditions of women's lives. "Feminisms" denotes inclusion of a range of issues, perspectives and methods, avoiding a single, unifying, stifling definition.

> Feminism is a multifaceted social movement, ... a politics that is dedicated to transforming those social and domestic arrangements that deliberately or unwittingly penalize women because of their sex ... feminists focus seriously on the ways that gender—social construction of masculinity and femininity—organizes political, personal, and intellectual life. The feminist assumption is that gender divisions of work, pleasure, power, and sensibility are socially created, detrimental to women and, to a lesser degree, to men, and therefore can and should be changed. (Ruddick, 1989, pp. 234-235)

For our purposes, in this chapter, we use Marshall's (1999) categories and delineations—from liberal feminisms, to women's ways and socialist feminisms, to power and politics feminisms to describe the evolution to critical feminist theory (CFT).

Liberal Feminism

Liberal feminists focus on rights. The nineteenth and twentieth century suffragists in the United States, and women, still, in other countries, act to gain political rights. Alongside struggles for votes and political representation are struggles for rights and equal access to educational opportunity, to employment, to own property and to control their children, money and bodies. In the United States, liberal feminist causes have gained the most credibility when couched as citizenship rights and civil and property rights, since those fit most closely with dominant and legitimized discourses in

The Handbook of Educational Theories, pp. 975–984

legal and policy arenas and arguably are covered by the Constitution and the 14th Amendment equal protection clause. Liberal feminisms' early successes include attaining voting rights for women and much later exploring the divergent routes girls and boys took in education and careers as well as the consequences of sex stereotyping and gender differentiation in our instructional and curricular practices (Arnot & Weiler, 1993). Moreover, their framing of these inequities led to the passage of Title IX to eliminate educational barriers based on gender.

Women's Ways and Socialist Feminisms

Drawing from Women's Ways feminism—labeled variously as, maternal and difference feminism—feminist scholars of this tradition focus on ways to hear and represent women's different life trajectories, values, ways of knowing and ethics. Recommendations for relationship-building, caring, community, and nonhierarchical leadership emerged from the work of difference feminists (Gilligan, 1982; Noddings, 1992). A different framing is needed focusing specifically on "women's ways" of valuing, knowing, meaning-making, living, and working, focusing solely on women, who had been left out of researching and theorizing, and developing new theories of relationship and ethics, most famously, in *Women's Ways of Knowing* (Belenkey, Clinchy, Goldberger & Tarrule, 1986) and *In a Different Voice* (Gilligan, 1982).

Feminist scholars widened the questions on differential access and treatment by gender and revealed consequences in a way that incorporates both the public and private spheres (Chowdhury, 1996; Kelly, Burton, & Reagan, 1996). This expansion beyond the public sphere issues of rights, to incorporate the private sphere, embraces women's voices, lives, values, and emphasizes (for all genders) passions, and relationships. This, along with the evolution of a women's culture and consciousness-raising, a global women's movement made visible, lent credence to theorizing that recognized realities of women's lives, incorporated women's voices, including their talk about sexuality, sexual orientation and their choices and dilemmas regarding motherhood, careers.

Feminism and Social Constructions of Gender

In feminist theory and methods gender has been one of the primary categories used for analysis and critique of social and political relations and systems (Harding, 1987; Hartsock, 1974; Smith, 1987; Reinharz, 1992). Feminists use gender in their efforts to account for and overturn patriarchal domination and to work for social change. In most feminist research gender and sexism are given position of prominence. Some caution, however, that focusing on gender reifies it as a social construction.

> … in a certain sense there are no "women" or "men" in the world—there is no "gender"—but only women, men, and gender constructed through particular historical struggles over just what races, classes, sexualities, cultures, religious groups, and so forth, will have access to resources and power. (Harding, 1991, p. 151)

Fuss (1989) explains that any discussion of women as a group is open to criticisms of essentialism and universalism. Thus, the glaring need is for identifying the powerful forces in the social construction of gender, revealing gendered power dynamics in employment, families, religions, schools, businesses, and politics. Locating the gender questions in larger policy arenas reveals how governments provide legitimacy to patriarchal institutions and reify oppressive gender relations (Connell, 1987; Marshall, 1997; Pateman, 1988; Stromquist, 1997). Ergo, the origins of power and politics feminism.

Power and Politics Feminism

Power and politics feminists have worked on multiple fronts to expose the politics of knowledge, arguing that traditional epistemologies have systematically excluded the possibility that women can be knowers (Harding, 1987). Power and politics feminisms incorporate a more radical insight and purpose. They have focused on a critique of the patriarchal state and its power to regulate the lives and bodies of women and girls—as teachers, mothers, daughters, and students (Connell, 1987). Some early work in this tradition drew on Marxist insights and acknowledged the interplay of market economies and class. However, early Marxist analyses in education were often focused on working class boys whose blue collar futures were fading (e.g. MacLeod, 1987; Willis, 1977) and missed the influences of patriarchy and of gender hierarchies on women's roles and opportunities. Scholars like Weiler (1988), Weis (1988), and Fine (1992) now provide insights about postindustrial forces combining with patriarchal traditions to limit females' futures. This integration of macro and micro power and politics benefits from liberal and women's ways feminisms as well as from critical theory and critical race theory (CRT), yielding CFT.

Critical Feminist Theory

CFT frames the gender/power dynamics in political, social and organizational lives. It builds on critical theory's focus on organizational, social, and political structures that perpetuate the power of some, to the detriment and oppression of others. CFT scholars have incorporated concentrated their theoretical and methodological efforts on to dismantling intersecting and interrelated race-, class-, and gender-based systems of oppression and subordination.

CFT benefits from critical theory's focuses on issues of power and justice and the way social systems are constructed and reproduced. It enables the search for how our thinking is mediated by historically constituted power relations. It enables the search for the embedded "facts" and assumptions that were once constructed, in some historical context, and then perpetuated as aspects of reality. It enables us to identify how some groups have gained and maintained privilege. Thus, when feminist and critical theory are merged, even farther-reaching discussions regarding epistemology emerge—i.e., who gets to define what counts as knowledge and knowing. Having a stance of critique, challenge, agency, and action, CFT promotes theoretical analysis and research aimed at re-framing policy to eliminate oppressive practice and empowering those whose voices and standpoints have been silenced. It requires "a rethinking and an unthinking of our current practices" (Pillow, 1997, p. 145).

CFT, then, frames research focusing on power and patriarchy to "out" hegemony, showing power sources that maintain control over the generation, legitimation, and interpretation of research, and the politics of maneuvers that advance the interests of dominants, usually White males. Research designs, then, focus on arenas of power and dominance, like boards of trustees, courts, and legislators and also on powerful policy artifacts, like curriculum guidelines, and unobtrusive policies in practices, like the understandings of deference to male voices in faculty meetings (Marshall, 1997). CFT provides strategies for examining how dominant discourses work by setting up the terms of reference and by disallowing or marginalizing alternatives. It offers a way to question every assumption that has reigned over organizational and social reality by examining what is being ignored or suppressed and then asking questions about women and girls.

CFT also shares some of the central tenets of CRT. For example, both perspectives highlight the ways that political arenas and courts have based decisions on the centrality of property rights, and how by doing so individuals who are White and male are privileged, while those who are neither White nor male (the other) are not. Indeed, like CFT, CRT creates an analytic tool through which we can understand the powerful forces that perpetuate inequities (Ladson-Billings & Tate, 1995). CRT "challenges the traditional claims that the educational system and its institution make toward objectivity, meritocracy, color-blindedness, race neutrality and equal opportunity ... traditional claims act as a camouflage for the self-interest, power, and privilege of dominant groups" (Solorzano & Yosso, 2002, p. 26).

Generalizability of Critical Feminist Theory

The question of whether feminist theory is generalizable to all female populations has been the subject of much debate (Reinharz, 1992; Sawicki, 1994). In large measure, feminist theory emphasizes the shared experiences of women across the divisions of race, class, age and/or culture. In such theories, the diversity of women's lives and activities have often been lumped into the category "women's experience," presumably in an effort to provide a basis for a collective feminist subject, emancipatory theory, and identity politics. More recently, however, it is the differences among women (e.g., differences of race, class, sexual orientation) that have moved to the forefront of theoretical discussions.

Diverse Women: Diverse Concerns

De Beauvoir (1973) is often quoted as saying "one is not born a woman, one becomes a woman." Women learn continuously from birth the behavior appropriate to their position, and as they grow older their behavior and attitudes are subtly and profoundly molded by their cultural milieu (p. 301). However, the effects of culture on socialization are apparent in cross-cultural comparisons of women's behavior. The issue of race illustrates well the need to be concerned with the generalizability of feminist theory. Although feminism and feminist research was developed "for women," (Harding, 1987) it has been argued that "academic feminism is part of White culture" (Reinharz, 1992), that too many feminist studies claiming to represent "women's experiences" are rooted in Anglo populations and samples (Stanfield, 1993), and that the appellation "feminism" misrepresents women as a whole and unified group. Portraying feminism and the female experience as singular, while useful to some researchers such as Jean Kelly-Gadol (1987) in her research on Women's history, is regarded as problematic by others (Sawicki, 1991).

Women of color, in particular, have raised concerns about the generalizability of traditional feminist perspectives and have demanded that their diversity and concerns be recognized, respected, and appreciated. Chicanas are often misrepresented as resigned, quiet women, dependent on macho men; however, their oppression is a function not only of cultural tradition but also of contemporary institutional discrimination that excludes them from many aspects of public life (Zinn, 1982). Malveaux (1985) has noted important differences between the concerns of the Black woman and her Anglo counterpart. In a study of Black adolescents, Ladner (1987) found that "the resources which adolescent girls have at their disposal combined with the cultural heritage of their communities, are crucial factors in determining what kind of women they become" (p. 80).

Similarly, Green (1980) argued that Native American women must be seen within the context of Native American life, in which they are largely responsible for maintaining "the resilient intratribal and pan-Indian networks ... on and off reservation, networks which keep migratory and urban Indians working, educated and in touch with their Indian identities" (p. 266). Women from developing countries are similarly concerned with misrepresentation. Gayatri Spivak (1992) notes that the "paradigms of academic intelligibility of feminism in Algeria and in the Maghreb have been, for the large part, modulated in the intellectual configurations of Western thought: They have offered the frame and the genesis" (pp. 54-55).

The Lesbian-Gay-BiSexual-Transgendered-Queer (LGBTQ) critique, too, emanates from the concern that a generic feminist theory does not generalize well to their population and that it marginalizes those whose sexual orientation is already marginalized. For some, the very meaning of gender comes into question, framing it as performative and socially ascribed (Butler, 1990). The challenge for CFT is to incorporate sexual orientation among the intersections of gender, race, and class.

Scholars have also raised issues concerning the impact of culture and perspective on the research process (Anderson, 1993; Stanfield, 1993). Similarly, feminist scholars such as bell hooks (1990) have argued that female members of subordinated groups have had unique experiences that would be inadequately interpreted by White women. This argument is not unlike of feminists who exclude men from feminist research, arguing that men can support feminists, but, lacking the perspective of the women's experience, they cannot be feminists.

The Emergence of Feminist Standpoints

In a voice of their own, diverse groups of women have brought forth epistemologies from their culturally embedded experiences as women. Feminist critical researchers are defining and using endarkened feminist epistemologies (Dillard, 2000), Black Feminist Epistemology (Collins, 1991), and Chicana Feminist Epistemology, (Mendez-Morse, 2003). Critical feminist insights have informed educational studies on issues such as teacher unions (Marshall, 2002), sexual harassment (Laible, 1997), teen pregnancy (Pillow, 1997), on Chicana student resistance (Bernal, 1998), mothers and school choice (Andre-Bechely, 2005), women's access to higher education (Shaw; 2004) and women in school leadership as exemplified by Sanders-Lawson, Smith-Campbell and Benham (2010). Each of the above evolving feminist perspectives foreground different issues for the study of women vis-à-vis important educational, societal, economic and political issues.

Questions of Validity

Those who scrutinize feminist research are concerned foremost with the objectivity of the research and the adequacy and credibility of the research results. How feminist researchers address the issue of validity or "trustworthiness" depends primarily on their research approaches. For those using more traditional research strategies, reflecting positivism, techniques used to ensure validity will be traditional as well (Olesen, 2000). For those who use postpositivist or critical approaches, their efforts to ensure trustworthiness will involve activities such as audit trails and member checks. Some feminist researchers take this even further, searching for what Lather describes as transformational and transgressive validity in feminist deconstructive approach (Lather, 1991).

Beyond presenting the notion that to be valid research samples must include women and girls before drawing conclusions about health, leadership, moral reasoning, feminist research has moved to another stance: studying women in their own right in order to develop versions of reality that more accurately reflect their experiences. For most feminist researchers their approach is also highly sensitive to the ethical issues of research including issues of harm, consent, deception, privacy and the confidentiality of data as well as representation or misrepresentation of the "other." As discussed in an earlier section, the issue of representation is extremely complex. Morris Punch (1994) pointed out "feminist research by women on women implies a 'standpoint epistemology' that not only colors the ethical and moral component of research related to the power imbalances in a sexist and racist environment, but also inhibits deception of the research 'subjects'" (p. 89).

Feminists have used varied traditions and methodologies to extend their influence and impact across a wide range of issues (Marshall & Young, 2007). Although there is no real consensus regarding what counts as feminist methodology (DeVault, 1999; Gorelick, 1991; Oakley, 1981; Ramazanoglu, 1989), Marshall and Young (2007) provide an overview of methods that use and or develop feminist insights, including survey and experimental methods. Bruner and Grogan's (2005) national survey of women in the superintendency is a good example of a feminist survey. More common, is the use of interview research, inductive fieldwork, Marxist and ethno-methodological approaches, phenomenology, action/participatory approaches, oral history, among others. A range of tools and processes has been used to research a variety of topics from feminist and critical feminist perspectives. However, researchers who use quantitative approaches are much less likely to describe their methodology as feminist (Marshall & Young, 2007).

The methodological and theoretical leaps of the past 3 decades challenge overly-narrow social science, with radical reexaminations of assumptions, and reconstructions of previously accepted interpretations. CFT and research heralds and legitimizes the challenges, highlighting repressed realities about gender inequities and exclusions. Research and action framed by CFT can assert the evolving right of scholars to insert values, like "the desire to eliminate institutional evil," into their research agendas (Laible, 2003). The possibility that researchers can use CFT for framing openly ideological research (Lather, 1991) and for reframing policies (Marshall& Gerstl-Pepin 2005) to envision the lives of women and girls in ways that free them from hegemony asserts the transformational validity of CFT.

THE USE OF CRITICAL FEMINIST THEORY

CFT moves to encompass a range of topics that were previously considered not important, too personal, or nonacademic (e.g., sexuality, the private sphere of family) (Olesen, 2000).

VOICES ON THE MARGINS

CFT researchers seek to better understand both the forces of domination that affect the lives of women and their worldviews. CFT centers on the experience of girls and women and looks for how their issues are defined from without. Framing, then, can identify the gender/power dynamics in political, social and organizational lives seeking those phenomena as expressed in women's voices, eliciting often—marginalized. Research in this area includes Gilligan's research on moral development. Previous to her work, women's moral development was understood by male standards, which were not only inaccurate but also damaging to women. Feminist research, in fact, has exposed a large amount of female marginalization within science (e.g., Devault, 1999) and how such science was used to control women. Thus, CFT ploughed the fertile field for women's studies.

AREAS OF SILENCE

CFT has raised questions previously ignored. In education, the paucity of women in educational leadership was ignored, undiscussed (Tyack & Hansot, 1982; Blount, 1998). Most states and professional associations did not even keep statistics on gender in education. CFT uncovered the informal curriculum of schooling, which taught boys and girls that men are in charge and reified differentiated sex role socialization in the formal curriculum in home economics and shop. CFT highlights the repressed realities about persistent underrepresentation of women in educational administrative positions, and the ways scholars, the knowledge base and professional culture have perpetuated this repression. CFT helps reframe these historically embedded practices.

REFRAMING TO FOCUS ON WOMEN

CFT shifts policy and research questions by highlighting effects on women. In inquiry regarding development efforts with Third World women (e.g., near India's Narmada River), CFT focuses on how women benefit from their involvement (O'Bannon, 1994). This reframing exposes women earning less income than men for similar work and women's earnings going to their family, not to them—where household resources are controlled by men.

Analyses of welfare policy (U.S. and international) provide examples of CFT reframing policy. Shaw (2004), exploring women's motivation and perseverance in higher education, especially those who are single mothers and poor, asked those (few) women to describe their challenges. These include barriers emanating from the assumptions in welfare reform policies. CFT policy analyses show that gender- and race-neutral policies—are blind to the reality that people on welfare are, indeed women, often with small children. They ignore the complications of childcare and the biases of agency caseworkers, and their formulation ignores women's realities. This all points to the question: who benefits and who continues to be disadvantaged. Orloff (1993) notes "the character of public social provision affects women's material situations, shapes gender relationships, structures political conflict and participation" (pp. 303-304). Her CFT critique identifies the power- and market-forces at work and asserts "fundamental to full social participation and self determination are control over ones' body and bodily capacities (including sexuality and reproduction) and the right to political participation" (p. 307). Thus, CFT reframes policy to encompass the sexual division of labor, women's access to paid work, the treatment of care work and care workers, women's political and labor market rights and marriage and family relations.

CHALLENGING HEGEMONY

CFT identifies hegemonic realities, equips people with agency to resist oppression, and moves people to struggle. CFT can challenge assumptions dominating programs, evaluations, and research methods. In the context where dominant education policy focused on accountability, MacDonnell 's (2004) examination of suicide prevention programs asked different questions. Canadian adolescents' suicides increased drastically over 3 decades, especially among Aboriginal and sexual minority youth. MacDonnell problematized the programs' isolation from the curriculum, education professionals' avoidance of sexual minorities' issues, and insensitivity to the ways sexual orientation intersects with racism and sexism. Her CFT questioning of the evaluations of programs, revealed how the canons of systematic reviews, based on focused questions, actually exacerbated that insensitivity. Hegemony over research questions and methods prevented useful evaluations. Positivist assumptions about the nature of truth and validity and demand for controls, resulted in decontextualized issues. As Bensimone and Marshall assert, the belief that bias is neutralized results in failures to embrace local context and differences, like gender, sexuality, race and historicity (Bensimon & Marshall, 1997; 2003).

Hegomony is challenged when women recognize their issues are not being represented and then create alternative modes of power. Several studies demonstrate women, knowing they are outsiders within, gingerly assessing, managing the maneuvering in organizational and political systems. Studies of Australian "femocrats"— (also nicknamed "tall poppies in silk shirts") found women who attained high positions in bureaucracies ,who knew how to jolly along with powerful males so they could advocate women's issues (Franzway, Court, Connell, 1989; Marshall, 2000; Watson, 1990).

Pointing to the Elephant in the Room

Sometimes it is blindness to reality: In the midst of tremendous attention to concerns about recruitment and retention of teachers, analyses of the pipeline for leadership rarely includes acknowledgement of the female majority in that pipeline (Rowan, 1994; Young, 2003). Policymakers, while labeling crisis in the shortage of school administrators, fail to ask, where are the women? Feminist scholars have, for decades, documented issues such as: (a) the male-normed profession and the outdated androcentric and corporate models of leadership; (b) the assumption that all is gender-neutral (i.e., women's careers, like males in the past, are unencumbered by childbearing and child-rearing choices).

Blindness to women's realities in legal proceedings is highlighted in CFT. In legal studies, MacKinnon (1989) demonstrates, using examples of incest, rape, abortion, birth control, domestic battery, prostitution, and pornography, ways in which the legal and political system protects prerogatives, propensities, freedoms, rights, and property of men, leaving women at the mercy of judges and politicians to decide whether to extend protections to them. Those judges' and politicians' face "he said, she said" situations. These are situations where a woman lacking the symbolic and tangible social capital mix of class, race, and family backing have few protections. Such highlighting of women's oppression within hegemonic forces brings to the surface the intermix of power, gender, and sexuality so that one can see women in prostitution or pornography as part of an economic, political, legal system which uses women's sexuality within a system that subjugates women.

One study of organizational sociology stands out as an exemplar of CFT. In *Men and Women of the Corporation*, Kanter (1977) uncovered the unwritten messages people receive in their workplace regarding gendered hierarchies and "opportunity positions." This expanded understanding of women's loss of motivation and unwillingness to make extra efforts, as a response to the message that they are not and probably won't be in opportunity positions.

Women's unpaid work is another elephant. In economics, Waring (1988) conducts CFT calculations of the value, globally, of women's unpaid work as volunteers, caretakers, nurturers of extended family, teachers of the very young, and then demonstrates how the world's economies would be altered if "women's work" were given monetary value.

Critiques of the Critical Feminist Theory

With the discourse of scientific research along with an increasingly conservative sociopolitical environment have come a crisis of legitimacy for feminist research and an abundance of CFT critiques.

It Is Irrelevant and no Longer Needed

Certainly the strongest silent critique is CFT being simply ignored, underutilized, and otherwise marginalized. This is the bane of critical researchers and, as Marshall and Anderson (1995) state, the critical consultant is an oxymoron. Usually those with power are not prone to invite the insight of people who suggest their way of framing issues is overly narrow, or even wrong!

A variant of this critique is that raising gender issues is a diversion from topics that are of crisis dimension, like the achievement gap, immigration, the economy, etc. A related critique is the argument that gender issues have been taken care of already, with liberal feminist policies that require equal access, equal pay, and equal political participation, like, in the U.S., Title IX and the Equal Pay Act and the 2008 ascension of Hillary

Clinton to the stature of Secretary of State, and such parallels in other countries. This critique obfuscates gender questions under the umbrella of liberal politics and antidiscrimination law moving attention elsewhere, ignoring evidence of unequal access and leaving women with liberal, feminist framing of solutions, Band-aid and token quick fixes and still vulnerable to the ignored power dynamics.

It Is Unsettling, Disruptive, and Offers no Cure

As with all critical theories, the insights uncovered are startling and upsetting but leave one feeling hopeless. For example, Ferguson's (1984) *Feminist Critique of Bureaucracy* lays bare the disadvantaged positioning of women in seemingly sanitized bureaucratic practices. But she offers few immediately workable alternatives. Studies reveal how universities promise support in careers in math, sciences, engineering, etc, and then leave women academics with the large burdens of caring and mentoring students. Similarly, studies guided by CFT reveal how family structures, teaching practices, and the hidden curriculum of schooling tracks pretty girls into cheerleading and athletic boys into football, reinforcing and accentuating societal gendered valuation messages. Yet, how does one begin to carve out the messages intertwined in societal context, including media, consumer goods, family, religion, and laws? Finding cures for institutional practices embedded in centuries of patriarchy is a daunting challenge! Further, what entity has the power and will to listen, embrace the issues, and search for cures? They may demand, for example, in developing countries, that international aid go to girls' schooling, which looks good, without ever touching the family dynamic that keeps girls home to care for the littlest ones while their brothers go to school. Powers that be are not inviting this critique so they are not prone to seek solutions that disrupt their ways of thinking. As Audre Lorde (1984) said, "the master's tools will never dismantle the master's house" (p. 112).

This critique would maintain the existing gendered order in institutions and society. Arguing that CFT disrupts gender roles and that gender roles are more biologically based than socially constructed, this logic wins the day when questions are framed with those assumptions. CFT that demonstrates the social construction of gender roles, then, is discredited as ideological.

It Is Just Ideology

Critics of CFT assert that CFT ideologues study practices, programs, research agendas, and then initiate value-based analyses to discover findings that fit with their ideology. So, findings about women getting cooled out of higher paying jobs, girls' internalized low self-esteem when their bodies are not the media ideal, or findings about women feeling pressure to act like men in order to get administrative positions—are considered illegitimate, tainted by slanted ideology. Other critiques assert that CFT methodological stances seeking to give voice and to empower the heretofore silenced and marginalized—are unscientific. Critics ask: where are the control groups, random samples, and experiments? If women and girls in these case studies expressed a disempowering force in the hidden curriculum, how do we know findings are generalizable?

It Is Antiboy

The critique above continues with the assertion that CFT's agenda is to set up new institutional practices that privilege women and girls—that the values base of CRT is centered on identifying what male-normed practices set up advantages for men and then to tear those down. (Would that CFT were so powerful!) This critique ignores CFT research assumptions that gender roles are social constructions and that they limit possibilities for everyone. Some examples include research on men in careers that are traditionally female, like nursing, and on boys in postindustrial societies who drop out of school when their model identities and employment possibilities seem to have no fit with realities they see (Weis, 1993).

This critique seems to emanate from an unfounded fear and backlash. An analysis of journals searching for policy studies with a feminist framing (examination of 4,000+ articles between 1980 and 1996) found only 58 that made gender central to the interpretation of the research problem (Parsons & Ward, 2001).

CFT Actually Makes Women More Vulnerable

Arguments that women and girls need, and benefit from protections built into institutions gain tremendous credence. One of us watched Phyllis Shafly testify and win over a state legislature contemplating ratification of the U.S. Constitutional amendment guaranteeing rights to women and girls. Assertions that women and girls need special protections from military service, special public bathrooms, protections against strenuous taxing labor, are paternalistic yet appealing. That military service and taxing labor are, for men, stepping stones to good pay, careers, pensions, and other benefits, and that women actually regularly do dangerous and taxing labor, be it defending their children in ghettos, washing floors or giving birth—are arguments that do not penetrate the views seen in dominant male, White, middle class understandings of those who think women and girls have to have and do have protections in existing gender regimes.

The Antifemininity and Antimarriage Critique

CFT is criticized for having an agenda that undermines traditional marriage, motherhood, and that seeks to make women and men alike. This critique is appealing and powerful, having media support. Media messages trumpeted that women would be alone and poor if they did not work harder at finding a husband and curving their bodies to comply with dominant beauty norms and with motherhood (Faludi, 1991). Media announced the "death" of feminism and schools' history curricula gave little to no attention to the women's movement. In the twenty-first century, few girls and women have knowledge of the suffrage struggles, never mind the jailing of Margaret Sanger for helping poor women get information so that they could limit the number of babies they bore. Young women are known to say "I'm not a feminist" but then act and benefit from the achievements of the feminist movements.

CFT is "guilty" in this critique in that it does frame research that can uncover unequal power dynamics in intimate relationships and in institutions like marriage and religion, courts, bureaucracies.

It Is Narrow and Essentializes Women

Critiques of CFT come from equity-oriented activists and scholars too—for inadequately recognizing global, race, class, age, sexual orientation, life choices, ability and a range of nuanced differences among women. CFT does center on women's experiences and voices, leading to viewing women as a category, as if there were one prototypical woman with a universalized life trajectory. Feminisms of the 1970s and 1980s were criticized for being the province of White, educated, middle class, heterosexual women with leisure time. The allegation was that these feminist activists went to meetings while their ironing and childcare was done by often by low-paid women of color. These were seen as feminists who were insensitive to Black women's situation where in the struggle was, in part, about supporting the men and boys in their families whose political and socioeconomic struggles were about survival and avoiding prison and death.

A nuance of this critique in that CFT is colonialist and ethnocentric because of the mobilization of CFT in developed countries. *Ms.* Magazine, though, is a constant source of journalistic presentations of what is happening with women and girls, ranging from Afghanistan to Indonesia to Kenya, offering expanded views. Mount-Cors' (2010) study of literacy and home life, for example, is situated with realizations that women's rights may be less important than access to water, and charcoal for fire. Thus, the challenge is to expand CFT through studies that incorporate much wider cultural and political contexts.

Conclusion

Notwithstanding the above critiques of feminist research and perspectives, it is a perspective that is stronger than ever before due to the commitment of theorists and researchers to apply, revise and refine methods and perspectives. Feminist researchers are committed to both feminism and social science, and they use the tool of the discipline to "talk back… in a spirited critique aimed at improving the ways we know society" (Devault, 1999, p. 27). Ground breaking feminist theorizing has laid bare the ways traditions in academies, theory, research, methodology and in the politics of knowledge have historically excluded women's issues and perspectives (Smith, 1987). Thus, research on girls and women, "women's issues," "women's work," and "the private sphere," a wide and contextual context of personal and political and economic, have become topics worthy of incorporation for research and theory.

CFT still faces hurtles, however, in the public sphere, such as policy arenas. Many feminists have critiqued the traditional way that policy is framed (Devault, 1999; Marshall, 1997; Pillow, 1997; Young, 2003). In the policy arena, which favors the question framing, insights, values, and experiences of the powerful, and favors quantitative over qualitative research, feminist research has made less progress, particularly in terms of how policy issues emerge, how they are constructed, and how policy goals are defined and accomplished (Marshall, 1997; Olesen, 2000; Young, 2000). So, "we must take our work public with extraordinary levels of reflexivity, caution and semiotic and rhetorical sophistication" (Stacey, 2003, p. 28). Thus we conclude with our CFT work plan:

Vigilant monitoring of how gender-research questions and data are framed, collected and reported (or silences) requires activists researcher stances with feminist voices challenging academia, media, foundations, and government agencies to ask that gendered data be collected, and 'spun' reports debunked. (Marshall & Young, 2006, p. 74)

References

Anderson, M. (1993). Studying across difference: Race, class and gender in qualitative research. In J. Stanfield & R. Dennis (Eds.), *Race and ethnicity in research methods* (pp. 39-52). Thousand Oaks, CA: SAGE.

Andre-Becheley, L. (2005). *Could it be otherwise? Parents and the inequalities of public school choice.* New York, NY: Routledge/Falmer.

Arnot, M., & Weiler, K. (1993). *Feminism and social justice in education: International perspectives.* London, England: Falmer Press.

Belenky, M., Clinchy, B., Goldberger, N., & Tarule, J. (1986). *Women's ways of knowing.* New York, NY: Basic Books.

Bensimone, E., & Marshall, C. (2003). Like it or not: Feminist critical policy analysis matters. *Journal of Higher Education, 74*(3), 3-15.

Bernal, D. (1998). Grassroots leadership reconceptualized: Chicana oral histories and the 1968 East Los Angeles School Blowouts. *Frontiers: A Journal of Women's Studies, 19*(2), 113-142.

Blount, J. (1998). *Destined to rule the schools: Women and the superintendency,* (pp. 1873-1995). Albany, NY: State University of New York Press.

Bruner, C., & Grogan, M. (2005, April). *National study of women in the superintendency.* Paper presented at the annual meeting of the American Educational Research Association, Montreal, Canada.

Butler, J. (1990). *Gender trouble: Feiminism and the subversion of identity.* New York, NY: Routledge.

Chowdhury, K. P. (1997). Pakistan. In G. C. L. Mak (Ed.), *Women, education, and development in Asia.* New York, NY: Garland.

Collins, P. (1990). *Black feminist thought: Knowledge, consciousness, and the politics of empowerment.* Boston, MA: Unwin Hyman.

Connell, R. W. (1987). *Gender and power.* Cambridge, England: Polity Press.

De Beauvoir, S. (1973). *The second sex.* New York, NY: Vintage.

Derrida, J. (1974). *Of grammatology* (G. C. Spivak, Trans.). Baltimore, MD: Johns Hopkins University Press. (Original work published 1967)

DeVault, M. (1999). *Liberating method: Feminism and social research.* Philadelphia, PA: Temple University Press.

Dillard, C. B. (2000). The substance of things hoped for, the evidence of things not seen: Examining an endarkened feminist epistemology in educational research and leadership. *International Journal of Qualitative Studies in Education, 13*(6), 661-681.

Faludi, S. (1991). *Backlash: The undeclared war against American women.* New York, NY: Doubleday Press.

Ferguson, N. (1984). *The feminist case against bureaucracy.* Philadelphia, PA: Temple University Press.

Fine, M. (1992). *Disruptive voices: The possibilities of feminist research.* Ann Arbor, MI: University of Michigan Press.

Franzway, S., Court, D., & Connell, R. (1989). *Staking a claim: Feminism, bureaucracy and the state.* Oxford, England: Polity Press.

Fuss, D. (1989). *Essentially speaking: Feminism nature and difference.* New York, NY: Routledge.

Gilligan, C. (1982). *In a different voice.* Cambridge, MA: Harvard University Press.

Gorelick, S. (1991). Contradictions of feminist methodology. *Gender and Society, 5,* 459-477.

Green, R. (1980). Native American women. *Signs, 6,* 248-267.

Group for Collaborative Inquiry. (1993). The democratization of knowledge. *The Adult Education Quarterly, 43*(4), 1-8.

Harstock, N. (1974). Political change: Two perspectives on power. *Quest: A Feminist Quarterly, 1*(1), 3-19.

Harding, S. (Ed.). (1987). Introduction: Is there a feminist method? In *Feminism and methodology* (pp. 1-14). Bloomington, IN: Indiana University Press.

hooks, b. (Ed.). (1990). The politics of radical black subjectivity. In *Yearning: Race, gender, and cultural politics* (pp. 15-22). Boston, MA: South End.

Kanter, R. M. (1977). *Men and women of the corporation.* New York, NY: Basic Books.

Kelly, L., Burton, S., & Reagan, L. (1994). Rescuing women's lives or studying women's oppression: What constitutes feminist research? In M. Maynard & J. Purvis (Eds.), *Researching women's lives from a feminist perspective* (pp. 27-48). London, England: Taylor & Francis.

Kelly-Gadol, J. (1987). The social relation of the sexes: Methodological implications of women's history. In S. Harding (Ed.), *Feminism and methodology* (pp. 15-28). Bloomington, IN: Indiana University Press.

Ladner, J. (1987). Tomorrow's tomorrow: The Black woman. In S. Harding (Ed.), *Feminism and methodology* (pp. 74-83). Bloomington, IN: Indiana University Press.

Ladson-Billings, G., & Tate, W. F. (1995). Toward a critical race theory of education. *Teachers College Record, 97,* 47–68.

Laible, J. (1997). Feminist analysis of sexual harassment policy; A critique of the ideal community. In C. Marshall (Ed.), *Feminist critical policy analysis* (pp. 201-215). Bristol, PA: The Falmer Press.

Laible, J. (2003). A loving epistemology: What I hold critical in my life, faith, and profession. In M. Young & L. Skrla (Eds.), *Reconsidering feminist research in educational leadership.* Albany, NY: State University of New York Press.

Lather, P. (1991). *Getting smart: Feminist research and pedagogy with/in the postmodern.* New York, NY: Routledge.

Lorde, A. (1984). *Sister outsider.* Freedom, CA: The Crossing Press.

MacDonnell, J. (2004). *Examining the construction of evidence for adolescent suicide prevention: A feminist policy analysis.* Paper presented at the annual conference of the American Educational Research Association.

MacKinnon, C. (1989). *Toward a feminist theory of the state.* Cambridge, MA: Harvard University Press.

MacLeod, J. (1987). *Ain't no makin' it: Leveled aspirations in a low-income neighborhood.* Boulder, CO: Westview Press.

Malveaux, J. (1985). Current economic trends and Black feminist consciousness. *Black Scholar, 16*(2), 26-31.

Marshall, C. (1996). Undomesticated gender policy. In B. J. Bank & P. M. Hall (Eds.), *Gender, equity, and schooling.* New York, NY: Garland.

Marshall, C. (1997). *Feminist critical policy analysis.* London, England: Falmer Press.

Marshall, C. (1999). Researching the margins: Feminist critical policy analysis. *Educational Policy, 13*(1), 59-76.

Marshall, C. (2000). Policy mechanisms for education gender equality in Australia. *Education Policy, 14*(3), 357-384.

Marshall, C., & Anderson, G. (1995). Rethinking the public and private spheres: Feminist and cultural studies perspectives on politics of education. In J. Scribner & D. Layton (Eds.), *The study of educational policies* (pp. 169-182). London, England: Falmer Press.

Marshall, C., & Gerstl-Pepin, C. (2005). *Re-framing educational politics for social justice.* Boston, MA: Allyn & Bacon, Pearson Education.

Marshall, C., & Young, M. (2006). Gender and methodology. In C. Skelton (Ed.), *The SAGE handbook of gender in education* (pp. 63-78). Thousand Oaks, CA: SAGE.

Mendez-Morse, S. (2003). Chicana feminism and educational leadership. In M. Young & L. Skrla (Eds.), *Reconsidering feminist research in educational leadership.* Albany, NY: State University of New York Press.

Mount-Cors, C. (2010). *Homing in: Mothers at the heart of health and literacy in costal Kenya* (Unpublished dissertation). The University of North Carolina at Chapel Hills.

Noddings, N. (1992). *The challenge to care in schools: An alternative approach to education.* New York, NY: Teachers College Press.

O'Bannon, B. (1994). The Narmada River project: Toward a feminist model of women in development. *Policy Sciences 27,* 247-267. Dordrecht, The Netherlands: Kluwer Academic.

Oakley, A. (1981). Interviewing women. In H. Roberts (Ed.), *Doing feminist research* (pp. 30-61). New York, NY: Routledge.

Olesen, V. (2000). Feminisms and qualitative research into the millennium. In N. K. Denzin & Y. S. Lincoln (Eds.), *Handbook of qualitative research* (pp. 215-255). Thousand Oaks, CA: SAGE.

Orloff, A. S. (1993). Gender and the social rights of citizenship: The comparative analysis of gender relations and welfare states. *American Sociological Review, 58,* 303-328.

Parsons, M., & Ward, E. (2001). The roaring silence: Feminist revisions in the educational policy literature. *Policy Studies Review, 18*(2), 46-64.

Pateman, C. (1988). The patriarchal welfare state. In A. Gutmann (Ed.), *Democracy and the state* (pp. 231-278). Princeton, NJ: Princeton University Press.

Pillow, W. S. (1997). Decentering silences/troubling irony: Teen pregnancy's challenge to policy analysis. In C. Marshall (Ed.), *Feminist critical policy analysis* (pp. 134-152). Bristol, PA: The Falmer Press.

Punch, M. (1994). Politics and ethics in qualitative research. In N. K. Denzin & Y. S. Lincoln (Eds.), *Handbook of qualitative research* (pp. 83-97). Thousand Oaks, CA: SAGE.

Ramazanoglu, C. (1989). Improving on sociology: The problems of taking a feminist standpoint. *Sociology, 23*(23), 247-42.

Reinharz, S. (1992). *Feminist methods in social research.* New York, NY: Oxford University Press.

Rowan, B. (1994). Comparing teachers' work with work in other occupations: Notes on the professional status of teaching. *Educational Researcher, 23*(6), 4-17.

Ruddick, S. (1989). *Maternal thinking: Toward a politics of peace.* Toronto, Ontario, Canada: Random House.

Sanders-Lawson, E., Smith-Campbell, S., & Benham, M. (2010). Wholistic visioning for social justice: Black women theorizing practice. In C. Marshall & M. Oliva (Eds.), *Leadership for social justice* (pp. 74-98). New York, NY: Allyn & Bacon.

Sawicki, J. (1991). Foucault and feminism: Toward a politics of difference. In M. Shanley & C. Pateman (Eds.), *Feminist interpretations and political theory* (pp. 217-231). University Park, PA: Pennsylvania State University Press.

Sawicki, J. (1994). Foucault, feminism and questions of identity. In G. Gutting (Ed.), *The Cambridge companion to Foucault* (pp. 286-312). Cambridge, England: Cambridge University Press.

Shaw, K. (2004). Using feminist critical policy analysis in the realm of higher education. *The Journal of Higher Education, 75*(1), 56-79.

Smith, D. E. (1987). *The everyday world as problematic: A feminist sociology.* Toronto, Ontario, Canada: University of Toronto Press.

Solorzano, D., & Yosso, T. (2002). Critical race methodology: Counter-storytelling as an analytical framework for education research. *Qualitative Inquiry, 8,* 23-44.

Spivak, G. (1974). Translators introduction. In J. Derrida, *Of grammatorlgy* (G. C. Spivak, Trans.). Baltimore, MD: Johns Hopkins University Press. (Original work published 1967)

Stacey, J. (2003). In the name of the family. In M. A. Mason & S. Sugarman (Eds.), *All our families: New policies for a new century* (pp. 105-128). New York, NY: Oxford University Press.

Stanfield, J. (1993). Epistemological considerations. In J. Stanfield & R. Dennis (Eds.), *Race and ethnicity in research methods* (pp. 16-36). Thousand Oaks, CA: SAGE.

Stromquist, N. P. (1997). State policies and gender equity: Comparative perspectives. In J. Bank & P. Hall (Eds.), *Gender, equity, and schooling: Policy and practice* (pp. 31-62). New York, NY: Garland.

Tyack, D., & Hansot, E. (1982). *Managers of virtue: Public school leadership in the U.S.* (pp. 1890-1980). New York, NY: Basic Books.

Waring, M. (1988). *If women counted: A new feminist economics.* San Francisco, CA: Harper & Row.

Watson, S. (1990). The state of play: An introduction. In *Playing the state: Australian feminist interventions* (pp. 1-20). London, England: Verso.

Weiler, K. (1988). *Women teaching for change: Gender, class, and power.* South Hadley, MA: Bergin & Garvey.

Weis, L. (Ed.). (1988). High school girls in a de-industrializing economy. In *Class, race, and gender in American education* (pp. 183-208). Albany, NY: State University of New York Press.

Weis, L. (1993). White male working-class youth: An exploration of relative privilege and loss. In L. Weis & M. Fine (Vol. Eds.), *Beyond silenced voices: Class, race, and gender in United States schools* (pp. 237-258). Albany, NY: State University of New York Press.

Willis, P. E. (1977). *Learning to labor: How working class kids get working class jobs.* New York, NY: Columbia University Press.

Young, M. D. (2000). Considering irreconcilable contradictions in cross-group feminist research. *International Journal of Qualitative Studies in Education, 13*(6), 558-588.

Young, M. D. (2003) The leadership crisis: Gender and the shortage of school administrators. In M. D. Young & L. Skrla (Eds.), *Reconsidering feminist research in educational leadership.* Albany, NY: State University of New York Press.

Zinn, M. (1982). Mexican-American women in the social sciences. *Signs, 8,* 259-272.

Author Contact Information: Michelle D. Young, University of Virginia. Telephone: 434-243-1040. E-mail: mdy8n@eservices .virgina.edu

CHAPTER 88

The Synergistic Leadership Theory

An Inclusive Theory in the Twenty-First Century

Beverly J. Irby, Genevieve Brown, and LingLing Yang
Sam Houston State University

Founded on equity and socially just underpinnings (Brown & Irby, 2006), the synergistic leadership theory (SLT; Irby, Brown, Duffy, & Trautman, 2002) adds a new theory to existing theoretical discussions in leadership. Shapiro (2009) pointed out that the SLT was "the first [leadership] theory in the [twenty-first] century" (p. 84). The SLT adds to existing leadership theories by (a) describing the systemic relationship and the interconnectedness of the SLT's four factors—leadership behavior, organizational structure, external forces, and attitudes, beliefs, and values, (b) promoting transformative reflection related to self, others, context, and situations, (c) encompassing the holistic nature of leadership and interactions internal and external to an organization, (d) considering contextual, situational, and changing dynamics of educational organizations, (e) exemplifying cultural relevance through the recognition that culture is an external force that significantly impacts leadership and organizations, (f) offering a framework for describing collaborative interdependence, and (g) embracing inclusivity via the inclusion of female leaders' voices and their experiences alongside those of male leaders (Irby, Brown, & Yang, 2009). Additionally, unlike some of the existing, earlier leadership theories, the SLT has numerous validation studies including "national and international samples and nonmajority populations" (Lunenburg & Ornstein, 2012, p. 125).

The Description of the Synergistic Leadership Theory

A tetrahedral model (Figure 88.1) depicts the SLT's four equal and interactive factors which are identified by four stellar points with six interaction pairs. This model can be rotated on any apex and still maintain its shape, thereby indicating no structural hierarchy or linear connotation; rather, suggesting that each factor equally affects the success of the leader in context as well as of the organization (Irby et al., 2002).

Factor 1: Leadership behavior. Leadership behaviors, within the SLT, are defined as daily professional actions exhibited by an administrator. Researchers have indicated that specific leadership behaviors may be of a masculine or feminine nature (Avila, 1993; Chaffins, Forbes, Fuqua, & Cangemi, 1995; Grogan, 1996, 1998; Helgeson, 1990; Shakeshaft, 1986, 1989). For example, leadership behaviors that have been traditionally associated with male leaders are self-assertion, separation, supervision, task orientation, independence, control, and competition (Brunner, 1999; Deal & Peterson, 1990; Marshall, 1993). Behaviors that have been ascribed to female leaders are interdependence, cooperation, receptivity, acceptance, and awareness of patterns, gestalt, and context (Aburdene & Naisbitt, 1992; Brunner, 1999; Funk, 1998; Gilligan, 1982; Grogan, 1998; Irby, et al., 2002; Matusak, 2001; Reagan & Brooks, 1995; Rosener, 1990). The SLT encompasses leadership behaviors ranging from autocratic to nurturer and includes gender-neutral behaviors (Irby et al., 2002). Further, the SLT does not endorse a particular leadership behavior as a determinant or indicator for success or failure (Schlosberg, 2003).

Although leadership often has been defined in terms of style (Kowalski, 1999); in the SLT, it is specific behaviors or actions of the leader in relation to other factors rather than *style* that result in perceived success or failure of the leaders and/or the organization. According to Irby, Brown, and Yang (2009), the twenty-first century

The Handbook of Educational Theories, pp. 985–995

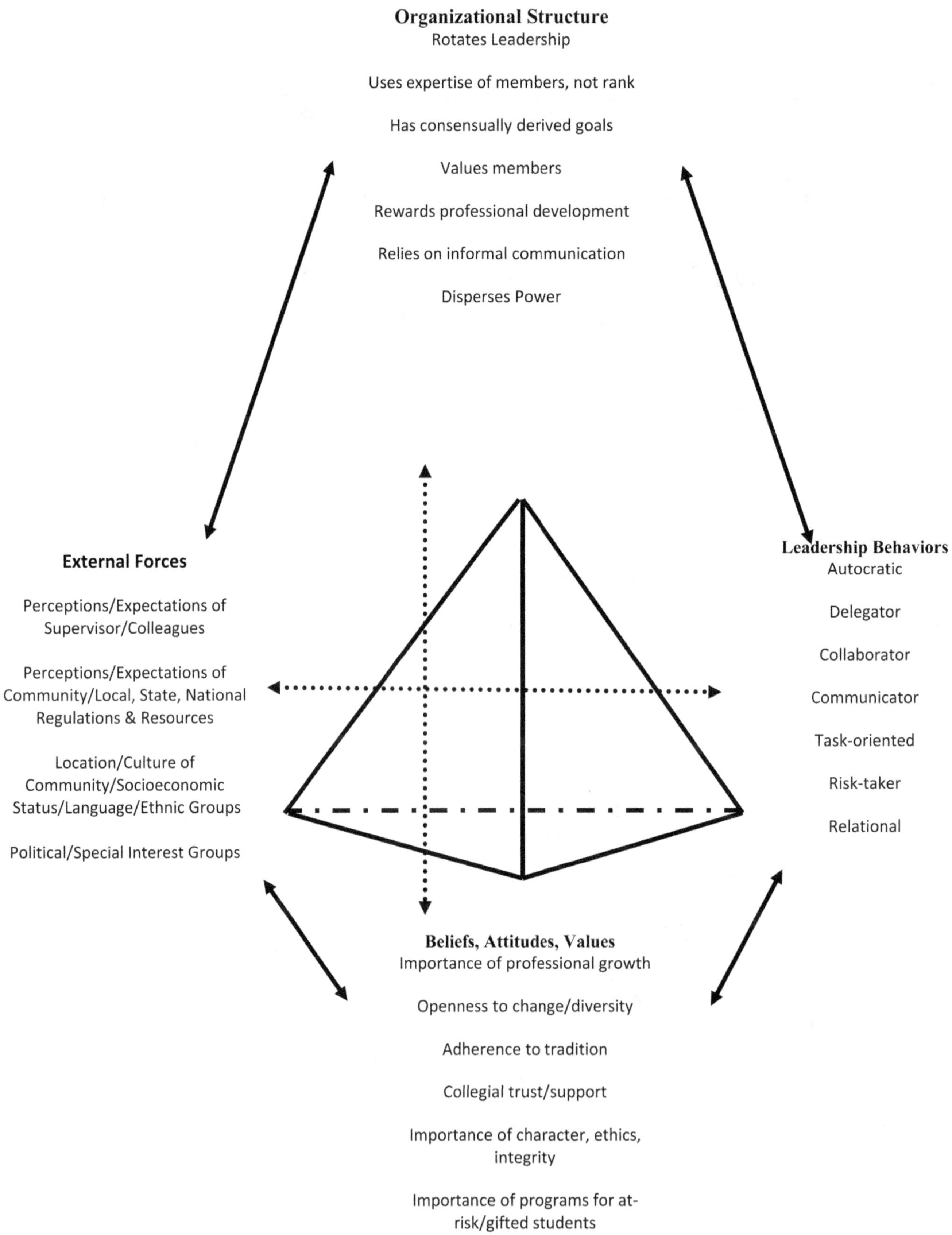

Figure 88.1. Tetrahedral model of the SLT.

necessitates that leaders be not only decisive, but also insightful and reflective. Additionally, such leaders need to be adaptable as they find themselves frequently faced with challenges to traditional practices in schools. Leadership behaviors such as decisiveness, visioning, facilitation, team building, capacity building, community building, ongoing reflection, and conflict management all support the agility necessary to lead change in the twenty-first century.

Factor 2: Organizational structure. The SLT exemplifies organizational structures ranging from rigid bureaucratic composites to open, flexible ones. The structure of the organization includes how the system operates and the organization's characteristics, as well as how the structure influences behaviors, the exchange of communication, relationships among the organization's members, and the values of the group. For example, in a bureaucratic, closed organization rules, division of labor, hierarchy of authority, impersonality, and competence are emphasized (Lunenburg & Ornstein, 2008), while in open organizational structures, practices such as collaborative decision making, systems of rotating leadership, power sharing, and a community of cooperation are promoted (Irby et al., 2002). Within the SLT, organizational structures interact with the other three to impact leadership and organizational progress.

Factor 3: External forces. In the SLT, external forces are pressures outside the organization over which leaders have no control; however, leaders must attend to such constantly changing external environments or influencers, particularly in the arena of the twenty-first century. Contextual examples of significant external forces are local, state, and national and international community and conditions, governmental regulations, laws, demographics, cultural climate, technological advances, economic situations, geography, political climate, and family conditions (Irby et al., 2002). Such external influencers are impactful on an organization's structure, on leaders' decisions and their decision-making processes, and on employers' attitudes toward employees (Irby et al.). The sources of external forces can range from the global level to the national and local community level. In the SLT, external forces interact in nontrivial ways with the other three factors.

Factor 4: Attitudes, beliefs, and values. How individuals see the world is based on their attitudes, assumptions, values, and beliefs. Thus, attitudes, beliefs, and values directly impact the choices and decisions made by individuals, communities, and organizations. Daresh (2001) recognized the interconnectedness of attitudes, values, and beliefs with a leader and the organization.

In the SLT, attitudes, beliefs, and values are described as dichotomous, meaning that an organization's member or group of members either adhere or do not adhere to specific attitudes, beliefs, or values at a given time. Examples of the dichotomous representations of attitudes, beliefs, and values included in the SLT are: openness to change or diversity, importance of professional growth, adherence to tradition, role of teachers/administration, and the purpose of school (Irby et al., 2002).

Attitudes, beliefs, and values form the foundation for principles of norms, ideas, and teachings (Irby et al., 2002). While beliefs may change as new information is processed, attitudes and values remain constant. Daresh (2001) described attitudes as "clusters of individual beliefs that survive the immediate moment" (p. 31). Irby et al. (2002) emphasized that values are "the permanent realization of beliefs and attitudes" (p. 314). In the SLT, tensions may arise if attitudes, beliefs, and values are not congruent with the other three factors of the theory (Irby et al.). According to Irby, Brown, and Yang (2009), "for [twenty-first] century leaders, understanding the attitudes, values, and beliefs of themselves and of the individuals they lead is critical to moving the vision of the organization forward" (p. 97).

Goals of the SLT

The goal of the SLT is to add to existing leadership theory by (a) including female leaders and their experiences (Irby et al., 2002), (b) recognizing that culture is an external force that significantly impacts leadership and organizations (Irby et al., 2002; Schlosberg, 2003), (c) considering contextual and situational dynamics, (d) describing the systemic relationship and the interconnectedness of leadership behavior, organizational structure, external forces and attitude, beliefs, and values, (e) promoting reflection related to self, others, and situations, (f) determining fit for individual leaders within an organization, (g) offering a nonlinear framework for describing collaborative interdependence (Irby et al, 2002), and (h) promoting equity and social justice (Brown & Irby, 2006). A secondary goal of the SLT is to enhance relevancy of theories presented in leadership training programs. This goal is accomplished by (a) providing a socially just leadership theory that has been empirically tested and found valid for both males and females and among ethnic minority groups and (b) including female voices and experiences in the development of the theory.

Assumptions and Aspects of the SLT

Nine major aspects are foundational to the SLT. First, the SLT assumes that leadership is based on the positive interaction among the four factors of attitudes, beliefs, and values; leadership behaviors; external forces; and organizational structure. Second, an alignment of all four factors leads to the leader and the organization being perceived as effective or successful, while a misalignment among the four factors negatively impacts the perceived effectiveness of the leader and the organization (Irby et al., 2002). Third, reflection and location of self in relation to all four factors is critical to attaining desired factor alignment (Irby, Brown, & Yang, 2009). Fourth, leaders at various positions or levels, that is, teacher leaders to superintendents, are impacted differently by the interactions of the factors of the theory. Fifth, female leaders may be impacted by external forces, organizational structures, and beliefs, attitudes, and values in ways male leaders are not, and vice versa. Sixth, leadership behaviors purported as female may interact with the factors in ways unlike the purported leadership behaviors of males (Irby et al., 2002). Seventh, unlike any leadership theories to date, female leaders purposefully were included in the theory development. Eighth, the theory is accompanied by an instrument, the Organizational and Leadership Effectiveness Inventory (OLEI; Irby, Brown, & Duffy, 2000) that encourages self assessment in relationship to the four factors in order to determine an individual's *fit* within an organization. Ninth, the SLT offers a theory of practice in which the leader can analyze specific tensions among the four factors and can be better positioned to address the lack of congruence, and thus, determine inhibitors to the progress of the organization or of individuals in order to prevent or alter negative perceptions related to leadership and the organization.

The Original Development of the SLT

Theory, according to Lunenburg and Ornstein (2012), is defined as "an organized body of interrelated concepts, assumptions, and generalizations that systematically explains and predicts some phenomena" (p. 2), with more well-developed theories enabling the ability "to make predictions and to control phenomena" (p. 2). Morse (1997) pointed out there is a difference in quantitatively (QNT) and qualitatively (QLT) derived theories. QNT is created by investigators through processes of reasoning and deduction using available knowledge, the wisdom of personal experience, and responding—a process known as *theorizing*. The theory is created apart from empirical data, but the results of previous empirical research may comprise some components of the theory. QLT is constructed from the empirical world during the process of inquiry and is as accurate as possible, representing the empirical world. Data analysis consists of organizing reality with inferences that are subsequently systematically confirmed in the process of inquiry. Theories developed through QLT are rich in description, and the theoretical boundaries have been derived from the context and not from the researcher's arbitrary goals for delimiting the scope. QLT produces a theory that resembles reality. The QLT was employed in the development of the SLT.

Development, Initial Validation, and Procedural Fidelity

In order to address questions of initial validity, triangulation (Lincoln & Guba, 1985) was used in the development of the SLT. Denzin (1978) identified four basic types of triangulation; we employed three of these:

- data triangulation—the use of a variety of data sources in a study;
- investigator triangulation—the use of several different researchers or evaluators; and
- methodological triangulation—the use of multiple methods to study a single problem.

Data triangulation (see Irby, Brown, Duffy, & Trautman, 2002 for full information) occurred by using multiple sources of data—current books regarding females' realities, current research reflective of women's voices, and data from interviews with women school executives and scholars in the field of educational and management leadership preparation programs. As conceptualizations emerged, interplay of the data occurred in recursive discourse and investigation. Investigator triangulation occurred using three principal investigators in the coding and interpretation of data. Methodological triangulation occurred with document content analysis of textbooks and research studies, interviews of female school executives, and open-ended surveys.

Procedural fidelity was monitored by recording times and processes of major changes in the database, providing a history of the analysis processes. First, data were gathered from an exhaustive review of the literature, books and research studies related to females in leadership or management positions. Both educational and trade books were used. Next, we developed a list of behaviors and characteristics of female-lead organizations. Third, we selected purposive sample of 30 women, nationally, from education and business for inclusion in the initial development phase. Included were: 10 women school executives from urban (3), suburban (4), and rural (3) school districts (must have been in this position for 3 years); 10 women executives of corporations (must have been in the position for 3 years); 5 women from educational leadership programs and 5 women from business leadership programs at senior level professorships. These women ranked the listed items from the exhaustive review of literature as to importance in leading that came. Additionally, data were used from books and research studies regarding women's ways of leading. In browsing of documents or the coding of data, the researchers created categories (each investigator separately at first, then combined in consensus, after discussion). As new understandings developed, 20 women leaders were asked to review the data and provide feedback. Explorations of meanings were further explored through open-ended interviews (transcribed and entered as additional data for further exploration) with ten female scholars—school executives—and with ten women who were teaching in leadership preparation programs. These explorations of meanings, linking them with wider data, were reflected upon in context. We made notes and discussed those among the theory developers, furthering the development of the data. Those data discussions illuminated the concept and provided clarification, exploration, and *dimensionalizing* of concepts. As a result, additional annotations were added to the concept formation. All results became the basis of further questioning and further in-depth recursive dialogue among the theory developers and scholars in the field.

These processes supported the principle of qualitative research and grounded theory method in which inquiry is interactive, building on the results of previous inquiries and constructing new ideas out of old ones.

The Accompanying Instrument: OLEI

The OLEI consists of five sections requiring agreement or disagreement with certain statements about leadership and organization on a Likert-type rating scale of one to four for each statement, with a rating of one indicating strong disagreement and a rating of four indicating strong agreement. Comprised of a total of 96 items, the OLEI includes four subscales that address the four factors of the SLT: (a) leadership behavior, with management behavior and interpersonal behavior as subfactors, (b) external forces, (c) organizational structure, and (d) attitudes, beliefs, and values. A demographic section encompassing gender, ethnicity, and years of experience is included at the end of the instrument.

The OLEI is a revision of the original OLEI, on which Brown and Irby (2004) reworded 11 items into positive statements. For example, item #96 on the original OLEI "goals not defined" was changed to "well-defined goals." Such revisions allowed for the creation of a scale of optimal scores for the revised OLEI. Results of a factor analysis conducted on the revised OLEI evidenced that the data from the OLEI were aligned with the four factors of the SLT and confirmed the revised instrument as a valid measure of the SLT. As a result of the factor analysis, modifications were made to the OLEI optimal factor scores as two items were excluded from the revised OLEI participant responses. Revalidating the instrument was necessary due to the revisions made to the instrument by Brown and Irby (2004). A full review of the instrument may be read in Holtkamp, Irby, Brown, and Yang (2007) and in Hernandez (2004).

Validation Studies

Since its development, the SLT has been validated for both males and females and at various management levels across American ethnic cultural and geographic locations in the United States and in international settings (Ardovini, Brown, & Irby, 2006; Bamberg, 2004; Glenn, 2008; Hernandez, 2004; Holtkamp, 2001; Holtkamp et al., 2006; Schlosberg, 2003; Trautman, 2000; Truslow, 2004; Yang, Irby, & Brown; 2008).

Trautman Study

Trautman (2000) conducted a mixed method study to validate the SLT nationally with male and female superintendents, assistant superintendents, and secondary (Grades 6-12) and elementary principals (Grades K-5). For the quantitative study, a total sample of 800 was randomly selected from four levels of management; at each level of management 100 females and 100 males were chosen. The qualitative sample was composed of 34 participants, including 7 superintendents, 4 assistant superintendents, 4 secondary principals, and 7 elementary principals. Her quantitative study, applying the OLEI, found that males and females acknowledge use of a wide range of male and female leadership behaviors. With the researcher-developed open-ended interview data, her qualitative findings revealed that although males and females saw the four factors of the SLT interacting in different ways, they did acknowledge that all four factors of the SLT are interactive.

Holtkamp Study

Holtkamp (2001) examined the psychometric properties of the OLEI to determine if the OLEI was a valid measure of the SLT. Utilizing data collected from 374 randomly selected public male and female school leaders, including 90 superintendents, 102 assistant superintendents, 76 secondary principals, and 94 elementary principals, a confirmatory factor analysis was conducted with varimax rotation with a four-factor solution to verify whether the items of the OLEI aligned with the four constructs presented in the SLT model. The results of this quantitative study evidenced the OLEI as a statistically valid measure of the SLT. Additionally, because the OLEI data aligned with the four factors of the SLT, the OLEI and the theory can be applied to male and female leaders from the four management levels, as well as leaders from different ethnic groups.

SCHLOSBERG STUDY

Schlosberg (2003) employed the SLT as a theoretical framework to examine the extent of applicability of the SLT to selected educational leaders in a Mexican non-profit school setting. The researcher collected multiple sources of data, utilizing semistructured open-ended interview and focus group questions and various techniques, including face-to-face individual interviews, focus group, and the researcher's observation and reflection, among a purposeful sample of 56 participants. The 56 participants were: 2 school cofounders (1 female, 1 male), 5 instructional coordinators (4 females, 1 male), 21 school teachers (16 females, 5 males), 6 high school student leaders (5 females, 1 male), 6 community educational leaders (5 females, 1 male), 15 parents (13 females, 2 males), and 1 male university professor. The qualitative case study revealed that each of the four factors of the SLT has cross-cultural applicability to the selected Mexican leaders, that the SLT is a helpful tool for understanding leadership practice in another culture, and that culture exerts a significant impact on leadership practice and perceived success.

BAMBERG STUDY

Bamberg (2004) examined and analyzed the leadership experiences of five female superintendents leading five successful school districts nationwide through the lens of the SLT. The leadership experiences of each superintendent was investigated by interviewing 15 participants (i.e., five superintendents, five administrative team members, and five school board members), with semistructured, open-ended interview questions created through reviewing the OLEI. The 15 participants were purposefully chosen and represented five school districts in five different states (i.e., Texas, Minnesota, Rhode Island, California, and Maryland). To collect additional data, a follow-up survey study was conducted using a revised OLEI (Hernandez, 2004; Irby, Brown, Holtkamp, 2001). Bamberg, via the qualitative case studies, found three of the five superintendents had aligned factors in their districts. Two superintendents did not have alignment with their external forces; however, one used her leadership behaviors to marginalize the impact of the misalignment, while the other did not take corrective actions and the factors continued to be misaligned. As a result, the superintendent was perceived as unsuccessful and subsequently left the position.

HERNANDEZ STUDY

Hernandez's (2004) study was designed to revalidate the revised OLEI (completed by Brown and Irby in 2004) which was used as a measure of the SLT and to examine the perceptions of superintendents and school boards with regards to the applicability of the four factors of the SLT. The sample consisted of a national, stratified random sample of 2,000 public school superintendents and their respective school board presidents. The total 423 returned instruments represented 260 superintendents (118 female and 142 male) and 163 school board presidents (79 for female superintendents and 84 for male superintendents). The analyses revealed that the perceptions of superintendents and school boards were congruent with regard to the four factors of the SLT, though some disagreements existed between the superintendents and board presidents in the perceptions of risk taking, external forces, and change agents.

TRUSLOW STUDY

The purpose of the Truslow's (2004) study, involving a mixed method, was to identify the differences in conflict management modes of male and female public school superintendents in relation to the SLT. Both quantitative and qualitative data were collected through two instruments: the Thomas-Kilmann Inventory, an open-ended interview protocol, and the OLEI, among a stratified random sample of 500 female and 500 male superintendents. According to the data, male and female superintendents have significantly different conflict management modes. Additionally, a relationship was identified between the four factors of the SLT and each conflict management mode. There was no difference between gender and the SLT within each conflict management mode. The identification of the same factors as sources of incongruence within each conflict mode among male and female superintendents suggests that gender is related to each conflict management mode; however, gender is not related to perceived incongruence among factors of the SLT and conflict within each conflict management mode.

KASPER STUDY

Kasper (2006) utilized phenomenological case study method to examine the relationship of the SLT to the experiences of four elementary principals leading exemplary, low socioeconomic schools. The four campuses were purposefully selected from 80 exemplary elementary campuses in Texas, based upon the criteria of greater than 50% of their students identified as economically disadvantaged. A total of 20 participants were involved in the study, including 4 principals, their four direct supervisors, 8 campus staff members (2 per campus), and 4 parents (1 from each campus). The data were gathered through participants' completing face-to-face interviews and the OLEI. Qualitative case study results revealed that the principals in the study acted purposefully and proactively through the use of their leadership behaviors to positively impact the organizational structures, external forces, and attitudes, values and beliefs of their organization to produce exemplary student achievement. Kasper further indicated that it was critical to the effective leadership and success of the campuses that all four factors of the SLT were in alignment.

Justice Study

The purpose of Justice's (2007) study was to determine whether there exist significant differences between the perceptions of male and female secondary school principals in relation to the four factors of SLT. The target population consisted of 36 principals of public schools in Western North Carolina counties. All 36 principals were invited to participate in the study, and 20 (12 males and 8 females) responded. Utilizing the OLEI, with an added sociodemographic component designed to collect principal and school demographic data, Justice examined (a) these principals' leadership behaviors, beliefs, attitudes, and values, (b) how their leadership is impacted by external forces and organizational structure, and (c) their perceptions of how the four factors of the SLT interact. Justice concluded that there are no significant differences in male and female secondary school principals' perceptions of the interactions of the SLT factors of leadership behavior, external forces, organizational structure, and attitudes, beliefs, and values. Further, both male and female secondary school leaders shared congruent perceptions with regard to four factors of the SLT.

Glenn Study

Glenn (2008) employed a mixed method to examine superintendent search consultants' perceptions of school boards' expectations of superintendent candidates in relation to the SLT. Data for the study were collected among a snowballing sample of 108 superintendent search consultants in Texas, utilizing the OLEI as the quantitative instrument and open-ended questions as the qualitative instrument. Data analyses revealed multiple career path barriers for aspiring superintendents; among them, experience was the most significant barrier for candidates. In addition, Glenn found that (a) excellent interpersonal and communication skills as a component of the SLT are essential for superintendent candidates and that the SLT can assist in determining fit for such a position via external search firms, (b) the career positions most likely to benefit superintendent candidates, and (c) the most beneficial preparatory position for candidates was the high school principalship.

Yang Study

Yang, Irby, and Brown (2008) conducted a theoretical validation test on the applicability and transcendence of the SLT to leaders in East Asian cultures. By examining and comparing the SLT and East Asian cultural values and traditions that impact leadership practices in East Asian cultures, researchers found some linkages and congruence existing between the Western-developed SLT and Confucian Asian values and traditions. Specifically, the linkages and congruence deal with ethics of care and the transformational nature of the SLT. Because of the congruence, the study confirmed the possibility of the transcendence of the SLT to leaders in East Asian cultures.

Summary of Validation Studies

All these validation studies indicated the SLT is a useful theory for understanding leadership practices and educational organizations because, foundationally, the SLT

1. is gender inclusive (Irby et al., 2002; Schlosberg, 2003; Trautman, 2000);
2. is contextual and situational (Kaspar, 2006; Irby et al., 2002; Trautman, 2000; Holtkamp, 2001);
3. is cultural transcendent (Irby et al., 2002; Schlosberg, 2003, Yang, Irby & Brown, 2008);
4. possesses explanatory power across a range of leadership positions and by gender (Justice, 2007; Kaspar, 2004; Trautman et al., 2006; Truslow, 2004);
5. is practical and useful for understanding interactive systems (Trautman et al., 2006); and
6. is applicable by external search firms in determining fit for executive school positions (Glenn, 2008).

Generalizability Considerations

Gender-Inclusive Leadership Consideration

The SLT is the first gender-inclusive leadership theory that addresses the female perspective and includes attributes, experiences, and abilities inherent in both male and female leaders (Irby, Brown, & Duffy, 1999). Focusing on gender inclusivity and seeking gender equity, the SLT included female leaders in theory development. By acknowledging a range of behaviors and organizational structures inclusive of those considered feminine, the SLT reflects females' leadership experiences (Brown & Irby, 2006). The theory states that female leaders may be impacted by external forces, organizational structures, beliefs, attitudes, and values in different ways from male leaders. As a result, female leadership behaviors may interact with the factors of the theory in ways unlike the leadership behavior of males (Brown & Irby, 2006).

Contextual and Situational Leadership Consideration

Leadership is not a *one size fits all* pursuit. Contextual leadership emphasizes that within different settings and context, a leader needs to adapt to a variety of scenarios by applying different behaviors. Situational leadership assumes that leadership behaviors depend on a range of situational factors, including the structures and culture of a group (Hersey & Blanchard, 1982; Yukl, 1989); thus, situational leadership theory implies a transcendence across contexts and cultures, requiring the leader to determine and adopt the appropriate leadership behavior in a given situation taking many situational (including cultural) factors into consideration. The SLT is contextual and situational (Holtkamp, 2001; Irby et al., 2002; Schlosberg, 2003; Trautman, 2000; Yang, 2008), incorporates the characteristics of situational leadership, and furthers the concept of situational leadership by acknowledging multiple vantage points and taking in account multiple perspectives and cultures.

Systemic and Holistic Leadership Consideration

Based upon a systems theory approach, the SLT's model portraits a complex interrelational system. The model of the theory reflects the work of Fuller (1979) who employed synergy to describe interactions of systems. Irby et al. (2002) described the SLT as "relational and interactive, rather than linear, with four factors interacting in substantial ways" (p. 312). The SLT calls for attention to a number of interconnected behaviors, attitudes, beliefs, values, external forces, and organizational structures (Irby et al., 2002) and stresses the dynamic interactions of the four factors. Emphasizing the importance of the alignment among the four factors, the SLT implies that regardless of "values, beliefs, attitudes, leadership behaviors, organizational structures, and external forces, the leader and organization can be perceived as effective if there is an alignment among the four factors" (Yang et al., 2008, p. 18). Additionally, the SLT has multiple vantage points and takes a macro perspective of interactions among values, beliefs, external forces, individuals, and organizations. Thus, the SLT provides complete and holistic pictures of the realities of leadership.

Explanatory Power Consideration

Explanatory power is the capacity to account for events and phenomena. A theory gains explanatory power from inherent logical consistency and is tested by how well it describes and predicts reality (Schmalleger, 2007). The SLT's explanatory power is reflected in its broad applicability in explaining a range of related or unrelated phenomena. For example, Trautman (2000) employed the SLT as a theoretical framework in her quantitative study to explain the interactions of the four factors. Her findings validated the SLT as an interactive theory for both male and female leaders at four levels of school management: elementary principals, secondary principals, central office administrators, and superintendents. Further, studies conducted by Bamberg (2004), Hernandez (2004), Holtkamp (2001), Truslow (2004), and Kaspar (2006) demonstrated the explanatory power of the SLT through the alignment or misalignment of the four factors as the interaction impacted the perceived effectiveness or ineffectiveness of the leader and the organization. Their findings also indicated explanatory power across different levels of management, including principals, superintendents, and school boards as well as by gender.

Cultural leadership consideration

Culture is defined as "The totality of socially transmitted behavior patterns, arts, beliefs, institutions, and all other products of human work and thought" (American Heritage Dictionary, 2006, p. 442). These patterns, traits, attitudes, beliefs, and values are expressions of a particular period, class, community, or society. Culture (e.g., organizational culture, and societal culture) plays a strong role in the content of leadership prototypes (Lord & Maher, 1991). According to the project GLOBE (House, Javidan, Hanges, & Dorfman, 2002), both organizational culture and societal culture affect what leaders do. Specifically, societal culture becomes an important concept in the development of theory and practice within a globalizing context (Dimmock, 2000). According to Dimmock (2000), societal culture is the enduring set of beliefs, values, and practices that differentiate one group of people from another. Societal culture serves as a filter of ideas and practices from across the globe, resulting in adoption, adaptation and rejection of these ideas. For example, when evaluating leadership behavior, followers use implicit prototypes that are heavily influenced by national culture (Lord & Maher). This implies that an individual will rate the leader's effectiveness based on a match with his own cultural prototype (Nye & Forsyth, 1991). The SLT considers culture as one of the external forces exerting important impact on leadership. The close attention to the role of culture in the SLT significantly implies that in a cross-cultural context, the leaders' personal awareness of cultural values and the need for adaptation to cultural contexts are necessary for the effective practice of leadership and the growth of the organization.

USE AND APPLICATION OF THE THEORY

The SLT can be practically applied to educational settings in a variety of ways:

1. The SLT is not focused on just the leader or just the organization; rather, the theory calls attention to a number of interconnected behaviors, beliefs, values, structures, and forces that impact the leader, the people within the organization, and the structure and success of the organization. As a result, one can analyze and describe particular interactions that may account for tension, conflict, or harmony at specific points in time or over time. If, in an analysis of all factors it is discovered that tension exists between even two of the factors, then the effectiveness of the leader or the organization itself can be negatively impacted.

2. Descriptive of the holistic environment of leading and of those lead within an organization, the SLT can serve to build an understanding of that environment in order to aid in the leader's decision making. For example, leaders cannot make decisions in isolation, failing to take into account the impact their decisions will have upon the organization (the people within) and external forces.

3. The SLT is beneficial in analyzing why or why not an individual is perceived as successful within the organization. For example, if an individual's leadership behaviors are more inclusive of the perceived feminine dimensions of leadership, but the organization is a closed bureaucratic one, with external forces also supporting such, then the tetrahedron, with the SLT's four factors as shown in the model in Figure 88.1, will be distorted, out of shape, and misaligned, resulting in perceptions that the leader is unsuccessful. If the leader is able to determine the specific tension or lack of congruence among in the four factors of the SLT, he/she is better positioned to alter those negative perceptions by:

- setting in motion a plan to alter the organizational structure and/or the external forces;
- exploring and adopting alternative another leadership behaviors;
- altering attitudes, values, and beliefs of others, and
- realigning personal values and belief structures to that of the organization and/or the external forces. It is possible that the individual will determine that he/she does not "fit" within the organization or that the change effort is too great—subsequently, exiting the organization may the best decision.

4. Not only is the SLT beneficial in determining the *fit* of an individual within a particular environment or organization, it can also be of assistance in job selection. The theory can be used in organizational and personal leadership analysis prior to accepting a particular leadership position. Once the individual analyzes his/her own leadership behaviors, the prospective organizational structure, the external forces, and his/her own values, beliefs, and attitudes, as well as those held by key people in the organization, the individual can then determine whether he/she can maximize his/her personal success as well as that of the organization's success. The lack of congruency among the four factors would indicate a lack of *fit* for the specific position.

5. Further analysis of the factors of the SLT can be used in personal and organizational growth efforts, team building, and conflict resolution.

6. The SLT fosters reflective practice, as it encourages individuals to engage in self-assessment. Specifically, the SLT requires the individual to assess his/her leadership behaviors in relation to the organizational structure, external forces, and attitudes, beliefs, and values. Constant vigilance in the engagement of reflection on whether or not the four factors are aligned is critical to leadership and organizational success.

CONCLUDING REMARKS

In conclusion, new leadership concepts and/or leadership organizational theories have emerged since the early 1990s which describe leadership approaches or philosophies that differ from traditional leadership models and theories developed and cultivated through the early 1980s (Irby, Brown, & Yang, 2009). Following a comprehensive study of 450 studies and books on leadership, Rost (1991) determined that leadership definitions through the 1980s were (a) structural-functionalist in a hierarchical linear mode, (b) management oriented considering leadership and management equivalent, (c) personalistic in focusing only on the leader while paying no attention to the follower, (d) goal achievement dominated, (e) self-interested and individualistic in outlook, (f) male oriented, (g) utilitarian and materialistic in ethical perspective, and (h) rationalistic, technocratic, linear, quantitative, and scientific in language and methodology. In contrast to these older leadership definitions and theories which are guided by outdated recipes, contemporary leadership concepts, styles, and philosophies include (a) interactive leadership (Rosener, 1990), (b) caring leadership (Grogan, 1998), (c) relational leadership (Reagan & Brooks, 1995), (d) power-shared leadership (Brunner, 1999), (e) learning-focused leadership (Beck & Murphy, 1996), (f) social justice leadership (Theoharis, 2007), and (g) authentic, moral, servant, or value-added leadership (Sergiovanni, 1991, 1992, 1994). Although the aforementioned concepts, styles, and philosophies have provided valid considerations for leaders over the past 20-plus years, only two leadership theories in the twenty-first century have emerged: (a) constructivist leadership (Lambert et al., 2002; Shapiro, 2003, 2008) and (b) the synergistic leadership theory (Irby, Brown, Duffy, & Trautman, 2002).

The SLT is the only educational leadership theory that was developed to include, purposefully, female leadership experiences and perspectives. Numerous validation studies, which include both male and female educational leaders, various levels of leadership, management, and/or administration, as well as different ethnicities and cultures, have been conducted on the SLT. The SLT also has an accompanying instrument, the OLEI, which has been validated.

REFERENCES

Aburdene, P., & Naisbitt, J. (1992). *Megatrends for women*. New York, NY: Villard.

American Heritage Dictionary (4th ed.). (2006). Boston, MA: Houghton Mifflin.

Ardovini, J., Trautman, D., Brown, G., & Irby, B.J. (2006). Validating synergistic leadership theory in education: The importance of including female leadership experiences and behaviors. *Journal of Practical Leadership, 1*(1), 23-44.

Avila, L. (1993). Why women are ready for educational leadership positions. In G. Brown & Irby, B. J. (Ed.), *Women as school executives: A powerful paradigm* (pp. 47-51). Huntsville, TX: Sam Houston State University, Texas Council of Women School Executives.

Bamberg, W. (2004). An application of the synergistic leadership theory to the leadership experiences of five female superintendents leading successful school districts (Doctoral dissertation, Sam Houston State University, 2004). *Dissertation Abstracts International, 65*(08A), 2824. (UMI No. 3143574)

Beck, L. G., & Murphy, J. (1996). *The four imperatives of a successful school*. Newbury Park, CA: Corwin/SAGE.

Brown, G., & Irby, B. J. (2004). OLEI revision. Revised for Hernandez Dissertation Research for Center for Research in Educational Leadership, Sam Houston State University. Used with permission in Hernandez (2004) dissertation.

Brown, G., & Irby, B. J, (2006). Expanding the knowledge base: socially just theory in educational leadership program. In F. L. Dembowski & L. K. Lemasters (Eds.), *Unbridled spirit: Best practices in educational administration* (pp. 7-13). Lancaster, PA: DES*tech* Publications.

Brunner, C. C. (1999). Power, gender and superintendent selection. In C.C. Brunner (Ed.), *Sacred dreams: Women and the superintendency* (pp. 63-78). Albany, NY: State University of New York Press.

Chaffins, S., Forbes, M., Fuqua, H., & Cangemi, J. (1995). The glass ceiling: are women where they should be? *Education, 115*(3), 380-386.

Daresh, J. C. (2001). *Supervision as proactive leadership*. Prospect Heights, IL: Waveland Press.

Deal, T. E., & Peterson, K. D. (1990). *The principal's role in school culture*. Washington, DC: Office of Educational Research Improvement.

Denzin, N. K. (1978). *Sociological methods*. New York, NY: McGraw-Hill.

Dimmock, C. (2000). Globalization and societal culture: Redefining schooling and school leadership in the twenty-first century. *Compare: A Journal of Comparative Education, 30*, 303-313.

Fuller, B. (1979). *Synergetics 2: Further explorations in the geometry of thinking*. New York, NY: Macmillan.

Funk, C. (1998). What women bring to executive school positions. In B. J. Irby & G. Brown (Eds.), *Structuring leaders: Structuring success* (pp. 33-42). Dubuque, IA: Kendall/Hunt.

Gilligan, C. (1982). *In a difference voice*. Cambridge, MA: Harvard University Press.

Glenn, J. (2008). *Superintendent search consultants' perceptions of school boards' expectations of superintendent candidates* (Unpublished doctoral dissertation). Sam Houston State University, Huntsville, TX.

Grogan, M. (1996). *Voices of women aspiring to the superintendency*. Albany, NY: State University of New York Press.

Grogan, M. (1998). Equity/equality issues of gender, race, and class. *Educational Administration Quarterly, 36*, 518-536.

Helgeson, S. (1990). *The female advantage: Women's ways of leadership*. New York, NY: Doubleday.

Hernandez, R. (2004). An analysis and school board's perception of the factors of the synergistic leadership theory (Doctoral dissertation, Sam Houston State University, 2004). *Dissertation Abstracts International, 65*(08A), 2848. (UMI No. 3143582)

Hershey, P., & Blanchard, K. H. (1982). *Management of organizational behavior* (4th ed.). Englewood Cliffs, NJ: Prentice Hall.

Holtkamp, L. W. (2001). The validation of the organizational and leadership effectiveness inventory (Doctoral dissertation, Sam Houston State University, 2001). *Dissertation Abstracts International, 62*(07A), 2300. (UMI No. 3020890)

Holtkamp, L., Irby, B. J., Brown, G., & Yang, LL. (2007). Validation of the synergistic leadership theory. *Journal of Research for Educational Leadership, 4*, 75-111.

House, R. J., Javidan, M., Hanges, P. J., & Dorfman, P. W. (2002). Understanding cultures and implicit leadership theories across the globe: An introduction to project GLOBE. *Journal of World Business, 37*, 3-10.

Irby, B. J., Brown, G., & Duffy, J. (1999). *A feminine inclusive leadership theory*. Paper presented at the Annual Meeting of the American Educational Research Association, New Orleans, LA.

Irby, B. J., Brown, G., & Duffy, J. (2000). *Organizational and leadership effectiveness inventory*. Huntsville, TX: Sam Houston Press.

Irby, B. J., Brown, G., Duffy, J. A., & Trautman, D. (2002). The synergistic leadership theory. *Journal of Educational Administration, 40*(4), 304-322.

Irby, B. J., Brown, G., & Holtkamp, L. (2001). The adapted organizational and leadership effectiveness inventory. In L. Holtkamp (Ed.), *The validation of the organizational and leadership effectiveness inventory* (pp. 98-104). (Doctoral dissertation, Sam Houston State University, 2001). *Dissertation Abstracts International, 62*(07A), 2300.

Irby, B. J., Brown, G., & Yang, L. L. (2009). The synergistic leadership theory: A 21st century leadership theory. In C. Achilles & B. J. Irby (Eds.), *Remembering our mission: The 2009 NCPEA Yearbook*. Lancaster, PA: ProActive.

Justice, P. P. (2007). Secondary school leaders in western North Carolina: The impact of place and gender on selection and behavior. (Doctoral dissertation, Western Carolina University, 2007). *Dissertation Abstracts International, 68*(03A). (UMI No. 3255360)

Kaspar, K. A. (2006). The relationship of the synergistic leadership theory to the experiences of four elementary principals leading exemplary, low socio-economic campuses (Doctoral dissertation, Sam Houston State University, 2006). *Dissertation Abstracts International, 68*(02A). (UMI No. 3250648)

Kowalski, T. (1999). *The school superintendent: Theory, practice, and cases*. Upper Saddle River, NJ: Prentice-Hall.

Lambert, L., Walker, D., Zimmerman, D. P., Cooper, J. E., Lambert, M. D., Gardiner, M. E., & Slack, P. J. (2002). *The constructivist leader* (2nd ed.). New York, NY: Teachers College Press.

Lincoln, Y. S., & Guba, E. G. (1985). *Naturalistic inquiry*. Beverly Hills, CA: Sage Publications.

Lord, R. G., & Maher, K. J. (1991). *Leadership and information processing: Linking perceptions and performance*. Boston, MA: Unwin Hayman.

Lunenburg, F. C., & Ornstein, A, C. (2012). *Educational administration: Concepts and practices* (6th ed.). Belmont, CA: Wadsworth.

Marshall, C. (1993). *The new politics of race and gender*. Bristol, PA: Falmer.

Matusak, L. R. (2001). *Leadership: Gender related, not gender specific*. Washington, DC: The Academy of Leadership, University of Maryland.

Morse, J. M. (Ed.). (1997). *Completing a qualitative project: Details and dialogue*. Newbury Park, CA: SAGE.

Nye, J. L., & Forsyth, D. R. (1991). The effects of prototype-based biases on leadership appraisals: A test of leadership categorization theory. *Small Group Research, 22*, 360-379.

Regan, H., & Brooks, G. (1995). *Out of women's experiences: Creating relational leadership*. Thousand Oaks, CA: Corwin Press.

Rosener, J. (1990). Ways women lead. *Harvard Business Review, 68*(4), 28-49.

Rost, J. C. (1991). *Leadership for the twenty-first century*. New York, NY: Praeger.

Schlosberg, T. V. (2003). Synergistic leadership: An international case study (Doctoral dissertation, Sam Houston State University, 2003). *Dissertation Abstracts International, 64*(07A), 2337. (UMB No. 3098504)

Schmalleger, F. (2007). *Criminal justice: A brief introduction* (7th ed.). Englewood Cliffs, NJ: Prentice Hall.

Shapiro, A. (2003). *Case studies in constructivist leadership and teaching*. Lanham, MD: Scarecrow.

Shapiro, A. (2008). *The constructivist leader: A guide to the successful approaches*. Lanham, MD: Roman & Littlefield.

Sergiovanni, T. (1991). *The principalship: A reflective practice perspective* (2nd ed.). Boston, MA: Allyn & Bacon.

Sergiovanni, T. (1992). *Moral leadership: Getting to the heart of leadership*. San Francisco, CA: Jossey-Bass.

Sergiovanni, T. (1994). *Building community in schools*. San Francisco, CA: Jossey-Bass.

Shakeshaft, C. (1986). *Women in education administration*. Beverly Hills, CA: SAGE.

Shakeshaft, C. (1989). *Women in educational administration*. Newbury Park, CA: Corwin Press.

Shapiro, A. (2009, January). *A comprehensive theory and practice of constructivist leadership*. Paper presented at the International Congress for School Effectiveness and Improvement, Vancouver, Canada.

Theoharis, G. T. (2007). Social justice educational leaders and resistance: Toward a theory of social justice leadership. *Educational Administration Quarterly, 43*, 221-258.

Trautman, D. (2000). A validation of the synergistic leadership theory: A gender-inclusive leadership theory (Doctoral dissertation, Sam Houston State University, 2000). *Dissertation Abstracts International, 62*(07A), 2598. (UMI No. 3020899)

Truslow, K. O. (2004). Effects of the synergistic leadership theory: A gender-inclusive Leadership theory (Doctoral dissertation, Sam Houston State University, 2004). *Dissertation Abstracts International, 65*(08A), 2859. (UMI No. 3143586).

Yang, L.- L., Irby, B. J. & Brown, G., (2008, May 6). *Applicability of the synergistic leadership theory to leaders in East Asian cultures*. Paper presented at 2008 Global Leadership Conference, Shanghai, China.

Yukl, G. A. (1989). *Leadership in organizations*. Englewood Cliffs, NJ: Prentice Hall.

Author Contact Information: Beverly J. Irby, EdD, Professor and Chair, Department of Educational Leadership and Counseling, Sam Houston State University, Huntsville, TX 77341. E-mail: edu_bid@shsu.edu

Section 12: Social Justice Theory

INTRODUCTION

SECTION EDITOR
Jill Blackmore
Deakin University Melbourne, Australia

Social justice has again emerged as a major theoretical, research and policy issue in the past decades as evidence as to the detrimental effects of neoliberal reforms of the late twentieth century are emerging. Market and managerial approaches informing policies based on efficiency, narrow measures of effectiveness, and parental choice have exacerbated old inequalities in new ways in most Anglophone nation states. Given the failure of neoliberal policies to deliver greater educational equity, and because of the promises promoted in the policy rhetoric about the need for more self-reliant citizens and adaptable workers in globalized societies characterized by cultural diversity, mobility and fluidity, strong theories of social justice offering alternative ways of imagining our shared educational futures are important.

The selection of theorists of social justice to include in this section was complex:-whether to include only the mainstream theorists of social justice that have dominated liberal thought and approaches to education such as Rawls (1971); or to focus on marginalized discourses where debates over social justice have often been located and explicitly integrated into theoretical frameworks in education, including critical theory, the liberation theology of Freire, feminist theory and critical race theory. Given that feminism produced the greatest theoretical resurgence in the 1980s, which feminist theories about social justice would be most appropriate—Nancy Fraser, Iris Young or Martha Nussbaum? Furthermore, does one recognize the shift towards post structuralism in educational thought in the late twentieth century and its critique of universals? What would Foucault, who refused to do theory or promote social justice, have to offer a theory of social justice? The selection of papers therefore provides a range of epistemological and political perspectives on social justice.

In an overview, Jill Blackmore provides an historical account of the primary theories of social justice that have informed educational thinking and practice. She considers a range of theories, starting with dominant liberal theories such as Rawls theory of "justice as fairness," and Habermasian critical theory through to Critical race theory, and Foucault's rejection of universal theory. Her feminist perspective provides the analytical tools to identify each theory's strengths and weakness in terms of addressing the complexities arising from various forms of oppression. She suggests that the feminist theories of Nancy Fraser which focus on three principles of redistribution, recognition and association together with capability theories of Sen and Nussbaum provide alternative ways of addressing justice from a pluralist perspective.

As Richard Bates outlines in his chapter, there were two strands of critical theory that emerged during the 1980s in education. Critical theory (CT) from the European liberationist tradition of the Frankfurt School was informed by Jurgen Habermas who sought to deconstruct the relationship through *dialogical analysis* between forms of knowledge, power and freedom. As Bates has argued, Habermas sought to transform capitalism to make it more democratic based on encouraging *communicative practices* that would lead to consensus for action, thus displaying a faith in the capacity of dialogue to inform democratic practice. This view was developed through the notion of an *ideal speech situation* that was based on particular rules of involvement to encourage dialogue, without coercion or intimidation. Habermas also recognized the power of ideology to distort discourse in the *lifeworld* and encouraged a critique of discourse to unpack how *systems* of media, power and discourse work to advantage some and not others. Bates suggests that new technologies that have produced new forms of social media and communication promise other ways in which the lifeworld can better respond to inequality.

The second strand of critical theory, developed initially in the United States, was based on Freire's (1970)

The Handbook of Educational Theories, pp. 997–999

Pedagogy of the Oppressed (1970) which drew from Liberation Theology and the pragmatism of Dewey. In education, Freire's writings and activism stimulated numerous emancipatory educational and political projects in the Third World. He focused on adult literacy as the means of emancipation for those living in poverty and under oppression as literacy facilitated processes of *conscientiazatio*n that could develop a sense of agency and action. In particular, Freire's notion of changing education from a view of the "banking" of knowledge into a view of learners as producers of knowledge has informed progressive thinking into the twenty-first century.

Emerging out of the civil rights movement is critical race theory (CRT) that argues "race" is socially constituted. Chapman Dixson, Gillborn, and Ladson-Billings identify the numerous antiracist strategies that CRT has developed, such as producing counternarratives that unpack how everyday racism is normalized through the law, structures, policies and practices in education as in the case of streaming according to ability or in terms of what counts as merit. Context was critical to wins and losses as CRT scholars have been politically pro-active. CRT critiqued civil rights laws, in particular explicating how blacks gained rights only when they were in the interests of the dominant whites as with the landmark *Brown vs Board of Education* desegregation case at the time of the Cold War. CRT strategically assumes a position of racial realism: aiming to not just do what ought to be done, but also what could be done within current constraints. At the same time, their chapter charts the growing recognition of CRT in the academy, although not without its critics because if its questioning of the category of race (Anthias & Lloyd, 2002).

In the chapter on Nancy Fraser, Martin Mills indicates how Fraser works through the tensions between economic redistribution and cultural recognition as analytical tools with particular regard to gender and race where these tensions are most evident, and why and how she argues the case for *affirmative* and *transformative remedies*. Affirmative remedies seek to rectify inequalities without altering the structural and cultural relations from which they are produced, whereas transformative remedies seek to radically reform these structures and cultures.

Finally, Carolyn Shields indicates in her chapter, notions of democracy and social justice are themselves contested and context specific. Therefore, she argues one needs to work from a set of social justice principles that may lead to different local practices. Shields usefully distinguishes between a *socially just education* and *social justice education*. The former implies that the learning environment, organizational structures, and educational opportunities experienced by students offer equity of both access and outcomes to all students has to be premised upon a set of principles, as cited below

- All persons in a given organization shall be treated respectfully
- The education institution will ensure equitable access for all
- The education institution will promote equitable outcomes for all
- The practices of the organization should emphasize mutual benefit
- The norms and practices of the organization shall be equally inclusive of all members
- All members of a designated group (society, community, school) shall have equal civil, political, and social rights as citizens

Socially just education recognizes a wide range of capabilities in a proactive and positive rather than negative view of difference. *Social justice education* means students are educated about issues of social justice and how they can aware of how to work towards a fairer and more just society.

Kari Dehli's chapter on whether, and how, Foucault as a poststructuralist would consider social justice as an issue provides a counterpoint to the above positions which assume that a theory of social justice is desirable for, and possible in, education. Drawing from teaching Foucault to graduate students, Dehli indicates how his thinking tools regarding the archeology of knowledge, genealogy and governmentality have informed educational thinking about power as being dispersed with both positive and negative possibilities, the role of discourse and how deconstruction leads to the questioning of truth claims, and how these approaches informed new ways of thinking about social justice in diverse areas such as pedagogy, policy, leadership, and curriculum.

Collectively these papers provide a comprehensive overview of how theories of social justice have been mobilized in education to advance thinking about the possibilities of creating a more equitable society and quality of life for all. As Blackmore points out, because of the complexity of globalized societies and recognition of cultural difference the need for more complex ways of theorizing social justice has produced pluralist notions of social justice. The question that remains is whether our current democratic processes are capable of making use of these theories to inform policy and practice, as political will at the national and international level as well as a sense of localized agency is critical.

REFERENCES

Anthias, F., & Lloyd, C. (2002) *Rethinking racisms: From theory to practice.* London, England: Routledge.

Freire, P. (1970). *Pedagogy of the oppressed.* New York, NY: Seabury.

Rawls, J. (1971). *A theory of justice.* Cambridge, MA: The Belknap Press of Harvard University Press.

Author Content Information: Jill Blackmore, PhD, School of Education, Deakin University Melbourne, Australia, Phone: + 61 392 446396. E-mail: jillb@deakin.edu.au

CHAPTER 89

Social Justice in Education

A Theoretical Overview

Jill Blackmore
Deakin University

Social justice is about what constitutes "fairness" in a "good" society. Therefore, social justice is central to analyzing the role of the state with regard to the individual and different social groups in terms of the provision of education. Social justice has therefore been at the core of influential educational theories. Theorizing social justice requires us to both understand the different forms of inequality arising out of different forms of oppression, whether exploitation, marginalization, powerlessness, cultural imperialism, or violence (Young, 1990). Such inequality can be based on gender, race, class, sexuality or disability and is often the unintentional consequence of systematic and everyday practice. Focusing on social justice encourages us to consider the "institutional conditions necessary for the development and exercise of individual capacities and collective communication and cooperation" as well as imagine what constitutes a good society (Young, 1990, p. 39). It also requires us to think about who should make claims (an individual or a group), upon what institution should these claims be made (state, courts) and on what basis such claims can be made—rights, interests or needs?

The following narrative charts broad historical themes in education that contextualize each theorist historically and conceptually within wider debates over the changing ways in which social justice has been understood. Theories of social justice emerge out of specific historical conditions, discourses and epistemological legacies, each taking on different imperatives and trajectories. There has always been a strong discourse of social justice evident in educational theory from various perspectives—philosophy, psychology, history, politics, and sociology. Piaget and Dewey's work during the early twentieth century indicated a "strong correlation between learning and rights" premised upon a naturalist view that considered there were strong environmental influences on individual character and consciences (Burke, 2007, p. 337). Dewey's influence on progressive educational thinking in Western democracies is paramount (see Shields in this section). Dewey argued that education focus on the authentic needs of the individual child in order he or she become an active participant in a social democracy, a perspective not backed up by legal rights until the 1924 Geneva Declaration of the Rights of the Child (Burke, 2007).

Human rights were also closely tied up with the post 1945 desire to protect individual freedom without distinction as to race, sex, language, or religion across continents. Social justice therefore raises issues about the nature of the democratic state and dominant political theories in Western societies such as liberalism. Cultural traditions are embedded within theories of social justice, in terms of how liberalism is understood and enacted through legislation and practice, as well as how each views the role of the state and international bodies such as the United Nations, Organization for Economic Cooperation and Development (OECD), and World Bank (see Blackmore, 2005, 2006). Scandinavian states have a more social democratic focus and equality discourse which has seen greater state investment in child care, family friendly workplaces, and so on. Sawer (2003) points to how historically contractarian liberalism is stronger in the United States compared to social liberalism in the United Kingdom or Australia, although there is now a convergence among the Anglophone nations states due to the intellectual hegemony

The Handbook of Educational Theories, pp. 1001–1009

of United States and new public administration reforms since the 1980s (Blackmore, 2007). Contractarian liberalism in the United States sees the state as separate from nongovernment organizations, such as the women's and civil rights movements, which are often oppositional rather than complimentary. A big state from this perspective means less individual freedom, rather than a state supportive of individual freedoms, a position held in the United Kingdom, Australia, and New Zealand. Social liberals are more concerned about the division between the private market sphere dominated by self-interest (market liberalism) and citizenship, which requires both state and nonstate activities in civil sphere or "third sector" voluntarism (social liberalism). Different theories get mobilized in different contexts by different traditions of critical theory.

Claims for children's rights are also informed by, and inform, educational theory, each with different conceptualizations of the child (Burke, 2007). A behaviorist approach tends to derive from the psychological traditions that are teacher-centered and focus on the transmission of knowledge. More critical perspectives have focused on meaning-centered education that is about nurturing the individual capacities of the child to encourage the individual to learn to be responsible and autonomous based on a feeling of belonging. The latter approach addresses social and material contexts and thus requires basic needs to be met as preconditions to learning, including freedom from poverty and poor nutrition as well as access to equal schooling, and therefore foregrounds notions of social justice that go beyond the psychological. This requires theorists of social justice to address the role of the state and the courts when considering how social justice can be enacted in specific national contexts.

STATE WELFARISM

Schooling has long been considered to be an institution of both social control and or emancipation by political, religious and philanthropic institutions, whether with the Poor Laws in England, Ireland and Scotland; the New Deal in the USA inspired by a democratic urge in response to the Great Depression of the 1930s; liberation theology in South America; or recent "development" theory in Africa and South-East Asia. Since the move toward government funded universal primary education in the 1870s in most Western democracies, education has been considered integral to nation-state building and industrialized economies. The post-1945 expansion of secondary education for all was seen to be critical to rebuilding postwar national economies. Social and economic inequality was foregrounded in the 1960s by the student and civil rights movements with the focus on race in the United States, and gender inequality by the women's movement. Education was considered by the 1970s from a neo-Marxist perspective to be a primary site of the economic, cultural and social reproduction of capitalism (Bourdieu & Passeron, 1977; Bowles & Gintis, 1976). Yet the welfare state in most Western liberal democracies during the late twentieth century was premised upon a shared belief that equitable systems of education were central to social democratic life. Indeed, under various weak and strong forms of state-welfarism in North America, Europe, Scandinavia, and Australasia, the gap between rich and poor decreased during the 1980s. Funding individual equal opportunity within largely government funded meritocratic education systems was seen to contribute to the public good (Blackmore, 2007).

The focus of social theory in the 1960s, influenced by neo-Marxism, was primarily on distributive justice, on how to redistribute wealth more evenly. Educational reform was about remediating economic inequality as exemplified in the great reforms in the United States, the United Kingdom, and Australia. In the most part, the strategy was to provide equality of access to, and participation in, rather than equality of outcomes, in education, contextualized by debates over whether schools "could make a difference" such as the Coleman Report (1966) in the United States. Highly influential after writing *A Theory of Justice* (1971), the philosopher John Rawls, drawing on the social contract theory of Hobbes, Locke, Rousseau, and Kant, sought to elaborate within liberal theory the principle of distributive justice to balance between liberty and equality premised upon the notion of "justice as fairness." He proposed that within constraints, decisions have to be based as if from an original position where one assumes a "veil of ignorance" in which they do not know their class position, race, gender, physical, or psychological dispositions. Rawls' assumption was that if individuals did not know what decision was in their own interests then they would make a fairer decision because they themselves could be in a position to benefit *or* lose.

Such a theory would therefore assume each would desire equal opportunity in terms of access to education, inclusion within but not necessarily equal outcomes, as individuals would like to think that there was some merit in merit. Rawl's first principle is that all people are free and equal. The second principle was that any social and economic inequalities required first, all offices be open to all under conditions of fair equal opportunity; and second, they any decisions were based on the greatest benefit to the least advantaged to society or the difference principle (Rawls 2001, pp. 42-43). In *Justice as Fairness: A Restatement* Rawls (2001) views social justice as a political concept embedded in a democratic liberalism that is premised upon social cooperation and not as a moral doctrine. Justice as fairness does not necessarily promote a particular point of religious or political view, but resorts to dialogue within a reasonable pluralist liberal democracy to produce a rational consensus. Criticisms of Rawl's theory from feminists and others are that it is a hypothetical and ahistorical position in ways that do not address human failings of self-interest. Furthermore, Martha Nussbaum (2011) argues that social contract theories do not include those who are roughly equal in capacity, such as women seeking to be leaders in schools and universities. Focusing on difference often means treating difference as a deficiency.

Critical theory developed out of neo-Marxist and later feminist critiques of liberalism. The Frankfurt School of critical theory (CT) that emerged from postwar Europe and in particular the work of Jurgen Habermas sought to reinstate as central to democratic societies the notion of communicative action and dialogue as a way of arriving at political consensus. Habermas focused on the rise of the media and its relationship to political power, knowledge, and discourse in ways that privileged elite groups. Education was critical to the democratic anticapitalist project in order to identify and challenge through communicative competence how privilege worked. The second tradition of critical theory drew from the liberation theology of Paolo Freire located in South America. Freire, in *Pedagogy of the Oppressed*, saw adult literacy education as a primary source of "conscientization" or raising awareness as to the nature of the oppression in many rural South American communities. Social justice was to be achieved through education that rejected the "banking" view of knowledge which privileged the teacher and official knowledge (refer to Bates in this section for elaborations on CT).

Both Habermas and Freire relied on notions of respect and communication in developing democratic practices and individual agency, capacities that were developed through education and processes of individual and collective self-reflection or conscientization, although each had different historical trajectories. Habermas had greater influence in the emergence of critical theory in Australia around notions of the socially critical schooling and action research, classroom practices and leadership while drawing eclectically from the new sociology of knowledge as well as multiculturalist, democratic, labour process and feminist theory. Freire informed North American debates over race, gender, and class drawing on notions of social reproduction, the hidden curriculum, and pedagogy. These traditions intersected/interacted cross-nationally in terms of their shared concerns around democratic schooling, critiquing power/knowledge relations as well as promoting teacher and student agency. Critical theorists of social justice therefore questioned the universal claims of liberalism as to its neutrality, objectivity, and universality and therefore its capacity to produce social justice.

The second wave women's movement emerged in the 1970s, alienated by the failure of the civil rights and student movements as well as male social theorists in the academy to address gender inequality. Feminism is a series of interconnected epistemological as well as social and political cross-cultural movements that have familial resemblances. Western feminist political, sociological and philosophical theory during the 1980s and 1990s, at the forefront in theorizing social justice, regarded liberalism as a political philosophy was fatally flawed because it assumed a neutral state and a disembodied abstract individual premised on the assumption that the experience of universal man was the same as that of women (Sawer, 2003).

In an important text, the Australian political theorist Carole Pateman (1980) referred to the invisible sexual contract underpinning social contract theory. Embedded in all forms of contractual relations (family, work, voluntarism), social contract theory positioned women's claims, such as for childcare, as a private matter without public benefits (Yeatman, 1994). In particular, there was a focus on the unequal effects of the social contract premised upon a public/private binary, with male rationality dominating the "public" domain of paid work and politics, and female emotionality (positioned as irrational) supporting the "private" domain of the family and care. Debates about paid family leave continue around whether having children is an individual's choice (private) or a state (taxpayer or public) responsibility.

Feminists have responded through collectivist action with nongovernment organizations to make claims upon the state and legal systems or as in Australia and Scandinavia through feminists located within the state (femocrats). Feminist activists developed equal opportunity policies for girls and women during the 1970s and 1980s on the basis of their collective interests but which initial focused on changing women and girls while claiming equal access to and participation in the same education as boys (Blackmore, 2006, 2007). Interestingly, social justice discourses for women have been premised less on rights as individuals and more upon needs as mothers and caregivers, similar to claims made around disability. Implicitly, this positions women as having different interests to men (and the nation state) and also as being deficient (as needy). Therefore, women as a social group tend to gain improved distribution of rewards and status when their interests coincide with the nation's interests, such as getting mothers back into work when there are skill shortages.

Through the women's movement after the 1960s, feminists remained critical of other critical theories. For example, Habermas drew on those Enlightenment traditions of science of which many feminists were wary because of the ways Enlightenment science traditionally positioned women by taking the position of the dislocated or disinterested observer. Making gender (or race) invisible was seen to obliterate how inequality was produced (as for example Rawls "veil of ignorance") and therefore was inadequate as an explanatory theory of injustice and led to weak theories of social justice. Feminist standpoint theorists such as Sandra Harding (1987), therefore sought to develop a feminist science and epistemology to provide an alternative perspective as to what counts as valued knowledge, thereby utilizing science for its emancipatory possibilities. In that sense, Habermas and feminist standpoint theorists sought to elaborate or expand on Enlightenment's belief in the capacity of different sciences to create antiracist, free, and democratic societies.

Likewise, while recognizing the positive influence of Frierian pedagogy, a feminist critical pedagogy tradition emerged premised not on the role of the teacher, or the media or social institutions, but on women's and girl's experiences (Weiler, 1991). Feminists too had mobilized conscience-raising groups, and developed feminist pedagogies through women's studies and education programs in community colleges, universities and schools as a means of encouraging voice and legitimating different ways of seeing and knowing (Luke & Gore, 1993). Feminists also were critical of any presumption that women could be "empowered" by another as some critical pedagogy approaches implied (Ellsworth, 1993). Given that much research and theory of the Enlightenment was done by men on men, making women's voices and experiences visible was central to producing comprehensive theories of social justice that addressed gender inequality and all its forms of exploitation, oppression and domination.

New perspectives on social justice emerged from within feminist and neo-Marxist perspectives and the civil rights movements around issues of race and class during the 1970s as different cultural groupings based on race, ethnicity in what has been called the politics of recognition made claims upon the nation state and challenged White-centric social movements and theory (Fraser, 1977). Chapman, Dixson, Gillborn, and Ladson-Billings (in this section) chart how critical race theory (CRT) developed as an antioppressive theory. Deeply critical of the color-blindness of liberalism, CRT emerged from the work of U.S. Black legal scholars in the 1970s and was brought into education through the work of Gloria Ladson-Billings and Tate (1995) and the feminist Patricia Hill Collins (1990) where it received mainstream opposition because of its focus on white dominance and everyday racist practices. CRT drew from multiple disciplines to critique the notion of race as fixed, immutable, biological, and essentialized and argued that race is socially and historically constructed. CRT focuses on the representations, structures, cultures, and processes of education that socially constitute "race." Particular "racialized" subjectivities and collectivities have been marginalized, discriminated against, and pathologized, not only within dominant "White," a color of "naturalized" privilege, societies. CRT considers how "race" is a marker of difference in multiracial contexts where cultural ("racial") purism is no longer possible, and the complexities of race, gender, class, and religion produce different synchronicities of disadvantage in particular contexts.

Social justice for CRT theorists have led to a focus on how geography, identity, and culture work to disadvantage particular racialized groups in gaining access to the same opportunities through education, the same sense of belonging through participation in education, and similar educational outcomes. Curriculum and pedagogy have been a focus in terms of creating inclusive educational environments in terms of whose knowledge is valued and whose experience heard and legitimated, as well as creating cultures of inclusion. Feminist indigenous scholars have also challenged white feminists as to how they are complicit in maintaining certain power/knowledge hierarchies which negates indigenous ways of being and knowing (Moreton-Robinson 2000).

Feminist theoretical debates about social justice from the 1990s have been dominated by debates between Nancy Fraser and her critics (e.g., Fraser & Honneth, 2003) and among feminist scholars such as Judith Butler and Iris Marion Young (1997) around the competing principles of economic redistribution and cultural recognition (see Mills chapter in this section). Feminist theorists have identified a dilemma in that while seeking to problematize categories such as women as a unitary and fixed category and recognizing the complexity of how gender intersects with race, class, religion, and disability, this tends to undermine the ways in which women can make claims as a group upon the state. Gender is inextricably linked to economic injustice in terms of the ongoing embedded gender division of labour which devalues women's work (unpaid and paid), including teaching.

Feminists have fully understood how women indeed embody culture; thus changing women's roles and recognizing their rights challenges cultural traditions. Reducing gender inequality means changing the social, economic and political relations of gender regimes that are embedded in all forms of social, political, and economic organization, and thus challenges individual and cultural identity. Fraser indicates how gender, as race, confuse what may be universal principles that could be the basis of social justice. The issue of cultural recognition is often premised on a localization (sometimes based on nation state or cultural group) of rights discourse that challenges universal human rights. But respecting and recognizing difference at the local level means that dominant claims about culture and tradition can impose reduced freedom on women and girls or particular social groups, for example, caste system in India and particularly in religious states, but increasingly in Western nation states in particular regions as a result of migration and refugee movements.

Children's rights are also complicated by the proliferation of, and reliance of many local economies, on child labor, sex trafficking, and child soldiers. Girls' rights are particularly impacted on by fundamentalist religious beliefs that significantly reduce their freedom of choice, movement and education. Human rights advocates can therefore, paradoxically, be in opposition to individual choice (as exercised by parents) as a right that must give way to other principles, for example, right to have an education free from oppression (Blackmore, 2005). Therefore, as Fraser points out, women's and girls' rights often come into conflict with the principle of recognition of difference and the diversity of religions, cultures, and languages now found in most societies as social justice also requires cognitive justice which requires that we recognize different forms of knowing and being in the world. Likewise, individual choice is dependent on material circumstance often without regard for consequences for the other, and therefore some form of distributive justice is required as well to facilitate individual choice.

Throughout, these theories have assumed the imaginary of democratic life as offering the greatest potential for social justice. Schools are where students are educated into democratic process (see Shields in this section), but only if students themselves have a sense of belonging and voice—Nancy Fraser's third principle of associational justice. The dominance of neoliberal policies of choice, commodification, and privatization in education hold little promise that education can provide the social cohesion that they promised in the twentieth century where the state invested in "the public" as national project. While democracy is itself a contested notion cross-nationally, democracy has become an imaginary fuelling, for example, the fall of the Berlin wall of 1989, the Arab Spring protests, and the Occupy movements in Western nations in 2011 in response to the lack of political will for social justice. As Shields argues, *social justice educat*ion goes further and argues that social justice principles should be taught to students, and they should be prepared to take a stance on such principles (Blackmore, 2002).

All the above perspectives share opposition to the "banking" concept of education in which the teacher is the authority, and propose instead a synergy between theory and practice, the authenticity of individual experience, and the right for students—children, young people and adults—to have a voice and agency in one's own education and society. Education within a democratic framework provides the individual with the capacity for agency, to be able to reflect upon, understand and to change one's own position to greater benefit oneself as an individual or collectively. The capacity of education to produce shared benefits has been central as are the democratic relations that underpin educational work. The role of education is to provide the individual with the tools to engage with others for collective wellbeing and a shared vision of "a good society." Access to equal forms of education is therefore seen to be integral to a fair and just society as it is a moral and ethical as well as a relational enterprise, arguably a broad tenet of social liberalism but not necessarily contract liberalism.

Neoliberal Moves

It has been contract liberalism that took on new vigor in the 1990s. With the speed of economic globalization after the 1980s as fast global capital rapidly sought cheaper labor and massive profits to feed financial markets and individual wealth, the gap between rich and poor rapidly expanded, and together with moves towards more devolved governance in education with self managing schools working within education markets, producing greater educational inequality (Teese, Lamb, & Duru-Bellat, 2007). Third World governments were pressured by the International Monetary Fund (IMF) and World Bank to repay national debt rather than investing in their own people's health, education and wellbeing. Spurred on by neoliberal economic orthodoxies of marketization and privatization, women and children, particularly in South America, South East Asia, and Africa, bore the greatest burden of rising economic uncertainty, war, poverty and disease globally (Unterhalter, 2006).

In Western education systems since the 1980s, there were also significant moves towards market liberalism focusing on parental choice informed by an individual rights-oriented claim upon the state (Mitchell, 2001). This move to postwelfarism in most Anglophone states assumes a greater capacity for self-help, yet the state has not addressed new "pockets" of "racialized" poverty. Educational inequality is increasingly closely associated with intergenerational unemployment, inadequate government services, poor health and wellbeing, and high levels of crime in specific locations eg. inner city predominantly black suburbs or isolated indigenous regions (Teese et al., 2007). Risk is more not less unevenly distributed (Beck, 1994) as a shrinking global elite have amassed unbelievable wealth while protected from global recession (Wilkinson & Pickett, 2009).

Middle class anxiety has intensified, particularly over education, as the insecurity of global markets has increased the chance of everyone experiencing unemployment and underemployment, poor health and wellbeing (Brantlinger, 2003). This insecurity, together with new technologies have fed the media frenzy over ranking and comparing individuals, schools, systems and nations using narrow measures of educational achievement, further fueling the neoliberal discourse of individual choice (Ball, 2003). Postwelfarism has meant responsibility and risk have been passed on to the individual without the safety net of the welfare state. Market liberalism means that individuals bear a greater responsibility for, and consequences of, their choices regardless of any material circumstances that may limit their choices.

At the same time, education policies such as that of lifelong learning have assumed the same gender, class and race neutral human capital theory assumptions that educational credentials have the same rewards in the labour market for all. As a positional private good, user pays has entered education policy. Yet as feminists show, women do not receive the same benefits in the labor market as their male equivalents despite over-achieving in education, with gender disparities in pay emerging immediately on women entering into an historically discriminating workplace (Leathwood & Francis, 2006).

Poststructuralist theory sought to theorize complexity and make sense of the experiences of contradiction, ambiguity and insecurity under these rapidly changing historical conditions. Foucault did not claim to develop a universal theory or indeed a theory at all and refused to address issues such as social justice. Foucault has been at the foreground of poststructuralist theory mobilized in education. Regardless of his refusal to accept metanarratives, to develop universal theories or indeed make recommendation, his work and methodological tools of genealogy and deconstruction led to a closer focus on discourse in terms of the production of multiple subjectivities and the self-governing subject through disciplinary technologies of power. These notions together with the power of discourse and text from cultural and communication studies, themselves offshoots of CT, were particularly taken up in the new policy sociology of the 1990s. Policy sociology has provided significant capacity to understand the power of policy to utilise social justice theory and research and how social justice policies are positioned within particular historical contexts.

Indeed, Dehli points out Foucault questions whether the "we" who are the basis of collective claims or action are a product rather than origin of the claim—a point troubling feminist and critical race theorists. Feminists themselves question how categories (such as woman) are problematic when fixed. Women are not a unified group with similar interests because of cultural, class, and racial difference. But without the category of "woman" it is difficult to promote women's interests or make claims for women. Hence CRT's pragmatic realism—when to claim as a unitary group and when to recognize difference within the category.

Globalization has highlighted these tensions when it comes to social justice with the realization that the nation state cannot alone be held responsible for action. Cultural globalization with the more rapid movement of people increased claims as to the pluralism of knowledge and interests that troubled psychological notions of a unified and fixed identity during the 1980s. Indigenous groups thus made claims upon 'settler nation' states (United States, New Zealand, Canada, Australia) on the basis of their unique relationship to (as well as their prior ownership of) the land (Moreton-Robinson, 2007; Tuhiwa-Smith, 1999). Charles Mills (1997) referred to the racial contract embedded in liberal theory, and assumptions about the naturalness of European world domination. Colonialism and racial domination asserted through coercion or economics has produced a racial divide both globally and within nation states.

With economic globalization, as with gender, there is a growing not reducing gap between blacks and whites as intergenerational transmission of wealth not income has become the primary determinant of educational opportunities. Economic globalization has also highlighted gender injustice, as women and girls are the majority of the new poor even in Western societies and most impacted in the Third World by global economic restructuring. Interestingly, epidemiological studies show income inequality between nation states is reducing as income inequality within the nation state increases. Yet social and economic inequality are strongly linked to the "strength" of the social fabric of societies (Wilkinson & Pickett, 2009). Poor health and wellbeing impacts on educational achievement that in turn impacts on long term economic and social opportunities, health and wellbeing and participation within a democratic society (Wilkinson and Pickett, 2009).

Future Thinking on Social Justice

After three decades of neoliberal policy orthodoxies focusing on individual choice and reduced investment in public education, education has become more of a positional good funded increasingly by the individual or family. At the same time, nation states have linked education more closely to the nation state's economic interests as post-industrial economies strive to become knowledge-based economies, making education a trans-national project. Finally, citizenship and identity no longer necessarily coincide with geographic boundaries (Mohanty, 2003).

Within a globalized world, education is now considered a fundamental and universal human right and a key indicator of economic stability and social maturity of nation states as argued in the Millenium Development Goals 2000 (Unterhalter, 2006). The United Nations Universal Declaration of the Rights of the Child 1990 states that children have *negative* rights of freedom from restriction of speech and religion, and *positive* social, cognitive and physical developmental rights such as right to survival, right to protection, and right to develop (Burke, 2007, p. 338). Amaryta Sen (1999) and Martha Nussbaum (2011) have in this context sought to theorize social justice in ways that address human rights and local context through capability theory. Sen and Nussbaum argue that there is a human right to equal access to education but that it is also in the individuals and communal best interests for the capabilities of each individual to be developed to their fullest. Disadvantage exists, for example, when education does not provide the capability to develop and *enhance other capabilities* for example, capabilities of reasoning, problem solving, evaluating evidence, respect for difference, sense of self and efficacy. Thus basic numeracy and literacy are insufficient as an enabling or facilitating education which provides an individual the capabilities to assess on one's capacities and goals, to weigh up evidence, assess truth claims and imagine one's future and the good life. "Capability" is about the freedom to achieve those functionings or what a person values doing and being (Walker, 2006, p. 104). The capability approach is premised upon the notion of positive liberty or "agency freedom" as choice requires a level of capability that is neither equally distributed nor innate. Education therefore should provide the freedom to develop those capabilities that impart a range of options and choices for individuals. For this reason, children need to be educated in a context that provides more than one view of the world and that encourages active participation to learn to be agentic and reflexive. From this reasoning, the state, for example, can intervene to prioritize over parental choice in order that the child has that freedom.

The issue all the above theories highlight is the nature of democratic governance within a globalized context. What are the consequences of prioritizing economic globalization, as privileging the economic usually undermines local equality, for example, transnational trade agreements. But there are many versions of democracy and modes of governance, each with a different sense of the synergy between individual rights and responsibilities and the collective. Each has different approaches to how claims can be made by individuals and groups upon the state. For example, children's rights are tied up with traditional views around children as property of parents and notions of guardianship. This raises the issue as to whose responsibility it is to provide the resources to guarantee children's developmental rights (or capabilities)—parents or the state—which in turn raises the issue of funding, whether public and private education, and what the nation state can bear in cost to provide education for all.

There are common storylines in these theories of social justice in education. While all critique the universal claims of liberalism and the damage of neoliberal orthodoxies, the complexity of theorizing social justice in a globalized interdependent world where context increasingly matters means there is no one theory of social justice that is adequate. There are also the unintentional, if systematic, forms of injustice arising from the practices of everyday life and institutional practices that normalize racism, sexism, and other forms of injustice. With regard to interventions, there is the dilemma about the power of categories to perpetuate inequality but how categories are important to make collective claims upon the state. Strategically, the issue is to whether to mobilize unitary collectivism on the basis of shared interests (gender, ethnicity, race) while developing counter-narratives based on experience that unpack how different forms of injustice around gender, race, class work differently.

Some theorists are working through concepts such as intersectionality. All espoused the need for strategic pragmatism in any activist movement or historical moment; to be constantly reflexive on prior strategies as no discourse is safe; and realize that key wins can be more symbolic than real. Notions such as equality, social justice, and democracy are themselves ideologically mobilized in different contexts as various social groups from both conservative and radical movements claim to be promoting social justice by promoting quite contradictory policies. All recognize the real politic that often marginalized groups interests have to be seen to be in the national or dominant groups interests to achieve even incremental change. Finally, a constant worry evident across all these discussions is the superficial adoption of particular theories of social justice without understanding their distinctive histories, legacies and implications.

What is central to theorizing social justice is the significance of agency that gets beyond the limitations of equal access and participation. Agency implies the necessity for education to provide the conditions to improve one's position. Shields posits as one of her principles that a socially just education should provide social mobility. Agency is the central concept of capability theory, just as it was for Dewey and Freire. Agency raises the notion of meaningful participation that gets beyond representational participation where a token woman or person of color is positioned as representing a group but marginalized or ignored in any decision-making. This is the key test for critical theories notion of communicative practice and the capacity of reasoned dialogue and a fair outcome within democratic practice. Fraser added representation to her principles of social justice as a consequence of debates over how her theory of social justice did not address agency. Associational justice is necessary in order to achieve relative parity of participation.

Cribb and Gewirtz (2007) argue that recent debates now concentrate on a conception of social justice as plural. This is because of the rise of multicultural societies, in which racial, cultural, religious, gender diversity is now the norm and in which there are contradictions and competing grounds for claims around the key principles of redistribution, recognition and representation. In other words, social justice is viewed as having a variety of facets. For example, it is viewed as "simultaneously concerning the distribution of material goods and resources on the one hand and the valorization of a range of social collectivities and cultural identities on the other" (Cribb & Gewirtz, 2007, p. 15). They offer a diagrammatic representation of plural models of social justice in Figure 89.1. The struggle now is between how to better conceptualize the site (central, local, international) and role of government in terms of providing the conditions of access with regard to the relationship between structuring structures and what Sen refers to as "agency freedom" for the individual citizen (Sen, 1999, p. 19).

As social theorists such as Bauman (2000) and Beck (1992) have commented, processes of individualization arising from the nature of globalized economies and societies interacting with neoliberal policies of choice now offer an array of possibilities for many but not all. Awareness as to the social, political and economic implications of widening inequalities between nation states and populations has led to international agreements and intranational bodies to focus on education as a source of economic and social cohesion and equal opportunity for women and girls in particular as indicators of national maturity and economic stability. Some propose forms of citizenship that go beyond the state, a global citizenship that recognizes the multilayered notion of citizenship. Seyla Benhabib (2002) argues that theories about the nature of citizenship (and therefore how citizen make claims for social justice) have been too statecentric, and that in complex worlds we participate in and through complex network of associations above and beyond the nation state. The nation state is no longer the "privileged apex of collective identity but instead, along with Rawls, view it as a 'union of unions', then citizenship should also be understood as a form of collective identity mediated in and through the institutions of civil society" (pp. 169-170). But a tension still arises between national sovereignty and human rights claims because there has been a "de-territorialisation of citizenship, a pluralisation of cultural identities which demand a decentering of administrative uniformity and creation of multiple legal and jurisdictional hierarchies at national and international level" (p. 181).

This raises an issue for social theorists about how to develop principles of social justice that consider what constitutes a good society beyond the nation-state. The question is now who is responsible for social justice—the nation state, national, or international legal systems, the civil sector and transnational nongovernmental organizations and social movements? Who does one make claim to—transnational bodies, such as the United Nations or the nation state? (Blackmore, 1999). And what should be the basis of such claims—rights, needs, and/or interests? These questions require new ways of understanding educational inequality and theorizing social justice. At the same time, some things seem to stay the same: education is expected to resolve wider social, economic, and political problems. But education cannot do this without significant transformation of social economic and political conditions and political will within both the polity and civic spheres.

Table 89.1. Plural Models of Justice-Dimensions of Pluralism

Monism	*Pluralism*
Unified conceptions of justice (e.g., distributive OR procedural etc.)	Justice as multidimensional (e.g., distributive AND cultural AND associational)
A single currency of relevant goods Single account, that is, the relevant criteria for claims to justice (e.g., needs OR desert OR ability to benefit)	Different, possibly incommensurable kinds of good
Transcontextual model of justice (i.e., one model of justice for all goods and settings)	"Pluralistic" model of relevant claims (e.g., needs AND desert AND ability to benefit, etc.)
Universal model—"recipients" of justice treated the same	Context-dependent model—model depends on nature of good and setting Differentiated models—differences between recipients are relevant for justice
Centralized model of justice—central agent with responsibility for arbitration and "dispensing;" of justice	Diffused and centralized model, that is, agency and responsibility shared between all, including center and periphery

Source: Cribb and Gewirtz (2007, p. 16).

REFERENCES

Anthias, F., & Lloyd, C. (Eds.). (2002). *Rethinking antiracisms: From theory to practice.* London, England: Routledge.

Ball, S. (2002). *Class strategies and the education market. The middle classes and social advantage.* London, England: RoutledgeFalmer.

Bauman, Z (2000). *The individualized society* Cambridge, MA: Polity Press.

Beck, U. (1992). *A risk society.* Cambridge, MA: Polity Press.

Benhabib, S. (2002). *The claims of culture: equality and diversity in the global era.* Princeton, NJ: Princeton University Press.

Blackmore, J. (1999). Globalisation\localisation: Strategic dilemmas for state feminism and gender equity policy [Special Issue on Globalisation and Education]. *Journal of Education Policy, 14*(1), 33-54.

Blackmore, J. (2007). Equity and social justice in Australian education systems: Retrospect and prospect. In W. Pink & G. Noblit (Eds.), *International handbook for urban education.* (pp. 249-64). Dordrecht, The Netherlands: Springer.

Blackmore, J. (2006). Localization/globalization and the midwife state: strategic dilemmas for state feminism in education? In A Halsey, H. Lauder, P. Brown, & J. Dillabough (Eds.), *Education, globalization and social change* (pp. 212-27) Oxford, England: Oxford University Press.

Blackmore, J. (2005). Feminist strategic rethinking of human rights discourses in education. In W. Hesford & W. Kozol (Eds.), *Just advocacy? Women's human rights, transnational feminism and the politics of representation* (pp. 243-65). New Brunswick, NJ: Rutgers University Press.

Blackmore, J. (2002, March,). Leadership for socially just schooling: more substance and less style in high risk low trust times? (Special Issue). *Journal of School Leadership, 12,* 198-219.

Bourdieu, P., & Passeron, J. (1977). *Reproduction in education society and culture.* London, England: SAGE.

Bowles, S., & Gintis, H. (1976). *Schooling in Capitalist America: Educational reform and the contradictions of economic life.*

Brantlinger, E. (2003) *Dividing classes. How the middle class negotiates and rationalises school advantage.* London, England: RoutledgeFalmer.

Burke, K. (2007). Human rights and the rights of a child: A panoramic view. *Globalisation, Societies and Education, 5*(3), 333-349.

Butler, J. (1990) *Gender trouble: Feminism and the subversion of identity.* New York, NY: Routledge.

Coleman, J. S., Campbell, E., Holson, C. J., McPartland, J., & Mood, A. (1966). *Equity of educational opportunity.* Washington, DC: U.S. Government Printing Office.

Cribb, A., & Gewirtz, S. (2003). Towards a sociology of just practices: an analysis of plural conceptions of justice. In C. Vincent (Ed.), *Social justice, education and identity* (pp. 15-30). London, England: Routledge.

Ellsworth, E. (1992). Why isn't this empowering? In C. Luke & J. Gore (Eds.), *Feminisms and critical pedagogy.* London, England: Routledge

Fraser, N. (1977). *Justice interruptus: Critical reflections on the "postsocialist" condition.* London, England: Routledge.

Fraser, N., & Honneth, A. (2003). *Redistribution or recognition? A political-philosophical exchange.* Essex, England: Verso Press.

Freire, P. (1970). *Pedagogy of the oppressed.* New York, NY: Seabury.

Harding, S. (1987). *Feminism and methodology.* Milton Keynes, England: Open University Press.

Hill Collins, P. (1990). *Black feminist thought. Knowledge consciousness and the politics of empowerment.* New York, NY: Routledge.

Ladson-Billings, G., & Tate, W. F., IV. (1995). Toward a critical race theory of education. *Teachers College Record, 97*(1), 47-55.

Leathwood, C., & Francis, B. (Ed.). (2006) *Gender and lifelong learning: Critical feminist engagements.* London, England: Routledge.

Luke, C., & Gore, J. (Eds.). (1992). *Feminisms and critical pedagogy.* London, England: Routledge.

Mills, C. (1997). *The racial contract.* New York, NY: Cornell University Press.

Mitchell. K. (2001) Education for democratic citizenship: trans-nationalism, multiculturalism and the limits of liberalism *Harvard Educational Review, 71*(1), 51-78.

Mohanty, C. (2003). *Feminism without Borders. Decolonising theory, practicing solidarity.* Durham, NC: Duke University Press.

Moreton- Robinson, A. (Ed.). (2007). *Sovereign subjects. Indigenous sovereignty matters.* Sydney, Australia: Allen & Unwin.

Nussbaum M. (2011) *Creating capabilities: The human development approach.* Cambridge, MA: Harvard University Press.

Rawls, J. (1971). *A theory of justice.* Cambridge, MA: Harvard University Press.

Rawls, J. (2001). *Justice as fairness: a restatement.* Cambridge, MA: Harvard University Press.

Sawer, M. (2003). *The ethical state?* Melbourne, Australia: Melbourne University Press.

Sen, A. (1999). *Development as freedom.* Oxford, England: Oxford University Press.

Teese, R. Lamb, S., & Duru-Bellat, M. (Eds.). (2007). *International studies in educational inequality, theory and policy. Inequality: educational theory and public policy* (Vol. 3). Dordrecht, The Netherlands: Springer.

Tuhiwa-Smith, T. (1999). *Decolonising methodologies.* London, England: Routledge.

Unterhalter, E. (2006). *Gender, schooling and global social justice.* London, England: Routledge.

Walker, M. (2006). Towards a capability-based theory of social justice for education policy-making. *Journal of Education Policy, 21*(2), 163-185.

Weiler, K. (1991). Freire and a feminist pedagogy of difference. *Harvard Educational Review, 61*(4), 339-475.

Wilkinson R., & Pickett, K. (2009). *The spirit level. Why greater equality makes societies stronger.* New York, NY: Bloomsbury Press.

Yeatman, A. (1994). *Postmodern revisionings of the political.* London, England: Routledge.

Young, I. M. (1990). *Justice and the politics of difference.* Princeton, NJ: Princeton University Press.

Author Content Information: Jill Blackmore, Professor and Director of the Centre for Research in Educational Futures and Innovation, Deakin University. E-mail: jillb@deakin.edu.au

CHAPTER 90

Education and Social Justice

A Critical Social Theory Perspective

Richard Bates
Deakin University

Concerns over social justice lie at the heart of critical social theory, or, perhaps more precisely, critical social theory is fundamentally concerned with the possibility of emancipation from social *in*justices, especially those inscribed in institutional and cultural practices that constrain the practice of deliberative democracy and discursive will formation. Similarly concerns over social justice lie at the heart of the educational process.

This coincidence of concerns makes critical social theory particularly apposite in the consideration of educational ideals, procedures, and practices. It is somewhat surprising, then, that critical social theory has played only a marginal role in their formation.

Contemporary approaches to critical theory fall into two broad traditions. The first is European in origin and has its roots in the work of the Frankfurt Institute of Social Research, which was established in 1923 and became influential in its reinterpretation and critique of Marxism under the direction on Max Horkheimer from 1930. Its application to education has been developed mainly by a group of Australians—Kemmis, Young, Grundy, Smyth, and Bates. The second approach, known as critical pedagogy, although marginally influenced by the Frankfurt School through the work of Henry Giroux, was much more influenced by American traditions of progressive education and more recently by Marxist liberation theology and in particular the work of Paulo Freire. Both traditions were indebted to Marxist social theory as well as American pragmatism via John Dewey. In what follows, each of these traditions will be considered before turning to their educational implications.

CRITICAL THEORY AND THE FRANKFURT SCHOOL

Critical theory, said Horkeimer, seeks to "liberate human beings from the circumstances that enslave them" (1982, p. 244) by transforming capitalism into a truly democratic form of life where "all conditions of social life that are controllable by human beings" are subject to modification through 'real consensus' in a rational society" (pp. 249-50). In order to do so the key Frankfurt School theorists (especially Horkheimer, Adorno, Marcuse and Fromm) committed themselves to the Marxist objective of making philosophy practical: that is to the combination of both materialist (realist) and idealist (normative) theories through a critique of existing social relations. In this they adopted the Hegelian/Marxist notion of dialectical analysis, situating both knowledge and critique within particular historical circumstances. However, the Second World War and its consequences persuaded the Frankfurt School (relocated to Geneva and then New York during the War before returning to Frankfurt in 1953) that the processes of historical materialism and the Enlightenment assumption of the triumph of reason (and, in Marxist theory, of the working class) were rather less than inevitable.

While building on the work of the early Frankfurt School, Jurgen Habermas proclaimed a rather more modest objective for critical theory where knowledge, especially in the social sciences, was seen not as transcendental but as hypothetical and fallible. Moreover, practical knowledge or reason was argued to be: "embodied in cognition, speech and action" (Habermas 1984, p. 10). Here, Habermas suggested that the

The Handbook of Educational Theories, pp. 1011–1018

preconditions for appropriate tests of knowledge are implicit in the very speech act itself. Often these tests remain implicit in conversation, but when made explicit they form the basis of *discourse* through which validity claims are put to the test. The object of discourse is to reach consensus by examining arguments put forward against the criteria of truth, comprehensibility, sincerity and rightness. Moreover, implicit in the very giving and questioning of reasons through discourse, is the idea of unconstrained communication in an *ideal speech situation*. In such a situation each participant is regarded as an autonomous person where:

Each subject who is capable of speech and action is allowed to participate in discourses:

1. Each is allowed to call into question any proposal.
2. Each is allowed to introduce any proposal into the discourse.
3. Each is allowed to express his attitudes, desires, and needs.

No speaker ought to be hindered by compulsion—whether arising from inside the discourse or outside of it (Habermas, 1990a, p. 99).

There is an ineluctable relationship between such discourse and ideas of democracy, for to insist that discourse be free of compulsion is to insist that coercion of whatever kind—physical, emotional, economic, institutional, ideological—provides for a situation of distorted communication which runs counter to the rules of engagement implicit in discourse itself. As Habermas insists

> the conditions for ideal discourse are connected with conditions for an ideal form of life; they include linguistic conceptualizations of the traditional ideas of freedom and justice. "Truth" therefore, cannot be analysed independently of "freedom" and "justice" (Habermas, 1975, p. xvii).

Typically, however, much communication is in practice distorted by the exercise of power of one kind or another either directly or through ideology. Here processes of communication are undermined, as are the social conditions under which democratic discussion might take place. Habermas's theory of ideology therefore also makes possible critique of the ways in which language is used to "encode, produce, and reproduce relations of power and domination, even within institutional spheres of communication and interaction governed by norms that make democratic ideals explicit in normative procedures and constraints" (Bohman, 2010, p. 8).

Such critique is especially potent in examining the ways in which the "system" encroaches on the "lifeworld" through the media of power and money. In everyday life, concerned as it is with the socialization of individuals, the transmission of culture and issues of social integration and solidarity, communicative action is imperative and indispensible. Here, practical discourse provides the mechanism through which ideas of the good life can be articulated. Such ideas "are not representations, which hover above us as an abstract ought; they stamp the identity of groups and individuals in such a way that they form an integrated component of the particular culture or personality" (Habermas, 1990a, p. 108).

This is not to say that cultures are immutable, rather that in the modern world they are increasingly reflexive in that they both *bind* their members "while at the same time allowing members to subject the traditions to critical examination ... leaving later generations the *option* of learning from other traditions or converting and setting out for other shores" (Habermas, 1998, p. 222). This is especially important in multicultural societies where the individual has both the opportunity to grow up within a cultural heritage and perpetuate it in its conventional form "or to transform it, as well as ... to turn away from its commands with indifference or break with it self-critically and then live spurred on by having made a conscious break with tradition, or even with a divided identity" (Habermas, 1998, p. 223).

The world of culture is very much the life-world where the continuation, recreation and creation of identity and shared values, ideals and collective commitments are formed and re-formed through "democratic and participatory processes of forming a collective will" (Habermas, 1988, p. 64). Such processes encourage the formation of common orientations "within which more subjectivity and more sentiment can find expression, in which affective conduct is more taken into account" (Habermas, 1988, p. 64).

However, systems such as the capitalist economy operate through the steering media of money and power that do not require a common orientation among individuals. Systems demand the increasing commodification (through money) and bureaucratization (through power) of society, thus operating against the grain of the lifeworld within which individuals find meaning and express their collective identities and purposes. The increasing efficiency of systems as they apply *scientific/technical* knowledge and procedures in the pursuit of control of both natural and (increasingly) social worlds threatens the ability of individuals and cultures to make meaning of their subjective *practical* experience.

The resolution of the resulting conflict between system and lifeworld can only be achieved through democratization and the development of counterpublic spheres: "centers of concentrated communication which arise naturally out of the microdomains of everyday practice" (Habermas, 1990b, p. 67). Such public centers of communication can provide for expressions of an *emancipatory* interest in social justice through democratic politics (Habermas, 1984, 1996).

Habermas has been particularly interested in the role that new social movements play in this process, arguing that contemporary controversies over genetic engineering, ecological threats, and threats from the spiralling nuclear arms race, for instance "were not brought up by exponents of the state apparatus, large organizations, or functional systems. Instead, they were broached by intellectuals, concerned citizens, radical professionals, self-proclaimed 'advocates'" (Habermas, 1996, p. 381). Such social movements serve both to articulate concerns from the margins into the center of the public sphere, and to serve as radical democratic learning sites.

Through debates within the public sphere such centers of concentrated communication articulate concerns that become widely recognized.

> Discourses in the autonomous public spheres supply the production and application discourses with arguments, while formulating social needs and defining what issues are relevant at a given moment.... Public debates produce "communicative power" which is "transformed into administrative power" by law. (Guibentif, 1996, p. 58)

Law becomes the formally recognized process through which it is able to "transform the weak force of ... intersubjectively shared convictions into a social integrative power, which is ultimately able to dominate all kinds of naked violence" (Habermas, 1996, p. 187). Law, therefore, is the mechanism through which processes of *social* integration produced in the lifeworld can become recognized and institutionalized in ways that may constrain the processes of *system* integration pursued by economy and state (Habermas, 1996, pp. 399-476).

However, previously available areas for public debate such as public media (freedoms of speech and assembly, access to a free press, rights of participation in the political process) have been increasingly coopted by corporations through the privatization of traditional media (through private ownership of radio, television, newspapers, journals, etc.). Thus the economy and the private interests that constitute it encroaches on the lifeworld, displacing mechanisms of *social* integration and substituting mechanisms of *system* integration by restricting what can be discussed and by whom. Contemporary commentary, however, suggests that new technologies originating in the corporate/military sphere as mechanisms of system integration may well provide the mechanisms for the emergence of a new democratic politics. Kellner, for instance, argued that

> A new democratic politics will thus be concerned that the new media and computer technologies be used to serve the interests of the people and not corporate elites. A democratic politics will strive to see that broadcast media and computers are used to inform and enlighten individuals rather than manipulate them. A democratic politics will teach individuals how to use the new technologies, to articulate their own experiences and interests, and to promote democratic debate and diversity, allowing a full range of voices and ideas to become part of the cyber democracy of the future. (Kellner, 2000, p. 280)

The emergence of a new public sphere through new technologies may well have the potential to reassert the potency of social integration via the pivot of the law into the administrative processes of system integration. In this way, both the importance of communicative rationality and the notion of social justice as a historically contingent set of agreements articulated through law into binding agreements that shape the activities of both system and lifeworld can be seen. As we shall see, the issues of communicative rationality and discursive will formation centered on issues of emancipation and social justice that are the basis for the learning society in critical social theory are also central to the educative process.

PAULO FREIRE AND CRITICAL PEDAGOGY

Although coming from a quite different background, Paulo Freire, like Habermas, insisted on the importance of communication as a fundamental of human emancipation. "Only through communication can human life hold meaning" (Freire, 1972, p. 50). Drawing on Dewey's commitment to education for democracy, Marxist ideas of revolutionary praxis and liberation theology's commitment to social transformation, Freire articulated a practice of adult literacy that saw *critical* literacy as a means of emancipation. Such critical literacy was contrasted with the "culture of silence" created through the imposition of a particular consciousness—that of the dominant social class—whereby knowledge and meaning are "given" rather than "made." The transmission of consciousness and meaning under such a system maintained relations of power and prevented the development of human agency among the poor and oppressed (Freire, 1972, 1985). Under such conditions meaning is treated as something predetermined, something to be "deposited" in individuals through a "banking" process that denies human agency and the intimate relationship between language, meaning and action. By such means, reality is made to seem other than what it is. "The mystification of reality consists of making the world appear different from what it is and, in the process and by necessity, of imparting an artificial consciousness" (Freire, 1985, p. 116).

In developing literacy programs, particularly in his native Brazil as well as in Chile during a period of exile, Freire insisted that the learning of language, of reading and writing, was an active process directed toward the agency of the individual and that this was part of the development of revolutionary consciousness.

> If learning to read and write is to constitute an act of knowing, the learners must assume from the beginning the role of creative subjects. It is not a matter of memorizing and repeating given syllables, words and phrases, but rather, of reflecting critically on the process of reading and writing itself, and on the profound significance of language.... The cognitive dimensions of the literacy process must include the relationships of men with their world. These relationships are the source of the dialectic between the products men achieve in transforming the world and the conditioning these products in turn exercise on men (Freire, 1985, p. 50)

This process of awakening a critical stance toward the world as a made reality and of the possibility of exercising agency within it Freire called "conscientization" whose purpose "is to provoke recognition of the world, not as a 'given' world, but as a world dynamically 'in the making'" (1985, p. 106). This is a revolutionary project that begins with "a struggle against oppressive and dehumanising structures" (1985, p. 83) and becomes a process "in which the people assume the role of subject in the precarious adventure of transforming and recreating the world" (1985, p. 82). In short "there can be no conscientization of the people without a radical denunciation of dehumanizing structures, accompanied by the proclamation of a new reality to be created by men" (1985 p. 85).

At the heart of this revolutionary process is the dialogic relationship between individuals which substitutes democracy for bureaucracy, mutual respect for domination.

> A dialogic relationship—communication and intercommunication among active subjects who are immune to the bureaucratization of their minds and open to discovery and to knowing more—is indispensable to knowledge. The social nature of this process makes a dialogical relationship a natural element of it. In that sense, authoritarian dialogue violates the nature of human beings, their process of discovery, and it contradicts democracy. (Freire, 1997, p. 99)

Democratization as an ideal and a process is thus linked with a pedagogical process of dialogue and critique and with a politics of everyday life through which the complex dynamics of social movements arise as challenges to existing forms of domination. Social justice depends upon such a democratic process.

Critical Social Theory and Critical Pedagogy: Habermas and Freire

As Morrow and Torres (2002) have pointed out, both Habermas and Freire are concerned with a "shared critical theory of the dialogical and developmental subject" (p. ix). The objective of both analyses is the democratization and revitalization of the public sphere. In fact three common themes emerge: a crisis theory of society; a theory of the dominated democratic subject; and a model of fundamental, radical democratization (Morrow & Torres, 2002, p. 84). Moreover Friere and Habermas shared an interest in communication as a fundamental mechanism of challenge to the dominating "culture of silence" (Friere) and forms of "distorted communication" (Habermas). This challenge is mounted through processes of "concientization" (Friere) and "self-reflection" (Habermas). It results in the development of ethical discourse and the capacity for "social criticism" (Friere) and "communicative ethics" (Habermas).

There are, of course, differences between the two approaches as well as similarities. For instance, while Friere's approach was developed out of engagement with political struggle and social action among the campesinos of Brazil in their fight against underdevelopment and dependency, Habermas developed his theory with respect to problems in advanced, democratic, pluralist societies. Friere expresses a more existential perspective than that embraced by Habermas's cognitive concern in that Friere insists upon developmental processes requiring a balance between cognitive, ego, moral and interactional development. There is also a significant difference between Friere's direct concern with pedagogy as a mechanism for "conscientization" and Habermas's very limited direct concern with pedagogy.

It is not, however, these differences that have given rise to different educational traditions, but rather that serendipitous concentrations of scholars in Australia (with an interest in Habermas) and the United States (with an interest in Friere) have developed in response to particular social and intellectual challenges. In the United States the predominant emphasis was on the extension of the tradition of progressive education through the utilization of Friere's insights in challenging established structures of race, class and gender relations through education (Darder, Baltondano, & Torres, 2009). In Australia, the focus was much more directly on the development of action research, the socially critical school, critical theory and classroom talk, curriculum as praxis and a critical approach to educational leadership. Not that these concerns were mutually exclusive and there were overlaps, but the emphases were different, as were the conceptions of the relationship between education and social justice.

CRITICAL SOCIAL THEORY, EDUCATION, AND SOCIAL JUSTICE

The beginning point for what Kemmis, Cole, and Suggett call the socially critical approach to education is the belief that "If social justice is to be achieved in society, then the curriculum of schools must be changed so that the processes of schooling are compatible with the processes of a socially just society" (1983, p. 19). In such a pursuit Young argues the need for specific critique "of the present forms of schooling, pedagogy, curriculum development, administration, research and so on" and the development of "organizational forms and practices which offer the possibility of transcending existing inadequacies and permit a vision of a concretely realisable state of affairs which represents an improvement on the existing state of affairs" (1990, p. 82).

Such an orientation takes the concrete situations of students and teachers into account, but situates them within the broader society whose social and ideological structures are seen to shape schools in ways that are not necessarily educational. By this the socially critical theorists mean that traditionally the knowledge presented in schools tends

> toward an ahistorical, value-free view of knowledge as a finished product, toward a mistaking of the contemporary surface of things for their full range of possible states and toward a view that critique is not a matter of method, but of personal and nonrational decision. (Young, 1990, p. 82)

Moreover,

> it is only by taking the structures and concerns of society to be problematic, rather than as given, that the school can perform an educational task. Taking social structures for granted is to deny the essentially critical function of education and ultimately to lose the possibility of education itself. Once this occurs, the school becomes merely a training ground for production and consumption, and the critical educational function—that of penetrating and understanding the nature of our society and its work—is lost. Unless schools have this critical function ... they do not educate, they only train students to participate in the given structures of society. (Kemmis et al., 1983, p. 19)

But critical social theory is not simply about critique. Its intention is to bring about improvement in actual concrete situations inhabited by real people: teachers, students, parents. Its goal must be to bring about

> actual improvements of concrete educational practices by their practitioners, and in the improvement of concrete situations in which these practices occur.... To improve actual educational situations, therefore, we must transform the interacting webs of practices that constitute them. (Carr & Kemmis 1983, p. 160)

This does not mean, however, a myopic concentration on the minutiae of classroom life but the search for connections between the daily lives of students and teachers and the wider social issues of the day. For instance, the critique provided by the women's movement of the inequalities of the social and economic position of women points also to the socialization processes of the family and the school which encourage acceptance of such inequalities not only among girls and women, but among boys and men as well. As Kemmis et al. point out

> The social position of women can only be improved by changing the way girls and women are treated; the social processes of socialization must be changed for men and women, boys and girls, if social justice is to be achieved. (1983, p. 9)

Here the relationship between a social movement and the reconstruction of schooling around the interests of those being socialized in classrooms intersect. Moreover, as Young points out, this requires a reconstruction of classroom discourse around a notion of inquiry that is concerned not only with description but also with the nature and justice of relationships and their possible reconstruction (Young, 1992).

However, the centrality of inquiry in the educational process is threatened by the industrialization of schooling through which system imperatives overwhelm the pedagogical relationship.

> The penetration of classroom life by system imperatives steered by bureaucratic power and market incentives can only destroy the pedagogical relationship by industrialising it.... There is an irreducible field of pedagogic freedom without which the pedagogical relationship is not possible. Indeed, without such freedom there can be no act of teaching as such, and no need for teachers. (Young , 1990, p. 131)

Critical social theory observes that "different understandings of learning are realized through different patterns of classroom communication" (Young, 1992, p. 21) and that the learning that results from the application of methods of inquiry that are context free and disconnected from the lives of pupils and the problems of the wider society result in an impoverished form of learning that is of little practical (as opposed to technical) use. The alternative is a form of pedagogy that considers learning as a joint product of the active inquiry of teachers and pupils—a form of collective learning (Young, 1992, p. 25).

Grundy took this point seriously in her discussion of curriculum as praxis, contrasting the preformed ideals of a *technical* approach to curriculum and learning and its interests in predictability and control with the *emancipatory* approach as a form of praxis directed toward the recognition and reconstruction of social arrangements toward greater social justice. Praxis is, in her terms

> the act of reflectively constructing or reconstructing the social world … informed by an emancipatory interest which would preserve for all groups the freedom to act within their own social situations in ways which enable the participants to be in control of that situation, rather than the ultimate control of their actions residing elsewhere. (Grundy, 1987, p. 113).

Translated into the work of teachers and pupils this means that the quality of an educational situation must be judged, not solely by technical outcomes, but also by the agency of those involved and the adequacy of the processes through which learning occurs.

> Thus, evaluation does not simply look at the work of learning, but embraces a critique of what is learnt as well as of the interactions that comprise the learning situation. All the time the criteria by which the quality of learning is to be judged are those relating to the degree of autonomy and equality experienced by the members of the learning group. (Grundy, 1987, p. 139)

Curriculum as praxis, therefore, sees knowledge as a coconstruction of teachers and students, both of whom are learners as they apply available ideas to the situating of their experience and understanding within the wider social context, incorporating both an active pedagogy and an emancipatory commitment to social justice.

Such a perspective on pedagogy and curriculum opens up the possibility of reconceptualizing traditional approaches to educational administration and leadership. In a groundbreaking book, Smyth and his colleagues explore the implications of thinking of educational administration as a technology of control and posit the alternatives that arise from thinking of leadership as a process of mediation between interests and values in the pursuit of a pedagogical and educative practice of educational leadership directed toward democracy and social justice (Smyth, 1989a). Considering the relationships between power and leadership (Watkins, 1989); a critical approach to leadership (Foster, 1989); leadership and educational reform (Angus, 1989); feminist critique and reconstruction (Blackmore, 1989); leadership as reflective action (Codd, 1989); a pedagogical view of leadership (Smyth, 1989b); and the necessity of organizational democracy (Rizvi, 1989), these authors suggest that rather than conceive of leadership and administration as a technology of control

> the perspective sketched here suggests that leaders might better be thought of as located in space and time, within particular discourses of power and knowledge, within particular definitions of agency and structure, and within particular discourses which address issues involved in the rationalization of culture and ethics on the one hand and power and organization on the other, as well as within the dialectic between them. (Bates, 1989, p. 154)

Such a position allows for the conceptualization of educational leadership based upon pedagogical and social principles informed by what Habermas identifies as technical, practical and emancipatory interests (Habermas, 1979) in the pursuit of social justice through education, a position elaborated at some length by Foster (1986).

These connections between pedagogy, curriculum and leadership are brought together by Carr and Kemmis (1983) in their advocacy of action research as praxis and a means for participatory educational and social change. Improvements are not to be directed simply toward greater "efficiency" but toward greater understanding and the transformation of pedagogical and social situations through action. Educational action research is therefore directed toward "creating the conditions under which … participants can take collaborative responsibility for the development and reform of education" (Carr & Kemmis 1983, p. 211). The purpose of such reform was a move toward greater social justice within schools and society.

Critical Pedagogy, Progressive Education, and Social Justice

While the Australian application of critical social theory to education was derived mainly from the application of Habermas's insights to schools and classrooms, the American development of critical pedagogy was rooted in a tradition of progressive education associated in particular with Dewey's concerns over the relationship of education with democracy (Dewey, 1916) and with the radical educators of the mid-twentieth century—Kohl (2009), Kozol (1967), Illich (1971) and especially Friere (1972) who saw existing educational practices as unjust and as institutionalizing power relations in class, gender and race that deprived disadvantaged groups in particular of understanding and acting on their world in ways that would bring about greater social justice. As Darder et al. (2009) argued a critical pedagogy

> seeks to contest mainstream practices of schooling and explore democratic strategies and interventions that can shift relations of power and alter meaning…. The purpose of critique then, within critical pedagogy, is to serve as a powerful lens of analysis from which social inequalities and oppressive institutional structures can be unveiled, critiqued and, most importantly, trans-

> formed through processes of political engagement and social action. (Darder et al., 2009, p. 23)

This is not simply an internal project for the school but one that links what goes on in schools with the wider social context so that "students should study the world around them, in the process learning who they are and what has shaped them" (Kincheloe, 2010, p. 11). This is an overtly political process directed toward the transformation of unjust social practices and the unwarranted, unjustifiable exercise of power, as McLaren makes clear in his advocacy of schools as democratic public spheres.

> Viewing schools as democratic public spheres means regarding schools as sites dedicated to forms of self- and social empowerment, where students have the opportunity to learn the knowledge and skills necessary to live in an authentic democracy. Instead of defining schools as extensions of the workplace, or as frontline institutions in the battle for international markets and foreign competition, schools as democratic public spheres function to dignify meaningful dialogue and action and to give students the opportunity to learn the language of social responsibility. Such a language seeks to recapture the idea of democracy as a *social movement* grounded in respect for *individual freedom* and *social justice.* (McLaren, 2003, p. 254)

McLaren's concept of critical pedagogy owes much to the work of Henry Giroux, in particular to his discussion of the relevance of the work of Habermas, Friere, Bernstein, Bourdieu, Bowles and Gintis, but extends the ideas of social reproduction into consideration of the hidden curriculum (Apple, 1979, 1982) and of the relationships between power and knowledge (Foucault, 1980).

The importance of epistemology in the construction of school knowledge is taken up especially by Kincheloe (2010) in his discussion of the relationship between knowledge and power.

> All knowledge ... is produced within power-driven social and cultural practices and cannot easily be removed from the denotations and connotations that power renders attainable in a particular historical moment. A critical complex epistemology works to expose and challenge the might-makes-right dimensions of knowledge production in a colonialistic, corporate-driven, globalized empire. (Kincheloe, 2010, p. 221)

Pedagogy, from this point of view is about "the production of meaning and the primacy of the ethical and political as a fundamental part of this process" (Giroux, 1992, p. 162). Critical pedagogy is therefore also a pedagogy of resistance and a political act directed toward the amelioration of social injustice (Giroux, 1983).

Critical Theory, Critical Pedagogy, and Social Justice Through Education

The Habermasian perspective on language, reason, ethics and democracy and the Friereian perspective of revolutionary praxis can thus be seen to come together in the development of critical approaches to curriculum, pedagogy, policy and administration in education. While there are differences in emphasis in the various increasingly differentiated perspectives there are common concerns with the importance of language and literacy as an active democratic discourse directed toward emancipation; with the importance of discourse within the construction of the public sphere; with the unmasking of institutional and ideological constraints on democratic discourse; with the remedy of social injustice through critique coupled with action. Moreover there is agreement over the importance of such ideas being the driving force behind a pedagogy that is not simply reproductive of existing social and political relations, but transformative of political, economic and institutional structures in the name of social justice. In this, critical social theory makes a significant contribution to the ongoing debate over social justice, education and identity (Vincent, 2003) and the emerging emphasis on leadership for social justice (Marshall & Oliva, 2006) within what Wrigley identifies as "a cultural struggle for the meaning of school learning and for personal and collective futures" (2003, p. 178). Or, as Connell and her colleagues put it:

> The education we are speaking of is plainly more than a mere reflection of existing social life; it bears on its reconstitution.... Education has fundamental connections with the idea of human emancipation, though it is constantly in danger of being captured for other interests. In a society disfigured by class exploitation, sexual and racial oppression, and in chronic danger of war and environmental destruction, the only education worth the name is one that forms people capable of taking part in their own liberation. (Connell, Ashenden, Kessler, & Dowsett, 1982, cited in Bates, 2006, p. 156)

References

Angus, L. (1989). New leadership and the possibility of educational reform. In J. Smyth (Ed.), *Critical perspectives on educational leadership* (pp. 63-92). London, England: Falmer Press.

Apple, M. (1979). *Ideology and curriculum.* London, England: Routledge.

Bates, R. (1989). Leadership and the rationalization of society. In J. Smyth (Ed.), *Critical perspectives on educational leadership* (pp. 131-156). London, England: Falmer Press.

Bates, R. (2006). Educational administration and social justice education. *Citizenship and Social Justice, 1(2)*, 141-156

Blackmore, J. (1989). Educational Leadership: a feminist critique and reconstruction. In J. Smyth (Ed.), *Critical perspectives on educational leadership* (pp. 93-130). London, England: Falmer Press.

Bohman, J. (2010, Spring). Critical theory. *The Stanford Encyclopaedia of Philosophy.* Retrieved from http://plato .stanford.edu/archives/spr2010/entries/critica-theory/

Carr, W., & Kemmis, S. (1983). *Becoming critical: Education, knowledge and action research.* Geelong, Australia: Deakin University Press.

Codd, J. (1989). Educational leadership as reflective action. In J. Smyth (Ed.), *Critical perspectives on educational leadership* (pp. 157-178). London, England: Falmer Press.

Darder, A., Baltodano, M. & Torres, D. (2009). Critical pedagogy: An introduction. In A. Darder, A, M. Baltodano & D. Torres (Eds.), *The critical pedagogy reader* (pp. 1-20). New York, NY: Routledge.

Dewey, J. (1916). *Democracy and education.* New York, NY. Macmillan.

Foster, W. (1986). *Paradigms and promises.* Buffalo, NY: Prometheus Books.

Foster, W. (1989). Toward a critical practice of educational leadership. In J. Smyth (Ed.), *Critical perspectives on educational leadership* (pp. 39-62). London, England: Falmer Press.

Foucault, M. (1980). *Power and knowledge* (C. Gordon, Ed.). New York, NY: Pantheon.

Freire, P. (1972). *Pedagogy of the oppressed.* London, England: Penguin.

Freire, P. (1985). *The politics of education.* South Hadley, MA: Bergin & Garvey.

Freire, P. (1997). *Pedagogy of the heart.* New York, NY: Continuum.

Giroux, H. (1983). *Theory and resistance in education.* South Hadley, MA: Bergin & Garvey.

Giroux, H. (1992). *Border crossings.* New York, NY: Routledge.

Grundy, S. (1987). *Curriculum as praxis.* London, England: Falmer Press.

Guibentif, P. (1996). Approaching the production of law through Habermas's concept of communicative action. In M. Deflem (Ed.), *Habermas, modernity and law* (pp. 45-70). London, England: SAGE.

Habermas, J. (1975). *Legitimation crisis* (T. McCarthy, Trans.). Boston, MA: Beacon Press.

Habermas, J. (1979). *Communication and the evolution of society* (J. McCarthy, Trans.). London, England: Heinemann.

Habermas, J. (1984). *The theory of communicative action.* Boston, MA: Beacon Press.

Habermas, J. (1988). *Autonomy and solidarity* (P. Drews, Trans. & Ed.). London, England: Verso.

Habermas, J. (1990a). *Moral consciousness and communicative action* (C. Lenhardt & S. Nicholsen, Trans.). Cambridge, MA: MIT Press.

Habermas, J. (1990b). *The philosophical discourse of modernity* (F. Lawrence, Trans.)., Cambridge, MA: MIT Press.

Habermas, J. (1996). *Between facts and norms.* Cambridge, MA: MIT Press.

Habermas, J. (1998). *The inclusion of the other: Studies in political theory* (C. Cronin & P. De Greiff, Eds.). Cambridge, MA: MIT Press.

Horkheimer, M. (1982). *Critical theory.* New York, NY: Seabury Press.

Illich, I. (1971). *Deschooling society.* New York, NY: Harper & Row.

Kellner, D. (2000). Habermas, the public sphere and democracy. In L. Hahn (Ed.), *Perspectives on Habermas* (pp. 259-287). Chicago, IL: Open Court.

Kemmis, S., Cole, P., & Suggett, D. (1983). *The socially critical school.* Melbourne, Australia: Victorian Institute of Secondary Education.

Kincheloe, J. (2008). *Knowledge and critical pedagogy.* London, England. Springer

Kohl, H. (2009). *The Herb Kohl reader.* New York, NY: New Press.

Kozol, J. (1967). *Death at an early age.* Boston, MA: Houghton Mifflin.

Marshall, C., & Oliva, M. (Eds.). (2006). *Leadership for social justice.* Boston, MA: Allyn & Bacon.

McLaren, P. (2003). *Life in schools* (4th ed.). Boston, MA: Allyn & Bacon.

Morrow, R. & Torres C. (2002). *Reading Freire and Habermas.* New York, NY: Teachers College Press.

Rizvi, F. (1989). In defence of organizational democracy. In J. Smyth (Ed.). *Critical perspectives on educational leadership* (pp. 205-234). London, England: Falmer Press.

Smyth, J. (1989a). *Critical perspectives on educational leadership.* London, England: Falmer Press.

Smyth, J. (Ed.). (1989b). A pedagogical and educative view of leadership. In *Critical perspectives on educational leadership* (pp. 179-204). London, England: Falmer Press.

Vincent, C. (Ed.). (2003). *Social justice, education and identity.* London, England: Routledge.

Watkins, P. (1989). Leadership, power and symbols in educational administration. In J. Smyth (Ed.). *Critical perspectives on educational leadership* (pp. 9-38). London, England: Falmer Press.

Wrigley, T. (2003). *Schools of hope.* Stoke-on-Trent, England: Trentham Books.

Young, R. (1990). *A critical theory of education: Habermas and our children's future.* New York, NY: Teachers College Press.

Young, R. (1992). *Critical theory and classroom talk.* Philadelphia, PA: Multilingual Matters.

Author Contact Information: **Richard Bates**, PhD, Professor of Education (Social and Administrative Studies), Faculty of Education, Deakin University. E-mail: rbates@deakin.edu.au

CHAPTER 91

Critical Race Theory

Thandeka K. Chapman
University of Wisconsin, Milwaukee

Adrienne Dixson
Ohio State University

David Gillborn
Institute of Education, London

Gloria Ladson-Billings
University of Wisconsin

"Race" is a social construct; the characteristics that are usually taken to denote "racial" phenomena (especially physical markers such as skin tone) are assigned different meanings in particular historical and social contexts. Far from being a fixed and natural system of genetic difference, race is a system of socially constructed and enforced categories that are constantly recreated and modified through human interaction. In the United States, for example, any physical marker of African American ancestry is usually taken as sufficient to identify a person as "Black"—that same person, however, could board a flight to Brazil and, on disembarking, would find that he was viewed very differently by most Brazilians because the conventional race categories in that society are markedly different to the "common-sense" assumptions in North America. Despite its contested, changing, and ultimately deceitful character, however, race remains one of the most important characteristics in relation to how people experience education and the kinds of outcome that they are likely to achieve. Critical race theory (CRT) is a relatively new, fast growing, and radical perspective that places an understanding of race and racism at the very heart of its approach but also seeks to understand how racism intersects with other forms of oppression such as class, gender, and disability. In this chapter we outline the tenets of CRT in education and discuss recent developments as CRT scholars seek to establish the approach and offer support to colleagues within a hostile and discriminatory system. We begin by describing the origins of the approach, as a radical activist perspective that has had to fight for recognition from its very inception to the present day.

The Origins of Critical Race Theory

CRT is a relative newcomer as a discrete approach to understanding and opposing inequalities in education, but the approach has its roots in the centuries old diasporic experiences and struggles of people of color, especially (but not exclusively) enslaved Africans and their descendents in the United States. The perspective builds on this tradition in numerous ways, including the central role it devotes to political struggle, its concern for storytelling, and the significant position accorded to key Black intellectual figures of the nineteenth and twentieth centuries such as Frederick Douglass and W. E. B. Du Bois (Baszile, 2008; Mills, 2003).

As a self-consciously new and oppositional form of antioppressive theory, CRT began in the 1970s and 1980s in the work of legal scholars. Derrick Bell is fre-

The Handbook of Educational Theories, pp. 1019–1026

quently "credited as the originator and force behind the movement" (Lee, 1995, p. 390): not only through his ground-breaking scholarship on the law's role in protecting and legitimating race inequality (Bell, 1980a) but also through his personal campaigns and sacrifices as he challenged the raced and gendered status quo of the academy in general and his then employer, Harvard Law School, in particular (see Crenshaw, 2002; Ladson-Billings, 2011; Lee, 1995; Tate, 1997) "Having been the first black professor tenured by Harvard Law School," Bell wrote, "I became one of the few of any race to be fired" (as cited in Lee, 1995, p. 387).

CRT emerged as an alternative to dominant perspectives, not only the conservative mainstream but also the ostensibly radical tradition of *critical legal studies* (CLS) which, in the words of Cornel West (1995) deconstructed liberalism, yet seldom addressed the role of deep-seated racism in American life. Frustration with the silence on racism prompted CRT scholars to foreground race and to challenge not only the foci of existing analyses, but also the methods and forms of argumentation that were considered legitimate. Their attempts to position race/racism as a central feature were met with a visceral reaction, especially by "some of the White male heavies of CLS who portrayed the "race turn" as a threat to the movement's very existence" (Crenshaw, 2002, p. 1355).

In addition to Derrick Bell, the foundational critical race theorists in law include Kimberlé Crenshaw, Richard Delgado, Alan Freeman, Angela Harris, Charles Lawrence, Mari Matsuda, and Patricia Williams. These writers represent a range of racial/ethnic heritages (including people of African American, Latina/o, Asian American, and White backgrounds) but share a commitment to analyses and oppose the workings of race inequality in legal culture and, more generally, in U.S. society as a whole.

There is no single canonical statement of CRT; the perspective is built upon a series of key insights which are constantly refined through their application analytically and practically. In this sense, critical race theorists view social theory as a work in progress. But this does not mean that CRT is any less serious about the importance of theory—quite the contrary. From its first iteration as a new approach, critical race scholars have staked a claim to the conceptual importance of their work. Kimberlé Crenshaw, for example, describes how she and colleagues sought to find a form of words that could be used to describe (and provide a rallying point for) the new ideas they were developing as they began to organize what was to become the first ever CRT workshop (held at the University of Wisconsin, Madison in July 1989):

> Turning this question over, I began to scribble down words associated with our objectives, identities, and perspectives, drawing arrows and boxes around them to capture various aspects of who "we" were and what we were doing ... we settled on what seemed to be the most telling marker for this peculiar subject. We would signify the specific political and intellectual location of the project through "critical," the substantive focus through "race," and the desire to develop a coherent account of race and law through the term "theory." (Crenshaw, 2002, pp. 1360-1361)

This practical and strategic orientation reflects a perspective that Derrick Bell (1992) terms "racial realism," that is, a determination to continually interrogate the workings of race and racism in the real world rather than as hypotheticals in an abstract analytic context. The real world focus of CRT should not be seen as in any way lessening its claim to be taken seriously as a major innovation in social theory. From its inception CRT has encountered patronizing and dismissive responses from academics who find its focus on racism distasteful and/or threatening (Crenshaw, 2002); unfortunately this same response was encountered when CRT moved into education (Gillborn, 2009; Ladson-Billings, 2011).

CRT quickly began to move beyond law schools and was introduced into educational studies in the mid-1990s by Gloria Ladson-Billings and William Tate IV (1995). Subsequently the approach has been adopted by numerous scholars, especially people of color working with qualitative methods, most notably Thandeka Chapman, Adrienne Dixon, Marvin Lynn, Laurence Parker, Celia Rousseau, Daniel Solórzano, David Stovall, Edward Taylor, and Tara Yosso. CRT is also building an international presence, and has begun to grow especially quickly in the United Kingdom (Gillborn, 2005, 2008; Hylton, 2008; Preston, 2007).

Tenets of Critical Race Theory

There is no single dogmatic statement of CRT but the approach is broadly characterized by a focus on the central importance of White racism and the need for active struggle towards greater equity:

> Although Critical Race scholarship differs in object, argument, accent, and emphasis, it is nevertheless unified by two common interests. The first is to understand how a regime of white supremacy and its subordination of people of color have been created and maintained.... The second is a desire not merely to understand the vexed bond between law and racial power but to change it. (Crenshaw, Gotando, Peller, & Thomas, 1995, p. xiii)

White Supremacy

In CRT the phrase "White supremacy" is used very differently to its common meaning—the term usually refers to individuals and groups who engage in the crudest, most obvious acts of race hatred. But for critical race theorists the more important, hidden, and pervasive form of White supremacy lies in the operation of forces that saturate the everyday mundane actions and policies that shape the world in the interests of White people:

> a political, economic, and cultural system in which whites overwhelmingly control power and material resources, conscious and unconscious ideas of white superiority and entitlement are widespread, and relations of white dominance and non-white subordination are daily reenacted across a broad array of institutions and social settings. (Ansley, 1997, p. 592)

White supremacy, understood in this way, is as central to CRT as the notion of capitalism is to Marxist theory and patriarchy to feminism (Mills, 2003; Stovall, 2006). This perspective on the nature and extent of contemporary racism is one of the key defining elements of critical race theory. CRT views racism as more than just the most obvious and crude acts of race hatred; it focuses on the subtle and hidden processes which have the effect of discriminating, regardless of their stated intent:

> CRT begins with a number of basic insights. One is that racism is normal, not aberrant, in American society. Because racism is an ingrained feature of our landscape, it looks ordinary and natural to persons in the culture. (Delgado & Stefancic, 2000, p. xvi)

Racism

When White people hear the word racism, they tend to imagine acts of conscious and deliberate race-hatred—discrimination is assumed to be an abnormal and relatively unusual facet of the education system. In contrast, CRT suggests that racism operates much more widely, through the routine, mundane activities and assumptions that are unquestioned by most practitioners and policymakers: what Delgado and Stefancic (2000) call "business-as-usual forms of racism" (p. xvi). For example, racism is figured in the selection and training of teachers (where minoritized teachers tend to have less secure jobs and to teach less advanced classes); in the identification of ability in school (where both formal and informal forms of assessment encode the assumptions and experiences of White people, thereby disadvantaging minoritized students); and through the selection of curricula (that celebrate a false notion of society as color-blind, where anyone can succeed on the basis of their individual merit and where racist violence is presented as an historical aberration committed by bad men disconnected from wider structures and institutions of White racial domination): see Brown and Brown (2010); Gillborn (2008); Tate (1997). This is part of what is sometimes called CRT's *critique of liberalism*.

CRT portrays dominant legal claims of neutrality, objectivity, color blindness, and meritocracy as camouflages for the self-interest of powerful entities of society (Tate, 1997).

CRT is not critical of the *idea* of a meritocracy (a place where people rise according solely to their efforts and talents) but rather it attacks the *ideology* of meritocracy, that is, the false belief that such a state actually exists in places like the United States and the United Kingdom. In these systems, characterized by deep and recurring race inequity, the pretence of a meritocracy disguises the continued benefit that White people draw from racism and allows race inequities to be presented as just and necessary, as a mere reflection of the deficiencies of the people who suffer racism (Delgado & Stafancic, 2001).

In addition to a focus on racism, CRT is also distinguished by certain other themes. For example, there is a *call to context* which challenges researchers to pay close attention to the historical location of particular events and, in particular, to recognise *the experiential knowledge of people of color.* CRT does not assume that any group of people can simply read off one "true" view of reality but there is a belief that people who experience racism are uniquely positioned to understand certain elements of its operation and power (Tate, 1997). This belief finds powerful expression in the use of *storytelling*.

Richard Delgado (1989) is one of the leading advocates of the need to "name one's own reality." Inspired by the scholarship of Derrick Bell, and the centuries old traditions of storytelling in minoritized communities, Delgado has argued forcefully for the use of narrative and counterstorytelling as a means of presenting a different reading of the world; one that questions taken for granted assumptions and destabilizes the framework that currently sustains, and masks, racial injustice. Both Bell and Delgado have produced rich narratives that span numerous publications, where their invented characters explore and challenge the operation of racism in society.

One of the greatest contributions of CRT is its emphasis on narratives and counterstories told from the vantage point of the oppressed. In doing so, CRT exposes the contradictions inherent in the dominant storyline that, among other things, blames people of color for their own condition of inequality. Critical race theorists understand that narratives are not neutral, but rather political expressions of power relationships. (Zamudio, Russell, Rios, & Bridgeman, 2011).

This approach makes CRT an easy target for those who are willing to oversimplify and seize the opportunity to accuse the approach of merely inventing its data (see Taylor, Gillborn, & Ladson-Billings, 2009). Mainstream critics frequently misunderstand the nature of counterstorytelling and ignore the fact that most CRT "chronicles" are tightly footnoted so that detailed evidence is marshalled to back up each substantive part of the argument. CRT scholars are not making up stories—they are constructing narratives out of the historical, sociocultural and political realities of their lives and those of people of color (Ladson-Billings, 2006, p. xi).

Another distinctive CRT theme is its *revisionist critique of civil rights laws* as fundamentally limited as a means of addressing inequality. Detractors have sought to present CRT as disrespectful of civil rights campaigns and victories but this is a misrepresentation. CRT is not critical of the campaigns, nor the people who sacrificed so much to advance race equality (see Crenshaw et al., 1995). Rather, CRT exposes the limits to law and policymaking, and shows how even apparently radical changes are reclaimed and often turned back over time. A key element here is the concept of *interest convergence* (Bell, 1980b). Put simply, this view argues that advances in race equality come about only when White elites see the changes as in their own interest. Derrick Bell (2004), the leading African American legal scholar, coined the idea of interest convergence and has summarized the notion like this: Justice for blacks versus racism = racism. Racism versus obvious perceptions of White self-interest = justice for Blacks (p. 59)

It is important to note that interest convergence does not envisage a rational negotiation, between minoritized groups and White power holders, where change is achieved through the mere force of reason and logic. Rather, history suggests that advances in racial justice must be won, through protest and mobilization, so that taking action against racism becomes the lesser of two evils for White interests.

Bell (2004) argued that a study of the civil rights movement reveals that time and again the "perceived self-interest by whites rather than the racial injustices suffered by blacks has been the major motivation in racial-remediation policies" (p. 59). For example, the moves to outlaw segregation in the 1960s are usually presented as a sign of growing enlightenment, but they have to be understood within the context of the "cold war" and the fact that the United States was having difficulty recruiting friendly African states when Soviet interests could point to the forms of apartheid that operated in the Southern United States. As W. E. B. Du Bois noted of the famous *Brown vs Board of Education* desegregation case: "No such decision would have been possible without the world pressure of communism" which made it "simply impossible for the United States to continue to lead a 'Free World' with race segregation kept legal over a third of its territory" (as cited in Bell, 2004, p. 67). The obvious signs of segregation have gone—such as separate toilets and lunch counters —but the reality continues in economic, residential, and educational terms.

Similarly, in the United Kingdom, the racist murder of Stephen Lawrence (a Black teenager stabbed by a White gang as he waited for a London bus) is widely hailed as a landmark case that changed race relations forever. An official inquiry into the police's failure to prosecute Stephen's killers revealed gross incompetence, disregard and deep-rooted racism. Much of the inquiry was held in public and the nightly coverage in the news media meant that the catalogue of police errors and racism was broadcast nationally, initially to a sceptical public but eventually to a growing sense of outrage. When the inquiry report was published, in 1999, the revelations about the police's arrogance, incompetence and racism were such that inaction by policymakers was inconceivable (Macpherson, 1999). The Prime Minister, Tony Blair, promised changes in the law and said that the report signaled "a new era in race relations … a new more tolerant and more inclusive Britain" ("Prime Minister's Questions," 1999, column 380-381). Radical changes were made to race relations legislation; more than 45,000 public bodies faced a new legal duty to pro-actively ensure race equality. All state-funded schools had to design a race equality policy, monitor achievements for signs of bias, and publicly plan to eradicate any signs of race inequity. On paper these are some of the most far reaching equality duties anywhere on Earth but in practice they have been largely ineffective because most schools have ignored their duties while the national education department has paid lip-service to race equality but continued to press ahead with key reforms (such as expanding the use of hierarchical teaching groups and promoting a national "gifted and talented" scheme) that have *increased* the institutional barriers to success facing most Black students in school (Gillborn, 2005, 2008; Gillborn & Youdell, 2000; Tomlinson, 2008).

The Stephen Lawrence case in the United Kingdom, like the *Brown* decision in the United States, exemplifies the way in which apparently radical civil rights breakthroughs have uncertain consequences in practice. Delgado and Stefancic (2001) argue that such events can be seen as *contradiction closing cases* which heal the gulf between the reality of racism in practice and the public rhetoric of equal opportunities and social justice: "after the celebration dies down, the great victory is quietly cut back by narrow interpretation, administrative obstruction, or delay. In the end, the minority group is left little better than it was before, if not worse" (p. 24).

CRT is not only concerned with race/racism, but with the intersection of race with other categories of oppression and exclusion, including social class, gender and disability. This concern with *intersectionality* is especially strong in critical race feminism (Wing, 1997). Indeed, building on Crenshaw's work, United Kingdom scholars Avtar Brah and Ann Phoenix (2004) argue that intersectionality itself can provide a useful focus that offers numerous advances on current single-issue thinking (see, also, Loutzenheiser & MacIntosh, 2004). As Crenshaw (1995) indicated, rather than viewing intersectionality as a kind of problem to be solved, the best way ahead may be to use intersectionality as a key means of understanding how White supremacy operates and how to mount effective resistance (see African American Policy Forum, n.d.).

NEW DEVELOPMENTS AND CONTINUING STRUGGLES

> Then he said to them all: "f anyone would come after me, he must deny himself and take up his cross daily and follow me." (Luke 9:23)

The Gospel of Luke is considered one of the most complete accounts of the life of Jesus Christ (Knight, 2003). In this instance, informing followers that they must be willing to view Christianity as the central aspect of their lives, not merely an add-on. Similarly, *race work*, especially race work done through the lens of CRT, requires that scholars be mindful of, and willing to accept, the important responsibility of directly challenging racism and White supremacy, especially as it manifests in the daily realities of education and education policy. CRT calls for embracing interdisciplinary scholarship and applying a more specific set of concepts and tenets that separate CRT from the commonly used critical theories and sociocultural theories in education. The charge to "take up your cross daily" is important for CRT scholars in that it reminds them that serious race work is always already activist in nature; that they must commit and recommit to it daily, fully cognizant of the possible costs to their relationships with peers and, indeed, their professional trajectories.

In the years that have elapsed since the publication of Ladson-Billings and Tate's (1995) groundbreaking article, CRT in education has established itself as an important theoretical framework for scholars who are concerned with race and educational equality. Many edited books with social justice frameworks host one or two chapters that utilize CRT and an increasing number of books have been published, both edited and sole authored, with an overarching focus informed by critical race theory (e.g., Dixson & Rousseau, 2006; Epstein, 2006; Ladson-Billings, 2003; Ladson-Billings & Tate, 2006; Lopez & Parker, 2003; Parker, Deyhle, & Villenas, 1999; Prendergast, 2003; Taylor et al., 2009; Yosso, 2006; Zamudio et al. 2011). CRT scholars have also used special issues of numerous well established peer-reviewed journals to explore and develop the approach (including *Cultural Politics of Education* 2007; *Educational Administration Quarterly* 2007; *Educational Philosophy and Theory* 2004; *Educational Studies* 2003; *Equity and Excellence* 2002; *Qualitative Inquiry* 2002; *Qualitative Studies in Education* 1998; *Race Ethnicity and Education* 2005, 2009; and *Teachers College Record* 2011). Special issues have proven to be particularly significant in offering CRT scholars a supportive and extended context within which to develop a diverse set of articles focused on different articulations of CRT. While the status of the journals has helped to bolster the standing of CRT, the special issues have also provided a way forward free from the conservative (sometimes reactionary) attitudes of the academic *mainstream* which still tends to view CRT as at best *specialist* and at worst as a threat to established standards.

Scholars in the millennium have employed various tenets of CRT to highlight past and present educational conditions and events. Some have used the interest convergence principle to examine how marginalized groups have struggled with the political power bloc to gain greater, more equitable access to education (Alemán & Alemán, 2010; Irvine & Irvine, 2007; Milner & Howard, 2004). These struggles often yield some measure of access for minority groups but simultaneously create larger gains for White majority political stakeholders. White scholars have increasingly contributed to CRT analyses of the centrality of race/racism, especially around questions of Whiteness, to unpack issues of White supremacy and colorblind ideologies among teachers and, indeed, within the academy (Allen, 2009; Marx, 2004; Pennington, 2007; Preston, 2007; Rogers & Mosley, 2006).

NONTRADITIONAL MOVES AND CRT SCHOLARSHIP

As noted above, critical race theorists do not define themselves solely through their academic scholarship measured in publications, presentations, and organizational leadership in academic spaces. Critical race scholars typically view activism as a key part of their role (Stovall, 2006; Stovall, Lynn, Danley, & Martin, 2009) and, in education, they have increasingly moved to collectivist forms of activism and support that mirror the initial workshops and conferences that gave birth to the approach. The U.S. has seen the greatest number of such innovations, including an annual CRT conference, the development of the Critical Race Studies in Education Association (CRSEA) and a dedicated professional development course on CRT in education at the annual meeting of the American Educational Research

Association (AERA)—the largest scholarly association for educational researchers in North America. In this way, CRT scholars have heeded the charge to "take up thy cross" within the often hostile and fraught arena of the academy. In the UK similar moves have taken place with the aim of establishing CRT as a distinctive approach to social theory (Pilkington, Housee, & Hylton, 2009 and to offer dedicated spaces for support, e.g. through a national network of CRT practitioners and the first ever U.K.-wide conference on CRT in education (held in London in 2009). These developments have proven vital as a means of offering support to colleagues who face academic persecution in the forms of emotional and institutional isolation and ideological marginalization: for example, we have worked with published scholars who have been warned that community activism might jeopardize their tenure applications (by detracting from their standing as "serious" academics) and graduate students who have been told that they *cannot* use CRT because it's not a real theory.

In 2009 Dixson and Chapman facilitated the first CRT professional development workshop for educational researchers at the AERA annual meeting in San Diego, CA. In addition to offering support to beginning researchers, the workshop was designed to address the growing misuse of CRT in education research where researchers sometimes claim to be following the path of CRT (and examining racialized educational inequity) but are often carving their own personalized path without understanding, or applying, key elements of the theory. Returning to our original metaphor, the call to use CRT should not be taken up in discreet parts and presented as acontextual, undertheorized, and underanalyzed in a way that disregards the multifaceted theoretical framework developed by CRT scholars to date. Many graduate students and new scholars hail from colleges and universities with few seasoned scholars who have built a body of work using CRT. This means that new scholars are not receiving the close professional mentoring they need to move their work, and the field, forward with new instantiations of CRT. In order to help educational researchers who were interested in CRT to develop a more substantive understanding, Dixson and Chapman invited senior and midcareer scholars who have published significant CRT work in education to serve as mentors to graduate students and new scholars seeking to use CRT. The response to the seminar was extremely positive: the course was oversubscribed and participants' reactions were so positive that a second course was invited the following year.

The need to mentor new scholars has been extended into the annual conference held by the CRSEA. Looking towards its fifth conference in May 2011, the conference has integrated sessions on the dissertation process, cultivating an area of scholarship, publications, and building coalitions which have gained in popularity each year. The CRSEA is working toward institutionalizing forms of mentoring to support new and existing CRT scholars. Sharing these experiences, making the information available to a wider breadth of scholars, and creating transparent pathways are ways in which CRT scholars are seeking to promote the tenet of social justice located in CRT.

Despite the increasing intensification and marketization of higher education, CRT scholars continue to push the boundaries of traditional academic forms of work by asserting the value of their work with local education agencies, community organizations, families, and children. Scholars have documented their social justice efforts in various publication formats, helped influence district and local policies, worked alongside legal challenges to educational inequity, and changed programs and practices in teacher education. Although the path is often difficult, as new scholars insist on a more balanced integration of service, teaching, and research in the field of education, CRT holds the promise of serving children and families of color in multiple ways that we have yet to envision and cannot wait to behold.

CONCLUSION

CRT represents a dramatic break with previous approaches to studying racism in education and is being taken up by a growing array of scholars internationally. The approach goes a good deal further than previous perspectives (such as multicultural and antiracist education) by developing a coherent body of conceptual tools that draws on an interdisciplinary perspective, values educational activism alongside groundbreaking analyses, and places White racism at the very centre of its work. Perhaps predictably, the approach has faced criticism from both sides of the political spectrum. CRT's usefulness will be limited not by the weakness of its constructs but by the degree that many Whites will not accept its assumptions; I anticipate critique from both left and right (Taylor, 1998, p. 124). CRT is a dynamic and changing field that offers a framework for critical analysis of educational inequality that is both insightful and inclusive; it remains to be seen whether the field of education is capable of sustaining, and even embracing, such a radical challenge.

REFERENCES

African American Policy Forum. (n.d.). *Primer on intersectionality.* Retrieved from http://aapf.org/wp/uploads/2009/03/aapf_intersectionality_primer.pdf

Alemán E., Jr., & Alemán, S. M. (2010). "Do Latin@ interests always have to 'converge' with White interests?":

(Re)claiming racial realism and interest-convergence in critical race theory praxis. *Race Ethnicity & Education, 13*(1), 1-21.

Allen, R. L. (2009)."What about poor White people?" In W. Ayers, T. Quinn, & D. Stovall (Eds.), *Handbook of social justice in education* (pp. 209-230). New York, NY: Routledge.

Ansley, F. L. (1997). White supremacy (and what we should do about it). In R. Delgado & J. Stefancic (Eds.), *Critical White studies: Looking behind the mirror* (pp. 592-595). Philadelphia, PA: Temple University Press.

Baszile, D. T. (2008). Beyond all reason indeed: the pedagogical promise of critical race testimony. *Race Ethnicity & Education, 11*(3), 251-265.

Bell, D. (1980a). *Race, racism and American Law.* Boston, MA: Little Brown.

Bell, D. (1980b). Brown v. Board of Education and the interest convergence dilemma. *Harvard Law Review, 93,* 518-533.

Bell, D. (1992). *Faces at the bottom of the well: the permanence of racism.* New York, NY: Basic Books.

Bell, D. (2004). *Silent covenants.* New York, NY: Oxford University Press.

Brah, A., & Phoenix, A. (2004). Ain't I a woman? Revisiting Intersectionality. *Journal of International Women's Studies, 5*(3), 75-86.

Brown, A. L., & Brown, K. D. (2010). Strange fruit indeed: Interrogating contemporary textbook representations of racial violence toward African Americans. *Teachers College Record, 112*(1), 31-67.

Crenshaw, K. W. (1995). Mapping the margins: Intersectionality, identity politics, and violence against women of color. In K. Crenshaw, N. Gotanda, G. Peller, & K. Thomas (Eds.), *Critical race theory: The key writings that formed the movement* (pp. 357-383). New York, NY: New Press.

Crenshaw, K. W. (2002). The first decade: critical reflections, or "a foot in the closing door." *UCLA Law Review, 49,* 1343-1372.

Crenshaw, K., Gotanda, N., Peller, G., & Thomas, K. (Eds.). (1995). *Critical race theory: The key writings that formed the movement.* New York, NY: New Press.

Delgado, R. (1989). Storytelling for oppositionists and others: a plea for narrative. *Michigan Law Review, 87,* 2411-2441.

Delgado, R., & Stefancic, J. (2000). *Introduction: Critical race theory: The cutting edge* (2nd ed.), Philadelphia, PA: Temple University Press.

Delgado, R., & Stefancic, J. (2001). *Critical race theory: An introduction.* New York, NY: New York University Press.

Dixson, A. D., & Rousseau, C. K. (Eds.). (2006). *Critical race theory in education: All God's children got a song.* New York, NY: Routledge.

Epstein, K. K. (2006). A different view of urban schools: Civil rights, critical race theory, and unexplored realities. *Counterpoints: Studies in the Postmodern Theory of Education* (Vol. 291). Oxford England: Peter Lang.

Gillborn, D. (2005). Education policy as an act of white supremacy: Whiteness, critical race theory and education reform. *Journal of Education Policy, 20*(4), 485-505.

Gillborn, D. (2008). *Racism and education: Coincidence or conspiracy?* London: Routledge.

Gillborn, D. (2009). Who's afraid of critical race theory in education? A reply to Mike Cole's "The Color-Line and the Class Struggle." *Power and Education, 1*(1), 125-131.

Gillborn, D., & Youdell, D. (2000). *Rationing education: Policy, practice, reform and equity.* Buckingham, England: Open University Press.

Hylton, K. (2008). *"Race" and sport: Critical race theory.* London: Routledge.

Irvine, J. J., & Irvine, R. W. (2007). The impact of the desegregation process on the education of Black Students: A retrospective analysis. *Journal of Negro Education,* 76(3), 297-305.

Knight, G. W. (2003). *The layman's Bible handbook.* Uhrichsville, OH: Barbour.

Ladson-Billings, G. (2011). Race still matters: Critical race theory in education In M. W. Apple, W. Au, & L. A. Gandin (Eds.), *The Routledge international handbook of critical education.* New York, NY: Routledge.

Ladson-Billings, G. (2006). They're trying to wash us away: The adolescence of critical race theory in education. In A. D. Dixson & C. K. Rousseau (Eds.), *Critical race theory in education: ALL God's children got a song* (pp. v-xiii). New York, NY: Routledge.

Ladson-Billings, G. (Ed.). (2003). *Critical race perspectives on social studies education: The profession, policies, and curriculum.* Charlotte, NC: Information Age Publishing.

Ladson-Billings, G., & Tate, W. F., IV. (1995). Toward a critical race theory of education. *Teachers College Record, 97,* 47-68.

Ladson-Billings, G., & Tate, W. F., IV. (Eds). (2006). *Education Research in the Public Interest: Social justice, action, and policy.* New York, NY: Teachers College Press

Lee, I. (1995). Nomination of Derrick A. Bell, Jr., to be an Associate Justice of the Supreme Court of the United States: The chronicles of Civil Rights activist. *Ohio Northern University Law Review, 22,* 363-448.

Lopez, G. R., & Parker, L. (Eds.). (2003) *Interrogating racism in qualitative research methodology.* New York, NY: Peter Lang.

Loutzenheiser, L. W., & MacIntosh, L. B. (2004). Citizenships, sexualities, and education. *Theory Into Practice, 43,* 151-158. Columbus, OH: Ohio State University.

Macpherson, W. (1999). *The Stephen Lawrence inquiry: CM 4262-I.* London: The Stationery Office.

Marx, S. (2004). Regarding Whiteness: Exploring and intervening in the effects of White racism in teacher education. *Equity and Excellence in Education, 37*(1), 31-43.

Mills, C.W. (2003). *From class to race.* New York, NY: Rowman & Littlefield.

Milner, H. R., & Howard, T. C. (2004). Black teachers, Black students, Black communities, and Brown: Perspectives and insights from experts. *Journal of Negro Education, 73*(3), 285-297.

Parker, L., Deyhle, D., & Villenas, S. (1999). *Race is ... race isn't: Critical race theory and qualitative studies in education.* Boulder, CO: Westview.

Pennington, J. L. (2007). Silence in the classroom/whispers in the halls: Autoethnography as pedagogy in White pre-service teacher education. *Race Ethnicity and Education, 10*(1), 93-113.

Pilkington, A., Housee, S., & Hylton, S. (Eds.). (2009). *Race(ing) forward: Transitions in theorising "race" in education.* Birmingham, England: Higher Education Academy, Sociology, Anthropology, Politics.

Prendergast, C. (2003). *Literacy and racial justice: The Politics of learning after Brown v. Board of Education.* Carbondale, IL: Southern Illinois University Press.

Preston, J. (2007). *Whiteness and class in education.* Dordrecht, The Netherlands: Springer.

Prime minister's questions. (1999, Feb). *Hansard,* column 379-387. Retrieved from http://www.publications .parliament.uk/pa/cm199899/cmhansrd/vo990224/debtext/ 90224-20.htm#90224-20_spmin0

Rogers, R., & Mosley, M. (2006). Racial literacy in a second-grade classroom: Critical race theory, Whiteness studies, and literacy research. *Reading Research Quarterly, 41*(4), 462-495.

Stovall, D. (2006). Forging community in race and class. *Race Ethnicity & Education, 9*(3), 243-259.

Stovall, D., Lynn, M., Danley, L., & Martin, D. (2009). Critical Race Praxis In Education: Introduction. *Race Ethnicity and Education, 12*(2), 131-132.

Tate, W.F. (1997). Critical race theory and education: History, theory, and implications. In M. W. Apple (Ed.), *Review of Research in Education* (Vol. 22, pp. 195-247). Washington DC: AERA.

Taylor, E. (1998). A primer on critical race theory: Who are the critical race theorists and what are they saying? *Journal of Blacks in Higher Education, 19,* 122-124.

Taylor, E., Gillborn, D., & Ladson-Billings, G. (Eds.). (2009). *Foundations of Critical race theory in education.* New York, NY: Routledge.

Tomlinson, S. (2008). *Race and education.* Maidenhead, England: Open University Press.

West, C. (1995). Foreword. In K. Crenshaw, N. Gotanda, G. Peller, & K. Thomas (Eds.), *Critical race theory: The key writings that formed the movement* (pp. xi-xii). New York, NY: New Press

Wing, A. K. (Ed.). (1997). *Critical race feminism: A reader.* New York, NY: New York University Press.

Yosso, T. J. (2006). *Critical race counterstories along the Chicana/Chicano educational pipeline.* New York, NY: Routledge.

Zamudio, M. M., Russell, C., Rios, F. A., & Bridgeman, J. L. (2011). *Critical race theory matters: Education and ideology.* New York, NY: Routledge.

Author Contact Information: Adrienne Dixson, Education Policy, Organization, & Leadership, 351 Education Building, 1310 S. Sixth Street, Champaign, IL 61820, E-mail: addixson@illinois.edu

CHAPTER 92

The Work of Nancy Fraser and a Socially Just Education System

Martin Mills
The University of Queensland

The work of Nancy Fraser has been critical for those working in research fields concerned with social justice and education (see for example, Cribb & Gewirtz, 2003; Keddie, 2008; Lipman, 2008; Power & Frandji, 2010). This chapter outlines key concepts within her theories of justice, traces some of the challenges posed to her work and through the use of a case study on male teachers shows how some of her work can be used to promote an understanding of social justice problematics in the field of education.

Nancy Fraser's theorizing of social justice has occurred in both the Cold War and post-Cold War era. This chapter focuses on her work in the latter period. However, her (1989) collected essays *Unruly Practices* provide an indication of the tensions and debates that surround her later work. This set of essays originated from her engagements with New Left and socialist feminist theorizing. Throughout this body of work is a consideration of the implications of her theorizing for activism. The various chapters in this book all come from articles published prior to the end of the Cold War and at a time when identity politics and poststructural theorizing were impacting upon justice debates within the academy in significant ways. In this book she begins her later task of: "developing a critical theory of recognition, one that identifies and defends only those versions of the cultural politics of difference that can be combined with the social politics of equality" (Fraser, 1997a, p. 12).

Central to her contributions to debates about social justice have been her attempts to work together understandings of distribution and recognition, and later representation, to theorize contemporary issues of social justice. Fraser's (1997a) book *Justice Interruptus* sought to come to terms with how justice could be understood in a period considered by some to have become dominated by concerns with identity politics. In this work her socialist concerns with the distribution of economic resources were evident. However, her feminist politics also ensured that a concern with recognition was present in her theorizing of justice.

In *Justice Interruptus* Fraser sought to outline a theory of justice that did not treat concerns with distribution and concerns with recognition as operating within two distinct paradigms. Instead she suggested that while these concerns are at times at odds with each other, it is possible to develop an integrated theory that is concerned with both distribution and recognition (see also, Fraser, 1995a, 1995b). Such a theory, she suggested, is critical to the demands of our age. In later work (2009) she expanded on this theorizing to include a consideration of representation as a matter of political justice.

KEY CONCEPTS

With the end of the Cold War, the disintegration of the Soviet Union and the demise of communism in Eastern Europe, socialist politics appeared to go out of fashion, and justice concerns appeared to be linked to calls to "recognize difference" rather than to claims about the redistribution or resources. Conflicts between those arguing for a justice agenda grounded in a politics of cultural recognition and those arguing for a justice

The Handbook of Educational Theories, pp. 1027–1034

agenda focussing on economic matters appeared irreconcilable. Nancy Fraser's (1995a) essay "From Redistribution to Recognition" was one of the first attempts to provide an integrated theory of justice that worked across both paradigms.

Fraser acknowledged that there were two distinct forms of injustice: economic injustice and cultural injustice. The former has been the valid concern of those she refers to as egalitarian theorists (e.g., Marx, Rawls, Sen). Such theorists were troubled by acts of maldistribution which saw people's futures and life opportunities being restricted (or advantaged) by their levels of income, by people having their labor exploited for the benefit of others, by people experiencing high levels of economic deprivation and marginalization. For many of these egalitarian theorists the political economy is the primary source of injustice. Hence, addressing this form of injustice would require some form of redistribution of economic resources, including a restructure of the economic division of labor.

In terms of the injustices growing out of a lack of recognition she suggested that misrecognition occurs when people experience cultural domination, that is, are forced to subjugate their own cultural ways of being and communicating to the (often hostile) norms of the dominant culture, are made invisible or are disrespected as a consequence of being from a particular cultural group. She indicates that these are the primary concerns of difference theorists (e.g., Honneth, 1995; Young, 1990, 1997; Taylor, 1992). Fraser's concern in this early work was to try and work these two concerns of justice together into one theory. She suggested that many injustices tended to entail a mixture of these types. However, she also indicated that on a spectrum of injustices there are some that are more clearly one than the other.

She began by outlining cases of injustice that fall clearly into one or other of these two paradigms. For her purposes she indicated that these categories were only used for analytical purposes. She suggested that there are certain injustices that are clearly socioeconomic and some that are cultural. In the first instance she used the case of class and the exploitation of labor. She suggested in this instance, that the remedy is located within changes to the political economy. In other words redresses to this injustice would involve redistribution of income and resources. I n terms of cultural injustice she suggests that those who experience a despised sexuality are suffering from a cultural injustice. As such the remedy lies in "the cultural-valuational structure of society." In other words, redresses to this injustice would involve recognition. The apparent distinction between these two groups is that in the first instance the purpose of redistributing material resources is so that the collectivity of "class" can do away with itself, whereas the purpose of recognition is to valorize groups constructed around nonheteronormative sexualities. She stresses that these two collectivities are analytical and that in practice they are somewhat entwined. For instance, some gays and lesbians do experience socioeconomic injustices due to discrimination in the workplace and some working class people experience cultural injustices based on a denigration of particular working class attributes, such as accent. However for the purposes of analysis, she suggested that at each end of the spectrum the remedies are easy to determine. However, she indicated that the situation is less clear when the cases are bivalent, as with, for example, gender and race.

If we just take the case of gender here, she suggested that gender injustices are of both forms, economic and cultural. For example, women clearly earn less income than men in most occupations, have greater difficulty in securing promotions and high status positions in public and private organizations, and are often expected to forgo income during, at least, the early years of parenthood. However, women also experience cultural injustice. This is evident in the way that women are depicted in the media, and how they are the primary victims of sexual assault, rape and violence in the home. Thus tackling injustices against women would involve both economic and cultural remedies. However, it is here that the postsocialist dilemma presents itself. One remedy may very well negate the other remedy, or indeed exacerbate the other injustice.

Staying with gender in order to explain, she suggested that the intent of remedying economic injustices against women is eradicating difference. In a situation where economic gender justice occurs, gender would be irrelevant as gender would have no bearing upon income levels, promotional opportunities or occupation. Thus, as with class, she suggested the task of challenging such injustice is to *put gender out of business.* However, the intent of remedying cultural injustice would be to foreground and celebrate women's difference from men. In this instance, justice requires not eradicating difference but valorizing it. This she indicated is the *feminist version of the redistribution-recognition dilemma*. How can social justice remedies both eradicate gender differences that cause socioeconomic injustices while also valorizing nonmasculinist ways of being?

In navigating a pathway through this dilemma, she identifies two broad approaches to remedying injustices—affirmative and transformative remedies. She detailed what each of these might look like in terms of addressing both economic and cultural injustices. She claimed that affirmative remedies are designed to correct inequitable outcomes without substantially disrupting the structures underpinning them. Affirmative economic remedies include, for instance, welfare policies and targeted employment policies. However, she explained that such policies whist working to negate some economic injustices often work to reinforce cultural injustices. For example, she suggests that they work to produce difference rather than negating difference and that in the process create the perception that oppressed groups are actually privileged, as such often attracting resentment. Colloquial terms such as "dole bludge," "welfare cheat," and "sit-down money" are all indicative of this resentment. Affirmative cultural injustice policies include concerns with the ways in which people belonging to certain groups are portrayed in textbooks, offering various multicultural foods in schools and offering special spaces in organizations for cultural groups to gather, for example women's rooms. Such remedies maintain the groups and work to value difference. However, they do not challenge the underlying structures, such as, patriarchy, heteronormativity and Eurocentricism that underpin the existence of cultural injustice.

Transformative remedies, however, work to reform those structures which generate injustice. In relation to cultural injustices, Fraser suggested that "queer theory" provides examples of the kind of remedies that are transformative. While affirmative remedies would be linked to gay and lesbian identity politics that seek to valorize various despised sexual collectivities, transformative queer politics work to destabilize all sexual identities. Such politics attribute injustice to the construction of groups and argue, not for a universal liberal notion of the individual, but for a pluralizing ever-changing understanding of difference. In terms of socioeconomic injustice she suggested that transformative remedies lie within a socialist politics. Socialism she argued seeks to undermine the structures of the capitalist state which perpetuate economic inequalities. The transformative politics of socialism would include a universal public social welfare program, which would remove, for instance, private schooling, private health funds and services, and private communication services. This politics would also promote practices that value all people's labor and occupations through, in particular, minimizing wage differentials. She suggested that as with affirmative remedies there is an underpinning concern with the moral worth of all human beings. However, while affirmative economic policies entrench difference, usually in negative, patronizing and despised ways, transformative approaches tend to make class differences less distinct. Thus, with transformative remedies for cultural injustice there is a focus on multiplying difference, while with transformative remedies for economic injustice there is an undermining of difference. As a consequence, she indicated that justice remedies are clear when addressing pure cases of economic or cultural injustice, but less so when addressing injustices of both types at the same time.

Using the examples of bivalent differentiations—where oppression is experienced on both the axes of economic and cultural injustice, she argued that what is required is both transformative redistribution and transformative recognition. Using the example of gender, she provided a case for the ways in which both sets of politics can avoid "interfering" with each other. She argued that the goal of a transformative politics relating to gender justice is to deconstruct gender binaries and to destabilize existing categories to produce a plurality of gender differences. She suggested that this aligns with a feminist socialist politics that seeks to challenge those constructions of femininity (and masculinity) that facilitate discrimination of women in the workplace and labor market and that structure various gendered practices in public and private organizations. Recognizing that axes of injustice are not exclusive, she argued that a politics is needed that recognizes the multiple oppressions a person faces at any one time and that this will require a deep restructuring both of the economy and of culture. This concern with multiple oppressions has been evident in all her later work and led her to modify her theory.

In Fraser's more recent publications, for example, "Reframing Justice in a Globalizing World" (2007), and *Scales of Justice* (2009), she recognizes that globalization has entailed a need to rethink the meanings of justice. She argues that her previously understood two-dimensional model of justice was located within a global north state—what she calls the Westphalian state—frame and that the current era requires another dimension of justice—representation. Her argument is that previous claims for redistribution and recognition were located within a nation state and that those who could make justice claims were the citizens of those countries. However, increasingly it has become obvious that actions affecting particular collectivities can occur outside the nation state. For example, economic distribution is affected by the movement of transnational corporations across locations to minimize wage costs; and cultural recognition is affected by global media. As a consequence, in making justice claims the modern state may not be the most the appropriate frame within which its citizens can make such claims. Fraser thus argues that alongside justice concerns with economics and culture there has to be a concern with political injustice.

For Fraser, politics represents the stage on which claims over distribution and recognition are made. However, on this stage, set in an era of globalization, it is not clear who can make claims and against whom such claims can be made. She argues that political injustice, which she refers to as *misrepresentation*, occurs when some are denied the opportunity to make justice claims when they are experiencing economic or cultural injustice. However, she also argues that misrepresentation can occur (although unlikely) in the absence of economic and cultural injustices. Thus, she argues that as with her earlier argument that neither a theory focussing on economic justice or a theory focussing on cultural justice is adequate for understanding justice claims in modern capitalist societies, so too, she suggests, her earlier theory is inadequate for explaining injustice in, what she refers to as, a post-Keynesian-Westphalian era. While she argues that her claims regarding recognition and redistribution stand, she also argues that there has to be a complex understanding of the political misrepresentation added to this theory.

For Fraser there are two forms of misrepresentation: ordinary political misrepresentation and *misframing*. In the first instance, misrepresentation occurs when a system fails to ensure that all its members have parity of participation. This can come about, for instance, through electoral practices shaped by a gerrymander or that work against particular groups (for example, women, Indigenous people and nonnative language speakers). Claims about such injustices are generally located within a nation state frame. However, whist such claims are familiar, less recognizable are those occurring in an era of globalization where the frame appears indeterminate. In such instances "the frame" becomes an issue of justice.

Misframing occurs when people who are affected by particular injustices are excluded from the frame in which justice claims can be made. Fraser identifies the consequential inability to make claims for redress as a major social justice concern as claims for redistribution or recognition are denied an audience. She suggests that globalization has made misframing and the injustices associated with it visible. The nation state frame, or as she refers to it, the Keynesian-Westphalian frame, works to exclude, for instance, workers from the poorest nations making claims against multinational companies that exploit their poverty to profit those living in affluent countries. Other issues that have highlighted the inadequacy of the nation state frame for making justice claims include: climate change, global media, the weapon and drug trades, and financial markets. Thus, the politics of framing—that is the process whereby the distinctions between members and nonmembers of the frame are determined—is a social justice matter in that it identifies who can make justice claims. Fraser suggests that what is required to address misrepresentation is a transformative politics of framing. Such a politics would recognize that the grammar of framing needs to change. She indicates that what this might look like is uncertain at this stage, but that the all affected principle may serve as a means to democratize the politics of framing.

Thus, Fraser's current theory of justice indicates that the three conditions of recognition, redistribution and representation all need to be met in order for justice to be achieved. For Nancy Fraser the general meaning of justice is "parity of participation" (2009, p. 16). Parity of participation ensures that all are able to participate in social life as peers. As indicated, she suggests that such participation is hindered by economic, cultural and political injustices. A socially just education system would thus work to ensure that barriers to such participation are removed, both within the practices of schooling and beyond. Examples from the field of education are used in a following section of this chapter to indicate some of the implications for her theory in addressing injustices in and through schooling. However, it is first necessary to provide a brief account of some of the critiques of Fraser.

Critiques

Nancy Fraser has not been without her critics. Fortunately many of them have been brought together in one text (Olsen, 2008), including the famous *New Left Review* debate with the late Iris Marion Young. The critiques of Fraser's work have included that she is either too focussed on distribution or on recognition; that her theorizing is inadequate for addressing the distribution-recognition dilemma; that there are forms of injustice other than maldistribution and misrecognition; and that misrepresentation is not an injustice of the same order as maldistribution and misrecognition. A full coverage of the extent of these critiques is not possible here. However, the concerns raised about her focus on either difference or distribution, and the inadequacy of her original framework require some mention.

The critiques that Fraser has received from "difference" theorists have included people such as Judith Butler (2008), Alex Honneth (Fraser & Honneth, 2003) and Iris Marion Young (1990, 1997). Butler, for instance, argued that Fraser's theory has misconstrued issues of recognition as merely cultural. She suggested that Fraser subordinates her concerns with recognition to those of distribution. She critiqued Fraser's use of heterosexism and her suggestion that the damages this causes those performing or identifying with diverse sexualities are cultural rather than material. Butler instead argued that the existence of the capitalist economy and heterosexism are linked. Butler did not suggest that sexual politics were located in either concerns about culture or the economy, she claimed rather that they make the distinction between the two blurred. Fraser's response was that she had never suggested that material consequences did not flow from misrecognition. Her point was that, and one with which Butler would disagree, concerns with distribution and recognition provide the need for two distinct, nonreducible, social justice claims; and that she was providing a framework for theorizing the ways in which these claims could be worked together in ways that did not interfere with each other.

Fraser's most well known debate was with Iris Marion Young in the 1990s. Young (1990) in *Justice and the Politics of Difference* sought to provide a theory of social justice which broke out of the recognition/distribution paradigms. In this book she identified five faces of oppression: exploitation, marginalization, powerlessness, cultural imperialism and violence. These oppressions, she suggested, do not sit easily within either a recognition or distribution framework and provide a more complex understanding of the kinds of injustice faced by various social groups. Fraser (1995b), in a critique of Young, disagreed. She sought to indicate how the various "faces of oppression" can be accounted for through either a distribution or recognition framework. According to Young (1997), however, Fraser polarized claims for recognition and redistribution and simplified the claims being made by feminists, antiracists and gay and lesbian activists, suggesting that in all but the most extreme cases, such groups recognize issues of distribution alongside recognition. She asked what the justification was for reducing her five analytical concepts to two. Further, she contended that Fraser's framework, in valorizing transformative remedies over affirmative ones, played in to the hands of the right which attacks affirmative action politics as racist and sexist (by discriminating against white men!) (see also Anderson, 2008). In turn, Fraser (1997b) responded that Young had trivialized her arguments and that she was not dichotomizing redistribution and recognition. She indicated that her intent had been to bring together the best of both sets of politics in order to articulate a theory of justice that recognized the potential for addressing the redistribution-recognition dilemma.

Fraser also receives criticism for her focus on recognition. For example, Rorty (2008), who supports her position in relation to Young and Butler, was concerned with ensuring that a politics focussed on economic injustice is at the forefront of social justice claims. In a critique of leftist politics in the academy, Rorty suggests that prejudice has been replaced by recognition as a means of legitimizing areas of study to university and funding bodies. This he suggests has been damaging to the formation of political alliances to reduce inequalities. He makes the claim that rather than seeking to valorize difference, social justice would be better served by eradicating prejudice. The latter would shift the focus from valorizing group difference to valuing individual difference and valuing what people have in common. However, Fraser argues that misrecognition comes in multiple forms and that prejudice does not fully capture these differences. The approach by Rorty, she suggests, belongs to a bygone era and that current accounts of social justice, and the proposed transformative remedies to tackle them, have been made richer by considerations of difference.

Fraser was also critiqued for the inadequacy, in her early theorizing, of using just recognition and distribution to understand contemporary forms of injustice. For instance, Feldman (2008) argued that an adequate "critical theory of the state" was absent from her work. He argued for the need to consider the ways in which the liberal state contributed to the production of status hierarchies. This was recognized elsewhere, for instance, in education Cribb and Gewirtz (2003) added associational justice to Fraser's earlier model of justice in order to take in to account the ways in which "patterns of association" prevent some people and some groups from obtaining parity of participation. Such criticisms of her work were not ignored by Fraser, and indeed she expressed some of her own uncomfortableness with the two dimensions she had been working with in her earlier work. It was these critiques and her engagement with the politics of a changing political world being brought about by globalization that caused her to add a political dimension to her work and a consideration of representation.

The various critiques of Fraser's work have been important for the development of her theory and for refining various aspects of it. Some of these critiques have been valuable for focussing on the significance of her various concepts, for extending her theory, for providing a language to address injustices, and for developing a lens through which various practices can be examined to consider their social justice implications. In so doing her work creates questions about: "what" constitutes justice (and injustice); "how" to achieve justice and tackle injustice; and "who" can make justice claims and to whom these claims can be made. While the critiques of Fraser's work cannot be ignored, the questions her work raises are all of critical concern in working toward a socially just education systems.

The following section provides an example of how Nancy Fraser's work can inform current debates in education and indicates how various concepts constructed and used by Fraser can provoke further discussion.

A Case Study: Where Are all the Male Teachers?

The male primary school teacher debate has been constructed as a contested social justice issue in a number of English speaking countries (see for example, Education Queensland, 2002; Maurer, 2006; Torney, 2006; see Francis & Skelton, 2001 for critique), although not restricted to such countries (Jóhannesson, Lingard, & Mills, 2009). In summary, a key argument in this debate has been that there is a significant disproportionate ratio of male to female primary school teachers in many countries. As such, male teachers in these schools are constructed as a minority whose work is undertaken in an environment not supportive of men. The assumed feminized environment is said to deter men from entering the profession. It is claimed that the victims of this state of affairs, along with the male teachers and men who would like to become teachers, are boys. The suggestion is that boys' results are suffering at school because of a lack of male teachers who understand what it is to be male. This construction of male teachers as a despised group, the effects of which are said to impact negatively upon both men and boys in primary schools, is identified as a gender justice issue.

A counter argument is that far from being a feminized environment that favors women, it is men who are advantaged in the primary school system. They, as a collectivity, are given preferential employment opportunities and experience rapid advancement into principal positions (Mills, Martino, & Lingard, 2004). Similarly, the claim that boys are not performing as well as girls in schools is also contested (Lingard, Martino, & Mills, 2009). The argument is often put that it does not matter to students whether or not they are being taught by a man or a woman, and that it is the quality of the pedagogy that is important. Hence, rather than initiating policies to encourage men into teaching the focus should be on improving pedagogy. Furthermore, there is the claim that men in teaching are already advantaged in that primary school structures enable male teachers to experience what Williams (1992) has referred to as the "glass escalator effect," that is rapid promotion. Thus it can be argued that policies seeking to attract more men into teaching will perpetuate gender injustice. How can Fraser help here?

The existence of professions that are numerically dominated by either women or men is an indication that society has some way to go in destabilizing dominant gender constructions that shore up patriarchal privileges. A primary schooling sector that is primarily staffed by women, with a disproportionate number of male headteachers, suggests that the same binary constructions of gender that shapes broader forms of inequity also shapes the primary teaching profession. It is clear that there is an issue of economic injustice within primary teaching. As a profession, given the number of years of study involved, expectations of further professional development, responsibility and autonomy (despite the increasing accountability pressures), primary school teaching is not well paid compared to equivalent professions largely occupied by men suggesting an issue of maldistribution based on gender. A central cause of this, it can be argued, is that this is because it is a profession largely occupied by women, and that other professions largely occupied by women, like nursing and social work, are also poorly paid in comparison to those predominantly occupied by men. At the heart of this is a devaluing of those attributes and practices associated with femininity, for example, care and work with young children. It is this devaluing that also works to make the profession unattractive to men. Hence, one suggestion that has been mooted that would attract more men and increase the status of primary teaching is increasing the salaries of teachers (House of Representatives Standing Committee on Education and Training, 2002).

This treats the gender injustice here as a matter of maldistribution: because primary school teaching is a profession that is primarily occupied by women, the pay is lower, and thus a remedy is required that redistributes income to increase the pay of primary teachers. However, there is also a gender injustice here that entails matters of misrecognition—primary school teaching involves working with young children; this is constructed as a feminine activity; feminine activities are devalued in relation to those constructed as masculine, and thus a remedy is required that works to recognize and value attributes considered feminine. As Fraser indicates, in the first instance, gender as an influence on income levels requires eradication, while in the second, recognizing gender becomes imperative to valuing women's labor. However, this dilemma can be tackled through transformative remedies which take into account matters of redistribution and recognition. These remedies are more likely to bring lasting change than many of the mooted affirmative action policies such as scholarships for male teachers. In the first instance, there has to be a restructuring of the economy in ways that do not make major differentiations in income between occupations, this has to be for all professions so that the dominance of one gender in a profession is not a predictor of income levels. This remedy will complement those recognition remedies which seek to destabilize behaviors considered masculine and feminine and to revalue those behaviors and attributes constructed as feminine.

This is just one area of education where the work of Fraser can help to provide some insights into educational in/justice. Her earlier theory focussing on redistribution and recognition are clearly relevant to this issue. The frame within which justice claims about policy initiatives addressing male teacher shortages can be made are clear. However, it is worth noting that the calls for more male teachers reach across countries and the backlash discourses they draw upon are not easily challenged. This can be seen in the way that the boys' debate has been taken up in countries where girls experience severe discrimination (see for example, Jha & Kelleher, 2006). Such global discourses, thus, also raise issues of misrepresentation.

Conclusion

Nancy Fraser is clearly one of the great thinkers in the field of social justice and has been a major contributor to ongoing debates about the nature of social injustice and its remedies. In particular, her work has provided a framework to consider the multiple oppressions and injustices that face diverse communities. Her theorizing has not remained static and has engaged with major political shifts over the last 30 years, for example: (a) the pre- and post-Cold War era; (b) the rise of identity politics; and (c) globalization. However, consistent throughout her writings has been a commitment to bringing about change that improves "parity of participation" for all experiencing one form of oppression or another. Indeed, her work has been testament to the intent in *Unruly Practices* to demonstrate that "the radical academic is not an oxymoron" (Fraser, 1989, p. 1).

That her work has had an impact is demonstrated by the way it has framed up concerns with social justice in multiple fields. This impact is also highlighted by the engagement of multiple theorists with her work, many of whom who have taken issue with one or more aspects of her theories (see Olsen, 2008). These critiques have been critical for extending her theorizing and for opening up new areas of inquiry. Indeed, Nancy Fraser's responses to these critiques have been a major contribution to her body of work.

The frameworks that she has developed, along with the responses to her critics, have provoked significant questions about social justice for researchers in many fields. For those working in education, Fraser's work forces one to think about the following types of questions:

- How much inequality in terms of economic resources and distribution of academic outcomes can a socially just education system tolerate?
- How much redistribution of resources and academic outcomes is required to create a socially just education system and how should this redistribution occur?
- What kinds of despised differences warrant valuing and recognizing?
- How do schools contribute to the oppression of certain cultural groups and how can they play a role in providing remedies to these oppressions?
- What is the appropriate frame for making justice claims through schooling? And who can make these claims?

While the ways in which Fraser has tried to make sense of these questions can be contested, there is no doubt that the questions themselves are critical for moving toward a more socially just education system. These are questions that researchers working within diverse educational fields cannot ignore.

References

Anderson, E. (2008) Affirmative action and Fraser's redistribution-recognition dilemma. In K. Olsen (Ed.), *Adding insult to injury: Nancy Fraser debates her critics* (pp. 164-175.). London, England: Verso.

Butler, J. (2008). Merely cultural. In K. Olsen (Ed.), *Adding insult to injury: Nancy Fraser debates her critics* (pp. 42-56). London, England: Verso.

Cribb, A., & Gewirtz, S. (2003). Towards a sociology of just practices. In C. Vincent (Ed.), *Social justice education and identity* (pp. 15-29). London, England: Routledge.

Education Queensland. (2002). *Male teachers' strategy: strategic plan for the attraction, recruitment and retention of male teachers in Queensland state schools 2002-2005.* Brisbane, Australia: Queensland Government.

Feldman, L. (2008) Status injustice: The role of the state. In K. Olsen (Ed.), *Adding insult to injury: Nancy Fraser debates her critics* (pp. 221-245). London, England: Verso.

Francis, B., & Skelton, C. (2001). Men teachers and the construction of heterosexual masculinity in the classroom. *Sex Education*, 1(1), 9-21.

Fraser, N. (1989). *Unruly practices: Power, discourse and gender in contemporary social theory.* Cambridge, MA: Polity Press.

Fraser, N. (1995a). From redistribution to recognition? Dilemmas of justice in a 'post-socialist' age. *New Left Review, 212,* 68-93.

Fraser, N. (1995b). Recognition or redistribution? A critical reading of Iris Young's *Justice and the politics of difference, Journal of Political Philosophy,* 3(2), 166-180.

Fraser, N. (1997a). *Justice interruptus: Critical reflections on the "postsocialist" condition.* New York, NY: Routledge.

Fraser, N. (1997b) A Rejoinder to Iris Young, *New Left Review, 223,* 126-129.

Fraser, N. (2007). Reframing justice in a globalizing world. In T. Lovell (Ed.), *(Mis)recognition, social inequality and social justice: Nancy Fraser and Pierre Bourdieu* (pp. 17-35). Abington, England: Routledge.

Fraser, N. (2009). *Scales of justice: Reimagining political space in a globalizing world.* New York, NY: Columbia University Press.

Fraser, N., & Honneth, A. (2003). *Redistribution or recognition? a political-philosophical exchange.* London, England: Verso.

Honneth, A. (1995). *The struggle for recognition: The moral grammar of social conflicts* (J. Anderson, Trans.). Cambridge, MA: Polity Press.

House of Representatives Standing Committee on Education and Training. (2002). *Boys' education: Getting it right,* Canberra, Australia: Commonwealth Government.

Jóhannesson, I., Lingard, B., & Mills, M. (2009). Problems and possibilities in the boy turn: Comparative lessons from Australia and Iceland. *Scandinavian Journal of Educational Research, 53*(2), 309-325.

Jha, J., & Kelleher, F. (2006) *Boys' underachievement in education: An exploration in selected commonwealth countries.* Vancouver, British Columbia, Candida: Commonwealth of Learning.

Keddie, A. (2008). Gender justice and the English citizenship curriculum: A consideration of post-September 11 national imperatives and issues of "Britishness." *International Journal of Educational Reform, 17*(1), 3-18.

Lingard B., Martino, W., & Mills, M. (2009). *Boys and schooling: Contexts, issues and practices*. Basingstoke, England: Palgrave Macmillan.

Lipman, P. (2008). Mixed-income schools and housing: advancing the neoliberal urban agenda. *Journal of Education Policy, 23*(2), 119 -134.

Maurer, P. (2006, September 28). Schools need male teachers in classrooms, *The Detroit News*, p. 15.

Mills, M., Martino, W., & Lingard, B. (2004). Issues in the male teacher debate: Masculinities, misogyny and homophobia. *British Journal of Sociology of Education, 25*(3), 354-369.

Olsen, K. (Ed.). (2008). *Adding insult to injury: Nancy Fraser debates her critics*. London, England: Verso.

Power, S., & Frandji, D. (2010). Education markets, the new politics of recognition and the increasing fatalism towards inequality. *Journal of Education Policy, 25*(3), 385-396.

Rorty, R. (2008). Is "cultural recognition" a useful notion for leftist politics? In K. Olsen (Ed.), *Adding insult to injury: Nancy Fraser debates her critics* (pp. 69-81). London, England: Verso.

Taylor, C. (1992). *Multiculturalism and the politics of recognition: An essay*. Princeton, NJ: Princeton University Press.

Torney, K. (2006, January 4). Pupils 'miss out due to lack of male teachers' [electronic version]. *Belfast Telegraph*. Retrieved from Factiva Database.

Williams, C. (1992). The glass escalator: Hidden advantages for men in the female professions. *Social Problems, 39*, 253-267.

Young, I. (1990). *Justice and the politics of difference*, Princeton, NJ: Princeton University Press.

Young, I. (1997). Unruly categories: A critique of Nancy Fraser's dual systems theory. *New Left Review, 222*, 147-160.

Author Contact Information: Martin Mills, Professor, School of Education, The University of Queensland. Telephone: +61 7 33656484. E-mail: m.mills@uq.edu.au

CHAPTER 93

Theorizing Democratic and Social Justice Education

Conundrum or Impossibility?

Carolyn M. Shields
Wayne State University

> No man is an island, entire of itself; every man is a piece of the continent, a part of the main; … any man's death diminishes me, because I am involved in mankind.
>
> —Meditation (XVII, 1624)

Despite John Donne's assertion that we live in interdependence with others and are diminished by their suffering or death, disparities among rich and poor, powerful and less powerful, those who live in countries with abundant resources and others whose lands are (or have been) impoverished, all suggest that somehow, we permit inequity to exist without allowing ourselves to feel diminished. Because freedoms, resources, material goods, and opportunities are still remarkably inequitably distributed, it is necessary to develop robust ways to theorize and advance education for democracy and social justice.

Despite the need to clarify what is meant by democratic and social justice education, it is challenging, indeed likely impossible to develop a one-size-fits-all—good-for-all-contexts—theory. The task is compounded by the prevalence of competing ideological definitions of both social justice and democracy. Both *social justice* and *democracy*, for our purposes here, imply the prevalence of certain values and not particular systems of distribution of goods or of participatory or representative government.

The language of "social justice education" is highly contested *within* jurisdictions, and so views of what constitutes social justice may sometimes be diametrically opposed. For example, in America, "experts" from both the right and the left argue for and against universal health care, increased taxation, or government intervention in various sectors—all in the name of social justice. Additionally, because equitable distribution of one "good" does not imply equity of others, context becomes critically important. One can, for example, have an advanced educational degree but be unemployed; one can have more than enough food and material goods, but because of a lack of medical insurance, become quickly stressed in the advent of a health crisis. Similarly, it is possible to claim equity of *access* to education in countries like the United States or Australia, but at the same time, to recognize that educational *outcomes* and *achievements* may still be inequitably distributed based on access to good teachers, advanced educational resources, high performance expectations, and so forth. One may be able to demonstrate equitable distribution of access to a free elementary education in a particular country, but experience barriers to accessing adequate nutrition and, hence, not be healthy enough to attend or profit from school. Moreover, although a right, such as school attendance, may be equitably distributed in countries like Zimbabwe or Iran, the presence of coercion, political corruption, or a bias against educating women may mediate its actual distribution.

Tackling issues of equity, inclusion, and social justice becomes even more complex when one compounds the challenges by introducing concepts of democracy into the conversation, for democracy (with a small "d") is neither normative or uniform. Yet, including theories of

The Handbook of Educational Theories, pp. 1035–1046

citizenship such as Marshall's (1950) conception of civil, political, and social rights, enriched by understandings from critical feminism (Hill-Collins, 2008; Mohanty, 2000) or critical race theory (Bell, 1975; Ladson-Billings & Tate, 1995; Parker & Villapando, 2007) may also hold utility for deepening our understanding. The difficulties of theorizing concepts that are vast, disparate, and context-dependent (in terms of geographic, cultural, and socioeconomic contexts) are considerable. However, an eclectic and holistic examination of theories that may comprise a framework for a more robust conception of democratic and social justice education is needed.

In a chapter such as this, one could, for example, draw on theories of social and cultural capital (Bourdieu, 1977; Putnam, 2001) for their power to explain people's apparent differential abilities to participate fully in social institutions. Alternatively, one could advance the capabilities theories of Sen (1992) or Nussbaum (2006) as ways of thinking about requisite conditions for increasing social justice. Indigenous theories of place (Read, 2000) might appropriately address the inequitable distribution of natural resources related to famine, poverty, access to health care and so on. One could also be seen to be remiss in attempting to discuss social (in)justice without addressing issues of ecological and economic sustainability as they either reflect the current neoliberal emphases (Giroux, 2005) or provide promising ways of advancing justice.

In this chapter, I approach social justice in an integrative fashion. I will not attempt to provide either a comprehensive or a historical theory, but will suggest some key ideas that, together, might provide the necessary scaffolding for the construction of locally-relevant and contextually-appropriate theorizing. To do so, I identify some underlying principles useful for theorizing democratic and social justice education. The discussion of the principles will include consideration of a number of theories that have gained currency both outside of and within education, theories that hold promise for promoting critical reflection and for enhancing educational practices related to overcoming injustice and advancing equity for all.

Caveats and Definitions

Three caveats are in order. First, it is important to note the use of the term *democratic*—used here intentionally with a small "d." This concept of "democratic" is not confined to processes of governance; it recognizes that one person, one vote, is not sufficient, for it always leaves open the possibility that the majority can override the rights, wishes, or needs of the minority. As used here, *democracy* represents a way of organizing social life that is respectful, inclusive, and mutually beneficial—one in which the principles to be developed clearly guide both beliefs and actions. Here, we start from the premise, articulated by Dewey, almost a century ago, that "the purpose [of education] is to set free and to develop the capacities of human individuals without respect to race, sex, class, or economic status" (Green, 1999, p. 56). According to this definition, one could conceivably have the paradoxical situation of democratic education within a state that is not democratic in governance as well as educational institutions that are clearly not democratic within a state that purports to be a democracy. Second, when we reflect on democratic education, a common approach is to argue that schools should be "more democratic"—and I certainly believe they should. Although the question of degree is always open to interpretation, my position is that schools (in which the population is never totally voluntary) neither are, nor can be, full democracies, but training grounds for democracy—sites where (as I have argued elsewhere, see Shields, 2009) students learn *about*, receive apprenticeship *in*, and are prepared *for*—democratic citizenship.

The third caveat here is the need to distinguish between a *socially just* education, and *social justice education*. The former implies that the learning environment, organizational structures, and educational opportunities experienced by students offer equity of both access and outcomes to all students. The latter incorporates these elements, but goes further, implying that students are again taught *in* a socially just institution, taught *about* social (in) justice in the world, and are prepared *for* taking a stance against injustice wherever it may be encountered. A *democratic social justice education* therefore is one that balances individual academic excellence and the welfare of the group; it promotes both public and private good.

The Centrality of Context

Examining the foregoing caveats and assertions, it becomes clear that one cannot discuss either individual excellence or public good without attending to context. For example, any educational theorist wanting to advance the concepts of a democratic and social justice education would likely find himself or herself readily arguing the fundamental principle of equitable and respectful treatment of individuals, regardless of gender, ethnicity, color, religious background, or primary language. At the same time, in almost any context, there would be considerable dispute over what such treatment might entail. Should students whose families have entered a country "illegally" and without proper documentation have access to the same high quality education as those who were born there? Does it show adequate respect to taxpayers and homeowners if "illegal aliens" are permitted to access educational resources without having paid for them? What of people who have landed on the shores of a foreign country after a long and arduous sea-journey, as in the case of numerous refugees? Does respect for their human rights require that they be given access to health care, legal services, and an immigration hearing? Or does the fact that others have been in the queue, waiting months or even years, to be processed, require that recent arrivals be denied entry? The complex myriad responses all purport to arise from a deep concern for human rights and for the safety and security of those already in the country.

As another example, consider the debate over child labor in countries such as India or Pakistan. Although few (if any) would claim to be proponents of child labor, understanding the social and economic complexities of the situation might lead those who claim adherence to the same principles of respect and absolute regard to reach quite different practical conclusions. Someone might argue that despite the undesirability of child labor, shutting it down would lead to increased starvation or to child prostitution, as destitute minor children sought ways to support themselves and their families; hence, arguing first for large-scale social reform. Another person might stand on principle, arguing that despite the need for societal reform in order to provide for children's basic needs, we need to eliminate the practice. The foregoing examples are provided, not in any attempt to take a position on the topics (although obviously I have one), but to demonstrate the ongoing difficulties of developing a practical theory of democratic and social justice education.

Creating a Scaffolding

Because of the centrality of context, I argue that scaffolding for democratic and social justice education may clarify some likely to-be-agreed-upon principles, but permit the details to be worked out *in context,* and *with* those most to be affected by the policies or practices under discussion. And, although the following list is by no means exhaustive, the key principles to be developed here, that could undergird a theory of democratic and social justice education, are the following:

- All persons in a given organization shall be treated respectfully.
- The education institution will ensure equitable access for all.
- The education institution will promote equitable outcomes for all.
- The practices of the organization should emphasize mutual benefit.
- The norms and practices of the organization shall be equally inclusive of all members.
- All members of a designated group (society, community, school) shall have equal civil, political, and social rights as citizens.
- Competition for funds to ensure basic needs is undemocratic.

It is important to acknowledge from the outset that only if taken together will these principles begin to form a basis for theorizing democratic and social justice education; they rely on, interact with, and extend each other as the threads of an intricately woven tapestry; separately they signify little; together they form a complex whole. In the following sections, although I consider each principle separately, drawing from various relevant theories as I develop it, each is completed as it interacts with the others. I conclude with a section in which I further reflect on how context informs our understandings and helps to determine the specifics for a given situation.

Considering the Principles

Seven principles that may serve to ground considerations of democratic and social justice education are presented here. Although these principles will not provide answers to thorny questions such as, "Is affirmative action socially just?" or "What type of discipline policies are most equitable?" they are intended to prompt critical reflection and ongoing dialogue.

Dignity, Respect, and Absolute Regard

Human dignity and respect are basic to many different kinds of institutions and organizations and to many disparate conceptions of justice. Nevertheless, they are so foundational that they comprise the first principle of democratic, social justice education. Nussbaum (2006) acknowledged that each person is worthy of respect and dignity regardless of the kind of life he or se lives. Starratt (1991) called for "absolute regard" for others—perhaps especially for those who are, in some ways, different from ourselves. In society, as in educational organizations and institutions, regardless of whether a person has the physical or intellectual capacity to fully understand and/or to participate in a given activity, that person still has intrinsic worth and dignity and is worthy of respect. Too often, democratic principles advance the need for inclusive participation (Dahl, 1989) on the part of all members or citizens, but ignore the fact that a few may not be able to participate fully or express an informed opinion on a decision that may affect them. Although, as Nussbaum (2006) asserted persuasively, many kinds of impairments and disabilities do not prevent full participation in political choice, it is clear that some others may not be able to speak out for themselves; yet, it is necessary that we make all possible efforts to accommodate and include both groups. When we treat all persons with absolute regard, a possible limitation itself does not and must not diminish anyone's personal dignity or worth.

Thus Nussbaum's (2006) critique of Hobbes' social contract or of Rawl's notion of justice among individuals who are "free, equal, and independent" is important. She argued that social contract theories do not include those who are not "roughly equal in capacity," and hence, I submit that these theories are not adequate as a basis for a democratic, social justice education in which each person is accepted as the equal of others. Nussbaum advocated what she and economist Amartya Sen (1992) have called a *capabilities approach*—an approach that relies on the intuitive idea of human dignity, that the abilities and capabilities of each person should be developed as ends and not as instrumental abilities to be used for the benefit of others.

In education, to treat each person with absolute regard requires that we take into account two additional theories. The first, the theory known as deficit thinking, must be rejected. This is the approach that implies a medical model of education that pathologizes difference and ascribes deficiency to the differentiated characteristics of members of a group. Shields, Bishop, and Mazawi (2005) explained it as follows:

> pathologizing the lived experiences of children becomes a process of treating differences (achievement levels, abilities, ethnic origin, knowledge perspectives, etc.) as deficits that locate the responsibility in the lived experiences of children (home life, home culture, socioeconomic status) rather than locating responsibility within classroom interactions and relationships, or indeed, within the education system itself. (p. 19)

Yet, as West (2002) argued, cultural differences do not "exist independent of social contexts and power relations; they are, rather, signs of struggle, interpretations of human tendencies, practices, features, and customs defined in relationships and struggles among groups of people in particular contexts for particular reasons" (p. 1).

A democratic and social justice education, then, will strive to ensure that difference is not interpreted as deficiency, and will promote equitable, respectful, relationships, and interactions among all members of the school community. Theorizing such an education must start with a theory of dignity and respect such that the lived experiences of all children are valued and their abilities and capabilities deemed to be a useful basis for making connections in ways that help to make sense of the formal curriculum. Social exclusion and pathologizing the lived experiences and social and cultural capital of children are not bases for democratic education and its sense-making classroom conversations; conversely, absolute regard for each person is a mandatory starting point.

Equity of Access

The principle of equity of access requires that all members of the community have equal (and similar) opportunities for individual growth as well as to learn about, in, and for democracy and social justice. This implies, as Dahl (2000) might have argued, that all students have similar opportunities to learn about themselves and the world around them. Dahl termed this basis for being able to fully participate in democratic life "enlightened understanding." Although he recognizes that "full understanding" is not possible, he argues for the fullest understanding possible of both our own interests and those of others, calling for "enlightened sympathy in which we try to grasp the desires, wants, needs, and values of other human beings" (p. 181). For Dahl, enlightened understanding requires an "expansion of the institutional protections for many fundamental rights and interests" (p. 187). This, it seems to me, is the necessary response of educational institutions in a democracy—an expansion of protections to ensure that the fundamental rights of all children to access an equitable and high quality education are protected.

In education, equity of access has multiple implications and applications. In still developing countries, such as Pakistan or Afghanistan and many others, where education is not yet universally available (or even compulsory), many barriers present themselves to young people striving not only to benefit themselves but their communities. Moreover, in a number of countries, (including Angola, Bangladesh, Burma, Iran, Laos, Pakistan), children can finish school by age 10—well below legal age for employment include (Tomasevski, 2006, p. xx). For them, equity of access to education itself becomes critically important.

Elsewhere, equity of access must mean that all educational programs are open to all students regardless of their ethnicity, home language, or socioeconomic status. In more developed countries, equity of access might require that no students or group of students on the basis of their group affiliation (economic situation, minority status, disability, sexual orientation, home language, and so forth) are either automatically entitled to participate in, or are prevented from accessing, specific courses, concepts, opportunities or activities, simply on the basis of their group identification. Instead of those students often identified as "gifted" being given opportunities for advanced understandings, professional job shadowing or internships, trips to college campuses, international exchanges and so forth, these opportunities must be open to all students based on encouraging their interests and abilities.

Education that is democratic provides opportunities for all students regardless of their material conditions. Income disparities must not be the basis on which educational activities are available; parental levels of education should not predetermine opportunities for engagement; home language that is other than the language of instruction should be seen as a benefit rather than detrimental to learning. Indeed, Cummins' (1989) notion of empowerment education that is respectful and inclusive of minoritized cultures and is additive rather than subtractive, is central to a theory of democratic and social justice education.

An emphasis on social justice education will promote what some have called "global curiosity"—piquing curiosity and awareness of the conditions under which others live and of the huge disparities in income, wealth, and social conditions that exist within, between, and among countries. Further, global curiosity must lead to equity, respect, and global understanding. On occasion I have heard educators commenting that their concept of social justice includes "realistic" expectations for all kids, hence, offering some job training, rather than offering false hope and encouraging all students to dream of university. This statement is not reflective of social justice but is inherently unjust, making arbitrary decisions to limit and restrict the opportunities of some students for reasons of assumption and tradition.

Kincheloe and Steinberg (1995) wrote that the systems of meaning we construct in our education systems must be "just, optimistic, empathetic, and democratic" (p. 2). For this to occur, it is important, they say, "to understand the way power regulates discourses" (p. 4) and to critique how schools "identify, often unconsciously, conceptions of what it means to be educated in the terms of the upper middle-class white culture" (p. 4). To overcome this framing, and expand our conception of democratic and social justice education, we must constantly remind ourselves of Barber's (2001) notion that education, as the "enabler of democracy," must create equitable opportunities to achieve "both liberty and equality" (p. 13).

Equity of Outcomes

The third principle of democratic and social justice education is that it must "level up and never down" (Barber, 2001, p. 19)—focusing not only on the provision of equitable access, but on equitable outcomes as well. In other words, education should be one catalyst for social mobility, for opening life's chances and choices for all children. Nussbaum (2006) stated that inequalities between rich and poor nations affect the life chances of their citizens. Thus, social justice education must take seriously the need to redress such inequities by offering educational experiences in every country that promote social mobility. Although the United Nations' goal of a free and universal public education remains elusive for many children throughout the world, with more than 75 million not having access to education of any quality, in most developed countries, disparity takes a different form—disparity of outcomes, rather than of access. The long-repeated and well-known litany related to achievement gaps between students from the dominant culture and language and those who are learning in alternative languages and contexts is well-known.

To achieve equity of outcomes, Farrell (1999) posited the need to change from a conception of educational opportunity centered on access to a conception focused on results; thus ensuring that all children are able to avail themselves of similar educational opportunities regardless of their social location in society. He argued that educational inequality or inequity may operate across different dimensions of education, including *access* (the ability to get into a certain class or school), *survival* (the ability of students to remain), *output* (the probability that all children will learn the same things to the same levels), and *outcome* (the probability that all children will have equal life opportunities as a result of schooling). He then raised the question of what "equity of results" might mean in societies that are fundamentally differentiated and stratified across markers of difference.

Statistics show clearly that equitable outcomes rarely exist in most developed democratic countries and almost never in less developed countries. Many policy makers and parents argue for the maintenance of programs and policies that promote the interests of their elite group and ignore the interests of outsiders. Perpetuating gifted classes and magnet programs that over-identify students from dominant groups and deny access to bright and talented students from different backgrounds and cultures is still too common. Drop-out (or push-out) rates, completion rates, and achievement levels too often vary with socioeconomic background, ethnicity, or home language, depending primarily on the sociocultural and economic capital with which students enter school. Moreover, scholars have noted that, often, efforts to redress this situation have not been successful, focusing on technical rather than significant and substantive reforms (Farrell, 1999; Oaks & Rogers, 2006).

Yet, Darling-Hammond (2010), Bishop, Berryman, Tiakiwai, and Richardson (2003), and others from many countries have demonstrated repeatedly that where educators focus on the rejection of deficit thinking (Shields, Bishop, & Mazawi, 2005; Valencia, 1997) and incorporate high expectations, meaningful pedagogical strategies (Grumet, 1995; Ladson-Billings, 1994), and a strong focus on the creation of a positive and inclusive school environment (Ryan, 2006; Shields, 2009) then it is possible to reverse these trends.

This is also confirmed by the 2001 Organization for Economic Cooperation and Development (OECD) report of international achievement. It demonstrates, for example, that both high quality education and high equity for all students is achieved in Korea. There "students whose parents have lower levels of occupational status perform well both in relative terms … and in absolute terms, i.e., when compared with students whose parents have similar occupational status in other countries" (OECD, 2001, p. 139). In contrast, students in Belgium, Germany, the United States, and the United Kingdom "who are in the bottom quarter of the occupational index are more than twice as likely as other students also to be among the bottom 25 per cent of their country's performers" (p. 140). The authors of the report explain that many factors likely contribute to this situation, but that in some other countries there is much less correlation between students being from low-income families and performing in the bottom quartile of their class. The goal towards which socially just leaders must work is equity of outcomes and results for all students regardless of their family situation.

Mutual Benefit

This fourth principle emphasizes the notion of mutual benefit and asserts that neither members of the majority nor members of the minority should have the ability to make decisions that disregard the rights of others. Here Green's (1999) rejection of "thin democracy" comes into play. She argued that purely formal democracy, grounded in participatory processes such as voting, is "essentially unsustaining and culturally unsustainable" (p. vi); moreover,

> a limited, formal conception of democracy contrasts with *a deeper conception of democracy* that expresses the experience-based possibility of more equal, respectful, and mutually beneficial ways of community life. (p. vi, italics in original)

Note that here the concept of mutual benefit envisioned is not that of economic benefit (as is often advocated) but instead, a form of communal benefit evident in the life lived in common with others.

The promotion of mutual benefit is informed by an examination of Bourdieu's concepts of habitus, fields, and cultural capital. Swartz (1997) stated that Bourdieu thinks of "school systems as the institutionalized context where the intellectual habitus of a culture develops" (p. 102). Educational systems are therefore fields in which, over time, durable dispositions develop and become entrenched to the point where they begin to operate as organizing principles that constrain our thinking, define what can and cannot be seen as acceptable, and hence, perpetuate societal norms, often at a subconscious level. Such norms and dispositions comprise the *habitus* of education, often making White-middle-class norms, values, beliefs, and cultural practices the benchmark against which all others are measured (and generally found wanting).

To implement democratic and social justice education, one must, therefore, expand one's concepts of what is valuable, useful, or normal. We must recognize, for example, that all children enter school with abilities, capabilities, and knowledge—some of which are congruent with that expected by schools and on which the curriculum is based and some of which relate to life in the *outside world*. The more the home preparation of children is congruent with the norms and expectations of the school, the more likely it is that they will perform well, and become successful students. *The more their cultural capital differs from that of the school, the more likely they are to be seen as deficient, and to be funneled into a special education class or lower level program. Broadening our understanding of the possible contributions of each group is one way to promote the democratic excellence advocated by Barber* (2001)—*"an inherent virtue that does not depend on comparative standing"* (p. 13).

Mutual benefit suggests that those who are stronger have a civic responsibility to care for those who are weak; those who are more economically advantaged have a responsibility to share (at a minimum, through a redistribution of taxed income) with those who are less advantaged; those who are richer to share with those who are poor, and so forth. It also requires that those who are materially advantaged recognize that they have much to learn from those who have different (and often complementary) strengths and positions. Thus power will need to be reconceptualized to include the concept of mutual benefit. Those who have traditionally held power to sway decisions, to prevent (or permit) change, or to ensure that policies and practices perpetuate their personal advantage will have to recognize mutual benefit as broader and more inclusive of those who are, in some ways, different from themselves.

As an example, parents whose children benefit from advanced college prep classes and the strongest teachers have sometimes resisted attempts to open these classes to children from minoritized groups who have been traditionally under-represented in such classes, purporting that this will both "water down" expectations and enlarge the pool of successful applicants competing for university admission, scholarships, and ultimately positions. Obviously this position perpetuates hegemonic divides rather than ensuring a more equitable distribution of educational resources that will ultimately result in a healthier and more prosperous society overall. In other contexts, the focus of mutual benefit might be on renewed efforts to make education compulsory as well as free and accessible for all children, and in the process, reducing crime, and ensuring the safety and security of all citizens.

Here perhaps Green's (2001) concept of egalitarian solidarity is useful. He described solidarity as the "disposition to ally oneself with others not because they are similar to oneself in social background or agree with one's own tastes and values but precisely because they are different and yet have permanently common human interests" (p. 197). It is this kind of solidarity that the principle of mutual benefit calls forth.

EQUITABLE INCLUSION

Related to previous principles is the right to expect a democratic and socially just institution to be equally inclusive of each group's norms. This is a difficult principle, for it does not and cannot imply a relativistic stance in which there are no preferred norms, no acceptable values, and no desirable courses of action. It does, however, suggest that the norms of an institution must not be predetermined, but should likely be negotiated as a result of dialogue among those with multiple perspectives in order to be as inclusive as possible of all cultural backgrounds. At the same time, inclusion here must once again be meaningful, firmly grounded on the concept of *absolute regard*, and not on superficial, one-time-only celebrations such as multicultural fairs.

One way of thinking about equitable inclusion is to consider Fraser's (1995) model of democracy that combines "a struggle for an antiessentialist multiculturalism with the struggle for social equality" (Fraser & Naples, 2004, p. 1104). She argues for an integrated and interrelated conception of inclusion that is rooted in both the political-economic and the cultural-symbolic structures of society, each of which requires a different type of "remedy." She argues that both recognition of cultural inequities (such as the current rejection and punishment of gays and lesbians in many societies) and redistribution of resources (income, health care, and educational opportunity) are necessary to achieve justice. Her call is for both reinterpreting and changing the world, emphasizing the need to address and provide redress for "class hierarchies" which deny "some actors the resources they need to interact with others as peers" and "status hierarchy, which denies some the requisite social standing" (p. 1115). In education, overcoming the hierarchical organization of subject matter instruction and of learning opportunities may exemplify both.

The principle of equitable inclusion raises difficult questions related to both policy and practice. On one level, the principle of recognition may require rethinking some of the *political correctness* that dominates in this present age. Somehow it has become necessary in many venues to reject acknowledgement of the dominant culture's Christmas celebration, requiring its replacement with such empty phrases as "Happy Holidays"; in those same spaces, however, it seems perfectly acceptable for minority religious beliefs to be recognized and validated, thus, permitting acknowledgement of Eid Mubarak, or Hannukah, or other such holy days. This is a sensitive and tricky issue for again, the power of the majority to exclude others must be overcome, while the equal right of all to celebrate from their own perspective must be preserved.

At the same time, the principle of redistribution may need to be invoked to ensure equitable inclusion. Hence, an educator might find herself arguing that not every child has the same ability to fund-raise for a class trip but that nevertheless, each child should have the right to participate through a reallocation of funds. To be equitable, this policy might also require that each child learn the appropriate material, take some responsibility for the preparations, (planning for accommodation, making travel arrangements, keeping track of funds and so forth). In another situation, ensuring that each child who wishes to do so (and not just those selected by a teacher) has an opportunity to participate in an extramural leadership program may constitute equitable inclusion. A democratic and social justice education will ensure that no group is advantaged within the institution to the exclusion of others.

EQUAL CITIZENSHIP RIGHTS

This sixth principle requires that citizenship rights be extended equally and equitably to all members of an educational institution (society, community, or school). Using Marshall's (1950) theoretical distinctions among civil, political, and social rights as a starting point, it is incumbent on those wishing to foster democratic and social justice education to ensure that all individuals and groups within an organization have equal rights as citizens. Marshall describes these fundamental rights, respectively, as the right to individual freedoms (such as those outlined in the U.S. Bill of Rights), the right to be involved in the exercise of power (including voting and other decision-making mechanisms), and the right to a degree of economic security, health services, and educational provision. There is no doubt that in this regard, because educational institutions are embedded in the norms, beliefs, and practices of a wider society, they have followed some of the exclusionary practices of that wider society. Just as the culture of power (Delpit, 1990) within Western society has been largely shaped by White middle-class norms, so the norms of schooling, including curriculum, have reflected these same dominant values. In turn, this has made the successful negotiation of schooling more readily available to those whose cultural capital most closely resembles that valued by the institution. For that reason, some (see for example, Torres, 1998) argued that citizenship rights need to be continuously reinterpreted; he writes,

> The question of citizenship and democratic education cannot, and should not, be separated from the questions of who are the citizens to be educated, how these citizens change over time in terms of their own demographic, political, cultural, even symbolic configuration, and, in turn, in terms of how citizens perceive these changes. (p. 149)

For example, during previous centuries in America, when in society, women, and girls were considered chattel rather than citizens, they would have had fewer civil rights related to education as well. Similarly, prior to reconstitution, legislation pertaining to education often excluded African Americans. Other examples include the deprivation of rights for Native Americans, and for Chinese and Japanese immigrants. Many countries have similar histories of depriving certain groups, perhaps especially their indigenous populations, of equal citizenship rights. For these reasons, to advance this principle of equitable citizenship rights, it is useful to expand and inform Marshall's three rights with additional critical theoretical perspectives including (but not limited to) those advanced by critical feminism (Capper, 1998; Hill-Collins, 2008; Miller, 2000), critical race theory (Aleman & Aleman, 2010; Bell, 1975; Ladson-Billings & Tate, 1995; Parker & Villalpando, 2007), queer theory (Capper, 1998; Katz, 1997; Seidman, 1995) and so forth. This expansion makes explicit the inclusion of various and often marginalized groups and, hence, permits a more inclusive conceptualization of citizenship rights.

In educational institutions as in the wider society, civil rights may be deemed to be equal protection of personal liberties as given to citizens under the law. Unlike in previous eras, equal legal protection now extends to male and female students, as well as to members of all ethnic groups; however, there are still sometimes denied students with nonheteronormative sexual orientations, for example, and well-known cases in which students have not been permitted to attend school events with a partner of their choice.

Similarly, in many communities, parental membership on either school advisory councils or elected school boards fails to proportionately represent the demographics of many diverse communities, thus indicating a failure to distribute political rights equitably in many instances. Another important issue in the consideration of political citizenship rights is the question of school choice. Some would argue that opportunities such as charter schools, magnet schools, and vouchers promote equitable participation through choice, as these options offer autonomy and alternatives to all families. To others, it becomes patently obvious that the choice is only symbolic. As observed by many scholars (Apple, 2006; Giroux, 2005), when choice is offered in a marketplace in which people are unequally positioned, despite the rhetoric, some cannot avail themselves of the proffered goods.

Equally disturbing in today's schools are the incidents when social rights are limited and some students exposed to name-calling and slurs related to their social location, cultural background, or ability/disability. The frequency with which school administrators report requests from parents not to have their children in classes with "that Black teacher," or with "those Latino kids" is not only disturbing, but a powerful indication of the persistence of inequity related to the social right to feel welcome and secure within the educational institution. Similarly, disproportionate representation of some groups in disciplinary incidents, school suspensions, or identification of certain groups of students for special education services are further indication of a lack of equitable distribution of citizenship rights.

In other countries of course, context determines which citizenship rights are inequitably distributed and need to be addressed. For example, Dahar (2010) stated that "according to the Government of Pakistan (2009), out of 9587 secondary schools, 1340 have no toilets or latrine facility" (p. 28); moreover the preponderance of schools with no facilities are girls' schools—an issue, undoubtedly, of safety and respect as well as equity. Further, in many countries, where curriculum is reduced to rote learning in large groups with undereducated teachers and in unacceptable facilities, these issues must be addressed. Failure to provide appropriate education for all is clearly an indication of inequitable citizenship rights.

As can be seen, Fraser's (1995) framework for social justice assigns injustices to the two distinct but interrelated positions of maldistribution and misrecognition, and calls for remedies that integrate the politics of redistribution and the politics of recognition. Some have critiqued her paradigm, claiming that it is dualistic and that one or other dimension is inappropriately predominant. Honneth, for example, noted that recognition is a fundamental_and overarching "moral and social category" (Huttunen, 2007, pp. 423 & 428); and therefore he calls for redistribution to be considered a fundamental and irreducible dimension of justice (Huttunen, 2007). The principle of equitable citizenship, as well as the previously discussed principles for inclusive and equitable educational opportunities, seem to reflect his primary concern with the need for a politics of recognition. They provide evidence of the need for a recognitive perspective, in that, as Fraser (2001) posited that "injustice appears in the guise of status insubordination, rooted in institutionalized hierarchies of cultural value. Injustice occurs through misrecognition, which must also be broadly understood to encompass cultural domination, non-recognition, and disrespect"

(p. 5). These injustices must be overcome if we are to realize the goal of distributing citizenship rights and responsibilities in equitable ways.

Noncompetitive and Equitable Resource Distribution

This final principle emphasizes that where resources are inequitably distributed, redistribution must occur on the basis of need and not based on successful competition for scarce resources. Here, the reality of economic disparity attests to the salience of Fraser's (2001) second perspective—the need for economic redistribution. In fact, although Fraser argues that the two dimensions are separate but necessarily interrelated, from a redistributive perspective, "injustice appears in the guise of class-like inequalities, rooted in the economic structure of society. Here the quintessential injustice is maldistribution" (p. 5) and the proposed remedy is redistribution and economic restructuring. This is important because, in many educational situations, as reflected in this principle, although one can never totally separate the implicit cultural values from policy, there are times when the injustice is overtly economic. In fact, the neoliberal emphasis on market-driven reforms that permeates education in both explicit and implicit ways often promotes a competitive reform agenda that is both undemocratic and unjust. Although allocating additional resources is always a welcome political gesture, making these awards competitive instead of providing funds to address the most pressing needs, once again rewards those who have the fiscal and human resources to spend on preparing grant proposals, and who have the most expertise to frame their arguments persuasively for the peer reviewers.

For example, in America, funds from the recent 2010 competitive grants, known as Race To The Top (RTTT), from a $4.35 billion fund, were awarded to 11 states and the District of Columbia — jurisdictions that most successfully advanced reforms in four specific areas, including "turning around our lowest-achieving schools" ("Nine States," 2010). In announcing the second group of successful bidders, Secretary of Education Duncan stated that

> The 10 winning applicants have adopted rigorous common, college- and career-ready standards in reading and math, created pipelines and incentives to put the most effective teachers in high-need schools, and all have alternative pathways to teacher and principal certification. (para. 13)

And yet, if one examines a data base from the 2007 U.S. Census, one finds that the states with the lowest high school graduation rate are: Louisiana, Mississippi, and Texas—all of whose rates are below 80% (U.S. Census Bureau, 2010), and none of which was successful in capturing a share of the RTTT funds.

In other countries, as we have seen, redistribution will be fundamental to providing equitable access and educational outcomes. Thus, in some countries with large numbers of unschooled children, consideration must be given to redistribution of resources to increase access. For instance, in Pakistan, a country in which 5 million children never attend school, in which there are 50% more soldiers than teachers and in which 7.8% of the budget is expended on education compared to 29.9% on the military (Tomasevski, 2006), redistribution could be an important first step. The Sudan, as well, which commits almost 47% of its budget to military expenditures compared with less than 2% on education might well begin with redistribution. In fact, Sudan might well follow the example of Nigeria (Tomasevski, 2006) where, in 1999, with the change from military to civilian government that ended 33 years of military rule, the government re-instituted free primary education.

Young (1997) is correct in her claim that "redistributive remedies for economic injustice, ... do not change the conditions that produce this injustice, and in some ways, tend to reinforce these conditions" (p. 153). Nevertheless, in many cases, redistribution of available funds based on need would be a step forward.

Integrating Principles—A Contextual Challenge

In the foregoing pages, I have identified seven principles that can form the basis for democratic and social justice education. No doubt there are additional elements, concepts, or situations that do not neatly fall into these categories; nevertheless, taken together, these principles form the basis for both reflection and action. In the spirit of Fraser's call for "no recognition without redistribution" (Fraser & Naples, 2004, p. 1122), the call here is for no education without principles of democracy and social justice. And yet, as discussed at the outset, this call becomes challenging and conflictual in practice. A brief reflection on how they might play out in very different contexts will make this point well.

Even the first principle of respect and absolute regard, one that seems straight-forward, is dependent on ideological interpretations of who is included in a given organization and hence, who is deemed a worthy recipient of respect. If education is not compulsory, as is the case in at least 25 countries (Tomasevski, 2006), or if countries have established a minimal definition of the right to education, considering it more a form of poverty reduction and hence a "hand-out" than a right, respect for students will generally be restricted to those who have the where-with-all to attend schools.

Evidence that this is not simply an issue for developing countries was startlingly presented in a July 2010 posting by a blogger, calling himself "froivinber," that appeared in the Vincenton Post; he wrote in opposition to free education in the United States, saying, "I am primarily against this notion—that the state, according to our semi-socialist Constitution, has the eternal duty to 'protect and promote the right of all citizens to quality education at all levels' and 'to make such education accessible to all'—simply because it is against economic and political realities and because it will only lead to our own collective destruction" (Froivinber, 2010, para. 7). Clearly here there is no understanding of education as a mutually beneficial public good, no sense that when one increases the level of education, society as a whole benefits, not only in economic terms, but increased health, lower crime and so forth.

One key, perhaps, to extending the regard deserving all people with respect to education as well as other social goods, is to recall the principle of mutual benefit. Kaplan (2001) argued that for a democracy to develop, a country requires an educated middle-class as well as civil institutions. Barber (2001) extended this notion and claimed that

> the literacy required to live in civil society, the competence to participate in democratic communities, the ability to think critically and act deliberately in a pluralistic world, the empathy that permits us to hear and thus accommodate others, all involve skills that must be acquired. (p. 12)

These scholars and others promote the notion that the skills required to live in mutual benefit, in civil society, are the skills that education can and must promote. Indeed, many, including myself, would argue this is the fundamental task of education in a democracy.

Nevertheless, what this looks like, how it plays out, will differ from community to community and country to country. As stated at the outset, context matters profoundly when one begins to implement general principles. In developed countries in which schooling is neither compulsory nor universal, the civil right to education may take precedence over a more nuanced dialogue about cultural inclusion and opening avenues for participation and decision making. This is not to say issues of race, ethnicity, or gender will not be salient in each context—in fact, quite the contrary. Finding ways to educate girls in countries like Iran or Afghanistan, to encourage more males to avail themselves of educational opportunities in the United Arab Emirates or Saudi Arabia, and to provide equity to the ethnic expat workers from Pakistan, Bangladesh, and the Philippines in these same Muslim countries may have the same starting point and underlying concerns about respect, but again, will manifest in different policies and strategies.

Further, a discussion of the importance of redistributing material and fiscal goods in the above-mentioned situation in which schools in Pakistan have no latrines seems quantitatively and qualitatively different from a discussion of reforming the base of support for schools in the American state of Illinois, emphasizing the need to move to a more equitable formula than one based on local taxation. A discussion of equitable education in a sub-Saharan African country may take a very different form from a discussion on equity in the United States which is likely to focus on schools not achieving adequate yearly progress under No Child Left Behind (2002), or on the continued gap in achievement between White and African American or Latino students. In one country, equitable outcomes might well focus on a discussion of enhancing the country's literacy rate, while in another, it might focus on increasing student preparation for success in career and college.

Concluding Thoughts

The responsibility for ensuring a democratic social justice education must be shared by governments, policymakers, educators, and families themselves. Moreover, the close ties among education policy and economic policies and exigencies must be recognized and addressed. Universal access; inclusive policies related to outcomes, school cultures, decision making; and equitable citizenship rights cannot co-exist with child-labor, relatively costly school fees, high transportation costs, inadequate facilities or poorly trained teachers. Neither can they coexist with beliefs and values of elitism, racism, sexism, classism, and the like.

To be "involved in mankind" as Donne (1624) phrased it almost 4 centuries ago, requires us to acknowledge that where educational policies or practices do not further democratic and social justice teaching, increased global awareness, and a disposition to act for the betterment of all, we are still diminished. Where they are not built on the dignity and worth of every human being, we are diminished. Where schooling fails to work towards the additional principles of mutual benefit; equitable inclusion, access, outcomes, and rights; we are diminished. When we fail to recognize the hegemony of culture, beliefs, and values that continue to marginalize and exclude some students and to privilege others, we are diminished. And when our beliefs permit us to justify the status quo, failing to achieve a more equitable redistribution of material goods and resources, we are all diminished. It is my hope that this attempt to identify some principles on which to begin a more complete theorizing of democratic and social justice education will move us forward, prompting us and the schools and educators with which we work, to be more fully involved in all of mankind.

REFERENCES

Aleman, E., Jr., & Aleman, S. M. (2010). Do Latin/a interests always have to "converge" with White interests?: (Re)claiming racial realism and interest-convergence in critical race theory praxis. *Race, Ethnicity & Education, 13*(1), 1-21.

Apple, M. (2006, January). Keynote address, presented at the annual conference of the International Congress of School Effectiveness and School Improvement, Fort Lauderdale.

Barber, B. R., (2001). An aristocracy of everyone. In S. J. Goodlad (Ed.), *The last best hope: A democracy reader* (pp. 11-22) San Francisco, CA: Jossey-Bass.

Bell, D. (1975). Serving two masters: Integration ideals and client interests in school desegregation litigation. *Yale Law Journal, 85*, 470–516.

Bishop, R., Berryman, M., Tiakiwai, S., & Richardson, C. (2003). *Te Kotahitanga: The experiences of Year 9 and 10 Maori students in mainstream classrooms.* Wellington, New Zealand: Ministry of Education. Retrieved from www.minedu.govt.nz/goto/tekotahitanga

Bourdieu, P., (1977). *Reproduction in education, society and culture.* London: SAGE.

Capper, C. A. (1998). Critically oriented and postmodern perspectives. *Educational Administration Quarterly, 34*(3), 354-370.

Cummins, J. (1989). Empowering minority students: A framework for intervention. In N. M. Hidalgo, C. L. McDowell, & E. V. Siddle (Eds.), *Facing racism in education.* Cambridge, MA: Harvard Educational Review.

Dahar, M. A. (2010). *Relationship between the school resource inputs and academic achievement of students at secondary level in Pakistan* (Unpublished dissertation). International Islamic University, Islamabad.

Dahl, R. A. (1989). *Democracy and its critics.* New Haven, CT: Yale University Press.

Dahl, R. A. (2000). *On democracy.* New Haven, CT: Yale University Press.

Darling-Hammond, L. (2010). *The flat world and education.* New Haven, CT: Teachers College Press.

Delpit, L. D. (1990). The silenced dialogue: Power and pedagogy in educating other people's children. In N. M. Hidalgo, C. L. McDowell, & E. V. Siddle (Eds.), *Facing racism in education* (pp. 84-102). Cambridge, MA: Harvard Educational Review.

Donne, J. (1624). *Meditation XVII.* Retrieved from http://www.online-literature.com/donne/409/

Farrell, J. P., (1999). Changing conceptions of equality of education. In R. F. Arnove & C. A. Torres (Eds.), *Comparative education: The dialectic of the global and the local* (pp. 149-177), Lanham, MD: Rowman & Littlefield.

Fraser, N. (1995). From redistribution to recognition? Dilemmas of justice in a "post-socialist" age. *New Left Review, 212*, 68-93

Fraser, N. (2001). Recognition without ethics? *Theory, Culture & Society, 18*(2/3), 21.

Fraser, N., & Naples, N. (2004). To interpret the world and to change it: An interview with Nancy Fraser. *Sign: Journal of Women in Culture and Society, 29*(5), 1103-1123.

Froivinber. (2010). The "Right to Education" is an invalid concept. *The Vincenton Post.* Retrieved from http://fvdb.wordpress.com/2010/07/26/the-right-to-education-is-an-invalid-concept/

Giroux, H. A. (2005). The terror of neoliberalism: Rethinking the significance of cultural politics. *College Literature, 32*(1), 10-19.

Green, J. M. (1999). *Deep democracy: Diversity, community, and transformation.* Lanham, MD: Rowman & Littlefield.

Green, P. (2001). Egalitarian solidarity, In S. J. Goodlad (Ed.), *The last best hope: A democracy reader* (pp. 194-203). San Francisco, CA: Jossey-Bass.

Grumet, M. R., (1995). The curriculum: What are the basics and are we teaching them? In J. L. Kincheloe & S. R. Steinberg (Eds.), *Thirteen questions* (2nd ed., pp. 15-21). New York, NY: Peter Lang.

Hill-Collins, P. (2008). *Black feminist thought: Knowledge, consciousness, and the politics of empowerment.* New York, NY: Routledge.

Huttunen, R. (2007). Critical adult education and the political-philosophical debate between Nancy Fraser and Axel Honneth. *Educational Theory, 57*(4), 423-433.

Kaplan, R. D. (2001). Was democracy just a moment? In S. J. Goodlad (Ed.), *The last best hope: A democracy reader* (pp. 49-74). San Francisco, CA: Jossey-Bass.

Katz, J. N. (1997). "Homosexual" and "heterosexual": Questioning the terms. In M. Duberman (Ed.), *A queer world: The Centre for Lesbian and Gay Studies reader* (pp. 177–180). New York, NY: New York University Press.

Kincheloe, J. L., & Steinberg, S. R. (1995). The more questions we ask, the more questions we ask. In *Thirteen questions* (2nd ed., pp. 1-12.). New York, NY: Peter Lang.

Ladson-Billings, G. (1994). What we can learn from multicultural education research. *Educational Leadership, 51*(8), 22.

Ladson-Billings, G., & Tate, W. F., IV. (1995). Toward a critical race theory of education. *Teachers College Record, 97*(1), 47.

Marshall, T. H. (1950). *Citizenship and social class and other essays.* Cambridge, MA: Cambridge University Press.

Miller, L. J. (2000). The poverty of truth-seeking: Postmodernism, discourse analysis and critical feminism. *Theory & Psychology, 10*(3), 313.

Mohanty, S. P. (2000). The epistemic status of cultural identity, In P. M. L. Moya & M. R. Hames-Garcia (Eds.), *Reclaiming identity.* Los Angeles, CA: University of California Press.

Nine States and the District of Columbia win second round race to the top grants. (2010, August 24). Race to the Top Fund. *ed.gov.* Retrieved from http://www.ed.gov/news/press-releases/nine-states-and-district-columbia-win-second-round-race-top-grants

No Child Left Behind. (2002). *ed.gov.* Retrieved from http://www.ed.gov/nclb/accountability/index.html?src=ov

Nussbaum, M. C. (2006). *Frontiers of justice* [Kindle version]. Retrieved from http://www.amazon.com/Frontiers-Justice-Disability-Nationality-ebook/dp/B002OEBO8M/ref=sr_1_4_title_1_ke?s=books&ie=UTF8&qid=1290615210&sr=1-4

Organization for Economic Cooperation and Development (2001). *Knowledge and skills for life: First results from the OECD programme for international student assessment (PISA), 2000.* Retrieved from http://www.oecd.org/dataoecd/44/53/33691596.pdf

Oaks, J., & Rogers, J. (2006). *Learning power: Organizing for education and justice,* New York, NY: Teachers College Press.

Parker, L., & Villalpando, O. (2007). A racial(ized) perspective on educational leadership: Critical race theory in educational administration. *Educational Administration Quarterly, 43*(5), 519-524.

Putnam, R. D. (2001). What makes democracy work? In S. J. Goodlad (Ed.), *The last best hope: A democracy reader* (pp. 25-32.) San Francisco, CA: Jossey-Bass.

Read, P. (2000), *Belonging: Australians, place and Aboriginal ownership.* Oakleigh, Victoria, Australia: Cambridge University Press.

Ryan, J. (2006). *Inclusive leadership.* San Francisco, CA: Jossey-Bass.

Seidman, S. (1995). Deconstructing queer theory or the under-theorization of the social and the ethical. In L. Nicholson & S. Seidman (Eds.), *Social postmodernism: Beyond identity politics,* (pp. 116–141.). Cambridge: MA: Cambridge University Press.

Sen, A. (1992). *Inequality reexamined* [Kindle edition]. Retrieved from http://www.amazon.com/gp/product/B002Y28QAS/sr=1-1/qid=1290615575/ref=sr_1_1_oe_1?ie=UTF8&s=books&qid=1290615575&sr=1-1

Shields, C. M. (2009). *Courageous leadership for transforming schools: Democratizing practice.* Norwood, MA: Christopher-Gordon.

Shields, C. M., Bishop, R., & Mazawi, A. E. (2005). *Pathologizing practices: Deficit thinking in education.* New York, NY: Peter Lang.

Starratt, R. J. (1991). Building an ethical school: A theory for practice in educational leadership. *Educational Administration Quarterly, 27*(2), 155-202.

Swartz, D. (1997). *Culture and power: The sociology of Pierre Bourdieu,* Chicago, IL: Chicago University Press.

Tomasevski, K. (2006). *The state of the right to education worldwide: Free or fee: 2006 global report.* Copenhagen, Denmark: Retrieved from www.katarinatomasevski.com

Torres, C. A. (1998). *Democracy, education, multiculturalism.* Lanham, MD: Rowman & Littlefield.

U.S. Census Bureau. (2010). 2010 statistical abstract: Educational Attainment by State. Retrieved from http://www.census.gov/compendia/statab/2010/tables/10s0228.pdf

Valencia, R. R. (Ed.). (1997). *The evolution of deficit thinking.* London: Falmer.

West, T. R. (2002). *Signs of struggle: The rhetorical politics of cultural difference.* New York, NY: State University of Buffalo Press.

Young, I. M. (1997). *Justice and the politics of difference,* Princeton, NJ: Princeton University Press.

Author Contact Information: **Carolyn M. Shields**, PhD, College of Education, 441 Education Bldg., Detroit, MI. E-mail: cshields@wayne.edu

CHAPTER 94

Michel Foucault

A Theorist of and for Social Justice in Education

Kari Dehli
University of Toronto

It is with a sense of irony and some trepidation that I embark on a chapter on the theoretical work of Michel Foucault for this collection. The task is ironic in that Foucault never claimed to generate theories of education (or anything else). Indeed, shortly before his death in 1984 Foucault offered a summary of his work, asserting that his ideas represented "neither a theory nor a methodology" (Foucault, 2003a, p. 126). He was deeply suspicious of theoretical pretensions, and one of his key contributions to knowledge was precisely to question what he called "the will to truth" in the human sciences and the theories and practices generated through them. Much of his work, which he labeled histories of "systems of thought," sought to disturb the taken for granted assumptions, rules, norms and practices that underpin and make possible modern forms of knowledge and power that take the human subject as their object and target. Writing a chapter about Foucault, therefore, attempting to fit his work into the format of a theory of education—an institutional domain and set of practices whose self-understanding is premised on the very knowledge his work sought to critique—is at best a contradictory exercise.

At the same time, any attempt to summarize Foucault's "theory" is an intimidating task because there are several *foucaults,* each pursuing distinct questions, reversing and contradicting arguments (Peters, 2004). It is not surprising, therefore, that education scholars have mobilized, interpreted or critiqued different parts of Foucault's work to analyze different questions in education research: some dealing with disciplinary practices and normalization, some focusing on archaeologies of schooling, others detailing how pedagogy operates as a form of power that shapes particular kinds of subjects or how techniques of self-government are integral to neoliberal regimes of education, to mention some. In this chapter, therefore, my aim is more modest, namely to discuss those aspects of Foucault's work that I find most generative for thinking through questions in critical education research, and particularly questions dealing with social justice in relation to racism in education.

To the extent that critical theories of social justice mobilize and rely on humanist discourses of progress, agency and emancipation, Foucault presents us with a further conundrum. His works perform a destabilizing critique of modern power-knowledge regimes and the humanist discourses of freedom and progress through which these regimes are rationalized and made effective. Much of his work sought to show that humanism is integral to, not set apart from, relations of modern power, and to introduce *discontinuity* into accepted narratives of history moving from a constrained and oppressive past to an emancipated present ("What is enlightenment?"). Where other critical theorists might propose that better, less ideological knowledge could enable moves toward a more democratic, equitable and socially just society, Foucault's critiques take at once more modest and more radical positions. They are modest in that he sought to critique relations of knowledge and power as they are actually exercised, without reference to an ideal or normative vision of freedom and justice beyond regimes of power. In this sense, his critiques operate from within to problematize claims to truth, arrangements of order and discipline, and tactics of government. Yet, his critiques are also more radical in that he insisted that knowledge and power are intertwined and mutually constituted in ways that both

The Handbook of Educational Theories, pp. 1047–1056

enable and constrain the very conditions in which human beings know the world and know themselves as subjects. Thus, his studies of psychiatry, medicine, prisons and sexuality sought to displace the subject from the center of explanation, whether as intending, conscious individual actors or authors, or as collective subjects of history, such as classes, elites or institutions. Foucault described the objective of his work as efforts "to create a history of the different modes by which, in our culture, human beings are made subjects" (Foucault, 2003a, p. 126). As I will discuss below, critics of his work have wondered whether such a decentered notion of the subject, accompanied by a rejection of normative foundations, can provide sufficient conceptual resources for scholarship and programs committed to social justice.

Had this been written 10 years ago, a quite comprehensive review might have been possible within the constraints of a book chapter. Writing in 2010, however, I find myself making difficult choices as I select from the large and growing number of publications in education theory and research that have been influenced by Foucault's writings. Rather than claim to present a comprehensive review, then, I will draw from works that have influenced my own thinking and writing, and works that I have found to be stimulating and effective in working with graduate students in education. In the first part of this chapter I discuss some of the key preoccupations, concepts and approaches in Foucault's work, particularly those that are generative for thinking about social justice in education. I then review how Foucault's work has been discussed and taken up by critical scholars in education and other fields publishing in English in North America, the United Kingdom, Australia and New Zealand.[1] I include a brief discussion of efforts to *police* and *correct* interpretations and uses of Foucault's work, and in the final section I turn to some of the critiques of his writings and their implications for scholars and practitioners committed to social justice. I limit my review to work that has mobilized his writing to critically analyze the present or past educational racial "order of things," as well as some who have offered important critiques of Foucault's writings and their implications for educators seeking to enable more socially just education.[2]

A Brief Overview

I find it useful to begin with Foucault's own summary of his works and aims, written in 1982. He wrote that his work "has dealt with three modes of objectification that transform human beings into subjects" (Foucault, 2003a, p. 126). First, he describes how his work examined "the modes of inquiry that try to give themselves the status of sciences." Here, in archaeological investigations of a cluster of human sciences, such as linguistics, political economy and biology, he traced the ways in which these disciplines emerged within, and relied upon, discursive regularities that made it possible to turn the speaking, productive or biological subject into objects of knowledge. *Madness and Civilization: A History of Insanity in the Age or Reason* (1967), *The Birth of the Clinic: An Archaeology of Medical Perception* (1973), *The Order of Things: An Archaeology of the Human Sciences* (1970), and *The Archaeology of Knowledge* (1972) are the main works investigating the formation, operations and effects of knowledge in these terms.[3]

In the second area of his work, Foucault wrote that he was studying "the objectivizing of the subject in what I shall call 'dividing practices'" (Foucault, 2003a, p. 126). He went on to say that his interest in these studies are to ask how the subject "is either divided inside himself or from others," such as the bad and the good, the sick and the healthy, and the mad and the sane. The key study where he pursued this line of inquiry was *Discipline and Punish: The Birth of the Prison* (1977). This book offers a genealogical account and critique of modern forms of punishment. While the move from punishment violently applied to the body toward forms of incarceration have been viewed as progressive and modern, Foucault shows that practices of confinement entailed increasingly detailed practices of surveillance and discipline, a new form of power as well as new forms of knowledge, that took the body and the soul as their target and extended far beyond the prison. As Foucault traces the emergence and distribution of 'dividing practices,' and the modes of surveillance, normalization and discipline in which they were instrumentalized, the school, along with the prison and the army, is viewed as central to the emergence of modern forms of governance and social discipline (Usher & Edwards, 1994).

Finally, Foucault was interested in "the way a human being turns him- or herself into a subject," and particularly how "men have learned to recognize themselves as subjects of 'sexuality'" (Foucault, 2003a, p. 126). These ideas are developed in the first volume of *The History of Sexuality: An Introduction* (1979), a series of studies of sexuality that remained incomplete, as Foucault turned his attention to how questions of ethical self-government were discussed in ancient Greek texts and to analyses of modern and liberal thought and practices of government, what became known as studies of governmentality. In this short book Foucault examines the way sexuality emerged in modern European history as a central object of knowledge, a target of social intervention, and a site of individual identity formation and (repressed) freedom. Here, too, he overturns several taken-for-granted understandings, not only of sexuality and its role in subject formation, but also of the nature and operation of modern power. In particular, he argues in a short chapter on "method" that modern power is not something that is possessed, rather it circulates; it is not only controlling and prohibitive, but also productive and enabling; and modern power is intertwined with freedom and resistance, and it is effective only to the extent that it acts upon free subjects (Foucault, 1979).

Archaeology of Knowledge

One of Foucault's key insights is the observation that when we speak and write, much of what we say is made possible by the language we are employing rather than a product of our distinctive insight or ability (Gutting, 2005). Through archaeological investigations, Foucault turned to the rules and conditions of language to ask how it was that, of all the statements that could be made about something, only *some* came to be regarded as scientific truth? According to the conventional view, change and innovation in scientific thought could be attributed either to brilliant individual thinkers or to the progressive development of better theories. In contrast, Foucault regarded scientific statements as "events," whose emergence and conditions of existence could be examined by tracing the implicit rules and procedures that organize scientific discourses. His archaeological inquiries of the human sciences—of biology, linguistics, political economy, medicine, psychiatry—were not concerned with uncovering a *real* meaning hidden within texts, nor was he focused on authors and their intentions. Rather, he worked "archaeologically" with documents or texts as objects that can bring into view the discursive, social and material conditions of a particular period and domain that allow some statements, rather than others, to come into "the true" (Foucault, 1991a). Thus, while his archeological method is historical, it does not aim to make general assertions about what was said or written about human beings in the past. Instead, the aim is to discover the rules, logics, conditions and constraints that enabled some questions, objects and relations to become knowable and sayable. Furthermore, Foucault's history of systems of thought asserts that such rules, logics, conditions and constraints are themselves historically constituted; in other words, they are not universal or transhistorical truths about the human. Instead, his archaeological works traces the emergence of sciences that placed the human subject at the center of knowledge, as both an object and subject of knowledge. How was it, he asked in *The Order of Things* (1970) that the human—the speaking, biological or labouring subject—emerged at the center of knowledge in modern European society?

Archaeology examines written *statements* in order to discover conditions and regularities beyond the subjective consciousness, intentions and expression of the speaker and writer. Foucault's archaeology can be viewed as an historical "method" that can trace the linguistic "unconscious" or episteme of a particular period and society. According to Gutting, every "mode of thinking involves implicit rules (maybe not even formable by those following them) that materially restrict the range of thought" (Gutting, 2005, p. 33). If these rules can be uncovered, apparently arbitrary constraints might appear sensible in the framework defined by those rules. Language, according to Gutting's reading of Foucault, is "a source of thought in its own right, not merely an instrument for expressing the ideas of those who use it" (p. 32). The task of the archaeologist is not a matter of letting language speak for itself, but to analyze the constraints that, at any given time and in any given domain, shape how people are able to think, know, speak and write.

Michael Peters suggested that Foucault "treated truth as a product of the *regimentation* of statements within discourses that had progressed or were in the process of progressing to the stage of a scientific discipline" (Peters, 2004, p. 54). While Peters goes on to argue that this treatment is indicative of a tendency in Foucault's archaeological work to deny freedom and effective agency to the subject, I would agree with Gutting that analyzing the rules of discourse that allow and constrain what individuals can write and speak, does not entail a total dismissal of subject from history. Rather, it allows us to focus on the conditions and regularities of discourse, rather than remain fixed on the consciousness, intentions and identity of speakers and writers. This shift in attention is from the subject who is speaking or writing, to the practices and conditions in which statements in language come to form true discourses. It is in this sense that archaeology treats language as a material practice and statements as historical events in their own right.

Genealogy of Power and the Subject

In his genealogical studies, Foucault complicates relation between power and truth, arguing that they are always mutually constituted. One consequence of this is that there is no place of *better* truth beyond the reach of power. Truth is always implicated in relations of power, and there is no power that is not, at the same time, embedded in and constituted through forms of knowledge. In his genealogies Foucault did not try to generalize about what people thought, said or did, but sought instead to "construct the general mode of thinking (episteme) that lay behind what was not doubt a very diverse range of beliefs and practices" (Gutting 2005, p. 40). He pursues this form of analysis in *Discipline and Punish*, and extends it in the introductory volume to *The History of Sexuality*, a slim book that also attends to relations between power and the subject. These two texts are probably the most widely read and cited works by Foucault among education students and researchers who have turned to the chapters in *Discipline and Punish* where Foucault details the operation and effects of hierarchical observation, normalizing judgment, and the examination, as well as to his observations about the organization of space and time in that text (Ball, 1990; Ball & Tamboukou, 2003). Rather than treating sexuality as an essential and repressed part of individuality, Foucault treats sexuality as a network of power and knowledge that generates sexual identities and sexual subjects. He details how sexuality operates as a field, instrument and target of power/knowledge relations that functions to normalize individuals and regulate populations (McWhorter, 2004, 2009). Readings of *The History of Sexuality* have encountered contrasting accounts of the subject that emphasize individuals' own engagement in their formation, while at the same time offering an analysis of systematic forms of government, such as biopower, that target the population, dividing bodies free subjects within and among themselves (Ball & Tamboukou, 2003; Baker & Heyning, 2004)

The paradoxical accounts of *docile bodies,* and the biopolitics of populations in these two books provide ample and challenging discussions in graduate classrooms and conference seminars, discussions that are further extended and complicated by reading shorter articles and interviews such as "The Subject and Power," "Questions of Method," "Truth and Power," "What is an Author," and "Nietzsche, Genealogy, History."[4] In these texts, Foucault shows that the modern subject is "made" and remade through relations of power and knowledge. His account is an explicit rejection of all notions of a human essence or transhistorical consciousness. This rejection entails critical scrutiny of some of education theories' central assumptions and concepts—the developing child, cognitive development, stages of learning, ranges of ability; the division between students and teachers. Rather than treating such concepts as foundational, Foucault invites us to view them as historically constituted, contested and variable. Moreover, as discussed earlier, his analytic questions do not attempt to answer whether or not a particular concept or assumption offers an accurate representation of real children and their learning. Instead, by examining knowledge that claims to offer true statements about *the child, the learner, the parent*, and so on, he draws our attention to the conditions in which these knowledges (rather than others) appear, the relations in which they come to operate as truth, and the ways in which they come to have effects in people's lives (Popkewitz, 1998). How is it, Foucault might ask, that educators came to believe that knowing "the child" in these, often normative and normalizing ways, would enable the emergence of "better children"? His analysis potentially undercuts many of the foundational claims of human sciences that have shaped education and schooling, "sciences" that purport to distill the structure and operation of consciousness, cognition, emotions, development, ability, personality and so forth within the individual (Henriques, Hollway, Unwin, Venn, & Walkerdine, 1984).

GOVERNMENTALITY

Education scholars interested in social justice have been particularly interested in Foucault's varied writings on power, and power's relation to knowledge and subject formation. In addition to the books discussed above, his lectures on governmentality have also been mined for their innovative analytical perspective on contemporary forms of power. These lectures sought to specify and historicize the changing conditions, terms, strategies, technologies and effects of modern forms of power, particularly the emergence and distribution of power concerned with ways to "introduce economy, that is to say, the correct way of managing individuals, goods, and wealth within the family" (Foucault, 2003b, p. 234). As objects and targets of rule shifted from territories to populations, three questions inform what Foucault called the "art of government": first, the government of oneself, or the regulation and personal conduct through right habits and dispositions; second, the government of souls and conscience, or the elaboration of pastoral doctrine and confessional relations whereby self-reflection and self-critique might be cultivated; and third, the government of children, or how to bring out capacities for improvement, reason and maturity, the problematic of pedagogy (Foucault, 1991b; Gordon, 1991).

Foucault labeled his work on liberal governmentality an analytic of government, rather than a theory of politics or the state. His investigations were concerned with changes in how governing as a matter of knowledge and practice addresses questions of security, territory and population. With regard to liberal government, he was interested in how this heterogeneous form of government is thought into being (through rationalities or mentalities of rule) and how it is worked out in diverse and specific ways in relation to particular targets and aims (through governing techniques and practices). One of the questions that interested him about liberalism as a mode of government, was the emergence of what he called "the governmentalization of the state" (Foucault, 2003b, p. 244). Here the analytical question is not to identify the nature or logic of "the state," but to trace the articulation of particular "rationalities" and knowledge about how to govern effectively within and beyond the state. The problem for liberal government in this regard is not that there is too much government, but that the state is doing too much of the governing.

According to Lemke (2002), the critical contribution of governmentatlity as an analytic concept is its capacity to bridge the dualisms of state and market, individual and society "by coupling forms of knowledge, strategies of power and technologies of the self" (p. 54). Philosopher of education, Michael Peters (2004), suggests likewise *that* one of Foucault's great insights of liberalism was to identify the link between the governance of the self and government of the state (Peters, 1996). In contrast to theories of the state, governmentality allows for "a more comprehensive account of the current political and social transformations since it makes visible the depth and breadth of processes of domination and exploitation" (Lemke 2002, p. 54).

Biopolitics and Liberal (and Neoliberal) Rule

Foucault wrote that biopolitics is "the endeavor, begun in the eighteenth century, to rationalize problems presented to governmental practice by the phenomena characteristic of a group of living human beings constituted as a population: health, sanitation, birth rate, longevity, race" (cited in Dean 1999, p. 99). Dean argues that it is within biopolitics that we can find divisions of populations into subgroups, allowing for the identifying and managing of those who 'retard' the health, progress and improvement of the population, such as those identified as feeble-minded, retarded, disabled, criminal and dangerous, indolent and imbecile (Dean, 1999). It is in these *dividing practices* that Foucault locates "the modern form of racism as a racism of the state in which the notion of race appears as a defense of the life and welfare of the population against internal and external enemies" (Dean, 1999, p. 100). The concepts of biopolitics or biopower, and their relation to Foucault's notion of dividing practices can be used effectively in education studies of racism and social justice, inviting an analysis that is focused on practices and strategies, rather than on the (bad) intentions of particular groups or the failures of individuals (Scheurich, 1994).

Mitchell Dean has drawn attention to the continuing tension within Western liberal (and neoliberal) governmentality (2002) where distinctions are routinely made between and within subjects, and between and within populations, with regard to the capacity for improvement and self-government: those who are deemed capable of liberal self-government, and those who are not; those who can be expected to benefit from education and guidance, and those who cannot. Running as a double set of *dividing practices*, initially organized around notions of demoralization, later in terms of degeneracy and race, these divisions are at the heart of liberal governance both *at home* and *in the colonies* from the eighteenth century onward. According to Dean they operate in the space between sovereignty and discipline, rights and biopolitics, freedom and obedience, entangled in a complex set of organizations, programs, interventions, regulations and laws. Some sought to intervene directly in the daily life of populations, through housing, nutrition and public health interventions, while others sought to identify and separate individuals or groups whose degeneracy posed a threat to the health, morality or security of others. Social or public hygiene, on the one hand, and eugenics, on the other, stand as opposite end of a continuum of 'positive' and 'negative' forms of biopower; but both were integral to liberal rule (Dean, 2002).

Foucault as a "Theorist" of Education?

While Foucault did not specifically study education or schooling as an institution, there are numerous references to education and pedagogy in some of his major texts, including *Discipline and Punish* and *The History of Sexuality.* Usher and Edwards argued in the mid-1990s that an assessment of Foucault's writings "in terms of their implications for educational theory and practice is problematic," in part because Foucault himself refused categorizations and because he himself suggested that his works did not constitute a theory (1994, p. 82). Ten years later Michael Peters (2004) could write that "Foucault's impact on educational research is still in the process of development and assessment." With that caveat, he went on to suggest that, "it is clear that his influence, nearly 20 years after his death, is extensive" (p. 51). More recently, Baker (2007a, 2007b) has argued that the constitution of education research and education as a domain have produced troubling encounters and take-ups of Foucault's work. This is because educational thought frequently relies upon and generates a "dualistic and moralistic sense," whereby bodies of knowledge and thought are judged according to the identities of their authors. She argues further that Foucault's work in particular has tended to be reduced to "scientized and template" schemas in the how-to mode, attempts to normalize and govern particular approaches or methodologies as correct understanding and uses of Foucault, or moralistic and dualistic judgments about his work's utility, frequently framed in terms of its possibilities versus dangers.

Schools and education policies generate both formal and informal norms, standards, and expectations, and they develop practices of qualification, recognition, and correction in relation to students who adapt to or deviate from them. An early collection that profoundly affected my thinking about education and my practice as a researcher and teacher was written by Julian Henriques and colleagues in 1984. Moving across the conceptual and methodological space of Foucault and Lacanian psychoanalysis, I read the papers in this collection as part of a graduate course. I was especially taken with Valerie Walkerdine's (2006) paper on child-centered pedagogy and child psychology, as well as her and the other contributors' careful account the operation and effects of normative thinking and ordering of schools (Henriques et al., 1984). What was particularly compelling—and disturbing—about this collection was its insistence on attending to the power effects of interventions in schools that are framed as benevolent responses to individual need or as corrections histories of collective exclusion and disadvantage (see also Popkewitz, 1998; Popkewitz, & Brennan, 2008). These authors detail how norms operate to position some individuals and populations as embodying the problems to be addressed, and others as subjects who are capable of action and intervention. While appearing to address inequality and exclusion, normative thinking leaves the structures of schooling and society, as well as the terms and effects of norms themselves, unexamined.

Karen Jones and Kevin Williamson's paper, "The Birth of the Schoolroom," published in 1979 in the journal *Ideology and Consciousness*, was an early attempt to deploy Foucault's archaeological approach to write a different history of education. The article's opening sentence announces their archeological approach by suggesting that they will

> approach English popular education in the nineteenth century from the point of view of its discursive conditions ... from the standpoint of how the pedagogy of popular schools is formulated and in terms of how the field of political discourses, in which popular education is stated as a need, is constituted. (Jones & Williamson 1979, p. 59).

They go on to distinguish their archaeological account from causal and social histories of education as social control, as well as from functionalist claims about schooling meeting transhistorical needs for children's socialization toward adult capacity for freedom and responsibility. In contrast to such histories, Jones and Williamson frame their project a "description of a discontinuous series of discursive unities, where each forms conditions of possibility of certain educational practices, and of certain other nondiscursive practices too" (1979, p. 60). By attending to shifting discursive unities and relations among them, their analysis suggests that early nineteenth century schooling sought to develop principles and practices that aimed to form "a population with useful habits" that would, in turn, "secure a moral foundation for governmental and religious authority" (Jones & Williamson, 1979, p. 60). Their aim is not to investigate the past for its own sake but to uncover the changing and enduring layers of conditions that continue to shape pedagogical practices as matters of forming students as moral subjects. Ian Hunter (1996) adopted a similar archaeological approach in his studies if schooling in Australia.

In a much later, and very different paper that graduate students in our program have found very illuminating and helpful for their questions, James Scheurich (1994) drew on and extended Foucault's archaeological approach to analyze how some social experiences and populations become "policy problems." In particular, he asks how social problems come to be studied and represented, how interventions are formulated and targeted in relation to specific populations, and how policy researchers contribute to these processes. Scheurich developed the term "social regularities arena" (1994, p. 306) to show how education policy discourse reproduces, and operates within, limits that define what or who can be conceived of as a problem, while also providing the means or terms through which the problem can be known and addressed. Thus social regularities are ontological, in that they construct "who the problem group is," and epistemological, in that they regulate "how the group is seen or known as a problem" (Scheurich 1994, p. 306).

In a series of articles, book chapters and books, Tom Popkewitz has made use of archeological and genealogical methods to examine what he terms the *rules of reason* and the techniques of power by which the terms and truths of education politics and policy discourses are organized (Popkewitz, 1998, 2000, 2008). Locating Foucault in the tradition of critical inquiry, Popkewitz and Brennan invited education scholars to consider his "disciplined questioning of the ways in which power works through the discursive practices and performances of schooling" (Popkewitz & Brennan, 1998, p. 4). Two related questions follow from this type of analysis. The first asks how norms, and normative forms of reason and rationality, are expressed in education policy and governance in ways that organize inclusion and exclusion (Popkewitz, 1998). The second asks how such norms and forms of reason are taken up (or not) in the practices of those who act in the field of education politics. In other words, how is it that some individuals and groups come to be recognized and even respected as political agents or subjects, while others are cast as members of populations to be managed?

In my own work I have taken up part of this to trace some of the ways in which the category of "parents" came to the attention of educators in new ways in the 1970s and 1980s (Dehli, 1996), asking how, at the end of the twentieth century, did "the parent" come to be seen as a topic for education researchers and as both a problem and a resource for education policymakers? I argue that parents were deliberately brought into education policy discourse, as a category of education knowledge, as a resource in curriculum and pedagogy, and as subjects who are invited to relate to schools as partners, stakeholders, or consumers (Dehli, 2004).

Policing the Field of Foucaultian Studies: What Counts?

From time to time, education scholars have been caught up in discussions about the *correct* interpretation of or response to Foucault. Bernadette Baker characterizes three such responses—vilification, discipleship and agnosticism—in a long paper published in *Foucault Studies* in 2007. She identifies the vilification response with Francis Schrag, while Jim Marshall's (2007) approach to Foucault receives the label agnostic. Baker's review of Lynn Fendler's intervention as a discussant during a session of the Foucault in Education Special Interest Group of AERA in Montreal in 2005 is particularly illuminating. Fendler, identified by Baker as a *disciple*, was seemingly alarmed by "incorrect" appropriations of Foucault in a paper submitted to her for review by a journal. In her response to this paper she enumerates several reasons and instances in which "Foucault is not useful." I should also point out that she presented these corrective points while responding to the papers of a group of young scholars at the conference, including a doctoral student that I supervised. As an audience member I was among those who experienced her intervention as both as chilling and moralizing. Included in Fendler's list of *not useful* take-ups of Foucault, were those who mobilize his ideas in scholarship dedicated toward social justice, particularly those "dependent on a 'demographics identifiable groups'" (Fendler cited in Baker 2007, p. 109). While taking issue with Fendler's arguments, Baker's paper draws attention to the corrective and polemical form of her argumentation, viewing it as an instance of policing and purifying Foucault, calling for adherence to rules rather than creatively mobilizing his work to perform critiques of social and educational arrangements (Baker, 2007).

Critical Interventions: Foucault and Social Justice

Do we need foundational norms and coherent subjects in order to make convincing arguments about social injustice and to work to bring about social justice in education? Many critics of Foucault believe that we do, that without such norms and coherence the very idea of working for justice is impossible, first because we're left unable to evaluate particular programs or policies in terms that exceed their own specific aims and experiences (an alternative school program may serve social justice ends for teachers and students participating in it, but contribute little or nothing to the broader communities of students). Foucault argued that the "we" in political assertion is an outcome, rather than a presupposition of political discussion. It could be argued that his writings suggest an approach to politics that pursues "pragmatic reform rather than fundamental revolution" (Gutting 2005, p. 29) and that he rejected principled *for or against* propositions in relation to particular political programs. In their place he offered the notion of critique as a mode of living, suggesting persistent vigilance in relation modes of thought that rationalize, authorize and organize political programs, not because *everything is bad*, but because everything is potentially dangerous. At the same time, Foucault cautioned about an intellectual stance presuming to know better than people who experienced oppression how to understand and act in their situation.

With respect to questions of racial injustice in schooling, Foucault's investigations of normalization, dividing practices, biopolitics and governmentality do have much to offer. Yet, it would be an overstatement to suggest that he provides a comprehensive theory of racism or that he presents us with concrete strategies for addressing racism in education. For example, while the notions of biopower and governmentality are productive in analyzing racial knowledge and the racialization of subjects and populations, there are limitations as well. Some of these limitations can be traced to the way Foucault developed the notion of governmentality to historicize the complex and changing interactions of different forms of government in Europe. While his lectures on governmentality dealt in detail with changes in what he called the art of government from the sixteenth century onward, and while he elaborated an argument about internal war and security as central to modern social formations in the West, he did not link those observations to the genealogies of state racism, and the interrelation of sexuality and race, that he begun in the first volume of *The History of Sexuality.*

Moreover, as Stoler (1995) pointed out, Foucault's genealogy of forms of sovereignty, discipline and biopower, is focused narrowly on Europe, even though the very forms of power that he discussed there emerged in conditions of colonial expansion and were articulated in, and in many ways contingent upon, the government of colonial populations (Scott, 1999; Stoler, 1995). Indeed, as I have suggested, on Stoler's reading, Foucault's preoccupations with governmentality *replaced* his interest in race and racism. Yet, as Stoler herself, and scholars such as David Scott (1999), Gail Lewis (2000) and Barnor Hesse (2004) have demonstrated in their own studies of colonial governmentality and racism, Foucault's work can provide a rich conceptual resource.

A more general critique of governmentality studies was offered by O'Malley, Weir, and Shearing in a paper published in 1997. One of their concerns at that time was to recover the criticality of Foucault's project for justice-seeking social movements, and to situate governmentality thinking within an explicitly critical perspective. They argued that the lack of attention to social and political theory, and to histories of struggle against oppression and violence in much governmentality work, could lead to an absence of effective critique of power relations, on the one hand, while eschewing positive consideration of "forms of work on the capacities of individuals or groups that we might want to defend" (Ivison 1998, p. 562), on the other.

O'Malley, Weir, and Shearing (1997) called for incorporation of Foucault's notions of discontinuities and difference in governmentality studies in order to break with the monotony of accounts of how expert authorities envision the problems, objects and targets of rule. In place of, or in supplement to, such studies, they argue for a resituating of governmentality studies in Foucault's notion of critique where, beyond description and diagnosis of terms, forms and techniques of rule, scholars seek to generate critical and effective studies of power, rule and resistance as they are engaged "on the ground" in the "messy actualities" by people organizing and working for justice. These suggestions could, in my view, be very fruitfully developed studies and proactive intervention into struggles for social justice in education.

Concluding Thoughts

Foucault's decentered perspectives of power, knowledge and the subject lend themselves to examination of the forms and practices of schooling—the rules, standards, and categories that regulate, control and normalize the experiences and effects of schooling. His works also enable analyses of how educational knowledge and educational practices give meaning to terms such as student, teacher or parent. Schooling not only provides knowledge for children to acquire, it positions them as particular kinds of subjects, divided within and among themselves. While the main subject position of schooling is that of student, children also learn to see themselves through categories such as bright, smart, slow or learning disabled, or as a C or A student. Working with Foucault's forms of analysis, we can investigate the historical formation and effects of the terms we use to identify ourselves, and we can recognize that they are effects of power.

The scholarship of Michel Foucault is notoriously difficult to pin down: his intellectual interests ranged over several areas, he developed and used different strategies in his research, writing, lectures and interviews, and he engaged in political polemics with his contemporaries that may seem paradoxical from the perspective of our present. As I hope to have shown in this paper, it is useful to organize his extensive contributions into three broad areas. First, he was concerned to rethink what he called the "history of systems of thought" and particularly to examine knowledge and discourse in terms of the conditions, rules and procedures of their formation, dissemination and effects. We may call this the "archaeological Foucault." Second, his work offers important approaches to studies of power, expanding the study of power beyond the law, the state and its institutions, while attending to the ways everyday existence is regulated, normalized and disciplined. This second, "genealogical Foucault," argued that power takes many forms, some operate as sovereign, negative and controlling, while others enable, encourage and authorize. In his later works—we may call this the "governmental" or "ethical Foucault"—he discussed specific "techniques" of power through which human beings make themselves as free and ethical subjects and he challenged conventional ways of thinking about the individual, the self and the subject. Throughout his work he sought to "decenter" the idea of the subject as source and foundation of meaning (so prevalent in much modern social and political theory), suggesting instead that while the subject is free and capable of acting ethically, it is also a condition and an effect of power/knowledge. In this sense, the subject comprises ongoing, incomplete and historically situated practices, open to inscription and reinscription. Foucault returned to these areas, and throughout his life he often subjected his thinking on these (and other) questions to reflection and revision.

It would be paradoxical to claim that this review, or any other summary could distil "the true" Foucault. Yet, attempts to do just that have generated a veritable industry of *foucauldian* studies. To propose that there are many Foucaults is not to suggest that there are no consistent themes or questions in his work. While ranging widely in the sense of crossing disciplinary fields and subjects, Foucault's work remained preoccupied with quite specific questions, and his own research involved detailed and systematic, meticulous archival investigations and reflections. Versions of the question, Who are we?, Who are we today?, and Who are we becoming?, run through most of his work. These questions are ones that could inform projects of critiquing the past and present, while imagining more just futures.

Foucault did not propose a singular theory of education or of society. Rather, his analytics provides resources for rethinking schools, and educational practices, as sites of disciplinary practices, regimes of truth and power, and modes of regulation of the social and the self, and as technologies for the production of subjects. Foucault did not offer us a total theory that critical education scholars must adhere to in order to think correctly about social justice. Rather he opens questions, provides conceptual tools, and presents a sensibility or ethic of critique. While these ideas are powerful and effective, they do not give us answers. Foucault leaves us with a set of incisive and imaginative tools that we may adapt to our own critiques and questions. There is much work to be done.

Notes

1. The limitation to publications in the English language is an obvious limitation due to my inability to read French sufficiently well to study Foucault's texts in the language in which he wrote. As well, it means that my reading of education research is confined to publications in the English-speaking global north.

2. Another limitation of my review is that it regrettably excludes Foucault's work on ethics and what he termed "care of the self." While these writings might be very suggestive for thinking about social justice in education, their "take up" among education scholars has been more recent. Furthermore my own learning and appreciation of this work are, at this point, too rudimentary to do it justice here.

3. In this section I insert the original publication dates to provide a sense of chronology. English translations appeared later and have been published in new editions several times.

4. These papers and interviews have been published in several collections. In this paper I reference their publication in *The Essential Foucault: Selections from Essential Works of Foucault, 1954-1984*, compiled and edited by Paul Rabinow and Nikolas Rose (2003c).

References

Baker, B. (2007a). Normalizing Foucault? A rhizomatic approach to plateaus in Anglophone educational research. *Foucault Studies, 4*, 78-119.

Baker, B. (2007b). Hypnotic inductions: On the persistence of the subject. *Foucault Studies, 4*, 127-148.

Baker, B., & Heyning, K. L. (Eds.). (2004). *Dangerous coagulations? The uses of Foucault for the study of education.* New York, NY: Peter Lang.

Ball, S. J. (Ed.). (1990). *Foucault and education.* London, England: Routledge.

Ball, S. J., & Tamboukou, M. (Eds.). (2003). *Dangerous encounters: Geneology and ethnography.* New York, NY: Peter Lang.

Dean, M. (1999). *Governmentality: Power and rule in modern society.* London, England: Sage Publications.

Dean, M. (2002). Liberal government and authoritarianism. *Economy and Society, 31*(1), 37-61.

Dehli, K. (1996) Travelling tales: Education reform and parental 'choice' in postmodern times. *Journal of Education Policy, 11*(1), 75-88.

Dehli, K. (2004) Parental involvement and neo-liberal government: Critical analyses of contemporary education. *Canadian and International Education, 33*(1), 45-75.

Foucault, M. (1967). *Madness and civilization: A history of insanity in the age of reason.* London, England: Tavistock.

Foucault, M. (1970). *The order of things: An archaeology of the human sciences.* London, England: Tavistock.

Foucault, M. (1972). *The archaeology of knowledge.* London, England: Tavistock.

Foucault, M. (1973). *The birth of the clinic: An archaeology of medical perception.* New York, NY: Pantheon Books.

Foucault, M. (1977). *Discipline and punish: The birth of the prison.* New York, NY: Vintage Books.

Foucault, M. (1979). *The history of sexuality (Vol. 1): An introduction.* London, England: Allen Lane.

Foucault, M. (1980). Two Lectures. In C. Gordon (Ed.), *Power/knowledge: Selected interviews and other writings 1972-1977* (pp. 78-108). London, England: Harvester Press.

Foucault, M. (1991a). Politics and the study of discourse. In G. Burchell, P. Miller, & C. Gordon (Eds.), *The Foucault effect: Studies in governmentality* (pp. 53-72). Chicago, IL: The University of Chicago Press.

Foucault, M. (1991b). Governmentality. In G. Burchell, P. Miller, & C. Gordon (Eds.), *The Foucault effect: Studies in governmentality* (pp. 87-104). Chicago, IL: The University of Chicago Press.

Foucault, M. (1994). Truth and power. In P. Rabinow (Ed.), *The Foucault reader* (pp. 51-100). New York, NY: Pantheon Books.

Foucault, M. (2003a). The subject and power. In P. Rabinow & N. Rose (Eds.), *The essential Foucault: Selections from essential works of Foucault, 1954-1984* (pp. 126-144). New York, NY: The New Press.

Foucault, M. (2003b). Governmentality. In P. Rabinow & N. Rose (Eds.), *The essential Foucault: Selections from essential works of Foucault, 1954-1984* (pp. 229-245). New York, NY: The New Press.

Foucault, M. (2003c). Questions of method. In P. Rabinow & N. Rose (Eds.), *The essential Foucault: Selections from essential works of Foucault, 1954-1984* (pp. 246-258). New York, NY: The New Press.

Foucault, M. (2003d). Truth and power. In P. Rabinow & N. Rose (Eds.), *The essential Foucault: Selections from essential works of Foucault, 1954-1984* (pp. 300-318). New York, NY: The New Press.

Foucault, M. (2003e). Nietzsche, genealogy, history. In P. Rabinow & N. Rose (Eds.), *The essential Foucault: Selections from essential works of Foucault, 1954-1984* (pp. 351-369). New York, NY: The New Press.

Foucault, M. (2003f). *Society must be defended: Lectures at the College de France, 1975-1976.* New York, NY: Picador.

Foucault, M. (2003g). What is an author? In P. Rabinow & N. Rose (Eds.), *The essential Foucault: Selections from essential works of Foucault, 1954-1984* (pp. 377-391). New York, NY: The New Press.

Gordon, C. (1991). Introduction. In G. Burchell, C. Gordon, & P. Miller (Eds.), *The Foucault effect: Studies in governmentality* (pp. 1-51). Chicago, IL: The University of Chicago Press.

Gutting, G. (2005). *Foucault: A very short introduction.* Oxford, England: Oxford University Press.

Henriques, J., Hollway, W., Unwin, C., Venn, C., & Walkerdine, V. (1984). *Changing the subject: Psychology, social regulation and subjectivity.* London, England: Methuen.

Hesse, B. (2004) Im/plausible deniability: Racism's conceptual double bind. *Social Identities, 10*(1), 9-29.

Hunter, I. (1996). Assembling the school. In A. Barry, T. Osborne, & N. Rose (Eds.), *Foucault and political reason: Liberalism, neo-liberalism and rationalities of government* (pp. 143-166). Chicago, IL: University of Chicago Press.

Ivison, D. (1998). The technical and the political: Discourses of race, reasons of state. *Social and Legal Studies, 7*(4), 561-566

Jones, K., & Williamson, K. (1979). The birth of the schoolroom. *Ideology & Consciousness, 6,* 59-110.

Lemke, T. (2002). Foucault, governmentality and critique. *Rethinking Marxism, 14*(3), 49-64.

Lewis, G. (2000). *'Race,' gender, social welfare: Encounters in a postcolonial society.* Cambridge, MA: Cambridge University Press.

Marshall, J. (2007). On being agnostic: A response to Bernadette Baker. *Foucault Studies, 4,* 120-127.

McWhorter, L. (2004). Sex, race, and biopower: A Foucauldian genealogy. *Hypatia, 19*(3), 38-62.

McWhorter, L. (2009). *Racism and sexual oppression in Anglo-America.* Bloomington, IN: Indiana University Press.

O'Malley, P. , Weir, L., & Shearing, C. (1997). Governmentality, criticism, politics. *Economy & Society, 26*(4), 501-517.

Peters, M. (1996). *Poststructuralism, politics and education.* Westport, CT: Bergin & Garvey.

Peters, M. (2004). Educational research: 'games of truth' and the ethics of subjectivity. *Journal of Educational Enquiry, 5*(2), 50-63.

Popkewitz, T. (1998). *Struggling for the soul: The politics of schooling and the construction of the teacher.* New York, NY: Teachers College Press.

Popkewitz, T. (Ed.). (2000). *Educational knowledge: Changing relationships between the state, civil society, and the educational community.* Albany, NY: State University of New York Press.

Popkewitz, T. (2008). Education sciences, schooling, and abjection: Recognizing difference and the making of inequality? *South African Journal of Education, 28,* 301-319.

Popkewitz, T., & Brennan, M. (Eds.). (1998). *Foucault's challenge: Discourse, knowledge, and power in education.* New York, NY: Teachers' College Press.

Rabinow, P., & Rose, N. (Eds.). (2003). *The Essential foucault: Selections from essential works of Foucault, 1954-1984.* New York, NY: The New Press.

Rose, N. (1996). Governing "advanced" liberal democracies. In A. Barry, T. Osborne, & N. Rose (Eds.), *Foucault and Political reason: Liberalism, neo-liberalism and rationalities of government* (pp. 37-64). Chicago, IL: University of Chicago Press.

Scheurich, J. (1994). Policy archaeology: A new policy studies methodology. *Journal of Educational Policy, 9*(4), 297-316.

Scott, D. (1999). *Refashioning futures: Criticism after postcoloniality.* Princeton, NY: Princeton University Press.

Stoler, A. L. (1995). *Race and the education of desire: Foucault's history of sexuality and the colonial order of things.* Durham, NC: Duke University Press,

Usher, R., & Edwards, R. (1994). *Postmodernism and Education.* London, England: Routledge.

Walkerdine, V. (2006). Workers in the new economy: Transformation as border crossing. *Ethos, 34*(1), 10-41.

Author Contact Information: Kari Dehli, Professor, Department of Sociology and Equity Studies in Education, Ontario Institute for Studies in Education, University of Toronto, 252 Bloor Street West, Toronto, Ontario M5S 1V6. E-mail: kari.dehli@utoronto.ca

Section 13: Teaching and Education Delivery Theory

INTRODUCTION

SECTION EDITOR
Shirley Jackson
Sam Houston State University

Goethe in *Elective Affinities* (1808) wrote, "A teacher who can arouse a feeling for one single good action, for one single good poem, accomplishes more than he who fills our memory with rows on rows of natural objects classified with name and form." Unfortunately, Goethe did not go on to fully explain what it is a teacher must do to arouse such feelings. Even so, we all remember one or more teachers who aroused such feelings for us—teachers who made a difference. Maybe, even one whose influence was so great it altered the path we chose as an adult. Was it what they taught us, or was it how they taught us? Was it their content, or was it their delivery?

The most effective teachers are always those who use theory to teach students rather than to teach content. They understand the importance of considering the individual needs of each learner rather than just what students must know and be able to do. They are able to individualize their instruction because they understand how humans learn, and they are the ones we are able to relate to because we believe they have our interests at heart.

Teachers who address students' difference take into account their students' strengths and weaknesses as well as their interests. They create a safe environment where students are challenged, want to learn and are able to retain new learning. Teachers who are student-centered know that students learn at different rates and that the same assignment for everyone may be too difficult for some and too easy for others. They also know that students have preferred ways of learning and that while some stress can be helpful, too much stress can be damaging.

Too often teachers confuse the meaning of the words *teach* and *learn*. A teacher's responsibility is not to teach content. A teacher's responsibility is to first teach the students, while making sure that all students learn new content every day (Winebrenner, 2001). No easy task in a time of increased accountability and standardized testing. According to the Comprehensive School Reform Program Guidance (U.S. Department of Education, 2002) and supported by current researchers, students are an eclectic bunch and too many of them continue to be at risk (Ravitch, 2007). What a teacher does in the day-to-day interaction with the students as well as the strategies used to teach them make an enormous difference in individual student achievement (Bulach & Lunenburg, 2008; Gage, 2010). Additionally, research shows that within some schools there can exist a climate that will marginalize African American, Hispanic, and the economically disadvantaged and/or suffers from the belief that only the gifted can benefit from challenging instruction. Fortunately, there are also schools with excellent teachers, the ones who make a difference in the lives of the children they teach, and who require their students to think critically while developing an in-depth understanding of complex problems (Newmann & Wehlage, 2010). From my own experience as a public school teacher, I never met a child who could not wait to start school or many fourth graders who displayed the same enthusiasm.

If students can lose their enthusiasm, so can teachers. The classroom has become just as stressful for the educators as it often is for the students. As a result, not only do we find students dropping out of school, but we find teachers *dropping out* as well. The pressures resulting from the accountability that accompanies standardized testing are often more than young educators are willing to contend with—especially when coupled with a diverse student body, discipline problems, empowered parents, long hours and low pay. Is it any wonder we lose qualified teachers to the corporate world?

It is with the needs of the teacher as well as the student that the chapters in this section look at not just how we learn but how we learn best. We begin with

The Handbook of Educational Theories, pp. 1057–1059

Janice Taylor's study, "Teaching Through the Lens of Resilience Theory and Black Feminist Theory." Taylor puts forth the premise that if we are going to keep qualified teachers in the classroom, it is essential that education preparation programs include resiliency. Resiliency training provides personal strategies to cope with the stress associated with the classroom and can be the difference between staying in the profession and leaving it. While it is important to keep all qualified teachers in education, it may be even more important that we keep qualified teachers of color in the classroom because they provide essential role models for Black and Hispanic children who are most often at risk. Black feminist theory provides an historical perspective to the unique experiences of Black women educators and how that perspective can serve them in today's classroom.

The second chapter, "Teaching for How People Learn Naturally" by Geoffrey and Renate Caine directs our attention to education delivery as it bridges the gap between theoretical knowledge and performance knowledge. To bridge this gap it is important to understand what they call *natural learning* or learning that is brain/mind friendly and engages the entire person. Brain-based learning has powerful implications for teachers because it reframes our understanding of instruction. More specifically it shows that instruction needs to blend three elements: an optimal state of mind which they call relaxed alertness, the immersion of the learner in complex experience, and the ongoing processing of that experience. When these elements are present, deep learning occurs.

In the third chapter of the section, Miki Henderson introduces "The Reggio Emilia Approach to Early Childhood Education." Originating in Italy, the focus is on early childhood and capitalizes on the enormous potential and natural curiosity of young children to understand and make meaning of their world. Closely related to constructivist theory, it is driven by children's rights. The teacher is seen as merely a facilitator to assist in a child's ability to learn naturally.

Also having its roots in Italy is the Montessori model of human development where the focus is on the spontaneous interaction of children with a prepared environment. Drs. Rodriguez, Irby, Lara-Alecio, and Brown, in this next chapter, discuss the Montessori approach and how it too is able to meet individual needs thus allowing students to develop at their own rate. Montessori schools enjoy a world wide reputation and can serve children from birth to 18 years of age. Research has shown that Montessori, rich in meaningful content, is also beneficial in language acquisition.

Carol Ann Tomlinson and Marcia B. Imbeau, strong advocates for differentiating instruction, follow with "Differentiated Instruction: An Integration of Theory and Practice." Tomlinson's focus is on the individual learner understanding that people differ as learners, that those differences matter, and that teachers are most effective when their lessons take into consideration those differences, and they plan accordingly." Tomlinson and Imbeau remind us that learning to differentiate instruction to meet individual needs is a delivery process that places the instruction on the student rather than on the content. While it begins with collective lessons to introduce new content, Tomlinson and Imbeau advocate that teachers use a variety of teaching and learning modes based on students readiness levels, interests, and approaches to learning, using formative assessment to guide their decision making.

The next chapter, while still stressing the need for individualization, shifts our focus to the identified gifted and talented. Joseph Renzulli's "What Makes Giftedness? A Four-Part Theory for the Development of Creative Productive Giftedness in Young People," presents differentiated opportunities and services designed to provide appropriate educational opportunities for the brightest among us. He wrote,

> from preschool through college and even at graduate and professional school levels, there is a range of learning potentials that justifies an examination of differentiated opportunities and services based on theoretical constructs designed to guide appropriate educational experiences for targeted individuals and groups.

The final chapter in this section, "The Four-Dimensional Bilingual Pedagogical Theory," by Drs. Lara-Alecio, Irby, and Tong, presents in detail Lara-Alecio and Parker's model designed to improve the pedagogical teaching of second language learners. The Lara-Alecio and Parker (1994) model attempts to incorporate and operationalize elements of classroom instruction supported by commonly espoused principles of bilingual education to specify and integrate those theoretical notions which show most promise for pedagogical utility, identify classroom elements which teachers have the ability to adjust to enhance student learning; and to develop a pedagogical model which can be can be translated into reliably observable and codable elements, and to provide an observational tool with potential use for formative program evaluation via the presence and absence of valued elements specified by the model.

The Lara-Alecio and Parker model is but one example of educational research that can provide a basis for good teaching and student learning. The chapters in this section continually demonstrate that trying to separate learning theory from instructional theory or curriculum theory from literacy and language acquisition theory is difficult because by their nature they will overlap just as organizational theory and management theory must; for the same reasons it is difficult to separate teaching theory from delivery theory. Yet, the way a teacher delivers content impacts the ability of the students to learn. The decisions a teacher makes when planning a lesson must take into account all those factors that affect learning. Remembering how we learn and providing for differentiation based on individual needs will ensure a more productive classroom. A teacher's delivery is not dependent upon time, money or materials but rather an understanding of how we learn and that every student has the potential to learn beyond that which he already knows.

Successful teachers, learn early on to balance their careers with their personal lives. Always open to new instructional theories, they work with their students, parents and their own peers to provide quality instruction with sound classroom practice. Successful teachers demonstrate resiliency and their positive attitude becomes contagious. They understand the advantages of a brain friendly environment and that students have preferred learning styles that can enhance their strengths and compensate for weaknesses. Successful teachers continue to be life-long learners themselves as they study the theories behind what they do and plan accordingly. When their students succeed, they have the satisfaction of knowing they make a difference.

REFERENCES

Bulach, C., & Lunenburg, F. C. (2008). *Creating a culture for high-performing schools: A comprehensive approach to school reform*. Lanham, MD: Rowman & Littlefield.

Gage, N. L. (2010). *A conception of teaching*. New York, NY: Springer.

Goethe, J. W. V. (1808). Elective affinities. In E. M. Beck (Ed.), *Bartlett's familiar quotations* (p. 395). Boston, MA: Little, Brown and Company.

Lara-Alecio, R., & Parker, R. (1994). A pedagogical model for transitional English bilingual classrooms. *Bilingual Research Journal, 18*(3&4), 119-133.

Newmanan, F., & Wehlage, G. (2010). *Teaching for authentic intellectual work: Standards and scoring criteria for teachers' tasks, student performance, and instruction*. New York, NY: Tasara Books.

Ravitch, D. (2007, July/August). Questions and answers: The truth about America's schools. *The American Online Magazine*. Retrieved from http://www.ael.org/

United States Department of Education. (2002). *Comprehensive school reform (CSR) program guidance*. Retrieved from http://www.ed.gov/offices/OESE.compreform/chiefltr.html

Winebrenner, S. (2001). *Teaching gifted kids in the regular classroom*. Minneapolis, MN: Free Spirit.

Author Contact Information: Shirley Jackson, EdD, Researcher, Center for Research and Doctoral Studies, Sam Houston State University, Huntsville, TX. Mailing address: 337 Elkins Lake, Huntsville, TX 77340. Telephone: 936-291-0952. E-mail: jackson337@msn.com

CHAPTER 95

Teaching Through the Lens of Resilience Theory and Black Feminist Theory

Janice L. Taylor
Sam Houston State University and University of St. Thomas

As teachers are faced with the challenges to be successful in diverse classroom settings and to meet federal and state accountability standards, they must have the ability and the competence to adjust to changing situations. Resiliency is a critical element in helping teachers to meet these challenges and in retaining them in the education profession. To prepare teachers for the challenges they will face in the classroom, Bernshausen and Cunningham (2001) stated that teacher preparation programs must be collaboratively designed to build resilience, and thus equip teachers with the personal strategies they need in order to remain in the profession beyond 5 years. Bernshausen and Cunningham also advocated that efforts to maintain resilience in novice teachers occur by: (a) providing formal mentor support, (b) assigning reasonable teaching assignments, (c) developing targeted and relevant professional development, (d) establishing cohort meetings and activities for novice teachers, and (e) follow up by university faculty in order to provide ongoing support. Sagor (1996) indicated that attributes of resilience that provide people with strength and fortitude to confront overwhelming situations in life are competence, belonging, usefulness, potency, and optimism.

Recent studies have indicated that many teachers do not remain in the education profession. Ingersoll (2007) indicated that as many as half of those trained to be teachers never enter teaching, and that 40-50% of those who do enter teaching leave the occupation altogether in the first 5 years on the job. Included in this group are African American teachers. The shortage of African American teachers can be attributed to high failure rates on teacher competency tests, noncompetitive teacher salaries, the lack of status in the teaching profession, and increases of job opportunities for African Americans in other career areas (Hunter-Boykin, 1992). Banks (1988) stated that more African Americans had chosen professions as lawyers, engineers or scientists. A group of African American teachers in a study by King (1992) indicated that some of their initial attractions to the teaching profession included the subjects they teach, vacation time, their relationships with students, their influence as a role model, and their potential contribution to communities composed of people of color. King further indicated that these same attractions, specifically opportunities to serve as role models for African American youth and to improve conditions of minority communities, could serve as catalysts to retain African Americans in the teaching profession.

THE CONCEPT OF RESILIENCE

Walsh (2006) defined resilience as the capacity to rebound from adversity strengthened and more resourceful, and an active process of endurance and growth in response to challenge. Related to the field of education, resilience may be defined as the ability of teachers to adjust to varied situations and increase one's competence in the face of adverse conditions (Gordon & Coscarelli, 1996; Masten, Best, & Garmezy, 1990). During one's teaching career, there will be situations that involve conflict and stress that can affect physical health and psychological well being that may lead to life-altering changes in self-esteem and sleeping

The Handbook of Educational Theories, pp. 1061–1069

patterns, in addition to job dissatisfaction (Brooks, 1994; Linville, 1987). The prevailing conditions associated with teaching make it necessary for all teachers to be resilient (Bobek, 2002). Bobek stated that a teacher's resilience is enhanced when he is capable of assessing adverse situations, recognizing options for coping, and arriving at appropriate resolutions. Bobek recommended that individuals be provided with the necessary resources to develop resilience: (a) significant adult relationships; (b) a sense of personal responsibility; (c) social and problem solving skills; (d) a sense of competence, expectations and goals, confidence, a sense of humor; (e) and a sense of accomplishment.

RESILIENCE THEORY

Polidore (2004) developed a theory on resilience with African American female teachers, which focused on how individuals continued careers in education despite subjugation to significant adversity. Polidore's theory on resilience was developed using data obtained from three individuals who participated in a qualitative research study. Polidore's theory on resilience was based on an ecological and developmental perspective. Developmental perspective is based on the premise that adults develop resilience over a lifetime through their relationships. Ecological perspective is based on the way adults develop resiliency and adapt to their external processes such as their environment and social customs. The themes that resulted from Polidore's study and ultimately yielded an original model on Resilience theory includes the following: religion, flexible locus of control, an individual's ability to view adverse situations positively, autonomy, commitment, change, positive relationships, and education viewed as important.

RESILIENCE THEMES

Religion. The first theme of resilience is religion. Many of our fundamental beliefs are founded in religion and spirituality (Walsh, 1998). Religion and spirituality can be powerful therapeutic resources for resilience (Walsh). Studies about resiliency in individuals include beliefs about religion, spirituality, or faith. In studies on resilience, all three terms refer to a similar concept, or may be used synonymously, but may be independent of each other, depending on the beliefs of the individual. In individuals who are resilient, faith is not necessarily tied to a religious affiliation, but resilient individuals are no less devout.

Flexible Locus of Control. The second theme of resilience is the concept of flexible locus of control. The concept has its foundation in social learning theory that was developed by Rotter (1966). As stated by Rotter, individuals with a belief in external locus of control perceive that what happens to them is primarily due to reinforcements such as luck, chance, fate, or the power of others. These individuals are less likely to change their behavior. In contrast to individuals with external locus of control, Rotter stated that individuals with internal locus of control are more likely to change their behavior following a positive or negative reinforcement, if the reinforcement is of value and meaning to the person. As Polidore (2004) stated, a person with an internal locus of control may attribute an unpleasant experience in life to the lack of a specific skill, and will then work to acquire the skill, while a person with external locus of control might attribute an unpleasant life experience to fate or the power of others, and therefore sees no need to effect change. Walsh (1998) indicated that flexible use of each locus of control is beneficial for resilient individuals.

Bias for Optimism. The third theme is an individual's ability to view adverse situations positively, also referred to as optimistic bias (Seligman, 1990). Seligman stated that optimism could be learned through experiences of mastery, as individuals come to believe that their efforts can yield success. Teachers who were confident and optimistic were likely to look for their student's strengths rather than their deficiencies (Bondy & McKenzie, 1999).

Autonomy. The fourth theme of resilience is autonomy. The development of well-differentiated identity and autonomy is important for competence and coping with adverse situations (Walsh, 1998). Resilient individuals take responsibility for their own thoughts, feelings, and actions, in addition to respecting the unique qualities and views of others (Walsh).

Commitment. Commitment is the fifth theme of resilience. The theme of commitment is often intertwined with faith or religion and human relationships in the lives of resilient individuals. In Higgins' (1994) study of resilient individuals, the overarching themes of commitment and positive human relationships that resulted included:

> a dedication to creating a depth of contact in all important relationships; the restorative power of their human bonds; the value of relating to others in a manner that includes each person in the relationship while embracing the broader human context that includes us all; their determination to "make the world a home" for themselves and others; and the recognition that creating irreplaceable attachments is fundamentally humanizing to them, capturing the depth of their investment in life itself. (p. 201)

Fairclough (2004) indicated that African American teachers brought a special sense of dedication and commitment to their classrooms.

Change. Change is the sixth theme of resilience. The capacity to change when necessary fosters high functioning in resilient individuals (Walsh, 1998). As Polidore (2004) stated, change was a critical theme in the lives of the three informants in her study as it pertained to the events leading up to and after the desegregation of schools. This theme may be a key attribute when adapting to adverse situations and developing resilience.

Positive Relationships. The seventh theme found in the life of a resilient individual is having a positive relationship. Werner (1993) found that resilient individuals, who despite being raised in adverse situations, became successful because they had at least one unconditional relationship. Bobek (2002) indicated that new teachers may enhance their resilience by fostering productive relationships with people who understand the trials and tribulations of teaching, and can offer insight on options available for dealing with various situations.

Education Viewed as Important. Finally, the eighth theme of resilience, which specifically focused on the experiences of African American teachers, is education is viewed as important. Polidore's study concluded that both ecological and developmental factors contributed to a resilient teacher's ideology that education was not just a concept that one pursued personally or encouraged others to pursue, rather, viewing education as important was a way of life. Polidore's Resilience theory model is shown in Figure 95.1.

THE CONCEPT OF BLACK FEMINIST THEORY

The concept of Black feminist theory is relevant to the unique perspectives and self-defined standpoint of African American women. Collins (1989) defined Black feminist theory "as a process of self-conscious struggle that empowers women and men to actualize human vision of community" (p. 30). According to hooks (1981), the Black feminist movement, which advocates feminist ideology, had its inception in the nineteenth century by African American women who were choosing between supporting the interests of the African American male patriarchs of the Black movement, and

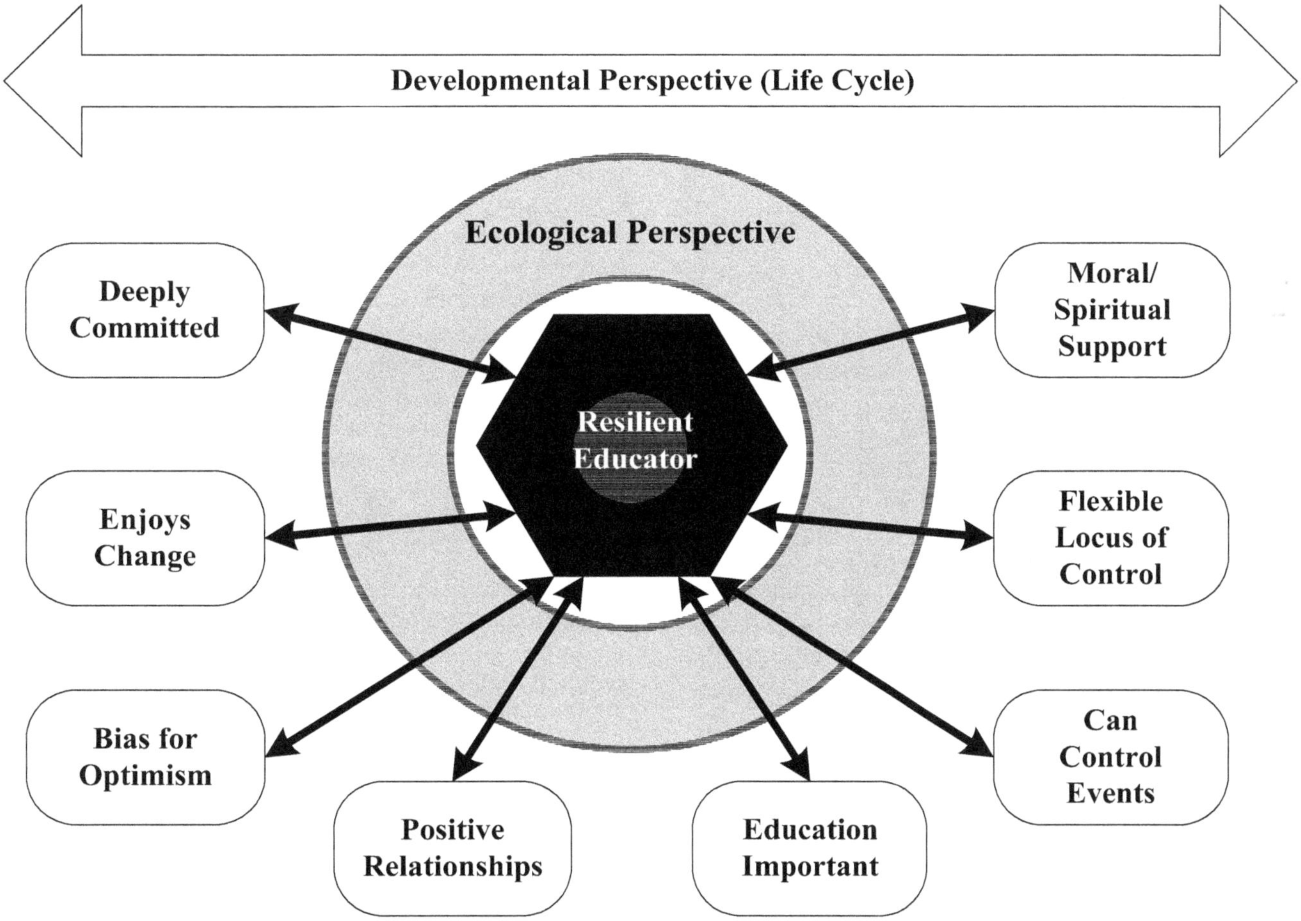

Source: Polidore (2004, p. 28). Reprinted with permission.

Figure 95.1. Graphic conceptualization of resilience in education theoretical framework.

the women's movement, which primarily served the interest of White women. The concept of Black feminist theory resulted from Black feminist activists' and scholars' perceptions of not fitting in or experiencing a disconnect to White, middle class, liberal feminist discourses (Few, 2007). Collins (2003) argued, "at the core of Black feminist thought lie theories created by African American women which clarify a Black woman's standpoint—in essence, an interpretation of Black women's experiences and ideas by those who participate in them" (p. 15). Collins (1998) also stated that the concept of Black feminist thought had not been without challenges; however, deconstruction methodologies, which typically dismantle truths and refute knowledge, have been used by African American female sociologists to benefit Black feminist thought by exposing the narrow views associated with Black feminist traditions, and by allowing the redefinition of African American women and the legitimization of their knowledge. Emanating from a Black feminist standpoint, African American women have affirmed some modicum of authority by using their ability to speak in self-defined voices as knowledge creators (Collins, 1990). "Black women's ability to forge these individual, often unarticulated, yet potentially powerful expressions of everyday consciousness into an articulated, self-defined, collective standpoint is key to Black women's survival" (Collins, 2000, p. 36).

Knowledge Levels of Black Feminist Thought

Black feminist thought represents two levels of knowledge, the knowledge of experts who are part of the group and support the group's standpoint, and the knowledge of African American women that is taken for granted, yet encourages African American women to create a self-definition and validate their own standpoint (Collins, 1989). Collins (2000) stated that Black feminists are able to acknowledge and examine the historical struggles and oppressors faced by African American women and their families as related to race, gender, and class. According to hooks (1984), Black women have a lived experience that may shape the consciousness and worldview of Black women in a way that is different from the prevailing racial, sexist, and classist social groups that are associated with privilege. Essential in the feminist struggle, hooks also stated that Black women should recognize the special vantage point, unique and valuable perspectives that their marginality gives them.

Themes of Black Feminist Thought

Although there is no one Black feminist platform that exists from which one can measure the thoughts of all African American women, there is a long and rich tradition of Black feminist thought that has been produced by ordinary African American women in their roles as mothers and teachers (Collins, 1989). Black feminist thought supports an African American woman's standpoint, assumes that African American women have a unique perspective of their experiences with certain commonalities shared by other African American women, and is predicated upon four themes (Collins, 1989). While commonalities in the themes as described by Collins (1989) exist, there are different expressions of the themes that are based on the diversity that exists among African American women, such as age, religion, and class. The themes, as described by Collins (1989) are: (a) African American women are able to empower themselves and repel negative stereotypes of African American womanhood through self-definition and self-valuation; (b) African American women do not allow themselves to become oppressed by race, class, or gender dominance; (c) African American women are able to merge their intelligence and political ambition; and (d) African American women have the skills necessary to resist daily discrimination. Collins (1989) stated that Black feminist theory, therefore, specializes in formulating and articulating the distinctive, self-defined standpoint of African American women.

Advancing Intellectual Discourse With Black Feminist Thought

The Black feminist concept allows for fostering dialogues among African American women; however, what is most important is that Black feminist concept reconceptualizes the intellectual writings and history of African American women who have struggled with injustices (Collins, 1998). As African American women continue to listen to and be influenced by those African American women who have come before them, they are empowered to prepare an intellectual space for African American women who will confront future injustices that have been veiled, disguised, or reconfigured (Collins, 1998). By maintaining a collective voice after many years of silence, Collins (1998) stated that "Black women teachers and administrators who publish little but who hold positions of power and authority in higher education, school districts, publishing avenues, and the media may have far greater impact on Black women's intellectual production" (p. 76).

Resilience Theory and Black Feminist Theory—Intersecting Phenomena

I conducted a qualitative research study to capture the stories of four African American female teachers as related to their teaching experiences and the characteristics of resilience that influenced their retention in education in a rural community before, during, and after desegregation in the South. Polidore's (2004) Resilience theory, which was undergirded by Black feminist theory (Collins, 1989; Few, 2007; hooks, 1984), served as the theoretical framework of my study. This theoretical framework was chosen because no study had paired Black feminist theory and Resilience theory as the theoretical framework in which to examine the natural correlation between African American female educators and the phenomena of resilience. Combining the tenets of both Poldiore's Resilience theory and the Black feminist theory in a qualitative study allowed me to: (a) give the African American female informants an authoritative voice about their experiences; (b) allow a more thorough and comprehensive examination of their perspectives about their teaching experiences before, during, and after desegregation in the South; and (c) gain an understanding about who or what caused them to remain in education, and how they were influenced to continue their careers despite subjugation to adverse experiences during a historical and life-altering transition period in their lives. From my own self-concept as an African American woman, the Black feminist theory concept provided an additional dynamic in which to examine the perspectives of the informants. Additionally, using Black feminist theory provided intellectual space and allowed me, the primary research instrument, to navigate the challenges of misrepresentation and substitution of my own experiences (Few, 2007), in lieu of the informants, that may occur in this type of qualitative study.

Purpose and Significance of the Study

The purpose of my historical, biographical research study was to examine the perspectives of African American female teachers related to their (a) teaching experiences and (b) the characteristics of resilience that influenced their retention in education in a rural community before, during, and after desegregation in the South. My study undergirded the educational importance of teachers' stories and how teachers' stories provide "theoretical ideas about the nature of human life as lived to bear on educational experience as lived" (Connelly & Clandinin, 1990, p. 3).

The significance of my study was two-fold. First, I wanted to give others an opportunity to look through the *lenses* of the four informants in order to become more aware through first-hand accounts of the changes that took place in education in a rural community before, during, and after desegregation in the South, and to see how these women were impacted. These stories may be of tremendous personal, professional and sociological benefit to current teachers, in addition to the historical benefit for future generations. "By giving voice to those not heard before" (Ambert, Adler, Adler, & Detzner, 1995, p. 166), my study was a tribute to the stories of the four teachers. Second, the challenges that some African American female teachers faced during desegregation in rural communities in the South parallel the challenges that some current African American teachers face as they migrate from urban school districts to suburban school districts. The stories of the women in my study could assist them during their transition.

Research Questions

Research questions were developed based on the purpose, problem and significance of this study. The questions were developed to ascertain characteristics of resilience that may have led to career longevity in education for the African American female teachers. The two questions were:

1. What were the teaching experiences of African American female teachers in a rural community before, during, and after desegregation in the South?
2. What characteristics of resilience emerged as themes that influenced the retention and longevity of African American female teachers in education in a rural community before, during, and after desegregation in the South?

Method

In order to understand the perspectives of the African American female teachers related to their teaching experiences and the characteristics of resilience that influenced their retention in education in a rural community before, during, and after desegregation in the South, I used the historical biography method (Denzin & Lincoln, 2000) with a narrative inquiry technique. Using narrative inquiry technique, a viable and practical research method, that involves a naturalistic and interpretive approach for this type of study, contributed to the advancement of qualitative methodology by using the experiences and stories of a purposive sample to advance the discourse on the issue of teacher retention and teacher resilience. The use of narrative inquiry technique also contributes to qualitative methodology by validating the use of reflexivity as integral in the role of the constructivist researcher. This qualitative technique could be further applied to the epistemological perspectives currently being used by educational researchers to gather and analyze qualitative data for the purpose of addressing other contemporary issues in education, the progression of social justice, and research currently being pursued that pertain to other disciplines. A secondary research instru-

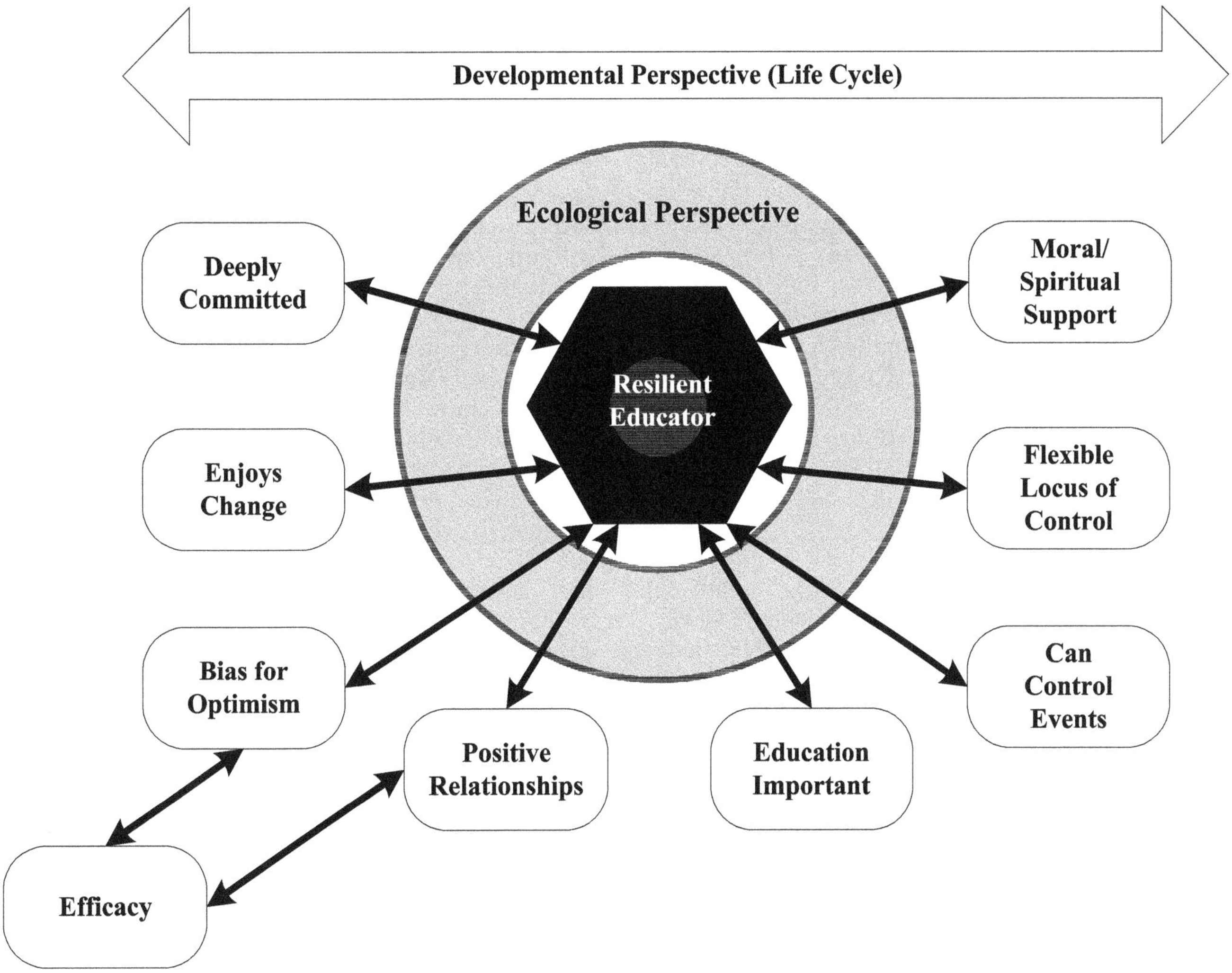

Source: Polidore (2004, p. 28). Adapted with permission.

Figure 95.2. Graphic conceptualization of resilience in education theoretical framework modified.

girded by the resilience themes positive relationships and optimistic bias. Figure 95.2 is a graphic conceptualization of resilience in education theoretical framework (Polidore 2004) with efficacy as an overarching theme of positive relationships and optimistic bias.

Efficacy helped to shape the worldview and consciousness of the African American female teachers in my study, validated their roles in society, and helped them to determine where they fit in their teaching careers during a crucial period in history, the desegregation of schools. The African American female teachers believed that they were competent in their chosen career, which allowed them to empower their students through teaching. Efficacy allowed the teachers to empower their students to take responsibility for their learning and for parents to assist responsibly in the education of their children. When explaining her commitment to her teaching career, Ms. Sutton stated,

> Being in touch with parents, making sure the children understood their assignments.... If the child needed assistance with their homework, if they were out of order in any way—homework, discipline—you had no problems because all you had to do was call the parents. When you called the parents, they were right there. I never had any parents that weren't cooperative with what we were doing or what we had to do.

As the research on Black feminist theory indicated, the African American women in my study respectively took their place as uplifters (Collins, 2000) within their schools and communities, a strong belief held by some African American female educators. Within the community, each of the teachers—Ms. Sammie Sutton, Ms. Willie R. Scott, Ms. Johnetta Cooper, and Ms. Jean Birmingham—was committed to helping people. Ms. Sutton stated, "I care about people. I share, care, and reach out." In the workplace, Ms. Birmingham's efforts to uplift teachers of other cultures and races were demonstrated through her jovial personality and positive attitude when she went into the teachers' lounge at the school where she was transferred during the pivotal 1970-71 school year. Ms. Birmingham stated, "When I was in there, I would smile and say, how ya'll doing today? Can I help ya'll do something?"

The four retired African American female teachers strongly believed that their lives and teaching careers would be successful. The belief that they held about themselves was absolute. As they navigated two worlds, first as women and second as African Americans, their efficacy helped them to carve out respected positions as successful educators within their community, despite subjugation to adversity.

Discussion

The teaching experiences and the lives of the four informants in my study were abundant with the themes of resilience as identified in Polidore's (2004) Resilience theory model. Their stories clearly depicted that their teaching experiences did not focus on what was lost during the desegregation of schools, rather, the informants focused on what could be gained from the desegregation experience by everyone affected. The informants never lost their focus on doing the best job possible for the benefit of children. Their current perspectives about the desegregation of schools still convey more benefit than not for all children of all races and cultures. Although some of the resilience themes were more dominant than others in my study, resilience themes such as autonomy, change, optimistic bias, flexible locus of control and positive relationships, it was apparent that each theme of resilience was influential and played a role in helping the African American female teachers to remain in education for many years.

The adversities that the African American female teachers experienced may never be entirely comprehended; however, they prevailed in their profession during extremely negative conditions, as indicated by their tenure in the profession. Their voices, full of integrity, richness, depth, breadth, and resilience, resonated from a unique standpoint as African American women whose self-validation compelled them to be conscientious and contributing members to the education profession and within their own communities.

Through the lens of four retired African American female teachers, their storied lives of resilience and self-empowerment, as validated by Polidore's (2004) Resilience theory and Black feminist theory have provided a wealth of information and significant insight about their teaching experiences before, during, and after desegregation in a rural community in the South. Their stories of resilience have value for educators today.

Implications

Teacher efficacy, a type of self-efficacy, and a powerful construct, pertains to the beliefs that an individual has about their capacity to achieve at a certain level. Bandura (1997) stated that the individual beliefs a person has can influence how much effort is put forth, how long they will persist when faced with obstacles, and how resilient they are when attempting to cope with demands and challenges. The concept of teacher efficacy has far reaching effects that can impact student beliefs and achievement, parental relations, teacher performance, collegiality, and the school organization as a whole. Administrators and teacher preparation programs must view their role seriously in developing efficacious teachers. As accountability standards continue to increase and more pressure is placed on teachers, teachers with a high degree of efficacy are likely to embrace the changes that must occur to improve student achievement. Administrators must develop efficacy beliefs among both experienced and novice teachers by providing opportunities for them to acquire new skills and knowledge through professional development and by providing specific feedback about job performances. Applying these themes of resilience may lead to an increase in teacher retention for teachers of all races and ethnicities.

The data from my study can serve as the impetus for recommendations to be made to campus administrators, local and state policy makers, researchers, and college preparation programs to develop systems that foster resilience. Implementation of the recommendations could ultimately empower and encourage teachers to remain in the education profession. The informants' experiences can also be used to contribute to the empirical body of research on the on-going issue of teacher retention, and positively impact the current discourse, development, and evolution of best practices that pertain to properly equipping teachers with the intangible, yet necessary tools, needed to remain in the education profession.

As challenges that impact teacher retention continue to plague schools, support systems that foster resilience become imperative. In order to sustain quality teachers over time and increase the recruitment and retention of more teachers in the education profession, regardless of race or ethnicity, developing resilience in teachers must become a priority. Polidore's (2004) model of resilience can be used for this important purpose.

References

Ambert, A., Adler, P., Adler, P. A., & Detzner, D. F. (1995). Understanding and evaluating qualitative research. *Journal of Marriage and the Family, 57*, 879-893.

Bandura, A. (1997). *Self-efficacy: The exercise of control.* New York, NY: Cambridge University.

Banks, J. A. (1988). Ethnicity, class, cognitive, and motivational styles: Research and teaching implication. *Journal of Negro Education, 57*(4), 452-466.

Bernshausen, D., & Cunningham, C. (2001, March). *The role of resilience in teacher preparation and retention.* Paper presented at the 53rd annual meeting of the American Association of Colleges for Teacher Education, Dallas, TX.

Bobek, B. (2002). Teacher resiliency: A key to career longevity. *Clearing House, 75*(4), 202.

Bogdan, R. C., & Biklen, S. K. (2007). *Qualitative research for education: An introduction to theories and methods* (5th ed.). Boston, MA: Allyn & Bacon.

Bondy, E., & McKenzie, J. (1999). Resilience building and social reconstructionist teaching: A first-year teacher's story. *The Elementary School Journal, 100*(2), 129-150.

Brooks, R. B. (1994). Children at risk: Fostering resilience and hope. *American Journal of Orthopsychiatry, 64,* 172-79.

Collins, P. H. (1989). The social construction of Black feminist thought. *Signs, 14*(4), 745-773.

Collins, P. H. (1990). *Black feminist thought: Knowledge, consciousness, and the politics of empowerment.* New York, NY: Routledge, Chapman & Hall.

Collins, P. H. (1998). *Fighting words—Black women & the search for justice.* Minneapolis, MN: University of Minnesota Press.

Collins, P. H. (2000). *Black feminist thought: Knowledge, consciousness, and the politics of empowerment* (2nd ed.). New York, NY: Routledge.

Collins, P. H. (2003). The politics of Black feminist thought. In C. R. McCann & S. Kim (Eds.), *Feminist theory reader: Local and global perspectives* (pp. 318-333). New York, NY: Routledge.

Connelly, F. M., & Clandinin, D. J. (1990). Stories of experience and narrative inquiry. *Educational Researcher, 19*(5), 2-14.

Creswell, J. (1998). *Qualitative inquiry and research design: Choosing among five traditions.* Thousand Oaks, CA: SAGE.

Denzin, N. K., & Lincoln, Y. S. (2000). *Handbook of qualitative research* (2nd ed.). Thousand Oaks, CA: SAGE.

Denzin, N. K., & Lincoln, Y. S. (2005). *Handbook of qualitative research* (3rd ed.). Thousand Oaks, CA: SAGE.

Dexter, L. A. (1970). *Elite and specialized interviewing.* Evanston, IL: Northwestern University Press.

Few, A. L. (2007). Integrating Black consciousness and critical race feminism into family studies research. *Journal of Family Issues, 8*(4), 452-473.

Fairclough, A. (2004). The costs of *Brown*: Black teachers and school integration. *The Journal of American History, 91*(1), 43-55.

Gordon, K. A., & Coscarelli, W. C. (1996). Recognizing and fostering resilience. *Performance Improvement, 35*(9), 14-17.

Higgins, G. O. (1994). *Resilient adult overcoming a cruel past.* San Francisco, CA: Jossey-Bass.

hooks, b. (1981). *Ain't I a woman: Black women and feminism.* Boston, MA: South End Press.

hooks, b. (1984). *Feminist theory from margin to center.* Boston, MA: South End Press.

Hunter-Boykin, H. S. (1992). Responses to the African American teacher shortage: "We grow our own" through the teacher preparation program at Coolidge High School. *The Journal of Negro Education, 61*(4), 483-495.

Ingersoll, R. (2007). *Misdiagnosing the teacher quality problem* (CPRE Research Brief No. RB-49). Philadelphia, PA: The Consortium for Policy Research in Education.

King, S. H. (1992, March). *Why did we choose teaching careers and what will enable us to stay? Recruitment and retention insights from one cohort of the African-American teaching pool.* Paper presented at the annual meeting of the American Educational Research Association, San Francisco, CA.

Lincoln, Y. S., & Guba, E. G. (1985). *Naturalistic inquiry.* Newbury Park, CA: SAGE

Linville, P. W. (1987). Self-complexity as a cognitive buffer against stress-related illness and depression. *Journal of Personality and Social Psychology, 52*(4),663-76.

Masten, A. K., Best, M., & Garmezy, N. (1990). Resilience and development: Contributions from the study of children who overcome adversity. *Development and Psychopathology, 2,* 425-44.

Patton, M. Q. (2002). *Qualitative research & evaluation methods* (3rd ed.). Thousand Oaks, CA: SAGE.

Polidore, E. (2004). The teaching experiences of Lucille Bradley, Maudester Hicks, and Algeno McPherson before, during, and after desegregation in the rural south: A theoretical model of adult resilience among three African American female educators (Doctoral dissertation, Sam Houston State University, 2004). *Dissertation Abstracts International, 65*(08), 2924A.

Rotter, J. B. (1966). Generalized expectancies for internal versus external control of reinforcement. *Psychological Monographs: General and Applied, 80*(1), Whole No. 609.

Sagor, R. (1996). Building resiliency in students. *Educational Leadership, 54*(1), 38-43.

Seligman, M. (1990). *Learned optimism.* New York, NY: Random House.

Walsh, F. (1998). *Strengthening family resilience.* New York, NY: Guilford Press.

Walsh, F. (2006). *Strengthening family resilience* (2nd ed.). New York, NY: Guilford Press.

Werner, E. E. (1993). Risk, resilience, and recovery: Perspectives from Kauai longitudinal study. *Development and Psychopathology, 5,* 503-515.

Author Contact Information: Janice L. Taylor, EdD, Sam Houston State University. Mailing address: 7702 Dayhill Drive, Spring, Texas 77379. Telephone: 713-854-9531. E-mail: janiceltaylor54@msn.com

CHAPTER 96

Teaching for How People Learn Naturally

Geoffrey Caine and Renate N. Caine
Caine Learning Center

The goal of our work is for both students and educators to improve their everyday, real world performance. We stress this point because there is a fundamental difference between intellectually understanding a concept or mastering a strategy in a classroom, and being able to use concepts and strategies naturally and spontaneously in the real world. That gap between theoretical knowledge and performance knowledge is the gap that sound education has to bridge.

The foundation for attaining this goal, and our consuming interest, has always been with how people learn. And it would seem obvious that some of the issues could be resolved by science. The problem is that for many decades the science of learning has muddied the waters as much as it has helped. So that is where we begin.

The Limits of Science

In the limited space available we will drop down into a few of the thickets of thorns to which educators have been exposed, more to taste the confusion than to analyze it in depth.

- *Some science, though initially persuasive, turns out to have made some totally unwarranted claims. Behaviorism is an example.* The essence of behaviorism is that all learning can be reduced to changes in behavior, and these changes can be induced by the manipulation of rewards and punishments. The extreme view essentially dismisses the notion that people have minds, and almost totally ignores the existence of an inner world, save for working with largely reflexive pleasure and pain—the basis for the impact of rewards and punishments.

The impact on education has been enormous. It helped to end progressive education, outcome based education, and humanistic education (to name a few); it was the foundation for programmed instruction and behavior modification; it supported the notion that clusters of students could be treated in the same way for long periods of time (in batches, as Sir Ken Robinson says [2010]; it helped to consolidate the widely held view that children have to be externally motivated to learn. And some of the core ideas still permeate popular culture, as evident, for instance, in the notion that students should be paid to study (Gingrich, 2007). Of course, behavior modification does work in some limited circumstances, and sometimes external rewards and punishments do play a role. But both are small parts of a much larger picture of education and what it means to learn, one that the science of behaviorism muddied almost beyond recognition.

- *Some science is sadly limited. Traditional cognitive science is an example.* Cognitive science proper began to gain a major foothold in the 1950s. It marked a huge advance over behaviorism, simply because it dealt with thought and mind, and with the fact that people can form internal mental representations of the world, that concepts can be understood, and that minds can change.

From the perspective of educators and all those interested in education, however, traditional cognitive science suffered from at least one enormous weakness. It ignored much of what is now known to be involved in

The Handbook of Educational Theories, pp. 1071–1079

human learning. Thus, it largely ignored the fact that people think with their feelings and their emotions, they think with their bodies, they think by means of their interactions with others, some of their thinking and functioning is unconscious, and more. The point is that great educators know and knew much of this, but the most high profile "science" of learning often categorically dismissed them. Many researchers have been investigating these issues, some for a long time, and they are finally being incorporated into the mainstream. But for the most part they have not informed education.

- *Many scientists working in the same field disagree with each other. Neuroscience is an example.* The two of us became interested in neuroscience in the 1980s. Naively, we believed that neuroscience would help to reconcile the conflicting messages of other disciplines and provide a solid foundation for how people learn that could benefit every educator (R. Caine & Caine, 1990, 1994). Yet the fact is that neuroscientists do not talk with one voice, nor do they share the same views of how the brain functions and how people learn and grow.

Perhaps the most fundamental conflict has been spelled out by Joaquin Fuster (2003). He points out that the bulk of neuroscience is grounded in a modular view of the brain—separate (though interconnected) functions for different parts. An alternative view, however, treats the brain as essentially holistic and integrated. Although all the differing regions have their roles, each is interpenetrated by the others. And it is in the way that all the regions and functions interact, and in the many layers of such interaction, that people learn, act, and grow. And these differences matter to educators, because they lend support to different modes of instruction.

What, then, is an educator or policy maker to do when he or she comes across competing views of what science purports to explain or support? On the one hand, the findings and the rigors of science are important and need to be respected. On the other hand, largely because of a consistently narrow view of the problem, many influential scientists have regularly adopted a very narrow focus, and missed what great educators have known. So the challenge is to find a way to think about science and other fields of endeavor that incorporate the huge diversity of findings, in a way that is understandable and useful to both policy makers and educators in the trenches, while not suppressing the art that great educators have mastered.

Understanding "Natural Learning"

In our view, the place to begin is with a basic understanding of how the brain/mind learns naturally *outside school,* because natural learning is the way in which people at all times in the history of the human race have come to improve their performance in the real world.

It plays out in all ethnic groups, at all ages, and in very location from the desert to the forest, from the mall to the oil field, from factory floor to high tech think tanks.

The essential question, then, is to ask what sort of learning is at the core of life? And the answer is that every organism (and therefore every one of us) has to develop in two basic and interconnected ways that are indispensable aspects of survival and success—of the continuation of life itself. This is the dance of perception and action—a focus that has been emerging slowly from several different perspectives in recent times (Fuster, 2003; Maturana, Varela, & Paolucci, 1998; Noe, 2004; Thompson, 2007).

- On the one hand, individuals need to change and expand the ways they come to see and interpret things, situations, and themselves—that is, how and what they perceive. So people develop different ways to "read" their worlds. Infants are doing this all the time. But so is anyone who immigrates to a new country, or becomes highly skilled in some profession such as interior design or neuroscience or politics.
- On the other hand, and this happens in parallel, people must also develop new ways of acting on their worlds. They need to acquire new and additional skills. One way to observe this development is to follow the path of someone mastering a sport—say beginning with kicking a ball in the street and going on to become a professional soccer player.

The process of coming to see and act in new ways occurs as a result of multiple iterations of what scientists call the perception/action cycle (R. Caine & Caine, 2011; Fuster, 2003). These play out continuously in ordinary, everyday experience. These cycles recur throughout life as people test, and either confirm or change, the ways in which they do things. In a general sense, therefore, "natural learning" can be defined as making sense of experience and acquiring what we have called "performance knowledge" (G. Caine & Caine, 2001, 2011). Performance knowledge is a blend of the capacities to perceive and act appropriately in the real world.

How to Use Research

We have been persuaded by the view that each person is an integrated living system (Damasio, 2005; Fuster, 2003). The entire organism—the whole person—interacts with its world. That means that body, brain, heart and mind are all involved in learning. And given that researchers from many different domains are essentially investigating the same underlying phenomenon from their different perspectives, our approach has been to synthesize research across many disciplines, ranging from neuroscience to cognitive psychology, for the purpose of eliciting a set of useful and accurate principles that together underlie and clarify the dance of perception and action. They are foundations of natural learning.

In our view, such principles need to meet four basic criteria (R. Caine 2004):

- *The phenomena described by a principle should be universal.* A brain/mind learning principle must be true for all human beings, despite individual genetic variations, unique experiences, and developmental differences.
- *Research documenting any specific Principle should span more than one field or discipline.* Since a learning principle describes a system's property, one would expect validation and confirmation from research across multiple fields and disciplines.
- *A principle should anticipate future research.* It should be expected that emerging research will refine and confirm each principle. For example, much of the brain research on the links between emotion and cognition was published after we first formulated our principles in 1990.
- *The principle should provide implications for practice.* Learning principles ought, as a minimum, provide the basis for an effective general framework to guide decisions about teaching and training, and help in the identification and selection of appropriate methods and strategies.

An Example

When we first embarked on this journey, one of our primary interests was in the impact of stress on learning. And one of the facts that garnered our attention was that researchers in different domains were pointing to a common set of behaviors and phenomena, often without being aware of each other. So writing in the late 1980s, we drew on the following sources, amongst others:

- Hans Selye (1954), an endicronologist who is the "father" of stress theory, noticed how the body's reserves are depleted by excessive stress;
- Paul MacLean (1978), a neuroscientist who developed the theory that all humans have a brain of three brains (the triune brain theory)—a reptilian brain that deals with instinctual responses, a limbic system that is the seat of emotions, and a neocortex that houses higher order functions. He posited that when the survival response (fight of flight) is activated, the "lower" brains tend to prevail;
- Les Hart (1983), businessman turned educator and founder of brain compatible learning, called upon McClean's work. Hart coined the term "downshifting" to convey the notion that a threatened brain "downshifts" into more primitive functioning.
- Neuroscientists John O'Keefe and Lynn Nadel (1978), who worked in part on the role of the hippocampus in memory and looked at how its indexing function seemed to be impaired under stress.
- Educational psychologist Art Combs (1999) who developed a field theory of perception and noticed that the perceptual field "narrows" when a person is threatened; and
- Social scientists Edward Deci and Richard Ryan (1987), whose theory of self-determination deals with the power of intrinsic motivation and the ways that it can be nurtured or undermined by extrinsic factors.

Although most of these researchers were unfamiliar with each other, they seemed to be describing the same sort of response to stressful experiences. With these commonalities in mind we therefore suggested that they were in fact addressing the same issue from different perspectives. We framed our conclusion in terms of a general principle that applies to life and to learning. More specifically, that complex learning is inhibited by threat associated with helplessness and/or fatigue. This became the bulk of our principle.

In the ensuing years, the picture was both rendered more complex and became clearer, and the overall premise has been fully substantiated. MacLean's theory of how the brain evolved and is organized is clearly oversimplistic (though still very valuable, see, i.e., LeDoux, 1996; Sagan, 1986). And the relationship between extrinsic and intrinsic motivation is more complex than we first described. Nevertheless, the overall notion has been powerfully confirmed. For instance:

- Neurobiologist Robert Sapolsky (1998) has documented the debilitating impact of stress quite conclusively. See for example, the report of his work on the National Geographic DVD "Stress: Portrait of a Killer" (Bredar & Bean, 2008).
- Neuroscientist Joseph LeDoux (1996) has rigorously researched the pathways of fear in the brain. On the basis of his research, he demonstrated that the brain has a low road and a high road. When people are in survival mode, the low road is activated, fight or flight is triggered, and higher order functioning is literally hijacked. This is classic downshifting. The high road, where higher order functions can be accessed, requires a different and more self-assured state of mind.

- Bruce Perry (2003), a physician working with traumatized children, reached a similar conclusion coming from a different direction. He expanded on the notion by showing that the response to stress and threat is not black or white but occurs along a continuum. In brief, Perry demonstrated that all of us have a range of states of mind, ranging from the calm (what we have called relaxed alertness) to the terrified (where very primitive modes of responding prevail).

Accordingly, the overall point is now extremely clear. When people are in survival mode, complex learning is compromised—both in the real world and in school. That is why it is so essential to develop an appropriate state of mind in students, their educators, and the school as a whole. It is a combination of high intrinsic challenge and low threat which we call it relaxed alertness. We describe it in a little more depth below.

Brain/Mind Principles of Natural Learning

All of our principles were approached in a similar (though nonlinear) way. Most of the research in support of the principles can be found elsewhere (see, e.g., G. Caine & Caine, 2001, 2008, 2011; www.Naturallearninginstitute.org). Each principle contributes to the picture of how people of all ages and ethnic origins learn naturally. As a practical matter, each Principle also reveals capacities for learning that are shared by everyone and that can be activated by educators and accessed by students. Here are the principles in capsule form:

1. *Learning is physiological.* Body and brain change as a result of experience, and new learning is literally structured in the physiology. This is sometimes called "embodied cognition" (Thompson, 2007; Varella, Thompson, & Rosch, 1991).

   Implication: Learning is enhanced if there is adequate sensory engagement, physical movement and action. This applies both to soft skills and to abstract ideas and concepts.
2. *The brain/mind is social.* The recent discovery of what are called "mirror neurons" (Rizzolatti & Sinigaglia, 2006). Confirms that at a biological level we are all innately social creatures, and the brain/mind is designed to learn by imitation and from modeling. Learning is also influenced by social context and relationships. This is sometimes described as situated cognition (Lave & Wenger, 1991).

   Implication: Ensure that learning is both an individual and a social process. Create opportunities to introduce material through informal conversations between friends, colleagues, and others. In addition, ensure that learners see and experience the new material being used appropriately and naturally by others.
3. *The search for meaning is innate.* We all have what has been called "an explanatory drive" (Gopnik, Meltsoff, & Kuhl, 1999). So students want to understand what is happening in their lives. They want to belong. And at a deeper level there is a hunger for meaningfulness and purpose (Frankl, 2006; Hillman, 1996).

   Implication: Find ways to relate the standards and curriculum to authentic learner interests and questions. And explore ways of allowing the intrinsic motivation of students to drive what happens in classrooms and schools.
4. *The search for meaning occurs through patterning.* The brain and mind naturally extract patterns from, and impose patterns on, reality (Restak, 1995). Cognitive psychologists use many different terms to describe these patterns, terms such as categories, frames, and schemata. So meaning is grounded in how things are both separate and connected with each other.

   Implication: Find ways to assist learners to make connections by way of metaphor, identifying common elements, and relating to their own prior experience by discovering links to what is already known.
5. *Emotions are critical to patterning.* Cognition and emotion interact. Thus neuroscientist Antonia Damasio (1999) talks of "the feeling of what happens." This means that the way a person feels about an idea or skill always influences how well it is understood or mastered. Organizational theorist Dan Ariely (2010) makes this point the foundation of his work on how people and organizations function.

   Implication: Introduce new material in ways that are inviting, and make it possible for learners to establish a genuinely positive emotional link to that material.
6. *The brain/mind processes parts and wholes simultaneously.* The brain has modules for discerning specific and separate features of reality. There is also a constant ongoing synthesis of experience in the prefrontal cortex, sometimes called the integrative cortex (Fuster, 2003). This means that every skill and concept is better understood and mastered when there is an interplay between the specific elements and the concept or skill as a whole.

   Implication: Introduce and organize new material in terms of natural wholes such as projects, stories and big ideas.
7. *Learning involves both focused attention and peripheral perception.* Part of what is learned comes from paying full attention and being emotionally engaged. And part is a matter of picking things up indirectly

from the context. Claxton (1999) describes this as "learning by osmosis."

Implication: In addition to finding ways to help learners stay engaged through projects and exploration of their own questions, use the larger environment and design the physical context so that it indirectly conveys information and suggestions that support what is being dealt with.

8. *Learning is both conscious and unconscious.* In addition to intentionally trying to make sense of things and master them, the brain/mind also processes information and experiences below the level of awareness. This can be called the cognitive unconscious (see, e.g., Lakoff & Johnson, 1999).

   Implication: Incorporate processes, such as the arts, that prime unconscious incubation. And help learners develop their metacognitive capacities and executive functions (such as the ability to plan, work with others and make decisions) so that they become more conscious of, and take better charge of, the ways in which they process and digest experience.

9. *There are at least two types of memory.* Scientists have identified several different memory systems, and there have been many different approaches to memory (Danziger, 2008). A key practical distinction for educators, first formulated by O'Keefe and Nadel (1978) is between systems that are used to archive and store information and routines (sometimes by rote memory) and systems that naturally register, make sense of, and store ongoing experience.

   Implication: In addition to sometimes using techniques for memorization, introduce new ideas and skills in the context of everyday experiences and projects, and use tools such as deep observation and extended questioning to process those experiences.

10. *Learning is developmental.* There are at least two different dimensions of development. First, there are many stage theories about the development of identity and general capacities such as the shift from concrete to abstract thinking. Second, there is a rough progression in the mastery of a discipline or subject, from novice to expert.

    Implication: Teaching should be scaffolded to take into consideration the capacities of the learner and his or her current state of knowledge and competence, while incorporating expectations for ongoing improvement.

11. *Complex learning is enhanced by challenge and inhibited by threat associated with helplessness and/or fatigue.* The brain/mind literally becomes less effective and people lose access to their own capacities for higher order functioning and creativity when the survival response kicks in. (See discussion above.)

    Implication: Create conditions in which individuals and groups feel safe and relaxed at the same time as they feel challenged and engaged.

12. *Each brain is uniquely organized.* Although all people have many capacities and qualities in common, everyone is also a unique blend of experience and genetics. There are many ways of identifying individual differences. A good example is Gardner's theory of multiple intelligences (1993). Another is the Myers-Briggs personality typology.

    Implication: Teachers need to both treat everyone equally and at the same time, helps individuals to capitalize on their own strengths. It helps to use a good learning style inventory so that participants can grasp some of their own predispositions and preferences. (We should add that when we use our own inventory with adolescents, www.cainelearning.com, they love exploring their similarities and differences!).

THE THREE ELEMENTS OF EFFECTIVE TEACHING

Every principle leads to some practical implications for improving learning. More power comes, however, when we find ways to integrate the principles simultaneously so that they are mutually reinforcing in support of the overall dance of enhancing perception and action.

When one takes a bird's eye view of all the principles from the perspective of what educators need to know, three core elements of great teaching stand out. We should add that they are not separate. Rather they function as a sort of triple helix, because each is ongoing all the time, and each impacts the other two. Collectively they are the foundations of what we call the *Guided Experience Approach* (Caine and Caine, 2011). When they are integrated, the result is teaching that is a dynamic and not a static process.

1. There is an optimal state of mind for individuals and the learning community. We call it relaxed alertness.

Relaxed alertness is a blend of low threat and high challenge. Low threat is important because learning is inhibited when people are threatened to the point where they feel helpless (Principle 11). And motivation is increased when people can tap into their own search for meaning (Principle 3) so that they are doing what really matters to them. Another way to describe this state of mind is that it is a blend of competence, confidence, and intrinsic motivation. So a teacher or leader should be constantly alert to the state of mind of learners, and needs to know how to adjust his or her practice accordingly.

It is important for learners to feel safe, to enjoy the process, to be interested in becoming more effective, to actually look forward to trying new things out and learning from mistakes as well as successes, and to exploring and discussing all this with fellow students and others in a rigorous but low environment. That is one reason why a good learning community is so important.

2. The overall frame for teaching is the orchestrated immersion of participants in complex experience in which the content is embedded.

The principles tell us that meaningful learning is influenced by emotions, relationships, the physical context and more. The only way to integrate all these aspects of learning is through a combination of experiences in which the content is embedded. That is why Roger Schank (Engines4Education; http://engines4ed.org/) works with what he used to call "goal-based scenarios" and now calls a "story-based curriculum." This frame is at the heart of sophisticated project based teaching, experiential education, constructivist methodologies and more. Note, in addition, that the guided experience approach *includes* direct instruction and a host of instructional strategies as needed, but always in the service of the orchestration of complex experience.

The use of a wide range of procedures integrated through ongoing experience should not be surprising. Any young child mastering its native language, or its culture, is exposed to all of these elements. And anyone who becomes an expert in any field ranging from scientific research to high level competence in any sport also taps into all these elements.

The key is to have a systematic process that is sustained over time.

3. Infused throughout the entire experience is the constant active processing of that experience.

Experience by itself is never enough. Experience has to be adequately digested—or processed. Without this third element, the many elegant activities that many teachers generate are much less effective than they could be. And that is why constant, ongoing active processing is the third indispensable element of this approach to education and professional development. The patterns are there in the experiences that learners have—but they are often hidden

The key is for educators is to assure that students have many opportunities to receive feedback, digest, think about, question, examine, and continuously process what they are experiencing—sometimes self-directed and sometimes guided.

Active processing includes, where appropriate, such activities as:

- detailed sensory observation;
- deliberate (selective and mindful) practice and rehearsal;
- multiple modes of questioning;
- analysis of data and sources;
- ongoing responses to and reflection on feedback; and
- expansion of capacities for self-discipline and self-regulation.

Note that active processing naturally supplies ongoing formative assessment.

NATURAL LEARNING AND LEARNING OUTCOMES

Our rule of thumb is that the fewer aspects of the three elements that are engaged, the more superficial is the knowledge and skill that is acquired and the less real world capacity is developed. It does not matter whether educators or the public talk about "understanding" or "mastery" or "high standards." The key is the type of processes that are used in teaching. For example, if there is insufficient active processing it is most unlikely that students will develop in depth understanding, irrespective of what teachers try to do or the system purports to assess.

Here, in slightly artificial form (because things are not really as neat and clean as this) are five different sorts of outcome.

1. *Surface knowledge.* Surface knowledge consists of facts "about" things and basic routines that have been memorized. It can be recalled in different contexts. It can be copious. But much of what is remembered in this way tends to be only shallowly understood. The acquisition of surface knowledge requires little relaxed alertness, immersion is limited to presentations and transmission of information and procedures, and processing is limited to simple memorization and shallow problem solving.
2. *Technical/scholastic knowledge.* Technical/scholastic knowledge consists of theoretical understanding and routine skills. It is generated when the three elements discussed above are expanded to include the solving of more complex problems, opportunities to work on small projects, practice and rehearsal, group interactions including discussion and debate, and more. In essence, students have multiple opportunities to make sense of things and try things out for themselves (a constructivist approach), with feedback and guidance. However,

the core limitation of this type of knowledge is revealed in the difficulty with which it is transferred to the real world. That is because something else is still needed.

3. *Dynamical or performance knowledge.* Performance knowledge is developed when there is a perceptual shift so that a person can see and act in the real world in new ways. The new knowledge becomes a lens with which a person can "read" the real world context. He or she acquires what has been called "a new organ of cognition." And the new skills can be adapted in the moment and appropriately to unplanned situations. For new cognitive lenses and complex skills to develop, immersion in real world experience is essential. That is why complex projects, including whole school programs, can be so powerful. Good service learning is a great example.
4. *Maturity, self-knowledge and the capacity to self-regulate.* Much of self-knowledge is what Goleman calls emotional (2006) and social (2007) intelligence. In order to develop self-knowledge, people need to find out how to observe themselves in multiple ways. This calls for the development of the metacognitive capacities and executive functions of the brain that we refer to in Principle 8). In effect, people develop the capacity to process their own processing.
5. *Creativity and the capacity to deal with change.* Creativity is often characterized as a skill. That is partly true. It is also contingent on the actual knowledge base that a person has. But creativity is also the byproduct of a state of mind. Deep relaxed alertness is essential. This is the message, for instance, of cognitive psychologist Guy Claxton (1999). In essence, the sort of learning that produces creativity requires the occasional unrushed, enthusiastic exploration of possibility (sometimes called "play"!), in a context where outcomes are not tightly bound and prespecified, in such a way that new insights or ways of seeing can emerge.

If we are genuinely preparing students to be successful in the real world then education needs to focus on all the five outcomes listed above. And both science and experience suggest to us that the only way to address all of the outcomes in parallel, over the duration of a student's school life, is to for individual teachers, a school as a whole, and the surrounding community, to implement the guided experience approach. We hasten to add that this is our own term for an approach that many educators and theorists have been exploring from many perspectives. Examples include the wide field of constructivism, self-directed learning, self-regulated learning, service learning, project based teaching and learning, experiential learning and others. We also wish to reiterate that these approaches do *not* exclude direct instruction. Explanations, modeling, the provision of some information and so on are all part of great teaching. The important point is that the guided experience approach *transcends but includes* direct instruction.

That leads, finally, to a word about assessment. One of the great sources of confusion in the debate about education lies in the myopic concentration on test scores. Some of the outcomes mentioned above are related to test scores, but in ways that are too complex to discuss here. The general point, however, is that multiple modes of appropriate assessment are needed, at a variety of different times, and for formative and summative purposes, to adequately deal with the continuous development of the different sorts of learning outcomes. Scores on standardized tests, for instance, simply do not adequately reveal depth of understanding, and are hopeless at revealing real world competence. Here are some possible indicators of competence:

- The ability to use the language of a discipline or subject in social interaction;
- the ability to perform appropriately in unanticipated situations;
- the ability of learners to ask their own pertinent questions;
- the ability to solve real problems using the skills and concepts; and
- the ability to show, explain, or teach an idea or skill to another who has a real interest or need to know.

It Can Be Done Because it Is Being Done

Over the last 20 years we have developed our own terminology and approach both to the science of learning and the art of teaching. As we note above, there are many kindred spirits, however, who use different terms and frames of reference, and who are clearly and unequivocally very successful at the multiple levels that we talk about. While we cannot describe them here, we invite readers to follow up the references and find out more about them. We have written about some of them elsewhere.

- *Reggio Emilia* a region in Northern Italy, is generally regarded as having the most sophisticated early childhood program in the world (G. Caine & Caine, 2001; Edwards, Gandini, & Forman. 1998).
- *Bridgewater Elementary* is a superb primary school in South Australia. It is one of several hundred schools that was involved in one of the world's leading edge programs of system change, *Learning to Learn*, which

has now become the foundation of curriculum and pedagogy for the entire state (R. Caine & Caine, 2011; South Australian teaching for effective learning framework guide).

- High Tech High began as a single charter high school. It is now the only charter district in California and consists of a set of nine schools, including elementary, middle, and high schools, all of which implement the sorts of processes described here (R. Caine & Caine, 2011; Wagner, 2008).
- A superb example of this approach in homeschooling can be found in a book by the Colfaxes (1988). We came across their work in a story in the *LA Times* with the title: "Third Home Schooled Child Off to Harvard" (R. Caine & Caine, 1994).
- Service learning is an approach to education in which students participate in extensive community based projects into which the standards and formal curriculum are incorporated (see, e.g., The Providers' Network: http://www.slprovidersnetwork.org/index.php).

Conclusion and a Word of Caution

Learning for all people, irrespective of gender, nationality, or any other factor, can be dramatically enhanced when the natural capacities of the brain and mind are accessed. Implementing a sound process, however, is more than a matter of just adding new strategies because great teaching is just as difficult as rocket science or brain surgery. Teachers and leaders need a high degree of knowledge and skill. They need to have or develop some personal qualities and attributes, such as patience, an appreciation of the uneven development of mastery, and a grasp of how different aspects of the curriculum and real life are connected. They need to larger be able to make education genuinely learner centered.

It is not easy. It is not simple. It is not neat. In short, great education is like life itself. It requires very sophisticated professional development for educators that lives and models what is being taught. And even then the system has to be configured so that it supports and does not undermine the complex approach to instruction that is advocated here. Fortunately, the return on investment for students, the community, and educators themselves, is well worth the price.

Acknowledgment

Much of this chapter first appeared in Caine, G., & Caine, R. (2010). "How People Learn: The Brain/Mind Principles of Natural Learning" in N. Lazeron (Ed.). *Brain Based Learning*. Dutch Association of Training and Development.

References

Ariely, D. (2010). Predictably irrational. *The hidden forces that shape our decisions.* New York, NY: Harper Perennial

Bredar, J., & Bean, R. (2008). *Stress: Portrait of a killer.* Washington, DC: National Geographic Television and Stanford University.

Caine, G., & Caine, R. (2001). *The brain, education and the competitive edge.* Lanham, MD: Rowman & Littlefield.

Caine, G., & Caine, R. (2008). *Natural learning: The basis for raising and sustaining high standards of real world performance.* Retrieved from www.naturallearninginstitute.org

Caine, R. (2004, April). *How systems principles can serve as foundation for constructivist learning and teaching.* Paper presented at the annual meeting of the American Education Research Association, San Diego, CA.

Caine, R. (2008). How neuroscience informs our teaching of elementary students. In C. Block, S. Parris, & P. Afflerbach (Eds.), *Comprehension instruction* (2nd ed., pp. 127-141). New York, NY: Guilford Press.

Caine, R., & Caine G. (1990). Understanding a brain based approach to learning and teaching. *Educational Leadership, 48*(2), 66-70.

Caine, R., & Caine, G. (1994). *Making connections: Teaching and the human brain.* Menlo Park, CA: Addison-Wesley-Longman.

Caine, R., & Caine, G. (2011). *Natural learning for a connected world: Education, technology and the human brain.* New York, NY: Teachers College Press.

Caine, R., Caine, G., McClintic, C., & Klimek, K. (2008). *The 12 brain/mind learning principles in action* (2nd ed.). Thousand Oaks, CA: Corwin Press.

Claxton, G. (1999). *Hare brain, tortoise mind: How intelligence increases when you think less.* New York, NY: Harper Perennial.

Colfax, D., & Colfax, M. (1988). *Homeschooling for excellence.* New York, NY: Grand Central.

Combs, A. W. (1999). *Being and becoming: A field approach to psychology.* New York, NY: Springer.

Damasio, A. R. (1999). *The feeling of what happens: Body and emotion in the making of consciousness.* New York, NY: Harcourt Brace.

Damasio, A. (2005). *Descartes' error: Emotion, reason, and the human brain.* New York, NY: Penguin.

Danziger, K. (2008). *Marking the mind: A history of memory.* Cambridge, England: Cambridge University Press.

Deci, E. L., & Ryan, R. M. (1987). The support of autonomy and the control of behavior. *Journal of Personality and Social Psychology, 53*(6), 1024-1037.

Edwards, C., Gandini , L., & Forman, G. (1998). *The hundred languages of children: The Reggio Emilia approach advanced reflections* (2nd ed.). Atlanta, GA: Elsevier Science

Frankl, V. (2006). *Man's search for meaning.* Boston, MA: Beacon Press.

Fuster, J. M. (2003). *Cortex and mind: Unifying cognition.* New York, NY: Oxford University Press.

Gardner, H. (2006). *Multiple intelligences: New horizons in theory and practice.* Westfield, MA: Basic Books.

Gingrich, N. 2007, *On the issues.* Retrieved from http://www.ontheissues.org/2008/Newt_Gingrich_Education.htm

Goleman, D. (2006). *Emotional intelligence: Why it can matter more than IQ.* New York, NY: Bantam Books.

Goleman, D. (2007). *Social intelligence: The new science of human relationships*. New York, NY: Bantam Books.

Gopnik, A., Meltsoff, A. N., & Kuhl, P. (1999). *The scientist in the crib: Minds, brains, and how children learn*. New York, NY: William Morrow.

Hart, L.A. (1983). *Human brain and human learning*. White Plains, NY: Longman.

Hillman, J. (1996). *The soul's code: In search of character and calling*. New York, NY: Warner Books.

Lakoff, G., & Johnson, M. (1999). *Philosophy in the flesh: The embodied mind and its challenge to Western thought*. New York, NY: Basic Books.

Lave, J., & Wenger, E. (1991). *Situated learning: Legitimate peripheral participation (Learning in doing: Social, cognitive and computational perspectives)*. Cambridge, England: Cambridge University Press.

LeDoux, J. (1996). *The emotional brain*. New York, NY: Simon & Schuster.

MacLean, P. D. (1978). A mind of three minds: Educating the triune brain. In J. Chall & A. Mirsky (Eds.), *Education and the brain* (pp. 308-342). Chicago, IL: University of Chicago Press.

Maturana, H. R., Varela, F. J., & Paolucci, R. (1998). *The tree of knowledge: The biological roots of human understanding*. Boston, MA: Shambhala Publications.

Noe, A. (2004). *Action in perception*. Cambridge, MA: MIT Press.

O'Keefe, J., & Nadel, L. (1978). *The hippocampus as a cognitive map*. Oxford, England: Clarendon Press.

Perry, B. D. (2003). *Effects of traumatic events on children*. Retrieved from www.mentalhealthconnection.org/pdfs/perry-handout-effects-of-trauma.pdf

Restak, R. (1995). *Brainscapes*. New York, NY: Hyperion.

Rizzolatti, G., & Sinigaglia, C. (2006). *Mirrors in the brain: How our minds share actions and emotions*. Oxford, England: Oxford University Press.

RSA Animate: (2010). Changing education paradigms—Sir Ken Robinson. Retrieved May 9, 2010, from http://www.youtube.com/watch?w=zD2FcDGpL4U

Sagan, C. (1986). *The dragons of eden: Speculations on the evolution of human intelligence*. New York, NY: Ballantine Books.

Sapolsky, R. (1998). *Why zebras don't get ulcers: An updated guide to stress, stress-related diseases, and coping*. New York, NY: W.H. Freeman

Selye, H. (1956). *The stress of life*. New York, NY: McGraw Hill.

Schank, R. (2011). *Engines for education*. Retrieved from http://www.engines4ed.org/hyperbook/

Thompson, E. (2007). *Mind in life: Biology, phenomemology, and the sciences of mind*. Cambridge, MA: Harvard University Press.

Varella, F. J., Thompson, E., & Rosch, E. (1991) *The embodied mind: Cognitive science and human experience*. Cambridge, MA: MIT Press.

Wagner, T. (2008). *The global achievement gap*. New York, NY: Basic Books.

Author Contact Information: **Geoffrey Caine**, LLM, and **Renate N. Caine**, PhD, Caine Learning Center, P.O. Box 1847, Idyllwild, CA 92549. Phone: 951-659-0152. E-mail: www.Cainelearning.com

CHAPTER 97

The Reggio Emilia Approach to Early Childhood Education

C. Miki Henderson
Sam Houston State University

Reggio Emilia is a municipality in northern Italy with an international reputation for its revolutionary philosophy and practices with respect to early childhood education. The fundamental philosophical basis of the Reggio Emilia approach to early childhood education is that all children have rights and are deserving of respect (Malaguzzi, 2000). However, other ideas which are important and have garnered the world's attention are the teacher's documentation of children's development (Wurm, 2005), the uses of children's interests to help guide instruction (Cadwell, 2003), and the support for individual and group work while embracing the idea that there are multiple forms of knowing (Giudici, Rinaldi, & Krechevsky, 2001), and an unprecedented commitment to family participation in all aspects of the program (Gandini & Edwards, 2001). These aspects of the Reggio approach have inspired whole countries such as Sweden and New Zealand to reevaluate their systems of early care and education. In the United States many early childhood practitioners have found parts of the Reggio philosophy to implement in their own settings as well.

In this chapter, we will attempt to inform scholars about the Reggio Emilia approach to early childhood education and the influences which helped shape this philosophy into a worldwide example of quality programming for young children. We will consider political and societal issues in Italy, the view of children and childhood, the perceptions about families and their role in education, and finally the profession of teaching and the environment with regards to their impact on the Reggio philosophy.

Italian Politics and Societal Values

Reggio Emilia is a small, affluent city in the Emilia Romagna region of northern Italy approximately 35 miles northwest of Bologna. It has a long history of political activism and engaging citizens in the town's operations and politics. According to Sahlberg and Moss (2007), this region was a stronghold of the Italian Communist Party, but is currently held by center-left coalitions. This area also housed an anti-fascist resistance around the time of World War II stemming from a history of anticlericalism dating from the nineteenth century, when parts of Emilia–Romagna belonged of the Papal States. Around 1945, just at the end of the Fascist dictatorship and World War II when the Italian people began to consider the importance of early childhood as way to bring about lasting change and a new world of social justice, they began to build their own preschools. Some of them continued until 1967 when they were transferred over to the city, in part due to the Union of Italian Women (Edwards, Gandini, & Forman, 1998).

Loris Malaguzzi was born in 1920 and died in 1994. He was the inspiration behind the extraordinary educational approach that would be named after the town of Reggio Emilia. He studied psychology and merged that with his work in education (Day, 2001). The first school was built by the people of Villa Cella in northern Italy and about 20 miles from Reggio Emilia. Eventually, this school was absorbed by the municipality. By most accounts he worked tirelessly for children and was respected for his commitment and his creativity. In Malaguzzi's obituary in *The Independent*, a British newspaper out of London, Wolfgang Achtner writes:

> Malaguzzi had little time for "success" or awards; his was a labour of love. Although he had retired in 1985, until the day he died he dedicated all his energy to the school system he had helped create, participating in conventions, meetings with parents, teachers and local administrators and lengthy visits to Reggio's preschools, on an almost daily basis.

The Handbook of Educational Theories, pp. 1081–1084

ment consisted of some questions used in Polidore's (2004) study. More questions were added to the secondary instrument and were used to guide the stories told by the informants during semistructured interviews. As suggested by Dexter (1970), an interview is a conversation with a purpose. "Narrative researchers base their inquiry on intensive interviews about specific aspects of people's lives rather than on conversations in specific organizational contexts" (Denzin & Lincoln, 2005, p. 659). As Lincoln and Guba (1985) suggested, using a semistructured interview in my study allowed the informants to reconstruct their past experiences that were focused on the central purpose of the study. Purposeful dialogue was used to acquire an understanding of perspectives shared by the informants in their natural setting. The open-ended nature of the approach allowed the informants to answer from their own time frame of reference (Bogdan & Biklen, 2007). The semistructured interview format also (a) ensured that the same course of inquiry was used with each informant interviewed; (b) provided topics in which I was free to explore, probe, and establish a conversation with the focus on a particular subject that had been predetermined; and (c) systematically maximized the time for comprehensive interviews to be conducted (Patton, 2002). Probing questions were also used to solicit elaboration to some responses provided by the informants.

Informants and Context of the Study

A purposive sample of four African American female teachers was chosen for this study. Bogdan and Biklen (2007) indicated that when the researcher wants the informants to freely express their thoughts around a particular subject, small samples are used. Creswell (1998) stated that researchers designing qualitative studies need clear criteria in mind and need to provide rationales for their decisions. The sole criterion for the informants in this study was that they had taught in a public school in the rural community of Marshall, Texas before 1970, and continued their career in teaching after 1970 until they resigned or retired from education. Three of the informants, Ms. Sammie Sutton, Ms. Willie R. Scott, and Ms. Johnetta Cooper, were interviewed in their natural setting—their home. The fourth informant, Ms. Jean Birmingham was interviewed while on a visit to Houston, Texas.

Data collection and Results

The teaching experiences of the four African American female teachers in my historical, biographical research study were revealed through their stories, and the data collected were analyzed to understand emergent themes of resilience that influenced the teachers' retention and longevity in education. The qualitative data collected yielded each of Polidore's (2004) eight themes; however, there was one additional theme that resonated throughout the narratives of the four informants. The resilience theme efficacy, not identified in Polidore's Resilience theory model, echoed throughout the dramatic narratives of the four African American female teachers.

Efficacy—An Additional Resilience Theme

The term efficacy refers to the strong beliefs held by some African American female educators about their competence, confidence, and purpose to serve as uplifters within African American communities (Collins, 2000). A pattern of efficacy was more challenging to discern from the eight themes of resilience in Polidore's (2004) model because efficacy is based on a person's belief in oneself. Ms. Cooper stated, "I had to plan more in-depth because there were some sharp kids in my classes, and I felt the need to be able to challenge them. So, I had to dig deeper in my studying in order to be able to challenge them."

Efficacy is an abstract concept that is intrinsically based and was not easily culled from among two similar themes of resilience, positive relationships and optimistic bias. Although several of Polidore's resilience themes are also abstract in nature—flexible locus of control, commitment, and autonomy—the presence of these themes is more easily distinguished from observations of one's actions. The theme of efficacy was not initially identified because it may have been intertwined with the themes positive relationships and optimistic bias. When I probed deeper, the theme of efficacy emerged from my data; it was especially noteworthy and distinguishable throughout the lives of my informants. Ms. Scott stated,

> The teachers, parents, and students from other races respected me because they recognized my intelligence, my knowledge of the subject matter, the ideas that I projected. They knew that I wanted to help and they saw that I looked upon students first as human beings. I often told them [students] that I am here to teach you and I am as interested in you as my very own children.

The theme of efficacy is different from the theme positive relationships because positive relationships are a more tangible part of one's life; however, positive relationships can influence the development of one's efficacy. The theme of optimistic bias is also similar to efficacy. Optimistic bias, like efficacy, is abstract in nature. Optimistic bias is a perception or a belief that allows one to view adverse situations positively, and as a result, perform or behave in a manner that will yield success (Seligman, 1990). I determined that the theme of efficacy was an overarching theme and was under-

Throughout the latter half of the twentieth century Italy underwent many social and political movements that shaped the Reggio system of early care. The policies which required free schooling for young children and demanded equal pay for women helped Reggio centers flourish and grow (Reggio Children, 2007). Reggio Emilia's system of care and the philosophy behind it gained world acclaim as the gold standard of care for young children and the model drew researchers and educators from around the globe to Italy. Reggio Emilia has become a source of national pride for the country.

The question of sustainability in today's economic climate must be given serious consideration. There are over fifty centers for infants and preschoolers that are part of the *Istituzione Scuole e Nidi d'Infanzia* which manages the programs (Reggio Children, 2007). This system requires a massive financial investment and a social commitment to young children that unprecedented. As of yet, there are no plans to privatize these municipal centers, but there is little doubt that it may have to be considered in the future.

THEORETICAL PERSPECTIVE

The Reggio Emilia Approach is related to constructivist theorists such as Piaget and Vygotsky (Edwards, Gandini, & Forman, 1998; Rinaldi, 2006). Piaget and Vygotsky offer theories on ways children think cognitively in a developmental manner. Piaget believed children to be competent, when they learn new things it just enhances their skills further. Vygotsky also believed children are competent, however, when they learn new things, it helps them in the process of the zone of proximal development (ZPD). According to Piaget, children who are in the preoperational thought stage are innately motivated to learn. They ask questions constantly and try to get answers. They move from an simple thought process to a more complex ways of expressing themselves. In time they learn to use symbols to express their ideas. Reggio Emilia has developed the concept that children have many different ways of expressing their knowledge of the world around them called the hundred languages (Malaguzzi, 2000). Piaget's stage of preoperational thought and symbolic function relates to the Reggio Emilia approach to symbolic representation. Eventually, however, Malaguzzi rejected Piaget's stages as too limiting and worked to infuse a much more powerful view of children and childhood into the Reggio philosophy.

Vygotsky believed that the ZPD assists children develop cognitively through their social interactions with teachers and with their families. Reggio also supports this concept in that parents, teachers and the environment impact learning (Gandini, 1993). Scaffolding, another Vygotsky premise, can be clearly seen in the way teachers try to limit their interference in children's work. They make themselves available to children when their assistance is likely to be welcomed and appreciated.

It is clear that Malaguzzi was influenced by the constructivists movement in education and that he drew upon those theories that enhanced his perspective of the child as a person with rights and the need to develop their own voice in order to become civically engaged and effective agents for change. In turn, the Reggio philosophies and theories now impact many researchers, early childhood teachers and preschools around the world.

THE CONCEPT OF CHILDHOOD

The concept of children's rights drives the Reggio philosophy. Since children have the right to be heard and to participate in the greater world, no one should be allowed to interfere. They should not only be free to develop their voice, but adults are bound by moral and ethical obligations to enhance their development of voice (Rinaldi, 2006). This is why it is necessary to provide free and public preschool for children—to teach them to use their voice through creative thinking and artistic endeavors.

Another part of the foundation of the Reggio approach is to acknowledge that children have enormous potentiality and curiosity. Children have an innate drive to understand their world; therefore they tend to hypothesize about the world they live in out of curiosity. There is great potential in young children to solve problems and construct their own knowledge to appease this curiosity. In the book, *The Hundred Languages of Children: The Reggio Emilia Approach—Advanced Reflections*, Loris Malaguzzi (2000) is quoted expressing this sentiment:

> Each child is unique and the protagonist of his or her own growth. Children desire to acquire knowledge, have much capacity for curiosity and amazement, and yearn to create relationships with others and communicate. (p. 67)

In Reggio programming the child's primary role is to satisfy their curiosity, daydream, think creatively, and express their thoughts and ideas through the arts.

THE HUNDRED LANGUAGES OF CHILDREN

As children engage in investigations, they generate and test their hypotheses, they are expected to depict their understandings through one of many symbolic languages, and this will include drawing, sculpting, singing, dancing, dramatizing, and writing (Malaguzzi, 2000). The products produced by children help them develop their voice and are used to document that growth along the way.

The Role of Families in Education

Families are a vital component to the Reggio philosophy and reflects the Italian view that children are a collective responsibility (Gandini & Edwards, 2001). Families are considered to be partners with the school as well as advocates for their children. Reggio teachers respect parents as each child's first teacher and seek ways to involve them in every aspect of the curriculum. Family members are welcomed and encouraged to volunteer within Reggio Emilia classrooms. Families are expected to take part in regular discussions about school policy, child development concerns, and curriculum planning and evaluation. Teachers work with the families to educate and support them in children's development. Families often extend what they learn at Reggio to their home lives (Gandini, 1993).

The advocacy role of families is deliberately cultivated (Hendrick, 2003). They are viewed as essential partners in the collaboration to sustain Reggio programming for the children in the community. They hold crucial information, dispositions, and other resources that make the effort essential. They play an important role as liaisons to the greater community.

The Role of Early Childhood Educators

The teacher in Reggio Emilia is a researcher, a collector of data, a learner, and must finesse the child's capacity to learn. The responsibility is on the teacher to provide contexts for learning to take place. Malaguzzi (2000) sets forth a purpose for the early childhood educator in his interview transcribed in *The Hundred Languages Of Children: The Reggio Emilia approach—Advanced Reflections*:

> The central act of adults, therefore, is to activate, especially indirectly, the meaning-making competencies of children as a basis of all learning. They must try to capture the right moments, and then find the right approaches, for bringing together, into a fruitful dialogue, their meanings and interpretations with those children. (p. 81)

The teacher's role is a very complex one. Working alongside with children, the teacher is a resource and guide through the creative processes (Edwards, Gandini, & Forman, 1998). Within such a teacher as researcher role, educators must actively listen, observe, and document children's work while also stimulating thought and collaboration with peers in the classroom (Fu, Hill, & Stremmel, 2001). In addition, while all of this is taking place, a teacher must pay careful attention to their own growth and development through reflection (Hendrick, 2003; Wurm, 2005).

The most time consuming and challenging roles of the teacher is the documentation process. However, many schools around the world are engaging in these processes that have been inspired by Reggio Emilia practices. Portfolios, cooperative learning, individual and group project-based learning are all akin to the Reggio approach. According to Malaguzzi (2000), if documentation is collected, reviewed, and then shared only at the end of a learning experience, but not during, the opportunity may be lost to gain new meanings that could enhance the experience being documented. Much is still to be learned about documentation and the educator's role in the process. Documentation communicates what is going on in the children's days in care to families and other visitors, even more important are opportunities for children to revisit their experiences (Kinney & Wharton, 2008).

Documentation is an involved process that includes observation, reflection, collaboration, interpretation, analysis, and is made a part of the classroom (Fraser, 2000). Multiple forms of documentation including photos, audio recordings and transcripts, video, anecdotal notes and the creative products by children create a multifaceted view of what takes place in the Reggio center for all of the parties involved in the care of the children and for the children themselves (Cadwell, 1997; Giudici, Rinaldi, & Krechevsky, 2001). In her book, *In Dialogue with Reggio Emilia* Rinaldi (2006) asserts that:

> The construction of traces (through notes, slides, videos, and so on) that not only testify to the children's learning paths and processes, but also make them possible because they are visible. (p. 83)

The expectations placed on the teachers as collectors of data are high and require a great amount of knowledge and skill in order to meet. The necessity of documentation is indeed the crux of the Reggio approach and so much emphasis is placed on this aspect of the teacher's job.

Researchers in Stirling, Scotland who implemented a documentation system based upon Reggio principles found working with faculty in an early childhood setting is one of the most challenging aspects (Cadwell, 2003). As in Scotland, the U.S. also has a childcare workforce that varies widely in age, years of service and experience, levels of dedication to the field and education. Added to this is that the U.S. system of childcare is just as diverse as the country itself, there is no uniform system of service provision as it is market driven. Therefore, the turnover rate for early care teachers is very high in comparison to those in Reggio Emilia centers (Gandini & Edwards, 2001).

The Environment as Teacher

Much emphasis is placed on the aesthetics of the classrooms in a Reggio school. In fact, the Environment is considered to be the "third teacher." Space is intentionally planned to meet the physical and social needs of children. Documentation of children's work, photographs, plants, and collections that have been made from excursions are displayed at the children's and adult eye level. Malaguzzi discusses the importance of the environment in his book and during an interview with Lella Gandini offers:

> The wider the range of possibilities we offer children, the more intense will be their motivations and the richer their experiences. We must widen the range of topics and goals, the types of situations we offer and their degree of structure, the kinds and combinations of resources and materials, and the possible interactions with things, peers, and adults. (Edwards, Gandini, & Forman, 1998, p. 79)

A welcoming environment encourages a child to engage in activity and discovery. The Reggio Emilia approach, much like Montessori integrates nature into the curriculum and environment so that the child learns to appreciate the aesthetics of the environment.

The "Atelier" or art studio is a key feature of a Reggio-inspired classroom, as is an "atelerista" or art specialist trained in early childhood education and fine arts (Gandini, 2005). The atelier is a beautiful and inspiring studio space that is developed to allow children to actively investigate, explore and solve problems.

CONCLUSION

Reggio Emilia is a unique example of programming for young children. Born out of socialist political views and historical changes over several decades, Reggio is distinctly Italian. However, many ideas have been deemed universal and important such at the rights of children, the necessity of documenting children's development, using of children's interests to guide instruction, and the concept of the hundred languages, as well as the need to cultivate family participation in young children's educational experiences. There is much to be gleaned from studying the Reggio Emilia approach and seeking to apply its most important universal elements to early childhood education programs outside of Italy.

REFERENCES

Achtner, W. (1994, April 1). Obituary: Loris Malaguzzi. *The Independent*, p. 23.

Cadwell, L. (2003) *Bringing learning to life: The Reggio approach to early childhood education*, New York, NY: Teachers College Press.

Cadwell, L. (1997). *Bringing Reggio Emilia home: An innovative approach to early childhood education.* New York, NY: Teachers College Press.

Dahlberg, G., & Moss, P. (2007). *Ethics and politics in early childhood education* (Contesting early childhood). New York, NY: RoutledgeFalmer.

Day, C. (2001, May). Pioneers in our field: Loris Malaguzzi—founder of The Reggio Emilia Approach. *Early Childhood Today.* Retrieved from http://www.scholastic.com/teachers/article/pioneers-our-field-loris-malaguzzi-founder-reggio-emilia-approach

Edwards, C., Gandini, L., & Forman, G. (Eds.). (1998). *The hundred languages of children: The Reggio Emilia approach—Advanced reflections* (2nd ed.). Norwood, NJ: Ablex.

Fraser, S. (2000). *Authentic childhood: Experiencing Reggio Emilia in the classroom.* Scarborough, ON: Nelson Thomas Learning.

Fu, V., Hill L., & Stremmel, A. (2001). *Teaching and learning, collaborative exploration of the Reggio Emilia approach.* Upper Saddle River, NJ: Prentice Hall.

Gandini, L. (1993). *Fundamentals of the Reggio Emilia approach to early childhood education. Young Children*, Washington, DC: National Association for the Education of Young Children.

Gandini, L. (2005). *In the spirit of the studio: Learning from the atelier of Reggio Emilia.* New York, NY: Teachers College Press.

Gandini, L., & Edwards, C. (Eds.). (2001). *Bambini: The Italian approach to infant/toddler care.* New York, NY: Teachers College Press.

Giudici, C., Rinaldi, C., & Krechevsky, M. (Eds.). (2001). *Making learning visible: Children as individuals and group learners.* Reggio Emilia, Italy: Reggio Children.

Hendrick, J. (Ed.). (2003). *Next steps in teaching the Reggio way: Accepting the challenge to change* (2nd ed.). Upper Saddle River, NJ: Pearson Merrill Prentice-Hall.

Kinney, L., & Wharton, P. (2008). *An encounter with Reggio Emilia: Children's early learning made visible.* New York, NY: Routledge.

Malaguzzi, L. (2000). *The hundred languages of children: The Reggio Emilia approach—Advanced reflections.* Reggio Emilia, Italy: Elsevier Science.

Reggio Children. (2007). Retrieved from http://zerosei.comune.re.it/inter/reggiochildren.htm

Rinaldi, C. (2006) *In dialogue with Reggio Emilia.* London: Routledge.

Wurm, J. P. (2005). *Working in the Reggio way: A beginner's guide for American teachers.* St. Paul, MN: Red Leaf Press.

Author Contact Information: C. Miki Henderson, EdD, Sam Houston State University, 3008 Manor Lane, Apartment B, Huntsville, Texas 77340, Phone: 936-668-6776. E-mail: cmh055@shsu.edu

CHAPTER 98

Montessori Philosophy, Education, and Bilingual Education

Linda Rodriguez, Beverly J. Irby,
Rafael Lara-Alecio, and Genevieve Brown
Sam Houston State University

The Montessori method of education was developed in Italy by Dr. Maria Montessori in 1906 to serve disadvantaged children (Kahn, 1995). Her first school, Casa dei Bambini, served 50 very poor children from a Roman slum (Ruenzel, 1997). Montessori stated:

> The poor have not yet had proper consideration, and always there remains one class that was yet more completely ignored, even among the rich. Such was childhood! All social problems are considered from the point of view of the adult and his needs ... Far more important are the needs of the child. (Montessori, 1961, p. 120)

She continued in the same essay, "suppose we set up in schools the same social improvement that we are so proud of achieving! Let us feed the children, give them playground, clothing, freedom of speech" (Montessori, 1961, p. 121). Although the pedagogy introduced by Maria Montessori is over a century old, it is remarkably relevant for low socioeconomic preschool children of the twenty-first century. According to Kramer (1988), Montessori was deeply concerned with social injustices for women and children; therefore, she concentrated her efforts on those women and children from poor socioeconomic status and initially on those children with apparent mental deficiencies (Standing, 1957).

According to the National Center for Educational Statistics, in 1999, only 50% of children living in households with incomes of $10,000 or less receive care and education from persons other than their parents, in comparison to 77% of children in households with incomes in excess of $75,000 (National Center for Educational Statistics, 1999). By 2009, according to Flanagan and McPhee, in terms of participation in nonparental early care and education the year *prior* to kindergarten, about four out of five (83.2%) had a regular early care and education arrangement. Over 2 decades ago, Kagan (1989) hailed inequities in early childhood education, indicating, "there are vast inequities regarding children's eligibility an access to programs. Children are segregated by income, with limited choices and resources for low-income families" (Kagan, 1989, p. 234), and, this situation "does not reflect the law or spirit or our nation" (Kagan, 1989, p. 235). In 2009, she continued her admonition (Kagan, 2009).

Published literature is limited in its references to Montessori and low socioeconomic status, much less to Montessori and English language learners Hispanic students and corresponding bilingual educational programs. In an exhaustive review of Montessori literature, only three studies were found which related to low socioeconomic status (Clements & Sarama, 2008; Jackson, 1980; Wheeler, 1998), while only three studies were found related to English language learners students (Barrera, Rule, & Stewart, 2004; Jackson, 1980; Rodriguez, Irby, Brown, Lara-Alecio, & Galloway, 2003; Wheeler, 1998).

HISTORY OF MONTESSORI

Dr. Maria Montessori revolutionized the notion of early education through the establishment of "Children's Houses," Casa dei Bambini, in Roman slums in 1907. She worked with children from the age of 2½ years at a time when American educators were discussing the rel-

The Handbook of Educational Theories, pp. 1085–1095

evance of her ideas for 4- and 5-year-olds in public school kindergartens (Kramer, 1988).

Maria Montessori came to the study of education as a clinician. The young physician's successful work with the retarded led her to 7 years of further study in anthropology and psychology as preparation for work with normal children (Kramer, 1988; Standing, 1957). A supervisor of a schoolroom project in 1907, she brought to the first Casa dei Bambini (Casa) some of the materials she had been using with mentally retarded children. She instructed the teacher in the Casa to allow the children to react to those materials without interfering with the children. Her observations of the children's behaviors began to build a method that would revolutionize education (Kramer, 1988).

Montessori projected on the educational world a charismatic image. Her medical background as the first female physician in Italy, her understanding of the scientific method, and her option in favor of the environment as crucial in the determination of the organism, combined to produce a unique educational theory that outlined new revolutionary roles to both teacher and learner (Kramer, 1988).

In the Montessori method the teacher was expected to prepare an environment responsive to the needs of the learner. Montessori believed that the main need of the learners was their liberty to develop their personalities. Therefore, she thought that the teacher's role was to prepare the learners to meet their own needs (Kramer, 1988).

Montessori designed a "didactic apparatus" as a means to the achievement of sensory, motor, and intellectual development through the free exercise of the child's interest (Kramer, 1988; Standing, 1957). Much of her "didactic apparatus" she derived from her French medical predecessor, Edouard Seguin. Despite the attention focused upon the Montessori didactic apparatus by both disciples and admirers, the apparatus, Montessori firmly believed, remains dependent for its effectiveness on her view of the total environment in which learning occurs (Kramer, 1988).

The teacher's role in the preparation and mediation of the learner's learning environment was primarily one of observation. Montessori recognized that the capacity of the adult for accurate observation determines much of what the child was free to do. Montessori used observation as her principle tool to develop her method. Her own clinical background convinced her of the importance of detecting even minimal differences in individual behavior of the child, which cued the adult to an appropriate response (Kramer, 1988).

Since the first training course she offered in Rome in 1913, Montessori repeatedly emphasized the role of observation as a critical part of her method. She believed that skill in observation was a function of repeated exposure to it, as she reminded her students that a teacher in her method was more of an observer than a teacher. In other words, a teacher must know how to observe. Montessori believed that a teacher who could not observe could not teach (Kramer, 1988).

Maria Montessori (1964) stated that two of the greatest influences in her work were Itard and Seguin.

> Itard was the first educator to practice the observation of the pupil in the way in which the sick are observed in the hospitals, especially those suffering from diseases of the nervous system. The pedagogic writings of Itard are most interesting and minute descriptions of educational efforts and experiences, and anyone reading them today must admit that they were practically the first attempts at experimental psychology. But the merit of having completed a genuine educational system for deficient children was due to Edward Seguin, first a teacher and then a physician. He took the experiences of Itard as his starting point, applying these methods, modifying and completing them during a period of 10 years experience with children taken from the insane asylums and placed in a little school in Rue Pigalle in Paris. (Montessori, 1964, p. 34)

Later, Seguin went to the United States, where he continued to work with children, published his method, and defined it as the physiological method. Following him, Montessori created her own method. "Montessori observed the morphological growth of the pupils and developed her own method, whose fundamental base was the liberty of the pupils in their spontaneous manifestations" (Montessori, 1964, p. 80).

Kramer (1988) stated that while one of the influences on Montessori's thinking was the work done by the physicians, Itard and Seguin, on the training of mentally defective children. Another influence consisted of the ideas about the education of all children from the philosophy of educators such as Froebel, Pestalozzi, and Rousseau. However, it is safe to note that Montessori never believed, like Rousseau, that all civilization corrupted the child. On the contrary, she believed that work, the systematic mastery of the environment, met an innate need of the developing human being from the earliest age and was the key to both individual development and the progress of civilization (Kramer, 1988). Unlike Rousseau, Montessori did not believe in turning the young child out to school into the world of nature, but to use nature to perfect schools. She did not believe in the "destructuring" of education, but in the idea of developing the senses as a prior basis for abstract learning in a school that was structured the right way (Kramer, 1988).

Pestalozzi also had a big influence on Montessori's philosophy (Kramer, 1988). His main educational principle was the importance of training the senses, based on his belief that all thinking began with accurate observation of concrete objects. By the time of his death in 1827, Pestalozzi was a formidable influence in European and American schools (Kramer, 1988).

Friedrich Froebel's work was identified as the bridge between Pestalozzi and Montessori. A young teacher who followed Pestalozzi's ideas, Froebel was the German schoolmaster who gave the world the kindergarten. Froebel's stated aim as an educator was to discover universal principles of life and apply them scientifically so as to fully develop "man's divine spiritual nature" (Kramer, 1988 p. 66). He focused on the child's experience of the real world, the unfolding of his natural capacities, on learning as a process of self-discovery as the child passes through successive stages of development. Froebel saw this process of self-fulfillment through self-activity possible only where the adult does not interfere with the child's spontaneous activity, providing guidance rather than coercion. Kramer (1988) indicated that Montessori once was questioned by an interviewer as to the difference between her system and Froebel's kindergarten system (where children should "work in freedom"). She replied that while Froebel imposed his philosophy of the child on the child, she went to the child to get hers. It was through observation of the child that Montessori came up with the principles that guided her method.

Description of Montessori Prekindergarten Education

Montessori's Philosophy

According to Standing (1957), Montessori's official biographer, one of the basic principles behind her method was "the fundamental difference between the child and the adult" (p. 87). Further explained, "the child was a continual state of growth and metamorphosis, whereas the adult had reached the norm of the species" (Standing, 1957, p. 87). Ungerer (2011) the Executive Director of the American Montessori Society, having observed many Montessori classrooms found a level of respect that could be applied to all levels of learners. He determined the Montessori philosophy:

- supports the freedom of each child to pursue her or his own interests, while at the same time encouraging responsible choices;
- uses mixed-age classrooms as a vehicle for providing time for the development of relationships between younger and older children;
- respects and follows the child;
- promotes cooperation and peaceful behaviors—seeing children as capable 'peace builders';
- deals with conflict by using conflict as a source of creativity;
- encourages self-control, self-discipline, and self-regulation;
- copes with bullying (physical, verbal, and relational) and gossiping;
- provides opportunities for intentional conversations;
- creates a safe environment where children are not intimidated by others;
- acts on trust;
- understands how decisions are made, and teaching decision making;
- skills and the art of making good choices;
- supports rather than attempts to control children;
- helps children to value differences and to be open to contrasting;
- points of view;
- practices listening skills—guiding children to listen and to learn from one another; and
- Builds positive self-esteem. (p. 3)

Stages of Mental Metamorphosis

Montessori identified three main stages of mental metamorphosis or mental development. The first epoch of development (0-6 years) was the epoch of "the absorbent mind," which subdivides in two stages: unconscious (0-3 years) and conscious (3-6 years). In the first stage, the child absorbs the world through his unconscious intelligence. In the second stage, the child takes in consciously from the environment, using their hands, which become the instruments of the brain (Standing, 1957).

In the second epoch of development (6-12 years), Montessori identified a "herd instinct" in children (Standing, 1957). While the first epoch was devoted to the construction of the human individual, in the second epoch children develop a group instinct. This second stage of childhood was marked by the strengthening of the reasoning faculty. On the moral plane, for instance, it examines the rightness and wrongness of actions (Standing, 1957).

Montessori called the third epoch of development adolescence (12-18 years). She subdivides this period into two stages: puberty (12-15) and adolescence (15-18). Standing (1957) noted that while "in the preceding epoch the individual tended to be an extrovert, the adolescent tends to look inward [...and thus] the creation of the socially conscious individual [takes place]" (Standing, 1957, p. 97).

Sensitive Periods in Development

The term "sensitive periods" was discovered by the Dutch scholar, Hugo De Vries, who in 1900 confirmed the Mendelian laws of heredity (Kramer, 1988). Struck by the parallels between Montessori's theory and his own theories of the development of plants, De Vries (as cited in Kramer, 1988) suggested Montessori make use of this term to describe her observations about the stages of children's growth and learning (Kramer, 1988).

Standing (1957) noted that "during the development of certain organisms there come periods of special sensibility. These [transitory] periods of sensibility are related to certain elements in the environment toward which the organism was directed with an irresistible impulse and a well-defined activity" (Standing, 1957, p. 100). The intense and prolonged activity aroused and sustained by a sensitive period does not cause fatigue; rather the reverse. In each sensitive period, the children are endowed with special powers, which help them to construct their personality through the acquisition of some well-defined characteristic or function (Montessori, 1914).

One of the earliest sensitive periods in the child's development was the one concerned with the acquisition of spoken language. Transitory as all sensitive periods, once gone, it never returns (Standing, 1957).

Another sensitive period was that of order (2-4 years of age). This period was of great practical significance in the running of a Montessori school. According to Standing (1957), children get a sense of the position of everything in the classroom very quickly just because of this sensitive period of order. In the Montessori school, this sensitive period was acknowledged by providing children with learning environments where everything had its proper place and must be kept.

EDUCATION OF THE SENSES

Montessori identified a sensitive period for refinement of the senses. She thought there was a period (2 ½ -6 years of age) where the child refined senses and impressions of all kinds, in color, sound, shape, and texture. Montessori believed in the education of the senses, which aimed at "the refinement of the differential perception of stimuli by means of repeated exercises" (Montessori, 1964, p. 173). This was the period where Montessori gave the children the sensorial materials designed to stimulate and refine the senses (Standing, 1957). Rippa (1997) noted that Montessori thought that sensory education was the basis of her method. To Montessori, it was necessary to begin the education of the senses in the formative period. To translate her ideas into practice, Montessori invented some ingenious and varied educational "games" (Rippa, 1997). The "didactic apparatus" for these games consisted of twenty-six separate items (cylinders, geometric insects, rectangular blocks, and colored tablets). Each piece of material was carefully graded and self-corrective. In addition, she designed and had manufactured lightweight, movable furniture; small chairs and tables replaced the then-customary large stationary desks. She also planned special activities to develop auditory skills (the "game of silence") and to encourage vocabulary enrichment and the use of correct and fluent speech (Rippa, 1997).

Another period identified by Montessori was the sensitive period for learning good manners (also 2 ½-6 years of age). This period was perfect for learning good manners such as opening and closing a door, handing a sharp instrument to another person, eating correctly, saluting, or being excused.

Standing (1957) noted that according to Montessori, "when the education of children was organized in relation to their sensitive periods, they work with a sustained enthusiasm which had to be seen in order to be believed" (Standing, 1957, p. 133).

THE NORMAL CHILD

Through experience, Montessori discovered the characteristics of the normal child. These characteristics did not vary from country to country; they remained the same regardless of race, climate, religion, or civilization. Montessori's "new" children presented the following characteristics: a love of order, love of work, profound spontaneous concentration, attachment to reality, love of silence and of working alone, sublimation of the possessive instinct, power to act from real choice and not from curiosity, obedience, independence and initiative, spontaneous self-discipline, and joy (Standing, 1957). Montessori was committed to bringing out the "new, normal" child in the children she taught. In this sense, she stated that her schools may be compared to "sanatoria; for the first thing that happens in them was that the children are restored to mental health" (Standing, 1957, p. 178).

MONTESSORI'S CLASSROOM FURNISHINGS

Montessori (1964) literally abolished desks and benches or stationary chairs that impeded children's free movement. Montessori's little tables and various types of chairs were light, easily transported, and permitted the children to "select the position which [the children found] most comfortable. [They could] make [themselves] comfortable as well as seat [themselves] in [their] own place" (Montessori, 1964, p. 84). Montessori went on to explain why her classroom's special furnishing promoted freedom while being a means of education. She stated:

> If by an awkward movement a child upsets a chair, which falls noisily to the floor, he would have an evident proof of his own incapacity; the same movement had it taken place amid stationary benches would have passed unnoticed by him. Thus the child had some means by which he could correct himself, and having

done so he had before him the actual proof of the power he had gained: the little tables and chairs remained firm and silent each in its own place. (Montessori, 1964, p. 84)

Montessori's Didactic Material

Guided by the work of Itard and Seguin, Montessori created a variety of didactic materials. These materials did not represent Montessori's method by themselves. As Montessori noted, these materials "became in the hands of those who knew how to apply them, a most remarkable and efficient means, but unless rightly presented, they failed to attract the attention of the [children]" (Montessori, 1964, p. 36).

Further, Montessori stated her belief that not the didactic materials, but her voice "awakened the children, and encouraged them to use the didactic material and through it, to educate themselves" (Montessori, 1964, p. 37). Montessori's didactic materials were carefully designed to control every error thus allowing the children to correct themselves.

Discipline

To Montessori, discipline must come through liberty. She stated that, "we call an individual disciplined when he was master of himself, and can, therefore, regulate his own conduct" (Montessori, 1964, p. 86). It is through activity and movement that children learn to regulate their conduct and be independent.

Montessori's concept of active discipline implied that the teacher bring "not only the capacity but the desire to observe natural phenomena" (Montessori, 1964, p. 87). The teacher's "anxious scientific curiosity, and absolute respect for the phenomenon which she wishes to observe" (Montessori, 1964, p. 87) are essential components of Montessori's method.

Montessori's Lessons

Collective lessons in the Montessori method are very rare, since the children being free are not obliged to remain in their places quiet and ready to listen to the teacher, or watch what she was doing. The collective lessons, in fact, are of very secondary importance, and have been almost abolished by us (Montessori, 1964, p. 108). Lessons in the Montessori method should be individual, concise, simple and objective, and must allow for teacher observation while promoting the children's liberty. According to Lillard (2007), when cognition and movement within lessons are integrated, children's thinking and learning are enhanced. In the Montessori classroom, children create knowledge and learn with and from their peers; they learn in rich and meaningful contexts, and in an environment that is orderly.

Exercises of Practical Life

In Montessori's Casas, the exercises of practical life (cleanliness, order, poise, and conversation) formed the beginning of the day. An inspection of cleanliness takes place as soon as children arrive at school. Teachers call the attention to the child in case of buttons missing, garments torn, or shoes not clean. It was expected that children "become accustomed to observing themselves and take an interest in their own appearance" (Montessori, 1964, p. 122). Children are taught how to take care of themselves and older children are taught to help the younger ones. After the previous exercise, the children proceed to put on their aprons and inspect the classroom. They make sure the materials are clean and in order. When the children are ready with their materials in order, they are taught "poise and equilibrium" while sitting and working. Next, the teacher invites the children to talk with her. These conversations among the children and the teacher "encouraged the unfolding or development of the language." They are also "of great educational value" (Montessori, 1964, p. 124) since children learn through these conversations proper themes and ways to communicate with each other.

Language and How Language Calls the Child

In *The Absorbent Mind*, Montessori (1949) presented her thoughts on language. She claimed that language grows in children "organically," following natural developmental patterns that appear to be common to all children in all languages. Montessori asserted that from birth, children are engaged in developing the essential skills for whatever human language exists around them. Montessori also suggested that whether children's potential was limited to one language or was more fully developed depends very much on how early and how effectively children are exposed to other languages (Renton, 1998).

Reading and Writing

Kramer (1988) noted that Montessori grew more and more interested in the possibility that the children in the first Casa might be able to learn reading and writing effortlessly through methods similar to those where they gained perceptual skills (making increasingly subtle discriminations of size, shape, pattern, and color by themselves). She thought about the results of her work with deficient children, whom she had managed to teach to read and write using her three-dimensional models of letters.

According to Kramer (1988), although it was not possible for Montessori to afford her three-dimensional original materials for the children in the Casa dei Bambini, she herself elaborated letters that she cut out of paper. Her assistants colored one set of letters blue, and she cut another set out of sandpaper and glued these onto smooth cards. The children of the Casa handled this sensorial apparatus (Montessori, 1955) and traced the letter with their fingers and later with pencil or chalk, learning the sounds, first vowels and then consonants. They took enormous pleasure in the game by means of which they were teaching themselves what other children two and three years older were learning so laboriously in the regular school (Kramer, 1988).

The next accomplishment of the children of the Casa was reading, which was learned after writing. This was contrary to the accepted idea of the time. The children already knew the individual sounds of the letters. They put the sounds together and connected them with names of things. This way, the children started to read from small slips on which the names of familiar objects were written. Later, the children read short sentences indicating actions to be performed. The small reading slips used were brief, easy, clear, and at the same time interesting, especially as they are also accompanied by motor activities, not of the hand only but of the whole body (Kramer, 1988). As Kramer (1988) noted, the idea of children of 4 or 5 years old learning to write in less than 2 months and to read in a few days was certainly revolutionary in 1907.

Research on Montessori Prekindergarten Education

Hainstock (1997) stated that truly conclusive results to determine the advantages of a Montessori education have been difficult to obtain because of the wide variety of teaching styles within Montessori. Additionally, he noted the high cost of research and the time factors involved are other aspects hampering significant research. There was a great need for more testing and research to determine the true long-range value of Montessori early education. Several tests have suggested that children with some kind of educational preschool experience tend to show an overwhelming advantage throughout their fourteen years of schooling over those without such early training. Those with Montessori schooling are only slightly ahead of the groups with some other kind of preprimary experience.

According to Hainstock (1997), possibilities for research of the method are extensive and can cover a wide range of specialties such as: the normal child, the gifted child, emotionally, physically, and mentally handicapped, culturally deprived, application of the method in day care centers, etc. Due to cost and lack of personnel, such studies have not been done (Heinstock, 1997).

In 1965, the Cincinnati Montessori Society, the Carnegie Foundation, and the Cincinnati Board of Education began a 6-year study, using children from three different communities. Children from Montessori schools and children from traditional urban public school classrooms participated in this study. This was the first scientifically designed research project to study the Montessori method of education (Hainstock, 1997).

The report, known as The Sands School Project Report, examined performance on several variables including self-concept, social competence, curiosity, creativity, motor impulse control, innovative behavior, and some aspects of conventional intelligence. Academic achievement, per se, was not examined. The conclusion drawn from this research suggested that considerable promise for the Montessori approach in fostering a wide range of desirable behavior in elementary school age children.

A 6-year follow-up program evaluated whether or not continued and early exposure to Montessori education made a difference in later academic life. Verbal and mathematic skills were measured by the Metropolitan Achievement Test in third-grade children of varied preschool and primary school experiences. The groups studied included (a) children with four years of Montessori preschool and primary school education; (b) children with 2 years of Montessori preschool; (c) children with 1 year of Head Start prior to kindergarten; and (d) children who no school experience prior to kindergarten (Hainstock, 1997). Hainstock (1997) stated that the results of this test were not really conclusive enough to formulate anything more than a probable generalization. Age was a significant factor in correlating achievement, and all the children were from low socioeconomic groupings.

While the children in group one (4 years of Montessori) achieved high scores, it was apparent that to maintain the effect of a higher level of proficiency, it was necessary to continue the method of learning beyond prekindergarten years. The groups rated in predictable prehypothesis fashion, that is children who attended Montessori preschool would score higher than would children who attended no preschool or attended Head Start, and children who attended preschool would score higher than children who did not attend preschool. Group 1 children achieved higher minimum scores overall with a large differential between the highest minimum score of the next group (Hainstock, 1997).

In summary, a small group of children who attended Montessori classes for at least 4 years beginning during preschool scored first of four groups in all seven of the Metropolitan Achievement Test subscores while they were in the third grade. The children were compared with children who had Montessori preschool, Head Start, or no prekindergarten experience. The Montessori children scored significantly higher in Word Analysis and Math Problem-Solving, two areas considered important in the Montessori philosophy. Thus, the influence of the Montessori program on academic achievement had been shown to be strong. Age was a factor in influencing scores. A wide range of further studies was needed, but this material indicated that the Montessori approach with primary school children of lower socioeconomic status were more effective than regular public school primary grade programs, regardless of the previous preschool experience (Hainstock, 1997).

MONTESSORI IN BILINGUAL EDUCATION

Today's society has promoted Montessori primarily for an exclusive private education, even though Montessori focused her initial work toward poor children. For example, according to Ruenzel (1997), only 4% (200) of the approximately 5000 schools in the United States are funded under public education. Thus, the social injustice for which Montessori worked continues to be evidenced in the schools of her namesake in which general access to her methodology or philosophy is limited to those who have the resources to afford private school education. In 2007, Shapiro indicated that of the 4200 Montessori schools in the United States, not even 300 were operated in the public schools. Furthermore, Rosanova (2000) indicated that for bilingual education, Montessori education in combination with bilingual education has been virtually ignored and unexplored.

According to Ceo-DiFrancesco (2007), the combination of the Montessori method and foreign language instruction began in the 1960s in the United States and began with thematic units. She said, "Montessori educators around the world have for years employed strategies and techniques in the Montessori environment that can significantly enhance the child's acquisition of another language" (p. 197). Furthermore, Renton (1998) indicated that Montessori spoke of young children as natural linguists. In Montessori's view, children unconsciously learn about the language itself and how it operates. It was the exposure that children have to one or more languages what determines whether their linguistic potential was developed (Renton, 1998).

Renton (1998) stated that in the cases of some children, a natural linguist was awakened by their family context, where the child might grow up with two or more languages being spoken at home. In the case of other children, their potential was developed at school, where their native language was used to introduce a second, dominant language. Yet other children in many Montessori programs are exposed to two or more languages with the purpose of developing true bilingual skills.

In her study, Renton (1998) stated that the complex multicultural and multilingual reality of American education today was affecting Montessori programs, especially in the public schools. Issues in early childhood education are of concern in an increasingly changing society. This was why, as Renton (1998) indicated, Montessorians worldwide are developing creative responses to this challenge. These responses include Montessori schools' support for home language maintenance, second language, bilingual multicultural, and immersion programs whose aim are to utilize the sensitive period for language development more fully, from prekindergarten through elementary.

To Renton (1998), the home and the language of culturally and linguistically diverse learners should not only be respected, but also maintained and developed as fully as possible. For these children, the mastery of the dominant language was also of vital importance. Culturally and linguistically diverse children should consider themselves functional in two cultures and in two languages.

With the belief that primary language skills in a first language was the base for developing skills in a second language, Renton (1998) presented five basic principles of current second language acquisition approaches that she suggested can be successfully implemented in a Montessori environment.

First, Renton (1998) stated that second language acquisition happens most naturally when the process closely resembles first-language acquisition. Renton adheres to the notion that effective second-language acquisition takes place when children are exposed to natural interactions, and when the goal was communicative competence (Krashen, 1988).

Second, the environment that should promote second language acquisition must provide comprehensible input (Krashen, 1988) and a supportive affective climate. This principle means that language should be understandable and meaningful. Undoubtedly, the concept of context plays a critical role in making language understandable and meaningful. According to Renton (1998), the concrete materials used in the Montessori method have proved attractive to children while at the same time they "embody specific concepts, and invite exploration through movement and the senses" (Renton 1998, p. 31).

Third, second language acquisition should foster a basic communicative proficiency and a cognitive academic proficiency. In a Montessori learning environment, both levels of language are continually being constructed and practiced (Renton, 1998). Social conversations among the learners and the teacher and lessons that target concept development are combined in the instruction of children.

Fourth, second language acquisition requires time. The 3-year cycle proposed by Montessori programs provides time for children to move through various levels of second language development. Finally, the fifth principle presented by Renton (1998) stated that languages are inseparable from culture, and the former are always learned most effectively in a cultural context. Indeed, as Renton indicated, "culture shapes the child's first experiences, from which language arises" (Renton, 1998, p. 31).

Jackson (1980) conducted a study in which the purpose was twofold. He purported to describe and evaluate the first year of a Montessori bilingual early childhood program. This program involved 77 children in two kindergarten classrooms from four classes in two communities in central Texas. Four teachers who had been trained and certified by the Association Montessori Internationale participated in this study. They used materials and techniques developed by Maria Montessori. The evaluation of the program included language testing for comprehension and production of Spanish and English as well as observational data from the spring and fall semesters of 1980.

Three research questions guided Jackson's study. The first question asked what happened the first year that the Montessori method was tried in a bilingual setting. The second question asked what changes, if any, took place in the ability of children involved to understand and speak Spanish and English, and the third question asked what changes, if any, took place in the behavior of the children involved.

Regarding the first research question, Jackson (1980) described the oral language development component of the program, which included instructional activities for vocabulary enrichment, isolating the sounds of language, and clarifying the function of words. He also described the adaptations of the Montessori method for their implementation in a bilingual setting.

The description of the classroom management component of the program included the preparation of the environment, observation and recordkeeping practices, the basic techniques for presenting materials, and "grace and courtesy lessons." Then, Jackson discussed Montessori's views on the nature of education, the role of the teacher, and the concept of discipline and behavior change.

Two instruments were used in this study to respond to questions two and three: the James Language Dominance Test and a modified version of the Coping Analysis Schedule for Educational Setting (Jackson, 1980). The obtained results suggested that regarding English and Spanish comprehension and production, the gains made in each case (English/Spanish) were highly significant, using the correlated t-tests. However, given the lack of a comparison group, these changes cannot necessarily be attributed to the Montessori bilingual treatment. Behavior changes observed included positive shifts in percentage of time spent in self-directed activity, in paying attention to the task at hand, and in positive social interaction. The results indicated that the program goals for the first year were met. The study also pointed to a number of possible changes for program improvement, including the use of Spanish, the recruitment of more Spanish-dominant students, the development of separate sets of materials for Spanish and English instruction, and the sharing by teachers of their particular classroom management strategies.

In her study, Farmer (1998), director of the Gloria F. Montejano Montessori Teacher Education Program, discussed the program's objectives. These objectives are (a) to ensure the expansion of Montessori in a multicultural and multilingual world; (b) to participate and support national and state reform movements of public education and teacher education through the Montessori philosophy and method; (c) to take Montessori education back to its roots by assisting publicly funded organizations in their efforts to convert existing programs to Montessori and to initiate new programs for poor children; (d) to promote contact and dialogue among traditional and nontraditional Montessori program teachers; (e) to support the Montessori commitment to educational excellence; and (f) to continue to assert the power of a child's home culture and language.

Farmer (1998) noted that while these objectives might be similar to those of other so called "bilingual education programs," replacing Spanish with English was the real objective of these programs. Children who have been pushed to English by these pseudobilingual programs usually attain a fragmented education and are more likely to drop out before they complete high school. Conversely, in Montessori preschool programs, children who are from Spanish-speaking homes are guided by teachers who are native Spanish speakers. These children master the content in Spanish and then transition to English; they have a positive self-image and self-confidence to attempt new challenges.

According to the Montessori's philosophy, children construct their identity from what was offered in the environment (Standing, 1957). Hence the importance that their first school experience be a smooth transition from home, where teachers speak the children's native language and understand children's native culture. Farmer (1998) stated that if the school program was in a language and a culture dissimilar to the children's, the vital cognitive and socializing experiences at school do not connect with the home experiences. The result of an education of this sort was what Farmer (1998) called "an unfinished and confused" individual.

A child's self-image is affected by the values of the dominant culture in schools. If the dominant culture devalues the children's native language, the one in which they have constructed themselves, children would eventually learn to devalue their own identity. Children learn to reject their native language and the associations to their native culture (Farmer, 1998). As

Farmer stated, "the self was weakened because its base was emotionally and psychologically cut off. The individual no longer attempts to access the deposit of early understandings and skills, which were framed in the home language" (Farmer, 1998, p. 22).

The director of the InterCultura Foreign Language Immersion Montessori School in Oak Park, Illinois, Rosanova (1998), described his program for children of ages two through 6 years. His school had been identified by the Illinois Resource Center of Bilingual Education as the only true immersion school in the state of Illinois. Here, teachers refrain from speaking the majority language under any circumstances for at least the first 3 years of the program. InterCultura's purpose is to help speakers of the majority language to become bilingual. Most of the children in InterCultura speak English as their native language. The program also includes a few children who are native speakers of the various targeted minority languages.

Rosanova (1998) stated that what makes InterCultura unique among immersion Montessori schools was the fact that English was not one of the primary target languages in his school. The targeted languages are Spanish, French, Italian, and Japanese. An educational model like InterCultura's was certainly not common in a country where American-born individuals are not encouraged to become functionally bilingual (Rosanova, 1998).

According to Rosanova (1998), if a healthy child from a supportive and at least minimally literate family participates in a Montessori immersion program "consistently enough, and long enough, then it was not normal for the child to remain monolingual" (Rosanova, 1998, p. 37). What would be normal for this child was to become functionally bilingual.

Teachers in InterCultura look for critical signs that reflect children's emotional and social progress. One of these signs was a blank stare, which begins to disappear within a few weeks for most children. Also, Rosanova (1998) noticed that within 8 to 10 months after entering InterCultura, most of the children begin to talk or sing to themselves in the target language. This behavior occurs more often while children are engaged in what Montessori termed "exercises of practical life." To Rosanova (1998), this behavior that children show was an important landmark in their progress toward bilingualism in his program.

Rosanova (1998) noted that perhaps the most critical aspect of children's motivation in any Montessori program was "the child's ability and willingness to tolerate ambiguity and to search for meaning; that was, a child's ability and willingness to guess" (Rosanova, 1998, p. 37) so as to become engaged in their own critical development.

A guiding principle of the InterCultura program was that children's emotional development correlates with language development. Bearing this principle in mind, Rosanova (1998) identifies four developmental stages of a Montessori community, namely the preproduction, the early production, the speech emergence, and the intermediate fluency stages.

In their first year of the program, children would only say isolated words, phrases, routine expressions, or would not speak in the target language at all. According to Rosanova (1998), children's first task was to develop social and cognitive strategies that enabled them to understand and eventually to develop a receptive vocabulary. However, until this happens, children "get distracted easily, often would not follow directions ... and rely heavily on contextual cues for understanding" (Rosanova, 1998, p. 37). The teacher's role at this point was to provide a lot of demonstration and repetition, even more than in a monolingual Montessori setting.

In the early production stage, many children have begun to produce a variety of simple words and short phrases in the target language, and they are also able to respond with one-word answers to questions. Contextual cues continue to be critical to children's understanding. Also, the children's community gets stronger with children helping their peers interpret and understand. As Rosanova (1998) suggested, the emergence of interpreting among the children was critical for classroom behavior.

In the speech emergence stage, coherent dialogues begin to emerge. Some children begin to speak the target language in longer phrases and more fluently. A few of them, however, would still struggle with the pronunciation or the grammar. Despite these differences, most of the children would be able to get the message across.

Finally, in the intermediate fluency stage, the children who become more capable of structuring cooperative work usually create roles for at least some of the younger children. Younger children are exposed to episodes of full sentences and connected narrative, which are provided by models different from the teacher. This way, children become the models for their younger peers.

Rosanova's (1998) study concluded with a few recommendations for language immersion programs. First, survival vocabulary goals need to be established. It was important that children be exposed to richer vocabulary than the traditional noun lists. Further, children who attain their goals also need to be identified.

Second, repetition of key grammatical forms working in context was critical. This does not mean identification of parts of speech, but the actual use of words in real communication.

Third, presentation of new material should be done utilizing key phrases that children can identify easily. The teacher should decide in advance what key phrases she decides to utilize, and these should be emphasized constantly and consistently.

Fourth, rhyme and movement are essential. As Rosanova (1998) indicated, young children love to sing and they love to move; rhythmic singing and movement are the physical embodiment of their capacity for memory.

From his experience in InterCultura, Rosanova (1998) concluded that young children's growth to bilingualism was both resilient and robust under the right circumstances. In his view, the basic Montessori curriculum and standard Montessori practices supply the rudiments of what most children need. He further suggested that the three to classrooms was an exceptionally good environment for the development of what, in second language acquisition theory, was termed as "basic interpersonal skills" and "cognitive academic language."

Montessori, herself, worked in a bilingual setting. During her years in India, Montessori trained teachers and helped to establish schools in parts of this multicultural and multilingual country. Montessori referred to the schools founded in India as "English medium schools " because the language of instruction was English. Today, these schools are referred to as "English-language immersion Montessori schools" (Rosanova, 1998, p. 31).

The maturational/linguistic worldview of the young child with special foci on bilingualism was advocated by Saville-Troike (1973), McLaughlin (1978, 1987), and Chaudron (1988). The child begins to develop sounds and place those sounds in such an order until they may elicit a response from a parent or other significant adult. The child's primary language was used as a mode of instruction. Additive English occurred when the child had mastered concepts in his primary language. Private schools have used the Montessorian/ maturational worldview quite successfully with young and older children in the United States (Montessori, 1966). The best match maximizes the potential for thought and language development with ongoing curricular experiences. Cummins (1986) showed that content areas of instruction provide a rich source of comprehensible input for English language learner children, who often experience anxiety and hostility toward learning in general and toward English in particular. Such attitudes reduce the amount of input that can be acquired and slow down the development of English as a second language (Chomsky, 1988; Cummins, 1986; Krashen, 1985). To overcome these obstacles, teachers and administrators must appeal to the child's affect, demonstrating that they value their language and culture (Rodriguez et al., 2003).

REFERENCES

Barrera, M. T., Rule, A. C., & Stewart, R. A. (2004). Using descriptive adjective object boxes to improve science vocabulary. *Montessori Life, 16*(2), 28-33.

Ceo-DiFrancesco, D. (2007). A Montessori approach to learning another language. *The NAMTA Journal, 32*(1), 197-210.

Chaudron, C. (1988). *Second language classrooms.* Cambridge, England: Press Syndicate of the University of Cambridge.

Chomsky, N. (1988). *Language and problems of knowledge*. Cambridge, MA: MIT Press.

Clements, D., & Sarama, J. (2008). Experimental evaluation of the effects of a research-based preschool mathematics curriculum. *American Educational Research Journal, 45*(2), 443-494.

Cummins, J. (1986). Empowering minority students: A framework for intervention. *Harvard Educational Review, 56, 18-36.*

Farmer, M. (1998). Creating Montessori bilingual programs. *Montessori Life, 10*(2), 22-25.

Flanagan, K. D., & McPhee, C. (2009). *The children born in 2001 at kindergarten entry: First findings From the kindergarten data collections of the early childhood longitudinal study, Birth cohort (ECLS-B).* (NCES 2010-005). Washington, DC: National Center for Education Statistics.

Hainstock, E. G. (1997). *The essential Montessori.* New York, NY: Plume.

Jackson, S. (1980). *Formative evaluation of a Montessori bilingual preschool program* (Unpublished doctoral dissertation). University of Texas at Austin.

Kagan, S. L. (2009). *American early childhood education: Preventing or perpetuating inequity?* Retrieved from http://www.tc.columbia.edu/i/a/document/13797_EquityMatters_Kagan_Final.pdf

Kagan, S. L. (1989). Normalizing preschool education: The illusive imperative. In E. Flaxman & A. H. Passow (Eds.), *Changing populations/changing schools: Ninety-fourth yearbook of the National Society for the Study of Education* (840-101). Chicago, IL: National Society for the Study of Education.

Kahn, D. (1995). *What is Montessori preschool?* Cleveland, OH: North American Montessori Teachers' Association.

Kramer, R. (1988). *Maria Montessori. A biography.* Chicago, IL: University of Chicago.

Krashen, S. (1985). *The input hypothesis: Issues and implications.* New York, NY: Longman.

Krashen, S. (1988). *Second language acquisition and second language learning.* Oxford, England: Pergamon Press.

Lillard, A. S. (2007). *Montessori: The science behind the genius.* New York, NY: Oxford University Press.

McLaughlin, B. (1978). *Second-language acquisition in childhood.* Hillside, NJ: Erlbaum.

McLaughlin, B. (1987). *Theories of second-language learning.* London, England: Edward Arnold.

Montessori, M. (1914). *Dr. Montessori's own handbook.* New York, NY: Shocken Books.

Montessori, M. (1949). *The absorbent mind.* Adyar, India: Vasanta Press.

Montessori, M. (1955). *Childhood education* (F. Dell'uomo, Trans.). Chicago, IL: Henry Regnery.

Montessori, M. (1961). *To educate the human potential.* Madras, India: Kalakshetra Publications.

Montessori, M. (1964). *The Montessori method.* New York, NY: Schocken Books.

Montessori, M. (1966). *The secret of childhood* (J. Costelloe, Trans.). Notre Dame, IN: Fides.

National Center for Education Statistics. (1999, August). *Enrollment: U.S. Department of Education, National Center for Education Statistics, preprimary enrollment, various years;* and *U.S. Department of Commence, Bureau of the Census, current population survey.* Unpublished data.

Renton, A. (1998). Cultivating the natural linguist. *Montessori Life, 10*(2), 31-33.

Rippa, S. A. (1997). *Education in a free society: An American history.* New York, NY: Longman.

Rosanova, M. (1998). Early childhood bilingualism in the Montessori children's house. *Montessori Life, 10*(2), 37-48.

Rosanova, M. (2000). Demand grows for bilingual programs: In U.S. and internationally, Montessorians are moving forward. *Public School Montessorian, 12*(2), 14-15.

Rodriguez, L., Irby, B. J., Brown, G., Lara-Alecio, R., & Galloway, M. (2003, April). *An analysis of a public school prekindergarten bilingual Montessori program.* Paper presented at the annual meeting of the American Educational Research Association, Chicago, IL. Retrieved from http://eric.ed.gov/ERICWebPortal/search/detailmini.jsp?_nfpb=true&_&ERICExtSearch_SearchValue_0=ED478568&ERICExtSearch_SearchType_0=no&accno=ED478568

Ruenzel, D. (1997). *The Montessori method.* Retrieved from http://www.edweek.org/tm/1997/07mont.h08

Saville-Troike, M. (1973). *Bilingual children: A resource document,* 2. Washington, DC: Center for Applied Linguistics.

Shapiro, D. (2007). *100 years of Montessori.* Retrieved from the Public School Montesorian website: http://www.jolamontessori.com.psm/75/articles/centenary75.html

Standing, E. M. (1957). *Maria Montessori. Her life and work.* New York, NY: Plume.

Ungerer, R. A. (2011). Treating each other with respect. *Montesorri Life, 23*(2), 3, 5.

Wheeler, K. (1998). *Bilingualism and bilinguality: An exploration of parental values and expectations in an american sponsored overseas school* (Unpublished doctoral dissertation). University of Minnesota.

Author Contact Information: Linda Rodriguez, EdD, Area Superintendent Aldine ISD, Researcher Center for Research and Doctoral Studies Sam Houston State University, Huntsville, TX. 1430 Bodart, Houston, TX. Telephone: 281-985-7308. E-mail: Rrodriguez4@aldine.k12.tx.us

CHAPTER 99

Differentiated Instruction

An Integration of Theory and Practice

Carol Ann Tomlinson
University of Virginia

Marcia B. Imbeau
University of Arkansas

Differentiated Instruction is a model stemming from theory, research, and classroom practice and designed to guide planning for teaching and learning. The three-part premise of the model is an ancient one: (a) people differ as learners, (b) those differences matter in learning, and (c) teachers are more effective when they seek to understand those differences and plan with them in mind.

The idea of differentiation, or addressing individual variance in teaching, is a very old one. Its underlying tenet is found in the writings of Confucius, in the texts of Judaism, and in the ancient writings of Islam. More recently, a form of what we have come to call "differentiated instruction" was accepted practice in many of the one-room schoolhouses commonly found in the United States, Canada, the United Kingdom, Australia, New Zealand, Spain, and Ireland in the late nineteenth and early twentieth centuries. They are still used in some developing nations and in remote areas in many countries.

The model of differentiation referenced in this chapter was developed as a classroom practice during the 1970s and 80s by Carol Tomlinson and some of her colleagues in the Fauquier County (Virginia) Public Schools. From its inception, the model has been informed both by research findings and by current and evolving theories in psychology, pedagogy, and, more recently, the emerging field of neuroscience. The evolution of the model will be discussed in greater detail later in the chapter.

The current model of differentiation is a synthesis model in that it draws and distills practices from a variety of educational specialties such as reading, special education, multicultural education, and gifted education, as well as from curriculum and instruction, psychology, and child development. It unifies insights and practices from multiple fields for coherent and ready access for practitioners.

DESCRIPTION OF THE MODEL

This model of differentiation envisions the classroom elements as a system of interdependent parts, with each element affected by and affecting the others. Those key elements are: learning environment, curriculum, assessment, instruction, and management of routines. While differentiated instruction is, at its core, an instructional approach, it addresses all of the classroom elements based on the proposition that attending to one of the elements without attention to all of them and to their interaction diminishes learning for most students. Figure 99.1 depicts the principle-driven model which reflects that proposition.

The model proposes that:

- Differentiating instruction is a process that evolves over time in teacher development. It is not a particular act or event. Rather, it is a way of thinking about teaching and learning.

The Handbook of Educational Theories, pp. 1097–1117

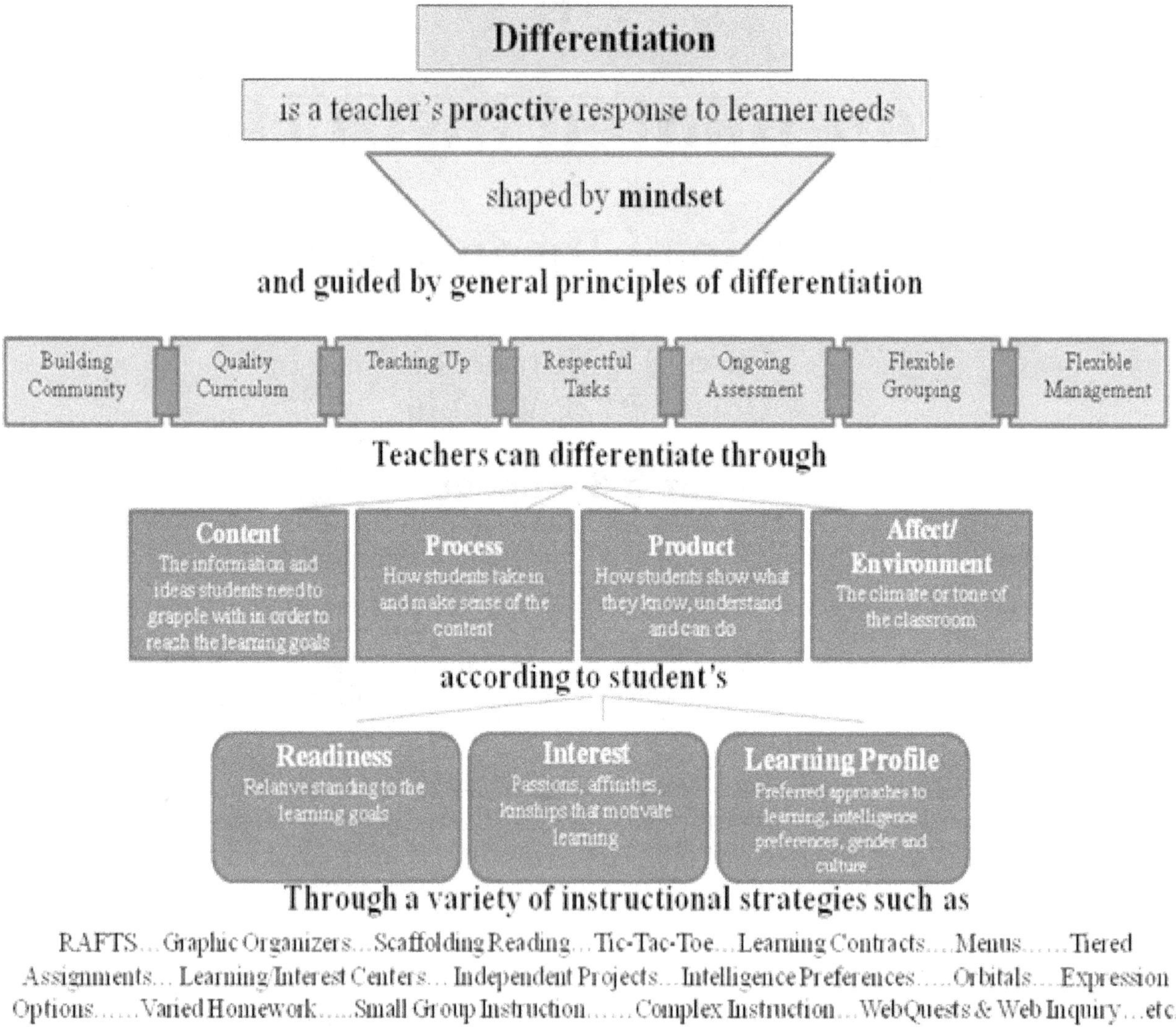

Figure 99.1. A flowchart of the elements of differentiated instruction.

- The process begins when a teacher reaches out in some way to address the needs of particular students which, at the time, appear somewhat different from the needs of others in the class.
- The teacher's capacity to attend to learner variance is shaped by the teacher's "mindset" (Dweck, 2000)—or beliefs about the malleability of human potential. A teacher's mindset impacts students' mindsets.
- The most effective differentiation is likely to be proactively planned rather than reactive or improvisational. Although improvisation plays a role in understanding and attending to learner needs, solely or largely improvisational differentiation is not powerful enough to address the learning needs of many students.
- Developing the classroom as a community of learners in which students support one another's growth makes the environment safe for students to risk learning and helps students achieve a sense of belonging or affiliation.
- The power of what a teacher differentiates (quality of curriculum) impacts the power of the differentiation (quality of instruction).
- Quality curriculum includes: (a) clarity about precisely what students must know, understand, and be able to do as the result of any segment of learning, (b) a plan to engage students, (c) and an emphasis on student understanding of content.
- Persistent use of preassessment and ongoing assessment that are tightly aligned with essential knowledge, understanding, and skill should inform teacher understanding about student learning needs, teacher planning to address those needs, and students' ability to address their own success.

- Student outcomes are most robust when teachers "teach up"—that is, when they plan tasks that require students to work at high levels and scaffold the success of students who are not yet able to function independently at those levels rather than "teaching down" or diluting goals and opportunities for those students.
- Teachers should design and all students should work with "respectful tasks"—that is tasks that are focused on essential understandings, require students to reason, and that look equally interesting and appealing to students.
- Classrooms that facilitate attention to student variance balance structure and flexibility. In such classrooms, students understand the reason for and contribute to the success of routines that provide predictability while allowing for variability.
- Teachers can modify content (what students learn or how they access what they learn), process (how students make sense of or come to "own" content), products (how students demonstrate what they have learned at summative points in a unit of study), affect/learning environment (the physical environment in the classroom as well as how students feel about or respond to learning and the classroom environment),
- There are many instructional strategies that facilitate attending to students' varied learning needs. No specific set of strategies is required for differentiation. Rather teachers should develop and draw from an extensive repertoire of strategies suited to the nature and needs of the students and content requirements of the subjects they teach.

Original Development and Iterations of the Model

"Differentiated instruction" was born of a practical need. During the early part of her 20-plus year teaching career, Tomlinson was hired in Warrenton, Virginia to develop and teach in a middle school language arts program. A typical class of 35-40 students included 10-15 students who read 4 to 6 years below grade level and 15-18 students who read 4-5 years above grade level. In most classes, students working at or near grade level numbered no more than five or six. It was immediately apparent that selecting a single "target" group of students as the focus of instructional planning was ineffective. With that approach it was not only impossible to move the diverse learners ahead academically, but also very difficult to maintain their engagement with course content. Tomlinson and colleagues, therefore, developed classroom routines that allowed students to work together on common tasks at some points, while working independently or working in small groups with either common or differentiated tasks at other times. Simultaneously, the teachers used formative assessment of student proficiency with specified learning goals to learn how to target instruction for varied learner needs.

From the outset of their work with this approach (which would only receive the name "differentiated instruction" some 2 years later), Tomlinson and her colleagues also emphasized high engagement curriculum that focused on student understanding and on developing a community of learners that functioned like a team in shared responsibility for supporting one another's academic growth and for establishing and executing flexible classroom processes and routines.

Also part of the original iteration of the model, of course, was the use of a broad range of instructional strategies that facilitated attention to a range of learning needs. Many of these were drawn from the field of reading, which Tomlinson studied at the masters and doctoral levels as she taught in public school. Use of flexible versus stable instructional groupings of students was also an important feature of the model in its early stages of development in order to help establish a cohesive community of learners rather than classes in which readiness or economic background became the predictor of student instructional or work groups and thus became divisive.

During the early years of implementing differentiation in the classroom, Tomlinson and her colleagues were awarded funds from the Virginia Department of Education to test and ultimately disseminate the principles and practices of their classes, called Communications Core, within and beyond their school district. A part of the grant called for measuring impacts of their approach on students. For 3 years, Communications Core students served as a treatment group and seventh graders in peer schools without Communications Core served as a control group in assessing student growth in reading comprehension, vocabulary, spelling, and attitude about English. In every instance, communications core students performed significantly better than students in the control group in every category measured.

Based on those findings, communications core ultimately provided both the curriculum and pedagogical approach for all seventh grade language arts classes in the school district for the next 2 decades. "differentiation" was also used in other middle school English classes in the district. During that time, Communications Core teachers met regularly to ensure a shared understanding of the curriculum and the instructional approach they shared. Throughout that time they refined and extended their practices and assessed its impacts on both student growth and their own work.

In the early 1990s, Tomlinson joined the faculty at the University of Virginia. It was not her intent to further develop or share the approach to teaching she and her colleagues had developed. In working with teachers in the field, however, she found two common themes. First, teachers saw a clear need to plan differently for different students—for example, students with reading problems, learning disabilities, advanced levels of performance, and so on. Second, they had difficulty envisioning how the class would function in terms of curriculum, instruction, and management if they attempted to address more than one set of student needs at a time. Hearing about a framework for academically responsive instruction appeared both interesting and helpful to the teachers with whom she often worked and it therefore seemed worthwhile to develop the framework further.

At the same time, she was engaged in research projects with university colleagues. In designing one of the early research projects, Tomlinson named the instructional approach she had used in the classroom and developed the first graphic depiction of the model. Over time, a number of these projects provided an opportunity for the research group to extend their understanding of differentiation as both a theory and a practice. Tomlinson's work in the field informed the direction of her research interests and her research findings informed her work with practitioners. In combination, these two venues contributed to an evolving conception of differentiation.

The following key publications reflect some key steps and stages in informing the model's iterations between 1990 and 2011.

- *Deciding to Differentiate Instruction in Middle School: One School's Journey* (Tomlinson, 1995) is a case study of the understanding and application of differentiation in a middle school in the Midwest. It is a first look at how educators understand and misunderstand the concept of differentiation, how teachers' beliefs impact their practice regarding students' learning differences, and the origin of the concept of proactive versus reactive differentiation.
- *How to Differentiate Instruction in Mixed Ability Classrooms* (1st ed.) (Tomlinson, 1995) delineates and defines the model of differentiation for practitioners for the first time.
- *The Differentiated Classroom: Responding to the Needs of All Learners* (Tomlinson, 1999) elaborated on the framework of differentiation and provides additional examples of differentiated instruction in K-12 classrooms with particular emphasis on teacher rationales for differentiating content, process, and product based on students' readiness levels, interests, and learning profiles.
- *Leadership for Schoolwide Differentiation* (Tomlinson & Allan, 2000) begins to explore the role of school leaders in developing teacher attitudes and practices that are more responsive to academically diverse student populations.
- *Fulfilling the Promise of the Differentiated Classroom* (Tomlinson, 2003) introduces the affective underpinnings of differentiation as well as providing extended examples of classroom differentiation.
- *Differentiation in Practice: A Resource Guide for Differentiating Curriculum* is a three-volume set for K-5 (Tomlinson & Eidson, 2003), 5-9 (2003), and 9-12 (Tomlinson & Strickland, 2005) that provides examples of fully developed, differentiated units of study in the core content areas of math, science, language arts, and history/social studies. Teachers who designed the units annotate their work with the thinking behind the units' design.
- *Integrating Differentiated Instruction and Understanding by Design: Connecting Content and Kids* (Tomlinson & McTighe, 2006) details important connections between curriculum quality and differentiation, delineating ways in which curriculum and instruction work in tandem to connect a wide range of students with meaningful content.
- *The Differentiated School: Making Revolutionary Changes in Teaching and Learning* (Tomlinson, Brimijoin, & Narvaez, 2008) documents the work of an elementary principal, a high school principal, and their faculties in moving to differentiation throughout the schools. The book synthesizes literature related to the nature of school leaders whose work results in extensive change as a means of analyzing the work of the two principals. It also includes student outcome data during the period of the study.
- *Leading and Managing a Differentiated Classroom* (Tomlinson & Imbeau, 2010) for the first time expands on the philosophy or rationale for differentiation. It also provides specific guidance for teachers who seek to work with their students in establishing classroom communities of learning built around that philosophy and in which teacher and students work together to support the academic growth of all students in the classroom.
- *Differentiation and the Brain: How Neuroscience Supports the Learner-Friendly Classroom* (Sousa & Tomlinson, 2011) examines how an emerging knowledge of the brain relates to the key principles of differentiated instruction and provides support beyond the fields of education and psychology for those principles.

The progression of writing on differentiation as an instructional model demonstrates an intent to present the model as a whole as well as exploring each of its key elements in greater detail. Writings also reflect an intent to update the model and its components based on emerging research on relevant aspects of learning and pedagogy.

Generalizability of the Theory

The model of differentiated instruction discussed in this chapter was developed to attend to student variance of any kind in a classroom, including variance related to gender, culture, ethnicity, and economic status. A primary aim of the model is to support equity of access to excellent instruction for the broadest possible range of learners. The model is heuristic or principle-driven rather than algorithmic or recipe-like. Its principles apply to varied cultures, economic groups, ethnicities, and genders while making room for differences that exist within groups as well.

The culture of a classroom may or may not align with the cultural, economic, or gender perspectives of a given learner. When there is a mismatch between what any student brings to class in terms of skills and expectations, it is likely that student achievement suffers. That is particularly problematic if the school or classroom is centered in the patterns of a dominant culture while some students in the classroom are more comfortable with the patterns and expectations of other cultures.

While differentiation cautions that generalizing *across* cultures or ethnicities in terms of instructional design and implementation is unwise, it does not generalize *within* a culture, gender, or economic group either. In other words, while it points to some differences in learning that can exist between males and females, for example, it cautions educators against assuming that all males will learn alike or that all females will approach learning in the same way. Likewise, it cautions against generalizing within ethnic, cultural, ethnic, and economic groups as well. Differentiation encourages and supports teachers in learning about students' backgrounds and learning preferences in order to provide a range of approaches to learning and to help students develop awareness of conditions that facilitate their learning.

In terms of culture, ethnicity, and economic status, experts in the area of multicultural education note particular concern for students from nondominant groups and students from any group that is judged by peers to be of low status. Figure 99.1 lists, according to classroom elements, some conditions that can impede achievement of students from nondominant groups and low status students (Cohen & Lotan, 2004; Knapp & Woolverton, 2004). Table 99.1 also notes principles and practices of differentiation that address those concerns.

Use and Application of the Theory

Differentiation is an instructional model intended for use in a broad range of classroom settings. It is currently used in classrooms from preschool through the university level, including general education, special education, gifted education, English language learning, and teacher education in the United States. However, when used with fidelity to the model, differentiation enables educators to drastically reduce the need for tracked and ability grouped classes by attending to learners' varied needs in heterogeneous settings. That the books on differentiation noted in the previous section are available in 13 languages suggests broad international use of the theories as well. However, it is not possible to determine with precision either the pervasiveness of the model's use or, more saliently, the degree of fidelity of its implementation.

Use of the principles of differentiation (generically, vs. a particular model of differentiation) is advocated by the National Association for the Education of Young Children, *Turning Points 2000* (a Carnegie Foundation document focusing on effective teaching in the middle grades), *This We Believe: Successful Schools for Young Adolescents*, a 2003 position paper of the National Middle School Association; *Breaking Ranks II* (a high school reform agenda produced by the National Association of Secondary School Principals in 2004); the core standards of the National Board for Professional Teaching Standards; and a 1997 document prepared by the American Psychological Association called *Learner-Centered Psychological Principles: A Framework For School Reform And Re-design.*

Critiques of the Theory

One criticism of the theory is that this model of differentiation is complex—in other words, that it asks teachers to attend to a variety of elements simultaneously. In fact, the model discussed here *is* a multifaceted model intended to help teachers grow in understanding of the interconnectedness of classroom environment, curriculum, assessment, instruction, and classroom management.

For many teachers, learning to differentiate instruction requires second order or pervasive change rather than first order or incremental change. Making such change requires time, intelligent support, leaders that understands the both the change initiative and the change process, leaders who are effective in guiding teachers to understand the importance of the change, and diligent use of formative assessment to inform the change process. *The Differentiated School: Making Revolutionary Changes in Teaching and Learning* documents the work of two schools in which leaders exemplified those attributes (Tomlinson, Brimijoin, & Narvaez, 2008). Failure to understand the complexity of second order change and failure of leaders to provide the degree of support necessary enact second order change often results in the downfall of the change (Marzano, Waters, & McNulty, 2005). The following study demonstrates negative impacts and outcomes of an ill-informed and ill-supported attempt to implement differentiation in a large school district.

Table 99.1. Experts' Concerns for Students From Nondominant Groups and Low Status Students From Any Group in Classrooms

Classroom Element	Concerns for Students From Nondominant Groups and Low Status Students	Principles and Practices From Differentiation That Address the Concerns
View of ability	In schools and classrooms, ability is often viewed from the perspective of the dominant culture. Students from other groups are then viewed as deficient if they display abilities other than those expected for success.	Differentiation emphasizes the dignity and worth of each student. It approaches ability from a growth mindset perspective, proposing that most students can learn most things if they work hard and are supported by teachers and peers in their work and notes the impact of mindset on teacher effectiveness and student outcomes.
Grouping students for instruction	Students are often tracked and labeled based on perceptions of their ability. This transmits negative messages about perceptions of and expectations for students in low tracks.	Differentiation strongly advocates maximum feasible heterogeneity and minimum student labeling. The raison d'etre of the model is to facilitate equity of access to high quality curriculum and instruction in heterogeneous settings.
Nature of the learning environment	In low track classes, the environment is often teacher-focused and controlling, displays few positive student-teacher connections, and isolates students from one another.	Differentiation supports teachers in developing environments in which each student experiences affirmation, affiliation, challenge, and support. Teachers make decisions based on knowledge of and concern for students as individually and as a group.
Quality of curriculum	Within and across classes, curriculum for students from nondominant groups and low status students tends to be low level, low relevance, and less preparatory for future options than for other students.	Two key principles of differentiation are teaching up (planning for advanced learners and differentiating to support access of all students to that level of challenge) and respectful tasks (ensuring that all student work is equally engaging, requires complex thought, and focuses on understanding).
Instructional arrangements	Students from nondominant groups and low status students often move around less in class, participate less, work with a narrow range of peers, and are cast in dependent roles in the classroom.	Instructional environments include movement in the classroom, student decision- making.
Management of the classroom	Management in low track classes is often rigid, authoritarian, and conveys to students a lack of adult trust in their ability to guide their own learning and behave responsibly.	Differentiation advocates classroom management in which teachers guide students to work as a community of learners and in partnership with the teacher to create and implement classroom routines and procedures that support learning success for each member of the community.

- Valli, L. and Buese, D. (2007). *The Changing Roles Of Teachers in an Era of High-stakes Accountability.*

This multiyear, mixed-method study of fourth and fifth grade reading and math teachers from a large urban school district found that the teachers' use of a differentiated instruction was overwhelming within the climate of pressure on teachers to ensure that students met AYP (adequately yearly progress) on mandated standardized tests while they were simultaneously asked to implement newly mandated reading and math curricula as well as differentiated instruction. The authors noted that learning to differentiate instruction while also adhering to what was teachers perceived to be district mandates for strict adherence to new curriculum caused the sample of teachers to use less cognitively complex instruction and to maintain or increase assignments that placed little cognitive demand on students. In addition, teachers' relationships with students were negatively impacted by the press to prepare the students for the end of grade test, resulting in tension for many teachers between caring for students and focusing on mandates. A result was debilitating stress for teachers, causing them to feel that they had too many expectations to address in too short a period of time. The authors concluded that there were so many changes thrust upon teachers in a brief time without ample support to achieve them that it was difficult for teachers to feel any ownership in the initiatives they were expected to accept. Additionally, teachers did not have ample time and support to achieve a level of skill with the initiatives to make implementation feasible.

In recent years, some experts in psychology, neuroscience, and sociology have been critical of both the concept and use of "learning styles" in classrooms, one element in the model of differentiation. While few, if any, experts assert that all students learn in the same ways, they are sharply critical of several aspects of teacher use of learning styles. Chief among criticisms are that: (1) the concept of learning style is poorly defined—with over 70 major learning styles models that frequently conflict in terms of the meaning of the concept, (2) most instruments used to determine students' learning styles lack reliability and validity, (3) much research that has been done on application learning styles in the classroom is weak and therefore fails to provide robust evidence of its effectiveness in supporting student learning, (4) suggesting that a student only learns in a specific way is unwarranted, and (5) labeling students by learning style is potentially limiting to individual students and may result in stereotyping of groups of students (Coffield, Moseley, Hall, & Ecclestone, 2004; Pashler, McDaniel, Rohrer, & Bjork, 2008).

Some key researchers and authors on this topic note that: (1) there is widespread face validity to the idea of learning preferences, (2) not all research supporting the concept has been found lacking, (3) there is a need for additional research to be conducted with sound methodology to explore the topic further, (5) there is some evidence to support a visual-auditory-kinesthetic model of learning, and (6) it is likely that it is beneficial for students to experience multimodal learning in order to improve retention of content and storage in long-term memory (Lisle, 2006; Pashler, McDaniel, Rohrer, & Bjork, 2008; Willis, 2006, 2007).

Based on current knowledge, it would appear that judicious application of "learning styles" in the classroom would exclude use of surveys to determine a student's learning style, categorizing students by learning style, and assignment of students to tasks based on their perceived learning style. Appropriate attention to students' varied approaches to learning would likely include teachers presenting information in a variety of ways, offering students options for taking in, exploring, and demonstrating key content, planning for multimodal student learning, and helping students become more self-aware in determining which approaches to learning work for them in specific contexts and understanding how to adjust their approach to learning when the approach does not seem to be facilitating their learning.

Studies Using the Theory as a Framework

Among studies using the model of differentiation discussed in this chapter as a theoretical framework are the following dissertations and a provincial-level study from Canada.

- Doubet, K. (2007). *Teacher Fidelity and Student Response to a Model of Differentiation as implemented in One High School.*

(This qualitative study investigated how faculty in one high school implemented differentiated instruction as a result of a school wide detracking and differentiation initiative, as well as examining the degree of fidelity with which teachers used the model. The study also examined how students in the high school responded to differentiated instruction as enacted by their teachers. Qualitative research methods of observation, interview, and document analysis were used to investigate (1) how teachers of various grades and subjects (n = 29) thought about and implemented differentiation; (2) how teachers (n = 29) and administrators (n = 7) perceived that students responded to differentiation; and (3) how high school students of all grade levels (n = 80) thought about and responded to differentiated instruction. Study findings included evidence of the interdependence of the elements in the model of differentiation and emphasized the importance of effective use of all the model's elements for maximum benefit. Formative assessment emerged as centrally important in the model, driving all other elements.

- Hockett, J. (2010). *The Influence of Lesson Study on How Teachers Plan for, Implement, and Understand Differentiated Instruction.*

A qualitative study using grounded theory methodology, this dissertation examined the influence of Lesson Study on one group of fourth grade math teachers understanding of, planning for, and implementation of differentiation in four elementary classrooms. Findings indicated that Lesson Study enhanced the flexibility of teachers' planning and instructional frameworks, use of new instructional strategies, and proactive management of differentiation in their classrooms. The teachers' conceptions of differentiation also grew more sophisticated over the course of the Lesson Study cycle. Among factors that appeared to influence teacher growth were the lesson study team's willingness to engage in conflict throughout the process, the nature of the interaction of the Lesson Study team's cofacilitators with the group, and pre- and post-Lesson Study cycle observations and interviews.)

- Maeng, J. (2011). *Differentiating Science Instruction: Success Stories of High School Science Teachers.*

Using intensive observation and teacher interviews, this qualitative case study researched the experiences of seven high school science teachers who sought to differentiate instruction in their classrooms. Each classroom observation was scored using a validated differentiated instruction implementation matrix-modified [DIIM-M]. One teacher was selected for more in-depth study based on the results from the DIIM-M. Results indicated that all teachers could use some low-prep differentiation learning profile strategies with the in-depth case study participant using more complex strategies for learning profile and fewer strategies for student readiness and interest.

- Quarrie, L. M., and McRae, P. (2010). *A Provincial Perspective on Differentiated Instruction: The Alberta Initiative for School Improvement (AISI).*

This article reviews site-based research project reports determined by Alberta Education's School Improvement Branch (SIB) to have had "significant impacts on student learning" (p. 4) based on calculated effect sizes. This article was based on data obtained from 25 schools and/or districts in Alberta, Canada that demonstrated positive impact on student learning and sought to address challenges posed by increasing learner diversity in the classroom utilizing DI practices. The schools had worked for a 3-year period with over 70,000 students representing various school settings and all school divisions in the province. Over 60% of the projects involved implementation of differentiated instruction in inclusive classrooms, while the remaining projects focused on differentiation for specific groups of learners (e.g., special education students, English language learners, etc.). The two major findings from this review are that (1) effective pedagogies and learning supports and (2) effective project supports accounted for the positive results. Using assessment data to monitor student progress, determine student interests and learning preferences, and to have students self-evaluate the degree to which personal learning goals had been reached was noted at a factor in positive outcomes. Use of technology to aid in the instruction and monitoring of student learning and small group instruction targeted to learners who were more at risk were additional examples of effective pedagogies. Support from district leaders (both formal and informal) was noted as an important component in both beginning and continuing the differentiation initiative.

- Rasmussen, F. (2006). *Differentiated instruction as a means for improving achievement as measured by the American College Testing (ACT).*

A dissertation submitted to the School of Education, Loyola University of Chicago, Chicago, IL. (This quantitative study examined the frequency of use of differentiation by teachers in a Chicago high school and the ACT achievement scores of 226 high school students in the classes of those teachers. Students receiving more instruction from a differentiated instructional methodology outperformed students receiving less instruction from a differentiated methodology on ACT English, ACT Mathematics, ACT Reading, and ACT Composite by as much as .48 sigma.)

Instruments Associated With the Theory

Following are two instruments useful in understanding effective differentiated instruction. The first is a tool designed to help school leaders and instructional coaches sharpen their own understanding of differentiation as well as for use in guiding teachers to set goals for their own growth in addressing varied student needs in academically diverse classrooms. The second is an observation matrix created to assist with systematic classroom observation for a research study on teacher use of differentiation in secondary science classrooms (Maeng, 2011).

References

American Psychological Association. (1997). *Learner-centered psychological principles: A framework for school reform and redesign.* Washington, DC: The Learner-Centered Principles Workgroup of the American Psychological Association. Retrieved from http://www.apa.org/ed/governance/bea/learner-centered.pdf

This document provides 14 principles designed to guide educators in developing student-centered learning contexts that take into account the diversity of students in classrooms and in ways that promote learning. Among descriptors of the principles are: assisting students in becoming self-directed, developing learning goals that are engaging and motivating to learners, guiding students to construct their own understanding, creating a nurturing environment, and use of instructional approaches that account for students varied abilities and entry points. These descriptors align directly with the principles of differentiation.

Coffield, F., Moseley, D., Hall, E., & Ecclestone, K. (2004). *Should we be using learning styles; What research has to say to practice.* London: The Learning and Skills Research Centre.

These authors reviewed literature on learning styles to determine what was credible regarding use in classrooms. After closer examination of 13 models, the authors concluded that research on these models failed to support their use to benefit student achievement. They caution that too much is still unknown about learning styles to support use in classrooms.

Cohen, E., & Lotan, R. (2004). Equity in heterogeneous classes. In J. Banks & C. Banks (Eds.), *Handbook of research on multicultural education* (2nd ed., pp. 736-752). San Francisco, CA: Jossey-Bass.

The authors detail several factors that work together to assist all learners in heterogeneous classrooms in becoming academically successful, while also attending to needs of low status students. Research on cooperative learning tasks often carried out in small intercultural groups was found to have a positive impact on student learning and to produce "equal-status interactions" among group members.

Doubet, K. (2007). *Teacher fidelity and student response to a model of differentiation as implemented in one high school* (Unpublished doctoral dissertation). University of Virginia, Charlottesville, VA.

See text in this chapter for annotation.

Dweck, C. (2000). *Self-theories: Their role in motivation, personality, and development.* Philadelphia, PA: Psychology Press.

Dweck describes the difference between fixed and growth mindset approaches to achievement and success. She emphasizes that extraordinary accomplishments come from individuals dedicated to working hard to develop their abilities rather than relying on "being smart."

Hockett, J. (2010). *The influence of lesson study on how teachers plan for, implement, and understand differentiated instruction* (Unpublished doctoral dissertation). University of Virginia, Charlottesville, VA

See text in this chapter for annotation.

Jackson, A., & Davis, G. (2000). *Turning Points 2000: Educating adolescents in the 21st century, A report of the Carnegie Corporation.* New York, NY: Teachers College Press.

This report is a follow-up to *Turning Points: Preparing American youth for the 21st Century* which made broad recommendations for reforming education for young adolescents. Turning Points 2000 seeks to document what works to benefit learning for young adolescents and to present both guidance and a vision for high-achieving schools that are equitable and developmentally appropriate.

Knapp, M., & Woolverton, S. (2004). Social class and schooling. In J. Banks & C. Banks (Eds.), *Handbook of research on multicultural education* (2nd ed., pp. 656-681). San Francisco, CA: Jossey-Bass.

The authors argue that the relationship of social class and schooling is complex and far-reaching and continues to impact the expectations and outcomes for many students throughout their school years. The chapter explores the influence of community, student population, teachers, peers, and instruction on the school experience.

Lisle, A. M. (2006). *Cognitive neuroscience in education: Mapping neuro-cognitive processes and structures to learning styles, can it be done?* Retrieved from http://www.leeds.ac.uk/educol/documents/157290.htm

This paper presented to the British Educational Research Association examines feasibility of learning styles theory based on brain activity observed with imaging equipment. Some evidence suggests that using multimodal instruction and visual-auditory-kinesthetic approaches may benefit learning but the author cautioned educators that limiting students to learning in a "preferred" approach can be detrimental.

Marzano, R., Waters, T., & McNulty, B. (2005). *School leadership that works: From research to results.* Alexandria, VA: ASCD.

The authors share the results of a meta-analysis of 69 studies to determine the correlation of leadership behavior of building principals and overall student achievement in those building and offer practical suggestions regarding 21 leader responsibilities.

Maeng, J. (2011). *Differentiating science instruction: Success stories of high school science teachers* (Unpublished doctoral dissertation). University of Virginia, Charlottesville, VA.

See text in this chapter for annotation.

National Association of Secondary School Principals. (2004). *Breaking ranks II: Strategies for leading high school reform.* Reston, VA: Author.

This reform document advocates seven strategies as key to improving the performance of each student in high school. Among the strategies forging teacher-student connections, personalized planning for students' high school experiences, teaching that responds to student differences, and flexible use of instructional time. These strategies align directly with the core principles of differentiation.

National Board of Professional Teaching Standards. (n.d.). *The five core propositions.* Retrieved from http://www.nbpts.org/the_standards/the_five_core_propositions

The five core standards of NBPTS frame the knowledge, skills, beliefs, and dispositions of excellent teaching. The 5 standards include the belief that every student can succeed, equitable treatment of all students, teaching with individual learning differences in mind, attending to students cultural backgrounds, use of a wide range of instructional strategies, and use of varied formative assessments to guide instructional planning. These elements align directly with the principles of differentiation.

National Middle School Association. (2003). *This we believe: Successful schools for young adolescents.* Westerville, OH: Author.

One of a sequence of position papers published by NMSA, this document briefly describes both school cultures and classrooms that are successful for young adolescents. In the latter category, the paper calls for curriculum that is relevant, integrative challenging and exploratory, multiple approaches to teaching and learning that respond to the diversity of middle grade students, and assessment and evaluation that promote learning. These areas of focus align directly with the core principles of differentiation.

Quarrie, L. M., & McRae, P. (2010). A provincial perspective on differentiated instruction: The Alberta Initiative for School Improvement (AISI). *Journal of Applied Research on Learning, 3*(4), 1-18.

See text in this chapter for annotation.

Pashler, H., McDaniel, M., Rohrer, D., & Bjork R. (2008). Learning styles: Concepts and evidence. *Psychological Science in the Public Interest, 9(3)*, 106-119.

The authors reviewed research on teaching to students' preferred learning styles and found little substantial evidence to support the approach. They note that few studies used sound research methodology and advise that while learning preferences may exist, use of instruments to determine a student's preference followed by teaching to that preference lacks research support.

Rasmussen, F. (2006). *Differentiated instruction as a means for improving achievement as measured by the American College Testing* (Unpublished doctoral dissertation). Loyola University of Chicago, Chicago, IL.

See text in this chapter for annotation.

Sousa, D., & Tomlinson, C. (2011). *Differentiation and the brain: How neuroscience supports the learner-friendly classroom.* Indianapolis, IN: Solution Tree.

Sousa and Tomlinson describe links between current brain research and key principles of differentiated instruction. Specifically, it explores neuroscience/differentiation connections related to teacher mindset, curriculum, assessment, instruction and classroom management in addressing the various learning needs of students in typical school settings.

Tomlinson, C. (1995). Deciding to differentiate instruction in middle school: One school's journey. *Gifted Child Quarterly, 39*(2), 77-87.

This case study documents one school's early implemented a district's mandate for differentiating instruction, detailing factors that enhanced and hindered their progress.

Tomlinson, C. (1995). *How to differentiate instruction in mixed ability classrooms* (1st ed.). Alexandria, VA: ASCD.

This brief book outlines what differentiated instruction is and is not, and provides a rationale for supporting the learning needs of academically diverse student groups. Practical suggestions are offered for teachers to address student readiness, interest and learning profile through attending to the curricular elements of content, process, and product.

Tomlinson, C. (1999). *The differentiated classroom: Responding to the needs of all learners*. Alexandria, VA: ASCD.

This volume extends the rationale for differentiation by relating the teaching practice to current views of intelligence, brain research and motivation. Several sample lessons are offered illustrating *what* was differentiated, *how* it was differentiated and *why* to assist teachers who are new to differentiation understand its logic.

Tomlinson, C. (2003). *Fulfilling the promise of the differentiated classroom*. Alexandria, VA: ASCD.

Tomlinson presents differentiation as a system of interdependent parts or "cogs" that work together to support success for a range of learners. The three "cogs" are student needs, teacher response to those needs, and curriculum as a vehicle to assist teachers in addressing student needs. The text also contains a teacher toolkit containing several examples of differentiated lessons.

Tomlinson, C., & Allan, S. (2000). *Leadership for differentiating schools and classrooms*. Alexandria, VA: ASCD.

This text provides guideline for school leaders working for successful implementation of differentiation within a school or district. The authors caution that leaders need to understand the complexity of change in schools as they plan for differentiation. The book also presents several areas in which teachers often need support along with several implementation tools to guide school leaders in their work with differentiation.

Tomlinson, C., Brimijoin, K., & Narvaez, L. (2008). *The differentiated school: Making revolutionary changes in teaching and learning*. Alexandria, VA: ASCD.

The authors detail the work of an elementary school and a high school moving to school wide differentiation, discussing the obstacles and successes they encountered. The book discusses the attributes of leaders who guided the successful work in the two schools.

Tomlinson, C., & Eidson, C. (Eds.). (2003). *Differentiation in practice: A resource guide for differentiating curriculum, K-5*. Alexandria, VA: ASCD.

This edited volume contains 6 differentiated units of study including a language arts unit concerning the alphabet for young learners and the core content areas. A two column format allows the reader to see both the details of the lessons and the teachers' thinking in designing and implementing the units.

Tomlinson, C., & Eidson, C. (Eds.). (2003). *Differentiation in practice: A resource guide for differentiating curriculum, 5-9*. Alexandria, VA: ASCD.

This edited volume contains 6 differentiated units of study in math, science, social studies, math, and language. A two column format allows the reader to see both the details of the lessons and the teachers' thinking in designing and implementing the units.

Tomlinson, C., & Imbeau, M. B. (2010). *Leading and managing a differentiated classroom*. Alexandria, VA: ASCD.

The authors propose that leading and managing effectively differentiated classrooms first requires teachers to examine their beliefs about human learning and their impact on that learning. Part I of the book deals with elements necessary to lead a differentiated classroom. Part II discusses how to manage details such as assigning students to groups, handling noise, and designing thoughtful anchoring activities. A toolkit provides classroom examples.

Tomlinson, C., & McTighe, J. (2006). *Integrating differentiated instruction and understanding by design: Connecting content and kids*. Alexandria, VA: ASCD.

Tomlinson and McTighe describe intersections between understanding by design, a curriculum model, and differentiated instruction, an instructional model. The authors discuss how to addressing diverse learner needs while teaching essential content for understanding.

Tomlinson, C., & Strickland, C. (Ed.). (2005). *Differentiation in practice: A resource guide for differentiating curriculum, 9-12*. Alexandria, VA: ASCD.

This edited volume contains nine differentiated units of study from math, history, literature, earth science, art and world languages for use with high school students, focusing on key principles of the disciplines. It also highlights teachers' thinking about unit design and differentiation.

Valli, L., & Buese, D. (2007). The changing roles of teachers in an era of high-stakes accountability. *American Educational Research Journal, 44*(3), 519-558.

See text of this chapter for annotation.

Willis, J. (2006). *Research-based strategies to ignite student learning: Insights from a neurologist and classroom teacher.* Alexandria, VA: ASCD.

Based on background as a neurologist and classroom teacher, Willis offers educators practical instructional strategies that support student learning and shares, in lay terms, brain function behind the suggestions.

Willis, J. (2007). *Brain-friendly strategies for the inclusion classroom*. Alexandria, VA: ASCD.

Willis offers educators several teaching strategies backed by brain-research to promote academic success for students with learning challenges. She provides specific recommendations for addressing students' diverse learning styles, teaching for meaning and understanding, using various grouping arrangements, and creating learning environments conducive to student achievement.

Author Contact Information: Carol Ann Tomlinson, EdD, Curry School of Education, University of Virginia, Charlottesville, VA512-A Worthington Drive, Charlottesville, VA 22903. Phone: 434-242-7551

Look-Fors in an Effectively Differentiated Classroom

Developed by Carol Ann Tomlinson & Jessica Hockett

Background

This tool is designed to help school coaches and leaders better understand how differentiation might look when it is effectively implemented in classrooms. It is also designed to help teachers reflect on their own practice and set goals for continuing growth as they work to meet the needs of varied learners in their classrooms.

No teacher should be expected to display all of these attributes at a given time. Rather these are elements toward which strong teachers persistently work and many of which strong teachers regularly demonstrate in their teaching. Guiding questions in this document are useful in conversations with teachers as catalysts for their thinking about their work with differentiation.

Differentiated instruction is a proactively planned, **interdependent system** marked by a positive community of learners; focused, high-quality curriculum; frequent formative assessment; flexible instructional arrangements; and respectful tasks.

- Student needs are the motivation for differentiated instruction.
- Building a sense community among students and the teacher in a positive learning environment is the foundation for differentiated instruction.
- Focused, high-quality provides the compass for differentiated instruction. (High-quality differentiation is necessary for high-quality differentiation.)
- Frequent formative assessment is the primary tool for gathering information about how and why to differentiate instruction.
- Well-managed, flexible grouping provides a mechanism for differentiated instruction.
- A variety of low-prep and high-prep strategies can be used to design and deliver respectful tasks that adjust content, process, and products for students' readiness, interests, and learning profiles.

Categories, Look-Fors, Rubrics, and Guiding Questions

Look for 1: Classroom Environment

Category: The teacher builds a foundation for differentiated instructed on a solid classroom community and a positive learning environment.

Indicators:

- The physical and affective characteristics of the classroom set a positive tone for learning.
- The teacher fosters respect for individual differences and preferences.
- The teacher and students share ownership of and responsibility for the classroom.

Evidence:

- The teacher communicates explicitly and implicitly to students that they are multi-faceted individuals whose needs, preferences, and strengths are dynamic.
- The teacher communicates implicitly and explicitly to students that they and their contributions are valuable and necessary in order for the classroom to function well.
- The teacher helps students get to know one another well.
- The teacher encourages creativity of thought and expression.
- The teacher structures activities so that students see one another in varied contexts and in varied roles.
- The teacher assists students in setting their own personal and class goals for learning and behavior.
- The teacher solicits student input in making decisions that will affect the whole class.
- The teacher frequently asks students for feedback on how the class is working for them, and for suggestions about how they and the teacher could work together toward improvement.
- The teacher designs and assigns roles for students to assume in making the routines and systems flow smoothly.

RUBRIC:

	Classroom Environment
Advanced 4	a. The affective and physical attributes of the classroom environment inspire students to achieve their personal best and to take initiative in learning. b. The teacher empowers students to view their and each other's differences as assets to the classroom community such that students view one another as equals. c. The teacher and students are equal partners in sharing responsibility for the classroom.
Proficient 3	a. The affective and physical attributes of the classroom environment equip students to succeed in achieving the teacher's high expectations. b. The teacher honors student differences, nurtures student strengths and preferences, and provides opportunities for students to compensate for their weaknesses. c. The teacher shares his/her roles and responsibilities with students, allowing them to control many aspects of classroom routines
Basic 2	a. The affective and physical attributes of the classroom environment convey ambiguous messages about how the teacher views the student's role in the learning process. b. The teacher recognizes student differences, but does not build on them to foster a positive classroom environment. c. The teacher allows students to share some of his/her roles and responsibilities.

	Classroom Community—Questions for Reflection
Advanced 4	Compare the way your current classroom looks and feels with how it looked and felt in your first year of teaching. How do you encourage students to apply and transfer what they learn in your classroom about student differences to the real world? What would it look like to allow students to have even more control over the classroom?
Proficient 3	How do student differences impact your decisions about the physical aspects of your classroom (e.g., how the room is set-up, the messages students see on the walls)? How do you capitalize on the strengths and maturity level of this age group to help daily routines run more smoothly?
Basic 2	How do you help students see one another as equally valuable to the classroom community? In what ways do you communicate to students that this is their classroom? How do you decide which classroom roles responsibilities to give to students, and which to keep in your control?
Below Basic 1	What are some ways that students in your class differ from one another, and from you? What are some concrete ways you communicate to them that those differences are assets to the classroom community? What are the most flexible aspects of your physical classroom space?

LOOK FOR 2: CURRICULUM

CATEGORY: THE TEACHER USES HIGH-QUALITY, COHERENT CURRICULUM AS A COMPASS FOR DIFFERENTIATED INSTRUCTION.

INDICATORS:

- The teacher plans curriculum so that important conceptual ideas are at the forefront of a unit of study. Essential facts and skills are used to help students make sense of these ideas.
- The teacher uses the curriculum as a point of engagement, of motivation, and of access to powerful ideas.
- The teacher ensures that the curriculum is an authentic reflection of the discipline being studied.

EVIDENCE:

- Tasks give all students access to the same clear, high-quality lesson/unit goals.

- Tasks require students to mimic or approximate the skills, thinking, habits, dispositions, or work of real-world professionals (e.g., mathematicians, biologists, writers).
- Tasks require all students to use higher-level thinking skills (e.g., analyzing, judging, defending).
- Tasks are equally appealing and engaging from the students' perspective.
- The teacher scaffolds tasks using a variety of techniques.

RUBRIC:

	Respectful Tasks
Advanced 4	a. The teacher plans tasks that are focused on the same learning goals and mimic the work of an expert/professional in the discipline. b. The teacher articulates a continuum of criteria based on student readiness and provides multiple scaffolds to ensure successful, high-quality completion of the tasks by the full range of students. c. Side-by-side, the tasks are equally challenging and intriguing.
Proficient 3	a. The teacher plans tasks that are focused on similar learning goals and suggest the work of an expert/professional in the discipline. b. The teacher articulates clear criteria and provides scaffolding to ensure successful, high-quality completion of the tasks. c. Side-by-side, the tasks are comparatively challenging and intriguing.
Basic 2	a. The teacher plans tasks that are not aligned to the same learning goals and are loosely tied to the work of an expert/professional in the discipline. b. The teacher's criteria for successful completion are confusing or incomplete. The teacher provides some scaffolding, if students compel a need for it. c. Side-by-side, one task may be more/less challenging and intriguing than another.
Below Basic 1	a. The teacher plans tasks without considering what all students should know, understand, and be able to do, or how an expert/professional in the discipline works. Tasks may be tangential to unit content. b. The teacher does not articulate criteria for quality or provide scaffolding for success. c. Tasks bore or frustrate students.

	Respectful Tasks—Questions for Reflection
Advanced 4	What steps do you take in planning differentiated tasks to make sure each student is optimally challenged? How do you involve students in the process of determining task criteria? How do you decide what supports students might need?
Proficient 3	What are the similarities between what the students are doing and what practicing professionals in the discipline (e.g., writers) do? If you have two or more versions of a task, which version do you design first? Why? How do you adjust the tasks for readiness, interest, or learning profile?
Basic 2	Describe your process for planning a task or lesson that is differentiated for student readiness. How do ensure all students produce work that is high-quality and meets your expectations? When you give a choice between differentiated tasks, how do you prevent your students from choosing an "easy" option?
Below Basic 1	What do you want all students to know, understand, and be able to do upon completing these tasks? How do you decide what makes a worthwhile task? How might students' differences in readiness, interest, and learning profile affect their capacity to complete a task successfully?

DIFFERENTIATED INSTRUCTION IMPLEMENTATION MATRIX-MODIFIED

Developed by and used with permission of Jennifer Maeng (2011)

Criteria	Novice (1)	Apprentice (2)	Practitioner (3)	Expert (4)
1. Quality and clarity of the lesson objectives: What students should know, understand, and be able to do.	Objectives are not clearly articulated for the lesson.	Lesson objectives might be informed by national or state standards, but do not include big ideas meaningful to the content area.	Lesson objectives include big ideas, issues, or problems specific and meaningful to the content area. Objectives are informed by national or state standards.	Lesson objectives are informed by national or state standards and the important ideas, issues, or problems specific and meaningful to the content area. Objectives extend learning in authentic ways.
2. Alignment of lesson objectives and lesson activities	The activities are mildly related to the objectives, It is not likely that students will master the objectives.	The activities of the lesson are unevenly related to the objectives. It is likely that only some students will master the objectives after successful completion of the activities.	The activities of the lesson are clearly related to the objectives. Most students are likely to master the objectives after successful completion of the activities.	The activities of the lesson are clearly and strongly related to the objectives. All students will master the objectives after successful completion of the activities.
3.Communication of learning goals and outcomes to students	Lesson objectives and desired outcomes are not communicated to the students.	Lesson objectives and desired outcomes are listed for students but not referred to during the lesson or connected to lesson components.	Lesson objectives and desired outcomes are clearly articulated to students, but the connection between the objectives, desired outcomes, and the lesson components is not evident to students.	Lesson objectives and desired outcomes are clearly articulated to students, and it is clear to students how the lesson components are related to these goals.

Domain 2: Planning and Response to Learner Needs

Criteria	Novice (1)	Apprentice (2)	Practitioner (3)	Expert (4)
1. Preassessment and Proactive Preparation	The lesson demonstrates very little consideration of student needs.	The lesson demonstrates that the teacher considered various student needs when planning the lesson.	The lesson demonstrates that the teacher used preassessment data in advance of the lesson to plan for the needs of the students.	The lesson demonstrates that the teacher used multiple sources of preassessment data and student learning profiles in advance of the lesson to plan for the needs of the students.

2. Scaffolding for Struggling Learners; Spec. Ed., ELL, reading, etc.	Struggling learners are given irrelevant tasks of poor quality that do not require higher order thinking. Struggling learners may be grouped together most of the time.	Struggling learners are given tasks of moderate quality or better quality tasks with little or no scaffolding and may not reach the lesson's learning goals, especially the big ideas and understandings of the lesson. Struggling students may be grouped together a lot of the time.	Struggling learners are given tasks of good quality and thoughtfulness with appropriate scaffolding and are expected to approximate the lesson's learning goals. Struggling learners experience may experience variety of grouping strategies.	Struggling learners are given tasks of high-quality and thoughtfulness with appropriate scaffolding to reach the same learning goals as other students. Multiple indicators are used when grouping students so that struggling learners experience a variety of grouping strategies.
3. Challenging Advanced Students	Academically advanced students are assigned more or irrelevant work. They are used to tutor less advanced students.	Advanced students may be challenged with probing questions and challenging tasks, but are sometimes assigned more work. They may be used to tutor less advanced students.	Academically advanced students are appropriately challenged at higher levels of quality, not quantity. Occasionally, they are used to academically anchor a flexible group.	Academically advanced students are appropriately challenged at higher levels of complexity and quality, not quantity. Experiences as an academic anchor in a flexible group enhance their understanding. Options are available for compacting into independent study on the topic.

Domain 3: Instructional Practices

Criteria	Novice (1)	Apprentice (2)	Practitioner (3)	Expert (4)
1. Lesson Organization	The lesson is unfocused and/or disorganized. The activities do not follow a logical progression.	The lesson has an identifiable structure, although the logic of that structure may be unclear. Progression of the activities is uneven.	The lesson is organized in a sensible manner, progressing in a fairly even manner.	The lesson is organized in a coherent (organized, unified, and sensible) manner, producing a unified whole.
2. Modes of Instruction	The lesson uses a single mode of instruction that may meet the needs of some students in the class.	The lesson uses multiple modes of instruction on a limited basis, some of which may encourage active learning with the intention of providing variety for the students.	The lesson uses multiple modes of instruction that encourage active learning and match the perceived learning profiles of the students.	The lesson uses multiple modes of instruction that require active learning and the exploration of the lesson's understandings and intentionally matches the learning profiles of the students.

(Domain 3 continues on next page)

Domain 3: Instructional Practices Continued

Criteria	Novice (1)	Apprentice (2)	Practitioner (3)	Expert (4)
3. Instructional Strategies and Best Practice	The lesson may focus on one or more strategies or activities which are not based on best practices in that content area.	Some of the strategies and activities used in the lesson reflect best practices in that content area.	The strategies and activities are used during instruction to meet the learning needs of the students and to promote higher order thinking. Most strategies and activities reflect best practices in that content area.	The strategies and activities are used flexibly during instruction to meet the learning needs of the students and to promote higher order thinking for all students. The strategies and activities reflect best practices in that content area.
4. Engagement Capacity of Activities	Lesson components are not engaging and do not connect to the students lives.	Lesson components are somewhat interesting to learners, but do not necessarily connect with students prior learning, experiences, and/or goals.	Lesson components are engaging to learners and may be linked to students prior learning or experience, and may connect with their lives and/or goals. The teacher helps students make connections between lesson content, practical applications, current events, the real world, or other aspects of the content area.	Lesson components are stimulating, motivating, and engaging to learners, linked to students' prior learning or experiences, and clearly connect to their lives and/or goals. Students explicate connections between lesson content, practical applications, current events, the real world, or other aspects of the content area.
5. Intellectual Development[1]	Activities are designed with little regard to student readiness, interest, and/or learning profile. Few students are likely to learn as a result of the activities. The lesson design does not provide work that is challenging for most of the students.	Students with a particular readiness, interest, and/or learning profile will likely learn, but other students will find it difficult or impossible to learn. The lesson design is inconsistent in its ability to challenge students at the highest level of which they are capable.	Students with varied readiness, interest, and/or learning profiles have an opportunity to learn at some point during the lesson. A few students are able to find loopholes in the lesson design which permits them to avoid completing their highest quality work.	Each student works at levels of readiness, interest, and/or learning profile that are appropriately challenging. The lesson is designed so that all students are compelled to do their best and complete high-quality work.

1. Levels of performance are paraphrased from Strickland, C. (2006). *Differentiated lesson observation rubric.* Unpublished manuscript.

Domain 4: Classroom Routines

Criteria	Novice (1)	Apprentice (2)	Practitioner (3)	Expert (4)
1. Flexible Grouping * Grouping practices may not be observed in every lesson. If it is not observed, it should be rated N/O not novice.	Lesson may use a grouping strategy, but groups are not differentiated in any intentional way. Student groupings, which may have been created using some student data, are not flexible, but remain static over time.	Lesson uses at least one grouping strategy that differentiates content, process, or product by readiness, interest, or learning profile. Flexibility is to accommodate variety in the lesson as opposed to matching student needs to the lesson's learning goals.	Lesson uses at least one grouping strategy that differentiates content, process, or product by readiness, interest, or learning profile. Flexibility in grouping strategies is a planned response to student needs.	Lesson uses various student groupings: individual, pairs, small groups. Students are grouped for a great variety of reasons to differentiate content, process, and/or product by readiness, interest, and/or learning profile. The lesson may combine grouping rationales (i.e. readiness and interest). Flexibility in grouping strategies is in response to a clear analysis of student needs.
2. Flexible Use of Space, Time, and Materials *Student movement should take into consideration the physical space in which the observation is occurring. In some classrooms, it may be unfeasible for great mobility in the classroom due to space constraints. This warrants a N/O, not a "novice" rating.	Students all use the same materials, resources, or technologies as designated by the teacher. Students rarely move out of their seats and where applicable, have no flexibility in product completion.	Students have some access, as permitted by the teacher, to a variety of materials, resources. Teacher has an effective strategy for distribution of materials. Students have limited flexibility to move out of their seats and where applicable, have limited flexibility in timelines for product completion.	Students have access to a variety of materials, resources, and technologies. Students are given some flexibility to move about the room and where applicable, have some flexibility in timelines for product completion.	Students have access to and are encouraged to use a variety of materials, resources, and technologies. Students move about the room as needed and where applicable, are given flexibility in the timeframes for product completion.
3. Clear Directions for Multiple Tasks[2]	Directions and procedures are confusing to students to the point of challenging classroom management.	Directions and procedures are mildly confusing and require clarification and/or are excessively detailed.	Directions and procedures for each activity are clear to students with appropriate levels of detail. Written directions for various groups are clear.	Directions and procedures for each activity are clear to students. Anticipated student misunderstandings are planned and accounted for. Written directions for various groups are crystal clear to limit confusion.

(Domain 4 continues on next page)

Domain 4: Classroom Routines Continued

Criteria	Novice (1)	Apprentice (2)	Practitioner (3)	Expert (4)
4. Classroom Leadership and Management[3]	Students who are not directly engaged with the teacher are not productively learning. Much instructional time is lost due to poorly executed transitions and management routines. Student behavior is not monitored and attempts to respond to misbehavior are inconsistent, too severe, and/or do not respect the student's dignity.	Students working in groups are somewhat organized so that some off-task behavior is observed when the teacher is involved with another group. Movement through transitions and management routines is irregular and results in some lost instructional time. Teacher is largely aware of student behavior, but may not notice some misbehavior. Attempts to respond to misbehavior have uneven results.	Students working in groups are organized so that most students are engaged most of the time. Transitions between differentiated and nondifferentiated activities and management routines are smooth with little loss of instructional time. Teacher is aware of student behavior at all times and responds to misbehavior in a way that preserves the student's dignity.	Students working in groups are independently and productively engaged at all times with students taking responsibility for productivity. Transitions between differentiated and nondifferentiated activities and management routines are seamless. Monitoring of behavior is subtle and preventative while interventions are sensitive to student's individual needs.

2 . Levels of performance are paraphrased from Danielson, C. (1996). Enhancing professional practice: A framework for teaching. Alexandria, VA: ASCD.

3. Levels of performance are paraphrased from Danielson, C. (1996). Enhancing professional practice: A framework for teaching. Alexandria, VA: ASCD.

Domain 5: Student Assessment

Criteria	Novice (1)	Apprentice (2)	Practitioner (3)	Expert (3)
1. Formative Assessment	Teacher does not make use of formative assessment during or at the end of the lesson.	Teacher may use some general informal assessment during the lesson (e.g., class poll) or at the end of the lesson (e.g., quiz, exit card). The data are used to gauge understanding of the lesson objectives and/or to plan for future whole-class instruction.	Teacher uses formative assessments embedded within the body of the lesson to make minor modifications to instruction (e.g. reviewing, clarifying misconceptions, adjusting lesson pacing) and to gauge student understanding. Assessment data are used to plan whole-class instruction.	Teacher regularly uses formative assessments throughout the lesson. Data from these lessons is used to: make modifications to instruction within a lesson, to gauge student understanding, and to plan future instruction for individuals and groups.

2. Existence and Quality of Rubrics and Guidelines[4]	Rubrics and guidelines have not been developed.	Rubrics and guidelines have been developed, but are not clear or are not clearly shared with students.	Rubrics and guidelines of clearly articulated assessment criteria and standards are shared with students.	Rubrics and guidelines of clearly articulated assessment criteria and standards are shared with students. Students have participated in the creation of the rubric and guidelines and are aware of how they are meeting the standards and actively plan next steps for learning.

4 Levels of performance are paraphrased from Danielson, C. (1996). Enhancing professional practice: A framework for teaching. Alexandria, VA: ASCD.

Domain 6: Positive, Supportive Learning Environment

Criteria	Novice (1)	Apprentice (2)	Practitioner (3)	Expert (4)
1. Sense of Community[5]	Environment is physically and emotionally unsafe. Students recognize and comment negatively on differences. Disrespect for one another is apparent. There are no discussions about the rationale for differentiation or related concerns.	Environment is physically safe, but some students occasionally feel as though they do not belong or are not valued. Occasional negative comments about differences are heard, although the teacher attempts to address these issues when they arise and encourage respect for each other.	Environment is physically and emotionally safe. In general, students feel as they belong and are valued. Students recognize and acknowledge similarities and differences and respect one another and the teacher.	Environment is physically and emotionally safe. There are consistent affirmations of belonging, value, and respect for each other and the teacher. Students and teacher recognize, acknowledge, and celebrate similarities and differences.

(Domain 6 continues on next page)

Domain 6: Positive, Supportive Learning Environment Continues

Criteria	Novice (1)	Apprentice (2)	Practitioner (3)	Expert (4)
2. Teacher's Role	The teacher's only role is to deliver content and/or direct student activity. Teacher takes the lead in most classroom activities.	Teacher's role is primarily deliverer of information and/or director of student activity. Teacher invites occasional student input into lesson content and activities.	Teacher plays the role of deliverer of information and/or director of student activity, but also acts as coach or facilitator of learning at some point in the lesson. Students have some input into lesson content and activities.	Teacher's overall role is primarily that of coach or facilitator in learning. Both students and teacher have consistent input into lesson content.
3. Respectful Behavior Toward Students	Teacher behavior and response to students discourages participation. Students are hesitant to ask questions and are unaware of each other's strengths, successes, and contributions. Teacher does not seek to connect individually with students.	Teacher behavior and response to students does not encourage participation from a broad range of students. Some students seem hesitant to ask questions or request assistance. Teacher does not make an attempt to make students aware of each other's strengths, successes, and contributions. Teacher only connects individually with the more outgoing students. Teacher is somewhat aware of some students' learning profiles and interests.	Teacher behavior and response to students fosters participation from most students. Students are generally comfortable asking questions or requesting assistance. Teacher attempts to make students aware of each other's strengths, successes, and contributions. Teacher seeks to connect with individual students as time permits. Teacher is aware of students learning profiles and interests.	Teacher behavior and response to students fosters active participation from all students. All students are comfortable asking questions or requesting assistance. Awareness of students' strengths, successes, and contributions are cultivated and celebrated. Teacher talks with students as they enter and exit class and seeks to connect with individual students during class. Teacher is highly aware of students' learning profiles and interests.

4. Facilitation of Learner Independence and Student Choice	The teacher sets goals and assesses student progress toward these goals. Students have no input or choice in lesson components.	The teacher sets goals and assesses student progress toward these goals, but invites limited student input in what the goals are or the progress being made. Students have an opportunity to make a choice at some point in the lesson OR Students make all the choices with no teach input.	Students take on increasing responsibility for their own learning in terms of setting goals for learning and assessing progress toward those goals. There is a balance of student and teacher choice.	Students are consistently involved in setting goals for learning and assessing progress toward those goals, taking on increasing responsibility for their own learning. There is a perfect balance of student and teacher choice.

5. Levels of performance are taken directly from Strickland, C. (2006). *Differentiated lesson observation rubric.* Unpublished manuscript.

6. Levels of performance are taken directly from Strickland, C. (2006). *Differentiated lesson observation rubric.* Unpublished manuscript.

Domain 7: Evidence of Differentiation[7]

Criteria	Novice (1)	Apprentice (2)	Practitioner (3)	Expert (4)
1. Content "The input of teaching and learning," adapting *what* is taught and modifying *how students are given access* to the information and understandings. (Tomlinson, 2001, p. 72)	Lesson is mostly about learning discrete facts and does little to address concept-based instruction. All students are working with the same materials.	Lesson is designed to be roughly a 50/50 split between concept-based instruction and learning discrete facts. There may be two options for material use that vary in readability, complexity, and/or interest. Lesson may include one of the strategies listed in the Expert column.	Lesson is concept-based, but may contain some learning of discrete facts. There are several options for material use that vary in readability, complexity, and/or interest. Lesson includes at least one or more of the strategies listed in the Expert column.	Lesson is highly concept-based and makes use of diverse materials at various levels of readability, complexity, and/or interest. Lesson includes, but is not limited to, one or more of the following strategies: multiple ways to access and organize information, learning contracts, curriculum compacting, flex-group minilessons, and varied support systems such as audio/video recorders, note-taking organizers, highlighted print materials, digests of key ideas, peer/adult mentors.

7. Descriptors and strategies are taken from Tomlinson, C.A. How to differentiate instruction in mixed-ability classrooms. Alexandria, VA: ASCD.

CHAPTER 100

What Makes Giftedness?

A Four-Part Theory for the Development of Creative Productive Giftedness in Young People

Joseph S. Renzulli
The University of Connecticut

> *He who loves practice without theory is like the sailor who boards a ship without a rudder and compass, and never knows where he may land.*
>
> —Leonardo da Vinci

The field of gifted education is based on the almost universally accepted reality that some learners demonstrate outstanding performance or potential for superior performance in academic, creative, leadership, or artistic domains when compared with their peers. From preschool through college and even at graduate and professional school levels, there is a range of learning potentials that justifies an examination of differentiated opportunities and services based on theoretical constructs designed to guide appropriate educational experiences for targeted individuals and groups. As the quotation above points out, if we are not guided by a unified theory we are likely to fall for anything! Theory is, indeed, the rudder and compass that should guide us toward the practices that avoid randomness in the goals we pursue.

When it comes to educational programs of any type, the absence of theory usually results in services that are piecemeal, fragmented, and patched-up practices rather than integrated theory-driven programs that provide internal consistency from goal setting to services and evaluation. Without sound underlying theory and the will to stick to a charted course, what happens in classrooms is often a reaction to political and/or commercial interests, the whims of bureaucratic policymakers far removed from classrooms, questionable research and scholarship, the latest fads or flavor-of-the-month *innovations*, the predilections of gurus without credentials, or well intentioned but unapprised local sages, or a combination of the above. But theory alone will not make substantial differences unless it has generated a strong research base, it is translatable into logically derivative practices that are relatively easy for practitioners to understand and implement, and it has the flexibility to adapt theory driven practices to variations in local demographics and resources.

When it comes to theories for educating gifted and talented students two additional and related caveats must be taken into account. The first caveat is that there should be a logical relationship between the theory-guided services provided to students and the conception of giftedness that serves as a rationale for the development of that theory. An acceleration-based theory that recommends the use of advanced mathematics courses, for example, should obviously be related to a conception of gifted that targets students with high aptitudes in math. The second caveat is derivative of the first and pertains to the enrichment-based theory presented in this chapter. This theory argues that services should be provided for both advanced cognitive development and what are referred to below to as "intelligences outside the normal curve." A rationale for this conception of giftedness is provided in the various subsections that follow.

This chapter is an overview of a theory that has been developed over the past 3 decades to guide the imple-

The Handbook of Educational Theories, pp. 1119–1128

mentation of school programs designed to develop giftedness and talents in young people. The overall theory is composed of four interrelated subtheories and is based on the belief that when one is reexamining the role of theory in gifted education we should always begin the why question—why should a society devote special resources to the development of giftedness in young people? Although there are two generally accepted purposes for providing special education for young people with high potentials, I believe that these two purposes in combination give rise to a third purpose that is intimately related to the conception of giftedness question. The first purpose of gifted education is to provide young people with maximum opportunities for self-fulfillment through the development and expression of one or a combination of performance areas where superior potential may be present. The second purpose is to increase society's reservoir of persons who will help to solve the problems of contemporary civilization by becoming producers of knowledge and art rather than mere consumers of existing information. Although there may be some arguments for and against both of the above purposes, most people would agree that goals related to self-fulfillment and/or societal contributions are generally consistent with democratic philosophies of education. What is even more important is that the two goals are highly interactive and mutually supportive of each other. In other words, the self-satisfying work of scientists, artists, writers, entrepreneurs, and leaders in all walks of life has the potential to produce results that might be valuable contributions to society. If, as I have argued, the purpose of gifted programs is to increase the size of society's supply of potentially creative and productive adults, then the argument for special education programs that focus on creative productivity (rather than lesson-learning giftedness) is a very simple one.

If we agree with these two goals of gifted education, and if we believe that our programs should produce the next generation of leaders, problem solvers, and persons who will make important contributions to all areas of human productivity, then the third purpose is to show the sensibility in modeling special programs and services after the *modus operandi* of these persons rather than after those of good lesson learners. This view is not an argument against good lesson learning and high levels of achievement and text consumption. But good lesson learning should be the province of the best quality general education that schooling can provide to all students according to their individual needs and aptitudes. A focus on creative productivity, however, is especially important because the most efficient lesson learners are not necessarily those persons who go on to make important contributions to knowledge. And in this day and age, when rampant knowledge expansion exists, it would seem wise to consider a model that focuses on how our most able students access and make use of information rather than merely on how they accumulate, store, and retrieve it.

A Few Words About Terminology

In both education and psychology the term giftedness has evolved into a theoretical construct (something to be studied); however, most writers use the word "gifted" as a noun. In my work, I have consistently used the term gifted as an adjective (e.g., gifted behaviors, a gifted writer) rather than a noun (e.g., referring to an individual or group as "the gifted"); and when I refer to gifted education or gifted programs, the adjective is in the context of the root meaning of the word—that which is given. Thus, I have consistently argued that we should label the services necessary to develop high potentials rather than labeling the students as gifted or not gifted. Accordingly, when we identify traits or aptitudes in students, we should focus on specific behavioral manifestations (e.g., superior memory for important dates in history, generates creative ideas, high task commitment in film making, advanced analytic abilities in mathematics).

I have also purposely made a distinction between two types of giftedness. The first is called high achieving or schoolhouse giftedness, referring to students who are good lesson learners in traditional school achievement. The second is creative productive giftedness, referring to the traits that inventors, designers, authors, artists, and others *apply* to selected areas of economic, cultural, and social capital. These two types of giftedness are not mutually exclusive but the distinction is important because of its implications for the ways in which we develop gifted behaviors in educational settings.

In the sections that follow I will describe the four parts of my work that contribute to the overall theory depicted in Figure 100.1. These subtheories, taken collectively, are designed to point out both the ways in which we identify talent potential in young people and how we develop both academic talent and what I refer to as *intelligences outside the normal curve.* These nonintellective traits are as important in promoting the development of fully functioning high potential individuals as traditionally measured cognitive traits.

The Four-Part Theory

For over 4 decades, I have been examining and reexamining the meaning of the age-old questions of *What makes giftedness?* and *How do we develop it in young people?* In the early 1970s I raised the first part of this question in an article that reexamined existing conceptions of giftedness (Renzulli, 1978). Emerging research led to subsequent updates over the next few decades (Ren-

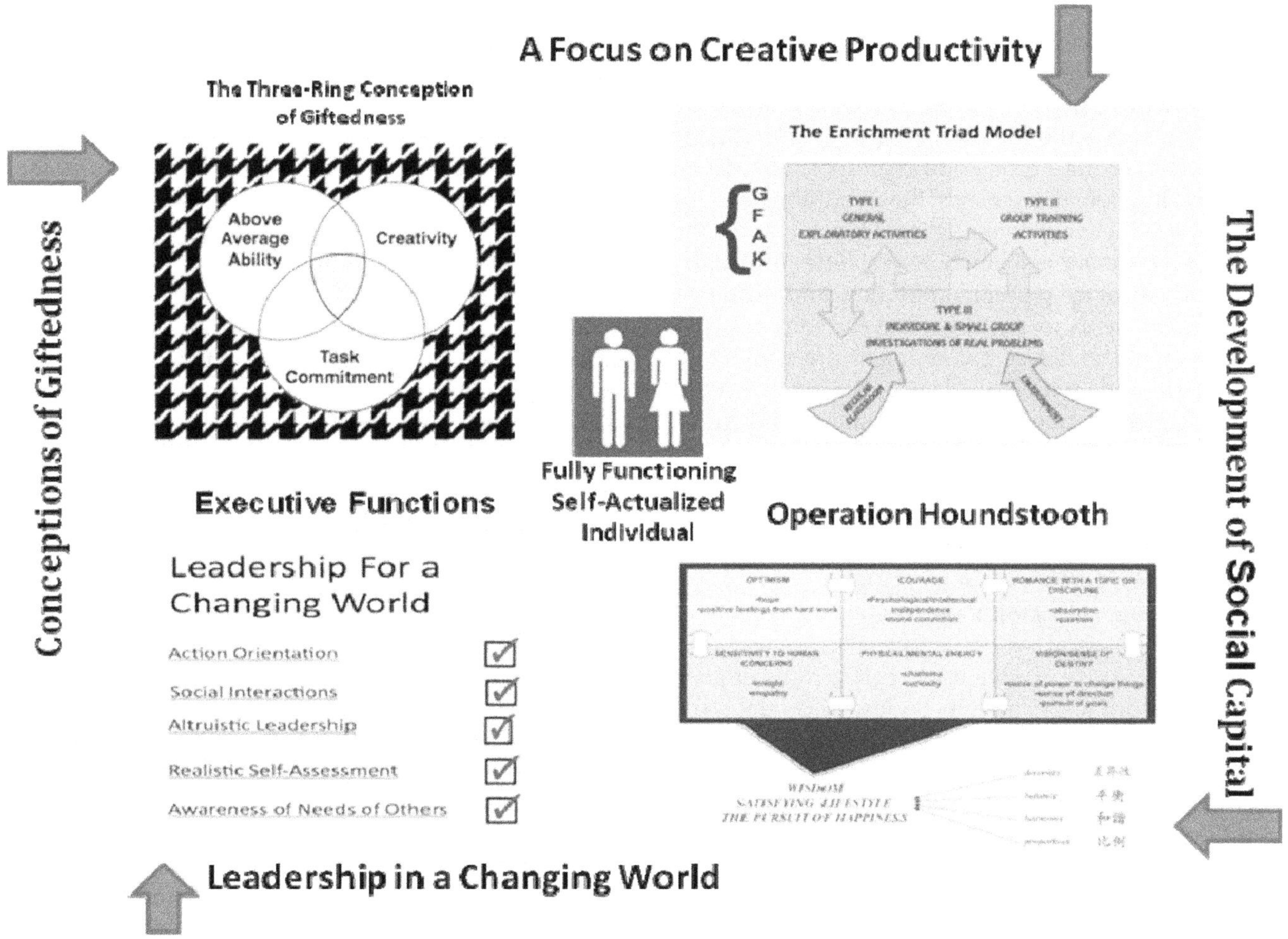

Figure 100.1. A four-part theory of talent development.

zulli, 1986, 2005) as I continued to explore what causes some people to use their intellectual, motivational, and creative assets in ways that lead to outstanding manifestations of achievement and creative productivity, while others with similar or perhaps even greater potential fail to achieve high levels of accomplishment. I continue to wonder what causes the development of only a minuscule number of Thomas Edisons or Rachel Carsons or Langston Hughes or Isadora Duncans, while millions of persons with equal "equipment" and educational advantages (or disadvantages) never rise above mediocrity. Why do some people who have not enjoyed the advantages of special educational opportunities achieve high levels of accomplishment, whereas others who have benefitted from the best of educational opportunities and enriching lifestyles fade into obscurity (Dai & Renzulli, 2008; Renzulli, 1982b)? Subsequent questions have also attempted to frame the nature of giftedness. Is giftedness an absolute or a relative concept? That is, is a person either gifted or not gifted (the absolute view) or can varying kinds and degrees of gifted behaviors be displayed in certain people, at certain times, and under certain circumstances (the relative view)? Is gifted a static concept (i.e., you have it or you don't have it) or is it a dynamic concept (i.e., it varies both within persons and within learning-performance situations) (Renzulli, 1986, p. 62)?

This chapter represents a synthesis of all that I have learned up to this point in time about the questions addressed above and the purposes of gifted education that form the rationale for recommended approaches to developing giftedness. Although I refer to this work as a general theory for the development of human potential, it is made up of four subtheories that I have worked on over the years and that are presented in graphic form in Figure 100.1.

Subtheory I: The Three-Ring Conception of Giftedness

The three-ring conception of giftedness is a theory that attempts to portray the main dimensions of human potential for creative productivity. The name derives from the conceptual framework of the theory—

namely, three interacting clusters of traits (above average ability, task commitment, and creativity) and their relationship with general and specific areas of human performance. Perhaps the most salient aspect of this theory is that it is the interaction between and among these clusters of traits brought to bear upon a particular problem situation that creates the conditions for the creative productive process to commence. A second aspect of the theory is that whereas abilities (especially general intelligence, specific aptitudes, and academic achievement) tend to remain relatively constant over time, creativity and task commitment are contextual, situational, and temporal. These clusters of traits emerge in certain people, at certain times, and under certain circumstances. The enrichment triad (described below) is the compatible learning theory that attempts to prescribe educational conditions that create the conditions for stimulating interaction between and among the three rings, described below.

Above average ability encompasses both general (e.g., verbal and numerical reasoning, spatial relations, memory) and specific (e.g., chemistry, ballet, musical composition, experimental design) performance areas and is the most constant of the rings. That is, any student's performance within the parameters of this ring is minimally variable, as it is linked most closely with traditional cognitive/intellectual traits. The reason that this ring makes reference to "above average ability" (as opposed to, for example, "the top 5%" or "exceptional ability") derives from research that highlights minimal criterion validity between academic aptitude and professional accomplishments.[1] In other words, research suggests that, beyond a certain level of cognitive ability, real-world achievement is less dependent upon ever increasing performance on skills assessment than upon other personal and dispositional factors (e.g., task commitment and creativity). This realization highlights the limitations of intelligence tests and innumerable aptitude and achievement tests that are used to identify candidates for "gifted programs."

Task commitment represents a nonintellective cluster of traits found consistently in creative productive individuals (e.g., perseverance, determination, will power, positive energy). It may best be summarized as a focused or refined form of motivation—energy brought to bear on a particular problem or specific performance area. The significance of this cluster of traits in any definition of giftedness derives from myriad research studies as well as autobiographical sketches of creative productive individuals. Simply stated, one of the primary ingredients for success among persons who have made important contributions to their respective performance areas is their ability to immerse themselves fully in a problem or area for an extended period of time and to persevere even in the face of obstacles that may inhibit others.

Creativity is that cluster of traits that encompasses curiosity, originality, ingenuity, and a willingness to challenge convention and tradition. For example, there have been many gifted scientists throughout history, but the scientists whose work we revere, whose names have remained recognizable in scholarly communities and among the general public, are those scientists who used their creativity to envision, analyze, and ultimately help resolve scientific questions in new, original ways.

In summary, the most salient point to make in discussing and generalizing about the three-ring conception of giftedness is that the overlap and the interaction between and among the three clusters of traits that create the conditions for making giftedness. Giftedness is not viewed as an absolute or fixed state of being (i.e., "you have it or you don't have it"). Rather, it is viewed as a developmental set of behaviors that can be applied to problem solving situations. Varying kinds and degrees of gifted behaviors can be developed and displayed in certain people, at certain times, and under certain circumstances. The rationale for the three-ring conception of giftedness draws upon the previously mentioned anticipated social roles that are played in society by persons with high potential.

Subtheory II: The Enrichment Triad Model

All learning exists on a continuum ranging from deductive, didactic, and prescriptive approaches at one end to inductive, investigative, and constructivist-based approaches at the other. This continuum exists for learners of all ages—from toddlers to doctoral students—and it exists in all areas of curricular activity. The continuum also exists for learning that takes place in the nonschool world, the kind of experiences that young people and adults pursue as they acquire new skills for their jobs or work in the kitchen, the garden, or the workshop in the basement. (There are, of course, occasions when a particular approach falls between the two ends of the continuum, but for purposes of clarifying the main features of deductive and inductive learning, I will treat the two models as polar opposites.) Both models of learning and teaching are valuable in the overall process of schooling, and a well-balanced school program must make use of basic and high-end approaches as well as the combined approaches between the two ends of the continuum.

The deductive model of learning. Although many names have been used to describe the theories that define the ends of the continuum, I simply refer to them as the deductive model and the inductive model. The deductive model is familiar to most educators and guides most of the learning that takes place in classrooms and other places in which formal learning is pursued. The inductive model, on the other hand, represents the kind of learning that typically takes place outside formal school situations. A good way to understand the difference between these two types of learning is to compare how learning takes place in a typical classroom with how someone learns new material or skills in real-world situations. Classrooms are characterized by relatively fixed time schedules, segmented subjects or topics, predetermined sets of information and activities, tests and grades to determine progress, and a pattern of organization that is largely driven by the need to acquire and assimilate information and skills that are deemed important by curriculum developers, textbook publishers, and committees who prepare lists of standards. This model assumes that current learning will have transfer value for some future problem, course, occupational pursuit, or life activity.

Deductive learning is based mainly on the factory model or human engineering conception of schooling. The underlying psychological theory is behaviorism, and the theorists most frequently associated with this model are Ivan Pavlov, E. L. Thorndike, and B. F. Skinner. At the center of this ideology is the ability to produce desirable responses by presenting selected stimuli. In educational settings, these theories translate into a form of structured training for purposes of knowledge and skill acquisition. A curriculum based on the deductive model must be examined in terms of both what and how something is taught.

The instructional effects of the deductive model are those directly achieved by leading the learner in prescribed directions. As indicated above, there is nothing inherently "wrong" with the deductive model; however, it is based on a limited conception of the role of the learner and fails to consider variations in interests and learning styles. Also, in this approach, students are always cast in the roles of lesson-learners and exercise-doers rather than authentic, first-hand inquirers.

The inductive model of learning. The inductive model, on the other hand, represents the kinds of learning that ordinarily occur outside formal classrooms in places such as research laboratories, artists' studios, theaters, film and video production sets, business offices, service agencies, and within almost any extracurricular activity in which products, performances, or services are pursued. The theorists most closely associated with inductive learning are John Dewey, Maria Montessori, and Jerome Bruner. The type of learning advocated by these theorists can be summarized as knowledge and skill acquisition gained from investigative and creative activities that are characterized by three requirements (Renzulli, 1977, 1982a). First, there is a personalization of the topic or problem—the students are doing the work because they want to. Second, students are using methods of investigation or creative production that approximate the modus operandi of the practicing professional, even if the methodology is at a more junior level than that used by adult researchers, film makers, or business entrepreneurs. Third, the work is always geared toward the production of a product or service that is intended to have an impact on a particular audience.

The information (content) and the skills (process) derived in inductive learning situations are based on need-to-know and need-to-do requirements. For example, if a group of students is interested in examining differences in attitudes toward dress codes or teenage dating between and within various groups (e.g., gender, grade, students versus adults), they need certain background information. What have other studies on these topics revealed? Are there any national trends? Have other countries examined dress code or teenage dating issues? Where can these studies be found? Students will need to learn how to design authentic questionnaires, rating scales, and interview schedules and how to record, analyze, and report their findings in the most appropriate format (e.g., written, statistical, graphic, oral, dramatized). Finally, they will need to know how to identify potentially interested audiences, the most appropriate presentation formats (based on a particular audience's level of comprehension), and how to open doors for publication and presentation opportunities. Information used in inductive learning is based on just-in-time knowledge as opposed to the to-be-presented knowledge that characterizes most deductive learning situations. The advent of the Internet has now made just-in-time knowledge easily available to today's young learners; and the interactive capacity of today's technology allows students to go beyond simple text consumption and worksheets-on-line.[2]

This example demonstrates how knowledge and skills that might otherwise be considered trivial or unimportant become instantaneously relevant because they are necessary to prepare a high-quality product. All resources, information, schedules, and sequences of events are directed toward this goal, and evaluation (rather than grading) is a function of the quality of the product or service as viewed through the eyes of a client, consumer, or other type of audience member. Everything that results in learning in a research laboratory, for example, is for present use. Therefore, looking up new information, conducting an experiment, analyzing results, or preparing a report or presentation is an action-oriented and investigative act of learning. We can see here the relevance of the just-in-time knowledge mentioned above. This kind of learning differs from deductive learning, and the skills developed in investigative learning are the best payoff for preparing young people for creative and productive futures.

In summary, the deductive model has dominated the ways in which most formal education is pursued, and the track record of the model has been less than impressive. One need only reflect for a moment on his or her own school experience to realize that with the exception of some basic language and mathematics skills, much of the compartmentalized material learned for some remote and ambiguous future situation is seldom used in the conduct of daily activities. The names of famous generals, geometric formulas, the periodic table, and parts of a plant learned outside an applicable, real-world situation are generally quickly forgotten. This is not to say that previously learned information is unimportant, but its relevancy, meaningfulness, and endurance for future use is minimized when it is almost always learned apart from situations that have personalized meaning for the learner.

The three types of enrichment in the triad model are designed to work in harmony with one another and it is the *interaction* between and among the types of enrichment that produce the dynamic properties represented by the arrows which are as important as the individual components in achieving the goals of this inductive approach to learning. Type I enrichment includes general, exploratory activities that expose students to problems, issues, ideas, notions, theories, skills—in sum, *possibilities*. Often, this type of enrichment serves as a catalyst for curiosity and internal motivation. Type I enrichment may be the method for externally stimulating students toward internal commitment and purpose. These activities should be made available to all students—a highlight of the model that underscores the philosophy behind the three-ring conception of giftedness is that task commitment and creativity are crucial to the development of potentially gifted students, who may "rise to the challenge" in unexpected ways or at unexpected times, given the proper environment.

Type II enrichment involves both individual and group training activities in a variety of cognitive, metacognitive, methodological and affective skills. This type of enrichment prepares the students to produce tangible products and/or generate resolutions to real-world problems through its emphasis on skill development and information gathering. It is not enough to be curious and moved toward action; one must also be equipped to tap and utilize resources in order to take action. Type I activities endeavor to capture students' interests—to inspire—whereas Type II activities endeavor to teach students how to move from inspiration to action. Type II activities are contingent upon the students' developmental levels and, as such, should vary in complexity and sophistication with personal and academic maturity. Generally, there are five categories of Type II activities, all of which may be considered *process skills*: (a) cognitive training, (b) affective training, (c) learning-how-to-learn training, (d) research and reference procedures, and (e) written, oral, and visual communication procedures. Type II enrichment activities can also serve as points of entry into Type III involvement.

Type III activities are individual and small group investigations of real-world problems. Real-world problems are here defined as those with a personal frame of reference for students with no existing or unique resolution and that are designed to have an impact on a targeted audience. As with Type II activities, the sophistication and depth of Type III activities is contingent upon students' developmental levels. Regardless of the level of influence and breadth of reach of solutions to real-world problems generated by Type III activities, all such activities encompass four objectives: (a) to acquire advanced-level understanding of the knowledge and methodology used within particular disciplines, artistic areas of expression, and interdisciplinary studies; (b) to develop authentic products or services that are primarily directed toward bringing about a desired impact on one or more specified audiences; (c) to develop self-directed learning skills in the areas of planning, problem finding, and focusing, management, cooperativeness, decision making, and self-evaluation; and (d) to develop task commitment, self-confidence, feelings of creative accomplishment, and the ability to interact effectively with other students and adults who share common goals and interests.

Type III experiences are the culmination of natural learning, representing synthesis and an application of content, process, and personal involvement through self-motivated work. These activities serve as the vehicles within the total school experience through which everything from basic skills to advanced content and processes *come together* in the form of student-developed products and services. In this regard, I sometimes refer to them as *the assembly plant of the mind*. Clearly, the student's role is transformed from one of lesson-learner to first-hand investigator or creator, and the teacher's role must shift from that of instructor or disseminator of knowledge to some combination of coach, promoter, manager, mentor, agent, guide, and sometimes even colleague.

Subtheory III: Operation Houndstooth—Gifted Education and Social Capital

The rationale for this subtheory and the one that follows is based on the anticipated roles that high potential play in society. Whether we like it or not, history has shown us that highly able people emerge to important positions in all walks of life—government, law, science, religion, politics, business, and the arts and humanities. What kinds of leaders will these people be? What kinds of life experiences created the difference between a Nelson Mandela and an Idi Amin? This subpart of the overall theory addresses the question: "Why do some people mobilize their interpersonal, political, ethical, and moral realms of being in such ways that they place human concerns and the common good above materialism, ego enhancement, and self-indulgence?" The abundance of folk wisdom, research literature, and biographical and anecdotal accounts about creativity and giftedness are nothing short of mind boggling; and yet, we are still unable to answer this fundamental question about persons who have devoted their lives to improving the human condition. Several theorists have speculated about the necessary ingredients for giftedness and creative productivity, and their related theories have called attention to important components and conditions for high-level accomplishment. Most of these theories have dwelt only on cognitive characteristics, and by so doing, they have failed to explain how the confluence of desirable traits result in commitments for making the lives of all people more rewarding, environmentally safe, economically viable, peaceful, and politically free.

Work related to this topic examines the scientific research that defines several categories of personal characteristics associated with an individual's commitment to the production of social capital, briefly defined here as using one's talents to improve human conditions, whether that improvement is directed toward one person or larger audiences or conditions. These characteristics include: optimism, courage, romance *with* a topic or discipline, physical and mental energy, vision and a sense of destiny, and sense of power to change things (Renzulli, 2002). These factors and their subcomponents are portrayed in the lower right quadrant of Figure 100.1. They are represented in the three-ring conception figure by the houndstooth background in which the three clusters of traits are found. I call these "houndstooth" traits cocognitive factors because they interact with and enhance the cognitive traits that are ordinarily associated with the development of human abilities. A number of researchers have suggested that constructs of this type, including social, emotional, and inter/intrapersonal intelligence are related to each other and are independent from traditional measures of ability. The two-directional arrows in this diagram point out the many interactions that take place between and among the factors.

The general goal of this work and a related intervention model is designed to infuse into the overall process of schooling experiences that promote the houndstooth components and that ultimately give highly able young people a sense of their responsibility to society at large. It would be naïve to think that a redirection of educational goals can take place without a commitment at all levels to examine the purposes of education in a democracy. It is also naïve to think that experiences directed toward the production of social capital can, or are even intended to, replace our present-day focus on material productivity and intellectual capital. Rather, this work seeks to enhance the development of wisdom and a satisfying lifestyle that are paralleled by concerns for diversity, balance, harmony, and proportion in all of the choices and decisions that young people make in the process of growing up. What people think and decide to do drives some of society's best ideas and achievements. If we want leaders who will promote ideas and achievements that take into consideration the components we have identified in Operation Houndstooth, then giftedness in the new century will have to be redefined in ways that take these cocognitive components into account. And the strategies that are used to develop giftedness in young people will need to give as much attention to the cocognitive conditions of development as we presently give to cognitive development.

Subtheory IV: Executive Functions—Leadership for a Changing World

The fourth and final theory may very well be the "yeast" that enables all constructs described above to actually be used to pursue a desired goal in an efficient and effective way. I sometimes describe this final subtheory as simply "getting your act together." The most creative ideas, advanced analytic skills, and the noblest of motives may not result in positive action unless leadership skills such as organization, sequencing, and sound judgment are brought to bear on problem situations. Landmark research (e.g., Barnett et al., 2008; Borghans, Duckworth, Heckman, & ter Weel, 2008; Duckworth, 2009; Duckworth, Peterson, Matthews, & Kelly, 2007; Duckworth & Quinn, 2009; Duckworth & Seligman, 2005) has shown that students who persist in college were not necessarily the ones who excelled academically, but the ones with exceptional character strengths such as optimism, persistence, and social intelligence. This research showed that measures of self-control can be more reliable predictors of students' grade point averages than their IQ scores. Including this focus in the overall theory represents a distinctly different approach to talent development than most of the models focusing primarily on cognitive development. Both IQ and self-discipline are correlated with grade point average, but self-discipline is a much more important contributor: Those with low self-discipline have substantially lower college grades than those with low IQs, while high-discipline students received much better grades than high-IQ students. Even after adjusting for the student's grades during the first marking period of the year, students with higher self-discipline still had higher grades at the end of the year. The same could not be said for IQ. Further, these studies found no correlation between IQ and self-discipline—these two traits varied independently.

Our work in this area has been an investigation into what are commonly referred to in the business and human resource literature as executive functions. Executive functions are broadly defined as the ability to engage in *novel* situations that require planning, decision making, troubleshooting, and compassionate and ethical leadership that is not dependent on routine or well-rehearsed responses to challenging combinations of conditions. These traits also involve organizing, integrating, and managing information, emotions, and other cognitive and affective functions that lead to "doing the right thing" in situations that do not have a predetermined or formulaic driven response. These functions are especially important to highly capable people because of the positions of power to which they typically ascend.

A number of researchers have pointed out the importance of incorporating these noncognitive skills into everything from curricular experiences (Bodrova, & Leong, 1996; Diamond, 2010) to educational assessments (Levin, 2011; Sedlack, 2005) and college admission considerations (Sternberg, 2005). These skills have important implications for the academic success of students, career decisions, and even the economic productivity of nations. While not minimizing the importance of traditional cognitive ability, these authors point out that conventional assessments account for a small portion of the variance when examining long term academic and career accomplishment, especially as it relates to the advancement of adult competencies in highly demanding professions where leadership skills and creative productivity are the criteria for success.

A good deal of the background material that led to the inclusion of executive functions in this overall talent development model comes from the field of human resources (Durlak, Weissberg, Dymnicki, Taylor, & Schellinger, 2011; Heckman & Rubenstein, 2001). These authors point out the importance of noncognitive skills in personal and social as well as academic development and—more importantly for this overall theory—a meta-analysis showed that these skills can be taught. Initial input was also derived from the literature on social, behavioral, and "emotional intelligence" (Goleman, 2006). Goleman argued that great leadership works through noncognitive traits such as self-awareness, self-management, motivation, empathy, and social skills. Although the research literature on these types of noncognitive traits is massive, there is general agreement that the following so-called Big Five personality traits (Almlund, Duckworth, Heckman, & Kautz, 2011) are the basis around which education intervention programs should focus:

1. **Openness—**inventive and curious as opposed to consistent and cautious;
2. **Conscientiousness—**efficient and organized as opposed to easy-going and careless;
3. **Extraversion—**outgoing and energetic as opposed to solitary and reserved;
4. **Agreeableness—**friendly and compassionate as opposed to cold and unkind; and
5. **Neuroticism—**sensitive and nervous as opposed to secure and confident.

Our research to date on this subtheory has included the development of an instrument called *Rating the Executive Functions of Young People* (Renzulli & Mitchell, 2011). The instrument is designed to assist in research dealing with the types and degrees of executive function traits in young people. The instrument is intended to be diagnostic in nature and can be used both to identify potential leadership traits in young people and help teachers determine which curricular experiences can be provided to develop desirable leadership traits in individuals or groups. Subsequent diagnostic techniques may include simulations to determine successful performance in demanding problem-solving situations.

While developing this instrument, an initial review of research identified several constructs including mindfulness, ethical/moral, social, motivational, and leadership traits as well as the so-called Big Five personality traits or factors mentioned above. Also identified were specific traits such as being eager to learn, studious, intelligent, interested, and industrious and other variables such as positive and realistic self-appraisal, preference for long-range goals, successful leadership experience, and community service. Researchers in other domains have also identified noncognitive variables of persons who lead and make a difference. For example, in reports on the characteristics possessed by some of the most altruistic persons in American society, common traits that were demonstrated by most of these individuals included passion, determination, talent, self-discipline, and faith. Leadership, ethics, accountability, adaptability, personal productivity, personal responsibility, people skills, self-direction, and social responsibility have also been identified as critical skills in the literature dealing with twenty-first century skills, as were professionalism, enthusiasm, leadership, positive work ethic, values, decisiveness, teamwork, character, support, conformity, openness, self-concept, anxiety, and life-long learning.

This overwhelming list of traits that emerged from the literature review has been grouped into five general categories as a result of a factor analysis conducted with several hundred respondents using the instrument mentioned above. The first factor is action orientation, which includes specific characteristics that motivate an individual to succeed. The second factor is Social Interactions and it includes traits that enable someone to successfully interact with others. The third factor is Altruistic Leadership, and it includes characteristics relating to both empathy and dependability. The fourth factor is called realistic self-assessment and it includes characteristics that demonstrate awareness of one's own abilities, realistic self-appraisal, and self-efficacy. The fifth factor, Awareness of the needs of others, subsumes sensitivity, approachableness, and strong communication skills. Taken collectively, all of these behaviors reflect not only the characteristics of highly effective persons, but also include traits that cause people who have emerged as leaders in their respective fields to "do the right thing" in the arenas and domains over which they have had an influence.

The most salient point to make when discussing and generalizing about the study of giftedness in the twenty-first century is that there is an overlap and an interaction between and among cognitive, affective, and motivational characteristics. We cannot divorce these numerous and interactive characteristics from the ways we should go about developing gifted behaviors in young people. Developing the intelligences outside the normal curve is as important to the contributions that our field can make as have been the traditional academic markers of successful gifted programs.

A second and final consideration deals with how we should go about producing leaders for the twenty-first century. This consideration deals directly with how gifted education should differ *qualitatively* from general education. People who have gained recognition as gifted contributors in the beyond-the-school world have always done so because of something they did—an invention, a sonata, a design, a solution to a political or economic problem. They brought myriad traits to bear on their respective challenges, and it is these types of experiences that should be the core of our efforts to educate tomorrow's people of great promise. The anticipated social roles that people of high potential will play should be the main rationale for both supporting special programs and designing learning experiences that will prepare today's students for responsible leadership roles in the future.

In my opinion, the biggest challenge in gifted education is to extend our traditional investment in the production of intellectual and creative capital to include an equal investment in social capital and the development of executive function skills. I believe that experiences designed to develop these skills should begin at early ages and focus mainly on direct involvement rather than *teaching-and-preaching* experiences. If we can have an impact on social capital and effective and empathetic leadership, then we will be preparing the kinds of leaders who are as sensitive to human and environmental and democratic concerns as they are to the traditional materialistic markers of success in today's world. And the greatest payoff from focusing gifted education on investigative learning and using knowledge wisely will be a dramatic increase in the reservoir of people who will use their talents to create a better world.

Notes

1. A comprehensive summary of this work can be found in full-length descriptions of the theories (Renzulli, 1978, 1986; 2005).

2. For a discussion of what I refer to as "Going Beyond Gutenberg" see http://www.gifted.uconn.edu/sem/Going_Beyond_Gutenberg.html.

References

Almlund, M., Duckworth, A. L., Heckman, J. & Kautz, T. (2011). *Personality psychology and economics*. (IZA DP No. 5500). Retrieved from the University of Chicago website: http://ftp.iza.org/dp5500.pdf

Barnett, W. S., Jung, K., Yarosz, D. J., Thomas, J., Hornbeck, A., Stechuk, R., & Burns, S. (2008). Educational effects of the tools of the mind curriculum: A randomized trial. *Early Childhood Research Quarterly, 23*, 299-313.

Bodrova, E., & Leong, D. J. (1996). *Tools of the mind: The Vygotskian approach to early childhood education*. Englewood Cliffs, NJ: Merrill.

Borghans, L., Duckworth, A. L., Heckman, J. J., & ter Weel, B. (2008). The economics and psychology of personality traits. *Journal of Human Resources, 43*(4), 972-1059.

Dai, D. Y., & Renzulli, J. S. (2008). Snowflakes, living systems, and the mystery of giftedness. *Gifted Child Quarterly, 52*, 114-130.

Diamond, A. (2010). The evidence base for improving school outcomes by addressing the whole child and by addressing skills and attitudes, not just content. *Early Education and Development, 21(5)*, 780-793.

Duckworth, A. L. (2009). Backtalk: Self-discipline is empowering. *Phi Delta Kappan, 90(7)*, 536.

Duckworth, A. L., Peterson, C., Matthews, M. D., & Kelly, D. R. (2007). Grit: Perseverance and passion for long-term goals. *Journal of Personality and Social Psychology, 92(6)*, 1087-1101.

Duckworth, A. L., & Quinn, P. D. (2009). Development and validation of the Short Grit scale (Grit-S). *Journal of Personality Assessment, 91*, 166-174.

Duckworth, A. L., & Seligman, M. E. P. (2005). Self-discipline outdoes IQ predicting academic performance of adolescents. *Psychological Science, 16*(12), 939-944.

Durlak, J. A., Weissberg, R. P., Dymnicki, A. B., Taylor, R. D., & Schellinger, K. B. (2011). The impact of enhancing students' social and emotional learning: A meta-analysis of school-based universal interventions. *Child Development, 82*(1), . 405-432.

Heckman, J., & Rubenstein, Y. (2001). The importance of noncognitive skills: Lessons from the GED testing program. *American Economic Review, 91*(2), 145-149.

Levin, H. M. (2011). *The utility and need for incorporating noncognitive skills into large scale educational assessments.*

Retrieved from http://cpr.maxwell.syr.edu/efap/Papers_reports/Levin_paper.pdf

Goleman, D. (2006). *Emotional intelligence: Why it can matter more than IQ.* New York, NY: Bantam Press.

Renzulli, J. S. (1977). *The enrichment triad model: A guide for developing defensible programs for the gifted and talented.* Mansfield Center, CT: Creative Learning Press.

Renzulli, J. S. (1978). What makes giftedness: Reexamining a definition. *Phi Delta Kappan, 60,* 180-184.

Renzulli, J. S. (1982a). What makes a problem real: Stalking the illusive meaning of qualitative differences in gifted education. *Gifted Child Quarterly, 26*(3), 147-156.

Renzulli, J. S. (1982b). Dear Mr. and Mrs. Copernicus: We regret to inform you. *Gifted Child Quarterly 26*(1), 11-14.

Renzulli, J. S. (1986). The three ring conception of giftedness: A developmental model for creative productivity. In R. J. Sternberg & J. Davidson (Eds.), *Conceptions of giftedness* (pp. 246-279). New York, NY: Cambridge University Press.

Renzulli, J. S. (2002). Expanding the conception of giftedness to include co-cognitive traits and to promote social capital. *Phi Delta Kappan, 84*(1), 33-40, 57-58.

Renzulli, J. S. (2005). The three-ring conception of giftedness: A developmental model for promoting creative productivity. In R. J. Sternberg & J. E. Davidson (Eds.), *Conceptions of giftedness* (2nd ed., pp. 53-92). New York, NY: Cambridge University Press.

Renzulli, J. S., & Mitchell, M. S. (2011). *Rating the executive functions of young people.* Stores, CT: The National Research Center on the Gifted and Talented.

Sedlack, W. E. (2005). The case for noncognitive measures. In W. J. Camara & E. W. Kimmel (Eds.), *Choosing students: Higher education admission tools for the 21st century* (pp. 177-191). Mahwah, NJ: Erlbaum.

Sternberg, R. J. (2005). Augmenting the SAT through assessments of analytic, practical, and creative skills. In W. J. Camara & E. W. Kimmel (Eds.), *Choosing students: higher education admission tools for the 21st century* (pp. 159-176). Mahwah, NJ: Erlbaum.

Author Contact Information: Joseph S. Renzulli, Director, The National Research Center on the Gifted and Talented, The University of Connecticut. URL: www.gifted.uconn.edu/nrcgt.html. Storrs, CT 06269. Telephone: 860-486-5279. E-mail: joseph.renzulli@uconn.edu

CHAPTER 101

The Four-Dimensional Bilingual Pedagogical Theory

Rafael Lara-Alecio
Texas A&M University

Beverly J. Irby
Sam Houston State University

Fuhui Tong
Texas A&M University

In 1994, the four-dimensional bilingual pedagogical theory was published by Lara-Alecio and Parker in *The Bilingual Research Journal*. This theory today continues as the only pedagogical theory to be used to improve the pedagogy of teachers of second language learners. The theory has provided the theoretical foundation to over $20,000,000 in grant funding for school districts and the university over the past 17 years. In this chapter, the theory is shared, along with the instrument that accompanies it (Transitional Bilingual Observation Protocol/Bilingual Observation Protocol).

Lara-Alecio and Parker (1994) indicated that pedagogical guidance from bilingual theory to classroom practice had been general in nature (Cummins, 1986; Díaz, Moll, & Mehan, 1970; Fishman, 1976; Krashen, 1981; Trueba & Barnett-Mizrahi, 1979; Trueba & Delgado-Gaitán, 1988; Trueba, 1979); not much has changed in almost 20 years. The following have been employed as general pedagogical issues within bilingual education:

- provide an emotionally supportive environment;
- emphasize quality of social interaction between teacher and student;
- ensure bilingual status is not considered a disability;
- provide quality social interactions between teacher and student;
- provide multimodality interactions with student;
- incorporate minority students' culture in teaching;
- guide and facilitate rather than control student learning
- encourage student talk and independent learning;
- structure activities which facilitate quality interactions;
- encourage community participation in schooling;
- promote student intrinsic motivation;
- teach meaningful content;
- develop prior competency in the home language; and
- continue to develop competencies in both languages (Lara-Alecio & Parker, 1994, pp. 119-120).

The generality of these propositions is understandable in that the main theoretical underpinnings for bilingual education have been transported or extended from other fields (e.g., sociology, linguistics, anthropology). Furthermore, at the time of the Lara-Alecio and Parker theory, theoretical validation research typically was not generally emerging from classrooms; rather, research findings had been transposed onto the classroom environment from very different contexts. In most cases, studies on language development derive from communication in natural situations (Krashen, 1985). Unlike the natural contexts, classrooms are much more

The Handbook of Educational Theories, pp. 1129–1137

focused, directed, and more complex language learning environments. Lara-Alecio and Parker noted that the lack of instructional and curriculum guidance beyond these general principles had some predictable results, particularly, a lack of definitional clarity. Not all the classrooms are the same; even classrooms under the same theoretical label and the same set of guiding principles may look very different inside (Cziko, 1992; Lam, 1992; Slavin & Chueng, 2005; Trujo, 2004). In the field of bilingual education, Lara-Alecio and Parker stressed that, "[it] had failed to operationalize and particularize its propositions and principles to offer concrete guidance to teachers" (p. 120). Additionally, there had been a lack of demonstrable studies on the effectiveness of pedagogy in bilingual education. This is understandable, because without well-defined instructional activities for bilingual education, it is unlikely for their effectiveness to be accurately evaluated. In fact, in terms of comparing approaches in bilingual education and English-only, there have been very few studies according to Slavin and Cheung, and those should be interpreted with caution. August and Hakuta (1997) suggested that researchers investigate features of classrooms that would be effective in specific contexts, rather than assuming one size fits all context. Even over 20 years ago, similarly Trueba (1989) stated "researchers and practitioners ultimately need to find more useful theories and possible explanations that permit them to improve instructional design (p. 21).

With regard to the variation of classroom characteristics and instruction, it is critical to gather observational evidence related to quality instruction that contributes to students' school performance (Allington, 1991; Foorman et al., 2006; Protheroe, 2002; Waxman & Padrón, 2004). Researchers have also agreed that instructional practices and occurrences in the classroom are particularly critical for those students who are more susceptible to underachievement in bilingual and English as a second language (ESL) program models where students are English language learners (ELLs) (Foorman & Schatschneider, 2003; Hill & Flynn, 2006; Uribe, 2004). However, this issue becomes more complex and intricate when it is intertwined with the following: (a) language of instruction, (b) time allocation of the preferred language of instruction, (c) teachers' perceptions of the percentage of time allocation, and (d) the time-intensive nature and observer-school scheduling alignment issues. Studies targeting how teachers allocate their instructional time, and the quality of such instruction can provide valuable insights regarding effective teaching, which cannot be achieved by time on task, but by the effectiveness and quality of such tasks (Allington, 1991; de Felix, Waxman, Paige, & Huang, 1993). Unfortunately, there is a lack of research on the knowledge base and empirical studies on teachers' pedagogical delivery, as well as the documented quality of teaching as shaped by instructional intervention (August & Shanahan, 2006; Cheung & Slavin, 2005; Gersten & Baker, 2000; Lara-Alecio, Tong, Irby, & Mathes, 2009).

Bilingual and ESL Classroom Observational Studies

Researchers have agreed that effective classroom observation can provide information on (a) classroom occurrence in a comprehensive manner, (b) teachers' pedagogical competence, and (c) how to improve teaching practices that impact students' academic performance (Cirino, Pollard-Durodola, Foorman, Carlson, & Francis, 2007; Foorman et al., 2006; Foorman & Schatschneider, 2003; Lara-Alecio & Parker, 1994; Protheroe, 2002; Waxman & Padron, 2004). While extensive literature has been devoted to systematic observation in English-only classrooms (see Brophy & Good, 1974; Stallings, 1980; Waxman, Huang, Anderson, & Weinstein, 1997; Waxman, Rodriguez, Padrón, & Knight, 1988), only a few studies have been conducted exclusively in bilingual and ESL classrooms with ELLs (e.g., Breunig, 1998; Brisk, 1991; Bruce et al., 1997; Dolson & Mayer, 1992; Escamilla, 1992; Irby, Tong, Lara-Alecio, Meyer, & Rodriguez, 2007; Padrón, 1994; Ramírez, Yuen, Ramey, & Pasta, 1991; Strong, 1986). Among these observational studies, it was determined that teachers in transitional bilingual classrooms (a) spent an excessive amount of time instructing in English, resembling teachers in English-only classrooms and (b) used very small amounts of students' first language for instructional purposes (Dolson & Mayer, 1992; Escamilla, 1992; Strong, 1986). For example, Strong (1986) described 20 elementary school teachers' amount of language instruction and pedagogical activities in English-only classrooms and transitional bilingual education (TBE) with Spanish being students' first language [L1] and English, students' second language [L2]. The author employed a coding system to record the proportion of teacher language to silence, as well as the amount of language instruction by bilingual teachers in L1/L2. It was found that teachers spent the same amount of time using L2 in both TBE and English-only classrooms, although more L1 was expected in a TBE instructional setting. Similar findings were reported in maintenance two-way Spanish/English bilingual classrooms (Escamilla, 1992) and Spanish/ English TBE classrooms (Dolson & Mayer, 1992) where teachers failed to teach in students' Ll (Spanish in both of the studies).

While older studies have noted a lack of cognitively demanding and interactive instruction in teaching Hispanic ELLs (Padrón, 1994; Ramirez et al., 1991), more recent observational studies with ELLs have particularly focused on reading/language-arts instruction in elementary classrooms with preference given to a time-sampling/coding approach. For instance, Haager, Gersten, Baker, and Graves (2003) designed a moderate-inference instrument for teachers with beginning ELLs in early reading intervention. Their instrument allowed observers to evaluate the quality of classroom instruction on a 4-point Likert rating scale with a predetermined set of categories such as instructional practice, interactive teaching, adaptations for individual differences, English-language development, vocabulary development, and phonemic awareness and decoding. Classrooms observations were conducted during the entire reading/language arts period with a minimum of 2.5 hours. The authors suggested using this instrument in research instead of for evaluation purposes.

More recent studies include a multiyear multisite (i.e., California and Texas) project in which Foorman, Goldenberg, Carlson, Saunders, and Pollard-Durodola (2004) adapted a two-dimensional measure of time-by-activity to observe three representational models during reading/language arts and/or English language development (ELD) instruction: late-exit TBE, two-way dual language, and English immersion. The instrument consisted of language codes and content codes (e.g., oral language and listening comprehension, vocabulary, phonemic awareness, etc.) based on 1-5 scale to rate the overall quality of instruction at the end of each interval. It was observed that even in the same type of instruction program, that is, English immersion, teachers in California site taught exclusively in English, whereas teachers in Texas instructed primarily in English with a small portion of students' L1. Additionally, teachers in the California sites were observed instructing more frequently in oral-language development. Saunders, Foorman, and Carlson's (2006) subsequent study reported that regardless of program type, that is, TBE, English immersion, teachers with a separate English language development (ELD) block were more likely to allocate more instructional time in ELLs' oral language development.

Limitation of Current Literature

The review of literature has revealed several issues. First, there is a limitation regarding the instruments available to be applied with ELLs. The observation instrument used by Haager et al.'s (2003) study was a moderate inference scale format with Likert-type rating scale that required observers to make strong interferences or subjective judgments, hence, a higher interrater reliability for this instrument to be translated into wide use.

Second, few studies exclusively observed teachers' pedagogical behavior during an ESL or ELD block, particularly on oral language development for ELLs. As Lara-Alecio et al. (2009) pointed out, the emphases largely rested on reading/language arts (e.g., Foorman & Schatschneider, 2003), content reading in science and social studies (e.g., Irby et al., 2007), or a mixture of reading/language arts and ELD (e.g., Foorman et al., 2006). Such limitation should be immediately addressed, because oral language ability is the foundation for subsequent reading achievement (Reese, Garnier, Gallimore, & Goldenberg, 2000; Riches & Genesee, 2006; Saunders & O'Brien, 2006). Because of the fact that English oral proficiency occurs at early grade levels, that is, kindergarten for ELLs, a clear understanding of teachers' time allotment in classroom activities during ESL or ELD block is much desired so as to identify effective practices to enhance students' oral abilities. Such information can be valuable particularly for professional development programs.

Finally, there is a lack of connection between observational research and instructional intervention comparing pedagogical differences among various program models serving ELLs. As Gersten and Baker (2000) claimed, little is known on how instructional intervention can shape teachers' pedagogical delivery. In summary, the lack of reliable and valid instruments, and therefore, the corresponding empirical evidence, masks the actual classroom practice in transitional bilingual/ESL programs with Spanish-speaking ELLs.

The Four-Dimensional Bilingual Pedagogical Theory and Model

The Lara-Alecio and Parker (1994) model attempts to incorporate and operationalize elements of classroom instruction supported by commonly espoused principles of bilingual education. According to Lara-Alecio and Parker, the purposes of their research were to: (a) specify and integrate those theoretical notions which show most promise for pedagogical utility (i.e., notions which can be translated into manipulable elements of the classroom environment), (b) identify classroom elements which teachers have the ability to adjust to enhance student learning; and to develop a pedagogical model which can be can be translated into reliably observable and codable elements, and (c) provide an observational tool with potential use for formative program evaluation via the presence and absence of valued elements specified by the model. There are four dimensions of the theory as follows and as represented in Figure 101.1.

Language of instruction. This dimension of the theory can be controlled by the teachers in their content area instruction with a mixture of students' L1 and L2. For ELLs, content areas such as science can serve as the content vehicle and provide a rich source of input for language learning (Cummins, 1986; Krashen, 1985). In this dimension, four progressive uses of students' L1

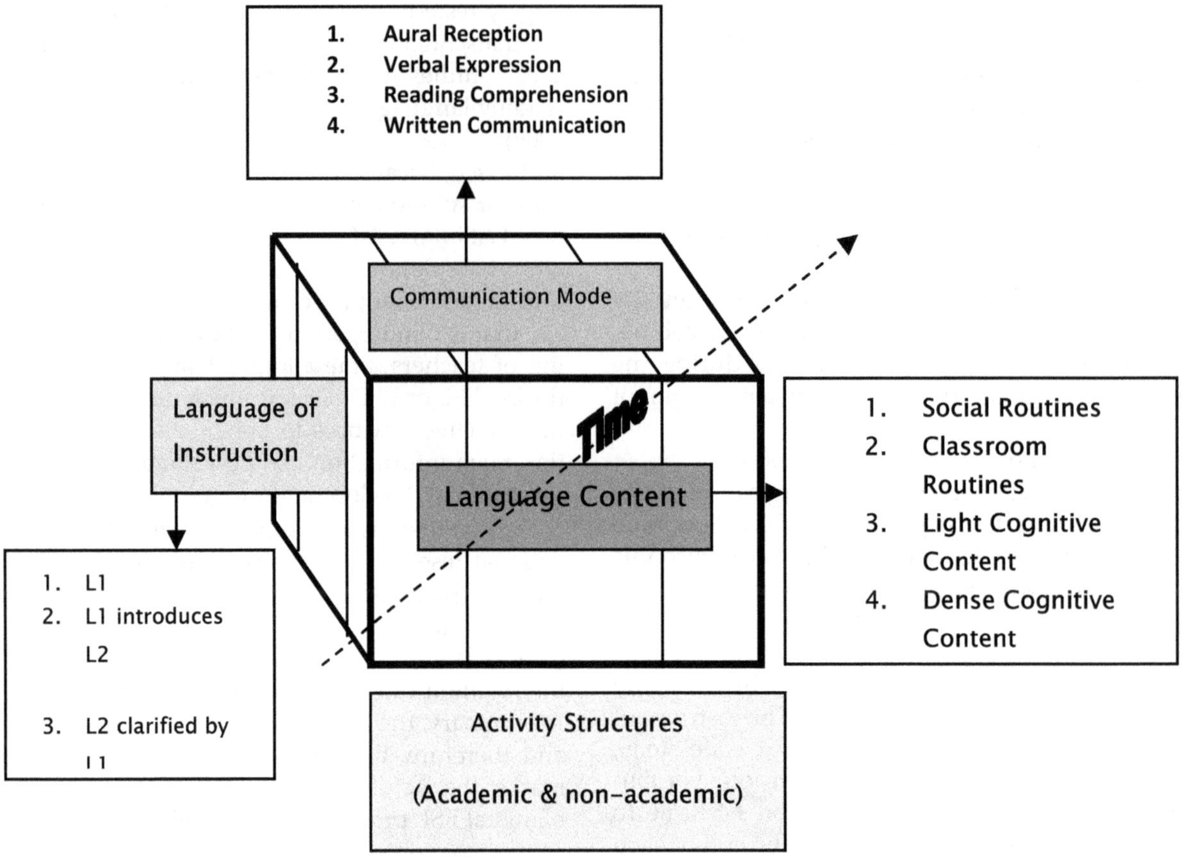

Source: Lara-Alecio and Parker (1994).

Figure 101.1. Model of the four-dimensional bilingual pedagogical theory.

and L2 in the classroom are included: (a) content presented in L1, (b) L1 introducing L2, (c) L2 supported and clarified by L1, and (d) content presented in L2. This dimension acknowledges the concept of transition (as in *transitional bilingual*), and affirms the importance of content areas as rich sources of language input for ELL students and as vehicles for language learning. Language of instruction usually refers to the teacher's use of language. However, it may also refer to the reading text used, or the language used by students in cooperative learning groups.

Language content. The second dimension of the pedagogical model, language content, derives directly from Cummins's (1986) second language acquisition theory. He proposed a distinction between basic interpersonal communications skills (BICS), which takes 1 to 3 years to acquire, and cognitive-academic language proficiency (CALP) language competencies, which normally requires a period of 5 to 7 years to master. Cummins' postulation has been challenged by some researchers for the isolation of social and cognitive factors (Genesee, 1984) and for the overgeneralization of the complex concept of language proficiency (Edelsky, 1996; Trueba, 1989; Wiley, 1996). Based on their observation of a range of activities in Texas bilingual classrooms, Lara-Alecio and Parker also agreed with the charge that the two-tiered BICS/CALP distinction is too simplistic to describe varying student abilities in these activities. Therefore, in the four-dimensional bilingual pedagogical theory, rather than being fixed or long-term abilities, BICS and CALP were reformulated as malleable levels of discourse. Further, two additional levels were included to create a total of four levels of language content: (a) social routines (i.e., social exchanges and conversation); (b) academic routines (i.e., preparing for recess, returning books, learning strategies, handing in assignments, structuring homework); (c) light cognitive content (i.e., current events, discussion of the school fiesta, multicultural education issues, also repetitive drill or skills practice); and (d) dense cognitive content (i.e., new content-area information, conceptually loaded communication with specialized vocabulary and procedures).

It is commonly inferred that CALP in L1 must precede BICS in L2, and that L1 CALP accelerates later CALP in L2. But for ELLs, will English CALP readily occur after native language CALP is established, presumably over several years? The notion of prerequisite development offers little guidance to teachers in how the L1 to L2 CALP may be accelerated. The model proposed by Lara-Alecio and Parker implies not general developmental prerequisites, but rather strategic incremental shifts in emphasis over time. It suggests that the transition from L1 to L2 occurs incrementally, and possibly at different rates and times for different activity structures or language modes. example, students may be ready for English instruction for Level II, academic routines, but maintained in their L1 for Level III, light cognitive content. The teacher identifies the level for each activity structure (see next section for discussion of activity structure), and accordingly uses L2 or L1. This suggestion to select the language by activity structure does not violate the warning against frequent code-switching, which can produce confusion (Hoffman, 1991). Additionally, there is a definite difference between what is considered code-switching and what Lara-Alecio and Parker have defined as clarifications (L1 introducing L2 and L2 supported and clarified by L1). Selection of the language of instruction by activity structure is possible because activity structures are relatively stable, commonly changing 2 to 5 times per hour (Doyle, 1981).

Activity structures. The third dimension is known as Activity Structures. From a sociocognitive perspective, Vygotsky (1978) proposed his influential notion of zone of proximal development that required educators' attention to and participation in the social and task structure of each learning activity (Cole & Griffin, 1983). The emphasis is on the context of instruction, in addition to the traditional content of instruction. Erickson (1982) stated that classroom ethnographers focus on the structure of events each structure type with its own opportunities, implied values and expectations for student participation. Unfortunately, traditional pedagogy in classrooms with emphasis on the lesson, with its objectives, curriculum content, and assignments, often ignored these activity structures. Nevertheless, such concept of activity structures has received considerable amount of attention in research (Doyle, 1986). As defined by Brophy and Evertson (1978) and Doyle (1981), activity structures are teacher-structured learning situations, each with its own expectations for teacher and student communication. They are relatively stable, recurring periods of activity, each with a recognized purpose and opportunities for communication. Communication which is expected, appropriate, and fostered in one activity structure may be inappropriate and discouraged in a second. Activity structures are intuitively appealing to teachers, though practitioners rarely referred to them by name. Activity structures are the essential building blocks of teacher planning and organization, playing a larger role than "goals and objectives" (Berliner, 1983; Doyle, 1981; Gump, 1987) in coding activity structures (Parker, Tindal, & Hasbrouck, 1994).

Communication mode. Both Cummins' (1986) reciprocal interaction model and the context-specific model (Díaz et al., 1970) support the practice of multiple modalities within particular activity structures. These modalities (especially reading, writing, and verbal expression) also are meaningful to teachers as curriculum content areas. These modalities can be mutually supportive, and are often integrated within a lesson. Their differentiation within the model, however, is to indicate that English facility may vary greatly by mode, and that each mode should be permitted to progress at the fastest rate possible. This may mean that students are permitted to produce an essay exam in L1 on a difficult topic following a lecture presented in English. It may mean that students are expected to read an assignment in English, but follow-up discussion is conducted in L1. This flexible procedure permits maximum progress in content curriculum coverage. The two previous examples demonstrate the overlap between this Communication Mode dimension and the Language of Instruction dimension discussed earlier.

THEORY AND MODEL VALIDATION AND APPLICATION

An observation instrument, The Transitional Bilingual Observation Protocol (TBOP), developed by Lara-Alecio and Parker has been validated and used in numerous studies and funded grants (Bruce et al., 1997; Breunig, 1998). This protocol consists of four domains previously discussed (for detailed information on conceptual framework, examples, coding procedures and categories, see Bruce et al., 1997, as well as Lara-Alecio & Parker, 1994). The protocol was used in an longitudinal randomized trial study, Project English Language and Literacy Acquisition (funded by Institute for Education Sciences, R305P030032) and in a National Science Foundation randomized trial study, Project MSSELL (DRL-0822343) and provided data as to how well the teachers were implementing the intervention pedagogically and the differences between the control and experimental classrooms. In addition, a comprehensive ESL checklist of 50 strategies, based on the work of Herrell and Jordan (2004), was added to the protocol to observe inclusion and frequency of implementation of ESL strategies in the typical practice classroom versus specified research-based ESL strategies as determined effective in Project ELLA. The TBOP was tested and used with a technology based handheld device, a personal digital assistant as shown in Figure 101.2. The data are downloaded to an Excel file.

In a field with a surplus of theoretical and advocacy literature and a deficit of empirical data, validation of

Figure 101.2. PDA version of TBOP.

the theory and model were essential. Lara-Alecio and Parker contended that such validation involves the determination of a model that demonstrates (a) explanatory and predictive power, stability (i.e., over time), and generalizability (across a range of classroom situations), (b) instructional usage (positively affects student growth when used for lesson planning), (c) parsimony (simply integrates a large number of variables), and (d) interrelation with other pedagogical models. Classroom learning activities can unambiguously be classified as model dimensions by independent raters. Reliability for the observation instrument is established by in situ observation in transitional bilingual classrooms and coding of individual activity structures on each model dimension.

The explanatory and predictive power of the model can be established in at least five ways. First, data collected over time from a given classroom and teacher has provided sufficient stability to permit a given classroom to be described in terms of the model. Second, a macrolevel, model-based empirical description of the classroom mirrors the espoused philosophy of the program and teacher. Third, on a microlevel, teacher intentions and plans for a particular lesson reflects in observed data. Fourth, model-based observation data reflects students' English language skill levels in the four modes. The fifth and possibly the most powerful form of model validation has involved testing its instructional validity (i.e. its prescriptive use to increase teaching efficiency within experimental designs). Observations of pedagogy have been compared to the assessment of student skill growth. Thus, the theory and model can serve as an intervention, a means of feeding classroom observational data back to teachers.

The Lara-Alecio and Parker theory/model has been applied successfully in evaluation research with ELLs in various settings with reported Kappa values ranging from 0.65 to 0.98 (Breunig, 1998; Irby et al., 2007; Lara-Alecio et al., 2009). For example, to contribute to the understanding of the relationship between bilingual teachers' actual use of language of instruction and their perception of such usage, Irby et al. (2007) utilized the low-inference TBOP instrument to investigate 17 third-grade English/Spanish TBE teachers' perceived instructional time allocation in two languages in relation to their students' academic performance. A 20-second timed interval of teachers' language of instruction was coded and repeated during the class period, and calculated for the frequency of occurrence. An inconsistency was reported between teachers' instructional time in

English (44.9%) and Spanish (38.2%) and the required district's TBE model (50% in both languages), and these teachers were not even aware of such discrepancy.

In a related study, to respond to the need of exploring and reporting pedagogical occurrences in the classrooms with ELLs, Lara-Alecio, Tong, Irby, and Mathes (2009) applied TBOP to gather data on teachers' pedagogical behaviors within a specifically designed English language and literacy intervention for kindergarten ELLs. During the ESL class period, teachers who were in the treatment condition were observed to devote to a higher percentage of instructional time in developing students' cognitive ability, higher order thinking skills, and oral language proficiency through intensive English instruction.

In summary, in the field of bilingual education, theory without validation or only language development theory and advocacy have sometimes substituted for solid, empirical data. This has resulted both in the lack of a data-base of knowledge and in lack of solid, detailed feedback and guidance to bilingual teachers. Lara-Alecio's and Parker's four-dimensional theoretical model is a theory that provides consistent, yet specific, concrete data to teachers on the process of transitional bilingual instruction (and other bilingual education models).

REFERENCES

Allington, R. L. (1991). Children who find learning to read difficult: School responses to diversity. In E. H. Hiebert (Ed.), *Literacy for a diverse society* (pp. 237-252). New York, NY: Teachers College Press.

August, D., & Hakuta, K. (1997). Improving schooling for language-minority children: A research agenda. Washington, DC: National Research Council.

August, D., & Shanahan, T. (2006). *Developing literacy in second-language learners. Report of the national literacy panel on language-minority children and youth.* Mahwah, NJ: Erlbaum.

Berliner, D. (1983). Developing conceptions of classroom environments: Some light on the T in classroom studies of ATI. *Educational Psychologist, 18*(1), 1-13.

Breunig, N. A. (1998). Measuring the instructional use of Spanish and English in elementary transitional bilingual classrooms. *Dissertation Abstracts International,* 59(04), 1046A.

Brisk, M. (1991). Toward multiingual and multicultural mainstream education. *Journal of Education, 173,* 1 14-129.

Brophy, J. E., & Good, T. L. (1974). *Teacher-student relationships: Causes and consequences.* New York, NY: Holt, Rinehart, & Winston.

Brophy, J. E., & Evertson, C. (1978). Context variables in teaching. *Educational Psychologist, 12,* 310-316.

Bruce, K., Lara-Alecio, R., Parker, R., Hasbrouck, J., Weaver, L., & Irby, B. J. (1997). Inside transitional bilingual classrooms: Accurately describing the language learning process. *Bilingual Research Journal, 21*(2&3), 123-142.

Cheung, A., & Slavin, R E. (2005). Effective reading programs for English language learners and other language minority students. *Bilingual Research Journal, 29*(2), 241-267.

Cirino, P., Pollard-Durodola, S. D., Foorman, B. R, Carlson, C. D., & Francis, D. J. (2007). Teacher characteristics, classroom instruction, and student literacy and language outcomes in bilingual kindergartners. *Elementary School Journal, 107*(4), 341-364.

Cole, M., & Griffin, P. (1983). A socio-historical approach to remediation. *The Quarterly Newsletter of the Laboratory of Comparative Human Cognition, 5*(4), 69-74.

Cummins, J. (1986). Empowering minority students: A framework for intervention. *Harvard Educational Review, 56*(1), 18-36.

Cziko, G. A. (1992). The evaluation of bilingual education: From necessity and probability to possibility. *Educational Researcher, 21,* 10-15.

de Felix, J. W., Waxman, H. C., Paige, S., & Huang, S. L. (1993). A comparison of classroom instruction in bilingual and monolingual secondary school classrooms. *Peabody Journal of Education, 69*(1), 102-116. Retrieved from Questia database: http://www.questia.com/PM.qst?a=o&d=95241868

Diaz, S., Moll, L. C., & Mehan, H. (1970). Sociocultural resources in instruction: A context-specific approach. In The California Office of Bilingual Bicultural Education (Ed.), *Beyond language: Social and cultural factors in schooling language minority students* (pp. 187-230). Sacramento, CA: Bilingual Education Office, California State Department of Education.

Dolson, D. P., & Mayer, J. (1992). Longitudinal study of three program models for language-minority students: A critical examination of reported findings. *Bilingual Research Journal, 16*(1-2), 105-157.

Doyle, W. (1986). Classroom organization and management. In M. Wittrock (Ed.), *Handbook of research on teaching* (pp. 392-431). New York, NY: Macmillan.

Edelsky, C. (1996). *With literacy and justice for all: Rethinking the social in language and education* (2nd ed.). London, England: Taylor & Francis.

Erickson, F. (1982). Classroom discourse as improvisation: Relationships between academic task structure and social participation structure in lessons. In L. C. Wilkinson (Ed.) *Communicating in the classroom* (pp. 119-158). New York, NY: Macmillan.

Escamilla, K. (1992). Classroom discourse as improvisation: Relationships between academic task structure and social participation structure in lessons. In L. C. Wilkinson (Ed.), *Communicating in the classroom* (pp. 19-158). New York, NY: MacMillan.

Fishman, J. (1976). *Bilingual education: An international sociological perspective.* Rowley, MA: Newbury House.

Foorman, B. R, Goldenberg, C, Carlson, C. D., Saunders, W. M., & Pollard-Durodola, S. D. (2004). How teachers allocate time during literacy instruction in primary-grade English language learner classrooms. In P. McCardle & V. Chhabra (Eds.), *The voice of evidence in reading research.* Baltimore, MD: Paul H. Brookes.

Foorman, B. R, & Schatschneider, C. (2003). Measurement of teaching practices during reading/language arts instruction and its relationship to student achievement. In S. Vaughn & K. L. Briggs (Eds.), *Reading in the classroom: Sys-*

tems for the observation of teaching and learning (pp. 1-30). Baltimore, MD: Brookes.

Foorman, B. R, Schatschneider, C., Eakin, M. N., Fletcher, J. M., Moats, L. C., & Francis, D. J. (2006). The impact of instructional practices in Grades 1 and 2 on reading and spelling achievement in high poverty schools. *Contemporary Educational Psychology, 31*, 1-29.

Genesee, F. (1984). On Cummins' theoretical framework. In C. Rivera (Ed.), *Language proficiency and academic achievement.* Clevedon, England: Multilingual Matters.

Gersten, R., & Baker, S. (2000). What we know about effective instructional practices for English-language learners. *Exceptional Children, 66*(4), 454-470.

Gump, P. V. (1987). School and classroom environments. In I. Altman & D. Stokols (Eds.), *Handbook of environmental psychology* (pp. 691-732). New York, NY: Wiley.

Haager, D., Gersten, R., Baker, S., & Graves, A. W. (2003). The English-language learner classroom observation instrument for beginning readers. In S. Vaughn & K. L. Briggs (Eds.), *Reading in the classroom: Systems for the observation of teaching and learning* (pp. 111-144). Baltimore, MD: Brookes.

Herrell, A., & Jordan, M. (2004). *Fifty strategies for teaching English language learners* (2nd ed.). Upper Saddle River, NJ: Pearson Education.

Hill, J., & Flynn, K. (2006). *Classroom instruction that works: Research-based strategies for increasing student achievement.* Alexandria, VA: Association for Supervision and Curriculum Development.

Irby, B., Tong, F., Lara-Alecio, R., Meyer, D., & Rodriguez, L. (2007). The critical nature of language of instruction compared to observed practices and high stakes tests in transitional bilingual classroom. *Research in the Schools, 14*(2), 27-36.

Krashen, S. D. (1981). Bilingual education and second language acquisition theory. In C. F. Leyba (Ed.), *Schooling and language minority students: A theoretical framework.* Los Angeles, CA: California State University.

Krashen, S. D. (1985). *The input hypothesis: Issues and implications.* New York, NY: Longman.

Lam, T. C. M. (1992). Review of practices and problems in the evaluation of bilingual education. *Review of Educational Research, 62*, 181-203.

Lara-Alecio, R., & Parker, R. (1994). A pedagogical model for transitional English bilingual classrooms. *Bilingual Research Journal, 18*(3&4), 119-133.

Lara-Alecio, R., Tong, F., Irby, B.J., & Mathes, P. (2009). Teachers' pedagogical differences among bilingual and structured English immersion kindergarten classrooms in a randomized trial study. *Bilingual Research Journal, 32*(1), 77-100.

Padrón, Y. (1994). Comparing reading instruction in Hispanic/limited English proficient schools and other inner-city schools. *Bilingual Research Journal, 18*, 49-66.

Parker, R., Tindal, G., & Hasbrouck, J. (1994). Teachers' pedagogical differences among bilingual and structured English immersion kindergarten classrooms in a randomized trial study. *Bilingual Research Journal, 32*(1), 77-100.

Protheroe, N. (2002). Improving instruction through teacher observation. *Principal, 82*(1), 48-51.

Ramirez, J. D., Yuen, S. D., Ramey, D. R, & Pasta, D. J. (1991). *Final report: Longitudinal study of structured English immersion strategy, early-exit and late-exit transitional bilingual education programs for language-minority children* (Report No. 300-87-0156). San Mateo, CA: Aguirre International.

Reese, L., Garnier, H., Gallimore, R, & Goldenberg, C. (2000). Longitudinal analysis of the antecedents of emergent Spanish literacy and middle-school English reading achievement of Spanish-speaking students. *American Educational Research Journal, 37*(3), 633-662.

Riches, C., & Genesee, F. (2006). Crosslinguistic and crossmodal issues. In F. Genesee, K. J. Lindholm, W. M. Saunders, & D. Christian (Eds.), *Educating English language learners: A synthesis of research evidence* (pp. 64-108). New York, NY: Cambridge University Press.

Saunders, W. M., Foorman, B. R., & Carlson, C. D. (2006). Is a separate block of time for oral English language development in programs for English learners needed? *Elementary School Journal, 107*(2), 181-198.

Saunders, W. M., & O'Brien, G. (2006). Oral language. In F. Genesee, K. Lindholm-Leary, W. M. Saunders, & D. Christian (Eds.), *Educating English language learners: A synthesis of research evidence* (pp. 14-63). New York, NY: Cambridge University Press.

Slavin, R., & Cheung, A. (2005). A synthesis of research on language of reading instruction for English language learners. *Review of Educational Research 75*(2), 247-284.

Stallings, J. (1980). Allocated academic learning time revisited, or beyond time on task. *Educational Researcher, 9*, 11-16.

Strong, M. (1986). Teacher language to limited English speakers in bilingual and submersion classrooms. In R. R. Day (Ed.), *Talking to learn: Conversation in second language acquisition* (pp. 53-63). Rowley, MA: Newbury House.

Trueba, H. (1979). Bilingual education models: Types and designs. In H. Trueba & C. Barnett-Mizrahi (Eds.) *Bilingual multicultural education and the professional: From theory to practice* (pp. 54-73). Rowley, MA: Newbury House.

Trueba, H. T. (1989). *Raising silent voices. Educating linguistic minorities for the 21st century.* Boston, MA: Heinle & Heinle.

Trueba, H., & Barnett-Mizrahi, C. (1970). *Bilingual multicultural education and the professional. From theory to practice.* Rowley, MA: Newbury House.

Trueba, H., & Delgado-Gaitan, C. (1988). *School and society. Learning content through culture.* New York, NY: Praeger Publishers.

Trujo, S. (2004, September/October). Differentiated instruction: We can no longer just aim down the middle. *ELL Outlook.* Retrieved from http://coursecrafters.com/ELL-Outlook/index.html

Uribe, M. (2004). Effective literacy strategies in the transitional classroom. *Dissertation Abstracts International, 65* (07), 2467A. (UMINo. 3138722)

Vygotsky, L. S. (1978). *Mind and society: The development of higher mental processes.* Cambridge, MA: Harvard University Press.

Waxman, H., Huang, S. L., Anderson, L. W., & Weinstein, T. (1997). Classroom process differences in inner-city elementary schools. *Journal of Educational Research, 91*, 49-59.

Waxman, H. C., & Padrón, Y. N. (2004). The uses of the Classroom Observation Schedule to improve classroom instruction. In H. C. Waxman, R. G. Tharp, & R. S. Hilberg (Eds.), *Observational research in U.S. classrooms: New approaches for understanding cultural and linguistic diversity* (pp. 72-96). New York, NY: Cambridge University Press.

Waxman, H., Rodriguez, J., Padrón, Y. N., & Knight, S. L. (1988). The use of systematic classroom observations during field experience components of teacher education programs. *The College Student Journal, 22*, 199-202.

Wiley, T. G. (1996). *Literacy and language diversity in the United States*. McHenry, IL: Center for Applied Linguistics and Delta Systems.

Author Contact Information: **Rafael Lara-Alecio**, PhD, Professor and Director of Bilingual Programs, Education Psychology Department, College of Education and Human Development, Texas A&M University, 107 H Harrington Tower, College Station, TX 77843-4225. Telephone: 979-845-3467. E-mail: a-lara@tamu.edu

About the Editors and Section Editors

Beverly J. Irby is associate dean for graduate programs in the College of Education at Sam Houston State University. She also holds the distinction of the Texas State University System Regents' Professor. Her primary areas of research and expertise focus around social responsibility, particularly related to early childhood, women's leadership, and gifted and bilingual education. She also holds expertise in research and theory development and in educational administration. She has served as a teacher PK-8, an educational diagnostician, a special education director, an elementary principal, an assistant superintendent, and superintendent of schools. Her work at the university level spans 21 years as professor, director of a doctoral program, director of student teaching and field experiences, and chair of the Department of Educational Leadership and Counseling, and she has over 200 scholarly publications, including book chapters, technical reports, journal articles, and books. She is a published children's book author, as well as editor or founding editor of professional journals.

Genevieve Brown is professor and dean of the College of Education at Sam Houston State University, Huntsville, Texas. She has extensive experience as an administrator in public schools, including 10 years as assistant superintendent. Her research, writing, and presentations have focused on administrator preparation and evaluation, administration portfolio development, leadership theory, and women's leadership. Coauthor and coeditor of numerous articles and books on leadership, she is the codeveloper of *The Synergistic Leadership Theory*, the first leadership theory particularly inclusive of women's voices and reflective of women's experiences. Additionally, she is cofounder and coeditor of *Advancing Women in Leadership Journal*, the first international, online refereed journal for professional women. At the 2005 annual conference of the American Educational Research Association, Dr. Brown, along with her colleague Dr. Beverly J. Irby, was named recipient of the Willystine Goodsell Award for distinguished scholarship in the field of gender equity.

Rafael Lara-Alecio is a professor and director of the bilingual programs in the Department of Educational Psychology at Texas A&M University. He holds the distinction of TAMU Former Students Association Teaching Scholar and College Mentor. Additionally, he is one of a few at TAMU who hold the TAMU Outreach Award. His primary areas of research and expertise include assessment and evaluation, bilingual and ESL methodologies and content area instruction, biliteracy, and parental involvement. His research efforts have garnered over $20,000,000 for TAMU or for public schools from the Institute of Educational Sciences, National Science Foundation, Office of English Language Acquisition at the United States Department of Education, Texas Educational Agency, and Intercontinental Development Bank and Costa Rica/USA Foundation. He is an experienced early childhood, elementary, and secondary school bilingual teacher, and had served at the university provost and presidency levels in the national university in Guatemala. For the past 20 years he has been directing the undergraduate, master, and doctoral bilingual programs at Texas A&M University.

Shirley Jackson returned to college after 25 years as a secondary school English teacher and department chair to enroll in a doctoral program in educational leadership at Sam Houston State University. Following graduation, she became an adjunct lecturer and researcher in the Center for Research and Doctoral Studies at SHSU. In addition, with a masters in gifted education, she conducts workshops in the 30 hours of training required by Texas for teachers of the identified gifted and talented. As a classroom teacher, Dr. Jackson received numerous teaching awards including a Teacher of Excellence by the University of Texas Ex-Students Association and Teacher of the Year for Region 6. More importantly, her students have received academic recognition at the local, state and national levels. She has written several grants designed to improve student learning; presented at state and national educational conferences, as well as having written a variety of journal articles.

SECTION 1: PHILOSOPHICAL EDUCATION

Section Editor: Barbara J. Thayer-Bacon teaches graduate courses on philosophy and history of education, social philosophy and cultural diversity at the University of Tennessee. Her primary research areas are: philosophy of education, pragmatism, feminist theory and pedagogy, and cultural studies in education. She is program coordinator for the Cultural Studies in Education, Master's Degree and editor of the journal, *International Education.* She is an active member in numerous professional organizations, such as American Educational Research Association, American Educational Studies Association, and Philosophy of Education Society, and presents papers regularly at their annual conferences. She is past president for the Ohio Valley Philosophy of Education Society, and the Philosophical Studies in Education and the Research on Women and Education Special Interest Groups for AERA. She is the author of more than 15 chapters in essay collections and more than 70 journal articles published in professional journals such as *The Journal of Thought, Educational Theory, Studies in Philosophy and Education, Inquiry, Educational Foundations,* and *Educational Studies.* She has presented more than 85 conference papers to various professional organizations. She has written four books, *Philosophy Applied to Education: Nurturing a Democratic Community in the Classroom,* with Dr. Charles S. Bacon as contributing author (Merrill Publishing, Prentice-Hall, Inc., 1998); *Transforming Critical Thinking: Constructive Thinking* (Teachers College Press, 2000); *Relational "(e)pistemologies"* (Peter Lang, 2003), and *Beyond Liberal Democracy in Schools: The Power of Pluralism* (Teachers College Press.

SECTION 2: LEARNING THEORY

Section Editor: Patrick M. Jenlink is a professor of doctoral studies in the Department of Secondary Education and Educational Leadership and director of the Educational Research Center at Stephen F. Austin State University. Dr. Jenlink has served as a classroom teacher at the junior high and high school level as well a K-12 counselor. He has also served as building administrator and school district superintendent in Oklahoma. His university teaching experience includes Northwestern Oklahoma State University, Western Michigan University, and assignments in Europe with University of Oklahoma and NATO. Dr. Jenlink's teaching emphasis in doctoral studies at Stephen F. Austin State University includes courses in ethics and philosophy of leadership, research methods and design, and leadership theory and practice. Dr. Jenlink's research interests include learning theory with an emphasis in cultural-historical activity theory and situated cognition, politics of identity, democratic education and leadership, and critical theory. He has authored numerous articles, guest edited journals, authored or coauthored numerous chapters in books, and edited or coedited several books. Currently Dr. Jenlink serves as editor of *Teacher Education & Practice* and coeditor of *Scholar-Practitioner Quarterly,* both refereed journals. Books published include *Dialogue as a Means of Collective Communication* (Kluwer Academic/Plenum Publishing), *Dialogue as a Collective Means of Design Conversation* (Springer Publishing), *Equity Issues for Today's Educational Leaders: Meeting the Challenge of Creating Equitable Schools for All* (Rowman & Littlefield), *Dewey's Democracy and Education Revisited: Contemporary Discourses for Democratic Education and Leadership* (Rowman & Littlefield). Dr. Jenlink's current book projects include a coauthored book, *Developing Scholar-Practitioner Leaders: The Empowerment of Educators* (forthcoming from Falmer Press), *Ethics and the Educational Leader: A Casebook of Ethical Dilemmas* (forthcoming from Rowman & Littlefield Publishing Group), and *Educational Leadership, Moral Literacy, and the Dispositions of Moral Leaders* (forthcoming from Rowman & Littlefield Publishing Group).

SECTION 3: INSTRUCTIONAL THEORY

Section Editor: Janice Koch is professor emerita of science education at Hofstra University on Long Island, New York where she directed IDEAS-the Institute for the Development of Education in the Advanced Sciences. This outreach institute fosters the public understanding of science as well as furthering the professional development of precollege teachers of science. Dr. Koch is the past president (2007-2009) of the Association for Science Teacher Education. She has taught courses addressing introduction to education, action research, science education, qualitative research and gender issues and education. Dr. Koch earned her PhD in education at New York University where her cognate area was environmental science. Her research explores furthering the science experiences of girls and women and minorities through science teacher education. She is the author of *TEACH* (2nd ed., 2013), an introduction to education textbook and *Science Stories: Science Methods for Elementary and Middle School Teacher* (5th ed., 2013).

SECTION 4: CURRICULUM THEORY

Section Editor: Arthur Shapiro has been a teacher, high school principal, director of secondary education, assistant superintendent, and superintendent of schools in nationally prominent urban, suburban, and rural districts. He is a professor at the University of South Florida. He was professor of education at George

Peabody College of Vanderbilt University, directed the first off-campus doctoral center, the University of Tennessee, and has been department chair of Leadership and Policy Studies at the University of South Florida five times. He writes and consultants internationally and nationally in policy, leadership, curriculum, and supervision, lately decentralizing large schools into small learning communities, and was lead consultant for improving the Republic of Macedonia's schools.

SECTION 5: LITERACY AND LANGUAGE ACQUISITION THEORY

Section Editor: Fuhui Tong is an assistant professor in the Department of Educational Psychology, Texas A&M University (College Station, TX). Her research interests are instructional and teacher factors in the language and literacy development and academic achievement for students in bilingual and ESL settings. Dr. Tong's work has appeared in peer-reviewed journals, including *American Educational Research Journal*, *Elementary School Journal*, *Hispanic Journal of Behavioral Science*, *Bilingual Research Journal*, and *Journal of Educational Research*. She has been engaged as key personnel on multiple U.S. Department of Education funded projects, including Field Initiated Research and an Institute of Education Sciences longitudinal research. She is also the coprincipal investigator for a National Science Foundation research grant; all of which aimed to promote English language/literacy and content knowledge acquisition for culturally and linguistically diverse and low socioeconomic status children and youth.

SECTION 6: COUNSELING THEORY

Section Editors: Richard C. Henriksen Jr. is an associate professor in the Counseling Program at Sam Houston State University in Huntsville, TX. He is a Licensed Professional Counselor and Supervisor, National Certified Counselor, and Board Approved Supervisor. Dr. Henriksen has been a counselor educator for 12 years. Dr. Henriksen has experience as a substance abuse counselor, a community counselor and an acute care counselor. He has experience in clinical practice working as a licensed professional counselor in private practice, hospitals, and community agencies. Dr. Henriksen's research interests include multicultural counseling, counseling individuals, couples and families with multiple heritage backgrounds, and religious and spiritual issues in counseling.

Mary Nichter is a professor and coordinator of the Counseling Program at Sam Houston State University in Huntsville, TX. She is a licensed professional counselor and supervisor, licensed marriage and family therapist and board approved supervisor and a certified school counselor. Dr. Nichter has been a counselor educator for 13 years. Dr. Nichter has experience as an elementary school counselor and a high school counselor. She has experience in clinical practice working as a marriage and family therapist in private practice, hospitals, and at a clinic for pain stress and depression. Dr. Nichter's research interests include development of theoretical orientation for beginning counselors, identifying student impairment, and supervision.

SECTION 7: MORAL DEVELOPMENT THEORY

Section Editor: Rebecca A. Robles-Piña is a professor at Sam Houston State University in Huntsville, TX. She is the editor for *The Journal of At-Risk Issues*, a journal dedicated to empirical research that improves the status of populations that are at-risk of dropping out of school due to issues including achievement, absenteeism, pregnancy, substance abuse, bullying, and violence. Her research interests are depression in adolescent Hispanic students, school retention, bullying, school climate, and educational and psychological issues that affect the achievement gap of minority students. Regarding scholarly work, Rebecca has published more than 50 scholarly publications and has made more than 100 scholarly presentations. She has developed *The Bullying Survey* to be used for assessing knowledge and bullying interventions that educational leaders have and use to intervene in school bullying incidents. Further, she received a Department of Education grant to develop a bilingual school bullying program. Rebecca is a practicing school psychologist and licensed psychologist who works primarily with children and adolescents. Rebecca received the Sam Houston State University Faculty Excellence in Research Award.

SECTION 8: CLASSROOM MANAGEMENT THEORY

Section Editors: Patricia Williams, a faculty member at Sam Houston State University in Huntsville, Texas, for the past 32 years, holds a bachelor's degree in English and political science and a master's degree in English from Sam Houston State University, along with a doctorate in English education from the University of Houston. While as SHSU, she has served as faculty senate chair and SHSU Alumni Association president. She currently serves as the Phi Delta Kappa International president-elect, and the association includes the Future Educators Association and Pi Lambda Theta. In addition, she is a member of the Alpha Chi National College

Honor Scholarship Society's National Council, and previously served as the national president for 4 years. During her career, Patricia has authored/coauthored approximately 100 publications, including articles in *Kappan, Delta Kappa Gamma International Bulletin, Action in Teacher Education, Clearing House*, and books, such as *Secondary Classroom Management* (Allyn & Bacon), *Why Didn't I Think of That?* (Scott Foresman), and *Responsibilities of the Professional Educator* (McGraw-Hill). She has made over 300 presentations, including ones at the International Association of Special Education Conference in Hong Kong, the Oxford Round Table at Oxford University, the Association of Teacher Educators Meeting, the National Council of Teachers of English Conference, the International Reading Association Conference, the Future Educators Association National Conference, and the Writing across the Curriculum International Conference. While at Sam Houston State University, she has previously served as the Across-the-University Writing Program director and the Academic Enrichment Center executive director (the University writing/reading/math/technology center). In 2009, *Self Magazine* named Patricia as a runner-up for the "Women Doing Good Award," and she felt she was in good company. The next year, Beyoncé Knowles received the award.

Sandra Harris earned her doctoral degree in educational leadership from the University of Texas at Austin. A former teacher and administrator in private and public K-12 schools, she currently directs the Center for Doctoral Studies in Educational Leadership at Lamar University. Sandra has published over 125 papers in peer-reviewed journals and book chapters. She has authored or coauthored 14 books, including *Bravo Teacher, Bravo Principal* (both published by Eye on Education), a series of three books on best practices of elementary principals, secondary principals and superintendents (Corwin Press) and a series of case study books on the principalship, assistant principalship, and superintendency (R & L Publishing). Sandra's primary research interests include leadership topics that improve social justice for all and result in school communities where all are treated with respect and mentoring. She presents widely on these topics. Sandra is the recipient of the Texas Council of Professors of Educational Administration Living Legend Award and the National Council of Professors of Educational Administration Living Legend Award.

Vicky R. Farrow received her PhD from Purdue University in educational psychology. Formerly, Dr. Farrow taught high school math, psychology, and business. She has been at Lamar University for 14 years where she has served as chair of the Department of Professional Pedagogy, teaching educational psychology and working with postbaccalaureate students in the alternative certification program. Additionally, Vicky has taught in the EdD program in educational leadership and has served on numerous dissertation committees. Vicky currently serves as the executive director for the Office of Planning and Assessment and also continues her role as professor teaching courses in the online teacher leadership program. Vicky's main research interest is induction and retention of novice teachers.

SECTION 9: ASSESSMENT THEORY

Section Editors: Samuel Ortiz is a professor of psychology at St. John's University, New York. He holds a PhD in clinical psychology from the University of Southern California and a credential in school psychology with postdoctoral training in bilingual school psychology from San Diego State University. He has served as a visiting professor and research fellow at Nagoya University, Japan, as vice president for Professional Affairs of APA Division 16 (School Psychology), and is currently serving third terms as a member of APA's, Committee on Psychological Tests and Assessment, Coalition for Psychology in Schools and Education, the New York State Committee of Practitioners on English Language Learners and Limited English Proficient Students, and recently completed service on the APA Presidential Task Force on Educational Disparities. Dr. Ortiz serves or has served on various editorial boards including *Journal of School Psychology, School Psychology Quarterly, Journal of Applied School Psychology, Psychology in the Schools*, and *Journal of Cognitive Education.* Dr. Ortiz trains and consults nationally and internationally (e.g., Japan, Mexico, Vietnam) for various federal, state, regional, and local educational agencies, conducts and supervises research in the schools, and has published widely on a variety of topics including nondiscriminatory assessment, evaluation of English learners, cross-battery assessment, and learning disabilities. He has authored or coauthored 16 journal articles, nine books, and 36 book chapters, as well as several software products including the Culture-Language Interpretive Matrix (C-LIM v2.0), the Processing Strengths and Weaknesses Analyzer (PSW-A v1.0), the XBA Data Management and Interpretive System (XBA DMIA 2.0), the SLD Assistant (v1.0), and the School Psychology Service Delivery Analyzer (SPSDA). His recent books include *Assessment of Culturally and Linguistically Diverse Students: A Practical Guide*, and *Essentials of Cross-Battery Assessment* (3rd ed.), which is due out in January 2013. Dr. Ortiz is bilingual, Spanish, and bicultural, Puerto Rican.

Dawn P. Flanagan is professor of psychology and director of the School Psychology training programs at St. John's University in Queens, NY. She is also a clinical assistant professor at Yale Child Study Center, Yale University School of Medicine. In addition to her teaching responsibilities in the areas of intellectual assessment, psychoeducational assessment, learning disability, and professional issues in school psychology, she serves as an expert witness, learning disability consultant, and psychoeducational test/measurement consultant and trainer for organizations both nationally and internationally. She is a widely published author of books, book chapters, and articles. Her most recent books include the *Essentials of WISC-IV Assessment* and the second editions of *Contemporary Intellectual Assessment: Theories, Tests, and Issues; The Achievement Test Desk Reference: A Guide to Learning Disability Identification*; and *Essentials of Cross-Battery Assessment*. Dr. Flanagan is a fellow of both APA and the American Board of Psychological Specialties. She is a past recipient of APA's Lightner Witmer Award—in recognition of her early contributions to the field of school psychology. Dr. Flanagan also received an "Outstanding Faculty Achievement Award" from her university in recognition of her dedication to teaching, mentoring students, publishing, and conducting research. Dr. Flanagan is perhaps best known for the development of the CHC Cross-Battery Approach and the development of an operational definition of specific learning disability. Dr. Flanagan's most recent contribution to the field is a 6-hour multimedia professional development course entitled, "Agora: The Marketplace of Ideas. Best Practices: Applying Response to Intervention (RTI) and Comprehensive Assessment for the Identification of Specific Learning Disabilities" [DVD].

Section 10: Organizational Theory

Section Editor: Fred C. Lunenburg is the Merchant Professor of Education at Sam Houston State University. He has taught at Loyola University Chicago, the University of Louisville, and Southern Utah University, where he also served as dean of the College of Education. Prior to moving to the university, he served as a teacher, principal, and superintendent of schools. He is coauthor with Allan Ornstein of *Educational Administration: Concepts and Practices* (1991, 1996, 2000, 2004, 2008, 2012); with CleteBulach, *Creating a Culture for High-Performing Schools* (2008, 2011); with Beverly Irby, *Writing a Successful Thesis or Dissertation* (2008); with Beverly Irby, *The Principalship: Vision to Action* (2006); with Carolyn Carr, *Shaping the Future* (2003); with George Perreault, *The Changing World of School Administration* (2002); and with Beverly Irby, *High Expectations: An Action Plan for Implementing Goals 2000* (2000).

Section 11: Leadership and Management Theory

Section Editor: Fenwick W. English currently teaches at the graduate level in the educational leadership area. He has served in administrative capacities in higher education as department chair, dean, and vice chancellor of academic affairs. English has held leadership positions throughout the country and has served in an executive capacity at the national level with the American Association of School Administrators in Arlington, Virginia, and with KPMG Peat Marwick, a private accounting and consulting firm in Washington, D.C. English has lived or worked in all 50 states and two U.S. territories during his career. He has headed task forces sponsored by the National Secondary School Principals, and by the Association for Supervision and Curriculum Development. He is now serving on the executive board of the National Council of Professors of Educational Administration. English's scholarship includes more than 25 books and over 100 articles published in both practitioner and academic journals. He is considered a leading advocate of the application of postmodern analysis in educational leadership. These insights have helped redefine the field of educational leadership. His 2008 book *The Art of Educational Administration* explores leadership as drama and the long arc of the humanities from Plutarch to Shakespeare as the source of determining the challenges of morality in school administration. Also in 2008 he published *Anatomy of Professional Practice: Promising Research Perspectives in Educational Leadership* (Roman and Littlefield). In 2009 he released *Restoring Human Agency in Educational Administration* with Rosemary Papa (Pro-Active Publishers). He is currently serving as editor of the second edition of the SAGE *Handbook of Educational Leadership.*

Section 12: Social Justice Theory

Section Editor: Jill Blackmore joined Deakin University in 1987 as a lecturer in education. She was appointed to a personal chair in 2002 and to the position of director of the Centre for Research in Educational Futures and Innovation in the School of Education, Faculty of Arts and Education, in 2009. The center aims to become the preeminent centre for educational research in the Asia Pacific region and is committed to theoretically informed, and practice oriented, research that informs educational policy and practice. Professor Blackmore's current work focuses on global restructuring and how it articulates locally in terms of organizational change and the production of teacher, academic and student identities. The dominant research question throughout all her work is; "What do changing relations between structures, organizations and identities mean for more equitable education systems and a more equitable society?" She currently holds three Australian Research Council (ARC) grants and two Category 2 grants to support this work which involves teams across different faculties and universities. Professor Blackmore has a long history of successfully gaining external competitive grants to support her research. Throughout her research career, promoting equity has been a constant, producing works such as *Performing and Re-Forming Leaders: Gender, Educational Restructuring and Organisational Change* (with Judyth Sachs, 2007, SUNY Press) which won the Critics Choice Award from the American Educational Studies Association in the year it was published. From her earliest publications, Professor Blackmore has used feminist theory to inform the field of leadership and educational administration, and now edits a Routledge book series with Professor Pat Thomson (University of Nottingham) and Professor Helen Gunter (University of Manchester) on critical theories and educational leadership. As director of the Centre for Research in Educational Futures and Innovation, Professor Blackmore has provided strong leadership in building an education research profile at Deakin by leading teams that have successfully built a research grant profile as well as a publication and impact profile. In addition, she has also been very successful in building future capacity by working closely with early career researchers and successfully supervising a large cohort of PhD students who consistently seek out Professor Blackmore to be the supervisor of their doctoral work. She carries a large load in PhD supervision and to date 24 of her doctoral students have successfully graduated. Many are now in successful academic positions across Australia and internationally.

SECTION 13: TEACHING AND EDUCATION DELIVERY THEORY

Section Editor: Shirley Jackson returned to college after 25 years as a secondary school English teacher and department chair to enroll in a doctoral program in educational leadership at Sam Houston State University. Following graduation, she became an adjunct lecturer and researcher in the Center for Research and Doctoral Studies at SHSU. In addition, with a masters in gifted education, she conducts workshops in the 30 hours of training required by Texas for teachers of the identified gifted and talented. As a classroom teacher, Dr. Jackson received numerous teaching awards including a Teacher of Excellence by the University of Texas Ex-Students Association and Teacher of the Year for Region 6. More importantly, her students have received academic recognition at the local, state and national levels. She has written several grants designed to improve student learning; presented at state and national educational conferences, as well as having written a variety of journal articles.

CPSIA information can be obtained
at www.ICGtesting.com
Printed in the USA
LVHW061612021020
667743LV00023B/2772

9 781617 358654